NATIONAL ACCOUNTS STATISTICS: MAIN AGGREGATES AND DETAILED TABLES, 1991

PART II

UNITED NATIONS
NEW YORK, 1993

NOTE

Symbols of United Nations documents are composed of capital letters combined with figures. Mention of such a symbol indicates a reference to a United Nations document. The first 14 editions of the *Yearbook* were issued without series symbols.

ST/ESA/STAT/SER.X/20, Part II

UNITED NATIONS PUBLICATION
Sales No. E.94.XVII.5, Part II

ISBN 92-1-161361-2

Inquiries should be directed to:
SALES SECTION
UNITED NATIONS
NEW YORK, NY 10017

CONTENTS

Page

Introduction v

   I. System of National Accounts (SNA) ix
  II. System of Material Product Balances (MPS) xxi
 III. Country tables... 1121

	Page			Page
Latvia	1121		Rwanda	1607
Lebanon	1125		Saint Kitts and Nevis	1618
Lesotho	1126		Saint Lucia	1620
Liberia	1134		Saint Vincent and the Grenadines	1622
Libyan Arab Jamahiriya	1137		Sao Tome and Principe	1625
Lithuania	1145		Saudi Arabia	1626
Luxembourg	1146		Senegal	1629
Madagascar	1163		Seychelles	1632
Malawi	1165		Sierra Leone	1643
Malaysia	1169		Singapore	1655
Maldives	1175		Slovakia	1659
Mali	1177		Slovenia	1660
Malta	1181		Solomon Islands	1661
Martinique	1202		Somalia	1666
Mauritania	1205		South Africa	1670
Mauritius	1208		Spain	1682
Mexico	1225		Sri Lanka	1712
Mongolia	1235		Sudan	1733
Montserrat	1236		Suriname	1747
Morocco	1240		Swaziland	1750
Mozambique	1243		Sweden	1760
Myanmar	1244		Switzerland	1824
Nepal	1249		Syrian Arab Republic	1829
Netherlands	1253		Tajikistan	1837
Netherlands Antilles	1299		Thailand	1838
New Caledonia	1305		Togo	1861
New Zealand	1308		Tonga	1863
Nicaragua	1329		Trinidad and Tobago	1868
Niger	1330		Tunisia	1878
Nigeria	1332		Turkey	1882
Norway	1344		Uganda	1888
Oman	1409		Ukraine	1890
Pakistan	1415		United Arab Emirates	1893
Panama	1425		United Kingdom	1900
Papua New Guinea	1441		United Rep. of Tanzania	1956
Paraguay	1449		United States	1960
Peru	1459		Uruguay	2022
Philippines	1507		USSR (Former)	2035
Poland	1522		Vanuatu	2038
Portugal	1531		Venezuela	2044
Puerto Rico	1583		Viet Nam	2066
Qatar	1589		Yemen	2073
Republic of Moldova	1590		Yugoslavia (Former)	2086
Reunion	1594		Zaire	2088
Romania	1597		Zambia	2089
Russian Federation	1605		Zimbabwe	2099

INTRODUCTION

This is the thirty-fifth issue of *National Accounts Statistics: Main Aggregates and Detailed Tables*[1/], showing detailed national accounts estimates for 178 countries and areas. Like the previous issues, it has been prepared by the Statistical Division of the Department for Economic and Social Information and Policy Analysis of the United Nations Secretariat with the generous co-operation of national statistical services. It is issued in accordance with the request of the Statistical Commission[2/] that the most recent available data on national accounts for as many countries and areas as possible be published regularly.

The present publication (Parts I and II) forms part of a National Accounts Statistics series. Another publication which is a special supplement to the National Accounts series, *Trends in International Distribution of Gross World Product* [3/] is the first of several specialized publications designed to apply a variety of analyses to the integrated national accounts database maintained by the Statistical Division. The specialized issues will replace the annual publication *National Accounts Statistics: Analysis of Main Aggregates* [4/], which presented in the form of analytical tables a summary of main national accounts aggregates extracted from the database and supplemented by estimates made by the Statistical Division where official data are not available.

SCOPE OF PUBLICATION

National accounts estimates for countries or areas whose data are in terms of the United Nations System of National Accounts (SNA) are shown, where available, for each of the following tables:

Part 1. Summary information

1.1 Expenditures on the gross domestic product (current prices)

1.2 Expenditures on the gross domestic product (constant prices)

1.3 Cost components of the gross domestic product

1.4 General government current receipts and expenditures, summary

1.5 Current income and outlay of corporate and quasi-corporate enterprises, summary

1.6 Current income and outlay of households and non-profit institutions, summary

1.7 External transactions on current account, summary

1.8 Capital transactions of the nation, summary

1.9 Gross domestic product by institutional sector of origin

1.10 Gross domestic product by kind of activity (current prices)

1.11 Gross domestic product by kind of activity (constant prices)

1.12 Relations among national accounting aggregates

Part 2. Final expenditures on gross domestic product: detailed breakdowns and supporting tables

2.1 General government final consumption expenditure by function (current prices)

2.2 General government final consumption expenditure by function (constant prices)

2.3 Total government outlays by function and type (current prices)

2.4 Composition of general government social security benefits and social assistance grants to households

2.5 Private final consumption expenditure by type (current prices)

2.6 Private final consumption expenditure by type (constant prices)

2.7 Gross capital formation by type of good and owner (current prices)

2.8 Gross capital formation by type of good and owner (constant prices)

2.9 Gross capital formation by kind of activity of owner, ISIC major divisions (current prices)

2.10 Gross capital formation by kind of activity of owner, ISIC major divisions (constant prices)

2.11 Gross fixed capital formation by kind of activity of owner, ISIC divisions (current prices)

2.12 Gross fixed capital formation by kind of activity of owner, ISIC divisions (constant prices)

2.13 Stocks of reproducible fixed assets, by type of good and owner (current prices)

2.14 Stocks of reproducible fixed assets, by type of good and owner (constant prices)

2.15 Stocks of reproducible fixed assets by kind of activity (current prices)

2.16 Stocks of reproducible fixed assets by kind of activity (constant prices)

2.17 Exports and imports of goods and services, detail

Part 3. Institutional sector accounts: detailed flow accounts[5]

1. General government

3.11 Production account

3.12 Income and outlay account

3.13 Capital accumulation account

3.14 Capital finance account

2. Corporate and quasi-corporate enterprises

3.21 Production account: total and subsectors

3.22 Income and outlay account: total and subsectors

3.23 Capital accumulation account: total and subsectors

3.24 Capital finance account: total and subsectors

3. Households and private unincorporated enterprises

3.31 Production account: total and subsectors

3.32 Income and outlay account: total and subsectors

3.33 Capital accumulation account: total and subsectors

3.34 Capital finance account: total and subsectors

4. Private non-profit institutions serving households

3.41 Production account

3.42 Income and outlay account

3.43 Capital accumulation account

3.44 Capital finance account

5. External transactions

3.51 Current account, detail

3.52 Capital accumulation account

3.53 Capital finance account

Part 4. Production by kind of activity: detailed breakdowns and supporting tables

4.1 Derivation of value added by kind of activity (current prices)

4.2 Derivation of value added by kind of activity (constant prices)

4.3 Cost components of value added

For the countries or areas whose data are in terms of the System of Material Product Balances (MPS), the estimates are shown, where available, for each of the following tables:

1. Net material product by use

2. Net material product by kind of activity of the material sphere

3. Primary incomes by kinds of activity of the material sphere

4. Primary incomes from net material product

5. Supply and disposition of goods and material services

6. Capital formation by kind of activity of the material and non-material spheres

7. Final consumption

8. Personal consumption according to source of supply of goods and material services

9. Total consumption of the population by object, commodity and service, and mode of acquisition

Estimates for all tables are shown for the years 1980 through 1991.

CONCEPTUAL REFERENCES

The form and concepts of the statistical tables in the present publication generally conform, for the countries or areas with SNA data, to the recommendations in *A System of National Accounts* [6], Studies in Methods, Series F, No. 2, Rev. 3. For the countries or areas with MPS data, the form and concepts generally conform to the recommendations in *Basic Methodological Principles Governing the Compilation of the System of Statistical Balances of the National Economy: Vol. I and Vol. II* [7], Series F, No. 17/Rev. 1, New York 1989. A summary of the conceptual framework of both systems, their classifications and definitions of transactions is provided in chapters I and II of the present publication.

COMPILATION OF DATA

To compile the large volume of national accounts data, the Statistical Division each year sends to countries or areas prefilled SNA questionnaire and/or MPS questionnaire. The recipients are requested to update the questionnaire with the latest available national accounts estimates and to indicate where the scope and coverage of the country estimates differ for conceptual or statistical reasons from the definitions and classifications recommended in SNA or in MPS. Data obtained from these replies are supplemented by information gathered from correspondence with the national statistical services and from national and international source publications.

In the present publication, the data for each country or area are presented in separate chapters, as far as possible, under uniform table headings and classifications of SNA and/or MPS, as the case may be. Important deviations from the two systems, where known, are described in the general note, while differences in definition and coverage of specific items are indicated in footnotes to the relevant tables.

Country data in chapter III are presented in alphabetical order. Unless otherwise stated, the data in the country tables relate to the calendar year against which they are shown.

COMPARABILITY OF THE NATIONAL ESTIMATES

Every effort has been made to present the estimates of the various countries or areas in a form designed to facilitate international comparability. To this end, important differences in concept, scope,

coverage and classification have been described in the notes which precede and accompany the country tables. Such differences should be taken into account if misleading comparisons among countries or areas are to be avoided.

REVISIONS

The figures shown are the most recent estimates and revisions available at the time of compilation. In general, figures for the most recent year are to be regarded as provisional. For more up to date information, reference is made to selected issues of the United Nations *Monthly Bulletin of Statistics* [8]

NOMENCLATURE

The information for the countries and areas shown in this publication reflect what is available to the Statistical Division of the United Nations as of 30 September 1993.

Designations which have changed in recent years are as follows:

Czech Republic , Slovakia - Data for Czech Republic and Slovakia are shown separately under the approrpiate country name. For period prior to 1 January 1993, data for the former Czechoslovakia are shown under the country name "Czechoslovakia (Former)".

USSR (Former) - In 1991, the Union of Soviet Socialist republics formally dissolved into fifteen independent republics (Armenia, Azerbaijan, Belarus, Estonia, Georgia, Kazakhstan, Kyrgyzstan, Latvia, Lithuania, Republic of Moldova, Russina Federation, Tajikistan, Turkmenistan, Ukraine and Uzbekistan). When available, data are shown for the individual republics. All data for the former USSR are shown under the contry name "USSR (Former)

Yugoslavia (Former) - All data for Yugoslavia prior to 1 January 1992 refer to the Socialist Federal Republic of Yugoslavia which was composed ot six republics . After that date, when available, data for the republics, Bosnia and Herzegovina, Croatia, Slovania The Former Republiic of Macedonia, and the Federal Republic of Yugoslavia which is composed of two republics (Sebia and Montenegro) are shown separately.

EXPLANATION OF SYMBOLS

The following symbols have been employed:

Data not available ....

Category not applicable ....

Magnitude nil or less than half of the unit employed .... -

Decimal figures are always preceded by a point (.)

When a series is not homogeneous, it is indicated by presenting the data in separate rows.

Decimals and percentages in tables do not necessarily add to totals shown because of rounding.

GENERAL DISCLAIMER

The designations employed and the presentation of material in this publication do not imply the expression of any opinion whatsoever on the part of the Secretariat of the United Nations concerning the legal status of any country, territory, city or area or of its authorities, or concerning the delimitation of its frontiers and boundaries.

Where the designation "country or area" appears in the headings of tables, it covers countries, territories, cities or areas. In prior issues of this publication, where the designation "country" appears in the headings of tables, it covers countries, territories, cities or areas.

In some tables, the designations "developed" and "developing" economies are intended for statistical convenience and do not, necessarily, express a judgement about the stage reached by a particular country or area in the development process.

1/United Nations publication. The first 25 editions of this publication were issued under the title Yearbook of National Accounts Statistics under the following sales number: 1957, 58. XVII3; 1958, 59. XVII.3; 1959, 60. XVII.3; 1960, 61. XVII.4; 1961, 62. XVII.2; 1962, 63. XVII.2; 1963, 64. XVII.4; 1964, 65. XVII.2; 1965, 66. XVII.2; 1966, 67. XVII.14; 1967, 69. XVII.6; 1968, vol. 1, 70. XVII.2, vol. II, 70. XVII.3; 1969, vol. 1, 71. XVII.2, vol. II, 71. XVII.3; 1970, 72. XVII.3, vol. 1, 72. XVII.3, vol. II; 1971, (3 volumes), E.73.XVII.3; 1972, (3 volumes), E.74.XVII.3; 1973, (3 volumes), E.75.XVII.2; 1975, (3 volumes), E.75.XVII.5, 1975, (3 volumes), 1976.XVII.2; 1976 (2 volumes), E.77.XVII.2; 1977, (2 volumes), E.78 XVII.2; 1978, (2 volumes) E.79.XVII.8; 1979, (2 volumes), E.80.XVII, 11; 1980, (2 volumes) E.82.XVII.6; 1981 (2 volumes), E.83.XVII.3. Beginning with the twenty-sixth edition, this publication replaced Volume 1, individual country data, of the Yearbook and it was issued under the following sales number: 1982, E.85.XVII.4; 1983, E.86.XVII.3; 1984, E.86.XVII.26; 1985, E.87.XVII.10; 1986, E.89.XVII.7 (Parts I and II), 1987, E.90.XVII.2 (Parts I and II), 1988, E.90.XVII.18 (Part I and II), 1989,E.91XVII.16(Part I and Part II)1990, E.93.XVII..3 (Part I and II).

2/See Official Records of the Economic and Social Council, First Year. Second Session, (E/39), annex III, chap. IV.

3/United Nations publications, Sales No. E.92.XVII..7

4/United Nations publication, Sales No. E.91.XVII.17.

5/Institutional sector accounts are shown only for those countries which have tables for all the institutional sectors.

6/United Nations publication, Sales No. E.69.XVII.3. The first addition of the report, published in 1953, was prepared by an expert committee appointed by the Secretary-General of the United Nations.

7/United Nations publication, Sales No. E.89.XVII.5.

8/United Nations publication, ST/ESA/STAT/SER.Q.

I. SYSTEM OF NATIONAL ACCOUNTS (SNA)

The revised System of National Accounts (SNA) was adopted by the Statistical Commission at its fifteenth session [1] for the use of national statistical authorities and in the international reporting of comparable national accounting data. The present System [2] is a revision and extension of the former SNA which was first formulated in 1952.

A. STRUCTURE OF SNA

SNA provides a comprehensive and detailed framework for the systematic and integrated recording of transaction flows in an economy. It brings together into an articulated and coherent system data ranging in degree of aggregation from consolidated accounts of the nation to detailed input-output and flow-of-funds tables. It includes production and goods and services and outlay and capital finance accounts for institutional sectors and subsectors.

The country tables are divided into four parts. These are listed in the above introduction. Part 1 contains summary but comprehensive information, at current and, where appropriate, constant prices. This part includes not only the basic gross domestic product (final expenditures and cost composition) but also summary information on government receipts and disbursements, enterprise and household income and outlay, and external transactions, a summary capital transactions account, information on gross product by institutional sector of origin and kind of activity and, finally, a table showing the relations among the aggregate concepts used in the revised SNA and also commonly in national statistical systems. Tables 1.1, 1.3, 1.4, 1.5, 1.6, 1.7 and 1.8 form a simple, closed and balancing set of flow accounts, drawn from the much more complex and elaborate standard accounts of SNA; these tables can therefore be used not only to provide an overview of the operation of the economic system but also as a guide to the more detailed data that follow and as a framework to enforce conceptual and statistical consistency.

Part 2 shows detailed breakdowns of the final expenditure components on gross domestic product (consumption, capital formation, imports and exports), in current and constant prices, together with supporting tables giving additional information on government outlays and capital stock. This part also shows tables relating to stocks of reproducible tangible assets at current and constant prices.

Part 3 shows detailed institutional sector accounts. For each sector and subsector, five accounts are given: a production account, an income and outlay account, a capital formation account, a capital finance account, and a balance sheet. The latter four are standard SNA accounts, as shown in annex 8.3 to *A System of National Accounts* [2] and in annex 8.2 to *Provisional Guidelines on National and Sector Balance Sheets and Reconciliation Accounts of the System of National Accounts.* [4]

The SNA standard accounts do not include institutional sector production accounts, but provision is made for this information in the supporting tables.

The sectors and subsectors distinguished in part 3 are: general government (central, state or provincial, local, social security funds), corporate and quasi-corporate enterprises (non-financial, financial), households and private unincorporated enterprises (farm entrepreneurial, other farm, non-farm entrepreneurial, non-farm wage earner, other) and non-profit institutions serving households.

Part 4 contains kind-of-activity breakdowns. Two levels of detail are employed. All of the information is asked for at the major division (1-digit) level of the *International Standard Industrial Classification of All Economic Activities* [5] (ISIC). In some cases, data are also asked for at the ISIC division (2-digit) level, with a very small amount of further breakdown to the 3-digit level. Where appropriate, both current and constant prices are specified. The tables show the derivation of value added (gross output less intermediate consumption), the cost components of value added, and employment.

B. STANDARD CLASSIFICATIONS OF THE SNA

Detailed discussions of definitions and classifications are to be found in *A System of National Accounts*, [2] and in the other publications on SNA cited above. SNA distinguishes between transactor and transaction classifications. Below is a short summary of the main characteristics of each of the classifications used by the system.

I. *Classifications of transactors*

1. *Kind of activity*

The kind-of-activity classification employed is the major division (1-digit) level or, in some tables the division (2-digit) level of ISIC.

In SNA, this classification is intended to be applied to establishment-type units, defined as the smallest units for which separate production accounts can be compiled. SNA also employs a much broader kind of activity classification which divides producers into "industries" and three categories of "other producers". Industries are, broadly, establishments whose activities are intended to be self-sustaining, whether through production for the market or for own use, and it is to this category that the ISIC breakdown is generally applied.

All establishments falling into ISIC major divisions 1-8 should be classed as industries. Producers of government services, private non-profit services to households, and domestic services are classed as "other producers"; all of these should fall into ISIC category 9 "Community, social and personal services". ISIC category 9 also may, of course, include some establishments classed as industries. Where countries consider, however, that some establishments classed as other producers should appear in ISIC categories other than 9, the nature of the exceptions would be specified in footnotes to tables 1.10 and 1.11.

2. *Institutional sectors*

The basic SNA institutional sectoring is given in *A System of National Accounts*, [3/] table 5.1.

Institutional sectoring, in SNA, is intended to be applied to enterprise-type units, that is, units for which complete accounts can be compiled, as opposed to the establishment-type units employed in the kind-of-activity classification. This distinction is applicable mainly to the corporate and quasi-corporate enterprise sector.

The sectoring and subsectoring employed in the institutional sector accounts in part 3 is as follows:

General government

    Central
    State or provincial
    Local
    Social security funds

Corporate and quasi-corporate enterprises

    Non-financial
    Financial

Households and private unincorporated enterprises

    Farm entrepreneurial
    Other farm
    Non-farm entrepreneurial
    Non-farm wage earner
    Other

Non-profit institutions serving households

Rest of the world

(a) *General government.* This sector includes (1) *producers of government services*, all bodies, departments and establishments of any level of government that engage in administration, defence, regulation of the public order and health, cultural, recreational and other social services and social security arrangements that are furnished but not normally sold to the public; and (2) *industries of government*, ancillary departments and establishments mainly engaged in supplying goods and services to other units of government, such as printing plants, central transport pools and arsenals, and agencies mainly selling goods and services to the public but operating on a small scale and financially integrated with general government, such as government restaurant facilities in public buildings.

Non-profit institutions which, while not an official part of any organ of government, are wholly or mainly financed and controlled by it should be included in producers of government services. Ancillary agencies may occur in any kind of activity. Producers of government services normally occur only in major division 9 (which of course may also include ancillary agencies).

Provision is made for four subsectors of general government, all of which may include the two components noted above. However, it is not intended that artificial distinctions should be introduced where they do not exist in the institutions of a particular country. It will, for instance, usually be desirable to separate state or provincial government from local government only in countries in which state or provincial governments exercise a considerable degree of autonomy. Similarly, social security funds should in general be distinguished separately only where they are organized separately from the other activities of general government and exercise substantial autonomy in their operations.

(b) *Corporate and quasi-corporate enterprises.* SNA defines this sector to include enterprises which meet any one of the following criteria: (1) they are incorporated; (2) they are owned by a non-resident; (3) they are relatively large partnerships or proprietorships with complete income statements and balance sheets; (4) they are non-profit institutions mainly serving business and financed and controlled by business; or (5) they are engaged in financial activities. Because of the difficulty that may be encountered in compiling separate production account data for incorporated and unincorporated units, a combined production account for these two sectors has also been provided for.

(c) *Households and private unincorporated enterprises.* This sector includes all private unincorporated enterprises not classed as quasi-corporations. SNA also includes in this sector private non-profit institutions serving households that employ less than the equivalent of two full-time persons.

The criterion for classifying the subsectors of the household sector in these tables differs slightly from that tentatively proposed in SNA. There, the subsectoring is based on the occupational status of the person designated "head of household". Here, the classification is based on the most important source of household income, taking all household members into account. It is considered that this criterion more accurately reflects both changing social views and changing labour force participation practices; it also responds to recent directives relating to the elimination of sex-based stereotypes.

(d) *Private non-profit institutions serving households.* This sector includes institutions, not mainly financed and controlled by general governments and employing the equivalent of two or more persons, that furnish educational, health, cultural, recreational and other social and community services to households free of charge or at prices that do not fully cover their costs of production.

As in the case of general government, SNA includes two components in this sector: (1) *producers of private non-profit services to households*, which engage in the activities enumerated above, and (2) *commercial activities* of these institutions, such as owning and letting dwellings, operating eating and lodging facilities, and publishing and selling books, for which it is possible to compile separate production accounts but not complete separate financial accounts. (Where separate financial accounts can be compiled, such activities would be classed as ordinary quasi-corporations.) In SNA, these commercial activities are considered to be "industries" and should be classed in the appropriate ISIC categories, whereas the non-profit services proper will all fall into ISIC category 9.

II. *Classifications of transactions*

1. *Classification of the functions of government*

Table 5.3 of *A System of National Accounts* [3/] contains a classification of the purposes of government, the l-digit level of which was used in previous publications for classifying general government outlays. This classification has now been superseded by the *Classification of the Functions of Government.* [6/]

2. *Household consumption expenditure*

Table 6.1 of SNA provides a classification of household goods and services. The classification used in the present publication is a slightly condensed version of the second level of this classification, in which some second-level categories have been combined.

3. *Purposes of private non-profit bodies serving households*

This classification appears in table 5.4 of SNA. It is used for classifying the final consumption expenditures of private non-profit institutions serving households.

4. *Gross capital formation*

Table 6.2 of SNA classifies stocks according to type, and table 6.3 classifies gross fixed capital formation according to type. These classifications are used in the present publication in slightly modified form, calling for less detail in some areas and slightly more detail in others (specifically, transport equipment).

5. *Exports and imports of goods and services*

This classification is given in table 6.4 of SNA.

6. *Transfers*

Table 7.1 of SNA contains a classification of unrequired current transfers, including direct taxes. This classification is not employed directly in the present publication but it is the source of the definitions of a number of flows, and will be referred to in that connection.

7. *Financial assets and liabilities*

Table 7.2 of SNA gives a classification of items appearing in the capital finance account.

8. *Balance sheet categories*

Classifications of the various types of assets not included in the previous classification are given in tables 5.1 and 5.2 of *Provisional Guidelines on National and Sector Balance Sheets and Reconciliation Accounts of the System of National Accounts,* [4/], which deal respectively, with stocks and fixed assets, and non-reproducible tangible assets. These classifications are used in the capital stock tables in part 2 and the balance sheet tables in part 3 of the present publication.

C. DEFINITIONS OF FLOWS

The following section briefly defines the content of the flows appearing in the SNA tables of chapter III of the present publication.

I. *Total supply of goods and services*

1. *Gross output of goods and services*

Gross output of goods and services covers both the value of goods and services produced for sale and the value of goods and services produced for own use. It includes (a) the domestic production of goods and services which are either for sale or for transfer to others, (b) net additions to work in progress valued at cost and to stocks of finished goods valued in producers' prices; (c) products made on own account for government or private consumption or for gross fixed capital formation; and (d) rents received on structures, machinery and equipment (but not on land) and imputed rent for owner-occupied dwellings.

Production for own consumption of households includes all own-account production of primary products (agricultural, fishing, forestry, mining and quarrying), own-account production of such items as butter, flour, wine, cloth or furniture made from primary products, and other goods and services that are also commonly sold. Gross output of the distributive trades is defined as the difference between sales and purchase values of goods sold. Gross output of banks and similar financial institutions is defined as the sum of actual service charges and imputed service charges; the latter is equal to the excess of property income received over interest paid out on deposits. For casualty insurance companies, gross output is defined as the excess of premiums received over claims paid, and for life insurance schemes it is the excess of premiums received over the sum of claims paid and net additions to actuarial reserves, excluding the accrued interest of the policy-holders in these reserves. Gross output of general government includes the market value of sales and goods and services produced for own use. The latter should be valued at cost, that is, the sum of net purchases of goods and services for intermediate consumption (at purchasers' prices), consumption of fixed capital, compensation of employees and any indirect taxes paid.

The concept of gross output appears in the tables in both part 3 and part 4. In part 3, each sector production account aggregates to its gross output. In part 4, gross output of various kind-of-activity sectors appears in tables 4.1 - 4.2 and 4.5 - 4.10. In the sector production accounts (tables 3.11, 3.21, 3.31 and 3.41) and the supply tables (4.5, 4.6, 4.9 and 4.10), gross output is divided into marketed and non-marketed components. The marketed component includes all output offered for sale (whether or not a buyer is actually found) or valued on the basis of a market transaction, even if it reaches the ultimate recipient through a transfer.

2. *Imports of goods and services*

Imports of goods and services include broadly the equivalent of general imports of merchandise as defined in external trade statistics, plus imports of services and direct purchases abroad made by resident households and by the government on current account. Transfer of migrants' household and personal effects and gifts between households are also included. The following additions and deductions are required, however, to move from the general trade concept to the national accounting concept. Additions required include (1) the value of purchases of bankers, stores and ballast for ships, aircraft, etc., (2) fish and salvage purchased from foreign vessels, and (3) purchases from abroad of gold ore and gold for industrial uses Deductions required include (4) goods imported solely for improvement or repair and subsequently re-exported; and (5) leased or rented machinery, equipment and other goods; the value of the repairs or leasing and rental services is included, however. The valuation of imports is c.i.f. In principle, transactions should be recorded at the moment the transfer of ownership takes place and not when goods physically enter the domestic territory, but in practice the time of recording used in the national accounts usually must follow that used in the external trade statistics.

Total imports of goods and services appear in tables 1.1, 1.2, 1.7 and 3.51. A detailed breakdown is given in table 2.17.

II. *Disposition of total supply: intermediate and final uses*

1. *Intermediate consumption*

Intermediate consumption covers non-durable goods and services used up in production, including repair and maintenance, research and development and exploration costs. It also includes indirect outlays on financing capital formation, such as flotation costs for loans and transfer costs involved in the purchase and sale of intangible assets and financial claims. Intermediate consumption is, as far as possible, valued in purchasers' prices at the moment of use.

For producers of government services and private non-profit services to households, intermediate consumption includes (1) purchases of goods and services on current account *less* sales of similar second-hand goods and scraps and wastes, (2) value of goods in kind received as transfers or gifts from foreign governments, except those received for distribution to households without renovation or alteration, (3) durable goods acquired primarily for military purposes, and (4) goods and services paid for by government but furnished by private suppliers to individuals (e.g., medical services), provided that the individuals have no choice of supplier. However, intermediate consumption of these producers does not include (1) goods and services acquired for use in constructing capital assets, such as roads or buildings, (2) goods and services paid for by government but furnished by private suppliers to individuals, when the individuals can choose the supplier and (3) purchases of strategic materials for government stockpiles.

Intermediate consumption appears in each institutional sector production account in part 3, and in tables 4.1-4.2 by kind of activity. In addition to the flow numbers assigned in SNA, flow numbers have been introduced for two categories of intermediate consumption not separately numbered in *A System of National Accounts*. [3] The first is imputed bank service charges. The imputed bank service charge is defined as the excess of property income accruing to banks and similar financial institutions from the investment of deposits over the interest accruing to their depositors. This imputation is made because of the view that banks perform services for depositors for which no explicit payment is made, in return for the use of the deposits as earning assets. It is not possible to allocate the imputation to specific recipients of the services, however, so that it cannot be included, as would be desirable, as part of the intermediate consumption of each reception. It is therefore deducted as a lump-sum adjustment. The adjustment appears in the tables showing kind-of-activity breakdowns of value added or intermediate consumption, including tables 1.10, 1.11 and 4.1-4.2. The second addition is intermediate consumption of industries of government, required for constructing a production account for general government (table 3.11).

2. *Government final consumption expenditure*

Government final consumption expenditure is equal to the service produced by general government for its own use. Since these services are not sold, they are valued in the gross domestic product at their cost to the government. This cost is defined as the sum of (1) intermediate consumption, (2) compensation of employees, (3) consumption of fixed capital and (4) payments of indirect taxes, *less* (5) the value of own-account production of fixed assets, and *less* (6) sales of goods and services.

The latter item, government sales, includes all payments made by individuals for services received (whether nominal or full cost) and it also includes the provision of second-hand goods from government stores as transfers in kind to foreign governments. Sales of such items as timber from forest preserves, seeds from agricultural experiment stations and government publications would also appear here. Compensation of employees, consumption of fixed capital and indirect taxes paid (if any) should preferably relate to all general government activity, with intra-governmental purchases and sales of goods and services eliminated in order to avoid double counting. With this treatment, there will be no operating surplus for any general government unit. Where countries consider that ancillary agencies and/or unincorporated government enterprises selling to the general public are operated on commercial principles and that the prices charged reflect market values, treatment of these entities on a net basis is an acceptable alternative. In this treatment, their sales to other government agencies will appear as intermediate consumption of the latter, and their operating surplus will appear as an item of general government income. This treatment has a number of disadvantages: the boundary between ancillary agencies and other government agencies is very difficult to specify precisely, and variations in treatment are likely to lead to incomparability among countries. Also, the net treatment makes it impossible to obtain figures for such flows as total compensation of general government employees. Finally, the level of gross domestic product will vary when the government's internal transfer prices are altered, a result that is somewhat incongruous.

Total government consumption expenditures appear in tables 1.1, 1.2, 4.7 and 4.8. A breakdown by government subsectors appears in table 3.12. Tables 2.1-2.2 show detailed breakdowns by function.

3. *Private final consumption expenditure*

Private consumption expenditure measures the final consumption expenditure of all resident non-governmental units. Thus, it is the sum of final consumption expenditure of households and that of private non-profit institutions serving households.

(a) *Private non-profit institutions serving households.* Final consumption expenditure of these units, as in the case of government, is equal to services they produce for their own use and is valued at cost. Cost includes purchases and the value (in purchasers' prices) of transfers of goods and services received in kind, compensation of employees, consumption of fixed capital, and indirect taxes paid by these institutions, *less* their sales of goods and services. The definitions of purchases and sales on current account are much the same as those for general government. Private non-profit

institutions serving households are defined to include units employing the equivalent of two or more full-time persons and providing educational, health, cultural, recreational, and other social and community services to households free of charge or at prices that are not intended to cover the full costs of their production. Units mainly financed and controlled by general government, however, are included in general government rather than here. Units primarily serving business, such as trade associations, are included with corporate and quasi-corporate enterprises. In applying these definitions, some judgement is required, and it will often be necessary to examine intent, as well as outcome. A normally profit-making unit that sustains a loss does not thereby become a non-profit institution.

Final expenditures of private non-profit institutions serving households appear in tables 1.1, 1.2 and 3.42, and a breakdown by purpose appears in tables 2.5 and 2.6. Definitions of the purpose categories are given in SNA classification 5.4

(b) *Resident households.* What is wanted as a component of the final uses of gross domestic product is the final consumption expenditure of resident households. What is most commonly available in the statistics, however, is not expenditure of resident units but expenditure in the domestic market. To adjust expenditure in the domestic market to expenditure of resident units, purchases abroad and net gifts in kind received from abroad have been added, and subtracted are purchases in the domestic market of non-resident units. Corresponding adjustments are made to exports (to ensure that they include purchases of non-residents in the domestic market) and to imports (to ensure that they include purchases of residents abroad). These adjustments include expenditures by tourists, ships' crews, border and seasonal workers and diplomatic and military personnel on goods and services, including local transportation, but they exclude expenditures reimbursible as travel expenses (which are counted as intermediate consumption). These adjustments are shown in tables 2.5 and 2.6.

Household final consumption expenditure includes outlays on non-durable and durable goods and services, *less* sales of second-hand goods and of scraps and wastes. In addition to market purchases, household final consumption expenditure includes the imputed gross rent of owner-occupied dwellings, food and other items produced on own account and consumed, and items provided as wages and salaries in kind by an employer, such as food, shelter or clothing, and other fringe benefits included in compensation of employees, except those considered to add to household saving. The imputed gross rent of owner-occupied dwellings should, in principle, be valued at the rent of similar facilities on the market but has been approximated by costs, including operating maintenance and repair charges, depreciation, mortgage interest, and interest on the owner's equity. Other non-marketed output included in final consumption is valued at producers' prices.

Total resident final consumption expenditure appears in tables 1.1, 1.2, 1.6 and 1.12. It is broken down by institutional subsectors in tables 3.32, and in tables 4.7 and 4.8 it is broken down by industrial origin. A detailed breakdown by type of good is shown in tables 2.5 and 2.6. The type-of-good categories are defined in SNA classification 6.1.

4. Gross capital formation

Gross capital formation is the sum of the increase in stocks and gross fixed capital formation, defined below. It appears in tables 1.1, 1.2 and 1.8. Breakdowns of gross capital formation appear in tables 2.7-2.12, 4.7 and 4.8. Gross capital formation of individual institutional sectors appears in tables 3.13, 3.23, 3.33, and 3.43.

(a) *Increase in stocks.* This flow includes the value of the physical change in (a) stocks of raw materials, work in progress and finished goods held by private producers, and (b) stocks of strategic materials held by the government. Work put in place on buildings and other structures, roads and other construction projects is treated as gross fixed capital formation rather than increase in stocks but is distinguished separately there to facilitate analysis. Increases in livestock raised for slaughter should be included in the increase in stocks, but breeding and draft animals, dairy cattle, and animals raised for wool clips are treated as fixed capital. The physical change in stocks during a period of account should be valued at average purchasers' prices during the period. In some cases, the available data relate to the change in the value of stocks held rather than the value of the physical change.

A classification of the increase in stocks by type is given in tables 2.7 and 2.8, and defined in SNA classification 6.2. The increase in stocks by kind of activity of owner is shown in tables 2.9 and 2.10.

(b) *Gross capital formation.* This flow is defined to include purchases and own-account production of new producers' durable goods, reduced by net sales to the rest of the world of similar second-hand or scrapped goods. Outlays of producers of government services for military purposes (except on land and certain civilian-type items, such as schools, hospitals, family-type housing and, in some cases, roads when for civilian use) are, however, considered to be current expenditures. "Military purposes" are here construed in terms of final expenditures: they include the military airport, but not the bulldozer used in constructing the airport. Gross fixed capital formation includes outlays on reclamation and improvement of land and development and extension of timber tracts, mines, plantations, orchards,

vineyards etc., and on breeding and dairy cattle, draft animals, and animals raised for wool. Outlays on alteration or extension of fixed assets, which significantly extend their life or increase their productivity, are included, but outlays on repair and maintenance to keep fixed assets in good working order are not. All costs are included that are directly connected with the acquisition and installation of the fixed assets, such as customs duties and other indirect taxes, transport, delivery and installation charges, site clearing, planning and designing costs, legal fees and other transfer costs with respect to transactions in land, mineral deposits, timber tracts etc. However, the costs of financing, such as flotation costs, underwriters' commissions and the cost of advertising bond issues, are excluded; these items are included in intermediate consumption. The acquisition of fixed assets is to be recorded at the moment that the ownership of the goods passes to the buyer. In the case of construction projects, this is taken to be the time that the work is put in place but, as noted above, uncompleted construction projects are shown separately from completed ones.

A classification of fixed assets by type is given in tables 2.7 and 2.8, and the categories are defined in SNA classification 6.3. A classification by kind of activity of purchaser is given in tables 2.9, 2.10, 2.11 and 2.12, and a classification by producing industry is given in tables 4.7 and 4.8. Breakdowns by institutional sector are given in tables 3.13, 3.23, 3.33 and 3.43.

5. Exports of goods and services

Exports of goods and services are defined to be parallel to the definition of imports given above, and they are shown in the same tables and classifications. Exports are, however, valued f.o.b., whereas imports are valued c.i.f.

III. Cost components and income shares

1. Value added and gross domestic product

The value added of industries at producers' prices is equal to the gross output of the industries at producers' prices *less* the value of their intermediate consumption at purchasers' prices. Value added for the total of all domestic producers (*plus* import duties and value added tax which are not included in the value added of any domestic producer, and *less* imputed bank service charges which are deducted in a single line) is equal to the gross domestic product is shown in tables 1.9-1.11, and 4.1 - 4.2. Gross domestic product may be defined alternatively as the sum of final expenditures in the domestic economy (tables 1.1 and 1.2) or as the sum of incomes received in the domestic economy (tables 1.3, 1.9 and 4.3). In principle, all three methods should yield the same result but in statistical practice there are likely to be small discrepancies. Such statistical discrepancies are shown where they exist.

2. *Compensation of employees*

Compensation of employees appears in SNA as a domestic concept and as a national concept. Table 1.3 employs the domestic concept, that is, compensation of employees paid by resident producers. This includes payments to non-resident employees working in the country but excludes payments to resident employees temporarily working abroad. In order to show the relation of this concept to compensation received by resident households (shown in tables 1.6 and 3.32) and compensation paid to the rest of the world (shown in tables 1.7 and 3.51), the two components are shown separately in table 1.3. Each component includes (a) wages and salaries, (b) employers' contributions to social security schemes and (c) employers' contributions to private pension, insurance and similar schemes. The national concept of compensation of employees is shown in the household sector income and outlay account (tables 1.6 and 3.31), where compensation received by resident households from domestic producers and that received from the rest of the world are gathered together. The portion paid by resident producers appears in table 1.3; that paid by the rest of the world appears in table 1.7.

Wages and salaries include all payments to employees for their labour, whether in cash or in kind, before deduction of employee contributions to social security schemes, withholding taxes and the like. They include commissions, bonuses and tips, and cost of living, vacation and sick leave allowances paid directly by the employers to the employee but exclude reimbursement for travel and other expenses incurred by employees for business purposes, which is included in intermediate consumption. The pay and allowances of members of the armed forces, the fees, salaries and bonuses of members of boards of directors, managing directors, executives and other employees of incorporated enterprises and the fees of ministers of religion are included. Wages and salaries in kind are valued at their cost to the employer, and include goods and services furnished to employees free of charge or at markedly reduced cost that are clearly and primarily of benefit to the employees as consumers.

Employers' contributions to social security schemes include all social security contributions that employers make on behalf of their employees, but not the employees' own share of such contributions. Social security contributions may be broader than payments to social security funds, since not all social security arrangements are funded.

Employers' contributions to pension, insurance and similar schemes include paid and imputed contributions by employers on behalf of their employees to private funds, reserves or other schemes for providing pensions, family allowances, lay-off and severance pay, maternity leave, workmen's compensation, health and other casualty insurance life insurance and the like. Where employers make payments to employees for such benefits without the establishment a formal fund for this purpose, the contributions that would be required to support such a fund are imputed both here and subsequently as an imputed transfer from households to their employers, since of course the employees do not control the use of the fund.

3. *Operating surplus*

Operating surplus is the balancing item in the SNA production account. For an individual establishment, it is defined as the excess of value added over the sum of compensation of employees, consumption of fixed capital, and net indirect taxes. The operating surplus of all types of establishments -- corporate, quasi-corporate, and unincorporated, public and private -- is included in the figure shown in table 1.3. Operating surplus for each of the institutional sectors individually is shown in tables 3.11, 3.21 and 3.31; its breakdown by kind of activity is shown in table 4.3 . It is also included in the totals for property and entrepreneurial income shown in tables 1.4, 1.5 and 1.6.

4. *Consumption of fixed capital*

Consumption of fixed capital includes allowances for normal wear and tear, foreseen obsolescence and probable (normally expected) accidental damage to fixed capital not made good by repair, all valued at current replacement cost. Unforeseen obsolescence, damages due to calamities, and depletion of natural resources are not included, since these are capital losses and should appear as changes in the balance sheet. Also not included is the revaluation of past allowances for consumption of fixed capital due to changes in the current replacement cost of fixed assets; this also will appear as part of the change in accumulated allowances shown in the balance sheet. Total consumption of fixed capital appears in tables 1.3, 1.8 and 1.12, consumption of fixed capital of individual institutional sectors in tables 3.11, 3.21, 3.31 and 3.41, and consumption of fixed capital by kind of activity in table 4.3. The accumulated consumption of fixed capital for specific types of assets and kind-of-activity sectors appears as the difference between the gross and net capital stock in tables 2.13-2.16, and for individual institutional sectors it appears in tables 3.15, 3.25, 3.35 and 3.45.

5. *Indirect taxes*

Indirect taxes are defined as taxes chargeable to the cost of production or sale of goods and services. They include (a) import and export duties, (b) excise, sales, entertainment and turnover taxes, (c) real estate and land taxes, unless they are merely an administrative device for collecting income tax, (d) levies on value added and the employment of labour (but not social security contributions), (e) motor-vehicle, driving-test, licence, airport and passport fees, when paid by producers, and (f) the operating surplus of government fiscal monopolies on such items as alcoholic beverages and tobacco (in principle reduced by the normal profit margin of similar business units). In the present publication, indirect taxes paid and subsidies received from supranational organizations (e.g., the European Economic Community) are shown separately. Also, the net treatment of value added taxes recommended by the European Economic Community has been employed.

Unlike all other indirect taxes, SNA does not allocate import duties among producers in tables by kind of activity. Indirect taxes are only allocated to a particular kind of activity where they are levied directly on the output of that activity (e.g., excise duties) or on the process of producing that output (e.g., employment taxes). Import duties, however, are levied on the output of foreign rather than domestic producers, and are therefore shown separately in tables by kind of activity, including tables 1.10, 1.11, 4.1, 4.2, 4.3, 4.5 and 4.6.

Total indirect taxes appear in table 1.3. Indirect taxes paid by individual institutional sectors appear in tables 3.11, 3.21, 3.31, and 3.41. Indirect taxes paid to supranational organizations appear in tables 1.7 and 1.12. Indirect taxes retained by government are shown in table 3.12.

6. Subsidies

Subsidies are grants on current account by the government to (a) private enterprises and public corporations, or (b) unincorporated public enterprises when clearly intended to compensate for losses resulting from the price policies of government. Total subsidies, including those paid by supranational organizations, as well as by government, appear in table 1.3; subsidies paid by supranational organizations in tables 1.7 and 1.12; and those paid by government in tables 1.4 and 3.12. Subsidies received by individual institutional sectors appear in tables 3.21, 3.31 and 3.41.

7. Withdrawals from quasi-corporations

Withdrawals from the entrepreneurial income of quasi-corporations consist of the actual payments made to the proprietors of quasi-corporations from the entrepreneurial income of these units. Entrepreneurial income of quasi-corporations is equal to their income from production (net operating surplus) *plus* their net income (receipts *less* payments) from property. In some cases, the whole of the entrepreneurial income will be treated as if paid out to the proprietors; in other cases, some of it is retained as net saving within the quasi-corporation. Withdrawals from quasi-corporations also include withdrawals from foreign branches

of domestic companies or from domestic branches of foreign companies, since both of these categories are treated as quasi-corporations. The withdrawals may be negative, since proprietors may provide funds to the enterprises to compensate for losses.

SNA assigns separate flow numbers to withdrawals as they appear in the paying sectors (flow 4.4) and in the receiving sectors (flow 4.5). As disbursements, they appear in table 3.22 and as part of a larger total in table 1.5. As receipts, they appear in tables 3.12, 3.22, 3.32 and 3.42, and as parts of the larger total in tables 1.4, 1.5 and 1.6

8. Property income

Property income consists of payments of interest, dividends and land rents and royalties, all of which are assigned separate SNA flow numbers, both as payments and as receipts. Interest is defined as income payable and receivable on financial claims, such as bank and other deposits, bills and bonds, including public debt, and the equity of households in life insurance actuarial reserves and pension funds. Dividends consist of income payable and receivable on corporate equity securities and other forms of participation in the equity of private incorporated enterprises, public corporations and co-operatives. Rent payments include, in addition to net land rent, royalty payments for concessions to exploit mineral deposits or for the use of patents, copyrights, trademarks and the like. They exclude rent payments on machinery and equipment or buildings, which are treated as the purchase of a service rather than property income and appear in gross output of the seller and intermediate consumption of the purchaser. Payments of land rent are always treated as a domestic flow since the foreign owners are, for national accounting purposes, dealt with as residents of the country in which the land is located. When it is not possible to separate rent of buildings and rent of the land on which the buildings stand, the whole flow is attributed to the buildings, that is, excluded from property income and included in intermediate consumption.

Property income paid and received by individual institutional sectors is shown in tables 3.12, 3.22, 3.32 and 3.42. As part of a larger total it appears in the summary tables 1.4, 1.5 and 1.6.

IV. Taxes and unrequited transfers

The categories of taxes and unrequited transfers are classified and defined in SNA classification 7.1. SNA does not provide the full articulation of the to-whom from-whom relationships of these flows, but assigns flow numbers to the various combinations of them used in specific standard tables and accounts. In order to define less ambiguosly the flows used in the present publication, a somewhat fuller listing of individual flow components is used.

xvi

1. *Casualty insurance transactions*

Casualty insurance transactions refer to health, accident fire, theft, unemployment and similar insurance schemes. The total of net premiums for the economy as a whole is equal to the total premiums payable *less* an imputed service charge which in turn is defined to be equal to the difference between premiums and claims. As a consequence, for the economy as a whole, net premiums and claims are equal. However, the total service charge is distributed to sectors of receipt and disbursement in proportion to the total (not net) premiums paid, so that net premiums and claims are not necessarily equal for each sector. In the former SNA, these insurance transactions were considered to be in part capital items, and this practice continues in the accounts of a number of countries. In the revised SNA, however, all casualty insurance transactions, including compensation for capital losses, are considered to be current flows. They are shown in detail in tables 3.12, 3.22, 3.32 and 3.42.

2. *Taxes and other government receipts*

Taxes and other government receipts include direct taxes, compulsory fees, fines and penalties, social security contributions, and other current transfers received by general government.

Direct taxes include two components. Direct taxes on income cover levies by public authorities at regular intervals (except social security contributions) on income from employment, property, capital gains or any other source. Real estate and land taxes are included only if they are merely administrative procedures for the assessment and collection of income tax. Other direct taxes cover levies by public authorities at regular intervals on the financial assets and the net of total worth of enterprises, private non-profit institutions and households, and on the possession or use of goods by households. Direct taxes received are shown in tables 1.4 and 3.2; payments of other sectors are shown in tables 3.22, 3.32 and 3.42.

Compulsory fees are payments to public authorities by households for services that are obligatory and unavoidable in the only circumstances in which they are useful. Examples of such fees are payments by households for driving tests and licenses, airport and court fees and the like. Similar payments by business units are treated as indirect taxes. Fines and penalties, however, include not only those paid by households but also those paid by corporate and quasi-corporate enterprises and private non-profit institutions serving households. They appear in the same tables as direct taxes.

Social security contributions consist of contributions for the account of employees, whether made by employees or by employers on their behalf, to the social security arrangements that are imposed, controlled or financed by the government for the purpose of providing social security benefits for the community or large sections of the community. They appear as receipts in tables 1.4 and 3.12, and as payments in tables 1.6 and 3.32.

Current transfers n.e.c. received by general government consist primarily of transfers received from the rest of the world and imputed employee welfare contributions. Transfers from the rest of the world include grants between governments to finance military outlays, outlays for health and educational purposes, and similar transfers in kind of military equipment, food, clothing etc. Payments and assessments and other periodic contributions to international organizations are also included. In addition to actual transfers, this item also includes imputed transfers arising from the obligation of the government as an employer to pay directly to its employees pensions, family allowances, severance and lay-off pay and other welfare benefits when there is no special fund, reserve or insurance for these purposes. In these circumstances, SNA provides for the establishment of an imputed fund to which imputed contributions are made, of a magnitude sufficient to support the unfunded benefit payments. The imputed contributions are included in compensation of employees, as an addition to actual payments, and are then shown as an imputed payment by the employees back to the government as an employer. These transfers appear in table 1.4 as an aggregate, and in table 3.12 in more detail.

3. *Household transfer receipts*

Household transfer receipts include social security benefits, social assistance grants, and unfunded employee welfare benefits. These flows, in varying detail, are shown in tables 1.6, 2.4 and 3.32.

Social security benefits are payments to individuals under the social security arrangements described above. The payments are often made out of a special fund and may be related to the income of individuals from employment or to contributions to social security arrangements made on their behalf. Examples are unemployment insurance benefits, old-age, disability and survivors' pensions, family allowances and reimbursements for medical and hospital expenses. It may be difficult to distinguish social security benefits from social assistance grants, on the one hand, and insurance benefits, on the other. The main criterion is method of finance; the actual content will vary from country to country. Medical services, for instance, may be supplied as social assistance, as a part of social security, as a casualty insurance benefit, or as a free government service.

Social assistance grants are cash grants to individuals and households, except social security benefits and unfunded employee welfare benefits. They may be made by public authorities, private non-profit institutions, or corporate and quasi-corporate enterprises. Examples are relief payments;

widows', guardians' and family allowances and payments of medical and dental expenses which are not part of social insurance schemes; war bonuses, pensions and service grants; and scholarships, fellowships and maintenance allowances for educational, training and similar purposes. They include payments made by public authorities for services provided by business enterprises and private non-profit institutions directly and individually to persons, whether these payments are made to the individuals or directly to the providers of the services that the persons are considered to have purchased. They exclude, however, transfers to persons or households as indemnities for property losses during floods, wars and similar calamities; these are considered to be capital items.

Unfunded employee welfare benefits are pensions, family allowances, severance and lay-off pay, maternity leave pay, workmen's and disability compensation and reimbursements for medical expenses and other casualties which employers pay directly to their former or present employees when there is no special fund, reserve or insurance for these purposes.

4. *Transfers received by private non-profit institutions*

Transfers received by private non-profit institutions serving households include grants and gifts, in cash and in kind, to non-profit institutions serving households which are intended to cover partially the cost of the provision of services by these institutions. They also include membership dues paid to political organizations, fraternal bodies and the like. They appear as a receipt in table 3.42, and as payments sometimes as part of a larger total, in tables 3.12, 3.22 and 3.32.

5. *Other current transfers n.e.c.*

Other current transfers n.e.c. include transfers to and from resident sectors that are not specifically included in any other flows. They may include migrants' remittances, transfers of immigrants' personal and household goods, and transfers between resident and non-resident households, in cash and in kind. They include allowances for bad debts.

V. *Finance of gross accumulation*

1. *Net saving*

Net saving is the balancing item in the SNA income and outlay account. It is defined as the difference between current receipts and current disbursements. Net saving for the nation as a whole appears in tables 1.8 and 1.12. Net saving for individual institutional sectors appears in tables 3.12, 3.13, 3.22, 3.23, 3.32, 3.33, 3.42 and 3.43.

2. *Surplus of the nation on current transactions*

The surplus of the nation on current transactions is the balancing item in the external transactions current accounts (tables 1.7 and 3.51). It also appears in table 1.8, the capital transactions account, in table 1.12, the table showing relationships among the national accounting aggregates, and table 3.52, the external transactions capital accumulation account.

3. *Purchases of land, net*

Purchases of land, net, include purchases *less* sales of land, subsoil deposits, forests and inland waters, including any improvements that are an integral part of these assets except buildings and other structures. The purchases and sales are valued at the transaction (sales) price of the land, forests etc., not including the transfer costs involved; such transfer costs are included in gross capital formation. Purchases and sales are assumed to take place when the legal title to the land is passed. They are considered to take place between resident institutions only. Where the land is purchased by a non-resident, a nominal resident institution is considered to be the owner of the land. The foreign owner is assigned equity in the resident institution equivalent to the purchase price of the land. The value recorded in the flow is the same for both the buyer and the seller. For the country as a whole, therefore, purchases and sales will cancel out. If the sales value of the structures situated on the land cannot be separated from the sales value of the land itself, the entire transaction should be recorded as a purchase and sale of structures (i.e., of second-hand assets), unless the structures are intended for immediate demolition. Purchases of land appear in the capital accumulation accounts of the individual institutional sectors, (tables 3.13, 3.23, 3.33 and 3.43.

4. *Purchases of intangible assets, net*

Purchases of intangible assets, net, are defined as purchases, *less* sales, of exclusive rights to mineral, fishing and other concessions and of patents, copyrights etc. These transactions involve the once-and-for-all relinquishment and acquisition of the exclusive rights, although they may be paid for over a period of years; they do not include concessions, leases, licences to use patents and permission to publish copyrighted materials which involve the periodic payment of royalties or rents, with eventual reversion of the rights to the seller. The purchases and sales are valued at the transaction (sales) value of the mineral concession, lease, patent, etc., not including any transfer costs involved. (The transfer costs are included in gross capital formation.) Purchases of intangible assets appear in the individual institutional sector capital accumulation accounts (tables 3.13, 3.23, 3.33, and 3.43) as a part of gross accumulation. Purchases from the rest of the world appear in table 3.52.

5. *Capital transfers*

Capital transfers are defined as unrequited transfers, in cash or in kind, which are used for purposes of capital formation or other forms of capital accumulation, are made out of wealth, or are non-recurrent. Examples of capital transfers are grants from one government to another to finance deficits in external trade, investment grants, unilateral transfers of capital goods, legacies, death duties and inheritance taxes, migrants' transfers of financial assets and indemnities in respect of calamities. Mixed transfers, considered by one party to the transaction as capital and the other as current, are treated as capital. Capital transfers appear in tables 3.13, 3.23, 3.33, 3.43 and 3.52.

6. *Net lending*

Net lending is defined as the excess of the sources of finance of accumulation (i.e., net saving, consumption of fixed capital and capital transfers received) over the uses of these funds for gross capital formation, net purchases of land and intangibles, and capital transfers paid. It appears in the capital accumulation accounts of the individual institutional sectors (tables 3.13, 3.23, 3.33 and 3.43), and in the external transactions capital accumulation account (table 3.52). Net lending is also equal to the difference between a sector's net acquisition of financial assets and its net incurrence of financial liabilities. It thus also appears in the institutional sector capital finance accounts (tables 3.14, 3.24, 3.34, 3.44 and 3.53). Although not for all countries, net lending derived in these two different ways are statistically identical.

VI. *Financial assets and liabilities*

Net acquisition of financial assets is defined as the difference between, on the one hand, acquisitions or purchases and, on the other, relinquishment or sales by given transactors of financial claims on second parties. Net incurrence of liabilities is equal to the issue or sale *less* redemption or payment of financial claims of second parties. A classification and definitions of financial assets and liabilities is given in SNA classification 7.2. Changes in financial assets and liabilities for individual institutional sectors appear in the capital finance accounts (tables 3.14, 3.24, 3.34, 3.44 and 3.53). Their total amount is shown in the sector balance sheets (tables 3.15, 3.25, 3.35 and 3.45).

VII. *Other assets*

1. *Reproducible tangible assets*

Reproducible tangible assets are classified and defined in table 5.1 of the *Provisional Guidelines on National and Sector Balance Sheets and Reconciliation Accounts of the System of National Accounts.* [4] They appear, classified by type of asset and broad sector, in tables 2.13 and 2.14, by kind of activity in tables 2.15 and 2.16 and for individual institutional sectors, in the sector balance sheets in tables 3.15, 3.25, 3.35 and 3.45

2. *Non-reproducible tangible assets*

Non-reproducible tangible assets are classified and defined in table 5.2 of the *Provisional Guidelines* (see above). Only the total appears in the tables, in the sector balance sheets (tables 3.15, 3.25, and 3.45).

3. *Non-financial intangible assets*

Non-financial intangible assets include the mineral, fishing and other concessions, leases, patents, copyrights etc., the purchase and sale of which is recorded in the capital accumulation account. These intangible assets are created at the time of the purchase or sale, that is, when a once-and-for-all lump-sum payment has been made for the lease, concession, patent or copyright. They appear in the sector balance sheets (tables 3.15, 3.25, 3.35 and 3.45).

---

[1]   *Official records of the Economic and Social Council, Forty-fourth Session, Supplement No. 10,* (E/4471), paras. 8-24.

[2]   The present system is published in *A System of National Accounts,* Studies in Methods, Series F, No. 2, Rev. 3 (United Nations publication, Sales No. E.69.XVII.3).

[3]   *Ibid*

[4]   Statistical Papers, Series M, No. 60 United Nations publication, Sales No. 77.XVII.10.

[5]   Statistical Papers, Series M, No. 4, Rev. 2, Add. 1 (United Nations publication, Sales No. E.71.XVII.8).

[6]   Statistical Papers, Series M, No. 70 (United Nations publication, Sales No. 80.XVII.17).

II. SYSTEM OF MATERIAL PRODUCT BALANCES (MPS)

The System of Material Product Balances (MPS) furnishes the means for standardizing the national accounting data which the Statistical Office of the the Department of International Economic and Social Affairs of the United Nations Secretariat receives from countries with centrally planned economies. Data collection follows the principles found in the *Basic Methodological Rules for the Compilation of the Statistical Balance of the National Economy.* [1] This system is also described in the *Basic Principles of the System of Balances of the National Economy.* [2]

A. STRUCTURE OF MPS

MPS is based on a system of balances. It includes material and financial balances, the balance of manpower resources and the balance of fixed capital and indicators of national wealth. The material balance is a presentation of the volume of the supply of goods and material services originating in domestically produced global product and imports and their disposition to consumption, capital formation and exports, classified by different production activity categories. The financial balance is a presentation of income flows generated in production in the material sphere, their redistribution through transactions in the non-material sphere and through other transfers flows and, finally, their disbursement to consumption and capital formation. The income flows of the financial balance are classified by institutional (social) sectors. The presentation is therefore comparable to that of production, income and outlay and capital finance accounts by institutional sectors in the System of National Accounts (SNA). The third type of balance, that is, the manpower balance, presents the allocation of available manpower to production activities and institutional or social sectors. This balance is expressed in the number of persons employed. The last balance is the one of national wealth and capital assets. It is a presentation of the volume of the stocks of tangible fixed and other assets available at the beginning and the end of the year and the increase that has taken place during the year. The tangible assets are classified by type of asset and by form of ownership and production activities of the national economy.

The MPS tables that are presented in chapter III and are listed in the introduction provide further detail on the material balances. Table 1 on net material product by use is similar to the SNA table on gross domestic product by kind of economic activity. Data regarding the production and goods and services transactions are included in tables 2, 3, 4 and 5 which present, respectively, activity breakdowns of net material product and of primary incomes, of the population and of enterprises, a breakdown by socio-economic sectors of these two types of primary incomes, and a breakdown of

supply and disposition of goods and material services by kind of activity of the producers. Tables 6, 7, 8 and 9 present further details on the expenditure categories, such as a breakdown of fixed capital formation by kind of economic activity and by socio-economic sector and of increases in material circulating assets and of stocks by kind of activity, and a classification of final consumption, personal consumption and of total consumption of the population by type of expenditure.

B. DIFFERENCES BETWEEN MPS AND SNA

Apart from the differences in structure of the two systems, there are considerable differences between the coverage of the concepts used in MPS and in SNA. Since these differences limit the use of MPS and SNA data in cross-country types of analyses, a summary of those that are relevant to the MPS data published in chapter III of the present publication is reproduced below. [3]

1. *The treatment of material and non-material services*

In MPS there is a distinction different to that made in SNA, between the production of material and non-material services. Only the production of material services, together with that of goods, is covered by the gross output (global product) concept of MPS. The production of non-material services is excluded. Material goods and services used as input in the production of non-material services are considered to be a part of final consumption expenditure, while income flows resulting from this type of production are treated as income transfers. The material services are those that are directly linked to the production of goods and cover the services related to the repair, transportation and distribution of goods. All other services are treated as non-material services. This important difference between MPS and the present SNA results in the following concrete differences between the two systems:

(a) Expenditures by enterprises on cultural, sports and similar facilities for their employees are excluded in MPS from intermediate consumption. Instead, a transfer between enterprises and households is included, while the material goods and services involved in the above expenditures are allocated to final consumption of the population. SNA treats these expenditures as intermediate consumption;

(b) Depreciation of dwellings and other material goods and services involved in the provision of housing are allocated in MPS to final consumption expenditure. Since these are non-material services, no value-added contribution is included in net material product. In SNA, this contribution is included in gross domestic product;

(c) Travel expenses in connection with business are not included in intermediate consumption in MPS as they are in the present SNA. Instead, they are treated as a part of compensation of employees and the material goods and services involved are allocated to private final consumption expenditure;

(d) In SNA and MPS a different distinction is drawn between uniforms to be treated as intermediate consumption and those to be included in compensation of employees and final consumption expenditure of households. In SNA, the distinction is drawn between civilian (intermediate consumption) and military uniforms and in MPS, between dress and working uniforms;

(e) Tips are treated in SNA as a part of compensation of employees, while in MPS they are treated as income transfers, when they exceed the normal service charge.

2. *Capital formation*

The MPS and SNA guidelines differ, on the one hand, with regard to the treatment of capital gains and losses and the coverage of depreciation and, on the other, in the coverage of fixed capital formation and increases in stocks. The main differences are the following:

(a) In MPS, depreciation, as well as the replacement for losses due to certain foreseeable and non-forseeable damages to fixed assets and stocks, including those caused by accidents and calamities, are deducted in order to arrive at net fixed capital formation. In SNA, generally uses the concept of gross fixed capital formation only is generally used. However, if net capital formation were to be estimated, only depreciation on fixed assets would have to be deducted in that system. Losses in stocks or fixed assets would never be considered for deduction. Losses on fixed assets would be treated as capital losses and dealt with outside the national accounts flows, while losses in stocks would be treated as a part of intermediate consumption or as capital losses, depending on whether they are due to normal events in production or to calamities. The dividing line between losses and depreciation of fixed assets also differs in the two systems. In SNA, depreciation is assumed to cover, among other things, the average amount of accidental damage to fixed assets that is not made good by repair or replacement of parts--for example, damage arising from fire and accidents. In MPS, such damages are not reflected in depreciation but covered under losses;

(b) Depreciation in MPS is based on the original cost of the assets. However, every eight to ten years, adjustments to replacement cost are made to this asset value and these adjustments are also reflected in a corrected value of depreciation. Furthermore, differences that arise between the actual value and the written-off book value at the moment the assets are scrapped or sold are included in the value of depreciation for the year in which the sale or scrapping occurs. In SNA, instead, the replacement value of the assets is used as a basis for depreciation. Any change in this value, whether it happens at the moment the asset is sold or during the time it is used, is considered to be a capital gain or loss and is not accounted for in the national accounting flows;

(c) In addition, in MPS, depreciation includes capital consumption allowances with respect to afforestation, land improvements, roads, bridges and similar structures. In SNA, no imputations for depreciation of this type of asset are included;

(d) Expenditures on fixed assets for military purposes are treated in MPS as a part of net fixed capital formation. In SNA, these outlays are allocated to government final consumption expenditure, except for outlays by government on the construction and alteration of family dwellings for personnel of the armed forces, which are included in gross fixed capital formation;

(e) Transfer cost with regard to purchases and sales of existing fixed assets are treated in MPS as transfers since these are non-material services. In SNA, these costs are included in gross fixed capital formation;

(f) Work put in place on structures, roads, dams, ports and other forms of construction is allocated in MPS to increases in material circulating assets and stocks. Only when the construction is finished is its total value transferred to net fixed capital formation. In SNA, these outlays are immediately allocated to gross fixed capital formation.

3. *External transactions*

The third area in which MPS and SNA differ is in the coverage of exports and imports of goods and services, in the distinction between residents and non-residents and in the treatment of monetary, as opposed to non-monetary gold. The differences are the following:

(a) In MPS, embassies, consulates and international bodies are treated as residents of the country in which they are located, while in SNA they are treated as residents of the country they represent. This difference in the residence concept has consequences for the allocation between countries of capital formation and government final consumption expenditure and also for the allocation of the income flows. Wages and salaries paid to local employees of these extraterritorial bodies are not included in SNA concept of gross domestic product. They are dealt with, however, as factor income from abroad and therefore accounted for in the national income concept in SNA. In MPS, such wages and salaries, if earned in the sphere of material production, are included in primary incomes of the population, as well as in net material product;

(b) In MPS, the territorial concept of final consumption expenditure, which includes purchases by non-residents in the domestic market and excludes purchases abroad by residents, is used. As a result, such flows are not accounted for in exports or imports. On the other hand, it does include, in exports and imports, transactions that, though they take place in the domestic market, are conducted in foreign currency. These transactions are treated as if they were transactions with non-residents. In SNA, the national concept of final consumption expenditure is used; taken into account in exports and imports, respectively, are the direct purchases in the domestic market by non-residents and the direct purchases abroad by non-residents. Furthermore, no distinction is made in SNA between transactions that are conducted in local or in foreign currency;

(c) Purchases and sales by external trade organizations of goods that do not cross the border of the country in question and also imported goods that are re-exported without being processed are treated in MPS as part of respectively, imports and exports. In SNA, they are not accounted for in the export and import flows, except for the margins received by resident units as payments for services rendered;

(d) Gifts in kind by households to and from abroad are included in exports and imports in SNA. In MPS, they are excluded from these flows;

(e) Transactions in intangible assets (patents, copyrights, trade-marks, exclusive rights to exploit mineral deposits etc.) with the rest of the world are included in MPS in exports and imports. In SNA, they are treated as property income or as sales or purchases of intangible assets to or from abroad, depending on whether the payment is for the use of the rights or for the outright transfer of those rights;

(f) Transactions with the rest of the world in monetary and non-monetary gold are included in MPS in exports and imports. In SNA, included in exports and imports are actual transactions in non-monetary gold only. Exports in addition include newly mined gold (whether actually exported or not) in order to transform gold as a commodity into a financial asset.

C. STANDARD CLASSIFICATIONS OF MPS

Two classifications are used in the MPS standard tables presented, that is, the kind-of-activity classification and the classification by socio-economic group. Contrary to SNA usage with respect to the activity and institutional classifications for different groups of transactions, the two MPS classifications are parallel ones that are applied to the same transaction categories: net material product and its component primary incomes and capital formation. Each of these classifications is described briefly below.

1. *Kind of activity*

All forms of activity in production are classified according to groups or branches, depending on the nature and

results of the application of labour. The two major categories constitute branches of the material sphere and branches of the non-material sphere. The first category covers the production of goods, and services that are related to the production of goods, such as repair services, transportation services and goods distribution services. The second category includes the remaining services-producing activities. Each of the two categories is further broken down by branches which are similar in character to the ISIC categories used in SNA. The unit of classification is not the organizational unit (i.e., enterprise) but a smaller unit that performs one type of activity (i.e., establishment). If an enterprise or institution or other organizational unit carries on more than one type of economic activity, it is considered to consist of two or more establishments that perform different activities.

For the subclassification of net material product by kind of activity, only the activity breakdown of the material sphere is used since net material product originates in this sphere only. For capital formation, however, the activity categories of the non-material sphere are also used, since capital formation relates not only to the material sphere but also to non-material branches.

A rough correspondence based on the names of the activity categories can be established between the activity categories presented in SNA and in the MPS branches. The user should be aware, however, of the limitations that such a linkage may entail, as indicated in the following points:

(a) Mining and quarrying, manufacturing, and electricity, gas and water are shown as three separate categories in the SNA presentation and as one category (industrial production), in the MPS presentation;

(b) Hunting and the collection of forestry products is treated as a part of agriculture in the SNA presentation and as a part of forestry and logging in MPS;

(c) The distribution of gas, electricity and water to households is treated in MPS as a non-material service (including in housing). This activity is therefore not reflected in net material product, while its capital formation is dealt with as capital formation of the non-material sphere. In SNA, these distribution activities are an integral part of the activity category for electricity, gas and water;

(d) Printing and publishing, which is treated as a material activity in MPS, is allocated to the MPS category known as "other activities of the material sphere". In SNA, this activity is included with manufacturing;

(e) Cleaning, dyeing and repair services are included with industrial activity (manufacturing) in the MPS presentation and with community, social and personal services in SNA;

(f) In comparing the activity breakdown of net material product and gross domestic product, the user should be aware that the coverage of the MPS category known as "other activities of the material sphere" falls far short of the combined coverage of the two SNA categories for finance, insurance, real estate and business services and for community, social and personal services. The SNA categories include all non-material activities that are excluded from the MPS coverage of net material product. In addition, the shifts between activity categories that were outlined in the previous points affect this group. Other activities in the presentation of net material product include telegraph, news-gathering and editorial agencies, industrial services other than architectural design services, printing and publishing services, the production of motion pictures, phonograph records and prerecorded tapes, data-processing and tabulating services, waterway-maintenance services and the operation of flood-control systems, and services related to the conservation of natural resources and the protection of the environment.

2. Socio-economic sectors

The rates of development of the national economy and the basic features of production that support this development are largely determined by the social structure of the community. In order to study the process, the various activities involved in the production of material goods and services are classified in MPS by socio-economic sector. This classification is based on the form of ownership of the fixed and circulating capital. The form of ownership of the means of production determines the forms of ownership of the product and of the incomes generated by its disposal.

The basic socio-economic sectors are the socialist sector and the private sector.

The socialist sector embraces the enterprises and institutions in public, socialist ownership. The fixed and circulating assets of these enterprises are public property. The socialist sector also includes the personal plots of employees and members of co-operatives.

Within the socialist sector, the following socio-economic subsectors are distinguished: the state subsector; the co-operative subsector, which includes agricultural producers' co-operatives; associations; personal plots of employees; personal plots of members of co-operatives.

The state subsector includes the enterprises and institutions in state ownership. The State furnishes them with the fixed and circulating assets required for their operation. These economic units are administratively subordinated to central or local organs of state authority. The production of the state subsector and the income generated in it belong to the people as a country.

The co-operative subsector embraces the enterprises and institutions in collective or group onwership. The fixed and circulating assets of these economic bodies are originally built up from the entrance fees (initiation fees) of their members and the proceeds of sales of shares to them; and are later supplemented from part of their operating surplus. The output and income of the enterprises and institutions of the co-operative subsector are the property of their members.

The association subsector includes the enterprises and institutions owned by voluntary or semi-voluntary associations. The fixed and circulating assets of the economic bodies of this subsector are built up from the voluntary contributions of their members and from part of the operating surplus of such bodies. The output and income of this subsector belong to the associations.

The personal plots of employees and members of co-operatives embrace agricultural output, construction and other forms of activity (gathering of wild fruits and berries, scrap collection etc.).

The private sector includes the enterprises and institutions, the fixed and circulating assets of which are privately owned. The classification of enterprises and institutions of the private sector is based on the specific economic conditions in the country concerned. Within this sector, the subsector of craftsmen, artisans and peasants who are not members of co-operatives may be distinguished.

Peasants, craftsmen and artisans who do not belong to co-operatives operate small private ventures in which the productive process is carried out by their owners in person, as a rule without recourse to hired labour. This group also includes the subsidiary activities of the population occupied in the private sector of the national economy.

D. DEFINITIONS OF FLOWS

Given below are the definitions of the flows that appear in the MPS standard tables of chapter III. To make possible a comparison between SNA and MPS data, a description of the differences between the MPS and the SNA coverage is added to each of the sections. The items needed in order to convert the MPS coverage into a coverage that conforms to the SNA definition are only summarily indicated. For more information on these items, the user is therefore referred to the description of the differences between the two systems in section B above. The items described below have been grouped together into categories similar to those used for the SNA flows (see chap. I above, sect. C).

I. Total supply and disposition of goods and material services

1. Gross output

Global product covers the value of goods and material services produced. Deliveries of goods and material services within the same enterprise are generally excluded. Included are, among other things, the value of own-account constructed capital goods and capital repairs to fixed assets, the value of work-in-progress and the value of finished goods added to stocks. Covered is, furthermore, the value of goods and material services provided free to employees (the material services are valued at the material cost involved). Included in the contribution to global product by agriculture are seeds and feed produced and consumed at the same farm and agricultural and other goods produced on personal plots for own consumption or for sale, including the cost of their processing. This concept of gross output appears in MPS table 5.

To derive gross output in producers' prices as defined in SNA, global product as described above needs to be increased by:

plus: the gross output value of non-material services (including those of government), including the transfer cost on purchases and sales of existing second-hand fixed assets and land.

2. *Trade margins and transport charges*

The gross output of material goods and services is valued at both producers' and purchasers' values. The difference between the two sets of values gives the distributive trade margins (including restaurants, cafés and other catering) and the transportation margins. The gross output of the distributive-trade units is equal to the value of their gross margins on internal and external trade.

The gross margins on external trade are equivalent to the sum in domestic currency of (a) the value of imports of goods and material services in the domestic market *less* the actual value at which these imports are purchased from abroad and (b) the actual value at which exports of goods and material services are sold to abroad *less* the value of these exports in the domestic market. Trade margins and transport charges appear in MPS table 5.

3. *Intermediate material consumption, including depreciation*

Intermediate material consumption consists of the value of the goods and material services used up in the process of production during a period of account by units of the material sphere, including the consumption of fixed assets during the period. Consistent with the scope of the gross output of goods and material services included in intermediate consumption are certain items, for example, seeds and animal feed, which are produced and used by the same unit. The intermediate output of raw materials etc., is valued net of the value of scraps and wastes originating in the process of production. Purchased items are valued at purchasers' values; items produced on own account are valued at cost in the case of state and co-operative enterprises and at average pur-

chasers' prices in the case of personal plots of households. This concept of intermediate material consumption appears in MPS table 5.

Depreciation or consumption of fixed assets includes an allowance for normal wear and tear and foreseen obsolescence of fixed assets based on standard rates of depreciation and, furthermore, the difference between the book value of scrapped fixed assets and their scrap value. The allowances for depreciation are often based on the original cost of the assets which may be periodically adjusted to replacement cost.

To arrive from intermediate material consumption, including depreciation as defined above, at the SNA concept of intermediate consumption, the MPS coverage needs to be increased and decreased by the following items:

plus: (i) material cost of non-material services;

plus: (ii) material expenditures by enterprises on cultural, sports and similar facilities for their employees;

plus: (iii) reimbursable expenditures for material goods and services purchased during business trips;

minus: (iv) consumption of fixed capital in the material sphere.

4. *Personal consumption*

This consists of all consumer goods, irrespective of durability, and material services (repair, transport, communication and similar services) which are purchased by households, received in kind as payment for work in state and collective enterprises and in private plots, or produced on own account on personal plots. Excluded is the purchase by households of dwellings (which is dealt with as capital formation) but included is the maintenance and depreciation of dwellings. Also included are reimbursable expenditures for material goods and services purchased during business trips. This concept of personal consumption appears in MPS tables 1 and 7. It appears according to source of supply of goods and material services in MPS table 8. In MPS, the domestic concept of consumption is used, so that direct purchases by foreign tourists, diplomatic personnel and other non-residents in the domestic market are included, while similar purchases abroad by residents are excluded.

5. *Material consumption in the units of the non-material sphere serving individuals*

This flow covers expenditures on non-durable goods and material services by units of the non-material sphere serving individuals, reduced by the increases in their stocks of goods. Also included is consumption of fixed assets used by these units. It appears in MPS tables 1 and 7.

6. *Material consumption in the units of the non-material sphere serving the community as a whole*

This flow consists of non-durable goods and material services purchased during a period of account by units of the non-material sphere serving the community as a whole, reduced by the increases in their stocks of goods during the period of account. Also included is consumption of fixed assets of these units. It appears in MPS tables 1 and 7.

To arrive from this concept at government final consumption expenditure as defined in SNA, the following additions to and subtraction from the MPS concept have to be made:

plus: (i) the difference between the value of non-material services produced by government and their material cost and depreciation

plus: (ii) government expenditures on fixed assets that have military uses;

plus: (iii) the difference between consumption expenditures (i.e., material and non-material cost, depreciation and compensation of employees) of extraterritorial bodies that represent the country abroad *minus* consumption expenditures incurred by extraterritorial bodies of other countries and international organizations located in the country in question;

plus: (iv) material expenditures by government (units in the non-material sphere serving individuals) on education, health, culture and other services provided free to individuals.

7. *Final consumption*

This flow is equal to the sum of personal consumption and material consumption in the units of the non-material sphere serving individuals and of those serving the community as a whole. Each of these concepts has been defined above. They appear in MPS tables 5 and 7.

8. *Consumption of the population*

Consumption of the population is the sum of personal consumption and material consumption in the units of the non-material sphere serving individuals. This concept is comparable to private final consumption expenditure in SNA, which can be derived from this MPS concept by adding and subtracting the following items:

plus: (i) the difference between the value of non-material services purchased by households, including housing services and the material cost and depreciation included in the value of these services;

minus: (ii) material expenditures by government (units in the non-material sphere serving individuals) on education, health, culture and other services provided free to individuals;

plus: (iii) the difference between direct purchases abroad by resident households and direct purchases in the domestic market by non-resident households as well as the difference between gifts sent abroad by household *minus* gifts received from abroad;

minus: (iv) reimbursable expenditures for material goods and services purchased during business trips;

minus: (v) material expenditures by enterprises on cultural sports and similar facilities for their employees.

9. *Total consumption of the population*

Total consumption of the population covers the consumption by the population of goods and material services and of non-material services, whether purchased by households or furnished free of charge. It therefore exceeds the consumption of the population (i.e., the sume of personal consumption and material consumption in the units of the non-material sphere serving individuals) by the value of the services of the units of the non-material sphere serving individuals, reduced by the consumption of goods and material services by these units. The value of the services of the units is equivalent to their costs of production, including operating surplus in some instances. In the case of dwellings provided by these units, their depreciation is not included when evaluating costs of production, since charges in respect of depreciation of these dwellings are included in personal consumption. Total consumption of the population appears classified by object in MPS table 9.

10. *Net fixed capital formation*

Net fixed capital formation consists of the value of new fixed assets purchased or constructed on own account and of completed capital repairs to these assets reduced by consumption of fixed assets for renewal of assets and capital repairs, and capital losses due to fire, floods and other calamities and furthermore reduced by the remaining value of scrappled fixed assets. Thus, it measures the net increase in the value of fixed assets during a period of account. This flow appears in MPS tables 5 and 6.

Fixed assets include completed dwellings, buildings and other structures; machinery, equipment and other durable goods acquired by units of the material and non-material sphere; cattle, excluding young cattle and cattle raised for meat; perennial plants; and expenditures on the improvement of land, forests and other natural resources. New fixed assets put into use are generally valued inclusive of acquisition and installation cost.

Capital repairs cover outlays on repairs that make up at least in part for the physical depreciation of the fixed assets and/or significantly raise the capacity and productivity of the fixed assets.

In order to convert the MPS concept of net fixed capital formation into gross fixed capital formation as defined in SNA, the following additions to and substractions from the MPS concept have to be made:

plus: (i) consumption of fixed capital in the material and non-material sphere, including that on afforestation, roads, bridges and similar structures;

plus: (ii) losses due to foreseeable as well as non-foreseeable damages to fixed assets;

plus: (iii) transfer cost with regard to purchases and sales of existing second-hand fixed assets, including land;

plus: (iv) work in progress on the construction of structures, roads, dams and ports on other forms of construction;

plus: (v) the difference between outlays on fixed capital formation by extraterritorial bodies representing the country in question abroad, *less* similar outlays by extraterritorial bodies of other countries and international organizations located in the country in question;

minus: (vi) government expenditures on fixed assets that have military uses.

11. *Gross fixed capital formation*

Gross fixed capital formation is equal to net fixed capital formation as defined above *plus* depreciation. Depreciation is defined in section 3 above, together with intermediate material consumption. Gross fixed capital formation classified by kind of activity appears in MPS table 6.

12. *Increases in material circulating assets and stocks*

This item consists of increases during the period of account in the stocks of enterprises in the material sphere, including wholesale and retail trade units, reduced by losses. Also covered are increases in government stockpiles, including stocks of defense items and state reserves of precious metals and precious stones. The stocks in the material sphere consist of raw materials, fuels, supplies and other non-durable goods; young cattle and cattle raised for meat; work in progress, including uncompleted construction projects; and finished goods not yet sold. Increases in material circulating assets and stocks appear in MPS tables 1 and 6.

In order to convert the MPS concept of increases in material circulating assets and stocks into increases in stocks as defined in SNA, the following addition to and subtractions from the MPS concept are needed:

plus: (i) losses due to foreseeable and non-foreseeable damages to stocks;

minus: (ii) work in progress on the construction of structures, roads, dams and ports and on other forms of construction;

minus: (iii) net increases in the holdings of gold ingots and other monetary gold.

13. *Losses*

This item is the sum of the value of the losses in fixed assets and losses in material circulating assets and stocks.

Included are losses (a) due to fires, floods and other calamities, (b) in adult productive and working cattle, (c) due to abandoned or interrupted construction works and (d) in agricultural products in storage at state and co-operative agricultural enterprises and at farms. This flow appears in MPS tables 1 and 5.

In SNA, this final demand category is not identified separately from gross capital formation.

14. *Exports and imports of goods and material services*

Exports are defined to include: (a) outward-bound goods thast cross the border of the country, including imported goods which are exported without being processed; (b) goods which are purchased outside the country by an external trade organization of the country in question and shipped directly to a third country; (c) outward-bound monetary and non-monetary gold and other precious metals; (d) unilateral transfers of goods by the government and public organizations of the country (uncompensated foreign aid); (e) material services, such as transport, forwarding and communication services, rental, including rental payments for time-charter of ships and other transport equipment and, furthermore, export contract services rendered to other countries. The imports cover the same categories of goods and material services which are inward bound. Exports are valued f.o.b. while imports are valued c.i.f. They appear in MPS tables 1 and 5.

To arrive at the SNA coverage of exports of goods and services, the following additions to and subtractions from the MPS concept are needed:

plus: (i) the difference between the export value of non-material services and the material cost and depreciation included in these services;

plus: (ii) consumption expenditure (material and non-material cost, depreciation and compensation of employees) and outlays on fixed capital formation by extraterritorial bodies of foreign governments and international organizations located in the country in question;

plus: (iii) direct purchases in the domestic market by non-resident households and gifts sent abroad by households;

minus: (iv) sales abroad by an external trade organization of the country of goods that have not crossed the border of the country in question; as well as of goods that have crossed the border but that are re-exported without being processed;

minus: (v) the difference between exported monetary gold and the value of sales of newly produced gold ingots and bars.

MPS imports have to be adjusted in a similar manner. To be added are the import value of non-material services *minus* material cost and depreciation, consumption expenditure and fixed capital formation of extraterritorial bodies that represent the country abroad and direct purchases abroad by residents. To be deducted are re-exports and purchases abroad by external trade organizations of goods that do not cross the border of the country, and also the value of imported monetary gold and gifts received households from abroad.

III. *Cost components and income shares*

1. *Net material product*

Net material product is defined in MPS and is used in countries with centrally planned economies. It can be estimated from the production income and expenditure side in the same manner, as is indicated in chapter I above, section C.III, in which the SNA coverage of gross domestic product is described. Following the production approach, net material product is the difference between global product (i.e., gross output) of goods and material services and intermediate material consumption, including consumption of fixed assets. Net material product defined from the income side is the sum of primary incomes of the population (comparable to compensation of employees in SNA) and primary incomes of enterprises (comparable to operating surplus in SNA). The expenditure approach finally defines net material product as the sum of the final uses of goods and material services, that is, personal consumption, and material consumption of units in the non-material sphere serving individuals and that of similar units serving the community as a whole, net capital formation (i.e., net of depreciation), replacement for losses and the balance between exports and imports of goods and material services. These three different methods for deriving net material product are shown in MPS tables 1, 2 and 4.

To arrive at the SNA concept of gross domestic product, net material product needs to be increased and reduced as follows:

plus: (i) the excess value of non-material services (i.e., the gross output value *minus* material cost and depreciation) consumed by households and by government *plus* the difference between these excess values of exported and imported non-material services;

minus: (ii) material expenditures by enterprises on cultural, sports and similar facilities for their employees;

minus: (iii) reimbursable expenditures for material goods and services purchased during business trips;

plus: (iv) consumption of fixed capital in the material and non-material sphere, including that on afforestation, roads, bridges and similar structures;

plus: (v) losses of fixed assets and stocks due to accidental damage, such as fire, accidents etc.;

plus: (vi) transfer cost with regard to purchases and sales of existing second-hand fixed assets, including land.

2. *Primary income of the population*

The primary income of the population consists of (a) wages and salaries, including receipts in kind, and related income, such as bonuses and reimbursements of expenses on business trips received from state, co-operative and private units of the material sphere; (b) the net material product (net value added) originating from the personal plots of households; and (c) the net material product of self-employed craftsmen, artisans and peasants. This flow appears in MPS tables 3 and 4.

Primary income of the population is roughly comparable to the SNA concept of compensation of employees. However, several differences remain and in order to arrive from the MPS concept at compensation of employees as defined in SNA, the following additions and subtractions are needed:

plus: (i) compensation of employees, including employers' contributions to social security funds, paid out in connection with non-material activities, inclusive of those that are paid out in connection with the provision of cultural, sports and similar facilities by industries in the material sphere;

plus: (ii) employers' contributions to social security funds paid out in connection with material activities;

minus: (iii) income from private enterprises;

minus: (iv) reimbursable expenditures for material goods and services purchased during business trips.

3. *Primary income of enterprises*

Primary income of enterprises consists of the sum of the net material product of the units of the material sphere which have employees *less* the wages and salaries and related incomes which they pay out. The primary incomes of these units are the source of such items as their net income, turnover taxes, contributions to social insurance, payments of taxes, fines and other compulsory items, finance of purchases of non-material services, insurance premiums, interest on bank loans and other business costs. This flow appears in MPS tables 3 and 4.

Although the coverage of primary income of enterprises is similar to that of operating surplus in SNA, the following additions to and subtractions from the MPS concept are needed in order to arrive at operating surplus as defined in SNA:

plus: (i) the remaining value of non-material services (i.e., the gross output value *minus* material cost, depreciation and compensation of employees) consumed by households and government, *plus* the difference between the remaining values of exported and imported non-material services;

minus: (ii) material expenditures by enterprises on cultural, sports and similar facilities for their employees;

plus: (iii) consumption of fixed capital in the material and non-material sphere, including that on afforestation, roads, bridges and similar structures;

plus: (iv) losses of fixed assets and stocks due to accidental damage, such as fire, accidents etc.;

plus: (v) transfer cost with regard to purchases and sales of existing fixed assets, including land;

minus: (vi) employers'contributions to social security funds, paid out in connection with material activities;

plus: (vii) income from private plots and private enterprises.

1/ Standing Statistical Commission. Council of Mutual Economic Assistance (Moscow, 1969).

2/ Studies in Methods. Series F, No. 17 (United Nations publication, Sales No. E.71.XVII.10).

3/ For a more exhaustive list of differences between MPS and SNA, the user should refer to *Comparisons of the System of National Accounts and the System of Balances of the National Economy*, part One, *Conceptual Relationships* (United Nations publication, Sales No. 77.XVII.6).

III. COUNTRY TABLES

Latvia

Source. Reply to the United Nations National Accounts Questionnaire from the State Committee for Statistics of the Republic of Latvia, Riga.
General note. The estimates shown in the following tables for the years 1970-1990 have been prepared in accordance with the System of Material Product Balances (MPS). Since 1990, the calculation of the estimates within the MPS framework had been discontinued. Thus, beginning 1990, the estimates are in accordance with the System of National Accounts (SNA) so far as the existing data would permit.

1.1 Expenditure on the Gross Domestic Product, in Current Prices

Million Roubles

	1980	1981	1982	1983	1984	1985	1986	1987	1988	1989	1990	1991
1 Government final consumption expenditure	...	...	...	...	...	...	...	...	...	...	1069	2948
2 Private final consumption expenditure	...	...	...	...	...	...	...	...	...	...	6578	13250
A Households	...	...	...	...	...	...	...	...	...	...	6578	13250
B Private non-profit institutions serving households											...	...
3 Gross capital formation	...	...	...	...	...	...	...	...	...	...	5006	9669
A Increase in stocks	...	...	...	...	...	...	...	...	...	...	2134	7901
B Gross fixed capital formation	...	...	...	...	...	...	...	...	...	...	2872	1768
4 Exports of goods and services	...	...	...	...	...	...	...	...	...	...	5957	10104
5 Less: Imports of goods and services	...	...	...	...	...	...	...	...	...	...	6122	7306
Equals: Gross Domestic Product	7459	7994	8352	8381	8724	8444	8725	8853	9320	10292	12488	28665

1.2 Expenditure on the Gross Domestic Product, in Constant Prices

Million Roubles

	1980	1981	1982	1983	1984	1985	1986	1987	1988	1989	1990	1991
At constant prices of:1990												
1 Government final consumption expenditure	...	...	...	...	...	...	...	...	...	...	1069	1017
2 Private final consumption expenditure	...	...	...	...	...	...	...	...	...	...	6578	4868
A Households	...	...	...	...	...	...	...	...	...	...	6578	4868
B Private non-profit institutions serving households	...	...	...	...	...	...	...	...	...	...	...	...
3 Gross capital formation	...	...	...	...	...	...	...	...	...	...	5006	4520
A Increase in stocks	...	...	...	...	...	...	...	...	...	...	2134	3817
B Gross fixed capital formation	...	...	...	...	...	...	...	...	...	...	2872	703
4 Exports of goods and services	...	...	...	...	...	...	...	...	...	...	5957	4040
5 Less: Imports of goods and services	...	...	...	...	...	...	...	...	...	...	6122	3432
Statistical discrepancy	...	...	...	...	...	...	...	...	...	...	-	442
Equals: Gross Domestic Product	...	...	...	...	...	...	...	...	...	...	12488	11455

1.3 Cost Components of the Gross Domestic Product

Million Roubles

	1980	1981	1982	1983	1984	1985	1986	1987	1988	1989	1990	1991
1 Indirect taxes, net	...	...	...	...	...	...	...	...	...	...	825	1922
A Indirect taxes	...	...	...	...	...	...	...	...	...	...	2734	3655
B Less: Subsidies	...	...	...	...	...	...	...	...	...	...	1909	1733
2 Consumption of fixed capital	...	...	...	...	...	...	...	...	...	...	1042	1138
3 Compensation of employees paid by resident producers to:	...	...	...	...	...	...	...	...	...	...	5982	12238
A Resident households	...	...	...	...	...	...	...	...	...	...	5982	12238
B Rest of the world	...	...	...	...	...	...	...	...	...	...	...	...
4 Operating surplus	...	...	...	...	...	...	...	...	...	...	4639	13367
A Corporate and quasi-corporate enterprises	...	...	...	...	...	...	...	...	...	...	3982	11391
B Private unincorporated enterprises	...	...	...	...	...	...	...	...	...	...	657	1976
C General government	...	...	...	...	...	...	...	...	...	...	...	...
Equals: Gross Domestic Product	...	...	...	...	...	...	...	...	...	...	12488	28665

Latvia

1.8 Capital Transactions of The Nation, Summary

Million Roubles

	1980	1981	1982	1983	1984	1985	1986	1987	1988	1989	1990	1991
Finance of Gross Capital Formation												
Gross saving	...	...	...	...	...	...	...	...	...	...	5006	13097
1 Consumption of fixed capital	...	...	...	...	...	...	...	...	...	...	1042	1138
A General government	...	...	...	...	...	...	...	...	...	...	...	...
B Corporate and quasi-corporate enterprises	...	...	...	...	...	...	...	...	...	...	1032	1126
C Other	...	...	...	...	...	...	...	...	...	...	10	12
2 Net saving	...	...	...	...	...	...	...	...	...	...	3964	11959
A General government	...	...	...	...	...	...	...	...	...	...	1274	2417
B Corporate and quasi-corporate enterprises	...	...	...	...	...	...	...	...	...	...	2106	8696
C Other	...	...	...	...	...	...	...	...	...	...	584	846
Less: Surplus of the nation on current transactions	...	...	...	...	...	...	...	...	...	...	-	3428
Finance of Gross Capital Formation	...	...	...	...	...	...	...	...	...	...	5006	9669
Gross Capital Formation												
Increase in stocks	...	...	...	...	...	...	...	...	...	...	2134	7901
Gross fixed capital formation	...	...	...	...	...	...	...	...	...	...	2872	1768
1 General government	...	...	...	...	...	...	...	...	...	...	163	551
2 Corporate and quasi-corporate enterprises	...	...	...	...	...	...	...	...	...	...	2655	1132
3 Other	...	...	...	...	...	...	...	...	...	...	54	85
Gross Capital Formation	...	...	...	...	...	...	...	...	...	...	5006	9669

1.10 Gross Domestic Product by Kind of Activity, in Current Prices

Million Roubles

	1980	1981	1982	1983	1984	1985	1986	1987	1988	1989	1990	1991
1 Agriculture, hunting, forestry and fishing	...	...	...	...	...	...	...	...	...	...	2357	5739
2 Mining and quarrying	...	...	...	...	...	...	...	...	...	...	25	54
3 Manufacturing	...	...	...	...	...	...	...	...	...	...	2762	9853
4 Electricity, gas and water	...	...	...	...	...	...	...	...	...	...	212	583
5 Construction	...	...	...	...	...	...	...	...	...	...	1167	1604
6 Wholesale and retail trade, restaurants and hotels	...	...	...	...	...	...	...	...	...	...	812	3212
7 Transport, storage and communication	...	...	...	...	...	...	...	...	...	...	1309	2001
8 Finance, insurance, real estate and business services	...	...	...	...	...	...	...	...	...	...	735	1406
9 Community, social and personal services	...	...	...	...	...	...	...	...	...	...	585	1099
Total, Industries	...	...	...	...	...	...	...	...	...	...	9964	25551
Producers of Government Services	...	...	...	...	...	...	...	...	...	...	397	1273
Other Producers	...	...	...	...	...	...	...	...	...	...	-	22
Subtotal	...	...	...	...	...	...	...	...	...	...	10361	26846
Less: Imputed bank service charge	...	...	...	...	...	...	...	...	...	...	...	...
Plus: Import duties	...	...	...	...	...	...	...	...	...	...	3	11
Plus: Value added tax	...	...	...	...	...	...	...	...	...	...	2124	1808
Equals: Gross Domestic Product	...	...	...	...	...	...	...	...	...	...	12488	28665
Memorandum Item: Mineral fuels and power	...	...	...	...	...	...	...	...	...	...	199	553

1.11 Gross Domestic Product by Kind of Activity, in Constant Prices

Million Roubles

	1980	1981	1982	1983	1984	1985	1986	1987	1988	1989	1990	1991
At constant prices of:1990												
1 Agriculture, hunting, forestry and fishing	...	...	...	...	...	...	...	...	...	...	2357	2306
2 Mining and quarrying	...	...	...	...	...	...	...	...	...	...	25	22
3 Manufacturing	...	...	...	...	...	...	...	...	...	...	2762	2753
4 Electricity, gas and water	...	...	...	...	...	...	...	...	...	...	212	206
5 Construction	...	...	...	...	...	...	...	...	...	...	1167	693

1.11 Gross Domestic Product by Kind of Activity, in Constant Prices
(Continued)

Million Roubles

	1980	1981	1982	1983	1984	1985	1986	1987	1988	1989	1990	1991
					At constant prices of:1990							
6 Wholesale and retail trade, restaurants and hotels	...	...	...	...	...	...	...	...	...	...	812	665
7 Transport, storage and communication	...	...	...	...	...	...	...	...	...	...	1309	1103
8 Finance, insurance, real estate and business services	...	...	...	...	...	...	...	...	...	...	735	652
9 Community, social and personal services	...	...	...	...	...	...	...	...	...	...	585	509
Total, Industries	...	...	...	...	...	...	...	...	...	...	9964	8909
Producers of Government Services	...	...	...	...	...	...	...	...	...	...	397	377
Other Producers	...	...	...	...	...	...	...	...	...	...	-	7
Subtotal	...	...	...	...	...	...	...	...	...	...	10361	9293
Less: Imputed bank service charge	...	...	...	...	...	...	...	...	...	...	...	...
Plus: Import duties	...	...	...	...	...	...	...	...	...	...	3	3
Plus: Value added tax	...	...	...	...	...	...	...	...	...	...	2124	2159
Equals: Gross Domestic Product	...	...	...	...	...	...	...	...	...	...	12488	11455
Memorandum Item: Mineral fuels and power	...	...	...	...	...	...	...	...	...	...	199	190

1.12 Relations Among National Accounting Aggregates

Million Roubles

	1980	1981	1982	1983	1984	1985	1986	1987	1988	1989	1990	1991
Gross Domestic Product	7459	7994	8352	8381	8724	8444	8725	8853	9320	10292	...	...
Plus: Net factor income from the rest of the world	-294	-328	-318	-368	-440	-427	-456	-558	-524	-378	...	...
Factor income from the rest of the world	213	223	207	197	190	190	208	264	291	349	...	...
Less: Factor income to the rest of the world	507	550	524	565	630	616	664	822	814	727	...	...
Equals: Gross National Product	7165	7667	8035	8012	8284	8017	8268	8295	8797	9914	...	...
Less: Consumption of fixed capital	661	701	738	787	833	879	924	981	1039	1101	...	...
Equals: National Income	6504	6966	7297	7226	7451	7138	7344	7314	7758	8813	...	...
Plus: Net current transfers from the rest of the world	...	...	...	...	...	...	...	...	...	...	...	...
Equals: National Disposable Income	...	...	...	...	...	...	...	...	...	...	...	...
Less: Final consumption	...	...	...	...	...	...	...	...	...	...	...	...
Equals: Net Saving	...	...	...	...	...	...	...	...	...	...	...	...
Less: Surplus of the nation on current transactions	...	...	...	...	...	...	...	...	...	...	...	...
Equals: Net Capital Formation	...	...	...	...	...	...	...	...	...	...	...	...

1a Net Material Product by Use at Current Market Prices

Million Roubles

	1980	1981	1982	1983	1984	1985	1986	1987	1988	1989	1990	1991
1 Personal consumption	4045	4244	4308	4333	4434	4572	4684	4779	5044	5323	5996	...
2 Material consumption in the units of the non-material sphere serving individuals	409	428	457	482	501	527	553	595	616	641	706	...
Consumption of the Population	4454	4672	4765	4816	4935	5099	5237	5373	5660	5964	6701	...
3 Material consumption in the units of the non-material sphere serving the community as a whole	86	88	92	96	106	123	130	137	143	145	288	...
4 Net fixed capital formation	492	529	622	582	690	864	933	1007	800	803	799	...
5 Increase in material circulating assets and in stocks	240	643	659	702	780	657	715	644	850	1024	975	...
6 Losses	38	50	53	57	43	69	63	70	66	73	137	...
7 Exports of goods and material services [a]	5290	5515	5949	6155	6325	6444	6649	4693	4896	5413	5283	...
8 Less: Imports of goods and material services [a]	5138	5633	6064	6299	6534	6867	7141	5593	5591	6030	6327	...
Statistical discrepancy [a]	329	435	468	345	399	-40	-41	211	197	238	993	...
Net Material Product	5790	6300	6544	6454	6743	6350	6545	6543	7021	7630	8849	...

a) Exports and imports data were not elaborated separately. The export/import balance was obtained as difference between the produced Net Material Product (NMP) in the country (Table 2a) and the NMP utilized in the national economy (Table 1a, lines 1-7). Therefore, data on exports and imports are extracted from interbranch balance sheets which were prepared applying different principles. These differences are reflected in item 'Statistical Discrepancy'.

Latvia

1b Net Material Product by Use at Constant Market Prices

Million Roubles

	1980	1981	1982	1983	1984	1985	1986	1987	1988	1989	1990	1991
					At constant prices of:1980							
1 Personal consumption	4045	4177	4047	4089	4234	4364	4385	4429	4652	4767	4803	...
2 Material consumption in the units of the non-material sphere serving individuals	409	428	452	479	499	526	552	593	613	629	659	...
Consumption of the Population	4454	4605	4498	4568	4733	4889	4937	5022	5265	5396	5462	...
3 Material consumption in the units of the non-material sphere serving the community as a whole	86	88	91	94	104	109	115	122	127	128	228	...
4 Net fixed capital formation	492	536	614	560	565	682	730	754	581	462	359	...
5 Increase in material circulating assets and in stocks	240	572	554	574	621	589	705	687	817	870	620	...
6 Losses	38	54	57	64	49	50	47	54	47	52	92	...
7 Exports of goods and material services												...
8 Less: Imports of goods and material services	480	240	470	672	765	503	604	604	856	1357	1380	...
Statistical discrepancy												...
Net Material Product	5790	6095	6285	6532	6837	6822	7137	7244	7693	8264	8141	...

2a Net Material Product by Kind of Activity of the Material Sphere in Current Market Prices

Million Roubles

	1980	1981	1982	1983	1984	1985	1986	1987	1988	1989	1990	1991
1 Agriculture and forestry	706	912	1142	1382	1633	1649	1579	1392	1822	1826	1955	...
A Agriculture and livestock	697	903	1130	1369	1620	1629	1559	1372	1802	1805	1931	...
B Forestry	9	9	12	13	12	20	20	20	20	21	25	...
C Other	...	...	...	...	...	...	...	...	...	...	...	...
2 Industrial activity	3254	3409	3306	2887	2796	2855	3109	3241	3099	3437	4534	...
3 Construction	412	440	449	463	525	548	513	559	640	744	717	...
4 Wholesale and retail trade and restaurants and other eating and drinking places	335	351	346	344	348	349	365	372	410	479	557	...
5 Transport and communication	321	343	373	410	447	459	466	475	527	551	668	...
A Transport	306	327	356	392	428	432	445	451	500	524	638	...
B Communication	15	16	17	18	19	26	22	24	26	26	31	...
6 Other activities of the material sphere	762	845	928	969	994	490	512	504	523	593	417	...
Net material product	5790	6300	6544	6454	6743	6350	6545	6543	7021	7630	8849	...

2b Net Material Product by Kind of Activity of the Material Sphere in Constant Market Prices

Million Roubles

	1980	1981	1982	1983	1984	1985	1986	1987	1988	1989	1990	1991
					At constant prices of:1980							
1 Agriculture and forestry	706	771	786	852	962	869	923	860	859	903	752	...
A Agriculture and livestock	697	762	777	842	953	860	913	851	849	893	739	...
B Forestry	9	9	10	10	10	10	10	10	10	11	12	...
C Other	...	...	...	...	...	...	...	...	...	...	...	...
2 Industrial activity	3254	3392	3480	3555	3612	3627	3870	4105	4380	4623	4964	...
3 Construction	412	435	430	441	494	489	487	487	563	630	642	...
4 Wholesale and retail trade and restaurants and other eating and drinking places	335	342	330	330	343	361	359	358	392	460	496	...
5 Transport and communication	321	338	345	379	414	408	415	426	469	481	458	...
A Transport	306	322	329	362	396	388	394	403	445	455	427	...
B Communication	15	16	17	17	18	20	20	23	24	26	31	...
6 Other activities of the material sphere	762	828	929	1006	1075	1110	1121	1122	1158	1366	1101	...
Statistical discrepancy	-	-11	-15	-32	-64	-42	-38	-114	-127	-198	-271	...
Net material product	5790	6095	6285	6532	6837	6822	7137	7244	7693	8264	8141	...

Lebanon

Source. Reply to the United Nations National Accounts Questionnaire from the Direction Centrale de la Statistique, Ministere du plan, Beyrouth. The official estimates are published annually by the Direction Centrale de la Statistique in 'Les Comptes Economiques'.

General note. The official estimates of Lebanon have been adjusted by the Direction Centrale de la Statistique to conform to the United Nations System of National Accounts so far as the existing data would permit.

1.1 Expenditure on the Gross Domestic Product, in Current Prices

Million Lebanese pounds

	1980	1981	1982	1983	1984	1985	1986	1987	1988	1989	1990	1991
1 Government final consumption expenditure	3515	4219	4850	...	...	...	...	...	...	...	...	...
2 Private final consumption expenditure	12905	15488	15840	...	...	...	...	...	...	...	...	...
3 Gross capital formation	2196	3459	1179	...	...	...	...	...	...	...	...	...
4 Exports of goods and services	5460	5724	5255	...	...	...	...	...	...	...	...	...
5 Less: Imports of goods and services	10076	12090	14525	...	...	...	...	...	...	...	...	...
Equals: Gross Domestic Product	14000	16800	12599	...	...	...	...	...	...	...	...	...

1.3 Cost Components of the Gross Domestic Product

Million Lebanese pounds

	1980	1981	1982	1983	1984	1985	1986	1987	1988	1989	1990	1991
1 Indirect taxes, net	683	436	306	...	...	...	...	...	...	...	...	...
2 Consumption of fixed capital	...	...	...	...	...	...	...	...	...	...	...	...
3 Compensation of employees paid by resident producers to:	...	...	...	...	...	...	...	...	...	...	...	...
4 Operating surplus	...	...	...	...	...	...	...	...	...	...	...	...
Equals: Gross Domestic Product	14000	16800	12599	...	...	...	...	...	...	...	...	...

1.10 Gross Domestic Product by Kind of Activity, in Current Prices

Million Lebanese pounds

	1980	1981	1982	1983	1984	1985	1986	1987	1988	1989	1990	1991
1 Agriculture, hunting, forestry and fishing	1288	1435	1076	...	...	...	...	...	...	...	...	...
2 Mining and quarrying	...	...	...	...	...	...	...	...	...	...	...	...
3 Manufacturing	1702	2192	1644	...	...	...	...	...	...	...	...	...
4 Electricity, gas and water	708	911	683	...	...	...	...	...	...	...	...	...
5 Construction	447	575	431	...	...	...	...	...	...	...	...	...
6 Wholesale and retail trade, restaurants and hotels	4008	4753	3565	...	...	...	...	...	...	...	...	...
7 Transport, storage and communication	530	628	471	...	...	...	...	...	...	...	...	...
8 Finance, insurance, real estate and business services	2349	2785	2089	...	...	...	...	...	...	...	...	...
9 Community, social and personal services	1526	1809	1357	...	...	...	...	...	...	...	...	...
Total, Industries	12557	15087	11316	...	...	...	...	...	...	...	...	...
Producers of Government Services	1443	1712	1284	...	...	...	...	...	...	...	...	...
Other Producers	...	...	...	...	...	...	...	...	...	...	...	...
Subtotal	14000	16800	12600	...	...	...	...	...	...	...	...	...
Less: Imputed bank service charge	...	...	...	...	...	...	...	...	...	...	...	...
Plus: Import duties	...	...	...	...	...	...	...	...	...	...	...	...
Plus: Value added tax	...	...	...	...	...	...	...	...	...	...	...	...
Equals: Gross Domestic Product	14000	16800	12600	...	...	...	...	...	...	...	...	...

Lesotho

General note. The preparation of national accounts statistics in Lesotho is undertaken by the Bureau of Statistics, Maseru. The official estimates together with methodological notes on sources and methods are published in a series of reports entitled 'National Accounts'. Beginning 1980, the estimates have been revised utilizing new sources of information. The most important of which is the 1986/87 Household Budget Survey. The estimates are generally in accordance with the classifications and definitions recommended in the United Nations System of National Accounts (SNA). The following tables have been prepared from successive replies to the United Nations national accounts questionnaire. When the scope and coverage of the estimates differ for conceptual or statistical reasons from the definitions and classifications recommended in SNA, a footnote is indicated to the relevant tables.

Sources and methods :

(a) Gross domestic product. Gross domestic product is estimated mainly through the production approach.

(b) Expenditure on the gross domestic product. All items of GDP by expenditure type are estimated through the expenditure approach. Government final consumption expenditure, consisting of wages and salaries and purchases of goods and services, is obtained from government accounts. The government expenditure is classified by the type of service provided by the central authorities. The estimates of private final consumption expenditure are based on the rural household survey undertaken in 1967-1969 and on the urban household survey carried out in six district towns from May 1972 to May 1973. Recently, this item has been estimated as a residual. For the new series, household consumption is also obtained as a residual. Increase in stocks is estimated mainly from questionnaires and surveys carried out for the agricultural sector. Gross fixed capital formation consists of the value of purchases and own-account construction of fixed assets by government, private and public enterprises, individuals and non-profit institutions. Various sources such as questionnaires and imports of building materials are used to collect the information. The gross capital formation in plant machinery and vehicles of the new series is assumed to be 1.2 times the imports of capital goods. Estimates of exports and imports of merchandise are obtained from foreign trade statistics with adjustments made for differences in coverage and valuation. Exports are recorded f.o.b. at the border of Lesotho and imports are also recorded f.o.b. at the point of dispatch. For the estimates of GDP at constant prices, household consumption is obtained as a residual. The estimates of gross capital formation and the imports and exports of goods and services are calculated by using the relevant import price indexes.

(c) Cost-structure of the gross domestic product. Wages and salaries are derived from the government accounts and other returns. Estimates of operating surplus are derived as residuals from the production accounts of all sectors. Depreciation is obtained from returned questionnaires and no estimate is available for the government or subsistence sectors. Indirect taxes consist mainly of revenue received by Lesotho as a member of the customs agreement with Botswana, South Africa and Swaziland. Subsidy figures consist of government contributions to defray part of the operating expenses of government and other enterprises.

(d) Gross domestic product by kind of economic activity. The table of GDP by kind of economic activity is prepared in factor values. The production approach is used to estimate the value added of the different industries except for producers of government services in which case the income approach is used. The Agricultural Division of the Bureau of Statistics carries out regular annual surveys. The 1970 census of agriculture and the 1973 agricultural survey are used to derive estimates of cereal production, assuming a wastage of 6 per cent during the various stages of harvest. The 1967-69 rural household survey is used for fruit and vegetable production estimates. For livestock, balance sheets prepared by the Agricultural Division of the Bureau of Statistics provide changes in stock estimates, to which the average values for different types of livestock are applied. For the new series, the annual crop survey and annual livestock survey supply information on quantities produced. The price information for the crop is available from the Ministrey of Agriculture while the price movement for livestock is deducted from retail price index. For meat production, average carcass weights are applied to the number of livestock slaughtered which are obtained from the Ministry of Health and annual production surveys. The value of diamonds sold to licenced dealers by diggers is regarded as the value of diamonds exported from Lesotho. The receipts from diamonds are regarded as a contribution by the mining sector to GDP. Data on quantities and values of diamonds are obtained monthly from the Department of Mines and Geology. For manufacturing, data are derived from questionnaires prepared specially for manufacturing enterprises while data for handicrafts are based on the 1967-1969 rural household consumption and expenditure survey. For years 1980-1985, the estimates of manufacturing have been reconciled with the Yearbook of Industrial Statistics 1987. The estimates of the years after 1985 are based on industrial survey and survey of industrial production. Data for electricity and water are obtained from the balance sheets of the electricity corporation and accounts of the concerned ministry. Special questionnaires filled in by building contractors are used for the construction sector. Estimates of own-account contribution are included. For the new series, value added of construction is a fixed proportion of the input of building material which is based on import statistics. For the trade sector, questionnaires are used for large enterprises while the results of a survey conducted in 1970-1971 are used for small enterprises. Estimates of the public transport and communication sector are based on government accounts supplemented by inquiries while estimates of private transport are obtained from the concerned enterprises. For the financial sector, special inquiries directed at the banks and the headquarters of insurance companies are used. For ownership of dwellings, government accounts provide information for the public sector while questionnaires returned by businesses and institutions are used for the private sector. The 1972-73 urban household survey is used to estimate imputed rent. Information relating to general government services is obtained from the government accounts. Data on other services are obtained through questionnaires and special inquiries. The estimates of GDP by kind of economic activity at constant prices are calculated by using relevant price indexes for most of the industries.

1.1 Expenditure on the Gross Domestic Product, in Current Prices

Million Lesotho maloti

	1980	1981	1982	1983	1984	1985	1986	1987	1988	1989	1990	1991
1 Government final consumption expenditure	74.0	81.0	89.9	91.7	98.6	135.9	159.3	171.5	215.8	222.2	234.6	278.6
2 Private final consumption expenditure	383.2	471.0	557.1	686.2	782.9	837.9	935.9	1109.3	1494.9	1667.4	1605.7	2175.9
A Households	355.0	442.5	527.6	654.4	746.7	792.0	884.7	1056.1	1426.6	1589.5	1520.3	...
B Private non-profit institutions serving households	28.2	28.5	29.5	31.8	36.2	45.9	51.2	53.2	68.3	77.9	85.4	...
3 Gross capital formation	122.1	141.5	183.9	131.5	189.8	272.4	290.9	342.2	506.2	829.0	1162.4	1228.8
A Increase in stocks	6.3	8.3	-2.9	0.6	5.2	-0.9	13.6	5.1	2.0	5.3	-	-
B Gross fixed capital formation	115.8	133.2	186.8	130.9	184.7	273.3	277.3	337.2	504.2	823.7	1162.4	1228.8
Residential buildings												...
Non-residential buildings	74.8	79.9	125.7	84.7	109.9	171.3	158.1	215.7	317.2	634.2	957.7	...
Other construction and land improvement etc.												...
Other	41.0	53.3	61.1	46.2	74.8	102.0	119.2	121.5	187.0	189.5	204.7	...
4 Exports of goods and services	58.0	58.2	55.4	50.8	60.5	70.2	80.4	122.8	185.2	227.0	214.9	224.5
5 Less: Imports of goods and services	350.2	423.3	513.4	569.6	676.8	765.2	835.3	992.5	1375.6	1658.3	1712.6	2264.0
Equals: Gross Domestic Product	287.0	328.4	372.9	390.6	455.0	551.1	631.2	753.2	1026.4	1287.3	1504.9	1643.8

1.2 Expenditure on the Gross Domestic Product, in Constant Prices

Million Lesotho maloti

	1980	1981	1982	1983	1984	1985	1986	1987	1988	1989	1990	1991
					At constant prices of:1980							
1 Government final consumption expenditure	74.0	74.3	78.4	76.7	79.7	84.5	93.2	94.5	97.0	91.3	92.7	...
2 Private final consumption expenditure	383.2	418.4	428.1	465.4	474.1	441.1	421.0	445.6	524.1	491.2	409.9	...
A Households	355.0	388.9	398.1	433.6	441.8	408.2	387.3	411.4	488.5	454.9	372.5	...
B Private non-profit institutions serving households	28.2	29.5	30.0	31.8	32.3	32.9	33.7	34.2	35.6	36.3	37.4	...
3 Gross capital formation	122.1	122.9	140.0	84.7	104.0	131.9	112.7	113.6	149.3	222.2	274.8	...

1.2 Expenditure on the Gross Domestic Product, in Constant Prices
(Continued)

Million Lesotho maloti

	1980	1981	1982	1983	1984	1985	1986	1987	1988	1989	1990	1991
	At constant prices of:1980											
A Increase in stocks	6.3	6.5	-1.6	0.4	2.8	-0.5	6.8	2.4	0.8	1.5	-	...
B Gross fixed capital formation	115.8	116.5	141.6	84.3	101.2	132.4	105.9	111.2	148.5	220.7	274.8	...
Residential buildings												...
Non-residential buildings	74.8	69.7	93.1	52.7	62.0	84.8	64.6	77.3	102.2	180.8	237.0	...
Other construction and land improvement etc.												...
Other	41.0	46.7	48.5	31.6	39.2	47.7	41.2	33.8	46.3	39.8	37.8	...
4 Exports of goods and services	58.0	49.7	50.2	35.0	38.0	38.9	40.8	54.9	68.6	79.4	63.4	...
5 Less: Imports of goods and services	350.2	375.4	396.6	387.5	398.3	388.4	353.7	378.5	465.7	469.9	410.1	...
Equals: Gross Domestic Product	287.0	289.8	300.2	274.4	297.6	308.0	314.1	330.1	373.2	414.3	430.7	...

1.3 Cost Components of the Gross Domestic Product

Million Lesotho maloti

	1980	1981	1982	1983	1984	1985	1986	1987	1988	1989	1990	1991
1 Indirect taxes, net	39.1	45.8	64.3	82.4	89.1	98.4	121.9	155.5	200.6	260.3	286.3	...
2 Consumption of fixed capital	...	...	...	...	...	...	...	...	...	...	...	...
3 Compensation of employees paid by resident producers to:	...	...	...	...	...	...	...	...	...	...	...	...
4 Operating surplus	...	...	...	...	...	...	...	...	...	...	...	...
Equals: Gross Domestic Product	287.0	328.4	372.9	390.6	455.0	551.1	631.2	753.2	1026.4	1287.3	1504.9	...

1.4 General Government Current Receipts and Disbursements

Fiscal year beginning 1 April

Thousand Lesotho maloti

	1980	1981	1982	1983	1984	1985	1986	1987	1988	1989	1990	1991
	Receipts											
1 Operating surplus	...	...	...	...	...	...	...	...	...	...	...	...
2 Property and entrepreneurial income	4105	2530	2641	3324	...	...	...	...	...	...	...	...
3 Taxes, fees and contributions	77873	77556	91828	121618	...	...	...	...	...	...	...	...
A Indirect taxes	56779	58737	61000	100028	...	...	...	...	...	...	...	...
B Direct taxes	18215	16691	18249	18276	...	...	...	...	...	...	...	...
C Social security contributions	...	...	...	...	...	...	...	...	...	...	...	...
D Compulsory fees, fines and penalties	2879	2128	12579	3314	...	...	...	...	...	...	...	...
4 Other current transfers	23448	25568	27291	39372	...	...	...	...	...	...	...	...
Total Current Receipts of General Government	105426	105654	121760	164314	...	...	...	...	...	...	...	...
	Disbursements											
1 Government final consumption expenditure	113546	106903	96369	116182	...	...	...	...	...	...	...	...
A Compensation of employees	74341	73808	70474	77239	...	...	...	...	...	...	...	...
B Consumption of fixed capital	...	...	...	...	...	...	...	...	...	...	...	...
C Purchases of goods and services, net	39205	33095	25895	38943	...	...	...	...	...	...	...	...
D Less: Own account fixed capital formation	...	...	...	...	...	...	...	...	...	...	...	...
E Indirect taxes paid, net	...	...	...	...	...	...	...	...	...	...	...	...
2 Property income	3800	3803	4049	19624	...	...	...	...	...	...	...	...
A Interest	3800	3803	4049	19624	...	...	...	...	...	...	...	...
B Net land rent and royalties	...	...	...	...	...	...	...	...	...	...	...	...
3 Subsidies	1175	190	...	...	...	...	...	...	...	...	...	...
4 Other current transfers	5301	6711	5610	8763	...	...	...	...	...	...	...	...
A Social security benefits	2329	3037	1843	2004	...	...	...	...	...	...	...	...
B Social assistance grants	1197	1316	1857	3291	...	...	...	...	...	...	...	...
C Other	1775	2358	1910	3468	...	...	...	...	...	...	...	...
5 Net saving	-18396	-11953	15732	19745	...	...	...	...	...	...	...	...
Total Current Disbursements and Net Saving of General Government	105426	105654	121760	164314	...	...	...	...	...	...	...	...

Lesotho

1.7 External Transactions on Current Account, Summary

Million Lesotho maloti

	1980	1981	1982	1983	1984	1985	1986	1987	1988	1989	1990	1991
Payments to the Rest of the World												
1 Imports of goods and services	350.2	423.3	513.4	569.6	676.8	765.2	835.3	992.5	1375.6	1658.3	1712.6	...
A Imports of merchandise c.i.f.	331.5	405.5	497.8	539.7	634.5	720.9	776.9	929.5	1310.3	1594.0	1657.9	...
B Other	18.7	17.8	15.6	29.9	42.3	44.3	58.4	63.1	65.3	64.2	54.7	...
2 Factor income to the rest of the world	5.7	7.7	16.4	13.9	16.3	20.1	23.8	30.4	36.4	57.0	58.9	...
A Compensation of employees	...	...	...	...	...	...	...	...	...	...	...	...
B Property and entrepreneurial income	5.7	7.7	16.4	13.9	16.3	20.1	23.8	30.4	36.4	57.0	58.9	...
3 Current transfers to the rest of the world	3.4	3.6	4.5	4.1	6.0	8.5	14.4	12.5	19.0	26.0	40.4	...
4 Surplus of the nation on current transactions	-8.7	-42.9	-41.8	-11.7	2.2	-16.4	-20.0	-19.2	-154.5	-57.0	137.6	...
Payments to the Rest of the World and Surplus of the Nation on Current Transactions	350.6	391.7	492.5	575.9	701.3	777.4	853.4	1016.1	1276.4	1684.2	1949.5	...
Receipts From The Rest of the World												
1 Exports of goods and services	58.0	58.2	55.4	50.8	60.5	70.2	80.4	122.8	185.2	227.0	214.9	...
A Exports of merchandise f.o.b.	46.6	44.6	40.6	34.6	41.8	50.0	58.2	94.2	144.9	178.4	152.7	...
B Other	11.4	13.6	14.8	16.2	18.7	20.2	22.2	28.5	40.3	48.6	62.3	...
2 Factor income from rest of the world	210.7	262.5	389.3	437.0	503.5	534.3	607.1	736.3	866.1	984.8	1160.8	...
A Compensation of employees	205.0	255.0	378.0	421.0	475.9	499.0	583.6	718.5	844.3	956.8	1106.2	...
B Property and entrepreneurial income	5.7	7.5	11.3	16.0	27.6	35.3	23.5	17.8	21.8	28.0	54.6	...
3 Current transfers from rest of the world	81.9	71.0	47.8	88.1	137.3	172.9	165.9	157.1	225.1	472.5	573.9	...
Receipts from the Rest of the World on Current Transactions	350.6	391.7	492.5	575.9	701.3	777.4	853.4	1016.1	1276.4	1684.2	1949.5	...

1.8 Capital Transactions of The Nation, Summary

Million Lesotho maloti

	1980	1981	1982	1983	1984	1985	1986	1987	1988	1989	1990	1991
Finance of Gross Capital Formation												
Gross saving	113.4	98.6	142.2	119.8	192.1	256.0	270.8	323.0	351.7	771.9	1300.0	...
Less: Surplus of the nation on current transactions	-8.7	-42.9	-41.8	-11.7	2.2	-16.4	-20.0	-19.2	-154.5	-57.0	137.6	...
Finance of Gross Capital Formation	122.1	141.5	183.9	131.5	189.8	272.4	290.9	342.2	506.2	829.0	1162.4	...
Gross Capital Formation												
Increase in stocks	6.3	8.3	-2.9	0.6	5.2	-0.9	13.6	5.1	2.0	5.3	-	...
Gross fixed capital formation	115.8	133.2	186.8	130.9	184.7	273.3	277.3	337.2	504.2	823.7	1162.4	...
1 General government	44.4	61.0	64.3	59.2	69.0	73.7	84.8	102.0	123.1	123.1	-	...
2 Corporate and quasi-corporate enterprises	71.4	72.2	122.5	71.7	115.7	199.6	192.5	235.2	381.1	700.6	1162.4	...
A Public	...	...	...	...	...	...	...	...	...	...	...	...
B Private	71.4	72.2	122.5	71.7	115.5	199.6	192.5	235.2	381.1	700.6	1162.4	...
3 Other	...	...	...	...	...	...	...	...	...	...	...	...
Gross Capital Formation	122.1	141.5	183.9	131.5	189.8	272.4	290.9	342.2	506.2	829.0	1162.4	...

1.10 Gross Domestic Product by Kind of Activity, in Current Prices

Million Lesotho maloti

	1980	1981	1982	1983	1984	1985	1986	1987	1988	1989	1990	1991
1 Agriculture, hunting, forestry and fishing	59.2	77.0	67.7	73.7	88.6	97.2	107.7	119.9	201.5	215.0	249.9	...
2 Mining and quarrying	20.7	16.0	13.5	0.9	0.6	1.6	1.9	1.9	0.8	4.4	6.2	...
3 Manufacturing [a]	16.2	20.2	27.4	33.2	43.3	50.4	66.0	89.0	120.3	150.3	166.7	...
4 Electricity, gas and water	1.6	1.6	1.8	1.9	2.5	3.7	5.5	4.7	9.0	13.3	24.8	...
5 Construction	33.1	36.0	56.2	39.8	50.8	78.3	71.5	98.5	134.3	214.2	291.7	...

Lesotho

1.10 Gross Domestic Product by Kind of Activity, in Current Prices
(Continued)

Million Lesotho maloti

	1980	1981	1982	1983	1984	1985	1986	1987	1988	1989	1990	1991
6 Wholesale and retail trade, restaurants and hotels	22.3	25.2	30.0	35.0	42.6	51.6	61.2	71.8	85.3	100.7	123.0	...
7 Transport, storage and communication	6.1	7.9	9.2	11.0	11.8	14.5	17.5	22.7	29.6	39.1	46.7	...
8 Finance, insurance, real estate and business services	31.7	38.0	49.2	57.6	68.7	72.2	77.7	83.1	108.5	139.4	158.6	...
9 Community, social and personal services	4.5	5.1	5.9	7.0	7.8	9.3	11.4	13.2	15.0	17.9	19.2	...
Total, Industries	195.4	227.0	260.9	260.1	316.7	378.8	420.4	504.8	704.3	894.3	1086.8	...
Producers of Government Services	29.5	35.1	33.7	36.2	39.1	54.1	60.3	61.0	82.1	90.2	96.9	...
Other Producers	31.0	31.8	32.6	35.2	39.9	50.9	57.3	59.8	81.4	93.6	100.2	...
Subtotal b	255.9	293.9	327.2	331.5	395.7	483.8	538.0	625.6	867.8	1078.1	1283.9	...
Less: Imputed bank service charge	8.1	11.4	18.7	23.5	29.9	31.1	28.7	27.8	42.0	51.1	65.0	...
Plus: Import duties	...	...	...	...	...	...	...	...	...	...	...	...
Plus: Value added tax	...	...	...	...	...	...	...	...	...	...	...	...
Plus: Other adjustments c	39.1	45.8	64.3	82.4	89.1	98.4	121.9	155.5	200.6	260.3	286.3	...
Equals: Gross Domestic Product	287.0	328.4	372.9	390.6	455.0	551.1	631.2	753.2	1026.4	1287.3	1504.9	...

a) Item 'Manufacturing' includes handicrafts.
b) Gross domestic product in factor values.
c) Item 'Other adjustments' refers to indirect taxes net of subsidies.

1.11 Gross Domestic Product by Kind of Activity, in Constant Prices

Million Lesotho maloti

	1980	1981	1982	1983	1984	1985	1986	1987	1988	1989	1990	1991
						At constant prices of:1980						
1 Agriculture, hunting, forestry and fishing	59.2	62.3	49.9	48.5	54.0	52.2	56.4	52.5	67.3	69.1	73.3	...
2 Mining and quarrying	20.7	11.5	15.7	1.5	1.5	2.6	2.1	1.7	1.0	4.5	2.6	...
3 Manufacturing a	16.2	17.1	21.1	23.1	27.5	28.7	33.2	39.1	46.7	53.2	51.1	...
4 Electricity, gas and water	1.6	1.9	2.1	2.2	2.3	2.4	2.5	2.2	3.1	2.1	3.5	...
5 Construction	33.1	31.4	41.6	24.9	29.3	38.4	30.3	36.0	41.5	63.2	73.5	...
6 Wholesale and retail trade, restaurants and hotels	22.3	22.3	23.8	24.6	27.2	29.1	30.4	32.1	33.9	34.9	38.2	...
7 Transport, storage and communication	6.1	6.6	6.7	7.1	7.1	7.4	8.6	9.8	10.6	10.9	13.5	...
8 Finance, insurance, real estate and business services	31.7	35.0	38.1	39.1	41.9	43.8	47.4	52.7	60.3	71.9	76.5	...
9 Community, social and personal services	4.5	4.5	4.7	4.7	4.8	5.0	5.2	5.4	5.5	5.7	5.8	...
Total, Industries	195.4	192.6	203.7	175.7	195.6	209.7	216.1	231.5	269.9	316.5	338.0	...
Producers of Government Services	29.5	32.8	31.5	33.8	36.6	36.1	40.2	40.7	41.3	42.0	45.1	...
Other Producers	31.0	32.8	33.7	36.1	37.4	37.3	39.4	40.4	43.1	44.4	46.0	...
Subtotal b	255.9	258.2	268.9	245.6	269.6	283.1	295.7	312.6	354.3	402.9	429.1	...
Less: Imputed bank service charge	8.1	10.8	13.6	14.1	15.9	18.2	20.9	24.9	30.1	38.3	42.3	...
Plus: Import duties	...	...	...	...	...	...	...	...	...	...	...	...
Plus: Value added tax	...	...	...	...	...	...	...	...	...	...	...	...
Plus: Other adjustments c	39.1	42.2	45.0	42.9	43.8	43.2	39.3	42.4	49.1	49.9	43.8	...
Equals: Gross Domestic Product	287.0	289.8	300.2	274.4	297.6	308.0	314.1	330.1	373.2	414.3	430.7	...

a) Item 'Manufacturing' includes handicrafts.
b) Gross domestic product in factor values.
c) Item 'Other adjustments' refers to indirect taxes net of subsidies.

1.12 Relations Among National Accounting Aggregates

Million Lesotho maloti

	1980	1981	1982	1983	1984	1985	1986	1987	1988	1989	1990	1991
Gross Domestic Product	287.0	328.4	372.9	390.6	455.0	551.1	631.2	753.2	1026.4	1287.3	1504.9	...
Plus: Net factor income from the rest of the world	205.0	254.8	372.9	423.1	487.2	514.3	583.3	705.9	829.7	927.8	1101.8	...
Factor income from the rest of the world	210.7	262.5	389.3	437.0	503.5	534.3	607.1	736.3	866.1	984.8	1160.8	...
Less: Factor income to the rest of the world	5.7	7.7	16.4	13.9	16.3	20.1	23.8	30.4	36.4	57.0	58.9	...
Equals: Gross National Product	492.0	583.2	745.8	813.7	942.1	1065.4	1214.6	1459.1	1856.2	2215.1	2606.7	...
Less: Consumption of fixed capital	...	...	...	...	...	...	...	...	...	...	...	...

Lesotho

1.12 Relations Among National Accounting Aggregates
(Continued)

Million Lesotho maloti

	1980	1981	1982	1983	1984	1985	1986	1987	1988	1989	1990	1991
Equals: National Income b	492.0	583.2	745.8	813.7	942.1	1065.4	1214.6	1459.1	1856.2	2215.1	2606.7	...
Plus: Net current transfers from the rest of the world	78.5	67.4	43.3	84.0	131.3	164.4	151.5	144.6	206.1	446.5	533.5	...
Current transfers from the rest of the world	81.9	71.0	47.8	88.1	137.3	172.9	165.9	157.1	225.1	472.5	573.9	...
Less: Current transfers to the rest of the world	3.4	3.6	4.5	4.1	6.0	8.5	14.4	12.5	19.0	26.0	40.4	...
Equals: National Disposable Income c	570.5	650.6	789.2	897.8	1073.5	1229.8	1366.1	1603.7	2062.3	2661.6	3140.2	...
Less: Final consumption	457.1	552.0	647.0	777.9	881.4	973.8	1095.2	1280.7	1710.6	1889.6	1840.2	...
Equals: Net Saving d	113.4	98.6	142.2	119.8	192.1	256.0	270.8	323.0	351.7	771.9	1300.0	...
Less: Surplus of the nation on current transactions	-8.7	-42.9	-41.8	-11.7	2.2	-16.4	-20.0	-19.2	-154.5	-57.0	137.6	...
Equals: Net Capital Formation e	122.1	141.5	183.9	131.5	189.8	272.3	290.9	342.2	506.2	829.0	1162.4	...

b) Item 'National income' includes consumption of fixed capital.
c) Item 'National disposable income' includes consumption of fixed capital.
d) Item 'Net saving' includes consumption of fixed capital.
e) Item 'Net capital formation' includes consumption of fixed capital.

2.1 Government Final Consumption Expenditure by Function, in Current Prices

Million Lesotho maloti

	1980	1981	1982	1983	1984	1985	1986	1987	1988	1989	1990	1991
1 General public services	16.9	17.2	14.5	18.7	20.4	30.9	35.5	32.5	37.5	43.9	57.0	...
2 Defence	...	...	...	...	...	...	...	...	...	...	...	...
3 Public order and safety	21.1	22.1	36.3	30.0	30.7	43.0	52.3	57.3	66.4	70.9	74.3	...
4 Education	3.7	4.1	3.4	3.9	4.0	5.6	5.5	6.5	9.0	9.4	9.5	...
5 Health	7.5	7.4	8.7	11.4	12.0	15.5	20.3	20.9	26.5	28.0	25.7	...
6 Social security and welfare												...
7 Housing and community amenities	4.2	5.8	4.8	4.1	6.2	9.2	12.8	14.7	19.7	18.2	16.9	...
8 Recreational, cultural and religious affairs	...	...	...	...	...	...	...	...	...	...	...	...
9 Economic services	20.7	24.4	22.2	23.8	25.3	31.6	32.8	39.8	56.7	51.8	51.2	...
A Fuel and energy	...	...	...	...	...	...	...	...	...	...	...	...
B Agriculture, forestry, fishing and hunting	11.0	12.2	10.0	10.3	11.8	14.8	14.0	16.0	20.9	20.8	21.6	...
C Mining, manufacturing and construction, except fuel and energy	...	...	...	...	...	...	...	...	...	...	...	...
D Transportation and communication	6.3	8.0	8.2	8.6	8.4	9.6	11.1	12.7	22.6	17.7	16.1	...
E Other economic affairs	3.4	4.2	4.0	4.9	5.1	7.2	7.7	11.1	13.2	13.3	13.5	...
10 Other functions	...	...	...	...	...	...	...	...	...	...	...	...
Total Government Final Consumption Expenditure	74.0	81.0	89.9	91.9	98.6	135.9	159.3	171.5	215.8	222.2	234.6	...

2.2 Government Final Consumption Expenditure by Function, in Constant Prices

Million Lesotho maloti

	1980	1981	1982	1983	1984	1985	1986	1987	1988	1989	1990	1991
				At constant prices of:1980								
1 General public services	16.9	15.9	13.1	16.1	16.9	19.3	20.7	18.3	17.4	18.4	22.9	...
2 Defence	...	...	...	...	...	...	...	...	...	...	...	...
3 Public order and safety	21.1	20.2	30.9	24.4	24.1	26.3	30.1	30.0	29.0	28.2	27.9	...
4 Education	3.7	3.8	3.1	3.4	3.5	3.7	3.5	3.9	4.3	4.1	4.0	...
5 Health	7.5	6.8	7.6	9.2	9.4	9.6	11.8	11.7	12.1	11.6	10.6	...
6 Social security and welfare												...
7 Housing and community amenities	4.2	5.3	4.3	3.8	5.4	5.9	7.8	8.7	9.2	7.9	7.2	...
8 Recreational, cultural and religious affairs	...	...	...	...	...	...	...	...	...	...	...	...
9 Economic services	20.7	22.3	19.4	19.8	20.4	19.7	19.3	21.9	25.0	21.1	20.1	...
A Fuel and energy	...	...	...	...	...	...	...	...	...	...	...	...
B Agriculture, forestry, fishing and hunting	11.0	11.3	9.0	9.0	10.1	9.5	8.6	9.4	9.8	9.0	9.1	...
C Mining, manufacturing and construction, except fuel and energy	...	...	...	...	...	...	...	...	...	...	...	...
D Transportation and communication	6.3	7.2	6.9	6.6	6.2	5.8	6.2	6.6	9.3	6.7	5.8	...
E Other economic affairs	3.4	3.8	3.5	4.2	4.1	4.4	4.5	5.9	5.9	5.4	5.2	...
10 Other functions	...	...	...	...	...	...	...	...	...	...	...	...
Total Government Final Consumption Expenditure	74.0	74.3	78.4	76.7	79.7	84.5	93.2	94.5	97.0	91.3	92.7	...

2.3 Total Government Outlays by Function and Type

Thousand Lesotho maloti

Fiscal year beginning 1 April

	Final Consumption Expenditures			Subsidies	Other Current Transfers & Property Income	Total Current Disbursements	Gross Capital Formation	Other Capital Outlays	Total Outlays
	Total	Compensation of Employees	Other						
1980									
1 General public services	30189	19568	10621	...	...	...	14525	...	...
2 Defence	...	...	...	...	...	...	...	...	...
3 Public order and safety	23828	13331	10497	...	...	...	2845	...	...
4 Education	29654	26748	2906	...	...	...	3452	...	...
5 Health	8207	4538	3669	...	...	...	740	...	...
6 Social security and welfare	...	...	...	...	...	...	...	...	...
7 Housing and community amenities	...	...	...	...	...	...	...	...	...
8 Recreation, culture and religion	...	...	...	...	...	...	...	...	...
9 Economic services	21668	10156	11512	...	...	...	22777	...	...
A Fuel and energy	...	...	...	...	...	...	...	...	...
B Agriculture, forestry, fishing and hunting	11930	6686	5244	...	...	...	2784	...	...
C Mining (except fuels), manufacturing and construction	...	...	...	...	...	...	...	...	...
D Transportation and communication	...	...	...	...	...	...	3082	...	...
E Other economic affairs	9738	3470	6268	...	...	...	16911	...	...
10 Other functions	...	...	...	...	...	...	...	...	...
Total	113546	74341	39205	1175	9101	123822	44339	...	168161
1981									
1 General public services	37116	26115	11001	...	...	...	21818	...	...
2 Defence	...	...	...	...	...	...	...	...	...
3 Public order and safety	19631	11918	7713	...	...	...	4273	...	...
4 Education	23213	21055	2158	...	...	...	5185	...	...
5 Health	6765	4286	2479	...	...	...	1111	...	...
6 Social security and welfare	...	...	...	...	...	...	...	...	...
7 Housing and community amenities	...	...	...	...	...	...	...	...	...
8 Recreation, culture and religion	...	...	...	...	...	...	...	...	...
9 Economic services	20178	10434	9744	...	...	...	34213	...	...
A Fuel and energy	...	...	...	...	...	...	...	...	...
B Agriculture, forestry, fishing and hunting	8774	6603	2171	...	...	...	4182	...	...
C Mining (except fuels), manufacturing and construction	...	...	...	...	...	...	...	...	...
D Transportation and communication	...	...	...	...	...	...	4629	...	...
E Other economic affairs	11404	3831	7573	...	...	...	25402	...	...
10 Other functions	...	...	...	...	...	...	...	...	...
Total	106903	73808	33095	190	10514	117607	66600	...	184207
1982									
1 General public services	15962	17342	-1380	...	...	...	3216	...	...
2 Defence	...	...	...	...	...	...	...	...	...
3 Public order and safety	26561	15589	10972	...	...	...	957	...	...
4 Education	24696	22548	2148	...	...	...	2279	...	...
5 Health	8817	4714	4103	...	...	...	811	...	...
6 Social security and welfare	...	...	...	...	...	...	...	...	...
7 Housing and community amenities	...	...	...	...	...	...	...	...	...
8 Recreation, culture and religion	...	...	...	...	...	...	...	...	...
9 Economic services	20333	10281	10052	...	...	...	56237	...	...
A Fuel and energy	...	...	...	...	...	...	...	...	...
B Agriculture, forestry, fishing and hunting	9123	6311	2812	...	...	...	12471	...	...
C Mining (except fuels), manufacturing and construction	...	...	...	...	...	...	11436	...	...
D Transportation and communication	...	...	...	...	...	...	4824	...	...
E Other economic affairs	11210	3970	7240	...	...	...	27506	...	...
10 Other functions	...	...	...	...	...	...	...	...	...
Total	96369	70474	25895	-	9659	106028	63500	...	169528

Lesotho

2.3 Total Government Outlays by Function and Type
(Continued)

Thousand Lesotho maloti   Fiscal year beginning 1 April

	Final Consumption Expenditures			Subsidies	Other Current Transfers & Property Income	Total Current Disbursements	Gross Capital Formation	Other Capital Outlays	Total Outlays
	Total	Compensation of Employees	Other						
1983									
1 General public services	32192	20897	11295	...	...	...	9634	...	...
2 Defence	...	...	...	...	...	...	...	...	...
3 Public order and safety	23764	14232	9532	...	...	...	3592	...	...
4 Education	27963	25434	2529	...	...	...	4421	...	...
5 Health	11084	4965	6119	...	...	...	1395	...	...
6 Social security and welfare	...	...	...	...	...	...	...	...	...
7 Housing and community amenities	...	...	...	...	...	...	...	...	...
8 Recreation, culture and religion	...	...	...	...	...	...	...	...	...
9 Economic services	21179	11711	9468	...	...	...	38758	...	...
A Fuel and energy	...	...	...	...	...	...	...	...	...
B Agriculture, forestry, fishing and hunting	9505	6835	2670	...	...	...	4761	...	...
C Mining (except fuels), manufacturing and construction	...	...	...	...	...	...	5547	...	...
D Transportation and communication	...	...	...	...	...	...	16532	...	...
E Other economic affairs	11674	4876	6798	...	...	...	11918	...	...
10 Other functions	...	...	...	...	...	...	...	...	...
Total	116182	77239	38943	-	28387	144569	57800	...	202369

4.3 Cost Components of Value Added

Thousand Lesotho maloti   Fiscal year beginning 1 April

	1980						1981					
	Compensation of Employees	Capital Consumption	Net Operating Surplus	Indirect Taxes	Less: Subsidies Received	Value Added	Compensation of Employees	Capital Consumption	Net Operating Surplus	Indirect Taxes	Less: Subsidies Received	Value Added
All Producers												
1 Agriculture, hunting, forestry and fishing	2899	1380	64733	...	...	69012	3455	1645	77157	...	...	82257
2 Mining and quarrying	11515	...	9199	...	...	20714	8915	...	7121	...	...	16036
3 Manufacturing	8013	570	6135	...	...	14718	9340	733	7855	...	...	17928
4 Electricity, gas and water	656	407	784	...	...	1847	921	461	343	...	...	1725
5 Construction	7714	400	20148	...	...	28262	8705	3538	19544	...	...	31787
6 Wholesale and retail trade, restaurants and hotels	13756	1947	17503	...	...	33206	15441	1669	21481	...	...	38591
A Wholesale and retail trade	8470	950	14494	...	...	23914	9555	986	17339	...	...	27880
B Restaurants and hotels	5286	997	3009	...	...	9292	5886	683	4142	...	...	10711
7 Transport, storage and communication	1968	976	854	...	...	3798	2221	1066	1263	...	...	4550
A Transport and storage	1361	976	847	...	...	3184	1463	1066	1240	...	...	3769
B Communication	607	-	7	...	...	614	758	-	23	...	...	781
8 Finance, insurance, real estate and business services	7155	766	18495	...	...	26416	7451	988	27606	...	...	36045
A Financial institutions	3731	334	1459	...	...	5524	3521	338	6081	...	...	9940
B Insurance	...	...	...	...	...	...	...	...	...	...	...	...
C Real estate and business services	3424	432	17036	...	...	20892	3930	650	21525	...	...	26105
Real estate, except dwellings	3424	432	3070	...	...	6926	3930	650	5248	...	...	9828
Dwellings	...	...	13966	...	...	13966	...	...	16277	...	...	16277
9 Community, social and personal services	1869	232	719	...	...	2820	3224	311	-60	...	...	3475
Total, Industries	55545	6678	138570	...	...	200793	59673	10411	162310	...	...	232394
Producers of Government Services	43804	...	...	...	...	43804	48467	...	...	...	...	48467
Other Producers	30983	...	...	...	...	30983	31609	...	...	...	...	31609
Total	130332	6678	138570	...	...	275580	139749	10411	162310	...	...	312470
Less: Imputed bank service charge	...	...	2830	...	...	2830	...	...	7549	...	...	7549
Import duties	...	...	...	...	...	...	...	...	...	...	...	...
Value added tax	...	...	...	...	...	...	...	...	...	...	...	...
Other adjustments	...	...	...	56779	1175	55604	...	...	...	58737	190	58547
Total	130332	6678	135740	56779	1175	328354	139749	10411	154761	58737	190	363468

4.3 Cost Components of Value Added

Thousand Lesotho maloti
Fiscal year beginning 1 April

	1982						1983					
	Compensation of Employees	Capital Consumption	Net Operating Surplus	Indirect Taxes	Less: Subsidies Received	Value Added	Compensation of Employees	Capital Consumption	Net Operating Surplus	Indirect Taxes	Less: Subsidies Received	Value Added
All Producers												
1 Agriculture, hunting, forestry and fishing	3410	1624	76170	...	...	81204	3955	1884	88324	...	...	94163
2 Mining and quarrying	8098	675	4723	...	...	13496	...	...	811	...	...	811
3 Manufacturing	15531	2201	6460	...	...	24192	20265	1030	3689	...	...	24984
4 Electricity, gas and water	1053	586	438	...	...	2077	2071	752	954	...	...	3777
5 Construction	29598	1932	6900	...	...	38430	33695	2504	7731	...	...	43930
6 Wholesale and retail trade, restaurants and hotels	21737	2769	21681	...	...	46187	22838	3075	25795	...	...	51708
A Wholesale and retail trade	14144	1913	18626	...	...	34683	14784	1717	20161	...	...	36662
B Restaurants and hotels	7593	856	3055	...	...	11504	8054	1358	5634	...	...	15046
7 Transport, storage and communication	3241	1371	998	...	...	5610	3419	1718	1457	...	...	6594
A Transport and storage	2572	1371	991	...	...	4934	2745	1718	1454	...	...	5917
B Communication	669	-	7	...	...	676	674	-	3	...	...	677
8 Finance, insurance, real estate and business services	12132	1033	29488	...	...	42653	12951	1112	33751	...	...	47814
A Financial institutions	5123	328	7292	...	...	12743	5750	397	8008	...	...	14155
B Insurance	...	...	...	...	...	...	...	...	...	...	...	...
C Real estate and business services	7009	705	22196	...	...	29910	7201	715	25743	...	...	33659
Real estate, except dwellings	7009	705	3852	...	...	11566	7201	715	5657	...	...	13573
Dwellings	...	...	18344	...	...	18344	...	...	20086	...	...	20086
9 Community, social and personal services	2148	325	1492	...	...	3965	1978	298	1015	...	...	3291
Total, Industries	96948	12516	148350	...	...	257814	101172	12373	163527	...	...	277072
Producers of Government Services	43212	...	...	...	...	43212	46840	...	...	...	...	46840
Other Producers	27856	...	...	...	...	27856	31096	...	...	...	...	31096
Total	168016	12516	148350	...	...	328882	179108	12373	163527	...	...	355008
Less: Imputed bank service charge	...	...	7879	...	...	7879	...	...	9309	...	...	9309
Import duties	...	...	...	...	...	...	...	...	...	...	...	...
Value added tax	...	...	...	...	...	...	...	...	...	...	...	...
Other adjustments	...	...	...	61000	...	61000	...	...	...	100028	...	100028
Total	168016	12516	140471	61000	...	382003	179108	12373	154218	100028	...	445727

Liberia

General note. The preparation of national accounts statistics in Liberia is undertaken by the Ministry of Planning and Economic Affairs, Monrovia. The official estimates are published annually in 'Economic Survey of Liberia'. A description of the sources and methods used for the national accounts estimation is found in 'Sources and Methods of Estimation of National Product, 1970-1973' and 'The New Series and Methodology for Estimating Gross Domestic Product, 1973' published in 1975 and 1978 respectively. The estimates are generally in accordance with the classifications and definitions recommended in the United Nations System of National Accounts (SNA). The following tables have been prepared from successive replies to the United Nations national accounts questionnaire. When the scope and coverage of the estimates differ for conceptual or statistical reasons from the definitions and classifications recommended in SNA, a footnote is indicated to the relevant tables.

Sources and methods :

(a) Gross domestic product. Gross domestic product is estimated mainly through the income approach.

(b) Expenditure on the gross domestic product. The expenditure approach is used to estimate government final consumption expenditure, increase in stocks and exports and imports of goods and services. The commodity-flow approach is used to estimate private final consumption expenditure and gross fixed capital formation. The main sources used for estimating government final consumption expenditure are the monthly revenue and expenditure reports contained in 'Government Accounts of Liberia'. For private expenditure on imported goods, the c.i.f. value and import duties are obtained directly from the import statistics of consumer goods while the trade and transport margin is put at 35 per cent of the c.i.f. value. For local production, estimates are obtained from the production statistics of goods and services. Changes in stocks are estimated for iron-ore only. The sources used are the annual reports of the iron-ore companies and an analysis based on the difference between production and exports. The estimate is obtained by finding the difference between the quantities produced and the quantities exported and applying the average export prices. Gross fixed capital formation is estimated as value of local production plus imports minus exports plus transport costs, trade mark-ups, duties paid, etc. For machinery and equipment, the estimates are based on foreign trade statistics. For construction, the estimates are prepared by analysing import and local production of construction materials, the data of which are obtained from import statistics and the survey of establishments. The estimates of imports and exports of goods and services are based on the foreign trade statistics. Figures on exports and imports are supplemented by estimates for non-factor services. Constant price series of government expenditure is estimated by using employment data to extrapolate the base-year figures. The base-year value for stocks of iron-ore is extrapolated by using a volume indicator. For the remaining components of GDP by expenditure type, the current values are deflated by price indexes.

(c) Cost-structure of the gross domestic product. The estimates of compensation of employees, operating surplus and consumption of fixed capital are obtained from income tax files, replies to the national accounts questionnaires and from annual reports and financial accounts. The estimates of indirect taxes and subsidies are based on income tax returns for the main activities.

(d) Gross domestic product by kind of economic activity. The table of GDP by kind of economic activity is prepared in factor values. The income approach is used to estimate the value added of most industries. When data are available, the production and expenditure approaches are also used. For the agricultural sector, value added of rubber production is estimated from the financial accounts of the rubber concessions, the income tax statements of all rubber companies, and from information obtained from local rubber farmers. For other agricultural crops and fishing, value added is obtained from the income tax files. The value added of forestry is arrived at from an input-output study of the industry, based on the national accounts surveys. For the mining of iron-ore, value added is obtained directly from the financial accounts of the companies. Information of production components of manufacturing is obtained from income tax files, semi-annual questionnaires and other supplementary series. An extrapolation is made for non-reporting establishments. The value added of electricity, gas and water is obtained directly from the annual reports and accounts of concerned enterprises and their replies to the national accounts questionnaires. Estimates of the construction sector are derived mainly by using the commodity-flow approach. Domestic production of commodities used in construction is estimated and adjusted for exports, imports and changes in stocks and supplementary data on transport costs, dealers' margins, etc. is added. The value of imported construction materials and production statistics of locally produced construction are obtained. Information on substantial development of land undertaken by the companies. A combination of the production approach and the income approach is used for the trade sector. The output is equal to the gross margin. The income tax data and the technique of extrapolation are used to arrive at value added. The extrapolation process involves separating the large establishments from the others, extrapolating the value added by the change registered by comparable establishments and finally indentifying new establishments and treating them as an additional contributor to value added. The estimates of the transport sector are derived from various sources such as national accounts questionnaire, income tax files and reports of the Motor Vehicle Division. The gross output of the financial sector is equal to the sum of actual service charges and imputed service charges. The data required for the value added are obtained through a questionnaire. The estimates of real estate and ownership of dwellings are obtained by extrapolating the 1967 estimate by means of the population growth rate and the rent component of the consumer price index. For producers of government services, the main source is the detailed analysis of the government accounts. The value added of other private services are extrapolated by the change in compensation of employees, interest, depreciation and operating surplus obtained from the income tax files. For the constant price estimates, price deflation is used for manufacturing, construction and trade sectors. For the remaining sectors, value added is extrapolated by using volume indexes.

1.1 Expenditure on the Gross Domestic Product, in Current Prices

Million Liberian dollars

	1980	1981	1982	1983	1984	1985	1986	1987	1988	1989	1990	1991
1 Government final consumption expenditure	182.0	200.1	222.4	169.1	160.2	137.3	142.8	143.9	136.3	141.6	...	...
2 Private final consumption expenditure	430.0	647.2	650.4	723.0	710.2	706.8	662.6	713.9	733.3	656.8	...	...
3 Gross capital formation	245.2	198.1	236.0	190.8	194.6	134.3	122.8	127.4	118.8	100.8	...	...
A Increase in stocks a	49.1	18.5	42.9	7.7	25.7	7.8	7.8	7.0	3.5	4.0	...	...
B Gross fixed capital formation	196.1	179.6	193.1	183.1	168.9	126.5	115.0	120.4	115.3	96.8	...	...
4 Exports of goods and services	613.5	540.7	510.6	463.5	489.0	470.2	459.4	438.2	452.3	521.4	...	...
5 Less: Imports of goods and services	614.0	560.9	478.5	479.2	411.5	322.8	325.2	356.8	321.5	275.2	...	...
Statistical discrepancy	59.9	29.1	-47.6	18.4	-72.3	-70.5	-25.2	22.9	39.1	48.2	...	...
Equals: Gross Domestic Product	916.6	1054.3	1093.3	1085.6	1070.2	1055.3	1037.2	1089.5	1158.3	1193.6	...	...

a) Item 'Increase in stocks' includes only increase in iron ore stocks. Beginning 1981, it includes increase in iron ore and rubber stocks.

1.2 Expenditure on the Gross Domestic Product, in Constant Prices

Million Liberian dollars

	1980	1981	1982	1983	1984	1985	1986	1987	1988	1989	1990	1991
		At constant prices of:										
		1971					1981					
1 Government final consumption expenditure	61.0	58.5 / 200.1	218.9	169.0	156.8	136.9	141.2	142.3	134.8	140.0	...	...
2 Private final consumption expenditure	171.0	163.5 / 647.2	620.9	650.0	621.1	625.0	593.4	628.9	646.0	576.8	...	...
3 Gross capital formation	116.9	87.1 / 198.1	234.3	193.4	173.3	120.2	104.4	102.9	87.0	82.3	...	...
A Increase in stocks	21.7a	-4.5a / 18.5	40.5	5.4	20.6	6.5	6.5	5.8	3.8	4.2	...	...
B Gross fixed capital formation	95.2	91.6 / 179.6	193.8	188.0	152.7	113.7	97.9	97.1	83.2	78.1	...	...
4 Exports of goods and services	237.0	217.4 / 540.7	471.0	460.1	489.5	473.0	449.0	471.8	480.7	534.1	...	...
5 Less: Imports of goods and services	187.0	169.0 / 560.9	454.0	473.1	375.1	317.4	413.6	315.1	265.7	227.4	...	...
Statistical discrepancy	12.5	17.9 / 29.1	-18.3	36.5	-35.8	-28.7	122.7	-15.8	-39.1	-33.0	...	...
Equals: Gross Domestic Product	411.4	395.4 / 1054.3	1072.8	1035.9	1029.8	1009.0	997.1	1015.0	1043.7	1072.8	...	...

a) Item 'Increase in stocks' includes only increase in iron ore stocks. Beginning 1981, it includes increase in iron ore and rubber stocks.

1.10 Gross Domestic Product by Kind of Activity, in Current Prices

Million Liberian dollars

	1980	1981	1982	1983	1984	1985	1986	1987	1988	1989	1990	1991
1 Agriculture, hunting, forestry and fishing	159.0	297.0	284.8	334.5	358.7	351.3	343.6	381.8	412.0	410.7	...	...
2 Mining and quarrying	153.0	127.4	150.3	123.2	107.4	128.3	118.5	105.0	115.0	122.3	...	...
3 Manufacturing	77.0	62.9	65.2	59.6	65.8	64.8	59.8	73.1	80.4	81.6	...	...
4 Electricity, gas and water	19.1	22.7	25.0	28.9	22.5	16.6	18.8	19.0	18.8	19.0	...	...
5 Construction	32.5	37.0	39.7	39.8	34.6	32.2	28.9	32.7	28.8	26.3	...	...
6 Wholesale and retail trade, restaurants and hotels	79.0	59.1	74.9	70.4	62.5	60.2	56.7	60.1	64.2	63.3	...	...
7 Transport, storage and communication	61.0	76.2	77.0	80.4	80.7	71.4	75.3	75.3	79.1	79.1	...	...
8 Finance, insurance, real estate and business services	76.6	85.8	90.2	100.9	110.3	109.0	112.9	119.2	136.1	141.8	...	...
9 Community, social and personal services	31.5	28.6	29.6	31.7	27.7	31.4	31.0	34.4	35.5	35.5	...	...
Total, Industries	688.7	796.7	836.7	869.4	870.2	865.2	845.5	900.6	969.9	979.6	...	...
Producers of Government Services	123.6	154.4	154.9	127.1	121.7	114.4	109.7	108.5	109.7	139.4	...	...
Other Producers	...	...	...	...	...	...	...	...	...	...	...	...
Subtotal a	812.3	951.1	991.6	996.5	991.9	979.6	955.2	1009.1	1079.6	1119.0	...	...
Less: Imputed bank service charge	11.5	13.3	16.5	17.7	24.7	20.3	19.7	18.3	27.1	36.5	...	...
Plus: Import duties	67.6	80.3	67.3	60.3	57.0						...	...
Plus: Value added tax	...	...	...	...	...	96.0	101.6	99.0	105.8	111.3	...	...
Plus: Other adjustments b	48.2	36.2	50.9	46.5	46.0						...	...
Equals: Gross Domestic Product	916.6	1054.3	1093.3	1085.6	1070.2	1055.3	1037.2	1089.5	1158.3	1193.6	...	...

a) Gross domestic product in factor values.
b) Item 'Other adjustments' refers to net indirect taxes other than import duties.

1.11 Gross Domestic Product by Kind of Activity, in Constant Prices

Million Liberian dollars

	1980	1981	1982	1983	1984	1985	1986	1987	1988	1989	1990	1991
		At constant prices of:										
		1971					1981					
1 Agriculture, hunting, forestry and fishing	63.0	49.4 / 297.0	297.9	305.0	323.2	339.2	340.4	365.3	379.5	379.5	...	...
2 Mining and quarrying	111.0	100.8 / 127.4	120.9	96.0	99.4	92.0	91.0	81.5	81.1	82.5	...	...
3 Manufacturing	26.0	23.6 / 62.9	66.0	65.4	68.3	67.2	65.1	66.1	72.7	73.8	...	...
4 Electricity, gas and water	7.8	7.9 / 22.7	26.9	23.4	23.6	24.0	24.0	25.3	25.4	25.6	...	...
5 Construction	15.0	18.0 / 37.0	33.3	38.2	29.8	30.5	26.7	26.6	27.9	25.5	...	...

Liberia

1.11 Gross Domestic Product by Kind of Activity, in Constant Prices
(Continued)

Million Liberian dollars

	1980	1981	1982	1983	1984	1985	1986	1987	1988	1989	1990	1991
	1971				At constant prices of:		**1981**					
6 Wholesale and retail trade, restaurants and hotels	25.0	23.0 / 59.1	68.9	67.1	56.9	57.4	51.5	51.7	51.0	50.3	...	...
7 Transport, storage and communication	35.0	33.4 / 76.2	88.8	86.4	84.7	72.7	71.7	69.5	71.6	71.6	...	...
8 Finance, insurance, real estate and business services	30.0	31.1 / 85.8	83.6	88.7	86.3	86.5	87.3	95.9	99.9	104.1	...	...
9 Community, social and personal services	17.0	16.0 / 28.6	30.5	31.4	27.1	30.0	28.0	28.9	24.5	24.5	...	...
Total, Industries	330.3	303.2 / 796.7	816.8	801.6	799.3	799.5	785.7	810.8	833.6	837.4	...	...
Producers of Government Services	39.6	50.4 / 154.4	154.9	152.5	146.0	137.3	131.7	130.3	130.3	165.0	...	...
Other Producers	...	... / ...	...	...	...	...	...	...	...	...	...	...
Subtotal	369.9[a]	353.6[a] / 951.1	971.7	954.1	945.3	936.8	917.4	941.1	963.9	1002.4	...	...
Less: Imputed bank service charge	3.7	4.3 / 13.3	12.4	14.7	11.1	13.0	13.7	15.9	16.5	12.3	...	...
Plus: Import duties	...	... / ...	...	...	...	...	...	...	...	...	...	...
Plus: Value added tax	...	... / ...	...	...	...	...	...	...	...	...	...	...
Plus: Other adjustments	45.2[b]	45.8[b] / 116.5	113.5	96.5	95.6	85.2	93.2	90.1	96.3	82.7	...	...
Equals: Gross Domestic Product	411.4	395.4 / 1054.3	1072.8	1035.9	1029.8	1009.0	997.1	1015.0	1043.7	1072.8	...	...

a) Gross domestic product in factor values.
b) Item 'Other adjustments' refers to net indirect taxes other than import duties.

1.12 Relations Among National Accounting Aggregates

Million Liberian dollars

	1980	1981	1982	1983	1984	1985	1986	1987	1988	1989	1990	1991
Gross Domestic Product	...	1054.3	1093.3	1085.6	1070.2	1055.3	1037.2	1089.5	1158.3	1193.6	...	...
Plus: Net factor income from the rest of the world	...	-125.2	-175.5	-141.9	-170.1	-123.6	-180.5	-183.1	-183.1	-180.3	...	...
Equals: Gross National Product	...	929.1	917.8	943.7	900.1	931.7	856.7	906.4	975.2	1013.3	...	...
Less: Consumption of fixed capital	...	118.3	115.8	115.8	98.6	85.2	90.8	93.2	96.0	101.9	...	...
Equals: National Income	...	810.8	802.0	827.9	801.5	846.5	765.9	813.2	879.2	911.4	...	...
Plus: Net current transfers from the rest of the world	...	...	...	...	...	...	...	...	...	...	...	...
Equals: National Disposable Income	...	...	...	...	...	...	...	...	...	...	...	...
Less: Final consumption	...	...	...	...	...	...	...	...	...	...	...	...
Equals: Net Saving	...	...	...	...	...	...	...	...	...	...	...	...
Less: Surplus of the nation on current transactions	...	...	...	...	...	...	...	...	...	...	...	...
Equals: Net Capital Formation	...	...	...	...	...	...	...	...	...	...	...	...

Libyan Arab Jamahiriya

General note. The preparation of national accounts statisticis in Libyan Arab Jamahiriya is undertaken by the Ministry of Planning, Tripoli. The official estimates are published in a series of publications entitled 'National Accounts of Libya'. A detailed description of the sources and methods used for the national accounts estimation is contained in a publication entitled 'National Accounts Statistics of the Libyan Arab Republic - Sources and Methods' published in 1972. The estimates are generally in accordance with the classifications and definitions recommended in the United Nations System of National Accounts (SNA). The following tables have been prepared from successive replies to the United Nations national accounts questionnaire. When the scope and coverage of the estimates differ for conceptual or statistical reasons from the definitions and classifications recommended in SNA, a footnote is indicated to the relevant tables.

Sources and methods :

(a) Gross domestic product. Gross domestic product is estimated mainly through the production approach.

(b) Expenditure on the gross domestic product. The expenditure approach is used to estimate government final consumption expenditure and imports and exports of goods and services. This approach is also used for gross fixed capital formation, although supported by the commodity-flow method for machinery and equipment. The commodity-flow method is used for the estimation of private expenditure on goods while other approaches are used for the estimation of expenditure on services. For government final consumption expenditure, the estimates are obtained from actual revenue and expenditure data supplied by the Ministry of Finance, by municipalities and by the National Social Insurance Institutions. The estimates are classified both by purpose and by kind of expenditure. The estimates of private expenditures on goods are obtained from the external trade statistics by commodity and from data on locally produced goods, import duties, trade margins and average retail prices. The estimates of capital formation for the petroleum sector are obtained from Annual Survey of Petroleum Mining Industry and for the general government, the most important source is the data on actual expenditure in the central government development budgets. For machinery and equipment, external trade data are used, adding duties paid and other costs and deducting value of re-export from c.i.f. value of imports. Exports and imports of goods and services are estimated from data supplied by the Bank of Libya. For the constant price estimates, price deflation is used for most of the expenditure items, the current values being deflated by various price indexes such as nation-wide cost of living index, price index of imported consumer goods and appropriate unit value indexes for different capital goods. Personal expenditures on items such as food and transport equipment are extrapolated by quantity indicators.

(c) Cost-structure of the gross domestic product. In estimating the cost-structure components of GDP, depreciation of the petroleum sector is obtained from the Annual Survey of Petroleum Mining Industry. For other sectors, depreciation is estimated as a certain percentage of gross domestic product according to international experience and judgement about the prevailing situation in the Libyan economy. Indirect taxes are estimated from the central government and local authorities' annual accounts, while subsidies are estimated on the basis on the ordinary and the development budgets. No information for compensation of employees and operating surplus is available about the methods of estimation.

(d) Gross domestic product by kind of economic activity. The table of gross domestic product by kind of economic activity is prepared at market prices, i.e.

producers' values. The production approach is used to estimate value added of the majority of industries. The income approach is used for transport, storage and communication, public administration and defence and other services. The expenditure approach is used for the construction sector, whereas value added of the trade sectors is based upon the use of the commodity-flow method. All data required for the estimation of the agriculture sector are supplied by the Ministry of Agriculture. The agricultural statistics are based on reports made by the local authorities of the Ministry of Agriculture and data derived from the reporting system are verified by the agricultural census held in 1974. Petroleum mining, which accounts for more than two-thirds of GDP, is carried out by petroleum mining concession holding units and by non-concession holding units which are engaged in prospecting and drilling activities on a contract basis. Gross output of the concession holding units is made up of value of exports, value of changes in stocks, cost of surveys and exploration, value of work done for others and miscellaneous sources of income. The value of exports based on f.o.b. values, is reported by crude petroleum exporting companies, while the value of the other output is contained in the Annual Survey of Petroleum Mining Industry. The total value of inputs consists of the cost of materials consumed and the value of services purchased. For the activities of the non-concession holding units, a survey is undertaken on an annual basis since 1970. The basic source of information for manufacturing is the annual survey conducted since 1965 and published in 'Report of the Annual Survey of Large Manufacturing Establishments'. The data derived from the surveys are adjusted to exclude trade activity. Estimates for gross output and value added are then worked out for all establishments, including those engaging less than 20 persons which are not covered by the annual surveys. The main sources of information for the construction sector are the government budgets, statements by the municipalities and the annual surveys of the petroleum mining industry and of the large manufacturing establishments. The value added of construction is estimated as a percentage of the total expenditure on construction made by all sectors of the economy. There are no comprehensive statistics which could be used for a direct compilation of value added originating in trade. The estimation is instead based on an indirect method, according to which the income accruing to the trade sector is estimated as a percentage of the value of goods transacted during the year. The value added of road transport is based on the number of vehicles in operation and the value added per vehicle. Transport data are supplied by Ministry of Communication Road Department and Libyan Arab Airline. Data for banking and insurance are supplied by Bank of Libya. The income accrued from ownership of dwellings is based on the estimation of the number of dwelling units existing each year and on the application of an average annual rent per unit. Estimates for the producers of government services are based on actual revenue and expenditure of the government sectors. Other services estimates are derived by applying an average gross income per person to the number of persons engaged in the different activities. For the constant price estimates, double deflation is used for the agricultural sector with the quantity of output and input valued at average 1963-1965 prices. Value added of crude oil production, electricity, gas and water, construction and transport is extrapolated by quantity indexes of output. For other activities in the petroleum sector, the current value is deflated by a price index roughly reflecting changes in the cost of its main goods and services. For manufacturing, trade, financial sector and other services, different kinds of price indexes are used, such as cost of living index and price index of domestic manufacturing goods.

1.1 Expenditure on the Gross Domestic Product, in Current Prices

Million Libyan dinars

	1980	1981	1982	1983	1984	1985	1986	1987	1988	1989	1990	1991
1 Government final consumption expenditure	2350.5	2990.5	2900.8	2883.4	2690.0	2622.4	...	...	...	...	...	...
2 Private final consumption expenditure	2868.9	3887.4	3617.9	3453.8	3094.2	3108.9	...	...	...	...	...	...
3 Gross capital formation	2570.0	3100.3	2393.1	2107.8	2071.2	1663.1	...	...	...	...	...	...
A Increase in stocks	95.0	200.0	-75.0	-100.0	40.0	35.0	...	...	...	...	...	...
B Gross fixed capital formation	2475.0	2900.3	2468.1	2207.8	2031.2	1628.1	...	...	...	...	...	...
4 Exports of goods and services	6537.9	4409.5	4104.5	3703.3	3315.2	3093.9	...	...	...	...	...	...
5 Less: Imports of goods and services	3752.1	5127.7	3920.1	3343.1	3157.3	2211.3	...	...	...	...	...	...
Equals: Gross Domestic Product	10575.2	9260.0	9096.2	8805.2	8013.3	8277.0	...	...	...	...	...	...

1.2 Expenditure on the Gross Domestic Product, in Constant Prices

Million Libyan dinars

	1980	1981	1982	1983	1984	1985	1986	1987	1988	1989	1990	1991
						At constant prices of:1980						
1 Government final consumption expenditure	2350.5	2886.0	2766.6	2728.6	2477.1	2285.2	...	...	...	...	...	...
2 Private final consumption expenditure	2868.9	3845.5	3419.6	3557.0	3500.2	3602.4	...	...	...	...	...	...
3 Gross capital formation	2570.0	2924.6	2194.9	1897.0	1842.0	1467.9	...	...	...	...	...	...
A Increase in stocks	95.0	196.0	-72.5	-95.5	38.5	36.5	...	...	...	...	...	...
B Gross fixed capital formation	2475.0	2728.6	2267.4	1992.5	1804.5	1431.4	...	...	...	...	...	...
4 Exports of goods and services	6537.9	3965.4	4108.6	3829.7	3886.5	3867.3	...	...	...	...	...	...
5 Less: Imports of goods and services	3752.1	5075.7	3704.1	3443.9	3570.4	2408.9	...	...	...	...	...	...
Equals: Gross Domestic Product	10575.2	8545.8	8785.6	8568.4	8136.4	8813.9	...	...	...	...	...	...

Libyan Arab Jamahiriya

1.3 Cost Components of the Gross Domestic Product

Million Libyan dinars

	1980	1981	1982	1983	1984	1985	1986	1987	1988	1989	1990	1991
1 Indirect taxes, net	297.9	390.9	315.6	323.3	332.2	226.8	...	...	...	...	...	...
A Indirect taxes	509.4	575.8	528.0	470.0	462.2	389.0	...	...	...	...	...	...
B Less: Subsidies	211.5	184.9	212.4	146.7	130.0	162.2	...	...	...	...	...	...
2 Consumption of fixed capital	345.8	390.6	412.7	436.1	457.5	481.6	...	...	...	...	...	...
3 Compensation of employees paid by resident producers to:	2184.7	2489.8	2622.5	2763.1	2865.8	2996.2	...	...	...	...	...	...
4 Operating surplus	7746.8	5988.7	5745.4	5282.7	4357.8	4572.4	...	...	...	...	...	...
Equals: Gross Domestic Product	10575.2	9260.0	9096.2	8805.2	8013.3	8277.0	...	...	...	...	...	...

1.4 General Government Current Receipts and Disbursements

Million Libyan dinars

	1980	1981	1982	1983	1984	1985	1986	1987	1988	1989	1990	1991
Receipts												
1 Operating surplus	15.9	...	...	...	...	...	...	...	...	...	...	...
2 Property and entrepreneurial income	6497.9	...	...	...	...	...	...	...	...	...	...	...
3 Taxes, fees and contributions	919.8	...	...	...	...	...	...	...	...	...	...	...
A Indirect taxes	509.4	...	...	...	...	...	...	...	...	...	...	...
B Direct taxes	283.9	...	...	...	...	...	...	...	...	...	...	...
C Social security contributions	86.0	...	...	...	...	...	...	...	...	...	...	...
D Compulsory fees, fines and penalties	40.5	...	...	...	...	...	...	...	...	...	...	...
4 Other current transfers	1.7	...	...	...	...	...	...	...	...	...	...	...
Total Current Receipts of General Government	7435.4											
Disbursements												
1 Government final consumption expenditure	2350.5	...	...	...	...	...	...	...	...	...	...	...
2 Property income	...	...	...	...	...	...	...	...	...	...	...	...
3 Subsidies	211.5	...	...	...	...	...	...	...	...	...	...	...
4 Other current transfers	337.6	...	...	...	...	...	...	...	...	...	...	...
A Social security benefits	49.9	...	...	...	...	...	...	...	...	...	...	...
B Social assistance grants	81.3	...	...	...	...	...	...	...	...	...	...	...
C Other	206.4	...	...	...	...	...	...	...	...	...	...	...
5 Net saving	4535.7	...	...	...	...	...	...	...	...	...	...	...
Total Current Disbursements and Net Saving of General Government	7435.4	...	...	...	...	...	...	...	...	...	...	...

1.7 External Transactions on Current Account, Summary

Million Libyan dinars

	1980	1981	1982	1983	1984	1985	1986	1987	1988	1989	1990	1991
Payments to the Rest of the World												
1 Imports of goods and services	3752.1	5127.7	3920.1	3343.1	3157.3	2211.3	...	...	...	...	...	...
A Imports of merchandise c.i.f.	3411.2	4790.4	3610.4	2953.0	2784.1	1879.1	...	...	...	...	...	...
B Other	340.9	337.3	309.7	390.1	373.2	332.2	...	...	...	...	...	...
2 Factor income to the rest of the world	679.0	871.7	842.9	989.0	727.7	397.9	...	...	...	...	...	...
A Compensation of employees	322.3	464.9	472.7	605.3	367.2	238.3	...	...	...	...	...	...
B Property and entrepreneurial income	356.7	406.9	370.2	383.7	360.5	159.6	...	...	...	...	...	...
3 Current transfers to the rest of the world	19.3	30.1	32.5	25.2	27.9	16.0	...	...	...	...	...	...
4 Surplus of the nation on current transactions	2472.8	-1130.9	-424.6	-445.2	-452.6	593.8	...	...	...	...	...	...
Payments to the Rest of the World and Surplus of the Nation on Current Transactions	6923.2	4898.7	4370.9	3912.1	3460.3	3219.0	...	...	...	...	...	...
Receipts From The Rest of the World												
1 Exports of goods and services	6537.9	4409.5	4104.5	3703.3	3315.2	3093.9	...	...	...	...	...	...

1.7 External Transactions on Current Account, Summary
(Continued)

Million Libyan dinars

	1980	1981	1982	1983	1984	1985	1986	1987	1988	1989	1990	1991
A Exports of merchandise f.o.b.	6498.3	4370.4	4065.5	3662.3	3272.8	3072.3	...	...	...	...	...	...
B Other	39.6	39.1	39.0	41.0	42.4	21.6	...	...	...	...	...	...
2 Factor income from rest of the world	379.5	481.6	256.9	200.2	142.8	122.5	...	...	...	...	...	...
A Compensation of employees	-	-	-	-	-	-	...	...	...	...	...	...
B Property and entrepreneurial income	...	...	...	...	...	...	...	...	...	...	...	...
3 Current transfers from rest of the world	5.8	7.6	9.5	8.6	2.3	2.6	...	...	...	...	...	...
Receipts from the Rest of the World on Current Transactions	6923.2	4898.7	4370.9	3912.1	3460.3	3219.0	...	...	...	...	...	...

1.8 Capital Transactions of The Nation, Summary

Million Libyan dinars

	1980	1981	1982	1983	1984	1985	1986	1987	1988	1989	1990	1991
Finance of Gross Capital Formation												
Gross saving	5042.8	1969.4	1968.5	1662.6	1618.6	2256.9	...	...	...	...	...	...
1 Consumption of fixed capital	345.8	390.6	412.7	436.1	457.5	481.6	...	...	...	...	...	...
A General government	63.7	...	...	...	...	...	...	...	...	...	...	...
B Corporate and quasi-corporate enterprises	...	...	...	...	...	...	...	...	...	...	...	...
C Other	...	...	...	...	...	...	...	...	...	...	...	...
2 Net saving	4697.0	1578.8	1555.8	1226.5	1161.1	1775.3	...	...	...	...	...	...
A General government	4535.7	...	...	...	...	...	...	...	...	...	...	...
B Corporate and quasi-corporate enterprises	...	...	...	...	...	...	...	...	...	...	...	...
C Other	...	...	...	...	...	...	...	...	...	...	...	...
Less: Surplus of the nation on current transactions	2472.8	-1130.9	-424.6	-445.2	-452.6	593.8	...	...	...	...	...	...
Finance of Gross Capital Formation	2570.0	3100.3	2393.1	2107.8	2071.2	1663.1	...	...	...	...	...	...
Gross Capital Formation												
Increase in stocks	95.0	200.0	-75.0	-100.0	40.0	35.0	...	...	...	...	...	...
Gross fixed capital formation	2475.0	2900.3	2468.1	2207.8	2031.2	1628.1	...	...	...	...	...	...
1 General government	2223.3	...	...	...	...	...	...	...	...	...	...	...
2 Corporate and quasi-corporate enterprises	...	...	...	...	...	...	...	...	...	...	...	...
3 Other	...	...	...	...	...	...	...	...	...	...	...	...
Gross Capital Formation	2570.0	3100.3	2393.1	2107.8	2071.2	1663.1	...	...	...	...	...	...

1.10 Gross Domestic Product by Kind of Activity, in Current Prices

Million Libyan dinars

	1980	1981	1982	1983	1984	1985	1986	1987	1988	1989	1990	1991
1 Agriculture, hunting, forestry and fishing	183.0	210.7	220.7	255.0	258.8	283.2	...	...	...	...	...	...
2 Mining and quarrying a	6620.0	4688.4	4532.6	4138.7	3144.5	3345.9	...	...	...	...	...	...
3 Manufacturing	192.2	219.3	243.7	274.6	298.3	365.1	...	...	...	...	...	...
4 Electricity, gas and water	49.7	55.7	69.2	80.0	92.0	101.5	...	...	...	...	...	...
5 Construction	935.7	1002.5	914.9	879.0	851.4	920.5	...	...	...	...	...	...
6 Wholesale and retail trade, restaurants and hotels	489.8	625.7	632.1	515.1	605.7	560.5	...	...	...	...	...	...
7 Transport, storage and communication	356.1	418.1	405.2	387.6	403.5	399.1	...	...	...	...	...	...
8 Finance, insurance, real estate and business services	456.8	515.6	479.2	549.3	530.5	524.9	...	...	...	...	...	...
9 Community, social and personal services	382.9	451.8	510.9	553.3	579.1	641.0	...	...	...	...	...	...
Total, Industries	9666.2	8187.8	8008.5	7632.6	6763.8	7141.7	...	...	...	...	...	...
Producers of Government Services	611.1	681.3	772.1	849.3	917.3	908.5	...	...	...	...	...	...

Libyan Arab Jamahiriya

1.10 Gross Domestic Product by Kind of Activity, in Current Prices
(Continued)

Million Libyan dinars

	1980	1981	1982	1983	1984	1985	1986	1987	1988	1989	1990	1991
Other Producers	...	...	...	...	...	...	...	...	...	...	...	...
Subtotal b	10277.3	8869.1	8780.6	8481.9	7681.1	8050.2	...	...	...	...	...	...
Less: Imputed bank service charge	...	...	...	...	...	...	...	...	...	...	...	...
Plus: Import duties	...	...	...	...	...	...	...	...	...	...	...	...
Plus: Value added tax	...	...	...	...	...	...	...	...	...	...	...	...
Plus: Other adjustments c	297.9	390.9	315.6	323.3	332.2	226.8	...	...	...	...	...	...
Equals: Gross Domestic Product	10575.2	9260.0	9096.2	8805.2	8013.3	8277.0	...	...	...	...	...	...

a) Item 'Mining and quarrying' includes oil and gas production.
b) Gross domestic product in factor values.
c) Item 'Other adjustments' refers to indirect taxes net of subsidies.

1.11 Gross Domestic Product by Kind of Activity, in Constant Prices

Million Libyan dinars

	1980	1981	1982	1983	1984	1985	1986	1987	1988	1989	1990	1991
					At constant prices of:1980							
1 Agriculture, hunting, forestry and fishing	183.0	207.9	213.0	244.3	234.8	244.3	...	...	...	...	...	...
2 Mining and quarrying a	6620.0	4215.4	4505.9	4247.9	3684.3	4178.5	...	...	...	...	...	...
3 Manufacturing	192.2	213.5	235.2	273.3	295.4	373.5	...	...	...	...	...	...
4 Electricity, gas and water	49.7	54.1	64.2	75.3	86.7	96.4	...	...	...	...	...	...
5 Construction	935.7	944.1	841.2	793.0	756.7	809.6	...	...	...	...	...	...
6 Wholesale and retail trade, restaurants and hotels	489.8	531.6	599.2	478.5	516.3	480.6	...	...	...	...	...	...
7 Transport, storage and communication	356.1	407.0	385.4	373.5	393.6	389.3	...	...	...	...	...	...
8 Finance, insurance, real estate and business services	456.4	509.0	457.5	522.7	509.3	503.6	...	...	...	...	...	...
9 Community, social and personal services	382.9	412.8	456.4	475.9	468.7	497.3	...	...	...	...	...	...
Total, Industries	9666.2	7495.4	7758.0	7484.4	6945.8	7573.1	...	...	...	...	...	...
Producers of Government Services	611.1	668.2	718.6	765.0	845.3	790.5	...	...	...	...	...	...
Other Producers	...	...	...	...	...	...	...	...	...	...	...	...
Subtotal	10277.3	8163.6	8476.6	8249.4	7791.1	8363.6	...	...	...	...	...	...
Less: Imputed bank service charge	...	...	...	...	...	...	...	...	...	...	...	...
Plus: Import duties	...	...	...	...	...	...	...	...	...	...	...	...
Plus: Value added tax	...	...	...	...	...	...	...	...	...	...	...	...
Equals: Gross Domestic Product b	10575.2	8545.8	8785.6	8568.4	8136.4	8813.9	...	...	...	...	...	...

a) Item 'Mining and quarrying' includes oil and gas production.
b) Gross domestic product in factor values.

1.12 Relations Among National Accounting Aggregates

Million Libyan dinars

	1980	1981	1982	1983	1984	1985	1986	1987	1988	1989	1990	1991
Gross Domestic Product	10575.2	9260.0	9096.2	8805.2	8013.3	8277.0	...	...	...	...	...	...
Plus: Net factor income from the rest of the world	-299.5	-390.2	-586.0	-788.8	-584.9	-275.4	...	...	...	...	...	...
Factor income from the rest of the world	379.5	481.6	256.9	200.2	142.8	122.5	...	...	...	...	...	...
Less: Factor income to the rest of the world	679.0	871.7	842.9	989.0	727.7	397.9	...	...	...	...	...	...
Equals: Gross National Product	10275.7	8869.8	8510.2	8016.4	7428.4	8001.6	...	...	...	...	...	...
Less: Consumption of fixed capital	345.8	390.6	412.7	436.1	457.5	481.6	...	...	...	...	...	...
Equals: National Income	9929.9	8479.2	8097.5	7580.3	6970.9	7520.0	...	...	...	...	...	...
Plus: Net current transfers from the rest of the world	-13.5	-22.5	-23.0	-16.6	-25.6	-13.4	...	...	...	...	...	...
Current transfers from the rest of the world	5.8	7.6	9.5	8.6	2.3	2.6	...	...	...	...	...	...
Less: Current transfers to the rest of the world	19.3	30.1	32.5	25.2	27.9	16.0	...	...	...	...	...	...
Equals: National Disposable Income	9916.4	8456.7	8074.5	7563.7	6945.3	7506.6	...	...	...	...	...	...
Less: Final consumption	5219.4	6877.9	6518.7	6337.2	5784.2	5731.3	...	...	...	...	...	...
Equals: Net Saving	4697.0	1578.8	1555.8	1226.5	1161.1	1775.3	...	...	...	...	...	...
Less: Surplus of the nation on current transactions	2472.8	-1130.9	-424.6	-445.2	-452.6	593.8	...	...	...	...	...	...
Equals: Net Capital Formation	2224.2	2709.7	1980.4	1671.7	1613.7	1181.5	...	...	...	...	...	...

2.11 Gross Fixed Capital Formation by Kind of Activity of Owner, ISIC Divisions, in Current Prices

Million Libyan dinars

	1980	1981	1982	1983	1984	1985	1986	1987	1988	1989	1990	1991
					All Producers							
1 Agriculture, hunting, forestry and fishing	334.2	375.9	247.7	237.4	241.5	173.5	...	...	...	...	...	...
2 Mining and quarrying	153.5	159.4	161.3	168.8	179.2	188.6	...	...	...	...	...	...
3 Manufacturing	431.8	442.9	342.7	396.5	347.2	274.5	...	...	...	...	...	...
4 Electricity, gas and water	370.8	261.3	252.0	238.9	240.0	212.3	...	...	...	...	...	...
5 Construction	22.8	25.0	30.0	33.0	40.0	50.0	...	...	...	...	...	...
6 Wholesale and retail trade, restaurants and hotels	83.2	107.0	90.0	55.7	51.1	30.0	...	...	...	...	...	...
7 Transport, storage and communication	439.4	703.8	690.4	507.3	421.7	286.2	...	...	...	...	...	...
8 Finance, insurance, real estate and business services	251.7	324.0	234.7	219.3	208.5	163.2	...	...	...	...	...	...
9 Community, social and personal services	197.5	305.3	265.1	214.2	185.5	122.3	...	...	...	...	...	...
Total Industries	2284.9	2704.6	2313.9	2071.1	1914.7	1500.6	...	...	...	...	...	...
Producers of Government Services	190.1	195.7	154.2	136.7	116.5	127.5	...	...	...	...	...	...
Private Non-Profit Institutions Serving Households	...	...	...	...	...	...	...	...	...	...	...	...
Total	2475.0	2900.3	2468.1	2207.8	2031.2	1628.1	...	...	...	...	...	...

2.12 Gross Fixed Capital Formation by Kind of Activity of Owner, ISIC Divisions, in Constant Prices

Million Libyan dinars

	1980	1981	1982	1983	1984	1985	1986	1987	1988	1989	1990	1991
					At constant prices of:1980							
					All Producers							
1 Agriculture, hunting, forestry and fishing	334.2	360.7	232.8	219.4	218.6	154.5	...	...	...	...	...	...
2 Mining and quarrying	153.5	152.1	148.9	153.4	160.0	165.6	...	...	...	...	...	...
3 Manufacturing	431.8	404.8	304.4	347.8	300.6	235.6	...	...	...	...	...	...
4 Electricity, gas and water	370.8	246.1	231.6	216.8	213.7	187.1	...	...	...	...	...	...
5 Construction	22.8	24.2	28.5	30.8	36.6	44.8	...	...	...	...	...	...
6 Wholesale and retail trade, restaurants and hotels	83.2	101.0	82.0	50.2	45.4	26.7	...	...	...	...	...	...
7 Transport, storage and communication	439.4	659.6	639.3	461.2	376.5	253.3	...	...	...	...	...	...
8 Finance, insurance, real estate and business services	251.7	305.6	217.4	199.5	186.2	144.5	...	...	...	...	...	...
9 Community, social and personal services	197.5	289.9	242.4	191.9	164.3	107.9	...	...	...	...	...	...
Total Industries	2284.9	2544.0	2127.3	1871.0	1701.9	1320.0	...	...	...	...	...	...
Producers of Government Services	190.1	184.6	140.1	121.5	102.6	111.4	...	...	...	...	...	...
Private Non-Profit Institutions Serving Households	...	...	...	...	...	...	...	...	...	...	...	...
Total	2475.0	2728.6	2267.4	1992.5	1804.5	1431.4	...	...	...	...	...	...

4.1 Derivation of Value Added by Kind of Activity, in Current Prices

Million Libyan dinars

	1980		
	Gross Output	Intermediate Consumption	Value Added
		All Producers	
1 Agriculture, hunting, forestry and fishing	233.7	68.8	164.9
A Agriculture and hunting	227.7	67.2	160.5
B Forestry and logging	1.1	0.2	0.9
C Fishing	4.9	1.4	3.5
2 Mining and quarrying [a]	6862.2	241.5	6620.7
A Coal mining	-	-	-
B Crude petroleum and natural gas production	6801.2	229.3	6571.9
C Metal ore mining	-	-	-
D Other mining	61.0	12.2	48.8

Libyan Arab Jamahiriya

4.1 Derivation of Value Added by Kind of Activity, in Current Prices
(Continued)

Million Libyan dinars

	1980		
	Gross Output	Intermediate Consumption	Value Added
3 Manufacturing	623.0	409.1	213.9
A Manufacture of food, beverages and tobacco	110.7	74.5	36.2
B Textile, wearing apparel and leather industries	26.9	17.7	9.2
C Manufacture of wood and wood products, including furniture	21.3	14.4	6.9
D Manufacture of paper and paper products, printing and publishing	12.5	4.9	7.6
E Manufacture of chemicals and chemical petroleum, coal, rubber and plastic products b	363.8	252.1	111.7
F Manufacture of non-metallic mineral products, except products of petroleum and coal b	41.6	21.2	20.4
G Basic metal industries	34.3	17.5	16.8
H Manufacture of fabricated metal products, machinery and equipment			
I Other manufacturing industries	11.9	6.8	5.1
4 Electricity, gas and water	107.4	57.7	49.7
A Electricity, gas and steam	106.0	57.3	48.7
B Water works and supply	1.4	0.4	1.0
5 Construction	1701.5	765.8	935.7
6 Wholesale and retail trade, restaurants and hotels	598.6	116.9	481.7
A Wholesale and retail trade	558.3	102.7	455.6
B Restaurants and hotels	40.3	14.2	26.1
7 Transport, storage and communication	455.5	120.2	335.3
A Transport and storage	454.3	119.9	334.4
B Communication	1.2	0.3	0.9
8 Finance, insurance, real estate and business services	457.5	16.2	441.3
A Financial institutions	204.4	10.5	193.9
B Insurance	19.4	1.8	17.6
C Real estate and business services	233.7	3.9	229.8
Real estate, except dwellings	21.0	1.6	19.4
Dwellings	212.7	2.3	210.4
9 Community, social and personal services	496.7	115.8	380.9
A Sanitary and similar services	-	-	-
B Social and related community services	445.6	110.1	335.5
Educational services	271.2	50.4	220.8
Medical, dental, other health and veterinary services	174.4	59.7	114.7
C Recreational and cultural services	5.3	1.1	4.2
D Personal and household services	45.8	4.6	41.2
Total, Industries	11536.1	1912.0	9624.2
Producers of Government Services	1934.7	1323.6	611.1
Other Producers	2.8	0.8	2.0
Total c	13473.6	3236.4	10237.3
Less: Imputed bank service charge	...	...	...
Import duties	...	...	...
Value added tax	...	...	...
Total	...	...	...

a) Item 'Mining and quarrying' includes oil and gas production.

b) Petroleum products and liquified gas industries are included in item 'Manufacture of non-metallic mineral products'.

c) Gross domestic product in factor values.

4.3 Cost Components of Value Added

Million Libyan dinars

		1980					
		Compensation of Employees	Capital Consumption	Net Operating Surplus	Indirect Taxes	Less: Subsidies Received	Value Added
					All Producers		
1	Agriculture, hunting, forestry and fishing	46.3	24.5	94.1	...	...	164.9
	A Agriculture and hunting	44.0	23.9	92.6	...	...	160.5
	B Forestry and logging	0.7	0.1	0.1	...	...	0.9
	C Fishing	1.6	0.5	1.4	...	...	3.5
2	Mining and quarrying a	128.5	73.3	6418.9	...	...	6620.7
	A Coal mining	...	...	...	...	...	...
	B Crude petroleum and natural gas production	108.8	63.5	6399.6	...	...	6571.9
	C Metal ore mining	...	...	...	...	...	...
	D Other mining	19.7	9.8	19.3	...	...	48.8
3	Manufacturing	71.6	24.8	117.5	...	...	213.9
	A Manufacture of food, beverages and tobacco	18.8	10.1	7.3	...	...	36.2
	B Textile, wearing apparel and leather industries	8.5	1.2	-0.5	...	...	9.2
	C Manufacture of wood and wood products, including furniture	6.5	1.4	-1.0	...	...	6.9
	D Manufacture of paper and paper products, printing and publishing	4.9	0.8	1.9	...	...	7.6
	E Manufacture of chemicals and chemical petroleum, coal, rubber and plastic products b	12.2	6.7	92.8	...	...	111.7
	F Manufacture of non-metallic mineral products, except products of petroleum and coal b	10.9	3.0	6.5	...	...	20.4
	G Basic metal industries	7.7	1.3	7.8	...	...	16.8
	H Manufacture of fabricated metal products, machinery and equipment	...	...	...	...	...	...
	I Other manufacturing industries	2.1	0.3	2.7	...	...	5.1
4	Electricity, gas and water	30.5	19.2	-	...	...	49.7
	A Electricity, gas and steam	29.7	19.0	-	...	...	48.7
	B Water works and supply	0.8	0.2	-	...	...	1.0
5	Construction	692.1	53.9	189.7	...	...	935.7
6	Wholesale and retail trade, restaurants and hotels	80.6	10.4	390.7	...	...	481.7
	A Wholesale and retail trade	69.5	7.0	379.1	...	...	455.6
	B Restaurants and hotels	11.1	3.4	11.6	...	...	26.1
7	Transport, storage and communication	152.2	53.8	129.3	...	...	335.3
	A Transport and storage	152.0	53.7	128.7	...	...	334.4
	B Communication	0.2	0.1	0.6	...	...	0.9
8	Finance, insurance, real estate and business services	22.7	36.4	382.2	...	...	441.3
	A Financial institutions	15.6	1.7	176.6	...	...	193.9
	B Insurance	2.5	0.4	14.7	...	...	17.6
	C Real estate and business services	4.6	34.3	190.9	...	...	229.8
	Real estate, except dwellings	3.5	1.9	14.0	...	...	19.4
	Dwellings	1.1	32.4	176.9	...	...	210.4
9	Community, social and personal services	339.6	27.9	13.5	...	...	381.0
	A Sanitary and similar services	-	-		...	...	-
	B Social and related community services	308.7	26.8	-	...	...	335.5
	Educational services	206.3	14.5	-	...	...	220.8
	Medical, dental, other health and veterinary services	102.4	12.3	-	...	...	114.7
	C Recreational and cultural services	1.1	0.5	2.6	...	...	4.2
	D Personal and household services	29.8	0.5	10.9	...	...	41.2

Libyan Arab Jamahiriya

4.3 Cost Components of Value Added
(Continued)

Million Libyan dinars

	Compensation of Employees	Capital Consumption	Net Operating Surplus	Indirect Taxes	Less: Subsidies Received	Value Added
	1980					
Total, Industries c	1564.1	324.2	7735.9	...	...	9624.2
Producers of Government Services	...	...	...	...	...	...
Other Producers	...	...	...	...	...	...
Total	...	...	...	...	...	...
Less: Imputed bank service charge	...	...	...	...	...	...
Import duties	...	...	...	...	...	...
Value added tax	...	...	...	...	...	...
Total	...	...	...	...	...	...

a) Item 'Mining and quarrying' includes oil and gas production.

b) Petroleum products and liquified gas industries are included in item 'Manufacture of non-metallic mineral products'.

c) Gross domestic product in factor values.

Lithuania

Source. Reply to the United Nations national accounts questionnaire from the Department of Statistics.

General note. The estimates shown in the following table have been prepared in accordance with the United Nations System of National Accounts (SNA) so far as the existing data would permit.

1.12 Relations Among National Accounting Aggregates

Million Roubles

	1980	1981	1982	1983	1984	1985	1986	1987	1988	1989	1990	1991
Gross Domestic Product	...	...	...	...	...	...	...	...	...	...	...	...
Plus: Net factor income from the rest of the world	...	...	...	.	...	...	...	...	...	...	...	...
Equals: Gross National Product	...	...	...	...	...	...	...	...	...	...	...	...
Less: Consumption of fixed capital	...	...	...	...	...	...	...	...	...	...	...	...
Equals: National Income	5867	6464	7011	7241	7424	7514	7922	8280	8913	9550	9997	...
Plus: Net current transfers from the rest of the world	...	...	...	...	...	...	...	...	...	...	...	...
Equals: National Disposable Income	...	...	...	...	...	...	...	...	...	...	...	...
Less: Final consumption	...	...	...	...	...	...	...	...	...	...	...	...
Equals: Net Saving	...	...	...	...	...	...	...	...	...	...	...	...
Less: Surplus of the nation on current transactions	...	...	...	...	...	...	...	...	...	...	...	...
Equals: Net Capital Formation	...	...	...	...	...	...	...	...	...	...	...	...

Luxembourg

Source. Reply to the United Nations National Accounts Questionnaire from the Service Central de la Statistique et des Etudes Economiques, Ministere de L'Economie Nationale, Luxembourg. The official estimates and descriptions are published by the Service in 'Cahiers Economiques, Serie B, Comptes Nationaux'. **General note.** The official estimates have been adjusted by the Service to conform to the United Nations System of National Accounts so far as the existing data would permit. It should be noted that in the National Accounts published by the Service Central de la Statistique et des Etudes Economiques of Luxembourg, imputed bank services provided to non-residents are not deducted in calculating GDP. For this reason estimates of GDP published by the Luxembourg authorities are somewhat higher than those shown here, particularly for the recent years.

1.1 Expenditure on the Gross Domestic Product, in Current Prices

Million Luxembourg francs

	1980	1981	1982	1983	1984	1985	1986	1987	1988	1989	1990	1991
1 Government final consumption expenditure	22182	24668	26097	27556	29756	32306	34958	38243	40326	43574	49333	54368
2 Private final consumption expenditure a	78085	86252	95756	104180	112602	120523	126180	134716	143667	154612	166543	182597
3 Gross capital formation	33518	34761	39437	42514	47879	41614	52380	56447	67682	78042	84920	100141
A Increase in stocks	-2516	-1258	-234	5420	9060	5350	3053	-1672	103	1425	4200	7748
B Gross fixed capital formation	36034	36019	39671	37094	38819	36264	49327	58119	67579	76617	80720	92393
Residential buildings	7278	7325	6840	5992	6240	6555	7470	8856	11017	13892	16115	17400
Non-residential buildings	15490	16547	18253	16743	16650	16639	17995	20171	22687	26780	30067	35478
Other construction and land improvement etc.												
Other	13266	12147	14578	14359	15929	13070	23862	29092	33875	35945	34538	39515
4 Exports of goods and services	117659	122760	141313	157616	195762	222892	224810	223819	249193	285928	290953	300634
5 Less: Imports of goods and services	118515	126750	143817	157183	192333	212080	215024	225679	250660	279331	291340	318936
Equals: Gross Domestic Product	132929	141691	158786	174683	193666	205255	223304	227546	250208	282825	300409	318804

a) Item 'Private consumption expenditure' refers to expenditure in the domestic market only.

1.2 Expenditure on the Gross Domestic Product, in Constant Prices

Million Luxembourg francs

	1980	1981	1982	1983	1984	1985	1986	1987	1988	1989	1990	1991
					At constant prices of:1985							
1 Government final consumption expenditure	29573	29987	30431	31008	31682	32306	33301	34209	35514	36183	37323	38754
2 Private final consumption expenditure	112749	114710	115162	115729	117402	120523	124565	130806	135858	141115	146748	156309
3 Gross capital formation	43933	43798	44953	42746	45148	41614	52167	53811	62440	69941	75791	85715
A Increase in stocks	-5298	-1783	-413	2717	5070	5350	4578	-796	153	2137	6299	9409
B Gross fixed capital formation	49231	45581	45366	40029	40078	36264	47589	54607	62287	67804	69492	76306
Residential buildings	9937	9261	7975	6581	6477	6555	7190	8177	9899	11813	13017	13411
Non-residential buildings	20050	19823	20432	18044	17225	16639	17224	18359	19955	22149	23375	26239
Other construction and land improvement etc.												
Other	19244	16497	16959	15404	16376	13070	23175	28071	32433	33842	33100	36656
4 Exports of goods and services	172588	164264	163749	172411	203494	222892	229970	244942	263237	281387	288669	299135
5 Less: Imports of goods and services	177520	172435	171931	174079	198291	212080	224933	242377	263010	279006	290970	314458
Equals: Gross Domestic Product	181323	180324	182364	187815	199435	205255	215070	221391	234039	249620	257561	265455

1.3 Cost Components of the Gross Domestic Product

Million Luxembourg francs

	1980	1981	1982	1983	1984	1985	1986	1987	1988	1989	1990	1991
1 Indirect taxes, net	14029	13862	16526	20465	23623	27920	30036	30942	35151	41056	43014	47568
A Indirect taxes	19024	20542	24118	30132	32638	35157	37677	39203	43597	49177	52164	56696
B Less: Subsidies	4995	6680	7592	9667	9015	7237	7641	8261	8446	8121	9150	9128
2 Consumption of fixed capital	15921	16961	18144	20180	22610	23980	25100	26400	27780	30310	31750	34000
3 Compensation of employees paid by resident producers to:	85181	93545	100045	106757	115276	122387	130853	141614	151248	168123	188533	206329
A Resident households	76699	84289	89931	95514	103010	108772	115416	123941	130823	142749	157323	168471
B Rest of the world	8482	9256	10114	11243	12266	13615	15437	17673	20425	25374	31210	37858
4 Operating surplus	17798	17323	24071	27281	32157	30968	37315	28590	36029	43336	37112	30907
A Corporate and quasi-corporate enterprises	...	...	...	...	...	...	...	...	...	...	...	...
B Private unincorporated enterprises	...	...	...	...	...	...	...	...	...	...	...	...
C General government	2679	2729	3009	3139	3257	3342	3816	3931	4120	4339	...	...
Equals: Gross Domestic Product	132929	141691	158786	174683	193666	205255	223304	227546	250208	282825	300409	318804

1.4 General Government Current Receipts and Disbursements

Million Luxembourg francs

		1980	1981	1982	1983	1984	1985	1986	1987	1988	1989	1990	1991
	Receipts												
1	Operating surplus	2679	2729	3009	3139	3257	3342	3816	...	...	...	...	...
2	Property and entrepreneurial income	5331	5923	6376	6228	6192	7227	6269	...	...	...	...	...
3	Taxes, fees and contributions	60120	64408	72550	85322	91539	99864	103496	...	...	...	...	...
	A Indirect taxes	18094	19233	22552	27921	30045	32797	34346	...	...	...	...	...
	B Direct taxes	24015	25699	28844	35060	36953	41485	41812	...	...	...	...	...
	C Social security contributions	18011	19476	21154	22341	24541	25582	27338	...	...	...	...	...
	D Compulsory fees, fines and penalties	...	...	...	...	...	...	...	...	...	...	...	...
4	Other current transfers	2712	3226	3423	3515	3946	4390	4554	...	...	...	...	...
	Total Current Receipts of General Government [a]	70842	76286	85358	98204	104934	114823	118135	...	...	...	...	...
	Disbursements												
1	Government final consumption expenditure	22182	24668	26097	27556	29756	32306	35521	...	...	...	...	...
2	Property income	1127	1281	1650	1844	2099	2305	2363	...	...	...	...	...
	A Interest	1127	1281	1650	1844	2099	2305	2363	...	...	...	...	...
	B Net land rent and royalties	-	-	-	-	-	-	-	...	...	...	...	...
3	Subsidies	4484	6460	7370	9376	8766	8956	9495	...	...	...	...	...
4	Other current transfers	33449	37562	40796	43282	46862	49580	53192	...	...	...	...	...
	A Social security benefits	30245	33855	37028	39606	42840	45127	48768	...	...	...	...	...
	B Social assistance grants	...	...	...	...	...	...	...	...	...	...	...	...
	C Other	3204	3707	3768	3676	4022	4453	4424	...	...	...	...	...
5	Net saving	9600	6315	9445	16146	17451	21676	17564	...	...	...	...	...
	Total Current Disbursements and Net Saving of General Government [a]	70842	76286	85358	98204	104934	114823	118135	...	...	...	...	...

a) Data for this table have not been revised, therefore, data for some years are not comparable with those of other tables.

1.7 External Transactions on Current Account, Summary

Million Luxembourg francs

		1980	1981	1982	1983	1984	1985	1986	1987	1988	1989	1990	1991
	Payments to the Rest of the World												
1	Imports of goods and services	118515	126750	143817	157183	192333	212080	215024	225679	250660	279331	291340	318936
	A Imports of merchandise c.i.f.	105622	111461	124638	136168	168990	186696	188110	195597	215962	244696	253830	279837
	B Other	12893	15289	19179	21015	23343	25384	26914	30082	34698	34635	37510	39099
2	Factor income to the rest of the world	317615	523064	532971	423202	489077	484099	432669	446283	504679	769690	947304	992457
	A Compensation of employees	8482	9256	10114	11243	12266	13615	15437	17673	20425	25374	31210	37858
	B Property and entrepreneurial income	309133	513808	522857	411959	476811	470484	417232	428610	484254	744316	916094	954599
3	Current transfers to the rest of the world	5636	6321	7344	8217	9342	9992	11533	12445	13928	14673	15880	16858
	A Indirect taxes to supranational organizations	923	1301	1607	2182	2575	2360	3331	3395	3330	3269	3431	4409
	B Other current transfers	4713	5020	5737	6035	6767	7632	8202	9050	10598	11404	12449	12449
4	Surplus of the nation on current transactions	25202	30172	54654	68951	75707	89922	86581	68982	77060	96298	103133	89350
	Payments to the Rest of the World and Surplus of the Nation on Current Transactions	466968	686307	738786	657553	766459	796093	745807	753389	846327	1159992	1357657	1417601
	Receipts From The Rest of the World												
1	Exports of goods and services	117659	122760	141313	157616	195762	222892	224810	223819	249193	285928	290953	300634
	A Exports of merchandise f.o.b.	88598	89394	102865	112243	146240	168707	166925	163995	187029	213902	211376	215053

Luxembourg

1.7 External Transactions on Current Account, Summary
(Continued)

Million Luxembourg francs

	1980	1981	1982	1983	1984	1985	1986	1987	1988	1989	1990	1991
B Other	29061	33366	38448	45373	49522	54185	57885	59824	62164	72026	79577	85581
2 Factor income from rest of the world	345616	559651	593121	495394	565797	567636	514998	523465	590428	865646	1056429	1106744
A Compensation of employees	7835	8957	10424	11217	12391	13035	14615	15702	17235	18401	19473	20287
B Property and entrepreneurial income	337781	550694	582697	484177	553406	554601	500383	507763	573193	847245	1036956	1086457
3 Current transfers from rest of the world	3693	3896	4352	4543	4900	5565	5999	6105	6706	8418	10275	10223
A Subsidies from supranational organisations	511	220	222	291	249	295	197	151	229	248	273	221
B Other current transfers	3182	3676	4130	4252	4651	5270	5802	5954	6477	8170	10002	10002
Receipts from the Rest of the World on Current Transactions	466968	686307	738786	657553	766459	796093	745807	753389	846327	1159992	1357657	1417601

1.10 Gross Domestic Product by Kind of Activity, in Current Prices

Million Luxembourg francs

	1980	1981	1982	1983	1984	1985	1986	1987	1988	1989	1990	1991
1 Agriculture, hunting, forestry and fishing	3311	3723	5150	4703	4866	5240	5244	5088	5326	5924	5807	4477
2 Mining and quarrying	501	468	177	192	180	172	177	578	678	803	956	997
3 Manufacturing	37819	39346	46776	49834	57410	61634	66048	59484	68264	79081	77406	77303
4 Electricity, gas and water	3097	3638	4129	4183	4479	4894	4858	4596	4693	4845	5094	5264
5 Construction	10026	10184	10104	10872	10942	11006	12512	13982	17113	18901	21626	23905
6 Wholesale and retail trade, restaurants and hotels	22264	24381	27248	29692	31703	33970	35294	37603	40690	45691	49541	52285
7 Transport, storage and communication	7149	7523	7644	9129	10839	11122	13251	13774	15537	18741	20379	22139
8 Finance, insurance, real estate and business services a	13927	18161	36506	49699	47767	49993	50444	48500	45191	37744	39855	44236
9 Community, social and personal services a	20609	22076	24633	26855	29224	30369	32508	36056	38390	42074	45496	48656
Total, Industries	118703	129500	162367	185159	197410	208400	220336	219661	235882	253804	266160	279262
Producers of Government Services	17121	19104	20100	21707	23517	25167	27558	30006	31231	34021	38754	43133
Other Producers	960	1093	1195	1328	1616	1730	1914	2230	2478	2874	3234	3667
Subtotal	136784	149697	183662	208194	222543	235297	249808	251897	269591	290699	308148	326062
Less: Imputed bank service charge	14849	19784	38459	50807	48641	50917	48802	47639	45673	36317	37870	42017
Plus: Import duties	4422	4072	4509	6788	7274	7645	7996	8148	9276	9848	9793	11760
Plus: Value added tax	6572	7706	9074	10508	12490	13230	14302	15140	17014	18595	20338	22999
Equals: Gross Domestic Product b	132929	141691	158786	174683	193666	205255	223304	227546	250208	282825	300409	318804

a) Business services are included in item 'Community, social and personal services'.
b) The branch breakdown used in this table (GDP by kind of activity) is according to the classification NACE/CLIO.

1.11 Gross Domestic Product by Kind of Activity, in Constant Prices

Million Luxembourg francs

	1980	1981	1982	1983	1984	1985	1986	1987	1988	1989	1990	1991
					At constant prices of:1985							
1 Agriculture, hunting, forestry and fishing	4791	5039	5778	5044	5309	5240	5236	4971	5056	5208	5183	4378
2 Mining and quarrying	727	623	256	226	195	172	170	543	589	679	782	751
3 Manufacturing	52900	49760	50649	52400	58416	61634	62763	61799	68281	73462	73373	74419
4 Electricity, gas and water	5357	5340	5078	4719	4616	4894	5149	4946	5124	5214	5355	5580
5 Construction	12383	12315	11611	11768	11531	11006	11963	13017	15196	15982	17201	17889
6 Wholesale and retail trade, restaurants and hotels	30948	31338	32333	32698	32964	33970	35048	37221	39512	43170	45464	46695
7 Transport, storage and communication	8932	9100	9250	9548	10830	11122	11844	12706	13617	14495	15220	15573
8 Finance, insurance, real estate and business services	45735	47970	47791	47653	47584	49993	55568	60861	65278	75517	83564	85223
9 Community, social and personal services	26639	26742	27610	28113	29545	30369	32285	34523	35096	36207	37879	38972
Total, Industries	188412	188227	190356	192169	200990	208400	220026	230587	247749	269934	284021	289480
Producers of Government Services	22268	22612	23217	24518	25185	25167	25929	26021	26610	27129	27654	28851
Other Producers	1448	1524	1601	1663	1718	1730	1778	1871	1967	2026	2094	2213
Subtotal	212128	212363	215174	218350	227893	235297	247733	258479	276326	299089	313769	320544
Less: Imputed bank service charge	47465	50186	50445	49184	48811	50917	54392	60204	66248	74800	82289	83713
Plus: Import duties	6506	7166	6926	7049	7400	7645	7554	8323	8012	8181	7952	8783
Plus: Value added tax	10154	10981	10709	11600	12953	13230	14175	14793	15949	17150	18129	19841
Equals: Gross Domestic Product	181323	180324	182364	187815	199435	205255	215070	221391	234039	249620	257561	265455

1.12 Relations Among National Accounting Aggregates

Million Luxembourg francs

	1980	1981	1982	1983	1984	1985	1986	1987	1988	1989	1990	1991
Gross Domestic Product	132929	141691	158786	174683	193666	205255	223304	227546	250208	282825	300409	318804
Plus: Net factor income from the rest of the world	28001	36587	60150	72192	76720	83537	82329	77182	85749	95955	109125	114287
Factor income from the rest of the world	345616	559651	593121	495394	565797	567636	514998	523465	590428	865646	1056429	1106744
Less: Factor income to the rest of the world	317615	523064	532971	423202	489077	484099	432669	446283	504679	769691	947304	992457
Equals: Gross National Product	160930	178278	218936	246875	270386	288792	305633	304728	335957	378780	409534	433091
Less: Consumption of fixed capital	15921	16961	18144	20180	22610	23980	25100	26400	27780	30310	31750	34000
Equals: National Income	145009	161317	200792	226695	247776	264812	280533	278328	308177	348470	377784	399091
Plus: Net current transfers from the rest of the world	-1943	-2425	-2992	-3674	-4442	-4427	-5534	-6340	-7222	-6255	-5605	-6635
Current transfers from the rest of the world	3693	3896	4352	4543	4900	5565	5999	6105	6706	8418	10275	10223
Less: Current transfers to the rest of the world	5636	6321	7344	8217	9342	9992	11533	12445	13928	14673	15880	16858
Equals: National Disposable Income	143066	158892	197800	223021	243334	260385	274999	271988	300955	342216	372179	392456
Less: Final consumption	100267	110920	121853	131736	142358	152829	161138	172959	183993	198186	215876	236965
Equals: Net Saving	42799	47972	75947	91285	100976	107556	113861	99029	116962	144030	156303	155491
Less: Surplus of the nation on current transactions	25202	30172	54654	68951	75707	89922	86581	68982	77060	96298	103133	89350
Equals: Net Capital Formation	17597	17800	21293	22334	25269	17634	27280	30047	39902	47732	53170	66141

2.5 Private Final Consumption Expenditure by Type and Purpose, in Current Prices

Million Luxembourg francs

	1980	1981	1982	1983	1984	1985	1986	1987	1988	1989	1990	1991
Final Consumption Expenditure of Resident Households												
1 Food, beverages and tobacco	18480	20440	24159	26872	27782	29294	29571	29489	30017	31352	33123	34896
A Food	13103	14202	15681	16832	18014	18697	18938	18794	19139	19433	20270	20555
B Non-alcoholic beverages	355	426	511	560	567	685	787	863	962	1058	1076	1209
C Alcoholic beverages	1423	1620	1750	1784	1787	1884	2055	1983	1922	2101	2096	2357
D Tobacco	3599	4192	6217	7696	7414	8028	7791	7849	7994	8760	9681	10775
2 Clothing and footwear	5875	6400	6745	7373	7460	8270	8690	9363	9634	10141	10486	11018
3 Gross rent, fuel and power	15200	17262	19406	22068	24364	26403	26697	28234	30370	32468	33818	37246
A Fuel and power	5610	6538	7792	9108	9979	10803	9923	9818	10221	10146	10601	11506
B Other	9590	10724	11614	12960	14385	15600	16774	18416	20149	22322	23217	25740
4 Furniture, furnishings and household equipment and operation	7498	8191	8741	9412	10581	11565	12386	14154	15234	16864	18543	20303
5 Medical care and health expenses	5863	6362	7043	7287	7941	8390	9155	10208	10977	11946	12803	13792
6 Transport and communication	13359	15454	17818	18976	20028	21282	21328	22248	24537	27410	29946	35894
7 Recreational, entertainment, education and cultural services	2707	2930	3457	3833	4193	4336	4915	5387	5823	6602	7413	7849
8 Miscellaneous goods and services	11310	11740	12563	13793	15226	16293	17513	19035	20130	21899	24850	26963
Total Final Consumption Expenditure in the Domestic Market by Households, of which	80292	88779	99932	109614	117575	125833	130255	138118	146722	158682	170982	187961
Plus: Direct purchases abroad by resident households	3770	4324	5033	5540	5980	6458	6626	6974	7379	7941	8516	9334
Less: Direct purchases in the domestic market by non-resident households	5977	6851	9209	10974	10953	11768	10701	10376	10434	12011	12955	14698
Equals: Final Consumption Expenditure of Resident Households a	78085	86252	95756	104180	112602	120523	126180	134716	143667	154612	166543	182597
Final Consumption Expenditure of Private Non-profit Institutions Serving Households												
Equals: Final Consumption Expenditure of Private Non-profit Organisations Serving Households	...	...	...	...	...	...	...	...	...	...	...	...
Private Final Consumption Expenditure	78085	86252	95756	104180	112602	120523	126180	134716	143667	154612	166543	182597

a) Item 'Final consumption expenditure of resident households' includes consumption expenditure of private non-profit institutions serving households.

Luxembourg

2.6 Private Final Consumption Expenditure by Type and Purpose, in Constant Prices

Million Luxembourg francs

	1980	1981	1982	1983	1984	1985	1986	1987	1988	1989	1990	1991
	At constant prices of:1985											
	Final Consumption Expenditure of Resident Households											
1 Food, beverages and tobacco	27062	27483	29195	30094	28938	29294	28531	28381	28334	28519	28968	29504
A Food	18576	18622	18632	18607	18631	18697	18544	18547	18689	18364	18361	18022
B Non-alcoholic beverages	462	503	584	596	585	685	743	812	899	966	967	1054
C Alcoholic beverages	2078	2149	2090	1952	1845	1884	1958	1864	1781	1879	1804	1968
D Tobacco	5946	6209	7889	8939	7877	8028	7286	7158	6965	7310	7836	8460
2 Clothing and footwear	7863	7974	7945	8126	7823	8270	8230	8634	8695	8949	8997	9171
3 Gross rent, fuel and power	22720	23385	23594	24463	25365	26403	27121	28043	28684	28959	28758	30930
A Fuel and power	9118	9330	9678	10203	10349	10803	11153	11590	11965	11568	11652	12538
B Other	13602	14055	13916	14260	15016	15600	15968	16453	16719	17391	17106	18392
4 Furniture, furnishings and household equipment and operation	10586	10866	10542	10319	10913	11565	11920	13367	14209	15398	16422	17437
5 Medical care and health expenses	7925	8024	8363	8119	8452	8390	8616	9208	9714	9851	10360	10823
6 Transport and communication	19922	20963	20935	20852	20721	21282	22798	23650	25347	27750	29479	34088
7 Recreational, entertainment, education and cultural services	3778	3914	4278	4322	4341	4336	4834	5234	5640	6355	6928	7115
8 Miscellaneous goods and services	16079	15461	15332	15470	16034	16293	16538	17592	18124	19048	20747	21833
Total Final Consumption Expenditure in the Domestic Market by Households, of which	115935	118070	120184	121765	122587	125833	128588	134109	138747	144829	150659	160901
Plus: Direct purchases abroad by resident households	5444	5751	6053	6154	6235	6458	6541	6772	6978	7248	7504	7990
Less: Direct purchases in the domestic market by non-resident households	8630	9111	11075	12190	11420	11768	10564	10075	9867	10962	11415	12582
Equals: Final Consumption Expenditure of Resident Households	112749	114710	115162	115729	117402	120523	124565	130806	135858	141115	146748	156309
	Final Consumption Expenditure of Private Non-profit Institutions Serving Households											
Equals: Final Consumption Expenditure of Private Non-profit Organisations Serving Households	...	...	...	...	...	...	...	...	...	...	...	...
Private Final Consumption Expenditure	112749	114710	115162	115729	117402	120523	124565	130806	135858	141115	146748	156309

2.11 Gross Fixed Capital Formation by Kind of Activity of Owner, ISIC Divisions, in Current Prices

Million Luxembourg francs

	1980	1981	1982	1983	1984	1985	1986	1987	1988	1989	1990	1991
	All Producers											
1 Agriculture, hunting, forestry and fishing	1166	1310	1693	1987	1600	1361	1121	1408	1625	1888	1940	2158
2 Mining and quarrying	55	4	12	15	4	10	20	21	2	192	99	142
A Coal mining	-	-	-	-	-	-	-	-	-	-	-	-
B Crude petroleum and natural gas production	-	-	-	-	-	-	-	-	-	-	-	-
C Metal ore mining	1	-	-	-	-	-	-	-	-	-	-	-
D Other mining	54	4	12	15	4	10	20	21	2	192	99	142

2.11 Gross Fixed Capital Formation by Kind of Activity of Owner, ISIC Divisions, in Current Prices
(Continued)

Million Luxembourg francs

	1980	1981	1982	1983	1984	1985	1986	1987	1988	1989	1990	1991
3 Manufacturing	7834	8737	7609	7859	7706	9146	12879	12835	10679	10323	12245	13213
A Manufacturing of food, beverages and tobacco	514	699	542	606	627	864	819	740	994	938	946	1621
B Textile, wearing apparel and leather industries	54	43	88	35	21	182	1877	3910	2052	220	557	421
C Manufacture of wood, and wood products, including furniture a	...	...	...	...	...	...	...	...	...	...	...	...
D Manufacture of paper and paper products, printing and publishing	157	157	178	182	241	160	241	291	442	586	159	120
E Manufacture of chemicals and chemical petroleum, coal, rubber and plastic products	988	814	1523	1688	1891	2346	3845	2435	1476	1876	3359	3926
F Manufacture of non-metalic mineral products except products of petroleum and coal	814	2229	589	837	449	673	761	407	949	1203	365	522
G Basic metal industries	4498	3416	3417	3716	3167	3443	3620	3728	3615	2860	4849	3957
H Manufacture of fabricated metal products, machinery and equipment	726	1330	1232	733	1226	1435	1659	1290	1068	2471	1900	2488
I Other manufacturing industries a	83	49	40	62	84	43	57	34	83	169	110	158
4 Electricity, gas and water	1011	1115	1073	1223	1090	1233	1139	1369	1420	1761	2139	2439
5 Construction	884	686	790	766	795	619	901	914	1269	1555	1667	1858
6 Wholesale and retail trade, restaurants and hotels	2530	2748	3250	3670	5303	4477	4625	5457	6497	6388	6192	6888
A Wholesale and retail trade	1962	2033	2216	2475	3190	3337	3658	3815	4466	5276	5200	5784
B Restaurants and hotels	568	715	1034	1195	2113	1140	967	1642	2031	1112	992	1104
7 Transport, storage and communication	4090	2038	2820	2199	1769	-1956	3108	5999	10060	10151	5756	8259
A Transport and storage	3288	1280	1846	1746	1334	-2741	1589	4798	2528	8105	3466	3855
B Communication	802	758	974	453	435	785	1519	1201	7532	2046	2290	4404
8 Finance, insurance, real estate and business services b	1587	1936	2947	2616	3196	3704	6491	8008	9409	11145	12845	14293
9 Community, social and personal services b	8469	8522	10085	7614	8396	8953	9840	11929	15066	20395	23600	25741
Total Industries	27626	27096	30279	27949	29859	27547	40124	47940	56027	63798	66483	74991
Producers of Government Services	8398	8909	9358	9097	8881	8677	9172	10112	11509	12774	14184	17343
Private Non-Profit Institutions Serving Households	10	14	34	48	79	40	31	67	43	45	53	59
Total	36034	36019	39671	37094	38819	36264	49327	58119	67579	76617	80720	92393

a) Item 'Manufacture of wood and wood products, including furniture' is included in item 'Other manufacturing industries'.
b) Business services are included in item 'Community, social and personal services'.

2.12 Gross Fixed Capital Formation by Kind of Activity of Owner, ISIC Divisions, in Constant Prices

Million Luxembourg francs

	1980	1981	1982	1983	1984	1985	1986	1987	1988	1989	1990	1991
					At constant prices of:1985							
					All Producers							
1 Agriculture, hunting, forestry and fishing	1557	1694	1993	2201	1671	1361	1052	1297	1456	1620	1616	1723
2 Mining and quarrying	79	5	14	16	4	10	19	20	2	172	87	120
A Coal mining	-	-	-	-	-	-	-	-	-	-	-	-
B Crude petroleum and natural gas production	-	-	-	-	-	-	-	-	-	-	-	-
C Metal ore mining	2	-	-	-	-	-	-	-	-	-	-	-
D Other mining	77	5	14	16	4	10	19	20	2	172	87	120

Luxembourg

2.12 Gross Fixed Capital Formation by Kind of Activity of Owner, ISIC Divisions, in Constant Prices
(Continued)

Million Luxembourg francs

	1980	1981	1982	1983	1984	1985	1986	1987	1988	1989	1990	1991
					At constant prices of:1985							
3 Manufacturing	11160	11675	8842	8475	7992	9146	12375	12095	9809	9137	10538	10799
A Manufacturing of food, beverages and tobacco	735	928	632	654	649	864	788	699	914	829	823	1356
B Textile, wearing apparel and leather industries	78	57	103	38	22	182	1798	3682	1891	196	491	357
C Manufacture of wood, and wood products, including furniture	...	...	...	...	...	...	...	...	...	...	...	...
D Manufacture of paper and paper products, printing and publishing	220	212	208	197	250	160	232	274	405	508	138	101
E Manufacture of chemicals and chemical petroleum, coal, rubber and plastic products	1400	1079	1767	1823	1961	2346	3694	2296	1360	1669	2701	2955
F Manufacture of non-metalic mineral products except products of petroleum and coal	1109	2979	681	904	466	673	732	382	862	1049	318	437
G Basic metal industries	6456	4584	3975	3999	3285	3443	3480	3515	3322	2537	4347	3420
H Manufacture of fabricated metal products, machinery and equipment	1044	1770	1429	793	1272	1435	1596	1215	978	2200	1624	2041
I Other manufacturing industries	118	66	47	67	87	43	55	32	77	149	96	132
4 Electricity, gas and water	1274	1293	1160	1293	1124	1233	1086	1240	1243	1442	1649	1798
5 Construction	1282	933	937	832	826	619	864	862	1168	1375	1457	1562
6 Wholesale and retail trade, restaurants and hotels	3450	3523	3699	3923	5434	4477	4512	5270	6221	5859	5677	6107
A Wholesale and retail trade	2688	2616	2527	2639	3273	3337	3568	3686	4312	4825	4735	5090
B Restaurants and hotels	762	907	1172	1284	2161	1140	944	1584	1909	1034	942	1017
7 Transport, storage and communication	5771	2490	3174	2345	1818	-1956	3001	5632	9244	8968	4970	6899
A Transport and storage	4728	1580	2100	1868	1373	-2741	1519	4489	2295	7114	2929	3132
B Communication	1043	910	1074	477	445	785	1482	1143	6949	1854	2041	3767
8 Finance, insurance, real estate and business services	2191	2508	3418	2817	3271	3704	6339	7675	8987	10354	11830	12732
9 Community, social and personal services	11538	10777	11656	8287	8679	8953	9516	11200	13904	18146	20360	21368
Total Industries	38302	34898	34893	30189	30819	27547	38764	45291	52034	57073	58184	63108
Producers of Government Services	10915	10665	10433	9787	9177	8677	8795	9254	10213	10692	11264	13151
Private Non-Profit Institutions Serving Households	14	18	40	53	82	40	30	62	40	39	44	47
Total	49231	45581	45366	40029	40078	36264	47589	54607	62287	67804	69492	76306

2.17 Exports and Imports of Goods and Services, Detail

Million Luxembourg francs

	1980	1981	1982	1983	1984	1985	1986	1987	1988	1989	1990	1991
					Exports of Goods and Services							
1 Exports of merchandise, f.o.b.	88598	89394	102865	112243	146240	168707	166925	163995	187029	213902	211376	215053
2 Transport and communication												
3 Insurance service charges	23084	26515	29239	34399	38569	42417	47184	49448	51730	60015	66622	70883
4 Other commodities												
5 Adjustments of merchandise exports to change-of-ownership basis												
6 Direct purchases in the domestic market by non-residential households	5977	6851	9209	10974	10953	11768	10701	10376	10434	12011	12955	14698
7 Direct purchases in the domestic market by extraterritorial bodies	...	...	...	...	...	...	...	...	...	...	...	...
Total Exports of Goods and Services	117659	122760	141313	157616	195762	222892	224810	223819	249193	285928	290953	300634
					Imports of Goods and Services							
1 Imports of merchandise, c.i.f.	105622	111461	124638	136168	168990	186696	188110	195597	215962	244696	253830	279837

2.17 Exports and Imports of Goods and Services, Detail
(Continued)

Million Luxembourg francs

	1980	1981	1982	1983	1984	1985	1986	1987	1988	1989	1990	1991
2 Adjustments of merchandise imports to change-of-ownership basis												
3 Other transport and communication												
4 Other insurance service charges	9123	10965	14146	15475	17363	18926	20288	23108	27319	26694	28994	29765
5 Other commodities												
6 Direct purchases abroad by government												
7 Direct purchases abroad by resident households	3770	4324	5033	5540	5980	6458	6626	6974	7379	7941	8516	9334
Total Imports of Goods and Services	118515	126750	143817	157183	192333	212080	215024	225679	250660	279331	291340	318936
Balance of Goods and Services	-856	-3990	-2504	433	3429	10812	9786	-1860	-1467	6597	-387	-18302
Total Imports and Balance of Goods and Services	117659	122760	141313	157616	195762	222892	224810	223819	249193	285928	290953	300634

4.2 Derivation of Value Added by Kind of Activity, in Constant Prices

Million Luxembourg francs

	1980 Gross Output	1980 Intermediate Consumption	1980 Value Added	1981 Gross Output	1981 Intermediate Consumption	1981 Value Added	1982 Gross Output	1982 Intermediate Consumption	1982 Value Added	1983 Gross Output	1983 Intermediate Consumption	1983 Value Added
At constant prices of:1985												
All Producers												
1 Agriculture, hunting, forestry and fishing	...	...	4791	...	...	5039	...	...	5778	...	...	5044
2 Mining and quarrying	...	...	727	...	...	623	...	...	256	...	...	226
A Coal mining	...	...	...	...	...	...	...	...	...	...	...	...
B Crude petroleum and natural gas production	...	...	...	...	...	...	...	...	...	...	...	...
C Metal ore mining	...	...	515	...	...	381	...	...	...	...	...	...
D Other mining	...	...	212	...	...	242	...	...	256	...	...	226
3 Manufacturing	...	...	52900	...	...	49760	...	...	50649	...	...	52400
A Manufacture of food, beverages and tobacco	...	...	4254	...	...	4252	...	...	4824	...	...	5291
B Textile, wearing apparel and leather industries	...	...	1365	...	...	1369	...	...	1245	...	...	1216
C Manufacture of wood and wood products, including furniture	...	...	...	...	...	...	...	...	...	...	...	...
D Manufacture of paper and paper products, printing and publishing	...	...	1620	...	...	1730	...	...	1689	...	...	1801
E Manufacture of chemicals and chemical petroleum, coal, rubber and plastic products	...	...	7242	...	...	7433	...	...	8382	...	...	9754
F Manufacture of non-metallic mineral products, except products of petroleum and coal	...	...	2792	...	...	2909	...	...	3727	...	...	3895
G Basic metal industries	...	...	27591	...	...	23979	...	...	22642	...	...	22182
H Manufacture of fabricated metal products, machinery and equipment	...	...	7626	...	...	7674	...	...	7702	...	...	7842
I Other manufacturing industries	...	...	410	...	...	414	...	...	438	...	...	419
4 Electricity, gas and water	...	...	5357	...	...	5340	...	...	5078	...	...	4719
5 Construction	...	...	12383	...	...	12315	...	...	11611	...	...	11768
6 Wholesale and retail trade, restaurants and hotels	...	...	30948	...	...	31338	...	...	32333	...	...	32698
A Wholesale and retail trade	...	...	26529	...	...	26935	...	...	27794	...	...	27996
B Restaurants and hotels	...	...	4419	...	...	4403	...	...	4539	...	...	4702
7 Transport, storage and communication	...	...	8932	...	...	9100	...	...	9250	...	...	9548
A Transport and storage	...	...	5918	...	...	6036	...	...	6022	...	...	6139
B Communication	...	...	3014	...	...	3064	...	...	3228	...	...	3409
8 Finance, insurance, real estate and business services	...	...	45735	...	...	47970	...	...	47791	...	...	47653
A Financial institutions	...	...	44970	...	...	47153	...	...	46958	...	...	46826
B Insurance	...	...	765	...	...	817	...	...	833	...	...	827
C Real estate and business services	...	...	...	...	...	...	...	...	...	...	...	...
9 Community, social and personal services	...	...	26639	...	...	26742	...	...	27610	...	...	28113

Luxembourg

4.2 Derivation of Value Added by Kind of Activity, in Constant Prices
(Continued)

Million Luxembourg francs

	1980			1981			1982			1983		
	Gross Output	Intermediate Consumption	Value Added	Gross Output	Intermediate Consumption	Value Added	Gross Output	Intermediate Consumption	Value Added	Gross Output	Intermediate Consumption	Value Added
					At constant prices of:1985							
Total, Industries	...	...	188412	...	...	188227	...	...	190356	...	...	192169
Producers of Government Services	...	...	22268	...	...	22612	...	...	23217	...	...	24518
Other Producers	...	...	1448	...	...	1524	...	...	1601	...	...	1663
Total	...	...	212128	...	...	212363	...	...	215174	...	...	218350
Less: Imputed bank service charge	...	...	47465	...	...	50186	...	...	50445	...	...	49184
Import duties	...	...	6506	...	...	7166	...	...	6926	...	...	7049
Value added tax	...	...	10154	...	...	10981	...	...	10709	...	...	11600
Total	...	...	181323	...	...	180324	...	...	182364	...	...	187815

	1984			1985			1986			1987		
	Gross Output	Intermediate Consumption	Value Added	Gross Output	Intermediate Consumption	Value Added	Gross Output	Intermediate Consumption	Value Added	Gross Output	Intermediate Consumption	Value Added
					At constant prices of:1985							
					All Producers							
1 Agriculture, hunting, forestry and fishing	...	...	5309	...	...	5240	...	...	5236	...	...	4971
2 Mining and quarrying	...	...	195	...	...	172	...	...	170	...	...	543
A Coal mining	...	...	...	...	...	...	...	...	...	...	...	...
B Crude petroleum and natural gas production	...	...	...	...	...	...	...	...	...	...	...	...
C Metal ore mining	...	...	...	...	...	...	...	...	...	...	...	...
D Other mining	...	...	195	...	...	172	...	...	170	...	...	543
3 Manufacturing	...	...	58416	...	...	61634	...	...	62763	...	...	61799
A Manufacture of food, beverages and tobacco	...	...	5184	...	...	5505	...	...	5504	...	...	5607
B Textile, wearing apparel and leather industries	...	...	1154	...	...	1171	...	...	1073	...	...	1091
C Manufacture of wood and wood products, including furniture	...	...	...	...	...	...	...	...	...	...	...	...
D Manufacture of paper and paper products, printing and publishing	...	...	1824	...	...	1962	...	...	2020	...	...	2051
E Manufacture of chemicals and chemical petroleum, coal, rubber and plastic products	...	...	10258	...	...	10575	...	...	11570	...	...	12267
F Manufacture of non-metallic mineral products, except products of petroleum and coal	...	...	4032	...	...	3924	...	...	4276	...	...	4324
G Basic metal industries	...	...	26450	...	...	28527	...	...	27757	...	...	26857
H Manufacture of fabricated metal products, machinery and equipment	...	...	9094	...	...	9570	...	...	10150	...	...	9171
I Other manufacturing industries	...	...	420	...	...	400	...	...	413	...	...	431
4 Electricity, gas and water	...	...	4616	...	...	4894	...	...	5149	...	...	4946
5 Construction	...	...	11531	...	...	11006	...	...	11963	...	...	13017
6 Wholesale and retail trade, restaurants and hotels	...	...	32964	...	...	33970	...	...	35048	...	...	37221
A Wholesale and retail trade	...	...	28107	...	...	28897	...	...	29996	...	...	31826
B Restaurants and hotels	...	...	4857	...	...	5073	...	...	5052	...	...	5395
7 Transport, storage and communication	...	...	10830	...	...	11122	...	...	11844	...	...	12706
A Transport and storage	...	...	7206	...	...	7237	...	...	7678	...	...	8303
B Communication	...	...	3624	...	...	3885	...	...	4166	...	...	4403
8 Finance, insurance, real estate and business services	...	...	47584	...	...	49993	...	...	55568	...	...	60861
A Financial institutions	...	...	46694	...	...	49051	...	...	54572	...	...	59813
B Insurance	...	...	890	...	...	942	...	...	996	...	...	1048
C Real estate and business services	...	...	...	...	...	...	...	...	...	...	...	...
9 Community, social and personal services	...	...	29545	...	...	30369	...	...	32285	...	...	34523

4.2 Derivation of Value Added by Kind of Activity, in Constant Prices
(Continued)

Million Luxembourg francs

	1984			1985			1986			1987		
	Gross Output	Intermediate Consumption	Value Added	Gross Output	Intermediate Consumption	Value Added	Gross Output	Intermediate Consumption	Value Added	Gross Output	Intermediate Consumption	Value Added
					At constant prices of:1985							
Total, Industries	...	...	200990	...	...	208400	...	...	220026	...	...	230587
Producers of Government Services	...	...	25185	...	...	25167	...	...	25929	...	...	26021
Other Producers	...	...	1718	...	...	1730	...	...	1778	...	...	1871
Total	...	...	227893	...	...	235297	...	...	247733	...	...	258479
Less: Imputed bank service charge	...	...	48811	...	...	50917	...	...	54392	...	...	60204
Import duties	...	...	7400	...	...	7645	...	...	7554	...	...	8323
Value added tax	...	...	12953	...	...	13230	...	...	14175	...	...	14793
Total	...	...	199435	...	...	205255	...	...	215070	...	...	221391

	1988			1989			1990			1991		
	Gross Output	Intermediate Consumption	Value Added	Gross Output	Intermediate Consumption	Value Added	Gross Output	Intermediate Consumption	Value Added	Gross Output	Intermediate Consumption	Value Added
					At constant prices of:1985							
					All Producers							
1 Agriculture, hunting, forestry and fishing	...	...	5056	...	...	5208	...	...	5183	...	...	4378
2 Mining and quarrying	...	...	589	...	...	679	...	...	782	...	...	751
A Coal mining	...	...	...	...	...	...	...	...	...	...	...	...
B Crude petroleum and natural gas production	...	...	...	...	...	...	...	...	...	...	...	...
C Metal ore mining	...	...	...	...	...	...	...	...	...	...	...	...
D Other mining	...	...	589	...	...	679	...	...	782	...	...	751
3 Manufacturing	...	...	68281	...	...	73462	...	...	73373	...	...	74419
A Manufacture of food, beverages and tobacco	...	...	5609	...	...	5747	...	...	5874	...	...	5882
B Textile, wearing apparel and leather industries	...	...	1413	...	...	2189	...	...	2511	...	...	2555
C Manufacture of wood and wood products, including furniture	...	...	...	...	...	...	...	...	...	...	...	...
D Manufacture of paper and paper products, printing and publishing	...	...	2138	...	...	2224	...	...	2537	...	...	2659
E Manufacture of chemicals and chemical petroleum, coal, rubber and plastic products	...	...	13399	...	...	14591	...	...	13955	...	...	14828
F Manufacture of non-metallic mineral products, except products of petroleum and coal	...	...	4319	...	...	5838	...	...	6554	...	...	6742
G Basic metal industries	...	...	30922	...	...	31428	...	...	30049	...	...	28933
H Manufacture of fabricated metal products, machinery and equipment	...	...	10038	...	...	10938	...	...	11318	...	...	12184
I Other manufacturing industries	...	...	443	...	...	507	...	...	575	...	...	636
4 Electricity, gas and water	...	...	5124	...	...	5214	...	...	5355	...	...	5580
5 Construction	...	...	15196	...	...	15982	...	...	17201	...	...	17889
6 Wholesale and retail trade, restaurants and hotels	...	...	39512	...	...	43170	...	...	45464	...	...	46695
A Wholesale and retail trade	...	...	33923	...	...	37363	...	...	39266	...	...	40492
B Restaurants and hotels	...	...	5589	...	...	5807	...	...	6198	...	...	6203
7 Transport, storage and communication	...	...	13617	...	...	14495	...	...	15220	...	...	15573
A Transport and storage	...	...	8980	...	...	9435	...	...	9793	...	...	10002
B Communication	...	...	4637	...	...	5060	...	...	5427	...	...	5571
8 Finance, insurance, real estate and business services	...	...	65278	...	...	75517	...	...	83564	...	...	85223
A Financial institutions	...	...	64166	...	...	74258	...	...	82194	...	...	83819
B Insurance	...	...	1112	...	...	1259	...	...	1370	...	...	1404
C Real estate and business services	...	...	...	...	...	...	...	...	...	...	...	...
9 Community, social and personal services	...	...	35096	...	...	36207	...	...	37879	...	...	38972

Luxembourg

4.2 Derivation of Value Added by Kind of Activity, in Constant Prices
(Continued)

Million Luxembourg francs

	1988			1989			1990			1991		
	Gross Output	Intermediate Consumption	Value Added	Gross Output	Intermediate Consumption	Value Added	Gross Output	Intermediate Consumption	Value Added	Gross Output	Intermediate Consumption	Value Added
					At constant prices of:1985							
Total, Industries	...	...	247749	...	...	269934	...	...	284021	...	...	289480
Producers of Government Services	...	...	26610	...	...	27129	...	...	27654	...	...	28851
Other Producers	...	...	1967	...	...	2026	...	...	2094	...	...	2213
Total	...	...	276326	...	...	299089	...	...	313769	...	...	320544
Less: Imputed bank service charge	...	...	66248	...	...	74800	...	...	82289	...	...	83713
Import duties	...	...	8012	...	...	8181	...	...	7952	...	...	8783
Value added tax	...	...	15949	...	...	17150	...	...	18129	...	...	19841
Total	...	...	234039	...	...	249620	...	...	257561	...	...	265455

4.3 Cost Components of Value Added

Million Luxembourg francs

	1980						1981					
	Compensation of Employees	Capital Consumption	Net Operating Surplus	Indirect Taxes	Less: Subsidies Received	Value Added	Compensation of Employees	Capital Consumption	Net Operating Surplus	Indirect Taxes	Less: Subsidies Received	Value Added
					All Producers							
1 Agriculture, hunting, forestry and fishing	447	...	3130	...	...	3311	493	...	3443	...	...	3723
2 Mining and quarrying	428	...	70	...	...	501	418	...	106	...	...	468
A Coal mining	...	...	...	...	...	...	...	...	...	...	...	...
B Crude petroleum and natural gas production	...	...	...	...	...	...	...	...	...	...	...	...
C Metal ore mining	301	...	22	...	...	323	292	...	42	...	...	273
D Other mining	127	...	48	...	...	178	126	...	64	...	...	195
3 Manufacturing	27004	...	9521	...	...	37819	28183	...	9928	...	...	39346
A Manufacture of food, beverages and tobacco	1555	...	1250	...	...	3517	1720	...	1281	...	...	3858
B Textile, wearing apparel and leather industries	402	...	559	...	...	976	446	...	547	...	...	1037
C Manufacture of wood and wood products, including furniture	...	...	...	...	...	...	...	...	...	...	...	...
D Manufacture of paper and paper products, printing and publishing	853	...	341	...	...	1210	925	...	439	...	...	1388
E Manufacture of chemicals and chemical petroleum, coal, rubber and plastic products	3423	...	1859	...	...	5438	3674	...	2276	...	...	6193
F Manufacture of non-metallic mineral products, except products of petroleum and coal	1319	...	917	...	...	2300	1477	...	835	...	...	2388
G Basic metal industries	14942	...	2901	...	...	18067	15079	...	2679	...	...	17610
H Manufacture of fabricated metal products, machinery and equipment	4270	...	1548	...	...	5916	4617	...	1737	...	...	6484
I Other manufacturing industries	240	...	146	...	...	395	245	...	134	...	...	388
4 Electricity, gas and water	1149	...	1816	...	...	3097	1224	...	2269	...	...	3638
5 Construction	7287	...	2565	...	...	10026	7460	...	2546	...	...	10184
6 Wholesale and retail trade, restaurants and hotels	11289	...	10260	...	...	22264	12349	...	11290	...	...	24381
A Wholesale and retail trade	9858	...	8657	...	...	19111	10747	...	9567	...	...	20923
B Restaurants and hotels	1431	...	1603	...	...	3153	1602	...	1723	...	...	3458
7 Transport, storage and communication	7753	...	2491	...	...	7149	8427	...	2743	...	...	7523
A Transport and storage	6146	...	1732	...	...	4776	6644	...	1850	...	...	4838
B Communication	1607	...	759	...	...	2373	1783	...	893	...	...	2685
8 Finance, insurance, real estate and business services [a]	7750	...	3744	...	...	13927	9091	...	6200	...	...	18161
A Financial institutions	7217	...	3767	...	...	13190	...	...	...	...	...	17536
B Insurance	533	...	-23	...	...	737	...	...	...	...	...	625
C Real estate and business services	...	...	...	...	...	...	...	...	...	...	...	...
9 Community, social and personal services [a]	5602	...	13426	...	...	20609	7549	...	13769	...	...	22076

Luxembourg

4.3 Cost Components of Value Added
(Continued)

Million Luxembourg francs

	1980						1981					
	Compensation of Employees	Capital Consumption	Net Operating Surplus	Indirect Taxes	Less: Subsidies Received	Value Added	Compensation of Employees	Capital Consumption	Net Operating Surplus	Indirect Taxes	Less: Subsidies Received	Value Added
Total, Industries [b]	68709	...	47023	...	...	118703	75194	...	52294	...	...	129500
Producers of Government Services	15558	...	1499	...	...	17121	17310	...	1722	...	...	19104
Other Producers	914	...	46	...	...	960	1041	...	52	...	...	1093
Total [b]	85181	...	48568	...	...	136784	93545	...	54068	...	...	149697
Less: Imputed bank service charge	...	...	14849	...	...	14849	...	...	19784	...	...	19784
Import duties	...	...	...	...	...	4422	...	...	...	...	...	4072
Value added tax	...	...	...	...	...	6572	...	...	...	...	...	7706
Total [cb]	85181	...	33719	...	...	132929	93545	...	34284	...	...	141691

	1982						1983					
	Compensation of Employees	Capital Consumption	Net Operating Surplus	Indirect Taxes	Less: Subsidies Received	Value Added	Compensation of Employees	Capital Consumption	Net Operating Surplus	Indirect Taxes	Less: Subsidies Received	Value Added
All Producers												
1 Agriculture, hunting, forestry and fishing	524	...	4862	...	...	5150	561	...	4450	...	...	4703
2 Mining and quarrying	132	...	42	...	...	177	135	...	53	...	...	192
A Coal mining	...	...	...	...	...	...	...	...	...	...	...	...
B Crude petroleum and natural gas production	...	...	...	...	...	...	...	...	...	...	...	...
C Metal ore mining	-	...	-	...	...	-	-	...	-	...	...	-
D Other mining	132	...	42	...	...	177	135	...	53	...	...	192
3 Manufacturing	29936	...	15398	...	...	46776	29893	...	19760	...	...	49834
A Manufacture of food, beverages and tobacco	1820	...	1625	...	...	4570	1951	...	1880	...	...	5170
B Textile, wearing apparel and leather industries	453	...	480	...	...	988	492	...	538	...	...	1071
C Manufacture of wood and wood products, including furniture	...	...	...	...	...	...	...	...	...	...	...	...
D Manufacture of paper and paper products, printing and publishing	988	...	463	...	...	1475	1116	...	500	...	...	1641
E Manufacture of chemicals and chemical petroleum, coal, rubber and plastic products	3916	...	3505	...	...	7711	4327	...	4198	...	...	8900
F Manufacture of non-metallic mineral products, except products of petroleum and coal	1684	...	1389	...	...	3174	1863	...	1553	...	...	3535
G Basic metal industries	15774	...	6045	...	...	21511	14632	...	9021	...	...	21803
H Manufacture of fabricated metal products, machinery and equipment	5058	...	1721	...	...	6927	5261	...	1896	...	...	7280
I Other manufacturing industries	243	...	170	...	...	420	251	...	174	...	...	434
4 Electricity, gas and water	1318	...	2646	...	...	4129	1418	...	2561	...	...	4183
5 Construction	7633	...	2295	...	...	10104	7780	...	2892	...	...	10872
6 Wholesale and retail trade, restaurants and hotels	13427	...	13045	...	...	27248	14276	...	14576	...	...	29692
A Wholesale and retail trade	11635	...	11204	...	...	23469	12322	...	12495	...	...	25490
B Restaurants and hotels	1792	...	1841	...	...	3779	1954	...	2081	...	...	4202
7 Transport, storage and communication	8777	...	2919	...	...	7644	9373	...	4297	...	...	9129
A Transport and storage	6869	...	2042	...	...	4850	7298	...	3064	...	...	5812
B Communication	1908	...	877	...	...	2794	2075	...	1233	...	...	3317
8 Finance, insurance, real estate and business services [a]	10609	...	22502	...	...	36506	12390	...	33951	...	...	49699
A Financial institutions	...	...	...	...	...	35568	...	...	...	...	...	48651
B Insurance	...	...	...	...	...	938	...	...	...	...	...	1048
C Real estate and business services	...	...	...	...	...	...	...	...	...	...	...	...
9 Community, social and personal services [a]	8167	...	15255	...	...	24633	9592	...	14108	...	...	26855

Luxembourg

4.3 Cost Components of Value Added
(Continued)

Million Luxembourg francs

	1982						1983					
	Compensation of Employees	Capital Consumption	Net Operating Surplus	Indirect Taxes	Less: Subsidies Received	Value Added	Compensation of Employees	Capital Consumption	Net Operating Surplus	Indirect Taxes	Less: Subsidies Received	Value Added
Total, Industries b	80523	...	78964	...	...	162367	85418	...	96648	...	...	185159
Producers of Government Services	18383	...	1654	...	...	20100	20074	...	1557	...	...	21707
Other Producers	1139	...	56	...	...	1195	1265	...	63	...	...	1328
Total b	100045	...	80674	...	...	183662	106757	...	98268	...	...	208194
Less: Imputed bank service charge	...	...	38459	...	...	38459	...	...	50807	...	...	50807
Import duties	...	...	...	...	...	4509	...	...	...	...	...	6788
Value added tax	...	...	...	...	...	9074	...	...	...	...	...	10508
Total cb	100045	...	42215	...	...	158786	106757	...	47461	...	...	174683

	1984						1985					
	Compensation of Employees	Capital Consumption	Net Operating Surplus	Indirect Taxes	Less: Subsidies Received	Value Added	Compensation of Employees	Capital Consumption	Net Operating Surplus	Indirect Taxes	Less: Subsidies Received	Value Added
					All Producers							
1 Agriculture, hunting, forestry and fishing	636	...	4527	...	...	4866	681	...	4809	...	...	5240
2 Mining and quarrying	135	...	41	...	...	180	125	...	42	...	...	172
A Coal mining	...	...	...	...	...	...	...	...	...	...	...	...
B Crude petroleum and natural gas production	...	...	...	...	...	...	...	...	...	...	...	...
C Metal ore mining	-	...	-	...	...	-	-	...	-	...	...	-
D Other mining	135	...	41	...	...	180	125	...	42	...	...	172
3 Manufacturing	32251	...	23888	...	...	57410	34363	...	24184	...	...	61634
A Manufacture of food, beverages and tobacco	2065	...	1792	...	...	5344	2135	...	1844	...	...	5505
B Textile, wearing apparel and leather industries	494	...	516	...	...	1047	503	...	604	...	...	1171
C Manufacture of wood and wood products, including furniture	...	...	...	...	...	...	...	...	...	...	...	...
D Manufacture of paper and paper products, printing and publishing	1249	...	509	...	...	1790	1406	...	524	...	...	1962
E Manufacture of chemicals and chemical petroleum, coal, rubber and plastic products	5111	...	4132	...	...	9716	5556	...	4497	...	...	10575
F Manufacture of non-metallic mineral products, except products of petroleum and coal	2075	...	1826	...	...	4021	2115	...	1704	...	...	3924
G Basic metal industries	15060	...	12235	...	...	26235	15656	...	12202	...	...	28527
H Manufacture of fabricated metal products, machinery and equipment	5930	...	2712	...	...	8814	6708	...	2703	...	...	9570
I Other manufacturing industries	267	...	166	...	...	443	284	...	106	...	...	400
4 Electricity, gas and water	1517	...	2722	...	...	4479	1594	...	3061	...	...	4894
5 Construction	8232	...	2437	...	...	10942	8132	...	2663	...	...	11006
6 Wholesale and retail trade, restaurants and hotels	15433	...	15352	...	...	31703	16525	...	16447	...	...	33970
A Wholesale and retail trade	13132	...	13195	...	...	27059	13824	...	14283	...	...	28897
B Restaurants and hotels	2301	...	2157	...	...	4644	2701	...	2164	...	...	5073
7 Transport, storage and communication	10078	...	5274	...	...	10839	10597	...	5246	...	...	11122
A Transport and storage	7864	...	3739	...	...	7080	8309	...	3660	...	...	7237
B Communication	2214	...	1535	...	...	3759	2288	...	1586	...	...	3885
8 Finance, insurance, real estate and business services a	13702	...	30375	...	...	47767	15383	...	30165	...	...	49993
A Financial institutions	...	...	...	...	...	46611	14392	...	30650	...	...	49051
B Insurance	...	...	...	...	...	1156	991	...	-485	...	...	942
C Real estate and business services	...	...	...	...	...	...	...	...	...	...	...	...
9 Community, social and personal services a	10157	...	16877	...	...	29224	10336	...	17086	...	...	30369

4.3 Cost Components of Value Added
(Continued)

Million Luxembourg francs

	Compensation of Employees	Capital Consumption	Net Operating Surplus	Indirect Taxes	Less: Subsidies Received	Value Added	Compensation of Employees	Capital Consumption	Net Operating Surplus	Indirect Taxes	Less: Subsidies Received	Value Added
	1984						**1985**					
Total, Industries b	92141	...	101493	...	...	197410	97736	...	103703	...	...	208400
Producers of Government Services	21596	...	1838	...	...	23517	23003	...	2080	...	...	25167
Other Producers	1539	...	77	...	...	1616	1648	...	82	...	...	1730
Total b	115276	...	103408	...	...	222543	122387	...	105865	...	...	235297
Less: Imputed bank service charge	...	...	48641	...	...	48641	...	...	50917	...	...	50917
Import duties	...	...	...	...	...	7274	...	...	...	...	...	7645
Value added tax	...	...	...	...	...	12490	...	...	...	...	...	13230
Total cb	115276	...	54767	...	...	193666	122387	...	54948	...	...	205255

	Compensation of Employees	Capital Consumption	Net Operating Surplus	Indirect Taxes	Less: Subsidies Received	Value Added	Compensation of Employees	Capital Consumption	Net Operating Surplus	Indirect Taxes	Less: Subsidies Received	Value Added
	1986						**1987**					
	All Producers											
1 Agriculture, hunting, forestry and fishing	718	...	4761	...	...	5244	752	...	4571	...	...	5088
2 Mining and quarrying	126	...	44	...	...	177	325	...	235	...	...	578
A Coal mining	...	...	...	...	...	...	...	...	...	...	...	...
B Crude petroleum and natural gas production	...	...	...	...	...	...	...	...	...	...	...	...
C Metal ore mining	-	...	-	...	...	-	-	...	-	...	...	-
D Other mining	126	...	44	...	...	177	325	...	235	...	...	578
3 Manufacturing	36427	...	27112	...	...	66048	36702	...	20819	...	...	59484
A Manufacture of food, beverages and tobacco	2226	...	2161	...	...	5995	2274	...	2096	...	...	5852
B Textile, wearing apparel and leather industries	540	...	507	...	...	1101	701	...	201	...	...	933
C Manufacture of wood and wood products, including furniture	...	...	...	...	...	...	...	...	...	...	...	...
D Manufacture of paper and paper products, printing and publishing	1482	...	654	...	...	2176	1589	...	647	...	...	2261
E Manufacture of chemicals and chemical petroleum, coal, rubber and plastic products	5885	...	5532	...	...	11951	6162	...	5085	...	...	11678
F Manufacture of non-metallic mineral products, except products of petroleum and coal	2273	...	2463	...	...	4876	2231	...	3023	...	...	5427
G Basic metal industries	16394	...	11966	...	...	28321	15953	...	6684	...	...	22349
H Manufacture of fabricated metal products, machinery and equipment	7353	...	3692	...	...	11208	7537	...	2903	...	...	10545
I Other manufacturing industries	274	...	137	...	...	420	255	...	180	...	...	439
4 Electricity, gas and water	1670	...	2949	...	...	4858	1761	...	2749	...	...	4596
5 Construction	8806	...	3464	...	...	12512	9999	...	3795	...	...	13982
6 Wholesale and retail trade, restaurants and hotels	17508	...	16742	...	...	35294	18619	...	17867	...	...	37603
A Wholesale and retail trade	14662	...	14402	...	...	29884	15567	...	15251	...	...	31693
B Restaurants and hotels	2846	...	2340	...	...	5410	3052	...	2616	...	...	5910
7 Transport, storage and communication	11546	...	6587	...	...	13251	12633	...	6363	...	...	13774
A Transport and storage	8936	...	4327	...	...	8369	9799	...	4113	...	...	8656
B Communication	2610	...	2260	...	...	4882	2834	...	2250	...	...	5118
8 Finance, insurance, real estate and business services a	17627	...	28269	...	...	50444	19931	...	24037	...	...	48500
A Financial institutions	16570	...	28317	...	...	48936	18765	...	24353	...	...	47113
B Insurance	1057	...	-48	...	...	1508	1166	...	-316	...	...	1387
C Real estate and business services	...	...	...	...	...	...	...	...	...	...	...	...
9 Community, social and personal services a	9803	...	18534	...	...	32508	11622	...	19228	...	...	36056

Luxembourg

4.3 Cost Components of Value Added
(Continued)

Million Luxembourg francs

	1986						1987					
	Compensation of Employees	Capital Consumption	Net Operating Surplus	Indirect Taxes	Less: Subsidies Received	Value Added	Compensation of Employees	Capital Consumption	Net Operating Surplus	Indirect Taxes	Less: Subsidies Received	Value Added
Total, Industries [b]	104231	...	108462	...	...	220336	112344	...	99664	...	...	219661
Producers of Government Services	24799	...	2664	...	...	27558	27146	...	2859	...	...	30006
Other Producers	1823	...	91	...	...	1914	2124	...	106	...	...	2230
Total [b]	130853	...	111217	...	...	249808	141614	...	102629	...	...	251897
Less: Imputed bank service charge	...	...	48802	...	...	48802	...	...	47639	...	...	47639
Import duties	...	...	...	...	...	7996	...	...	...	...	...	8148
Value added tax	...	...	...	...	...	14302	...	...	...	...	...	15140
Total [cb]	130853	...	62415	...	...	223304	141614	...	54990	...	...	227546

	1988						1989					
	Compensation of Employees	Capital Consumption	Net Operating Surplus	Indirect Taxes	Less: Subsidies Received	Value Added	Compensation of Employees	Capital Consumption	Net Operating Surplus	Indirect Taxes	Less: Subsidies Received	Value Added
All Producers												
1 Agriculture, hunting, forestry and fishing	793	...	4878	...	...	5326	878	...	5580	...	...	5924
2 Mining and quarrying	339	...	319	...	...	678	414	...	365	...	...	803
A Coal mining	...	...	...	...	...	...	...	...	...	...	...	...
B Crude petroleum and natural gas production	...	...	...	...	...	...	...	...	...	...	...	...
C Metal ore mining	-	...	-	...	...	-	-	...	-	...	...	...
D Other mining	339	...	319	...	...	678	414	...	365	...	...	803
3 Manufacturing	37849	...	27789	...	...	68264	39913	...	35968	...	...	79081
A Manufacture of food, beverages and tobacco	2275	...	2355	...	...	6164	2369	...	2507	...	...	6480
B Textile, wearing apparel and leather industries	891	...	422	...	...	1367	913	...	1243	...	...	2253
C Manufacture of wood and wood products, including furniture	...	...	...	...	...	...	...	...	...	...	...	...
D Manufacture of paper and paper products, printing and publishing	1656	...	751	...	...	2446	1797	...	836	...	...	2675
E Manufacture of chemicals and chemical petroleum, coal, rubber and plastic products	6370	...	6375	...	...	13219	6744	...	7212	...	...	14467
F Manufacture of non-metallic mineral products, except products of petroleum and coal	2386	...	2576	...	...	5545	2874	...	3796	...	...	7672
G Basic metal industries	16296	...	11507	...	...	27595	16707	...	15090	...	...	31565
H Manufacture of fabricated metal products, machinery and equipment	7727	...	3614	...	...	11480	8243	...	5035	...	...	13442
I Other manufacturing industries	248	...	189	...	...	448	266	...	249	...	...	527
4 Electricity, gas and water	1843	...	2762	...	...	4693	1989	...	2767	...	...	4845
5 Construction	11436	...	5439	...	...	17113	12783	...	5860	...	...	18901
6 Wholesale and retail trade, restaurants and hotels	20136	...	19340	...	...	40690	22522	...	21812	...	...	45691
A Wholesale and retail trade	16802	...	16612	...	...	34374	18762	...	19012	...	...	38860
B Restaurants and hotels	3334	...	2728	...	...	6316	3760	...	2800	...	...	6831
7 Transport, storage and communication	13551	...	7083	...	...	15537	14953	...	9191	...	...	18741
A Transport and storage	10521	...	4665	...	...	10074	11634	...	5477	...	...	11692
B Communication	3030	...	2418	...	...	5463	3319	...	3714	...	...	7049
8 Finance, insurance, real estate and business services [a]	21691	...	18223	...	...	45191	25956	...	6919	...	...	37744
A Financial institutions	20424	...	18232	...	...	43322	24539	...	6736	...	...	35455
B Insurance	1267	...	-9	...	...	1869	1417	...	183	...	...	2289
C Real estate and business services	...	...	...	...	...	...	...	...	...	...	...	...
9 Community, social and personal services [a]	13162	...	20389	...	...	38390	15626	...	17696	...	...	42074

4.3 Cost Components of Value Added
(Continued)

Million Luxembourg francs

	1988						1989					
	Compensation of Employees	Capital Consumption	Net Operating Surplus	Indirect Taxes	Less: Subsidies Received	Value Added	Compensation of Employees	Capital Consumption	Net Operating Surplus	Indirect Taxes	Less: Subsidies Received	Value Added
Total, Industries [b]	120800	...	106222	...	...	235882	135034	...	106158	...	...	253804
Producers of Government Services	28088	...	3142	...	...	31231	30352	...	3668	...	...	34021
Other Producers	2360	...	118	...	...	2478	2737	...	137	...	...	2874
Total [b]	151248	...	109482	...	...	269591	168123	...	109963	...	...	290699
Less: Imputed bank service charge	...	...	45673	...	...	45673	...	...	36317	...	...	36317
Import duties	...	...	...	...	...	9276	...	...	...	...	...	9848
Value added tax	...	...	...	...	...	17014	...	...	...	...	...	18595
Total [cb]	151248	...	63809	...	...	250208	168123	...	73646	...	...	282825

	1990						1991					
	Compensation of Employees	Capital Consumption	Net Operating Surplus	Indirect Taxes	Less: Subsidies Received	Value Added	Compensation of Employees	Capital Consumption	Net Operating Surplus	Indirect Taxes	Less: Subsidies Received	Value Added

All Producers

	Compensation of Employees	Capital Consumption	Net Operating Surplus	Indirect Taxes	Less: Subsidies Received	Value Added	Compensation of Employees	Capital Consumption	Net Operating Surplus	Indirect Taxes	Less: Subsidies Received	Value Added
1 Agriculture, hunting, forestry and fishing	968	...	5358	...	...	5807	1074	...	4735	...	...	4477
2 Mining and quarrying	447	...	481	...	...	956	458	...	510	...	...	997
A Coal mining	...	...	...	...	...	...	...	...	...	...	...	...
B Crude petroleum and natural gas production	...	...	...	...	...	...	...	...	...	...	...	...
C Metal ore mining	-	...	...	...	...	-	-	...	-	...	...	-
D Other mining	447	...	481	...	...	956	458	...	510	...	...	997
3 Manufacturing	42524	...	31638	...	...	77406	43907	...	30101	...	...	77303
A Manufacture of food, beverages and tobacco	2568	...	2607	...	...	6781	2771	...	2565	...	...	7050
B Textile, wearing apparel and leather industries	956	...	1371	...	...	2433	1035	...	1395	...	...	2542
C Manufacture of wood and wood products, including furniture	...	...	...	...	...	...	...	...	...	...	...	...
D Manufacture of paper and paper products, printing and publishing	2023	...	1101	...	...	3177	2234	...	1191	...	...	3483
E Manufacture of chemicals and chemical petroleum, coal, rubber and plastic products	7027	...	5750	...	...	13262	7782	...	6083	...	...	14353
F Manufacture of non-metallic mineral products, except products of petroleum and coal	3295	...	3786	...	...	8112	3434	...	3407	...	...	7762
G Basic metal industries	17291	...	11812	...	...	28881	16694	...	9666	...	...	26168
H Manufacture of fabricated metal products, machinery and equipment	9069	...	4889	...	...	14129	9625	...	5449	...	...	15253
I Other manufacturing industries	295	...	322	...	...	631	332	...	345	...	...	692
4 Electricity, gas and water	2190	...	2811	...	...	5094	2332	...	2849	...	...	5264
5 Construction	14546	...	6783	...	...	21626	16148	...	7426	...	...	23905
6 Wholesale and retail trade, restaurants and hotels	24804	...	23263	...	...	49541	26693	...	24036	...	...	52285
A Wholesale and retail trade	20682	...	20120	...	...	41976	22196	...	20822	...	...	44258
B Restaurants and hotels	4122	...	3143	...	...	7565	4497	...	3214	...	...	8027
7 Transport, storage and communication	16692	...	10044	...	...	20379	16574	...	11697	...	...	22139
A Transport and storage	13056	...	5736	...	...	12418	13094	...	6479	...	...	13424
B Communication	3636	...	4308	...	...	7961	3480	...	5218	...	...	8715
8 Finance, insurance, real estate and business services [a]	29809	...	5649	...	...	39855	33098	...	6714	...	...	44236
A Financial institutions	28350	...	5459	...	...	37447	31288	...	6757	...	...	41710
B Insurance	1459	...	190	...	...	2408	1810	...	-43	...	...	2526
C Real estate and business services	...	...	...	...	...	...	...	...	...	...	...	...
9 Community, social and personal services [a]	18686	...	16585	...	...	45496	23834	...	14268	...	...	48656

Luxembourg

4.3 Cost Components of Value Added
(Continued)

Million Luxembourg francs

	1990						1991					
	Compensation of Employees	Capital Consumption	Net Operating Surplus	Indirect Taxes	Less: Subsidies Received	Value Added	Compensation of Employees	Capital Consumption	Net Operating Surplus	Indirect Taxes	Less: Subsidies Received	Value Added
Total, Industries b	150666	...	102612	...	...	266160	164118	...	102336	...	...	279262
Producers of Government Services	34787	...	3966	...	...	38754	38719	...	4413	...	...	43133
Other Producers	3080	...	154	...	...	3234	3492	...	175	...	...	3667
Total b	188533	...	106732	...	...	308148	206329	...	106924	...	...	326062
Less: Imputed bank service charge	...	...	37870	...	...	37870	...	...	42017	...	...	42017
Import duties	...	...	...	...	...	9793	...	...	...	...	...	11760
Value added tax	...	...	...	...	...	20338	...	...	...	...	...	22999
Total cb	188533	...	68862	...	...	300409	206329	...	64907	...	...	318804

a) Business services are included in item 'Community, social and personal services'.
b) Column 'Consumption of fixed capital' is included in column 'Net operating surplus'.
c) The branch breakdown used in this table (GDP by kind of activity) is according to the classification NACE/CLIO.

Madagascar

Source. Reply to the United Nations National Accounts Questionnaire from the Institut National de la Statistique et de la Recherche Economique, Ministere des Finances et du Commerce, Tananarive.
General note. The official estimates of Madagascar have been adjusted by the Institut National de la Statistique et de la Recherche Economique to conform to the United Nations System of National Accounts so far as the existing data would permit.

1.1 Expenditure on the Gross Domestic Product, in Current Prices

Million Malagasy francs

	1980	1981	1982	1983	1984	1985	1986	1987	1988	1989	1990	1991
1 Government final consumption expenditure	117800	129100	149500	165300	185000	209700	...	...	...	...	...	...
2 Private final consumption expenditure a	526100	604600	799000	973400	1058100	1208600	...	...	...	...	...	...
3 Gross capital formation	162400	142500	133000	160700	185700	217700	...	...	...	...	...	...
A Increase in stocks	4800	-5800	3600	...	...	...						
B Gross fixed capital formation	157600	148300	129400	...	...	...						
4 Exports of goods and services	96800	96400	125700	139700	214200	225000	...	...	...	...	...	...
5 Less: Imports of goods and services	213300	183600	211100	218000	273900	307600	...	...	...	...	...	...
Equals: Gross Domestic Product	689800	789000	996100	1221100	1369100	1553400	2203800	2743100	3436700	4005300	4601600	4906400

a) Item 'Private final consumption expenditure' has been obtained as a residual.

1.2 Expenditure on the Gross Domestic Product, in Constant Prices

Million Malagasy francs

	1980	1981	1982	1983	1984	1985	1986	1987	1988	1989	1990	1991
			At constant prices of:									
			1970					1984				
1 Government final consumption expenditure	59600	59500	57700	57900	... 185000	189600	...	...	...	...	...	...
2 Private final consumption expenditure a	175800	157400	161700	162700	... 1058100	1070500	...	...	...	...	...	...
3 Gross capital formation	49200	34300	28000	27800	... 185700	189300	...	...	...	...	...	...
4 Exports of goods and services	48700	37300	38100	33400	... 214200	223300	...	...	...	...	...	...
5 Less: Imports of goods and services	58000	37000	38600	32900	... 273900	272500	...	...	...	...	...	...
Equals: Gross Domestic Product	275300	251500	246900	248900	... 1369100	1400200	...	...	...	...	...	...

a) Item 'Private final consumption expenditure' has been obtained as a residual.

1.10 Gross Domestic Product by Kind of Activity, in Current Prices

Million Malagasy francs

	1980	1981	1982	1983	1984	1985	1986	1987	1988	1989	1990	1991
1 Agriculture, hunting, forestry and fishing	249100	313600	409700	525300	580600	653200	...	...	...	...	...	...
2 Mining and quarrying							...	...	...	...	...	...
3 Manufacturing	124300	125300	149900	185400	213900	254100	...	...	...	...	...	...
4 Electricity, gas and water												
5 Construction							...	...	...	...	...	...
6 Wholesale and retail trade, restaurants and hotels							...	...	...	...	...	...
7 Transport, storage and communication	197700	230100	298700	361500	400600	451300						
8 Finance, insurance, real estate and business services							...	...	...	...	...	...
9 Community, social and personal services							...	...	...	...	...	...
Total, Industries	571100	669000	858300	1072200	1195100	1358600	...	...	...	...	...	...
Producers of Government Services	83600	90400	107600	115200	128000	142000	...	...	...	...	...	...
Other Producers a	...	...	...	...	...	...	...	...	...	...	...	...
Subtotal	654700	759400	965900	1187400	1323100	1500600	...	...	...	...	...	...
Less: Imputed bank service charge	...	...	...	...	...	...	...	...	...	...	...	...
Plus: Import duties	35100	29600	30200	33700	46000	52800	...	...	...	...	...	...
Plus: Value added tax	...	...	...	...	...	...	...	...	...	...	...	...
Equals: Gross Domestic Product	689800	789000	996100	1221100	1369100	1553400	...	...	...	...	...	...

a) Item 'Other producers' is included in item 'Community, social and personal services'.

Madagascar

1.11 Gross Domestic Product by Kind of Activity, in Constant Prices

Million Malagasy francs

	1980	1981	1982	1983	1984	1985	1986	1987	1988	1989	1990	1991
			1970		At constant prices of:			1984				
1 Agriculture, hunting, forestry and fishing	78300	74800	77800	79700	580600	591700	...	...	...	...	...	...
2 Mining and quarrying							...	...	...	...	...	...
3 Manufacturing	55000	42400	36400	36900	213900	223500	...	...	...	...	...	...
4 Electricity, gas and water							...	...	...	...	...	...
5 Construction							...	...	...	...	...	...
6 Wholesale and retail trade, restaurants and hotels							...	...	...	...	...	...
7 Transport, storage and communication	90700	84500	83600	82900	400600	409200	...	...	...	...	...	...
8 Finance, insurance, real estate and business services							...	...	...	...	...	...
9 Community, social and personal services							...	...	...	...	...	...
Total, Industries	224000	201700	197800	199500	1195100	1224400	...	...	...	...	...	...
Producers of Government Services	41700	43800	44200	44700	128000	129200	...	...	...	...	...	...
Other Producers a	...	...	...	...	...	...	...	...	...	...	...	...
Subtotal	265700	245500	242000	244200	1323100	1353600	...	...	...	...	...	...
Less: Imputed bank service charge	...	...	...	...	...	...	...	...	...	...	...	...
Plus: Import duties	9600	6000	4900	4700	46000	46600	...	...	...	...	...	...
Plus: Value added tax	...	...	...	...	...	...	...	...	...	...	...	...
Equals: Gross Domestic Product	275300	251500	246900	248900	1369100	1400200	...	...	...	...	...	...

a) Item 'Other producers' is included in item 'Community, social and personal services'.

1.12 Relations Among National Accounting Aggregates

Million Malagasy francs

	1980	1981	1982	1983	1984	1985	1986	1987	1988	1989	1990	1991
Gross Domestic Product	689800	...	...	...	...	...	...	...	...	...	...	...
Plus: Net factor income from the rest of the world	-1000	...	...	...	...	...	...	...	...	...	...	...
Equals: Gross National Product	688800	...	...	...	...	...	...	...	...	...	...	...
Less: Consumption of fixed capital	...	...	...	...	...	...	...	...	...	...	...	...
Equals: National Income	...	...	...	...	...	...	...	...	...	...	...	...
Plus: Net current transfers from the rest of the world	...	...	...	...	...	...	...	...	...	...	...	...
Equals: National Disposable Income	...	...	...	...	...	...	...	...	...	...	...	...
Less: Final consumption	...	...	...	...	...	...	...	...	...	...	...	...
Equals: Net Saving	...	...	...	...	...	...	...	...	...	...	...	...
Less: Surplus of the nation on current transactions	...	...	...	...	...	...	...	...	...	...	...	...
Equals: Net Capital Formation	...	...	...	...	...	...	...	...	...	...	...	...

Malawi

General note. The preparation of national accounts statistics in Malawi is undertaken by the National Statistical Office, Zomba. The official estimates are published in a series of reports entitled 'National Accounts Report'. A detailed description of the sources and methods used for national accounts estimates is found in 'National Accounts Handbook, Sources and Methods' published in 1985. The estimates are generally in accordance with the classifications and definitions recommended in the United Nations System of National Accounts (SNA). The following tables have been prepared from successive replies to the United Nations national accounts questionnaire. When the scope and coverage of the estimates differ for conceptual or statistical reasons from the definitions and classifications recommended in SNA, a footnote is indicated to the relevant tables.

Sources and methods :

(a) Gross domestic product. Gross domestic product is estimated mainly through the production approach.

(b) Expenditure on the gross domestic product. The expenditure approach is used to estimate government final consumption expenditure, increase in stocks, investment in building and construction and exports and imports of goods and services. The commodity-flow approach is used to estimate the gross capital formation of transport equipment, plant and machinery whereas private final consumption expenditure is estimated as a residual. Government expenditure is estimated by netting out rent from the total of Malawi Government Revenue Expenditure on Revenue and Development Account Expenditure and final consumption as shown in 'Public Sector Financial Statistics'. Changes in recorded stocks of the monetary sector are obtained from the annual economic surveys and annual reports of the Agricultural Development and Marketing Corporation. Unrecorded stocks, i.e., imported goods, are estimated on the basis of information received from businessmen and the Ministry of Trade and Industry. Estimates of non-monetary stocks are estimated from annual economic surveys, reports of the Veterinary Department and from the Agricultural Development and Marketing Corporation. Estimates of investments in building and construction are obtained directly from large enterprises and government. For fixed operating and auxiliary equipment, installation costs are estimated at 25 per cent of the price of deliveries. Other equipment is valued at estimated delivered prices. 15 per cent of the private cars and bicyles are assumed to be imported by government and private industry and are treated as capital formation. Export and imports of goods and services are based on the balance of payments report. For the constant price estimates, price deflation is used to estimate all items of GDP by expenditure type.

(c) Cost-structure of the gross domestic product. Estimates of compensation of employees, operating surplus and consumption of fixed capital are based on data obtained from the annual survey of ecomomic activities. Data on indirect taxes and subsidies are taken from the financial statistics of the public sector.

(d) Gross domestic product by kind of economic activity. The table of GDP by kind of economic activity is prepared in factor values. The production approach is used to estimate the value added of most industries. The value added of large and medium-scale establishments, was generally taken from the Annual Economic Survey 1973-1979 and from the Medium Business Annual Review. Estimates of agricultural output are based mainly on the annual reports of the Agricultural Development and Marketing Corporation and on agricultural surveys undertaken by the National Statistical Office. Net income of farmers from sales of crops to the corporation is derived by deducting from total farm receipts the expenditure on cotton spraying and 50 per cent of the expenditure on fertilizers, seeds and tools. Income from sales of crops to other dealers is calculated as 50 per cent of the free-on-rail export value of the crops, whereas income from sales in local village and urban markets is calculated from estimates of the annual consumption of main food crops by the African population. For livestock production, estimates are based on live-weight purchases by butchers and the Cold Storage Commission which are published in the annual reports of the Veterinary Department. Increase in herds is estimated from the annual livestock censuses and the national sample survey of agriculture. For forestry, the National Statistical Office makes estimates of the retail value of firewood sales less the cost of axes and hatchets. An assumption on the quantities of firewood consumed per household is made for nonmarketed firewood. The Fisheries Department provides estimates for the fishing sector. Own-consumption of fish is estimated as 10 per cent of the landed value of the total fish catch. The estimates of large mining entreprises are based on the annual economic survey. For large manufacturing enterprises employing 20 persons or more, the annual economic survey is used to estimate gross output and intermediate consumption. The estimates of enterprises such as grain-milling, tailoring, fish-curing, handicrafts, etc. are based on agricultural sample surveys, information from the Ministry of Trade and Industry, data supplied by the Buildings Department, etc. The sources for the estimates of electricity, gas and water are the annual ecomomic surveys and the public sector financial statistics. For government construction, the annual reports of the Ministry of Works and Supplies and the estimates prepared by the National Statisticial Office are used as sources. For private construction, the quarterly building inquiries and the annual economic surveys are used for the larger enterprises while data from agricultural surveys are used for other construction including own-account construction. It is assumed that the ratio of value added to total receipts for the large construction enterprises also applies to small operators. The annual economic survey is the source used to estimate activity of larger trade enterprises while the annual reviews of small businesses are used for other enterprises. The wage component of gross output is derived from data on average employment per store and minimum wage rates. For the transport sector, the annual economic survey is also used for the larger enterprises while the annual reports of the Road Traffic Commissioner are used for the small transport operators. It is assumed that average value added per vehicle for the larger operators applies equally to the small enterprises. Value added of the financial institutions is estimated on the basis of the quarterly employment inquiries, documents of banks, information from the Ministry of Finance and the Accountant-General's annual reports. Rental value are obtained from various sources such as the public sector financial statistics, the Accountant-General's annual reports and reports of the Commissioner for Taxes.ng income survey, respectively. Value added of public administration and defence is obtained from the detailed analysis of government accounts. For private services, estimates are based on quarterly employment and earnings inquiries, agricultural surveys, annual inquiries of domestic servants, annual economic surveys and information supplied by the Ministry of Trade and Industry. GDP by kind of economic activity is not estimated at constant prices.

1.1 Expenditure on the Gross Domestic Product, in Current Prices

Million Malawi kwacha

	1980	1981	1982	1983	1984	1985	1986	1987	1988	1989	1990	1991
1 Government final consumption expenditure	193.9	198.0	213.2	235.1	264.7	345.4	434.6	487.7	570.9	712.4	773.1	...
2 Private final consumption expenditure a	728.6	806.5	918.9	1109.2	1167.3	1430.3	1535.8	1932.6	2770.9	3764.0	4380.8	...
3 Gross capital formation	...	...	...	...	...	...	...	...	...	...	...	...
A Increase in stocks a	...	...	...	...	...	...	...	...	...	...	...	...
B Gross fixed capital formation	223.1	167.8	181.7	197.3	222.7	259.5	264.1	352.9	524.0	699.6	700.0	...
4 Exports of goods and services	249.7	284.4	280.2	298.2	484.4	470.5	504.7	665.1	824.3	817.0	1029.9	...
5 Less: Imports of goods and services	390.1	348.6	359.3	407.1	451.2	576.4	551.8	726.6	1184.8	1456.6	1730.7	...
Equals: Gross Domestic Product b	1005.1	1108.1	1234.7	1432.7	1687.9	1929.2	2187.4	2711.8	3505.3	4536.4	5853.9	...

a) Beginning 1980, item 'Increase in stocks' is included in item 'Private final consumption expenditure'. b) Data in this table have been revised, therefore they are not strictly comparable with the unrevised data in the other tables.

1.2 Expenditure on the Gross Domestic Product, in Constant Prices

Million Malawi kwacha

	1980	1981	1982	1983	1984	1985	1986	1987	1988	1989	1990	1991
					At constant prices of:1978							
1 Government final consumption expenditure	157.2	150.6	150.9	153.0	164.2	213.6	230.9	238.9	247.6	245.1	253.8	...
2 Private final consumption expenditure a	543.1	547.0	569.1	601.6	548.4	599.6	556.6	555.6	599.3	773.0	742.4	...
3 Gross capital formation	...	...	...	...	...	...	...	...	...	...	...	...
A Increase in stocks a	...	...	...	...	...	...	...	...	...	...	...	.
B Gross fixed capital formation	174.0	117.9	114.8	112.0	108.5	108.0	80.9	88.2	101.2	115.7	102.5	...
4 Exports of goods and services	273.6	224.7	202.3	209.0	277.4	291.6	281.1	284.3	290.0	245.3	...	...
5 Less: Imports of goods and services	308.8	239.7	228.7	232.8	217.5	262.7	195.6	190.0	235.9	267.1	...	...
Equals: Gross Domestic Product	839.1	800.4	808.4	848.9	881.0	950.1	953.8	976.9	1002.2	1052.0	1098.8	...

a) Beginning 1980, item 'Increase in stocks' is included in item 'Private final consumption expenditure'.

Malawi

1.3 Cost Components of the Gross Domestic Product

Million Malawi kwacha

	1980	1981	1982	1983	1984	1985	1986	1987	1988	1989	1990	1991
1 Indirect taxes, net	103.5	107.8	116.1	139.6	178.1	216.0	216.4	268.3	349.4	415.5	...	...
2 Consumption of fixed capital a	60.9	75.0	82.3	88.3	91.8	109.5	140.2	...	...	...	...	...
3 Compensation of employees paid by resident producers to:	233.7	263.1	295.1	316.1	327.2	394.3	455.8	...	...	...	...	...
4 Operating surplus a	607.0	662.2	751.6	892.9	1109.9	1230.1	1382.0	...	...	...	...	...
Equals: Gross Domestic Product	1005.1	1108.1	1245.1	1436.9	1707.0	1949.9	2194.4	2731.5	3574.2	4081.7	5023.5	...

a) Item 'Operating surplus' includes consumption of fixed capital.

1.4 General Government Current Receipts and Disbursements

Million Malawi kwacha

	1980	1981	1982	1983	1984	1985	1986	1987	1988	1989	1990	1991
Receipts												
1 Operating surplus	...	...	...	...	...	...	...	...	...	...	...	...
2 Property and entrepreneurial income	...	...	...	...	...	...	...	...	...	...	...	...
3 Taxes, fees and contributions	180.2	179.0	202.5	...	...	...	...	...	...	...	...	...
A Indirect taxes	103.5	107.8	116.1	139.6	178.1	216.0	216.4	268.3	349.4	468.5	565.0	...
B Direct taxes	64.9	61.9	79.9	...	...	...	...	...	...	...	...	...
C Social security contributions	...	...	...	...	...	...	...	...	...	...	...	...
D Compulsory fees, fines and penalties	11.8	9.3	6.5	...	...	...	...	...	...	...	...	...
4 Other current transfers	40.6	41.4	34.5	...	...	...	...	...	...	...	...	...
Total Current Receipts of General Government	220.8	220.4	237.0	...	...	...	...	...	...	...	...	...
Disbursements												
1 Government final consumption expenditure	193.9	198.0	218.3	235.9	268.0	344.0	433.8	488.6	540.2	577.8	773.1	...
A Compensation of employees	74.1	84.4	99.0	111.7	127.3	149.5	186.9	231.7	248.5	311.2	346.9	...
B Consumption of fixed capital	119.8	113.6	119.3	124.2	140.7	194.5	246.9	256.9	291.7	266.6	426.2	...
C Purchases of goods and services, net												...
D Less: Own account fixed capital formation	...	...	...	...	...	...	...	...	...	...	...	...
E Indirect taxes paid, net	...	...	...	...	...	...	...	...	...	...	...	...
2 Property income	...	...	...	...	...	...	...	...	...	...	...	...
3 Subsidies	...	...	...	...	...	...	...	...	...	...	...	...
4 Other current transfers	...	...	...	...	...	...	...	...	...	...	...	...
5 Net saving	26.9	22.4	18.7	...	...	...	...	...	...	...	...	...
Total Current Disbursements and Net Saving of General Government	220.8	220.4	237.0	...	...	...	...	...	...	...	...	...

1.10 Gross Domestic Product by Kind of Activity, in Current Prices

Million Malawi kwacha

	1980	1981	1982	1983	1984	1985	1986	1987	1988	1989	1990	1991
1 Agriculture, hunting, forestry and fishing a	335.9	315.7	353.2	402.0	494.3	535.1	584.0	...	...	...	...	...
2 Mining and quarrying	...	...	...	...	...	...	...	...	...	...	...	...
3 Manufacturing	158.3	161.1	155.9	155.4	245.3	270.1	343.3	...	...	...	...	...
4 Electricity, gas and water	15.0	17.1	19.1	23.6	23.9	23.8	20.6	...	...	...	...	...
5 Construction	55.9	42.0	41.2	35.4	26.1	33.9	34.1	...	...	...	...	...
6 Wholesale and retail trade, restaurants and hotels	92.2	98.3	171.6	129.2	89.5	197.6	195.0	...	...	...	...	...
7 Transport, storage and communication	40.4	56.1	39.5	40.8	64.5	73.2	58.5	...	...	...	...	...
8 Finance, insurance, real estate and business services	63.2	76.0	80.2	83.0	116.1	102.4	91.7	...	...	...	...	...
9 Community, social and personal services	12.7	34.1	5.3	41.7	36.4	40.2	42.4	...	...	...	...	...

1.10 Gross Domestic Product by Kind of Activity, in Current Prices
(Continued)

Million Malawi kwacha

	1980	1981	1982	1983	1984	1985	1986	1987	1988	1989	1990	1991
Total, Industries	773.6	800.4	866.0	911.1	1096.1	1276.1	1369.6	...	...	...	...	...
Producers of Government Services	81.3	91.4	105.7	121.0	137.3	164.2	213.6	...	...	...	...	...
Other Producers	42.1	48.9	53.6	61.0	88.4	99.7	110.7	...	...	...	...	...
Subtotal	897.0	940.7	1025.3	1093.1	1321.8	1540.2	1693.9	...	...	...	...	...
Less: Imputed bank service charge	25.5	30.6	32.2	33.2	46.5	38.0	34.0	...	...	...	...	...
Plus: Import duties	73.5	72.9	74.1	78.3	110.9	134.6	132.3	...	...	...	...	...
Plus: Value added tax	6.2	7.0	10.7	17.9	11.5	17.9	1.2	...	...	...	...	...
Equals: Gross Domestic Product	951.1	990.2	1077.9	1156.1	1397.7	1654.7	1793.4	...	...	...	...	...

a) Item 'Agriculture, hunting, forestry and fishing' includes all non-monetary output.

1.11 Gross Domestic Product by Kind of Activity, in Constant Prices

Million Malawi kwacha

	1980	1981	1982	1983	1984	1985	1986	1987	1988	1989	1990	1991
					At constant prices of:1978							
1 Agriculture, hunting, forestry and fishing	284.2	261.0	277.6	289.9	306.5	308.1	310.1	312.4	318.7	326.6	319.7	...
2 Mining and quarrying	...	...	...	...	...	...	...	...	...	...	...	...
3 Manufacturing	88.8	95.3	88.6	97.4	95.8	95.2	102.4	101.0	102.8	111.5	127.1	...
4 Electricity, gas and water	14.2	14.4	14.6	15.8	16.1	16.4	17.3	18.7	19.1	20.7	23.1	...
5 Construction	43.5	36.4	35.8	33.1	30.2	39.5	34.1	32.9	38.1	40.5	40.4	...
6 Wholesale and retail trade, restaurants and hotels	110.4	99.4	94.4	97.3	100.6	108.5	103.8	104.6	102.0	112.7	129.0	...
7 Transport, storage and communication	52.3	48.6	47.0	46.0	46.7	51.1	53.7	50.6	51.6	53.4	57.0	...
8 Finance, insurance, real estate and business services	52.0	48.4	47.8	49.9	49.4	56.3	56.0	53.3	54.8	59.6	66.2	...
9 Community, social and personal services	29.1	30.5	31.7	33.7	34.7	35.2	37.7	38.4	39.8	41.1	42.5	...
Total, Industries	674.5	634.0	637.5	663.1	680.0	710.3	715.1	711.9	726.9	766.1	805.0	...
Producers of Government Services	78.4	101.8	108.4	114.4	127.8	136.0	148.0	172.3	182.8	181.1	187.2	...
Other Producers	32.4	32.1	32.5	33.6	34.2	35.5	36.1	36.6	37.7	39.8	41.0	...
Subtotal	785.3	767.9	778.4	811.1	842.0	881.8	899.2	920.8	947.4	987.0	1033.2	...
Less: Imputed bank service charge	21.1	19.5	19.2	20.0	19.8	20.9	20.8	20.6	21.1	23.0	25.6	...
Plus: Import duties	...	...	...	...	...	...	...	...	...	...	...	...
Plus: Value added tax	...	...	...	...	...	...	...	...	...	...	...	...
Plus: Other adjustments	74.7	...	...	...	...	...	...	...	...	...	...	...
Equals: Gross Domestic Product a	839.1	748.4	759.2	791.2	822.2	860.9	878.4	900.2	926.4	964.0	1007.6	...

a) Gross domestic product in factor values.

1.12 Relations Among National Accounting Aggregates

Million Malawi kwacha

	1980	1981	1982	1983	1984	1985	1986	1987	1988	1989	1990	1991
Gross Domestic Product	1005.1	1108.1	1234.7	1432.7	1687.9	1929.2	2187.4	2711.8	3505.3	4536.4	5853.9	...
Plus: Net factor income from the rest of the world	-81.1	-74.3	-101.3	-139.0	-78.8	-90.9	-112.9	-125.7	-137.9	-137.6	-155.7	...
Equals: Gross National Product	924.0	1033.8	1133.4	1293.7	1609.1	1838.3	2074.5	2586.1	3367.4	4398.8	5698.2	...
Less: Consumption of fixed capital	60.9	75.0	82.3	88.3	91.8	109.5	140.2	...	...	...	...	...
Equals: National Income	863.1	958.8	1051.1	1205.4	1517.3	1728.8	1934.3	...	...	...	...	...
Plus: Net current transfers from the rest of the world	...	...	...	...	...	...	...	...	...	...	...	...
Equals: National Disposable Income	...	...	...	...	...	...	...	...	...	...	...	...
Less: Final consumption	...	...	...	...	...	...	...	...	...	...	...	...
Equals: Net Saving	...	...	...	...	...	...	...	...	...	...	...	...
Less: Surplus of the nation on current transactions	...	...	...	...	...	...	...	...	...	...	...	...
Equals: Net Capital Formation	...	...	...	...	...	...	...	...	...	...	...	...

2.11 Gross Fixed Capital Formation by Kind of Activity of Owner, ISIC Divisions, in Current Prices

Million Malawi kwacha

	1980	1981	1982	1983	1984	1985	1986	1987	1988	1989	1990	1991
					All Producers							
1 Agriculture, hunting, forestry and fishing	2.5	7.9	8.0	7.4	7.7	14.2	14.3	...	...	...	...	...
2 Mining and quarrying	...	...	...	...	...	...	...	...	...	...	...	...
3 Manufacturing	8.2	19.3	17.1	34.4	18.0	39.6	39.7	...	...	...	...	...
4 Electricity, gas and water	38.4	20.2	12.7	10.0	9.8	16.8	31.5	...	...	...	...	...

Malawi

Million Malawi kwacha

	1980	1981	1982	1983	1984	1985	1986	1987	1988	1989	1990	1991
5 Construction	1.0	1.4	1.6	1.7	1.6	3.0	3.1	...	...	...	...	...
6 Wholesale and retail trade, restaurants and hotels	9.5	10.6	14.1	11.7	22.6	22.8	21.8	...	...	...	...	...
7 Transport, storage and communication	3.4	35.9	19.0	19.4	28.2	42.8	46.5	...	...	...	...	...
8 Finance, insurance, real estate and business services	9.4	17.8	23.9	17.3	24.4	20.3	22.2	...	...	...	...	...
9 Community, social and personal services	2.0	1.4	0.4	0.2	0.3	0.4	0.6	...	...	...	...	...
Total Industries	74.4	114.5	96.8	102.1	112.6	159.9	179.7	...	...	...	...	...
Producers of Government Services	11.4	13.1	13.6	13.9	14.0	14.0	14.0	...	...	...	...	...
Private Non-Profit Institutions Serving Households	129.7	47.8	63.3	86.3	59.1	90.5	70.4	...	...	...	...	...
Total	215.5	175.4	173.7	202.3	185.7	264.4	264.1	...	...	...	...	...

Malaysia

General note. The preparation of national accounts statistics in Malaysia is undertaken by the Department of Statistics, Kuala Lumpur. The official estimates are published in a series of reports entitled 'Malaysian National Accounts Statistics'. The estimates are generally in accordance with the classifications and definitions recommended in the United Nations System of National Accounts (SNA, 1968). Since 1970, the publication of estimates of national accounts have been on a Malaysia basis and is in both current and constant prices. The initial constant price series published were valued in 1970 prices, for the period 1971 to 1983. Subsequently, the valuation of the constant series were updated to 1978 prices and are available from 1978 up to the present.

Sources and methods :

(a) Gross domestic product. Gross domestic product is estimated mainly through the production approach.

(b) Expenditure on the gross domestic product. The expenditure approach in combination with the commodity with the commodity-flow approach are used to estimate the expenditure aggregates. Government final consumption expenditure is based on public accounts and financial records and statements of the government bodies. Benchmark estimates of private final consumption expenditure are derived from detailed commodity balancing for the final accounts years. Between final accounts years, estimates of private consumption expenditure have been made by allocating the available supply of consumer goods and services from import and local production to the various consumption component items. Gross fixed capital formation includes not only construction, machinery and equipment but also investment in plantation and smallholders' perennial crops. Exports and imports of goods and services are estimated from customs returns and balance-of-payments returns. In the process of compiling the constant price series, extensive use is made of the Producer Price Index and the Consumer Price Index as deflators. For the producers of government services, an average price index for material inputs as well as a weighted index for salary revisions have been utilized.

(c) Cost-structure of the gross domestic product. Estimates for compensation of employees are derived from statistical surveys and from government accounts. Indirect taxes are obtained from government accounts. Operating surplus including depreciation is obtained as a residual. The cost structure of the gross domestic product is only estimated for final accounts years.

(d) Gross domestic product by kind of economic activity. The production approach is used to estimate the value added by kind of economic activity. A detailed commodity-flow approach has been adopted for the reference years 1971, 1973, 1978 and 1983, to derive value added by sector. For those years in between, national accounts estimates in constant prices are compiled based extensively on volume indicators of production. The indicators are used to extrapolate base year value added by sector/sub-sectors. Current monthly/annual statistics for agricultural crops, manufacturing, mining and other service sectors form the basis for computation of the appropriate volume indices. For producers of government services, the value added is derived from preliminary estimates of the expenditure obtained from the Accountant General's Office.

1.1 Expenditure on the Gross Domestic Product, in Current Prices

Million Malaysian ringgit

	1980	1981	1982	1983	1984	1985	1986	1987	1988	1989	1990	1991
1 Government final consumption expenditure	8811	10425	11469	11015	11741	11844	12127	12239	12997	14769	16191	18392
2 Private final consumption expenditure	26946	30594	33226	36458	39594	40283	36499	37685	44856	52889	61732	70850
3 Gross capital formation	16217	20157	23358	26466	26697	21367	18604	18455	23584	29779	37073	47056
A Increase in stocks	-380	-602	613	1253	1306	-1757	-261	175	1662	-284	-417	1035
B Gross fixed capital formation	16597	20759	22745	25213	25391	23124	18865	18280	21922	30063	37490	46021
Residential buildings	...	...	...	2702	...	...	...	...	...	...	...	...
Non-residential buildings	...	...	...	3067	...	...	...	...	...	...	...	...
Other construction and land improvement etc.	...	...	...	7064	...	...	...	...	...	...	...	...
Other	...	...	...	12380	...	...	...	...	...	...	...	...
4 Exports of goods and services	30676	30154	31846	35795	43171	42537	40305	50838	61259	75030	89378	105914
5 Less: Imports of goods and services	29342	33717	37300	39793	41653	38561	35941	39592	51835	69933	88805	112671
Equals: Gross Domestic Product	53308	57613	62599	69941	79550	77470	71594	79625	90861	102534	115569	129541

1.2 Expenditure on the Gross Domestic Product, in Constant Prices

Million Malaysian ringgit

	1980	1981	1982	1983	1984	1985	1986	1987	1988	1989	1990	1991
					At constant prices of:1978							
1 Government final consumption expenditure	7750	8784	9552	9989	9500	9417	9536	9676	10149	10914	11514	12937
2 Private final consumption expenditure	24445	25686	26531	27376	29142	29269	26315	26857	31189	35616	40280	44281
3 Gross capital formation	13612	15952	18261	19638	20713	16626	14389	14016	17312	21017	25535	32032
A Increase in stocks	-319	-498	494	445	952	-1262	-212	62	1228	-195	-337	780
B Gross fixed capital formation	13931	16450	17767	19193	19761	17888	14601	13954	16084	21212	25872	31252
4 Exports of goods and services	22619	22431	24826	27889	31733	31875	35632	40819	45637	53903	63763	73332
5 Less: Imports of goods and services	23914	25251	28724	31310	33347	30067	28122	30505	37984	49045	61662	76280
Equals: Gross Domestic Product	44512	47602	50446	53582	57741	57120	57750	60863	66303	72405	79430	86302

1.3 Cost Components of the Gross Domestic Product

Million Malaysian ringgit

	1980	1981	1982	1983	1984	1985	1986	1987	1988	1989	1990	1991
1 Indirect taxes, net	9066	8836	8758	10882	12066	11650	9943	9972	12021	14149	15877	18109
A Indirect taxes	9714	9712	9754	11635	12069	11653	9945	9974	12024	14151	15987	18281
B Less: Subsidies	648	876	996	753	3	3	2	2	3	2	110	172
2 Consumption of fixed capital	...	...	...	...	...	...	...	...	...	...	...	...
3 Compensation of employees paid by resident producers to:	...	...	...	23396	...	...	...	...	...	...	...	...
4 Operating surplus	...	...	...	35663	...	...	...	...	...	...	...	...
Equals: Gross Domestic Product	53308	57613	62599	69941	79550	77470	71594	79625	90861	102534	115569	129541

Malaysia

1.7 External Transactions on Current Account, Summary

Million Malaysian ringgit

	1980	1981	1982	1983	1984	1985	1986	1987	1988	1989	1990	1991
Payments to the Rest of the World												
1 Imports of goods and services	29342	33717	37300	39793	41653	38561	35941	39592	51835	69933	88805	112671
A Imports of merchandise c.i.f.	22804	27160	29788	33466	31546	28762	26646	30095	40173	56284	73214	93933
B Other	6538	6557	7512	6327	10107	9799	9295	9497	11661	13649	15591	18738
2 Factor income to the rest of the world	3620	3928	4508	5815	6940	7155	6299	7047	7939	9077	10065	10194
A Compensation of employees	193	267	313	302	247	254	284	246	326	344	493	399
B Property and entrepreneurial income	3427	3661	4196	5513	6693	6901	6015	6801	7613	8733	9572	9795
3 Current transfers to the rest of the world	205	249	259	200	255	245	289	325	360	355	526	462
4 Surplus of the nation on current transactions	-629	-5652	-8418	-8430	-3940	-1546	-320	6648	4735	-587	-4344	-12465
Payments to the Rest of the World and Surplus of the Nation on Current Transactions	32538	32242	33649	37378	44908	44415	42209	53612	64869	78778	95052	110862
Receipts From The Rest of the World												
1 Exports of goods and services	30676	30154	31846	35795	43171	42537	40305	50838	61259	75030	89378	105914
A Exports of merchandise f.o.b.	28082	26985	28019	31432	38509	37622	35015	44802	54695	66870	78424	93477
B Other	2594	3169	3827	4363	4662	4915	5290	6036	6564	8160	10954	12437
2 Factor income from rest of the world	1702	1917	1619	1404	1572	1647	1519	2101	2855	3174	5001	4183
A Compensation of employees	94	92	102	99	134	180	104	123	281	376	501	497
B Property and entrepreneurial income	1608	1825	1517	1305	1438	1467	1415	1978	2574	2798	4500	3686
3 Current transfers from rest of the world	160	171	184	179	165	231	385	673	755	574	673	765
Receipts from the Rest of the World on Current Transactions	32538	32242	33649	37378	44908	44415	42209	53612	64869	78778	95052	110862

1.10 Gross Domestic Product by Kind of Activity, in Current Prices

Million Malaysian ringgit

	1980	1981	1982	1983	1984	1985	1986	1987	1988	1989	1990	1991
1 Agriculture, hunting, forestry and fishing	...	...	...	13100	...	...	...	...	...	...	...	...
2 Mining and quarrying	...	...	...	9756	...	...	...	...	...	...	...	...
3 Manufacturing	...	...	...	13376	...	...	...	...	...	...	...	...
4 Electricity, gas and water	...	...	...	1024	...	...	...	...	...	...	...	...
5 Construction	...	...	...	3846	...	...	...	...	...	...	...	...
6 Wholesale and retail trade, restaurants and hotels	...	...	...	8084	...	...	...	...	...	...	...	...
7 Transport, storage and communication	...	...	...	3656	...	...	...	...	...	...	...	...
8 Finance, insurance, real estate and business services	...	...	...	6587	...	...	...	...	...	...	...	...
9 Community, social and personal services	...	...	...	1905	...	...	...	...	...	...	...	...
Total, Industries	...	...	...	61334	...	...	...	...	...	...	...	...
Producers of Government Services	...	...	...	7171	...	...	...	...	...	...	...	...
Other Producers	...	...	...	185	...	...	...	...	...	...	...	...
Subtotal	...	...	...	68690	...	...	...	...	...	...	...	...
Less: Imputed bank service charge	...	...	...	1895	...	...	...	...	...	...	...	...
Plus: Import duties	...	...	...	3146	...	...	...	...	...	...	...	...
Plus: Value added tax	...	...	...	...	...	...	...	...	...	...	...	...
Equals: Gross Domestic Product	...	...	...	69941	...	...	...	...	...	...	...	...

1.11 Gross Domestic Product by Kind of Activity, in Constant Prices

Million Malaysian ringgit

	1980	1981	1982	1983	1984	1985	1986	1987	1988	1989	1990	1991
	At constant prices of:1978											
1 Agriculture, hunting, forestry and fishing	10189	10684	11393	11302	11623	11854	12348	13216	13933	14768	14813	14818
2 Mining and quarrying	4487	4289	4617	5342	6073	5985	6362	6408	6803	7383	7743	7936
3 Manufacturing	8742	9155	9671	10429	11711	11263	12111	13734	16151	18444	21340	24307
4 Electricity, gas and water	640	689	721	798	890	948	1027	1109	1211	1344	1526	1690
5 Construction	2066	2367	2598	2867	2988	2738	2354	2077	2133	2380	2835	3250

1.11 Gross Domestic Product by Kind of Activity, in Constant Prices
(Continued)

Million Malaysian ringgit

	1980	1981	1982	1983	1984	1985	1986	1987	1988	1989	1990	1991
	At constant prices of:1978											
6 Wholesale and retail trade, restaurants and hotels	5383	5694	6104	6583	7107	6911	6147	6423	6988	7687	8825	10098
7 Transport, storage and communication	2542	2847	2984	3138	3464	3630	3851	4055	4412	4839	5477	6038
8 Finance, insurance, real estate and business services	3687	3953	4226	4570	4892	5121	5078	5483	6088	6770	7750	8726
9 Community, social and personal services	912	950	1022	1076	1130	1182	1231	1278	1329	1393	1541	1686
Total, Industries	38648	40628	43337	46105	49878	49632	50509	53783	59048	65008	71850	78549
Producers of Government Services	4563	5649	6027	6328	6817	6957	7253	7543	7819	8185	8579	8964
Other Producers	109	115	117	117	119	120	121	122	125	126	130	135
Subtotal	43320	46392	49481	52550	56814	56709	57883	61448	66992	73319	80559	87648
Less: Imputed bank service charge	854	877	1152	1397	1595	1834	1891	2235	2820	3356	4076	4804
Plus: Import duties	2046	2087	2116	2429	2522	2245	1759	1650	2131	2442	2947	3458
Plus: Value added tax	...	...	...	...	...	...	...	...	...	...	...	...
Equals: Gross Domestic Product	44512	47602	50445	53582	57741	57120	57751	60863	66303	72405	79430	86302

1.12 Relations Among National Accounting Aggregates

Million Malaysian ringgit

	1980	1981	1982	1983	1984	1985	1986	1987	1988	1989	1990	1991
Gross Domestic Product	53308	57613	62599	69941	79550	77470	71594	79625	90861	102534	115569	129541
Plus: Net factor income from the rest of the world	-1918	-2011	-2889	-4411	-5368	-5508	-4780	-4946	-5084	-5903	-5064	-6011
Factor income from the rest of the world	1702	1917	1619	1404	1572	1647	1519	2101	2855	3174	5001	4183
Less: Factor income to the rest of the world	3620	3928	4508	5815	6940	7155	6299	7047	7939	9077	10065	10194
Equals: Gross National Product	51390	55602	59710	65530	74182	71962	66814	74679	85777	96631	110505	123530
Less: Consumption of fixed capital	...	...	...	...	...	...	...	...	...	...	...	...
Equals: National Income [a]	51390	55602	59710	65530	74182	71962	66814	74679	85777	96631	110505	123530
Plus: Net current transfers from the rest of the world	-45	-78	-75	-21	-90	-14	96	348	395	219	147	303
Current transfers from the rest of the world	160	171	184	179	165	231	385	673	755	574	673	765
Less: Current transfers to the rest of the world	205	249	259	200	255	245	289	325	360	355	526	462
Equals: National Disposable Income [b]	51345	55524	59635	65509	74092	71948	66910	75027	86172	96850	110653	123833
Less: Final consumption	35757	41019	44695	47473	51335	52127	48626	49924	57853	67658	77923	89242
Equals: Net Saving [c]	15588	14505	14940	18036	22757	19821	18284	25103	28319	29192	32730	34591
Less: Surplus of the nation on current transactions	-629	-5652	-8418	-8430	-3940	-1546	-320	6648	4735	-587	-4344	-12465
Equals: Net Capital Formation [d]	16217	20157	23358	26466	26697	21367	18604	18455	23584	29779	37074	47056

a) Item 'National income' includes consumption of fixed capital.
b) Item 'National disposable income' includes consumption of fixed capital.
c) Item 'Net saving' includes consumption of fixed capital.
d) Item 'Net capital formation' includes consumption of fixed capital.

2.1 Government Final Consumption Expenditure by Function, in Current Prices

Million Malaysian ringgit

	1980	1981	1982	1983	1984	1985	1986	1987	1988	1989	1990	1991
1 General public services	1058	1257	1343	1336	1966	1933	1776	1814	1845	2035	2207	2400
2 Defence	2984	3333	3694	3371	2774	2410	2338	2093	2244	2830	3118	4349
3 Public order and safety	744	902	1020	1010	1061	1119	1186	1271	1344	1482	1615	1690
4 Education	2100	2535	2726	2649	3117	3267	3510	3698	3844	4312	4820	5297
5 Health	745	935	1014	961	1023	1104	1190	1176	1272	1443	1558	1635
6 Social security and welfare												
7 Housing and community amenities	257	357	377	315	472	531	568	582	595	687	769	812
8 Recreational, cultural and religious affairs												
9 Economic services	923	1106	1295	1373	1328	1480	1559	1605	1853	1980	2104	2209
10 Other functions	...	...	...	...	...	...	...	...	...	...	...	...
Total Government Final Consumption Expenditure	8811	10425	11469	11015	11741	11844	12127	12239	12997	14769	16191	18392

Malaysia

2.2 Government Final Consumption Expenditure by Function, in Constant Prices

Million Malaysian ringgit

	1980	1981	1982	1983	1984	1985	1986	1987	1988	1989	1990	1991
	At constant prices of:1978											
1 General public services	939	1079	1125	1178	1575	1507	1375	1405	1405	1470	1536	1636
2 Defence	2614	2791	3065	3200	2263	1956	1886	1710	1827	2199	2339	3229
3 Public order and safety	709	757	846	850	867	898	944	1021	1066	1105	1159	1197
4 Education	1825	2154	2297	2497	2508	2583	2731	2888	2964	3122	3356	3657
5 Health	649	793	856	834	853	904	950	949	1012	1081	1129	1160
6 Social security and welfare												
7 Housing and community amenities	222	293	306	345	373	410	432	447	449	489	523	537
8 Recreational, cultural and religious affairs												
9 Economic services	792	917	1057	1085	1061	1159	1218	1256	1426	1448	1472	1521
10 Other functions	...	...	...	...	...	...	...	...	...	...	...	...
Total Government Final Consumption Expenditure	7750	8784	9552	9989	9500	9417	9536	9676	10149	10914	11514	12937

2.5 Private Final Consumption Expenditure by Type and Purpose, in Current Prices

Million Malaysian ringgit

	1980	1981	1982	1983	1984	1985	1986	1987	1988	1989	1990	1991
	Final Consumption Expenditure of Resident Households											
1 Food, beverages and tobacco	...	...	...	11546	...	...	...	...	...	...	...	...
A Food	...	...	...	9113	...	...	...	...	...	...	...	...
B Non-alcoholic beverages	...	...	...	309	...	...	...	...	...	...	...	...
C Alcoholic beverages	...	...	...	752	...	...	...	...	...	...	...	...
D Tobacco	...	...	...	1372	...	...	...	...	...	...	...	...
2 Clothing and footwear	...	...	...	1540	...	...	...	...	...	...	...	...
3 Gross rent, fuel and power	...	...	...	3628	...	...	...	...	...	...	...	...
4 Furniture, furnishings and household equipment and operation	...	...	...	2742	...	...	...	...	...	...	...	...
A Household operation	...	...	...	670	...	...	...	...	...	...	...	...
B Other	...	...	...	2072	...	...	...	...	...	...	...	...
5 Medical care and health expenses	...	...	...	902	...	...	...	...	...	...	...	...
6 Transport and communication	...	...	...	7410	...	...	...	...	...	...	...	...
A Personal transport equipment	...	...	...	2967	...	...	...	...	...	...	...	...
B Other	...	...	...	4443	...	...	...	...	...	...	...	...
7 Recreational, entertainment, education and cultural services	...	...	...	4123	...	...	...	...	...	...	...	...
A Education	...	...	...	219	...	...	...	...	...	...	...	...
B Other	...	...	...	3904	...	...	...	...	...	...	...	...
8 Miscellaneous goods and services	...	...	...	3512	...	...	...	...	...	...	...	...
A Personal care	...	...	...	1062	...	...	...	...	...	...	...	...
B Expenditures in restaurants, cafes and hotels	...	...	...	1904	...	...	...	...	...	...	...	...
C Other	...	...	...	546	...	...	...	...	...	...	...	...
Total Final Consumption Expenditure in the Domestic Market by Households, of which	...	...	...	35403	...	...	...	...	...	...	...	...
A Durable goods	...	...	...	5787	...	...	...	...	...	...	...	...
B Semi-durable goods	...	...	...	4505	...	...	...	...	...	...	...	...
C Non-durable goods	...	...	...	16534	...	...	...	...	...	...	...	...
D Services	...	...	...	8577	...	...	...	...	...	...	...	...
Plus: Direct purchases abroad by resident households	...	...	...	2630	...	...	...	...	...	...	...	...
Less: Direct purchases in the domestic market by non-resident households	...	...	...	1575	...	...	...	...	...	...	...	...
Equals: Final Consumption Expenditure of Resident Households a	...	...	...	36458	...	...	...	...	...	...	...	...
	Final Consumption Expenditure of Private Non-profit Institutions Serving Households											
Equals: Final Consumption Expenditure of Private Non-profit Organisations Serving Households	...	...	...	...	...	...	...	...	...	...	...	...
Private Final Consumption Expenditure	...	...	...	36458	...	...	...	...	...	...	...	...

a) Item 'Final consumption expenditure of resident households' includes consumption expenditure of private non-profit institutions serving households.

2.17 Exports and Imports of Goods and Services, Detail

Million Malaysian ringgit

	1980	1981	1982	1983	1984	1985	1986	1987	1988	1989	1990	1991
Exports of Goods and Services												
1 Exports of merchandise, f.o.b.	28082	26985	28019	31432	38509	37622	35015	44802	54695	66870	78424	93477
2 Transport and communication	811	1001	1075	1097	1081	1135	1267	1413	1615	1878	2250	2679
3 Insurance service charges	899	1067	1307	1690	1903	1988	2135	2567	2680	3227	3917	4619
4 Other commodities												
5 Adjustments of merchandise exports to change-of-ownership basis	...	...	...	...	...	...	...	...	...	...	...	...
6 Direct purchases in the domestic market by non-residential households	691	891	1209	1326	1425	1544	1672	1799	2016	2807	4555	4903
7 Direct purchases in the domestic market by extraterritorial bodies	193	210	236	250	253	248	216	257	253	248	232	236
Total Exports of Goods and Services	30676	30154	31846	35795	43171	42537	40305	50838	61259	75030	89378	105914
Imports of Goods and Services												
1 Imports of merchandise, c.i.f.	22804	27160	29788	33466	31546	28762	26646	30095	40173	56284	73214	93933
2 Adjustments of merchandise imports to change-of-ownership basis	...	...	...	...	...	...	...	...	...	...	...	...
3 Other transport and communication	867	994	920	1044	1180	1071	1120	1368	1659	1883	2207	2620
4 Other insurance service charges	3895	3797	4402	2653	6023	5572	4729	4554	6113	7559	9216	11514
5 Other commodities												
6 Direct purchases abroad by government	200	203	207	214	230	279	406	450	471	509	245	266
7 Direct purchases abroad by resident households	1576	1563	1983	2416	2674	2876	3040	3125	3419	3698	3923	4338
Total Imports of Goods and Services	29342	33717	37300	39793	41653	38560	35941	39592	51835	69933	88805	112671
Balance of Goods and Services	1334	-3563	-5454	-3998	1518	3977	4364	11246	9424	5097	573	-6757
Total Imports and Balance of Goods and Services	30676	30154	31846	35795	43171	42537	40305	50838	61259	75030	89378	105914

4.3 Cost Components of Value Added

Million Malaysian ringgit

	1983					
	Compensation of Employees	Capital Consumption	Net Operating Surplus	Indirect Taxes	Less: Subsidies Received	Value Added
All Producers						
1 Agriculture, hunting, forestry and fishing	2721	...	8931	...	...	13100
A Agriculture and hunting	1896	...	5962	...	...	8155
B Forestry and logging	568	...	1569	...	...	3271
C Fishing	257	...	1400	...	...	1674
2 Mining and quarrying	742	...	6432	...	...	9756
3 Manufacturing	3877	...	6503	...	...	13376
A Manufacture of food, beverages and tobacco	535	...	1503	...	...	2686
B Textile, wearing apparel and leather industries	341	...	210	...	...	620
C Manufacture of wood and wood products, including furniture	522	...	323	...	...	1079
D Manufacture of paper and paper products, printing and publishing	286	...	278	...	...	612
E Manufacture of chemicals and chemical petroleum, coal, rubber and plastic products	555	...	1566	...	...	3067
F Manufacture of non-metallic mineral products, except products of petroleum and coal	232	...	418	...	...	676
G Basic metal industries	344	...	471	...	...	940
H Manufacture of fabricated metal products, machinery and equipment	1062	...	1734	...	...	3696
I Other manufacturing industries		...		...	...	
4 Electricity, gas and water	241	...	773	...	...	1024

Malaysia

Million Malaysian ringgit

	Compensation of Employees	Capital Consumption	Net Operating Surplus	Indirect Taxes	Less: Subsidies Received	Value Added
	1983					
5 Construction	2544	...	1264	...	...	3846
6 Wholesale and retail trade, restaurants and hotels	2606	...	5289	...	...	8084
A Wholesale and retail trade	...	...	...	...	...	6930
B Restaurants and hotels	...	...	...	...	...	1154
7 Transport, storage and communication	1446	...	2174	...	...	3656
8 Finance, insurance, real estate and business services	1438	...	5083	...	...	6587
9 Community, social and personal services	610	...	926	...	...	1905
Total, Industries	16225	...	37375	...	...	61334
Producers of Government Services	6988	183	...	...	...	7171
Other Producers	185	...	...	...	...	185
Total	23398	183	37375	...	...	68690
Less: Imputed bank service charge	...	...	1895	...	...	1895
Import duties	...	...	...	...	...	3146
Value added tax	...	...	...	...	...	...
Total a	23396	183	35480	10882	...	69941

a) Column 4 refers to indirect taxes less subsidies received.

Maldives

Source. Reply to the United Nations National Accounts Questionnaire from the Department of information and broadcasting, Male. Official estimates are published by the ministry of planning and development in the Statistical Yearbook.

General note. The estimates shown in the following tables have been prepared in accordance with the United Nations System of National Accounts so far as the existing data would permit.

1.1 Expenditure on the Gross Domestic Product, in Current Prices

Million Maldivian Rufiyaa

	1980	1981	1982	1983	1984	1985	1986	1987	1988	1989	1990	1991
1 Government final consumption expenditure	56.8	49.0	65.0	76.0	94.8	...	...	...	...	...	...	...
2 Private final consumption expenditure	270.3	344.0	367.0	385.0	416.0	...	...	...	...	...	...	...
3 Gross capital formation	117.4	99.0	105.0	178.0	220.0	...	...	...	...	...	...	...
A Increase in stocks	...	...	1.6	12.0	8.0	...	...	...	...	...	...	...
B Gross fixed capital formation	...	...	103.0	166.0	212.0							
4 Exports of goods and services	142.4	196.0	240.0	288.0	300.0	...	...	...	...	...	...	...
5 Less: Imports of goods and services	231.3	313.0	345.0	464.0	495.0	...	...	...	...	...	...	...
Equals: Gross Domestic Product	355.6	376.0	432.0	466.0	537.0	596.0	...	...	...	...	...	...

1.2 Expenditure on the Gross Domestic Product, in Constant Prices

Million Maldivian Rufiyaa

	1980	1981	1982	1983	1984	1985	1986	1987	1988	1989	1990	1991
				At constant prices of:								
			1982					1984				
1 Government final consumption expenditure	45.0	46.0	60.0	70.0 / 83.6	94.8	...	...	...	...	...	...	...
2 Private final consumption expenditure	321.0	354.0	363.0	374.0 / 380.8	416.0	...	...	...	...	...	...	...
3 Gross capital formation	87.0	105.0	105.0	109.0 / 178.0	220.0	...	...	...	...	...	...	...
A Increase in stocks	...	...	...	... / 12.0	8.0	...	...	...	...	...	...	...
B Gross fixed capital formation	...	...	...	... / 166.0	212.0	...	...	...	...	...	...	...
4 Exports of goods and services	175.0	225.0	239.0	261.0 / 288.0	300.0	...	...	...	...	...	...	...
5 Less: Imports of goods and services	254.0	312.0	322.0	352.0 / 464.0	495.0	...	...	...	...	...	...	...
Equals: Gross Domestic Product	374.0	418.0	445.0	462.0 / 475.4	537.0	...	...	...	...	...	...	...

1.10 Gross Domestic Product by Kind of Activity, in Current Prices

Million Maldivian Rufiyaa

	1980	1981	1982	1983	1984	1985	1986	1987	1988	1989	1990	1991
1 Agriculture, hunting, forestry and fishing	111.5	130.5	130.3	149.3	167.5	176.3	212.7	...	...	...	...	...
2 Mining and quarrying	5.8	10.3	10.7	11.1	11.4	11.7	12.0	...	...	...	...	...
3 Manufacturing	14.3	16.8	21.4	27.2	30.4	33.5	38.1	...	...	...	...	...
4 Electricity, gas and water								...	...	...	...	...
5 Construction	30.2	27.7	32.8	34.2	40.7	48.9	52.9	...	...	...	...	...
6 Wholesale and retail trade, restaurants and hotels	40.0	36.6	49.5	69.4	87.7	97.2	103.5	...	...	...	...	...
7 Transport, storage and communication	17.2	84.2	41.6	58.7	101.3	135.7	159.3	...	...	...	...	...
8 Finance, insurance, real estate and business services	8.2	11.7	13.4	15.4	19.6	26.0	29.3	...	...	...	...	...
9 Community, social and personal services	54.5	7.7	9.6	16.5	41.5	38.0	34.1	...	...	...	...	...
Total, Industries	281.1	325.6	309.3	381.8	500.1	567.3	641.9	...	...	...	...	...
Producers of Government Services	39.5	18.5	22.2	37.6	42.7	45.8	55.5	...	...	...	...	...
Other Producers	...	...	...	...	...	...	...	...	...	...	...	...
Subtotal	320.6	344.1	331.5	381.8	542.8	613.1	697.4	...	...	...	...	...
Less: Imputed bank service charge	...	...	...	...	...	...	...	...	...	...	...	...
Plus: Import duties	...	...	...	...	...	...	...	...	...	...	...	...
Plus: Value added tax	...	...	...	...	...	...	...	...	...	...	...	...
Equals: Gross Domestic Product	320.6	344.1	331.5	381.8	542.8	613.1	697.4	...	...	...	...	...

Maldives

1.11 Gross Domestic Product by Kind of Activity, in Constant Prices

Million Maldivian Rufiyaa

	1980	1981	1982	1983	1984	1985	1986	1987	1988	1989	1990	1991
		1982			At constant prices of:		1985					
1 Agriculture, hunting, forestry and fishing	128.7	138.9 / 150.2	140.7	145.6	157.3	176.4	184.1	194.5	204.0	214.9	234.7	...
2 Mining and quarrying	5.6	5.4 / 9.0	9.6	10.4	11.0	11.7	12.4	13.2	14.0	14.9	17.9	...
3 Manufacturing	12.7	16.0 / 19.3	25.9	29.8	32.1	33.5	36.1	39.7	43.6	48.2	55.6	...
4 Electricity, gas and water												...
5 Construction	39.6	28.6 / 28.5	33.4	34.4	40.8	48.9	52.8	58.1	63.9	70.5	83.9	...
6 Wholesale and retail trade, restaurants and hotels	44.0	44.3 / 36.6	49.5	69.4	87.7	97.2	103.6	115.5	128.8	144.1	166.8	...
7 Transport, storage and communication	19.4	21.0 / 82.8	39.7	53.6	92.6	122.7	145.6	159.5	174.7	192.3	234.8	...
8 Finance, insurance, real estate and business services	12.5	14.7 / 15.3	16.2	17.5	20.9	26.0	28.3	30.9	33.7	36.9	40.6	...
9 Community, social and personal services	58.4	72.1 / 8.2	10.0	17.1	42.3	38.0	33.4	37.9	42.9	49.2	55.6	...
Total, Industries	320.9	340.9 / 349.9	325.2	377.9	484.8	554.5	596.4	649.1	705.6	771.0	889.9	...
Producers of Government Services	44.9	54.9 / 18.6	22.2	37.6	42.8	45.9	55.5	60.5	66.0	72.2	80.4	...
Other Producers	...	...	...	...	...	...	...	...	...	...	...	...
Subtotal	365.8	395.8 / 368.5	347.4	415.5	527.5	600.3	651.9	709.7	771.6	843.2	970.3	...
Less: Imputed bank service charge	...	...	...	...	...	...	...	...	...	...	...	...
Plus: Import duties	...	...	...	...	...	...	...	...	...	...	...	...
Plus: Value added tax	...	...	...	...	...	...	...	...	...	...	...	...
Equals: Gross Domestic Product	365.8	395.8 / 368.5	347.4	415.5	527.5	600.3	651.9	709.7	771.6	843.2	970.3	...

2.1 Government Final Consumption Expenditure by Function, in Current Prices

Million Maldivian Rufiyaa

	1980	1981	1982	1983	1984	1985	1986	1987	1988	1989	1990	1991
1 General public services	...	...	19.6	27.5	31.3	36.2	44.9	...	...	...	...	...
2 Defence	...	...	11.4	14.1	16.1	18.1	22.6	...	...	...	...	...
3 Public order and safety	...	...						...	...	...	...	...
4 Education	...	...	9.7	13.1	15.0	17.5	22.5	...	...	...	...	...
5 Health	...	...	7.4	7.1	8.1	9.5	11.5	...	...	...	...	...
6 Social security and welfare	...	...	27.1	13.7	7.0	6.8	7.4	...	...	...	...	...
7 Housing and community amenities	...	...	4.4	5.2	6.0	9.7	10.8	...	...	...	...	...
8 Recreational, cultural and religious affairs	...	...						...	...	...	...	...
9 Economic services	...	...	9.0	10.1	14.3	14.3	7.8	...	...	...	...	...
A Fuel and energy	...	...	...	...	...	...	...	...	...	...	...	...
B Agriculture, forestry, fishing and hunting	...	...	1.2	1.5	1.8	1.7	2.6	...	...	...	...	...
C Mining, manufacturing and construction, except fuel and energy	...	...	...	...	...	...	...	...	...	...	...	...
D Transportation and communication	...	...	6.8	6.9	10.2	10.4	2.3	...	...	...	...	...
E Other economic affairs	...	...	1.0	1.7	2.3	2.2	2.9	...	...	...	...	...
10 Other functions	...	...	4.2	4.4	5.1	8.8	11.3	...	...	...	...	...
Total Government Final Consumption Expenditure	...	...	92.8	95.2	102.9	120.9	138.8	...	...	...	...	...

Mali

Source. Reply to the United Nations National Accounts Questionnaire from the Direction Nationale de la Statistique et de l'informatique, Ministere du Plan, Bamako, Mali. Official estimates are published by the same office annually in 'Comptes Economiques du Mali'. On 1 June 1984, Mali joined the French Community in Africa of which the legal tender is CFA francs. Two Mali francs is equivalent to one CFA franc.

General note. The estimates shown in the following tables have been prepared in accordance with the United Nations System of National Accounts so far as the existing data would permit.

1.1 Expenditure on the Gross Domestic Product, in Current Prices

Thousand Million CFA francs

	1980	1981	1982	1983	1984	1985	1986	1987	1988	1989	1990	1991
1 Government final consumption expenditure	12.6	... 36.6	39.6	44.9	50.1	104.9	106.3	94.8	100.1	109.8	104.2	105.6
2 Private final consumption expenditure	246.5	... 315.6	360.4	386.5	423.8	436.4	448.5	453.1	509.9	523.9	540.0	588.7
3 Gross capital formation	50.6	... 93.0	71.0	59.9	70.5	87.5	129.0	120.4	123.7	139.0	151.4	121.8
A Increase in stocks	3.0	... ...	-0.4	-15.1	-14.1	-12.3	10.0	5.3	7.0	12.5	15.0	-16.6
B Gross fixed capital formation	47.6	... ...	71.4	75.0	84.6	99.8	119.0	115.1	116.7	126.5	136.4	138.4
4 Exports of goods and services	53.3	... 55.6	62.6	78.6	107.2	96.3	88.6	93.9	98.7	103.2	118.2	120.9
5 Less: Imports of goods and services	90.0	... 120.6	130.0	158.6	188.1	204.9	187.3	161.5	216.5	214.5	230.5	245.2
Equals: Gross Domestic Product a	300.6	... 380.2	403.6	411.3	463.5	520.2	585.1	600.7	615.8	661.4	683.3	691.4

a) Data in this table have been revised, therefore they are not strictly comparable with the unrevised data in the other tables.

1.2 Expenditure on the Gross Domestic Product, in Constant Prices

Thousand Million CFA francs

	1980	1981	1982	1983	1984	1985	1986	1987	1988	1989	1990	1991
					At constant prices of:1987							
1 Government final consumption expenditure	...	...	...	...	...	...	...	94.8	88.6	97.2	92.3	91.2
2 Private final consumption expenditure	...	...	...	...	...	...	...	453.1	451.4	472.6	483.0	509.1
3 Gross capital formation	...	...	...	...	...	...	...	120.4	131.1	142.3	152.7	118.4
A Increase in stocks	...	...	...	...	...	...	...	5.3	12.1	17.0	19.0	-15.3
B Gross fixed capital formation	...	...	...	...	...	...	...	115.1	119.0	125.3	133.7	133.7
4 Exports of goods and services	...	...	...	...	...	...	...	93.9	92.6	100.8	106.3	120.2
5 Less: Imports of goods and services	...	...	...	...	...	...	...	161.5	161.5	165.5	171.3	177.3
Equals: Gross Domestic Product	461.6	481.5	511.5	485.0	488.3	529.8	615.2	600.7	602.2	647.3	662.9	661.6

1.3 Cost Components of the Gross Domestic Product

Thousand Million CFA francs

	1980	1981	1982	1983	1984	1985	1986	1987	1988	1989	1990	1991
1 Indirect taxes, net	14.5	... 28.9	30.6	...	...	...	...	...	...	...	...	...
A Indirect taxes	17.3	... 30.9	33.0	...	...	...	...	...	...	...	...	...
B Less: Subsidies	2.8	... 2.0	2.5	...	...	...	...	...	...	...	...	...
2 Consumption of fixed capital	...	... 22.6	24.3	...	...	...	...	...	...	...	...	...
3 Compensation of employees paid by resident producers to:	68.5	... 81.0	90.7	...	...	...	...	...	...	...	...	...
4 Operating surplus a	208.6	... 197.6	221.0	...	...	...	...	...	...	...	...	...
Equals: Gross Domestic Product	300.6	... 330.0	366.5	...	...	...	...	...	...	...	...	...

a) Item 'Operating surplus' includes consumption of fixed capital.

1.4 General Government Current Receipts and Disbursements

Thousand Million CFA francs

	1980	1981	1982	1983	1984	1985	1986	1987	1988	1989	1990	1991
					Receipts							
1 Operating surplus	...	-	-	...	...	...	...	...	...	...	...	...
2 Property and entrepreneurial income	...	-	0.3	...	...	...	...	...	...	...	...	...
3 Taxes, fees and contributions	...	45.8	48.5	...	...	...	...	...	...	...	...	...
A Indirect taxes	...	30.9	33.0	...	...	...	...	...	...	...	...	...

Mali

1.4 General Government Current Receipts and Disbursements
(Continued)

Thousand Million CFA francs

	1980	1981	1982	1983	1984	1985	1986	1987	1988	1989	1990	1991
B Direct taxes	...	10.0	10.8	...	...	...	...	...	...	...	...	...
C Social security contributions	...	4.4	4.1	...	...	...	...	...	...	...	...	...
D Compulsory fees, fines and penalties	...	0.6	0.7	...	...	...	...	...	...	...	...	...
4 Other current transfers	...	30.8	31.8	...	...	...	...	...	...	...	...	...
Total Current Receipts of General Government	...	76.7	80.7	...	...	...	...	...	...	...	...	...
Disbursements												
1 Government final consumption expenditure	...	35.0	38.1	...	...	...	...	...	...	...	...	...
2 Property income	...	3.9	7.0	...	...	...	...	...	...	...	...	...
3 Subsidies	...	2.0	2.5	...	...	...	...	...	...	...	...	...
4 Other current transfers	...	12.8	11.2	...	...	...	...	...	...	...	...	...
A Social security benefits	...	1.7	1.9	...	...	...	...	...	...	...	...	...
B Social assistance grants	...	...	...	...	...	...	...	...	...	...	...	...
C Other	...	11.2	9.3	...	...	...	...	...	...	...	...	...
5 Net saving	...	22.9	21.9	...	...	...	...	...	...	...	...	...
Total Current Disbursements and Net Saving of General Government	...	76.7	80.7	...	...	...	...	...	...	...	...	...

1.7 External Transactions on Current Account, Summary

Thousand Million CFA francs

	1980	1981	1982	1983	1984	1985	1986	1987	1988	1989	1990	1991
Payments to the Rest of the World												
1 Imports of goods and services	...	120.6	130.0	158.6	188.1	204.9	187.3	...	216.5	214.5	230.5	245.2
A Imports of merchandise c.i.f.	...	104.6	109.2	134.6	160.9	187.7	167.7	...	152.8	156.6	172.1	185.4
B Other	...	16.0	20.8	24.0	27.2	31.1	19.6	...	63.7	57.9	58.4	59.8
2 Factor income to the rest of the world		8.0	12.6	13.7	17.2	15.5	16.2	...	10.5	10.2	11.5	12.0
A Compensation of employees	...	4.1	4.7	5.0	5.1	6.2	7.7	...	...	...	...	...
B Property and entrepreneurial income	...	3.9	7.9	8.7	12.1	9.3	8.5	...	10.5	10.2	11.5	12.0
3 Current transfers to the rest of the world	...	1.3	1.7	2.0	1.8	2.0	2.0	...	48.1	55.7	46.2	51.3
4 Surplus of the nation on current transactions	...	-31.0	-44.3	-49.7	-39.2	-52.7	-65.6	...	-70.7	-68.1	-41.7	-42.9
Payments to the Rest of the World and Surplus of the Nation on Current Transactions	...	98.9	100.0	124.6	167.9	169.7	139.9	...	204.4	212.3	246.5	265.6
Receipts From The Rest of the World												
1 Exports of goods and services	...	55.6	62.6	78.6	107.2	96.3	88.6	...	98.7	103.2	118.2	120.9
A Exports of merchandise f.o.b.	...	42.0	47.9	63.0	89.4	78.5	70.7	...	74.2	77.2	92.0	95.8
B Other	...	13.6	14.7	15.6	17.8	17.8	17.9	...	24.5	26.0	26.2	25.1
2 Factor income from rest of the world	...	12.5	12.9	13.9	14.2	15.8	14.0	...	1.3	2.8	3.2	3.3
A Compensation of employees	...	12.5	12.9	13.9	14.2	15.8	14.0	...	...	...	...	...
B Property and entrepreneurial income	...	...	...	...	...	...	...	...	1.3	2.8	3.2	3.3
3 Current transfers from rest of the world	...	30.8	24.5	32.1	46.5	57.6	37.3	...	104.4	106.3	125.1	141.4
Receipts from the Rest of the World on Current Transactions	...	98.9	100.0	124.6	167.9	169.7	139.9	...	204.4	212.3	246.5	265.6

1.10 Gross Domestic Product by Kind of Activity, in Current Prices

Thousand Million CFA francs

	1980	1981	1982	1983	1984	1985	1986	1987	1988	1989	1990	1991
1 Agriculture, hunting, forestry and fishing	...	224.5	232.0	219.9	233.4	198.8	246.7	269.7	275.4	311.9	313.2	305.2
2 Mining and quarrying	...	...	5.7	7.4	7.2	14.2	14.9	13.9	7.1	7.1	10.2	11.3
3 Manufacturing a	...	15.9	19.1	22.0	33.9	36.6	37.8	43.4	40.2	48.7	53.4	45.7
4 Electricity, gas and water	...	20.8	14.2	16.2	18.7	21.7	24.0	22.0	26.4	22.4	24.6	28.4
5 Construction	...											

1.10 Gross Domestic Product by Kind of Activity, in Current Prices
(Continued)

Thousand Million CFA francs

	1980	1981	1982	1983	1984	1985	1986	1987	1988	1989	1990	1991
6 Wholesale and retail trade, restaurants and hotels	...	53.6	61.3	65.8	75.8	91.0	94.6	94.0	122.0	119.2	123.2	133.6
7 Transport, storage and communication	...	13.0	12.9	15.0	21.0	26.8	27.3	27.2	28.8	30.3	32.1	32.8
8 Finance, insurance, real estate and business services	...	16.4	16.5	18.0	19.8	32.3	33.5	33.8	51.8	54.8	56.3	59.1
9 Community, social and personal services	...											
Statistical discrepancy	...	-4.3	-3.8	-4.0	-4.4	...	...	...	...	...	...	...
Total, Industries	...	339.8	357.9	360.3	405.4	421.4	478.8	504.0	551.6	594.4	613.1	616.0
Producers of Government Services	...	26.6	29.3	33.6	37.9	72.2	77.5	69.6	41.5	41.9	42.5	46.5
Other Producers	...	...	...	...	...	...	...	...	...	...	...	...
Subtotal	...	366.4	387.2	393.9	443.3	493.6	556.3	573.6	593.1	636.3	655.6	662.5
Less: Imputed bank service charge	...	...	...	...	...	4.0	4.1	4.2	4.2	4.8	4.9	4.9
Plus: Import duties	...	13.8	16.3	17.5	20.0	30.7	32.7	31.1	26.9	29.8	32.7	33.6
Plus: Value added tax	...	...	...	...	...	...	...	...	...	...	...	...
Equals: Gross Domestic Product b	...	380.2	403.6	411.3	463.5	520.2	585.1	600.7	615.8	661.4	683.3	691.4

a) Item 'Manufacturing' includes handicrafts.
b) Data in this table have been revised, therefore they are not strictly comparable with the unrevised data in the other tables.

1.11 Gross Domestic Product by Kind of Activity, in Constant Prices

Thousand Million CFA francs

	1980	1981	1982	1983	1984	1985	1986	1987	1988	1989	1990	1991
					At constant prices of:1987							
1 Agriculture, hunting, forestry and fishing	...	...	...	...	...	...	...	269.7	268.2	331.6	318.1	304.4
2 Mining and quarrying	...	...	...	...	...	...	...	13.9	13.9	7.6	7.4	9.6
3 Manufacturing	...	...	...	...	...	...	...	43.4	47.2	46.8	45.7	46.6
4 Electricity, gas and water	...	...	...	...	...	...	...	22.0	21.8	22.4	21.8	21.8
5 Construction	...	...	...	...	...	...	...					
6 Wholesale and retail trade, restaurants and hotels	...	...	...	...	...	...	...	94.0	96.8	77.5	109.1	119.4
7 Transport, storage and communication	...	...	...	...	...	...	...	27.2	29.3	30.9	30.2	30.9
8 Finance, insurance, real estate and business services	...	...	...	...	...	...	...	33.8	34.6	36.3	36.9	37.6
9 Community, social and personal services	...	...	...	...	...	...	...					
Total, Industries	...	...	...	...	...	...	...	504.0	511.8	553.1	569.2	570.3
Producers of Government Services	...	...	...	...	...	...	...	69.6	65.1	65.8	64.1	61.3
Other Producers	...	...	...	...	...	...	...	...	...	...	...	...
Subtotal	...	...	...	...	...	...	...	573.6	576.9	618.9	633.3	631.6
Less: Imputed bank service charge	...	...	...	...	...	...	...	4.2	4.1	4.1	4.9	4.9
Plus: Import duties	...	...	...	...	...	...	...	31.1	25.5	32.8	34.4	34.6
Plus: Value added tax	...	...	...	...	...	...	...	...	...	...	...	...
Equals: Gross Domestic Product	...	...	...	...	...	...	...	600.7	602.2	647.3	662.9	661.6

1.12 Relations Among National Accounting Aggregates

Thousand Million CFA francs

	1980	1981	1982	1983	1984	1985	1986	1987	1988	1989	1990	1991
Gross Domestic Product	300.6	... 380.2	403.6	411.3	463.5	520.2	585.1	...	615.8	661.4	683.3	691.4
Plus: Net factor income from the rest of the world	-7.4	... 4.5	0.3	0.2	-3.0	0.3	-2.2	...	-9.2	-7.4	-8.3	-8.7
Factor income from the rest of the world	...	... 12.5	12.9	13.9	14.2	15.8	14.0	...	1.3	2.8	3.2	3.3
Less: Factor income to the rest of the world	...	... 8.0	12.6	13.7	17.2	15.5	16.2	...	10.5	10.2	11.5	12.0
Equals: Gross National Product	293.2	... 384.7	403.9	411.5	460.5	520.5	582.9	...	606.6	654.0	675.0	682.7
Less: Consumption of fixed capital	...	...	...	...	...	...	...	...	24.2	25.8	26.6	27.4

Mali

Thousand Million CFA francs

	1980	1981	1982	1983	1984	1985	1986	1987	1988	1989	1990	1991
Equals: National Income [a]	...	384.7	403.9	...	...	...	...	...	582.4	628.2	648.4	655.3
Plus: Net current transfers from the rest of the world	...	29.5	22.8	30.1	44.7	55.6	35.3	...	56.3	50.6	78.9	91.3
Current transfers from the rest of the world	...	30.8	24.5	32.1	46.5	57.6	37.3	...	104.4	106.3	125.1	141.4
Less: Current transfers to the rest of the world	...	1.3	1.7	2.0	1.8	2.0	2.0	...	48.1	55.7	46.2	51.3
Equals: National Disposable Income [b]	...	414.2	426.7	...	...	...	...	...	638.7	678.8	727.3	746.6
Less: Final consumption	...	352.2	400.0	431.4	473.9	541.3	554.8	...	610.0	633.7	644.2	694.3
Equals: Net Saving [c]	...	62.0	26.7	...	...	...	...	...	28.7	45.1	83.1	52.3
Less: Surplus of the nation on current transactions	...	-31.0	-44.3	-49.7	-39.2	-52.7	-65.6	...	-70.7	-68.1	-41.7	-42.9
Equals: Net Capital Formation [d]	...	93.0	71.0	...	...	...	...	...	99.4	113.2	124.8	95.2

a) Item 'National income' includes consumption of fixed capital.
b) Item 'National disposable income' includes consumption of fixed capital.

c) Item 'Net saving' includes consumption of fixed capital.
d) Item 'Net capital formation' includes consumption of fixed capital.

Malta

General note. The preparation of national accounts statistics in Malta is undertaken by the Central Office of Statistics, Valetta. The offical estimates and methodological notes are published annually in 'National Accounts of the Maltese Islands'. The estimates are generally in accordance with the definitions and classifications recommended in the United Nations System of National Accounts (SNA). Input-output tables are published in the above-mentioned publication. The following tables have been prepared from successive replies to the United Nations national accounts questionaire. When the scope and coverage of the estimates differ for conceptual or statistical reasons from the definitions and classification recommended in SNA, a footnote is indicated to the relevant tables.

Sources and methods :

(a) Gross domestic product. Gross domestic product is estimated mainly through the income approach.

(b) Expenditure on the gross domestic product. The expenditure approach is used to estimate government final consumption expenditure and exports and imports of goods and services. This approach, in combination with the commodity-flow approach is used for gross fixed capital formation and private final consumption expenditure. Increase in stocks is obtained as a residual. The estimates of government consumption expenditure is based on returns from all government departments. Excluded are current expenditure on national insurance benefits, subsidies and grants to persons and expenditure on fixed capital assets and on addition to stocks. Private consumption expenditure represents expenditure on consumer goods and services by persons and non-profit making bodies at market prices. Gross fixed capital formation constitutes expenditure on fixed assets for the replacement of and addition to existing assets. The estimates are based on an analysis of government expenditure, import data and censuses of production. The estimates of exports and imports of goods and services are based on data available from trade returns, banking statistics and estimates of expenditure on services, supplemented by ad hoc inquiries. For the constant price estimates, government

final consumption expenditure, gross fixed capital formation and exports and imports of goods and services are deflated by appropriate indexes. For private consumption expenditure, extensive use is made of the various subindexes that make up the retail price index.

(c) Cost-structure of the gross domestic product. Compensation of employees includes employers' contributions to national insurance. For the private sector, employees' incomes are taken from annual reports of labours inspectors except in the manufacturing, quarrying and construction sectors, for which data are taken from the censuses of production. Government wages and salaries are estimated on the basis of department returns, while the services submit actual figures of their wage and salary bill. Profits are estimated from income tax data for professionals, annual censuses of production for manufacturing and ad hoc inquiries for other activities. For trade, gross profits are arrived at by assessing wholesale and retail profits on the basis of calculated turnovers. Income from property is estimated on the basis of actual rents received by the government plus rents earned by the private sector which is based on data obtained in the census of population, housing and employment in 1967 and interest earned from local sources. Indirect taxes cover items such as customs and excise duties, business licenses, stamp duties, motor vehicle licenses, etc. While subsidies include grants to farmers, price-stabilization payment, loss incurred on water and milk supplies, etc.

(d) Gross domestic product by kind of economic activity. The table of GDP by kind of economic activity is prepared in factor values. The income approach is used to estimate the value added of most industries except agriculture and fishing, for which the production approach is used. For most sectors of GDP by economic activity, separate estimates are available for wages and salaries, income from self-employment and other trading income. The contribution of each industry also includes provision for depreciation. The sources of these estimates are described in the cost-structure of GDP above. GDP by kind of economic activity is not estimated at constant prices.

1.1 Expenditure on the Gross Domestic Product, in Current Prices

Thousand Maltese pounds

	1980	1981	1982	1983	1984	1985	1986	1987	1988	1989	1990	1991
1 Government final consumption expenditure	63364	75407	85216	82257	80321	84309	89508	98249	105185	119613	129153	...
2 Private final consumption expenditure	253485	279434	305724	306705	317475	333239	343369	351187	387567	425515	460845	...
3 Gross capital formation	96457	118154	145625	137090	133233	133754	130506	151076	174555	198340	245279	...
A Increase in stocks a	9383	12557	25504	5460	6780	7883	8179	-2377	8150	9903	12668	...
B Gross fixed capital formation	87074	105597	120121	131630	126453	125871	122327	153453	166405	188437	232611	...
Residential buildings	20875	30155										...
Non-residential buildings			50020	50960	48661	41197	44779	49103	50168	55294	64672	...
Other construction and land improvement etc.	10658	11215										...
Other	55541	64227	70101	80670	77792	84674	77548	104350	116237	133143	167939	...
4 Exports of goods and services	356647	355918	319799	307647	323539	345155	370228	429593	480024	543463	626415	...
5 Less: Imports of goods and services	377989	392462	394578	376143	393516	420475	421742	480934	540880	616792	726947	...
Equals: Gross Domestic Product	391964	436451	461786	457556	461052	475982	511869	549171	606451	670139	734745	...

a) Item 'Increase in stocks' includes a statistical discrepancy.

1.2 Expenditure on the Gross Domestic Product, in Constant Prices

Thousand Maltese pounds

	1980	1981	1982	1983	1984	1985	1986	1987	1988	1989	1990	1991
					At constant prices of:1973							
1 Government final consumption expenditure	38900	41800	44300	43800	42700	45100	47100	51400	54500	61400	...	...
2 Private final consumption expenditure	149100	154000	158500	160700	167100	175400	177900	178800	194900	212900	...	...
3 Gross capital formation	48900	58900	78500	67000	64000	62800	58300	63100	77700	80100	...	...
A Increase in stocks a	9400	12600	25400	5500	6800	7900	8200	-2400	8200	9900	...	...
B Gross fixed capital formation	39500	46300	53100	61500	57200	54900	50100	65500	69500	70200	...	...
4 Exports of goods and services	192000	170100	146600	143900	149700	160800	172000	193700	205600	227600	...	...
5 Less: Imports of goods and services	166200	153400	150400	139500	145000	158400	158500	178000	197700	219600	...	...
Equals: Gross Domestic Product	262700	271400	277600	275900	278500	285700	296800	309000	335000	362400	...	...

a) Item 'Increase in stocks' includes a statistical discrepancy.

Malta

1.3 Cost Components of the Gross Domestic Product

Thousand Maltese pounds

	1980	1981	1982	1983	1984	1985	1986	1987	1988	1989	1990	1991
1 Indirect taxes, net	43352	45917	44041	40426	39675	45432	50103	53721	63817	73290	85154	...
A Indirect taxes	45744	47897	46852	43794	43706	49452	54885	58595	69392	79362	92155	...
B Less: Subsidies	2392	1980	2811	3368	4031	4020	4782	4874	5575	6072	7001	...
2 Consumption of fixed capital	12896	14363	15738	19753	20990	21423	23200	25977	28854	32023	35273	...
3 Compensation of employees paid by resident producers to:	180553	203805	228625	223584	217928	222942	231617	254706	269569	288234	318990	...
4 Operating surplus	155163	172366	173382	173793	182459	186185	206949	214767	244211	276592	295328	...
A Corporate and quasi-corporate enterprises	77597	73736	74167	69052	69425	73345	76513	79604	94593	108914	116934	...
B Private unincorporated enterprises	71287	83587	88491	92466	97810	101151	108507	109863	114715	129506	145011	...
C General government a	6279	15043	10724	12275	15224	11689	21929	25300	34903	38172	33383	...
Equals: Gross Domestic Product	391964	436451	461786	457556	461052	475982	511869	549171	606451	670139	734745	...

a) Public enterprises is included in general government.

1.4 General Government Current Receipts and Disbursements

Thousand Maltese pounds

	1980	1981	1982	1983	1984	1985	1986	1987	1988	1989	1990	1991
Receipts												
1 Operating surplus	2295	7581	3566	2997	6250	2752	14290	18645	26846	28165	23854	...
2 Property and entrepreneurial income	50911	56584	59969	46139	52434	48276	39825	33075	33266	43320	51838	...
3 Taxes, fees and contributions	108634	121039	127618	123744	118437	126801	131338	130681	152197	167443	194980	...
A Indirect taxes a	45744	47897	46852	43794	43706	49452	54885	58595	69392	79362	92155	...
B Direct taxes	36521	40908	45994	44974	41310	42666	41570	36425	44179	49156	55295	...
C Social security contributions	26369	32234	34772	34976	33421	34683	34883	35661	38626	38925	47530	...
D Compulsory fees, fines and penalties a	...	...	...	...	...	...	...	...	...	...	...	...
4 Other current transfers	4001	4558	4603	5081	5697	5792	5695	5683	6477	6909	7147	...
Total Current Receipts of General Government b	165841	189762	195756	177961	182818	183621	191148	188084	218786	245837	277819	...
Disbursements												
1 Government final consumption expenditure	63364	75407	85216	82257	80321	84309	89508	98249	105185	119613	129153	...
A Compensation of employees	44444	51513	58152	57348	56090	58534	62317	68862	74370	82736	92673	...
B Consumption of fixed capital	...	...	...	...	...	...	...	...	...	...	...	...
C Purchases of goods and services, net	18920	23894	27064	24909	24231	25775	27191	29387	30815	36877	36480	...
D Less: Own account fixed capital formation	...	...	...	...	...	...	...	...	...	...	...	...
E Indirect taxes paid, net	...	...	...	...	...	...	...	...	...	...	...	...
2 Property income	1666	1641	1630	1611	1700	1705	1716	1717	1783	4261	4349	...
A Interest	1666	1641	1630	1611	1700	1705	1716	1717	1783	4261	4349	...
B Net land rent and royalties	...	...	...	...	...	...	...	...	...	...	...	...
3 Subsidies	2392	1980	2811	3368	4031	4020	4782	4874	5575	6072	7001	...
4 Other current transfers	40312	51410	59402	61484	65351	65021	66668	68392	72870	77574	87263	...
A Social security benefits	40035	51125	59130	61211	65100	64726	66412	68075	72301	77203	86576	...
B Social assistance grants												...
C Other	277	285	272	273	251	295	256	317	569	371	687	...
5 Net saving	58107	59324	46697	29241	31415	28566	28474	14852	33373	38317	50053	...
Total Current Disbursements and Net Saving of General Government b	165841	189762	195756	177961	182818	183621	191148	188084	218786	245837	277819	...

a) Item 'Fees, fines and penalties' is included in item 'Indirect taxes'.
b) Public enterprises is included in general government.

1.5 Current Income and Outlay of Corporate and Quasi-Corporate Enterprises, Summary

Thousand Maltese pounds

	1980	1981	1982	1983	1984	1985	1986	1987	1988	1989	1990	1991
					Receipts							
1 Operating surplus	52235	59863	68790	69703	72729	76329	74824	82851	96122	115080	130778	...
2 Property and entrepreneurial income received	4618	5474	5412	3826	3876	4209	4387	5719	6130	7301	7606	...
3 Current transfers	...	...	...	...	...	...	...	...	...	...	...	...
Total Current Receipts a	56853	65337	74202	73529	76605	80538	79211	88570	102252	122381	138384	...
					Disbursements							
1 Property and entrepreneurial income	29296	31397	33484	32107	35279	38009	35066	32556	43504	50572	58824	...
2 Direct taxes and other current payments to general government	10260	11376	17065	16032	14728	15194	15354	16612	18191	21014	21804	...
3 Other current transfers	...	...	...	...	...	...	...	...	...	...	...	...
4 Net saving	17297	22564	23653	25390	26598	27335	28791	39402	40557	50795	57756	...
Total Current Disbursements and Net Saving a	56853	65337	74202	73529	76605	80538	79211	88570	102252	122381	138384	...

a) Public enterprises is included in general government.

1.6 Current Income and Outlay of Households and Non-Profit Institutions

Thousand Maltese pounds

	1980	1981	1982	1983	1984	1985	1986	1987	1988	1989	1990	1991
					Receipts							
1 Compensation of employees	180553	203805	228625	223584	217928	222942	231617	254706	269569	288234	318990	...
2 Operating surplus of private unincorporated enterprises	57940	66268	72020	73370	75774	79082	84042	83352	89372	102023	111126	...
3 Property and entrepreneurial income	48676	50878	50767	49599	53845	54036	54419	56059	66105	71299	88316	...
4 Current transfers	53668	64994	74126	77252	81334	79638	80236	83476	92474	102657	110443	...
A Social security benefits	40035	51125	59130	61211	65100	64726	66412	68075	72301	77203	86576	...
B Social assistance grants												...
C Other	13633	13869	14996	16041	16234	14912	13824	15401	20173	25454	23867	...
Total Current Receipts	340837	385945	425538	423805	428881	435698	450314	477593	517520	564213	628875	...
					Disbursements							
1 Private final consumption expenditure	253485	279434	305724	306705	317475	333239	343369	351187	387567	425515	460845	...
2 Property income	...	...	...	...	...	...	...	...	...	...	...	...
3 Direct taxes and other current transfers n.e.c. to general government	52968	62042	64060	64347	60471	62603	61483	55762	64993	67473	81453	...
A Social security contributions	23464	28450	30482	31304	29492	30766	31466	32396	35282	34956	40548	...
B Direct taxes	29166	33316	33219	32614	30511	31389	29633	23078	29332	32111	40473	...
C Fees, fines and penalties	338	276	359	429	468	448	384	288	379	406	432	...
4 Other current transfers	6095	7053	6308	6499	8095	7420	7530	8114	9094	11603	13303	...
5 Net saving	28289	37416	49446	46254	42840	32436	37932	62530	55866	59622	73274	...
Total Current Disbursements and Net Saving	340837	385945	425538	423805	428881	435698	450314	477593	517520	564213	628875	...

1.7 External Transactions on Current Account, Summary

Thousand Maltese pounds

	1980	1981	1982	1983	1984	1985	1986	1987	1988	1989	1990	1991
					Payments to the Rest of the World							
1 Imports of goods and services	377989	392462	394578	376143	393516	420475	421742	480934	540880	616792	726947	...
2 Factor income to the rest of the world	19929	19679	11801	9874	9199	10758	17195	8850	17564	22429	23762	...
A Compensation of employees	...	...	...	...	...	...	...	...	...	...	...	...
B Property and entrepreneurial income	19929	19679	11801	9874	9199	10758	17195	8850	17564	22429	23762	...
3 Current transfers to the rest of the world	2915	3156	2383	2173	3185	2465	2560	3108	3678	5582	7347	...
4 Surplus of the nation on current transactions	20132	15513	-10091	-16452	-11390	-23994	-12109	-8315	-15905	-17583	-28923	...
Payments to the Rest of the World and Surplus of the Nation on Current Transactions	420965	430810	398671	371738	394510	409704	429388	484577	546217	627220	729133	...

Malta

1.7 External Transactions on Current Account, Summary
(Continued)

Thousand Maltese pounds

	1980	1981	1982	1983	1984	1985	1986	1987	1988	1989	1990	1991
Receipts From The Rest of the World												
1 Exports of goods and services	356647	355918	319799	307647	323539	345155	370228	429593	480024	543463	626415	...
2 Factor income from rest of the world	50479	60923	63829	47997	54669	49543	45251	39511	45907	58192	78779	...
A Compensation of employees	...	...	...	...	...	...	...	...	...	...	...	...
B Property and entrepreneurial income	50479	60923	63829	47997	54669	49543	45251	39511	45907	58192	78779	...
3 Current transfers from rest of the world	13839	13969	15043	16094	16302	15006	13909	15473	20286	25565	23939	...
Receipts from the Rest of the World on Current Transactions	420965	430810	398671	371738	394510	409704	429388	484577	546217	627220	729133	...

1.8 Capital Transactions of The Nation, Summary

Thousand Maltese pounds

	1980	1981	1982	1983	1984	1985	1986	1987	1988	1989	1990	1991
Finance of Gross Capital Formation												
Gross saving	116589	133667	135534	120638	121843	109760	118397	142761	158650	180757	216356	...
1 Consumption of fixed capital	12896	14363	15738	19753	20990	21423	23200	25977	28854	32023	35273	...
A General government a	3127	3746	4996	5624	5972	5917	6778	7569	7945	8284	9021	...
B Corporate and quasi-corporate enterprises	6718	7087	7285	10097	11594	12269	12946	15077	17490	19740	22014	...
Public	...	...	...	...	...	...	...	...	...	...	...	...
Private	6718	7087	7285	10097	11594	12269	12946	15077	17490	19740	22014	...
C Other	3051	3530	3457	4032	3424	3237	3476	3331	3419	3999	4238	...
2 Net saving	103693	119304	119796	100885	100853	88337	95197	116784	129796	148734	181083	...
A General government	58107	59324	46697	29241	31415	28566	28474	14852	33373	38317	50053	...
B Corporate and quasi-corporate enterprises	17297	22564	23653	25390	26598	27335	28791	39402	40557	50795	57756	...
Public	...	...	...	...	...	...	...	...	...	...	...	...
Private	17297	22564	23653	25390	26598	27335	28791	39402	40557	48395	57756	...
C Other	28289	37416	49446	46254	42840	32436	37932	62530	55866	59622	73274	...
Less: Surplus of the nation on current transactions	20132	15513	-10091	-16452	-11390	-23994	-12109	-8315	-15905	-17583	-28923	...
Finance of Gross Capital Formation	96457	118154	145629	137090	133233	133754	130506	151076	174555	198340	245279	...
Gross Capital Formation												
Increase in stocks b	9383	12557	25504	5460	6780	7883	8179	-2377	8150	9903	12668	...
Gross fixed capital formation	87074	105597	120121	131630	126453	125871	122327	153453	166405	188437	232611	...
1 General government a	25543	30609	33375	23747	25124	25330	25795	33093	33297	48918	76933	...
2 Corporate and quasi-corporate enterprises	38903	44043	43354	72964	60601	57982	53344	78596	85200	90722	105770	...
A Public	...	...	...	...	...	...	...	...	...	...	...	...
B Private	38903	44043	43354	72964	60601	57982	53344	78596	85200	90722	105770	...
3 Other	22628	30945	43392	34919	40728	42559	43188	41764	47908	48797	49908	...
Gross Capital Formation	96457	118154	145625	137090	133233	133754	130506	151076	174555	198340	245279	...

a) Public enterprises is included in general government.
b) Item 'Increase in stocks' includes a statistical discrepancy.

1.10 Gross Domestic Product by Kind of Activity, in Current Prices

Thousand Maltese pounds

	1980	1981	1982	1983	1984	1985	1986	1987	1988	1989	1990	1991
1 Agriculture, hunting, forestry and fishing	13289	15038	16767	18731	19346	19375	20419	21429	21108	22355	22537	...
2 Mining and quarrying a	15655	17073	23546	23511	19660	20758	18869	21051	21353	22257	22882	...
3 Manufacturing	115358	121384	125024	120036	124706	126929	134676	136427	146557	163663	175634	...
4 Electricity, gas and water b	15635	23586	21958	21119	24985	22278	34704	42119	51878	54034	53426	...
5 Construction a	...	...	...	...	...	...	...	...	...	...	...	...
6 Wholesale and retail trade, restaurants and hotels c	51001	57421	63184	64010	66077	66696	67647	70847	76899	84846	93772	...
7 Transport, storage and communication	22230	22596	20396	24050	23391	23955	26240	30204	34527	34602	37131	...
8 Finance, insurance, real estate and business services d	37269	45519	50303	51475	53517	57131	61255	62782	69713	80226	93336	...
9 Community, social and personal services cde	33731	36404	38415	36850	33605	34894	35639	41729	46229	52130	58200	...
Total, Industries	304168	339021	359593	359782	365287	372016	399449	426588	468264	514113	556918	...
Producers of Government Services	44444	51513	58152	57348	56090	58534	62317	68862	74370	82736	92673	...

1.10 Gross Domestic Product by Kind of Activity, in Current Prices
(Continued)

Thousand Maltese pounds

	1980	1981	1982	1983	1984	1985	1986	1987	1988	1989	1990	1991
Other Producers e	...	...	...	...	...	...	...	...	...	...	...	...
Subtotal f	348612	390534	417745	417130	421377	430550	461766	495450	542634	596849	649591	...
Less: Imputed bank service charge	...	...	...	...	...	...	...	...	...	...	...	...
Plus: Import duties	...	...	...	...	...	...	...	...	...	...	...	...
Plus: Value added tax	...	...	...	...	...	...	...	...	...	...	...	...
Plus: Other adjustments g	43352	45917	44041	40426	39675	45432	50103	53721	63817	73290	85154	...
Equals: Gross Domestic Product	391964	436451	461786	457556	461052	475982	511869	549171	606451	670139	734745	...

a) Item 'Construction' is included in item 'Mining and quarrying'.
b) Item 'Electricity, gas and water' refers to all government enterprises.
c) Restaurants and hotels are included in item 'Community, social and personal services'.
d) Business services are included in item 'Community, social and personal services'.
e) Beginning 1980, item 'Other producers' is included in item 'Community, social and personal services'.
f) Gross domestic product in factor values.
g) Item 'Other adjustments' refers to indirect taxes net of subsidies.

1.12 Relations Among National Accounting Aggregates

Thousand Maltese pounds

	1980	1981	1982	1983	1984	1985	1986	1987	1988	1989	1990	1991
Gross Domestic Product	391964	436451	461786	457556	461052	475982	511869	549171	606451	670139	734745	...
Plus: Net factor income from the rest of the world	30550	41244	52028	38123	45470	38785	28056	30661	28343	35763	55017	...
Factor income from the rest of the world	50479	60923	63829	47997	54669	49543	45251	39511	45907	58192	78779	...
Less: Factor income to the rest of the world	19929	19679	11801	9874	9199	10758	17195	8850	17564	22429	23762	...
Equals: Gross National Product	422514	477695	513814	495679	506522	514767	539925	579832	634794	705902	789762	...
Less: Consumption of fixed capital	12896	14363	15738	19753	20990	21423	23200	25977	28854	32023	35273	...
Equals: National Income	409618	463332	498076	475926	485532	493344	516725	553855	605940	673879	754489	...
Plus: Net current transfers from the rest of the world	10924	10813	12660	13921	13117	12541	11349	12365	16608	19983	16592	...
Current transfers from the rest of the world	13839	13969	15043	16094	16302	15006	13909	15473	20286	25565	23939	...
Less: Current transfers to the rest of the world	2915	3156	2383	2173	3185	2465	2560	3108	3678	5582	7347	...
Equals: National Disposable Income	420542	474145	510736	489847	498649	505885	528074	566220	622548	693862	771081	...
Less: Final consumption	316849	354841	390940	388962	397796	417548	432877	449436	492752	545128	589998	...
Equals: Net Saving	103693	119304	119796	100885	100853	88337	95197	116784	129796	148734	181083	...
Less: Surplus of the nation on current transactions	20132	15513	-10091	-16452	-11390	-23994	-12109	-8315	-15905	-17583	-28923	...
Equals: Net Capital Formation	83561	103791	129887	117337	112243	112331	107306	125099	145701	166317	210006	...

2.1 Government Final Consumption Expenditure by Function, in Current Prices

Thousand Maltese pounds

	1980	1981	1982	1983	1984	1985	1986	1987	1988	1989	1990	1991
1 General public services	9583	9819	10887	10718	9575	10804	11478	12844	13525	15271	16323	...
2 Defence	9264	11419	14339	14169	13826	14636	15265	17366	17229	17876	17805	...
3 Public order and safety												...
4 Education	15500	18252	20266	19666	18528	19484	20197	22885	26412	30652	32543	...
5 Health	15133	17587	20731	20723	20680	21108	22980	25565	26282	29245	32862	...
6 Social security and welfare	1449	1950	1792	1704	2160	2146	2385	2009	3902	7558	8612	...
7 Housing and community amenities	10711	14265	14428	12606	12768	13314	14041	14014	14282	15227	16948	...
8 Recreational, cultural and religious affairs	...	...	...	...	...	...	...	...	...	...	...	...
9 Economic services	1724	2115	2773	2671	2784	2817	3162	3566	3553	3784	4060	...
10 Other functions	-	-	-	-	-	-	-	-	-	-	-	...
Total Government Final Consumption Expenditure	63364	75407	85216	82257	80321	84309	89508	98249	105185	119613	129153	...

2.5 Private Final Consumption Expenditure by Type and Purpose, in Current Prices

Thousand Maltese pounds

	1980	1981	1982	1983	1984	1985	1986	1987	1988	1989	1990	1991
				Final Consumption Expenditure of Resident Households								
1 Food, beverages and tobacco	114993	127180	133047	131847	131301	141513	140887	150799	157545	169607	182665	...
A Food	74501	83668	92140	93762	92954	101225	98285	107015	111182	122185	130429	...
B Non-alcoholic beverages	5248	6932	9938	9907	10811	12920	13599	15066	15159	15316	15699	...
C Alcoholic beverages	21626	22559	17354	15545	14810	14840	16224	15458	17119	17763	20867	...
D Tobacco	13618	14021	13615	12633	12726	12528	12779	13260	14085	14343	15670	...
2 Clothing and footwear	29375	29725	25951	25184	27014	33039	36247	37000	39427	41831	42798	...
3 Gross rent, fuel and power	25042	26296	21867	22225	22423	22828	24102	25560	28291	30279	31671	...
A Fuel and power	8232	8827	6730	7196	8102	8032	8525	8676	9696	9860	10473	...

Malta

2.5 Private Final Consumption Expenditure by Type and Purpose, in Current Prices
(Continued)

Thousand Maltese pounds

	1980	1981	1982	1983	1984	1985	1986	1987	1988	1989	1990	1991
B Other	16810	17469	15137	15029	14321	14796	15577	16884	18595	20419	21198	...
4 Furniture, furnishings and household equipment and operation	37639	35917	35771	35141	35517	33534	35252	37754	42779	45464	52536	...
A Household operation	8966	9037	10310	9766	10925	10888	9544	10129	10935	11107	13521	...
B Other	28673	26880	25461	25375	24592	22646	25708	27625	31844	34357	39015	...
5 Medical care and health expenses	10675	10404	12198	12593	13404	12524	14620	15268	17318	19288	20577	...
6 Transport and communication	50689	50870	51151	50726	51042	57969	60127	66126	79036	84842	95101	...
A Personal transport equipment	32420	31796	32819	31425	33893	37189	38974	43249	52467	56734	64654	...
B Other	18269	19074	18332	19301	17149	20780	21153	22877	26569	28108	30447	...
7 Recreational, entertainment, education and cultural services	21953	23169	23114	21009	22527	21490	24949	26392	30461	35773	42220	...
A Education	1731	1342	1470	1406	1547	1547	1677	1721	1661	1950	2504	...
B Other	20222	21827	21644	19603	20980	19943	23272	24671	28800	33823	39716	...
8 Miscellaneous goods and services	56717	61696	55498	52976	54457	56749	63976	77075	91086	104903	107190	...
A Personal care	11421	12020	13109	10645	11048	10777	10903	11790	13596	15851	19028	...
B Expenditures in restaurants, cafes and hotels	41083	46490	37455	38181	39240	41531	48744	60681	72492	83740	79324	...
C Other	4213	3186	4934	4150	4169	4441	4329	4604	4998	5312	8838	...
Total Final Consumption Expenditure in the Domestic Market by Households, of which	347083	365257	358597	351701	357685	379646	400160	435974	485943	531987	574758	...
Plus: Direct purchases abroad by resident households	18336	19591	23707	22804	22890	23443	27085	35310	39782	37313	43493	...
Less: Direct purchases in the domestic market by non-resident households	111934	105414	76580	67800	63100	69850	83876	120097	138158	143785	157406	...
Equals: Final Consumption Expenditure of Resident Households [a]	253485	279434	305724	306705	317475	333239	343369	351187	387567	425515	460845	...

Final Consumption Expenditure of Private Non-profit Institutions Serving Households

	1980	1981	1982	1983	1984	1985	1986	1987	1988	1989	1990	1991
Equals: Final Consumption Expenditure of Private Non-profit Organisations Serving Households	...	...	...	...	...	...	...	...	...	...	...	
Private Final Consumption Expenditure	253485	279434	305724	306705	317475	333239	343369	351187	387567	425515	460845	...

a) Item 'Final consumption expenditure of resident households' includes consumption expenditure of private non-profit institutions serving households.

2.6 Private Final Consumption Expenditure by Type and Purpose, in Constant Prices

Thousand Maltese pounds

	1980	1981	1982	1983	1984	1985	1986	1987	1988	1989	1990	1991
At constant prices of:1973												
Final Consumption Expenditure of Resident Households												
1 Food, beverages and tobacco	71139	69605	67851	68081	68583	74885	72805	77093	79875	86595	...	...
A Food	49096	48375	48370	50067	50433	56105	53027	56836	58692	66491	...	...
B Non-alcoholic beverages	2581	2507	3490	3482	3799	4541	4779	5295	5328	5383	...	...
C Alcoholic beverages	10585	9954	7578	6816	6468	6481	7086	6751	7350	6830	...	...
D Tobacco	8877	8769	8413	7716	7883	7758	7913	8211	8505	7891	...	...
2 Clothing and footwear	24392	24026	19323	18730	20156	24540	25590	25910	27349	29018	...	...
3 Gross rent, fuel and power	18526	19043	16102	16329	16120	16501	17434	18632	20583	21194	...	...
A Fuel and power	3418	3515	2689	3013	3457	3426	3661	3710	4143	4413	...	...
B Other	15108	15528	13413	13316	12663	13075	13773	14922	16440	16781	...	...
4 Furniture, furnishings and household equipment and operation	24330	21869	20766	20976	20963	19723	20943	22371	25336	26595	...	...
A Household operation	4577	4366	4838	4752	5321	5303	4560	4849	5271	5351	...	...
B Other	19753	17503	15928	16224	15642	14420	16383	17522	20065	21244	...	...
5 Medical care and health expenses	8036	8376	7488	7421	7904	7415	8577	8705	9607	10639	...	...
6 Transport and communication	18854	16823	15292	15326	15437	17698	18549	21147	25594	25757	...	...
A Personal transport equipment	11163	9692	9369	8786	9166	10603	11132	12834	16009	15934	...	...
B Other	7691	7131	5923	6540	6271	7095	7417	8313	9585	9823	...	...
7 Recreational, entertainment, education and cultural services	15012	14089	13874	12538	13482	12854	14489	15217	17277	20001	...	...
A Education	1265	981	1075	1028	1131	1131	1226	1258	1214	1425	...	...

2.6 Private Final Consumption Expenditure by Type and Purpose, in Constant Prices
(Continued)

Thousand Maltese pounds

	1980	1981	1982	1983	1984	1985	1986	1987	1988	1989	1990	1991
					At constant prices of:1973							
B Other	13747	13108	12799	11510	12351	11723	13263	13959	16063	18576	...	...
8 Miscellaneous goods and services	34978	32701	31538	31159	32016	33367	37615	45317	53555	59565	...	...
Total Final Consumption Expenditure in the Domestic Market by Households, of which	215267	207252	192234	190559	194661	206983	216002	234392	259176	279364	...	...
Plus: Direct purchases abroad by resident households	6739	6660	7141	6602	6489	6182	6725	8382	8956	7885	...	...
Less: Direct purchases in the domestic market by non-resident households	72940	59956	40862	36422	34027	37761	44820	64011	73227	74384	...	...
Equals: Final Consumption Expenditure of Resident Households a	149066	153956	158513	160739	167123	175404	177907	178763	194905	212865	...	...
Final Consumption Expenditure of Private Non-profit Institutions Serving Households												
Equals: Final Consumption Expenditure of Private Non-profit Organisations Serving Households	...	...	...	...	...	...	...	...	...	...	...	...
Private Final Consumption Expenditure	149066	153956	158513	160739	167123	175404	177907	178763	194905	212865	...	...

a) Item 'Final consumption expenditure of resident households' includes consumption expenditure of private non-profit institutions serving households.

2.7 Gross Capital Formation by Type of Good and Owner, in Current Prices

Thousand Maltese pounds

	1980				1981				1982			
	TOTAL	Total Private	Public Enterprises	General Government	TOTAL	Total Private	Public Enterprises	General Government	TOTAL	Total Private	Public Enterprises	General Government
Increase in stocks, total	9383	2036	6971	376	12557	7160	5856	-459	25504	19229	3096	3179
Gross Fixed Capital Formation, Total	87074	61531	5070	20473	105597	74988	13466	17143	120121	86746	19214	14161
1 Residential buildings	20875	...	...	...	30155	25760	...	4395				
2 Non-residential buildings		...	...	...			...		50020	33366	5635	11019
3 Other construction	10658	...	...	...	11215	...	...	...				
4 Land improvement and plantation and orchard development		...	...	...		...	...	...				
5 Producers' durable goods	55541	44782	3115	7644	64227	49228	10004	4995	70101	53380	13579	3142
A Transport equipment	13153	13040			13828	13595			14508	14273	...	...
B Machinery and equipment	42388	31742	...	...	50399	35633	...	...	55593	39107	...	...
6 Breeding stock, dairy cattle, etc.	...	...	...	...	...	...	...	...	...	...	...	...
Total Gross Capital Formation	96457	63567	12041	20849	118154	82148	19322	16684	145625	105975	22310	17340

	1983				1984				1985			
	TOTAL	Total Private	Public Enterprises	General Government	TOTAL	Total Private	Public Enterprises	General Government	TOTAL	Total Private	Public Enterprises	General Government
Increase in stocks, total	5460	9479	-7588	3569	6780	-1372	5197	2955	7883	9446	-5000	3437
Gross Fixed Capital Formation, Total	131630	107883	11371	12376	126453	101329	14199	10925	125871	100541	16453	8877
1 Residential buildings												
2 Non-residential buildings	50960	37400	4035	9527	48661	37076	2964	8621	41197	30806	3382	7009
3 Other construction												
4 Land improvement and plantation and orchard development												
5 Producers' durable goods	80670	70483	7338	2849	77792	64253	11235	2304	84674	69735	13071	1868
A Transport equipment	33135	32972	...	...	14559	14449	...	...	15939	15755	...	...
B Machinery and equipment	47535	37511	...	...	63233	49804	...	...	68735	53980	...	...
6 Breeding stock, dairy cattle, etc.	...	...	...	...	...	...	...	...	...	...	...	...
Total Gross Capital Formation	137090	117362	3783	15945	133233	99957	19396	13880	133754	109987	11453	12314

Malta

2.7 Gross Capital Formation by Type of Good and Owner, in Current Prices

Thousand Maltese pounds

	1986				1987				1988			
	TOTAL	Total Private	Public Enterprises	General Government	TOTAL	Total Private	Public Enterprises	General Government	TOTAL	Total Private	Public Enterprises	General Government
Increase in stocks, total	8179	3500	324	4355	-2377	-1783	-214	-380	8150	5950	815	1385
Gross Fixed Capital Formation, Total	122327	96532	16210	9585	153453	120360	14652	18441	166405	133108	12724	20573
1 Residential buildings												
2 Non-residential buildings	44779	32925	3607	8247	49103	25608	6645	16850	50168	27923	3743	18502
3 Other construction												
4 Land improvement and plantation and orchard development												
5 Producers' durable goods	77548	63607	12603	1338	104350	94752	8007	1591	116237	105185	8981	2071
A Transport equipment	16676	16491	...	...	41515	41382	...	...	38063	37766	...	...
B Machinery and equipment	60872	47116	...	...	62835	53370	...	...	78174	67419	...	...
6 Breeding stock, dairy cattle, etc.	...	...	...	...	...	...	...	...	...	...	...	...
Total Gross Capital Formation	130506	100032	16534	13940	151076	118577	14438	18061	174555	139058	13539	21958

	1989				1990			
	TOTAL	Total Private	Public Enterprises	General Government	TOTAL	Total Private	Public Enterprises	General Government
Increase in stocks, total	9903	7328	891	1684	12668	9375	1140	2153
Gross Fixed Capital Formation, Total	188437	139519	20838	28080	232611	155678	42693	34240
1 Residential buildings								
2 Non-residential buildings	55294	25774	5640	23880	64672	24985	9999	29688
3 Other construction								
4 Land improvement and plantation and orchard development								
5 Producers' durable goods	133143	113745	15198	4200	167939	130693	32694	4552
A Transport equipment	34336	33949	...	...	66180	65250	...	...
B Machinery and equipment	98807	79796	...	...	101759	65443	...	...
6 Breeding stock, dairy cattle, etc.	...	...	...	...	...	...	...	...
Total Gross Capital Formation	198340	146847	21729	29764	245279	165053	43833	36393

2.11 Gross Fixed Capital Formation by Kind of Activity of Owner, ISIC Divisions, in Current Prices

Thousand Maltese pounds

	1980	1981	1982	1983	1984	1985	1986	1987	1988	1989	1990	1991
					All Producers							
1 Agriculture, hunting, forestry and fishing	1180	1270	1447	1363	1603	1355	1697	1404	1684	2202	1677	...
2 Mining and quarrying a	1432	2692	4976	4761	6340	5743	5598	6116	9149	7417	6605	...
3 Manufacturing	22693	28095	24882	23301	26298	30578	23620	28836	34888	43747	33707	...
4 Electricity, gas and water	...	...	...	...	...	...	...	...	...	...	...	...
5 Construction a	...	...	...	...	...	...	...	...	...	...	...	...
6 Wholesale and retail trade, restaurants and hotels	12085	7912	6721	4143	4606	4829	10000	16591	11080	13308	13232	...
7 Transport, storage and communication	11184	14415	15582	37345	31486	32016	27326	44185	45788	44596	72886	...
8 Finance, insurance, real estate and business services b	9792	18179	29274	32985	26898	22821	24195	19377	22154	20654	18279	...
9 Community, social and personal services b	2165	2425	3864	3985	4098	3199	4096	3851	8365	7595	9292	...
Total Industries	61531	74988	86746	107883	101329	100541	96532	120360	133108	139519	155678	...
Producers of Government Services	25543	30609	33375	23747	25124	25330	25795	33093	33297	48918	76933	...
Private Non-Profit Institutions Serving Households	...	...	...	...	...	...	...	...	...	...	...	...
Total	87074	105597	120121	131630	126453	125871	122327	153453	166405	188437	232611	...

a) Item 'Construction' is included in item 'Mining and quarrying'.
b) Finance, insurance and business services are included in item 'Community, social and personal services'.

3.13 General Government Capital Accumulation Account: Total and Subsectors

Thousand Maltese pounds

	1980					1981				
	Total General Government	Central Government	State or Provincial Government	Local Government	Social Security Funds	Total General Government	Central Government	State or Provincial Government	Local Government	Social Security Funds
Finance of Gross Accumulation										
1 Gross saving	61234	...	...	...	...	63070	...	...	...	...
A Consumption of fixed capital	3127	...	...	...	...	3746	...	...	...	...
B Net saving	58107	...	...	...	...	59324	...	...	...	...
2 Capital transfers	6351	...	...	...	...	19995	...	...	...	...
A From other government subsectors	...	...	...	...	...	...	...	...	...	...
B From other resident sectors	1753	...	...	...	...	1955	...	...	...	...
C From rest of the world	4598	...	...	...	...	18040	...	...	...	...
Finance of Gross Accumulation [a]	67585	...	...	...	...	83065	...	...	...	...
Gross Accumulation										
1 Gross capital formation	32890	...	...	...	...	36006	...	...	...	...
A Increase in stocks	7347	...	...	...	...	5397	...	...	...	...
B Gross fixed capital formation	25543	...	...	...	...	30609	...	...	...	...
2 Purchases of land, net	-	...	...	...	...	-	...	...	...	...
3 Purchases of intangible assets, net	-	...	...	...	...	-	...	...	...	...
4 Capital transfers	759	...	...	...	...	1086	...	...	...	...
A To other government subsectors	...	...	...	...	...	1	...	...	...	...
B To other resident sectors	759	...	...	...	...	1085	...	...	...	...
C To rest of the world	...	...	...	...	...	...	...	...	...	...
Net lending	33936	...	...	...	...	45973	...	...	...	...
Gross Accumulation [a]	67585	...	...	...	...	83065	...	...	...	...

	1982					1983				
	Total General Government	Central Government	State or Provincial Government	Local Government	Social Security Funds	Total General Government	Central Government	State or Provincial Government	Local Government	Social Security Funds
Finance of Gross Accumulation										
1 Gross saving	51693	...	...	...	...	34865	...	...	...	...
A Consumption of fixed capital	4996	...	...	...	...	5624	...	...	...	...
B Net saving	46697	...	...	...	...	29241	...	...	...	...
2 Capital transfers	10776	...	...	...	...	9393	...	...	...	...
A From other government subsectors	...	...	...	...	...	...	...	...	...	...
B From other resident sectors	1721	...	...	...	...	1824	...	...	...	...
C From rest of the world	9055	...	...	...	...	7569	...	...	...	...
Finance of Gross Accumulation [a]	62469	...	...	...	...	44258	...	...	...	...
Gross Accumulation										
1 Gross capital formation	39650	...	...	...	...	19728	...	...	...	...
A Increase in stocks	6275	...	...	...	...	-4019	...	...	...	...
B Gross fixed capital formation	33375	...	...	...	...	23747	...	...	...	...
2 Purchases of land, net	-	...	...	...	...	-	...	...	...	...
3 Purchases of intangible assets, net	-	...	...	...	...	-	...	...	...	...
4 Capital transfers	591	...	...	...	...	435	...	...	...	...
A To other government subsectors	...	...	...	...	...	...	...	...	...	...
B To other resident sectors	591	...	...	...	...	435	...	...	...	...
C To rest of the world	...	...	...	...	...	...	...	...	...	...
Net lending	22228	...	...	...	...	24095	...	...	...	...
Gross Accumulation [a]	62469	...	...	...	...	44258	...	...	...	...

	1984					1985				
	Total General Government	Central Government	State or Provincial Government	Local Government	Social Security Funds	Total General Government	Central Government	State or Provincial Government	Local Government	Social Security Funds
Finance of Gross Accumulation										
1 Gross saving	37387	...	...	...	...	34483	...	...	...	...
A Consumption of fixed capital	5972	...	...	...	...	5917	...	...	...	...
B Net saving	31415	...	...	...	...	28566	...	...	...	...
2 Capital transfers	9298	...	...	...	...	2040	...	...	...	...

Malta

3.13 General Government Capital Accumulation Account: Total and Subsectors
(Continued)

Thousand Maltese pounds

	1984					1985				
	Total General Government	Central Government	State or Provincial Government	Local Government	Social Security Funds	Total General Government	Central Government	State or Provincial Government	Local Government	Social Security Funds
A From other government subsectors	...	...	...	...	...	...	...	...	...	...
B From other resident sectors	2116	...	...	...	...	1596	...	...	...	...
C From rest of the world	7182	...	...	...	...	444	...	...	...	...
Finance of Gross Accumulation a	46685	...	...	...	...	36523	...	...	...	...
Gross Accumulation										
1 Gross capital formation	33276	...	...	...	...	23767	...	...	...	...
A Increase in stocks	8152	...	...	...	...	-1563	...	...	...	...
B Gross fixed capital formation	25124	...	...	...	...	25330	...	...	...	...
2 Purchases of land, net	-	...	...	...	...	-	...	...	...	...
3 Purchases of intangible assets, net	-	...	...	...	...	-	...	...	...	...
4 Capital transfers	543	...	...	...	...	246	...	...	...	...
A To other government subsectors	...	...	...	...	...	...	...	...	...	...
B To other resident sectors	543	...	...	...	...	246	...	...	...	...
C To rest of the world	...	...	...	...	...	...	...	...	...	...
Net lending	12866	...	...	...	...	12510	...	...	...	...
Gross Accumulation a	46685	...	...	...	...	36523	...	...	...	...

	1986					1987				
	Total General Government	Central Government	State or Provincial Government	Local Government	Social Security Funds	Total General Government	Central Government	State or Provincial Government	Local Government	Social Security Funds
Finance of Gross Accumulation										
1 Gross saving	35252	...	...	...	...	22421	...	...	...	...
A Consumption of fixed capital	6778	...	...	...	...	7569	...	...	...	...
B Net saving	28474	...	...	...	...	14852	...	...	...	...
2 Capital transfers	2923	...	...	...	...	2033	...	...	...	...
A From other government subsectors	...	...	...	...	...	...	...	...	...	...
B From other resident sectors	1584	...	...	...	...	1972	...	...	...	...
C From rest of the world	1339	...	...	...	...	61	...	...	...	...
Finance of Gross Accumulation a	38175	...	...	...	...	24454	...	...	...	...
Gross Accumulation										
1 Gross capital formation	30474	...	...	...	...	32499	...	...	...	...
A Increase in stocks	4679	...	...	...	...	-594	...	...	...	...
B Gross fixed capital formation	25795	...	...	...	...	33093	...	...	...	...
2 Purchases of land, net	-	...	...	...	...	-	...	...	...	...
3 Purchases of intangible assets, net	-	...	...	...	...	-	...	...	...	...
4 Capital transfers	206	...	...	...	...	2648	...	...	...	...
A To other government subsectors	...	...	...	...	...	...	...	...	...	...
B To other resident sectors	691	...	...	...	...	2648	...	...	...	...
C To rest of the world	...	...	...	...	...	...	...	...	...	...
Net lending	7010	...	...	...	...	-10693	...	...	...	...
Gross Accumulation a	38175	...	...	...	...	24454	...	...	...	...

	1988					1989				
	Total General Government	Central Government	State or Provincial Government	Local Government	Social Security Funds	Total General Government	Central Government	State or Provincial Government	Local Government	Social Security Funds
Finance of Gross Accumulation										
1 Gross saving	41318	...	...	...	...	46601	...	...	...	...
A Consumption of fixed capital	7945	...	...	...	...	8284	...	...	...	...
B Net saving	33373	...	...	...	...	38317	...	...	...	...
2 Capital transfers	16362	...	...	...	...	10807	...	...	...	...
A From other government subsectors	...	...	...	...	...	...	...	...	...	...
B From other resident sectors	2043	...	...	...	...	2457	...	...	...	...
C From rest of the world	14319	...	...	...	...	8350	...	...	...	...
Finance of Gross Accumulation a	57680	...	...	...	...	57408	...	...	...	...

3.13 General Government Capital Accumulation Account: Total and Subsectors
(Continued)

Thousand Maltese pounds

	1988					1989				
	Total General Government	Central Government	State or Provincial Government	Local Government	Social Security Funds	Total General Government	Central Government	State or Provincial Government	Local Government	Social Security Funds
					Gross Accumulation					
1 Gross capital formation	35497	...	...	...	...	51493	...	...	...	...
A Increase in stocks	2200	...	...	...	...	2575	...	...	...	...
B Gross fixed capital formation	33297	...	...	...	...	48918	...	...	...	...
2 Purchases of land, net	-	...	...	...	...	-	...	...	...	...
3 Purchases of intangible assets, net	-	...	...	...	...	-	...	...	...	...
4 Capital transfers	3453	...	...	...	...	11977	...	...	...	...
A To other government subsectors		...	...	...	...		...	...	...	...
B To other resident sectors	3453	...	...	...	...	11977	...	...	...	...
C To rest of the world	...	...	...	...	...	...	...	...	...	...
Net lending	18730	...	...	...	...	-6062	...	...	...	...
Gross Accumulation a	57680	...	...	...	...	57408	...	...	...	...

a) Public enterprises is included in general government.

3.22 Corporate and Quasi-Corporate Enterprise Income and Outlay Account: Total and Sectors

Thousand Maltese pounds

	1980			1981			1982			1983		
	TOTAL	Non-Financial	Financial	TOTAL	Non-Financial	Financial	TOTAL	Non-Financial	Financial	TOTAL	Non-Financial	Financial
						Receipts						
1 Operating surplus	52235	43201	9034	59863	53807	6056	68790	59316	9474	69703	62505	7198
2 Property and entrepreneurial income	4618	4618	-	5474	5474	-	5412	5412	-	3826	3826	-
A Withdrawals from quasi-corporate enterprises	4618	4618	-	5474	5474	-	5412	5412	-	3826	3826	-
B Interest	...	...	...	...	...	...	...	...	...	...	...	...
C Dividends	...	...	...	...	...	...	...	...	...	...	...	...
D Net land rent and royalties	...	...	...	...	...	...	...	...	...	...	...	...
3 Current transfers	...	...	...	...	...	...	...	...	...	...	...	...
Total Current Receipts	56853	47819	9034	65337	59281	6056	74202	64728	9474	73529	66331	7198
						Disbursements						
1 Property and entrepreneurial income	29296	26315	2981	31397	28852	2545	33484	29460	4024	32107	28497	3610
A Withdrawals from quasi-corporations	9970	9970	-	6129	6129	-	6268	6268	-	3547	3547	-
B Interest	19326	16345	2981	25268	22723	2545	27216	23192	4024	28560	24950	3610
C Dividends												
D Net land rent and royalties	...	...	...	...	...	...	...	...	...	...	...	...
2 Direct taxes and other current transfers n.e.c. to general government	10260	7324	2936	11376	9408	1968	17065	13986	3079	16032	13693	2339
A Direct taxes	10260	7324	2936	11376	9408	1968	17065	13986	3079	16032	13693	2339
On income	10260	7324	2936	11376	9408	1968	17065	13986	3079	16032	13693	2339
Other	...	...	...	...	...	...	...	...	...	...	...	...
B Fines, fees, penalties and other current transfers n.e.c.												
3 Other current transfers	...	...	...	...	...	...	...	...	...	...	...	...
Net saving	17297	14180	3117	22564	21021	1543	23653	21282	2371	25390	24141	1249
Total Current Disbursements and Net Saving	56853	47819	9034	65337	59281	6056	74202	64728	9474	73529	66331	7198

	1984			1985			1986			1987		
	TOTAL	Non-Financial	Financial	TOTAL	Non-Financial	Financial	TOTAL	Non-Financial	Financial	TOTAL	Non-Financial	Financial
						Receipts						
1 Operating surplus	72729	65309	7420	76329	67289	9040	74824	65722	9102	82851	76726	6125
2 Property and entrepreneurial income	3876	3876	-	4209	4209	-	4387	4387	-	5719	5719	-
A Withdrawals from quasi-corporate enterprises	3876	3876	-	4209	4209	-	4387	4387	-	5719	5719	-
B Interest	...	...	...	...	...	...	...	...	...	...	...	...
C Dividends	...	...	...	...	...	...	...	...	...	...	...	...
D Net land rent and royalties	...	...	...	...	...	...	...	...	...	...	...	...

Malta

3.22 Corporate and Quasi-Corporate Enterprise Income and Outlay Account: Total and Sectors
(Continued)

Thousand Maltese pounds

	1984			1985			1986			1987		
	TOTAL	Non-Financial	Financial	TOTAL	Non-Financial	Financial	TOTAL	Non-Financial	Financial	TOTAL	Non-Financial	Financial
3 Current transfers	...	...	...	...	...	...	...	...	...	...	...	...
Total Current Receipts	76605	69185	7420	80538	71498	9040	79211	70109	9102	88570	82445	6125
Disbursements												
1 Property and entrepreneurial income	35279	30774	4505	38009	35239	2770	35066	32480	2586	32556	31003	1553
A Withdrawals from quasi-corporations	4820	4820	-	6842	6842	-	4743	4743	-	5207	5207	-
B Interest	30459	25954	4505	31167	28397	2770	30323	27737	2586	27349	25796	1553
C Dividends												
D Net land rent and royalties	...	...	...	...	...	...	...	...	...	...	...	...
2 Direct taxes and other current transfers n.e.c. to general government	14728	12317	2411	15194	12256	2938	15354	12396	2958	16612	14621	1991
A Direct taxes	14728	12317	2411	15194	12256	2938	15354	12396	2958	16612	14621	1991
On income	14728	12317	2411	15194	12256	2938	15354	12396	2958	16612	14621	1991
Other	...	...	...	...	...	...	...	...	...	...	...	...
B Fines, fees, penalties and other current transfers n.e.c.	...	...	...	...	...	...	...	...	...	...	...	...
3 Other current transfers	...	...	...	...	...	...	...	...	...	...	...	...
Net saving	26598	26094	504	27335	24003	3332	28791	25233	3558	39402	36821	2581
Total Current Disbursements and Net Saving	76605	69185	7420	80538	71498	9040	79211	70109	9102	88570	82445	6125

	1988			1989			1990		
	TOTAL	Non-Financial	Financial	TOTAL	Non-Financial	Financial	TOTAL	Non-Financial	Financial
Receipts									
1 Operating surplus	96122	86749	9373	115080	102467	12613	130778	117544	13234
2 Property and entrepreneurial income	6130	6130	-	7301	7301	-	7606	7606	-
A Withdrawals from quasi-corporate enterprises	6130	6130	-	7301	7301	-	7606	7606	-
B Interest	...	...	...	...	...	...	...	...	...
C Dividends	...	...	...	...	...	...	...	...	...
D Net land rent and royalties	...	...	...	...	...	...	...	...	...
3 Current transfers	...	...	...	...	...	...	...	...	...
Total Current Receipts	102252	92879	9373	122381	109768	12613	138384	125150	13234
Disbursements									
1 Property and entrepreneurial income	43504	41831	1673	50572	49094	1478	58824	57471	1353
A Withdrawals from quasi-corporations	5058	5058	-	8713	8713	-	7790	7790	-
B Interest	38446	36773	1673	41859	40381	1478	51034	49681	1353
C Dividends									
D Net land rent and royalties	...	...	...	...	...	...	...	...	...
2 Direct taxes and other current transfers n.e.c. to general government	18191	15144	3047	21014	16914	4100	21804	17172	4632
A Direct taxes	18191	15144	3047	21014	16914	4100	21804	17172	4632
On income	18191	15144	3047	21014	16914	4100	21804	17172	4632
Other	...	...	...	...	...	...	...	...	...
B Fines, fees, penalties and other current transfers n.e.c.	...	...	...	...	...	...	...	...	...
3 Other current transfers	...	...	...	...	...	...	...	...	...
Net saving	40557	35904	4653	50795	43760	7035	57756	50507	7249
Total Current Disbursements and Net Saving	102252	92879	9373	122381	109768	12613	138384	125150	13234

Malta

3.23 Corporate and Quasi-Corporate Enterprise Capital Accumulation Account: Total and Sectors

Thousand Maltese pounds

	1980			1981			1982			1983		
	TOTAL	Non-Financial	Financial	TOTAL	Non-Financial	Financial	TOTAL	Non-Financial	Financial	TOTAL	Non-Financial	Financial
Finance of Gross Accumulation												
1 Gross saving	24015	20415	3600	29651	27899	1752	30938	28325	2613	35487	33983	1504
A Consumption of fixed capital	6718	6575	143	7087	6878	209	7285	7043	242	10097	9842	255
B Net saving	17297	13840	3457	22564	21021	1543	23653	21282	2371	25390	24141	1249
2 Capital transfers	...	...	...	...	...	...	...	...	...	...	...	...
Finance of Gross Accumulation	24015	20415	3600	29651	27899	1752	30938	28325	2613	35487	33983	1504
Gross Accumulation												
1 Gross capital formation	40914	40914	-	50782	50782	-	62394	62394	-	82193	82193	-
A Increase in stocks	2011	2011	-	6739	6739	-	19040	19040	-	9229	9229	-
B Gross fixed capital formation	38903	38903	-	44043	44043	-	43354	43354	-	72964	72964	-
2 Purchases of land, net	...	...	...	...	...	...	...	...	...	...	...	...
3 Purchases of intangible assets, net	...	...	...	...	...	...	...	...	...	...	...	...
4 Capital transfers	...	...	...	...	...	...	...	...	...	...	...	...
Net lending	-16899	-20499	3600	-21131	-22883	1752	-31456	-34069	2613	-46706	-48210	1504
Gross Accumulation	24015	20415	3600	29651	27899	1752	30938	28325	2613	35487	33983	1504

	1984			1985			1986			1987		
	TOTAL	Non-Financial	Financial	TOTAL	Non-Financial	Financial	TOTAL	Non-Financial	Financial	TOTAL	Non-Financial	Financial
Finance of Gross Accumulation												
1 Gross saving	38192	37397	795	39604	35961	3643	41737	37836	3901	54479	51460	3019
A Consumption of fixed capital	11594	11303	291	12269	11958	311	12946	12603	343	15077	14639	438
B Net saving	26598	26094	504	27335	24003	3332	28791	25233	3558	39402	36821	2581
2 Capital transfers	...	...	...	-	-	-	606	606	-	2611	2611	-
Finance of Gross Accumulation	38192	37397	795	39604	35961	3643	42343	38442	3901	57090	54071	3019
Gross Accumulation												
1 Gross capital formation	59271	59271	-	67028	67028	-	56344	56344	-	77526	77526	-
A Increase in stocks	-1330	-1330	-	9046	9046	-	3000	3000	-	-1070	-1070	-
B Gross fixed capital formation	60601	60601	-	57982	57982	-	53344	53344	-	78596	78596	-
2 Purchases of land, net	...	...	...	...	...	...	...	...	...	...	...	...
3 Purchases of intangible assets, net	...	...	...	...	...	...	...	...	...	...	...	...
4 Capital transfers	...	...	...	...	...	...	...	...	...	...	...	...
Net lending	-21079	-21874	795	-27424	-31067	3643	-14001	-17902	3901	-20436	-23455	3019
Gross Accumulation	38192	37397	795	39604	35961	3643	42343	38442	3901	57090	54071	3019

	1988			1989			1990		
	TOTAL	Non-Financial	Financial	TOTAL	Non-Financial	Financial	TOTAL	Non-Financial	Financial
Finance of Gross Accumulation									
1 Gross saving	58047	52881	5166	70535	62597	7938	79770	70910	8860
A Consumption of fixed capital	17490	16977	513	19740	18837	903	22014	20403	1611
B Net saving	40557	35904	4653	50795	43760	7035	57756	50507	7249
2 Capital transfers	2679	2679	-	9669	9669	-	10145	10145	-
Finance of Gross Accumulation	60726	55560	5166	80204	72266	7938	89915	81055	8860
Gross Accumulation									
1 Gross capital formation	88868	88868	-	95178	95178	-	111471	111471	-
A Increase in stocks	3668	3668	-	4456	4456	-	5701	5701	-
B Gross fixed capital formation	85200	85200	-	90722	90722	-	105770	105770	-
2 Purchases of land, net	...	...	...	...	...	...	...	...	...
3 Purchases of intangible assets, net	...	...	...	...	...	...	...	...	...
4 Capital transfers	...	...	...	...	...	...	...	...	...
Net lending	-28142	-33308	5166	-14974	-22912	7938	-21556	-30416	8860
Gross Accumulation	60726	55560	5166	80204	72266	7938	89915	81055	8860

Malta

3.32 Household and Private Unincorporated Enterprise Income and Outlay Account

	1980	1981	1982	1983	1984	1985	1986	1987	1988	1989	1990	1991
Receipts												
1 Compensation of employees	180553	203805	228625	223584	217928	222942	231617	254706	269569	288234	318990	...
A Wages and salaries	168821	189580	213384	207932	203182	207559	215884	238508	251928	270755	298716	...
B Employers' contributions for social security	11732	14225	15241	15652	14746	15383	15733	16198	17641	17479	20274	
C Employers' contributions for private pension & welfare plans	...	...	...	...	...	...	...	...	...	...	...	
2 Operating surplus of private unincorporated enterprises	57940	66268	72020	73370	75774	79082	84042	83352	89372	102023	111126	
3 Property and entrepreneurial income	48676	50878	50767	49599	53845	54036	54419	56059	66105	71299	88316	
A Withdrawals from private quasi-corporations	...	...	...	...	...	...	...	...	...	...	...	...
B Interest												...
C Dividends	48676	50878	50767	49599	53845	54036	54419	56059	66105	71299	88316	
D Net land rent and royalties												...
3 Current transfers	53668	64994	74126	77252	81334	79638	80236	83476	92474	102657	110443	...
A Casualty insurance claims	...	...	...	...	...	...	...	...	...	...	...	
B Social security benefits	40035	51125	59130	61211	65100	64726	66412	68075	72301	77203	86576	
C Social assistance grants												
D Unfunded employee pension and welfare benefits	-	-	-	-	-	-	...	...	-	-	-	...
E Transfers from general government	...	...	...	...	...	...	...	...	...	...	...	
F Transfers from the rest of the world	13633	13869	14996	16041	16234	14912	13824	15401	20173	25454	23867	
G Other transfers n.e.c.	...	...	...	...	...	...	...	...	...	...	...	...
Total Current Receipts	340837	385945	425538	423805	428881	435698	450314	477593	517520	564213	628875	...
Disbursements												
1 Final consumption expenditures	253485	279434	305724	306705	317475	333239	343369	351187	387567	425515	460845	...
A Market purchases	...	...	...	...	...	...	...	...	...	...	...	
B Gross rents of owner-occupied housing	2965	3586	3758	3884	3932	4184	4307	4455	4626	4875	5171	
C Consumption from own-account production	...	...	...	...	...	...	...	...	...	...	...	
2 Property income	...	...	...	...	...	...	...	...	...	...	...	...
3 Direct taxes and other current transfers n.e.c. to government	52968	62042	64060	64347	60471	62603	61483	55762	64993	67473	81453	...
A Social security contributions	23464	28450	30482	31304	29492	30766	31466	32396	35282	34958	40548	
B Direct taxes	29166	33316	33219	32614	30511	31389	29633	23078	29332	32109	40473	
Income taxes	29166	33316	33219	32614	30511	31389	26216	19812	25989	28142	33492	
Other	...	...	...	...	...	...	3417	3266	3343	3967	6981	
C Fees, fines and penalties	338	276	359	429	468	448	384	288	379	406	432	...
4 Other current transfers	6095	7053	6308	6499	8095	7420	7530	8114	9094	11603	13303	...
A Net casualty insurance premiums	...	...	...	...	...	...	...	...	...	...	...	
B Transfers to private non-profit institutions serving households	...	...	...	...	...	...	...	...	...	...	...	
C Transfers to the rest of the world	2638	2871	2111	1900	2934	2170	2304	2791	3109	5211	6660	...
D Other current transfers, except imputed	3457	4182	4197	4599	5161	5250	5226	5323	5985	6392	6643	...
E Imputed employee pension and welfare contributions	-	-	-	-	-	-	-	-	-	-	-	
Net saving	28289	37416	49446	46254	42840	32436	37932	62530	55866	59622	73274	...
Total Current Disbursements and Net Saving	340837	385945	425538	423805	428881	435698	450314	477593	517520	564213	628875	...

3.33 Household and Private Unincorporated Enterprise Capital Accumulation Account

	1980	1981	1982	1983	1984	1985	1986	1987	1988	1989	1990	1991
Finance of Gross Accumulation												
1 Gross saving	31340	40946	52903	50286	46264	35673	41408	65861	59285	63621	77512	...
A Consumption of fixed capital	3051	3530	3457	4032	3424	3237	3476	3331	3419	3999	4238	...
B Net saving	28289	37416	49446	46254	42840	32436	37932	62530	55866	59622	73274	...
2 Capital transfers a	3389	5228	7960	5829	7802	11376	13913	15454	22855	7886	4271	...

3.33 Household and Private Unincorporated Enterprise Capital Accumulation Account
(Continued)

Thousand Maltese pounds

	1980	1981	1982	1983	1984	1985	1986	1987	1988	1989	1990	1991
Total Finance of Gross Accumulation	34729	46174	60863	56115	54066	47049	55321	81315	82140	71507	81783	...
Gross Accumulation												
1 Gross Capital Formation	22653	31366	43581	35169	40686	42959	43688	41051	50190	51669	53582	...
A Increase in stocks	25	421	189	250	-42	400	500	-713	2282	2872	3674	...
B Gross fixed capital formation	22628	30945	43392	34919	40728	42559	43188	41764	47908	48797	49908	...
2 Purchases of land, net	...	...	...	...	...	...	...	...	...	...	...	...
3 Purchases of intangibles, net	...	...	...	...	...	...	...	...	...	...	...	...
4 Capital transfers	...	...	...	...	...	...	...	...	...	...	...	...
Net lending	12076	14808	17282	20946	13380	4090	11633	40264	31950	19838	28201	...
Total Gross Accumulation	34729	46174	60863	56115	54066	47049	55321	81315	82140	71507	81783	...

a) Capital transfers received are recorded net of capital transfers paid.

3.51 External Transactions: Current Account: Detail

Thousand Maltese pounds

	1980	1981	1982	1983	1984	1985	1986	1987	1988	1989	1990	1991
Payments to the Rest of the World												
1 Imports of goods and services	377989	392462	394578	376143	393516	420475	421742	480934	540880	616792	726947	...
2 Factor income to the rest of the world	19929	19679	11801	9874	9199	10758	17195	8850	17564	22429	23762	...
A Compensation of employees	...	...	...	...	...	...	...	...	...	...	...	...
B Property and entrepreneurial income	19929	19679	11801	9874	9199	10758	17195	8850	17564	22429	23762	...
3 Current transfers to the rest of the world	2915	3156	2383	2173	3185	2465	2560	3108	3678	5582	7347	...
A Indirect taxes by general government to supranational organizations	...	...	...	...	...	...	...	...	...	...	...	...
B Other current transfers	2915	3156	2383	2173	3185	2465	2560	3108	3678	5582	7347	...
By general government	277	285	272	273	251	295	256	317	569	371	687	...
By other resident sectors	2638	2871	2111	1900	2934	2170	2304	2791	3109	5211	6660	...
4 Surplus of the nation on current transactions	20132	15513	-10091	-16452	-11390	-23994	-12109	-8315	-15905	-17583	-28923	...
Payments to the Rest of the World, and Surplus of the Nation on Current Transfers	420965	430810	398671	371738	394510	409704	429388	484577	546217	627220	729133	...
Receipts From The Rest of the World												
1 Exports of goods and services	356647	355918	319799	307647	323539	345155	370228	429593	480024	543463	626415	...
2 Factor income from the rest of the world	50479	60923	63829	47997	54669	49543	45251	39511	45907	58192	78779	...
A Compensation of employees	...	...	...	...	...	...	...	...	...	...	...	...
B Property and entrepreneurial income	50479	60923	63829	47997	54669	49543	45251	39511	45907	58192	78779	...
3 Current transfers from the rest of the world	13839	13969	15043	16094	16302	15006	13909	15473	20286	25565	23939	...
A Subsidies to general government from supranational organizations	...	...	...	...	...	...	...	...	...	...	...	...
B Other current transfers	13839	13969	15043	16094	16302	15006	13909	15473	20286	25565	23939	...
To general government	206	100	47	53	68	94	85	72	113	111	72	...
To other resident sectors	13633	13869	14996	16041	16234	14912	13824	15401	20173	25454	23867	...
Receipts from the Rest of the World on Current Transfers	420965	430810	398671	371738	394510	409704	429388	484577	546217	627220	729133	...

Malta

3.52 External Transactions: Capital Accumulation Account

Thousand Maltese pounds

	1980	1981	1982	1983	1984	1985	1986	1987	1988	1989	1990	1991
Finance of Gross Accumulation												
1 Surplus of the nation on current transactions	20132	15513	-10091	-16452	-11390	-23994	-12109	-8315	-15905	-17583	-28923	...
2 Capital transfers from the rest of the world	8981	24138	18145	14787	16557	13170	16751	17450	38443	16385	11204	...
A By general government	4598	18040	9055	7569	7182	444	1339	61	14319	8350	7932	...
B By other resident sectors	4383	6098	9090	7218	9375	12726	15412	17389	24124	8035	3272	...
Total Finance of Gross Accumulation	29113	39651	8054	-1664	5167	-10824	4642	9135	22538	-1198	-17719	...
Gross Accumulation												
1 Capital transfers to the rest of the world	...	...	...	...	...	...	...	...	...	...	...	...
2 Purchases of intangible assets, n.e.c., net, from the rest of the world	-	-	-	-	-	-	-	-	-	-	-	-
Net lending to the rest of the world	29113	39651	8054	-1665	5167	-10824	4642	9135	22538	-1198	-17719	...
Total Gross Accumulation	29113	39651	8054	-1665	5167	-10824	4642	9135	22538	-1198	-17719	...

4.1 Derivation of Value Added by Kind of Activity, in Current Prices

Thousand Maltese pounds

	1980			1981			1982			1983		
	Gross Output	Intermediate Consumption	Value Added	Gross Output	Intermediate Consumption	Value Added	Gross Output	Intermediate Consumption	Value Added	Gross Output	Intermediate Consumption	Value Added
All Producers												
1 Agriculture, hunting, forestry and fishing	...	...	13289	...	...	15038	...	...	16767	...	...	18731
2 Mining and quarrying [a]	...	...	15655	...	...	17073	...	...	23546	...	...	23511
3 Manufacturing	...	...	115358	...	...	121384	...	...	125024	...	...	120036
A Manufacture of food, beverages and tobacco	...	...	15543	...	...	18413	...	...	20814	...	...	19903
B Textile, wearing apparel and leather industries	...	...	36559	...	...	36531	...	...	36189	...	...	33665
C Manufacture of wood and wood products, including furniture	...	...	5306	...	...	5622	...	...	6223	...	...	5466
D Manufacture of paper and paper products, printing and publishing	...	...	8266	...	...	7790	...	...	6829	...	...	6979
E Manufacture of chemicals and chemical petroleum, coal, rubber and plastic products	...	...	7423	...	...	6879	...	...	6325	...	...	7005
F Manufacture of non-metallic mineral products, except products of petroleum and coal	...	...	2786	...	...	2957	...	...	3448	...	...	3965
G Basic metal industries	...	...	4319	...	...	-	...	...	-	...	...	-
H Manufacture of fabricated metal products, machinery and equipment	...	...	25558	...	...	34823	...	...	35710	...	...	32537
I Other manufacturing industries	...	...	9598	...	...	8369	...	...	9486	...	...	10516
4 Electricity, gas and water [b]	...	...	15635	...	...	23586	...	...	21958	...	...	21119
5 Construction [a]	...	...	...	...	...	...	...	...	...	...	...	...
6 Wholesale and retail trade, restaurants and hotels [c]	...	...	51001	...	...	57421	...	...	63184	...	...	64010
7 Transport, storage and communication	...	...	22230	...	...	22596	...	...	20396	...	...	24050
8 Finance, insurance, real estate and business services [d]	...	...	37269	...	...	45519	...	...	50303	...	...	51475
9 Community, social and personal services [cde]	...	...	33731	...	...	36404	...	...	38415	...	...	36850
Total, Industries	...	...	304168	...	...	339021	...	...	359593	...	...	359782
Producers of Government Services	...	...	44444	...	...	51513	...	...	58152	...	...	57348
Other Producers [e]	...	...	...	...	...	...	...	...	...	...	...	...
Total [f]	...	...	348612	...	...	390534	...	...	417745	...	...	417130
Less: Imputed bank service charge	...	...	...	...	...	...	...	...	...	...	...	...
Import duties	...	...	...	...	...	...	...	...	...	...	...	...
Value added tax	...	...	...	...	...	...	...	...	...	...	...	...
Other adjustments [g]	...	...	43352	...	...	45917	...	...	44041	...	...	40426
Total	...	...	391964	...	...	436451	...	...	461786	...	...	457556

4.1 Derivation of Value Added by Kind of Activity, in Current Prices

Thousand Maltese pounds

	1984			1985			1986			1987		
	Gross Output	Intermediate Consumption	Value Added	Gross Output	Intermediate Consumption	Value Added	Gross Output	Intermediate Consumption	Value Added	Gross Output	Intermediate Consumption	Value Added
All Producers												
1 Agriculture, hunting, forestry and fishing	...	...	19346	...	...	19375	...	...	20419	...	...	21429
2 Mining and quarrying a	...	...	19660	...	...	20758	...	...	18869	...	...	21051
3 Manufacturing	...	...	124706	...	...	126929	...	...	134676	...	...	136427
A Manufacture of food, beverages and tobacco	...	...	20431	...	...	22813	...	...	25390	...	...	27374
B Textile, wearing apparel and leather industries	...	...	35052	...	...	35091	...	...	35809	...	...	33499
C Manufacture of wood and wood products, including furniture	...	...	5065	...	...	4220	...	...	4994	...	...	5233
D Manufacture of paper and paper products, printing and publishing	...	...	8661	...	...	8383	...	...	7818	...	...	8862
E Manufacture of chemicals and chemical petroleum, coal, rubber and plastic products	...	...	7962	...	...	8352	...	...	8314	...	...	10128
F Manufacture of non-metallic mineral products, except products of petroleum and coal	...	...	4891	...	...	3626	...	...	2887	...	...	2950
G Basic metal industries	...	...	-	...	...	-	...	...	-	...	...	-
H Manufacture of fabricated metal products, machinery and equipment	...	...	31607	...	...	33431	...	...	35653	...	...	31574
I Other manufacturing industries	...	...	11037	...	...	11013	...	...	13811	...	...	16807
4 Electricity, gas and water b	...	...	24985	...	...	22278	...	...	34704	...	...	42119
5 Construction a	...	...	...	...	...	...	...	...	...	...	...	...
6 Wholesale and retail trade, restaurants and hotels c	...	...	66077	...	...	66696	...	...	67647	...	...	70847
7 Transport, storage and communication	...	...	23391	...	...	23955	...	...	26240	...	...	30204
8 Finance, insurance, real estate and business services d	...	...	53517	...	...	57131	...	...	61255	...	...	62782
9 Community, social and personal services cde	...	...	33605	...	...	34894	...	...	35639	...	...	41729
Total, Industries	...	...	365287	...	...	372016	...	...	399449	...	...	426588
Producers of Government Services	...	...	56090	...	...	58534	...	...	62317	...	...	68862
Other Producers e	...	...	...	...	...	...	...	...	...	...	...	...
Total f	...	...	421377	...	...	430550	...	...	461766	...	...	495450
Less: Imputed bank service charge	...	...	...	...	...	...	...	...	...	...	...	...
Import duties	...	...	...	...	...	...	...	...	...	...	...	...
Value added tax	...	...	...	...	...	...	...	...	...	...	...	...
Other adjustments g	...	...	39675	...	...	45432	...	...	50103	...	...	53721
Total	...	...	461052	...	...	475982	...	...	511869	...	...	549171

	1988			1989			1990		
	Gross Output	Intermediate Consumption	Value Added	Gross Output	Intermediate Consumption	Value Added	Gross Output	Intermediate Consumption	Value Added
All Producers									
1 Agriculture, hunting, forestry and fishing	...	...	21108	...	...	22355	...	...	22537
2 Mining and quarrying a	...	...	21353	...	...	22257	...	...	22882
3 Manufacturing	...	...	146557	...	...	163663	...	...	175634
A Manufacture of food, beverages and tobacco	...	...	27187	...	...	31792	...	...	...

Malta

Thousand Maltese pounds

	1988			1989			1990		
	Gross Output	Intermediate Consumption	Value Added	Gross Output	Intermediate Consumption	Value Added	Gross Output	Intermediate Consumption	Value Added
B Textile, wearing apparel and leather industries	...	...	29950	...	...	33994	...	...	...
C Manufacture of wood and wood products, including furniture	...	...	6435	...	...	8759	...	...	...
D Manufacture of paper and paper products, printing and publishing	...	...	8540	...	...	11417	...	...	...
E Manufacture of chemicals and chemical petroleum, coal, rubber and plastic products	...	...	10946	...	...	12965	...	...	...
F Manufacture of non-metallic mineral products, except products of petroleum and coal	...	...	3230	...	...	4094	...	...	...
G Basic metal industries			-			-			
H Manufacture of fabricated metal products, machinery and equipment	...	...	44076	...	...	48812	...	...	...
I Other manufacturing industries	...	...	16193	...	...	11830	...	...	...
4 Electricity, gas and water b	...	...	51878	...	...	54034	...	...	53426
5 Construction a	...	...	...	...	...	...	...	...	...
6 Wholesale and retail trade, restaurants and hotels c	...	...	76899	...	...	84846	...	...	93772
7 Transport, storage and communication	...	...	34527	...	...	34602	...	...	37131
8 Finance, insurance, real estate and business services d	...	...	69713	...	...	80226	...	...	93336
9 Community, social and personal services cde	...	...	46229	...	...	52130	...	...	58200
Total, Industries	...	...	468264	...	...	514113	...	...	556918
Producers of Government Services	...	...	74370	...	...	82736	...	...	92673
Other Producers e	...	...	...	...	...	...	...	...	...
Total f	...	...	542634	...	...	596849	...	...	649591
Less: Imputed bank service charge	...	...	...	...	...	...	...	...	...
Import duties	...	...	...	...	...	...	...	...	...
Value added tax	...	...	...	...	...	...	...	...	...
Other adjustments g	...	...	63817	...	...	73290	...	...	85154
Total	...	...	606451	...	...	670139	...	...	734745

a) Item 'Construction' is included in item 'Mining and quarrying'.
b) Item 'Electricity, gas and water' refers to all government enterprises.
c) Restaurants and hotels are included in item 'Community, social and personal services'.
d) Business services are included in item 'Community, social and personal services'.
e) Beginning 1980, item 'Other producers' is included in item 'Community, social and personal services'.
f) Gross domestic product in factor values.
g) Item 'Other adjustments' refers to indirect taxes net of subsidies.

4.3 Cost Components of Value Added

Thousand Maltese pounds

	1980						1981					
	Compensation of Employees	Capital Consumption	Net Operating Surplus	Indirect Taxes	Less: Subsidies Received	Value Added	Compensation of Employees	Capital Consumption	Net Operating Surplus	Indirect Taxes	Less: Subsidies Received	Value Added
				All Producers								
1 Agriculture, hunting, forestry and fishing	1366	...	11923	...	...	13289	1699	...	13339	...	...	15038
2 Mining and quarrying a	12337	...	3318	...	...	15655	12936	...	4137	...	...	17073
3 Manufacturing	67560	...	47798	...	...	115358	73420	...	47964	...	...	121384
4 Electricity, gas and water b	10213	...	5422	...	...	15635	12259	...	11327	...	...	23586
5 Construction a	...	...	...	...	...	...	...	...	...	...	...	...
6 Wholesale and retail trade, restaurants and hotels c	8253	...	42748	...	...	51001	10282	...	47139	...	...	57421
7 Transport, storage and communication	9757	...	12473	...	...	22230	11215	...	11381	...	...	22596
8 Finance, insurance, real estate and business services d	5137	...	32132	...	...	37269	5839	...	39680	...	...	45519
9 Community, social and personal services cde	21486	...	12245	...	...	33731	24642	...	11762	...	...	36404
Total, Industries	136109	...	168059	...	...	304168	152292	...	186729	...	...	339021
Producers of Government Services	44444	...	...	...	...	44444	51513	...	...	...	...	51513

4.3 Cost Components of Value Added
(Continued)

Thousand Maltese pounds

	1980						1981					
	Compensation of Employees	Capital Consumption	Net Operating Surplus	Indirect Taxes	Less: Subsidies Received	Value Added	Compensation of Employees	Capital Consumption	Net Operating Surplus	Indirect Taxes	Less: Subsidies Received	Value Added
Other Producers e	...	...	...	...	...	...	...	...	...	...	...	...
Total fg	180553	...	168059	...	...	348612	203805	...	186729	...	...	390534
Less: Imputed bank service charge	...	...	...	...	...	...	...	...	...	...	...	...
Import duties	...	...	...	...	...	...	...	...	...	...	...	...
Value added tax	...	...	...	...	...	...	...	...	...	...	...	...
Other adjustments h	...	...	...	45744	2392	43352	...	...	...	47897	1980	45917
Total	180553	...	168059	45744	2392	391964	203805	...	186729	47897	1980	436451

	1982						1983					
	Compensation of Employees	Capital Consumption	Net Operating Surplus	Indirect Taxes	Less: Subsidies Received	Value Added	Compensation of Employees	Capital Consumption	Net Operating Surplus	Indirect Taxes	Less: Subsidies Received	Value Added
						All Producers						
1 Agriculture, hunting, forestry and fishing	2072	...	14695	...	...	16767	1975	...	16756	...	...	18731
2 Mining and quarrying a	16804	...	6742	...	...	23546	16923	...	6588	...	...	23511
3 Manufacturing	78328	...	46696	...	...	125024	75103	...	44933	...	...	120036
4 Electricity, gas and water b	13396	...	8562	...	...	21958	12498	...	8621	...	...	21119
5 Construction a	...	...	...	...	...	...	...	...	...	...	...	...
6 Wholesale and retail trade, restaurants and hotels c	11668	...	51516	...	...	63184	11931	...	52079	...	...	64010
7 Transport, storage and communication	11674	...	8722	...	...	20396	11945	...	12105	...	...	24050
8 Finance, insurance, real estate and business services d	7942	...	42361	...	...	50303	7933	...	43542	...	...	51475
9 Community, social and personal services cde	28589	...	9826	...	...	38415	27928	...	8922	...	...	36850
Total, Industries	170473	...	189120	...	...	359593	166236	...	193546	...	...	359782
Producers of Government Services	58152	...	...	...	...	58152	57348	...	...	...	...	57348
Other Producers e	...	...	...	...	...	...	...	...	...	...	...	...
Total fg	228625	...	189120	...	...	417745	223584	...	193546	...	...	417130
Less: Imputed bank service charge	...	...	...	...	...	...	...	...	...	...	...	...
Import duties	...	...	...	...	...	...	...	...	...	...	...	...
Value added tax	...	...	...	...	...	...	...	...	...	...	...	...
Other adjustments h	...	...	...	46852	2811	44041	...	...	...	43794	3368	40426
Total	228625	...	189120	46852	2811	461786	223584	...	193546	43794	3368	457556

	1984						1985					
	Compensation of Employees	Capital Consumption	Net Operating Surplus	Indirect Taxes	Less: Subsidies Received	Value Added	Compensation of Employees	Capital Consumption	Net Operating Surplus	Indirect Taxes	Less: Subsidies Received	Value Added
						All Producers						
1 Agriculture, hunting, forestry and fishing	1830	...	17516	...	...	19346	1783	...	17592	...	...	19375
2 Mining and quarrying a	14224	...	5436	...	...	19660	14495	...	6263	...	...	20758
3 Manufacturing	75470	...	49236	...	...	124706	76029	...	50900	...	...	126929
4 Electricity, gas and water b	12763	...	12222	...	...	24985	13609	...	8669	...	...	22278
5 Construction a	...	...	...	...	...	...	...	...	...	...	...	...
6 Wholesale and retail trade, restaurants and hotels c	12294	...	53783	...	...	66077	12452	...	54244	...	...	66696
7 Transport, storage and communication	12491	...	10900	...	...	23391	12901	...	11054	...	...	23955
8 Finance, insurance, real estate and business services d	7988	...	45529	...	...	53517	8254	...	48877	...	...	57131
9 Community, social and personal services cde	24778	...	8827	...	...	33605	24885	...	10009	...	...	34894
Total, Industries	161838	...	203449	...	...	365287	164408	...	207608	...	...	372016
Producers of Government Services	56090	...	...	...	...	56090	58534	...	...	...	...	58534
Other Producers e	...	...	...	...	...	...	...	...	...	...	...	...
Total fg	217928	...	203449	...	...	421377	222942	...	207608	...	...	430550
Less: Imputed bank service charge	...	...	...	...	...	...	...	...	...	...	...	...
Import duties	...	...	...	...	...	...	...	...	...	...	...	...
Value added tax	...	...	...	...	...	...	...	...	...	...	...	...
Other adjustments h	...	...	...	43706	4031	39675	...	...	...	49452	4020	45432
Total	217928	...	203449	43706	4031	461052	222942	...	207608	49452	4020	475982

Malta

4.3 Cost Components of Value Added

Thousand Maltese pounds

All Producers

	1986						1987					
	Compensation of Employees	Capital Consumption	Net Operating Surplus	Indirect Taxes	Less: Subsidies Received	Value Added	Compensation of Employees	Capital Consumption	Net Operating Surplus	Indirect Taxes	Less: Subsidies Received	Value Added
1 Agriculture, hunting, forestry and fishing	1774	...	18645	...	...	20419	2054	...	19375	...	...	21429
2 Mining and quarrying a	13676	...	5193	...	...	18869	15518	...	5533	...	...	21051
3 Manufacturing	80856	...	53820	...	...	134676	85879	...	50548	...	...	136427
4 Electricity, gas and water b	13636	...	21068	...	...	34704	15905	...	26214	...	...	42119
5 Construction a	...	...	...	...	...	...	...	...	...	...	...	...
6 Wholesale and retail trade, restaurants and hotels c	12834	...	54813	...	...	67647	13005	...	57842	...	...	70847
7 Transport, storage and communication	12569	...	13671	...	...	26240	14441	...	15763	...	...	30204
8 Finance, insurance, real estate and business services d	8983	...	52272	...	...	61255	10660	...	52122	...	...	62782
9 Community, social and personal services cde	24972	...	10667	...	...	35639	28382	...	13347	...	...	41729
Total, Industries	169300	...	230149	...	...	399449	185844	...	240744	...	...	426588
Producers of Government Services	62317	...	...	...	...	62317	68862	...	...	...	...	68862
Other Producers e	...	...	...	...	...	...	...	...	...	...	...	...
Total fg	231617	...	230149	...	...	461766	254706	...	240744	...	...	495450
Less: Imputed bank service charge	...	...	...	...	...	...	...	...	...	...	...	...
Import duties	...	...	...	...	...	...	...	...	...	...	...	...
Value added tax	...	...	...	...	...	...	...	...	...	...	...	...
Other adjustments h	...	...	...	54885	4782	50103	...	...	...	58595	4874	53721
Total	231617	...	230149	54885	4782	511869	254706	...	240744	58595	4874	549171

All Producers

	1988						1989					
	Compensation of Employees	Capital Consumption	Net Operating Surplus	Indirect Taxes	Less: Subsidies Received	Value Added	Compensation of Employees	Capital Consumption	Net Operating Surplus	Indirect Taxes	Less: Subsidies Received	Value Added
1 Agriculture, hunting, forestry and fishing	2213	...	18895	...	...	21108	2215	...	20140	...	...	22355
2 Mining and quarrying a	16353	...	5000	...	...	21353	16168	...	6089	...	...	22257
3 Manufacturing	88629	...	57928	...	...	146557	91961	...	71702	...	...	163663
4 Electricity, gas and water b	17087	...	34791	...	...	51878	17585	...	36449	...	...	54034
5 Construction a	...	...	...	...	...	...	...	...	...	...	...	...
6 Wholesale and retail trade, restaurants and hotels c	13678	...	63221	...	...	76899	14502	...	70344	...	...	84846
7 Transport, storage and communication	15121	...	19406	...	...	34527	16183	...	18419	...	...	34602
8 Finance, insurance, real estate and business services d	11185	...	58528	...	...	69713	12333	...	67893	...	...	80226
9 Community, social and personal services cde	30933	...	15296	...	...	46229	34551	...	17579	...	...	52130
Total, Industries	195199	...	273065	...	...	468264	205498	...	308615	...	...	514113
Producers of Government Services	74370	...	...	...	...	74370	82736	...	...	...	...	82736
Other Producers e	...	...	...	...	...	...	...	...	...	...	...	...
Total fg	269569	...	273065	...	...	542634	288234	...	308615	...	...	596849
Less: Imputed bank service charge	...	...	...	...	...	...	...	...	...	...	...	...
Import duties	...	...	...	...	...	...	...	...	...	...	...	...
Value added tax	...	...	...	...	...	...	...	...	...	...	...	...
Other adjustments h	...	...	...	69392	5575	63817	...	...	...	79362	6072	73290
Total	269569	...	273065	69392	5575	606451	288234	...	308615	79362	6072	670139

All Producers

	1990					
	Compensation of Employees	Capital Consumption	Net Operating Surplus	Indirect Taxes	Less: Subsidies Received	Value Added
1 Agriculture, hunting, forestry and fishing	2264	...	20273	...	...	22537
2 Mining and quarrying a	15892	...	6990	...	...	22882
3 Manufacturing	100660	...	74974	...	...	175634
4 Electricity, gas and water b	20551	...	32875	...	...	53426

4.3 Cost Components of Value Added
(Continued)

Thousand Maltese pounds

	Compensation of Employees	Capital Consumption	Net Operating Surplus	Indirect Taxes	Less: Subsidies Received	Value Added
	1990					
5 Construction a	...	...	...	...	...	...
6 Wholesale and retail trade, restaurants and hotels c	16457	...	77315	...	...	93772
7 Transport, storage and communication	18502	...	18629	...	...	37131
8 Finance, insurance, real estate and business services d	14551	...	78785	...	...	93336
9 Community, social and personal services cde	37440	...	20760	...	...	58200
Total, Industries	226317	...	330601	...	...	556918
Producers of Government Services	92673	...	-	...	...	92673
Other Producers e	...	...	...	...	...	...
Total fg	318990	...	330601	...	...	649591
Less: Imputed bank service charge	...	...	...	...	...	...
Import duties	...	...	...	...	...	...
Value added tax	...	...	...	...	...	...
Other adjustments h	...	...	...	...	...	85154
Total	318990	...	330601	92155	7001	734745

a) Item 'Construction' is included in item 'Mining and quarrying'.
b) Item 'Electricity, gas and water' refers to all government enterprises.
c) Restaurants and hotels are included in item 'Community, social and personal services'.
d) Business services are included in item 'Community, social and personal services'.
e) Beginning 1980, item 'Other producers' is included in item 'Community, social and personal services'.
f) Gross domestic product in factor values.
g) Column 'Consumption of fixed capital' is included in column 'Net operating surplus'.
h) Item 'Other adjustments' refers to indirect taxes net of subsidies.

Martinique

Source. Reply to the United Nations National Accounts Questionnaire from the Institute national de la statistique et des studes economiques (INSEE), Paris. **General note.** The estimates shown in the following tables have been adjusted by the INSEE to conform to the United Nations System of National Accounts so far as the existing data would permit.

1.1 Expenditure on the Gross Domestic Product, in Current Prices

Million French francs

		1980	1981	1982	1983	1984	1985	1986	1987	1988	1989	1990	1991
1	Government final consumption expenditure	2236.5	2567.9	3039.3	3484.5	3909.4	4206.2	4426.1	4649.3	5035.8	...	...	...
2	Private final consumption expenditure	5499.4	6549.5	8013.4	9160.3	9632.9	10908.5	11730.7	12964.5	14292.8	...	...	...
3	Gross capital formation	1461.5	1460.3	1698.6	2083.4	2061.1	2019.6	2290.3	3586.1	4236.9	...	...	...
	A Increase in stocks	187.4	92.3	13.6	3.6	41.7	-61.4	-158.4	119.6	215.0			
	B Gross fixed capital formation	1274.1	1368.0	1685.0	2079.8	2019.4	2081.0	2448.7	3466.5	4021.9			
4	Exports of goods and services	528.6	894.6	992.8	1261.8	1356.2	1457.7	1502.2	1181.1	1253.2			
5	Less: Imports of goods and services	3624.4	4227.3	4896.4	5723.8	6039.4	6108.4	6125.7	6621.8	7922.6			
	Equals: Gross Domestic Product	6101.6	7245.0	8847.7	10266.2	10920.2	12483.6	13823.6	15759.2	16896.1		...	...

1.3 Cost Components of the Gross Domestic Product

Million French francs

		1980	1981	1982	1983	1984	1985	1986	1987	1988	1989	1990	1991
1	Indirect taxes, net	687.7	790.5	958.6	1078.1	1231.8	1553.2	1612.7	1806.3	2051.1	...	...	...
	A Indirect taxes [a]	775.3	939.2	1123.4	1277.0	1439.0	1742.7	1800.9	2003.1	2251.4	...	...	...
	B Less: Subsidies	87.6	148.7	164.8	198.9	207.2	189.5	188.2	196.8	200.3	...	...	...
2	Consumption of fixed capital [b]	...	...	...	...	...	...	...	...	...			
3	Compensation of employees paid by resident producers to:	4432.1	5092.0	6133.0	7105.7	7782.8	8749.2	9384.6	10307.1	11533.7	...	...	...
4	Operating surplus [b]	981.8	1362.5	1756.1	2082.4	1905.6	2181.2	2826.3	3645.8	3311.3	...	...	...
	Equals: Gross Domestic Product	6101.6	7245.0	8847.7	10266.2	10920.2	12483.6	13823.6	15759.2	16896.1	...	...	...

a) Item 'Subsidies' in table 1.3 includes subsidies from the government and from the rest of the world.
b) Item 'Operating surplus' includes consumption of fixed capital.

1.4 General Government Current Receipts and Disbursements

Million French francs

		1980	1981	1982	1983	1984	1985	1986	1987	1988	1989	1990	1991
	Receipts												
1	Operating surplus	...	...	...	...	...	...	...	...	...	...	...	...
2	Property and entrepreneurial income	43.6	67.2	64.2	64.2	78.7	82.4	65.6	61.6	67.6	...	...	...
3	Taxes, fees and contributions	2313.2	2767.3	3378.7	4028.5	4611.7	5083.5	5452.6	6000.1	6623.6	...	...	...
4	Other current transfers	2595.3	2946.9	3442.4	3563.6	3768.2	4089.9	4613.4	4495.9	4887.8	...	...	...
	Total Current Receipts of General Government	4952.1	5781.4	6885.3	7656.3	8458.6	9255.8	10131.6	10557.6	11579.0	...	...	...
	Disbursements												
1	Government final consumption expenditure	2236.5	2567.9	3039.3	3484.5	3909.4	4206.1	4426.1	4649.3	5035.8	...	...	...
2	Property income	64.6	97.4	119.4	147.5	172.2	196.1	235.7	270.7	306.7	...	...	...
3	Subsidies [a]	61.7	89.9	106.5	112.7	136.2	167.2	173.4	181.4	198.6	...	...	...
4	Other current transfers	1938.6	2414.1	2942.8	3408.9	3742.1	3990.7	4507.8	4762.8	5200.6	...	...	...
5	Net saving	650.7	612.1	677.3	502.7	498.7	695.7	788.6	693.4	837.3	...	...	...
	Total Current Disbursements and Net Saving of General Government	4952.1	5781.4	6885.3	7656.3	8458.6	9255.8	10131.6	10557.6	11579.0	...	...	...

a) Item 'Subsidies' in table 1.3 includes subsidies from the government and from the rest of the world.

1.7 External Transactions on Current Account, Summary

Million French francs

		1980	1981	1982	1983	1984	1985	1986	1987	1988	1989	1990	1991
	Payments to the Rest of the World												
1	Imports of goods and services	3624.4	4227.3	4896.4	5723.8	6039.4	6108.4	6125.7	6621.8	7922.6	...	...	...
2	Factor income to the rest of the world	213.4	275.3	322.3	402.1	448.5	562.6	595.1	682.8	723.9	...	...	...
	A Compensation of employees	-	-	-	-	-	-	-	-	-	...	...	...
	B Property and entrepreneurial income	213.4	275.3	322.3	402.1	448.5	562.6	595.1	682.8	723.9	...	...	...

1.7 External Transactions on Current Account, Summary
(Continued)

Million French francs

	1980	1981	1982	1983	1984	1985	1986	1987	1988	1989	1990	1991
3 Current transfers to the rest of the world	80.9	104.8	117.9	102.9	101.6	72.9	82.1	90.1	98.0	...	...	...
4 Surplus of the nation on current transactions	-639.3	-513.2	-617.0	-1075.2	-1153.3	-1023.8	-500.8	-1503.3	-2419.8	...	...	...
Payments to the Rest of the World and Surplus of the Nation on Current Transactions	3279.4	4094.2	4719.6	5153.7	5436.2	5720.1	6302.1	5891.4	6324.7	...	...	...
Receipts From The Rest of the World												
1 Exports of goods and services	528.6	894.6	992.8	1261.8	1356.2	1457.7	1502.2	1181.1	1253.2	...	...	...
2 Factor income from rest of the world	114.2	174.7	201.0	212.3	207.9	115.4	140.0	175.9	147.6	...	...	...
A Compensation of employees	-	-	-	-	-	-	-	-	-	...	...	...
B Property and entrepreneurial income	114.2	174.7	201.0	212.3	207.9	115.4	140.0	175.9	147.6	...	...	...
3 Current transfers from rest of the world	2636.6	3024.9	3525.8	3679.6	3872.1	4147.0	4659.9	4534.5	4923.9	...	...	...
Receipts from the Rest of the World on Current Transactions	3279.4	4094.2	4719.6	5153.7	5436.2	5720.1	6302.1	5891.4	6324.7	...	...	...

1.8 Capital Transactions of The Nation, Summary

Million French francs

	1980	1981	1982	1983	1984	1985	1986	1987	1988	1989	1990	1991
Finance of Gross Capital Formation												
Gross saving	822.2	947.0	1081.6	1008.2	907.8	995.8	1789.5	2082.8	1817.2	...	...	...
Less: Surplus of the nation on current transactions	-639.3	-513.3	-617.0	-1075.2	-1153.3	-1023.8	-500.8	-1503.3	-2419.2	...	...	...
Finance of Gross Capital Formation	1461.5	1460.2	1698.6	2083.4	2061.1	2019.6	2290.3	3586.1	4237.0	...	...	...
Gross Capital Formation												
Increase in stocks	187.4	92.2	13.6	3.6	41.7	-61.4	-158.4	119.6	215.0	...	...	...
Gross fixed capital formation	1274.1	1368.1	1685.0	2079.8	2019.4	2081.0	2448.7	3466.5	4021.9	...	...	...
1 General government	498.3	442.5	548.0	469.1	628.3	655.2	687.7	673.2	906.8	...	...	...
2 Corporate and quasi-corporate enterprises	603.5	703.8	864.2	1314.7	1103.7	1038.7	1190.5	2018.1	2318.0	...	...	...
3 Other	172.3	221.8	271.8	296.0	287.4	387.1	570.5	774.6	797.1	...	...	...
Gross Capital Formation	1461.5	1460.2	1698.6	2083.4	2061.1	2019.6	2290.3	3586.1	4236.9	...	...	...

1.10 Gross Domestic Product by Kind of Activity, in Current Prices

Million French francs

	1980	1981	1982	1983	1984	1985	1986	1987	1988	1989	1990	1991
1 Agriculture, hunting, forestry and fishing	372.9	531.2	691.1	871.0	850.8	974.5	1092.1	940.4	1047.4	...	...	...
2 Mining and quarrying	303.5	419.7	527.9	575.8	619.1	752.3	937.3	1232.5	1269.0	...	...	...
3 Manufacturing										...	...	...
4 Electricity, gas and water	97.9	87.8	89.6	125.9	98.9	255.2	537.1	537.3	438.2	...	...	...
5 Construction	225.8	258.5	310.4	410.3	407.1	462.8	550.1	748.6	741.5	...	...	...
6 Wholesale and retail trade, restaurants and hotels	1037.3	1196.3	1478.2	1726.4	1742.5	2094.0	2245.2	2700.3	3186.8	...	...	...
7 Transport, storage and communication	220.3	269.2	372.5	438.2	502.6	600.1	723.4	864.7	953.3	...	...	...
8 Finance, insurance, real estate and business services	427.8	627.6	762.6	780.9	863.7	981.8	1074.7	1337.5	1452.1	...	...	...
9 Community, social and personal services	1118.4	1288.9	1512.9	1741.0	1897.9	2065.7	2214.7	2648.8	2687.0	...	...	...
Total, Industries	3803.9	4679.2	5745.2	6669.5	6982.6	8186.4	9374.6	11010.1	11775.3	...	...	...
Producers of Government Services	1985.6	2254.4	2686.3	3043.7	3386.0	3649.9	3822.1	3995.2	4263.1	...	...	...
Other Producers	115.4	137.4	162.0	188.9	196.2	214.5	208.3	245.9	279.1	...	...	...
Subtotal	5904.9	7071.0	8593.6	9902.1	10564.8	12050.8	13405.0	15251.2	16317.5	...	...	...
Less: Imputed bank service charge	308.6	418.0	479.8	468.2	514.1	553.4	613.9	679.0	781.5	...	...	...
Plus: Import duties	247.5	284.2	344.5	396.7	415.3	478.0	499.2	592.3	697.1	...	...	...
Plus: Value added tax	257.8	307.8	389.5	435.6	454.2	508.2	533.3	594.7	663.0	...	...	...
Equals: Gross Domestic Product	6101.6	7245.0	8847.7	10266.2	10920.2	12483.6	13823.6	15759.2	16896.1	...	...	...

Martinique

1.12 Relations Among National Accounting Aggregates

Million French francs

	1980	1981	1982	1983	1984	1985	1986	1987	1988	1989	1990	1991
Gross Domestic Product	6101.6	7245.0	8847.7	10266.2	10920.2	12483.6	13823.6	15759.2	16896.1	...	...	...
Plus: Net factor income from the rest of the world	-99.2	-100.6	-121.3	-189.8	-240.6	-447.2	-455.1	-506.9	-576.3	...	...	...
Factor income from the rest of the world	114.2	174.7	201.0	212.3	207.9	115.4	140.0	175.9	147.6	...	...	...
Less: Factor income to the rest of the world	213.4	275.3	322.3	402.1	448.5	562.6	595.1	682.8	723.9	...	...	...
Equals: Gross National Product	6002.4	7144.4	8726.4	10076.4	10679.6	12036.4	13368.5	15252.3	16319.8	...	...	...
Less: Consumption of fixed capital	...	...	...	...	...	...	...	...	...	...	...	...
Equals: National Income	...	...	...	...	...	...	...	...	...	...	...	...
Plus: Net current transfers from the rest of the world	2555.7	2920.1	3407.9	3576.7	3770.5	4074.1	4577.8	4444.4	4825.9	...	...	...
Current transfers from the rest of the world	2636.6	3024.9	3525.8	3679.6	3872.1	4147.0	4659.9	4534.5	4923.9	...	...	...
Less: Current transfers to the rest of the world	80.9	104.8	117.9	102.9	101.6	72.9	82.1	90.1	98.0	...	...	...
Equals: National Disposable Income	...	...	...	...	...	...	...	...	...	...	...	...
Less: Final consumption	7735.9	9117.4	11052.7	12644.8	13542.3	15114.7	16156.8	17613.8	19328.6	...	...	...
Equals: Net Saving	...	...	...	...	...	...	...	...	...	...	...	...
Less: Surplus of the nation on current transactions	-639.3	-513.3	-617.0	-1075.2	-1153.3	-1023.8	-500.8	-1503.3	-2419.8	...	...	...
Equals: Net Capital Formation	...	...	...	...	...	...	...	...	...	...	...	...

Mauritania

Source. Reply to the United Nations National Accounts Questionnaire from the Direction de la Statistique et des Etudes Economiques, Ministere de la Planification et du Developpement Industriel, Nouakchott. The official estimates are published annually in 'Comptes Economiques'.

General note. The estimates shown in the following tables have been prepared in accordance with the United Nations System of National Accounts so far as the existing data would permit.

1.1 Expenditure on the Gross Domestic Product, in Current Prices

Million Mauritanian ouguiyas

	1980	1981	1982	1983	1984	1985	1986	1987	1988	1989	1990	1991
1 Government final consumption expenditure	9183	9224	9885	10127	10189	11740	8537	9137	10297	...	...	...
2 Private final consumption expenditure	28331	32176	30504	27690	31183	35432	50985	55544	57783	...	...	...
3 Gross capital formation	10200	15925	18708	19682	16280	17071	14486	15089	13368	...	...	...
A Increase in stocks	2400	6353	8108	8317	1580	2051	910	1114	994	...	...	...
B Gross fixed capital formation	7800	9572	10600	11365	14700	15020	13576	13975	12374	...	...	...
4 Exports of goods and services	11566	12128	15434	19675	21006	30954	33092	32487	35681	...	...	...
5 Less: Imports of goods and services	21210	26214	31862	32275	32531	42532	47385	45041	44494	...	...	...
Equals: Gross Domestic Product	38070	43239	42669	44899	46127	52665	59715	67216	72635	...	...	...

1.7 External Transactions on Current Account, Summary

Million Mauritanian ouguiyas

	1980	1981	1982	1983	1984	1985	1986	1987	1988	1989	1990	1991
Payments to the Rest of the World												
1 Imports of goods and services	21210	26214	31862	32275	32531	42532	47385	45041	44494	45852	...	...
A Imports of merchandise c.i.f.	14751	18653	22083	20732	19276	25739	29839	26536	26255	29012	...	...
B Other	6459	7561	9779	11543	13255	16793	17546	18505	18239	16840	...	...
2 Factor income to the rest of the world	1023	2076	1874	2373	1325	5689	6024	3769	4560	3677	...	...
A Compensation of employees	18	16	15	17	10	13	91	91	192	88	...	...
B Property and entrepreneurial income	1005	2060	1859	2356	1315	5676	5933	3678	4368	3589	...	...
3 Current transfers to the rest of the world	2375	1714	2384	2212	2017	2402	3078	3098	3542	3291	...	...
4 Surplus of the nation on current transactions	-6171	-10747	-14324	-11706	-7095	-8470	-13534	-10569	-7174	-1392	...	...
Payments to the Rest of the World and Surplus of the Nation on Current Transactions	18437	19257	21796	25154	28778	42153	42953	41339	45422	51428	...	...
Receipts From The Rest of the World												
1 Exports of goods and services	11566	12128	15434	19675	21006	30954	33092	32487	35681	39987	...	...
A Exports of merchandise f.o.b.	9013	9411	12426	17286	18745	28639	31145	29729	32935	37198	...	...
B Other	2553	2717	3008	2389	2261	2315	1947	2758	2746	2789	...	...
2 Factor income from rest of the world	815	1018	1008	550	595	360	305	317	480	663	...	...
A Compensation of employees	46	46	50	50	55	55	133	133	169	199	...	...
B Property and entrepreneurial income	769	972	958	500	540	305	172	184	311	464	...	...
3 Current transfers from rest of the world	6056	6111	5354	4929	7177	10839	9556	8535	9261	10778	...	...
Receipts from the Rest of the World on Current Transactions	18437	19257	21796	25154	28778	42153	42953	41339	45422	51428	...	...

1.10 Gross Domestic Product by Kind of Activity, in Current Prices

Million Mauritanian ouguiyas

	1980	1981	1982	1983	1984	1985	1986	1987	1988	1989	1990	1991
1 Agriculture, hunting, forestry and fishing	12262	15223	13028	11305	8630	10544	14238	19485	21082	25818	...	...
2 Mining and quarrying	4505	4831	5342	4369	5426	5684	5995	5034	4981	7887	...	...
3 Manufacturing	1997	2337	2408	3685	4049	6033	7001	7283	8483	7782	...	...
4 Electricity, gas and water											...	...
5 Construction	2314	2726	2888	3175	3505	3666	3655	3816	4093	4815	...	...
6 Wholesale and retail trade, restaurants and hotels	3424	3100	3834	4708	6588	6880	7081	7868	8577	...	...	...
7 Transport, storage and communication	2584	2710	3007	3179	3188	3237	2976	3066	3342	3729	...	...
8 Finance, insurance, real estate and business services	2632	2500	2500	2585	3185	3292	3588	3803	3891		...	...
9 Community, social and personal services										...	...	...

Mauritania

1.10 Gross Domestic Product by Kind of Activity, in Current Prices
(Continued)

Million Mauritanian ouguiyas

	1980	1981	1982	1983	1984	1985	1986	1987	1988	1989	1990	1991
Total, Industries	29718	33427	33007	33006	34571	39336	44534	50355	54449	64561	...	...
Producers of Government Services	5943	6938	6166	7720	7400	7492	8930	9947	10620	10925		
Other Producers	...	...	...	...	...				...			
Subtotal a	35661	40365	39173	40726	41971	46828	53464	60302	65069	75486		
Less: Imputed bank service charge	...	...	...	...	...	...	...	...	...	...		
Plus: Import duties	...	...	...	...	...	...	...	...	...	...		
Plus: Value added tax	...	...	...	...	...	...	...	...	...	...		
Plus: Other adjustments b	2409	2874	3496	4173	4156	5837	6251	6914	7566	8034	...	...
Equals: Gross Domestic Product	38070	43239	42669	44899	46127	52665	59715	67216	72635	83520		

a) Gross domestic product in factor values.
b) Item 'Other adjustments' refers to indirect taxes net of subsidies.

1.11 Gross Domestic Product by Kind of Activity, in Constant Prices

Million Mauritanian ouguiyas

	1980	1981	1982	1983	1984	1985	1986	1987	1988	1989	1990	1991
			At constant prices of:									
		1973						1983				
1 Agriculture, hunting, forestry and fishing	3317	4464	3884	3398 / 11305	8378	9989	10749	11305	11629	12329	...	...
2 Mining and quarrying	2189	2336	2115	2127 / 4369	5464	4393	4906	4483	4574	5953	...	...
3 Manufacturing	997	1297	1216	1412 / 3685	3438	4210	4458	4497	4408	4084	...	...
4 Electricity, gas and water											...	
5 Construction	1157	1250	1162	1280 / 3175	3463	3772	4121	4203	4478	4632		
6 Wholesale and retail trade, restaurants and hotels	1712	1670	1706	1803 / 4708	6105	6187	5900	6062	6311	...		
7 Transport, storage and communication	1119	1320	1310	1325 / 3179	3110	2832	2655	2762	2876	3005		
8 Finance, insurance, real estate and business services	1316	-	-	- / 2585	3040	2866	2873	2722	2638	...		
9 Community, social and personal services										...		
Total, Industries	11807	12337	11393	11345 / 33006	32998	34249	35662	36034	36914	39540	...	...
Producers of Government Services	3552	3304	2680	3027 / 7720	7400	6911	8238	9176	9350	9397	...	...
Other Producers	...	...	...	...	...	...	...	...	...	...		
Subtotal	15359a	15641a	14073a	14372a / 40726	40398	41160	43900	45210	46264	48937		
Less: Imputed bank service charge	...	...	...	...	...	...	...	...	...	...		
Plus: Import duties				...								
Plus: Value added tax	...	...	...	...								
Plus: Other adjustments	1456b	1844b	2076b	2179b / 4173	3543	4254	4153	3954	3930	3828		
Equals: Gross Domestic Product	16815	17485	16149	16551 / 44899	43941	45414	48053	49164	50194	52764		

a) Gross domestic product in factor values.
b) Item 'Other adjustments' refers to indirect taxes net of subsidies.

1.12 Relations Among National Accounting Aggregates

Million Mauritanian ouguiyas

	1980	1981	1982	1983	1984	1985	1986	1987	1988	1989	1990	1991
Gross Domestic Product	38070	43239	42669	44899	46127	52665	59715	67216	72635	83520	...	...
Plus: Net factor income from the rest of the world	-208	-1058	-866	-1823	-730	-5329	-5719	-3452	-4080	-3014		
Factor income from the rest of the world	815	1018	1008	550	595	360	305	317	480	663	...	...
Less: Factor income to the rest of the world	1023	2076	1874	2373	1325	5689	6024	3769	4560	3677		
Equals: Gross National Product	37862	42181	41803	43076	45397	47336	53996	63764	68555	80506		
Less: Consumption of fixed capital	...	...	...	...	...	...	...	...	...	...		

1.12 Relations Among National Accounting Aggregates
(Continued)

Million Mauritanian ouguiyas

	1980	1981	1982	1983	1984	1985	1986	1987	1988	1989	1990	1991
Equals: National Income [a]	37862	42181	41803	43076	45397	47336	53996	63764	68555	80506	...	...
Plus: Net current transfers from the rest of the world	3681	4397	2970	2717	5160	8437	6478	5437	5719	7487	...	...
Current transfers from the rest of the world	6056	6111	5354	4929	7177	10839	9556	8535	9261	10778		
Less: Current transfers to the rest of the world	2375	1714	2384	2212	2017	2402	3078	3098	3542	3291	...	
Equals: National Disposable Income [b]	41543	46578	44773	45793	50557	55773	60474	69201	74274	87993	...	...
Less: Final consumption	37514	41400	40389	37817	41372	47172	59522	64681	68080		...	
Equals: Net Saving	4029	5178	4384	7976	9185	8601	952	4520	6194	...		
Less: Surplus of the nation on current transactions	-6171	-10747	-14324	-11706	-7095	-8470	-13534	-10569	-7174	-1392	...	
Equals: Net Capital Formation	10200	15925	18708	19682	16280	17071	14486	15089	13368		...	...

a) Item 'National income' includes consumption of fixed capital.
b) Item 'National disposable income' includes consumption of fixed capital.

2.17 Exports and Imports of Goods and Services, Detail

Million Mauritanian ouguiyas

	1980	1981	1982	1983	1984	1985	1986	1987	1988	1989	1990	1991
Exports of Goods and Services												
1 Exports of merchandise, f.o.b.	9013	9411	12426	17286	18745	28639	31145	29729	32935	...		...
2 Transport and communication	725	1001	1046	566	559	679	544	679	547	...		...
A In respect of merchandise imports	1	-	-	-	-	-	-	-	-	...	...	...
B Other	724	1001	1046	566	559	679	544	679	547	...	...	...
3 Insurance service charges	...	...	...	...	...	...	...	...	...	...	...	...
4 Other commodities	99	435	693	922	593	388	383	455	539	...	...	...
5 Adjustments of merchandise exports to change-of-ownership basis	-	-	-	-	-	-	-	-	-	...	...	...
6 Direct purchases in the domestic market by non-residential households	1420	960	840	519	670	845	434	604	760	...	...	...
7 Direct purchases in the domestic market by extraterritorial bodies	309	321	429	382	439	403	586	1020	900	...	...	...
Total Exports of Goods and Services	11566	12128	15434	19675	21006	30954	33092	32487	35681	...	...	...
Imports of Goods and Services												
1 Imports of merchandise, c.i.f.	14751	18653	22083	20732	19276	25739	29839	26536	26255	29012	...	...
A Imports of merchandise, f.o.b.	14751	18653	22083	20732	19276	25739	29839	26536	26255	29012	...	
B Transport of services on merchandise imports	...	...	...	...	...	...	...	...	...	...		
C Insurance service charges on merchandise imports	...	...	...	...	...	...	...	...	...	...		
2 Adjustments of merchandise imports to change-of-ownership basis	...	...	...	...	...	...	...	...	...	...		
3 Other transport and communication	3689	4488	4708	5863	6421	10293	9623	8737	9196	8431	...	...
4 Other insurance service charges											...	...
5 Other commodities	1584	2145	3617	4366	5194	4979	6398	7765	7006	5656	...	...
6 Direct purchases abroad by government	587	245	497	354	791	459	463	483	659	584	...	...
7 Direct purchases abroad by resident households	599	683	957	960	849	1062	1062	1520	1378	2169	...	...
Total Imports of Goods and Services	21210	26214	31862	32275	32531	42532	47385	45041	44494	45852	...	...
Balance of Goods and Services	-9644	-14086	-16428	-12600	-11525	-11578	-14293	-12554	-8813	...	...	...
Total Imports and Balance of Goods and Services	11566	12128	15434	19675	21006	30954	33092	32487	35681	...	...	...

Mauritius

General note. The preparation of national accounts statistics in Mauritius is undertaken by the Central statistical Office, Rose Hill. The official estimates are published periodically in 'National Accounts of Mauritius'. The following presentation on sources and methods is mainly based on information received from the central Statistical Office. The estimates are generally in accordance with the Clasifications and definitions recommended in the United Nations System of National Accounts (SNA). The following tables have been prepared from successive replies to the United Nations national accounts questionnaire. When the scope and coverage of the estimates differ for conceptual or statistical reasons from the definitions and classifications recommended in SNA, a footnote is indicated to the relevant tables.

Sources and methods :

(a) Gross domestic product. Gross domestic product is estimated mainly through the production approach.

(b) Expenditure on the gross domestic product. The expenditure approach is used to estimate government final consumption expenditure and exports and imports of goods and services. This approach, in combination with the commodity-flow approach is used to estimate gross fixed capital formation. The commodity-flow approach is used for private final consumption expenditure supplemented by the expenditure approach for expenditure on services. Government consumption expenditure is estimated on the basis of the annual financial reports of the government and the municipal and town councils. The sources of data for private expenditure on goods include the 1990 census of population, the 1985/86 household budget survey, the annual trade reports of the Customs Department, the annual financial reports of the government and special surveys of wholesale and retail margins, costs and profits. Figures of imported goods are extracted and reclassified from the foreign trade statistics and added to the figures for local production, both valued at market prices. Expenditure on services and private expenditure abroad are estimated on the basis of data from financial reports of the government, the censuses, records of income Tax Office and annual reports of the Ministry of Education. Information of investment on new buildings is obtained from records of building permits issued, records of the municipal and town councils and from returns of industrial and building companies. Investment on plantations is estimated from the returns of agricultural concerns and reports of the Chamber of Agriculture and the Tobacco Board. For machinery and equipment, figures on imports are derived from the annual trade reports and returns from industrial firms. Charges for transport, trade margins and installation costs are added to the c.i.f. values. Domestic production figures are obtained from the annual returns of manufacturing firms. Estimates of exports and imports of goods and services are based on sources such as the annual trade reports of the Customs Department, monthly returns from banks, records of Post Office and balance-of-payments. Current price estimates of the different components of GDP from the expenditure side are deflated by appropriate indices and added to obtain GDP at constant price. All discrepancies with GDP at constant price obtained from the production approach are included in increase in stock.

(c) Cost-structure of the gross domestic product. Information on compensation of employees for large establishments of all sectors, except the sugar industry is available from questionnaires sent out in connexion with the census of production and income tax returns. For the sugar sector, detailed figures of payments in cash and in kind are supplied by all sugar estates with factories while figures from employment records, statutory wage rates and the quantity of canes produced are used for the remaining sugar industry. Wages and salaries for the public sector are obtained from a bi-annual survey of all government departments and ministries. Operating surplus is estimated through the use of questionnaires and income-tax statistics for the private sector and production accounts for the government sector. No attempt has been made to estimate the consumption of fixed capital because of the lack of data on capital stock. Consequently all aggregates are given on a gross basis. Data on indirect taxes and subsidies are obtained from government and municipal council records.

(d) Gross domestic product by kind of economic activity. The table of GDP by kind of economic activity is prepared in factor values. The production approach is used to estimate value added of most industries. The income approach is used for some private services and for public administration and defence. For the agricultural sector, estimates are made on an item-by-item basis using annual statistical returns, annual surveys and reports supplemented by direct inquiries among producers and distributors. Sources used for sugar production are reports of the Chamber of Agriculture and financial statements of the Mauritius Sugar Syndicate. The estimates for mining and quarrying refer only to salt production and sand quarries and are provided directly by the concerned enterprises. The estimates for manufacturing are obtained through similar methods as those used for the agricultural sector. For sugar and related products, data are obtained from returns furnished by the factories and distilleries, reports and statistics of the Chamber of Agriculture and financial statements of the Mauritius Sugar Syndicate. The estimates of electricity and water are based on information provided by the concerned enterprises and the financial reports of the government. Information on private construction is obtained from records of building permits issued and from the municipal and town councils. Information furnished by the building contractors and financial reports of the government are used for public construction. For trade, information is obtained from the Income Tax Office and from imports and local production statistics. Special questionnaires on receipts and expenditure are sent to large hotel and restaurant enterprises as well as to large transport enterprises. Informatiom on public transport is available from the Accountant-General's records. For the financial sector, the most important sources are the Central Bank, income-tax returns of commercial banks and annual reports of the Registrar of insurance Companies. Special questionnaires are also sent to insurance companies. The estimates for ownership of dwellings are based on the 1990 Housing Census and records of building permits issued. For public administration and de fence, detailed information is available from treasury records. For the private services, information is obtained from the population census and special questionnaires sent to large enterprises. For the constant price estimates, current values are generally deflated by appropriate price indexes. In cases where production is homogeneous, e.g. Sugar production value added is extrapolated by volume indexes.

1.1 Expenditure on the Gross Domestic Product, in Current Prices

Million Mauritius rupees

	1980	1981	1982	1983	1984	1985	1986	1987	1988	1989	1990	1991
1 Government final consumption expenditure	1224	1422	1624	1706	1835	1915	2076	2722	3509	3936	4456	4930
2 Private final consumption expenditure	6562	7269	8301	8874	9841	11118	12000	14395	17215	20850	24840	27500
3 Gross capital formation	1803	2578	2130	2229	3165	3900	4312	5961	8502	9918	11559	12624
A Increase in stocks	-225	338	30	-71	570	800	422	871	512	1353	-306	239
B Gross fixed capital formation	2028	2240	2100	2300	2595	3100	3890	5090	7990	8565	11865	12385
Residential buildings	685	730	735	700	740	730	775	850	1075	1495	2060	2700
Non-residential buildings	223	248	245	277	350	635	660	800	1215	1620	2140	2425
Other construction and land improvement etc.	327	402	480	527	495	425	635	715	915	1025	1370	1450
Other	793	860	640	796	1010	1310	1820	2725	4785	4425	6295	5810
4 Exports of goods and services	4450	4566	5529	5953	6989	8895	11919	15639	18565	21363	25669	27597
5 Less: Imports of goods and services	5342	5626	5859	5999	7470	9210	10607	15141	19988	23802	28534	29901
Equals: Gross Domestic Product	8697	10209	11725	12763	14360	16618	19700	23576	27803	32265	37990	42750

1.2 Expenditure on the Gross Domestic Product, in Constant Prices

Million Mauritius rupees

	1980	1981	1982	1983	1984	1985	1986	1987	1988	1989	1990	1991
		1976		At constant prices of: 1982						1987		
1 Government final consumption expenditure	688	713	727 / 1624	1665	1727	1727	1755	1878 / 2722	2863	2966	3162	3270
2 Private final consumption expenditure	3059	2965	3071 / 8301	8463	8844	9295	9945	11904 / 14395	15633	16759	17595	18207
3 Gross capital formation	988	1213	908 / 2130	2097	2520	2690	3267	4124 / 5961	7300	6948	8392	8187
A Increase in stocks	-132	173	14 / 30	-70	220	160	232	339 / 871	125	278	167	197
B Gross fixed capital formation	1120	1040	894 / 2100	2167	2300	2530	3035	3785 / 5090	7175	6670	8225	7990
Residential buildings	418	382	348 / 735	667	665	630	650	685 / 850	975	1190	1440	1765
Non-residential buildings	130	120	107 / 245	263	310	540	545	630 / 800	1100	1270	1445	1505
Other construction and land improvement etc.	185	189	204 / 480	502	445	365	520	560 / 715	820	815	945	910
Other	387	349	235 / 640	735	880	995	1320	1910 / 2725	4280	3395	4395	3810
4 Exports of goods and services	2843	2701	2971 / 5529	5580	5810	6504	8258	9761 / 15639	17531	18074	19552	20162
5 Less: Imports of goods and services	2733	2462	2265 / 5859	6035	6578	7031	9000	12195 / 15141	18154	18426	20498	20362
Statistical discrepancy	...	...	... / -	-	9	-5	239	462 / -	-	-	-	-
Equals: Gross Domestic Product	4845	5130	5412 / 11725	11770	12332	13180	14464	15934 / 23576	25173	26321	28203	29464

1.3 Cost Components of the Gross Domestic Product

Million Mauritius rupees

	1980	1981	1982	1983	1984	1985	1986	1987	1988	1989	1990	1991
1 Indirect taxes, net	1308	1444	1705	2150	2310	2738	3250	3881	4622	5191	6200	6800
A Indirect taxes	1326	1455	1717	2180	2355	2784	3348	4071	4890	5535	6589	7215
B Less: Subsidies	18	11	12	30	45	46	98	190	268	344	389	415
2 Consumption of fixed capital a	...	...	...	...	...	...	...	...	...	...	...	...
3 Compensation of employees paid by resident producers to:	3953	4482	4972	5400	5915	6570	7365	8895	10915	12815	14890	16975
4 Operating surplus a	3436	4283	5048	5213	6135	7310	9085	10800	12266	14259	16900	18975
A Corporate and quasi-corporate enterprises	...	...	2067	1925	2522	3125	3947	4707	5387	6278	7335	...
B Private unincorporated enterprises	...	...	2939	3227	3546	4093	5040	5990	6800	7940	9500	...
C General government	...	...	43	62	67	92	98	103	79	41	65	...
Equals: Gross Domestic Product	8697	10209	11725	12763	14360	16618	19700	23576	27803	32265	37990	42750

a) Item 'Operating surplus' includes consumption of fixed capital.

1.4 General Government Current Receipts and Disbursements

Million Mauritius rupees

	1980	1981	1982	1983	1984	1985	1986	1987	1988	1989	1990	1991
					Receipts							
1 Operating surplus	...	23	43	62	67	92	98	103	79	41	65	...
2 Property and entrepreneurial income	125	129	176	180	135	303	328	404	425	409	474	...
3 Taxes, fees and contributions	1845	2193	2492	3042	3263	3754	4483	5546	6789	7943	9478	...
A Indirect taxes	1326	1455	1717	2180	2355	2784	3347	4071	4889	5535	6589	...
B Direct taxes	379	464	457	509	529	545	650	918	1223	1544	1967	...
C Social security contributions	115	248	287	322	344	387	432	491	606	782	819	...
D Compulsory fees, fines and penalties	25	26	31	31	35	38	54	66	71	82	103	...

Mauritius

1.4 General Government Current Receipts and Disbursements
(Continued)

Million Mauritius rupees

	1980	1981	1982	1983	1984	1985	1986	1987	1988	1989	1990	1991
4 Other current transfers	3	14	72	29	51	30	30	28	91	134	115	...
Total Current Receipts of General Government	1973	2359	2783	3313	3516	4179	4939	6081	7384	8527	10132	...
Disbursements												
1 Government final consumption expenditure	1224	1422	1624	1706	1835	1915	2076	2722	3509	3936	4456	
A Compensation of employees	1043	1242	1421	1471	1522	1598	1723	2249	2928	3260	3560	
B Consumption of fixed capital	...	...	...	...	...	...	...	...	...	...	...	
C Purchases of goods and services, net	180	180	203	235	313	317	353	473	581	676	896	
D Less: Own account fixed capital formation	...	...	...	...	...	...	...	...	...	...	...	
E Indirect taxes paid, net	...	...	...	...	...	...	...	...	...	...	...	
2 Property income	332	410	866	759	848	929	965	917	897	1161	1454	...
3 Subsidies	18	11	12	30	45	46	98	190	267	344	389	
4 Other current transfers	478	659	825	860	774	880	865	955	1161	1407	1631	
A Social security benefits a	...	328	389	449	503	563	640	724	857	1061	1197	
B Social assistance grants	...											...
C Other	...	331	436	411	271	317	225	231	304	346	434	
Statistical discrepancy	...	...	...	...	...	...	...	...	...	...	11	
5 Net saving	-79	-143	-544	-42	14	409	935	1297	1550	1679	2191	
Total Current Disbursements and Net Saving of General Government	1973	2359	2783	3313	3516	4179	4939	6081	7384	8527	10132	...

a) Item 'Social security benefits' includes unfunded employee welfare benefits.

1.5 Current Income and Outlay of Corporate and Quasi-Corporate Enterprises, Summary

Million Mauritius rupees

	1980	1981	1982	1983	1984	1985	1986	1987	1988	1989	1990	1991
Receipts												
1 Operating surplus	...	...	2067	1925	2522	3125	3947	4707	5387	6278	7335	...
2 Property and entrepreneurial income received	...	...	666	699	740	1156	1313	1934	2727	3826	4723	...
3 Current transfers	...	...	346	396	472	436	441	545	843	1154	1197	...
Total Current Receipts	...	...	3079	3020	3734	4717	5701	7186	8957	11258	13255	...
Disbursements												
1 Property and entrepreneurial income	...	...	777	923	1049	1604	1986	2946	4043	5038	6444	...
2 Direct taxes and other current payments to general government	...	...	181	204	188	233	327	485	653	811	1064	...
3 Other current transfers	...	...	302	363	462	371	349	440	818	1230	1185	...
4 Net saving	...	...	1819	1530	2035	2509	3039	3315	3443	4179	4562	...
Total Current Disbursements and Net Saving	...	...	3079	3020	3734	4717	5701	7186	8957	11258	13255	...

1.6 Current Income and Outlay of Households and Non-Profit Institutions

Million Mauritius rupees

	1980	1981	1982	1983	1984	1985	1986	1987	1988	1989	1990	1991
Receipts												
1 Compensation of employees	...	...	4972	5400	5915	6570	7365	8895	10915	12815	14890	...
2 Operating surplus of private unincorporated enterprises	...	...	2939	3227	3546	4093	5040	5990	6800	7940	9500	
3 Property and entrepreneurial income	...	...	419	473	576	629	841	1513	1764	2370	3154	...
4 Current transfers	...	...	1052	1156	1162	1333	1369	1633	2364	2775	3189	...
A Social security benefits a	...	...	389	449	503	563	640	724	857	1061	1197	...
B Social assistance grants	...	...										...
C Other	...	...	663	707	659	770	729	909	1507	1714	1992	...
Total Current Receipts	...	...	9382	10256	11199	12625	14615	18031	21843	25900	30733	...
Disbursements												
1 Private final consumption expenditure	...	...	8301	8874	9841	11118	12000	14395	17215	20850	24840	...

Mauritius

1.6 Current Income and Outlay of Households and Non-Profit Institutions
(Continued)

Million Mauritius rupees

	1980	1981	1982	1983	1984	1985	1986	1987	1988	1989	1990	1991
2 Property income	...	...	110	161	180	255	260	520	569	696	792	...
3 Direct taxes and other current transfers n.e.c. to general government	...	...	595	658	720	737	809	990	1247	1597	1825	...
A Social security contributions	...	...	287	322	344	387	432	491	606	782	819	...
B Direct taxes	...	...	283	311	348	320	334	446	584	749	924	...
C Fees, fines and penalties	...	...	25	25	28	30	43	53	57	66	82	...
4 Other current transfers	...	...	122	147	146	194	217	293	316	346	426	...
5 Net saving	...	...	254	416	312	321	1329	1833	2496	2411	2850	...
Total Current Disbursements and Net Saving	...	...	9382	10256	11199	12625	14615	18031	21843	25900	30733	...

a) Item 'Social security benefits' includes unfunded employee welfare benefits.

1.7 External Transactions on Current Account, Summary

Million Mauritius rupees

	1980	1981	1982	1983	1984	1985	1986	1987	1988	1989	1990	1991
Payments to the Rest of the World												
1 Imports of goods and services	5342	5626	5859	5999	7470	9210	10607	15141	19988	23802	28534	29901
A Imports of merchandise c.i.f.	4661	4922	5008	5164	6528	8083	9292	13113	17191	20189	24008	24620
B Other	681	704	851	835	942	1127	1315	2028	2797	3613	4526	5281
2 Factor income to the rest of the world	216	470	541	514	666	730	805	713	950	1081	1170	1203
A Compensation of employees	-	-	-	-	-	-	-	-	-	-	-	-
B Property and entrepreneurial income	216	470	541	514	666	730	805	713	950	1081	1170	1203
3 Current transfers to the rest of the world	60	64	53	80	75	76	85	118	145	145	175	271
4 Surplus of the nation on current transactions	-911	-1321	-457	-237	-716	-459	1253	815	-770	-1593	-1766	-936
Payments to the Rest of the World and Surplus of the Nation on Current Transactions	4707	4839	5996	6356	7495	9557	12750	16787	20313	23435	28113	30439
Receipts From The Rest of the World												
1 Exports of goods and services	4450	4566	5529	5953	6989	8895	11919	15639	18565	21363	25669	27597
A Exports of merchandise f.o.b.	3332	2999	3985	4346	5201	6639	9056	11493	13455	15166	17914	18696
B Other	1118	1567	1544	1607	1788	2256	2863	4146	5110	6197	7755	8901
2 Factor income from rest of the world	38	62	43	29	40	30	76	180	357	778	831	1292
A Compensation of employees	-	-	-	-	-	-	-	-	-	-	-	-
B Property and entrepreneurial income	38	62	43	29	40	30	76	180	357	778	831	1292
3 Current transfers from rest of the world	219	211	424	374	466	632	755	968	1391	1294	1613	1550
Receipts from the Rest of the World on Current Transactions	4707	4839	5996	6356	7495	9557	12750	16787	20313	23435	28113	30439

1.10 Gross Domestic Product by Kind of Activity, in Current Prices

Million Mauritius rupees

	1980	1981	1982	1983	1984	1985	1986	1987	1988	1989	1990	1991
1 Agriculture, hunting, forestry and fishing	914	1257	1530	1465	1736	2123	2510	2884	3067	3370	3895	4060
2 Mining and quarrying	15	16	17	18	19	20	22	25	27	30	37	43
3 Manufacturing	1127	1377	1560	1678	2183	2864	3830	4841	5627	6365	7461	8325
4 Electricity, gas and water	209	188	260	245	296	397	462	490	517	577	507	775
5 Construction	561	588	625	655	690	775	880	1045	1370	1735	2220	2590
6 Wholesale and retail trade, restaurants and hotels	1050	1219	1290	1455	1640	1834	2300	2962	3785	4540	5455	6100
7 Transport, storage and communication	837	997	1112	1230	1372	1510	1775	2075	2365	2949	3490	4200
8 Finance, insurance, real estate and business services a	1416	1635	1883	2044	2232	2446	2641	2887	3275	3954	4752	5380
9 Community, social and personal services	361	442	525	569	593	624	674	748	895	1093	1376	1637
Total, Industries	6490	7719	8802	9359	10761	12593	15094	17957	20928	24613	29193	33110
Producers of Government Services	952	1104	1275	1327	1379	1447	1560	2035	2680	2987	3262	3600

Mauritius

1.10 Gross Domestic Product by Kind of Activity, in Current Prices
(Continued)

Million Mauritius rupees

	1980	1981	1982	1983	1984	1985	1986	1987	1988	1989	1990	1991
Other Producers	54	60	71	81	92	96	102	108	125	167	187	240
Subtotal [b]	7496	8883	10148	10767	12232	14136	16756	20100	23733	27767	32642	36950
Less: Imputed bank service charge [a]	107	118	128	154	182	256	306	405	552	693	852	1000
Plus: Import duties	...	...	...	...	...	...	...	...	...	...	...	...
Plus: Value added tax	...	...	...	...	...	...	...	...	...	...	...	...
Plus: Other adjustments [c]	1308	1444	1705	2150	2310	2738	3250	3881	4622	5191	6200	6800
Equals: Gross Domestic Product	8697	10209	11725	12763	14360	16618	19700	23576	27803	32265	37990	42750

a) Item 'Less: Imputed bank service charge' is netted out of item 'Finance, insurance, real estate and business services'.   b) Gross domestic product in factor values.   c) Item 'Other adjustments' refers to indirect taxes net of subsidies.

1.11 Gross Domestic Product by Kind of Activity, in Constant Prices

Million Mauritius rupees

	1980	1981	1982	1983	1984	1985	1986	1987	1988	1989	1990	1991
		1976	At constant prices of: 1982							1987		
1 Agriculture, hunting, forestry and fishing	643	784	936 / 1530	1331	1341	1492	1652	1601 / 2884	2732	2518	2764	2745
2 Mining and quarrying	7	7	7 / 17	17	17	17	18	19 / 25	26	27	29	31
3 Manufacturing	701	762	802 / 1560	1576	1768	2038	2450	2810 / 4841	5225	5478	5901	6237
4 Electricity, gas and water	97	97	117 / 250	243	267	315	343	360 / 490	509	569	581	636
5 Construction	307	292	280 / 625	633	646	698	768	834 / 1045	1223	1357	1527	1649
6 Wholesale and retail trade, restaurants and hotels	558	568	542 / 1290	1373	1455	1527	1677	2016 / 2962	3305	3552	3754	3912
7 Transport, storage and communication	423	434	454 / 1112	1151	1209	1260	1345	1486 / 2075	2262	2443	2580	2711
8 Finance, insurance, real estate and business services [a]	761	794	831 / 1765	1812	1872	1935	1993	2076 / 2482	2599	2778	2981	3144
9 Community, social and personal services	252	265	286 / 596	627	646	652	675	709 / 748	790	841	908	980
Total, Industries	3749	4003	4255 / 8745	8763	9221	9934	10921	11911 / 17552	18671	19563	21025	22045
Producers of Government Services	569	591	604 / 1275	1300	1320	1330	1343	1383 / 2035	2116	2193	2292	2360
Other Producers	...	...	... / ...	...	...	...	...	108	117	125	135	147
Subtotal [b]	4318	4594	4859 / 10020	10063	10541	11264	12264	13294 / 19695	20904	21881	23452	24552
Less: Imputed bank service charge [a]	...	...	... / ...	...	...	...	...	... / ...	...	...	...	...
Plus: Import duties	...	...	... / ...	...	...	...	...	... / ...	...	...	...	...
Plus: Value added tax	...	...	... / ...	...	...	...	...	... / ...	...	...	...	...
Plus: Other adjustments [c]	527	536	553 / 1705	1707	1791	1916	2200	2640 / 3881	4269	4440	4751	4912
Equals: Gross Domestic Product	4845	5130	5412 / 11725	11770	12332	13180	14464	15934 / 23576	25173	26321	28203	29464

a) Item 'Less: Imputed bank service charge' is netted out of item 'Finance, insurance, real estate and business services'.   b) Gross domestic product in factor values.   c) Item 'Other adjustments' refers to indirect taxes net of subsidies.

Mauritius

1.12 Relations Among National Accounting Aggregates

Million Mauritius rupees

	1980	1981	1982	1983	1984	1985	1986	1987	1988	1989	1990	1991
Gross Domestic Product	8697	10209	11725	12763	14360	16618	19700	23576	27803	32265	37990	42750
Plus: Net factor income from the rest of the world	-178	-408	-498	-485	-626	-700	-729	-533	-593	-303	-339	89
Factor income from the rest of the world	38	62	43	29	40	30	76	180	357	778	831	1292
Less: Factor income to the rest of the world	216	470	541	514	666	730	805	713	950	1081	1170	1203
Equals: Gross National Product	8519	9801	11227	12278	13734	15918	18971	23043	27210	31962	37651	42839
Less: Consumption of fixed capital	...	...	...	...	...	...	...	...	...	...	...	...
Equals: National Income a	8519	9801	11227	12278	13734	15918	18971	23043	27210	31962	37651	42839
Plus: Net current transfers from the rest of the world	159	147	371	294	391	556	670	850	1246	1149	1438	1279
Current transfers from the rest of the world	219	211	424	374	466	632	755	968	1391	1294	1613	1550
Less: Current transfers to the rest of the world	60	64	53	80	75	76	85	118	145	145	175	271
Equals: National Disposable Income b	8678	9948	11598	12572	14125	16474	19641	23893	28456	33111	39089	44118
Less: Final consumption	7786	8691	9925	10580	11676	13033	14076	17117	20724	24786	29296	32430
Equals: Net Saving c	892	1257	1673	1992	2449	3441	5565	6776	7732	8325	9793	11688
Less: Surplus of the nation on current transactions	-911	-1321	-457	-237	-716	-459	1253	815	-770	-1593	-1766	-936
Equals: Net Capital Formation d	1803	2578	2130	2229	3165	3900	4312	5961	8502	9918	11559	12624

a) Item 'National income' includes consumption of fixed capital.
b) Item 'National disposable income' includes consumption of fixed capital.
c) Item 'Net saving' includes consumption of fixed capital.
d) Data in this table have been revised, therefore they are not strictly comparable with the unrevised data in the other tables.

2.1 Government Final Consumption Expenditure by Function, in Current Prices

Million Mauritius rupees

	1980	1981	1982	1983	1984	1985	1986	1987	1988	1989	1990	1991
1 General public services	147	173	208	215	254	298	327	390	580	594	725	788
2 Defence	22	27	34	34	42	38	42	61	64	87	144	175
3 Public order and safety	157	171	193	208	221	247	269	361	473	586	625	739
4 Education	299	349	384	435	419	440	476	620	788	925	936	1027
5 Health	228	256	283	296	328	336	364	479	575	662	760	793
6 Social security and welfare	27	29	30	37	48	56	63	49	85	93	113	126
7 Housing and community amenities	84	90	105	116	105	72	79	173	196	196	219	266
8 Recreational, cultural and religious affairs	23	26	36	32	34	35	39	49	70	79	94	157
9 Economic services	237	301	351	333	384	393	417	540	678	714	839	859
A Fuel and energy	1	1	1	1	1	1	1	2	5	4	3	4
B Agriculture, forestry, fishing and hunting	82	88	135	123	145	169	178	224	304	316	359	375
C Mining, manufacturing and construction, except fuel and energy	108	160	172	167	172	164	177	174	209	215	273	287
D Transportation and communication	3	4	5	7	8	8	9	63	80	88	102	108
E Other economic affairs	43	48	38	35	58	51	52	77	80	91	102	85
10 Other functions	-	-	-	-	-	-	-	-	-	-	-	-
Total Government Final Consumption Expenditure	1224	1422	1624	1706	1835	1915	2076	2722	3509	3936	4455	4930

2.3 Total Government Outlays by Function and Type

Million Mauritius rupees

	Final Consumption Expenditures Total	Compensation of Employees	Other	Subsidies	Other Current Transfers & Property Income	Total Current Disbursements	Gross Capital Formation	Other Capital Outlays	Total Outlays
					1982				
1 General public services	208	141	67	4	9	221	...	...	...
2 Defence	34	28	6	-	-	34	...	...	...
3 Public order and safety	193	181	12	-	-	193	...	...	...
4 Education	384	368	16	-	130	514	...	...	...
5 Health	283	231	52	-	2	285	...	...	...
6 Social security and welfare	30	32	-2	-	392	422	...	...	...
7 Housing and community amenities	105	93	13	-	2	107	...	...	...
8 Recreation, culture and religion	36	30	6	3	5	44	...	...	...
9 Economic services	351	318	33	5	285	641	...	...	...

Mauritius

Million Mauritius rupees

	Final Consumption Expenditures			Subsidies	Other Current Transfers & Property Income	Total Current Disbursements	Gross Capital Formation	Other Capital Outlays	Total Outlays
	Total	Compensation of Employees	Other						
A Fuel and energy	1	1	-	-	-	1	...	...	...
B Agriculture, forestry, fishing and hunting	135	132	3	-	2	137	...	...	...
C Mining (except fuels), manufacturing and construction	172	149	23	5	-	177	...	...	...
D Transportation and communication	5	5	-	-	-	5	...	...	...
E Other economic affairs	38	31	7	-	283	321	...	...	...
10 Other functions	-	-	-	-	866	866	...	...	...
Total	1624	1421	203	12	1691	3327	...	...	...
1983									
1 General public services	215	148	67	-	9	224	...	...	...
2 Defence	34	30	4	-	-	34	...	...	...
3 Public order and safety	208	187	21	-	-	208	...	...	...
4 Education	435	387	48	-	125	560	...	...	...
5 Health	296	238	58	-	1	297	...	...	...
6 Social security and welfare	37	37	-	-	452	489	...	...	...
7 Housing and community amenities	116	106	10	-	1	117	...	...	...
8 Recreation, culture and religion	32	25	7	3	6	41	...	...	...
9 Economic services	333	313	20	27	266	627	...	...	...
A Fuel and energy	1	1	-	-	1	2	...	...	...
B Agriculture, forestry, fishing and hunting	123	128	-5	15	7	146	...	...	...
C Mining (except fuels), manufacturing and construction	167	145	22	8	-	175	...	...	...
D Transportation and communication	7	7	-	4	-	11	...	...	...
E Other economic affairs	35	32	3	-	258	293	...	...	...
10 Other functions	-	-	-	-	759	759	...	...	...
Total	1706	1471	235	30	1619	3355	...	...	...
1984									
1 General public services	254	162	92	-	18	272	...	...	...
2 Defence	42	31	11	-	-	42	...	...	...
3 Public order and safety	221	196	25	-	-	221	...	...	...
4 Education	419	393	26	-	144	563	...	...	...
5 Health	328	242	86	-	2	330	...	...	...
6 Social security and welfare	48	40	8	-	507	555	...	...	...
7 Housing and community amenities	105	96	9	-	9	114	...	...	...
8 Recreation, culture and religion	34	27	7	3	7	44	...	...	...
9 Economic services	384	335	49	42	87	513	...	...	...
A Fuel and energy	1	1	-	-	1	2	...	...	...
B Agriculture, forestry, fishing and hunting	145	148	-3	26	8	179	...	...	...
C Mining (except fuels), manufacturing and construction	172	146	26	11	-	183	...	...	...
D Transportation and communication	8	7	1	5	1	14	...	...	...
E Other economic affairs	58	33	25	-	77	135	...	...	...
10 Other functions	-	-	-	-	848	848	...	...	...
Total	1835	1522	313	45	1622	3502	...	...	...
1985									
1 General public services	298	195	103	-	10	308	...	...	...
2 Defence	38	31	7	-	-	38	...	...	...
3 Public order and safety	247	214	33	-	-	247	...	...	...
4 Education	440	414	26	-	147	587	...	...	...
5 Health	336	248	88	-	4	340	...	...	...
6 Social security and welfare	56	48	8	-	563	619	...	...	...
7 Housing and community amenities	72	70	2	9	1	82	...	...	...
8 Recreation, culture and religion	35	26	9	2	7	44	...	...	...
9 Economic services	393	352	41	35	148	576	...	...	...

2.3 Total Government Outlays by Function and Type
(Continued)

Million Mauritius rupees

	Final Consumption Expenditures			Subsidies	Other Current Transfers & Property Income	Total Current Disbursements	Gross Capital Formation	Other Capital Outlays	Total Outlays
	Total	Compensation of Employees	Other						
A Fuel and energy	1	1	-	-	1	2	...	...	...
B Agriculture, forestry, fishing and hunting	169	161	8	24	4	197	...	...	...
C Mining (except fuels), manufacturing and construction	164	149	15	5	-	169	...	...	...
D Transportation and communication	8	7	1	6	5	19	...	...	...
E Other economic affairs	51	34	17	-	138	189	...	...	...
10 Other functions	-	-	-	-	929	929	...	...	...
Total	1915	1598	317	46	1809	3770	...	...	...
1986									
1 General public services	327	208	119		17	344	...	...	...
2 Defence	42	32	10	-	-	42	...	...	...
3 Public order and safety	269	233	36	-	-	269	...	...	...
4 Education	476	446	30	-	147	623	...	...	...
5 Health	364	272	92	-	3	367	...	...	...
6 Social security and welfare	63	51	12	-	640	703	...	...	...
7 Housing and community amenities	79	76	3	9	-	88	...	...	...
8 Recreation, culture and religion	39	27	12	2	7	48	...	...	...
9 Economic services	417	378	39	87	51	555	...	...	...
A Fuel and energy	1	1	-	-	2	3	...	...	...
B Agriculture, forestry, fishing and hunting	180	176	4	77	1	254	...	...	...
C Mining (except fuels), manufacturing and construction	177	162	15	6	1	184	...	...	...
D Transportation and communication	9	8	1	6	1	16	...	...	...
E Other economic affairs	52	33	19	-	46	98	...	...	...
10 Other functions	-	-	-	-	965	965	...	...	...
Total	2076	1723	353	98	1830	4004	...	...	...
1987									
1 General public services	390	257	133		20	410	...	...	...
2 Defence	61	43	18	-	-	61	...	...	...
3 Public order and safety	361	312	49	-	2	363	...	...	...
4 Education	620	579	41	-	166	786	...	...	...
5 Health	479	363	116	-	3	482	...	...	...
6 Social security and welfare	49	39	10	-	732	781	...	...	...
7 Housing and community amenities	173	136	37	11	7	191	...	...	...
8 Recreation, culture and religion	49	36	13	2	9	60	...	...	...
9 Economic services	540	484	56	177	16	733	...	...	...
A Fuel and energy	2	2	-	-	2	4	...	...	...
B Agriculture, forestry, fishing and hunting	224	219	5	115	4	343	...	...	...
C Mining (except fuels), manufacturing and construction	174	176	-2	7	1	182	...	...	...
D Transportation and communication	63	47	16	5	6	74	...	...	...
E Other economic affairs	77	40	37	50	3	130	...	...	...
10 Other functions	-	-	-	-	917	917	...	...	...
Total	2722	2249	473	190	1872	4784	...	...	...
1988									
1 General public services	580	410	170	-	22	602	...	...	...
2 Defence	64	56	8	-	-	64	...	...	...
3 Public order and safety	473	408	65	-	6	479	...	...	...
4 Education	788	729	59	-	227	1015	...	...	...
5 Health	575	448	127	-	4	579	...	...	...
6 Social security and welfare	85	68	17	-	865	950	...	...	...
7 Housing and community amenities	196	158	38	11	-	207	...	...	...
8 Recreation, culture and religion	70	51	19	2	11	83	...	...	...
9 Economic services	678	600	78	254	26	958	...	...	...

Mauritius

Million Mauritius rupees

		Final Consumption Expenditures			Subsidies	Other Current Transfers & Property Income	Total Current Disbursements	Gross Capital Formation	Other Capital Outlays	Total Outlays
		Total	Compensation of Employees	Other						
A	Fuel and energy	5	3	2	-	-	5	...	...	...
B	Agriculture, forestry, fishing and hunting	304	280	24	106	15	425	...	...	...
C	Mining (except fuels), manufacturing and construction	209	204	5	9	-	218	...	...	...
D	Transportation and communication	80	60	20	10	1	91	...	...	...
E	Other economic affairs	80	53	27	129	10	219	...	...	...
10	Other functions	-	-	-	-	897	897	...	...	...
	Total	3509	2928	581	267	2058	5834	...	...	...
				1989						
1	General public services	594	407	187	3	20	617	...	...	...
2	Defence	87	59	28	-	-	87	...	...	...
3	Public order and safety	586	491	95	-	6	592	...	...	...
4	Education	925	857	68	-	281	1206	...	...	...
5	Health	662	522	140	-	6	668	...	...	...
6	Social security and welfare	93	78	15	-	1068	1161	...	...	...
7	Housing and community amenities	196	151	45	12	-	208	...	...	...
8	Recreation, culture and religion	79	57	22	2	13	94	...	...	...
9	Economic services	714	638	76	327	14	1055	...	...	...
A	Fuel and energy	4	2	2	-	-	4	...	...	...
B	Agriculture, forestry, fishing and hunting	316	299	17	73	2	391	...	...	...
C	Mining (except fuels), manufacturing and construction	215	213	2	11	1	227	...	...	...
D	Transportation and communication	88	66	22	13	1	102	...	...	...
E	Other economic affairs	91	58	33	230	10	331	...	...	...
10	Other functions	-	-	-	-	1161	1161	...	...	...
	Total	3936	3260	676	344	2569	6849	...	...	...
				1990						
1	General public services	725	506	219	4	30	759	...	...	...
2	Defence	144	67	77	-	-	144	...	...	...
3	Public order and safety	625	533	92	-	5	630	...	...	...
4	Education	936	861	75	-	358	1294	...	...	...
5	Health	760	565	195	-	3	763	...	...	...
6	Social security and welfare	113	92	21	-	1209	1322	...	...	...
7	Housing and community amenities	219	165	54	10	1	230	...	...	...
8	Recreation, culture and religion	94	64	30	2	6	102	...	...	...
9	Economic services	839	707	132	373	19	1231	...	...	...
A	Fuel and energy	3	3	-	-	4	7	...	...	...
B	Agriculture, forestry, fishing and hunting	359	332	27	78	3	440	...	...	...
C	Mining (except fuels), manufacturing and construction	273	251	22	18	-	291	...	...	...
D	Transportation and communication	102	68	34	19	2	123	...	...	...
E	Other economic affairs	102	53	49	258	10	370	...	...	...
10	Other functions	-	-	-	-	1454	1454	...	...	...
	Total	4455	3560	895	389	3085	7929	...	...	...
				1991						
1	General public services	788	532	256	5	40	833	...	...	...
2	Defence	175	85	90	-	-	175	...	...	...
3	Public order and safety	739	627	112	-	5	744	...	...	...
4	Education	1027	925	102	-	403	1430	...	...	...
5	Health	793	609	184	-	-	793	...	...	...
6	Social security and welfare	126	108	18	-	1510	1636	...	...	...
7	Housing and community amenities	266	189	77	11	1	278	...	...	...
8	Recreation, culture and religion	157	70	87	1	19	177	...	...	...
9	Economic services	859	755	104	398	20	1277	...	...	...

2.3 Total Government Outlays by Function and Type
(Continued)

Million Mauritius rupees

	Final Consumption Expenditures			Subsidies	Other Current Transfers & Property Income	Total Current Disbursements	Gross Capital Formation	Other Capital Outlays	Total Outlays
	Total	Compensation of Employees	Other						
A Fuel and energy	4	3	1	-	3	7	...	...	...
B Agriculture, forestry, fishing and hunting	375	345	30	103	4	482	...	...	
C Mining (except fuels), manufacturing and construction	287	263	24	22	1	310	...	...	
D Transportation and communication	108	73	35	28	3	139	...	...	...
E Other economic affairs	85	71	14	245	9	339	...	...	...
10 Other functions	-	-	-	-	1547	1547	...	...	...
Total	4930	3900	1030	415	3545	8890	...	...	...

2.7 Gross Capital Formation by Type of Good and Owner, in Current Prices

Million Mauritius rupees

	1980				1981				1982			
	TOTAL	Total Private	Public Enterprises	General Government	TOTAL	Total Private	Public Enterprises	General Government	TOTAL	Total Private	Public Enterprises	General Government
Increase in stocks, total	-225	...	...	...	338	...	...	...	30	...	...	...
Gross Fixed Capital Formation, Total	2028	1298	...	730	2240	1375	...	865	2100	1345	...	755
1 Residential buildings	685	573	...	112	730	637	...	93	735	655	...	80
2 Non-residential buildings	223	120	...	103	248	143	...	105	245	164	...	81
3 Other construction	327	27	...	300	402	31	...	371	480	46	...	434
4 Land improvement and plantation and orchard development	...	...	...	...	...	...	...	...	...	...	...	...
5 Producers' durable goods	793	578	...	215	860	564	...	296	640	480	...	160
A Transport equipment	246	208	...	38	242	136	...	106	120	86	...	34
Passenger cars	46	43	...	3	52	37	...	15	45	41	...	4
Other	200	165	...	35	190	99	...	91	75	45	...	30
B Machinery and equipment	547	370	...	177	618	428	...	190	520	394	...	126
6 Breeding stock, dairy cattle, etc.	...	...	...	...	...	...	...	...	...	...	...	...
Total Gross Capital Formation	1803	...	...	...	2578	...	...	...	2130	...	...	...

	1983				1984				1985			
	TOTAL	Total Private	Public Enterprises	General Government	TOTAL	Total Private	Public Enterprises	General Government	TOTAL	Total Private	Public Enterprises	General Government
Increase in stocks, total	-73	...	...	...	570	...	...	...	800	...	...	...
Gross Fixed Capital Formation, Total	2300	1485	...	815	2595	1770	...	825	3100	2100	...	1000
1 Residential buildings	700	634	...	66	740	685	...	55	730	678	...	52
2 Non-residential buildings	277	207	...	70	350	260	...	90	635	375	...	260
3 Other construction	527	50	...	477	495	74	...	421	425	60	...	365
4 Land improvement and plantation and orchard development	...	...	...	...	...	...	...	...	...	...	...	...
5 Producers' durable goods	796	594	...	202	1010	751	...	259	1310	987	...	323
A Transport equipment	151	89	...	62	201	159	...	42	270	197	...	73
Passenger cars	40	35	...	5	56	47	...	9	85	75	...	10
Other	111	54	...	57	145	112	...	33	185	122	...	63
B Machinery and equipment	645	505	...	140	809	592	...	217	1040	790	...	250
6 Breeding stock, dairy cattle, etc.	...	...	...	...	...	...	...	...	...	...	...	...
Total Gross Capital Formation	2229	...	...	...	3165	...	...	...	3900	...	...	...

	1986				1987				1988			
	TOTAL	Total Private	Public Enterprises	General Government	TOTAL	Total Private	Public Enterprises	General Government	TOTAL	Total Private	Public Enterprises	General Government
Increase in stocks, total	422	...	...	...	871	...	...	...	512	...	...	...
Gross Fixed Capital Formation, Total	3890	2515	...	1375	5090	3375	...	1715	7990	4610	...	3380
1 Residential buildings	775	761	...	14	850	839	...	11	1075	1058	...	17
2 Non-residential buildings	660	372	...	288	800	535	...	265	1215	812	...	403
3 Other construction	635	55	...	580	715	50	...	665	915	50	...	865

Mauritius

2.7 Gross Capital Formation by Type of Good and Owner, in Current Prices
(Continued)

Million Mauritius rupees

	1986				1987				1988			
	TOTAL	Total Private	Public Enterprises	General Government	TOTAL	Total Private	Public Enterprises	General Government	TOTAL	Total Private	Public Enterprises	General Government
4 Land improvement and plantation and orchard development	...	...	...	...	...	...	...	...	...	...	...	...
5 Producers' durable goods	1820	1327	...	493	2725	1951	...	774	4785	2690	...	2095
A Transport equipment	470	257	...	213	725	545	...	180	2265	765	...	1500
Passenger cars	155	135	...	20	255	235	...	20	295	249	...	46
Other	315	122	...	193	470	310	...	160	1970	516	...	1454
B Machinery and equipment	1350	1070	...	280	2000	1406	...	594	2520	1925	...	595
6 Breeding stock, dairy cattle, etc.	...	...	...	...	...	...	...	...	...	...	...	...
Total Gross Capital Formation	4312	...	...	...	5961	...	...	...	8502	...	...	...

	1989				1990				1991			
	TOTAL	Total Private	Public Enterprises	General Government	TOTAL	Total Private	Public Enterprises	General Government	TOTAL	Total Private	Public Enterprises	General Government
Increase in stocks, total	1353	...	...	...	-306	...	...	...	239	...	...	...
Gross Fixed Capital Formation, Total	8565	6280	...	2285	11865	7500	...	4365	12385	8870	3515	...
1 Residential buildings	1495	1477	...	18	2060	2047	...	13	2700	2679	21	...
2 Non-residential buildings	1620	1373	...	247	2140	1582	...	558	2425	1816	609	...
3 Other construction	1025	65	...	960	1370	123	...	1247	1450	143	1307	...
4 Land improvement and plantation and orchard development	...	...	...	...	...	...	...	...	...	...	...	...
5 Producers' durable goods	4425	3365	...	1060	6295	3748	...	2547	5810	4232	1578	...
A Transport equipment	1195	1056	...	139	2595	1163	...	1432	1275	1086	189	...
Passenger cars	380	323	...	57	475	433	...	42	490	414	76	...
Other	815	733	...	82	2120	730	...	1390	785	672	113	...
B Machinery and equipment	3230	2309	...	921	3700	2585	...	1115	4535	3146	1389	...
6 Breeding stock, dairy cattle, etc.	...	...	...	...	...	...	...	...	...	...	...	...
Total Gross Capital Formation	9918	...	...	...	11559	...	...	...	12624	...	...	...

2.11 Gross Fixed Capital Formation by Kind of Activity of Owner, ISIC Divisions, in Current Prices

Million Mauritius rupees

	1980	1981	1982	1983	1984	1985	1986	1987	1988	1989	1990	1991
					All Producers							
1 Agriculture, hunting, forestry and fishing	102	127	135	102	123	130	130	290	230	200	270	480
2 Mining and quarrying	-	-	-	-	-	-	-	-	-	-	-	-
3 Manufacturing	279	302	315	337	503	740	1070	1460	1875	2130	2070	2280
4 Electricity, gas and water	170	243	350	467	316	285	230	310	455	605	385	1305
5 Construction	62	74	45	36	29	80	135	115	165	250	615	205
6 Wholesale and retail trade, restaurants and hotels	101	111	90	131	184	330	300	485	750	1305	1930	2005
7 Transport, storage and communication	380	374	235	330	453	435	930	1180	2860	1855	3235	2020
8 Finance, insurance, real estate and business services	760	773	780	744	788	815	875	960	1205	1690	2300	3035
9 Community, social and personal services	40	50	70	63	95	135	75	90	175	205	215	320
Total Industries	1894	2054	2020	2210	2491	2950	3745	4890	7715	8240	11020	11650
Producers of Government Services	134	186	80	90	104	150	145	200	275	325	845	735
Private Non-Profit Institutions Serving Households	...	...	...	...	...	...	...	...	...	...	...	...
Total	2028	2240	2100	2300	2595	3100	3890	5090	7990	8565	11865	12385

2.12 Gross Fixed Capital Formation by Kind of Activity of Owner, ISIC Divisions, in Constant Prices

Million Mauritius rupees

	1980	1981	1982	1983	1984	1985	1986	1987	1988	1989	1990	1991
		1976	At constant prices of: **1982**							**1987**		
			All Producers									
1 Agriculture, hunting, forestry and fishing	58	60	53 135	107	122	120	115	250 290	205	155	185	310
2 Mining and quarrying	-	-	- -		-	-	-	- -	-	-	-	-
3 Manufacturing	141	127	117 315	314	442	580	805	1060 1460	1680	1635	1435	1485
4 Electricity, gas and water	88	104	136 350	438	280	231	180	235 310	405	470	265	835
5 Construction	30	30	18 45	33	25	60	95	60 115	150	195	435	135
6 Wholesale and retail trade, restaurants and hotels	56	50	40 90	123	162	269	235	350 485	680	1025	1325	1275
7 Transport, storage and communication	192	158	92 235	300	388	341	705	855 1180	2560	1440	2250	1300
8 Finance, insurance, real estate and business services	458	401	367 780	708	704	697	725	750 960	1095	1345	1610	1985
9 Community, social and personal services	22	26	34 70	60	86	110	60	70 90	155	155	145	200
Total Industries	1045	956	857 2020	2083	2209	2408	2920	3630 4890	6930	6420	7650	7525
Producers of Government Services	75	84	37 80	84	91	122	115	155 200	245	250	575	465
Private Non-Profit Institutions Serving Households	...	...	... ...	...	...	...	...	... ...	...	...	...	...
Total	1120	1040	894 2100	2167	2300	2530	3035	3785 5090	7175	6670	8225	7990

2.17 Exports and Imports of Goods and Services, Detail

Million Mauritius rupees

	1980	1981	1982	1983	1984	1985	1986	1987	1988	1989	1990	1991
					Exports of Goods and Services							
1 Exports of merchandise, f.o.b.	3332	2999	3985	4346	5201	6639	9056	11493	13455	15166	17914	18696
2 Transport and communication	449	507	669	712	777	985	1143	1618	1859	2357	2931	3352
A In respect of merchandise imports	20	35	33	34	26	30	38	43	49	62	70	77
B Other	429	472	636	678	751	955	1105	1575	1810	2295	2861	3275
3 Insurance service charges	17	214	11	12	14	10	13	42	33	43	84	73
A In respect of merchandise imports	-	-	-	-	-	-	-	-	-	-	-	-
B Other	17	214	11	12	14	10	13	42	33	43	84	73
4 Other commodities	267	344	334	327	302	342	467	628	762	924	1020	1444
5 Adjustments of merchandise exports to change-of-ownership basis	-	-	-	-	-	-	-	-	-	-	-	-
6 Direct purchases in the domestic market by non-residential households	325	433	450	503	631	845	1190	1786	2381	2796	3630	3940
7 Direct purchases in the domestic market by extraterritorial bodies	60	69	80	53	64	74	50	72	75	77	90	92
Total Exports of Goods and Services	4450	4566	5529	5953	6989	8895	11919	15639	18565	21363	25669	27597
					Imports of Goods and Services							
1 Imports of merchandise, c.i.f.	4661	4922	5008	5164	6528	8083	9292	13113	17191	20189	24008	24620

Mauritius

2.17 Exports and Imports of Goods and Services, Detail
(Continued)

Million Mauritius rupees

	1980	1981	1982	1983	1984	1985	1986	1987	1988	1989	1990	1991
A Imports of merchandise, f.o.b.	3965	4260	4313	4516	5727	7056	8294	11701	15628	18385	21921	22479
B Transport of services on merchandise imports	696	662	695	648	801	1027	998	1412	1563	1804	2087	2141
C Insurance service charges on merchandise imports	...	...	...	...	...	...	...	...	...	...	...	...
2 Adjustments of merchandise imports to change-of-ownership basis	...	...	...	...	...	...	...	...	...	...	...	...
3 Other transport and communication	296	305	342	302	349	468	460	754	1029	1293	1745	1849
4 Other insurance service charges	68	57	98	83	95	128	129	140	178	177	206	214
5 Other commodities	95	119	143	173	183	198	306	390	612	820	972	1294
6 Direct purchases abroad by government	222	223	268	277	315	333	420	744	978	1323	1603	1924
7 Direct purchases abroad by resident households												
Total Imports of Goods and Services	5342	5626	5859	5999	7470	9210	10607	15141	19988	23802	28534	29901
Balance of Goods and Services	-892	-1060	-330	-46	-481	-315	1312	498	-1423	-2439	-2865	-2304
Total Imports and Balance of Goods and Services	4450	4566	5529	5953	6989	8895	11919	15639	18565	21363	25669	27597

4.1 Derivation of Value Added by Kind of Activity, in Current Prices

Million Mauritius rupees

	1980			1981			1982			1983		
	Gross Output	Intermediate Consumption	Value Added	Gross Output	Intermediate Consumption	Value Added	Gross Output	Intermediate Consumption	Value Added	Gross Output	Intermediate Consumption	Value Added
All Producers												
1 Agriculture, hunting, forestry and fishing	1523	609	914	1984	727	1257	2345	815	1530	2316	861	1455
2 Mining and quarrying	34	19	15	35	19	16	38	21	17	40	22	18
3 Manufacturing	5008	3397	1611	6198	4210	1988	7038	4789	2249	7498	5104	2394
4 Electricity, gas and water	381	172	209	456	268	188	502	242	260	558	313	245
5 Construction	1558	997	561	1653	1065	588	1700	1075	625	1780	1124	656
6 Wholesale and retail trade, restaurants and hotels	1839	737	1102	2076	802	1274	2254	902	1352	2617	928	1689
7 Transport, storage and communication	1514	666	848	1760	748	1012	1962	839	1123	2201	960	1241
8 Finance, insurance, real estate and business services	1734	299	1436	1982	325	1657	2296	383	1913	2470	397	2073
9 Community, social and personal services	633	222	411	729	229	500	829	229	600	892	231	661
Total, Industries	14225	7118	7107	16873	8393	8480	18964	9295	9669	20372	9940	10432
Producers of Government Services	1170	218	952	1328	224	1104	1520	245	1275	1608	281	1327
Other Producers	58	5	54	66	7	60	76	5	71	86	5	81
Total	15454	7341	8113	18267	8624	9644	20560	9545	11015	22066	10226	11840
Less: Imputed bank service charge	...	-107	107	...	-118	118	...	-128	128	...	-154	154
Import duties	691	...	691	684	...	684	839	...	839	1076	...	1076
Value added tax	...	...	...	...	...	...	...	...	...	...	...	...
Total	16145	7448	8697	18951	8742	10210	21399	9673	11726	23142	10380	12762

	1984			1985			1986			1987		
	Gross Output	Intermediate Consumption	Value Added	Gross Output	Intermediate Consumption	Value Added	Gross Output	Intermediate Consumption	Value Added	Gross Output	Intermediate Consumption	Value Added
All Producers												
1 Agriculture, hunting, forestry and fishing	2607	886	1721	3098	990	2108	3438	982	2456	3864	1092	2772
2 Mining and quarrying	42	23	19	44	24	20	49	27	22	55	30	25
3 Manufacturing	9160	6323	2837	11610	7999	3611	14428	9741	4687	17663	11850	5813
4 Electricity, gas and water	648	351	297	797	400	397	847	385	462	912	422	490
5 Construction	1910	1226	684	2148	1380	768	2400	1527	873	2765	1729	1036
6 Wholesale and retail trade, restaurants and hotels	2754	842	1912	2849	941	1908	3639	1253	2386	4680	1624	3056
7 Transport, storage and communication	2512	1129	1383	2891	1372	1519	3258	1470	1788	4051	1960	2091
8 Finance, insurance, real estate and business services	2799	532	2267	3056	573	2483	3258	576	2682	3547	623	2924
9 Community, social and personal services	964	275	689	1036	310	726	1101	311	790	1196	316	880

4.1 Derivation of Value Added by Kind of Activity, in Current Prices
(Continued)

Million Mauritius rupees

	1984			1985			1986			1987		
	Gross Output	Intermediate Consumption	Value Added	Gross Output	Intermediate Consumption	Value Added	Gross Output	Intermediate Consumption	Value Added	Gross Output	Intermediate Consumption	Value Added
Total, Industries	23396	11587	11809	27529	13989	13540	32418	16272	16146	38733	19646	19087
Producers of Government Services	1717	338	1379	1785	338	1447	1933	373	1560	2541	506	2035
Other Producers	97	5	92	100	4	96	112	11	101	115	7	108
Total	25210	11930	13280	29414	14331	15083	34463	16656	17807	41389	20159	21230
Less: Imputed bank service charge	...	-181	181	...	-256	256	...	-306	306	...	-405	405
Import duties	1261	...	1261	1791	...	1791	2199	...	2199	2751	...	2751
Value added tax	...	...	...	...	...	...	...	...	...	...	...	...
Total	26471	12111	14360	31205	14587	16618	36662	16962	19700	44140	20564	23576

	1988			1989			1990		
	Gross Output	Intermediate Consumption	Value Added	Gross Output	Intermediate Consumption	Value Added	Gross Output	Intermediate Consumption	Value Added
All Producers									
1 Agriculture, hunting, forestry and fishing	4201	1241	2960	4622	1323	3299	5328	1509	3819
2 Mining and quarrying	60	33	27	66	36	30	79	42	37
3 Manufacturing	20230	13490	6740	23047	15661	7386	26781	18118	8663
4 Electricity, gas and water	1017	500	517	1120	543	577	1262	755	507
5 Construction	3730	2370	1360	4698	2970	1728	6310	4095	2215
6 Wholesale and retail trade, restaurants and hotels	5862	2016	3846	6915	2385	4530	8565	3065	5500
7 Transport, storage and communication	4763	2384	2379	6071	3105	2966	7584	4070	3514
8 Finance, insurance, real estate and business services	3998	687	3311	4979	975	4004	5979	1177	4802
9 Community, social and personal services	1437	391	1046	1690	425	1265	2163	562	1601
Total, Industries	45298	23112	22186	53208	27423	25785	64051	33393	30658
Producers of Government Services	3289	609	2680	3711	724	2987	4200	937	3263
Other Producers	134	9	125	176	10	166	203	17	186
Total	48721	23730	24991	57095	28157	28938	68454	34347	34107
Less: Imputed bank service charge	...	-552	552	...	-693	693	...	-852	852
Import duties	3364	...	3364	4020	...	4020	4735	...	4735
Value added tax	...	...	...	...	...	...	...	...	...
Total	52085	24282	27803	61115	28850	32265	73189	35199	37990

4.3 Cost Components of Value Added

Million Mauritius rupees

	1980						1981					
	Compensation of Employees	Capital Consumption	Net Operating Surplus	Indirect Taxes	Less: Subsidies Received	Value Added	Compensation of Employees	Capital Consumption	Net Operating Surplus	Indirect Taxes	Less: Subsidies Received	Value Added
All Producers												
1 Agriculture, hunting, forestry and fishing	737	...	177	-	...	914	840	...	417	-	...	1257
2 Mining and quarrying	8	...	7	-	...	15	8	...	8	-	...	16
3 Manufacturing	589	...	538	484	...	1611	684	...	694	610	...	1988
4 Electricity, gas and water	114	...	95	-	...	209	121	...	67	-	...	188
5 Construction	376	...	185	-	...	561	380	...	208	-	...	588
6 Wholesale and retail trade, restaurants and hotels	333	...	717	52	...	1102	377	...	842	55	...	1274
7 Transport, storage and communication	485	...	352	11	...	848	556	...	441	15	...	1012
8 Finance, insurance, real estate and business services	152	...	1264	20	...	1436	177	...	1458	22	...	1657
9 Community, social and personal services	153	...	208	50	...	411	175	...	267	58	...	500
Total, Industries [ab]	2947	...	3543	617	...	7107	3318	...	4402	760	...	8480
Producers of Government Services	952	...	...	...	...	952	1104	...	...	...	...	1104
Other Producers	54	...	...	...	...	54	60	...	...	...	...	60
Total [ab]	3953	...	3543	617	...	8113	4482	...	4402	760	...	9644
Less: Imputed bank service charge	...	...	107	...	...	107	...	...	118	...	...	118
Import duties	...	...	...	691	...	691	...	...	...	684	...	684
Value added tax	...	...	...	...	...	...	...	...	...	...	...	...
Total [ab]	3953	...	3436	1308	...	8697	4482	...	4284	1444	...	10210

Mauritius

4.3 Cost Components of Value Added

Million Mauritius rupees

1982 / 1983

All Producers

	Compensation of Employees	Capital Consumption	Net Operating Surplus	Indirect Taxes	Less: Subsidies Received	Value Added	Compensation of Employees	Capital Consumption	Net Operating Surplus	Indirect Taxes	Less: Subsidies Received	Value Added
1 Agriculture, hunting, forestry and fishing	900	...	630	-	...	1530	974	...	491	-10	...	1455
2 Mining and quarrying	9	...	8	-	...	17	9	...	9	-	...	18
3 Manufacturing	754	...	806	689	...	2249	841	...	836	717	...	2394
4 Electricity, gas and water	140	...	120	-	...	260	150	...	95	-	...	245
5 Construction	400	...	225	-	...	625	420	...	235	1	...	656
6 Wholesale and retail trade, restaurants and hotels	420	...	870	61	...	1351	469	...	986	234	...	1689
7 Transport, storage and communication	596	...	515	12	...	1123	660	...	570	11	...	1241
8 Finance, insurance, real estate and business services	205	...	1678	30	...	1913	248	...	1796	29	...	2073
9 Community, social and personal services	202	...	324	74	...	600	221	...	348	92	...	661
Total, Industries ab	3626	...	5176	866	...	9668	3992	...	5366	1074	...	10432
Producers of Government Services	1275	...	...	...	...	1275	1327	...	...	...	...	1327
Other Producers	71	...	...	...	...	71	81	...	...	...	...	81
Total ab	4972	...	5176	866	...	11014	5400	...	5366	1074	...	11840
Less: Imputed bank service charge	...	...	128	...	...	128	...	...	154	...	...	154
Import duties	...	...	...	839	...	839	...	...	...	1076	...	1076
Value added tax	...	...	...	...	...	...	...	...	...	...	...	...
Total ab	4972	...	5048	1705	...	11725	5400	...	5212	2150	...	12762

1984 / 1985

All Producers

	Compensation of Employees	Capital Consumption	Net Operating Surplus	Indirect Taxes	Less: Subsidies Received	Value Added	Compensation of Employees	Capital Consumption	Net Operating Surplus	Indirect Taxes	Less: Subsidies Received	Value Added
1 Agriculture, hunting, forestry and fishing	994	...	742	-15	...	1721	1043	...	1080	-15	...	2108
2 Mining and quarrying	10	...	9	-	...	19	10	...	10	-	...	20
3 Manufacturing	1043	...	1139	655	...	2837	1320	...	1543	748	...	3611
4 Electricity, gas and water	156	...	141	-	...	297	155	...	242	-	...	397
5 Construction	450	...	240	-6	...	684	480	...	295	-7	...	768
6 Wholesale and retail trade, restaurants and hotels	523	...	1116	273	...	1912	650	...	1184	74	...	1908
7 Transport, storage and communication	753	...	619	11	...	1383	791	...	719	9	...	1519
8 Finance, insurance, real estate and business services	284	...	1947	36	...	2267	329	...	2117	37	...	2483
9 Community, social and personal services	231	...	363	95	...	689	249	...	376	101	...	726
Total, Industries ab	4444	...	6316	1049	...	11809	5027	...	7566	947	...	13540
Producers of Government Services	1379	...	...	...	...	1379	1447	...	...	...	...	1447
Other Producers	92	...	...	...	...	92	96	...	...	...	...	96
Total ab	5915	...	6316	1049	...	13280	6570	...	7566	947	...	15083
Less: Imputed bank service charge	...	...	181	...	...	181	...	...	256	...	...	256
Import duties	...	...	...	1261	...	1261	...	...	...	1791	...	1791
Value added tax	...	...	...	...	...	...	...	...	...	...	...	...
Total ab	5915	...	6135	2310	...	14360	6570	...	7310	2738	...	16618

1986 / 1987

All Producers

	Compensation of Employees	Capital Consumption	Net Operating Surplus	Indirect Taxes	Less: Subsidies Received	Value Added	Compensation of Employees	Capital Consumption	Net Operating Surplus	Indirect Taxes	Less: Subsidies Received	Value Added
1 Agriculture, hunting, forestry and fishing	1059	...	1451	-54	...	2456	1188	...	1696	-112	...	2772
2 Mining and quarrying	11	...	11	-	...	22	12	...	13	-	...	25
3 Manufacturing	1696	...	2134	857	...	4687	2085	...	2756	972	...	5813
4 Electricity, gas and water	161	...	301	-	...	462	193	...	297	-	...	490

4.3 Cost Components of Value Added
(Continued)

Million Mauritius rupees

	Compensation of Employees	Capital Consumption	Net Operating Surplus	Indirect Taxes	Less: Subsidies Received	Value Added	Compensation of Employees	Capital Consumption	Net Operating Surplus	Indirect Taxes	Less: Subsidies Received	Value Added
	1986						**1987**					
5 Construction	545	...	335	-7	...	873	640	...	405	-9	...	1036
6 Wholesale and retail trade, restaurants and hotels	749	...	1551	86	...	2386	960	...	2002	94	...	3056
7 Transport, storage and communication	862	...	913	13	...	1788	935	...	1140	16	...	2091
8 Finance, insurance, real estate and business services	356	...	2285	41	...	2682	437	...	2450	37	...	2924
9 Community, social and personal services	265	...	410	115	...	790	302	...	446	132	...	880
Total, Industries	5704	...	9391	1051	...	16146	6752	...	11205	1130	...	19087
Producers of Government Services	1560	...	...	...	...	1560	2035	...	...	...	...	2035
Other Producers	101	...	...	...	...	101	108	...	...	...	...	108
Total ab	7365	...	9391	1051	...	17807	8895	...	11205	1130	...	21230
Less: Imputed bank service charge	...	...	306	...	...	306	...	...	405	...	...	405
Import duties	...	...	...	2199	...	2199	...	...	...	2751	...	2751
Value added tax	...	...	...	...	...	...	...	...	...	...	...	...
Total ab	7365	...	9085	3250	...	19700	8895	...	10800	3881	...	23576

	Compensation of Employees	Capital Consumption	Net Operating Surplus	Indirect Taxes	Less: Subsidies Received	Value Added	Compensation of Employees	Capital Consumption	Net Operating Surplus	Indirect Taxes	Less: Subsidies Received	Value Added
	1988						**1989**					
	All Producers											
1 Agriculture, hunting, forestry and fishing	1394	...	1672	-106	...	2960	1515	...	1855	-71	...	3299
2 Mining and quarrying	13	...	14	-	...	27	15	...	15	-	...	30
3 Manufacturing	2544	...	3083	1113	...	6740	2906	...	3459	1021	...	7386
4 Electricity, gas and water	233	...	284	-	...	517	278	...	299	-	...	577
5 Construction	750	...	621	-11	...	1360	960	...	775	-7	...	1728
6 Wholesale and retail trade, restaurants and hotels	1210	...	2575	61	...	3846	1510	...	3030	-10	...	4530
7 Transport, storage and communication	1015	...	1350	14	...	2379	1285	...	1665	16	...	2966
8 Finance, insurance, real estate and business services	516	...	2759	36	...	3311	655	...	3299	50	...	4004
9 Community, social and personal services	435	...	460	151	...	1046	528	...	565	172	...	1265
Total, Industries ab	8110	...	12818	1258	...	22186	9662	...	14952	1171	...	25785
Producers of Government Services	2680	...	...	...	...	2680	2987	...	...	...	...	2987
Other Producers	125	...	...	...	...	125	166	...	...	...	...	166
Total ab	10915	...	12818	1258	...	24991	12815	...	14952	1171	...	28938
Less: Imputed bank service charge	...	...	552	...	...	552	...	...	693	...	...	693
Import duties	...	...	...	3364	...	3364	...	...	...	4020	...	4020
Value added tax	...	...	...	...	...	...	...	...	...	...	...	...
Total ab	10915	...	12266	4622	...	27803	12815	...	14259	5191	...	32265

	Compensation of Employees	Capital Consumption	Net Operating Surplus	Indirect Taxes	Less: Subsidies Received	Value Added
	1990					
	All Producers					
1 Agriculture, hunting, forestry and fishing	1755	...	2140	-76	...	3819
2 Mining and quarrying	17	...	20	-	...	37
3 Manufacturing	3439	...	4023	1201	...	8663
4 Electricity, gas and water	317	...	190	-	...	507
5 Construction	1160	...	1060	-5	...	2215
6 Wholesale and retail trade, restaurants and hotels	1838	...	3617	45	...	5500
7 Transport, storage and communication	1529	...	1961	24	...	3514
8 Finance, insurance, real estate and business services	835	...	3917	50	...	4802
9 Community, social and personal services	551	...	824	226	...	1601

Mauritius

4.3 Cost Components of Value Added
(Continued)

Million Mauritius rupees

	Compensation of Employees	Capital Consumption	Net Operating Surplus	Indirect Taxes	Less: Subsidies Received	Value Added
	1990					
Total, Industries ab	11441	...	17752	1465	...	30658
Producers of Government Services	3263	...	...	...	...	3263
Other Producers	186	...	...	...	...	186
Total ab	14890	...	17752	1465	...	34107
Less: Imputed bank service charge	...	...	852	...	...	852
Import duties	...	...	...	4735	...	4735
Value added tax	...	...	...	...	...	...
Total ab	14890	...	16900	6200	...	37990

a) Column 4 refers to indirect taxes less subsidies received.
b) Column 'Consumption of fixed capital' is included in column 'Net operating surplus'.

Mexico

General note. The preparation of national accounts statistics in Mexico is undertaken by the Direccion General de Estadistica of the Instituto Nacional de Estadistica, Geografia e Informatica (Ministry of Programming and the Budget). The official estimates are published annually in 'Sistema de Cuentas Naconales de Mexico'. The estimates are generally in accordance with the classifications and definitions recommended in the United Nations System of National Accounts (SNA). Input-output tables for 1950, 1960, 1970 and 1975 have been published. The following tables have been prepared from successive replies to the United Nations national accounts questionnaire. A revision of the national accounts estimates is presently undertaken by the Direccion General de Estadistica. The new series will be published in the 1981 edition of this publication. When the scope and coverage of the estimates differ for conceptual or statistical reasons from the definitions and classifications recommended in SNA, a footnote is indicated to the relevant tables.

Sources and methods :

(a) Gross domestic product. The main approach used to estimate GDP is the production approach.

(b) Expenditure on the gross domestic product. The expenditure approach is used to estimate government final consumption expenditure, increase in stocks, and exports and imports of goods and services. The estimates of gross fixed capital formation is largely based on the commodity-flow approach, whereas private final consumption expenditure is calculated as a residual. The estimates of government consumption expenditure are based on government accounts. For gross fixed capital formation the values from the input-output table of 1960 are extrapolated by value indexes for each of the principal components. The indexes are constructed by using special quantity and price indexes. Exports and imports of goods are estimated from the table of external transactions, which is based on the balance of payments. For the calculation of constant prices, general government expenditure is deflated by a specially constructed price index covering wages and salaries as well as prices of goods and services. As in the case of current prices, private consumption expenditure in constant prices is calculated as a residual. Gross domestic investment is first estimated in constant prices and later converted into current prices. Exports and imports of goods and services are deflated by specially constructed price indexes.

(c) Cost-structure of the gross domestic product. The estimates of compensation of employees for general government, petroleum and electricity production, financial institutions and partly for the transport sector, are based on direct current information on wages, salaries, etc. In the case of manufacturing, mining and private services the estimates are based on ratios of wages and salaries to gross output taken from sample surveys. For construction, trade and agriculture, employment indexes are constructed on the basis of data on occupation from the population censuses of 1960 and 1970, projected by production indexes and indexes of average wages. The estimates of consumption of fixed capital, are based on an approximation to the perpetual inventory method. Each year depreciation of the capital stock, valued at replacement cost, is estimated, based on assumptions regarding the economic life of the fixed assets. The price indexes required are derived implicitly from the estimation of gross fixed capital at 1960 prices. Government accounts are used in the estimation of indirect taxes and subsidies. Operating surplus is estimated as a residual.

(d) Gross domestic product by kind of economic activity. The table of GDP by kind of economic activity is prepared at market prices, i.e. producers' values. The production approach is used to estimate value added of all industries with direct relation to the input-output table of 1960. The income approach or the expenditure approach are used for some sectors. The estimation of gross output, intermediate consumption and value added is based on the 1960 input-output table, from which extrapolations are made by means of value indexes. These value indexes are, in general, the products of price indexes and volume indexes. The volume index for agricultural production is based on statistics of gross output of more than 60 commodities. The index for livestock production is based on statistics of animals slaughtered for domestic consumption and export, live animals exported and inventory changes. The intermediate consumption of crop and livestock production in 1960 is extrapolated by value indexes for the principal components and commodities used. For petroleum and other mining, the volume indexes are based on data from the concerned authorities. The intermediate consumption of 1960 is extrapolated by value indexes for the principal components and commodities used, based on various surveys. The volume index for manufacturing, which covers 200 products, is based on data from several authorities and through direct inquiries to industry associations and manufacturers. Input is extrapolated by value indicators. The index for construction is compiled on the basis of the apparent consumption of a few construction materials. Fixed input-output coefficients of 1960 are used. The volume index for trade is based on estimates of trade margins on locally produced and imported goods. Gross margins are based on data from the commercial censuses and special surveys. Input is extrapolated by a weighed value index. The volume index for transport and communications is based on data from the concerned authorities and companies. Input is extrapolated by quantity indexes. Value added of financial institutions and insurance is estimated through the income approach. For real estate output is extrapolated by value index for housing construction and industrial rents. Fixed input-output coefficients are used at constant prices. Current prices are obtained through the use of a specially constructed price index of principal commodities. The population censuses and household budget surveys are used to impute the rents of owner-occupied dwellings. The volume index for public administration and defense is obtained by compiling an index of wages, salaries and other compensation paid to the government employees. For the computation of constant prices, double deflation is used for all sectors, except the community, social and personal services sector. Output is extrapolated by means of output or volume indexes in all sectors in which double deflation is used. The input of the base-year is extrapolated by quantity indexes in all sectors except for the electricity, construction, restaurants and hotels, financing and services sectors, in which cases either deflation by price indexes is done or constant input-output coefficients are assumed. In the community, social and personal services sector, various approaches are used to estimate output in constant prices, such as double deflation, extrapolation of value added and deflation by price indexes.

1.1 Expenditure on the Gross Domestic Product, in Current Prices

Thousand Million Mexican pesos

	1980	1981	1982	1983	1984	1985	1986	1987	1988	1989	1990	1991
1 Government final consumption expenditure	449	660	1026	1574	2722	4374	7208	16995	33741	42915	57798	77971
2 Private final consumption expenditure	2909	3945	6036	10882	18590	30575	54209	127268	270998	356900	486354	620215
3 Gross capital formation	1214	1678	2244	3710	5853	10035	14681	37233	79700	108700	150272	193473
A Increase in stocks	107	61	-4	573	566	987	-734	1566	4501	16480	22544	25459
B Gross fixed capital formation	1107	1617	2249	3137	5287	9048	15415	35667	75199	92220	127728	168014
Residential buildings	199	276	431	744	1231	2079	3638	8792	18338	22518	28274	37790
Non-residential buildings	144	209	322	397	713	1080	1514	4202	9174	11060	15295	18974
Other construction and land improvement etc.	278	422	600	737	1146	1887	3164	6572	12620	14497	20277	26099
Other	486	710	896	1259	2197	4003	7098	16101	35067	44144	63882	85150
4 Exports of goods and services	479	638	1502	3397	5122	7305	13732	37692	65568	81148	108299	120682
5 Less: Imports of goods and services	580	793	1011	1684	2815	4897	10639	25877	59555	82045	116318	147176
Equals: Gross Domestic Product	4470	6128	9798	17879	29472	47392	79191	193312	390451	507618	686406	865166

1.2 Expenditure on the Gross Domestic Product, in Constant Prices

Thousand Million Mexican pesos

	1980	1981	1982	1983	1984	1985	1986	1987	1988	1989	1990	1991
					At constant prices of:1980							
1 Government final consumption expenditure	449	495	505	519	553	558	566	559	556	555	569	591
2 Private final consumption expenditure	2909	3123	3046	2883	2977	3083	2995	2991	3046	3252	3450	3610
3 Gross capital formation	1214	1393	1055	770	817	901	726	768	858	898	995	1068
A Increase in stocks	107	107	-16	2	-	20	-51	-9	36	25	7	-
B Gross fixed capital formation	1107	1286	1070	768	817	881	777	776	821	874	988	1068

Mexico

1.2 Expenditure on the Gross Domestic Product, in Constant Prices
(Continued)

Thousand Million Mexican pesos

	1980	1981	1982	1983	1984	1985	1986	1987	1988	1989	1990	1991
	At constant prices of:1980											
Residential buildings	199	214	218	205	215	232	229	239	236	256	260	271
Non-residential buildings	144	164	159	103	116	115	88	104	111	114	126	125
Other construction and land improvement etc.	278	329	285	204	201	204	181	163	153	147	167	174
Other	486	580	409	255	284	329	280	270	321	358	435	497
4 Exports of goods and services	479	534	650	739	781	746	788	862	912	933	967	1019
5 Less: Imports of goods and services	580	683	424	281	331	367	339	357	488	592	709	825
Equals: Gross Domestic Product	4470	4862	4832	4629	4796	4920	4736	4824	4884	5047	5272	5463

1.3 Cost Components of the Gross Domestic Product

Thousand Million Mexican pesos

	1980	1981	1982	1983	1984	1985	1986	1987	1988	1989	1990	1991
1 Indirect taxes, net	343	458	858	1326	2375	4435	6319	18728	35612	47789	66213	86109
A Indirect taxes	432	579	1135	1924	3164	5688	8541	23523	42548	56245	74873	93852
B Less: Subsidies	89	122	277	598	789	1254	2222	4795	6937	8455	8660	7743
2 Consumption of fixed capital	384	527	956	2176	3359	5331	10871	25284	46763	53637	66239	82436
3 Compensation of employees paid by resident producers to:	1611	2295	3450	5248	8445	13590	22605	51878	102179	130490	171415	222960
4 Operating surplus	2133	2847	4533	9129	15293	24036	39396	97421	205898	275701	382538	473662
Equals: Gross Domestic Product	4470	6128	9798	17879	29472	47392	79191	193312	390451	507618	686406	865166

1.7 External Transactions on Current Account, Summary

Thousand Million Mexican pesos

	1980	1981	1982	1983	1984	1985	1986	1987	1988	1989	1990	1991
	Payments to the Rest of the World											
1 Imports of goods and services	580	793	1011	1684	2815	4897	10639	25877	59555	82045	116318	147176
A Imports of merchandise c.i.f.	456	615	722	1141	2000	3535	7801	19343	47507	65427	92525	120575
B Other	124	178	288	544	815	1362	2838	6533	12048	16618	23793	26601
2 Factor income to the rest of the world	157	257	640	1269	2042	2753	5374	12139	21318	25057	28688	28792
A Compensation of employees	...	...	...	...	...	...	...	...	...	...	...	...
B Property and entrepreneurial income	157	257	640	1269	2042	2753	5374	12139	21318	25057	28688	28792
3 Current transfers to the rest of the world	1	1	1	5	4	8	8	26	34	39	40	57
4 Surplus of the nation on current transactions	-224	-365	-50	704	765	615	-291	5298	-4257	-13262	-18466	-39705
Payments to the Rest of the World and Surplus of the Nation on Current Transactions	514	686	1602	3661	5627	8273	15730	43340	76651	93879	126580	136320
	Receipts From The Rest of the World											
1 Exports of goods and services	479	638	1502	3397	5122	7305	13732	37692	65568	81148	108299	120682
A Exports of merchandise f.o.b.	347	476	1211	2655	3994	5523	9840	27409	45517	55251	74825	81099
B Other	131	162	292	743	1128	1783	3892	10283	20051	25897	33474	39583
2 Factor income from rest of the world	29	40	82	214	424	632	1119	3289	6730	7546	8319	8815
A Compensation of employees	4	5	10	23	44	89	205	506	951	1126	1412	1641
B Property and entrepreneurial income	24	35	72	191	380	542	914	2783	5779	6420	6907	7174
3 Current transfers from rest of the world	7	8	18	50	80	336	879	2358	4352	5185	9962	6823
Receipts from the Rest of the World on Current Transactions	514	686	1602	3661	5627	8273	15730	43340	76651	93879	126580	136320

1.10 Gross Domestic Product by Kind of Activity, in Current Prices

Thousand Million Mexican pesos

	1980	1981	1982	1983	1984	1985	1986	1987	1988	1989	1990	1991
1 Agriculture, hunting, forestry and fishing	368	503	720	1392	2533	4307	7466	16825	30691	39246	54810	66682
2 Mining and quarrying [a]	141	144	298	1264	1647	2190	2868	9744	12609	13454	17515	17950
3 Manufacturing [a]	991	1329	2037	3780	6633	11096	19477	49617	105547	124228	156360	192697
4 Electricity, gas and water	44	56	88	167	282	449	994	2090	4959	6785	9480	13068
5 Construction	287	427	635	804	1298	2070	3383	7887	15726	19588	27230	36217

1.10 Gross Domestic Product by Kind of Activity, in Current Prices
(Continued)

Thousand Million Mexican pesos

	1980	1981	1982	1983	1984	1985	1986	1987	1988	1989	1990	1991
6 Wholesale and retail trade, restaurants and hotels	1250	1695	2903	5073	8362	13306	21185	52425	106622	135438	178783	214150
7 Transport, storage and communication	286	395	606	1172	2004	3165	5708	13767	29528	37610	56505	76545
8 Finance, insurance, real estate and business services	396	554	843	1440	2310	3659	6458	14308	31742	54390	83154	111310
9 Community, social and personal services	401	569	926	1700	2693	4410	7399	16617	34603	47374	66734	88564
Total, Industries	4165	5673	9055	16793	27762	44652	74938	183280	372028	478112	650572	817184
Producers of Government Services	353	521	830	1232	2065	3293	5279	12561	24157	32512	43386	58997
Other Producers	...	...	...	...	...	...	...	...	...	...	...	...
Subtotal	4518	6194	9884	18025	29827	47945	80217	195841	396185	510624	693958	876181
Less: Imputed bank service charge	48	66	86	146	355	554	1026	2529	5734	3006	7552	11015
Plus: Import duties	...	...	...	...	...	...	...	...	...	...	...	...
Plus: Value added tax	...	...	...	...	...	...	...	...	...	...	...	...
Equals: Gross Domestic Product	4470	6128	9798	17879	29472	47392	79191	193312	390451	507618	686406	865166

a) Basic petroleum manufacturing is included in item 'Mining and quarrying'.

1.11 Gross Domestic Product by Kind of Activity, in Constant Prices

Thousand Million Mexican pesos

	1980	1981	1982	1983	1984	1985	1986	1987	1988	1989	1990	1991
					At constant prices of:1980							
1 Agriculture, hunting, forestry and fishing	368	391	383	391	401	416	405	410	395	386	409	413
2 Mining and quarrying a	141	162	177	175	179	179	172	181	182	181	186	188
3 Manufacturing a	991	1055	1026	946	993	1054	998	1028	1061	1137	1206	1254
4 Electricity, gas and water	44	49	54	55	58	62	65	67	71	76	79	81
5 Construction	287	329	305	247	260	267	240	246	245	250	268	274
6 Wholesale and retail trade, restaurants and hotels	1250	1382	1370	1267	1298	1312	1227	1234	1255	1302	1355	1414
7 Transport, storage and communication	286	314	291	283	298	306	296	305	312	325	347	367
8 Finance, insurance, real estate and business services	396	421	440	456	481	499	517	535	543	559	580	603
9 Community, social and personal services	401	428	433	435	431	430	411	411	411	420	430	445
Total, Industries	4165	4532	4480	4254	4400	4525	4330	4418	4475	4637	4859	5038
Producers of Government Services	353	385	409	434	459	458	470	471	476	480	486	505
Other Producers	...	...	...	...	...	...	...	...	...	...	...	...
Subtotal	4518	4916	4889	4688	4858	4983	4800	4889	4951	5117	5346	5543
Less: Imputed bank service charge	48	54	57	59	62	63	64	66	68	69	74	80
Plus: Import duties	...	...	...	...	...	...	...	...	...	...	...	...
Plus: Value added tax	...	...	...	...	...	...	...	...	...	...	...	...
Equals: Gross Domestic Product	4470	4862	4832	4629	4796	4920	4736	4824	4884	5047	5272	5463

a) Basic petroleum manufacturing is included in item 'Mining and quarrying'.

1.12 Relations Among National Accounting Aggregates

Thousand Million Mexican pesos

	1980	1981	1982	1983	1984	1985	1986	1987	1988	1989	1990	1991
Gross Domestic Product	4470	6128	9798	17879	29472	47392	79191	193312	390451	507618	686406	865166
Plus: Net factor income from the rest of the world	-129	-217	-558	-1055	-1618	-2122	-4255	-8849	-14588	-17511	-20369	-19977
Factor income from the rest of the world	29	40	82	214	424	632	1119	3289	6730	7546	8319	8815
Less: Factor income to the rest of the world	157	257	640	1269	2042	2753	5374	12139	21318	25057	28688	28792
Equals: Gross National Product	4341	5911	9240	16824	27854	45270	74936	184462	375864	490107	666037	845189
Less: Consumption of fixed capital	384	527	956	2176	3359	5331	10871	25284	46763	53637	66239	82436

Mexico

1.12 Relations Among National Accounting Aggregates
(Continued)

Thousand Million Mexican pesos

	1980	1981	1982	1983	1984	1985	1986	1987	1988	1989	1990	1991
Equals: National Income	3958	5383	8283	14648	24495	39939	64065	159178	329101	436470	599798	762753
Plus: Net current transfers from the rest of the world	6	7	17	45	76	329	871	2332	4318	5145	9922	6766
Current transfers from the rest of the world	7	8	18	50	80	336	879	2358	4353	5185	9962	6823
Less: Current transfers to the rest of the world	1	1	1	5	4	8	8	26	34	39	40	57
Equals: National Disposable Income	3964	5390	8300	14693	24571	40268	64936	161510	333419	441615	609720	769519
Less: Final consumption	3358	4605	7062	12455	21312	34949	61417	144263	304739	399815	544153	698187
Equals: Net Saving	607	785	1238	2238	3260	5319	3519	17247	28681	41800	65567	71332
Less: Surplus of the nation on current transactions	-224	-365	-50	704	765	615	-291	5298	-4257	-13262	-18466	-39705
Equals: Net Capital Formation	830	1150	1288	1534	2494	4704	3810	11948	32938	55063	84033	111037

2.5 Private Final Consumption Expenditure by Type and Purpose, in Current Prices

Thousand Million Mexican pesos

	1980	1981	1982	1983	1984	1985	1986	1987	1988	1989	1990	1991
Final Consumption Expenditure of Resident Households												
1 Food, beverages and tobacco	1035	1383	2127	3956	7100	11782	21472	49676	101850	132462	174385	216494
2 Clothing and footwear	313	410	578	1049	1758	2966	4892	10843	23525	28515	36467	45112
3 Gross rent, fuel and power	267	360	572	1003	1623	2566	4394	8414	20196	36299	55680	76874
4 Furniture, furnishings and household equipment and operation	410	545	835	1553	2509	4075	7166	18028	37519	45010	55668	67919
5 Medical care and health expenses	115	158	263	460	762	1215	2087	4998	9987	13233	19153	25249
6 Transport and communication	268	367	564	987	1673	2823	5070	13240	28188	34097	52947	71469
7 Recreational, entertainment, education and cultural services	189	259	382	587	995	1695	2995	6811	14488	18465	24178	30588
8 Miscellaneous goods and services	321	452	754	1485	2419	3719	6816	17397	38244	51292	69196	88782
Total Final Consumption Expenditure in the Domestic Market by Households, of which	2918	3933	6074	11080	18838	30840	54890	129407	273997	359373	487673	622487
A Durable goods	383	513	688	1094	1879	3283	5585	14037	30188	35477	46741	59161
B Semi-durable goods	1600	2119	3256	6077	10716	17803	31755	74777	154329	196988	255735	316797
C Non-durable goods												
D Services	934	1300	2130	3910	6243	9754	17551	40593	89480	126908	185198	246530
Plus: Direct purchases abroad by resident households	71	101	129	241	409	694	1425	3441	7358	10644	15766	17386
Less: Direct purchases in the domestic market by non-resident households	80	89	167	440	657	959	2106	5581	10357	13116	17084	19658
Equals: Final Consumption Expenditure of Resident Households [a]	2909	3945	6036	10882	18590	30575	54209	127268	270998	356900	486354	620215
Final Consumption Expenditure of Private Non-profit Institutions Serving Households												
Equals: Final Consumption Expenditure of Private Non-profit Organisations Serving Households	...	...	...	...	...	...	...	...	...	...	...	...
Private Final Consumption Expenditure	2909	3945	6036	10882	18590	30575	54209	127268	270998	356900	486354	620215

a) Item 'Final consumption expenditure of resident households' includes consumption expenditure of private non-profit institutions serving households.

2.6 Private Final Consumption Expenditure by Type and Purpose, in Constant Prices

Thousand Million Mexican pesos

	1980	1981	1982	1983	1984	1985	1986	1987	1988	1989	1990	1991
At constant prices of:1980												
Final Consumption Expenditure of Resident Households												
1 Food, beverages and tobacco	1035	1077	1107	1101	1132	1161	1161	1169	1165	1231	1284	1341
2 Clothing and footwear	313	350	318	279	289	299	281	249	253	271	293	297
3 Gross rent, fuel and power	267	281	297	303	327	349	360	376	390	419	445	476
4 Furniture, furnishings and household equipment and operation	410	431	419	389	389	405	392	390	395	416	430	441

2.6 Private Final Consumption Expenditure by Type and Purpose, in Constant Prices
(Continued)

Thousand Million Mexican pesos

	1980	1981	1982	1983	1984	1985	1986	1987	1988	1989	1990	1991
					At constant prices of:1980							
5 Medical care and health expenses	115	124	128	131	134	138	124	120	118	125	131	134
6 Transport and communication	268	294	262	230	242	260	247	255	271	298	336	360
7 Recreational, entertainment, education and cultural services	189	208	192	167	178	190	184	167	176	182	191	196
8 Miscellaneous goods and services	321	346	359	350	340	328	321	336	334	361	381	401
Total Final Consumption Expenditure in the Domestic Market by Households, of which	2917	3110	3082	2951	3030	3131	3070	3062	3101	3303	3489	3645
A Durable goods	383	423	353	275	292	326	280	267	291	309	343	365
B Semi-durable goods	1600	1687	1703	1647	1704	1762	1731	1717	1711	1839	1933	2015
C Non-durable goods												
D Services	934	1000	1026	1029	1034	1043	1043	1077	1100	1155	1213	1265
Plus: Direct purchases abroad by resident households	71	85	44	30	39	39	37	39	50	63	78	78
Less: Direct purchases in the domestic market by non-resident households	80	72	79	98	93	87	96	110	106	114	117	113
Equals: Final Consumption Expenditure of Resident Households	2909	3123	3046	2883	2977	3083	2995	2991	3046	3252	3450	3610
				Final Consumption Expenditure of Private Non-profit Institutions Serving Households								
Equals: Final Consumption Expenditure of Private Non-profit Organisations Serving Households	...	...	...	...	...	...	...	...	...	...	...	...
Private Final Consumption Expenditure	2909	3123	3046	2883	2977	3083	2995	2991	3046	3252	3450	3610

4.1 Derivation of Value Added by Kind of Activity, in Current Prices

Thousand Million Mexican pesos

	1980			1981			1982			1983		
	Gross Output	Intermediate Consumption	Value Added	Gross Output	Intermediate Consumption	Value Added	Gross Output	Intermediate Consumption	Value Added	Gross Output	Intermediate Consumption	Value Added
						All Producers						
1 Agriculture, hunting, forestry and fishing	511	142	368	690	187	503	1005	286	720	1983	591	1392
2 Mining and quarrying a	186	45	141	197	53	144	380	82	298	1467	203	1264
A Coal mining	3	1	2	4	1	3	6	2	4	17	5	12
B Crude petroleum and natural gas production	94	12	82	102	18	83	220	23	196	1097	58	1039
C Metal ore mining	61	27	34	55	28	26	97	49	48	249	123	126
D Other mining	27	4	23	37	5	31	58	9	49	104	17	87
3 Manufacturing a	2391	1400	991	3160	1830	1329	4810	2774	2037	8825	5045	3780
A Manufacture of food, beverages and tobacco	707	464	243	929	607	322	1467	945	522	2763	1784	979
B Textile, wearing apparel and leather industries	293	157	136	371	196	175	539	282	257	1049	558	491
C Manufacture of wood and wood products, including furniture	90	48	42	111	57	54	163	82	80	278	137	141
D Manufacture of paper and paper products, printing and publishing	117	62	54	153	79	74	231	118	113	437	223	214
E Manufacture of chemicals and chemical petroleum, coal, rubber and plastic products	379	226	153	499	292	206	849	510	339	1652	936	716
F Manufacture of non-metallic mineral products, except products of petroleum and coal	117	48	69	164	69	95	246	100	146	440	171	269
G Basic metal industries	172	111	61	220	141	80	316	203	113	618	403	214
H Manufacture of fabricated metal products, machinery and equipment	487	271	216	671	373	298	935	507	428	1483	787	696
I Other manufacturing industries	30	13	17	41	16	25	64	26	38	105	46	59
4 Electricity, gas and water	79	35	44	88	32	56	146	58	88	276	109	167

Mexico

4.1 Derivation of Value Added by Kind of Activity, in Current Prices
(Continued)

Thousand Million Mexican pesos

	1980 Gross Output	1980 Intermediate Consumption	1980 Value Added	1981 Gross Output	1981 Intermediate Consumption	1981 Value Added	1982 Gross Output	1982 Intermediate Consumption	1982 Value Added	1983 Gross Output	1983 Intermediate Consumption	1983 Value Added
5 Construction	608	321	287	888	461	427	1325	690	635	1826	1023	804
6 Wholesale and retail trade, restaurants and hotels	1486	236	1250	2034	339	1695	3457	554	2903	6139	1066	5073
7 Transport, storage and communication	405	119	286	559	164	395	865	259	606	1692	520	1172
8 Finance, insurance, real estate and business services	451	55	396	629	75	554	971	128	843	1677	237	1440
9 Community, social and personal services	540	139	401	757	188	569	1238	313	926	2318	618	1700
Total, Industries	6657	2492	4165	9003	3330	5673	14198	5143	9055	26204	9411	16793
Producers of Government Services	449	96	353	660	139	521	1026	196	830	1574	342	1232
Other Producers	...	...	...	...	...	...	...	...	...	...	...	...
Total	7106	2588	4518	9663	3470	6194	15224	5339	9884	27778	9753	18025
Less: Imputed bank service charge	...	-48	48	...	-66	66	...	-86	86	...	-146	146
Import duties	...	...	...	...	...	...	...	...	...	...	...	...
Value added tax	...	...	...	...	...	...	...	...	...	...	...	...
Total	7106	2636	4470	9663	3535	6128	15224	5426	9798	27778	9899	17879

	1984 Gross Output	1984 Intermediate Consumption	1984 Value Added	1985 Gross Output	1985 Intermediate Consumption	1985 Value Added	1986 Gross Output	1986 Intermediate Consumption	1986 Value Added	1987 Gross Output	1987 Intermediate Consumption	1987 Value Added
All Producers												
1 Agriculture, hunting, forestry and fishing	3591	1058	2533	6060	1753	4307	10618	3152	7466	24044	7218	16825
2 Mining and quarrying a	1957	309	1647	2723	534	2190	3908	1040	2868	12364	2620	9744
A Coal mining	34	8	26	56	12	44	82	25	57	247	63	184
B Crude petroleum and natural gas production	1404	93	1312	1889	217	1672	2193	380	1814	7815	873	6942
C Metal ore mining	325	178	147	426	254	172	944	539	406	2802	1457	1345
D Other mining	193	30	163	352	50	302	688	97	591	1501	227	1274
3 Manufacturing a	15610	8976	6633	25817	14781	11036	45399	25922	19477	114312	64695	49617
A Manufacture of food, beverages and tobacco	4921	3202	1719	8102	5218	2884	14607	9032	5575	33285	20477	12808
B Textile, wearing apparel and leather industries	1668	898	770	2644	1407	1237	4484	2388	2096	11171	6027	5144
C Manufacture of wood and wood products, including furniture	485	240	245	870	441	429	1444	715	729	3380	1637	1744
D Manufacture of paper and paper products, printing and publishing	777	398	379	1302	664	639	2349	1194	1154	6465	3306	3159
E Manufacture of chemicals and chemical petroleum, coal, rubber and plastic products	2811	1603	1208	4618	2685	1933	8738	5164	3574	23302	13412	9890
F Manufacture of non-metallic mineral products, except products of petroleum and coal	752	290	461	1296	495	801	2262	855	1408	5887	2224	3663
G Basic metal industries	1243	800	443	1780	1141	638	3064	1979	1085	8374	5265	3109
H Manufacture of fabricated metal products, machinery and equipment	2766	1471	1295	4884	2605	2278	7909	4377	3532	21201	11827	9374
I Other manufacturing industries	187	74	112	320	124	196	542	218	324	1247	521	726
4 Electricity, gas and water	512	231	282	832	383	449	1887	894	994	4153	2063	2090
5 Construction	3002	1703	1298	4898	2828	2070	8040	4657	3383	18911	11025	7887
6 Wholesale and retail trade, restaurants and hotels	10154	1792	8362	16014	2708	13306	26184	4999	21185	64764	12338	52425
7 Transport, storage and communication	2931	927	2004	4596	1431	3165	8624	2916	5708	20920	7153	13767
8 Finance, insurance, real estate and business services	2715	405	2310	4323	663	3659	7772	1314	6458	17741	3433	14308
9 Community, social and personal services	3695	1002	2693	5955	1546	4410	10232	2832	7399	23473	6857	16617
Total, Industries	44165	16403	27762	71219	26627	44592	122664	47726	74938	300682	117402	183280
Producers of Government Services	2722	657	2065	4374	1081	3293	7208	1929	5279	16995	4435	12561
Other Producers	...	...	...	...	...	...	...	...	...	...	...	...
Total	46886	17059	29827	75593	27708	47885	129872	49655	80217	317678	121837	195841
Less: Imputed bank service charge	...	-355	355	...	-554	554	...	-1026	1026	...	-2529	2529
Import duties	...	...	...	...	...	...	...	...	...	...	...	...
Value added tax	...	...	...	...	...	...	...	...	...	...	...	...
Total	46886	17415	29472	75593	28262	47331	129872	50681	79191	317678	124366	193312

4.1 Derivation of Value Added by Kind of Activity, in Current Prices

Thousand Million Mexican pesos

	1988			1989			1990			1991		
	Gross Output	Intermediate Consumption	Value Added	Gross Output	Intermediate Consumption	Value Added	Gross Output	Intermediate Consumption	Value Added	Gross Output	Intermediate Consumption	Value Added
All Producers												
1 Agriculture, hunting, forestry and fishing	46956	16265	30691	59148	19903	39246	79040	24230	54810	95315	28632	66682
2 Mining and quarrying a	17904	5296	12609	19365	5911	13454	24915	7399	17515	25689	7740	17950
A Coal mining	687	120	566	693	117	576	855	138	717	870	157	713
B Crude petroleum and natural gas production	8167	1648	6519	8099	1797	6302	11729	2420	9309	11539	2707	8832
C Metal ore mining	5985	3060	2925	7076	3484	3592	8183	4235	3948	7570	4171	3400
D Other mining	3065	466	2598	3496	512	2983	4148	607	3541	5711	706	5006
3 Manufacturing a	244140	138592	105547	290097	165869	124228	365723	209363	156360	447655	254957	192697
A Manufacture of food, beverages and tobacco	68711	42662	26049	85088	53680	31408	109242	68646	40596	138020	87914	50106
B Textile, wearing apparel and leather industries	22560	11882	10678	25997	13628	12369	31248	16320	14928	36540	18866	17673
C Manufacture of wood and wood products, including furniture	7479	3597	3883	8455	4085	4370	9926	4746	5180	11311	5392	5919
D Manufacture of paper and paper products, printing and publishing	13701	7043	6658	16415	8324	8091	19340	9568	9772	22324	10671	11653
E Manufacture of chemicals and chemical petroleum, coal, rubber and plastic products	50494	29132	21362	57287	33117	24170	70541	40771	29770	81909	46006	35903
F Manufacture of non-metallic mineral products, except products of petroleum and coal	12014	4520	7493	13765	5117	8648	18053	6775	11279	23386	8781	14605
G Basic metal industries	19213	11938	7275	21640	13458	8182	26020	16375	9645	27124	16985	10139
H Manufacture of fabricated metal products, machinery and equipment	47433	26794	20639	58350	33246	25104	77175	44578	32597	101994	58513	43481
I Other manufacturing industries	2534	1025	1509	3099	1213	1886	4178	1585	2593	5047	1829	3218
4 Electricity, gas and water	9405	4445	4959	12685	5900	6785	16858	7379	9480	21876	8808	13068
5 Construction	38782	23055	15726	46545	26958	19588	61902	34672	27230	80427	44211	36217
6 Wholesale and retail trade, restaurants and hotels	133109	26487	106622	169338	33900	135438	223487	44705	178783	269083	54932	214150
7 Transport, storage and communication	43664	14136	29528	54499	16889	37609	81142	24637	56505	108325	31780	76545
8 Finance, insurance, real estate and business services	39177	7435	31742	63732	9342	54390	95980	12826	83154	129094	17784	111310
9 Community, social and personal services	49676	15073	34603	66559	19185	47374	91555	24821	66734	121511	32946	88564
Total, Industries	622812	250784	372028	781968	303856	478112	1040603	390032	650572	1298975	481791	817184
Producers of Government Services	33741	9584	24157	42915	10402	32512	57798	14413	43386	77971	18974	58997
Other Producers	...	...	...	...	...	...	...	...	...	...	...	...
Total	656553	260368	396185	824883	314259	510624	1098402	404444	693958	1376946	500765	876181
Less: Imputed bank service charge	...	-5734	5734	...	-3006	3006	...	-7552	7552	...	-11015	11015
Import duties	...	...	...	...	...	...	...	...	...	...	...	...
Value added tax	...	...	...	...	...	...	...	...	...	...	...	...
Total	656553	266102	390451	824883	317265	507618	1098402	411996	686406	1376946	511780	865166

a) Basic petroleum manufacturing is included in item 'Mining and quarrying'.

4.2 Derivation of Value Added by Kind of Activity, in Constant Prices

Thousand Million Mexican pesos

	1980			1981			1982			1983		
	Gross Output	Intermediate Consumption	Value Added	Gross Output	Intermediate Consumption	Value Added	Gross Output	Intermediate Consumption	Value Added	Gross Output	Intermediate Consumption	Value Added
At constant prices of:1980												
All Producers												
1 Agriculture, hunting, forestry and fishing	511	142	368	542	151	391	537	154	383	546	155	391
2 Mining and quarrying a	186	45	141	213	51	162	230	53	177	231	56	175
A Coal mining	3	1	2	4	1	3	3	1	3	4	1	3
B Crude petroleum and natural gas production	94	12	82	111	15	96	128	17	111	124	16	108
C Metal ore mining	61	27	34	69	31	39	70	31	39	77	35	43
D Other mining	27	4	23	29	4	25	29	4	24	26	4	22

Mexico

4.2 Derivation of Value Added by Kind of Activity, in Constant Prices
(Continued)

Thousand Million Mexican pesos

	1980			1981			1982			1983		
	Gross Output	Intermediate Consumption	Value Added	Gross Output	Intermediate Consumption	Value Added	Gross Output	Intermediate Consumption	Value Added	Gross Output	Intermediate Consumption	Value Added
	At constant prices of:1980											
3 Manufacturing ᵃ	2391	1400	991	2554	1499	1055	2484	1458	1026	2307	1361	946
A Manufacture of food, beverages and tobacco	707	464	243	743	489	254	778	513	265	772	511	262
B Textile, wearing apparel and leather industries	293	157	136	309	165	144	291	154	137	275	146	130
C Manufacture of wood and wood products, including furniture	90	48	42	89	47	42	88	47	41	80	42	38
D Manufacture of paper and paper products, printing and publishing	117	62	54	122	65	57	123	65	57	115	62	53
E Manufacture of chemicals and chemical petroleum, coal, rubber and plastic products	379	226	153	415	248	167	424	253	171	421	253	168
F Manufacture of non-metallic mineral products, except products of petroleum and coal	118	48	69	122	51	71	118	49	69	107	43	64
G Basic metal industries	172	111	60	180	116	64	163	105	58	155	100	54
H Manufacture of fabricated metal products, machinery and equipment	487	271	216	537	300	237	465	256	208	356	193	163
I Other manufacturing industries	30	13	17	36	16	20	34	15	19	26	11	15
4 Electricity, gas and water	79	35	44	85	35	49	90	35	54	89	34	55
5 Construction	608	321	287	692	364	329	647	342	305	499	252	247
6 Wholesale and retail trade, restaurants and hotels	1486	236	1250	1653	270	1382	1647	277	1370	1525	259	1267
7 Transport, storage and communication	405	119	286	446	132	314	420	129	291	400	117	283
8 Finance, insurance, real estate and business services	451	55	396	481	60	421	501	61	440	513	58	456
9 Community, social and personal services	540	139	401	578	150	428	592	159	433	593	158	435
Total, Industries	6657	2492	4165	7244	2713	4532	7148	2669	4480	6703	2449	4254
Producers of Government Services	449	96	353	495	110	385	505	96	409	519	84	434
Other Producers	...	...	...	...	...	...	...	...	...	...	...	...
Total	7106	2588	4518	7739	2823	4916	7653	2764	4889	7222	2533	4688
Less: Imputed bank service charge	...	-48	48	...	-54	54	...	-57	57	...	-59	59
Import duties	...	...	...	...	...	...	...	...	...	...	...	...
Value added tax	...	...	...	...	...	...	...	...	...	...	...	...
Total	7106	2636	4470	7739	2877	4862	7653	2821	4832	7222	2593	4629

	1984			1985			1986			1987		
	Gross Output	Intermediate Consumption	Value Added	Gross Output	Intermediate Consumption	Value Added	Gross Output	Intermediate Consumption	Value Added	Gross Output	Intermediate Consumption	Value Added
	At constant prices of:1980											
	All Producers											
1 Agriculture, hunting, forestry and fishing	562	160	401	582	166	416	570	166	405	575	165	410
2 Mining and quarrying ᵃ	236	57	179	237	58	179	229	58	172	243	62	181
A Coal mining	4	1	3	4	1	3	4	1	3	5	1	4
B Crude petroleum and natural gas production	126	17	109	123	16	107	114	15	99	119	16	103
C Metal ore mining	78	35	43	80	36	44	82	37	45	89	40	49
D Other mining	27	4	23	30	5	25	28	4	24	30	5	25

4.2 Derivation of Value Added by Kind of Activity, in Constant Prices
(Continued)

Thousand Million Mexican pesos

	1984			1985			1986			1987		
	Gross Output	Intermediate Consumption	Value Added	Gross Output	Intermediate Consumption	Value Added	Gross Output	Intermediate Consumption	Value Added	Gross Output	Intermediate Consumption	Value Added
				At constant prices of:1980								
3 Manufacturing [a]	2427	1433	993	2562	1508	1054	2434	1435	998	2505	1476	1028
A Manufacture of food, beverages and tobacco	786	521	265	809	533	275	806	532	274	803	527	276
B Textile, wearing apparel and leather industries	281	150	131	286	152	134	269	141	128	258	136	122
C Manufacture of wood and wood products, including furniture	83	44	40	86	45	41	83	43	40	86	45	41
D Manufacture of paper and paper products, printing and publishing	121	65	56	131	70	61	126	67	59	129	69	60
E Manufacture of chemicals and chemical petroleum, coal, rubber and plastic products	448	269	179	472	283	189	461	279	183	489	297	192
F Manufacture of non-metallic mineral products, except products of petroleum and coal	113	45	68	123	50	73	113	45	68	125	50	75
G Basic metal industries	172	111	61	173	112	61	163	106	57	180	116	63
H Manufacture of fabricated metal products, machinery and equipment	392	215	177	448	249	200	381	208	173	407	224	183
I Other manufacturing industries	31	13	17	34	15	19	30	13	17	28	12	16
4 Electricity, gas and water	91	34	58	94	32	62	96	32	65	101	34	67
5 Construction	518	258	260	537	269	267	482	242	240	491	245	246
6 Wholesale and retail trade, restaurants and hotels	1563	265	1298	1573	261	1312	1490	264	1227	1505	272	1234
7 Transport, storage and communication	424	126	298	430	124	306	424	128	296	438	133	305
8 Finance, insurance, real estate and business services	539	59	481	559	60	499	580	63	517	604	69	535
9 Community, social and personal services	583	152	431	585	155	430	559	148	411	562	150	411
Total, Industries	6943	2543	4400	7159	2634	4525	6866	2536	4330	7024	2606	4418
Producers of Government Services	553	94	459	558	100	458	566	96	470	559	88	471
Other Producers	...	...	...	...	...	...	...	...	...	...	...	...
Total	7496	2637	4858	7717	2733	4983	7432	2632	4800	7583	2694	4889
Less: Imputed bank service charge	...	-62	62	...	-63	63	...	-64	64	...	-66	66
Import duties	...	...	...	...	...	...	...	...	...	...	...	...
Value added tax	...	...	...	...	...	...	...	...	...	...	...	...
Total	7496	2700	4796	7717	2796	4920	7432	2696	4736	7583	2759	4824

	1988			1989			1990			1991		
	Gross Output	Intermediate Consumption	Value Added	Gross Output	Intermediate Consumption	Value Added	Gross Output	Intermediate Consumption	Value Added	Gross Output	Intermediate Consumption	Value Added
				At constant prices of:1980								
				All Producers								
1 Agriculture, hunting, forestry and fishing	558	163	395	546	160	386	573	164	409	581	168	413
2 Mining and quarrying [a]	244	62	182	242	61	181	249	63	186	249	61	188
A Coal mining	5	1	4	4	1	3	4	1	3	4	1	3
B Crude petroleum and natural gas production	118	15	103	119	16	103	121	16	105	126	17	110
C Metal ore mining	91	41	50	88	40	48	92	41	51	88	39	49
D Other mining	30	4	26	31	5	26	31	5	27	31	5	26

Mexico

Thousand Million Mexican pesos

	1988			1989			1990			1991		
	Gross Output	Intermediate Consumption	Value Added	Gross Output	Intermediate Consumption	Value Added	Gross Output	Intermediate Consumption	Value Added	Gross Output	Intermediate Consumption	Value Added
				At constant prices of:1980								
3 Manufacturing [a]	2584	1522	1061	2759	1622	1137	2930	1724	1206	3056	1802	1254
A Manufacture of food, beverages and tobacco	805	528	277	851	553	298	872	565	307	914	591	323
B Textile, wearing apparel and leather industries	259	137	122	267	140	127	274	144	130	266	141	125
C Manufacture of wood and wood products, including furniture	84	43	40	82	43	40	82	42	39	82	43	39
D Manufacture of paper and paper products, printing and publishing	134	72	62	143	76	67	149	80	70	147	79	69
E Manufacture of chemicals and chemical petroleum, coal, rubber and plastic products	497	301	196	541	328	213	573	348	225	588	357	231
F Manufacture of non-metallic mineral products, except products of petroleum and coal	122	49	73	128	51	77	137	56	82	142	58	84
G Basic metal industries	188	121	67	193	124	68	209	135	74	200	129	71
H Manufacture of fabricated metal products, machinery and equipment	466	259	207	522	292	229	598	339	259	681	390	291
I Other manufacturing industries	29	13	16	32	14	18	35	15	20	36	16	20
4 Electricity, gas and water	105	34	71	113	36	76	117	39	79	121	41	81
5 Construction	485	240	245	501	250	250	537	269	268	554	280	274
6 Wholesale and retail trade, restaurants and hotels	1529	275	1255	1593	291	1302	1677	322	1355	1761	347	1414
7 Transport, storage and communication	445	133	312	468	143	325	500	153	347	529	162	367
8 Finance, insurance, real estate and business services	617	74	543	637	78	559	663	83	580	692	89	603
9 Community, social and personal services	563	152	411	579	159	420	594	164	430	618	173	445
Total, Industries	7130	2656	4475	7437	2800	4637	7840	2981	4859	8160	3122	5038
Producers of Government Services	556	80	476	556	76	480	569	82	486	591	86	505
Other Producers	...	...	...	...	...	...	...	...	...	...	...	...
Total	7687	2735	4951	7993	2876	5117	8409	3063	5346	8751	3208	5543
Less: Imputed bank service charge	...	-68	68	...	-69	69	...	-74	74	...	-80	80
Import duties	...	...	...	...	...	...	...	...	...	...	...	...
Value added tax	...	...	...	...	...	...	...	...	...	...	...	...
Total	7687	2803	4884	7993	2946	5047	8409	3137	5272	8751	3288	5463

a) Basic petroleum manufacturing is included in item 'Mining and quarrying'.

Mongolia

Source. The official data are published annually in 'National Economy of the Mongolian People's Republic'.
General note. The estimates shown in the following tables have been prepared in accordance with the System of Material Product Balances. Therefore, these estimates are not comparable in concept and coverage with those conforming to the United Nations System of National Accounts.

1a Net Material Product by Use at Current Market Prices

Million Mongolian tugriks

	1980	1981	1982	1983	1984	1985	1986	1987	1988	1989	1990	1991
1 Personal consumption	3500.5	3647.1	3856.4	4068.1	4262.5	4429.5	4618.7	4844.4	5066.7	5348.3	5746.1	...
2 Material consumption in the units of the non-material sphere serving individuals	768.5	924.1	909.5	957.7	1007.6	1078.6	1173.0	1222.9	1368.7	1431.1	1326.3	...
Consumption of the Population	4269.0	4571.2	4765.9	5025.8	5270.1	5508.1	5791.7	6067.3	6435.4	6779.4	7072.4	...
3 Material consumption in the units of the non-material sphere serving the community as a whole	360.1	464.4	536.5	585.5	624.7	660.9	755.5	774.1	779.2	743.6	714.0	...
4 Net fixed capital formation	2882.5	2358.4	2642.6	2544.4	4298.5	4759.0	2505.8	3213.3	2824.9	3195.5	806.6	...
5 Increase in material circulating assets and in stocks	-267.2	1282.1	986.7	1313.4	-679.7	-618.2	1599.7	1.0	290.4	394.5	1477.3	...
6 Losses	...	...	...	...	...	...	...	...	...	...	...	...
7 Exports of goods and material services	1343.2	1583.4	1923.6	2082.1	2343.5	2237.2	2508.6	2670.4	2616.7	2309.2	2238.9	...
8 Less: Imports of goods and material services	3173.0	4230.9	4241.6	4386.5	4694.6	5126.9	6078.1	5627.7	5454.5	4968.7	4439.8	...
Statistical discrepancy	162.3	122.0	212.0	160.6	215.6	216.4	164.4	380.3	407.5	192.5	458.1	...
Net Material Product	5576.9	6150.6	6825.7	7325.3	7378.1	7636.5	7247.6	7478.7	7899.6	8646.0	8327.5	...

2a Net Material Product by Kind of Activity of the Material Sphere in Current Market Prices

Percentages

	1980	1981	1982	1983	1984	1985	1986	1987	1988	1989	1990	1991
1 Agriculture and forestry	15.0	16.4	17.9	18.0	17.0	16.2	21.0	18.8	...	...	...	...
2 Industrial activity	29.3	29.4	30.9	32.2	32.3	32.6	33.7	33.7	...	...	...	...
3 Construction	6.1	5.6	5.1	4.8	5.0	5.0	5.8	6.7	...	...	...	...
4 Wholesale and retail trade and restaurants and other eating and drinking places	36.3	35.9	33.8	32.8	33.0	33.0	25.7	27.2	...	...	...	...
5 Transport and communication	11.2	10.9	10.5	10.5	11.0	11.5	11.7	11.5	...	...	...	...
A Transport	10.1	9.7	9.3	9.2	9.6	10.1	10.2	10.0	...	...	...	...
B Communication	1.1	1.2	1.2	1.3	1.4	1.4	1.5	1.5	...	...	...	...
6 Other activities of the material sphere	2.0	1.8	1.8	1.7	1.7	1.7	2.1	2.1	...	...	...	...
Net material product	100.0	100.0	100.0	100.0	100.0	100.0	100.0	100.0	...	...	...	...

2b Net Material Product by Kind of Activity of the Material Sphere in Constant Market Prices

Index numbers 1970=100

	1980	1981	1982	1983	1984	1985	1986	1987	1988	1989	1990	1991
					At constant prices of:1970							
1 Agriculture and forestry	81	95	109	109	99	109	115	108	...	...	...	...
2 Industrial activity	295	321	355	390	424	447	457	470	...	...	...	...
3 Construction	188	188	190	193	202	210	232	276	...	...	...	...
4 Wholesale and retail trade and restaurants and other eating and drinking places a	160	171	179	187	194	200	211	230	...	...	...	...
5 Transport and communication	266	285	306	327	347	376	422	430	...	...	...	...
A Transport	262	277	295	312	330	359	404	409	...	...	...	...
B Communication	313	379	426	493	532	559	621	657	...	...	...	...
6 Other activities of the material sphere	157	157	171	176	175	175	198	200	...	...	...	...
Net material product	181	196	213	226	236	249	262	272	...	...	...	...

a) Item 'Other activities of the material sphere' is included in item 'Wholesale and retail trade and restaurants and other eating and drinking places'.

Montserrat

Source. Government of Montserrat, Statistics Office, 'National Accounts Statistics 1975-82'.
General note. The estimates shown in the following tables have been prepared in accordance with the United Nations System of National Accounts so far as the existing data would permit.

1.1 Expenditure on the Gross Domestic Product, in Current Prices

Million East Caribbean dollars

	1980	1981	1982	1983	1984	1985	1986	1987	1988	1989	1990	1991
1 Government final consumption expenditure	12.2	14.1	16.9	17.9	19.3	20.3	21.3	...	...	...	...	...
2 Private final consumption expenditure	71.2	76.5	81.9	83.7	90.2	96.4	102.1	...	...	...	...	...
3 Gross capital formation	26.8	33.7	32.1	25.6	24.7	26.2	40.8	...	...	...	...	...
A Increase in stocks	5.2	4.3	1.5	2.0	2.5	1.5	3.2	...	...	...	...	...
B Gross fixed capital formation	21.6	29.4	30.6	23.6	22.2	24.7	37.6	...	...	...	...	...
Residential buildings								...	...	...	...	...
Non-residential buildings	11.4	14.4	18.6	12.9	13.9	16.0	19.1	...	...	...	...	...
Other construction and land improvement etc.								...	...	...	...	...
Other	10.2	15.0	12.0	10.7	8.3	8.7	18.5	...	...	...	...	...
4 Exports of goods and services	4.8	8.9	10.5	18.5	12.7	11.7	11.5	...	...	...	...	...
5 Less: Imports of goods and services	49.7	59.9	60.4	59.2	53.3	54.5	61.5	...	...	...	...	...
Equals: Gross Domestic Product	65.4	73.3	81.0	86.5	93.6	100.1	114.1	...	...	...	...	...

1.2 Expenditure on the Gross Domestic Product, in Constant Prices

Million East Caribbean dollars

	1980	1981	1982	1983	1984	1985	1986	1987	1988	1989	1990	1991
					At constant prices of:1977							
1 Government final consumption expenditure	7.5	8.3	9.1	9.4	9.4	10.1	9.8	...	...	...	...	...
2 Private final consumption expenditure	40.4	38.8	40.0	38.2	38.9	42.4	41.4	...	...	...	...	...
3 Gross capital formation	18.0	20.6	18.6	13.2	12.3	13.5	20.2	...	...	...	...	...
A Increase in stocks	3.0	2.3	0.8	1.1	0.7	0.8	1.6	...	...	...	...	...
B Gross fixed capital formation	15.0	18.3	17.6	12.1	11.6	12.7	18.6	...	...	...	...	...
Residential buildings								...	...	...	...	...
Non-residential buildings	8.2	8.9	10.6	6.9	7.4	8.5	10.2	...	...	...	...	...
Other construction and land improvement etc.								...	...	...	...	...
Other	6.8	9.4	7.0	5.2	4.1	4.2	8.4	...	...	...	...	...
4 Exports of goods and services	3.3	5.8	6.0	9.2	6.3	5.8	5.6	...	...	...	...	...
5 Less: Imports of goods and services	29.3	32.4	30.7	28.4	24.6	27.5	30.4	...	...	...	...	...
Equals: Gross Domestic Product	39.9	41.1	42.8	41.6	42.3	44.3	46.6	...	...	...	...	...

1.4 General Government Current Receipts and Disbursements

Thousand East Caribbean dollars

	1980	1981	1982	1983	1984	1985	1986	1987	1988	1989	1990	1991
					Receipts							
1 Operating surplus	...	...	...	...	...	...	...	...	...	...	...	...
2 Property and entrepreneurial income	1090	1994	...	...	...	...	...	...	...	...	...	...
3 Taxes, fees and contributions	12840	15453	...	...	...	...	...	...	...	...	...	...
A Indirect taxes	7948	9807	10020	9980	10554	11890	...	...	...	...	...	...
B Direct taxes	2853	3299	4040	5210	5686	5100	...	...	...	...	...	...
C Social security contributions	-	-	-	...	...	...	...	...	...	...	...	...
D Compulsory fees, fines and penalties	2039	2347	...	...	...	...	...	...	...	...	...	...
4 Other current transfers	763	570	785	865	1099	349	...	...	...	...	...	...
Total Current Receipts of General Government	14693	18017	19776	20920	21559	22119	...	...	...	...	...	...
					Disbursements							
1 Government final consumption expenditure	12242	14119	16877	17929	19279	20279	...	...	...	...	...	...

1.4 General Government Current Receipts and Disbursements
(Continued)

Thousand East Caribbean dollars

	1980	1981	1982	1983	1984	1985	1986	1987	1988	1989	1990	1991
A Compensation of employees	8700	8828	10792	12109	13400	14068	...	...	...	...	...	...
B Consumption of fixed capital	...	...	...	...	...	...	...	...	...	...	...	...
C Purchases of goods and services, net	3542	5291	6085	5820	5879	6211	...	...	...	...	...	...
D Less: Own account fixed capital formation	...	...	...	...	...	...	...	...	...	...	...	...
E Indirect taxes paid, net	...	...	...	...	...	...	...	...	...	...	...	...
2 Property income	57	303	370	326	268	257	...	...	...	...	...	...
A Interest	57	303	370	326	268	257	...	...	...	...	...	...
B Net land rent and royalties	-	-	-	-	-	-	...	...	...	...	...	...
3 Subsidies	120	135	-	130	139	155	...	...	...	...	...	...
4 Other current transfers	1096	1175	1378	1593	1668	1105	...	...	...	...	...	...
5 Net saving	1178	2285	1151	942	205	323	...	...	...	...	...	...
Total Current Disbursements and Net Saving of General Government	14693	18017	19776	20920	21559	22119	...	...	...	...	...	...

1.10 Gross Domestic Product by Kind of Activity, in Current Prices

Million East Caribbean dollars

	1980	1981	1982	1983	1984	1985	1986	1987	1988	1989	1990	1991
1 Agriculture, hunting, forestry and fishing	2.4	3.0	3.3	3.3	3.9	4.3	4.4	4.9	...	...	...	...
2 Mining and quarrying	0.4	0.5	1.1	0.7	1.1	1.2	1.4	1.5	...	...	...	...
3 Manufacturing	3.4	4.1	4.0	5.3	5.6	5.1	5.8	6.8	...	...	...	...
4 Electricity, gas and water	1.9	2.0	2.1	3.0	3.3	3.3	3.8	3.8	...	...	...	...
5 Construction	5.3	6.4	8.3	5.7	6.2	7.1	11.6	13.6	...	...	...	...
6 Wholesale and retail trade, restaurants and hotels	10.6	15.0	16.2	16.1	16.0	16.2	19.2	26.2	...	...	...	...
7 Transport, storage and communication	4.3	5.2	6.5	8.5	9.7	10.4	11.9	13.1	...	...	...	...
8 Finance, insurance, real estate and business services	17.7	15.7	15.5	19.8	20.7	19.9	20.9	21.7	...	...	...	...
9 Community, social and personal services	8.6	10.0	11.9	11.4	13.1	15.0	15.3	16.9	...	...	...	...
Total, Industries	54.6	61.9	68.9	73.8	79.6	82.5	94.3	108.5	...	...	...	...
Producers of Government Services	4.9	4.9	5.8	6.6	7.7	7.7	8.4	9.9	...	...	...	...
Other Producers	...	...	...	...	...	...	...	...	...	...	...	...
Subtotal a	59.5	66.8	74.7	80.4	87.3	90.2	102.7	118.4	...	...	...	...
Less: Imputed bank service charge	1.9	2.8	3.7	3.6	4.0	4.3	4.5	5.0	...	...	...	...
Plus: Import duties	...	...	...	...	...	...	...	...	...	...	...	...
Plus: Value added tax	...	...	...	...	...	...	...	...	...	...	...	...
Plus: Other adjustments b	7.8	9.3	10.0	9.7	10.3	...	...	...	...	...	...	...
Equals: Gross Domestic Product	65.4	73.3	81.0	86.5	93.6	...	...	...	...	...	...	...

a) Gross domestic product in factor values.
b) Item 'Other adjustments' refers to indirect taxes net of subsidies.

1.11 Gross Domestic Product by Kind of Activity, in Constant Prices

Million East Caribbean dollars

	1980	1981	1982	1983	1984	1985	1986	1987	1988	1989	1990	1991
				At constant prices of:1977								
1 Agriculture, hunting, forestry and fishing	1.5	1.7	1.6	1.4	1.7	1.8	1.7	1.8	...	...	...	...
2 Mining and quarrying	0.3	0.3	0.7	0.3	0.5	0.5	0.5	0.5	...	...	...	...
3 Manufacturing	3.1	3.5	3.4	3.6	3.5	3.5	3.6	3.7	...	...	...	...
4 Electricity, gas and water	1.1	1.1	1.1	1.2	1.3	1.3	1.4	1.5	...	...	...	...
5 Construction	3.6	4.0	4.7	3.1	3.3	3.8	4.7	6.5	...	...	...	...
6 Wholesale and retail trade, restaurants and hotels	7.7	8.1	8.2	8.0	7.6	8.0	9.1	10.7	...	...	...	...
7 Transport, storage and communication	2.8	2.9	3.1	3.2	3.2	3.5	3.7	4.0	...	...	...	...
8 Finance, insurance, real estate and business services	8.5	8.7	8.8	8.9	9.2	9.4	8.9	9.0	...	...	...	...
9 Community, social and personal services	5.0	4.9	4.7	4.5	4.6	4.7	5.7	5.7	...	...	...	...
Total, Industries	33.7	35.2	36.3	34.2	34.9	36.5	39.3	43.4	...	...	...	...
Producers of Government Services	3.2	3.1	3.3	3.6	3.9	4.1	4.0	4.4	...	...	...	...

Montserrat

1.11 Gross Domestic Product by Kind of Activity, in Constant Prices
(Continued)

Million East Caribbean dollars

	1980	1981	1982	1983	1984	1985	1986	1987	1988	1989	1990	1991
					At constant prices of:1977							
Other Producers	...	...	...	...	...	...	...	...	...	...	...	...
Subtotal a	36.9	38.3	39.6	37.8	38.8	40.6	43.3	47.8	...	...	...	...
Less: Imputed bank service charge	1.6	1.6	1.6	1.6	1.7	1.7	1.8	1.9	...	...	...	...
Plus: Import duties	...	...	...	...	...	...	...	...	...	...	...	...
Plus: Value added tax	...	...	...	...	...	...	...	...	...	...	...	...
Plus: Other adjustments b	4.6	4.4	4.8	5.4	5.2	5.3	...	...	...	...	...	...
Equals: Gross Domestic Product	39.9	41.1	42.8	41.6	42.3	44.2	...	...	...	...	...	...

a) Gross domestic product in factor values.
b) Item 'Other adjustments' refers to indirect taxes net of subsidies.

2.1 Government Final Consumption Expenditure by Function, in Current Prices

Thousand East Caribbean dollars

		1980	1981	1982	1983	1984	1985	1986	1987	1988	1989	1990	1991
1	General public services	2281	2378	3109	2715	3786	3802	...	...	...	...	...	...
2	Defence	71	43	56	63	59	59	...	...	...	...	...	...
3	Public order and safety	1373	1486	1752	1961	2031	2301	...	...	...	...	...	...
4	Education	2222	2513	2772	3170	3727	4533	...	...	...	...	...	...
5	Health	2298	2502	2822	3121	3063	3093	...	...	...	...	...	...
6	Social security and welfare	1225	1174	1522	1652	1275	982	...	...	...	...	...	...
7	Housing and community amenities	75	148	141	135	-45	188	...	...	...	...	...	...
8	Recreational, cultural and religious affairs	64	75	175	249	120	341	...	...	...	...	...	...
9	Economic services	2500	3793	4475	4832	5250	4963	...	...	...	...	...	...
	A Fuel and energy	54	63	69	191	-	-	...	...	...	...	...	...
	B Agriculture, forestry, fishing and hunting	732	661	732	914	1380	1569	...	...	...	...	...	...
	C Mining, manufacturing and construction, except fuel and energy	457	956	1416	2436	3391	2433	...	...	...	...	...	...
	D Transportation and communication	1173	1641	1959	868	420	927	...	...	...	...	...	...
	E Other economic affairs	84	472	299	423	59	34	...	...	...	...	...	...
10	Other functions	133	7	38	-	13	17	...	...	...	...	...	...
	Total Government Final Consumption Expenditure	12242	14119	16862	17929	19279	20279	...	...	...	...	...	...

4.1 Derivation of Value Added by Kind of Activity, in Current Prices

Million East Caribbean dollars

		1980			1981		
		Gross Output	Intermediate Consumption	Value Added	Gross Output	Intermediate Consumption	Value Added
				All Producers			
1	Agriculture, hunting, forestry and fishing	...	...	2.4	...	...	3.0
	A Agriculture and hunting	...	...	1.7	...	...	2.3
	B Forestry and logging	...	...	0.4	...	...	0.4
	C Fishing	...	...	0.3	...	...	0.3
2	Mining and quarrying	...	...	0.4	...	...	0.5
3	Manufacturing	...	...	3.5	...	...	4.1
4	Electricity, gas and water	...	...	1.9	...	...	2.0
5	Construction	...	...	5.3	...	...	6.4
6	Wholesale and retail trade, restaurants and hotels	...	...	10.7	...	...	15.0
	A Wholesale and retail trade	...	...	8.9	...	...	12.6
	B Restaurants and hotels	...	...	1.7	...	...	2.4
	Restaurants	...	...	0.1	...	...	0.2
	Hotels and other lodging places	...	...	1.6	...	...	2.2
7	Transport, storage and communication	...	...	4.3	...	...	5.2
	A Transport and storage	...	...	3.5	...	...	4.3
	B Communication	...	...	0.8	...	...	0.9
8	Finance, insurance, real estate and business services	...	...	17.7	...	...	15.7
	A Financial institutions	...	...	2.3	...	...	2.7

4.1 Derivation of Value Added by Kind of Activity, in Current Prices
(Continued)

Million East Caribbean dollars

	1980			1981		
	Gross Output	Intermediate Consumption	Value Added	Gross Output	Intermediate Consumption	Value Added
B Insurance	...	...	0.4	...	...	0.8
C Real estate and business services	...	...	15.0	...	...	12.2
Real estate, except dwellings	...	...	1.2	...	...	1.5
Dwellings	...	...	13.8	...	...	10.7
9 Community, social and personal services	...	...	8.6	...	...	10.0
A Sanitary and similar services	...	...	-	...	...	-
B Social and related community services	...	...	5.8	...	...	7.2
C Recreational and cultural services	...	...	2.0	...	...	1.9
D Personal and household services	...	...	0.8	...	...	0.9
Total, Industries	...	...	54.6	...	...	61.9
Producers of Government Services	...	...	4.9	...	...	4.9
Other Producers	...	...	...	...	...	...
Total a	...	...	59.5	...	...	66.8
Less: Imputed bank service charge	...	...	1.9	...	...	2.8
Import duties	...	...	...	...	...	...
Value added tax	...	...	...	...	...	...
Other adjustments b	...	...	7.8	...	...	9.3
Total	...	...	65.4	...	...	73.3
Memorandum Item: Mineral fuels and power	...	...	1.4	...	...	

a) Gross domestic product in factor values.
b) Item 'Other adjustments' refers to indirect taxes net of subsidies.

Morocco

Source. Reply to the United Nations National Accounts Questionnaire from the Division du Plan et des Etudes Economiques, Rabat. Official estimates are published by the Division in 'Comptes de la Nation'.
General note. The estimates have been adjusted by the Division du Plan et des Etudes Economiques to conform to the United Nations System of National Accounts so far as the existing data would permit. It should be noted that the domestic territory is defined to include all de facto residents, such as foreign diplomats and troops.

1.1 Expenditure on the Gross Domestic Product, in Current Prices

Thousand Million Moroccan Dirhams

	1980	1981	1982	1983	1984	1985	1986	1987	1988	1989	1990	1991
1 Government final consumption expenditure	13.59	15.08	17.00	16.63	17.48	20.52	23.75	24.63	28.03	30.41	32.98	36.80
2 Private final consumption expenditure	49.50	53.70	61.49	66.55	77.42	84.48	104.19	104.73	115.01	127.20	138.71	160.74
3 Gross capital formation	17.93	20.64	26.22	23.78	28.40	35.13	35.27	33.04	38.26	45.93	53.57	55.06
A Increase in stocks	1.45	0.13	0.84	-0.45	2.45	5.20	2.28	1.41	1.03	1.76	2.57	1.27
B Gross fixed capital formation	16.48	20.51	25.38	24.23	25.95	29.93	32.99	31.63	37.23	44.17	51.00	53.79
4 Exports of goods and services	13.04	16.22	18.14	21.10	26.95	32.20	33.02	35.52	44.88	42.75	52.26	53.60
5 Less: Imports of goods and services	19.97	26.60	29.94	28.92	37.91	42.81	41.94	41.58	44.93	52.36	63.55	65.45
Equals: Gross Domestic Product	74.09	79.03	92.90	99.14	112.34	129.51	154.29	156.34	181.25	193.93	213.99	240.76

1.7 External Transactions on Current Account, Summary

Thousand Million Moroccan Dirhams

	1980	1981	1982	1983	1984	1985	1986	1987	1988	1989	1990	1991
Payments to the Rest of the World												
1 Imports of goods and services	19.97	26.60	29.94	28.92	37.91	42.81	41.94	41.58	44.93	52.36	63.55	65.45
A Imports of merchandise c.i.f.	18.39	24.54	27.48	26.38	35.13	39.57	37.19	37.87	40.50	48.10	58.78	60.70
B Other	1.58	2.06	2.46	2.54	2.78	3.24	4.75	3.71	4.43	4.26	4.77	4.75
2 Factor income to the rest of the world	2.79	4.32	5.00	5.09	5.46	8.17	6.81	6.89	9.21	10.85	9.68	12.65
A Compensation of employees	0.01	0.01	0.01	0.01	0.02	0.02	0.03	0.03	0.06	0.06	0.07	0.08
B Property and entrepreneurial income	2.78	4.31	4.99	5.08	5.44	8.15	6.78	6.86	9.15	10.79	9.61	12.57
3 Current transfers to the rest of the world a	0.63	0.71	0.69	0.73	0.82	0.68	0.25	0.35	0.23	0.11	0.23	0.39
4 Surplus of the nation on current transactions	-5.30	-9.15	-10.92	-6.05	-8.32	-8.05	-1.32	1.98	4.33	-6.09	-0.83	-2.58
Payments to the Rest of the World and Surplus of the Nation on Current Transactions	18.10	22.45	24.73	28.70	35.90	43.62	47.68	50.80	58.70	57.23	72.62	75.91
Receipts From The Rest of the World												
1 Exports of goods and services	13.04	16.22	18.14	21.10	26.95	32.20	33.02	35.52	44.88	42.75	52.26	53.60
A Exports of merchandise f.o.b.	9.65	12.00	12.47	14.76	19.12	21.75	22.11	23.39	29.76	28.27	34.86	37.29
B Other	3.39	4.22	5.67	6.34	7.83	10.45	10.91	12.13	15.12	14.48	17.40	16.31
2 Factor income from rest of the world	0.25	0.31	0.33	0.23	0.37	0.52	0.49	0.44	1.15	1.26	1.75	2.77
A Compensation of employees	0.03	0.04	0.05	0.05	0.07	0.08	0.10	0.10	0.11	0.10	0.11	0.11
B Property and entrepreneurial income	0.22	0.27	0.28	0.18	0.30	0.44	0.39	0.34	1.04	1.16	1.64	2.66
3 Current transfers from rest of the world	4.79	5.96	6.25	7.37	8.55	10.88	14.19	14.85	12.67	13.22	18.61	19.53
Receipts from the Rest of the World on Current Transactions	18.10	22.45	24.73	28.70	35.90	43.62	47.70	50.81	58.70	57.23	72.62	75.91

a) Item 'Current transfers to the rest of the world' includes net casualty insurance premiums and claims.

1.10 Gross Domestic Product by Kind of Activity, in Current Prices

Thousand Million Moroccan Dirhams

	1980	1981	1982	1983	1984	1985	1986	1987	1988	1989	1990	1991
1 Agriculture, hunting, forestry and fishing	13.65	10.21	14.22	15.03	16.85	21.50	29.52	24.07	31.35	33.37	35.87	45.51
2 Mining and quarrying a	3.41	4.41	3.95	4.11	5.31	5.63	4.54	3.99	5.24	5.45	5.65	4.94
3 Manufacturing	12.47	14.30	16.09	18.22	20.74	24.03	26.59	28.59	31.89	34.55	40.27	42.99
4 Electricity, gas and water ba	2.40	2.36	3.01	4.05	4.96	6.19	10.72	11.19	13.87	13.78	12.77	15.14
5 Construction	4.65	5.85	6.58	6.57	6.38	7.39	7.67	7.39	9.14	10.54	11.49	12.20
6 Wholesale and retail trade, restaurants and hotels	10.61	11.38	13.46	13.33	15.57	18.25	22.60	23.57	24.92	25.32	28.12	30.62
7 Transport, storage and communication	3.88	4.46	5.14	5.98	7.20	8.32	9.00	10.51	12.03	12.74	14.13	14.86
8 Finance, insurance, real estate and business services	1.88	2.02	2.11	2.41	3.25	3.86	4.57	5.19	5.90	6.23	6.93	9.95
9 Community, social and personal services	8.14	8.93	10.11	11.06	12.58	14.13	15.97	17.03	18.42	19.45	21.18	23.14

1.10 Gross Domestic Product by Kind of Activity, in Current Prices
(Continued)

Thousand Million Moroccan Dirhams

	1980	1981	1982	1983	1984	1985	1986	1987	1988	1989	1990	1991
Total, Industries	61.09	63.92	74.67	80.76	92.84	109.30	131.18	131.53	152.76	161.43	176.41	199.35
Producers of Government Services	8.79	10.43	11.77	13.18	14.01	14.84	16.16	17.81	19.91	22.81	25.34	28.48
Other Producers	...	...	...	...	...	...	...	...	...	...	...	...
Subtotal	69.88	74.35	86.44	93.94	106.85	124.14	147.34	149.34	172.67	184.24	201.75	227.83
Less: Imputed bank service charge	1.57	1.80	1.78	2.39	2.97	3.67	4.20	5.03	5.46	6.54	6.90	9.99
Plus: Import duties	5.79	6.48	8.24	7.59	8.48	9.05	11.15	12.03	14.04	16.22	19.14	22.91
Plus: Value added tax	...	...	...	...	...	...	...	...	...	...	...	...
Equals: Gross Domestic Product	74.09	79.03	92.90	99.14	112.34	129.51	154.29	156.34	181.25	193.92	213.99	240.75

a) Petroleum refining is included in item 'Electricity, gas and water'.
b) Item 'Electricity, gas and water' excludes gas.

1.11 Gross Domestic Product by Kind of Activity, in Constant Prices

Thousand Million Moroccan Dirhams

	1980	1981	1982	1983	1984	1985	1986	1987	1988	1989	1990	1991
					At constant prices of:1980							
1 Agriculture, hunting, forestry and fishing	13.65	9.75	13.15	11.79	12.23	14.48	19.80	15.13	19.88	20.80	19.40	23.35
2 Mining and quarrying a	3.41	3.47	3.29	3.42	3.64	3.62	3.52	3.48	3.89	3.29	3.62	3.28
3 Manufacturing	12.47	12.65	13.32	13.88	14.48	15.50	15.69	16.17	17.30	17.03	19.06	19.48
4 Electricity, gas and water ba	2.40	2.36	2.44	2.56	2.62	2.75	2.74	3.01	3.23	3.43	3.66	3.73
5 Construction	4.65	5.03	5.12	4.64	4.10	4.40	4.40	4.18	4.77	5.10	5.23	5.04
6 Wholesale and retail trade, restaurants and hotels	10.61	10.32	11.27	11.05	11.57	12.23	12.88	12.90	13.80	14.61	15.31	15.87
7 Transport, storage and communication	3.88	4.04	4.25	4.54	4.67	4.86	4.86	5.12	5.31	5.38	5.68	5.67
8 Finance, insurance, real estate and business services	1.88	1.80	1.69	1.82	2.19	2.41	2.63	2.90	3.22	3.30	3.45	4.56
9 Community, social and personal services	8.14	8.12	8.40	8.67	8.85	9.22	9.63	9.96	10.49	10.71	10.98	11.19
Total, Industries	61.09	57.54	62.93	62.37	64.35	69.47	76.15	72.85	81.88	83.65	86.39	92.17
Producers of Government Services	8.79	9.87	10.74	12.02	12.78	13.30	14.17	15.03	15.52	16.30	16.57	17.34
Other Producers	...	...	...	...	...	...	...	...	...	...	...	...
Subtotal	69.88	67.41	73.67	74.39	77.13	82.77	90.32	87.88	97.40	99.95	102.96	109.51
Less: Imputed bank service charge	1.57	1.60	1.44	1.81	2.01	2.30	2.41	2.81	2.99	3.46	3.43	4.58
Plus: Import duties	5.79	6.24	6.73	5.94	6.82	6.63	6.26	6.76	7.10	7.54	8.37	8.52
Plus: Value added tax	...	...	...	...	...	...	...	...	...	...	...	...
Equals: Gross Domestic Product	74.09	72.04	78.97	78.53	81.93	87.11	94.17	91.83	101.51	104.03	107.90	113.45

a) Petroleum refining is included in item 'Electricity, gas and water'.
b) Item 'Electricity, gas and water' excludes gas.

1.12 Relations Among National Accounting Aggregates

Thousand Million Moroccan Dirhams

	1980	1981	1982	1983	1984	1985	1986	1987	1988	1989	1990	1991
Gross Domestic Product	74.09	79.03	92.90	99.14	112.34	129.51	154.29	156.34	181.25	193.93	213.99	240.76
Plus: Net factor income from the rest of the world	-2.54	-4.01	-4.67	-4.86	-5.09	-7.65	-6.32	-6.45	-8.06	-9.59	-7.93	-9.87
Factor income from the rest of the world	0.25	0.31	0.33	0.23	0.37	0.52	0.48	0.44	1.15	1.26	1.75	2.77
Less: Factor income to the rest of the world	2.79	4.32	5.00	5.09	5.46	8.17	6.81	6.89	9.21	10.85	9.68	12.64
Equals: Gross National Product	71.55	75.02	88.23	94.28	107.25	121.86	147.97	149.89	173.19	184.34	206.06	230.89
Less: Consumption of fixed capital	...	...	...	...	...	...	...	...	...	...	...	...
Equals: National Income a	71.55	75.02	88.23	94.28	107.25	121.86	147.97	149.89	173.19	184.34	206.06	230.89
Plus: Net current transfers from the rest of the world	4.16	5.25	5.56	6.64	7.73	10.20	13.94	14.50	12.44	13.11	18.38	19.14
Current transfers from the rest of the world	4.79	5.96	6.25	7.37	8.55	10.88	14.19	14.85	12.67	13.22	18.61	19.53
Less: Current transfers to the rest of the world b	0.63	0.71	0.69	0.73	0.82	0.68	0.25	0.35	0.23	0.11	0.23	0.39
Equals: National Disposable Income c	75.71	80.26	93.79	100.92	114.98	132.06	161.91	164.39	185.63	197.45	224.44	250.03
Less: Final consumption	63.09	68.77	78.49	83.18	94.90	104.99	127.94	129.36	143.04	157.61	171.69	197.54
Equals: Net Saving d	12.63	11.49	15.30	17.74	20.08	27.07	33.95	35.02	42.59	39.85	52.75	52.49
Less: Surplus of the nation on current transactions	-5.30	-9.15	-10.92	-6.05	-8.32	-8.05	-1.32	1.97	4.32	-6.09	-0.83	-2.58
Equals: Net Capital Formation e	17.93	20.64	26.22	23.78	28.40	35.13	35.27	33.05	38.27	45.93	53.57	55.06

a) Item 'National income' includes consumption of fixed capital.
b) Item 'Current transfers to the rest of the world' includes net casualty insurance premiums and claims.
c) Item 'National disposable income' includes consumption of fixed capital.
d) Item 'Net saving' includes consumption of fixed capital.
e) Item 'Net capital formation' includes consumption of fixed capital.

Morocco

2.17 Exports and Imports of Goods and Services, Detail

Thousand Million Moroccan Dirhams

	1980	1981	1982	1983	1984	1985	1986	1987	1988	1989	1990	1991
Exports of Goods and Services												
1 Exports of merchandise, f.o.b.	9.65	12.00	12.47	14.76	19.12	21.75	22.11	23.39	29.76	28.27	34.86	37.29
2 Transport and communication	1.16	1.37	1.86	1.65	1.88	2.21	2.40	2.45	3.06	2.41	2.92	3.48
3 Insurance service charges	0.03	0.04	0.06	0.06	0.05	0.07	0.07	0.07	0.10	0.10	0.09	0.09
4 Other commodities	0.20	0.50	0.90	1.01	1.21	1.55	1.13	1.22	2.03	2.57	2.96	3.06
5 Adjustments of merchandise exports to change-of-ownership basis	...	...	...	...	...	...	...	...	...	...	...	...
6 Direct purchases in the domestic market by non-residential households a	1.91	2.20	2.70	3.46	4.49	6.39	6.99	8.06	9.50	9.01	11.01	9.26
7 Direct purchases in the domestic market by extraterritorial bodies	0.09	0.12	0.16	0.17	0.20	0.24	0.33	0.33	0.43	0.37	0.43	0.41
Total Exports of Goods and Services	13.04	16.22	18.14	21.10	26.95	32.20	33.02	35.52	44.88	42.75	52.26	53.60
Imports of Goods and Services												
1 Imports of merchandise, c.i.f.	18.39	24.54	27.48	26.38	35.13	39.57	37.19	37.87	40.50	48.10	58.78	60.70
2 Adjustments of merchandise imports to change-of-ownership basis	...	...	...	...	...	...	...	...	...	...	...	...
3 Other transport and communication	0.27	0.29	0.36	0.25	0.25	0.34	0.33	0.36	0.46	0.52	0.55	0.48
4 Other insurance service charges	0.01	0.02	0.02	0.01	0.02	0.03	0.03	0.03	0.04	0.04	0.04	0.04
5 Other commodities	0.74	1.08	1.36	1.46	1.64	1.72	3.14	1.83	2.14	1.94	2.14	1.96
6 Direct purchases abroad by government	0.08	0.09	0.11	0.11	0.11	0.12	0.16	0.17	0.22	0.23	0.24	0.28
7 Direct purchases abroad by resident households	0.48	0.58	0.62	0.71	0.76	1.03	1.10	1.31	1.58	1.54	1.79	1.98
Total Imports of Goods and Services	19.97	26.60	29.94	28.92	37.91	42.81	41.94	41.58	44.93	52.36	63.55	65.45
Balance of Goods and Services	-6.93	-10.38	-11.80	-7.82	-10.96	-10.61	-8.92	-6.06	-0.06	-9.61	-11.28	-11.85
Total Imports and Balance of Goods and Services	13.04	16.22	18.14	21.10	26.95	32.20	33.02	35.52	44.87	42.75	52.26	53.60

a) Item 'Direct purchases in the domestic market by non-resident households' refers to foreign tourists and agencies.

Mozambique

Source. The estimates are published by the Direccao Nacional de Estatistica in 'Infermacao Estadistica'.
General note. The estimates shown in the following tables have been prepared in accordance with the United Nations System of National Accounts so far as the existing data would permit.

1.1 Expenditure on the Gross Domestic Product, in Current Prices

Thousand Million Mozambique Meticais

	1980	1981	1982	1983	1984	1985	1986	1987	1988	1989	1990	1991
1 Government final consumption expenditure	14	17	19	21	23	23	27	68	112	195	271	378
2 Private final consumption expenditure	64	65	77	80	93	128	142	403	645	931	1290	1663
A Households	64	65	77	80	93	128	142	403	645	931	1290	1663
B Private non-profit institutions serving households	...	...	...	...	...	...	...	...	...	...	...	...
3 Gross capital formation	15	16	18	9	11	10	16	102	214	343	511	799
4 Exports of goods and services	-14	-16	-21	-19	-18	-15	6	51	99	149	213	438
5 Less: Imports of goods and services							24	202	427	652	868	1407
Statistical discrepancy	-1	-	-1	-	-	1	-	4	16	-	-29	-
Equals: Gross Domestic Product	78	82	92	91	109	147	167	426	659	966	1388	1871

1.2 Expenditure on the Gross Domestic Product, in Constant Prices

Thousand Million Mozambique Meticais

	1980	1981	1982	1983	1984	1985	1986	1987	1988	1989	1990	1991
	At constant prices of:1980											
1 Government final consumption expenditure	14	16	16	16	14	11	11	11	12	...	...	...
2 Private final consumption expenditure	64	63	63	58	60	55	55	56	58	...	...	...
A Households	64	63	63	58	60	55	55	56	58	...	...	...
B Private non-profit institutions serving households	...	...	...	...	...	...	...	...	...	...	...	...
3 Gross capital formation	15	15	15	7	9	7	11	13	15	...	...	...
4 Exports of goods and services	-14	-15	-17	-15	-15	-11	-14	-14	-15	...	...	...
5 Less: Imports of goods and services										...	...	...
Equals: Gross Domestic Product	78	79	76	66	68	62	63	66	69	...	...	...

1.3 Cost Components of the Gross Domestic Product

Thousand Million Mozambique Meticais

	1980	1981	1982	1983	1984	1985	1986	1987	1988	1989	1990	1991
1 Indirect taxes, net	5	5	3	1	2	2	5	25	...	...	...	...
A Indirect taxes	10	10	10	11	9	10	15	38	...	...	...	...
B Less: Subsidies	4	5	7	10	6	7	10	13	...	...	...	...
2 Consumption of fixed capital	5	5	5	4	4	4	4	...	...	...	...	...
3 Compensation of employees paid by resident producers to:	65	69	79	79	96	137	...	...	...	...	...	...
4 Operating surplus							...	...	...	...	...	...
Equals: Gross Domestic Product	78	82	92	91	109	147	167	426	...	...	...	...

1.12 Relations Among National Accounting Aggregates

Thousand Million Mozambique Meticais

	1980	1981	1982	1983	1984	1985	1986	1987	1988	1989	1990	1991
Gross Domestic Product	78	82	92	91	109	147	167	...	...	...	...	...
Plus: Net factor income from the rest of the world	1	-	-1	1	-	-	1	...	...	...	...	...
Equals: Gross National Product	79	81	91	92	109	147	168	...	...	...	...	...
Less: Consumption of fixed capital	5	5	5	4	4	4	...	...	...	...	...	...
Equals: National Income	74	76	86	88	105	143	...	...	...	...	...	...
Plus: Net current transfers from the rest of the world	...	...	...	...	...	...	...	...	...	...	...	...
Equals: National Disposable Income	...	...	...	...	...	...	...	...	...	...	...	...
Less: Final consumption	...	...	...	...	...	...	...	...	...	...	...	...
Equals: Net Saving	...	...	...	...	...	...	...	...	...	...	...	...
Less: Surplus of the nation on current transactions	...	...	...	...	...	...	...	...	...	...	...	...
Equals: Net Capital Formation	...	...	...	...	...	...	...	...	...	...	...	...

Myanmar

Source. Reply to the United Nations National Accounts Questionnaire from the Planning Department, Ministry of Planning and Finance, Rangoon. The official estimates and descriptions are published annually in the 'National Income of Myanmar' and 'Review of the Financial Economic and Social Conditions', by the same Department.

General note. The estimates shown in the following tables have been prepared in accordance with the United Nations System of National Accounts so far as the existing data would permit.

1.1 Expenditure on the Gross Domestic Product, in Current Prices

Million Myanmarese kyats — Fiscal year beginning 1 April

	1980	1981	1982	1983	1984	1985	1986	1987	1988	1989	1990	1991
1 Government final consumption expenditure	31775	35217	39747	42685	47395	49532	53067	63168	67754	113726	132006	152073
2 Private final consumption expenditure												
3 Gross capital formation	8293	9841	10375	8962	8110	8693	7478	7941	9763	11501	20190	26735
A Increase in stocks	1065	1206	331	-95	-367	44	-1139	-742	2467	-326	-2005	-1448
B Gross fixed capital formation	7228	8635	10044	9057	8477	8649	8617	8683	7296	11827	22195	28183
4 Exports of goods and services	3176	3432	3003	3373	3133	2566	2419	1655	2169	2834	3057	3211
5 Less: Imports of goods and services	4635	5611	6314	5197	5041	4802	3936	4066	3443	3395	5279	5448
Equals: Gross Domestic Product	38609	42879	46811	49823	53597	55989	59028	68698	76243	124666	149974	176571

1.2 Expenditure on the Gross Domestic Product, in Constant Prices

Million Myanmarese kyats — Fiscal year beginning 1 April

At constant prices of:1985

	1980	1981	1982	1983	1984	1985	1986	1987	1988	1989	1990	1991
1 Government final consumption expenditure	37481	39802	42879	44916	48522	49532	49053	47629	41065	41826	41849	42238
2 Private final consumption expenditure												
3 Gross capital formation	9103	10289	10533	9034	8163	8693	7189	6978	6423	6375	8215	8543
A Increase in stocks	1223	1326	355	-108	-383	44	-1083	-578	1024	-77	-630	-843
B Gross fixed capital formation	7880	8963	10178	9142	8546	8649	8272	7556	5399	6452	8845	9386
4 Exports of goods and services	2800	2888	2729	3153	2819	2566	3068	2495	2762	3528	4189	4160
5 Less: Imports of goods and services	5022	5822	6427	5225	5067	4802	3913	3924	3109	2846	4027	4039
Equals: Gross Domestic Product	44362	47157	49714	51878	54437	55989	55397	53178	47141	48883	50226	50902

1.3 Cost Components of the Gross Domestic Product

Million Myanmarese kyats — Fiscal year beginning 1 April

	1980	1981	1982	1983	1984	1985	1986	1987	1988	1989	1990	1991
1 Indirect taxes, net	3709	4063	4363	4336	4288	4253	3903	3893	2811	4435	6610	6461
A Indirect taxes	3709	4063	4363	4336	4288	4253	3903	3893	2811	4435	6610	6461
B Less: Subsidies	...	...	...	...	...	...	...	...	...	...	...	...
2 Consumption of fixed capital	3415	3784	4166	4484	4871	5056	5318	6245	6850	7519	8309	9251
3 Compensation of employees paid by resident producers to:	14596	16190	17812	18998	20637	21950	23711	28154	32816	52535	64414	76526
4 Operating surplus	16889	18842	20470	22005	23801	24731	26096	30406	33766	60177	70641	84333
Equals: Gross Domestic Product	38609	42879	46811	49823	53597	55989	59028	68698	76243	124666	149974	176571

1.10 Gross Domestic Product by Kind of Activity, in Current Prices

Million Myanmarese kyats — Fiscal year beginning 1 April

	1980	1981	1982	1983	1984	1985	1986	1987	1988	1989	1990	1991
1 Agriculture, hunting, forestry and fishing	17970	20330	22319	23711	25795	26983	29633	37990	43739	71069	86807	103598
2 Mining and quarrying	427	430	501	504	545	533	483	478	512	988	1040	1076
3 Manufacturing	3683	4009	4350	4775	5280	5561	5450	5337	5723	10731	11115	12206
4 Electricity, gas and water [a]	135	167	210	227	263	278	289	289	321	435	402	372
5 Construction	647	692	833	872	946	945	976	970	833	1538	2478	3073
6 Wholesale and retail trade, restaurants and hotels [b]	10121	10714	11512	12273	12886	13389	13526	14581	15849	27156	33731	40096
7 Transport, storage and communication	1357	1612	1834	1985	2106	2218	2311	2459	2240	3346	4052	4316
8 Finance, insurance, real estate and business services [c]	829	1039	1096	1172	1254	1332	1421	1498	1538	222	270	295
9 Community, social and personal services [bca]	1603	1854	1941	2038	2125	2182	2266	2326	2491	3434	3984	5062
Total, Industries	36772	40847	44596	47557	51200	53421	56355	65928	73246	118919	143879	170094
Producers of Government Services	1837	2032	2215	2266	2397	2568	2673	2770	2997	5747	6095	6477

1.10 Gross Domestic Product by Kind of Activity, in Current Prices
(Continued)

Million Myanmarese kyats

	1980	1981	1982	1983	1984	1985	1986	1987	1988	Fiscal year beginning 1 April 1989	1990	1991
Other Producers	...	...	...	...	...	...	...	...	...	...	...	...
Subtotal	38609	42879	46811	49823	53597	55989	59028	68698	76243	124666	149974	176571
Less: Imputed bank service charge	...	...	...	...	...	...	...	...	...	...	...	...
Plus: Import duties	...	...	...	...	...	...	...	...	...	...	...	...
Plus: Value added tax	...	...	...	...	...	...	...	...	...	...	...	...
Equals: Gross Domestic Product	38609	42879	46811	49823	53597	55989	59028	68698	76243	124666	149974	176571
Memorandum Item: Mineral fuels and power	4269	4909	5242	...	...	...	...	...	...	...	...	...

a) Item 'Electricity, gas and water' refers to electricity only. Gas and water are included in item 'Community, social and personal services'.
b) Restaurants and hotels are included in item 'Community, social and personal services'.
c) Insurance, real estate and business services are included in item 'Community, social and personal services'.

1.11 Gross Domestic Product by Kind of Activity, in Constant Prices

Million Myanmarese kyats

	1980	1981	1982	1983	1984	1985	1986	1987	1988	Fiscal year beginning 1 April 1989	1990	1991
					At constant prices of:1985							
1 Agriculture, hunting, forestry and fishing	21262	22904	24307	25443	26424	26983	27120	25819	22595	23589	24060	24381
2 Mining and quarrying	382	399	432	446	513	533	498	430	344	449	423	409
3 Manufacturing	4237	4529	4770	4968	5403	5561	5123	4870	4094	4555	4557	4541
4 Electricity, gas and water a	150	181	212	229	264	278	289	301	283	323	339	360
5 Construction	674	783	836	879	953	945	947	898	688	913	1185	1294
6 Wholesale and retail trade, restaurants and hotels b	11256	11493	11892	12358	12910	13389	12820	11993	10558	11118	11365	11381
7 Transport, storage and communication	1560	1759	1937	2046	2166	2218	2259	2328	1989	2188	2278	2287
8 Finance, insurance, real estate and business services c	988	1080	1116	1175	1256	1332	1421	1498	1604	229	268	294
9 Community, social and personal services bca	1878	1929	1969	2050	2136	2182	2261	2296	2199	2232	2284	2335
Total, Industries	42387	45057	47471	49594	52025	53421	52738	50433	44354	45596	46759	47282
Producers of Government Services	1975	2100	2243	2284	2412	2568	2659	2745	2787	3287	3467	3620
Other Producers	...	...	...	...	...	...	...	...	...	...	...	...
Subtotal	44362	47157	49714	51878	54437	55989	55397	53178	47141	48883	50226	50902
Less: Imputed bank service charge	...	...	...	...	...	...	...	...	...	...	...	...
Plus: Import duties	...	...	...	...	...	...	...	...	...	...	...	...
Plus: Value added tax	...	...	...	...	...	...	...	...	...	...	...	...
Equals: Gross Domestic Product	44362	47157	49714	51878	54437	55989	55397	53178	47141	48883	50226	50902

a) Item 'Electricity, gas and water' refers to electricity only. Gas and water are included in item 'Community, social and personal services'.
b) Restaurants and hotels are included in item 'Community, social and personal services'.
c) Insurance, real estate and business services are included in item 'Community, social and personal services'.

1.12 Relations Among National Accounting Aggregates

Million Myanmarese kyats

	1980	1981	1982	1983	1984	1985	1986	1987	1988	Fiscal year beginning 1 April 1989	1990	1991
Gross Domestic Product	38609	42879	46811	49823	53597	55989	59028	68698	76243	124666	149974	176571
Plus: Net factor income from the rest of the world	-160	-168	-347	-510	-517	-581	-658	-520	-261	-304	47	-269
Equals: Gross National Product	38449	42711	46464	49313	53080	55408	58370	68178	75982	124362	150021	176302
Less: Consumption of fixed capital	3415	3784	4166	4484	4871	5056	5318	6245	6850	7519	8309	9251
Equals: National Income	35034	38927	42298	44829	48209	50352	53052	61933	69132	116843	141712	167051
Plus: Net current transfers from the rest of the world	...	...	...	...	...	...	...	...	...	...	...	...
Equals: National Disposable Income	...	...	...	...	...	...	...	...	...	...	...	...
Less: Final consumption	...	...	...	...	...	...	...	...	...	...	...	...
Equals: Net Saving	...	...	...	...	...	...	...	...	...	...	...	...
Less: Surplus of the nation on current transactions	...	...	...	...	...	...	...	...	...	...	...	...
Equals: Net Capital Formation	...	...	...	...	...	...	...	...	...	...	...	...

Myanmar

4.1 Derivation of Value Added by Kind of Activity, in Current Prices

Million Myanmarese kyats

Fiscal year beginning 1 April

	1980			1981			1982			1983		
	Gross Output	Intermediate Consumption	Value Added	Gross Output	Intermediate Consumption	Value Added	Gross Output	Intermediate Consumption	Value Added	Gross Output	Intermediate Consumption	Value Added
All Producers												
1 Agriculture, hunting, forestry and fishing	21847	3877	17970	24769	4439	20330	26898	4579	22319	28648	4937	23711
2 Mining and quarrying	790	363	427	803	373	430	846	345	501	850	346	504
3 Manufacturing	20534	16851	3683	22275	18266	4009	24061	19711	4350	26438	21663	4775
4 Electricity, gas and water a	214	79	135	264	97	167	313	103	210	338	111	227
5 Construction	2099	1452	647	2248	1556	692	2729	1896	833	2859	1987	872
6 Wholesale and retail trade, restaurants and hotels b	13066	2945	10121	14159	3445	10714	15259	3747	11512	16244	3971	12273
7 Transport, storage and communication	2358	1001	1357	2775	1163	1612	3178	1344	1834	3344	1359	1985
8 Finance, insurance, real estate and business services c	1230	401	829	1551	512	1039	1804	708	1096	1919	747	1172
9 Community, social and personal services abc	1874	271	1603	2177	323	1854	2278	337	1941	2388	350	2038
Total, Industries	64012	27240	36772	71021	30174	40847	77366	32770	44596	83028	35471	47557
Producers of Government Services	3491	1654	1837	3970	1938	2032	4211	1996	2215	4298	2032	2266
Other Producers	...	...	...	...	...	...	...	...	...	...	...	...
Total	67503	28894	38609	74991	32112	42879	81577	34766	46811	87326	37503	49823
Less: Imputed bank service charge	...	...	...	...	...	...	...	...	...	...	...	...
Import duties	...	...	...	...	...	...	...	...	...	...	...	...
Value added tax	...	...	...	...	...	...	...	...	...	...	...	...
Total	67503	28894	38609	74991	32112	42879	81577	34766	46811	87326	37503	49823

	1984			1985			1986			1987		
	Gross Output	Intermediate Consumption	Value Added	Gross Output	Intermediate Consumption	Value Added	Gross Output	Intermediate Consumption	Value Added	Gross Output	Intermediate Consumption	Value Added
All Producers												
1 Agriculture, hunting, forestry and fishing	31566	5771	25795	33242	6259	26983	35924	6291	29633	46551	8561	37990
2 Mining and quarrying	959	414	545	904	371	533	823	340	483	810	332	478
3 Manufacturing	29254	23974	5280	31191	25630	5561	30906	25456	5450	30561	25224	5337
4 Electricity, gas and water a	379	116	263	398	120	278	425	136	289	443	154	289
5 Construction	3096	2150	946	3078	2133	945	3202	2226	976	3183	2213	970
6 Wholesale and retail trade, restaurants and hotels b	17227	4341	12886	18112	4723	13389	18297	4771	13526	19782	5201	14581
7 Transport, storage and communication	3536	1430	2106	3694	1476	2218	3827	1516	2311	4059	1600	2459
8 Finance, insurance, real estate and business services c	2051	797	1254	2147	815	1332	2328	907	1421	2397	899	1498
9 Community, social and personal services abc	2498	373	2125	2571	389	2182	2684	418	2266	2736	410	2326
Total, Industries	90566	39366	51200	95337	41916	53421	98416	42061	56355	110522	44594	65928
Producers of Government Services	4547	2150	2397	4886	2318	2568	5067	2394	2673	5234	2464	2770
Other Producers	...	...	...	...	...	...	...	...	...	...	...	...
Total	95113	41516	53597	100223	44234	55989	103483	44455	59028	115756	47058	68698
Less: Imputed bank service charge	...	...	...	...	...	...	...	...	...	...	...	...
Import duties	...	...	...	...	...	...	...	...	...	...	...	...
Value added tax	...	...	...	...	...	...	...	...	...	...	...	...
Total	95113	41516	53597	100223	44234	55989	103483	44455	59028	115756	47058	68698

	1988			1989			1990			1991		
	Gross Output	Intermediate Consumption	Value Added	Gross Output	Intermediate Consumption	Value Added	Gross Output	Intermediate Consumption	Value Added	Gross Output	Intermediate Consumption	Value Added
All Producers												
1 Agriculture, hunting, forestry and fishing	53396	9657	43739	86526	15457	71069	107444	20637	86807	128511	24913	103598
2 Mining and quarrying	870	358	512	1706	718	988	1779	739	1040	1863	787	1076
3 Manufacturing	32971	27248	5723	63211	52480	10731	65409	54294	11115	72020	59814	12206
4 Electricity, gas and water a	532	211	321	747	312	435	787	385	402	833	461	372
5 Construction	2731	1898	833	5043	3505	1538	8127	5649	2478	10079	7006	3073
6 Wholesale and retail trade, restaurants and hotels b	22216	6367	15849	38167	11011	27156	47479	13748	33731	56690	16594	40096
7 Transport, storage and communication	3826	1586	2240	5625	2279	3346	6866	2814	4052	7343	3027	4316
8 Finance, insurance, real estate and business services c	2566	1028	1538	1175	953	222	1315	1045	270	1319	1024	295
9 Community, social and personal services abc	2913	422	2491	4038	604	3434	4698	714	3984	5878	816	5062

1246

4.1 Derivation of Value Added by Kind of Activity, in Current Prices
(Continued)

Million Myanmarese kyats

Fiscal year beginning 1 April

	1988			1989			1990			1991		
	Gross Output	Intermediate Consumption	Value Added	Gross Output	Intermediate Consumption	Value Added	Gross Output	Intermediate Consumption	Value Added	Gross Output	Intermediate Consumption	Value Added
Total, Industries	122021	48775	73246	206238	87319	118919	243904	100025	143879	284536	114442	170094
Producers of Government Services	5693	2696	2997	11728	5981	5747	12700	6605	6095	14996	8519	6477
Other Producers	...	...	...	...	...	...	...	...	...	...	...	...
Total	127714	51471	76243	217966	93300	124666	256604	106630	149974	299532	122961	176571
Less: Imputed bank service charge	...	...	...	...	...	...	...	...	...	...	...	...
Import duties	...	...	...	...	...	...	...	...	...	...	...	...
Value added tax	...	...	...	...	...	...	...	...	...	...	...	...
Total	127714	51471	76243	217966	93300	124666	256604	106630	149974	299532	122961	176571

a) Item 'Electricity, gas and water' refers to electricity only. Gas and water are included in item 'Community, social and personal services'.
b) Restaurants and hotels are included in item 'Community, social and personal services'.
c) Insurance, real estate and business services are included in item 'Community, social and personal services'.

4.2 Derivation of Value Added by Kind of Activity, in Constant Prices

Million Myanmarese kyats

Fiscal year beginning 1 April

	1980			1981			1982			1983		
	Gross Output	Intermediate Consumption	Value Added	Gross Output	Intermediate Consumption	Value Added	Gross Output	Intermediate Consumption	Value Added	Gross Output	Intermediate Consumption	Value Added
	At constant prices of:1985											
	All Producers											
1 Agriculture, hunting, forestry and fishing	26241	4979	21262	28324	5420	22904	29735	5428	24307	31134	5691	25443
2 Mining and quarrying	644	262	382	686	287	399	702	270	432	727	281	446
3 Manufacturing	24097	19860	4237	25856	21327	4529	27083	22313	4770	28351	23383	4968
4 Electricity, gas and water a	214	64	150	264	83	181	314	102	212	338	109	229
5 Construction	2366	1692	674	2408	1625	783	2745	1909	836	2880	2001	879
6 Wholesale and retail trade, restaurants and hotels b	14893	3637	11256	15779	4286	11493	16161	4269	11892	16654	4296	12358
7 Transport, storage and communication	2690	1130	1560	2994	1235	1759	3335	1398	1937	3443	1397	2046
8 Finance, insurance, real estate and business services c	1414	426	988	1623	543	1080	1812	696	1116	1925	750	1175
9 Community, social and personal services abc	2201	323	1878	2268	339	1929	2309	340	1969	2402	352	2050
Total, Industries	74760	32373	42387	80202	35145	45057	84196	36725	47471	87854	38260	49594
Producers of Government Services	3694	1719	1975	4008	1908	2100	4239	1996	2243	4321	2037	2284
Other Producers	...	...	...	...	...	...	...	...	...	...	...	...
Total	78454	34092	44362	84210	37053	47157	88435	38721	49714	92175	40297	51878
Less: Imputed bank service charge	...	...	...	...	...	...	...	...	...	...	...	...
Import duties	...	...	...	...	...	...	...	...	...	...	...	...
Value added tax	...	...	...	...	...	...	...	...	...	...	...	...
Total	78454	34092	44362	84210	37053	47157	88435	38721	49714	92175	40297	51878

	1984			1985			1986			1987		
	Gross Output	Intermediate Consumption	Value Added	Gross Output	Intermediate Consumption	Value Added	Gross Output	Intermediate Consumption	Value Added	Gross Output	Intermediate Consumption	Value Added
	At constant prices of:1985											
	All Producers											
1 Agriculture, hunting, forestry and fishing	32538	6114	26424	33242	6259	26982	33306	6186	27120	31933	6114	25819
2 Mining and quarrying	865	352	513	908	375	533	838	340	498	741	311	430
3 Manufacturing	30381	24978	5403	31191	25630	5561	29071	23948	5123	27921	23051	4870
4 Electricity, gas and water a	380	116	264	398	120	278	425	136	289	443	143	300
5 Construction	3121	2169	952	3078	2133	945	3105	2158	947	2947	2048	899
6 Wholesale and retail trade, restaurants and hotels b	17452	4542	12910	18112	4723	13389	17339	4519	12820	16238	4245	11993
7 Transport, storage and communication	3624	1458	2166	3693	1475	2218	3739	1480	2259	3836	1508	2328
8 Finance, insurance, real estate and business services c	2053	797	1256	2148	816	1332	2328	907	1421	2397	899	1498
9 Community, social and personal services abc	2509	373	2136	2571	389	2182	2669	408	2261	2694	398	2296

Myanmar

4.2 Derivation of Value Added by Kind of Activity, in Constant Prices
(Continued)

Million Myanmarese kyats Fiscal year beginning 1 April

	1984			1985			1986			1987		
	Gross Output	Intermediate Consumption	Value Added	Gross Output	Intermediate Consumption	Value Added	Gross Output	Intermediate Consumption	Value Added	Gross Output	Intermediate Consumption	Value Added
At constant prices of:1985												
Total, Industries	92923	40899	52024	95341	41920	53421	92820	40082	52738	89150	38717	50433
Producers of Government Services	4571	2158	2413	4886	2318	2568	5046	2387	2659	5202	2457	2745
Other Producers	...	...	...	...	...	...	...	...	...	...	...	...
Total	97494	43057	54437	100227	44238	55989	97866	42469	55397	94352	41174	53178
Less: Imputed bank service charge	...	...	...	...	...	...	...	...	...	...	...	...
Import duties	...	...	...	...	...	...	...	...	...	...	...	...
Value added tax	...	...	...	...	...	...	...	...	...	...	...	...
Total	97494	43057	54437	100227	44238	55989	97866	42469	55397	94352	41174	53178

	1988			1989			1990			1991		
	Gross Output	Intermediate Consumption	Value Added	Gross Output	Intermediate Consumption	Value Added	Gross Output	Intermediate Consumption	Value Added	Gross Output	Intermediate Consumption	Value Added
At constant prices of:1985												
All Producers												
1 Agriculture, hunting, forestry and fishing	28082	5487	22595	29022	5433	23589	29541	5481	24060	30021	5640	24381
2 Mining and quarrying	582	238	344	787	338	449	745	322	423	722	313	409
3 Manufacturing	24182	20088	4094	26866	22311	4555	26895	22338	4557	26802	22261	4541
4 Electricity, gas and water a	418	135	283	472	149	323	510	171	339	546	186	360
5 Construction	2257	1569	688	2995	2082	913	3887	2702	1185	4243	2949	1294
6 Wholesale and retail trade, restaurants and hotels b	14078	3520	10558	14852	3734	11118	15209	3844	11365	15254	3873	11381
7 Transport, storage and communication	3258	1269	1989	3581	1393	2188	3785	1507	2278	3808	1521	2287
8 Finance, insurance, real estate and business services c	2566	962	1604	1102	873	229	1291	1023	268	1296	1002	294
9 Community, social and personal services abc	2560	361	2199	2626	394	2232	2697	413	2284	2748	413	2335
Total, Industries	77983	33629	44354	82303	36707	45596	84560	37801	46759	85440	38158	47282
Producers of Government Services	5322	2535	2787	6802	3515	3287	7239	3772	3467	8395	4775	3620
Other Producers	...	...	...	...	...	...	...	...	...	...	...	...
Total	83305	36164	47141	89105	40222	48883	91799	41573	50226	93835	42933	50902
Less: Imputed bank service charge	...	...	...	...	...	...	...	...	...	...	...	...
Import duties	...	...	...	...	...	...	...	...	...	...	...	...
Value added tax	...	...	...	...	...	...	...	...	...	...	...	...
Total	83305	36164	47141	89105	40222	48883	91799	41573	50226	93835	42933	50902

a) Item 'Electricity, gas and water' refers to electricity only. Gas and water are included in item 'Community, social and personal services'.
b) Restaurants and hotels are included in item 'Community, social and personal services'.
c) Insurance, real estate and business services are included in item 'Community, social and personal services'.

Nepal

Source. Reply to the United Nations National Accounts Questionnaire from the National Income Division, Central Bureau of Statistics, Kathmandu.
General note. The official estimates of Nepal have been prepared in accordance with the United Nations System of National Accounts so far as the existing data would permit.

1.1 Expenditure on the Gross Domestic Product, in Current Prices

Million Nepalese rupees

	1980	1981	1982	1983	1984	1985	1986	1987	1988	1989	1990	1991
1 Government final consumption expenditure	1565	1922	2638	3416	3644	4371	5133	6570	8511	9186	10394	...
2 Private final consumption expenditure	19195	22411	25272	27458	31860	33807	39408	45355	52345	61372	70067	...
A Households	19040	22190	...	...	...	...	...	...	...	...	...	...
B Private non-profit institutions serving households	155	221	...	...	...	...	...	...	...	...	...	...
3 Gross capital formation	4270	4808	5314	6628	7351	10184	10599	12898	14717	17179	16124	...
A Increase in stocks	589	509	-151	52	444	798	1168	1073	1823	3023	2074	...
B Gross fixed capital formation	3681	4299	5465	6576	6907	9386	9431	11825	12894	14156	14050	...
Residential buildings	1021	1203	...	...	...	...	...	...	...	...	...	...
Non-residential buildings	1765	2140	...	...	...	...	...	...	...	...	...	...
Other construction and land improvement etc.			...	...	...	...	...	...	...	...	...	...
Other	895	956	...	...	...	...	...	...	...	...	...	...
4 Exports of goods and services	2695	3523	3592	3455	4196	5372	6506	7555	8749	9878	7744	...
5 Less: Imports of goods and services	4374	5357	5828	7196	7661	9317	11218	13132	15464	19356	15618	...
Equals: Gross Domestic Product	23351	27307	30988	33761	39390	44417	50428	59246	68858	78259	88711	...

1.3 Cost Components of the Gross Domestic Product

Million Nepalese rupees

	1980	1981	1982	1983	1984	1985	1986	1987	1988	1989	1990	1991
1 Indirect taxes, net	1465	1841	1951	2117	2386	2861	3364	3888	5258	5437	6245	...
2 Consumption of fixed capital	1091	1283	1427	1583	1748	2055	2387	2627	...	...	...	...
3 Compensation of employees paid by resident producers to:	13251	16328	16665	18603	...	...	...	...	...	...	...	...
4 Operating surplus	7544	7855	10945	11458	...	...	...	...	...	...	...	...
Equals: Gross Domestic Product	23351	27307	30988	33761	39390	44417	50428	59246	68858	78259	88711	...

1.4 General Government Current Receipts and Disbursements

Million Nepalese rupees

	1980	1981	1982	1983	1984	1985	1986	1987	1988	1989	1990	1991
Receipts												
1 Operating surplus	...	...	...	...	...	...	...	...	...	...	...	...
2 Property and entrepreneurial income	93	...	...	...	...	...	...	...	...	...	...	...
3 Taxes, fees and contributions	2216	...	...	...	...	...	...	...	...	...	...	...
A Indirect taxes	1465	...	...	...	...	...	...	...	...	...	...	...
B Direct taxes	115	...	...	...	...	...	...	...	...	...	...	...
C Social security contributions	413	...	...	...	...	...	...	...	...	...	...	...
D Compulsory fees, fines and penalties	223	...	...	...	...	...	...	...	...	...	...	...
4 Other current transfers	319	...	...	...	...	...	...	...	...	...	...	...
Total Current Receipts of General Government	2628	...	...	...	...	...	...	...	...	...	...	...
Disbursements												
1 Government final consumption expenditure	1565	...	...	...	...	...	...	...	...	...	...	...
A Compensation of employees	867	...	...	...	...	...	...	...	...	...	...	...
B Consumption of fixed capital	...	...	...	...	...	...	...	...	...	...	...	...
C Purchases of goods and services, net	699	...	...	...	...	...	...	...	...	...	...	...
D Less: Own account fixed capital formation	...	...	...	...	...	...	...	...	...	...	...	...
E Indirect taxes paid, net	...	...	...	...	...	...	...	...	...	...	...	...
2 Property income	...	...	...	...	...	...	...	...	...	...	...	...
3 Subsidies	5	...	...	...	...	...	...	...	...	...	...	...
4 Other current transfers	67	...	...	...	...	...	...	...	...	...	...	...
5 Net saving	991	...	...	...	...	...	...	...	...	...	...	...
Total Current Disbursements and Net Saving of General Government	2628	...	...	...	...	...	...	...	...	...	...	...

Nepal

1.7 External Transactions on Current Account, Summary

Million Nepalese rupees

	1980	1981	1982	1983	1984	1985	1986	1987	1988	1989	1990	1991
Payments to the Rest of the World												
1 Imports of goods and services	4374	5357	5828	7196	7662	9318	11218	13132	15464	19356	15618	...
A Imports of merchandise c.i.f.	3569	4443	4948	6333	6534	7769	9373	10927	13893	16297	...	...
B Other	805	914	880	863	1128	1549	1845	2205	1571	3059	...	...
2 Factor income to the rest of the world	53	57	59	56	84	124	164	190	229	397	501	...
3 Current transfers to the rest of the world	-	-	-	-	-	-	-	-	-	2	-	...
4 Surplus of the nation on current transactions	-341	-296	-393	-1671	-1343	-1850	-2471	-2904	-3705	-6400	-4695	
Payments to the Rest of the World and Surplus of the Nation on Current Transactions	4086	5118	5494	5581	6403	7592	8911	10418	11988	13355	11424	
Receipts From The Rest of the World												
1 Exports of goods and services	2695	3523	3592	3455	4196	5371	6506	7555	8749	9878	7744	...
A Exports of merchandise f.o.b.	1166	1613	1496	1136	1710	2746	3086	3003	4127	4211	...	...
B Other	1529	1910	2096	2319	2486	2625	3420	4552	4622	5667	...	...
2 Factor income from rest of the world	547	644	674	753	709	785	873	1394	1804	2111	2435	
3 Current transfers from rest of the world	844	951	1228	1373	1498	1436	1532	1469	1435	1366	1245	
Receipts from the Rest of the World on Current Transactions	4086	5118	5494	5581	6403	7592	8911	10418	11988	13355	11424	

1.10 Gross Domestic Product by Kind of Activity, in Current Prices

Million Nepalese rupees

	1980	1981	1982	1983	1984	1985	1986	1987	1988	1989	1990	1991
1 Agriculture, hunting, forestry and fishing	13520	15510	17715	19082	22570	23927	26555	30448	35477	41833	49704	...
2 Mining and quarrying	42	58	66	85	111	140	120	100	93	95	97	...
3 Manufacturing a	936	1049	1243	1460	1816	1998	2622	3065	3646	3834	4320	...
4 Electricity, gas and water	60	67	82	127	158	196	342	415	467	516	655	...
5 Construction	1570	1974	2342	2377	2576	3583	3989	5040	5396	6008	6392	...
6 Wholesale and retail trade, restaurants and hotels	889	953	1068	1199	1520	1837	2207	2905	3365	3747	3759	
7 Transport, storage and communication	1541	1889	1992	2129	2468	2764	3123	3594	3686	4171	3848	
8 Finance, insurance, real estate and business services	1833	2077	2366	2594	2937	3420	3942	4715	5519	6274	6776	
9 Community, social and personal services b	284	315	416	475	561	656	776	867	951	1056	1158	
Total, Industries	20675	23892	27290	29528	34717	38521	43676	51149	58680	67534	76709	
Producers of Government Services b	1211	1574	1747	2116	2287	3035	3388	4209	4920	5288	5757	
Other Producers b	...	...	...	...	...	...	...	...	...	...	...	...
Subtotal c	21886	25466	29037	31644	37004	41556	47064	55358	63600	72822	82466	
Less: Imputed bank service charge	...	...	...	...	...	...	...	...	...	...	...	...
Plus: Import duties	...	...	...	...	...	...	...	...	...	...	...	...
Plus: Value added tax	...	...	...	...	...	...	...	...	...	...	...	...
Plus: Other adjustments d	1465	1841	1951	2117	2386	2861	3364	3888	5258	5437	6245	...
Equals: Gross Domestic Product	23351	27307	30988	33761	39390	44417	50428	59246	68858	78259	88711	...

a) Item 'Manufacturing' includes cottage industries.
b) Items 'Other producers' and 'Producers of government services' are included in item 'Community, social and personal services'.
c) Gross domestic product in factor values.
d) Item 'Other adjustments' refers to indirect taxes net of subsidies.

1.11 Gross Domestic Product by Kind of Activity, in Constant Prices

Million Nepalese rupees

	1980	1981	1982	1983	1984	1985	1986	1987	1988	1989	1990	1991
At constant prices of:1975												
1 Agriculture, hunting, forestry and fishing	10933	12066	12616	12478	13668	13990	14705	14789	15993	17194	18444	...
2 Mining and quarrying	...	...	...	...	...	...	...	...	...	...	...	...
3 Manufacturing	...	...	...	...	...	...	...	...	...	...	...	...
4 Electricity, gas and water	...	...	...	...	...	...	...	...	...	...	...	...
5 Construction	...	...	...	...	...	...	...	...	...	...	...	...

1.11 Gross Domestic Product by Kind of Activity, in Constant Prices
(Continued)

Million Nepalese rupees

Fiscal year ending 15 July

	1980	1981	1982	1983	1984	1985	1986	1987	1988	1989	1990	1991
					At constant prices of:1975							
6 Wholesale and retail trade, restaurants and hotels	...	...	...	...	...	...	...	...	...	...	...	...
7 Transport, storage and communication	...	...	...	...	...	...	...	...	...	...	...	...
8 Finance, insurance, real estate and business services	...	...	...	...	...	...	...	...	...	...	...	...
9 Community, social and personal services	...	...	...	...	...	...	...	...	...	...	...	...
Total, Industries	...	...	...	...	...	...	...	...	...	...	...	...
Producers of Government Services	...	...	...	...	...	...	...	...	...	...	...	...
Other Producers	...	...	...	...	...	...	...	...	...	...	...	...
Subtotal	...	...	...	...	...	...	...	...	...	...	...	...
Less: Imputed bank service charge	...	...	...	...	...	...	...	...	...	...	...	...
Plus: Import duties	...	...	...	...	...	...	...	...	...	...	...	...
Plus: Value added tax	...	...	...	...	...	...	...	...	...	...	...	...
Equals: Gross Domestic Product	18606	20158	20920	20297	22262	23630	24645	25617	27475	28536	29560	...

1.12 Relations Among National Accounting Aggregates

Million Nepalese rupees

Fiscal year ending 15 July

	1980	1981	1982	1983	1984	1985	1986	1987	1988	1989	1990	1991
Gross Domestic Product	23351	27307	30988	33761	39390	44417	50428	59246	68858	78259	88711	...
Plus: Net factor income from the rest of the world	494	587	615	697	625	661	709	1204	1575	1714	1934	...
Factor income from the rest of the world	547	644	674	753	709	785	873	1394	1804	2111	2435	...
Less: Factor income to the rest of the world	53	57	59	56	84	124	164	190	229	397	501	...
Equals: Gross National Product	23845	27894	31603	34458	40015	45078	51137	60450	70433	79973	90645	...
Less: Consumption of fixed capital	...	...	...	...	...	...	...	...	...	...	...	...
Equals: National Income a	23845	27894	31603	34458	40015	45078	51137	60450	70433	79973	90645	...
Plus: Net current transfers from the rest of the world	844	951	1228	1373	1498	1436	1532	1469	1435	1364	1245	...
Current transfers from the rest of the world	844	951	1228	1373	1498	1436	1532	1469	1435	1366	1245	...
Less: Current transfers to the rest of the world	-	-	-	-	-	-	-	-	-	2	-	...
Equals: National Disposable Income b	24689	28845	32831	35831	41513	46514	52669	61919	71868	81337	91890	...
Less: Final consumption	20760	24333	27910	30874	35504	38178	44541	51925	60856	70558	80461	...
Equals: Net Saving c	3929	4512	4921	4957	6009	8336	8128	9994	11012	10779	11429	...
Less: Surplus of the nation on current transactions	-341	-296	-393	-1671	-1343	-1850	-2471	-2904	-3705	-6400	-4695	...
Equals: Net Capital Formation d	4270	4808	5314	6628	7352	10186	10599	12898	14717	17179	16124	...

a) Item 'National income' includes consumption of fixed capital.
b) Item 'National disposable income' includes consumption of fixed capital.
c) Item 'Net saving' includes consumption of fixed capital.
d) Item 'Net capital formation' includes consumption of fixed capital.

2.1 Government Final Consumption Expenditure by Function, in Current Prices

Million Nepalese rupees

Fiscal year ending 15 July

	1980	1981	1982	1983	1984	1985	1986	1987	1988	1989	1990	1991
1 General public services	...	...	...	503	540	579	745	979	1048	...	...	...
2 Defence	...	...	...	431	468	551	595	757	514	...	...	...
3 Public order and safety	...	...	...	293	321	458	492	472	759	...	...	...
4 Education	...	...	...	975	1038	1247	1211	1596	1655	...	...	...
5 Health	...	...	...	159	195	236	405	503	263	...	...	...
6 Social security and welfare	...	...	...	50	53	2	33	28	118	...	...	...
7 Housing and community amenities	...	...	...	135	141	108	127	183	271	...	...	...
8 Recreational, cultural and religious affairs	...	...	...	68	73	39	306	48	112	...	...	...
9 Economic services	...	...	...	748	848	1072	1169	2005	2552	...	...	...

2.1 Government Final Consumption Expenditure by Function, in Current Prices
(Continued)

Million Nepalese rupees

Fiscal year ending 15 July

	1980	1981	1982	1983	1984	1985	1986	1987	1988	1989	1990	1991
A Fuel and energy	...	...	...	146	153	95	261	302	652	...	...	...
B Agriculture, forestry, fishing and hunting	...	...	...	275	348	593	506	838	874	...	...	...
C Mining, manufacturing and construction, except fuel and energy	...	...	...	137	134	83	183	212	96	...	...	...
D Transportation and communication	...	...	...	143	178	146	154	424	741	...	...	...
E Other economic affairs	...	...	...	47	35	155	65	229	189	...	...	...
10 Other functions	...	...	...	...	...	...	...	...	...	...	...	
Total Government Final Consumption Expenditure	...	...	...	3362	3689	4445	5083	6571	7303	8033	10372	...

2.11 Gross Fixed Capital Formation by Kind of Activity of Owner, ISIC Divisions, in Current Prices

Million Nepalese rupees

Fiscal year ending 15 July

	1980	1981	1982	1983	1984	1985	1986	1987	1988	1989	1990	1991
					All Producers							
1 Agriculture, hunting, forestry and fishing	752	669	803	893	1019	1144	1245	1202	1430	1379	1580	...
2 Mining and quarrying	1	1	1	1	2	4	7	54	45	48	54	...
3 Manufacturing	47	61	208	363	201	284	472	430	1074	497	385	...
4 Electricity, gas and water	11	94	31	130	168	1517	258	1122	778	435	129	...
5 Construction	95	135	193	158	183	264	301	455	443	421	472	...
6 Wholesale and retail trade, restaurants and hotels	104	136	119	123	149	184	236	298	303	329	330	...
7 Transport, storage and communication	155	139	167	200	241	289	350	624	462	555	894	...
8 Finance, insurance, real estate and business services	1025	1207	1414	1716	1743	1995	2386	2869	2830	3468	3800	...
9 Community, social and personal services	10	9	12	14	17	21	26	28	29	31	35	...
Total Industries	2200	2451	2948	3598	3723	5702	5281	7082	7394	7163	7679	...
Producers of Government Services	1466	1823	2487	2941	3139	3629	3909	4727	5483	6728	6395	...
Private Non-Profit Institutions Serving Households	15	25	30	37	45	55	57	16	17	17	18	...
Total	3681	4299	5465	6576	6907	9386	9247	11825	12894	13908	14092	...

Netherlands

General note. The preparation of national accounts statistics in the Netherlands is undertaken by the Central Bureau of Statistics, Voorburg. The official estimates together with methodological notes are published annually in 'Nationale Rekeningen' (National Accounts). The estimates are generally in accordance with the classifications and definitions recommended in the United Nations System of National Accounts (SNA). The first annual publication on input-output tables, covering the years 1948-1957, was issued in 1960. The following tables have been prepared from successive replies to the United Nations national accounts questionnaire. When the scope and coverage of the estimates differ for conceptual or statistical reasons from the definitions and classifications recommended in SNA, a footnote is indicated to the relevant tables.

Sources and methods :
(a) Gross domestic product. The main approach used to estimate GDP is the production approach.
(b) Expenditure on the gross domestic product. The expenditure approach is used to estimate government final consumption expenditure, gross fixed capital formation and exports and imports of goods and services. A combination of the commodity-flow approach and the expenditure approach is used for the estimation of private final consumption expenditure, private gross fixed capital formation and increase in stocks. The main sources for estimating general government consumption expenditure are the final accounts of the various agencies. The data sources for exports and imports of goods and services are foreign trade statistics for merchandise and balance of payments data and survey data for services. Constant prices are obtained through deflation with price indexes for all expenditure components, except government consumption expenditure referring to wages and salaries, which is extrapolated by employment data.
(c) Cost-structure of the gross domestic product. The main sources for the compilation of compensation of employees are data from the social security institutions and data from annual production statistics in the case of employees in enterprises and accounts data in the case of general government employees. Operating surplus is obtained as a residual within the framework Statistics of the annual input-output tables. Estimates of the consumption of fixed capital are made by the Central Bureau of Statistics, based on the perpetual inventory method. Information on indirect taxes and subsidies is provided by government agencies.
(d) Gross domestic product by kind of economic activity. The table on GDP by kind of economic activity is prepared at market prices net of value added tax for which breakdown by kind of economic activity is not available. The production approach is used to estimate value added of most industries. This is done within the framework of detailed input-output tables using the commodity-flow approach. The income approach is used to estimate value added of producers of government services, business services and most community, social and personal services. For the

agricultural sector, the main sources of information are the annual surveys of crop production and unpublished reports of statutory trade offices. Data on the structure of production costs are provided by annual farm management surveys. Statistics on sales of horticulture produce in special markets are also available. Net increase of livestock is evaluated on the basis of frequent samples, and on average annual prices per category. Regarding crude petroleum and natural gas production the information base consists of data supplied by all individual enterprises. The information base for manufacturing consists mainly of an annual survey of all enterprises with more than 10 employees. Recent bench-mark information is given by a census of establishments conducted for 1978. The census covers all establishments and collects information on kind of economic activity and employment. For the private construction sector, annual production surveys are available. For general government, data are available on the capital expenditure. The production of buildings is covered by quarterly progress reports from the municipalities. The production value is estimated on the basis of the production of work completed. Bench-mark data for wholesale and retail trade are available for certain years. For some parts of the trade sector annual production surveys are available. Surveys are planned to be held for other parts. Annual surveys are carried out for the transport sector. Information on railways and communications is derived directly from the few existing enterprises. Inter-urban public transportation by bus is covered by statements by government agencies. For the estimation of value added of credit institutions, the required data are collected on the basis of an annual survey. Data of insurance companies are obtained both from an annual survey and from the companies' accounts. The value of dwellings corresponds to total rents, including the imputed rents of owner-occupied houses. Cost accounts for houses are published by housing corporations. For producers of government services the main sources are the accounts of the agencies. Considerable gaps exist regarding some sub-sectors of private services. In these cases date are collected from various sources such as income tax data and social security information. For the constant price estimates, double deflation is used for agriculture and fishing. Current output quantities are valued at base-year prices where quantities are available, otherwise deflated by representative price indexes. Some input categories are valued at base year prices while others are deflated by price index. Value added of mining and quarrying, manufacturing, electricity, gas, water, transport and communication is calculated by double deflation. For trade, output at constant prices is extrapolated by quantity indicators for output, input categories are deflated by price indexes. Value added at constant prices of financing, insurance and business services is generally extrapolated by means of volume indexes of material output and factor input. For producers of government services, net value added at constant prices is extrapolated by means of a value added index based on quantity data of factor services. For private services value added is extrapolated by indexes of employment.

1.1 Expenditure on the Gross Domestic Product, in Current Prices

Million Netherlands guilders

	1980	1981	1982	1983	1984	1985	1986	1987	1988	1989	1990	1991
1 Government final consumption expenditure	60260	62750	65120	66580	66390	67670	68550	70590 / 69780	70200	71760	74680	77910
2 Private final consumption expenditure	205780	213230	221830	229860	236750	247720	256150	263930 / 267940	271640	284490	302820	323070
3 Gross capital formation	72510	64490	66140	70020	76300	82750	84400	82310 / 91160	97700	109510	114330	114700
A Increase in stocks	1720	-3090	-1020	560	1990	2500	-1780	-4790 / -420	310	5430	4490	1700
B Gross fixed capital formation	70790	67580	67160	69460	74310	80250	86180	87100 / 91580	97390	104080	109840	113000
Residential buildings	20840	20130	19540	19470	20400	20380	21210	21940 / 23160	26470	27020	26750	25330
Non-residential buildings	15120	13710	12900	11960	12310	12480	13570	14540 / 14170	15910	17560	20000	21400
Other construction and land improvement etc.	8030	8010	7630	7360	7960	8030	8070	7530 / 9750	10480	10630	11240	11740
Other	26800	25730	27090	30670	33640	39360	43330	43090 / 44500	44530	48870	51850	54530
4 Exports of goods and services	176810	204620	212600	219770	248560	265540	232520	226650 / 219260	240250	267670	280990	293880
5 Less: imports of goods and services	178620	192240	196830	205210	227750	245500	213010	213310 / 207560	222380	248760	256500	266000
Equals: Gross Domestic Product	336740	352850	368860	381020	400250	418180	428610	430170 / 440580	457410	484670	516320	543560

Netherlands

1.2 Expenditure on the Gross Domestic Product, in Constant Prices

Million Netherlands guilders

	1980	1981	1982	1983	1984	1985	1986	1987	1988	1989	1990	1991
					At constant prices of: 1980				1987			
1 Government final consumption expenditure	60260	61460	61860	62630	62260	63090	64340	65880 / 69780	70770	71850	73330	74500
2 Private final consumption expenditure	205780	200610	198260	199990	201990	206930	212510	219950 / 267940	270200	279620	291080	300540
3 Gross capital formation	72510	60920	60000	62430	66420	71150	72550	69170 / 91160a	95530a	105190a	108160a	105400a
A Increase in stocks	1720	-2500	-840	330	970	1260	-2480	-6670 / -420	-190	4830	4210	1350
B Gross fixed capital formation	70790	63420	60840	62100	65450	69890	75030	75840 / 91580a	95720a	100440a	104020a	104080a
Residential buildings	20840	18840	17790	17720	18510	18430	19120	19480 / 23160	25770	25940	25020	23110
Non-residential buildings	15120	12920	11910	11070	11340	11600	12550	13290 / 14170	15510	16730	18520	19260
Other construction and land improvement etc.	8030	7540	6990	6670	7040	6940	7020	6470 / 9750	10390	10150	10370	10390
Other	26800	24120	24150	26640	28560	32920	36340	36600 / 44500	44050	47630	50120	51360
4 Exports of goods and services	176810	179540	179510	185820	199560	210310	216430	224010 / 219260	238940	254830	268910	281370
5 Less: Imports of goods and services	178620	168160	169970	176580	185380	197540	204690	214890 / 207560	223340	238390	250080	259400
Equals: Gross Domestic Product	336740	334370	329660	334290	344850	353940	361140	364120 / 440580a	452100a	473260a	491640a	502660a

a) The estimates in constant prices of the fixed base year 1987 have been calculated on the basis of figures in constant prices of the preceding year. Because of this, the sum of the sub-items do not add-up to the main aggregate. However, for the constant price 1980, the differences were eliminated by adding them proportionally to the details.

1.3 Cost Components of the Gross Domestic Product

Million Netherlands guilders

	1980	1981	1982	1983	1984	1985	1986	1987	1988	1989	1990	1991
1 Indirect taxes, net	32020	32900	32700	33920	35380	37190	39800	40590 / 39430	41710	43630	48990	51680
A Indirect taxes	41120	41720	42760	45140	47990	50700	53700	57420 / 58620	60560	60370	64850	69270
B Less: Subsidies	9100	8820	10060	11220	12610	13510	13900	16830 / 19190	18850	16740	15860	17590
2 Consumption of fixed capital	32490	35620	37860	39190	41190	42870	43800	45480 / 48540	51190	54880	58250	61560
3 Compensation of employees paid by resident producers to:	197840	201530	207480	209640	210000	216770	225240	232060 / 239360	245740	252850	269990	285630
A Resident households	196930	200520	206340	208520	208880	215550	224030	230990 / 238290	244540	251590	268860	284470
B Rest of the world	910	1010	1140	1120	1120	1220	1210	1070 / 1070	1200	1260	1130	1160
4 Operating surplus	74390	82800	90820	98270	113680	121350	119770	112040 / 113250	118770	133310	139090	144690
A Corporate and quasi-corporate enterprises	74390	82800	90820	98270	113680	121350	119770	112040a / 63110	66000	75150	78630	81140
B Private unincorporated enterprises								... / 50140	52770	58160	60460	63550
C General government	...	...	...	...	...	...	...	... / ...	...	...	...	...
Equals: Gross Domestic Product	336740	352850	368860	381020	400250	418180	428610	430170 / 440580	457410	484670	516320	543560

a) Including item 'Private unincorporated enterprises'.

1.4 General Government Current Receipts and Disbursements

Million Netherlands guilders

	1980	1981	1982	1983	1984	1985	1986	1987	1988	1989	1990	1991
					Receipts							
1 Operating surplus	...	...	...	...	...	...	...	... / ...	...	...	...	...
2 Property and entrepreneurial income	20000	25290	26950	28170	32530	35790	29540	21120 / 20460	17800	18890	21180	24020
3 Taxes, fees and contributions	153570	159040	167330	178160	179390	186870	192880	204320 / 211760	221060	219850	233440	258380
A Indirect taxes a	37450	37990	38710	41000	43400	45690	48060	51530 / 58620	60560	60370	64850	69270

1.4 General Government Current Receipts and Disbursements
(Continued)

Million Netherlands guilders

	1980	1981	1982	1983	1984	1985	1986	1987	1988	1989	1990	1991
B Direct taxes	53500	53280	54290	51890	51030	52870	57610	60780 62320	65980	67510	80040	91660
C Social security contributions	61220	66140	72490	83300	82860	85990	84740	89140 90310	93950	91330	87910	96780
D Compulsory fees, fines and penalties	1400	1630	1840	1970	2100	2320	2470	2870 510	570	640	640	670
4 Other current transfers [a]	4270	4300	4320	4220	4440	4530	4610	4920 12930	13140	13760	13100	13270
Total Current Receipts of General Government	177840	188630	198600	210550	216360	227190	227030	230360 245150	252000	252500	267720	295670

Disbursements

	1980	1981	1982	1983	1984	1985	1986	1987	1988	1989	1990	1991
1 Government final consumption expenditure	60260	62750	65120	66580	66390	67670	68550	70590 69780	70200	71760	74680	77910
A Compensation of employees	44080	45020	46720	46950	46410	46910	47450	48510 48900	48610	48800	50680	52480
B Consumption of fixed capital	2400	2560	2420	2300	2620	2750	2780	3030 3400	3550	3740	3910	4080
C Purchases of goods and services, net	14000	15390	16170	17490	17580	18170	18370	19050 17630	18200	19400	20280	21530
D Less: Own account fixed capital formation	580	580	570	560	640	590	510	480 620	620	660	700	720
E Indirect taxes paid, net	360	360	380	400	420	430	460	480 470	460	480	510	540
2 Property income	15660	19340	23180	26500	29860	32170	32620	31070 28170	29010	29060	30840	33530
A Interest	15660	19340	23180	26500	29860	32170	32620	31070 28140	28980	29040	30810	33500
B Net land rent and royalties	...	...	...	...	...	...	...	... 30	30	20	30	30
3 Subsidies [b]	4980	5520	6220	6710	7410	7860	8120	10590 19190	18850	16740	15860	17590
4 Other current transfers	94260	102730	112860	118420	119370	121360	123660	126190 135510	139190	143630	157390	168090
A Social security benefits	70920	75690	80610	81400	81570	82960	84540	86910 86990	89650	88560	101280	108760
B Social assistance grants	12700	15600	20490	24730	24870	22510	22750	22800 20510	20490	24710	24950	25650
C Other [b]	10640	11440	11760	12290	12930	15890	16370	16480 28010	29050	30360	31160	33680
5 Net saving	2680	-1710	-8780	-7660	-6670	-1870	-5920	-8080 -7500	-5250	-8690	-11050	-1450
Total Current Disbursements and Net Saving of General Government	177840	188630	198600	210550	216360	227190	227030	230360 245150	252000	252500	267720	295670

a) The import duties of non-resident enterprises paid by the Netherlands to the European Community are not included in these figures (1987:190; 1988:220; 1989:300; 1990:430; 1991:570 million N. Guilders).   b) The subsidies from the European Community paid to the Netherlands but destined for non-resident enterprises are not included in these figures (1987:370; 1988:2780; 1989:2560; 1990:1310; 1991:610 million N. guilders).

Netherlands

1.5 Current Income and Outlay of Corporate and Quasi-Corporate Enterprises, Summary

Million Netherlands guilders

	1980	1981	1982	1983	1984	1985	1986	1987	1988	1989	1990	1991
Receipts												
1 Operating surplus	74390	82800	90820	98270	113680	121350	119770	112040 / 63110	66000	75150	78630	81140
2 Property and entrepreneurial income received	73520	89240	93600	91000	97200	102070	99890	102000 / 114560	121390	145550	163690	175010
3 Current transfers	11540	12840	12710	13210	13600	14210	15260	16480 / 17720	18510	20010	24000	22180
Total Current Receipts	159450	184880	197130	202480	224480	237630	234920	230520 / 195390	205900	240710	266320	278330
Disbursements												
1 Property and entrepreneurial income	132540	154080	165560	165370	179920	189810	185680	183240 / 143000	149190	173930	196770	211330
2 Direct taxes and other current payments to general government	10170	11100	11340	10850	10300	13060	14370	16030 / 16380	16100	15870	17570	18730
3 Other current transfers	11540	12840	12710	13210	13600	14210	15260	16480 / 17360	17460	18680	23030	21800
4 Net saving	5200	6860	7520	13050	20660	20550	19610	14770 / 18650	23150	32230	28950	26470
Total Current Disbursements and Net Saving	159450	184880	197130	202480	224480	237630	234920	230520 / 195390	205900	240710	266320	278330

1.6 Current Income and Outlay of Households and Non-Profit Institutions

Million Netherlands guilders

	1980	1981	1982	1983	1984	1985	1986	1987	1988	1989	1990	1991
Receipts												
1 Compensation of employees	197960	201640	207690	209810	210150	216850	225220	232180 / 239480	245730	252710	269710	285290
A From resident producers	196930	200520	206340	208520	208880	215550	224030	230990 / 238290	244540	251590	268860	284470
B From rest of the world	1030	1120	1350	1290	1270	1300	1190	1190 / 1190	1190	1120	850	820
2 Operating surplus of private unincorporated enterprises	...	...	...	...	...	...	...	50140	52770	58160	60460	63550
3 Property and entrepreneurial income	55850	59890	69490	74830	81100	86380	89620	92060 / 53400	54960	59480	65860	71230
4 Current transfers	98960	107570	117480	123270	123920	126190	128720	132220 / 137060	140700	145390	160180	169370
A Social security benefits	70370	75100	79900	80730	80870	82230	83740	86120 / 86200	88790	87670	100400	107730
B Social assistance grants	12820	15710	20600	24840	25010	22640	22880	22940 / 20510	20490	24710	24950	25650
C Other	15770	16760	16980	17700	18040	21320	22100	23160 / 30350	31420	33010	34830	35990
Total Current Receipts	352770	369100	394660	407910	415170	429420	443560	456460 / 480080	494160	515740	556210	589440
Disbursements												
1 Private final consumption expenditure	205780	213230	221830	229860	236750	247720	256150	263930 / 267940	271640	284490	302820	323070
2 Property income	1910	2070	1890	1740	1700	1660	1710	1720 / 18520	19440	20990	23420	25950
3 Direct taxes and other current transfers n.e.c. to general government	105950	109950	117280	126310	125690	128120	130450	136760 / 136110	143490	142820	150230	169490
A Social security contributions	61220	66140	72490	83300	82860	85990	84740	89140 / 90310	93950	91330	87910	96780
B Direct taxes	43330	42180	42950	41040	40730	39810	43240	44750 / 45100	48810	50700	61520	71920
C Fees, fines and penalties	1400	1630	1840	1970	2100	2320	2470	2870 / 700	730	790	800	790
4 Other current transfers	11890	12370	12480	12700	13280	13930	14550	15700 / 17480	18120	19440	20850	21670
5 Net saving	27240	31480	41180	37300	37750	37990	40700	38350 / 40030	41470	48000	58890	49260
Total Current Disbursements and Net Saving	352770	369100	394660	407910	415170	429420	443560	456460 / 480080	494160	515740	556210	589440

1.7 External Transactions on Current Account, Summary

Million Netherlands guilders

	1980	1981	1982	1983	1984	1985	1986	1987	1988	1989	1990	1991
Payments to the Rest of the World												
1 Imports of goods and services	178620	192240	196830	205210	227750	245500	213010	213310 / 207560	222380	248760	256500	266000
A Imports of merchandise c.i.f.	156120	168420	171710	179580	200240	216610	185240	185300 / 177820	190820	214500	220320	226710
B Other	22500	23820	25120	25630	27510	28890	27770	28010 / 29740	31560	34260	36180	39290
2 Factor income to the rest of the world	22710	31090	32400	27810	31370	32200	29500	30390 / 32030	36730	48490	50080	50760
A Compensation of employees	910	1010	1140	1120	1120	1220	1210	1070 / 1070	1200	1260	1130	1160
B Property and entrepreneurial income	21800	30080	31260	26690	30250	30980	28290	29320 / 30960	35530	47230	48950	49600
By general government	...	...	...	...	...	...	...	... / 2770	3580	3720	3750	4360
By corporate and quasi-corporate enterprises	21800	30080	31260	26690	30250	30980	28290	29320 / 28190	31950	43510	45200	45240
By other	...	...	...	...	...	...	...	... / ...	...	...	...	...
3 Current transfers to the rest of the world	8400	9160	9600	9830	10860	11790	12710	13040 / 12000	12580	13550	14150	16080
A Indirect taxes to supranational organizations a	3670	3730	4050	4140	4590	5010	5640	5890 / 5700	6140	6430	6260	7480
B Other current transfers b	4730	5430	5550	5690	6270	6780	7070	7150 / 6300	6440	7120	7890	8600
4 Surplus of the nation on current transactions c	-4900	7760	11640	11860	16630	17310	11630	5930 / 8560	12860	16910	20710	21140
Payments to the Rest of the World and Surplus of the Nation on Current Transactions	204830	240250	250470	254710	286610	306800	266850	262670 / 260150	284550	327710	341440	353980
Receipts From The Rest of the World												
1 Exports of goods and services	176810	204620	212600	219770	248560	265540	232520	226650 / 219260	240250	267670	280990	293880
A Exports of merchandise f.o.b.	147080	171330	177620	185010	210630	225950	195850	188780 / 181560	199180	222080	230330	239770
B Other	29730	33290	34980	34760	37930	39590	36670	37870 / 37700	41070	45590	50660	54110
2 Factor income from rest of the world	22090	30130	32020	28370	30870	32880	28520	29660 / 30880	33230	48290	49500	49870
A Compensation of employees	1030	1120	1350	1290	1270	1300	1190	1190 / 1190	1190	1120	850	820
B Property and entrepreneurial income	21060	29010	30670	27080	29600	31580	27330	28470 / 29690	32040	47170	48650	49050
By general government	40	110	100	80	70	130	70	70 / 40	80	90	50	60
By corporate and quasi-corporate enterprises	20100	27830	29140	25470	27940	29520	25450	26490 / 28520	30670	45670	47150	47490
By other	920	1070	1430	1530	1590	1930	1810	1910 / 1130	1290	1410	1450	1500
3 Current transfers from rest of the world	5930	5500	5850	6570	7180	7860	7970	8640 / 10010	11070	11750	10950	10230
A Subsidies from supranational organisations b	4120	3300	3840	4510	5200	5650	5780	6240 / 6370	6380	6660	5540	5690
B Other current transfers a	1810	2200	2010	2060	1980	2210	2190	2400 / 3640	4690	5090	5410	4540
Statistical discrepancy d	...	...	...	...	...	520	-2160	-2280 / -	-	-	-	-
Receipts from the Rest of the World on Current Transactions	204830	240250	250470	254710	286610	306800	266850	262670 / 260150	284550	327710	341440	353980

a) The import duties of non-resident enterprises paid by the Netherlands to the European Community are not included in these figures (1987:190; 1988:220; 1989:300; 1990:430; 1991:570 million N. Guilders).

b) The subsidies from the European Community paid to the Netherlands but destined for non-resident enterprises are not included in these figures (1987:370; 1988:2780; 1989:2560; 1990:1310; 1991:610 million N. guilders).

c) As a result of definition and measuring differences, this surplus differs from the surplus on current transactions according to the balance of payments on a transaction basis, estimated by the Dutch Central Bank in cooperation with the Central Bureau of Statistics.

d) The surplus of the nation on current transactions corresponds to gross national saving less gross capital formation, plus from 1985 onwards a statistical discrepancy. This discrepancy is a consequence of the difference between on the one hand the surplus of the nation on current transactions (estimated by the Dutch Central Bank in cooperation with the Central Bureau of Statistics) and on the other hand the sum of the balance of exports and imports and the net current distributive transactions with the rest of the world. For the years 1983 and 84 there were also statistical discrepancies. However, these have been eliminated by altering the imports with destination increase in stocks.

Netherlands

1.8 Capital Transactions of The Nation, Summary

Million Netherlands guilders

	1980	1981	1982	1983	1984	1985	1986	1987	1988	1989	1990	1991
Finance of Gross Capital Formation												
Gross saving	67610	72250	77780	81880	92930	99540	98190	90520 / 99720	110560	126420	135040	135840
1 Consumption of fixed capital	32490	35620	37860	39190	41190	42870	43800	45480 / 48540	51190	54880	58250	61560
A General government	2400	2560	2420	2300	2620	2750	2780	3030 / 3400	3550	3740	3910	4080
B Corporate and quasi-corporate enterprises a	30090	33060	35440	36890	38570	40120	41020	42450 / 34210	36050	39120	41340	43930
C Other a	...	...	...	...	...	...	...	... / 10930	11590	12020	13000	13550
2 Net saving	35120	36630	39920	42690	51740	56670	54390	45040 / 51180	59370	71540	76790	74280
A General government	2680	-1710	-8780	-7660	-6670	-1870	-5920	-8080 / -7500	-5250	-8690	-11050	-1450
B Corporate and quasi-corporate enterprises	5200	6860	7520	13050	20660	20550	19610	14770 / 18650	23150	32230	28950	26470
C Other	27240	31480	41180	37300	37750	37990	40700	38350 / 40030	41470	48000	58890	49260
Less: Surplus of the nation on current transactions b	-4900	7760	11640	11860	16630	17310	11630	5930 / 8560	12860	16910	20710	21140
Statistical discrepancy c	...	...	...	...	...	520	-2160	-2280 / -	-	-	-	-
Finance of Gross Capital Formation	72510	64490	66140	70020	76300	82750	84400	82310 / 91160	97700	109510	114330	114700
Gross Capital Formation												
Increase in stocks	1720	-3090	-1020	560	1990	2500	-1780	-4790 / -420	310	5430	4490	1700
Gross fixed capital formation	70790	67580	67160	69460	74310	80250	86180	87100 / 91580	97390	104080	109840	113000
1 General government	10970	11100	10620	10190	11190	10940	10570	10240 / 11480	12210	12530	13540	13990
2 Corporate and quasi-corporate enterprises a	59820	56480	56540	59270	63120	69310	75610	76860 / 54280	55710	61320	65030	67860
3 Other a	...	...	...	...	...	...	...	... / 25820	29470	30230	31270	31150
Gross Capital Formation	72510	64490	66140	70020	76300	82750	84400	82310 / 91160	97700	109510	114330	114700

a) Item 'Other' is included in item 'Corporate and quasi-corporate enterprises'.
b) As a result of definition and measuring differences, this surplus differs from the surplus on current transactions according to the balance of payments on a transaction basis, estimated by the Dutch Central Bank in cooperation with the Central Bureau of Statistics.
c) The surplus of the nation on current transactions corresponds to gross national saving less gross capital formation, plus from 1985 onwards a statistical discrepancy. This discrepancy is a consequence of the difference between on the one hand the surplus of the nation on current transactions (estimated by the Dutch Central Bank in cooperation with the Central Bureau of Statistics) and on the other hand the sum of the balance of exports and imports and the net current distributive transactions with the rest of the world. For the years 1983 and 84 there were also statistical discrepancies. However, these have been eliminated by altering the imports with destination increase in stocks.

1.9 Gross Domestic Product by Institutional Sectors of Origin

Million Netherlands guilders

	1980	1981	1982	1983	1984	1985	1986	1987	1988	1989	1990	1991
Domestic Factor Incomes Originating												
1 General government	44080	45020	46720	46950	46410	46910	47450	48510 / 48900	48610	48800	50680	52480
2 Corporate and quasi-corporate enterprises a	228150	239310	251580	260960	277270	291210	297560	295590 / 234270	242880	258350	275060	289810
A Non-financial	224630	236070	248570	257900	273950	287750	293580	291200 / 231520	240420	254210	271680	286790
B Financial	3520	3240	3010	3060	3320	3460	3980	4390 / 2750	2460	4140	3380	3020

1.9 Gross Domestic Product by Institutional Sectors of Origin
(Continued)

Million Netherlands guilders

	1980	1981	1982	1983	1984	1985	1986	1987	1988	1989	1990	1991
3 Households and private unincorporated enterprises ab	...	...	...	...	...	...	...	... 69440	73020	79010	83340	88030
4 Non-profit institutions serving households ab	...	...	...	...	...	...	...	...	...	...	...	...
Subtotal: Domestic Factor Incomes	272230	284330	298300	307910	323680	338120	345010	344100 352610	364510	386160	409080	430320
Indirect taxes, net	32020	32900	32700	33920	35380	37190	39800	40590 39430	41710	43630	48990	51680
A Indirect taxes	41120	41720	42760	45140	47990	50700	53700	57420 58620	60560	60370	64850	69270
B Less: Subsidies	9100	8820	10060	11220	12610	13510	13900	16830 19190	18850	16740	15860	17590
Consumption of fixed capital	32490	35620	37860	39190	41190	42870	43800	45480 48540	51190	54880	58250	61560
Gross Domestic Product	336740	352850	368860	381020	400250	418180	428610	430170 440580	457410	484670	516320	543560

a) The estimates of Households and private unincorporated enterprises and Non-profit institutions serving households are included in item 'Corporate and quasi-corporate enterprises'.

b) Beginning 1987 of the new series, the estimates of item 'Non-profit institutions serving households' are included in item 'Households and private unincorporated enterprises'.

1.10 Gross Domestic Product by Kind of Activity, in Current Prices

Million Netherlands guilders

	1980	1981	1982	1983	1984	1985	1986	1987	1988	1989	1990	1991
1 Agriculture, hunting, forestry and fishing	11676	14557	15932	16124	17259	17141	18454	17694 17478	17955	20671	20589	21264
2 Mining and quarrying	19151	25563	25972	27328	31091	35372	23525	15727 15511	12504	13288	15249	18796
3 Manufacturing	60365	59780	64670	67463	72569	75231	83214	81407 79308	85896	92547	99545	101979
4 Electricity, gas and water	7172	7606	8159	8412	8367	8551	8819	8520 7957	7999	8149	8648	9295
5 Construction	23760	23056	22444	21413	21357	21264	22295	23026 21842	24724	25898	27934	28926
6 Wholesale and retail trade, restaurants and hotels ab	43437	44575	47051	48461	51175	53743	53715	56132 63793	66238	70376	76125	78881
7 Transport, storage and communication	21298	22265	22395	23152	24590	26083	28038	28366 27717	29141	30773	32030	34606
8 Finance, insurance, real estate and business services b	46893	50314	54273	60108	63012	65836	70248	72998 82723	87528	96575	101390	108907
9 Community, social and personal services a	37528	39452	41626	42776	43278	44390	46684	48173 47176	48628	49823	52817	56475
Statistical discrepancy	-	12	8	13	12	9	-2	-13	-	-	-	-
Total, Industries	271280	287180	302530	315250	332710	347620	354990	352030 363505	380613	408100	434327	459129
Producers of Government Services	46840	47940	49520	49650	49450	50090	50690	52020 49473	49279	49745	51770	53440
Other Producers c	1050	1060	1090	1070	1090	1140	1160	1170 1413	1510	1610	1696	1778
Subtotal	319170	336180	353140	365970	383250	398850	406840	405220 414390	431400	459450	487800	514340
Less: Imputed bank service charge	11460	12660	14080	16150	16420	16730	16760	16300 16540	17450	18030	18060	19930
Plus: Import duties d	4440	4220	4580	4770	5130	5650	6260	7050 5940	5590	6370	7100	7520
Plus: Value added tax e	24590	25110	25220	26430	28290	30410	32270	34200 36420	37450	36480	39140	41260
Plus: Other adjustments f	...	...	...	...	...	...	...	... 370	420	400	340	370
Equals: Gross Domestic Product	336740	352850	368860	381020	400250	418180	428610	430170 440580	457410	484670	516320	543560
Memorandum Item: Mineral fuels and power	...	...	...	...	...	...	...	... 27538	25245	26042	30701	36327

a) For the first series, repair services are included in item 'Community, social and personal services'.
b) For the years 1990 and 1991, real estate brokers are included in item 'Wholesale and retail trade, restaurants and hotels'.
c) Beginning 1987 of the second series, item 'Other producers' includes only domestic services of households; private non-profit services to households are included in various industries above.

d) Beginning 1987 of the new series, item 'Import duties' includes all taxes linked to imports (excluding VAT) less import subsidies.
e) For the first series, item 'Value added tax' includes selective investment levy.
f) Beginning 1987 of the new series, item 'Other adjustments' includes only levies on fixed capital goods.

Netherlands

1.11 Gross Domestic Product by Kind of Activity, in Constant Prices

Million Netherlands guilders

	1980	1981	1982	1983	1984	1985	1986	1987	1988	1989	1990	1991
					At constant prices of: 1980							
								1987				
1 Agriculture, hunting, forestry and fishing	11680	13290	14270	14740	15650	15220	16620	15500 / 17480	18240	19500	20960	21390
2 Mining and quarrying								90440a / 15510	13660	14130	14170	15820
3 Manufacturing	86680	85070	80980	83980	87140	90480	90850	... / 79310	82610	87220	90510	91550
4 Electricity, gas and water								... / 7960	8150	8170	8260	8670
5 Construction	23760	21860	20730	20110	20730	20890	21340	21400 / 21840	23970	24290	25110	25010
6 Wholesale and retail trade, restaurants and hotels								168940bd / 63800c	65770c	69240c	73670c	75300c
7 Transport, storage and communication	149160	149610	150090	151720	157430	162160	165670	... / 27710	28730	30560	31620	32880
8 Finance, insurance, real estate and business services								... / 82720c	85480c	91410c	94450c	97270c
9 Community, social and personal services								... / 47180	48060	48320	49600	51160
Total, Industries	271280	269830	266070	270550	280950	288750	294480	296280 / 363510e	374670e	392870e	408410e	419040e
Producers of Government Services	46840	47680	47820	47690	47760	48230	48640	49140 / 49470	49900	50430	51220	51270
Other Producers	1050	1030	1000	980	990	1020	1010	1010 / 1410f	1490f	1540f	1540f	1560f
Subtotal	319170	318540	314890	319220	329700	338000	344130	346430 / 414390e	426060e	444880e	461300e	472040e
Less: Imputed bank service charge	11460	11910	12380	12360	12330	12450	12810	12930 / 16540	17010	16810	17360	17980
Plus: Import duties	4440	4250	4400	4550	4380	4770	5050	5150 / 5940g	5390g	6150g	6680g	6650g
Plus: Value added tax	24590h	23490h	22750h	22880h	23100h	23620h	24770h	25470h / 36420	37240	38620	40690	41600
Plus: Other adjustments	...	...	...	...	...	...	...	... / 370i	420i	400i	340i	370i
Equals: Gross Domestic Product	336740	334370	329660	334290	344850	353940	361140	364120 / 440580e	452100e	473260e	491640e	502660e
Memorandum Item: Mineral fuels and power	...	...	...	...	...	...	...	... / 27540	26320	26740	27310	29440

a) Including item 'Mining and quarrying' through 'Electricity, gas and water'.
b) For the first series, repair services are included in item 'Community, social and personal services'.
c) For the years 1990 and 1991, real estate brokers are included in item 'Wholesale and retail trade, restaurants and hotels'.
d) Including item 'Wholesale and retail trade, restaurants and hotels' through 'Community, social and personal services'.
e) The estimates in constant prices of the fixed base year 1987 have been calculated on the basis of figures in constant prices of the preceding year. Because of this, the sum of the sub-items do not add-up to the main aggregate. However, for the constant price 1980, the differences were eliminated by adding them proportionally to the details.
f) Beginning 1987 of the second series, item 'Other producers' includes only domestic services of households; private non-profit services to households are included in various industries above.
g) Beginning 1987 of the new series, item 'Import duties' includes all taxes linked to imports (excluding VAT) less import subsidies.
h) For the first series, item 'Value added tax' includes selective investment levy.
i) Beginning 1987 of the new series, item 'Other adjustments' includes only levies on fixed capital goods.

1.12 Relations Among National Accounting Aggregates

Million Netherlands guilders

	1980	1981	1982	1983	1984	1985	1986	1987	1988	1989	1990	1991
Gross Domestic Product	336740	352850	368860	381020	400250	418180	428610	430170 / 440580	457410	484670	516320	543560
Plus: Net factor income from the rest of the world	-620	-960	-380	560	-500	680	-980	-730 / -1150	-3500	-200	-580	-890
Factor income from the rest of the world	22090	30130	32020	28370	30870	32880	28520	29660 / 30880	33230	48290	49500	49870
Less: Factor income to the rest of the world	22710	31090	32400	27810	31370	32200	29500	30390 / 32030	36730	48490	50080	50760
Equals: Gross National Product	336120	351890	368480	381580	399750	418860	427630	429440 / 439430	453910	484470	515740	542670
Less: Consumption of fixed capital	32490	35620	37860	39190	41190	42870	43800	45480 / 48540	51190	54880	58250	61560

1.12 Relations Among National Accounting Aggregates
(Continued)

Million Netherlands guilders

	1980	1981	1982	1983	1984	1985	1986	1987	1988	1989	1990	1991
Equals: National Income	303630	316270	330620	342390	358560	375990	383830	383960 390890	402720	429590	457490	481110
Plus: Net current transfers from the rest of the world	-2470	-3660	-3750	-3260	-3680	-3930	-4740	-4400 -1990	-1510	-1800	-3200	-5850
Current transfers from the rest of the world ab	5930	5500	5850	6570	7180	7860	7970	8640 10010	11070	11750	10950	10230
Less: Current transfers to the rest of the world ab	8400	9160	9600	9830	10860	11790	12710	13040 12000	12580	13550	14150	16080
Equals: National Disposable Income	301160	312610	326870	339130	354880	372060	379090	379560 388900	401210	427790	454290	475260
Less: Final consumption	266040	275980	286950	296440	303140	315390	324700	334520 337720	341840	356250	377500	400980
Equals: Net Saving	35120	36630	39920	42690	51740	56670	54390	45040 51180	59370	71540	76790	74280
Less: Surplus of the nation on current transactions c	-4900	7760	11640	11860	16630	17310	11630	5930 8560	12860	16910	20710	21140
Statistical discrepancy d	...	...	...	...	...	520	-2160	-2280	-	-	-	-
Equals: Net Capital Formation	40020	28870	28280	30830	35110	39880	40600	36830 42620	46510	54630	56080	53140

a) The subsidies from the European Community paid to the Netherlands but destined for non-resident enterprises are not included in these figures (1987:370; 1988:2780; 1989:2560; 1990:1310; 1991:610 million N. guilders).
b) The import duties of non-resident enterprises paid by the Netherlands to the European Community are not included in these figures (1987:190; 1988:220; 1989:300; 1990:430; 1991:570 million N. Guilders).
c) As a result of definition and measuring differences, this surplus differs from the surplus on current transactions according to the balance of payments on a transaction basis, estimated by the Dutch Central Bank in cooperation with the Central Bureau of Statistics.

d) The surplus of the nation on current transactions corresponds to gross national saving less gross capital formation, plus from 1985 onwards a statistical discrepancy. This discrepancy is a consequence of the difference between on the one hand the surplus of the nation on current transactions (estimated by the Dutch Central Bank in cooperation with the Central Bureau of Statistics) and on the other hand the sum of the balance of exports and imports and the net current distributive transactions with the rest of the world. For the years 1983 and 84 there were also statistical discrepancies. However, these have been eliminated by altering the imports with destination increase in stocks.

2.1 Government Final Consumption Expenditure by Function, in Current Prices

Million Netherlands guilders

	1980	1981	1982	1983	1984	1985	1986	1987	1988	1989	1990	1991
1 General public services a	...	...	...	...	...	...	...	...	...	...	...	...
2 Defence	10170	10790	11430	12360	12230	11920	12260	12790	12970	13050	...	...
3 Public order and safety	...	...	...	...	...	...	...	...	...	...	...	...
4 Education b	21130	21650	21970	21480	21200	21550	21860	22030	21880	21980	...	...
5 Health a	...	...	...	...	...	...	...	...	...	...	...	...
6 Social security and welfare c	2400	2650	2890	2990	3070	3120	3210	3370	3460	3560	...	...
7 Housing and community amenities a											...	...
8 Recreational, cultural and religious affairs	26560	27660	28830	29750	29890	31080	31220	32400	32850	33900	...	...
9 Economic services d											...	...
10 Other functions a											...	...
Total Government Final Consumption Expenditure	60260	62750	65120	66580	66390	67670	68550	70590	71160	72490	...	...

a) Items 'General public service' and 'Health' are included in items 'Housing and community amenities' through 'Other functions'.
b) Item 'Education' refers to school only.

c) Item 'Social security and welfare' refers to social security only.
d) Data for this table have not been revised, therefore, data for some years are not comparable with those of other tables.

2.3 Total Government Outlays by Function and Type

Million Netherlands guilders

	Final Consumption Expenditures			Subsidies	Other Current Transfers & Property Income	Total Current Disbursements	Gross Capital Formation	Other Capital Outlays	Total Outlays
	Total	Compensation of Employees	Other						
					1980				
1 General public services a	...	...	...	...	...	...	...	...	...
2 Defence	10170	6460	3710	...	500	10670	...	10	10680
3 Public order and safety	...	...	...	...	...	...	...	...	...
4 Education b	21130	17160	3970	...	1400	22530	1630	10	24170
5 Health a	...	...	...	...	...	...	...	...	...
6 Social security and welfare c	2400	1510	890	...	70940	73340	...	90	73430
7 Housing and community amenities a									
8 Recreation, culture and religion	26560	18950	7610	4980	33860	65400	9340	8750	83490
9 Economic services d									
10 Other functions a									
Total	60260	44080	16180	4980	106700	171940	10970	8860	191770

Netherlands

2.3 Total Government Outlays by Function and Type
(Continued)

Million Netherlands guilders

	Final Consumption Expenditures			Subsidies	Other Current Transfers & Property Income	Total Current Disbursements	Gross Capital Formation	Other Capital Outlays	Total Outlays
	Total	Compensation of Employees	Other						
1981									
1 General public services [a]	...	...	...	...	...	...	...	...	...
2 Defence	10790	6640	4150	...	520	11310	...	200	11510
3 Public order and safety	...	...	...	...	...	...	...	...	...
4 Education [b]	21650	17470	4180	...	1450	23100	1510	-	24610
5 Health [a]	...	...	...	...	...	...	...	...	...
6 Social security and welfare [c]	2650	1640	1010	...	75790	78440	...	80	78520
7 Housing and community amenities [a]									
8 Recreation, culture and religion	27660	19270	8390	5520	40630	73810	9590	10150	93550
9 Economic services [d]									
10 Other functions [a]									
Total	62750	45020	17730	5520	118390	186660	11100	10430	208190
1982									
1 General public services [a]	...	...	...	...	...	...	...	...	...
2 Defence	11430	6840	4590	...	540	11970	...	110	12080
3 Public order and safety	...	...	...	...	...	...	...	...	...
4 Education [b]	21970	17890	4080	...	1420	23390	1460	10	24860
5 Health [a]	...	...	...	...	...	...	...	...	...
6 Social security and welfare [c]	2890	1840	1050	...	80720	83610	...	70	83680
7 Housing and community amenities [a]									
8 Recreation, culture and religion	28830	20150	8680	6220	49220	84270	9160	10450	103880
9 Economic services [d]									
10 Other functions [a]									
Total	65120	46720	18400	6220	131900	203240	10620	10640	224500
1983									
1 General public services [a]	...	...	...	...	...	...	...	...	...
2 Defence	12360	6840	5520	...	510	12870	...	10	12880
3 Public order and safety	...	...	...	...	...	...	...	...	...
4 Education [b]	21480	17600	3880	...	1440	22920	1210	-	24130
5 Health [a]	...	...	...	...	...	...	...	...	...
6 Social security and welfare [c]	2990	1900	1090	...	81500	84490	...	70	84560
7 Housing and community amenities [a]									
8 Recreation, culture and religion	29750	20610	9140	6710	56630	93090	8980	10290	112360
9 Economic services [d]									
10 Other functions [a]									
Total	66580	46950	19630	6710	140080	213370	10190	10370	233930
1984									
1 General public services [a]	...	...	...	...	...	...	...	...	...
2 Defence	12230	6930	5300	...	570	12800	...	10	12810
3 Public order and safety	...	...	...	...	...	...	...	...	...
4 Education [b]	21200	17170	4030	...	1480	22680	1300	-	23980
5 Health [a]	...	...	...	...	...	...	...	...	...
6 Social security and welfare [c]	3070	1930	1140	...	81690	84760	...	80	84840
7 Housing and community amenities [a]									
8 Recreation, culture and religion	29890	20380	9510	7410	59490	96790	9890	11780	118460
9 Economic services [d]									
10 Other functions [a]									
Total	66390	46410	19980	7410	143230	217030	11190	11870	240090

2.3 Total Government Outlays by Function and Type
(Continued)

Million Netherlands guilders

	Final Consumption Expenditures			Subsidies	Other Current Transfers & Property Income	Total Current Disbursements	Gross Capital Formation	Other Capital Outlays	Total Outlays
	Total	Compensation of Employees	Other						
1985									
1 General public services a	...	...	...	...	...	...	...	...	...
2 Defence	11920	6800	5120	...	580	12500	...	20	12520
3 Public order and safety	...	...	...	...	...	...	...	...	...
4 Education b	21550	17390	4160	...	1590	23140	1270	-	24410
5 Health a	...	...	...	...	...	...	...	...	...
6 Social security and welfare c	3120	1990	1130	...	83090	86210	...	90	86300
7 Housing and community amenities a									
8 Recreation, culture and religion	31080	20730	10350	7860	62260	101200	9670	11770	122640
9 Economic services d									
10 Other functions a									
Total	67670	46910	20760	7860	147520	223050	10940	11880	245870
1986									
1 General public services a	...	...	...	...	...	...	...	...	...
2 Defence	12260	6850	5410	...	610	12870	...	30	12900
3 Public order and safety	...	...	...	...	...	...	...	...	...
4 Education b	21860	17730	4130	...	1760	23620	1350	-	24970
5 Health a	...	...	...	...	...	...	...	...	...
6 Social security and welfare c	3210	2090	1120	...	84660	87870	...	100	87970
7 Housing and community amenities a									
8 Recreation, culture and religion	31220	20780	10440	8120	63230	102570	9220	14080	125870
9 Economic services d									
10 Other functions a									
Total	68550	47450	21100	8120	150260	226930	10570	14210	251710
1987									
1 General public services a	...	...	...	...	...	...	...	...	...
2 Defence	12790	7140	5650	...	600	13390	...	70	13460
3 Public order and safety	...	...	...	...	...	...	...	...	...
4 Education b	22030	18090	3940	...	1970	24000	1540	-	25540
5 Health a	...	...	...	...	...	...	...	...	...
6 Social security and welfare c	3370	2160	1210	...	87030	90400	...	100	90500
7 Housing and community amenities a									
8 Recreation, culture and religion	32400	21120	11280	10590	63000	105990	8700	15730	130420
9 Economic services d									
10 Other functions a									
Total	70590	48510	22080	10590	152600	233780	10240	15900	259920
1988									
1 General public services a	...	...	...	...	...	...	...	...	...
2 Defence	12970	7110	5860	...	630	13600	...	40	13640
3 Public order and safety	...	...	...	...	...	...	...	...	...
4 Education b	21880	17780	4100	...	2070	23950	1550	-	25500
5 Health a	...	...	...	...	...	...	...	...	...
6 Social security and welfare c	3460	2190	1270	...	89520	92980	...	90	93070
7 Housing and community amenities a									
8 Recreation, culture and religion	32850	21390	11460	10520	63800	107170	9020	12290	128480
9 Economic services d									
10 Other functions a									
Total	71160	48470	22690	10520	156020	237700	10570	12420	260690

Netherlands

2.3 Total Government Outlays by Function and Type
(Continued)

Million Netherlands guilders

	Final Consumption Expenditures			Subsidies	Other Current Transfers & Property Income	Total Current Disbursements	Gross Capital Formation	Other Capital Outlays	Total Outlays
	Total	Compensation of Employees	Other						
					1989				
1 General public services a	...	...	...	...	...	...	...	...	...
2 Defence	13050	7110	5940	...	660	13710	...	40	13750
3 Public order and safety	...	...	...	...	...	...	...	...	...
4 Education b	21980	17860	4120	...	2200	24180	1590	-	25770
5 Health a	...	...	...	...	...	...	...	...	...
6 Social security and welfare c	3560	2210	1350	...	88070	91630	...	-	91630
7 Housing and community amenities a									
8 Recreation, culture and religion	33900	21680	12220	8420	69370	111690	9410	11770	132870
9 Economic services d									
10 Other functions a									
Total	72490	48860	23630	8420	160300	241210	11000	11810	264020

a) Items 'General public service' and 'Health' are included in items 'Housing and community amenities' through 'Other functions'.
b) Item 'Education' refers to school only.
c) Item 'Social security and welfare' refers to social security only.
d) Data for this table have not been revised, therefore, data for some years are not comparable with those of other tables.

2.5 Private Final Consumption Expenditure by Type and Purpose, in Current Prices

Million Netherlands guilders

	1980	1981	1982	1983	1984	1985	1986	1987	1988	1989	1990	1991
					Final Consumption Expenditure of Resident Households							
1 Food, beverages and tobacco	39610	41840	43860	44750	46510	47200	47800	48480 / 42350	42750	44370	46630	49050
A Food	30630	32390	33910	34520	36020	36700	37160	37770 / 32630	32920	34190	35870	37700
B Non-alcoholic beverages	1090	1140	1310	1360	1300	1330	1400	1380 / 1290	1410	1510	1630	1780
C Alcoholic beverages	4060	4340	4620	4690	4790	4740	4870	4820 / 4180	4210	4410	4710	5000
D Tobacco	3830	3970	4020	4180	4400	4430	4370	4510 / 4250	4210	4260	4420	4570
2 Clothing and footwear	16170	15770	15690	15690	15770	17010	18090	18800 / 19660	19200	19700	21200	22240
3 Gross rent, fuel and power a	32640	36410	39670	42540	44820	48000	48540	47730 / 46640	47490	49560	53250	58680
A Fuel and power	10530	12150	12770	13200	14000	15870	14510	11930 / 9700	8360	8210	9260	11330
B Other	22110	24260	26900	29340	30820	32130	34030	35800 / 36940	39130	41350	43990	47350
4 Furniture, furnishings and household equipment and operation	18590	17590	17190	17400	17260	17920	19050	20490 / 18540	19140	20310	21960	22970
A Household operation	3940	4070	4300	4310	4460	4630	4740	4920 / 4360	4560	4940	5220	5570
B Other	14650	13520	12890	13090	12800	13290	14310	15570 / 14180	14580	15370	16740	17400
5 Medical care and health expenses	24830	26560	28410	29220	29750	30640	31610	32320 / 33320	34410	35700	37900	40650
6 Transport and communication	21810	22500	23070	24330	24710	26580	27840	29620 / 34070	33480	34880	36980	40430
A Personal transport equipment	6760	6630	6950	7990	7960	8950	10470	11160 / 11750	10310	10590	11270	11770
B Other	15050	15870	16120	16340	16750	17630	17370	18460 / 22320	23170	24290	25710	28660
7 Recreational, entertainment, education and cultural services	20050	20300	20380	21250	21960	22590	23510	24640 / 26790	27960	29190	31640	33600
A Education	660	700	710	730	740	760	740	760 / 1720	1840	1870	2020	2190
B Other	19390	19600	19670	20520	21220	21830	22770	23880 / 25070	26120	27320	29620	31410
8 Miscellaneous goods and services	27310	28180	29150	30050	31820	32970	34530	35890 / 41880	42470	46110	48920	51270
A Personal care	5100	5190	5150	5390	5650	5830	6130	6330 / 6940	7190	7620	8200	8580
B Expenditures in restaurants, cafes and hotels	9660	10050	10560	10880	11770	12020	12360	12630 / 12230	12530	13750	14850	16110

1264

2.5 Private Final Consumption Expenditure by Type and Purpose, in Current Prices
(Continued)

Million Netherlands guilders

	1980	1981	1982	1983	1984	1985	1986	1987	1988	1989	1990	1991
C Other	12550	12940	13440	13780	14400	15120	16040	16930 22710	22750	24740	25870	26580
Total Final Consumption Expenditure in the Domestic Market by Households, of which	201010	209150	217420	225230	232600	242910	250970	257970 263250	266900	279820	298480	318890
A Durable goods	23270	21830	21550	22740	22250	23600	26200	28170 28580	27780	28810	31100	32380
B Semi-durable goods	33120	32850	32410	32870	33570	35790	38160	40340 41920	42360	44070	47550	51110
C Non-durable goods	64790	69560	72670	74210	77550	80540	79140	77900 72170	71840	74710	79570	85450
D Services	79830	84910	90790	95410	99230	102980	107470	111560 120580	124920	132230	140260	149950
Plus: Direct purchases abroad by resident households	9450	9410	9630	9870	10200	10940	11280	12070 9630	9900	10640	10350	11370
Less: Direct purchases in the domestic market by non-resident households	4680	5330	5220	5240	6050	6130	6100	6110 4940	5160	5970	6010	7190
Equals: Final Consumption Expenditure of Resident Households [b]	205780	213230	221830	229860	236750	247720	256150	263930 267940	271640	284490	302820	323070

Final Consumption Expenditure of Private Non-profit Institutions Serving Households

	1980	1981	1982	1983	1984	1985	1986	1987	1988	1989	1990	1991
Equals: Final Consumption Expenditure of Private Non-profit Organisations Serving Households	...	...	...	...	...	...	...	... ...	...	...	...	...
Private Final Consumption Expenditure	205780	213230	221830	229860	236750	247720	256150	263930 267940	271640	284490	302820	323070

a) Item 'Gross rent, fuel and power' includes maintenance expenditure.
b) Item 'Final consumption expenditure of resident households' includes consumption expenditure of private non-profit institutions serving households.

2.6 Private Final Consumption Expenditure by Type and Purpose, in Constant Prices

Million Netherlands guilders

	1980	1981	1982	1983	1984	1985	1986	1987	1988	1989	1990	1991
					At constant prices of: 1980					1987		
					Final Consumption Expenditure of Resident Households							
1 Food, beverages and tobacco	39610	39770	39620	40040	40100	40320	41080	42070 42350	42720	44040	45920	47040
A Food	30630	30790	30720	31080	31510	31920	32630	33750 32630	32970	33840	35400	36250
B Non-alcoholic beverages	1090	1140	1180	1260	1170	1140	1220	1220 1290	1370	1580	1690	1750
C Alcoholic beverages	4060	4160	4120	4170	4140	4040	4040	3970 4180	4180	4350	4500	4640
D Tobacco	3830	3680	3600	3530	3280	3220	3190	3130 4250	4200	4260	4320	4400
2 Clothing and footwear	16170	15180	14500	14320	14180	14780	15140	15860 19660	19770	20320	22000	22490
3 Gross rent, fuel and power [a]	32640	32610	32730	33330	34170	35630	36130	37240 46640	46590	47970	49480	51890
A Fuel and power	10530	9880	9240	9230	9410	10210	10030	10300 9700	8570	8670	8850	10020
B Other	22110	22730	23490	24100	24760	25420	26100	26940 36940	38020	39290	40610	41880
4 Furniture, furnishings and household equipment and operation	18590	16720	15750	15740	15490	15760	16350	17450 18540[b]	19040[b]	19940[b]	21260[b]	21710[b]
A Household operation	3940	3930	3970	3940	4010	4090	4070	4190 4360	4510	4680	4820	4980
B Other	14650	12790	11780	11800	11480	11670	12280	13260 14180	14530	15260	16450	16740
5 Medical care and health expenses	24830	25120	25490	25760	26360	26910	27460	28140 33320	34330	35390	36320	37460
6 Transport and communication	21810	21000	20710	21060	20960	21930	23200	23780 34070[b]	33050[b]	33870[b]	34600[b]	36510[b]
A Personal transport equipment	6760	6380	6250	6830	6680	7250	7870	7970 11750	9920	10160	10560	10610

Netherlands

2.6 Private Final Consumption Expenditure by Type and Purpose, in Constant Prices
(Continued)

Million Netherlands guilders

	1980	1981	1982	1983	1984	1985	1986	1987	1988	1989	1990	1991
					At constant prices of: 1980					1987		
B Other	15050	14620	14460	14230	14280	14680	15330	15810 / 22320	23130	23710	24040	25890
7 Recreational, entertainment, education and cultural services	20050	19510	18860	19080	19440	19550	20130	21180 / 26790b	28100b	29290b	31350b	32600b
A Education	660	650	610	590	570	570	580	580 / 1720	1820	1830	1930	2020
B Other	19390	18860	18250	18490	18870	18980	19550	20600 / 25070	26280	27470	29420	30580
8 Miscellaneous goods and services	27310	27060	26900	26890	27810	28350	29030	29610 / 41880b	41930b	44370b	46330b	47360b
A Personal care	5100	5060	4920	5070	5290	5370	5600	5770 / 6940	7160	7530	8080	8260
B Expenditures in restaurants, cafes and hotels	9660	9450	9440	9350	9740	9760	9770	9810 / 12230	12310	13240	13950	14650
C Other	12550	12550	12540	12470	12780	13220	13660	14030 / 22710	22460	23600	24310	24470
Total Final Consumption Expenditure in the Domestic Market by Households, of which	201010	196970	194560	196220	198510	203230	208520	215330 / 263250b	265530b	275190b	287190b	297060b
A Durable goods	23270	21040	19990	20640	20120	20850	22390	23760 / 28580	27630	28700	30670	30980
B Semi-durable goods ...	33120	31570	30130	30010	30260	31330	32450	34290 / 41920	42820	44700	48050	50720
C Non-durable goods ...	64790	63880	63020	63220	63720	64750	65660	67040 / 72170	72250	74480	76970	79680
D Services	79830	80480	81420	82350	84410	86300	88020	90240 / 120580	122830	127310	131580	135800
Plus: Direct purchases abroad by resident households	9450	8630	8320	8290	8370	8550	8800	9410 / 9630	9790	10180	9590	10140
Less: Direct purchases in the domestic market by non-resident households	4680	4990	4620	4520	4890	4850	4810	4790 / 4940	5130	5750	5680	6630
Equals: Final Consumption Expenditure of Resident Households cb	205780	200610	198260	199990	201990	206930	212510	219950 / 267940	270200	279620	291080	300540

Final Consumption Expenditure of Private Non-profit Institutions Serving Households

	1980	1981	1982	1983	1984	1985	1986	1987	1988	1989	1990	1991
Equals: Final Consumption Expenditure of Private Non-profit Organisations Serving Households	...	...	...	...	...	...	...	... / ...	...	...	...	...
Private Final Consumption Expenditure	205780	200610	198260	199990	201990	206930	212510	219950 / 267940	270200	279620	291080	300540

a) Item 'Gross rent, fuel and power' includes maintenance expenditure.
b) The estimates in constant prices of the fixed base year 1987 have been calculated on the basis of figures in constant prices of the preceding year. Because of this, the sum of the sub-items do not add-up to the main aggregate. However, for the constant price 1980, the differences were eliminated by adding them proportionally to the details.
c) Item 'Final consumption expenditure of resident households' includes consumption expenditure of private non-profit institutions serving households.

2.7 Gross Capital Formation by Type of Good and Owner, in Current Prices

Million Netherlands guilders

	1987				1988				1989			
	TOTAL	Total Private	Public Enterprises	General Government	TOTAL	Total Private	Public Enterprises	General Government	TOTAL	Total Private	Public Enterprises	General Government
Increase in stocks, total a	-420	-420	...	...	310	310	...	...	5430	5430	...	...
Gross Fixed Capital Formation, Total a	91580	80100	...	11480	97390	85180	...	12210	104080	91550	...	12530
1 Residential buildings	23160	23160	...	...	26470	26470	...	...	27020	27020	...	...
2 Non-residential buildings ...	14170	11260	...	2910	15910	12570	...	3340	17560	13870	...	3690
3 Other construction	9750	2790	...	6960	10480	3200	...	7280	10630	3610	...	7020
4 Land improvement and plantation and orchard development			...				...				...	
5 Producers' durable goods	44940	43130	...	1810	44540	42680	...	1860	48860	46650	...	2210
A Transport equipment	10570	10310	...	260	9880	9600	...	280	12440	12110	...	330
Passenger cars	5540	...	...	...	5010	...	...	...	5640	...	...	...
Other	5030	...	...	...	4870	...	...	...	6800	...	...	...
B Machinery and equipment	34370	32820	...	1550	34660	33080	...	1580	36420	34540	...	1880
6 Breeding stock, dairy cattle, etc.	-540	-540	...	...	-130	-130	...	...	80	80	...	...
Statistical discrepancy bc	100	300	...	-200	120	390	...	-270	-70	320	...	-390
Total Gross Capital Formation a	91160	79680	...	11480	97700	85490	...	12210	109510	96980	...	12530

2.7 Gross Capital Formation by Type of Good and Owner, in Current Prices

Million Netherlands guilders

	1990				1991			
	TOTAL	Total Private	Public Enterprises	General Government	TOTAL	Total Private	Public Enterprises	General Government
Increase in stocks, total [a]	4490	4490	...	...	1700	1700	...	...
Gross Fixed Capital Formation, Total [a]	109840	96300	...	13540	113000	99010	...	13990
1 Residential buildings	26750	26750	...	...	25330	25330	...	...
2 Non-residential buildings	20000	16140	...	3860	21400	17300	...	4100
3 Other construction	11240	3870	...	7370	11740	4180	...	7560
4 Land improvement and plantation and orchard development			...				...	
5 Producers' durable goods	52310	49810	...	2500	54580	52080	...	2500
A Transport equipment	13140	12790	...	350	13870	13490	...	380
Passenger cars	6180	...	...	...	6780	...	...	...
Other	6960	...	...	...	7090	...	...	...
B Machinery and equipment	39170	37020	...	2150	40710	38590	...	2120
6 Breeding stock, dairy cattle, etc.	40	40	...	...	30	30	...	...
Statistical discrepancy [bc]	-500	-310	...	-190	-80	90	...	-170
Total Gross Capital Formation [a]	114330	100790	...	13540	114700	100710	...	13990

a) Column 'Public enterprises' is included in column 'Total private'.
b) Item 'Statistical discrepancy' refers to transfers costs on existing fixed capital goods.
c) Item 'Statistical discrepancy' includes net sales of used capital goods.

2.8 Gross Capital Formation by Type of Good and Owner, in Constant Prices

Million Netherlands guilders

	1987				1988				1989			
	TOTAL	Total Private	Public Enterprises	General Government	TOTAL	Total Private	Public Enterprises	General Government	TOTAL	Total Private	Public Enterprises	General Government
	At constant prices of:1987											
Increase in stocks, total [a]	-420	-420	...	...	-190	-190	...	...	4830	4830	...	...
Gross Fixed Capital Formation, Total [ab]	91580	80100	...	11480	95720	83640	...	12080	100440	88300	...	12140
1 Residential buildings	23160	23160	...	...	25770	...	...	...	25940	...	...	...
2 Non-residential buildings	14170	11260	...	2910	15510	...	...	...	16730	...	...	...
3 Other construction	9750	2790	...	6960	10390	...	...	...	10150	...	...	...
4 Land improvement and plantation and orchard development			...				...			...	...	...
5 Producers' durable goods [b]	44940	43130	...	1810	44070	...	...	...	47650	...	...	...
A Transport equipment	10570	10310	...	260	9620	...	...	...	11880	...	...	...
Passenger cars	5540	...	...	...	4820	...	...	...	5380	...	...	...
Other	5030	...	...	...	4800	...	...	...	6510	...	...	...
B Machinery and equipment	34370	32820	...	1550	34450	...	...	...	35740	...	...	...
6 Breeding stock, dairy cattle, etc.	-540	-540	...	...	-100	...	...	...	70	...	...	...
Total Gross Capital Formation [ab]	91160	79680	...	11480	95530	83450	...	12080	105190	93040	...	12140

	1990				1991			
	TOTAL	Total Private	Public Enterprises	General Government	TOTAL	Total Private	Public Enterprises	General Government
	At constant prices of:1987							
Increase in stocks, total [a]	4210	4210	...	...	1350	1350	...	...
Gross Fixed Capital Formation, Total [ab]	104020	91280	...	12730	104080	91360	...	12710
1 Residential buildings	25020	...	...	...	23110	...	...	...
2 Non-residential buildings	18520	...	...	...	19260	...	...	...
3 Other construction	10370	...	...	...	10390	...	...	...
4 Land improvement and plantation and orchard development		...	...	...		...	...	...
5 Producers' durable goods [b]	50540	...	...	...	51460	...	...	...
A Transport equipment	12260	...	...	...	12560	...	...	...
Passenger cars	5740	...	...	...	6120	...	...	...
Other	6530	...	...	...	6450	...	...	...
B Machinery and equipment	38260	...	...	...	38880	...	...	...
6 Breeding stock, dairy cattle, etc.	60	...	...	...	50	...	...	...
Total Gross Capital Formation [ab]	108160	95410	...	12730	105400	92670	...	12710

a) Column 'Public enterprises' is included in column 'Total private'.
b) The estimates in constant prices of the fixed base year 1987 have been calculated on the basis of figures in constant prices of the preceding year. Because of this, the sum of the sub-items do not add-up to the main aggregate. However, for the constant price 1980, the differences were eliminated by adding them proportionally to the details.

Netherlands

2.11 Gross Fixed Capital Formation by Kind of Activity of Owner, ISIC Divisions, in Current Prices

Million Netherlands guilders

	1980	1981	1982	1983	1984	1985	1986	1987	1988	1989	1990	1991
					All Producers							
1 Agriculture, hunting, forestry and fishing	3870	3120	3390	3820	3760	4170	4820	4560 3915	4609	5281	5740	6078
A Agriculture and hunting	3810	2970	3160	3470	...	...	...	... ...	...	...	...	...
B Forestry and logging	...	...	...	...	...	...	...	... ...	...	...	...	...
C Fishing	60	150	120	150	...	...	...	... ...	...	...	...	...
2 Mining and quarrying	1060	1370	1690	1470	1530	2230	1910	1510 1418	1147	1159	24930	26165
A Coal mining	-	-	-	...	...	...	...	... ...	...	...	...	...
B Crude petroleum and natural gas production	1060	1370	1700	...	...	...	...	... ...			...	...
C Metal ore mining	...	...	...	...	...	...	...	...	...	...		
D Other mining	...	...	...	...	...	...	...	...	...	...		
3 Manufacturing	11970	11230	11260	11730	13980	16350	17420	18180 16511	15657	16070	...	...
A Manufacturing of food, beverages and tobacco	3050	2660	2590	...	...	...	...	... 2903	2721	2680		
B Textile, wearing apparel and leather industries	310	240	310	...	...	...	...	... 335	365	403		
C Manufacture of wood, and wood products, including furniture	280	200	200	...	...	...	...	... 272	311	313	...	...
D Manufacture of paper and paper products, printing and publishing	1120	1190	1140	...	...	...	...	... 2196	1821	1676		
E Manufacture of chemicals and chemical petroleum, coal, rubber and plastic products	2750	2900	3140	...	...	...	...	... 4853	5065	5336	...	...
F Manufacture of non-metalic mineral products except products of petroleum and coal	830	640	450	...	...	...	...	... 618	602	669	...	...
G Basic metal industries	430	490	420	...	...	...	...	... 781	730	738		
H Manufacture of fabricated metal products, machinery and equipment	3050	2740	2930	...	...	...	...	... 4299	3739	3972	...	...
I Other manufacturing industries	150	170	160	...	...	...	...	... 254	303	283	...	...
4 Electricity, gas and water	3070	3080	2540	2280	2440	2530	4100	4210 4030	3835	3833		
5 Construction	1150	1040	890	1120	1250	1600	1660	1610 1455	1697	1918	...	...
6 Wholesale and retail trade, restaurants and hotels	4240	3700	3600	3630	4120	4800	5550	5900 8566	9535	9687	10795	11528
A Wholesale and retail trade	...	...	...	...	...	...	...	... 7597	8114	8410	...	...
B Restaurants and hotels	...	...	...	...	...	...	...	... 969	1421	1277	...	...
7 Transport, storage and communication	6020	5540	6530	8110	7590	8380	8730	8140 8497	9303	12091	12775	13187
A Transport and storage	4560	4150	5130	6340	...	...	...	... 5999	6315	8519	...	...
B Communication	1460	1390	1380	1450	...	...	...	... 2498	2988	3572	...	...
8 Finance, insurance, real estate and business services [a]	22470	21520	20890	21070	21990	22080	23290	24160 25071	28451	29153	29030	27697
A Financial institutions	210	230	250	270	300	320	360	390 ...	...	...	...	...

2.11 Gross Fixed Capital Formation by Kind of Activity of Owner, ISIC Divisions, in Current Prices
(Continued)

Million Netherlands guilders

	1980	1981	1982	1983	1984	1985	1986	1987	1988	1989	1990	1991
B Insurance	100	110	120	130	140	150	160	170 / ...	...	...	...	...
C Real estate and business services	22160	21180	20520	20670	21550	21610	22770	23600 / 25071	28451	29153	29030	27697
Real estate except dwellings	...	...	...	...	...	...	...	... / ...	...	...	...	...
Dwellings	22160	21180	20520	20670	21550	21610	22770	23600 / 25071	28451	29153	29030	27697
9 Community, social and personal services a	5970	5880	5750	6040	6460	7170	8130	8590 / 13563	14026	15651	17208	18300
Total Industries b	59820	56480	56540	59270	63120	69310	75610	76860 / 83026	88260	94843	100478	102955
Producers of Government Services	10970	11100	10620	10190	11190	10940	10570	10240 / 10874	11616	12072	12832	13208
Private Non-Profit Institutions Serving Households b	...	...	...	...	...	...	...	... / ...	...	...	...	...
Statistical discrepancy c	...	...	...	...	...	...	...	... / -2318	-2486	-2841	-3467	-3160
Total	70790	67580	67160	69460	74310	80250	86180	87100 / 91580	97390	104080	109840	113000

a) Finance, insurance, real estate (except owner-occupied dwellings) and business services are included in item 'Community, social and personal services'.
b) Item 'Private non-profit institutions serving households' is included with various industries above.
c) Item 'Statistical discrepancy' includes net sales of used capital goods.

2.12 Gross Fixed Capital Formation by Kind of Activity of Owner, ISIC Divisions, in Constant Prices

Million Netherlands guilders

	1980	1981	1982	1983	1984	1985	1986	1987	1988	1989	1990	1991
	At constant prices of: 1980							1987				
	All Producers											
1 Agriculture, hunting, forestry and fishing	3870	2930	3060	3390	3240	3560	4070	3840 / 3920	4560	5060	5410	5570
2 Mining and quarrying								21950a / 1420	1140	1130	23730	24290
3 Manufacturing								... / 16510	15470	15560	...	...
A Manufacturing of food, beverages and tobacco								... / 2900	2680	2590	...	...
B Textile, wearing apparel and leather industries								... / 340	360	390	...	...
C Manufacture of wood, and wood products, including furniture								... / 270	310	300	...	...
D Manufacture of paper and paper products, printing and publishing	17250	15510	14430	14350	16330	19070	21260	... / 2200	1800	1620	...	...
E Manufacture of chemicals and chemical petroleum, coal, rubber and plastic products								... / 4850	5010	5150	...	...
F Manufacture of non-metalic mineral products except products of petroleum and coal								... / 620	590	650	...	...
G Basic metal industries								... / 780	720	720	...	...
H Manufacture of fabricated metal products, machinery and equipment								... / 4300	3700	3860	...	...
I Other manufacturing industries								... / 250	300	280	...	...
4 Electricity, gas and water								... / 4030	3780	3650	...	...

2.12 Gross Fixed Capital Formation by Kind of Activity of Owner, ISIC Divisions, in Constant Prices
(Continued)

Million Netherlands guilders

	1980	1981	1982	1983	1984	1985	1986	1987	1988	1989	1990	1991
	At constant prices of: 1980									1987		
5 Construction	...	...	...	...	...	...	...	... / 1450	1670	1840	...	...
6 Wholesale and retail trade, restaurants and hotels	4240	3510	3260	3210	3580	4110	4660	4920 / 8560	9380	9360	10230	10640
A Wholesale and retail trade	...	...	...	...	...	...	...	... / 7590	7990	8140	...	...
B Restaurants and hotels	...	...	...	...	...	...	...	... / 970	1390	1220	...	...
7 Transport, storage and communication	6020	5150	5770	6920	6410	6960	7330	6930 / 8500	9170	11630	12110	12150
A Transport and storage	...	...	...	...	...	...	...	... / 6000	6220	8130	...	...
B Communication	...	...	...	...	...	...	...	... / 2500	2950	3500	...	...
8 Finance, insurance, real estate and business services [b]								29300c / 25070	27730	27990	27140	25190
A Financial institutions								... / ...	...	...	...	...
B Insurance								... / ...	...	...	...	...
C Real estate and business services	28440	25860	24600	24960	25920	26600	28430	... / 25070	27730	27990	27140	25190
Real estate except dwellings								... / ...	...	...	...	...
Dwellings								... / 25070	27730	27990	27140	25190
9 Community, social and personal services [b]								... / 13570	13820	15330	16620	17220
Total Industries [d]	59820	52960	51120	52830	55480	60300	65750	66940 / 83030	86720	91530	95210	94980
Producers of Government Services	10970	10460	9720	9270	9970	9590	9280	8900 / 10870	11490	11690	12080	12010
Private Non-Profit Institutions Serving Households [d]	...	...	...	...	...	...	...	... / ...	...	...	...	...
Statistical discrepancy	...	...	...	...	...	...	...	... / -2320e	-2490e	-2790e	-3290e	-2920e
Total	70790	63420	60840	62100	65450	69890	75030	75840 / 91580	95720	100440	104020	104080

a) Including item '2/Mining and quarrying' through '4/Electricity, gas and water'.
b) Finance, insurance, real estate (except owner-occupied dwellings) and business services are included in item 'Community, social and personal services'.
c) Including item '8/Finance, insurance, real estate and business services' through '9/Community, social and personal services'.
d) Item 'Private non-profit institutions serving households' is included with various industries above.
e) Item 'Statistical discrepancy' includes net sales of used capital goods.

2.17 Exports and Imports of Goods and Services, Detail

Million Netherlands guilders

	1980	1981	1982	1983	1984	1985	1986	1987	1988	1989	1990	1991
	**Exports of Goods and Services**											
1 Exports of merchandise, f.o.b.	147080	171330	177620	185010	210630	225950	195850	188780 / 181560	199180	222080	230330	239770
2 Transport and communication	13760	15350	15180	15560	16930	17890	16640	16480 / 17000	18520	20070	20910	22540
A In respect of merchandise imports	380	430	430	400	500	550	430	420 / 620	680	760	740	610
B Other	13380	14920	14750	15160	16430	17340	16210	16060 / 16380	17840	19310	20170	21930
3 Insurance service charges	830	1100	920	1030	860	910	950	1090 / 1100	1080	1140	1950	1420

2.17 Exports and Imports of Goods and Services, Detail
(Continued)

Million Netherlands guilders

	1980	1981	1982	1983	1984	1985	1986	1987	1988	1989	1990	1991
4 Other commodities	10460	11510	13660	12930	14090	14660	12980	14190 / 14590	16240	17850	21580	22570
5 Adjustments of merchandise exports to change-of-ownership basis [a]	...	...	...	...	...	...	...	... / 70	70	560	210	390
6 Direct purchases in the domestic market by non-residential households	4680	5330	5220	5240	6050	6130	6100	6110 / 4940	5160	5970	6010	7190
7 Direct purchases in the domestic market by extraterritorial bodies												
Total Exports of Goods and Services	176810	204620	212600	219770	248560	265540	232520	226650 / 219260	240250	267670	280990	293880

Imports of Goods and Services

	1980	1981	1982	1983	1984	1985	1986	1987	1988	1989	1990	1991
1 Imports of merchandise, c.i.f.	156120	168420	171710	179580	200240	216610	185240	185300 / 177820	190820	214500	220320	226710
A Imports of merchandise, f.o.b.	147200	158330	161810	170390	188700	203770	175200	175610 / 168580	180390	203370	209630	215450
B Transport of services on merchandise imports	8480	9620	9460	8770	11030	12320	9620	9280 / 8830	9980	10640	10230	10820
By residents	380	430	430	400	500	550	430	420 / 620	680	760	740	610
By non-residents	8100	9190	9030	8370	10530	11770	9190	8860 / 8210	9300	9880	9490	10210
C Insurance service charges on merchandise imports	440	470	440	420	510	520	420	410 / 410	450	490	460	440
By residents	...	...	...	...	...	...	...	... / ...	...	...	...	...
By non-residents	440	470	440	420	510	520	420	410 / 410	450	490	460	440
2 Adjustments of merchandise imports to change-of-ownership basis [a]	...	...	...	...	...	...	...	... / ...	...	...	...	...
3 Other transport and communication	960	1040	1140	1120	1200	1260	1060	1030 / 1030	1140	1300	1380	1440
4 Other insurance service charges	930	1000	1040	1050	1090	1160	1240	1280 / 1220	1270	1330	1410	1460
5 Other commodities	11160	12370	13310	13590	15020	15530	14190	13630 / 17860	19250	20990	23040	25020
6 Direct purchases abroad by government												
7 Direct purchases abroad by resident households	9450	9410	9630	9870	10200	10940	11280	12070 / 9630	9900	10640	10350	11370
Total Imports of Goods and Services	178620	192240	196830	205210	227750	245500	213010	213310 / 207560	222380	248760	256500	266000
Balance of Goods and Services	-1810	12380	15770	14560	20810	20040	19510	13340 / 11700	17870	18910	24490	27880
Total Imports and Balance of Goods and Services	176810	204620	212600	219770	248560	265540	232520	226650 / 219260	240250	267670	280990	293880

a) The figures on adjustments of merchandise exports to change-of-ownership basis are net of imports to change-of-ownership basis.

3.11 General Government Production Account: Total and Subsectors

Million Netherlands guilders

	1987					1988				
	Total General Government	Central Government	State or Provincial Government	Local Government	Social Security Funds	Total General Government	Central Government	State or Provincial Government	Local Government	Social Security Funds
Gross Output										
1 Sales	11440	3090	...	8010	340	11850	3420	...	8090	340
2 Services produced for own use	69780	31940	...	34510	3330	70200	32350	...	34360	3490
3 Own account fixed capital formation	620	-	...	620	-	620	-	...	620	-
Gross Output [a]	81840	35030	...	43140	3670	82670	35770	...	43070	3830
Gross Input										
Intermediate Consumption	29070	14430	...	13350	1290	30050	15010	...	13780	1260
Subtotal: Value Added	52770	20600	...	29790	2380	52620	20760	...	29290	2570

Netherlands

3.11 General Government Production Account: Total and Subsectors
(Continued)

Million Netherlands guilders

	1987					1988				
	Total General Government	Central Government	State or Provincial Government	Local Government	Social Security Funds	Total General Government	Central Government	State or Provincial Government	Local Government	Social Security Funds
1 Indirect taxes, net	470	120	...	350	-	460	130	...	330	-
A Indirect taxes	470	120	...	350	-	460	130	...	330	-
B Less: Subsidies	...	...	...	...	...	...	...	...	...	...
2 Consumption of fixed capital	3400	1000	...	2320	80	3550	1050	...	2410	90
3 Compensation of employees	48900	19480	...	27120	2300	48610	19580	...	26550	2480
A To residents	48900	19480	...	27120	2300	48610	19580	...	26550	2480
B To the rest of the world	-	-	...	-	-	-	-	...	-	-
4 Net Operating surplus	...	...	...	...	...	...	...	...	...	...
Gross Input a	81840	35030	...	43140	3670	82670	35770	...	43070	3830

	1989					1990				
	Total General Government	Central Government	State or Provincial Government	Local Government	Social Security Funds	Total General Government	Central Government	State or Provincial Government	Local Government	Social Security Funds
Gross Output										
1 Sales	12260	3470	...	8300	490	12610	3640	...	8560	410
2 Services produced for own use	71760	33240	...	34980	3540	74680	34480	...	36320	3880
3 Own account fixed capital formation	660	-	...	660	-	700	-	...	700	-
Gross Output a	84680	36710	...	43940	4030	87990	38120	...	45580	4290
Gross Input										
Intermediate Consumption	31660	15730	...	14580	1350	32890	16490	...	14990	1410
Subtotal: Value Added	53020	20980	...	29360	2680	55100	21630	...	30590	2880
1 Indirect taxes, net	480	140	...	340	-	510	140	...	370	-
A Indirect taxes	480	140	...	340	-	510	140	...	370	-
B Less: Subsidies	...	...	...	...	...	...	...	...	...	...
2 Consumption of fixed capital	3740	1120	...	2520	100	3910	1190	...	2620	100
3 Compensation of employees	48800	19720	...	26500	2580	50680	20300	...	27600	2780
A To residents	48800	19720	...	26500	2580	50680	20300	...	27600	2780
B To the rest of the world	-	-	...	-	-	...	...	...	...	...
4 Net Operating surplus	...	...	...	...	...	...	...	...	...	...
Gross Input a	84680	36710	...	43940	4030	87990	38120	...	45580	4290

	1991				
	Total General Government	Central Government	State or Provincial Government	Local Government	Social Security Funds
Gross Output					
1 Sales	13230	3930	...	8850	450
2 Services produced for own use	77910	35860	...	37770	4280
3 Own account fixed capital formation	720	-	...	720	-
Gross Output a	91860	39790	...	47340	4730
Gross Input					
Intermediate Consumption	34760	17620	...	15430	1710
Subtotal: Value Added	57100	22170	...	31910	3020
1 Indirect taxes, net	540	140	...	400	-
A Indirect taxes	540	140	...	400	-
B Less: Subsidies	...	...	...	...	...
2 Consumption of fixed capital	4080	1250	...	2720	110
3 Compensation of employees	52480	20780	...	28790	2910
A To residents	52480	20780	...	28790	2910
B To the rest of the world	...	...	...	...	...
4 Net Operating surplus	...	...	...	...	...
Gross Input a	91860	39790	...	47340	4730

a) Local Government includes provincial government and other regional government entities.

3.12 General Government Income and Outlay Account: Total and Subsectors

Million Netherlands guilders

	1987 Total General Government	1987 Central Government	1987 State or Provincial Government	1987 Local Government	1987 Social Security Funds	1988 Total General Government	1988 Central Government	1988 State or Provincial Government	1988 Local Government	1988 Social Security Funds
Receipts										
1 Operating surplus	...	...	...	...	...	...	...	...	...	...
2 Property and entrepreneurial income	20460	14930	...	9520	790	17800	11620	...	9450	850
A Withdrawals from public quasi-corporations	3860	1200	...	2660	...	3480	1210	...	2270	...
B Interest	6370	4850	...	5510	790	6550	4190	...	5630	850
C Dividends	3990	3760	...	230	...	2940	2670	...	270	...
D Net land rent and royalties	6240	5120	...	1120		4830	3550	...	1280	
3 Taxes, fees and contributions	211760	115250	...	6200	90310	221060	120620	...	6490	93950
A Indirect taxes a	58620	55100	...	3520	-	60560	56900	...	3660	-
B Direct taxes	62320	59760	...	2560	-	65980	63280	...	2700	-
Income	57280	57280	...	-	-	60690	60690	...	-	-
Other	5040	2480	...	2560	-	5290	2590	...	2700	-
C Social security contributions	90310	-	...	-	90310	93950	-	...	-	93950
D Fees, fines and penalties	510	390	...	120	-	570	440	...	130	-
4 Other current transfers	12930	11280	...	60180	1990	13140	11430	...	59130	3550
A Casualty insurance claims	100	30	...	70	-	100	30	...	70	-
B Transfers from other government subsectors	...	980	...	57610	1930	...	960	...	56510	3500
C Transfers from the rest of the world a	6820	6820	...	-	-	6870	6870	...	-	-
D Other transfers, except imputed	220	120	...	70	30	180	80	...	80	20
E Imputed unfunded employee pension and welfare contributions	5790	3330	...	2430	30	5990	3490	...	2470	30
Total Current Receipts b	245150	141460	...	75900	93090	252000	143670	...	75070	98350
Disbursements										
1 Government final consumption expenditure	69780	31940	...	34510	3330	70200	32350	...	34360	3490
2 Property income c	28170	21660	...	11220	70	29010	22460	...	10600	70
A Interest	28140	21630	...	11220	70	28980	22430	...	10600	70
B Net land rent and royalties	30	30	...	...	...	30	30	...	...	...
3 Subsidies d	19190	14450	...	4740	...	18850	14260	...	4590	...
4 Other current transfers	135510	83370	...	24600	88060	139190	85200	...	24250	90710
A Casualty insurance premiums, net	100	30	...	70	-	100	30	...	70	-
B Transfers to other government subsectors	...	59510	...	-	1010	...	59980	...	-	990
C Social security benefits	86990	-	...	-	86990	89650	-	...	-	89650
D Social assistance grants	20510	4600	...	15910	-	20490	5120	...	15370	-
E Unfunded employee pension and welfare benefits	5790	3330	...	2430	30	5990	3490	...	2470	30
F Transfers to private non-profit institutions serving households	1280	120	...	1160	-	1390	120	...	1270	-
G Other transfers n.e.c.	12850	7790	...	5030	30	13070	7960	...	5070	40
H Transfers to the rest of the world d	7990	7990	...	-	-	8500	8500	...	-	-
Net saving	-7500	-9960	...	830	1630	-5250	-10600	...	1270	4080
Total Current Disbursements and Net Saving b	245150	141460	...	75900	93090	252000	143670	...	75070	98350

	1989 Total General Government	1989 Central Government	1989 State or Provincial Government	1989 Local Government	1989 Social Security Funds	1990 Total General Government	1990 Central Government	1990 State or Provincial Government	1990 Local Government	1990 Social Security Funds
Receipts										
1 Operating surplus	...	...	...	...	...	...	...	...	...	...
2 Property and entrepreneurial income	18890	11960	...	9840	1160	21180	13610	...	10150	1390
A Withdrawals from public quasi-corporations	2310	170	...	2140	...	2100	150	...	1950	...
B Interest	7640	4650	...	5900	1160	8260	4540	...	6300	1390

Netherlands

3.12 General Government Income and Outlay Account: Total and Subsectors
(Continued)

Million Netherlands guilders

	1989					1990				
	Total General Government	Central Government	State or Provincial Government	Local Government	Social Security Funds	Total General Government	Central Government	State or Provincial Government	Local Government	Social Security Funds
C Dividends	4270	3930	...	340	...	5100	4700	...	400	...
D Net land rent and royalties	4670	3210	...	1460	...	5720	4220	...	1500	...
3 Taxes, fees and contributions	219850	121690	...	6830	91330	233440	138510	...	7020	87910
A Indirect taxes [a]	60370	56560	...	3810	-	64850	60960	...	3890	-
B Direct taxes	67510	64630	...	2880	-	80040	77050	...	2990	-
Income	61920	61920	...	-	-	74170	74170	...	-	-
Other	5590	2710	...	2880	-	5870	2880	...	2990	-
C Social security contributions	91330	-	...	-	91330	87910	-	...	-	87910
D Fees, fines and penalties	640	500	...	140	-	640	500	...	140	-
4 Other current transfers	13760	11870	...	59130	2970	13100	10880	...	60320	16740
A Casualty insurance claims	100	10	...	90	-	90	10	...	80	-
B Transfers from other government subsectors	...	970	...	56330	2910	...	990	...	57180	16670
C Transfers from the rest of the world [a]	7070	7070	...	-	-	5860	5860	...	-	-
D Other transfers, except imputed	180	80	...	70	30	190	100	...	60	30
E Imputed unfunded employee pension and welfare contributions	6410	3740	...	2640	30	6960	3920	...	3000	40
Total Current Receipts [b]	252500	145520	...	75800	95460	267720	163000	...	77490	106040

Disbursements

	Total General Government	Central Government	State or Provincial Government	Local Government	Social Security Funds	Total General Government	Central Government	State or Provincial Government	Local Government	Social Security Funds
1 Government final consumption expenditure	71760	33240	...	34980	3540	74680	34480	...	36320	3880
2 Property income [c]	29060	22450	...	10610	70	30840	23870	...	10890	50
A Interest	29040	22430	...	10610	70	30810	23840	...	10890	50
B Net land rent and royalties	20	20	...	...	...	30	30	...	...	...
3 Subsidies [d]	16740	11770	...	4970	...	15860	10820	...	5040	...
4 Other current transfers	143630	90620	...	23570	89650	157390	105820	...	24000	102410
A Casualty insurance premiums, net	100	10	...	90	-	90	10	...	80	-
B Transfers to other government subsectors	...	59190	...	-	1020	...	73790	...	-	1050
C Social security benefits	88560	-	...	-	88560	101280	-	...	-	101280
D Social assistance grants	24710	10210	...	14500	-	24950	10450	...	14500	-
E Unfunded employee pension and welfare benefits	6410	3740	...	2640	30	6960	3920	...	3000	40
F Transfers to private non-profit institutions serving households	1380	130	...	1250	-	1320	120	...	1200	-
G Other transfers n.e.c.	13220	8090	...	5090	40	13790	8530	...	5220	40
H Transfers to the rest of the world [d]	9250	9250	...	-	-	9000	9000	...	-	-
Net saving	-8690	-12560	...	1670	2200	-11050	-11990	...	1240	-300
Total Current Disbursements and Net Saving [b]	252500	145520	...	75800	95460	267720	163000	...	77490	106040

	1991				
	Total General Government	Central Government	State or Provincial Government	Local Government	Social Security Funds

Receipts

	Total General Government	Central Government	State or Provincial Government	Local Government	Social Security Funds
1 Operating surplus	...	...	...	...	...
2 Property and entrepreneurial income	24020	16280	...	10440	1310
A Withdrawals from public quasi-corporations	2040	190	...	1850	...
B Interest	8540	4670	...	6570	1310
C Dividends	5850	5360	...	490	...
D Net land rent and royalties	7590	6060	...	1530	...
3 Taxes, fees and contributions	258380	154030	...	7570	96780
A Indirect taxes [a]	69270	65120	...	4150	-
B Direct taxes	91660	88390	...	3270	-
Income	85350	85350	...	-	-

3.12 General Government Income and Outlay Account: Total and Subsectors
(Continued)

Million Netherlands guilders

	1991				
	Total General Government	Central Government	State or Provincial Government	Local Government	Social Security Funds
Other	6310	3040	...	3270	-
C Social security contributions	96780	-	...	-	96780
D Fees, fines and penalties	670	520	...	150	-
4 Other current transfers	13270	11050	...	63130	17300
A Casualty insurance claims	90	10	...	80	-
B Transfers from other government subsectors	...	990	...	59990	17230
C Transfers from the rest of the world a	6030	6030	...	-	
D Other transfers, except imputed	150	70	...	50	30
E Imputed unfunded employee pension and welfare contributions	7000	3950	...	3010	40
Total Current Receipts b	295670	181360	...	81140	115390

Disbursements

	Total General Government	Central Government	State or Provincial Government	Local Government	Social Security Funds
1 Government final consumption expenditure	77910	35860	...	37770	4280
2 Property income c	33530	26160	...	11320	60
A Interest	33500	26130	...	11320	60
B Net land rent and royalties	30	30	...	...	...
3 Subsidies d	17590	12180	...	5410	...
4 Other current transfers	168090	112160	...	24240	109900
A Casualty insurance premiums, net	90	10	...	80	-
B Transfers to other government subsectors	...	77150	...	-	1060
C Social security benefits	108760	-	...	-	108760
D Social assistance grants	25650	11020	...	14630	-
E Unfunded employee pension and welfare benefits	7000	3950	...	3010	40
F Transfers to private non-profit institutions serving households	1330	130	...	1200	-
G Other transfers n.e.c.	14230	8870	...	5320	40
H Transfers to the rest of the world d	11030	11030	...	-	-
Net saving	-1450	-5000	...	2400	1150
Total Current Disbursements and Net Saving b	295670	181360	...	81140	115390

a) The import duties of non-resident enterprises paid by the Netherlands to the European Community are not included in these figures (1987:190; 1988:220; 1989:300; 1990:430; 1991:570 million N. Guilders).
b) Local Government includes provincial government and other regional government entities.
c) Item 'Property income' includes payments and receipts of property income from other subsectors of general government.
d) The subsidies from the European Community paid to the Netherlands but destined for non-resident enterprises are not included in these figures (1987:370; 1988:2780; 1989:2560; 1990:1310; 1991:610 million N. guilders).

3.13 General Government Capital Accumulation Account: Total and Subsectors

Million Netherlands guilders

	1987					1988				
	Total General Government	Central Government	State or Provincial Government	Local Government	Social Security Funds	Total General Government	Central Government	State or Provincial Government	Local Government	Social Security Funds
	Finance of Gross Accumulation									
1 Gross saving	-4100	-8960	...	3150	1710	-1700	-9550	...	3680	4170
A Consumption of fixed capital	3400	1000	...	2320	80	3550	1050	...	2410	90
B Net saving	-7500	-9960	...	830	1630	-5250	-10600	...	1270	4080
2 Capital transfers	1430	1390	...	4820	170	1350	1240	...	5960	180
A From other government subsectors	...	30	...	4750	170	...	10	...	5840	180
B From other resident sectors	1320	1250	...	70	-	1260	1140	...	120	-
C From rest of the world	110	110	...	-	-	90	90	...	-	-
Finance of Gross Accumulation a	-2670	-7570	...	7970	1880	-350	-8310	...	9640	4350
	Gross Accumulation									
1 Gross capital formation	11480	2980	...	8360	140	12210	2700	...	9390	120
A Increase in stocks	-	-	...	-	-	-	-	...	-	-
B Gross fixed capital formation	11480	2980	...	8360	140	12210	2700	...	9390	120
Own account	620	-	...	620	...	620	-	...	620	...
Other	10860	2980	...	7740	140	11590	2700	...	8770	120

Netherlands

Million Netherlands guilders

	1987 Total General Government	Central Government	State or Provincial Government	Local Government	Social Security Funds	1988 Total General Government	Central Government	State or Provincial Government	Local Government	Social Security Funds
2 Purchases of land, net	-2370	70	...	-2440	...	-2780	40	...	-2820	...
3 Purchases of intangible assets, net	...	...	...	...	...	...	...	...	...	...
4 Capital transfers	14320	17770	...	1380	120	11250	14910	...	2240	130
A To other government subsectors	...	4920	...	30	-	...	6020	...	10	-
B To other resident sectors	13650	12180	...	1350	120	10520	8160	...	2230	130
C To rest of the world	670	670	...	-	-	730	730	...	-	-
Net lending [b]	-26100	-28390	...	670	1620	-21030	-25960	...	830	4100
Gross Accumulation [a]	-2670	-7570	...	7970	1880	-350	-8310	...	9640	4350

	1989 Total General Government	Central Government	State or Provincial Government	Local Government	Social Security Funds	1990 Total General Government	Central Government	State or Provincial Government	Local Government	Social Security Funds
Finance of Gross Accumulation										
1 Gross saving	-4950	-11440	...	4190	2300	-7140	-10800	...	3860	-200
A Consumption of fixed capital	3740	1120	...	2520	100	3910	1190	...	2620	100
B Net saving	-8690	-12560	...	1670	2200	-11050	-11990	...	1240	-300
2 Capital transfers	1580	1390	...	5920	250	1570	1450	...	6090	170
A From other government subsectors	...	-	...	5810	170	...	-	...	5970	170
B From other resident sectors	1460	1270	...	110	80	1440	1320	...	120	-
C From rest of the world	120	120	...	-	-	130	130	...	-	-
Finance of Gross Accumulation [a]	-3370	-10050	...	10110	2550	-5570	-9350	...	9950	-30
Gross Accumulation										
1 Gross capital formation	12530	2940	...	9300	290	13540	3120	...	10100	320
A Increase in stocks	-	-	...	-	-	-	-	...	-	-
B Gross fixed capital formation	12530	2940	...	9300	290	13540	3120	...	10100	320
Own account	660	-	...	660	...	700	-	...	700	...
Other	11870	2940	...	8640	290	12840	3120	...	9400	320
2 Purchases of land, net	-2860	50	...	-2910	...	-3030	-130	...	-2900	...
3 Purchases of intangible assets, net	...	...	...	...	...	...	...	...	...	...
4 Capital transfers	9960	13280	...	2550	110	9260	12550	...	2490	360
A To other government subsectors	...	5980	...	-	-	...	6140	...	-	-
B To other resident sectors	9160	6500	...	2550	110	8460	5610	...	2490	360
C To rest of the world	800	800	...	-	-	800	800	...	-	-
Net lending [b]	-23000	-26320	...	1170	2150	-25340	-24890	...	260	-710
Gross Accumulation [a]	-3370	-10050	...	10110	2550	-5570	-9350	...	9950	-30

	1991 Total General Government	Central Government	State or Provincial Government	Local Government	Social Security Funds
Finance of Gross Accumulation					
1 Gross saving	2630	-3750	...	5120	1260
A Consumption of fixed capital	4080	1250	...	2720	110
B Net saving	-1450	-5000	...	2400	1150
2 Capital transfers	1960	1840	...	6310	170
A From other government subsectors	...	-	...	6190	170
B From other resident sectors	1820	1700	...	120	-
C From rest of the world	140	140	...	-	-
Finance of Gross Accumulation [a]	4590	-1910	...	11430	1430
Gross Accumulation					
1 Gross capital formation	13990	3300	...	10520	170
A Increase in stocks	-	-	...	-	-
B Gross fixed capital formation	13990	3300	...	10520	170
Own account	720	-	...	720	...
Other	13270	3300	...	9800	170

3.13 General Government Capital Accumulation Account: Total and Subsectors
(Continued)

Million Netherlands guilders

		1991			
	Total General Government	Central Government	State or Provincial Government	Local Government	Social Security Funds
2 Purchases of land, net	-3130	-140	...	-2990	...
3 Purchases of intangible assets, net	...	...	...	...	...
4 Capital transfers	7380	11070	...	2500	170
A To other government subsectors	...	6360	...	-	-
B To other resident sectors	6430	3760	...	2500	170
C To rest of the world	950	950	...	-	-
Net lending b	-13650	-16140	...	1400	1090
Gross Accumulation a	4590	-1910	...	11430	1430

a) Local Government includes provincial government and other regional government entities.
b) Net lending of the capital accumulation account and the capital finance account have not been reconciled and are different due to different statistical sources.

3.14 General Government Capital Finance Account, Total and Subsectors

Million Netherlands guilders

	1987					1988				
	Total General Government	Central Government	State or Provincial Government	Local Government	Social Security Funds	Total General Government	Central Government	State or Provincial Government	Local Government	Social Security Funds
Acquisition of Financial Assets										
1 Gold and SDRs	...	...	...	...	...	...	...	...	...	...
2 Currency and transferable deposits	-1530	-2450	...	400	520	-130	280	...	-270	-140
3 Other deposits	-1880	60	...	-460	-1480	4450	-10	...	1070	3390
4 Bills and bonds, short term	-250	...	...	...	-250	380	...	...	...	380
A Corporate and quasi-corporate enterprises, resident	...	...	...	...	...	480	...	...	...	480
B Other government subsectors	-250	...	...	...	-250	-100	...	...	...	-100
C Rest of the world	...	...	...	...	...	...	...	...	...	...
5 Bonds, long term	220	...	...	...	220	120	10	...	...	110
A Corporations	270	...	...	...	270	100	10	...	...	90
B Other government subsectors	-40	...	...	...	-40	40	20	...	...	20
C Rest of the world	-10	...	...	...	-10	-20	-20	...	...	...
6 Corporate equity securities	1160	960	...	210	-10	600	960	...	-370	10
7 Short-term loans, n.e.c.	30	-490	...	190	330	-1250	80	...	-1000	-330
8 Long-term loans, n.e.c.	-11120	-7890	...	-3990	760	5280	1000	...	3340	940
A Mortgages	-30	...	...	...	-30	10	...	...	...	10
B Other	-11090	-7890	...	-3990	790	5270	1000	...	3340	930
9 Other receivables a	-480	-2820	...	1300	1040	-3240	-3240	...	420	-420
10 Other assets	...	...	...	...	...	...	...	...	...	...
Total Acquisition of Financial Assets b	-13850	-12630	...	-2350	1130	6210	-920	...	3190	3940
Incurrence of Liabilities										
1 Currency and transferable deposits	60	60	...	...	...	400	400	...	...	...
2 Other deposits	...	...	...	...	...	...	...	...	...	...
3 Bills and bonds, short term	-1640	-2170	...	530	...	-1000	-900	...	-100	...
4 Bonds, long term	12780	12800	...	-20	...	17850	17720	...	130	...
5 Short-term loans, n.e.c.	-1300	700	...	-1380	-620	-900	140	...	-990	-50
6 Long-term loans, n.e.c.	2280	4270	...	-1970	-20	11100	7930	...	3230	-60
7 Other payables a	...	...	...	...	...	...	...	...	...	...
8 Other liabilities	...	...	...	...	...	...	...	...	...	...
Total Incurrence of Liabilities	12180	15660	...	-2840	-640	27450	25290	...	2270	-110
Statistical discrepancy	70	100	...	-180	150	-210	-250	...	90	-50
Net Lending c	-26100	-28390	...	670	1620	-21030	-25960	...	830	4100
Incurrence of Liabilities and Net Worth b	-13850	-12630	...	-2350	1130	6210	-920	...	3190	3940

Netherlands

3.14 General Government Capital Finance Account, Total and Subsectors

Million Netherlands guilders

	1989					1990				
	Total General Government	Central Government	State or Provincial Government	Local Government	Social Security Funds	Total General Government	Central Government	State or Provincial Government	Local Government	Social Security Funds
Acquisition of Financial Assets										
1 Gold and SDRs	...	...	...		...	...	...		...	...
2 Currency and transferable deposits	-3600	-3410	...	-340	150	1620	1230	...	40	350
3 Other deposits	2670	...	...	1180	1490	-2940	...	...	100	-3040
4 Bills and bonds, short term	-40	...	...	...	-40	...	...	...	...	...
A Corporate and quasi-corporate enterprises, resident	-40	...	...	...	-40	...	...	...	...	...
B Other government subsectors	...	...	...	...	...	...	...	...	...	...
C Rest of the world	...	...	...	...	...	...	...	...	...	...
5 Bonds, long term	420	20	...	...	400	680	30	...	...	650
A Corporations	-90	10	...	...	-100	100	...	...	...	100
B Other government subsectors	510	10	...	...	500	580	30	...	...	550
C Rest of the world	...	...	...	...	...	...	...	...	...	...
6 Corporate equity securities	-26580	-26780	...	190	10	-620	-800	...	180	...
7 Short-term loans, n.e.c.	-1370	-800	...	-330	-240	-80	-130	...	130	-80
8 Long-term loans, n.e.c.	9230	7440	...	1800	-10	820	600	...	280	-60
A Mortgages	20	...	...	10	10	...	...	...	...	...
B Other	9210	7440	...	1790	-20	820	600	...	280	-60
9 Other receivables a	680	-230	...	770	140	-1440	-2420	...	370	610
10 Other assets	...	...	...	...	...	...	...	...	...	...
Total Acquisition of Financial Assets b	-18590	-23760	...	3270	1900	-1960	-1490	...	1100	-1570
Incurrence of Liabilities										
1 Currency and transferable deposits	360	360	...	...	...	200	200	...	...	...
2 Other deposits	...	...	...	...	...	...	...	...	...	...
3 Bills and bonds, short term	-3720	-3470	...	-250	...	-1520	-1700	...	180	...
4 Bonds, long term	20630	20490	...	140	...	21600	21610	...	-10	...
5 Short-term loans, n.e.c.	1100	680	...	550	-130	-10	40	...	550	-600
6 Long-term loans, n.e.c.	-14000	-15290	...	1300	-10	3190	3050	...	150	-10
7 Other payables a	...	...	...	...	...	...	...	...	...	...
8 Other liabilities	...	...	...	...	...	...	...	...	...	...
Total Incurrence of Liabilities	4370	2770	...	1740	-140	23460	23200	...	870	-610
Statistical discrepancy	40	-210	...	360	-110	-80	200	...	-30	-250
Net Lending c	-23000	-26320	...	1170	2150	-25340	-24890	...	260	-710
Incurrence of Liabilities and Net Worth b	-18590	-23760	...	3270	1900	-1960	-1490	...	1100	-1570

a) Item 'Other receivables' is registered net, it includes trade credit and advances and all other amounts receivable and payable.
b) Local Government includes provincial government and other regional government entities.
c) Net lending of the capital accumulation account and the capital finance account have not been reconciled and are different due to different statistical sources.

3.21 Corporate and Quasi-Corporate Enterprise Production Account: Total and Sectors

Million Netherlands guilders

	1987			ADDENDUM: Total,	1988			ADDENDUM: Total,	1989			ADDENDUM: Total,
	Corporate and Quasi-Corporate Enterprises			including Unincorporated	Corporate and Quasi-Corporate Enterprises			including Unincorporated	Corporate and Quasi-Corporate Enterprises			including Unincorporated
	TOTAL	Non-Financial	Financial		TOTAL	Non-Financial	Financial		TOTAL	Non-Financial	Financial	
Gross Output												
1 Output for sale	...	...	...	744330	...	...	...	780380	...	...	...	840090
2 Imputed bank service charge	16540	...	16540	16540	17450	...	17450	17450	18030	...	18030	18030
3 Own-account fixed capital formation	...	...	...	2200	...	...	...	2040	...	...	...	2060
Gross Output a	...	...	...	763070	...	...	...	799870	...	...	...	860180
Gross Input												
Intermediate consumption	...	...	...	375260	...	...	...	395080	...	...	...	428530
1 Imputed banking service charge	16540	...	16540	16540	17450	...	17450	17450	18030	...	18030	18030
2 Other intermediate consumption	...	...	...	358720	...	...	...	377630	...	...	...	410500
Subtotal: Value Added	...	...	...	387810	...	...	...	404790	...	...	...	431650
1 Indirect taxes, net	...	...	...	38960	...	...	...	41250	...	...	...	43150
A Indirect taxes	...	...	...	58150	...	...	...	60100	...	...	...	59890

3.21 Corporate and Quasi-Corporate Enterprise Production Account: Total and Sectors
(Continued)

Million Netherlands guilders

	1987			ADDENDUM: Total, including Unincorporated	1988			ADDENDUM: Total, including Unincorporated	1989			ADDENDUM: Total, including Unincorporated
	Corporate and Quasi-Corporate Enterprises				Corporate and Quasi-Corporate Enterprises				Corporate and Quasi-Corporate Enterprises			
	TOTAL	Non-Financial	Financial		TOTAL	Non-Financial	Financial		TOTAL	Non-Financial	Financial	
B Less: Subsidies	...	...	...	19190	...	...	...	18850				16740
2 Consumption of fixed capital	34210	33240	970	45140	36050	35060	990	47640	39120	38080	1040	51140
3 Compensation of employees	171160	159770	11390	190460	176880	165050	11830	197130	183200	171110	12090	204050
A To residents	...	...	...	189390	...	...	...	195930	...	...	...	202790
B To the rest of the world	...	...	...	1070	...	...	...	1200	...	...	...	1260
4 Net operating surplus	63110	71750	-8640	113250	66000	75370	-9370	118770	75150	83100	-7950	133310
Gross Input a	...	...	...	763070	...	...	...	799870	...	...	...	860180

	1990			ADDENDUM: Total, including Unincorporated	1991			ADDENDUM: Total, including Unincorporated
	Corporate and Quasi-Corporate Enterprises				Corporate and Quasi-Corporate Enterprises			
	TOTAL	Non-Financial	Financial		TOTAL	Non-Financial	Financial	
Gross Output								
1 Output for sale	...	...	...	885490	...	...	...	926800
2 Imputed bank service charge	18060	...	18060	18060	19930	...	19930	19930
3 Own-account fixed capital formation	...	...	...	2090	...	...	...	2090
Gross Output a	...	...	...	905640	...	...	...	948820
Gross Input								
Intermediate consumption	...	...	...	444420	...	...	...	462360
1 Imputed banking service charge	18060	...	18060	18060	19930	...	19930	19930
2 Other intermediate consumption	...	...	...	426360	...	...	...	442430
Subtotal: Value Added	...	...	...	461220	...	...	...	486460
1 Indirect taxes, net	...	...	...	48480	...	...	...	51140
A Indirect taxes	...	...	...	64340	...	...	...	68730
B Less: Subsidies	...	...	...	15860	...	...	...	17590
2 Consumption of fixed capital	41340	40280	1060	54340	43930	42860	1070	57480
3 Compensation of employees	196430	183720	12710	219310	208670	195140	13530	233150
A To residents	...	...	...	218180	...	...	...	231990
B To the rest of the world	...	...	...	1130	...	...	...	1160
4 Net operating surplus	78630	87960	-9330	139090	81140	91650	-10510	144690
Gross Input a	...	...	...	905640	...	...	...	948820

a) Column 'Total, including unincorporated' includes also private non-profit institutions serving households.

3.22 Corporate and Quasi-Corporate Enterprise Income and Outlay Account: Total and Sectors

Million Netherlands guilders

	1987			1988			1989			1990		
	TOTAL	Non-Financial	Financial	TOTAL	Non-Financial	Financial	TOTAL	Non-Financial	Financial	TOTAL	Non-Financial	Financial
Receipts												
1 Operating surplus	63110	71750	-8640	66000	75370	-9370	75150	83100	-7950	78630	87960	-9330
2 Property and entrepreneurial income	114560	15470	99090	121390	16070	105320	145550	21150	124400	163690	22490	141200
A Withdrawals from quasi-corporate enterprises	2540	...	2540	2640	...	2640	2810	...	2810	2970	...	2970
B Interest	102240	9200	93040	108480	10260	98220	128060	11620	116440	147500	15350	132150
C Dividends	8220	4710	3510	8430	3970	4460	12540	7390	5150	11080	5000	6080
D Net land rent and royalties	1560	1560	...	1840	1840	...	2140	2140	...	2140	2140	...
3 Current transfers	17720	5110	12610	18510	5730	12780	20010	6470	13540	24000	7690	16310
A Casualty insurance claims	3630	3280	350	3430	3140	290	3640	3330	310	5790	4690	1100
B Casualty insurance premiums, net, due to be received by insurance companies	11960	-	11960	12140	-	12140	12940	-	12940	14900	-	14900
C Current transfers from the rest of the world	270	270	...	980	980	...	1270	1270	...	920	920	...
D Other transfers except imputed	90	90	-	70	70	-	60	60	-	50	50	-
E Imputed unfunded employee pension and welfare contributions	1770	1470	300	1890	1540	350	2100	1810	290	2340	2030	310
Total Current Receipts	195390	92330	103060	205900	97170	108730	240710	110720	129990	266320	118140	148180
Disbursements												
1 Property and entrepreneurial income	143000	58950	84050	149190	60410	88780	173930	66070	107860	196770	71700	125070

Netherlands

3.22 Corporate and Quasi-Corporate Enterprise Income and Outlay Account: Total and Sectors
(Continued)

Million Netherlands guilders

	1987			1988			1989			1990		
	TOTAL	Non-Financial	Financial	TOTAL	Non-Financial	Financial	TOTAL	Non-Financial	Financial	TOTAL	Non-Financial	Financial
A Withdrawals from quasi-corporations	6400	6390	10	6120	6110	10	5120	5110	10	5070	5060	10
B Interest	107580	28150	79430	113860	29610	84250	136370	34350	102020	157310	38790	118520
C Dividends	20140	15830	4310	21130	17040	4090	23240	18040	5200	24860	18880	5980
D Net land rent and royalties	8880	8580	300	8080	7650	430	9200	8570	630	9530	8970	560
2 Direct taxes and other current transfers n.e.c. to general government	16380	15000	1380	16100	14660	1440	15870	14180	1690	17570	15650	1920
A Direct taxes	16350	15000	1350	16080	14660	1420	15840	14180	1660	17540	15650	1890
On income	16350	15000	1350	16080	14660	1420	15840	14180	1660	17540	15650	1890
Other	-	-	-	-	-	-	-	-	-	-	-	-
B Fines, fees, penalties and other current transfers n.e.c.	30	-	30	20	-	20	30	-	30	30	-	30
3 Other current transfers	17360	4750	12610	17460	4680	12780	18680	5140	13540	23030	6720	16310
A Casualty insurance premiums, net	3630	3280	350	3430	3140	290	3640	3330	310	5790	4690	1100
B Casualty insurance claims liability of insurance companies	11960	-	11960	12140	-	12140	12940	-	12940	14900	-	14900
C Transfers to private non-profit institutions	-	-	-	-	-	-	-	-	-	-	-	-
D Unfunded employee pension and welfare benefits	1770	1470	300	1890	1540	350	2100	1810	290	2340	2030	310
E Social assistance grants	-	-	-	-	-	-	-	-	-	-	-	-
F Other transfers n.e.c.	...	...	...	...	...	...	...	...	...	...	...	...
G Transfers to the rest of the world	-	-	-	-	-	-	-	-	-	-	-	-
Net saving	18650	13630	5020	23150	17420	5730	32230	25330	6900	28950	24070	4880
Total Current Disbursements and Net Saving	195390	92330	103060	205900	97170	108730	240710	110720	129990	266320	118140	148180

	1991		
	TOTAL	Non-Financial	Financial

Receipts

1 Operating surplus	81140	91650	-10510
2 Property and entrepreneurial income	175010	25970	149040
A Withdrawals from quasi-corporate enterprises	3270	...	3270
B Interest	156530	17430	139100
C Dividends	12270	5600	6670
D Net land rent and royalties	2940	2940	...
3 Current transfers	22180	6490	15690
A Casualty insurance claims	4630	4080	550
B Casualty insurance premiums, net, due to be received by insurance companies	14810	-	14810
C Current transfers from the rest of the world	330	330	...
D Other transfers except imputed	50	50	-
E Imputed unfunded employee pension and welfare contributions	2360	2030	330
Total Current Receipts	278330	124110	154220

Disbursements

1 Property and entrepreneurial income	211330	80000	131330
A Withdrawals from quasi-corporations	5310	5300	10
B Interest	167050	43330	123720
C Dividends	26500	19500	7000
D Net land rent and royalties	12470	11870	600
2 Direct taxes and other current transfers n.e.c. to general government	18730	16940	1790
A Direct taxes	18700	16940	1760
On income	18700	16940	1760

3.22 Corporate and Quasi-Corporate Enterprise Income and Outlay Account: Total and Sectors
(Continued)

Million Netherlands guilders

	1991		
	TOTAL	Non-Financial	Financial
Other	-	-	-
B Fines, fees, penalties and other current transfers n.e.c.	30	-	30
3 Other current transfers	21800	6110	15690
A Casualty insurance premiums, net	4630	4080	550
B Casualty insurance claims liability of insurance companies	14810	-	14810
C Transfers to private non-profit institutions	-	-	-
D Unfunded employee pension and welfare benefits	2360	2030	330
E Social assistance grants	-	-	-
F Other transfers n.e.c.	...	...	...
G Transfers to the rest of the world	-	-	-
Net saving	26470	21060	5410
Total Current Disbursements and Net Saving	278330	124110	154220

3.23 Corporate and Quasi-Corporate Enterprise Capital Accumulation Account: Total and Sectors

Million Netherlands guilders

	1987			1988			1989			1990		
	TOTAL	Non-Financial	Financial	TOTAL	Non-Financial	Financial	TOTAL	Non-Financial	Financial	TOTAL	Non-Financial	Financial
	Finance of Gross Accumulation											
1 Gross saving	52860	46870	5990	59200	52480	6720	71350	63410	7940	70290	64350	5940
A Consumption of fixed capital	34210	33240	970	36050	35060	990	39120	38080	1040	41340	40280	1060
B Net saving	18650	13630	5020	23150	17420	5730	32230	25330	6900	28950	24070	4880
2 Capital transfers	11800	10970	830	8540	7830	710	7520	6880	640	7140	6560	580
A From resident sectors	11800	10970	830	8540	7830	710	7520	6880	640	7140	6560	580
B From the rest of the world	-	-	-	-	-	-	-	-	-	-	-	-
Finance of Gross Accumulation	64660	57840	6820	67740	60310	7430	78870	70290	8580	77430	70910	6520
	Gross Accumulation											
1 Gross capital formation	53570	52540	1030	55280	54010	1270	66320	64670	1650	69220	67550	1670
A Increase in stocks	-710	-710	-	-430	-430	-	5000	5000	-	4190	4190	-
B Gross fixed capital formation	54280	53250	1030	55710	54440	1270	61320	59670	1650	65030	63360	1670
2 Purchases of land, net	1090	1040	50	1380	1330	50	1410	1350	60	1370	1310	60
3 Purchases of intangible assets, net	...	...	...	...	...	...	...	...	...	...	...	...
4 Capital transfers	620	190	430	590	170	420	660	260	400	720	290	430
A To resident sectors a	620	190	430	590	170	420	660	260	400	720	290	430
B To the rest of the world	-	-	-	-	-	-	-	-	-	-	-	-
Net lending b	9380	4070	5310	10490	4800	5690	10480	4010	6470	6120	1760	4360
Gross Accumulation	64660	57840	6820	67740	60310	7430	78870	70290	8580	77430	70910	6520

	1991		
	TOTAL	Non-Financial	Financial
	Finance of Gross Accumulation		
1 Gross saving	70400	63920	6480
A Consumption of fixed capital	43930	42860	1070
B Net saving	26470	21060	5410
2 Capital transfers	5500	4810	690
A From resident sectors	5500	4810	690
B From the rest of the world	-	-	-
Finance of Gross Accumulation	75900	68730	7170
	Gross Accumulation		
1 Gross capital formation	69460	67750	1710
A Increase in stocks	1600	1600	-
B Gross fixed capital formation	67860	66150	1710

Netherlands

3.23 Corporate and Quasi-Corporate Enterprise Capital Accumulation Account: Total and Sectors
(Continued)

Million Netherlands guilders

	1991		
	TOTAL	Non-Financial	Financial
2 Purchases of land, net	1430	1360	70
3 Purchases of intangible assets, net	...	...	...
4 Capital transfers	1060	510	550
A To resident sectors a	1060	510	550
B To the rest of the world	-	-	-
Net lending b	3950	-890	4840
Gross Accumulation	75900	68730	7170

a) Capital transfers from financial enterprises to resident sectors on imputed transaction that is equal to the capital transfer received by pension funds from general government in order to supplement the net equity of households in life insurance and pension funds.   b) Net lending of the capital accumulation account and the capital finance account have not been reconciled and are different due to different statistical sources.

3.24 Corporate and Quasi-Corporate Enterprise Capital Finance Account: Total and Sectors

Million Netherlands guilders

	1987			1988			1989			1990		
	TOTAL	Non-Financial	Financial	TOTAL	Non-Financial	Financial	TOTAL	Non-Financial	Financial	TOTAL	Non-Financial	Financial
Acquisition of Financial Assets												
1 Gold and SDRs	-720	...	-720	780	...	780	730	...	730	750	...	750
2 Currency and transferable deposits	2270	140	2130	5320	3100	2220	5930	4990	940	5980	4440	1540
3 Other deposits	8680	-30	8710	28730	8430	20300	33710	14060	19650	27590	9500	18090
4 Bills and bonds, short term	2180	-240	2420	2220	-50	2270	-3360	-80	-3280	420	20	400
A Corporate and quasi-corporate, resident	1530	-180	1710	2050	-50	2100	-540	-80	-460	240	20	220
B Government	-1390	-60	-1330	-900	...	-900	-3720	...	-3720	-2150	...	-2150
C Rest of the world	2040	...	2040	1070	...	1070	900	...	900	2330	...	2330
5 Bonds, long term	7600	510	7090	21310	590	20720	9040	540	8500	18170	640	17530
A Corporate, resident	1270	-360	1630	3450	120	3330	5150	800	4350	3690	840	2850
B Government	-60	870	-930	7710	470	7240	7840	-260	8100	12080	-200	12280
C Rest of the world	6390	...	6390	10150	...	10150	-3950	...	-3950	2400	...	2400
6 Corporate equity securities	17100	3730	13370	20490	7740	12750	23480	4110	19370	26870	10390	16480
7 Short term loans, n.e.c.	3400	5720	-2320	12850	2310	10540	26540	10260	16280	27790	5810	21980
8 Long term loans, n.e.c.	49250	9360	39890	58800	10750	48050	30800	-10010	40810	34550	11400	23150
A Mortgages	10010	...	10010	12100	...	12100	13500	...	13500	11090	...	11090
B Other	39240	9360	29880	46700	10750	35950	17300	-10010	27310	23460	11400	12060
9 Trade credits and advances a	...	...	...	...	...	...	...	...	...	...	...	...
10 Other receivables a	5970	4640	1330	7190	4640	2550	6260	10410	-4150	4810	-1310	6120
11 Other assets	...	...	...	...	...	...	...	...	...	...	...	...
Total Acquisition of Financial Assets	95730	23830	71900	157690	37510	120180	133130	34280	98850	146930	40890	106040
Incurrence of Liabilities												
1 Currency and transferable deposits	5630	...	5630	6400	...	6400	7230	...	7230	7660	...	7660
2 Other deposits	8410	...	8410	37890	...	37890	36520	...	36520	47410	...	47410
3 Bills and bonds, short term	2180	230	1950	4460	100	4360	-1410	50	-1460	-2640	70	-2710
4 Bonds, long term	2540	770	1770	10570	2420	8150	2330	1000	1330	4840	930	3910
5 Corporate equity securities	11930	6010	5920	15910	8030	7880	-10540	-17650	7110	8970	7490	1480
6 Short-term loans, n.e.c.	250	220	30	6140	1860	4280	16690	17970	-1280	16950	13130	3820
7 Long-term loans, n.e.c.	26560	15700	10860	36260	24790	11470	36730	28290	8440	24700	21410	3290
8 Net equity of households in life insurance and pension fund reserves	32240	...	32240	34050	...	34050	34720	...	34720	37070	...	37070
9 Proprietors' net additions to the accumulation of quasi-corporations	...	...	...	...	...	...	...	...	...	...	...	...
10 Trade credit and advances a	...	...	...	...	...	...	...	...	...	...	...	...
11 Other accounts payable a	...	...	...	...	...	...	...	...	...	...	...	...
12 Other liabilities	...	...	...	...	...	...	...	...	...	...	...	...
Total Incurrence of Liabilities	89740	22930	66810	151680	37200	114480	122270	29660	92610	144960	43030	101930
Statistical discrepancy	-3390	-3170	-220	-4480	-4490	10	380	610	-230	-4150	-3900	-250
Net Lending b	9380	4070	5310	10490	4800	5690	10480	4010	6470	6120	1760	4360
Incurrence of Liabilities and Net Lending	95730	23830	71900	157690	37510	120180	133130	34280	98850	146930	40890	106040

a) Item 'Other receivables' is registered net, it includes trade credit and advances and all other amounts receivable and payable.   b) Net lending of the capital accumulation account and the capital finance account have not been reconciled and are different due to different statistical sources.

3.32 Household and Private Unincorporated Enterprise Income and Outlay Account

Million Netherlands guilders

	1980	1981	1982	1983	1984	1985	1986	1987	1988	1989	1990	1991
Receipts												
1 Compensation of employees	197960	201640	207690	209810	210150	216850	225220	232180 / 239480	245730	252710	269710	285290
A Wages and salaries	152080	155080	160320	159850	160550	166100	172870	178860 / 184840	190430	198620	231360	244780
B Employers' contributions for social security	31350	32300	33250	35360	35410	37040	38640	39900 / 36180	36800	35760	18680	19880
C Employers' contributions for private pension & welfare plans	14530	14260	14120	14600	14190	13710	13710	13420 / 18460	18500	18330	19670	20630
2 Operating surplus of private unincorporated enterprises	...	...	...	...	...	...	...	... / 50140	52770	58160	60460	63550
3 Property and entrepreneurial income	55850	59890	69490	74830	81100	86380	89620	92060 / 53400	54960	59480	65860	71230
A Withdrawals from private quasi-corporations	...	...	...	...	...	...	...	... / ...	...	...	...	...
B Interest	12530	14220	15910	14460	14610	15930	14430	14820 / 48850	50080	53290	58810	63800
C Dividends	43320	45670	53580	60370	66490	70450	75190	77240 / 3850	4050	5060	5950	6200
D Net land rent and royalties	...	...	...	...	...	...	...	... / 700	830	1130	1100	1230
3 Current transfers	98960	107570	117480	123270	123920	126190	128720	132220 / 137060	140700	145390	160180	169370
A Casualty insurance claims	4870	5190	5360	5570	5860	6400	7060	7810 / 7820	8110	8680	9260	9750
B Social security benefits	70370	75100	79900	80730	80870	82230	83740	86120 / 86200	88790	87670	100400	107730
C Social assistance grants	12820	15710	20600	24840	25010	22640	22880	22940 / 20510	20490	24710	24950	25650
D Unfunded employee pension and welfare benefits	4730	4690	4660	4580	4610	4710	4710	4940 / 7560	7880	8510	9300	9360
E Transfers from general government	5210	5810	5970	6580	6620	9170	9330	9380 / 14040	14390	14540	15060	15510
F Transfers from the rest of the world	960	1070	990	970	950	1040	1000	1030 / 930	1040	1280	1210	1370
G Other transfers n.e.c.	...	...	...	...	...	...	...	... / ...	...	...	...	...
Total Current Receipts [a]	352770	369100	394660	407910	415170	429420	443560	456460 / 480080	494160	515740	556210	589440
Disbursements												
1 Final consumption expenditures	205780	213230	221830	229860	236750	247720	256150	263930 / 267940	271640	284490	302820	323070
A Market purchases	...	...	...	...	...	...	...	... / ...				
B Gross rents of owner-occupied housing	...	...	...	...	...	...	...	... / 18670	20010	20970	22310	24070
C Consumption from own-account production	...	...	...	...	...	...	...	... / ...	...	...	...	...
2 Property income	1910	2070	1890	1740	1700	1660	1710	1720 / 18520	19440	20990	23420	25950
A Interest	1910	2070	1890	1740	1700	1660	1710	1720 / 17840	18670	20100	22510	25010
B Net land rent and royalties	...	...	...	...	...	...	...	... / 680	770	890	910	940
3 Direct taxes and other current transfers n.e.c. to government	105950	109950	117280	126310	125690	128120	130450	136760 / 136110	143490	142820	150230	169490
A Social security contributions	61220	66140	72490	83300	82860	85990	84740	89140 / 90310	93950	91330	87910	96780
B Direct taxes	43330	42180	42950	41040	40730	39810	43240	44750 / 45100	48810	50700	61520	71920
Income taxes	40510	39310	39960	38000	37490	36420	39760	41070 / 40060	43520	45110	55650	65610
Other	2820	2870	2990	3040	3240	3390	3480	3680 / 5040	5290	5590	5870	6310
C Fees, fines and penalties	1400	1630	1840	1970	2100	2320	2470	2870 / 700	730	790	800	790

Netherlands

3.32 Household and Private Unincorporated Enterprise Income and Outlay Account
(Continued)

Million Netherlands guilders

	1980	1981	1982	1983	1984	1985	1986	1987	1988	1989	1990	1991
4 Other current transfers	11890	12370	12480	12700	13280	13930	14550	15700 17480	18120	19440	20850	21670
A Net casualty insurance premiums	4870	5190	5360	5570	5860	6400	7060	7810 7820	8110	8680	9260	9750
B Transfers to private non-profit institutions serving households	...	...	...	...	...	...	...	... ...	...	...	...	...
C Transfers to the rest of the world	1960	2150	2140	2230	2410	2530	2500	2650 2100	2130	2250	2290	2560
D Other current transfers, except imputed	330	340	320	320	400	290	280	300 -	-	-	-	-
E Imputed employee pension and welfare contributions	4730	4690	4660	4580	4610	4710	4710	4940 7560	7880	8510	9300	9360
Net saving	27240	31480	41180	37300	37750	37990	40700	38350 40030	41470	48000	58890	49260
Total Current Disbursements and Net Saving a	352770	369100	394660	407910	415170	429420	443560	456460 480080	494160	515740	556210	589440

a) Private non-profit institutions serving households are included in household and private
unincorporated enterprises.

3.33 Household and Private Unincorporated Enterprise Capital Accumulation Account

Million Netherlands guilders

	1980	1981	1982	1983	1984	1985	1986	1987	1988	1989	1990	1991
Finance of Gross Accumulation												
1 Gross saving	27240	31480	41180	37300	37750	37990	40700	38350 50960	53060	60020	71890	62810
A Consumption of fixed capital	...	...	...	...	...	...	...	... 10930	11590	12020	13000	13550
Owner-occupied housing	...	...	...	...	...	...	...	... 3810	4070	4290	4540	4790
Other unincorported enterprises	...	...	...	...	...	...	...	... 7120	7520	7730	8460	8760
B Net saving	27240	31480	41180	37300	37750	37990	40700	38350 40030	41470	48000	58890	49260
2 Capital transfers	1150	1230	1540	1600	1930	2010	1850	1960 3070	3140	2770	2510	2310
A From resident sectors a	840	840	1000	1060	1430	1340	1170	1170 2280	2400	1960	1750	1480
B From the rest of the world	310	390	540	540	500	670	680	790 790	740	810	760	830
Total Finance of Gross Accumulation b	28390	32710	42720	38900	39680	40000	42550	40310 54030	56200	62790	74400	65120
Gross Accumulation												
1 Gross Capital Formation	...	...	...	...	...	...	...	26110	30210	30660	31570	31250
A Increase in stocks	...	...	...	...	...	...	...	... 290	740	430	300	100
B Gross fixed capital formation	...	...	...	...	...	...	...	... 25820	29470	30230	31270	31150
Owner-occupied housing	...	...	...	...	...	...	...	... 16130	18700	18670	18600	17740
Other gross fixed capital formation	...	...	...	...	...	...	...	... 9690	10770	11560	12670	13410
2 Purchases of land, net	...	...	...	...	...	...	...	... 1280	1400	1450	1660	1700
3 Purchases of intangibles, net	...	...	...	...	...	...	...	... ...	...	...	...	...
4 Capital transfers	1330	1410	1470	1290	1430	1480	2030	2450 2450	2160	2540	2400	2640
A To resident sectors	740	780	710	680	810	820	980	1140 1130	1090	1120	1150	1310
B To the rest of the world	590	630	760	610	620	660	1050	1310 1320	1070	1420	1250	1330
Net lending c	27060	31300	41250	37610	38250	38520	40520	37860 24190	22430	28140	38770	29530
Total Gross Accumulation b	28390	32710	42720	38900	39680	40000	42550	40310 54030	56200	62790	74400	65120

a) Capital transfers from financial enterprises to resident sectors on imputed transaction that is
equal to the capital transfer received by pension funds from general government in order to
supplement the net equity of households in life insurance and pension funds.
b) Private non-profit institutions serving households are included in household and private
unincorporated enterprises.
c) Net lending of the capital accumulation account and the capital finance account have not been
reconciled and are different due to different statistical sources.

3.34 Household and Private Unincorporated Enterprise Capital Finance Account

Million Netherlands guilders

	1980	1981	1982	1983	1984	1985	1986	1987	1988	1989	1990	1991
Acquisition of Financial Assets												
1 Gold	...	...	...	...	...	...	...	...	...	...	...	
2 Currency and transferable deposits	...	...	...	...	...	...	...	5830	3040	4730	2070	...
3 Other deposits	...	...	...	...	...	...	...	3840	7670	10240	15770	...
4 Bills and bonds, short term	...	...	...	...	...	...	...	-10	-70	-640	-1710	
A Corporate and quasi-corporate	...	...	...	...	...	...	...	-10	-70	-640	-1710	...
B Government	...	...	...	...	...	...	...	...	...	...	...	
C Rest of the world	...	...	...	...	...	...	...	...	...	...	...	
5 Bonds, long term	...	...	...	...	...	...	...	860	-740	-2260	7610	
A Corporate	...	...	...	...	...	...	...	-2690	400	-5930	590	
B Government	...	...	...	...	...	...	...	4360	-1440	3380	7580	
C Rest of the world	...	...	...	...	...	...	...	-810	300	290	-560	
6 Corporate equity securities	...	...	...	...	...	...	...	410	1200	320	-3580	
7 Short term loans, n.e.c.	...	...	...	...	...	...	...	180	-130	-	-20	...
8 Long term loans, n.e.c.	...	...	...	...	...	...	...	-20	160	-80	200	...
A Mortgages	...	...	...	...	...	...	...	...	...	...	...	
B Other	...	...	...	...	...	...	...	-20	160	-80	200	
9 Trade credit and advances [a]	...	...	...	...	...	...	...	...	...	...	...	...
10 Net equity of households in life insurance and pension fund reserves	...	...	...	...	...	...	...	32600	34440	35210	37550	...
11 Proprietors' net additions to the accumulation of quasi-corporations	...	...	...	...	...	...	...	...	...	...	...	
12 Other [a]	...	...	...	...	...	...	...	-5330	-2360	-240	-1490	...
Total Acquisition of Financial Assets [b]	...	...	...	...	...	...	...	38360	43210	47280	56400	...
Incurrence of Liabilities												
1 Short term loans, n.e.c.	...	...	...	...	...	...	...	350	2260	-480	820	...
2 Long term loans, n.e.c.	...	...	...	...	...	...	...	12480	16490	17520	15660	...
A Mortgages	...	...	...	...	...	...	...	11540	14110	13830	...	...
B Other	...	...	...	...	...	...	...	940	2380	3690	...	...
3 Trade credit and advances [a]	...	...	...	...	...	...	...	...	...	...	...	
4 Other accounts payable [a]	...	...	...	...	...	...	...	...	...	...	...	
5 Other liabilities	...	...	...	...	...	...	...	...	...	...	...	
Total Incurrence of Liabilities	...	...	...	...	...	...	...	12830	18750	17040	16480	...
Statistical discrepancy	...	...	...	...	...	...	...	1340	2030	2100	1150	...
Net Lending [c]	...	...	...	...	...	...	...	24190	22430	28140	38770	...
Incurrence of Liabilities and Net Lending [b]	...	...	...	...	...	...	...	38360	43210	47280	56400	...

a) Item 'Other receivables' is registered net, it includes trade credit and advances and all other amounts receivable and payable.
b) Private non-profit institutions serving households are included in household and private unincorporated enterprises.
c) Net lending of the capital accumulation account and the capital finance account have not been reconciled and are different due to different statistical sources.

3.51 External Transactions: Current Account: Detail

Million Netherlands guilders

	1980	1981	1982	1983	1984	1985	1986	1987	1988	1989	1990	1991
Payments to the Rest of the World												
1 Imports of goods and services	178620	192240	196830	205210	227750	245500	213010	213310 / 207560	222380	248760	256500	266000
A Imports of merchandise c.i.f.	156120	168420	171710	179580	200240	216610	185240	185300 / 177820	190820	214500	220320	226710
B Other	22500	23820	25120	25630	27510	28890	27770	28010 / 29740	31560	34260	36180	39290
2 Factor income to the rest of the world	22710	31090	32400	27810	31370	32200	29500	30390 / 32030	36730	48490	50080	50760
A Compensation of employees	910	1010	1140	1120	1120	1220	1210	1070 / 1070	1200	1260	1130	1160
B Property and entrepreneurial income	21800	30080	31260	26690	30250	30980	28290	29320 / 30960	35530	47230	48950	49600
By general government	...	...	...	...	...	...	...	2770	3580	3720	3750	4360
By corporate and quasi-cororate enterprises	21800	30080	31260	26690	30250	30980	28290	29320 / 28190	31950	43510	45200	45240

Netherlands

3.51 External Transactions: Current Account: Detail
(Continued)

Million Netherlands guilders

	1980	1981	1982	1983	1984	1985	1986	1987	1988	1989	1990	1991
By other	...	...	...	...	...	...	...	...	...	...	...	...
3 Current transfers to the rest of the world	8400	9160	9600	9830	10860	11790	12710	13040 / 12000	12580	13550	14150	16080
A Indirect taxes by general government to supranational organizations a	3670	3730	4050	4140	4590	5010	5640	5890 / 5700	6140	6430	6260	7480
B Other current transfers	4730	5430	5550	5690	6270	6780	7070	7150 / 6300	6440	7120	7890	8600
By general government b	2060	2290	2580	2530	3100	3440	3720	3490 / 3080	3220	3710	3620	4580
By other resident sectors	2670	3140	2970	3160	3170	3340	3350	3660 / 3220	3220	3410	4270	4020
4 Surplus of the nation on current transactions c	-4900	7760	11640	11860	16630	17310	11630	5930 / 8560	12860	16910	20710	21140
Payments to the Rest of the World, and Surplus of the Nation on Current Transfers	204830	240250	250470	254710	286610	306800	266850	262670 / 260150	284550	327710	341440	353980

Receipts From The Rest of the World

	1980	1981	1982	1983	1984	1985	1986	1987	1988	1989	1990	1991
1 Exports of goods and services	176810	204620	212600	219770	248560	265540	232520	226650 / 219260	240250	267670	280990	293880
A Exports of merchandise f.o.b.	147080	171330	177620	185010	210630	225950	195850	188780 / 181560	199180	222080	230330	239770
B Other	29730	33290	34980	34760	37930	39590	36670	37870 / 37700	41070	45590	50660	54110
2 Factor income from the rest of the world	22090	30130	32020	28370	30870	32880	28520	29660 / 30880	33230	48290	49500	49870
A Compensation of employees	1030	1120	1350	1290	1270	1300	1190	1190 / 1190	1190	1120	850	820
B Property and entrepreneurial income	21060	29010	30670	27080	29600	31580	27330	28470 / 29690	32040	47170	48650	49050
By general government	40	110	100	80	70	130	70	70 / 40	80	90	50	60
By corporate and quasi-corporate enterprises	20100	27830	29140	25470	27940	29520	25450	26490 / 28520	30670	45670	47150	47490
By other	920	1070	1430	1530	1590	1930	1810	1910 / 1130	1290	1410	1450	1500
3 Current transfers from the rest of the world	5930	5500	5850	6570	7180	7860	7970	8640 / 10010	11070	11750	10950	10230
A Subsidies to general government from supranational organizations b	4120	3300	3840	4510	5200	5650	5780	6240 / 6370	6380	6660	5540	5690
B Other current transfers	1810	2200	2010	2060	1980	2210	2190	2400 / 3640	4690	5090	5410	4540
To general government a	140	140	190	160	270	360	340	360 / 1430	1690	1520	1440	1520
To other resident sectors	1670	2060	1820	1900	1710	1850	1850	2040 / 2210	3000	3570	3970	3020
Statistical discrepancy	...	...	...	...	...	520	-2160	-2280 / -	-	-	-	-
Receipts from the Rest of the World on Current Transfers	204830	240250	250470	254710	286610	306800	266850	262670 / 260150	284550	327710	341440	353980

a) The import duties of non-resident enterprises paid by the Netherlands to the European Community are not included in these figures (1987:190; 1988:220; 1989:300; 1990:430; 1991:570 million N. Guilders).
b) The subsidies from the European Community paid to the Netherlands but destined for non-resident enterprises are not included in these figures (1987:370; 1988:2780; 1989:2560; 1990:1310; 1991:610 million N. guilders).
c) As a result of definition and measuring differences, this surplus differs from the surplus on current transactions according to the balance of payments on a transaction basis, estimated by the Dutch Central Bank in cooperation with the Central Bureau of Statistics.

3.52 External Transactions: Capital Accumulation Account

Million Netherlands guilders

	1980	1981	1982	1983	1984	1985	1986	1987	1988	1989	1990	1991
					Finance of Gross Accumulation							
1 Surplus of the nation on current transactions	-4900	7760	11640	11860	16630	17310	11630	5930 / 8560	12860	16910	20710	21140
2 Capital transfers from the rest of the world	410	490	620	680	620	820	780	970 / 900	830	930	890	970
A By general government	100	100	80	140	120	150	100	180 / 110	90	120	130	140
B By other resident sectors	310	390	540	540	500	670	680	790 / 790	740	810	760	830

3.52 External Transactions: Capital Accumulation Account
(Continued)

Million Netherlands guilders

	1980	1981	1982	1983	1984	1985	1986	1987	1988	1989	1990	1991
Total Finance of Gross Accumulation	-4490	8250	12260	12540	17250	18130	12410	6900 / 9460	13690	17840	21600	22110

Gross Accumulation

	1980	1981	1982	1983	1984	1985	1986	1987	1988	1989	1990	1991
1 Capital transfers to the rest of the world	1200	1390	1570	1230	1110	1170	1710	1980 / 1990	1800	2220	2050	2280
A By general government	610	760	810	620	490	510	660	670 / 670	730	800	800	950
B By other resident sectors	590	630	760	610	620	660	1050	1310 / 1320	1070	1420	1250	1330
2 Purchases of intangible assets, n.e.c., net, from the rest of the world	...	...	...	...	...	...	...	... / ...	...	...	...	...
Net lending to the rest of the world a	-5690	6860	10690	11310	16140	16960	10700	4920 / 7470	11890	15620	19550	19830
Total Gross Accumulation	-4490	8250	12260	12540	17250	18130	12410	6900 / 9460	13690	17840	21600	22110

a) Net lending of the capital accumulation account and the capital finance account have not been reconciled and are different due to different statistical sources.

3.53 External Transactions: Capital Finance Account

Million Netherlands guilders

	1980	1981	1982	1983	1984	1985	1986	1987	1988	1989	1990	1991
Acquisitions of Foreign Financial Assets												
1 Gold and SDR's	249	276	-	-	...	...	...	...	...	...	...	...
2 Currency and transferable deposits	226	2803	1578	628	...	...	...	990	-490	1960	-620	...
3 Other deposits	28782	21702	-811	5373	...	...	...	5870	16440	8180	21050	...
4 Bills and bonds, short term	...	...	...	...	...	...	...	660	2000	-200	-540	...
5 Bonds, long term	4240	1826	2119	1352	...	...	...	12220	18170	12100	1820	...
6 Corporate equity securities	2496	1617	3769	1670	...	...	...	690	3400	10430	3290	...
7 Short-term loans, n.e.c.	178	1325	-1032	-2310	...	...	...	2110	3530	11390	7740	...
8 Long-term loans	3466	5022	2355	6834	...	...	...	4840	8860	12240	17110	...
9 Prproietors' net additions to accumulation of quasi-corporate, non-resident enterprises	...	...	...	...	...	...	...	...	...	...	...	...
10 Trade credit and advances a	...	...	...	...	...	...	...	...	...	...	...	...
11 Other a	-190	-320	-290	-240	...	...	...	-160	-1590	-6700	-1880	...
Statistical discrepancy b	...	...	...	...	...	...	...	-470	-460	-570	-520	...
Total Acquisitions of Foreign Financial Assets	39447	34251	7688	13307	...	...	...	26750	49860	48830	47450	...
Incurrence of Foreign Liabilities												
1 Currency and transferable deposits	2732	-825	3962	851	...	...	...	1870	940	1430	1190	...
2 Other deposits	17406	18227	-2864	-253	...	...	...	8100	19400	18280	14060	...
3 Bills and bonds, short term	...	...	...	...	...	...	...	2040	1070	890	2330	...
4 Bonds, long term	693	886	2718	2997	...	...	...	5580	10440	-3660	1840	...
5 Corporate equity securities	2022	3123	2056	2164	...	...	...	7430	9780	18190	16990	...
6 Short-term loans, n.e.c.	3991	9808	4998	4248	...	...	...	6420	7500	19250	17670	...

Netherlands

3.53 External Transactions: Capital Finance Account
(Continued)

Million Netherlands guilders

	1980	1981	1982	1983	1984	1985	1986	1987	1988	1989	1990	1991
7 Long-term loans	9167	12441	8927	11740	...	...	...	... 1630	9250	11940	9130	...
8 Non-resident proprietors' net additions to accumulation of resident quasi-corporate enterprises	...	...	...	...	...	...	...	... ...	...	...	...	...
9 Trade credit and advances a	...	...	...	...	...	...	...	... ...	...	...	...	...
10 Other a	96	422	532	-732	...	...	...	... -720	780	730	750	...
Statistical discrepancy b								-110	-70	-80	-40	...
Total Incurrence of Liabilities	36107	44082	20329	21015	...	...	...	... 32240	59090	66970	63920	
Statistical discrepancy b	-2660	-3211	-3141	2762	...	...	...	... 1980	2660	-2520	3080	...
Net Lending c	6000	-6620	-9500	-10470	...	...	...	... -7470	-11890	-15620	-19550	...
Total Incurrence of Liabilities and Net Lending	39447	34251	7688	13307	...	...	...	... 26750	49860	48830	47450	...

a) Item 'Other receivables' is registered net, it includes trade credit and advances and all other amounts receivable and payable.
b) Item 'Statistical discrepancy' refers to net equity of households in life insurance and pension fund reserves.
c) Net lending of the capital accumulation account and the capital finance account have not been reconciled and are different due to different statistical sources.

4.1 Derivation of Value Added by Kind of Activity, in Current Prices

Million Netherlands guilders

	1987			1988			1989			1990		
	Gross Output	Intermediate Consumption	Value Added	Gross Output	Intermediate Consumption	Value Added	Gross Output	Intermediate Consumption	Value Added	Gross Output	Intermediate Consumption	Value Added
All Producers												
1 Agriculture, hunting, forestry and fishing	38875	21397	17478	39694	21739	17955	43524	22853	20671	42298	21709	20589
A Agriculture and hunting	37825	21025	16800	38778	21362	17416	42541	22463	20078	41312	21314	19998
B Forestry and logging												
C Fishing	1050	372	678	916	377	539	983	390	593	986	395	591
2 Mining and quarrying	18623	3112	15511	15543	3039	12504	16305	3017	13288	19428	4179	15249
A Coal mining	...	...	...	...	...	...	...	...	...	...	...	...
B Crude petroleum and natural gas production	16987	2444	14543	13909	2429	11480	14754	2535	12219	17770	3654	14116
C Metal ore mining	...	...	...	...	...	...	...	...	...	...	...	...
D Other mining	1636	668	968	1634	610	1024	1551	482	1069	1658	525	1133
3 Manufacturing	257907	178599	79308	272780	186884	85896	298648	206101	92547	308878	209333	99545
A Manufacture of food, beverages and tobacco	67133	56936	10197	70237	59742	10495	75695	62439	13256	76761	60313	16448
B Textile, wearing apparel and leather industries	8247	5418	2829	8341	5372	2969	8809	5766	3043	9252	6022	3230
C Manufacture of wood and wood products, including furniture	5916	3687	2229	6369	3911	2458	6703	4205	2498	7051	4397	2654
D Manufacture of paper and paper products, printing and publishing	23098	14019	9079	24909	15168	9741	26771	16478	10293	28211	17168	11043
E Manufacture of chemicals and chemical petroleum, coal, rubber and plastic products	67799	46988	20811	72151	47516	24635	79997	54891	25106	82816	56808	26008
F Manufacture of non-metallic mineral products, except products of petroleum and coal	7056	4060	2996	7824	4530	3294	8363	4915	3448	8712	5171	3541
G Basic metal industries	8039	5070	2969	9468	5817	3651	11119	6883	4236	9977	6499	3478
H Manufacture of fabricated metal products, machinery and equipment	66986	40511	26475	69629	42737	26892	76803	48115	28688	81570	50457	31113
I Other manufacturing industries	3633	1910	1723	3852	2091	1761	4388	2409	1979	4528	2498	2030
4 Electricity, gas and water	20852	12895	7957	19724	11725	7999	19814	11665	8149	21919	13271	8648
A Electricity, gas and steam	18884	12284	6600	17704	11117	6587	17729	11027	6702	19776	12623	7153
B Water works and supply	1968	611	1357	2020	608	1412	2085	638	1447	2143	648	1495
5 Construction	59546	37704	21842	67502	42778	24724	72469	46571	25898	76728	48794	27934
6 Wholesale and retail trade, restaurants and hotels	102111	38318	63793	106553	40315	66238	114682	44306	70376	124326	48201	76125
A Wholesale and retail trade	88331	31584	56747	92112	33246	58866	98701	36657	62044	107093	40215	66878
B Restaurants and hotels	13780	6734	7046	14441	7069	7372	15981	7649	8332	17233	7986	9247
7 Transport, storage and communication	46318	18601	27717	49357	20216	29141	52755	21982	30773	55197	23167	32030
A Transport and storage	35234	16009	19225	37548	17317	20231	40169	18890	21279	41820	19866	21954

1288

4.1 Derivation of Value Added by Kind of Activity, in Current Prices
(Continued)

Million Netherlands guilders

	1987 Gross Output	1987 Intermediate Consumption	1987 Value Added	1988 Gross Output	1988 Intermediate Consumption	1988 Value Added	1989 Gross Output	1989 Intermediate Consumption	1989 Value Added	1990 Gross Output	1990 Intermediate Consumption	1990 Value Added
B Communication	11084	2592	8492	11809	2899	8910	12586	3092	9494	13377	3301	10076
8 Finance, insurance, real estate and business services a	111617	28894	82723	118416	30888	87528	129847	33272	96575	137561	36171	101390
A Financial institutions	20500	5152	15348	21571	5441	16130	23036	5816	17220	22882	6200	16682
B Insurance	12377	6640	5737	12715	7000	5715	14745	7642	7103	15168	8196	6972
C Real estate and business services	78740	17102	61638	84130	18447	65683	92066	19814	72252	99511	21775	77736
Real estate, except dwellings	7670	1231	6439	7636	1338	6298	8489	1363	7126	9230	1433	7797
Dwellings	32818	3934	28884	34757	4431	30326	36735	4503	32232	38934	4737	34197
9 Community, social and personal services	67808	20632	47176	70128	21500	48628	72125	22302	49823	76200	23383	52817
A Sanitary and similar services	...	...	...	...	...	...	...	...	...	...	...	...
B Social and related community services	48224	12593	35631	49529	13193	36336	50952	13612	37340	53842	14271	39571
Educational services	...	...	...	...	...	...	...	...	...	...	...	...
Medical, dental, other health and veterinary services	29972	7313	22659	30856	7675	23181	31899	8056	23843	33804	8475	25329
C Recreational and cultural services	11428	5190	6238	11874	5381	6493	12132	5584	6548	12684	5810	6874
D Personal and household services	8156	2849	5307	8725	2926	5799	9041	3106	5935	9674	3302	6372
Statistical discrepancy	1593	1593	-	1640	1640	-	1725	1725	-	1725	1725	-
Total, Industries	725250	361745	363505	761337	380724	380613	821894	413794	408100	864260	429933	434327
Producers of Government Services	75519	26046	49473	76238	26959	49279	78109	28364	49745	81086	29316	51770
Other Producers b	1413	...	1413	1510	...	1510	1610	...	1610	1696	...	1696
Total	802180	387790	414390	839080	407680	431400	901610	442160	459450	947050	459250	487800
Less: Imputed bank service charge	...	-16540	16540	...	-17450	17450	...	-18030	18030	...	-18060	18060
Import duties c	5940	...	5940	5590	...	5590	6370	...	6370	7100	...	7100
Value added tax	36420	...	36420	37450	...	37450	36480	...	36480	39140	...	39140
Other adjustments d	370	...	370	420	...	420	400	...	400	340	...	340
Total	844910	404330	440580	882540	425130	457410	944860	460190	484670	993630	477310	516320
Memorandum Item: Mineral fuels and power	58549	31011	27538	52960	27715	25245	58262	32220	26042	66795	36094	30701

All Producers

	1991 Gross Output	1991 Intermediate Consumption	1991 Value Added
1 Agriculture, hunting, forestry and fishing	43849	22585	21264
A Agriculture and hunting	42828	22197	20631
B Forestry and logging			
C Fishing	1021	388	633
2 Mining and quarrying	23555	4759	18796
A Coal mining	...	...	...
B Crude petroleum and natural gas production	21804	4221	17583
C Metal ore mining	...	...	...
D Other mining	1751	538	1213

Netherlands

Million Netherlands guilders

	1991		
	Gross Output	Intermediate Consumption	Value Added
3 Manufacturing	315242	213263	101979
A Manufacture of food, beverages and tobacco	78026	62355	15671
B Textile, wearing apparel and leather industries	9357	6125	3232
C Manufacture of wood and wood products, including furniture	7373	4398	2975
D Manufacture of paper and paper products, printing and publishing	29179	17563	11616
E Manufacture of chemicals and chemical petroleum, coal, rubber and plastic products	83911	56638	27273
F Manufacture of non-metallic mineral products, except products of petroleum and coal	8946	5256	3690
G Basic metal industries	9266	6373	2893
H Manufacture of fabricated metal products, machinery and equipment	84246	51916	32330
I Other manufacturing industries	4938	2639	2299
4 Electricity, gas and water	24909	15614	9295
A Electricity, gas and steam	22697	14949	7748
B Water works and supply	2212	665	1547
5 Construction	77695	48769	28926
6 Wholesale and retail trade, restaurants and hotels	130651	51770	78881
A Wholesale and retail trade	112036	43045	68991
B Restaurants and hotels	18615	8725	9890
7 Transport, storage and communication	59190	24584	34606
A Transport and storage	44895	21019	23876
B Communication	14295	3565	10730
8 Finance, insurance, real estate and business services [a]	147638	38731	108907
A Financial institutions	24915	6627	18288
B Insurance	15689	8712	6977
C Real estate and business services	107034	23392	83642
Real estate, except dwellings	9825	1495	8330
Dwellings	41322	4945	36377
9 Community, social and personal services	81249	24774	56475
A Sanitary and similar services	...	...	...
B Social and related community services	57631	15169	42462
Educational services	...	...	...
Medical, dental, other health and veterinary services	36477	9105	27372
C Recreational and cultural services	13348	6110	7238
D Personal and household services	10270	3495	6775
Statistical discrepancy	1755	1755	-
Total, Industries	905733	446604	459129
Producers of Government Services	84022	30582	53440
Other Producers [b]	1778	...	1778

4.1 Derivation of Value Added by Kind of Activity, in Current Prices
(Continued)

Million Netherlands guilders

	1991		
	Gross Output	Intermediate Consumption	Value Added
Total	991530	477190	514340
Less: Imputed bank service charge	...	-19930	19930
Import duties c	7520	...	7520
Value added tax	41260	...	41260
Other adjustments d	370	...	370
Total	1040680	497120	543560
Memorandum Item: Mineral fuels and power	74980	38653	36327

a) For the years 1990 and 1991, real estate brokers are included in item 'Wholesale and retail trade, restaurants and hotels'.
b) Beginning 1987 of the second series, item 'Other producers' includes only domestic services of households; private non-profit services to households are included in various industries above.
c) Beginning 1987 of the new series, item 'Import duties' includes all taxes linked to imports (excluding VAT) less import subsidies.
d) Beginning 1987 of the new series, item 'Other adjustments' includes only levies on fixed capital goods.

4.2 Derivation of Value Added by Kind of Activity, in Constant Prices

Million Netherlands guilders

	1987			1988			1989			1990		
	Gross Output	Intermediate Consumption	Value Added	Gross Output	Intermediate Consumption	Value Added	Gross Output	Intermediate Consumption	Value Added	Gross Output	Intermediate Consumption	Value Added

At constant prices of:1987

All Producers

1 Agriculture, hunting, forestry and fishing a	38870	21390	17480	39630	21390	18240	40910	21440	19500	42140	21200	20960
A Agriculture and hunting	37820	21020	16800	38630	20980	17650	39830	21050	18790	41040	20830	20230
B Forestry and logging												
C Fishing	1050	370	680	1000	410	590	1090	380	710	1100	370	730
2 Mining and quarrying a	18620	3110	15510	16770	3110	13660	17280	3160	14130	18550	4370	14170
A Coal mining	...	...	...	...	...	...	...	...	...	...	...	...
B Crude petroleum and natural gas production	16980	2440	14540	15200	2470	12730	15920	2610	13310	17040	3710	13270
C Metal ore mining	...	...	...	...	...	...	...	...	...	...	...	...
D Other mining	1640	670	970	1570	640	930	1390	550	840	1540	640	910
3 Manufacturing a	257910	178600	79310	269380	186770	82610	282380	195130	87220	291900	201360	90510
A Manufacture of food, beverages and tobacco	67130	56930	10200	68850	58420	10430	70400	58490	11940	73880	60560	13300
B Textile, wearing apparel and leather industries	8250	5420	2830	8300	5350	2950	8710	5700	3010	9090	6000	3090
C Manufacture of wood and wood products, including furniture	5920	3690	2230	6300	3880	2420	6460	4000	2470	6540	4080	2460
D Manufacture of paper and paper products, printing and publishing	23100	14020	9080	24590	14980	9610	25760	15750	10010	26880	16490	10400
E Manufacture of chemicals and chemical petroleum, coal, rubber and plastic products	67810	47000	20810	72480	50110	22370	75420	52280	23160	76580	53020	23580
F Manufacture of non-metallic mineral products, except products of petroleum and coal	7050	4060	2990	7680	4470	3210	8030	4750	3290	8140	4830	3310
G Basic metal industries	8040	5070	2970	8630	5390	3240	9180	5770	3420	9000	5660	3340
H Manufacture of fabricated metal products, machinery and equipment	66980	40500	26480	68720	42090	26630	74090	46060	28030	77490	48360	29130
I Other manufacturing industries	3630	1910	1720	3830	2080	1750	4300	2360	1940	4370	2420	1950
4 Electricity, gas and water a	20850	12890	7960	20330	12180	8150	20390	12220	8170	21080	12830	8260
A Electricity, gas and steam	18880	12280	6600	18310	11560	6750	18320	11580	6740	18960	12190	6780
B Water works and supply	1970	610	1360	2020	620	1400	2070	640	1430	2120	640	1480
5 Construction	59550	37710	21840	65990	42020	23970	68530	44250	24290	70390	45290	25110
6 Wholesale and retail trade, restaurants and hotels ab	102110	38310	63800	105650	39880	65770	112000	42760	69240	119710	46040	73670
A Wholesale and retail trade	88330	31580	56750	91440	32860	58580	96640	35350	61290	103570	38240	65320
B Restaurants and hotels	13780	6730	7050	14210	7020	7190	15360	7410	7950	16140	7800	8340
7 Transport, storage and communication a	46320	18610	27710	48920	20190	28730	51830	21270	30560	53580	21960	31620
A Transport and storage	35240	16020	19220	37140	17350	19790	39190	18290	20890	40410	18850	21560
B Communication	11080	2590	8490	11780	2840	8940	12640	2970	9670	13170	3100	10070
8 Finance, insurance, real estate and business services ca	111620	28900	82720	115960	30480	85480	123450	32040	91410	128430	33980	94450
A Financial institutions	20500	5150	15350	21030	5380	15650	21450	5680	15780	21950	5920	16030

Netherlands

Million Netherlands guilders

	1987			1988			1989			1990		
	Gross Output	Intermediate Consumption	Value Added	Gross Output	Intermediate Consumption	Value Added	Gross Output	Intermediate Consumption	Value Added	Gross Output	Intermediate Consumption	Value Added
	At constant prices of:1987											
B Insurance	12380	6640	5740	12740	6970	5770	13800	7260	6550	14150	7560	6590
C Real estate and business services	78740	17110	61630	82190	18130	64060	88200	19090	69100	92360	20500	71860
Real estate, except dwellings	...	...	...	...	...	...	...	...	...	...	...	...
Dwellings	40490	5170	35320	41200	5620	35580	42880	5590	37290	44250	5730	38520
9 Community, social and personal services a	67810	20630	47180	69370	21310	48060	70210	21890	48320	72070	22470	49600
A Sanitary and similar services	...	...	...	...	...	...	...	...	...	...	...	...
B Social and related community services	48220	12590	35630	49040	13090	35950	49810	13400	36410	50970	13800	37170
Educational services	...	...	...	...	...	...	...	...	...	...	...	...
Medical, dental, other health and veterinary services	29970	7310	22660	30570	7610	22960	31230	7950	23280	31870	8220	23640
C Recreational and cultural services	11430	5190	6240	11700	5320	6380	11700	5450	6250	12020	5540	6480
D Personal and household services	8160	2850	5310	8630	2900	5730	8700	3040	5660	9080	3130	5950
Statistical discrepancy	1590	1590	...	1640	1640	...	1710	1710	...	1710	1710	...
Total, Industries a	725250	361740	363510	753640	378970	374670	788760	395880	392870	819490	411070	408410
Producers of Government Services	75520	26050	49470	76610	26710	49900	77800	27370	50430	79130	27900	51220
Other Producers d	1410	...	1410	1490	...	1490	1540	...	1540	1560	...	1540
Total a	802180	387790	414390	831740	405680	426060	868140	423250	444880	900270	438980	461300
Less: Imputed bank service charge	...	-16540	16540	...	-17010	17010	...	-16810	16810	...	-17360	17360
Import duties e	5940	...	5940	5390	...	5390	6150	...	6150	6680	...	6680
Value added tax	36420	...	36420	37240	...	37240	38620	...	38620	40690	...	40690
Other adjustments f	370	...	370	420	...	420	400	...	400	340	...	340
Total a	844910	404330	440580	874790	422690	452100	913310	440050	473260	947950	456310	491640
Memorandum Item: Mineral fuels and power	58550	31010	27540	57230	30910	26320	58930	32220	26740	61370	34080	27310

	1991		
	Gross Output	Intermediate Consumption	Value Added
	At constant prices of:1987		
	All Producers		
1 Agriculture, hunting, forestry and fishing a	42810	21450	21390
A Agriculture and hunting	41720	21080	20660
B Forestry and logging			
C Fishing	1100	370	730
2 Mining and quarrying a	20620	4770	15820
A Coal mining	...	...	...
B Crude petroleum and natural gas production	19090	4100	14920
C Metal ore mining	...	...	...
D Other mining	1560	650	920

4.2 Derivation of Value Added by Kind of Activity, in Constant Prices
(Continued)

Million Netherlands guilders

	1991			
	Gross Output	Intermediate Consumption	Value Added	
3 Manufacturing a	296980	205440	91550	At constant prices of:1987
A Manufacture of food, beverages and tobacco	75110	61950	13220	
B Textile, wearing apparel and leather industries	9080	5990	3090	
C Manufacture of wood and wood products, including furniture	6740	4070	2670	
D Manufacture of paper and paper products, printing and publishing	27410	16780	10620	
E Manufacture of chemicals and chemical petroleum, coal, rubber and plastic products	78400	54510	23910	
F Manufacture of non-metallic mineral products, except products of petroleum and coal	8130	4800	3320	
G Basic metal industries	9100	5720	3380	
H Manufacture of fabricated metal products, machinery and equipment	78460	49160	29290	
I Other manufacturing industries	4620	2500	2110	
4 Electricity, gas and water a	22670	14020	8670	
A Electricity, gas and steam	20550	13380	7190	
B Water works and supply	2110	640	1470	
5 Construction	69400	44390	25010	
6 Wholesale and retail trade, restaurants and hotels ab	123190	47880	75300	
A Wholesale and retail trade	106220	39610	66590	
B Restaurants and hotels	16960	8270	8690	
7 Transport, storage and communication a	55740	22860	32880	
A Transport and storage	41870	19600	22270	
B Communication	13880	3270	10620	
8 Finance, insurance, real estate and business services ca	132440	35190	97270	
A Financial institutions	22520	6160	16370	
B Insurance	14390	7690	6700	
C Real estate and business services	95560	21340	74220	
Real estate, except dwellings	...	...	...	
Dwellings	45410	5810	39590	
9 Community, social and personal services a	74240	23080	51160	
A Sanitary and similar services	...	...	...	
B Social and related community services	52600	14210	38390	
Educational services	...	...	...	
Medical, dental, other health and veterinary services	32920	8540	24380	
C Recreational and cultural services	12340	5650	6690	
D Personal and household services	9310	3230	6080	
Statistical discrepancy	1700	1700	...	
Total, Industries a	839640	420580	419040	
Producers of Government Services	79690	28400	51270	
Other Producers d	1560	...	1560	

Netherlands

4.2 Derivation of Value Added by Kind of Activity, in Constant Prices
(Continued)

Million Netherlands guilders

	1991			
	Gross Output	Intermediate Consumption	Value Added	
				At constant prices of:1987
Total a	921010	448970	472040	
Less: Imputed bank service charge	...	-17980	17980	
Import duties e	6650	...	6650	
Value added tax	41600	...	41600	
Other adjustments f	370	...	370	
Total a	969590	466930	502660	
Memorandum Item: Mineral fuels and power	66210	36790	29440	

a) The estimates in constant prices of the fixed base year 1987 have been calculated on the basis of figures in constant prices of the preceding year. Because of this, the sum of the sub-items do not add-up to the main aggregate. However, for the constant price 1980, the differences were eliminated by adding them proportionally to the details.
b) For the first series, repair services are included in item 'Community, social and personal services'.
c) For the years 1990 and 1991, real estate brokers are included in item 'Wholesale and retail trade, restaurants and hotels'.
d) Beginning 1987 of the second series, item 'Other producers' includes only domestic services of households; private non-profit services to households are included in various industries above.
e) Beginning 1987 of the new series, item 'Import duties' includes all taxes linked to imports (excluding VAT) less import subsidies.
f) Beginning 1987 of the new series, item 'Other adjustments' includes only levies on fixed capital goods.

4.3 Cost Components of Value Added

Million Netherlands guilders

	1987						1988					
	Compensation of Employees	Capital Consumption	Net Operating Surplus	Indirect Taxes	Less: Subsidies Received	Value Added	Compensation of Employees	Capital Consumption	Net Operating Surplus	Indirect Taxes	Less: Subsidies Received	Value Added
					All Producers							
1 Agriculture, hunting, forestry and fishing	2833	...	14003	964	322	17478	2999	...	14387	985	416	17955
A Agriculture and hunting	2608	...	13554	960	322	16800	2781	...	14071	980	416	17416
B Forestry and logging								...				
C Fishing	225		449	4	-	678	218	...	316	5	-	539
2 Mining and quarrying	872	...	14569	73	3	15511	875	...	11560	72	3	12504
A Coal mining	...	...	...	...	...	...	...	...	...	...	...	...
B Crude petroleum and natural gas production	681	...	13797	66	1	14543	682	...	10734	65	1	11480
C Metal ore mining	...	...	...	...	...	...	...	...	...	...	...	...
D Other mining	191	...	772	7	2	968	193	...	826	7	2	1024
3 Manufacturing	52765	...	25995	8570	8022	79308	53416	...	31278	8616	7414	85896
A Manufacture of food, beverages and tobacco	8482	...	5323	3914	7522	10197	8482	...	5116	3772	6875	10495
B Textile, wearing apparel and leather industries	1990	...	813	48	22	2829	2045	...	896	45	17	2969
C Manufacture of wood and wood products, including furniture	1498	...	697	42	8	2229	1608	...	816	43	9	2458
D Manufacture of paper and paper products, printing and publishing	6002	...	2984	132	39	9079	6272	...	3381	128	40	9741
E Manufacture of chemicals and chemical petroleum, coal, rubber and plastic products	8969	...	7987	3937	82	20811	9304	...	11262	4159	90	24635
F Manufacture of non-metallic mineral products, except products of petroleum and coal	1793	...	1156	58	11	2996	1870	...	1381	61	18	3294
G Basic metal industries	2116	...	825	47	19	2969	2134	...	1491	52	26	3651
H Manufacture of fabricated metal products, machinery and equipment	20688	...	5716	373	302	26475	20427	...	6444	342	321	26892
I Other manufacturing industries	1227	...	494	19	17	1723	1274	...	491	14	18	1761
4 Electricity, gas and water	2874	...	5068	50	35	7957	2950	...	5060	50	61	7999
A Electricity, gas and steam	2352	...	4232	46	30	6600	2380	...	4210	48	51	6587
B Water works and supply	522	...	836	4	5	1357	570	...	850	2	10	1412
5 Construction	17063	...	4716	244	181	21842	18368	...	6323	245	212	24724
6 Wholesale and retail trade, restaurants and hotels a	33693	...	29478	864	242	63793	35229	...	30399	888	278	66238
A Wholesale and retail trade	30575	...	25639	763	230	56747	31945	...	26391	794	264	58866
B Restaurants and hotels	3118	...	3839	101	12	7046	3284	...	4008	94	14	7372
7 Transport, storage and communication	18762	...	11968	413	3426	27717	19136	...	12997	459	3451	29141
A Transport and storage	14219	...	8051	374	3419	19225	14555	...	8700	420	3444	20231
B Communication	4543	...	3917	39	7	8492	4581	...	4297	39	7	8910
8 Finance, insurance, real estate and business services b	29480	...	53603	4507	4867	82723	31079	...	56458	4802	4811	87528
A Financial institutions	7482	...	8097	219	450	15348	7765	...	8611	216	462	16130

1294

4.3 Cost Components of Value Added
(Continued)

Million Netherlands guilders

	1987						1988					
	Compensation of Employees	Capital Consumption	Net Operating Surplus	Indirect Taxes	Less: Subsidies Received	Value Added	Compensation of Employees	Capital Consumption	Net Operating Surplus	Indirect Taxes	Less: Subsidies Received	Value Added
B Insurance	4026	...	1023	688	-	5737	4200	...	759	756	-	5715
C Real estate and business services	17972	...	44483	3600	4417	61638	19114	...	47088	3830	4349	65683
Real estate, except dwellings	581	...	5606	252	...	6439	595	...	5368	335	...	6298
Dwellings	1059	...	30884	1221	4280	28884	1131	...	32192	1262	4259	30326
9 Community, social and personal services	33559	...	14146	494	1023	47176	34449	...	14555	582	958	48628
A Sanitary and similar services	...	...	...	...	...	...	...	...	...	...	...	...
B Social and related community services	25740	...	10535	245	889	35631	26272	...	10636	281	853	36336
Educational services	...	...	...	...	...	...	...	...	...	...	...	...
Medical, dental, other health and veterinary services	14643	...	8614	189	787	22659	14908	...	8813	205	745	23181
C Recreational and cultural services	4019	...	2161	164	106	6238	4155	...	2238	163	63	6493
D Personal and household services	3800	...	1450	85	28	5307	4022	...	1681	138	42	5799
Statistical discrepancy	-	...	-	-	-	-	-	...	-	-	-	-
Total, Industries c	191901	...	173546	16179	18121	363505	198501	...	183017	16699	17604	380613
Producers of Government Services	46048	...	3074	351	...	49473	45725	...	3197	357	...	49279
Other Producers d	1413	...	...	...	...	1413	1510	...	...	...	...	1510
Total c	239360	...	176620	16530	18120	414390	245740	...	186210	17050	17600	431400
Less: Imputed bank service charge	...	...	16540	...	...	16540	...	...	17450	...	...	17450
Import duties e	...	...	...	7010	1070	5940	...	...	...	6840	1250	5590
Value added tax	...	...	1710	34710	...	36420	...	...	1200	36250	...	37450
Other adjustments f	...	...	...	370	...	370	...	...	...	420	...	420
Total c	239360	...	161790	58620	19190	440580	245740	...	169960	60560	18850	457410

	1989						1990					
	Compensation of Employees	Capital Consumption	Net Operating Surplus	Indirect Taxes	Less: Subsidies Received	Value Added	Compensation of Employees	Capital Consumption	Net Operating Surplus	Indirect Taxes	Less: Subsidies Received	Value Added
All Producers												
1 Agriculture, hunting, forestry and fishing	3036	...	17022	1213	600	20671	3260	...	16729	1070	470	20589
A Agriculture and hunting	2827	...	16642	1208	599	20078	3028	...	16377	1063	470	19998
B Forestry and logging		...						...				
C Fishing	209	...	380	5	1	593	232	...	352	7	...	591
2 Mining and quarrying	895	...	12322	74	3	13288	963	...	14204	85	3	15249
A Coal mining	...	...	...	...	...	...	...	...	...	...	...	...
B Crude petroleum and natural gas production	702	...	11451	67	1	12219	747	...	13292	78	1	14116
C Metal ore mining	...	...	...	...	...	...	...	...	...	...	...	...
D Other mining	193	...	871	7	2	1069	216	...	912	7	2	1133

Netherlands

Million Netherlands guilders

	Compensation of Employees	Capital Consumption	Net Operating Surplus	Indirect Taxes	Less: Subsidies Received	Value Added	Compensation of Employees	Capital Consumption	Net Operating Surplus	Indirect Taxes	Less: Subsidies Received	Value Added
	1989						1990					
3 Manufacturing	54367	...	34628	8754	5202	92547	57676	...	36340	9877	4348	99545
A Manufacture of food, beverages and tobacco	8365	...	5597	3808	4514	13256	8810	...	7402	3850	3614	16448
B Textile, wearing apparel and leather industries	2048	...	977	39	21	3043	2133	...	1087	32	22	3230
C Manufacture of wood and wood products, including furniture	1657	...	808	45	12	2498	1775	...	851	41	13	2654
D Manufacture of paper and paper products, printing and publishing	6560	...	3662	116	45	10293	6938	...	4049	105	49	11043
E Manufacture of chemicals and chemical petroleum, coal, rubber and plastic products	9494	...	11506	4230	124	25106	10008	...	10692	5431	123	26008
F Manufacture of non-metallic mineral products, except products of petroleum and coal	1938	...	1472	62	24	3448	2040	...	1472	55	26	3541
G Basic metal industries	2161	...	2042	64	31	4236	2244	...	1216	51	33	3478
H Manufacture of fabricated metal products, machinery and equipment	20788	...	7942	362	404	28688	22287	...	8971	294	439	31113
I Other manufacturing industries	1356	...	622	28	27	1979	1441	...	600	18	29	2030
4 Electricity, gas and water	3018	...	5128	62	59	8149	3169	...	5368	170	59	8648
A Electricity, gas and steam	2424	...	4271	56	49	6702	...	...	...	...	...	7153
B Water works and supply	594	...	857	6	10	1447	...	...	...	...	...	1495
5 Construction	19022	...	6887	265	276	25898	20360	...	7603	269	298	27934
6 Wholesale and retail trade, restaurants and hotels a	36742	...	32913	954	233	70376	40437	...	34959	969	240	76125
A Wholesale and retail trade	33168	...	28247	843	214	62044	36457	...	29787	853	219	66878
B Restaurants and hotels	3574	...	4666	111	19	8332	3980	...	5172	116	21	9247
7 Transport, storage and communication	19820	...	13907	519	3473	30773	21163	...	14163	520	3816	32030
A Transport and storage	14790	...	9472	483	3466	21279	15849	...	9428	485	3808	21954
B Communication	5030	...	4435	36	7	9494	5314	...	4735	35	8	10076
8 Finance, insurance, real estate and business services b	33260	...	63553	5048	5286	96575	35771	...	65831	5074	5286	101390
A Financial institutions	7918	...	9499	241	438	17220	8354	...	8559	200	431	16682
B Insurance	4317	...	1987	799	-	7103	4515	...	1644	813	-	6972
C Real estate and business services	21025	...	52067	4008	4848	72252	22902	...	55628	4061	4855	77736
Real estate, except dwellings	589	...	6204	333	...	7126	644	...	6813	340	...	7797
Dwellings	1141	...	34524	1307	4740	32232	1225	...	36383	1335	4746	34197
9 Community, social and personal services	35094	...	15192	561	1024	49823	37634	...	15703	543	1063	52817
A Sanitary and similar services	...	...	...	...	...	...	...	...	...	...	...	...
B Social and related community services	26823	...	11138	266	887	37340	28748	...	11503	240	920	39571
Educational services	...	...	...	...	...	...	...	...	...	...	...	...
Medical, dental, other health and veterinary services	15268	...	9158	183	766	23843	16316	...	9657	159	803	25329
C Recreational and cultural services	4174	...	2278	178	82	6548	4470	...	2311	181	88	6874
D Personal and household services	4097	...	1776	117	55	5935	4416	...	1889	122	55	6372
Statistical discrepancy	-	...	-	-	-	-	-	...	-	-	-	-
Total, Industries c	205254	...	201552	17450	16156	408100	220433	...	210900	18577	15583	434327
Producers of Government Services	45991	...	3367	387	...	49745	47865	...	3522	383	...	51770
Other Producers d	1610	...	...	...	...	1610	1696	...	...	...	...	1696
Total c	252850	...	204920	17840	16160	459450	269990	...	214430	18960	15580	487800
Less: Imputed bank service charge	...	...	18030	...	...	18030	...	...	18060	...	...	18060
Import duties e	...	...	...	6950	580	6370	...	...	...	7380	280	7100
Value added tax	...	...	1300	35180	...	36480	...	...	970	38170	...	39140
Other adjustments f	...	...	...	400	...	400	...	...	...	340	...	340
Total c	252850	...	188190	60370	16740	484670	269990	...	197340	64850	15860	516320

4.3 Cost Components of Value Added

Million Netherlands guilders

		1991				
	Compensation of Employees	Capital Consumption	Net Operating Surplus	Indirect Taxes	Less: Subsidies Received	Value Added
				All Producers		
1 Agriculture, hunting, forestry and fishing	3464	...	17276	1101	577	21264
A Agriculture and hunting	3218	...	16896	1094	577	20631
B Forestry and logging		...				
C Fishing	246	...	380	7	...	633
2 Mining and quarrying	1010	...	17680	109	3	18796
A Coal mining	...	...	...	...	...	...
B Crude petroleum and natural gas production	799	...	16685	100	1	17583
C Metal ore mining	...	...	...	...	...	...
D Other mining	211	...	995	9	2	1213
3 Manufacturing	59862	...	36437	10951	5271	101979
A Manufacture of food, beverages and tobacco	9293	...	7094	3941	4657	15671
B Textile, wearing apparel and leather industries	2183	...	1033	35	19	3232
C Manufacture of wood and wood products, including furniture	1900	...	1038	47	10	2975
D Manufacture of paper and paper products, printing and publishing	7346	...	4192	117	39	11616
E Manufacture of chemicals and chemical petroleum, coal, rubber and plastic products	10469	...	10568	6342	106	27273
F Manufacture of non-metallic mineral products, except products of petroleum and coal	2104	...	1542	65	21	3690
G Basic metal industries	2314	...	550	58	29	2893
H Manufacture of fabricated metal products, machinery and equipment	22730	...	9642	325	367	32330
I Other manufacturing industries	1523	...	778	21	23	2299
4 Electricity, gas and water	3360	...	5690	305	60	9295
A Electricity, gas and steam	...	...	...	...	...	7748
B Water works and supply	...	...	...	...	...	1547
5 Construction	20981	...	7900	291	246	28926
6 Wholesale and retail trade, restaurants and hotels [a]	43613	...	34425	1050	207	78881
A Wholesale and retail trade	39352	...	28907	922	190	68991
B Restaurants and hotels	4261	...	5518	128	17	9890
7 Transport, storage and communication	22545	...	15461	557	3957	34606
A Transport and storage	16730	...	10578	518	3950	23876
B Communication	5815	...	4883	39	7	10730
8 Finance, insurance, real estate and business services [b]	38831	...	70387	5397	5708	108907
A Financial institutions	8877	...	9680	163	432	18288
B Insurance	4816	...	1278	883	-	6977
C Real estate and business services	25138	...	59429	4351	5276	83642
Real estate, except dwellings	713	...	7245	372	...	8330
Dwellings	1383	...	38697	1464	5167	36377
9 Community, social and personal services	40811	...	16276	632	1244	56475
A Sanitary and similar services	...	...	...	...	...	...
B Social and related community services	31214	...	12079	273	1104	42462
Educational services	...	...	...	...	...	...
Medical, dental, other health and veterinary services	17779	...	10400	181	988	27372
C Recreational and cultural services	4692	...	2406	224	84	7238
D Personal and household services	4905	...	1791	135	56	6775
Statistical discrepancy	-	...	-	-		-

Netherlands

4.3 Cost Components of Value Added
(Continued)

Million Netherlands guilders

	1991					
	Compensation of Employees	Capital Consumption	Net Operating Surplus	Indirect Taxes	Less: Subsidies Received	Value Added
Total, Industries c	234477	...	221532	20393	17273	459129
Producers of Government Services	49374	...	3666	400	...	53440
Other Producers d	1778	...	...	...	...	1778
Total c	285630	...	225190	20790	17270	514340
Less: Imputed bank service charge	...	...	19930	...	...	19930
Import duties e	...	...	...	7840	320	7520
Value added tax	...	...	990	40270	...	41260
Other adjustments f	...	...	...	370	...	370
Total c	285630	...	206250	69270	17590	543560

a) For the first series, repair services are included in item 'Community, social and personal services'.

b) For the years 1990 and 1991, real estate brokers are included in item 'Wholesale and retail trade, restaurants and hotels'.

c) Column 'Consumption of fixed capital' is included in column 'Net operating surplus'.

d) Beginning 1987 of the second series, item 'Other producers' includes only domestic services of households; private non-profit services to households are included in various industries above.

e) Beginning 1987 of the new series, item 'Import duties' includes all taxes linked to imports (excluding VAT) less import subsidies.

f) Beginning 1987 of the new series, item 'Other adjustments' includes only levies on fixed capital goods.

Netherlands Antilles

Source. Reply to the United Nations National Accounts Questionnaire from the Bureau Voor de Statistiek, Curacao. Official estimates together with detailed information on concepts, definitions, sources and methods of estimation utilized are published in 'Nationale Rekeningen, 1975'. The estimates beginning 1979 exclude Aruba.

General note. The official estimates have been adjusted by the Bureau to conform to the United Nations System of National Accounts so far as the existing data would permit. It should be noted that estimates for Aruba and Windward Islands are not included.

1.1 Expenditure on the Gross Domestic Product, in Current Prices

Million Netherlands Antillian guilders

	1980	1981	1982	1983	1984	1985	1986	1987	1988	1989	1990	1991
1 Government final consumption expenditure	420.3	474.9	534.6	574.4	613.2	626.5	...	...	...	...	...	...
2 Private final consumption expenditure	1120.1	1266.6	1390.5	1391.5	1386.4	1375.5	...	...	...	...	...	...
3 Gross capital formation	287.4	329.6	310.2	283.4	258.4	310.2	...	...	...	...	...	...
A Increase in stocks	39.4	51.9	28.2	-10.5	-5.8	15.4	...	...	...	...	...	...
B Gross fixed capital formation	248.0	277.7	282.0	293.9	264.2	294.8	...	...	...	...	...	...
4 Exports of goods and services a	1456.9	1547.3	1587.0	1404.6	1319.5	1308.4	...	...	...	...	...	...
5 Less: Imports of goods and services a	1726.2	1823.6	1903.1	1744.3	1648.7	1655.0	...	...	...	...	...	...
Equals: Gross Domestic Product	1558.5	1794.8	1919.2	1909.6	1928.8	1965.6	...	...	...	...	...	...

a) Exports and imports of merchandise are recorded on the basis of the crossing of frontiers. No data are available on the basis of changes in the ownership of the goods. Imports and exports are recorded on a cash basis and the imports and exports of oil refineries are not included in the estimates.

1.3 Cost Components of the Gross Domestic Product

Million Netherlands Antillian guilders

	1980	1981	1982	1983	1984	1985	1986	1987	1988	1989	1990	1991
1 Indirect taxes, net	137.5	131.8	123.3	...	...	...	...	...	...	...	...	...
A Indirect taxes	188.2	183.2	200.7	...	...	...	...	...	...	...	...	...
B Less: Subsidies	50.7	51.4	77.4	...	...	...	...	...	...	...	...	...
2 Consumption of fixed capital	158.1	187.4	206.1	...	...	...	...	...	...	...	...	...
3 Compensation of employees paid by resident producers to: a	1442.1	1681.5	1865.8	...	...	...	...	...	...	...	...	...
A Resident households	1403.3	1645.0	1823.6	...	...	...	...	...	...	...	...	...
B Rest of the world	38.8	36.5	42.2	...	...	...	...	...	...	...	...	...
4 Operating surplus	336.3	403.4	362.7	...	...	...	...	...	...	...	...	...
Equals: Gross Domestic Product a	2074.0	2404.1	2557.9	...	...	...	...	...	...	...	...	...

a) The oil refineries in the Netherlands Antilles are now considered non-resident producers. Consequently, their compensation of employees to resident households is treated as wages and salaries paid by the rest of the world. Other cost components of these oil refineries are not included in GDP.

1.4 General Government Current Receipts and Disbursements

Million Netherlands Antillian guilders

	1980	1981	1982	1983	1984	1985	1986	1987	1988	1989	1990	1991
Receipts												
1 Operating surplus	-	-	-	...	...	...	...	...	...	...	...	...
2 Property and entrepreneurial income	8.2	28.5	12.7	...	...	...	...	...	...	...	...	...
3 Taxes, fees and contributions	608.5	707.6	741.1	...	...	...	...	...	...	...	...	...
A Indirect taxes	188.2	183.2	200.7	...	...	...	...	...	...	...	...	...
B Direct taxes a	328.7	409.7	410.7	...	...	...	...	...	...	...	...	...
C Social security contributions	86.1	107.5	124.4	...	...	...	...	...	...	...	...	...
D Compulsory fees, fines and penalties	5.5	7.2	5.3	...	...	...	...	...	...	...	...	...
4 Other current transfers a	215.3	289.1	434.5	...	...	...	...	...	...	...	...	...
Total Current Receipts of General Government	832.0	1025.2	1188.3	...	...	...	...	...	...	...	...	...
Disbursements												
1 Government final consumption expenditure	568.3	649.1	726.7	...	...	...	...	...	...	...	...	...
A Compensation of employees	395.5	469.1	536.4	...	...	...	...	...	...	...	...	...
B Consumption of fixed capital	8.1	9.9	11.1	...	...	...	...	...	...	...	...	...
C Purchases of goods and services, net	173.3	179.9	191.0	...	...	...	...	...	...	...	...	...
D Less: Own account fixed capital formation	9.1	10.4	12.4	...	...	...	...	...	...	...	...	...
E Indirect taxes paid, net	0.5	0.6	0.6	...	...	...	...	...	...	...	...	...
2 Property income	31.0	33.4	39.4	...	...	...	...	...	...	...	...	...
A Interest	31.0	33.4	39.4	...	...	...	...	...	...	...	...	...
B Net land rent and royalties	-	-	-	...	...	...	...	...	...	...	...	...

Netherlands Antilles

1.4 General Government Current Receipts and Disbursements
(Continued)

	1980	1981	1982	1983	1984	1985	1986	1987	1988	1989	1990	1991
3　Subsidies	50.7	51.4	77.4	...	...	...	...	...	...	...	...	...
4　Other current transfers	172.3	206.0	236.1	...	...	...	...	...	...	...	...	...
A　Social security benefits	80.4	102.2	116.3	...	...	...	...	...	...	...	...	...
B　Social assistance grants	25.2	30.2	35.6	...	...	...	...	...	...	...	...	...
C　Other	66.7	73.6	84.2	...	...	...	...	...	...	...	...	...
5　Net saving	9.7	85.3	108.7	...	...	...	...	...	...	...	...	...
Total Current Disbursements and Net Saving of General Government	832.0	1025.2	1188.3	...	...	...	...	...	...	...	...	...

a) The profit taxes paid by the petroleum refineries and the off-shore companies are now considered as current transfers from the rest of the world.

1.7 External Transactions on Current Account, Summary

	1980	1981	1982	1983	1984	1985	1986	1987	1988	1989	1990	1991
Payments to the Rest of the World												
1　Imports of goods and services [a]	2186.6	2313.9	2311.1	...	...	...	...	...	...	...	...	...
A　Imports of merchandise c.i.f.	1610.0	1531.2	1636.4	...	...	...	...	...	...	...	...	...
B　Other	576.6	782.7	674.7	...	...	...	...	...	...	...	...	...
2　Factor income to the rest of the world	141.0	110.8	111.8	...	...	...	...	...	...	...	...	...
A　Compensation of employees	38.8	36.5	42.2	...	...	...	...	...	...	...	...	...
B　Property and entrepreneurial income	102.2	74.3	69.6	...	...	...	...	...	...	...	...	...
By general government	21.8	17.9	17.2	...	...	...	...	...	...	...	...	...
By corporate and quasi-corporate enterprises	80.4	56.4	52.4	...	...	...	...	...	...	...	...	...
By other	-	-	-	...	...	...	...	...	...	...	...	...
3　Current transfers to the rest of the world	57.4	69.4	90.9	...	...	...	...	...	...	...	...	...
A　Indirect taxes to supranational organizations	-	-	-	...	...	...	...	...	...	...	...	...
B　Other current transfers	57.4	69.4	90.9	...	...	...	...	...	...	...	...	...
4　Surplus of the nation on current transactions	-89.0	44.0	109.2	...	...	...	...	...	...	...	...	...
Payments to the Rest of the World and Surplus of the Nation on Current Transactions	2296.0	2538.1	2623.0	...	...	...	...	...	...	...	...	...
Receipts From The Rest of the World												
1　Exports of goods and services [a]	1791.2	1886.5	1787.6	...	...	...	...	...	...	...	...	...
A　Exports of merchandise f.o.b.	243.8	191.7	179.0	...	...	...	...	...	...	...	...	...
B　Other	1547.4	1694.8	1608.6	...	...	...	...	...	...	...	...	...
2　Factor income from rest of the world	288.6	360.1	416.6	...	...	...	...	...	...	...	...	...
A　Compensation of employees [b]	231.6	255.4	287.5	...	...	...	...	...	...	...	...	...
B　Property and entrepreneurial income	57.0	104.7	129.1	...	...	...	...	...	...	...	...	...
By general government	-	-	-	...	...	...	...	...	...	...	...	...
By corporate and quasi-corporate enterprises	39.2	33.5	41.9	...	...	...	...	...	...	...	...	...
By other	17.8	71.2	87.2	...	...	...	...	...	...	...	...	...
3　Current transfers from rest of the world	216.2	291.5	418.8	...	...	...	...	...	...	...	...	...
A　Subsidies from supranational organisations	-	-	-	...	...	...	...	...	...	...	...	...
B　Other current transfers	216.2	291.5	418.8	...	...	...	...	...	...	...	...	...
Receipts from the Rest of the World on Current Transactions	2296.0	2538.1	2623.0	...	...	...	...	...	...	...	...	...

a) Exports and imports of merchandise are recorded on the basis of the crossing of frontiers. No data are available on the basis of changes in the ownership of the goods. Imports and exports are recorded on a cash basis and the imports and exports of oil refineries are not included in the estimates.

b) The oil refineries in the Netherlands Antilles are now considered non-resident producers. Consequently, their compensation of employees to resident households is treated as wages and salaries paid by the rest of the world. Other cost components of these oil refineries are not included in GDP.

1.8 Capital Transactions of The Nation, Summary

Million Netherlands Antillian guilders

	1980	1981	1982	1983	1984	1985	1986	1987	1988	1989	1990	1991
Finance of Gross Capital Formation												
Gross saving	344.3	523.5	572.6	...	...	...	...	...	...	...	...	...
1 Consumption of fixed capital	158.1	187.4	206.1	...	...	...	...	...	...	...	...	...
A General government	8.1	9.9	11.1	...	...	...	...	...	...	...	...	...
B Corporate and quasi-corporate enterprises	150.0	177.5	195.0	...	...	...	...	...	...	...	...	...
C Other	...	...	...	...	...	...	...	...	...	...	...	...
2 Net saving	186.2	336.1	366.5	...	...	...	...	...	...	...	...	...
A General government	9.7	85.3	108.8	...	...	...	...	...	...	...	...	...
B Corporate and quasi-corporate enterprises	176.5	250.8	257.7	...	...	...	...	...	...	...	...	...
C Other	...	...	...	...	...	...	...	...	...	...	...	...
Less: Surplus of the nation on current transactions	-89.0	44.0	109.2	...	...	...	...	...	...	...	...	...
Finance of Gross Capital Formation	433.3	479.5	463.4	...	...	...	...	...	...	...	...	...
Gross Capital Formation												
Increase in stocks	49.3	64.9	35.3	...	...	...	...	...	...	...	...	...
Gross fixed capital formation	384.0	414.6	428.1	...	...	...	...	...	...	...	...	...
1 General government	44.9	39.4	51.0	...	...	...	...	...	...	...	...	...
2 Corporate and quasi-corporate enterprises	339.1	375.2	377.1	...	...	...	...	...	...	...	...	...
3 Other	...	...	...	...	...	...	...	...	...	...	...	...
Gross Capital Formation	433.3	479.5	463.4	...	...	...	...	...	...	...	...	...

1.9 Gross Domestic Product by Institutional Sectors of Origin

Million Netherlands Antillian guilders

	1980	1981	1982	1983	1984	1985	1986	1987	1988	1989	1990	1991
Domestic Factor Incomes Originating												
1 General government	395.5	469.1	536.4	...	...	...	...	...	...	...	...	...
2 Corporate and quasi-corporate enterprises				...	...	...	...	...	...	...	...	...
3 Households and private unincorporated enterprises	1382.9	1615.8	1692.1	...	...	...	...	...	...	...	...	...
4 Non-profit institutions serving households				...	...	...	...	...	...	...	...	...
Subtotal: Domestic Factor Incomes	1778.4	2084.9	2228.5	...	...	...	...	...	...	...	...	...
Indirect taxes, net	137.5	131.8	123.3	...	...	...	...	...	...	...	...	...
A Indirect taxes	188.2	183.2	200.7	...	...	...	...	...	...	...	...	...
B Less: Subsidies	50.7	51.4	77.4	...	...	...	...	...	...	...	...	...
Consumption of fixed capital	158.1	187.4	206.1	...	...	...	...	...	...	...	...	...
Gross Domestic Product	2074.0	2404.1	2557.9	...	...	...	...	...	...	...	...	...

1.10 Gross Domestic Product by Kind of Activity, in Current Prices

Million Netherlands Antillian guilders

	1980	1981	1982	1983	1984	1985	1986	1987	1988	1989	1990	1991
1 Agriculture, hunting, forestry and fishing	10.1	9.7	10.4	14.8	19.8	18.5	...	...	...	...	...	...
2 Mining and quarrying							...	...	...	...	...	...
3 Manufacturing	135.8	147.1	152.9	144.6	137.2	138.9	...	...	...	...	...	...
4 Electricity, gas and water	20.4	44.6	48.7	62.6	71.5	66.2	...	...	...	...	...	...
5 Construction	157.5	145.9	160.5	170.5	174.9	156.4	...	...	...	...	...	...
6 Wholesale and retail trade, restaurants and hotels	328.4	402.5	446.0	415.6	416.8	453.5	...	...	...	...	...	...
7 Transport, storage and communication	313.2	328.5	281.5	244.5	214.6	212.6	...	...	...	...	...	...
8 Finance, insurance, real estate and business services	232.2	283.1	314.4	340.4	343.5	341.9	...	...	...	...	...	...
9 Community, social and personal services	103.2	128.0	156.2	167.3	175.3	177.1	...	...	...	...	...	...

Netherlands Antilles

1.10 Gross Domestic Product by Kind of Activity, in Current Prices
(Continued)

Million Netherlands Antillian guilders

	1980	1981	1982	1983	1984	1985	1986	1987	1988	1989	1990	1991
Total, Industries	1300.8	1489.4	1570.6	1560.3	1553.6	1565.1	...	...	...	...	...	...
Producers of Government Services	303.3	356.3	405.2	419.8	444.5	466.9	...	...	...	...	...	...
Other Producers	...	...	...	...	...	...	...	...	...	...	...	...
Subtotal	1604.1	1845.7	1975.8	1980.1	1998.1	2032.0	...	...	...	...	...	...
Less: Imputed bank service charge	45.6	50.9	56.6	70.5	69.3	66.4	...	...	...	...	...	...
Plus: Import duties	...	...	...	...	...	...	...	...	...	...	...	...
Plus: Value added tax	...	...	...	...	...	...	...	...	...	...	...	...
Equals: Gross Domestic Product	1558.5	1794.8	1919.2	1909.6	1928.8	1965.6	...	...	...	...	...	...

1.12 Relations Among National Accounting Aggregates

Million Netherlands Antillian guilders

	1980	1981	1982	1983	1984	1985	1986	1987	1988	1989	1990	1991
Gross Domestic Product	2074.0	2404.1	2557.9	...	...	...	...	...	...	...	...	...
Plus: Net factor income from the rest of the world	147.6	249.3	304.8	...	...	...	...	...	...	...	...	...
Factor income from the rest of the world	288.6	360.1	416.6	...	...	...	...	...	...	...	...	...
Less: Factor income to the rest of the world	141.0	110.8	111.8	...	...	...	...	...	...	...	...	...
Equals: Gross National Product	2221.6	2653.4	2862.7	...	...	...	...	...	...	...	...	...
Less: Consumption of fixed capital	158.1	187.4	206.1	...	...	...	...	...	...	...	...	...
Equals: National Income	2063.5	2466.0	2656.6	...	...	...	...	...	...	...	...	...
Plus: Net current transfers from the rest of the world	158.8	222.1	327.9	...	...	...	...	...	...	...	...	...
Current transfers from the rest of the world	216.2	291.5	418.8	...	...	...	...	...	...	...	...	...
Less: Current transfers to the rest of the world	57.4	69.4	90.9	...	...	...	...	...	...	...	...	...
Equals: National Disposable Income	2222.3	2688.1	2984.5	...	...	...	...	...	...	...	...	...
Less: Final consumption	2036.1	2352.0	2618.0	...	...	...	...	...	...	...	...	...
Equals: Net Saving	186.2	336.1	366.5	...	...	...	...	...	...	...	...	...
Less: Surplus of the nation on current transactions	-89.0	44.0	109.2	...	...	...	...	...	...	...	...	...
Equals: Net Capital Formation	275.2	292.1	257.3	...	...	...	...	...	...	...	...	...

2.1 Government Final Consumption Expenditure by Function, in Current Prices

Million Netherlands Antillian guilders

	1980	1981	1982	1983	1984	1985	1986	1987	1988	1989	1990	1991
1 General public services	82.1	106.6	130.3	...	...	...	...	...	...	...	...	...
2 Defence	20.5	10.9	1.7	...	...	...	...	...	...	...	...	...
3 Public order and safety	49.7	69.1	81.6	...	...	...	...	...	...	...	...	...
4 Education	150.9	179.7	198.4	...	...	...	...	...	...	...	...	...
5 Health a	42.0	48.2	51.6	...	...	...	...	...	...	...	...	...
6 Social security and welfare	101.2	114.7	130.1	...	...	...	...	...	...	...	...	...
7 Housing and community amenities a	...	...	...	...	...	...	...	...	...	...	...	...
8 Recreational, cultural and religious affairs	12.3	14.8	16.6	...	...	...	...	...	...	...	...	...
9 Economic services	66.0	66.2	69.5	...	...	...	...	...	...	...	...	...
A Fuel and energy				...	...	...	...	...	...	...	...	...
B Agriculture, forestry, fishing and hunting	37.5	45.2	44.2	...	...	...	...	...	...	...	...	...
C Mining, manufacturing and construction, except fuel and energy				...	...	...	...	...	...	...	...	...
D Transportation and communication	28.5	21.0	25.3	...	...	...	...	...	...	...	...	...
E Other economic affairs	-	-	-	...	...	...	...	...	...	...	...	...
10 Other functions	43.6	38.9	46.9	...	...	...	...	...	...	...	...	...
Total Government Final Consumption Expenditure b	568.3	649.1	726.7	...	...	...	...	...	...	...	...	...

a) Housing and community amenities are included in health.
b) The estimates of government final consumption expenditure include estimates of non-commodity sales and commodities produced for which there is no available breakdown.

2.3 Total Government Outlays by Function and Type

Million Netherlands Antillian guilders

	Final Consumption Expenditures			Subsidies	Other Current Transfers & Property Income	Total Current Disbursements	Gross Capital Formation	Other Capital Outlays	Total Outlays
	Total	Compensation of Employees	Other						
1980									
1 General public services a	82.1	67.3	14.8	-	38.1	120.2	9.4	...	...
2 Defence	20.5	-	20.5	-		20.5	-	...	...
3 Public order and safety	49.7	43.4	6.3	-	-	49.7	5.2	...	...
4 Education	150.9	131.6	19.3	-	14.8	165.7	10.5	...	...
5 Health b	42.0	28.4	13.6	1.4	-	43.4	3.1	...	...
6 Social security and welfare	101.2	43.0	58.2	-	108.7	209.9	0.3	...	...
7 Housing and community amenities b	...	...	...	...	...	...	...	...	...
8 Recreation, culture and religion	12.3	6.9	5.4	-	2.1	14.4	2.0	...	...
9 Economic services	66.0	32.5	33.5	49.2	-	115.2	13.1	...	...
A Fuel and energy								...	...
B Agriculture, forestry, fishing and hunting	37.5	24.4	13.1	48.5	-	86.0	6.0		
C Mining (except fuels), manufacturing and construction								...	...
D Transportation and communication	28.5	8.1	20.4	0.7	-	29.2	7.1	...	...
E Other economic affairs	-	-	-	-	-	-	-	...	...
10 Other functions	43.6	35.7	7.9	0.1	39.6	83.3	1.3	...	...
Total c	568.3	388.8	179.5	50.7	203.3	822.3	44.9	64.9	932.1
1981									
1 General public services a	106.6	84.7	21.9	-	41.6	148.2	8.5	...	...
2 Defence	10.9	0.1	10.8	-	-	10.9	-	...	...
3 Public order and safety	69.1	60.0	9.1	-	-	69.1	2.0	...	...
4 Education	179.7	157.3	22.4	-	16.8	196.5	6.8	...	...
5 Health b	48.2	33.4	14.8	-	-	48.2	4.8	...	...
6 Social security and welfare	114.7	45.0	69.7	0.4	136.7	251.8	1.2	...	...
7 Housing and community amenities b	...	...	...	...	...	...	...	...	...
8 Recreation, culture and religion	14.8	8.0	6.8	0.2	2.0	17.0	3.6	...	...
9 Economic services	66.2	38.6	27.6	50.5	-	116.7	9.7	...	...
A Fuel and energy								...	...
B Agriculture, forestry, fishing and hunting	45.2	28.3	16.9	45.3	-	90.5	6.6		
C Mining (except fuels), manufacturing and construction								...	...
D Transportation and communication	21.0	10.3	10.7	5.2	-	26.2	3.1	...	...
E Other economic affairs	-	-	-	-	-	-	-	...	...
10 Other functions	38.9	34.1	4.8	0.3	42.3	81.5	2.8	...	...
Total c	649.1	461.2	187.9	51.4	239.4	939.9	39.4	63.3	1042.6
1982									
1 General public services a	130.2	103.1	27.1	-	50.2	180.4	7.3	...	...
2 Defence	1.7	0.1	1.6	-	-	1.7	-	...	...
3 Public order and safety	81.6	69.4	12.2	-	-	81.6	2.5	...	...
4 Education	198.4	172.9	25.5	-	15.8	214.2	6.0	...	...
5 Health b	51.7	38.5	13.2	5.5	-	57.2	10.2	...	...
6 Social security and welfare	130.1	52.1	78.0	-	156.8	286.9	0.4	...	...
7 Housing and community amenities b	...	...	...	...	...	...	...	...	...
8 Recreation, culture and religion	16.6	9.6	7.0	0.3	2.4	19.3	8.4	...	...
9 Economic services	69.5	43.7	25.8	70.7	-	140.2	13.3	...	...

Netherlands Antilles

2.3 Total Government Outlays by Function and Type
(Continued)

Million Netherlands Antillian guilders

	Final Consumption Expenditures			Subsidies	Other Current Transfers & Property Income	Total Current Disbursements	Gross Capital Formation	Other Capital Outlays	Total Outlays
	Total	Compensation of Employees	Other						
A Fuel and energy								...	...
B Agriculture, forestry, fishing and hunting	44.2	31.0	13.2	63.9	-	108.1	9.6		
C Mining (except fuels), manufacturing and construction								...	...
D Transportation and communication	25.3	12.7	12.6	6.8	-	32.1	3.7	...	...
E Other economic affairs	-	-	-	-	-	-	-	...	...
10 Other functions	46.9	38.5	8.4	0.9	50.3	98.1	2.9		...
Total c	726.7	527.9	198.8	77.4	275.5	1079.6	51.0	72.4	1203.0

a) General public services of column 5 includes the total amount of unfunded employee pension and welfare benefits for which there is no available breakdown.
b) Housing and community amenities are included in health.
c) The estimates of government final consumption expenditure include estimates of non-commodity sales and commodities produced for which there is no available breakdown.

2.17 Exports and Imports of Goods and Services, Detail

Million Netherlands Antillian guilders

	1980	1981	1982	1983	1984	1985	1986	1987	1988	1989	1990	1991
Exports of Goods and Services												
1 Exports of merchandise, f.o.b.	243.8	191.7	179.0	...	...	...	...	...	...	...	...	...
2 Transport and communication	493.2	474.2	377.3	...	...	...	...	...	...	...	...	...
3 Insurance service charges				...	...	...	...	...	...	...	...	...
4 Other commodities	188.8	239.9	247.4	...	...	...	...	...	...	...	...	...
5 Adjustments of merchandise exports to change-of-ownership basis	...	...	...	...	...	...	...	...	...	...	...	...
6 Direct purchases in the domestic market by non-residential households	714.7	785.7	759.4	...	...	...	...	...	...	...	...	...
7 Direct purchases in the domestic market by extraterritorial bodies	150.7	195.0	224.5	...	...	...	...	...	...	...	...	...
Total Exports of Goods and Services a	1791.2	1886.5	1787.6	...	...	...	...	...	...	...	...	...
Imports of Goods and Services												
1 Imports of merchandise, c.i.f.	1610.0	1531.2	1636.4	...	...	...	...	...	...	...	...	...
2 Adjustments of merchandise imports to change-of-ownership basis	...	...	...	...	...	...	...	...	...	...	...	...
3 Other transport and communication	113.3	165.6	153.9	...	...	...	...	...	...	...	...	...
4 Other insurance service charges	...	...	...	...	...	...	...	...	...	...	...	...
5 Other commodities	346.6	485.7	366.4	...	...	...	...	...	...	...	...	...
6 Direct purchases abroad by government	12.7	13.4	12.9	...	...	...	...	...	...	...	...	...
7 Direct purchases abroad by resident households	104.0	118.0	141.5	...	...	...	...	...	...	...	...	...
Total Imports of Goods and Services a	2186.6	2313.9	2311.1	...	...	...	...	...	...	...	...	...
Balance of Goods and Services	-395.4	-427.4	-523.5	...	...	...	...	...	...	...	...	...
Total Imports and Balance of Goods and Services	1791.2	1886.5	1787.6	...	...	...	...	...	...	...	...	...

a) Exports and imports of merchandise are recorded on the basis of the crossing of frontiers. No data are available on the basis of changes in the ownership of the goods.

New Caledonia

Source. Reply to the United Nations National Accounts Questionnaire from the Institute national de la statistique et des etudes economiques (INSEE), Paris.

the INSEE to conform to the United Nations System of National Accounts so far as the existing data would permit.

General note. The estimates shown in the following tables have been adjusted by

1.1 Expenditure on the Gross Domestic Product, in Current Prices

Million CFP francs

	1980	1981	1982	1983	1984	1985	1986	1987	1988	1989	1990	1991
1 Government final consumption expenditure ab	25334	29473	35631	39773	46037	52831	61526	62868	69654	70041	...	...
2 Private final consumption expenditure a	49575	57147	65935	68606	72488	76497	88805	92845	101420	131340	...	...
3 Gross capital formation	19772	16362	19637	19145	18405	19579	31572	40588	46590	58551	...	...
A Increase in stocks	-619	-904	-1247	-817	-2933	-1963	843	794	1006	4684	...	...
B Gross fixed capital formation	20391	17266	20884	19962	21338	21542	30729	39794	45584	53867	...	...
4 Exports of goods and services	31908	33794	30295	30964	42951	46680	27814	28547	71209	80477	...	...
5 Less: Imports of goods and services	37050	40631	43719	44763	53211	55484	58739	62524	64645	87390	...	...
Statistical discrepancy bc	1308	159	314	436	-181	-453	303	303	270	456	...	...
Equals: Gross Domestic Product	90847	96304	108093	114161	126489	139650	151281	162627	224498	253475	...	...

a) Beginning 1972, education and health are included in item 'Government final consumption expenditure' rather than in item 'Private final consumption expenditure'.
b) Government final consumption expenditure estimates are under-estimated since the system of national accounts used treats the government sector separately. Therefore this under estimation is rectified as a statistical discrepancy.
c) The accounting reconciliation is done at the level of the gross domestic production instead of gross domestic product. Therefore the statistical discrepancy reflects mainly the domestic salaries not accounted for elsewhere.

1.3 Cost Components of the Gross Domestic Product

Million CFP francs

	1980	1981	1982	1983	1984	1985	1986	1987	1988	1989	1990	1991
1 Indirect taxes, net	3159	3708	3611	3543	4400	2837	5847	9258	11028	15181	...	...
A Indirect taxes	...	7312	8036	8372	9617	8567	12439	16415	19592	22434	...	...
B Less: Subsidies	...	3604	4425	4829	5217	5730	6592	7157	8564	7253	...	...
2 Consumption of fixed capital	13694	9881	11594	10083	11482	11887	17948	20395	20357	27193	...	...
3 Compensation of employees paid by resident producers to:	55190	51492	61318	66930	73810	82201	88671	95184	105453	110493	...	...
4 Operating surplus	18804	31223	31570	33605	36797	42725	38815	37790	87660	100605	...	...
Equals: Gross Domestic Product	90847	96304	108093	114161	126489	139650	151281	162627	224498	253475	...	...

1.4 General Government Current Receipts and Disbursements

Million CFP francs

	1980	1981	1982	1983	1984	1985	1986	1987	1988	1989	1990	1991
Receipts												
1 Operating surplus	...	...	...	...	...	...	...	...	...	...	...	...
2 Property and entrepreneurial income	...	...	...	...	...	...	...	...	...	...	...	...
3 Taxes, fees and contributions	...	19268	21359	24217	28279	29095	34707	41904	52278	68480	...	...
A Indirect taxes	...	7312	8036	8372	9617	8567	12439	16415	19592	22434	...	...
B Direct taxes	...	4983	5082	6490	7417	8177	8505	9502	13689	25104	...	...
C Social security contributions	...	6973	8241	9355	11245	12351	13763	15987	18997	20942	...	...
D Compulsory fees, fines and penalties	...	...	...	...	...	...	...	...	...	...	...	...
4 Other current transfers	...	30013	35952	40370	42875	50694	63285	60449	70414	70952	...	...
Total Current Receipts of General Government	...	49281	57311	64587	71154	79789	97992	102353	122692	139432	...	...
Disbursements												
1 Government final consumption expenditure	...	29473	35631	39773	46037	52831	61526	62868	69654	70041	...	...
A Compensation of employees	...	21703	26084	29337	33679	38177	41989	43566	47924	47225	...	...
B Consumption of fixed capital	...	...	...	...	...	...	...	...	...	...	...	...
C Purchases of goods and services, net	...	6339	7840	8236	9185	11424	15449	13787	15793	15519	...	...
D Less: Own account fixed capital formation	...	...	...	...	...	...	...	...	...	...	...	...
E Indirect taxes paid, net	...	1431	1707	2200	3173	3230	4088	5515	5937	7297	...	...
2 Property income	...	...	...	...	...	...	...	...	...	...	...	...

New Caledonia

1.4 General Government Current Receipts and Disbursements
(Continued)

Million CFP francs	1980	1981	1982	1983	1984	1985	1986	1987	1988	1989	1990	1991
3 Subsidies	...	3604	4425	4829	5217	5730	6592	7157	8564	7253	...	...
4 Other current transfers	...	11663	14307	16938	18403	20746	23674	22664	29611	33605	...	...
A Social security benefits	...	3921	4713	5936	7021	7785	8165	8196	10301	11565	...	...
B Social assistance grants	...	5107	6116	6698	7588	7933	8667	9388	11734	12779	...	...
C Other	...	2635	3478	4304	3794	5028	6842	5080	7576	9261	...	...
5 Net saving	...	4541	2948	3047	1497	482	6200	9664	14863	28533	...	...
Total Current Disbursements and Net Saving of General Government		49281	57311	64587	71154	79789	97992	102353	122692	139432	...	...

1.5 Current Income and Outlay of Corporate and Quasi-Corporate Enterprises, Summary

Million CFP francs	1980	1981	1982	1983	1984	1985	1986	1987	1988	1989	1990	1991
Receipts												
1 Operating surplus	...	41104	43164	43688	48279	54612	56763	58185	108017	127798	...	...
2 Property and entrepreneurial income received	...	717	784	1675	2193	2469	2411	2628	2986	3290	...	...
3 Current transfers	...	...	...	...	...	...	...	...	...	...	...	...
Total Current Receipts	...	41821	43948	45363	50472	57081	59174	60813	111003	131088	...	...
Disbursements												
1 Property and entrepreneurial income	...	18383	20995	22286	22616	22275	24800	29231	32850	39133	...	...
2 Direct taxes and other current payments to general government	...	5534	5100	5442	5296	7372	8503	8093	12157	24022	...	...
3 Other current transfers	...	1479	2056	2192	2605	4293	3524	4872	5512	6146	...	...
4 Net saving	...	16425	15797	15443	19955	23141	22347	18617	60484	61787	...	...
Total Current Disbursements and Net Saving	...	41821	43948	45363	50472	57081	59174	60813	111003	131088	...	...

1.6 Current Income and Outlay of Households and Non-Profit Institutions

Million CFP francs	1980	1981	1982	1983	1984	1985	1986	1987	1988	1989	1990	1991
Receipts												
1 Compensation of employees	...	43801	52226	56677	61563	68901	73528	77659	84771	87716	...	...
2 Operating surplus of private unincorporated enterprises	...	18383	20995	22286	22616	22275	24800	29231	32850	39133	...	...
3 Property and entrepreneurial income	...	...	...	...	...	...	...	...	...	...	...	...
4 Current transfers	...	13070	16281	19082	20948	24992	27182	27536	35123	39559	...	...
A Social security benefits	...	3921	4713	5936	7021	7785	8165	8196	10301	11565	...	...
B Social assistance grants	...	5107	6116	6698	7588	7933	8667	9388	11734	12779	...	...
C Other	...	4042	5452	6448	6339	9274	10350	9952	13088	15215	...	...
Statistical discrepancy a	...	718	851	898	1002	949	1380	1538	1685	1838	...	...
Total Current Receipts	...	75972	90353	98943	106129	117117	126890	135964	154429	168246	...	...
Disbursements												
1 Private final consumption expenditure	...	57147	65935	68606	72488	76497	88805	92845	101420	131340	...	...
2 Property income	...	...	...	...	...	...	...	...	...	...	...	...
3 Direct taxes and other current transfers n.e.c. to general government	...	1208	2070	3010	4074	3952	3568	4216	4941	6325	...	...
A Social security contributions	...	204	241	266	327	318	402	448	494	538	...	...
B Direct taxes	...	1004	1829	2744	3747	3634	3166	3768	4447	5787	...	...
C Fees, fines and penalties	...	...	...	...	...	...	...	...	...	...	...	...
4 Other current transfers	...	2193	2955	3932	4240	5611	7109	5811	7097	8211	...	...
Statistical discrepancy a	...	718	851	898	1002	949	1380	1538	1685	1838	...	...
5 Net saving	...	14706	18542	22497	24325	30108	26028	31554	39286	20532	...	...
Total Current Disbursements and Net Saving	...	75972	90353	98943	106129	117117	126890	135964	154429	168246	...	...

a) Item 'Statistical discrepancy' refers to salaries paid by the households to their employees.

1.7 External Transactions on Current Account, Summary

Million CFP francs

	1980	1981	1982	1983	1984	1985	1986	1987	1988	1989	1990	1991
Payments to the Rest of the World												
1 Imports of goods and services	37050	40631	43719	44763	53211	55484	58739	62524	64645	87390	...	...
2 Factor income to the rest of the world	...	...	...	...	...	...	...	...	...	...	...	...
3 Current transfers to the rest of the world	470	...	...	...	...	...	...	...	...	...	...	...
4 Surplus of the nation on current transactions	18952	20238	18612	21842	27372	34152	23004	19247	68043	52301	...	...
Payments to the Rest of the World and Surplus of the Nation on Current Transactions	56472	60869	62331	66605	80583	89636	81743	81771	132688	139691	...	...
Receipts From The Rest of the World												
1 Exports of goods and services	31908	33794	30295	30964	42951	46680	27814	28547	71209	80477	...	...
2 Factor income from rest of the world	...	...	...	...	...	...	...	...	...	...	...	...
3 Current transfers from rest of the world	24565	27075	32036	35641	37632	42956	53929	53224	61479	59214	...	...
Receipts from the Rest of the World on Current Transactions	56472	60869	62331	66605	80583	89636	81743	81771	132688	139691	...	...

1.10 Gross Domestic Product by Kind of Activity, in Current Prices

Million CFP francs

	1980	1981	1982	1983	1984	1985	1986	1987	1988	1989	1990	1991
1 Agriculture, hunting, forestry and fishing	2719	1429	1820	2155	2252	2581	2831	3156	3575	4511	...	...
2 Mining and quarrying	14472	15901	13476	10591	16379	21739	11880	11445	51796	59920	...	...
3 Manufacturing	5231	4030	4985	5892	6215	6497	7812	8599	11222	11262	...	...
4 Electricity, gas and water	2319	2332	2091	2318	2491	3239	3789	4363	5723	5715	...	...
5 Construction	8279	5432	6782	5290	5301	4749	6698	6982	10712	11581	...	...
6 Wholesale and retail trade, restaurants and hotels [a]	19351	24287	28395	30483	31274	33277	40496	43167	46794	55599	...	...
7 Transport, storage and communication	3395	4288	4761	4917	4227	4741	6969	7502	8806	11443	...	...
8 Finance, insurance, real estate and business services	13377	14549	16900	19814	20169	20153	22947	26346	29830	36546	...	...
9 Community, social and personal services [a]											...	...
Total, Industries	69142	72248	79210	81460	88308	96976	103422	111560	168458	196577	...	...
Producers of Government Services	20447	23134	27791	31537	36852	41407	46077	49081	53861	54522	...	...
Other Producers	1258	922	1092	1164	1329	1267	1782	1986	2179	2376	...	...
Subtotal	90847	96304	108093	114161	126489	139650	151281	162627	224498	253475	...	...
Less: Imputed bank service charge	...	...	...	...	...	...	...	...	...	...	...	...
Plus: Import duties	...	...	...	...	...	...	...	...	...	...	...	...
Plus: Value added tax	...	...	...	...	...	...	...	...	...	...	...	...
Equals: Gross Domestic Product	90847	96304	108093	114161	126489	139650	151281	162627	224498	253475	...	...

a) Restaurants and hotels are included in item 'Community, social and personal services'.

New Zealand

Source. Reply to the United Nations National Accounts Questionnaire from the Department of Statistics, Wellington. The official estimates and descriptions are published by the Department in the 'Annual Series National Income and Expenditure' and as appendices to the 'Monthly Abstract of Statistics'.

General note. The official estimates of New Zealand have been adjusted by the Department of Statistics to conform to the United Nations System of National Accounts so far as the existing data would permit.

1.1 Expenditure on the Gross Domestic Product, in Current Prices

Million New Zealand dollars — Fiscal year beginning 1 April

	1980	1981	1982	1983	1984	1985	1986	1987	1988	1989	1990	1991
1 Government final consumption expenditure	4134	4989	5566	5858	6334	7345	8930	10128	11052	11759	12295	12138
2 Private final consumption expenditure	14181	16639	19123	20689	23395	27712	32570	37225	40733	43876	46250	46960
A Households	13961	16360	18829	20401	23076	27339	32108	36697	40156	...	...	...
B Private non-profit institutions serving households	221	278	293	288	318	373	462	528	576	...	...	...
3 Gross capital formation	4797	6887	8134	8991	11186	12004	13279	13544	13286	16717	15475	12355
A Increase in stocks a	43	290	380	544	1333	264	1171	281	396	2036	1025	313
B Gross fixed capital formation	4754	6597	7754	8447	9853	11740	12108	13263	12890	14681	14450	12042
Residential buildings	881	1180	1311	1562	1783	2057	2413	2754	2833	...	...	...
Non-residential buildings	821	1034	1165	1246	1458	1959	2402	2948	2915	...	...	...
Other construction and land improvement etc.	808	1136	1307	1363	1345	1464	1496	1254	1416	...	...	...
Other	2244	3247	3971	4277	5266	6260	5798	6306	5726	...	...	...
4 Exports of goods and services	7003	8249	9266	10507	13229	13947	15122	16663	18064	19162	20086	21470
5 Less: Imports of goods and services	7272	9168	10318	11063	14536	15325	15293	15968	16141	19670	20496	20108
Statistical discrepancy	246	394	-234	-86	-79	-248	480	274	-592	-338	-267	397
Equals: Gross Domestic Product b	23089	27990	31537	34896	39529	45435	55088	61866	66402	71506	73343	73212

a) From 1977-1981, stock valuation adjustment is made for the estimates of value of physical increase in stocks. b) Data in this table have been revised, therefore they are not strictly comparable with the unrevised data in the other tables.

1.2 Expenditure on the Gross Domestic Product, in Constant Prices

Million New Zealand dollars — Fiscal year beginning 1 April

	1980	1981	1982	1983	1984	1985	1986	1987	1988	1989	1990	1991
					At constant prices of:1982							
1 Government final consumption expenditure	5435	5535	5566	5702	5816	5905	6016	6073	6028	6023	6109	6061
2 Private final consumption expenditure	18898	19284	19123	19695	20506	20743	21516	22118	22464	22713	22535	22603
3 Gross capital formation	6309	7611	8134	8417	9603	9063	9162	9074	8818	10591	10068	7887
A Increase in stocks a	284	342	380	331	970	-83	549	-68	-112	787	466	-182
B Gross fixed capital formation	6025	7269	7754	8086	8633	9146	8613	9142	8930	9804	9602	8069
4 Exports of goods and services	8918	9124	9266	9701	10451	10592	11080	11649	11895	11517	12623	13259
5 Less: Imports of goods and services	9164	10170	10318	10290	11415	11697	12041	13450	13312	15312	15720	14916
Statistical discrepancy	-849	-403	-234	-837	-964	-294	-538	-16	-855	-53	-262	-109
Equals: Gross Domestic Product b	29547	30981	31537	32388	33997	34312	35195	35448	35038	35479	35353	34785

a) From 1977-1981, stock valuation adjustment is made for the estimates of value of physical increase in stocks. b) Data in this table have been revised, therefore they are not strictly comparable with the unrevised data in the other tables.

1.3 Cost Components of the Gross Domestic Product

Million New Zealand dollars — Fiscal year beginning 1 April

	1980	1981	1982	1983	1984	1985	1986	1987	1988	1989	1990	1991
1 Indirect taxes, net	1996	2336	2684	3214	3926	4492	6381	8618	9122	10681	10788	10472
A Indirect taxes	2344	2914	3440	3874	4524	4854	6683	8934	9297	10883	10982	10644
B Less: Subsidies	348	578	756	660	598	362	302	316	175	202	194	172
2 Consumption of fixed capital	1684	1922	2237	2661	3182	3712	4336	5051	5540	6033	6490	6861
3 Compensation of employees paid by resident producers to:	13068	15747	17237	17577	19242	22661	26824	30258	32004	32733	33180	32705
A Resident households	13068	15747	17237	17577	19242	22661	26824	30258	32004	32733	33180	32705
B Rest of the world	-	-	-	-	-	-	-	-	-	-	-	-
4 Operating surplus	6341	7986	9379	11444	13178	14570	17547	17940	19737	22057	22885	23175
Equals: Gross Domestic Product ab	23089	27991	31537	34896	39528	45435	55088	61867	66403	71504	73343	73213

a) From 1977-1981, stock valuation adjustment is made for the estimates of value of physical increase in stocks. b) Data in this table have been revised, therefore they are not strictly comparable with the unrevised data in the other tables.

1.6 Current Income and Outlay of Households and Non-Profit Institutions

Million New Zealand dollars

	1980	1981	1982	1983	1984	1985	1986	1987	1988	1989	1990	1991
									Fiscal year beginning 1 April			
Receipts												
1 Compensation of employees	...	...	17143	17443	18932	22099	26076	28857	30124	...	...	...
2 Operating surplus of private unincorporated enterprises	...	...	931	1066	1281	1990	2399	2637	3251	...	...	...
3 Property and entrepreneurial income	...	...	5482	6102	6916	8020	9077	10690	12306	...	...	...
4 Current transfers	...	...	5260	5793	6451	7970	9343	10849	12177	...	...	...
A Social security benefits	...	...	227	260	313	417	531	620	771	...	...	...
B Social assistance grants	...	...	4006	4331	4817	5986	7068	8376	9466	...	...	...
C Other	...	...	1027	1202	1321	1567	1744	1853	1940	...	...	...
Total Current Receipts a	...	...	28816	30404	33580	40079	46895	53033	57858	...	...	...
Disbursements												
1 Private final consumption expenditure	...	...	18716	20198	22857	27054	31367	35587	39143	...	...	...
2 Property income	...	...	920	1103	1350	1785	2135	2817	2872	...	...	...
3 Direct taxes and other current transfers n.e.c. to general government	...	...	6842	7040	7483	9442	11304	12238	13442	...	...	...
A Social security contributions	...	...	171	203	155	173	201	666	831	...	...	...
B Direct taxes	...	...	6608	6768	7251	9179	10992	11432	12426	...	...	...
C Fees, fines and penalties	...	...	63	69	77	90	111	140	185	...	...	...
4 Other current transfers	...	...	952	1050	1127	1371	1577	1679	1768	...	...	...
5 Net saving	...	...	1385	1013	761	426	512	713	631	...	...	...
Total Current Disbursements and Net Saving a	...	...	28815	30404	33578	40078	46895	53034	57856	...	...	...

a) The estimates refer to households only.

1.7 External Transactions on Current Account, Summary

Million New Zealand dollars

	1980	1981	1982	1983	1984	1985	1986	1987	1988	1989	1990	1991
									Fiscal year beginning 1 April			
Payments to the Rest of the World												
1 Imports of goods and services	7272	9168	10318	11063	14536	15327	15293	15968	16140	19563	20595	...
A Imports of merchandise c.i.f.	5576	7086	7887	8604	11679	11947	11397	11976	11583	14871	15498	...
B Other	1696	2082	2463	2459	2857	3380	3896	3992	4557	4692	5097	...
2 Factor income to the rest of the world	604	803	1068	1513	2152	2938	3375	3995	3839	4662	4724	...
A Compensation of employees	-	-	-	-	-	-	-	-	-	-	-	...
B Property and entrepreneurial income	604	803	1068	1513	2152	2938	3375	3995	3839	4662	4724	...
3 Current transfers to the rest of the world a	262	311	214	251	329	462	498	521	489	586	707	...
A Indirect taxes to supranational organizations	...	...	...	...	...	...	...	...	...	...	...	...
B Other current transfers	262	311	214	251	329	462	498	521	489	586	707	...
4 Surplus of the nation on current transactions	-740	-1502	-1799	-1709	-3051	-3673	-2690	-2223	-965	-4108	-3935	...
Payments to the Rest of the World and Surplus of the Nation on Current Transactions	7398	8780	9801	11118	13966	15054	16476	18261	19503	20703	22091	...
Receipts From The Rest of the World												
1 Exports of goods and services	7003	8249	9265	10506	13229	13949	15122	16663	18064	19231	20091	...
A Exports of merchandise f.o.b.	5715	6624	7360	8239	10290	10771	11529	12752	13994	15054	15822	...
B Other	1288	1625	1905	2267	2939	3178	3593	3911	4070	4177	4269	...
2 Factor income from rest of the world	93	188	210	238	150	418	608	789	610	480	920	...
A Compensation of employees	-	-	-	-	-	-	-	-	-	-	-	...
B Property and entrepreneurial income	93	188	210	238	150	418	608	789	610	480	920	...
3 Current transfers from rest of the world a	302	343	325	374	587	687	746	809	829	992	1080	...
A Subsidies from supranational organisations	...	...	...	...	...	...	...	...	...	...	...	...
B Other current transfers	302	343	325	374	587	687	746	809	829	992	1080	...
Receipts from the Rest of the World on Current Transactions	7398	8780	9800	11118	13966	15054	16476	18261	19503	20703	22091	...

a) Item 'Current transfers to/from the rest of the world' includes also capital transfers.

New Zealand

1.10 Gross Domestic Product by Kind of Activity, in Current Prices

Million New Zealand dollars

Fiscal year beginning 1 April

	1980	1981	1982	1983	1984	1985	1986	1987	1988	1989	1990	1991
1 Agriculture, hunting, forestry and fishing	2492	2638	2539	2960	3793	4004	4359	4983	5574	6157	...	...
2 Mining and quarrying	188	227	369	280	422	582	607	671	747	897	...	...
3 Manufacturing	5082	6517	7298	7787	9016	9589	11126	11509	11869	12662	...	...
4 Electricity, gas and water	715	828	962	1077	1116	1442	1710	1753	2004	2095	...	...
5 Construction	1238	1625	1852	2034	2334	2687	2945	3248	3282	3419	...	...
6 Wholesale and retail trade, restaurants and hotels	4400	5334	6189	7069	7437	8643	10247	9855	10429	10992	...	...
7 Transport, storage and communication	1854	2145	2500	2914	3177	3528	4369	5199	5536	5768	...	...
8 Finance, insurance, real estate and business services	3236	4078	4822	5626	6642	8644	11022	13234	15061	15865	...	...
9 Community, social and personal services	863	1035	1189	1294	1486	1766	1907	2076	2310	2324	...	...
Total, Industries	20068	24427	27720	31041	35423	40886	48294	52529	56812	60179		
Producers of Government Services	3106	3715	4088	4202	4388	5136	6366	7195	7890	8460		
Other Producers	251	289	293	282	308	349	419	488	562	607		
Subtotal	23425	28431	32101	35525	40119	46371	55079	60212	65264	69246		
Less: Imputed bank service charge	603	834	977	1121	1276	1574	2198	2671	2708	2818		
Plus: Import duties	231	337	362	432	604	535	570	847	507	629		
Plus: Value added tax	...	...	...	...	...	...	1467	3250	3454	4411		
Plus: Other adjustments a	37	55	51	62	81	103	169	211	89	82		
Equals: Gross Domestic Product b	23090	27989	31537	34898	39528	45435	55087	61849	66606	71550		

a) Item 'Other adjustments' relates to other indirect taxes and import duties not allocated to industries. b) From 1977-1981, stock valuation adjustment is made for the estimates of value of physical increase in stocks.

1.11 Gross Domestic Product by Kind of Activity, in Constant Prices

Million New Zealand dollars

Fiscal year beginning 1 April

	1980	1981	1982	1983	1984	1985	1986	1987	1988	1989	1990	1991
					At constant prices of:1982							
1 Agriculture, hunting, forestry and fishing	2467	2457	2561	2460	2412	2921	3067	3501	3257	3143	3275	...
2 Mining and quarrying	228	250	367	288	385	555	577	496	617	724	663	...
3 Manufacturing	6612	7183	7235	7435	8223	7864	8044	7703	7478	7585	7215	...
4 Electricity, gas and water	935	954	962	1068	1076	1107	1139	1145	1180	1122	1153	...
5 Construction	1491	1606	1620	1751	1813	1865	1804	1879	1670	1664	1556	...
6 Wholesale and retail trade, restaurants and hotels	6037	6359	6205	6399	6490	6237	6452	6333	6180	6260	6176	...
7 Transport, storage and communication	2433	2503	2527	2736	3031	3058	3194	3261	3469	3661	3768	...
8 Finance, insurance, real estate and business services	4499	4627	4630	4962	5245	5541	5921	6242	6311	6442	6387	...
9 Community, social and personal services	1420	1478	1466	1531	1598	1671	1704	1707	1656	1652	1656	...
Total, Industries	26121	27419	27573	28627	30270	30820	31900	32265	31818	32255	31850	...
Producers of Government Services	3992	4060	4088	4132	4108	4085	4075	4029	3957	3889	3858	
Other Producers	...	...	...	...	...	...	...	...	...	...	...	
Subtotal	30113	31479	31661	32759	34378	34905	35975	36294	35775	36144	35708	
Less: Imputed bank service charge	946	965	977	1158	1296	1457	1673	1855	1788	1831	1863	
Plus: Import duties	...	...	...	...	...	...	...	...	...	...	...	
Plus: Value added tax	...	...	...	...	...	...	...	...	...	...	...	
Plus: Other adjustments a	380	467	413	406	489	498	522	570	567	705	719	
Equals: Gross Domestic Product b	29547	30981	31097	32007	33571	33946	34824	35009	34554	35018	34564	...

a) Item 'Other adjustments' relates to other indirect taxes and import duties not allocated to industries. b) From 1977-1981, stock valuation adjustment is made for the estimates of value of physical increase in stocks.

1.12 Relations Among National Accounting Aggregates

Million New Zealand dollars

Fiscal year beginning 1 April

	1980	1981	1982	1983	1984	1985	1986	1987	1988	1989	1990	1991
Gross Domestic Product	23089	27990	31537	34896	39529	45435	55088	61867	66403	71505	73343	73213
Plus: Net factor income from the rest of the world	-511	-615	-858	-1275	-2002	-2520	-2767	-3206	-3229	-4260	-3809	-3513
Factor income from the rest of the world	93	188	210	238	150	418	608	789	610	...	...	...
Less: Factor income to the rest of the world	604	803	1068	1513	2152	2938	3375	3995	3839	...	...	...
Equals: Gross National Product	22578	27376	30678	33621	37526	42915	52321	58661	63174	67245	69534	69700
Less: Consumption of fixed capital	1684	1922	2237	2661	3182	3712	4336	5051	5540	6033	6490	6861

1.12 Relations Among National Accounting Aggregates
(Continued)

	1980	1981	1982	1983	1984	1985	1986	1987	1988	1989	1990	1991
Equals: National Income	20894	25454	28441	30960	34344	39203	47985	53610	57634	61212	63044	62839
Plus: Net current transfers from the rest of the world a	40	32	111	124	259	224	249	289	340	390	336	356
Current transfers from the rest of the world	302	343	325	374	587	687	746	809	829	...	...	...
Less: Current transfers to the rest of the world	262	311	214	251	329	462	498	521	489	...	...	...
Equals: National Disposable Income	20934	25486	28552	31084	34603	39427	48234	53899	57974	61602	63380	63195
Less: Final consumption	18315	21628	24689	26547	29729	35057	41500	47353	51785	55635	58545	59098
Equals: Net Saving	2619	3858	3864	4537	4875	4370	6734	6546	6188	5967	4835	4097
Less: Surplus of the nation on current transactions	-740	-1502	-1799	-1707	-3050	-3674	-2689	-2222	-966	-4378	-3883	-1795
Statistical discrepancy	-246	-394	234	86	79	248	-480	-274	592	338	267	-397
Equals: Net Capital Formation bc	3113	4965	5897	6330	8004	8292	8943	8494	7746	10683	8985	5495

a) Item 'Current transfers to/from the rest of the world' includes also capital transfers.
b) From 1977-1981, stock valuation adjustment is made for the estimates of value of physical increase in stocks.
c) Data in this table have been revised, therefore they are not strictly comparable with the unrevised data in the other tables.

2.5 Private Final Consumption Expenditure by Type and Purpose, in Current Prices

Final Consumption Expenditure of Resident Households

	1980	1981	1982	1983	1984	1985	1986	1987	1988	1989	1990	1991
1 Food, beverages and tobacco	...	...	3549	3833	4233	4831	5707	6574	7034	7737	8458	...
A Food	...	...	2525	2682	2952	3373	3932	4561	4846	5276	5648	...
B Non-alcoholic beverages	...	...	618	687	769	895	1088	1144	1257	1375	1647	...
C Alcoholic beverages	...	...	...	...	...	...	...	...	...	...	...	...
D Tobacco	...	...	406	464	512	563	687	869	931	1086	1163	...
2 Clothing and footwear	...	...	1363	1434	1619	1848	2239	2383	2255	2407	2371	...
3 Gross rent, fuel and power	...	...	3079	3401	3935	5143	6210	7298	8673	9403	10152	...
A Fuel and power	...	...	440	462	482	572	716	838	923	1011	1087	...
B Other	...	...	2639	2939	3453	4571	5494	6460	7750	8392	9065	...
4 Furniture, furnishings and household equipment and operation	...	...	1703	1812	2036	2276	2739	2949	3020	3135	3131	...
5 Medical care and health expenses	...	...	869	954	1086	1351	1728	2100	2390	2555	2908	...
6 Transport and communication	...	...	3414	3699	4338	5200	5462	6131	6606	7251	7129	...
A Personal transport equipment	...	...	1176	1230	1549	1796	1854	2044	2016	2285	2063	...
B Other a	...	...	2238	2469	2789	3404	3608	4087	4590	4966	5066	...
7 Recreational, entertainment, education and cultural services	...	...	1679	1817	2006	2249	2673	3009	3285	3475	3544	...
8 Miscellaneous goods and services	...	...	2938	3283	3834	4637	5616	6474	6771	7315	7602	...
A Personal care	...	...	603	657	744	898	1106	1255	1364	1452	1555	...
B Expenditures in restaurants, cafes and hotels b	...	...	1492	1690	2005	2418	2859	3232	3220	3378	3392	...
C Other a	...	...	843	936	1085	1321	1651	1987	2187	2485	2655	...
Total Final Consumption Expenditure in the Domestic Market by Households, of which	...	...	18593	20234	23085	27537	32374	36917	40034	43277	45296	...
A Durable goods	...	...	5716	6075	7004	7961	9126	9845	9988	10673	10434	...
B Semi-durable goods	...	...	...	...	...	...	...	...	...	...	...	...
C Non-durable goods	...	...	5587	6035	6706	7838	9115	10472	11236	12371	13440	...
D Services a	...	...	7290	8124	9375	11738	14133	16600	18810	20233	21422	...
Plus: Direct purchases abroad by resident households	...	...	...	...	...	...	...	...	...	...	...	...
Less: Direct purchases in the domestic market by non-resident households	...	...	-236	-166	9	198	266	220	-122	-45	-79	...
Equals: Final Consumption Expenditure of Resident Households	...	...	18829	20401	23076	27339	32108	36697	40156	43322	45376	...

Final Consumption Expenditure of Private Non-profit Institutions Serving Households

	1980	1981	1982	1983	1984	1985	1986	1987	1988	1989	1990	1991
Equals: Final Consumption Expenditure of Private Non-profit Organisations Serving Households	...	...	293	288	318	373	462	528	576	630	700	...
Private Final Consumption Expenditure	...	...	19122	20689	23394	27712	32570	37225	40732	43952	46076	...

a) Item 'Other' includes fringe benefits received by households.
b) Item 'Expenditures in restaurants, cafes and hotels' includes expenditure on alcohol consumed in chartered clubs, taverns and hotels and restaurants.

New Zealand

2.6 Private Final Consumption Expenditure by Type and Purpose, in Constant Prices

Million New Zealand dollars

At constant prices of:1982

Final Consumption Expenditure of Resident Households

	1980	1981	1982	1983	1984	1985	1986	1987	1988	1989	1990	1991
1 Food, beverages and tobacco	...	...	3549	3630	3694	3640	3809	3905	3952	...	...	...
A Food	...	...	2525	2578	2628	2610	2671	2841	2846	...	...	...
B Non-alcoholic beverages	...	...	618	638	655	650	797	707	742	...	...	...
C Alcoholic beverages	...	...	...	...	...	...	...	...	...	...	...	...
D Tobacco	...	...	406	414	411	380	341	357	364	...	...	...
2 Clothing and footwear	...	...	1363	1326	1405	1404	1470	1368	1235	1277	1202	...
3 Gross rent, fuel and power	...	...	2945	3007	3054	3086	3159	3208	3255	...	...	...
A Fuel and power	...	...	440	465	470	455	484	494	503	...	...	...
B Other	...	...	2505	2542	2584	2631	2675	2714	2752	...	...	...
4 Furniture, furnishings and household equipment and operation	...	...	1703	1757	1865	1838	1914	1862	1838	...	...	...
5 Medical care and health expenses	...	...	858	892	938	980	1024	1056	1103	1071	1090	...
6 Transport and communication	...	...	3482	3550	3744	3766	3701	3883	4119	...	...	...
A Personal transport equipment	...	...	1202	1160	1289	1250	1158	1165	1262	...	...	...
B Other	...	...	2280	2390	2455	2516	2543	2718	2857	...	...	...
7 Recreational, entertainment, education and cultural services	...	...	1679	1738	1797	1858	1999	2027	2124	2138	2159	...
8 Miscellaneous goods and services	...	...	2902	3090	3221	3312	3387	3491	3482	...	...	...
A Personal care	...	...	603	636	672	702	755	788	828	...	...	...
B Expenditures in restaurants, cafes and hotels	...	...	1492	1598	1651	1695	1683	1646	1554	...	...	...
C Other	...	...	807	856	898	915	949	1057	1100	...	...	...
Total Final Consumption Expenditure in the Domestic Market by Households, of which	...	...	18480	18987	19719	19870	20421	20750	21034	21333	21316	...
A Durable goods	...	...	5743	5755	5813	5838	6115	6230	6413	6509	6701	...
B Semi-durable goods	...	...	...	...	...	...	...	...	...	...	...	...
C Non-durable goods	...	...	5586	5784	6209	6178	6317	6224	6223	6468	6247	...
D Services	...	...	7150	7450	7697	7855	7987	8295	8400	8355	8370	...
Plus: Direct purchases abroad by resident households	...	...	...	...	...	...	...	...	...	...	...	...
Less: Direct purchases in the domestic market by non-resident households	...	...	-211	-183	-195	-169	-272	-459	-530	-452	-425	...
Equals: Final Consumption Expenditure of Resident Households	...	...	18690	19170	19914	20039	20693	21209	21564	21785	21741	...

Final Consumption Expenditure of Private Non-profit Institutions Serving Households

	1980	1981	1982	1983	1984	1985	1986	1987	1988	1989	1990	1991
Equals: Final Consumption Expenditure of Private Non-profit Organisations Serving Households	...	...	293	294	306	326	359	359	375	356	351	...
Private Final Consumption Expenditure	...	...	18983	19464	20220	20365	21052	21568	21939	22141	22092	...

2.7 Gross Capital Formation by Type of Good and Owner, in Current Prices

Million New Zealand dollars

	1980				1981				1982			
	TOTAL	Total Private	Public Enterprises	General Government	TOTAL	Total Private	Public Enterprises	General Government	TOTAL	Total Private	Public Enterprises	General Government
Increase in stocks, total a	43	...	...	...	290	...	...	...	380	...	...	...
Gross Fixed Capital Formation, Total	4754	3289	...	...	6597	4617	...	...	7754	5087	...	...
1 Residential buildings	881	828	...	...	1180	1142	...	...	1311	1245	...	...
2 Non-residential buildings	821	460	...	...	1034	634	...	...	1165	678	...	...
3 Other construction	592	115	...	...	862	258	...	...	1051	201	...	...
4 Land improvement and plantation and orchard development	216	166	...	...	274	211	...	...	256	180	...	...
5 Producers' durable goods	2244	1720	...	...	3247	2373	...	...	3971	2784	...	...
A Transport equipment	812	674	...	...	1217	883	...	...	1223	968	...	...
B Machinery and equipment	1432	1046	...	...	2030	1490	...	...	2748	1816	...	...
6 Breeding stock, dairy cattle, etc.	...	...	...	...	...	...	...	...	...	...	...	...
Total Gross Capital Formation	4797	...	...	...	6887	...	...	...	8134	...	...	...

2.7 Gross Capital Formation by Type of Good and Owner, in Current Prices

Million New Zealand dollars

Fiscal year beginning 1 April

	1983				1984				1985			
	TOTAL	Total Private	Public Enterprises	General Government	TOTAL	Total Private	Public Enterprises	General Government	TOTAL	Total Private	Public Enterprises	General Government
Increase in stocks, total [a]	544	...	...	...	1333	...	...	...	264	...	...	...
Gross Fixed Capital Formation, Total	8447	5452	...	...	9853	7157	...	...	11740	7972	...	...
1 Residential buildings	1562	1488	...	...	1783	1711	...	...	2057	1925	...	...
2 Non-residential buildings	1246	699	...	...	1458	905	...	...	1959	1219	...	...
3 Other construction	1120	216	...	...	1100	256	...	...	1276	225	...	...
4 Land improvement and plantation and orchard development	243	174	...	...	245	168	...	...	188	123	...	...
5 Producers' durable goods	4277	2874	...	...	5266	4117	...	...	6260	4479	...	...
A Transport equipment	1178	979	...	...	1664	1518	...	...	1996	1458	...	...
B Machinery and equipment	3099	1895	...	...	3602	2599	...	...	4264	3021	...	...
6 Breeding stock, dairy cattle, etc.	...	...	...	...	...	...	...	...	...	...	...	...
Total Gross Capital Formation	8991	...	...	...	11186	...	...	...	12004	...	...	...

	1986				1987				1988			
	TOTAL	Total Private	Public Enterprises	General Government	TOTAL	Total Private	Public Enterprises	General Government	TOTAL	Total Private	Public Enterprises	General Government
Increase in stocks, total [a]	1171	...	...	...	281	...	...	...	396	...	...	...
Gross Fixed Capital Formation, Total	12108	8598	...	...	13263	10011	...	...	12890	9634	...	...
1 Residential buildings	2413	2287	...	...	2754	2622	...	...	2833	2707	...	...
2 Non-residential buildings	2402	1675	...	...	2948	2237	...	...	2915	1905	...	...
3 Other construction	1365	237	...	...	1127	159	...	...	1254	212	...	...
4 Land improvement and plantation and orchard development	131	82	...	...	127	88	...	...	162	107	...	...
5 Producers' durable goods	5798	4317	...	...	6306	4906	...	...	5726	4703	...	...
A Transport equipment	1691	1486	...	...	1736	1532	...	...	1064	996	...	...
B Machinery and equipment	4107	2831	...	...	4570	3374	...	...	4662	3707	...	...
6 Breeding stock, dairy cattle, etc.	...	...	...	...	...	...	...	...	...	...	...	...
Total Gross Capital Formation	13279	...	...	...	13544	...	...	...	13286	...	...	...

	1989				1990			
	TOTAL	Total Private	Public Enterprises	General Government	TOTAL	Total Private	Public Enterprises	General Government
Increase in stocks, total [a]	1998	...	...	...	1306	...	...	...
Gross Fixed Capital Formation, Total	14481	11328	...	...	14574	11154	...	...
1 Residential buildings	3355	3181	...	...	3503	3260	...	...
2 Non-residential buildings	2463	1736	...	...	2109	1228	...	...
3 Other construction	1399	172	...	...	1507	376	...	...
4 Land improvement and plantation and orchard development	197	147	...	...	185	135	...	...
5 Producers' durable goods	7068	6092	...	...	7272	6155	...	...
A Transport equipment	1799	1653	...	...	1785	1625	...	...
B Machinery and equipment	5269	4439	...	...	5487	4530	...	...
6 Breeding stock, dairy cattle, etc.	...	...	...	...	...	...	...	...
Total Gross Capital Formation	16479	...	...	...	15880	...	...	...

a) From 1977-1981, stock valuation adjustment is made for the estimates of value of physical increase in stocks.

New Zealand

2.8 Gross Capital Formation by Type of Good and Owner, in Constant Prices

	1982 TOTAL	1982 Total Private	1982 Public Enterprises	1982 General Government	1983 TOTAL	1983 Total Private	1983 Public Enterprises	1983 General Government	1984 TOTAL	1984 Total Private	1984 Public Enterprises	1984 General Government
				At consta	nt prices	of:1982						
Increase in stocks, total	319	...	...	...	380	...	...	...	949	...	...	...
Gross Fixed Capital Formation, Total	7743	5087	...	...	8153	5238	...	...	8605	6156	...	...
1 Residential buildings	1311	1244	...	...	1511	1429	...	...	1587	1514	...	...
2 Non-residential buildings	1165	677	...	...	1207	678	...	...	1333	827	...	...
3 Other construction	1050	200	...	...	1090	212	...	...	997	234	...	...
4 Land improvement and plantation and orchard development	256	180	...	...	239	172	...	...	224	155	...	...
5 Producers' durable goods	3962	2784	...	...	4107	2750	...	...	4466	3428	...	...
A Transport equipment	1220	968	...	...	1088	902	...	...	1356	1215	...	...
B Machinery and equipment	2742	1816	...	...	3019	1848	...	...	3110	2213	...	...
6 Breeding stock, dairy cattle, etc.	...	...	...	...	...	...	...	...	...	...	...	...
Total Gross Capital Formation	8062	5087	...	...	8533	5238	...	...	9554	6156	...	...

	1985 TOTAL	1985 Total Private	1985 Public Enterprises	1985 General Government	1986 TOTAL	1986 Total Private	1986 Public Enterprises	1986 General Government	1987 TOTAL	1987 Total Private	1987 Public Enterprises	1987 General Government
				At consta	nt prices	of:1982						
Increase in stocks, total	36	...	...	...	340	...	...	...	-299	...	...	...
Gross Fixed Capital Formation, Total	9134	6102	...	...	8735	5846	...	...	9446	6862	...	...
1 Residential buildings	1595	1489	...	...	1535	1441	...	...	1562	1457	...	...
2 Non-residential buildings	1596	989	...	...	1740	1205	...	...	1991	1502	...	...
3 Other construction	1032	181	...	...	1007	164	...	...	734	97	...	...
4 Land improvement and plantation and orchard development	151	99	...	...	93	59	...	...	84	55	...	...
5 Producers' durable goods	4760	3344	...	...	4360	2977	...	...	5075	3751	...	...
A Transport equipment	1376	1028	...	...	1061	933	...	...	1116	994	...	...
B Machinery and equipment	3384	2316	...	...	3299	2044	...	...	3959	2757	...	...
6 Breeding stock, dairy cattle, etc.	...	...	...	...	...	...	...	...	...	...	...	...
Total Gross Capital Formation	9170	6102	...	...	9075	5846	...	...	9147	6862	...	...

	1988 TOTAL	1988 Total Private	1988 Public Enterprises	1988 General Government	1989 TOTAL	1989 Total Private	1989 Public Enterprises	1989 General Government	1990 TOTAL	1990 Total Private	1990 Public Enterprises	1990 General Government
				At consta	nt prices	of:1982						
Increase in stocks, total	-323	...	...	...	784	...	...	...	626	...	...	...
Gross Fixed Capital Formation, Total	9214	6729	...	...	10313	7958	...	...	10421	8311	...	...
1 Residential buildings	1656	1533	...	...	1806	1711	...	...	1809	1695	...	...
2 Non-residential buildings	1800	1194	...	...	1536	1056	...	...	1242	867	...	...
3 Other construction	691	134	...	...	756	89	...	...	825	184	...	...
4 Land improvement and plantation and orchard development	86	57	...	...	96	67	...	...	93	65	...	...
5 Producers' durable goods	4981	3811	...	...	6122	5033	...	...	6454	5500	...	...
A Transport equipment	827	738	...	...	1386	1283	...	...	1539	1423	...	...
B Machinery and equipment	4154	3073	...	...	4736	3750	...	...	4915	4077	...	...
6 Breeding stock, dairy cattle, etc.	...	...	...	...	...	...	...	...	...	...	...	...
Total Gross Capital Formation	8891	6729	...	...	11097	7958	...	...	11047	8311	...	...

2.9 Gross Capital Formation by Kind of Activity of Owner, ISIC Major Divisions, in Current Prices

	1980 Total Gross Capital Formation	1980 Increase in Stocks	1980 Gross Fixed Capital Formation	1981 Total Gross Capital Formation	1981 Increase in Stocks	1981 Gross Fixed Capital Formation	1982 Total Gross Capital Formation	1982 Increase in Stocks	1982 Gross Fixed Capital Formation	1983 Total Gross Capital Formation	1983 Increase in Stocks	1983 Gross Fixed Capital Formation
					All Pr	oducers						
1 Agriculture, hunting, fishing and forestry	967	329	638	1165	345	820	1004	223	781	1446	609	837
2 Mining and quarrying	65	-5	70	65	14	51	61	-4	65	122	7	115
3 Manufacturing	550	-183	733	1264	-41	1305	2233	10	2223	2040	-159	2199
4 Electricity, gas and water	379	-27	406	493	-17	510	584	6	578	640	45	595

2.9 Gross Capital Formation by Kind of Activity of Owner, ISIC Major Divisions, in Current Prices
(Continued)

Million New Zealand dollars

Fiscal year beginning 1 April

	1980			1981			1982			1983		
	Total Gross Capital Formation	Increase in Stocks	Gross Fixed Capital Formation	Total Gross Capital Formation	Increase in Stocks	Gross Fixed Capital Formation	Total Gross Capital Formation	Increase in Stocks	Gross Fixed Capital Formation	Total Gross Capital Formation	Increase in Stocks	Gross Fixed Capital Formation
5 Construction	154	4	150	215	2	213	192	21	171	193	16	177
6 Wholesale and retail trade, restaurants and hotels	368	-96	464	621	-6	627	769	90	679	793	-32	825
7 Transport, storage and communication	424	-1	425	721	-3	724	772	35	737	765	45	720
8 Finance, insurance, real estate and business services	1149	-	1149	1545	-	1545	1664	-	1664	2039	-	2039
9 Community, social and personal services	70	-2	72	83	-6	89	92	-3	95	128	10	118
Total Industries	4128	20	4108	6172	288	5884	7370	377	6993	8168	542	7626
Producers of Government Services	602	23	579	635	2	633	691	4	687	734	3	731
Private Non-Profit Institutions Serving Households	67	-	67	81	-	81	73	-	73	90	-	90
Total a	4797	43	4754	6888	290	6598	8134	381	7753	8992	545	8447

	1984			1985			1986			1987		
	Total Gross Capital Formation	Increase in Stocks	Gross Fixed Capital Formation	Total Gross Capital Formation	Increase in Stocks	Gross Fixed Capital Formation	Total Gross Capital Formation	Increase in Stocks	Gross Fixed Capital Formation	Total Gross Capital Formation	Increase in Stocks	Gross Fixed Capital Formation

All Producers

1 Agriculture, hunting, fishing and forestry	1687	763	924	1837	1220	617	1400	878	522	1569	1083	486
2 Mining and quarrying	128	3	125	186	6	180	308	4	304	85	-18	103
3 Manufacturing	2410	262	2148	2268	-86	2354	1969	68	1901	1481	-154	1635
4 Electricity, gas and water	566	18	548	546	4	542	612	29	583	560	-30	590
5 Construction	201	24	177	187	-5	192	216	-3	219	245	13	232
6 Wholesale and retail trade, restaurants and hotels	1359	169	1190	377	-994	1371	1588	307	1281	938	-640	1578
7 Transport, storage and communication	995	80	915	1719	144	1575	1286	-121	1407	1385	42	1343
8 Finance, insurance, real estate and business services	2725	-	2725	3507	-	3507	4379	-	4379	5704	-	5704
9 Community, social and personal services	220	10	210	264	-24	288	311	3	308	394	-14	408
Total Industries	10292	1329	8963	10892	264	10628	12067	1164	10903	12363	282	12081
Producers of Government Services	800	5	795	1010	1	1009	1094	7	1087	1038	-1	1039
Private Non-Profit Institutions Serving Households	95	-	95	102	-	102	118	-	118	143	-	143
Total a	11187	1334	9853	12004	265	11739	13279	1171	12108	13544	281	13263

	1988			1989			1990		
	Total Gross Capital Formation	Increase in Stocks	Gross Fixed Capital Formation	Total Gross Capital Formation	Increase in Stocks	Gross Fixed Capital Formation	Total Gross Capital Formation	Increase in Stocks	Gross Fixed Capital Formation

All Producers

1 Agriculture, hunting, fishing and forestry	1704	1124	580	2078	1291	787	...	1259	...
2 Mining and quarrying	121	9	112	83	-9	92	...	5	...
3 Manufacturing	867	-476	1343	1627	131	1496	...	403	...
4 Electricity, gas and water	547	-18	565	564	-7	571	...	-8	...
5 Construction	175	-44	219	204	-	204	...	9	...
6 Wholesale and retail trade, restaurants and hotels	1258	-198	1456	2467	592	1875	...	-402	...
7 Transport, storage and communication	1057	-23	1080	1567	-26	1593	...	5	...
8 Finance, insurance, real estate and business services	5834	-	5834	6051	-	6051	...	-	...
9 Community, social and personal services	321	18	303	430	20	410	...	6	...
Total Industries	11884	393	11491	15075	1994	13081	...	1305	...
Producers of Government Services	1239	4	1235	1219	4	1215	...	1	...
Private Non-Profit Institutions Serving Households	164	-	164	185	-	185	...	-	...
Total a	13287	397	12890	16479	1998	14481	...	1306	...

a) From 1977-1981, stock valuation adjustment is made for the estimates of value of physical increase in stocks.

New Zealand

2.10 Gross Capital Formation by Kind of Activity of Owner, ISIC Major Divisions, in Constant Prices

Million New Zealand dollars — Fiscal year beginning 1 April

At constant prices of:1982 — All Producers

	1982			1983			1984			1985		
	Total Gross Capital Formation	Increase in Stocks	Gross Fixed Capital Formation	Total Gross Capital Formation	Increase in Stocks	Gross Fixed Capital Formation	Total Gross Capital Formation	Increase in Stocks	Gross Fixed Capital Formation	Total Gross Capital Formation	Increase in Stocks	Gross Fixed Capital Formation
1 Agriculture, hunting, fishing and forestry	...	223	...	...	376	...	...	416	...	...	649	...
2 Mining and quarrying	...	-4	...	...	1	...	...	-8	...	...	-	...
3 Manufacturing	...	-53	...	...	-202	...	...	268	...	...	-38	...
4 Electricity, gas and water	...	6	...	...	41	...	...	5	...	...	-21	...
5 Construction	...	21	...	...	16	...	...	21	...	...	15	...
6 Wholesale and retail trade, restaurants and hotels	...	90	...	...	80	...	...	158	...	...	-666	...
7 Transport, storage and communication	...	35	...	...	47	...	...	67	...	...	112	...
8 Finance, insurance, real estate and business services	...	-	...	...	-	...	...	-	...	...	-	...
9 Community, social and personal services	...	-3	...	...	10	...	...	8	...	...	-13	...
Total Industries	...	315	...	...	369	...	...	935	...	...	38	...
Producers of Government Services	...	4	...	...	3	...	...	3	...	...	-7	...
Private Non-Profit Institutions Serving Households	...	-	...	...	-	...	...	-	...	...	-	...
Total	...	319	...	...	372	...	...	938	...	...	31	...

At constant prices of:1982 — All Producers

	1986			1987			1988		
	Total Gross Capital Formation	Increase in Stocks	Gross Fixed Capital Formation	Total Gross Capital Formation	Increase in Stocks	Gross Fixed Capital Formation	Total Gross Capital Formation	Increase in Stocks	Gross Fixed Capital Formation
1 Agriculture, hunting, fishing and forestry	...	186	...	...	523	...	...	330	...
2 Mining and quarrying	...	8	...	...	-1	...	...	-	...
3 Manufacturing	...	-193	...	...	-112	...	...	-347	...
4 Electricity, gas and water	...	57	...	...	-29	...	...	-44	...
5 Construction	...	-12	...	...	17	...	...	-9	...
6 Wholesale and retail trade, restaurants and hotels	...	443	...	...	-631	...	...	-393	...
7 Transport, storage and communication	...	-95	...	...	-58	...	...	-61	...
8 Finance, insurance, real estate and business services	...	-	...	...	-	...	...	-	...
9 Community, social and personal services	...	2	...	...	1	...	...	4	...
Total Industries	...	396	...	...	-290	...	...	-520	...
Producers of Government Services	...	-18	...	...	-1	...	...	-2	...
Private Non-Profit Institutions Serving Households	...	-	...	...	-	...	...	-	...
Total	...	378	...	...	-291	...	...	-522	...

2.11 Gross Fixed Capital Formation by Kind of Activity of Owner, ISIC Divisions, in Current Prices

Million New Zealand dollars — Fiscal year beginning 1 April

All Producers

	1980	1981	1982	1983	1984	1985	1986	1987	1988	1989	1990	1991
1 Agriculture, hunting, forestry and fishing	638	820	781	837	924	617	522	486	580	787	...	...
A Agriculture and hunting	593	770	740	783	865	554	466	419	523	682	...	...
B Forestry and logging	36	43	27	31	34	28	26	16	29	34	...	...
C Fishing	9	7	14	23	25	35	30	51	28	71	...	...
2 Mining and quarrying	70	51	65	115	125	180	304	103	112	92	...	...

2.11 Gross Fixed Capital Formation by Kind of Activity of Owner, ISIC Divisions, in Current Prices
(Continued)

Million New Zealand dollars

Fiscal year beginning 1 April

	1980	1981	1982	1983	1984	1985	1986	1987	1988	1989	1990	1991
3 Manufacturing	733	1305	2223	2199	2148	2354	1901	1635	1343	1496	...	...
A Manufacturing of food, beverages and tobacco	348	393	394	393	400	358	478	571	443	574	...	...
B Textile, wearing apparel and leather industries	31	35	68	65	89	107	58	61	41	46	...	...
C Manufacture of wood, and wood products, including furniture	32	27	42	41	121	158	109	45	56	57	...	...
D Manufacture of paper and paper products, printing and publishing	86	115	137	141	212	228	345	261	354	419	...	...
E Manufacture of chemicals and chemical petroleum, coal, rubber and plastic products	98	382	1067	1009	779	649	297	102	103	122	...	...
F Manufacture of non-metallic mineral products except products of petroleum and coal	20	53	63	39	48	45	47	78	82	52	...	...
G Basic metal industries	29	172	301	343	268	529	316	252	83	62	...	...
H Manufacture of fabricated metal products, machinery and equipment	86	125	148	160	222	270	237	259	177	159	...	...
I Other manufacturing industries	3	3	3	8	9	10	14	6	4	5	...	...
4 Electricity, gas and water	406	510	578	595	548	542	583	590	565	571	...	...
5 Construction	150	213	171	177	177	192	219	232	219	204	...	...
6 Wholesale and retail trade, restaurants and hotels	464	627	679	825	1190	1371	1281	1578	1456	1875	...	...
7 Transport, storage and communication	425	724	737	720	915	1575	1407	1343	1080	1593	...	...
A Transport and storage	327	605	542	443	617	1131	811	861	447	829	...	...
B Communication	98	119	195	277	298	444	596	482	633	764	...	...
8 Finance, insurance, real estate and business services	1149	1545	1664	2039	2725	3507	4379	5704	5834	6051	...	...
Real estate except dwellings	...	...	...	...	...	...	...	...	...	...	...	...
Dwellings	784	1095	1177	1412	1638	1850	2199	2559	2588	3045	...	...
9 Community, social and personal services	72	89	95	118	210	288	308	408	303	410	...	...
Total Industries	4108	5884	6993	7626	8963	10628	10903	12081	11491	13081	...	...
Producers of Government Services	579	633	687	731	795	1009	1087	1039	1235	1215	...	...
Private Non-Profit Institutions Serving Households	67	81	73	90	95	102	118	143	164	185	...	...
Total	4754	6598	7753	8447	9853	11739	12108	13263	12890	14481	...	...

4.1 Derivation of Value Added by Kind of Activity, in Current Prices

Million New Zealand dollars

Fiscal year beginning 1 April

	1980			1981			1982			1983		
	Gross Output	Intermediate Consumption	Value Added	Gross Output	Intermediate Consumption	Value Added	Gross Output	Intermediate Consumption	Value Added	Gross Output	Intermediate Consumption	Value Added
All Producers												
1 Agriculture, hunting, forestry and fishing	5184	2692	2492	5760	3122	2638	6029	3489	2539	7067	4108	2960
A Agriculture and hunting a	4502	2366	2136	4944	2724	2220	5074	2974	2101	5942	3513	2430
B Forestry and logging	502	206	296	593	252	341	685	334	349	777	351	426
C Fishing a	180	120	60	223	146	77	270	181	89	348	244	104
2 Mining and quarrying	431	243	188	540	313	227	761	392	369	868	589	280

New Zealand

4.1 Derivation of Value Added by Kind of Activity, in Current Prices
(Continued)

Million New Zealand dollars

	1980			1981			1982			1983		
	Gross Output	Intermediate Consumption	Value Added	Gross Output	Intermediate Consumption	Value Added	Gross Output	Intermediate Consumption	Value Added	Gross Output	Intermediate Consumption	Value Added
3 Manufacturing	15732	10652	5082	19932	13414	6517	21835	14537	7298	23204	15418	7787
A Manufacture of food, beverages and tobacco	4701	3307	1394	5767	4119	1647	6484	4436	2048	6949	4620	2329
B Textile, wearing apparel and leather industries	1605	1046	560	1931	1216	716	2132	1376	756	2140	1436	704
C Manufacture of wood and wood products, including furniture	1043	676	367	1377	905	472	1374	932	442	1453	939	514
D Manufacture of paper and paper products, printing and publishing	1710	1104	606	2049	1325	724	2175	1372	803	2381	1538	844
E Manufacture of chemicals and chemical petroleum, coal, rubber and plastic products	1748	1278	470	2168	1573	595	2320	1651	668	2531	1840	691
F Manufacture of non-metallic mineral products, except products of petroleum and coal	539	312	227	764	427	337	872	499	373	905	508	397
G Basic metal industries	606	433	173	773	556	217	873	575	298	998	681	317
H Manufacture of fabricated metal products, machinery and equipment	3645	2416	1229	4913	3186	1726	5404	3565	1839	5628	3717	1911
I Other manufacturing industries	135	80	56	190	107	83	201	131	71	219	139	80
4 Electricity, gas and water	1468	753	715	1667	839	828	1991	1030	962	2143	1066	1077
5 Construction	4103	2866	1238	5268	3643	1625	6140	4288	1852	6744	4710	2034
6 Wholesale and retail trade, restaurants and hotels	9973	5573	4400	11972	6638	5334	13657	7468	6189	15415	8346	7069
7 Transport, storage and communication	3493	1639	1854	4110	1965	2145	4770	2268	2500	5189	2276	2914
A Transport and storage	2749	1517	1232	3253	1811	1442	3703	2086	1616	4015	2081	1934
B Communication	744	122	622	857	154	703	1067	182	884	1174	195	980
8 Finance, insurance, real estate and business services	4903	1667	3236	6143	2065	4078	7403	2581	4822	8480	2855	5626
Real estate, except dwellings	...	...	...	...	...	...	...	...	...	...	...	...
Dwellings	1368	486	882	1652	540	1112	2015	667	1348	2282	679	1604
9 Community, social and personal services	1750	887	863	2121	1085	1035	2401	1212	1189	2615	1321	1294
Total, Industries	47040	26972	20068	57514	33084	24427	64984	37265	27720	71726	40689	31041
Producers of Government Services	4482	1376	3106	5398	1682	3715	6026	1942	4088	6356	2154	4202
Other Producers	439	188	251	507	218	289	539	246	293	536	254	282
Total	51962	28536	23425	63419	34984	28431	71552	39453	32101	78621	43097	35525
Less: Imputed bank service charge	...	-603	603	...	-834	834	...	-977	977	...	-1121	1121
Import duties	231	...	231	337	...	337	362	...	362	432	...	432
Value added tax	...	...	...	...	...	...	...	...	...	...	...	...
Other adjustments b	37	...	37	55	...	55	51	...	51	62	...	62
Total c	52230	29139	23090	63811	35818	27989	71965	40430	31537	79115	44218	34898

	1984			1985			1986			1987		
	Gross Output	Intermediate Consumption	Value Added	Gross Output	Intermediate Consumption	Value Added	Gross Output	Intermediate Consumption	Value Added	Gross Output	Intermediate Consumption	Value Added
All Producers												
1 Agriculture, hunting, forestry and fishing	8545	4751	3793	8535	4533	4004	8915	4556	4359	9865	4884	4983
A Agriculture and hunting a	7183	4143	3040	6761	3806	2956	6822	3776	3046	7365	3851	3515
B Forestry and logging	984	360	623	1344	474	871	1574	484	1090	1875	631	1245
C Fishing a	378	248	130	430	253	177	519	296	223	625	402	223
2 Mining and quarrying	1050	629	422	1360	778	582	1433	826	607	1439	768	671

4.1 Derivation of Value Added by Kind of Activity, in Current Prices
(Continued)

Million New Zealand dollars

Fiscal year beginning 1 April

	1984			1985			1986			1987		
	Gross Output	Intermediate Consumption	Value Added	Gross Output	Intermediate Consumption	Value Added	Gross Output	Intermediate Consumption	Value Added	Gross Output	Intermediate Consumption	Value Added
3 Manufacturing	27748	18734	9016	30098	20508	9589	32612	21486	11126	34032	22521	11509
A Manufacture of food, beverages and tobacco	7976	5328	2648	8685	6174	2511	9572	6595	2976	10117	6795	3322
B Textile, wearing apparel and leather industries	2492	1714	779	2629	1743	886	2931	1900	1031	2992	2142	850
C Manufacture of wood and wood products, including furniture	1701	1108	593	1899	1228	671	1927	1238	689	1957	1294	663
D Manufacture of paper and paper products, printing and publishing	2939	1802	1138	3246	2005	1241	3738	2307	1431	4286	2590	1695
E Manufacture of chemicals and chemical petroleum, coal, rubber and plastic products	3083	2296	787	3463	2489	973	3888	2518	1370	3901	2545	1356
F Manufacture of non-metallic mineral products, except products of petroleum and coal	1010	604	406	1144	736	408	1218	802	417	1207	797	409
G Basic metal industries	1304	920	385	1263	871	392	1296	891	405	1283	903	380
H Manufacture of fabricated metal products, machinery and equipment	6938	4759	2178	7419	5047	2372	7704	5021	2683	7970	5233	2737
I Other manufacturing industries	305	203	102	350	215	135	338	214	124	319	222	97
4 Electricity, gas and water	2354	1238	1116	2922	1479	1442	3414	1704	1710	3719	1967	1753
5 Construction	7666	5333	2334	9681	6994	2687	10559	7613	2945	11988	8740	3248
6 Wholesale and retail trade, restaurants and hotels	17512	10075	7437	20107	11464	8643	23560	13313	10247	22242	12387	9855
7 Transport, storage and communication	5994	2817	3177	6955	3427	3528	8135	3766	4369	9512	4313	5199
A Transport and storage	4680	2537	2143	5429	3057	2372	6069	3283	2786	6791	3666	3125
B Communication	1314	280	1034	1526	370	1156	2066	483	1583	2721	647	2074
8 Finance, insurance, real estate and business services	9988	3345	6642	12728	4083	8644	16298	5276	11022	19346	6112	13234
Real estate, except dwellings	...	...	...	...	...	...	...	...	...	...	...	...
Dwellings	2711	781	1929	3614	858	2756	4380	938	3442	5173	1104	4069
9 Community, social and personal services	3013	1527	1486	3540	1774	1766	3648	1741	1907	4044	1968	2076
Total, Industries	83870	48449	35423	95924	55040	40886	108573	60281	48294	116187	63660	52529
Producers of Government Services	6891	2503	4388	8013	2877	5136	9984	3618	6366	11233	4038	7195
Other Producers	581	273	308	680	331	349	820	401	419	950	462	488
Total	91342	51225	40119	104617	58248	46371	119378	64300	55079	128370	68160	60212
Less: Imputed bank service charge	...	-1276	1276	...	-1574	1574	...	-2198	2198	...	-2671	2671
Import duties	604	...	604	535	...	535	570	...	570	847	...	847
Value added tax	...	...	...	...	...	...	1467	...	1467	3250	...	3250
Other adjustments [b]	81	...	81	103	...	103	169	...	169	211	...	211
Total [c]	92027	52501	39528	105255	59822	45435	121584	66498	55087	132678	70831	61849

	1988			1989		
	Gross Output	Intermediate Consumption	Value Added	Gross Output	Intermediate Consumption	Value Added

All Producers

	1988			1989		
1 Agriculture, hunting, forestry and fishing	10970	5398	5574	...	...	6157
A Agriculture and hunting [a]	8162	4271	3892	...	...	4405
B Forestry and logging	2144	702	1442	...	...	1539
C Fishing [a]	664	425	240	...	...	213
2 Mining and quarrying	1396	649	747	...	...	897

New Zealand

4.1 Derivation of Value Added by Kind of Activity, in Current Prices
(Continued)

Million New Zealand dollars

	1988			1989		
	Gross Output	Intermediate Consumption	Value Added	Gross Output	Intermediate Consumption	Value Added
3 Manufacturing	34670	22799	11869	...	...	12662
A Manufacture of food, beverages and tobacco	11623	7800	3823	...	...	3913
B Textile, wearing apparel and leather industries	2496	1681	814	...	...	886
C Manufacture of wood and wood products, including furniture	2026	1264	761	...	...	822
D Manufacture of paper and paper products, printing and publishing	4232	2548	1684	...	...	1841
E Manufacture of chemicals and chemical petroleum, coal, rubber and plastic products	4027	2599	1428	...	...	1575
F Manufacture of non-metallic mineral products, except products of petroleum and coal	1185	797	388	...	...	378
G Basic metal industries	1486	1145	341	...	...	485
H Manufacture of fabricated metal products, machinery and equipment	7332	4783	2549	...	...	2659
I Other manufacturing industries	263	182	81	...	...	103
4 Electricity, gas and water	4090	2086	2004	...	...	2095
5 Construction	11676	8394	3282	...	...	3419
6 Wholesale and retail trade, restaurants and hotels	23876	13446	10429	...	...	10992
7 Transport, storage and communication	10237	4701	5536	...	...	5768
A Transport and storage	7347	3961	3386	...	...	3602
B Communication	2890	740	2150	...	...	2166
8 Finance, insurance, real estate and business services	22016	6955	15061	...	...	15865
Real estate, except dwellings	...	...	...	...	...	...
Dwellings	6240	1320	4920	...	...	5293
9 Community, social and personal services	4393	2083	2310	...	...	2324
Total, Industries	123324	66511	56812	...	...	60179
Producers of Government Services	12132	4242	7890	...	...	8460
Other Producers	1042	480	562	...	...	607
Total	136498	71233	65264	...	...	69246
Less: Imputed bank service charge	...	-2708	2708	...	...	2818
Import duties	507	...	507	...	...	629
Value added tax	3454	...	3454	...	...	4411
Other adjustments b	89	...	89	...	...	82
Total c	140548	73941	66606	...	...	71550

a) Hunting is included in item 'Fishing'.
b) Item 'Other adjustments' relates to other indirect taxes and import duties not allocated to industries.

c) From 1977-1981, stock valuation adjustment is made for the estimates of value of physical increase in stocks.

4.2 Derivation of Value Added by Kind of Activity, in Constant Prices

Million New Zealand dollars

	1980			1981			1982			1983		
	Gross Output	Intermediate Consumption	Value Added	Gross Output	Intermediate Consumption	Value Added	Gross Output	Intermediate Consumption	Value Added	Gross Output	Intermediate Consumption	Value Added
				At constant prices of:1982								
				All Producers								
1 Agriculture, hunting, forestry and fishing	...	...	2467	...	...	2457	...	...	2561	...	...	2460
A Agriculture and hunting a	...	...	2038	...	...	2015	...	...	2117	...	...	1998
B Forestry and logging	...	...	349	...	...	358	...	...	356	...	...	365
C Fishing a	...	...	80	...	...	84	...	...	88	...	...	97
2 Mining and quarrying	...	...	228	...	...	250	...	...	367	...	...	288

4.2 Derivation of Value Added by Kind of Activity, in Constant Prices
(Continued)

Million New Zealand dollars   Fiscal year beginning 1 April

	1980			1981			1982			1983		
	Gross Output	Intermediate Consumption	Value Added	Gross Output	Intermediate Consumption	Value Added	Gross Output	Intermediate Consumption	Value Added	Gross Output	Intermediate Consumption	Value Added
At constant prices of:1982												
3 Manufacturing	...	...	6612	...	...	7183	...	...	7235	...	...	7435
A Manufacture of food, beverages and tobacco	...	...	1824	...	...	1872	...	...	1986	...	...	1998
B Textile, wearing apparel and leather industries	...	...	701	...	...	745	...	...	756	...	...	736
C Manufacture of wood and wood products, including furniture	...	...	436	...	...	489	...	...	442	...	...	468
D Manufacture of paper and paper products, printing and publishing	...	...	815	...	...	832	...	...	803	...	...	871
E Manufacture of chemicals and chemical petroleum, coal, rubber and plastic products	...	...	642	...	...	689	...	...	668	...	...	716
F Manufacture of non-metallic mineral products, except products of petroleum and coal	...	...	298	...	...	360	...	...	373	...	...	377
G Basic metal industries	...	...	257	...	...	285	...	...	298	...	...	334
H Manufacture of fabricated metal products, machinery and equipment	...	...	1639	...	...	1911	...	...	1909	...	...	1935
I Other manufacturing industries	...	...	...	...	...	...	...	...	...	...	...	...
4 Electricity, gas and water	...	...	935	...	...	954	...	...	962	...	...	1068
5 Construction	...	...	1491	...	...	1606	...	...	1620	...	...	1751
6 Wholesale and retail trade, restaurants and hotels	...	...	6037	...	...	6359	...	...	6205	...	...	6399
7 Transport, storage and communication	...	...	2433	...	...	2503	...	...	2527	...	...	2736
A Transport and storage	...	...	1604	...	...	1627	...	...	1616	...	...	1771
B Communication	...	...	829	...	...	876	...	...	911	...	...	965
8 Finance, insurance, real estate and business services	...	...	4499	...	...	4627	...	...	4630	...	...	4962
Real estate, except dwellings	...	...	...	...	...	...	...	...	...	...	...	...
Dwellings	...	...	1166	...	...	1187	...	...	1214	...	...	1238
9 Community, social and personal services	...	...	1420	...	...	1478	...	...	1466	...	...	1531
Total, Industries	...	...	26121	...	...	27419	...	...	27573	...	...	28627
Producers of Government Services	...	...	3992	...	...	4060	...	...	4088	...	...	4132
Other Producers	...	...	...	...	...	...	...	...	...	...	...	...
Total	...	...	30113	...	...	31479	...	...	31661	...	...	32759
Less: Imputed bank service charge	...	...	946	...	...	965	...	...	977	...	...	1158
Import duties	...	...	...	...	...	...	...	...	...	...	...	...
Value added tax	...	...	...	...	...	...	...	...	...	...	...	...
Other adjustments b	...	...	380	...	...	467	...	...	413	...	...	406
Total c	...	...	29547	...	...	30981	...	...	31097	...	...	32007

	1984			1985			1986			1987		
	Gross Output	Intermediate Consumption	Value Added	Gross Output	Intermediate Consumption	Value Added	Gross Output	Intermediate Consumption	Value Added	Gross Output	Intermediate Consumption	Value Added
At constant prices of:1982												
All Producers												
1 Agriculture, hunting, forestry and fishing	...	...	2412	...	...	2921	...	...	3067	...	...	3501
A Agriculture and hunting a	...	...	1938	...	...	2429	...	...	2589	...	...	2988
B Forestry and logging	...	...	378	...	...	390	...	...	376	...	...	404
C Fishing a	...	...	96	...	...	102	...	...	102	...	...	109
2 Mining and quarrying	...	...	385	...	...	555	...	...	577	...	...	496

New Zealand

Million New Zealand dollars   Fiscal year beginning 1 April

	1984			1985			1986			1987		
	Gross Output	Intermediate Consumption	Value Added	Gross Output	Intermediate Consumption	Value Added	Gross Output	Intermediate Consumption	Value Added	Gross Output	Intermediate Consumption	Value Added
						At constant prices of:1982						
3 Manufacturing	...	...	8223	...	...	7864	...	...	8044	...	...	7703
A Manufacture of food, beverages and tobacco	...	...	2085	...	...	1925	...	...	2176	...	...	2009
B Textile, wearing apparel and leather industries	...	...	819	...	...	797	...	...	841	...	...	781
C Manufacture of wood and wood products, including furniture	...	...	521	...	...	505	...	...	469	...	...	460
D Manufacture of paper and paper products, printing and publishing	...	...	986	...	...	990	...	...	1044	...	...	1096
E Manufacture of chemicals and chemical petroleum, coal, rubber and plastic products	...	...	817	...	...	790	...	...	803	...	...	754
F Manufacture of non-metallic mineral products, except products of petroleum and coal	...	...	412	...	...	427	...	...	424	...	...	385
G Basic metal industries	...	...	371	...	...	315	...	...	307	...	...	324
H Manufacture of fabricated metal products, machinery and equipment	...	...	2212	...	...	2115	...	...	1980	...	...	1894
I Other manufacturing industries	...	...	...	...	...	...	...	...	...	...	...	...
4 Electricity, gas and water	...	...	1076	...	...	1107	...	...	1139	...	...	1145
5 Construction	...	...	1813	...	...	1865	...	...	1804	...	...	1879
6 Wholesale and retail trade, restaurants and hotels	...	...	6490	...	...	6237	...	...	6452	...	...	6333
7 Transport, storage and communication	...	...	3031	...	...	3058	...	...	3194	...	...	3261
A Transport and storage	...	...	1983	...	...	1922	...	...	1962	...	...	1957
B Communication	...	...	1048	...	...	1136	...	...	1232	...	...	1304
8 Finance, insurance, real estate and business services	...	...	5245	...	...	5541	...	...	5921	...	...	6242
Real estate, except dwellings	...	...	...	...	...	...	...	...	...	...	...	...
Dwellings	...	...	1263	...	...	1292	...	...	1321	...	...	1346
9 Community, social and personal services	...	...	1598	...	...	1671	...	...	1704	...	...	1707
Total, Industries	...	...	30270	...	...	30820	...	...	31900	...	...	32265
Producers of Government Services	...	...	4108	...	...	4085	...	...	4075	...	...	4029
Other Producers	...	...	...	...	...	...	...	...	...	...	...	...
Total	...	...	34378	...	...	34905	...	...	35975	...	...	36294
Less: Imputed bank service charge	...	...	1296	...	...	1457	...	...	1673	...	...	1855
Import duties	...	...		...	...		...	...		...	...	
Value added tax	...	...	...	...	...	...	...	...	...	...	...	...
Other adjustments [b]	...	...	489	...	...	498	...	...	522	...	...	570
Total [c]	...	...	33571	...	...	33946	...	...	34824	...	...	35009

	1988			1989			1990		
	Gross Output	Intermediate Consumption	Value Added	Gross Output	Intermediate Consumption	Value Added	Gross Output	Intermediate Consumption	Value Added
				At constant prices of:1982					
				All Producers					
1 Agriculture, hunting, forestry and fishing	...	...	3257	...	...	3143	...	...	3275
A Agriculture and hunting [a]	...	...	2708	...	...	2576	...	...	2673
B Forestry and logging	...	...	418	...	...	442	...	...	470
C Fishing [a]	...	...	131	...	...	125	...	...	132
2 Mining and quarrying	...	...	617	...	...	724	...	...	663

4.2 Derivation of Value Added by Kind of Activity, in Constant Prices
(Continued)

Million New Zealand dollars

	1988			1989			1990		
	Gross Output	Intermediate Consumption	Value Added	Gross Output	Intermediate Consumption	Value Added	Gross Output	Intermediate Consumption	Value Added
	At constant prices of:1982								
3 Manufacturing	...	...	7478	...	...	7585	...	...	7215
A Manufacture of food, beverages and tobacco	...	...	2138	...	...	2063	...	...	2065
B Textile, wearing apparel and leather industries	...	...	623	...	...	667	...	...	588
C Manufacture of wood and wood products, including furniture	...	...	437	...	...	423	...	...	408
D Manufacture of paper and paper products, printing and publishing	...	...	1012	...	...	1064	...	...	1062
E Manufacture of chemicals and chemical petroleum, coal, rubber and plastic products	...	...	769	...	...	748	...	...	725
F Manufacture of non-metallic mineral products, except products of petroleum and coal	...	...	350	...	...	330	...	...	278
G Basic metal industries	...	...	441	...	...	516	...	...	517
H Manufacture of fabricated metal products, machinery and equipment	...	...	1708	...	...	1774	...	...	1572
I Other manufacturing industries	...	...	...	...	...	...	...	...	...
4 Electricity, gas and water	...	...	1180	...	...	1122	...	...	1153
5 Construction	...	...	1670	...	...	1664	...	...	1556
6 Wholesale and retail trade, restaurants and hotels	...	...	6180	...	...	6260	...	...	6176
7 Transport, storage and communication	...	...	3469	...	...	3661	...	...	3768
A Transport and storage	...	...	2051	...	...	2115	...	...	2155
B Communication	...	...	1418	...	...	1546	...	...	1613
8 Finance, insurance, real estate and business services	...	...	6311	...	...	6442	...	...	6387
Real estate, except dwellings	...	...	...	...	...	...	...	...	...
Dwellings	...	...	1372	...	...	1399	...	...	1430
9 Community, social and personal services	...	...	1656	...	...	1652	...	...	1656
Total, Industries	...	...	31818	...	...	32255	...	...	31850
Producers of Government Services	...	...	3957	...	...	3889	...	...	3858
Other Producers	...	...	...	...	...	...	...	...	...
Total	...	...	35775	...	...	36144	...	...	35708
Less: Imputed bank service charge	...	...	1788	...	...	1831	...	...	1863
Import duties	...	...	...	...	...	...	...	...	...
Value added tax	...	...	...	...	...	...	...	...	...
Other adjustments b	...	...	567	...	...	705	...	...	719
Total c	...	...	34554	...	...	35018	...	...	34564

a) Hunting is included in item 'Fishing'.
b) Item 'Other adjustments' relates to other indirect taxes and import duties not allocated to industries.
c) From 1977-1981, stock valuation adjustment is made for the estimates of value of physical increase in stocks.

4.3 Cost Components of Value Added

Million New Zealand dollars

	1980						1981					
	Compensation of Employees	Capital Consumption	Net Operating Surplus	Indirect Taxes	Less: Subsidies Received	Value Added	Compensation of Employees	Capital Consumption	Net Operating Surplus	Indirect Taxes	Less: Subsidies Received	Value Added
	All Producers											
1 Agriculture, hunting, forestry and fishing	501	310	1635	86	40	2492	600	343	1864	104	274	2638
A Agriculture and hunting a	373	288	1427	81	33	2136	446	320	1618	98	262	2220
B Forestry and logging	110	11	177	4	6	296	135	13	198	4	10	341
C Fishing a	18	11	31	1	1	60	19	10	48	2	2	77
2 Mining and quarrying	55	33	80	22	1	188	66	30	105	27	-	227

4.3 Cost Components of Value Added
(Continued)

Million New Zealand dollars

	1980						1981					
	Compensation of Employees	Capital Consumption	Net Operating Surplus	Indirect Taxes	Less: Subsidies Received	Value Added	Compensation of Employees	Capital Consumption	Net Operating Surplus	Indirect Taxes	Less: Subsidies Received	Value Added
3 Manufacturing	3422	393	948	416	101	5082	4184	446	1486	512	107	6517
A Manufacture of food, beverages and tobacco	916	119	145	256	42	1394	1091	140	156	301	40	1647
B Textile, wearing apparel and leather industries	407	30	123	6	7	560	494	32	194	7	11	716
C Manufacture of wood and wood products, including furniture	246	24	95	3	2	367	314	26	131	3	2	472
D Manufacture of paper and paper products, printing and publishing	387	63	140	19	4	606	470	72	162	23	3	724
E Manufacture of chemicals and chemical petroleum, coal, rubber and plastic products	326	52	97	36	40	470	385	54	153	44	41	595
F Manufacture of non-metallic mineral products, except products of petroleum and coal	121	18	85	3	1	227	151	21	163	4	2	337
G Basic metal industries	104	15	53	1	-	173	129	16	72	2	1	217
H Manufacture of fabricated metal products, machinery and equipment	880	69	198	87	5	1229	1105	81	427	121	7	1726
I Other manufacturing industries	35	3	12	5	-	56	45	4	28	7	-	83
4 Electricity, gas and water	213	85	419	4	6	715	263	97	469	5	6	828
5 Construction	791	63	382	14	13	1238	949	74	593	18	9	1625
6 Wholesale and retail trade, restaurants and hotels	2041	227	1192	983	44	4400	2435	269	1486	1173	28	5334
7 Transport, storage and communication	1355	211	341	83	135	1854	1584	247	356	101	143	2145
A Transport and storage	910	162	215	78	133	1232	1061	194	232	94	140	1442
B Communication	445	49	126	5	2	622	523	53	124	7	3	703
8 Finance, insurance, real estate and business services	931	293	1628	386	2	3236	1161	336	2097	488	3	4078
Real estate, except dwellings	...	...	...	...	...	...	...	...	...	...	...	...
Dwellings	...	135	558	189	...	882	...	154	728	231	...	1112
9 Community, social and personal services	445	42	318	64	8	863	554	53	365	73	9	1035
Total, Industries	9754	1659	6944	2057	348	20068	11793	1896	8820	2498	578	24427
Producers of Government Services	3094	-	-	12	-	3106	3700	-	-	15	-	3715
Other Producers	220	25	-	7	-	251	254	27	-	8	-	289
Total	13068	1684	6944	2076	348	23425	15747	1923	8820	2521	578	28431
Less: Imputed bank service charge	...	...	603	...	...	603	...	...	834	...	...	834
Import duties	...	...	...	231	...	231	...	...	...	337	...	337
Value added tax	...	...	...	...	...	...	...	...	...	...	...	...
Other adjustments b	...	...	...	37	...	37	...	...	...	55	...	55
Total cd	13068	1684	6341	2344	348	23090	15747	1923	7986	2913	578	27989

	1982						1983					
	Compensation of Employees	Capital Consumption	Net Operating Surplus	Indirect Taxes	Less: Subsidies Received	Value Added	Compensation of Employees	Capital Consumption	Net Operating Surplus	Indirect Taxes	Less: Subsidies Received	Value Added
					All Producers							
1 Agriculture, hunting, forestry and fishing	623	377	1864	121	447	2539	645	416	2136	128	365	2960
A Agriculture and hunting a	476	350	1597	114	437	2101	488	386	1783	120	347	2430
B Forestry and logging	126	13	214	5	9	349	132	12	294	5	17	426
C Fishing a	21	14	53	2	1	89	25	18	59	3	1	104
2 Mining and quarrying	78	39	208	43	-	369	88	59	86	47	-	280

4.3 Cost Components of Value Added
(Continued)

Million New Zealand dollars

	1982						1983					
	Compensation of Employees	Capital Consumption	Net Operating Surplus	Indirect Taxes	Less: Subsidies Received	Value Added	Compensation of Employees	Capital Consumption	Net Operating Surplus	Indirect Taxes	Less: Subsidies Received	Value Added
3 Manufacturing	4561	519	1746	571	99	7298	4466	623	2126	646	76	7787
A Manufacture of food, beverages and tobacco	1225	160	356	343	37	2048	1191	186	558	416	23	2329
B Textile, wearing apparel and leather industries	514	38	207	8	11	756	492	47	165	8	8	704
C Manufacture of wood and wood products, including furniture	325	29	86	4	2	442	315	36	160	5	2	514
D Manufacture of paper and paper products, printing and publishing	509	86	186	25	3	803	540	98	180	29	3	844
E Manufacture of chemicals and chemical petroleum, coal, rubber and plastic products	405	60	194	47	37	668	405	86	205	27	32	691
F Manufacture of non-metallic mineral products, except products of petroleum and coal	173	26	172	4	2	373	160	31	201	7	2	397
G Basic metal industries	146	25	126	2	1	298	150	32	134	2	1	317
H Manufacture of fabricated metal products, machinery and equipment	1220	91	403	131	6	1839	1169	102	502	143	5	1911
I Other manufacturing industries	44	4	16	7	-	71	44	5	21	9	-	80
4 Electricity, gas and water	277	109	575	5	5	962	294	137	646	5	5	1077
5 Construction	1077	96	666	21	7	1852	1129	118	770	23	6	2034
6 Wholesale and retail trade, restaurants and hotels	2630	322	1821	1445	28	6189	2689	397	2400	1618	34	7069
7 Transport, storage and communication	1701	290	549	121	159	2500	1738	357	849	131	162	2914
A Transport and storage	1148	226	286	113	156	1616	1192	270	508	123	159	1934
B Communication	553	64	263	8	3	884	546	87	341	8	3	980
8 Finance, insurance, real estate and business services	1334	391	2509	590	2	4822	1428	453	3085	661	2	5626
Real estate, except dwellings	...	...	...	...	...	...	...	...	...	...	...	...
Dwellings	...	169	897	282	...	1348	...	192	1100	311	...	1604
9 Community, social and personal services	631	67	419	82	9	1189	671	75	466	91	10	1294
Total, Industries	12913	2209	10356	2999	756	27720	13150	2633	12565	3351	660	31041
Producers of Government Services	4068	-	-	18	-	4088	4183	-	-	20	-	4202
Other Producers	256	28	-	9	-	293	244	28	-	10	-	282
Total	17237	2237	10356	3026	756	32101	17577	2661	12565	3380	660	35525
Less: Imputed bank service charge	...	...	977	...	...	977	...	...	1121	...	...	1121
Import duties	...	...	...	362	...	362	...	...	...	432	...	432
Value added tax	...	...	...	...	...	...	...	...	...	...	...	...
Other adjustments b	...	...	...	51	...	51	...	...	...	62	...	62
Total cd	17237	2237	9379	3439	756	31537	17577	2661	11444	3874	660	34898

	1984						1985					
	Compensation of Employees	Capital Consumption	Net Operating Surplus	Indirect Taxes	Less: Subsidies Received	Value Added	Compensation of Employees	Capital Consumption	Net Operating Surplus	Indirect Taxes	Less: Subsidies Received	Value Added
	All Producers											
1 Agriculture, hunting, forestry and fishing	729	476	2769	142	322	3793	780	478	2686	161	99	4004
A Agriculture and hunting a	561	440	2148	130	239	3040	603	425	1875	145	91	2956
B Forestry and logging	143	14	543	6	82	623	149	24	699	7	7	871
C Fishing a	25	22	78	6	1	130	28	29	112	9	1	177
2 Mining and quarrying	100	82	183	57	-	422	111	117	277	77	-	582

New Zealand

4.3 Cost Components of Value Added
(Continued)

Million New Zealand dollars   Fiscal year beginning 1 April

	1984						1985					
	Compensation of Employees	Capital Consumption	Net Operating Surplus	Indirect Taxes	Less: Subsidies Received	Value Added	Compensation of Employees	Capital Consumption	Net Operating Surplus	Indirect Taxes	Less: Subsidies Received	Value Added
3 Manufacturing	4980	764	2626	726	79	9016	5709	928	2191	810	48	9589
A Manufacture of food, beverages and tobacco	1345	238	653	441	29	2648	1406	267	371	481	14	2511
B Textile, wearing apparel and leather industries	544	53	177	10	5	779	626	58	194	13	4	886
C Manufacture of wood and wood products, including furniture	344	38	208	6	2	593	400	45	219	7	1	671
D Manufacture of paper and paper products, printing and publishing	596	120	389	36	4	1138	735	139	328	43	4	1241
E Manufacture of chemicals and chemical petroleum, coal, rubber and plastic products	455	112	218	33	31	787	566	167	216	42	17	973
F Manufacture of non-metallic mineral products, except products of petroleum and coal	173	36	191	8	2	406	207	46	146	10	1	408
G Basic metal industries	168	35	180	2	1	385	196	37	157	3	2	392
H Manufacture of fabricated metal products, machinery and equipment	1306	126	575	177	5	2178	1515	161	505	196	5	2372
I Other manufacturing industries	49	6	35	13	-	102	58	8	55	15	-	135
4 Electricity, gas and water	305	163	645	7	3	1116	389	181	859	13	1	1442
5 Construction	1249	141	919	28	4	2334	1450	149	1053	39	4	2687
6 Wholesale and retail trade, restaurants and hotels	3027	458	2117	1864	28	7437	3686	528	2549	1898	19	8643
7 Transport, storage and communication	1842	411	881	190	148	3177	2148	491	826	238	176	3528
A Transport and storage	1263	310	534	182	146	2143	1457	356	507	225	173	2372
B Communication	579	101	347	8	2	1034	691	135	319	13	1	1156
8 Finance, insurance, real estate and business services	1620	569	3765	690	2	6642	2097	702	5020	827	2	8644
Real estate, except dwellings	...	...	...	...	...	...	...	...	...	...	...	...
Dwellings	...	218	1383	328	...	1929	...	255	2116	385	...	2756
9 Community, social and personal services	761	90	548	98	11	1486	890	105	683	100	12	1766
Total, Industries	14614	3150	14454	3803	598	35423	17262	3678	16144	4164	362	40886
Producers of Government Services	4362	-	-	26	-	4388	5096	-	-	40	-	5136
Other Producers	266	32	-	10	-	308	303	34	-	12	-	349
Total	19242	3182	14454	3839	598	40119	22661	3712	16144	4216	362	46371
Less: Imputed bank service charge	...	...	1276	...	...	1276	...	...	1574	...	...	1574
Import duties	...	...	...	604	...	604	...	...	...	535	...	535
Value added tax	...	...	...	...	...	...	...	...	...	...	...	...
Other adjustments [b]	...	...	...	81	...	81	...	...	...	103	...	103
Total [cd]	19242	3182	13178	4524	598	39528	22661	3712	14570	4854	362	45435

	1986						1987					
	Compensation of Employees	Capital Consumption	Net Operating Surplus	Indirect Taxes	Less: Subsidies Received	Value Added	Compensation of Employees	Capital Consumption	Net Operating Surplus	Indirect Taxes	Less: Subsidies Received	Value Added
						All Producers						
1 Agriculture, hunting, forestry and fishing	816	490	2884	208	39	4359	833	480	3503	205	38	4983
A Agriculture and hunting [a]	622	437	1856	162	31	3046	701	429	2244	173	33	3515
B Forestry and logging	161	25	898	12	7	1090	97	20	1117	15	4	1245
C Fishing [a]	33	28	130	34	1	223	35	31	142	17	1	223
2 Mining and quarrying	183	121	213	93	3	607	202	129	225	115	-	671

New Zealand

4.3 Cost Components of Value Added
(Continued)

Million New Zealand dollars

Fiscal year beginning 1 April

	1986						1987					
	Compensation of Employees	Capital Consumption	Net Operating Surplus	Indirect Taxes	Less: Subsidies Received	Value Added	Compensation of Employees	Capital Consumption	Net Operating Surplus	Indirect Taxes	Less: Subsidies Received	Value Added
3 Manufacturing	6284	1125	2787	954	24	11126	6903	1271	2119	1241	21	11509
A Manufacture of food, beverages and tobacco	1479	297	606	600	6	2976	1761	323	332	912	6	3322
B Textile, wearing apparel and leather industries	659	63	300	13	3	1031	692	69	84	10	4	850
C Manufacture of wood and wood products, including furniture	423	56	198	12	1	689	432	58	165	10	1	663
D Manufacture of paper and paper products, printing and publishing	881	158	364	30	2	1431	975	178	528	18	4	1695
E Manufacture of chemicals and chemical petroleum, coal, rubber and plastic products	643	277	425	33	8	1370	663	327	348	20	1	1356
F Manufacture of non-metallic mineral products, except products of petroleum and coal	236	44	125	12	-	417	262	48	89	11	-	409
G Basic metal industries	210	38	153	5	-	405	234	42	100	5	1	380
H Manufacture of fabricated metal products, machinery and equipment	1692	183	570	241	4	2683	1824	217	447	253	4	2737
I Other manufacturing industries	61	9	46	8	-	124	60	9	26	2	-	97
4 Electricity, gas and water	479	203	1010	18	1	1710	551	259	931	11	1	1753
5 Construction	1556	175	1176	41	2	2945	1681	214	1337	45	29	3248
6 Wholesale and retail trade, restaurants and hotels	4493	645	3310	1808	9	10247	4884	733	2849	1406	16	9855
7 Transport, storage and communication	2517	617	1247	197	210	4369	3023	850	1285	230	189	5199
A Transport and storage	1671	430	695	180	190	2786	1963	477	640	215	170	3125
B Communication	846	187	552	17	20	1583	1060	373	645	15	19	2074
8 Finance, insurance, real estate and business services	2794	807	6436	986	2	11022	3474	942	7591	1230	3	13234
Real estate, except dwellings	...	...	...	...	...	...	...	...	...	...	...	...
Dwellings	...	284	2704	454	...	3442	...	320	3194	555	...	4069
9 Community, social and personal services	1021	113	683	103	12	1907	1145	127	726	97	19	2076
Total, Industries	20143	4296	19745	4413	302	48294	22695	5006	20567	4577	316	52529
Producers of Government Services	6315	-	-	51	-	6366	7142	-	-	54	-	7195
Other Producers	366	40	-	13	-	419	426	46	-	16	-	488
Total	26824	4336	19745	4477	302	55079	30262	5052	20567	4646	316	60212
Less: Imputed bank service charge	...	...	2198	...	...	2198	...	...	2671	...	...	2671
Import duties	...	...	...	570	...	570	...	...	...	847	...	847
Value added tax	...	...	...	1467	...	1467	...	...	...	3250	...	3250
Other adjustments b	...	...	...	168	...	169	...	...	...	210	...	211
Total cd	26824	4336	17547	6682	302	55087	30262	5052	17896	8953	316	61849

	1988					
	Compensation of Employees	Capital Consumption	Net Operating Surplus	Indirect Taxes	Less: Subsidies Received	Value Added
All Producers						
1 Agriculture, hunting, forestry and fishing	889	499	3973	224	13	5574
A Agriculture and hunting a	751	451	2513	188	12	3892
B Forestry and logging	104	19	1305	14	-	1442
C Fishing a	34	29	155	22	1	240
2 Mining and quarrying	193	159	263	132	-	747

New Zealand

Million New Zealand dollars

Fiscal year beginning 1 April

	Compensation of Employees	Capital Consumption	Net Operating Surplus	Indirect Taxes	Less: Subsidies Received	Value Added
	1988					
3 Manufacturing	6996	1326	2354	1204	14	11869
A Manufacture of food, beverages and tobacco	1937	324	652	914	5	3823
B Textile, wearing apparel and leather industries	660	73	71	13	3	814
C Manufacture of wood and wood products, including furniture	429	59	259	15	1	761
D Manufacture of paper and paper products, printing and publishing	1017	206	437	25	2	1684
E Manufacture of chemicals and chemical petroleum, coal, rubber and plastic products	673	344	383	27	1	1428
F Manufacture of non-metallic mineral products, except products of petroleum and coal	260	55	60	14	-	388
G Basic metal industries	266	58	12	6	-	341
H Manufacture of fabricated metal products, machinery and equipment	1698	200	465	188	2	2549
I Other manufacturing industries	56	7	15	2	-	81
4 Electricity, gas and water	569	268	1134	33	-	2004
5 Construction	1725	230	1263	66	2	3282
6 Wholesale and retail trade, restaurants and hotels	5175	829	2892	1546	13	10429
7 Transport, storage and communication	3248	964	1166	278	121	5536
A Transport and storage	2079	557	629	241	121	3386
B Communication	1169	407	537	37	-	2150
8 Finance, insurance, real estate and business services	3888	1074	8639	1463	2	15061
Real estate, except dwellings	...	...	...	...	...	...
Dwellings	...	342	3944	635	...	4920
9 Community, social and personal services	1236	142	805	138	11	2310
Total, Industries	23918	5494	22489	5086	175	56812
Producers of Government Services	7708	-	-	181	-	7890
Other Producers	493	52	-	17	-	562
Total	32119	5546	22489	5284	175	65264
Less: Imputed bank service charge	...	...	2708	...	...	2708
Import duties	...	...	...	507	...	507
Value added tax	...	...	...	3454	...	3454
Other adjustments b	...	...	...	89	...	89
Total cd	32119	5546	19781	9334	175	66606

a) Hunting is included in item 'Fishing'.
b) Item 'Other adjustments' relates to other indirect taxes and import duties not allocated to industries.

c) From 1977-1981, stock valuation adjustment is made for the estimates of value of physical increase in stocks.
d) For year 1986, fringe benefits and fringe benefits tax are not included.

Nicaragua

Source. Reply to the United Nations National Accounts Questionnaire from the Departamento de Estudios Economicos, Banco Central de Nicaragua, Managua. The official estimates are published by the Banco Central in the 'Informe Anual'.

General note. The estimates shown in the following tables have been prepared in accordance with the United Nations System of National Accounts so far as the existing data would permit.

1.1 Expenditure on the Gross Domestic Product, in Current Prices

Million Nicaraguan cordobas

	1980	1981	1982	1983	1984	1985	1986	1987	1988	1989	1990	1991
1 Government final consumption expenditure	4107	5371	6646	10351	15913	41235	154039	589130	...	...	...	...
2 Private final consumption expenditure	18381	18094	19237	18655	24965	55616	243194	1387850	...	...	...	...
3 Gross capital formation	3364	5777	5323	7401	10010	26702	73609	259270	...	...	...	...
A Increase in stocks	482	539	624	1011	1273	2782	13293	71420	...	...	...	...
B Gross fixed capital formation	2882	5238	4699	6390	8737	23920	60316	187850	...	...	...	...
4 Exports of goods and services	5039	5470	4530	6387	7404	17041	55672	527910	...	...	...	...
5 Less: Imports of goods and services	8999	10229	7386	9874	13262	25188	90770	374650	...	...	...	...
Equals: Gross Domestic Product	21892	24483	28350	32920	45030	115404	435742	2389500	...	...	...	...

1.12 Relations Among National Accounting Aggregates

Million Nicaraguan cordobas

	1980	1981	1982	1983	1984	1985	1986	1987	1988	1989	1990	1991
Gross Domestic Product	21892.0	24483.0	28350.0	32920.0	...	...	...	...	...	...	...	...
Plus: Net factor income from the rest of the world	-922.0	-1016.0	-1380.0	-671.0	...	...	...	...	...	...	...	...
Equals: Gross National Product	20970.0	23467.0	26970.0	32249.0	...	...	...	...	...	...	...	...
Less: Consumption of fixed capital	876.0	1038.0	1182.0	1473.0	...	...	...	...	...	...	...	...
Equals: National Income	20094.0	22429.0	25788.0	30776.0	...	...	...	...	...	...	...	...
Plus: Net current transfers from the rest of the world	...	...	...	...	...	...	...	...	...	...	...	...
Equals: National Disposable Income	...	...	...	...	...	...	...	...	...	...	...	...
Less: Final consumption	...	...	...	...	...	...	...	...	...	...	...	...
Equals: Net Saving	...	...	...	...	...	...	...	...	...	...	...	...
Less: Surplus of the nation on current transactions	...	...	...	...	...	...	...	...	...	...	...	...
Equals: Net Capital Formation	...	...	...	...	...	...	...	...	...	...	...	...

Niger

Source. Reply to the United Nations National Accounts Questionnaire from the Service de la Statistique et de la Mecanographie, Niamey.
General note. The estimates shown in the following tables have been adjusted by the Service to conform to the United Nations System of National Accounts so far as the existing data would permit.

1.1 Expenditure on the Gross Domestic Product, in Current Prices

Million CFA francs

	1980	1981	1982	1983	1984	1985	1986	1987	1988	1989	1990	1991
1 Government final consumption expenditure	53958	70230	81031	87512	89706	97200	102300	103600	105000	124400	117600	...
2 Private final consumption expenditure	381735	410608	483160	522824	524600	510200	505300	514000	446700	505300	505300	...
3 Gross capital formation	169104	168355	181191	106994	33300	99000	87500	70800	134600	84900	87300	...
A Increase in stocks	32389	4501	25975	-12370	-21700	6600	3400	-23300	53600	-500	7300	...
B Gross fixed capital formation	136715	163854	155216	119364	55000	92400	84100	94100	81000	85400	80000	...
4 Exports of goods and services	128824	141805	139817	143729	147300	135900	130900	139100	140500	129100	114500	...
5 Less: Imports of goods and services	197413	189539	222177	173917	156500	195000	166500	156400	148600	151100	142400	...
Equals: Gross Domestic Product a	536208	601459	663022	687142	638406	647100	659600	671200	678200	692600	682300	...

a) Data in this table have been revised, therefore they are not strictly comparable with the unrevised data in the other tables.

1.3 Cost Components of the Gross Domestic Product

Million CFA francs

	1980	1981	1982	1983	1984	1985	1986	1987	1988	1989	1990	1991
1 Indirect taxes, net	50725	51708	50566	49063	...	...	...	...	...	...	...	...
A Indirect taxes	51079	54977	57105	52730	...	...	...	...	...	...	...	...
B Less: Subsidies	354	3269	6539	3667	...	...	...	...	...	...	...	...
2 Consumption of fixed capital	40951	48224	57583	64175	...	...	...	...	...	...	...	...
3 Compensation of employees paid by resident producers to:	86552	106882	119171	121084	...	...	...	...	...	...	...	...
4 Operating surplus	357980	394645	435702	452820	...	...	...	...	...	...	...	...
A Corporate and quasi-corporate enterprises	...	...	...	...	...	...	...	...	...	...	...	...
B Private unincorporated enterprises	...	...	...	...	...	...	...	...	...	...	...	...
C General government	-2	...	...	...	...	...	...	...	...	...	...	...
Equals: Gross Domestic Product	536208	601459	663022	687142	638406	647141	643362	649846	...	...	...	...

1.7 External Transactions on Current Account, Summary

Million CFA francs

	1980	1981	1982	1983	1984	1985	1986	1987	1988	1989	1990	1991
Payments to the Rest of the World												
1 Imports of goods and services	197413	189539	222177	173917	162500	...	...	...	...	...	...	...
2 Factor income to the rest of the world	18133	23057	26512	25713	30729	...	...	...	...	...	...	...
A Compensation of employees	231	256	193	283	...	...	...	...	...	...	...	...
B Property and entrepreneurial income	17902	22801	26319	25430	...	...	...	...	...	...	...	...
3 Current transfers to the rest of the world	14725	17038	20367	21206	21626	...	...	...	...	...	...	...
4 Surplus of the nation on current transactions	-76740	-60222	-92752	-43916	-33249	...	...	...	...	...	...	...
Payments to the Rest of the World and Surplus of the Nation on Current Transactions	153531	169412	176304	176920	181606	...	...	...	...	...	...	...
Receipts From The Rest of the World												
1 Exports of goods and services	128824	141805	139817	143729	143300	...	...	...	...	...	...	...
2 Factor income from rest of the world	6653	4792	6102	4417	6162	...	...	...	...	...	...	...
A Compensation of employees	2043	1097	1561	1336	...	...	...	...	...	...	...	...
B Property and entrepreneurial income	4610	3695	4541	3081	...	...	...	...	...	...	...	...
3 Current transfers from rest of the world	18054	22815	30385	28774	32144	...	...	...	...	...	...	...
Receipts from the Rest of the World on Current Transactions	153531	169412	176304	176920	181606	...	...	...	...	...	...	...

1.10 Gross Domestic Product by Kind of Activity, in Current Prices

Million CFA francs

	1980	1981	1982	1983	1984	1985	1986	1987	1988	1989	1990	1991
1 Agriculture, hunting, forestry and fishing	228097	246815	279121	285712	228312	237777	231901	219070	...	...	...	...
2 Mining and quarrying	67397	50633	50724	56818	52693	52242	47454	49386	...	...	...	...
3 Manufacturing	19819	36007	40585	42840	44819	46250	49320	56642	...	...	...	...
4 Electricity, gas and water	2361	4626	6906	9941	11048	14151	16130	17900	...	...	...	...
5 Construction	32120	36075	35667	29377	29309	22693	28893	33375	...	...	...	...
6 Wholesale and retail trade, restaurants and hotels	62101	92773	99093	104996	109732	101971	90661	88859	...	...	...	...
7 Transport, storage and communication	22632	20843	24780	26471	25432	27328	26428	26942	...	...	...	...
8 Finance, insurance, real estate and business services	33565	39963	42393	42729	41331	43431	45973	48426	...	...	...	...
9 Community, social and personal services	10985	5624	6242	6582	7000	8104	7882	8353	...	...	...	...
Total, Industries	479077	533359	585510	605466	549676	553947	544642	548953	...	...	...	...
Producers of Government Services	33809	47749	54243	62734	66139	69895	74290	79294	...	...	...	...
Other Producers	2536	2100	2211	2328	3002	3185	3494	4001	...	...	...	...
Subtotal	515422	583208	641964	670528	618817	627027	622426	632248	...	...	...	...
Less: Imputed bank service charge	6302	8828	9576	8673	6654	5530	3771	3436	...	...	...	...
Plus: Import duties	27088	27079	30633	25287	26243	25644	24707	21034	...	...	...	...
Plus: Value added tax	...	...	...	...	...	...	...	...	...	...	...	...
Equals: Gross Domestic Product	536208	601459	663022	687142	638406	647141	643362	649846	...	...	...	...

1.12 Relations Among National Accounting Aggregates

Million CFA francs

	1980	1981	1982	1983	1984	1985	1986	1987	1988	1989	1990	1991
Gross Domestic Product	536208	601459	663022	687142	638406	...	...	...	...	...	...	...
Plus: Net factor income from the rest of the world	-11480	-18265	-20410	-21296	-24567	...	...	...	...	...	...	...
Factor income from the rest of the world	6653	4792	6102	4417	6162	...	...	...	...	...	...	...
Less: Factor income to the rest of the world	18133	23057	26512	25713	30729	...	...	...	...	...	...	...
Equals: Gross National Product	524728	583194	642612	665846	613839	...	...	...	...	...	...	...
Less: Consumption of fixed capital	40951	48224	57583	64175	66604	...	...	...	...	...	...	...
Equals: National Income	483777	534970	585029	601671	547235	...	...	...	...	...	...	...
Plus: Net current transfers from the rest of the world	3329	5777	10018	7568	10518	...	...	...	...	...	...	...
Current transfers from the rest of the world	18054	22815	30385	28774	32144	...	...	...	...	...	...	...
Less: Current transfers to the rest of the world	14725	17038	20367	21206	21626	...	...	...	...	...	...	...
Equals: National Disposable Income	487106	540747	595047	609239	557753	...	...	...	...	...	...	...
Less: Final consumption	435693	480838	564191	610336	563006	...	...	...	...	...	...	...
Equals: Net Saving	51413	59909	30856	-1097	-5253	...	...	...	...	...	...	...
Less: Surplus of the nation on current transactions	-76740	-60222	-92752	-43916	-33249	...	...	...	...	...	...	...
Equals: Net Capital Formation	128153	120131	123608	42819	27996	...	...	...	...	...	...	...

Nigeria

General note. The preparation of national accounts statistics in Nigeria is undertaken by the Federal Office of Statistics, Abuja. The official estimates together with methodological notes on sources and methods are published in 'Gross Domestic Product of Nigeria'. Another publication 'National Accounts of Nigeria' with estimates dating back to 1958/59, was published in 1978. The estimates are generally in accordance with the definitions and classifications recommended in the United Nations System of National Accounts (SNA). Input-output tables have been published for the year 1959/60 in 'An Input-Output Analysis of the Nigerian Economy'. The following tables have been prepared from successive replies to the United Nations national accounts questionnaire. Estimates relate to fiscal year beginning 1 April. When the scope and coverage of the estimates differ for conceptual or statistical reasons from the definitions and classifications recommended in SNA, a footnote is indicated to the relevant tables.

Sources and methods :

(a) Gross domestic product. Gross domestic product is estimated mainly through the production approach.

(b) Expenditure on the gross domestic product. The expenditure approach is used to estimate government final consumption expenditure, exports and imports of goods and services and buildings and other construction of gross fixed capital formation. This approach, in combination with the commodity-flow approach is used to estimate investment in machinery and equipment. Private final consumption expenditure, which includes increase in stocks, is estimated as a residual. Government consumption expenditure is estimated from the annual economic analysis of the accounts of the public authorities. Useful information on private consumption expenditure will become available when the urban consumer survey and the rural consumption inquiry for 1974/75 are completed. The estimates of gross capital formation for machinery, transport and other equipment are based on foreign trade statistics supplemented by information on import duties. A mark-up for trade, transport and installation charges of 33.3 per cent and 10 per cent is added to the import values of machinery and transport equipment respectively. The values of small concrete buildings are based on the value of cement used and of mud-walled houses on the estimated population in need of such houses. For the oil sector, the estimates of gross capital formation are compiled from the returns obtained from the oil companies. Sources for other sectors include the accounts of the Nigerian Coal Corp., the reports of the Nigerian Steel Development Authority, the Nigerian Railway Corp.and the Nigerian Shipping Line Ltd., and the accounts of the government. The main sources of information for exports and imports of goods and services are the balance-of-payments accounts.

(c) Cost-structure of the gross domestic product. Compensation of employees, operating surplus, and consumption of fixed capital are obtained as a residual by deducting net indirect taxes from the GDP. For indirect taxes and subsidies, the annual government accounts are used.

(d) Gross domestic product by kind of economic activity. The table of GDP by kind of economic activity is prepared in factor values. The production approach is used to estimate the value added of most industries. The income approach is used for producers of government services. Production estimates for 13 harvested agricultural crops are obtained from the national agriculture sample census in

1974/75 and the annual rural economic surveys. Estimates of output for green vegetables, tomatoes, oranges, bananas, sugar cane, coconut, pawpaw and pineapple are based on the average expenditure per household contained in the reports on inquiries into the income and expenditure patterns of lower and middle income households supplemented by export data. The values are reduced by 50 per cent for trade and transport charges. Foreign trade statistics provide the information for all other crops, except cocoa and tobacco which is estimated from information supplied by the Nigerian Produce Marketing CO., and from manufacturing companies. For livestock and its products, estimates are based on such data as foreign trade statistics, number of animals slaughtered, number of cattle that are milked, Lagos retail prices, etc. Non-monetary activities are covered in the estimates. The output of timber is estimated from the data on logs exported or used locally. Data on the production of fish are obtained from the Federal Fisheries Department. The annual reports of the Petroleum Division in the Federal Ministry of Mines and Power furnish information on production and f.o.b. values of crude oil and the quantity of gas sold. The same Ministry also furnishes data on production of metalliferous ores. This output is valued at f.o.b. prices. Information on the values of manufacturing output and intermediate consumption are obtained from the annual surveys of large establishments. Adjustment is made of value added by 20 per cent to cover small establishments. The estimates of electricity are based on annual reports of the concerned companies The sources of information on water supply are the actual expenditure of the Government bodies and annual accounts of water boards of corporations. Data for estimating value added in construction are obtained from accounts of public authorities and corporations government enterprises and the survey of large establishments engaged in mining, manufacturing and distributive activities. For smaller construction activities, sources such as the value of cement used,questionaire and actual of approved expenditure of public authorities are used. Trade is assumed to be 12.5 per cent of GDP in the base year 1958/59. For other years, value added is extrapolated by indexes. The bench-mark value added of road transport is based on the number of commercial vehicles. Other years' estimates are made by projecting the 1958/59 figure by the estimated number of tractors and commercial vehicles and using the CPI of transport services for five urban centres. The value added of railways, harbours, water and air transports are estimated from annual reports of concerned enterprises. The sources of information for estimating the value added of government services are the Accountant-General's reports and budget of the public authorities. For education, estimates are based on information obtained from the Federal Ministry of Education and the National Universities Commission for private institutions and on the number of teachers and an assumed average salary per teacher for other institutions. For private health institutions, the expenditure on personal emoluments is regarded as value added and assumed to grow at the same rate as for government institutions. The value added of other services, which includes the financial sector, is assumed to grow at an average annual rate of 13.8 per cent. For the constant price estimates, price deflation is used for the manufacturing, construction, part of transport and services sectors. For agriculture, the production of corps is either revalued at 1962/63 prices or deflated by retail prices. Value added of mining, electricity, trade and transport relating to passenger-miles and ton-miles is extrapolated by appropriate indicators.

1.1 Expenditure on the Gross Domestic Product, in Current Prices

Million Nigerian naira

	1980	1981	1982	1983	1984	1985	1986	1987	1988	1989	1990	1991
1 Government final consumption expenditure	5051	5504 6619	6816	7489	6925	7342	7488	7395	9253	10076	11469	12689
2 Private final consumption expenditure a	28437	33853 34563	36284	41457	47962	54066	56204	78329	113074	138827	155274	222204
3 Gross capital formation	11566	13992 11594	9734	7479	4257	5126	7734	9605	9391	18424	31127	36474
A Increase in stocks a	590	674 -621	-1188	-656	-1160	-447	411	-1056	-2993	10	500	200
B Gross fixed capital formation	10976	13318 12215	10922	8135	5417	5573	7323	10661	12384	18414	30627	36274
Residential buildings												
Non-residential buildings	7460	9165 6173	6106	5188	3552	3218	3966	4515	5041	8064	10457	11473
Other construction and land improvement etc.												
Other	3516	4153 6042	4816	2947	1865	2355	3357	6146	7342	10350	20170	24801
4 Exports of goods and services	14909	11376 11478	9561	7963	9548	12083	9427	30013	31955	94959	112562	129691
5 Less: Imports of goods and services	11705	16082 13505	10686	7246	5084	6262	7791	16457	18430	37490	49795	76264
Equals: Gross Domestic Product b	48257	48643 50749	51709	57142	63608	72355	73062	108885	145243	224797	260637	324794

a) Item 'Increase in stocks' is included in item 'Private final consumption expenditure'.
b) For the years 1970-1981, the estimates relate to fiscal year beginning 1 April.

1.2 Expenditure on the Gross Domestic Product, in Constant Prices

Million Nigerian naira

	1980	1981	1982	1983	1984	1985	1986	1987	1988	1989	1990	1991
		1977			At constant prices of:		**1984**					
1 Government final consumption expenditure	2592	2930 / 8929	8585	8485	6925	7046	6546	5949	6566	6550	7263	7852
2 Private final consumption expenditure	14594	18031 / 53094	52472	48872	47962	53278	55071	53451	60034	60097	63132	69662
3 Gross capital formation	9218	10511 / 13893	10332	7580	4257	4405	4775	3571	3134	4292	5732	5844
A Increase in stocks	562	625 / -657	-1382	-819	-1160	-364	439	-314	-989	2	71	56
B Gross fixed capital formation	8656	9885 / 14550	11714	8399	5417	4769	4336	3885	4123	4290	5661	5788
Residential buildings												
Non-residential buildings	6112	6408 / 7402	6510	5376	3552	2758	2709	2975	3226	3441	4150	4205
Other construction and land improvement etc.												
Other	2544	3477 / 7148	5204	3023	1865	2011	1627	910	897	850	1511	1583
4 Exports of goods and services	13295	9606 / 10185	10281	9249	9548	10535	8978	10473	10582	15827	18100	16342
5 Less: Imports of goods and services	8613	10711 / 15372	11365	7357	5084	5483	3835	2410	2251	3079	3681	4805
Equals: Gross Domestic Product	31086a	30366a / 70729	70305	66828	63608	69781	71535	71034	78066	83687	90546	94895

a) For the years 1970-1981, the estimates relate to fiscal year beginning 1 April.

1.3 Cost Components of the Gross Domestic Product

Million Nigerian naira

	1980	1981	1982	1983	1984	1985	1986	1987	1988	1989	1990	1991
1 Indirect taxes, net	1216	1597 / 292	139	432	602	987	934	2002	2565	2339	2764	3679
A Indirect taxes	1424	1888 / 696	809	922	1052	1332	1383	2329	3147	2770	3220	4187
B Less: Subsidies	207	290 / 404	670	489	450	344	449	327	582	431	456	508
2 Consumption of fixed capital	1207	1465 / 2941	3103	3412	3859	4429	4736	6536	8453	10590	13357	15267
3 Compensation of employees paid by resident producers to:	11915	14003 / 12321	13097	14485	14661	15871	16790	20841	28036	35099	41050	46887
A Resident households	11481	13487 / ...	...	...	...	...	...	...	...	...	...	...
B Rest of the world	434	516 / ...	...	...	...	...	...	...	...	...	...	...
4 Operating surplus	33919	31577 / 35195	35370	38813	44487	51068	50602	79506	106190	176769	203466	258961
Equals: Gross Domestic Product a	48257	48643 / 50749	51709	57142	63608	72355	73062	108885	145243	224797	260637	324794

a) For the years 1970-1981, the estimates relate to fiscal year beginning 1 April.

1.7 External Transactions on Current Account, Summary

Million Nigerian naira

	1980	1981	1982	1983	1984	1985	1986	1987	1988	1989	1990	1991
					Payments to the Rest of the World							
1 Imports of goods and services	11705	16082 / 13505	10686	7246	5084	6262	7791	16457	18430	37490	49795	76264
2 Factor income to the rest of the world	1469	1349 / 1114	1206	971	1413	1830	4492	11856	12933	18991	24090	26600
A Compensation of employees	434	516 / 281	271	278	239	230	230	106	168	252	379	567
B Property and entrepreneurial income	1034	832 / 832	935	693	1174	1600	4262	11750	12765	18739	23711	26033
3 Current transfers to the rest of the world	333	367 / 367	308	299	911	885	1799	1837	2202	459	659	1280
4 Surplus of the nation on current transactions	1798	-5963 / -3048	-2464	-460	2280	3251	-4492	505	-577	40755	44015	36245
Payments to the Rest of the World and Surplus of the Nation on Current Transactions a	15305	11835 / 11937	9736	8056	9688	12227	9590	30655	32987	97695	118558	140389

Nigeria

1.7 External Transactions on Current Account, Summary
(Continued)

Million Nigerian naira

	1980	1981	1982	1983	1984	1985	1986	1987	1988	1989	1990	1991
Receipts From The Rest of the World												
1 Exports of goods and services	14909	11376 / 11478	9561	7963	9548	12083	9427	30013	31955	94959	112562	129691
2 Factor income from rest of the world	378	439 / 439	156	81	45	85	108	191	196	1137	1723	2127
A Compensation of employees	7	8 / 8	8	6	5	12	9	7	11	17	25	37
B Property and entrepreneurial income	372	431 / 431	148	75	40	73	99	184	185	1120	1698	2089
3 Current transfers from rest of the world	17	20 / 20	19	13	95	56	55	451	836	1599	4273	8572
Receipts from the Rest of the World on Current Transactions [a]	15305	11835 / 11937	9736	8056	9688	12227	9590	30655	32987	97695	118558	140389

a) For the years 1970-1981, the estimates relate to fiscal year beginning 1 April.

1.10 Gross Domestic Product by Kind of Activity, in Current Prices

Million Nigerian naira

	1980	1981	1982	1983	1984	1985	1986	1987	1988	1989	1990	1991
1 Agriculture, hunting, forestry and fishing	10079	9863 / 13580	15906	18837	23799	26625	27887	39204	57924	69713	84345	98617
2 Mining and quarrying	15067	12400 / 11103	9294	8451	10155	12539	10071	25709	30243	79379	86854	120850
3 Manufacturing	2354	2648 / 4630	4925	5612	4926	6238	6296	7224	10727	11775	14297	18559
4 Electricity, gas and water	245	310 / 455	483	544	515	519	467	496	547	1067	1178	1345
5 Construction	3671	4002 / 2773	2488	2256	1906	1532	1920	2175	2467	3854	4351	4900
6 Wholesale and retail trade, restaurants and hotels	9723	10565 / 6848	7017	8721	9089	9661	9980	15306	21243	32890	36390	42386
7 Transport, storage and communication	1763	2129 / 3050	2771	2712	2897	3904	4061	4325	4655	4923	5662	6388
8 Finance, insurance, real estate and business services	815	1162 / 3338	3828	4140	4478	4922	5768	6412	7689	11036	15912	18199
9 Community, social and personal services	1310	1398 / 465	491	554	635	593	651	716	768	832	932	1072
Total, Industries	45026	44476 / 46241	47204	51826	58401	66533	67102	101569	136264	215470	249920	312316
Producers of Government Services	2015	2570 / 4216	4366	4884	4606	4836	5027	5314	6414	6987	7953	8800
Other Producers	...	...	...	...	...	...	...	...	...	...	...	...
Subtotal [a]	47041	47045 / 50457	51570	56710	63006	71368	72128	106883	142678	222458	257873	321116
Less: Imputed bank service charge	...	...	...	...	...	...	...	...	...	...	...	...
Plus: Import duties	...	...	...	...	...	...	...	...	...	...	...	...
Plus: Value added tax	...	...	...	...	...	...	...	...	...	...	...	...
Plus: Other adjustments [b]	1216	1597 / 293	139	432	602	987	934	2002	2565	2339	2764	3678
Equals: Gross Domestic Product [c]	48257	48643 / 50749	51709	57142	63608	72355	73062	108885	145243	224797	260637	324794

a) Gross domestic product in factor values.
b) Item 'Other adjustments' refers to indirect taxes net of subsidies.
c) For the years 1970-1981, the estimates relate to fiscal year beginning 1 April.

1.11 Gross Domestic Product by Kind of Activity, in Constant Prices

Million Nigerian naira

	1980	1981	1982	1983	1984	1985	1986	1987	1988	1989	1990	1991
					At constant prices of:							
		1977					**1984**					
1 Agriculture, hunting, forestry and fishing	6071	5721										
		24461	25082	25009	23799	27794	30357	29389	32273	33845	35277	36698
2 Mining and quarrying	7407	5302										
		10749	9634	9147	10155	10743	10029	9088	9828	11289	11911	12992
3 Manufacturing	2245	2458										
		6964	7861	5549	4926	5904	5674	5963	6729	6840	7361	7904
4 Electricity, gas and water	143	170										
		479	475	556	515	473	367	389	415	450	501	525
5 Construction	3056	3204										
		3325	2652	2338	1906	1313	1311	1433	1579	1645	1727	1796
6 Wholesale and retail trade, restaurants and hotels	6533	6941										
		9892	10247	9903	9089	9391	9712	10299	11193	11627	11967	12339
7 Transport, storage and communication	1311	1458										
		4506	3571	3098	2897	3406	3009	3011	3041	3049	3110	3191
8 Finance, insurance, real estate and business services	690	933										
		4418	5069	5071	4478	4449	4965	5217	5922	7422	10224	10627
9 Community, social and personal services	1092	1106										
		813	820	769	635	606	631	638	644	654	668	678
Total, Industries	28548	27292										
		65606	65413	61440	58401	64079	66056	65426	71626	76821	82746	86750
Producers of Government Services	1688	2151										
		4790	4744	4950	4606	4838	5020	5314	6126	6674	7596	7913
Other Producers	...	...										
		...	...	...	...	...	...	...	...	...	...	...
Subtotal a	30235	29443										
		70396	70157	66390	63006	68916	71076	70741	77752	83495	90342	94663
Less: Imputed bank service charge	...	...										
		...	...	...	...	...	...	...	...	...	...	...
Plus: Import duties	...	...										
		...	...	...	...	...	...	...	...	...	...	...
Plus: Value added tax	...	...										
		...	...	...	...	...	...	...	...	...	...	...
Plus: Other adjustments b	851	923										
		333	148	438	602	865	459	293	314	192	204	231
Equals: Gross Domestic Product c	31086	30366										
		70729	70305	66828	63608	69781	71535	71034	78066	83687	90546	94895

a) Gross domestic product in factor values.
b) Item 'Other adjustments' refers to indirect taxes net of subsidies.
c) For the years 1970-1981, the estimates relate to fiscal year beginning 1 April.

1.12 Relations Among National Accounting Aggregates

Million Nigerian naira

	1980	1981	1982	1983	1984	1985	1986	1987	1988	1989	1990	1991
Gross Domestic Product a	48257	48643										
		50749	51709	57142	63608	72355	73062	108885	145243	224797	260637	324794
Plus: Net factor income from the rest of the world	-1090	-910										
		-675	-1050	-891	-1367	-1745	-4384	-11665	-12736	-17854	-22367	-24474
Factor income from the rest of the world	378	439										
		439	156	80	45	85	108	191	196	1137	1723	2126
Less: Factor income to the rest of the world	1469	1349										
		1114	1206	971	1413	1829	4492	11856	12933	18991	24090	26600
Equals: Gross National Product a	47167	47733										
		50074	50660	56251	62241	70611	68678	97220	132507	206942	238270	300320
Less: Consumption of fixed capital	1207	1465										
		2941	3103	3412	3859	4429	4736	6536	8453	10590	13357	15267

1.12 Relations Among National Accounting Aggregates
(Continued)

Million Nigerian naira

	1980	1981	1982	1983	1984	1985	1986	1987	1988	1989	1990	1991
Equals: National Income a	45960	46268 47133	47557	52839	58382	66181	63942	90684	124054	196353	224913	285053
Plus: Net current transfers from the rest of the world	-315	-347 -347	-290	-286	-816	-829	-1745	-1386	-1366	1141	3614	7292
Current transfers from the rest of the world	17	20 20	19	13	95	56	55	451	836	1599	4273	8572
Less: Current transfers to the rest of the world	333	367 367	308	299	911	885	1799	1837	2202	459	659	1280
Equals: National Disposable Income a	45644	45921 46786	47267	52554	57566	65352	62197	89298	122688	197494	228528	292345
Less: Final consumption	33488	39357 41182	43100	48946	54887	61408	63692	85724	122327	148904	166743	234893
Equals: Net Saving a	12156	6564 5604	4167	3608	2679	3944	-1495	3574	361	48590	61785	57452
Less: Surplus of the nation on current transactions	1798	-5963 -3048	-2464	-460	2280	3251	-4492	505	-577	40755	44015	36245
Statistical discrepancy	...	... -	-	-1	-	-	-	-	-	-	-	-
Equals: Net Capital Formation a	10358	12527 8653	6631	4067	398	694	2998	3069	938	7834	17770	21207

a) For the years 1970-1981, the estimates relate to fiscal year beginning 1 April.

4.1 Derivation of Value Added by Kind of Activity, in Current Prices

Million Nigerian naira

	1981			1982			1983			1984		
	Gross Output	Intermediate Consumption	Value Added	Gross Output	Intermediate Consumption	Value Added	Gross Output	Intermediate Consumption	Value Added	Gross Output	Intermediate Consumption	Value Added
All Producers												
1 Agriculture, hunting, forestry and fishing	15985	2584	13402	18775	2984	15792	22322	3583	18739	28198	4446	23752
A Agriculture and hunting	13813	2210	11603	16348	2522	13827	19171	2903	16268	25188	3856	21332
B Forestry and logging	1078	4	1075	1082	3	1079	1174	3	1171	1278	3	1275
C Fishing	1094	370	724	1345	459	886	1977	677	1300	1732	587	1145
2 Mining and quarrying	12200	1092	11109	10369	1069	9301	9318	863	8456	11048	895	10154
A Coal mining	2	1	1	1	1	-	1	1	1	2	1	1
B Crude petroleum and natural gas production	10848	622	10226	9044	607	8437	8298	508	7790	10150	582	9568
C Metal ore mining	20	3	17	15	3	12	12	2	10	11	2	9
D Other mining	1330	465	865	1309	458	850	1007	352	654	886	310	576
3 Manufacturing	12280	7086	5195	12854	7233	5621	13714	7291	6423	12675	6816	5859
4 Electricity, gas and water	637	183	455	674	190	483	794	250	544	739	225	515
A Electricity, gas and steam	406	104	302	429	107	322	436	128	308	417	115	302
B Water works and supply	232	79	152	244	83	161	358	122	236	323	110	213
5 Construction	5500	2723	2777	5700	3208	2492	4763	2505	2258	3418	1510	1908
6 Wholesale and retail trade, restaurants and hotels	9382	2531	6851	9616	2596	7020	11875	3150	8724	12467	3376	9092
A Wholesale and retail trade	8611	2152	6459	8824	2206	6618	11078	2769	8308	11462	2866	8597
B Restaurants and hotels	771	379	392	792	390	402	797	381	416	1005	510	495
7 Transport, storage and communication	5390	2431	2960	4529	2201	2328	4328	1893	2436	4539	1919	2620
A Transport and storage	4985	2282	2704	4074	1785	2289	3906	1706	2200	4121	1752	2369
B Communication	405	149	256	455	172	283	422	187	236	418	167	251
8 Finance, insurance, real estate and business services	3712	384	3326	4327	512	3815	4653	528	4125	5067	599	4467
A Financial institutions	1680	245	1435	1999	327	1672	2118	349	1769	2594	407	2187
B Insurance	208	35	172	309	47	262	209	38	170	259	56	203
C Real estate and business services	1823	103	1719	2019	138	1881	2328	142	2186	2214	136	2078
Real estate, except dwellings	224	76	147	325	110	215	317	108	209	308	104	204
Dwellings	1599	27	1572	1694	28	1666	2011	34	1977	1906	32	1874
9 Community, social and personal services	547	86	461	585	93	491	652	98	553	757	122	635

4.1 Derivation of Value Added by Kind of Activity, in Current Prices
(Continued)

Million Nigerian naira

	1981			1982			1983			1984		
	Gross Output	Intermediate Consumption	Value Added	Gross Output	Intermediate Consumption	Value Added	Gross Output	Intermediate Consumption	Value Added	Gross Output	Intermediate Consumption	Value Added
Total, Industries	65633	19100	46534	67429	20086	47343	72419	20161	52258	78908	19905	59002
Producers of Government Services	6681	2465	4216	6889	2522	4366	7563	2679	4884	6980	2374	4605
Other Producers	...	...	...	...	...	...	...	...	...	...	...	...
Total	72314	21565	50749	74318	22608	51709	79982	22840	57142	85887	22280	63608
Less: Imputed bank service charge	...	...	...	...	...	...	...	...	...	...	...	...
Import duties	...	...	...	...	...	...	...	...	...	...	...	...
Value added tax	...	...	...	...	...	...	...	...	...	...	...	...
Total	72314	21565	50749	74318	22608	51709	79982	22840	57142	85887	22280	63608

	1985			1986			1987			1988		
	Gross Output	Intermediate Consumption	Value Added	Gross Output	Intermediate Consumption	Value Added	Gross Output	Intermediate Consumption	Value Added	Gross Output	Intermediate Consumption	Value Added
	All Producers											
1 Agriculture, hunting, forestry and fishing	31379	4804	26575	33052	5188	27865	46513	7321	39192	69149	11235	57914
A Agriculture and hunting	28939	4435	24504	30084	4687	25397	43717	6873	36844	65108	10450	54658
B Forestry and logging	1361	4	1357	1457	4	1453	1475	4	1470	1723	6	1717
C Fishing	1079	365	714	1511	497	1015	1321	444	878	2318	779	1539
2 Mining and quarrying	13433	869	12564	11109	979	10131	28933	2399	26534	34028	2815	31213
A Coal mining	3	1	1	3	1	1	3	1	1	2	1	1
B Crude petroleum and natural gas production	12776	640	12136	10736	848	9888	28496	2248	26248	33535	2646	30889
C Metal ore mining	9	1	7	2	-	2	13	2	11	13	1	12
D Other mining	646	226	420	369	129	240	422	148	274	478	167	311
3 Manufacturing	16050	8631	7420	16200	8711	7489	18588	9995	8592	27613	14853	12760
4 Electricity, gas and water	745	226	519	860	409	452	908	427	481	992	461	532
A Electricity, gas and steam	464	130	334	533	297	236	562	315	247	599	349	250
B Water works and supply	281	96	185	328	112	216	345	112	233	394	112	282
5 Construction	2956	1423	1533	3692	1768	1924	4182	2005	2177	4743	2274	2469
6 Wholesale and retail trade, restaurants and hotels	13223	3559	9664	13661	3679	9983	21605	6296	15310	29868	8623	21246
A Wholesale and retail trade	12249	3062	9187	12654	3164	9491	20577	5762	14816	28817	8069	20748
B Restaurants and hotels	974	497	477	1007	515	492	1028	534	494	1051	554	498
7 Transport, storage and communication	6343	2605	3738	6597	2815	3783	7193	3036	4157	7779	3533	4246
A Transport and storage	5868	2418	3450	6206	2624	3583	6670	2834	3836	7219	3316	3903
B Communication	475	187	288	391	191	200	523	202	321	560	217	343
8 Finance, insurance, real estate and business services	5562	647	4914	6654	891	5760	7501	1089	6412	8754	1072	7681
A Financial institutions	2941	447	2494	3751	669	3082	4473	860	3614	5401	724	4678
B Insurance	260	56	204	290	63	228	332	59	273	396	70	325
C Real estate and business services	2361	144	2217	2611	159	2452	2695	169	2526	2956	278	2678
Real estate, except dwellings	329	110	219	365	122	243	407	131	276	446	141	305
Dwellings	2032	34	1998	2246	37	2209	2288	38	2250	2510	137	2373
9 Community, social and personal services	705	112	593	776	125	650	849	133	716	913	145	768
Total, Industries	90396	22876	67520	92601	24564	68037	136272	32701	103571	183839	45010	138829
Producers of Government Services	7567	2732	4836	7694	2667	5027	7213	1899	5314	9449	3036	6414
Other Producers	...	...	...	...	...	...	...	...	...	...	...	...
Total	97963	25607	72355	100296	27232	73064	143485	34600	108885	193288	48045	145243
Less: Imputed bank service charge	...	...	...	...	...	...	...	...	...	...	...	...
Import duties	...	...	...	...	...	...	...	...	...	...	...	...
Value added tax	...	...	...	...	...	...	...	...	...	...	...	...
Total	97963	25607	72355	100296	27232	73064	143485	34600	108885	193288	48045	145243

	1989			1990			1991		
	Gross Output	Intermediate Consumption	Value Added	Gross Output	Intermediate Consumption	Value Added	Gross Output	Intermediate Consumption	Value Added
	All Producers								
1 Agriculture, hunting, forestry and fishing	83650	13953	69696	101424	17051	84374	118494	19854	98640
A Agriculture and hunting	76751	12245	64506	92734	14801	77933	108988	17358	91630
B Forestry and logging	2093	85	2007	2304	93	2211	2386	92	2294
C Fishing	4806	1623	3183	6386	2157	4230	7119	2404	4715

4.1 Derivation of Value Added by Kind of Activity, in Current Prices
(Continued)

Million Nigerian naira

	1989			1990			1991		
	Gross Output	Intermediate Consumption	Value Added	Gross Output	Intermediate Consumption	Value Added	Gross Output	Intermediate Consumption	Value Added
2 Mining and quarrying	86857	7104	79753	95067	7783	87284	132018	10737	121280
A Coal mining	2	1	1	2	1	1	3	2	1
B Crude petroleum and natural gas production	85952	6790	79162	94048	7430	86618	130872	10339	120533
C Metal ore mining	13	1	12	13	1	12	12	1	11
D Other mining	890	311	578	1004	351	653	1131	396	735
3 Manufacturing	30295	16291	14004	36784	19923	16861	48785	26706	22079
4 Electricity, gas and water	2214	1163	1051	2440	1277	1163	2807	1476	1331
A Electricity, gas and steam	1785	1041	744	1951	1138	813	2264	1321	943
B Water works and supply	429	122	308	489	139	350	543	155	388
5 Construction	7406	3549	3858	8362	4005	4357	9422	4512	4910
6 Wholesale and retail trade, restaurants and hotels	46069	13176	32894	50957	14560	36397	59317	16922	42395
A Wholesale and retail trade	44959	12591	32368	49780	13941	35838	58049	16257	41792
B Restaurants and hotels	1110	585	526	1177	619	559	1267	664	603
7 Transport, storage and communication	8133	3440	4692	9426	4013	5413	10558	4462	6096
A Transport and storage	7712	3273	4438	8946	3823	5123	10088	4280	5808
B Communication	421	167	254	480	190	290	470	183	287
8 Finance, insurance, real estate and business services	13078	2041	11036	18891	2981	15911	21037	2838	18199
A Financial institutions	8547	1608	6939	13737	2477	11260	14817	2263	12554
B Insurance	461	82	379	483	101	382	515	89	426
C Real estate and business services	4071	352	3719	4672	403	4269	5705	486	5219
Real estate, except dwellings	503	156	347	575	178	397	678	210	468
Dwellings	3568	196	3372	4097	225	3872	5027	276	4751
9 Community, social and personal services	982	157	825	1103	178	925	1274	209	1065
Total, Industries	278684	60874	217809	324454	71771	252683	403711	87716	315995
Producers of Government Services	10292	3305	6987	11715	3762	7953	12902	4102	8800
Other Producers	...	...	...	...	...	...	...	...	...
Total	288976	64180	224797	336169	75533	260637	416613	91818	324795
Less: Imputed bank service charge	...	...	...	...	...	...	...	...	...
Import duties	...	...	...	...	...	...	...	...	...
Value added tax	...	...	...	...	...	...	...	...	...
Total	288976	64180	224797	336169	75533	260637	416613	91818	324795

4.3 Cost Components of Value Added

Million Nigerian naira

	1981						1982					
	Compensation of Employees	Capital Consumption	Net Operating Surplus	Indirect Taxes	Less: Subsidies Received	Value Added	Compensation of Employees	Capital Consumption	Net Operating Surplus	Indirect Taxes	Less: Subsidies Received	Value Added
					All Producers							
1 Agriculture, hunting, forestry and fishing	1622	417	11541	74	253	13402	1840	471	13595	70	184	15792
A Agriculture and hunting	1320	393	10082	...	192	11602	1477	441	12035	...	126	13827
B Forestry and logging	15	2	1045	73	61	1074	14	2	1052	69	58	1079
C Fishing	287	22	414	1	...	724	349	28	508	1	...	886
2 Mining and quarrying	166	229	10708	6	-	11109	171	259	8864	7	-	9301
A Coal mining	-	-	1	...	...	1	-	-	-	...	...	1
B Crude petroleum and natural gas production	121	209	9890	6	-	10226	118	234	8078	7	-	8437
C Metal ore mining	8	1	6	...	...	17	6	1	5	...	...	13
D Other mining	36	19	810	...	...	865	46	25	780	...	...	851
3 Manufacturing	1570	522	2538	565	-	5195	1589	626	2711	696	-	5621
4 Electricity, gas and water	195	138	121	-	-	455	224	153	106	-	-	483
A Electricity, gas and steam	115	65	121	...	-	302	140	76	106	...	-	322
B Water works and supply	80	73	...	...	...	152	84	77	...	...	...	161

4.3 Cost Components of Value Added
(Continued)

Million Nigerian naira

	1981						1982					
	Compensation of Employees	Capital Consumption	Net Operating Surplus	Indirect Taxes	Less: Subsidies Received	Value Added	Compensation of Employees	Capital Consumption	Net Operating Surplus	Indirect Taxes	Less: Subsidies Received	Value Added
5 Construction	1032	11	1730	4	...	2777	1165	12	1311	4	...	2492
6 Wholesale and retail trade, restaurants and hotels	1937	353	4558	3	...	6851	1992	362	4662	3	...	7020
A Wholesale and retail trade	1789	336	4334	...	...	6459	1833	344	4441	...	...	6618
B Restaurants and hotels	148	17	224	3	...	392	159	18	221	3	...	402
7 Transport, storage and communication	1092	756	1201	45	136	2960	1121	642	1009	29	473	2328
A Transport and storage	910	726	1158	45	136	2704	916	608	965	29	228	2289
B Communication	182	30	43	-	-	256	205	34	44	-	-	283
8 Finance, insurance, real estate and business services	468	480	2388	-	12	3326	604	544	2680	-	14	3815
A Financial institutions	337	463	635	...	...	1435	432	520	720	...	...	1672
B Insurance	50	3	120	...	...	172	58	3	200	...	...	262
C Real estate and business services	81	15	1634	-	12	1719	114	20	1760	-	14	1881
Real estate, except dwellings	81	15	62	-	12	147	114	20	94	-	14	215
Dwellings	...	...	1572	...	...	1572	...	...	1666	...	...	1666
9 Community, social and personal services	42	13	409	-	4	461	45	14	432	-	-	491
Total, Industries	8124	2922	35195	696	404	46534	8751	3083	35370	809	670	47343
Producers of Government Services	4196	19	-	-	-	4216	4347	20	-	-	-	4366
Other Producers	...	...	...	...	...	...	...	...	...	...	...	...
Total	12321	2941	35195	696	404	50749	13097	3103	35370	809	670	51709
Less: Imputed bank service charge	...	...	...	...	...	...	...	...	...	...	...	...
Import duties	...	...	...	...	...	...	...	...	...	...	...	...
Value added tax	...	...	...	...	...	...	...	...	...	...	...	...
Total	12321	2941	35195	696	404	50749	13097	3103	35370	809	670	51709

	1983						1984					
	Compensation of Employees	Capital Consumption	Net Operating Surplus	Indirect Taxes	Less: Subsidies Received	Value Added	Compensation of Employees	Capital Consumption	Net Operating Surplus	Indirect Taxes	Less: Subsidies Received	Value Added
All Producers												
1 Agriculture, hunting, forestry and fishing	2212	548	16076	73	171	18739	2698	709	20393	76	124	23752
A Agriculture and hunting	1690	504	14186	...	112	16268	2229	665	18501	...	63	21332
B Forestry and logging	12	2	1145	71	59	1171	13	2	1249	72	61	1275
C Fishing	510	42	745	2	...	1300	456	42	643	4	...	1145
2 Mining and quarrying	189	273	7988	5	-	8456	228	377	9550	11	12	10154
A Coal mining	-	-	-	...	-	...	-	-	1	...	...	1
B Crude petroleum and natural gas production	150	251	7385	5	-	7790	197	354	9017	11	12	9568
C Metal ore mining	5	1	4	...	...	10	5	1	4	...	...	9
D Other mining	34	22	599	...	...	654	26	22	528	...	...	576
3 Manufacturing	1659	702	3251	811	-	6423	1743	640	2543	933	-	5859
4 Electricity, gas and water	284	197	63	-	-	544	266	199	49	-	-	515
A Electricity, gas and steam	161	84	63	...	-	308	155	98	49	...	-	302
B Water works and supply	123	112	...	...	...	236	111	102	...	...	...	212
5 Construction	973	7	1276	2	...	2258	610	6	1290	...	...	1908
6 Wholesale and retail trade, restaurants and hotels	2462	450	5809	3	...	8724	2582	463	6045	3	...	9092
A Wholesale and retail trade	2301	432	5575	...	...	8308	2381	447	5769	...	...	8597
B Restaurants and hotels	161	18	234	3	...	416	201	16	276	3	...	495
7 Transport, storage and communication	1116	622	973	27	303	2436	1109	684	1104	27	304	2620
A Transport and storage	915	589	958	27	290	2200	916	649	1075	27	298	2369
B Communication	201	33	15	-	13	236	193	35	29	-	6	251
8 Finance, insurance, real estate and business services	679	577	2886	-	15	4126	781	741	2955	-	10	4468
A Financial institutions	516	554	698	...	...	1769	609	718	860	...	...	2187
B Insurance	49	2	119	...	...	170	68	5	129	...	...	202
C Real estate and business services	113	21	2067	-	15	2186	104	17	1967	-	10	2078
Real estate, except dwellings	113	21	90	-	15	209	104	17	93	-	10	204

Nigeria

4.3 Cost Components of Value Added
(Continued)

Million Nigerian naira

	1983						1984					
	Compensation of Employees	Capital Consumption	Net Operating Surplus	Indirect Taxes	Less: Subsidies Received	Value Added	Compensation of Employees	Capital Consumption	Net Operating Surplus	Indirect Taxes	Less: Subsidies Received	Value Added
Dwellings	...	...	1977	...	...	1977	...	...	1874	...	...	1874
9 Community, social and personal services	47	16	491	-	-	552	59	18	558	-	-	635
Total, Industries	9621	3392	38813	922	489	52258	10076	3837	44487	1052	450	59003
Producers of Government Services	4864	20	-	-	-	4884	4584	21	-	-	-	4606
Other Producers	...	...		...	...	...	...	...		...	...	...
Total	14485	3412	38813	922	489	57142	14661	3859	44487	1052	450	63608
Less: Imputed bank service charge	...	...		...		...	...	...		...		...
Import duties	...	...	...	...	...	...	...	...	...	...	...	...
Value added tax	...	...	...	...	...	...	...	...	...	...	...	...
Total	14485	3412	38813	922	489	57142	14661	3859	44487	1052	450	63608

	1985						1986					
	Compensation of Employees	Capital Consumption	Net Operating Surplus	Indirect Taxes	Less: Subsidies Received	Value Added	Compensation of Employees	Capital Consumption	Net Operating Surplus	Indirect Taxes	Less: Subsidies Received	Value Added
All Producers												
1 Agriculture, hunting, forestry and fishing	2888	806	22931	78	128	26575	3118	847	23923	81	104	27864
A Agriculture and hunting	2588	772	21211	...	67	24504	2698	806	21933	...	40	25397
B Forestry and logging	12	3	1329	74	61	1357	13	3	1424	77	64	1452
C Fishing	288	31	391	4	...	714	407	38	566	4	...	1015
2 Mining and quarrying	213	349	11977	26	-	12564	190	421	9460	60	-	10130
A Coal mining	-	-	1	...	...	1	-	-	1	...	...	1
B Crude petroleum and natural gas production	196	336	11578	26	-	12136	182	410	9236	60	-	9888
C Metal ore mining	4	-	3	...	...	7	1	-	1	...	...	2
D Other mining	13	12	395	...	...	420	7	10	222	...	...	240
3 Manufacturing	2208	810	3220	1181	-	7420	2228	818	3250	1192	-	7489
4 Electricity, gas and water	284	183	52	-	-	519	252	214	1	-	15	452
A Electricity, gas and steam	187	95	52	...	...	334	139	111	1	...	15	236
B Water works and supply	97	88	...	...	...	185	113	103	...	...	...	216
5 Construction	507	4	1021	1	...	1533	630	6	1286	2	...	1924
6 Wholesale and retail trade, restaurants and hotels	2741	495	6424	3	...	9664	2833	513	6634	3	...	9983
A Wholesale and retail trade	2545	478	6164	...	...	9187	2629	494	6368	...	...	9491
B Restaurants and hotels	196	17	260	3	...	477	204	19	266	3	...	492
7 Transport, storage and communication	1357	939	1608	43	209	3738	1388	989	1684	45	323	3783
A Transport and storage	1148	897	1568	43	206	3450	1173	943	1642	45	220	3583
B Communication	209	42	40	-	3	288	215	46	42	-	103	200
8 Finance, insurance, real estate and business services	805	804	3314	-	7	4914	1087	886	3794	-	7	5761
A Financial institutions	629	784	1081	...	...	2494	892	865	1324	...	...	3082
B Insurance	68	6	130	...	...	204	77	6	144	...	...	228
C Real estate and business services	107	15	2102	-	7	2217	117	16	2326	-	7	2452
Real estate, except dwellings	107	15	104	-	7	219	117	16	117	-	7	243
Dwellings	...	...	1998	...	...	1998	...	...	2209	...	...	2209
9 Community, social and personal services	54	17	521	-	-	593	61	19	572	-	-	651
Total, Industries	11057	4407	51068	1332	344	67520	11787	4713	50604	1383	449	68037
Producers of Government Services	4813	22	-	-	-	4836	5003	23	-	-	-	5027
Other Producers	...	...	...	...	...	...	...	...	...	...	...	...
Total	15871	4429	51068	1332	344	72355	16790	4736	50604	1383	449	73064
Less: Imputed bank service charge	...	...		...		...	...	...		...		...
Import duties	...	...	...	...	...	...	...	...	...	...	...	...
Value added tax	...	...	...	...	...	...	...	...	...	...	...	...
Total	15871	4429	51068	1332	...	72355	16790	4736	50604	1383	449	73064

4.3 Cost Components of Value Added

Million Nigerian naira

	1987						1988					
	Compensation of Employees	Capital Consumption	Net Operating Surplus	Indirect Taxes	Less: Subsidies Received	Value Added	Compensation of Employees	Capital Consumption	Net Operating Surplus	Indirect Taxes	Less: Subsidies Received	Value Added
All Producers												
1 Agriculture, hunting, forestry and fishing	4428	1235	33541	83	95	39192	6921	1914	49089	87	97	57914
A Agriculture and hunting	4070	1212	31592	...	30	36844	6302	1875	46511	...	30	54658
B Forestry and logging	14	3	1439	79	65	1470	15	4	1685	80	67	1717
C Fishing	344	20	510	4	...	878	604	35	893	7	...	1539
2 Mining and quarrying	497	1102	24111	824	-	26534	584	1296	28363	970	-	31213
A Coal mining	-	-	1	...	...	1	-	-	-	...	...	1
B Crude petroleum and natural gas production	482	1089	23851	824	-	26248	568	1282	28069	970	-	30889
C Metal ore mining	5	1	5	...	...	11	6	1	5	...	...	12
D Other mining	8	12	254	...	...	274	9	13	288	...	...	311
3 Manufacturing	2557	939	3729	1368	-	8592	3798	1394	5535	2032	-	12760
4 Electricity, gas and water	281	215	-	...	15	481	354	194	-	-	15	532
A Electricity, gas and steam	158	105	-	...	15	247	206	59	-	...	15	250
B Water works and supply	123	110	...	...	...	233	148	135	...	...	...	282
5 Construction	713	6	1456	2	...	2177	809	7	1651	2	...	2469
6 Wholesale and retail trade, restaurants and hotels	4309	788	10208	3	...	15310	5954	1098	14191	3	...	21245
A Wholesale and retail trade	4104	770	9941	...	...	14816	5747	1079	13922	...	...	20748
B Restaurants and hotels	205	18	267	3	...	494	207	19	269	3	...	497
7 Transport, storage and communication	1499	1067	1759	48	216	4157	1632	1152	1871	52	461	4246
A Transport and storage	1274	1018	1713	48	216	3836	1392	1099	1821	52	461	3903
B Communication	225	49	46	-	-	321	240	53	50	-	-	343
8 Finance, insurance, real estate and business services	1200	1137	4074	-	-	6412	1527	1345	4815	-	9	7682
A Financial institutions	980	1112	1521	...	...	3614	1273	1317	2088	...	...	4678
B Insurance	92	7	174	...	...	273	109	9	207	...	...	325
C Real estate and business services	129	18	2379	-	-	2526	146	20	2520	-	8	2678
Real estate, except dwellings	129	18	129	-	-	276	146	20	147	-	8	305
Dwellings	...	...	2250	...	...	2250	...	...	2373	...	...	2373
9 Community, social and personal services	68	21	628	-	-	716	73	22	673	-	-	768
Total, Industries	15552	6510	79506	2326	327	103571	21652	8422	106190	3147	582	138829
Producers of Government Services	5289	26	-	-	-	5314	6383	31	-	-	-	6414
Other Producers	...	...	...	...	...	...	...	...	...	...	...	...
Total	20841	6536	79506	2326	327	108885	28036	8453	106190	3147	582	145243
Less: Imputed bank service charge	...	...	...	...	...	...	...	...	...	...	...	...
Import duties	...	...	...	...	...	...	...	...	...	...	...	...
Value added tax	...	...	...	...	...	...	...	...	...	...	...	...
Total	20841	6536	79506	2326	327	108885	28036	8453	106190	3147	582	145243

	1989						1990					
	Compensation of Employees	Capital Consumption	Net Operating Surplus	Indirect Taxes	Less: Subsidies Received	Value Added	Compensation of Employees	Capital Consumption	Net Operating Surplus	Indirect Taxes	Less: Subsidies Received	Value Added
All Producers												
1 Agriculture, hunting, forestry and fishing	8621	2296	58796	104	120	69696	10554	2741	71048	153	124	84373
A Agriculture and hunting	7342	2184	55022	...	42	64506	8874	2640	66465	...	46	77933
B Forestry and logging	18	5	1970	94	78	2007	19	5	2125	140	78	2211
C Fishing	1262	107	1805	10	...	3182	1661	96	2458	13	...	4230
2 Mining and quarrying	725	1607	77047	374	-	79753	793	1759	84302	430	-	87284
A Coal mining	-	-	1	...	...	1	-	-	1	...	...	1
B Crude petroleum and natural gas production	701	1582	76505	374	-	79162	767	1730	83690	430	-	86618
C Metal ore mining	6	1	5	...	...	12	6	1	5	...	...	13
D Other mining	18	24	536	...	...	578	20	27	605	...	...	653
3 Manufacturing	4167	1530	6078	2230	-	14004	5060	1853	7383	2564	-	16861
4 Electricity, gas and water	751	315	-	-	16	1051	827	351	-	-	15	1163
A Electricity, gas and steam	590	169	-	...	16	744	644	184	-	...	14	813
B Water works and supply	160	147	...	...	...	308	183	167	...	...	...	350

4.3 Cost Components of Value Added
(Continued)

Million Nigerian naira

	1989						1990					
	Compensation of Employees	Capital Consumption	Net Operating Surplus	Indirect Taxes	Less: Subsidies Received	Value Added	Compensation of Employees	Capital Consumption	Net Operating Surplus	Indirect Taxes	Less: Subsidies Received	Value Added
5 Construction	1263	11	2579	3	...	3858	1427	12	2912	6	...	4357
6 Wholesale and retail trade, restaurants and hotels	9183	1703	22003	3	...	32894	10159	1886	24345	6	...	36397
A Wholesale and retail trade	8965	1683	21719	...	...	32368	9927	1864	24047	...	...	35838
B Restaurants and hotels	218	20	284	3	...	526	232	22	298	6	...	559
7 Transport, storage and communication	1645	1223	2054	57	287	4692	1855	1414	2393	60	308	5413
A Transport and storage	1397	1167	2003	57	185	4438	1578	1347	2330	60	191	5123
B Communication	248	56	51	-	102	254	277	67	63	-	117	290
8 Finance, insurance, real estate and business services	1707	1847	7482	-	-	11037	2370	3276	10267	-	-	15911
A Financial institutions	1418	1815	3706	-	...	6939	2092	3245	5923	...	...	11260
B Insurance	127	10	241	...	...	379	93	5	285	...	...	382
C Real estate and business services	162	22	3535	-	-	3719	185	25	4058	-	-	4269
Real estate, except dwellings	161	22	163	-	-	347	185	25	186	-	-	397
Dwellings	...	...	3372	...	...	3372	...	...	3872	...	...	3872
9 Community, social and personal services	79	24	729	-	7	825	90	27	816	-	7	925
Total, Industries	28145	10556	176769	2770	431	217809	33135	13319	203466	3220	455	252683
Producers of Government Services	6954	33	-	-	-	6987	7915	38	-	-	-	7953
Other Producers	...	...	...	...	...	...	...	...	...	...	...	...
Total	35099	10590	176769	2770	431	224797	41050	13357	203466	3220	455	260637
Less: Imputed bank service charge	...	...	...	...	...	...	...	...	...	...	...	...
Import duties	...	...	...	...	...	...	...	...	...	...	...	...
Value added tax	...	...	...	...	...	...	...	...	...	...	...	...
Total	35099	10590	176769	2770	431	224797	41050	13357	203466	3220	455	260637

	1991					
	Compensation of Employees	Capital Consumption	Net Operating Surplus	Indirect Taxes	Less: Subsidies Received	Value Added
All Producers						
1 Agriculture, hunting, forestry and fishing	12739	3063	82814	154	131	98640
A Agriculture and hunting	10867	2950	77867	...	53	91630
B Forestry and logging	20	5	2207	140	78	2294
C Fishing	1852	108	2741	14	...	4715
2 Mining and quarrying	1098	2443	117309	430	-	121280
A Coal mining	-	-	2	...	...	2
B Crude petroleum and natural gas production	1069	2411	116622	430	-	120533
C Metal ore mining	6	1	4	...	...	11
D Other mining	22	31	682	...	...	735
3 Manufacturing	5707	2033	10819	3521	-	22079
4 Electricity, gas and water	942	386	17	-	15	1331
A Electricity, gas and steam	741	202	15	...	15	943
B Water works and supply	201	184	2	...	...	387
5 Construction	1607	14	3279	10	...	4910
6 Wholesale and retail trade, restaurants and hotels	11323	2103	28960	10	...	42395
A Wholesale and retail trade	11073	2079	28640	...	...	41792
B Restaurants and hotels	249	24	320	10	...	603
7 Transport, storage and communication	1954	1500	2935	63	355	6096
A Transport and storage	1647	1422	2870	63	193	5809
B Communication	307	78	65	-	162	287
8 Finance, insurance, real estate and business services	2655	3654	11890	-	-	18198
A Financial institutions	2332	3618	6603	...	...	12553
B Insurance	104	5	317	...	...	426
C Real estate and business services	219	30	4970	-	-	5219
Real estate, except dwellings	219	30	219	-	-	468

4.3 Cost Components of Value Added
(Continued)

Million Nigerian naira

	1991					
	Compensation of Employees	Capital Consumption	Net Operating Surplus	Indirect Taxes	Less: Subsidies Received	Value Added
Dwellings	...	...	4751	...	...	4751
9 Community, social and personal services	105	31	936	-	7	1065
Total, Industries	38130	15227	258959	4188	508	315995
Producers of Government Services	8758	42	-	-	-	8800
Other Producers	...	...	...	...	...	...
Total	46888	15269	258959	4188	508	324795
Less: Imputed bank service charge	...	...	...	...	...	...
Import duties	...	...	...	...	...	...
Value added tax	...	...	...	...	...	...
Total	46888	15269	258959	4188	508	324794

Norway

General note. The preparation of national accounts statistics in Norway is undertaken by the Central Bureau of Statistics, Oslo. The official estimates are published annually in 'Nasjonalregnskap (National Accounts)'. A detailed description of the sources and methods is found in 'National Accounts of Norway - System and Methods of Estimation', No. 45 in the series Samfunnsokonomieske Studier (Norwegian text) and No. 81/1 in the series RAPPORTER (English text), published in 1981. The estimates are generally in accordance with the classifications and definitions recommended in the United Nations system of National Accounts (SNA). Estimates conforming to the present SNA were published for the first time in 'Okonomisk Utsyn (Economic Survey) 1972'. The corresponding changes of concepts and classifications were published in 'Revidert Nasjonalregnskap (Revised National Accounts)' in 1975. Input-output tables were published in 1968 in 'Input-output data 1954, 1959 and 1964'. The following tables have been prepared from successive replies to the United Nations national accounts questionnaire. When the scope and coverage of the estimates differ for conceptual or statistical reasons from the definitions and classifications recommended in SNA, a footnote is indicated to the relevant tables.

Sources and methods :

(a) Gross domestic product. The main approach used to estimate GDP is the production approach.

(b) Expenditure on the gross domestic product. The expenditure approach is used to estimate all components of GDP by expenditure type, within the framework of detailed input-output tables using the commodity-flow method. Change in stocks, however, is primarily calculated as the difference between supply and other uses for each commodity. Government final consumption expenditure is mainly based on government accounts. Estimates of private consumption expenditure relating to consumer goods are based on turnover statistics and extrapolated by value indexes. Gross fixed capital formation is recorded at purchasers' prices which includes investment levies, but excludes value added tax. Exports and imports of goods and services are mainly based on foreign exchange statistics from the Bank of Norway and external trade statistics of the Central Bureau of Statistics. For the constant price estimates, double deflation and the commodity-flow approach are used within the framework of detailed annual input-output tables for all expenditure components. Current values are deflated by appropriate price indexes.

(c) Cost-structure of the gross domestic product. The value of compensation of employees is obtained through adding up wages and salaries by branch of activity. Censuses provide bench-mark data, while data from government accounts, quarterly earnings statistics and annual industrial statistics are used as extrapolators for the inter-censal years. Operating surplus is arrived at as a residual. Consumption of fixed capital is estimated by using the perpetual inventory method. Time series of gross investment at constant prices provide the basis for calculating consumption of fixed capital. Commodity taxes and subsidies are calculated on accrual basis through the commodity-flow method.

(d) Gross domestic product by kind of economic activity. The table of GDP by kind of economic activity is prepared at market prices, i.e. producers' values. The production approach is used to estimate value added of almost all industries. This is done within the framework of detailed input-output tables using the commodity-flow method. The income approach is used for producers of government services and part of other private services. The expenditure approach is used in the case of the trade sector. Agricultural production is estimated from data prepared by the Agricultural Budgeting Board. Information on prices is obtained from the Agricultural Price Reporting Office and from the marketing cooperatives. For mining and quarrying estimates are extracted from the annual industrial statistics, which include crude oil and natural gas production in the North Sea. For manufacturing use is made of the annual industrial statistics which supply detailed information on gross output and intermediate consumption by industrial activity and by commodity for all establishments employing five or more persons. The annual statistics of building and construction work give information on the number of establishments, persons engaged, value of production, cost of materials and gross fixed capital formation. Gross output of the trade sector is measured as the total of trade and transport margins plus some minor items. The margins are estimated as the aggregate difference between purchasers' values and producers' values, except for bench-mark years when mark-ups are estimated from information from government agencies, business organizations, surveys of consumer expenditure or from price data. The estimation of intermediate consumption is to a large extent based on ratios from bench-mark years. The estimates for railway, tramway, subway and suburban railway transport as well as air transport are based on detailed accounting data. For other land transport the statistical sources are the annual scheduled road transport statistics, data from censuses of establishments, etc. Summary accounts for financial institutions exist in the annual credit market statistics. For insurance the annual insurance statistics and extracts of accounts are used. Operating surplus of dwellings in the bench-mark year has been fixed as a certain percentage of reduced replacement cost of the dwelling stock in the base-year. For subsequent years gross output is extrapolated by using information on investments, repairs and clearing of old dwellings. Bench-mark estimates for business services are made from the censuses of establishments held every ten years and extrapolated by value indices based on annual statistics on services. For government services data are obtained from the municipal accounts and central government accounts including social insurance administration. For private services bench-mark estimates are to a large extent based on the censuses of establishments, and extrapolated by use of employment estimates and components of consumer price index. For the estimation of constant prices, double deflation and the commodity-flow approach are used within the framework of detailed annual input-output tables. In most sectors output is deflated by appropriate price indexes. However, output of crop and livestock products is valued at base-year prices, and extrapolation by quantity indicators is undertaken for restaurants and hotels, transport of goods and financial institutions.

1.1 Expenditure on the Gross Domestic Product, in Current Prices

Million Norwegian kroner

	1980	1981	1982	1983	1984	1985	1986	1987	1988	1989	1990	1991
1 Government final consumption expenditure	53478	62616	70408	78214	84099	92653	101580	116045	122237	130998	139115	147478
2 Private final consumption expenditure	135242	155205	175310	192979	210921	245439	278909	298054	307499	311955	336065	349705
3 Gross capital formation	78902	84032	96071	99116	116267	121145	151610	158584	157828	151158	135201	129074
A Increase in stocks	8104	-7761	3809	-4332	-1300	11103	6070	1221	-12517	-18327	11055	2021
B Gross fixed capital formation	70798	91793	92262	103448	117567	110042	145540	157363	170345	169485	124146	127053
Residential buildings a	13535	15055	17465	18526	19171	20523	24871	28911	29199	23887	19749	14748
Non-residential buildings	14482	16138	16289	17047	17918	21326	28237	32394	35334	28371	23071	22033
Other construction and land improvement etc. b	17682	29112	24379	36175	46106	33527	51954	52096	52684	59007	36510	47185
Other	25098	31488	34130	31702	34372	34666	40479	43963	53128	58221	44816	43087
4 Exports of goods and services	134795	156288	165023	183921	214077	235564	194663	200224	213671	261863	293015	307528
5 Less: Imports of goods and services	117371	130467	144543	152031	172852	194602	213044	211427	217958	234591	242845	247098
Equals: Gross Domestic Product	285046	327674	362269	402199	452512	500199	513718	561480	583277	621383	660551	686687

a) Item 'Residential buildings' includes also summer cottages, temporary dwellings, logging camps, fishermens' quarters etc.. b) The estimates of 'Other construction' include oil drilling rigs, oil production platforms etc., pipelines for gas, oil and gas exploration and drilling.

1.2 Expenditure on the Gross Domestic Product, in Constant Prices

Million Norwegian kroner

	1980	1981	1982	1983	1984	1985	1986	1987	1988	1989	1990	1991
			At constant prices of:									
			1980					1984				
1 Government final consumption expenditure	53478	56763	58985	61727	63238 / 84099	86842	88779	92304	92752	95190	97146	99624
2 Private final consumption expenditure	135242	136784	139199	141303	145139 / 210921	231825	244804	242388	235561	229041	235373	235301
3 Gross capital formation	78902	76461	77337	75509	87173 / 116267	112004	131639	123988	116374	107505	95337	90623
A Increase in stocks	8104	-7024	3041	-3109	-51 / -1300	10834	6255	1229	-8342	-12318	7667	1503
B Gross fixed capital formation	70798	83485	74296	78618	87224 / 117567	101170	125384	122759	124716	119823	87670	89120

1344

1.2 Expenditure on the Gross Domestic Product, in Constant Prices
(Continued)

Million Norwegian kroner

	1980	1981	1982	1983	1984	1985	1986	1987	1988	1989	1990	1991
	At constant prices of:											
			1980					1984				
Residential buildings a	13535	13695	14533	14420	14255 19171	19696	22100	22925	21903	18306	15380	11748
Non-residential buildings	14482	14975	14016	13897	14068 17918	20135	24589	25152	25829	21172	17453	16904
Other construction and land improvement etc. b	17682	25289	17861	26366	31619 46106	31298	45787	41814	39865	43441	26254	33048
Other	25098	29526	27887	23935	27282 34372	30041	32908	32814	36809	36639	28250	26987
4 Exports of goods and services	134795	136651	136451	146786	158841 214077	228754	232309	235042	248067	274525	296784	314932
5 Less: Imports of goods and services	117371	119113	123467	123449	135177 172852	183044	201235	186620	183416	185098	189122	192425
Statistical discrepancy	...	...	...	...	...	-	-	-922	-5718	-14556	-20480	-24877
Equals: Gross Domestic Product	285046	287546	288505	301876	319214 452512c	476381c	496296c	506180c	503620c	506607c	515038c	523178c

a) Item 'Residential buildings' includes also summer cottages, temporary dwellings, logging camps, fishermens' quarters etc..
b) The estimates of 'Other construction' include oil drilling rigs, oil production platforms etc., pipelines for gas, oil and gas exploration and drilling.
c) Beginning 1987, the estimates at 1984 constant prices are derived from the series of constant prices based on T-1 prices. This resulted in some statistical discrepancies shown in the table.

1.3 Cost Components of the Gross Domestic Product

Million Norwegian kroner

	1980	1981	1982	1983	1984	1985	1986	1987	1988	1989	1990	1991
1 Indirect taxes, net	29064	33901	38085	45294	52491	64101	70353	75978	73215	69963	71097	72847
A Indirect taxes	49025	55695	61747	69733	78200	91037	99922	107493	106984	106562	111089	115617
B Less: Subsidies	19961	21794	23662	24439	25709	26936	29569	31515	33769	36599	39992	42770
2 Consumption of fixed capital	41358	48053	55007	59614	62513	66512	72561	83301	91194	96678	98823	102462
3 Compensation of employees paid by resident producers to:	145421	164165	183355	198235	216350	239667	271412	306327	324249	328600	342003	356381
A Resident households	145331	163920	183086	197974	216070	239347	271032	305887	323809	328130	341504	355881
B Rest of the world	90	248	270	261	280	320	380	440	440	470	500	500
4 Operating surplus	69201	81554	85823	99055	121159	129920	99392	95874	94619	126142	148626	154996
A Corporate and quasi-corporate enterprises	42423	50576	51361	62069	80354	88229	54144	48602	43111	73944	90103	95448
B Private unincorporated enterprises	26780	30977	34462	36985	40805	41691	45248	47273	51508	52198	58523	59548
C General government	-	-	-	-	-	-	-	-	-	-	-	-
Equals: Gross Domestic Product	285044	327673	362270	402198	452513	500200	513718	561480	583277	621383	660549	686686

1.4 General Government Current Receipts and Disbursements

Million Norwegian kroner

	1980	1981	1982	1983	1984	1985	1986	1987	1988	1989	1990	1991
	Receipts											
1 Operating surplus	-	-	-	-	-	-	-	-	-	-	-	-
2 Property and entrepreneurial income a	7049	9639	11508	14089	19928	23053	30855	33463	32942	42673	51099	53546
3 Taxes, fees and contributions	144657	160248	176333	194119	216898	249304	247164	275775	283841	291305	310628	320590
A Indirect taxes	49024	55696	61747	69733	78200	91037	99922	107493	106984	106562	111089	115617
B Direct taxes	61260	65655	70605	76721	87637	100600	79309	87951	96505	107395	118449	120067
C Social security contributions	34224	38699	43494	47149	50511	57304	67460	79718	79632	76604	80239	83698
D Compulsory fees, fines and penalties	149	198	487	516	550	363	473	613	720	744	851	1208
4 Other current transfers	...	...	...	...	3000	3078	3078	578	4573	7466	10153	5691
Total Current Receipts of General Government	151706	169887	187841	208208	239826	275435	281097	309816	321356	341444	371880	379827
	Disbursements											
1 Government final consumption expenditure	53478	62616	70409	78213	84099	92654	101580	116045	122237	130998	139115	147478
A Compensation of employees	36574	42504	48526	53655	58470	64173	71054	80722	86504	92090	98118	105611
B Consumption of fixed capital	2327	2658	2979	3186	3338	3742	4259	4845	5355	5678	5933	6220
C Purchases of goods and services, net	14577	17454	18904	21372	22291	24689	26209	30415	30307	33157	34990	35568
D Less: Own account fixed capital formation	...	...	...	...	...	...	...	...	...	...	...	...
E Indirect taxes paid, net	...	...	...	...	...	49	58	63	72	73	75	80
2 Property income	9664	10721	11529	13414	15018	17393	22325	24061	22670	24705	25805	24836

Norway

1.4 General Government Current Receipts and Disbursements
(Continued)

Million Norwegian kroner

	1980	1981	1982	1983	1984	1985	1986	1987	1988	1989	1990	1991
A Interest	9664	10721	11529	13414	15018	17393	22325	24061	22670	24705	25805	24836
B Net land rent and royalties	...	...	...	...	...	...	...	...	...	...	...	...
3 Subsidies	19960	21795	23662	24439	25709	26936	29569	31515	33769	36599	39992	42770
4 Other current transfers	43172	50255	57789	66076	71787	78029	86472	97355	111701	124447	136409	148501
A Social security benefits	40975	47636	54516	62212	67917	73819	81525	92072	105358	118151	128982	140871
B Social assistance grants	...	...	...	...	...	...	...	...	...	...	...	...
C Other b	2197	2619	3273	3864	3870	4210	4947	5283	6342	6296	7426	7630
5 Net saving	25432	24500	24452	26066	43213	60423	41151	40838	30979	24695	30560	16241
Total Current Disbursements and Net Saving of General Government	151706	169887	187841	208208	239826	275435	281097	309814	321356	341444	371881	379826

a) Public enterprise surplus are deducted from item 'Withdrawals from public quasi-corporations.
b) Item 'Other' of Other current transfers refers to transfers to the rest of the world.

1.5 Current Income and Outlay of Corporate and Quasi-Corporate Enterprises, Summary

Million Norwegian kroner

	1980	1981	1982	1983	1984	1985	1986	1987	1988	1989	1990	1991
					Receipts							
1 Operating surplus	42423	50576	51361	62069	80354	88229	54144	48602	43111	73944	90103	95448
2 Property and entrepreneurial income received	41881	53255	65208	73940	83903	102944	141711	176232	200371	196147	194422	186974
3 Current transfers	11720	14597	16923	19068	20419	20971	24195	26818	29998	31665	33808	33356
Total Current Receipts	96024	118428	133492	155077	184676	212144	220050	251652	273480	301756	318333	315778
					Disbursements							
1 Property and entrepreneurial income a	47263	60453	73856	83022	98095	113340	152269	181064	205936	211413	216805	213479
2 Direct taxes and other current payments to general government	23603	26097	27955	32614	39176	47817	20184	18881	15810	23051	31003	29200
3 Other current transfers a	12344	15242	17838	20096	24595	23536	27015	27206	34092	38775	43591	38781
4 Net saving	12814	16636	13843	19345	22810	27452	20582	24501	17642	28516	26934	34317
Total Current Disbursements and Net Saving	96024	118428	133492	155077	184676	212145	220050	251652	273480	301755	318333	315777

a) Beginning 1985, imputed interest paid by pension funds to households, which used to be included in item other transfers n.e.c., is now included in interest.

1.6 Current Income and Outlay of Households and Non-Profit Institutions

Million Norwegian kroner

	1980	1981	1982	1983	1984	1985	1986	1987	1988	1989	1990	1991
					Receipts							
1 Compensation of employees	145396	164004	183182	198070	216178	239467	271158	306019	323953	328286	341672	356061
A From resident producers	145331	163920	183086	197974	216070	239347	271032	305887	323809	328130	341504	355881
B From rest of the world	66	84	96	96	108	120	126	132	144	156	168	180
2 Operating surplus of private unincorporated enterprises	26780	30977	34462	36985	40805	41691	45248	47273	51508	52198	58523	59548
3 Property and entrepreneurial income a	9612	11792	13711	16886	20392	23706	30346	37779	43529	41567	43186	42798
4 Current transfers a	43575	50675	58014	65937	72098	77025	85509	96617	110441	123283	134329	146897
A Social security benefits	40975	47636	54516	62212	67917	73819	81525	92072	105358	118151	128982	140871
B Social assistance grants	...	...	...	...	...	...	...	...	...	...	...	...
C Other a	2600	3039	3498	3725	4181	3206	3985	4545	5083	5133	5347	6027
Total Current Receipts	225363	257448	289369	317878	349473	381889	432261	487688	529431	545334	577710	605304
					Disbursements							
1 Private final consumption expenditure	135241	155205	175310	192979	210921	245439	278909	298054	307499	311955	336065	349705
2 Property income	11230	14024	17572	21316	24081	28838	37489	51866	61974	62155	63383	62592
3 Direct taxes and other current transfers n.e.c. to general government	72030	78455	86631	91772	99522	110450	127058	149401	161047	161692	168536	175773
A Social security contributions	34224	38699	43494	47149	50511	57304	67460	79718	79632	76604	80239	83698
B Direct taxes	37657	39558	42650	44107	48652	52799	59125	69070	80695	84344	87446	90867
C Fees, fines and penalties	149	198	487	516	359	347	473	613	720	744	851	1208
4 Other current transfers	2116	2458	2940	3077	3291	3721	4933	5761	6117	6614	6723	8084
5 Net saving	4746	7306	6915	8734	11658	-6559	-16128	-17395	-7205	2919	3002	9151
Total Current Disbursements and Net Saving	225363	257448	289368	317878	349473	381889	432261	487687	529432	545335	577709	605305

a) Beginning 1985, imputed interest paid by pension funds to households, which used to be included in item other transfers n.e.c., is now included in interest.

1.7 External Transactions on Current Account, Summary

Million Norwegian kroner

Payments to the Rest of the World

	1980	1981	1982	1983	1984	1985	1986	1987	1988	1989	1990	1991
1 Imports of goods and services	117371	130467	144543	152031	172852	194602	213044	211427	217958	234591	242845	247098
A Imports of merchandise c.i.f.	84543	90516	100458	102520	116542	133927	153073	151011	155350	166505	171779	170305
B Other	32828	39951	44085	49511	56311	60675	59971	60417	62608	68086	71066	76793
2 Factor income to the rest of the world	14841	19319	23431	23394	26651	27733	29541	30441	35292	42249	42383	41086
A Compensation of employees	90	248	270	261	280	320	380	440	440	470	500	500
B Property and entrepreneurial income	14751	19071	23161	23133	26371	27413	29161	30001	34852	41779	41883	40586
3 Current transfers to the rest of the world	3212	3796	4791	5522	5506	6189	7278	8103	9177	9613	10904	12135
A Indirect taxes to supranational organizations	-	-	-	-	-	-	-	-	-	-	-	-
B Other current transfers	3212	3796	4791	5522	5506	6189	7278	8103	9177	9613	10904	12135
4 Surplus of the nation on current transactions	5448	12460	4146	14644	23927	26682	-33443	-27338	-25220	1652	24120	33098
Payments to the Rest of the World and Surplus of the Nation on Current Transactions	140872	166042	176911	195591	228936	255206	216420	222633	237207	288105	320252	333417

Receipts From The Rest of the World

	1980	1981	1982	1983	1984	1985	1986	1987	1988	1989	1990	1991
1 Exports of goods and services	134795	156288	165023	183921	214077	235563	194664	200224	213671	261863	293015	307528
A Exports of merchandise f.o.b.	92863	106899	114799	133249	156822	173255	135999	145182	152631	190054	215450	223420
B Other	41932	49390	50224	50672	57256	62309	58663	55041	61040	71809	77565	84108
2 Factor income from rest of the world	5321	8740	10727	10392	13509	18227	20449	20893	21750	24408	25201	23564
A Compensation of employees	66	84	96	96	108	120	126	132	144	156	168	180
B Property and entrepreneurial income	5255	8656	10631	10296	13401	18107	20323	20761	21606	24252	25033	23384
3 Current transfers from rest of the world	756	1016	1161	1278	1350	1415	1307	1515	1787	1832	2036	2325
A Subsidies from supranational organisations	-	-	-	-	-	-	-	-	-	-	-	-
B Other current transfers	756	1016	1161	1278	1350	1415	1307	1515	1787	1832	2036	2325
Receipts from the Rest of the World on Current Transactions	140872	166044	176911	195591	228936	255205	216420	222632	237208	288103	320252	333417

1.8 Capital Transactions of The Nation, Summary

Million Norwegian kroner

Finance of Gross Capital Formation

	1980	1981	1982	1983	1984	1985	1986	1987	1988	1989	1990	1991
Gross saving	84351	96495	100217	113760	140193	147828	118166	131244	132610	152808	159319	162171
1 Consumption of fixed capital	41358	48053	55007	59615	62512	66512	72561	83300	91194	96678	98823	102462
A General government	2327	2658	2979	3186	3338	3742	4259	4845	5355	5678	5933	6220
B Corporate and quasi-corporate enterprises	28553	32808	38099	41467	43903	46209	49210	56655	62638	67537	69592	73481
Public	6806	7955	9052	10493	11096	13993	17042	20152	22789	25189	25823	28477
Private	21747	24853	29047	30974	32808	32216	32168	36503	39849	42347	43769	45004
C Other a	10479	12587	13928	14962	15271	16561	19091	21800	23202	23464	23299	22762
2 Net saving	42993	48442	45210	54145	77681	81316	45605	47944	41416	56130	60496	59709
A General government	25432	24500	24452	26066	43213	60423	41151	40838	30979	24695	30560	16241
B Corporate and quasi-corporate enterprises	12814	16636	13843	19345	22810	27452	20582	24501	17642	28516	26934	34317
Public	6421	7990	12084	13118	12347	7020	9485	9681	5421	12473	13872	17461
Private	6393	8646	1759	6227	10463	20431	11097	14820	12221	16043	13062	16856
C Other a	4746	7306	6915	8734	11658	-6559	-16128	-17395	-7205	2919	3002	9151
Less: Surplus of the nation on current transactions	5448	12460	4146	14644	23927	26682	-33443	-27338	-25220	1652	24120	33098
Finance of Gross Capital Formation	78903	84035	96071	99116	116266	121146	151609	158582	157830	151156	135199	129073

Gross Capital Formation

	1980	1981	1982	1983	1984	1985	1986	1987	1988	1989	1990	1991
Increase in stocks	8104	-7761	3809	-4332	-1300	11103	6070	1221	-12517	-18327	11055	2021

Norway

1.8 Capital Transactions of The Nation, Summary
(Continued)

Million Norwegian kroner

	1980	1981	1982	1983	1984	1985	1986	1987	1988	1989	1990	1991
Gross fixed capital formation	70798	91793	92262	103448	117567	110042	145540	157363	170345	169485	124146	127053
1 General government	11454	11602	11525	12410	12858	13288	16457	20087	22650	23020	21423	24320
2 Corporate and quasi-corporate enterprises	39221	60595	56990	67353	78854	64934	91465	96056	109352	115245	77117	82063
A Public	14811	19761	17887	26650	23752	27856	44789	45750	43804	44950	21577	37428
B Private	24410	40834	39103	40704	55102	37078	46676	50307	65548	70295	55540	44635
3 Other a	20123	19595	23748	23684	25856	31819	37618	41221	38344	31221	25607	20670
Gross Capital Formation	78902	84032	96071	99116	116267	121145	151610	158584	157828	151158	135201	129074

a) Item 'Other' includes households and private unincorporated enterprises and non- profit institutions serving households.

1.9 Gross Domestic Product by Institutional Sectors of Origin

Million Norwegian kroner

	1980	1981	1982	1983	1984	1985	1986	1987	1988	1989	1990	1991
					Domestic Factor Incomes Originating							
1 General government	36574	42504	48526	53655	58470	64173	71054	80722	86504	92090	98118	105611
2 Corporate and quasi-corporate enterprises a	178049	203216	220652	243635	279039	305414	299750	321479	332365	362651	392511	405767
3 Households and private unincorporated enterprises	...	...	...	...	...	...	...	...	...	...	...	...
4 Non-profit institutions serving households	...	...	...	...	...	...	...	...	...	...	...	...
Subtotal: Domestic Factor Incomes	214622	245719	269178	297290	337509	369587	370804	402201	418869	454741	490630	511377
Indirect taxes, net	29064	33901	38085	45294	52491	64101	70353	75978	73215	69963	71097	72847
A Indirect taxes	49025	55695	61747	69733	78200	91037	99922	107493	106984	106562	111089	115617
B Less: Subsidies	19961	21794	23662	24439	25709	26936	29569	31515	33769	36599	39992	42770
Consumption of fixed capital	41358	48053	55007	59614	62513	66512	72561	83301	91194	96678	98823	102462
Gross Domestic Product	285044	327673	362270	402198	452513	500200	513718	561480	583278	621382	660550	686686

a) The estimates of Households and private unincorporated enterprises and Non-profit institutions serving households are included in item 'Corporate and quasi-corporate enterprises'.

1.10 Gross Domestic Product by Kind of Activity, in Current Prices

Million Norwegian kroner

	1980	1981	1982	1983	1984	1985	1986	1987	1988	1989	1990	1991
1 Agriculture, hunting, forestry and fishing	10969	12957	13437	13135	15042	15150	16021	17695	17689	17568	20330	20052
2 Mining and quarrying	42078	51185	56514	68231	84778	91009	52530	53398	45951	71620	88644	91372
3 Manufacturing	45635	48575	51383	56724	64524	70127	75651	84590	89506	91265	90369	92591
4 Electricity, gas and water	8237	10158	11981	14312	16571	18278	19578	21439	23555	25109	26809	27266
5 Construction	16952	19673	22711	23848	24353	27070	30550	36632	38340	32549	29295	26910
6 Wholesale and retail trade, restaurants and hotels	33264	38475	42765	45475	49445	53897	62565	68118	70231	69985	73218	75315
7 Transport, storage and communication	26890	30755	31289	33852	37077	37976	43532	44425	51367	59669	64693	71731
8 Finance, insurance, real estate and business services	28244	34155	40859	45633	49318	56383	67557	78004	83942	88616	91249	94029
9 Community, social and personal services	12478	14009	15722	17701	18750	21408	24821	27389	29448	29549	31943	34030
Total, Industries	224747	259941	286660	318912	359858	391297	392806	431687	450028	485929	516551	533297
Producers of Government Services	38901	45162	51505	56841	61808	67965	75371	85629	91930	97841	104126	111910
Other Producers	...	...	...	...	...	...	...	...	...	...	...	...
Subtotal	263648	305103	338165	375753	421667	459261	468177	517316	541958	583770	620676	645207
Less: Imputed bank service charge	8724	11349	14318	15960	15443	15431	20280	24328	24604	25611	25200	24249
Plus: Import duties a	3692	4248	5203	5764	6006	9320	11852	9912	7046	6466	7244	7031
Plus: Value added tax	24703	28024	31536	34623	37794	44150	50309	54466	54941	53953	55803	56871
Plus: Other adjustments b	1726	1649	1683	2017	2489	2900	3660	4113	3937	2805	2028	1826
Equals: Gross Domestic Product	285045	327675	362269	402197	452512	500201	513718	561479	583278	621383	660552	686686
Memorandum Item: Mineral fuels and power	49587	59777	67331	80842	99676	107846	70238	73095	68112	94838	114097	117643

a) Item 'Import duties' includes collection of customs duties, value added tax on imports and special excises or taxes on imports.   b) Item 'Other adjustments' refers to collection of investment levy on fixed capital formation and subsidies on residential and social buildings.

1.11 Gross Domestic Product by Kind of Activity, in Constant Prices

Million Norwegian kroner

	1980	1981	1982	1983	1984	1985	1986	1987	1988	1989	1990	1991
			At constant prices of:									
			1980					1984				
1 Agriculture, hunting, forestry and fishing	10969	11959	12446	12319	13356 / 15042	13682	12878	13478	13624	14022	15630	15772
2 Mining and quarrying	42078	40498	40719	47866	55141 / 84778	87815	93616	105663	117718	148583	152765	173778
3 Manufacturing	45635	45191	44887	44555	47113 / 64524	66893	66862	68143	64887	63840	64262	62898
4 Electricity, gas and water	8237	8954	9094	10287	10614 / 16571	16109	14959	15906	16942	18676	18823	17004
5 Construction	16952	16735	17031	17563	17768 / 24353	25319	26597	26996	26350	24332	23433	22553
6 Wholesale and retail trade, restaurants and hotels	33264	32521	31907	31823	33351 / 49445	53663	56933	56190	52938	51213	50980	50607
7 Transport, storage and communication	26890	27545	26530	27149	28501 / 37077	38374	43015	42860	45039	47963	51855	54161
8 Finance, insurance, real estate and business services	28244	29310	30209	30274	31494 / 49318	53417	55601	58537	60052	58532	56966	55385
9 Community, social and personal services	12478	12542	12699	13031	12965 / 18750	20093	21593	21684	21844	20990	21505	21743
Statistical discrepancy	...	...	...	...	-	1	1	-4080	-10915	-32078	-34577	-46603
Total, Industries	224747	225254	225521	234866	250302 / 359858	375366	392055	405377	408479	416073	421642	427298
Producers of Government Services	38901	41141	43393	44993	46248 / 61808	63768	64870	66701	68139	69347	71131	73436
Other Producers	...	...	...	...	...	...	...	...	...	...	...	...
Subtotal	263648	266396	268914	279858	296550 / 421667	439135	456925	472028	476726	485520	493023	501207
Less: Imputed bank service charge	8724	8985	9205	9543	10157 / 15443	16393	17832	18497	18371	17223	16967	16145
Plus: Import duties a	3692	3869	4253	4092	4189 / 6006	9141	9794	7292	5265	4591	5626	5118
Plus: Value added tax	24703	25000	25399	25951	27309 / 37794	41820	44782	44519	42648	40497	40389	40255
Plus: Other adjustments b	1726	1267	-855	1518	1324 / 2489	2680	2627	1791	437	-52	-45	-39
Equals: Gross Domestic Product	285045	287546	288506	301877	319215 / 452512c	476381c	496296c	506180c	503620c	506607c	515038c	523178c
Memorandum Item: Mineral fuels and power	49587	48837	49455	57607	65289 / 99676	102457	106812	120057	132366	159816	164526	177508

a) Item 'Import duties' includes collection of customs duties, value added tax on imports and special excises or taxes on imports.
b) Item 'Other adjustments' refers to collection of investment levy on fixed capital formation and subsidies on residential and social buildings.
c) Beginning 1987, the estimates at 1984 constant prices are derived from the series of constant prices based on T-1 prices. This resulted in some statistical discrepancies shown in the table.

1.12 Relations Among National Accounting Aggregates

Million Norwegian kroner

	1980	1981	1982	1983	1984	1985	1986	1987	1988	1989	1990	1991
Gross Domestic Product	285045	327674	362270	402198	452512	500200	513718	561480	583278	621383	660550	686686
Plus: Net factor income from the rest of the world	-9520	-10579	-12704	-13002	-13142	-9506	-9092	-9548	-13542	-17841	-17182	-17522
Factor income from the rest of the world	5321	8740	10727	10392	13509	18227	20449	20893	21750	24408	25201	23564
Less: Factor income to the rest of the world	14841	19319	23431	23394	26651	27733	29541	30441	35292	42249	42383	41086
Equals: Gross National Product	275525	317095	349566	389196	439370	490694	504626	551932	569736	603542	643368	669164
Less: Consumption of fixed capital	41358	48053	55007	59614	62513	66512	72561	83301	91194	96678	98823	102462
Equals: National Income	234167	269043	294559	329581	376857	424183	432065	468631	478542	506864	544545	566701
Plus: Net current transfers from the rest of the world	-2456	-2780	-3630	-4244	-4156	-4774	-5971	-6588	-7390	-7781	-8869	-9810
Current transfers from the rest of the world	756	1016	1161	1278	1350	1415	1307	1515	1787	1832	2036	2325
Less: Current transfers to the rest of the world	3212	3796	4791	5522	5506	6189	7278	8103	9177	9613	10904	12135
Equals: National Disposable Income	231711	266263	290929	325337	372701	419409	426094	462043	471152	499083	535676	556892
Less: Final consumption	188719	217821	245719	271192	295020	338093	380489	414099	429736	442953	475181	497183
Equals: Net Saving	42992	48442	45210	54145	77681	81316	45605	47944	41416	56130	60496	59709
Less: Surplus of the nation on current transactions	5448	12460	4146	14644	23927	26682	-33443	-27338	-25220	1652	24120	33098
Equals: Net Capital Formation	37544	35982	41064	39501	53754	54634	79048	75282	66636	54479	36376	26611

Norway

2.1 Government Final Consumption Expenditure by Function, in Current Prices

Million Norwegian kroner

	1980	1981	1982	1983	1984	1985	1986	1987	1988	1989	1990	1991
1 General public services	4001	4564	5088	5735	6270	6993	7714	8898	10046	10698	11009	11984
2 Defence	8033	10243	11160	12569	13011	14441	15340	17764	17548	20458	22050	22218
3 Public order and safety	2207	2598	2910	3169	3422	3736	4179	4955	5193	5549	5892	6405
4 Education	14419	16347	18578	20263	21790	24067	26122	29165	31326	33566	35722	37854
5 Health	11547	13471	15396	17699	19464	21507	24134	27819	28786	29492	31229	33350
6 Social security and welfare	4642	5524	6312	6745	7191	8167	9284	11098	12286	13342	13860	15483
7 Housing and community amenities	235	99	35	-1	-141	-185	-148	-213	-295	-555	-675	-559
8 Recreational, cultural and religious affairs	1641	1933	2241	2512	2732	3005	3282	3689	3899	4059	4225	5285
9 Economic services	6562	7495	8424	9340	10047	10641	11259	12372	12839	13798	14654	15022
A Fuel and energy	99	120	159	138	9	-42	98	204	266	351	392	84
B Agriculture, forestry, fishing and hunting	725	870	965	1063	1195	1257	1383	1497	1637	1713	1800	1557
C Mining, manufacturing and construction, except fuel and energy	46	64	91	99	69	73	83	96	90	60	88	96
D Transportation and communication	4854	5468	6079	6637	7118	7551	7951	8740	8973	9214	9445	10067
E Other economic affairs	838	974	1131	1403	1657	1802	1743	1835	1873	2460	2930	3218
10 Other functions	190	342	265	182	313	282	415	499	610	592	1148	437
Total Government Final Consumption Expenditure	53478	62616	70408	78214	84099	92653	101580	116045	122237	130998	139115	147478

2.2 Government Final Consumption Expenditure by Function, in Constant Prices

Million Norwegian kroner

	1980	1981	1982	1983	1984	1985	1986	1987	1988	1989	1990	1991
			At constant prices of:									
			1980					1984				
1 General public services	4001	4130	4259	4544	4710 / 6270	6605	6854	7240	7816	7962	7866	8284
2 Defence	8033	9250	9304	9913	10026 / 13011	13561	13501	14552	13687	15283	15834	15596
3 Public order and safety	2207	2353	2438	2511	2569 / 3422	3517	3709	4049	4045	4110	4178	4402
4 Education	14419	14939	15737	16100	16473 / 21790	22626	22861	23454	23699	24269	24718	25356
5 Health	11547	12136	12822	13811	14296 / 19464	20010	20794	21435	21402	20998	21335	21768
6 Social security and welfare	4642	4967	5240	5266	5300 / 7191	7674	8084	8638	9131	9466	9436	10095
7 Housing and community amenities	235	89	43	33	-35 / -141	-192	-155	-247	-275	-477	-606	-472
8 Recreational, cultural and religious affairs	1641	1754	1865	1928	1994 / 2732	2811	2855	2905	2948	2944	2981	3613
9 Economic services	6562	6835	7057	7476	7669 / 10047	9965	9907	9868	9791	10171	10561	10659
A Fuel and energy	99	109	133	110	7 / 9	-39	87	168	208	261	278	58
B Agriculture, forestry, fishing and hunting	725	791	812	846	902 / 1195	1180	1225	1221	1271	1268	1274	1066
C Mining, manufacturing and construction, except fuel and energy	46	57	75	78	50 / 69	68	72	76	68	43	61	64
D Transportation and communication	4854	4996	5091	5335	5477 / 7118	7067	6999	6935	6817	6811	6890	7292
E Other economic affairs	838	882	946	1108	1232 / 1657	1689	1524	1471	1433	1798	2068	2197
10 Other functions	190	309	222	145	235 / 313	265	369	404	473	441	820	302
Total Government Final Consumption Expenditure	53478	56763	58985	61727	63238 / 84099 a	86842 a	88779 a	92304 a	92752 a	95190 a	97146 a	99624 a

a) Beginning 1987, the estimates at 1984 constant prices are derived from the series of constant prices based on T-1 prices. This resulted in some statistical discrepancies shown in the table.

2.3 Total Government Outlays by Function and Type

Million Norwegian kroner

	Final Consumption Expenditures			Subsidies	Other Current Transfers & Property Income	Total Current Disbursements	Gross Capital Formation	Other Capital Outlays	Total Outlays
	Total	Compensation of Employees	Other						
1980									
1 General public services	4001	2709	1292	...	2442	6443	469	...	6912
2 Defence	8033	3674	4359	...	60	8093	66	...	8159
3 Public order and safety	2207	1836	371	...	28	2235	116	...	2351
4 Education	14419	10626	3793	...	1895	16314	2004	...	18318
5 Health	11547	9176	2371	...	5342	16889	1732	...	18621
6 Social security and welfare	4642	4089	553	...	34311	38953	577	...	39530
7 Housing and community amenities	235	295	-60	...	2314	2549	1752	...	4301
8 Recreation, culture and religion	1641	1019	622	...	1393	3034	611	...	3645
9 Economic services	6562	3037	3524	...	17565	24127	4124	...	28251
A Fuel and energy	99	84	15	...	860	959	36	...	995
B Agriculture, forestry, fishing and hunting	725	568	157	...	7323	8048	29	...	8077
C Mining (except fuels), manufacturing and construction	46	26	20	...	1190	1236	2	...	1238
D Transportation and communication	4854	1727	3127	...	2956	7810	3986	...	11796
E Other economic affairs	838	633	205	...	5236	6074	71	...	6145
10 Other functions	190	112	78	...	9667	9857	3	...	9860
Total a	53478	36572	16904	...	75013	128494	11456	...	139947
1981									
1 General public services	4564	3053	1511	...	2725	7289	474	...	7763
2 Defence	10243	4114	6129	...	47	10290	62	...	10352
3 Public order and safety	2598	2127	471	...	54	2652	133	...	2785
4 Education	16347	12051	4296	...	2118	18465	1993	...	20458
5 Health	13471	10818	2653	...	6017	19488	1692	...	21180
6 Social security and welfare	5524	4947	577	...	40198	45722	662	...	46384
7 Housing and community amenities	99	380	-282	...	2232	2331	1683	...	4014
8 Recreation, culture and religion	1933	1218	715	...	1580	3513	680	...	4193
9 Economic services	7495	3535	3961	...	18986	26482	4221	...	30703
A Fuel and energy	120	90	30	...	467	587	40	...	627
B Agriculture, forestry, fishing and hunting	870	676	194	...	8707	9577	55	...	9632
C Mining (except fuels), manufacturing and construction	64	37	27	...	1969	2033	4	...	2037
D Transportation and communication	5468	2008	3460	...	3263	8731	4061	...	12792
E Other economic affairs	974	724	250	...	4580	5554	61	...	5615
10 Other functions	342	259	82	...	10735	11077	5	...	11082
Total a	62616	42503	20113	...	84693	147309	11604	...	158913
1982									
1 General public services	5088	3418	1670	...	3596	8684	430	...	9114
2 Defence	11160	4748	6411	...	66	11225	86	...	11311
3 Public order and safety	2910	2386	524	...	65	2975	155	...	3130
4 Education	18578	13802	4776	...	2438	21016	1917	...	22933
5 Health	15396	12378	3018	...	6690	22086	1690	...	23776
6 Social security and welfare	6312	5739	573	...	46201	52513	660	...	53173
7 Housing and community amenities	35	422	-387	...	2031	2066	1440	...	3506
8 Recreation, culture and religion	2241	1400	841	...	1913	4154	732	...	4886
9 Economic services	8424	4055	4369	...	20724	29147	4404	...	33551
A Fuel and energy	159	127	32	...	599	757	45	...	802
B Agriculture, forestry, fishing and hunting	965	767	198	...	9827	10792	58	...	10850
C Mining (except fuels), manufacturing and construction	91	44	47	...	2177	2268	3	...	2271
D Transportation and communication	6079	2283	3796	...	3598	9676	4254	...	13931
E Other economic affairs	1131	834	297	...	4523	5654	43	...	5697
10 Other functions	265	180	86	...	11470	11735	12	...	11746
Total a	70408	48526	21882	...	95193	165601	11525	...	177126

Norway

2.3 Total Government Outlays by Function and Type
(Continued)

Million Norwegian kroner

	Final Consumption Expenditures			Subsidies	Other Current Transfers & Property Income	Total Current Disbursements	Gross Capital Formation	Other Capital Outlays	Total Outlays
	Total	Compensation of Employees	Other						
1983									
1 General public services	5735	3744	1991	...	4100	9835	452	...	10287
2 Defence	12569	5146	7423	...	63	12632	94	...	12726
3 Public order and safety	3169	2567	602	...	74	3243	177	...	3420
4 Education	20263	15053	5210	...	2885	23148	2190	...	25338
5 Health	17699	14294	3405	...	7540	25239	1656	...	26895
6 Social security and welfare	6745	6027	718	...	52723	59468	841	...	60309
7 Housing and community amenities	-1	486	-486	...	1704	1703	1369	...	3072
8 Recreation, culture and religion	2512	1568	944	...	2047	4559	825	...	5384
9 Economic services	9340	4602	4739	...	21475	30815	4789	...	35604
A Fuel and energy	138	143	-5	...	496	634	45	...	679
B Agriculture, forestry, fishing and hunting	1063	834	229	...	10173	11236	49	...	11285
C Mining (except fuels), manufacturing and construction	99	49	50	...	2291	2390	10	...	2400
D Transportation and communication	6637	2552	4085	...	4037	10674	4611	...	15286
E Other economic affairs	1403	1024	379	...	4478	5881	74	...	5954
10 Other functions	182	168	15	...	13355	13538	18	...	13556
Total a	78214	53655	24559	...	105966	184180	12411	...	196591
1984									
1 General public services	6270	4086	2183	...	4339	10609	542	...	11150
2 Defence	13011	5387	7624	...	60	13071	94	...	13164
3 Public order and safety	3422	2785	636	...	72	3494	210	...	3705
4 Education	21790	16390	5400	...	3437	25228	2172	...	27400
5 Health	19464	15639	3825	...	7758	27222	1514	...	28737
6 Social security and welfare	7191	6656	536	...	57939	65130	901	...	66031
7 Housing and community amenities	-141	518	-659	...	1518	1377	1337	...	2714
8 Recreation, culture and religion	2732	1726	1006	...	2278	5010	863	...	5873
9 Economic services	10047	5075	4973	...	22042	32089	5213	...	37302
A Fuel and energy	9	162	-152	...	468	477	93	...	570
B Agriculture, forestry, fishing and hunting	1195	897	298	...	10504	11700	84	...	11784
C Mining (except fuels), manufacturing and construction	69	44	25	...	2390	2458	4	...	2462
D Transportation and communication	7118	2761	4357	...	4141	11259	4961	...	16219
E Other economic affairs	1657	1212	445	...	4539	6196	72	...	6268
10 Other functions	313	209	104	...	15038	15351	11	...	15362
Total a	84099	58471	25629	...	114481	198581	12858	...	211438
1985									
1 General public services	6993	4491	2502	...	4962	11954	596	...	12550
2 Defence	14441	5759	8682	...	62	14503	90	...	14593
3 Public order and safety	3736	3024	712	...	66	3802	214	...	4016
4 Education	24067	18057	6010	...	3310	27377	2113	...	29490
5 Health	21507	17150	4358	...	8147	29654	1457	...	31111
6 Social security and welfare	8167	7523	644	...	63196	71363	992	...	72355
7 Housing and community amenities	-185	583	-767	...	1732	1547	1089	...	2637
8 Recreation, culture and religion	3005	1904	1100	...	2389	5394	956	...	6350
9 Economic services	10641	5455	5186	...	23896	34537	5765	...	40302
A Fuel and energy	-42	174	-216	...	1085	1043	107	...	1150
B Agriculture, forestry, fishing and hunting	1257	971	287	...	11182	12439	61	...	12500
C Mining (except fuels), manufacturing and construction	73	47	26	...	2340	2412	5	...	2417
D Transportation and communication	7551	2898	4653	...	4360	11911	5494	...	17405
E Other economic affairs	1802	1365	437	...	4929	6731	99	...	6830
10 Other functions	282	229	53	...	17410	17692	17	...	17709
Total a	92653	64174	28480	...	125170	217824	13289	...	231112

2.3 Total Government Outlays by Function and Type
(Continued)

Million Norwegian kroner

	Final Consumption Expenditures			Subsidies	Other Current Transfers & Property Income	Total Current Disbursements	Gross Capital Formation	Other Capital Outlays	Total Outlays
	Total	Compensation of Employees	Other						
1986									
1 General public services	7714	4955	2759	...	5829	13543	927	...	14470
2 Defence	15340	6262	9079	...	70	15410	51	...	15461
3 Public order and safety	4179	3379	800	...	82	4261	268	...	4529
4 Education	26122	19974	6148	...	3697	29818	2403	...	32222
5 Health	24134	19110	5024	...	8918	33052	1912	...	34964
6 Social security and welfare	9284	8554	729	...	70050	79334	1072	...	80406
7 Housing and community amenities	-148	635	-783	...	2351	2203	1774	...	3977
8 Recreation, culture and religion	3282	2107	1174	...	2579	5861	1223	...	7084
9 Economic services	11259	5772	5487	...	26505	37764	6820	...	44584
A Fuel and energy	98	193	-95	...	1690	1788	94	...	1882
B Agriculture, forestry, fishing and hunting	1383	1057	327	...	11083	12466	80	...	12546
C Mining (except fuels), manufacturing and construction	83	52	31	...	3276	3359	8	...	3367
D Transportation and communication	7951	3187	4764	...	5415	13366	6474	...	19841
E Other economic affairs	1743	1284	460	...	5042	6785	164	...	6949
10 Other functions	415	307	108	...	22337	22752	7	...	22760
Total a	101580	71055	30526	...	142418	243998	16458	...	260456
1987									
1 General public services	8898	5643	3255	...	6134	15032	1506	...	16538
2 Defence	17764	6930	10834	...	558	18321	88	...	18409
3 Public order and safety	4955	3936	1019	...	118	5073	322	...	5395
4 Education	29165	22425	6740	...	4368	33534	3094	...	36628
5 Health	27819	22204	5615	...	10207	38026	2631	...	40657
6 Social security and welfare	11098	9965	1134	...	78933	90031	1428	...	91459
7 Housing and community amenities	-213	717	-931	...	2709	2495	2038	...	4533
8 Recreation, culture and religion	3689	2381	1307	...	2994	6682	1614	...	8296
9 Economic services	12372	6247	6124	...	30476	42848	7361	...	50209
A Fuel and energy	204	225	-21	...	4935	5139	53	...	5193
B Agriculture, forestry, fishing and hunting	1497	1159	338	...	11988	13485	70	...	13555
C Mining (except fuels), manufacturing and construction	96	57	39	...	2583	2679	10	...	2688
D Transportation and communication	8740	3509	5231	...	5999	14738	7127	...	21865
E Other economic affairs	1835	1297	538	...	4972	6807	101	...	6908
10 Other functions	499	273	226	...	24074	24573	6	...	24579
Total a	116045	80722	35322	...	160571	276616	20086	...	296702
1988									
1 General public services	10046	6243	3803	...	7277	17323	2070	...	19392
2 Defence	17548	7369	10180	...	128	17676	87	...	17763
3 Public order and safety	5193	4204	989	...	153	5346	276	...	5623
4 Education	31326	24035	7292	...	4952	36278	3181	...	39459
5 Health	28786	23532	5254	...	11258	40044	3226	...	43270
6 Social security and welfare	12286	10965	1321	...	90887	103173	1812	...	104985
7 Housing and community amenities	-295	792	-1087	...	2899	2604	2206	...	4811
8 Recreation, culture and religion	3899	2533	1366	...	3251	7150	1646	...	8796
9 Economic services	12839	6533	6306	...	35277	48116	8145	...	56260
A Fuel and energy	266	232	34	...	8025	8291	90	...	8381
B Agriculture, forestry, fishing and hunting	1637	1220	417	...	12592	14229	87	...	14316
C Mining (except fuels), manufacturing and construction	90	59	31	...	2954	3044	5	...	3049
D Transportation and communication	8973	3699	5274	...	6503	15476	7858	...	23333
E Other economic affairs	1873	1322	551	...	5204	7077	105	...	7182
10 Other functions	610	300	311	...	22682	23293	1	...	23294
Total a	122237	86504	35733	...	178765	301002	22650	...	323652

Norway

2.3 Total Government Outlays by Function and Type
(Continued)

Million Norwegian kroner

		Final Consumption Expenditures			Subsidies	Other Current Transfers & Property Income	Total Current Disbursements	Gross Capital Formation	Other Capital Outlays	Total Outlays
		Total	Compensation of Employees	Other						
	1989									
1	General public services	10698	6627	4072	...	7304	18002	1971	...	19973
2	Defence	20458	7767	12690	...	124	20581	104	...	20686
3	Public order and safety	5549	4404	1146	...	178	5727	473	...	6199
4	Education	33566	25621	7945	...	6409	39975	3212	...	43187
5	Health	29492	24350	5142	...	11743	41235	3026	...	44261
6	Social security and welfare	13342	12270	1072	...	102480	115821	1595	...	117416
7	Housing and community amenities	-555	841	-1395	...	3209	2655	2674	...	5328
8	Recreation, culture and religion	4059	2635	1424	...	3310	7369	1171	...	8539
9	Economic services	13798	7251	6547	...	30132	43930	8793	...	52723
	A Fuel and energy	351	241	110	...	1370	1721	134	...	1855
	B Agriculture, forestry, fishing and hunting	1713	1335	378	...	13624	15337	106	...	15443
	C Mining (except fuels), manufacturing and construction	60	44	16	...	2488	2548	21	...	2570
	D Transportation and communication	9214	3880	5335	...	6678	15893	8325	...	24217
	E Other economic affairs	2460	1752	708	...	5971	8431	207	...	8638
10	Other functions	592	324	268	...	24734	25325	1	...	25327
	Total ª	130998	92090	38908	...	189622	320619	23020	...	343640
	1990									
1	General public services	11009	6817	4193	...	8631	19640	1742	...	21383
2	Defence	22050	8519	13532	...	167	22217	77	...	22294
3	Public order and safety	5892	4651	1241	...	217	6109	492	...	6601
4	Education	35722	27099	8623	...	7164	42886	3326	...	46212
5	Health	31229	26122	5108	...	12870	44099	2695	...	46794
6	Social security and welfare	13860	13148	712	...	111605	125465	1532	...	126997
7	Housing and community amenities	-675	890	-1566	...	2929	2254	2285	...	4539
8	Recreation, culture and religion	4225	2784	1442	...	3520	7745	977	...	8722
9	Economic services	14654	7643	7012	...	33276	47930	8283	...	56214
	A Fuel and energy	392	296	96	...	2008	2400	123	...	2523
	B Agriculture, forestry, fishing and hunting	1800	1381	419	...	14430	16230	133	...	16363
	C Mining (except fuels), manufacturing and construction	88	60	28	...	3564	3652	9	...	3661
	D Transportation and communication	9445	4014	5431	...	6955	16400	7861	...	24260
	E Other economic affairs	2930	1893	1038	...	6318	9249	158	...	9407
10	Other functions	1148	446	702	...	25831	26978	15	...	26993
	Total ª	139115	98118	40997	...	206209	345324	21423	...	366747
	1991									
1	General public services	11984	7296	4688	...	8943	20926	1702	...	22628
2	Defence	22218	8643	13576	...	148	22366	33	...	22398
3	Public order and safety	6405	4993	1412	...	254	6659	568	...	7227
4	Education	37854	28584	9270	...	8334	46188	3656	...	49844
5	Health	33350	29111	4239	...	15154	48504	3444	...	51948
6	Social security and welfare	15483	14288	1195	...	120624	136106	1498	...	137604
7	Housing and community amenities	-559	1647	-2206	...	3872	3313	2475	...	5788
8	Recreation, culture and religion	5285	3134	2152	...	3799	9084	1829	...	10913
9	Economic services	15022	7592	7430	...	34102	49124	9034	...	58158

2.3 Total Government Outlays by Function and Type
(Continued)

Million Norwegian kroner

	Final Consumption Expenditures			Subsidies	Other Current Transfers & Property Income	Total Current Disbursements	Gross Capital Formation	Other Capital Outlays	Total Outlays
	Total	Compensation of Employees	Other						
A Fuel and energy	84	262	-178	...	1908	1992	161	...	2153
B Agriculture, forestry, fishing and hunting	1557	1210	347	...	14387	15944	77	...	16021
C Mining (except fuels), manufacturing and construction	96	60	36	...	3110	3206	10	...	3216
D Transportation and communication	10067	3795	6272	...	6308	16374	8637	...	25011
E Other economic affairs	3218	2266	953	...	8390	11608	150	...	11757
10 Other functions	437	323	113	...	24920	25357	68	...	25425
Total a	147478	105611	41867	...	220149	367627	24307	...	391934

a) Column 'Subsidies', is included in column 'Other current transfers and property income'.

2.4 Composition of General Government Social Security Benefits and Social Assistance Grants to Households

Million Norwegian kroner

	1980		1981		1982		1983		1984		1985	
	Social Security Benefits	Social Assistance Grants	Social Security Benefits	Social Assistance Grants	Social Security Benefits	Social Assistance Grants	Social Security Benefits	Social Assistance Grants	Social Security Benefits	Social Assistance Grants	Social Security Benefits	Social Assistance Grants
1 Education benefits	1092	...	1096	...	1247	...	1486	...	1630	...	1847	...
A Pre-primary and primary	38	...	42	...	47	...	59	...	62	...	71	...
B Secondary	152	...	129	...	186	...	378	...	401	...	539	...
C Tertiary	10	...	13	...	11	...	17	...	14	...	13	...
D Other	892	...	912	...	1005	...	1032	...	1153	...	1224	...
2 Health benefits	5313	...	5985	...	6653	...	7505	...	7729	...	8112	...
A Hospital	222	...	311	...	295	...	297	...	438	...	674	...
B Clinics and practitioners	4286	...	4818	...	5360	...	6029	...	5953	...	5920	...
C Public health	-	...	8	...	4	...	11	...	59	...	84	...
D Medicaments, etc.	805	...	849	...	995	...	1168	...	1279	...	1435	...
3 Social security and welfare benefits	34162	...	40017	...	45967	...	52523	...	57731	...	62968	...
A Social security	33235	...	38919	...	44711	...	50994	...	56079	...	61167	...
Temporary sickness	5910	...	7103	...	7746	...	8787	...	9656	...	10624	...
Old age and permanent disability	22601	...	25780	...	29469	...	32746	...	35816	...	39718	...
Unemployment	681	...	922	...	1521	...	2711	...	2962	...	2553	...
Family assistance	3268	...	4449	...	4978	...	5536	...	5922	...	6348	...
Other	763	...	665	...	997	...	1214	...	1723	...	1924	...
B Welfare	927	...	1099	...	1255	...	1529	...	1652	...	1801	...
4 Housing and community amenities	40	...	51	...	63	...	86	...	78	...	129	...
5 Recreation and cultural benefits	27	...	34	...	42	...	62	...	63	...	108	...
6 Other	342	...	454	...	544	...	549	...	688	...	657	...
Total	40976	...	47637	...	54516	...	62212	...	67918	...	73819	...

	1986		1987		1988		1989		1990		1991	
	Social Security Benefits	Social Assistance Grants	Social Security Benefits	Social Assistance Grants	Social Security Benefits	Social Assistance Grants	Social Security Benefits	Social Assistance Grants	Social Security Benefits	Social Assistance Grants	Social Security Benefits	Social Assistance Grants
1 Education benefits	1827	...	2067	...	2155	...	2669	...	3053	...	3311	...
A Pre-primary and primary	79	...	106	...	97	...	95	...	102	...	59	...
B Secondary	482	...	483	...	514	...	253	...	940	...	246	...
C Tertiary	11	...	10	...	12	...	43	...	859	...	54	...
D Other	1255	...	1467	...	1532	...	2279	...	1152	...	2952	...
2 Health benefits	8883	...	10114	...	11142	...	11621	...	12765	...	15027	...
A Hospital	447	...	496	...	3878	...	3969	...	3860	...	3961	...
B Clinics and practitioners	6624	...	7340	...	4372	...	4729	...	5409	...	7264	...
C Public health	126	...	205	...	329	...	144	...	156	...	186	...
D Medicaments, etc.	1685	...	2073	...	2563	...	2779	...	3341	...	3616	...
3 Social security and welfare benefits	69802	...	78674	...	90573	...	102150	...	111289	...	120284	...
A Social security	67761	...	76258	...	87626	...	98738	...	107717	...	116931	...
Temporary sickness	12058	...	13860	...	15809	...	17333	...	19162	...	21548	...
Old age and permanent disability	44314	...	49459	...	55983	...	60725	...	65122	...	69221	...
Unemployment	2006	...	2034	...	3212	...	6474	...	7812	...	8545	...

Norway

2.4 Composition of General Government Social Security Benefits and Social Assistance Grants to Households
(Continued)

Million Norwegian kroner

	1986		1987		1988		1989		1990		1991	
	Social Security Benefits	Social Assistance Grants	Social Security Benefits	Social Assistance Grants	Social Security Benefits	Social Assistance Grants	Social Security Benefits	Social Assistance Grants	Social Security Benefits	Social Assistance Grants	Social Security Benefits	Social Assistance Grants
Family assistance	7049	...	7930	...	8962	...	10051	...	11245	...	12841	...
Other	2334	...	2975	...	3661	...	4156	...	4376	...	4775	...
B Welfare	2041	...	2416	...	2947	...	3411	...	3572	...	3353	...
4 Housing and community amenities	164	...	159	...	148	...	159	...	195	...	253	...
5 Recreation and cultural benefits	96	...	92	...	80	...	89	...	81	...	74	...
6 Other	755	...	968	...	1260	...	1463	...	1599	...	1922	...
Total	81525	...	92073	...	105358	...	118151	...	128982	...	140871	...

2.5 Private Final Consumption Expenditure by Type and Purpose, in Current Prices

Million Norwegian kroner

	1980	1981	1982	1983	1984	1985	1986	1987	1988	1989	1990	1991
Final Consumption Expenditure of Resident Households												
1 Food, beverages and tobacco	36201	41360	46420	50743	54932	61601	68518	75198	77619	79793	84908	88852
A Food	27285	31381	35744	38758	41858	46707	51597	55949	56846	58614	62256	64438
B Non-alcoholic beverages	1327	1377	1726	1824	2008	2309	2841	3284	3694	3388	3747	4091
C Alcoholic beverages	4826	5412	5393	6144	6629	7521	8173	9277	9848	10149	10598	11152
D Tobacco	2764	3190	3557	4017	4436	5064	5908	6688	7231	7642	8308	9171
2 Clothing and footwear	11934	12975	13950	14352	15802	19076	21352	22159	22443	22125	22961	23826
3 Gross rent, fuel and power	21271	24881	28769	32708	36611	40858	44961	49892	54896	58949	64333	67797
A Fuel and power	7406	8846	10285	11570	13114	14848	16043	17225	18137	18554	20619	21184
B Other	13864	16036	18484	21138	23497	26009	28918	32667	36759	40396	43714	46613
4 Furniture, furnishings and household equipment and operation	11878	13215	14099	15102	16507	19060	21633	22773	22745	22394	23283	23432
A Household operation a	3069	3418	3672	4055	4398	4884	5445	5691	5869	5852	6129	6265
B Other	8810	9798	10428	11047	12110	14177	16189	17082	16875	16542	17154	17167
5 Medical care and health expenses	5676	6387	7407	8180	8586	9298	10301	11252	12990	13890	15844	18270
6 Transport and communication	20220	23086	26502	29188	31811	41337	47136	44888	40821	40623	43938	43510
A Personal transport equipment	7406	8089	9694	10393	11363	18296	21860	17475	12540	11038	11205	9308
B Other	12814	14997	16808	18795	20448	23041	25276	27413	28281	29585	32733	34202
7 Recreational, entertainment, education and cultural services	11626	13403	14488	15979	17572	20196	23861	25896	27701	27717	29884	31877
A Education	647	618	695	775	850	980	1115	1199	1387	1478	1728	1862
B Other	10979	12785	13794	15204	16722	19215	22746	24697	26315	26240	28156	30015
8 Miscellaneous goods and services	12968	15174	17139	19511	21742	25078	30336	34330	35640	36222	38821	41936
A Personal care	2335	2710	3112	3546	3987	4602	5373	6131	6705	6906	7233	7642
B Expenditures in restaurants, cafes and hotels	5150	6042	6960	8066	9147	10488	12603	14773	14552	14048	13773	14140
C Other	5483	6421	7068	7899	8609	9988	12361	13427	14382	15269	17814	20154
Total Final Consumption Expenditure in the Domestic Market by Households, of which	131773	150481	168774	185762	203563	236503	268098	286386	294854	301714	323971	339500
A Durable goods	16932	18851	20809	22127	24495	33817	39934	36374	31325	28788	29996	28628
B Semi-durable goods	20766	23235	25163	26282	28800	34599	39380	41105	41393	40795	42564	44093
C Non-durable goods	54529	62683	70534	77533	84513	94732	104419	114233	119051	123251	132567	139130
D Services	39545	45713	52269	59820	65755	73356	84364	94676	103086	108879	118844	127649
Plus: Direct purchases abroad by resident households	7414	9411	11592	12535	13197	15918	19184	20738	22768	20333	22545	21867
Less: Direct purchases in the domestic market by non-resident households	3945	4687	5056	5319	5839	6982	8373	9071	10123	10092	10451	11663
Equals: Final Consumption Expenditure of Resident Households b	135242	155205	175310	192979	210921	245439	278909	298054	307499	311955	336065	349705
Final Consumption Expenditure of Private Non-profit Institutions Serving Households												
Equals: Final Consumption Expenditure of Private Non-profit Organisations Serving Households	...	...	...	...	...	...	...	...	...	...	...	...
Private Final Consumption Expenditure	135242	155205	175310	192979	210921	245439	278909	298054	307499	311955	336065	349705

a) Item 'Household operations' also includes repair of furniture and household goods.
b) Item 'Final consumption expenditure of resident households' includes consumption expenditure of private non-profit institutions serving households.

2.6 Private Final Consumption Expenditure by Type and Purpose, in Constant Prices

Million Norwegian kroner

	1980	1981	1982	1983	1984	1985	1986	1987	1988	1989	1990	1991
					At constant prices of:							
					1980				1984			

Final Consumption Expenditure of Resident Households

	1980	1981	1982	1983	1984	1985	1986	1987	1988	1989	1990	1991
1 Food, beverages and tobacco	36201	34998	34498	34741	35261 / 54932	58117	59305	60251	58516	58126	59385	60225
A Food	27285	27057	27203	27313	27566 / 41858	43821	44411	44896	43002	43087	44347	45096
B Non-alcoholic beverages	1327	1195	1313	1320	1371 / 2008	2177	2469	2642	2784	2427	2525	2631
C Alcoholic beverages	4826	4275	3752	3845	3961 / 6629	7285	7319	7588	7493	7299	7169	7071
D Tobacco	2764	2472	2230	2263	2363 / 4436	4834	5106	5131	5234	5306	5347	5436
2 Clothing and footwear	11934	11627	11585	11308	11776 / 15802	17785	18291	17441	16701	15979	16211	16476
3 Gross rent, fuel and power	21271	21817	22420	23068	23855 / 36611	38632	40430	41920	42519	43088	44177	44574
A Fuel and power	7406	7380	7354	7232	7434 / 13114	13993	14607	14819	14297	13989	14590	14476
B Other	13864	14437	15066	15836	16422 / 23497	24639	25823	27095	28189	29053	29550	30049
4 Furniture, furnishings and household equipment and operation	11878	11623	11246	11174	11649 / 16507	18218	19282	18717	17696	16835	17083	16838
A Household operation a	3069	3079	2972	3052	3122 / 4398	4621	4809	4639	4419	4096	4006	3974
B Other	8810	8544	8274	8122	8527 / 12110	13597	14473	14077	13277	12743	13096	12879
5 Medical care and health expenses	5676	5771	6126	6345	6271 / 8586	8672	8900	9128	10223	10485	11190	12221
6 Transport and communication	20220	20662	21663	21857	22514 / 31811	39575	42231	36375	31149	29419	30885	29917
A Personal transport equipment	7406	7708	8568	8290	8273 / 11363	17050	17794	12365	8168	6936	6950	5666
B Other	12814	12955	13095	13567	14241 / 20448	22525	24436	24567	24102	23783	25394	25931
7 Recreational, entertainment, education and cultural services	11626	12428	12128	12505	13162 / 17572	19205	21409	21653	22085	21263	21999	22587
A Education	647	563	564	586	604 / 850	916	961	953	1036	1038	1151	1200
B Other	10979	11865	11564	11919	12558 / 16722	18289	20448	20701	21046	20218	20834	21370
8 Miscellaneous goods and services	12968	13154	13191	13568	14393 / 21742	23494	25508	26968	26371	25862	25785	25900
A Personal care	2335	2372	2389	2468	2619 / 3987	4314	4669	4865	4918	4870	4944	5084
B Expenditures in restaurants, cafes and hotels	5150	5005	4812	4979	5319 / 9147	9927	10933	11719	10814	9985	9378	9257
C Other	5483	5777	5989	6121	6455 / 8609	9253	9906	10390	10631	10997	11458	11551
Statistical discrepancy	...	...	...	...	... / -	-1	-	146	50	42	10	-1
Total Final Consumption Expenditure in the Domestic Market by Households, of which	131773	132081	132856	134566	138881 / 203563	223697	235356	232599	225310	221099	226725	228737
A Durable goods	16932	17462	18019	17662	18438 / 24495	31949	34025	27792	22584	20194	20735	19439
B Semi-durable goods	20766	20840	20813	20596	21499 / 28800	32614	34598	33292	31841	30560	31159	31580
C Non-durable goods	54529	53342	52988	53402	54372 / 84513	89701	92736	94276	92182	91600	93852	94548

Norway

Million Norwegian kroner

	1980	1981	1982	1983	1984	1985	1986	1987	1988	1989	1990	1991
			1980					**1984**				
					At constant prices of:							
D Services	39545	40437	41036	42906	44572 / 65755	69433	73996	77442	79215	79385	81629	83820
Plus: Direct purchases abroad by resident households	7414	8829	10159	10385	10036 / 13197	14753	16755	17055	17884	15123	15790	14194
Less: Direct purchases in the domestic market by non-resident households	3945	4126	3816	3648	3778 / 5839	6625	7306	7268	7608	7223	7185	7666
Equals: Final Consumption Expenditure of Resident Households	135242b	136784b	139199b	141303b	145139b / 210921bc	231825bc	244804bc	242388bc	235561bc	229041bc	235373bc	235301bc

Final Consumption Expenditure of Private Non-profit Institutions Serving Households

	1980	1981	1982	1983	1984	1985	1986	1987	1988	1989	1990	1991
Equals: Final Consumption Expenditure of Private Non-profit Organisations Serving Households	...	...	...	...	...	...	...	...	...	...	...	...
Private Final Consumption Expenditure	135242	136784	139199	141303	145139 / 210921c	231825c	244804c	242388c	235561c	229041c	235373c	235301c

a) Item 'Household operations' also includes repair of furniture and household goods.
b) Item 'Final consumption expenditure of resident households' includes consumption expenditure of private non-profit institutions serving households.
c) Beginning 1987, the estimates at 1984 constant prices are derived from the series of constant prices based on T-1 prices. This resulted in some statistical discrepancies shown in the table.

2.7 Gross Capital Formation by Type of Good and Owner, in Current Prices

Million Norwegian kroner

	1980				1981				1982			
	TOTAL	Total Private	Public Enterprises	General Government	TOTAL	Total Private	Public Enterprises	General Government	TOTAL	Total Private	Public Enterprises	General Government
Increase in stocks, total	8104	8104	...	...	-7761	-7761	...	...	3809	3809	...	...
1 Goods producing industries	6369	6369	...	...	-4282	-4282	...	...	4231	4231	...	...
A Materials and supplies	...	...	...	...	...	...	...	...	...	...	...	...
B Work in progress a	6284	6284	...	...	-4191	-4191	...	...	4278	4278	...	...
C Livestock, except breeding stocks, dairy cattle, etc. b	85	85	...	...	-91	-91	...	...	-47	-47	...	...
D Finished goods	...	...	...	...	...	...	...	...	...	...	...	...
2 Wholesale and retail trade	...	...	...	...	...	...	...	...	...	...	...	...
3 Other, except government stocks	1735	1735	...	...	-3479	-3479	...	...	-422	-422	...	...
4 Government stocks	...	...	...	...	...	...	...	...	...	...	...	...
Gross Fixed Capital Formation, Total	70798	59344	...	11454	91793	80190	...	11602	92262	80737	...	11525
1 Residential buildings c	13535	13489	...	46	15055	14986	...	69	17465	17693	...	-228
2 Non-residential buildings	14482	9405	...	5078	16138	10985	...	5153	16289	10949	...	5340
3 Other construction d	17146	12482	...	4665	28536	23968	...	4568	23775	19308	...	4467
4 Land improvement and plantation and orchard development	536	536	...	...	576	576	...	...	605	605	...	...
5 Producers' durable goods	24978	23312	...	1666	31412	29600	...	1812	34176	32230	...	1946
A Transport equipment	7359	7179	...	179	12341	11876	...	465	15043	14838	...	205
Passenger cars e	1585	1547	...	38	2305	1987	...	318	2369	2325	...	44
Other	5774	5633	...	142	10036	9890	...	147	12673	12513	...	161
B Machinery and equipment	17620	16133	...	1487	19071	17724	...	1347	19133	17392	...	1741
6 Breeding stock, dairy cattle, etc.	120	120	...	...	76	76	...	...	-46	-46	...	...
Total Gross Capital Formation	78902	67448	...	11454	84032	72429	...	11602	96071	84546	...	11525

	1983				1984				1985			
	TOTAL	Total Private	Public Enterprises	General Government	TOTAL	Total Private	Public Enterprises	General Government	TOTAL	Total Private	Public Enterprises	General Government
Increase in stocks, total	-4332	-4332	...	...	-1300	-1300	...	...	11103	11103	...	...
1 Goods producing industries	2116	2116	...	...	-2613	-2613	...	...	10960	10960	...	...
A Materials and supplies	...	...	...	...	...	...	...	...	...	...	...	...
B Work in progress a	2112	2112	...	...	-2649	-2649	...	...	10987	10987	...	...
C Livestock, except breeding stocks, dairy cattle, etc. b	4	4	...	...	36	36	...	...	-27	-27	...	...

2.7 Gross Capital Formation by Type of Good and Owner, in Current Prices
(Continued)

Million Norwegian kroner

	1983				1984				1985			
	TOTAL	Total Private	Public Enterprises	General Government	TOTAL	Total Private	Public Enterprises	General Government	TOTAL	Total Private	Public Enterprises	General Government
D Finished goods	...	...	...	...	...	...	...	...	...	...	...	...
2 Wholesale and retail trade	...	...	...	...	...	...	...	...	...	...	...	...
3 Other, except government stocks	-6448	-6448	...	...	1313	1313	...	...	143	143	...	...
4 Government stocks	...	...	...	...	...	...	...	...	...	...	...	...
Gross Fixed Capital Formation, Total	103448	91037	...	12410	117567	104709	...	12858	110042	96754	...	13288
1 Residential buildings c	18526	19035	...	-509	19171	19636	...	-465	20523	21304	...	-781
2 Non-residential buildings	17047	11158	...	5889	17918	12098	...	5820	21326	15595	...	5732
3 Other construction d	35608	30689	...	4919	45579	40410	...	5169	33072	27571	...	5501
4 Land improvement and plantation and orchard development	567	567	...	...	527	527	...	...	455	455	...	...
5 Producers' durable goods	31700	29589	...	2111	34406	32071	...	2335	34750	31913	...	2836
A Transport equipment	13150	12932	...	219	11725	11484	...	241	7740	7482	...	258
Passenger cars e	2535	2483	...	52	2521	2467	...	54	3632	3563	...	69
Other	10615	10449	...	166	9204	9017	...	187	4108	3918	...	190
B Machinery and equipment	18550	16657	...	1893	22681	20587	...	2094	27010	24432	...	2578
6 Breeding stock, dairy cattle, etc.	...	...	...	...	-34	-34	...	...	-84	-84	...	...
Total Gross Capital Formation	99116	86705	...	12410	116267	103409	...	12858	121145	107857	...	13288

	1986				1987				1988			
	TOTAL	Total Private	Public Enterprises	General Government	TOTAL	Total Private	Public Enterprises	General Government	TOTAL	Total Private	Public Enterprises	General Government
Increase in stocks, total	6070	6070	...	...	1221	1221	...	...	-12517	-12517	...	...
1 Goods producing industries	-949	-949	...	...	1620	1620	...	...	-2636	-2636	...	...
A Materials and supplies	...	...	...	...	...	...	...	...	...	...	...	...
B Work in progress a	-1009	-1009	...	...	1591	1591	...	...	-2646	-2646	...	...
C Livestock, except breeding stocks, dairy cattle, etc. b	60	60	...	...	29	29	...	...	10	10	...	...
D Finished goods	...	...	...	...	...	...	...	...	...	...	...	...
2 Wholesale and retail trade	...	...	...	...	...	...	...	...	...	...	...	...
3 Other, except government stocks	7020	7020	...	...	-399	-399	...	...	-9882	-9882	...	...
4 Government stocks	...	...	...	...	...	...	...	...	...	...	...	...
Gross Fixed Capital Formation, Total	145540	129082	...	16457	157363	137277	...	20087	170345	147695	...	22650
1 Residential buildings c	24871	25219	...	-348	28911	29392	...	-482	29199	29890	...	-691
2 Non-residential buildings	28237	21110	...	7126	32394	22641	...	9754	35334	24107	...	11227
3 Other construction d	51515	45136	...	6379	51713	44492	...	7221	52306	43995	...	8311
4 Land improvement and plantation and orchard development	438	438	...	...	383	383	...	...	379	379	...	...
5 Producers' durable goods	40565	37266	...	3300	44044	40450	...	3594	53137	49335	...	3803
A Transport equipment	9323	9010	...	313	10710	10395	...	314	21759	21444	...	315
Passenger cars e	5442	5354	...	88	4865	4764	...	101	2518	2413	...	105
Other	3881	3657	...	225	5845	5631	...	214	19241	19031	...	211
B Machinery and equipment	31242	28255	...	2987	33334	30054	...	3280	31378	27891	...	3487
6 Breeding stock, dairy cattle, etc.	-87	-87	...	...	-81	-81	...	...	-10	-10	...	...
Total Gross Capital Formation	151610	135152	...	16457	158584	138498	...	20087	157828	135178	...	22650

	1989				1990				1991			
	TOTAL	Total Private	Public Enterprises	General Government	TOTAL	Total Private	Public Enterprises	General Government	TOTAL	Total Private	Public Enterprises	General Government
Increase in stocks, total	-18327	-18327	...	...	11055	11055	...	...	2021	2021	...	...
1 Goods producing industries	-6103	-6103	...	...	16066	16066	...	...	9775	9775	...	...
A Materials and supplies	...	...	...	...	...	...	...	...	...	...	...	...
B Work in progress a	-6218	-6218	...	...	16101	16101	...	...	9743	9743	...	...
C Livestock, except breeding stocks, dairy cattle, etc. b	115	115	...	...	-35	-35	...	...	32	32	...	...

Norway

2.7 Gross Capital Formation by Type of Good and Owner, in Current Prices
(Continued)

Million Norwegian kroner

	1989				1990				1991			
	TOTAL	Total Private	Public Enterprises	General Government	TOTAL	Total Private	Public Enterprises	General Government	TOTAL	Total Private	Public Enterprises	General Government
D Finished goods	...	...	...	...	...	...	...	...	...	...	...	...
2 Wholesale and retail trade	...	...	...	...	...	...	...	...	...	...	...	...
3 Other, except government stocks	-12224	-12224	...	...	-5011	-5011	...	...	-7754	-7754	...	...
4 Government stocks	...	...	...	...	...	...	...	...	...	...	...	...
Gross Fixed Capital Formation, Total	169485	146465	...	23020	124146	102723	...	21423	127053	102733	...	24320
1 Residential buildings c	23887	24269	...	-383	19749	19800	...	-51	14748	14070	...	678
2 Non-residential buildings	28371	18385	...	9985	23071	14365	...	8707	22033	12638	...	9395
3 Other construction d	58655	49544	...	9112	36200	27844	...	8356	46898	37941	...	8956
4 Land improvement and plantation and orchard development	352	352	...	...	310	310	...	...	288	288	...	...
5 Producers' durable goods	58094	53788	...	4306	44837	40425	...	4412	42975	37683	...	5291
A Transport equipment	30842	30495	...	347	18052	17694	...	358	15108	14693	...	415
Passenger cars e	1455	1356	...	99	2423	2328	...	95	2891	2738	...	153
Other	29387	29139	...	249	15629	15366	...	263	12217	11954	...	263
B Machinery and equipment	27252	23294	...	3958	26785	22731	...	4054	27867	22991	...	4876
6 Breeding stock, dairy cattle, etc.	127	127	...	...	-21	-21	...	...	113	113	...	...
Total Gross Capital Formation	151158	128138	...	23020	135201	113778	...	21423	129074	104754	...	24320

a) Item 'Work in progress' includes work in progress in mining and manufacturing, ships, oil drilling and oil production platforms.
b) Item 'Livestock except breeding stocks, dairy cattles etc.' includes increase in stocks of fodder, timber and firewood.
c) Item 'Residential buildings' includes also summer cottages, temporary dwellings, logging camps, fishermens' quarters etc..
d) The estimates of 'Other construction' include oil drilling rigs, oil production platforms etc., pipelines for gas, oil and gas exploration and drilling.
e) Item 'Passenger cars' includes station wagons.

2.8 Gross Capital Formation by Type of Good and Owner, in Constant Prices

Million Norwegian kroner

	1984				1985				1986			
	TOTAL	Total Private	Public Enterprises	General Government	TOTAL	Total Private	Public Enterprises	General Government	TOTAL	Total Private	Public Enterprises	General Government
				At constant prices of:1984								
Increase in stocks, total	-1300	-1300	...	...	10834	10834	...	...	6255	6255	...	...
1 Goods producing industries	-2613	-2613	...	...	10263	10263	...	...	-857	-857	...	...
A Materials and supplies	...	...	...	...	...	...	...	...	...	...	...	...
B Work in progress a	-2649	-2649	...	...	10288	10288	...	...	-906	-906	...	...
C Livestock, except breeding stocks, dairy cattle, etc. b	36	36	...	...	-25	-25	...	...	49	49	...	...
D Finished goods	...	...	...	...	...	...	...	...	...	...	...	...
2 Wholesale and retail trade	...	...	...	...	...	...	...	...	...	...	...	...
3 Other, except government stocks	1313	1313	...	...	571	571	...	...	7110	7110	...	...
4 Government stocks	...	...	...	...	...	...	...	...	...	...	...	...
Statistical discrepancy	-	-	...	-	-	-	...	-	2	2	...	-
Gross Fixed Capital Formation, Total	117567	104709	...	12858	101170	88778	...	12392	125384	111128	...	14257
1 Residential buildings c	19171	19636	...	-465	19696	20449	...	-754	22100	22412	...	-312
2 Non-residential buildings	17918	12098	...	5820	20135	14724	...	5412	24589	18375	...	6214
3 Other construction d	45579	40410	...	5169	30877	25807	...	5070	45405	39925	...	5479
4 Land improvement and plantation and orchard development	527	527	...	...	421	421	...	...	382	382	...	...
5 Producers' durable goods	34406	32071	...	2335	30112	27448	...	2664	32979	30104	...	2875
A Transport equipment	11725	11484	...	241	4455	4220	...	235	5190	4927	...	263
Passenger cars e	2521	2467	...	54	3208	3148	...	60	4496	4423	...	73
Other	9204	9017	...	187	1247	1072	...	174	694	504	...	190
B Machinery and equipment	22681	20587	...	2094	25657	23228	...	2429	27789	25177	...	2612
6 Breeding stock, dairy cattle, etc.	-34	-34	...	...	-71	-71	...	...	-71	-71	...	...
Statistical discrepancy	-	1	...	-1	-	-	...	-	-	1	...	1
Total Gross Capital Formation f	116267	103409	...	12858	112004	99612	...	12392	131639	117383	...	14257

2.8 Gross Capital Formation by Type of Good and Owner, in Constant Prices

Million Norwegian kroner

	1987				1988				1989			
	TOTAL	Total Private	Public Enterprises	General Government	TOTAL	Total Private	Public Enterprises	General Government	TOTAL	Total Private	Public Enterprises	General Government
At constant prices of:1984												
Increase in stocks, total	1229	1229	...	...	-8342	-8342	...	...	-12318	-12318	...	...
1 Goods producing industries	1356	1356	...	...	-2094	-2094	...	...	-4761	-4761	...	...
A Materials and supplies	...	...	...	...	...	...	...	...	...	...	...	...
B Work in progress [a]	1338	1338	...	...	-2092	-2092	...	...	-4741	-4741	...	...
C Livestock, except breeding stocks, dairy cattle, etc. [b]	18	18	...	...	-2	-2	...	...	-20	-20	...	...
D Finished goods	...	...	...	...	...	...	...	...	...	...	...	...
2 Wholesale and retail trade	...	...	...	...	...	...	...	...	...	...	...	...
3 Other, except government stocks	-1222	-1222	...	...	-26144	-26144	...	...	-31681	-31681	...	...
4 Government stocks	...	...	...	...	...	...	...	...	...	...	...	...
Statistical discrepancy	1095	1095	...	-	19896	19896	...	-	24124	24124	...	-
Gross Fixed Capital Formation, Total	122759	107083	...	15688	124716	107876	...	16852	119823	102872	...	16976
1 Residential buildings [c]	22925	23310	...	-386	21903	22425	...	-523	18306	18603	...	-296
2 Non-residential buildings	25152	17552	...	7604	25829	17587	...	8249	21172	13853	...	7329
3 Other construction [d]	41522	35952	...	5553	39589	33452	...	6081	43189	36572	...	6559
4 Land improvement and plantation and orchard development	294	294	...	...	277	277	...	...	254	254	...	...
5 Producers' durable goods	32900	29980	...	2923	36863	33803	...	3043	36620	33243	...	3417
A Transport equipment	5484	5227	...	246	9632	9309	...	233	11480	11121	...	233
Passenger cars [e]	3486	3404	...	83	1735	1661	...	79	1011	944	...	72
Other	1007	749	...	163	2824	2155	...	152	3590	2745	...	158
B Machinery and equipment	27233	24554	...	2678	24949	22135	...	2812	21352	18173	...	3190
6 Breeding stock, dairy cattle, etc.	-86	-86	...	...	-35	-35	...	...	335	335	...	...
Statistical discrepancy	52	81	...	-6	290	367	...	2	-53	12	...	-33
Total Gross Capital Formation [f]	123988	108312	...	15688	116374	99534	...	16852	107505	90554	...	16976

	1990				1991			
	TOTAL	Total Private	Public Enterprises	General Government	TOTAL	Total Private	Public Enterprises	General Government
At constant prices of:1984								
Increase in stocks, total	7667	7667	...	...	1503	1503	...	...
1 Goods producing industries	11851	11851	...	...	7082	7082	...	...
A Materials and supplies	...	...	...	...	...	...	...	...
B Work in progress [a]	11845	11845	...	...	7087	7087	...	...
C Livestock, except breeding stocks, dairy cattle, etc. [b]	6	6	...	...	-5	-5	...	...
D Finished goods	...	...	...	...	...	...	...	...
2 Wholesale and retail trade	...	...	...	...	...	...	...	...
3 Other, except government stocks	-14146	-14146	...	...	-20737	-20737	...	...
4 Government stocks	...	...	...	...	...	...	...	...
Statistical discrepancy	9962	9962	...	-	15158	15158	...	-
Gross Fixed Capital Formation, Total	87670	72082	...	15765	89120	71365	...	18030
1 Residential buildings [c]	15380	15422	...	-40	11748	11207	...	549
2 Non-residential buildings	17453	11066	...	6386	16904	9896	...	6967

Norway

2.8 Gross Capital Formation by Type of Good and Owner, in Constant Prices
(Continued)

Million Norwegian kroner

	1990				1991			
	TOTAL	Total Private	Public Enterprises	General Government	TOTAL	Total Private	Public Enterprises	General Government
				At constant prices of:1984				
3 Other construction d	26034	20005	...	5942	32848	26424	...	6327
4 Land improvement and plantation and orchard development	220	220	...	...	201	201	...	...
5 Producers' durable goods	28328	25009	...	3550	26983	23076	...	4351
A Transport equipment	6610	6350	...	233	5358	5106	...	263
Passenger cars e	1684	1620	...	68	2006	1904	...	109
Other	1874	1421	...	161	1408	1063	...	155
B Machinery and equipment	21296	17986	...	3326	22323	18256	...	4105
6 Breeding stock, dairy cattle, etc.	-129	-129	...	...	647	647	...	...
Statistical discrepancy	384	489	...	-73	-211	-86	...	-164
Total Gross Capital Formation f	95337	79749	...	15765	90623	72868	...	18030

a) Item 'Work in progress' includes work in progress in mining and manufacturing, ships, oil drilling and oil production platforms.
b) Item 'Livestock except breeding stocks, dairy cattles etc.' includes increase in stocks of fodder, timber and firewood.
c) Item 'Residential buildings' includes also summer cottages, temporary dwellings, logging camps, fishermens' quarters etc..

d) The estimates of 'Other construction' include oil drilling rigs, oil production platforms etc., pipelines for gas, oil and gas exploration and drilling.
e) Item 'Passenger cars' includes station wagons.
f) Beginning 1987, the estimates at 1984 constant prices are derived from the series of constant prices based on T-1 prices. This resulted in some statistical discrepancies shown in the table.

2.11 Gross Fixed Capital Formation by Kind of Activity of Owner, ISIC Divisions, in Current Prices

Million Norwegian kroner

	1980	1981	1982	1983	1984	1985	1986	1987	1988	1989	1990	1991
					All Producers							
1 Agriculture, hunting, forestry and fishing	5795	6258	5897	5186	5359	6135	7256	7793	7931	6284	5164	4791
A Agriculture and hunting	4812	5156	4776	3955	3867	4390	4434	3971	3975	3486	3599	3330
B Forestry and logging	326	369	361	386	415	442	526	624	692	671	568	551
C Fishing	657	733	760	845	1077	1303	2297	3198	3264	2127	998	911
2 Mining and quarrying	6833	18343	11578	15401	28388	20111	36148	31562	32680	42131	15653	26028
A Coal mining	41	111	19	22	34	44	41	20	9	28	13	16
B Crude petroleum and natural gas production	6360	17696	11145	15042	28039	19705	35695	31206	32232	41681	15256	25598
C Metal ore mining	205	300	200	136	119	109	194	97	69	189	103	80
D Other mining	226	237	215	201	195	253	218	240	369	234	282	334
3 Manufacturing	9031	10855	9105	8258	9311	11975	16224	20133	18170	13418	14234	13101
A Manufacturing of food, beverages and tobacco	1593	1946	1897	1880	1970	2054	2336	2998	3332	2859	2686	2578
B Textile, wearing apparel and leather industries	282	222	217	126	142	189	265	232	164	210	121	112
C Manufacture of wood, and wood products, including furniture	584	782	676	724	761	710	871	1160	932	862	971	736
D Manufacture of paper and paper products, printing and publishing	2155	2039	970	980	1304	1550	2115	2560	2180	1346	2033	2105
E Manufacture of chemicals and chemical petroleum, coal, rubber and plastic products	962	1177	1235	1150	1208	1835	3506	6593	6414	3089	3269	2600
F Manufacture of non-metalic mineral products except products of petroleum and coal	350	492	517	288	401	606	825	1270	790	690	915	761
G Basic metal industries	1181	1939	1511	967	1287	2108	2876	1929	1304	1520	1555	1428
H Manufacture of fabricated metal products, machinery and equipment	1870	2189	2056	2103	2207	2863	3363	3328	2973	2781	2630	2692
I Other manufacturing industries	55	68	24	40	32	60	67	63	80	61	56	90
4 Electricity, gas and water	7000	7721	7960	8073	8266	8079	8947	9784	10002	7880	6620	6471
A Electricity, gas and steam	6380	7130	7353	7469	7665	7541	8259	9014	9204	7172	5960	5685
B Water works and supply	620	591	608	604	601	538	688	770	799	708	660	787
5 Construction a	1588	1549	3165	3312	2382	3545	4728	3810	3090	1821	5780	2297
6 Wholesale and retail trade, restaurants and hotels b	3285	3770	4141	4467	4464	5791	7316	7322	5155	4154	4923	5368
A Wholesale and retail trade	3152	3618	3972	4286	4283	5565	7067	7074	4967	3984	4731	5149
B Restaurants and hotels	133	152	169	181	181	227	249	248	188	170	192	219
7 Transport, storage and communication c	7696	11595	15090	20250	18191	8054	7018	8368	21629	32453	18638	21277
A Transport and storage	4910	8720	11841	16709	14413	3918	2824	3608	16262	27903	15353	17629

2.11 Gross Fixed Capital Formation by Kind of Activity of Owner, ISIC Divisions, in Current Prices
(Continued)

Million Norwegian kroner

	1980	1981	1982	1983	1984	1985	1986	1987	1988	1989	1990	1991
B Communication	2785	2875	3249	3541	3778	4136	4194	4760	5367	4551	3285	3648
8 Finance, insurance, real estate and business services d	16952	18732	22293	24437	26611	30516	38644	45604	46265	36434	29243	21041
A Financial institutions	1299	1926	1341	2359	2840	3562	3767	4897	5651	3474	4264	3085
B Insurance												
C Real estate and business services	15653	16806	20952	22077	23770	26955	34877	40707	40614	32960	24979	17956
Real estate except dwellings	2169	1825	3264	3047	4139	5655	9662	11319	10728	8695	5183	3889
Dwellings	13484	14981	17688	19030	19631	21300	25215	29388	29886	24265	19796	14067
9 Community, social and personal services e	1166	1369	1509	1654	1737	2547	2801	2902	2774	1891	2469	2360
Total Industries	59344	80190	80737	91037	104709	96754	129082	137277	147695	146465	102723	102733
Producers of Government Services	11454	11602	11525	12410	12858	13288	16457	20087	22650	23020	21423	24320
Private Non-Profit Institutions Serving Households	...	...	...	...	...	...	...	...	...	...	...	...
Total	70798	91792	92262	103447	117567	110042	145539	157364	170345	169485	124146	127053

a) Item 'Construction' also includes oil and natural gas exploration and drilling.
b) Item 'Wholesale and retail trade, restaurants and hotels' includes producers' durable goods, otherwise included in real estate.
c) Item 'Transport, storage and communication' includes pipeline transport for crude oil and natural gas.
d) Business services are included in item 'Community, social and personal services'.
e) Item 'Community, social and personal services' includes other private and business services but excludes commercial buildings.

2.12 Gross Fixed Capital Formation by Kind of Activity of Owner, ISIC Divisions, in Constant Prices

Million Norwegian kroner

	1980	1981	1982	1983	1984	1985	1986	1987	1988	1989	1990	1991
			At constant prices of:									
			1980						1984			
					All Producers							
1 Agriculture, hunting, forestry and fishing	5795	5781	5042	4176	4181 / 5359	5730	6365	6176	6063	4661	3723	3425
A Agriculture and hunting	4812	4774	4126	3183	2991 / 3867	4111	3849	3063	2933	2464	2474	2278
B Forestry and logging	326	340	309	312	320 / 415	412	460	487	519	491	408	389
C Fishing	657	667	608	681	869 / 1077	1208	2057	2648	2636	1699	768	688
2 Mining and quarrying	6833	15334	7334	10522	19408 / 28388	18906	32052	25834	25113	31273	11359	18253
A Coal mining	41	103	16	18	28 / 34	41	36	16	7	22	10	13
B Crude petroleum and natural gas production	6360	14719	6954	10217	19082 / 28039	18525	31653	25552	24772	30936	11062	17929
C Metal ore mining	205	286	175	115	114 / 119	103	171	77	52	142	77	59
D Other mining	226	227	189	172	184 / 195	238	192	190	280	173	209	246

2.12 Gross Fixed Capital Formation by Kind of Activity of Owner, ISIC Divisions, in Constant Prices
(Continued)

Million Norwegian kroner

	1980	1981	1982	1983	1984	1985	1986	1987	1988	1989	1990	1991
			1980		At constant prices of:			**1984**				
3 Manufacturing	9031	10330	7997	7087	8718 9311	11360	14405	16046	13851	10087	10799	9895
A Manufacturing of food, beverages and tobacco	1593	1843	1659	1598	1801 1970	1945	2072	2386	2528	2142	2032	1942
B Textile, wearing apparel and leather industries	282	212	191	109	134 142	178	235	185	126	159	91	85
C Manufacture of wood, and wood products, including furniture	584	743	592	624	700 761	673	774	927	712	651	740	559
D Manufacture of paper and paper products, printing and publishing	2155	1950	856	848	1254 1304	1476	1885	2053	1676	1016	1546	1592
E Manufacture of chemicals and chemical petroleum, coal, rubber and plastic products	962	1124	1086	996	1132 1208	1739	3094	5211	4853	2287	2444	1936
F Manufacture of non-metalic mineral products except products of petroleum and coal	350	469	453	249	371 401	572	730	1009	600	523	697	575
G Basic metal industries	1181	1842	1334	831	1202 1287	1992	2556	1542	998	1151	1186	1084
H Manufacture of fabricated metal products, machinery and equipment	1870	2082	1806	1799	2092 2207	2728	2999	2665	2277	2112	2019	2060
I Other manufacturing industries	55	64	21	34	32 32	56	60	51	62	45	42	66
4 Electricity, gas and water	7000	7264	6917	6724	6581 8266	7696	7968	7842	7599	5993	5045	4905
A Electricity, gas and steam	6380	6718	6406	6231	6118 7665	7193	7359	7239	7004	5466	4551	4324
B Water works and supply	620	547	511	493	463 601	503	609	603	596	526	491	575
5 Construction a	1588	1460	2453	2179	1756 2382	3317	4154	3017	2307	1343	4056	1661
6 Wholesale and retail trade, restaurants and hotels b	3285	3612	3604	3836	4022 4464	5296	6218	5607	3835	3008	3606	3933
A Wholesale and retail trade	3152	3467	3464	3684	3853 4283	5087	6004	5414	3691	2878	3456	3761
B Restaurants and hotels	133	145	140	152	169 181	209	214	193	144	131	151	174
7 Transport, storage and communication c	7696	10460	10894	12575	9410 18191	4965	3448	3850	8593	11069	6309	6997
A Transport and storage	4910	7701	7931	9258	5733 14413	1083	-232	-288	-1076	-1541	-835	-924
B Communication	2785	2760	2963	3317	3676 3778	3883	3680	3803	4143	3529	2622	2935
8 Finance, insurance, real estate and business services d ..	16952	17152	18755	19459	20580 26611	29124	34085	35958	34519	27858	22790	16755
A Financial institutions	1299	1805	1179	2068	2610 2840	3355	3282	3886	4293	2721	3389	2507
B Insurance												
C Real estate and business services	15653	15347	17576	17391	17971 23770	25769	30802	32065	30233	25128	19445	14280
Real estate except dwellings	2169	1721	2863	2566	3354 4139	5324	8394	8759	7812	6529	4026	3076

2.12 Gross Fixed Capital Formation by Kind of Activity of Owner, ISIC Divisions, in Constant Prices
(Continued)

Million Norwegian kroner

	1980	1981	1982	1983	1984	1985	1986	1987	1988	1989	1990	1991
					At constant prices of:							
			1980		**1984**							
Dwellings	13484	13626	14713	14825	14617 / 19631	20445	22408	23306	22421	18599	15419	11204
9 Community, social and personal services e	1166	1324	1388	1635	1898 / 1737	2384	2432	2340	2196	1494	1997	1951
Statistical discrepancy	...	...	...	...	... / -	-	1	413	3800	6086	2398	3590
Total Industries	59344	72717	64384	68194	76553 / 104709	88778	111128	107083	107876	102872	72082	71365
Producers of Government Services	11454	10769	9913	10425	10671 / 12858	12392	14257	15688	16852	16976	15765	18030
Private Non-Profit Institutions Serving Households	...	...	...	...	... / ...	...	...	...	...	...	...	...
Statistical discrepancy	...	...	...	...	... / -	-	-	-11	-12	-26	-178	-274
Total	70798	83486	74297	78619	87224 / 117567f	101170f	125385f	122760f	124716f	119822f	87669f	89121f

a) Item 'Construction' also includes oil and natural gas exploration and drilling.
b) Item 'Wholesale and retail trade, restaurants and hotels' includes producers' durable goods, otherwise included in real estate.
c) Item 'Transport, storage and communication' includes pipeline transport for crude oil and natural gas.

d) Business services are included in item 'Community, social and personal services'.
e) Item 'Community, social and personal services' includes other private and business services but excludes commercial buildings.
f) Beginning 1987, the estimates at 1984 constant prices are derived from the series of constant prices based on T-1 prices. This resulted in some statistical discrepancies shown in the table.

2.13 Stocks of Reproducible Fixed Assets, by Type of Good and Owner, in Current Prices

Million Norwegian kroner

	TOTAL		Total Private		Public Enterprises		General Government	
	Gross	Net	Gross	Net	Gross	Net	Gross	Net
				1980				
1 Residential buildings a	...	238433	...	238433	...	...	...	...
2 Non-residential buildings	...	223155	...	142440	...	...	...	80715
3 Other construction b	...	282185	...	173976	...	...	...	108210
4 Land improvement and plantation and orchard development	...	42776	...	42776	...	...	...	...
5 Producers' durable goods	...	220515	...	210060	...	...	...	10455
A Transport equipment	...	91841	...	91169	...	...	...	672
Passenger cars c	...	5450	...	5346	...	...	...	103
Other	...	86391	...	85822	...	...	...	569
B Machinery and equipment	...	128674	...	118891	...	...	...	9783
6 Breeding stock, dairy cattle, etc.	...	3933	...	3933	...	...	...	...
Total	...	1010997	...	811618	...	...	...	199380
				1981				
1 Residential buildings a	...	269938	...	269938	...	...	...	...
2 Non-residential buildings	...	251193	...	159925	...	...	...	91269
3 Other construction b	...	329514	...	207611	...	...	...	121903
4 Land improvement and plantation and orchard development	...	53235	...	53235	...	...	...	...
5 Producers' durable goods	...	240516	...	228994	...	...	...	11523
A Transport equipment	...	99868	...	98936	...	...	...	933
Passenger cars c	...	5872	...	5536	...	...	...	336
Other	...	93996	...	93399	...	...	...	597
B Machinery and equipment	...	140648	...	130058	...	...	...	10590
6 Breeding stock, dairy cattle, etc.	...	4435	...	4435	...	...	...	...
Total	...	1148831	...	924138	...	...	...	224695

2.13 Stocks of Reproducible Fixed Assets, by Type of Good and Owner, in Current Prices
(Continued)

Million Norwegian kroner

	TOTAL		Total Private		Public Enterprises		General Government	
	Gross	Net	Gross	Net	Gross	Net	Gross	Net
1982								
1 Residential buildings a	...	314114	...	314114	...	...	...	...
2 Non-residential buildings	...	281116	...	179022	...	...	...	102094
3 Other construction b	...	379268	...	240741	...	...	...	138527
4 Land improvement and plantation and orchard development	...	56426	...	56426	...	...	...	...
5 Producers' durable goods	...	263458	...	250716	...	...	...	12742
A Transport equipment	...	108076	...	107110	...	...	...	966
Passenger cars c	...	7129	...	6771	...	...	...	358
Other	...	100947	...	100339	...	...	...	608
B Machinery and equipment	...	155382	...	143606	...	...	...	11776
6 Breeding stock, dairy cattle, etc.	...	4432	...	4432	...	...	...	...
Total	...	1298814	...	1045451	...	...	...	253363
1983								
1 Residential buildings a	...	346259	...	346259	...	...	...	...
2 Non-residential buildings	...	306603	...	194132	...	...	...	112471
3 Other construction b	...	407193	...	260251	...	...	...	146942
4 Land improvement and plantation and orchard development	...	53205	...	53205	...	...	...	...
5 Producers' durable goods	...	274326	...	261640	...	...	...	12686
A Transport equipment	...	114360	...	113398	...	...	...	962
Passenger cars c	...	7582	...	7244	...	...	...	339
Other	...	106778	...	106154	...	...	...	624
B Machinery and equipment	...	159966	...	148242	...	...	...	11723
6 Breeding stock, dairy cattle, etc.	...	4315	...	4315	...	...	...	...
Total	...	1391901	...	1119802	...	...	...	272099
1984								
1 Residential buildings a	...	376232	...	376232	...	...	...	...
2 Non-residential buildings	...	329161	...	208831	...	...	...	120331
3 Other construction b	...	461360	...	301499	...	...	...	159861
4 Land improvement and plantation and orchard development	...	62894	...	62894	...	...	...	...
5 Producers' durable goods	...	257396	...	244773	...	...	...	12623
A Transport equipment	...	101243	...	100322	...	...	...	921
Passenger cars c	...	7315	...	7039	...	...	...	276
Other	...	93928	...	93283	...	...	...	645
B Machinery and equipment	...	156153	...	144452	...	...	...	11701
6 Breeding stock, dairy cattle, etc.	...	4663	...	4663	...	...	...	...
Total	...	1491706	...	1198892	...	...	...	292815
1985								
1 Residential buildings a	...	407077	...	407077	...	...	...	...
2 Non-residential buildings	...	362952	...	232374	...	...	...	130578
3 Other construction b	...	506135	...	327034	...	...	...	179101
4 Land improvement and plantation and orchard development	...	66826	...	66826	...	...	...	...
5 Producers' durable goods	...	263265	...	248465	...	...	...	14801
A Transport equipment	...	87646	...	86734	...	...	...	913
Passenger cars c	...	8609	...	8372	...	...	...	237
Other	...	79038	...	78362	...	...	...	675
B Machinery and equipment	...	175619	...	161731	...	...	...	13888
6 Breeding stock, dairy cattle, etc.	...	5195	...	5195	...	...	...	...
Total	...	1611450	...	1286971	...	...	...	324480

2.13 Stocks of Reproducible Fixed Assets, by Type of Good and Owner, in Current Prices
(Continued)

Million Norwegian kroner

		TOTAL		Total Private		Public Enterprises		General Government	
		Gross	Net	Gross	Net	Gross	Net	Gross	Net
						1986			
1	Residential buildings a	...	457955	...	457955	...	...	...	...
2	Non-residential buildings	...	411747	...	266412	...	...	...	145335
3	Other construction b	...	566723	...	368311	...	...	...	198412
4	Land improvement and plantation and orchard development	...	72604	...	72604	...	...	...	...
5	Producers' durable goods	...	282303	...	264786	...	...	...	17517
	A Transport equipment	...	81273	...	80371	...	...	...	903
	Passenger cars c	...	10839	...	10652	...	...	...	187
	Other	...	70434	...	69719	...	...	...	715
	B Machinery and equipment	...	201030	...	184415	...	...	...	16615
6	Breeding stock, dairy cattle, etc.	...	5409	...	5409	...	...	...	...
	Total	...	1796741	...	1435477	...	...	...	361264
						1987			
1	Residential buildings a	...	534634	...	534634	...	...	...	...
2	Non-residential buildings	...	482304	...	313218	...	...	...	169086
3	Other construction b	...	652599	...	423776	...	...	...	228823
4	Land improvement and plantation and orchard development	...	80181	...	80181	...	...	...	...
5	Producers' durable goods	...	314481	...	293986	...	...	...	20495
	A Transport equipment	...	81767	...	80773	...	...	...	994
	Passenger cars c	...	12717	...	12473	...	...	...	244
	Other	...	69051	...	68300	...	...	...	750
	B Machinery and equipment	...	232714	...	213213	...	...	...	19501
6	Breeding stock, dairy cattle, etc.	...	5629	...	5629	...	...	...	...
	Total	...	2069828	...	1651424	...	...	...	418404
						1988			
1	Residential buildings a	...	586205	...	586205	...	...	...	...
2	Non-residential buildings	...	534280	...	347565	...	...	...	186715
3	Other construction b	...	710678	...	461891	...	...	...	248787
4	Land improvement and plantation and orchard development	...	85263	...	85263	...	...	...	...
5	Producers' durable goods	...	335022	...	312516	...	...	...	22506
	A Transport equipment	...	85652	...	84647	...	...	...	1005
	Passenger cars c	...	11481	...	11227	...	...	...	254
	Other	...	74172	...	73420	...	...	...	751
	B Machinery and equipment	...	249370	...	227869	...	...	...	21501
6	Breeding stock, dairy cattle, etc.	...	5627	...	5627	...	...	...	...
	Total	...	2257075	...	1799067	...	...	...	458008
						1989			
1	Residential buildings a	...	589177	...	589177	...	...	...	...
2	Non-residential buildings	...	542258	...	348741	...	...	...	193517
3	Other construction b	...	744196	...	482202	...	...	...	261994
4	Land improvement and plantation and orchard development	...	89223	...	89223	...	...	...	...
5	Producers' durable goods	...	350656	...	326131	...	...	...	24525
	A Transport equipment	...	91924	...	90847	...	...	...	1077
	Passenger cars c	...	9257	...	8998	...	...	...	259
	Other	...	82667	...	81849	...	...	...	818
	B Machinery and equipment	...	258731	...	235284	...	...	...	23448
6	Breeding stock, dairy cattle, etc.	...	5838	...	5838	...	...	...	...
	Total	...	2321348	...	1841312	...	...	...	480036

2.13 Stocks of Reproducible Fixed Assets, by Type of Good and Owner, in Current Prices
(Continued)

Million Norwegian kroner

	TOTAL		Total Private		Public Enterprises		General Government	
	Gross	Net	Gross	Net	Gross	Net	Gross	Net
1990								
1 Residential buildings a	...	590653	...	590653	...	...	...	...
2 Non-residential buildings	...	547369	...	348169	...	...	...	199200
3 Other construction b	...	756601	...	483063	...	...	...	273539
4 Land improvement and plantation and orchard development	...	93889	...	93889	...	...	...	...
5 Producers' durable goods	...	352488	...	326576	...	...	...	25912
A Transport equipment	...	92842	...	91766	...	...	...	1076
Passenger cars c	...	8323	...	8069	...	...	...	253
Other	...	84519	...	83697	...	...	...	823
B Machinery and equipment	...	259646	...	234810	...	...	...	24836
6 Breeding stock, dairy cattle, etc.	...	5207	...	5207	...	...	...	...
Total	...	2346207	...	1847557	...	...	...	498651
1991								
1 Residential buildings a	...	582661	...	582661	...	...	...	...
2 Non-residential buildings	...	551199	...	347270	...	...	...	203930
3 Other construction b	...	775574	...	491263	...	...	...	284312
4 Land improvement and plantation and orchard development	...	96569	...	96569	...	...	...	...
5 Producers' durable goods	...	352558	...	324459	...	...	...	28099
A Transport equipment	...	89694	...	88560	...	...	...	1134
Passenger cars c	...	8226	...	7931	...	...	...	295
Other	...	81467	...	80628	...	...	...	839
B Machinery and equipment	...	262865	...	235900	...	...	...	26965
6 Breeding stock, dairy cattle, etc.	...	5356	...	5356	...	...	...	...
Total	...	2363917	...	1847578	...	...	...	516341

a) Item 'Residential buildings' includes also summer cottages, temporary dwellings, logging camps, fishermens' quarters etc..
b) The estimates of 'Other construction' include oil drilling rigs, oil production platforms etc., pipelines for gas, oil and gas exploration and drilling.
c) Item 'Passenger cars' includes station wagons.

2.14 Stocks of Reproducible Fixed Assets, by Type of Good and Owner, in Constant Prices

Million Norwegian kroner

	TOTAL		Total Private		Public Enterprises		General Government	
	Gross	Net	Gross	Net	Gross	Net	Gross	Net
At constant prices of:1984								
1984								
1 Residential buildings a	...	376232	...	376232	...	...	...	...
2 Non-residential buildings	...	329161	...	208831	...	...	...	120331
3 Other construction b	...	461360	...	301499	...	...	...	159861
4 Land improvement and plantation and orchard development	...	62894	...	62894	...	...	...	...
5 Producers' durable goods	...	257396	...	244773	...	...	...	12623
A Transport equipment	...	101243	...	100322	...	...	...	921
Passenger cars c	...	7315	...	7039	...	...	...	276
Other	...	93928	...	93283	...	...	...	645
B Machinery and equipment	...	156153	...	144452	...	...	...	11701
6 Breeding stock, dairy cattle, etc.	...	4663	...	4663	...	...	...	...
Statistical discrepancy	...	-1	...	-1	...	...	...	-1
Total de	...	1491705	...	1198891	...	...	...	292814
1985								
1 Residential buildings a	...	390761	...	390761	...	...	...	...
2 Non-residential buildings	...	342094	...	219236	...	...	...	122858
3 Other construction b	...	471823	...	306892	...	...	...	164931
4 Land improvement and plantation and orchard development	...	63331	...	63331	...	...	...	...
5 Producers' durable goods	...	248506	...	234597	...	...	...	13908

2.14 Stocks of Reproducible Fixed Assets, by Type of Good and Owner, in Constant Prices
(Continued)

Million Norwegian kroner

	TOTAL		Total Private		Public Enterprises		General Government	
	Gross	Net	Gross	Net	Gross	Net	Gross	Net
At constant prices of:1984								
A Transport equipment	...	81572	...	80742	...	...	...	830
Passenger cars c	...	7645	...	7435	...	...	...	210
Other	...	73927	...	73307	...	...	...	620
B Machinery and equipment	...	166934	...	153856	...	...	...	13079
6 Breeding stock, dairy cattle, etc.	...	4611	...	4611	...	...	...	...
Statistical discrepancy	...	-	...	-	...	...	...	1
Total de	...	1521126	...	1219428	...	...	...	301698
1986								
1 Residential buildings a	...	407018	...	407018	...	...	...	...
2 Non-residential buildings	...	358351	...	231798	...	...	...	126553
3 Other construction b	...	495564	...	325153	...	...	...	170410
4 Land improvement and plantation and orchard development	...	63847	...	63847	...	...	...	...
5 Producers' durable goods	...	250103	...	234812	...	...	...	15290
A Transport equipment	...	70900	...	70139	...	...	...	761
Passenger cars c	...	8941	...	8787	...	...	...	154
Other	...	61959	...	61352	...	...	...	607
B Machinery and equipment	...	179202	...	164673	...	...	...	14529
6 Breeding stock, dairy cattle, etc.	...	4538	...	4538	...	...	...	...
Statistical discrepancy	...	-1	...	-	...	...	...	1
Total de	...	1579420	...	1267166	...	...	...	312254
1987								
1 Residential buildings a	...	424039	...	424039	...	...	...	...
2 Non-residential buildings	...	374207	...	242779	...	...	...	131428
3 Other construction b	...	514724	...	338796	...	...	...	175956
4 Land improvement and plantation and orchard development	...	64237	...	64237	...	...	...	...
5 Producers' durable goods	...	254909	...	238214	...	...	...	16678
A Transport equipment	...	64986	...	64233	...	...	...	751
Passenger cars c	...	9104	...	8930	...	...	...	175
Other	...	55822	...	55244	...	...	...	577
B Machinery and equipment	...	190081	...	174142	...	...	...	15928
6 Breeding stock, dairy cattle, etc.	...	4484	...	4484	...	...	...	...
Statistical discrepancy	...	34	...	28	...	...	...	-15
Total de	...	1636634	...	1312577	...	...	...	324047
1988								
1 Residential buildings a	...	439834	...	439834	...	...	...	...
2 Non-residential buildings	...	390519	...	253787	...	...	...	136731
3 Other construction b	...	530524	...	348489	...	...	...	182037
4 Land improvement and plantation and orchard development	...	64564	...	64564	...	...	...	...
5 Producers' durable goods	...	262232	...	244159	...	...	...	18059
A Transport equipment	...	64740	...	64018	...	...	...	721
Passenger cars c	...	7772	...	7601	...	...	...	171
Other	...	57075	...	56527	...	...	...	550
B Machinery and equipment	...	197713	...	180355	...	...	...	17347
6 Breeding stock, dairy cattle, etc.	...	4476	...	4476	...	...	...	...
Statistical discrepancy	...	156	...	170	...	...	...	-55
Total de	...	1692305	...	1355479	...	...	...	336772
1989								
1 Residential buildings a	...	451622	...	451622	...	...	...	...
2 Non-residential buildings	...	402232	...	260975	...	...	...	141257
3 Other construction b	...	548372	...	359765	...	...	...	188596
4 Land improvement and plantation and orchard development	...	64840	...	64840	...	...	...	...
5 Producers' durable goods	...	265326	...	245661	...	...	...	19688

Norway

2.14 Stocks of Reproducible Fixed Assets, by Type of Good and Owner, in Constant Prices
(Continued)

Million Norwegian kroner

	TOTAL		Total Private		Public Enterprises		General Government	
	Gross	Net	Gross	Net	Gross	Net	Gross	Net
At constant prices of:1984								
A Transport equipment	...	64478	...	63772	...	...	...	705
Passenger cars c	...	6178	...	6007	...	...	...	172
Other	...	58619	...	58089	...	...	...	534
B Machinery and equipment	...	201122	...	182134	...	...	...	19002
6 Breeding stock, dairy cattle, etc.	...	4504	...	4504	...	...	...	...
Statistical discrepancy	...	391	...	375	...	...	...	-142
Total de	...	1737287	...	1387742	...	...	...	349399
1990								
1 Residential buildings a	...	460074	...	460074	...	...	...	...
2 Non-residential buildings	...	410390	...	265380	...	...	...	144990
3 Other construction b	...	548774	...	354014	...	...	...	194538
4 Land improvement and plantation and orchard development	...	65231	...	65231	...	...	...	...
5 Producers' durable goods	...	267991	...	246769	...	...	...	21334
A Transport equipment	...	64418	...	63728	...	...	...	690
Passenger cars c	...	5534	...	5368	...	...	...	167
Other	...	59242	...	58723	...	...	...	524
B Machinery and equipment	...	203928	...	183322	...	...	...	20682
6 Breeding stock, dairy cattle, etc.	...	4439	...	4439	...	...	...	...
Statistical discrepancy	...	256	...	222	...	...	...	-240
Total de	...	1757155	...	1396129	...	...	...	360622
1991								
1 Residential buildings a	...	464204	...	464204	...	...	...	...
2 Non-residential buildings	...	418027	...	268183	...	...	...	149726
3 Other construction b	...	555617	...	354407	...	...	...	200865
4 Land improvement and plantation and orchard development	...	65585	...	65585	...	...	...	...
5 Producers' durable goods	...	267689	...	244336	...	...	...	23658
A Transport equipment	...	61342	...	60633	...	...	...	707
Passenger cars c	...	5443	...	5250	...	...	...	193
Other	...	56232	...	55720	...	...	...	515
B Machinery and equipment	...	207097	...	184289	...	...	...	23012
6 Breeding stock, dairy cattle, etc.	...	4527	...	4527	...	...	...	...
Statistical discrepancy	...	331	...	108	...	...	...	-445
Total de	...	1775980	...	1401350	...	...	...	373804

a) Item 'Residential buildings' includes also summer cottages, temporary dwellings, logging camps, fishermens' quarters etc..
b) The estimates of 'Other construction' include oil drilling rigs, oil production platforms etc., pipelines for gas, oil and gas exploration and drilling.
c) Item 'Passenger cars' includes station wagons.
d) Column 8 (General government, net) refers to stocks of reproducible fixed assets outside general government.
e) Beginning 1987, the estimates at 1984 constant prices are derived from the series of constant prices based on T-1 prices. This resulted in some statistical discrepancies shown in the table.

2.15 Stocks of Reproducible Fixed Assets by Kind of Activity, in Current Prices

Million Norwegian kroner

	1980		1981		1982		1983		1984		1985	
	Gross	Net	Gross	Net	Gross	Net	Gross	Net	Gross	Net	Gross	Net
1 Residential buildings a	...	238433	...	269938	...	314114	...	346259	...	376232	...	407077
2 Non-residential buildings	...	223155	...	251193	...	281116	...	306603	...	329161	...	362952
A Industries	...	142440	...	159925	...	179022	...	194132	...	208831	...	232374
1 Agriculture	...	35945	...	40362	...	44333	...	47237	...	49932	...	53539
2 Mining and quarrying	...	1224	...	1425	...	1549	...	1650	...	1722	...	4284
3 Manufacturing	...	44272	...	49831	...	55411	...	59460	...	63044	...	68071
4 Electricity, gas and water	...	15427	...	17222	...	19379	...	21248	...	22499	...	24242
5 Construction	...	2132	...	2513	...	3063	...	3659	...	4078	...	4734
6 Wholesale and retail trade	...	...	...	...	...	...	...	...	...	...	...	...
7 Transport and communication	...	2078	...	2355	...	2670	...	2910	...	3175	...	3527

2.15 Stocks of Reproducible Fixed Assets by Kind of Activity, in Current Prices
(Continued)

Million Norwegian kroner

	1980		1981		1982		1983		1984		1985	
	Gross	Net	Gross	Net	Gross	Net	Gross	Net	Gross	Net	Gross	Net
8 Finance, etc.	...	41362	...	46217	...	52617	...	57968	...	64381	...	73978
9 Community, social and personal services	...	...	...	...	...	...	...	...	...	...	...	...
B Producers of government services	...	80715	...	91269	...	102094	...	112471	...	120331	...	130578
C Other producers	...	...	...	...	...	...	...	...	...	...	...	...
3 Other construction b	...	282185	...	329514	...	379268	...	407193	...	461360	...	506135
A Industries	...	173976	...	207611	...	240741	...	260251	...	301499	...	327034
1 Agriculture c	...	2414	...	2745	...	3150	...	3429	...	3804	...	4411
2 Mining and quarrying d	...	44908	...	66040	...	81808	...	84607	...	103329	...	112787
3 Manufacturing	...	6179	...	6737	...	7442	...	8035	...	8469	...	10070
4 Electricity, gas and water	...	67330	...	75290	...	84526	...	89967	...	98339	...	105848
5 Construction e	...	6728	...	6925	...	8670	...	8515	...	11023	...	11037
6 Wholesale and retail trade	...	...	...	...	...	...	...	...	...	...	...	...
7 Transport and communication f	...	46416	...	49874	...	55145	...	65698	...	76535	...	82882
8 Finance, etc.	...	...	...	...	...	...	...	...	...	...	...	...
9 Community, social and personal services	...	...	...	...	...	...	...	...	...	...	...	...
B Producers of government services	...	108210	...	121903	...	138527	...	146942	...	159861	...	179101
C Other producers	...	...	...	...	...	...	...	...	...	...	...	...
4 Land improvement and development and plantation and orchard development	...	42776	...	53235	...	56426	...	53205	...	62894	...	66826
5 Producers' durable goods	...	220515	...	240516	...	263458	...	274326	...	257396	...	263265
A Industries	...	210060	...	228994	...	250716	...	261640	...	244773	...	248465
1 Agriculture c	...	21832	...	23984	...	25869	...	27193	...	27839	...	29957
2 Mining and quarrying d	...	3062	...	3516	...	3787	...	3750	...	5131	...	5886
3 Manufacturing	...	55564	...	60289	...	66346	...	66870	...	59868	...	65282
4 Electricity, gas and water	...	14664	...	16196	...	18673	...	20718	...	22411	...	24519
5 Construction e	...	6979	...	7118	...	7373	...	7318	...	6247	...	6975
6 Wholesale and retail trade	...	14827	...	15526	...	16940	...	17364	...	17348	...	20162
7 Transport and communication	...	85280	...	93560	...	101647	...	107887	...	94746	...	81141
8 Finance, etc. g	...	1535	...	1870	...	2380	...	2788	...	3422	...	4944
9 Community, social and personal services g	...	6318	...	6938	...	7701	...	7753	...	7760	...	9598
B Producers of government services	...	10455	...	11523	...	12742	...	12686	...	12623	...	14801
C Other producers	...	...	...	...	...	...	...	...	...	...	...	...
6 Breeding stock, dairy cattle, etc.	...	3933	...	4435	...	4432	...	4315	...	4663	...	5195
Total	...	1010997	...	1148831	...	1298814	...	1391901	...	1491706	...	1611450
Memorandum Item: Mineral Fuels and Power	...	133292	...	164919	...	193130	...	204709	...	235265	...	258257

	1986		1987		1988		1989		1990		1991	
	Gross	Net	Gross	Net	Gross	Net	Gross	Net	Gross	Net	Gross	Net
1 Residential buildings a	...	457955	...	534634	...	586205	...	589177	...	590653	...	582661
2 Non-residential buildings	...	411747	...	482304	...	534280	...	542258	...	547369	...	551199
A Industries	...	266412	...	313218	...	347565	...	348741	...	348169	...	347270
1 Agriculture	...	58110	...	64413	...	68272	...	68134	...	68107	...	67136
2 Mining and quarrying	...	5604	...	6420	...	6927	...	6877	...	6869	...	7136
3 Manufacturing	...	76807	...	88304	...	95268	...	93152	...	91532	...	90196
4 Electricity, gas and water	...	26941	...	31299	...	34166	...	33556	...	32792	...	32781
5 Construction	...	5691	...	6868	...	8238	...	8443	...	8581	...	8546
6 Wholesale and retail trade	...	...	...	...	...	...	...	...	...	...	...	...
7 Transport and communication	...	3939	...	4647	...	5144	...	5189	...	5210	...	5312
8 Finance, etc.	...	89321	...	111268	...	129549	...	133391	...	135077	...	136163
9 Community, social and personal services	...	...	...	...	...	...	...	...	...	...	...	...
B Producers of government services	...	145335	...	169086	...	186715	...	193517	...	199200	...	203930
C Other producers	...	...	...	...	...	...	...	...	...	...	...	...

2.15 Stocks of Reproducible Fixed Assets by Kind of Activity, in Current Prices
(Continued)

Million Norwegian kroner

	1986 Gross	1986 Net	1987 Gross	1987 Net	1988 Gross	1988 Net	1989 Gross	1989 Net	1990 Gross	1990 Net	1991 Gross	1991 Net
3 Other construction b	...	566723	...	652599	...	710678	...	744196	...	756601	...	775574
A Industries	...	368311	...	423776	...	461891	...	482202	...	483063	...	491263
1 Agriculture c	...	5475	...	6838	...	7602	...	7772	...	7745	...	7821
2 Mining and quarrying d	...	136246	...	158228	...	177935	...	200083	...	197074	...	199928
3 Manufacturing	...	11286	...	16833	...	20852	...	21370	...	23582	...	24454
4 Electricity, gas and water	...	116933	...	134319	...	143742	...	144822	...	145337	...	146824
5 Construction e	...	11500	...	11163	...	9468	...	7527	...	9957	...	8700
6 Wholesale and retail trade	...	...	...	...	...	...	...	...	...	...	...	...
7 Transport and communication f	...	86871	...	96395	...	102292	...	100628	...	99368	...	103537
8 Finance, etc.	...	...	...	...	...	...	...	...	...	...	...	...
9 Community, social and personal services	...	...	...	...	...	...	...	...	...	...	...	...
B Producers of government services	...	198412	...	228823	...	248787	...	261994	...	273539	...	284312
C Other producers	...	...	...	...	...	...	...	...	...	...	...	...
4 Land improvement and development and plantation and orchard development	...	72604	...	80181	...	85263	...	89223	...	93889	...	96569
5 Producers' durable goods	...	282303	...	314481	...	335022	...	350656	...	352488	...	352558
A Industries	...	264786	...	293986	...	312516	...	326131	...	326576	...	324459
1 Agriculture c	...	32894	...	37170	...	39099	...	40423	...	39646	...	37715
2 Mining and quarrying d	...	6672	...	7898	...	8345	...	8220	...	7749	...	8219
3 Manufacturing	...	73868	...	86571	...	93198	...	97882	...	97917	...	100345
4 Electricity, gas and water	...	27018	...	30234	...	32788	...	33671	...	33982	...	34168
5 Construction e	...	7972	...	9407	...	10045	...	10050	...	9532	...	8932
6 Wholesale and retail trade	...	23961	...	27683	...	27705	...	26665	...	25596	...	25306
7 Transport and communication	...	73864	...	72349	...	76482	...	84204	...	86845	...	84937
8 Finance, etc. g	...	6868	...	8968	...	10043	...	10267	...	10423	...	9925
9 Community, social and personal services g	...	11670	...	13707	...	14813	...	14750	...	14885	...	14913
B Producers of government services	...	17517	...	20495	...	22506	...	24525	...	25912	...	28099
C Other producers	...	...	...	...	...	...	...	...	...	...	...	...
6 Breeding stock, dairy cattle, etc.	...	5409	...	5629	...	5627	...	5838	...	5207	...	5356
Total	...	1796741	...	2069828	...	2257075	...	2321348	...	2346207	...	2363917
Memorandum Item: Mineral Fuels and Power	...	300022	...	350367	...	388441	...	411958	...	409011	...	413224

a) Item 'Residential buildings' includes also summer cottages, temporary dwellings, logging camps, fishermens' quarters etc..
b) The estimates of 'Other construction' include oil drilling rigs, oil production platforms etc., pipelines for gas, oil and gas exploration and drilling.
c) Item 'Agriculture' refers to agriculture, forestry and fishing.
d) Item 'Mining and quarrying' also includes crude petroleum and natural gas production.
e) Item 'Construction' also includes oil and natural gas exploration and drilling.
f) Item 'Transport, storage and communication' includes pipeline transport for crude oil and natural gas.
g) Business services are included in item 'Community, social and personal services'.

2.16 Stocks of Reproducible Fixed Assets by Kind of Activity, in Constant Prices

Million Norwegian kroner

	1984 Gross	1984 Net	1985 Gross	1985 Net	1986 Gross	1986 Net	1987 Gross	1987 Net	1988 Gross	1988 Net	1989 Gross	1989 Net
					At constant prices of:1984							
1 Residential buildings a	...	376232	...	390761	...	407018	...	424039	...	439834	...	451622
2 Non-residential buildings	...	329161	...	342094	...	358351	...	374207	...	390519	...	402232
A Industries	...	208831	...	219236	...	231798	...	242779	...	253787	...	260975
1 Agriculture	...	49932	...	50248	...	50266	...	49737	...	49666	...	49407
2 Mining and quarrying	...	1722	...	4055	...	4893	...	4992	...	5074	...	5196
3 Manufacturing	...	63044	...	64427	...	67013	...	68599	...	69718	...	70327
4 Electricity, gas and water	...	22499	...	22957	...	23508	...	24317	...	25005	...	25336
5 Construction	...	4078	...	4485	...	4968	...	5338	...	6031	...	6377
6 Wholesale and retail trade	...	...	...	...	...	...	...	...	...	...	...	...
7 Transport and communication	...	3175	...	3317	...	3468	...	3642	...	3798	...	3953
8 Finance, etc.	...	64381	...	69748	...	77682	...	86163	...	94503	...	100387
9 Community, social and personal services	...	...	...	...	...	...	...	...	...	...	...	...
B Producers of government services	...	120331	...	122858	...	126553	...	131428	...	136731	...	141257

2.16 Stocks of Reproducible Fixed Assets by Kind of Activity, in Constant Prices
(Continued)

Million Norwegian kroner

	1984		1985		1986		1987		1988		1989	
	Gross	Net	Gross	Net	Gross	Net	Gross	Net	Gross	Net	Gross	Net
At constant prices of:1984												
C Other producers	...	...	...	...	...	...	...	...	...	...	...	...
3 Other construction b	...	461360	...	471823	...	495564	...	514724	...	530524	...	548372
A Industries	...	301499	...	306892	...	325153	...	338796	...	348489	...	359765
1 Agriculture c	...	3804	...	4124	...	4842	...	5336	...	5644	...	5728
2 Mining and quarrying d	...	103329	...	105674	...	120981	...	129888	...	137045	...	149094
3 Manufacturing	...	8469	...	9048	...	9670	...	12854	...	15167	...	15512
4 Electricity, gas and water	...	98339	...	100531	...	102625	...	104594	...	106582	...	107643
5 Construction e	...	11023	...	10475	...	10416	...	9196	...	7349	...	5666
6 Wholesale and retail trade	...	...	...	...	...	...	...	...	...	...	...	...
7 Transport and communication f	...	76535	...	77040	...	76619	...	76841	...	76579	...	76169
8 Finance, etc.	...	...	...	...	...	...	...	...	...	...	...	...
9 Community, social and personal services	...	...	...	...	...	...	...	...	...	...	...	...
B Producers of government services	...	159861	...	164931	...	170410	...	175956	...	182037	...	188596
C Other producers	...	...	...	...	...	...	...	...	...	...	...	...
4 Land improvement and development and plantation and orchard development	...	62894	...	63331	...	63847	...	64237	...	64564	...	64840
5 Producers' durable goods	...	257396	...	248506	...	250103	...	254909	...	262232	...	265326
A Industries	...	244773	...	234597	...	234812	...	238214	...	244159	...	245661
1 Agriculture c	...	27839	...	28125	...	28834	...	29700	...	30374	...	29832
2 Mining and quarrying d	...	5131	...	5643	...	6043	...	6458	...	6579	...	6312
3 Manufacturing	...	59868	...	62482	...	66582	...	70416	...	73091	...	74392
4 Electricity, gas and water	...	22411	...	23519	...	24768	...	25642	...	26241	...	26469
5 Construction e	...	6247	...	6610	...	7013	...	7459	...	7665	...	7434
6 Wholesale and retail trade	...	17348	...	18614	...	20519	...	21595	...	20965	...	19660
7 Transport and communication	...	94746	...	75969	...	64909	...	58628	...	59504	...	61703
8 Finance, etc. g	...	3422	...	4639	...	5987	...	7273	...	8028	...	8237
9 Community, social and personal services g	...	7760	...	8997	...	10158	...	11109	...	11826	...	11790
B Producers of government services	...	12623	...	13908	...	15290	...	16678	...	18059	...	19688
C Other producers	...	...	...	...	...	...	...	...	...	...	...	...
6 Breeding stock, dairy cattle, etc.	...	4663	...	4611	...	4538	...	4484	...	4476	...	4504
Statistical discrepancy	...	-1	...	-	...	-1	...	34	...	156	...	391
Total h	...	1491705	...	1521126	...	1579420	...	1636634	...	1692305	...	1737287
Memorandum Item: Mineral Fuels and Power	...	235265	...	244321	...	265656	...	281770	...	294980	...	308648

	1990		1991	
	Gross	Net	Gross	Net
At constant prices of:1984				
1 Residential buildings a	...	460074	...	464204
2 Non-residential buildings	...	410390	...	418027
A Industries	...	265380	...	268183
1 Agriculture	...	49246	...	48967
2 Mining and quarrying	...	5314	...	5599
3 Manufacturing	...	70746	...	70706
4 Electricity, gas and water	...	25347	...	25700
5 Construction	...	6635	...	6703
6 Wholesale and retail trade	...	...	...	...
7 Transport and communication	...	4064	...	4202
8 Finance, etc.	...	104071	...	106403
9 Community, social and personal services	...	...	...	...
B Producers of government services	...	144990	...	149726
C Other producers	...	...	...	...
3 Other construction b	...	548774	...	555617
A Industries	...	354014	...	354407

2.16 Stocks of Reproducible Fixed Assets by Kind of Activity, in Constant Prices
(Continued)

Million Norwegian kroner

	1990		1991	
	Gross	Net	Gross	Net
				At constant prices of:1984
1 Agriculture c	...	5670	...	5619
2 Mining and quarrying d	...	141133	...	138675
3 Manufacturing	...	17098	...	17748
4 Electricity, gas and water	...	108165	...	108390
5 Construction e	...	6859	...	6388
6 Wholesale and retail trade	...	...	...	...
7 Transport and communication f	...	75096	...	77758
8 Finance, etc.	...	...	...	...
9 Community, social and personal services	...	...	...	...
B Producers of government services	...	194538	...	200865
C Other producers	...	...	...	...
4 Land improvement and development and plantation and orchard development	...	65231	...	65585
5 Producers' durable goods	...	267991	...	267689
A Industries	...	246769	...	244336
1 Agriculture c	...	28578	...	27202
2 Mining and quarrying d	...	6049	...	6381
3 Manufacturing	...	75094	...	76192
4 Electricity, gas and water	...	26536	...	26367
5 Construction e	...	7180	...	6697
6 Wholesale and retail trade	...	19086	...	19003
7 Transport and communication	...	63663	...	61976
8 Finance, etc. g	...	8585	...	8371
9 Community, social and personal services g	...	12201	...	12501
B Producers of government services	...	21334	...	23658
C Other producers	...	...	...	...
6 Breeding stock, dairy cattle, etc.	...	4439	...	4527
Statistical discrepancy	...	256	...	331
Total h	...	1757155	...	1775980
Memorandum Item: Mineral Fuels and Power	...	301616	...	299630

a) Item 'Residential buildings' includes also summer cottages, temporary dwellings, logging camps, fishermens' quarters etc..
b) The estimates of 'Other construction' include oil drilling rigs, oil production platforms etc., pipelines for gas, oil and gas exploration and drilling.
c) Item 'Agriculture' refers to agriculture, forestry and fishing.
d) Item 'Mining and quarrying' also includes crude petroleum and natural gas production.

e) Item 'Construction' also includes oil and natural gas exploration and drilling.
f) Item 'Transport, storage and communication' includes pipeline transport for crude oil and natural gas.
g) Business services are included in item 'Community, social and personal services'.
h) Beginning 1987, the estimates at 1984 constant prices are derived from the series of constant prices based on T-1 prices. This resulted in some statistical discrepancies shown in the table.

2.17 Exports and Imports of Goods and Services, Detail

Million Norwegian kroner

	1980	1981	1982	1983	1984	1985	1986	1987	1988	1989	1990	1991
					Exports of Goods and Services							
1 Exports of merchandise, f.o.b.	92863	106899	114799	133249	156822	173255	135999	145182	152631	190054	215450	223420
2 Transport and communication	31500	36506	35246	34921	40191	43342	38617	35126	38820	48947	52813	57376
A In respect of merchandise imports	505	516	517	551	580	610	520	544	525	621	913	762
B Other	30995	35990	34729	34370	39611	42732	38097	34582	38295	48326	51900	56614
3 Insurance service charges	168	186	206	204	234	282	305	300	284	289	317	347
A In respect of merchandise imports	168	179	200	197	226	265	300	289	278	274	302	303
B Other	-	7	6	7	7	17	5	11	6	15	16	44

Norway

2.17 Exports and Imports of Goods and Services, Detail
(Continued)

Million Norwegian kroner

		1980	1981	1982	1983	1984	1985	1986	1987	1988	1989	1990	1991
4	Other commodities	6287	8022	9729	10240	11004	11703	11368	10545	11813	12482	13984	14723
5	Adjustments of merchandise exports to change-of-ownership basis	...	...	...	...	...	...	...	...	...	...	...	...
6	Direct purchases in the domestic market by non-residential households	3977	4430	4727	4910	5388	6590	7949	8557	9691	9337	9822	10836
7	Direct purchases in the domestic market by extraterritorial bodies	...	245	317	397	440	392	424	514	432	755	629	827
	Total Exports of Goods and Services	134795	156288	165023	183921	214077	235563	194664	200224	213671	261863	293015	307528

Imports of Goods and Services

		1980	1981	1982	1983	1984	1985	1986	1987	1988	1989	1990	1991
1	Imports of merchandise, c.i.f.	84543	90516	100458	102520	116542	133927	153073	151011	155350	166505	171779	170305
	A Imports of merchandise, f.o.b.	82787	88586	98462	99945	113707	130617	149688	147525	151451	161482	165686	164902
	B Transport of services on merchandise imports	1255	1392	1397	1985	2155	2515	2484	2619	3066	4200	5187	4496
	By residents	505	516	517	551	580	610	520	544	525	621	913	762
	By non-residents	750	876	880	1434	1574	1905	1964	2075	2541	3579	4274	3734
	C Insurance service charges on merchandise imports	501	538	598	590	679	795	900	867	835	822	904	908
	By residents	501	538	598	590	679	795	900	867	835	822	904	908
	By non-residents	-	-	-	-	-	-	-	-	-	-	-	-
2	Adjustments of merchandise imports to change-of-ownership basis	...	...	...	...	...	...	...	...	...	...	...	...
3	Other transport and communication	17936	21056	22038	24360	28281	29047	25559	24338	25130	30349	31016	33703
4	Other insurance service charges	663	405	356	579	903	924	512	-102	49	23	404	-21
5	Other commodities	6709	9105	10122	12061	13954	14785	14285	14964	14134	16823	16477	20548
6	Direct purchases abroad by government	...	109	125	126	139	158	170	181	207	218	219	249
7	Direct purchases abroad by resident households	7520	9279	11443	12385	13034	15761	19446	21035	23088	20672	22951	22313
	Total Imports of Goods and Services	117371	130467	144543	152031	172852	194602	213044	211427	217958	234591	242845	247098
	Balance of Goods and Services	17424	25821	20480	31890	41225	40961	-18380	-11203	-4287	27272	50170	60430
	Total Imports and Balance of Goods and Services	134795	156288	165023	183921	214077	235563	194664	200224	213671	261863	293015	307528

3.11 General Government Production Account: Total and Subsectors

Million Norwegian kroner

	1980					1981				
	Total General Government	Central Government	State or Provincial Government	Local Government	Social Security Funds	Total General Government	Central Government	State or Provincial Government	Local Government	Social Security Funds
Gross Output										
1 Sales	3885	1208	...	2677	...	5010	1510	...	3500	...
2 Services produced for own use	53478	21253	...	32225	...	62616	25878	...	36738	...
3 Own account fixed capital formation	...	...	...	...	...	...	...	...	...	...
Gross Output	57363	22461	...	34902	...	67626	27388	...	40238	...
Gross Input										
Intermediate Consumption	18462	9377	...	9084	...	22464	12118	...	10346	...
Subtotal: Value Added	38901	13083	...	25818	...	45162	15270	...	29892	...
1 Indirect taxes, net	...	...	...	...	...	...	...	...	...	...
A Indirect taxes	...	...	...	...	...	...	...	...	...	...
B Less: Subsidies	...	...	...	...	...	...	...	...	...	...
2 Consumption of fixed capital	2327	610	...	1717	...	2658	686	...	1972	...
3 Compensation of employees	36574	12474	...	24100	...	42504	14584	...	27919	...
4 Net Operating surplus	...	...	...	...	...	...	...	...	...	...
Gross Input	57363	22461	...	34901	...	67626	27388	...	40237	...

1375

Norway

3.11 General Government Production Account: Total and Subsectors

Million Norwegian kroner

	1982					1983				
	Total General Government	Central Government	State or Provincial Government	Local Government	Social Security Funds	Total General Government	Central Government	State or Provincial Government	Local Government	Social Security Funds
Gross Output										
1 Sales	6170	1961	...	4209	...	7140	2182	...	4958	...
2 Services produced for own use	70408	28469	...	41939	...	78214	31578	...	46636	...
3 Own account fixed capital formation	...	...	...	...	...	...	...	...	...	...
Gross Output	76578	30430	...	46148	...	85354	33760	...	51594	...
Gross Input										
Intermediate Consumption	25073	13219	...	11854	...	28512	15168	...	13345	...
Subtotal: Value Added	51505	17211	...	34294	...	56841	18593	...	38249	...
1 Indirect taxes, net	...	...	...	...	...	...	...	...	...	...
A Indirect taxes	...	...	...	...	...	...	...	...	...	...
B Less: Subsidies	...	...	...	...	...	...	...	...	...	...
2 Consumption of fixed capital	2979	750	...	2229	...	3186	783	...	2404	...
3 Compensation of employees	48526	16461	...	32065	...	53655	17810	...	35845	...
4 Net Operating surplus	...	...	...	...	...	...	...	...	...	...
Gross Input	76578	30430	...	46148	...	85353	33761	...	51594	...

	1984					1985				
	Total General Government	Central Government	State or Provincial Government	Local Government	Social Security Funds	Total General Government	Central Government	State or Provincial Government	Local Government	Social Security Funds
Gross Output										
1 Sales	8150	2622	...	5528	...	9266	3150	...	6116	...
2 Services produced for own use	84099	33142	...	50958	...	92653	35835	...	56818	...
3 Own account fixed capital formation	...	...	...	...	...	...	...	...	...	...
Gross Output	92249	35764	...	56486	...	101919	38985	...	62934	...
Gross Input										
Intermediate Consumption	30441	16069	...	14371	...	33955	17846	...	16108	...
Subtotal: Value Added	61808	19694	...	42114	...	67965	21139	...	46826	...
1 Indirect taxes, net	...	...	...	...	...	49	34	...	15	...
A Indirect taxes	...	...	...	...	...	49	34	...	15	...
B Less: Subsidies	...	...	...	...	...	...	...	...	...	...
2 Consumption of fixed capital	3338	813	...	2526	...	3742	921	...	2821	...
3 Compensation of employees	58470	18882	...	39589	...	64173	20184	...	43989	...
4 Net Operating surplus	...	...	...	...	...	...	...	...	...	...
Gross Input	92249	35764	...	56486	...	101919	38985	...	62933	...

	1986					1987				
	Total General Government	Central Government	State or Provincial Government	Local Government	Social Security Funds	Total General Government	Central Government	State or Provincial Government	Local Government	Social Security Funds
Gross Output										
1 Sales	10690	3837	...	6853	...	11778	3745	...	8034	...
2 Services produced for own use	101580	38777	...	62803	...	116045	44281	...	71763	...
3 Own account fixed capital formation	...	...	...	...	...	...	...	...	...	...
Gross Output	112270	42614	...	69656	...	127823	48026	...	79797	...
Gross Input										
Intermediate Consumption	36899	19286	...	17614	...	42194	22019	...	20175	...
Subtotal: Value Added	75371	23329	...	52042	...	85629	26007	...	59622	...
1 Indirect taxes, net	58	40	...	18	...	63	43	...	20	...
A Indirect taxes	58	40	...	18	...	63	43	...	20	...
B Less: Subsidies	...	...	...	...	...	...	...	...	...	...
2 Consumption of fixed capital	4259	1047	...	3213	...	4845	1185	...	3660	...
3 Compensation of employees	71054	22243	...	48811	...	80722	24780	...	55942	...
4 Net Operating surplus	...	...	...	...	...	...	...	...	...	...
Gross Input	112270	42616	...	69656	...	127824	48027	...	79797	...

3.11 General Government Production Account: Total and Subsectors

Million Norwegian kroner

	1988					1989				
	Total General Government	Central Government	State or Provincial Government	Local Government	Social Security Funds	Total General Government	Central Government	State or Provincial Government	Local Government	Social Security Funds
Gross Output										
1 Sales	14772	4659	...	10112	...	16155	4525	...	11630	...
2 Services produced for own use	122237	46537	...	75700	...	130998	51854	...	79144	...
3 Own account fixed capital formation	...	...	...	...	...	...	...	...	...	...
Gross Output	137009	51196	...	85812	...	147153	56379	...	90774	...
Gross Input										
Intermediate Consumption	45078	23513	...	21566	...	49311	26904	...	22408	...
Subtotal: Value Added	91930	27684	...	64247	...	97841	29476	...	68366	...
1 Indirect taxes, net	72	49	...	23	...	73	49	...	24	...
A Indirect taxes	72	49	...	23	...	73	49	...	24	...
B Less: Subsidies	...	...	...	...	...	...	...	...	...	...
2 Consumption of fixed capital	5355	1289	...	4066	...	5678	1402	...	4276	...
3 Compensation of employees	86504	26346	...	60158	...	92090	28025	...	64066	...
4 Net Operating surplus	...	...	...	...	...	...	...	...	...	...
Gross Input	137009	51197	...	85813	...	147152	56380	...	90774	...

	1990					1991				
	Total General Government	Central Government	State or Provincial Government	Local Government	Social Security Funds	Total General Government	Central Government	State or Provincial Government	Local Government	Social Security Funds
Gross Output										
1 Sales	18499	5648	...	12851	...	21696	6207	...	15489	...
2 Services produced for own use	139115	56083	...	83032	...	147478	58380	...	89098	...
3 Own account fixed capital formation	...	...	...	...	...	...	...	...	...	...
Gross Output	157614	61731	...	95883	...	169174	64587	...	104587	...
Gross Input										
Intermediate Consumption	53489	30066	...	23423	...	57264	31361	...	25904	...
Subtotal: Value Added	104126	31665	...	72461	...	111910	33226	...	78684	...
1 Indirect taxes, net	75	50	...	24	...	80	53	...	27	...
A Indirect taxes	75	50	...	24	...	80	53	...	27	...
B Less: Subsidies	...	...	...	...	...	...	...	...	...	...
2 Consumption of fixed capital	5933	1491	...	4442	...	6220	1612	...	4608	...
3 Compensation of employees	98118	30124	...	67994	...	105611	31562	...	74049	...
4 Net Operating surplus	...	...	...	...	...	...	...	...	...	...
Gross Input	157615	61731	...	95883	...	169175	64588	...	104588	...

3.12 General Government Income and Outlay Account: Total and Subsectors

Million Norwegian kroner

	1980					1981				
	Total General Government	Central Government	State or Provincial Government	Local Government	Social Security Funds	Total General Government	Central Government	State or Provincial Government	Local Government	Social Security Funds
Receipts										
1 Operating surplus	-	...	...	-	...	-	...	...	-	...
2 Property and entrepreneurial income [a]	7049	5935	...	-336	1450	9639	8321	...	-334	1652
A Withdrawals from public quasi-corporations [a]	-2216	-1214	...	-1002	...	-1894	-845	...	-1049	...
B Interest	9132	7016	...	666	1450	11415	9048	...	715	1652
C Dividends	133	133	...	...	...	118	118	...	...	...
D Net land rent and royalties	...	...	...	...	...	...	...	...	...	...
3 Taxes, fees and contributions	144657	85220	...	27006	32431	160248	93380	...	30169	36699
A Indirect taxes	49024	48399	...	487	138	55696	54940	...	609	147
B Direct taxes	61260	34741	...	26519	...	65655	36095	...	29560	...
Income	58393	33293	...	25100	...	62286	34292	...	27994	...
Other	2867	1448	...	1419	...	3369	1803	...	1566	...
C Social security contributions	34224	1931	...	...	32293	38699	2147	...	...	36552
D Fees, fines and penalties	149	149	...	...	...	198	198	...	...	...

3.12 General Government Income and Outlay Account: Total and Subsectors
(Continued)

Million Norwegian kroner

	1980					1981				
	Total General Government	Central Government	State or Provincial Government	Local Government	Social Security Funds	Total General Government	Central Government	State or Provincial Government	Local Government	Social Security Funds
4 Other current transfers	...	942	...	17762	10921	...	1181	...	20623	12944
A Casualty insurance claims	...	-	...	...	...	...	-	...	...	...
B Transfers from other government subsectors	...	942	...	17762	10921	...	1181	...	20623	12944
C Transfers from the rest of the world	...	...	...	...	...	...	-	...	...	...
D Other transfers, except imputed	...	...	...	...	...	...	...	...	...	...
E Imputed unfunded employee pension and welfare contributions	...	...	...	...	...	...	...	...	...	...
Total Current Receipts	151706	92097	...	44432	44802	169887	102882	...	50458	51295

Disbursements

	1980					1981				
	Total General Government	Central Government	State or Provincial Government	Local Government	Social Security Funds	Total General Government	Central Government	State or Provincial Government	Local Government	Social Security Funds
1 Government final consumption expenditure	53478	20417	...	32225	836	62616	24929	...	36737	950
2 Property income	9664	7813	...	1851	...	10721	8435	...	2286	...
A Interest	9664	7813	...	1851	...	10721	8435	...	2286	...
B Net land rent and royalties	...	...	...	...	...	...	...	...	...	...
3 Subsidies	19960	18845	...	866	249	21795	19656	...	1831	308
4 Other current transfers	43172	27243	...	5238	40316	50255	32441	...	5734	46828
A Casualty insurance premiums, net	-	-	...	...	...	-	-	...	...	...
B Transfers to other government subsectors	...	21690	...	998	6937	...	26118	...	1186	7444
C Social security benefits	40975	3356	...	4240	33379	47636	3704	...	4548	39384
D Social assistance grants	...	...	...	...	...	...	...	...	...	...
E Unfunded employee pension and welfare benefits	...	...	...	...	...	...	...	...	...	...
F Transfers to private non-profit institutions serving households	...	...	...	...	...	...	...	...	...	...
G Other transfers n.e.c.	11	11	...	...	...	2	2	...	...	...
H Transfers to the rest of the world	2186	2186	...	...	...	2617	2617	...	...	...
Net saving	25432	17779	...	4252	3401	24500	17421	...	3870	3209
Total Current Disbursements and Net Saving	151706	92097	...	44432	44802	169887	102882	...	50458	51295

	1982					1983				
	Total General Government	Central Government	State or Provincial Government	Local Government	Social Security Funds	Total General Government	Central Government	State or Provincial Government	Local Government	Social Security Funds

Receipts

	1982					1983				
	Total General Government	Central Government	State or Provincial Government	Local Government	Social Security Funds	Total General Government	Central Government	State or Provincial Government	Local Government	Social Security Funds
1 Operating surplus	-	...	...	-	...	-	...	...	...	...
2 Property and entrepreneurial income a	11508	9757	...	-152	1903	14089	11816	...	37	2236
A Withdrawals from public quasi-corporations a	-2207	-1166	...	-1041	...	-1510	-589	...	-921	...
B Interest	13218	10426	...	889	1903	15085	11891	...	958	2236
C Dividends	497	497	...	...	...	514	514	...	...	...
D Net land rent and royalties	...	...	...	...	...	...	...	...	...	...
3 Taxes, fees and contributions	176333	102004	...	32975	41354	194119	113247	...	36091	44781
A Indirect taxes	61747	60794	...	771	182	69733	68600	...	931	202
B Direct taxes	70605	38401	...	32204	...	76721	41561	...	35160	...
Income	67043	36601	...	30442	...	72650	39586	...	33064	...
Other	3562	1800	...	1762	...	4071	1975	...	2096	...
C Social security contributions	43494	2322	...	...	41172	47149	2570	...	...	44579
D Fees, fines and penalties	487	487	...	...	...	516	516	...	...	...
4 Other current transfers	...	1390	...	24204	14995	...	1547	...	26445	18026
A Casualty insurance claims	...	-	...	...	...	...	-	...	...	...
B Transfers from other government subsectors	...	1390	...	24204	14995	...	1547	...	26445	18026
C Transfers from the rest of the world	...	-	...	...	...	...	-	...	...	...
D Other transfers, except imputed	...	...	...	...	...	...	...	...	...	...
E Imputed unfunded employee pension and welfare contributions	...	...	...	...	...	...	...	...	...	...

3.12 General Government Income and Outlay Account: Total and Subsectors
(Continued)

Million Norwegian kroner

	1982 Total General Government	Central Government	State or Provincial Government	Local Government	Social Security Funds	1983 Total General Government	Central Government	State or Provincial Government	Local Government	Social Security Funds
Total Current Receipts	187841	113151	...	57027	58252	208208	126610	...	62573	65043

Disbursements

1 Government final consumption expenditure	70409	27472	...	41940	997	78213	30456	...	46635	1122
2 Property income	11529	8767	...	2762	...	13414	10237	...	3177	...
A Interest	11529	8767	...	2762	...	13414	10237	...	3177	...
B Net land rent and royalties	...	...	...	...	...	...	...	...	...	...
3 Subsidies	23662	21326	...	2021	315	24439	22224	...	2209	6
4 Other current transfers	57789	37862	...	6595	53921	66076	43476	...	7474	61144
A Casualty insurance premiums, net	-	-	...	...	...	-	-	...	...	...
B Transfers to other government subsectors	...	30460	...	1376	8753	...	34918	...	1529	9571
C Social security benefits	54516	4129	...	5219	45168	62212	4694	...	5945	51573
D Social assistance grants	...	...	...	...	...	...	...	...	...	...
E Unfunded employee pension and welfare benefits	...	...	...	...	...	...	...	...	...	...
F Transfers to private non-profit institutions serving households	...	...	...	...	...	...	...	...	...	...
G Other transfers n.e.c.	2	2	...	...	...	14	14	...	...	...
H Transfers to the rest of the world	3271	3271	...	...	...	3850	3850	...	...	...
Net saving	24452	17724	...	3709	3019	26066	20217	...	3078	2771
Total Current Disbursements and Net Saving	187841	113151	...	57027	58252	208208	126610	...	62573	65043

	1984 Total General Government	Central Government	State or Provincial Government	Local Government	Social Security Funds	1985 Total General Government	Central Government	State or Provincial Government	Local Government	Social Security Funds

Receipts

1 Operating surplus	-	...	...	-	...		...	...	-	...
2 Property and entrepreneurial income [a]	19928	16934	...	418	2576	23053	19468	...	745	2840
A Withdrawals from public quasi-corporations [a]	-1595	-833	...	-762	...	-2776	-2080	...	-696	...
B Interest	20552	16796	...	1180	2576	24780	20498	...	1441	2840
C Dividends	971	971	...	...	...	1050	1050	...	...	...
D Net land rent and royalties	...	...	...	...	...	...	...	...	...	...
3 Taxes, fees and contributions	216898	129856	...	39042	48000	249304	149348	...	45324	54632
A Indirect taxes	78200	76936	...	1062	202	91037	89545	...	1283	209
B Direct taxes	87637	49657	...	37980	...	100600	56559	...	44041	...
Income	83082	47617	...	35465	...	95312	54275	...	41037	...
Other	4555	2040	...	2515	...	5288	2284	...	3004	...
C Social security contributions	50511	2713	...	...	47798	57304	2881	...	...	54423
D Fees, fines and penalties	550	550	...	...	...	363	363	...	...	...
4 Other current transfers	3000	4743	...	31050	21584	3078	4708	...	34493	21497
A Casualty insurance claims	...	-	...	...	...	...	-	...	...	...
B Transfers from other government subsectors	...	1743	...	31050	21584	...	1631	...	34493	21497
C Transfers from the rest of the world	...	-	...	...	...	...	-	...	...	...
D Other transfers, except imputed	3000	3000	...	...	...	3078	3078	...	...	...
E Imputed unfunded employee pension and welfare contributions	...	...	...	...	...	...	...	...	...	...
Total Current Receipts	239826	151533	...	70510	72160	275435	173524	...	80562	78969

Disbursements

1 Government final consumption expenditure	84099	31999	...	50958	1142	92654	34525	...	56819	1310
2 Property income	15018	11219	...	3799	...	17393	13300	...	4093	...
A Interest	15018	11219	...	3799	...	17393	13300	...	4093	...
B Net land rent and royalties	...	...	...	...	...	...	...	...	...	...
3 Subsidies	25709	23340	...	2363	6	26936	24355	...	2574	7

Norway

3.12 General Government Income and Outlay Account: Total and Subsectors
(Continued)

Million Norwegian kroner

	1984 Total General Government	Central Government	State or Provincial Government	Local Government	Social Security Funds	1985 Total General Government	Central Government	State or Provincial Government	Local Government	Social Security Funds
4 Other current transfers	71787	49702	...	8447	68015	78029	52661	...	9471	73518
A Casualty insurance premiums, net	-	-	...	...	...	-	-	...	...	...
B Transfers to other government subsectors	...	40921	...	1559	11897	...	43195	...	1531	12895
C Social security benefits	67917	4911	...	6888	56118	73819	5257	...	7940	60623
D Social assistance grants	...	...	...	...	...	...	...	...	...	...
E Unfunded employee pension and welfare benefits	...	...	...	...	...	...	...	...	...	...
F Transfers to private non-profit institutions serving households	...	...	...	...	...	...	...	...	...	...
G Other transfers n.e.c.	-	-	...	...	...	-	-	...	...	...
H Transfers to the rest of the world	3870	3870	...	...	...	4210	4210	...	...	...
Net saving	43213	35273	...	4943	2997	60423	48683	...	7605	4135
Total Current Disbursements and Net Saving	239826	151533	...	70510	72160	275435	173524	...	80562	78970

	1986 Total General Government	Central Government	State or Provincial Government	Local Government	Social Security Funds	1987 Total General Government	Central Government	State or Provincial Government	Local Government	Social Security Funds
					Receipts					
1 Operating surplus	-	...	...	-	...	-	...	...	-	...
2 Property and entrepreneurial income a	30855	26228	...	1227	3400	33463	27458	...	1745	4260
A Withdrawals from public quasi-corporations a	-4047	-3077	...	-970	...	-7630	-6878	...	-751	...
B Interest	33290	27693	...	2197	3400	39935	33179	...	2496	4260
C Dividends	1612	1612	...	...	...	1157	1157	...	...	...
D Net land rent and royalties	...	...	...	...	...	...	...	...	...	...
3 Taxes, fees and contributions	247164	131534	...	51195	64435	275775	142423	...	57252	76099
A Indirect taxes	99922	98178	...	1575	169	107493	105504	...	1803	185
B Direct taxes	79309	29689	...	49620	...	87951	32502	...	55449	...
Income	73364	27104	...	46260	...	80931	29400	...	51531	...
Other	5945	2585	...	3360	...	7020	3102	...	3918	...
C Social security contributions	67460	3194	...	...	64266	79718	3804	...	...	75914
D Fees, fines and penalties	473	473	...	...	...	613	613	...	...	...
4 Other current transfers	3078	3990	...	37062	18714	578	1369	...	40503	18659
A Casualty insurance claims	...	-	...	...	...	...	...	...	...	...
B Transfers from other government subsectors	...	913	...	37062	18714	...	792	...	40503	18659
C Transfers from the rest of the world	...	-	...	...	...	...	...	...	...	...
D Other transfers, except imputed	3078	3078	...	...	...	578	578	...	...	...
E Imputed unfunded employee pension and welfare contributions	...	...	...	...	...	...	...	...	...	...
Total Current Receipts	281097	161752	...	89484	86549	309816	171250	...	99500	99018
					Disbursements					
1 Government final consumption expenditure	101580	37395	...	62803	1383	116045	42839	...	71763	1443
2 Property income	22325	17811	...	4513	...	24061	18923	...	5138	...
A Interest	22325	17811	...	4513	...	24061	18923	...	5138	...
B Net land rent and royalties	...	...	...	...	...	...	...	...	...	...
3 Subsidies	29569	26211	...	3350	8	31515	27740	...	3766	9

3.12 General Government Income and Outlay Account: Total and Subsectors
(Continued)

Million Norwegian kroner

	1986					1987				
	Total General Government	Central Government	State or Provincial Government	Local Government	Social Security Funds	Total General Government	Central Government	State or Provincial Government	Local Government	Social Security Funds
4 Other current transfers	86472	54010	...	9774	79376	97355	55394	...	12088	89827
A Casualty insurance premiums, net	-	-		...	...	-	-		...	...
B Transfers to other government subsectors	...	43306	...	900	12483	...	43504	...	1621	14828
C Social security benefits	81525	5757	...	8875	66893	92072	6607	...	10467	74999
D Social assistance grants	...	...	...	...	...	...	...	...	...	...
E Unfunded employee pension and welfare benefits	...	...	...	...	...	...	...	...	...	...
F Transfers to private non-profit institutions serving households	...	...	...	...	...	...	...	...	...	...
G Other transfers n.e.c.	-	-	...	...	...	-	-	...	...	...
H Transfers to the rest of the world	4947	4947	...	...	...	5283	5283	...	...	...
Net saving	41151	26325	...	9043	5783	40838	26355	...	6745	7738
Total Current Disbursements and Net Saving	281097	161752	...	89483	86550	309814	171251	...	99500	99017

	1988					1989				
	Total General Government	Central Government	State or Provincial Government	Local Government	Social Security Funds	Total General Government	Central Government	State or Provincial Government	Local Government	Social Security Funds

Receipts

1 Operating surplus	-	...	...	-	...	-	...	...	-	...
2 Property and entrepreneurial income [a]	32942	26674	...	1564	4703	42673	35993	...	1743	4938
A Withdrawals from public quasi-corporations [a]	-10552	-9493	...	-1059	...	-3731	-3030	...	-701	...
B Interest	43149	35822	...	2623	4703	45980	38597	...	2444	4938
C Dividends	345	345	...	...	...	425	425	...	...	...
D Net land rent and royalties	...	...	...	...	...	...	...	...	...	...
3 Taxes, fees and contributions	283841	147956	...	60505	75380	291305	159057	...	60552	71695
A Indirect taxes	106984	104819	...	1991	174	106562	104016	...	2372	173
B Direct taxes	96505	37991	...	58514	...	107395	49215	...	58180	...
Income	88404	34451	...	53953	...	98484	45171	...	53312	...
Other	8101	3540	...	4561	...	8912	4044	...	4868	...
C Social security contributions	79632	4426	...	...	75206	76604	5082	...	...	71522
D Fees, fines and penalties	720	720	...	...	...	744	744	...	...	...
4 Other current transfers	4573	6599	...	43928	31503	7466	9062	...	49673	45798
A Casualty insurance claims	...	-	...	...	...	...	-	...	...	...
B Transfers from other government subsectors	...	2026	...	43928	31503	...	1597	...	49673	45798
C Transfers from the rest of the world	...	-	...	...	...	...	-	...	...	...
D Other transfers, except imputed	4573	4573	...	...	...	7466	7466	...	...	...
E Imputed unfunded employee pension and welfare contributions	...	...	...	...	...	...	...	...	...	...
Total Current Receipts	321356	181229	...	105997	111586	341444	204112	...	111968	122431

Disbursements

1 Government final consumption expenditure	122237	45039	...	75700	1498	130998	50278	...	79144	1576
2 Property income	22670	16442	...	6228	...	24705	17847	...	6859	...
A Interest	22670	16442	...	6228	...	24705	17847	...	6859	...
B Net land rent and royalties	...	...	...	...	...	...	...	...	...	...
3 Subsidies	33769	29687	...	4073	9	36599	32365	...	4224	10

Norway

3.12 General Government Income and Outlay Account: Total and Subsectors
(Continued)

Million Norwegian kroner

	1988					1989				
	Total General Government	Central Government	State or Provincial Government	Local Government	Social Security Funds	Total General Government	Central Government	State or Provincial Government	Local Government	Social Security Funds
4 Other current transfers	111701	67734	...	16628	104796	124447	85541	...	18833	117140
A Casualty insurance premiums, net	-	-	...	...	...	-	...	...	...	...
B Transfers to other government subsectors	...	54163	...	4781	18514	...	70713	...	6347	20008
C Social security benefits	105358	7229	...	11847	86282	118151	8532	...	12487	97132
D Social assistance grants	...	...	...	...	...	...	...	...	...	...
E Unfunded employee pension and welfare benefits	...	...	...	...	...	...	...	...	...	...
F Transfers to private non-profit institutions serving households	...	...	...	...	...	...	...	...	...	...
G Other transfers n.e.c.	47	47	...	...	...	47	47	...	...	...
H Transfers to the rest of the world	6295	6295	...	...	...	6249	6249	...	...	...
Net saving	30979	22328	...	3369	5283	24695	18081	...	2909	3706
Total Current Disbursements and Net Saving	321356	181230	...	105998	111586	341444	204112	...	111969	122432

	1990					1991				
	Total General Government	Central Government	State or Provincial Government	Local Government	Social Security Funds	Total General Government	Central Government	State or Provincial Government	Local Government	Social Security Funds
Receipts										
1 Operating surplus	-	...	...	-	...	-	...	...	-	...
2 Property and entrepreneurial income a	51099	42394	...	2403	6303	53546	44782	...	2737	6027
A Withdrawals from public quasi-corporations a	1273	1461	...	-188	...	1609	1819	...	-210	...
B Interest	48569	39675	...	2591	6303	49927	40953	...	2947	6027
C Dividends	1257	1257	...	...	...	2010	2010	...	...	...
D Net land rent and royalties	...	...	...	...	...	...	...	...	...	...
3 Taxes, fees and contributions	310628	171226	...	64456	74946	320590	175604	...	66268	78717
A Indirect taxes	111089	108277	...	2627	185	115617	112509	...	2674	433
B Direct taxes	118449	56620	...	61829	...	120067	56148	...	63594	325
Income	109240	52462	...	56778	...	109637	51537	...	58100	...
Other	9209	4158	...	5051	...	10430	4611	...	5494	325
C Social security contributions	80239	5478	...	...	74761	83698	5739	...	...	77959
D Fees, fines and penalties	851	851	...	...	...	1208	1208	...	...	...
4 Other current transfers	10153	11769	...	53768	45462	5691	7087	...	57452	27925
A Casualty insurance claims	...	-	...	...	...	...	-	...	...	...
B Transfers from other government subsectors	...	1615	...	53768	45462	...	1396	...	57452	27925
C Transfers from the rest of the world	...	...	...	...	...	...	-	...	...	...
D Other transfers, except imputed	10153	10153	...	...	...	5691	5691	...	...	...
E Imputed unfunded employee pension and welfare contributions	...	...	...	...	...	...	...	...	...	...
Total Current Receipts	371880	225389	...	120627	126711	379827	227473	...	126457	112669
Disbursements										
1 Government final consumption expenditure	139115	54480	...	83032	1603	147478	56618	...	89098	1762
2 Property income	25805	18660	...	7145	...	24836	17375	...	7461	...
A Interest	25805	18660	...	7145	...	24836	17375	...	7461	...
B Net land rent and royalties	...	...	...	...	...	...	...	...	...	...
3 Subsidies	39992	35381	...	4598	13	42770	37944	...	4813	13

3.12 General Government Income and Outlay Account: Total and Subsectors
(Continued)

Million Norwegian kroner

	1990					1991				
	Total General Government	Central Government	State or Provincial Government	Local Government	Social Security Funds	Total General Government	Central Government	State or Provincial Government	Local Government	Social Security Funds
4 Other current transfers	136409	99872	...	18557	118825	148501	113090	...	16900	105284
A Casualty insurance premiums, net	-	-	...	...	...	-	-	...	...	...
B Transfers to other government subsectors	...	74242	...	5674	20930	...	83048	...	3489	236
C Social security benefits	128982	18204	...	12883	97895	140871	22412	...	13411	105048
D Social assistance grants	...	...	...	...	...	...	...	...	...	...
E Unfunded employee pension and welfare benefits	...	...	...	...	...	...	...	...	...	...
F Transfers to private non-profit institutions serving households	...	...	...	...	...	...	...	...	...	...
G Other transfers n.e.c.	41	41	...	...	...	-	...	...	...	...
H Transfers to the rest of the world	7385	7385	...	...	...	7630	7630	...	...	...
Net saving	30560	16996	...	7294	6270	16241	2446	...	8186	5610
Total Current Disbursements and Net Saving	371881	225389	...	120626	126711	379826	227473	...	126458	112669

a) Public enterprise surplus are deducted from item 'Withdrawals from public quasi-corporations.

3.13 General Government Capital Accumulation Account: Total and Subsectors

Million Norwegian kroner

	1980					1981				
	Total General Government	Central Government	State or Provincial Government	Local Government	Social Security Funds	Total General Government	Central Government	State or Provincial Government	Local Government	Social Security Funds
Finance of Gross Accumulation										
1 Gross saving	27759	18389	...	5969	3401	27160	18107	...	5842	3209
A Consumption of fixed capital	2327	610	...	1717	...	2658	686	...	1972	...
B Net saving	25432	17779	...	4252	3401	24502	17421	...	3870	3209
2 Capital transfers	...	...	...	...	...	...	...	...	...	...
Finance of Gross Accumulation	27759	18389	...	5969	3401	27160	18107	...	5842	3209
Gross Accumulation										
1 Gross capital formation	11454	3627	...	7786	41	11602	3780	...	7787	36
A Increase in stocks	...	...	...	...	...	...	...	...	...	...
B Gross fixed capital formation	11454	3627	...	7786	41	11602	3780	...	7787	36
2 Purchases of land, net	...	...	...	...	...	...	...	...	...	...
3 Purchases of intangible assets, net	...	...	...	...	...	...	...	...	...	...
4 Capital transfers	...	...	...	...	...	...	...	...	...	...
Net lending	16305	14762	...	-1817	3360	15558	14327	...	-1945	3173
Gross Accumulation	27759	18389	...	5969	3401	27160	18107	...	5842	3209

	1982					1983				
	Total General Government	Central Government	State or Provincial Government	Local Government	Social Security Funds	Total General Government	Central Government	State or Provincial Government	Local Government	Social Security Funds
Finance of Gross Accumulation										
1 Gross saving	27430	18474	...	5938	3019	29254	21000	...	5482	2771
A Consumption of fixed capital	2979	750	...	2229	...	3187	783	...	2404	...
B Net saving	24451	17724	...	3709	3019	26067	20217	...	3078	2771
2 Capital transfers	...	...	...	...	...	...	...	...	...	...
Finance of Gross Accumulation	27430	18474	...	5938	3019	29254	21000	...	5482	2771
Gross Accumulation										
1 Gross capital formation	11525	3811	...	7694	20	12410	4254	...	8130	26
A Increase in stocks	...	...	...	...	...	...	...	...	...	...
B Gross fixed capital formation	11525	3811	...	7694	20	12410	4254	...	8130	26
2 Purchases of land, net	...	...	...	...	...	...	...	...	...	...
3 Purchases of intangible assets, net	...	...	...	...	...	...	...	...	...	...
4 Capital transfers	...	...	...	...	...	...	...	...	...	...
Net lending	15905	14663	...	-1756	2999	16844	16746	...	-2648	2745
Gross Accumulation	27430	18474	...	5938	3019	29254	21000	...	5482	2771

Norway

3.13 General Government Capital Accumulation Account: Total and Subsectors

Million Norwegian kroner

1984 / 1985

	1984					1985				
	Total General Government	Central Government	State or Provincial Government	Local Government	Social Security Funds	Total General Government	Central Government	State or Provincial Government	Local Government	Social Security Funds
Finance of Gross Accumulation										
1 Gross saving	46551	36086	...	7469	2997	64164	49604	...	10426	4135
A Consumption of fixed capital	3339	813		2526	...	3742	921	...	2821	...
B Net saving	43212	35273	...	4943	2997	60422	48683		7605	4135
2 Capital transfers	...	...	...	...	...	...	...	...	...	...
Finance of Gross Accumulation	46551	36086	...	7469	2997	64164	49604		10426	4135
Gross Accumulation										
1 Gross capital formation	12858	4691	...	8094	73	13288	5044		8105	139
A Increase in stocks	...	...		...	...	...	...	...	...	...
B Gross fixed capital formation	12858	4691	...	8094	73	13288	5044		8105	139
2 Purchases of land, net	...	...	...	...	...	...	...	...	...	...
3 Purchases of intangible assets, net	...	...	...	...	...	...	...	...	...	...
4 Capital transfers	...	...	...	...	...	...	...	...	...	...
Net lending	33693	31395	...	-625	2924	50876	44560		2321	3996
Gross Accumulation	46551	36086	...	7469	2997	64164	49604	...	10426	4135

1986 / 1987

	1986					1987				
	Total General Government	Central Government	State or Provincial Government	Local Government	Social Security Funds	Total General Government	Central Government	State or Provincial Government	Local Government	Social Security Funds
Finance of Gross Accumulation										
1 Gross saving	45410	27371	...	12256	5783	45683	27540	...	10405	7738
A Consumption of fixed capital	4259	1046	...	3213		4845	1185		3660	...
B Net saving	41151	26325	...	9043	5783	40838	26355		6745	7738
2 Capital transfers	...	...	...	...	...	...	...	...	...	...
Finance of Gross Accumulation	45410	27371	...	12256	5783	45683	27540	...	10405	7738
Gross Accumulation										
1 Gross capital formation	16458	5627	...	10754	77	20087	6686	...	13378	23
A Increase in stocks	...	...	...	...	...	...	...	...	...	...
B Gross fixed capital formation	16458	5627	...	10754	77	20087	6686	...	13378	23
2 Purchases of land, net	...	...	...	...	...	...	...	...	...	...
3 Purchases of intangible assets, net	...	...	...	...	...	...	...	...	...	...
4 Capital transfers	...	...	...	...	...	...	...	...	...	...
Net lending	28952	21744	...	1502	5706	25596	20854	...	-2973	7715
Gross Accumulation	45410	27371	...	12256	5783	45683	27540	...	10405	7738

1988 / 1989

	1988					1989				
	Total General Government	Central Government	State or Provincial Government	Local Government	Social Security Funds	Total General Government	Central Government	State or Provincial Government	Local Government	Social Security Funds
Finance of Gross Accumulation										
1 Gross saving	36334	23617	...	7435	5283	30373	19483	...	7184	3706
A Consumption of fixed capital	5355	1289	...	4066	...	5678	1402		4276	...
B Net saving	30979	22328	...	3369	5283	24695	18081		2908	3706
2 Capital transfers	...	...	...	...	...	...	...	...	...	...
Finance of Gross Accumulation	36334	23617	...	7435	5283	30373	19483	...	7184	3706
Gross Accumulation										
1 Gross capital formation	22650	7935	...	14680	35	23020	9341	...	13625	54
A Increase in stocks	...	...	...	...	...	...	...	...	...	...
B Gross fixed capital formation	22650	7935	...	14680	35	23020	9341	...	13625	54
2 Purchases of land, net	...	...	...	...	...	...	...	...	...	...
3 Purchases of intangible assets, net	...	...	...	...	...	...	...	...	...	...
4 Capital transfers	...	...	...	...	...	...	...	...	...	...
Net lending	13684	15682	...	-7245	5248	7353	10142	...	-6441	3652
Gross Accumulation	36334	23617	...	7435	5283	30373	19483	...	7184	3706

3.13 General Government Capital Accumulation Account: Total and Subsectors

Million Norwegian kroner

	1990					1991				
	Total General Government	Central Government	State or Provincial Government	Local Government	Social Security Funds	Total General Government	Central Government	State or Provincial Government	Local Government	Social Security Funds
Finance of Gross Accumulation										
1 Gross saving	36493	18487	...	11736	6270	22461	4058	...	12793	5610
A Consumption of fixed capital	5933	1491	...	4442	...	6220	1612	...	4608	...
B Net saving	30560	16996	...	7294	6270	16241	2446	...	8185	5610
2 Capital transfers	...	...	...	...	...	...	...	...	...	...
Finance of Gross Accumulation	36493	18487	...	11736	6270	22461	4058	...	12793	5610
Gross Accumulation										
1 Gross capital formation	21423	9291	...	12084	48	24321	11354	...	12916	51
A Increase in stocks	...	...	...	...	...	...	...	...	...	...
B Gross fixed capital formation	21423	9291	...	12084	48	24321	11354	...	12916	51
2 Purchases of land, net	...	...	...	...	...	...	...	...	...	...
3 Purchases of intangible assets, net	...	...	...	...	...	...	...	...	...	...
4 Capital transfers	...	...	...	...	...	...	...	...	...	...
Net lending	15070	9196	...	-348	6222	-1860	-7296	...	-123	5559
Gross Accumulation	36493	18487	...	11736	6270	22461	4058	...	12793	5610

3.22 Corporate and Quasi-Corporate Enterprise Income and Outlay Account: Total and Sectors

Million Norwegian kroner

	1980			1981			1982			1983		
	TOTAL	Non-Financial	Financial	TOTAL	Non-Financial	Financial	TOTAL	Non-Financial	Financial	TOTAL	Non-Financial	Financial
Receipts												
1 Operating surplus	42423	46075	-3652	50576	55015	-4439	51361	57140	-5779	62069	68944	-6875
2 Property and entrepreneurial income	41881	8005	33876	53255	10069	43186	65208	11963	53245	73940	13879	60061
A Withdrawals from quasi-corporate enterprises [a]	2220	2220	-	1921	1921	-	2210	2210	-	2037	2037	-
B Interest	37990	4295	33695	49225	6241	42984	61303	8316	52987	68784	9114	59670
C Dividends	1462	1281	181	1858	1656	202	1510	1252	258	2777	2386	391
D Net land rent and royalties	209	209	-	251	251	-	185	185	-	342	342	-
3 Current transfers	11720	6078	5642	14597	7739	6858	16923	8472	8451	19068	9815	9253
A Casualty insurance claims	4040	4040	-	5014	5014	-	6076	6076	-	6412	6412	-
B Casualty insurance premiums, net, due to be received by insurance companies	5130	-	5130	6293	-	6293	7623	-	7623	7969	-	7969
C Current transfers from the rest of the world	...	...	...	...	...	...	100	100	...	100	100	...
D Other transfers except imputed	2550	2038	512	3290	2725	565	3124	2296	828	4587	3303	1284
E Imputed unfunded employee pension and welfare contributions	...	...	...	...	...	...	...	...	...	...	...	...
Total Current Receipts	96024	60158	35866	118428	72823	45605	133492	77575	55917	155077	92638	62439
Disbursements												
1 Property and entrepreneurial income	47263	23416	23847	60453	30316	30137	73856	37082	36774	83022	41277	41745
A Withdrawals from quasi-corporations [b]	4	4	-	27	27	-	3	3	-	527	527	-
Public	4	4	-	27	27	-	3	3	-	527	527	-
Private	...	...	...	...	...	...	...	...	...	...	...	...
B Interest [c]	42153	18720	23433	54228	24561	29667	65931	29686	36245	73269	32223	41046
C Dividends	4756	4342	414	5759	5289	470	7438	6909	529	8588	7889	699
D Net land rent and royalties	350	350	-	439	439	-	484	484	-	638	638	-
2 Direct taxes and other current transfers n.e.c. to general government	23603	23337	266	26097	25800	297	27955	27625	330	32614	32026	588
A Direct taxes	23603	...	...	26097	...	...	27955	27625	330	32614	32026	588
On income	22910	...	...	25329	...	...	27176	26925	251	31728	31294	434
Other	693	...	...	768	...	...	779	700	79	886	732	154
B Fines, fees, penalties and other current transfers n.e.c.	...	...	...	...	...	...	...	...	...	...	...	...

Norway

3.22 Corporate and Quasi-Corporate Enterprise Income and Outlay Account: Total and Sectors
(Continued)

Million Norwegian kroner

	1980			1981			1982			1983		
	TOTAL	Non-Financial	Financial	TOTAL	Non-Financial	Financial	TOTAL	Non-Financial	Financial	TOTAL	Non-Financial	Financial
3 Other current transfers	12344	5457	6887	15242	7246	7996	17838	8137	9701	20096	9893	10203
A Casualty insurance premiums, net	4040	4040	-	5014	5014	-	6076	6076	-	6412	6412	-
B Casualty insurance claims liability of insurance companies	5130	-	5130	6293	-	6293	7623	-	7623	7969	-	7969
C Transfers to private non-profit institutions	...	...	...	...	...	...	...	...	...	...	...	...
D Unfunded employee pension and welfare benefits	...	...	...	...	...	...	...	...	...	...	...	...
E Social assistance grants	...	...	...	...	...	...	...	...	...	...	...	...
F Other transfers n.e.c. c	3174	1417	1757	3935	2232	1703	4012	1934	2078	5563	3329	2234
G Transfers to the rest of the world	...	...	...	...	...	...	127	127	...	152	152	...
Net saving	12814	7948	4866	16636	9463	7173	13843	4731	9112	19345	9442	9903
Total Current Disbursements and Net Saving	96024	60158	35866	118428	72825	45603	133492	77575	55917	155077	92638	62439

	1984			1985			1986			1987		
	TOTAL	Non-Financial	Financial	TOTAL	Non-Financial	Financial	TOTAL	Non-Financial	Financial	TOTAL	Non-Financial	Financial
						Receipts						
1 Operating surplus	80354	88191	-7836	88229	95707	-7478	54144	62114	-7971	48602	56468	-7866
2 Property and entrepreneurial income	83903	13782	70121	102944	19038	83906	141711	27566	114145	176232	32670	143562
A Withdrawals from quasi-corporate enterprises a	1967	1967	-	2811	2811	-	4052	4052	-	7640	7640	-
B Interest	78695	9044	69651	98201	14746	83455	135947	22348	113599	166258	23243	143015
C Dividends	2982	2512	470	1645	1194	451	1713	1167	546	2334	1787	548
D Net land rent and royalties	259	259	-	287	287	-	-	-	-	-	-	-
3 Current transfers	20419	10474	9945	20971	11100	9872	24195	12372	11823	26818	13790	13028
A Casualty insurance claims	6986	6986	-	7331	7331	-	8056	8056	-	9053	9053	-
B Casualty insurance premiums, net, due to be received by insurance companies	8777	-	8777	9134	-	9134	10773	-	10773	12083	-	12083
C Current transfers from the rest of the world	59	59	...	13	13	...	-	-	-	-	-	-
D Other transfers except imputed	4597	3429	1168	4494	3756	738	5366	4316	1050	5682	4737	945
E Imputed unfunded employee pension and welfare contributions	...	...	...	...	...	...	...	...	...	...	...	...
Total Current Receipts	184676	112447	72230	212144	125845	86300	220050	102052	117997	251652	102928	148724
						Disbursements						
1 Property and entrepreneurial income	98095	46122	51973	113340	46723	66617	152269	60656	91613	181064	64691	116372
A Withdrawals from quasi-corporations b	372	372	-	35	35	-	5	5	-	10	10	-
Public	372	372	-	35	35	-	5	5	-	10	10	-
Private	...	...	...	...	...	...	...	...	...	...	...	...
B Interest c	87325	36118	51207	103370	37666	65704	142517	51646	90871	171953	56031	115922
C Dividends	9736	8969	767	9233	8320	913	9245	8502	742	8230	7780	450
D Net land rent and royalties	663	663	-	701	701	-	503	503	-	870	870	-
2 Direct taxes and other current transfers n.e.c. to general government	39176	38587	589	47817	47206	611	20184	19545	639	18881	18297	584
A Direct taxes	38985	38396	589	47802	47191	611	20184	19545	639	18881	18297	584
On income	38088	37555	533	46305	45770	535	18538	17992	546	16980	16465	515
Other	897	841	56	1497	1421	76	1646	1553	93	1901	1833	68
B Fines, fees, penalties and other current transfers n.e.c.	191	191	...	16	16	...	-	-	...	-	-	...

3.22 Corporate and Quasi-Corporate Enterprise Income and Outlay Account: Total and Sectors
(Continued)

Million Norwegian kroner

	1984			1985			1986			1987		
	TOTAL	Non-Financial	Financial	TOTAL	Non-Financial	Financial	TOTAL	Non-Financial	Financial	TOTAL	Non-Financial	Financial
3 Other current transfers	24595	10313	14282	23536	9100	14436	27015	10737	16278	27206	13056	14151
A Casualty insurance premiums, net	6986	6986	-	7330	7330	-	8056	8056	-	9053	9053	-
B Casualty insurance claims liability of insurance companies	8777	-	8777	9134	-	9134	10773	-	10773	12083	-	12083
C Transfers to private non-profit institutions	...	...	...	...	...	...	...	...	...	...	...	...
D Unfunded employee pension and welfare benefits	...	...	...	...	...	...	...	...	...	...	...	...
E Social assistance grants	...	...	...	...	...	...	...	...	...	...	...	...
F Other transfers n.e.c. c	8696	3191	5505	7010	1708	5302	8110	2605	5505	5982	3914	2068
G Transfers to the rest of the world	136	136	...	62	62	...	76	76	...	89	89	...
Net saving	22810	17425	5386	27452	22816	4636	20582	11115	9467	24501	6884	17617
Total Current Disbursements and Net Saving	184676	112447	72230	212145	125845	86300	220050	102053	117997	251652	102928	148724

	1988			1989			1990			1991		
	TOTAL	Non-Financial	Financial	TOTAL	Non-Financial	Financial	TOTAL	Non-Financial	Financial	TOTAL	Non-Financial	Financial

Receipts

1 Operating surplus	43111	52419	-9309	73944	82117	-8174	90103	98302	-8198	95448	100885	-5438
2 Property and entrepreneurial income	200371	41622	158750	196147	37641	158506	194422	36075	158347	186974	35594	151380
A Withdrawals from quasi-corporate enterprises a	10625	10625	-	3870	3870	-	3980	3980	-	4054	4054	-
B Interest	187328	29113	158215	189162	31270	157891	187523	29987	157536	179673	28979	150694
C Dividends	2418	1884	534	3116	2501	615	2723	1912	811	3247	2561	686
D Net land rent and royalties	-	-	-	-	-	-	196	196	-	-	-	-
3 Current transfers	29998	15202	14796	31665	16715	14950	33808	18131	15676	33356	16308	17047
A Casualty insurance claims	9889	9889	-	9857	9857	-	9835	9835	-	10961	10961	-
B Casualty insurance premiums, net, due to be received by insurance companies	13185	-	13185	13143	-	13143	13113	-	13113	14615	-	14615
C Current transfers from the rest of the world	-	-	...	-	-	...	-	-	...	-	-	...
D Other transfers except imputed	6924	5313	1611	8664	6858	1807	10860	8297	2563	7779	5347	2432
E Imputed unfunded employee pension and welfare contributions	...	...	...	...	...	...	...	...	...	...	...	...
Total Current Receipts	273480	109243	164237	301756	136473	165282	318333	152508	165825	315778	152787	162989

Disbursements

1 Property and entrepreneurial income	205936	74722	131214	211413	81430	129984	216805	87443	129362	213479	89829	123650
A Withdrawals from quasi-corporations b	73	73	-	138	138	-	5254	5254	-	5663	5663	-
Public	73	73	-	138	138	-	5254	5254	-	5663	5663	-
Private	...	...	...	...	...	...	...	...	...	...	...	...
B Interest c	198358	67757	130601	202253	73687	128567	201332	72390	128942	194563	71593	122970
C Dividends	6991	6378	613	8854	7437	1417	9918	9499	420	12917	12237	680
D Net land rent and royalties	513	513	-	168	168	-	301	301	...	336	336	...
2 Direct taxes and other current transfers n.e.c. to general government	15810	15342	468	23051	22034	1017	31003	30373	630	29200	28707	493
A Direct taxes	15810	15342	468	23051	22034	1017	31003	30373	630	29200	28707	493
On income	13674	13260	414	20690	19808	881	28688	28138	551	26520	26102	418
Other	2136	2082	55	2362	2226	136	2315	2236	80	2680	2605	75
B Fines, fees, penalties and other current transfers n.e.c.	-	-	...	-	-	...	-	-	...	-	-	...

3.22 Corporate and Quasi-Corporate Enterprise Income and Outlay Account: Total and Sectors
(Continued)

Million Norwegian kroner

	1988			1989			1990			1991		
	TOTAL	Non-Financial	Financial	TOTAL	Non-Financial	Financial	TOTAL	Non-Financial	Financial	TOTAL	Non-Financial	Financial
3 Other current transfers	34092	14619	19473	38775	13488	25287	43591	15668	27923	38781	13524	25257
A Casualty insurance premiums, net	9889	9889	-	9857	9857	-	9834	9834	-	10961	10961	-
B Casualty insurance claims liability of insurance companies	13185	-	13185	13143	-	13143	13113	-	13113	14615	-	14615
C Transfers to private non-profit institutions	...	...	...	...	...	...	...	...	...	...	...	...
D Unfunded employee pension and welfare benefits	...	...	...	15	...	15	33	...	33	48	...	48
E Social assistance grants	...	...	...	...	...	...	...	...	...	...	...	...
F Other transfers n.e.c. c	10958	4670	6288	15724	3594	12130	20536	5759	14777	13083	2489	10594
G Transfers to the rest of the world	61	61	...	36	36	...	75	75	...	74	74	...
Net saving	17642	4560	13082	28516	19522	8995	26934	19023	7910	34317	20727	13590
Total Current Disbursements and Net Saving	273480	109243	164237	301755	136474	165283	318333	152507	165825	315777	152787	162990

a) Item 'Withdrawals from quasi-corporate enterprises' refers to central and local government enterprise surplus less local government enterprise deficit.
b) Item 'Withdrawals from quasi-corporate enterprises' refers to central government deficit only.
c) Beginning 1985, imputed interest paid by pension funds to households, which used to be included in item other transfers n.e.c., is now included in interest.

3.32 Household and Private Unincorporated Enterprise Income and Outlay Account

Million Norwegian kroner

	1980	1981	1982	1983	1984	1985	1986	1987	1988	1989	1990	1991
Receipts												
1 Compensation of employees	145396	164004	183182	198070	216178	239467	271158	306019	323953	328286	341672	356061
A Wages and salaries	124105	139800	156164	169236	185034	205209	232162	261439	275135	279496	290863	303327
B Employers' contributions for social security	21291	24204	27018	28834	31144	34258	38996	44580	48818	48790	50809	52734
C Employers' contributions for private pension & welfare plans	...	...	...	...	...	...	...	...	...	...	...	...
2 Operating surplus of private unincorporated enterprises	26780	30977	34462	36985	40805	41691	45248	47273	51508	52198	58523	59548
3 Property and entrepreneurial income	9612	11792	13711	16886	20392	23706	30346	37779	43529	41567	43186	42798
A Withdrawals from private quasi-corporations	-	-	-	-	-	-	-	-	-	-	-	-
B Interest a	8516	10376	12461	15296	18719	22349	28960	35965	42043	40475	41845	41523
C Dividends	1096	1416	1250	1590	1673	1357	1386	1814	1486	1092	1341	1276
D Net land rent and royalties	-	-	-	-	-	-	-	-	-	-	-	-
3 Current transfers	43575	50675	58014	65937	72098	77025	85509	96617	110441	123283	134329	146897
A Casualty insurance claims	1090	1279	1547	1557	1791	1804	2717	3030	3296	3286	3278	3654
B Social security benefits	40975	47636	54516	62212	67917	73819	81525	92072	105358	118151	128982	140871
C Social assistance grants										...	...	...
D Unfunded employee pension and welfare benefits	...	...	...	...	...	...	...	...	...	15	33	48
E Transfers from general government										...	...	...
F Transfers from the rest of the world	756	1016	1061	1178	1291	1402	1268	1515	1787	1832	2036	2325
G Other transfers n.e.c. a	754	744	890	990	1099	-	-	-	-	-	-	-
Total Current Receipts b	225363	257448	289369	317878	349473	381889	432261	487688	529431	545334	577710	605304
Disbursements												
1 Final consumption expenditures	135241	155205	175310	192979	210921	245439	278909	298054	307499	311955	336065	349705
2 Property income	11230	14024	17572	21316	24081	28838	37489	51866	61974	62155	63383	62592
A Interest	11230	14024	17572	21316	24081	28838	37489	51866	61974	62155	63383	62592
B Net land rent and royalties	-	-	-	-	-	-	-	-	-	-	-	-
3 Direct taxes and other current transfers n.e.c. to government	72030	78455	86631	91772	99522	110450	127058	149401	161047	161692	168536	175773
A Social security contributions	34224	38699	43494	47149	50511	57304	67460	79718	79632	76604	80239	83698
B Direct taxes	37657	39558	42650	44107	48652	52799	59125	69070	80695	84344	87446	90867
Income taxes	35483	36957	39867	40922	44994	49007	54826	63951	74730	77794	80552	83117
Other	2174	2601	2783	3185	3658	3792	4299	5119	5965	6550	6894	7750
C Fees, fines and penalties	149	198	487	516	359	347	473	613	720	744	851	1208

3.32 Household and Private Unincorporated Enterprise Income and Outlay Account
(Continued)

Million Norwegian kroner

	1980	1981	1982	1983	1984	1985	1986	1987	1988	1989	1990	1991
4 Other current transfers	2116	2458	2940	3077	3291	3721	4933	5761	6117	6614	6723	8084
A Net casualty insurance premiums	1090	1279	1547	1557	1791	1804	2717	3030	3296	3286	3278	3654
B Transfers to private non-profit institutions serving households	...	...	...	...	...	...	...	...	...	...	...	...
C Transfers to the rest of the world	1026	1179	1393	1520	1500	1918	2216	2731	2821	3328	3444	4430
D Other current transfers, except imputed	...	...	...	...	...	...	...	...	...	...	...	...
E Imputed employee pension and welfare contributions	...	...	...	...	...	...	...	...	...	...	...	...
Net saving b	4746	7306	6915	8734	11658	-6559	-16128	-17395	-7205	2919	3002	9151
Total Current Disbursements and Net Saving b	225363	257448	289368	317878	349473	381889	432261	487687	529432	545335	577709	605305

a) Beginning 1985, imputed interest paid by pension funds to households, which used to be included in item other transfers n.e.c., is now included in interest.
b) Column 'Farm' is included in column 'Non-farm entrepreneurial'.

3.51 External Transactions: Current Account: Detail

Million Norwegian kroner

	1980	1981	1982	1983	1984	1985	1986	1987	1988	1989	1990	1991
Payments to the Rest of the World												
1 Imports of goods and services	117371	130467	144543	152031	172852	194602	213044	211427	217958	234591	242845	247098
A Imports of merchandise c.i.f.	84543	90516	100458	102520	116542	133927	153073	151011	155350	166505	171779	170305
B Other	32828	39951	44085	49511	56311	60675	59971	60417	62608	68086	71066	76793
2 Factor income to the rest of the world	14841	19319	23431	23394	26651	27733	29541	30441	35292	42249	42383	41086
A Compensation of employees	90	248	270	261	280	320	380	440	440	470	500	500
B Property and entrepreneurial income	14751	19071	23161	23133	26371	27413	29161	30001	34852	41779	41883	40586
3 Current transfers to the rest of the world	3212	3796	4791	5522	5506	6189	7278	8103	9177	9613	10904	12135
A Indirect taxes by general government to supranational organizations	-	-	-	-	-	-	-	-	-	-	-	-
B Other current transfers	3212	3796	4791	5522	5506	6189	7278	8103	9177	9613	10904	12135
By general government	2186	2617	3271	3850	3870	4210	4947	5283	6295	6249	7385	7630
By other resident sectors	1026	1179	1520	1672	1636	1979	2331	2820	2882	3364	3519	4505
4 Surplus of the nation on current transactions	5448	12460	4146	14644	23927	26682	-33443	-27338	-25220	1652	24120	33098
Payments to the Rest of the World, and Surplus of the Nation on Current Transfers	140872	166042	176911	195591	228936	255206	216420	222633	237207	288105	320252	333417
Receipts From The Rest of the World												
1 Exports of goods and services	134795	156288	165023	183921	214077	235563	194664	200224	213671	261863	293015	307528
A Exports of merchandise f.o.b.	92863	106899	114799	133249	156822	173255	135999	145182	152631	190054	215450	223420
B Other	41932	49390	50224	50672	57256	62309	58663	55041	61040	71809	77565	84108
2 Factor income from the rest of the world	5321	8740	10727	10392	13509	18227	20449	20893	21750	24408	25201	23564
A Compensation of employees	66	84	96	96	108	120	126	132	144	156	168	180
B Property and entrepreneurial income	5255	8656	10631	10296	13401	18107	20323	20761	21606	24252	25033	23384
3 Current transfers from the rest of the world	756	1016	1161	1278	1350	1415	1307	1515	1787	1832	2036	2325
A Subsidies to general government from supranational organizations	-	-	-	-	-	-	-	-	-	-	-	-
B Other current transfers	756	1016	1161	1278	1350	1415	1307	1515	1787	1832	2036	2325
To general government	-	-	-	-	-	-	-	-	-	-	-	-
To other resident sectors	756	1016	1161	1278	1350	1415	1307	1515	1787	1832	2036	2325
Receipts from the Rest of the World on Current Transfers	140872	166044	176911	195591	228936	255205	216420	222632	237208	288103	320252	333417

Norway

3.52 External Transactions: Capital Accumulation Account

Million Norwegian kroner

	1980	1981	1982	1983	1984	1985	1986	1987	1988	1989	1990	1991
Finance of Gross Accumulation												
1 Surplus of the nation on current transactions	5448	12460	4146	14645	23929	26682	-33443	-27338	-25219	1652	24120	33098
2 Capital transfers from the rest of the world	...	...	...	...	...	...	...	...	...	...	...	...
Statistical discrepancy a	199	206	-	-	-	-	-	-	-	-	-	-
Total Finance of Gross Accumulation	5647	12666	4146	14645	23929	26682	-33443	-27338	-25219	1652	24120	33098
Gross Accumulation												
1 Capital transfers to the rest of the world	...	...	...	...	...	...	...	...	...	...	...	...
2 Purchases of intangible assets, n.e.c., net, from the rest of the world	-	-	-	-	-	-	-	-	-	-	-	-
Statistical discrepancy	-	-	-	-	-	-	-	-	-	-	-	-
Net lending to the rest of the world	5647	12666	4146	14645	23929	26682	-33443	-27338	-25219	1652	24120	33098
Total Gross Accumulation	5647	12666	4146	14645	23929	26682	-33443	-27338	-25219	1652	24120	33098

a) Item 'Statistical discrepancy' refers to allocation of SDRs.

3.53 External Transactions: Capital Finance Account

Million Norwegian kroner

	1980	1981	1982	1983	1984	1985	1986	1987	1988	1989	1990	1991
Acquisitions of Foreign Financial Assets												
1 Gold and SDR's	115	356	995	1117	501	-224	752	159	246	-418	-344	-285
2 Currency and transferable deposits	87	4	45	35	62	37	108	8	-94	-18	-24	-50
3 Other deposits	14701	6798	2450	-4253	14851	-4119	-10111	3960	5352	-10989	4506	5584
4 Bills and bonds, short term	512	741	4614	3197	12762	30072	-139	-766	-8619	17101	91	97
5 Bonds, long term	-	-	-	-	-	-	55	-	-	2	-	-
6 Corporate equity securities	178	890	538	1520	1330	3965	5927	3971	4819	10126	6421	10557
A Subsidiaries abroad	...	911	511	1187	1162	3790	4117	2614	5013	8088	4189	8979
B Other	...	-21	27	333	169	174	1810	1356	-195	2038	2232	1578
7 Short-term loans, n.e.c.	-514	1328	4033	2351	3972	2031	605	-2629	-2621	-3868	5290	-1409
A Subsidiaries abroad	...	-	-	-	-	524	375	-2344	776	-276	2075	2075
B Other	...	1328	4033	2351	3972	1507	230	-286	-3398	-3592	3214	-3484
8 Long-term loans	2013	1591	3282	4431	4286	12662	10908	15159	2027	10616	12247	2112
A Subsidiaries abroad	...	134	1342	1379	3807	6229	7317	5725	520	1522	2983	639
B Other	...	1458	1941	3052	479	6434	3592	9433	1507	9094	9264	1473
9 Prporietors' net additions to accumulation of quasi-corporate, non-resident enterprises	-	-	-	-	-	-	-	-	-	-	-	-
10 Trade credit and advances	781	1567	2394	2291	-841	516	-614	-1967	1322	-1568	612	-3453
11 Other	1941	484	941	1342	-1	1015	1079	2575	742	510	-1026	-990
Total Acquisitions of Foreign Financial Assets	19814	13759	19292	12031	36922	45955	8570	20470	3174	21494	27773	12163
Incurrence of Foreign Liabilities												
1 Currency and transferable deposits	-	-	-	-	-	-	-	-	-	-	-	-
2 Other deposits	7293	4661	7287	2693	12175	12900	7597	25288	-8663	-1810	-1730	-21219
3 Bills and bonds, short term	-	-	-	-	-	1178	1488	1994	1480	-3419	631	-5289
4 Bonds, long term	-149	-4109	-4425	-7256	3442	12913	30638	19821	26231	20892	2990	-185
5 Corporate equity securities	687	235	1029	1585	3838	1284	4520	5846	3006	12996	6143	5684
A Subsidiaries of non-resident incorporated units	...	148	650	484	1124	966	2063	4223	604	5827	2186	4292
B Other	...	87	379	1101	2714	317	2457	1624	2402	7169	3957	1391
6 Short-term loans, n.e.c.	1396	-254	-765	-3933	-1764	8970	4489	6138	4269	-8677	11650	-5858
A Subsidiaries of non-residents	...	-	-	-	-	1856	50	132	466	639	2719	1175
B Other	...	-254	-765	-3933	-1764	7115	4439	6006	3803	-9316	8931	-7033
7 Long-term loans	-1503	1993	10542	134	-2235	-10189	3760	-1383	8984	9524	5614	9627
A Subsidiaries of non-residents	...	3783	2087	1972	-2966	-6796	5441	-3115	786	3961	1218	-7805

3.53 External Transactions: Capital Finance Account
(Continued)

Million Norwegian kroner

	1980	1981	1982	1983	1984	1985	1986	1987	1988	1989	1990	1991
B Other	...	-1790	8455	-1838	731	-3393	-1680	1733	8198	5564	4396	17431
8 Non-resident proprietors' net additions to accumulation of resident quasi-corporate enterprises	-	-	-	-	-	-	-	-	-	-	-	-
9 Trade credit and advances	10	-880	1699	345	1620	1714	2449	-251	352	-912	-695	757
10 Other	1908	-561	521	999	-942	804	-734	-1175	-337	603	-3403	-3507
Total Incurrence of Liabilities	9642	1084	15887	-5433	16135	29573	54207	56279	35322	29197	21168	-19992
Statistical discrepancy a	4525	10	-740	2819	-3141	-10300	-12193	-8472	-6929	-9354	-17516	-943
Net Lending	5647	12665	4146	14646	23929	26682	-33443	-27338	-25220	1652	24120	33098
Total Incurrence of Liabilities and Net Lending	19814	13759	19293	12032	36923	45955	8571	20469	3173	21495	27772	12163

a) Item 'Statistical discrepancy' refers to other short-term capital transactions and a statistical discrepancy.

4.1 Derivation of Value Added by Kind of Activity, in Current Prices

Million Norwegian kroner

	1980			1981			1982			1983		
	Gross Output	Intermediate Consumption	Value Added	Gross Output	Intermediate Consumption	Value Added	Gross Output	Intermediate Consumption	Value Added	Gross Output	Intermediate Consumption	Value Added
All Producers												
1 Agriculture, hunting, forestry and fishing	22439	11469	10969	25510	12553	12957	27013	13576	13437	27599	14464	13135
A Agriculture and hunting	16465	9496	6969	18186	10339	7847	19650	11054	8597	19638	11688	7950
B Forestry and logging	2048	311	1737	2610	366	2244	2536	365	2171	2405	359	2046
C Fishing	3926	1662	2264	4714	1848	2866	4827	2157	2670	5556	2417	3139
2 Mining and quarrying	45905	3827	42078	56253	5068	51185	65140	8627	56514	78160	9929	68231
A Coal mining	111	79	32	186	125	61	186	130	55	191	108	84
B Crude petroleum and natural gas production	43523	2532	40991	53544	3565	49979	62436	7090	55346	75137	8282	66855
C Metal ore mining	1100	678	422	1258	767	492	1148	743	405	1263	792	470
D Other mining	1171	538	633	1265	611	654	1370	664	707	1569	747	822
3 Manufacturing	159133	113498	45635	176296	127721	48575	184297	132914	51383	193424	136699	56724
A Manufacture of food, beverages and tobacco	32824	27931	4894	38236	31800	6436	41740	34041	7699	44958	35924	9034
B Textile, wearing apparel and leather industries	4872	3017	1856	4811	2954	1857	4594	2892	1702	4293	2684	1609
C Manufacture of wood and wood products, including furniture	11812	7745	4067	12908	8716	4192	13367	9065	4303	13259	8964	4296
D Manufacture of paper and paper products, printing and publishing	16899	11322	5577	19725	13258	6467	20197	13476	6722	21859	13951	7908
E Manufacture of chemicals and chemical petroleum, coal, rubber and plastic products	26405	21031	5374	28746	24056	4689	29650	24520	5130	32801	27092	5709
F Manufacture of non-metallic mineral products, except products of petroleum and coal	4685	2860	1824	5271	3253	2019	5576	3456	2120	5744	3432	2312
G Basic metal industries	16273	10594	5679	15915	11430	4484	14792	10821	3971	18305	12137	6168
H Manufacture of fabricated metal products, machinery and equipment	44565	28528	16037	49924	31807	18117	53568	34171	19397	51340	32043	19297
I Other manufacturing industries	798	470	328	760	447	314	813	474	339	864	474	391
4 Electricity, gas and water	16401	8164	8237	19216	9058	10158	24062	12081	11981	28123	13811	14312
A Electricity, gas and steam	15824	7907	7917	18682	8803	9878	23425	11782	11643	27380	13485	13895
B Water works and supply	576	257	320	534	255	280	637	298	338	743	326	417
5 Construction	47590	30638	16952	53953	34281	19673	59555	36844	22711	63157	39309	23848
6 Wholesale and retail trade, restaurants and hotels	51992	18729	33264	59825	21350	38475	67956	25191	42765	73974	28499	45475
A Wholesale and retail trade	45300	15185	30115	51975	17279	34697	58913	20541	38372	63530	23201	40328
B Restaurants and hotels	6692	3544	3149	7850	4071	3779	9043	4650	4393	10445	5298	5147
7 Transport, storage and communication	56952	30062	26890	65811	35057	30755	69031	37742	31289	72963	39110	33852
A Transport and storage	49903	27722	22181	57149	32594	24556	58088	34703	23385	60096	35637	24459
B Communication	7049	2340	4709	8662	2463	6199	10943	3039	7904	12867	3473	9394
8 Finance, insurance, real estate and business services	41507	13263	28244	49638	15483	34155	59462	18604	40859	67441	21807	45633
A Financial institutions	11206	3059	8147	14409	3482	10926	18136	4283	13853	20781	5220	15562

4.1 Derivation of Value Added by Kind of Activity, in Current Prices
(Continued)

Million Norwegian kroner

	1980			1981			1982			1983		
	Gross Output	Intermediate Consumption	Value Added	Gross Output	Intermediate Consumption	Value Added	Gross Output	Intermediate Consumption	Value Added	Gross Output	Intermediate Consumption	Value Added
B Insurance	2183	1339	845	2047	1225	822	2053	1504	549	2339	1970	370
C Real estate and business services	28118	8865	19253	33182	10776	22406	39273	12816	26457	44320	14618	29702
Real estate, except dwellings	5071	2427	2644	6090	3030	3061	6761	3221	3539	7488	3492	3997
Dwellings	13389	3321	10067	15464	3855	11609	17784	4381	13402	20315	5314	15001
9 Community, social and personal services	16925	4447	12478	19048	5040	14009	21491	5770	15722	24232	6531	17701
A Sanitary and similar services	488	39	449	556	45	511	661	54	608	719	57	663
B Social and related community services	6924	2109	4815	7851	2455	5396	8987	2828	6159	10101	3238	6863
Educational services	1019	772	247	1109	947	162	1357	1159	198	1525	1345	180
Medical, dental, other health and veterinary services	4456	949	3508	5058	1064	3994	5818	1202	4616	6374	1318	5057
C Recreational and cultural services	2510	778	1732	2881	884	1997	3102	971	2131	3834	1210	2624
D Personal and household services	7003	1521	5482	7760	1656	6104	8741	1916	6824	9578	2027	7551
Total, Industries	458843	234096	224747	525550	265609	259941	578006	291347	286660	629072	310160	318912
Producers of Government Services	57363	18462	38901	67626	22464	45162	76579	25073	51505	85354	28512	56841
Other Producers	...	...	...	...	...	...	...	...	...	...	...	...
Total	516206	252558	263648	593176	288073	305103	654585	316420	338165	714425	338672	375753
Less: Imputed bank service charge	...	-8724	8724	...	-11349	11349	...	-14318	14318	...	-15960	15960
Import duties [a]	3692	...	3692	4248	...	4248	5203	...	5203	5764	...	5764
Value added tax	24703	...	24703	28024	...	28024	31536	...	31536	34623	...	34623
Other adjustments [b]	1726	...	1726	1649	...	1649	1683	...	1683	2017	...	2017
Total	546327	261282	285045	627097	299422	327675	693007	330738	362269	756829	354632	402197
Memorandum Item: Mineral fuels and power	70899	21312	49587	84428	24651	59777	98395	31064	67331	116008	35166	80842

of which General Government:

	1980			1981			1982			1983		
	Gross Output	Intermediate Consumption	Value Added	Gross Output	Intermediate Consumption	Value Added	Gross Output	Intermediate Consumption	Value Added	Gross Output	Intermediate Consumption	Value Added
1 Agriculture, hunting, forestry and fishing	16	6	10	17	7	10	18	7	11	23	10	13
2 Mining and quarrying	...	...	...	...	...	...	...	...	...	...	...	...
3 Manufacturing	...	...	...	...	...	...	...	...	...	...	...	...
4 Electricity, gas and water	...	...	...	...	...	...	...	...	...	...	...	...
5 Construction	...	...	...	...	...	...	...	...	...	...	...	...
6 Wholesale and retail trade, restaurants and hotels	...	...	...	...	...	...	...	...	...	...	...	...
7 Transport and communication	3695	2890	805	4178	3243	935	4653	3587	1066	5052	3929	1123
8 Finance, insurance, real estate and business services	298	141	157	368	169	199	343	107	236	395	121	273
9 Community, social and personal services	53353	15425	37928	63063	19045	44018	71565	21373	50192	79884	24452	55432
Total, Industries of General Government	57363	18462	38901	67626	22464	45162	76579	25073	51505	85354	28512	56841
Producers of Government Services	...	...	...	...	...	...	...	...	...	...	...	...
Total, General Government	...	...	...	...	...	...	...	...	...	...	...	...

	1984			1985			1986			1987		
	Gross Output	Intermediate Consumption	Value Added	Gross Output	Intermediate Consumption	Value Added	Gross Output	Intermediate Consumption	Value Added	Gross Output	Intermediate Consumption	Value Added

All Producers

	1984 GO	1984 IC	1984 VA	1985 GO	1985 IC	1985 VA	1986 GO	1986 IC	1986 VA	1987 GO	1987 IC	1987 VA
1 Agriculture, hunting, forestry and fishing	30397	15354	15042	32045	16895	15150	34442	18421	16021	38207	20512	17695
A Agriculture and hunting	21629	12249	9380	22364	13355	9009	23543	14462	9081	25413	15624	9789
B Forestry and logging	2880	420	2459	2880	437	2443	3231	455	2776	3690	518	3172
C Fishing	5888	2685	3203	6801	3103	3698	7668	3503	4164	9104	4370	4734
2 Mining and quarrying	96398	11621	84778	107612	16603	91009	73758	21228	52530	74617	21220	53398
A Coal mining	188	100	88	234	114	120	217	166	52	176	139	38
B Crude petroleum and natural gas production	93089	9702	83387	104071	14364	89706	69985	19019	50966	70700	18941	51759
C Metal ore mining	1390	941	449	1483	1173	309	1341	892	449	1318	880	437
D Other mining	1732	878	854	1825	951	874	2215	1151	1064	2423	1260	1164

4.1 Derivation of Value Added by Kind of Activity, in Current Prices
(Continued)

Million Norwegian kroner

	1984 Gross Output	1984 Intermediate Consumption	1984 Value Added	1985 Gross Output	1985 Intermediate Consumption	1985 Value Added	1986 Gross Output	1986 Intermediate Consumption	1986 Value Added	1987 Gross Output	1987 Intermediate Consumption	1987 Value Added
3 Manufacturing	217590	153066	64524	247337	177210	70127	260473	184822	75651	281870	197280	84590
A Manufacture of food, beverages and tobacco	48990	38744	10246	53129	41572	11556	59360	46196	13164	64953	49881	15072
B Textile, wearing apparel and leather industries	4643	2934	1709	5069	3215	1854	5340	3348	1992	5453	3430	2024
C Manufacture of wood and wood products, including furniture	13843	9431	4412	15240	10339	4901	17292	11747	5545	19133	13128	6005
D Manufacture of paper and paper products, printing and publishing	25266	15997	9269	28252	18094	10158	31112	19973	11139	34607	22209	12399
E Manufacture of chemicals and chemical petroleum, coal, rubber and plastic products	37358	30059	7299	39703	32120	7582	32266	24701	7566	36458	26609	9849
F Manufacture of non-metallic mineral products, except products of petroleum and coal	5867	3594	2272	6742	4238	2505	8136	5141	2995	8922	5492	3430
G Basic metal industries	23843	15471	8372	24576	17188	7388	23122	16264	6858	25104	17672	7432
H Manufacture of fabricated metal products, machinery and equipment	56826	36307	20519	73537	49808	23729	82664	56779	25886	85907	58090	27817
I Other manufacturing industries	955	529	427	1089	636	454	1179	674	506	1331	769	562
4 Electricity, gas and water	32772	16201	16571	38418	20141	18278	41481	21903	19578	44959	23521	21439
A Electricity, gas and steam	31953	15828	16124	37496	19699	17797	40472	21395	19077	43817	22926	20892
B Water works and supply	819	372	447	922	442	481	1009	508	501	1142	595	547
5 Construction	66660	42307	24353	73735	46665	27070	85842	55292	30550	100337	63705	36632
6 Wholesale and retail trade, restaurants and hotels	80850	31405	49445	89211	35315	53897	102991	40426	62565	113641	45523	68118
A Wholesale and retail trade	68973	25305	43668	75530	28232	47298	86777	32083	54694	94622	35729	58893
B Restaurants and hotels	11877	6100	5777	13681	7082	6599	16214	8343	7871	19019	9794	9225
7 Transport, storage and communication	82146	45069	37077	88693	50717	37976	92512	48979	43532	95784	51359	44425
A Transport and storage	67960	41146	26814	73433	45789	27645	74809	43221	31588	75208	43578	31630
B Communication	14186	3923	10263	15260	4929	10332	17703	5759	11944	20576	7782	12795
8 Finance, insurance, real estate and business services	75172	25853	49318	87361	30979	56383	102163	34606	67557	118576	40572	78004
A Financial institutions	21090	6076	15015	22931	7030	15901	30202	8689	21513	35865	10290	25575
B Insurance	2750	2659	91	3948	3224	724	4789	3510	1279	5023	2722	2301
C Real estate and business services	51332	17119	34213	60482	20725	39757	67173	22408	44765	77688	27560	50128
Real estate, except dwellings	8281	3978	4303	9516	4606	4910	10771	5219	5552	12809	6405	6404
Dwellings	22569	5913	16656	24984	6879	18105	27779	8069	19711	31392	9596	21796
9 Community, social and personal services	25730	6980	18750	29253	7845	21408	33963	9142	24821	37467	10078	27389
A Sanitary and similar services	770	57	714	927	74	854	1127	89	1038	1190	96	1093
B Social and related community services	10697	3501	7197	11650	3786	7864	12926	4225	8701	14307	4595	9713
Educational services	1672	1473	199	1891	1620	271	2152	1824	328	2362	1982	381
Medical, dental, other health and veterinary services	6668	1399	5269	7138	1462	5676	7808	1602	6207	8373	1703	6671
C Recreational and cultural services	4066	1283	2783	4618	1467	3151	5361	1677	3683	6136	1903	4233
D Personal and household services	10197	2140	8057	12058	2519	9539	14549	3150	11399	15835	3485	12350
Total, Industries	707714	347856	359858	793666	402369	391297	827624	434818	392806	905457	473770	431687
Producers of Government Services	92249	30441	61808	101919	33955	67965	112270	36899	75371	127823	42194	85629
Other Producers	...	...	...	...	...	...	...	...	...	...	...	...
Total	799963	378296	421667	895585	436324	459261	939894	471717	468177	1033280	515964	517316
Less: Imputed bank service charge	...	-15443	15443	...	-15431	15431	...	-20280	20280	...	-24328	24328
Import duties [a]	6006	...	6006	9320	...	9320	11852	...	11852	9912	...	9912
Value added tax	37794	...	37794	44150	...	44150	50309	...	50309	54466	...	54466
Other adjustments [b]	2489	...	2489	2900	...	2900	3660	...	3660	4113	...	4113
Total	846252	393739	452512	951955	451755	500201	1005715	491997	513718	1101771	540292	561479
Memorandum Item: Mineral fuels and power	140211	40535	99676	157571	49726	107846	118315	48077	70238	124138	51043	73095

Norway

4.1 Derivation of Value Added by Kind of Activity, in Current Prices
(Continued)

Million Norwegian kroner

	1984			1985			1986			1987		
	Gross Output	Intermediate Consumption	Value Added	Gross Output	Intermediate Consumption	Value Added	Gross Output	Intermediate Consumption	Value Added	Gross Output	Intermediate Consumption	Value Added
of which General Government:												
1 Agriculture, hunting, forestry and fishing	28	14	15	25	11	14	25	11	15	22	9	13
2 Mining and quarrying	...	...	...	...	...	...	...	...	...	...	...	...
3 Manufacturing	...	...	...	...	...	...	...	...	...	...	...	...
4 Electricity, gas and water	...	...	...	...	...	...	...	...	...	...	...	...
5 Construction	...	...	...	...	...	...	...	...	...	...	...	...
6 Wholesale and retail trade, restaurants and hotels	...									...	...	...
7 Transport and communication	5423	4248	1175	5797	4528	1270	6025	4627	1399	6711	5171	1540
8 Finance, insurance, real estate and business services	501	159	341	558	179	380	615	204	411	645	214	431
9 Community, social and personal services	86297	26020	60277	95539	29238	66301	105604	32058	73546	120445	36800	83645
Total, Industries of General Government	92249	30441	61808	101919	33955	67965	112270	36899	75371	127823	42194	85629
Producers of Government Services	...	...	...	...	...	...	...	...	...	...	...	...
Total, General Government	...	...	...	...	...	...	...	...	...	...	...	...

	1988			1989			1990			1991		
	Gross Output	Intermediate Consumption	Value Added	Gross Output	Intermediate Consumption	Value Added	Gross Output	Intermediate Consumption	Value Added	Gross Output	Intermediate Consumption	Value Added
All Producers												
1 Agriculture, hunting, forestry and fishing	39630	21941	17689	40703	23135	17568	43829	23499	20330	43526	23473	20052
A Agriculture and hunting	25588	15910	9678	26811	16212	10599	28218	16489	11729	27559	16113	11447
B Forestry and logging	4273	614	3659	4314	665	3650	4643	656	3987	4418	649	3769
C Fishing	9769	5417	4352	9577	6259	3319	10968	6354	4614	11548	6712	4836
2 Mining and quarrying	70970	25019	45951	97478	25859	71620	117781	29137	88644	124782	33409	91372
A Coal mining	127	128	-1	160	125	35	157	142	15	158	137	21
B Crude petroleum and natural gas production	66986	22603	44383	93100	23345	69755	113502	26590	86912	120543	30872	89671
C Metal ore mining	1241	864	377	1408	859	550	1408	913	496	1296	927	369
D Other mining	2617	1425	1192	2810	1530	1280	2715	1493	1222	2785	1473	1312
3 Manufacturing	296665	207159	89506	312892	221627	91265	321924	231555	90369	323358	230768	92591
A Manufacture of food, beverages and tobacco	68592	52483	16110	71973	55140	16833	75734	57956	17778	81170	60745	20425
B Textile, wearing apparel and leather industries	5071	3129	1942	4562	2867	1695	4906	3090	1816	5052	3148	1905
C Manufacture of wood and wood products, including furniture	18158	12360	5798	17460	11883	5576	18180	12359	5821	16631	11413	5218
D Manufacture of paper and paper products, printing and publishing	36987	23651	13337	39484	25336	14148	40113	25721	14392	39757	25395	14362
E Manufacture of chemicals and chemical petroleum, coal, rubber and plastic products	35806	25309	10497	40493	29692	10801	47315	35686	11629	44849	33794	11054
F Manufacture of non-metallic mineral products, except products of petroleum and coal	8750	5642	3107	8134	5112	3022	8339	5228	3110	7438	4535	2903
G Basic metal industries	33934	22613	11321	37611	25826	11784	31071	23565	7506	29079	22496	6582
H Manufacture of fabricated metal products, machinery and equipment	88100	61261	26838	91920	65077	26843	94798	67133	27665	97674	68299	29375
I Other manufacturing industries	1267	711	556	1257	693	563	1468	817	651	1710	944	766
4 Electricity, gas and water	49701	26146	23555	50181	25072	25109	51301	24492	26809	55860	28593	27266
A Electricity, gas and steam	48441	25529	22912	48780	24454	24326	49739	23831	25908	54341	27955	26386
B Water works and supply	1260	617	643	1401	618	783	1562	661	901	1519	639	880
5 Construction	105012	66672	38340	91062	58512	32549	82762	53468	29295	79461	52551	26910
6 Wholesale and retail trade, restaurants and hotels	117815	47584	70231	117321	47337	69985	121861	48643	73218	124867	49552	75315
A Wholesale and retail trade	99114	37916	61198	99361	37934	61427	104321	39386	64934	106625	39962	66663
B Restaurants and hotels	18701	9668	9033	17960	9402	8558	17541	9257	8284	18242	9591	8652
7 Transport, storage and communication	104707	53340	51367	119694	60025	59669	129598	64905	64693	138022	66291	71731
A Transport and storage	81719	45347	36372	95600	52107	43493	104747	56486	48261	112950	56967	55984

4.1 Derivation of Value Added by Kind of Activity, in Current Prices
(Continued)

Million Norwegian kroner

	1988			1989			1990			1991		
	Gross Output	Intermediate Consumption	Value Added	Gross Output	Intermediate Consumption	Value Added	Gross Output	Intermediate Consumption	Value Added	Gross Output	Intermediate Consumption	Value Added
B Communication	22988	7993	14995	24094	7918	16176	24852	8419	16433	25072	9324	15748
8 Finance, insurance, real estate and business services	126729	42787	83942	131665	43050	88616	136334	45085	91249	141189	47160	94029
A Financial institutions	35865	10642	25223	36714	10834	25880	34815	10793	24022	33565	10969	22596
B Insurance	5515	2972	2543	6121	3093	3028	8173	4166	4008	9338	4036	5302
C Real estate and business services	85349	29173	56176	88831	29123	59708	93346	30126	63220	98286	32155	66132
Real estate, except dwellings	14004	6937	7067	14451	7216	7234	15244	7683	7561	16215	8054	8161
Dwellings	35253	9886	25367	38608	9668	28940	41627	9340	32287	44060	10249	33811
9 Community, social and personal services	40094	10646	29448	40275	10726	29549	43573	11630	31943	46381	12351	34030
A Sanitary and similar services	1454	114	1339	1495	121	1374	1565	127	1439	1664	135	1530
B Social and related community services	15309	4917	10392	15798	5042	10757	17714	5442	12272	19035	5793	13242
Educational services	2575	2094	482	2662	2160	502	2999	2357	642	3180	2501	679
Medical, dental, other health and veterinary services	9019	1838	7181	9334	1902	7432	10807	2042	8765	11639	2196	9442
C Recreational and cultural services	6723	1953	4769	7160	2066	5094	7797	2280	5517	8335	2448	5887
D Personal and household services	16609	3662	12947	15822	3498	12324	16498	3782	12716	17347	3975	13371
Total, Industries	951320	501292	450028	1001272	515343	485929	1048963	532413	516551	1077446	544148	533297
Producers of Government Services	137009	45078	91930	147153	49311	97841	157614	53489	104126	169174	57264	111910
Other Producers	...	...	...	...	...	...	...	...	...	...	...	...
Total	1088329	546371	541958	1148424	564654	583770	1206577	585901	620676	1246620	601413	645207
Less: Imputed bank service charge	...	-24604	24604	...	-25611	25611	...	-25200	25200	...	-24249	24249
Import duties a	7046	...	7046	6466	...	6466	7244	...	7244	7031	...	7031
Value added tax	54941	...	54941	53953	...	53953	55803	...	55803	56871	...	56871
Other adjustments b	3937	...	3937	2805	...	2805	2028	...	2028	1826	...	1826
Total	1154253	570975	583278	1211648	590265	621383	1271652	611101	660552	1312348	625662	686686
Memorandum Item: Mineral fuels and power	123545	55433	68112	153450	58612	94838	180615	66518	114097	190012	72369	117643

of which General Government:

	1988			1989			1990			1991		
	Gross Output	Intermediate Consumption	Value Added	Gross Output	Intermediate Consumption	Value Added	Gross Output	Intermediate Consumption	Value Added	Gross Output	Intermediate Consumption	Value Added
1 Agriculture, hunting, forestry and fishing	26	12	14	24	13	11	5	2	3	5	2	2
2 Mining and quarrying	...	...	...	...	...	...	...	...	...	...	...	...
3 Manufacturing	...	...	...	...	...	...	...	...	...	...	...	...
4 Electricity, gas and water	...	...	...	...	...	...	...	...	...	...	...	...
5 Construction	...	...	...	...	...	...	...	...	...	...	...	...
6 Wholesale and retail trade, restaurants and hotels	...	...	...	...	...	...	...	...	...	...	...	...
7 Transport and communication	7017	5379	1639	7238	5523	1714	7586	5758	1828	8278	6350	1928
8 Finance, insurance, real estate and business services	662	227	435	784	271	513	840	268	573	908	273	635
9 Community, social and personal services	129303	39461	89842	139107	43504	95603	149183	47461	101722	159983	50639	109345
Total, Industries of General Government	137009	45078	91930	147153	49311	97841	157614	53489	104126	169174	57264	111910
Producers of Government Services	...	...	...	...	...	...	...	...	...	...	...	...
Total, General Government	...	...	...	...	...	...	...	...	...	...	...	...

a) Item 'Import duties' includes collection of customs duties, value added tax on imports and special excises or taxes on imports. b) Item 'Other adjustments' refers to collection of investment levy on fixed capital formation and subsidies on residential and social buildings.

4.2 Derivation of Value Added by Kind of Activity, in Constant Prices

Million Norwegian kroner

	1984			1985			1986			1987		
	Gross Output	Intermediate Consumption	Value Added	Gross Output	Intermediate Consumption	Value Added	Gross Output	Intermediate Consumption	Value Added	Gross Output	Intermediate Consumption	Value Added
						At constant prices of:1984						
						All Producers						
1 Agriculture, hunting, forestry and fishing	30397	15354	15042	29489	15806	13682	29735	16857	12878	31253	17784	13478
A Agriculture and hunting	21629	12249	9380	20724	12477	8247	20390	13114	7276	21093	13421	7656
B Forestry and logging	2880	420	2459	2675	412	2263	2799	416	2383	2883	426	2457
C Fishing	5888	2685	3203	6089	2917	3172	6546	3327	3219	7271	3958	3363
2 Mining and quarrying	96398	11621	84778	103365	15550	87815	112229	18613	93616	120310	17342	105663

4.2 Derivation of Value Added by Kind of Activity, in Constant Prices
(Continued)

Million Norwegian kroner

	1984			1985			1986			1987		
	Gross Output	Intermediate Consumption	Value Added	Gross Output	Intermediate Consumption	Value Added	Gross Output	Intermediate Consumption	Value Added	Gross Output	Intermediate Consumption	Value Added
	At constant prices of:1984											
A Coal mining	188	100	88	222	106	116	216	147	69	178	114	66
B Crude petroleum and natural gas production	93089	9702	83387	99968	13446	86522	108655	16590	92065	117068	15424	104271
C Metal ore mining	1390	941	449	1405	1105	300	1325	827	498	1220	757	466
D Other mining	1732	878	854	1770	893	877	2033	1048	984	2066	1051	1015
3 Manufacturing	217590	153066	64524	234804	167911	66893	242203	175341	66862	243507	175296	68143
A Manufacture of food, beverages and tobacco	48990	38744	10246	49719	39197	10522	51131	40672	10459	51999	41723	10310
B Textile, wearing apparel and leather industries	4643	2934	1709	4853	3044	1809	4860	3020	1840	4649	2933	1715
C Manufacture of wood and wood products, including furniture	13843	9431	4412	14460	9828	4632	15304	10479	4825	15508	10717	4793
D Manufacture of paper and paper products, printing and publishing	25266	15997	9269	26480	16937	9543	27609	17852	9758	27747	18092	9659
E Manufacture of chemicals and chemical petroleum, coal, rubber and plastic products	37358	30059	7299	38179	31229	6950	37664	31132	6532	40733	32242	8040
F Manufacture of non-metallic mineral products, except products of petroleum and coal	5867	3594	2272	6337	4056	2280	7069	4706	2363	7221	4733	2477
G Basic metal industries	23843	15471	8372	24707	16531	8176	24898	16965	7933	26479	18095	8378
H Manufacture of fabricated metal products, machinery and equipment	56826	36307	20519	69034	46461	22573	72618	49866	22752	69036	46626	22410
I Other manufacturing industries	955	529	427	1036	628	409	1051	652	400	1093	665	427
4 Electricity, gas and water	32772	16201	16571	32116	16006	16109	30530	15570	14959	32529	16620	15906
A Electricity, gas and steam	31953	15828	16124	31256	15596	15660	29642	15121	14521	31606	16141	15464
B Water works and supply	819	372	447	860	411	449	888	449	439	919	479	440
5 Construction	66660	42307	24353	69535	44216	25319	75546	48950	26597	78905	51925	26996
6 Wholesale and retail trade, restaurants and hotels	80850	31405	49445	86608	32945	53663	92176	35243	56933	92520	36290	56190
A Wholesale and retail trade	68973	25305	43668	73709	26321	47388	78176	27990	50186	77506	28293	49185
B Restaurants and hotels	11877	6100	5777	12899	6624	6275	14000	7254	6747	14974	7997	6982
7 Transport, storage and communication	82146	45069	37077	85745	47371	38374	92413	49397	43015	88994	46103	42860
A Transport and storage	67960	41146	26814	70174	42644	27530	74513	44095	30418	69465	39427	29943
B Communication	14186	3923	10263	15572	4727	10844	17899	5302	12597	19562	6506	12951
8 Finance, insurance, real estate and business services	75172	25853	49318	82882	29464	53417	86767	31165	55601	91762	33250	58537
A Financial institutions	21090	6076	15015	22414	6896	15517	24536	8002	16534	25676	8669	17056
B Insurance	2750	2659	91	3772	3129	643	3710	3324	386	3662	2461	642
C Real estate and business services	51332	17119	34213	56697	19439	37257	58521	19839	38682	62476	22053	40444
Real estate, except dwellings	8281	3978	4303	9017	4293	4724	9634	4781	4853	10657	5359	5302
Dwellings	22569	5913	16656	23682	6501	17180	24847	7110	17737	26120	7489	18630
9 Community, social and personal services	25730	6980	18750	27542	7450	20093	29665	8072	21593	29922	8239	21684
A Sanitary and similar services	770	57	714	882	73	810	984	82	902	908	85	824
B Social and related community services	10697	3501	7197	10922	3597	7325	11236	3755	7482	11569	3792	7775
Educational services	1672	1473	199	1766	1538	228	1843	1605	238	1864	1617	246
Medical, dental, other health and veterinary services	6668	1399	5269	6654	1385	5269	6757	1445	5312	6900	1425	5471
C Recreational and cultural services	4066	1283	2783	4444	1376	3068	4912	1497	3415	5332	1550	3786
D Personal and household services	10197	2140	8057	11293	2403	8890	12532	2738	9795	12137	2814	9326
Statistical discrepancy	-1	-	-	-1	-	1	-1	-	1	-1094	759	-4080
Total, Industries	707714	347856	359858	752085	376719	375366	791263	399208	392055	808608	403608	405377
Producers of Government Services	92249	30441	61808	95527	31759	63768	97997	33127	64870	101556	34878	66701
Other Producers	...	...	...	...	...	...	...	...	...	...	...	...
Total	799963	378296	421667	847612	408478	439135	889260	432336	456925	910281	438516	472028
Less: Imputed bank service charge	...	-15443	15443	...	-16393	16393	...	-17832	17832	...	-18497	18497
Import duties a	6006	...	6006	9141	...	9141	9794	...	9794	7292	...	7292

4.2 Derivation of Value Added by Kind of Activity, in Constant Prices
(Continued)

Million Norwegian kroner

	1984 Gross Output	1984 Intermediate Consumption	1984 Value Added	1985 Gross Output	1985 Intermediate Consumption	1985 Value Added	1986 Gross Output	1986 Intermediate Consumption	1986 Value Added	1987 Gross Output	1987 Intermediate Consumption	1987 Value Added
At constant prices of:1984												
Value added tax	37794	...	37794	41820	...	41820	44782	...	44782	44519	...	44519
Other adjustments b	2489	...	2489	2680	...	2680	2627	...	2627	1791	...	1791
Total c	846252	393739	452512	901253	424871	476381	946463	450168	496296	963883	457013	506180
Memorandum Item: Mineral fuels and power	140211	40535	99676	146931	44474	102457	153398	46586	106812	165733	47366	120057
of which General Government:												
1 Agriculture, hunting, forestry and fishing	28	14	15	23	10	13	21	8	13	17	6	10
2 Mining and quarrying	...	...	...	...	...	...	...	...	...	...	...	...
3 Manufacturing	...	...	...	...	...	...	...	...	...	...	...	...
4 Electricity, gas and water	...	...	...	...	...	...	...	...	...	...	...	...
5 Construction	...	...	...	...	...	...	...	...	...	...	...	...
6 Wholesale and retail trade, restaurants and hotels	...	...	...	...	...	...	...	...	...	...	...	...
7 Transport and communication	5423	4248	1175	5408	4222	1186	5268	4064	1204	5274	4063	1210
8 Finance, insurance, real estate and business services	501	159	341	519	161	358	521	165	355	496	154	342
9 Community, social and personal services	86297	26020	60277	89578	27367	62212	92188	28890	63298	95771	30662	65138
Statistical discrepancy	...	...	...	...	...	...	...	...	...	...	...	-1
Total, Industries of General Government	92249	30441	61808	95527	31759	63768	97997	33127	64870	101556	34878	66701
Producers of Government Services	...	...	...	...	...	...	...	...	...	...	...	...
Total, General Government	...	...	...	...	...	...	...	...	...	...	...	...

	1988 Gross Output	1988 Intermediate Consumption	1988 Value Added	1989 Gross Output	1989 Intermediate Consumption	1989 Value Added	1990 Gross Output	1990 Intermediate Consumption	1990 Value Added	1991 Gross Output	1991 Intermediate Consumption	1991 Value Added
At constant prices of:1984												
All Producers												
1 Agriculture, hunting, forestry and fishing	32167	18587	13624	33169	19195	14022	34584	18965	15630	34723	18958	15772
A Agriculture and hunting	20861	13177	7660	21329	13085	8203	22260	12953	9235	21891	12688	9133
B Forestry and logging	3105	486	2620	3096	506	2594	3151	479	2672	2932	465	2469
C Fishing	8160	4988	3346	8722	5729	3244	9169	5656	3800	9977	5966	4309
2 Mining and quarrying	134180	19393	117718	155071	18619	148583	160773	19748	152765	180600	21329	173778
A Coal mining	126	102	-2	153	94	65	145	102	28	145	96	42
B Crude petroleum and natural gas production	131568	17429	116950	152989	16683	148239	159079	17861	152610	179653	19479	174159
C Metal ore mining	1069	716	343	1111	676	432	1130	685	440	1073	681	382
D Other mining	2118	1141	974	2173	1164	1005	2067	1084	980	2002	1038	963
3 Manufacturing	239368	174631	64887	239465	175950	63840	242061	178163	64262	240109	177643	62898
A Manufacture of food, beverages and tobacco	51764	41786	10057	52872	42627	10315	53092	43211	10034	54866	44895	10187
B Textile, wearing apparel and leather industries	4165	2584	1580	3656	2300	1356	3853	2423	1429	3934	2476	1459
C Manufacture of wood and wood products, including furniture	13897	9474	4423	13103	8881	4220	12868	8893	3972	11747	8105	3638
D Manufacture of paper and paper products, printing and publishing	27602	18166	9448	27903	18518	9408	27685	18226	9469	27208	17881	9334
E Manufacture of chemicals and chemical petroleum, coal, rubber and plastic products	39509	31650	7545	41066	32935	7820	45665	36640	8684	43395	35443	7800
F Manufacture of non-metallic mineral products, except products of petroleum and coal	6826	4555	2274	6069	3929	2132	5984	3877	2100	5142	3401	1742
G Basic metal industries	29266	20164	9080	28515	20319	8241	27742	19564	8200	27700	19346	8435
H Manufacture of fabricated metal products, machinery and equipment	66896	46462	20430	67199	47057	20137	67116	46940	20173	67408	47310	20087
I Other manufacturing industries	965	576	386	918	538	375	1051	626	421	1198	720	476
4 Electricity, gas and water	34368	17428	16942	37062	18419	18676	37539	18749	18823	34457	17508	17004
A Electricity, gas and steam	33397	16943	16457	36032	17945	18119	36405	18244	18191	33381	17018	16415
B Water works and supply	966	482	484	1023	464	558	1126	495	629	1068	480	587

4.2 Derivation of Value Added by Kind of Activity, in Constant Prices
(Continued)

Million Norwegian kroner

	1988 Gross Output	1988 Intermediate Consumption	1988 Value Added	1989 Gross Output	1989 Intermediate Consumption	1989 Value Added	1990 Gross Output	1990 Intermediate Consumption	1990 Value Added	1991 Gross Output	1991 Intermediate Consumption	1991 Value Added
			At constant prices of:1984									
5 Construction	78056	51758	26350	68092	43631	24332	62053	38506	23433	59760	37095	22553
6 Wholesale and retail trade, restaurants and hotels	88819	35809	52938	85385	34103	51213	84912	33864	50980	84271	33595	50607
A Wholesale and retail trade	75090	28464	46542	72858	27194	45587	73253	27374	45801	72622	27239	45304
B Restaurants and hotels	13717	7327	6395	12537	6891	5663	11707	6465	5262	11693	6331	5370
7 Transport, storage and communication	92145	47121	45039	98704	50761	47963	105356	53487	51855	109490	55308	54161
A Transport and storage	70983	40565	30309	77384	44511	32774	82596	46927	35494	83864	47839	35869
B Communication	21225	6403	14846	21302	6169	15218	22741	6477	16378	25922	7331	18737
8 Finance, insurance, real estate and business services	93452	33385	60052	90900	32343	58532	89721	32840	56966	88999	33886	55385
A Financial institutions	25765	8455	17309	24022	8217	15849	23645	7830	15809	22503	7818	14712
B Insurance	4128	2614	773	4185	2620	794	4106	3434	512	4030	3401	498
C Real estate and business services	63617	22253	41388	62790	21456	41339	62071	21612	40488	62561	22682	40003
Real estate, except dwellings	10758	5608	5157	10404	5621	4808	10305	5787	4576	10450	5956	4569
Dwellings	27086	7377	19745	27800	7029	20832	28145	6758	21444	28398	7318	21179
9 Community, social and personal services	30143	8300	21844	28958	7968	20990	29815	8316	21505	30326	8597	21743
A Sanitary and similar services	1010	98	913	969	100	872	966	105	865	974	121	861
B Social and related community services	12104	3892	8207	12084	3794	8284	12856	3924	8928	13058	4083	8970
Educational services	1926	1670	254	1877	1633	244	1999	1716	274	2042	1763	274
Medical, dental, other health and veterinary services	7287	1451	5830	7283	1434	5844	7810	1466	6341	7873	1553	6316
C Recreational and cultural services	5583	1507	4091	5687	1524	4181	5944	1610	4351	6178	1689	4504
D Personal and household services	11517	2806	8722	10396	2557	7853	10306	2681	7657	10399	2710	7722
Statistical discrepancy	-7216	940	-10915	-20670	184	-32078	-24012	-161	-34577	-33147	-141	-46603
Total, Industries	815482	407352	408479	816136	401173	416073	822802	402477	421642	829588	403778	427298
Producers of Government Services	103822	35709	68139	106703	37431	69347	109898	38865	71131	114073	40764	73436
Other Producers	...	...	...	...	...	...	...	...	...	...	...	...
Total	919574	443106	476726	923432	438700	485520	933553	441470	493023	944878	444736	501207
Less: Imputed bank service charge		-18371	18371	...	-17223	17223	...	-16967	16967	...	-16145	16145
Import duties [a]	5265	...	5265	4591	...	4591	5626	...	5626	5118	...	5118
Value added tax	42648	...	42648	40497	...	40497	40389	...	40389	40255	...	40255
Other adjustments [b]	437	...	437	-52	...	-52	-45	...	-45	-39	...	-39
Total [c]	967924	461477	503620	968468	455923	506607	979523	458437	515038	990212	460881	523178
Memorandum Item: Mineral fuels and power	180175	50450	132366	203180	51952	159816	213446	56347	164526	223380	55841	177508
			of which General Government:									
1 Agriculture, hunting, forestry and fishing	19	8	11	16	8	8	3	1	2	3	1	1
2 Mining and quarrying	...	...	...	...	...	...	...	...	...	...	...	...
3 Manufacturing	...	...	...	...	...	...	...	...	...	...	...	...
4 Electricity, gas and water	...	...	...	...	...	...	...	...	...	...	...	...
5 Construction	...	...	...	...	...	...	...	...	...	...	...	...
6 Wholesale and retail trade, restaurants and hotels	...	...	...	...	...	...	...	...	...	...	...	...
7 Transport and communication	5273	4033	1238	5305	4057	1246	5516	4202	1313	6012	4658	1354
8 Finance, insurance, real estate and business services	489	160	327	548	182	364	577	181	395	607	182	423
9 Community, social and personal services	98046	31522	66562	100840	33206	67731	103810	34508	69424	107471	35952	71660
Statistical discrepancy	...	...	...	...	...	...	...	...	...	...	...	...
Total, Industries of General Government	103822	35709	68139	106703	37431	69347	109898	38865	71131	114073	40764	73436
Producers of Government Services	...	...	...	...	...	...	...	...	...	...	...	...
Total, General Government	...	...	...	...	...	...	...	...	...	...	...	...

a) Item 'Import duties' includes collection of customs duties, value added tax on imports and special excises or taxes on imports.
b) Item 'Other adjustments' refers to collection of investment levy on fixed capital formation and subsidies on residential and social buildings.
c) Beginning 1987, the estimates at 1984 constant prices are derived from the series of constant prices based on T-1 prices. This resulted in some statistical discrepancies shown in the table.

4.3 Cost Components of Value Added

Million Norwegian kroner

	1980						1981					
	Compensation of Employees	Capital Consumption	Net Operating Surplus	Indirect Taxes	Less: Subsidies Received	Value Added	Compensation of Employees	Capital Consumption	Net Operating Surplus	Indirect Taxes	Less: Subsidies Received	Value Added
All Producers												
1 Agriculture, hunting, forestry and fishing	1226	3564	9857	272	3950	10969	1401	3944	11748	409	4544	12957
A Agriculture and hunting	344	2358	7626	97	3457	6969	369	2628	8481	139	3771	7847
B Forestry and logging	634	202	1072	19	190	1737	736	223	1515	22	252	2244
C Fishing	248	1005	1159	156	303	2264	296	1093	1752	248	522	2866
2 Mining and quarrying	2225	5082	30619	4271	119	42078	2717	7490	35857	5494	372	51185
A Coal mining	80	20	27	1	95	32	104	22	57	1	123	61
B Crude petroleum and natural gas production	1413	4745	30594	4239	...	40991	1830	7120	35565	5464	...	49979
C Metal ore mining	421	176	-174	19	21	422	449	193	81	15	246	492
D Other mining	310	142	172	12	3	633	334	155	154	14	3	654
3 Manufacturing	34161	5552	8817	2671	5566	45635	37559	6068	7287	2991	5328	48575
A Manufacture of food, beverages and tobacco	4687	1010	1221	1883	3908	4894	5162	1097	1175	2181	3179	6436
B Textile, wearing apparel and leather industries	1489	184	274	22	113	1856	1485	196	284	21	128	1857
C Manufacture of wood and wood products, including furniture	2758	352	1007	59	109	4067	2990	390	921	64	173	4192
D Manufacture of paper and paper products, printing and publishing	4553	785	356	88	206	5577	4973	873	760	91	230	6467
E Manufacture of chemicals and chemical petroleum, coal, rubber and plastic products	3090	1038	1055	254	62	5374	3417	1107	-19	248	65	4689
F Manufacture of non-metallic mineral products, except products of petroleum and coal	1185	274	336	50	20	1824	1268	299	423	49	20	2019
G Basic metal industries	2975	741	2077	91	205	5679	3293	825	453	98	184	4484
H Manufacture of fabricated metal products, machinery and equipment	13151	1140	2443	222	920	16037	14699	1250	3255	237	1324	18117
I Other manufacturing industries	273	27	48	3	22	328	271	31	35	3	26	314
4 Electricity, gas and water	1943	2560	2239	1625	131	8237	2204	2842	3647	1644	180	10158
A Electricity, gas and steam	1840	2412	2149	1622	107	7917	2125	2675	3588	1641	151	9878
B Water works and supply	103	148	90	3	24	320	79	167	60	3	29	280
5 Construction	13268	2085	1485	192	78	16952	13984	2259	3290	207	66	19673
6 Wholesale and retail trade, restaurants and hotels	21343	3481	4805	6878	3242	33264	23893	3635	7185	7828	4065	38475
A Wholesale and retail trade	18800	3353	4301	6854	3193	30115	20938	3505	6466	7802	4014	34697
B Restaurants and hotels	2543	127	504	24	50	3149	2955	130	719	26	52	3779
7 Transport, storage and communication	18120	11033	-1470	881	1674	26890	20591	12827	-2073	942	1533	30755
A Transport and storage	14133	10107	-1177	792	1674	22181	16115	11780	-2669	863	1533	24556
B Communication	3987	927	-293	89	...	4709	4476	1047	596	80	...	6199
8 Finance, insurance, real estate and business services	8472	4785	16092	723	1828	28244	10269	5411	19574	831	1931	34155
A Financial institutions	3499	227	5788	24	1391	8147	4211	277	7835	27	1423	10926
B Insurance	1370	117	-646	4	1	845	1518	142	-842	5	1	822
C Real estate and business services	3604	4441	10951	695	437	19253	4540	4992	12581	800	508	22406
Real estate, except dwellings	17	778	1782	146	79	2644	19	854	2078	170	61	3061
Dwellings	152	3635	6372	246	337	10067	179	4106	7433	297	406	11609
9 Community, social and personal services	8089	889	5482	556	2539	12478	9045	920	6388	610	2955	14009
A Sanitary and similar services	329	...	120	...	...	449	355	...	156	...	...	511
B Social and related community services	3534	580	2395	2	1696	4815	4021	597	2735	3	1960	5396
Educational services	745	70	654	2	1223	247	846	71	687	3	1444	162
Medical, dental, other health and veterinary services	1308	476	1741	...	18	3508	1472	492	2048	...	18	3994
C Recreational and cultural services	589	173	1284	529	843	1732	686	188	1536	582	994	1997
D Personal and household services	3637	136	1683	25	...	5482	3983	135	1962	26	1	6104

4.3 Cost Components of Value Added
(Continued)

Million Norwegian kroner

	1980						1981					
	Compensation of Employees	Capital Consumption	Net Operating Surplus	Indirect Taxes	Less: Subsidies Received	Value Added	Compensation of Employees	Capital Consumption	Net Operating Surplus	Indirect Taxes	Less: Subsidies Received	Value Added
Total, Industries	108847	39031	77925	18069	19126	224747	121661	45395	92904	20955	20974	259941
Producers of Government Services	36574	2327	...	...	...	38901	42504	2658	...	...	...	45162
Other Producers	...	...	...	...	...	...	...	...	...	...	...	...
Total	145421	41358	77925	18069	19126	263648	164165	48053	92904	20955	20974	305103
Less: Imputed bank service charge [a]	...	...	8724	...	...	8724	...	...	11349	...	...	11349
Import duties	...	...	...	3693	1	3692	...	...	...	4249	1	4248
Value added tax [b]	...	...	...	24703	...	24703	...	...	...	28024	...	28024
Other adjustments	...	...	...	2560	834	1726	...	...	...	2468	819	1649
Total	145421	41358	69201	49025	19961	285045	164165	48053	81555	55696	21794	327675

of which General Government:

	Compensation of Employees	Capital Consumption	Net Operating Surplus	Indirect Taxes	Less: Subsidies Received	Value Added	Compensation of Employees	Capital Consumption	Net Operating Surplus	Indirect Taxes	Less: Subsidies Received	Value Added
1 Agriculture, hunting, forestry and fishing	10	...	...	...	...	10	10	...	...	...	...	10
2 Mining and quarrying	...	...	...	...	...	...	...	...	...	...	...	...
3 Manufacturing	...	...	...	...	...	...	...	...	...	...	...	...
4 Electricity, gas and water	...	...	...	...	...	...	...	...	...	...	...	...
5 Construction	...	...	...	...	...	...	...	...	...	...	...	...
6 Wholesale and retail trade, restaurants and hotels	...	...	...	...	...	...	...	...	...	...	...	...
7 Transport and communication	559	246	...	...	...	805	658	278	...	...	...	935
8 Finance, insurance, real estate & business services	153	5	...	...	...	157	194	5	...	...	...	199
9 Community, social and personal services	35852	2076	...	...	...	37928	41642	2375	...	...	...	44018
Total, Industries of General Government	36574	2327	...	...	...	38901	42504	2658	...	...	...	45162
Producers of Government Services	...	...	...	...	...	...	...	...	...	...	...	...
Total, General Government	...	...	...	...	...	...	...	...	...	...	...	...

	1982						1983					
	Compensation of Employees	Capital Consumption	Net Operating Surplus	Indirect Taxes	Less: Subsidies Received	Value Added	Compensation of Employees	Capital Consumption	Net Operating Surplus	Indirect Taxes	Less: Subsidies Received	Value Added

All Producers

	Compensation of Employees	Capital Consumption	Net Operating Surplus	Indirect Taxes	Less: Subsidies Received	Value Added	Compensation of Employees	Capital Consumption	Net Operating Surplus	Indirect Taxes	Less: Subsidies Received	Value Added
1 Agriculture, hunting, forestry and fishing	1413	4296	12484	368	5125	13437	1540	4511	12201	408	5526	13135
A Agriculture and hunting	394	2900	9694	127	4519	8597	427	3176	8936	147	4735	7950
B Forestry and logging	690	238	1465	27	250	2171	722	258	1322	33	288	2046
C Fishing	330	1157	1325	214	357	2670	391	1078	1944	229	502	3139
2 Mining and quarrying	3504	9690	37522	6199	402	56514	3946	10432	45392	8880	419	68231
A Coal mining	126	23	64	1	157	55	137	23	136	1	213	84
B Crude petroleum and natural gas production	2591	9295	37288	6172	...	55346	3007	10038	44961	8849	...	66855
C Metal ore mining	444	204	-16	15	241	405	419	198	38	18	203	470
D Other mining	344	169	186	12	4	707	384	173	257	12	4	822

4.3 Cost Components of Value Added
(Continued)

Million Norwegian kroner

	1982						1983					
	Compensation of Employees	Capital Consumption	Net Operating Surplus	Indirect Taxes	Less: Subsidies Received	Value Added	Compensation of Employees	Capital Consumption	Net Operating Surplus	Indirect Taxes	Less: Subsidies Received	Value Added
3 Manufacturing	39868	6714	7001	3422	5623	51383	41462	6956	10286	3758	5738	56724
A Manufacture of food, beverages and tobacco	5632	1216	1400	2691	3239	7699	6051	1266	1920	2984	3187	9034
B Textile, wearing apparel and leather industries	1452	211	143	19	122	1702	1353	212	206	18	180	1609
C Manufacture of wood and wood products, including furniture	3129	431	868	59	185	4303	3176	448	899	65	292	4296
D Manufacture of paper and paper products, printing and publishing	5152	962	790	73	254	6722	5866	996	1218	77	248	7908
E Manufacture of chemicals and chemical petroleum, coal, rubber and plastic products	3639	1217	106	232	65	5130	3836	1254	446	240	66	5709
F Manufacture of non-metallic mineral products, except products of petroleum and coal	1365	330	404	41	20	2120	1392	338	563	45	24	2312
G Basic metal industries	3269	929	50	73	349	3971	3334	955	2373	72	566	6168
H Manufacture of fabricated metal products, machinery and equipment	15954	1385	3188	233	1363	19397	16169	1454	2568	256	1149	19297
I Other manufacturing industries	278	33	53	3	27	339	286	34	94	3	26	391
4 Electricity, gas and water	2479	3224	4686	1750	157	11981	2675	3511	6394	1888	156	14312
A Electricity, gas and steam	2390	3034	4608	1747	136	11643	2573	3310	6250	1885	123	13895
B Water works and supply	89	189	78	3	20	338	102	201	144	3	33	417
5 Construction	15675	2600	4274	207	45	22711	17069	2733	3942	237	133	23848
6 Wholesale and retail trade, restaurants and hotels	26834	3897	8516	7990	4472	42765	28678	3999	8764	8449	4414	45475
A Wholesale and retail trade	23419	3748	7654	7963	4413	38372	24924	3847	7489	8419	4350	40328
B Restaurants and hotels	3414	149	862	27	59	4393	3754	152	1275	30	64	5147
7 Transport, storage and communication	22632	14347	-5056	1038	1671	31289	23958	16332	-5810	1228	1856	33852
A Transport and storage	17381	13162	-6447	959	1671	23385	18363	15091	-8270	1130	1856	24459
B Communication	5251	1185	1391	79	...	7904	5596	1241	2460	98	...	9394
8 Finance, insurance, real estate and business services	12225	6242	23480	941	2030	40859	13978	6933	25773	1164	2214	45633
A Financial institutions	4898	335	10046	30	1457	13853	5644	386	11066	41	1576	15562
B Insurance	1779	175	-1409	5	1	549	1995	206	-1837	6	1	370
C Real estate and business services	5548	5732	14843	907	573	26457	6339	6341	16544	1117	638	29702
Real estate, except dwellings	22	973	2457	177	89	3539	33	1063	2799	197	95	3997
Dwellings	205	4724	8561	370	457	13402	218	5243	9593	446	499	15001
9 Community, social and personal services	10199	1019	7233	708	3438	15722	11275	1020	8073	846	3512	17701
A Sanitary and similar services	410	...	198	...	...	608	464	...	198	...	...	663
B Social and related community services	4603	661	3097	3	2205	6159	5139	662	3306	4	2248	6863
Educational services	945	79	691	3	1519	198	1054	79	617	4	1574	180
Medical, dental, other health and veterinary services	1673	544	2406	...	7	4616	1836	545	2689	...	13	5057
C Recreational and cultural services	739	210	1736	678	1232	2131	830	209	2038	811	1264	2624
D Personal and household services	4447	148	2203	27	1	6824	4842	149	2530	31	1	7551
Total, Industries	134829	52028	100141	22624	22962	286660	144580	56428	115014	26857	23967	318912
Producers of Government Services	48526	2979	...	...	...	51505	53655	3186	...	...	...	56841
Other Producers	...	...	...	...	...	...	...	...	...	...	...	...
Total	183355	55007	100141	22624	22962	338165	198235	59614	115014	26857	23967	375753
Less: Imputed bank service charge [a]	...	...	14318	...		14318	...	...	15960	...		15960
Import duties	...	...	...	5204	1	5203	...	...	...	5765	1	5764
Value added tax [b]	...	...	...	31536	...	31536	...	...	...	34623	...	34623
Other adjustments	...	...	...	2383	700	1683	...	...	...	2489	472	2017
Total	183355	55007	85823	61747	23663	362269	198235	59614	99054	69734	24440	402197

of which General Government:

1 Agriculture, hunting, forestry and fishing	11	...	...	...	...	11	13	...	...	...	...	13

Norway

4.3 Cost Components of Value Added
(Continued)

Million Norwegian kroner

	1982						1983					
	Compensation of Employees	Capital Consumption	Net Operating Surplus	Indirect Taxes	Less: Subsidies Received	Value Added	Compensation of Employees	Capital Consumption	Net Operating Surplus	Indirect Taxes	Less: Subsidies Received	Value Added
2 Mining and quarrying	...	...	...	...	...	...	...	...	...	...	...	...
3 Manufacturing	...	...	...	...	...	...	...	...	...	...	...	...
4 Electricity, gas and water	...	...	...	...	...	...	...	...	...	...	...	...
5 Construction	...	...	...	...	...	...	...	...	...	...	...	...
6 Wholesale and retail trade, restaurants and hotels	...	...	...	...	...	...	...	...	...	...	...	...
7 Transport and communication	760	306	...	...	...	1066	811	311	...	...	...	1123
8 Finance, insurance, real estate & business services	231	6	...	...	...	236	268	6	...	...	...	273
9 Community, social and personal services	47524	2668	...	...	...	50192	52563	2869	...	...	...	55432
Total, Industries of General Government	48526	2979	...	...	...	51505	53655	3186	...	...	...	56841
Producers of Government Services	...	...	...	...	...	...	...	...	...	...	...	...
Total, General Government	...	...	...	...	...	...	...	...	...	...	...	...

	1984						1985					
	Compensation of Employees	Capital Consumption	Net Operating Surplus	Indirect Taxes	Less: Subsidies Received	Value Added	Compensation of Employees	Capital Consumption	Net Operating Surplus	Indirect Taxes	Less: Subsidies Received	Value Added
All Producers												
1 Agriculture, hunting, forestry and fishing	1711	4591	13877	419	5556	15042	1938	4977	14007	118	5889	15150
A Agriculture and hunting	449	3325	10156	184	4735	9380	485	3620	9908	90	5093	9009
B Forestry and logging	825	271	1621	38	296	2459	880	293	1574	19	323	2443
C Fishing	437	995	2100	197	525	3203	573	1063	2526	9	472	3698
2 Mining and quarrying	5139	12935	56112	11137	544	84778	6206	14595	59480	11214	485	91009
A Coal mining	124	21	197	1	254	88	136	22	43	1	82	120
B Crude petroleum and natural gas production	4117	12573	55604	11094	...	83387	5124	14217	59181	11184	...	89706
C Metal ore mining	488	180	40	27	286	449	495	184	14	15	399	309
D Other mining	410	161	272	16	5	854	451	172	242	13	4	874
3 Manufacturing	44940	6542	14581	4293	5832	64524	49454	7138	14985	4327	5777	70127
A Manufacture of food, beverages and tobacco	6488	1191	2370	3301	3104	10246	7011	1286	2925	3583	3249	11556
B Textile, wearing apparel and leather industries	1401	192	278	21	183	1709	1520	202	287	4	159	1854
C Manufacture of wood and wood products, including furniture	3316	423	866	72	265	4412	3622	461	1011	34	226	4901
D Manufacture of paper and paper products, printing and publishing	6450	935	2036	101	253	9269	7258	1016	1797	160	72	10158
E Manufacture of chemicals and chemical petroleum, coal, rubber and plastic products	4191	1165	1692	319	68	7299	4396	1263	1735	245	56	7582
F Manufacture of non-metallic mineral products, except products of petroleum and coal	1485	313	452	46	24	2272	1663	340	504	21	23	2505
G Basic metal industries	3761	908	4391	105	793	8372	3973	1012	2613	158	368	7388
H Manufacture of fabricated metal products, machinery and equipment	17543	1383	2379	325	1111	20519	19649	1524	4028	122	1594	23729
I Other manufacturing industries	306	30	118	3	30	427	363	35	86	1	31	454
4 Electricity, gas and water	2942	3804	7598	2387	159	16571	3307	4128	7739	3252	149	18278
A Electricity, gas and steam	2832	3584	7448	2383	121	16124	3185	3887	7620	3229	124	17797
B Water works and supply	111	220	150	4	38	447	122	241	120	23	25	481
5 Construction	18168	2695	3457	287	254	24353	19528	3306	3692	771	227	27070
6 Wholesale and retail trade, restaurants and hotels	31548	3800	9367	9473	4744	49445	35416	4290	8346	10817	4973	53897
A Wholesale and retail trade	27270	3660	7970	9435	4666	43668	30582	4133	6723	10756	4895	47298
B Restaurants and hotels	4278	140	1397	39	78	5777	4834	157	1623	62	78	6599
7 Transport, storage and communication	24968	16233	-3604	1434	1954	37077	26343	14745	-2810	1671	1973	37976
A Transport and storage	18990	14931	-6514	1312	1906	26814	19643	13233	-4786	1507	1953	27645
B Communication	5978	1303	2910	121	49	10263	6700	1512	1976	164	20	10332
8 Finance, insurance, real estate and business services	16380	7583	26630	1333	2607	49318	19820	8572	29825	1218	3052	56383
A Financial institutions	6301	449	10113	44	1892	15015	7321	580	10260	57	2317	15901

1402

4.3 Cost Components of Value Added
(Continued)

Million Norwegian kroner

1984 / 1985

	Compensation of Employees	Capital Consumption	Net Operating Surplus	Indirect Taxes	Less: Subsidies Received	Value Added	Compensation of Employees	Capital Consumption	Net Operating Surplus	Indirect Taxes	Less: Subsidies Received	Value Added
	1984						**1985**					
B Insurance	2223	238	-2377	7	1	91	2572	307	-2166	13	1	724
C Real estate and business services	7856	6895	18894	1282	714	34213	9927	7685	21731	1148	734	39757
Real estate, except dwellings	35	1171	2963	248	116	4303	38	1337	3409	230	104	4910
Dwellings	227	5689	10767	522	549	16656	246	6149	11872	417	578	18105
9 Community, social and personal services	12083	992	8584	991	3900	18750	13482	1019	10087	1185	4365	21408
A Sanitary and similar services	463	...	250	...	...	714	542	20	291	1	...	854
B Social and related community services	5551	643	3528	4	2529	7197	6121	637	4015	20	2929	7864
Educational services	1134	76	722	4	1737	199	1271	82	895	2	1978	271
Medical, dental, other health and veterinary services	1954	529	2807	...	21	5269	2048	511	3121	18	22	5676
C Recreational and cultural services	836	207	2165	945	1369	2783	1022	205	2225	1133	1434	3151
D Personal and household services	5232	142	2641	42	1	8057	5798	158	3556	30	2	9539
Total, Industries	157880	59174	136602	31753	25551	359858	175494	62770	145351	34572	26890	391297
Producers of Government Services	58470	3338	...	...	...	61808	64173	3742	...	49	...	67965
Other Producers	...	...	...	...	...	...	...	...	...	...	...	...
Total	216350	62513	136602	31753	25551	421667	239667	66512	145351	34621	26890	459261
Less: Imputed bank service charge a	...	...	15443	...	...	15443	...	...	15431	...	...	15431
Import duties	...	...	...	6006	...	6006	...	...	...	9320	...	9320
Value added tax b	...	...	...	37794	...	37794	...	...	...	44150	...	44150
Other adjustments	...	...	...	2647	159	2489	...	...	...	2946	46	2900
Total	216350	62513	121159	78200	25710	452512	239667	66512	129920	91037	26936	500201

of which General Government:

	Compensation of Employees	Capital Consumption	Net Operating Surplus	Indirect Taxes	Less: Subsidies Received	Value Added	Compensation of Employees	Capital Consumption	Net Operating Surplus	Indirect Taxes	Less: Subsidies Received	Value Added
1 Agriculture, hunting, forestry and fishing	15	...	...	...	...	15	14	...	...	...	...	14
2 Mining and quarrying	...	...	...	...	...	...	...	...	...	...	...	...
3 Manufacturing	...	...	...	...	...	...	...	...	...	...	...	...
4 Electricity, gas and water	...	...	...	...	...	...	...	...	...	...	...	...
5 Construction	...	...	...	...	...	...	...	...	...	...	...	...
6 Wholesale and retail trade, restaurants and hotels	...	...	...	...	...	...	...	...	...	...	...	...
7 Transport and communication	860	316	...	...	...	1175	904	366	...	...	...	1270
8 Finance, insurance, real estate & business services	336	6	...	...	...	341	373	7	...	...	...	380
9 Community, social and personal services	57260	3017	...	...	...	60277	62883	3370	...	49	...	66301
Total, Industries of General Government	58470	3338	...	...	...	61808	64173	3742	...	49	...	67965
Producers of Government Services	...	...	...	...	...	...	...	...	...	...	...	...
Total, General Government	...	...	...	...	...	...	...	...	...	...	...	...

1986 / 1987 — All Producers

	Compensation of Employees	Capital Consumption	Net Operating Surplus	Indirect Taxes	Less: Subsidies Received	Value Added	Compensation of Employees	Capital Consumption	Net Operating Surplus	Indirect Taxes	Less: Subsidies Received	Value Added
	1986						**1987**					
1 Agriculture, hunting, forestry and fishing	2160	5500	14345	155	6139	16021	2439	6287	15626	231	6888	17695
A Agriculture and hunting	532	3972	9667	115	5204	9081	555	4458	10583	187	5993	9789
B Forestry and logging	949	320	1839	23	355	2776	1083	362	2109	25	407	3172
C Fishing	679	1208	2840	18	580	4164	801	1467	2934	20	488	4734
2 Mining and quarrying	6922	17410	21807	6925	533	52530	7700	20107	19161	6906	476	53398
A Coal mining	154	25	4	2	133	52	132	28	36	2	161	38
B Crude petroleum and natural gas production	5760	17003	21306	6897	...	50966	6509	19657	18715	6878	...	51759
C Metal ore mining	500	198	136	9	394	449	467	217	55	9	310	437
D Other mining	509	184	361	17	6	1064	592	205	355	18	6	1164

Norway

Million Norwegian kroner

	1986						1987					
	Compensation of Employees	Capital Consumption	Net Operating Surplus	Indirect Taxes	Less: Subsidies Received	Value Added	Compensation of Employees	Capital Consumption	Net Operating Surplus	Indirect Taxes	Less: Subsidies Received	Value Added
3 Manufacturing	54865	7973	14839	5023	7049	75651	60802	9296	15437	5816	6761	84590
A Manufacture of food, beverages and tobacco	7898	1419	3126	4154	3432	13164	8876	1641	3143	4817	3405	15072
B Textile, wearing apparel and leather industries	1635	216	316	5	180	1992	1728	238	156	5	104	2024
C Manufacture of wood and wood products, including furniture	3970	511	1326	40	302	5545	4447	599	1230	45	314	6005
D Manufacture of paper and paper products, printing and publishing	8212	1140	1872	187	272	11139	9355	1329	1774	226	285	12399
E Manufacture of chemicals and chemical petroleum, coal, rubber and plastic products	4881	1413	1019	294	41	7566	5375	1699	2488	329	42	9849
F Manufacture of non-metallic mineral products, except products of petroleum and coal	1925	374	689	26	19	2995	2161	445	817	28	19	3430
G Basic metal industries	4340	1155	1910	179	726	6858	4614	1322	1403	216	122	7432
H Manufacture of fabricated metal products, machinery and equipment	21599	1706	4482	137	2037	25886	23778	1979	4345	150	2435	27817
I Other manufacturing industries	406	39	100	1	40	506	469	45	82	1	35	562
4 Electricity, gas and water	3720	4562	7949	3523	175	19578	4220	5204	8356	3868	209	21439
A Electricity, gas and steam	3593	4299	7836	3498	149	19077	4076	4898	8227	3840	148	20892
B Water works and supply	128	263	113	25	27	501	144	306	130	28	61	547
5 Construction	22989	3727	3127	915	208	30550	27756	4252	3743	1079	199	36632
6 Wholesale and retail trade, restaurants and hotels	41568	4989	7790	12472	4254	62565	46756	5839	4549	14966	3992	68118
A Wholesale and retail trade	35539	4810	6110	12404	4169	54694	39701	5633	2578	14886	3905	58893
B Restaurants and hotels	6029	179	1680	68	85	7871	7055	206	1971	80	86	9225
7 Transport, storage and communication	29046	13029	1676	2073	2291	43532	31035	14267	-866	2451	2462	44425
A Transport and storage	21467	11283	-740	1854	2276	31588	22170	12222	-2422	2111	2451	31630
B Communication	7579	1745	2416	219	15	11944	8865	2045	1556	340	11	12795
8 Finance, insurance, real estate and business services	23478	10103	36139	1494	3656	67557	27223	12221	41202	1968	4611	78004
A Financial institutions	8757	749	14659	73	2725	21513	9856	960	18219	98	3559	25575
B Insurance	2863	394	-1993	16	1	1279	3264	507	-1490	20	1	2301
C Real estate and business services	11857	8960	23473	1405	930	44765	14103	10754	24473	1850	1051	50128
Real estate, except dwellings	53	1609	3739	270	119	5552	62	1989	4120	363	131	6404
Dwellings	284	6905	12774	499	751	19711	312	8044	13667	628	854	21796
9 Community, social and personal services	15611	1011	11999	1451	5251	24821	17674	984	12994	1654	5918	27389
A Sanitary and similar services	632	21	384	2	...	1038	798	59	235	2	...	1093
B Social and related community services	7037	621	4609	23	3589	8701	8099	625	4993	26	4031	9713
Educational services	1471	79	1227	2	2452	328	1654	83	1420	3	2779	381
Medical, dental, other health and veterinary services	2345	488	3382	21	29	6207	2677	435	3572	23	38	6671
C Recreational and cultural services	1211	182	2561	1389	1660	3683	1417	83	3032	1585	1883	4233
D Personal and household services	6732	187	4445	37	2	11399	7361	217	4734	41	4	12350
Total, Industries	200358	68302	119672	34031	29556	392806	225605	78456	120202	38939	31515	431687
Producers of Government Services	71054	4259	...	58	...	75371	80722	4845	...	63	...	85629
Other Producers	...	...	...	...	...	...	...	...	...	...	...	...
Total	271412	72561	119672	34088	29556	468177	306327	83301	120202	39001	31515	517316
Less: Imputed bank service charge [a]	...	...	20280	...	...	20280	...	...	24328	...	...	24328
Import duties	...	...	...	11852	...	11852	...	...	...	9912	...	9912
Value added tax [b]	...	...	...	50309	...	50309	...	...	...	54466	...	54466
Other adjustments	...	...	...	3673	13	3660	...	...	...	4113	...	4113
Total	271412	72561	99392	99922	29569	513718	306327	83301	95874	107492	31515	561479

of which General Government:

	1986						1987					
1 Agriculture, hunting, forestry and fishing	15	...	...	...	...	15	13	...	...	...	...	13

4.3 Cost Components of Value Added
(Continued)

Million Norwegian kroner

	1986						1987					
	Compensation of Employees	Capital Consumption	Net Operating Surplus	Indirect Taxes	Less: Subsidies Received	Value Added	Compensation of Employees	Capital Consumption	Net Operating Surplus	Indirect Taxes	Less: Subsidies Received	Value Added
2 Mining and quarrying	...	...	...	...	...	...	...	...	...	...	...	...
3 Manufacturing	...	...	...	...	...	...	...	...	...	...	...	...
4 Electricity, gas and water	...	...	...	...	...	...	...	...	...	...	...	...
5 Construction	...	...	...	...	...	...	...	...	...	...	...	...
6 Wholesale and retail trade, restaurants and hotels	...			...		...	...	...				...
7 Transport and communication	973	426	...	...	...	1399	1058	482	...	...	...	1540
8 Finance, insurance, real estate & business services	404	8	...	...	...	411	422	9	...	...	...	431
9 Community, social and personal services	69663	3826	...	58	...	73546	79228	4355	...	63	...	83645
Total, Industries of General Government	71054	4259	...	58	...	75371	80722	4845	...	63	...	85629
Producers of Government Services	...	...	...	...	...	...	...	...	...	...	...	...
Total, General Government	...	...	...	...	...	...	...	...	...	...	...	...

	1988						1989					
	Compensation of Employees	Capital Consumption	Net Operating Surplus	Indirect Taxes	Less: Subsidies Received	Value Added	Compensation of Employees	Capital Consumption	Net Operating Surplus	Indirect Taxes	Less: Subsidies Received	Value Added
All Producers												
1 Agriculture, hunting, forestry and fishing	2496	6705	15327	256	7094	17689	2536	6985	15759	276	7987	17568
A Agriculture and hunting	582	4650	10445	199	6197	9678	602	4783	11929	211	6926	10599
B Forestry and logging	1021	377	2676	29	444	3659	1008	392	2695	29	475	3650
C Fishing	892	1679	2206	28	453	4352	925	1810	1134	36	586	3319
2 Mining and quarrying	8153	23134	9263	5930	528	45951	8728	26063	29282	7919	373	71620
A Coal mining	123	29	25	1	179	-1	105	30	72	1	173	35
B Crude petroleum and natural gas production	6952	22670	8863	5898	...	44383	7541	25591	28731	7892	...	69755
C Metal ore mining	431	219	62	9	344	377	435	217	85	7	194	550
D Other mining	648	216	313	22	6	1192	647	224	395	20	6	1280
3 Manufacturing	61744	10036	17651	6306	6231	89506	60276	10451	20366	6934	6763	91265
A Manufacture of food, beverages and tobacco	9372	1774	2787	5213	3037	16110	9544	1862	3153	5707	3433	16833
B Textile, wearing apparel and leather industries	1611	245	169	6	88	1942	1444	249	116	5	119	1695
C Manufacture of wood and wood products, including furniture	4541	641	819	49	252	5798	4278	666	866	47	280	5576
D Manufacture of paper and paper products, printing and publishing	9730	1428	2286	252	358	13337	9792	1474	3051	274	443	14148
E Manufacture of chemicals and chemical petroleum, coal, rubber and plastic products	5411	1899	2873	361	46	10497	5686	2003	2790	428	106	10801
F Manufacture of non-metallic mineral products, except products of petroleum and coal	2254	474	370	31	22	3107	1992	486	569	26	52	3022
G Basic metal industries	4893	1401	5006	248	228	11321	4683	1449	5488	274	109	11784
H Manufacture of fabricated metal products, machinery and equipment	23448	2125	3285	145	2165	26838	22404	2212	4236	173	2182	26843
I Other manufacturing industries	484	49	57	1	35	556	453	51	97	1	39	563
4 Electricity, gas and water	4455	5630	9491	4177	197	23555	4661	5739	10362	4485	138	25109
A Electricity, gas and steam	4300	5299	9291	4149	128	22912	4499	5398	10062	4459	93	24326
B Water works and supply	155	331	199	28	69	643	162	341	299	26	45	783
5 Construction	29979	4209	3125	1154	126	38340	27339	3969	325	1065	149	32549
6 Wholesale and retail trade, restaurants and hotels	50155	6090	2048	16250	4312	70231	51164	6075	1084	15807	4145	69985
A Wholesale and retail trade	42631	5878	740	16168	4219	61198	43488	5870	374	15743	4048	61427
B Restaurants and hotels	7525	213	1307	82	94	9033	7676	205	710	64	96	8558
7 Transport, storage and communication	32038	15356	4123	2712	2863	51367	32866	16769	10380	2708	3054	59669
A Transport and storage	22710	13103	1072	2339	2851	36372	23649	14418	6047	2388	3008	43493
B Communication	9328	2254	3051	374	11	14995	9218	2351	4334	320	47	16176
8 Finance, insurance, real estate and business services	30218	13656	43052	2406	5389	83942	30344	13891	48442	2288	6349	88616
A Financial institutions	10895	1122	17109	330	4233	25223	10690	1189	18972	166	5137	25880

1405

Norway

4.3 Cost Components of Value Added
(Continued)

Million Norwegian kroner

	1988						1989					
	Compensation of Employees	Capital Consumption	Net Operating Surplus	Indirect Taxes	Less: Subsidies Received	Value Added	Compensation of Employees	Capital Consumption	Net Operating Surplus	Indirect Taxes	Less: Subsidies Received	Value Added
B Insurance	3550	583	-1612	22	...	2543	3683	596	-1259	23	15	3028
C Real estate and business services	15773	11952	27554	2053	1156	56176	15970	12106	30730	2098	1197	59708
Real estate, except dwellings	64	2285	4473	393	148	7067	65	2354	4545	390	120	7234
Dwellings	337	8812	16445	695	922	25367	345	8869	19912	771	957	28940
9 Community, social and personal services	18508	1024	15145	1799	7028	29448	18596	1058	15753	1784	7642	29549
A Sanitary and similar services	879	67	391	2	...	1339	855	69	457	2	8	1374
B Social and related community services	8516	571	6273	30	4997	10392	8774	590	6817	32	5456	10757
Educational services	1682	170	2104	3	3477	482	1691	176	2463	4	3832	502
Medical, dental, other health and veterinary services	2751	282	4169	27	48	7181	2814	291	4354	28	55	7432
C Recreational and cultural services	1486	91	3497	1722	2027	4769	1500	94	3931	1710	2141	5094
D Personal and household services	7628	295	4984	45	5	12947	7467	305	4549	41	37	12324
Total, Industries	237745	85839	119223	40989	33769	450028	236509	91000	151753	43265	36599	485929
Producers of Government Services	86504	5355		72	...	91930	92090	5678	...	73	...	97841
Other Producers	...	...	...	...	...	...	...	...	...	...	...	...
Total	324249	91194	119223	41061	33769	541958	328600	96678	151753	43338	36599	583770
Less: Imputed bank service charge [a]	...	...	24604	...	...	24604	...	...	25611	...	...	25611
Import duties	...	...		7046	...	7046	...	...	...	6466	...	6466
Value added tax [b]	...	...	...	54941	...	54941	...	...	...	53953	...	53953
Other adjustments	...	...	...	3937	...	3937	...	...	...	2805	...	2805
Total	324249	91194	94619	106985	33769	583278	328600	96678	126142	106562	36599	621383

of which General Government:

	1988						1989					
	Compensation of Employees	Capital Consumption	Net Operating Surplus	Indirect Taxes	Less: Subsidies Received	Value Added	Compensation of Employees	Capital Consumption	Net Operating Surplus	Indirect Taxes	Less: Subsidies Received	Value Added
1 Agriculture, hunting, forestry and fishing	14	...	...	...	...	14	11	...	...	...	...	11
2 Mining and quarrying	...	...	...	...	...	...	...	...	...	...	...	...
3 Manufacturing	...	...	...	...	...	...	...	...	...	...	...	...
4 Electricity, gas and water	...	...	...	...	...	...	...	...	...	...	...	...
5 Construction	...	...	...	...	...	...	...	...	...	...	...	...
6 Wholesale and retail trade, restaurants and hotels	...	...	...	...	...	...	...	...	...	...	...	...
7 Transport and communication	1110	529	...	...	...	1639	1134	580	...	...	...	1714
8 Finance, insurance, real estate & business services	426	10	...	...	...	435	503	11	...	...	...	513
9 Community, social and personal services	84954	4816	...	72	...	89842	90443	5088	...	73	...	95603
Total, Industries of General Government	86504	5355	...	72	...	91930	92090	5678	...	73	...	97841
Producers of Government Services	...	...	...	...	...	...	...	...	...	...	...	...
Total, General Government	...	...	...	...	...	...	...	...	...	...	...	...

	1990						1991					
	Compensation of Employees	Capital Consumption	Net Operating Surplus	Indirect Taxes	Less: Subsidies Received	Value Added	Compensation of Employees	Capital Consumption	Net Operating Surplus	Indirect Taxes	Less: Subsidies Received	Value Added

All Producers

	1990						1991					
	Compensation of Employees	Capital Consumption	Net Operating Surplus	Indirect Taxes	Less: Subsidies Received	Value Added	Compensation of Employees	Capital Consumption	Net Operating Surplus	Indirect Taxes	Less: Subsidies Received	Value Added
1 Agriculture, hunting, forestry and fishing	2461	7076	18738	257	8202	20330	2390	6997	19217	264	8816	20052
A Agriculture and hunting	600	4847	13136	194	7048	11729	593	4773	13568	199	7686	11447
B Forestry and logging	971	392	3074	28	478	3987	897	385	2937	29	479	3769
C Fishing	890	1837	2528	35	676	4614	901	1839	2711	36	651	4836
2 Mining and quarrying	9076	27130	43509	9313	382	88644	10103	28750	42615	10168	264	91372
A Coal mining	97	30	91	1	204	15	101	29	14	1	125	21
B Crude petroleum and natural gas production	7907	26665	43052	9287	...	86912	8887	28281	42360	10143	...	89671
C Metal ore mining	422	210	26	7	170	496	436	206	-148	7	132	369
D Other mining	648	225	340	17	8	1222	679	234	389	18	7	1312

4.3 Cost Components of Value Added
(Continued)

Million Norwegian kroner

	1990						1991					
	Compensation of Employees	Capital Consumption	Net Operating Surplus	Indirect Taxes	Less: Subsidies Received	Value Added	Compensation of Employees	Capital Consumption	Net Operating Surplus	Indirect Taxes	Less: Subsidies Received	Value Added
3 Manufacturing	62511	10576	16781	7440	6940	90369	63566	10829	17731	7964	7499	92591
A Manufacture of food, beverages and tobacco	9866	1884	2628	6167	2767	17778	10158	1935	4565	6679	2911	20425
B Textile, wearing apparel and leather industries	1507	242	196	4	133	1816	1498	239	350	4	186	1905
C Manufacture of wood and wood products, including furniture	4317	679	1088	44	307	5821	4175	689	691	46	382	5218
D Manufacture of paper and paper products, printing and publishing	10129	1498	2890	283	407	14392	10350	1545	2618	287	438	14362
E Manufacture of chemicals and chemical petroleum, coal, rubber and plastic products	5928	2030	3355	460	145	11629	6103	2069	2621	457	196	11054
F Manufacture of non-metallic mineral products, except products of petroleum and coal	2070	492	587	25	64	3110	2143	501	313	27	81	2903
G Basic metal industries	4658	1462	1592	287	493	7506	4747	1498	184	292	138	6582
H Manufacture of fabricated metal products, machinery and equipment	23493	2239	4344	169	2579	27665	23912	2300	6100	172	3107	29375
I Other manufacturing industries	543	52	100	1	45	651	481	55	289	2	60	766
4 Electricity, gas and water	4798	5814	11741	4651	194	26809	4953	5928	11894	4672	180	27266
A Electricity, gas and steam	4627	5463	11311	4630	123	25908	4781	5563	11508	4650	116	26386
B Water works and supply	170	350	429	22	71	901	172	365	386	22	64	880
5 Construction	27151	4056	-2747	994	159	29295	26609	3519	-3958	924	183	26910
6 Wholesale and retail trade, restaurants and hotels	52830	5751	3286	16420	5069	73218	54210	5547	1091	18781	4315	75315
A Wholesale and retail trade	44739	5557	3239	16360	4961	64934	45650	5360	1149	18717	4212	66663
B Restaurants and hotels	8092	194	47	60	108	8284	8561	187	-57	64	102	8652
7 Transport, storage and communication	34230	17362	13704	2712	3315	64693	35538	19530	17345	2734	3416	71731
A Transport and storage	24680	14990	9423	2449	3281	48261	25678	17120	14125	2468	3407	55984
B Communication	9550	2372	4281	263	34	16433	9860	2411	3220	267	9	15748
8 Finance, insurance, real estate and business services	31121	14055	51311	2167	7405	91249	32213	14049	54978	2102	9314	94029
A Financial institutions	10950	1248	17689	107	5973	24022	10806	1272	18171	100	7754	22596
B Insurance	3818	604	-404	22	33	4008	3946	592	788	24	48	5302
C Real estate and business services	16353	12204	34025	2038	1399	63220	17461	12186	36020	1978	1512	66132
Real estate, except dwellings	68	2379	4933	362	180	7561	70	2404	5545	355	213	8161
Dwellings	375	8923	23181	831	1023	32287	396	8860	24800	829	1074	33811
9 Community, social and personal services	19708	1071	17506	1985	8326	31943	21188	1092	18333	2201	8784	34030
A Sanitary and similar services	950	68	430	2	10	1439	1048	68	475	2	64	1530
B Social and related community services	9479	600	8101	33	5941	12272	10301	613	8510	37	6219	13242
Educational services	1841	180	2580	4	3963	642	2006	185	2683	5	4199	679
Medical, dental, other health and veterinary services	3046	296	5522	29	127	8765	3323	302	5827	32	42	9442
C Recreational and cultural services	1622	96	4208	1910	2318	5517	1833	98	4277	2120	2440	5887
D Personal and household services	7658	307	4767	40	56	12716	8006	312	5072	42	62	13371
Total, Industries	243885	92891	173827	45940	39992	516551	250771	96242	179245	49809	42770	533297
Producers of Government Services	98118	5933	...	75	...	104126	105611	6220	...	80	...	111910
Other Producers	...	...	...	...	...	...	...	...	...	...	...	...
Total	342003	98823	173827	46014	39992	620676	356381	102462	179245	49889	42770	645207
Less: Imputed bank service charge [a]	...	...	25200	...	...	25200	...	...	24249	...	...	24249
Import duties	...	...	...	7244	...	7244	...	...	...	7031	...	7031
Value added tax [b]	...	...	...	55803	...	55803	...	...	...	56871	...	56871
Other adjustments	...	...	...	2028	...	2028	...	...	...	1826	...	1826
Total	342003	98823	148627	111089	39992	660552	356381	102462	154996	115617	42770	686686

of which General Government:

1 Agriculture, hunting, forestry and fishing	3	...	...	...	...	3	2	...	...	...	...	2

Norway

Million Norwegian kroner

	1990						1991					
	Compensation of Employees	Capital Consumption	Net Operating Surplus	Indirect Taxes	Less: Subsidies Received	Value Added	Compensation of Employees	Capital Consumption	Net Operating Surplus	Indirect Taxes	Less: Subsidies Received	Value Added
2 Mining and quarrying	...	...	...	...	...	...	...	...	...	...	...	...
3 Manufacturing	...	...	...	...	...	...	...	...	...	...	...	...
4 Electricity, gas and water	...	...	...	...	...	...	...	...	...	...	...	...
5 Construction	...	...	...	...	...	...	...	...	...	...	...	...
6 Wholesale and retail trade, restaurants and hotels	...	...	...	...	...	...	...	...	...	...	...	...
7 Transport and communication	1211	617	...	...	...	1828	1260	669	...	...	...	1928
8 Finance, insurance, real estate & business services	561	11	...	...	...	573	622	12	...	...	...	635
9 Community, social and personal services	96343	5304	...	75	...	101722	103726	5539	...	80	...	109345
Total, Industries of General Government	98118	5933	...	75	...	104126	105611	6220	...	80	...	111910
Producers of Government Services	...	...	...	...	...	...	...	...	...	...	...	...
Total, General Government	...	...	...	...	...	...	...	...	...	...	...	...

a) Item 'Import duties' includes collection of customs duties, value added tax on imports and special excises or taxes on imports.

b) Item 'Other adjustments' refers to collection of investment levy on fixed capital formation and subsidies on residential and social buildings.

Oman

Source. Reply to the United Nations National Accounts Questionnaire from the Directorate General of National Statistics, Development Council, Technical Secretariat, Muscat. Official estimates are published in the 'Statistical Yearbook, Fourth Issue, 1397 A.H., 1977 A.D.'.

General note. The estimates shown in the following tables have been adjusted by the United Nations Statistical Office to conform to the United Nations System of National Accounts so far as the existing data would permit.

1.1 Expenditure on the Gross Domestic Product, in Current Prices

Million Rials Omani

	1980	1981	1982	1983	1984	1985	1986	1987	1988	1989	1990	1991
1 Government final consumption expenditure	499.2	656.4	715.2	779.8	808.0	938.1	929.0	913.7	956.0	975.6	1544.9	1394.7
2 Private final consumption expenditure a	576.8	590.6	794.7	802.2	938.5	1125.6	1020.0	929.6	1179.8	1261.8	1080.6	1505.7
3 Gross capital formation	465.7	583.5	706.7	736.9	913.2	953.1	898.4	564.3	511.1	444.2	529.2	659.4
A Increase in stocks a	...	...	...	...	...	...	...	...	...	...	...	...
B Gross fixed capital formation	465.7	583.5	706.7	736.9	913.2	953.1	898.4	564.3	511.1	444.2	529.2	659.4
4 Exports of goods and services	1294.0	1625.0	1532.0	1475.0	1532.0	1722.0	1098.0	1468.0	1290.0	1565.0	2118.0	1873.0
5 Less: Imports of goods and services	772.2	965.0	1135.0	1054.0	1145.0	1285.0	1145.0	873.0	1011.0	1016.0	1222.0	1497.0
Equals: Gross Domestic Product	2063.5	2490.5	2613.6	2739.9	3046.7	3453.8	2800.4	3002.6	2925.9	3230.6	4050.7	3935.8

a) Item 'Increase in stocks' is included in item 'Private final consumption expenditure'.

1.3 Cost Components of the Gross Domestic Product

Million Rials Omani

	1980	1981	1982	1983	1984	1985	1986	1987	1988	1989	1990	1991
1 Indirect taxes, net	...	...	...	...	...	...	...	...	...	...	...	...
2 Consumption of fixed capital	...	...	...	...	...	...	...	...	...	...	...	...
3 Compensation of employees paid by resident producers to:	424.4	555.2	655.7	749.3	884.8	994.1	996.7	942.5	1007.6	1031.1	1212.9	1296.5
4 Operating surplus	...	...	...	...	...	...	...	...	...	...	...	...
Equals: Gross Domestic Product	2063.5	2490.5	2613.6	2739.9	3046.7	3453.8	2800.4	3002.6	2925.9	3230.6	4050.7	3935.8

1.4 General Government Current Receipts and Disbursements

Million Rials Omani

	1980	1981	1982	1983	1984	1985	1986	1987	1988	1989	1990	1991
Receipts												
1 Operating surplus	...	...	...	...	...	...	...	...	...	...	...	...
2 Property and entrepreneurial income a	1132.3	1399.1	1250.4	1308.9	1362.1	1568.2	994.3	1266.3	1047.6	1252.6	1761.2	1574.8
3 Taxes, fees and contributions b	28.3	39.5	43.9	63.1	82.3	105.8	104.4	87.4	88.7	88.2	89.3	101.6
4 Other current transfers c	27.4	39.5	39.5	51.8	68.3	89.0	89.3	125.6	104.5	121.0	171.8	169.0
Total Current Receipts of General Government	...	...	...	...	...	...	...	...	...	...	...	...
Disbursements												
1 Government final consumption expenditure	499.2	656.4	715.2	779.8	808.0	938.1	929.0	913.7	956.0	975.6	1544.9	1394.7
A Compensation of employees	194.6	260.5	305.0	360.0	423.9	477.9	495.8	509.9	535.2	548.7	658.6	669.5
B Consumption of fixed capital	...	...	...	...	...	...	...	...	...	...	...	...
C Purchases of goods and services, net	304.6	395.9	410.2	419.8	384.1	460.2	433.2	403.8	420.8	426.9	886.3	725.2
D Less: Own account fixed capital formation	...	...	...	...	...	...	...	...	...	...	...	...
E Indirect taxes paid, net	...	...	...	...	...	...	...	...	...	...	...	...
2 Property income	...	...	...	...	...	...	...	...	...	...	...	...
A Interest	21.1	15.5	17.5	19.2	36.0	45.0	75.9	72.9	84.0	95.0	93.0	70.0
B Net land rent and royalties	...	...	...	...	...	...	...	...	...	...	...	...
3 Subsidies	...	...	...	...	...	...	...	...	...	...	...	...
4 Other current transfers	...	...	...	...	...	...	...	...	...	...	...	...
5 Net saving	...	...	...	...	...	...	...	...	...	...	...	...
Total Current Disbursements and Net Saving of General Government	...	...	...	...	...	...	...	...	...	...	...	...

a) Item 'Property and entrepreneurial income' refers to oil and gas revenue and interest from investment and rent.
b) Item 'Taxes fees and contributions' includes indirect taxes and compulsory fees, fines and penalties only.
c) Item 'Other transfers' represents income accrued from sales and services.

Oman

1.7 External Transactions on Current Account, Summary

Million Rials Omani

	1980	1981	1982	1983	1984	1985	1986	1987	1988	1989	1990	1991
Payments to the Rest of the World												
1 Imports of goods and services	772.2	965.0	1135.0	1054.0	1145.0	1285.0	1145.0	873.0	1011.0	1016.0	1222.0	1497.0
A Imports of merchandise c.i.f.	661.2	833.0	991.0	906.0	1013.0	1162.0	980.0	756.0	900.0	910.0	1076.0	1279.0
B Other	111.0	132.0	144.0	148.0	132.0	123.0	165.0	117.0	111.0	106.0	146.0	218.0
2 Factor income to the rest of the world	234.0	310.0	363.0	418.0	484.0	539.0	579.0	496.0	522.0	545.0	582.0	561.0
A Compensation of employees	137.0	172.0	206.0	254.0	297.0	327.0	338.0	285.0	308.0	319.0	340.0	355.0
B Property and entrepreneurial income	97.0	138.0	157.0	164.0	187.0	212.0	241.0	211.0	214.0	226.0	242.0	206.0
3 Current transfers to the rest of the world	...	...	...	...	...	...	...	...	...	...	...	...
4 Surplus of the nation on current transactions	332.8	425.0	159.0	124.0	37.0	38.0	-383.0	314.0	-129.0	143.0	466.0	-32.0
Payments to the Rest of the World and Surplus of the Nation on Current Transactions	1339.0	1700.0	1657.0	1596.0	1666.0	1862.0	1341.0	1683.0	1404.0	1704.0	2270.0	2026.0
Receipts From The Rest of the World												
1 Exports of goods and services	1294.0	1625.0	1532.0	1475.0	1532.0	1722.0	1098.0	1468.0	1290.0	1565.0	2118.0	1873.0
2 Factor income from rest of the world	45.0	75.0	125.0	121.0	134.0	140.0	243.0	215.0	114.0	139.0	152.0	153.0
A Compensation of employees	12.0	14.0	15.0	15.0	15.0	15.0	15.0	15.0	15.0	15.0	15.0	15.0
B Property and entrepreneurial income	33.0	61.0	110.0	106.0	119.0	125.0	228.0	200.0	99.0	124.0	137.0	138.0
3 Current transfers from rest of the world	...	...	...	...	...	...	...	...	...	...	...	...
Receipts from the Rest of the World on Current Transactions	1339.0	1700.0	1657.0	1596.0	1666.0	1862.0	1341.0	1683.0	1404.0	1704.0	2270.0	2026.0

1.10 Gross Domestic Product by Kind of Activity, in Current Prices

Million Rials Omani

	1980	1981	1982	1983	1984	1985	1986	1987	1988	1989	1990	1991
1 Agriculture, hunting, forestry and fishing	52.6	62.1	66.1	80.6	89.0	93.7	95.9	105.4	123.6	117.1	133.8	143.9
2 Mining and quarrying	1280.5	1476.4	1424.7	1402.0	1468.6	1683.9	1072.4	1413.0	1202.1	1478.6	2002.2	1669.1
3 Manufacturing	15.6	27.0	39.6	49.7	72.1	82.3	103.1	111.5	122.7	137.1	152.4	168.3
4 Electricity, gas and water	16.0	18.7	21.3	24.0	32.7	36.8	40.3	43.5	46.2	48.2	59.7	62.7
5 Construction	117.8	144.9	169.8	187.4	226.9	242.2	220.8	137.0	126.0	106.0	123.3	164.1
6 Wholesale and retail trade, restaurants and hotels	188.3	251.3	299.5	315.7	369.0	428.0	383.2	327.3	388.8	393.6	468.5	540.6
7 Transport, storage and communication	38.3	53.8	64.9	72.9	84.5	99.6	103.4	97.7	108.3	112.3	129.3	146.8
8 Finance, insurance, real estate and business services	162.8	206.6	231.2	250.1	275.9	295.9	281.2	260.3	269.4	291.5	354.7	352.3
9 Community, social and personal services	13.0	16.9	20.7	25.4	31.6	36.0	38.5	40.4	45.7	49.1	57.1	71.5
Total, Industries	1884.9	2257.7	2337.8	2407.8	2650.3	2998.4	2338.8	2536.1	2432.8	2733.5	3481.0	3319.3
Producers of Government Services	194.6	260.5	305.0	360.0	423.9	477.9	495.8	509.9	535.2	548.7	658.6	669.5
Other Producers	...	...	...	...	...	...	...	...	...	...	...	...
Subtotal	2079.5	2518.2	2642.8	2767.8	3074.2	3476.3	2834.6	3046.0	2968.0	3282.2	4139.6	3988.8
Less: Imputed bank service charge	24.6	39.0	43.9	49.6	59.2	63.6	71.2	70.3	71.7	81.0	121.8	92.5
Plus: Import duties	8.6	11.3	14.7	21.7	31.7	41.1	37.0	26.9	29.6	29.4	32.9	39.5
Plus: Value added tax	...	...	...	...	...	...	...	...	...	...	...	...
Equals: Gross Domestic Product	2063.5	2490.5	2613.6	2739.9	3046.7	3453.8	2800.4	3002.6	2925.9	3230.6	4050.7	3935.8

1.11 Gross Domestic Product by Kind of Activity, in Constant Prices

Million Rials Omani

	1980	1981	1982	1983	1984	1985	1986	1987	1988	1989	1990	1991
At constant prices of:1978												
1 Agriculture, hunting, forestry and fishing	49.0	49.7	54.1	64.2	70.4	81.7	79.1	83.8	101.8	94.6	96.4	100.4
2 Mining and quarrying	438.4	501.6	505.3	599.8	645.5	775.6	880.9	935.1	1004.7	1032.4	1101.8	1133.5
3 Manufacturing	12.5	20.6	30.2	37.8	55.9	67.3	81.0	84.3	87.2	87.8	100.6	100.9
4 Electricity, gas and water	16.7	18.3	26.3	29.9	44.8	47.5	78.0	95.4	116.2	130.5	157.3	160.2
5 Construction	91.4	107.1	142.3	174.6	221.3	239.3	235.4	144.5	122.0	110.8	114.7	143.6

1.11 Gross Domestic Product by Kind of Activity, in Constant Prices
(Continued)

Million Rials Omani

	1980	1981	1982	1983	1984	1985	1986	1987	1988	1989	1990	1991
	\multicolumn{12}{c}{At constant prices of:1978}											
6 Wholesale and retail trade, restaurants and hotels	139.0	180.4	224.6	238.6	286.9	316.6	250.5	191.9	210.5	228.3	257.1	304.0
7 Transport, storage and communication	33.2	43.2	51.3	59.0	73.4	86.5	84.5	80.3	84.4	90.4	102.6	113.2
8 Finance, insurance, real estate and business services	125.5	143.5	162.4	179.1	215.6	239.6	248.3	226.1	227.4	243.4	280.8	271.1
9 Community, social and personal services	12.1	15.1	18.3	22.8	29.5	34.0	34.8	36.1	40.7	43.2	50.8	63.4
Total, Industries	917.8	1079.5	1214.8	1405.8	1643.3	1888.1	1972.5	1877.5	1994.9	2061.4	2262.1	2390.3
Producers of Government Services	144.6	170.2	176.6	203.9	235.6	248.1	239.1	259.6	263.0	277.4	281.5	308.3
Other Producers	...	...	...	...	...	...	...	...	...	...	...	...
Subtotal	1062.4	1249.7	1391.4	1609.7	1878.9	2136.2	2211.6	2137.1	2257.9	2338.8	2543.6	2698.6
Less: Imputed bank service charge	21.5	32.2	35.3	40.7	52.8	58.1	60.1	57.9	58.1	66.5	100.3	74.5
Plus: Import duties	6.3	8.1	11.0	16.3	24.5	27.1	23.9	16.2	15.6	16.6	17.7	22.0
Plus: Value added tax	...	...	...	...	...	...	...	...	...	...	...	...
Equals: Gross Domestic Product	1047.2	1225.6	1367.1	1585.3	1850.6	2105.2	2175.4	2095.4	2215.4	2288.9	2461.0	2646.1

1.12 Relations Among National Accounting Aggregates

Million Rials Omani

	1980	1981	1982	1983	1984	1985	1986	1987	1988	1989	1990	1991
Gross Domestic Product	2063.5	2490.5	2613.6	2739.9	3046.7	3453.8	2800.4	3002.6	2925.9	3230.6	4050.7	3935.8
Plus: Net factor income from the rest of the world	-189.0	-235.0	-238.0	-297.0	-350.0	-399.0	-336.0	-281.0	-408.0	-406.0	-430.0	-408.0
Factor income from the rest of the world	45.0	75.0	125.0	121.0	134.0	140.0	243.0	215.0	114.0	139.0	152.0	153.0
Less: Factor income to the rest of the world	234.0	310.0	363.0	418.0	484.0	539.0	579.0	496.0	522.0	545.0	582.0	561.0
Equals: Gross National Product	1875.4	2255.5	2375.6	2442.9	2696.7	3054.8	2464.4	2721.6	2517.9	2824.6	3620.7	3527.8
Less: Consumption of fixed capital	...	...	...	...	...	...	...	...	...	...	...	...
Equals: National Income	...	...	...	...	...	...	...	...	...	...	...	...
Plus: Net current transfers from the rest of the world	...	...	...	...	...	...	...	...	...	...	...	...
Equals: National Disposable Income	...	...	...	...	...	...	...	...	...	...	...	...
Less: Final consumption	...	...	...	...	...	...	...	...	...	...	...	...
Equals: Net Saving	...	...	...	...	...	...	...	...	...	...	...	...
Less: Surplus of the nation on current transactions	...	...	...	...	...	...	...	...	...	...	...	...
Equals: Net Capital Formation	...	...	...	...	...	...	...	...	...	...	...	...

2.1 Government Final Consumption Expenditure by Function, in Current Prices

Million Rials Omani

	1980	1981	1982	1983	1984	1985	1986	1987	1988	1989	1990	1991
1 General public services	...	...	...	...	...	...	...	...	...	...	...	...
2 Defence	430.0	565.4	605.2	654.0	665.2	773.5	749.4	723.9	763.3	777.6	1291.1	1113.5
3 Public order and safety												
4 Education	31.8	44.7	55.6	66.0	73.6	85.0	102.3	110.4	104.6	107.7	152.5	174.5
5 Health	18.5	24.6	29.6	32.5	39.2	45.8	47.1	52.1	60.2	62.0	68.0	73.1
6 Social security and welfare	...	...	...	...	...	...	...	...	...	...	...	...
7 Housing and community amenities	...	...	...	...	...	...	...	...	...	...	...	...
8 Recreational, cultural and religious affairs	...	...	...	...	...	...	...	...	...	...	...	...
9 Economic services	18.9	21.7	24.8	26.5	30.0	33.8	30.2	27.3	27.9	28.3	33.3	33.6
A Fuel and energy	...	...	...	...	...	...	...	...	...	...	...	...
B Agriculture, forestry, fishing and hunting	6.7	7.7	8.7	9.2	11.0	12.2	10.4	11.2	9.8	10.5	13.8	13.9
C Mining, manufacturing and construction, except fuel and energy	...	...	...	...	...	...	...	...	...	...	...	...
D Transportation and communication	12.2	14.0	16.1	17.3	19.0	21.6	19.8	16.1	18.1	17.8	19.5	19.7
E Other economic affairs	...	...	...	...	...	...	...	...	...	...	...	...
10 Other functions	...	...	...	...	...	...	...	...	...	...	...	...
Total Government Final Consumption Expenditure	499.2	656.4	715.2	779.0	808.0	938.1	929.0	913.7	956.0	975.6	1544.9	1394.7

Oman

4.1 Derivation of Value Added by Kind of Activity, in Current Prices

Million Rials Omani

All Producers

	1980 Gross Output	1980 Intermediate Consumption	1980 Value Added	1981 Gross Output	1981 Intermediate Consumption	1981 Value Added	1982 Gross Output	1982 Intermediate Consumption	1982 Value Added	1983 Gross Output	1983 Intermediate Consumption	1983 Value Added
1 Agriculture, hunting, forestry and fishing	73.0	20.3	52.6	86.7	24.6	62.1	91.8	25.7	66.1	112.4	31.8	80.6
A Agriculture and hunting	49.7	12.4	37.2	53.9	13.5	40.5	60.9	15.2	45.7	71.3	17.8	53.5
B Forestry and logging	...	...	...	...	...	...	...	...	...	...	...	...
C Fishing	23.3	7.9	15.4	32.8	11.2	21.7	30.9	10.5	20.4	41.1	14.0	27.1
2 Mining and quarrying	1329.1	48.7	1280.4	1544.3	67.9	1476.4	1506.1	81.4	1424.7	1483.9	81.9	1402.0
A Coal mining	...	...	...	...	...	...	...	...	...	...	...	...
B Crude petroleum and natural gas production	1327.1	47.7	1279.4	1539.1	65.3	1473.8	1498.6	77.7	1420.9	1471.3	74.8	1396.5
C Metal ore mining	...	...	...	...	...	...	...	...	...	...	...	...
D Other mining	2.0	1.0	1.0	5.2	2.6	2.6	7.5	3.7	3.8	12.6	7.1	5.5
3 Manufacturing	38.8	23.2	15.6	69.7	42.7	27.0	89.5	49.9	39.6	257.2	207.5	49.7
4 Electricity, gas and water	36.3	20.3	16.0	47.9	29.2	18.7	53.4	32.1	21.3	63.7	39.7	24.0
A Electricity, gas and steam	30.2	17.5	12.7	40.3	26.4	13.9	44.3	28.4	15.9	52.1	35.6	16.5
B Water works and supply	6.1	2.8	3.3	7.6	2.8	4.8	9.1	3.7	5.4	11.6	4.1	7.5
5 Construction	294.5	176.7	117.8	362.4	217.5	145.0	424.6	254.8	169.8	468.8	281.4	187.4
6 Wholesale and retail trade, restaurants and hotels	277.4	89.1	188.3	367.1	115.7	251.3	438.2	138.8	299.5	463.4	147.8	315.7
A Wholesale and retail trade	261.6	78.5	183.1	346.3	103.9	242.4	412.6	123.8	288.8	432.8	129.9	303.0
B Restaurants and hotels	15.8	10.6	5.2	20.7	11.8	8.9	25.7	15.0	10.7	30.6	17.9	12.7
7 Transport, storage and communication	70.9	32.6	38.3	91.2	37.4	53.8	108.5	43.6	64.9	121.1	48.2	72.9
A Transport and storage	57.0	24.9	32.1	74.3	32.3	42.0	87.6	38.0	49.6	94.4	41.1	53.3
B Communication	13.9	7.7	6.2	16.9	5.1	11.8	20.9	5.6	15.3	26.7	7.1	19.6
8 Finance, insurance, real estate and business services	187.4	24.5	162.9	234.4	27.8	206.6	261.7	30.5	231.2	285.3	35.2	250.1
A Financial institutions	39.3	8.2	31.1	53.7	9.0	44.7	62.2	10.4	51.8	69.3	12.9	56.4
B Insurance	5.4	2.1	3.3	5.7	1.3	4.4	11.3	1.3	10.0	8.8	1.6	7.2
C Real estate and business services	142.8	14.3	128.5	175.1	17.5	157.6	188.2	18.8	169.4	207.2	20.7	186.5
9 Community, social and personal services	17.4	4.4	13.0	22.4	5.5	16.8	27.5	6.8	20.7	33.7	8.3	25.4
A Sanitary and similar services	...	...	...	...	...	...	...	...	...	...	...	...
B Social and related community services	2.0	0.4	1.6	2.7	0.5	2.2	3.5	0.7	2.8	4.4	0.9	3.5
Educational services	1.5	0.3	1.2	1.9	0.4	1.5	2.4	0.5	1.9	3.0	0.6	2.4
Medical, dental, other health and veterinary services	0.5	0.1	0.4	0.8	0.2	0.7	1.1	0.2	0.9	1.4	0.3	1.1
C Recreational and cultural services	8.6	3.4	5.2	10.7	4.2	6.5	12.9	5.0	7.9	15.3	6.0	9.3
D Personal and household services	6.8	0.6	6.2	8.9	0.8	8.1	11.1	1.1	10.0	14.0	1.4	12.6
Total, Industries	2324.8	439.7	1884.9	2826.1	568.3	2257.7	3001.3	663.6	2337.8	3289.5	881.8	2407.8
Producers of Government Services	500.8	306.2	194.6	659.4	398.9	260.5	718.9	413.9	305.0	783.5	423.5	360.0
Other Producers	...	...	...	...	...	...	...	...	...	...	...	...
Total	2825.5	745.9	2079.5	3485.5	967.2	2518.2	3720.2	1077.5	2642.8	4073.0	1305.3	2767.8
Less: Imputed bank service charge	...	-24.6	24.6	...	-39.0	39.0	...	-43.9	43.9	...	-49.6	49.6
Import duties	8.6	...	8.6	11.3	...	11.3	14.7	...	14.7	21.7	...	21.7
Value added tax	...	...	...	...	...	...	...	...	...	...	...	...
Total	2834.2	770.5	2063.5	3496.8	1006.2	2490.5	3734.9	1121.4	2613.6	4094.7	1354.9	2739.9

All Producers

	1984 Gross Output	1984 Intermediate Consumption	1984 Value Added	1985 Gross Output	1985 Intermediate Consumption	1985 Value Added	1986 Gross Output	1986 Intermediate Consumption	1986 Value Added	1987 Gross Output	1987 Intermediate Consumption	1987 Value Added
1 Agriculture, hunting, forestry and fishing	124.5	35.5	89.0	129.7	36.0	93.7	132.9	37.0	95.9	147.9	42.5	105.4
A Agriculture and hunting	76.2	19.1	57.1	90.0	22.5	67.5	90.9	22.7	68.2	95.1	24.5	70.6
B Forestry and logging	...	...	...	...	...	...	...	...	...	...	...	...
C Fishing	48.3	16.4	31.9	39.7	13.5	26.2	42.0	14.3	27.7	52.8	18.0	34.8
2 Mining and quarrying	1561.5	92.9	1468.6	1791.2	107.3	1683.9	1191.5	119.1	1072.4	1509.3	96.3	1413.0
A Coal mining	...	...	...	...	...	...	...	...	...	...	...	...
B Crude petroleum and natural gas production	1544.4	83.1	1461.4	1770.7	95.6	1675.1	1172.8	109.7	1063.1	1492.1	87.4	1404.7
C Metal ore mining	...	...	...	...	...	...	...	...	...	...	...	...
D Other mining	17.0	9.8	7.2	20.5	11.7	8.8	18.7	9.4	9.3	17.2	8.8	8.3

4.1 Derivation of Value Added by Kind of Activity, in Current Prices
(Continued)

Million Rials Omani

	1984			1985			1986			1987		
	Gross Output	Intermediate Consumption	Value Added	Gross Output	Intermediate Consumption	Value Added	Gross Output	Intermediate Consumption	Value Added	Gross Output	Intermediate Consumption	Value Added
3 Manufacturing	319.0	246.9	72.1	372.0	289.7	82.3	392.3	289.1	103.1	380.1	268.6	111.5
4 Electricity, gas and water	77.7	45.0	32.7	92.5	55.7	36.8	97.2	56.8	40.4	108.6	65.1	43.5
A Electricity, gas and steam	65.1	39.9	25.2	76.2	49.1	27.1	80.6	50.8	29.8	86.6	58.6	28.0
B Water works and supply	12.6	5.1	7.5	16.3	6.6	9.7	16.6	6.0	10.6	22.0	6.5	15.5
5 Construction	567.2	340.3	226.9	605.5	363.3	242.2	551.9	331.1	220.8	342.5	205.5	137.0
6 Wholesale and retail trade, restaurants and hotels	541.9	172.8	369.1	626.8	198.9	427.9	563.9	180.8	383.2	483.9	156.6	327.3
A Wholesale and retail trade	506.2	151.8	354.3	588.8	176.6	412.2	523.4	157.0	366.4	444.3	133.3	311.0
B Restaurants and hotels	35.7	21.0	14.7	38.0	22.3	15.7	40.5	23.7	16.8	39.6	23.3	16.3
7 Transport, storage and communication	139.1	54.6	84.5	163.9	64.3	99.6	169.9	66.6	103.4	162.8	65.1	97.7
A Transport and storage	106.4	46.2	60.2	120.7	52.5	68.2	122.0	53.4	68.7	115.0	50.9	64.1
B Communication	32.7	8.4	24.3	43.2	11.8	31.4	47.9	13.2	34.7	47.8	14.2	33.6
8 Finance, insurance, real estate and business services	315.4	39.5	275.9	333.0	37.1	295.9	321.6	40.4	281.2	298.5	38.2	260.3
A Financial institutions	80.5	14.2	66.3	84.9	11.1	73.8	96.0	17.5	78.5	89.6	15.3	74.3
B Insurance	15.6	3.4	12.2	20.2	3.2	17.0	17.0	2.0	15.0	13.6	3.4	10.2
C Real estate and business services	219.3	21.9	197.4	227.8	22.8	205.0	208.6	20.9	187.7	195.3	19.5	175.8
9 Community, social and personal services	41.9	10.3	31.6	47.9	11.9	36.0	51.3	12.9	38.4	53.9	13.4	40.4
A Sanitary and similar services	...	...	...	...	...	...	...	...	...	...	...	...
B Social and related community services	5.9	1.2	4.8	8.0	1.6	6.4	8.9	1.8	7.1	9.1	1.8	7.3
Educational services	4.1	0.8	3.3	5.8	1.1	4.7	6.5	1.3	5.2	6.6	1.3	5.3
Medical, dental, other health and veterinary services	1.8	0.4	1.5	2.2	0.5	1.7	2.4	0.5	1.9	2.5	0.5	2.0
C Recreational and cultural services	17.4	6.8	10.6	19.9	7.8	12.1	21.4	8.4	13.0	22.2	8.7	13.5
D Personal and household services	18.5	2.3	16.3	19.9	2.5	17.4	21.0	2.7	18.4	22.5	2.8	19.6
Total, Industries	3688.2	1037.8	2650.4	4162.6	1164.2	2998.4	3472.5	1133.7	2338.8	3487.4	951.2	2536.2
Producers of Government Services	810.9	387.0	423.9	897.7	419.8	477.9	853.4	357.6	495.8	916.6	406.7	509.9
Other Producers	...	...	...	...	...	...	...	...	...	...	...	...
Total	4499.1	1424.8	3074.3	5060.3	1584.0	3476.3	4325.9	1491.3	2834.6	4404.0	1357.9	3046.1
Less: Imputed bank service charge	...	-59.2	59.2	...	-63.6	63.6	...	-71.2	71.2	...	-70.3	70.3
Import duties	31.7	...	31.7	41.1	...	41.1	37.0	...	37.0	26.9	...	26.9
Value added tax	...	...	...	...	...	...	...	...	...	...	...	...
Total	4530.8	1484.0	3046.8	5101.4	1647.6	3453.8	4362.9	1562.5	2800.4	4430.9	1428.2	3002.6

	1988			1989			1990			1991		
	Gross Output	Intermediate Consumption	Value Added	Gross Output	Intermediate Consumption	Value Added	Gross Output	Intermediate Consumption	Value Added	Gross Output	Intermediate Consumption	Value Added
						All Producers						
1 Agriculture, hunting, forestry and fishing	173.2	49.6	123.6	162.3	45.2	117.1	187.3	53.5	133.8	201.0	57.1	143.9
A Agriculture and hunting	103.8	26.0	77.8	110.9	27.7	83.2	112.9	28.2	84.7	124.4	31.1	93.3
B Forestry and logging	...	...	...	...	...	...	...	...	...	...	...	...
C Fishing	69.4	23.6	45.8	51.4	17.5	33.9	74.4	25.3	49.1	76.6	26.0	50.6
2 Mining and quarrying	1301.2	99.1	1202.1	1581.6	103.0	1478.6	2116.8	114.6	2002.2	1796.5	127.4	1669.1
A Coal mining	...	...	...	...	...	...	...	...	...	...	...	...
B Crude petroleum and natural gas production	1277.9	89.8	1188.1	1556.9	93.9	1462.0	2096.1	105.8	1990.3	1775.0	116.6	1658.4
C Metal ore mining	...	...	...	...	...	...	...	...	...	...	...	...
D Other mining	23.3	9.3	14.0	25.7	9.1	16.6	20.7	8.8	11.9	21.5	10.8	10.7
3 Manufacturing	429.1	306.4	122.7	464.7	327.6	137.1	538.2	385.8	152.4	574.5	406.2	168.3
4 Electricity, gas and water	114.0	67.8	46.2	117.0	68.8	48.2	125.0	65.3	59.7	130.9	68.2	62.7
A Electricity, gas and steam	90.5	62.0	28.4	91.1	63.7	27.4	97.1	59.7	37.4	94.7	61.0	33.7
B Water works and supply	23.6	5.8	17.8	25.9	5.1	20.8	27.9	5.6	22.3	36.2	7.2	29.0

Oman

4.1 Derivation of Value Added by Kind of Activity, in Current Prices
(Continued)

Million Rials Omani

	1988			1989			1990			1991		
	Gross Output	Intermediate Consumption	Value Added	Gross Output	Intermediate Consumption	Value Added	Gross Output	Intermediate Consumption	Value Added	Gross Output	Intermediate Consumption	Value Added
5 Construction	315.0	189.0	126.0	265.0	159.0	106.0	308.3	185.0	123.3	410.3	246.2	164.1
6 Wholesale and retail trade, restaurants and hotels	574.5	185.7	388.8	582.6	189.0	393.6	693.7	225.2	468.5	798.2	257.6	540.6
A Wholesale and retail trade	528.6	158.6	370.0	532.9	159.9	373.1	634.1	190.2	443.9	735.1	220.5	514.6
B Restaurants and hotels	45.9	27.1	18.8	49.7	29.2	20.5	59.6	35.0	24.6	63.1	37.1	26.0
7 Transport, storage and communication	174.6	66.3	108.3	178.8	66.5	112.3	203.2	73.9	129.3	230.6	83.8	146.8
A Transport and storage	127.7	56.1	71.6	127.8	56.5	71.2	145.0	63.8	81.2	164.8	72.2	92.6
B Communication	46.9	10.2	36.7	51.0	9.9	41.1	58.2	10.1	48.1	65.8	11.6	54.2
8 Finance, insurance, real estate and business services	307.8	38.4	269.4	332.7	41.2	291.5	399.8	45.1	354.7	399.8	47.5	352.3
A Financial institutions	91.8	14.8	77.0	103.8	16.1	87.7	140.1	16.6	123.5	112.8	16.0	96.8
B Insurance	15.0	3.5	11.5	16.8	3.9	12.9	18.9	4.4	14.5	21.1	4.9	16.2
C Real estate and business services	201.0	20.1	180.9	212.1	21.2	190.9	240.8	24.1	216.7	265.9	26.6	239.3
9 Community, social and personal services	59.7	14.0	45.7	64.7	15.6	49.1	75.5	18.4	57.1	92.2	20.7	71.5
A Sanitary and similar services	...	...	...	...	...	...	...	...	...	...	...	...
B Social and related community services	9.9	1.9	8.0	11.9	2.4	9.5	15.7	3.2	12.5	18.6	3.7	14.9
Educational services	7.2	1.4	5.8	7.8	1.6	6.2	10.8	2.2	8.6	12.4	2.5	9.9
Medical, dental, other health and veterinary services	2.7	0.5	2.2	4.1	0.8	3.3	4.9	1.0	3.9	6.2	1.2	5.0
C Recreational and cultural services	22.7	9.0	13.7	24.1	9.5	14.6	26.6	10.5	16.1	29.1	11.4	17.7
D Personal and household services	27.1	3.1	24.0	28.7	3.7	25.0	33.2	4.7	28.5	44.5	5.6	38.9
Total, Industries	3449.1	1016.3	2432.8	3749.4	1015.9	2733.5	4647.8	1166.8	3481.0	4634.0	1314.7	3319.3
Producers of Government Services	958.4	423.2	535.2	975.6	426.9	548.7	1549.0	890.4	658.6	1399.5	730.0	669.5
Other Producers	...	...	...	...	...	...	...	...	...	...	...	...
Total	4407.5	1439.5	2968.0	4725.0	1442.8	3282.2	6196.8	2057.2	4139.6	6033.5	2044.7	3988.8
Less: Imputed bank service charge	...	-71.7	71.7	...	-81.0	81.0	...	-121.8	121.8	...	-92.5	92.5
Import duties	29.6	...	29.6	29.4	...	29.4	32.9	...	32.9	39.5	...	39.5
Value added tax	...	...	...	...	...	...	...	...	...	...	...	...
Total	4437.1	1511.2	2925.9	4754.4	1523.8	3230.6	6229.7	2179.0	4050.7	6073.0	2137.2	3935.8

Pakistan

General note. The preparation of national accounts statistics in Pakistan is undertaken by the Federal Bureau of Statistics (FBS), Statistics Division of the Ministry of Finance and Economic Affairs, Islamabad. The official estimates and methodological notes on sources and methods are published in a series of reports entitled 'National Accounts of Pakistan'. The estimates are generally in accordance with the classifications and definitions recommended in the United Nations System of National Accounts (SNA). The following tables have been prepared from successive replies to the United Nations national accounts questionnaire. Estimates relate to fiscal year beginning 1 July. When the scope and coverge of the estimates differ for conceptual or statistical reasons from the definitions and classifications recommended in SNA, a footnote is indicated to the relevant tables.

Sources and methods Sources and methods:

(a) Gross domestic product. Gross domestic product is estimated mainly through the production approach.

(b) Expenditure on the gross domestic product. The expenditure approach is used to estimate government final consumption expenditure and exports and imports of goods and services. This approach, in combination with the commodity-flow approach is used to estimate gross capital formation. Private final consumption expenditure is derived as a residual. Government consumption expenditure is estimated by analysing the budgets of the government bodies with an element of estimation made for the local sector for which the budget are difficult to obtain. The basic information used in estimating increase in stocks is received from the Planning Commission. The estimates of gross fixed capital formation are classified by economic sectors. Benchmark estimates of agriculture are derived from 1980 Agriculture Census adjusted for 1980-81 and non-monetized investment are based on Survey results conducted by FBS. Investment in the mining and quarrying sector is estimated on the basis of data obtained from annual censuses of mining industries and from concerned source agencies. For large scale manufacturing, investment estimates are based on annual sample surveys while the small industries surveys in 1976-77 and 1983-84 provided data for investment in small industries. Investment in machinery and equipment of the agricultural and mining sectors is estimated by the commodity-flow method. For the service sector, estimates are prepared from trade and domestic production data, annual budgets and annual questionnaires. Estimates of private residential construction are based on the rural construction survey, census reports, population growth and number of persons per household. Capital expenditure for the government bodies are based on the classification of their budgets. The estimates of exports of goods and services are obtained from the trade statistics of the FBS and the balance-of-payments statistics. For constant price estimates, all items of GDP by expenditure type are deflated by appropriate price indexes except gross fixed capital formation which is extrapolated by quantity indicators. Private consumption expenditure is obtained as residual.

(c) Cost-structure of the gross domestic product. Domestic factor incomes consisting of compensation of employees and operating surplus, is obtained as a residual, i.e., after subtracting depreciation and net indirect taxes from GDP. For depreciation, a flat rate is applied for the different sectors, 5 per cent for agriculture, mining and quarrying, small-scale manufacturing, public administration and defence and other private services, 10 per cent for large-scale manufacturing and parts of road transport, 2.5 per cent for construction, 2 per cent for trade and 20 per cent for ownership of dwellings in the rural areas and 25 per cent in the urban areas. Data of indirect taxes and subsidies are derived from budgets of the government bodies.

(d) Gross domestic product by kind of economic activity. The table of GDP by kind of economic activity is prepared in factor values. The production approach is used to estimate value added in agriculture, mining and quarrying, manufacturing and electricity. The income approach is used for most of the remaining sectors. Production data of major agricultural crops are obtained from the Ministry of Agriculture. Corresponding harvest prices are obtained from the Provincial Directorates of Land Records. Minor crops harvest prices are taken at 80 per cent of the wholesale prices. Data on livestock products and wholesale prices are obtained from the Department of Agricultural Marketing and Grading. The current price estimates are derived indirectly by applying the wholesale price index to the constant price estimates. Production and price data of forestry and fishing are obtained from concerned departments. The Natural Resources Division and the Provincial Mineral Development Department provide production and price data for the mining sector. Gross value of output is obtained by multiplying the output of each mineral by pit-head or well-head prices in the benchmark year while annual output and index of wholesale prices are used for the current estimates. Benchmark estimates for large-scale manufacturing are mainly based on the adjusted figures of 1980-81 census of manufacturing industries. Other years' estimates are obtained by applying the quantum index of manufacturing to the benchmark value. For small-scale manufacturing, benchmark 1980-81 was computed on the basis of survey reports on SHMI for 1976-77 and 1983-84 and employment data from 1981 Population Census and Labour Force Surveys 1982-83 and 1984-85. The estimates for electricity and gas are based on data furnished by concerned companies while the estimates of water are included in public administration and defence sector. For construction estimates are based on gross fixed capital formation data in construction activity collected on annual basis by FBS, and its value added coefficients obtained from concerned construction agencies/companies. Value added at constant factor cost thus obtained are adjusted by wholesale price index for manufacturing to arrive at current estimates. The value added of the trade sector is measured by net trade margins earned by traders on various types of products entering into wholesale and retail trade. Trade margins are derived from distributive Trade Survey 1983-84. For the transport sector, estimates are based on data supplied by concerned enterprises and FBS surveys on mechanized and non-mechanized road transport. For the financial sector, value added is based on data provided by the State Bank of Pakistan and various financial institutions. Estimates of ownership of dwellings are based on Housing Census 1980, HED Survey 1973 and Construction Survey 1986. For government services, the budgets of the government bodies are used. For private services, the number of persons engaged in the different occupations is obtained from the 1981 Population Census and extrapolated by the intercensal growth rate in the working force of this sector. For constant price estimates, double deflation is used for agriculture. Price deflation is used for forestry and fishing, electricity and gas, transport, financial and community services. For mining, the annual output of each mineral is multipled by the base year pit-head and well-head prices. Value added of the trade sector is obtained from the distribution of agricultural produce, manufactured and imported goods. Value added of manufacturing construction and ownership of dwellings is extrapolated by quantum indexes.

1.1 Expenditure on the Gross Domestic Product, in Current Prices

Million Pakistan rupees — Fiscal year beginning 1 July

	1980	1981	1982	1983	1984	1985	1986	1987	1988	1989	1990	1991
1 Government final consumption expenditure	28276	33522	41606	50741	57126	65662	77482	104754	129201	129562	145575	155569
2 Private final consumption expenditure	224135	263658	291942	336747	385346	392532	415674	486565	543297	611710	701629	875010
3 Gross capital formation	52207	62447	68462	76701	86525	96545	109540	121666	145570	162076	190961	224560
A Increase in stocks	4500	7858	6701	7489	8600	9000	9500	10400	12400	14000	15800	18300
B Gross fixed capital formation	47707	54589	61761	69212	77925	87545	100040	111266	133170	148076	175161	206260
Residential buildings	1703	2333	2584	2812	3263	3938	3940	4389	16690	17130	19931	21924
Non-residential buildings	3209	3964	3678	4957	5568	6179	6834	7676	25089	18912	23704	26075
Other construction and land improvement etc.	16605	19110	21182	22478	25220	27624	32043	35560	27482	33595	44299	54776
Other	26189	29182	34317	38965	43874	49804	57223	63641	63909	78439	87227	103485
4 Exports of goods and services	35707	33033	44395	47835	49889	63268	79056	93601	108318	126583	172812	202963
5 Less: Imports of goods and services	62129	68501	82018	92222	106729	103475	109273	131197	156641	173293	188681	255756
Equals: Gross Domestic Product	278196	324159	364387	419802	472157	514532	572479	675389	769745	856638	1022296	1202346

Pakistan

1.2 Expenditure on the Gross Domestic Product, in Constant Prices

Million Pakistan rupees

	1980	1981	1982	1983	1984	1985	1986	1987	1988	1989	1990	1991
	At constant prices of:1980											
1 Government final consumption expenditure	28276	30744	36228	40716	43467	47826	54158	56518	68052	65895	65566	63804
2 Private final consumption expenditure	224135	234239	243703	258725	281173	278194	288006	317345	319912	337404	335754	389961
3 Gross capital formation	52207	59665	63426	66459	73218	76382	79575	78551	84447	86012	85996	90645
A Increase in stocks	4500	7319	5924	6018	6570	6572	6606	6574	7147	7520	7596	7995
B Gross fixed capital formation	47707	52346	57502	60441	66648	69807	72969	71977	77300	78492	78400	82650
4 Exports of goods and services	35707	33570	41819	40275	40130	53296	59868	57112	64979	65710	87700	96218
5 Less: Imports of goods and services	62129	61835	68703	73672	80241	78266	79825	77107	83524	80601	74639	101273
Equals: Gross Domestic Product	278196	296383	316473	332503	357747	377432	401782	432419	453866	474420	500377	539355

1.3 Cost Components of the Gross Domestic Product

Million Pakistan rupees

	1980	1981	1982	1983	1984	1985	1986	1987	1988	1989	1990	1991
1 Indirect taxes, net	30365	32006	35975	45453	47093	48213	57048	74364	86607	96092	112226	147515
A Indirect taxes	35562	37440	43487	53557	56396	58205	64422	84494	99361	108641	123437	155889
B Less: Subsidies	5197	5434	7512	8104	9303	9992	7374	10130	12754	12549	11211	8374
2 Consumption of fixed capital	16124	18923	21893	25563	28719	31526	34736	39242	43772	49871	60437	69989
3 Compensation of employees paid by resident producers to:	231707	273230	306519	348786	396345	434793	480695	561783	639366	710675	849633	984842
4 Operating surplus												
Equals: Gross Domestic Product	278196	324159	364387	419802	472157	514532	572479	675389	769745	856638	1022296	1202346

1.10 Gross Domestic Product by Kind of Activity, in Current Prices

Million Pakistan rupees

	1980	1981	1982	1983	1984	1985	1986	1987	1988	1989	1990	1991
1 Agriculture, hunting, forestry and fishing	76399	92216	99380	104550	121293	128801	135308	156375	184074	197441	233337	268103
2 Mining and quarrying	1053	1215	1342	1599	2064	3281	3681	4811	4932	5403	6507	7302
3 Manufacturing	37446	44197	50200	60398	67596	75881	85850	100917	113517	132329	158947	185546
4 Electricity, gas and water	5928	6436	7284	8270	8740	10639	11789	15690	17093	21470	29672	34034
5 Construction	11586	13172	13666	14716	17116	19052	22508	25109	27706	32052	38172	46199
6 Wholesale and retail trade, restaurants and hotels a	37330	44165	49957	58221	67632	72742	80886	100585	115810	129135	154609	177335
7 Transport, storage and communication	23927	27425	31092	35199	38219	41196	44624	51047	54316	60487	76463	94161
8 Finance, insurance, real estate and business services	16786	20405	25117	30915	34905	38317	41806	46272	50303	56255	67469	77222
9 Community, social and personal services ab	18119	21456	23907	27348	30785	34357	37961	42910	50208	56859	68376	80111
Total, Industries	228574	270687	301945	341216	388350	424266	464413	543716	617959	691431	833552	970013
Producers of Government Services	19257	21466	26467	33133	36714	42053	51018	57309	65179	69115	76518	84818
Other Producers b	...	...	...	...	...	...	...	...	...	...	...	...
Subtotal c	247831	292153	328412	374349	425064	466319	515431	601025	683138	760546	910070	1054831
Less: Imputed bank service charge	...	...	...	...	...	...	...	...	...	...	...	...
Plus: Import duties	...	...	...	...	...	...	...	...	...	...	...	...
Plus: Value added tax	...	...	...	...	...	...	...	...	...	...	...	...
Plus: Other adjustments d	30365	32006	35975	45453	47093	48213	57048	74364	86607	96092	112226	147515
Equals: Gross Domestic Product	278196	324159	364387	419802	472157	514532	572479	675389	769745	856638	1022296	1202346

a) Restaurants and hotels are included in item 'Community, social and personal services'.
b) Item 'Other producers' is included in item 'Community, social and personal services'.
c) Gross domestic product in factor values.
d) Item 'Other adjustments' refers to indirect taxes net of subsidies.

1.11 Gross Domestic Product by Kind of Activity, in Constant Prices

Million Pakistan rupees

	1980	1981	1982	1983	1984	1985	1986	1987	1988	1989	1990	1991
	At constant prices of:1980											
1 Agriculture, hunting, forestry and fishing	76399	80008	83532	79502	88187	93433	96473	99108	105917	109127	114649	121992
2 Mining and quarrying	1053	1167	1164	1181	1340	1657	1782	2029	2071	2269	2514	2624
3 Manufacturing	37446	42596	45592	49187	53166	57180	61484	67622	70300	74324	79023	85104
4 Electricity, gas and water	5928	6023	6425	7295	7486	8362	9207	10711	12125	13896	15337	16423
5 Construction	11586	12242	11910	12025	13155	14035	15784	16563	16937	17466	18462	19556

1.11 Gross Domestic Product by Kind of Activity, in Constant Prices
(Continued)

Million Pakistan rupees   Fiscal year beginning 1 July

	1980	1981	1982	1983	1984	1985	1986	1987	1988	1989	1990	1991
At constant prices of:1980												
6 Wholesale and retail trade, restaurants and hotels a	37330	40957	44397	46440	51876	55361	58661	63932	67305	69655	73520	79085
7 Transport, storage and communication	23927	25910	27971	30283	32688	34305	36785	39293	37716	40184	42378	45315
8 Finance, insurance, real estate and business services	16786	18832	21623	24967	26601	27848	28895	30280	31671	33197	34752	36225
9 Community, social and personal services ab	18119	19302	20563	21905	23336	24860	26483	28212	30054	32017	34108	36335
Total, Industries	228574	247037	263177	272785	297835	317041	335554	357750	374096	392135	414743	442659
Producers of Government Services	19257	19534	21490	23192	23916	25183	26556	27666	29852	30667	31679	32246
Other Producers b	...	...	...	...	...	...	...	...	...	...	...	...
Subtotal c	247831	266571	284667	295977	321751	342224	362110	385416	403948	422802	446422	474905
Less: Imputed bank service charge	...	...	...	...	...	...	...	...	...	...	...	...
Plus: Import duties	...	...	...	...	...	...	...	...	...	...	...	...
Plus: Value added tax	...	...	...	...	...	...	...	...	...	...	...	...
Plus: Other adjustments d	30365	29812	31806	36526	35996	35205	39672	47003	49918	51618	53955	64450
Equals: Gross Domestic Product	278196	296383	316473	332503	357747	377429	401782	432419	453866	474420	500377	539355

a) Restaurants and hotels are included in item 'Community, social and personal services'.
b) Item 'Other producers' is included in item 'Community, social and personal services'.
c) Gross domestic product in factor values.
d) Item 'Other adjustments' refers to indirect taxes net of subsidies.

1.12 Relations Among National Accounting Aggregates

Million Pakistan rupees   Fiscal year beginning 1 July

	1980	1981	1982	1983	1984	1985	1986	1987	1988	1989	1990	1991
Gross Domestic Product	278196	324159	364387	419802	472157	514532	572479	675389	769745	856638	1022296	1202346
Plus: Net factor income from the rest of the world	22692	25349	39395	39595	38311	41359	36378	29095	28005	36900	30795	23046
Equals: Gross National Product	300888	349508	403782	459397	510468	555891	608857	704484	797750	893538	1053091	1225392
Less: Consumption of fixed capital	16124	18923	21893	25563	28719	31526	34736	39242	43772	49871	60437	69989
Equals: National Income	284764	330585	381889	433834	481749	524365	574121	665242	753978	843667	992654	1155403
Plus: Net current transfers from the rest of the world	...	...	...	...	...	...	...	...	...	...	...	...
Equals: National Disposable Income	...	...	...	...	...	...	...	...	...	...	...	...
Less: Final consumption	...	...	...	...	...	...	...	...	...	...	...	...
Equals: Net Saving	...	...	...	...	...	...	...	...	...	...	...	...
Less: Surplus of the nation on current transactions	...	...	...	...	...	...	...	...	...	...	...	...
Equals: Net Capital Formation	...	...	...	...	...	...	...	...	...	...	...	...

2.1 Government Final Consumption Expenditure by Function, in Current Prices

Million Pakistan rupees   Fiscal year beginning 1 July

	1980	1981	1982	1983	1984	1985	1986	1987	1988	1989	1990	1991
1 General public services	16890	20630	25212	30769	34215	38805	45202	67290	72009	76373	83236	88540
2 Defence												
3 Public order and safety	2151	2225	2823	3766	4275	4934	5951	6514	8718	9308	10797	11800
4 Education	3280	3739	4882	6177	5440	6454	7992	8889	16049	12852	15202	16332
5 Health	1060	1214	1585	2055	2518	2949	3390	4107	6041	5637	6551	6986
6 Social security and welfare	905	1175	1538	1644	1695	1987	2486	2797	3799	4113	4794	5140
7 Housing and community amenities	668	783	750	959	958	1128	1319	1548	1746	1995	2197	2290
8 Recreational, cultural and religious affairs	122	130	157	201	229	268	376	493	590	616	673	702
9 Economic services	3102	3505	4109	4637	7244	8502	10018	12328	19451	17590	20855	22414
A Fuel and energy	124	143	159	202	232	271	308	386	437	440	477	481
B Agriculture, forestry, fishing and hunting	1755	1981	2737	3231	5633	6627	7860	9281	13502	13479	16156	17407
C Mining, manufacturing and construction, except fuel and energy	124	142	190	204	331	384	441	532	2076	762	900	976
D Transportation and communication	389	499	558	616	582	677	767	987	1212	1331	1563	1690
E Other economic affairs	710	740	465	384	466	543	642	1142	2224	1578	1759	1860
10 Other functions	98	121	550	533	552	635	748	788	798	1078	1270	1365
Total Government Final Consumption Expenditure	28276	33522	41606	50741	57126	65662	77482	104754	129201	129562	145575	155569

Pakistan

2.3 Total Government Outlays by Function and Type

Million Pakistan rupees

Fiscal year beginning 1 July

	Final Consumption Expenditures			Subsidies	Other Current Transfers & Property Income	Total Current Disbursements	Gross Capital Formation	Other Capital Outlays	Total Outlays
	Total	Compensation of Employees	Other						
1980									
1 General public services	16890	9067	7823	23	468	17381	1947	5	19333
2 Defence									
3 Public order and safety	2151	1612	539	-	722	2873	164	-	3037
4 Education	3280	2755	525	-	90	3370	698	2	4070
5 Health	1060	535	525	10	47	1117	642	-	1759
6 Social security and welfare	905	811	94	-	487	1392	19	-	1411
7 Housing and community amenities	668	441	227	6	-	674	639	-	1313
8 Recreation, culture and religion	122	56	66	164	82	368	203	-	571
9 Economic services	3102	1361	1741	4774	5637	13513	4943	18024	36480
A Fuel and energy	124	36	88	-	-	124	682	16	822
B Agriculture, forestry, fishing and hunting	1755	740	1015	4717	2013	8485	1452	14026	23963
C Mining (except fuels), manufacturing and construction	124	51	73	-	613	737	202	-	939
D Transportation and communication	389	124	265	32	2893	3314	2536	2464	8314
E Other economic affairs	710	410	300	25	118	853	71	1518	2442
10 Other functions	98	35	63	220	18923	19241	315	167612	187168
Total	28276	16673	11603	5197	26456	59929	9570	185643	255142
1981									
1 General public services	20630	10257	10373	37	1294	21961	3721	28	25710
2 Defence									
3 Public order and safety	2225	1563	662	-	15	2240	177	-	2417
4 Education	3739	3188	551	-	852	4591	935	1	5527
5 Health	1214	605	609	16	56	1286	894	-	2180
6 Social security and welfare	1175	803	372	-	36	1211	29	-	1240
7 Housing and community amenities	783	502	281	10	958	1751	813	1	2565
8 Recreation, culture and religion	130	66	64	-	58	188	254	-	442
9 Economic services	3505	1562	1943	5011	3909	12425	5569	13615	31609
A Fuel and energy	143	42	101	-	-	143	868	4	1015
B Agriculture, forestry, fishing and hunting	1981	857	1124	5009	1384	8374	1466	10595	20435
C Mining (except fuels), manufacturing and construction	142	65	77	-	448	590	91	-	681
D Transportation and communication	499	145	354	-	1993	2492	44	1608	4144
E Other economic affairs	740	453	287	2	84	826	3100	1408	5334
10 Other functions	121	39	82	360	4693	5174	287	314007	319468
Total	33522	18585	14937	5434	11871	50827	12679	327652	391158
1982									
1 General public services	25212	11919	13293	617	1751	27580	2449	44	30073
2 Defence									
3 Public order and safety	2823	2086	737	-	19	2842	268	2	3112
4 Education	4882	4023	859	-	1078	5960	871	-	6831
5 Health	1585	739	846	-	84	1669	694	29	2392
6 Social security and welfare	1538	1373	165	-	97	1635	22	-	1657
7 Housing and community amenities	750	456	294	10	566	1326	946	4	2276
8 Recreation, culture and religion	157	74	83	-	90	247	166	-	413
9 Economic services	4109	1893	2216	6635	2358	13102	6829	18054	37985
A Fuel and energy	159	68	91	15	-	174	656	6	836
B Agriculture, forestry, fishing and hunting	2737	1297	1440	3156	1111	7004	1877	15192	24073
C Mining (except fuels), manufacturing and construction	190	99	91	1723	385	2298	48	162	2508
D Transportation and communication	558	133	425	36	81	675	4098	156	4929
E Other economic affairs	465	296	169	1705	781	2951	150	2538	5639
10 Other functions	550	353	197	250	9398	10198	895	209441	220534
Total	41606	22916	18690	7512	15441	64559	13140	227574	305273

2.3 Total Government Outlays by Function and Type
(Continued)

Million Pakistan rupees

	Final Consumption Expenditures			Subsidies	Other Current Transfers & Property Income	Total Current Disbursements	Gross Capital Formation	Other Capital Outlays	Total Outlays
	Total	Compensation of Employees	Other						
1983									
1 General public services	30769	15142	15627	1595	1670	34034	2974	34	37042
2 Defence									
3 Public order and safety	3766	2866	900	-	8	3774	373	-	4147
4 Education	6177	5025	1152	1	1080	7258	1285	-	8543
5 Health	2055	1020	1035	-	172	2227	1037	-	3264
6 Social security and welfare	1644	1483	161	-	30	1674	20	-	1694
7 Housing and community amenities	959	486	473	-	515	1474	1097	-	2571
8 Recreation, culture and religion	201	90	111	-	123	324	215	-	539
9 Economic services	4637	2249	2388	6508	12725	23870	6948	12285	43103
A Fuel and energy	202	89	113	15	1132	1349	726	30	2105
B Agriculture, forestry, fishing and hunting	3231	1613	1618	4546	1954	9731	2188	12052	23971
C Mining (except fuels), manufacturing and construction	204	85	119	-	1151	1355	68	157	1580
D Transportation and communication	616	187	429	297	7213	8126	3847	-	11973
E Other economic affairs	384	275	109	1650	1275	3309	119	46	3474
10 Other functions	533	325	208	-	10833	11366	554	288167	300087
Total	50741	28686	22055	8104	27156	86001	14503	300486	400990
1984									
1 General public services	34215	16328	17887	2258	1866	38339	3340	38	41717
2 Defence									
3 Public order and safety	4275	3163	1112	-	9	4284	474	-	4758
4 Education	5440	4279	1161	-	1207	6647	1579	-	8226
5 Health	2518	1347	1171	-	192	2710	1132	-	3842
6 Social security and welfare	1695	1509	186	-	34	1729	23	-	1752
7 Housing and community amenities	958	521	437	-	576	1534	1181	-	2715
8 Recreation, culture and religion	229	135	94	-	137	366	241	-	607
9 Economic services	7244	4204	3040	5848	14221	27313	7681	13788	48782
A Fuel and energy	232	76	156	89	1265	1586	665	34	2285
B Agriculture, forestry, fishing and hunting	5633	3520	2113	4354	2184	12171	2415	13526	28112
C Mining (except fuels), manufacturing and construction	331	132	199	-	1286	1617	97	176	1890
D Transportation and communication	582	184	398	268	8061	8911	4365	-	13276
E Other economic affairs	466	292	174	1137	1425	3028	139	52	3219
10 Other functions	552	301	251	1197	12106	13855	598	323496	337949
Total	57126	31787	25339	9303	30348	96777	16249	337322	450348
1985									
1 General public services	38805	18104	20701	2968	2275	44048	3818	43	47909
2 Defence									
3 Public order and safety	4934	3662	1272	-	10	4944	542	-	5486
4 Education	6454	5111	1343	-	1432	7886	1801	-	9687
5 Health	2949	1606	1343	-	225	3174	1289	-	4463
6 Social security and welfare	1987	1773	214	-	40	2027	27	-	2054
7 Housing and community amenities	1128	620	508	-	678	1806	1325	-	3131
8 Recreation, culture and religion	268	157	111	-	160	428	270	-	698
9 Economic services	8502	5028	3474	5446	16692	30640	8722	15318	54680
A Fuel and energy	271	91	180	-	1607	1878	748	37	2663
B Agriculture, forestry, fishing and hunting	6627	4219	2408	3594	2570	12791	2754	15028	30573
C Mining (except fuels), manufacturing and construction	384	156	228	-	1730	2114	113	198	2425
D Transportation and communication	677	221	456	353	9126	10156	4956	-	15112
E Other economic affairs	543	341	202	1499	1659	3701	151	55	3907
10 Other functions	635	348	287	1578	13940	16153	675	356270	373098
Total	65662	36409	29253	9992	35452	111106	18469	371631	501206

Pakistan

Million Pakistan rupees

Fiscal year beginning 1 July

	Final Consumption Expenditures			Subsidies	Other Current Transfers & Property Income	Total Current Disbursements	Gross Capital Formation	Other Capital Outlays	Total Outlays
	Total	Compensation of Employees	Other						
1986									
1 General public services	45202	21964	23238	2190	3593	50985	4460	51	55496
2 Defence									
3 Public order and safety	5951	4443	1508	-	18	5969	869	-	6838
4 Education	7992	6249	1743	-	2296	10288	2045	-	12333
5 Health	3390	1900	1490	-	362	3752	1496	-	5248
6 Social security and welfare	2486	2161	325	-	65	2551	36	-	2587
7 Housing and community amenities	1319	742	577	-	1087	2406	1484	-	3890
8 Recreation, culture and religion	376	190	186	-	257	633	312	-	945
9 Economic services	10018	6101	3917	4019	26500	40537	9857	18258	68652
A Fuel and energy	308	110	198	...	2321	2629	833	44	3506
B Agriculture, forestry, fishing and hunting	7860	5120	2740	2652	4113	14625	3185	17912	35722
C Mining (except fuels), manufacturing and construction	441	189	252	...	2425	2866	135	236	3237
D Transportation and communication	767	268	499	261	14966	15994	5512	-	21506
E Other economic affairs	642	414	228	1106	2675	4423	192	66	4681
10 Other functions	748	422	326	1165	22537	24450	758	424253	449461
Total	77482	44172	33310	7374	56715	141571	21317	442562	605450
1987									
1 General public services	67290	25514	41776	2480	6129	75899	5767	55	81721
2 Defence									
3 Public order and safety	6514	4586	1928	-	30	6544	937	-	7481
4 Education	8889	6899	1990	-	3917	12806	2419	-	15225
5 Health	4107	2143	1964	-	617	4724	1834	-	6558
6 Social security and welfare	2797	2461	336	-	112	2909	39	-	2948
7 Housing and community amenities	1548	807	741	-	1856	3404	1935	-	5339
8 Recreation, culture and religion	493	214	279	-	440	933	387	-	1320
9 Economic services	12328	6706	5622	6331	45226	63885	10396	21842	96123
A Fuel and energy	386	121	265	-	3961	4347	841	54	5242
B Agriculture, forestry, fishing and hunting	9281	5593	3688	4783	7019	21083	3653	21435	46171
C Mining (except fuels), manufacturing and construction	532	244	288	-	4138	4670	111	273	5054
D Transportation and communication	987	295	692	296	25543	26826	5579	-	32405
E Other economic affairs	1142	453	689	1252	4565	6959	212	80	7251
10 Other functions	788	288	500	1319	38462	40569	897	483952	525418
Total	104754	49618	55136	10130	96789	211673	24611	505849	742133
1988									
1 General public services	72009	27265	44744	3788	6882	82679	6017	65	88761
2 Defence									
3 Public order and safety	8718	4901	3817	-	31	8749	977	-	9726
4 Education	16049	8235	7814	-	4014	20063	2523	-	22586
5 Health	6041	2476	3565	-	632	6673	1911	-	8584
6 Social security and welfare	3799	2827	972	-	115	3914	40	-	3954
7 Housing and community amenities	1746	867	879	-	1902	3648	2043	-	5691
8 Recreation, culture and religion	590	218	372	-	653	1243	406	-	1649
9 Economic services	19451	8130	11321	6951	46357	72759	11045	23883	107687
A Fuel and energy	437	148	289	-	4060	4497	895	59	5451
B Agriculture, forestry, fishing and hunting	13502	6779	6723	4587	7194	25283	3859	23438	52580
C Mining (except fuels), manufacturing and construction	2076	296	1780	-	4241	6317	116	297	6730
D Transportation and communication	1212	358	854	452	26183	27847	5950	-	33797
E Other economic affairs	2224	549	1675	1912	4679	8815	225	89	9129
10 Other functions	798	542	256	2015	39224	42037	941	529177	572155
Total	129201	55461	73740	12754	99810	241765	25903	553125	820793

2.3 Total Government Outlays by Function and Type
(Continued)

Million Pakistan rupees

Fiscal year beginning 1 July

	Final Consumption Expenditures			Subsidies	Other Current Transfers & Property Income	Total Current Disbursements	Gross Capital Formation	Other Capital Outlays	Total Outlays
	Total	Compensation of Employees	Other						
1989									
1 General public services	76373	28920	47453	...	7590	83963	6783	69	90815
2 Defence				...					
3 Public order and safety	9308	5198	4110	-	34	9342	1107	-	10449
4 Education	12852	9397	3455	-	4427	17279	2846	-	20125
5 Health	5637	2782	2855	-	697	6334	2156	-	8490
6 Social security and welfare	4113	3249	864	-	216	4329	46	-	4375
7 Housing and community amenities	1995	995	1000	-	2098	4093	2273	-	6366
8 Recreation, culture and religion	616	265	351	-	720	1336	455	-	1791
9 Economic services	17590	8902	8688	12722	51132	81444	12216	25388	119048
A Fuel and energy	440	162	278	1701	4478	6619	986	63	7668
B Agriculture, forestry, fishing and hunting	13479	7423	6056	7277	7938	28694	4290	24911	57895
C Mining (except fuels), manufacturing and construction	762	324	438	1786	4678	7226	130	316	7672
D Transportation and communication	1331	377	954	1958	28880	32169	6625	-	38794
E Other economic affairs	1578	616	962	-	5158	6736	185	98	7019
10 Other functions	1078	132	946	-	43213	44291	1054	562332	607677
Total	129562	59840	69722	12722	110127	252411	28936	587789	869136
1990									
1 General public services	83236	32018	51218	-	8273	91509	7575	76	99160
2 Defence									
3 Public order and safety	10797	5754	5043	-	37	10834	1080	-	11914
4 Education	15202	10403	4799	-	4825	20027	3580	-	23607
5 Health	6551	3080	3471	-	760	7311	2389	-	9700
6 Social security and welfare	4794	3597	1197	-	235	5029	82	-	5111
7 Housing and community amenities	2197	1102	1095	-	2287	4484	3213	-	7697
8 Recreation, culture and religion	673	293	380	-	785	1458	569	-	2027
9 Economic services	20855	9855	11000	11211	55734	87800	14714	27927	130441
A Fuel and energy	477	179	298	1498	4881	6856	1676	69	8601
B Agriculture, forestry, fishing and hunting	16156	8218	7938	6413	8652	31221	4734	27402	63357
C Mining (except fuels), manufacturing and construction	900	398	502	1574	5099	7573	1191	348	9112
D Transportation and communication	1563	417	1146	1726	31479	34768	6592	-	41360
E Other economic affairs	1759	643	1116	-	5623	7382	521	108	8011
10 Other functions	1270	147	1123	-	47102	48372	1483	618564	668419
Total	145575	66249	79326	11211	120038	276824	34685	646567	958076
1991									
1 General public services	88540	35948	52592	-	7664	96204	6837	80	103121
2 Defence									
3 Public order and safety	11800	8113	3687	-	38	11838	1007	-	12845
4 Education	16332	10730	5602	-	5110	21442	3469	-	24911
5 Health	6986	3176	3810	-	771	7757	2318	-	10075
6 Social security and welfare	5140	3709	1431	-	140	5280	88	-	5368
7 Housing and community amenities	2290	1136	1154	-	2319	4609	3070	-	7679
8 Recreation, culture and religion	702	303	399	-	795	1497	542	-	2039
9 Economic services	22414	10167	12247	8374	55891	86679	14231	30557	131467
A Fuel and energy	481	166	315	1119	4896	6496	1613	69	8178
B Agriculture, forestry, fishing and hunting	17407	8159	9248	4790	8672	30869	4676	30020	65565
C Mining (except fuels), manufacturing and construction	976	513	463	1176	5113	7265	935	343	8543
D Transportation and communication	1690	703	987	1289	31568	34547	6495	-	41042
E Other economic affairs	1860	626	1234	-	5642	7502	512	125	8139
10 Other functions	1365	153	1212	-	48308	49673	1435	617930	669038
Total	155569	73435	82134	8374	121036	284979	32997	648567	966543

Pakistan

2.7 Gross Capital Formation by Type of Good and Owner, in Current Prices

Million Pakistan rupees

	1980				1981				1982			
	TOTAL	Total Private	Public Enterprises	General Government	TOTAL	Total Private	Public Enterprises	General Government	TOTAL	Total Private	Public Enterprises	General Government
Increase in stocks, total	4500	...	...	...	7858	...	...	...	6701	...	...	...
Gross Fixed Capital Formation, Total	47707	21608	16529	9570	54589	23331	18579	12679	61761	26758	21863	13140
1 Residential buildings	1703	1233	-	459	2333	1387	-	595	2584	1539	-	580
2 Non-residential buildings	3209	{		3220	3964			4315	3678			4143
3 Other construction	15214	5908	4364	4942	17644	6208	5070	6366	19689	6798	5963	6928
4 Land improvement and plantation and orchard development	1392	1378	-	14	1466	1428	-	36	1493	1462	-	31
5 Producers' durable goods	22660	10237	11699	724	25288	11251	13002	1035	30046	13685	15310	1051
A Transport equipment	5610	2382	3073	155	6193	2431	3625	137	6581	2719	3626	236
B Machinery and equipment	17050	7855	8626	569	19095	8820	9377	898	23465	10966	11684	815
6 Breeding stock, dairy cattle, etc.	...	...	...	...	...	...	...	...	...	...	...	...
Statistical discrepancy a	3529	2852	466	211	3894	3057	507	330	4271	3274	590	407
Total Gross Capital Formation	52207	...	...	...	62447	...	...	...	68462	...	...	...

	1983				1984				1985			
	TOTAL	Total Private	Public Enterprises	General Government	TOTAL	Total Private	Public Enterprises	General Government	TOTAL	Total Private	Public Enterprises	General Government
Increase in stocks, total	7489	...	...	...	8600	...	...	...	9000	...	...	...
Gross Fixed Capital Formation, Total	69212	31419	23290	14503	77925	35840	25836	16249	87545	39959	29117	18469
1 Residential buildings	2812	1807	-	758	3263	2194	-	920	3938	2530	-	1050
2 Non-residential buildings	4957	{		5204	5568			5717	6179			6537
3 Other construction	20824	7626	6542	6656	23425	8287	7737	7401	25752	8879	8499	8374
4 Land improvement and plantation and orchard development	1654	1616	-	38	1795	1768	-	27	1872	1842	-	30
5 Producers' durable goods	34131	16737	16026	1368	38439	19441	17348	1650	43501	22063	19555	1882
A Transport equipment	7340	3110	3892	338	9181	3775	5054	352	10114	4408	5304	402
B Machinery and equipment	26791	13627	12134	1030	29258	15666	12294	1298	33387	17655	14252	1480
6 Breeding stock, dairy cattle, etc.	...	...	...	...	...	...	...	...	...	...	...	...
Statistical discrepancy a	4834	3633	722	479	5435	4150	751	534	6303	4645	1062	596
Total Gross Capital Formation	76701	...	...	...	86525	...	...	...	96545	...	...	...

	1986				1987				1988			
	TOTAL	Total Private	Public Enterprises	General Government	TOTAL	Total Private	Public Enterprises	General Government	TOTAL	Total Private	Public Enterprises	General Government
Increase in stocks, total	9500	...	...	...	10400	...	...	...	12400	...	...	...
Gross Fixed Capital Formation, Total	100040	44349	34374	21317	111266	51769	34886	24611	133170	64162	43105	25903
1 Residential buildings	3940	2006	-	1224	4389	1796	-	1414	41779	26584	4513	10682
2 Non-residential buildings	6834	{		7544	7674			8853				
3 Other construction	29458	9581	10212	9665	32701	11253	10382	11066	20290	3016	5466	11808
4 Land improvement and plantation and orchard development	2585	2550	-	35	2859	2820	-	39	7192	4202	2947	43
5 Producers' durable goods	50116	25067	22859	2190	55314	29594	23198	2522	57481	24995	29861	2625
A Transport equipment	11892	4991	6434	467	12634	6172	5924	538	13647	6360	6727	560
B Machinery and equipment	38224	20076	16425	1723	42680	23422	17274	1984	43834	18635	23134	2065
6 Breeding stock, dairy cattle, etc.	...	...	...	...	...	...	...	...	...	...	...	...
Statistical discrepancy a	7107	5145	1303	659	8329	6305	1307	717	6428	5365	318	745
Total Gross Capital Formation	109540	...	...	...	121666	...	...	...	145570	...	...	...

	1989				1990				1991			
	TOTAL	Total Private	Public Enterprises	General Government	TOTAL	Total Private	Public Enterprises	General Government	TOTAL	Total Private	Public Enterprises	General Government
Increase in stocks, total	14000	...	...	...	15800	...	...	...	18300	...	...	...
Gross Fixed Capital Formation, Total	148076	76563	42577	28936	175161	90962	49514	34685	206260	113581	59682	32997
1 Residential buildings	36042	19410	4568	12064	43635	24263	4911	14461	47999	28557	5863	13579
2 Non-residential buildings												
3 Other construction	26342	3943	9397	13002	36622	10924	10113	15585	46203	19366	11855	14982

2.7 Gross Capital Formation by Type of Good and Owner, in Current Prices
(Continued)

Million Pakistan rupees

Fiscal year beginning 1 July

	1989				1990				1991			
	TOTAL	Total Private	Public Enterprises	General Government	TOTAL	Total Private	Public Enterprises	General Government	TOTAL	Total Private	Public Enterprises	General Government
4 Land improvement and plantation and orchard development	7253	4526	2681	46	7677	3854	3768	55	8573	5738	2780	55
5 Producers' durable goods	73094	44496	25633	2965	80274	46570	30150	3554	95743	53615	38727	3401
A Transport equipment	16203	9807	5764	632	23659	13482	9419	758	26862	14934	11203	725
B Machinery and equipment	56891	34689	19869	2333	56615	33088	20731	2796	68881	38681	27524	2676
6 Breeding stock, dairy cattle, etc.	...	...	...	...	...	...	...	...	...	...	...	...
Statistical discrepancy a	5345	4188	298	859	6953	5351	572	1030	7742	6305	457	980
Total Gross Capital Formation	162076	...	...	...	190961	...	...	...	224560	...	...	...

a) Item 'Statistical discrepancy' refers to furniture and fixture.

2.11 Gross Fixed Capital Formation by Kind of Activity of Owner, ISIC Divisions, in Current Prices

Million Pakistan rupees

Fiscal year beginning 1 July

	1980	1981	1982	1983	1984	1985	1986	1987	1988	1989	1990	1991
					All Producers							
1 Agriculture, hunting, forestry and fishing a	5170	5704	7292	8719	9590	9907	10874	12275	13537	15537	17684	18563
2 Mining and quarrying	383	419	291	902	1040	2152	2873	2090	3286	1889	2561	3864
3 Manufacturing	9387	10156	11950	14265	13882	16889	16762	19604	25915	31875	38634	55100
A Manufacturing of food, beverages and tobacco	574	949	1113	1411	1901	1677	1664	1805	2386	2935	3557	5073
B Textile, wearing apparel and leather industries	1508	1276	1579	1655	2048	2936	2915	5084	6721	8267	10020	14291
C Manufacture of wood, and wood products, including furniture	156	200	172	102	142	187	187	201	266	327	396	565
D Manufacture of paper and paper products, printing and publishing	245	640	522	712	558	782	775	936	1237	1521	1844	2630
E Manufacture of chemicals and chemical petroleum, coal, rubber and plastic products	3376	1781	2845	4025	3698	3276	3251	4175	5519	6788	8227	11733
F Manufacture of non-metalic mineral products except products of petroleum and coal	1069	1299	1407	1898	1766	1593	1581	1183	1564	1924	2332	3326
G Basic metal industries	1756	2920	3135	2649	1522	3052	3029	684	904	1112	1348	1922
H Manufacture of fabricated metal products, machinery and equipment	574	716	858	1414	1797	2723	2702	4587	6064	7459	9041	12894
I Other manufacturing industries	129	375	319	399	450	663	658	949	1254	1542	1869	2666
4 Electricity, gas and water b	3382	3910	6195	6136	7949	8356	11687	13226	22411	23455	24103	31233
5 Construction	2037	2425	3666	2694	3088	3097	3884	4591	4894	5835	5127	4986
6 Wholesale and retail trade, restaurants and hotels	429	419	445	499	590	656	713	935	1028	1189	1708	1985
7 Transport, storage and communication c	6338	7152	6411	7758	10719	11289	13308	12462	13434	13969	20558	23834
8 Finance, insurance, real estate and business services d	8259	8695	9244	10307	11219	12263	13304	15053	16418	18579	21659	24407
9 Community, social and personal services d	2752	3030	3127	3429	3599	4467	5318	6419	6344	6812	8442	9291
Total Industries e	38137	41910	48621	54709	61676	69076	78723	86655	107267	119140	140476	173263
Producers of Government Services	9570	12679	13140	14503	16249	18469	21317	24611	25903	28936	34685	32997
Private Non-Profit Institutions Serving Households	...	...	...	...	...	...	...	...	...	...	...	...
Total	47707	54589	61761	69212	77925	87545	100040	111266	133170	148076	175161	206260

a) Item 'Agriculture, hunting, fishing and forestry' includes investment in Indus Basin Project made by WAPDA.
b) Item 'Electricity, gas and water' refers to electricity and gas only.
c) Item 'Transport, storage and communication' excludes storage.
d) Business services are included in item 'Community, social and personal services'.
e) The estimates of gross capital formation by kind of activity of owner refer to private and semi-public sector only.

2.12 Gross Fixed Capital Formation by Kind of Activity of Owner, ISIC Divisions, in Constant Prices

Million Pakistan rupees

Fiscal year beginning 1 July

	1980	1981	1982	1983	1984	1985	1986	1987	1988	1989	1990	1991
					At constant prices of:1980							
					All Producers							
1 Agriculture, hunting, forestry and fishing	5170	5570	6910	7866	8394	8053	8396	8314	8073	8541	8455	7972
2 Mining and quarrying	383	403	270	809	912	1764	2336	1530	2076	1128	1300	1732
3 Manufacturing	9387	9185	10500	11652	11797	12772	9702	9186	10668	12057	12768	16743
4 Electricity, gas and water	3382	3826	5878	5582	7016	6877	9453	9538	14158	13787	12157	13986

Pakistan

2.12 Gross Fixed Capital Formation by Kind of Activity of Owner, ISIC Divisions, in Constant Prices
(Continued)

Million Pakistan rupees

Fiscal year beginning 1 July

	1980	1981	1982	1983	1984	1985	1986	1987	1988	1989	1990	1991
					At constant prices of:1980							
5 Construction	2037	2021	2995	1977	2484	2172	1676	1525	1409	1549	1125	1060
6 Wholesale and retail trade, restaurants and hotels	429	397	406	435	492	521	550	664	649	702	866	907
7 Transport, storage and communication	6338	6904	6061	6838	9206	9341	10345	9078	9158	9016	9625	10152
8 Finance, insurance, real estate and business services	8259	8613	8927	9233	9431	9777	10012	10468	10442	10859	10810	11110
9 Community, social and personal services	2752	2925	2920	3072	3139	3656	4272	4660	4035	3967	4243	4151
Total Industries	38137	39844	44867	47464	52871	54934	56742	54963	60668	61606	61349	67813
Producers of Government Services	9570	12500	12636	12979	13777	14876	16229	17014	16632	16886	17051	14837
Private Non-Profit Institutions Serving Households	...	...	...	...	...	...	...	...	...	...	...	...
Total	47707	52344	57503	60443	66648	69807	72971	71977	77300	78492	78400	82650

Panama

General note. The preparation of national accounts statistics in Panama is undertaken by the Direccion de Estadistica y Censos Panama. Official estimates are published annually, from 1960 in 'Estadistica Panamena, Serie C, Ingreso Nacional' and from 1976 in the bulletin 'Situacion Economica'. The most detailed description of the sources and methods used for the national accounts estimation is found in 'Situacion Economica, Cuentas Nacionales: Anos 1973 a 1975', published in 1976. The estimates are generally in accordance with the classifications and definitions recommended in the United Nations System of National Accounts (SNA). The following tables have been prepared from successive replies to the United Nations national accounts questionnaire. When the scope and coverage of the estimates differ for conceptual or statistical reasons from the definitions and classifications recommended in SNA, a footnote is indicated to the relevant tables.

Sources and methods :

(a) Gross domestic product. Gross domestic product is estimated mainly through the income approach.

(b) Expenditure on the gross domestic product. The expenditure approach is used to estimate government final consumption expenditure as well as imports and exports of goods and services. The commodity-flow approach is used to estimate private final consumption expenditure and, to a large extent, gross capital formation. Data on government consumption expenditure are obtained from official documents and directly from the concerned agencies. Estimates of private consumption expenditure are based on data on locally produced and imported consumer goods. The gross value of construction is obtained by adding the cost of inputs of building materials to the estimated value added of the industry. Factor and non-factor services rendered by residents of Panama to the Former Canal Zone and to the Colon Free Zone are treated uniformly as non-factor services to the rest of the world. These services are, therefore, included in exports of goods and services. Constant prices are estimated by a combined use of extrapolation and price indexes. For government consumption expenditure, compensation of employees is extrapolated by the number of persons employed, whereas purchases of goods and services are deflated by a combination of price indexes. For private consumption expenditure, base-year estimates are extrapolated by means of indexes which refer to consumption at both current and constant prices. The final estimates are adjusted for the discrepancy between total demand and total supply. Current values of gross fixed capital formation are deflated by a price index for inputs in the case of buildings and other construction. The current value of transport equipment and machinery and equipment are extrapolated by a volume index obtained by deflating current values by an index based on the unit export value of machinery in supplier countries. Various price indexes are used for price deflation of exports and imports of goods and services.

(c) Cost-structure of the gross domestic product. Estimates of compensation of employees are based on data on average wages, and the percentage distribution of employees obtained from household surveys. To this informaton is added yearly estimates of salaries earned in the public and private sectors, employers' contribution to social security schemes and an estimate of the incomes of self-employed workers. Operating surplus is compiled from various items, such as property income, saving and direct taxes. The estimates on consumption of fixed capital, which exclude depreciation of government fixed capital, are based on accounting data of the private enterprises, obtained through direct surveys, and financial information of all autonomous and semi-autonomous entities included in the public sector. Estimates of indirect taxes are based on data from public finance, and on revenue figures from central government, municipalities and the Panamanian Institute of Tourism.

(d) Gross domestic product by kind of economic activity. The table of GDP by kind of economic activity is prepared in factor values. For the agriculture, forestry and fishing sector, value added is obtained by deducting inputs from gross value of production. Sources used to estimate agricultural production include the census of agriculture, agricultural surveys and, in the case of export products, external trade statistics. Price data are obtained from the current statistics on prices received by the agricultural producers. Value added in forestry is derived from a bench-mark estimate of sawn wood produced, the number of persons occupied and the ratio of output to employment, which is obtained from periodical industrial inquiries. In the case of fishing, estimates are based on fish landings in the Gulf of Panama, as published in 'Estadistica Panamena' and on the number of persons engaged in fishing, which is obtained from the latest population census. Value added of manufacturing is estimated by extrapolating the bench-mark estimate by an indicator based on the gross value of production by type of industrial activity. A similar approach is used for the electricity, gas and water sector, as well as the construction and the trade sectors. For the trade sector the indicator used is based on the current prices of products which are marketed through wholesale and retail trade. For transport, value added is estimated on the basis of the payments to factor of production. Value added for ownership of dwellings is obtained by aggregating estimates for different geographical areas of the country. For business services value added is estimated by utilizing an indicator of patent registrations in force for operating business at the end of each year. Financial reports relating to factor payments from central government, other government authorities and municipalities, form the data basis for estimates of public administration. A similar approach is applied for other public services, whereas for other private services value added is first estimated at constant prices and then inflated by price indices to arrive at value added at current prices. For the estimation of constant prices in the agricultural sector, the current quantities are valued at base-year prices. Base year estimates, for the manufacturing sector, are extrapolated by various indexes such as indexes of input quantities and quantum indexes of output. For construction, value added is extrapolated by a quantity index of inputs. For electricity, trade and transport value added is extrapolated by quantity indicators of output. For restaurants and hotels the indicators are based on tourist expenditure in Panama and on food and beverage quantities. For banks, value added is extrapolated using the balance of loans and deposits at the end of each year. For ownership of dwellings in urban areas, the construction of new dwellings is used as indicator, and for the rural areas the base-year estimate is extrapolated by an index of rural population growth. The value added of government services is extrapolated by an index of number of government employees. For other private services as well value added is extrapolated using various quantity indicators.

1.1 Expenditure on the Gross Domestic Product, in Current Prices

Million Panamanian balboas

	1980	1981	1982	1983	1984	1985	1986	1987	1988	1989	1990	1991
1 Government final consumption expenditure	680.5	812.9	962.6	941.5	1001.3	1043.6	1127.8	1226.9	1011.6	986.7	939.1	962.0
2 Private final consumption expenditure	1975.4	2060.7	2261.0	2423.8	2819.3	3020.0	2910.0	2966.1	2606.8	3005.8	3003.9	3458.4
3 Gross capital formation	986.9	1167.2	1184.6	934.1	761.0	753.0	859.2	928.0	313.7	158.7	859.1	1001.7
A Increase in stocks	120.5	87.6	-0.8	16.3	-18.9	-20.1	-37.5	-9.0	-94.0	-161.3	385.7	75.9
B Gross fixed capital formation	866.4	1079.6	1185.4	917.8	779.9	773.1	896.7	937.0	407.7	320.0	473.4	925.8
Residential buildings	93.3	117.4	121.7	119.7	128.9	182.3	207.0	212.7	74.4	38.6	42.5	99.2
Non-residential buildings	219.7	225.8	236.0	221.9	145.3	170.8	188.1	221.0	82.6	56.3	100.5	205.7
Other construction and land improvement etc.	251.4	339.0	493.6	272.4	225.7	125.2	147.7	106.7	49.6	47.8	27.4	116.0
Other	302.0	397.4	334.1	303.8	280.0	294.8	353.9	396.6	201.1	177.3	303.0	504.9
4 Exports of goods and services	1626.2	1711.3	1772.9	1804.7	1707.3	1822.1	1869.7	1851.8	1731.4	1724.2	1936.0	2054.4
5 Less: Imports of goods and services	1676.4	1830.7	1856.5	1676.1	1679.0	1690.4	1575.8	1609.5	1059.0	1236.1	1728.7	1985.4
Equals: Gross Domestic Product	3592.6	3921.4	4324.6	4428.0	4609.9	4948.3	5190.9	5363.3	4604.5	4639.3	5009.4	5491.1

1.2 Expenditure on the Gross Domestic Product, in Constant Prices

Million Panamanian balboas

	1980	1981	1982	1983	1984	1985	1986	1987	1988	1989	1990	1991
					At constant prices of:1970							
1 Government final consumption expenditure	284.8	334.9	365.5	343.8	348.4	354.0	384.1	403.4	327.7	331.3	305.4	310.9
2 Private final consumption expenditure	915.5	895.1	943.4	992.7	1116.5	1137.2	1094.6	1088.2	829.9	983.3	925.1	1153.3
3 Gross capital formation	411.6	463.4	430.6	340.9	303.3	323.9	351.8	360.1	131.0	74.0	309.2	318.1
A Increase in stocks	46.3	37.3	0.5	7.9	-6.9	-7.5	-11.7	-4.2	-34.7	-60.6	131.5	26.2
B Gross fixed capital formation	365.3	426.1	430.1	333.0	310.2	331.4	363.5	364.3	165.7	134.6	177.7	291.9

Panama

1.2 Expenditure on the Gross Domestic Product, in Constant Prices
(Continued)

Million Panamanian balboas

	1980	1981	1982	1983	1984	1985	1986	1987	1988	1989	1990	1991
					At constant prices of:1970							
Residential buildings	37.0	42.8	41.4	39.6	43.1	60.8	66.7	67.3	23.9	12.1	14.2	30.5
Non-residential buildings	87.2	82.3	80.2	73.4	48.6	57.0	60.6	69.9	26.5	17.7	33.6	63.3
Other construction and land improvement etc.	99.8	123.5	167.7	90.1	75.4	41.8	47.6	33.7	15.9	15.2	9.2	35.7
Other	141.3	177.5	140.8	129.9	143.1	171.8	188.6	193.4	99.4	89.6	120.7	162.4
4 Exports of goods and services	787.9	774.6	837.5	841.6	788.7	844.0	880.3	879.5	902.8	861.4	952.7	996.3
5 Less: Imports of goods and services	663.4	661.3	670.0	600.5	646.7	658.7	643.8	614.2	404.7	470.8	630.8	743.0
Equals: Gross Domestic Product	1736.4	1806.7	1907.0	1918.5	1910.2	2000.4	2067.0	2117.0	1786.7	1779.2	1861.6	2035.6

1.3 Cost Components of the Gross Domestic Product

Million Panamanian balboas

	1980	1981	1982	1983	1984	1985	1986	1987	1988	1989	1990	1991
1 Indirect taxes, net	268.2	281.6	307.9	331.4	353.7	384.7	427.9	444.6	318.8	338.4	433.7	488.7
A Indirect taxes	269.7	285.4	313.7	336.4	358.8	390.0	432.9	452.3	325.9	347.3	443.1	498.7
B Less: Subsidies	1.5	3.8	5.8	5.0	5.1	5.3	5.0	7.7	7.1	8.9	9.4	10.0
2 Consumption of fixed capital	252.1	279.7	320.9	335.5	374.6	398.8	424.4	434.9	411.9	403.1	422.1	445.9
3 Compensation of employees paid by resident producers to:	1624.6	1800.2	2049.5	2193.2	2301.1	2455.1	2582.1	2672.6	2380.0	2300.5	2288.0	2531.8
4 Operating surplus	1447.7	1559.9	1646.3	1567.9	1580.5	1709.7	1756.5	1811.2	1493.8	1597.3	1865.6	2024.7
Equals: Gross Domestic Product	3592.6	3921.4	4324.6	4428.0	4609.9	4948.3	5190.9	5363.3	4604.5	4639.3	5009.4	5491.1

1.4 General Government Current Receipts and Disbursements

Million Panamanian balboas

	1980	1981	1982	1983	1984	1985	1986	1987	1988	1989	1990	1991
					Receipts							
1 Operating surplus	-0.7	-0.9	-1.5	0.2	-0.1	-0.2	-	0.7	-1.3	-0.9	-0.4	-
2 Property and entrepreneurial income	89.2	97.7	107.1	133.6	141.0	188.1	167.9	165.2	145.0	170.9	210.1	239.2
3 Taxes, fees and contributions	833.2	951.4	1054.1	1159.5	1149.0	1250.7	1357.4	1423.1	1057.8	1003.7	1213.6	1365.6
A Indirect taxes	269.7	285.4	313.7	336.4	358.8	390.0	432.9	452.3	325.9	347.3	443.1	498.7
B Direct taxes	226.6	284.2	300.8	354.1	304.7	342.3	366.2	382.6	251.4	199.3	247.4	316.1
C Social security contributions	236.9	279.8	339.6	361.7	371.5	394.0	433.4	461.2	389.7	381.9	425.6	445.0
D Compulsory fees, fines and penalties	100.0	102.0	100.0	107.3	114.0	124.4	124.9	127.0	90.8	75.2	97.5	105.8
4 Other current transfers	137.0	173.2	173.9	194.0	219.4	222.9	254.9	242.5	175.4	178.4	308.5	310.6
Total Current Receipts of General Government	1058.7	1221.4	1333.6	1487.3	1509.3	1661.5	1780.2	1831.5	1376.9	1352.1	1731.8	1915.4
					Disbursements							
1 Government final consumption expenditure	680.5	812.9	962.6	941.5	1001.3	1043.6	1127.8	1226.9	1011.6	985.6	939.1	962.0
2 Property income	187.4	230.3	316.5	292.2	310.3	319.2	360.7	319.2	111.9	162.4	163.6	143.4
A Interest	187.4	230.3	316.5	292.2	310.3	319.2	360.7	319.2	111.9	162.4	163.6	143.4
B Net land rent and royalties	...	...	...	...	...	...	...	...	...	...	...	...
3 Subsidies	1.5	3.8	5.8	5.0	5.1	5.3	5.0	7.7	7.1	8.9	9.4	10.0
4 Other current transfers	197.8	239.9	281.4	306.7	327.7	362.8	381.6	401.7	375.1	466.9	463.8	538.3
A Social security benefits	99.1	121.7	134.6	156.4	174.4	198.6	212.4	230.0	234.9	278.9	296.6	333.5
B Social assistance grants	14.1	12.4	20.9	18.2	18.0	16.6	17.4	17.5	5.6	4.9	6.5	8.3
C Other	84.6	105.8	125.9	132.1	135.3	147.6	151.8	154.2	134.6	183.1	160.7	196.5
5 Net saving	-8.5	-65.5	-232.7	-58.1	-135.1	-69.4	-94.9	-124.0	-128.8	-271.7	155.9	261.7
Total Current Disbursements and Net Saving of General Government	1058.7	1221.4	1333.6	1487.3	1509.3	1661.5	1780.2	1831.5	1376.9	1352.1	1731.8	1915.4

1.7 External Transactions on Current Account, Summary

Million Panamanian balboas

	1980	1981	1982	1983	1984	1985	1986	1987	1988	1989	1990	1991
					Payments to the Rest of the World							
1 Imports of goods and services	1676.4	1830.7	1856.5	1676.1	1679.0	1690.4	1575.8	1609.5	1059.0	1236.1	1728.7	1985.4
A Imports of merchandise c.i.f.	1483.9	1620.0	1636.9	1474.4	1468.3	1451.0	1323.7	1372.3	872.5	1042.6	1532.9	1747.6
B Other	192.5	210.7	219.6	201.7	210.7	239.4	252.1	237.2	186.5	193.5	195.8	237.8
2 Factor income to the rest of the world	2760.6	3510.5	3793.5	2827.8	2620.9	2134.0	1870.0	1475.0	894.4	954.2	933.2	891.0

1.7 External Transactions on Current Account, Summary
(Continued)

Million Panamanian balboas

	1980	1981	1982	1983	1984	1985	1986	1987	1988	1989	1990	1991
3 Current transfers to the rest of the world	58.1	54.8	63.9	70.4	61.3	39.0	33.2	59.6	45.3	44.2	29.2	32.5
4 Surplus of the nation on current transactions	-145.9	-166.8	-186.5	170.6	-5.7	194.0	345.9	264.1	509.5	285.2	149.4	30.7
Payments to the Rest of the World and Surplus of the Nation on Current Transactions	4349.2	5229.2	5527.4	4744.9	4355.5	4057.4	3824.9	3408.2	2508.2	2519.7	2840.5	2939.6

Receipts From The Rest of the World

	1980	1981	1982	1983	1984	1985	1986	1987	1988	1989	1990	1991
1 Exports of goods and services	1626.2	1711.3	1772.9	1804.7	1707.3	1822.1	1869.7	1851.8	1731.4	1724.2	1936.0	2054.4
A Exports of merchandise f.o.b.	584.6	574.3	572.1	521.7	453.4	480.3	483.6	513.4	466.9	487.8	542.9	543.5
B Other	1041.6	1137.0	1200.8	1283.0	1253.9	1341.8	1386.1	1338.4	1264.5	1236.4	1393.1	1510.9
2 Factor income from rest of the world	2650.6	3431.9	3654.6	2830.0	2497.3	2087.6	1826.3	1433.9	660.0	681.2	679.6	659.4
A Compensation of employees	62.8	58.6	72.1	75.4	73.3	78.2	82.0	83.0	82.6	88.2	91.9	92.7
B Property and entrepreneurial income	2587.8	3373.3	3582.5	2754.6	2424.0	2009.4	1744.3	1350.9	577.4	593.0	587.7	566.7
3 Current transfers from rest of the world	72.4	86.0	99.9	110.2	150.9	147.7	128.9	122.5	116.8	114.3	224.9	225.8
Receipts from the Rest of the World on Current Transactions	4349.2	5229.2	5527.4	4744.9	4355.5	4057.4	3824.9	3408.2	2508.2	2519.7	2840.5	2939.6

1.10 Gross Domestic Product by Kind of Activity, in Current Prices

Million Panamanian balboas

	1980	1981	1982	1983	1984	1985	1986	1987	1988	1989	1990	1991
1 Agriculture, hunting, forestry and fishing	354.2	402.8	416.9	462.7	460.3	497.8	524.4	559.1	531.8	554.2	552.1	609.6
2 Mining and quarrying	6.8	8.7	9.3	7.9	6.0	5.7	6.0	6.3	3.8	3.6	4.3	5.6
3 Manufacturing	356.0	375.6	394.0	401.0	411.0	420.0	421.8	440.4	328.7	353.7	407.0	453.5
4 Electricity, gas and water	113.8	142.4	152.6	153.5	194.9	212.1	227.6	228.5	240.8	231.3	228.7	228.6
5 Construction	258.4	295.2	378.4	271.5	225.0	229.8	260.0	261.4	103.1	69.4	83.0	202.7
6 Wholesale and retail trade, restaurants and hotels	618.2	667.6	681.3	647.5	655.4	693.5	707.1	679.1	501.8	532.4	627.9	702.8
7 Transport, storage and communication	408.2	427.4	497.0	601.1	590.6	640.8	651.7	659.8	571.0	569.6	637.3	731.7
8 Finance, insurance, real estate and business services	503.2	587.4	663.7	725.0	791.3	886.7	957.2	1044.8	966.2	952.9	989.4	1051.5
9 Community, social and personal services	246.9	273.1	344.0	358.5	379.5	397.1	420.7	429.4	329.3	361.7	376.8	405.4
Statistical discrepancy ab	312.4	330.4	353.3	321.1	337.7	342.6	360.5	360.4	370.8	361.8	410.5	428.7
Total, Industries	3178.1	3510.6	3890.5	3949.8	4051.7	4326.1	4537.0	4669.2	3947.3	3990.6	4317.0	4820.1
Producers of Government Services	446.4	468.5	534.2	595.1	673.7	731.1	761.0	815.8	811.1	768.9	741.5	760.9
Other Producers	37.2	42.4	46.2	50.7	56.3	57.6	59.7	61.2	53.4	57.0	62.8	66.4
Subtotal	3661.7	4021.5	4470.9	4595.6	4781.7	5114.8	5357.7	5546.2	4811.8	4816.5	5121.3	5647.4
Less: Imputed bank service charge	147.5	183.7	237.4	263.9	280.6	285.1	309.4	318.3	261.7	241.6	236.8	279.8
Plus: Import duties	78.4	83.6	91.1	96.3	108.8	118.6	142.6	135.4	54.4	64.4	124.9	123.5
Plus: Value added tax	...	...	...	...	...	...	...	...	...	...	...	...
Equals: Gross Domestic Product	3592.6	3921.4	4324.6	4428.0	4609.9	4948.3	5190.9	5363.3	4604.5	4639.3	5009.4	5491.1

a) For 1970-1979, item 'Statistical discrepancy' refers to the services rendered to the area of the Panama Canal. Beginning 1980, the Treaty Torrijos-Carter was inforced, therefore all the activities of the area of the Panama Canal have been incorporated to the corresponding type of economic activity.

b) Beginning 1980, item 'Statistical discrepancy' refers to transport services sold by a resident enterprise 'Commission del Canal de Panama'. Due to the special characteristics of this enterprise it has been separated from the rest to facilitate the analysis of the estimates.

1.11 Gross Domestic Product by Kind of Activity, in Constant Prices

Million Panamanian balboas

	1980	1981	1982	1983	1984	1985	1986	1987	1988	1989	1990	1991
					At constant prices of:1970							
1 Agriculture, hunting, forestry and fishing	164.3	176.0	173.6	183.8	186.8	195.9	190.4	207.3	196.5	203.8	210.0	223.9
2 Mining and quarrying	3.1	3.8	4.1	3.4	2.6	2.4	2.5	2.7	1.7	1.5	2.0	3.3
3 Manufacturing	182.1	176.1	179.9	176.7	175.8	179.3	183.3	190.1	147.1	155.2	173.2	188.5
4 Electricity, gas and water	53.5	56.2	59.2	64.9	64.2	69.2	73.3	78.4	76.3	74.1	76.5	81.0
5 Construction	124.3	128.3	154.7	106.4	87.9	87.9	94.5	91.9	36.1	23.9	33.5	72.7
6 Wholesale and retail trade, restaurants and hotels	256.4	252.9	251.0	239.4	240.4	251.4	255.4	243.5	184.2	192.0	217.7	241.2
7 Transport, storage and communication	207.6	216.5	251.1	321.1	305.1	335.5	338.8	360.0	301.4	279.4	278.9	320.9
8 Finance, insurance, real estate and business services	227.2	243.5	252.6	262.7	271.9	283.2	301.3	309.7	279.1	270.7	279.1	297.3
9 Community, social and personal services	142.6	150.1	163.3	168.8	176.2	182.4	195.7	197.1	141.9	154.4	162.2	175.3
Statistical discrepancy ab	175.5	188.4	204.7	175.0	174.6	177.0	186.0	187.6	193.8	189.9	192.1	202.4

Panama

1.11 Gross Domestic Product by Kind of Activity, in Constant Prices
(Continued)

Million Panamanian balboas

	1980	1981	1982	1983	1984	1985	1986	1987	1988	1989	1990	1991
					At constant prices of:1970							
Total, Industries	1536.6	1591.8	1694.2	1702.2	1685.5	1764.2	1821.2	1868.3	1558.1	1544.9	1625.2	1806.5
Producers of Government Services	201.2	222.9	232.1	240.6	248.3	258.7	265.2	272.4	264.0	260.0	244.4	250.1
Other Producers	17.7	18.5	19.3	19.4	21.5	21.9	22.5	22.4	19.5	20.9	23.0	24.0
Subtotal	1755.5	1833.2	1945.6	1962.2	1955.3	2044.8	2108.9	2163.1	1841.6	1825.8	1892.6	2080.6
Less: Imputed bank service charge	47.2	54.2	68.2	76.4	78.5	80.5	84.2	85.7	70.2	63.5	62.0	74.5
Plus: Import duties	28.1	27.7	29.6	32.7	33.4	36.1	42.3	39.6	15.3	16.9	31.0	29.5
Plus: Value added tax	...	...	...	...	...	...	...	...	...	...	...	...
Equals: Gross Domestic Product	1736.4	1806.7	1907.0	1918.5	1910.2	2000.4	2067.0	2117.0	1786.7	1779.2	1861.6	2035.6

a) For 1970-1979, item 'Statistical discrepancy' refers to the services rendered to the area of the Panama Canal. Beginning 1980, the Treaty Torrijos-Carter was inforced, therefore all the activities of the area of the Panama Canal have been incorporated to the corresponding type of economic activity.

b) Beginning 1980, item 'Statistical discrepancy' refers to transport services sold by a resident enterprise 'Commission del Canal de Panama'. Due to the special characteristics of this enterprise it has been separated from the rest to facilitate the analysis of the estimates.

1.12 Relations Among National Accounting Aggregates

Million Panamanian balboas

	1980	1981	1982	1983	1984	1985	1986	1987	1988	1989	1990	1991
Gross Domestic Product	3592.6	3921.4	4324.6	4428.0	4609.9	4948.3	5190.9	5363.3	4604.5	4639.3	5009.4	5491.1
Plus: Net factor income from the rest of the world	-110.0	-78.6	-138.9	2.2	-123.6	-46.4	-43.7	-41.1	-234.4	-273.0	-253.6	-231.6
Factor income from the rest of the world	2650.6	3431.9	3654.6	2830.0	2497.3	2087.6	1826.3	1433.9	660.0	681.2	679.6	659.4
Less: Factor income to the rest of the world	2760.6	3510.5	3793.5	2827.8	2620.9	2134.0	1870.0	1475.0	894.4	954.2	933.2	891.0
Equals: Gross National Product	3482.6	3842.8	4185.7	4430.2	4486.3	4901.9	5147.2	5322.2	4370.1	4366.3	4755.8	5259.5
Less: Consumption of fixed capital	252.1	279.7	320.9	335.5	374.6	398.8	424.4	434.9	411.9	403.1	422.1	445.9
Equals: National Income	3230.5	3563.1	3864.8	4094.7	4111.7	4503.1	4722.8	4887.3	3958.2	3963.2	4333.7	4813.6
Plus: Net current transfers from the rest of the world	14.3	31.2	36.0	39.8	89.6	108.7	95.7	62.9	71.5	70.1	195.7	193.3
Current transfers from the rest of the world	72.4	86.0	99.9	110.2	150.9	147.7	128.9	122.5	116.8	114.3	224.9	225.8
Less: Current transfers to the rest of the world	58.1	54.8	63.9	70.4	61.3	39.0	33.2	59.6	45.3	44.2	29.2	32.5
Equals: National Disposable Income	3244.8	3594.3	3900.8	4134.5	4201.3	4611.8	4818.5	4950.2	4029.7	4033.3	4529.4	5006.9
Less: Final consumption	2655.9	2873.6	3223.6	3365.3	3820.6	4063.6	4037.8	4193.0	3618.4	3992.5	3943.0	4420.4
Equals: Net Saving	588.9	720.7	677.2	769.2	380.7	548.2	780.7	757.2	411.3	40.8	586.4	586.5
Less: Surplus of the nation on current transactions	-145.9	-166.8	-186.5	170.6	-5.7	194.0	345.9	264.1	509.5	285.2	149.4	30.7
Equals: Net Capital Formation	734.8	887.5	863.7	598.6	386.4	354.2	434.8	493.1	-98.2	-244.4	437.0	555.8

2.1 Government Final Consumption Expenditure by Function, in Current Prices

Million Panamanian balboas

	1980	1981	1982	1983	1984	1985	1986	1987	1988	1989	1990	1991
1 General public services	275.3	372.8	445.7	348.0	351.5	323.5	402.5	480.5	307.6	318.3	301.8	335.8
2 Defence												
3 Public order and safety	...	...	...	...	...	...	...	...	...	...	...	...
4 Education	157.0	174.8	191.3	211.2	232.3	258.5	260.1	271.9	266.5	266.9	247.9	259.0
5 Health	54.9	57.5	74.0	72.9	77.6	78.8	94.8	105.9	103.2	95.1	97.4	102.5
6 Social security and welfare	101.8	116.2	133.9	173.6	211.3	217.0	222.6	219.3	210.4	180.6	169.8	159.1
7 Housing and community amenities	14.8	12.2	16.6	21.3	27.8	28.8	25.6	24.6	21.5	24.3	25.3	21.8
8 Recreational, cultural and religious affairs	13.2	19.1	25.4	22.4	25.9	22.9	25.8	36.0	28.8	29.9	20.5	21.8
9 Economic services	63.5	60.3	75.7	92.1	74.9	114.0	96.3	88.6	73.5	71.5	76.3	61.9
10 Other functions	-	-	-	-	-	0.1	0.1	0.1	0.1	0.1	0.1	0.1
Total Government Final Consumption Expenditure	680.5	812.9	962.6	941.5	1001.3	1043.6	1127.8	1226.9	1011.6	986.7	939.1	962.0

2.2 Government Final Consumption Expenditure by Function, in Constant Prices

Million Panamanian balboas

	1980	1981	1982	1983	1984	1985	1986	1987	1988	1989	1990	1991
	At constant prices of:1970											
1 General public services	115.2	153.7	169.3	127.1	122.3	109.7	137.1	158.0	99.7	106.9	98.2	110.8
2 Defence												
3 Public order and safety	...	...	...	...	...	...	...	...	...	...	...	...
4 Education	65.7	72.0	72.6	77.1	80.8	87.7	88.6	89.4	86.3	89.6	80.6	83.7
5 Health	23.0	23.6	28.1	26.6	27.0	26.7	32.3	34.8	33.4	31.9	31.7	33.1
6 Social security and welfare	42.6	47.9	50.9	63.4	73.5	73.6	75.8	72.1	68.2	60.7	55.2	45.9
7 Housing and community amenities	6.2	5.0	6.3	7.8	9.7	9.8	8.7	8.1	7.0	8.2	8.2	7.0
8 Recreational, cultural and religious affairs	5.5	7.9	9.6	8.2	9.0	7.8	8.8	11.9	9.3	10.0	6.7	7.1
9 Economic services	26.6	24.8	28.7	33.6	26.1	38.7	32.8	29.1	23.8	24.0	24.8	23.3
10 Other functions	-	-	-	-	-	-	-	-	-	-	-	-
Total Government Final Consumption Expenditure	284.8	334.9	365.5	343.8	348.4	354.0	384.1	403.4	327.7	331.3	305.4	310.9

2.7 Gross Capital Formation by Type of Good and Owner, in Current Prices

Million Panamanian balboas

	1980				1981				1982			
	TOTAL	Total Private	Public Enterprises	General Government	TOTAL	Total Private	Public Enterprises	General Government	TOTAL	Total Private	Public Enterprises	General Government
Increase in stocks, total	120.5	93.3	27.2	...	87.6	84.0	3.6	...	-0.8	-14.5	13.7	...
1 Goods producing industries	64.1	...	...	...	84.0	...	...	...	7.3	...	...	...
2 Wholesale and retail trade	53.6	...	...	...	-0.2	...	...	...	-5.6	...	...	...
3 Other, except government stocks	...	...	...	...	...	...	...	...	...	...	...	...
4 Government stocks	2.8	...	...	...	3.8	...	...	...	-2.5	...	...	...
Gross Fixed Capital Formation, Total	866.4	513.8	352.6	...	1079.6	733.3	346.3	...	1185.4	712.5	472.9	...
1 Residential buildings	93.3	78.1	15.2	...	117.4	99.8	17.6	...	121.7	103.2	18.5	...
2 Non-residential buildings	219.7	199.2	20.5	...	225.8	204.8	21.0	...	236.0	187.5	48.5	...
3 Other construction	251.4	33.6	217.8	...	339.0	126.3	212.7	...	493.6	237.5	256.1	...
A Completed	...	...	...	...	...	...	...	...	...	...	...	...
B Uncompleted	...	...	...	...	...	...	...	...	...	...	...	...
4 Land improvement and plantation and orchard development	...	...	...	...	...	...	...	...	...	...	...	...
5 Producers' durable goods	302.0	202.9	99.1	...	397.4	302.4	95.0	...	334.1	184.3	149.8	...
A Transport equipment	113.3	88.2	25.1	...	133.7	99.9	33.8	...	129.3	92.0	37.3	...
B Machinery and equipment	188.7	114.7	74.0	...	263.7	202.5	61.2	...	204.8	92.3	112.5	...
6 Breeding stock, dairy cattle, etc.	...	...	...	...	...	...	...	...	...	...	...	...
Total Gross Capital Formation	986.9	607.1	379.8	...	1167.2	817.3	349.9	...	1184.6	698.0	486.6	...

	1983				1984				1985			
	TOTAL	Total Private	Public Enterprises	General Government	TOTAL	Total Private	Public Enterprises	General Government	TOTAL	Total Private	Public Enterprises	General Government
Increase in stocks, total	16.3	-3.8	20.1	...	-18.9	0.7	-19.6	...	-20.1	-12.8	-7.3	...
1 Goods producing industries	-2.7	...	...	...	-24.7	...	...	...	-8.9	...	...	...
2 Wholesale and retail trade	0.5	...	...	...	0.4	...	...	...	-3.5	...	...	...
3 Other, except government stocks	...	...	...	...	...	...	...	...	...	...	...	...
4 Government stocks	18.5	...	...	...	5.4	...	...	...	-7.7	...	...	...
Gross Fixed Capital Formation, Total	917.8	604.8	313.0	...	779.9	497.5	282.4	...	773.1	586.1	187.0	...
1 Residential buildings	119.7	108.8	10.9	...	128.9	111.8	17.1	...	182.3	163.9	18.4	...
2 Non-residential buildings	221.9	202.3	19.6	...	145.3	118.8	26.5	...	170.8	146.8	24.0	...
3 Other construction	272.4	62.3	210.1	...	225.7	38.6	187.1	...	125.2	45.9	79.3	...
A Completed	...	...	...	...	...	...	...	...	...	...	...	...
B Uncompleted	...	...	...	...	...	...	...	...	...	...	...	...
4 Land improvement and plantation and orchard development	...	...	...	...	...	...	...	...	...	...	...	...
5 Producers' durable goods	303.8	231.4	72.4	...	280.0	228.3	51.7	...	294.8	229.5	65.3	...
A Transport equipment	103.4	77.7	25.7	...	105.4	89.3	16.1	...	117.6	94.1	23.5	...
B Machinery and equipment	200.4	153.7	46.7	...	174.6	139.0	35.6	...	177.2	135.4	41.8	...
6 Breeding stock, dairy cattle, etc.	...	...	...	...	...	...	...	...	...	...	...	...
Total Gross Capital Formation	934.1	601.0	333.1	...	761.0	498.2	262.8	...	753.0	573.3	179.7	...

Panama

2.7 Gross Capital Formation by Type of Good and Owner, in Current Prices

Million Panamanian balboas

	1986				1987				1988			
	TOTAL	Total Private	Public Enterprises	General Government	TOTAL	Total Private	Public Enterprises	General Government	TOTAL	Total Private	Public Enterprises	General Government
Increase in stocks, total	-37.5	-28.9	-8.6	...	-9.0	-19.5	10.5	...	-94.0	-88.1	-5.9	...
1 Goods producing industries	-49.5	...	...	...	1.7	...	...	...	-12.9	...	...	...
2 Wholesale and retail trade	19.6	...	...	...	-16.3	...	...	...	-78.9	...	...	...
3 Other, except government stocks	...	...	...	...	...	...	...	...	...	...	...	...
4 Government stocks	-7.6	...	...	...	5.6	...	...	...	-2.2	...	...	...
Gross Fixed Capital Formation, Total	896.7	715.4	181.3	...	937.0	790.2	146.8	...	407.7	301.9	105.8	...
1 Residential buildings	207.0	191.8	15.2	...	212.7	209.0	3.7	...	74.4	74.1	0.3	...
2 Non-residential buildings	188.1	169.5	18.6	...	221.0	204.3	16.7	...	82.6	75.5	7.1	...
3 Other construction	147.7	53.6	94.1	...	106.7	60.4	46.3	...	49.6	21.1	28.5	...
A Completed	...	...	...	...	...	...	...	...	...	...	...	...
B Uncompleted	...	...	...	...	...	...	...	...	...	...	...	...
4 Land improvement and plantation and orchard development	...	...	...	...	...	...	...	...	...	...	...	...
5 Producers' durable goods	353.9	300.5	53.4	...	396.6	316.5	80.1	...	201.1	131.2	69.9	...
A Transport equipment	140.1	125.9	14.2	...	159.1	116.0	43.1	...	69.9	43.0	26.9	...
B Machinery and equipment	213.8	174.6	39.2	...	237.5	200.5	37.0	...	131.2	88.2	43.0	...
6 Breeding stock, dairy cattle, etc.	...	...	...	...	...	...	...	...	...	...	...	...
Total Gross Capital Formation	859.2	686.5	172.7	...	928.0	770.7	157.3	...	313.7	213.8	99.9	...

	1989				1990				1991			
	TOTAL	Total Private	Public Enterprises	General Government	TOTAL	Total Private	Public Enterprises	General Government	TOTAL	Total Private	Public Enterprises	General Government
Increase in stocks, total	-161.3	-156.0	-5.3	...	385.7	376.3	9.4	...	75.9	64.6	11.3	...
1 Goods producing industries	-44.4	...	...	...	307.6	...	...	...	22.9	...	...	...
2 Wholesale and retail trade	-114.5	...	...	...	72.2	...	...	...	44.6	...	...	...
3 Other, except government stocks	...	...	...	...	...	...	...	...	...	...	...	...
4 Government stocks	-2.4	...	...	...	5.6	...	...	...	8.4	...	...	...
Gross Fixed Capital Formation, Total	320.0	239.7	80.3	...	473.4	411.0	62.4	...	925.8	749.5	176.3	...
1 Residential buildings	38.6	38.2	0.4	...	42.5	42.5	-	...	99.2	83.7	15.5	...
2 Non-residential buildings	56.3	44.8	11.5	...	100.5	91.8	8.7	...	205.7	184.8	20.9	...
3 Other construction	47.8	10.8	37.0	...	27.4	16.0	11.4	...	116.0	33.0	83.0	...
A Completed	...	...	...	...	27.4	16.0	11.4	...	116.0	33.0	83.0	...
B Uncompleted	...	...	...	...	...	...	...	...	...	...	...	...
4 Land improvement and plantation and orchard development	...	...	...	...	...	...	...	...	...	...	...	...
5 Producers' durable goods	177.3	145.9	31.4	...	303.0	260.7	42.3	...	504.9	448.0	56.9	...
A Transport equipment	55.1	43.2	11.9	...	103.0	70.8	32.2	...	200.5	178.1	22.4	...
B Machinery and equipment	122.2	102.7	19.5	...	200.0	189.9	10.1	...	304.4	269.9	34.5	...
6 Breeding stock, dairy cattle, etc.	...	...	...	...	...	...	...	...	...	...	...	...
Total Gross Capital Formation	158.7	83.7	75.0	...	859.1	787.3	71.8	...	1001.7	814.1	187.6	...

2.8 Gross Capital Formation by Type of Good and Owner, in Constant Prices

Million Panamanian balboas

	1980				1981				1982			
	TOTAL	Total Private	Public Enterprises	General Government	TOTAL	Total Private	Public Enterprises	General Government	TOTAL	Total Private	Public Enterprises	General Government
	At constant prices of:1970											
Increase in stocks, total	46.3	34.0	12.3	...	37.3	37.6	-0.3	...	0.5	-2.0	2.5	...
1 Goods producing industries	22.9	...	...	...	36.2	...	...	...	3.4	...	...	...
2 Wholesale and retail trade	21.5	...	...	...	-0.5	...	...	...	-1.0	...	...	...
3 Other, except government stocks	...	...	...	...	...	...	...	...	...	...	...	...
4 Government stocks	1.9	...	...	...	1.6	...	...	...	-1.9	...	...	...
Gross Fixed Capital Formation, Total	365.3	215.3	150.0	...	426.1	292.1	134.0	...	430.1	258.5	171.6	...
1 Residential buildings	37.0	30.9	6.1	...	42.8	36.4	6.4	...	41.4	35.1	6.3	...
2 Non-residential buildings	87.2	79.1	8.1	...	82.3	74.6	7.7	...	80.2	63.7	16.5	...

2.8 Gross Capital Formation by Type of Good and Owner, in Constant Prices
(Continued)

Million Panamanian balboas

	1980				1981				1982			
	TOTAL	Total Private	Public Enterprises	General Government	TOTAL	Total Private	Public Enterprises	General Government	TOTAL	Total Private	Public Enterprises	General Government
	At constant prices of:1970											
3 Other construction	99.8	13.4	86.4	...	123.5	46.0	77.5	...	167.7	80.7	87.0	...
4 Land improvement and plantation and orchard development	...	...	...	...	...	...	...	...	...	...	...	...
5 Producers' durable goods	141.3	91.9	49.4	...	177.5	135.1	42.4	...	140.8	79.0	61.8	...
A Transport equipment	35.3	27.5	7.8	...	60.7	45.4	15.3	...	54.4	39.8	14.6	...
B Machinery and equipment	106.0	64.4	41.6	...	116.8	89.7	27.1	...	86.4	39.2	47.2	...
6 Breeding stock, dairy cattle, etc.	...	...	...	...	...	...	...	...	...	...	...	...
Total Gross Capital Formation	411.6	249.3	162.3	...	463.4	329.7	133.7	...	430.6	256.5	174.1	...

	1983				1984				1985			
	TOTAL	Total Private	Public Enterprises	General Government	TOTAL	Total Private	Public Enterprises	General Government	TOTAL	Total Private	Public Enterprises	General Government
	At constant prices of:1970											
Increase in stocks, total	7.9	-2.9	10.8	...	-6.9	0.4	-7.3	...	-7.5	-1.9	-5.6	...
1 Goods producing industries	-0.4	...	...	...	-5.6	...	...	...	-2.5	...	...	...
2 Wholesale and retail trade	-1.7	...	...	...	1.5	...	...	...	-1.0	...	...	...
3 Other, except government stocks	...	...	...	...	...	...	...	...	...	...	...	...
4 Government stocks	10.0	...	...	...	-2.8	...	...	...	-4.0	...	...	...
Gross Fixed Capital Formation, Total	333.0	222.5	110.5	...	310.2	214.7	95.5	...	331.4	252.9	78.5	...
1 Residential buildings	39.6	36.0	3.6	...	43.1	37.4	5.7	...	60.8	54.7	6.1	...
2 Non-residential buildings	73.4	66.9	6.5	...	48.6	39.7	8.9	...	57.0	49.0	8.0	...
3 Other construction	90.1	20.6	69.5	...	75.4	13.0	62.4	...	41.8	15.3	26.5	...
4 Land improvement and plantation and orchard development	...	...	...	...	...	...	...	...	...	...	...	...
5 Producers' durable goods	129.9	99.0	30.9	...	143.1	124.6	18.5	...	171.8	133.9	37.9	...
A Transport equipment	43.2	32.5	10.7	...	49.0	43.2	5.8	...	73.4	58.7	14.7	...
B Machinery and equipment	86.7	66.5	20.2	...	94.1	81.4	12.7	...	98.4	75.2	23.2	...
6 Breeding stock, dairy cattle, etc.	...	...	...	...	...	...	...	...	...	...	...	...
Total Gross Capital Formation	340.9	219.6	121.3	...	303.3	215.1	88.2	...	323.9	251.0	72.9	...

	1986				1987				1988			
	TOTAL	Total Private	Public Enterprises	General Government	TOTAL	Total Private	Public Enterprises	General Government	TOTAL	Total Private	Public Enterprises	General Government
	At constant prices of:1970											
Increase in stocks, total	-11.7	-7.7	-4.0	...	-4.2	-8.4	4.2	...	-34.7	-32.3	-2.4	...
1 Goods producing industries	-14.6	...	...	...	-0.4	...	...	...	-4.8	...	...	...
2 Wholesale and retail trade	6.6	...	...	...	-6.4	...	...	...	-28.8	...	...	...
3 Other, except government stocks	...	...	...	...	...	...	...	...	...	...	...	...
4 Government stocks	-3.7	...	...	...	2.6	...	...	...	-1.1	...	...	...
Gross Fixed Capital Formation, Total	363.5	294.1	69.4	...	364.3	316.6	47.7	...	165.7	132.0	33.7	...
1 Residential buildings	66.7	61.8	4.9	...	67.3	66.1	1.2	...	23.9	23.8	0.1	...
2 Non-residential buildings	60.6	54.6	6.0	...	69.9	64.6	5.3	...	26.5	24.2	2.3	...
3 Other construction	47.6	17.3	30.3	...	33.7	19.1	14.6	...	15.9	6.8	9.1	...
4 Land improvement and plantation and orchard development	...	...	...	...	...	...	...	...	...	...	...	...
5 Producers' durable goods	188.6	160.4	28.2	...	193.4	166.8	26.6	...	99.4	77.2	22.2	...
A Transport equipment	77.6	69.7	7.9	...	82.3	68.0	14.3	...	36.5	28.1	8.4	...
B Machinery and equipment	111.0	90.7	20.3	...	111.1	98.8	12.3	...	62.9	49.1	13.8	...
6 Breeding stock, dairy cattle, etc.	...	...	...	...	...	...	...	...	...	...	...	...
Total Gross Capital Formation	351.8	286.4	65.4	...	360.1	308.2	51.9	...	131.0	99.7	31.3	...

Panama

2.8 Gross Capital Formation by Type of Good and Owner, in Constant Prices

Million Panamanian balboas

	1989				1990				1991			
	TOTAL	Total Private	Public Enterprises	General Government	TOTAL	Total Private	Public Enterprises	General Government	TOTAL	Total Private	Public Enterprises	General Government
At constant prices of:1970												
Increase in stocks, total	-60.6	-58.4	-2.2	...	131.5	127.6	3.9	...	26.2	20.8	5.4	...
1 Goods producing industries	-16.8	...	...	...	102.2	...	...	...	7.7			
2 Wholesale and retail trade	-42.5	...	...	...	26.3	...	...	...	14.0	...	...	...
3 Other, except government stocks	...	...	...	...	...	...	...	...	...	...	...	...
4 Government stocks	-1.3	...	...	...	3.0	...	...	...	4.5	...	...	...
Gross Fixed Capital Formation, Total	134.6	109.4	25.2	...	177.7	158.0	19.7	...	291.9	238.0	53.9	...
1 Residential buildings	12.1	12.0	0.1	...	14.2	14.2	-	...	30.5	25.8	4.7	...
2 Non-residential buildings	17.7	14.1	3.6	...	33.6	30.7	2.9	...	63.3	56.9	6.4	...
3 Other construction	15.2	3.5	11.7	...	9.2	5.4	3.8	...	35.7	10.1	25.6	...
4 Land improvement and plantation and orchard development	...	...	...	...	...	...	...	...	...	...	...	...
5 Producers' durable goods	89.6	79.8	9.8	...	120.7	107.7	13.0	...	162.4	145.2	17.2	...
A Transport equipment	30.6	27.0	3.6	...	41.1	31.5	9.6	...	55.2	48.7	6.5	...
B Machinery and equipment	59.0	52.8	6.2	...	79.6	76.2	3.4	...	107.2	96.5	10.7	...
6 Breeding stock, dairy cattle, etc.	...	...	...	...	...	...	...	...	...	...	...	...
Total Gross Capital Formation	74.0	51.0	23.0	...	309.2	285.6	23.6	...	318.1	258.8	59.3	...

2.17 Exports and Imports of Goods and Services, Detail

Million Panamanian balboas

	1980	1981	1982	1983	1984	1985	1986	1987	1988	1989	1990	1991
Exports of Goods and Services												
1 Exports of merchandise, f.o.b.	584.6	574.3	572.1	521.7	453.4	480.3	483.6	513.4	466.9	487.8	542.9	543.5
2 Transport and communication	408.0	440.3	532.9	640.8	602.0	645.6	622.8	607.7	582.2	520.8	528.5	560.8
3 Insurance service charges	2.1	2.3	2.1	1.4	1.6	2.7	1.5	2.7	2.4	2.2	1.9	1.8
4 Other commodities	366.6	413.9	380.1	351.4	341.9	343.8	418.6	385.5	357.0	401.3	507.5	558.5
5 Adjustments of merchandise exports to change-of-ownership basis	...	...	...	...	...	...	...	...	...	...	...	...
6 Direct purchases in the domestic market by non-residential households	219.8	232.8	235.8	240.8	249.6	284.2	283.6	266.0	241.4	235.5	247.9	271.4
7 Direct purchases in the domestic market by extraterritorial bodies a	45.1	47.7	49.9	48.6	58.8	65.5	59.6	76.5	81.5	76.6	107.3	118.4
Statistical discrepancy	-	-	-	-	-	-	-	-	-	-	-	...
Total Exports of Goods and Services	1626.2	1711.3	1772.9	1804.7	1707.3	1822.1	1869.7	1851.8	1731.4	1724.2	1936.0	2054.4
Imports of Goods and Services												
1 Imports of merchandise, c.i.f.	1483.9	1620.0	1636.9	1474.4	1468.3	1451.0	1323.7	1372.3	872.5	1042.6	1532.9	1747.6
A Imports of merchandise, f.o.b.	1327.0	1453.0	1477.3	1329.5	1314.6	1301.5	1152.0	1221.5	786.1	941.9	1379.9	1573.1
B Transport of services on merchandise imports	149.3	161.2	154.4	139.7	147.5	146.7	168.0	146.6	83.6	97.5	147.5	168.9
C Insurance service charges on merchandise imports	7.6	5.8	5.2	5.2	6.2	2.8	3.7	4.2	2.8	3.2	5.5	5.6
2 Adjustments of merchandise imports to change-of-ownership basis	...	...	...	...	...	...	...	...	...	...	...	...
3 Other transport and communication	42.4	46.8	45.8	46.0	59.8	58.8	67.0	59.0	40.2	42.6	36.4	59.6
4 Other insurance service charges	13.0	17.1	20.8	19.7	19.4	30.3	31.9	29.9	20.4	19.2	19.1	18.6
5 Other commodities	66.7	64.0	48.1	38.1	41.8	56.1	50.2	34.8	21.8	31.1	22.8	32.7
6 Direct purchases abroad by government	15.3	16.4	20.9	23.4	20.9	24.9	27.3	18.5	10.7	10.6	13.6	16.6
7 Direct purchases abroad by resident households	55.1	66.4	84.0	74.5	68.8	69.3	75.7	95.0	93.4	90.0	103.9	110.3
Total Imports of Goods and Services	1676.4	1830.7	1856.5	1676.1	1679.0	1690.4	1575.8	1609.5	1059.0	1236.1	1728.7	1985.4
Balance of Goods and Services	-50.2	-119.4	-83.6	128.6	28.3	131.7	293.9	242.3	672.4	488.1	207.3	69.0
Total Imports and Balance of Goods and Services	1626.2	1711.3	1772.9	1804.7	1707.3	1822.1	1869.7	1851.8	1731.4	1724.2	1936.0	2054.4

a) Item 'Direct purchases in the domestic market by extra-territorial bodies' relates to compensation of employees and property and entrepreneurial income received by residents of Panama for services rendered in the Former Canal Zone and Colon Free Zone.

4.1 Derivation of Value Added by Kind of Activity, in Current Prices

Million Panamanian balboas

	1980			1981			1982			1983		
	Gross Output	Intermediate Consumption	Value Added	Gross Output	Intermediate Consumption	Value Added	Gross Output	Intermediate Consumption	Value Added	Gross Output	Intermediate Consumption	Value Added
All Producers												
1 Agriculture, hunting, forestry and fishing	...	...	354.2	...	...	402.8	...	...	416.9	...	...	462.7
A Agriculture and hunting	...	...	306.4	...	...	361.8	...	...	369.4	...	...	411.5
B Forestry and logging	...	...	8.7	...	...	8.9	...	...	9.9	...	...	11.8
C Fishing	...	...	39.1	...	...	32.1	...	...	37.6	...	...	39.4
2 Mining and quarrying	...	...	6.8	...	...	8.7	...	...	9.3	...	...	7.9
3 Manufacturing	...	...	356.0	...	...	375.6	...	...	394.0	...	...	401.0
A Manufacture of food, beverages and tobacco	...	...	143.2	...	...	155.6	...	...	160.3	...	...	169.0
B Textile, wearing apparel and leather industries	...	...	44.1	...	...	44.8	...	...	46.1	...	...	45.2
C Manufacture of wood and wood products, including furniture	...	...	14.8	...	...	16.2	...	...	17.8	...	...	18.2
D Manufacture of paper and paper products, printing and publishing	...	...	27.1	...	...	26.5	...	...	27.1	...	...	30.1
E Manufacture of chemicals and chemical petroleum, coal, rubber and plastic products	...	...	69.7	...	...	72.3	...	...	76.4	...	...	76.3
F Manufacture of non-metallic mineral products, except products of petroleum and coal	...	...	30.6	...	...	33.5	...	...	36.8	...	...	33.6
G Basic metal industries	...	...	6.1	...	...	6.3	...	...	6.0	...	...	4.1
H Manufacture of fabricated metal products, machinery and equipment	...	...	19.4	...	...	19.6	...	...	22.6	...	...	23.0
I Other manufacturing industries	...	...	1.0	...	...	0.8	...	...	0.9	...	...	1.5
4 Electricity, gas and water	...	...	113.8	...	...	142.4	...	...	152.6	...	...	153.5
A Electricity, gas and steam	...	...	101.6	...	...	131.0	...	...	134.1	...	...	133.8
B Water works and supply	...	...	12.2	...	...	11.4	...	...	18.5	...	...	19.7
5 Construction	...	...	258.4	...	...	295.2	...	...	378.4	...	...	271.5
6 Wholesale and retail trade, restaurants and hotels	...	...	618.2	...	...	667.6	...	...	681.3	...	...	647.5
A Wholesale and retail trade	...	...	544.4	...	...	592.1	...	...	602.2	...	...	574.3
B Restaurants and hotels	...	...	73.8	...	...	75.5	...	...	79.1	...	...	73.2
7 Transport, storage and communication	...	...	408.2	...	...	427.4	...	...	497.0	...	...	601.1
A Transport and storage	...	...	352.8	...	...	356.3	...	...	413.9	...	...	509.5
B Communication	...	...	55.4	...	...	71.1	...	...	83.1	...	...	91.6
8 Finance, insurance, real estate and business services	...	...	503.2	...	...	587.4	...	...	663.7	...	...	725.0
A Financial institutions	...	...	166.3	...	...	203.5	...	...	226.8	...	...	242.3
B Insurance	...	...	24.5	...	...	30.1	...	...	34.5	...	...	37.5
C Real estate and business services	...	...	312.4	...	...	353.8	...	...	402.4	...	...	445.2
Real estate, except dwellings	...	...	13.3	...	...	16.3	...	...	18.0	...	...	20.1
Dwellings	...	...	247.9	...	...	278.4	...	...	319.1	...	...	359.1
9 Community, social and personal services	...	...	246.9	...	...	273.1	...	...	344.0	...	...	358.5
A Sanitary and similar services	...	...	17.5	...	...	16.5	...	...	20.8	...	...	20.5
B Social and related community services	...	...	64.6	...	...	74.5	...	...	94.9	...	...	101.9
Educational services	...	...	16.3	...	...	17.2	...	...	22.1	...	...	22.5
Medical, dental, other health and veterinary services	...	...	48.3	...	...	57.3	...	...	72.8	...	...	79.4
C Recreational and cultural services	...	...	102.7	...	...	111.0	...	...	133.7	...	...	135.5
D Personal and household services	...	...	62.1	...	...	71.1	...	...	94.6	...	...	100.6
Statistical discrepancy ab	...	...	312.4	...	...	330.4	...	...	353.3	...	...	321.1

Panama

Million Panamanian balboas

	1980			1981			1982			1983		
	Gross Output	Intermediate Consumption	Value Added	Gross Output	Intermediate Consumption	Value Added	Gross Output	Intermediate Consumption	Value Added	Gross Output	Intermediate Consumption	Value Added
Total, Industries	...	...	3178.1	...	...	3510.6	...	...	3890.5	...	...	3949.8
Producers of Government Services	...	...	446.4	...	...	468.5	...	...	534.2	...	...	595.1
Other Producers	...	...	37.2	...	...	42.4	...	...	46.2	...	...	50.7
Total	...	...	3661.7	...	...	4021.5	...	...	4470.9	...	...	4595.6
Less: Imputed bank service charge	...	...	147.5	...	...	183.7	...	...	237.4	...	...	263.9
Import duties	...	...	78.4	...	...	83.6	...	...	91.1	...	...	96.3
Value added tax	...	...	...	...	...	...	...	...	...	...	...	...
Total	...	...	3592.6	...	...	3921.4	...	...	4324.6	...	...	4428.0

	1984			1985			1986			1987		
	Gross Output	Intermediate Consumption	Value Added	Gross Output	Intermediate Consumption	Value Added	Gross Output	Intermediate Consumption	Value Added	Gross Output	Intermediate Consumption	Value Added
						All Producers						
1 Agriculture, hunting, forestry and fishing	...	...	460.3	...	...	497.8	...	...	524.4	...	...	559.1
A Agriculture and hunting	...	...	410.5	...	...	440.2	...	...	429.7	...	...	469.6
B Forestry and logging	...	...	12.2	...	...	12.3	...	...	12.3	...	...	11.9
C Fishing	...	...	37.6	...	...	45.3	...	...	82.4	...	...	77.6
2 Mining and quarrying	...	...	6.0	...	...	5.7	...	...	6.0	...	...	6.3
3 Manufacturing	...	...	411.0	...	...	420.0	...	...	421.8	...	...	440.4
A Manufacture of food, beverages and tobacco	...	...	175.5	...	...	188.6	...	...	197.8	...	...	201.3
B Textile, wearing apparel and leather industries	...	...	47.0	...	...	48.6	...	...	47.3	...	...	47.7
C Manufacture of wood and wood products, including furniture	...	...	21.4	...	...	21.7	...	...	21.2	...	...	20.0
D Manufacture of paper and paper products, printing and publishing	...	...	32.1	...	...	34.9	...	...	34.3	...	...	34.9
E Manufacture of chemicals and chemical petroleum, coal, rubber and plastic products	...	...	76.5	...	...	69.8	...	...	60.2	...	...	67.8
F Manufacture of non-metallic mineral products, except products of petroleum and coal	...	...	27.6	...	...	26.9	...	...	31.0	...	...	33.5
G Basic metal industries	...	...	3.9	...	...	4.3	...	...	4.7	...	...	6.1
H Manufacture of fabricated metal products, machinery and equipment	...	...	24.1	...	...	22.4	...	...	22.0	...	...	25.3
I Other manufacturing industries	...	...	2.9	...	...	2.8	...	...	3.3	...	...	3.2
4 Electricity, gas and water	...	...	194.9	...	...	212.1	...	...	227.6	...	...	228.5
A Electricity, gas and steam	...	...	176.0	...	...	194.5	...	...	206.6	...	...	208.6
B Water works and supply	...	...	18.9	...	...	17.6	...	...	21.0	...	...	19.9
5 Construction	...	...	225.0	...	...	229.8	...	...	260.0	...	...	261.4
6 Wholesale and retail trade, restaurants and hotels	...	...	655.4	...	...	693.5	...	...	707.1	...	...	679.1
A Wholesale and retail trade	...	...	575.1	...	...	604.0	...	...	615.2	...	...	593.4
B Restaurants and hotels	...	...	80.3	...	...	89.5	...	...	91.9	...	...	85.7
7 Transport, storage and communication	...	...	590.6	...	...	640.8	...	...	651.7	...	...	659.8
A Transport and storage	...	...	489.9	...	...	533.7	...	...	529.5	...	...	518.9
B Communication	...	...	100.7	...	...	107.1	...	...	122.2	...	...	140.9
8 Finance, insurance, real estate and business services	...	...	791.3	...	...	886.7	...	...	957.2	...	...	1044.8
A Financial institutions	...	...	255.7	...	...	278.3	...	...	308.3	...	...	313.2
B Insurance	...	...	40.2	...	...	41.0	...	...	43.8	...	...	47.4
C Real estate and business services	...	...	495.4	...	...	567.4	...	...	605.1	...	...	684.2
Real estate, except dwellings	...	...	21.2	...	...	22.9	...	...	26.0	...	...	29.1
Dwellings	...	...	402.3	...	...	466.7	...	...	496.1	...	...	569.4
9 Community, social and personal services	...	...	379.5	...	...	397.1	...	...	420.7	...	...	429.4
A Sanitary and similar services	...	...	18.5	...	...	17.4	...	...	17.6	...	...	18.0
B Social and related community services	...	...	111.6	...	...	113.9	...	...	115.5	...	...	119.4

4.1 Derivation of Value Added by Kind of Activity, in Current Prices
(Continued)

Million Panamanian balboas

	1984			1985			1986			1987		
	Gross Output	Intermediate Consumption	Value Added	Gross Output	Intermediate Consumption	Value Added	Gross Output	Intermediate Consumption	Value Added	Gross Output	Intermediate Consumption	Value Added
Educational services	...	...	20.7	...	...	21.3	...	...	21.9	...	...	22.4
Medical, dental, other health and veterinary services	...	...	90.9	...	...	92.6	...	...	93.6	...	...	97.0
C Recreational and cultural services	...	...	136.7	...	...	141.0	...	...	148.8	...	...	145.8
D Personal and household services	...	...	112.7	...	...	124.8	...	...	138.8	...	...	146.2
Statistical discrepancy ab	...	...	337.7	...	...	342.6	...	...	360.5	...	...	360.4
Total, Industries	...	...	4051.7	...	...	4326.1	...	...	4537.0	...	...	4669.2
Producers of Government Services	...	...	673.7	...	...	731.1	...	...	761.0	...	...	815.8
Other Producers	...	...	56.3	...	...	57.6	...	...	59.7	...	...	61.2
Total	...	...	4781.7	...	...	5114.8	...	...	5357.7	...	...	5546.2
Less: Imputed bank service charge	...	...	280.6	...	...	285.1	...	...	309.4	...	...	318.3
Import duties	...	...	108.8	...	...	118.6	...	...	142.6	...	...	135.4
Value added tax	...	...	...	...	...	...	...	...	...	...	...	...
Total	...	...	4609.9	...	...	4948.3	...	...	5190.9	...	...	5363.3

	1988			1989			1990			1991		
	Gross Output	Intermediate Consumption	Value Added	Gross Output	Intermediate Consumption	Value Added	Gross Output	Intermediate Consumption	Value Added	Gross Output	Intermediate Consumption	Value Added
						All Producers						
1 Agriculture, hunting, forestry and fishing	...	...	531.8	...	...	554.2	...	...	552.1	...	...	609.6
A Agriculture and hunting	...	...	469.9	...	...	477.7	...	...	494.6	...	...	545.7
B Forestry and logging	...	...	11.0	...	...	11.6	...	...	12.0	...	...	12.1
C Fishing	...	...	50.9	...	...	64.9	...	...	45.5	...	...	51.8
2 Mining and quarrying	...	...	3.8	...	...	3.6	...	...	4.3	...	...	5.6
3 Manufacturing	...	...	328.7	...	...	353.7	...	...	407.0	...	...	453.5
A Manufacture of food, beverages and tobacco	...	...	172.7	...	...	183.2	...	...	201.5	...	...	218.8
B Textile, wearing apparel and leather industries	...	...	33.4	...	...	36.4	...	...	39.0	...	...	43.9
C Manufacture of wood and wood products, including furniture	...	...	9.5	...	...	11.8	...	...	16.2	...	...	17.8
D Manufacture of paper and paper products, printing and publishing	...	...	28.3	...	...	31.9	...	...	36.3	...	...	37.4
E Manufacture of chemicals and chemical petroleum, coal, rubber and plastic products	...	...	53.3	...	...	58.0	...	...	69.5	...	...	77.2
F Manufacture of non-metallic mineral products, except products of petroleum and coal	...	...	13.4	...	...	12.9	...	...	18.2	...	...	28.5
G Basic metal industries	...	...	2.4	...	...	2.1	...	...	3.4	...	...	5.6
H Manufacture of fabricated metal products, machinery and equipment	...	...	13.4	...	...	14.5	...	...	20.2	...	...	21.6
I Other manufacturing industries	...	...	2.3	...	...	2.9	...	...	2.7	...	...	2.7
4 Electricity, gas and water	...	...	240.8	...	...	231.3	...	...	228.7	...	...	228.6
A Electricity, gas and steam	...	...	218.7	...	...	208.7	...	...	207.4	...	...	207.1
B Water works and supply	...	...	22.1	...	...	22.6	...	...	21.3	...	...	21.5
5 Construction	...	...	103.1	...	...	69.4	...	...	83.0	...	...	202.7
6 Wholesale and retail trade, restaurants and hotels	...	...	501.8	...	...	532.4	...	...	627.9	...	...	702.8
A Wholesale and retail trade	...	...	427.9	...	...	451.8	...	...	537.9	...	...	599.7
B Restaurants and hotels	...	...	73.9	...	...	80.6	...	...	90.0	...	...	103.1
7 Transport, storage and communication	...	...	571.0	...	...	569.6	...	...	637.3	...	...	731.7
A Transport and storage	...	...	428.3	...	...	420.2	...	...	467.4	...	...	561.5
B Communication	...	...	142.7	...	...	149.4	...	...	169.9	...	...	170.2
8 Finance, insurance, real estate and business services	...	...	966.2	...	...	952.9	...	...	989.4	...	...	1051.5
A Financial institutions	...	...	251.9	...	...	235.0	...	...	259.5	...	...	307.3
B Insurance	...	...	37.2	...	...	28.9	...	...	26.2	...	...	26.3
C Real estate and business services	...	...	677.1	...	...	689.0	...	...	703.7	...	...	717.9
Real estate, except dwellings	...	...	20.4	...	...	17.8	...	...	18.1	...	...	19.9

Panama

4.1 Derivation of Value Added by Kind of Activity, in Current Prices
(Continued)

Million Panamanian balboas

	1988			1989			1990			1991		
	Gross Output	Intermediate Consumption	Value Added	Gross Output	Intermediate Consumption	Value Added	Gross Output	Intermediate Consumption	Value Added	Gross Output	Intermediate Consumption	Value Added
Dwellings	...	...	590.0	...	...	596.3	...	...	597.1	...	...	598.6
9 Community, social and personal services	...	...	329.3	...	...	361.7	...	...	376.8	...	...	405.4
A Sanitary and similar services	...	...	9.4	...	...	11.2	...	...	13.5	...	...	16.9
B Social and related community services	...	...	120.7	...	...	124.3	...	...	122.5	...	...	124.5
Educational services	...	...	20.7	...	...	22.3	...	...	23.1	...	...	23.7
Medical, dental, other health and veterinary services	...	...	100.0	...	...	102.0	...	...	99.4	...	...	100.8
C Recreational and cultural services	...	...	96.3	...	...	108.4	...	...	112.8	...	...	125.3
D Personal and household services	...	...	102.9	...	...	117.8	...	...	128.0	...	...	138.7
Statistical discrepancy ab	...	...	370.8	...	...	361.8	...	...	410.5	...	...	428.7
Total, Industries	...	...	3947.3	...	...	3990.6	...	...	4317.0	...	...	4820.1
Producers of Government Services	...	...	811.1	...	...	768.9	...	...	741.5	...	...	760.9
Other Producers	...	...	53.4	...	...	57.0	...	...	62.8	...	...	66.4
Total	...	...	4811.8	...	...	4816.5	...	...	5121.3	...	...	5647.4
Less: Imputed bank service charge	...	...	261.7	...	...	241.6	...	...	236.8	...	...	279.8
Import duties	...	...	54.4	...	...	64.4	...	...	124.9	...	...	123.5
Value added tax	...	...	...	...	...	...	...	...	...	...	...	...
Total	...	...	4604.5	...	...	4639.3	...	...	5009.4	...	...	5491.1

a) For 1970-1979, item 'Statistical discrepancy' refers to the services rendered to the area of the Panama Canal. Beginning 1980, the Treaty Torrijos-Carter was inforced, therefore all the activities of the area of the Panama Canal have been incorporated to the corresponding type of economic activity.

b) Beginning 1980, item 'Statistical discrepancy' refers to transport services sold by a resident enterprise 'Commission del Canal de Panama'. Due to the special characteristics of this enterprise it has been separated from the rest to facilitate the analysis of the estimates.

4.2 Derivation of Value Added by Kind of Activity, in Constant Prices

Million Panamanian balboas

	1980			1981			1982			1983		
	Gross Output	Intermediate Consumption	Value Added	Gross Output	Intermediate Consumption	Value Added	Gross Output	Intermediate Consumption	Value Added	Gross Output	Intermediate Consumption	Value Added

At constant prices of:1970

All Producers

1 Agriculture, hunting, forestry and fishing	...	...	164.3	...	...	176.0	...	...	173.6	...	...	183.8
A Agriculture and hunting	...	...	152.0	...	...	164.3	...	...	161.7	...	...	171.4
B Forestry and logging	...	...	5.0	...	...	4.9	...	...	5.1	...	...	5.5
C Fishing	...	...	7.3	...	...	6.8	...	...	6.8	...	...	6.9
2 Mining and quarrying	...	...	3.1	...	...	3.8	...	...	4.1	...	...	3.4
3 Manufacturing	...	...	182.1	...	...	176.1	...	...	179.9	...	...	176.7
A Manufacture of food, beverages and tobacco	...	...	91.1	...	...	88.9	...	...	91.2	...	...	91.1
B Textile, wearing apparel and leather industries	...	...	22.3	...	...	21.9	...	...	21.1	...	...	16.8
C Manufacture of wood and wood products, including furniture	...	...	6.3	...	...	6.0	...	...	6.0	...	...	5.6
D Manufacture of paper and paper products, printing and publishing	...	...	12.5	...	...	11.0	...	...	11.6	...	...	13.0
E Manufacture of chemicals and chemical petroleum, coal, rubber and plastic products	...	...	23.6	...	...	22.1	...	...	23.2	...	...	24.7
F Manufacture of non-metallic mineral products, except products of petroleum and coal	...	...	13.4	...	...	12.7	...	...	13.3	...	...	12.1
G Basic metal industries	...	...	1.3	...	...	1.2	...	...	1.2	...	...	1.0
H Manufacture of fabricated metal products, machinery and equipment	...	...	10.2	...	...	10.1	...	...	10.5	...	...	9.9
I Other manufacturing industries	...	...	1.4	...	...	2.2	...	...	1.8	...	...	2.5
4 Electricity, gas and water	...	...	53.5	...	...	56.2	...	...	59.2	...	...	64.9
A Electricity, gas and steam	...	...	45.0	...	...	47.5	...	...	50.1	...	...	56.0
B Water works and supply	...	...	8.5	...	...	8.7	...	...	9.1	...	...	8.9

4.2 Derivation of Value Added by Kind of Activity, in Constant Prices
(Continued)

Million Panamanian balboas

	1980 Gross Output	1980 Intermediate Consumption	1980 Value Added	1981 Gross Output	1981 Intermediate Consumption	1981 Value Added	1982 Gross Output	1982 Intermediate Consumption	1982 Value Added	1983 Gross Output	1983 Intermediate Consumption	1983 Value Added
					At constant prices of:1970							
5 Construction	...	...	124.3	...	...	128.3	...	...	154.7	...	...	106.4
6 Wholesale and retail trade, restaurants and hotels	...	...	256.4	...	...	252.9	...	...	251.0	...	...	239.4
A Wholesale and retail trade	...	...	218.9	...	...	217.4	...	...	218.0	...	...	207.6
B Restaurants and hotels	...	...	37.5	...	...	35.5	...	...	33.0	...	...	31.8
7 Transport, storage and communication	...	...	207.6	...	...	216.5	...	...	251.1	...	...	321.1
A Transport and storage	...	...	.187.4	...	...	195.0	...	...	228.2	...	...	297.5
B Communication	...	...	20.2	...	...	21.5	...	...	22.9	...	...	23.6
8 Finance, insurance, real estate and business services	...	...	227.2	...	...	243.5	...	...	252.6	...	...	262.7
A Financial institutions	...	...	60.3	...	...	67.1	...	...	70.5	...	...	76.3
B Insurance	...	...	12.3	...	...	14.2	...	...	14.0	...	...	14.3
C Real estate and business services	...	...	154.6	...	...	162.2	...	...	168.1	...	...	172.1
Real estate, except dwellings	...	...	9.0	...	...	11.9	...	...	12.8	...	...	12.9
Dwellings	...	...	121.9	...	...	125.2	...	...	129.2	...	...	102.8
9 Community, social and personal services	...	...	142.6	...	...	150.1	...	...	163.3	...	...	168.8
A Sanitary and similar services	...	...	6.3	...	...	6.3	...	...	6.7	...	...	6.2
B Social and related community services	...	...	31.1	...	...	32.5	...	...	35.6	...	...	36.8
Educational services	...	...	8.3	...	...	7.9	...	...	8.7	...	...	8.6
Medical, dental, other health and veterinary services	...	...	22.8	...	...	24.6	...	...	26.9	...	...	28.2
C Recreational and cultural services	...	...	76.0	...	...	80.1	...	...	86.5	...	...	89.1
D Personal and household services	...	...	29.2	...	...	31.2	...	...	34.5	...	...	36.7
Statistical discrepancy [ab]	...	...	175.5	...	...	188.4	...	...	204.7	...	...	175.0
Total, Industries	...	...	1536.6	...	...	1591.8	...	...	1694.2	...	...	1702.2
Producers of Government Services	...	...	201.2	...	...	222.9	...	...	232.1	...	...	240.6
Other Producers	...	...	17.7	...	...	18.5	...	...	19.3	...	...	19.4
Total	...	...	1755.5	...	...	1833.2	...	...	1945.6	...	...	1962.2
Less: Imputed bank service charge	...	...	47.2	...	...	54.2	...	...	68.2	...	...	76.4
Import duties	...	...	28.1	...	...	27.7	...	...	29.6	...	...	32.7
Value added tax	...	...	...	...	...	...	...	...	...	...	...	...
Total	...	...	1736.4	...	...	1806.7	...	...	1907.0	...	...	1918.5

	1984 Gross Output	1984 Intermediate Consumption	1984 Value Added	1985 Gross Output	1985 Intermediate Consumption	1985 Value Added	1986 Gross Output	1986 Intermediate Consumption	1986 Value Added	1987 Gross Output	1987 Intermediate Consumption	1987 Value Added
			At constant prices of:1970									
			All Producers									
1 Agriculture, hunting, forestry and fishing	...	...	186.8	...	...	195.9	...	...	190.4	...	...	207.3
A Agriculture and hunting	...	...	174.6	...	...	180.9	...	...	171.7	...	...	189.7
B Forestry and logging	...	...	5.6	...	...	5.6	...	...	5.5	...	...	5.4
C Fishing	...	...	6.6	...	...	9.4	...	...	13.2	...	...	12.2
2 Mining and quarrying	...	...	2.6	...	...	2.4	...	...	2.5	...	...	2.7

Panama

4.2 Derivation of Value Added by Kind of Activity, in Constant Prices
(Continued)

Million Panamanian balboas

	1984			1985			1986			1987		
	Gross Output	Intermediate Consumption	Value Added	Gross Output	Intermediate Consumption	Value Added	Gross Output	Intermediate Consumption	Value Added	Gross Output	Intermediate Consumption	Value Added
					At constant prices of:1970							
3 Manufacturing	...	...	175.8	...	...	179.3	...	...	183.3	...	...	190.1
A Manufacture of food, beverages and tobacco	...	...	90.4	...	...	93.7	...	...	95.4	...	...	97.0
B Textile, wearing apparel and leather industries	...	...	18.2	...	...	18.6	...	...	18.8	...	...	18.7
C Manufacture of wood and wood products, including furniture	...	...	6.0	...	...	6.2	...	...	6.4	...	...	5.7
D Manufacture of paper and paper products, printing and publishing	...	...	13.1	...	...	14.0	...	...	13.3	...	...	13.9
E Manufacture of chemicals and chemical petroleum, coal, rubber and plastic products	...	...	24.6	...	...	24.2	...	...	24.5	...	...	27.5
F Manufacture of non-metallic mineral products, except products of petroleum and coal	...	...	10.5	...	...	10.1	...	...	11.7	...	...	12.7
G Basic metal industries	...	...	0.9	...	...	1.1	...	...	1.3	...	...	1.7
H Manufacture of fabricated metal products, machinery and equipment	...	...	9.6	...	...	8.9	...	...	9.0	...	...	10.2
I Other manufacturing industries	...	...	2.5	...	...	2.5	...	...	2.9	...	...	2.7
4 Electricity, gas and water	...	...	64.2	...	...	69.2	...	...	73.3	...	...	78.4
A Electricity, gas and steam	...	...	55.1	...	...	59.7	...	...	63.4	...	...	68.0
B Water works and supply	...	...	9.1	...	...	9.5	...	...	9.9	...	...	10.4
5 Construction	...	...	87.9	...	...	87.9	...	...	94.5	...	...	91.9
6 Wholesale and retail trade, restaurants and hotels	...	...	240.4	...	...	251.4	...	...	255.4	...	...	243.5
A Wholesale and retail trade	...	...	206.7	...	...	215.9	...	...	219.6	...	...	209.1
B Restaurants and hotels	...	...	33.7	...	...	35.5	...	...	35.8	...	...	34.4
7 Transport, storage and communication	...	...	305.1	...	...	335.5	...	...	338.8	...	...	360.0
A Transport and storage	...	...	280.3	...	...	309.5	...	...	311.8	...	...	332.1
B Communication	...	...	24.8	...	...	26.0	...	...	27.0	...	...	27.9
8 Finance, insurance, real estate and business services	...	...	271.9	...	...	283.2	...	...	301.3	...	...	309.7
A Financial institutions	...	...	79.7	...	...	83.6	...	...	91.4	...	...	91.7
B Insurance	...	...	14.3	...	...	15.0	...	...	17.1	...	...	16.7
C Real estate and business services	...	...	177.9	...	...	184.6	...	...	192.8	...	...	201.3
Real estate, except dwellings	...	...	12.9	...	...	13.2	...	...	14.8	...	...	16.1
Dwellings	...	...	136.4	...	...	140.3	...	...	145.7	...	...	151.7
9 Community, social and personal services	...	...	176.2	...	...	182.4	...	...	195.7	...	...	197.1
A Sanitary and similar services	...	...	5.4	...	...	4.9	...	...	4.9	...	...	5.2
B Social and related community services	...	...	40.4	...	...	41.5	...	...	43.9	...	...	44.6
Educational services	...	...	8.6	...	...	8.6	...	...	8.8	...	...	9.0
Medical, dental, other health and veterinary services	...	...	31.8	...	...	32.9	...	...	35.1	...	...	35.6
C Recreational and cultural services	...	...	89.5	...	...	91.3	...	...	97.1	...	...	95.2
D Personal and household services	...	...	40.9	...	...	44.7	...	...	49.8	...	...	52.1
Statistical discrepancy [ab]	...	...	174.6	...	...	177.0	...	...	186.0	...	...	187.6
Total, Industries	...	...	1685.5	...	...	1764.2	...	...	1821.2	...	...	1868.3
Producers of Government Services	...	...	248.3	...	...	258.7	...	...	265.2	...	...	272.4
Other Producers	...	...	21.5	...	...	21.9	...	...	22.5	...	...	22.4
Total	...	...	1955.3	...	...	2044.8	...	...	2108.9	...	...	2163.1
Less: Imputed bank service charge	...	...	78.5	...	...	80.5	...	...	84.2	...	...	85.7
Import duties	...	...	33.4	...	...	36.1	...	...	42.3	...	...	39.6
Value added tax	...	...	...	...	...	...	...	...	...	...	...	...
Total	...	...	1910.2	...	...	2000.4	...	...	2067.0	...	...	2117.0

4.2 Derivation of Value Added by Kind of Activity, in Constant Prices

Million Panamanian balboas

	1988			1989			1990			1991		
	Gross Output	Intermediate Consumption	Value Added	Gross Output	Intermediate Consumption	Value Added	Gross Output	Intermediate Consumption	Value Added	Gross Output	Intermediate Consumption	Value Added
At constant prices of:1970												
All Producers												
1 Agriculture, hunting, forestry and fishing	...	...	196.5	...	...	203.8	...	...	210.0	...	...	223.9
A Agriculture and hunting	...	...	184.6	...	...	189.6	...	...	197.2	...	...	210.8
B Forestry and logging	...	...	5.3	...	...	5.6	...	...	5.7	...	...	5.8
C Fishing	...	...	6.6	...	...	8.6	...	...	7.1	...	...	7.3
2 Mining and quarrying	...	...	1.7	...	...	1.5	...	...	2.0	...	...	3.3
3 Manufacturing	...	...	147.1	...	...	155.2	...	...	173.2	...	...	188.5
A Manufacture of food, beverages and tobacco	...	...	85.1	...	...	90.3	...	...	98.2	...	...	104.0
B Textile, wearing apparel and leather industries	...	...	13.1	...	...	13.2	...	...	14.5	...	...	16.7
C Manufacture of wood and wood products, including furniture	...	...	2.5	...	...	3.2	...	...	4.2	...	...	4.4
D Manufacture of paper and paper products, printing and publishing	...	...	12.1	...	...	12.8	...	...	14.3	...	...	14.8
E Manufacture of chemicals and chemical petroleum, coal, rubber and plastic products	...	...	21.5	...	...	22.5	...	...	24.9	...	...	26.5
F Manufacture of non-metallic mineral products, except products of petroleum and coal	...	...	5.1	...	...	5.1	...	...	6.9	...	...	10.7
G Basic metal industries	...	...	0.6	...	...	0.5	...	...	0.9	...	...	1.3
H Manufacture of fabricated metal products, machinery and equipment	...	...	5.2	...	...	5.3	...	...	7.1	...	...	7.9
I Other manufacturing industries	...	...	1.9	...	...	2.3	...	...	2.2	...	...	2.2
4 Electricity, gas and water	...	...	76.3	...	...	74.1	...	...	76.5	...	...	81.0
A Electricity, gas and steam	...	...	65.0	...	...	62.7	...	...	64.9	...	...	69.5
B Water works and supply	...	...	11.3	...	...	11.4	...	...	11.6	...	...	11.5
5 Construction	...	...	36.1	...	...	23.9	...	...	33.5	...	...	72.7
6 Wholesale and retail trade, restaurants and hotels	...	...	184.2	...	...	192.0	...	...	217.7	...	...	241.2
A Wholesale and retail trade	...	...	155.3	...	...	162.2	...	...	185.1	...	...	204.2
B Restaurants and hotels	...	...	28.9	...	...	29.8	...	...	32.6	...	...	37.0
7 Transport, storage and communication	...	...	301.4	...	...	279.4	...	...	278.9	...	...	320.9
A Transport and storage	...	...	273.3	...	...	250.1	...	...	249.1	...	...	289.1
B Communication	...	...	28.1	...	...	29.3	...	...	29.8	...	...	31.8
8 Finance, insurance, real estate and business services	...	...	279.1	...	...	270.7	...	...	279.1	...	...	297.3
A Financial institutions	...	...	73.2	...	...	65.3	...	...	69.7	...	...	82.7
B Insurance	...	...	14.1	...	...	13.0	...	...	11.4	...	...	11.6
C Real estate and business services	...	...	191.8	...	...	192.4	...	...	198.0	...	...	203.0
Real estate, except dwellings	...	...	11.1	...	...	9.7	...	...	9.8	...	...	10.6
Dwellings	...	...	152.9	...	...	153.4	...	...	153.6	...	...	154.0
9 Community, social and personal services	...	...	141.9	...	...	154.4	...	...	162.2	...	...	175.3
A Sanitary and similar services	...	...	3.2	...	...	4.1	...	...	5.6	...	...	7.8
B Social and related community services	...	...	44.8	...	...	45.4	...	...	44.8	...	...	45.5
Educational services	...	...	8.5	...	...	8.8	...	...	9.0	...	...	9.1
Medical, dental, other health and veterinary services	...	...	36.3	...	...	36.6	...	...	35.8	...	...	36.4
C Recreational and cultural services	...	...	62.4	...	...	70.1	...	...	73.0	...	...	80.3
D Personal and household services	...	...	31.5	...	...	34.8	...	...	38.8	...	...	41.7
Statistical discrepancy ab	...	...	193.8	...	...	189.9	...	...	192.1	...	...	202.4

Panama

Million Panamanian balboas

	1988			1989			1990			1991		
	Gross Output	Intermediate Consumption	Value Added	Gross Output	Intermediate Consumption	Value Added	Gross Output	Intermediate Consumption	Value Added	Gross Output	Intermediate Consumption	Value Added
At constant prices of:1970												
Total, Industries	...	...	1558.1	...	...	1544.9	...	...	1625.2	...	...	1806.5
Producers of Government Services	...	...	264.0	...	...	260.0	...	...	244.4	...	...	250.1
Other Producers	...	...	19.5	...	...	20.9	...	...	23.0	...	...	24.0
Total	...	...	1841.6	...	...	1825.8	...	...	1892.6	...	...	2080.6
Less: Imputed bank service charge	...	...	70.2	...	...	63.5	...	...	62.0	...	...	74.5
Import duties	...	...	15.3	...	...	16.9	...	...	31.0	...	...	29.5
Value added tax	...	...	...	...	...	...	...	...	...	...	...	...
Total	...	...	1786.7	...	...	1779.2	...	...	1861.6	...	...	2035.6

a) For 1970-1979, item 'Statistical discrepancy' refers to the services rendered to the area of the Panama Canal. Beginning 1980, the Treaty Torrijos-Carter was inforced, therefore all the activities of the area of the Panama Canal have been incorporated to the corresponding type of economic activity.

b) Beginning 1980, item 'Statistical discrepancy' refers to transport services sold by a resident enterprise 'Commission del Canal de Panama'. Due to the special characteristics of this enterprise it has been separated from the rest to facilitate the analysis of the estimates.

Papua New Guinea

General note. The preparation of national accounts statistics in Papua New Guinea is undertaken by the National Statistical Office(formerly Bureau of Statistics), Port Moresby. The official estimates are published in 'Bross Domestic Product and Expenditure'. A detailed description of the sources and methods used for the national accounts estimation is found in 'National Accounts Statistics 1960/61 - 1973/74', published in 1974. The estimates are generally in accordance with the classifications and definitions recommended in the United Nations System of National Accounts (SNA). Input-output tables for the years 1969/70, 1972/73 and 1976/77 were published in 1973, 1974 and 1982 respectively. The following tables have been prepared from successive replies to the United Nations national accounts questionnaire. When the scope and coverage of the estimates differ for conceptual or statistical reasons from the definitions and classfications recommended in SNA, a footnote is indicated to the relevant tables.

Sources and methods :

(a) Gross domestic product. Gross domestic product is estimated mainly through the production approach.

(b) Expenditure on the gross domestic product. All components of GDP by expenditure type are estimated through the expenditure approach. However, the commodity-flow approach is used for checking purposes in the case of a few items included under private consumption expenditure. The estimates of government consumption expenditure are based on Budget Papers, Annual Reports of the Commissioner for Local Government, Financial Statements of Provincial Government and Australian Budget Papers. The market component of household consumption expenditure is estimated mainly from the results of the retail sales and selected services survey. Estimates for items not covered by this survey are obtained from sources such as Budget Papers, the population census, various surveys of urban markets and village industry and taxation data. For some selected items, the estimates are checked and supplemented by data from international trade statistics using the commodity-flow approach. The non-market component of household consumption consists of food and firewood for own consumption and services of owner-occupied dwellings. Estimates of food produced for own consumption are calculated by using data from the Rural Industrial Bulletin and the estimated consumption per head of population. The annual quantity of firewood used per family is multiplied by average price and the number of families gathering firewood for own use. Construction and maintenance of housing is estimated by multiplying population data by the time spent and the minimum wage rate. Estimates of increase in stocks are based mainly on the Taxation Statistics Bulletin. For gross fixed capital formation by private industries, the principal source of information is the capital expenditure survey and for the public industries, the annual reports of the public enterprises. Exports and imports of goods and services are estimated mainly from the international trade statistics. For the constant price estimates of parts of government expenditure, private expenditure, gross fixed capital formation, increase in stocks and exports of merchandise, the current quantities are revalued at base-year prices. Regarding the market component of private consumption expenditure, building and construction, government expenditure on goods and services and imports of merchandise, the current values are deflated by appropriate price indexes.

(c) Cost-structure of the gross domestic product. Estimates of compensation of employees are based on taxation statistics, statistics of religious organizations and the Labour Information Bulletin. Adjustments are made for wages and salaries not covered by the above sources. Imputed wages referring to work provided to government and mission authorities are shown separately. Estimates of operating surplus for the market component are based mainly on taxation returns with some adjustments made to cover imputed bank service charge and to include producers not required to submit returns. For owner-occupied dwellings, operating surplus is calculated from information contained in the Building Statistics Bulletin. Consumption of fixed capital is estimated based on taxation data supplemented by annual reports for producers not covered. The Papua New Guinea Budget papers and the annual reports of the Commissioner for Local Government provide all the information needed to estimate indirect taxes and subsidies.

(d) Gross domestic product by kind of economic activity. The table of gross domestic product by kind of economic activity is prepared at market prices, i.e., producers' values. The income approach is used to estimate value added of most industries. Value added is defined as the sum of compensation of employees, operating surplus, consumption of fixed capital and net indirect taxes. The principal source is the income tax statistics, supplemented by annual reports of public and private enterprises. The reporting unit in these statistics is the enterprise (legal entity) rather than the establishment. For the major activities such as mining and quarrying, electricity, gas and water, and communication, in which cases almost the whole production is concentrated in a few enterprise units, the establishment type data are used. In cases where surveys data are used, adjustments and supplementary data are taken into account to cover activities not included. For the non-marketed production and contributions of free and partially-paid labour, estimates are available separately as sub-divisions of the relevant items as the amounts involved are quite substantial. As mentioned above, estimates of GDP by kind of economic activity are arrived at by subdividing the cost-structure components of total GDP into the various kinds of activity. Compensation of employees is classified in accordance with the industry information on individuals' tax returns. If an individual has more than one source of income, he is allocated to the industry category corresponding to his major source of income and all of his income is classed to that category. Data on operating surplus of private enterprises are classified on the basis of information given in the company tax statistics and in the statistics of individuals' income other than wages and salaries, while the industry categories of the operating surplus of public enterprises are determined by the nature of their productive activities. For industry allocation of consumption of fixed capital, the taxation data supplemented by other information in respect of producers not covered by the taxation statistics provide the basis. In the case of indirect taxes and subsidies, the industry allocation is made on the basis of the nature of indirect taxes and subsidies. GDP by kind of economic activity at constant prices is not estimated.

1.1 Expenditure on the Gross Domestic Product, in Current Prices

Million Papua New Guinea kina

	1980	1981	1982	1983	1984	1985	1986	1987	1988	1989	1990	1991
1 Government final consumption expenditure	411.2	454.4	468.1	471.3 / 498.8	531.8	572.4	591.1	639.7	662.9	744.9	763.9	808.1
2 Private final consumption expenditure	1051.3	1104.2	1117.9	1245.0 / 1385.6	1445.7	1599.9	1673.6	1814.9	1919.4	1962.0	1816.3	2165.9
3 Gross capital formation	430.6	458.1	562.5	626.2 / 630.7	619.0	480.6	507.7	585.3	862.5	707.3	751.9	988.1
A Increase in stocks	36.4	7.4	-14.2	-6.2 / -6.2	71.5	33.8	-31.5	34.1	125.5	-83.4	-21.0	-22.0
B Gross fixed capital formation	394.2	450.7	576.7	632.4 / 636.9	547.5	446.8	539.2	551.2	737.0	790.7	772.9	1010.1
4 Exports of goods and services	737.6	642.9	644.3	766.1 / 775.5	904.7	1020.9	1121.0	1232.1	1371.1	1238.0	1249.7	1523.9
5 Less: Imports of goods and services	910.8	987.6	1058.2	1129.6 / 1145.2	1219.0	1271.2	1321.0	1417.8	1646.0	1606.5	1505.7	1880.5
Statistical discrepancy	-11.8	9.2	14.5	-5.4 / ...	...	...	...	...	...	...	...	...
Equals: Gross Domestic Product	1708.1	1681.2	1749.1	1973.7 / 2145.5	2282.2	2402.6	2572.4	2854.4	3169.9	3045.7	3076.1	3605.5

Papua New Guinea

1.2 Expenditure on the Gross Domestic Product, in Constant Prices

Million Papua New Guinea kina

	1980	1981	1982	1983	1984	1985	1986	1987	1988	1989	1990	1991
		1977	1981	At constant prices of:				1983				
1 Government final consumption expenditure	337.8	324.8 / 454.4	422.6	414.1 / 498.8	502.2	520.4	510.9	526.5	517.5	548.5	533.1	527.1
2 Private final consumption expenditure	794.1	768.8 / 1104.2	1075.3	1119.0 / 1385.6	1369.4	1469.0	1452.1	1500.0	1504.5	1486.4	1286.9	1434.7
3 Gross capital formation	368.5	353.1 / 458.1	518.8	541.9 / 630.7	577.2	415.0	435.1	478.0	674.3	512.7	515.9	634.5
A Increase in stocks	29.2	5.3 / 7.4	-12.8	-5.3 / -6.2	63.6	24.3	-23.7	25.1	102.2	-73.9	-17.2	-18.3
B Gross fixed capital formation	339.3	347.8 / 450.7	531.6	547.2 / 636.9	513.6	390.7	458.8	452.9	572.1	586.6	533.1	652.8
4 Exports of goods and services	635.3	669.6 / 642.9	640.5	653.1 / 775.5	799.9	897.9	1005.7	995.5	981.3	972.5	928.1	1075.0
5 Less: Imports of goods and services	723.5	724.7 / 987.6	976.0	969.7 / 1145.2	1124.5	1101.6	1079.2	1111.1	1219.3	1096.6	913.1	1096.5
Statistical discrepancy	-10.0	6.7 / 9.2	14.0	-4.8	...	...		...		...	...	...
Equals: Gross Domestic Product	1402.3	1398.3 / 1681.2	1695.2	1753.5 / 2145.5	2124.3	2200.7	2324.5	2388.9	2458.5	2423.4	2350.8	2574.8

1.3 Cost Components of the Gross Domestic Product

Million Papua New Guinea kina

	1980	1981	1982	1983	1984	1985	1986	1987	1988	1989	1990	1991
1 Indirect taxes, net	110.0	114.6	134.4	151.9 / 151.9	179.2	189.7	229.5	263.9	283.2	346.0	329.6	384.1
A Indirect taxes	114.6	119.2	138.5	153.7 / 153.7	182.2	191.6	231.2	265.8	285.1	347.6	331.6	386.1
B Less: Subsidies	4.6	4.6	4.1	1.8 / 1.8	3.0	1.9	1.7	1.9	1.9	1.6	2.0	2.0
2 Consumption of fixed capital a	124.9	137.6	150.0	162.6 / 172.8	217.9	223.4	241.5	262.0	279.2	315.5	339.4	416.8
3 Compensation of employees paid by resident producers to:	676.2	747.7	763.4	792.9 / 843.7	881.0	944.2	982.0	1052.1	1160.3	1268.5	1262.4	1348.7
A Resident households	675.4	747.1	762.5	792.2 / 842.9	880.4	943.6	981.4	1051.4	1159.5	1267.7	...	...
B Rest of the world	0.7	0.6	0.8	0.8 / 0.8	0.6	0.6	0.6	0.7	0.8	0.8	...	...
4 Operating surplus	797.1	681.4	701.2	866.4 / 977.1	1004.0	1045.3	1119.5	1276.2	1447.1	1115.6	1144.6	1455.8
Equals: Gross Domestic Product	1708.1	1681.2	1749.1	1973.7 / 2145.5	2282.2	2402.6	2572.4	2854.4	3169.9	3045.7	3076.1	3605.5

a) Item 'Consumption of fixed capital' excludes consumption of fixed capital of producers of government-owned houses and hostels.

1.6 Current Income and Outlay of Households and Non-Profit Institutions

Million Papua New Guinea kina

	1980	1981	1982	1983	1984	1985	1986	1987	1988	1989	1990	1991
					Receipts							
1 Compensation of employees	677.2	753.1	768.8	798.8	...	...	...	...	...	...	...	...
A From resident producers	675.4	747.1	762.5	792.2	...	...	...	...	...	...	...	...
B From rest of the world	1.8	6.0	6.3	6.6	...	...	...	...	...	...	...	...
2 Operating surplus of private unincorporated enterprises	...	...	...	...	...	...	...	...	...	...	...	...
3 Property and entrepreneurial income	...	...	...	...	...	...	...	...	...	...	...	...
4 Current transfers	...	...	...	...	...	...	...	...	...	...	...	...
Total Current Receipts	...	...	...	...	...	...	...	...	...	...	...	...

1.6 Current Income and Outlay of Households and Non-Profit Institutions
(Continued)

Million Papua New Guinea kina

	1980	1981	1982	1983	1984	1985	1986	1987	1988	1989	1990	1991
					Disbursements							
1 Private final consumption expenditure	1051.3	1104.2	1117.9	1245.0	...	...	...	...	...	...	...	...
2 Property income	...	...	...	...	...	...	...	...	...	...	...	...
3 Direct taxes and other current transfers n.e.c. to general government	...	...	...	...	...	...	...	...	...	...	...	...
4 Other current transfers	...	...	...	...	...	...	...	...	...	...	...	...
5 Net saving	...	...	...	...	...	...	...	...	...	...	...	...
Total Current Disbursements and Net Saving	...	...	...	...	...	...	...	...	...	...	...	...

1.7 External Transactions on Current Account, Summary

Million Papua New Guinea kina

	1980	1981	1982	1983	1984	1985	1986	1987	1988	1989	1990	1991
				Payments to the Rest of the World								
1 Imports of goods and services	910.8	987.6	1058.2	1129.6 / 1145.2	1219.0	1271.2	1321.0	1417.8	1646.0	1606.5	1505.7	1880.5
A Imports of merchandise c.i.f.	808.7	872.3	897.5	961.2 / 974.3	1026.2	1068.1	1098.2	1201.5	1413.5	1368.0	1273.7	1620.0
B Other	102.1	115.3	160.7	168.4 / 170.9	192.8	203.1	222.8	216.3	232.5	238.5	232.0	260.5
2 Factor income to the rest of the world	100.4	98.2	122.5	174.8 / 174.8	124.1	151.4	170.2	191.0	231.9	196.8	201.0	201.0
A Compensation of employees	0.7	0.6	0.8	0.8 / 0.8	0.6	0.6	0.6	0.7	0.8	0.9	1.0	1.0
B Property and entrepreneurial income	99.7	97.6	121.7	174.0 / 174.0	123.5	150.8	169.6	190.3	231.1	195.9	200.0	200.0
3 Current transfers to the rest of the world	45.1	30.9	36.9	36.7 / 108.6	111.3	116.6	107.6	125.5	132.4	134.0	136.0	136.2
4 Surplus of the nation on current transactions	-101.2	-242.8	-306.3	-277.8 / -355.9	-242.9	-208.1	-133.8	-209.4	-298.9	-385.6	-274.9	-350.7
Payments to the Rest of the World and Surplus of the Nation on Current Transactions	955.1	873.9	911.4	1063.3 / 1072.7	1211.6	1331.1	1465.0	1524.9	1711.4	1551.7	1567.8	1867.0
				Receipts From The Rest of the World								
1 Exports of goods and services	737.6	642.9	644.3	766.1 / 775.5	904.7	1020.9	1121.0	1232.1	1371.1	1238.0	1249.7	1523.9
A Exports of merchandise f.o.b.	640.3	555.6	552.7	674.3 / 674.5	797.0	909.1	1009.8	1118.5	1249.7	1111.4	1122.2	1374.9
B Other	97.3	87.4	91.6	91.8 / 101.0	107.7	111.8	111.2	113.6	121.4	126.6	127.5	149.0
2 Factor income from rest of the world	41.7	37.8	50.1	55.4 / 55.4	51.7	62.9	98.1	60.5	109.8	81.8	83.1	83.1
A Compensation of employees	1.8	6.0	6.3	6.6 / 6.6	6.9	7.2	7.5	7.7	7.9	8.0	8.1	8.1
B Property and entrepreneurial income	39.9	31.8	43.8	48.8 / 48.8	44.8	55.7	90.6	52.8	101.9	73.8	75.0	75.0
3 Current transfers from rest of the world	175.8	193.2	217.0	241.7 / 241.8	255.2	247.3	245.9	232.3	230.5	232.0	235.0	260.0
Receipts from the Rest of the World on Current Transactions	955.0	873.9	911.4	1063.3 / 1072.7	1211.6	1331.1	1465.0	1524.9	1711.4	1551.7	1567.8	1867.0

Papua New Guinea

1.10 Gross Domestic Product by Kind of Activity, in Current Prices

Million Papua New Guinea kina

	1980	1981	1982	1983	1984	1985	1986	1987	1988	1989	1990	1991
1 Agriculture, hunting, forestry and fishing	565.7	561.4	567.2	647.8 / 714.2	832.6	799.8	828.0	852.4	924.0	856.3	891.2	936.5
2 Mining and quarrying	225.7	133.7	140.4	210.8 / 225.1	150.3	239.2	329.8	490.0	609.5	352.7	452.2	612.9
3 Manufacturing	162.3	166.6	164.6	178.8 / 213.4	249.8	261.5	256.3	268.9	294.3	336.9	275.8	345.1
4 Electricity, gas and water	6.3	19.9	19.4	28.8 / 30.9	45.1	45.4	40.0	43.6	46.1	49.0	52.3	59.2
5 Construction	64.2	70.5	82.0	84.7 / 123.6	111.0	94.0	103.7	101.8	133.2	161.3	155.1	224.0
6 Wholesale and retail trade, restaurants and hotels a	135.2	140.3	142.4	156.6 / 218.0	224.4	237.5	259.5	285.7	307.7	328.2	296.8	358.5
7 Transport, storage and communication	78.1	97.6	72.9	68.3 / 87.7	103.0	120.0	130.5	141.0	151.9	163.5	190.9	243.0
8 Finance, insurance, real estate and business services	139.4	126.1	172.3	187.4 / 143.2	155.5	165.1	145.8	157.7	171.8	172.9	130.8	147.6
9 Community, social and personal services ab	182.8	199.8	212.7	225.8 / 360.6	378.7	409.7	431.1	460.0	484.6	543.4	551.3	588.2
Total, Industries	1559.7	1515.9	1573.9	1789.0 / 2116.7	2250.4	2372.2	2524.7	2801.1	3123.1	2964.3	2996.4	3515.0
Producers of Government Services b	125.7	143.0	144.5	147.1 / ...	...	...	...	...	...	...	...	...
Other Producers	...	...	...	...	...	...	...	...	...	...	...	...
Subtotal	1685.4	1658.9	1718.4	1936.1 / 2116.7	2250.4	2372.2	2524.7	2801.1	3123.1	2964.3	2996.4	3515.0
Less: Imputed bank service charge	41.3	45.7	49.1	53.5 / 57.8	65.2	73.7	73.8	89.2	109.0	121.5	108.2	110.5
Plus: Import duties	64.1	68.1	79.7	91.1 / 88.4	99.9	106.0	123.1	144.3	157.9	205.0	189.9	203.0
Plus: Value added tax	...	...	...	...								
Plus: Other adjustments	...	...	...	... / -1.8	-3.0	-1.9	-1.7	-1.9	-1.9	-2.0	-2.0	-2.0
Equals: Gross Domestic Product	1708.1	1681.2	1749.1	1973.7 / 2145.5	2282.2	2402.6	2572.4	2854.4	3169.9	3045.7	3076.1	3605.5

a) Restaurants and hotels are included in item 'Community, social and personal services'.
b) Item 'Other producers' is included in item 'Community, social and personal services'.

1.11 Gross Domestic Product by Kind of Activity, in Constant Prices

Million Papua New Guinea kina

	1980	1981	1982	1983	1984	1985	1986	1987	1988	1989	1990	1991
						At constant prices of:1983						
1 Agriculture, hunting, forestry and fishing	...	...	...	...	...	...	710.7	748.7	775.0	785.7	803.1	781.9
2 Mining and quarrying	...	...	...	...	...	...	364.5	354.4	363.5	225.8	277.3	393.4
3 Manufacturing	...	...	...	...	...	...	220.4	222.3	230.9	250.3	193.3	223.9
4 Electricity, gas and water	...	...	...	...	...	...	34.2	36.0	36.0	36.6	36.6	38.6
5 Construction	...	...	...	...	...	...	90.3	84.5	105.0	119.1	108.9	144.8
6 Wholesale and retail trade, restaurants and hotels	...	...	...	...	...	...	248.0	272.9	277.7	298.6	264.5	296.0
7 Transport, storage and communication	...	...	...	...	...	...	112.1	116.5	119.1	121.4	132.7	157.9
8 Finance, insurance, real estate and business services	...	...	...	...	...	...	127.2	131.3	137.0	126.3	99.8	103.5
9 Community, social and personal services	...	...	...	...	...	...	377.8	379.0	379.1	395.3	384.7	382.4
Total, Industries	...	...	...	...	...	...	2285.2	2345.6	2423.3	2359.1	2301.9	2522.4
Producers of Government Services	...	...	...	...	...	...	...	...	...	...	...	...
Other Producers	...	...	...	...	...	...	...	...	...	...	...	...
Subtotal	...	...	...	...	...	...	2285.2	2345.6	2423.3	2359.1	2301.9	2522.4
Less: Imputed bank service charge	...	...	...	...	...	...	64.0	74.1	86.8	87.6	82.7	78.8
Plus: Import duties	...	...	...	...	...	...	104.8	118.8	123.3	153.2	132.7	132.6
Plus: Value added tax	...	...	...	...	...	...	...	...	...	...	...	...
Plus: Other adjustments	...	...	...	...	...	...	-1.5	-1.5	-1.5	-1.5	-1.4	-1.3
Equals: Gross Domestic Product	...	...	...	...	...	...	2324.5	2388.9	2458.4	2423.2	2350.8	2574.8

1.12 Relations Among National Accounting Aggregates

Million Papua New Guinea kina

	1980	1981	1982	1983	1984	1985	1986	1987	1988	1989	1990	1991
Gross Domestic Product	1708.1	1681.2	1749.1	1973.7 / 2145.5	2282.2	2402.6	2572.4	2854.4	3169.9	3045.7	3076.1	3605.5
Plus: Net factor income from the rest of the world	-58.7	-60.4	-72.4	-119.4 / -119.4	-72.4	-88.5	-72.1	-130.5	-122.1	-115.0	-117.9	-117.9
Factor income from the rest of the world	41.7	37.8	50.1	55.4 / 55.4	51.7	62.9	98.1	60.5	109.8	81.8	83.1	83.1
Less: Factor income to the rest of the world	100.4	98.2	122.5	174.8 / 174.8	124.1	151.4	170.2	191.0	231.9	196.8	201.0	201.0
Equals: Gross National Product	1649.4	1620.8	1676.7	1854.3 / 2026.1	2209.8	2314.1	2500.4	2723.9	3047.8	2930.7	2958.2	3487.6
Less: Consumption of fixed capital b	124.9	137.6	150.0	162.6 / 172.8	217.9	223.4	241.5	262.0	279.2	315.5	339.4	416.8
Equals: National Income	1524.5	1483.2	1526.6	1691.7 / 1853.3	1991.9	2090.7	2258.9	2461.9	2768.6	2615.2	2618.7	3070.7
Plus: Net current transfers from the rest of the world	130.7	162.3	180.1	205.1 / 133.2	143.9	130.7	138.4	106.6	98.1	98.0	99.0	123.8
Current transfers from the rest of the world	175.8	193.2	217.0	241.7 / 241.8	255.2	247.3	245.9	232.3	230.5	232.0	235.0	260.0
Less: Current transfers to the rest of the world	45.1	30.9	36.9	36.7 / 108.6	111.3	116.6	107.6	125.5	132.4	134.0	136.0	136.2
Equals: National Disposable Income	1655.2	1645.5	1706.7	1896.8 / 1986.5	2135.7	2221.4	2397.3	2568.6	2866.7	2713.1	2717.7	3194.5
Less: Final consumption	1462.5	1558.6	1586.0	1716.3 / 1884.4	1977.5	2172.3	2264.7	2454.6	2582.3	2706.9	2580.2	2974.0
Equals: Net Saving	192.8	86.9	120.8	180.5 / 102.1	158.2	49.1	132.6	114.0	284.4	6.2	137.5	220.5
Less: Surplus of the nation on current transactions	-101.2	-242.8	-306.3	-277.8 / -355.9	-242.9	-208.1	-133.8	-209.4	-298.9	-385.6	-274.9	-350.7
Statistical discrepancy	11.8	-9.3	-14.5	5.4 / -0.1	-	-	-0.2	-0.1	-	0.3	-	-
Equals: Net Capital Formation	305.8	320.4	412.6	463.6 / 457.9	401.1	257.2	266.2	323.2	583.3	392.1	412.5	571.3

b) Item 'Consumption of fixed capital' excludes consumption of fixed capital of producers of government-owned houses and hostels.

2.17 Exports and Imports of Goods and Services, Detail

Million Papua New Guinea kina

	1980	1981	1982	1983	1984	1985	1986	1987	1988	1989	1990	1991
Exports of Goods and Services												
1 Exports of merchandise, f.o.b. a	640.3	555.6	552.7	674.3 / 674.5	797.0	909.1	1009.8	1118.5	1249.7	1111.4	1122.4	1374.9
2 Transport and communication	46.1	51.2	54.4	58.0 / 67.5	72.6	76.3	75.3	77.4	78.9	81.7	80.1	98.5
A In respect of merchandise imports	22.3	22.5	24.1	25.5 / 35.0	36.1	38.4	36.3	37.4	38.9	39.1	...	...
B Other	23.8	28.7	30.3	32.5 / 32.5	36.5	37.9	39.0	40.0	41.0	42.6	...	...
3 Insurance service charges	1.5	1.1	1.3	0.4 / 0.4	1.4	2.1	1.9	1.7	2.0	2.2	2.4	2.6
A In respect of merchandise imports	1.4	1.0	1.2	0.3 / 0.3	1.2	1.8	1.7	1.5	1.8	2.0	2.2	2.3
B Other	0.1	0.1	0.1	0.1 / 0.1	0.2	0.3	0.2	0.2	0.2	0.2	0.2	0.3
4 Other commodities	41.1	27.3	28.3	26.5 / 26.1	26.6	26.9	26.8	26.3	31.1	33.0	34.0	35.0
5 Adjustments of merchandise exports to change-of-ownership basis	...	...	...	... / ...	...	...	...	...	...	...	...	...
6 Direct purchases in the domestic market by non-residential households	8.7	7.8	7.7	6.9 / 6.9	7.1	6.5	7.2	8.1	9.4	9.7	11.0	13.0
7 Direct purchases in the domestic market by extraterritorial bodies	...	...	...	... / ...	...	...	...	...	...	...	...	...
Total Exports of Goods and Services	737.6	642.9	644.3	766.1 / 775.5	904.7	1020.9	1121.0	1232.1	1371.1	1238.0	1249.7	1523.9

2.17 Exports and Imports of Goods and Services, Detail
(Continued)

Million Papua New Guinea kina

	1980	1981	1982	1983	1984	1985	1986	1987	1988	1989	1990	1991
				Imports of Goods and Services								
1 Imports of merchandise, c.i.f. a	808.7	872.3	897.5	961.2 974.3	1026.2	1068.1	1098.2	1201.5	1413.5	1368.0	1273.7	1620.0
A Imports of merchandise, f.o.b.	687.3	751.5	760.0	817.3 817.5	856.8	876.2	903.4	996.4	1199.5	1152.0	1056.7	1335.0
B Transport of services on merchandise imports	117.8	117.0	133.6	139.6 152.5	164.9	187.3	190.0	199.8	208.3	209.9	210.9	277.9
By residents	22.3	22.5	24.1	26.5 35.0	36.1	38.4	36.3	37.4	37.9	...	...	...
By non-residents	95.5	94.5	109.5	113.1 117.5	128.7	148.8	153.6	162.4	170.4	...	...	...
C Insurance service charges on merchandise imports	3.6	3.9	4.0	4.3 4.3	4.5	4.6	4.8	5.4	5.8	6.1	6.1	7.1
By residents	1.4	1.0	1.2	0.3 0.3	1.2	1.8	1.7	1.5	1.8	...	...	...
By non-residents	2.2	2.9	2.8	4.0 4.0	3.4	2.8	3.1	3.8	4.0	...	...	...
2 Adjustments of merchandise imports to change-of-ownership basis	...	...	...	... ...	...	...	...	...	...	...	...	...
3 Other transport and communication	41.3	40.2	49.7	40.8 40.8	46.4	47.7	51.4	53.3	55.1	56.3	68.0	76.0
4 Other insurance service charges	9.5	9.9	10.4	9.6 9.6	9.8	10.2	10.6	10.8	10.9	11.2		
5 Other commodities	34.0	46.7	83.8	100.5 103.8	119.4	128.9	144.3	135.5	147.6	150.6	145.0	160.5
6 Direct purchases abroad by government	1.9	2.4	2.1	4.2 3.4	3.7	2.7	2.8	2.7	2.9	4.3	19.0	24.0
7 Direct purchases abroad by resident households	15.4	16.1	14.8	13.3 13.3	13.5	13.6	13.8	14.1	16.1	16.1		
Total Imports of Goods and Services	910.8	987.6	1058.2	1129.6 1145.2	1219.0	1271.2	1321.0	1417.8	1646.0	1606.5	1505.7	1880.5
Balance of Goods and Services	-173.2	-344.7	-413.9	-363.5 -369.7	-314.4	-250.3	-200.0	-185.7	-274.9	-368.5	-256.0	-356.6
Total Imports and Balance of Goods and Services	737.6	642.9	644.3	766.1 775.5	904.7	1020.9	1121.0	1232.1	1371.1	1238.0	1249.7	1523.9

a) Exports and imports of merchandise are recorded on the basis of the crossing of frontiers. No data are available on the basis of changes in the ownership of the goods.

4.3 Cost Components of Value Added

Million Papua New Guinea kina

	1983						1984					
	Compensation of Employees	Capital Consumption	Net Operating Surplus	Indirect Taxes	Less: Subsidies Received	Value Added	Compensation of Employees	Capital Consumption	Net Operating Surplus	Indirect Taxes	Less: Subsidies Received	Value Added
				All Producers								
1 Agriculture, hunting, forestry and fishing	48.4	19.3	641.6	4.9	...	714.2	52.6	15.9	751.2	12.9	...	832.6
2 Mining and quarrying	55.9	48.0	121.1	0.1	...	225.1	77.0	86.1	-12.8	-	...	150.3
3 Manufacturing	82.8	19.6	59.5	51.5	...	213.4	85.2	32.8	73.2	58.6	...	249.8
4 Electricity, gas and water	10.9	6.7	13.3	...	...	30.9	14.5	6.8	23.7	...	...	45.1
5 Construction	67.5	20.1	36.0	...	...	123.6	56.4	14.4	40.2	...	...	111.0
6 Wholesale and retail trade, restaurants and hotels a	119.4	17.6	79.7	1.4	...	218.0	114.6	17.9	90.4	1.5	...	224.4
7 Transport, storage and communication	60.8	20.6	3.9	2.3	...	87.7	61.9	22.7	15.5	3.0	...	103.0
8 Finance, insurance, real estate and business services	48.7	18.1	71.3	5.2	...	143.2	52.1	18.4	78.7	6.3	...	155.5
9 Community, social and personal services a	349.4	2.7	8.4	...	...	360.6	366.8	2.8	9.1	...	...	378.7
Total, Industries	843.7	172.8	1034.8	65.3	...	2116.7	881.0	217.9	1069.2	82.2	...	2250.4
Producers of Government Services	...	...	...	...	...	...	...	...	...	...	...	...

4.3 Cost Components of Value Added
(Continued)

Million Papua New Guinea kina

	1983						1984					
	Compensation of Employees	Capital Consumption	Net Operating Surplus	Indirect Taxes	Less: Subsidies Received	Value Added	Compensation of Employees	Capital Consumption	Net Operating Surplus	Indirect Taxes	Less: Subsidies Received	Value Added
Other Producers	...	...	...	...	...	...	...	...	...	...	...	...
Total	843.7	172.8	1034.8	65.3	...	2116.7	881.0	217.9	1069.2	82.2	...	2250.4
Less: Imputed bank service charge	...	...	57.8	...	...	57.8	...	...	65.2	...	...	65.2
Import duties	...	...	...	88.4	...	88.4	...	...	...	99.9	...	99.9
Value added tax	...	...	...	...	...	...	...	...	...	...	...	...
Other adjustments	...	...	...	...	1.8	-1.8	...	...	...	...	3.0	-3.0
Total	843.7	172.8	977.1	153.7	1.8	2145.5	881.0	217.9	1004.0	182.2	3.0	2282.2

	1985						1986					
	Compensation of Employees	Capital Consumption	Net Operating Surplus	Indirect Taxes	Less: Subsidies Received	Value Added	Compensation of Employees	Capital Consumption	Net Operating Surplus	Indirect Taxes	Less: Subsidies Received	Value Added
	All Producers											
1 Agriculture, hunting, forestry and fishing	56.5	16.3	714.2	12.8	...	799.8	50.2	22.5	740.9	14.3	...	828.0
2 Mining and quarrying	72.2	87.0	80.0	-	...	239.2	71.1	93.6	165.1	-	...	329.8
3 Manufacturing	91.0	34.4	74.3	61.8	...	261.5	98.4	32.0	60.7	65.3	...	256.3
4 Electricity, gas and water	14.2	7.9	23.4	...	...	45.4	14.9	9.2	16.0	...	...	40.0
5 Construction	48.6	12.0	33.4	...	...	94.0	52.5	13.8	37.5	...	...	103.7
6 Wholesale and retail trade, restaurants and hotels a	133.6	18.3	83.6	1.9	...	237.5	139.7	18.5	82.5	18.8	...	259.5
7 Transport, storage and communication	66.4	25.3	26.4	1.9	...	120.0	71.7	28.8	28.7	1.3	...	130.5
8 Finance, insurance, real estate and business services	61.9	19.1	76.8	7.2	...	165.1	64.7	20.0	52.7	8.3	...	145.8
9 Community, social and personal services a	399.9	3.0	6.8	...	...	409.7	418.8	3.1	9.2	...	...	431.1
Total, Industries	944.2	223.4	1119.0	85.6	...	2372.2	982.0	241.5	1193.3	108.0	...	2524.8
Producers of Government Services	...	...	...	...	...	...	...	...	...	...	...	...
Other Producers	...	...	...	...	...	...	...	...	...	...	...	...
Total	944.2	223.4	1119.0	85.6	...	2372.2	982.0	241.5	1193.3	108.0	...	2524.8
Less: Imputed bank service charge	...	...	73.7	...	...	73.7	...	...	73.8	...	...	73.8
Import duties	...	...	...	106.0	...	106.0	...	...	...	123.1	...	123.1
Value added tax	...	...	...	...	...	...	...	...	...	...	...	...
Other adjustments	...	...	...	...	1.9	-1.9	...	...	...	...	1.7	-1.7
Total	944.2	223.4	1045.3	191.6	1.9	2402.6	982.0	241.5	1119.5	231.1	1.7	2572.4

	1987						1988					
	Compensation of Employees	Capital Consumption	Net Operating Surplus	Indirect Taxes	Less: Subsidies Received	Value Added	Compensation of Employees	Capital Consumption	Net Operating Surplus	Indirect Taxes	Less: Subsidies Received	Value Added
	All Producers											
1 Agriculture, hunting, forestry and fishing	55.2	23.2	756.8	17.2	...	852.4	64.3	26.0	817.3	16.4	...	924.0
2 Mining and quarrying	90.2	99.0	300.8	-	...	490.0	102.3	103.7	403.4	-	...	609.5
3 Manufacturing	104.2	34.2	62.3	68.2	...	268.9	116.3	36.7	74.5	66.8	...	294.3
4 Electricity, gas and water	15.6	10.6	17.4	...	...	43.6	19.4	10.5	16.2	...	...	46.1
5 Construction	50.4	16.6	34.8	...	...	101.8	62.1	17.7	53.4	...	...	133.2
6 Wholesale and retail trade, restaurants and hotels a	140.5	20.4	99.5	25.2	...	285.7	151.1	21.6	104.1	31.0	...	307.7
7 Transport, storage and communication	78.5	33.2	26.5	2.7	...	141.0	84.0	36.0	29.2	2.7	...	151.9
8 Finance, insurance, real estate and business services	70.3	21.4	57.7	8.1	...	157.7	89.8	23.7	48.0	10.3	...	171.8
9 Community, social and personal services a	447.2	3.3	9.5	...	...	460.0	471.1	3.4	10.0	...	...	484.6
Total, Industries	1052.1	262.0	1365.4	121.4	...	2800.9	1160.3	279.2	1556.1	127.2	...	3122.8
Producers of Government Services	...	...	...	...	...	...	...	...	...	...	...	...
Other Producers	...	...	...	...	...	...	...	...	...	...	...	...
Total	1052.1	262.0	1365.4	121.4	...	2800.9	1160.3	279.2	1556.1	127.2	...	3122.8
Less: Imputed bank service charge	...	...	89.2	...	...	89.2	...	...	109.0	...	...	109.0
Import duties	...	...	...	144.3	...	144.3	...	...	...	157.9	...	157.9
Value added tax	...	...	...	...	...	...	...	...	...	...	...	...
Other adjustments	...	...	...	...	1.9	-1.9	...	...	...	...	1.9	-1.9
Total	1052.1	262.0	1276.2	265.7	1.9	2854.4	1160.3	279.2	1447.1	285.2	1.9	3169.9

Papua New Guinea

4.3 Cost Components of Value Added

Million Papua New Guinea kina

All Producers

	1989						1990					
	Compensation of Employees	Capital Consumption	Net Operating Surplus	Indirect Taxes	Less: Subsidies Received	Value Added	Compensation of Employees	Capital Consumption	Net Operating Surplus	Indirect Taxes	Less: Subsidies Received	Value Added
1 Agriculture, hunting, forestry and fishing	66.8	27.9	749.7	11.9	...	856.3	64.3	28.2	789.4	9.4	...	891.2
2 Mining and quarrying	92.8	122.8	137.1	-	...	352.7	73.1	140.5	238.6	-	...	452.2
3 Manufacturing	131.2	39.4	84.2	82.0	...	336.9	130.6	40.0	21.2	84.0	...	275.8
4 Electricity, gas and water	20.4	11.0	17.6	...	...	49.0	21.8	11.8	18.7	...	...	52.3
5 Construction	75.4	21.3	64.6	...	...	161.3	75.9	22.3	56.9	...	...	155.1
6 Wholesale and retail trade, restaurants and hotels a	161.1	23.0	110.9	33.2	...	328.2	148.5	23.7	89.5	35.1	...	296.8
7 Transport, storage and communication	94.4	40.4	25.6	3.0	...	163.5	102.8	43.0	41.9	3.2	...	190.9
8 Finance, insurance, real estate and business services	97.8	26.0	36.3	12.9	...	172.9	106.4	26.0	-11.6	10.0	...	130.8
9 Community, social and personal services a	528.6	3.8	11.0	...	...	543.4	539.1	4.0	8.2	...	...	551.3
Total, Industries	1268.5	315.5	1237.1	143.0	...	2964.1	1262.4	339.4	1252.8	141.7	...	2996.3
Producers of Government Services	...	...	...	...	...	...	...	...	...	...	...	...
Other Producers	...	...	...	...	...	...	...	...	...	...	...	...
Total	1268.5	315.5	1237.1	143.0	...	2964.1	1262.4	339.4	1252.8	141.7	...	2996.3
Less: Imputed bank service charge	...	...	121.5	...	...	121.5	...	...	108.2	...	...	108.2
Import duties	...	...	...	205.0	...	205.0	...	...	...	189.9	...	189.9
Value added tax	...	...	...	...	...	...	...	...	...	...	...	...
Other adjustments	...	...	...	...	2.0	-2.0	...	...	...	...	2.0	-2.0
Total	1268.5	315.5	1115.6	348.0	2.0	3045.7	1262.4	339.4	1144.6	331.6	2.0	3076.1

All Producers

	1991					
	Compensation of Employees	Capital Consumption	Net Operating Surplus	Indirect Taxes	Less: Subsidies Received	Value Added
1 Agriculture, hunting, forestry and fishing	67.8	29.2	828.9	10.6	...	936.5
2 Mining and quarrying	93.5	195.6	323.8	-	...	612.9
3 Manufacturing	137.7	43.6	60.8	103.0	...	345.1
4 Electricity, gas and water	22.0	12.1	25.1	...	...	59.2
5 Construction	95.3	25.4	103.4	...	...	224.0
6 Wholesale and retail trade, restaurants and hotels a	153.5	30.0	124.9	50.0	...	358.5
7 Transport, storage and communication	103.1	48.0	87.9	4.0	...	243.0
8 Finance, insurance, real estate and business services	108.1	28.0	-4.0	15.5	...	147.6
9 Community, social and personal services a	567.7	4.9	15.5	...	...	588.2
Total, Industries	1348.7	416.8	1566.3	183.1	...	3515.0
Producers of Government Services	...	...	...	...	...	...
Other Producers	...	...	...	...	...	...
Total	1348.7	416.8	1566.3	183.1	...	3515.0
Less: Imputed bank service charge	...	...	110.5	...	...	110.5
Import duties	...	...	...	203.0	...	203.0
Value added tax	...	...	...	...	...	...
Other adjustments	...	...	...	...	2.0	-2.0
Total	1348.7	416.8	1455.8	386.1	2.0	3605.5

a) Restaurants and hotels are included in item 'Community, social and personal services'.

Paraguay

General note. The preparation of national accounts statistics in Paraguay is undertaken by the Departamento de Estudios Economicos of the Banco Central del Paraguay, Asuncion. The official estimates are published by the Department in 'Cuentas Nacionales'. The following presentation is based mainly on a comprehensive description of sources and methods used in national accounting received from the Banco Central. The estimates are generally in accordance with the classifications and definitions recommended in the United Nations System of National Accounts (SNA). The following tables have been prepared from successive replies to the United Nations national accounts questionnaire. When the scope and coverage of the estimates differ for conceptual or statistical reasons from the definitions and classifications recommded in SNA, a footnote is indicated to the relevant tables.

Sources and methods :

(a) Gross domestic product. Gross domestic product is estimated mainly through the production approach.

(b) Expenditure on the gross domestic product. The expenditure approach is used to estimate government final consumption expenditure and exports and imports of goods and services. The commodity-flow approach is used for the estimation of gross fixed capital formation. Private final consumption expenditure is arrived at as a residual. The information needed to estimate government consumption expenditure is obtained from the Ministerio de Hacienda, which controls the budget of the public sector institutions. Increase in stock is estimated for livestock only. It is assumed to be the annual increase of the cattle production minus the number of cattle slaughtered. Gross fixed capital formation is estimated on the basis of import statistics for machinery, equipment, transport and communication. Estimates of the domestic production of these items as well as the gross value of production in the construction sector are also included. Exports and imports of goods and services are estimated on the basis of information furnished by the Division de Balanza de Pagos of the Banco Central. For the constant price estimates, the only information available is that the wholesale price index is used as a deflator.

(c) Cost-structure of the gross domestic product. Compensation of employees is estimated by combining the information on the number of persons employed, by economic sectors and the average wages paid in each productive sector. Depreciation is estimated on the basis of the average lifetime of each type of capital good established in the respective depreciation tables. Information on indirect taxes and subsidies are supplied by the Ministerio de Hacienda. Operating surplus is obtained as a residual.

(d) Gross domestic product by kind of economic activity. The table of GDP by kind of economic activity is prepared at market prices, i.e., producers' values. The production approach is used to estimate the value added of most industries. The income approach is used to estimate the value added of public administration and defence, part of transport and communication, and part of other private services. The gross output of the trade sector is based on the commodity-flow approach, applying a fixed percentage for value added. The value of agricultural production is obtained by multiplying quantities by prices. Information on prices and on most quantities are obtained from Ministerio de Agricultura y Ganaderia. Remaining quantities are estimated through the use of indirect indicators such as the rate of population growth. The value of livestock production is estimated by type of livestock. Slaughtering is estimated on the basis of information provided by the Direccion De Impuestos and the meat-processing industries while stocks of cattle are based on the 1956 agricultural census. Inputs for the agricultural section is assumed to be a certain percentage of the gross value of production. The production of mining and quarrying is estimated on the basis of the industrial production coefficients of lime and cement. Information on the manufacturing sector is obtained from the surveys of the Banco Central, and the 1955 and 1963 industrial censuses. The value added of each industrial group is determined on the basis of coefficients from the 1963 industrial census applied to the gross production values. The value added of electricity and water is mainly based on information from the concerned enterprises. For constuction, the source used is the production index for construction materials. This index is compared with permits granted by the municipalities expressed in quantitative measures, multiplied by the base-year value and inflated by the implicit price index of construction materials. Value added of the trade sector is assumed to be 30 percent of the values of locally manufactured goods, imported goods and agricultural products net of farm consumption. For motor transport, the number of vehicles by category is multiplied by the number of days worked and the gross income earned in the base year. The resulting amounts are then multiplied by value added coefficients for each category of vehicle. Non-mechanical transport is calculated on the basis of the index of agricultural production transported in rural areas by carts. For ownership of dwellings, the estimates are prepared on the basis of the number of dwellings by type of construction materials used. Value added is estimated by multiplying the paid and imputed rents by the number of dwellings. The value added of public administration and defence is estimated as the total compensation paid to government employees based on information furnished by the Presupuesto General de la Nacion. The value of public education is determined directly from the Presupuesto General de Gastos de la Nacion while that of private education is estimated at constant prices by multiplying the number of students enrolled by the annual education costs plus registration fees minus 20 percent for intermediate consumption. For health, information is obtained directly from the public health services and social security services and from the Ministerio de Salud Publica y Bienestar Social for the private sector. Estimates for domestic services are obtained by multiplying actual annual wages by employment figures which are assumed to increase at a rate of 3.3 percent in the urban area and 2.6 percent in the rural area. For other services, bench-mark estimates, based on the 1963 economic census, are projected by a specially constructed growth rate. For the constant price estimates, double deflation is used for the agricultural sector. The current quantities of mining and manufacturing are revalued at base-year prices. Value added of construction, transport and financial sectors is extrapolated by using quantity indicators. For electricity, gas and water, trade and services sectors, value added is deflated by using appropriate price indexes.

1.1 Expenditure on the Gross Domestic Product, in Current Prices

Million Paraguayan guaranies

	1980	1981	1982	1983	1984	1985	1986	1987	1988	1989	1990	1991
1 Government final consumption expenditure	34732	48625	52272	58024	69280	90214	121790	176600	209138	306698	401900	543300
2 Private final consumption expenditure	399296	504074	552019	642198	821968	1066915	1434840	1882612	2586679	3496982	4841800	6038400
3 Gross capital formation	161204	204283	188916	175229	245478	306451	458882	625815	808739	1098832	1480400	1887900
A Increase in stocks a	8550	10064	12045	10720	14300	18500	27072	34400	40576	53240	55000	77000
B Gross fixed capital formation	152654	194219	176871	164509	231178	287951	431810	591415	768163	1045592	1425400	1810900
Residential buildings										...	...	
Non-residential buildings	90308	123000	115632	128351	133746	165776	220274	292084	326746	518513	...	...
Other construction and land improvement etc.											...	...
Other b	62346	71219	61239	36158	97432	122175	211536	299331	441417	527079	...	...
4 Exports of goods and services	77599	79107	89461	70054	169991	355028	399014	704695	938952	1566656	1872200	1500300
5 Less: Imports of goods and services	112372	127400	145628	127391	236273	424718	580726	896121	1224384	1860768	2121800	2424600
Equals: Gross Domestic Product	560459	708689	737040	818114	1070444	1393890	1833800	2493601	3319124	4608400	6474400	7545300

a) Item 'Increase in stocks' includes livestock only.
b) Item 'Other' of gross capital formation includes communications equipments.

1.2 Expenditure on the Gross Domestic Product, in Constant Prices

Million Paraguayan guaranies

	1980	1981	1982	1983	1984	1985	1986	1987	1988	1989	1990	1991
					At constant prices of:1982							
1 Government final consumption expenditure	42803	51126	52272	53919	50755	52800	53950	59350	61310	64639	...	...
2 Private final consumption expenditure	472573	524562	552019	543425	566155	576210	595573	603515	652723	669827	...	...
3 Gross capital formation	194465	227503	188916	154587	156940	158640	164500	175490	182387	200747	...	...
A Increase in stocks a	10766	10741	12045	9404	10500	11700	13000	14500	15436	15976	...	...
B Gross fixed capital formation	183699	216762	176871	145183	146440	146940	151500	160990	166951	184771	...	...

Paraguay

1.2 Expenditure on the Gross Domestic Product, in Constant Prices
(Continued)

Million Paraguayan guaranies

	1980	1981	1982	1983	1984	1985	1986	1987	1988	1989	1990	1991
	At constant prices of:1982											
Residential buildings											...	...
Non-residential buildings	108673	137277	115632	113185	91208	90296	91200	93024	95484	92916	...	...
Other construction and land improvement etc.												
Other b	75026	79485	61239	31998	55232	56644	60300	67966	71467	91855		
4 Exports of goods and services	110070	83358	89461	75734	94749	109487	104963	143471	152021	190237		
5 Less: Imports of goods and services	135225	142188	145628	112736	131693	130979	152763	182444	198234	225950		
Equals: Gross Domestic Product	684686	744361	737040	714929	736906	766158	766223	799382	850207	899500		

a) Item 'Increase in stocks' includes livestock only.
b) Item 'Other' of gross capital formation includes communications equipments.

1.3 Cost Components of the Gross Domestic Product

Million Paraguayan guaranies

	1980	1981	1982	1983	1984	1985	1986	1987	1988	1989	1990	1991
1 Indirect taxes, net	34536	41894	48210	45120	50726	66240	89455	150650	176465	266199	...	...
A Indirect taxes	34578	41946	48297	45166	50778	66350	89570	150830	176703	266275	...	...
B Less: Subsidies	42	52	87	46	52	110	115	180	238	76		
2 Consumption of fixed capital	58630	77688	74285	72184	107900	145270	196530	289100	355635	459220	...	
3 Compensation of employees paid by resident producers to:	195300	242850	245900	258243	342205	432120	561756	761440	974457	1261794		
4 Operating surplus a	271993	346257	368645	442567	569613	750260	986059	1292411	1812567	2621187		
Equals: Gross Domestic Product	560459	708689	737040	818114	1070444	1393890	1833800	2493601	3319124	4608400	...	...

a) Item 'Operating surplus' has been obtained as a residual.

1.4 General Government Current Receipts and Disbursements

Million Paraguayan guaranies

	1980	1981	1982	1983	1984	1985	1986	1987	1988	1989	1990	1991
	Receipts											
1 Operating surplus	...	...	...	...	...	...	...	...	...	...	...	...
2 Property and entrepreneurial income	7609	8315	6561	7412	7800	9924	16396	21474	26122	90095	...	...
3 Taxes, fees and contributions	53255	66563	74383	75301	79755	105622	137416	211066	248443	374074	...	...
A Indirect taxes	34578	41946	48297	45166	50778	66350	89570	150830	176703	266275	...	...
B Direct taxes	9097	11496	11528	12542	10001	15715	20298	35039	41385	57018	...	...
C Social security contributions a	9580	13121	14558	17593	18976	23557	27548	25197	30355	50781		
D Compulsory fees, fines and penalties	...	...	...	...	...	...	...	...	...	...		
4 Other current transfers	1452	1952	2591	3348	7660	8504	7500	7183	6465	14046		
Total Current Receipts of General Government	62316	76830	83535	86061	95215	124050	161312	239723	281030	478215	...	...
	Disbursements											
1 Government final consumption expenditure	34732	48625	52272	58024	69280	90214	121790	176600	209138	306698	...	...
2 Property income b	126	107	87	91	988	1208	1600	1984	1373	920	...	...
3 Subsidies	42	52	87	46	52	110	115	180	238	76	...	...
4 Other current transfers	7047	9955	18923	17593	23260	29100	36329	47774	58762	93117	...	...
A Social security benefits	...	...	...	...	...	...	...	...	...	...	...	...
B Social assistance grants	...	...	...	...	...	...	...	...	...	...	...	...
C Other	7047	9955	18923	17593	23260	29100	36329	47774	58762	93117	...	...
5 Net saving	20369	18091	12166	10307	1635	3418	1478	13185	11519	77404	...	...
Total Current Disbursements and Net Saving of General Government	62316	76830	83535	86061	95215	124050	161312	239723	281030	478215	...	...

a) Item 'Social security contributions' refers to direct taxes on households.
b) Item 'Property income' relates to interest on public debt.

1.6 Current Income and Outlay of Households and Non-Profit Institutions

Million Paraguayan guaranies

	1980	1981	1982	1983	1984	1985	1986	1987	1988	1989	1990	1991
	Receipts											
1 Compensation of employees	195300	242850	245900	258243	342205	432120	561756	761440	974457	1261794	...	...
2 Operating surplus of private unincorporated enterprises	...	...	...	...	...	...	...	...	...	...	...	...
3 Property and entrepreneurial income a	251674	323321	347430	414301	531465	685437	905160	1124751	1616080	2366649	...	...
4 Current transfers	7047	9955	18923	17593	23260	29100	36329	47774	58762	93117	...	...

1.6 Current Income and Outlay of Households and Non-Profit Institutions
(Continued)

Million Paraguayan guaranies

	1980	1981	1982	1983	1984	1985	1986	1987	1988	1989	1990	1991
A Social security benefits	...	...	...	...	...	...	...	...	...	...	...	...
B Social assistance grants	...	...	...	...	...	...	...	...	...	...	...	...
C Other	7047	9955	18923	17593	23260	29100	36329	47774	58762	93117	...	...
Total Current Receipts	454021	576126	612253	690137	896930	1146657	1503245	1933965	2649299	3721560	...	...

Disbursements

	1980	1981	1982	1983	1984	1985	1986	1987	1988	1989	1990	1991
1 Private final consumption expenditure	399296	504074	552019	642198	821968	1066915	1434840	1882612	2586679	3496982	...	...
2 Property income a	...	...	...	...	...	...	...	...	...	...	...	...
3 Direct taxes and other current transfers n.e.c. to general government	9840	13430	14982	17593	18976	23557	27548	25197	30355	50781	...	...
4 Other current transfers	1452	1952	2591	3348	7660	8504	7500	7183	6465	14046	...	...
5 Net saving	43433	56670	42661	26998	48326	47681	33357	18973	25800	159751	...	...
Total Current Disbursements and Net Saving	454021	576126	612253	690137	896930	1146657	1503245	1933965	2649299	3721560	...	...

a) Item 'Property and entrepreneurial income' received is net of item 'Property income' paid.

1.8 Capital Transactions of The Nation, Summary

Million Paraguayan guaranies

	1980	1981	1982	1983	1984	1985	1986	1987	1988	1989	1990	1991
Finance of Gross Capital Formation												
Gross saving	131692	164749	141012	122882	176771	223815	267901	384328	467447	799008	...	...
1 Consumption of fixed capital	58630	77688	74285	72184	107900	145270	196530	289100	355635	459220	...	...
2 Net saving	73062	87061	66727	50698	68871	78545	71371	95228	111812	339788	...	...
A General government	20369	18091	12166	10307	1635	3418	1478	13185	11519	77404	...	...
B Corporate and quasi-corporate enterprises	9260	12300	11900	13393	18910	27446	36536	63070	74493	102633	...	...
C Other	43433	56670	42661	26998	48326	47681	33357	18973	25800	159751	...	...
Less: Surplus of the nation on current transactions	-29512	-39534	-47904	-52347	-68707	-82636	-190981	-241487	341292	299824	...	...
Finance of Gross Capital Formation	161204	204283	188916	175229	245478	306451	458882	625815	808739	1098832	...	...
Gross Capital Formation												
Increase in stocks	8550	10064	12045	10720	14300	18500	27072	34400	40576	53240	...	...
Gross fixed capital formation	152654	194219	176871	164509	231178	287951	431810	591415	768163	1045592	...	...
Gross Capital Formation	161204	204283	188916	175229	245478	306451	458882	625815	808739	1098832	...	...

1.10 Gross Domestic Product by Kind of Activity, in Current Prices

Million Paraguayan guaranies

	1980	1981	1982	1983	1984	1985	1986	1987	1988	1989	1990	1991
1 Agriculture, hunting, forestry and fishing	165137	196784	190645	211615	307113	403261	498923	681934	983268	1361798	...	...
2 Mining and quarrying	2285	2933	3142	3487	4359	5672	8350	11507	15707	21160	...	...
3 Manufacturing	92338	118469	120966	134273	172003	226115	296008	404051	556088	785589	...	...
4 Electricity, gas and water	12923	15271	18120	20638	26064	30896	44791	62609	83754	111838	...	...
5 Construction	34317	46740	49544	54994	66873	82888	110137	146042	163373	259256	...	...
6 Wholesale and retail trade, restaurants and hotels ab	144870	188378	196158	217210	272599	360391	489776	662177	913979	1262709	...	...
7 Transport, storage and communication	23784	29059	31107	34529	44059	57974	80083	109313	132094	174369	...	...
8 Finance, insurance, real estate and business services bc	14993	20091	22500	24976	30971	39163	52553	70368	77565	91852	...	...
9 Community, social and personal services ac	50697	64286	72000	79920	101178	129209	174917	240808	272481	367304	...	...
Total, Industries	541344	682012	704183	781642	1025219	1335569	1755538	2388809	3198309	4435875	...	...
Producers of Government Services	19115	26678	32858	36472	45225	58321	78262	104792	120815	172525	...	...
Other Producers	...	...	...	...	...	...	...	...	...	...	...	...
Subtotal	560459	708689	737041	818114	1070444	1393890	1833800	2493601	3319124	4608400	...	...
Less: Imputed bank service charge	...	...	...	...	...	...	...	...	...	...	...	...
Plus: Import duties	...	...	...	...	...	...	...	...	...	...	...	...
Plus: Value added tax	...	...	...	...	...	...	...	...	...	...	...	...
Equals: Gross Domestic Product	560459	708689	737041	818114	1070444	1393890	1833800	2493601	3319124	4608400	...	...

a) Restaurants and hotels are included in item 'Community, social and personal services'.
b) Finance is included in item 'Wholesale and retail trade, restaurants and hotels'.
c) Business services are included in item 'Community, social and personal services'.

Paraguay

1.11 Gross Domestic Product by Kind of Activity, in Constant Prices

Million Paraguayan guaranies

	1980	1981	1982	1983	1984	1985	1986	1987	1988	1989	1990	1991
					At constant prices of:1982							
1 Agriculture, hunting, forestry and fishing	172524	189876	190645	185991	196990	206042	193467	207021	231994	249827	...	...
2 Mining and quarrying	2669	3070	3142	2912	2942	3073	3440	3646	3920	4147	...	...
3 Manufacturing	120422	125613	120966	115861	121075	127129	125345	129732	137309	145410	...	...
4 Electricity, gas and water	14025	14746	18120	17779	18164	19248	21218	22821	24823	26315	...	...
5 Construction	45164	52707	49544	46720	45604	45148	45600	46512	47742	48936	...	...
6 Wholesale and retail trade, restaurants and hotels ab	185028	200570	196158	190171	193634	202759	209437	216767	225640	236136	...	...
7 Transport, storage and communication	29551	30497	31107	30742	31853	33468	35142	36899	39149	41028	...	...
8 Finance, insurance, real estate and business services bc	21479	22961	22500	21448	21448	21662	22096	22538	22989	23541	...	...
9 Community, social and personal services ac	68096	72727	72000	71133	72243	73688	75858	78134	80791	83566	...	...
Total, Industries	658958	712768	704182	682757	703953	732217	731603	764070	814357	858906	...	...
Producers of Government Services	25728	31594	32858	32172	32953	33941	34620	35312	35850	40594	...	...
Other Producers	...	...	...	...	...	...	...	...	...	...	...	...
Subtotal	684686	744361	737040	714929	736906	766158	766223	799382	850207	899500	...	...
Less: Imputed bank service charge	...	...	...	...	...	...	...	...	...	...	...	...
Plus: Import duties	...	...	...	...	...	...	...	...	...	...	...	...
Plus: Value added tax	...	...	...	...	...	...	...	...	...	...	...	...
Equals: Gross Domestic Product	684686	744361	737040	714929	736906	766158	766223	799382	850207	899500	...	...

a) Restaurants and hotels are included in item 'Community, social and personal services'.
b) Finance is included in item 'Wholesale and retail trade, restaurants and hotels'.
c) Business services are included in item 'Community, social and personal services'.

1.12 Relations Among National Accounting Aggregates

Million Paraguayan guaranies

	1980	1981	1982	1983	1984	1985	1986	1987	1988	1989	1990	1991
Gross Domestic Product	560459	708689	737040	818114	1070444	1393890	1833800	2493601	3319124	4608400	...	...
Plus: Net factor income from the rest of the world	5261	8759	8263	4990	-2425	-12946	-9269	-50061	-55860	-5712	...	...
Factor income from the rest of the world	17247	22282	22119	20860	22904	39147	45841	56819	70980	137200	...	...
Less: Factor income to the rest of the world	11986	13523	13856	15870	25329	52093	55110	106880	126840	142912	...	...
Equals: Gross National Product	565720	717448	745303	823104	1068019	1380944	1824531	2443540	3263264	4602688	...	...
Less: Consumption of fixed capital	58630	77688	74285	72184	107900	145270	196530	289100	355635	459220	...	...
Equals: National Income	507090	639760	671018	750920	960119	1235674	1628001	2154440	2907629	4143468	5708300	...
Plus: Net current transfers from the rest of the world	-	-	-	-	-	-	-	-	-	-		
Equals: National Disposable Income	507090	639760	671018	750920	960119	1235674	1628001	2154440	2907629	4143468	...	...
Less: Final consumption	434028	552699	604291	700222	891248	1157129	1556630	2059212	2795817	3803680	...	...
Equals: Net Saving	73062	87061	66727	50698	68871	78545	71371	95228	111812	339788	...	...
Less: Surplus of the nation on current transactions	-29512	-39534	-47904	-52347	-68707	-82636	-190981	-241487	-341292	-299824	...	...
Equals: Net Capital Formation	102574	126595	114632	103045	137578	161181	262352	336715	453104	639612	...	...

4.1 Derivation of Value Added by Kind of Activity, in Current Prices

Million Paraguayan guaranies

	1980			1981			1982			1983		
	Gross Output	Intermediate Consumption	Value Added	Gross Output	Intermediate Consumption	Value Added	Gross Output	Intermediate Consumption	Value Added	Gross Output	Intermediate Consumption	Value Added
					All Producers							
1 Agriculture, hunting, forestry and fishing	...	...	165137	...	...	196784	...	...	190645	...	...	211615
A Agriculture and hunting	...	...	148397	...	...	176087	...	...	171838	...	...	190740
B Forestry and logging	...	...	16402	...	...	20300	...	...	18370	...	...	20390
C Fishing	...	...	338	...	...	397	...	...	437	...	...	485
2 Mining and quarrying	...	...	2285	...	...	2933	...	...	3142	...	...	3487

4.1 Derivation of Value Added by Kind of Activity, in Current Prices
(Continued)

Million Paraguayan guaranies

	1980			1981			1982			1983		
	Gross Output	Intermediate Consumption	Value Added	Gross Output	Intermediate Consumption	Value Added	Gross Output	Intermediate Consumption	Value Added	Gross Output	Intermediate Consumption	Value Added
3 Manufacturing	...	...	92338	...	...	118469	...	...	120966	...	...	134273
A Manufacture of food, beverages and tobacco	...	...	31780	...	...	40520	...	...	48023	...	...	56380
B Textile, wearing apparel and leather industries	...	...	10349	...	...	15194	...	...	12473	...	...	13036
C Manufacture of wood and wood products, including furniture	...	...	14832	...	...	16734	...	...	17678	...	...	19276
D Manufacture of paper and paper products, printing and publishing	...	...	3506	...	...	4515	...	...	6334	...	...	6409
E Manufacture of chemicals and chemical petroleum, coal, rubber and plastic products	...	...	16709	...	...	21433	...	...	13866	...	...	14242
F Manufacture of non-metallic mineral products, except products of petroleum and coal	...	...	3826	...	...	4956	...	...	4526	...	...	5774
G Basic metal industries	...	...	172	...	...	348	...	...	446	...	...	530
H Manufacture of fabricated metal products, machinery and equipment	...	...	2326	...	...	3326	...	...	3842	...	...	4122
I Other manufacturing industries	...	...	8838	...	...	11442	...	...	13778	...	...	14504
4 Electricity, gas and water	...	...	12923	...	...	15271	...	...	18120	...	...	20638
A Electricity, gas and steam	...	...	11238	...	...	13148	...	...	15778	...	...	17514
B Water works and supply	...	...	1685	...	...	2123	...	...	2342	...	...	3124
5 Construction	...	...	34317	...	...	46740	...	...	49544	...	...	54994
6 Wholesale and retail trade, restaurants and hotels ab	...	...	144870	...	...	188378	...	...	196158	...	...	217210
7 Transport, storage and communication	...	...	23784	...	...	29059	...	...	31107	...	...	34529
8 Finance, insurance, real estate and business services bc	...	...	14993	...	...	20091	...	...	22500	...	...	24976
9 Community, social and personal services ac	...	...	50697	...	...	64286	...	...	72000	...	...	79920
Total, Industries	...	...	541344	...	...	682012	...	...	704183	...	...	781643
Producers of Government Services	...	...	19115	...	...	26678	...	...	32858	...	...	36472
Other Producers	...	...	...	...	...	...	...	...	...	...	...	...
Total	...	...	560459	...	...	708689	...	...	737040	...	...	818114
Less: Imputed bank service charge	...	...	...	...	...	...	...	...	...	...	...	...
Import duties	...	...	...	...	...	...	...	...	...	...	...	...
Value added tax	...	...	...	...	...	...	...	...	...	...	...	...
Total	...	...	560459	...	...	708689	...	...	737040	...	...	818114

	1984			1985			1986			1987		
	Gross Output	Intermediate Consumption	Value Added	Gross Output	Intermediate Consumption	Value Added	Gross Output	Intermediate Consumption	Value Added	Gross Output	Intermediate Consumption	Value Added
						All Producers						
1 Agriculture, hunting, forestry and fishing	...	...	307113	...	...	403261	...	...	498923	...	...	681934
A Agriculture and hunting	...	...	273860	...	...	359230	...	...	429977	...	...	586972
B Forestry and logging	...	...	32642	...	...	43243	...	...	67778	...	...	93398
C Fishing	...	...	611	...	...	788	...	...	1168	...	...	1564
2 Mining and quarrying	...	...	4359	...	...	5672	...	...	8350	...	...	11507

Paraguay

Million Paraguayan guaranies

	1984			1985			1986			1987		
	Gross Output	Intermediate Consumption	Value Added	Gross Output	Intermediate Consumption	Value Added	Gross Output	Intermediate Consumption	Value Added	Gross Output	Intermediate Consumption	Value Added
3 Manufacturing	...	...	172003	...	...	226115	...	...	296008	...	...	404051
A Manufacture of food, beverages and tobacco	...	...	76307	...	...	106369	...	...	152186	...	...	206246
B Textile, wearing apparel and leather industries	...	...	22086	...	...	28903	...	...	32408	...	...	40245
C Manufacture of wood and wood products, including furniture	...	...	22948	...	...	25539	...	...	34641	...	...	42532
D Manufacture of paper and paper products, printing and publishing	...	...	6077	...	...	7215	...	...	10231	...	...	12267
E Manufacture of chemicals and chemical petroleum, coal, rubber and plastic products	...	...	16049	...	...	20917	...	...	23125	...	...	36531
F Manufacture of non-metallic mineral products, except products of petroleum and coal	...	...	5770	...	...	6425	...	...	12229	...	...	17650
G Basic metal industries	...	...	663	...	...	745	...	...	996	...	...	2095
H Manufacture of fabricated metal products, machinery and equipment	...	...	6559	...	...	7819	...	...	9887	...	...	12151
I Other manufacturing industries	...	...	15544	...	...	22183	...	...	20305	...	...	34334
4 Electricity, gas and water	...	...	26064	...	...	30896	...	...	44791	...	...	62609
A Electricity, gas and steam	...	...	22127	...	...	25780	...	...	37681	...	...	52904
B Water works and supply	...	...	3937	...	...	5116	...	...	7110	...	...	9705
5 Construction	...	...	66873	...	...	82888	...	...	110137	...	...	146042
6 Wholesale and retail trade, restaurants and hotels ab	...	...	272599	...	...	360391	...	...	489776	...	...	662177
7 Transport, storage and communication	...	...	44059	...	...	57974	...	...	80083	...	...	109313
8 Finance, insurance, real estate and business services bc	...	...	30971	...	...	39163	...	...	52553	...	...	70368
9 Community, social and personal services ac	...	...	101178	...	...	129209	...	...	174917	...	...	240808
Total, Industries	...	...	1025219	...	...	1335569	...	...	1755538	...	...	2388809
Producers of Government Services	...	...	45225	...	...	58321	...	...	78262	...	...	104792
Other Producers	...	...	...	...	...	...	...	...	...	...	...	...
Total	...	...	1070444	...	...	1393890	...	...	1833800	...	...	2493601
Less: Imputed bank service charge	...	...	...	...	...	...	...	...	...	...	...	...
Import duties	...	...	...	...	...	...	...	...	...	...	...	...
Value added tax	...	...	...	...	...	...	...	...	...	...	...	...
Total	...	...	1070444	...	...	1393890	...	...	1833800	...	...	2493601

	1988			1989		
	Gross Output	Intermediate Consumption	Value Added	Gross Output	Intermediate Consumption	Value Added

All Producers

	1988			1989		
1 Agriculture, hunting, forestry and fishing	...	...	983268	...	...	1361799
A Agriculture and hunting	...	...	883881	...	...	1221797
B Forestry and logging	...	...	97755	...	...	137752
C Fishing	...	...	1632	...	...	2250
2 Mining and quarrying	...	...	15707	...	...	21160

4.1 Derivation of Value Added by Kind of Activity, in Current Prices
(Continued)

Million Paraguayan guaranies

	1988			1989		
	Gross Output	Intermediate Consumption	Value Added	Gross Output	Intermediate Consumption	Value Added
3 Manufacturing	...	...	556088	...	...	785589
A Manufacture of food, beverages and tobacco	...	...	260648	...	...	312651
B Textile, wearing apparel and leather industries	...	...	91237	...	...	105415
C Manufacture of wood and wood products, including furniture	...	...	52106	...	...	97308
D Manufacture of paper and paper products, printing and publishing	...	...	18099	...	...	25649
E Manufacture of chemicals and chemical petroleum, coal, rubber and plastic products	...	...	48304	...	...	107729
F Manufacture of non-metallic mineral products, except products of petroleum and coal	...	...	21171	...	...	36613
G Basic metal industries	...	...	3600	...	...	5945
H Manufacture of fabricated metal products, machinery and equipment	...	...	15719	...	...	29619
I Other manufacturing industries	...	...	45204	...	...	64660
4 Electricity, gas and water	...	...	83754	...	...	111838
A Electricity, gas and steam	...	...	72097	...	...	96610
B Water works and supply	...	...	11657	...	...	15228
5 Construction	...	...	163373	...	...	259256
6 Wholesale and retail trade, restaurants and hotels ab	...	...	913979	...	...	1262709
7 Transport, storage and communication	...	...	132094	...	...	174369
8 Finance, insurance, real estate and business services bc	...	...	77565	...	...	91852
9 Community, social and personal services ac	...	...	272481	...	...	367304
Total, Industries	...	...	3198309	...	...	4435875
Producers of Government Services	...	...	120815	...	...	172525
Other Producers	...	...	...	...	...	...
Total	...	...	3319124	...	...	4608400
Less: Imputed bank service charge	...	...	...	...	...	...
Import duties	...	...	...	...	...	...
Value added tax	...	...	...	...	...	...
Total	...	...	3319124	...	...	4608400

a) Restaurants and hotels are included in item 'Community, social and personal services'.
b) Finance is included in item 'Wholesale and retail trade, restaurants and hotels'.
c) Business services are included in item 'Community, social and personal services'.

4.2 Derivation of Value Added by Kind of Activity, in Constant Prices

Million Paraguayan guaranies

	1980			1981			1982			1983		
	Gross Output	Intermediate Consumption	Value Added	Gross Output	Intermediate Consumption	Value Added	Gross Output	Intermediate Consumption	Value Added	Gross Output	Intermediate Consumption	Value Added
At constant prices of: 1982												
All Producers												
1 Agriculture, hunting, forestry and fishing	...	...	172524	...	...	189876	...	...	190645	...	...	185991
A Agriculture and hunting	...	...	153692	...	...	169981	...	...	171838	...	...	167534
B Forestry and logging	...	...	18424	...	...	19471	...	...	18370	...	...	18039
C Fishing	...	...	408	...	...	424	...	...	437	...	...	418
2 Mining and quarrying	...	...	2669	...	...	3070	...	...	3142	...	...	2912

Paraguay

4.2 Derivation of Value Added by Kind of Activity, in Constant Prices
(Continued)

Million Paraguayan guaranies

	1980			1981			1982			1983		
	Gross Output	Intermediate Consumption	Value Added	Gross Output	Intermediate Consumption	Value Added	Gross Output	Intermediate Consumption	Value Added	Gross Output	Intermediate Consumption	Value Added
					At constant prices of:1982							
3 Manufacturing	...	...	120422	...	...	125613	...	...	120966	...	...	115861
A Manufacture of food, beverages and tobacco	...	...	40025	...	...	45456	...	...	48023	...	...	49523
B Textile, wearing apparel and leather industries	...	...	11276	...	...	13540	...	...	12473	...	...	11624
C Manufacture of wood and wood products, including furniture	...	...	22979	...	...	17655	...	...	17678	...	...	16977
D Manufacture of paper and paper products, printing and publishing	...	...	5261	...	...	5885	...	...	6334	...	...	3873
E Manufacture of chemicals and chemical petroleum, coal, rubber and plastic products	...	...	20816	...	...	20606	...	...	13866	...	...	13541
F Manufacture of non-metallic mineral products, except products of petroleum and coal	...	...	4645	...	...	5040	...	...	4526	...	...	4874
G Basic metal industries	...	...	377	...	...	430	...	...	446	...	...	445
H Manufacture of fabricated metal products, machinery and equipment	...	...	3609	...	...	3863	...	...	3842	...	...	3780
I Other manufacturing industries	...	...	11434	...	...	13138	...	...	13778	...	...	11224
4 Electricity, gas and water	...	...	14025	...	...	14746	...	...	18120	...	...	17779
A Electricity, gas and steam	...	...	12137	...	...	12623	...	...	15778	...	...	15014
B Water works and supply	...	...	1888	...	...	2123	...	...	2342	...	...	2765
5 Construction	...	...	45164	...	...	52707	...	...	49544	...	...	46720
6 Wholesale and retail trade, restaurants and hotels ab	...	...	185028	...	...	200570	...	...	196158	...	...	190171
7 Transport, storage and communication	...	...	29551	...	...	30497	...	...	31107	...	...	30742
8 Finance, insurance, real estate and business services bc	...	...	21479	...	...	22961	...	...	22501	...	...	21448
9 Community, social and personal services ac	...	...	68096	...	...	72727	...	...	72000	...	...	71133
Total, Industries	...	...	658958	...	...	712767	...	...	704182	...	...	682757
Producers of Government Services	...	...	25728	...	...	31594	...	...	32858	...	...	32172
Other Producers	...	...	...	...	...	...	...	...	...	...	...	...
Total	...	...	684686	...	...	744361	...	...	737041	...	...	714929
Less: Imputed bank service charge	...	...	...	...	...	...	...	...	...	...	...	...
Import duties	...	...	...	...	...	...	...	...	...	...	...	...
Value added tax	...	...	...	...	...	...	...	...	...	...	...	...
Total	...	...	684686	...	...	744361	...	...	737041	...	...	714929

	1984			1985			1986			1987		
	Gross Output	Intermediate Consumption	Value Added	Gross Output	Intermediate Consumption	Value Added	Gross Output	Intermediate Consumption	Value Added	Gross Output	Intermediate Consumption	Value Added
					At constant prices of:1982							
					All Producers							
1 Agriculture, hunting, forestry and fishing	...	...	196990	...	...	206042	...	...	193467	...	...	207021
A Agriculture and hunting	...	...	178074	...	...	186954	...	...	172178	...	...	184468
B Forestry and logging	...	...	18490	...	...	18649	...	...	20837	...	...	22087
C Fishing	...	...	426	...	...	439	...	...	452	...	...	466
2 Mining and quarrying	...	...	2942	...	...	3073	...	...	3440	...	...	3646

4.2 Derivation of Value Added by Kind of Activity, in Constant Prices
(Continued)

Million Paraguayan guaranies

	1984			1985			1986			1987		
	Gross Output	Intermediate Consumption	Value Added	Gross Output	Intermediate Consumption	Value Added	Gross Output	Intermediate Consumption	Value Added	Gross Output	Intermediate Consumption	Value Added
					At constant prices of:1982							
3 Manufacturing	...	...	121075	...	...	127129	...	...	125345	...	...	129732
A Manufacture of food, beverages and tobacco	...	...	52664	...	...	53588	...	...	57195	...	...	59359
B Textile, wearing apparel and leather industries	...	...	12523	...	...	15352	...	...	12783	...	...	10300
C Manufacture of wood and wood products, including furniture	...	...	16724	...	...	15302	...	...	15661	...	...	17404
D Manufacture of paper and paper products, printing and publishing	...	...	4407	...	...	4487	...	...	4136	...	...	4217
E Manufacture of chemicals and chemical petroleum, coal, rubber and plastic products	...	...	12470	...	...	14006	...	...	12838	...	...	15284
F Manufacture of non-metallic mineral products, except products of petroleum and coal	...	...	4555	...	...	4003	...	...	5261	...	...	6076
G Basic metal industries	...	...	519	...	...	550	...	...	553	...	...	826
H Manufacture of fabricated metal products, machinery and equipment	...	...	4794	...	...	6253	...	...	5406	...	...	5303
I Other manufacturing industries	...	...	12419	...	...	13588	...	...	11512	...	...	10963
4 Electricity, gas and water	...	...	18164	...	...	19248	...	...	21218	...	...	22821
A Electricity, gas and steam	...	...	15344	...	...	16255	...	...	18060	...	...	19505
B Water works and supply	...	...	2820	...	...	2993	...	...	3158	...	...	3316
5 Construction	...	...	45604	...	...	45148	...	...	45600	...	...	46512
6 Wholesale and retail trade, restaurants and hotels ab	...	...	193634	...	...	202759	...	...	209437	...	...	216767
7 Transport, storage and communication	...	...	31853	...	...	33468	...	...	35142	...	...	36899
8 Finance, insurance, real estate and business services bc	...	...	21448	...	...	21662	...	...	22096	...	...	22538
9 Community, social and personal services ac	...	...	72243	...	...	73688	...	...	75858	...	...	78134
Total, Industries	...	...	703953	...	...	732217	...	...	731603	...	...	764070
Producers of Government Services	...	...	32953	...	...	33941	...	...	34620	...	...	35312
Other Producers	...	...	...	...	...	...	...	...	...	...	...	...
Total	...	...	736906	...	...	766158	...	...	766223	...	...	799382
Less: Imputed bank service charge	...	...	...	...	...	...	...	...	...	...	...	...
Import duties	...	...	...	...	...	...	...	...	...	...	...	...
Value added tax	...	...	...	...	...	...	...	...	...	...	...	...
Total	...	...	736906	...	...	766158	...	...	766223	...	...	799382

	1988			1989		
	Gross Output	Intermediate Consumption	Value Added	Gross Output	Intermediate Consumption	Value Added
		At constant prices of:1982				
		All Producers				
1 Agriculture, hunting, forestry and fishing	...	...	231994	...	...	249827
A Agriculture and hunting	...	...	208124	...	...	224988
B Forestry and logging	...	...	23390	...	...	24349
C Fishing	...	...	480	...	...	490
2 Mining and quarrying	...	...	3920	...	...	4147

Paraguay

Million Paraguayan guaranies

	1988			1989		
	Gross Output	Intermediate Consumption	Value Added	Gross Output	Intermediate Consumption	Value Added
3 Manufacturing	...	...	137309	At constant prices of:1982		
				...	...	145410
A Manufacture of food, beverages and tobacco	...	...	51490	...	...	54429
B Textile, wearing apparel and leather industries	...	...	17725	...	...	18127
C Manufacture of wood and wood products, including furniture	...	...	18092	...	...	18915
D Manufacture of paper and paper products, printing and publishing	...	...	4510	...	...	4547
E Manufacture of chemicals and chemical petroleum, coal, rubber and plastic products	...	...	18328	...	...	18723
F Manufacture of non-metallic mineral products, except products of petroleum and coal	...	...	6173	...	...	6166
G Basic metal industries	...	...	809	...	...	928
H Manufacture of fabricated metal products, machinery and equipment	...	...	5264	...	...	5462
I Other manufacturing industries	...	...	14918	...	...	18113
4 Electricity, gas and water	...	...	24823	...	...	26315
A Electricity, gas and steam	...	...	21368	...	...	22732
B Water works and supply	...	...	3455	...	...	3582
5 Construction	...	...	47742	...	...	48936
6 Wholesale and retail trade, restaurants and hotels ab	...	...	225640	...	...	236136
7 Transport, storage and communication	...	...	39149	...	...	41028
8 Finance, insurance, real estate and business services bc	...	...	22989	...		23541
9 Community, social and personal services ac	...	...	80791	...	...	83566
Total, Industries	...	...	814357	...	...	858906
Producers of Government Services	...	...	35850	...	...	40594
Other Producers	...	...	...	...	...	...
Total	...	...	850207	...	...	899500
Less: Imputed bank service charge	...	...	...	...	...	...
Import duties	...	...	...	...	...	...
Value added tax	...	...	...	...	...	...
Total	...	...	850207	...	...	899500

a) Restaurants and hotels are included in item 'Community, social and personal services'.
b) Finance is included in item 'Wholesale and retail trade, restaurants and hotels'.
c) Business services are included in item 'Community, social and personal services'.

Peru

Source. Reply to the United Nations National Accounts Questionnaire from the Instituto Nacional de Estadistica, Lima. The official estimates are published in 'Cuentas Nacionales del Peru: Tablas Insumo Producto y Sectores Institucionales', Instituto Nacional de Estadistica del Peru, Lima

General note. The estimates shown in the following tables have been prepared by the Instituto Nacional de Estadistica in accordance with the United Nations System of National Accounts so far as the existing data would permit. On February 1, 1985, the Inti, equal to 1,000 soles, was introduced. On July 1, 1991, the new sole, equal to one million Intis, replaced the Inti as the currency units.

1.1 Expenditure on the Gross Domestic Product, in Current Prices

New soles

	1980	1981	1982	1983	1984	1985	1986	1987	1988	1989	1990	1991
1 Government final consumption expenditure	667	1215	2260	4077	8104	22457	43336	93853	474630	12046	514296	2085984
2 Private final consumption expenditure	3659	6738	11070	21099	45532	123412	254987	497603	3214245	79090	5018069	6015904
3 Gross capital formation	1640	3347	5603	7617	16083	42727	83767	168686	1292250	23825	1434695	7839609
A Increase in stocks	239	575	664	172	-221	414	3232	11409	73024	119	11560	219223
B Gross fixed capital formation	1402	2772	4939	7445	16304	42313	80535	157278	1219226	23706	1423135	7620386
Residential buildings	469	982	1955	3161	7081	19124	35036	70417	477208	9371	...	...
Non-residential buildings											...	...
Other construction and land improvement etc.	284	561	1055	1613	3611	9474	19432	36563	367413	6733	...	...
Other	649	1228	1928	2672	5611	13715	26066	50298	374605	7602	482811	2223984
4 Exports of goods and services	1332	1735	2806	5880	13486	39611	45420	68527	564016	14261	765114	3325292
5 Less: Imports of goods and services	1329	2378	3829	6224	10794	30304	53534	89230	602824	14107	691174	4115082
Equals: Gross Domestic Product a	5968	10658	17909	32448	72410	197903	373976	739439	4942317	115115	7041000	15151707

a) Beginning 1989, the estimates are in thousand New Soles.

1.2 Expenditure on the Gross Domestic Product, in Constant Prices

New soles

	1980	1981	1982	1983	1984	1985	1986	1987	1988	1989	1990	1991
						At constant prices of:1979						
1 Government final consumption expenditure	368	362	410	374	357	370	382	405	341	316	286	289
2 Private final consumption expenditure	2236	2356	2376	2167	2209	2256	2593	2847	2636	2186	2133	2159
3 Gross capital formation	1031	1242	1151	704	634	564	749	959	869	586	604	724
A Increase in stocks	149	218	150	4	-23	-19	59	141	165	21	28	103
B Gross fixed capital formation	882	1024	1001	700	657	582	689	818	704	565	576	621
Residential buildings	272	300	311	251	249	225	264	325	305	256	...	...
Non-residential buildings											...	...
Other construction and land improvement etc.	191	225	222	172	176	153	199	226	216	182	...	...
Other	419	499	468	276	233	205	226	267	183	126	131	168
4 Exports of goods and services	879	854	906	812	886	925	831	771	715	849	804	767
5 Less: Imports of goods and services	868	1006	1028	723	592	541	651	747	680	508	572	608
Equals: Gross Domestic Product	3647	3808	3816	3334	3495	3574	3904	4235	3881	3429	3255	3331

Peru

1.3 Cost Components of the Gross Domestic Product

New soles

	1980	1981	1982	1983	1984	1985	1986	1987	1988	1989	1990	1991
1 Indirect taxes, net	573	1025	1710	2747	6197	19838	30492	50083	240624	... 5398	482004	2331363
A Indirect taxes	726	1195	1974	3152	6815	21608	33651	56657	313412	... 6495	517980	2359192
B Less: Subsidies	153	170	264	405	618	1770	3159	6574	72788	... 1097	35976	27829
2 Consumption of fixed capital	321	553	945	1886	4253	11005	21545	38853	358830	... 7818	431058	2180329
3 Compensation of employees paid by resident producers to:	1772	3286	5703	10700	21681	54321	114488	242634	1342121	... 31356	1719943	5533638
A Resident households	1767	3275	5675	10631	21564	54071	114075	241976	1341230	... 31291	1713128	
B Rest of the world	5	11	28	70	118	250	413	658	891	... 65	6815	...
4 Operating surplus	3303	5795	9551	17115	40279	112739	207451	407870	3000742	... 70543	4407995	5106377
Equals: Gross Domestic Product a	5968	10658	17909	32448	72410	197903	373976	739439	4942317	... 115115	7041000	15151707

a) Beginning 1989, the estimates are in thousand New Soles.

1.4 General Government Current Receipts and Disbursements

New soles

	1980	1981	1982	1983	1984	1985	1986	1987	1988	1989	1990	1991
Receipts												
1 Operating surplus	5	8	20	37	147	582	789	1357	26090	... 860	23892	...
2 Property and entrepreneurial income	213	399	571	939	1938	5652	2203	2041	9672	... 115	15323	...
3 Taxes, fees and contributions	1333	2097	3338	5440	11528	33356	61455	106179	569160	... 11639	789046	...
A Indirect taxes	726	1195	1974	3152	6815	21608	33651	56657	313412	... 6495	517980	...
B Direct taxes	424	512	782	1060	2115	4795	13343	17762	120622	... 1993	115999	...
C Social security contributions	168	332	513	1033	2053	5582	12370	27924	116601	... 2688	133617	...
D Compulsory fees, fines and penalties	15	58	69	195	545	1371	2091	3836	18525	... 463	21450	...
4 Other current transfers	136	207	82	373	707	1663	4009	9219	48992	... 1881	64493	...
Total Current Receipts of General Government a	1687	2712	4011	6789	14321	41253	68457	118795	653914	... 14495	892754	...
Disbursements												
1 Government final consumption expenditure	667	1215	2260	4077	8104	22457	43336	93853	474630	... 12046	514296	...
2 Property income	228	357	519	1411	3075	8175	8831	13225	101054	... 1421	163461	...
A Interest	228	357	519	1411	3075	8175	8831	13225	101054	... 1421	163461	...
B Net land rent and royalties	...	...	...	...	...	...	...	...	...	...	...	...
3 Subsidies	153	170	264	405	618	1770	3159	6574	72788	... 1097	35976	...
4 Other current transfers	527	897	1098	2195	4342	10389	14907	35337	169763	... 3671	193738	...
A Social security benefits	150	281	481	918	1926	4462	10482	25637	117907	... 2636	129158	...
B Social assistance grants	...	...	...	...	...	...	...	...	...	...	...	...
C Other	377	616	617	1277	2416	5927	4425	9700	51856	... 1035	64580	...
5 Net saving b	111	73	-130	-1299	-1818	-1538	-1776	-30193	-164321	-3740	-14717	...
Total Current Disbursements and Net Saving of General Government a	1687	2712	4011	6789	14321	41253	68457	118795	653914	... 14495	892754	...

a) Beginning 1989, the estimates are in thousand New Soles.
b) Item 'Net saving' includes consumption of fixed capital.

1.5 Current Income and Outlay of Corporate and Quasi-Corporate Enterprises, Summary

New soles

	1980	1981	1982	1983	1984	1985	1986	1987	1988	1989	1990	1991
Receipts												
1 Operating surplus	914	1359	2073	4014	11158	32617	43800	69752	786092	-3321	-305682	...
2 Property and entrepreneurial income received	583	1357	2280	4624	10492	25247	33283	69670	692098	20242	673426	...
3 Current transfers	298	538	741	1355	2551	6068	3361	5504	51266	705	31137	...
Total Current Receipts a	1794	3253	5095	9992	24202	63932	80445	144925	1529456	17626	398881	...
Disbursements												
1 Property and entrepreneurial income	914	2052	3368	6498	15125	39439	44483	86202	896478	20090	614837	...
2 Direct taxes and other current payments to general government	381	441	680	892	1831	4321	12910	16608	114042	598	44176	...
3 Other current transfers	65	137	232	552	969	2329	3339	6567	56262	737	42581	...
4 Net saving b	435	622	814	2049	6279	17842	19713	35550	462674	-3799	-302713	...
Total Current Disbursements and Net Saving a	1794	3253	5095	9992	24202	63932	80445	144924	1529456	17626	398881	...

a) Beginning 1989, the estimates are in thousand New Soles.
b) Item 'Net saving' includes consumption of fixed capital.

1.6 Current Income and Outlay of Households and Non-Profit Institutions

New soles

	1980	1981	1982	1983	1984	1985	1986	1987	1988	1989	1990	1991
Receipts												
1 Compensation of employees	1776	3290	5706	10703	21729	54617	114778	243343	1348929	...	...	...
A From resident producers	1767	3275	5675	10631	21564	54071	114075	241976	1341230	...	...	...
B From rest of the world	9	15	31	72	165	546	703	1367	7699	...	...	...
2 Operating surplus of private unincorporated enterprises	2704	4981	8402	14950	33227	90546	184407	375613	2547390	...	...	...
3 Property and entrepreneurial income	191	493	864	1625	3316	9563	12932	29580	266938	...	...	...
4 Current transfers	308	551	900	1693	3025	7126	14578	34041	159031	...	...	...
A Social security benefits	162	307	526	1021	2112	4682	10784	26373	122822	...	...	...
B Social assistance grants	...	...	...	...	...	...	...	...	...	...	...	...
C Other	147	244	374	672	913	2444	3794	7668	36209	...	...	...
Total Current Receipts	4980	9314	15872	28972	61296	161853	326694	682577	4322288	...	...	...
Disbursements												
1 Private final consumption expenditure	3659	6738	11070	21099	45532	123412	254987	497603	3214245	...	...	...
2 Property income	126	258	507	1054	1572	3151	5856	12425	85290	...	...	...
3 Direct taxes and other current transfers n.e.c. to general government	236	486	728	1499	3069	7647	15198	33651	146621	...	...	...
A Social security contributions	179	358	557	1136	2240	5802	12673	28660	121516	...	...	...
B Direct taxes	48	108	134	231	540	1092	1393	2575	11625	...	...	...
C Fees, fines and penalties	9	20	37	132	289	753	1132	2416	13480	...	...	...
4 Other current transfers	20	24	60	122	251	898	1626	3307	20099	...	...	...
5 Net saving a	938	1807	3507	5197	10871	26744	49028	135592	856033	...	...	...
Total Current Disbursements and Net Saving	4980	9314	15872	28972	61296	161853	326694	682577	4322288	...	...	...

a) Item 'Net saving' includes consumption of fixed capital.

1.7 External Transactions on Current Account, Summary

New soles

	1980	1981	1982	1983	1984	1985	1986	1987	1988	1989	1990	1991
Payments to the Rest of the World												
1 Imports of goods and services	1329	2377	3829	6224	10794	30304	53534	89231	602824	14107	691174	...
2 Factor income to the rest of the world	354	516	795	2031	4687	11999	12541	12848	121800	2498	212567	...
A Compensation of employees	5	11	28	70	118	250	413	658	891	65	6815	...
B Property and entrepreneurial income	349	505	767	1961	4569	11749	12128	12190	120909	2433	205752	...

Peru

1.7 External Transactions on Current Account, Summary
(Continued)

New soles

	1980	1981	1982	1983	1984	1985	1986	1987	1988	1989	1990	1991
3 Current transfers to the rest of the world	3	4	5	17	47	209	132	348	5942	... 55	834	...
4 Surplus of the nation on current transactions	-155	-844	-1413	-1669	-751	321	-16802	-27738	-138195	... -683	-57058	...
Payments to the Rest of the World and Surplus of the Nation on Current Transactions a	1531	2053	3216	6602	14777	42833	49406	74689	592371	... 15977	847517	...
Receipts From The Rest of the World												
1 Exports of goods and services	1332	1735	2806	5880	13486	39611	45420	68527	564016	... 14261	765114	...
2 Factor income from rest of the world	76	101	117	257	709	1993	2079	2996	14494	... 881	35086	...
A Compensation of employees	9	15	31	72	165	546	703	1367	7699	... 262	12602	...
B Property and entrepreneurial income	67	86	86	185	544	1447	1376	1629	6795	... 619	22484	...
3 Current transfers from rest of the world	123	216	294	464	582	1230	1907	3166	13861	... 835	47317	...
Receipts from the Rest of the World on Current Transactions a	1531	2053	3216	6602	14777	42833	49406	74689	592371	... 15977	847517	...

a) Beginning 1989, the estimates are in thousand New Soles.

1.9 Gross Domestic Product by Institutional Sectors of Origin

New soles

	1980	1981	1982	1983	1984	1985	1986	1987	1988	1989	1990	1991
Domestic Factor Incomes Originating												
1 General government	509	996	1715	3415	7350	18052	37853	84111	409304	... 10395	492942	...
2 Corporate and quasi-corporate enterprises	1707	2844	4678	8809	20615	56921	93473	173195	1449000	... 99322	6066053	...
A Non-financial	1678	2784	4560	8632	19987	56414	93349	171120	1420000	... 99170	6082911	...
Public	52	166	503	1140	2841	9074	16764	31742	243283	4242	150743	...
Private	1626	2618	4057	7492	17146	47340	76585	139378	1177000	... 94928	5932168	...
B Financial	29	60	118	177	628	507	126	2075	28943	152	-16858	...
3 Households and private unincorporated enterprises	3180	5793	9804	17477	38249	103092	212156	432050	2844000	... ...		
4 Non-profit institutions serving households	...	...	...	...	...	...	...	...	...	... ...		
Subtotal: Domestic Factor Incomes a	5396	9633	16197	29701	66214	178065	343482	689357	4701693	... 109717	6558996	...
Indirect taxes, net	573	1025	1710	2747	6197	19838	30492	50083	240624	... 5398	482004	...
A Indirect taxes	726	1195	1974	3152	6815	21608	33651	56657	313412	6495	517980	...
B Less: Subsidies	153	170	264	405	618	1770	3159	6574	72788	... 1097	35976	...
Consumption of fixed capital	...	...	...	...	...	...	...	...	...	... ...	...	...
Gross Domestic Product b	5968	10658	17909	32448	72410	197903	373976	739439	4942317	... 115115	7041000	...

a) Item 'Domestic factor incomes' includes consumption of fixed capital.
b) Beginning 1989, the estimates are in thousand New Soles.

1.10 Gross Domestic Product by Kind of Activity, in Current Prices

New soles

	1980	1981	1982	1983	1984	1985	1986	1987	1988	1989	1990	1991
1 Agriculture, hunting, forestry and fishing	610	1098	1709	3426	7982	18634	41930	76126	409452	... 9256	476633	2323413
2 Mining and quarrying	905	1257	1873	3589	7702	19513	11953	15758	110284	... 3212	191241	847737
3 Manufacturing	1206	1956	3275	5949	14424	48066	90681	172795	1474931	... 29090	1939762	8782634
4 Electricity, gas and water	51	111	191	270	824	2344	3588	6381	22738	... 404	40185	201532
5 Construction	342	737	1589	2172	4744	14087	28244	58329	446250	... 8948	533512	3012457
6 Wholesale and retail trade, restaurants and hotels	1060	1932	3131	6145	13240	35564	76484	150842	924873	... 21963	1315720	6584540
7 Transport, storage and communication	396	712	1089	1817	4266	12183	20333	40142	246467	... 5706	338626	2086149
8 Finance, insurance, real estate and business services	591	1238	2248	3836	8118	19454	39963	80478	598553	... 15081	1018692	6179769
9 Community, social and personal services	242	523	905	1749	3921	11019	23913	55515	341031	... 10263	677046	3472164
Total, Industries	5403	9564	16010	28953	65221	180864	337089	656366	4574579	... 103922	6531417	3490395
Producers of Government Services	461	916	1567	3020	6438	16103	33874	77058	374324	... 9579	468630	959763
Other Producers	62	150	316	536	975	2604	6798	13345	69175	... 1738	119239	598710
Subtotal	5926	10630	17893	32509	72634	199571	377761	746769	5018078	... 115239	7119286	5048868
Less: Imputed bank service charge	118	284	404	767	1624	5716	11687	20430	131631	... 1340	145452	207578
Plus: Import duties	160	312	419	705	1400	4048	7903	13100	55870	... 1215	67166	310417
Plus: Value added tax	...	...	...	...	...	...	...	...	...	...	...	...
Equals: Gross Domestic Product a	5968	10658	17909	32448	72410	197903	373977	739439	4942317	... 115115	7041000	15151707

a) Beginning 1989, the estimates are in thousand New Soles.

1.11 Gross Domestic Product by Kind of Activity, in Constant Prices

New soles

	1980	1981	1982	1983	1984	1985	1986	1987	1988	1989	1990	1991
					At constant prices of:1979							
1 Agriculture, hunting, forestry and fishing	382	416	428	382	427	443	471	495	534	508	466	471
2 Mining and quarrying	469	454	460	415	435	453	433	420	357 .	340	325	313
3 Manufacturing	867	873	862	706	746	780	902	1017	903	762	709	750
4 Electricity, gas and water	39	42	45	38	38	41	48	51	52	51	51	56
5 Construction	202	225	230	182	183	164	199	234	218	186	192	189
6 Wholesale and retail trade, restaurants and hotels	654	689	689	590	604	618	705	773	689	580	555	588
7 Transport, storage and communication	236	251	248	230	231	238	258	284	268	243	226	235
8 Finance, insurance, real estate and business services	386	411	410	391	391	424	448	485	442	427	422	436
9 Community, social and personal services	127	134	132	128	133	138	147	155	141	125	117	119
Total, Industries	3362	3495	3504	3062	3188	3299	3611	3914	3604	3222	3063	3157
Producers of Government Services	233	240	242	258	278	279	302	317	288	247	227	208
Other Producers	33	34	35	37	39	39	41	43	40	37	34	35
Subtotal	3628	3769	3781	3357	3505	3617	3954	4274	3932	3506	3324	3400
Less: Imputed bank service charge	82	89	90	98	88	111	125	127	125	118	120	123
Plus: Import duties	102	128	124	76	77	68	76	88	74	41	51	54
Plus: Value added tax	...	...	...	...	...	...	...	...	...	...	...	...
Equals: Gross Domestic Product	3647	3808	3816	3334	3495	3574	3904	4234	3881	3429	3255	3331

Peru

1.12 Relations Among National Accounting Aggregates

New soles

	1980	1981	1982	1983	1984	1985	1986	1987	1988	1989	1990	1991
Gross Domestic Product	5968	10658	17909	32448	72410	197903	373976	739439	4942317	115115	7041000	15151707
Plus: Net factor income from the rest of the world	-278	-415	-678	-1773	-3977	-10006	-10462	-9852	-107306	-1617	-177481	-751738
Factor income from the rest of the world	76	101	117	257	709	1992	2079	2996	14494	881	35086	...
Less: Factor income to the rest of the world	354	516	795	2030	4686	11998	12541	12848	121800	2498	212567	...
Equals: Gross National Product	5690	10244	17231	30675	68433	187897	363514	729587	4835011	113498	6863519	14399969
Less: Consumption of fixed capital	321	553	945	1886	4253	11005	21545	38853	358830	7818	431058	2180328
Equals: National Income	5369	9691	16286	28790	64180	176892	341969	690734	4476182	105680	6432461	1 2219641
Plus: Net current transfers from the rest of the world	120	213	289	448	535	1020	1775	2818	7918	780	46482	174731
Current transfers from the rest of the world	122	216	294	464	582	1230	1907	3166	13861	835	47317	...
Less: Current transfers to the rest of the world	3	4	5	17	47	209	132	348	5942	55	834	...
Equals: National Disposable Income	5489	9904	16575	29237	64715	177912	343744	693551	4484100	106460	6478943	1 2394372
Less: Final consumption	4325	7954	13329	25176	53636	145870	298323	591456	3688875	91136	5532365	8101888
Equals: Net Saving	1164	1950	3246	4061	11079	32042	45421	102095	795225	15324	946578	4292484
Less: Surplus of the nation on current transactions	-155	-844	-1413	-1669	-751	321	-16802	-27738	-138195	-683	-57058	-1366797
Equals: Net Capital Formation a	1318	2794	4658	5731	11830	31722	62222	129833	933420	16007	1003636	5659281

a) Beginning 1989, the estimates are in thousand New Soles.

2.1 Government Final Consumption Expenditure by Function, in Current Prices

New soles

	1980	1981	1982	1983	1984	1985	1986	1987	1988	1989	1990	1991
1 General public services	359	642	1347	2334	4388	12895	24530	52051	257000	5906	310755	974961
2 Defence												
3 Public order and safety	...	...	...	...	...	...	...	...	...	...	...	...
4 Education	167	325	530	1008	2206	5551	10818	25589	124000	2826	99661	687664
5 Health	52	101	152	346	685	1866	3984	6661	36000	1270	36986	181231
6 Social security and welfare	14	26	52	72	160	427	893	2706	13000	269	10968	43872
7 Housing and community amenities	1	2	5	8	10	47	72	153	1000	23	583	2623
8 Recreational, cultural and religious affairs	24	23	42	76	58	319	564	1712	12000	435	26966	80537
9 Economic services	50	96	133	233	596	1352	2477	4980	32000	1317	28377	115096
10 Other functions	...	...	...	...	...	...	...	...	...	...	...	...
Total Government Final Consumption Expenditure a	667	1215	2260	4077	8104	22457	43336	93853	474630	12046	514296	2085984

a) Beginning 1989, the estimates are in thousand New Soles.

2.5 Private Final Consumption Expenditure by Type and Purpose, in Current Prices

New soles

	1980	1981	1982	1983	1984	1985	1986	1987	1988	1989	1990	1991
Final Consumption Expenditure of Resident Households												
1 Food, beverages and tobacco	1356	2502	4005	8646	18373	47126	97196	172663	1018910	26416	1475877	42139
2 Clothing and footwear	501	830	1212	1565	3413	10403	23816	50336	374130	8225	428091	2029240
3 Gross rent, fuel and power	154	243	404	698	1232	2726	4591	7142	27006	712	52004	650398
4 Furniture, furnishings and household equipment and operation	484	866	1354	2230	4974	14614	31675	62349	436740	8463	506947	2029240
5 Medical care and health expenses	132	251	432	919	1844	4943	9921	21923	146647	3559	351903	1092668
6 Transport and communication	266	495	891	1693	3781	11497	18934	32211	224121	4271	374819	2003225
7 Recreational, entertainment, education and cultural services	263	542	934	1755	3923	11316	22840	50200	342158	10282	663517	3043861
8 Miscellaneous goods and services	565	1063	1896	3688	8181	21534	46575	102861	630424	17079	1162037	5125133
Total Final Consumption Expenditure in the Domestic Market by Households, of which	3721	6791	11130	21194	45721	124159	255549	499684	3200136	79007	5015195	6015904
Plus: Direct purchases abroad by resident households	27	67	126	274	596	2748	4216	6428	81600	1714	79161	...
Less: Direct purchases in the domestic market by non-resident households	90	120	186	369	785	3495	4778	8509	67491	1631	76287	...
Equals: Final Consumption Expenditure of Resident Households	3658	6738	11070	21099	45532	123412	254987	497603	3214245	79090	5018069	6015904
Final Consumption Expenditure of Private Non-profit Institutions Serving Households												
Equals: Final Consumption Expenditure of Private Non-profit Organisations Serving Households	...	...	...	...	...	...	...	...	...	...	...	...
Private Final Consumption Expenditure a	3658	6738	11070	21099	45532	123412	254987	497603	3214245	79089	5018069	6015904

a) Beginning 1989, the estimates are in thousand New Soles.

2.6 Private Final Consumption Expenditure by Type and Purpose, in Constant Prices

New soles

	1980	1981	1982	1983	1984	1985	1986	1987	1988	1989	1990	1991
At constant prices of:1979												
Final Consumption Expenditure of Resident Households												
1 Food, beverages and tobacco	862	914	941	910	931	930	1078	1178	1156	951	938	953
2 Clothing and footwear	279	277	281	224	221	234	260	289	277	242	218	217
3 Gross rent, fuel and power	112	115	117	119	121	126	143	142	141	140	138	146
4 Furniture, furnishings and household equipment and operation	291	307	283	214	220	227	288	312	242	178	180	163

Peru

2.6 Private Final Consumption Expenditure by Type and Purpose, in Constant Prices
(Continued)

New soles

	1980	1981	1982	1983	1984	1985	1986	1987	1988	1989	1990	1991
At constant prices of:1979												
5 Medical care and health expenses	83	87	89	76	73	76	80	87	78	62	53	59
6 Transport and communication	174	185	188	163	166	164	183	203	197	171	154	163
7 Recreational, entertainment, education and cultural services	147	154	160	156	159	162	178	199	188	144	152	157
8 Miscellaneous goods and services	328	336	331	315	328	348	386	439	360	289	273	301
Total Final Consumption Expenditure in the Domestic Market by Households, of which	2276	2376	2389	2177	2219	2266	2597	2849	2639	2177	2106	2159
Plus: Direct purchases abroad by resident households	23	34	37	34	35	37	43	51	51	63	76	...
Less: Direct purchases in the domestic market by non-resident households	63	54	50	44	45	47	47	53	54	54	49	...
Equals: Final Consumption Expenditure of Resident Households	2236	2356	2376	2167	2209	2256	2593	2847	2636	2186	2133	2159
Final Consumption Expenditure of Private Non-profit Institutions Serving Households												
Equals: Final Consumption Expenditure of Private Non-profit Organisations Serving Households	...	...	...	...	...	...	...	...	...	...	...	...
Private Final Consumption Expenditure	2236	2356	2376	2167	2209	2256	2593	2847	2636	2186	2133	2159

2.7 Gross Capital Formation by Type of Good and Owner, in Current Prices

New soles

	1980				1981				1982			
	TOTAL	Total Private	Public Enterprises	General Government	TOTAL	Total Private	Public Enterprises	General Government	TOTAL	Total Private	Public Enterprises	General Government
Increase in stocks, total	239	204	35	-	575	471	105	-	664	479	185	-
Gross Fixed Capital Formation, Total	1402	1059	164	179	2772	2133	291	348	4939	3585	739	615
1 Residential buildings	469	419	6	44	982	864	49	70	1955	1775	37	143
2 Non-residential buildings												
3 Other construction	239	60	124	55	470	240	85	145	907	198	472	237
4 Land improvement and plantation and orchard development	45	2	-	43	91	3	-	88	148	4	-	144
5 Producers' durable goods	649	579	34	36	1228	1027	157	45	1928	1608	230	90
A Transport equipment	173	159	2	12	417	388	18	11	629	581	24	25
B Machinery and equipment	476	419	32	25	811	639	139	33	1299	1028	205	66
6 Breeding stock, dairy cattle, etc.	...	...	...	...	...	...	...	...	...	...	...	...
Total Gross Capital Formation [a]	1640	1263	199	179	3347	2604	395	348	5603	4064	924	615

	1983				1984				1985			
	TOTAL	Total Private	Public Enterprises	General Government	TOTAL	Total Private	Public Enterprises	General Government	TOTAL	Total Private	Public Enterprises	General Government
Increase in stocks, total	172	123	48	-	-221	-1062	842	-	414	-1441	1855	-
Gross Fixed Capital Formation, Total	7445	5125	1375	945	16304	11769	2024	2510	42313	31493	5833	4987
1 Residential buildings	3161	2892	70	199	7081	6422	210	448	19124	17963	186	975
2 Non-residential buildings												
3 Other construction	1291	285	681	325	3000	250	1584	1166	8045	1371	4766	1908
4 Land improvement and plantation and orchard development	322	7	-	315	611	15	-	596	1429	47	-	1382
5 Producers' durable goods	2672	1941	624	106	5611	5082	230	300	13715	12111	881	722
A Transport equipment	770	724	16	30	1643	1546	19	78	3719	3437	118	164
B Machinery and equipment	1902	1217	609	76	3969	3536	211	222	9996	8675	763	558
6 Breeding stock, dairy cattle, etc.	...	...	...	...	...	...	...	...	...	...	...	...
Total Gross Capital Formation [a]	7617	5248	1423	945	16083	10707	2866	2510	42727	30051	7688	4987

2.7 Gross Capital Formation by Type of Good and Owner, in Current Prices

New soles

	1986				1987				1988			
	TOTAL	Total Private	Public Enterprises	General Government	TOTAL	Total Private	Public Enterprises	General Government	TOTAL	Total Private	Public Enterprises	General Government
Increase in stocks, total	3232	2460	772	-	11409	4738	6670	-	73024	-6127	79151	-
Gross Fixed Capital Formation, Total	80535	61872	7372	11291	157278	120438	18917	17922	1219226	1027506	102049	89671
1 Residential buildings	35037	31743	191	3103	70417	64965	255	5196	477206	461187	1851	14170
2 Non-residential buildings												
3 Other construction	16953	7345	5630	3978	32228	10974	15967	5287	324849	236818	67742	20289
4 Land improvement and plantation and orchard development	2479	91	-	2388	4335	582	-	3754	42564	1415	...	41149
5 Producers' durable goods	26066	22694	1552	1821	50298	43917	2695	3686	374605	328086	32456	14063
A Transport equipment	6895	6472	205	218	14145	13550	205	389	114756	107859	5345	1552
B Machinery and equipment	19172	16222	1346	1603	36153	30367	2489	3297	259849	220227	27111	12511
6 Breeding stock, dairy cattle, etc.	...	...	...	...	...	...	...	...	...	...	...	...
Total Gross Capital Formation a	83767	64333	8144	11291	168686	125176	25587	17922	1292250	1021379	181200	89671

	1989				1990				1991			
	TOTAL	Total Private	Public Enterprises	General Government	TOTAL	Total Private	Public Enterprises	General Government	TOTAL	Total Private	Public Enterprises	General Government
Increase in stocks, total	119	-754	873	-	11560	-53118	64678	-	219223	...	...	...
Gross Fixed Capital Formation, Total	23706	17546	2984	3176	1423135	1172143	158755	92237	7620386	...	...	...
1 Residential buildings	9371	...	...	...	...	...	...	...	...	...	...	...
2 Non-residential buildings		...	...	...	...	...	...	...	...	...	...	...
3 Other construction	5848	...	...	...	...	...	...	...	...	...	...	...
4 Land improvement and plantation and orchard development	885	...	...	...	...	...	...	...	...	...	...	...
5 Producers' durable goods	7602	...	...	...	...	...	...	...	...	...	...	...
A Transport equipment	...	...	...	...	...	...	...	...	...	...	...	...
B Machinery and equipment	...	...	...	...	...	...	...	...	...	...	...	...
6 Breeding stock, dairy cattle, etc.	...	...	...	...	...	...	...	...	...	...	...	...
Total Gross Capital Formation a	23825	16792	3857	3176	1434695	1119025	223433	92237	7839609	...	...	...

a) Beginning 1989, the estimates are in thousand New Soles.

2.8 Gross Capital Formation by Type of Good and Owner, in Constant Prices

New soles

	1980				1981				1982			
	TOTAL	Total Private	Public Enterprises	General Government	TOTAL	Total Private	Public Enterprises	General Government	TOTAL	Total Private	Public Enterprises	General Government
	At constant prices of:1979											
Increase in stocks, total	149	...	...	...	218	...	...	...	150	...	...	...
Gross Fixed Capital Formation, Total	882	658	110	114	1024	778	116	130	1001	716	165	122
1 Residential buildings	272	243	4	25	300	263	15	21	311	283	6	23
2 Non-residential buildings												
3 Other construction	163	41	84	38	193	98	35	60	195	43	101	51
4 Land improvement and plantation and orchard development	28	1	-	27	32	1	-	31	27	1	-	26
5 Producers' durable goods	419	373	22	23	499	415	66	18	468	389	58	21
A Transport equipment	110	101	1	8	162	151	7	4	142	132	5	5
B Machinery and equipment	309	272	21	16	337	264	59	14	326	257	53	16
6 Breeding stock, dairy cattle, etc.	...	...	...	...	...	...	...	...	...	...	...	...
Total Gross Capital Formation	1031	...	...	...	1242	...	...	...	1151	...	...	...

Peru

2.8 Gross Capital Formation by Type of Good and Owner, in Constant Prices

New soles

	1983				1984				1985			
	TOTAL	Total Private	Public Enterprises	General Government	TOTAL	Total Private	Public Enterprises	General Government	TOTAL	Total Private	Public Enterprises	General Government
	At constant prices of:1979											
Increase in stocks, total	4	...	...	...	-23	...	...	...	-19	...	...	...
Gross Fixed Capital Formation, Total	700	463	146	91	657	450	95	111	582	416	93	73
1 Residential buildings	252	230	6	16	249	226	7	16	225	212	2	11
2 Non-residential buildings												
3 Other construction	143	32	75	36	149	12	78	58	132	22	78	31
4 Land improvement and plantation and orchard development	29	1	-	28	27	1	-	26	21	1	-	20
5 Producers' durable goods	277	200	65	11	233	211	9	12	205	182	13	10
A Transport equipment	79	74	2	3	69	65	1	3	59	55	2	2
B Machinery and equipment	198	126	64	8	164	146	9	5	146	126	11	8
6 Breeding stock, dairy cattle, etc.	...	...	...	...	...	...	...	...	...	...	...	...
Total Gross Capital Formation	704	...	...	...	634	...	...	...	564	...	...	...

	1986				1987				1988			
	TOTAL	Total Private	Public Enterprises	General Government	TOTAL	Total Private	Public Enterprises	General Government	TOTAL	Total Private	Public Enterprises	General Government
	At constant prices of:1979											
Increase in stocks, total	59	...	...	...	141	...	...	...	165	...	...	...
Gross Fixed Capital Formation, Total	689	515	73	102	818	608	106	104	704	580	61	63
1 Residential buildings	264	239	2	23	325	300	1	25	305	293	1	11
2 Non-residential buildings												
3 Other construction	176	76	59	41	200	70	90	40	191	119	49	24
4 Land improvement and plantation and orchard development	23	1	-	22	26	1	-	25	24	1	-	23
5 Producers' durable goods	226	199	13	15	267	236	15	15	184	167	12	5
A Transport equipment	60	57	2	2	73	70	1	2	49	46	2	1
B Machinery and equipment	166	142	11	13	194	166	14	13	135	121	10	4
6 Breeding stock, dairy cattle, etc.	...	...	...	...	...	...	...	...	...	...	...	...
Total Gross Capital Formation	749	...	...	...	959	...	...	...	870	...	...	...

	1989				1990				1991			
	TOTAL	Total Private	Public Enterprises	General Government	TOTAL	Total Private	Public Enterprises	General Government	TOTAL	Total Private	Public Enterprises	General Government
	At constant prices of:1979											
Increase in stocks, total	21	...	...	...	28	...	...	...	103	...	...	...
Gross Fixed Capital Formation, Total	565	428	55	82	576	467	69	40	621	...	...	...
1 Residential buildings	256	243	1	12	...	...	...	...	...	...	...	...
2 Non-residential buildings					...	...	...	...	...	...	...	...
3 Other construction	159	77	47	35	...	...	...	...	...	...	...	...
4 Land improvement and plantation and orchard development	24	1	-	23	...	...	...	...	...	...	...	...
5 Producers' durable goods	126	107	7	12	...	...	...	...	...	...	...	...
A Transport equipment	32	29	1	2	30	...	...	...	...	...	...	...
B Machinery and equipment	99	84	9	6	111	...	...	...	...	...	...	...
6 Breeding stock, dairy cattle, etc.	...	...	...	...	...	...	...	...	...	...	...	...
Total Gross Capital Formation	586	...	...	...	604	...	...	...	724	...	...	...

3.11 General Government Production Account: Total and Subsectors

New soles

	1980					1981				
	Total General Government	Central Government	State or Provincial Government	Local Government	Social Security Funds	Total General Government	Central Government	State or Provincial Government	Local Government	Social Security Funds
	Gross Output									
1 Sales	5	4	...	2	...	11	7	...	4	...
2 Services produced for own use	667	517	...	139	11	1215	946	...	247	22
3 Own account fixed capital formation	137	55	...	29	53	263	116	...	46	101
Gross Output	809	575	...	170	64	1489	1069	...	297	124

3.11 General Government Production Account: Total and Subsectors
(Continued)

New soles

1980 / 1981

	Total General Government	Central Government	State or Provincial Government	Local Government	Social Security Funds	Total General Government	Central Government	State or Provincial Government	Local Government	Social Security Funds
Gross Input										
Intermediate Consumption	288	234	...	30	23	452	362	...	47	43
Subtotal: Value Added	521	341	...	139	41	1037	707	...	250	80
1 Indirect taxes, net	12	8	...	3	1	41	32	...	7	2
A Indirect taxes	12	8	...	3	1	41	32	...	7	2
B Less: Subsidies	...	...	...	...	...	...	...	...	...	...
2 Consumption of fixed capital	...	...	...	...	...	...	...	...	...	...
3 Compensation of employees	504	330	...	134	39	988	670	...	239	78
4 Net Operating surplus	5	3	...	2	-	8	4	...	3	1
Gross Input	809	575	...	170	64	1489	1069	...	297	124

1982 / 1983

	Total General Government	Central Government	State or Provincial Government	Local Government	Social Security Funds	Total General Government	Central Government	State or Provincial Government	Local Government	Social Security Funds
Gross Output										
1 Sales	19	16	...	3	...	31	25	...	6	...
2 Services produced for own use	2260	2116	...	98	46	4077	3821	...	195	61
3 Own account fixed capital formation	445	201	...	90	154	944	416	...	264	264
Gross Output	2724	2333	...	191	200	5052	4262	...	465	325
Gross Input										
Intermediate Consumption	956	820	...	67	69	1610	1317	...	191	102
Subtotal: Value Added	1769	1513	...	125	131	3442	2945	...	273	223
1 Indirect taxes, net	53	48	...	2	3	26	19	...	3	4
A Indirect taxes	53	48	...	2	3	26	19	...	3	4
B Less: Subsidies	...	...	...	...	...	...	...	...	...	...
2 Consumption of fixed capital	...	...	...	...	...	...	...	...	...	...
3 Compensation of employees	1696	1454	...	114	128	3379	2907	...	254	218
4 Net Operating surplus	20	10	...	9	1	37	19	...	16	1
Gross Input	2724	2333	...	191	200	5052	4262	...	465	325

1984 / 1985

	Total General Government	Central Government	State or Provincial Government	Local Government	Social Security Funds	Total General Government	Central Government	State or Provincial Government	Local Government	Social Security Funds
Gross Output										
1 Sales	65	53	...	11	...	165	131	...	33	-
2 Services produced for own use	8104	7543	...	437	124	22457	21062	...	1089	307
3 Own account fixed capital formation	2126	946	...	709	471	4858	2309	...	1399	1150
Gross Output	10294	8542	...	1157	595	27481	23502	...	2521	1457
Gross Input										
Intermediate Consumption	2886	2222	...	498	166	9357	7815	...	1043	499
Subtotal: Value Added	7408	6320	...	659	429	18124	15687	...	1478	958
1 Indirect taxes, net	58	46	...	7	5	72	50	...	15	7
A Indirect taxes	58	46	...	7	5	72	50	...	15	7
B Less: Subsidies	...	...	...	...	...	...	...	...	...	...
2 Consumption of fixed capital	...	...	...	...	...	...	...	...	...	...
3 Compensation of employees	7203	6182	...	610	411	17470	15225	...	1332	912
4 Net Operating surplus	147	92	...	43	12	582	412	...	131	39
Gross Input	10294	8542	...	1157	595	27481	23502	...	2521	1457

1986 / 1987

	Total General Government	Central Government	State or Provincial Government	Local Government	Social Security Funds	Total General Government	Central Government	State or Provincial Government	Local Government	Social Security Funds
Gross Output										
1 Sales	432	299	...	133	-	699	615	...	84	...
2 Services produced for own use	43336	40167	...	2522	647	93853	85106	...	6707	2040
3 Own account fixed capital formation	10826	4193	...	3719	2914	18267	6875	...	3597	7795
Gross Output	54596	44660	...	6375	3561	112820	92596	...	10389	9835
Gross Input										
Intermediate Consumption	16095	12248	...	2622	1225	26833	20512	...	3754	2567

Peru

3.11 General Government Production Account: Total and Subsectors
(Continued)

New soles

	1986					1987				
	Total General Government	Central Government	State or Provincial Government	Local Government	Social Security Funds	Total General Government	Central Government	State or Provincial Government	Local Government	Social Security Funds
Subtotal: Value Added	38500	32412	...	3752	2336	85987	72084	...	6635	7268
1 Indirect taxes, net	646	545	...	48	53	1876	1577	...	91	208
A Indirect taxes	646	545	...	48	53	1876	1577	...	91	208
B Less: Subsidies	...	...	...	...	...	...	...	...	...	...
2 Consumption of fixed capital	...	...	...	...	...	...	...	...	...	...
3 Compensation of employees	37064	31429	...	3454	2181	82753	69747	...	6010	6996
4 Net Operating surplus	789	437	...	250	102	1357	760	...	534	63
Gross Input	54596	44660	...	6375	3561	112820	92596	...	10389	9835

	1988				
	Total General Government	Central Government	State or Provincial Government	Local Government	Social Security Funds
Gross Output					
1 Sales	2716	2319	...	397	...
2 Services produced for own use	481926	416911	...	55951	9064
3 Own account fixed capital formation	91107	37267	...	16526	37314
Gross Output	575749	456497	...	72874	46378
Gross Input					
Intermediate Consumption	147882	112681	...	23493	11708
Subtotal: Value Added	427868	343817	...	49381	34670
1 Indirect taxes, net	8444	6609	...	828	1007
A Indirect taxes	8444	6609	...	828	1007
B Less: Subsidies	...	...	...	...	...
2 Consumption of fixed capital	...	...	...	...	...
3 Compensation of employees	407202	331350	...	43656	32196
4 Net Operating surplus	12220	5858	...	4896	1466
Gross Input	575749	456497	...	72874	46378

3.12 General Government Income and Outlay Account: Total and Subsectors

New soles

	1980					1981				
	Total General Government	Central Government	State or Provincial Government	Local Government	Social Security Funds	Total General Government	Central Government	State or Provincial Government	Local Government	Social Security Funds
Receipts										
1 Operating surplus	5	2	...	2	-	8	4	...	3	1
2 Property and entrepreneurial income	213	202	...	1	11	399	368	...	3	28
A Withdrawals from public quasi-corporations	...	...	...	...	...	...	...	...	...	...
B Interest	14	3	...	1	11	39	8	...	3	28
C Dividends	19	19	...	-	-	5	5	...	-	-
D Net land rent and royalties	180	180	...	-	-	355	355	...	-	-
3 Taxes, fees and contributions	1333	1197	...	20	116	2097	1814	...	51	231
A Indirect taxes	726	721	...	5	...	1195	1181	...	14	...
B Direct taxes	424	421	...	4	-	512	501	...	10	-
C Social security contributions	168	46	...	6	116	332	90	...	12	230
D Fees, fines and penalties	15	9	...	5	-	58	42	...	15	1
4 Other current transfers	136	15	...	120	-	207	20	...	188	-
A Casualty insurance claims	-	-	...	-	-	1	1	...	-	-
B Transfers from other government subsectors	...	...	...	...	...	...	...	...	...	...
C Transfers from the rest of the world	...	...	...	...	...	...	...	...	...	...
D Other transfers, except imputed	136	15	...	120	-	206	19	...	188	-
E Imputed unfunded employee pension and welfare contributions	...	...	...	...	...	...	...	...	...	...
Total Current Receipts [a]	1687	1417	...	143	127	2712	2207	...	246	260
Disbursements										
1 Government final consumption expenditure	667	517	...	139	11	1215	946	...	247	22

3.12 General Government Income and Outlay Account: Total and Subsectors
(Continued)

New soles

	1980					1981				
	Total General Government	Central Government	State or Provincial Government	Local Government	Social Security Funds	Total General Government	Central Government	State or Provincial Government	Local Government	Social Security Funds
2 Property income	228	228	...	-	-	357	357	...	-	-
A Interest	228	228	...	-	-	357	357	...	-	-
B Net land rent and royalties	...	...	...	...	...	...	...	...	...	...
3 Subsidies	153	153	...	-	-	170	170	...	-	-
4 Other current transfers	527	423	...	6	98	897	697	...	17	183
A Casualty insurance premiums, net	3	3	...	-	-	5	5	...	-	-
B Transfers to other government subsectors	...	...	...	...	...	...	...	...	...	...
C Social security benefits	150	46	...	6	98	281	90	...	12	179
D Social assistance grants	...	...	...	...	...	...	...	...	...	...
E Unfunded employee pension and welfare benefits	...	...	...	...	...	...	...	...	...	...
F Transfers to private non-profit institutions serving households	...	...	...	...	...	...	...	...	...	...
G Other transfers n.e.c.	374	374	...	-	-	611	602	...	5	4
H Transfers to the rest of the world	...	...	...	...	...	...	...	...	...	...
Net saving b	111	96	...	-3	18	73	38	...	-19	54
Total Current Disbursements and Net Saving a	1687	1417	...	143	127	2712	2207	...	246	260

	1982					1983				
	Total General Government	Central Government	State or Provincial Government	Local Government	Social Security Funds	Total General Government	Central Government	State or Provincial Government	Local Government	Social Security Funds
Receipts										
1 Operating surplus	20	10	...	9	1	37	19	...	16	1
2 Property and entrepreneurial income	571	510	...	6	55	939	852	...	13	74
A Withdrawals from public quasi-corporations	...	...	...	...	...	...	...	...	...	...
B Interest	68	7	...	6	55	91	4	...	13	74
C Dividends	15	15	...	-	-	6	6	...	-	-
D Net land rent and royalties	488	488	...	-	-	842	842	...	-	-
3 Taxes, fees and contributions	3338	2942	...	54	343	5440	4517	...	211	712
A Indirect taxes	1974	1953	...	20	...	3152	2999	...	154	...
B Direct taxes	782	770	...	13	-	1060	1038	...	22	-
C Social security contributions	513	182	...	3	328	1033	387	...	8	638
D Fees, fines and penalties	69	37	...	18	15	195	93	...	27	74
4 Other current transfers	82	36	...	46	-	373	291	...	82	-
A Casualty insurance claims	1	1	...	-	-	7	7	...	-	-
B Transfers from other government subsectors	...	...	...	...	...	...	...	...	...	...
C Transfers from the rest of the world	...	...	...	...	...	...	...	...	...	...
D Other transfers, except imputed	81	35	...	46	-	366	284	...	82	-
E Imputed unfunded employee pension and welfare contributions	...	...	...	...	...	...	...	...	...	...
Total Current Receipts a	4011	3498	...	115	398	6789	5680	...	322	787
Disbursements										
1 Government final consumption expenditure	2260	2116	...	98	46	4077	3821	...	195	61
2 Property income	519	518	...	-	1	1411	1403	...	-	8
A Interest	519	518	...	-	1	1411	1403	...	-	8
B Net land rent and royalties	...	...	...	...	...	...	...	...	...	...
3 Subsidies	264	264	...	-	-	405	405	...	-	-

3.12 General Government Income and Outlay Account: Total and Subsectors
(Continued)

New soles

	1982					1983				
	Total General Government	Central Government	State or Provincial Government	Local Government	Social Security Funds	Total General Government	Central Government	State or Provincial Government	Local Government	Social Security Funds
4 Other current transfers	1098	783	...	9	306	2195	1634	...	21	540
A Casualty insurance premiums, net	9	9	...	-	-	18	18	...	-	-
B Transfers to other government subsectors	...	...	...	...	...	...	...	...	...	...
C Social security benefits	481	182	...	3	296	918	387	...	8	523
D Social assistance grants	...	...	...	...	...	...	...	...	...	...
E Unfunded employee pension and welfare benefits	...	...	...	...	...	...	...	...	...	...
F Transfers to private non-profit institutions serving households	...	...	...	...	...	...	...	...	...	...
G Other transfers n.e.c.	609	592	...	6	10	1259	1229	...	13	17
H Transfers to the rest of the world	...	...	...	...	...	...	...	...	...	...
Net saving b	-130	-182	...	7	45	-1299	-1583	...	106	178
Total Current Disbursements and Net Saving a	4011	3498	...	115	398	6789	5680	...	322	787

	1984					1985				
	Total General Government	Central Government	State or Provincial Government	Local Government	Social Security Funds	Total General Government	Central Government	State or Provincial Government	Local Government	Social Security Funds
Receipts										
1 Operating surplus	147	92	...	43	12	582	412	...	131	39
2 Property and entrepreneurial income	1938	1740	...	35	163	5652	5170	...	141	341
A Withdrawals from public quasi-corporations	...	...	...	...	...	...	...	...	...	...
B Interest	206	8	...	35	163	492	19	...	135	338
C Dividends	128	128	...	-	-	362	356	...	6	-
D Net land rent and royalties	1604	1604	...	-	-	4798	4795	...	-	3
3 Taxes, fees and contributions	11528	9752	...	459	1317	33356	27836	...	1695	3825
A Indirect taxes	6815	6516	...	299	...	21608	20632	...	976	...
B Direct taxes	2115	2034	...	81	-	4795	4321	...	474	-
C Social security contributions	2053	881	...	19	1154	5582	2065	...	38	3479
D Fees, fines and penalties	545	321	...	60	163	1371	818	...	207	346
4 Other current transfers	707	560	...	147	1	1663	1508	...	155	-
A Casualty insurance claims	1	1	...	-	-	12	12	...	-	-
B Transfers from other government subsectors	...	...	...	...	...	...	...	...	...	...
C Transfers from the rest of the world	...	...	...	...	...	...	...	...	...	...
D Other transfers, except imputed	706	559	...	147	1	1651	1496	...	155	-
E Imputed unfunded employee pension and welfare contributions	...	...	...	...	...	...	...	...	...	...
Total Current Receipts a	14321	12143	...	684	1493	41253	34926	...	2122	4204
Disbursements										
1 Government final consumption expenditure	8104	7543	...	437	124	22457	21062	...	1089	307
2 Property income	3075	3054	...	3	18	8175	8142	...	3	30
A Interest	3075	3054	...	3	18	8175	8142	...	3	30
B Net land rent and royalties	...	...	...	...	...	...	...	...	...	...
3 Subsidies	618	618	...	-	-	1770	1770	...	-	-

3.12 General Government Income and Outlay Account: Total and Subsectors
(Continued)

New soles

	1984					1985				
	Total General Government	Central Government	State or Provincial Government	Local Government	Social Security Funds	Total General Government	Central Government	State or Provincial Government	Local Government	Social Security Funds
4 Other current transfers	4342	3241	...	51	1050	10389	7904	...	85	2399
A Casualty insurance premiums, net	51	50	...	-	-	116	115	...	-	-
B Transfers to other government subsectors	...	...	...	...	...	...	...	...	...	...
C Social security benefits	1926	881	...	19	1027	4462	2065	...	38	2359
D Social assistance grants	...	...	...	...	...	...	...	...	...	...
E Unfunded employee pension and welfare benefits	...	...	...	...	...	...	...	...	...	...
F Transfers to private non-profit institutions serving households	...	...	...	...	...	...	...	...	...	...
G Other transfers n.e.c.	2365	2310	...	32	23	5811	5724	...	47	40
H Transfers to the rest of the world	...	...	...	...	...	...	...	...	...	...
Net saving b	-1818	-2313	...	193	303	-1538	-3950	...	944	1468
Total Current Disbursements and Net Saving a	14321	12143	...	684	1493	41253	34926	...	2122	4204

	1986					1987				
	Total General Government	Central Government	State or Provincial Government	Local Government	Social Security Funds	Total General Government	Central Government	State or Provincial Government	Local Government	Social Security Funds
Receipts										
1 Operating surplus	789	437	...	250	102	1357	760	...	534	63
2 Property and entrepreneurial income	2203	1732	...	136	335	2041	1323	...	107	611
A Withdrawals from public quasi-corporations	...	...	...	...	...	...	...	...	...	...
B Interest	478	26	...	117	335	783	78	...	94	611
C Dividends	352	341	...	11	-	972	972	...	-	-
D Net land rent and royalties	1373	1365	...	8	-	284	272	...	12	-
3 Taxes, fees and contributions	61455	50070	...	3235	8151	106179	83210	...	5668	17301
A Indirect taxes	33651	32034	...	1617	...	56657	53412	...	3245	...
B Direct taxes	13343	12362	...	981	-	17762	16600	...	1162	-
C Social security contributions	12370	4712	...	95	7564	27924	11761	...	253	15910
D Fees, fines and penalties	2091	962	...	542	587	3836	1437	...	1008	1391
4 Other current transfers	4009	3489	...	520	-	9219	7767	...	1448	4
A Casualty insurance claims	224	223	...	1	-	282	279	...	2	1
B Transfers from other government subsectors	...	...	...	...	...	...	...	...	...	...
C Transfers from the rest of the world	...	...	...	...	...	...	...	...	...	...
D Other transfers, except imputed	3785	3266	...	519	...	8937	7488	...	1446	3
E Imputed unfunded employee pension and welfare contributions	...	...	...	...	...	...	...	...	...	...
Total Current Receipts a	68457	55728	...	4142	8588	118795	93060	...	7757	17978
Disbursements										
1 Government final consumption expenditure	43336	40167	...	2522	647	93853	85106	...	6707	2040
2 Property income	8831	8804	...	6	20	13225	13195	...	29	1
A Interest	8831	8804	...	6	20	13225	13195	...	29	1
B Net land rent and royalties	...	...	...	...	...	...	...	...	...	...
3 Subsidies	3159	3159	...	-	-	6574	6574	...	-	-

Peru

3.12 General Government Income and Outlay Account: Total and Subsectors
(Continued)

New soles

	1986 Total General Government	1986 Central Government	1986 State or Provincial Government	1986 Local Government	1986 Social Security Funds	1987 Total General Government	1987 Central Government	1987 State or Provincial Government	1987 Local Government	1987 Social Security Funds
4 Other current transfers	14907	9002	...	185	5720	35337	21112	...	493	13732
A Casualty insurance premiums, net	128	128	...	-	-	253	252	...	1	-
B Transfers to other government subsectors	...	...	...	...	...	...	...	...	...	...
C Social security benefits	10482	4712	...	95	5675	25637	11761	...	253	13623
D Social assistance grants	...	...	...	...	...	...	...	...	...	...
E Unfunded employee pension and welfare benefits	...	...	...	...	...	...	...	...	...	...
F Transfers to private non-profit institutions serving households	...	...	...	...	...	...	...	...	...	...
G Other transfers n.e.c.	4297	4162	...	90	45	9447	9099	...	239	109
H Transfers to the rest of the world	...	...	...	...	...	...	...	...	...	...
Net saving b	-1776	-5404	...	1428	2201	-30193	-32927	...	528	2206
Total Current Disbursements and Net Saving a	68458	55728	...	4141	8588	118795	93060	...	7757	17978

	1988 Total General Government	1988 Central Government	1988 State or Provincial Government	1988 Local Government	1988 Social Security Funds	1989 Total General Government	1989 Central Government	1989 State or Provincial Government	1989 Local Government	1989 Social Security Funds
Receipts										
1 Operating surplus	26090	16147	...	8283	1660	860	694	...	140	26
2 Property and entrepreneurial income	9672	7168	...	1107	1397	115	58	...	20	37
A Withdrawals from public quasi-corporations	...	...	...	...	...	...	...	...	...	...
B Interest	4125	1643	...	1085	1397	93	37	...	19	37
C Dividends	4177	4177	...	-	-	20	20	...	-	-
D Net land rent and royalties	1370	1348	...	22	-	2	1	...	1	-
3 Taxes, fees and contributions	569160	469373	...	29561	70226	11639	9686	...	520	1433
A Indirect taxes	313412	295790	...	17622	...	6495	6179	...	316	-
B Direct taxes	120622	114088	...	6534	-	1993	1875	...	118	-
C Social security contributions	116601	50103	...	1280	65218	2688	1316	...	26	1346
D Fees, fines and penalties	18525	9392	...	4125	5008	463	316	...	60	87
4 Other current transfers	48992	39206	...	9775	11	1881	1495	...	385	1
A Casualty insurance claims	5392	5346	...	35	11	207	205	...	1	1
B Transfers from other government subsectors	...	...	...	...	...	...	...	...	...	...
C Transfers from the rest of the world	...	...	...	...	...	...	...	...	...	...
D Other transfers, except imputed	43600	33860	...	9740	-	1674	1290	...	384	-
E Imputed unfunded employee pension and welfare contributions	...	...	...	...	...	...	...	...	...	...
Total Current Receipts a	653914	531894	...	48726	73294	14495	11933	...	1065	1497
Disbursements										
1 Government final consumption expenditure	474630	425840	...	39565	9225	12046	10845	...	1008	193
2 Property income	101054	98538	...	272	2244	1421	1354	...	40	27
A Interest	101054	98538	...	272	2244	1421	1354	...	40	27
B Net land rent and royalties	...	...	...	...	...	...	...	...	...	...
3 Subsidies	72788	72788	...	-	-	1097	1097	...	-	-

3.12 General Government Income and Outlay Account: Total and Subsectors
(Continued)

New soles

	1988					1989				
	Total General Government	Central Government	State or Provincial Government	Local Government	Social Security Funds	Total General Government	Central Government	State or Provincial Government	Local Government	Social Security Funds
4 Other current transfers	169763	100772	...	2193	66798	3671	2300	...	64	1307
A Casualty insurance premiums, net	3611	3599	...	8	4	31	31	...	-	-
B Transfers to other government subsectors	...	...	...	...	...	...	...	...	...	...
C Social security benefits	117907	50104	...	1280	66523	2636	1316	...	26	1294
D Social assistance grants	...	...	...	...	...	...	...	...	...	...
E Unfunded employee pension and welfare benefits	...	...	...	...	...	...	...	...	...	...
F Transfers to private non-profit institutions serving households	...	...	...	...	...	...	...	...	...	...
G Other transfers n.e.c.	48245	47069	...	905	271	1004	953	...	38	13
H Transfers to the rest of the world	...	...	...	...	...	...	...	...	...	...
Net saving b	-164321	-166044	...	6696	-4973	-3740	-3663	...	-47	-30
Total Current Disbursements and Net Saving a	653914	531894	...	48726	73294	14495	11933	...	1065	1497

	1990				
	Total General Government	Central Government	State or Provincial Government	Local Government	Social Security Funds
				Receipts	
1 Operating surplus	23892	17595	...	5731	566
2 Property and entrepreneurial income	15323	12061	...	1218	2044
A Withdrawals from public quasi-corporations	...	...	...	...	...
B Interest	15171	11909	...	1218	2044
C Dividends	140	140	...	...	...
D Net land rent and royalties	12	12	...	...	...
3 Taxes, fees and contributions	789046	696341	...	27078	65627
A Indirect taxes	517980	500667	...	17313	...
B Direct taxes	115999	109826	...	6173	...
C Social security contributions	133617	66267	...	3293	64057
D Fees, fines and penalties	21450	19581	...	299	1570
4 Other current transfers	64493	32755	...	31714	24
A Casualty insurance claims	11423	11326	...	73	24
B Transfers from other government subsectors	...	...	...	...	...
C Transfers from the rest of the world	...	...	...	...	...
D Other transfers, except imputed	53070	21429	...	31641	-
E Imputed unfunded employee pension and welfare contributions	...	...	...	...	...
Total Current Receipts a	892754	758752	...	65741	68261
				Disbursements	
1 Government final consumption expenditure	514296	456597	...	50093	7606
2 Property income	163461	160139	...	387	2935
A Interest	163461	160139	...	387	2935
B Net land rent and royalties	...	...	...	...	...
3 Subsidies	35976	35976	...	-	-

Peru

3.12 General Government Income and Outlay Account: Total and Subsectors
(Continued)

New soles

	1990				
	Total General Government	Central Government	State or Provincial Government	Local Government	Social Security Funds
4 Other current transfers	193738	128091	...	5551	60096
A Casualty insurance premiums, net	2175	2165	...	8	2
B Transfers to other government subsectors	...	...	...	...	...
C Social security benefits	129158	66272	...	3293	59593
D Social assistance grants	...	...	...	...	...
E Unfunded employee pension and welfare benefits	...	...	...	...	...
F Transfers to private non-profit institutions serving households	...	...	...	...	...
G Other transfers n.e.c.	62405	59654	...	2250	501
H Transfers to the rest of the world	...	...	...	...	...
Net saving b	-14717	-22051	...	9710	-2376
Total Current Disbursements and Net Saving a	892754	758752	...	65741	68261

a) Beginning 1989, the estimates are in thousand New Soles.
b) Item 'Net saving' includes consumption of fixed capital.

3.13 General Government Capital Accumulation Account: Total and Subsectors

New soles

	1980					1981				
	Total General Government	Central Government	State or Provincial Government	Local Government	Social Security Funds	Total General Government	Central Government	State or Provincial Government	Local Government	Social Security Funds
Finance of Gross Accumulation										
1 Gross saving	111	96	...	-3	18	73	38	...	-19	54
2 Capital transfers	61	6	...	55	-	102	13	...	88	-
Finance of Gross Accumulation a	172	102	...	52	18	175	51	...	70	54
Gross Accumulation										
1 Gross capital formation	179	101	...	67	12	348	213	...	110	25
A Increase in stocks	...	...	...	...	...	...	...	...	...	...
B Gross fixed capital formation	179	101	...	67	12	348	213	...	110	25
2 Purchases of land, net	6	7	...	-	-	-1	-	...	-1	-
3 Purchases of intangible assets, net	...	...	...	...	...	...	...	...	...	...
4 Capital transfers	89	89	...	-	-	164	162	...	2	-
Net lending b	-103	-94	...	-15	6	-337	-325	...	-41	29
Gross Accumulation a	172	102	...	52	18	175	51	...	70	54

	1982					1983				
	Total General Government	Central Government	State or Provincial Government	Local Government	Social Security Funds	Total General Government	Central Government	State or Provincial Government	Local Government	Social Security Funds
Finance of Gross Accumulation										
1 Gross saving	-130	-182	...	7	45	-1299	-1583	...	106	178
2 Capital transfers	127	26	...	101	-	296	68	...	227	-
Finance of Gross Accumulation a	-3	-156	...	108	45	-1003	-1515	...	334	178
Gross Accumulation										
1 Gross capital formation	616	455	...	127	34	945	540	...	381	24
A Increase in stocks	...	...	...	...	...	...	...	...	...	...
B Gross fixed capital formation	616	455	...	127	34	945	540	...	381	24
2 Purchases of land, net	-1	1	...	-2	-	-	1	...	-1	-
3 Purchases of intangible assets, net	...	...	...	...	...	...	...	...	...	...
4 Capital transfers	191	189	...	2	-	358	354	...	4	-
Net lending b	-808	-800	...	-19	11	-2306	-2410	...	-50	154
Gross Accumulation a	-3	-156	...	108	45	-1003	-1515	...	334	178

3.13 General Government Capital Accumulation Account: Total and Subsectors

New soles

	1984					1985				
	Total General Government	Central Government	State or Provincial Government	Local Government	Social Security Funds	Total General Government	Central Government	State or Provincial Government	Local Government	Social Security Funds
Finance of Gross Accumulation										
1 Gross saving	-1818	-2313	...	193	303	-1538	-3950	...	945	1468
2 Capital transfers	697	206	...	491	-	1477	444	...	1033	-
Finance of Gross Accumulation a	-1120	-2107	...	684	303	-61	-3507	...	1978	1468
Gross Accumulation										
1 Gross capital formation	2510	1582	...	896	32	4987	3247	...	1691	49
A Increase in stocks	...	...	...	...	...	...	...	...	...	...
B Gross fixed capital formation	2510	1582	...	896	32	4987	3247	...	1691	49
2 Purchases of land, net	-4	7	...	-11	-	-19	-6	...	-13	-
3 Purchases of intangible assets, net	...	...	...	...	...	...	...	...	...	...
4 Capital transfers	713	710	...	3	-	1464	1409	...	55	-
Net lending b	-4339	-4406	...	-204	270	-6492	-8157	...	245	1420
Gross Accumulation a	-1120	-2107	...	684	303	-61	-3507	...	1978	1468

	1986					1987				
	Total General Government	Central Government	State or Provincial Government	Local Government	Social Security Funds	Total General Government	Central Government	State or Provincial Government	Local Government	Social Security Funds
Finance of Gross Accumulation										
1 Gross saving	-1776	-5404	...	1428	2201	-30193	-32927	...	528	2206
2 Capital transfers	4983	1616	...	3366	1	11750	6089	...	5661	-
Finance of Gross Accumulation a	3207	-3789	...	4794	2202	-18443	-26838	...	6189	2206
Gross Accumulation										
1 Gross capital formation	11291	6261	...	4580	450	17923	10756	...	5829	1338
A Increase in stocks	...	...	...	...	...	...	...	...	...	...
B Gross fixed capital formation	11291	6261	...	4580	450	17923	10756	...	5829	1338
2 Purchases of land, net	-10	3	...	-14	-	-101	-13	...	-88	-
3 Purchases of intangible assets, net	...	...	...	...	...	...	...	...	...	...
4 Capital transfers	5959	5835	...	124	-	16354	15866	...	488	-
Net lending b	-14033	-15888	...	104	1751	-52618	-53447	...	-39	868
Gross Accumulation a	3207	-3789	...	4794	2202	-18443	-26838	...	6189	2206

	1988					1989				
	Total General Government	Central Government	State or Provincial Government	Local Government	Social Security Funds	Total General Government	Central Government	State or Provincial Government	Local Government	Social Security Funds
Finance of Gross Accumulation										
1 Gross saving	-164321	-166044	...	6696	-4973	-3740	-3663	...	-47	-30
2 Capital transfers	51093	34441	...	16652	-	1720	1187	...	533	-
Finance of Gross Accumulation a	-113228	-131603	...	23348	-4973	-2020	-2476	...	486	-30
Gross Accumulation										
1 Gross capital formation	89671	65831	...	21528	2312	3176	2426	...	730	20
A Increase in stocks	-	-	...	-	-	-	-	...	-	-
B Gross fixed capital formation	89671	65831	...	21528	2312	3176	2426	...	730	20
2 Purchases of land, net	-638	-83	...	-555	-	1	1	...	-	-
3 Purchases of intangible assets, net	...	...	...	...	...	...	...	...	...	...
4 Capital transfers	69448	69117	...	331	-	1637	1627	...	10	-
Net lending b	-271709	-266468	...	2044	-7285	-6834	-6530	...	-254	-50
Gross Accumulation a	-113228	-131603	...	23348	-4973	-2020	-2476	...	486	-30

	1990				
	Total General Government	Central Government	State or Provincial Government	Local Government	Social Security Funds
Finance of Gross Accumulation					
1 Gross saving	-14717	-22051	...	9710	-2376
2 Capital transfers	33454	21013	...	12441	-
Finance of Gross Accumulation a	18737	-1038	...	22151	-2376
Gross Accumulation					
1 Gross capital formation	92237	74375	...	17484	378

Peru

3.13 General Government Capital Accumulation Account: Total and Subsectors
(Continued)

New soles

	1990				
	Total General Government	Central Government	State or Provincial Government	Local Government	Social Security Funds
A Increase in stocks	...	...	...	...	...
B Gross fixed capital formation	92237	74375	...	17484	378
2 Purchases of land, net	2	2	...	...	...
3 Purchases of intangible assets, net	...	...	...	...	...
4 Capital transfers	52566	51770	...	796	-
Net lending b	-126068	-127185	...	3871	-2754
Gross Accumulation a	18737	-1038	...	22151	-2376

a) Beginning 1989, the estimates are in thousand New Soles.
b) Net lending of the capital accumulation account and the capital finance account have not been reconciled and are different due to different statistical sources.

3.14 General Government Capital Finance Account, Total and Subsectors

New soles

	1980					1981				
	Total General Government	Central Government	State or Provincial Government	Local Government	Social Security Funds	Total General Government	Central Government	State or Provincial Government	Local Government	Social Security Funds
Acquisition of Financial Assets										
1 Gold and SDRs	...	...	...	...	...	...	...	...	...	...
2 Currency and transferable deposits	-25	-33	...	-4	12	74	46	...	20	7
3 Other deposits	16	13	...	2	2	162	147	...	4	11
4 Bills and bonds, short term	-	-	...	-	-	2	-	...	1	1
5 Bonds, long term	1	-	...	-	1	7	-	...	-	7
6 Corporate equity securities	...	...	...	...	...	...	...	...	...	...
7 Short-term loans, n.e.c.	1	-	...	-	-	3	-	...	2	1
8 Long-term loans, n.e.c.	1	-	...	-	1	19	1	...	-	17
9 Other receivables	117	92	...	8	18	-83	-99	...	1	14
10 Other assets	223	222	...	1	-	187	186	...	1	-
Total Acquisition of Financial Assets	334	294	...	7	33	370	282	...	30	58
Incurrence of Liabilities										
1 Currency and transferable deposits	...	...	...	...	...	...	...	...	...	...
2 Other deposits	2	-1	...	2	1	29	29	...	-	-
3 Bills and bonds, short term	-	-	...	-	-	1	1	...	-	-
4 Bonds, long term	67	67	...	-	-	120	120	...	-	-
5 Short-term loans, n.e.c.	-22	-23	...	1	-	208	198	...	9	1
6 Long-term loans, n.e.c.	335	335	...	-	-	170	159	...	10	-
7 Other payables	42	3	...	13	26	131	97	...	9	25
8 Other liabilities	15	9	...	5	1	36	27	...	7	2
Total Incurrence of Liabilities	439	390	...	22	27	695	631	...	37	27
Net Lending a	-104	-96	...	-15	6	-325	-349	...	-6	30
Incurrence of Liabilities and Net Worth	334	294	...	7	33	370	282	...	30	58

	1982					1983				
	Total General Government	Central Government	State or Provincial Government	Local Government	Social Security Funds	Total General Government	Central Government	State or Provincial Government	Local Government	Social Security Funds
Acquisition of Financial Assets										
1 Gold and SDRs	...	...	...	...	...	...	...	...	...	...
2 Currency and transferable deposits	-7	-7	...	9	-9	312	296	...	14	2
3 Other deposits	64	14	...	24	26	323	242	...	80	1
4 Bills and bonds, short term	2	1	...	1	1	68	2	...	2	64
5 Bonds, long term	-8	-	...	-	-8	98	-	...	1	97
6 Corporate equity securities	...	...	...	...	...	...	...	...	...	...
7 Short-term loans, n.e.c.	1	2	...	-	-1	3	-	...	4	-1
8 Long-term loans, n.e.c.	-9	-	...	2	-11	41	37	...	3	-
9 Other receivables	11	-201	...	26	186	-262	-564	...	-78	380
10 Other assets	310	309	...	1	-	860	851	...	9	-
Total Acquisition of Financial Assets	364	118	...	62	184	1444	864	...	35	544
Incurrence of Liabilities										
1 Currency and transferable deposits	...	...	...	...	...	...	...	...	...	...

3.14 General Government Capital Finance Account, Total and Subsectors
(Continued)

New soles

	1982					1983				
	Total General Government	Central Government	State or Provincial Government	Local Government	Social Security Funds	Total General Government	Central Government	State or Provincial Government	Local Government	Social Security Funds
2 Other deposits	78	76	...	2	-	-56	-56	...	-	-
3 Bills and bonds, short term	1	1	...	-	-	-1	-1	...	-	-
4 Bonds, long term	59	59	...	-	-	100	100	...	-	-
5 Short-term loans, n.e.c.	-68	-79	...	-9	20	681	636	...	25	20
6 Long-term loans, n.e.c.	1058	1070	...	-11	-	2625	2637	...	-8	-4
7 Other payables	-20	-262	...	95	148	190	-226	...	52	365
8 Other liabilities	70	62	...	4	5	228	204	...	15	8
Total Incurrence of Liabilities	1180	926	...	81	173	3767	3294	...	84	389
Net Lending [a]	-816	-808	...	-19	11	-2324	-2429	...	-49	155
Incurrence of Liabilities and Net Worth	364	118	...	62	184	1444	864	...	35	544

	1984					1985				
	Total General Government	Central Government	State or Provincial Government	Local Government	Social Security Funds	Total General Government	Central Government	State or Provincial Government	Local Government	Social Security Funds
Acquisition of Financial Assets										
1 Gold and SDRs	...	...	...	...	...	...	...	...	...	...
2 Currency and transferable deposits	368	312	...	12	44	1802	1316	...	213	273
3 Other deposits	264	149	...	126	-11	649	264	...	283	102
4 Bills and bonds, short term	54	9	...	6	39	815	440	...	55	320
5 Bonds, long term	-11	1	...	1	-13	204	-2	...	5	202
6 Corporate equity securities	...	...	...	...	...	...	...	...	...	...
7 Short-term loans, n.e.c.	7	5	...	1	1	479	439	...	13	27
8 Long-term loans, n.e.c.	72	6	...	2	64	74	7	...	35	32
9 Other receivables	-3590	-4031	...	-278	718	-181	-1803	...	-291	1913
10 Other assets	1263	1245	...	19	-	1109	1037	...	72	-
Total Acquisition of Financial Assets	-1573	-2305	...	-111	842	4951	1698	...	384	2869
Incurrence of Liabilities										
1 Currency and transferable deposits	...	...	...	...	...	...	...	...	...	...
2 Other deposits	5	5	...	1	-1	55	48	...	8	-
3 Bills and bonds, short term	-	-	...	-	-	-	-	...	-	-
4 Bonds, long term	320	320	...	-	-	1151	1152	...	-	-
5 Short-term loans, n.e.c.	490	469	...	4	17	631	589	...	24	18
6 Long-term loans, n.e.c.	5348	5286	...	6	56	16889	16875	...	6	9
7 Other payables	-3971	-4460	...	18	471	-8179	-9579	...	35	1365
8 Other liabilities	563	471	...	64	28	958	835	...	65	57
Total Incurrence of Liabilities	2756	2091	...	93	572	11508	9920	...	138	1450
Net Lending [a]	-4329	-4395	...	-204	270	-6556	-8221	...	246	1419
Incurrence of Liabilities and Net Worth	-1573	-2305	...	-111	842	4951	1698	...	384	2869

	1986					1987				
	Total General Government	Central Government	State or Provincial Government	Local Government	Social Security Funds	Total General Government	Central Government	State or Provincial Government	Local Government	Social Security Funds
Acquisition of Financial Assets										
1 Gold and SDRs	...	...	...	...	...	...	...	...	...	...
2 Currency and transferable deposits	3129	2596	...	211	322	5315	3550	...	404	1361
3 Other deposits	2327	369	...	989	969	1073	1159	...	566	-652
4 Bills and bonds, short term	-404	-439	...	-39	74	3114	65	...	10	3039
5 Bonds, long term	-1	-	...	-	-1	514	800	...	60	-346
6 Corporate equity securities	...	...	...	...	...	...	...	...	...	...
7 Short-term loans, n.e.c.	97	94	...	1	2	-36	-88	...	17	35
8 Long-term loans, n.e.c.	196	33	...	90	73	1379	859	...	41	479
9 Other receivables	-2599	-6734	...	866	3269	-13249	-24411	...	2198	8964
10 Other assets	2043	2023	...	20	-	4402	4395	...	6	1
Total Acquisition of Financial Assets	4789	-2057	...	2138	4708	2511	-13672	...	3302	12881
Incurrence of Liabilities										
1 Currency and transferable deposits	...	...	...	...	...	...	...	...	...	...
2 Other deposits	40	12	...	28	-	2751	2767	...	-14	-2
3 Bills and bonds, short term	-	-	...	-	-	1	1	...	-	-

Peru

3.14 General Government Capital Finance Account, Total and Subsectors
(Continued)

New soles

	1986					1987				
	Total General Government	Central Government	State or Provincial Government	Local Government	Social Security Funds	Total General Government	Central Government	State or Provincial Government	Local Government	Social Security Funds
4 Bonds, long term	1082	1082	...	-	-	-918	-918	...	-	-
5 Short-term loans, n.e.c.	1766	1701	...	21	44	2075	1770	...	68	237
6 Long-term loans, n.e.c.	2011	1946	...	53	12	8496	8402	...	26	68
7 Other payables	12506	8009	...	1707	2790	38489	24582	...	2531	11376
8 Other liabilities	1845	1507	...	226	112	4922	3855	...	732	335
Total Incurrence of Liabilities	19249	14257	...	2034	2958	55816	40459	...	3343	12014
Net Lending a	-14460	-16313	...	102	1751	-53303	-54130	...	-41	868
Incurrence of Liabilities and Net Worth	4789	-2057	...	2138	4708	2511	-13672	...	3302	12881

	1988					1989				
	Total General Government	Central Government	State or Provincial Government	Local Government	Social Security Funds	Total General Government	Central Government	State or Provincial Government	Local Government	Social Security Funds
	Acquisition of Financial Assets									
1 Gold and SDRs	...	...	...	...	...	...	...	...	...	...
2 Currency and transferable deposits	60006	55711	...	3116	1179	710	580	...	70	59
3 Other deposits	12297	7289	...	1630	3378	231	145	...	43	43
4 Bills and bonds, short term	24249	818	...	45	23386	720	1	...	2	716
5 Bonds, long term	911	803	...	12	96	-	-	...	-	-
6 Corporate equity securities	...	...	...	...	...	...	...	...	...	...
7 Short-term loans, n.e.c.	388	388	...	123	-123	6	6	...	4	-3
8 Long-term loans, n.e.c.	28681	28130	...	253	298	26	10	...	6	10
9 Other receivables	2816	-31500	...	-13562	47878	3122	1595	...	89	1438
10 Other assets	1853	2920	...	48	-1115	921	915	...	-	6
Total Acquisition of Financial Assets	131201	64559	...	-8335	74977	5734	3252	...	214	2269
	Incurrence of Liabilities									
1 Currency and transferable deposits	...	...	...	...	...	...	...	...	...	...
2 Other deposits	1290	1017	...	249	24	18	13	...	6	-
3 Bills and bonds, short term	-	-	...	-	-	...	...	...	...	...
4 Bonds, long term	16333	16333	...	-	-	1891	1891	...	-	-
5 Short-term loans, n.e.c.	41414	27773	...	1184	12457	232	129	...	33	71
6 Long-term loans, n.e.c.	72510	69278	...	2772	460	45237	45098	...	128	10
7 Other payables	260949	212091	...	-20142	69000	-35633	-37938	...	82	2222
8 Other liabilities	11929	6050	...	5558	321	892	658	...	218	15
Total Incurrence of Liabilities	404425	332542	...	-10379	82262	12638	9852	...	468	2319
Net Lending a	-273224	-267983	...	2044	-7285	-6903	-6600	...	-253	-50
Incurrence of Liabilities and Net Worth	131201	64559	...	-8335	74977	5734	3252	...	214	2269

a) Net lending of the capital accumulation account and the capital finance account have not been reconciled and are different due to different statistical sources.

3.21 Corporate and Quasi-Corporate Enterprise Production Account: Total and Sectors

New soles

	1980				1981				1982			
	Corporate and Quasi-Corporate Enterprises			ADDENDUM: Total,	Corporate and Quasi-Corporate Enterprises			ADDENDUM: Total,	Corporate and Quasi-Corporate Enterprises			ADDENDUM: Total,
	TOTAL	Non-Financial	Financial	including Unincorporated	TOTAL	Non-Financial	Financial	including Unincorporated	TOTAL	Non-Financial	Financial	including Unincorporated
	Gross Output											
1 Output for sale	...	...	...	...	...	...	...	...	...	...	...	...
2 Imputed bank service charge	...	...	...	...	...	...	...	...	...	...	...	...
3 Own-account fixed capital formation	...	...	...	...	...	...	...	...	...	...	...	...
Gross Output	5019	4802	217	...	8549	8074	474	...	14057	13290	767	...
	Gross Input											
Intermediate consumption	2957	2777	180	...	5117	4724	393	...	8224	7612	612	...
1 Imputed banking service charge	119		119	...	284	...	284	...	404		404	...
2 Other intermediate consumption	62	...	62	...	108	...	108	...	208	...	208	...
Subtotal: Value Added	2063	2026	37	...	3431	3350	81	...	5832	5677	155	...

1480

3.21 Corporate and Quasi-Corporate Enterprise Production Account: Total and Sectors
(Continued)

New soles

	1980				1981				1982			
	Corporate and Quasi-Corporate Enterprises			ADDENDUM: Total,	Corporate and Quasi-Corporate Enterprises			ADDENDUM: Total,	Corporate and Quasi-Corporate Enterprises			ADDENDUM: Total,
	TOTAL	Non-Financial	Financial	including Unincorporated	TOTAL	Non-Financial	Financial	including Unincorporated	TOTAL	Non-Financial	Financial	including Unincorporated
1 Indirect taxes, net	356	349	7	...	587	567	20	...	1152	1116	36	...
A Indirect taxes	503	492	11	...	749	725	23	...	1391	1354	37	...
B Less: Subsidies	147	143	4	...	162	159	3	...	239	238	1	...
2 Consumption of fixed capital	...	...	...	...	...	...	...	...	...	...	...	...
3 Compensation of employees	793	710	83	...	1486	1315	171	...	2606	2302	304	...
4 Net operating surplus	914	968	-54	...	1359	1469	-110	...	2073	2259	-186	...
Gross Input	5019	4802	217	...	8549	8074	474	...	14057	13290	767	...

	1983				1984				1985			
	Corporate and Quasi-Corporate Enterprises			ADDENDUM: Total,	Corporate and Quasi-Corporate Enterprises			ADDENDUM: Total,	Corporate and Quasi-Corporate Enterprises			ADDENDUM: Total,
	TOTAL	Non-Financial	Financial	including Unincorporated	TOTAL	Non-Financial	Financial	including Unincorporated	TOTAL	Non-Financial	Financial	including Unincorporated
Gross Output												
1 Output for sale	...	...	...	...	...	...	...	...	...	...	...	...
2 Imputed bank service charge	...	...	...	...	...	...	...	...	...	...	...	...
3 Own-account fixed capital formation	...	...	...	...	...	...	...	...	...	...	...	...
Gross Output	26174	24733	1441	...	60781	57477	3304	...	177344	167519	9825	...
Gross Input												
Intermediate consumption	15491	14289	1202	...	35716	33157	2559	...	105370	96355	9015	...
1 Imputed banking service charge	767	...	767	...	1624	...	1624	...	5716	...	5716	...
2 Other intermediate consumption	435	...	435	...	935	...	935	...	3299	...	3299	...
Subtotal: Value Added	10683	10444	239	...	25065	24320	745	...	71974	71164	810	...
1 Indirect taxes, net	1875	1813	62	...	4450	4333	117	...	15053	14751	302	...
A Indirect taxes	2256	2194	62	...	4993	4876	117	...	16605	16303	302	...
B Less: Subsidies	381	381	-	...	543	543	-	...	1552	1552	-	...
2 Consumption of fixed capital	...	...	...	...	...	...	...	...	...	...	...	...
3 Compensation of employees	4795	4232	563	...	9456	8074	1382	...	24305	21234	3071	...
4 Net operating surplus	4014	4400	-386	...	11158	11912	-754	...	32617	35180	-2563	...
Gross Input	26174	24733	1441	...	60781	57477	3304	...	177344	167519	9825	...

	1986				1987				1988			
	Corporate and Quasi-Corporate Enterprises			ADDENDUM: Total,	Corporate and Quasi-Corporate Enterprises			ADDENDUM: Total,	Corporate and Quasi-Corporate Enterprises			ADDENDUM: Total,
	TOTAL	Non-Financial	Financial	including Unincorporated	TOTAL	Non-Financial	Financial	including Unincorporated	TOTAL	Non-Financial	Financial	including Unincorporated
Gross Output												
1 Output for sale	...	...	...	...	...	...	...	...	...	...	...	...
2 Imputed bank service charge	...	...	...	...	...	...	...	...	...	...	...	...
3 Own-account fixed capital formation	...	...	...	...	...	...	...	...	...	...	...	...
Gross Output	279501	261630	17871	...	...	...	34337	...	...	...	222191	...
Gross Input												
Intermediate consumption	165221	148031	17190	...	...	...	31192	...	...	...	201381	...
1 Imputed banking service charge	11687	...	11687	...	...	...	20430	...	...	...	124085	...
2 Other intermediate consumption	5503	...	5503	...	...	...	10762	...	...	...	77296	...
Subtotal: Value Added	114280	113599	681	...	...	...	3145	...	...	...	20810	...
1 Indirect taxes, net	20805	20250	555	...	...	...	1069	...	...	...	8296	...
A Indirect taxes	23664	23076	588	...	...	...	1069	...	...	...	8296	...
B Less: Subsidies	2859	2826	33	...	...	...	-	...	...	...	-	...
2 Consumption of fixed capital	...	...	...	...	...	...	...	...	...	...	...	...
3 Compensation of employees	49673	43723	5950	...	...	...	12954	...	...	...	98773	...
4 Net operating surplus	43800	49625	-5825	...	...	...	-10879	...	...	...	-86258	...
Gross Input	279501	261630	17871	...	...	...	34337	...	...	...	222191	...

Peru

3.22 Corporate and Quasi-Corporate Enterprise Income and Outlay Account: Total and Sectors

New soles

	1980 TOTAL	1980 Non-Financial	1980 Financial	1981 TOTAL	1981 Non-Financial	1981 Financial	1982 TOTAL	1982 Non-Financial	1982 Financial	1983 TOTAL	1983 Non-Financial	1983 Financial
Receipts												
1 Operating surplus	914	968	-54	1359	1469	-110	2073	2259	-186	4014	4400	-386
2 Property and entrepreneurial income	582	135	447	1356	219	1137	2280	413	1867	4624	1061	3563
A Withdrawals from quasi-corporate enterprises	...	...	...	...	...	...	...	...	...	...	...	...
B Interest	572	127	445	1335	203	1132	2237	383	1854	4517	967	3550
C Dividends	8	5	3	15	9	6	31	18	13	81	68	13
D Net land rent and royalties	3	3	-	6	6	-	12	12	-	26	26	-
3 Current transfers	298	271	27	538	481	57	741	642	99	1355	1116	239
A Casualty insurance claims	44	19	25	91	41	50	145	58	87	314	98	216
B Casualty insurance premiums, net, due to be received by insurance companies	...	...	...	...	...	...	...	...	...	...	...	...
C Current transfers from the rest of the world	...	...	...	...	...	...	...	...	...	...	...	...
D Other transfers except imputed	242	242	-	421	421	-	552	552	-	938	938	-
E Imputed unfunded employee pension and welfare contributions	12	10	2	26	19	7	44	32	12	103	80	23
Total Current Receipts a	1794	1374	421	3253	2169	1084	5095	3315	1780	9992	6576	3416
Disbursements												
1 Property and entrepreneurial income	915	570	345	2052	1198	853	3368	1900	1468	6498	3699	2799
A Withdrawals from quasi-corporations	...	...	...	...	...	...	...	...	...	...	...	...
B Interest	567	245	322	1483	643	840	2590	1151	1439	4721	1957	2764
C Dividends	156	133	23	195	181	14	256	227	29	864	829	35
D Net land rent and royalties	192	192	-	374	374	-	522	522	-	913	913	-
2 Direct taxes and other current transfers n.e.c. to general government	381	363	18	441	390	51	680	640	40	892	813	79
A Direct taxes	376	358	18	403	354	49	648	610	38	829	751	78
B Fines, fees, penalties and other current transfers n.e.c.	5	5	-	38	36	2	32	30	2	63	62	1
3 Other current transfers	64	36	28	137	78	59	232	126	106	552	293	259
A Casualty insurance premiums, net	41	16	25	88	38	50	138	56	82	298	110	188
B Casualty insurance claims liability of insurance companies	...	...	...	...	...	...	...	...	...	...	...	...
C Transfers to private non-profit institutions	...	...	...	...	...	...	...	...	...	...	...	...
D Unfunded employee pension and welfare benefits	12	10	2	26	19	7	44	32	12	103	80	23
E Social assistance grants	...	...	...	...	...	...	...	...	...	...	...	...
F Other transfers n.e.c.	10	9	1	23	20	3	50	38	12	151	103	48
G Transfers to the rest of the world	...	...	...	...	...	...	...	...	...	...	...	...
Net saving b	436	406	30	622	503	119	814	649	165	2049	1771	278
Total Current Disbursements and Net Saving a	1795	1374	421	3253	2169	1084	5095	3315	1780	9992	6576	3416

	1984 TOTAL	1984 Non-Financial	1984 Financial	1985 TOTAL	1985 Non-Financial	1985 Financial	1986 TOTAL	1986 Non-Financial	1986 Financial	1987 TOTAL	1987 Non-Financial	1987 Financial
Receipts												
1 Operating surplus	11158	11912	-754	32617	35180	-2563	43800	49625	-5825	69752	80631	-10879
2 Property and entrepreneurial income	10492	2340	8152	25247	5158	20089	33283	5343	27940	69670	14042	55628
A Withdrawals from quasi-corporate enterprises	...	...	...	...	...	...	...	...	...	...	...	...
B Interest	10139	2043	8096	24322	4310	20012	31824	4233	27591	66521	11446	55075
C Dividends	309	253	56	817	740	77	1289	940	349	2804	2252	552
D Net land rent and royalties	45	45	-	108	108	-	170	170	-	345	345	

3.22 Corporate and Quasi-Corporate Enterprise Income and Outlay Account: Total and Sectors
(Continued)

New soles

	1984			1985			1986			1987		
	TOTAL	Non-Financial	Financial	TOTAL	Non-Financial	Financial	TOTAL	Non-Financial	Financial	TOTAL	Non-Financial	Financial
3 Current transfers	2551	2091	460	6068	4937	1131	3361	1791	1570	5504	2862	2642
A Casualty insurance claims	628	221	407	1710	611	1099	2049	510	1539	3836	1279	2557
B Casualty insurance premiums, net, due to be received by insurance companies	...	...	...	...	...	...	...	...	...	...	...	...
C Current transfers from the rest of the world	...	...	...	...	...	...	...	...	...	...	...	...
D Other transfers except imputed	1737	1737	-	4138	4138	-	1010	1007	3	931	922	9
E Imputed unfunded employee pension and welfare contributions	186	133	53	220	188	32	302	274	28	737	661	76
Total Current Receipts a	24202	16344	7858	63932	45274	18658	80445	56760	23685	144925	97535	47390
Disbursements												
1 Property and entrepreneurial income	15125	8560	6565	39439	24794	14645	44483	28127	16356	86202	50945	35257
A Withdrawals from quasi-corporations	...	...	...	...	...	...	...	...	...	...	...	...
B Interest	11442	5016	6426	26813	12667	14146	31986	16355	15631	62216	28038	34178
C Dividends	1933	1795	138	7491	6993	498	10533	9810	723	22461	21387	1074
D Net land rent and royalties	1748	1748	-	5135	5134	1	1964	1962	2	1524	1520	4
2 Direct taxes and other current transfers n.e.c. to general government	1831	1597	234	4321	3445	876	12910	11834	1076	16608	14249	2359
A Direct taxes	1575	1343	232	3702	2830	872	11951	10881	1070	15188	12983	2205
B Fines, fees, penalties and other current transfers n.e.c.	256	254	2	618	614	4	959	953	6	1420	1266	154
3 Other current transfers	969	479	490	2329	1102	1227	3339	1579	1760	6567	3264	3303
A Casualty insurance premiums, net	599	212	387	1649	588	1061	1952	659	1293	3418	1145	2273
B Casualty insurance claims liability of insurance companies	...	...	...	...	...	...	...	...	...	...	...	...
C Transfers to private non-profit institutions	...	...	...	...	...	...	...	...	...	...	...	...
D Unfunded employee pension and welfare benefits	186	133	53	220	188	32	302	274	28	737	661	76
E Social assistance grants	...	...	...	...	...	...	...	...	...	...	...	...
F Other transfers n.e.c.	184	134	50	460	326	134	1085	646	439	2412	1458	954
G Transfers to the rest of the world	...	...	...	...	...	...	...	...	...	...	...	...
Net saving b	6279	5709	570	17842	15933	1909	19713	15220	4494	35550	29078	6472
Total Current Disbursements and Net Saving a	24202	16344	7858	63932	45274	18658	80445	56760	23685	144924	97534	47390

	1988			1989			1990					
	TOTAL	Non-Financial	Financial	TOTAL	Non-Financial	Financial	TOTAL	Non-Financial	Financial			
Receipts												
1 Operating surplus	786092	855551	-69459	-3321	-1381	-1940	-305682	-142369	-163313			
2 Property and entrepreneurial income	692098	204504	487594	20242	553	19689	673426	19025	654401			
A Withdrawals from quasi-corporate enterprises	...	...	...	...	...	...	...	...	...			
B Interest	663720	177529	486191	20173	551	19622	672839	18867	653972			
C Dividends	25911	24508	1403	68	1	67	518	89	429			
D Net land rent and royalties	2467	2467	-	1	1	-	69	69	-			
3 Current transfers	51266	25008	26258	705	133	572	31137	4445	26692			
A Casualty insurance claims	34971	9230	25741	668	101	567	28794	2254	26540			
B Casualty insurance premiums, net, due to be received by insurance companies	...	...	...	...	...	...	...	...	...			
C Current transfers from the rest of the world	...	...	...	...	...	...	...	...	...			
D Other transfers except imputed	11380	11316	64	3	2	1	5	-	5			
E Imputed unfunded employee pension and welfare contributions	4915	4462	453	34	30	4	2338	2191	147			
Total Current Receipts a	1529456	1085063	444393	17626	-695	18321	398881	-118899	517780			

3.22 Corporate and Quasi-Corporate Enterprise Income and Outlay Account: Total and Sectors
(Continued)

New soles

	1988			1989			1990			
	TOTAL	Non-Financial	Financial	TOTAL	Non-Financial	Financial	TOTAL	Non-Financial	Financial	
	Disbursements									
1 Property and entrepreneurial income	896478	534815	361663	20090	1788	18302	614837	105917	508920	
A Withdrawals from quasi-corporations	...	...	...	...	...	...	...	...	...	
B Interest	627008	276230	350778	19969	1747	18222	611042	105420	505622	
C Dividends	258335	247475	10860	120	40	80	3564	284	3280	
D Net land rent and royalties	11135	11110	25	1	1	-	231	213	18	
2 Direct taxes and other current transfers n.e.c. to general government	114042	84878	29164	598	221	377	44176	17578	26598	
A Direct taxes	108997	80126	28871	487	200	287	31250	12532	18718	
B Fines, fees, penalties and other current transfers n.e.c.	5045	4752	293	111	21	90	12926	5046	7880	
3 Other current transfers	56262	27172	29090	737	95	642	42581	6690	35891	
A Casualty insurance premiums, net	33128	10724	22404	527	38	489	24496	2017	22479	
B Casualty insurance claims liability of insurance companies	...	...	...	...	...	...	...	...	...	
C Transfers to private non-profit institutions	...	...	...	...	...	...	...	...	...	
D Unfunded employee pension and welfare benefits	4915	4462	453	34	30	4	2338	2191	147	
E Social assistance grants	...	...	...	...	...	...	...	...	...	
F Other transfers n.e.c.	18219	11986	6233	176	27	149	15747	2482	13265	
G Transfers to the rest of the world	...	...	...	...	...	...	...	...	...	
Net saving b	462674	438198	24476	-3799	-2799	-1000	-302713	-249084	-53629	
Total Current Disbursements and Net Saving a	1529456	1085063	444393	17626	-695	18321	398881	-118899	517780	

a) Beginning 1989, the estimates are in thousand New Soles.
b) Item 'Net saving' includes consumption of fixed capital.

3.23 Corporate and Quasi-Corporate Enterprise Capital Accumulation Account: Total and Sectors

New soles

	1980			1981			1982			1983		
	TOTAL	Non-Financial	Financial	TOTAL	Non-Financial	Financial	TOTAL	Non-Financial	Financial	TOTAL	Non-Financial	Financial
	Finance of Gross Accumulation											
1 Gross saving	436	406	30	622	503	119	814	649	165	2049	1771	278
2 Capital transfers	47	12	35	97	15	82	142	32	110	760	287	473
Finance of Gross Accumulation a	483	418	65	719	518	201	955	680	275	2809	2058	751
	Gross Accumulation											
1 Gross capital formation	895	864	31	1753	1714	39	2933	2857	76	3740	3808	-68
A Increase in stocks	171	156	15	400	405	-5	469	458	11	43	223	-180
B Gross fixed capital formation	724	708	16	1353	1309	44	2464	2399	65	3698	3585	113
2 Purchases of land, net	1	-	1	7	1	6	4	-2	6	8	2	6
3 Purchases of intangible assets, net	...	...	...	...	...	...	...	...	...	...	...	...
4 Capital transfers	8	-	8	11	2	9	32	14	18	286	25	261
Net lending b	-422	-447	25	-1050	-1198	148	-2013	-2188	175	-1225	-1777	552
Gross Accumulation a	483	418	65	719	518	201	955	680	275	2809	2058	751

	1984			1985			1986			1987		
	TOTAL	Non-Financial	Financial	TOTAL	Non-Financial	Financial	TOTAL	Non-Financial	Financial	TOTAL	Non-Financial	Financial
	Finance of Gross Accumulation											
1 Gross saving	6279	5709	570	17842	15933	1909	19714	15220	4494	35551	29078	6472
2 Capital transfers	519	106	413	1321	477	844	2061	454	1607	8400	1237	7163
Finance of Gross Accumulation a	6798	5815	983	19163	16410	2753	21774	15674	6100	43950	30315	13635
	Gross Accumulation											
1 Gross capital formation	7835	7224	611	22327	21325	1002	40655	38290	2365	85947	80489	5458

3.23 Corporate and Quasi-Corporate Enterprise Capital Accumulation Account: Total and Sectors
(Continued)

New soles

	1984			1985			1986			1987		
	TOTAL	Non-Financial	Financial	TOTAL	Non-Financial	Financial	TOTAL	Non-Financial	Financial	TOTAL	Non-Financial	Financial
A Increase in stocks	311	99	212	1065	873	192	2284	2066	218	10306	8094	2212
B Gross fixed capital formation	7523	7124	399	21262	20452	810	38370	36224	2146	75640	72394	3246
2 Purchases of land, net	16	-4	20	23	7	16	16	-	16	29	-14	43
3 Purchases of intangible assets, net	...	...	...	...	...	...	...	...	...	...	...	...
4 Capital transfers	122	122	-	356	268	88	353	166	187	470	77	393
Net lending b	-1174	-1526	352	-3543	-5190	1647	-19250	-22782	3532	-42496	-50237	7741
Gross Accumulation a	6798	5815	983	19163	16410	2753	21774	15674	6100	43950	30315	13635

	1988			1989			1990		
	TOTAL	Non-Financial	Financial	TOTAL	Non-Financial	Financial	TOTAL	Non-Financial	Financial
Finance of Gross Accumulation									
1 Gross saving	462343	438218	24125	-3799	-2799	-1000	-302713	-249084	-53629
2 Capital transfers	36001	20164	15837	894	290	604	33189	10964	22225
Finance of Gross Accumulation a	498344	458382	39962	-2905	-2509	-396	-269524	-238120	-31404
Gross Accumulation									
1 Gross capital formation	714549	659884	54665	5221	3857	1364	285546	223433	62113
A Increase in stocks	83270	65344	17926	1524	873	651	108440	64678	43762
B Gross fixed capital formation	631279	594540	36739	3697	2984	713	177106	158755	18351
2 Purchases of land, net	655	573	82	11	1	10	2161	20	2141
3 Purchases of intangible assets, net	...	...	...	...	...	...	...	...	...
4 Capital transfers	6075	2091	3984	287	-	287	15758	54	15704
Net lending b	-222935	-204166	-18769	-8424	-6367	-2057	-572989	-461627	-111362
Gross Accumulation a	498344	458382	39962	-2905	-2509	-396	-269524	-238120	-31404

a) Beginning 1989, the estimates are in thousand New Soles.
b) Net lending of the capital accumulation account and the capital finance account have not been reconciled and are different due to different statistical sources.

3.24 Corporate and Quasi-Corporate Enterprise Capital Finance Account: Total and Sectors

New soles

	1980			1981			1982			1983		
	TOTAL	Non-Financial	Financial	TOTAL	Non-Financial	Financial	TOTAL	Non-Financial	Financial	TOTAL	Non-Financial	Financial
Acquisition of Financial Assets												
1 Gold and SDRs	-19	-	-19	119	-	119	7	-	7	4	8	-4
2 Currency and transferable deposits	100	-38	138	131	12	119	-14	15	-29	540	91	449
3 Other deposits	465	-1	467	-263	-30	-233	891	86	805	1976	118	1858
4 Bills and bonds, short term	8	3	5	5	8	-3	21	-4	25	60	44	16
A Corporate and quasi-corporate, resident	8	3	5	5	8	-3	...	...	...	...	...	...
B Government	...	...	...	...	...	...	...	...	...	...	...	...
C Rest of the world	...	...	...	...	...	...	...	...	...	...	...	...
5 Bonds, long term	-19	-4	-15	145	1	144	77	3	74	-15	5	-20
6 Corporate equity securities	...	...	...	...	...	...	...	...	...	...	...	...
7 Short term loans, n.e.c.	176	-	176	981	4	977	681	81	600	2169	17	2152
8 Long term loans, n.e.c.	352	-	352	671	-	671	822	-	822	3233	-	3233
9 Trade credits and advances	...	...	...	...	...	...	...	...	...	...	...	...
10 Other receivables	106	59	47	405	177	229	699	376	324	4099	837	3262
11 Other assets	65	23	42	9	70	-61	127	90	37	66	18	48
Total Acquisition of Financial Assets a	1234	42	1192	2204	242	1962	3312	647	2665	12130	1137	10993
Incurrence of Liabilities												
1 Currency and transferable deposits	347	-	347	399	-	399	511	-	511	2514	-	2514
2 Other deposits	491	-	491	844	-9	853	1309	3	1306	4084	5	4079
3 Bills and bonds, short term	76	-	76	-83	-	-83	19	-	19	2	-	2
4 Bonds, long term	11	4	7	31	-2	33	43	3	40	39	3	36
5 Corporate equity securities	...	...	...	...	...	...	...	...	...	...	...	...
6 Short-term loans, n.e.c.	-75	-3	-72	211	57	154	406	295	111	1411	186	1225

Peru

3.24 Corporate and Quasi-Corporate Enterprise Capital Finance Account: Total and Sectors
(Continued)

New soles

	1980			1981			1982			1983		
	TOTAL	Non-Financial	Financial	TOTAL	Non-Financial	Financial	TOTAL	Non-Financial	Financial	TOTAL	Non-Financial	Financial
7 Long-term loans, n.e.c.	77	29	48	317	110	207	425	214	211	1085	279	806
8 Net equity of households in life insurance and pension fund reserves	...	...	...	...	...	...	...	...	...	...	...	...
9 Proprietors' net additions to the accumulation of quasi-corporations	...	...	...	...	...	...	...	...	...	...	...	...
10 Trade credit and advances	...	...	...	...	...	...	...	...	...	...	...	...
11 Other accounts payable	157	-34	191	333	200	132	659	467	192	2131	587	1544
12 Other liabilities	252	169	83	284	160	124	463	361	102	1443	1215	228
Total Incurrence of Liabilities	1336	165	1171	2334	516	1818	3835	1343	2492	12708	2275	10433
Net Lending [b]	-102	-123	21	-131	-274	143	-523	-696	173	-577	-1138	561
Incurrence of Liabilities and Net Lending [a]	1234	42	1192	2204	242	1962	3312	647	2665	12130	1137	10993

	1984			1985			1986			1987		
	TOTAL	Non-Financial	Financial	TOTAL	Non-Financial	Financial	TOTAL	Non-Financial	Financial	TOTAL	Non-Financial	Financial

Acquisition of Financial Assets

	TOTAL	Non-Financial	Financial	TOTAL	Non-Financial	Financial	TOTAL	Non-Financial	Financial	TOTAL	Non-Financial	Financial
1 Gold and SDRs	27	23	4	-9	-20	11	21	-20	41	965	10	955
2 Currency and transferable deposits	229	221	8	1104	1100	4	621	633	-12	1484	1239	245
3 Other deposits	173	127	46	2744	2129	615	-887	-796	-91	4501	3308	1193
4 Bills and bonds, short term	198	79	120	24	24	...	-138	-138	...	405	405	...
A Corporate and quasi-corporate, resident	...	...	...	...	...	...	...	...	...	...	...	...
B Government	...	...	...	...	...	...	...	...	...	...	...	...
C Rest of the world	...	...	...	...	...	...	...	...	...	...	...	...
5 Bonds, long term	25	19	6	-9	3	-12	167	119	48	81	-12	93
6 Corporate equity securities	...	...	...	...	...	...	...	...	...	...	...	...
7 Short term loans, n.e.c.	34	34	...	133	133	...	269	269	...	347	347	...
8 Long term loans, n.e.c.	3	-	3	9	-	9	14	...	14	63	-	63
9 Trade credits and advances	...	...	...	...	...	...	...	...	...	...	...	...
10 Other receivables	2477	2117	360	8482	7127	1355	7745	6986	759	19815	19276	539
11 Other assets	1473	1454	19	-23	-173	150	642	295	347	920	605	315
Total Acquisition of Financial Assets [a]	4639	4074	565	12456	10323	2133	8454	7348	1106	28580	25176	3404

Incurrence of Liabilities

	TOTAL	Non-Financial	Financial	TOTAL	Non-Financial	Financial	TOTAL	Non-Financial	Financial	TOTAL	Non-Financial	Financial
1 Currency and transferable deposits	...	...	...	...	...	...	...	...	...	...	-	-
2 Other deposits	4	4	...	32	32	...	29	26	3	42	15	27
3 Bills and bonds, short term	...	-	...	...	-	...	...	...	...	...	-	-
4 Bonds, long term	6	6	...	17	17	...	22	22	...	196	196	-
5 Corporate equity securities	...	...	...	...	...	...	...	...	...	...	...	...
6 Short-term loans, n.e.c.	191	191	...	-215	-215	...	244	244	...	1373	1373	-
7 Long-term loans, n.e.c.	1563	1563	...	858	858	...	2120	2120	...	15615	15615	-
8 Net equity of households in life insurance and pension fund reserves	...	...	...	...	...	...	...	...	...	...	...	...
9 Proprietors' net additions to the accumulation of quasi-corporations	...	...	...	...	...	...	...	...	...	...	...	...
10 Trade credit and advances	...	...	...	...	...	...	...	...	...	...	...	...
11 Other accounts payable	2333	2070	263	11100	9624	1476	6997	6379	618	19576	18476	1100
12 Other liabilities	1846	1828	18	3885	3807	78	5505	5411	94	11898	11588	310
Total Incurrence of Liabilities	5944	5663	281	15677	14123	1554	14917	14202	715	48700	47263	1437
Net Lending [b]	-1305	-1589	284	-3220	-3799	579	-6463	-6854	391	-20120	-22087	1967
Incurrence of Liabilities and Net Lending [a]	4639	4074	565	12456	10323	2133	8454	7348	1106	28580	25176	3404

	1988			1989		
	TOTAL	Non-Financial	Financial	TOTAL	Non-Financial	Financial

Acquisition of Financial Assets

	TOTAL	Non-Financial	Financial	TOTAL	Non-Financial	Financial
1 Gold and SDRs	68625	973	67652	32	-	31
2 Currency and transferable deposits	53381	36033	17348	732	323	408
3 Other deposits	92555	22877	69678	944	385	560
4 Bills and bonds, short term	8519	8519	-	78	78	-

1486

3.24 Corporate and Quasi-Corporate Enterprise Capital Finance Account: Total and Sectors
(Continued)

New soles

	1988			1989		
	TOTAL	Non-Financial	Financial	TOTAL	Non-Financial	Financial
A Corporate and quasi-corporate, resident	...	...	...	...	...	...
B Government	...	...	...	...	...	...
C Rest of the world	...	...	...	...	...	...
5 Bonds, long term	846	533	313	257	273	-17
6 Corporate equity securities	...	...	...	...	...	...
7 Short term loans, n.e.c.	8030	8030	-	209	202	7
8 Long term loans, n.e.c.	2468	-	2468	27	-	27
9 Trade credits and advances	...	...	...	...	...	...
10 Other receivables	1386025	484798	901227	14608	4031	10576
11 Other assets	8594	3595	4999	231	182	48
Total Acquisition of Financial Assets [a]	1629043	565358	1063685	17117	5475	11642
Incurrence of Liabilities						
1 Currency and transferable deposits	-	-	-	...	...	...
2 Other deposits	712	573	139	48	47	1
3 Bills and bonds, short term	-	-	-	...	...	...
4 Bonds, long term	709	709	-	7	7	-
5 Corporate equity securities	32011	32011	-	...	...	...
6 Short-term loans, n.e.c.	...	...	...	788	787	-
7 Long-term loans, n.e.c.	110744	110744	-	2809	2809	-
8 Net equity of households in life insurance and pension fund reserves	...	...	...	...	...	...
9 Proprietors' net additions to the accumulation of quasi-corporations	...	...	...	...	...	...
10 Trade credit and advances	...	...	...	...	...	...
11 Other accounts payable	1577990	510604	1067386	15649	4147	11502
12 Other liabilities	141202	132309	8893	4299	4200	99
Total Incurrence of Liabilities	1863368	786950	1076418	23599	11997	11602
Net Lending [b]	-234325	-221592	-12733	-6482	-6522	39
Incurrence of Liabilities and Net Lending [a]	1629043	565358	1063685	17117	5475	11642

a) Beginning 1989, the estimates are in thousand New Soles.
b) Net lending of the capital accumulation account and the capital finance account have not been reconciled and are different due to different statistical sources.

3.31 Household and Private Unincorporated Enterprise Production Account

New soles

	1980	1981	1982	1983	1984	1985	1986	1987	1988	1989	1990	1991
Gross Output												
1 Output for sale	5348	9538	15869	29067	64964	175166	342388	...	...	...	...	...
2 Non-marketed output	76	158	332	575	1059	3075	7571	...	...	...	...	...
Gross Output	5424	9696	16201	29641	66023	178241	349959	...	...	...	...	...
Gross Input												
Intermediate consumption	2199	3819	6312	12023	27485	74483	136666	...	...	...	...	...
Subtotal: Value Added	3225	5877	9890	17618	38538	103757	213293	...	...	...	...	...
1 Indirect taxes net liability of unincorporated enterprises	45	85	86	141	289	665	1137	...	...	...	...	...
A Indirect taxes	51	94	111	166	364	883	1437	...	...	...	...	...
B Less: Subsidies	6	9	25	25	75	218	300	...	...	...	...	...
2 Consumption of fixed capital	...	...	...	...	...	...	...	...	...	...	...	...
3 Compensation of employees	476	812	1401	2527	5022	12547	27749	...	...	...	...	...
4 Net operating surplus	2704	4981	8402	14950	33227	90546	184407	...	...	...	...	...
Gross Input	5424	9696	16201	29641	66023	178241	349959	...	...	...	...	...

Peru

3.32 Household and Private Unincorporated Enterprise Income and Outlay Account

New soles

	1980	1981	1982	1983	1984	1985	1986	1987	1988	1989	1990	1991
Receipts												
1 Compensation of employees	1776	3290	5706	10703	21729	54617	114778	243343	1348929	31553	1725729	...
A Wages and salaries	1597	2932	5149	9567	19489	48815	102105	214683	1227413	28794	1588200	...
B Employers' contributions for social security	116	230	328	638	1154	3479	7564	15910	65218	1346	64057	...
C Employers' contributions for private pension & welfare plans	64	128	229	498	1086	2323	5109	12750	56298	1412	73471	...
2 Operating surplus of private unincorporated enterprises	2704	4981	8402	14950	33227	90546	184407	375613	2547390	80821	5120843	...
3 Property and entrepreneurial income	191	493	864	1625	3316	9563	12932	29580	266938	11839	305235	...
A Withdrawals from private quasi-corporations	...	...	...	...	...	...	...	...	...	...	...	...
B Interest	118	395	683	956	1818	3271	3563	9878	30707	8172	162033	...
C Dividends	63	81	153	612	1378	5977	8807	18657	228197	3302	115334	...
D Net land rent and royalties	9	16	27	57	120	316	562	1044	8034	365	27868	...
3 Current transfers	308	551	900	1693	3025	7126	14578	34041	159031	3760	244524	...
A Casualty insurance claims	4	5	11	32	79	161	77	85	827	32	2415	...
B Social security benefits	162	307	526	1021	2112	4682	10784	26373	122822	2743	133837	...
C Social assistance grants	...	...	...	...	...	...	...	...	...	...	...	...
D Unfunded employee pension and welfare benefits	...		...				...			...	...	...
E Transfers from general government	...		...				...			...	...	...
F Transfers from the rest of the world	...		...		...		...			...	...	...
G Other transfers n.e.c.	142	239	363	640	834	2283	3717	7583	35382	985	108272	...
Total Current Receipts [a]	4980	9314	15872	28972	61296	161853	326694	682577	4322288	127973	7396331	...
Disbursements												
1 Final consumption expenditures	3659	6738	11070	21099	45532	123412	254987	497603	3214245	79089	5018069	...
2 Property income	126	258	507	1054	1572	3151	5856	12425	85290	12499	398955	...
A Interest	123	252	498	1035	1534	3052	5673	12090	82783	8895	257671	...
B Net land rent and royalties	3	6	9	18	38	99	184	335	2507	3604	141284	...
3 Direct taxes and other current transfers n.e.c. to government	236	486	728	1499	3069	7647	15198	33651	146621	4653	231568	...
A Social security contributions	179	358	557	1136	2240	5802	12673	28660	121516	2794	138296	...
B Direct taxes	48	108	134	231	540	1092	1393	2575	11625	1506	84749	...
Income taxes	...	...	...	...	...	...	...	...	...	...	...	...
Other	...	...	...	...	...	...	...	...	...	...	...	...
C Fees, fines and penalties	9	20	37	132	289	753	1132	2416	13480	353	8523	...

3.32 Household and Private Unincorporated Enterprise Income and Outlay Account
(Continued)

New soles

	1980	1981	1982	1983	1984	1985	1986	1987	1988	1989	1990	1991
4 Other current transfers	20	24	60	122	251	899	1626	3308	20099	1051	52674	...
A Net casualty insurance premiums	4	4	11	38	75	206	338	634	6151	371	16579	...
B Transfers to private non-profit institutions serving households	...	...	...	...	...	...	...	...	...	...	...	...
C Transfers to the rest of the world	...	...	...	...	...	...	...	...	...	...	...	...
D Other current transfers, except imputed	16	20	49	84	176	693	1288	2674	13948	681	36095	...
E Imputed employee pension and welfare contributions	...	...	...	...	...	...	...	...	...	...	...	...
Net saving b	938	1807	3507	5197	10871	26744	49028	135592	856033	30681	1695065	...
Total Current Disbursements and Net Saving a	4980	9314	15872	28972	61296	161853	326694	682577	4322288	127973	7396331	...

a) Beginning 1989, the estimates are in thousand New Soles.
b) Item 'Net saving' includes consumption of fixed capital.

3.33 Household and Private Unincorporated Enterprise Capital Accumulation Account

New soles

	1980	1981	1982	1983	1984	1985	1986	1987	1988	1989	1990	1991
Finance of Gross Accumulation												
1 Gross saving	938	1807	3507	5197	10871	26744	49028	135592	856033	30681	1695	...
2 Capital transfers	9	11	16	78	89	207	217	98	...	191	14	...
Total Finance of Gross Accumulation a	947	1818	3523	5275	10960	26950	49244	135690	856033	30872	1709	...
Gross Accumulation												
1 Gross Capital Formation	566	1246	2055	2931	5738	15413	31822	64817	488660	15427	1057	...
A Increase in stocks	67	176	195	129	-532	-651	948	1103	-9616	-1406	-97	...
B Gross fixed capital formation	499	1071	1860	2802	6270	16064	30874	63714	498276	16833	1154	...
2 Purchases of land, net	-8	-6	-3	-7	-11	-4	-7	72	-17	-12	-2	...
3 Purchases of intangibles, net	...	...	...	...	...	...	...	...	146	29	...	...
4 Capital transfers	3	3	-	-	-	47	-	...	...	...	2	...
Net lending	386	575	1471	2352	5233	11494	17429	70801	367244	15428	652	...
Total Gross Accumulation a	947	1818	3523	5275	10960	26950	49244	135690	856033	30872	1709	...

a) Beginning 1989, the estimates are in thousand New Soles.

3.51 External Transactions: Current Account: Detail

New soles

	1980	1981	1982	1983	1984	1985	1986	1987	1988	1989	1990	1991
Payments to the Rest of the World												
1 Imports of goods and services	1329	2378	3829	6224	10794	30304	53534	89231	602824	14107	691174	...
2 Factor income to the rest of the world	354	516	795	2031	4687	12000	12541	12848	121800	2498	212567	...
A Compensation of employees	5	11	28	69	118	251	413	658	891	65	6815	...
B Property and entrepreneurial income	349	505	767	1961	4569	11749	12128	12190	120909	2433	205752	...

Peru

New soles

	1980	1981	1982	1983	1984	1985	1986	1987	1988	1989	1990	1991
3 Current transfers to the rest of the world	3	4	5	16	47	207	132	348	5942	... 55	834	...
4 Surplus of the nation on current transactions	-155	-844	-1413	-1669	-751	321	-16802	-27738	-138195	... -683	-57058	...
Payments to the Rest of the World, and Surplus of the Nation on Current Transfers a	1531	2053	3216	6602	14777	42833	49406	74689	592371	... 15977	847517	...

Receipts From The Rest of the World

	1980	1981	1982	1983	1984	1985	1986	1987	1988	1989	1990	1991
1 Exports of goods and services	1332	1735	2806	5880	13486	39611	45420	68527	564016	... 14261	765114	...
2 Factor income from the rest of the world	76	101	117	257	709	1992	2079	2996	14494	... 881	35086	...
A Compensation of employees	9	15	31	72	165	546	703	1367	7699	... 262	12602	...
B Property and entrepreneurial income	67	86	86	185	544	1447	1376	1629	6795	... 619	22484	...
3 Current transfers from the rest of the world	123	216	294	464	582	1230	1907	3166	13861	... 835	47317	...
Receipts from the Rest of the World on Current Transfers a	1531	2053	3216	6602	14777	42833	49406	74689	592371	... 15977	847517	...

a) Beginning 1989, the estimates are in thousand New Soles.

3.52 External Transactions: Capital Accumulation Account

New soles

	1980	1981	1982	1983	1984	1985	1986	1987	1988	1989	1990	1991
Finance of Gross Accumulation												
1 Surplus of the nation on current transactions	-155	-844	-1413	-1669	-751	321	-16801	-27738	-138195	... -683	-57058	...
2 Capital transfers from the rest of the world	17	32	63	490	470	1138	947	3224	10425	... 852	10229	...
Total Finance of Gross Accumulation a	-138	-812	-1350	-1179	-281	1459	-15854	-24514	-126770	... 169	-46829	...
Gross Accumulation												
1 Capital transfers to the rest of the world	...	...	...	...	...	...	...	...	...	...	...	...
2 Purchases of intangible assets, n.e.c., net, from the rest of the world	...	...	...	...	...	...	...	...	...	...	...	...
Net lending to the rest of the world	...	...	...	...	...	...	...	...	...	...	...	...
Total Gross Accumulation a	-138	-812	-1350	-1179	-281	1459	-15854	-24514	-126770	... 169	-46829	...

a) Beginning 1989, the estimates are in thousand New Soles.

3.53 External Transactions: Capital Finance Account

New soles

	1980	1981	1982	1983	1984	1985	1986	1987	1988	1989	1990	1991
Acquisitions of Foreign Financial Assets												
1 Gold and SDR's	...	...	...	...	...	...	...	...	...	...	...	...
2 Currency and transferable deposits	62	-9	178	741	124	...	...	...	...	...	...	...
3 Other deposits	-3	-2	-213	128	-206	...	...	...	...	...	...	...
4 Bills and bonds, short term	-	11	-19	-	-	...	...	...	...	...	...	...
5 Bonds, long term	-	-	-	-	1	...	...	...	...	...	...	...
6 Corporate equity securities	68	123	88	174	-171	...	...	...	...	...	...	...
7 Short-term loans, n.e.c.	-31	-13	641	-541	-2406	...	...	...	...	...	...	...
8 Long-term loans	202	211	1243	1821	6026	...	...	...	...	...	...	...
9 Prporietors' net additions to accumulation of quasi-corporate, non-resident enterprises	...	...	...	...	...	...	...	...	...	...	...	...
10 Trade credit and advances	...	...	...	...	...	...	...	...	...	...	...	...
11 Other	100	41	21	52	3	...	...	...	...	...	...	...
Total Acquisitions of Foreign Financial Assets	397	362	1947	2374	3370	...	...	...	...	...	...	...

3.53 External Transactions: Capital Finance Account
(Continued)

New soles

	1980	1981	1982	1983	1984	1985	1986	1987	1988	1989	1990	1991
				Incurrence of Foreign Liabilities								
1 Currency and transferable deposits	-19	119	7	3	178	...	...	...	...	...	...	...
2 Other deposits	339	-345	258	205	1953	...	...	...	...	...	...	...
3 Bills and bonds, short term	-	-	-	-	...	...	...	...	...	...	...	...
4 Bonds, long term	1	-	-2	6	-	...	...	...	...	...	...	...
5 Corporate equity securities	7	5	31	72	62	...	...	...	...	...	...	...
6 Short-term loans, n.e.c.	-1	-1	-1	-10	-3	...	...	...	...	...	...	...
7 Long-term loans	5	-13	13	-9	-14	...	...	...	...	...	...	...
8 Non-resident proprietors' net additions to accumulation of resident quasi-corporate enterprises	...	...	...	...	...	...	...	...	...	...	...	...
9 Trade credit and advances	...	...	...	...	...	...	...	...	...	...	...	...
10 Other	42	46	118	552	353	...	...	...	...	...	...	...
Total Incurrence of Liabilities	374	-188	425	820	2529	...	...	...	...	...	...	...
Net Lending	23	550	1522	1554	842	...	...	...	...	...	...	...
Total Incurrence of Liabilities and Net Lending	397	362	1947	2374	3370	...	...	...	...	...	...	...

4.1 Derivation of Value Added by Kind of Activity, in Current Prices

New soles

	1980			1981			1982			1983		
	Gross Output	Intermediate Consumption	Value Added	Gross Output	Intermediate Consumption	Value Added	Gross Output	Intermediate Consumption	Value Added	Gross Output	Intermediate Consumption	Value Added
						All Producers						
1 Agriculture, hunting, forestry and fishing	817	207	610	1466	368	1098	2311	602	1709	4672	1246	3426
A Agriculture and hunting	777	196	581	1388	346	1042	2178	556	1622	4448	1171	3277
B Forestry and logging												
C Fishing	41	12	29	79	22	57	133	46	88	225	75	150
2 Mining and quarrying	1096	191	904	1576	319	1257	2430	557	1873	4751	1162	3589
A Coal mining a	...	...	...	...	...	...	...	...	...	...	...	...
B Crude petroleum and natural gas production	660	54	606	1078	92	986	1694	156	1538	2876	318	2558
C Metal ore mining	436	137	299	498	227	271	736	401	335	1875	844	1031
D Other mining a												
3 Manufacturing	4162	2956	1206	6794	4838	1956	10699	7424	3275	19738	13789	5949
A Manufacture of food, beverages and tobacco	1113	797	316	2060	1453	607	3198	2212	986	6356	4507	1849
B Textile, wearing apparel and leather industries	730	448	282	1049	618	431	1468	899	569	2109	1392	718
C Manufacture of wood and wood products, including furniture	163	90	73	259	137	122	454	250	204	813	446	368
D Manufacture of paper and paper products, printing and publishing	215	129	86	361	214	147	497	278	219	850	528	322
E Manufacture of chemicals and chemical petroleum, coal, rubber and plastic products	747	776	-29	1286	1357	-71	2233	2159	74	4663	3962	701
F Manufacture of non-metallic mineral products, except products of petroleum and coal	129	66	63	254	121	133	438	208	230	916	405	511
G Basic metal industries	549	327	221	650	404	246	977	625	352	2200	1455	745
H Manufacture of fabricated metal products, machinery and equipment	425	267	158	722	455	267	1191	693	498	1479	973	506
I Other manufacturing industries	91	56	35	153	79	74	259	115	144	413	182	230
4 Electricity, gas and water	74	23	51	152	41	111	287	96	191	484	214	270
A Electricity, gas and steam	...	...	44	...	...	95	...	...	158	...	...	208
B Water works and supply	...	...	8	...	...	16	...	...	33	...	...	61

Peru

New soles

	1980			1981			1982			1983		
	Gross Output	Intermediate Consumption	Value Added	Gross Output	Intermediate Consumption	Value Added	Gross Output	Intermediate Consumption	Value Added	Gross Output	Intermediate Consumption	Value Added
5 Construction	777	435	342	1590	853	737	3130	1541	1589	4941	2769	2172
6 Wholesale and retail trade, restaurants and hotels	1656	596	1060	3030	1098	1932	4981	1850	3131	9545	3400	6145
A Wholesale and retail trade	1234	415	819	2226	764	1463	3527	1301	2225	6538	2207	4331
B Restaurants and hotels	422	181	241	803	334	469	1454	549	905	3007	1193	1814
7 Transport, storage and communication	752	356	396	1375	663	712	2300	1211	1089	4323	2505	1818
8 Finance, insurance, real estate and business services	820	229	591	1649	411	1238	2973	725	2248	5279	1443	3836
A Financial institutions	175	39	136	402	72	330	655	143	512	1253	316	937
B Insurance	42	23	19	72	37	35	111	65	46	188	119	69
C Real estate and business services	603	167	436	1175	302	873	2207	517	1690	3838	1008	2830
Real estate, except dwellings	472	157	315	974	284	690	1875	481	1395	3283	930	2353
Dwellings	131	10	121	201	18	183	332	36	296	555	78	477
9 Community, social and personal services	321	79	242	671	148	523	1184	279	905	2286	536	1750
A Sanitary and similar services	...	...	...	...	...	...	...	...	...	...	...	...
B Social and related community services	109	30	79	215	52	163	396	91	305	837	182	655
Educational services	28	7	21	55	12	43	110	23	88	226	46	180
Medical, dental, other health and veterinary services	81	23	58	160	40	120	286	68	217	611	136	475
C Recreational and cultural services	212	49	163	456	96	360	788	188	600	1449	354	1095
D Personal and household services												
Total, Industries	10475	5072	5403	18303	8739	9564	30295	14285	16010	56019	27065	28953
Producers of Government Services	701	240	461	1273	356	917	2355	789	1567	4273	1253	3020
Other Producers	76	14	63	158	8	150	332	16	316	575	39	536
Total	11252	5326	5926	19734	9103	10631	32982	15090	17893	60867	28357	32509
Less: Imputed bank service charge	...	-119	119	...	-284	284	...	-404	404	...	-767	767
Import duties	160	...	160	312	...	312	419	...	419	705	...	705
Value added tax	...	...	...	...	...	...	...	...	...	...	...	...
Total b	11412	5444	5968	20046	9387	10658	33401	15494	17909	61572	29124	32448

	1984			1985			1986			1987		
	Gross Output	Intermediate Consumption	Value Added	Gross Output	Intermediate Consumption	Value Added	Gross Output	Intermediate Consumption	Value Added	Gross Output	Intermediate Consumption	Value Added
	All Producers											
1 Agriculture, hunting, forestry and fishing	10964	2982	7982	28029	9395	18634	58152	16222	41930	100498	24372	76126
A Agriculture and hunting	10344	2760	7583	25975	8541	17434	53424	14682	38742	93976	22324	71652
B Forestry and logging												
C Fishing	621	222	399	2054	854	1199	4728	1540	3188	6522	2048	4474
2 Mining and quarrying	10439	2737	7702	27770	8258	19513	23613	11660	11953	34263	18504	15758
A Coal mining a	...	...	...	...	...	...	...	...	...	...	...	...
B Crude petroleum and natural gas production	6808	775	6033	18014	2230	15784	11531	3132	8399	12571	4664	7907
C Metal ore mining	3631	1962	1669	9755	6027	3728	12083	8528	3554	21692	13840	7851
D Other mining a												

4.1 Derivation of Value Added by Kind of Activity, in Current Prices
(Continued)

New soles

	1984			1985			1986			1987		
	Gross Output	Intermediate Consumption	Value Added	Gross Output	Intermediate Consumption	Value Added	Gross Output	Intermediate Consumption	Value Added	Gross Output	Intermediate Consumption	Value Added
3 Manufacturing	46987	32563	14424	138576	90510	48066	235601	144920	90681	433660	260865	172795
A Manufacture of food, beverages and tobacco	15124	10655	4469	40654	27705	12949	74014	52140	21874	137994	94062	43932
B Textile, wearing apparel and leather industries	5341	3602	1739	17363	11093	6270	34217	18691	15526	68411	37584	30827
C Manufacture of wood and wood products, including furniture	1911	1032	879	5767	3085	2682	12719	6034	6685	27897	12134	15763
D Manufacture of paper and paper products, printing and publishing	2035	1197	838	5675	3300	2375	9699	5750	3949	19127	10933	8194
E Manufacture of chemicals and chemical petroleum, coal, rubber and plastic products	10538	9357	1180	33637	25112	8525	47064	28378	18686	70169	45582	24587
F Manufacture of non-metallic mineral products, except products of petroleum and coal	2008	862	1146	6243	2597	3646	11814	5105	6709	23740	9951	13789
G Basic metal industries	4814	3125	1689	13937	9328	4609	17045	12248	4797	27981	19528	8452
H Manufacture of fabricated metal products, machinery and equipment	4207	2466	1741	13201	7972	5229	24430	14588	9843	49393	26720	22673
I Other manufacturing industries	1174	431	743	2884	1101	1783	4598	1986	2612	8947	4369	4578
4 Electricity, gas and water	1198	374	824	3766	1421	2344	5936	2348	3588	10122	3741	6381
A Electricity, gas and steam	...	...	698	...	...	2052	...	...	2957	...	...	4444
B Water works and supply	...	...	126	...	...	292	...	...	631	...	...	1937
5 Construction	11117	6372	4745	29677	15590	14087	56812	28568	28244	111798	53469	58329
6 Wholesale and retail trade, restaurants and hotels	20605	7365	13240	55616	20053	35563	115486	39003	76483	227629	76786	150842
A Wholesale and retail trade	14245	4820	9425	38452	12592	25860	76291	25313	50978	137756	47730	90026
B Restaurants and hotels	6361	2545	3816	17164	7461	9703	39195	13690	25505	89873	29056	60816
7 Transport, storage and communication	9735	5469	4266	28838	16655	12183	47450	27117	20333	87926	47783	40142
8 Finance, insurance, real estate and business services	11416	3298	8118	29823	10369	19454	57200	17238	39962	113281	32804	80478
A Financial institutions	2911	685	2226	8236	2213	6023	14823	3661	11162	29283	7861	21421
B Insurance	393	250	143	1589	1087	502	3048	1842	1206	5054	2900	2154
C Real estate and business services	8112	2363	5749	19998	7069	12929	39329	11735	27594	78945	22042	56903
Real estate, except dwellings	7196	2235	4961	18173	6717	11456	36486	11140	25346	74410	20965	53445
Dwellings	917	128	788	1826	352	1473	2843	595	2248	4535	1077	3458
9 Community, social and personal services	5084	1164	3920	14369	3350	11019	30240	6328	23912	69410	13895	55515
A Sanitary and similar services	...	...	...	...	...	...	...	...	...	...	...	...
B Social and related community services	1861	368	1493	4999	1093	3906	10893	2056	8837	26499	3677	22822
Educational services	584	113	471	1666	324	1342	3462	543	2919	8661	1054	7607
Medical, dental, other health and veterinary services	1277	255	1022	3333	769	2564	7431	1513	5918	17838	2623	15215
C Recreational and cultural services	3223	796	2427	9370	2257	7113	19347	4272	15075	42913	10218	32695
D Personal and household services												
Total, Industries	127545	62324	65221	356463	175601	180864	630491	293404	337089	1188586	532220	656366
Producers of Government Services	8493	2055	6438	23526	7424	16103	45991	12118	33874	98178	21120	77058
Other Producers	1059	84	975	3075	471	2604	7571	774	6798	14784	1439	13345
Total	137097	64463	72634	383064	183496	199571	684053	306296	377761	1301548	554779	746769
Less: Imputed bank service charge	...	-1624	1624	...	-5716	5716	...	-11687	11687	...	-20430	20430
Import duties	1400	...	1400	4048	...	4048	7903	...	7903	13100	...	13100
Value added tax	...	...	...	...	...	...	...	...	...	...	...	...
Total b	138497	66087	72410	387112	189212	197903	691956	317983	373976	1314648	575209	739439

Peru

4.1 Derivation of Value Added by Kind of Activity, in Current Prices

	1988			1989			1990			1991		
	Gross Output	Intermediate Consumption	Value Added	Gross Output	Intermediate Consumption	Value Added	Gross Output	Intermediate Consumption	Value Added	Gross Output	Intermediate Consumption	Value Added
All Producers												
1 Agriculture, hunting, forestry and fishing	624671	215219	409452	13502	4246	9256	658019	181386	476633	...	...	2323414
A Agriculture and hunting	551404	198359	353045	12139	3905	8234	607607	168822	438785	...	...	2145942
B Forestry and logging										...	...	
C Fishing	73267	16860	56407	1363	341	1022	50412	12564	37848	...	...	177472
2 Mining and quarrying	235408	125124	110284	5848	2635	3213	316308	125067	191241	...	...	847738
A Coal mining a	...	...	...	...	...	...	...	...	...			
B Crude petroleum and natural gas production	65487	30132	35355	1596	717	879	113062	46208	66854	...	...	399492
C Metal ore mining	169921	94992	74929	4252	1918	2334	203246	78859	124387	...	...	448246
D Other mining a										...	...	
3 Manufacturing	3267323	1792392	1474931	64718	35630	29088	4185723	2245961	1939762	...	...	8782634
A Manufacture of food, beverages and tobacco	1055773	651012	404761	21632	13969	7663	1502652	928150	574502	...	...	2994573
B Textile, wearing apparel and leather industries	491242	259436	231806	11094	5884	5210	529268	254084	275184	...	...	990679
C Manufacture of wood and wood products, including furniture	202498	83891	118607	4121	1572	2549	241438	79540	161898	...	...	730266
D Manufacture of paper and paper products, printing and publishing	169845	89373	80472	2259	784	1475	189251	66216	123035	...	...	470826
E Manufacture of chemicals and chemical petroleum, coal, rubber and plastic products	525980	310133	215847	9866	5719	4147	885643	557422	328221	...	...	1707085
F Manufacture of non-metallic mineral products, except products of petroleum and coal	164795	68310	96485	3406	1408	1998	185080	65678	119402	...	...	479697
G Basic metal industries	238214	128454	109760	5755	3049	2706	299093	139165	159928	...	...	661853
H Manufacture of fabricated metal products, machinery and equipment	351937	169268	182669	5373	2714	2659	275521	124677	150844	...	...	562016
I Other manufacturing industries	67039	32515	34524	1212	531	681	77777	31029	46748	...	...	185639
4 Electricity, gas and water	51374	28636	22738	924	520	404	94833	54648	40185	...	...	201532
A Electricity, gas and steam	...	...	16041	...	...	298	...	...	33953	...	...	159267
B Water works and supply	...	...	6697	...	...	106	...	...	6232	...	...	42265
5 Construction	881093	434843	446250	16607	7659	8948	991096	457584	533512	...	...	3012457
6 Wholesale and retail trade, restaurants and hotels	1472132	547259	924873	35478	13515	21963	2053279	737558	1315721	...	...	6584540
A Wholesale and retail trade	941381	312213	629168	20559	6401	14158	1162094	341367	820727	...	...	3428236
B Restaurants and hotels	530751	235046	295705	14919	7114	7805	891185	396191	494994	...	...	3156304
7 Transport, storage and communication	608414	361947	246467	11716	6008	5708	715542	376916	338626	...	...	2086148
8 Finance, insurance, real estate and business services	864558	266005	598553	20614	5534	15080	1391104	372411	1018693	...	...	6179770
A Financial institutions	213845	56475	157370	2485	1268	1217	201063	72018	129045	...	...	669446
B Insurance	35447	25175	10272	1055	468	587	45320	24768	20552	...	...	87136
C Real estate and business services	615266	184355	430911	17074	3798	13276	1144721	275625	869096	...	...	5423188
Real estate, except dwellings	600056	180744	419312	16668	3701	12967	1115756	268709	847047	...	...	4892508
Dwellings	15210	3611	11599	406	97	309	28965	6916	22049	...	...	530680
9 Community, social and personal services	431711	90680	341031	13750	3487	10263	903585	226539	677046	...	...	3472164
A Sanitary and similar services	...	...	...	...	...	...	...	...	...			...
B Social and related community services	177287	25705	151582	6901	1631	5270	445772	106193	339579	...	...	1623092
Educational services	68332	8468	59864	3176	745	2431	186620	44523	142097	...	...	930559
Medical, dental, other health and veterinary services	108955	17237	91718	3725	886	2839	259152	61670	197482	...	...	692533
C Recreational and cultural services	254424	64975	189449	6849	1856	4993	457813	120346	337467	...	...	1849072
D Personal and household services										...	...	

1494

4.1 Derivation of Value Added by Kind of Activity, in Current Prices
(Continued)

New soles

	1988			1989			1990			1991		
	Gross Output	Intermediate Consumption	Value Added	Gross Output	Intermediate Consumption	Value Added	Gross Output	Intermediate Consumption	Value Added	Gross Output	Intermediate Consumption	Value Added
Total, Industries	8436684	3862105	4574579	183157	79234	103923	11309489	4778070	6531419	...	...	1 3490396
Producers of Government Services	495455	121131	374324	12265	2686	9579	591260	122630	468630	...	...	959762
Other Producers	79776	10601	69175	2172	434	1737	152172	32935	119237	...	...	598710
Total	9011915	3993837	5018078	197593	82354	115239	12052921	4933635	7119286	...	...	1 5048868
Less: Imputed bank service charge	...	-131631	131631	...	-1339	1339	...	-145452	145452	...	...	207578
Import duties	55870	...	55870	1215	...	1215	67166	...	67166	...	...	310417
Value added tax	...	...	...	...	...	...	...	...	...	...	...	...
Total b	9067785	4125468	4942317	198809	83693	115115	1 2120087	5079087	7041000	...	...	1 5151707

a) 'Coal mining' is included in 'Other mining'.
b) Beginning 1989, the estimates are in thousand New Soles.

4.2 Derivation of Value Added by Kind of Activity, in Constant Prices

New soles

	1980			1981			1982			1983		
	Gross Output	Intermediate Consumption	Value Added	Gross Output	Intermediate Consumption	Value Added	Gross Output	Intermediate Consumption	Value Added	Gross Output	Intermediate Consumption	Value Added
	At constant prices of:1979											
	All Producers											
1 Agriculture, hunting, forestry and fishing	515	133	382	562	146	416	578	150	428	516	134	382
A Agriculture and hunting	488	125	363	532	137	395	544	140	404	492	127	365
B Forestry and logging												
C Fishing	27	8	19	30	9	21	34	10	24	24	7	17
2 Mining and quarrying	596	127	469	577	123	454	585	125	460	534	119	415
A Coal mining a	...	...	...	...	...	...	...	...	...	...	...	...
B Crude petroleum and natural gas production	327	35	292	317	34	284	319	34	285	270	29	241
C Metal ore mining	269	92	177	260	89	171	266	91	175	264	90	174
D Other mining a												
3 Manufacturing	2706	1840	867	2751	1878	873	2706	1842	862	2295	1577	706
A Manufacture of food, beverages and tobacco	778	551	227	813	581	232	823	586	237	758	549	209
B Textile, wearing apparel and leather industries	430	290	140	404	273	131	387	261	126	316	208	108
C Manufacture of wood and wood products, including furniture	100	60	39	101	61	40	107	65	42	88	53	35
D Manufacture of paper and paper products, printing and publishing	134	83	52	135	82	53	111	65	46	103	60	43
E Manufacture of chemicals and chemical petroleum, coal, rubber and plastic products	510	410	100	534	427	107	538	431	107	452	373	79
F Manufacture of non-metallic mineral products, except products of petroleum and coal	79	43	36	84	46	39	82	44	38	72	39	33
G Basic metal industries	358	196	162	337	184	153	343	184	159	303	162	141
H Manufacture of fabricated metal products, machinery and equipment	267	174	93	293	191	102	269	176	91	169	111	46
I Other manufacturing industries	50	33	17	50	33	17	46	30	16	34	22	11
4 Electricity, gas and water	54	15	39	58	16	42	62	17	45	52	14	38
5 Construction	478	276	202	542	317	225	556	326	230	440	259	182
6 Wholesale and retail trade, restaurants and hotels	1023	369	654	1102	413	689	1105	416	689	950	360	590
A Wholesale and retail trade	782	253	529	855	293	562	853	294	559	695	237	458
B Restaurants and hotels	241	116	125	247	120	127	252	122	130	255	123	132
7 Transport, storage and communication	467	231	236	496	245	251	493	245	248	457	227	230
8 Finance, insurance, real estate and business services	535	149	386	571	160	411	572	162	410	543	152	391
A Financial institutions	123	25	98	136	28	108	146	32	115	151	34	117
B Insurance	25	14	11	24	13	11	21	13	8	17	12	6
C Real estate and business services	387	110	277	411	119	292	405	117	288	375	106	269
Real estate, except dwellings	292	104	188	315	113	202	307	111	196	276	100	176

Peru

New soles

At constant prices of:1979

	1980			1981			1982			1983		
	Gross Output	Intermediate Consumption	Value Added	Gross Output	Intermediate Consumption	Value Added	Gross Output	Intermediate Consumption	Value Added	Gross Output	Intermediate Consumption	Value Added
Dwellings	95	6	89	96	6	91	98	6	92	99	6	93
9 Community, social and personal services	176	49	127	186	52	134	185	53	132	176	48	128
A Sanitary and similar services	...	...	...	...	...	...	...	...	...	...	...	...
B Social and related community services	63	20	43	66	21	45	67	22	45	66	20	46
Educational services	17	4	13	17	4	13	17	4	13	18	5	13
Medical, dental, other health and veterinary services	46	16	31	49	17	32	50	18	32	48	15	33
C Recreational and cultural services	113	29	83	120	31	88	118	31	87	110	28	82
D Personal and household services												
Total, Industries	6550	3189	3362	6845	3350	3495	6842	3336	3504	5963	2890	3062
Producers of Government Services	388	155	233	381	141	240	430	188	242	393	135	258
Other Producers	42	9	33	38	4	34	39	4	35	41	4	37
Total	6980	3353	3628	7264	3495	3769	7311	3528	3781	6397	3029	3357
Less: Imputed bank service charge	...	-82	82	...	-89	89	...	-90	90	...	-98	98
Import duties	102	...	102	128	...	128	124	...	124	76		76
Value added tax	...	...	...	...	...	...	...	...	...	...	...	...
Total	7082	3435	3647	7392	3584	3808	7435	3618	3816	6473	3127	3334

At constant prices of:1979

All Producers

	1984			1985			1986			1987		
	Gross Output	Intermediate Consumption	Value Added	Gross Output	Intermediate Consumption	Value Added	Gross Output	Intermediate Consumption	Value Added	Gross Output	Intermediate Consumption	Value Added
1 Agriculture, hunting, forestry and fishing	577	150	427	599	156	443	638	167	471	670	175	495
A Agriculture and hunting	542	140	403	558	144	414	583	151	432	622	161	461
B Forestry and logging												
C Fishing	35	10	25	41	12	29	55	16	39	48	14	34
2 Mining and quarrying	559	124	435	586	133	453	563	130	433	550	130	420
A Coal mining a	...	...	...	...	...	...	...	...	...	...	...	...
B Crude petroleum and natural gas production	286	31	255	290	31	259	274	30	244	252	27	225
C Metal ore mining	273	93	179	296	102	194	289	100	189	298	103	195
D Other mining a												
3 Manufacturing	2419	1662	746	2518	1723	780	2913	1985	902	3227	2210	1017
A Manufacture of food, beverages and tobacco	781	565	216	788	565	223	917	646	271	1028	733	295
B Textile, wearing apparel and leather industries	347	230	117	388	258	130	422	280	142	449	300	149
C Manufacture of wood and wood products, including furniture	91	55	36	95	58	37	115	70	45	121	74	47
D Manufacture of paper and paper products, printing and publishing	102	59	43	96	56	40	111	66	46	134	80	54
E Manufacture of chemicals and chemical petroleum, coal, rubber and plastic products	488	401	87	497	406	91	568	456	112	639	508	131
F Manufacture of non-metallic mineral products, except products of petroleum and coal	69	37	32	69	37	32	95	52	43	132	72	60
G Basic metal industries	331	177	154	353	190	163	346	191	155	355	200	155
H Manufacture of fabricated metal products, machinery and equipment	175	115	49	202	133	54	300	198	75	318	209	109
I Other manufacturing industries	35	23	12	30	20	10	39	26	13	52	34	18
4 Electricity, gas and water	52	14	38	56	15	41	66	18	48	71	20	51

4.2 Derivation of Value Added by Kind of Activity, in Constant Prices
(Continued)

New soles

	1984 Gross Output	1984 Intermediate Consumption	1984 Value Added	1985 Gross Output	1985 Intermediate Consumption	1985 Value Added	1986 Gross Output	1986 Intermediate Consumption	1986 Value Added	1987 Gross Output	1987 Intermediate Consumption	1987 Value Added
					At constant prices of:1979							
5 Construction	443	260	183	398	234	164	488	289	199	579	345	234
6 Wholesale and retail trade, restaurants and hotels	955	351	604	973	355	618	1119	414	705	1235	460	775
A Wholesale and retail trade	691	223	468	690	218	472	803	260	543	888	291	597
B Restaurants and hotels	264	128	136	283	137	146	316	154	162	347	169	178
7 Transport, storage and communication	459	228	231	474	236	238	520	262	258	578	294	284
8 Finance, insurance, real estate and business services	543	151	392	595	171	424	634	186	448	696	211	485
A Financial institutions	148	33	115	171	39	132	170	39	130	185	46	140
B Insurance	17	11	6	25	17	8	29	19	10	31	20	11
C Real estate and business services	378	107	271	399	115	284	435	128	307	479	145	334
Real estate, except dwellings	277	101	176	297	108	189	330	121	209	370	138	232
Dwellings	101	6	95	102	7	95	105	7	98	109	7	102
9 Community, social and personal services	180	47	133	188	50	138	201	52	149	214	59	155
A Sanitary and similar services	...	...	...	...	...	...	...	...	...	...	...	...
B Social and related community services	67	18	49	70	20	51	73	19	54	79	23	56
Educational services	19	5	14	21	6	15	21	5	16	23	6	17
Medical, dental, other health and veterinary services	48	13	35	49	14	36	52	14	38	56	17	39
C Recreational and cultural services / D Personal and household services	113	29	84	118	30	87	128	33	94	135	36	99
Total, Industries	6187	2987	3188	6387	3073	3299	7142	3503	3611	7816	3902	3914
Producers of Government Services	375	97	278	389	110	279	417	114	302	435	118	317
Other Producers	43	4	39	47	8	39	50	9	41	52	9	43
Total	6605	3088	3505	6823	3191	3617	7609	3626	3954	8303	4029	4274
Less: Imputed bank service charge	...	-88	88	...	-111	111	...	-125	125	...	-127	127
Import duties	77	...	77	68	...	68	76	...	76	88	...	88
Value added tax	...	...	...	...	...	...	...	...	...	...	...	...
Total	6682	3176	3495	6891	3302	3574	7685	3751	3904	8390	4156	4234

	1988 Gross Output	1988 Intermediate Consumption	1988 Value Added	1989 Gross Output	1989 Intermediate Consumption	1989 Value Added	1990 Gross Output	1990 Intermediate Consumption	1990 Value Added	1991 Gross Output	1991 Intermediate Consumption	1991 Value Added
			At constant prices of:1979									
			All Producers									
1 Agriculture, hunting, forestry and fishing	722	189	533	686	178	508	630	164	466	...	...	472
A Agriculture and hunting	665	172	493	626	160	466	570	146	424	...	...	434
B Forestry and logging										...	...	
C Fishing	57	17	40	60	18	42	60	18	42	...	...	38
2 Mining and quarrying	466	109	357	446	106	340	423	97	326	...	...	313
A Coal mining a	...	...	...	...	...	...	...	...	...	...	...	...
B Crude petroleum and natural gas production	220	24	196	199	21	178	195	19	176	...	...	159
C Metal ore mining	246	85	161	247	85	162	228	78	150	...	...	154
D Other mining a										...	...	

Peru

New soles

	1988			1989			1990			1991		
	Gross Output	Intermediate Consumption	Value Added	Gross Output	Intermediate Consumption	Value Added	Gross Output	Intermediate Consumption	Value Added	Gross Output	Intermediate Consumption	Value Added
				At constant prices of:1979								
3 Manufacturing	2938	2035	903	2458	1697	761	2329	1619	710	...	...	750
A Manufacture of food, beverages and tobacco	1004	729	275	836	606	230	819	596	223	...	...	243
B Textile, wearing apparel and leather industries	452	302	150	411	272	139	353	235	118	...	...	115
C Manufacture of wood and wood products, including furniture	108	66	42	102	62	40	93	57	36	...	...	34
D Manufacture of paper and paper products, printing and publishing	130	76	54	75	44	31	82	48	34	...	...	29
E Manufacture of chemicals and chemical petroleum, coal, rubber and plastic products	575	462	113	468	387	81	458	378	80	...	...	80
F Manufacture of non-metallic mineral products, except products of petroleum and coal	126	69	57	83	45	38	82	45	37	...	...	39
G Basic metal industries	281	159	122	325	177	148	281	156	125	...	...	148
H Manufacture of fabricated metal products, machinery and equipment	215	142	73	130	86	44	134	87	47	...	...	51
I Other manufacturing industries	45	30	15	28	18	10	29	19	10	...	...	11
4 Electricity, gas and water	72	20	52	71	20	51	72	21	51	...	...	56
5 Construction	547	329	218	471	284	187	488	295	193	...	...	189
6 Wholesale and retail trade, restaurants and hotels	1115	426	689	929	349	580	897	342	555	...	...	588
A Wholesale and retail trade	811	277	534	672	225	447	650	223	427	...	...	455
B Restaurants and hotels	304	149	155	257	124	133	247	119	128	...	...	133
7 Transport, storage and communication	554	286	268	507	264	243	471	246	225	...	...	235
8 Finance, insurance, real estate and business services	644	201	443	609	182	427	591	171	420	...	...	436
A Financial institutions	178	40	138	163	36	127	62	34	128	...	...	132
B Insurance	31	25	6	31	24	7	25	18	7	...	...	8
C Real estate and business services	435	136	299	415	122	293	404	119	285	...	...	296
Real estate, except dwellings	326	129	197	305	115	190	294	112	182	...	...	192
Dwellings	109	7	102	110	7	103	110	7	103	...	...	104
9 Community, social and personal services	191	51	140	168	43	125	156	39	117	...	...	118
A Sanitary and similar services	...	...	...	...	...	...	...	...	...	...	...	...
B Social and related community services	71	19	52	66	17	49	61	16	45	...	...	44
Educational services	22	6	16	21	5	16	22	6	16	...	...	17
Medical, dental, other health and veterinary services	49	13	36	45	12	33	39	10	29	...	...	27
C Recreational and cultural services	120	32	88	102	26	76	95	23	72	...	...	74
D Personal and household services										...	...	
Total, Industries	7247	3643	3604	6345	3123	3222	6059	2996	3063	...	...	3157
Producers of Government Services	362	74	288	321	74	247	298	71	227	...	...	208
Other Producers	48	8	40	44	7	37	41	7	34	...	...	35
Total	7657	3725	3932	6710	3204	3506	6398	3074	3324	...	...	3400
Less: Imputed bank service charge	...	-125	125	...	-118	118	...	-120	120	...	...	123
Import duties	74	...	74	41	...	41	51	...	51	...	...	54
Value added tax	...	...	...	...	...	...	...	...	...	...	...	...
Total	7731	3850	3881	6751	3322	3429	6449	3194	3255	...	...	3331

a) 'Coal mining' is included in 'Other mining'.

4.3 Cost Components of Value Added

New soles

	1980						1981					
	Compensation of Employees	Capital Consumption	Net Operating Surplus	Indirect Taxes	Less: Subsidies Received	Value Added	Compensation of Employees	Capital Consumption	Net Operating Surplus	Indirect Taxes	Less: Subsidies Received	Value Added
All Producers												
1 Agriculture, hunting, forestry and fishing	129	16	464	1	...	610	223	29	845	1	...	1098
A Agriculture and hunting	118	10	452	1	...	581	202	18	821	1	...	1042
B Forestry and logging					...						...	
C Fishing	11	6	12	...	...	29	21	11	24	...	...	56
2 Mining and quarrying	89	37	690	89	...	905	162	70	933	92	...	1257
A Coal mining a	...	...	...	...	...	...	...	...	...	...	...	...
B Crude petroleum and natural gas production	21	1	531	53	...	606	46	35	847	58	...	986
C Metal ore mining a	68	36	159	36	...	299	116	35	86	34	...	271
D Other mining					...						...	
3 Manufacturing	343	101	494	341	73	1206	553	148	794	507	46	1956
A Manufacture of food, beverages and tobacco	81	25	156	98	44	316	134	42	300	146	15	607
B Textile, wearing apparel and leather industries	53	18	189	37	15	282	79	22	300	46	16	431
C Manufacture of wood and wood products, including furniture	14	3	53	4	1	73	23	5	89	6	1	122
D Manufacture of paper and paper products, printing and publishing	22	5	55	4	-	86	36	11	92	8	...	147
E Manufacture of chemicals and chemical petroleum, coal, rubber and plastic products	56	15	-224	127	3	-29	92	21	-403	225	6	-71
F Manufacture of non-metallic mineral products, except products of petroleum and coal	16	5	37	8	3	63	25	7	93	10	2	133
G Basic metal industries	36	15	137	35	1	222	65	23	131	29	2	246
H Manufacture of fabricated metal products, machinery and equipment	59	14	62	26	3	158	90	15	133	33	4	267
I Other manufacturing industries	6	1	29	2	3	35	9	2	59	4	-	74
4 Electricity, gas and water	27	13	6	5	...	51	58	25	17	11	...	111
A Electricity, gas and steam	...	...	...	...	...	...	...	...	...	...	...	...
B Water works and supply	...	...	...	...	...	...	...	...	...	...	...	...
5 Construction	114	20	201	7	...	342	197	42	487	11	...	737
6 Wholesale and retail trade, restaurants and hotels	186	12	871	63	72	1060	348	23	1552	122	113	1932
A Wholesale and retail trade	163	7	661	60	72	819	310	14	1134	118	113	1463
B Restaurants and hotels	23	5	210	3	...	241	38	9	418	4	...	469
7 Transport, storage and communication	108	57	215	18	2	396	201	98	385	34	6	712
8 Finance, insurance, real estate and business services	144	46	382	23	4	591	284	84	828	45	3	1238
A Financial institutions	77	6	51	5	3	136	160	8	153	11	2	330
B Insurance	6	-	7	6	...	19	11	1	11	12	...	35
C Real estate and business services	61	40	324	12	1	436	113	75	664	22	1	873
Real estate, except dwellings	61	28	216	11	1	315	113	56	501	21	1	690
Dwellings	...	12	108	1	...	121	...	19	163	1	...	183
9 Community, social and personal services	126	12	98	8	2	242	245	22	238	20	2	523
A Sanitary and similar services	...	...	...	...	...	...	...	...	...	...	...	...
B Social and related community services	55	4	20	2	2	79	110	5	46	4	2	163
Educational services	21	1	...	1	2	21	42	1	1	1	2	43
Medical, dental, other health and veterinary services	34	3	20	1	...	58	68	4	45	3	...	120
C Recreational and cultural services	71	8	78	6	...	163	135	17	192	16	...	360
D Personal and household services					...						...	

Peru

4.3 Cost Components of Value Added
(Continued)

New soles

	1980						1981					
	Compensation of Employees	Capital Consumption	Net Operating Surplus	Indirect Taxes	Less: Subsidies Received	Value Added	Compensation of Employees	Capital Consumption	Net Operating Surplus	Indirect Taxes	Less: Subsidies Received	Value Added
Total, Industries	1266	314	3421	555	153	5403	2271	541	6079	843	170	9564
Producers of Government Services	446	4	...	11	...	461	872	5	...	40	...	917
Other Producers	60	2	...	...	...	62	143	6	...	1	...	150
Total	1772	320	3421	566	153	5926	3286	552	6079	884	170	10631
Less: Imputed bank service charge	...	...	118	...	...	118	...	...	284	...	...	284
Import duties	...	...	...	160	...	160	...	...	...	312	...	312
Value added tax	...	...	...	...	...	...	...	...	...	...	...	...
Total b	1772	320	3303	726	153	5968	3286	552	5795	1196	170	10659

	1982						1983					
	Compensation of Employees	Capital Consumption	Net Operating Surplus	Indirect Taxes	Less: Subsidies Received	Value Added	Compensation of Employees	Capital Consumption	Net Operating Surplus	Indirect Taxes	Less: Subsidies Received	Value Added
All Producers												
1 Agriculture, hunting, forestry and fishing	348	46	1314	1	...	1709	724	84	2617	1	...	3426
A Agriculture and hunting	310	28	1283	1	...	1622	665	55	2556	1	...	3277
B Forestry and logging					...						...	
C Fishing	38	18	31	...	...	88	59	29	61	...	...	150
2 Mining and quarrying	271	115	1365	122	...	1873	505	304	2588	192	...	3589
A Coal mining a	...	...	...	...	...	...	...	...	...	...	...	...
B Crude petroleum and natural gas production	81	63	1294	100	...	1538	194	173	2020	171	...	2558
C Metal ore mining a	190	52	71	22	...	335	311	131	568	21	...	1031
D Other mining					...						...	
3 Manufacturing	940	239	1240	926	70	3275	1678	507	2308	1576	120	5949
A Manufacture of food, beverages and tobacco	222	70	474	234	14	986	372	143	990	373	29	1849
B Textile, wearing apparel and leather industries	134	34	380	43	22	569	243	81	375	58	40	717
C Manufacture of wood and wood products, including furniture	40	9	150	7	2	204	72	17	272	9	3	367
D Manufacture of paper and paper products, printing and publishing	61	16	122	20	...	219	99	24	172	27	...	322
E Manufacture of chemicals and chemical petroleum, coal, rubber and plastic products	162	33	-518	412	15	74	328	66	-516	852	29	701
F Manufacture of non-metallic mineral products, except products of petroleum and coal	47	13	144	29	3	230	75	41	366	30	1	511
G Basic metal industries	98	37	181	40	4	352	160	89	461	40	5	745
H Manufacture of fabricated metal products, machinery and equipment	162	24	251	112	10	539	303	39	153	141	13	623
I Other manufacturing industries	15	3	97	29	...	144	26	7	152	46	-	231
4 Electricity, gas and water	143	45	-10	12	...	191	239	81	-68	20	...	270
A Electricity, gas and steam	...	...	...	...	...	...	...	...	...	...	...	...
B Water works and supply	...	...	...	...	...	...	...	...	...	...	...	...
5 Construction	359	82	1137	11	...	1589	530	130	1494	18	...	2172
6 Wholesale and retail trade, restaurants and hotels	580	39	2480	213	181	3131	1014	75	5039	267	250	6145
A Wholesale and retail trade	518	22	1659	207	181	2225	895	41	3387	258	250	4331
B Restaurants and hotels	62	17	821	6	...	906	119	34	1652	9	...	1814
7 Transport, storage and communication	337	164	540	57	9	1089	775	304	641	123	26	1817
8 Finance, insurance, real estate and business services	491	157	1482	119	1	2248	917	293	2455	171	...	3836
A Financial institutions	285	16	192	20	1	512	526	33	347	31	...	937
B Insurance	18	2	9	17	...	46	37	5	-4	31	...	69
C Real estate and business services	188	139	1281	82	...	1690	354	255	2112	109	...	2830
Real estate, except dwellings	188	108	1016	82	...	1394	354	203	1687	109	...	2353

4.3 Cost Components of Value Added
(Continued)

New soles

	1982						1983					
	Compensation of Employees	Capital Consumption	Net Operating Surplus	Indirect Taxes	Less: Subsidies Received	Value Added	Compensation of Employees	Capital Consumption	Net Operating Surplus	Indirect Taxes	Less: Subsidies Received	Value Added
Dwellings	...	31	265	...	...	296	...	52	425	...	...	477
9 Community, social and personal services	422	36	408	42	3	905	821	73	808	55	7	1750
A Sanitary and similar services	...	...	...	...	...	...	...	...	...	...	...	...
B Social and related community services	201	10	91	6	3	305	412	23	217	10	7	655
Educational services	85	2	2	1	3	87	173	7	4	3	7	180
Medical, dental, other health and veterinary services	116	8	89	5	...	218	239	16	213	7	...	475
C Recreational and cultural services	221	26	317	36	...	600	409	50	591	45	...	1095
D Personal and household services					...						...	
Total, Industries	3891	923	9956	1504	264	16010	7203	1851	17882	2423	405	28953
Producers of Government Services	1508	9	...	50	...	1567	2982	15	...	22	...	3020
Other Producers	303	12	...	1	...	316	516	19	...	1	...	536
Total	5702	944	9956	1555	264	17893	10701	1886	17882	2446	405	32509
Less: Imputed bank service charge	...	...	404	...		404	...	...	767	...		767
Import duties	...	...	...	419		419	...	...	...	705		705
Value added tax	...	...	...	...	...	...	...	...	...	...	...	...
Total [b]	5702	944	9552	1974	264	17909	10700	1886	17115	3151	405	32448

	1984						1985					
	Compensation of Employees	Capital Consumption	Net Operating Surplus	Indirect Taxes	Less: Subsidies Received	Value Added	Compensation of Employees	Capital Consumption	Net Operating Surplus	Indirect Taxes	Less: Subsidies Received	Value Added
					All Producers							
1 Agriculture, hunting, forestry and fishing	1391	207	6380	4	...	7982	3272	490	14862	10	...	18634
A Agriculture and hunting	1276	127	6179	2	...	7583	2971	292	14166	5	...	17434
B Forestry and logging					...						...	
C Fishing	115	80	202	2		399	301	198	696	5		1199
2 Mining and quarrying	1087	476	5829	310	...	7702	2990	1032	14545	946	...	19513
A Coal mining [a]	...	...	...	...	...	...	...	...	...	...	...	...
B Crude petroleum and natural gas production	424	264	5083	262	...	6033	1222	374	13430	758	...	15784
C Metal ore mining [a]	663	212	746	48	...	1669	1767	658	1115	188	...	3728
D Other mining					...						...	
3 Manufacturing	3132	1292	6653	3704	358	14424	8312	3040	24319	13675	1277	48066
A Manufacture of food, beverages and tobacco	646	374	2737	822	110	4469	1576	727	8423	2550	327	12949
B Textile, wearing apparel and leather industries	451	176	1124	113	125	1739	1196	497	4800	239	462	6270
C Manufacture of wood and wood products, including furniture	122	58	685	18	4	879	340	144	2177	37	16	2682
D Manufacture of paper and paper products, printing and publishing	205	76	507	53	3	838	523	170	1584	110	12	2375
E Manufacture of chemicals and chemical petroleum, coal, rubber and plastic products	725	172	-1710	2055	61	1181	2022	434	-2728	9006	209	8525
F Manufacture of non-metallic mineral products, except products of petroleum and coal	126	114	850	62	6	1146	327	300	2906	134	21	3646
G Basic metal industries	329	194	1122	55	11	1689	919	509	2989	300	108	4609
H Manufacture of fabricated metal products, machinery and equipment	480	101	1259	372	37	2175	1261	225	4909	894	118	7171
I Other manufacturing industries	49	28	513	154	1	743	147	35	1200	405	4	1783
4 Electricity, gas and water	443	220	114	47	...	824	1456	657	114	118	...	2344
A Electricity, gas and steam	...	...	...	...	...	...	...	...	...	...	...	...
B Water works and supply	...	...	...	...	...	...	...	...	...	...	...	...

Peru

4.3 Cost Components of Value Added
(Continued)

New soles

	1984						1985					
	Compensation of Employees	Capital Consumption	Net Operating Surplus	Indirect Taxes	Less: Subsidies Received	Value Added	Compensation of Employees	Capital Consumption	Net Operating Surplus	Indirect Taxes	Less: Subsidies Received	Value Added
5 Construction	1055	292	3358	40	...	4745	2541	430	11031	86	...	14087
6 Wholesale and retail trade, restaurants and hotels	1888	159	10893	513	213	13240	4327	428	30437	797	426	35563
A Wholesale and retail trade	1668	87	7396	487	213	9425	3848	233	21473	732	426	25860
B Restaurants and hotels	220	72	3497	26	...	3815	479	195	8964	65	...	9703
7 Transport, storage and communication	1562	685	1798	259	38	4266	4118	2444	4959	717	55	12183
8 Finance, insurance, real estate and business services	2117	624	5019	358	...	8118	4897	1450	12270	837	-	19454
A Financial institutions	1308	88	775	55	...	2226	2872	215	2848	88	-	6023
B Insurance	74	12	-4	61	...	143	198	25	66	213	...	502
C Real estate and business services	735	524	4248	242	...	5749	1827	1210	9356	536	...	12929
Real estate, except dwellings	735	438	3546	242	...	4961	1827	1049	8044	536	...	11456
Dwellings	...	86	702	...	...	788	...	161	1312	...	...	1473
9 Community, social and personal services	1767	176	1860	126	9	3920	4302	503	5918	309	13	11019
A Sanitary and similar services	...	...	...	...	...	...	...	...	...	...	...	...
B Social and related community services	921	65	497	19	9	1493	2254	182	1443	40	12	3907
Educational services	444	18	12	6	9	471	1186	52	104	13	13	1342
Medical, dental, other health and veterinary services	477	47	485	13	...	1022	1068	130	1339	27	...	2564
C Recreational and cultural services	846	111	1363	107	...	2427	2048	321	4475	269	...	7113
D Personal and household services					...						...	
Total, Industries	14443	4132	41904	5361	618	65221	36215	10473	118455	17493	1771	180864
Producers of Government Services	6291	95	...	52	...	6438	15577	463	...	63	...	16103
Other Producers	946	26	...	2	...	975	2529	70	...	5	...	2604
Total	21681	4253	41904	5415	618	72634	54321	11006	118455	17561	1771	199571
Less: Imputed bank service charge	...	...	1624	...	...	1624	...	...	5716	...	...	5716
Import duties	...	...	...	1400	...	1400	...	...	...	4048	...	4048
Value added tax	...	...	...	...	...	...	...	...	...	...	...	...
Total b	21681	4253	40280	6815	618	72410	54321	11005	112739	21608	1771	197903

	1986						1987					
	Compensation of Employees	Capital Consumption	Net Operating Surplus	Indirect Taxes	Less: Subsidies Received	Value Added	Compensation of Employees	Capital Consumption	Net Operating Surplus	Indirect Taxes	Less: Subsidies Received	Value Added
						All Producers						
1 Agriculture, hunting, forestry and fishing	6090	1174	34649	17	...	41930	12380	1813	61887	46	...	76126
A Agriculture and hunting	5519	649	32566	8	...	38742	11236	1134	59259	22	...	71652
B Forestry and logging					...						...	
C Fishing	571	525	2083	9	...	3188	1144	679	2628	24	...	4474
2 Mining and quarrying	4545	1404	5169	836	...	11954	8186	2127	4929	517	...	15758
A Coal mining a	...	...	...	...	...	...	...	...	...	...	...	...
B Crude petroleum and natural gas production	1740	947	5112	600	...	8399	2898	1116	3560	333	...	7907
C Metal ore mining a	2805	457	57	236	...	3555	5288	1011	1369	184	...	7851
D Other mining					...						...	

4.3 Cost Components of Value Added
(Continued)

New soles

	1986						1987					
	Compensation of Employees	Capital Consumption	Net Operating Surplus	Indirect Taxes	Less: Subsidies Received	Value Added	Compensation of Employees	Capital Consumption	Net Operating Surplus	Indirect Taxes	Less: Subsidies Received	Value Added
3 Manufacturing	17258	6074	48667	20114	1431	90681	34375	9693	99318	29408	...	172795
A Manufacture of food, beverages and tobacco	3530	1572	12120	4966	314	21874	7198	3072	22827	10837	...	43934
B Textile, wearing apparel and leather industries	2643	1116	11962	322	517	15526	5463	1625	24002	-263	...	30827
C Manufacture of wood and wood products, including furniture	731	231	5687	48	12	6685	1442	378	13873	70	...	15763
D Manufacture of paper and paper products, printing and publishing	1109	397	2309	151	17	3949	2320	789	4803	283	...	8195
E Manufacture of chemicals and chemical petroleum, coal, rubber and plastic products	3564	799	2891	11780	348	18686	6756	877	2804	14150	...	24587
F Manufacture of non-metallic mineral products, except products of petroleum and coal	768	665	5115	183	22	6709	1540	847	11093	308	...	13788
G Basic metal industries	1806	703	1896	478	86	4797	3284	1109	3970	89	...	8452
H Manufacture of fabricated metal products, machinery and equipment	2805	522	8974	1592	111	13782	5724	898	13279	2773	...	22674
I Other manufacturing industries	303	69	1650	594	4	2612	649	100	2668	1161	...	4578
4 Electricity, gas and water	2641	1806	-1148	290	...	3588	5384	2440	-1907	465	...	6382
A Electricity, gas and steam	...	...	...	...	...	...	...	...	...	...	...	...
B Water works and supply	...	...	...	...	...	...	...	...	...	...	...	...
5 Construction	5836	862	21398	148	...	28244	12549	1683	43717	381	...	58329
6 Wholesale and retail trade, restaurants and hotels	9779	982	65990	1173	1441	76483	20416	2084	129187	-845	...	150842
A Wholesale and retail trade	8682	469	42257	1011	1441	50978	18082	819	72908	-1783	...	90026
B Restaurants and hotels	1097	512	23733	163	...	25505	2334	1265	56279	938	...	60816
7 Transport, storage and communication	9007	4090	6725	715	204	20333	17538	7788	13303	1514	...	40142
8 Finance, insurance, real estate and business services	10177	3227	25341	1250	33	39962	21133	6931	50047	2366	...	80478
A Financial institutions	5581	575	4845	194	33	11162	12167	1082	7804	368	...	21421
B Insurance	369	86	357	394	...	1206	788	137	527	701	...	2153
C Real estate and business services	4227	2566	20139	662	...	27594	8178	5712	41716	1297	...	56902
Real estate, except dwellings	4227	2321	18136	662	...	25346	8178	5339	38630	1297	...	53444
Dwellings	...	245	2003	...	...	2248	...	373	3086	...	...	3458
9 Community, social and personal services	9915	1097	12346	602	48	23912	23550	2736	27769	1462	...	55517
A Sanitary and similar services	...	...	...	...	...	...	...	...	...	...	...	...
B Social and related community services	5198	418	3198	71	48	8837	13114	843	8707	158	...	22822
Educational services	2696	112	136	23	48	2919	5936	281	1413	-23	...	7607
Medical, dental, other health and veterinary services	2502	306	3062	48	...	5918	7178	562	7294	181	...	15215
C Recreational and cultural services	4717	679	9148	531	...	15075	10436	1893	19062	1304	...	32695
D Personal and household services					...						...	
Total, Industries	75249	20716	219137	25144	3157	337089	155510	37294	428300	35263	...	656366
Producers of Government Services	32635	646	...	593	...	33874	74172	1192	...	1693	...	77058
Other Producers	6605	183	...	10	...	6798	12952	367	...	26	...	13345
Total	114488	21545	219137	25747	3157	377761	242634	38853	428300	36982	...	746769
Less: Imputed bank service charge	...	...	11687	...	...	11687	...	...	20430	...	...	20430
Import duties	...	...	...	7903	...	7903	...	...	...	13100	...	13100
Value added tax	...	...	...	...	...	...	...	...	...	...	...	...
Total b	114488	21545	207451	33650	3157	373976	242634	38853	407870	50082	...	739439

Peru

4.3 Cost Components of Value Added

New soles

	1988						1989					
	Compensation of Employees	Capital Consumption	Net Operating Surplus	Indirect Taxes	Less: Subsidies Received	Value Added	Compensation of Employees	Capital Consumption	Net Operating Surplus	Indirect Taxes	Less: Subsidies Received	Value Added
All Producers												
1 Agriculture, hunting, forestry and fishing	74013	17661	317481	297	...	409452	1393	397	7456	10	...	9256
A Agriculture and hunting	65720	10813	276413	99	...	353045	1233	266	6731	4	...	8234
B Forestry and logging					...						...	
C Fishing	8293	6848	41068	198	...	56407	160	131	725	6	...	1022
2 Mining and quarrying	60823	10522	35090	3849	...	110284	1846	287	940	140	...	3213
A Coal mining a	...	...	...	...	...	...	...	...	...	...	...	...
B Crude petroleum and natural gas production	34273	2957	-5038	3163	...	35355	990	70	-299	118	...	879
C Metal ore mining a	26550	7565	40128	686	...	74929	856	217	1239	22	...	2334
D Other mining					...						...	
3 Manufacturing	207613	85233	1019205	162880	...	1474931	4805	1788	19692	2803	...	29088
A Manufacture of food, beverages and tobacco	45167	27255	270538	61801	...	404761	942	572	4974	1175	...	7663
B Textile, wearing apparel and leather industries	31411	14725	186208	-538	...	231806	684	354	4191	-19	...	5210
C Manufacture of wood and wood products, including furniture	6214	3029	108846	518	...	118607	142	74	2322	11	...	2549
D Manufacture of paper and paper products, printing and publishing	11071	6711	60144	2546	...	80472	204	110	1121	40	...	1475
E Manufacture of chemicals and chemical petroleum, coal, rubber and plastic products	49965	6675	96159	63048	...	215847	1307	130	1747	963	...	4147
F Manufacture of non-metallic mineral products, except products of petroleum and coal	9621	7188	77286	2390	...	96485	188	150	1603	57	...	1998
G Basic metal industries	23727	13431	67891	4711	...	109760	686	302	1635	83	...	2706
H Manufacture of fabricated metal products, machinery and equipment	27487	5306	129620	20256	...	182669	591	82	1624	362	...	2659
I Other manufacturing industries	2950	913	22513	8148	...	34524	61	14	475	131	...	681
4 Electricity, gas and water	34555	30155	-43610	1638	...	22738	1165	306	-1124	57	...	404
A Electricity, gas and steam	...	...	...	...	...	...	...	...	...	...	...	...
B Water works and supply	...	...	...	...	...	...	...	...	...	...	...	...
5 Construction	66280	14163	363516	2291	...	446250	1282	306	7285	75	...	8948
6 Wholesale and retail trade, restaurants and hotels	117532	16398	832830	-41888	...	924873	2459	426	19374	-296	...	21963
A Wholesale and retail trade	100587	6560	564626	-42605	...	629168	2050	152	12265	-309	...	14158
B Restaurants and hotels	16945	9838	268204	717	...	295705	409	274	7109	13	...	7805
7 Transport, storage and communication	89505	67715	63774	25473	...	246467	1857	1514	1904	433	...	5708
8 Finance, insurance, real estate and business services	162719	64881	354012	16941	...	598553	3538	1324	9606	612	...	15080
A Financial institutions	93106	13194	49752	1318	...	157370	1969	99	-919	68	...	1217
B Insurance	5296	2339	-3113	5750	...	10272	123	98	122	244	...	587
C Real estate and business services	64317	49348	307373	9873	...	430911	1446	1127	10403	300	...	13276
Real estate, except dwellings	64317	45989	299133	9873	...	419312	1446	1101	10120	300	...	12967
Dwellings	...	3359	8240	...	...	11599	...	26	283	...	...	309
9 Community, social and personal services	118914	24641	190075	7401	...	341031	2791	550	6749	173	...	10263
A Sanitary and similar services	...	...	...	...	...	...	...	...	...	...	...	...
B Social and related community services	58714	6411	85381	1076	...	151582	1339	154	3732	45	...	5270
Educational services	24901	2535	32255	173	...	59864	600	68	1745	18	...	2431
Medical, dental, other health and veterinary services	33813	3876	53126	903	...	91718	739	86	1987	27	...	2839
C Recreational and cultural services	60200	18230	104694	6325	...	189449	1452	396	3017	128	...	4993
D Personal and household services					...						...	

1504

4.3 Cost Components of Value Added
(Continued)

New soles

	1988						1989					
	Compensation of Employees	Capital Consumption	Net Operating Surplus	Indirect Taxes	Less: Subsidies Received	Value Added	Compensation of Employees	Capital Consumption	Net Operating Surplus	Indirect Taxes	Less: Subsidies Received	Value Added
Total, Industries	931954	331370	3132370	178882	...	4574579	21136	6898	71882	4007	...	103923
Producers of Government Services	344461	24110	...	5753	...	374324	8570	838	...	171	...	9579
Other Producers	65706	3350	...	119	...	69175	1650	82	...	5	...	1737
Total	1342121	358830	3132373	184754	...	5018078	31356	7818	71882	4183	...	115239
Less: Imputed bank service charge	...	...	131631	...	...	131631	...	...	1339	...		1339
Import duties	...	...	...	55870	...	55870	...	...	...	1215	...	1215
Value added tax	...	...	...	...	...	...	...	...	...	...	...	...
Total b	1342121	358830	3000742	240624	...	4942317	31356	7818	70543	·5398	...	115115

	1990						1991					
	Compensation of Employees	Capital Consumption	Net Operating Surplus	Indirect Taxes	Less: Subsidies Received	Value Added	Compensation of Employees	Capital Consumption	Net Operating Surplus	Indirect Taxes	Less: Subsidies Received	Value Added
					All Producers							
1 Agriculture, hunting, forestry and fishing	77659	18385	379525	1064	...	476633	...	...	...	...	...	2323414
A Agriculture and hunting	70012	13705	354419	649	...	438785	...	...	...	...	...	2145942
B Forestry and logging					...		...	...	...	...	...	
C Fishing	7647	4680	25106	415	...	37848	...	...	...	...	...	177472
2 Mining and quarrying	89259	16391	61374	24217	...	191241	...	...	...	...	...	847738
A Coal mining a	...	...	...	...	...	...	...	...	...	...	...	...
B Crude petroleum and natural gas production	38199	5074	8601	14980	...	66854	...	...	...	...	...	399492
C Metal ore mining a	51060	11317	52773	9237	...	124387	...	...	...	...	...	448246
D Other mining					...		...	...	...	...	...	
3 Manufacturing	262136	101915	1266271	309440	...	1939762	...	...	...	...	...	8782634
A Manufacture of food, beverages and tobacco	53719	35726	402896	82161	...	574502	...	...	...	...	...	2994573
B Textile, wearing apparel and leather industries	32836	16807	223533	2008	...	275184	...	...	...	...	...	990679
C Manufacture of wood and wood products, including furniture	8026	3671	149728	473	...	161898	...	...	...	...	...	730266
D Manufacture of paper and paper products, printing and publishing	12818	8899	99262	2056	...	123035	...	...	...	...	...	470826
E Manufacture of chemicals and chemical petroleum, coal, rubber and plastic products	58806	7964	85550	175901	...	328221	...	...	...	...	...	1707085
F Manufacture of non-metallic mineral products, except products of petroleum and coal	10334	8647	99058	1363	...	119402	...	...	...	...	...	479697
G Basic metal industries	51542	14590	77550	16246	...	159928	...	...	...	...	...	661853
H Manufacture of fabricated metal products, machinery and equipment	30244	4756	95443	20401	...	150844	...	...	...	...	...	562016
I Other manufacturing industries	3811	855	33251	8831	...	46748	...	...	...	...	...	185639
4 Electricity, gas and water	66243	27711	-60589	6820	...	40185	...	...	...	...	...	201532
A Electricity, gas and steam	...	...	...	...	...	...	...	...	...	...	...	159267
B Water works and supply	...	...	...	...	...	...	...	...	...	...	...	42265
5 Construction	79685	17562	433674	2591	...	533512	...	...	...	...	...	3012457
6 Wholesale and retail trade, restaurants and hotels	121132	23804	1182552	-11767	...	1315721	...	...	...	...	...	6584540
A Wholesale and retail trade	98204	7644	727223	-12344	...	820727	...	...	...	...	...	3428236
B Restaurants and hotels	22928	16160	455329	577	...	494994	...	...	...	...	...	3156304
7 Transport, storage and communication	120965	80174	103642	33845	...	338626	...	...	...	...	...	2086148
8 Finance, insurance, real estate and business services	206131	87185	695166	30211	...	1018693	...	...	...	...	...	6179770
A Financial institutions	138260	17965	-38597	11417	...	129045	...	...	...	...	...	669446
B Insurance	8195	2604	167	9586	...	20552	...	...	...	...	...	87136
C Real estate and business services	59676	66616	733596	9208	...	869096	...	...	...	...	...	5423188
Real estate, except dwellings	59676	64875	713288	9208	...	847047	...	...	...	...	...	4892508

Peru

New soles

	1990						1991					
	Compensation of Employees	Capital Consumption	Net Operating Surplus	Indirect Taxes	Less: Subsidies Received	Value Added	Compensation of Employees	Capital Consumption	Net Operating Surplus	Indirect Taxes	Less: Subsidies Received	Value Added
Dwellings	-	1741	20308	-	...	22049	...	...	...	...	...	530680
9 Community, social and personal services	147252	31172	491832	6790	...	677046	...	...	...	...	...	3472164
A Sanitary and similar services	...	...	...	...	...	...	...	...	...	...	...	...
B Social and related community services	70608	7901	259660	1410	...	339579	...	...	...	...	...	1623092
Educational services	34095	3728	103520	754	...	142097	...	...	...	...	...	930559
Medical, dental, other health and veterinary services	36513	4173	156140	656	...	197482	...	...	...	...	...	692533
C Recreational and cultural services	76644	23271	232172	5380	...	337467	...	...	...	...	...	1849072
D Personal and household services					...						...	
Total, Industries	1170462	404299	4553447	403211	...	6531419	...	...	...	...	...	1 3490396
Producers of Government Services	435195	22031	-	11404	...	468630	...	...	...	...	...	959762
Other Producers	114286	4728	-	223	...	119237	...	...	...	...	...	598710
Total	1719943	431058	4553447	414838	...	7119286	...	...	...	...	...	1 5048868
Less: Imputed bank service charge	...	...	145452	...	...	145452	...	...	...	...	...	207578
Import duties	...	...	...	67166	...	67166	...	...	...	...	...	310417
Value added tax	...	...	...	...	...	...	...	...	...	...	...	...
Total b	1719943	431058	4407995	482004	...	7041000	...	...	...	...	...	1 5151707

a) 'Coal mining' is included in 'Other mining'.
b) Beginning 1989, the estimates are in thousand New Soles.

Philippines

General note. The preparation of national accounts statistics in the Philippines is undertaken by the National Economic and Development Authority (NEDA), Manila. The official estimates with methodological notes are published in the annual NEDA National Income Series entitled 'The National Income Accounts'. An over-all revision was completed in 1976 and a detailed description of the framework, sources and methods used in national income estimation is found in 'Manual on the Philippine System of National Accounts: Framework, Sources and Methods' published in 1978 by NEDA. The estimates are generally in accordance with the classifications and definitions recommended in the United Nations System of National Accounts (SNA). In 1961, the first input-output study was published by the Office of Statistical Coordination and Standards. The following tables have been prepared from successive replies to the United Nations national accounts questionnaire. When the scope and coverage of the estimates differ for conceptual or statistical reasons from the definitions and classifications recommended in SNA, a footnote is indicated to the relevant tables.

Sources and methods :

(a) Gross domestic product. Gross domestic product is estimated mainly through the production approach.

(b) Expenditure on the gross domestic product. The expenditure approach is used to estimate all components of GDP by expenditure type except capital formation in machinery and equipment for which the commodity-flow approach is used. The commodity-flow approach and income-elasticity approach are also used for private consumption expenditure. Estimates of government consumption expenditure are taken from the Commission on Audit reports for national and local government and for the social security system from the Budget Commission and the two offices administering it. For personal consumption of goods, for which the statistics are available in quantity terms, the value of final consumption is obtained by multiplying consumption quantities by the appropriate retail prices. Consumption expenditure on each broad expenditure group is estimated by using the commodity-flow method. Since the required data lag by at least a year, preliminary estimates are computed by using the income-elasticity approach. Bench-mark information on the levels and patterns of household expenditure are available from the family income and expenditure surveys for 1961, 1965 and 1971. Current data on supply are derived from production figures available from various sources such as censuses, surveys and concerned companies. The sources of data for increase in stocks include the integrated agricultural surveys and establishment surveys and censuses. For gross fixed capital formation, the net supply of durable equipment for domestic use is divided between consumption and capital formation by means of allocation ratios for each type of equipment. The 1969 survey of importers of durable equipment provided bench-mark data on importer-dealer ratios as well as trade and transport mark-up ratios. The ratios are updated by using the results of the annual trade establishments surveys. The primary sources of data for exports and imports of goods and services are the foreign trade statistics and the balance of payments. For the constant price estimates, wages and salaries of the government sector are extrapolated by an index of employment of government services. All the other components of GDP by expenditure type are deflated by appropriate price indexes.

(c) Cost-structure of the gross domestic product. Estimates of compensation of employees, operating surplus and depreciation are available from the annual surveys of establishments and reports of financial institutions and public utilities for the

non-agricultural sectors and from studies on production costs for the agricultural sector. For depreciation, a global estimate for all sectors is derived by estimating the cost of replacement of existing stock by the use of the perpetual inventory method. The global estimate is then allocated to each sector, using a sectoral structure based on the reported levels of depreciation. The estimates of indirect taxes and subsidies are made on the basis of reports of the Commission on Audit, the Bureau of Internal Revenue, the Bureau of Customs, the Central Bank and other government agencies.

(d) Gross domestic product by kind of economic activity. The table of GDP by kind of economic activity is prepared at market prices, i.e., producers' values. The production approach is used to estimate value added of most industries. The income approach is used for producers of government services and a large part of private services. The expenditure approach is also used for construction. The sources used for the estimation of the agricultural sector are the 1971 census of agriculture, the integrated agricultural surveys which are conducted five times a year, the family income and expenditure surveys and data collected through administrative agencies and producers' associations. The value of agricultural and livestock production is obtained by multiplying the volume of output by the average prices received by the farmers. The cost ratios are obtained from cost-of-production studies and from the 1969 input-output tables. For fishery, the sources are the monthly reports from the operators and sustenance estimates based on growth-rates in selected municipalities. Estimates for mining are based on the annual reports from the Bureau of Mines, the surveys of establishments, the 1972 economic census and the financial statements of mining firms. For the organized sector of manufacturing, the sources of data include the economic census and the survey of establishments. For 5 out of 20 major industry groups, the commodity-flow approach is used, taking the supply and disposition ratios from the 1969 input-output tables. Basic data for electricity, gas and water are collected from concerned companies, government agencies and the surveys of establishments. Gross output of private construction is estimated on the basis of building construction statistics and building permits issued. Data for public construction are obtained from the annual report of the Commission on Audit and from quarterly questionnaires. Bench-mark estimates for trade are taken from the 1972 economic census. These are extrapolated by using the results of the surveys of trade establishments. An undercoverage allowance is made for trade activities not covered using employment data from the labour force survey and an estimate of value added per worker. The main sources of data for the transport sector are the 1972 economic census, the surveys of establishments and the financial reports of the concerned companies. Data for the financial sector are derived from financial statements compiled by the Central Bank. Bench-mark estimates for the real estate sector are based on the results of the economic census and are extrapolated by the growth rates of real estate sales and mortgages. For the producers of government services, data are obtained from the annual report of the Commission on Audit. Bench-mark estimates for the private services are based on the economic census and are extrapolated by using appropriate price indexes for other years. For the domestic services, the value added is taken as the product of the number of persons employed and an estimate of value added per worker. For the constant price estimates, the value added of the agricultural and mining sectors are obtained by applying the base-year unit values to the volume of production. For the manufacturing, transport, financial and services sectors, value added is deflated by appropriate price indexes. Double deflation is used for electricity, gas and water, construction and trade.

1.1 Expenditure on the Gross Domestic Product, in Current Prices

Million Philippine pesos

	1980	1981	1982	1983	1984	1985	1986	1987	1988	1989	1990	1991
1 Government final consumption expenditure	22099	24661	28929	30552	36880	43520	48431	57333	72183	85376	108843	127053
2 Private final consumption expenditure	156824	181546	208104	237479	362257	420832	444529	482330	558765	649276	767061	916367
3 Gross capital formation	70898	77334	88414	109227	114303	87697	97441	123186	147515	202113	241333	246761
A Increase in stocks	4548	-813	1089	-940	-14284	-12121	-4933	6813	4331	8932	7084	2117
B Gross fixed capital formation	66350	78147	87325	110167	128587	99818	102374	116373	143184	193181	234249	244644
Residential buildings	16843	17952	20711	25696	26537	20951	20524	31188	32637	41798	38708	...
Non-residential buildings a	20216	27684	29238	40511	55931	35543	32786	30718	39038	55464	74382	114355
Other construction and land improvement etc.	216	342	406	491	480	398	823	1137	1509	1675	1829	...
Other b	29075	32169	36970	43469	45639	42926	48241	53330	70000	94244	119330	130289
4 Exports of goods and services	57458	67094	64526	79813	126682	137030	160187	182179	226431	263880	299211	373286
5 Less: Imports of goods and services	69398	76514	82897	103641	131504	125205	136235	179030	215292	280118	358548	391856
Statistical discrepancy	5868	7475	10101	15647	15863	8009	-5466	19070	12917	4634	13000	-27574
Equals: Gross Domestic Product	243749	281596	317177	369077	524481	571883	608887	685068	802519	925161	1070900	1244037

a) Beginning 1980, item 'Non-residential buildings' includes all government construction.
b) Item 'Other' includes also land improvement, plantation and orchard development.

1.2 Expenditure on the Gross Domestic Product, in Constant Prices

Million Philippine pesos

	1980	1981	1982	1983	1984	1985	1986	1987	1988	1989	1990	1991
	At constant prices of:1985											
1 Government final consumption expenditure	50177	48675	52328	49854	43971	43520	43669	45792	49943	52755	57042	57432
2 Private final consumption expenditure	397404	407958	422067	424634	425767	420832	434815	452386	480562	504619	531772	543637
3 Gross capital formation	161070	165659	179574	190243	127564	87697	94925	111588	124504	153887	162645	139855
A Increase in stocks	10354	-3369	1942	-1567	-17063	-12121	-4782	6458	5452	7689	5611	1110
B Gross fixed capital formation	150716	169028	177632	191810	144627	99818	99707	105130	119052	146198	157034	138745

Philippines

1.2 Expenditure on the Gross Domestic Product, in Constant Prices
(Continued)

Million Philippine pesos

	1980	1981	1982	1983	1984	1985	1986	1987	1988	1989	1990	1991
At constant prices of:1985												
Residential buildings	35030	34825	37515	41852	28911	20951	20004	27197	26147	28645	23786	...
Non-residential buildings a	44179	55528	54536	67908	60982	35543	31556	26964	31780	39771	44026	57575
Other construction and land improvement etc.	548	768	827	909	591	398	817	1087	1327	1348	1301	...
Other b	70959	77907	84754	81141	54143	42926	47330	49882	59798	76434	87921	81170
4 Exports of goods and services	154748	164698	151489	158252	164327	137030	160453	170889	195997	216980	219703	234152
5 Less: Imports of goods and services	179477	178057	182414	176841	145934	125205	138021	177532	212357	244590	269148	264889
Statistical discrepancy	25846	21709	30423	19575	1267	8009	-4418	16584	19814	14731	15241	2402
Equals: Gross Domestic Product	609768	630642	653467	665717	616962	571883	591423	619707	658463	698382	717255	712589

a) Beginning 1980, item 'Non-residential buildings' includes all government construction.
b) Item 'Other' includes also land improvement, plantation and orchard development.

1.3 Cost Components of the Gross Domestic Product

Million Philippine pesos

	1980	1981	1982	1983	1984	1985	1986	1987	1988	1989	1990	1991
1 Indirect taxes, net	20132	21634	24554	29520	38366	40856	43488	59625	56736	76497	87885	114227
A Indirect taxes	20739	22169	25119	30102	38691	41793	45778	61913	59454	82705	101185	122473
B Less: Subsidies	607	535	565	582	325	937	2290	2288	2718	6208	13300	8246
2 Consumption of fixed capital	17113	19997	22743	29080	48374	56674	60017	63966	67162	72001	82249	101782
3 Compensation of employees paid by resident producers to:	77013	90077	101392	112341	152182	172864	188078	215541	278874	324386	363078	427035
A Resident households	76945	90006	101323	112267	152162	172845	187955	215479	278664	324299	362956	426787
B Rest of the world	68	71	69	74	20	19	123	62	210	87	122	248
4 Operating surplus	129491	149888	168488	198136	285559	301489	317304	345936	399747	452977	537688	600993
A Corporate and quasi-corporate enterprises a	26717	27904	28477	33646	50170	22906	31712	56564	84061	99449	119207	127309
B Private unincorporated enterprises a	102897	122124	140068	164518	235357	278831	285712	289662	316239	354238	419090	474479
C General government	-123	-140	-57	-28	32	-248	-120	-290	-553	-710	-609	-795
Equals: Gross Domestic Product	243749	281596	317177	369077	524481	571883	608887	685068	802519	925161	1070900	1244037

a) Beginning 1980, corporate and quasi-enterprises refer to public and private corporations and private unincorporated enterprises refers to households and unincorporated enterprises.

1.4 General Government Current Receipts and Disbursements

Million Philippine pesos

	1980	1981	1982	1983	1984	1985	1986	1987	1988	1989	1990	1991
Receipts												
1 Operating surplus	-123	-140	-57	-28	32	-248	-120	-290	-553	-710	-609	-795
2 Property and entrepreneurial income	5044	6326	5867	6638	7729	10563	9434	13123	22786	32647	25575	41114
3 Taxes, fees and contributions	33611	36529	41173	46989	60408	69156	75051	96432	101104	138558	177333	214802
A Indirect taxes	20739	22169	25119	30102	38691	41793	45778	61913	59454	82705	101185	122473
B Direct taxes	8414	9255	10144	10669	15069	19717	20778	24844	29743	40880	54507	67158
C Social security contributions	3266	3678	3970	4235	4249	4585	4805	6218	8681	10462	14667	17770
D Compulsory fees, fines and penalties	1192	1427	1940	1983	2399	3061	3690	3457	3226	4511	6974	7401
4 Other current transfers	387	461	496	676	593	886	1091	2300	5236	3940	6438	6226
Total Current Receipts of General Government	38919	43176	47479	54275	68762	80357	85456	111565	128573	174435	208737	261347
Disbursements												
1 Government final consumption expenditure	22099	24661	28929	30552	36880	43520	48431	57333	72183	85376	108843	127053
A Compensation of employees	11362	13906	15878	16969	21402	26219	30925	36963	48638	58120	73661	86009
B Consumption of fixed capital	625	704	820	1010	1442	1658	1777	1833	1929	2142	2767	3026
C Purchases of goods and services, net	10101	10039	12208	12554	14015	15616	15711	18534	21612	25104	31812	37173
D Less: Own account fixed capital formation	...	...	...	...	...	...	...	...	...	...	...	...
E Indirect taxes paid, net	11	12	23	19	21	27	18	3	4	10	603	845
2 Property income	1104	918	1265	2745	5736	10275	12915	18769	23655	34714	47840	43550
A Interest	1104	918	1265	2745	5736	10275	12915	18769	23655	34714	47840	43550
B Net land rent and royalties	...	...	...	...	...	...	...	...	...	...	...	...

1.4 General Government Current Receipts and Disbursements
(Continued)

Million Philippine pesos

	1980	1981	1982	1983	1984	1985	1986	1987	1988	1989	1990	1991
3 Subsidies	607	535	565	582	325	937	2290	2288	2718	6208	13300	8246
4 Other current transfers	3645	4341	4978	5512	8428	9121	13476	13039	18358	19108	28718	32991
A Social security benefits	1411	1633	2025	2344	2714	3176	3439	4595	6059	6876	9294	12981
B Social assistance grants	303	521	211	469	511	711	924	1943	364	1517	1592	954
C Other	1931	2187	2742	2699	5203	5234	9113	6501	11935	10715	17832	19056
5 Net saving	11464	12721	11742	14884	17393	16504	8344	20136	11659	29029	10036	49507
Total Current Disbursements and Net Saving of General Government	38919	43176	47479	54275	68762	80357	85456	111565	128573	174435	208737	261347

1.5 Current Income and Outlay of Corporate and Quasi-Corporate Enterprises, Summary

Million Philippine pesos

	1980	1981	1982	1983	1984	1985	1986	1987	1988	1989	1990	1991
					Receipts							
1 Operating surplus	26717	27904	28477	33646	50170	22906	31712	56564	84061	99449	119207	127309
2 Property and entrepreneurial income received	2438	3857	5344	5750	10968	25021	15222	11893	15589	17235	21073	28675
3 Current transfers	1791	1867	2002	2206	2624	2822	2602	2848	3598	4308	5931	6424
Total Current Receipts a	30946	33628	35823	41602	63762	50749	49536	71305	103248	120992	146211	162408
					Disbursements							
1 Property and entrepreneurial income	21886	31457	37700	47442	67844	80629	63094	71553	75118	96180	105426	128921
2 Direct taxes and other current payments to general government	3217	3240	4599	3077	6200	8058	8817	13037	14918	15751	20740	27419
3 Other current transfers	1930	1906	2096	2336	3940	3577	4306	3008	3947	4669	9906	9387
4 Net saving	3913	-2975	-8572	-11253	-14222	-41515	-26681	-16293	9265	4392	10139	-3319
Total Current Disbursements and Net Saving a	30946	33628	35823	41602	63762	50749	49536	71305	103248	120992	146211	162408

a) Beginning 1980, corporate and quasi-enterprises refer to public and private corporations and private unincorporated enterprises refers to households and unincorporated enterprises.

1.6 Current Income and Outlay of Households and Non-Profit Institutions

Million Philippine pesos

	1980	1981	1982	1983	1984	1985	1986	1987	1988	1989	1990	1991
					Receipts							
1 Compensation of employees	81671	96444	111183	124692	165606	190900	208219	239278	304941	355444	404301	484431
A From resident producers	76945	90006	101323	112267	152162	172845	187955	215479	278664	324299	362956	426787
B From rest of the world	4726	6438	9860	12425	13444	18055	20264	23799	26277	31145	41345	57644
2 Operating surplus of private unincorporated enterprises	102897	122124	140068	164518	235357	278831	285712	289662	316239	354238	419090	474479
3 Property and entrepreneurial income	12867	18616	18387	24292	31447	28977	23783	34912	33486	47947	86712	80287
4 Current transfers	5936	6742	6989	8808	11714	12486	16248	18625	24157	27616	30913	39645
A Social security benefits	1411	1633	2025	2344	2714	3176	3439	4595	6059	6876	9294	12981
B Social assistance grants	4364	4938	4762	6216	8696	8958	12381	13594	17577	20186	20980	26070
C Other	161	171	202	248	304	352	428	436	521	554	639	594
Total Current Receipts	203371	243926	276627	322310	444124	511194	533962	582477	678823	785245	941016	1078842
					Disbursements							
1 Private final consumption expenditure	156824	181546	208104	237479	362257	420832	444529	482330	558765	649276	767061	916367
2 Property income a	2496	3844	4057	4653	5984	7502	5182	5281	6515	10011	16007	17384
3 Direct taxes and other current transfers n.e.c. to general government	9655	11120	11455	13810	15517	19305	20456	21482	26732	40102	55408	64910
A Social security contributions	3266	3678	3970	4235	4249	4585	4805	6218	8681	10462	14667	17770
B Direct taxes	5197	6015	5545	7592	8869	11659	11961	11807	14825	25129	33767	39739
C Fees, fines and penalties	1192	1427	1940	1983	2399	3061	3690	3457	3226	4511	6974	7401
4 Other current transfers	567	619	649	926	853	1273	1291	1519	4288	3195	2973	3305
5 Net saving	33829	46797	52362	65442	59513	62282	62504	71865	82523	82661	99567	76876
Total Current Disbursements and Net Saving	203371	243926	276627	322310	444124	511194	533962	582477	678823	785245	941016	1078842

a) Interest payment and public and consumer debts are treated as property income/payments.

Philippines

1.7 External Transactions on Current Account, Summary

Million Philippine pesos

	1980	1981	1982	1983	1984	1985	1986	1987	1988	1989	1990	1991
Payments to the Rest of the World												
1 Imports of goods and services	69398	76514	82897	103641	131504	125205	136235	179030	215292	280118	358548	391856
A Imports of merchandise c.i.f.	61087	65896	69932	87515	105817	98550	106345	142898	175129	237450	311040	348295
B Other	8311	10618	12965	16126	25687	26655	29890	36132	40163	42668	47508	43561
2 Factor income to the rest of the world	7757	11612	16627	22244	34979	40535	37656	41903	39874	50256	45536	52454
A Compensation of employees	68	71	69	74	20	19	123	62	210	87	122	248
B Property and entrepreneurial income	7689	11541	16558	22170	34959	40516	37533	41841	39664	50169	45414	52206
3 Current transfers to the rest of the world	1392	1608	2477	2419	4829	4970	8153	5608	10268	9155	15773	16388
4 Surplus of the nation on current transactions	-10447	-8269	-20240	-26721	-19108	-1761	12209	-2582	10177	-18664	-52342	5659
Payments to the Rest of the World and Surplus of the Nation on Current Transactions	68100	81465	81761	101583	152204	168949	194253	223959	275611	320865	367515	466357
Receipts From The Rest of the World												
1 Exports of goods and services	57458	67094	64526	79813	126682	137030	160187	182179	226431	263880	299211	373286
A Exports of merchandise f.o.b.	43449	48198	44526	56453	90883	88020	101148	121557	152637	174098	199458	249344
B Other	14009	18896	20000	23360	35799	49010	59039	60622	73794	89782	99753	123942
2 Factor income from rest of the world	7278	10559	12994	16435	18983	24726	25045	29965	32514	38938	50846	70071
A Compensation of employees	4726	6438	9860	12425	13444	18055	20264	23799	26277	31145	41345	57644
B Property and entrepreneurial income	2552	4121	3134	4010	5539	6671	4781	6166	6237	7793	9501	12427
3 Current transfers from rest of the world	3364	3812	4241	5335	6539	7193	9021	11815	16666	18047	17458	23000
Receipts from the Rest of the World on Current Transactions	68100	81465	81761	101583	152204	168949	194253	223959	275611	320865	367515	466357

1.8 Capital Transactions of The Nation, Summary

Million Philippine pesos

	1980	1981	1982	1983	1984	1985	1986	1987	1988	1989	1990	1991
Finance of Gross Capital Formation												
Gross saving	66319	76540	78275	98153	111058	93945	104184	139674	170609	188083	201991	224846
1 Consumption of fixed capital	17113	19997	22743	29080	48374	56674	60017	63966	67162	72001	82249	101782
A General government	625	704	820	1010	1442	1658	1777	1833	1929	2142	2767	3026
B Corporate and quasi-corporate enterprises	11025	12741	16599	20928	29709	23815	25127	26936	32423	38638	50587	60470
Public	1507	1444	2087	2621	5050	6381	8462	9531	11804	12327	15652	17416
Private	9518	11297	14512	18307	24659	17434	16665	17405	20619	26311	34935	43054
C Other	5463	6552	5324	7142	17223	31201	33113	35197	32810	31221	28895	38286
2 Net saving	49206	56543	55532	69073	62684	37271	44167	75708	103447	116082	119742	123064
A General government	11464	12721	11742	14884	17393	16504	8344	20136	11659	29029	10036	49507
B Corporate and quasi-corporate enterprises	3913	-2975	-8572	-11253	-14222	-41515	-26681	-16293	9265	4392	10139	-3319
Public	3551	2940	645	-27	-7451	-13143	-17560	-11762	-6360	-1692	-764	-17409
Private	362	-5915	-9217	-11226	-6771	-28372	-9121	-4531	15625	6084	10903	14090
C Other	33829	46797	52362	65442	59513	62282	62504	71865	82523	82661	99567	76876
Less: Surplus of the nation on current transactions	-10447	-8269	-20240	-26721	-19108	-1761	12209	-2582	10177	-18664	-52342	5659
Statistical discrepancy	-5868	-7475	-10101	-15647	-15863	-8009	5466	-19070	-12917	-4634	-13000	27574
Finance of Gross Capital Formation	70898	77334	88414	109227	114303	87697	97441	123186	147515	202113	241333	246761
Gross Capital Formation												
Increase in stocks	4548	-813	1089	-940	-14284	-12121	-4933	6813	4331	8932	7084	2117
Gross fixed capital formation	66350	78147	87325	110167	128587	99818	102374	116373	143184	193181	234249	244644
Gross Capital Formation	70898	77334	88414	109227	114303	87697	97441	123186	147515	202113	241333	246761

1.10 Gross Domestic Product by Kind of Activity, in Current Prices

Million Philippine pesos

	1980	1981	1982	1983	1984	1985	1986	1987	1988	1989	1990	1991
1 Agriculture, hunting, forestry and fishing	61219	70092	74055	82545	129824	140554	145807	163927	183515	210009	235956	263201
2 Mining and quarrying	5460	5173	4882	6182	8142	11893	14144	14354	15275	15446	16659	17504
3 Manufacturing	62654	71829	79608	89472	129171	143851	149958	169627	206728	233192	267485	315938
4 Electricity, gas and water	3806	4945	6577	8955	12779	15767	16642	16313	20120	21748	24299	30625
5 Construction	22625	28362	32087	40192	48727	29037	29784	37104	42814	57281	64903	62083
6 Wholesale and retail trade, restaurants and hotels	32175	36483	43531	51899	77031	89960	96011	106235	124646	142159	160594	189508
7 Transport, storage and communication	11319	13268	14680	17848	28117	31666	34307	36827	40762	43840	54345	73909
8 Finance, insurance, real estate and business services	24435	26311	32165	37984	46594	54733	60141	68069	79079	95623	114709	134862
9 Community, social and personal services	7185	9394	11713	14629	19880	24880	27709	31981	37002	43437	52605	63756
Total, Industries	230878	265857	299298	349706	500265	542341	574503	644437	749941	862735	991555	1151386
Producers of Government Services	11998	14622	16721	17998	22865	27904	32720	38799	50571	60272	77031	89880
Other Producers	873	1117	1158	1373	1351	1638	1664	1832	2007	2154	2314	2771
Subtotal	243749	281596	317177	369077	524481	571883	608887	685068	802519	925161	1070900	1244037
Less: Imputed bank service charge	...	...	...	...	...	...	...	...	...	...	...	...
Plus: Import duties	...	...	...	...	...	...	...	...	...	...	...	...
Plus: Value added tax	...	...	...	...	...	...	...	...	...	...	...	...
Equals: Gross Domestic Product	243749	281596	317177	369077	524481	571883	608887	685068	802519	925161	1070900	1244037

1.11 Gross Domestic Product by Kind of Activity, in Constant Prices

Million Philippine pesos

	1980	1981	1982	1983	1984	1985	1986	1987	1988	1989	1990	1991
					At constant prices of:1985							
1 Agriculture, hunting, forestry and fishing	143295	148479	149641	144586	143247	140554	145725	150414	155292	159964	160734	162193
2 Mining and quarrying	9128	9350	9165	9244	8959	11893	12313	11232	11704	11389	11091	10770
3 Manufacturing	168292	171569	174315	173756	156195	143851	146453	154604	167681	178396	183925	183111
4 Electricity, gas and water	12389	14205	17367	15783	16857	15767	17851	18595	19880	20412	20423	20609
5 Construction	57250	63421	64110	70204	56027	29037	28547	31742	33235	41384	42639	35700
6 Wholesale and retail trade, restaurants and hotels	85273	86163	93547	98325	91041	89960	94037	97705	102845	107833	109857	111211
7 Transport, storage and communication	29175	30629	31415	32622	32060	31666	33075	35086	37898	40243	41217	41407
8 Finance, insurance, real estate and business services	61772	58937	63402	67701	58885	54733	57285	61476	65918	71765	75766	75139
9 Community, social and personal services	15770	18454	20081	23222	24184	24880	25852	27438	29875	31659	33260	33208
Total, Industries	582344	601207	623043	635443	587455	542341	561138	588292	624328	663045	678912	673348
Producers of Government Services	25350	27122	28191	27844	27779	27904	28700	29712	32322	33459	36405	37293
Other Producers	2074	2313	2233	2430	1728	1638	1585	1703	1813	1878	1938	1948
Subtotal	609768	630642	653467	665717	616962	571883	591423	619707	658463	698382	717255	712589
Less: Imputed bank service charge	...	...	...	...	...	...	...	...	...	...	...	...
Plus: Import duties	...	...	...	...	...	...	...	...	...	...	...	...
Plus: Value added tax	...	...	...	...	...	...	...	...	...	...	...	...
Equals: Gross Domestic Product	609768	630642	653467	665717	616962	571883	591423	619707	658463	698382	717255	712589

1.12 Relations Among National Accounting Aggregates

Million Philippine pesos

	1980	1981	1982	1983	1984	1985	1986	1987	1988	1989	1990	1991
Gross Domestic Product	243749	281596	317177	369077	524481	571883	608887	685068	802519	925161	1070900	1244037
Plus: Net factor income from the rest of the world	-479	-1053	-3633	-5809	-15996	-15809	-12611	-11938	-7360	-11318	5310	17617
Factor income from the rest of the world	7278	10559	12994	16435	18983	24726	25045	29965	32514	38938	50846	70071
Less: Factor income to the rest of the world	7757	11612	16627	22244	34979	40535	37656	41903	39874	50256	45536	52454
Equals: Gross National Product	243270	280543	313544	363268	508485	556074	596276	673130	795159	913843	1076210	1261654
Less: Consumption of fixed capital	17113	19997	22743	29080	48374	56674	60017	63966	67162	72001	82249	101782

Philippines

1.12 Relations Among National Accounting Aggregates
(Continued)

Million Philippine pesos

	1980	1981	1982	1983	1984	1985	1986	1987	1988	1989	1990	1991
Equals: National Income	226157	260546	290801	334188	460111	499400	536259	609164	727997	841842	993961	1159872
Plus: Net current transfers from the rest of the world	1972	2204	1764	2916	1710	2223	868	6207	6398	8892	1685	6612
Current transfers from the rest of the world	3364	3812	4241	5335	6539	7193	9021	11815	16666	18047	17458	23000
Less: Current transfers to the rest of the world	1392	1608	2477	2419	4829	4970	8153	5608	10268	9155	15773	16388
Equals: National Disposable Income	228129	262750	292565	337104	461821	501623	537127	615371	734395	850734	995646	1166484
Less: Final consumption	178923	206207	237033	268031	399137	464352	492960	539663	630948	734652	875904	1043420
Equals: Net Saving	49206	56543	55532	69073	62684	37271	44167	75708	103447	116082	119742	123064
Less: Surplus of the nation on current transactions	-10447	-8269	-20240	-26721	-19108	-1761	12209	-2582	10177	-18664	-52342	5659
Statistical discrepancy	-5868	-7475	-10101	-15647	-15863	-8009	5466	-19070	-12917	-4634	-13000	27574
Equals: Net Capital Formation	53785	57337	65671	80147	65929	31023	37424	59220	80353	130112	159084	144979

2.5 Private Final Consumption Expenditure by Type and Purpose, in Current Prices

Million Philippine pesos

	1980	1981	1982	1983	1984	1985	1986	1987	1988	1989	1990	1991
Final Consumption Expenditure of Resident Households												
1 Food, beverages and tobacco	94090	109241	123566	140326	215748	249171	260590	281789	330349	390134	457105	532448
A Food	86141	99826	112450	128032	197115	226618	235584	253427	297830	354210	416276	483872
B Non-alcoholic beverages	3603	4272	4907	5402	7864	9632	10628	11582	13378	14930	17470	21145
C Alcoholic beverages												
D Tobacco	4346	5143	6209	6892	10769	12921	14378	16780	19141	20994	23359	27431
2 Clothing and footwear	5879	6711	7604	8845	13006	16113	17292	18860	21811	24590	28049	33488
3 Gross rent, fuel and power	4730	5850	6774	8162	12311	15448	15730	17409	20582	23051	30195	38880
A Fuel and power	19702	23682	10315	12209	17947	21461	20902	23627	26134	28561	...	...
B Other	...	...	...	...	...	...	...	...	...	...	...	...
4 Furniture, furnishings and household equipment and operation	20590	23508	27699	31264	46957	56015	60126	65362	74277	85470	100121	120798
A Household operation	15394	17753	21410	24429	37055	44290	47683	51906	58773	67604	79298	96262
B Other	5196	5755	6289	6835	9902	11725	12443	13456	15504	17866	20823	24536
5 Medical care and health expenses	...	...	...	...	...	...	...	...	...	...	...	...
6 Transport and communication	7020	8398	9851	11657	18377	20484	20778	22269	25191	26085	34281	48969
7 Recreational, entertainment, education and cultural services	...	...	...	...	...	...	...	...	...	...	...	...
8 Miscellaneous goods and services	24515	27838	32610	37225	55858	63601	70013	76641	86555	99946	117310	141784
Total Final Consumption Expenditure in the Domestic Market by Households, of which	156824	181546	208104	237479	362257	420832	444529	482330	558765	649276	767061	916367
Plus: Direct purchases abroad by resident households	...	...	...	...	...	...	...	...	...	...	...	...
Less: Direct purchases in the domestic market by non-resident households	...	...	...	...	...	...	...	...	...	...	...	...
Equals: Final Consumption Expenditure of Resident Households a	156824	181546	208104	237479	362257	420832	444529	482330	558765	649276	767061	916367
Final Consumption Expenditure of Private Non-profit Institutions Serving Households												
Equals: Final Consumption Expenditure of Private Non-profit Organisations Serving Households	...	...	...	...	...	...	...	...	...	...	...	...
Private Final Consumption Expenditure	156824	181546	208104	237479	362257	420832	444529	482330	558765	649276	767061	916367

a) Item 'Final consumption expenditure of resident households' includes consumption expenditure of private non-profit institutions serving households.

2.6 Private Final Consumption Expenditure by Type and Purpose, in Constant Prices

Million Philippine pesos

	1980	1981	1982	1983	1984	1985	1986	1987	1988	1989	1990	1991
At constant prices of:1985												
Final Consumption Expenditure of Resident Households												
1 Food, beverages and tobacco	235770	242161	250225	252066	252754	249171	258514	267655	283005	296752	315019	323137
A Food	215192	220658	228034	229828	230701	226618	234865	243179	256729	269115	286530	294332
B Non-alcoholic beverages	8895	9287	9622	9428	9471	9632	10123	10597	11355	11922	12554	12734
C Alcoholic beverages												

2.6 Private Final Consumption Expenditure by Type and Purpose, in Constant Prices
(Continued)

Million Philippine pesos

	1980	1981	1982	1983	1984	1985	1986	1987	1988	1989	1990	1991
					At constant prices of:1985							
D Tobacco	11683	12216	12569	12810	12582	12921	13526	13879	14921	15715	15935	16071
2 Clothing and footwear	15805	16054	16563	16748	16329	16113	16563	17528	19149	20172	21097	21590
3 Gross rent, fuel and power	14920	15154	15466	15879	15408	15448	16019	17357	19406	20769	21774	22341
4 Furniture, furnishings and household equipment and operation	51418	52686	54092	54411	55444	56015	57149	58897	62336	66493	69648	71053
A Household operation	39724	40737	41857	42378	43528	44290	45046	46165	48473	51688	53932	55115
B Other	11694	11949	12235	12033	11916	11725	12103	12732	13863	14805	15716	15938
5 Medical care and health expenses	...	...	...	...	...	...	...	...	...	...	...	...
6 Transport and communication	18720	19722	20653	21080	20802	20484	21137	22336	24990	26087	26956	27297
7 Recreational, entertainment, education and cultural services	...	...	...	...	...	...	...	...	...	...	...	...
8 Miscellaneous goods and services	60771	62181	65068	64450	65030	63601	65433	68613	71676	74346	77278	78219
Total Final Consumption Expenditure in the Domestic Market by Households, of which	397404	407958	422067	424634	425767	420832	434815	452386	480562	504619	531772	543637
Plus: Direct purchases abroad by resident households	...	...	...	...	...	...	...	...	...	...	...	...
Less: Direct purchases in the domestic market by non-resident households	...	...	...	...	...	...	...	...	...	...	...	...
Equals: Final Consumption Expenditure of Resident Households a	397404	407958	422067	424634	425767	420832	434815	452386	480562	504619	531772	543637
Final Consumption Expenditure of Private Non-profit Institutions Serving Households												
Equals: Final Consumption Expenditure of Private Non-profit Organisations Serving Households	...	...	...	...	...	...	...	...	...	...	...	...
Private Final Consumption Expenditure	397404	407958	422067	424634	425767	420832	434815	452386	480562	504619	531772	543637

a) Item 'Final consumption expenditure of resident households' includes consumption expenditure of private non-profit institutions serving households.

2.17 Exports and Imports of Goods and Services, Detail

Million Philippine pesos

	1980	1981	1982	1983	1984	1985	1986	1987	1988	1989	1990	1991
					Exports of Goods and Services							
1 Exports of merchandise, f.o.b.	43449	48198	44526	56453	90883	88020	101148	121557	152637	174098	199458	249344
2 Transport and communication	2387	2819	2599	2936	3662	4991	4796	4712	6194	7902	8994	9816
A In respect of merchandise imports	873	933	1160	1472	1152	1271	1545	1233	1520	2748	2997	2954
B Other	1514	1886	1439	1464	2510	3720	3251	3479	4674	5154	5997	6862
3 Insurance service charges	90	72	82	99	104	127	148	163	260	290	371	571
A In respect of merchandise imports	8	8	14	11	9	15	27	19	13	66	94	73
B Other	82	64	68	88	95	112	121	144	247	224	277	498
4 Other commodities	5152	7642	7625	9756	14921	21364	26809	25139	29394	40733	52574	68833
5 Adjustments of merchandise exports to change-of-ownership basis	...	...	...	...	...	...	...	...	...	...	...	...
6 Direct purchases in the domestic market by non-residential households	4634	6461	7363	8401	13741	16767	18579	23643	29943	28257	31391	36814
7 Direct purchases in the domestic market by extraterritorial bodies	1746	1902	2331	2168	3371	5761	8707	6965	8003	7063	6423	7908
Total Exports of Goods and Services	57458	67094	64526	79813	126682	137030	160187	182179	226431	263880	299211	373286
					Imports of Goods and Services							
1 Imports of merchandise, c.i.f.	61087	65896	69932	87515	105817	98550	106345	142898	175129	237450	311040	348295
A Imports of merchandise, f.o.b.	57063	61929	64849	81183	99943	92627	98762	134167	167366	226995	290701	321243
B Transport of services on merchandise imports	3945	3852	4908	6223	5623	5836	7471	8556	7608	10149	19729	26240
By residents	873	933	1160	1472	1152	1271	1545	1233	1520	2748	2997	2954
By non-residents	3072	2919	3748	4751	4471	4565	5926	7323	6088	7401	16732	23286
C Insurance service charges on merchandise imports	79	115	175	109	251	87	112	175	155	306	610	812
By residents	8	8	14	11	9	15	27	19	13	66	94	73

Philippines

2.17 Exports and Imports of Goods and Services, Detail
(Continued)

Million Philippine pesos

	1980	1981	1982	1983	1984	1985	1986	1987	1988	1989	1990	1991
By non-residents	71	107	161	98	242	72	85	156	142	240	516	739
2 Adjustments of merchandise imports to change-of-ownership basis	...	...	...	...	...	...	...	...	...	...	...	...
3 Other transport and communication	1454	1980	1891	1747	1533	715	1062	2262	3456	3414	4394	7745
4 Other insurance service charges	151	159	189	249	380	394	265	494	497	519	561	665
5 Other commodities	3235	4712	6263	6771	9304	8104	7150	9276	9793	11323	14047	17272
6 Direct purchases abroad by government	916	868	920	1521	714	414	427	629	146	614	989	586
7 Direct purchases abroad by resident households	2555	2899	3702	5838	13756	17028	20986	23471	26271	26798	27517	17293
Total Imports of Goods and Services	69398	76514	82897	103641	131504	125205	136235	179030	215292	280118	358548	391856
Balance of Goods and Services	-11940	-9420	-18371	-23828	-4822	11825	23952	3149	11139	-16238	-59337	-18570
Total Imports and Balance of Goods and Services	57458	67094	64526	79813	126682	137030	160187	182179	226431	263880	299211	373286

4.1 Derivation of Value Added by Kind of Activity, in Current Prices

Million Philippine pesos

	1980			1981			1982			1983		
	Gross Output	Intermediate Consumption	Value Added	Gross Output	Intermediate Consumption	Value Added	Gross Output	Intermediate Consumption	Value Added	Gross Output	Intermediate Consumption	Value Added
						All Producers						
1 Agriculture, hunting, forestry and fishing	...	...	61219	...	...	70092	...	...	74055	...	...	82545
A Agriculture and hunting	...	...	44973	...	...	48951	...	...	52587	...	...	56048
B Forestry and logging	...	...	6317	...	...	7968	...	...	7384	...	...	8917
C Fishing	...	...	9929	...	...	13173	...	...	14084	...	...	17580
2 Mining and quarrying	...	...	5460	...	...	5173	...	...	4882	...	...	6182
A Coal mining	...	...	...	...	...	...	...	...	...	...	...	...
B Crude petroleum and natural gas production	...	...	...	...	...	...	...	...	...	...	...	...
C Metal ore mining	...	...	4698	...	...	4073	...	...	3559	...	...	4549
D Other mining	...	...	762	...	...	1100	...	...	1323	...	...	1633
3 Manufacturing	...	...	62654	...	...	71829	...	...	79608	...	...	89472
A Manufacture of food, beverages and tobacco	...	...	26156	...	...	31637	...	...	36946	...	...	42297
B Textile, wearing apparel and leather industries	...	...	6967	...	...	8734	...	...	9033	...	...	8633
C Manufacture of wood and wood products, including furniture	...	...	4177	...	...	3862	...	...	4050	...	...	4106
D Manufacture of paper and paper products, printing and publishing	...	...	1870	...	...	1935	...	...	2028	...	...	2316
E Manufacture of chemicals and chemical petroleum, coal, rubber and plastic products	...	...	13280	...	...	14326	...	...	15915	...	...	18535
F Manufacture of non-metallic mineral products, except products of petroleum and coal	...	...	2088	...	...	2213	...	...	2335	...	...	2560
G Basic metal industries	...	...	1201	...	...	1090	...	...	1246	...	...	2049
H Manufacture of fabricated metal products, machinery and equipment	...	...	6279	...	...	7234	...	...	7161	...	...	8059
I Other manufacturing industries	...	...	636	...	...	798	...	...	894	...	...	917
4 Electricity, gas and water	...	...	3806	...	...	4945	...	...	6577	...	...	8955
A Electricity, gas and steam	...	...	3466	...	...	4492	...	...	5998	...	...	8189
B Water works and supply	...	...	340	...	...	453	...	...	579	...	...	766
5 Construction	...	...	22625	...	...	28362	...	...	32087	...	...	40192
6 Wholesale and retail trade, restaurants and hotels	...	...	32175	...	...	36483	...	...	43531	...	...	51899
A Wholesale and retail trade	...	...	29681	...	...	33299	...	...	39683	...	...	46743
B Restaurants and hotels	...	...	2494	...	...	3184	...	...	3848	...	...	5156
7 Transport, storage and communication	...	...	11319	...	...	13268	...	...	14680	...	...	17848
A Transport and storage	...	...	9857	...	...	11478	...	...	12540	...	...	14701
B Communication	...	...	1462	...	...	1790	...	...	2140	...	...	3147
8 Finance, insurance, real estate and business services	...	...	24435	...	...	26311	...	...	32165	...	...	37984
A Financial institutions	...	...	6908	...	...	6428	...	...	7645	...	...	10019

Philippines

4.1 Derivation of Value Added by Kind of Activity, in Current Prices
(Continued)

Million Philippine pesos

	1980 Gross Output	1980 Intermediate Consumption	1980 Value Added	1981 Gross Output	1981 Intermediate Consumption	1981 Value Added	1982 Gross Output	1982 Intermediate Consumption	1982 Value Added	1983 Gross Output	1983 Intermediate Consumption	1983 Value Added
B Insurance	...	...	2549	...	...	2825	...	...	3117	...	...	3465
C Real estate and business services	...	...	14978	...	...	17058	...	...	21403	...	...	24500
Real estate, except dwellings	...	...	5900	...	...	6487	...	...	8122	...	...	9156
Dwellings	...	...	9078	...	...	10571	...	...	13281	...	...	15344
9 Community, social and personal services	...	...	7185	...	...	9394	...	...	11713	...	...	14629
A Sanitary and similar services	...	...	...	...	...	...	...	...	...	...	...	...
B Social and related community services	...	...	3548	...	...	4276	...	...	5194	...	...	6105
Educational services	...	...	2056	...	...	2318	...	...	2736	...	...	3073
Medical, dental, other health and veterinary services	...	...	1492	...	...	1958	...	...	2458	...	...	3032
C Recreational and cultural services	...	...	1091	...	...	1330	...	...	1818	...	...	2580
D Personal and household services	...	...	2546	...	...	3788	...	...	4701	...	...	5944
Total, Industries	...	...	230878	...	...	265857	...	...	299298	...	...	349706
Producers of Government Services	...	...	11998	...	...	14622	...	...	16721	...	...	17998
Other Producers	...	...	873	...	...	1117	...	...	1158	...	...	1373
Total	...	...	243749	...	...	281596	...	...	317177	...	...	369077
Less: Imputed bank service charge	...	...	...	...	...	...	...	...	...	...	...	...
Import duties	...	...	...	...	...	...	...	...	...	...	...	...
Value added tax	...	...	...	...	...	...	...	...	...	...	...	...
Total	...	...	243749	...	...	281596	...	...	317177	...	...	369077

All Producers

	1984 Gross Output	1984 Intermediate Consumption	1984 Value Added	1985 Gross Output	1985 Intermediate Consumption	1985 Value Added	1986 Gross Output	1986 Intermediate Consumption	1986 Value Added	1987 Gross Output	1987 Intermediate Consumption	1987 Value Added
1 Agriculture, hunting, forestry and fishing	...	...	129824	...	...	140554	...	...	145807	...	...	163927
A Agriculture and hunting	...	...	93865	...	...	104499	...	...	104456	...	...	119415
B Forestry and logging	...	...	13293	...	...	8997	...	...	9332	...	...	13256
C Fishing	...	...	22666	...	...	27058	...	...	32019	...	...	31256
2 Mining and quarrying	...	...	8142	...	...	11893	...	...	14144	...	...	14354
A Coal mining	...	...	...	...	...	...	...	...	...	...	...	...
B Crude petroleum and natural gas production	...	...	...	...	...	...	...	...	...	...	...	...
C Metal ore mining	...	...	6072	...	...	9574	...	...	11709	...	...	11912
D Other mining	...	...	2070	...	...	2319	...	...	2435	...	...	2442
3 Manufacturing	...	...	129171	...	...	143851	...	...	149958	...	...	169627
A Manufacture of food, beverages and tobacco	...	...	63975	...	...	75823	...	...	80802	...	...	88391
B Textile, wearing apparel and leather industries	...	...	11006	...	...	11152	...	...	12092	...	...	15878
C Manufacture of wood and wood products, including furniture	...	...	5533	...	...	4481	...	...	4850	...	...	6128
D Manufacture of paper and paper products, printing and publishing	...	...	3136	...	...	2922	...	...	3500	...	...	3876
E Manufacture of chemicals and chemical petroleum, coal, rubber and plastic products	...	...	26699	...	...	30534	...	...	27955	...	...	31183
F Manufacture of non-metallic mineral products, except products of petroleum and coal	...	...	2933	...	...	2701	...	...	2844	...	...	3423
G Basic metal industries	...	...	3650	...	...	4384	...	...	4266	...	...	5048
H Manufacture of fabricated metal products, machinery and equipment	...	...	10354	...	...	9879	...	...	11094	...	...	12774
I Other manufacturing industries	...	...	1885	...	...	1975	...	...	2555	...	...	2926
4 Electricity, gas and water	...	...	12779	...	...	15767	...	...	16642	...	...	16313
A Electricity, gas and steam	...	...	11846	...	...	14427	...	...	14934	...	...	14378
B Water works and supply	...	...	933	...	...	1340	...	...	1708	...	...	1935

Philippines

Million Philippine pesos

	1984			1985			1986			1987		
	Gross Output	Intermediate Consumption	Value Added	Gross Output	Intermediate Consumption	Value Added	Gross Output	Intermediate Consumption	Value Added	Gross Output	Intermediate Consumption	Value Added
5 Construction	...	...	48727	...	...	29037	...	...	29784	...	...	37104
6 Wholesale and retail trade, restaurants and hotels	...	...	77031	...	...	89960	...	...	96011	...	...	106235
A Wholesale and retail trade	...	...	70822	...	...	82835	...	...	87825	...	...	96518
B Restaurants and hotels	...	...	6209	...	...	7125	...	...	8186	...	...	9717
7 Transport, storage and communication	...	...	28117	...	...	31666	...	...	34307	...	...	36827
A Transport and storage	...	...	22963	...	...	25764	...	...	27235	...	...	29302
B Communication	...	...	5154	...	...	5902	...	...	7072	...	...	7525
8 Finance, insurance, real estate and business services	...	...	46594	...	...	54733	...	...	60141	...	...	68069
A Financial institutions	...	...	12234	...	...	12672	...	...	13937	...	...	17443
B Insurance	...	...	4101	...	...	4451	...	...	4721	...	...	5003
C Real estate and business services	...	...	30259	...	...	37610	...	...	41483	...	...	45623
Real estate, except dwellings	...	...	10219	...	...	11080	...	...	12320	...	...	13366
Dwellings	...	...	20040	...	...	26530	...	...	29163	...	...	32257
9 Community, social and personal services	...	...	19880	...	...	24880	...	...	27709	...	...	31981
A Sanitary and similar services												...
B Social and related community services	...	...	7959	...	...	9867	...	...	10349	...	...	11836
Educational services	...	...	3756	...	...	4685	...	...	5106	...	...	5480
Medical, dental, other health and veterinary services	...	...	4203	...	...	5182	...	...	5243	...	...	6356
C Recreational and cultural services	...	...	3642	...	...	4687	...	...	5331	...	...	6648
D Personal and household services	...	...	8279	...	...	10326	...	...	12029	...	...	13497
Total, Industries	...	...	500265	...	...	542341	...	...	574503	...	...	644437
Producers of Government Services	...	...	22865	...	...	27904	...	...	32720	...	...	38799
Other Producers	...	...	1351	...	...	1638	...	...	1664	...	...	1832
Total	...	...	524481	...	...	571883	...	...	608887	...	...	685068
Less: Imputed bank service charge	...	...	...	...	...	...	...	...	...	...	...	...
Import duties	...	...	...	...	...	...	...	...	...	...	...	...
Value added tax	...	...	...	...	...	...	...	...	...	...	...	...
Total	...	...	524481	...	...	571883	...	...	608887	...	...	685068

	1988			1989			1990			1991		
	Gross Output	Intermediate Consumption	Value Added	Gross Output	Intermediate Consumption	Value Added	Gross Output	Intermediate Consumption	Value Added	Gross Output	Intermediate Consumption	Value Added
All Producers												
1 Agriculture, hunting, forestry and fishing	...	...	183515	...	...	210009	...	...	235956	...	...	263201
A Agriculture and hunting	...	...	135751	...	...	162408	...	...	186216	...	...	207246
B Forestry and logging	...	...	13056	...	...	11141	...	...	8907	...	...	8679
C Fishing	...	...	34708	...	...	36460	...	...	40833	...	...	47276
2 Mining and quarrying	...	...	15275	...	...	15446	...	...	16659	...	...	17504
A Coal mining	...	...	...	...	...	...	...	...	...	...	...	...
B Crude petroleum and natural gas production	...	...	...	...	...	...	...	...	...	...	...	...
C Metal ore mining	...	...	12083	...	...	11458	...	...	12610	...	...	13077
D Other mining	...	...	3192	...	...	3988	...	...	4049	...	...	4427

4.1 Derivation of Value Added by Kind of Activity, in Current Prices
(Continued)

Million Philippine pesos

	1988			1989			1990			1991		
	Gross Output	Intermediate Consumption	Value Added	Gross Output	Intermediate Consumption	Value Added	Gross Output	Intermediate Consumption	Value Added	Gross Output	Intermediate Consumption	Value Added
3 Manufacturing	...	...	206728	...	...	233192	...	...	267485	...	...	315938
A Manufacture of food, beverages and tobacco	...	...	105348	...	...	115811	...	...	132063	...	...	148538
B Textile, wearing apparel and leather industries	...	...	19030	...	...	23232	...	...	26236	...	...	31128
C Manufacture of wood and wood products, including furniture	...	...	7196	...	...	8629	...	...	10020	...	...	11070
D Manufacture of paper and paper products, printing and publishing	...	...	5000	...	...	5766	...	...	6243	...	...	7178
E Manufacture of chemicals and chemical petroleum, coal, rubber and plastic products	...	...	39433	...	...	40943	...	...	49973	...	...	66638
F Manufacture of non-metallic mineral products, except products of petroleum and coal	...	...	4454	...	...	6937	...	...	7547	...	...	9953
G Basic metal industries	...	...	6664	...	...	7905	...	...	8539	...	...	9553
H Manufacture of fabricated metal products, machinery and equipment	...	...	15942	...	...	19458	...	...	21753	...	...	25335
I Other manufacturing industries	...	...	3661	...	...	4511	...	...	5111	...	...	6545
4 Electricity, gas and water	...	...	20120	...	...	21748	...	...	24299	...	...	30625
A Electricity, gas and steam	...	...	17906	...	...	19038	...	...	21374	...	...	27043
B Water works and supply	...	...	2214	...	...	2710	...	...	2925	...	...	3582
5 Construction	...	...	42814	...	...	57281	...	...	64903	...	...	62083
6 Wholesale and retail trade, restaurants and hotels	...	...	124646	...	...	142159	...	...	160594	...	...	189508
A Wholesale and retail trade	...	...	113477	...	...	128528	...	...	145102	...	...	171699
B Restaurants and hotels	...	...	11169	...	...	13631	...	...	15492	...	...	17809
7 Transport, storage and communication	...	...	40762	...	...	43840	...	...	54345	...	...	73909
A Transport and storage	...	...	31898	...	...	33622	...	...	42305	...	...	58984
B Communication	...	...	8864	...	...	10218	...	...	12040	...	...	14925
8 Finance, insurance, real estate and business services	...	...	79079	...	...	95623	...	...	114709	...	...	134862
A Financial institutions	...	...	21513	...	...	27642	...	...	34658	...	...	38921
B Insurance	...	...	5577	...	...	6659	...	...	7873	...	...	9651
C Real estate and business services	...	...	51989	...	...	61322	...	...	72178	...	...	86290
Real estate, except dwellings	...	...	15397	...	...	18071	...	...	21688	...	...	26172
Dwellings	...	...	36592	...	...	43251	...	...	50490	...	...	60118
9 Community, social and personal services	...	...	37002	...	...	43437	...	...	52605	...	...	63756
A Sanitary and similar services	...	...	...	...	...	...	...	...	...	...	...	...
B Social and related community services	...	...	13663	...	...	16723	...	...	19942	...	...	25543
Educational services	...	...	6459	...	...	8353	...	...	10281	...	...	13075
Medical, dental, other health and veterinary services	...	...	7204	...	...	8370	...	...	9661	...	...	12468
C Recreational and cultural services	...	...	7790	...	...	8573	...	...	9921	...	...	11377
D Personal and household services	...	...	15549	...	...	18141	...	...	22742	...	...	26836
Total, Industries	...	...	749941	...	...	862735	...	...	991555	...	...	1151386
Producers of Government Services	...	...	50571	...	...	60272	...	...	77031	...	...	89880
Other Producers	...	...	2007	...	...	2154	...	...	2314	...	...	2771
Total	...	...	802519	...	...	925161	...	...	1070900	...	...	1244037
Less: Imputed bank service charge	...	...	...	...	...	...	...	...	...	...	...	...
Import duties	...	...	...	...	...	...	...	...	...	...	...	...
Value added tax	...	...	...	...	...	...	...	...	...	...	...	...
Total	...	...	802519	...	...	925161	...	...	1070900	...	...	1244037

Philippines

4.2 Derivation of Value Added by Kind of Activity, in Constant Prices

Million Philippine pesos

	1980			1981			1982			1983		
	Gross Output	Intermediate Consumption	Value Added	Gross Output	Intermediate Consumption	Value Added	Gross Output	Intermediate Consumption	Value Added	Gross Output	Intermediate Consumption	Value Added
At constant prices of:1985												
All Producers												
1 Agriculture, hunting, forestry and fishing	...	...	143295	...	...	148479	...	...	149641	...	...	144586
A Agriculture and hunting	...	...	103518	...	...	106776	...	...	108920	...	...	101202
B Forestry and logging	...	...	18265	...	...	16452	...	...	13734	...	...	13416
C Fishing	...	...	21512	...	...	25251	...	...	26987	...	...	29968
2 Mining and quarrying	...	...	9128	...	...	9350	...	...	9165	...	...	9244
A Coal mining	...	...	...	...	...	...	...	...	...	...	...	...
B Crude petroleum and natural gas production	...	...	...	...	...	...	...	...	...	...	...	...
C Metal ore mining	...	...	7213	...	...	7290	...	...	6881	...	...	6596
D Other mining	...	...	1915	...	...	2060	...	...	2284	...	...	2648
3 Manufacturing	...	...	168292	...	...	171569	...	...	174315	...	...	173756
A Manufacture of food, beverages and tobacco	...	...	84154	...	...	88014	...	...	90988	...	...	90180
B Textile, wearing apparel and leather industries	...	...	15252	...	...	17638	...	...	16974	...	...	15680
C Manufacture of wood and wood products, including furniture	...	...	8951	...	...	7830	...	...	7068	...	...	6705
D Manufacture of paper and paper products, printing and publishing	...	...	3978	...	...	3961	...	...	3942	...	...	3977
E Manufacture of chemicals and chemical petroleum, coal, rubber and plastic products	...	...	31544	...	...	29239	...	...	31941	...	...	32371
F Manufacture of non-metallic mineral products, except products of petroleum and coal	...	...	4626	...	...	4390	...	...	4347	...	...	4312
G Basic metal industries	...	...	2684	...	...	2390	...	...	2619	...	...	4023
H Manufacture of fabricated metal products, machinery and equipment	...	...	15099	...	...	15875	...	...	14166	...	...	14378
I Other manufacturing industries	...	...	2004	...	...	2232	...	...	2270	...	...	2130
4 Electricity, gas and water	...	...	12389	...	...	14205	...	...	17367	...	...	15783
A Electricity, gas and steam	...	...	11692	...	...	13467	...	...	16583	...	...	14740
B Water works and supply	...	...	697	...	...	738	...	...	784	...	...	1043
5 Construction	...	...	57250	...	...	63421	...	...	64110	...	...	70204
6 Wholesale and retail trade, restaurants and hotels	...	...	85273	...	...	86163	...	...	93547	...	...	98325
A Wholesale and retail trade	...	...	79335	...	...	79511	...	...	86338	...	...	89739
B Restaurants and hotels	...	...	5938	...	...	6652	...	...	7209	...	...	8586
7 Transport, storage and communication	...	...	29175	...	...	30629	...	...	31415	...	...	32622
A Transport and storage	...	...	24851	...	...	25534	...	...	25735	...	...	26634
B Communication	...	...	4324	...	...	5095	...	...	5680	...	...	5988
8 Finance, insurance, real estate and business services	...	...	61772	...	...	58937	...	...	63402	...	...	67701
A Financial institutions	...	...	17533	...	...	14429	...	...	15567	...	...	18544
B Insurance	...	...	6470	...	...	6341	...	...	6347	...	...	6413
C Real estate and business services	...	...	37769	...	...	38167	...	...	41488	...	...	42744
Real estate, except dwellings	...	...	15141	...	...	14843	...	...	17056	...	...	17339
Dwellings	...	...	22628	...	...	23324	...	...	24432	...	...	25405
9 Community, social and personal services	...	...	15770	...	...	18454	...	...	20081	...	...	23222
A Sanitary and similar services	...	...	...	...	...	...	...	...	...	...	...	...
B Social and related community services	...	...	7591	...	...	8346	...	...	8802	...	...	9453
Educational services	...	...	4437	...	...	4539	...	...	4651	...	...	4766
Medical, dental, other health and veterinary services	...	...	3154	...	...	3807	...	...	4151	...	...	4687
C Recreational and cultural services	...	...	2315	...	...	2507	...	...	3199	...	...	4224
D Personal and household services	...	...	5864	...	...	7601	...	...	8080	...	...	9545

4.2 Derivation of Value Added by Kind of Activity, in Constant Prices
(Continued)

Million Philippine pesos

	1980			1981			1982			1983		
	Gross Output	Intermediate Consumption	Value Added	Gross Output	Intermediate Consumption	Value Added	Gross Output	Intermediate Consumption	Value Added	Gross Output	Intermediate Consumption	Value Added
				At constant prices of:1985								
Total, Industries	...	...	582344	...	...	601207	...	...	623043	...	...	635443
Producers of Government Services	...	...	25350	...	...	27122	...	...	28191	...	...	27844
Other Producers	...	...	2074	...	...	2313	...	...	2233	...	...	2430
Total	...	...	609768	...	...	630642	...	...	653467	...	...	665717
Less: Imputed bank service charge	...	...	...	...	...	...	...	...	...	...	...	...
Import duties	...	...	...	...	...	...	...	...	...	...	...	...
Value added tax	...	...	...	...	...	...	...	...	...	...	...	...
Total	...	...	609768	...	...	630642	...	...	653467	...	...	665717

	1984			1985			1986			1987		
	Gross Output	Intermediate Consumption	Value Added	Gross Output	Intermediate Consumption	Value Added	Gross Output	Intermediate Consumption	Value Added	Gross Output	Intermediate Consumption	Value Added
				At constant prices of:1985								
				All Producers								
1 Agriculture, hunting, forestry and fishing	...	...	143247	...	...	140554	...	...	145725	...	...	150414
A Agriculture and hunting	...	...	102204	...	...	104499	...	...	106240	...	...	107155
B Forestry and logging	...	...	11660	...	...	8997	...	...	10239	...	...	12339
C Fishing	...	...	29383	...	...	27058	...	...	29246	...	...	30920
2 Mining and quarrying	...	...	8959	...	...	11893	...	...	12313	...	...	11232
A Coal mining	...	...	...	...	...	...	...	...	...	...	...	...
B Crude petroleum and natural gas production	...	...	...	...	...	...	...	...	...	...	...	...
C Metal ore mining	...	...	6436	...	...	9574	...	...	9838	...	...	8708
D Other mining	...	...	2523	...	...	2319	...	...	2475	...	...	2524
3 Manufacturing	...	...	156195	...	...	143851	...	...	146453	...	...	154604
A Manufacture of food, beverages and tobacco	...	...	81229	...	...	75823	...	...	78700	...	...	78754
B Textile, wearing apparel and leather industries	...	...	12776	...	...	11152	...	...	11510	...	...	13582
C Manufacture of wood and wood products, including furniture	...	...	6116	...	...	4481	...	...	4553	...	...	5184
D Manufacture of paper and paper products, printing and publishing	...	...	3554	...	...	2922	...	...	3164	...	...	3421
E Manufacture of chemicals and chemical petroleum, coal, rubber and plastic products	...	...	29607	...	...	30534	...	...	28717	...	...	32217
F Manufacture of non-metallic mineral products, except products of petroleum and coal	...	...	3489	...	...	2701	...	...	2722	...	...	3041
G Basic metal industries	...	...	4507	...	...	4384	...	...	4143	...	...	4623
H Manufacture of fabricated metal products, machinery and equipment	...	...	12421	...	...	9879	...	...	10549	...	...	11168
I Other manufacturing industries	...	...	2496	...	...	1975	...	...	2395	...	...	2614
4 Electricity, gas and water	...	...	16857	...	...	15767	...	...	17851	...	...	18595
A Electricity, gas and steam	...	...	15662	...	...	14427	...	...	16416	...	...	17127
B Water works and supply	...	...	1195	...	...	1340	...	...	1435	...	...	1468
5 Construction	...	...	56027	...	...	29037	...	...	28547	...	...	31742
6 Wholesale and retail trade, restaurants and hotels	...	...	91041	...	...	89960	...	...	94037	...	...	97705
A Wholesale and retail trade	...	...	83637	...	...	82835	...	...	86917	...	...	90038
B Restaurants and hotels	...	...	7404	...	...	7125	...	...	7120	...	...	7667
7 Transport, storage and communication	...	...	32060	...	...	31666	...	...	33075	...	...	35086
A Transport and storage	...	...	26014	...	...	25764	...	...	26484	...	...	28075
B Communication	...	...	6046	...	...	5902	...	...	6591	...	...	7011
8 Finance, insurance, real estate and business services	...	...	58885	...	...	54733	...	...	57285	...	...	61476
A Financial institutions	...	...	15061	...	...	12672	...	...	13832	...	...	16681
B Insurance	...	...	5049	...	...	4451	...	...	4685	...	...	4784
C Real estate and business services	...	...	38775	...	...	37610	...	...	38768	...	...	40011
Real estate, except dwellings	...	...	13129	...	...	11080	...	...	11802	...	...	11917

Philippines

4.2 Derivation of Value Added by Kind of Activity, in Constant Prices
(Continued)

Million Philippine pesos

	1984			1985			1986			1987		
	Gross Output	Intermediate Consumption	Value Added	Gross Output	Intermediate Consumption	Value Added	Gross Output	Intermediate Consumption	Value Added	Gross Output	Intermediate Consumption	Value Added
					At constant prices of:1985							
Dwellings	...	...	25646	...	...	26530	...	...	26966	...	...	28094
9 Community, social and personal services	...	...	24184	...	...	24880	...	...	25852	...	...	27438
A Sanitary and similar services	...	...	...	...	...	...	...	...	...	...	...	...
B Social and related community services	...	...	9532	...	...	9867	...	...	9559	...	...	10179
Educational services	...	...	4542	...	...	4685	...	...	4648	...	...	4561
Medical, dental, other health and veterinary services	...	...	4990	...	...	5182	...	...	4911	...	...	5618
C Recreational and cultural services	...	...	4528	...	...	4687	...	...	5099	...	...	5772
D Personal and household services	...	...	10124	...	...	10326	...	...	11194	...	...	11487
Total, Industries	...	...	587455	...	...	542341	...	...	561138	...	...	588292
Producers of Government Services	...	...	27779	...	...	27904	...	...	28700	...	...	29712
Other Producers	...	...	1728	...	...	1638	...	...	1585	...	...	1703
Total	...	...	616962	...	...	571883	...	...	591423	...	...	619707
Less: Imputed bank service charge	...	...	...	...	...	...	...	...	...	...	...	...
Import duties	...	...	...	...	...	...	...	...	...	...	...	...
Value added tax	...	...	...	...	...	...	...	...	...	...	...	...
Total	...	...	616962	...	...	571883	...	...	591423	...	...	619707

	1988			1989			1990			1991		
	Gross Output	Intermediate Consumption	Value Added	Gross Output	Intermediate Consumption	Value Added	Gross Output	Intermediate Consumption	Value Added	Gross Output	Intermediate Consumption	Value Added
					At constant prices of:1985							
					All Producers							
1 Agriculture, hunting, forestry and fishing	...	...	155292	...	...	159964	...	...	160734	...	...	162193
A Agriculture and hunting	...	...	115447	...	...	121066	...	...	122631	...	...	123573
B Forestry and logging	...	...	11264	...	...	9270	...	...	7320	...	...	6640
C Fishing	...	...	28581	...	...	29628	...	...	30783	...	...	31980
2 Mining and quarrying	...	...	11704	...	...	11389	...	...	11091	...	...	10770
A Coal mining	...	...	...	...	...	...	...	...	...	...	...	...
B Crude petroleum and natural gas production	...	...	...	...	...	...	...	...	...	...	...	...
C Metal ore mining	...	...	8077	...	...	8100	...	...	7837	...	...	7367
D Other mining	...	...	3627	...	...	3289	...	...	3254	...	...	3403
3 Manufacturing	...	...	167681	...	...	178396	...	...	183925	...	...	183111
A Manufacture of food, beverages and tobacco	...	...	80270	...	...	81898	...	...	82138	...	...	81049
B Textile, wearing apparel and leather industries	...	...	15112	...	...	17208	...	...	16913	...	...	17429
C Manufacture of wood and wood products, including furniture	...	...	5634	...	...	6260	...	...	6714	...	...	6430
D Manufacture of paper and paper products, printing and publishing	...	...	4289	...	...	4954	...	...	5147	...	...	5160
E Manufacture of chemicals and chemical petroleum, coal, rubber and plastic products	...	...	37332	...	...	39145	...	...	44298	...	...	43845
F Manufacture of non-metallic mineral products, except products of petroleum and coal	...	...	3811	...	...	5014	...	...	4552	...	...	5004
G Basic metal industries	...	...	5532	...	...	5446	...	...	4893	...	...	4936
H Manufacture of fabricated metal products, machinery and equipment	...	...	12575	...	...	14762	...	...	15521	...	...	15278
I Other manufacturing industries	...	...	3126	...	...	3709	...	...	3749	...	...	3980
4 Electricity, gas and water	...	...	19880	...	...	20412	...	...	20423	...	...	20609
A Electricity, gas and steam	...	...	18405	...	...	18812	...	...	18786	...	...	18958
B Water works and supply	...	...	1475	...	...	1600	...	...	1637	...	...	1651

1520

4.2 Derivation of Value Added by Kind of Activity, in Constant Prices
(Continued)

Million Philippine pesos

	1988			1989			1990			1991		
	Gross Output	Intermediate Consumption	Value Added	Gross Output	Intermediate Consumption	Value Added	Gross Output	Intermediate Consumption	Value Added	Gross Output	Intermediate Consumption	Value Added
					At constant prices of:1985							
5 Construction	...	...	33235	...	...	41384	...	...	42639	...	...	35700
6 Wholesale and retail trade, restaurants and hotels	...	...	102845	...	...	107833	...	...	109857	...	...	111211
A Wholesale and retail trade	...	...	94645	...	...	99283	...	...	101354	...	...	102877
B Restaurants and hotels	...	...	8200	...	...	8550	...	...	8503	...	...	8334
7 Transport, storage and communication	...	...	37898	...	...	40243	...	...	41217	...	...	41407
A Transport and storage	...	...	29871	...	...	31184	...	...	31329	...	...	30711
B Communication	...	...	8027	...	...	9059	...	...	9888	...	...	10696
8 Finance, insurance, real estate and business services	...	...	65918	...	...	71765	...	...	75766	...	...	75139
A Financial institutions	...	...	18902	...	...	21951	...	...	24422	...	...	23341
B Insurance	...	...	4912	...	...	5284	...	...	5546	...	...	5773
C Real estate and business services	...	...	42104	...	...	44530	...	...	45798	...	...	46025
Real estate, except dwellings	...	...	12383	...	...	13032	...	...	13549	...	...	13650
Dwellings	...	...	29721	...	...	31498	...	...	32249	...	...	32375
9 Community, social and personal services	...	...	29875	...	...	31659	...	...	33260	...	...	33208
A Sanitary and similar services	...	...	...	...	...	...	...	...	...	...	...	...
B Social and related community services	...	...	10957	...	...	11860	...	...	12162	...	...	12624
Educational services	...	...	4951	...	...	5217	...	...	5303	...	...	5366
Medical, dental, other health and veterinary services	...	...	6006	...	...	6643	...	...	6859	...	...	7258
C Recreational and cultural services	...	...	6725	...	...	6949	...	...	7197	...	...	7263
D Personal and household services	...	...	12193	...	...	12850	...	...	13901	...	...	13321
Total, Industries	...	...	624328	...	...	663045	...	...	678912	...	...	673348
Producers of Government Services	...	...	32322	...	...	33459	...	...	36405	...	...	37293
Other Producers	...	...	1813	...	...	1878	...	...	1938	...	...	1948
Total	...	...	658463	...	...	698382	...	...	717255	...	...	712589
Less: Imputed bank service charge	...	...	...	...	...	...	...	...	...	...	...	...
Import duties	...	...	...	...	...	...	...	...	...	...	...	...
Value added tax	...	...	...	...	...	...	...	...	...	...	...	...
Total	...	...	658463	...	...	698382	...	...	717255	...	...	712589

Poland

Source. Reply to the United Nations national accounts questionnaire from the Central Statistical Office of Poland, Warsaw. The official estimates are published annually in 'Rocznik Statystyczny' (Statistical Yearbook). Concepts, definitions and methods of estimation are described in the above Yearbook and also in 'Concise Statistical Yearbook of Poland' and in 'Rocznik Dochodu Narodowego, 1960-1965' (Yearbook of National Income, 1960-1965). The above publications are issued by the Central Statistical Office.

General note. The estimates shown in the following tables have been prepared in accordance with the United Nations System of National Accounts (SNA) so far as the existing data would permit. The SNA have replaced the System of Material Product Balances (MPS) since 1991. However, tables prepared in accordance with the MPS are also shown. The MPS estimates are not comparable in concept and coverage with those conforming to the SNA.

1.1 Expenditure on the Gross Domestic Product, in Current Prices

Thousand Million Polish zlotych

	1980	1981	1982	1983	1984	1985	1986	1987	1988	1989	1990	1991
1 Government final consumption expenditure	432	504	891	1196	1548	1927 1890	2303	2938	4744	16445	109052 108900	167973
2 Private final consumption expenditure	1478	1798	3040	3901	4680	5493 5509	6792	8736	14600	51839	263261 268734	480388
3 Gross capital formation	662	508	1550	1734	2257	2888 2888	3740	4884	9657	45533	184378 162887	177284
A Increase in stocks	41	-6	433	339	476	677 677	905	1063	2994	26182	68646 46821	22258
B Gross fixed capital formation	621	514	1117	1395	1781	2211 2211	2835	3821	6663	19351	115732 116066	155026
4 Exports of goods and services	707	638	1078	1192	1516	1901 1901	2358	3625	6745	22570	156211 160509	190257
5 Less: Imports of goods and services	780	696	962	1070	1346	1753 1761	2174	3218	5934	17608	106703 110500	187791
Statistical discrepancy	12	1	-52	-29	-79	-89 18	-66	-25	-183	-460	527 987	-3781
Equals: Gross Domestic Product	2511	2753	5546	6924	8576	10367 10445	12953	16940	29629	118319	606726 591517	824330

1.2 Expenditure on the Gross Domestic Product, in Constant Prices

Thousand Million Polish zlotych

	1980	1981	1982	1983	1984	1985	1986	1987	1988	1989	1990	1991
				At constant prices of:								
			1982					1984			1990	
1 Government final consumption expenditure	875	855	901	910	956	1001 1669	1692	1704	1707	1629	1636 113316	105898
2 Private final consumption expenditure	3797	3644	3102	3299	3448	3543 4874	5114	5260	5438	5421	4590 268669	288557
3 Gross capital formation	1714	1333	1287	1357	1443	1532 2341	2446	2449	2658	2795	2102 140714	120781
A Increase in stocks	108	33	165	136	102	133 469	490	412	497	680	212 24837	10089
B Gross fixed capital formation	1606	1300	1122	1221	1341	1399 1872	1956	2037	2161	2115	1890 115877	110692
4 Exports of goods and services	1241	1015	1078	1177	1316	1320 1520	1584	1663	1820	1868	2149 160509	157855
5 Less: Imports of goods and services	1383	1111	962	1018	1114	1190 1441	1518	1588	1743	1818	1631 110500	145449
Statistical discrepancy	24	-93	-32	-52	-56	5 54	80	94	98	99	-6 1472	2941
Equals: Gross Domestic Product	6268	5643	5374	5673	5993	6211 9017	9398	9582	9978	9994	8840 574180	530583

1a Net Material Product by Use at Current Market Prices

Thousand Million Polish zlotych

	1980	1981	1982	1983	1984	1985	1986	1987	1988	1989	1990	1991
1 Personal consumption	1409	1721	2929	3750	4456	5190 / 5206	6403	8255	13822	50071	249588	...
2 Material consumption in the units of the non-material sphere serving individuals [a]	...	...	...	...	...	... / 623	793	1034	1680	4819	42706	...
Consumption of the Population	1409	1721	2929	3750	4456	5190 / 5829	7196	9288	15501	54890	292294	...
3 Material consumption in the units of the non-material sphere serving the community as a whole [a]	255	276	526	688	885	1120 / 460	529	667	1087	2683	18357	...
4 Net fixed capital formation	348	225	800	1054	1275	1540 / 1534	1950	2612	4785	16695	76922	...
5 Increase in material circulating assets and in stocks	41	-6	433	339	476	678 / 678	905	1063	2994	26182	68646	...
6 Losses [b]						59[c] / 18	-66	-25	-184	-460	527	...
7 Exports of goods and material services	-61	-57	65	94	90	... / 1901	2358	3625	6745	22570	156211	...
8 Less: Imports of goods and material services						... / 1761	2174	3218	5934	17608	106704	...
Net Material Product [d]	1992	2160	4753	5924	7182	8586 / 8658	10697	14013	24995	104952	506253	...

a) Item 'Material consumption in units of the non-material sphere serving individuals' is included in item 'Material consumption in the units of the non-material sphere serving the community as a whole'.
b) Item 'Losses', includes also statistical discrepancy.
c) Including item 'Losses' through 'Less: Imports of goods and material services'.

d) Beginning 1975 the estimates of net material product shown in table 1a (Net Material Product by Use) differ from those shown in table 4 (Primary Income from Net Material Product). This is because net material product in table 1a is computed by means of the kind of activity method for which there was no possibility to single out elements of primary distribution while in table 4 there is primary distribution of net material product computed by means of the enterprise method.

1b Net Material Product by Use at Constant Market Prices

Thousand Million Polish zlotych

	1980	1981	1982	1983	1984	1985	1986	1987	1988	1989	1990	1991
At constant prices of:			1982						1984			
1 Personal consumption	3651	3502	2989	3176	3295	3368 / 4624	4855	5000	5164	5206	4383	...
2 Material consumption in the units of the non-material sphere serving individuals	...	...	...	...	...	... / 558	592	612	622	566	591	...
Consumption of the Population	3651	3502	2989	3176	3295	3368 / 5182	5447	5612	5786	5772	4975	...
3 Material consumption in the units of the non-material sphere serving the community as a whole	525[a]	483[a]	538[a]	555[a]	601[a]	640[a] / 393	398	399	402	312	316	...
4 Net fixed capital formation	1326	1005	805	881	990	1038 / 838	888	933	1019	944	682	...
5 Increase in material circulating assets and in stocks	108	33	165	136	102	133 / 469	490	412	498	680	211	...
6 Losses [b]						123[c] / 68	87	88	104	111	-7	...
7 Exports of goods and material services	-102	-175	83	107	140	... / 1520	1584	1663	1820	1868	2150	...
8 Less: Imports of goods and material services						... / 1441	1518	1588	1743	1818	1632	...
Net Material Product	5509	4848	4581	4856	5128	5301 / 7030	7376	7520	7885	7869	6695	...

a) Item 'Material consumption in units of the non-material sphere serving individuals' is included in item 'Material consumption in the units of the non-material sphere serving the community as a whole'.
b) Item 'Losses', includes also statistical discrepancy.
c) Including item 'Losses' through 'Less: Imports of goods and material services'.

2a Net Material Product by Kind of Activity of the Material Sphere in Current Market Prices

Thousand Million Polish zlotych

	1980	1981	1982	1983	1984	1985	1986	1987	1988	1989	1990	1991
1 Agriculture and forestry	315	638	925	1089	1256	1399 / 1399	1650	1849	3543	15089	45515	...
A Agriculture and livestock [a]	261	577	759	908	1050	1156 / 1156	1353	1454	2891	12610	33603	...
B Forestry	24	25	73	86	94	116 / 116	140	189	311	1312	7268	...
C Other	30	37	93	95	113	127 / 127	158	207	341	1168	4643	...
2 Industrial activity [a]	1039	910	2388	2968	3562	4182 / 4117	5061	6804	12031	52672	273900	...

Poland

2a Net Material Product by Kind of Activity of the Material Sphere in Current Market Prices
(Continued)

Thousand Million Polish zlotych

	1980	1981	1982	1983	1984	1985	1986	1987	1988	1989	1990	1991
3 Construction	202	158	510	644	833	1065 1064	1379	1801	3207	10055	54091	...
4 Wholesale and retail trade and restaurants and other eating and drinking places	254	270	656	802	982	1207 1344	1708	2385	4111	19502	90452	...
5 Transport and communication	143	141	207	318	420	579 563	667	851	1462	5184	26075	...
A Transport	116	114	167	261	356	489 473	562	709	1247	4522	20552	...
B Communication	27	28	40	57	65	91 91	105	143	215	663	5523	...
6 Other activities of the material sphere	39	43	68	103	128	155 171	232	323	641	2450	16221	...
Net material product	1992	2160	4753	5924	7182	8586 8658	10697	14013	24995	104952	506253	...

a) Inland water fishing is included in item 'Agriculture and livestock'. Ocean and coastal fishing and factory-vessel fishing are included in item 'Industrial activity'.

2b Net Material Product by Kind of Activity of the Material Sphere in Constant Market Prices

Thousand Million Polish zlotych

	1980	1981	1982	1983	1984	1985	1986	1987	1988	1989	1990	1991
			At constant prices of:									
			1982						1984			
1 Agriculture and forestry	774 ᵉ	787	829	877	926	928 1107	1176	1084	1098	1107	1080	...
A Agriculture and livestock a	602	626	662	717	760	763 918	982	884	889	901	932	...
B Forestry	63	67	73	83	89	90 95	100	103	105	100	78	...
C Other	109	95	95	77	77	75 94	94	98	103	105	71	...
2 Industrial activity a	2763	2361	2254	2384	2512	2611 3419	3571	3690	3868	3773	2850	...
3 Construction	732	548	502	541	585	610 844	880	899	954	948	808	...
4 Wholesale and retail trade and restaurants and other eating and drinking places	894	828	720	751	777	810 1163	1224	1294	1385	1447	1455	...
5 Transport and communication	262	239	207	227	249	259 363	382	405	424	431	363	...
A Transport	225	201	167	177	195	203 300	313	329	342	345	279	...
B Communication	38	37	40	50	54	56 64	69	77	82	86	84	...
6 Other activities of the material sphere	84	85	68	75	79	82 134	142	148	156	163	140	...
Net material product	5509	4848	4581	4856	5128	5301 7030	7376	7520	7885	7869	6695	...

a) Inland water fishing is included in item 'Agriculture and livestock'. Ocean and coastal fishing and factory-vessel fishing are included in item 'Industrial activity'.

3 Primary Incomes by Kind of Activity of the Material Sphere in Current Market Prices

Thousand Million Polish zlotych

	1980		1981	
	Primary Income of the Population	Primary Income of Enterprises	Primary Income of the Population	Primary Income of Enterprises
1 Agriculture and forestry	293	22	602	36
A Agriculture and livestock a	256	5	553	23
B Forestry	10	14	14	11
C Other	26	4	35	2
2 Industrial activity a	409	629	515	395
3 Construction	134	62	163	-12
4 Wholesale and retail trade and restaurants and other eating and drinking places	90	165	131	140
5 Transport and communication	91	53	114	27
6 Other activities of the material sphere	38	1	46	-3
Total b	1055	932	1572	583

a) Inland water fishing is included in item 'Agriculture and livestock'. Ocean and coastal fishing and factory-vessel fishing are included in item 'Industrial activity'.   b) Column 'Primary income of the population', includes net income of the owner of private farms and other private enterprises (equivalent to unincorporated enterprises in SNA).

4 Primary Incomes From Net Material Product

Thousand Million Polish zlotych

	1980	1981	1982	1983	1984	1985	1986	1987	1988	1989	1990	1991
a) Primary Incomes of the Population												
1 Socialist sector	755	972	...	...	...	...	...	...	...	...	...	...
A State sector	619	793	...	...	...	...	...	...	...	...	...	...
B Co-operative sector	133	175	...	...	...	...	...	...	...	...	...	...
C Personal plots of households	3	3	...	...	...	...	...	...	...	...	...	...
2 Private sector	300	600	...	...	...	...	...	...	...	...	...	...
Sub-total	1055	1572	...	...	...	...	...	...	...	...	...	...
b) Primary incomes of the enterprises												
1 Socialist sector	889	533	...	...	...	...	...	...	...	...	...	...
A State sector	824	528	...	...	...	...	...	...	...	...	...	...
B Co-operative sector	65	5	...	...	...	...	...	...	...	...	...	...
2 Private sector	43	50	...	...	...	...	...	...	...	...	...	...
Sub-total	932	583	...	...	...	...	...	...	...	...	...	...
Total net material product	1987	2155	...	...	...	...	...	...	...	...	...	...

5a Supply and Disposition of Goods and Material Services in Current Market Prices

Thousand Million Polish zlotych

	Gross Output at Producers Prices	Trade Margins and Transport Charges	Gross Output at Market Prices	Imports	Total Supply and Disposition	Intermediate Material Consumption including Depreciation	Final Consumption	Net Capital Formation	Losses	Exports
1982										
1 Agriculture and forestry a	1965	85	2050	81	2131	1646	477	-15	-	23
2 Industrial activity a	7088	726	7814	824	8638	4453	2589	802	-65	859
3 Construction	1114	1	1115	2	1117	202	91	756	-	68
4 Transport and communication	664	-	664	53	717	455	130	1	5	126
5 Other activities of the material sphere	249	4	253	2	255	143	104	6	-	2
Total b	11080	816	11896	962	12858	6899	3391	1550	-60	1078
1983										
1 Agriculture and forestry a	2232	105	2337	63	2400	1843	512	15	-	30
2 Industrial activity a	8656	975	9631	938	10569	5514	3407	728	-55	975
3 Construction	1415	2	1417	3	1420	268	113	985	-	54
4 Transport and communication	890	-	890	63	953	604	209	1	8	131
5 Other activities of the material sphere	317	5	322	3	325	186	133	4	-	2
Total b	13510	1087	14597	1070	15667	8415	4374	1733	-47	1192
1984										
1 Agriculture and forestry a	2484	136	2620	75	2695	2016	572	61	-	46
2 Industrial activity a	10453	1110	11563	1173	12736	6621	4074	922	-91	1210
3 Construction	1789	9	1798	1	1799	332	132	1267	-	68
4 Transport and communication	1102	-	1102	92	1194	745	259	2	8	180
5 Other activities of the material sphere	401	8	409	5	414	223	174	5	-	12
Total b	16229	1263	17492	1346	18838	9937	5211	2257	-83	1516

a) Inland water fishing is included in item 'Agriculture and livestock'. Ocean and coastal fishing and factory-vessel fishing are included in item 'Industrial activity'.
b) Column 2 (Trade margins and transport charges) refers to trade margins only, column 6 (Intermediate consumption including depreciation) excludes depreciation and column 9 (Losses) includes scraps and statistical discrepancies.

6a Capital Formation by Kind of Activity of the Material and Non-Material Spheres in Current Market Prices

Thousand Million Polish zlotych

	1980	1981	1982	1983	1984	1985	1986	1987	1988	1989	1990	1991
Net Fixed Capital Formation												
1 Agriculture and forestry	51	49	135	187	202	195 / 195	219	289	490	1991	5656	...
2 Industrial activity	76	17	144	199	249	332 / 327	432	654	1248	5409	23561	...
3 Construction	6	-6	-1	6	11	18 / 17	26	42	96	262	433	...
4 Wholesale and retail trade, restaurants and other eating and drinking places	5	4	17	25	30	34 / 34	60	83	151	571	2569	...

Poland

6a Capital Formation by Kind of Activity of the Material and Non-Material Spheres in Current Market Prices
(Continued)

Thousand Million Polish zlotych

	1980	1981	1982	1983	1984	1985	1986	1987	1988	1989	1990	1991
5 Transport and communication	14	-6	13	21	43	68 73	93	84	232	745	2271	...
6 Other activities of the material sphere	19	17	58	75	96	121 116	157	207	381	1106	4738	...
Total Material Sphere	170	74	365	514	632	768 762	987	1358	2597	10082	39228	...
7 Housing except owner-occupied, communal and miscellaneous personal services	94	73	190	240	292	345 345	425	530	899	2870	17340	
8 Education, culture and art	13	12	37	49	63	86 86	113	153	276	773	4071	...
9 Health and social welfare services and sports	20	18	43	56	74	98 98	129	172	295	821	3940	...
Total Non-Material Sphere Serving Individuals	127	103	271	344	428	529 529	667	855	1470	4464	25351	...
10 Government	...	...	...	...	...	... ...	...	...	...	...	...	
11 Finance, credit and insurance	...	...	...	...	...	... ...	...	...	...	...	...	
12 Research, scientific and technological institutes	...	...	...	...	...	... ...	...	...	...	...	...	...
13 Other activities of the non-material sphere	...	...	...	...	...	... ...	...	...	...	...	...	...
Total Non-Material Sphere Serving the Community as a Whole	30	29	73	79	96	111 110	146	198	370	938	5603	...
14 Owner-occupied dwellings	21	20	92	117	119	133 133	150	202	349	1211	6741	...
Total Net Fixed Capital Formation [a]	348	225	800	1054	1275	1540 1534	1950	2612	4785	16695	76922	...

Gross Fixed Capital Formation

	1980	1981	1982	1983	1984	1985	1986	1987	1988	1989	1990	1991
1 Agriculture and forestry	93	94	192	251	301	332 332	397	530	895	2495	13142	...
2 Industrial activity	202	151	293	353	469	615 613	804	1133	1988	6502	39130	...
3 Construction	27	15	18	25	36	47 47	63	89	169	382	1700	...
4 Wholesale and retail trade and restaurants and other eating and drinking places	11	11	24	34	41	49 52	82	111	193	651	3991	...
5 Transport and communication	55	35	53	67	105	146 146	190	264	485	1066	7172	...
6 Other activities of the material sphere	27	25	69	89	117	149 149	199	259	464	1238	6796	...
Total Material Sphere	415	332	650	818	1070	1338 1338	1735	2387	4195	12334	71932	...
7 Housing except owner-occupied, communal and miscellaneous personal services	103	82	200	251	312	376 376	468	586	990	3000	19276	...
8 Education, culture and art	18	17	43	54	70	94 94	123	166	296	803	4528	...
9 Health and social welfare services and sports	21	19	44	57	76	101 101	133	177	303	833	4113	...
Total Non-Material Sphere Serving Individuals	141	118	287	362	458	571 571	723	929	1588	4635	27916	...

6a Capital Formation by Kind of Activity of the Material and Non-Material Spheres in Current Market Prices
(Continued)

Thousand Million Polish zlotych

	1980	1981	1982	1983	1984	1985	1986	1987	1988	1989	1990	1991
10 Government	...	...	...	...	...	... ...	...	...	...	...	...	...
11 Finance, credit and insurance	...	...	...	...	...	... ...	...	...	...	...	...	...
12 Research, scientific and technological institutes	...	...	...	...	...	... ...	...	...	...	...	...	
13 Other activities of the non-material sphere	...	...	...	...	...	... ...	...	...	...	...	...	
Total Non-Material Sphere Serving the Community as a Whole	31	29	73	80	97	112 112	148	200	374	948	5778	...
14 Owner-occupied dwellings	35	35	108	135	156	190 190	229	305	506	1434	10106	...
Total Gross Fixed Capital Formation	621	514	1117	1395	1781	2211 2211	2836	3821	6663	19351	115732	...

a) Computing of amortization according to spheres and divisions in 1972 and 1973 is not possible, therefore the sum of spheres is not equal to the total net investment outlays for fixed capital formation.

6b Capital Formation by Kind of Activity of the Material and Non-Material Spheres in Constant Market Prices

Thousand Million Polish zlotych

	1980	1981	1982	1983	1984	1985	1986	1987	1988	1989	1990	1991
			At constant prices of:									
			1982						1984			
			Net Fixed Capital Formation									
1 Agriculture and forestry	217	198	139	150	152	127 62	53	62	76	52	-63	...
2 Industrial activity	339	204	145	160	199	229 84	104	119	129	173	116	...
3 Construction	40	14	-1	4	10	12 -8	-4	-3	-1	-14	-23	...
4 Wholesale and retail trade, restaurants and other eating and drinking places	20	19	17	22	24	24 23	28	30	31	42	31	...
5 Transport and communication	85	39	13	16	40	53 12	17	22	33	-9	1	...
6 Other activities of the material sphere	64	57	58	64	75	82 85	92	91	102	93	64	...
Total Material Sphere	764	530	370	415	500	527 257	291	321	369	336	125	...
7 Housing except owner-occupied, communal and miscellaneous personal services	289	229	190	210	222	226 271	270	264	273	282	285	...
8 Education, culture and art	42	40	37	42	48	55 69	74	78	85	77	71	...
9 Health and social welfare services and sports	52	46	43	49	55	63 82	88	92	94	88	70	...
Total Non-Material Sphere Serving Individuals	384	315	271	301	325	344 422	432	434	452	447	426	...
10 Government	...	...	...	...	...	... ...	...	...	...	...	...	...
11 Finance, credit and insurance	...	...	...	...	...	... ...	...	...	...	...	...	...
12 Research, scientific and technological institutes	...	...	...	...	...	... ...	...	...	...	...	...	...
13 Other activities of the non-material sphere	...	...	...	...	...	... ...	...	...	...	...	...	
Total Non-Material Sphere Serving the Community as a Whole	84	78	72	69	73	95 93	101	106	121	107	100	...
14 Owner-occupied dwellings	95	82	92	97	93	71 66	65	72	77	54	30	...
Total Net Fixed Capital Formation	1326	1005	805	881	990	1038 838	888	933	1019	944	682	...
			Gross Fixed Capital Formation									
1 Agriculture and forestry	264	247	197	214	218	196 284	282	299	316	299	191	...
2 Industrial activity	465	338	293	314	357	393 507	541	571	599	653	609	...

Poland

6b Capital Formation by Kind of Activity of the Material and Non-Material Spheres in Constant Market Prices
(Continued)

Thousand Million Polish zlotych

At constant prices of: 1982 / 1984

	1980	1981	1982	1983	1984	1985	1986	1987	1988	1989	1990	1991
3 Construction	61	35	18	22	29	31 / 40	44	46	52	40	29	...
4 Wholesale and retail trade and restaurants and other eating and drinking places	27	26	24	30	33	33 / 49	56	60	62	73	72	...
5 Transport and communciation	125	80	53	60	85	98 / 123	132	140	155	116	128	...
6 Other activities of the material sphere	73	68	69	78	90	98 / 128	137	138	152	144	117	...
Total Material Sphere	1015	794	655	717	812	848 / 1130	1192	1254	1335	1325	1145	...
7 Housing except owner-occupied, communal and miscellaneous personal services	298	238	200	221	233	239 / 321	322	319	330	340	347	...
8 Education, culture and art	47	45	43	48	53	61 / 80	86	90	97	91	86	...
9 Health and social welfare services and sports	53	47	44	50	57	64 / 85	92	96	99	92	74	...
Total Non-Material Sphere Serving Individuals	398	330	287	318	343	364 / 487	501	505	526	523	507	...
10 Government	...	...	...	...	...	... / ...	...	...	...	...	...	...
11 Finance, credit and insurance	...	...	...	...	...	... / ...	...	...	...	...	...	...
12 Research, scientific and technological institutes	...	...	...	...	...	... / ...		...	...	...	...	...
13 Other activities of the non-material sphere	...	...	...	...	...	... / ...	...	...	...	...	...	...
Total Non-Material Sphere Serving the Community as a Whole	84	79	73	70	74	72 / 95	103	108	124	110	104	...
14 Owner-occupied dwellings	109	97	108	115	113	115 / 160	161	169	176	156	135	...
Total Gross Fixed Capital Formation	1606	1300	1122	1221	1341	1399 / 1872	1957	2037	2161	2115	1890	...

7a Final Consumption at Current Market Prices

Thousand Million Polish zlotych

	1980	1981	1982	1983	1984	1985	1986	1987	1988	1989	1990	1991
1 Personal consumption	1409	1721	2929	3750	4456	5190 / 5206	6403	8255	13822	50071	249588	...

a) Material Consumption in the Units of the Non-Material Sphere Serving Individuals

	1980	1981	1982	1983	1984	1985	1986	1987	1988	1989	1990	1991
2 Total non-material sphere serving individuals	...	...	...	...	...	... / 623	793	1034	1680	4819	42706	...

b) Material Consumption in the Units of the Non-Material Sphere Serving the Community as a Whole

	1980	1981	1982	1983	1984	1985	1986	1987	1988	1989	1990	1991
3 Total non-material sphere serving the community as a whole	255	276	526	688	885	1120 / 460	529	667	1087	2683	18357	...
Final consumption	1664	1998	3455	4438	5341	6310 / 6290	7725	9956	16588	57573	310651	...

7b Final Consumption at Constant Market Prices

Thousand Million Polish zlotych

	1980	1981	1982	1983	1984	1985	1986	1987	1988	1989	1990	1991
					At constant prices of:							
			1982						1984			
1 Personal consumption	3651	3502	2989	3176	3295	3368 4624	4855	5000	5164	5206	4383	...

a) Material Consumption in the Units of the Non-Material Sphere Serving Individuals

	1980	1981	1982	1983	1984	1985	1986	1987	1988	1989	1990	1991
2 Total non-material sphere serving individuals	...	...	...	...	...	... 558	592	612	622	566	591	...

b) Material Consumption in the Units of the Non-Material Sphere Serving the Community as a Whole

	1980	1981	1982	1983	1984	1985	1986	1987	1988	1989	1990	1991
3 Total non-material sphere serving the community as a whole	525	483	538	555	601	640 393	398	399	402	312	316	...
Final consumption	4176	3985	3528	3731	3896	4008 5575	5845	6011	6187	6084	5291	...

8 Personal Consumption According to Source of Supply of Goods and Material Services in Current Market Prices

Thousand Million Polish zlotych

	1980	1981	1982	1983	1984	1985	1986	1987	1988	1989	1990	1991
1 Purchases of goods in state and co-operative retail trade	1101	1273	2216	2903	3441	4002 4009	4961	6423	10543	38046	...	...
2 Purchases of goods in the free market and from private retail trade	69	133	211	232	280	312 331	386	490	918	4479	...	...
3 Goods produced on own account and received in kind	85	136	219	236	257	286 286	334	387	737	2463	10237	...
4 Payments for transport and communication services	55	63	83	139	167	209 209	256	346	600	1834	...	...
5 Purchases of electricity, gas and water	14	15	31	33	39	46 46	58	78	141	305	...	...
6 Purchases directly from handicrafts, repair shops and the like	71	87	154	188	234	278 268	330	427	726	2722	...	...
7 Consumption of fixed assets in respect of all dwellings	14	15	16	19	38	57 58	79	104	158	223	3365	...
8 Other	...	...	...	...	...	... ...	...	...	...	...	...	...
Personal consumption	1409	1721	2929	3750	4456	5190 5206	6403	8255	13822	50071	249588	...

9a Total Consumption of the Population in Current Market Prices

Thousand Million Polish zlotych

	1980	1981	1982	1983	1984	1985	1986	1987	1988	1989	1990	1991
					By Object							
1 Housing except owner-occupied, communal and miscellaneous personal services	20	22	30	39	57	77 77	102	131	230	523	...	...
2 Education, culture and art	15	16	23	31	37	44 44	58	73	122	374	...	...
3 Health and social welfare services and sport	20	21	31	48	66	84 84	100	133	224	687	...	...
Statistical discrepancy a	11	14	16	24	33	44 44	59	81	118	181	...	...
Total consumption of non-material services	66	73	100	141	193	249 249	318	419	695	1766	14203	...
4 Personal consumption of goods and material services excluding depreciation of dwellings	1395	1706	2913	3731	4418	5133 5148	6324	8151	13664	49849	246223	...
Statistical discrepancy b	208	250	453	612	787	973 973	1178	1496	2431	9682	66641	...
Total consumption of the population	1668	2030	3466	4484	5398	6354 6370	7820	10066	16790	61296	327067	...
					By Commodity and Service							
1 Food c	479	629	1274	1427	1652	1920 1928	2338	2846	4645	18028	...	...
2 Beverages, coffee and tea	233	235	463	645	777	883 883	1065	1370	2270	7214	...	...
3 Tobacco	41	61	77	98	107	114 114	148	186	254	891	...	...

Poland

Thousand Million Polish zlotych

	1980	1981	1982	1983	1984	1985	1986	1987	1988	1989	1990	1991
4 Clothing and footwear	187	222	260	375	471	556 557	746	1021	1702	6658	...	...
5 Gross rent	44	49	99	126	165	204 204	260	346	584	1711	...	...
6 Fuel, electricity, water and gas	22	22	77	74	79	88 88	123	182	371	616	...	...
7 Furniture and household equipment	160	190	285	398	517	629 633	757	928	1402	5087		
8 Health	134	159	257	326	389	483 483	602	770	1276	4995	...	...
9 Transport and communication	140	176	253	387	429	486 487	629	824	1455	5466	...	...
10 Education, recreation, sport	196	230	370	541	709	868 869	1051	1399	2353	9167	...	...
11 Other	32	58	52	86	102	123 123	100	196	477	1464	...	...
Total consumption of the population	1668	2030	3466	4484	5398	6354 6370	7820	10066	16790	61296	327067	...
By Mode of Acquisition												
1 Purchased	1375	1643	2795	3636	4354	5095 5112	6309	8183	13623	49151	250189	...
2 Free of charge	208	250	453	612	787	973 973	1178	1496	2431	9682	66641	...
3 From own production	85	136	219	236	257	286 286	334	387	737	2463	10237	...
Total consumption of the population	1668	2030	3466	4484	5398	6354 6370	7820	10066	16790	61296	327067	...

a) Item 'Statistical discrepancy' refers to other non-material services.
b) Except for an amount of 8.1 for 1970 which refers to statistical discrepancy, item 'Statistical discrepancy' refers to consumption from social funds, (benefits in kind).

c) For series 1, including consumption of food in schools, health institutions, sports institutions etc.

Portugal

General note. The preparation of national accounts statistics in Portugal is undertaken by the Instituto Nacional de Estatistica, Lisbon. The official estimates are published annually in the 'Annuario Estatistico'. A detailed description of the sources and methods used for the national accounts estimation is found in 'As Contas Nacionais Portuguesas 1958-1971', published by the Institute in 1972. The estimates are generally in accordance with the classification and definitions recommended in the United Nations System of National Accounts (SNA). Input-output table for 1959 has been published in 'Algunas Aplicacoes de Analise Input-Output a Matriz Portuguesa de 1959'. The following tables have been prepared from successive replies to the United Nations national accounts questionnaire. When the scope and coverage of the estimates differ for conceptual or statistical reasons from the definitions and classifications recommended in SNA, a footnote is indicated to the relevant tables.

Sources and methods :

(a) Gross domestic product. Gross domestic product is estimated mainly through the production approach.

(b) Expenditure on the gross domestic product. All items of GDP by expenditure type are estimated through the expenditure approach. The commodity-flow approach is also used for part of private final consumption expenditure. The estimates of government consumption expenditure are obtained from the government accounts. For private consumption expenditure, only estimates for food, beverages, tobacco, gross rent, fuel and power are made. For other components an estimate is derived as a residual between GDP and other final uses. The estimates of food, beverages and tobacco are based on retail prices and quantities consumed. Quantities consumed of other consumer products are available either through direct information or from production and foreign trade statistics, taking into account changes in producers' and wholesalers' stocks. Expenditures on house rent are estimated on the basis of information published in Estatisticas das Contribucoes e Impostos, adding 12 per cent for repairs. The calculation of increase in stocks is based on information on stock values supplied by corporations. Fixed capital formation in the private sector is estimated on the basis of annual surveys of corporation, the results of which are used to calculate increasing coefficients to be applied to total fixed capital formation. The annual construction surveys are used for the estimations of expenditure on new dwellings. For the public sector, investment is estimated from the revenue and expenditure data of the central government and other state organizations. Data for estimating exports and imports of goods and services are obtained from the balance of payments. For the constant price estimates, current values of government consumption expenditure, gross capital formation and exports and imports of goods and services are deflated by appropriate price indexes. For private consumption expenditure, the current quantities of the items estimated are revalued at base-year prices.

(c) Cost-structure of the gross domestic product. Wages and salaries for private sector are calculated per capita and applied to the number of employees which are obtained from the employment surveys submitted by the enterprises. Remuneration data for the government sector are obtained from government accounts. The data on employers' contributions to social security schemes are taken from 'seguro social'. Mathematical formulae are used to calculate consumption of fixed capital. Indirect taxes and subsidies are obtained directly from the government accounts.

(d) Gross domestic product by kind of economic activity. The table of GDP by kind of economic activity is prepared in factor values. Since 1977, the Portuguese National Institute of Statistics has followed the European System of Integrated Economic Accounts (ESA) in the national accounts estimates. The data reported according to ISIC Major divisions have been approximated from the Portuguese Branch and Product Nomenclature. The production approach is used to estimate value added of goods-production sectors whereas the income approach is used for the service sectors. The principal sources used to estimate agricultural production are Estadistica Agricolas and the monthly Estado das Culturas e Previsao das Colheitas which contain data on quantities and prices. Data on intermediate consumption are supplied by the entities that supply the products. For products of forestry and logging not covered by statistics on agriculture, estimates are based on per capita data on consumption. For fishery, quantity and price data are obtained from fishery statistics while intermediate consumtpion is calculated as a percentage of the gross value of production. For the industrial activity sectors estimates are obtained directly from Estatisticas Industriais and the Anuario Estatistico. Adjustments are made for activities in the manufacturing sector not covered in these two sources by using the industrial census of 1957. Value added of electricity, gas and water is obtained directly from annual surveys of corporatons, non-corporations and local government services. The construction estimates are based on annual surveys of enterprises. For dwellings taxation statistics are used and the figures relating to floor area of new buildings are multiplied by the average cost of construction by region. For the trade sector, the annual surveys of corporations are used for the corporations while data on the economically active population and the value added per capita for the retail trade is used for the individual enterprises. Taxation statistics and information provided by corporation are used for restaurants and hotels. The value added of the transport sector is obtained from the concerned companies and from annual surveys. The estimates for the financial institutions are based on direct information whereas data published in 'Estatisticas das Contribucoes e Impostoa' are used for ownership of dwellings. For government services, value added is obtained through government accounts. For private services, estimates are obtained through the use of data from 'Estatisticas de Educacao' for education, inquiries held in various cities for domestic servants, number of tickets sold for recreational services and taxation statistics for other personal services. For the constant price estimates, double deflation is used for the agricultural sector. Value added for construction, trade, restaurants, services incidental to transport, financial institutions, and community services is deflated by appropriate price indexes. For industrial activity sectors, hotels, transport and ownership of dwellings, value added is extrapolated by quantity indexes.

1.1 Expenditure on the Gross Domestic Product, in Current Prices

Million Portuguese escudos

	1980	1981	1982	1983	1984	1985	1986	1987	1988	1989	1990	1991
1 Government final consumption expenditure	182608	225892	276165	348355	423078	546899	678841	787829	962190	1147416	1422833	1765900
2 Private final consumption expenditure	845522	1045445	1287061	1596207	1990334	2393244	2876199	3335676	3909887	4527091	5368706	6273800
A Households	840705	1040145	1280929	1587597	1980398	2381389	2861836	3319972	3891594	4505997	5343020	...
B Private non-profit institutions serving households	4817	5300	6132	8610	9936	11855	14363	15704	18293	21094	25686	...
3 Gross capital formation	412011	518815	631152	650661	625971	727184	987556	1421785	1781055	2077239	2474556	2806100
A Increase in stocks	53164	55803	56383	-20845	-37723	-40775	10562	170967	169807	192222	231211	231200
B Gross fixed capital formation	358847	463012	574769	671506	663694	767959	976994	1250818	1611248	1885017	2243345	2574900
Residential buildings	77004	95811	114597	131425	140356	168035	210457	247954	283049	327226	379268	...
Non-residential buildings	28676	36871	52539	63461	65111	68587	107695	129223	163857	193408	241260	...
Other construction and land improvement etc.	86441	110882	139935	168926	177072	199421	226611	271040	343134	405022	505380	...
Other	166726	219448	267698	307694	281155	331916	432231	602601	821208	959361	1117437	...
4 Exports of goods and services	343950	389515	488482	721243	1048633	1315210	1466573	1774670	2129516	2671147	3100167	3166300
5 Less: Imports of goods and services	528040	678536	832453	1014753	1272288	1458592	1588769	2145228	2779897	3292633	3858828	4098700
Equals: Gross Domestic Product	1256051	1501131	1850407	2301713	2815728	3523945	4420400	5174732	6002751	7130260	8507434	9913400

1.2 Expenditure on the Gross Domestic Product, in Constant Prices

Million Portuguese escudos

	1980	1981	1982	1983	1984	1985	1986	1987	1988	1989	1990	1991
					At constant prices of:1985							
1 Government final consumption expenditure	451443	476269	494018	512737	513867	546899	586075	614561	647229	665043	674708	694900
2 Private final consumption expenditure	2359396	2427845	2484947	2449308	2377173	2393244	2527046	2663131	2838343	2932064	3088033	3248200
A Households	2346991	2416313	2473639	2436356	2365092	2381389	2514120	2650288	2824603	2918366	3074388	...
B Private non-profit institutions serving households	12405	11532	11308	12952	12081	11855	12926	12843	13740	13698	13645	...
3 Gross capital formation	1097625	1137279	1151946	932027	741969	727184	857537	1105012	1222289	1311509	1411205	1442500

Portugal

1.2 Expenditure on the Gross Domestic Product, in Constant Prices
(Continued)

Million Portuguese escudos

	1980	1981	1982	1983	1984	1985	1986	1987	1988	1989	1990	1991
					At constant prices of:1985							
A Increase in stocks	135699	122414	114171	-31735	-54231	-40775	6095	125264	95976	121731	150807	151300
B Gross fixed capital formation	961926	1014865	1037775	963762	796200	767959	851442	979748	1126313	1189778	1260398	1291200
Residential buildings	197033	199524	199420	184856	169297	168035	181147	192013	199991	200385	201295	...
Non-residential buildings	73374	76783	91427	89261	78537	68587	92697	100069	115775	118438	128048	...
Other construction and land improvement etc.	229638	241842	236743	235913	215764	199421	200387	226127	254323	271519	292159	...
Other	461881	496716	510185	453732	332602	331916	377211	461539	556224	599436	638896	...
4 Exports of goods and services	972054	928866	972233	1104507	1233018	1315210	1404061	1525021	1680212	1903408	2084081	2107800
5 Less: Imports of goods and services	1508793	1543976	1603697	1505190	1438313	1458592	1704849	2045110	2373993	2591016	2852436	2993300
Equals: Gross Domestic Product	3371725	3426283	3499447	3493389	3427714	3523945	3669870	3862615	4014080	4221008	4405591	4500100

1.3 Cost Components of the Gross Domestic Product

Million Portuguese escudos

	1980	1981	1982	1983	1984	1985	1986	1987	1988	1989	1990	1991
1 Indirect taxes, net	111544	133645	195795	266711	316660	407032	628839	676118	852487	973111	1162218	1327700
A Indirect taxes	176915	215073	275397	358507	436761	534160	778189	826806	1026626	1133055	1338947	1539800
B Less: Subsidies a	65371	81428	79602	91796	120101	127128	149350	150688	174139	159944	176729	212100
2 Consumption of fixed capital	...	...	...	...	...	...	...	...	...	...	...	...
3 Compensation of employees paid by resident producers to:	642966	788599	963576	1174167	1385852	1669807	2009235	2380810	2725389	3147886	3814438	4501000
A Resident households	639987	786066	960176	1169103	1379615	1661686	1997951	2369905	2712825	3130611	3785815	...
B Rest of the world	2979	2533	3400	5064	6237	8121	11284	10905	12564	17275	28623	...
4 Operating surplus b	501541	578887	691036	860835	1113216	1447106	1782326	2117804	2424875	3009263	3530778	4084700
A Corporate and quasi-corporate enterprises	...	...	...	...	...	...	637457	774462	905405	1116299	1267937	...
B Private unincorporated enterprises	...	...	...	...	...	...	1138396	1334444	1508953	1877247	2243002	...
C General government	...	...	...	...	...	...	6473	8898	10517	15717	19839	...
Equals: Gross Domestic Product	1256051	1501131	1850407	2301713	2815728	3523945	4420400	5174732	6002751	7130260	8507434	9913400

a) The 1973, 1975, 1976 and 1986-1988 estimates for item 'Subsidies' in table 1.3 differ from those   are entered on a cash payment basis.
of table 1.4. In the first case they are entered on an accrual payment basis, in the second case they b) Item 'Operating surplus' includes consumption of fixed capital.

1.4 General Government Current Receipts and Disbursements

Million Portuguese escudos

	1980	1981	1982	1983	1984	1985	1986	1987	1988	1989	1990	1991
					Receipts							
1 Operating surplus	1092	1710	1834	1707	4550	3021	6473	8898	10517	15717	19839	...
2 Property and entrepreneurial income	10173	14793	24915	45965	49684	43162	70405	86480	72663	99127	117271	
3 Taxes, fees and contributions	368528	466207	604207	793128	961603	1178016	1509441	1685340	2103237	2511965	2955225	...
A Indirect taxes	176915	215073	275397	358507	436761	534160	767876	804800	1002781	1104517	1308798	
B Direct taxes	81993	113224	146937	206687	246744	313274	321972	319445	463255	667979	764615	
C Social security contributions	109620	137910	181873	227934	278098	330582	419593	561095	637201	739469	881812	
D Compulsory fees, fines and penalties	...	...	...	...	...	...	...	...	...	...	...	
4 Other current transfers	14300	16494	23475	28420	35299	42488	73897	92453	99158	129333	104043	
Total Current Receipts of General Government	394093	499204	654431	869220	1051136	1266687	1660216	1873171	2285575	2756142	3196378	
					Disbursements							
1 Government final consumption expenditure	182608	225892	276165	348355	423078	546899	678841	787829	962190	1147416	1422833	
A Compensation of employees	144647	176711	214636	269114	327301	410257	498933	...	...	...	...	
B Consumption of fixed capital	...	...	...	...	...	...	...	...	...	...	...	
C Purchases of goods and services, net	37925	49167	61507	79218	95754	136619	179710	...	...	...	...	
D Less: Own account fixed capital formation	...	...	...	...	...	...	...	...	...	...	...	
E Indirect taxes paid, net	36	14	22	23	23	29	198	...	...	...	...	
2 Property income	38755	80122	97910	141365	231042	329014	428104	452961	467561	507447	692293	
A Interest	38749	80115	97896	141348	231004	328966	428049	452882	467481	507349	692175	
B Net land rent and royalties	6	7	14	17	38	48	55	79	80	98	118	...

1.4 General Government Current Receipts and Disbursements
(Continued)

Million Portuguese escudos

	1980	1981	1982	1983	1984	1985	1986	1987	1988	1989	1990	1991
3 Subsidies a	65371	81428	79602	91796	120101	127128	131058	98361	109517	105519	106460	...
4 Other current transfers	137435	177082	215614	253846	310729	386491	549431	684714	802725	923294	1125806	...
A Social security benefits	100557	133493	168677	209590	255324	315451	402912	486208	581976	665176	804769	...
B Social assistance grants	25072	32026	30511	25575	30531	42266	78815	115305	113635	139339	180619	...
C Other	11806	11563	16426	18681	24874	28774	67704	83201	107114	118779	140418	...
5 Net saving b	-30076	-65320	-14860	33858	-33814	-122845	-127218	-150694	-56418	72466	-151014	...
Total Current Disbursements and Net Saving of General Government	394093	499204	654431	869220	1051136	1266687	1660216	1873171	2285575	2756142	3196378	...

a) The 1973, 1975, 1976 and 1986-1988 estimates for item 'Subsidies' in table 1.3 differ from those   are entered on a cash payment basis.
of table 1.4. In the first case they are entered on an accrual payment basis, in the second case they b) Item 'Net saving' includes consumption of fixed capital.

1.5 Current Income and Outlay of Corporate and Quasi-Corporate Enterprises, Summary

Million Portuguese escudos

	1980	1981	1982	1983	1984	1985	1986	1987	1988	1989	1990	1991
Receipts												
1 Operating surplus	151159	165501	172833	245115	358837	500760	637457	774462	905405	1116299	1267937	...
2 Property and entrepreneurial income received	242937	347826	477179	674833	960450	1273702	1267561	1245309	1413789	1723369	2178472	...
3 Current transfers	38057	44353	56017	66251	70933	89193	96448	130222	163324	207436	251195	...
Total Current Receipts	432153	557680	706029	986199	1390220	1863655	2001466	2149993	2482518	3047104	3697604	...
Disbursements												
1 Property and entrepreneurial income	334635	487953	716150	1016975	1445374	1805973	1625126	1490740	1705408	2073164	2376189	...
2 Direct taxes and other current payments to general government	22670	30852	38050	45373	58124	68447	72945	101376	139242	199102	252398	...
3 Other current transfers	40386	47217	63047	76343	81523	89231	105698	147496	173236	229819	266879	...
Statistical discrepancy	1492	1929	2956	3422	3451	-930	3234	4330	5425	8302	7734	...
4 Net saving a	32970	-10271	-114174	-155914	-198252	-99066	194463	406051	459207	536717	794404	...
Total Current Disbursements and Net Saving	432153	557680	706029	986199	1390220	1863655	2001466	2149993	2482518	3047104	3697604	...

a) Item 'Net saving' includes consumption of fixed capital.

1.6 Current Income and Outlay of Households and Non-Profit Institutions

Million Portuguese escudos

	1980	1981	1982	1983	1984	1985	1986	1987	1988	1989	1990	1991
Receipts												
1 Compensation of employees	642028	788893	963012	1173328	1386837	1674003	2008898	2386602	2733821	3153390	3816241	...
A From resident producers	639987	786066	960176	1169103	1379615	1661686	1997951	2369905	2712825	3130611	3785815	...
B From rest of the world	2041	2827	2836	4225	7222	12317	10947	16697	20996	22779	30426	...
2 Operating surplus of private unincorporated enterprises	349290	411676	516369	614013	749829	943325	1138396	1334444	1508953	1877247	2243002	...
3 Property and entrepreneurial income	141575	205120	280824	403374	614069	777375	713436	648096	722726	848459	995957	...
4 Current transfers	304977	377589	460442	541256	688002	810361	1001634	1253844	1412659	1620547	1895841	...
A Social security benefits	132634	173239	214072	253486	308884	380072	481533	587502	704021	802362	975043	...
B Social assistance grants												...
C Other	172343	204350	246370	287770	379118	430289	520101	666342	708638	818185	920798	...
Statistical discrepancy	1492	1929	2956	3422	3451	-930	3234	4330	5425	8302	7734	...
Total Current Receipts	1439362	1785207	2223603	2735393	3442188	4204134	4865598	5627316	6383584	7507945	8958775	...
Disbursements												
1 Private final consumption expenditure	845522	1045445	1287061	1596207	1990334	2393244	2876199	3335676	3909887	4527091	5368706	...
2 Property income	52935	62148	74281	88435	126757	160037	155550	177037	176817	211682	271895	...
3 Direct taxes and other current transfers n.e.c. to general government	173932	226852	299859	400309	479451	585871	685749	800731	986909	1238757	1433235	...
A Social security contributions	114609	144480	190972	238995	290831	341044	436722	582668	662902	769889	921026	...
B Direct taxes	59323	82372	108887	161314	188620	244827	249027	218063	324007	468868	512209	...
C Fees, fines and penalties	...	...	...	...	...	...	...	...	...	...	...	...
4 Other current transfers	32553	38880	52846	68420	84283	103447	122526	168064	193420	225722	262471	...
5 Net saving a	334420	411882	509556	582022	761363	961535	1025574	1145808	1116551	1304693	1622468	...
Total Current Disbursements and Net Saving	1439362	1785207	2223603	2735393	3442188	4204134	4865598	5627316	6383584	7507945	8958775	...

a) Item 'Net saving' includes consumption of fixed capital.

Portugal

1.7 External Transactions on Current Account, Summary

Million Portuguese escudos

	1980	1981	1982	1983	1984	1985	1986	1987	1988	1989	1990	1991
Payments to the Rest of the World												
1 Imports of goods and services	528040	678536	832453	1014753	1272288	1458592	1588769	2145228	2779897	3292633	3858828	...
A Imports of merchandise c.i.f.	488209	630478	772651	939000	1171135	1356383	1469791	1997944	2585948	3056346	3559277	...
B Other	39831	48058	59802	75753	101153	102209	118978	147284	193949	236287	299551	...
2 Factor income to the rest of the world	41736	74865	119064	143080	209709	244978	204414	194902	199259	231879	242517	...
A Compensation of employees	2979	2533	3400	5064	6237	8121	11284	10905	12564	17275	28623	
B Property and entrepreneurial income	38757	72332	115664	138016	203472	236857	193130	183997	186695	214604	213894	
3 Current transfers to the rest of the world	6864	5650	9263	13116	17367	21313	65689	95299	104336	126345	157976	...
A Indirect taxes to supranational organizations	...	...	...	...	...	...	10313	22006	23845	28538	30149	...
B Other current transfers	6864	5650	9263	13116	17367	21313	55376	73293	80491	97807	127827	
4 Surplus of the nation on current transactions	-74697	-182524	-250630	-190695	-96674	12440	105263	-20620	-261715	-163363	-208698	
Payments to the Rest of the World and Surplus of the Nation on Current Transactions	501943	576527	710150	980254	1402690	1737323	1964135	2414809	2821777	3487494	4050623	
Receipts From The Rest of the World												
1 Exports of goods and services	343950	389515	488482	721243	1048633	1315210	1466573	1774670	2129516	2671147	3100167	...
A Exports of merchandise f.o.b.	247564	275979	357465	536423	790234	1005286	1124168	1357098	1635076	2069053	2386109	...
B Other	96386	113536	131017	184820	258399	309924	342405	417572	494440	602094	714058	
2 Factor income from rest of the world	9158	12675	13077	19638	31724	48389	46699	59841	67083	116045	195643	...
A Compensation of employees	2041	2827	2836	4225	7222	12317	10947	16697	20996	22779	30426	
B Property and entrepreneurial income	7117	9848	10241	15413	24502	36072	35752	43144	46087	93266	165217	
3 Current transfers from rest of the world	148835	174337	208591	239373	322333	373724	450863	580298	625178	700302	754813	...
A Subsidies from supranational organisations	563	1095	...	...	...	...	18292	52327	64622	54425	70269	
B Other current transfers	148272	173242	208591	239373	322333	373724	432571	527971	560556	645877	684544	
Receipts from the Rest of the World on Current Transactions	501943	576527	710150	980254	1402690	1737323	1964135	2414809	2821777	3487494	4050623	...

1.8 Capital Transactions of The Nation, Summary

Million Portuguese escudos

	1980	1981	1982	1983	1984	1985	1986	1987	1988	1989	1990	1991
Finance of Gross Capital Formation												
Gross saving	337314	336291	380522	459966	529297	739624	1092819	1401165	1519340	1913876	2265858	2514600
1 Consumption of fixed capital	...	...	...	...	...	...	...	...	...	...	...	...
2 Net saving a	337314	336291	380522	459966	529297	739624	1092819	1401165	1519340	1913876	2265858	2514600
A General government a	-30076	-65320	-14860	33858	-33814	-122845	-127218	-150694	-56418	72466	-151014	...
B Corporate and quasi-corporate enterprises a	32970	-10271	-114174	-155914	-198252	-99066	194463	406051	459207	536717	794404	
C Other a	334420	411882	509556	582022	761363	961535	1025574	1145808	1116551	1304693	1622468	
Less: Surplus of the nation on current transactions	-74697	-182524	-250630	-190695	-96674	12440	105263	-20620	-261715	-163363	-208698	-291500
Finance of Gross Capital Formation	412011	518815	631152	650661	625971	727184	987556	1421785	1781055	2077239	2474556	2806100
Gross Capital Formation												
Increase in stocks	53164	55803	56383	-20845	-37723	-40775	10562	170967	169807	192222	231211	231200
Gross fixed capital formation	358847	463012	574769	671506	663694	767959	976994	1250818	1611248	1885017	2243345	2574900
1 General government	51605	74617	79923	88553	90656	108926	143957	170949	216944	246070	290924	...
2 Corporate and quasi-corporate enterprises	190220	239765	303083	370554	342234	379385	493435	679446	892358	1064366	1283259	
3 Other	117022	148630	191763	212399	230804	279648	339602	400423	501946	574581	669162	...
Gross Capital Formation	412011	518815	631152	650661	625971	727184	987556	1421785	1781055	2077239	2474556	2806100

a) Gross savings.

1.10 Gross Domestic Product by Kind of Activity, in Current Prices

Million Portuguese escudos

	1980	1981	1982	1983	1984	1985	1986	1987	1988	1989	1990	1991
1 Agriculture, hunting, forestry and fishing	129899	134560	162895	183321	234448	281203	328722	379025	365145	441014	490787	...
2 Mining and quarrying	388982	470161	545369	675744	862101	1070626	1290121	1514197	1707316	2055923	2373090	...
3 Manufacturing												...
4 Electricity, gas and water	26502	16097	33031	57330	91767	123049	136407	168055	211218	209762	261311	...
5 Construction	88852	113022	149451	175197	166841	200368	245720	296450	368504	452708	585382	...
6 Wholesale and retail trade, restaurants and hotels	272419	326190	416709	520187	615172	788545	904686	1034457	1185020	1397819	1681487	
7 Transport, storage and communication	69341	93804	121685	166490	214185	272262	297134	324486	361260	412995	462412	
8 Finance, insurance, real estate and business services a	131409	166562	211840	256567	290106	357453	427079	548654	685497	841636	1112586	
9 Community, social and personal services ab	30209	41011	52862	67106	85294	112966	139234	172436	201854	242524	294756	
Total, Industries	1137613	1361407	1693842	2101942	2559914	3206472	3769103	4437760	5085814	6054381	7261811	
Producers of Government Services	144683	176725	214658	269137	327324	410280	499131	629587	759704	926340	1156989	...
Other Producers	13282	16379	19120	23451	28344	34316	38799					...
Subtotal	1295578	1554511	1927620	2394530	2915582	3651068	4307033	5067347	5845518	6980721	8418800	...
Less: Imputed bank service charge	55553	77588	107420	135775	139753	179388	222787	305847	382586	472299	627863	
Plus: Import duties	16026	24208	30207	42958	39899	52265	54802	79969	117081	124671	146439	
Plus: Value added tax	...	...	...	...	...	...	281352	333263	422738	497167	570058	...
Equals: Gross Domestic Product	1256051	1501131	1850407	2301713	2815728	3523945	4420400	5174732	6002751	7130260	8507434	...
Memorandum Item: Mineral fuels and power	29654	20823	...	...	...	...	157975	187666	254938	223590	250628	

a) Business services and real estate except dwellings are included in item 'Community, social and services'. personal services'.

b) For the first series, repair services are included in item 'Community, social and personal

1.11 Gross Domestic Product by Kind of Activity, in Constant Prices

Million Portuguese escudos

	1980	1981	1982	1983	1984	1985	1986	1987	1988	1989	1990	1991
						At constant prices of:1985						
1 Agriculture, hunting, forestry and fishing	255600	228109	242095	238788	260332	281203	289959	302070	267192	302329	297563	...
2 Mining and quarrying	1079194	1113126	1101504	1087055	1044649	1070626	1137418	1170238	1199583	1296337	1355919	...
3 Manufacturing												...
4 Electricity, gas and water	84348	68931	92924	103482	111628	123049	112262	117943	132953	122051	134383	
5 Construction	217875	228106	232582	234232	212319	200368	204889	221048	245166	255077	265289	
6 Wholesale and retail trade, restaurants and hotels	820102	834978	842015	817771	779144	788545	832726	886725	927531	965441	1000300	
7 Transport, storage and communication	229964	233611	249629	264621	264869	272262	286117	300238	320795	338409	372540	
8 Finance, insurance, real estate and business services	335973	353165	374415	375813	340887	357453	364603	422882	445019	478207	574362	...
9 Community, social and personal services	99055	102809	105042	106111	106560	112966	114129	121740	123315	125381	124478	
Total, Industries	3122111	3162835	3240206	3227873	3120388	3206472	3342103	3542884	3661554	3883232	4124834	
Producers of Government Services	374006	392409	405654	424832	431897	444596	458725	479950	491524	506146	496358	...
Other Producers												...
Subtotal	3496117	3555244	3645860	3652705	3552285	3651068	3800828	4022834	4153078	4389378	4621192	...
Less: Imputed bank service charge	163285	181159	199831	203249	166431	179388	195502	243543	258714	282637	342414	
Plus: Import duties	38893	52198	53418	43933	41860	52265	64544	83324	119716	114267	126813	...
Plus: Value added tax	...	...	...	...	...	...	...	...	...	...	...	
Equals: Gross Domestic Product	3371725	3426283	3499447	3493389	3427714	3523945	3669870	3862615	4014080	4221008	4405591	
Memorandum Item: Mineral fuels and power	100139	102655	115328	114619	120558	135144	126666	131502	150020	141353	154147	...

1.12 Relations Among National Accounting Aggregates

Million Portuguese escudos

	1980	1981	1982	1983	1984	1985	1986	1987	1988	1989	1990	1991
Gross Domestic Product	1256051	1501131	1850407	2301713	2815728	3523945	4420400	5174732	6002751	7130260	8507434	9913400
Plus: Net factor income from the rest of the world	-32578	-62190	-105987	-123442	-177985	-196589	-157715	-135061	-132176	-115834	-46874	-54600
Factor income from the rest of the world	9158	12675	13077	19638	31724	48389	46699	59841	67083	116045	195643	...
Less: Factor income to the rest of the world	41736	74865	119064	143080	209709	244978	204414	194902	199259	231879	242517	...
Equals: Gross National Product	1223473	1438941	1744420	2178271	2637743	3327356	4262685	5039671	5870575	7014426	8460560	9858800
Less: Consumption of fixed capital	...	...	...	...	...	...	...	...	...	...	...	

Portugal

Million Portuguese escudos

	1980	1981	1982	1983	1984	1985	1986	1987	1988	1989	1990	1991
Equals: National Income a	1223473	1438941	1744420	2178271	2637743	3327356	4262685	5039671	5870575	7014426	8460560	9858800
Plus: Net current transfers from the rest of the world	141971	168687	199328	226257	304966	352411	385174	484999	520842	573957	596837	695500
Current transfers from the rest of the world	148835	174337	208591	239373	322333	373724	450863	580298	625178	700302	754813	...
Less: Current transfers to the rest of the world	6864	5650	9263	13116	17367	21313	65689	95299	104336	126345	157976	...
Equals: National Disposable Income b	1365444	1607628	1943748	2404528	2942709	3679767	4647859	5524670	6391417	7588383	9057397	554300
Less: Final consumption	1028130	1271337	1563226	1944562	2413412	2940143	3555040	4123505	4872077	5674507	6791539	8039700
Equals: Net Saving c	337314	336291	380522	459966	529297	739624	1092819	1401165	1519340	1913876	2265858	2514600
Less: Surplus of the nation on current transactions	-74697	-182524	-250630	-190695	-96674	12440	105263	-20620	-261715	-163363	-208698	-291500
Equals: Net Capital Formation d	412011	518815	631152	650661	625971	727184	987556	1421785	1781055	2077239	2474556	2806100

a) Item 'National income' includes consumption of fixed capital.
b) Item 'National disposable income' includes consumption of fixed capital.
c) Item 'Net saving' includes consumption of fixed capital.
d) Item 'Net capital formation' includes consumption of fixed capital.

2.3 Total Government Outlays by Function and Type

Million Portuguese escudos

	Final Consumption Expenditures			Subsidies	Other Current Transfers & Property Income	Total Current Disbursements	Gross Capital Formation	Other Capital Outlays	Total Outlays
	Total	Compensation of Employees	Other						
				1980					
1 General public services	24705	21209	3496	-	999	25704	5394	115	31213
2 Defence	36057	23023	13034	-	156	36213	115	4	36332
3 Public order and safety	15834	14798	1036	-	301	16135	602	18	16755
4 Education	42997	40433	2564	2	3936	46935	8490	455	55880
5 Health	32467	22266	10201	2	16758	49227	4138	73	53438
6 Social security and welfare	11099	9300	1799	-	110986	122085	1316	1042	124443
7 Housing and community amenities	3304	2874	430	1687	10	5001	7892	5006	17899
8 Recreation, culture and religion	1980	1404	576	-	1359	3339	1039	221	4599
9 Economic services	14120	9313	4807	63680	2681	80481	22607	9650	112738
A Fuel and energy	11	-	11	367	-	378	3259	503	4140
B Agriculture, forestry, fishing and hunting	5374	4042	1332	1202	28	6604	3540	347	10491
C Mining (except fuels), manufacturing and construction a	1046	710	336	15975	9	17030	169	3547	20746
D Transportation and communication	1698	630	1068	8112	2491	12301	14351	3523	30175
E Other economic affairs	5991	3931	2060	38024	153	44168	1288	1730	47186
10 Other functions	45	27	18	-	39004	39049	12	4100	43161
Total	182608	144647	37961	65371	176190	424169	51605	20684	496458
				1981					
1 General public services	29539	25403	4136	-	2093	31632	5790	-1150	36272
2 Defence	43001	26662	16339	-	5544	48545	1372	14	49931
3 Public order and safety	19232	18208	1024	-	1731	20963	1559	135	22657
4 Education	55279	51050	4229	11	3124	58414	10461	394	69269
5 Health	42661	28925	13736	36	18435	61132	6851	163	68146
6 Social security and welfare	12748	10136	2612	-	136713	149461	1082	1459	152002
7 Housing and community amenities	4230	3494	736	2087	85	6402	9190	848	16440
8 Recreation, culture and religion	2507	1860	647	-	1997	4504	1588	246	6338
9 Economic services	16693	10973	5720	79294	6388	102375	36724	13658	152757
A Fuel and energy	15	-	15	816	-	831	4989	1326	7146
B Agriculture, forestry, fishing and hunting	6251	4685	1566	1465	243	7959	3192	408	11559
C Mining (except fuels), manufacturing and construction a	1362	946	416	22940	110	24412	561	9261	34234
D Transportation and communication	2217	760	1457	7567	5415	15199	26357	1672	43228
E Other economic affairs	6848	4582	2266	46506	620	53974	1625	991	56590
10 Other functions	2	-	2	-	81094	81096	-	6458	87554
Total	225892	176711	49181	81428	257204	564524	74617	22225	661366

2.3 Total Government Outlays by Function and Type
(Continued)

Million Portuguese escudos

	Final Consumption Expenditures			Subsidies	Other Current Transfers & Property Income	Total Current Disbursements	Gross Capital Formation	Other Capital Outlays	Total Outlays
	Total	Compensation of Employees	Other						
1982									
1 General public services	34189	...	...	2	3941	38132	7587	128	45847
2 Defence	51829	...	...	-	6998	58827	535	32	59394
3 Public order and safety	24878	...	...	-	2102	26980	2377	573	29930
4 Education	67743	...	...	-	3039	70782	13123	474	84379
5 Health	53876	...	...	-	12746	66622	6278	51	72951
6 Social security and welfare	17260	...	...	1529	177308	196097	630	1749	198476
7 Housing and community amenities	4208	...	...	1760	103	6071	8593	9186	23850
8 Recreation, culture and religion	2914	...	...	814	2240	5968	2207	748	8923
9 Economic services	19268	...	...	75497	5786	100551	38593	30088	169232
A Fuel and energy	8	...	...	886	5	899	6236	1370	8505
B Agriculture, forestry, fishing and hunting	6904	...	...	2039	443	9386	3498	661	13545
C Mining (except fuels), manufacturing and construction [a]	1566	...	...	29753	106	31425	771	23201	55397
D Transportation and communication	3204	...	...	8747	4642	16593	27031	1786	45410
E Other economic affairs	7586	...	...	34072	590	42248	1057	3070	46375
10 Other functions	-	...	...	-	99261	99261	-	32147	131408
Total	276165	...	...	79602	313524	669291	79923	75176	824390
1983									
1 General public services	39613	...	...	-	2919	42532	8632	179	51343
2 Defence	66871	...	...	-	9983	76854	687	-	77541
3 Public order and safety	31167	...	...	-	2959	34126	2059	620	36805
4 Education	87331	...	...	7	4809	92147	15127	278	107552
5 Health	71944	...	...	-	1379	73323	6476	17	79816
6 Social security and welfare	17626	...	...	-	224973	242599	1230	2110	245939
7 Housing and community amenities	6304	...	...	383	123	6810	6964	6616	20390
8 Recreation, culture and religion	4119	...	...	-	2741	6860	2385	751	9996
9 Economic services	23305	...	...	91406	1348	116059	44993	166048	327100
A Fuel and energy	17	...	...	559	-	576	5473	884	6933
B Agriculture, forestry, fishing and hunting	2979	...	...	2228	180	5387	5353	1213	11953
C Mining (except fuels), manufacturing and construction [a]	1939	...	...	29363	81	31383	675	19864	51922
D Transportation and communication	2925	...	...	9114	20	12059	30389	4337	46785
E Other economic affairs	15445	...	...	50142	1067	66654	3103	139750	209507
10 Other functions	75	...	...	-	143977	144052	-	31711	175763
Total	348355	...	...	91796	395211	835362	88553	208330	1132245
1984									
1 General public services	53601	...	...	-	3647	57248	7586	-807	64027
2 Defence	74214	...	...	-	12583	86797	599	64	87460
3 Public order and safety	40375	...	...	-	4506	44881	2045	785	47711
4 Education	105877	...	...	1	5414	111292	15359	1674	128325
5 Health	84868	...	...	-	5423	90291	6437	100	96828
6 Social security and welfare	20779	...	...	3800	272106	296685	1883	1603	300171
7 Housing and community amenities	7306	...	...	406	139	7851	7184	6072	21107
8 Recreation, culture and religion	5246	...	...	1322	2951	9519	2879	1250	13648
9 Economic services	30243	...	...	111592	2172	144007	46684	152238	342929
A Fuel and energy	8	...	...	407	-	415	4759	1301	6475
B Agriculture, forestry, fishing and hunting	5028	...	...	3214	381	8623	9532	885	19040
C Mining (except fuels), manufacturing and construction [a]	2687	...	...	84487	81	87255	1316	2964	91535
D Transportation and communication	3185	...	...	8987	24	12196	26421	6861	45478
E Other economic affairs	19335	...	...	14497	1686	35518	4656	140227	180401
10 Other functions	569	...	...	2980	232830	236379	-	31778	268157
Total	423078	...	...	120101	541771	1084950	90656	194757	1370363

2.3 Total Government Outlays by Function and Type
(Continued)

Million Portuguese escudos

		Final Consumption Expenditures		Subsidies	Other Current Transfers & Property Income	Total Current Disbursements	Gross Capital Formation	Other Capital Outlays	Total Outlays
		Total	Compensation of Employees	Other						

		Total	Compensation of Employees	Other	Subsidies	Other Current Transfers & Property Income	Total Current Disbursements	Gross Capital Formation	Other Capital Outlays	Total Outlays
	1985									
1	General public services	67621	...	...	3	4707	72331	10500	-947	81884
2	Defence	88786	...	...	-	13309	102095	757	163	103015
3	Public order and safety	53116	...	...	-	5877	58993	2417	804	62214
4	Education	135196	...	...	2	6728	141926	16258	1287	159471
5	Health	123044	...	...	9	7901	130954	7298	132	138384
6	Social security and welfare	26037	...	...	2998	337351	366386	1980	2014	370380
7	Housing and community amenities	9846	...	...	470	184	10500	8325	45118	63943
8	Recreation, culture and religion	7253	...	...	1642	4215	13110	4672	1964	19746
9	Economic services	35764	...	...	119177	2307	157248	56719	241985	455952
	A Fuel and energy	467	...	...	207	41	715	4746	1372	6833
	B Agriculture, forestry, fishing and hunting	3440	...	...	12930	497	16867	11917	914	29698
	C Mining (except fuels), manufacturing and construction a	3136	...	...	67815	189	71140	1041	26939	99120
	D Transportation and communication	4509	...	...	18497	40	23046	32905	10723	66674
	E Other economic affairs	24212	...	...	19728	1540	45480	6110	202037	253627
10	Other functions	236	...	...	2827	332926	335989	-	37653	373642
	Total	546899	...	...	127128	715505	1389532	108926	330173	1828631
	1986									
1	General public services	82572	...	...	84	37939	120595	11729	-154	132170
2	Defence	116392	...	...	-	16402	132794	3147	328	136269
3	Public order and safety	65206	...	...	-	7431	72637	3769	1720	78126
4	Education	171751	...	...	-	8033	179784	25439	1361	206584
5	Health	147382	...	...	591	11455	159428	9001	194	168623
6	Social security and welfare	32180	...	...	4929	430048	467157	2772	2299	472228
7	Housing and community amenities	10801	...	...	984	25015	36800	9886	26468	73154
8	Recreation, culture and religion	9273	...	...	3113	6044	18430	5055	2762	26247
9	Economic services	43284	...	...	119174	2540	164998	73159	94859	333016
	A Fuel and energy	288	...	...	948	59	1295	5159	1679	8133
	B Agriculture, forestry, fishing and hunting	12579	...	...	12169	1090	25838	11347	4746	41931
	C Mining (except fuels), manufacturing and construction a	3544	...	...	52606	133	56283	1240	19893	77416
	D Transportation and communication	5697	...	...	31823	44	37564	46780	2695	87039
	E Other economic affairs	21176	...	...	21628	1214	44018	8633	65846	118497
10	Other functions	-	...	...	2183	432628	434811	-	53765	488576
	Total	678841	...	...	131058	977535	1787434	143957	183602	2114993

a) Item 'Mining, manufacturing and construction, except fuel and energy' includes fuel.

2.5 Private Final Consumption Expenditure by Type and Purpose, in Current Prices

Million Portuguese escudos

		1980	1981	1982	1983	1984	1985	1986	1987	1988	1989	1990	1991
	Final Consumption Expenditure of Resident Households												
1	Food, beverages and tobacco	320460	392837	489425	618890	786763	946473	1111562	...	...	...	...	...
	A Food	278473	342130	426554	543204	691743	833653	977043	...	...	...	...	...
	B Non-alcoholic beverages	2073	3052	3187	3429	4545	5767	7252	...	...	...	...	...
	C Alcoholic beverages	22839	26700	31531	35928	42536	49439	57700	...	...	...	...	...
	D Tobacco	17075	20955	28153	36329	47939	57614	69567	...	...	...	...	...
2	Clothing and footwear	91220	108766	130169	149840	195013	235383	307081	...	...	...	...	...
3	Gross rent, fuel and power	51722	59424	68880	86193	104213	124234	148261	...	...	...	...	...
	A Fuel and power	20073	25607	32027	46182	61671	77262	88446	...	...	...	...	...
	B Other	31649	33817	36853	40011	42542	46972	59815	...	...	...	...	...
4	Furniture, furnishings and household equipment and operation	87077	103457	121524	146122	183416	217791	257713	...	...	...	...	...
	A Household operation	28214	34103	40350	50638	66911	82436	91425	...	...	...	...	...

2.5 Private Final Consumption Expenditure by Type and Purpose, in Current Prices
(Continued)

Million Portuguese escudos

	1980	1981	1982	1983	1984	1985	1986	1987	1988	1989	1990	1991
B Other	58863	69354	81174	95484	116505	135355	166288	...	...	...	...	...
5 Medical care and health expenses	37141	45972	56870	72564	92141	115242	134585	...	...	...	...	...
6 Transport and communication	122577	164613	199456	253416	299433	371885	459673	...	...	...	...	...
A Personal transport equipment	82705	110566	134561	168832	185403	225789	293470	...	...	...	...	...
B Other	39872	54047	64895	84584	114030	146096	166203	...	...	...	...	...
7 Recreational, entertainment, education and cultural services	43384	57666	73400	92213	119253	145459	171628	...	...	...	...	...
A Education	7943	10788	14762	18939	25999	33331	40735	...	...	...	...	...
B Other	35441	46878	58638	73274	93254	112128	130893	...	...	...	...	...
8 Miscellaneous goods and services	114825	139498	173968	214174	275287	334932	401878	...	...	...	...	...
A Personal care	9780	12481	14882	17168	21881	28167	32229	...	...	...	...	...
B Expenditures in restaurants, cafes and hotels	82052	98089	122601	153370	195414	239122	289039	...	...	...	...	...
C Other	22993	28928	36485	43636	57992	67643	80610	...	...	...	...	...
Total Final Consumption Expenditure in the Domestic Market by Households, of which	868406	1072233	1313692	1633412	2055519	2491399	2992381	3498127	4088482	4747005	...	...
A Durable goods	68817	93413	...	...	...	...	241814	...	...	...	...	...
B Semi-durable goods	169565	205546	...	...	...	...	562400	...	...	...	...	...
C Non-durable goods	406152	496010	...	...	...	...	1403313	...	...	...	...	...
D Services	223872	277264	...	...	...	...	784854	...	...	...	...	...
Plus: Direct purchases abroad by resident households	17785	18814	23993	30890	39652	46662	56145	71450	91266	109503	...	...
Less: Direct purchases in the domestic market by non-resident households	45486	50902	56756	76705	114773	156672	186690	249605	288154	350511	...	...
Equals: Final Consumption Expenditure of Resident Households	840705	1040145	1280929	1587597	1980398	2381389	2861836	3319972	3891594	4505997	...	...

Final Consumption Expenditure of Private Non-profit Institutions Serving Households

	1980	1981	1982	1983	1984	1985	1986	1987	1988	1989	1990	1991
1 Research and science	-	-	-	-	-	-	-	...	...	...	...	...
2 Education	18	26	30	36	33	34	76	...	...	...	...	...
3 Medical and other health services	42	42	49	64	59	91	89	...	...	...	...	...
4 Welfare services								...	...	...	...	...
5 Recreational and related cultural services								...	...	...	...	...
6 Religious organisations	4757	5232	6053	8510	9844	11730	14198	...	...	...	...	...
7 Professional and labour organisations serving households								...	...	...	...	...
8 Miscellaneous								...	...	...	...	...
Equals: Final Consumption Expenditure of Private Non-profit Organisations Serving Households	4817	5300	6132	8610	9936	11855	14363	15704	18293	21094	...	...
Private Final Consumption Expenditure	845522	1045445	1287061	1596207	1990334	2393244	2876199	3335676	3909887	4527091	...	...

2.6 Private Final Consumption Expenditure by Type and Purpose, in Constant Prices

Million Portuguese escudos

At constant prices of:1985

Final Consumption Expenditure of Resident Households

	1980	1981	1982	1983	1984	1985	1986	1987	1988	1989	1990	1991
1 Food, beverages and tobacco	914201	931776	955791	951294	934797	946473	1000627	...	...	...	...	...
A Food	806221	820782	840925	834464	819869	833653	885402	...	...	...	...	...
B Non-alcoholic beverages	6413	6793	6290	5992	5938	5767	6019	...	...	...	...	...
C Alcoholic beverages	51058	52515	53220	53034	50471	49439	50562	...	...	...	...	...
D Tobacco	50509	51686	55356	57804	58519	57614	58644	...	...	...	...	...
2 Clothing and footwear	249755	249585	252045	239791	234254	235383	253573	...	...	...	...	...
3 Gross rent, fuel and power	109546	110910	113321	118146	118696	124234	131135	...	...	...	...	...
A Fuel and power	65568	66280	67709	71887	72386	77262	81934	...	...	...	...	...
B Other	43978	44630	45612	46259	46310	46972	49201	...	...	...	...	...
4 Furniture, furnishings and household equipment and operation	227541	229756	228567	262294	217936	217791	225769	...	...	...	...	...
A Household operation	79979	81063	81563	83790	81138	82436	83022	...	...	...	...	...

Portugal

2.6 Private Final Consumption Expenditure by Type and Purpose, in Constant Prices
(Continued)

Million Portuguese escudos

	1980	1981	1982	1983	1984	1985	1986	1987	1988	1989	1990	1991
					At constant prices of:1985							
B Other	147562	148693	147004	178504	136798	135355	142747	...	...	...	...	...
5 Medical care and health expenses	107117	109402	110446	93321	110866	115242	111217	...	...	...	...	...
6 Transport and communication	351624	382712	388178	383151	360004	371885	406272	...	...	...	...	...
A Personal transport equipment	207562	234977	242585	238930	212477	225789	258108	...	...	...	...	...
B Other	144062	147735	145593	144221	147527	146096	148164	...	...	...	...	...
7 Recreational, entertainment, education and cultural services	137068	145134	149699	146151	145259	145459	147636	...	...	...	...	...
A Education	33011	33655	33861	32145	33467	33331	33712	...	...	...	...	...
B Other	104057	111479	115838	114006	111792	112128	113924	...	...	...	...	...
8 Miscellaneous goods and services	317459	323287	331028	329959	334077	334932	349237	...	...	...	...	...
A Personal care	25534	27583	28350	27438	27343	28167	31601	...	...	...	...	...
B Expenditures in restaurants, cafes and hotels	225742	228081	232517	234200	235634	239122	248742	...	...	...	...	...
C Other	66183	67623	70161	68321	71100	67643	68894	...	...	...	...	...
Total Final Consumption Expenditure in the Domestic Market by Households, of which	2414311	2482562	2529075	2524107	2455889	2491399	2625466	2784004	2959806	3051684	...	...
Plus: Direct purchases abroad by resident households	...	...	...	...	...	...	...	...	...	...	...	...
Less: Direct purchases in the domestic market by non-resident households	...	...	...	...	...	...	...	...	...	...	...	...
Equals: Final Consumption Expenditure of Resident Households	2346991	2416313	2473639	2436356	2365092	2381389	2514120	2650288	2824603	2918366	...	...

Final Consumption Expenditure of Private Non-profit Institutions Serving Households

	1980	1981	1982	1983	1984	1985	1986	1987	1988	1989	1990	1991
Equals: Final Consumption Expenditure of Private Non-profit Organisations Serving Households	12405	11532	11308	12952	12081	11855	12926	12843	13740	13698	...	...
Private Final Consumption Expenditure	2359396	2427845	2484947	2449308	2377173	2393244	2527046	2663131	2838343	2932064	...	...

2.11 Gross Fixed Capital Formation by Kind of Activity of Owner, ISIC Divisions, in Current Prices

Million Portuguese escudos

	1980	1981	1982	1983	1984	1985	1986	1987	1988	1989	1990	1991
					All Producers							
1 Agriculture, hunting, forestry and fishing	17049	19704	21371	22384	27809	32013	44409	...	...	...	...	...
A Agriculture and hunting	13847	16801	16718	18558	23763	28271	39300	...	...	...	...	...
B Forestry and logging	944	1184	1448	753	1558	1741	2228	...	...	...	...	...
C Fishing	2258	1719	3205	3073	2488	2001	2881	...	...	...	...	...
2 Mining and quarrying	...	...	...	...	...	...	...	...	...	...	...	...
3 Manufacturing	82754	110069	154923	165595	156247	137682	166159	...	...	...	...	...
A Manufacturing of food, beverages and tobacco	8729	12019	14321	17624	19849	22447	26429	...	...	...	...	...
B Textile, wearing apparel and leather industries	13316	21565	26537	26813	29288	31078	40662	...	...	...	...	...
C Manufacture of wood, and wood products, including furniture	3878	4690	4208	5018	5178	3071	6938	...	...	...	...	...
D Manufacture of paper and paper products, printing and publishing	4550	9654	12509	30218	16660	13072	20982	...	...	...	...	...
E Manufacture of chemicals and chemical petroleum, coal, rubber and plastic products	26003	23330	30011	23872	26699	14865	14354	...	...	...	...	...
F Manufacture of non-metalic mineral products except products of petroleum and coal	7221	10199	21166	18496	15813	17388	25255	...	...	...	...	...
G Basic metal industries	2956	2993	7527	7078	4992	6251	2318	...	...	...	...	...
H Manufacture of fabricated metal products, machinery and equipment	14638	23735	36964	33887	35092	27347	27573	...	...	...	...	...
I Other manufacturing industries	1463	1884	1680	2589	2676	2163	1648	...	...	...	...	...
4 Electricity, gas and water	26982	23729	26916	40364	49029	150198	118100	...	...	...	...	...

2.11 Gross Fixed Capital Formation by Kind of Activity of Owner, ISIC Divisions, in Current Prices
(Continued)

Million Portuguese escudos

	1980	1981	1982	1983	1984	1985	1986	1987	1988	1989	1990	1991
5 Construction	23421	23415	31615	24185	20173	19410	31303	...	...	...	...	...
6 Wholesale and retail trade, restaurants and hotels	25918	31091	47200	47668	45888	44176	60742	...	...	...	...	...
A Wholesale and retail trade	22903	27914	37312	40292	40025	38893	52946	...	...	...	...	...
B Restaurants and hotels	3015	3177	9888	7376	5863	5283	7796	...	...	...	...	...
7 Transport, storage and communication	31427	46939	42157	82473	55376	35657	70250	...	...	...	...	...
A Transport and storage	23178	37512	35431	64140	31935	21363	36710	...	...	...	...	...
B Communication	8249	9427	6726	18333	23441	14294	33540	...	...	...	...	...
8 Finance, insurance, real estate and business services	109024	137752	173118	200102	218552	236246	329620	...	...	...	...	...
A Financial institutions	7715	10003	11069	16104	18663	17139	29239	...	...	...	...	...
B Insurance	2042	2813	3138	3399	3357	3953	4718	...	...	...	...	...
C Real estate and business services	99267	124936	158911	180599	196532	215154	295663	...	...	...	...	...
Real estate except dwellings	10299	11949	27814	26747	22925	14912	37958	...	...	...	...	...
Dwellings	88968	112987	131097	153852	173607	200242	257705	...	...	...	...	...
9 Community, social and personal services	3508	4200	5795	7919	7239	10222	24651	...	...	...	...	...
A Sanitary and similar services	...	...	...	...	...	...	...	...	...	...	...	...
B Social and related community services	1091	1802	1322	2310	1937	2549	4731	...	...	...	...	...
Educational services	162	403	153	844	869	491	2242	...	...	...	...	...
Medical, dental, other health and veterinary services	929	1399	1169	1466	1068	2058	2489	...	...	...	...	...
C Recreational and cultural services	2417	2398	4473	5609	5302	7673	19920	...	...	...	...	...
D Personal and household services	...	...	...	...	...	...	...	...	...	...	...	...
Total Industries	320083	396899	503095	590690	580313	665604	845234	...	...	...	...	...
Producers of Government Services	38764	66113	71674	80816	83381	102355	131760	...	...	...	...	...
Private Non-Profit Institutions Serving Households	...	...	...	...	...	...	...	...	...	...	...	...
Total	358847	463012	574769	671506	663694	767959	976994	...	...	...	...	...

2.17 Exports and Imports of Goods and Services, Detail

Million Portuguese escudos

	1980	1981	1982	1983	1984	1985	1986	1987	1988	1989	1990	1991
Exports of Goods and Services												
1 Exports of merchandise, f.o.b.	247564	275979	357465	536423	790234	1005286	1124168	1357098	1635076	2069053	2386109	...
2 Transport and communication	38810	47617	...	...	...	...	134022	144387	168347	194979	218235	...
A In respect of merchandise imports	13262	...	...	...	...	...	40263	54604	69293	83685	99762	...
B Other	25548	...	...	...	...	...	93759	89783	99054	111294	118473	...
3 Insurance service charges	999	874	...	...	...	...	2051	2163	5420	7010	8284	...
4 Other commodities	11091	14143	...	...	...	...	19642	21417	32519	49594	71540	...
5 Adjustments of merchandise exports to change-of-ownership basis	...	...	...	...	...	...	...	...	...	...	...	...
6 Direct purchases in the domestic market by non-residential households	45486	50902	...	...	...	...	186690	249605	288154	350511	415999	...
7 Direct purchases in the domestic market by extraterritorial bodies	...	...	...	...	...	...	...	...	...	...	...	...
Total Exports of Goods and Services	343950	389515	488482	721243	1048633	1315210	1466573	1774670	2129516	2671147	3100167	...
Imports of Goods and Services												
1 Imports of merchandise, c.i.f.	488209	630478	772651	939000	1171135	1356383	1469791	1997944	2585948	3056346	3559277	...
A Imports of merchandise, f.o.b.	432343	573372	...	...	...	...	1334478	1814402	2353072	2775105	3224005	...
B Transport of services on merchandise imports	50721	51491	...	...	...	...	122008	165463	209976	253589	302306	...
By residents	13262	16994	...	...	...	...	40263	54604	69293	83685	99762	...
By non-residents	37459	34497	...	...	...	...	81745	110859	140683	169904	202544	...
C Insurance service charges on merchandise imports	5145	5615	...	...	...	...	13305	18079	22900	27652	32966	...
By residents	1316	1685	...	...	...	...	3992	5424	6871	8296	9891	...

Portugal

2.17 Exports and Imports of Goods and Services, Detail
(Continued)

Million Portuguese escudos

	1980	1981	1982	1983	1984	1985	1986	1987	1988	1989	1990	1991
By non-residents	3829	3930	...	...	...	...	9313	12655	16029	19356	23075	...
2 Adjustments of merchandise imports to change-of-ownership basis	...	...	...	...	...	...	...	...	...	...	...	...
3 Other transport and communication	14554	18832	...	...	...	...	27159	33984	45408	55787	62731	...
4 Other insurance service charges	257	560	...	...	...	...	4823	1574	3621	927	1288	...
5 Other commodities	7235	9852	...	...	...	...	30851	40276	53654	70070	90801	...
6 Direct purchases abroad by government	...	...					...	...	...	...	...	...
7 Direct purchases abroad by resident households	17785	18814	...	...	...	...	56145	71450	91266	109503	144731	...
Total Imports of Goods and Services	528040	678536	832453	1014753	1272288	1458592	1588769	2145228	2779897	3292633	3858828	...
Balance of Goods and Services	-184090	-289021	-343971	-293510	-223655	-143382	-122196	-370558	-650381	-621486	-758661	...
Total Imports and Balance of Goods and Services	343950	389515	488482	721243	1048633	1315210	1466573	1774670	2129516	2671147	3100167	...

3.11 General Government Production Account: Total and Subsectors

Million Portuguese escudos

	1980					1981				
	Total General Government	Central Government	State or Provincial Government	Local Government	Social Security Funds	Total General Government	Central Government	State or Provincial Government	Local Government	Social Security Funds
Gross Output										
1 Sales	15843	13258	...	2253	332	19280	15950	...	2894	436
2 Services produced for own use	183809	160323	...	14471	9015	227812	198709	...	18648	10455
3 Own account fixed capital formation	...	...	...	...	...	...	...	...	...	...
Gross Output	199652	173581	...	16724	9347	247092	214659	...	21542	10891
Gross Input										
Intermediate Consumption	48752	42486	...	4771	1495	62164	54142	...	5946	2076
Subtotal: Value Added	150900	131095	...	11953	7852	184928	160517	...	15596	8815
1 Indirect taxes, net	4142	4135	...	5	2	5151	5166	...	-18	3
A Indirect taxes	4188	4142	...	44	2	5197	5174	...	20	3
B Less: Subsidies	46	7	...	39	-	46	8	...	38	-
2 Consumption of fixed capital	...	...	...	...	...	...	...	...	...	...
3 Compensation of employees	145666	126186	...	11859	7621	178067	154196	...	15308	8563
4 Net Operating surplus a	1092	774	...	89	229	1710	1155	...	306	249
Gross Input	199652	173581	...	16724	9347	247092	214659	...	21542	10891
	1982					1983				
	Total General Government	Central Government	State or Provincial Government	Local Government	Social Security Funds	Total General Government	Central Government	State or Provincial Government	Local Government	Social Security Funds
Gross Output										
1 Sales	23971	19921	...	3645	405	30358	25917	...	4031	410
2 Services produced for own use	279412	244215	...	22849	12348	352219	309934	...	28557	13728
3 Own account fixed capital formation	...	...	...	...	...	...	...	...	...	...
Gross Output	303383	264136	...	26494	12753	382577	335851	...	32588	14138
Gross Input										
Intermediate Consumption	78707	69424	...	6738	2545	101608	90588	...	7679	3341
Subtotal: Value Added	224676	194712	...	19756	10208	280969	245263	...	24909	10797
1 Indirect taxes, net	6485	6589	...	-107	3	8027	8111	...	-89	5
A Indirect taxes	6637	6604	...	30	3	8168	8136	...	27	5
B Less: Subsidies	152	15	...	137	-	141	25	...	116	-
2 Consumption of fixed capital	...	...	...	...	...	...	...	...	...	...
3 Compensation of employees	216357	186898	...	19457	10002	271235	235815	...	24789	10631
4 Net Operating surplus a	1834	1225	...	406	203	1707	1337	...	209	161
Gross Input	303383	264136	...	26494	12753	382577	335851	...	32588	14138

3.11 General Government Production Account: Total and Subsectors

Million Portuguese escudos

	1984					1985				
	Total General Government	Central Government	State or Provincial Government	Local Government	Social Security Funds	Total General Government	Central Government	State or Provincial Government	Local Government	Social Security Funds
Gross Output										
1 Sales	39090	33687	...	4974	429	51077	43953	...	6587	537
2 Services produced for own use	427190	375197	...	36498	15495	552595	483590	...	48985	20020
3 Own account fixed capital formation	...	...	...	...	...	...	...	...	...	...
Gross Output	466280	408884	...	41472	15924	603672	527543	...	55572	20557
Gross Input										
Intermediate Consumption	122893	107484	...	11039	4370	175351	152804	...	17147	5400
Subtotal: Value Added	343387	301400	...	30433	11554	428321	374739	...	38425	15157
1 Indirect taxes, net	8353	8577	...	-227	3	11236	11537	...	-304	3
A Indirect taxes	8626	8602	...	21	3	11565	11537	...	25	3
B Less: Subsidies	273	25	...	248	-	329	-	...	329	-
2 Consumption of fixed capital	...	...	...	...	...	...	...	...	...	...
3 Compensation of employees	330484	288763	...	30174	11547	414064	361090	...	37818	15156
4 Net Operating surplus a	4550	4060	...	486	4	3021	2112	...	911	-2
Gross Input	466280	408884	...	41472	15924	603672	527543	...	55572	20557

	1986					1987				
	Total General Government	Central Government	State or Provincial Government	Local Government	Social Security Funds	Total General Government	Central Government	State or Provincial Government	Local Government	Social Security Funds
Gross Output										
1 Sales	63173	52733	...	9707	733	74528	...	...	...	...
2 Services produced for own use	684742	600557	...	59832	24353	795301	...	...	...	...
3 Own account fixed capital formation	...	...	...	...	...	...	...	...	...	...
Gross Output	747915	653290	...	69539	25086	869829	...	...	...	...
Gross Input										
Intermediate Consumption	224235	195739	...	21138	7358	253605	...	...	...	...
Subtotal: Value Added	523680	457551	...	48401	17728	616224	...	...	...	...
1 Indirect taxes, net	13432	13803	...	-372	1	17474	...	...	...	...
A Indirect taxes	13840	13803	...	36	1	17916	...	...	...	...
B Less: Subsidies	408	-	...	408	-	442	...	...	...	...
2 Consumption of fixed capital	...	...	...	...	...	...	...	...	...	...
3 Compensation of employees	503775	439602	...	46569	17604	589852	...	...	...	...
4 Net Operating surplus a	6473	4146	...	2204	123	8898	...	...	...	...
Gross Input	747915	653290	...	69539	25086	869829	...	...	...	...

	1988					1989				
	Total General Government	Central Government	State or Provincial Government	Local Government	Social Security Funds	Total General Government	Central Government	State or Provincial Government	Local Government	Social Security Funds
Gross Output										
1 Sales	92848	...	...	...	...	112056	...	...	...	...
2 Services produced for own use	970902	...	...	...	...	1157577	...	...	...	...
3 Own account fixed capital formation	...	...	...	...	...	...	...	...	...	...
Gross Output	1063750	...	...	...	...	1269633	...	...	...	...
Gross Input										
Intermediate Consumption	311304	...	...	...	...	348826	...	...	...	...
Subtotal: Value Added	752446	...	...	...	...	920807	...	...	...	...
1 Indirect taxes, net	26110	...	...	...	...	30858	...	...	...	...
A Indirect taxes	26590	...	...	...	...	31546	...	...	...	...
B Less: Subsidies	480	...	...	...	...	688	...	...	...	...
2 Consumption of fixed capital	...	...	...	...	...	...	...	...	...	...
3 Compensation of employees	715819	...	...	...	...	874232	...	...	...	...
4 Net Operating surplus a	10517	...	...	...	...	15717	...	...	...	...
Gross Input	1063750	...	...	...	...	1269633	...	...	...	...

Portugal

3.11 General Government Production Account: Total and Subsectors

	1990 Total General Government	Central Government	State or Provincial Government	Local Government	Social Security Funds
Gross Output					
1 Sales	135920	...	...	...	...
2 Services produced for own use	1434684	...	...	...	...
3 Own account fixed capital formation	...	...	...	...	...
Gross Output	1570604	...	...	...	...
Gross Input					
Intermediate Consumption	418694	...	...	...	...
Subtotal: Value Added	1151910	...	...	...	...
1 Indirect taxes, net	40060	...	...	...	...
A Indirect taxes	40861	...	...	...	...
B Less: Subsidies	801	...	...	...	...
2 Consumption of fixed capital	...	...	...	...	...
3 Compensation of employees	1092011	...	...	...	...
4 Net Operating surplus a	19839	...	...	...	...
Gross Input	1570604	...	...	...	...

a) Item 'Operating surplus' includes consumption of fixed capital.

3.12 General Government Income and Outlay Account: Total and Subsectors

Million Portuguese escudos

	1980 Total General Government	Central Government	State or Provincial Government	Local Government	Social Security Funds	1981 Total General Government	Central Government	State or Provincial Government	Local Government	Social Security Funds
Receipts										
1 Operating surplus ab	1092	774	...	89	229	1710	1155	...	306	249
2 Property and entrepreneurial income	10173	9384	...	462	385	14793	13863	...	774	771
A Withdrawals from public quasi-corporations b	-	-	...	-	-	-	-	...	-	-
B Interest	3110	2508	...	275	385	8560	7876	...	528	771
C Dividends	6843	6831	...	12	-	5930	5930	...	-	-
D Net land rent and royalties	220	45	...	175	-	303	57	...	246	-
3 Taxes, fees and contributions	368528	249896	...	8526	110115	466207	318134	...	9621	138475
A Indirect taxes	176915	175225	...	1195	495	215073	212992	...	1516	565
B Direct taxes	81993	74671	...	7331	-	113224	105142	...	8105	-
Income	79587	73121	...	6475	...	...	...	...	...	...
Other	2406	1550	...	856	...	...	...	...	...	...
C Social security contributions	109620	-	...	-	109620	137910	-	...	-	137910
D Fees, fines and penalties	...	...	...	...	...	...	...	...	...	...
4 Other current transfers	14300	15131	...	14181	8208	16494	16595	...	16817	7713
A Casualty insurance claims	37	-	...	8	29	46	-	...	18	28
B Transfers from other government subsectors	...	2291	...	12942	7987	...	1118	...	16160	7353
C Transfers from the rest of the world	857	841	...	-	16	1095	1077	...	-	18
D Other transfers, except imputed	6252	5628	...	563	61	6623	6406	...	67	150
E Imputed unfunded employee pension and welfare contributions	7154	6371	...	668	115	8730	7994	...	572	164
Total Current Receipts	394093	275185	...	23258	118937	499204	349747	...	27518	147208
Disbursements										
1 Government final consumption expenditure	182608	159453	...	14285	8870	225892	197233	...	18361	10298
2 Property income	38755	38515	...	298	-	80122	79847	...	586	304
A Interest	38749	38511	...	296	-	80115	79843	...	583	304
B Net land rent and royalties	6	4	...	2	-	7	4	...	3	-
3 Subsidies	65371	65068	...	303	-	81428	80942	...	486	-

3.12 General Government Income and Outlay Account: Total and Subsectors
(Continued)

Million Portuguese escudos

	1980					1981				
	Total General Government	Central Government	State or Provincial Government	Local Government	Social Security Funds	Total General Government	Central Government	State or Provincial Government	Local Government	Social Security Funds
4 Other current transfers	137435	51145	...	3617	105902	177082	61372	...	2692	137672
A Casualty insurance premiums, net	70	20	...	44	6	82	24	...	53	5
B Transfers to other government subsectors	...	20915	...	1986	328	...	23397	...	761	496
C Social security benefits	100557	-	...	-	100557	133493	-	...	-	133493
D Social assistance grants c	25072	20837	...	918	3317	32026	27206	...	1306	3514
E Unfunded employee pension and welfare benefits	7154	6371	...	668	115	8730	7994	...	572	164
F Transfers to private non-profit institutions serving households	282	282	...	-	-	584	584	...	-	-
G Other transfers n.e.c.	-	-	...	...	...	-	-	...	...	...
H Transfers to the rest of the world	4300	2720	...	1	1579	2167	2167	...	-	-
Net saving d	-30076	-38996	...	4755	4165	-65320	-69647	...	5393	-1066
Total Current Disbursements and Net Saving	394093	275185	...	23258	118937	499204	349747	...	27518	147208

	1982					1983				
	Total General Government	Central Government	State or Provincial Government	Local Government	Social Security Funds	Total General Government	Central Government	State or Provincial Government	Local Government	Social Security Funds

Receipts

1 Operating surplus ab	1834	1225	...	406	203	1707	1337	...	209	161
2 Property and entrepreneurial income	24915	23238	...	1190	487	45965	43718	...	1742	505
A Withdrawals from public quasi-corporations b	-	-	...	-	-	-	-	...	-	-
B Interest	9514	8205	...	822	487	10680	9161	...	1014	505
C Dividends	15047	15015	...	32	-	34638	34523	...	115	-
D Net land rent and royalties	354	18	...	336	-	647	34	...	613	-
3 Taxes, fees and contributions	604207	410151	...	11486	182574	793128	551041	...	13358	228731
A Indirect taxes	275397	272799	...	1897	701	358507	355283	...	2427	797
B Direct taxes	146937	137352	...	9589	-	206687	195758	...	10931	-
Income	...	...	...	...	...	...	...	...	...	...
Other	...	...	...	...	...	...	...	...	...	...
C Social security contributions	181873	-	...	-	181873	227934	-	...	-	227934
D Fees, fines and penalties	...	...	...	...	...	...	...	...	...	...
4 Other current transfers	23475	22757	...	24827	9761	28420	28541	...	30157	19062
A Casualty insurance claims	26	1	...	23	2	21	-	...	21	-
B Transfers from other government subsectors	...	1744	...	22865	9261	...	2602	...	28107	18631
C Transfers from the rest of the world	757	668	...	-	89	80	20	...	-	60
D Other transfers, except imputed	9672	8266	...	1225	181	11672	10276	...	1216	180
E Imputed unfunded employee pension and welfare contributions	13020	12078	...	714	228	16647	15643	...	813	191
Total Current Receipts	654431	457371	...	37909	193025	869220	624637	...	45466	248459

Disbursements

1 Government final consumption expenditure	276165	241524	...	22501	12140	348355	306746	...	28201	13408
2 Property income	97910	95716	...	1674	520	141365	137728	...	2946	691
A Interest	97896	95702	...	1674	520	141348	137713	...	2944	691
B Net land rent and royalties	14	14	...	-	-	17	15	...	2	-
3 Subsidies	79602	78716	...	886	-	91796	91641	...	155	-

Portugal

3.12 General Government Income and Outlay Account: Total and Subsectors
(Continued)

Million Portuguese escudos

	1982					1983				
	Total General Government	Central Government	State or Provincial Government	Local Government	Social Security Funds	Total General Government	Central Government	State or Provincial Government	Local Government	Social Security Funds
4 Other current transfers	215614	71673	...	2953	174862	253846	82436	...	3153	217599
A Casualty insurance premiums, net	123	33	...	83	7	118	30	...	84	4
B Transfers to other government subsectors	...	32023	...	442	1409	...	46654	...	381	2307
C Social security benefits	168677	-	...	-	168677	209590			-	209590
D Social assistance grants c	30511	24256	...	1714	4541	25575	18193	...	1875	5507
E Unfunded employee pension and welfare benefits	13020	12078	...	714	228	16647	15643	...	813	191
F Transfers to private non-profit institutions serving households	752	752	...	-	-	865	865	...	-	-
G Other transfers n.e.c.	-	-	...	-	-	...	...	...	...	...
H Transfers to the rest of the world	2531	2531	...	-	-	1051	1051	...	-	-
Net saving d	-14860	-30258	...	9895	5503	33858	6086	...	11011	16761
Total Current Disbursements and Net Saving	654431	457371	...	37909	193025	869220	624637	...	45466	248459

	1984					1985				
	Total General Government	Central Government	State or Provincial Government	Local Government	Social Security Funds	Total General Government	Central Government	State or Provincial Government	Local Government	Social Security Funds
Receipts										
1 Operating surplus ab	4550	4060	...	486	4	3021	2112	...	911	-2
2 Property and entrepreneurial income	49684	46771	...	2330	583	43162	38764	...	2484	1914
A Withdrawals from public quasi-corporations b	-	-	...	-	-	-	-	...	-	-
B Interest	34975	32728	...	1666	581	32631	28834	...	1883	1914
C Dividends	14041	13910	...	129	2	9783	9765	...	18	-
D Net land rent and royalties	668	133	...	535	-	748	165	...	583	-
3 Taxes, fees and contributions	961603	665454	...	17123	279030	1178016	824704	...	20272	333049
A Indirect taxes	436761	432392	...	3437	932	534160	527276	...	4417	2467
B Direct taxes	246744	233062	...	13686	-	313274	297428	...	15855	-
Income	...	...	...	...	...	...	...	...	...	...
Other	...	...	...	...	...	...	...	...	...	...
C Social security contributions	278098	-	...	-	278098	330582	-	...	-	330582
D Fees, fines and penalties	...	...	...	...	...	...	...	...	...	...
4 Other current transfers	35299	34759	...	36185	43990	42488	40520	...	45993	48225
A Casualty insurance claims	12	-	...	12	-	25	-	...	25	-
B Transfers from other government subsectors	...	2884	...	33302	43449	...	3050	...	41972	47228
C Transfers from the rest of the world	250	200	...	-	50	65	12	...	-	53
D Other transfers, except imputed	14655	12619	...	1834	202	19002	15647	...	2854	501
E Imputed unfunded employee pension and welfare contributions	20382	19056	...	1037	289	23396	21811	...	1142	443
Total Current Receipts	1051136	751044	...	56124	323607	1266687	906100	...	69660	383186
Disbursements										
1 Government final consumption expenditure	423078	372124	...	35884	15070	546899	479218	...	48143	19538
2 Property income	231042	225803	...	4653	586	329014	323027	...	5509	478
A Interest	231004	225775	...	4643	586	328966	322998	...	5490	478
B Net land rent and royalties	38	28	...	10	-	48	29	...	19	-
3 Subsidies	120101	119677	...	424	-	127128	126852	...	276	-

3.12 General Government Income and Outlay Account: Total and Subsectors
(Continued)

Million Portuguese escudos

	1984					1985				
	Total General Government	Central Government	State or Provincial Government	Local Government	Social Security Funds	Total General Government	Central Government	State or Provincial Government	Local Government	Social Security Funds
4 Other current transfers	310729	122017	...	3555	264796	386491	146607	...	4610	327533
A Casualty insurance premiums, net	69	39	...	26	4	65	40	...	22	3
B Transfers to other government subsectors	...	76750	...	485	2404	...	89122	...	648	2489
C Social security benefits	255324	-	...	-	255324	315451	-	...	-	315451
D Social assistance grants c	30531	21749	...	2007	6775	42266	30321	...	2798	9147
E Unfunded employee pension and welfare benefits	20382	19056	...	1037	289	23396	21811	...	1142	443
F Transfers to private non-profit institutions serving households	1056	1056	...	-	-	1964	1964	...	-	-
G Other transfers n.e.c.	-	-	...	...	...	-	...	...	...	...
H Transfers to the rest of the world	3367	3367	...	-	-	3349	3349	...	-	-
Net saving d	-33814	-88577	...	11608	43155	-122845	-169604	...	11122	35637
Total Current Disbursements and Net Saving	1051136	751044	...	56124	323607	1266687	906100	...	69660	383186

	1986					1987				
	Total General Government	Central Government	State or Provincial Government	Local Government	Social Security Funds	Total General Government	Central Government	State or Provincial Government	Local Government	Social Security Funds
Receipts										
1 Operating surplus ab	6473	4146	...	2204	123	8898	...	...	...	...
2 Property and entrepreneurial income	70405	62438	...	2483	5484	86480	...	...	...	...
A Withdrawals from public quasi-corporations b	-	-	...	-	-	-	...	...	...	...
B Interest	39733	32743	...	1507	5483	48575	...	...	...	...
C Dividends	29529	29510	...	18	1	36534	...	...	...	...
D Net land rent and royalties	1143	185	...	958	-	1371	...	...	...	...
3 Taxes, fees and contributions	1509441	1061595	...	24584	423273	1685340	...	...	...	...
A Indirect taxes	767876	759225	...	4971	3680	804800	...	...	...	...
B Direct taxes	321972	302370	...	19613	-	319445	...	...	...	...
Income	...	...	...	...	...	...	...	...	...	...
Other	...	...	...	...	...	...	...	...	...	...
C Social security contributions	419593	-	...	-	419593	561095	...	...	...	...
D Fees, fines and penalties	...	...	...	...	...	...	...	...	...	...
4 Other current transfers	73897	83600	...	54725	35101	92453	...	...	...	...
A Casualty insurance claims	40	-	...	40	-	48	...	...	...	...
B Transfers from other government subsectors	...	13745	...	51750	34034	...	...	...	...	...
C Transfers from the rest of the world	26061	25735	...	-	326	23790	...	...	...	...
D Other transfers, except imputed	18147	16572	...	1352	223	27570	...	...	...	...
E Imputed unfunded employee pension and welfare contributions	29649	27548	...	1583	518	41045	...	...	...	...
Total Current Receipts	1660216	1211779	...	83996	463981	1873171	...	...	...	...
Disbursements										
1 Government final consumption expenditure	678841	596343	...	58678	23820	787829	...	...	...	...
2 Property income	428104	421896	...	6207	1	452961	...	...	...	...
A Interest	428049	421858	...	6190	1	452882	...	...	...	...
B Net land rent and royalties	55	38	...	17	-	79	...	...	...	...
3 Subsidies	131058	121067	...	428	9563	98361	...	...	...	...

Portugal

Million Portuguese escudos

	1986 Total General Government	Central Government	State or Provincial Government	Local Government	Social Security Funds	1987 Total General Government	Central Government	State or Provincial Government	Local Government	Social Security Funds
4 Other current transfers	549431	213287	...	5392	430292	684714	...	...	...	...
A Casualty insurance premiums, net	74	46	...	25	3	101	...	...	...	...
B Transfers to other government subsectors	...	85692	...	509	13339	...	...	...	...	...
C Social security benefits	402912	-	...	-	402912	486208	...	...	...	...
D Social assistance grants c	78815	62020	...	3275	13520	115305	...	...	...	...
E Unfunded employee pension and welfare benefits	29649	27548	...	1583	518	41045	...	...	...	...
F Transfers to private non-profit institutions serving households	2248	2248	...	-	-	2908	...	...	...	...
G Other transfers n.e.c.	-	-	...	...	...	...	...	...	...	...
H Transfers to the rest of the world	35733	35733	...	-	-	39147	...	...	...	...
Net saving d	-127218	-140814	...	13291	305	-150694	...	...	...	...
Total Current Disbursements and Net Saving	1660216	1211779	...	83996	463981	1873171	...	...	...	...

	1988 Total General Government	Central Government	State or Provincial Government	Local Government	Social Security Funds	1989 Total General Government	Central Government	State or Provincial Government	Local Government	Social Security Funds
Receipts										
1 Operating surplus ab	10517	...	...	...	...	15717	...	...	...	...
2 Property and entrepreneurial income	72663	...	...	...	...	99127	...	...	...	...
A Withdrawals from public quasi-corporations b	-	...	...	...	...	-	...	...	...	...
B Interest	41142	...	...	...	...	51594	...	...	...	...
C Dividends	29905	...	...	...	...	40855	...	...	...	...
D Net land rent and royalties	1616	...	...	...	...	6678	...	...	...	...
3 Taxes, fees and contributions	2103237	...	...	...	...	2511965	...	...	...	...
A Indirect taxes	1002781	...	...	...	...	1104517	...	...	...	...
B Direct taxes	463255	...	...	...	...	667979	...	...	...	...
Income	...	...	...	...	...	...	...	...	...	...
Other	...	...	...	...	...	...	...	...	...	...
C Social security contributions	637201	...	...	...	...	739469	...	...	...	...
D Fees, fines and penalties	...	...	...	...	...	...	...	...	...	...
4 Other current transfers	99158	...	...	...	...	129333	...	...	...	...
A Casualty insurance claims	56	...	...	...	...	73	...	...	...	...
B Transfers from other government subsectors	...	...	...	...	...	...	...	...	...	...
C Transfers from the rest of the world	22962	...	...	...	...	40313	...	...	...	...
D Other transfers, except imputed	22087	...	...	...	...	31398	...	...	...	...
E Imputed unfunded employee pension and welfare contributions	54053	...	...	...	...	57549	...	...	...	...
Total Current Receipts	2285575	...	...	...	...	2756142	...	...	...	...
Disbursements										
1 Government final consumption expenditure	962190	...	...	...	...	1147416	...	...	...	...
2 Property income	467561	...	...	...	...	507447	...	...	...	...
A Interest	467481	...	...	...	...	507349	...	...	...	...
B Net land rent and royalties	80	...	...	...	...	98	...	...	...	...
3 Subsidies	109517	...	...	...	...	105519	...	...	...	...

3.12 General Government Income and Outlay Account: Total and Subsectors
(Continued)

Million Portuguese escudos

	1988					1989				
	Total General Government	Central Government	State or Provincial Government	Local Government	Social Security Funds	Total General Government	Central Government	State or Provincial Government	Local Government	Social Security Funds
4 Other current transfers	802725	...	...	...	...	923294	...	...	...	...
A Casualty insurance premiums, net	118	...	...	...	...	154	...	...	...	...
B Transfers to other government subsectors	...	...	...	...	...	...	...	...	...	...
C Social security benefits	581976	...	...	...	...	665176	...	...	...	...
D Social assistance grants c	113635	...	...	...	...	139339	...	...	...	...
E Unfunded employee pension and welfare benefits	54053	...	...	...	...	57549	...	...	...	...
F Transfers to private non-profit institutions serving households	3199	...	...	...	...	3810	...	...	...	...
G Other transfers n.e.c.	...	...	...	...	...	...	...	...	...	...
H Transfers to the rest of the world	49744	...	...	...	...	57266	...	...	...	...
Net saving d	-56418	...	...	...	...	72466	...	...	...	...
Total Current Disbursements and Net Saving	2285575	...	...	...	...	2756142	...	...	...	...

	1990				
	Total General Government	Central Government	State or Provincial Government	Local Government	Social Security Funds
Receipts					
1 Operating surplus ab	19839	...	...	...	...
2 Property and entrepreneurial income	117271	...	...	...	...
A Withdrawals from public quasi-corporations b	-	...	...	...	...
B Interest	65936	...	...	...	...
C Dividends	44183	...	...	...	...
D Net land rent and royalties	7152	...	...	...	...
3 Taxes, fees and contributions	2955225	...	...	...	...
A Indirect taxes	1308798	...	...	...	...
B Direct taxes	764615	...	...	...	...
Income	...	...	...	...	...
Other	...	...	...	...	...
C Social security contributions	881812	...	...	...	...
D Fees, fines and penalties	...	...	...	...	...
4 Other current transfers	104043	...	...	...	...
A Casualty insurance claims	99	...	...	...	...
B Transfers from other government subsectors	...	...	...	...	...
C Transfers from the rest of the world	21562	...	...	...	...
D Other transfers, except imputed	14401	...	...	...	...
E Imputed unfunded employee pension and welfare contributions	67981	...	...	...	...
Total Current Receipts	3196378	...	...	...	...
Disbursements					
1 Government final consumption expenditure	1422833	...	...	...	...
2 Property income	692293	...	...	...	...
A Interest	692175	...	...	...	...
B Net land rent and royalties	118	...	...	...	...
3 Subsidies	106460	...	...	...	...

Portugal

3.12 General Government Income and Outlay Account: Total and Subsectors
(Continued)

Million Portuguese escudos

	1990				
	Total General Government	Central Government	State or Provincial Government	Local Government	Social Security Funds
4 Other current transfers	1125806	...	...	...	...
A Casualty insurance premiums, net	197	...	...	...	...
B Transfers to other government subsectors	...	...	...	...	...
C Social security benefits	804769	...	...	...	...
D Social assistance grants c	180619	...	...	...	...
E Unfunded employee pension and welfare benefits	67981	...	...	...	...
F Transfers to private non-profit institutions serving households	4522	...	...	...	...
G Other transfers n.e.c.	...	...	...	...	...
H Transfers to the rest of the world	67718	...	...	...	...
Net saving d	-151014	...	...	...	...
Total Current Disbursements and Net Saving	3196378	...	...	...	...

a) Item 'Operating surplus' includes consumption of fixed capital.
b) Item 'Withdrawal from public quasi-corporate enterprises' is included in item 'Operating surplus'.
c) Item 'Social assistance grants' includes also transfers to households n.e.c.
d) Item 'Net saving' includes consumption of fixed capital.

3.13 General Government Capital Accumulation Account: Total and Subsectors

Million Portuguese escudos

	1980					1981				
	Total General Government	Central Government	State or Provincial Government	Local Government	Social Security Funds	Total General Government	Central Government	State or Provincial Government	Local Government	Social Security Funds
Finance of Gross Accumulation										
1 Gross saving	-30076	-38996	...	4755	4165	-65320	-69647	...	5393	-1066
A Consumption of fixed capital	...	...	...	...	...	...	...	...	...	...
B Net saving a	-30076	-38996	...	4755	4165	-65320	-69647	...	5393	-1066
2 Capital transfers	171688	171265	...	21133	1666	2627	2202	...	25089	1694
A From other government subsectors	-	14	...	20696	1666	-	137	...	24527	1694
B From other resident sectors	171577	171232	...	345	-	2560	2057	...	503	-
C From rest of the world	111	19	...	92	-	67	8	...	59	-
Finance of Gross Accumulation	141612	132269	...	25888	5831	-62693	-67445	...	30482	628
Gross Accumulation										
1 Gross capital formation	51605	26442	...	24359	804	74617	40822	...	33170	625
A Increase in stocks	...	...	...	...	...	...	...	...	...	...
B Gross fixed capital formation	51605	26442	...	24359	804	74617	40822	...	33170	625
2 Purchases of land, net	1296	864	...	417	15	837	708	...	134	-5
3 Purchases of intangible assets, net	...	...	...	...	...	...	...	...	...	...
4 Capital transfers	19387	40210	...	568	985	21388	44658	...	1490	1598
A To other government subsectors	-	22354	...	11	11	-	26206	...	7	145
B To other resident sectors	14980	13450	...	556	974	15812	12876	...	1483	1453
C To rest of the world	4407	4406	...	1	-	5576	5576	...	-	-
Net lending	69323	64753	...	543	4027	-159535	-153633	...	-4312	-1590
Gross Accumulation	141612	132269	...	25888	5831	-62693	-67445	...	30482	628

	1982					1983				
	Total General Government	Central Government	State or Provincial Government	Local Government	Social Security Funds	Total General Government	Central Government	State or Provincial Government	Local Government	Social Security Funds
Finance of Gross Accumulation										
1 Gross saving	-14860	-30258	...	9895	5503	33858	6086	...	11011	16761
A Consumption of fixed capital	...	...	...	...	...	...	...	...	...	...
B Net saving a	-14860	-30258	...	9895	5503	33858	6086	...	11011	16761
2 Capital transfers	28904	4659	...	22340	1905	29886	6233	...	21852	1801
A From other government subsectors	...	...	...	...	...	...	...	...	...	...
B From other resident sectors	...	...	...	...	...	...	...	...	...	...
C From rest of the world	...	...	...	...	...	...	...	...	...	...
Finance of Gross Accumulation	14044	-25599	...	32235	7408	63744	12319	...	32863	18562

3.13 General Government Capital Accumulation Account: Total and Subsectors
(Continued)

Million Portuguese escudos

	1982					1983				
	Total General Government	Central Government	State or Provincial Government	Local Government	Social Security Funds	Total General Government	Central Government	State or Provincial Government	Local Government	Social Security Funds
Gross Accumulation										
1 Gross capital formation	79923	41982	...	37834	107	88553	51123	...	36472	958
A Increase in stocks	...	...	...	...	...	...	...	...	...	...
B Gross fixed capital formation	79923	41982	...	37834	107	88553	51123	...	36472	958
2 Purchases of land, net	558	956	...	-398	-	324	1604	...	-1280	-
3 Purchases of intangible assets, net	...	...	...	...	...	...	...	...	...	...
4 Capital transfers	74618	71175	...	1663	1780	208006	204998	...	1177	1831
A To other government subsectors	...	...	...	...	...	...	...	...	...	...
B To other resident sectors	...	...	...	...	...	...	...	...	...	...
C To rest of the world	...	...	...	...	...	...	...	...	...	...
Net lending	-141055	-139712	...	-6864	5521	-233139	-245406	...	-3506	15773
Gross Accumulation	14044	-25599	...	32235	7408	63744	12319	...	32863	18562

	1984					1985				
	Total General Government	Central Government	State or Provincial Government	Local Government	Social Security Funds	Total General Government	Central Government	State or Provincial Government	Local Government	Social Security Funds
Finance of Gross Accumulation										
1 Gross saving	-33814	-88577	...	11608	43155	-122845	-169604	...	11122	35637
A Consumption of fixed capital	...	...	...	...	...	...	...	...	...	...
B Net saving [a]	-33814	-88577	...	11608	43155	-122845	-169604	...	11122	35637
2 Capital transfers	120810	94254	...	24785	1771	300615	270494	...	28091	2030
A From other government subsectors	...	...	...	...	...	...	...	...	...	...
B From other resident sectors	...	...	...	...	...	...	...	...	...	...
C From rest of the world	...	...	...	...	...	...	...	...	...	...
Finance of Gross Accumulation	86996	5677	...	36393	44926	177770	100890	...	39213	37667
Gross Accumulation										
1 Gross capital formation	90656	54542	...	34986	1128	108926	65551	...	42298	1077
A Increase in stocks	...	...	...	...	...	...	...	...	...	...
B Gross fixed capital formation	90656	54542	...	34986	1128	108926	65551	...	42298	1077
2 Purchases of land, net	1542	1825	...	-283	-	1236	2428	...	-1192	-
3 Purchases of intangible assets, net	...	...	...	...	...	...	...	...	...	...
4 Capital transfers	193215	189906	...	1910	1399	328937	325377	...	1947	1613
A To other government subsectors	...	...	...	...	...	...	...	...	...	...
B To other resident sectors	...	...	...	...	...	...	...	...	...	...
C To rest of the world	...	...	...	...	...	...	...	...	...	...
Net lending	-198417	-240596	...	-220	42399	-261329	-292466	...	-3840	34977
Gross Accumulation	86996	5677	...	36393	44926	177770	100890	...	39213	37667

	1986					1987				
	Total General Government	Central Government	State or Provincial Government	Local Government	Social Security Funds	Total General Government	Central Government	State or Provincial Government	Local Government	Social Security Funds
Finance of Gross Accumulation										
1 Gross saving	-127218	-140814	...	13291	305	-150694	...	...	...	...
A Consumption of fixed capital	...	...	...	...	...	...	...	...	...	...
B Net saving [a]	-127218	-140814	...	13291	305	-150694	...	...	...	...
2 Capital transfers	173266	131734	...	39171	2361	105244	...	...	...	...
A From other government subsectors	...	...	...	...	...	...	...	...	...	...
B From other resident sectors	...	...	...	...	...	...	...	...	...	...
C From rest of the world	...	...	...	...	...	...	...	...	...	...
Finance of Gross Accumulation	46048	-9080	...	52462	2666	-45450	...	...	...	...
Gross Accumulation										
1 Gross capital formation	143957	94216	...	47717	2024	170949	...	...	...	...
A Increase in stocks	...	...	...	...	...	...	...	...	...	...
B Gross fixed capital formation	143957	94216	...	47717	2024	170949	...	...	...	...

Portugal

3.13 General Government Capital Accumulation Account: Total and Subsectors
(Continued)

Million Portuguese escudos

	1986					1987				
	Total General Government	Central Government	State or Provincial Government	Local Government	Social Security Funds	Total General Government	Central Government	State or Provincial Government	Local Government	Social Security Funds
2 Purchases of land, net	2380	3149	...	-769	-	2766	...	...	...	...
3 Purchases of intangible assets, net	...	...	...	...	...	...	...	...	...	...
4 Capital transfers	181222	171550	...	2287	7385	158710	...	...	...	...
A To other government subsectors	...	...	...	...	...	...	...	...	...	...
B To other resident sectors	...	...	...	...	...	...	...	...	...	...
C To rest of the world	...	...	...	...	...	...	...	...	...	...
Net lending	-281511	-277995	...	3227	-6743	-377875	...	...	...	...
Gross Accumulation	46048	-9080	...	52462	2666	-45450	...	...	...	...

	1988					1989				
	Total General Government	Central Government	State or Provincial Government	Local Government	Social Security Funds	Total General Government	Central Government	State or Provincial Government	Local Government	Social Security Funds
Finance of Gross Accumulation										
1 Gross saving	-56418	...	...	...	...	72466	...	...	...	...
A Consumption of fixed capital	...	...	...	...	...	...	...	...	...	...
B Net saving [a]	-56418	...	...	...	...	72466	...	...	...	...
2 Capital transfers	94465	...	...	...	...	103165	...	...	...	...
A From other government subsectors	...	...	...	...	...	...	...	...	...	...
B From other resident sectors	...	...	...	...	...	...	...	...	...	...
C From rest of the world	...	...	...	...	...	...	...	...	...	...
Finance of Gross Accumulation	38047	...	...	...	...	175631	...	...	...	...
Gross Accumulation										
1 Gross capital formation	216944	...	...	...	...	246070	...	...	...	...
A Increase in stocks	...	...	...	...	...	...	...	...	...	...
B Gross fixed capital formation	216944	...	...	...	...	246070	...	...	...	...
2 Purchases of land, net	2563	...	...	...	...	3108	...	...	...	...
3 Purchases of intangible assets, net	...	...	...	...	...	...	...	...	...	...
4 Capital transfers	145389	...	...	...	...	144768	...	...	...	...
A To other government subsectors	...	...	...	...	...	...	...	...	...	...
B To other resident sectors	...	...	...	...	...	...	...	...	...	...
C To rest of the world	...	...	...	...	...	...	...	...	...	...
Net lending	-326849	...	...	...	...	-218315	...	...	...	...
Gross Accumulation	38047	...	...	...	...	175631	...	...	...	...

	1990				
	Total General Government	Central Government	State or Provincial Government	Local Government	Social Security Funds
Finance of Gross Accumulation					
1 Gross saving	-151014	...	...	...	...
A Consumption of fixed capital	...	...	...	...	...
B Net saving [a]	-151014	...	...	...	...
2 Capital transfers	112752	...	...	...	...
A From other government subsectors	...	...	...	...	...
B From other resident sectors	...	...	...	...	...
C From rest of the world	...	...	...	...	...
Finance of Gross Accumulation	-38262	...	...	...	...
Gross Accumulation					
1 Gross capital formation	290924	...	...	...	...
A Increase in stocks	...	...	...	...	...
B Gross fixed capital formation	290924	...	...	...	...

3.13 General Government Capital Accumulation Account: Total and Subsectors
(Continued)

Million Portuguese escudos

	1990					
	Total General Government	Central Government	State or Provincial Government	Local Government	Social Security Funds	
2 Purchases of land, net	3920	...	...	...	...	
3 Purchases of intangible assets, net	...	...	...	...	...	
4 Capital transfers	120839	...	...	...	...	
A To other government subsectors	...	...	...	...	...	
B To other resident sectors	...	...	...	...	...	
C To rest of the world	...	...	...	...	...	
Net lending	-453945	...	...	...	...	
Gross Accumulation	-38262	...	...	...	...	

a) Item 'Net saving' includes consumption of fixed capital.

3.14 General Government Capital Finance Account, Total and Subsectors

Million Portuguese escudos

	1980					1981				
	Total General Government	Central Government	State or Provincial Government	Local Government	Social Security Funds	Total General Government	Central Government	State or Provincial Government	Local Government	Social Security Funds
Acquisition of Financial Assets										
1 Gold and SDRs	-5413	-5413	...	-	-	-2099	-2099	...	-	-
2 Currency and transferable deposits	1168	295	...	86	787	2025	809	...	90	1126
3 Other deposits	22596	20831	...	1704	640	30104	26813	...	1552	960
4 Bills and bonds, short term	-	-	...	-	-	-	-	...	-	-
5 Bonds, long term	3529	-1384	...	5	4908	-304	-208	...	-1	-95
6 Corporate equity securities	96851	101885	...	-	-5034	33438	33438	...	-	-
7 Short-term loans, n.e.c.	50	50	...	-	-	218	3221	...	-3	-
8 Long-term loans, n.e.c.	3743	3716	...	-	-	9802	9774	...	294	-163
9 Other receivables	3165	-1083	...	-	4248	2912	808	...	-7	2111
10 Other assets	28	23	...	5	-	16	10	...	5	1
Total Acquisition of Financial Assets	125717	118920	...	1800	5549	76112	72566	...	1930	3940
Incurrence of Liabilities										
1 Currency and transferable deposits	26371	1381	...	-	-	584	584	...	-	-
2 Other deposits	-580	-1	...	-	-	1283	504	...	-	-
3 Bills and bonds, short term	8419	8419	...	-	-	21543	21543	...	-	-
4 Bonds, long term	15747	15801	...	-54	-	156519	156519	...	-	-
5 Short-term loans, n.e.c.	-478	-1245	...	-11	778	4241	4233	...	8	3000
6 Long-term loans, n.e.c.	21541	20743	...	773	-2	40670	33259	...	6442	1072
7 Other payables	...	...	...	...	...	...	...	...	...	...
8 Other liabilities	7126	7126	...	-	-	10488	8898	...	-	1590
Total Incurrence of Liabilities	78146	52224	...	708	776	235328	225540	...	6450	5662
Statistical discrepancy	-21752	1943	...	549	746	319	659	...	-208	-132
Net Lending	69323	64753	...	543	4027	-159535	-153633	...	-4312	-1590
Incurrence of Liabilities and Net Worth	125717	118920	...	1800	5549	76112	72566	...	1930	3940

	1982					1983				
	Total General Government	Central Government	State or Provincial Government	Local Government	Social Security Funds	Total General Government	Central Government	State or Provincial Government	Local Government	Social Security Funds
Acquisition of Financial Assets										
1 Gold and SDRs	-686	-686	...	-	-	4643	4643	...	-	-
2 Currency and transferable deposits	-5261	-4883	...	-330	-48	10743	9505	...	-179	1417
3 Other deposits	838	2500	...	773	-2273	51433	54460	...	-718	-2309
4 Bills and bonds, short term	-	-	...	-	-	-	-	...	-	-
5 Bonds, long term	-132	-	...	-	-5100	-369	-138	...	-72	-159
6 Corporate equity securities	21205	21205	...	-	-	24246	24246	...	-	-
7 Short-term loans, n.e.c.	535	534	...	-	1	298	299	...	-	-1
8 Long-term loans, n.e.c.	15862	13673	...	631	-175	46542	46235	...	120	-193
9 Other receivables	34380	21142	...	-	13238	81914	64256	...	-	17658
10 Other assets	12	4	...	7	1	12	3	...	8	1
Total Acquisition of Financial Assets	66753	53489	...	1081	5644	219462	203509	...	-841	16414
Incurrence of Liabilities										
1 Currency and transferable deposits	735	735	...	-	-	1320	1320	...	-	-

Portugal

3.14 General Government Capital Finance Account, Total and Subsectors
(Continued)

Million Portuguese escudos

	1982 Total General Government	Central Government	State or Provincial Government	Local Government	Social Security Funds	1983 Total General Government	Central Government	State or Provincial Government	Local Government	Social Security Funds
2 Other deposits	528	690	...	-	-	4518	4518	...	-	-
3 Bills and bonds, short term	19933	19933	...			...	...	...		...
4 Bonds, long term	116843	111875	...	-	-	160945	160954	...	-9	-
5 Short-term loans, n.e.c.	17657	17721	...	-64	-	841	850	...	-9	-
6 Long-term loans, n.e.c.	62065	52738	...	7762	-168	96550	88565	...	3258	4347
7 Other payables	...	...	...	...	...	...	...	...	...	...
8 Other liabilities	-9670	-10087	...	-	417	184955	182779	...	414	1762
Total Incurrence of Liabilities	208091	193605	...	7698	249	449129	438986	...	3654	6109
Statistical discrepancy	-283	-404	...	247	-126	3472	9929	...	-989	-5468
Net Lending	-141055	-139712	...	-6864	5521	-233139	-245406	...	-3506	15773
Incurrence of Liabilities and Net Worth	66753	53489	...	1081	5644	219462	203509	...	-841	16414

	1984 Total General Government	Central Government	State or Provincial Government	Local Government	Social Security Funds	1985 Total General Government	Central Government	State or Provincial Government	Local Government	Social Security Funds
Acquisition of Financial Assets										
1 Gold and SDRs	17394	17394	...	-	-	15391	15391	...	-	-
2 Currency and transferable deposits	19940	15590	...	1167	3183	32493	27959	...	2675	1859
3 Other deposits	32603	22872	...	3479	7724	19726	18869	...	511	1100
4 Bills and bonds, short term	-	-	...	-	-	-4	-4	...	-	-
5 Bonds, long term	-498	-525	...	1	26	1135	-749	...	-104	1988
6 Corporate equity securities	34577	34565	...	12	-	24677	24657	...	20	-
7 Short-term loans, n.e.c.	231	226	...	-3	-	1259	160	...	-	-1
8 Long-term loans, n.e.c.	83287	82605	...	61	-216	86680	87571	...	87	-225
9 Other receivables	114615	92165	...	-	22241	574	-18557	...	-1971	21102
10 Other assets	29	7	...	22	-	41	27	...	14	-
Total Acquisition of Financial Assets	302178	264899	...	4739	32958	181972	155324	...	1232	25823
Incurrence of Liabilities										
1 Currency and transferable deposits	773	773	...	-	-	850	850	...	-	-
2 Other deposits	2431	3903	...	-	-	1008	1762	...	-	-
3 Bills and bonds, short term	-	-	...	-	-	109040	109040	...	-	-
4 Bonds, long term	238097	238102	...	-5	-	472155	471811	...	344	-
5 Short-term loans, n.e.c.	-3200	-3178	...	-23	-7	3599	2549	...	-50	-
6 Long-term loans, n.e.c.	79589	77287	...	2537	-1072	111130	114683	...	3306	-6106
7 Other payables	...	...	...	...	...	...	...	...	...	...
8 Other liabilities	171614	172617	...	-	-1212	-255880	-250590	...	279	-5569
Total Incurrence of Liabilities	489304	489504	...	2509	-2291	441902	450105	...	3879	-11675
Statistical discrepancy	11291	15991	...	2450	-7150	1399	-2315	...	1193	2521
Net Lending	-198417	-240596	...	-220	42399	-261329	-292466	...	-3840	34977
Incurrence of Liabilities and Net Worth	302178	264899	...	4739	32958	181972	155324	...	1232	25823

	1986 Total General Government	Central Government	State or Provincial Government	Local Government	Social Security Funds	1987 Total General Government	Central Government	State or Provincial Government	Local Government	Social Security Funds
Acquisition of Financial Assets										
1 Gold and SDRs	-1305	-1305	...	-	-	-5075	...	...	...	...
2 Currency and transferable deposits	-12105	-17075	...	3559	1411	38076	...	...	...	...
3 Other deposits	-27357	-68462	...	6211	36693	...	...	...	...	...
4 Bills and bonds, short term	1718	1707	...	-	11	...	...	...	...	...
5 Bonds, long term	-1155	-1389	...	-10	244	27053	...	...	...	...
6 Corporate equity securities	50774	50665	...	24	85	...	...	...	...	...
7 Short-term loans, n.e.c.	17317	17620	...	-	-	...	...	...	...	...
8 Long-term loans, n.e.c.	205921	206548	...	77	-246	199033	...	...	...	...
9 Other receivables	150003	128734	...	-	21269	...	...	...	...	...
10 Other assets	74	37	...	12	25	72	...	...	...	...
Total Acquisition of Financial Assets	383885	317080	...	9873	59492	259159	...	...	...	...
Incurrence of Liabilities										
1 Currency and transferable deposits	2024	2024	...	-	-	3701	...	...	...	...

Portugal

3.14 General Government Capital Finance Account, Total and Subsectors
(Continued)

Million Portuguese escudos

	1986					1987				
	Total General Government	Central Government	State or Provincial Government	Local Government	Social Security Funds	Total General Government	Central Government	State or Provincial Government	Local Government	Social Security Funds
2 Other deposits	20252	22051	...	-	-	...	...	...	...	...
3 Bills and bonds, short term	108742	108742	...	-	-	...	...	...	...	...
4 Bonds, long term	310809	310849	...	-40	-	...	...	...	...	...
5 Short-term loans, n.e.c.	7047	6312	...	986	52	...	...	...	...	...
6 Long-term loans, n.e.c.	149927	148196	...	2192	-3	137607	...	...	...	...
7 Other payables	...	...	...	...	...	...	...	...	...	...
8 Other liabilities	63403	-5946	...	3679	65670	...	...	...	...	...
Total Incurrence of Liabilities	662204	592228	...	6817	65719	...	...	...	...	...
Statistical discrepancy	3192	2847	...	-171	516	...	...	...	...	...
Net Lending	-281511	-277995	...	3227	-6743	-377875	...	...	...	...
Incurrence of Liabilities and Net Worth	383885	317080	...	9873	59492	259159	...	...	...	...

	1988					1989				
	Total General Government	Central Government	State or Provincial Government	Local Government	Social Security Funds	Total General Government	Central Government	State or Provincial Government	Local Government	Social Security Funds
Acquisition of Financial Assets										
1 Gold and SDRs	-836	...	...	...	...	-847	...	...	...	...
2 Currency and transferable deposits	16786	...	...	...	...	39870	...	...	...	...
3 Other deposits	...	...	...	...	...	...	...	...	...	...
4 Bills and bonds, short term	...	...	...	...	...	...	...	...	...	...
5 Bonds, long term	35381	...	...	...	...	-30722	...	...	...	...
6 Corporate equity securities	...	...	...	...	...	...	...	...	...	...
7 Short-term loans, n.e.c.	...	...	...	...	...	...	...	...	...	...
8 Long-term loans, n.e.c.	463175	...	...	...	...	280813	...	...	...	...
9 Other receivables	...	...	...	...	...	...	...	...	...	...
10 Other assets	89	...	...	...	...	1222	...	...	...	...
Total Acquisition of Financial Assets	514595	...	...	...	...	290336	...	...	...	...
Incurrence of Liabilities										
1 Currency and transferable deposits	1208	...	...	...	...	127917	...	...	...	...
2 Other deposits	...	...	...	...	...	...	...	...	...	...
3 Bills and bonds, short term	...	...	...	...	...	...	...	...	...	...
4 Bonds, long term	...	...	...	...	...	...	...	...	...	...
5 Short-term loans, n.e.c.	...	...	...	...	...	...	...	...	...	...
6 Long-term loans, n.e.c.	375980	...	...	...	...	-40498	...	...	...	...
7 Other payables	...	...	...	...	...	...	...	...	...	...
8 Other liabilities	...	...	...	...	...	...	...	...	...	...
Total Incurrence of Liabilities	...	...	...	...	...	...	...	...	...	...
Statistical discrepancy	...	...	...	...	...	...	...	...	...	...
Net Lending	-326849	...	...	...	...	-218315	...	...	...	...
Incurrence of Liabilities and Net Worth	514595	...	...	...	...	290336	...	...	...	...

	1990				
	Total General Government	Central Government	State or Provincial Government	Local Government	Social Security Funds
Acquisition of Financial Assets					
1 Gold and SDRs	3086	...	...	...	...
2 Currency and transferable deposits	224169	...	...	...	...
3 Other deposits	...	...	...	...	...
4 Bills and bonds, short term	...	...	...	...	...
5 Bonds, long term	-90980	...	...	...	...
6 Corporate equity securities	...	...	...	...	...
7 Short-term loans, n.e.c.	...	...	...	...	...
8 Long-term loans, n.e.c.	109469	...	...	...	...
9 Other receivables	...	...	...	...	...
10 Other assets	194	...	...	...	...
Total Acquisition of Financial Assets	245938	...	...	...	...
Incurrence of Liabilities					
1 Currency and transferable deposits	126147	...	...	...	...

Portugal

3.14 General Government Capital Finance Account, Total and Subsectors
(Continued)

Million Portuguese escudos

	1990				
	Total General Government	Central Government	State or Provincial Government	Local Government	Social Security Funds
2 Other deposits	...	...	...	...	...
3 Bills and bonds, short term	...	...	...	...	...
4 Bonds, long term	...	...	...	...	...
5 Short-term loans, n.e.c.	...	...	...	...	...
6 Long-term loans, n.e.c.	-49667	...	...	...	...
7 Other payables	...	...	...	...	...
8 Other liabilities	...	...	...	...	...
Total Incurrence of Liabilities	...	...	...	...	...
Statistical discrepancy	...	...	...	...	...
Net Lending	-453945	...	...	...	...
Incurrence of Liabilities and Net Worth	245938	...	...	...	...

3.21 Corporate and Quasi-Corporate Enterprise Production Account: Total and Sectors

Million Portuguese escudos

	1980			ADDENDUM:	1981			ADDENDUM:	1982			ADDENDUM:
	Corporate and Quasi-Corporate Enterprises			Total, including Unincorporated	Corporate and Quasi-Corporate Enterprises			Total, including Unincorporated	Corporate and Quasi-Corporate Enterprises			Total, including Unincorporated
	TOTAL	Non-Financial	Financial		TOTAL	Non-Financial	Financial		TOTAL	Non-Financial	Financial	
Gross Output												
1 Output for sale	1724834	1697559	27275	2405678	2144388	2109615	34773	2953244	2660773	2617214	43559	3653471
2 Imputed bank service charge	55553	-	55553	55553	77588	-	77588	77588	107420	-	107420	107420
3 Own-account fixed capital formation	...	...	...	...	...	...	...	...	...	...	...	...
Gross Output	1780387	1697559	82828	2461231	2221976	2109615	112361	3030832	2768193	2617214	150979	3760891
Gross Input												
Intermediate consumption	1144780	1076803	67977	1375568	1456845	1362581	94264	1743180	1818927	1689935	128992	2170761
1 Imputed banking service charge	55553	-	55553	55553	77588	-	77588	77588	107420	-	107420	107420
2 Other intermediate consumption	1089227	1076803	12424	1320015	1379257	1362581	16676	1665592	1711507	1689935	21572	2063341
Subtotal: Value Added	635607	620756	14851	1085663	765131	747034	18097	1287652	949266	927279	21987	1590130
1 Indirect taxes, net	83274	73650	9624	91347	93740	81267	12473	104232	147803	127258	20545	159026
A Indirect taxes	147706	138042	9664	156672	174450	161977	12473	185614	225541	204996	20545	238476
B Less: Subsidies	64432	64392	40	65325	80710	80710	-	81382	77738	77738	-	79450
2 Consumption of fixed capital	...	...	...	...	...	...	...	...	...	...	...	...
3 Compensation of employees	401174	371952	29222	493858	505890	468975	36915	606214	628630	581133	47497	741880
4 Net operating surplus a	151159	175154	-23995	500458	165501	196792	-31291	577206	172833	218888	-46055	689224
Gross Input	1780387	1697559	82828	2461231	2221976	2109615	112361	3030832	2768193	2617214	150979	3760891

	1983			ADDENDUM:	1984			ADDENDUM:	1985			ADDENDUM:
	Corporate and Quasi-Corporate Enterprises			Total, including Unincorporated	Corporate and Quasi-Corporate Enterprises			Total, including Unincorporated	Corporate and Quasi-Corporate Enterprises			Total, including Unincorporated
	TOTAL	Non-Financial	Financial		TOTAL	Non-Financial	Financial		TOTAL	Non-Financial	Financial	
Gross Output												
1 Output for sale	3439927	3386500	53427	4670441	4291399	4218571	72828	5791612	5223446	5134668	88778	7034770
2 Imputed bank service charge	135775	-	135775	135775	139753	-	139753	139753	179388	-	179388	179388
3 Own-account fixed capital formation	...	...	...	...	...	...	...	...	...	...	...	...
Gross Output	3575702	3386500	189202	4806216	4431152	4218571	212581	5931365	5402834	5134668	268166	7214158
Gross Input												
Intermediate consumption	2376347	2210991	165356	2835899	2939986	2759426	180560	3507895	3521362	3290557	230805	4182133
1 Imputed banking service charge	135775	-	135775	135775	139753	-	139753	139753	179388	-	179388	179388
2 Other intermediate consumption	2240572	2210991	29581	2700124	2800233	2759426	40807	3368142	3341974	3290557	51417	4002745
Subtotal: Value Added	1199355	1175509	23846	1970317	1491166	1459145	32021	2423470	1881472	1844111	37361	3032025
1 Indirect taxes, net	201642	174295	27347	215635	247951	211772	36179	268210	325372	280553	44819	343506
A Indirect taxes	290828	263481	27347	307290	364852	325367	39485	388038	440976	396157	44819	470305
B Less: Subsidies	89186	89186	-	91655	116901	113595	3306	119828	115604	115604	-	126799
2 Consumption of fixed capital	...	...	...	...	...	...	...	...	...	...	...	...
3 Compensation of employees	752598	689250	63348	895664	884378	807005	77373	1046747	1055340	957869	97471	1244558
4 Net operating surplus a	245115	311964	-66849	859018	358837	440368	-81531	1108513	500760	605689	-104929	1443961
Gross Input	3575702	3386500	189202	4806216	4431152	4218571	212581	5931365	5402834	5134668	268166	7214158

3.21 Corporate and Quasi-Corporate Enterprise Production Account: Total and Sectors

Million Portuguese escudos

	1986				1987				1988			
	Corporate and Quasi-Corporate Enterprises			ADDENDUM: Total, including Unincorporated	Corporate and Quasi-Corporate Enterprises			ADDENDUM: Total, including Unincorporated	Corporate and Quasi-Corporate Enterprises			ADDENDUM: Total, including Unincorporated
	TOTAL	Non-Financial	Financial		TOTAL	Non-Financial	Financial		TOTAL	Non-Financial	Financial	
Gross Output												
1 Output for sale	5675114	5577025	98089	7746743	6492378	6381255	111123	8881973	7394149	7258965	135184	68996
2 Imputed bank service charge	222787	-	222787	222787	305847	-	305847	305847	382586	-	382586	382586
3 Own-account fixed capital formation	...	...	...	...	...	...	...	...	...	...	...	...
Gross Output	5897901	5577025	320876	7969530	6798225	6381255	416970	9187820	7776735	7258965	517770	451582
Gross Input												
Intermediate consumption	3715158	3428699	286459	4422703	4260985	3887344	373641	5058107	4860712	4392180	468532	5758497
1 Imputed banking service charge	222787	-	222787	222787	305847	-	305847	305847	382586	-	382586	382586
2 Other intermediate consumption	3492371	3428699	63672	4199916	3955138	3887344	67794	4752260	4478126	4392180	85946	5375911
Subtotal: Value Added	2182743	2148326	34417	3546827	2537240	2493911	43329	4129713	2916023	2866785	49238	4693085
1 Indirect taxes, net	273941	219140	54801	279233	246774	184888	61886	245395	295484	194762	100722	286539
A Indirect taxes	411705	356895	54810	428175	382062	320176	61886	395641	445663	344941	100722	460198
B Less: Subsidies	137764	137755	9	148942	135288	135288	-	150246	150179	150179	-	173659
2 Consumption of fixed capital	...	...	...	...	...	...	...	...	...	...	...	...
3 Compensation of employees	1271345	1152379	118966	1492209	1516004	1376623	139381	1776171	1715134	1557628	157506	1993029
4 Net operating surplus a	637457	776807	-139350	1775385	774462	932400	-157938	2108147	905405	1114395	-208990	2413517
Gross Input	5897901	5577025	320876	7969530	6798225	6381255	416970	9187820	7776735	7258965	517770	451582

	1989				1990			
	Corporate and Quasi-Corporate Enterprises			ADDENDUM: Total, including Unincorporated	Corporate and Quasi-Corporate Enterprises			ADDENDUM: Total, including Unincorporated
	TOTAL	Non-Financial	Financial		TOTAL	Non-Financial	Financial	
Gross Output								
1 Output for sale	8681962	8500974	180988	2193773	99511	9856228	243283	3701621
2 Imputed bank service charge	472299	-	472299	472299	627863	-	627863	627863
3 Own-account fixed capital formation	...	...	...	...	...	...	...	...
Gross Output	9154261	8500974	653287	2666072	727374	9856228	871146	4329484
Gross Input								
Intermediate consumption	5739578	5152073	587505	6694185	6681562	5906303	775259	7715060
1 Imputed banking service charge	472299	-	472299	472299	627863	-	627863	627863
2 Other intermediate consumption	5267279	5152073	115206	6221886	6053699	5906303	147396	7087197
Subtotal: Value Added	3414683	3348901	65782	5971887	4045812	3949925	95887	6614424
1 Indirect taxes, net	326496	202679	123817	280439	410512	261762	148750	405641
A Indirect taxes	469551	345734	123817	470299	571339	420501	150838	582370
B Less: Subsidies	143055	143055	-	189860	160827	158739	2088	176729
2 Consumption of fixed capital	...	...	...	...	...	...	...	...
3 Compensation of employees	1971888	1788620	183268	2253951	2367363	2140171	227192	2699154
4 Net operating surplus a	1116299	1357602	-241303	3437497	1267937	1547992	-280055	3509629
Gross Input	9154261	8500974	653287	2666072	727374	9856228	871146	4329484

a) Item 'Operating surplus' includes consumption of fixed capital.

3.22 Corporate and Quasi-Corporate Enterprise Income and Outlay Account: Total and Sectors

Million Portuguese escudos

	1980			1981			1982			1983		
	TOTAL	Non-Financial	Financial	TOTAL	Non-Financial	Financial	TOTAL	Non-Financial	Financial	TOTAL	Non-Financial	Financial
Receipts												
1 Operating surplus a	151159	175154	-23995	165501	196792	-31291	172833	218888	-46055	245115	311964	-66849
2 Property and entrepreneurial income	242937	22861	220076	347826	33485	314341	477179	38180	438999	674833	49278	625555
A Withdrawals from quasi-corporate enterprises	423	423	-	466	466	-	591	591	-	621	621	-
B Interest	240841	21192	219649	344936	31423	313513	473905	35501	438404	671245	46744	624501
C Dividends	1381	954	427	2053	1226	827	2238	1643	595	2634	1581	1053
D Net land rent and royalties	292	292	-	371	370	1	445	445	-	333	332	1

Portugal

3.22 Corporate and Quasi-Corporate Enterprise Income and Outlay Account: Total and Sectors
(Continued)

Million Portuguese escudos

	1980			1981			1982			1983		
	TOTAL	Non-Financial	Financial	TOTAL	Non-Financial	Financial	TOTAL	Non-Financial	Financial	TOTAL	Non-Financial	Financial
3 Current transfers	38057	17066	20991	44353	19427	24926	56017	23132	32885	66251	26266	39985
A Casualty insurance claims	5690	5641	49	6189	6133	56	7892	7822	70	9018	8920	98
B Casualty insurance premiums, net, due to be received by insurance companies	14286	-	14286	16019	-	16019	20704	-	20704	25025	-	25025
C Current transfers from the rest of the world	-	-	-	-	-	-	-	-	-	-	-	-
D Other transfers except imputed	11521	6279	5242	13995	6905	7090	17152	7376	9776	18571	6807	11764
E Imputed unfunded employee pension and welfare contributions	6560	5146	1414	8150	6389	1761	10269	7934	2335	13637	10539	3098
Total Current Receipts	432153	215081	217072	557680	249704	307976	706029	280200	425829	986199	387508	598691
Disbursements												
1 Property and entrepreneurial income	334635	166457	168178	487953	248762	239191	716150	372793	343357	1016975	496467	520508
A Withdrawals from quasi-corporations	...	...	...	...	...	...	...	...	...	...	...	...
B Interest	315164	152620	162544	468701	234365	234336	683175	354553	328622	964194	478367	485827
C Dividends	15771	10137	5634	14862	10074	4788	26677	11942	14735	45800	11121	34679
D Net land rent and royalties	3700	3700	-	4390	4323	67	6298	6298	-	6981	6979	2
2 Direct taxes and other current transfers n.e.c. to general government	22670	21278	1392	30852	28943	1909	38050	35705	2345	45373	42379	2994
A Direct taxes	22670	21278	1392	30852	28943	1909	38050	35705	2345	45373	42379	2994
B Fines, fees, penalties and other current transfers n.e.c.	...	...	...	...	...	...	...	...	...	...	...	...
3 Other current transfers	40386	12904	27482	47217	14040	33177	63047	21439	41608	76343	24684	51659
A Casualty insurance premiums, net	5904	5790	114	6175	6120	55	8712	8649	63	9058	8988	70
B Casualty insurance claims liability of insurance companies	14286	-	14286	16019	-	16019	20704	-	20704	25025	-	25025
C Transfers to private non-profit institutions	365	365	-	551	551	-	608	608	-	713	713	-
D Unfunded employee pension and welfare benefits	...	...	...	...	...	...	...	...	...	...	...	...
E Social assistance grants	10057	5146	4911	12791	6389	6402	16412	7934	8478	21276	10539	10737
F Other transfers n.e.c.	9774	1603	8171	11681	980	10701	16611	4248	12363	20271	4444	15827
G Transfers to the rest of the world	...	...	...	...	...	...	...	...	...	...	...	...
Statistical discrepancy b	1492	-	1492	1929	-	1929	2956	-	2956	3422	-	3422
Net saving c	32970	14442	18528	-10271	-42041	31770	-114174	-149737	35563	-155914	-176022	20108
Total Current Disbursements and Net Saving	432153	215081	217072	557680	249704	307976	706029	280200	425829	986199	387508	598691

	1984			1985			1986			1987		
	TOTAL	Non-Financial	Financial	TOTAL	Non-Financial	Financial	TOTAL	Non-Financial	Financial	TOTAL	Non-Financial	Financial
Receipts												
1 Operating surplus a	358837	440368	-81531	500760	605689	-104929	637457	776807	-139350	774462	932400	-157938
2 Property and entrepreneurial income	960450	67956	892494	1273702	92152	1181550	1267561	109148	1158413	1245309	96447	1148862
A Withdrawals from quasi-corporate enterprises	1013	1013	-	1050	1050	-	1156	1156	-	1152	1152	-
B Interest	954489	63097	891392	1264452	84393	1180059	1259272	102223	1157049	1218129	71215	1146914
C Dividends	4336	3235	1101	7471	5980	1491	6154	4790	1364	24963	23015	1948
D Net land rent and royalties	612	611	1	729	729	-	979	979	-	1065	1065	-
3 Current transfers	70933	27488	43445	89193	41423	47770	96448	30603	65845	130222	39874	90348
A Casualty insurance claims	9312	9261	51	7514	7450	64	6569	6489	80	9375	9249	126
B Casualty insurance premiums, net, due to be received by insurance companies	25863	-	25863	30760	-	30760	39989	-	39989	57001	-	57001
C Current transfers from the rest of the world	-	-	-	-	-	-	-	-	-	-	-	-
D Other transfers except imputed	18177	4710	13467	28146	16706	11440	22786	3758	19028	29614	5963	23651
E Imputed unfunded employee pension and welfare contributions	17581	13517	4064	22773	17267	5506	27104	20356	6748	34232	24662	9570

3.22 Corporate and Quasi-Corporate Enterprise Income and Outlay Account: Total and Sectors
(Continued)

Million Portuguese escudos

	1984			1985			1986			1987		
	TOTAL	Non-Financial	Financial	TOTAL	Non-Financial	Financial	TOTAL	Non-Financial	Financial	TOTAL	Non-Financial	Financial
Total Current Receipts	1390220	535812	854408	1863655	739264	1124391	2001466	916558	1084908	2149993	1068721	1081272
Disbursements												
1 Property and entrepreneurial income	1445374	687589	757785	1805973	805518	1000455	1625126	674247	950879	1490740	632624	858116
A Withdrawals from quasi-corporations	...	...	...	...	...	...	...	...	...	...	...	...
B Interest	1412112	666752	745360	1770140	778568	991572	1568919	645435	923484	1392563	562700	829863
C Dividends	24646	12221	12425	25187	16304	8883	47294	19899	27395	85298	57045	28253
D Net land rent and royalties	8616	8616	-	10646	10646	-	8913	8913	-	12879	12879	-
2 Direct taxes and other current transfers n.e.c. to general government	58124	49300	8824	68447	62147	6300	72945	67573	5372	101376	95035	6341
A Direct taxes	58124	49300	8824	68447	62147	6300	72945	67573	5372	101376	95035	6341
B Fines, fees, penalties and other current transfers n.e.c.	...	...	...	...	...	...	...	...	...	...	...	...
3 Other current transfers	81523	26866	54657	89231	28939	60292	105698	36092	69606	147496	53254	94242
A Casualty insurance premiums, net	10457	10379	78	9121	8976	145	13591	13421	170	19344	19126	218
B Casualty insurance claims liability of insurance companies	25863	-	25863	30760	-	30760	39989	-	39989	57001	-	57001
C Transfers to private non-profit institutions	896	896	-	889	889	-	1080	1080	-	1106	1106	-
D Unfunded employee pension and welfare benefits	...	...	...	...	...	...	...	...	...	...	...	...
E Social assistance grants	26863	13517	13346	34165	17267	16898	40999	20356	20643	51475	24662	26813
F Other transfers n.e.c.	17444	2074	15370	14296	1807	12489	10039	1235	8804	18570	8360	10210
G Transfers to the rest of the world	...	...	...	...	...	...	...	...	...	...	...	...
Statistical discrepancy b	3451	-	3451	-930	-	-930	3234	-	3234	4330	-	4330
Net saving c	-198252	-227943	29691	-99066	-157340	58274	194463	138646	55817	406051	287808	118243
Total Current Disbursements and Net Saving	1390220	535812	854408	1863655	739264	1124391	2001466	916558	1084908	2149993	1068721	1081272

	1988			1989			1990		
	TOTAL	Non-Financial	Financial	TOTAL	Non-Financial	Financial	TOTAL	Non-Financial	Financial
Receipts									
1 Operating surplus a	905405	1114395	-208990	1116299	1357602	-241303	1267937	1547992	-280055
2 Property and entrepreneurial income	1413789	158588	1255201	1723369	192335	1531034	2178472	255672	1922800
A Withdrawals from quasi-corporate enterprises	1282	1282	-	1698	1698	-	2360	2360	-
B Interest	1345240	93648	1251592	1641541	117331	1524210	2078905	163771	1915134
C Dividends	66332	62723	3609	78990	72166	6824	95610	87944	7666
D Net land rent and royalties	935	935	-	1140	1140	-	1597	1597	-
3 Current transfers	163324	49965	113359	207436	59763	147673	251195	65897	185298
A Casualty insurance claims	17902	17757	145	23772	23577	195	28447	28214	233
B Casualty insurance premiums, net, due to be received by insurance companies	73819	-	73819	97324	-	97324	116515	-	116515
C Current transfers from the rest of the world	-	-	-	-	-	-	-	-	-
D Other transfers except imputed	34114	5394	28720	41437	5442	35995	51981	995	50986
E Imputed unfunded employee pension and welfare contributions	37489	26814	10675	44903	30744	14159	54252	36688	17564
Total Current Receipts	2482518	1322948	1159570	3047104	1609700	1437404	3697604	1869561	1828043
Disbursements									
1 Property and entrepreneurial income	1705408	811728	893680	2073164	1012591	1060573	2376189	1085308	1290881
A Withdrawals from quasi-corporations	...	...	...	...	...	...	...	...	...
B Interest	1532675	674784	857891	1869777	829599	1040178	2158856	887248	1271608

Portugal

3.22 Corporate and Quasi-Corporate Enterprise Income and Outlay Account: Total and Sectors
(Continued)

Million Portuguese escudos

	1988 TOTAL	1988 Non-Financial	1988 Financial	1989 TOTAL	1989 Non-Financial	1989 Financial	1990 TOTAL	1990 Non-Financial	1990 Financial
C Dividends	160479	124690	35789	191121	170726	20395	199158	179885	19273
D Net land rent and royalties	12254	12254	-	12266	12266	-	18175	18175	-
2 Direct taxes and other current transfers n.e.c. to general government	139242	129520	9722	199102	186033	13069	252398	234559	17839
A Direct taxes	139242	129520	9722	199102	186033	13069	252398	234559	17839
B Fines, fees, penalties and other current transfers n.e.c.	...	...	...	...	...	...	...	...	...
3 Other current transfers	173236	54467	118769	229819	84300	145519	266879	83425	183454
A Casualty insurance premiums, net	25861	25605	256	34221	33938	283	42142	41792	350
B Casualty insurance claims liability of insurance companies	73819	-	73819	97324	-	97324	116515	-	116515
C Transfers to private non-profit institutions	1216	1216	-	1448	1448	-	1719	1719	-
D Unfunded employee pension and welfare benefits	...	...	...	...	...	...	...	...	...
E Social assistance grants	57765	26814	30951	67021	30744	36277	85732	36688	49044
F Other transfers n.e.c.	14575	832	13743	29805	18170	11635	20771	3226	17545
G Transfers to the rest of the world	...	...	...	...	...	...	...	...	...
Statistical discrepancy b	5425	-	5425	8302	-	8302	7734	-	7734
Net saving c	459207	327233	131974	536717	326776	209941	794404	466269	328135
Total Current Disbursements and Net Saving	2482518	1322948	1159570	3047104	1609700	1437404	3697604	1869561	1828043

a) Item 'Operating surplus' includes consumption of fixed capital.
b) Item 'Statistical discrepancy' refers to increase in technical reserves of pension funds.
c) Item 'Net saving' includes consumption of fixed capital.

3.23 Corporate and Quasi-Corporate Enterprise Capital Accumulation Account: Total and Sectors

Million Portuguese escudos

	1980 TOTAL	1980 Non-Financial	1980 Financial	1981 TOTAL	1981 Non-Financial	1981 Financial	1982 TOTAL	1982 Non-Financial	1982 Financial	1983 TOTAL	1983 Non-Financial	1983 Financial
Finance of Gross Accumulation												
1 Gross saving	32970	14442	18528	-10271	-42041	31770	-114174	-149737	35563	-155914	-176022	20108
A Consumption of fixed capital	...	...	...	...	...	...	...	...	...	...	...	...
B Net saving a	32970	14442	18528	-10271	-42041	31770	-114174	-149737	35563	-155914	-176022	20108
2 Capital transfers	16260	16168	92	17129	17102	27	45325	45149	176	177189	176905	284
Finance of Gross Accumulation	49230	30610	18620	6858	-24939	31797	-68849	-104588	35739	21275	883	20392
Gross Accumulation												
1 Gross capital formation	243698	233941	9757	292271	279455	12816	353909	338949	14960	358755	339252	19503
A Increase in stocks	53478	53478	-	52506	52506	-	50826	50826	-	-11799	-11799	-
B Gross fixed capital formation	190220	180463	9757	239765	226949	12816	303083	288123	14960	370554	351051	19503
2 Purchases of land, net	6392	5320	1072	5952	4670	1282	9134	8116	1018	6529	5371	1158
3 Purchases of intangible assets, net												
4 Capital transfers	173936	2481	171455	6753	3174	3579	11417	6206	5211	9331	4392	4939
Net lending	-374796	-211132	-163664	-298118	-312238	14120	-443309	-457859	14550	-353340	-348132	-5208
Gross Accumulation	49230	30610	18620	6858	-24939	31797	-68849	-104588	35739	21275	883	20392

	1984 TOTAL	1984 Non-Financial	1984 Financial	1985 TOTAL	1985 Non-Financial	1985 Financial	1986 TOTAL	1986 Non-Financial	1986 Financial	1987 TOTAL	1987 Non-Financial	1987 Financial
Finance of Gross Accumulation												
1 Gross saving	-198252	-227943	29691	-99066	-157340	58274	194463	138646	55817	406051	287808	118243
A Consumption of fixed capital	...	...	...	...	...	...	...	...	...	...	...	...
B Net saving a	-198252	-227943	29691	-99066	-157340	58274	194463	138646	55817	406051	287808	118243
2 Capital transfers	162721	162367	354	250027	247998	2029	141097	140874	223	122868	121926	942
Finance of Gross Accumulation	-35531	-65576	30045	150961	90658	60303	335560	279520	56040	528919	409734	119185
Gross Accumulation												
1 Gross capital formation	312798	290778	22020	347922	326830	21092	503381	469426	33955	828139	779781	48358

3.23 Corporate and Quasi-Corporate Enterprise Capital Accumulation Account: Total and Sectors
(Continued)

Million Portuguese escudos

	1984			1985			1986			1987		
	TOTAL	Non-Financial	Financial	TOTAL	Non-Financial	Financial	TOTAL	Non-Financial	Financial	TOTAL	Non-Financial	Financial
A Increase in stocks	-29436	-29436	-	-31463	-31463	-	9946	9946	-	148693	148693	-
B Gross fixed capital formation	342234	320214	22020	379385	358293	21092	493435	459480	33955	679446	631088	48358
2 Purchases of land, net	8623	7366	1257	6565	5261	1304	4863	1708	3155	10041	1771	8270
3 Purchases of intangible assets, net												
4 Capital transfers	93310	88855	4455	272811	139696	133115	116356	101591	14765	44238	22246	21992
Net lending	-450262	-452575	2313	-476337	-381129	-95208	-289040	-293205	4165	-353499	-394064	40565
Gross Accumulation	-35531	-65576	30045	150961	90658	60303	335560	279520	56040	528919	409734	119185

	1988			1989			1990			
	TOTAL	Non-Financial	Financial	TOTAL	Non-Financial	Financial	TOTAL	Non-Financial	Financial	

Finance of Gross Accumulation

	TOTAL	Non-Financial	Financial	TOTAL	Non-Financial	Financial	TOTAL	Non-Financial	Financial	
1 Gross saving	459207	327233	131974	536717	326776	209941	794404	466269	328135	
A Consumption of fixed capital	...	...	...	...	...	...	...	...	...	
B Net saving a	459207	327233	131974	536717	326776	209941	794404	466269	328135	
2 Capital transfers	125790	114167	11623	124708	123430	1278	118429	97647	20782	
Finance of Gross Accumulation	584997	441400	143597	661425	450206	211219	912833	563916	348917	

Gross Accumulation

	TOTAL	Non-Financial	Financial	TOTAL	Non-Financial	Financial	TOTAL	Non-Financial	Financial	
1 Gross capital formation	1038342	981869	56473	1231000	1177943	53057	1483692	1403590	80102	
A Increase in stocks	145984	145984	-	166634	166634	-	200433	200433	-	
B Gross fixed capital formation	892358	835885	56473	1064366	1011309	53057	1283259	1203157	80102	
2 Purchases of land, net	6246	2202	4044	9160	2593	6567	6722	3159	3563	
3 Purchases of intangible assets, net										
4 Capital transfers	53074	11668	41406	51953	10913	41040	53192	6777	46415	
Net lending	-512665	-554339	41674	-630688	-741243	110555	-630773	-849610	218837	
Gross Accumulation	584997	441400	143597	661425	450206	211219	912833	563916	348917	

a) Item 'Net saving' includes consumption of fixed capital.

3.24 Corporate and Quasi-Corporate Enterprise Capital Finance Account: Total and Sectors

Million Portuguese escudos

	1980			1981			1982			1983		
	TOTAL	Non-Financial	Financial	TOTAL	Non-Financial	Financial	TOTAL	Non-Financial	Financial	TOTAL	Non-Financial	Financial

Acquisition of Financial Assets

	TOTAL	Non-Financial	Financial	TOTAL	Non-Financial	Financial	TOTAL	Non-Financial	Financial	TOTAL	Non-Financial	Financial
1 Gold and SDRs	14438	-	14438	3036	-	3036	7053	-	7053	-43626	-	-43626
2 Currency and transferable deposits	36722	33125	3597	7265	5108	2157	32616	29302	3314	24382	23357	1025
3 Other deposits	1339	10326	-8987	-10242	14204	-24446	24936	28840	-3904	12768	8548	4220
4 Bills and bonds, short term	4959	-	4959	15024	-	15024	13940	-	13940	-	-	-
5 Bonds, long term	-59896	499	-60395	156290	1274	155016	138474	6	138468	196325	1183	195142
6 Corporate equity securities	-5020	-	-5020	-119	-	-119	1030	-	1030	-2012	770	-2782
7 Short term loans, n.e.c.	95944	7708	88236	139733	8	139725	119998	-593	120591	200727	-9	200736
8 Long term loans, n.e.c.	145948	716	145232	145360	-1750	147110	246516	855	245661	264367	1200	263167
9 Trade credits and advances	15024	6768	8256	41142	20974	20168	888	3908	-3020	189913	159306	30607
10 Other receivables	-	-	-	-	-	-	-	-	-	-	-	-
11 Other assets a	2224	2205	19	1888	1874	14	2660	2640	20	2479	2457	22
Total Acquisition of Financial Assets	251682	61347	190335	499377	41692	457685	588111	64958	523153	845323	196812	648511

Incurrence of Liabilities

	TOTAL	Non-Financial	Financial	TOTAL	Non-Financial	Financial	TOTAL	Non-Financial	Financial	TOTAL	Non-Financial	Financial
1 Currency and transferable deposits	62190	-	62190	43985	-	43985	60832	-	60832	63907	-	63907
2 Other deposits	273384	-	273384	369059	-	369059	379225	-	379225	435665	-	435665
3 Bills and bonds, short term	-	-	-	-	-	-	-	-	-	-	-	-
4 Bonds, long term	-809	-755	-54	11854	10909	945	19978	19978	-	17191	12585	4606
5 Corporate equity securities	37337	36538	799	33289	32562	727	38607	37835	772	34551	33760	791
6 Short-term loans, n.e.c.	103416	134270	-30854	116886	120845	-3959	142835	153115	-10280	116119	130388	-14269

Portugal

3.24 Corporate and Quasi-Corporate Enterprise Capital Finance Account: Total and Sectors
(Continued)

Million Portuguese escudos

	1980			1981			1982			1983		
	TOTAL	Non-Financial	Financial	TOTAL	Non-Financial	Financial	TOTAL	Non-Financial	Financial	TOTAL	Non-Financial	Financial
7 Long-term loans, n.e.c.	130274	121809	8465	146466	124442	22024	350847	288700	62147	375162	276914	98248
8 Net equity of households in life insurance and pension fund reserves	8058	-	8058	8508	-	8508	11324	-	11324	11866	-	11866
9 Proprietors' net additions to the accumulation of quasi-corporations	...	...	...	...	...	...	...	...	...	...	...	...
10 Trade credit and advances	-11879	-21308	9429	91703	87431	4272	40882	32752	8130	101766	94668	7098
11 Other accounts payable	...	...	...	...	...	...	...	...	...	...	...	...
12 Other liabilities	-3930	...	-3930	-2126	...	-2126	-3173	...	-3173	45718		45718
Total Incurrence of Liabilities	598041	270554	327487	819624	376189	443435	1041357	532380	508977	1201945	548315	653630
Statistical discrepancy	28437	1925	26512	-22129	-22259	130	-9937	-9563	-374	-3282	-3371	89
Net Lending	-374796	-211132	-163664	-298118	-312238	14120	-443309	-457859	14550	-353340	-348132	-5208
Incurrence of Liabilities and Net Lending	251682	61347	190335	499377	41692	457685	588111	64958	523153	845323	196812	648511

	1984			1985			1986			1987		
	TOTAL	Non-Financial	Financial	TOTAL	Non-Financial	Financial	TOTAL	Non-Financial	Financial	TOTAL	Non-Financial	Financial
	Acquisition of Financial Assets											
1 Gold and SDRs	32752	-	32752	81617	-	81617	-68031	-	-68031	7384	-	7384
2 Currency and transferable deposits	54475	34356	20119	62934	64084	-1150	174049	173452	597	1380663	114320	1266343
3 Other deposits	67086	33647	33439	165647	122851	42796	-114302	-131945	17643	...	...	...
4 Bills and bonds, short term	-	-	-	69493	41338	28155	104125	-4656	108781	...	...	...
5 Bonds, long term	245304	866	244438	502828	-110	502938	310201	22782	287419	7216	113584	-106368
6 Corporate equity securities	2670	-	2670	46727	15573	31154	71643	40014	31629	...	...	...
7 Short term loans, n.e.c.	261412	10	261402	98654	-	98654	117041	53	116988	...	...	...
8 Long term loans, n.e.c.	216966	4478	212488	154988	6475	148513	308582	32393	276189	212004	6489	205515
9 Trade credits and advances	136861	125594	11267	-139355	-137577	-1778	5242	9663	-4421	...	...	...
10 Other receivables	-	-	-	-	-	-	-	-	-	...	...	...
11 Other assets a	2040	2027	13	2505	2484	21	4090	4055	35	4513	4475	38
Total Acquisition of Financial Assets	1019566	200978	818588	1046038	115118	930920	912640	145811	766829	1611780	238868	1372912
	Incurrence of Liabilities											
1 Currency and transferable deposits	114844	-	114844	207381	-	207381	369293	-	369293	1695014	-	1695014
2 Other deposits	635000	-	635000	832039	-	832039	249623	-	249623	...	...	...
3 Bills and bonds, short term	-	-	-	20902	-4	20906	6038	-	6038	...	...	...
4 Bonds, long term	28998	15988	13010	46504	46504	-	4749	6107	-1358	-190904	200655	-391559
5 Corporate equity securities	54828	52682	2146	91794	60141	31653	138394	81422	56972	...	...	...
6 Short-term loans, n.e.c.	135888	213606	-77718	22664	47905	-25241	-44020	-61010	16990	...	...	...
7 Long-term loans, n.e.c.	410418	332119	78299	245371	320255	-74884	290738	269273	21465	...	...	...
8 Net equity of households in life insurance and pension fund reserves	11224	-	11224	10287	-	10287	-	-	-	463230	420628	42602
9 Proprietors' net additions to the accumulation of quasi-corporations	...	...	...	...	...	...	...	...	...	...	...	...
10 Trade credit and advances	36882	31901	4981	44684	20273	24411	177029	156621	20408	...	...	...
11 Other accounts payable	...	...	...	...	...	...	...	...	...	...	...	...
12 Other liabilities	33332	...	33332	377	...	377	21893	-	21893	-3719	-	-3719
Total Incurrence of Liabilities	1461414	646296	815118	1522003	495074	1026929	1213737	452413	761324	1963621	621283	1342338
Statistical discrepancy	8414	7257	1157	372	1173	-801	-12057	-13397	1340	1658	11649	-9991
Net Lending	-450262	-452575	2313	-476337	-381129	-95208	-289040	-293205	4165	-353499	-394064	40565
Incurrence of Liabilities and Net Lending	1019566	200978	818588	1046038	115118	930920	912640	145811	766829	1611780	238868	1372912

	1988			1989			1990		
	TOTAL	Non-Financial	Financial	TOTAL	Non-Financial	Financial	TOTAL	Non-Financial	Financial
	Acquisition of Financial Assets								
1 Gold and SDRs	277734	-	277734	745433	-	745433	-16366	...	-16366
2 Currency and transferable deposits	868078	159747	708331	1226879	320768	906111	308245	-38535	346780
3 Other deposits	...	...	...	...	...	...	...	...	...
4 Bills and bonds, short term	...	...	...	...	...	...	...	...	...
5 Bonds, long term	127909	65690	62219	526442	234475	291967	1544030	413791	1130239
6 Corporate equity securities	...	...	...	...	...	...	...	...	...
7 Short term loans, n.e.c.	...	...	...	...	...	...	...	...	...

1562

3.24 Corporate and Quasi-Corporate Enterprise Capital Finance Account: Total and Sectors
(Continued)

Million Portuguese escudos

	1988 TOTAL	1988 Non-Financial	1988 Financial	1989 TOTAL	1989 Non-Financial	1989 Financial	1990 TOTAL	1990 Non-Financial	1990 Financial
8 Long term loans, n.e.c.	443715	36432	407283	904298	54454	849844	929697	57559	872138
9 Trade credits and advances	...	...	...	...	...	...	...	...	...
10 Other receivables	...	...	...	...	...	...	...	...	...
11 Other assets a	5385	5339	46	7051	6991	60	10159	10071	88
Total Acquisition of Financial Assets	1722821	267208	1455613	3410103	616688	2793415	2775765	442886	2332879

Incurrence of Liabilities

	1988 TOTAL	1988 Non-Financial	1988 Financial	1989 TOTAL	1989 Non-Financial	1989 Financial	1990 TOTAL	1990 Non-Financial	1990 Financial
1 Currency and transferable deposits	1299665	-	1299665	1880668	-	1880668	1136713	39216	1097497
2 Other deposits	...	...	...	...	...	...	...	...	...
3 Bills and bonds, short term	...	...	...	...	...	...	...	...	...
4 Bonds, long term	71382	148384	-77002	783911	473961	309950	1373472	556421	817051
5 Corporate equity securities	...	...	...	...	...	...	...	...	...
6 Short-term loans, n.e.c.	...	...	...	...	...	...	...	...	...
7 Long-term loans, n.e.c.	...	...	...	...	...	...	...	...	...
8 Net equity of households in life insurance and pension fund reserves	699890	660215	39675	1308102	887022	421080	805399	698755	106644
9 Proprietors' net additions to the accumulation of quasi-corporations	...	...	...	...	...	...	...	...	...
10 Trade credit and advances	...	...	...	...	...	...	...	...	...
11 Other accounts payable	...	...	...	...	...	...	...	...	...
12 Other liabilities	158361	-	158361	67294	-	67294	91754	-	91754
Total Incurrence of Liabilities	2229298	808599	1420699	4039975	1360983	2678992	3407338	1294392	2112946
Statistical discrepancy	6188	12948	-6760	816	-3052	3868	-800	-1896	1096
Net Lending	-512665	-554339	41674	-630688	-741243	110555	-630773	-849610	218837
Incurrence of Liabilities and Net Lending	1722821	267208	1455613	3410103	616688	2793415	2775765	442886	2332879

a) Item 'Other assets' refers to insurance reserves.

3.31 Household and Private Unincorporated Enterprise Production Account

Million Portuguese escudos

	1980	1981	1982	1983	1984	1985	1986	1987	1988	1989	1990	1991
Gross Output												
1 Output for sale	670924	796676	978783	1214149	1480341	1787645	2045343	2358222	2639723	3064940	3548796	...
2 Non-marketed output	9920	12180	13915	16365	19872	23679	26286	31373	35124	41872	53314	...
Gross Output	680844	808856	992698	1230514	1500213	1811324	2071629	2389595	2674847	3106812	3602110	...
Gross Input												
Intermediate consumption	230788	286335	351834	459552	567909	660771	707545	797122	897785	954607	1033498	...
Subtotal: Value Added	450056	522521	640864	770962	932304	1150553	1364084	1592473	1777062	2152205	2568612	...
1 Indirect taxes net liability of unincorporated enterprises	8073	10492	11223	13993	20259	18134	5292	-1379	-8945	-6100	-4871	...
A Indirect taxes	8966	11164	12935	16462	23186	29329	16470	13579	14535	10101	11031	...
B Less: Subsidies	893	672	1712	2469	2927	11195	11178	14958	23480	16201	15902	...
2 Consumption of fixed capital	...	...	...	...	...	...	...	...	...	...	...	...
3 Compensation of employees	92684	100324	113250	143066	162369	189218	220864	260167	277895	282063	331791	...
4 Net operating surplus a	349299	411705	516391	613903	749676	943201	1137928	1333685	1508112	1876242	2241692	...
Gross Input	680844	808856	992698	1230514	1500213	1811324	2071629	2389595	2674847	3106812	3602110	...

a) Item 'Operating surplus' includes consumption of fixed capital.

3.32 Household and Private Unincorporated Enterprise Income and Outlay Account

Million Portuguese escudos

	1980	1981	1982	1983	1984	1985	1986	1987	1988	1989	1990	1991
Receipts												
1 Compensation of employees	642028	788893	963012	1173328	1386837	1674003	2008898	2386602	2733821	3153390	3816241	...
2 Operating surplus of private unincorporated enterprises	349299	411705	516391	613903	749676	943201	1137928	1333685	1508112	1876242	2241692	...
3 Property and entrepreneurial income	139532	202101	276806	397800	606619	768896	703750	638853	715786	839256	986529	...
A Withdrawals from private quasi-corporations	-	-	-	-	-	-	-	-	-	-	-	...
B Interest	128416	191779	262761	384963	592913	753140	686677	609221	644451	756426	906221	...
C Dividends	7312	6491	8965	7966	6187	7771	11060	23565	64224	75111	71954	...
D Net land rent and royalties	3804	3831	5080	4871	7519	7985	6013	6067	7111	7719	8354	...

Portugal

3.32 Household and Private Unincorporated Enterprise Income and Outlay Account
(Continued)

Million Portuguese escudos

	1980	1981	1982	1983	1984	1985	1986	1987	1988	1989	1990	1991
3 Current transfers	301347	371743	453445	533192	678171	799376	988256	1239202	1396450	1601217	1872770	...
A Casualty insurance claims	9217	10665	13493	17271	18445	25104	35502	49709	58908	75257	90389	...
B Social security benefits	132634	173239	214072	253486	308884	380072	481533	587502	704021	802362	975043	...
C Social assistance grants												...
D Unfunded employee pension and welfare benefits	180	175	177	163	170	210	232	266	220	246	288	
E Transfers from general government	...	...	...	...	...	...	...	...	...	...	...	
F Transfers from the rest of the world	...	...	...	...	...	...	...	...	...	...	...	
G Other transfers n.e.c.	159316	187664	225703	262272	350672	393990	470989	601725	633301	723352	807050	
Statistical discrepancy a	1492	1929	2956	3422	3451	-930	3234	4330	5425	8302	7734	
Total Current Receipts	1433698	1776371	2212610	2721645	3424754	4184546	4842066	5602672	6359594	7478407	8924966	...

Disbursements

	1980	1981	1982	1983	1984	1985	1986	1987	1988	1989	1990	1991
1 Final consumption expenditures	840705	1040145	1280929	1587597	1980398	2381389	2861836	3319972	3891594	4505997	5343020	...
2 Property income	52933	62050	74132	88149	126439	159725	155180	176661	176542	211341	271467	...
A Interest	50863	59942	71562	85319	122320	155567	148647	169920	168639	197972	257149	...
B Net land rent and royalties	2070	2108	2570	2830	4119	4158	6533	6741	7903	13369	14318	...
3 Direct taxes and other current transfers n.e.c. to government	173932	226846	299858	400307	479444	585865	685749	800731	986909	1238757	1433235	...
A Social security contributions	114609	144480	190972	238995	290831	341044	436722	582668	662902	769889	921026	...
B Direct taxes	59323	82366	108886	161312	188613	244821	249027	218063	324007	468868	512209	...
Income taxes	...	...	...	...	...	...	...	...	...	...	...	...
Other	...	...	...	...	...	...	...	...	...	...	...	...
C Fees, fines and penalties	...	...	...	...	...	...	...	...	...	...	...	...
4 Other current transfers	31309	37565	50616	66120	81137	99441	118428	163545	188022	219648	257979	...
A Net casualty insurance premiums	7972	8849	11479	13908	11967	17748	23093	36588	46901	61317	72659	...
B Transfers to private non-profit institutions serving households	2700	4317	5074	5880	7544	7650	9291	9506	10449	12448	14776	...
C Transfers to the rest of the world	1792	1653	2634	7498	11044	12910	15920	26085	23856	25863	35491	...
D Other current transfers, except imputed	4933	5665	7909	8315	12380	14649	13006	15687	14900	17139	12316	...
E Imputed employee pension and welfare contributions	13912	17081	23520	30519	38202	46484	57118	75679	91916	102881	122737	...
Net saving b	334819	409765	507075	579472	757336	958126	1020873	1141763	1116527	1302664	1619265	...
Total Current Disbursements and Net Saving	1433698	1776371	2212610	2721645	3424754	4184546	4842066	5602672	6359594	7478407	8924966	...

a) Item 'Statistical discrepancy' refers to increase in technical reserves of pension funds.
b) Item 'Net saving' includes consumption of fixed capital.

3.33 Household and Private Unincorporated Enterprise Capital Accumulation Account

Million Portuguese escudos

	1980	1981	1982	1983	1984	1985	1986	1987	1988	1989	1990	1991
Finance of Gross Accumulation												
1 Gross saving	334819	409765	507075	579472	757336	958126	1020873	1141763	1116527	1302664	1619265	1302664
A Consumption of fixed capital	...	...	...	...	...	...	...	...	...	...	...	...
B Net saving a	334819	409765	507075	579472	757336	958126	1020873	1141763	1116527	1302664	1619265	1302664
2 Capital transfers	2020	4623	6611	6929	7293	51686	14026	19246	47080	62415	70672	62415
Total Finance of Gross Accumulation	336839	414388	513686	586401	764629	1009812	1034899	1161009	1163607	1365079	1689937	1365079
Gross Accumulation												
1 Gross Capital Formation	117427	150521	194845	200991	219947	266786	335456	419424	521678	595639	694690	595639
A Increase in stocks	-314	3297	5557	-9046	-8287	-9312	616	22274	23823	25588	30778	25588
B Gross fixed capital formation	117741	147224	189288	210037	228234	276098	334840	397150	497855	570051	663912	570051
2 Purchases of land, net	-7786	-6952	-9771	-7103	-10473	-7968	-7743	-13284	-9350	-12934	-11642	-12934
3 Purchases of intangibles, net												
4 Capital transfers	1045	1798	2010	5393	8035	9938	13979	13775	12761	6858	14685	6858
Net lending	226153	269021	326602	387120	547120	741056	693207	741094	638518	775516	992204	775516
Total Gross Accumulation	336839	414388	513686	586401	764629	1009812	1034899	1161009	1163607	1365079	1689937	1365079

a) Item 'Net saving' includes consumption of fixed capital.

3.34 Household and Private Unincorporated Enterprise Capital Finance Account

Million Portuguese escudos

	1980	1981	1982	1983	1984	1985	1986	1987	1988	1989	1990	1991
Acquisition of Financial Assets												
1 Gold	-801	-	-	-	-	-	-	-	-	-	...	...
2 Currency and transferable deposits	49428	34477	33377	28548	38125	111014	203024	510714	516827	614436	689737	...
3 Other deposits	238169	326196	346550	378575	560383	690152	411193	...	...	...	...	...
4 Bills and bonds, short term	3460	6519	5991	-	-	60442	8976	...	...	...	...	...
5 Bonds, long term	69928	12505	-3854	-20312	8914	-	-	178405	298390	351243	490921	...
6 Corporate equity securities	-59163	-5996	10976	3508	-	14980	1633	...	...	...	...	...
7 Short term loans, n.e.c.	-	-	-	-	-	3	-4	-	-	-	...	...
8 Long term loans, n.e.c.	-	-	-	8	-4	-	123699	65414	15378	-8106	68423	...
A Mortgages	...	...	...	...	...	...	...	65414	15378	-8106	68423	...
B Other	...	...	...	...	...	...	...	...	...	...	...	...
9 Trade credit and advances	5114	2960	2961	36061	57660	-105801	78407	...	...	...	...	...
10 Net equity of households in life insurance and pension fund reserves	5805	6603	8650	9374	9152	7738	...	...	...	...	...	...
11 Proprietors' net additions to the accumulation of quasi-corporations	-	-	-	-	-	-	...	...	...	...	...	...
12 Other	-	-	-	-	-	-	17723	27817	39829	59012	81401	...
Total Acquisition of Financial Assets	311940	383264	404651	435762	674230	778528	844651	782350	870424	1016585	1330482	...
Incurrence of Liabilities												
1 Short term loans, n.e.c.	21908	12587	5234	4436	10929	11232	11331	...	...	...	...	...
2 Long term loans, n.e.c.	47017	56832	62904	46401	29835	42218	123150	45040	213957	238714	...	...
A Mortgages	...	...	...	...	...	...	...	...	...	...	338928	...
B Other	...	...	...	...	...	...	...	...	...	...	...	...
3 Trade credit and advances	8977	4092	6261	3869	89017	-21883	206	...	...	...	...	...
4 Other accounts payable	...	...	...	...	...	...	...	...	...	...	...	...
5 Other liabilities	-	-	-	-	-	1635	-	-	14348	-	...	...
Total Incurrence of Liabilities	77902	73511	74399	54706	129781	33202	134687	45040	228305	238714	338928	...
Statistical discrepancy	7885	40732	3650	-6064	-2671	4270	16757	-3784	3601	2355	-650	...
Net Lending	226153	269021	326602	387120	547120	741056	693207	741094	638518	775516	992204	...
Incurrence of Liabilities and Net Lending	311940	383264	404651	435762	674230	778528	844651	782350	870424	1016585	1330482	...

3.41 Private Non-Profit Institutions Serving Households: Production Account

Million Portuguese escudos

	1980	1981	1982	1983	1984	1985	1986	1987	1988	1989	1990	1991
Gross Output												
1 Sales	552	1060	1196	1866	2377	3699	4435	5603	6662	7841	9423	...
2 Non-marketed output	5961	6858	8309	11217	13385	15913	18740	21165	24191	28021	33410	...
A Services produced for own use	5961	6858	8309	11217	13385	15913	18740	21165	24191	28021	33410	...
B Own account fixed capital formation	...	...	...	...	...	...	...	...	...	...	...	...
Gross Output	6513	7918	9505	13083	15762	19612	23175	26768	30853	35862	42833	...
Gross Input												
Intermediate consumption	3051	3575	4111	5614	6790	8278	9436	11205	13452	15135	18230	...
Subtotal: Value Added	3462	4343	5394	7469	8972	11334	13739	15563	17401	20727	24603	...
1 Indirect taxes, net	29	54	77	91	198	25	20	17	19	19	20	...
2 Consumption of fixed capital	...	...	...	...	...	...	...	...	...	...	...	...
3 Compensation of employees	3442	4318	5339	7268	8621	11185	13251	14787	16541	19703	23273	...
4 Net operating surplus a	-9	-29	-22	110	153	124	468	759	841	1005	1310	...
Gross Input	6513	7918	9505	13083	15762	19612	23175	26768	30853	35862	42833	...

a) Item 'Operating surplus' includes consumption of fixed capital.

3.42 Private Non-Profit Institutions Serving Households: Income and Outlay Account

Million Portuguese escudos

	1980	1981	1982	1983	1984	1985	1986	1987	1988	1989	1990	1991
Receipts												
1 Operating surplus a	-9	-29	-22	110	153	124	468	759	841	1005	1310	...
2 Property and entrepreneurial income	2043	3019	4018	5574	7450	8479	9686	9243	6940	9203	9428	...
A Withdrawals from quasi-corporations	-	-	-	-	-	-	-	...	...	...	...	...
B Interest	960	1407	1609	1426	2075	2760	1828	...	...	...	...	...

Portugal

3.42 Private Non-Profit Institutions Serving Households: Income and Outlay Account
(Continued)

Million Portuguese escudos

	1980	1981	1982	1983	1984	1985	1986	1987	1988	1989	1990	1991
C Dividends	1083	1611	2408	4147	5372	5719	7854	...	...	...	...	...
D Net land rent and royalties	-	1	1	1	3	-	4	...	...	...	...	...
3 Current transfers	3630	5846	6997	8064	9831	10985	13378	14642	16209	19330	23071	...
A Casualty insurance claims	-	-	-	-	-	-	-	...	...	...	...	...
B Current transfers from general government	3612	5815	6943	7992	9762	10880	13245	...	...	...	...	...
C Other transfers from resident sectors	...	...	...	...	...	...	...	...	...	...	...	...
D Current transfers received from the rest of the world	...	...	...	...	...	...	...	...	...	...	...	...
E Imputed unfunded employee pension and welfare contributions	18	26	54	72	69	105	133	...	...	...	...	...
Total Current Receipts	5664	8836	10993	13748	17434	19588	23532	24644	23990	29538	33809	...

Disbursements

	1980	1981	1982	1983	1984	1985	1986	1987	1988	1989	1990	1991
1 Final consumption expenditures	4817	5300	6132	8610	9936	11855	14363	15704	18293	21094	25686	...
A Compensation of employees	3333	4145	...	...	...	...	...	...	...	...	...	...
B Consumption of fixed capital	...	...	...	...	...	...	...	...	...	...	...	...
C Purchases of goods and services, net	1484	1155	...	...	...	...	...	...	...	...	...	...
Purchases	2932	3402	...	...	...	...	...	...	...	...	...	...
Less: Sales	1448	2247	...	...	...	...	...	...	...	...	...	...
2 Property income	2	98	149	286	318	312	370	376	275	341	428	...
A Interest	2	98	149	286	318	311	370	376	275	341	428	...
B Net land rent and royalties	-	-	-	-	-	1	-	...	...	...	...	...
3 Direct taxes and other transfers to general government	-	6	1	2	7	6	-	...	...	...	...	...
A Direct taxes	-	6	1	2	7	6	-	...	...	...	...	...
B Fees, fines and penalties	...	...	...	...	...	...	...	...	...	...	...	...
4 Other current transfers	1244	1315	2230	2300	3146	4006	4098	4519	5398	6074	4492	...
A Net casualty insurance premiums	18	8	10	11	13	31	28	...	...	...	...	...
B Social assistance grants	225	373	374	599	913	1162	1262	...	...	...	...	...
C Unfunded employee pension and welfare benefits	-	-	-	-	-	-	-	...	...	...	...	...
D Current transfers to the rest of the world	267	234	541	797	942	1016	920	...	...	...	...	...
E Other current transfers n.e.c.	734	700	1305	893	1278	1797	1888	...	...	...	...	...
Net saving b	-399	2117	2481	2550	4027	3409	4701	4045	24	2029	3203	...
Total Current Disbursements	5664	8836	10993	13748	17434	19588	23532	24644	23990	29538	33809	...

a) Item 'Operating surplus' includes consumption of fixed capital.
b) Item 'Net saving' includes consumption of fixed capital.

3.43 Private Non-Profit Institutions Serving Households: Capital Accumulation Account

Million Portuguese escudos

	1980	1981	1982	1983	1984	1985	1986	1987	1988	1989	1990	1991
				Finance of Gross Accumulation								
1 Gross saving	-399	2117	2481	2550	4027	3409	4701	4045	24	2029	3203	...
A Consumption of fixed capital	...	...	...	...	...	...	...	...	...	...	...	...
B Net saving a	-399	2117	2481	2550	4027	3409	4701	4045	24	2029	3203	...
2 Capital transfers	104	103	396	486	497	695	743	617	809	844	332	...
Finance of Gross Accumulation	-295	2220	2877	3036	4524	4104	5444	4662	833	2873	3535	...
				Gross Accumulation								
1 Gross capital formation	-719	1406	2475	2362	2570	3550	4762	3273	4091	4530	5250	...
A Increase in stocks	-	-	-	-	-	-	-	-	-	-	...	...
B Gross fixed capital formation	-719	1406	2475	2362	2570	3550	4762	3273	4091	4530	5250	...
2 Purchases of land, net	...	...	...	...	...	...	...	...	...	...	...	...
3 Purchases of intangible assets, net	-2	2	-84	26	48	-161	61	-	-	-	...	...
4 Capital transfers	-	52	62	77	-	-	-	310	507	739	...	...
Net lending	426	760	424	571	1906	715	621	1079	-3765	-2396	-1715	...
Gross Accumulation	-295	2220	2877	3036	4524	4104	5444	4662	833	2873	3535	...

a) Item 'Net saving' includes consumption of fixed capital.

Portugal

3.44 Private Non-Profit Institutions Serving Households: Capital Finance Account

Million Portuguese escudos

	1980	1981	1982	1983	1984	1985	1986	1987	1988	1989	1990	1991
Acquisition of Financial Assets												
1 Gold	165	73	99	19	459	24	-363	...	...	...	...	...
2 Currency and transferable deposits	512	856	1002	819	2286	-64	340	...	...	...	...	...
3 Other deposits	1013	678	900	66	4221	163	-3025	...	...	...	...	...
4 Bills and bonds, short term	-	-	2	-	-	11	-39	...	...	...	...	...
5 Bonds, long term	-130	698	-209	1747	-33	58	-	...	...	...	...	...
6 Corporate equity securities	231	-1139	-1927	-1414	-3605	1454	5621	...	...	...	...	...
7 Short-term loans, n.e.c.	266	68	789	174	156	63	-	...	...	...	...	...
8 Long-term loans, n.e.c.	68	18	5	5	20	4	117	...	...	...	...	...
9 Other receivables	-	2	14	-4	30	19	309	...	...	...	...	...
10 Proprietors' net additions to the accumulation of quasi-corporations	...	...	...	...	...	...	...	...	...	...	...	...
11 Other assets	1	1	2	1	3	3	6	...	...	...	...	...
Total Acquisition of Financial Assets	2126	1255	677	1413	3537	1735	2966	...	...	...	...	...
Incurrence of Liabilities												
1 Short-term loans	1675	545	-153	628	1155	170	181	...	...	...	...	...
2 Long-term loans	127	-95	359	11	175	470	-171	...	...	...	...	...
3 Other liabilities	2	3	16	-7	24	253	2203	...	...	...	...	...
Total Incurrence of Liabilities	1804	453	222	632	1354	893	2213	...	...	...	...	...
Statistical discrepancy	-104	42	31	210	277	127	132	...	...	...	...	...
Net Lending	426	760	424	571	1906	715	621	...	...	...	...	...
Incurrence of Liabilities and Net Lending	2126	1255	677	1413	3537	1735	2966	...	...	...	...	...

3.51 External Transactions: Current Account: Detail

Million Portuguese escudos

	1980	1981	1982	1983	1984	1985	1986	1987	1988	1989	1990	1991
Payments to the Rest of the World												
1 Imports of goods and services	528040	678536	832453	1014753	1272288	1458592	1588769	2145228	2779897	3292633	3858828	...
A Imports of merchandise c.i.f.	488209	630478	772651	939000	1171135	1356383	1469791	1997944	2585948	3056346	3559277	...
B Other	39831	48058	59802	75753	101153	102209	118978	147284	193949	236287	299551	...
2 Factor income to the rest of the world	41736	74865	119064	143080	209709	244978	204414	194902	199259	231879	242517	...
A Compensation of employees	2979	2533	3400	5064	6237	8121	11284	10905	12564	17275	28623	...
B Property and entrepreneurial income	38757	72332	115664	138016	203472	236857	193130	183997	186695	214604	213894	...
3 Current transfers to the rest of the world	6864	5650	9263	13116	17367	21313	65689	95299	104336	126345	157976	...
A Indirect taxes by general government to supranational organizations	...	...	...	...	...	...	10313	22006	23845	28538	30149	...
B Other current transfers	6864	5650	9263	13116	17367	21313	55376	73293	80491	97807	127827	...
4 Surplus of the nation on current transactions	-74697	-182524	-250630	-190695	-96674	12440	105263	-20620	-261715	-163363	-208698	...
Payments to the Rest of the World, and Surplus of the Nation on Current Transfers	501943	576527	710150	980254	1402690	1737323	1964135	2414809	2821777	3487494	4050623	...
Receipts From The Rest of the World												
1 Exports of goods and services	343950	389515	488482	721243	1048633	1315210	1466573	1774670	2129516	2671147	3100167	...
A Exports of merchandise f.o.b.	247564	275979	357465	536423	790234	1005286	1124168	1357098	1635076	2069053	2386109	...
B Other	96386	113536	131017	184820	258399	309924	342405	417572	494440	602094	714058	...
2 Factor income from the rest of the world	9158	12675	13077	19638	31724	48389	46699	59841	67083	116045	195643	...
A Compensation of employees	2041	2827	2836	4225	7222	12317	10947	16697	20996	22779	30426	...
B Property and entrepreneurial income	7117	9848	10241	15413	24502	36072	35752	43144	46087	93266	165217	...
3 Current transfers from the rest of the world	148835	174337	208591	239373	322333	373724	450863	580298	625178	700302	754813	...
A Subsidies to general government from supranational organizations	563	1095	...	...	...	...	18292	52327	64622	54425	70269	...
B Other current transfers	148272	173242	208591	239373	322333	373724	432571	527971	560556	645877	684544	...
Receipts from the Rest of the World on Current Transfers	501943	576527	710150	980254	1402690	1737323	1964135	2414809	2821777	3487494	4050623	...

Portugal

3.52 External Transactions: Capital Accumulation Account

Million Portuguese escudos

	1980	1981	1982	1983	1984	1985	1986	1987	1988	1989	1990	1991
Finance of Gross Accumulation												
1 Surplus of the nation on current transactions	-74697	-182524	-250630	-190695	-96674	12440	105263	-20620	-261715	-163363	-208698	...
2 Capital transfers from the rest of the world	111	67	32	1191	3211	820	28732	44109	69347	105906	132558	...
Total Finance of Gross Accumulation	-74586	-182457	-250598	-189504	-93463	13260	133995	23489	-192368	-57457	-76140	...
Gross Accumulation												
1 Capital transfers to the rest of the world	4407	5576	6903	9508	6450	9483	11157	13167	12934	19092	19089	...
2 Purchases of intangible assets, n.e.c., net, from the rest of the world a	-99	-161	-163	-224	-260	-328	-439	-477	-541	-666	-1000	...
Net lending to the rest of the world	-78894	-187872	-257338	-198788	-99653	4105	123277	10799	-204761	-75883	-94229	...
Total Gross Accumulation	-74586	-182457	-250598	-189504	-93463	13260	133995	23489	-192368	-57457	-76140	...

a) Item 'Purchase of intangible assets, n.e.c. net, from the rest of the world' refers to sales of land.

3.53 External Transactions: Capital Finance Account

Million Portuguese escudos

	1980	1981	1982	1983	1984	1985	1986	1987	1988	1989	1990	1991
Acquisitions of Foreign Financial Assets												
1 Gold and SDR's a	-3930	-2126	-3173	45718	33332	377	-	-36202	103737	11823	...	...
2 Currency and transferable deposits	731	-54	-167	735	791	1854	6009	14272	7962	187651	313973	...
3 Other deposits	896	-409	3111	2595	2556	-2331	21135	...	...	...	...	...
4 Bills and bonds, short term	...	...	...	...	...	...	...	...	...	...	...	...
5 Bonds, long term	1480	326	2493	733	13379	13070	9314	107438	121686	388202	461174	...
6 Corporate equity securities	5010	7287	7461	11236	22598	33056	26654	...	...	...	...	...
7 Short-term loans, n.e.c.	38082	-3959	42086	-78082	-119440	-67847	-158603	...	...	...	...	...
8 Long-term loans	52527	90219	215625	212184	242111	183917	-68247	...	...	...	...	...
9 Prporietors' net additions to accumulation of quasi-corporate, non-resident enterprises	...	...	...	...	...	...	...	160413	440019	332463	69405	...
10 Trade credit and advances	...	...	...	...	...	...	...	...	...	...	...	...
11 Other	-21717	72154	10012	-7501	-5523	9930	-6067	...	...	...	...	...
Total Acquisitions of Foreign Financial Assets	73079	163438	277448	187618	189804	172026	-169805	245921	673404	920139	844552	...
Incurrence of Foreign Liabilities												
1 Currency and transferable deposits	8389	1010	6466	-38964	50605	97032	...	247262	114906	63866	273264	...
2 Other deposits	-8791	-24015	-3418	5254	29418	40310	17769	...	...	...	...	...
3 Bills and bonds, short term	...	...	...	...	...	...	...	...	...	...	...	...
4 Bonds, long term	-27	1142	-49	-18	-29	-1568	2802	2836	20043	19330	408005	...
5 Corporate equity securities	572	182	138	1012	1412	27465	17931	...	...	...	...	...
6 Short-term loans, n.e.c.	7821	1801	-2165	1100	-2413	-5533	1212	...	...	...	...	...
7 Long-term loans	3327	1526	1833	4982	22363	26400	6428	-143	73343	16003	82334	...
8 Non-resident proprietors' net additions to accumulation of resident quasi-corporate enterprises	...	...	...	...	...	...	...	...	...	...	...	...
9 Trade credit and advances	-2640	12884	10766	9800	6106	-1807	-14947	...	...	...	...	...
10 Other	...	...	...	...	...	...	-69699	674	268384	744586	-13280	...
Total Incurrence of Liabilities	8651	-5470	13571	-16834	107462	182299	-38504	250629	476676	843785	750323	...
Statistical discrepancy	-14466	-18964	6539	5664	-17311	-6168	2232	6091	-8033	471	...	...
Net Lending	78894	187872	257338	198788	99653	-4105	-133533	-10799	204761	75883	94229	...
Total Incurrence of Liabilities and Net Lending	73079	163438	277448	187618	189804	172026	-169805	245921	673404	920139	844552	...

a) Item 'Gold and SDRs' includes also foreign currency.

4.1 Derivation of Value Added by Kind of Activity, in Current Prices

Million Portuguese escudos

	1980			1981			1982			1983		
	Gross Output	Intermediate Consumption	Value Added	Gross Output	Intermediate Consumption	Value Added	Gross Output	Intermediate Consumption	Value Added	Gross Output	Intermediate Consumption	Value Added
All Producers												
1 Agriculture, hunting, forestry and fishing	207060	77161	129899	231975	97415	134560	280383	117488	162895	339566	156245	183321
A Agriculture and hunting	159831	68681	91150	184398	88322	96076	230625	107887	122738	280378	143003	137375
B Forestry and logging	28168	1602	26566	25512	1493	24019	27512	1815	25697	31857	2468	29389
C Fishing	19061	6878	12183	22065	7600	14465	22246	7786	14460	27331	10774	16557

4.1 Derivation of Value Added by Kind of Activity, in Current Prices
(Continued)

Million Portuguese escudos

	1980			1981			1982			1983		
	Gross Output	Intermediate Consumption	Value Added	Gross Output	Intermediate Consumption	Value Added	Gross Output	Intermediate Consumption	Value Added	Gross Output	Intermediate Consumption	Value Added
2 Mining and quarrying	1220979	831997	388982	1490834	1020673	470161	1820948	1275579	545369	2348609	1672865	675744
3 Manufacturing												
A Manufacture of food, beverages and tobacco	278005	206456	71549	342156	254654	87502	424373	317421	106952	560500	419087	141413
B Textile, wearing apparel and leather industries	238806	150905	87901	264679	164543	100136	310925	196090	114835	416902	266892	150010
C Manufacture of wood and wood products, including furniture	63260	38604	24656	66213	39730	26483	68751	41156	27595	83765	49476	34289
D Manufacture of paper and paper products, printing and publishing	55178	33780	21398	71701	43568	28133	83993	53164	30829	106952	69121	37831
E Manufacture of chemicals and chemical petroleum, coal, rubber and plastic products	223488	188349	35139	304681	261406	43275	408385	358595	49790	547016	482063	64953
F Manufacture of non-metallic mineral products, except products of petroleum and coal	62945	30448	32497	81362	40048	41314	98732	51103	47629	120487	63667	56820
G Basic metal industries	44549	33554	10995	46294	32838	13456	59194	40314	18880	73766	51682	22084
H Manufacture of fabricated metal products, machinery and equipment	195212	109728	85484	240359	135640	104719	281352	162004	119348	331039	197784	133255
I Other manufacturing industries	59536	40173	19363	73389	48246	25143	85243	55732	29511	108182	73093	35089
4 Electricity, gas and water	63786	37284	26502	89732	73635	16097	122612	89581	33031	186918	129588	57330
5 Construction	222967	134115	88852	287330	174308	113022	362236	212785	149451	438680	263483	175197
6 Wholesale and retail trade, restaurants and hotels	406779	134360	272419	491231	165041	326190	618855	202146	416709	771263	251076	520187
A Wholesale and retail trade	316344	81467	234877	382483	102327	280156	482964	125574	357390	600381	154560	445821
B Restaurants and hotels	90435	52893	37542	108748	62714	46034	135891	76572	59319	170882	96516	74366
7 Transport, storage and communication	133189	63848	69341	173399	79595	93804	217339	95654	121685	298564	132074	166490
A Transport and storage	109975	60666	49309	140876	75114	65762	178640	90096	88544	240514	124005	116509
B Communication	23214	3182	20032	32523	4481	28042	38699	5558	33141	58050	8069	49981
8 Finance, insurance, real estate and business services [a]	161666	30257	131409	207160	40598	166562	263906	52066	211840	328328	71761	256567
A Financial institutions	69580	7312	62268	96610	10334	86276	132724	13700	119024	166164	18104	148060
B Insurance	12784	5112	7672	15156	6342	8814	17435	7872	9563	22061	11477	10584
C Real estate and business services	79302	17833	61469	95394	23922	71472	113747	30494	83253	140103	42180	97923
Real estate, except dwellings	55119	12415	42704	70324	17051	53273	88076	21919	66157	113901	31255	82646
Dwellings	24183	5418	18765	25070	6871	18199	25671	8575	17096	26202	10925	15277
9 Community, social and personal services [ab]	42172	11963	30209	56231	15220	41011	71907	19045	52862	91539	24433	67106
A Sanitary and similar services	...	...	...	...	...	...	...	...	...	...	...	...
B Social and related community services	24591	5743	18848	33563	7326	26237	44625	9052	35573	59201	12239	46962
Educational services	7605	2135	5470	10570	2701	7869	14537	3165	11372	18701	3848	14853
Medical, dental, other health and veterinary services	16986	3608	13378	22993	4625	18368	30088	5887	24201	40500	8391	32109
C Recreational and cultural services	17581	6220	11361	22668	7894	14774	27282	9993	17289	32338	12194	20144
D Personal and household services	...	...	...	...	...	...	...	...	...	...	...	...
Total, Industries	2458598	1320985	1137613	3027892	1666485	1361407	3758186	2064344	1693842	4803467	2701525	2101942
Producers of Government Services	192613	47930	144683	238223	61498	176725	292617	77959	214658	369760	100623	269137
Other Producers	16185	2903	13282	19727	3348	16379	22976	3856	19120	28649	5198	23451
Total	2667396	1371818	1295578	3285842	1731331	1554511	4073779	2146159	1927620	5201876	2807346	2394530
Less: Imputed bank service charge	...	-55553	55553	...	-77588	77588	...	-107420	107420	...	-135775	135775
Import duties	16026	...	16026	24208	...	24208	30207	...	30207	42958	...	42958
Value added tax	...	...	...	...	...	...	...	...	...	...	...	...
Total	2683422	1427371	1256051	3310050	1808919	1501131	4103986	2253579	1850407	5244834	2943121	2301713
Memorandum Item: Mineral fuels and power	169728	140074	29654	250540	229717	20823	...	...	...	...	...	...

Portugal

4.1 Derivation of Value Added by Kind of Activity, in Current Prices

Million Portuguese escudos

	1984			1985			1986			1987		
	Gross Output	Intermediate Consumption	Value Added	Gross Output	Intermediate Consumption	Value Added	Gross Output	Intermediate Consumption	Value Added	Gross Output	Intermediate Consumption	Value Added
All Producers												
1 Agriculture, hunting, forestry and fishing	441288	206840	234448	523700	242497	281203	605377	276655	328722	683886	304861	379025
A Agriculture and hunting	365278	189120	176158	426931	219354	207577	489254	251511	237743	555282	278467	276815
B Forestry and logging	41628	3490	38138	55426	4469	50957	63260	4760	58500	75624	5155	70469
C Fishing	34382	14230	20152	41343	18674	22669	52863	20384	32479	52980	21239	31741
2 Mining and quarrying	2967985	2105884	862101	3603012	2532386	1070626	3833795	2543674	1290121	4392466	2878269	1514197
3 Manufacturing												
A Manufacture of food, beverages and tobacco	685427	513014	172413	846959	633180	213779	946673	703641	243032	1074716	804221	270495
B Textile, wearing apparel and leather industries	588278	378452	209826	744412	468101	276311	857189	502718	354471	998063	573699	424364
C Manufacture of wood and wood products, including furniture	101471	62207	39264	120963	76139	44824	143322	89134	54188	174695	109133	65562
D Manufacture of paper and paper products, printing and publishing	153617	94164	59453	187849	120693	67156	215580	129347	86233	257070	144405	112665
E Manufacture of chemicals and chemical petroleum, coal, rubber and plastic products	693952	602524	91428	813273	697977	115296	673606	531982	141624	706933	559454	147479
F Manufacture of non-metallic mineral products, except products of petroleum and coal	138609	74436	64173	157225	82838	74387	178730	87903	90827	212375	101714	110661
G Basic metal industries	89323	64400	24923	102524	72369	30155	104528	67286	37242	117820	72691	45129
H Manufacture of fabricated metal products, machinery and equipment	389362	233986	155376	479365	280405	198960	527957	312036	215921	640292	375247	265045
I Other manufacturing industries	127946	82701	45245	150442	100684	49758	186210	119627	66583	210502	137705	72797
4 Electricity, gas and water	240068	148301	91767	288603	165554	123049	336227	199820	136407	381607	213552	168055
5 Construction	461899	295058	166841	528516	328148	200368	605458	359738	245720	711423	414973	296450
6 Wholesale and retail trade, restaurants and hotels	929656	314484	615172	1168389	379844	788545	1338182	433496	904686	1536931	502474	1034457
A Wholesale and retail trade	712566	190215	522351	902426	231886	670540	1038153	264698	773455	1181762	304796	876966
B Restaurants and hotels	217090	124269	92821	265963	147958	118005	300029	168798	131231	355169	197678	157491
7 Transport, storage and communication	386698	172513	214185	470434	198172	272262	503256	206122	297134	560121	235635	324486
A Transport and storage	312898	160953	151945	372729	183607	189122	393123	190132	202991	435416	216362	219054
B Communication	73800	11560	62240	97705	14565	83140	110133	15990	94143	124705	19273	105432
8 Finance, insurance, real estate and business services a	385082	94976	290106	476473	119020	357453	566135	139056	427079	702350	153696	548654
A Financial institutions	178728	24288	154440	224938	30050	194888	275461	40091	235370	369272	44828	324444
B Insurance	32568	16519	16049	41659	21367	20292	43602	23581	20021	45389	22966	22423
C Real estate and business services	173786	54169	119617	209876	67603	142273	247072	75384	171688	287689	85902	201787
Real estate, except dwellings	146753	40486	106267	182491	51029	131462	212420	56041	156379	247335	64532	182803
Dwellings	27033	13683	13350	27385	16574	10811	34652	19343	15309	40354	21370	18984
9 Community, social and personal services ab	116992	31698	85294	151927	38961	112966	182890	43656	139234	224041	51605	172436
A Sanitary and similar services	...	...	...	...	...	...	...	...	...	...	...	...
B Social and related community services	77211	16168	61043	100377	19457	80920	122202	20886	101316	153139	24874	128265
Educational services	26123	5249	20874	33462	6058	27404	40952	6745	34207	51527	7789	43738
Medical, dental, other health and veterinary services	51088	10919	40169	66915	13399	53516	81250	14141	67109	101612	17085	84527
C Recreational and cultural services	39781	15530	24251	51550	19504	32046	60688	22770	37918	70902	26731	44171
D Personal and household services	...	...	...	...	...	...	...	...	...	...	...	...

4.1 Derivation of Value Added by Kind of Activity, in Current Prices
(Continued)

Million Portuguese escudos

	1984			1985			1986			1987		
	Gross Output	Intermediate Consumption	Value Added	Gross Output	Intermediate Consumption	Value Added	Gross Output	Intermediate Consumption	Value Added	Gross Output	Intermediate Consumption	Value Added
Total, Industries	5929668	3369754	2559914	7211054	4004582	3206472	7971320	4202217	3769103	9192825	4755065	4437760
Producers of Government Services	449032	121708	327324	584345	174065	410280	721591	222460	499131	891592	262005	629587
Other Producers	34707	6363	28344	42043	7727	34316	47709	8910	38799			
Total	6413407	3497825	2915582	7837442	4186374	3651068	8740620	4433587	4307033	84417	5017070	5067347
Less: Imputed bank service charge	...	-139753	139753	...	-179388	179388	...	-222787	222787	...	-305847	305847
Import duties	39899	...	39899	52265	...	52265	54802	...	54802	79969	...	79969
Value added tax	...	...	...	...	...	...	281352	...	281352	333263	...	333263
Total	6453306	3637578	2815728	7889707	4365762	3523945	9076774	4656374	4420400	497649	5322917	5174732
Memorandum Item: Mineral fuels and power	...	...	...	...	...	...	558946	400971	157975	601422	413756	187666

	1988			1989			1990		
	Gross Output	Intermediate Consumption	Value Added	Gross Output	Intermediate Consumption	Value Added	Gross Output	Intermediate Consumption	Value Added

All Producers

	Gross Output	Intermediate Consumption	Value Added	Gross Output	Intermediate Consumption	Value Added	Gross Output	Intermediate Consumption	Value Added
1 Agriculture, hunting, forestry and fishing	689018	323873	365145	807270	366256	441014	890373	399586	490787
A Agriculture and hunting	546418	296101	250317	644713	337837	306876	716085	370985	345100
B Forestry and logging	82912	5236	77676	99821	5658	94163	112550	6025	106525
C Fishing	59688	22536	37152	62736	22761	39975	61738	22576	39162
2 Mining and quarrying	4938006	3230690	1707316	5757643	3701720	2055923	6535000	4161910	2373090
3 Manufacturing									
A Manufacture of food, beverages and tobacco	1175651	875713	299938	1371322	980853	390469	1550654	1041616	509038
B Textile, wearing apparel and leather industries	1105241	646512	458729	1309342	756940	552402	1472300	857920	614380
C Manufacture of wood and wood products, including furniture	209427	130324	79103	261710	160441	101269	304227	191880	112347
D Manufacture of paper and paper products, printing and publishing	297520	161669	135851	355241	188135	167106	375198	221867	153331
E Manufacture of chemicals and chemical petroleum, coal, rubber and plastic products	816799	617449	199350	886897	688009	198888	982593	807238	175355
F Manufacture of non-metallic mineral products, except products of petroleum and coal	249214	119254	129960	285485	137636	147849	320097	157182	162915
G Basic metal industries	132209	82487	49722	166660	93688	72972	210461	110490	99971
H Manufacture of fabricated metal products, machinery and equipment	713425	436969	276456	830311	505925	324386	976351	555340	421011
I Other manufacturing industries	238520	160313	78207	290675	190093	100582	343119	218377	124742
4 Electricity, gas and water	431579	220361	211218	524527	314765	209762	602749	341438	261311
5 Construction	869476	500972	368504	1019960	567252	452708	1237948	652566	585382
6 Wholesale and retail trade, restaurants and hotels	1759280	574260	1185020	2052701	654882	1397819	2459346	777859	1681487
A Wholesale and retail trade	1359554	351025	1008529	1550779	397828	1152951	1814075	462044	1352031
B Restaurants and hotels	399726	223235	176491	501922	257054	244868	645271	315815	329456
7 Transport, storage and communication	643621	282361	361260	733944	320949	412995	849770	387358	462412
A Transport and storage	495977	257965	238012	562681	291153	271528	630643	349830	280813
B Communication	147644	24396	123248	171263	29796	141467	219127	37528	181599
8 Finance, insurance, real estate and business services [a] ..	874221	188724	685497	1076466	234830	841636	1411950	299364	1112586
A Financial institutions	460071	54724	405347	578565	78328	500237	788591	100712	687879
B Insurance	54932	31222	23710	71768	36878	34890	78842	46684	32158
C Real estate and business services	359218	102778	256440	426133	119624	306509	544517	151968	392549
Real estate, except dwellings	311268	78680	232588	365879	92189	273690	472675	120425	352250
Dwellings	47950	24098	23852	60254	27435	32819	71842	31543	40299
9 Community, social and personal services [a]	260064	58210	201854	307454	64930	242524	366601	71845	294756
A Sanitary and similar services	...	...	...	...	...	...	...	...	...
B Social and related community services	176908	27918	148990	209915	30760	179155	251178	34297	216881

Portugal

4.1 Derivation of Value Added by Kind of Activity, in Current Prices
(Continued)

Million Portuguese escudos

	1988			1989			1990		
	Gross Output	Intermediate Consumption	Value Added	Gross Output	Intermediate Consumption	Value Added	Gross Output	Intermediate Consumption	Value Added
Educational services	57228	8749	48479	65196	9256	55940	74905	10010	64895
Medical, dental, other health and veterinary services	119680	19169	100511	144719	21504	123215	176273	24287	151986
C Recreational and cultural services	83156	30292	52864	97539	34170	63369	115423	37548	77875
D Personal and household services	...	...	...	...	...	...	...	...	...
Total, Industries	465265	5379451	5085814	2279965	6225584	6054381	14353737	7091926	7261811
Producers of Government Services	1080920	321216	759704	1286603	360263	926340	1589184	432195	1156989
Other Producers									
Total	1546185	5700667	5845518	3566568	6585847	6980721	15942921	7524121	8418800
Less: Imputed bank service charge	...	-382586	382586	...	-472299	472299	...	-627863	627863
Import duties	117081	...	117081	124671	...	124671	146439	...	146439
Value added tax	422738	...	422738	497167	...	497167	570058	...	570058
Total	2086004	6083253	6002751	4188406	7058146	7130260	16659418	8151984	8507434
Memorandum Item: Mineral fuels and power	686607	431669	254938	799977	576387	223590	913004	662376	250628

a) Business services and real estate except dwellings are included in item 'Community, social and personal services'.

4.2 Derivation of Value Added by Kind of Activity, in Constant Prices

Million Portuguese escudos

	1980			1981			1982			1983		
	Gross Output	Intermediate Consumption	Value Added	Gross Output	Intermediate Consumption	Value Added	Gross Output	Intermediate Consumption	Value Added	Gross Output	Intermediate Consumption	Value Added
	At constant prices of:1985											
	All Producers											
1 Agriculture, hunting, forestry and fishing	511803	256203	255600	480136	252027	228109	495593	253498	242095	485111	246323	238788
A Agriculture and hunting	410276	232523	177753	392661	230427	162234	412278	234028	178250	398706	225848	172858
B Forestry and logging	60370	4630	55740	48106	3694	44412	48840	3787	45053	50001	3918	46083
C Fishing	41157	19050	22107	39369	17906	21463	34475	15683	18792	36404	16557	19847
2 Mining and quarrying	3417276	2338082	1079194	3495407	2382281	1113126	3575431	2473927	1101504	3603903	2516848	1087055
3 Manufacturing												
A Manufacture of food, beverages and tobacco	848902	630741	218161	892323	667820	224503	895300	664114	231186	887681	649901	237780
B Textile, wearing apparel and leather industries	642460	403771	238689	627833	382853	244980	633140	388118	245022	660474	406379	254095
C Manufacture of wood and wood products, including furniture	153178	92842	60336	136567	83978	52589	123197	76593	46604	124350	76640	47710
D Manufacture of paper and paper products, printing and publishing	157266	95981	61285	163687	101465	62222	166043	103538	62505	170817	108927	61890
E Manufacture of chemicals and chemical petroleum, coal, rubber and plastic products	656964	543721	113243	693775	564406	129369	773412	652387	121025	815206	698902	116304
F Manufacture of non-metallic mineral products, except products of petroleum and coal	158293	90637	67656	168443	95918	72525	170372	96687	73685	168032	94426	73606
G Basic metal industries	123628	90347	33281	112089	78185	33904	114542	79119	35423	111628	78839	32789
H Manufacture of fabricated metal products, machinery and equipment	515791	281370	234421	536152	298193	237959	534906	305261	229645	498200	292518	205682
I Other manufacturing industries	160794	108672	52122	164538	109463	55075	164519	108110	56409	167515	110316	57199
4 Electricity, gas and water	232789	148441	84348	226567	157636	68931	245946	153022	92924	272923	169441	103482
5 Construction	581360	363485	217875	613011	384905	228106	625262	392680	232582	614620	380388	234232
6 Wholesale and retail trade, restaurants and hotels	1186020	365918	820102	1212314	377336	834978	1229323	387308	842015	1198039	380268	817771
A Wholesale and retail trade	936075	226950	709125	958549	235793	722756	970842	241714	729128	937203	234152	703051
B Restaurants and hotels	249945	138968	110977	253765	141543	112222	258481	145594	112887	260836	146116	114720
7 Transport, storage and communication	424491	194527	229964	430656	197045	233611	444644	195015	249629	467656	203035	264621
A Transport and storage	353934	185431	168503	355619	186601	169018	359204	184262	174942	371943	190881	181062
B Communication	70557	9096	61461	75037	10444	64593	85440	10753	74687	95713	12154	83559
8 Finance, insurance, real estate and business services	426226	90253	335973	450142	96977	353165	477724	103309	374415	487280	111467	375813
A Financial institutions	203121	22164	180957	224517	24780	199737	246682	27844	218838	249842	28575	221267

4.2 Derivation of Value Added by Kind of Activity, in Constant Prices
(Continued)

Million Portuguese escudos

	1980 Gross Output	1980 Intermediate Consumption	1980 Value Added	1981 Gross Output	1981 Intermediate Consumption	1981 Value Added	1982 Gross Output	1982 Intermediate Consumption	1982 Value Added	1983 Gross Output	1983 Intermediate Consumption	1983 Value Added
					At constant prices of:1985							
B Insurance	36778	15140	21638	35391	14856	20535	33672	15527	18145	34895	17775	17120
C Real estate and business services	186327	52949	133378	190234	57341	132893	197370	59938	137432	202543	65117	137426
Real estate, except dwellings	161238	37768	123470	164482	41752	122730	171415	44227	127188	176183	49161	127022
Dwellings	25089	15181	9908	25752	15589	10163	25955	15711	10244	26360	15956	10404
9 Community, social and personal services	134288	35233	99055	139728	36919	102809	142717	37675	105042	143942	37831	106111
A Sanitary and similar services	...	...	...	...	...	...	...	...	...	...	...	...
B Social and related community services	85769	17116	68653	89917	18102	71815	92853	18475	74378	95014	19034	75980
Educational services	31954	6119	25835	33185	6457	26728	33461	6298	27163	31769	5944	25825
Medical, dental, other health and veterinary services	53815	10997	42818	56732	11645	45087	59392	12177	47215	63245	13090	50155
C Recreational and cultural services	48519	18117	30402	49811	18817	30994	49864	19200	30664	48928	18797	30131
D Personal and household services	...	...	...	...	...	...	...	...	...	...	...	...
Total, Industries	6914253	3792142	3122111	7047961	3885126	3162835	7236640	3996434	3240206	7273474	4045601	3227873
Producers of Government Services	517741	143735	374006	543694	151285	392409	564588	158934	405654	586506	161674	424832
Other Producers												
Total	7431994	3935877	3496117	7591655	4036411	3555244	7801228	4155368	3645860	7859980	4207275	3652705
Less: Imputed bank service charge	...	-163285	163285	...	-181159	181159	...	-199831	199831	...	-203249	203249
Import duties	38893	...	38893	52198	...	52198	53418	...	53418	43933	...	43933
Value added tax	...	...	...	...	...	...	...	...	...	...	...	...
Total	7470887	4099162	3371725	7643853	4217570	3426283	7854646	4355199	3499447	7903913	4410524	3493389
Memorandum Item: Mineral fuels and power	555118	454979	100139	581163	478508	102655	618016	502688	115328	656162	541543	114619

	1984 Gross Output	1984 Intermediate Consumption	1984 Value Added	1985 Gross Output	1985 Intermediate Consumption	1985 Value Added	1986 Gross Output	1986 Intermediate Consumption	1986 Value Added	1987 Gross Output	1987 Intermediate Consumption	1987 Value Added
					At constant prices of:1985							
					All Producers							
1 Agriculture, hunting, forestry and fishing	503070	242738	260332	523700	242497	281203	546093	256134	289959	569297	267227	302070
A Agriculture and hunting	411646	221088	190558	426931	219354	207577	441295	232072	209223	465929	243490	222439
B Forestry and logging	53206	4248	48958	55426	4469	50957	57980	4595	53385	59396	4706	54690
C Fishing	38218	17402	20816	41343	18674	22669	46818	19467	27351	43972	19031	24941
2 Mining and quarrying / 3 Manufacturing	3513066	2468417	1044649	3603012	2532386	1070626	3797516	2660098	1137418	3923237	2752999	1170238
A Manufacture of food, beverages and tobacco	841501	625778	215723	846959	633180	213779	875929	645465	230464	924387	688676	235711
B Textile, wearing apparel and leather industries	696727	433183	263544	744412	468101	276311	796351	500457	295894	808223	510601	297622
C Manufacture of wood and wood products, including furniture	121795	77109	44686	120963	76139	44824	129040	80478	48562	138688	87728	50960
D Manufacture of paper and paper products, printing and publishing	173489	113120	60369	187849	120693	67156	198849	123910	74939	204072	127109	76963
E Manufacture of chemicals and chemical petroleum, coal, rubber and plastic products	792011	680563	111448	813273	697977	115296	889217	765944	123273	861365	740927	120438
F Manufacture of non-metallic mineral products, except products of petroleum and coal	160347	87739	72608	157225	82838	74387	163045	83606	79439	178297	93031	85266
G Basic metal industries	107229	77550	29679	102524	72369	30155	102606	67546	35060	117014	75471	41543
H Manufacture of fabricated metal products, machinery and equipment	469809	275271	194538	479365	280405	198960	484184	285332	198852	528933	318451	210482
I Other manufacturing industries	150158	98104	52054	150442	100684	49758	158295	107360	50935	162258	111005	51253
4 Electricity, gas and water	284088	172460	111628	288603	165554	123049	297773	185511	112262	305884	187941	117943

Portugal

4.2 Derivation of Value Added by Kind of Activity, in Constant Prices
(Continued)

Million Portuguese escudos

At constant prices of:1985

	1984			1985			1986			1987		
	Gross Output	Intermediate Consumption	Value Added	Gross Output	Intermediate Consumption	Value Added	Gross Output	Intermediate Consumption	Value Added	Gross Output	Intermediate Consumption	Value Added
5 Construction	559812	347493	212319	528516	328148	200368	539173	334284	204889	584566	363518	221048
6 Wholesale and retail trade, restaurants and hotels	1153813	374669	779144	1168389	379844	788545	1229580	396854	832726	1309432	422707	886725
A Wholesale and retail trade	891869	227659	664210	902426	231886	670540	950919	242723	708196	1015826	259612	756214
B Restaurants and hotels	261944	147010	114934	265963	147958	118005	278661	154131	124530	293606	163095	130511
7 Transport, storage and communication	471929	207060	264869	470434	198172	272262	489042	202925	286117	519464	219226	300238
A Transport and storage	374585	193135	181450	372729	183607	189122	381815	188657	193158	401310	203387	197923
B Communication	97344	13925	83419	97705	14565	83140	107227	14268	92959	118154	15839	102315
8 Finance, insurance, real estate and business services	456852	115965	340887	476473	119020	357453	488115	123512	364603	548455	125573	422882
A Financial institutions	212682	29871	182811	224938	30050	194888	238904	35236	203668	290708	36574	254134
B Insurance	39414	19989	19425	41659	21367	20292	37948	20179	17769	35844	17964	17880
C Real estate and business services	204756	66105	138651	209876	67603	142273	211263	68097	143166	221903	71035	150868
Real estate, except dwellings	177642	49695	127947	182491	51029	131462	183385	51074	132311	193746	53712	140034
Dwellings	27114	16410	10704	27385	16574	10811	27878	17023	10855	28157	17323	10834
9 Community, social and personal services	144885	38325	106560	151927	38961	112966	154447	40318	114129	165961	44221	121740
A Sanitary and similar services	...	...	...	...	...	...	...	...	...	...	...	...
B Social and related community services	96517	19554	76963	100377	19457	80920	97764	18939	78825	103780	20844	82936
Educational services	33645	6351	27294	33462	6058	27404	33888	6137	27751	36196	6579	29617
Medical, dental, other health and veterinary services	62872	13203	49669	66915	13399	53516	63876	12802	51074	67584	14265	53319
C Recreational and cultural services	48368	18771	29597	51550	19504	32046	56683	21379	35304	62181	23377	38804
D Personal and household services	...	...	...	...	...	...	...	...	...	...	...	...
Total, Industries	7087515	3967127	3120388	7211054	4004582	3206472	7541739	4199636	3342103	7926296	4383412	3542884
Producers of Government Services	586766	154869	431897	626388	181792	444596	667626	208901	458725	700932	220982	479950
Other Producers												
Total	7674281	4121996	3552285	7837442	4186374	3651068	8209365	4408537	3800828	8627228	4604394	4022834
Less: Imputed bank service charge	...	-166431	166431	...	-179388	179388	...	-195502	195502	...	-243543	243543
Import duties	41860		41860	52265	...	52265	64544	...	64544	83324	...	83324
Value added tax	...	...	...	...	...	...	...	...	...	...	...	...
Total	7716141	4288427	3427714	7889707	4365762	3523945	8273909	4604039	3669870	8710552	4847937	3862615
Memorandum Item: Mineral fuels and power	624857	504299	120558	637713	502569	135144	704699	578033	126666	677624	546122	131502

At constant prices of:1985

All Producers

	1988			1989			1990		
	Gross Output	Intermediate Consumption	Value Added	Gross Output	Intermediate Consumption	Value Added	Gross Output	Intermediate Consumption	Value Added
1 Agriculture, hunting, forestry and fishing	527081	259889	267192	574450	272121	302329	583373	285810	297563
A Agriculture and hunting	427985	236625	191360	477767	249929	227838	491520	265907	225613
B Forestry and logging	55556	4402	51154	55644	4403	51241	56034	4334	51700
C Fishing	43540	18862	24678	41039	17789	23250	35819	15569	20250

4.2 Derivation of Value Added by Kind of Activity, in Constant Prices
(Continued)

Million Portuguese escudos

	1988			1989			1990		
	Gross Output	Intermediate Consumption	Value Added	Gross Output	Intermediate Consumption	Value Added	Gross Output	Intermediate Consumption	Value Added
				At constant prices of:1985					
2 Mining and quarrying	4072360	2872777	1199583	4317346	3021009	1296337	4571365	3215446	1355919
3 Manufacturing									
A Manufacture of food, beverages and tobacco	937102	696559	240543	995477	729917	265560	1031875	755631	276244
B Textile, wearing apparel and leather industries	816463	518008	298455	898222	568563	329659	933738	608843	324895
C Manufacture of wood and wood products, including furniture	146963	92779	54184	156026	98200	57826	158953	102509	56444
D Manufacture of paper and paper products, printing and publishing	206385	128211	78174	213297	132976	80321	228205	147709	80496
E Manufacture of chemicals and chemical petroleum, coal, rubber and plastic products	930945	804888	126057	949640	825646	123994	1012068	888518	123550
F Manufacture of non-metallic mineral products, except products of petroleum and coal	191274	100492	90782	205519	106716	98803	223020	115863	107157
G Basic metal industries	121751	79292	42459	131457	80617	50840	168163	94241	73922
H Manufacture of fabricated metal products, machinery and equipment	549945	334296	215649	586511	351120	235391	623812	366541	257271
I Other manufacturing industries	171532	118252	53280	181197	127254	53943	191531	135591	55940
4 Electricity, gas and water	323367	190414	132953	355621	233570	122051	390650	256267	134383
5 Construction	645724	400558	245166	671546	416469	255077	705873	440584	265289
6 Wholesale and retail trade, restaurants and hotels	1371005	443474	927531	1426403	460962	965441	1506731	506431	1000300
A Wholesale and retail trade	1065435	273101	792334	1097948	281601	816347	1141366	304089	837277
B Restaurants and hotels	305570	170373	135197	328455	179361	149094	365365	202342	163023
7 Transport, storage and communication	566038	245243	320795	593763	255354	338409	651809	279269	372540
A Transport and storage	432621	227247	205374	443911	235345	208566	476359	256060	220299
B Communication	133417	17996	115421	149852	20009	129843	175450	23209	152241
8 Finance, insurance, real estate and business services	581752	136733	445019	630546	152339	478207	753880	179518	574362
A Financial institutions	307984	39793	268191	342749	50632	292117	425747	60055	365692
B Insurance	36935	21339	15596	42704	22687	20017	42753	27534	15219
C Real estate and business services	236833	75601	161232	245093	79020	166073	285380	91929	193451
Real estate, except dwellings	208358	58034	150324	216277	61115	155162	256189	73574	182615
Dwellings	28475	17567	10908	28816	17905	10911	29191	18355	10836
9 Community, social and personal services	168183	44868	123315	170910	45529	125381	170962	46484	124478
A Sanitary and similar services	...	...	...	...	...	...	...	...	...
B Social and related community services	105160	21108	84052	106588	21329	85259	107298	21802	85496
Educational services	36810	6697	30113	35736	6520	29216	35404	6485	28919
Medical, dental, other health and veterinary services	68350	14411	53939	70852	14809	56043	71894	15317	56577
C Recreational and cultural services	63023	23760	39263	64322	24200	40122	63664	24682	38982
D Personal and household services	...	...	...	...	...	...	...	...	...
Total, Industries	8255510	4593956	3661554	8740585	4857353	3883232	9334643	5209809	4124834
Producers of Government Services	734480	242956	491524	753652	247506	506146	765006	268648	496358
Other Producers									
Total	8989990	4836912	4153078	9494237	5104859	4389378	99649	5478457	4621192
Less: Imputed bank service charge	...	-258714	258714	...	-282637	282637	...	-342414	342414
Import duties	119716	...	119716	114267	...	114267	126813	...	126813
Value added tax	...	...	...	...	...	...	...	...	...
Total	9109706	5095626	4014080	9608504	5387496	4221008	226462	5820871	4405591
Memorandum Item: Mineral fuels and power	764317	614297	150020	834103	692750	141353	902824	748677	154147

Portugal

4.3 Cost Components of Value Added

Million Portuguese escudos

	1980						1981					
	Compensation of Employees	Capital Consumption	Net Operating Surplus	Indirect Taxes	Less: Subsidies Received	Value Added	Compensation of Employees	Capital Consumption	Net Operating Surplus	Indirect Taxes	Less: Subsidies Received	Value Added
All Producers												
1 Agriculture, hunting, forestry and fishing	26602	...	102532	1967	1202	129899	28767	...	104991	2267	1465	134560
A Agriculture and hunting	16464	...	74097	1418	829	91150	16902	...	78631	1664	1121	96076
B Forestry and logging	543	...	25797	226	-	26566	678	...	23116	227	2	24019
C Fishing	9595	...	2638	323	373	12183	11187	...	3244	376	342	14465
2 Mining and quarrying	205666	...	147691	51761	16136	388982	249307	...	177908	62781	19835	470161
3 Manufacturing		...						...				
A Manufacture of food, beverages and tobacco	24094	...	33164	20154	5863	71549	29705	...	39003	25140	6346	87502
B Textile, wearing apparel and leather industries	59750	...	24787	3808	444	87901	69402	...	27194	4526	986	100136
C Manufacture of wood and wood products, including furniture	12560	...	10782	1392	78	24656	14379	...	10474	1734	104	26483
D Manufacture of paper and paper products, printing and publishing	10128	...	10280	1283	293	21398	12659	...	14180	1762	468	28133
E Manufacture of chemicals and chemical petroleum, coal, rubber and plastic products	18213	...	14578	9320	6972	35139	22814	...	18096	9850	7485	43275
F Manufacture of non-metallic mineral products, except products of petroleum and coal	16106	...	14745	1776	130	32497	19797	...	19479	2434	396	41314
G Basic metal industries	6938	...	3679	569	191	10995	8581	...	4465	688	278	13456
H Manufacture of fabricated metal products, machinery and equipment	48060	...	26767	12780	2123	85484	60245	...	32885	15292	3703	104719
I Other manufacturing industries	9817	...	8909	679	42	19363	11725	...	12132	1355	69	25143
4 Electricity, gas and water	10845	...	15283	741	367	26502	13668	...	2118	1127	816	16097
5 Construction	60010	...	26604	2716	478	88852	75583	...	37837	3242	3640	113022
6 Wholesale and retail trade, restaurants and hotels	78550	...	149210	81165	36506	272419	96742	...	181258	92700	44510	326190
A Wholesale and retail trade	67412	...	124177	79744	36456	234877	82656	...	150875	90861	44236	280156
B Restaurants and hotels	11138	...	25033	1421	50	37542	14086	...	30383	1839	274	46034
7 Transport, storage and communication	55680	...	17245	3914	7498	69341	70769	...	25935	4667	7567	93804
A Transport and storage	42264	...	11638	2802	7395	49309	53557	...	16751	2968	7514	65762
B Communication	13416	...	5607	1112	103	20032	17212	...	9184	1699	53	28042
8 Finance, insurance, real estate and business services [a]	37119	...	82083	14649	2442	131409	46973	...	103887	18525	2823	166562
A Financial institutions	22991	...	31955	7362	40	62268	29397	...	47504	9375	-	86276
B Insurance	6231	...	-861	2302	-	7672	7518	...	-1802	3098	-	8814
C Real estate and business services	7897	...	50989	4985	2402	61469	10058	...	58185	6052	2823	71472
Real estate, except dwellings	7816	...	30743	4839	694	42704	9971	...	38143	5895	736	53273
Dwellings	81	...	20246	146	1708	18765	87	...	20042	157	2087	18199
9 Community, social and personal services [ab]	10594	...	16446	3911	742	30209	13754	...	22541	5488	772	41011
A Sanitary and similar services	...	...	...	...	...	...	...	...	...	...	...	...
B Social and related community services	5479	...	13120	253	4	18848	7131	...	18782	371	47	26237
Educational services	2525	...	2853	94	2	5470	3206	...	4536	138	11	7869
Medical, dental, other health and veterinary services	2954	...	10267	159	2	13378	3925	...	14246	233	36	18368
C Recreational and cultural services	5115	...	3326	3658	738	11361	6623	...	3759	5117	725	14774
D Personal and household services	...	...	...	...	...	...	...	...	...	...	...	...
Total, Industries [c]	485066	...	557094	160824	65371	1137613	595563	...	656475	190797	81428	1361407
Producers of Government Services	144647	...	36	-	-	144683	176711	...	-	14	-	176725
Other Producers	13253	...	-	29	-	13282	16325	...	-	54	-	16379
Total [c]	642966	...	557094	160889	65371	1295578	788599	...	656475	190865	81428	1554511
Less: Imputed bank service charge	...	...	55553	...	...	55553	...	...	77588	...	...	77588
Import duties	...	...	...	16026	...	16026	...	...	...	24208	...	24208
Value added tax	...	...	...	...	...	...	...	...	...	...	...	...
Total	642966	...	501541	176915	65371	1256051	788599	...	578887	215073	81428	1501131

4.3 Cost Components of Value Added

Million Portuguese escudos

	1982						1983					
	Compensation of Employees	Capital Consumption	Net Operating Surplus	Indirect Taxes	Less: Subsidies Received	Value Added	Compensation of Employees	Capital Consumption	Net Operating Surplus	Indirect Taxes	Less: Subsidies Received	Value Added
All Producers												
1 Agriculture, hunting, forestry and fishing	31619	...	130709	3139	2572	162895	36087	...	146201	3261	2228	183321
A Agriculture and hunting	18637	...	103867	2481	2247	122738	20817	...	116190	2477	2109	137375
B Forestry and logging	886	...	24576	237	2	25697	1014	...	28122	277	24	29389
C Fishing	12096	...	2266	421	323	14460	14256	...	1889	507	95	16557
2 Mining and quarrying	300070	...	198057	74814	27572	545369	356048	...	255406	93282	28992	675744
3 Manufacturing		...						...				
A Manufacture of food, beverages and tobacco	35527	...	46629	31116	6320	106952	42685	...	68301	38656	8229	141413
B Textile, wearing apparel and leather industries	81044	...	29115	5824	1148	114835	99129	...	44742	7211	1072	150010
C Manufacture of wood and wood products, including furniture	16387	...	10266	1076	134	27595	18835	...	13269	2323	138	34289
D Manufacture of paper and paper products, printing and publishing	15754	...	14286	1255	466	30829	19584	...	16112	2655	520	37831
E Manufacture of chemicals and chemical petroleum, coal, rubber and plastic products	28478	...	24236	12336	15260	49790	34501	...	27801	14417	11766	64953
F Manufacture of non-metallic mineral products, except products of petroleum and coal	24098	...	20948	2994	411	47629	28350	...	26147	3595	1272	56820
G Basic metal industries	10949	...	7241	904	214	18880	12182	...	9118	1000	216	22084
H Manufacture of fabricated metal products, machinery and equipment	73335	...	31827	17677	3491	119348	83196	...	34283	21437	5661	133255
I Other manufacturing industries	14498	...	13509	1632	128	29511	17586	...	15633	1988	118	35089
4 Electricity, gas and water	17616	...	14696	1830	1111	33031	22406	...	33433	2050	559	57330
5 Construction	98862	...	46926	4200	537	149451	122016	...	51078	5022	2919	175197
6 Wholesale and retail trade, restaurants and hotels	114654	...	213701	119906	31552	416709	137672	...	271379	156974	45838	520187
A Wholesale and retail trade	97405	...	173332	117646	30993	357390	116755	...	220542	153766	45242	445821
B Restaurants and hotels	17249	...	40369	2260	559	59319	20917	...	50837	3208	596	74366
7 Transport, storage and communication	89235	...	36463	5872	9885	121685	107223	...	57122	8779	6634	166490
A Transport and storage	67112	...	27052	4222	9842	88544	79770	...	36899	6473	6633	116509
B Communication	22123	...	9411	1650	43	33141	27453	...	20223	2306	1	49981
8 Finance, insurance, real estate and business services a	60271	...	128957	28149	5537	211840	78298	...	145292	36879	3902	256567
A Financial institutions	37908	...	64782	16334	-	119024	51391	...	74180	22489	-	148060
B Insurance	9589	...	-4237	4211	-	9563	11957	...	-6229	4858	2	10584
C Real estate and business services	12774	...	68412	7604	5537	83253	14950	...	77341	9532	3900	97923
Real estate, except dwellings	12679	...	49776	7449	3747	66157	14845	...	61912	9366	3477	82646
Dwellings	95	...	18636	155	1790	17096	105	...	15429	166	423	15277
9 Community, social and personal services ab	17570	...	28947	7181	836	52862	21943	...	36699	9188	724	67106
A Sanitary and similar services	...	...	...	...	...	...	...	...	...	...	...	...
B Social and related community services	9432	...	25673	489	21	35573	11988	...	34261	720	7	46962
Educational services	3945	...	7268	180	21	11372	4917	...	9700	243	7	14853
Medical, dental, other health and veterinary services	5487	...	18405	309	-	24201	7071	...	24561	477	-	32109
C Recreational and cultural services	8138	...	3274	6692	815	17289	9955	...	2438	8468	717	20144
D Personal and household services	...	...	...	...	...	...	...	...	...	...	...	...
Total, Industries c	729897	...	798456	245091	79602	1693842	881693	...	996610	315435	91796	2101942
Producers of Government Services	214636	...	-	22	-	214658	269114	...	-	23	-	269137
Other Producers	19043	...	-	77	-	19120	23360	...	-	91	-	23451
Total c	963576	...	798456	245190	79602	1927620	1174167	...	996610	315549	91796	2394530
Less: Imputed bank service charge	...	...	107420	...	...	107420	...	...	135775	...	...	135775
Import duties	...	...	...	30207	...	30207	...	...	...	42958	...	42958
Value added tax	...	...	...	...	...	...	...	...	...	...	...	...
Total	963576	...	691036	275397	79602	1850407	1174167	...	860835	358507	91796	2301713

Portugal

4.3 Cost Components of Value Added

Million Portuguese escudos

	1984						1985					
	Compensation of Employees	Capital Consumption	Net Operating Surplus	Indirect Taxes	Less: Subsidies Received	Value Added	Compensation of Employees	Capital Consumption	Net Operating Surplus	Indirect Taxes	Less: Subsidies Received	Value Added
All Producers												
1 Agriculture, hunting, forestry and fishing	42110	...	189564	5584	2810	234448	49707	...	238113	6182	12799	281203
A Agriculture and hunting	24125	...	150322	4399	2688	176158	29173	...	186425	4623	12644	207577
B Forestry and logging	1530	...	36174	440	6	38138	2118	...	48241	607	9	50957
C Fishing	16455	...	3068	745	116	20152	18416	...	3447	952	146	22669
2 Mining and quarrying	414094	...	372516	113292	37801	862101	496839	...	484858	137739	48810	1070626
3 Manufacturing								...				
A Manufacture of food, beverages and tobacco	49467	...	82959	46591	6604	172413	58216	...	105432	56445	6314	213779
B Textile, wearing apparel and leather industries	115905	...	86353	9097	1529	209826	142803	...	122650	12661	1803	276311
C Manufacture of wood and wood products, including furniture	21203	...	15516	2755	210	39264	25057	...	16450	3590	273	44824
D Manufacture of paper and paper products, printing and publishing	24323	...	32056	3881	807	59453	28069	...	35324	4631	868	67156
E Manufacture of chemicals and chemical petroleum, coal, rubber and plastic products	41016	...	47051	19604	16243	91428	49766	...	68072	22154	24696	115296
F Manufacture of non-metallic mineral products, except products of petroleum and coal	31877	...	29227	4040	971	64173	35953	...	35127	4756	1449	74387
G Basic metal industries	14045	...	9668	1460	250	24923	17564	...	11209	1863	481	30155
H Manufacture of fabricated metal products, machinery and equipment	95274	...	47968	23166	11032	155376	114073	...	69201	28394	12708	198960
I Other manufacturing industries	20984	...	21718	2698	155	45245	25338	...	21393	3245	218	49758
4 Electricity, gas and water	31353	...	58942	2788	1316	91767	37862	...	81900	4215	928	123049
5 Construction	124809	...	37889	5396	1253	166841	139494	...	54071	7833	1030	200368
6 Wholesale and retail trade, restaurants and hotels	168214	...	312312	195909	61263	615172	200467	...	398707	235116	45745	788545
A Wholesale and retail trade	143454	...	248348	191210	60661	522351	172057	...	314491	228962	44970	670540
B Restaurants and hotels	24760	...	63964	4699	602	92821	28410	...	84216	6154	775	118005
7 Transport, storage and communication	128669	...	83116	11989	9589	214185	152318	...	119110	14184	13350	272262
A Transport and storage	95140	...	57355	8976	9526	151945	111605	...	80981	9859	13323	189122
B Communication	33529	...	25761	3013	63	62240	40713	...	38129	4325	27	83140
8 Finance, insurance, real estate and business services a	95455	...	149930	49982	5261	290106	118384	...	183295	58765	2991	357453
A Financial institutions	63043	...	62031	32672	3306	154440	78974	...	79135	36779	-	194888
B Insurance	14379	...	-5143	6813	-	16049	18497	...	-6245	8040	-	20292
C Real estate and business services	18033	...	93042	10497	1955	119617	20913	...	110405	13946	2991	142273
Real estate, except dwellings	17909	...	79549	10290	1481	106267	20766	...	99635	13730	2669	131462
Dwellings	124	...	13493	207	474	13350	147	...	10770	216	322	10811
9 Community, social and personal services ab	25701	...	48700	11701	808	85294	30194	...	66440	17807	1475	112966
A Sanitary and similar services	...	...	...	...	...	...	...	...	...	...	...	...
B Social and related community services	14084	...	45946	1018	5	61043	15987	...	63680	1289	36	80920
Educational services	5657	...	14850	369	2	20874	5912	...	21054	468	30	27404
Medical, dental, other health and veterinary services	8427	...	31096	649	3	40169	10075	...	42626	821	6	53516
C Recreational and cultural services	11617	...	2754	10683	803	24251	14207	...	2760	16518	1439	32046
D Personal and household services	...	...	...	...	...	...	...	...	...	...	...	...
Total, Industries c	1030405	...	1252969	396641	120101	2559914	1225265	...	1626494	481841	127128	3206472
Producers of Government Services	327301	...	-	23	-	327324	410253	...	-	27	-	410280
Other Producers	28146	...	-	198	-	28344	34289	...	-	27	-	34316
Total c	1385852	...	1252969	396862	120101	2915582	1669807	...	1626494	481895	127128	3651068
Less: Imputed bank service charge	...	...	139753	...	...	139753	...	...	179388	...	...	179388
Import duties	...	...	...	39899	...	39899	...	...	...	52265	...	52265
Value added tax	...	...	...	...	...	...	...	...	...	...	...	...
Total	1385852	...	1113216	436761	120101	2815728	1669807	...	1447106	534160	127128	3523945

1578

4.3 Cost Components of Value Added

Million Portuguese escudos

	1986						1987					
	Compensation of Employees	Capital Consumption	Net Operating Surplus	Indirect Taxes	Less: Subsidies Received	Value Added	Compensation of Employees	Capital Consumption	Net Operating Surplus	Indirect Taxes	Less: Subsidies Received	Value Added
All Producers												
1 Agriculture, hunting, forestry and fishing	56061	...	283089	4341	14769	328722	64338	...	327215	3301	15829	379025
A Agriculture and hunting	32483	...	216408	3064	14212	237743	37554	...	251656	2477	14872	276815
B Forestry and logging	2325	...	55789	436	50	58500	3491	...	66684	395	101	70469
C Fishing	21253	...	10892	841	507	32479	23293	...	8875	429	856	31741
2 Mining and quarrying	598170	...	640727	111768	60544	1290121	699986	...	778638	92487	56914	1514197
3 Manufacturing		...						...				
A Manufacture of food, beverages and tobacco	69755	...	139563	50312	16598	243032	81341	...	153640	54686	19172	270495
B Textile, wearing apparel and leather industries	180288	...	166261	9912	1990	354471	213592	...	207997	6720	3945	424364
C Manufacture of wood and wood products, including furniture	30835	...	23153	1911	1711	54188	35828	...	31346	1201	2813	65562
D Manufacture of paper and paper products, printing and publishing	34374	...	50632	2263	1036	86233	40650	...	73884	1511	3380	112665
E Manufacture of chemicals and chemical petroleum, coal, rubber and plastic products	59676	...	81498	24279	23829	141624	69045	...	83424	10176	15166	147479
F Manufacture of non-metallic mineral products, except products of petroleum and coal	43173	...	47912	2143	2401	90827	50903	...	62541	1112	3895	110661
G Basic metal industries	20194	...	20113	1416	4481	37242	23561	...	21560	978	970	45129
H Manufacture of fabricated metal products, machinery and equipment	128831	...	77664	17652	8226	215921	146928	...	109927	15117	6927	265045
I Other manufacturing industries	31044	...	33931	1880	272	66583	38138	...	34319	986	646	72797
4 Electricity, gas and water	42587	...	92208	3574	1962	136407	49891	...	118221	1519	1576	168055
5 Construction	165377	...	77026	6064	2747	245720	195946	...	101946	2646	4088	296450
6 Wholesale and retail trade, restaurants and hotels	244578	...	462776	218941	21609	904686	306486	...	570584	191425	34038	1034457
A Wholesale and retail trade	209291	...	369315	215796	20947	773455	259374	...	460585	190147	33140	876966
B Restaurants and hotels	35287	...	93461	3145	662	131231	47112	...	109999	1278	898	157491
7 Transport, storage and communication	181785	...	143337	6794	34782	297134	219132	...	123731	8189	26566	324486
A Transport and storage	130627	...	100645	6177	34458	202991	159057	...	81852	3938	25793	219054
B Communication	51158	...	42692	617	324	94143	60075	...	41879	4251	773	105432
8 Finance, insurance, real estate and business services a	144786	...	218236	70332	6275	427079	170667	...	300614	80496	3123	548654
A Financial institutions	96521	...	93848	45009	8	235370	113133	...	159818	51493	-	324444
B Insurance	22445	...	-12224	9801	1	20021	26248	...	-14218	10393	-	22423
C Real estate and business services	25820	...	136612	15522	6266	171688	31286	...	155014	18610	3123	201787
Real estate, except dwellings	25640	...	121095	15370	5726	156379	31089	...	136223	18501	3010	182803
Dwellings	180	...	15517	152	540	15309	197	...	18791	109	113	18984
9 Community, social and personal services ab	38179	...	87714	20003	6662	139234	45012	...	102702	33276	8554	172436
A Sanitary and similar services	...	...	...	...	...	...	...	...	...	...	...	...
B Social and related community services	20029	...	82754	1139	2606	101316	23278	...	108425	490	3928	128265
Educational services	7374	...	28419	398	1984	34207	8595	...	38062	166	3085	43738
Medical, dental, other health and veterinary services	12655	...	54335	741	622	67109	14683	...	70363	324	843	84527
C Recreational and cultural services	18150	...	4960	18864	4056	37918	21734	...	-5723	32786	4626	44171
D Personal and household services	...	...	...	...	...	...	...	...	...	...	...	...
Total, Industries c	1471523	...	2005113	441817	149350	3769103	1751458	...	2423651	413339	150688	4437760
Producers of Government Services	499084	...	-	47	-	499131	...	...	...	...	...	629587
Other Producers	38628	...	-	171	-	38799	...	...	...	...	...	
Total c	2009235	...	2005113	442035	149350	4307033	2380810	...	2423651	413574	150688	5067347
Less: Imputed bank service charge	...	...	222787	...	...	222787	...	...	305847	...	...	305847
Import duties	...	...	...	54802	...	54802	...	...	...	79969	...	79969
Value added tax	...	...	...	281352	...	281352	...	...	...	333263	...	333263
Total	2009235	...	1782326	778189	149350	4420400	2380810	...	2117804	826806	150688	5174732

Portugal

4.3 Cost Components of Value Added

Million Portuguese escudos

	1988						1989					
	Compensation of Employees	Capital Consumption	Net Operating Surplus	Indirect Taxes	Less: Subsidies Received	Value Added	Compensation of Employees	Capital Consumption	Net Operating Surplus	Indirect Taxes	Less: Subsidies Received	Value Added
All Producers												
1 Agriculture, hunting, forestry and fishing	70314	...	311673	3470	20312	365145	...	...	...	...	...	441014
A Agriculture and hunting	42204	...	224695	2534	19116	250317	...	...	...	...	...	306876
B Forestry and logging	4641	...	72700	469	134	77676	...	...	...	...	...	94163
C Fishing	23469	...	14278	467	1062	37152	...	...	...	...	...	39975
2 Mining and quarrying	762471	...	893500	95379	44034	1707316	...	...	...	...	...	2055923
3 Manufacturing							...	...	...	...	...	
A Manufacture of food, beverages and tobacco	86239	...	172797	56617	15715	299938	...	...	...	...	...	390469
B Textile, wearing apparel and leather industries	232394	...	224041	7147	4853	458729	...	...	...	...	...	552402
C Manufacture of wood and wood products, including furniture	38950	...	42072	1371	3290	79103	...	...	...	...	...	101269
D Manufacture of paper and paper products, printing and publishing	44319	...	93397	1767	3632	135851	...	...	...	...	...	167106
E Manufacture of chemicals and chemical petroleum, coal, rubber and plastic products	73402	...	117381	10999	2432	199350	...	...	...	...	...	198888
F Manufacture of non-metallic mineral products, except products of petroleum and coal	56226	...	76896	1266	4428	129960	...	...	...	...	...	147849
G Basic metal industries	26344	...	23405	1099	1126	49722	...	...	...	...	...	72972
H Manufacture of fabricated metal products, machinery and equipment	160748	...	109380	14004	7676	276456	...	...	...	...	...	324386
I Other manufacturing industries	43849	...	34131	1109	882	78207	...	...	...	...	...	100582
4 Electricity, gas and water	51664	...	159803	1772	2021	211218	...	...	...	...	...	209762
5 Construction	232612	...	138083	3134	5325	368504	...	...	...	...	...	452708
6 Wholesale and retail trade, restaurants and hotels	361878	...	666878	216589	60325	1185020	...	...	...	...	...	1397819
A Wholesale and retail trade	304286	...	548499	215239	59495	1008529	...	...	...	...	...	1152951
B Restaurants and hotels	57592	...	118379	1350	830	176491	...	...	...	...	...	244868
7 Transport, storage and communication	236605	...	147811	5643	28799	361260	...	...	...	...	...	412995
A Transport and storage	170566	...	89807	5175	27536	238012	...	...	...	...	...	271528
B Communication	66039	...	58004	468	1263	123248	...	...	...	...	...	141467
8 Finance, insurance, real estate and business services [a]	198124	...	362861	128172	3660	685497	...	...	...	...	...	841636
A Financial institutions	128065	...	191424	85858	-	405347	...	...	...	...	...	500237
B Insurance	29441	...	-20595	14864	-	23710	...	...	...	...	...	34890
C Real estate and business services	40618	...	192032	27450	3660	256440	...	...	...	...	...	306509
Real estate, except dwellings	40390	...	168408	27325	3535	232588	...	...	...	...	...	273690
Dwellings	228	...	23624	125	125	23852	...	...	...	...	...	32819
9 Community, social and personal services [ab]	52280	...	126852	32385	9663	201854	...	...	...	...	...	242524
A Sanitary and similar services	...	...	...	...	...	...	...	...	...	...	...	...
B Social and related community services	25959	...	127202	563	4734	148990	...	...	...	...	...	179155
Educational services	10531	...	41348	183	3583	48479	...	...	...	...	...	55940
Medical, dental, other health and veterinary services	15428	...	85854	380	1151	100511	...	...	...	...	...	123215
C Recreational and cultural services	26321	...	-350	31822	4929	52864	...	...	...	...	...	63369
D Personal and household services	...	...	...	...	...	...	...	...	...	...	...	...
Total, Industries [c]	1965948	...	2807461	486544	174139	5085814	...	...	3481562	...	159944	6054381
Producers of Government Services	...	...	...	...	...	759704	...	...	...	...	...	926340
Other Producers	...	...	...	...	...		...	...	...	...	...	
Total [c]	2725389	...	2807461	486807	174139	5845518	3147886	...	3481562	511217	159944	6980721
Less: Imputed bank service charge	...	...	382586	...	...	382586	...	...	472299	...	...	472299
Import duties	...	...	...	117081	...	117081	...	...	...	124671	...	124671
Value added tax	...	...	...	422738	...	422738	...	...	...	497167	...	497167
Total	2725389	...	2424875	1026626	174139	6002751	3147886	...	3009263	1133055	159944	7130260

4.3 Cost Components of Value Added

Million Portuguese escudos

	1990					
	Compensation of Employees	Capital Consumption	Net Operating Surplus	Indirect Taxes	Less: Subsidies Received	Value Added
			All Producers			
1 Agriculture, hunting, forestry and fishing	...	...	...	...	...	490787
A Agriculture and hunting	...	...	...	...	...	345100
B Forestry and logging	...	...	...	...	...	106525
C Fishing	...	...	...	...	...	39162
2 Mining and quarrying	...	...	...	...	...	⎧ 2373090 ⎫
3 Manufacturing	...	...	...	...	...	⎩ ⎭
A Manufacture of food, beverages and tobacco	...	...	...	...	...	509038
B Textile, wearing apparel and leather industries	...	...	...	...	...	614380
C Manufacture of wood and wood products, including furniture	...	...	...	...	...	112347
D Manufacture of paper and paper products, printing and publishing	...	...	...	...	...	153331
E Manufacture of chemicals and chemical petroleum, coal, rubber and plastic products	...	...	...	...	...	175355
F Manufacture of non-metallic mineral products, except products of petroleum and coal	...	...	...	...	...	162915
G Basic metal industries	...	...	...	...	...	99971
H Manufacture of fabricated metal products, machinery and equipment	...	...	...	...	...	421011
I Other manufacturing industries	...	...	...	...	...	124742
4 Electricity, gas and water	...	...	...	...	...	261311
5 Construction	...	...	...	...	...	585382
6 Wholesale and retail trade, restaurants and hotels	...	...	...	...	...	1681487
A Wholesale and retail trade	...	...	...	...	...	1352031
B Restaurants and hotels	...	...	...	...	...	329456
7 Transport, storage and communication	...	...	...	...	...	462412
A Transport and storage	...	...	...	...	...	280813
B Communication	...	...	...	...	...	181599
8 Finance, insurance, real estate and business services [a] ..	...	...	...	...	...	1112586
A Financial institutions	...	...	...	...	...	687879
B Insurance	...	...	...	...	...	32158
C Real estate and business services	...	...	...	...	...	392549
Real estate, except dwellings	...	...	...	...	...	352250
Dwellings	...	...	...	...	...	40299
9 Community, social and personal services [ab]	...	...	...	...	...	294756
A Sanitary and similar services	...	...	...	...	...	...
B Social and related community services	...	...	...	...	...	216881
Educational services	...	...	...	...	...	64895
Medical, dental, other health and veterinary services	...	...	...	...	...	151986
C Recreational and cultural services	...	...	...	...	...	77875
D Personal and household services	...	...	...	...	...	...

Portugal

Million Portuguese escudos

	1990					
	Compensation of Employees	Capital Consumption	Net Operating Surplus	Indirect Taxes	Less: Subsidies Received	Value Added
Total, Industries c	...	...	4158641	...	176729	7261811
Producers of Government Services	...	...	-	...	-	1156989
Other Producers	...	...	...	...	...	...
Total c	3814438	...	4158641	622450	176729	8418800
Less: Imputed bank service charge	...	...	627863	...	...	627863
Import duties	...	...	...	146439	...	146439
Value added tax	...	...	...	570058	...	570058
Total	3814438	...	3530778	1338947	176729	8507434

a) Business services and real estate except dwellings are included in item 'Community, social and personal services'.

b) For the first series, repair services are included in item 'Community, social and personal services'.

c) Column 'Consumption of fixed capital' is included in column 'Net operating surplus'.

Puerto Rico

General note. The preparation of national accounts statistics in Puerto Rico is undertaken by the Puerto Rico Planning Board, San Juan. The official estimates are published periodically in 'Ingreso y Producto-Puerto Rico Income and Product'. The following presentation of sources and methods is mainly based on information received from the Puerto Rico Planning Board. The estimates are generally in accordance with the classifications and definitions recommended in the United Nations System of National Accounts (SNA). The following tables have been prepared from successive replies to the United Nations national accounts questionnaire. When the scope and coverage of the estimates differ for conceptual or statistical reasons from the definitions and classifications recommended in SNA, a footnote is indicated to the relevant tables.

Sources and methods :

(a) Gross domestic product. Gross domestic product is estimated mainly through the expnditure approach.

(b) Expenditure on the gross domestic product. All components of GDP by expenditure type are estimated through the expenditure approach except private final consumption expenditure of goods and private investment in machinery and equipment which are estimated through the commodity-flow approach. Estimates of government consumption expenditure are based on special tabulations prepared by the Accounting Division of the Department of the Treasury. For personal consumption expenditure on goods, import data in f.o.b. values are obtained from the trade statistics whereas transport costs by commodity are computed by the Division of Economic Accounts. Estimates of locally produced goods are prepared by using the Puerto Rican censuses of manufactures as bench-marks and extrapolating these data for other years. Estimates of local sales of agricultural products are furnished by the Division of Agricultural Statistics. Adjustments for changes in trade inventories and mark-ups are made on the basis of data obtained from income tax returns and from the firms concerned. For some goods, the estimated quantity consumed is multiplied by the average price believed to have been paid by the consumer. Estimates of services are based on the gross receipts of the firms or organizations providing the services. Estimates of changes in stocks for the manufacturing sector are obtained through the use of census data which are extrapolated for the non-census years. For sugar and tobacco, quantity data from official sources are multiplied by the average export prices. For trade, inventories are calculated as percentages of sales from a sample of income tax returns. These percentages are then applied to the estimated total sales. Farm inventories of livestock are computed from data supplied by the Department of Agriculture. Estimates of gross fixed domestic investment in construction are obtained directly

through surveys among the contractors. For those not covered by the surveys, data from building permits are used. Private investment in machinery and equipment is estimated on the basis of import statistics. For the government sector, capital expenditure estimates are based on direct surveys within the agencies and on special tabulations prepared by the Accounting Division of the Department of the Treasury. Sales to the rest of the world, i.e., to the federal government and other non-residents of Puerto Rico, include wages and salaries paid to federal employees and all purchases of goods and services by the federal government. These data are obtained from the records of the agencies themselves. Data on imports are obtained from the trade statistics issued by the United States Department of Commerce. For the constant price estimates, private final consumption expenditure is obtained by multiplying quantities by base-year prices where quantity data are available. Otherwise, the current estimates are deflated by appropriate price indexes. For all other components of GDP by expenditure type, price defaltion is used.

(c) Cost-structure of the gross domestic product. Basic data on wages and salaries are derived from records of the Bureau of Unemployment Insurance, from censuses of business and manufacturers and from income tax returns and other financial reports of private businesses and public corporations. The method used for estimating operating surplus in manufacturing, construction and some services consists in calculating, from a sample of income tax returns, ratios of profits and other property income to wages and salaries. These ratios are then applied to total wages and salaries. For some industries, the method is based on ratios of profits to gross receipts as reported in the income tax returns. Rental income of prsons is estimated by deducting from the total rent paid the rent received by businesses, government and the rest of the world. Depreciation is estimated by applying to the total wages and salaries the ratio of depreciation charges to wages and salaries or to gross receipts, in the case of trade, derived from income tax returns. Data on indirect taxes and subsidies are obtained in detail from government reports.

(d) Gross domestic product by kind of economic activity. The table of gross domestic product by kind of economic activity is prepared at market prices, i.e., producers' values. The income approach by distributive shares is used to estimate the value added of each industrial sector. The net income by distributive shares is available by industrial sector. Business transfer payments, depreciation and subsidies are distributed using direct methods. Indirect business taxes are obtained from government reports and are broken down by industrial sector, using economic indicators such as data on local production and imports. For the constant price estimates, price deflation is used for the different economic activities of GDP.

1.1 Expenditure on the Gross Domestic Product, in Current Prices

Million United States dollars — Fiscal year beginning 1 July

	1980	1981	1982	1983	1984	1985	1986	1987	1988	1989	1990	1991
1 Government final consumption expenditure	2505	2420	2567	2888	3065	3235	3438	3716	4079	4431	4647	4877
2 Private final consumption expenditure	11898	12542	13299	14063	15057	15746	16795	18012	18873	19827	20599	21040
3 Gross capital formation	2288	1515	1746	2636	2501	2259	3275	4080	4884	5189	5222	5405
A Increase in stocks	126	-336	24	535	155	-69	245	186	473	418	217	251
B Gross fixed capital formation	2162	1851	1722	2100	2346	2327	3030	3894	4411	4771	5006	5154
Residential buildings	417	387	360	331	374	361	452	522	558	670	754	632
Non-residential buildings	192	193	172	260	277	285	322	362	406	457	482	562
Other construction and land improvement etc.	768	656	502	637	665	567	874	1277	1343	1367	1397	1556
Other	786	615	689	873	1030	1114	1382	1733	2104	2277	2373	2404
4 Exports of goods and services	10908	11805	11412	12915	13704	14632	15840	17563	20269	23163	24723	24434
5 Less: Imports of goods and services	11643	11517	11747	13339	14038	13903	15470	17192	19838	22006	22601	21787
Equals: Gross Domestic Product	15956	16764	17277	19163	20289	21969	23878	26178	28267	30604	32591	33969

1.2 Expenditure on the Gross Domestic Product, in Constant Prices

Million United States dollars — Fiscal year beginning 1 July

	1980	1981	1982	1983	1984	1985	1986	1987	1988	1989	1990	1991
					At constant prices of:1954							
1 Government final consumption expenditure	905	865	902	968	1024	1077	1142	1225	1332	1374	1366	1398
2 Private final consumption expenditure	3926	3919	4033	4222	4412	4596	4861	5054	5111	5216	5214	5310
3 Gross capital formation	629	397	434	633	591	541	757	915	1038	1053	1014	1036
A Increase in stocks	53	-55	21	141	46	2	70	62	121	110	56	70
B Gross fixed capital formation	577	453	412	492	545	540	688	853	918	943	958	966
Residential buildings	102	87	79	71	80	77	97	107	109	127	141	114
Non-residential buildings	47	44	38	56	59	61	88	75	80	87	90	102
Other construction and land improvement etc.	187	148	110	137	142	121	164	263	263	260	260	281
Other	241	173	187	228	264	281	338	408	466	469	467	469
4 Exports of goods and services	2346	2382	2278	2508	2615	2832	3040	3299	3709	4124	4292	4115
5 Less: Imports of goods and services	3094	2994	3056	3404	3614	3608	4095	4417	4814	5149	5115	4875
Equals: Gross Domestic Product	4712	4569	4590	4926	5027	5438	5705	6077	6377	6618	6772	6984

Puerto Rico

1.3 Cost Components of the Gross Domestic Product

Million United States dollars

	1980	1981	1982	1983	1984	1985	1986	1987	1988	1989	1990	1991
1 Indirect taxes, net	1075	1105	1212	1340	1346	1244	1484	1586	1564	1678	1600	1725
A Indirect taxes	1282	1334	1449	1674	1650	1564	1799	1920	1904	2029	2030	2157
B Less: Subsidies	207	229	237	334	304	320	315	334	340	350	430	432
2 Consumption of fixed capital	936	1042	1086	1146	1276	1328	1375	1703	1788	1920	1987	2046
3 Compensation of employees paid by resident producers to:	7538	7711	7877	8560	9082	9537	10297	11350	12362	13151	13751	14324
A Resident households	7481	7653	7817	8502	9022	9477	10225	11295	12306	13090	13677	14244
B Rest of the world	57	58	59	59	60	60	73	55	56	61	75	80
4 Operating surplus	5905	6526	6940	7931	8495	9714	10992	12180	12851	13975	15159	15902
Statistical discrepancy	502	380	162	186	91	145	-271	-640	-298	-121	94	-28
Equals: Gross Domestic Product	15956	16764	17277	19163	20289	21969	23878	26178	28267	30604	32591	33969

1.7 External Transactions on Current Account, Summary

Million United States dollars

	1980	1981	1982	1983	1984	1985	1986	1987	1988	1989	1990	1991
Payments to the Rest of the World												
1 Imports of goods and services	11643	11517	11747	13339	14038	13903	15470	17192	19838	22006	22601	21787
A Imports of merchandise c.i.f.	10435	10175	10336	11801	12379	12221	13684	15243	17821	20104	20328	19443
B Other	1208	1341	1411	1538	1659	1682	1785	1949	2017	1902	2272	2344
2 Factor income to the rest of the world	4861	5396	5645	6386	7045	7765	8685	9727	10314	11060	11769	12221
A Compensation of employees	57	58	59	59	60	61	73	55	56	61	75	80
B Property and entrepreneurial income	4804	5338	5586	6327	6985	7705	8612	9672	10258	10999	11694	12142
By general government	132	139	171	200	205	200	188	188	198	203	231	246
By corporate and quasi-corporate enterprises	...	...	...	...	...	...	...	...	...	...	...	...
By other	...	...	...	...	...	...	...	...	...	...	...	...
3 Current transfers to the rest of the world	942	965	1053	1168	1246	1345	1420	1605	1753	1897	1947	2048
4 Surplus of the nation on current transactions	-1479	-616	-1250	-2112	-2344	-1633	-2772	-3701	-4195	-3541	-3251	-3089
Payments to the Rest of the World and Surplus of the Nation on Current Transactions	15967	17262	17195	18780	19984	21381	22803	24823	27710	31422	33065	32968
Receipts From The Rest of the World												
1 Exports of goods and services	10908	11805	11412	12915	13704	14632	15840	17563	20269	23163	24723	24434
A Exports of merchandise f.o.b.	9644	10449	9971	11388	12026	13048	13971	15429	17932	20644	21992	21518
B Other	1264	1356	1441	1527	1678	1584	1869	2134	2338	2519	2731	2916
2 Factor income from rest of the world	1008	1218	1288	1247	1596	1665	1814	1940	1831	1922	1877	1705
A Compensation of employees	319	337	361	390	420	453	456	491	511	548	577	589
B Property and entrepreneurial income	688	881	927	857	1176	1213	1358	1449	1321	1374	1300	1117
By general government	23	32	42	40	44	55	42	30	28	50	74	80
By corporate and quasi-corporate enterprises	...	...	...	...	...	...	...	...	...	...	...	...
By other	...	...	...	...	...	...	...	...	...	...	...	...
3 Current transfers from rest of the world	4051	4239	4496	4619	4684	5083	5148	5320	5610	6337	6466	6828
Receipts from the Rest of the World on Current Transactions	15967	17262	17195	18780	19984	21381	22803	24823	27710	31422	33065	32968

1.10 Gross Domestic Product by Kind of Activity, in Current Prices

Million United States dollars

	1980	1981	1982	1983	1984	1985	1986	1987	1988	1989	1990	1991
1 Agriculture, hunting, forestry and fishing	367	388	391	345	357	373	411	399	443	434	449	462
2 Mining and quarrying	13	11	12	10	11	15	18	26	28	31	31	31
3 Manufacturing	5793	6124	6406	7371	7909	8549	9483	10513	11133	12126	12762	13155
4 Electricity, gas and water	489	619	612	634	625	677	755	784	809	888	951	1026
5 Construction a	426	365	289	315	323	316	400	526	634	689	740	758

1.10 Gross Domestic Product by Kind of Activity, in Current Prices
(Continued)

Million United States dollars — Fiscal year beginning 1 July

	1980	1981	1982	1983	1984	1985	1986	1987	1988	1989	1990	1991
6 Wholesale and retail trade, restaurants and hotels	2615	2712	2722	3065	3331	3552	3961	4380	4665	5049	5142	5350
7 Transport, storage and communication	861	919	988	1080	1084	1228	1290	1478	1505	1581	1726	1815
8 Finance, insurance, real estate and business services	1869	2256	2529	2753	2901	3248	3604	4034	4308	4500	4849	5163
9 Community, social and personal services	856	923	998	1094	1158	1264	1381	1569	1653	1882	2053	2201
Total, Industries	13290	14316	14947	16667	17699	19222	21302	23709	25178	27179	28703	29959
Producers of Government Services	2052	1952	2040	2174	2346	2445	2680	2918	3187	3337	3538	3738
Other Producers	112	116	128	136	155	157	167	191	200	208	257	300
Subtotal	15454	16384	17115	18976	20199	21823	24149	26818	28565	30725	32497	33997
Less: Imputed bank service charge	...	...	...	...	...	...	...	...	...	...	...	...
Plus: Import duties	...	...	...	...	...	...	...	...	...	...	...	...
Plus: Value added tax	...	...	...	...	...	...	...	...	...	...	...	...
Plus: Other adjustments	502	380	162	186	91	147	-271	-640	-298	-121	94	-28
Equals: Gross Domestic Product	15956	16764	17277	19163	20289	21969	23878	26178	28267	30604	32591	33969

a) Item 'Construction' refers to contract construction only.

1.11 Gross Domestic Product by Kind of Activity, in Constant Prices

Million United States dollars — Fiscal year beginning 1 July

	1980	1981	1982	1983	1984	1985	1986	1987	1988	1989	1990	1991
					At constant prices of:1954							
1 Agriculture, hunting, forestry and fishing	165	172	168	152	155	161	186	183	200	195	203	209
2 Mining and quarrying	5	4	4	3	3	4	5	7	7	7	7	7
3 Manufacturing	2123	2097	2084	2309	2338	2401	2564	2751	2775	2865	2839	2838
4 Electricity, gas and water	133	142	143	148	146	176	208	214	229	211	224	257
5 Construction a	104	82	63	68	69	68	84	108	124	131	138	137
6 Wholesale and retail trade, restaurants and hotels	826	800	781	864	919	972	1063	1133	1156	1205	1181	1224
7 Transport, storage and communication	293	306	306	335	342	388	402	459	463	457	470	487
8 Finance, insurance, real estate and business services	648	719	774	837	843	975	1165	1226	1185	1192	1316	1381
9 Community, social and personal services	272	283	287	305	315	336	356	386	395	421	426	433
Total, Industries	4569	4605	4609	5021	5129	5482	6033	6467	6535	6682	6803	6974
Producers of Government Services	756	719	743	756	815	848	927	1006	1095	1091	1093	1121
Other Producers	29	29	31	33	37	37	39	43	46	45	53	62
Subtotal	5354	5353	5383	5810	5981	6366	6998	7516	7676	7819	7949	8155
Less: Imputed bank service charge	...	...	...	...	...	...	...	...	...	...	...	...
Plus: Import duties	...	...	...	...	...	...	...	...	...	...	...	...
Plus: Value added tax	...	...	...	...	...	...	...	...	...	...	...	...
Plus: Other adjustments	-642	-784	-793	-884	-954	-929	-1292	-1439	-1299	-1201	-1177	-1171
Equals: Gross Domestic Product	4712	4569	4590	4926	5027	5438	5705	6077	6377	6618	6772	6984

a) Item 'Construction' refers to contract construction only.

1.12 Relations Among National Accounting Aggregates

Million United States dollars — Fiscal year beginning 1 July

	1980	1981	1982	1983	1984	1985	1986	1987	1988	1989	1990	1991
Gross Domestic Product	15956	16764	17277	19163	20289	21969	23878	26178	28267	30604	32591	33969
Plus: Net factor income from the rest of the world	-3853	-4178	-4357	-5139	-5449	-6100	-6871	-7787	-8483	-9138	-9892	-10516
Factor income from the rest of the world	1008	1218	1288	1247	1596	1665	1814	1940	1831	1922	1877	1705
Less: Factor income to the rest of the world	4861	5396	5645	6386	7045	7765	8685	9727	10314	11060	11769	12221
Equals: Gross National Product	12103	12586	12920	14023	14840	15869	17007	18392	19784	21466	22699	23453
Less: Consumption of fixed capital	936	1042	1086	1146	1276	1328	1375	1703	1788	1920	1987	2046

Puerto Rico

1.12 Relations Among National Accounting Aggregates
(Continued)

Million United States dollars										Fiscal year beginning 1 July		
	1980	1981	1982	1983	1984	1985	1986	1987	1988	1989	1990	1991
Equals: National Income	11167	11544	11833	12877	13565	14541	15632	16689	17996	19546	20712	21408
Plus: Net current transfers from the rest of the world	3109	3274	3443	3451	3438	3738	3729	3715	3857	4440	4519	4780
Current transfers from the rest of the world	4051	4239	4496	4619	4684	5083	5148	5320	5610	6337	6466	6828
Less: Current transfers to the rest of the world	942	965	1053	1168	1246	1345	1420	1605	1753	1897	1947	2048
Equals: National Disposable Income	14276	14818	15276	16328	17003	18279	19360	20404	21853	23986	25231	26188
Less: Final consumption	14403	14961	15866	16951	18123	18981	20233	21727	22952	24258	25246	25917
Equals: Net Saving	-127	-143	-590	-623	-1120	-702	-872	-1324	-1099	-272	-16	271
Less: Surplus of the nation on current transactions	-1479	-616	-1250	-2112	-2344	-1633	-2772	-3701	-4195	-3541	-3251	-3089
Equals: Net Capital Formation	1352	473	660	1489	1225	931	1899	2378	3095	3269	3236	3360

2.5 Private Final Consumption Expenditure by Type and Purpose, in Current Prices

Million United States dollars										Fiscal year beginning 1 July		
	1980	1981	1982	1983	1984	1985	1986	1987	1988	1989	1990	1991

Final Consumption Expenditure of Resident Households

	1980	1981	1982	1983	1984	1985	1986	1987	1988	1989	1990	1991
1 Food, beverages and tobacco	3395	3605	3810	3766	4036	4157	4433	4575	4707	4816	4931	4781
A Food	2737	2921	3025	3049	3261	3355	3557	3648	3757	3779	3922	3781
B Non-alcoholic beverages	...	...	...	...	...	...	...	...	...	...	...	...
C Alcoholic beverages	446	447	535	477	496	531	573	625	658	694	682	700
D Tobacco	212	237	250	240	279	271	304	302	292	344	326	301
2 Clothing and footwear	1010	1038	1154	1265	1165	1351	1446	1471	1590	1696	1735	1774
3 Gross rent, fuel and power	1802	1962	2075	2188	2320	2429	2556	2702	2828	3066	3234	3346
4 Furniture, furnishings and household equipment and operation	848	931	922	994	1083	1151	1304	1368	1431	1475	1422	1510
A Household operation	258	276	287	294	311	311	347	377	403	384	419	437
B Other	589	656	635	700	772	840	956	991	1028	1092	1004	1073
5 Medical care and health expenses	599	641	700	788	938	1012	1147	1281	1421	1602	1685	1832
6 Transport and communication	2048	1976	1986	2240	2393	2474	2515	2733	2808	2761	2871	2947
A Personal transport equipment	520	398	493	751	876	965	1029	1094	1024	923	848	826
B Other	1528	1578	1493	1489	1517	1509	1486	1640	1784	1838	2023	2121
7 Recreational, entertainment, education and cultural services	800	853	923	953	1027	1036	1088	1207	1306	1439	1483	1599
A Education	236	267	305	335	362	399	434	501	573	644	678	711
B Other	564	587	618	618	666	637	654	706	733	795	805	888
8 Miscellaneous goods and services	1343	1503	1648	1754	1960	2012	2216	2655	2808	3047	3234	3274
A Personal care	327	391	403	427	451	443	464	521	543	575	559	546
B Expenditures in restaurants, cafes and hotels	423	434	475	492	532	498	550	685	748	816	858	914
C Other	593	678	770	835	977	1071	1202	1449	1517	1657	1816	1814
Total Final Consumption Expenditure in the Domestic Market by Households, of which	11844	12509	13219	13948	14922	15622	16705	17993	18897	19903	20594	21063
Plus: Direct purchases abroad by resident households	468	488	497	513	539	533	620	676	730	773	881	896
Less: Direct purchases in the domestic market by non-resident households	663	734	732	730	774	810	977	1148	1284	1400	1468	1549
Equals: Final Consumption Expenditure of Resident Households	11650	12263	12983	13731	14688	15345	16348	17521	18343	19276	20007	20411

Final Consumption Expenditure of Private Non-profit Institutions Serving Households

	1980	1981	1982	1983	1984	1985	1986	1987	1988	1989	1990	1991
1 Research and science	...	...	...	...	...	...	...	...	...	...	...	...
2 Education	...	...	...	...	...	...	...	...	...	...	...	...
3 Medical and other health services	229	258	291	304	330	370	411	449	484	505	536	559

2.5 Private Final Consumption Expenditure by Type and Purpose, in Current Prices
(Continued)

Million United States dollars   Fiscal year beginning 1 July

	1980	1981	1982	1983	1984	1985	1986	1987	1988	1989	1990	1991
4 Welfare services	...	...	...	...	...	...	...	...	...	...	...	...
5 Recreational and related cultural services	...	...	...	...	...	...	...	...	...	...	...	...
6 Religious organisations	20	21	25	29	39	31	35	42	45	46	56	71
7 Professional and labour organisations serving households	...	...	...	...	...	...	...	...	...	...	...	...
8 Miscellaneous	...	...	...	...	...	...	...	...	...	...	...	...
Equals: Final Consumption Expenditure of Private Non-profit Organisations Serving Households	249	279	316	333	369	402	446	491	530	552	593	630
Private Final Consumption Expenditure	11898	12542	13299	14063	15057	15746	16795	18012	18873	19827	20599	21040

2.6 Private Final Consumption Expenditure by Type and Purpose, in Constant Prices

Million United States dollars   Fiscal year beginning 1 July

	1980	1981	1982	1983	1984	1985	1986	1987	1988	1989	1990	1991
At constant prices of:1954												
Final Consumption Expenditure of Resident Households												
1 Food, beverages and tobacco	931	926	951	916	970	986	1029	1032	1022	989	951	890
A Food	742	754	758	744	787	799	829	826	815	777	759	704
B Non-alcoholic beverages	...	...	...	...	...	...	...	...	...	...	...	...
C Alcoholic beverages	131	115	136	119	122	130	137	145	149	151	140	141
D Tobacco	58	57	57	54	61	57	63	61	58	62	53	46
2 Clothing and footwear	434	438	484	530	480	563	608	622	664	734	754	804
3 Gross rent, fuel and power	683	685	691	700	713	728	746	763	787	800	813	841
4 Furniture, furnishings and household equipment and operation	369	388	377	401	430	453	513	529	538	561	514	535
A Household operation	84	84	84	83	87	83	92	99	105	93	94	92
B Other	285	304	293	318	344	370	421	430	433	468	420	443
5 Medical care and health expenses	161	162	165	179	205	210	225	240	257	274	271	276
6 Transport and communication	580	528	541	626	671	695	694	723	722	714	713	727
A Personal transport equipment	161	115	142	211	239	254	243	240	218	194	187	186
B Other	420	413	399	415	431	440	451	483	505	520	526	542
7 Recreational, entertainment, education and cultural services	359	374	383	392	417	404	423	468	485	486	497	574
A Education	75	81	88	93	95	102	105	117	132	138	134	138
B Other	284	293	295	299	321	303	318	351	353	349	363	435
8 Miscellaneous goods and services	376	395	415	442	492	531	612	688	663	695	739	722
A Personal care	126	139	138	145	150	145	149	166	170	178	170	162
B Expenditures in restaurants, cafes and hotels	93	84	86	87	92	86	93	108	109	114	119	116
C Other	158	172	191	211	249	301	370	415	385	403	450	444
Total Final Consumption Expenditure in the Domestic Market by Households, of which	3894	3896	4006	4186	4376	4571	4850	5065	5137	5253	5252	5368
Plus: Direct purchases abroad by resident households	150	141	140	144	146	143	164	173	175	177	174	166
Less: Direct purchases in the domestic market by non-resident households	177	181	179	176	184	193	231	262	284	297	296	306
Equals: Final Consumption Expenditure of Resident Households	3867	3856	3967	4154	4338	4521	4783	4976	5029	5133	5129	5228
Final Consumption Expenditure of Private Non-profit Institutions Serving Households												
1 Research and science	...	...	...	...	...	...	...	...	...	...	...	...
2 Education	...	...	...	...	...	...	...	...	...	...	...	...
3 Medical and other health services	53	57	59	59	63	67	68	68	71	71	72	66

Puerto Rico

2.6 Private Final Consumption Expenditure by Type and Purpose, in Constant Prices
(Continued)

Million United States dollars — Fiscal year beginning 1 July

	1980	1981	1982	1983	1984	1985	1986	1987	1988	1989	1990	1991
					At constant prices of:1954							
4 Welfare services	...	...	...	...	...	...	...	...	...	...	...	...
5 Recreational and related cultural services	...	...	...	...	...	...	...	...	...	...	...	...
6 Religious organisations	6	6	7	8	11	9	10	11	12	12	13	16
7 Professional and labour organisations serving households	...	...	...	...	...	...	...	...	...	...	...	...
8 Miscellaneous	...	...	...	...	...	...	...	...	...	...	...	...
Equals: Final Consumption Expenditure of Private Non-profit Organisations Serving Households	59	63	66	67	74	75	78	80	83	83	85	82
Private Final Consumption Expenditure	3926	3919	4033	4222	4412	4596	4861	5054	5111	5217	5214	5310

2.17 Exports and Imports of Goods and Services, Detail

Million United States dollars — Fiscal year beginning 1 July

	1980	1981	1982	1983	1984	1985	1986	1987	1988	1989	1990	1991
					Exports of Goods and Services							
1 Exports of merchandise, f.o.b.	9644	10449	9971	11388	12026	13048	13971	15429	17932	20644	21992	21518
2 Transport and communication	348	375	403	425	426	422	448	520	505	560	594	604
A In respect of merchandise imports	74	83	85	88	87	91	83	96	84	116	128	122
B Other	274	292	318	337	339	331	365	423	421	444	466	482
3 Insurance service charges	3	3	5	5	5	6	7	7	7	-33	-1	3
A In respect of merchandise imports	3	3	5	5	5	6	7	7	7	-33	-1	3
B Other	-	-	-	-	-	-	-	-	-	-	-	-
4 Other commodities	250	243	300	367	473	346	437	459	541	593	670	761
5 Adjustments of merchandise exports to change-of-ownership basis	...	...	...	...	...	...	...	...	...	...	...	...
6 Direct purchases in the domestic market by non-residential households	663	734	732	730	774	810	977	1148	1284	1400	1468	1549
7 Direct purchases in the domestic market by extraterritorial bodies	...	...	...	...	...	...	...	...	...	...	...	...
Total Exports of Goods and Services	10908	11805	11412	12915	13704	14632	15840	17563	20269	23163	24723	24434
					Imports of Goods and Services							
1 Imports of merchandise, c.i.f.	10435	10175	10336	11801	12379	12221	13684	15243	17821	20104	20328	19443
A Imports of merchandise, f.o.b.	10016	9782	9877	11247	11715	11579	13013	14523	17015	19199	19460	18578
B Transport of services on merchandise imports	388	364	430	522	630	608	635	680	758	852	815	814
By residents	...	...	...	...	...	...	...	...	...	...	...	...
By non-residents	388	364	430	522	630	608	635	680	758	852	815	814
C Insurance service charges on merchandise imports	31	29	29	32	34	34	36	40	48	53	54	52
By residents	...	...	...	...	...	...	...	...	...	...	...	...
By non-residents	31	29	29	32	34	34	36	40	48	53	54	52
2 Adjustments of merchandise imports to change-of-ownership basis	...	...	...	...	...	...	...	...	...	...	...	...
3 Other transport and communication	321	392	429	460	466	434	421	467	494	523	562	554
4 Other insurance service charges	...	...	...	...	...	...	...	...	...	...	...	...
5 Other commodities	395	429	459	529	612	675	701	768	747	558	768	828
6 Direct purchases abroad by government	24	32	25	36	42	40	43	38	46	48	62	66
7 Direct purchases abroad by resident households	468	488	497	513	539	533	620	676	730	773	881	896
Total Imports of Goods and Services	11643	11517	11747	13339	14038	13903	15470	17192	19838	22006	22601	21787
Balance of Goods and Services	-735	288	-336	-424	-334	729	371	371	431	1157	2122	2647
Total Imports and Balance of Goods and Services	10908	11805	11412	12915	13704	14632	15840	17563	20269	23163	24723	24434

Qatar

Source. Reply to the United Nations National Accounts Questionnaire from the Central Statistical Organization, Doha.
General note. The estimates shown in the following tables have been prepared in accordance with the United Nations System of National Accounts so far as the existing data would permit.

1.1 Expenditure on the Gross Domestic Product, in Current Prices

Million Qatari riyals

	1980	1981	1982	1983	1984	1985	1986	1987	1988	1989	1990	1991
1 Government final consumption expenditure	5622	8143	7236	8203	9021	7882	8384	8776	...	...	...	...
2 Private final consumption expenditure	4509	5424	5921	5769	5927	5626	5437	6362	...	...	...	...
3 Gross capital formation	4883	5596	7606	5176	4147	3998	3409	2858	...	...	...	...
A Increase in stocks	117	284	215	-544	-155	30	7	-126	...	...	...	...
B Gross fixed capital formation	4766	5312	7391	5720	4302	3968	3402	2984	...	...	...	...
4 Exports of goods and services	21127	21468	16753	12753	13450	11502	7330	8188	...	...	...	...
5 Less: Imports of goods and services	7478	9063	9811	8296	7537	6610	6167	6359	...	...	...	...
Equals: Gross Domestic Product	28663	31568	27705	23605	25008	22398	18393	19825	21979	23616	26792	24289

1.10 Gross Domestic Product by Kind of Activity, in Current Prices

Million Qatari riyals

	1980	1981	1982	1983	1984	1985	1986	1987	1988	1989	1990	1991
1 Agriculture, hunting, forestry and fishing	150	172	190	195	206	213	237	237	243	...	...	...
2 Mining and quarrying	19245	20175	15001	10790	11330	9595	5395	5869	5644	...	...	...
3 Manufacturing	943	1491	1391	1464	1829	1770	1777	2100	2462	...	...	...
4 Electricity, gas and water	64	83	89	133	165	191	363	362	366	...	...	...
5 Construction	1556	1632	1829	1395	1411	1313	1054	993	1015	...	...	...
6 Wholesale and retail trade, restaurants and hotels	1293	1858	1775	1587	1506	1186	1149	1319	1374	...	...	...
7 Transport, storage and communication	399	409	458	450	480	450	410	508	518	...	...	...
8 Finance, insurance, real estate and business services	1705	2022	2308	2030	1919	1899	1972	1988	2239	...	...	...
9 Community, social and personal services	128	176	242	227	222	201	214	214	217	...	...	...
Total, Industries	25483	28018	23283	18272	19068	16818	12571	13590	14078	...	...	...
Producers of Government Services	3367	3865	4727	5553	6189	5748	6047	6425	6900	...	...	...
Other Producers	132	143	157	168	176	187	198	213	233	...	...	...
Subtotal	28982	32026	28167	23993	25433	22753	18816	20228	21211	...	...	...
Less: Imputed bank service charge	406	561	569	492	543	484	553	533	540	...	...	...
Plus: Import duties	87	103	107	104	118	129	130	130	139	...	...	...
Plus: Value added tax	...	...	...	...	...	...	...	...	...	...	...	...
Equals: Gross Domestic Product	28663	31568	27705	23605	25008	22398	18393	19825	20810	...	...	...

1.11 Gross Domestic Product by Kind of Activity, in Constant Prices

Million Qatari riyals

	1980	1981	1982	1983	1984	1985	1986	1987	1988	1989	1990	1991
				At constant prices of:1981								
1 Agriculture, hunting, forestry and fishing	148	172	189	184	192	193	218	203	...	...	...	...
2 Mining and quarrying	23524	20175	16342	14647	16071	15252	16685	14607	...	...	...	...
3 Manufacturing	1470	1491	1622	1792	2141	2219	2438	2406	...	...	...	...
4 Electricity, gas and water	61	83	105	143	173	201	216	216	...	...	...	...
5 Construction	1600	1632	1795	1369	1481	1406	1128	1084	...	...	...	...
6 Wholesale and retail trade, restaurants and hotels	1272	1858	1702	1428	1362	1017	1010	1120	...	...	...	...
7 Transport, storage and communication	409	409	428	436	446	408	369	432	...	...	...	...
8 Finance, insurance, real estate and business services	1839	2022	2197	2052	2122	2108	2201	2162	...	...	...	...
9 Community, social and personal services	139	176	228	209	202	180	189	182	...	...	...	...
Total, Industries	30462	28018	24608	22260	24190	22984	24454	22412	...	...	...	...
Producers of Government Services	3436	3865	4089	4422	4434	4476	4480	4553	...	...	...	...
Other Producers	143	143	148	155	160	167	174	181	...	...	...	...
Subtotal	34041	32026	28845	26837	28784	27627	29108	27146	...	...	...	...
Less: Imputed bank service charge	441	561	537	453	495	432	486	452	...	...	...	...
Plus: Import duties	89	103	103	81	81	65	52	55	...	...	...	...
Plus: Value added tax	...	...	...	...	...	...	...	...	...	...	...	...
Equals: Gross Domestic Product	33689	31568	28411	26465	28370	27260	28674	26749	...	...	...	...

Republic of Moldova

Source. Reply to the United Nations national accounts questionnaire from the State Department of Statistics of the Republic of Moldova.

General note. The estimates in the following tables have been prepared in accordance with the United Nations System of National Accounts (SNA) so far as the existing data would permit. In addition, same tables have been prepared in accordance with the System of Material Product Balances. Therefore, these estimates are not comparable in concept and coverage with those conforming to the SNA.

1.1 Expenditure on the Gross Domestic Product, in Current Prices

Million Roubles

	1980	1981	1982	1983	1984	1985	1986	1987	1988	1989	1990	1991
1 Government final consumption expenditure	...	...	...	...	...	...	...	...	...	...	...	...
2 Private final consumption expenditure	...	...	...	...	...	...	...	...	...	...	...	...
3 Gross capital formation	...	...	...	...	...	...	...	...	...	...	...	...
4 Exports of goods and services	292	-5	139	746	434	-275	-519	-89	-875	-992	-364	-1555
5 Less: Imports of goods and services												
Equals: Gross Domestic Product	7526	7826	8828	9527	9596	8560	9143	9433	9830	11218	12681	23000

1.2 Expenditure on the Gross Domestic Product, in Constant Prices

Million Roubles

	1980	1981	1982	1983	1984	1985	1986	1987	1988	1989	1990	1991
					At constant prices of:1983							
1 Government final consumption expenditure	...	...	...	...	...	...	...	...	...	...	...	...
2 Private final consumption expenditure	...	...	...	...	...	...	...	...	...	...	...	...
3 Gross capital formation	...	...	...	...	...	...	...	...	...	...	...	...
4 Exports of goods and services	-43	-607	-408	59	61	79	-205	85	-479	-305	-187	-1410
5 Less: Imports of goods and services												
Equals: Gross Domestic Product	...	...	...	...	...	...	...	...	...	...	...	...

1.12 Relations Among National Accounting Aggregates

Million Roubles

	1980	1981	1982	1983	1984	1985	1986	1987	1988	1989	1990	1991
Gross Domestic Product	7526	7826	8828	9527	9596	8560	9143	9433	9830	11218	12681	23000
Plus: Net factor income from the rest of the world	...	...	...	...	...	...	...	...	...	...	...	...
Equals: Gross National Product	...	...	...	...	...	...	...	...	...	...	...	...
Less: Consumption of fixed capital	1016	1079	1165	1256	1316	1526	1514	1575	1661	1729	1813	...
Equals: National Income	6510	6747	7663	8271	8280	7034	7629	7858	8169	9489	10868	18753
Plus: Net current transfers from the rest of the world	...	...	...	...	...	...	...	...	...	...	...	...
Equals: National Disposable Income	...	...	...	...	...	...	...	...	...	...	...	...
Less: Final consumption	...	...	...	...	...	...	...	...	...	...	...	...
Equals: Net Saving	...	...	...	...	...	...	...	...	...	...	...	...
Less: Surplus of the nation on current transactions	...	...	...	...	...	...	...	...	...	...	...	...
Equals: Net Capital Formation	...	...	...	...	...	...	...	...	...	...	...	...

1a Net Material Product by Use at Current Market Prices

Million Roubles

	1980	1981	1982	1983	1984	1985	1986	1987	1988	1989	1990	1991
1 Personal consumption	4004	4269	4370	4506	4680	4808	4905	5077	5473	6102	6907	13862
2 Material consumption in the units of the non-material sphere serving individuals	386	415	450	474	499	509	547	572	585	629	680	1109
Consumption of the Population	4390	4684	4820	4980	5179	5317	5452	5649	6058	6731	7587	14971
3 Material consumption in the units of the non-material sphere serving the community as a whole	60	65	72	75	86	102	99	102	110	129	190	170
4 Net fixed capital formation	738	626	684	762	952	960	838	1148	1230	1295	1065	1280
5 Increase in material circulating assets and in stocks	374	720	1327	1014	987	360	1024	270	755	1057	824	3661
6 Losses	56	70	62	76	60	73	75	110	83	52	141	226
7 Exports of goods and material services	292	-5	139	746	434	-275	-519	-89	-875	-992	-364	-1555
8 Less: Imports of goods and material services												
Net Material Product	5910	6160	7104	7653	7698	6537	6969	7190	7361	8272	9443	18753

1b Net Material Product by Use at Constant Market Prices

Million Roubles

	1980	1981	1982	1983	1984	1985	1986	1987	1988	1989	1990	1991
				At constant prices of:1983								
1 Personal consumption	4303	4475	4475	4620	4851	4957	5067	5254	5585	6088	6199	5868
2 Material consumption in the units of the non-material sphere serving individuals	385	415	444	471	498	509	575	572	584	618	638	941
Consumption of the Population	4688	4890	4919	5091	5349	5466	5642	5826	6169	6706	6837	6809
3 Material consumption in the units of the non-material sphere serving the community as a whole	68	73	80	83	96	103	99	103	112	129	181	143
4 Net fixed capital formation	979	840	867	960	980	953	843	1138	1158	1149	821	489
5 Increase in material circulating assets and in stocks	276	679	2208	920	832	278	1081	334	690	883	555	1472
6 Losses	82	110	93	119	90	83	81	119	85	52	122	81
7 Exports of goods and material services	-43	-607	-408	59	61	79	-205	85	-479	-305	-187	-1410
8 Less: Imports of goods and material services												
Statistical discrepancy	25	93	-771	143	209	-	-28	-	-	-198	-37	-783
Net Material Product	6075	6078	6988	7375	7617	6962	7513	7606	7735	8416	8292	6801

2a Net Material Product by Kind of Activity of the Material Sphere in Current Market Prices

Million Roubles

	1980	1981	1982	1983	1984	1985	1986	1987	1988	1989	1990	1991
1 Agriculture and forestry	1778	1763	2315	2704	2710	2159	2708	2638	2738	3321	3943	7836
A Agriculture and livestock	1771	1757	2309	2698	2705	2151	2700	2630	2730	3312	3934	7822
B Forestry	7	6	6	6	5	8	8	8	8	9	9	14
C Other	...	...	...	...	...	...	...	...	...	...	...	...
2 Industrial activity	2504	2682	2943	3015	2925	2750	2572	2918	2872	2913	3245	7048
3 Construction	484	397	434	423	466	490	608	655	687	826	852	1296
4 Wholesale and retail trade and restaurants and other eating and drinking places	951	1123	1187	1271	1359	882	803	708	706	817	871	1756
5 Transport and communication	163	164	194	204	206	218	231	221	292	316	452	711
A Transport	155	156	186	193	195	206	218	207	276	299	432	671
B Communication	8	8	8	11	11	12	13	14	16	17	20	40
6 Other activities of the material sphere	30	31	32	36	32	38	47	50	66	79	80	106
Net material product	5910	6160	7105	7653	7698	6537	6969	7190	7361	8272	9443	18753

2b Net Material Product by Kind of Activity of the Material Sphere in Constant Market Prices

Million Roubles

	1980	1981	1982	1983	1984	1985	1986	1987	1988	1989	1990	1991
				At constant prices of:1983								
1 Agriculture and forestry	2699	2374	3128	3066	3176	2487	3084	2980	2996	3215	2579	1856
A Agriculture and livestock	2688	2364	3119	3057	3168	2479	3076	2972	2988	3206	2570	1850
B Forestry	11	10	9	9	8	8	8	8	8	9	9	6
C Other	...	...	...	...	...	...	...	...	...	...	...	...
2 Industrial activity	2279	2404	2613	2859	2933	2798	2753	2958	2995	3257	3895	3078
3 Construction	564	539	564	638	627	631	614	654	646	773	810	838
4 Wholesale and retail trade and restaurants and other eating and drinking places	603	643	690	721	744	784	785	744	741	790	828	756
5 Transport and communication	183	183	204	212	213	219	231	221	292	301	239	212
A Transport	175	174	195	201	202	206	218	207	276	284	226	190
B Communication	8	9	9	11	11	13	13	14	16	17	13	22
6 Other activities of the material sphere	38	40	38	44	38	43	46	49	65	78	87	155
Statistical discrepancy	-291	-105	-249	-165	-114	-	-	-	-	2	-146	-94
Net material product	6075	6078	6988	7375	7617	6962	7513	7606	7735	8416	8292	6801

Republic of Moldova

8 Personal Consumption According to Source of Supply of Goods and Material Services in Current Market Prices

Million Roubles

	1980	1981	1982	1983	1984	1985	1986	1987	1988	1989	1990	1991
1 Purchases of goods in state and co-operative retail trade	3289	...	...	...	...	3962	4024	4189	4496	4874	5604	10546
2 Purchases of goods in the free market and from private retail trade	130	...	...	...	...	171	196	196	217	284	313	807
3 Goods produced on own account and received in kind	388	...	...	...	...	417	411	410	488	631	727	2222
4 Payments for transport and communication services	...	...	...	...	...	...	...	...	...	...	...	...
5 Purchases of electricity, gas and water	53	...	...	...	...	72	76	78	84	89	75	104
6 Purchases directly from handicrafts, repair shops and the like	-	...	...	...	...	-	-	-	-	28	-	10
7 Consumption of fixed assets in respect of all dwellings	84	...	...	...	...	107	114	124	124	135	132	117
8 Other	60	...	...	...	...	79	83	80	64	61	56	56
Personal consumption	4004	...	...	...	...	4808	4904	5077	5473	6102	6907	13862

9a Total Consumption of the Population in Current Market Prices

Million Roubles

	1980	1981	1982	1983	1984	1985	1986	1987	1988	1989	1990	1991
By Object												
1 Housing except owner-occupied, communal and miscellaneous personal services	...	...	...	...	...	...	...	...	...	...	...	...
2 Education, culture and art	...	...	...	...	...	...	...	...	...	...	...	...
3 Health and social welfare services and sport	...	...	...	...	...	...	...	...	...	...	...	...
Total consumption of non-material services	1043	...	...	...	...	1310	1366	1463	1582	1709	1873	3239
4 Personal consumption of goods and material services excluding depreciation of dwellings	3963	...	...	...	...	4750	4843	5010	5413	6037	6847	13820
Total consumption of the population	5006	...	...	...	...	6060	6209	6473	6995	7746	8720	17059
By Commodity and Service												
1 Food	...	...	...	...	...	...	...	...	...	...	...	...
2 Beverages, coffee and tea	...	...	...	...	...	...	...	...	...	...	...	...
3 Tobacco	...	...	...	...	...	...	...	...	...	...	...	...
4 Clothing and footwear	...	...	...	...	...	...	...	...	...	...	...	...
5 Gross rent	...	...	...	...	...	...	...	...	...	...	...	...
6 Fuel, electricity, water and gas	...	...	...	...	...	...	...	...	...	...	...	...
7 Furniture and household equipment	...	...	...	...	...	...	...	...	...	...	...	...
8 Health	...	...	...	...	...	...	...	...	...	...	...	...
9 Transport and communication	...	...	...	...	...	...	...	...	...	...	...	...
10 Education, recreation, sport	...	...	...	...	...	...	...	...	...	...	...	...
11 Other	...	...	...	...	...	...	...	...	...	...	...	...
Total consumption of the population	5006	...	...	...	...	6060	6209	6473	6995	7746	8720	17059
By Mode of Acquisition												
1 Purchased	3828	...	...	...	...	4644	4761	4958	5351	5918	6622	12414
2 Free of charge	790	...	...	...	...	999	1037	1105	1156	1197	1371	2423
3 From own production	388	...	...	...	...	417	411	410	488	631	727	2222
Total consumption of the population	5006	...	...	...	...	6060	6209	6473	6995	7746	8720	17059

9b Total Consumption of the Population in Constant Market Prices

Million Roubles

	1980	1981	1982	1983	1984	1985	1986	1987	1988	1989	1990	1991
	At constant prices of:1983											
	By Object											
1 Housing except owner-occupied, communal and miscellaneous personal services	...	...	...	...	...	...	...	...	...	...	...	...
2 Education, culture and art	...	...	...	...	...	...	...	...	...	...	...	...
3 Health and social welfare services and sport	...	...	...	...	...	...	...	...	...	...	...	...
Total consumption of non-material services	1043	...	...	...	...	1310	1366	1464	1582	1628	1678	1360
4 Personal consumption of goods and material services excluding depreciation of dwellings	4117	...	...	...	...	4726	5005	5187	5525	6023	6138	5774
Statistical discrepancy	-6	...	...	...	...	-	-	-	-	-2	-76	-11
Total consumption of the population	5154	...	...	...	...	6036	6371	6651	7107	7649	7740	7123

Reunion

Source. Reply to the United Nations National Accounts Questionnaire from the Institute national de la statistique et des etudes economiques (INSEE), Paris. Official estimates and descriptions are published by the same Institute in 'Comptes Economiques de la Reunion'.

General note. The estimates shown in the following tables have been adjusted by the INSEE to conform to the United Nations System of National Accounts so far as the existing data would permit.

1.1 Expenditure on the Gross Domestic Product, in Current Prices

Million French francs

	1980	1981	1982	1983	1984	1985	1986	1987	1988	1989	1990	1991
1 Government final consumption expenditure	2827	3248	3915	4287	4958	5592	5877	6092	6520	...	...	...
2 Private final consumption expenditure	7161	8374	10440	12059	13290	14690	15939	17435	18864	...	...	...
A Households	7120	8291	10297	11818	13064	14444	15656	17112	18541	...	...	...
B Private non-profit institutions serving households	41	82	144	240	225	246	283	323	322	...	...	...
3 Gross capital formation	1875	2085	2571	3064	3445	3306	4095	6308	7468	...	...	...
A Increase in stocks	130	92	73	88	-215	-432	-264	344	402	...	...	...
B Gross fixed capital formation	1745	1993	2498	2977	3660	3738	4359	5964	7066	...	...	...
4 Exports of goods and services	556	763	787	882	876	1083	968	996	1001	...	...	...
5 Less: Imports of goods and services	3971	4342	5427	6556	7047	7617	8021	8932	10250	...	...	...
Equals: Gross Domestic Product	8449	10128	12286	13735	15522	17054	18858	21899	23604	...	...	...

1.3 Cost Components of the Gross Domestic Product

Million French francs

	1980	1981	1982	1983	1984	1985	1986	1987	1988	1989	1990	1991
1 Indirect taxes, net	872	1022	1262	1526	1536	1809	1945	2281	2615	...	...	...
A Indirect taxes	1114	1222	1491	1830	2056	2250	2403	2745	3144	...	...	...
B Less: Subsidies	242	201	228	304	520	441	458	464	529	...	...	...
2 Consumption of fixed capital a ...	...	...	...	...	...	...	...	...	...	...	...	...
3 Compensation of employees paid by resident producers to:	5481	6478	7682	8921	10025	11181	11797	12962	13925	...	...	...
4 Operating surplus a	2096	2629	3341	3287	3960	4063	5116	6656	7063	...	...	...
A Corporate and quasi-corporate enterprises	347	521	832	707	1305	1243	1909	3110	3237	...	...	...
B Private unincorporated enterprises	1743	2175	2511	2568	2646	2811	3196	3533	3811	...	...	...
C General government	6	-68	-1	12	9	10	12	13	15	...	...	...
Equals: Gross Domestic Product	8449	10128	12286	13735	15522	17054	18858	21899	23604	...	...	...

a) Item 'Operating surplus' includes consumption of fixed capital.

1.4 General Government Current Receipts and Disbursements

Million French francs

	1980	1981	1982	1983	1984	1985	1986	1987	1988	1989	1990	1991
Receipts												
1 Operating surplus	6	-68	-1	12	9	10	12	13	15	...	...	...
2 Property and entrepreneurial income	37	56	61	55	60	60	97	58	73	...	...	...
3 Taxes, fees and contributions	2933	3297	4198	4918	5804	6254	6813	7582	8388	...	...	...
A Indirect taxes	1050	1157	1412	1757	1990	2189	2338	2669	3055	...	...	...
B Direct taxes	565	585	793	833	1167	1161	1246	1454	1522	...	...	...
C Social security contributions	1318	1555	1993	2327	2647	2903	3229	3459	3810	...	...	...
D Compulsory fees, fines and penalties	...	...	...	...	...	...	...	...	...	...	...	...
4 Other current transfers	3678	4473	5055	5547	6881	7643	8613	8816	9288	...	...	...
Total Current Receipts of General Government	6654	7759	9313	10531	12754	13967	15535	16470	17764	...	...	...
Disbursements												
1 Government final consumption expenditure	2827	3248	3915	4287	4958	5592	5877	6092	6520	...	...	...
A Compensation of employees	2602	3038	3567	4073	4514	5080	5258	5509	5888	...	...	...
B Consumption of fixed capital	...	...	...	...	...	...	...	...	...	...	...	...
C Purchases of goods and services, net	218	200	333	195	422	483	584	550	601	...	...	...
D Less: Own account fixed capital formation	...	...	...	...	...	...	...	...	...	...	...	...
E Indirect taxes paid, net	7	10	14	19	22	29	34	33	31	...	...	...
2 Property income	112	145	170	239	290	347	420	469	508	...	...	...

1.4 General Government Current Receipts and Disbursements
(Continued)

Million French francs

	1980	1981	1982	1983	1984	1985	1986	1987	1988	1989	1990	1991
A Interest	112	145	170	239	290	347	420	469	508	...	...	...
B Net land rent and royalties	...	...	...	...	...	...	...	...	...	...	...	...
3 Subsidies	101	136	148	172	261	265	280	148	363	...	...	...
4 Other current transfers	2881	3535	4678	5417	6378	6758	7653	8249	8682	...	...	...
A Social security benefits	2690	3285	4361	4940	5974	6408	7262	7790	8223	...	...	...
B Social assistance grants	...	...	...	...	...	...	...	...	...	...	...	...
C Other	192	250	317	477	404	350	391	459	459	...	...	...
5 Net saving	733	695	402	417	867	1005	1305	1512	1691	...	...	...
Total Current Disbursements and Net Saving of General Government	6654	7759	9313	10531	12754	13967	15535	16470	17764	...	...	...

1.7 External Transactions on Current Account, Summary

Million French francs

	1980	1981	1982	1983	1984	1985	1986	1987	1988	1989	1990	1991
Payments to the Rest of the World												
1 Imports of goods and services	3971	4342	5427	6556	7047	7617	8021	8932	10250	...	...	...
A Imports of merchandise c.i.f.	3971	4342	5427	6556	7047	7617	8021	8932	10250	...	...	...
B Other	...	...	...	...	...	...	...	...	...	...	...	...
2 Factor income to the rest of the world	279	316	401	438	427	520	671	768	891	...	...	...
A Compensation of employees	...	...	...	...	...	...	...	...	...	...	...	...
B Property and entrepreneurial income	279	316	401	438	427	520	671	768	891	...	...	...
3 Current transfers to the rest of the world	131	156	187	216	156	82	92	103	119	...	...	...
A Indirect taxes to supranational organizations	64	65	79	72	66	61	65	76	89	...	...	...
B Other current transfers	67	91	108	143	90	21	27	27	29	...	...	...
4 Surplus of the nation on current transactions	-73	442	-66	-784	174	490	757	10	-1141	...	...	...
Payments to the Rest of the World and Surplus of the Nation on Current Transactions	4308	5255	5948	6427	7804	8710	9541	9812	10118	...	...	...
Receipts From The Rest of the World												
1 Exports of goods and services	556	763	787	882	876	1083	968	995	1001	...	...	...
2 Factor income from rest of the world	198	275	416	354	283	297	334	261	307	...	...	...
A Compensation of employees	...	...	...	...	...	...	...	...	...	...	...	...
B Property and entrepreneurial income	...	...	...	354	283	297	334	261	307	...	...	...
3 Current transfers from rest of the world	3554	4217	4744	5192	6645	7330	8238	8556	8810	...	...	...
Receipts from the Rest of the World on Current Transactions	4308	5255	5948	6427	7804	8710	9541	9812	10118	...	...	...

1.8 Capital Transactions of The Nation, Summary

Million French francs

	1980	1981	1982	1983	1984	1985	1986	1987	1988	1989	1990	1991
Finance of Gross Capital Formation												
Gross saving	1802	2527	2505	2281	3619	3796	4852	6318	6326	...	...	...
1 Consumption of fixed capital	...	...	...	...	...	...	...	...	...	...	...	...
2 Net saving	1802	2527	2505	2281	3619	3796	4852	6318	6326	...	...	...
Less: Surplus of the nation on current transactions	-73	442	-66	-784	174	490	757	10	-1141	...	...	...
Finance of Gross Capital Formation	1875	2085	2571	3064	3445	3306	4095	6308	7468	...	...	...
Gross Capital Formation												
Increase in stocks	130	92	73	88	-215	-432	-264	344	402	...	...	...
Gross fixed capital formation	1745	1993	2498	2977	3660	3738	4359	5964	7066	...	...	...
1 General government	420	529	705	917	902	1001	1205	1457	1848	...	...	...
2 Corporate and quasi-corporate enterprises	906	928	1059	1228	1625	1697	1695	2178	2697	...	...	...
3 Other	418	536	734	831	1132	1040	1458	2328	2520	...	...	...
Gross Capital Formation	1875	2085	2571	3064	3445	3306	4095	6308	7468	...	...	...

Reunion

1.9 Gross Domestic Product by Institutional Sectors of Origin

Million French francs

	1980	1981	1982	1983	1984	1985	1986	1987	1988	1989	1990	1991
					Domestic Factor Incomes Originating							
1 General government	2607	2971	3566	4085	4523	5090	5270	5521	5903	...	...	...
2 Corporate and quasi-corporate enterprises	2531	3127	4027	4443	5481	5860	6888	8772	9341	...	...	...
A Non-financial	2504	3101	4015	4451	5467	5863	6895	8756	9349	...	...	...
B Financial	26	26	13	-9	14	-3	-7	17	-8	...	...	...
3 Households and private unincorporated enterprises	2392	2925	3295	3468	3774	4067	4506	5014	5452	...	...	...
4 Non-profit institutions serving households	46	83	136	213	208	227	249	310	293	...	...	...
Subtotal: Domestic Factor Incomes	7577	9106	11024	12209	13986	15244	16913	19617	20989	...	...	...
Indirect taxes, net	872	1022	1262	1526	1536	1809	1945	2281	2615	...	...	...
A Indirect taxes	1114	1222	1491	1830	2056	2250	2402	2745	3144	...	...	...
B Less: Subsidies	242	201	228	304	520	441	458	464	529	...	...	...
Consumption of fixed capital	...	...	...	...	...	...	...	...	...			
Gross Domestic Product	8449	10128	12286	13735	15522	17054	18858	21899	23604	...	...	...

1.10 Gross Domestic Product by Kind of Activity, in Current Prices

Million French francs

	1980	1981	1982	1983	1984	1985	1986	1987	1988	1989	1990	1991
1 Agriculture, hunting, forestry and fishing	500	646	828	790	678	691	855	963	1166	...	...	...
2 Mining and quarrying	833	985	1126	1158	1110	1301	1538	1876	1830	...	...	...
3 Manufacturing										...	...	...
4 Electricity, gas and water	129	185	225	237	584	703	807	894	971	...	...	...
5 Construction	385	487	639	655	988	933	1115	1434	1529	...	...	...
6 Wholesale and retail trade, restaurants and hotels	1395	1525	1751	2037	2415	2734	2969	3757	4246	...	...	...
7 Transport, storage and communication	333	460	561	664	756	806	927	1083	1228	...	...	...
8 Finance, insurance, real estate and business services	1848	2417	2899	3168	3498	3791	4321	5153	5449	...	...	...
9 Community, social and personal services										...	...	...
Total, Industries	5423	6705	8029	8709	10029	10960	12531	15160	16419	...	...	...
Producers of Government Services	2735	3161	3797	4436	4892	5500	5727	5976	6369	...	...	...
Other Producers										...	...	...
Subtotal	8158	9866	11826	13145	14921	16460	18258	21136	22788	...	...	...
Less: Imputed bank service charge	383	520	539	582	722	808	902	953	1106	...	...	...
Plus: Import duties	335	379	488	558	620	646	730	836	958	...	...	...
Plus: Value added tax	339	403	511	614	702	756	773	881	963	...	...	...
Equals: Gross Domestic Product	8449	10128	12286	13735	15522	17054	18858	21899	23604	...	...	...

1.12 Relations Among National Accounting Aggregates

Million French francs

	1980	1981	1982	1983	1984	1985	1986	1987	1988	1989	1990	1991
Gross Domestic Product	8449	10128	12286	13735	15522	17054	18858	21899	23604	...	...	...
Plus: Net factor income from the rest of the world	-81	-41	16	-85	-144	-223	-337	-507	-585	...	...	...
Factor income from the rest of the world	198	275	416	354	283	297	334	261	307	...	...	...
Less: Factor income to the rest of the world	279	316	401	438	427	520	671	768	892	...	...	...
Equals: Gross National Product	8368	10088	12302	13650	15378	16831	18521	21393	23019	...	...	...
Less: Consumption of fixed capital	...	...	...	...	...	...	...	...	...	...	...	...
Equals: National Income	8368	10088	12302	13650	15378	16831	18521	21393	23019	...	...	...
Plus: Net current transfers from the rest of the world	3423	4061	4557	4976	6489	7248	8147	8452	8691	...	...	...
Current transfers from the rest of the world	3554	4217	4744	5192	6645	7330	8238	8556	8810	...	...	...
Less: Current transfers to the rest of the world	131	156	187	216	156	82	92	103	119	...	...	...
Equals: National Disposable Income	11790	14148	16859	18626	21867	24078	26668	29845	31710	...	...	...
Less: Final consumption	9988	11621	14355	16345	18248	20282	21816	23527	25384	...	...	...
Equals: Net Saving	1802	2527	2504	2281	3619	3796	4852	6318	6326	...	...	...
Less: Surplus of the nation on current transactions	-73	442	-66	-784	174	490	757	10	-1141	...	...	...
Equals: Net Capital Formation	1875	2085	2571	3064	3445	3306	4095	6308	7468	...	...	...

Romania

Source. Communication from the Central Statistical Board of Romania, Bucharest. Official estimates and descriptions are published annually in 'Anuarul Statistic' (Statistical Yearbook).
General note. The estimates shown in the following tables have been prepared in accordance with the United Nations System of National Accounts (SNA) so far as the existing data would permit. Estimates in accordance with the System of Material Product Balances (MPS) are also shown. These estimates are not comparable in concept and coverage with those conforming to the SNA. Beginning 1991, the calculation of the estimates within the MPS framework had been discontinued.

1.1 Expenditure on the Gross Domestic Product, in Current Prices

Thousand Million Romanian lei

	1980	1981	1982	1983	1984	1985	1986	1987	1988	1989	1990	1991
1 Government final consumption expenditure	72.5	76.6	76.6	76.0	80.2	83.5	80.5	75.0	77.7	82.3	105.3	281.3
2 Private final consumption expenditure	315.9	335.1	391.8	387.6	413.6	408.4	416.7	441.9	454.7	459.5	547.6	1205.7
A Households	315.9	335.1	391.8	387.6	413.6	408.4	416.7	441.9	454.7	459.5	547.6	1193.6
B Private non-profit institutions serving households	-	-	-	-	-	-	-	-	-	-	-	12.1
3 Gross capital formation	245.7	226.4	245.3	261.6	278.8	269.9	288.4	268.9	243.3	213.2	289.3	707.6
A Increase in stocks	32.9	17.1	28.9	30.9	34.1	23.6	39.4	23.4	3.1	-23.2	120.9	393.5
B Gross fixed capital formation	212.8	209.3	216.4	230.7	244.7	246.3	249.0	245.5	240.2	236.4	168.4	314.1
4 Exports of goods and services	-34.8	-22.7	4.0	32.4	29.3	33.2	35.5	52.8	80.1	46.6	-96.3	-84.9
5 Less: Imports of goods and services												
Statistical discrepancy	17.6	8.3	9.7	11.1	14.2	22.4	17.5	6.5	1.2	-3.6	-1.9	-
Equals: Gross Domestic Product	616.9	623.7	727.4	768.7	816.1	817.4	838.6	845.1	857.0	798.0	844.0	2109.7

1.2 Expenditure on the Gross Domestic Product, in Constant Prices

Thousand Million Romanian lei

	1980	1981	1982	1983	1984	1985	1986	1987	1988	1989	1990	1991
			At constant prices of:									
			1981						1983			
1 Government final consumption expenditure	72.9	76.6	75.7	69.0	77.3	83.9	80.4	75.0	77.6	82.3	104.7	89.9
2 Private final consumption expenditure	328.6	335.1	330.8	328.6	402.5	406.5	413.8	439.1	450.2	457.4	490.2	435.9
A Households	328.6	335.1	330.8	328.6	402.5	406.5	413.8	439.1	450.2	457.4	490.2	432.5
B Private non-profit institutions serving households	-	-	-	-	... / -	-	-	-	-	-	-	3.4
3 Gross capital formation	262.6	226.4	230.8	238.3	273.8	272.7	288.7	269.4	243.7	213.2	218.1	234.3
A Increase in stocks	37.3	17.1	29.4	32.0	29.1	23.8	39.7	23.9	3.5	-23.2	72.3	114.4
B Gross fixed capital formation	225.3	209.3	201.4	206.3	244.7	248.9	249.0	245.5	240.2	236.4	145.8	119.9
4 Exports of goods and services	-58.7	-22.7	3.3	28.1	28.2	31.0	33.9	58.1	80.3	50.6	-73.9	-31.7
5 Less: Imports of goods and services												
Statistical discrepancy	17.6	8.3	7.7	23.5	32.8	21.2	19.7	4.0	-10.9	3.9	0.2	-
Equals: Gross Domestic Product [a]	623.0	623.7	648.3	687.5	814.6	815.3	836.5	845.6	840.9	807.4	739.3	728.4

a) For the period 1980-1983, base year in prices 1981 and for the years beginning 1984, base year in prices of the previous years as against the years in which calculations were carried out.

1.3 Cost Components of the Gross Domestic Product

Thousand Million Romanian lei

	1980	1981	1982	1983	1984	1985	1986	1987	1988	1989	1990	1991
1 Indirect taxes, net	106.8	99.7	130.2	132.0	145.3	159.6	172.4	162.0	171.4	161.9	95.6	...
2 Consumption of fixed capital	61.4	67.0	71.9	76.8	83.6	89.0	90.0	98.6	105.5	110.0	109.2	...
3 Compensation of employees paid by resident producers to:	357.2	384.5	437.3	436.2	459.5	463.0	477.1	469.6	481.2	522.7	601.5	...
4 Operating surplus	91.5	72.5	88.0	123.7	127.7	105.8	99.1	114.9	98.9	3.4	37.7	...
Equals: Gross Domestic Product	616.9	623.7	727.4	768.7	816.1	817.4	838.6	845.1	857.0	798.0	844.0	...

Romania

1.10 Gross Domestic Product by Kind of Activity, in Current Prices

Thousand Million Romanian lei

	1980	1981	1982	1983	1984	1985	1986	1987	1988	1989	1990	1991
1 Agriculture, hunting, forestry and fishing	78.0	91.6	125.7	107.9	110.7	114.3	106.8	103.4	115.6	110.9	151.9	391.2
2 Mining and quarrying												
3 Manufacturing	325.3	311.2	365.4	411.4	445.1	433.0	460.5	461.8	459.9	421.9	407.0	919.5
4 Electricity, gas and water												
5 Construction	47.4	44.7	47.2	52.2	53.5	57.9	59.5	60.8	60.4	50.6	47.9	104.6
6 Wholesale and retail trade, restaurants and hotels	36.4	38.1	39.5	33.3	35.3	39.9	39.5	43.2	46.9	48.2	59.3	178.5
7 Transport, storage and communication	43.6	44.8	48.9	49.9	53.1	55.4	57.0	58.0	60.3	60.0	56.5	95.6
8 Finance, insurance, real estate and business services	15.1	16.3	18.1	30.3	31.4	21.0	18.7	20.2	18.3	11.6	13.4	49.3
9 Community, social and personal services	14.0	14.4	12.8	13.4	13.5	13.2	13.6	13.8	15.1	12.1	13.1	71.0
Total, Industries	559.8	561.1	657.6	698.4	742.6	734.7	755.6	761.2	776.5	715.3	749.1	1809.7
Producers of Government Services	40.2	43.3	46.2	46.9	49.6	56.3	53.5	53.7	53.3	56.5	67.3	202.8
Other Producers	16.9	19.3	23.6	23.4	23.9	26.4	29.5	30.2	27.2	26.2	27.6	97.2
Subtotal	616.9	623.7	727.4	768.7	816.1	817.4	838.6	845.1	857.0	798.0	844.0	2109.7
Less: Imputed bank service charge	...	...	...	...	...	...	...	...	...	...	...	...
Plus: Import duties	...	...	...	...	...	...	...	...	...	...	...	...
Plus: Value added tax	...	...	...	...	...	...	...	...	...	...	...	...
Equals: Gross Domestic Product	616.9	623.7	727.4	768.7	816.1	817.4	838.6	845.1	857.0	798.0	844.0	2109.7

1.11 Gross Domestic Product by Kind of Activity, in Constant Prices

Thousand Million Romanian lei

	1980	1981	1982	1983	1984	1985	1986	1987	1988	1989	1990	1991
			At constant prices of:									
			1981					1983				
1 Agriculture, hunting, forestry and fishing	92.2	91.6	94.7	93.9	... 117.4	112.1	106.3	96.4	112.9	108.8	122.4	144.9
2 Mining and quarrying												
3 Manufacturing	314.0	311.2	328.4	359.5	... 434.4	434.3	458.3	464.6	447.0	435.3	351.8	324.8
4 Electricity, gas and water												
5 Construction	49.0	44.7	46.2	51.5	... 53.4	56.4	59.4	58.9	60.4	50.8	45.8	38.9
6 Wholesale and retail trade, restaurants and hotels	38.4	38.1	38.3	35.2	... 34.8	37.7	39.0	39.8	46.4	48.9	59.4	52.7
7 Transport, storage and communication	42.8	44.8	45.9	49.3	... 52.9	54.6	56.3	57.9	61.1	59.4	53.9	41.6
8 Finance, insurance, real estate and business services	15.1	16.3	18.0	18.9	... 35.4	29.7	20.7	31.4	18.1	9.7	3.5	15.0
9 Community, social and personal services	14.0	14.4	12.5	13.1	... 13.4	13.0	13.6	13.8	15.1	12.1	13.3	14.0
Total, Industries	565.5	561.1	584.0	621.4	... 741.7	737.8	753.6	762.8	761.0	725.0	650.1	631.9
Producers of Government Services	40.2	43.3	43.5	43.3	... 47.6	51.1	53.5	53.7	53.0	56.3	64.7	71.3
Other Producers	17.3	19.3	20.8	22.8	... 25.3	26.4	29.4	29.1	26.9	26.1	24.5	25.2
Subtotal	623.0	623.7	648.3	687.5	... 814.6	815.3	836.5	845.6	840.9	807.4	739.3	728.4
Less: Imputed bank service charge	...	...	...	...	...	...	...	...	...	...	...	...
Plus: Import duties	...	...	...	...	...	...	...	...	...	...	...	...
Plus: Value added tax	...	...	...	...	...	...	...	...	...	...	...	...
Equals: Gross Domestic Product a	623.0	623.7	648.3	687.5	... 814.6	815.3	836.5	845.6	840.9	807.4	739.3	728.4

a) For the period 1980-1983, base year in prices 1981 and for the years beginning 1984, base year in prices of the previous years as against the years in which calculations were carried out.

1a Net Material Product by Use at Current Market Prices

Thousand Million Romanian lei

	1980	1981	1982	1983	1984	1985	1986	1987	1988	1989	1990	1991
1 Personal consumption	310.2	331.0	387.3	383.6	407.0	400.9	409.0	430.4	445.5	450.8	542.1	...
2 Material consumption in the units of the non-material sphere serving individuals	17.2	17.7	19.0	17.9	20.2	18.2	17.7	15.2	14.9	15.4	23.3	...
Consumption of the Population	327.4	348.7	406.3	401.5	427.2	419.1	426.7	445.6	460.4	466.2	565.4	...
3 Material consumption in the units of the non-material sphere serving the community as a whole	13.2	12.1	10.6	13.4	13.5	13.3	13.3	11.9	12.0	12.1	15.9	...
4 Net fixed capital formation	156.8	146.0	148.0	157.5	166.0	162.2	167.3	154.1	140.9	132.9	67.9	...
5 Increase in material circulating assets and in stocks	32.9	17.1	28.9	30.8	34.1	23.5	39.4	23.4	3.1	-23.2	120.9	...
6 Losses a	-16.7	-11.6	15.7	36.8	43.0	53.9	47.6	62.2	81.0	44.6	-98.6	...
7 Exports of goods and material services	...	...	...	...	...	...	...	...	...	...	...	...
8 Less: Imports of goods and material services	...	...	...	...	...	...	...	...	...	...	...	...
Net Material Product	513.6	512.3	609.5	640.0	683.8	672.0	694.3	697.2	697.4	632.6	671.5	...

a) The estimate includes net foreign balance and unallocated items.

1b Net Material Product by Use at Constant Market Prices

Thousand Million Romanian lei

	1980	1981	1982	1983	1984	1985	1986	1987	1988	1989	1990	1991
				At constant prices of:1981								
1 Personal consumption	322.8	331.0	326.1	324.6	416.4	398.8	406.1	427.6	441.7	448.8	497.1	...
2 Material consumption in the units of the non-material sphere serving individuals	17.7	17.7	18.2	15.5	19.9	18.2	17.7	15.2	14.9	15.4	22.8	...
Consumption of the Population	340.5	348.7	344.3	340.1	436.3	417.0	423.8	442.8	456.6	464.2	519.9	...
3 Material consumption in the units of the non-material sphere serving the community as a whole	13.2	12.1	10.3	12.3	12.8	13.3	13.3	12.0	12.0	12.0	15.8	...
4 Net fixed capital formation	169.4	146.0	133.0	133.0	166.0	164.7	167.3	154.1	140.9	132.9	45.3	...
5 Increase in material circulating assets and in stocks	37.3	17.1	29.4	31.9	29.1	23.8	39.7	23.9	3.5	-23.2	72.3	...
6 Losses a	-46.1	-11.6	16.4	47.8	37.6	57.5	48.1	66.6	70.2	56.2	-83.7	...
7 Exports of goods and material services	...	...	...	...	...	...	...	...	...	...	...	...
8 Less: Imports of goods and material services	...	...	...	...	...	...	...	...	...	...	...	...
Net Material Product b	514.3	512.3	533.4	565.1	681.8	676.3	692.2	699.4	683.2	642.1	569.6	...

a) The estimate includes net foreign balance and unallocated items.
b) For the period 1970-1974, base year in prices 1963, for the period 1975-1979, base year in prices 1977, for the period 1980-1983, base year in prices 1981, and for the years beginning 1984, base year in prices of the previous years as against the years in which calculations were carried out.

2a Net Material Product by Kind of Activity of the Material Sphere in Current Market Prices

Percentages

	1980	1981	1982	1983	1984	1985	1986	1987	1988	1989	1990	1991
1 Agriculture and forestry	14.2	16.8	19.6	15.9	15.7	16.0	14.9	14.2	15.3	15.7	21.1	...
A Agriculture and livestock	13.8	16.3	19.2	15.4	15.2	15.5	14.4	13.7	14.8	15.2	20.6	...
B Forestry	0.4	0.5	0.4	0.5	0.5	0.5	0.5	0.5	0.5	0.5	0.5	...
C Other	...	...	...	...	...	...	...	...	...	...	...	...
2 Industrial activity	59.5	56.6	55.9	60.1	60.8	59.0	60.0	59.8	59.0	58.1	53.5	...
3 Construction	8.6	8.2	7.4	7.8	7.8	8.3	8.3	8.4	8.2	7.2	6.9	...
4 Wholesale and retail trade and restaurants and other eating and drinking places	7.6	7.8	6.8	6.4	6.2	6.5	6.2	6.8	7.0	7.5	8.2	...
5 Transport and communication	6.9	7.0	6.5	6.3	6.1	6.4	6.5	6.6	6.8	7.5	6.4	...
A Transport	6.0	6.1	5.3	4.9	4.8	4.9	5.0	5.0	5.2	5.6	4.7	...
B Communication	0.9	0.9	1.2	1.4	1.3	1.5	1.5	1.6	1.6	1.9	1.7	...
6 Other activities of the material sphere	3.2	3.6	3.8	3.5	3.4	3.8	4.1	4.2	3.7	4.0	3.9	...
Net material product	100.0	100.0	100.0	100.0	100.0	100.0	100.0	100.0	100.0	100.0	100.0	...

Romania

2b Net Material Product by Kind of Activity of the Material Sphere in Constant Market Prices

Index numbers 1970=100

	1980	1981	1982	1983	1984	1985	1986	1987	1988	1989	1990	1991
					At constant prices of:1970							
1 Agriculture and forestry	154	153	157	154	173	171	165	153	161	147	164	...
A Agriculture and livestock	154	153	158	155	175	173	167	155	163	149	166	...
B Forestry	124	133	123	118	118	119	108	107	108	108	109	...
C Other	...	...	...	...	...	...	...	...	...	...	...	...
2 Industrial activity	279	278	291	314	332	320	336	341	327	302	244	...
3 Construction	178	165	174	191	204	212	221	223	218	173	165	...
4 Wholesale and retail trade and restaurants and other eating and drinking places	329	328	331	326	340	360	352	390	398	389	450	...
5 Transport and communication	288	300	306	330	344	347	358	363	384	376	316	...
6 Other activities of the material sphere	234	261	282	310	334	366	407	401	354	339	315	...
Net material product	245	244	254	269	287	284	292	295	289	266	239	...

3 Primary Incomes by Kind of Activity of the Material Sphere in Current Market Prices

Thousand Million Romanian lei

	1980		1981		1982		1983		1984		1985	
	Primary Income of the Population	Primary Income of Enterprises	Primary Income of the Population	Primary Income of Enterprises	Primary Income of the Population	Primary Income of Enterprises	Primary Income of the Population	Primary Income of Enterprises	Primary Income of the Population	Primary Income of Enterprises	Primary Income of the Population	Primary Income of Enterprises
1 Agriculture and forestry	85.9	-13.1	101.7	-15.7	131.8	-12.3	121.6	-19.9	123.1	-15.9	129.6	-21.9
A Agriculture and livestock	84.3	-13.5	99.9	-16.5	130.2	-13.3	119.7	-21.3	121.0	-17.3	127.7	-23.6
B Forestry	1.6	0.4	1.8	0.8	1.6	1.0	1.9	1.4	2.1	1.4	1.9	1.7
C Other	...	...	...	...	...	...	...	...	...	...	...	...
2 Industrial activity	136.7	169.1	143.9	146.1	153.9	186.8	162.2	222.6	178.6	237.1	163.8	232.4
3 Construction	35.9	7.8	34.0	7.8	36.6	8.5	37.6	12.1	39.8	13.2	40.0	15.4
4 Wholesale and retail trade and restaurants and other eating and drinking places	18.2	21.1	19.2	20.7	20.4	21.0	20.5	20.3	19.4	23.2	20.7	23.2
5 Transport and communication	23.7	11.8	27.0	8.8	29.0	10.6	28.5	11.6	29.9	12.1	30.1	13.0
A Transport	21.2	9.8	24.3	6.8	26.1	6.0	25.6	5.9	26.7	6.0	26.9	6.4
B Communication	2.5	2.0	2.7	2.0	2.9	4.6	2.9	5.7	3.2	6.1	3.2	6.6
6 Other activities of the material sphere	13.5	3.0	15.5	3.3	19.5	3.7	18.7	4.2	18.9	4.4	21.5	4.1
Total	313.9	199.7	341.3	171.0	391.2	218.3	389.1	250.9	409.7	274.1	405.7	266.2

	1986		1987		1988		1989		1990	
	Primary Income of the Population	Primary Income of Enterprises	Primary Income of the Population	Primary Income of Enterprises	Primary Income of the Population	Primary Income of Enterprises	Primary Income of the Population	Primary Income of Enterprises	Primary Income of the Population	Primary Income of Enterprises
1 Agriculture and forestry	123.2	-19.7	119.7	-21.0	129.9	-23.3	136.5	-37.0	165.2	-23.3
A Agriculture and livestock	121.0	-20.8	117.6	-22.2	127.9	-24.6	134.4	-38.2	162.3	-23.7
B Forestry	2.2	1.1	2.1	1.2	2.0	1.3	2.1	1.2	2.9	0.4
C Other	...	...	...	...	...	...	...	...	...	...
2 Industrial activity	178.9	237.8	179.1	238.2	181.4	230.0	206.6	161.2	232.1	127.3
3 Construction	40.8	16.5	40.1	18.3	39.3	17.7	42.5	2.6	40.9	5.5
4 Wholesale and retail trade and restaurants and other eating and drinking places	23.6	19.4	22.7	24.9	24.8	23.9	25.2	22.4	28.6	26.3
5 Transport and communication	30.4	14.8	29.9	15.9	29.8	17.8	31.8	15.7	41.6	1.0
A Transport	27.1	7.6	26.6	8.4	26.5	9.7	28.1	7.6	36.8	-5.2
B Communication	3.3	7.2	3.3	7.5	3.3	8.1	3.7	8.1	4.8	6.2
6 Other activities of the material sphere	23.6	5.0	23.9	5.4	20.6	5.5	20.5	4.6	23.0	3.3
Total	420.5	273.8	415.4	281.7	425.8	271.6	463.1	169.5	531.4	140.1

4 Primary Incomes From Net Material Product

Thousand Million Romanian lei

	1980	1981	1982	1983	1984	1985	1986	1987	1988	1989	1990	1991
					a) Primary Incomes of the Population							
1 Socialist sector	313.9	341.3	391.2	389.1	409.7	405.7	420.5	415.4	425.8	463.1	531.4	...
A State sector	219.7	228.9	246.6	253.2	272.6	261.0	280.3	277.8	288.2	316.1	351.8	...
B Co-operative sector	34.7	41.2	45.9	46.3	45.4	45.2	43.3	45.1	42.5	49.6	48.8	...
C Personal plots of households	59.5	71.2	98.7	89.6	91.7	99.5	96.9	92.5	95.1	97.4	130.8	...
2 Private sector	-	-	-	-	-	-	-	-	-	-	-	...
Sub-total	313.9	341.3	391.2	389.1	409.7	405.7	420.5	415.4	425.8	463.1	531.4	...

4 Primary Incomes From Net Material Product
(Continued)

Thousand Million Romanian lei

	1980	1981	1982	1983	1984	1985	1986	1987	1988	1989	1990	1991
b) Primary incomes of the enterprises												
1 Socialist sector	199.7	171.0	218.3	250.9	274.1	266.2	273.8	281.7	271.6	169.5	140.1	...
A State sector	195.1	171.0	216.0	252.3	272.3	267.1	271.7	281.8	266.9	173.2	139.6	...
B Co-operative sector	4.6	-	2.3	-1.4	1.8	-0.9	2.1	-0.1	4.7	-3.7	0.5	...
2 Private sector	-	-	-	-	-	-	-	-	-	-	-	...
Sub-total	199.7	171.0	218.3	250.9	274.1	266.2	273.8	281.7	271.6	169.5	140.1	...
Total net material product	513.6	512.3	609.5	640.0	683.8	671.9	694.3	697.1	697.4	632.6	671.5	...

6a Capital Formation by Kind of Activity of the Material and Non-Material Spheres in Current Market Prices

Million Romanian lei

	1980	1981	1982	1983	1984	1985	1986	1987	1988	1989	1990	1991
Net Fixed Capital Formation												
1 Agriculture and forestry	20926	24596	24157	27130	29424	33218	31726	28852	25598	26743	17397	...
2 Industrial activity	77052	71993	64934	71484	79912	71477	76727	61763	55518	39307	11826	...
3 Construction	4890	2755	3619	2989	4242	5542	5645	5466	4566	4017	778	...
4 Wholesale and retail trade, restaurants and other eating and drinking places	2861	3363	3622	3242	2948	3080	3600	3214	2583	2985	1154	...
5 Transport and communication	19502	13611	19191	21163	18194	20095	14970	15618	13502	15495	6672	...
6 Other activities of the material sphere	1767	992	1075	780	1097	1441	1339	1138	897	1891	883	...
Total Material Sphere	126998	117310	116598	126788	135817	134853	134007	116051	102664	90438	38710	...
7 Housing except owner-occupied, communal and miscellaneous personal services	...	...	...	...	...	...	...	...	...	...	...	...
8 Education, culture and art	...	...	...	...	...	...	...	...	...	...	...	...
9 Health and social welfare services and sports	...	...	...	...	...	...	...	...	...	...	...	...
Total Non-Material Sphere Serving Individuals	...	...	...	...	...	...	...	...	...	...	...	...
10 Government	...	...	...	...	...	...	...	...	...	...	...	...
11 Finance, credit and insurance	...	...	...	...	...	...	...	...	...	...	...	...
12 Research, scientific and technological institutes	...	...	...	...	...	...	...	...	...	...	...	...
13 Other activities of the non-material sphere	...	...	...	...	...	...	...	...	...	...	...	...
Total Non-Material Sphere Serving the Community as a Whole	29794	28674	31362	30668	30180	27322	33292	38023	38194	42465	29200	...
14 Owner-occupied dwellings	...	...	...	...	...	...	...	...	...	...	...	...
Total Net Fixed Capital Formation	156792	145984	147960	157456	165997	162175	167299	154074	140858	132903	67910	...
Gross Fixed Capital Formation												
1 Agriculture and forestry	28008	32821	33687	37481	40963	44814	43308	41758	39649	40917	30091	...
2 Industrial activity	107058	105490	101545	111684	124094	119121	124668	116047	114592	102527	74513	...
3 Construction	9652	7218	8312	8142	9542	11347	11304	11623	11269	11001	6672	...
4 Wholesale and retail trade and restaurants and other eating and drinking places	4567	4866	5701	5237	5059	5233	5648	5686	5273	5722	4303	...
5 Transport and communication	25286	20631	26983	29183	26321	26369	22532	24064	23896	25019	17648	...
6 Other activities of the material sphere	...	...	...	...	...	...	...	...	...	...	...	...
Total Material Sphere	174571	171026	176228	191727	205979	206884	207460	199178	194679	185186	133227	...
7 Housing except owner-occupied, communal and miscellaneous personal services [a]	28391	30822	33405	34311	33638	31970	33569	38798	38578	34964	28387	...
8 Education, culture and art	2761	1977	2048	1082	771	917	948	849	909	2655	1638	...
9 Health and social welfare services and sports	1050	1091	1286	1099	1052	1030	775	514	562	688	1280	...
Total Non-Material Sphere Serving Individuals	32202	33890	36739	36492	35461	33917	35292	40161	40049	38307	31305	...

Romania

6a Capital Formation by Kind of Activity of the Material and Non-Material Spheres in Current Market Prices
(Continued)

Million Romanian lei

	1980	1981	1982	1983	1984	1985	1986	1987	1988	1989	1990	1991
10 Government	1218	1117	1440	900	1110	1475	1462	2152	2112	9688	1669	...
11 Finance, credit and insurance												...
12 Research, scientific and technological institutes	1349	1239	1135	1064	1380	1416	1609	1404	1344	2256	768	...
13 Other activities of the non-material sphere	...	...	...	...	...	...	...	...	...	...	...	...
Total Non-Material Sphere Serving the Community as a Whole	2567	2356	2575	1964	2490	2891	3071	3556	3456	11944	2437	...
14 Owner-occupied dwellings	1111	682	812	560	784	2610	3178	2578	2024	974	1441	...
Total Gross Fixed Capital Formation	210451	207954	216354	230743	244714	246302	249001	245473	240208	236411	168410	...

Increases in Material Circulating Assets and Stocks

	1980	1981	1982	1983	1984	1985	1986	1987	1988	1989	1990	1991
1 Agriculture and forestry	-48	-1342	8056	8068	8470	-10	7966	-2075	4370	-11829	9502	...
2 Industrial activity	8570	20349	16341	429	5163	8427	-466	2240	-13485	-22519	78450	...
3 Construction	5615	-3977	-3155	-2482	-764	2944	4587	900	-1227	-1532	2826	...
4 Wholesale and retail trade and restaurants and other eating and drinking places	7533	-7550	-5467	15753	4168	-6906	2096	1387	-4311	-6806	13992	...
5 Transport and communication	799	227	-308	179	220	300	-26	-198	381	-77	1042	...
6 Other activities of the non-material sphere	216	537	-95	432	696	-227	340	131	190	473	358	...
Total increase in material circulating assets	22685	8244	15372	22379	17953	4528	14497	2385	-14082	-42290	106170	...
Statistical discrepancy	...	...	...	...	...	...	...	...	...	...	...	...
Increase in stocks of the non-material sphere	10255	8827	13560	8480	16178	19042	24861	21074	17190	19077	14705	...

Gross Fixed Capital Formation by Socio-economic Sector and Industrial Use

	1980	1981	1982	1983	1984	1985	1986	1987	1988	1989	1990	1991
1 State and co-operative (excluding collective farms)	194535	191683	199597	214227	229444	231351	236418	233924	229569	226077	157452	...
2 Collective farms	7671	7468	7946	8212	8230	8221	7287	6931	6962	5940	3677	...
3 Other	8245	8803	8811	8304	7040	6730	5296	4618	3677	4394	7281	...
Gross Fixed Capital Formation	210451	207954	216354	230743	244714	246302	249001	245473	240208	236411	168410	...

a) Item 'Owner-occupied dwellings' is included in item 'Housing except owner-occupied, communal, and miscellaneous personal services'.

6b Capital Formation by Kind of Activity of the Material and Non-Material Spheres in Constant Market Prices

Million Romanian lei

	1980	1981	1982	1983	1984	1985	1986	1987	1988	1989	1990	1991
At constant prices of:1981												
Net Fixed Capital Formation												
1 Agriculture and forestry	22456	24596	22676	24603	29424	33815	31726	28852	25868	26743	13356	...
2 Industrial activity	81942	71993	58755	60416	79912	73037	76727	61763	55518	39307	1821	...
3 Construction	5148	2755	3299	2536	4242	5542	5645	5466	4566	4017	-118	...
4 Wholesale and retail trade, restaurants and other eating and drinking places	3220	3363	2852	2330	2948	3080	3600	3214	2583	2985	576	...
5 Transport and communication	20688	13611	16936	17508	18194	20507	14970	15618	13502	15495	3904	...
6 Other activities of the material sphere	1857	992	1036	722	1097	1441	1339	1138	897	1891	614	...
Total Material Sphere a	135311	117310	105554	108115	135817	137422	134007	116051	102934	90438	20153	...
7 Housing except owner-occupied, communal and miscellaneous personal services	...	...	...	...	...	...	...	...	...	...	...	...
8 Education, culture and art	...	...	...	...	...	...	...	...	...	...	...	...
9 Health and social welfare services and sports	...	...	...	...	...	...	...	...	...	...	...	...
Total Non-Material Sphere Serving Individuals	...	...	...	...	...	...	...	...	...	...	...	...
10 Government	...	...	...	...	...	...	...	...	...	...	...	...
11 Finance, credit and insurance	...	...	...	...	...	...	...	...	...	...	...	...
12 Research, scientific and technological institutes	...	...	...	...	...	...	...	...	...	...	...	...
13 Other activities of the non-material sphere	...	...	...	...	...	...	...	...	...	...	...	...
Total Non-Material Sphere Serving the Community as a Whole a	34053	28674	27462	24893	30180	27297	33292	38023	37924	42465	25142	...
14 Owner-occupied dwellings	...	...	...	...	...	...	...	...	...	...	...	...
Total Net Fixed Capital Formation a	169364	145984	133016	133008	165997	164719	167299	154074	140858	132903	45295	...
Gross Fixed Capital Formation												
1 Agriculture and forestry	29848	32821	32219	37481	40963	44814	43308	41758	39649	40917	26100	...

6b Capital Formation by Kind of Activity of the Material and Non-Material Spheres in Constant Market Prices
(Continued)

Million Romanian lei

		1980	1981	1982	1983	1984	1985	1986	1987	1988	1989	1990	1991
						At constant prices of:1981							
2	Industrial activity	111948	105490	95358	111684	124094	119121	124668	116047	114592	102527	64153	...
3	Construction	9910	7218	7991	8142	9542	11347	11304	11623	11269	11001	6311	...
4	Wholesale and retail trade and restaurants and other eating and drinking places	4926	4866	4929	5237	5059	5233	5648	5686	5273	5722	3938	...
5	Transport and communication	26472	20631	25010	29183	26321	26369	22532	24064	23896	25019	15650	...
6	Other activities of the material sphere	...	...	...	...	...	...	...	...	...	...	...	...
	Total Material Sphere a	183104	171026	165507	191727	205979	206884	207460	199178	194679	185186	116152	
7	Housing except owner-occupied, communal and miscellaneous personal services b	33025	30822	29588	34311	33638	31970	33569	38798	38578	34964	23559	...
8	Education, culture and art	2972	1977	1853	1082	771	917	948	849	909	2655	1432	...
9	Health and social welfare services and sports	1150	1091	1205	1099	1052	1030	775	514	562	688	1248	...
	Total Non-Material Sphere Serving Individuals a	37147	33890	32646	36492	35461	33917	35292	40161	40049	38307	26239	...
10	Government	1347	1117	1372	900	1110	1475	1462	2152	2112	9688	1263	...
11	Finance, credit and insurance												...
12	Research, scientific and technological institutes	1401	1239	1104	1064	1380	1416	1609	1404	1344	2256	754	...
13	Other activities of the non-material sphere	...	...	...	...	...	...	...	...	...	...	...	
	Total Non-Material Sphere Serving the Community as a Whole	2748	2356	2476	1964	2490	2891	3071	3556	3456	11944	2017	
14	Owner-occupied dwellings	878	682	799	560	784	2610	3178	2578	2024	974	1364	
	Total Gross Fixed Capital Formation a	223877	207954	201428	230743	244714	246302	249001	245473	240208	236411	145772	...
	Increases in Material Circulating Assets and Stocks												
1	Agriculture and forestry	-50	-1342	7520	7498	7292	586	7700	-2208	4757	-11829	6743	...
2	Industrial activity	12476	20349	15100	4826	3702	7843	534	2917	-13485	-22519	44731	...
3	Construction	5924	-3977	-4849	-2189	-764	2944	4587	900	-1227	-1532	1611	...
4	Wholesale and retail trade and restaurants and other eating and drinking places	7533	-7550	-2089	12547	4168	-6906	2096	1387	-4311	-6806	7978	...
5	Transport and communication	882	227	-3	179	220	300	-26	-198	381	-77	594	...
6	Other activities of the non-material sphere	228	537	-63	286	696	-227	340	131	190	473	204	...
	Total increase in material circulating assets	26993	8244	15616	23147	15314	4540	15231	2929	-13695	-42290	61861	...
	Statistical discrepancy	...	...	...	...	...	...	...	...	...	...	...	
	Increase in stocks of the non-material sphere a	10276	8827	13769	8798	13784	19282	24513	21017	17159	19077	10464	...

a) For the period 1970-1974, base year in prices 1963, for the period 1975-1979, base year in prices 1977, for the period 1980-1983, base year in prices 1981, and for the years beginning 1984, base year in prices of the previous years as against the years in which calculations were carried out.

b) Item 'Owner-occupied dwellings' is included in item 'Housing except owner-occupied, communal, and miscellaneous personal services'.

7a Final Consumption at Current Market Prices

Thousand Million Romanian lei

		1980	1981	1982	1983	1984	1985	1986	1987	1988	1989	1990	1991
1	Personal consumption	310.2	331.0	387.3	383.6	407.0	400.9	409.0	430.4	445.5	450.8	542.1	...
	a) Material Consumption in the Units of the Non-Material Sphere Serving Individuals												
	Housing except owner-occupied, communal and miscellaneous personal services	0.4	0.4	0.7	0.4	0.5	0.4	0.4	0.3	0.2	0.2	0.2	...
	Education, culture and art	4.7	4.9	4.6	3.7	4.9	3.9	3.5	3.0	2.8	3.0	4.9	...
	Health and social welfare services and sports	6.9	6.8	7.6	7.5	8.5	7.7	7.8	6.6	6.4	6.8	8.7	...
	Other	5.2	5.6	6.1	6.3	6.3	6.1	6.0	5.3	5.5	5.4	9.5	...
2	Total non-material sphere serving individuals	17.2	17.7	19.0	17.9	20.2	18.1	17.7	15.2	14.9	15.4	23.3	...

Romania

7a Final Consumption at Current Market Prices
(Continued)

Thousand Million Romanian lei

	1980	1981	1982	1983	1984	1985	1986	1987	1988	1989	1990	1991
b) Material Consumption in the Units of the Non-Material Sphere Serving the Community as a Whole												
Government	1.0	1.1	1.2	1.1	1.0	1.0	1.1	1.1	1.2	1.2	1.7	...
Finance, credit and insurance	-	-	-	-	-	-	-	0.1	0.1	0.1	0.1	...
Research, scientific and technological institutes	0.7	0.6	0.7	0.9	0.9	0.9	0.9	1.0	0.9	0.9	1.7	...
Other activities of the non-material sphere	11.5	10.4	8.7	11.4	11.6	11.4	11.3	9.7	9.8	9.9	12.4	...
3 Total non-material sphere serving the community as a whole	13.2	12.1	10.6	13.4	13.5	13.3	13.3	11.9	12.0	12.1	15.9	...
Final consumption	340.6	360.8	416.9	414.9	440.7	432.3	440.0	457.5	472.4	478.3	581.3	...

7b Final Consumption at Constant Market Prices

Thousand Million Romanian lei

	1980	1981	1982	1983	1984	1985	1986	1987	1988	1989	1990	1991
At constant prices of:1981												
1 Personal consumption [a]	322.8	331.0	326.1	324.6	416.4	398.8	406.1	427.6	441.7	448.8	497.1	...
a) Material Consumption in the Units of the Non-Material Sphere Serving Individuals												
Housing except owner-occupied, communal and miscellaneous personal services	0.4	0.4	0.7	0.4	0.5	0.4	0.4	0.3	0.2	0.2	0.2	...
Education, culture and art	4.7	4.9	4.6	3.1	4.9	3.9	3.5	3.0	2.8	3.0	4.9	...
Health and social welfare services and sports	6.9	6.8	7.6	6.7	8.3	7.7	7.8	6.6	6.4	6.8	8.7	...
Other	5.7	5.6	5.3	5.3	6.2	6.2	6.0	5.3	5.5	5.4	9.0	...
2 Total non-material sphere serving individuals [a]	17.7	17.7	18.2	15.5	19.9	18.2	17.7	15.2	14.9	15.4	22.8	...
b) Material Consumption in the Units of the Non-Material Sphere Serving the Community as a Whole												
Government	1.0	1.1	1.1	1.0	1.0	1.0	1.1	1.1	1.2	1.2	1.7	...
Finance, credit and insurance	-	-	-	-	-	-	-	0.1	0.1	0.1	0.1	...
Research, scientific and technological institutes	0.7	0.6	0.7	1.1	0.9	0.9	0.9	1.0	0.9	0.9	1.7	...
Other activities of the non-material sphere	11.5	10.4	8.5	10.2	10.9	11.4	11.3	9.8	9.8	9.8	12.3	...
3 Total non-material sphere serving the community as a whole	13.2	12.1	10.3	12.3	12.8	13.3	13.3	12.0	12.0	12.0	15.8	...
Final consumption [a]	353.7	360.8	354.6	352.4	449.1	430.3	437.1	454.8	468.6	476.2	535.7	...

a) For the period 1980-1983, base year in prices 1981 and for the years beginning 1984, base year in prices of the previous years as against the years in which calculations were carried out.

8 Personal Consumption According to Source of Supply of Goods and Material Services in Current Market Prices

Thousand Million Romanian lei

	1980	1981	1982	1983	1984	1985	1986	1987	1988	1989	1990	1991
1 Purchases of goods in state and co-operative retail trade	199.6	209.0	235.1	244.8	257.8	262.9	270.3	278.3	278.5	283.2	341.4	...
2 Purchases of goods in the free market and from private retail trade	67.0	74.1	100.2	82.0	91.5	80.4	77.2	89.3	97.9	100.4	127.0	...
3 Goods produced on own account and received in kind												...
4 Payments for transport and communication services	15.4	16.5	17.5	17.9	17.9	19.3	20.3	20.8	22.3	22.5	24.5	...
5 Purchases of electricity, gas and water	6.9	7.3	9.2	11.6	12.0	11.7	12.1	12.7	16.4	15.4	12.6	...
6 Purchases directly from handicrafts, repair shops and the like	...	...	...	...	...	...	...	...	...	...	...	...
7 Consumption of fixed assets in respect of all dwellings	4.7	4.8	5.0	5.1	5.0	4.2	6.4	5.6	4.5	3.9	5.8	...
8 Other	16.6	19.3	20.3	22.2	22.8	22.4	22.7	23.7	25.9	25.4	30.8	...
Personal consumption	310.2	331.0	387.3	383.6	407.0	400.9	409.0	430.4	445.5	450.8	542.1	...

Russian Federation

Source. Reply to the United Nations national accounts questionnaire from the State Committee of Russian Federation on Statistics and Analysis.
General note. The estimates shown in the following tables are in accordance with the System of Material Product Balances (MPS). Therefore, these estimates are not comparable in concept amd coverage with those conforming to the United Nations System of National Accounts (SNA).

1a Net Material Product by Use at Current Market Prices

Million Roubles

	1980	1981	1982	1983	1984	1985	1986	1987	1988	1989	1990	1991
1 Personal consumption	170332	180483	186258	192787	199131	203104	206752	212938	223939	244143	276244	499922
2 Material consumption in the units of the non-material sphere serving individuals	20431	21334	22867	23964	24707	25247	26307	27672	29556	31750	34729	73016
Consumption of the Population	190762	201817	209125	216750	223838	228351	233059	240610	253495	275893	310973	572938
3 Material consumption in the units of the non-material sphere serving the community as a whole	10890	11585	12281	13396	14181	15094	15841	17471	19066	20339	22502	45779
4 Net fixed capital formation	45322	43487	46287	48595	51157	50424	55313	58280	58027	53861	50833	55201
5 Increase in material circulating assets and in stocks	24100	25761	37387	38837	40668	43181	36936	30625	44308	47662	44097	103233
6 Losses	2570	3376	3650	3590	3031	3903	4126	4978	4895	6033	7560	11571
7 Exports of goods and material services	-491	288	-3394	-3226	-6150	-11751	-13690	-12714	-5587	-8877	-8601	-21703
8 Less: Imports of goods and material services												
Statistical discrepancy a	983	-574	6787	6452	12299	23503	27379	25428	11173	17754	17201	43406
Net Material Product	274136	285740	312123	324394	339024	352705	358964	364678	385377	412665	444565	810425

a) The difference between the produced Net Material Product (NMP) in the country (Table 2) and the NMP used in the national economy (Table 1, lines 1-7) is shown in item 'Statistical Discrepancy' in table 1.

1b Net Material Product by Use at Constant Market Prices

Million Roubles

	1980	1981	1982	1983	1984	1985	1986	1987	1988	1989	1990	1991
	At constant prices of: 1973						1983			1988		
1 Personal consumption	162633	168773	169201	173444	180095	182630	... 202226	205351	212163	... 236141	247623	264218
2 Material consumption in the units of the non-material sphere serving individuals	19995	20884	22137	23315	24217	24991	... 26308	27672	29451	... 31305	33231	36361
Consumption of the Population	182628	189656	191338	196759	204312	207621	... 228534	233023	241614	... 267446	280854	300579
3 Material consumption in the units of the non-material sphere serving the community as a whole	11528	12012	12347	13468	14077	14955	... 16203	18421	19900	... 19903	21454	23771
4 Net fixed capital formation	46216	44528	46401	48128	43915	40926	... 54996	56941	55337	... 52000	44207	15026
5 Increase in material circulating assets and in stocks	22475	22933	30057	29480	30291	36878	... 36072	29261	43763	... 44073	34532	45540
6 Losses	...	...	...	...	...	...	... ...	...	...	... ...	...	...
7 Exports of goods and material services	...	...	...	...	...	...	... ...	...	...	... ...	...	...
8 Less: Imports of goods and material services	...	...	...	...	...	...	... ...	...	...	... ...	...	...
Statistical discrepancy ab	12167	13845	14132	17195	21111	19502	... 15020	15798	8179	... 9438	16743	10819
Net Material Product	275014	282975	294276	305030	313707	319882	... 350825	353444	368793	... 392860	397790	395735

a) The difference between the produced Net Material Product (NMP) in the country (Table 2) and the NMP used in the national economy (Table 1, lines 1-7) is shown in item 'Statistical Discrepancy' in table 1. b) Beginning 1989, the base year is the preceding year (T-1).

Russian Federation

2a Net Material Product by Kind of Activity of the Material Sphere in Current Market Prices

Million Roubles

	1980	1981	1982	1983	1984	1985	1986	1987	1988	1989	1990	1991
1 Agriculture and forestry	29380	29052	34658	52854	55029	52598	58389	59128	76076	82327	96381	132816
A Agriculture and livestock	26614	26225	31691	49723	51785	49724	55454	56044	72006	77517	88461	123353
B Forestry	452	451	680	689	692	405	410	413	417	467	541	1006
C Other	2313	2377	2287	2443	2552	2468	2526	2672	3652	4343	7379	8457
2 Industrial activity	153464	159458	173325	163643	171253	171304	167578	172219	171553	183597	187729	415773
3 Construction	28661	29427	31216	31843	35102	36937	43169	46574	50379	53549	56620	128354
4 Wholesale and retail trade and restaurants and other eating and drinking places	14617	15292	15442	15793	16067	16706	17095	16471	18335	20028	22639	38067
5 Transport and communication	17788	18474	20925	21928	22182	22769	24071	24247	25426	24062	30621	39058
A Transport	17067	17710	20117	20983	21200	21676	22913	22978	24072	22638	29113	...
B Communication	721	764	808	945	983	1093	1159	1269	1354	1423	1508	...
6 Other activities of the material sphere	30226	34037	36557	38331	39391	52392	48662	46038	43609	49102	50575	56357
Net material product	274136	285740	312123	324394	339024	352705	358964	364678	385377	412665	444565	810425

2b Net Material Product by Kind of Activity of the Material Sphere in Constant Market Prices

Million Roubles

	1980	1981	1982	1983	1984	1985	1986	1987	1988	1989	1990	1991
	At constant prices of: 1973						1983			1988		
1 Agriculture and forestry	21450	18662	21977	23916	21551	21037	48977	47660	49900	78273	75695	90184
A Agriculture and livestock	18699	15867	19373	21168	18734	18281	46036	44561	46365	73974	72682	82649
B Forestry	452	451	442	503	506	509	410	413	417	471	540	503
C Other	2299	2345	2162	2245	2311	2247	2531	2686	3118	3828	2473	7032
2 Industrial activity	165549	171601	175158	178931	184912	188070	169429	172378	182396	175119	179453	175340
3 Construction	29671	30546	31139	32308	33593	34382	43808	46883	50435	50759	51239	49542
4 Wholesale and retail trade and restaurants and other eating and drinking places	13032	13606	13632	13918	14453	14640	16347	15738	16928	19824	20592	21349
5 Transport and communication	18241	18912	19446	20227	20452	20831	24070	24256	25441	23105	22846	28313
A Transport	17520	18148	18643	19344	19534	19896	22912	22987	24086	...	...	...
B Communication	721	764	802	884	919	936	1159	1269	1354	...	...	...
6 Other activities of the material sphere	27071	29647	32925	35731	38747	40923	48193	46529	43693	45780	47965	31007
Net material product [a]	275014	282975	294276	305030	313707	319882	350825	353444	368793	392860	397790	395735

a) Beginning 1989, the base year is the preceding year (T-1).

Rwanda

Source. Reply to the United Nations National Accounts Questionnaire from the Ministry of Planning, Kigali. Some official estimates together with information on concepts, definitions and methods of estimation are published in 'Comptes Economiques du Rwanda, 1969 et 1970'.

General note. The estimates shown in the following tables have been prepared in accordance with the United Nations System of National Accounts so far as the existing data would permit.

1.1 Expenditure on the Gross Domestic Product, in Current Prices

Thousand Million Rwanda francs

	1980	1981	1982	1983	1984	1985	1986	1987	1988	1989	1990	1991
1 Government final consumption expenditure	13.49	22.96	16.91	16.71	16.25	19.58	20.13	20.55	24.28	24.46	33.10	46.00
2 Private final consumption expenditure	89.97	98.00	107.27	119.29	128.91	139.87	134.72	139.81	142.18	156.94	159.90	174.90
3 Gross capital formation	17.43	16.31	23.28	19.24	25.15	30.07	27.04	26.87	27.90	25.42	22.10	22.20
A Increase in stocks	4.24	0.33	4.50	-1.50	0.49	3.02	0.24	-0.07	0.98	0.14	-1.80	-3.20
B Gross fixed capital formation	13.19	15.98	18.78	20.74	24.66	27.05	26.80	26.94	26.92	25.28	23.90	25.40
4 Exports of goods and services	15.59	12.05	15.13	16.47	20.10	18.73	21.44	15.76	16.09	15.61	14.90	20.80
5 Less: Imports of goods and services	28.49	26.68	31.63	29.52	31.29	34.54	34.33	31.57	32.53	32.21	37.10	50.90
Equals: Gross Domestic Product	107.99	122.64	130.96	142.19	159.11	173.70	168.99	171.43	177.92	190.22	192.90	212.90

1.2 Expenditure on the Gross Domestic Product, in Constant Prices

Thousand Million Rwanda francs

	1980	1981	1982	1983	1984	1985	1986	1987	1988	1989	1990	1991
					At constant prices of:1985							
1 Government final consumption expenditure	...	...	19.32	17.93	16.53	19.58	20.35	19.66	21.39	22.57	...	...
2 Private final consumption expenditure	...	...	132.75	144.97	135.78	139.87	147.64	144.69	143.82	158.67	...	...
3 Gross capital formation	...	...	24.38	20.53	27.51	30.07	28.44	28.07	29.55	24.45	...	...
A Increase in stocks	...	...	5.00	-1.60	0.42	3.02	0.25	-0.11	1.50	0.21	...	...
B Gross fixed capital formation	...	...	19.38	22.13	27.09	27.05	28.19	28.18	28.05	24.24	...	...
4 Exports of goods and services	...	...	17.13	18.25	18.10	18.73	21.48	22.56	23.89	21.71	...	...
5 Less: Imports of goods and services	...	...	29.65	27.95	31.55	34.54	36.38	33.20	36.80	39.64	...	...
Equals: Gross Domestic Product	...	...	163.94	173.74	166.37	173.70	181.53	181.78	181.85	187.76	...	...

1.3 Cost Components of the Gross Domestic Product

Thousand Million Rwanda francs

	1980	1981	1982	1983	1984	1985	1986	1987	1988	1989	1990	1991
1 Indirect taxes, net	8.26	7.81	9.12	9.44	11.68	13.88	17.22	14.91	15.21	12.46	...	...
A Indirect taxes	...	9.40	9.63	10.20	12.05	13.88	17.21	14.91	15.46	...	...	...
B Less: Subsidies	...	1.59	0.39	0.74	0.38	-	-	-	0.25	...	...	...
2 Consumption of fixed capital	6.06	3.74	4.74	5.27	6.82	9.39	10.54	11.08	12.36	14.54	...	...
3 Compensation of employees paid by resident producers to:	17.82	26.86	27.94	30.34	30.62	41.35	41.91	42.53	45.05	46.97	...	...
4 Operating surplus	75.85	84.23	89.16	97.14	109.98	109.08	99.33	102.92	105.31	116.25	...	...
Equals: Gross Domestic Product	107.99	122.64	130.96	142.19	159.11	173.70	168.99	171.43	177.93	190.22	...	...

1.7 External Transactions on Current Account, Summary

Thousand Million Rwanda francs

	1980	1981	1982	1983	1984	1985	1986	1987	1988	1989	1990	1991
					Payments to the Rest of the World							
1 Imports of goods and services	28.49	26.68	31.63	29.52	31.29	34.54	34.33	31.57	32.53	32.21	...	...
2 Factor income to the rest of the world	1.45	1.30	1.78	2.63	3.24	2.75	4.19	3.54	4.26	2.98	...	...
A Compensation of employees	...	...	...	...	...	1.52	1.68	1.57	1.74	1.36	...	...
B Property and entrepreneurial income	...	...	...	...	...	1.23	2.52	1.97	2.52	1.62	...	...
3 Current transfers to the rest of the world	5.59	6.09	4.38	3.40	3.29	1.85	2.18	2.01	1.95	1.81	...	...
4 Surplus of the nation on current transactions	-9.49	-11.31	-12.85	-8.51	-7.96	-10.91	-9.98	-14.26	-14.84	-14.16	...	...
Payments to the Rest of the World and Surplus of the Nation on Current Transactions	26.04	22.76	24.94	27.04	29.86	28.23	30.72	22.89	23.90	22.84	...	...

Rwanda

1.7 External Transactions on Current Account, Summary
(Continued)

Thousand Million Rwanda francs

	1980	1981	1982	1983	1984	1985	1986	1987	1988	1989	1990	1991
					Receipts From The Rest of the World							
1 Exports of goods and services	15.59	12.05	15.13	16.47	20.10	18.73	21.44	15.76	16.09	15.61	...	...
2 Factor income from rest of the world	1.59	2.21	0.50	0.82	0.82	0.97	0.85	0.80	0.69	0.75	...	...
A Compensation of employees	...	...	...	0.02	0.02	0.06	0.06	0.04	0.05	0.04	...	...
B Property and entrepreneurial income	...	...	...	0.80	0.80	0.91	0.80	0.76	0.64	0.71	...	...
3 Current transfers from rest of the world	8.84	8.50	9.32	9.75	8.94	8.53	8.43	6.29	7.12	6.47	...	...
Receipts from the Rest of the World on Current Transactions	26.04	22.76	24.94	27.04	29.86	28.23	30.72	22.89	23.90	22.83	...	...

1.10 Gross Domestic Product by Kind of Activity, in Current Prices

Thousand Million Rwanda francs

	1980	1981	1982	1983	1984	1985	1986	1987	1988	1989	1990	1991
1 Agriculture, hunting, forestry and fishing	49.51	49.96	51.49	53.60	64.41	72.67	62.58	65.35	67.44	75.69	...	...
2 Mining and quarrying	1.84	0.81	0.62	0.72	0.57	0.46	0.33	0.34	0.36	0.79	...	...
3 Manufacturing	16.48	19.30	18.27	22.55	22.78	23.83	27.13	25.04	24.98	24.93	...	...
4 Electricity, gas and water	0.13	0.08	0.45	0.77	0.91	0.91	1.10	1.02	1.17	0.95	...	...
5 Construction	4.82	5.39	10.19	11.69	14.20	15.11	11.86	11.94	12.23	12.88	...	...
6 Wholesale and retail trade, restaurants and hotels	15.88	19.65	19.19	18.26	19.56	21.24	23.61	23.62	22.66	24.40		
7 Transport, storage and communication	2.30	3.24	7.42	8.67	8.19	8.47	10.17	11.90	12.64	12.93	...	...
8 Finance, insurance, real estate and business services [a]	4.11	5.34	8.00	10.04	11.82	13.25	12.52	12.94	14.56	16.05		
9 Community, social and personal services	9.17	15.39	11.46	12.20	12.04	12.28	13.96	14.61	15.66	15.76		
Total, Industries	104.24	119.16	127.09	138.51	154.47	168.23	163.26	166.76	171.70	184.38		
Producers of Government Services	...	...	...	...	...	...	...	...	...	...	...	...
Other Producers	...	...	...	...	...	...	...	...	...	...	...	...
Subtotal	104.24	119.16	127.09	138.51	154.47	168.23	163.26	166.76	171.70	184.38	...	...
Less: Imputed bank service charge [a]	...	...	...	...	...	...	...	...	...	...	...	...
Plus: Import duties	3.75	3.48	3.87	3.68	4.64	5.47	5.73	4.68	6.24	5.84		
Plus: Value added tax	...	...	...	...	...	...	...	...	...	...		
Equals: Gross Domestic Product	107.99	122.64	130.94	142.19	159.11	173.70	168.99	171.44	177.94	190.22	...	...

a) Item 'Less: Imputed bank service charge' is netted out of item 'Finance, insurance, real estate and business services'.

1.11 Gross Domestic Product by Kind of Activity, in Constant Prices

Thousand Million Rwanda francs

	1980	1981	1982	1983	1984	1985	1986	1987	1988	1989	1990	1991
					At constant prices of:1985							
1 Agriculture, hunting, forestry and fishing	...	...	74.65	77.91	71.04	72.67	73.11	73.25	71.84	74.50	...	...
2 Mining and quarrying	...	...	0.34	0.69	0.54	0.46	0.34	0.35	0.38	0.75	...	...
3 Manufacturing	...	...	22.77	26.26	22.28	23.83	28.29	30.12	28.92	25.35	...	...
4 Electricity, gas and water	...	...	0.49	0.87	1.04	0.91	1.04			1.26	...	...
5 Construction	...	...	10.20	11.99	14.62	15.11	12.45	12.43	13.25	12.19	...	...
6 Wholesale and retail trade, restaurants and hotels	...	...	21.94	19.59	19.90	21.24	23.87				...	...
7 Transport, storage and communication	...	...	7.94	9.09	8.30	8.47	10.04	46.77	47.70	47.19	...	...
8 Finance, insurance, real estate and business services [a]	...	...	8.64	10.58	11.77	13.25	12.55				...	...
9 Community, social and personal services	...	...	13.10	13.09	12.24	12.28	14.11	14.19	14.76	14.83	...	...
Total, Industries	...	...	160.06	170.06	161.73	168.23	175.80	177.11	176.86	176.07	...	...
Producers of Government Services	...	...	...	...	...	...	...	...	...	...	...	...
Other Producers	...	...	...	...	...	...	...	...	...	...	...	...
Subtotal	...	...	160.06	170.06	161.73	168.23	175.80	177.11	176.86	176.07	...	...
Less: Imputed bank service charge [a]	...	...	...	...	...	...	...	...	...	...	...	...
Plus: Import duties	...	...	3.87	3.68	4.64	5.47	5.73	4.68	6.24	5.84	...	...
Plus: Value added tax	...	...	...	...	...	...	...	...	...	...	...	...
Equals: Gross Domestic Product	...	...	163.94	173.74	166.37	173.70	181.53	181.78	183.10	181.91	...	...

a) Item 'Less: Imputed bank service charge' is netted out of item 'Finance, insurance, real estate and business services'.

1.12 Relations Among National Accounting Aggregates

Thousand Million Rwanda francs

	1980	1981	1982	1983	1984	1985	1986	1987	1988	1989	1990	1991
Gross Domestic Product	107.99	122.64	130.96	142.19	159.11	173.70	168.99	171.43	177.94	190.22	...	...
Plus: Net factor income from the rest of the world	0.14	0.91	-1.29	-1.81	-2.42	-1.78	-3.34	-2.74	-3.57	-2.23	...	...
Factor income from the rest of the world	1.59	2.21	0.50	0.82	0.82	0.97	0.85	0.80	0.69	0.75	...	...
Less: Factor income to the rest of the world	1.45	1.30	1.78	2.63	3.24	2.75	4.19	3.54	4.26	2.98	...	...
Equals: Gross National Product	108.13	123.55	129.67	140.38	156.69	171.92	165.65	168.69	174.36	187.99	...	...
Less: Consumption of fixed capital	6.06	3.74	4.74	5.27	6.82	9.39	10.53	11.08	12.36	14.54	...	...
Equals: National Income	102.07	119.81	124.93	135.11	149.87	162.53	155.12	157.61	162.00	173.45	...	...
Plus: Net current transfers from the rest of the world	3.26	2.40	4.94	6.35	5.65	6.68	6.25	4.28	5.17	4.66	...	...
Current transfers from the rest of the world	8.84	8.50	9.32	9.75	8.94	8.53	8.43	6.29	7.12	6.47	...	...
Less: Current transfers to the rest of the world	5.59	6.10	4.38	3.40	3.29	1.85	2.18	2.01	1.95	1.81	...	...
Equals: National Disposable Income	105.33	122.21	129.87	141.46	155.52	169.21	161.37	161.89	167.17	178.11	...	...
Less: Final consumption	103.46	120.96	124.17	136.00	145.14	159.45	154.85	160.36	166.47	181.40	...	...
Equals: Net Saving	1.87	1.25	5.70	5.46	10.37	9.76	6.52	1.53	0.71	-3.29	...	...
Less: Surplus of the nation on current transactions	-9.49	-11.31	-12.85	-8.51	-7.96	-10.91	-9.98	-14.26	-14.84	-14.16	...	...
Equals: Net Capital Formation	11.36	12.56	18.55	13.97	18.35	20.67	16.50	15.79	15.55	10.87	...	...

4.1 Derivation of Value Added by Kind of Activity, in Current Prices

Thousand Million Rwanda francs

	1980			1981			1982			1983		
	Gross Output	Intermediate Consumption	Value Added	Gross Output	Intermediate Consumption	Value Added	Gross Output	Intermediate Consumption	Value Added	Gross Output	Intermediate Consumption	Value Added
All Producers												
1 Agriculture, hunting, forestry and fishing	51.33	1.82	49.51	51.32	1.36	49.96	55.66	1.38	54.28	58.19	1.62	56.57
A Agriculture and hunting	...	...	...	...	...	...	54.66	1.38	53.28	57.14	1.62	55.52
B Forestry and logging	...	...	...	...	...	...	0.75	-	0.75	0.78	-	0.78
C Fishing	...	...	...	...	...	...	0.25	-	0.25	0.28	-	0.28
2 Mining and quarrying	2.98	1.14	1.84	2.08	1.27	0.81	1.59	0.97	0.62	1.80	1.08	0.72
A Coal mining	...	...	...	...	...	...	...	...	...	...	...	...
B Crude petroleum and natural gas production	...	...	...	...	...	...	-	0.05	-0.05	0.02	0.04	-0.02
C Metal ore mining	...	...	...	...	...	...	1.41	0.92	0.49	1.60	1.04	0.56
D Other mining	...	...	...	...	...	...	0.17	-	0.17	0.18	-	0.18
3 Manufacturing	46.86	30.38	16.48	53.96	34.66	19.30	55.02	34.21	20.81	60.59	34.60	25.99
A Manufacture of food, beverages and tobacco	...	...	...	...	...	...	44.69	28.89	15.80	49.54	28.74	20.80
B Textile, wearing apparel and leather industries	...	...	...	...	...	...	3.04	1.51	1.53	3.55	2.02	1.53
C Manufacture of wood and wood products, including furniture	...	...	...	...	...	...	0.87	0.24	0.63	0.89	0.22	0.67
D Manufacture of paper and paper products, printing and publishing	...	...	...	...	...	...	0.31	0.19	0.12	0.39	0.18	0.21
E Manufacture of chemicals and chemical petroleum, coal, rubber and plastic products	...	...	...	...	...	...	2.06	1.43	0.63	1.99	1.48	0.51
F Manufacture of non-metallic mineral products, except products of petroleum and coal	...	...	...	...	...	...	1.18	0.15	1.03	1.25	0.15	1.10
G Basic metal industries	...	...	...	...	...	...						
H Manufacture of fabricated metal products, machinery and equipment	...	...	...	...	...	...	2.86	1.81	1.05	2.98	1.81	1.17
I Other manufacturing industries	...	...	...	...	...	...	...	...	...	...	...	...
4 Electricity, gas and water	0.50	0.37	0.13	0.51	0.44	0.08	1.24	0.79	0.45	1.28	0.51	0.77
A Electricity, gas and steam	...	...	...	...	...	...	0.97	0.40	0.57	0.98	0.29	0.69
B Water works and supply	...	...	...	...	...	...	0.26	0.39	-0.13	0.30	0.22	0.09

4.1 Derivation of Value Added by Kind of Activity, in Current Prices
(Continued)

Thousand Million Rwanda francs

	1980 Gross Output	Intermediate Consumption	Value Added	1981 Gross Output	Intermediate Consumption	Value Added	1982 Gross Output	Intermediate Consumption	Value Added	1983 Gross Output	Intermediate Consumption	Value Added
5 Construction	9.39	4.57	4.82	9.48	4.09	5.39	8.93	3.27	5.66	10.47	3.98	6.49
6 Wholesale and retail trade, restaurants and hotels	17.57	1.69	15.88	21.56	1.91	19.65	23.40	2.09	21.31	22.32	2.04	20.28
A Wholesale and retail trade	...	...	...	...	...	...	22.76	1.82	20.94	21.59	1.74	19.85
B Restaurants and hotels	...	...	...	...	...	...	0.65	0.27	0.38	0.73	0.30	0.43
7 Transport, storage and communication	7.37	5.07	2.30	5.53	2.28	3.25	6.95	2.94	4.01	7.64	2.95	4.69
A Transport and storage	...	...	...	...	...	...	6.43	2.88	3.55	7.13	2.62	4.51
B Communication	...	...	...	...	...	...	0.51	0.06	0.45	0.51	0.33	0.18
8 Finance, insurance, real estate and business services a	7.90	3.79	4.11	9.40	4.06	5.34	8.45	3.71	4.74	9.11	3.68	5.43
A Financial institutions	...	...	...	...	...	...	3.09	2.78	0.31	2.91	2.48	0.43
B Insurance	...	...	...	...	...	...	-	-0.08	0.08	0.31	0.08	0.23
C Real estate and business services	...	...	...	...	...	...	5.36	1.02	4.34	5.88	1.12	4.76
Real estate, except dwellings	...	...	...	...	...	...	...	...	...	...	...	...
Dwellings	...	...	...	...	...	...	...	...	...	...	...	...
9 Community, social and personal services	15.68	6.51	9.17	24.57	9.18	15.39	26.32	9.63	16.69	26.22	8.29	17.93
Total, Industries	159.58	55.34	104.24	178.41	59.25	119.16	187.54	59.00	128.55	197.62	58.75	138.87
Producers of Government Services	...	...	...	...	...	...	...	...	...	...	...	...
Other Producers	...	...	...	...	...	...	...	...	...	...	...	...
Total	159.58	55.34	104.24	178.41	59.25	119.16	187.54	59.00	128.55	197.62	58.75	138.87
Less: Imputed bank service charge a	...	...	...	...	...	...	...	...	...	...	...	...
Import duties	3.75	...	3.75	3.48	...	3.48	3.87	...	3.87	3.68	...	3.68
Value added tax	...	...	...	...	...	...	...	...	...	...	...	...
Total b	163.33	55.34	107.99	181.89	59.25	122.64	191.41	59.00	132.42	201.30	58.75	142.55

	1984 Gross Output	Intermediate Consumption	Value Added	1985 Gross Output	Intermediate Consumption	Value Added	1986 Gross Output	Intermediate Consumption	Value Added	1987 Gross Output	Intermediate Consumption	Value Added
						All Producers						
1 Agriculture, hunting, forestry and fishing	70.75	2.06	68.69	76.71	4.04	72.67	66.23	3.65	62.58	69.12	9.02	60.10
A Agriculture and hunting	69.66	2.06	67.60	...	...	...	...	...	...	...	...	...
B Forestry and logging	0.81	-	0.81	...	...	...	...	...	...	...	...	...
C Fishing	0.28	-	0.28	...	...	...	...	...	...	...	...	...
2 Mining and quarrying	0.88	0.31	0.57	0.68	0.22	0.46	0.36	0.03	0.33	0.37	0.06	0.31
A Coal mining	...	...	...	...	...	...	...	...	...	...	...	...
B Crude petroleum and natural gas production	0.03	0.01	0.02	...	...	...	...	...	...	...	...	...
C Metal ore mining	0.66	0.30	0.36	...	...	...	...	...	...	...	...	...
D Other mining	0.19	-	0.19	...	...	...	...	...	...	...	...	...
3 Manufacturing	62.64	36.59	26.05	65.79	41.95	23.83	65.21	38.08	27.13	65.77	41.65	24.12
A Manufacture of food, beverages and tobacco	49.45	30.11	19.34	...	...	...	49.96	...	...	...	...	...
B Textile, wearing apparel and leather industries	3.54	1.86	1.68	...	...	...	4.09	...	...	...	...	...
C Manufacture of wood and wood products, including furniture	1.08	0.37	0.71	...	...	...	1.30	0.49	0.81	1.40	0.38	1.02
D Manufacture of paper and paper products, printing and publishing	0.35	0.19	0.16	...	...	...	0.52	0.20	0.32	0.52	0.20	0.32
E Manufacture of chemicals and chemical petroleum, coal, rubber and plastic products	2.50	1.60	0.90	...	...	...	2.72	1.88	0.84	2.95	2.18	0.77
F Manufacture of non-metallic mineral products, except products of petroleum and coal	2.61	0.60	2.01	...	...	...	3.62	1.03	2.59	3.40	0.89	2.51
G Basic metal industries	[		]	...	...	...	[					]
H Manufacture of fabricated metal products, machinery and equipment	3.11	1.86	1.25	...	...	...	3.00	2.05	0.95	3.51	1.86	1.65
I Other manufacturing industries	...	...	...	...	...	...	...	...	...	...	...	...
4 Electricity, gas and water	1.49	0.58	0.91	1.80	0.89	0.91	1.56	0.46	1.10	1.61	0.59	1.02
A Electricity, gas and steam	1.10	0.44	0.66	...	...	...	...	...	...	...	...	...
B Water works and supply	0.38	0.13	0.25	...	...	...	...	...	...	...	...	...

4.1 Derivation of Value Added by Kind of Activity, in Current Prices
(Continued)

Thousand Million Rwanda francs

	1984			1985			1986			1987		
	Gross Output	Intermediate Consumption	Value Added	Gross Output	Intermediate Consumption	Value Added	Gross Output	Intermediate Consumption	Value Added	Gross Output	Intermediate Consumption	Value Added
5 Construction	12.84	4.95	7.89	24.33	9.21	15.11	23.74	11.88	11.86	24.17	4.17	20.00
6 Wholesale and retail trade, restaurants and hotels	24.19	2.46	21.73	46.57	25.32	21.24	44.15	20.54	23.61	46.91	27.68	19.23
A Wholesale and retail trade	23.12	1.90	21.22	...	...	...	20.58	2.48	18.10	20.11	6.83	13.28
B Restaurants and hotels	1.07	0.57	0.50	...	...	...	23.57	18.07	5.50	26.80	20.85	5.95
7 Transport, storage and communication	9.92	5.50	4.42	16.53	8.06	8.47	19.14	8.97	10.17	22.66	10.75	11.91
A Transport and storage	9.33	5.34	3.99	...	...	...	18.31	8.86	9.45	21.66	10.61	11.05
B Communication	0.59	0.16	0.43	...	...	...	0.84	0.12	0.72	1.00	0.14	0.86
8 Finance, insurance, real estate and business services [a] ..	10.36	4.13	6.23	15.76	2.52	13.25	17.39	4.87	12.52	17.22	4.28	12.94
A Financial institutions	3.52	2.80	0.72	...	...	...	3.75	2.53	1.21	2.41	1.64	0.77
B Insurance	0.30	0.09	0.21	...	...	...	0.22	0.18	0.04	0.36	0.15	0.21
C Real estate and business services	6.54	1.24	5.30	...	...	...	13.43	2.16	11.27	14.45	2.49	11.96
Real estate, except dwellings	...	...	...	...	...	...	5.57	0.74	4.83	5.86	0.94	4.92
Dwellings	...	...	...	...	...	...	7.86	1.42	6.44	8.59	1.55	7.04
9 Community, social and personal services	26.63	8.83	17.80	20.49	8.20	12.28	22.55	8.59	13.96	22.55	7.94	14.61
Total, Industries	219.70	65.41	154.29	268.66	100.44	168.23	260.34	97.08	163.26	270.38	104.83	165.55
Producers of Government Services	...	...	...	...	...	...	...	...	...	...	...	...
Other Producers	...	...	...	...	...	...	...	...	...	...	...	...
Total	219.70	65.41	154.29	268.66	100.44	168.23	260.34	97.08	163.26	270.38	104.83	165.55
Less: Imputed bank service charge [a]	...	...	...	...	...	...	...	...	...	...	...	...
Import duties	4.64	...	4.64	5.47	...	5.47	5.73	...	5.73	4.68	...	4.68
Value added tax	...	...	...	...	...	...	...	...	...	...	...	...
Total [b]	224.34	65.41	158.93	274.13	100.44	173.70	266.07	97.08	168.99	275.06	104.83	170.23

	1988			1989		
	Gross Output	Intermediate Consumption	Value Added	Gross Output	Intermediate Consumption	Value Added
	All Producers					
1 Agriculture, hunting, forestry and fishing	71.78	4.34	67.44	79.87	4.18	75.69
A Agriculture and hunting	...	...	...	75.94	3.89	72.05
B Forestry and logging	...	...	...	3.77	0.24	3.53
C Fishing	...	...	...	0.16	0.05	0.11
2 Mining and quarrying	0.40	0.04	0.36	0.88	0.09	0.79
A Coal mining	...	...	...	...	...	...
B Crude petroleum and natural gas production	...	...	...	...	...	...
C Metal ore mining	...	...	...	...	...	...
D Other mining	...	...	...	...	...	...
3 Manufacturing	64.44	39.46	24.98	65.77	40.84	24.93
A Manufacture of food, beverages and tobacco	46.83	30.48	16.35	46.99	31.43	15.56
B Textile, wearing apparel and leather industries	5.58	3.42	2.16	5.96	3.52	2.44
C Manufacture of wood and wood products, including furniture	1.44	0.37	1.07	1.33	0.33	1.00
D Manufacture of paper and paper products, printing and publishing	0.52	0.22	0.30	0.78	0.48	0.30
E Manufacture of chemicals and chemical petroleum, coal, rubber and plastic products	3.17	2.14	1.03	3.40	2.15	1.25
F Manufacture of non-metallic mineral products, except products of petroleum and coal	3.33	0.94	2.39	3.48	0.88	2.60
G Basic metal industries						
H Manufacture of fabricated metal products, machinery and equipment	3.57	1.89	1.68	3.82	2.04	1.78
I Other manufacturing industries	...	...	...	...	...	...
4 Electricity, gas and water	2.09	0.92	1.17	2.10	1.15	0.95
A Electricity, gas and steam	...	...	...	...	...	...
B Water works and supply	...	...	...	...	...	...

Rwanda

4.1 Derivation of Value Added by Kind of Activity, in Current Prices
(Continued)

Thousand Million Rwanda francs

	1988			1989		
	Gross Output	Intermediate Consumption	Value Added	Gross Output	Intermediate Consumption	Value Added
5 Construction	24.80	12.56	12.23	26.03	13.15	12.88
6 Wholesale and retail trade, restaurants and hotels	44.84	22.18	22.66	49.64	25.24	24.40
A Wholesale and retail trade	20.28	2.45	17.83	21.99	2.68	19.31
B Restaurants and hotels	24.56	19.73	4.83	27.65	22.56	5.09
7 Transport, storage and communication	23.78	11.14	12.64	24.48	11.55	12.93
A Transport and storage	22.64	10.95	11.69	23.34	11.37	11.97
B Communication	1.14	0.19	0.95	1.14	0.18	0.96
8 Finance, insurance, real estate and business services a ..	20.39	5.83	14.56	21.86	5.81	16.05
A Financial institutions	3.96	2.94	1.02	4.14	3.29	0.85
B Insurance	0.36	0.15	0.21	0.32	0.11	0.21
C Real estate and business services	16.07	2.74	13.33	17.40	2.41	14.99
Real estate, except dwellings	6.26	0.97	5.29	...	...	...
Dwellings	9.81	1.77	8.04	...	...	...
9 Community, social and personal services	27.18	11.52	15.66	27.28	11.52	15.76
Total, Industries	279.70	107.99	171.70	297.91	113.53	184.38
Producers of Government Services	...	...	...	...	...	...
Other Producers	...	...	...	...	...	...
Total	279.70	107.99	171.70	297.91	113.53	184.38
Less: Imputed bank service charge a	...	...	...	...	...	...
Import duties	6.24	...	6.24	5.84	...	5.84
Value added tax	...	...	...	...	...	...
Total b	285.94	107.99	177.94	303.75	113.53	190.22

a) Item 'Less: Imputed bank service charge' is netted out of item 'Finance, insurance, real estate and business services'. b) Data for this table have not been revised, therefore, data for some years are not comparable with those of other tables.

4.3 Cost Components of Value Added

Thousand Million Rwanda francs

	1980						1981					
	Compensation of Employees	Capital Consumption	Net Operating Surplus	Indirect Taxes	Less: Subsidies Received	Value Added	Compensation of Employees	Capital Consumption	Net Operating Surplus	Indirect Taxes	Less: Subsidies Received	Value Added
					All Producers							
1 Agriculture, hunting, forestry and fishing	0.50	0.03	47.62	1.36	...	49.51	0.26	0.07	49.41	0.22	...	49.96
A Agriculture and hunting	...	...	...	...	...	...	...	...	...	...	...	...
B Forestry and logging	...	...	...	...	...	...	...	...	...	...	...	...
C Fishing	...	...	...	...	...	...	...	...	...	...	...	...
2 Mining and quarrying	0.95	0.33	0.47	0.09	...	1.84	1.07	0.30	-0.70	0.14	...	0.81
A Coal mining	...	...	...	...	...	...	...	...	...	...	...	...
B Crude petroleum and natural gas production	...	...	...	...	...	...	...	...	...	...	...	...
C Metal ore mining	...	...	...	...	...	...	...	...	...	...	...	...
D Other mining	...	...	...	...	...	...	...	...	...	...	...	...

4.3 Cost Components of Value Added
(Continued)

Thousand Million Rwanda francs

	1980						1981					
	Compensation of Employees	Capital Consumption	Net Operating Surplus	Indirect Taxes	Less: Subsidies Received	Value Added	Compensation of Employees	Capital Consumption	Net Operating Surplus	Indirect Taxes	Less: Subsidies Received	Value Added
3 Manufacturing	1.88	0.64	11.17	2.79	...	16.48	2.24	0.71	13.33	3.02	...	19.30
A Manufacture of food, beverages and tobacco	...	...	...	...	...	...	0.84	0.44	10.86	3.02	...	15.16
B Textile, wearing apparel and leather industries	...	...	...	...	...	...	0.30	0.02	1.07	0.01	...	3.30
C Manufacture of wood and wood products, including furniture	...	...	...	...	...	...	0.27	0.02	0.30	-	...	0.60
D Manufacture of paper and paper products, printing and publishing	...	...	...	...	...	...	0.07	0.01	0.08	-	...	0.16
E Manufacture of chemicals and chemical petroleum, coal, rubber and plastic products	...	...	...	...	...	...	0.21	0.12	0.22	-	...	3.44
F Manufacture of non-metallic mineral products, except products of petroleum and coal	...	...	...	...	...	...	0.30	-	0.67	-	...	0.97
G Basic metal industries	...	...	...	...	...	...						
H Manufacture of fabricated metal products, machinery and equipment	...	...	...	...	...	...	0.25	0.09	0.33	0.01	...	0.68
I Other manufacturing industries	...	...	...	...	...	...	...	...	...	...	...	...
4 Electricity, gas and water	0.06	0.26	-0.19	-	...	0.13	0.21	0.15	-0.28	-	...	0.08
A Electricity, gas and steam	...	...	...	...	...	...	...	...	...	...	...	...
B Water works and supply	...	...	...	...	...	...	...	...	...	...	...	...
5 Construction	3.85	0.97	-	-	...	4.82	4.71	0.23	0.44	0.01	...	5.39
6 Wholesale and retail trade, restaurants and hotels	1.27	0.67	13.88	0.06	...	15.88	1.71	0.39	16.82	0.73	...	19.65
A Wholesale and retail trade	...	...	...	...	...	...	1.52	0.28	16.71	0.72	...	19.24
B Restaurants and hotels	...	...	...	...	...	...	0.19	0.11	0.11	0.02	...	0.41
7 Transport, storage and communication	0.62	0.56	1.03	0.09	...	2.30	0.69	0.15	2.45	-0.04	...	3.25
A Transport and storage	...	...	...	...	...	...	0.36	0.15	2.32	0.08	...	2.91
B Communication	...	...	...	...	...	...	0.33	-	0.13	-0.12	...	0.34
8 Finance, insurance, real estate and business services	0.43	1.71	1.87	0.10	...	4.11	0.61	1.72	2.76	0.25	...	5.34
A Financial institutions	...	...	...	...	...	...	0.53	0.12	0.46	0.06	...	1.17
B Insurance	...	...	...	...	...	...	0.08	0.05	0.07	-	...	0.20
C Real estate and business services	...	...	...	...	...	...	-	1.55	2.23	0.19	...	3.97
Real estate, except dwellings	...	...	...	...	...	...	-	-	0.10	-	...	0.10
Dwellings	...	...	...	...	...	...	-	1.55	2.13	0.19	...	3.87
9 Community, social and personal services	8.26	0.91	-	-	...	9.17	15.37	0.02	-	-	...	15.39
Total, Industries	17.82	6.08	75.85	4.49	...	104.24	26.86	3.74	84.23	4.33	...	119.16
Producers of Government Services	...	...	...	...	...	...	...	...	...	...	...	...
Other Producers	...	...	...	...	...	...	...	...	...	...	...	...
Total	17.82	6.08	75.85	4.49	...	104.24	26.86	3.74	84.23	4.33	...	119.16
Less: Imputed bank service charge	...	...	...	...	...	...	...	...	...	...	...	...
Import duties	...	...	...	3.75	...	3.75	...	...	...	3.48	...	3.48
Value added tax	...	...	...	...	...	...	...	...	...	...	...	...
Total	17.82	6.08	75.85	8.24	...	107.99	26.86	3.74	84.23	7.81	...	122.64

	1982						1983					
	Compensation of Employees	Capital Consumption	Net Operating Surplus	Indirect Taxes	Less: Subsidies Received	Value Added	Compensation of Employees	Capital Consumption	Net Operating Surplus	Indirect Taxes	Less: Subsidies Received	Value Added
All Producers												
1 Agriculture, hunting, forestry and fishing	0.23	0.07	52.81	1.17	...	54.28	0.30	0.06	55.57	0.64	...	56.57
A Agriculture and hunting	...	...	...	...	...	...	0.30	0.06	54.51	0.64	...	55.51
B Forestry and logging	...	...	...	...	...	...	-	-	0.78	-	...	0.78
C Fishing	...	...	...	...	...	...	-	-	0.28	-	...	0.28
2 Mining and quarrying	1.09	0.29	-0.84	0.08	...	0.62	1.15	0.33	-0.85	0.09	...	0.72
A Coal mining	...	...	...	...	...	...	...	...	...	...	...	...
B Crude petroleum and natural gas production	...	...	...	...	...	...	0.01	0.01	-0.04	-	...	-0.02
C Metal ore mining	...	...	...	...	...	...	1.07	0.32	-0.92	0.09	...	0.56

Rwanda

Thousand Million Rwanda francs

	1982						1983					
	Compensation of Employees	Capital Consumption	Net Operating Surplus	Indirect Taxes	Less: Subsidies Received	Value Added	Compensation of Employees	Capital Consumption	Net Operating Surplus	Indirect Taxes	Less: Subsidies Received	Value Added
D Other mining	...	...	...	...	...	...	0.07	-	0.11	-	...	0.18
3 Manufacturing	2.65	0.72	14.16	3.28	...	20.81	2.81	0.91	18.38	3.90	...	25.99
A Manufacture of food, beverages and tobacco	0.31	0.29	1.19	0.01	...	1.54	0.94	0.56	15.40	3.90	...	20.80
B Textile, wearing apparel and leather industries	...	...	...	...	...	...	0.37	0.03	1.12	0.01	...	1.53
C Manufacture of wood and wood products, including furniture	0.29	0.02	0.32	-	...	0.63	0.31	0.02	0.34	-	...	0.67
D Manufacture of paper and paper products, printing and publishing	0.08	0.02	0.02	-	...	0.12	0.09	0.03	0.09	-	...	0.21
E Manufacture of chemicals and chemical petroleum, coal, rubber and plastic products	0.28	0.13	0.22	-	...	0.63	0.27	0.15	0.08	-	...	0.51
F Manufacture of non-metallic mineral products, except products of petroleum and coal	0.31	-	0.72	-	...	1.04	0.33	-	0.77	-	...	1.10
G Basic metal industries					...						...	
H Manufacture of fabricated metal products, machinery and equipment	0.48	0.12	0.44	0.02	...	1.05	0.50	0.11	0.57	-0.02	...	1.17
I Other manufacturing industries	...	...	...	...	...	...	...	...	...	...	...	...
4 Electricity, gas and water	0.11	0.35	-0.01	-	...	0.45	0.21	0.35	0.21	-	...	0.77
A Electricity, gas and steam	0.07	0.29	0.21		...	0.57	0.10	0.28	0.30	-	...	0.68
B Water works and supply	0.41	0.55	-0.22	-	...	-0.13	0.11	0.07	-0.09	-	...	0.09
5 Construction	4.92	0.26	0.47	0.01	...	5.66	5.55	0.30	0.63	0.01	...	6.49
6 Wholesale and retail trade, restaurants and hotels	1.82	0.94	17.77	0.78	...	21.31	1.92	0.90	16.62	0.84	...	20.28
A Wholesale and retail trade	1.62	0.81	17.72	0.78	...	20.94	1.67	0.81	16.53	0.84	...	19.85
B Restaurants and hotels	0.02	0.13	0.05	-	...	0.37	0.24	0.09	0.09	-	...	0.43
7 Transport, storage and communication	0.65	0.17	3.10	0.09	...	4.01	0.60	0.21	3.52	0.36	...	4.69
A Transport and storage	...	...	...	...	...	...	0.36	0.21	3.52	0.42	...	4.51
B Communication	...	...	...	...	...	...	0.23	-	-	-0.06	...	0.18
8 Finance, insurance, real estate and business services	0.70	1.99	2.10	-0.05	...	4.74	0.80	2.17	2.52	-0.06	...	5.43
A Financial institutions	0.62	0.28	-0.44	-0.05	...	0.41	0.71	0.30	-0.52	-0.06	...	0.44
B Insurance	0.08	0.01	-0.01	-	...	0.08	0.08	0.01	0.14	-	...	0.23
C Real estate and business services	-	1.70	2.54	-	...	4.25	-	1.87	2.90	-	...	4.77
Real estate, except dwellings	...	-	0.01	-	...	0.01	...	...	...	...	...	...
Dwellings	...	1.70	2.54		...	4.24	...	...	...	...	...	...
9 Community, social and personal services	16.67	0.02	-	-	...	16.69	17.08	0.06	0.79	-	...	17.93
Total, Industries	28.24	4.81	90.15	5.37	...	128.57	30.42	5.29	97.39	5.78	...	138.87
Producers of Government Services	...	...	...	...	...	...	...	...	...	...	...	...
Other Producers	...	...	...	...	...	...	...	...	...	...	...	...
Total	28.24	4.81	90.15	5.37	...	128.57	30.42	5.29	97.39	5.78	...	138.87
Less: Imputed bank service charge	...	...	...	...	...	...	...	...	...	...	...	...
Import duties	...	...	...	3.87	...	3.87	...	...	...	3.68	...	3.68
Value added tax	...	...	...	...	...	...	...	...	...	...	...	...
Total	28.24	4.81	90.15	9.24	...	132.44	30.42	5.29	97.39	9.46	...	142.55

	1984						1985					
	Compensation of Employees	Capital Consumption	Net Operating Surplus	Indirect Taxes	Less: Subsidies Received	Value Added	Compensation of Employees	Capital Consumption	Net Operating Surplus	Indirect Taxes	Less: Subsidies Received	Value Added
					All Producers							
1 Agriculture, hunting, forestry and fishing	0.31	0.06	66.75	1.58	...	68.69	4.59	0.77	67.08	0.23	...	72.67
A Agriculture and hunting	0.31	0.06	65.66	1.58	...	67.61	...	...	...	...	...	...
B Forestry and logging	-	-	0.81	-	...	0.81	...	...	...	...	...	...
C Fishing	-	-	0.28		...	0.28	...	...	...	...	...	...
2 Mining and quarrying	1.01	0.31	-0.89	0.14	...	0.57	0.32	0.08	-0.02	0.08	...	0.46
A Coal mining	...	...	...	...	...	...	...	...	...	...	...	...
B Crude petroleum and natural gas production	0.01	-	0.01	-	...	0.02	...	...	...	...	...	...

4.3 Cost Components of Value Added
(Continued)

Thousand Million Rwanda francs

	1984						1985					
	Compensation of Employees	Capital Consumption	Net Operating Surplus	Indirect Taxes	Less: Subsidies Received	Value Added	Compensation of Employees	Capital Consumption	Net Operating Surplus	Indirect Taxes	Less: Subsidies Received	Value Added
C Metal ore mining	0.92	0.31	-1.02	0.14	...	0.36	...	...	...	...	...	...
D Other mining	0.08	-	0.12		...	0.20						
3 Manufacturing	2.92	1.09	17.75	4.29	...	26.05	3.46	1.22	12.15	7.00	...	23.83
A Manufacture of food, beverages and tobacco	0.94	0.69	13.52	4.19	...	19.34	...	...	...	...	...	...
B Textile, wearing apparel and leather industries	0.36	0.02	1.29	0.01	...	1.68	...	...	...	...	...	...
C Manufacture of wood and wood products, including furniture	0.33	0.02	0.36	-	...	0.71	...	...	...	...	...	...
D Manufacture of paper and paper products, printing and publishing	0.09	0.04	0.02	0.02	...	0.16	...	...	...	...	...	...
E Manufacture of chemicals and chemical petroleum, coal, rubber and plastic products	0.32	0.15	0.46	-0.02	...	0.91	...	...	...	...	...	...
F Manufacture of non-metallic mineral products, except products of petroleum and coal	0.34	0.04	1.64	-	...	2.01	...	...	...	...	...	...
G Basic metal industries							...	...	...	...	...	...
H Manufacture of fabricated metal products, machinery and equipment	0.55	0.14	0.46	0.10	...	1.25	...	...	...	...	...	...
I Other manufacturing industries	...	...	...	...	...	...	...	...	...	...	...	...
4 Electricity, gas and water	0.24	0.53	0.15	-	...	0.91	0.34	0.55	0.02	-	...	0.91
A Electricity, gas and steam	0.16	0.46	0.04	-	...	0.66	...	...	...	...	...	...
B Water works and supply	0.08	0.07	0.11	-	...	0.25	...	...	...	...	...	...
5 Construction	5.97	0.99	0.86	0.06	...	7.89	8.78	0.31	5.98	0.05	...	15.11
6 Wholesale and retail trade, restaurants and hotels	2.07	0.96	17.79	0.90	...	21.72	5.16	0.48	15.23	0.36	...	21.24
A Wholesale and retail trade	1.73	0.87	17.73	0.89	...	21.22	...	...	...	...	...	...
B Restaurants and hotels	0.34	0.09	0.06	0.01	...	0.50	...	...	...	...	...	...
7 Transport, storage and communication	0.83	0.50	2.97	0.12	...	4.43	2.24	3.05	2.63	0.55	...	8.47
A Transport and storage	0.59	0.50	2.78	0.12	...	3.99	...	...	...	...	...	...
B Communication	0.24	-	0.19	-	...	0.43	...	...	...	...	...	...
8 Finance, insurance, real estate and business services	0.72	2.30	3.27	-0.07	...	6.23	4.25	2.87	6.01	0.12	...	13.25
A Financial institutions	0.63	0.22	-0.07	-	...	0.72	...	...	...	...	...	...
B Insurance	0.10	0.01	0.10	-	...	0.21	...	...	...	...	...	...
C Real estate and business services	-	2.07	3.23	-	...	5.30	...	...	...	...	...	...
Real estate, except dwellings	...	...	...	...	...	...	...	...	...	...	...	...
Dwellings	...	...	...	...	...	...	...	...	...	...	...	...
9 Community, social and personal services	16.51	0.07	1.21	-	...	17.80	12.22	0.07	-	-	...	12.28
Total, Industries	30.58	6.81	109.85	7.02	...	154.29	41.35	9.39	109.08	8.41	...	168.23
Producers of Government Services	...	...	...	...	...	...	...	...	...	...	...	...
Other Producers	...	...	...	...	...	...	...	...	...	...	...	...
Total	30.58	6.81	109.85	7.02	...	154.29	41.35	9.39	109.08	8.41	...	168.23
Less: Imputed bank service charge	...	...	...	...	...	...	...	...	...	...	...	...
Import duties	...	...	...	4.64	...	4.64	...	...	...	5.47	...	5.47
Value added tax	...	...	...	...	...	...	...	...	...	...	...	...
Total	30.58	6.81	109.85	11.66	...	158.93	41.35	9.39	109.08	13.88	...	173.70

	1986						1987					
	Compensation of Employees	Capital Consumption	Net Operating Surplus	Indirect Taxes	Less: Subsidies Received	Value Added	Compensation of Employees	Capital Consumption	Net Operating Surplus	Indirect Taxes	Less: Subsidies Received	Value Added
	All Producers											
1 Agriculture, hunting, forestry and fishing	4.01	0.70	57.41	0.45	...	62.58	4.75	1.03	62.18	1.32	...	69.26
A Agriculture and hunting	4.00	0.69	57.31	0.45	...	62.46	4.51	1.01	58.92	1.32	...	65.76
B Forestry and logging					...		0.20	-	3.13	-	...	3.33
C Fishing	0.01	0.01	0.10	-	...	0.12	0.02	0.02	0.13	-	...	0.17
2 Mining and quarrying	0.16	-	0.12	0.04	...	0.33	0.20	-	0.12	0.04	...	0.36

Rwanda

4.3 Cost Components of Value Added
(Continued)

Thousand Million Rwanda francs

	1986						1987					
	Compensation of Employees	Capital Consumption	Net Operating Surplus	Indirect Taxes	Less: Subsidies Received	Value Added	Compensation of Employees	Capital Consumption	Net Operating Surplus	Indirect Taxes	Less: Subsidies Received	Value Added
A Coal mining	...	...	...	...	...	...	...	...	...	...	...	...
B Crude petroleum and natural gas production	...	...	...	...	...	...	...	...	...	...	...	...
C Metal ore mining	...	...	...	...	...	...	0.20	0.03	0.12	0.04	...	0.36
D Other mining	...	...	...	...	...	...	...	...	...	...	...	...
3 Manufacturing	4.07	1.30	11.90	9.87	...	27.13	6.63	2.16	22.33	14.97	...	46.30
A Manufacture of food, beverages and tobacco	2.29	0.78	8.32	10.53	...	21.92	3.31	1.16	14.42	14.47	...	33.60
B Textile, wearing apparel and leather industries	0.46	0.12	0.41	0.05	...	1.03	1.02	0.24	2.47	0.21	...	3.92
C Manufacture of wood and wood products, including furniture	0.04	0.13	0.25	0.03	...	0.81	0.42	0.14	0.43	0.03	...	1.01
D Manufacture of paper and paper products, printing and publishing	0.10	0.03	0.19	0.01	...	0.32	0.10	0.03	0.19	0.05	...	0.32
E Manufacture of chemicals and chemical petroleum, coal, rubber and plastic products	0.32	0.18	0.22	0.12	...	0.83	0.30	0.17	0.21	0.10	...	0.78
F Manufacture of non-metallic mineral products, except products of petroleum and coal	0.54	0.12	1.30	-	...	1.97	1.18	0.33	3.49	0.02	...	5.02
G Basic metal industries					...						...	
H Manufacture of fabricated metal products, machinery and equipment	0.28	0.08	1.07	0.14	...	1.57	0.30	0.09	1.12	0.14	...	1.65
I Other manufacturing industries	...	...	...	...	...	...	...	...	...	...	...	...
4 Electricity, gas and water	0.55	0.61	-0.06	-	...	1.10	0.53	0.64	-0.16	-	...	1.02
A Electricity, gas and steam	...	...	...	...	...	...	...	...	...	...	...	...
B Water works and supply	...	...	...	...	...	...	...	...	...	...	...	...
5 Construction	6.65	0.74	4.37	0.11	...	11.86	13.17	1.47	9.03	0.21	...	23.88
6 Wholesale and retail trade, restaurants and hotels	5.10	0.50	17.67	0.33	...	23.61	5.04	0.49	17.76	0.33	...	23.62
A Wholesale and retail trade	3.41	0.45	13.93	0.31	...	18.10	3.35	0.44	13.58	0.30	...	17.68
B Restaurants and hotels	1.69	0.05	3.74	0.02	...	5.51	1.69	0.05	4.18	0.03	...	5.94
7 Transport, storage and communication	2.55	3.14	3.84	0.64	...	10.17	2.99	3.15	4.58	1.17	...	11.90
A Transport and storage	2.37	3.14	3.30	0.64	...	9.45	2.80	3.15	3.92	1.17	...	11.05
B Communication	0.18	-	0.54	-	...	0.72	0.19	-	0.66	-	...	0.85
8 Finance, insurance, real estate and business services	4.71	3.45	4.35	0.01	...	12.52	4.56	3.69	5.85	0.21	...	14.26
A Financial institutions	1.01	0.36	-0.26	0.10	...	1.21	0.62	0.30	1.07	0.10	...	2.08
B Insurance	0.15	0.02	-0.13	-	...	0.04	0.16	0.02	0.03	-	...	0.21
C Real estate and business services	3.55	3.07	4.74	-0.09	...	11.27	3.78	3.37	4.75	0.11	...	11.97
Real estate, except dwellings	3.55	0.71	0.66	-0.09	...	4.83	0.59	0.76	0.31	0.07	...	1.73
Dwellings	-	2.36	4.08	-	...	6.44	-	2.58	4.46	-	...	7.04
9 Community, social and personal services	14.11	0.09	-0.28	0.04	...	13.96	14.58	0.30	-0.36	0.10	...	14.61
Total, Industries	41.91	10.53	99.33	11.48	...	163.26	52.45	12.93	121.33	18.35	...	204.85
Producers of Government Services	...	...	...	...	...	...	...	...	...	...	...	...
Other Producers	...	...	...	...	...	...	...	...	...	...	...	...
Total	41.91	10.53	99.33	11.48	...	163.26	52.45	12.93	121.33	18.35	...	204.85
Less: Imputed bank service charge	...	...	...	...	...	...	...	...	...	...	...	...
Import duties	...	...	...	5.73	...	5.73	...	...	...	4.68	...	4.68
Value added tax	...	...	...	...	...	...	...	...	...	...	...	...
Total	41.91	10.53	99.33	17.21	...	168.99	52.45	12.93	121.33	14.91	...	171.43

	1988						1989					
	Compensation of Employees	Capital Consumption	Net Operating Surplus	Indirect Taxes	Less: Subsidies Received	Value Added	Compensation of Employees	Capital Consumption	Net Operating Surplus	Indirect Taxes	Less: Subsidies Received	Value Added
					All Producers							
1 Agriculture, hunting, forestry and fishing	4.33	0.84	61.90	0.37	...	67.44	4.96	0.81	71.53	-1.61	...	75.69
A Agriculture and hunting	4.11	0.82	58.65	0.37	...	63.95	4.73	0.79	68.14	-1.61	...	72.05
B Forestry and logging	0.20	-	3.16	-	...	3.36	0.22	-	3.31	-	...	3.53
C Fishing	0.02	0.02	0.09	-	...	0.13	0.01	0.02	0.08	-	...	0.11

4.3 Cost Components of Value Added
(Continued)

Thousand Million Rwanda francs

	1988						1989					
	Compensation of Employees	Capital Consumption	Net Operating Surplus	Indirect Taxes	Less: Subsidies Received	Value Added	Compensation of Employees	Capital Consumption	Net Operating Surplus	Indirect Taxes	Less: Subsidies Received	Value Added
2 Mining and quarrying	0.18	-	0.13	0.04	...	0.36	0.40	0.01	0.28	0.10	...	0.79
A Coal mining	...	...	...	...	...	...	...	...	...	...	...	...
B Crude petroleum and natural gas production	...	...	...	...	...	...	...	...	...	...	...	...
C Metal ore mining	...	...	...	...	...	...	...	...	...	...	...	...
D Other mining	...	...	...	...	...	...	...	...	...	...	...	...
3 Manufacturing	4.26	1.84	11.97	6.91	...	24.98	4.23	2.93	11.45	6.32	...	24.93
A Manufacture of food, beverages and tobacco	1.87	0.96	7.11	6.41	...	16.35	1.55	1.77	6.42	5.82	...	15.56
B Textile, wearing apparel and leather industries	0.54	0.15	1.36	0.11	...	2.16	0.66	0.27	1.40	0.11	...	2.44
C Manufacture of wood and wood products, including furniture	0.45	0.15	0.45	0.02	...	1.07	0.41	0.15	0.41	0.03	...	1.00
D Manufacture of paper and paper products, printing and publishing	0.10	0.02	0.17	0.01	...	0.30	0.17	0.11	0.02	-	...	0.30
E Manufacture of chemicals and chemical petroleum, coal, rubber and plastic products	0.38	0.22	0.30	0.13	...	1.03	0.40	0.28	0.43	0.14	...	1.25
F Manufacture of non-metallic mineral products, except products of petroleum and coal	0.62	0.25	1.44	0.08	...	2.39	0.71	0.25	1.58	0.06	...	2.60
G Basic metal industries					...						...	
H Manufacture of fabricated metal products, machinery and equipment	0.30	0.09	1.14	0.15	...	1.68	0.33	0.10	1.19	0.16	...	1.78
I Other manufacturing industries	...	...	...	...	...	...	...	...	...	...	...	...
4 Electricity, gas and water	0.42	0.81	-0.06	-	...	1.17	0.53	1.12	-0.70	-	...	0.95
A Electricity, gas and steam	...	...	...	...	...	...	...	...	...	...	...	...
B Water works and supply	...	...	...	...	...	...	...	...	...	...	...	...
5 Construction	6.74	0.74	4.64	0.11	...	12.23	6.89	0.82	5.05	0.12	...	12.88
6 Wholesale and retail trade, restaurants and hotels	4.75	0.49	17.10	0.32	...	22.66	5.29	0.53	18.23	0.35	...	24.40
A Wholesale and retail trade	3.38	0.45	13.70	0.30	...	17.83	3.72	0.48	14.78	0.33	...	19.31
B Restaurants and hotels	1.37	0.04	3.40	0.02	...	4.83	1.57	0.05	3.45	0.02	...	5.09
7 Transport, storage and communication	3.39	3.33	4.80	1.13	...	12.65	3.42	3.39	4.97	1.15	...	12.93
A Transport and storage	3.13	3.33	4.10	1.13	...	11.69	3.16	3.39	4.27	1.15	...	11.97
B Communication	0.26	-	0.70	-	...	0.96	0.26	-	0.70	-	...	0.96
8 Finance, insurance, real estate and business services	5.35	4.32	4.80	0.08	...	14.55	5.50	4.95	5.41	0.19	...	16.05
A Financial institutions	1.14	0.52	-0.64	-	...	1.02	1.21	0.30	-0.74	-0.06	...	0.85
B Insurance	0.16	0.02	0.02	0.01	...	0.21	0.21	0.04	-0.08	0.04	...	0.21
C Real estate and business services	4.05	3.78	5.42	0.07	...	13.32	4.08	4.61	6.23	0.07	...	14.99
Real estate, except dwellings	4.05	0.83	0.33	0.07		5.28	...	...	...	...		...
Dwellings	-	2.95	5.09	-		8.04	...	...	...	...		...
9 Community, social and personal services	15.66	-	-	-	...	15.66	15.76	-	-	-	...	15.76
Total, Industries	45.08	12.37	105.28	8.97	...	171.70	46.98	14.56	116.22	6.62	...	169.39
Producers of Government Services	...	...	...	...	...	...	...	...	...	...	...	...
Other Producers	...	...	...	...	...	...	...	...	...	...	...	...
Total	45.08	12.37	105.28	8.97	...	171.70	46.98	14.56	116.22	6.62	...	184.38
Less: Imputed bank service charge	...	...	...	...		...	...	...	...	...		...
Import duties	...	...	...	6.24		6.24	...	...	...	5.84	...	5.84
Value added tax	...	...	...	...		...	...	...	...	...		...
Total	45.08	12.37	105.28	15.20	...	177.94	46.98	14.56	116.22	12.46	...	190.22

Saint Kitts and Nevis

Source. Reply to the United Nations National Accounts Questionnaire from the Ministry of Finance, St. Kitts-Nevis.

General note. The estimates shown in the following tables have been prepared in accordance with the United Nations System of National Accounts so far as the existing data would permit.

1.1 Expenditure on the Gross Domestic Product, in Current Prices

Thousand E.C. dollars

	1980	1981	1982	1983	1984	1985	1986	1987	1988	1989	1990	1991
1 Government final consumption expenditure	26310	38780	35520	35520	37520	...	...	...	...	...	...	...
2 Private final consumption expenditure	92690	108950	117200	140150	129560	...	...	...	...	...	...	...
3 Gross capital formation	49440	46060	55120	49910	53270	...	...	...	...	...	...	...
A Increase in stocks	-	-	-	-	-							
B Gross fixed capital formation	49440	46060	55120	49910	53270	...	...	...	...	...	...	...
4 Exports of goods and services	86730	92240	80630	78840	92820	...	...	...	...	...	...	...
5 Less: Imports of goods and services	125930	136610	130370	150390	145980	...	...	...	...	...	...	...
Equals: Gross Domestic Product	129240	149420	158100	154030	167190	...	...	...	...	...	...	...

1.3 Cost Components of the Gross Domestic Product

Thousand E.C. dollars

	1980	1981	1982	1983	1984	1985	1986	1987	1988	1989	1990	1991
1 Indirect taxes, net	26130	28880	20340	21940	...	...	...	...	...	...	...	...
A Indirect taxes	32220	35020	27270	25220	26700	...	...	...	...	...	...	...
B Less: Subsidies	6090	6140	6930	3280	...	...	...	...	...	...	...	...
2 Consumption of fixed capital	...	...	...	...	...	...	...	...	...	...	...	...
3 Compensation of employees paid by resident producers to:	...	...	...	...	...	...	...	...	...	...	...	...
4 Operating surplus	...	...	...	...	...	...	...	...	...	...	...	...
Equals: Gross Domestic Product	129240	149420	158100	154030	167190	...	...	...	...	...	...	...

1.10 Gross Domestic Product by Kind of Activity, in Current Prices

Thousand E.C. dollars

	1980	1981	1982	1983	1984	1985	1986	1987	1988	1989	1990	1991
1 Agriculture, hunting, forestry and fishing	16510	13830	20310	16190	19220	16440	23040	25940	27820	27700	...	...
2 Mining and quarrying	320	330	410	450	380	450	500	640	860	1080	...	...
3 Manufacturing	15740	17880	18660	17550	22620	21940	32830	35370	44250	47380	...	...
4 Electricity, gas and water	880	1110	1430	1360	1600	1780	4400	2960	2710	2850	...	...
5 Construction	10580	10850	13600	14960	12820	15050	16680	21320	28740	35810	...	...
6 Wholesale and retail trade, restaurants and hotels	17480	19480	20830	22620	28040	35770	44110	54720	57290	62250	...	...
7 Transport, storage and communication	10000	15420	17450	16420	19540	21140	26290	29820	40510	43510	...	...
8 Finance, insurance, real estate and business services	11920	13320	16380	16310	19540	20870	28810	27180	33110	35700	...	...
9 Community, social and personal services	5200	6570	7300	7830	8400	9010	9650	10130	10530	11420	...	...
Total, Industries	88630	98790	116370	113690	132160	142450	186310	208080	245820	267700	...	...
Producers of Government Services	19200	26640	28550	29930	36080	37330	41230	44640	49540	54490	...	...
Other Producers	...	...	...	...	...	...	...	...	...	...	...	...
Subtotal a	107830	125430	144920	143620	168240	179780	227540	252720	295360	322190	...	...
Less: Imputed bank service charge	4360	3990	6180	7130	8920	8020	13160	12940	16800	19920		
Plus: Import duties	...	...	...	...	...	...	...	...	...	...	...	...
Plus: Value added tax	...	...	...	...	...	...	...	...	...	...		
Equals: Gross Domestic Product a	103460	121440	138740	136490	159320	171760	214380	239780	278560	302270	...	...

a) Gross domestic product in factor values.

1.11 Gross Domestic Product by Kind of Activity, in Constant Prices

Thousand E.C. dollars

	1980	1981	1982	1983	1984	1985	1986	1987	1988	1989	1990	1991
					At constant prices of:1977							
1 Agriculture, hunting, forestry and fishing	13440	14090	14090	11500	11990	11720	11390	11640	12060	11590	...	...
2 Mining and quarrying	230	240	280	310	260	290	320	370	430	510	...	...
3 Manufacturing	13530	12150	13170	11720	13150	12440	13460	13230	13680	13850	...	...
4 Electricity, gas and water	880	940	1000	1010	1070	1160	1270	1360	1500	1540	...	...
5 Construction	7720	7990	9490	10440	8720	9810	10300	12470	14470	16930	...	...

1.11 Gross Domestic Product by Kind of Activity, in Constant Prices
(Continued)

Thousand E.C. dollars

	1980	1981	1982	1983	1984	1985	1986	1987	1988	1989	1990	1991
	At constant prices of:1977											
6 Wholesale and retail trade, restaurants and hotels	11970	12110	12680	13430	15970	18450	20720	23400	24570	24940	...	...
7 Transport, storage and communication	6880	9290	9410	9640	10480	11460	13740	15220	19050	22140	...	...
8 Finance, insurance, real estate and business services	9780	9760	10580	10750	11360	11870	12630	13070	13540	14050	...	...
9 Community, social and personal services	3750	4290	4500	4720	4950	5200	5460	5680	5510	5680	...	...
Total, Industries	68180	70860	75200	73520	77950	82400	89290	96440	104810	111230	...	...
Producers of Government Services	15690	16580	17750	18500	22400	23520	23330	24390	24640	24810	...	...
Other Producers	...	...	...	...	...	...	...	...	...	...	...	...
Subtotal ᵃ	83870	87440	92950	92020	100350	105920	112620	120830	129450	136040	...	...
Less: Imputed bank service charge	3590	3060	3250	3300	3630	3810	4190	4400	4830	5070	...	...
Plus: Import duties	...	...	...	...	...	...	...	...	...	...	...	...
Plus: Value added tax	...	...	...	...	...	...	...	...	...	...	...	...
Equals: Gross Domestic Product ᵃ ..	80280	84380	89700	88720	96720	102110	108430	116430	124620	130970	...	...

a) Gross domestic product in factor values.

1.12 Relations Among National Accounting Aggregates

Thousand E.C. dollars

	1980	1981	1982	1983	1984	1985	1986	1987	1988	1989	1990	1991
Gross Domestic Product	...	...	158100	154030	167190	...	...	...	...	...	...	...
Plus: Net factor income from the rest of the world	...	...	-9100	-2200	-800	-2200	...	...	...	...	...	...
Equals: Gross National Product	...	...	149000	151830	166390	...	...	...	...	...	...	...
Less: Consumption of fixed capital	...	...	...	...	...	...	...	...	...	...	...	...
Equals: National Income	...	...	...	...	...	...	...	...	...	...	...	...
Plus: Net current transfers from the rest of the world	...	...	35100	30500	31600	...	...	...	...	...	...	...
Equals: National Disposable Income	...	...	...	...	...	...	...	...	...	...	...	...
Less: Final consumption	...	...	...	...	...	...	...	...	...	...	...	...
Equals: Net Saving	...	...	...	...	...	...	...	...	...	...	...	...
Less: Surplus of the nation on current transactions	...	...	...	...	...	...	...	...	...	...	...	...
Equals: Net Capital Formation	...	...	...	...	...	...	...	...	...	...	...	...

Saint Lucia

Source. 'Economic Survey and Projections', British Development Division in the Caribbean.
General note. The estimates shown in the following tables have been prepared in accordance with the United Nations System of National Accounts so far as the existing data would permit.

1.1 Expenditure on the Gross Domestic Product, in Current Prices

Million E.C. dollars

	1980	1981	1982	1983	1984	1985	1986	1987	1988	1989	1990	1991
1 Government final consumption expenditure	59.4	73.4	87.9	97.5	102.7	...	...	...	...	...	...	...
2 Private final consumption expenditure	225.3	280.1	274.6	243.7	266.7	...	...	...	...	...	...	...
3 Gross capital formation	159.1	164.8	145.3	113.8	126.0	...	...	...	...	...	...	...
A Increase in stocks	26.2	27.5	24.2	19.0	21.0	...	...	...	...	...	...	...
B Gross fixed capital formation	132.9	137.3	121.1	94.8	105.0	...	...	...	...	...	...	...
4 Exports of goods and services	213.0	191.7	200.1	241.4	261.4	...	...	...	...	...	...	...
5 Less: Imports of goods and services	351.5	369.1	344.3	316.4	348.6	...	...	...	...	...	...	...
Equals: Gross Domestic Product	305.3	340.9	363.6	380.0	408.2	...	...	...	...	...	...	...

1.10 Gross Domestic Product by Kind of Activity, in Current Prices

Million E.C. dollars

	1980	1981	1982	1983	1984	1985	1986	1987	1988	1989	1990	1991
1 Agriculture, hunting, forestry and fishing	31.0	28.9	36.1	42.3	46.2	58.3	70.7	64.1	...	...	...	...
2 Mining and quarrying	3.9	4.1	3.2	2.2	2.3	2.3	2.5	2.7	...	...	...	...
3 Manufacturing	24.7	25.3	26.8	30.2	31.1	33.0	34.0	35.0	...	...	...	...
4 Electricity, gas and water	5.5	7.3	8.6	11.2	13.6	15.0	16.5	18.5	...	...	...	...
5 Construction	31.5	37.9	33.1	19.6	23.2	27.0	31.9	36.1	...	...	...	...
6 Wholesale and retail trade, restaurants and hotels	67.2	72.9	72.8	75.8	83.0	88.4	94.1	104.4	...	...	...	...
7 Transport, storage and communication	30.9	34.5	35.3	37.6	38.7	40.4	42.2	42.7	...	...	...	...
8 Finance, insurance, real estate and business services	28.9	36.8	40.0	41.5	42.5	43.8	45.2	46.0	...	...	...	...
9 Community, social and personal services	11.4	13.5	14.9	16.2	17.9	19.0	20.5	20.7	...	...	...	...
Total, Industries	235.0	261.2	270.8	276.6	298.5	327.2	357.6	370.2	...	...	...	...
Producers of Government Services	41.2	56.1	62.3	67.8	76.3	84.0	92.0	98.4	...	...	...	...
Other Producers	...	...	...	...	...	...	...	...	...	...	...	...
Subtotal a	276.2	317.3	333.1	344.4	374.8	411.2	449.6	468.6	...	...	...	...
Less: Imputed bank service charge	12.0	17.9	20.6	21.0	21.8	22.4	23.0	23.1	...	...	...	...
Plus: Import duties	...	...	...	...	...	...	...	...	...	...	...	...
Plus: Value added tax	...	...	...	...	...	...	...	...	...	...	...	...
Equals: Gross Domestic Product a	264.2	299.4	312.5	323.4	353.0	388.8	426.6	445.5	...	...	...	...

a) Gross domestic product in factor values.

1.11 Gross Domestic Product by Kind of Activity, in Constant Prices

Million E.C. dollars

	1980	1981	1982	1983	1984	1985	1986	1987	1988	1989	1990	1991
					At constant prices of:1977							
1 Agriculture, hunting, forestry and fishing	22.1	18.8	25.0	28.7	31.0	34.8	39.1	37.4	...	...	...	...
2 Mining and quarrying	3.0	2.8	1.5	0.9	0.9	0.9	1.0	1.1	...	...	...	...
3 Manufacturing	15.5	15.8	17.0	18.8	18.8	19.3	19.6	19.8	...	...	...	...
4 Electricity, gas and water	5.7	5.8	6.0	6.6	7.1	7.6	8.0	8.5	...	...	...	...
5 Construction	18.7	19.8	17.2	9.7	10.9	12.5	14.5	16.4	...	...	...	...
6 Wholesale and retail trade, restaurants and hotels	46.0	44.3	43.5	45.3	48.0	49.6	51.9	53.5	...	...	...	...
7 Transport, storage and communication	19.0	18.7	19.1	22.0	23.0	24.9	27.0	28.5	...	...	...	...
8 Finance, insurance, real estate and business services	20.0	20.9	21.6	22.8	23.1	24.0	24.7	25.3	...	...	...	...
9 Community, social and personal services	7.9	8.2	8.6	9.3	10.0	10.4	10.6	10.9	...	...	...	...

1.11 Gross Domestic Product by Kind of Activity, in Constant Prices
(Continued)

Million E.C. dollars

	1980	1981	1982	1983	1984	1985	1986	1987	1988	1989	1990	1991
					At constant prices of:1977							
Total, Industries	157.9	155.1	159.5	164.1	172.8	184.0	196.4	201.4	...	...	...	...
Producers of Government Services	32.8	38.7	39.9	43.4	44.8	46.4	47.1	47.2	...	...	...	...
Other Producers	...	...	...	...	...	...	...	...	...	...	...	...
Subtotal a	190.7	193.8	199.4	207.5	217.6	230.4	243.5	248.6	...	...	...	...
Less: Imputed bank service charge	8.6	9.2	9.5	9.9	10.1	10.5	10.8	11.0	...	...	...	...
Plus: Import duties	...	...	...	...	...	...	...	...	...	...	...	...
Plus: Value added tax	...	...	...	...	...	...	...	...	...	...	...	...
Equals: Gross Domestic Product a ..	182.1	184.3	189.9	197.6	207.5	219.9	232.7	237.7	...	...	...	...

a) Gross domestic product in factor values.

Saint Vincent and the Grenadines

Source. 'The preparation of national accounts statistics in St. Vincent and the Grenadines is undertaken by the Statistical Office, Ministry of Finance, Planning and Development, Kingstown. The official estimates together with a description of the sources and methods used for the national accounts estimation are published in 'National Accounts of St. Vincent and the Grenadines'.

General note. The estimates shown in the following tables have been prepared in accordance with the United Nations System of National Accounts so far as the existing data would permit.

1.1 Expenditure on the Gross Domestic Product, in Current Prices

Million E.C. dollars

	1980	1981	1982	1983	1984	1985	1986	1987	1988	1989	1990	1991
1 Government final consumption expenditure	37.4	46.8	54.0	58.3	62.9	60.2	67.8	76.6	80.3	92.0	93.6	...
2 Private final consumption expenditure	140.2	147.9	177.4	195.4	175.6	175.7	197.5	250.3	252.8	349.3	352.9	...
3 Gross capital formation	62.8	64.2	64.7	62.9	77.4	86.1	101.7	124.9	134.6	138.0	166.2	...
A Increase in stocks	-	-	-	-	6.9	9.9	2.8	9.9	13.6	12.5	7.1	...
B Gross fixed capital formation	62.8	64.2	64.7	62.9	70.5	76.2	98.9	115.0	121.0	125.5	159.1	...
Residential buildings										...	...	
Non-residential buildings	40.5	46.6	45.7	41.7	37.7	44.1	64.7	71.5	75.4	81.4	...	
Other construction and land improvement etc.										...	...	
Other	22.3	17.6	19.0	21.2	39.7	42.0	37.0	53.4	59.2	56.6	...	
4 Exports of goods and services	89.5	116.0	135.9	155.7	193.0	222.5	257.2	245.2	334.6	299.5	370.5	...
5 Less: Imports of goods and services	170.9	178.8	204.7	217.5	231.6	239.9	280.7	313.3	368.6	409.4	458.2	...
Equals: Gross Domestic Product	159.7	196.1	227.3	254.8	277.3	304.6	343.7	383.7	433.7	469.4	524.9	...

1.7 External Transactions on Current Account, Summary

Million E.C. dollars

	1980	1981	1982	1983	1984	1985	1986	1987	1988	1989	1990	1991
Payments to the Rest of the World												
1 Imports of goods and services	...	...	...	...	...	...	280.7	313.3	368.6	409.5	...	...
A Imports of merchandise c.i.f.	...	...	...	...	...	...	235.6	266.4	330.1	344.2	...	...
B Other	...	...	...	...	...	...	45.1	46.9	38.5	65.3	...	...
2 Factor income to the rest of the world	...	...	...	...	...	...	17.3	19.1	26.7	31.0	...	...
A Compensation of employees	...	...	...	...	...	...	-	-	-	-	...	...
B Property and entrepreneurial income	...	...	...	...	...	...	17.3	19.1	26.7	31.0	...	...
By general government	...	...	...	...	...	...	3.0	2.2	2.7	4.5	...	...
By corporate and quasi-corporate enterprises	...	...	...	...	...	...	2.1	2.3	1.3	2.7	...	...
By other	...	...	...	...	...	...	12.2	14.6	22.7	23.8	...	...
3 Current transfers to the rest of the world	...	...	...	...	...	...	21.0	11.0	12.3	11.1	...	...
A Indirect taxes to supranational organizations	...	...	...	...	...	...	2.6	2.3	6.7	5.0	...	...
B Other current transfers	...	...	...	...	...	...	18.4	8.7	5.6	6.1	...	...
4 Surplus of the nation on current transactions	...	...	...	...	...	...	21.4	-41.7	-28.5	-44.3	...	...
Payments to the Rest of the World and Surplus of the Nation on Current Transactions	...	...	...	...	...	...	340.4	301.7	379.1	407.3	...	...
Receipts From The Rest of the World												
1 Exports of goods and services	...	...	...	...	...	...	257.2	246.8	334.6	299.5	...	...
A Exports of merchandise f.o.b.	...	...	...	...	...	...	172.4	141.3	230.2	201.4	...	...

1.7 External Transactions on Current Account, Summary
(Continued)

Million E.C. dollars

	1980	1981	1982	1983	1984	1985	1986	1987	1988	1989	1990	1991
B Other	...	...	...	...	...	...	84.8	105.5	104.4	98.1	...	...
2 Factor income from rest of the world	...	...	...	...	...	...	8.1	7.1	7.8	10.0	...	...
A Compensation of employees	...	...	...	...	...	...	-	-	-	-	...	...
B Property and entrepreneurial income	...	...	...	...	...	...	8.1	7.1	7.8	10.0	...	...
By general government	...	...	...	...	...	...	3.3	2.8	1.9	1.3	...	...
By corporate and quasi-corporate enterprises	...	...	...	...	...	...	2.4	4.3	5.9	8.7	...	...
By other	...	...	...	...	...	...	2.4	-	-	-	...	...
3 Current transfers from rest of the world	...	...	...	...	...	...	75.1	47.8	36.7	97.8	...	...
A Subsidies from supranational organisations	...	...	...	...	...	...	21.1	20.2	4.3	28.9	...	...
B Other current transfers	...	...	...	...	...	...	54.0	27.6	32.4	68.9	...	...
Statistical discrepancy	...	...	...	...	...	...	-	-	-	-	...	...
Receipts from the Rest of the World on Current Transactions	...	...	...	...	...	...	340.4	301.7	379.1	407.3	...	...

1.10 Gross Domestic Product by Kind of Activity, in Current Prices

Million E.C. dollars

	1980	1981	1982	1983	1984	1985	1986	1987	1988	1989	1990	1991
1 Agriculture, hunting, forestry and fishing	19.8	27.5	31.9	36.6	43.2	49.5	54.8	54.2	65.1	67.9	...	...
2 Mining and quarrying	0.5	0.6	0.6	0.6	0.5	0.5	0.8	0.9	1.0	1.0	...	...
3 Manufacturing	14.5	18.8	21.2	21.7	29.5	29.3	29.4	32.7	38.2	43.0	...	...
4 Electricity, gas and water	3.4	4.6	5.5	7.0	7.6	10.0	10.0	13.5	17.7	19.0	...	...
5 Construction	18.4	20.6	21.8	23.2	16.6	19.4	28.5	31.5	33.3	35.9	...	...
6 Wholesale and retail trade, restaurants and hotels	20.3	22.1	26.7	28.9	30.7	33.7	37.2	42.4	46.2	51.9	...	...
7 Transport, storage and communication	23.8	29.2	34.6	37.9	41.3	46.5	53.4	61.2	70.9	79.5	...	...
8 Finance, insurance, real estate and business services	15.1	18.3	20.5	22.9	27.1	26.0	29.4	32.1	34.8	42.6	...	...
9 Community, social and personal services	4.6	5.3	5.7	6.1	6.4	6.5	6.7	7.0	7.2	7.5	...	...
Total, Industries	120.4	147.0	168.5	184.9	202.9	221.4	250.2	275.5	314.4	348.3	...	...
Producers of Government Services	22.6	29.4	32.9	39.5	41.5	42.9	46.5	55.6	59.7	67.5	...	...
Other Producers	...	...	...	...	...	...	...	...	...	...	...	...
Subtotal a	143.0	176.4	201.4	224.4	244.4	264.3	296.7	331.1	374.1	415.8	...	...
Less: Imputed bank service charge	7.4	8.5	10.8	11.7	11.9	12.0	13.0	13.0	15.5	25.4	...	...
Plus: Import duties	...	...	...	...	...	...	...	...	...	...	...	...
Plus: Value added tax	...	...	...	...	...	...	...	...	...	...	...	...
Plus: Other adjustments b	24.2	28.2	36.8	42.2	44.7	52.3	58.9	65.7	75.3	79.0	...	...
Equals: Gross Domestic Product	159.8	196.1	227.4	254.9	277.2	304.6	342.6	383.8	433.9	469.4	...	...

a) Gross domestic product in factor values.
b) Item 'Other adjustments' refers to indirect taxes net of subsidies.

1.11 Gross Domestic Product by Kind of Activity, in Constant Prices

Million E.C. dollars

	1980	1981	1982	1983	1984	1985	1986	1987	1988	1989	1990	1991
					At constant prices of:1977							
1 Agriculture, hunting, forestry and fishing	12.5	17.7	18.7	20.2	21.5	23.3	24.2	23.1	28.9	29.2	...	...
2 Mining and quarrying	0.3	0.3	0.3	0.3	0.3	0.4	0.4	0.4	0.5	0.5	...	...
3 Manufacturing	11.4	11.6	12.2	12.6	13.6	13.8	14.6	16.0	16.8	18.9	...	...
4 Electricity, gas and water	3.3	3.4	3.8	3.8	4.1	4.3	4.7	5.3	5.9	6.0	...	...
5 Construction	11.2	11.4	11.5	12.2	12.1	12.4	14.3	16.1	16.7	17.9	...	...
6 Wholesale and retail trade, restaurants and hotels	15.7	14.3	16.1	16.6	17.2	18.5	20.3	22.4	23.9	25.9	...	...
7 Transport, storage and communication	19.8	21.7	23.4	26.0	27.7	29.3	31.9	34.9	38.2	43.8	...	...
8 Finance, insurance, real estate and business services	9.2	9.7	9.6	9.9	10.7	10.1	10.6	10.5	10.2	11.6	...	...
9 Community, social and personal services	3.1	3.2	3.4	3.4	3.5	3.5	3.6	3.6	3.7	3.7	...	...

Saint Vincent and the Grenadines

1.11 Gross Domestic Product by Kind of Activity, in Constant Prices
(Continued)

Million E.C. dollars

	1980	1981	1982	1983	1984	1985	1986	1987	1988	1989	1990	1991
					At constant prices of:1977							
Total, Industries	86.5	93.3	99.0	105.0	110.7	115.6	124.6	132.3	144.8	157.5	...	...
Producers of Government Services	17.1	17.5	17.5	17.8	18.4	18.9	19.5	20.1	20.6	21.2	...	...
Other Producers	...	...	...	...	...	...	...	...	...	...	...	...
Subtotal a	103.6	110.8	116.5	122.8	129.1	134.5	144.1	152.4	165.4	178.7	...	...
Less: Imputed bank service charge	4.3	4.2	4.4	4.3	3.9	3.8	3.8	3.3	3.3	5.2	...	...
Plus: Import duties	...	...	...	...	...	...	...	...	...	...	...	...
Plus: Value added tax	...	...	...	...	...	...	...	...	...	...	...	...
Equals: Gross Domestic Product a ..	99.3	106.6	112.1	118.5	125.2	130.7	140.3	149.1	162.1	173.5	...	...

a) Gross domestic product in factor values.

1.12 Relations Among National Accounting Aggregates

Million E.C. dollars

	1980	1981	1982	1983	1984	1985	1986	1987	1988	1989	1990	1991
Gross Domestic Product	159.7	196.1	227.4	254.9	277.2	304.6	343.5	383.7	433.7	469.4	...	...
Plus: Net factor income from the rest of the world	-2.4	-4.6	-7.3	-6.2	-8.1	-5.1	-9.2	-12.0	-18.9	-21.0	...	...
Factor income from the rest of the world	...	...	...	...	...	...	8.1	7.1	7.8	10.0	...	...
Less: Factor income to the rest of the world	...	...	...	...	...	...	17.3	19.1	26.7	31.0	...	...
Equals: Gross National Product	157.3	191.5	220.1	248.7	269.1	299.5	334.3	371.7	414.8	448.4	...	...
Less: Consumption of fixed capital	...	...	...	...	...	...	...	...	...	...	...	...
Equals: National Income	...	...	...	...	...	...	...	...	...	...	...	...
Plus: Net current transfers from the rest of the world	...	...	...	...	...	...	...	...	...	...	...	...
Equals: National Disposable Income	...	...	...	...	...	...	...	...	...	...	...	...
Less: Final consumption	...	...	...	...	...	...	...	...	...	...	...	...
Equals: Net Saving	...	...	...	...	...	...	...	...	...	...	...	...
Less: Surplus of the nation on current transactions	...	...	...	...	...	...	...	...	...	...	...	...
Equals: Net Capital Formation	...	...	...	...	...	...	...	...	...	...	...	...

2.1 Government Final Consumption Expenditure by Function, in Current Prices

Million E.C. dollars   Fiscal year beginning 1 July

	1980	1981	1982	1983	1984	1985	1986	1987	1988	1989	1990	1991
1 General public services	4.1	4.8	5.0	6.4	5.1	5.8	5.0	4.9	...	...	...	...
2 Defence	-	-	-	-	-	-	-	-	...	...	...	...
3 Public order and safety	4.4	5.9	6.4	7.6	7.4	8.1	8.9	9.9	...	...	...	...
4 Education	9.3	13.2	13.8	16.1	15.7	16.6	19.0	20.5	...	...	...	...
5 Health	6.0	8.3	9.4	10.9	11.4	11.7	13.5	15.7	...	...	...	...
6 Social security and welfare	2.2	2.7	3.1	3.4	3.4	4.3	4.4	4.7	...	...	...	...
7 Housing and community amenities	1.4	2.2	2.4	3.0	0.7	0.8	1.5	2.0	...	...	...	...
8 Recreational, cultural and religious affairs	-	-	-	-	-	-	-	-	...	...	...	...
9 Economic services	11.8	16.7	14.1	15.1	13.7	15.2	17.2	18.5	...	...	...	...
A Fuel and energy	...	...	...	...	...	...	...	...	...	...	...	...
B Agriculture, forestry, fishing and hunting	2.2	2.5	2.7	3.0	2.9	3.1	3.5	3.8	...	...	...	...
C Mining, manufacturing and construction, except fuel and energy	9.5	13.0	10.3	11.1	9.0	9.2	10.7	12.7	...	...	...	...
D Transportation and communication	-	-	-	-	-	-	-	-	...	...	...	...
E Other economic affairs	0.1	0.2	1.1	1.0	1.8	2.9	3.0	2.0	...	...	...	...
10 Other functions	...	...	...	...	...	...	...	...	...	...	...	...
Total Government Final Consumption Expenditure	39.2	53.8	54.2	62.5	57.4	62.5	69.5	76.2	...	...	...	...

Sao Tome and Principe

Source. National Accounts estimates are published in 'Comptes Nationaux'.
General note. The estimates shown in the following tables have been adjusted by the United Nations Statistical Office to conform to the United Nations System of National Accounts so far as the existing data would permit.

1.1 Expenditure on the Gross Domestic Product, in Current Prices

Million Sao Tome and Principe dobras

	1980	1981	1982	1983	1984	1985	1986	1987	1988	1989	1990	1991
1 Government final consumption expenditure	440.0	516.0	611.0	692.0	769.0	621.1	751.8	744.8	893.1	...	...	...
2 Private final consumption expenditure	1296.0	1277.0	1230.0	1091.0	1130.0	...	1884.3	1895.7	3032.2	...	...	...
3 Gross capital formation	550.0	360.0	646.0	899.0	426.0	...	358.2	493.6	662.0	...	...	...
A Increase in stocks	...	...	...	...	...	...	21.2	31.8	-	...	...	...
B Gross fixed capital formation	...	...	...	...	...	...	337.0	461.8	662.0	...	...	...
4 Exports of goods and services	624.0	307.0	400.0	406.0	589.0		...	...	...	...	...	...
5 Less: Imports of goods and services	1285.0	1050.0	1138.0	965.0	1305.0	...	1258.4	1293.5	2818.5	...	...	...
Equals: Gross Domestic Product	1625.0	1410.0	1549.0	1523.0	1609.0	...	2477.7	3003.4	4220.9	...	...	...

1.10 Gross Domestic Product by Kind of Activity, in Current Prices

Million Sao Tome and Principe dobras

	1980	1981	1982	1983	1984	1985	1986	1987	1988	1989	1990	1991
1 Agriculture, hunting, forestry and fishing	580.0	420.0	379.0	454.0	379.0	...	659.2	882.2	1219.7	...	...	...
2 Mining and quarrying	4.0	4.0	4.0	4.0	4.0	...	...	...	...	...	...	...
3 Manufacturing	118.0	95.0	112.0	130.0	142.0	...	51.8	37.3	65.6	...	...	...
4 Electricity, gas and water	31.0	32.0	37.0	40.0	46.0	...	6.6	39.6	39.0	...	...	...
5 Construction	105.0	118.0	156.0	114.0	137.0	...	77.3	106.4	159.3	...	...	...
6 Wholesale and retail trade, restaurants and hotels	90.0	76.0	106.0	114.0	142.0	...	438.2	478.0	715.2	...	...	...
7 Transport, storage and communication	106.0	90.0	125.0	133.0	166.0	...	119.6	156.5	154.5	...	...	...
8 Finance, insurance, real estate and business services	16.0	15.0	18.0	15.9	19.0	...	25.2	53.9	95.0	...	...	...
9 Community, social and personal services	...	...	...	...	...	...	24.0	26.9	32.5	...	...	...
Total, Industries	1050.0	850.0	937.0	1004.9	1035.0	...	1401.9	1780.8	2480.8	...	...	...
Producers of Government Services	248.0	281.0	331.0	381.0	418.0	...	632.8	751.6	972.4	...	...	...
Other Producers	...	...	...	...	...	...	224.6	265.0	347.1	...	...	...
Subtotal	1298.0	1131.0	1268.0	1385.9	1453.0	...	2259.3	2797.4	3800.3	...	...	...
Less: Imputed bank service charge	...	...	...	...	...	...	...	...	...	...	...	...
Plus: Import duties	...	...	...	...	...	...	218.4	206.0	420.6	...	...	...
Plus: Value added tax	...	...	...	...	...	...	...	...	...	...	...	...
Plus: Other adjustments	327.0	279.0	281.0	138.0	156.0	...	...	...	...	...	...	...
Equals: Gross Domestic Product	1625.0	1410.0	1549.0	1523.0	1609.0	...	2477.7	3003.4	4220.9	...	...	...

Saudi Arabia

General note. The preparation of national accounts statistics in Saudi Arabia is undertaken by the Central Department of Statistics, Ministry of Finance and National Economy, Riyadh. The official estimates are published in the National Income Series entitled 'National Accounts of Saudi Arabia'. The most detailed description of the sources and methods used for the national accounts estimation is found in 'National Accounts of Saudi Arabia 1386-87 through 1391-92, A.H.' published in 1973. The estimates are generally in accordance with the classifications and definitions recommended in the United Nations System of National Accounts (SNA). The following tables have been prepared from successive replies to the United Nations national accounts questionnaire. The national accounts estimates shown relate to Hejra fiscal years. A Hejra fiscal year covers the period from the beginning of the seventh month of one Hejra calendar year through the end of the sixth month of the following year. When the scope and coverage of the estimates differ for conceptual or statistical reasons from the definitions and classifications recommended in SNA, a footnote is indicated to the relevant tables.

Sources and methods :

(a) Gross domestic product. Gross domestic product is estimated mainly through the production approach.

(b) Expenditure on the gross domestic product. All components of GDP by expenditure type are estimated through the expenditure approach except private final consumption expenditure and gross fixed capital formation of private transport establishments which are estimated by using the commodity-flow approach. Government consumption expenditure is calculated as the sum of compensation of employees and net current purchases of goods and services. Data are obtained from the appropriations in the government budget rather than from actual expenditure data. The estimates are, however, adjusted for under-spending. Estimates of private consumption expenditure are based on imports in c.i.f. values and gross output of domestically produced goods and services. Import duties are based on the customs tariffs whereas transport and distribution margins are based on assumed margin rates. In order to estimate the gross fixed capital formation of transport establishments, a detailed classification of import statistics is used to estimate the capital formation in transport equipment. For general government, public enterprises and private industries the estimates are based on surveys of industrial production, which include information on fixed assets. Gross capital formation of the oil sector is based on data provided by the oil companies through their annual returns. Exports of crude petroleum and petroleum products constitute over 99 per cent of total exports of merchandise. The data are obtained from annual returns of the oil companies. Non-petroleum exports and imports of merchandise are obtained from foreign trade statistics and balance of payment estimates. GDP by expenditure type at constant prices is not estimated.

(c) Cost-structure of the gross domestic product. Compensation of employees for the crude petroleum and petroleum refining industries is obtained from the annual returns provided by the oil companies. For most of the other industries, the estimates are determined on the basis of an estimated ratio of wages to gross output. Estimates of indirect taxes are made from revenue figures of the central and local

governments while subsidies are calculated from information supplied by the Ministry of Finance. Gross operating surplus, including depreciation, is estimated as a residual.

(d) Gross domestic product by kind of economic activity. The table of GDP by kind of economic activity is prepared at market prices, i.e. producers' values. The production approach is used to estimate value added of the majority of industries. The income approach is used for mining other than extraction of crude petroleum and natural gas, mechanized road transport, ownership of dwellings, domestic services and producers of government services. For the agricultural sector, bench-mark estimates for 1967-68 on gross output and intermediate consumption were prepared based on the results of agricultural surveys conducted in the period 1960-1965. Other years' estimates are calculated by multiplying the 1967-68 figures by index numbers of physical output and producers' prices. The extraction of crude petroleum and natural gas are undertaken by Aramco, Getty, and Arabian Oil Company. The annual returns from these companies and from the Saudi Arabian Oil refineries provide details on sales, costs and capital expenditures which enable the calculation of gross output, intermediate consumption and compensation of employees for mining, manufacturing of petroleum products and construction. Internal prices of the oil companies are used for the calculation of sales figures and not the 'posted' prices which are used for calculating the payment of income tax. For other manufacturing, electricity, non-residential building construction, trade, water transport, financial services other than commercial banks, real estate, business services and private services, the estimates on gross output, intermediate consumption and compensation of employees for 1970 are available from the sample survey of establishments in 1971. Other years' estimates are calculated by multiplying the bench-mark year figures by quantity indexes, price indexes or assumed growth rates. Estimates on construction for the government sector are based on details of government appropriations. For the private sector, the value of construction of dwellings is derived by multiplying the estimated number of dwellings constructed by the estimated cost of construction per dwelling. For mechanized road transport, the estimated number of vehicles is multiplied by an estimated value added per vehicle while for the airlines, railways and the Tapline annual returns from the companies concerned provide data on gross output, intermediate consumption and compensation of employees. Commercial banks' figures for 1970 are obtained from a survey of the operations of commercial banks. An estimated index of growth of banking services is applied for other years. Estimates of government services are derived from a classification of government appropriations shown in the budget volumes. For the constant price estimates, the value added of the agricultural sector, manufacturing, electricity, trade, transport and other services is extrapolated by quantity indexes. Value added of crude petroleum and petroleum refining is extrapolated by quantity indexes compiled from figures on barrels produced. Different kinds of price indexes such as index of wage rates and cost of living index are used to deflate the value added of construction and the financial sectors.

1.1 Expenditure on the Gross Domestic Product, in Current Prices

Million Saudi Arabia riyals — Fiscal year beginning 1 July

	1980	1981	1982	1983	1984	1985	1986	1987	1988	1989	1990	1991
1 Government final consumption expenditure	82878	116115	131066	126568	121055	114388	106367	107707	97420	96560	...	...
2 Private final consumption expenditure	108563	131145	151218	159369	159354	158592	140148	135539	139400	145030	...	...
3 Gross capital formation	101593	109877	114831	129039	116095	65690	53826	52331	59650	67170	...	...
A Increase in stocks a	-1622	-10466	-4151	19637	19602	-10624	-12318	-12871	2730	6760	...	...
B Gross fixed capital formation b	103215	120343	118982	109402	96493	76314	66144	65202	56920	60410	...	...
4 Exports of goods and services	347345	391591	266511	171681	145530	113163	85989	99045	103079	118210	...	...
5 Less: Imports of goods and services	149437	187591	205502	212775	190639	137892	115239	119170	114400	116150	...	...
Equals: Gross Domestic Product c	490942	561136	458124	373882	351397	313941	271091	275452	285150	310820	...	...

a) Item 'Increase in stocks' includes a statistical discrepancy.
b) Beginning 1974, item 'gross capital formation' includes other not classified capital goods.

c) Data in this table have been revised, therefore they are not strictly comparable with the unrevised data in the other tables.

1.3 Cost Components of the Gross Domestic Product

Million Saudi Arabia riyals — Fiscal year beginning 1 July

	1980	1981	1982	1983	1984	1985	1986	1987	1988	1989	1990	1991
1 Indirect taxes, net	-2144	-3547	-7217	-5852	-5210	-5649	-5975	-4667	-620	...	...	...
2 Consumption of fixed capital a	...	...	...	...	...	...	...	...	...	...	...	...
3 Compensation of employees paid by resident producers to:	87748	107427	122577	128378	131300	133173	128422	126656	129810	...	...	...
4 Operating surplus a	405338	457256	342764	251356	225307	186417	148644	153464	152781	...	...	...
Equals: Gross Domestic Product	490942	561136	458124	373882	351397	313941	271091	275453	281971	...	...	...

a) Item 'Operating surplus' includes consumption of fixed capital.

1.7 External Transactions on Current Account, Summary

Million Saudi Arabia riyals

Fiscal year beginning 1 July

	1980	1981	1982	1983	1984	1985	1986	1987	1988	1989	1990	1991
Payments to the Rest of the World												
1 Imports of goods and services	157500	187700	181300	175900	159400	...	...	...	...	...	...	...
2 Factor income to the rest of the world	46400	39600	32900	31300	30300	...	...	...	...	...	...	...
A Compensation of employees	13900	18300	18100	18600	18400	...	...	...	...	...	...	...
B Property and entrepreneurial income	32500	21300	14800	12700	11900	...	...	...	...	...	...	...
3 Current transfers to the rest of the world	19300	...	...	...	...	...	...	...	...	...	...	...
4 Surplus of the nation on current transactions	182300	175800	60000	8300	-10300	...	...	...	...	...	...	...
Payments to the Rest of the World and Surplus of the Nation on Current Transactions	405500	403100	274200	215500	179400	...	...	...	...	...	...	...
Receipts From The Rest of the World												
1 Exports of goods and services	368400	354900	219400	168400	134700	...	...	...	...	...	...	...
2 Factor income from rest of the world	37100	48200	54800	47100	44700	...	...	...	...	...	...	...
A Compensation of employees	-	-	-	-	-	...	...	...	...	...	...	...
B Property and entrepreneurial income	37100	48200	54800	47100	44700	...	...	...	...	...	...	...
3 Current transfers from rest of the world	...	...	...	...	...	...	...	...	...	...	...	...
Receipts from the Rest of the World on Current Transactions	405500	403100	274200	215500	179400	...	...	...	...	...	...	...

1.10 Gross Domestic Product by Kind of Activity, in Current Prices

Million Saudi Arabia riyals

Fiscal year beginning 1 July

	1980	1981	1982	1983	1984	1985	1986	1987	1988	1989	1990	1991
1 Agriculture, hunting, forestry and fishing	5399	6255	8372	9643	11620	13789	15861	18312	20695	...	...	...
2 Mining and quarrying	324671	357669	237870	145714	122169	90098	63020	65113	63466	...	...	...
3 Manufacturing	19516	26520	21670	23604	27421	24499	19722	23852	24740	...	...	...
4 Electricity, gas and water	362	458	-454	-295	-586	301	523	681	722	...	...	...
5 Construction	47991	57525	57435	52479	44964	38745	33989	33250	31594	...	...	...
6 Wholesale and retail trade, restaurants and hotels	21287	26099	29018	30268	30386	30222	29072	27797	26654	...	...	...
7 Transport, storage and communication	17154	19980	22019	23210	23844	23719	22783	22087	22709	...	...	...
8 Finance, insurance, real estate and business services	21662	25849	30123	32298	30500	27184	22458	21472	22249	...	...	...
9 Community, social and personal services	5587	6904	8511	9292	9704	11033	10584	10507	10986	...	...	...
Total, Industries	463629	527259	414564	326213	300022	259590	218012	223071	223815	...	...	...
Producers of Government Services	14559	17378	22722	24950	26417	27757	27336	26792	27650	...	...	...
Other Producers	13818	17821	21954	23569	25655	27214	26802	26269	27108	...	...	...
Subtotal	492006	562458	459240	374732	352094	314561	272150	276132	278573	...	...	...
Less: Imputed bank service charge	3597	3960	4364	4526	4670	4529	4304	4132	4104	...	...	...
Plus: Import duties	2534	2637	3248	3677	3973	3910	3245	3453	7500	...	...	...
Plus: Value added tax	...	...	...	...	...	...	...	...	...	...	...	...
Equals: Gross Domestic Product	490943	561136	458124	373882	351398	313941	271091	275453	281971	...	...	...

1.11 Gross Domestic Product by Kind of Activity, in Constant Prices

Million Saudi Arabia riyals

Fiscal year beginning 1 July

	1980	1981	1982	1983	1984	1985	1986	1987	1988	1989	1990	1991
At constant prices of:1979												
1 Agriculture, hunting, forestry and fishing	4900	5200	5700	6200	6300	...	...	...	...	...	...	...
2 Mining and quarrying	248000	223900	134000	116700	96700	...	...	...	...	...	...	...
3 Manufacturing	20700	22100	24200	27400	27000	...	...	...	...	...	...	...
4 Electricity, gas and water	300	-400	-500	600	600	...	...	...	...	...	...	...
5 Construction	47500	52300	49100	45300	41200	...	...	...	...	...	...	...

1.11 Gross Domestic Product by Kind of Activity, in Constant Prices
(Continued)

Million Saudi Arabia riyals   Fiscal year beginning 1 July

	1980	1981	1982	1983	1984	1985	1986	1987	1988	1989	1990	1991
					At constant prices of:1979							
6 Wholesale and retail trade, restaurants and hotels	21000	24200	27300	27800	27600	...	...	...	...	...	...	...
7 Transport, storage and communication	17100	18500	20100	22400	22200	...	...	...	...	...	...	...
8 Finance, insurance, real estate and business services	20500	22200	23700	24100	23300	...	...	...	...	...	...	...
9 Community, social and personal services	5700	6300	6700	6700	6500	...	...	...	...	...	...	...
Total, Industries	385800	374300	290300	277200	251300	...	...	...	...	...	...	...
Producers of Government Services	25800	27600	29600	30400	32000	...	...	...	...	...	...	...
Other Producers	...	...	...	...	...	...	...	...	...	...	...	...
Subtotal	411500	401900	319900	307600	283400	...	...	...	...	...	...	...
Less: Imputed bank service charge	4100	4300	4500	4500	4600	...	...	...	...	...	...	...
Plus: Import duties	2200	1900	2200	2100	1900	...	...	...	...	...	...	...
Plus: Value added tax	...	...	...	...	...	...	...	...	...	...	...	...
Equals: Gross Domestic Product	409700	399500	317600	305100	280600	...	...	...	...	...	...	...

1.12 Relations Among National Accounting Aggregates

Million Saudi Arabia riyals   Fiscal year beginning 1 July

	1980	1981	1982	1983	1984	1985	1986	1987	1988	1989	1990	1991
Gross Domestic Product	520500	524700	415200	371200	330900	...	...	...	...	...	...	...
Plus: Net factor income from the rest of the world	-9300	8600	21900	15800	14400	...	...	...	...	...	...	...
Factor income from the rest of the world	37100	48200	54800	47100	44700	...	...	...	...	...	...	...
Less: Factor income to the rest of the world	46400	39600	32900	31300	30300	...	...	...	...	...	...	...
Equals: Gross National Product	511200	533300	437100	387000	345300	...	...	...	...	...	...	...
Less: Consumption of fixed capital	...	...	...	...	...	...	...	...	...	...	...	...
Equals: National Income [a]	511200	533300	437100	387000	345300	...	...	...	...	...	...	...
Plus: Net current transfers from the rest of the world	-19300	...	...	...	...	...	...	...	...	...	...	...
Current transfers from the rest of the world	...	...	...	...	...	...	...	...	...	...	...	...
Less: Current transfers to the rest of the world	19300	...	...	...	...	...	...	...	...	...	...	...
Equals: National Disposable Income [b]	491900	533300	437100	387000	345300	...	...	...	...	...	...	...
Less: Final consumption	196800	255000	264200	265300	261600	...	...	...	...	...	...	...
Equals: Net Saving [c]	295100	278300	172900	121700	83700	...	...	...	...	...	...	...
Less: Surplus of the nation on current transactions	182300	175800	60000	8300	-10300	...	...	...	...	...	...	...
Equals: Net Capital Formation [d]	112800	102500	112900	113400	94000	...	...	...	...	...	...	...

a) Item 'National income' includes consumption of fixed capital.
b) Item 'National disposable income' includes consumption of fixed capital.
c) Item 'Net saving' includes consumption of fixed capital.
d) Item 'Net capital formation' includes consumption of fixed capital.

Senegal

Source. Reply to the United Nations National Accounts Questionnaire from the Direction de la Statistique, Dakar.
General note. The estimates shown in the following tables have been adjusted by the United Nations Statistical Office to conform to the United Nations System of National Accounts so far as the existing data would permit.

1.1 Expenditure on the Gross Domestic Product, in Current Prices

Thousand Million CFA francs

	1980	1981	1982	1983	1984	1985	1986	1987	1988	1989	1990	1991
1 Government final consumption expenditure	128.2	137.6	154.5	170.3	188.8	194.5	200.8	215.6	218.1	227.5	...	...
2 Private final consumption expenditure	524.3	586.4	702.7	778.0	809.6	980.4	1029.5	1082.4	1154.5	1163.6	...	...
3 Gross capital formation	70.7	80.0	95.8	112.2	119.4	113.5	142.5	161.8	185.3	161.1	...	...
A Increase in stocks	-11.9	-4.5	-6.9	-10.1	-5.8	-19.5	-12.5	-9.1	-	-23.4	...	...
B Gross fixed capital formation	82.6	84.5	102.7	122.3	125.2	133.0	155.0	170.9	185.3	184.5	...	...
4 Exports of goods and services	176.1	216.4	290.5	311.1	387.4	343.9	345.6	345.5	373.3	397.3	...	...
5 Less: Imports of goods and services	267.9	346.6	394.6	426.9	484.1	474.1	416.2	423.1	447.9	474.1	...	...
Equals: Gross Domestic Product	631.4	673.7	848.8	944.7	1021.3	1158.1	1302.9	1382.3	1483.3	1475.4	...	...

1.2 Expenditure on the Gross Domestic Product, in Constant Prices

Thousand Million CFA francs

	1980	1981	1982	1983	1984	1985	1986	1987	1988	1989	1990	1991
					At constant prices of:1987							
1 Government final consumption expenditure	168.7	168.9	176.5	183.8	189.3	194.2	206.4	215.6	216.3	215.8	...	...
2 Private final consumption expenditure	919.2	948.7	988.2	989.9	961.4	1054.7	1044.2	1073.1	1121.7	1145.7	...	...
3 Gross capital formation	114.2	108.4	139.0	148.3	140.5	120.5	157.4	171.2	178.4	153.1	...	...
A Increase in stocks	-19.2	-13.2	9.0	8.6	6.6	-13.6	-4.1	0.3	-	-23.1	...	...
B Gross fixed capital formation	133.4	121.6	130.0	139.7	133.9	134.1	161.5	170.9	178.4	176.2	...	...
4 Exports of goods and services	253.5	252.4	336.9	341.3	351.3	295.6	340.4	345.4	362.7	356.7	...	...
5 Less: Imports of goods and services	360.1	393.2	390.3	387.2	417.5	393.8	418.6	423.1	426.7	441.2	...	...
Equals: Gross Domestic Product	1095.8	1082.8	1248.9	1276.1	1225.0	1271.3	1329.2	1382.3	1452.4	1430.1	...	...

1.3 Cost Components of the Gross Domestic Product

Thousand Million CFA francs

	1980	1981	1982	1983	1984	1985	1986	1987	1988	1989	1990	1991
1 Indirect taxes, net	95.2	113.7	...	...	...	...	...	...	...	...	...	...
2 Consumption of fixed capital	41.9	46.8	...	...	...	...	...	...	...	...	...	...
3 Compensation of employees paid by resident producers to:	...	...	...	...	...	...	...	...	...	...	...	...
A Resident households	...	...	10.9	12.0	13.1	14.5	16.3	17.6	19.1	...	...	...
B Rest of the world	...	...	...	...	...	...	...	...	...	...	...	...
4 Operating surplus	...	...	...	...	...	...	...	...	...	...	...	...
Equals: Gross Domestic Product	627.5	669.8	844.3	924.9	1015.5	1152.0	1307.0	1374.6	1558.1	...	...	...

1.7 External Transactions on Current Account, Summary

Thousand Million CFA francs

	1980	1981	1982	1983	1984	1985	1986	1987	1988	1989	1990	1991
					Payments to the Rest of the World							
1 Imports of goods and services	278.4	...	...	...	...	...	...	...	...	...	...	...
2 Factor income to the rest of the world	22.6	...	...	...	...	...	...	...	...	...	...	...
A Compensation of employees	7.4	...	...	...	...	...	...	...	...	...	...	...
B Property and entrepreneurial income	15.2	...	...	...	...	...	...	...	...	...	...	...
3 Current transfers to the rest of the world	11.9	...	...	...	...	...	...	...	...	...	...	...
4 Surplus of the nation on current transactions	-66.0	...	...	...	...	...	...	...	...	...	...	...
Payments to the Rest of the World and Surplus of the Nation on Current Transactions	246.9	...	...	...	...	...	...	...	...	...	...	...
					Receipts From The Rest of the World							
1 Exports of goods and services	164.3	...	...	...	...	...	...	...	...	...	...	...

Senegal

1.7 External Transactions on Current Account, Summary
(Continued)

Thousand Million CFA francs

	1980	1981	1982	1983	1984	1985	1986	1987	1988	1989	1990	1991
A Exports of merchandise f.o.b.	103.8	...	...	...	...	...	...	...	...	...	...	...
B Other	60.5	...	...	...	...	...	...	...	...	...	...	...
2 Factor income from rest of the world	23.9	...	...	...	...	...	...	...	...	...	...	...
A Compensation of employees	21.3	...	...	...	...	...	...	...	...	...	...	...
B Property and entrepreneurial income	2.6	...	...	...	...	...	...	...	...	...	...	...
3 Current transfers from rest of the world	58.7	...	...	...	...	...	...	...	...	...	...	...
Receipts from the Rest of the World on Current Transactions	246.9	...	...	...	...	...	...	...	...	...	...	...

1.10 Gross Domestic Product by Kind of Activity, in Current Prices

Thousand Million CFA francs

	1980	1981	1982	1983	1984	1985	1986	1987	1988	1989	1990	1991
1 Agriculture, hunting, forestry and fishing	119.1	120.2	184.3	203.1	172.8	217.1	290.6	299.5	333.0	281.7	...	...
2 Mining and quarrying	1.8	2.1	1.7	2.3	2.2	3.4	3.6	3.2	7.0	11.2	...	...
3 Manufacturing	66.8	77.5	88.2	100.0	123.8	148.3	163.4	177.5	197.8	193.3	...	...
4 Electricity, gas and water	12.5	8.9	12.0	13.8	17.5	20.3	25.0	26.9	25.3	28.0	...	...
5 Construction	15.9	18.1	25.4	30.1	30.6	33.0	35.7	39.3	43.2	39.7	...	...
6 Wholesale and retail trade, restaurants and hotels											...	...
7 Transport, storage and communication	296.3	320.2	395.5	439.8	503.3	560.5	627.7	667.6	705.6	741.9	...	...
8 Finance, insurance, real estate and business services											...	...
9 Community, social and personal services											...	...
Total, Industries	512.4	547.0	707.1	789.1	850.2	982.6	1146.0	1214.0	1311.9	1295.8	...	...
Producers of Government Services	106.6	113.6	126.3	138.7	154.3	155.8	135.5	145.1	147.6	155.1	...	...
Other Producers	12.3	13.2	15.4	17.0	16.8	19.7	21.8	23.2	23.9	24.5	...	...
Subtotal	631.4	673.7	848.8	944.7	1021.3	1158.1	1302.9	1382.3	1483.3	1475.4	...	...
Less: Imputed bank service charge	...	...	...	...	...	...	...	...	...	...	...	...
Plus: Import duties	...	...	...	...	...	...	...	...	...	...	...	...
Plus: Value added tax	...	...	...	...	...	...	...	...	...	...	...	...
Equals: Gross Domestic Product	631.4	673.7	848.8	944.7	1021.3	1158.1	1302.9	1382.3	1483.3	1475.4	...	...

1.11 Gross Domestic Product by Kind of Activity, in Constant Prices

Thousand Million CFA francs

	1980	1981	1982	1983	1984	1985	1986	1987	1988	1989	1990	1991
					At constant prices of: 1987							
1 Agriculture, hunting, forestry and fishing	241.0	227.2	283.5	297.2	245.2	264.7	291.5	299.5	328.2	293.0	...	...
2 Mining and quarrying	2.8	3.4	2.2	2.6	2.9	3.1	3.2	3.2	4.3	4.4	...	...
3 Manufacturing	120.8	135.7	150.5	152.3	152.0	154.6	163.0	177.5	195.1	189.4	...	...
4 Electricity, gas and water	23.2	15.2	25.2	26.4	24.2	24.9	25.7	26.9	25.4	27.4	...	...
5 Construction	28.7	31.2	35.4	36.8	35.0	35.8	37.1	39.3	42.1	37.9	...	...
6 Wholesale and retail trade, restaurants and hotels											...	...
7 Transport, storage and communication	533.8	519.5	593.8	600.4	585.5	597.5	646.3	667.7	688.0	709.9	...	...
8 Finance, insurance, real estate and business services											...	...
9 Community, social and personal services											...	...
Total, Industries	950.3	932.2	1090.6	1115.7	1044.8	1080.6	1166.8	1214.1	1283.1	1262.0	...	...
Producers of Government Services	127.5	134.3	142.2	148.8	157.6	163.0	139.9	145.1	145.4	144.8	...	...
Other Producers	18.0	16.3	16.1	11.5	22.6	27.7	22.5	23.2	23.9	23.4	...	...
Subtotal	1095.8	1082.8	1248.9	1276.1	1225.0	1271.3	1329.2	1382.3	1452.4	1430.1	...	...
Less: Imputed bank service charge	...	...	...	...	...	...	...	...	...	...	...	...
Plus: Import duties	...	...	...	...	...	...	...	...	...	...	...	...
Plus: Value added tax	...	...	...	...	...	...	...	...	...	...	...	...
Equals: Gross Domestic Product	1095.8	1082.8	1248.9	1276.1	1225.0	1271.3	1329.2	1382.3	1452.4	1430.1	...	...

1.12 Relations Among National Accounting Aggregates

Thousand Million CFA francs

	1980	1981	1982	1983	1984	1985	1986	1987	1988	1989	1990	1991
Gross Domestic Product	627.5	669.8	844.3	924.9	1015.5	1152.0	1307.0	1374.6	...	...	...	...
Plus: Net factor income from the rest of the world	24.3	23.4	-11.4	-10.1	-24.6	-36.8	-55.3	-67.6	...	...	...	...
Equals: Gross National Product	651.8	693.2	832.9	914.8	990.9	995.9	1174.9	1313.9	...	...	...	...
Less: Consumption of fixed capital	41.9	46.8	87.1	107.7	110.7	157.8	179.4	...	...	...	...	...
Equals: National Income	609.9	646.4	745.8	807.1	880.2	957.4	1072.3	1218.0	...	...	...	...
Plus: Net current transfers from the rest of the world	...	...	...	56.7	58.3	67.6	70.0	73.0	...	...	...	...
Equals: National Disposable Income	...	...	...	...	...	...	...	...	...	...	...	...
Less: Final consumption	...	...	...	...	...	...	...	...	...	...	...	...
Equals: Net Saving	...	...	...	...	...	...	...	...	...	...	...	...
Less: Surplus of the nation on current transactions	...	...	...	...	...	...	...	...	...	...	...	...
Equals: Net Capital Formation	...	...	...	...	...	...	...	...	...	...	...	...

Seychelles

Source. Reply to the United Nations National Accounts Questionnaire from the Ministry of Administration and Manpower, Victoria. The official estimates have been published in the annual National Accounts Bulletin which has been replaced in 1991 by the publication entitled 'National Income and Expenditure'.

General note. The estimates shown in the following tables have been prepared in accordance with the United Nations System of National Accounts so far as the existing data would permit.

1.1 Expenditure on the Gross Domestic Product, in Current Prices

Million Seychelles rupees

	1980	1981	1982	1983	1984	1985	1986	1987	1988	1989	1990	1991
1 Government final consumption expenditure	270.0	308.5	338.0	326.0	327.7	417.4	497.6	406.6	415.6	474.7	544.4	...
2 Private final consumption expenditure	519.0	490.7	595.5	673.3	653.0	700.7	700.3	870.5	909.9	988.4	1004.9	...
3 Gross capital formation	360.9	317.1	313.2	212.2	231.7	273.5	315.2	275.9	390.3	472.5	483.4	...
A Increase in stocks	16.7	-12.5	10.3	-9.5	4.6	-	5.6	15.8	33.0	54.5	31.5	...
B Gross fixed capital formation	344.2	329.6	302.9	219.9	226.9	273.5	309.6	260.1	357.3	418.0	451.9	...
Residential buildings	196.3	205.4	160.0	97.0	135.7	149.3	135.5	100.3	94.5	139.8	167.6	...
Non-residential buildings												...
Other construction and land improvement etc.	1.0	3.9	4.8	4.7	5.4	4.5	4.5	2.0	2.9	4.3	4.5	
Other	146.9	120.3	138.0	118.3	85.7	119.7	169.6	157.8	259.9	273.9	279.8	
4 Exports of goods and services	468.4	554.1	404.4	413.2	524.9	581.1	496.9	541.7	737.3	833.8	1056.2	...
5 Less: Imports of goods and services	676.4	705.6	686.0	635.3	669.2	767.8	720.0	698.8	925.2	1028.5	1098.2	...
Equals: Gross Domestic Product	941.9	964.8	965.1	989.4	1068.1	1204.9	1290.0	1395.9	1527.9	1740.9	1990.7	

1.2 Expenditure on the Gross Domestic Product, in Constant Prices

Million Seychelles rupees

	1980	1981	1982	1983	1984	1985	1986	1987	1988	1989	1990	1991
	At constant prices of:1986											
1 Government final consumption expenditure	392.8	403.3	424.0	386.7	372.0	400.5	497.6	393.2	399.5	470.1	518.8	...
2 Private final consumption expenditure	566.0	546.8	601.1	708.5	660.3	702.8	700.3	848.6	871.0	933.7	911.7	...
3 Gross capital formation	282.7	235.0	288.8	194.1	248.1	288.9	315.5	270.8	375.6	493.8	466.3	...
4 Exports of goods and services	437.7	368.0	282.1	272.2	429.7	552.6	496.6	540.5	724.9	784.0	935.7	...
5 Less: Imports of goods and services	495.8	448.3	507.8	491.9	554.8	670.6	720.0	706.6	952.8	1096.5	1127.5	...
Equals: Gross Domestic Product	1183.4	1104.8	1088.2	1069.6	1155.3	1274.2	1290.0	1346.5	1418.2	1585.1	1705.0	...

1.3 Cost Components of the Gross Domestic Product

Million Seychelles rupees

	1980	1981	1982	1983	1984	1985	1986	1987	1988	1989	1990	1991
1 Indirect taxes, net	152.9	169.0	183.1	186.4	190.6	204.6	212.4	252.4	350.6	370.6	465.8	...
2 Consumption of fixed capital	45.0	54.2	57.6	59.3	64.3	75.2	84.4	90.7	106.6	113.1	164.7	...
3 Compensation of employees paid by resident producers to:	356.9	399.6	409.0	401.8	419.5	447.4	461.3	531.6	547.0	614.1	703.3	...
4 Operating surplus	387.1	342.0	315.4	341.9	393.7	477.7	532.0	521.4	523.8	643.1	657.0	...
Equals: Gross Domestic Product	941.9	964.8	965.1	989.4	1068.1	1204.9	1290.0	1395.9	1527.9	1740.9	1990.7	...

1.7 External Transactions on Current Account, Summary

Million Seychelles rupees

	1980	1981	1982	1983	1984	1985	1986	1987	1988	1989	1990	1991
	Payments to the Rest of the World											
1 Imports of goods and services	745.4	705.6	686.0	635.3	669.2	767.8	720.0	698.8	925.2	1028.5	1098.2	...
A Imports of merchandise c.i.f.	631.4	589.0	639.3	592.1	616.7	702.7	650.0	631.9	854.6	928.2	991.8	...
B Other	114.0	116.6	46.7	43.2	52.5	65.1	70.0	66.9	70.6	100.3	106.4	...
2 Factor income to the rest of the world	56.3	34.2	44.5	48.6	56.0	57.6	65.1	93.3	110.2	104.0	125.1	...
A Compensation of employees	...	...	...	...	...	...	...	...	...	...	...	...
B Property and entrepreneurial income	56.3	34.2	44.5	48.6	56.0	57.6	65.1	93.3	110.2	104.0	125.1	...
3 Current transfers to the rest of the world	20.9	31.5	21.0	18.8	16.6	21.0	48.2	31.6	50.5	51.4	51.4	...
4 Surplus of the nation on current transactions	-58.0	-113.6	-264.8	-175.1	-95.4	-132.5	-205.2	-116.3	-152.8	-129.5	-3.0	...
Payments to the Rest of the World and Surplus of the Nation on Current Transactions	764.6	657.7	486.7	527.6	646.4	713.8	628.1	707.4	933.1	1054.4	1271.7	...
	Receipts From The Rest of the World											
1 Exports of goods and services	640.1	554.1	404.4	415.0	524.9	581.1	496.9	541.7	737.3	833.8	1056.2	...

1.7 External Transactions on Current Account, Summary
(Continued)

Million Seychelles rupees

	1980	1981	1982	1983	1984	1985	1986	1987	1988	1989	1990	1991
A Exports of merchandise f.o.b.	38.3	30.9	25.3	33.9	35.3	33.1	27.4	44.9	92.8	81.7	149.2	...
B Other	601.8	523.2	379.1	381.1	489.6	548.0	469.5	496.8	644.5	752.1	907.0	...
2 Factor income from rest of the world	22.2	19.6	18.3	16.0	14.8	15.4	12.7	15.1	16.6	19.8	21.6	...
A Compensation of employees	...	...	...	...	...	...	...	...	...	...	...	...
B Property and entrepreneurial income	22.2	19.6	18.3	16.0	14.8	15.4	12.7	15.1	16.6	19.8	21.6	...
3 Current transfers from rest of the world	102.3	84.0	64.0	96.6	106.7	117.4	118.5	150.6	179.2	200.8	193.9	...
Receipts from the Rest of the World on Current Transactions	764.6	657.7	486.7	527.6	646.4	713.8	628.1	707.4	933.1	1054.4	1271.7	...

1.10 Gross Domestic Product by Kind of Activity, in Current Prices

Million Seychelles rupees

	1980	1981	1982	1983	1984	1985	1986	1987	1988	1989	1990	1991
1 Agriculture, hunting, forestry and fishing	64.4	62.3	54.6	76.9	69.0	69.3	77.3	73.9	72.3	73.9	92.3	...
2 Mining and quarrying	0.7	0.2	-	-	-	-	-	-	-	-	-	...
3 Manufacturing	69.5	84.4	83.0	95.6	100.3	116.4	120.4	136.7	160.4	162.3	198.6	...
4 Electricity, gas and water	2.1	11.3	12.6	14.9	23.4	31.7	35.4	20.7	27.3	23.2	26.9	...
5 Construction	75.0	71.8	55.0	42.8	52.8	73.1	76.1	61.7	64.0	86.6	94.3	...
6 Wholesale and retail trade, restaurants and hotels	239.1	230.4	219.7	225.6	257.5	298.1	325.1	351.7	376.3	464.4	531.1	...
7 Transport, storage and communication	131.5	109.8	108.4	120.3	154.5	169.5	142.3	141.5	140.7	183.2	236.5	...
8 Finance, insurance, real estate and business services	117.6	115.7	120.4	111.2	106.3	119.2	135.2	166.1	189.9	203.3	214.6	...
9 Community, social and personal services [a]	24.4	28.1	29.3	28.6	28.0	33.3	34.4	36.9	38.1	46.0	46.6	...
Total, Industries	724.3	714.1	683.1	715.9	791.9	910.6	946.2	989.2	1069.0	1242.9	1440.9	...
Producers of Government Services	142.3	171.0	183.4	170.7	173.6	191.8	184.0	223.5	214.7	219.4	256.2	...
Other Producers [a]	...	...	...	...	...	...	...	...	...	...	...	...
Subtotal	866.6	885.1	866.5	886.6	965.5	1102.4	1130.2	1212.7	1283.7	1462.3	1697.1	...
Less: Imputed bank service charge	29.8	34.1	29.6	25.8	26.0	31.9	37.7	43.6	51.3	51.9	68.5	...
Plus: Import duties	105.1	113.7	128.2	128.6	128.6	134.5	197.6	226.8	295.6	330.4	362.2	...
Plus: Value added tax	...	...	...	...	...	...	...	...	...	...	...	...
Equals: Gross Domestic Product	941.9	964.8	965.1	989.4	1068.1	1205.0	1290.0	1395.9	1527.9	1740.9	1990.7	...

a) Item 'Other producers' is included in item 'Community, social and personal services'.

1.11 Gross Domestic Product by Kind of Activity, in Constant Prices

Million Seychelles rupees

	1980	1981	1982	1983	1984	1985	1986	1987	1988	1989	1990	1991
					At constant prices of:1986							
1 Agriculture, hunting, forestry and fishing	80.6	73.7	67.6	84.2	72.4	72.3	77.3	73.7	70.1	69.2	78.2	...
2 Mining and quarrying	0.7	0.3	-	-	-	-	-	-	-	-	-	...
3 Manufacturing	107.1	92.1	94.3	103.5	104.2	113.0	120.4	135.2	164.1	167.0	191.9	...
4 Electricity, gas and water	-5.8	-12.2	-12.1	-21.5	26.8	37.3	35.4	19.3	21.1	10.6	14.1	...
5 Construction	96.2	93.0	66.3	49.0	57.8	71.6	76.1	62.1	50.5	63.3	70.7	...
6 Wholesale and retail trade, restaurants and hotels	288.4	260.6	251.1	263.7	280.2	312.0	325.1	350.4	354.6	432.7	450.2	...
7 Transport, storage and communication	148.9	129.9	126.2	144.8	168.4	166.8	142.3	147.7	129.8	163.3	204.9	...
8 Finance, insurance, real estate and business services	136.4	119.9	126.0	114.7	102.9	114.5	135.2	164.4	185.1	194.9	197.5	...
9 Community, social and personal services [a]	43.1	42.3	40.5	34.5	31.1	34.4	34.4	34.7	33.6	36.7	26.1	...
Total, Industries	895.6	799.5	759.8	772.7	843.9	921.9	946.2	987.4	1008.9	1137.7	1233.6	...
Producers of Government Services	176.9	209.8	211.0	179.1	178.5	188.0	184.0	209.6	195.9	194.0	216.4	...
Other Producers [a]	...	...	...	...	...	...	...	...	...	...	...	...
Subtotal	1072.5	1009.3	970.8	951.8	1022.4	1109.9	1130.2	1197.0	1204.8	1331.7	1450.0	...
Less: Imputed bank service charge	30.0	30.9	27.1	22.3	22.7	23.2	37.7	42.4	50.9	52.4	67.9	...
Plus: Import duties	140.9	126.4	144.5	140.1	155.6	187.5	197.6	191.7	264.3	305.8	322.9	...
Plus: Value added tax												...
Equals: Gross Domestic Product	1183.4	1104.8	1088.2	1069.6	1155.3	1274.2	1290.0	1346.5	1418.2	1585.1	1705.0	...

a) Item 'Other producers' is included in item 'Community, social and personal services'.

Seychelles

1.12 Relations Among National Accounting Aggregates

Million Seychelles rupees

	1980	1981	1982	1983	1984	1985	1986	1987	1988	1989	1990	1991
Gross Domestic Product	941.9	964.8	965.1	989.4	1068.0	1204.9	1290.0	1395.9	1527.9	1740.9	1990.7	...
Plus: Net factor income from the rest of the world	-34.1	-14.6	-26.2	-32.6	-41.2	-42.2	-52.4	-78.2	-93.6	-84.2	-103.5	...
Factor income from the rest of the world	22.2	19.6	18.3	16.0	14.8	15.4	12.7	15.1	16.6	19.8	21.6	
Less: Factor income to the rest of the world	56.3	34.2	44.5	48.6	56.0	57.6	65.1	93.3	110.2	104.0	125.1	...
Equals: Gross National Product	907.8	950.2	938.9	956.8	1026.8	1162.7	1237.6	1317.7	1434.3	1656.7	1887.2	
Less: Consumption of fixed capital	45.0	54.2	57.6	59.3	64.3	75.2	84.3	90.6	106.5	113.0	164.7	
Equals: National Income	862.8	896.0	881.3	897.5	962.5	1087.5	1153.3	1227.1	1327.8	1543.7	1722.5	
Plus: Net current transfers from the rest of the world	81.4	52.5	43.0	77.8	90.1	96.4	70.3	119.0	128.7	149.4	142.5	
Current transfers from the rest of the world	102.3	84.0	64.0	96.6	106.7	117.4	118.5	150.6	179.2	200.8	193.9	
Less: Current transfers to the rest of the world	20.9	31.5	21.0	18.8	16.6	21.0	48.2	31.6	50.5	51.4	51.4	
Equals: National Disposable Income	944.2	948.5	924.3	975.3	1052.6	1183.9	1223.6	1346.2	1456.5	1693.0	1865.1	
Less: Final consumption	686.3	799.2	933.5	999.2	980.7	1118.1	1197.9	1277.1	1325.5	1463.1	1549.3	
Equals: Net Saving	257.9	149.3	-9.2	-23.9	71.9	65.8	25.7	69.0	131.0	229.9	315.8	
Less: Surplus of the nation on current transactions	-58.0	-113.6	-264.8	-175.1	-95.4	-132.5	-205.1	-116.3	-152.8	-129.5	-3.0	
Equals: Net Capital Formation	315.9	262.9	255.6	151.2	167.3	198.3	230.8	185.3	283.8	359.4	318.8	...

2.1 Government Final Consumption Expenditure by Function, in Current Prices

Million Seychelles rupees

	1980	1981	1982	1983	1984	1985	1986	1987	1988	1989	1990	1991
1 General public services	...	...	...	...	...	...	...	...	...	44.5	51.6	...
2 Defence	...	...	...	...	...	...	...	...	...	54.8	55.5	
3 Public order and safety	...	...	...	...	...	...	...	...	...	23.2	27.5	
4 Education	...	...	...	...	...	...	...	...	...	141.2	158.7	
5 Health	...	...	...	...	...	...	...	...	...	55.8	69.5	
6 Social security and welfare	...	...	...	...	...	...	...	...	...	12.2	19.3	
7 Housing and community amenities	...	...	...	...	...	...	...	...	...	9.9	14.2	
8 Recreational, cultural and religious affairs	...	...	...	...	...	...	...	...	...	14.6	31.9	
9 Economic services	...	...	...	...	...	...	...	...	...	81.2	99.8	
A Fuel and energy	...	...	...	...	...	...	...	...	...	1.8	3.8	
B Agriculture, forestry, fishing and hunting	...	...	...	...	...	...	...	...	...	8.9	20.3	
C Mining, manufacturing and construction, except fuel and energy										-	-	
D Transportation and communication	...	...	...	...	...	...	...	...	...	54.1	56.7	
E Other economic affairs	...	...	...	...	...	...	...	...	...	16.4	19.0	...
10 Other functions	...	...	...	...	...	...	...	...	...	37.3	16.4	
Total Government Final Consumption Expenditure	...	...	...	...	...	...	...	...	...	474.7	544.4	...

4.1 Derivation of Value Added by Kind of Activity, in Current Prices

Million Seychelles rupees

	1980			1981			1982			1983		
	Gross Output	Intermediate Consumption	Value Added	Gross Output	Intermediate Consumption	Value Added	Gross Output	Intermediate Consumption	Value Added	Gross Output	Intermediate Consumption	Value Added
						All Producers						
1 Agriculture, hunting, forestry and fishing	88.1	23.7	64.4	88.2	25.9	62.3	86.7	32.1	54.6	114.6	37.7	76.9
A Agriculture and hunting	52.5	17.3	35.2	53.8	18.0	35.8	48.0	22.0	26.0	70.3	24.5	45.8
B Forestry and logging	2.4	0.4	2.0	2.6	0.5	2.2	2.4	0.3	2.1	2.1	0.6	1.5
C Fishing	33.2	6.0	27.2	31.8	7.4	24.3	36.2	9.8	26.5	42.3	12.7	29.6
2 Mining and quarrying	1.4	0.7	0.7	0.4	0.2	0.2	-	-	-	-	-	-
3 Manufacturing	130.0	60.5	69.5	161.2	76.8	84.4	159.3	76.3	83.0	171.6	76.0	95.6
4 Electricity, gas and water	44.1	42.0	2.1	67.7	56.5	11.3	68.1	55.4	12.6	74.2	59.3	14.9
A Electricity, gas and steam	40.3	39.3	1.0	58.3	50.6	7.7	58.7	49.4	9.3	60.9	49.6	11.3
B Water works and supply	3.8	2.7	1.1	9.4	5.9	3.6	9.4	6.0	3.3	13.3	9.7	3.5

4.1 Derivation of Value Added by Kind of Activity, in Current Prices
(Continued)

Million Seychelles rupees

	1980			1981			1982			1983		
	Gross Output	Intermediate Consumption	Value Added	Gross Output	Intermediate Consumption	Value Added	Gross Output	Intermediate Consumption	Value Added	Gross Output	Intermediate Consumption	Value Added
5 Construction	196.3	121.3	75.0	209.3	137.5	71.8	160.0	104.9	55.0	98.0	55.2	42.8
6 Wholesale and retail trade, restaurants and hotels	407.4	168.3	239.1	386.6	156.2	230.4	335.8	116.1	219.7	373.2	147.6	225.6
A Wholesale and retail trade	207.4	48.4	158.9	207.5	47.6	159.9	207.3	44.6	162.7	211.1	46.5	164.6
B Restaurants and hotels	200.0	119.9	80.2	179.2	108.6	70.5	128.5	71.5	57.0	162.1	101.1	61.0
7 Transport, storage and communication	225.1	93.5	131.5	218.1	108.2	109.9	209.5	101.1	108.4	304.0	183.7	120.3
8 Finance, insurance, real estate and business services	139.1	21.5	117.6	144.4	28.7	115.7	147.7	27.3	120.4	135.7	24.5	111.2
A Financial institutions	53.0	11.1	41.9	44.9	17.1	27.9	49.5	15.7	33.8	44.6	16.4	28.2
B Insurance	10.2	3.4	6.8	8.8	3.7	5.1	12.0	4.2	7.8	5.7	1.1	4.6
C Real estate and business services	75.9	7.0	68.9	90.7	7.9	82.7	86.2	7.5	78.8	85.4	7.0	78.4
Real estate, except dwellings	15.3	1.5	13.6	16.3	1.6	14.7	15.5	1.6	14.0	15.8	1.6	14.3
Dwellings	50.8	1.5	49.3	61.1	1.9	59.2	58.5	1.8	56.7	58.7	1.7	57.1
9 Community, social and personal services a	37.6	13.2	24.5	42.9	14.8	28.1	47.1	17.8	29.3	41.5	12.9	28.6
Total, Industries	1269.1	544.7	724.4	1318.8	604.8	714.1	1214.0	531.0	683.1	1312.8	596.9	715.9
Producers of Government Services	282.3	140.0	142.3	322.8	151.8	171.0	356.0	172.6	183.4	341.9	171.2	170.7
Other Producers a	...	...	...	...	...	...	...	...	...	...	...	...
Total	1551.4	684.7	866.7	1641.6	756.6	885.1	1570.0	703.6	866.5	1654.7	768.1	886.6
Less: Imputed bank service charge	...	-29.8	29.8	...	-34.1	34.1	...	-29.6	29.6	...	-25.8	25.8
Import duties	105.1	...	105.1	113.7	...	113.7	128.2	...	128.2	128.6	...	128.6
Value added tax	...	...	...	...	...	...	...	...	...	...	...	...
Total	1656.4	714.5	941.9	1755.4	790.7	964.8	1698.2	733.2	965.1	1783.3	793.9	989.4

	1984			1985			1986			1987		
	Gross Output	Intermediate Consumption	Value Added	Gross Output	Intermediate Consumption	Value Added	Gross Output	Intermediate Consumption	Value Added	Gross Output	Intermediate Consumption	Value Added
						All Producers						
1 Agriculture, hunting, forestry and fishing	105.7	36.7	69.0	103.1	33.8	69.3	112.6	35.3	77.3	112.0	38.1	73.9
A Agriculture and hunting	68.9	25.8	43.1	71.3	27.0	44.3	75.0	28.3	46.7	82.2	31.0	51.2
B Forestry and logging	2.0	0.6	1.4	2.1	0.6	1.5	2.2	0.6	1.6	2.2	0.6	1.6
C Fishing	34.8	10.4	24.4	29.7	6.2	23.5	35.4	6.4	29.0	27.6	6.5	21.1
2 Mining and quarrying	-	-	-	-	-	-	-	-	-	-	-	-
3 Manufacturing	177.2	76.9	100.3	203.8	87.4	116.4	208.1	87.7	120.4	279.9	143.1	136.8
4 Electricity, gas and water	80.0	56.5	23.4	89.7	58.0	31.7	97.8	62.5	35.3	109.0	88.3	20.7
A Electricity, gas and steam	62.9	46.2	16.7	73.3	49.5	23.9	81.6	53.6	28.0	86.1	76.1	10.0
B Water works and supply	17.1	10.3	6.7	16.3	8.5	7.8	16.2	8.9	7.4	22.9	12.2	10.7
5 Construction	103.5	50.7	52.8	137.8	64.7	73.1	146.9	70.8	76.1	113.0	51.3	61.7
6 Wholesale and retail trade, restaurants and hotels	411.6	154.1	257.5	505.1	207.0	298.1	534.5	209.4	325.1	597.1	245.4	351.7
A Wholesale and retail trade	216.3	46.5	169.8	246.6	51.3	195.4	267.0	52.9	214.1	278.7	54.6	224.1
B Restaurants and hotels	195.4	107.6	87.7	258.5	155.7	102.7	267.5	156.5	111.0	318.4	190.8	127.6
7 Transport, storage and communication	346.6	192.1	154.5	382.2	212.7	169.5	476.0	333.7	142.3	514.1	372.6	141.5
8 Finance, insurance, real estate and business services	130.2	24.0	106.3	148.8	29.6	119.2	166.2	31.0	135.2	194.6	28.4	166.1
A Financial institutions	46.7	15.2	31.4	59.8	16.2	43.6	66.0	18.2	47.8	80.8	18.4	62.4
B Insurance	3.2	1.3	1.9	7.4	2.3	5.1	16.3	4.6	11.7	27.6	2.9	24.6
C Real estate and business services	80.3	7.5	73.0	81.6	11.1	70.5	83.9	8.2	75.6	86.2	7.1	79.1
Real estate, except dwellings	14.0	1.4	12.6	5.8	4.0	1.8	5.7	0.6	5.1	5.8	0.6	5.2
Dwellings	55.5	1.7	53.8	65.2	1.9	63.3	66.6	2.0	64.6	68.2	2.1	66.2
9 Community, social and personal services a	40.5	12.5	28.0	46.4	13.1	33.3	47.1	12.8	34.4	49.4	12.5	36.9

Seychelles

4.1 Derivation of Value Added by Kind of Activity, in Current Prices
(Continued)

Million Seychelles rupees

	1984			1985			1986			1987		
	Gross Output	Intermediate Consumption	Value Added	Gross Output	Intermediate Consumption	Value Added	Gross Output	Intermediate Consumption	Value Added	Gross Output	Intermediate Consumption	Value Added
Total, Industries	1395.3	603.5	791.9	1616.9	706.3	910.6	1789.2	843.2	946.0	1969.1	979.7	989.3
Producers of Government Services	345.2	171.6	173.6	417.4	225.6	191.8	497.6	313.6	184.0	406.6	183.1	223.5
Other Producers a	...	...	...	...	...	...	...	...	...	...	...	...
Total	1740.5	775.1	965.5	2034.3	931.9	1102.4	2286.8	1156.8	1130.0	2375.7	1162.8	1212.8
Less: Imputed bank service charge	...	-26.0	26.0	...	-31.9	31.9	...	-37.7	37.7	...	-43.6	43.6
Import duties	128.6	...	128.6	134.5	...	134.5	197.6	...	197.6	226.8	...	226.8
Value added tax	...	...	...	...	...	...	...	...	...	...	...	...
Total	1869.1	801.1	1068.1	2168.8	963.8	1205.0	2484.4	1194.5	1290.0	2602.5	1206.6	1395.9

	1988			1989			1990		
	Gross Output	Intermediate Consumption	Value Added	Gross Output	Intermediate Consumption	Value Added	Gross Output	Intermediate Consumption	Value Added
				All Producers					
1 Agriculture, hunting, forestry and fishing	113.9	41.5	72.3	114.5	40.5	74.0	140.0	47.7	92.3
A Agriculture and hunting	84.9	33.5	51.4	85.1	32.1	53.0	100.7	37.7	62.9
B Forestry and logging	2.1	0.6	1.4	2.4	0.7	1.6	2.6	0.8	1.8
C Fishing	26.9	7.4	19.5	27.0	7.7	19.3	36.8	9.2	27.6
2 Mining and quarrying	-	-	-	-	-	-	...	...	...
3 Manufacturing	347.3	186.9	160.4	354.6	192.3	162.3	407.9	209.3	198.6
4 Electricity, gas and water	131.2	103.9	27.3	147.0	123.7	23.2	152.4	125.4	26.9
A Electricity, gas and steam	99.4	90.7	8.7	112.5	103.7	8.8	117.9	105.1	12.7
B Water works and supply	31.9	13.2	18.6	34.5	20.0	14.5	34.5	20.3	14.2
5 Construction	119.5	55.5	64.0	164.4	77.8	86.6	172.1	77.8	94.3
6 Wholesale and retail trade, restaurants and hotels	696.4	320.1	376.3	829.4	365.1	464.4	942.8	411.8	531.1
A Wholesale and retail trade	297.7	75.8	221.9	375.7	92.8	283.0	413.5	97.6	315.9
B Restaurants and hotels	398.7	244.3	154.4	453.7	272.3	181.4	529.4	314.2	215.2
7 Transport, storage and communication	583.4	442.7	140.7	653.9	470.7	183.2	750.3	513.8	236.5
8 Finance, insurance, real estate and business services	218.7	28.9	189.8	237.4	34.1	203.3	250.1	35.5	214.6
A Financial institutions	105.2	19.4	85.8	108.6	23.7	84.9	114.2	25.1	89.1
B Insurance	28.7	2.5	26.2	38.3	2.8	35.5	43.7	3.7	40.0
C Real estate and business services	84.8	7.0	77.8	90.5	7.6	82.9	92.2	6.7	85.5
Real estate, except dwellings	5.9	0.6	5.3	6.0	0.6	5.4	6.1	0.6	5.5
Dwellings	67.6	2.0	65.6	69.9	2.1	67.8	71.7	2.1	69.6
9 Community, social and personal services a	49.0	11.0	38.0	62.1	16.1	46.0	62.2	15.6	46.6
Total, Industries	2259.4	1190.5	1068.8	2563.3	1320.3	1243.0	2877.8	1436.9	1440.9
Producers of Government Services	415.6	200.9	214.7	474.7	255.3	219.4	544.4	288.2	256.2
Other Producers a	...	...	...	...	...	...	...	...	...
Total	2675.0	1391.4	1283.5	3038.0	1575.6	1462.4	3422.2	1725.1	1697.1
Less: Imputed bank service charge	...	-51.3	51.3	...	-51.9	51.9	...	-68.5	68.5
Import duties	295.6	...	295.6	330.4	...	330.4	362.2	...	362.2
Value added tax	...	...	...	...	...	...	...	...	...
Total	2970.6	1442.6	1527.9	3368.4	1627.5	1740.9	3784.4	1793.6	1990.7

a) Item 'Other producers' is included in item 'Community, social and personal services'.

4.2 Derivation of Value Added by Kind of Activity, in Constant Prices

Million Seychelles rupees

	1980			1981			1982			1983		
	Gross Output	Intermediate Consumption	Value Added	Gross Output	Intermediate Consumption	Value Added	Gross Output	Intermediate Consumption	Value Added	Gross Output	Intermediate Consumption	Value Added
				At constant prices of:1986								
				All Producers								
1 Agriculture, hunting, forestry and fishing	103.3	22.8	80.6	98.8	25.1	73.7	98.6	31.0	67.6	115.6	31.4	84.2
A Agriculture and hunting	57.2	16.8	40.4	59.9	18.4	41.4	57.9	22.9	35.0	76.5	23.5	53.0
B Forestry and logging	2.6	0.6	2.1	3.2	0.9	2.4	2.3	0.5	1.9	1.7	0.5	1.1
C Fishing	43.5	5.4	38.1	35.7	5.8	29.9	38.4	7.6	30.7	37.4	7.4	30.1
2 Mining and quarrying	1.3	0.7	0.7	0.4	0.2	0.3	-	-	-	-	-	-

4.2 Derivation of Value Added by Kind of Activity, in Constant Prices
(Continued)

Million Seychelles rupees

	1980			1981			1982			1983		
	Gross Output	Intermediate Consumption	Value Added	Gross Output	Intermediate Consumption	Value Added	Gross Output	Intermediate Consumption	Value Added	Gross Output	Intermediate Consumption	Value Added
	At constant prices of:1986											
3 Manufacturing	164.5	57.5	107.1	156.8	64.7	92.1	161.5	67.3	94.3	170.1	66.6	103.5
4 Electricity, gas and water	56.1	61.9	-5.8	63.1	75.2	-12.2	64.3	76.4	-12.1	69.5	91.0	-21.5
A Electricity, gas and steam	51.6	58.6	-7.0	53.7	69.1	-15.4	56.6	71.2	-14.6	56.6	81.1	-24.5
B Water works and supply	4.5	3.3	1.2	9.4	6.1	3.2	7.7	5.2	2.5	12.9	9.9	3.0
5 Construction	218.5	122.3	96.2	229.7	136.6	93.0	163.3	97.0	66.3	100.0	51.0	49.0
6 Wholesale and retail trade, restaurants and hotels	442.5	154.1	288.4	400.6	140.1	260.6	368.0	116.9	251.1	407.0	143.4	263.7
A Wholesale and retail trade	234.8	40.1	194.7	213.9	37.0	177.0	220.5	36.0	184.5	214.6	37.8	176.9
B Restaurants and hotels	207.7	114.0	93.7	186.7	103.1	83.6	147.5	80.9	66.6	192.4	105.6	86.8
7 Transport, storage and communication	321.9	173.0	148.9	295.5	165.6	129.9	282.7	156.5	126.2	346.8	202.1	144.8
8 Finance, insurance, real estate and business services	158.6	22.1	136.4	146.9	27.1	119.9	152.6	26.5	126.0	136.0	21.4	114.7
A Financial institutions	63.2	12.2	51.0	48.8	17.0	31.8	53.6	15.7	37.9	46.3	14.9	31.5
B Insurance	12.2	3.8	8.4	9.6	3.7	5.9	13.0	4.2	8.8	5.3	1.0	4.3
C Real estate and business services	83.2	6.1	77.0	88.5	6.4	82.2	86.0	6.6	79.3	84.4	5.5	78.9
Real estate, except dwellings	18.8	1.8	17.0	19.0	1.8	17.2	17.2	1.6	15.6	18.5	1.8	16.7
Dwellings	56.9	1.6	55.3	61.8	1.7	60.1	59.7	1.7	58.0	60.0	1.6	58.4
9 Community, social and personal services [a]	66.6	23.5	43.1	66.0	23.7	42.3	62.6	22.1	40.5	57.6	23.0	34.5
Total, Industries	1533.4	637.8	895.6	1457.8	658.3	799.5	1353.7	593.8	759.8	1402.7	629.9	772.7
Producers of Government Services	340.1	163.2	176.9	346.9	137.1	209.8	368.0	157.0	211.0	334.8	155.7	179.1
Other Producers [a]	...	...	...	...	...	...	...	...	...	...	...	...
Total	1873.5	801.0	1072.5	1804.7	795.4	1009.3	1721.7	750.8	970.8	1737.5	785.6	951.8
Less: Imputed bank service charge	...	-30.0	30.0	...	-30.9	30.9	...	-27.1	27.1	...	-22.3	22.3
Import duties	140.9	...	140.9	126.4	...	126.4	144.5	...	144.5	140.1	...	140.1
Value added tax	...	...	...	...	...	...	...	...	...	...	...	...
Total	2014.4	831.0	1183.4	1931.1	826.3	1104.8	1866.2	777.9	1088.2	1877.6	807.9	1069.6

	1984			1985			1986			1987		
	Gross Output	Intermediate Consumption	Value Added	Gross Output	Intermediate Consumption	Value Added	Gross Output	Intermediate Consumption	Value Added	Gross Output	Intermediate Consumption	Value Added
	At constant prices of:1986											
	All Producers											
1 Agriculture, hunting, forestry and fishing	103.9	31.4	72.4	102.9	30.7	72.3	112.7	35.3	77.2	111.2	37.5	73.7
A Agriculture and hunting	71.0	24.8	46.2	71.3	25.5	45.8	75.0	28.3	46.7	81.1	30.6	50.5
B Forestry and logging	2.2	0.6	1.6	2.1	0.6	1.5	2.2	0.6	1.5	2.2	0.6	1.5
C Fishing	30.7	6.0	24.6	29.5	4.6	25.0	35.5	6.4	29.0	27.9	6.3	21.6
2 Mining and quarrying	-	-	-	-	-	-	-	-	-	-	-	-
3 Manufacturing	170.7	66.5	104.2	192.2	79.2	113.0	208.1	87.7	120.4	262.4	127.2	135.2
4 Electricity, gas and water	80.5	53.7	26.8	93.5	56.1	37.3	97.8	62.5	35.4	106.4	87.0	19.4
A Electricity, gas and steam	64.1	43.3	20.8	79.5	48.2	31.2	81.6	53.6	28.0	90.8	74.3	16.5
B Water works and supply	16.4	10.4	6.0	14.0	7.9	6.1	16.2	8.9	7.4	15.6	12.8	2.8
5 Construction	104.0	46.1	57.8	135.1	63.4	71.6	146.9	70.8	76.1	112.9	50.8	62.1
6 Wholesale and retail trade, restaurants and hotels	439.6	159.4	280.2	513.8	201.9	312.0	534.5	209.4	325.1	588.5	238.1	350.4
A Wholesale and retail trade	219.3	38.5	180.8	247.2	45.7	201.5	267.0	52.9	214.1	284.8	55.0	229.8
B Restaurants and hotels	220.3	120.9	99.4	266.6	156.2	110.5	267.5	156.5	111.0	303.7	183.1	120.6
7 Transport, storage and communication	381.0	212.6	168.4	380.6	213.8	166.8	476.0	333.7	142.3	515.6	368.0	147.6
8 Finance, insurance, real estate and business services	124.7	21.9	102.9	140.8	26.3	114.5	166.2	31.0	135.2	191.6	27.1	164.5
A Financial institutions	46.6	14.7	31.9	55.8	13.4	42.4	66.0	18.2	47.9	78.8	18.0	60.7
B Insurance	3.2	1.3	2.0	6.9	1.9	5.0	16.3	4.6	11.7	26.2	3.0	23.2
C Real estate and business services	74.9	5.9	69.0	78.1	11.0	67.1	83.9	8.2	75.6	86.6	6.1	80.5
Real estate, except dwellings	16.1	1.5	14.6	5.7	3.9	1.8	5.7	0.6	5.1	5.8	0.6	5.2
Dwellings	53.1	1.5	51.6	61.6	1.8	59.8	66.6	2.0	64.6	66.5	2.0	64.5
9 Community, social and personal services [a]	53.5	22.4	31.1	47.3	12.8	34.4	47.1	12.8	34.4	47.6	12.9	34.7

Seychelles

Million Seychelles rupees

	1984			1985			1986			1987		
	Gross Output	Intermediate Consumption	Value Added	Gross Output	Intermediate Consumption	Value Added	Gross Output	Intermediate Consumption	Value Added	Gross Output	Intermediate Consumption	Value Added
	At constant prices of:1986											
Total, Industries	1457.8	614.0	843.9	1606.1	684.2	921.9	1789.2	843.2	946.0	1936.2	948.6	987.6
Producers of Government Services	333.9	155.3	178.5	400.5	212.5	188.0	497.6	313.6	184.0	393.2	183.6	209.6
Other Producers a	...	...	...	...	...	...	...	...	...	...	...	...
Total	1791.7	769.3	1022.4	2006.6	896.7	1109.9	2286.8	1156.8	1130.0	2329.4	1132.2	1197.2
Less: Imputed bank service charge	...	-22.7	22.7	...	-23.2	23.2	...	-37.7	37.7	...	-42.4	42.4
Import duties	155.6	...	155.6	187.5	...	187.5	197.6	...	197.6	191.7	...	191.7
Value added tax	...	...	...	...	...	...	...	...	...	...	...	...
Total	1947.3	792.0	1155.3	2194.1	919.9	1274.2	2484.4	1194.5	1290.0	2521.0	1174.6	1346.5

	1988			1989			1990		
	Gross Output	Intermediate Consumption	Value Added	Gross Output	Intermediate Consumption	Value Added	Gross Output	Intermediate Consumption	Value Added
	At constant prices of:1986								
	All Producers								
1 Agriculture, hunting, forestry and fishing	105.1	35.0	70.1	103.6	34.4	69.2	118.6	40.4	78.2
A Agriculture and hunting	73.7	27.9	45.8	72.9	26.5	46.4	83.0	32.0	51.1
B Forestry and logging	2.0	0.6	1.4	2.1	0.6	1.5	2.0	0.6	1.5
C Fishing	29.4	6.5	22.9	28.6	7.3	21.3	33.5	7.9	25.7
2 Mining and quarrying	-	-	-	-	-	-	-	-	-
3 Manufacturing	325.2	161.1	164.1	319.4	152.4	166.9	362.0	170.1	191.9
4 Electricity, gas and water	122.5	101.3	21.2	137.2	126.6	10.6	142.0	127.9	14.1
A Electricity, gas and steam	106.6	87.2	19.3	119.7	103.9	15.8	127.2	104.0	23.2
B Water works and supply	15.9	14.1	1.8	17.5	22.8	-5.2	14.8	23.9	-9.1
5 Construction	107.9	57.4	50.5	138.4	75.1	63.3	139.9	69.2	70.7
6 Wholesale and retail trade, restaurants and hotels	674.3	319.7	354.6	796.5	363.7	432.8	857.9	407.7	450.2
A Wholesale and retail trade	316.2	78.0	238.2	399.9	93.8	306.1	415.3	97.5	317.9
B Restaurants and hotels	358.1	241.7	116.4	396.6	269.9	126.6	442.6	310.3	132.3
7 Transport, storage and communication	581.8	451.9	129.8	665.5	502.4	163.2	713.8	508.9	204.9
8 Finance, insurance, real estate and business services	213.1	28.0	185.1	228.7	33.8	194.9	232.6	35.0	197.5
A Financial institutions	100.1	19.5	80.7	102.6	24.2	78.4	103.1	25.1	77.9
B Insurance	26.5	2.5	24.0	35.2	2.9	32.2	38.4	3.8	34.5
C Real estate and business services	86.4	6.0	80.5	90.9	6.6	84.2	91.2	6.1	85.1
Real estate, except dwellings	6.0	0.6	5.4	6.0	0.6	5.4	6.0	0.6	5.4
Dwellings	67.2	2.0	65.2	68.0	2.0	66.0	63.7	2.0	66.7
9 Community, social and personal services a	46.2	12.7	33.5	55.0	18.3	36.8	48.3	22.1	26.1
Total, Industries	2176.1	1167.1	1008.9	2444.3	1306.7	1137.7	2615.1	1381.5	1233.6
Producers of Government Services	399.5	203.6	195.9	470.1	276.2	194.0	544.4	328.0	216.4
Other Producers a	...	...	...	...	...	...	...	...	...
Total	2575.6	1370.7	1204.8	2914.4	1582.9	1331.7	3159.5	1709.5	1450.0
Less: Imputed bank service charge	...	-50.9	50.9	...	-52.4	52.4	...	-67.9	67.9
Import duties	264.3	...	264.3	305.8	...	305.8	322.9	...	322.9
Value added tax	...	...	...	...	...	...	...	...	...
Total	2840.0	1421.7	1418.2	3220.3	1635.2	1585.1	3482.3	1777.4	1705.0

a) Item 'Other producers' is included in item 'Community, social and personal services'.

4.3 Cost Components of Value Added

Million Seychelles rupees

	1980						1981					
	Compensation of Employees	Capital Consumption	Net Operating Surplus	Indirect Taxes	Less: Subsidies Received	Value Added	Compensation of Employees	Capital Consumption	Net Operating Surplus	Indirect Taxes	Less: Subsidies Received	Value Added
	All Producers											
1 Agriculture, hunting, forestry and fishing	-	-	64.3	0.1	...	64.4	-	-	60.8	1.5	...	62.3
A Agriculture and hunting	-	-	35.1	0.1	...	35.2	-	-	34.6	1.2	...	35.8
B Forestry and logging	-	-	2.0	-	...	2.0	-	-	2.2	-	...	2.2
C Fishing	-	-	27.2	-	...	27.2	-	-	24.0	0.4	...	24.3
2 Mining and quarrying	0.5	0.2	-0.2	0.2	...	0.7	0.3	-	-0.2	0.1	...	0.2

4.3 Cost Components of Value Added
(Continued)

Million Seychelles rupees

	1980						1981					
	Compensation of Employees	Capital Consumption	Net Operating Surplus	Indirect Taxes	Less: Subsidies Received	Value Added	Compensation of Employees	Capital Consumption	Net Operating Surplus	Indirect Taxes	Less: Subsidies Received	Value Added
3 Manufacturing	18.1	5.4	21.6	24.3	...	69.5	22.1	8.1	22.5	31.8	...	84.4
4 Electricity, gas and water	9.2	...	-7.0	...	...	2.1	12.9	3.9	-5.5	-	...	11.3
A Electricity, gas and steam	3.6	-	-2.5	-	...	1.0	8.5	3.5	-4.3	-	...	7.7
B Water works and supply	5.6	-	-4.5	-	...	1.1	4.4	0.3	-1.2	-	...	3.6
5 Construction	48.5	2.7	23.8	-	...	75.0	46.1	3.0	22.7	-	...	71.8
6 Wholesale and retail trade, restaurants and hotels	50.9	6.1	162.1	20.0	...	239.1	53.7	6.4	151.6	18.6	...	230.4
A Wholesale and retail trade	...	...	...	...	...	...						
B Restaurants and hotels	...	...	...	...	...	...						
7 Transport, storage and communication	69.6	15.8	43.5	2.6	...	131.5	74.3	15.8	17.4	2.4	...	109.9
A Transport and storage	54.0	9.4	33.9	2.6	...	99.9	57.1	9.3	16.3	2.4	...	85.2
B Communication	15.6	6.3	9.6	-	...	31.5	17.1	6.5	1.1	-	...	24.7
8 Finance, insurance, real estate and business services	18.0	14.8	84.7	0.2	...	117.6	19.2	16.9	79.0	0.6	...	115.7
A Financial institutions	10.9	0.9	29.9	0.2	...	41.9	11.0	1.1	15.7	-	...	27.9
B Insurance	3.1	0.3	3.5	-	...	6.8	3.4	0.3	1.4	-	...	5.1
C Real estate and business services	4.0	13.6	51.3	-	...	68.9	4.9	15.5	61.8	0.5	...	82.7
Real estate, except dwellings	-	-	13.6	-	...	13.6	-	-	14.7	-	...	14.7
Dwellings	-	13.4	35.9	-	...	49.3	-	15.3	43.9	-	...	59.2
9 Community, social and personal services [a]	-	-	24.2	0.3	...	24.5	-	-	27.9	0.2	...	28.1
Total, Industries	214.7	44.9	416.9	47.8	...	724.4	228.7	54.1	376.1	55.3	...	714.1
Producers of Government Services	142.2	0.1	-	-	...	142.3	170.9	0.1	...	...	...	171.0
Other Producers [a]	...	...	...	...	...	...	...	...	...	...	...	...
Total	356.9	45.0	416.9	47.8	...	866.7	399.6	54.2	376.1	55.3	...	885.1
Less: Imputed bank service charge	...	...	29.8	...	...	29.8	...	...	34.1	...	...	34.1
Import duties	...	...	...	105.1	...	105.1	...	...	...	113.7	...	113.7
Value added tax	...	...	...	...	...	...	...	...	...	...	...	...
Total	356.9	45.0	387.1	152.9	...	941.9	399.6	54.2	342.0	169.0	...	964.8

	1982						1983					
	Compensation of Employees	Capital Consumption	Net Operating Surplus	Indirect Taxes	Less: Subsidies Received	Value Added	Compensation of Employees	Capital Consumption	Net Operating Surplus	Indirect Taxes	Less: Subsidies Received	Value Added
All Producers												
1 Agriculture, hunting, forestry and fishing	-	-	53.3	1.2	...	54.6	-	-	76.9	0.1	...	76.9
A Agriculture and hunting	-	-	25.4	0.6	...	26.0	-	-	45.8	-	...	45.8
B Forestry and logging	-	-	2.1	-	...	2.1	-	-	1.5	-	...	1.5
C Fishing	-	-	25.8	0.6	...	26.5	-	-	29.6	-	...	29.6
2 Mining and quarrying	-	-	...	...	...	-						
3 Manufacturing	24.5	8.5	15.4	34.5	...	83.0	27.3	9.6	21.0	37.7	...	95.6
4 Electricity, gas and water	12.2	6.5	-6.2	-	...	12.6	18.1	6.4	-10.5	1.0	...	14.9
A Electricity, gas and steam	7.1	5.8	-3.6	-	...	9.3	9.4	5.9	-4.7	0.7	...	11.3
B Water works and supply	5.1	0.8	-2.6	-	...	3.3	8.7	0.4	-5.8	0.3	...	3.5
5 Construction	36.1	3.3	15.6	-	...	55.0	27.1	2.2	13.5	-	...	42.8
6 Wholesale and retail trade, restaurants and hotels	41.8	7.0	157.1	13.8	...	219.7	50.3	7.4	154.5	13.4	...	225.6
A Wholesale and retail trade	...	...	...	...	...	...	-	7.4	154.4	2.6	...	164.4
B Restaurants and hotels	...	...	...	...	...	...	50.3	-	-0.1	10.8	...	61.0
7 Transport, storage and communication	67.4	14.7	22.6	3.7	...	108.4	65.8	14.5	36.8	3.3	...	120.3
A Transport and storage	49.2	9.2	12.0	3.7	...	74.2	44.7	8.2	26.9	0.9	...	80.8
B Communication	18.1	5.5	10.7	-	...	34.3	21.1	6.2	9.8	2.4	...	39.6
8 Finance, insurance, real estate and business services	20.6	17.4	80.9	1.4	...	120.4	21.3	18.2	69.8	1.9	...	111.2
A Financial institutions	13.4	1.9	18.3	0.2	...	33.8	15.2	1.6	11.4	-	...	28.2
B Insurance	3.5	0.3	4.0	-	...	7.8	1.4	0.1	1.2	1.8	...	4.6
C Real estate and business services	3.7	15.2	58.6	1.2	...	78.8	4.7	16.4	57.2	0.1	...	78.4
Real estate, except dwellings	-	-	14.0	-	...	14.0	-	-	14.3	-	...	14.3

Seychelles

4.3 Cost Components of Value Added
(Continued)

Million Seychelles rupees

	1982						1983					
	Compensation of Employees	Capital Consumption	Net Operating Surplus	Indirect Taxes	Less: Subsidies Received	Value Added	Compensation of Employees	Capital Consumption	Net Operating Surplus	Indirect Taxes	Less: Subsidies Received	Value Added
Dwellings	-	14.6	42.1	-	...	56.7	-	15.5	41.5	-	...	57.1
9 Community, social and personal services a	23.0	-	6.1	0.2	...	29.3	21.5	0.8	5.8	0.5	...	28.6
Total, Industries	225.6	57.5	344.8	54.9	...	683.1	231.2	59.2	367.7	57.8	...	715.9
Producers of Government Services	183.3	0.1	...	...	...	183.4	170.6	0.1	...	...	...	170.7
Other Producers a	...	...	...	...	...	...	...	...	...	...	...	...
Total	409.0	57.6	345.0	54.8	...	866.5	401.9	59.1	367.7	57.9	...	886.5
Less: Imputed bank service charge	...	...	29.6	...	...	29.6	...	...	25.8	...	...	25.8
Import duties	...	...	...	128.2	...	128.2	...	...	...	128.6	...	128.6
Value added tax	...	...	...	...	...	...	...	...	...	...	...	...
Total	409.0	57.6	315.4	183.1	...	965.1	401.8	59.3	341.9	186.4	...	989.4

	1984						1985					
	Compensation of Employees	Capital Consumption	Net Operating Surplus	Indirect Taxes	Less: Subsidies Received	Value Added	Compensation of Employees	Capital Consumption	Net Operating Surplus	Indirect Taxes	Less: Subsidies Received	Value Added
All Producers												
1 Agriculture, hunting, forestry and fishing	-	-	69.0	-	...	69.0	0.8	-	68.5	-	...	69.3
A Agriculture and hunting	-	-	43.1	-	...	43.1	-	-	44.3	-	...	44.3
B Forestry and logging	-	-	1.4	-	...	1.4	-	-	1.5	-	...	1.5
C Fishing	-	-	24.4	-	...	24.4	0.8	-	22.6	-	...	23.5
2 Mining and quarrying	-	-	-	-	...	-	...	...	...	...	...	...
3 Manufacturing	27.2	9.8	21.5	41.8	...	100.3	29.4	9.8	28.3	48.9	...	116.4
4 Electricity, gas and water	18.4	6.0	-3.5	2.6	...	23.4	16.4	6.4	6.3	2.6	...	31.7
A Electricity, gas and steam	9.6	5.7	-0.9	2.3	...	16.7	9.8	6.3	5.2	2.6	...	23.9
B Water works and supply	8.8	0.3	-2.6	0.3	...	6.7	6.6	0.1	1.2	-	...	7.8
5 Construction	30.9	4.7	17.1	-	...	52.8	26.5	10.2	36.4	-	...	73.1
6 Wholesale and retail trade, restaurants and hotels	53.1	6.2	186.4	11.8	...	257.5	66.3	6.5	212.7	12.6	...	298.1
A Wholesale and retail trade	-	6.2	160.8	2.7	...	169.7	-	6.5	185.7	3.1	...	195.4
B Restaurants and hotels	53.1	-	25.5	9.1	...	87.7	66.3	-	27.0	9.5	...	102.7
7 Transport, storage and communication	69.9	17.8	63.0	3.8	...	154.5	70.3	21.2	74.8	3.3	...	169.5
A Transport and storage	52.1	8.1	45.7	1.8	...	107.7	54.8	8.7	48.0	0.8	...	112.3
B Communication	17.8	9.8	17.2	2.0	...	46.8	15.5	12.5	26.8	2.4	...	57.2
8 Finance, insurance, real estate and business services	23.4	18.1	63.1	1.8	...	106.3	23.2	19.7	74.4	2.0	...	119.2
A Financial institutions	16.7	2.0	12.7	-	...	31.4	16.1	2.2	25.3	-	...	43.6
B Insurance	1.9	0.2	-1.9	1.8	...	1.9	1.9	0.1	1.1	1.9	...	5.1
C Real estate and business services	4.7	15.9	52.3	0.1	...	73.0	5.2	17.3	48.0	0.1	...	70.5
Real estate, except dwellings	-	-	12.6	-	...	12.6	0.8	0.7	0.1	-	...	1.8
Dwellings	-	15.0	38.8	-	...	53.9	-	16.3	47.0	-	...	63.3
9 Community, social and personal services a	23.1	1.5	3.1	0.3	...	28.0	22.8	1.3	8.3	0.8	...	33.3
Total, Industries	246.0	64.2	419.7	62.0	...	791.9	255.7	75.1	509.6	70.2	...	910.6
Producers of Government Services	173.5	0.1	...	...	...	173.6	191.7	0.1	-	-	...	191.8
Other Producers a	...	...	...	...	...	...	...	...	...	...	...	...
Total	419.5	64.3	419.7	62.0	...	965.5	447.4	75.2	509.6	70.2	...	1102.4
Less: Imputed bank service charge	...	...	26.0	...	...	26.0	...	...	31.9	...	...	31.9
Import duties	...	...	...	128.6	...	128.6	...	...	...	134.5	...	134.5
Value added tax	...	...	...	...	...	...	...	...	...	...	...	...
Total	419.5	64.3	393.7	190.6	...	1068.1	447.4	75.2	477.7	204.6	...	1204.9

	1986						1987					
	Compensation of Employees	Capital Consumption	Net Operating Surplus	Indirect Taxes	Less: Subsidies Received	Value Added	Compensation of Employees	Capital Consumption	Net Operating Surplus	Indirect Taxes	Less: Subsidies Received	Value Added
All Producers												
1 Agriculture, hunting, forestry and fishing	2.7	-	74.6	-	...	77.3	3.4	-	70.5	-	...	73.9
A Agriculture and hunting	-	-	46.7	-	...	46.7	-	-	51.2	-	...	51.2
B Forestry and logging	-	-	1.5	-	...	1.6	-	-	1.6	-	...	1.6
C Fishing	2.7	-	26.4	-	...	29.0	3.4	-	17.7	-	...	21.1

4.3 Cost Components of Value Added
(Continued)

Million Seychelles rupees

	Compensation of Employees	Capital Consumption	Net Operating Surplus	Indirect Taxes	Less: Subsidies Received	Value Added	Compensation of Employees	Capital Consumption	Net Operating Surplus	Indirect Taxes	Less: Subsidies Received	Value Added
	1986						1987					
2 Mining and quarrying	-	-	-	-	...	-	34.3	12.8	31.2	58.5	...	136.8
3 Manufacturing	31.9	11.0	30.9	46.6	...	120.4	34.3	12.8	31.2	58.5	...	136.8
4 Electricity, gas and water	22.1	5.6	4.2	3.4	...	35.3	21.5	5.2	-8.4	2.4	...	20.7
A Electricity, gas and steam	13.2	5.1	6.3	3.3	...	27.9	12.0	4.7	-8.0	1.3	...	10.0
B Water works and supply	8.9	0.5	-2.1	0.1	...	7.4	9.5	0.5	-0.4	1.1	...	10.7
5 Construction	29.5	9.6	37.0	-	...	76.1	23.6	7.3	30.8	-	...	61.7
6 Wholesale and retail trade, restaurants and hotels	67.6	10.2	244.4	2.8	...	325.1	85.2	20.5	238.8	7.2	...	351.7
A Wholesale and retail trade	-	6.1	207.9	-	...	214.1	-	6.6	217.5	-	...	224.1
B Restaurants and hotels	67.6	4.1	36.5	2.8	...	111.0	85.2	13.9	21.4	7.2	...	127.6
7 Transport, storage and communication	74.8	28.4	79.5	-40.5	...	142.3	87.2	23.1	81.9	-50.7	...	141.5
A Transport and storage	61.6	16.3	45.5	-43.3	...	80.1	73.4	10.5	45.6	-54.3	...	75.2
B Communication	13.2	12.1	34.0	2.8	...	62.1	13.8	12.6	36.3	3.6	...	66.3
8 Finance, insurance, real estate and business services	25.0	18.1	89.6	2.5	...	135.2	27.0	20.1	110.8	8.3	...	166.1
A Financial institutions	17.6	2.1	28.1	-	...	47.8	17.9	2.3	37.0	5.2	...	62.4
B Insurance	1.8	0.2	7.2	2.5	...	11.7	2.2	0.2	19.8	2.5	...	24.6
C Real estate and business services	5.5	15.8	54.3	-	...	75.6	6.9	17.6	54.0	0.5	...	79.1
Real estate, except dwellings	0.9	0.5	3.8	-	...	5.2	0.9	0.5	3.7	-	...	5.2
Dwellings	-	15.1	49.5	-	...	64.6	-	16.9	49.3	-	...	66.2
9 Community, social and personal services a	23.7	1.2	9.4	-	...	34.4	26.0	1.5	9.4	-	...	36.9
Total, Industries	277.3	84.1	569.6	14.8	...	946.1	308.2	90.5	565.0	25.6	...	989.3
Producers of Government Services	184.0	0.1	-	...	...	184.0	223.4	0.1	-	...	...	223.5
Other Producers a	...	...	...	...	...	...	...	...	...	...	...	...
Total	461.3	84.3	569.6	14.8	...	1130.1	531.6	90.6	565.0	25.6	...	1212.8
Less: Imputed bank service charge	...	...	37.7	...	...	37.7	...	...	43.6	...	...	43.6
Import duties	...	...	...	197.6	...	197.6	...	...	...	226.8	...	226.8
Value added tax	...	...	...	...	...	...	...	...	...	...	...	...
Total	461.3	84.4	532.0	212.4	...	1290.0	531.6	90.6	521.4	252.4	...	1395.9
	1988						1989					
				All Producers								
1 Agriculture, hunting, forestry and fishing	3.2	...	69.0	-	...	72.3	4.8	-	69.2	-	...	74.0
A Agriculture and hunting	-	-	51.4	-	...	51.4	-	-	53.0	-	...	53.0
B Forestry and logging	-	-	1.4	-	...	1.4	-	-	1.6	-	...	1.6
C Fishing	3.2	-	16.2	-	...	19.5	4.8	-	14.5	-	...	19.3
2 Mining and quarrying	-	-	-	-	...	-	-	-	-	-	...	-
3 Manufacturing	38.8	17.3	36.9	67.5	...	160.4	47.4	17.8	25.2	71.9	...	162.4
4 Electricity, gas and water	23.5	11.9	-13.9	5.8	...	27.3	24.6	11.6	-14.2	1.3	...	23.2
A Electricity, gas and steam	11.2	10.5	-17.3	4.3	...	8.7	11.2	10.8	-14.1	0.8	...	8.8
B Water works and supply	12.3	1.4	3.5	1.5	...	18.6	13.4	0.8	-0.1	0.5	...	14.5
5 Construction	27.2	10.7	26.2	-	...	64.0	35.6	9.7	41.3	-	...	86.6
6 Wholesale and retail trade, restaurants and hotels	97.3	18.2	251.8	9.0	...	376.3	113.2	18.8	322.9	9.5	...	464.4
A Wholesale and retail trade	-	6.9	215.0	-	...	221.9	-	8.0	274.9	-	...	283.0
B Restaurants and hotels	97.3	11.3	36.9	9.0	...	154.4	113.2	10.8	47.9	9.5	...	181.4
7 Transport, storage and communication	88.7	26.0	57.2	-31.2	...	140.7	116.6	32.8	84.5	-50.7	...	183.2
A Transport and storage	74.0	12.5	38.1	-36.1	...	88.5	100.2	17.6	52.5	-56.3	...	114.0
B Communication	14.7	13.5	19.1	4.9	...	52.2	16.5	15.1	32.0	5.6	...	69.2
8 Finance, insurance, real estate and business services	26.1	20.8	138.9	3.9	...	189.8	28.0	20.7	151.5	3.1	...	203.3
A Financial institutions	19.2	2.1	64.5	-	...	85.8	20.8	2.2	59.9	2.1	...	84.9
B Insurance	2.3	0.2	20.4	3.3	...	26.2	2.3	0.6	32.6	-	...	35.5
C Real estate and business services	4.7	18.5	54.0	0.6	...	77.8	5.0	17.9	59.1	0.9	...	82.9
Real estate, except dwellings	1.0	0.5	3.8	-	...	5.3	1.0	0.7	-0.5	-	...	5.4

Seychelles

4.3 Cost Components of Value Added
(Continued)

Million Seychelles rupees

	1988						1989					
	Compensation of Employees	Capital Consumption	Net Operating Surplus	Indirect Taxes	Less: Subsidies Received	Value Added	Compensation of Employees	Capital Consumption	Net Operating Surplus	Indirect Taxes	Less: Subsidies Received	Value Added
Dwellings	-	17.7	47.8	-	...	65.6	-	16.9	50.8	-	...	67.8
9 Community, social and personal services [a]	27.6	1.6	8.9	-	...	38.0	24.5	1.7	14.7	5.1	...	46.0
Total, Industries	332.4	106.5	575.0	55.0	...	1068.8	394.7	113.0	695.1	40.2	...	1243.1
Producers of Government Services	214.6	0.1	-	-	...	214.7	219.3	0.1	-	-	...	219.4
Other Producers [a]	...	...	...	...	...	...	...	...	...	...	...	...
Total	547.0	106.6	575.0	55.0	...	1283.5	614.1	113.1	695.1	40.2	...	1462.5
Less: Imputed bank service charge	...	...	51.3	...	...	51.3	...	...	51.9	...	...	51.9
Import duties	...	...	...	295.6	...	295.6	...	...	...	330.4	...	330.4
Value added tax	...	...	...	...	...	...	...	...	...	...	...	...
Total	547.0	106.5	523.8	350.6	...	1527.9	614.1	113.1	643.2	370.6	...	1740.9

	1990					
	Compensation of Employees	Capital Consumption	Net Operating Surplus	Indirect Taxes	Less: Subsidies Received	Value Added

All Producers

1 Agriculture, hunting, forestry and fishing	4.1	-	88.2	-	...	92.3
A Agriculture and hunting	-	-	62.9	-	...	62.9
B Forestry and logging	-	-	1.8	-	...	1.8
C Fishing	4.1	-	23.5	-	...	27.6
2 Mining and quarrying	...	...	...	...	...	...
3 Manufacturing	59.5	25.0	31.4	82.6	...	198.6
4 Electricity, gas and water	29.5	11.7	-21.4	7.2	...	26.9
A Electricity, gas and steam	12.7	10.8	-16.3	5.6	...	12.7
B Water works and supply	16.8	0.9	-5.1	1.6	...	14.2
5 Construction	40.0	9.2	45.1	-	...	94.3
6 Wholesale and retail trade, restaurants and hotels	127.3	33.8	353.1	16.9	...	531.1
A Wholesale and retail trade	-	9.0	306.9	-	...	315.9
B Restaurants and hotels	127.3	24.8	46.2	16.9	...	215.2
7 Transport, storage and communication	128.8	61.0	57.0	-10.3	...	236.5
A Transport and storage	107.2	43.8	27.7	-17.2	...	161.5
B Communication	21.6	17.2	29.3	7.0	...	75.0
8 Finance, insurance, real estate and business services	31.6	21.4	154.5	7.1	...	214.6
A Financial institutions	22.9	2.4	57.7	6.1	...	89.1
B Insurance	3.0	0.6	36.3	-	...	40.0
C Real estate and business services	5.7	18.3	60.5	0.9	...	85.5
Real estate, except dwellings	1.0	0.5	4.0	-	...	5.5
Dwellings	-	17.4	52.2	-	...	69.6
9 Community, social and personal services [a]	26.4	2.6	17.6	-	...	46.6
Total, Industries	447.2	164.7	725.5	103.5	...	1440.9
Producers of Government Services	256.1	0.1	-	-	...	256.2
Other Producers [a]	...	...	...	...	...	...
Total	703.3	164.8	725.5	103.5	...	1697.1
Less: Imputed bank service charge	-	-	68.5	-	...	68.5
Import duties	-	-	-	362.2	...	362.2
Value added tax	...	...	...	...	...	...
Total	703.3	164.7	657.0	465.8	...	1990.7

a) Item 'Other producers' is included in item 'Community, social and personal services'.

1642

Sierra Leone

General note. The preparation of national accounts statistics in Sierra Leone is undertaken by the Central Statistics Office, Freetown. Official estimates together with methodological notes are published in a series of reports entitled 'National Accounts of Sierra Leone'. The most detailed description of the sources and methods used for the national accounts estimation is found in the sixteenth edition of this report published in December 1987. The estimates are generally in accordance with the classifications and definitions recommended in the United Nations System of National Accounts (SNA). New and revised estimates for the years 1970/71 to 1975/76 were published in 1977, incorporating results of the 1974 population census and the Njala University survey on small-scale manufacturing in 1974. The following tables have been prepared from successive replies to the United Nations national accounts questionnaire. Estimates prior to 1967 relate to fiscal year beginning 1 April while estimates from 1966 relate to fiscal year beginning 1 July. When the scope and coverage of the estimates differ for conceptual or statistical reasons from the definitions and classifications recommended in SNA, a footnote is indicated to the relevant tables.

Sources and methods :

(a) Gross domestic product. Gross domestic product is estimated mainly through the income approach.

(b) Expenditure on the gross domestic product. The expenditure approach is used for the estimation of government final consumption expenditure and exports and imports of goods and services. A combination of the commodity-flow method and the expenditure approach is used to estimate private final consumption expenditure. The commodity-flow method is used to obtain estimates of gross capital formation. The actual expenditures incurred by the government are obtained from the government budget documents. The expenditure is classified by purpose, distinguishing between military and civilian purposes. Private final consumption expenditure estimates are compiled mainly by tracing the consumption goods through the distributive system to the ultimate consumer. Estimates for a few items of food and services are, however, prepared from data collected through the household expenditure survey and the report of the survey of business and industry. The figures on changes in stocks relate principally to diamonds, iron ore, bauxite, rice, export crops, stocks of all public companies, and all major manufacturing and trading establishments for which the completed questionnaires are received by the Central Statistics Office. The estimates of gross fixed capital formation are obtained through an analysis of production and imports of all capital goods classified by type and then marked up for distributive costs. Exports and imports of goods and services are estimated mainly from external trade statistics. GDP by expenditure type at constant prices is not estimated.

(c) Cost-structure of the gross domestic product. Estimates of domestic factor income are compiled from returns directly obtained from the companies concerned and then marked up for non-responding establishments. Analysis of indirect taxes and subsidies by industry was undertaken for the first time in 1976 to arrive at GDP by economic activity in producers' values. Information on depreciation is available only for some larger establishments.

(d) Gross domestic product by kind of economic activity. The table of gross domestic product by kind of economic activity is prepared at market prices, i.e. producers' values. Value added of the majority of industries is estimated through the income approach. The production approach is used to estimate the agricultural and mining sectors. Fairly reliable information on production of major agricultural crops is available only for 1970-71 and 1984-85 based on objective samples surveys. For other years the Ministry of Agriculture and Natural Resources estimate the production of these crops on the basis of reports received from their regional office. For other crops the main source is the Production Yearbook of the Food and Agriculture Organisation. The data required to estimate the value added of mining are obtained from the companies concerned while the value of diamonds smuggled out of the country is based on informal discussions with knowledgeable persons in the industry. The estimates of total income, wages and salaries, operating profits, etc. of a large sample of manufacturing establishments employing six or more persons are compiled from returns directly obtained from them, and then marked up for non-responding establishments using employment data as mark-up factors. The census of manufacturing establishments 1986-87 provided valuable data to strengthen the estimates for 1984 and 1985. The Njala University survey in 1974/75 was used to confirm estimates made for small-scale manufacturing which are based on employment projections and statistics of earnings. The commodity-flow method is used to estimate gross output and intermediate consumption of construction. Data from the government public works department and a number of private contractors are used for analysis of total construction expenditure. The commodity-flow method is also used for the trade sector, preparing aggregate trade margin estimates of all commodities marketed. Receipts and expenditure data are collected directly for national accounting purposes from a sample of trading establishments. For smaller trade establishments, estimates are obtained as a product of the number of persons engaged which is based on the 1974 census, and average earnings per person obtained from a bench-mark year and adjusted yearly. Transportation surveys and other data sources are used for bench-mark estimates in the transport sector. For the services sector, the imputed banking service charge is treated as a negative operating surplus of a nominal finance industry and deducted as a lump sum separately. The number of persons engaged in domestic services, obtained from the 1974 population census has been assumed to continue to grow at the average rate as indicated by the two censuses in 1963 and 1974. Government budgetary documents and unpublished records are used to obtain estimates for central government and local authorities. For the constant price estimates, double deflation is used for the agricultural components with current quantities valued at base-year prices of 1963/64 and 1972/73. Index of building costs is used for price deflation in the construction sector. For other industries, value added is extrapolated by quantity indexes of output obtained by price deflation or employment data. No single typical approach is used for mining and quarrying.

1.1 Expenditure on the Gross Domestic Product, in Current Prices

Million Sierra Leone leones

Fiscal year beginning 1 July

	1980	1981	1982	1983	1984	1985	1986	1987	1988	1989	1990	1991
1 Government final consumption expenditure	90	138	167	189	345	498	1210	1389	3311	5492	15676	...
2 Private final consumption expenditure	1172	1416	1647	2242	4002	6238	16267	25295	38117	70139	117036	...
3 Gross capital formation	247	215	268	347	477	839	2058	2297	5911	11637	17914	...
A Increase in stocks	11	10	33	15	53	109	205	22	336	415	2729	...
B Gross fixed capital formation	236	205	235	332	424	730	1854	2275	5575	11222	15185	...
Residential buildings	...	...	...	...	...	...	...	...	...	...	...	...
Non-residential buildings	131	128	125	188	253	426	988	1254	2879	4928	6199	...
Other construction and land improvement etc.												...
Other	105	77	110	144	171	304	866	1021	2696	5582	8987	...
4 Exports of goods and services [a]	297	253	208	290	463	855	2516	4491	6390	16343	38124	...
5 Less: Imports of goods and services	514	416	413	339	503	949	2350	4393	9782	20774	38574	...
Equals: Gross Domestic Product	1292	1605	1876	2730	4785	7481	19701	29080	43947	82837	150175	...

a) The estimates of exports of goods and services shown in table 1.1 include an upward adjustments for the estimated value of diamond smuggled out of the country.

1.2 Expenditure on the Gross Domestic Product, in Constant Prices

Million Sierra Leone leones

Fiscal year beginning 1 July

	1980	1981	1982	1983	1984	1985	1986	1987	1988	1989	1990	1991
				At constant prices of:1984								
1 Government final consumption expenditure	...	...	...	...	...	365	292	301	380	339	388	...
2 Private final consumption expenditure	...	...	...	...	...	3840	4236	4488	4463	4574	4371	...
3 Gross capital formation	...	...	...	...	...	547	375	328	533	498	443	...
A Increase in stocks	...	...	...	...	...	68	52	4	40	27	101	...
B Gross fixed capital formation	...	...	...	...	...	479	323	324	493	471	342	...

Sierra Leone

1.2 Expenditure on the Gross Domestic Product, in Constant Prices
(Continued)

Million Sierra Leone leones

Fiscal year beginning 1 July

	1980	1981	1982	1983	1984	1985	1986	1987	1988	1989	1990	1991
					At constant prices of:1984							
Residential buildings	...	...	...	...	...							
Non-residential buildings	...	...	...	...	...	266	248	216	344	321	229	
Other construction and land improvement etc.	...	...	...	...	...							
Other	...	...	...	...	...	213	75	108	149	149	111	...
4 Exports of goods and services	...	...	...	...	...	455	412	417	316	400	376	...
5 Less: Imports of goods and services	...	...	...	...	...	538	392	478	523	513	418	...
Equals: Gross Domestic Product	...	...	...	...	...	4668	4923	5055	5169	5298	5160	...

1.3 Cost Components of the Gross Domestic Product

Million Sierra Leone leones

Fiscal year beginning 1 July

	1980	1981	1982	1983	1984	1985	1986	1987	1988	1989	1990	1991
1 Indirect taxes, net	119	101	77	105	132	213	912	1088	2438	3293	11815	...
A Indirect taxes	119	101	77	106	139	223	913	1089	2445	3300	11815	...
B Less: Subsidies	1	-	-	1	7	11	1	1	6	7	-	...
2 Consumption of fixed capital	124	153	183	280	360	507	1385	1947	2537	4882	8411	...
3 Compensation of employees paid by resident producers to:	345	410	489	711	836	1351	3209	4668	6567	10594	20858	...
4 Operating surplus	704	942	1128	1634	3457	5410	14194	21377	32404	64068	109091	...
Equals: Gross Domestic Product	1292	1605	1876	2730	4785	7481	19701	29080	43947	82837	150175	...

1.4 General Government Current Receipts and Disbursements

Million Sierra Leone leones

Fiscal year beginning 1 July

	1980	1981	1982	1983	1984	1985	1986	1987	1988	1989	1990	1991
					Receipts							
1 Operating surplus	...	...	...	...	...	...	...	...	...	...	...	...
2 Property and entrepreneurial income	...	...	...	...	...	13	63	93	309	538	1520	...
3 Taxes, fees and contributions	...	...	...	...	...	331	1176	1871	3519	4374	16226	...
A Indirect taxes	...	...	...	...	...	222	911	1089	2445	3077	11815	...
B Direct taxes	...	...	...	...	...	95	254	697	1011	1185	4054	...
C Social security contributions	...	...	...	...	...	...	...	...	...	...	...	...
D Compulsory fees, fines and penalties	...	...	...	...	...	14	12	84	63	112	358	...
4 Other current transfers	...	...	...	...	...	3	6	29	33	58	90	...
Total Current Receipts of General Government	...	...	...	...	...	346	1245	1993	3861	4970	17836	...
					Disbursements							
1 Government final consumption expenditure	...	...	...	...	...	290	1168	1473	3311	5542	15692	...
A Compensation of employees	...	...	...	...	...	180	574	941	1065	1706	4287	...
B Consumption of fixed capital	...	...	...	...	...	-	-	-	-	-	...	...
C Purchases of goods and services, net	...	...	...	...	...	110	593	532	2246	3836	11406	...
D Less: Own account fixed capital formation	...	...	...	...	...	...	...	...	...	...	...	...
E Indirect taxes paid, net	...	...	...	...	...	...	...	...	...	...	...	...
2 Property income	...	...	...	...	...	195	-	-	-	1	-	...
A Interest	...	...	...	...	...	195	-	-	-	1	-	...
B Net land rent and royalties	...	...	...	...	...	...	...	...	...	...	...	...
3 Subsidies	...	...	...	...	...	10	1	1	6	7	-	...
4 Other current transfers	...	...	...	...	...	105	138	234	533	676	1190	...
5 Net saving	...	...	...	...	...	-254	-61	285	11	-1255	953	...
Total Current Disbursements and Net Saving of General Government	...	...	...	...	...	346	1245	1993	3861	4970	17836	...

1644

1.7 External Transactions on Current Account, Summary

Million Sierra Leone leones — Fiscal year beginning 1 July

	1980	1981	1982	1983	1984	1985	1986	1987	1988	1989	1990	1991
Payments to the Rest of the World												
1 Imports of goods and services	514	416	413	339	499	945	2350	5260	5631	12291	32576	...
A Imports of merchandise c.i.f.	405	360	369	287	376	720	1793	3821	4494	9590	21269	...
B Other	108	56	45	52	123	226	557	1439	1138	2700	11307	...
2 Factor income to the rest of the world	24	43	44	40	85	-56	-1860	1984	-389	-661	7728	...
A Compensation of employees	...	...	...	...	...	...	...	...	...	...	...	
B Property and entrepreneurial income	24	43	44	40	85	-56	-1860	1984	-389	-661	7728	...
3 Current transfers to the rest of the world	4	1	5	5	4	7	5	21	22	40	36	...
4 Surplus of the nation on current transactions	-192	-165	-199	-33	-57	38	2076	-748	147	-517	-7325	...
Payments to the Rest of the World and Surplus of the Nation on Current Transactions [a]	350	295	263	350	531	935	2572	6517	5411	11153	33015	...
Receipts From The Rest of the World												
1 Exports of goods and services	289	243	196	276	441	822	2466	6259	5101	10658	31776	...
A Exports of merchandise f.o.b.	224	177	137	202	333	672	2027	4753	3397	8344	21175	...
B Other	65	66	59	74	108	150	438	1507	1704	2314	10601	...
2 Factor income from rest of the world	1	1	-	1	3	4	2	5	5	20	156	...
A Compensation of employees	...	...	...	...	...	...	...	...	...	...	...	
B Property and entrepreneurial income	1	1	-	1	3	4	2	5	5	20	156	...
3 Current transfers from rest of the world	60	52	67	74	87	108	104	252	305	475	1082	...
Receipts from the Rest of the World on Current Transactions [a]	350	295	263	350	531	935	2572	6517	5411	11153	33015	...

a) Estimates are derived from Balance of Payment Accounts, therefore are not strictly comparable to those in other tables.

1.10 Gross Domestic Product by Kind of Activity, in Current Prices

Million Sierra Leone leones — Fiscal year beginning 1 July

	1980	1981	1982	1983	1984	1985	1986	1987	1988	1989	1990	1991
1 Agriculture, hunting, forestry and fishing	399	552	691	1062	2075	2925	7713	11673	16651	30553	52494	...
2 Mining and quarrying	122	95	101	141	296	1312	2154	2225	2688	5768	14133	...
3 Manufacturing	94	143	145	182	229	325	1118	1722	3267	5781	13000	...
4 Electricity, gas and water	7	8	11	14	6	13	109	108	134	194	78	...
5 Construction	56	55	48	71	128	174	419	501	1102	1555	1870	...
6 Wholesale and retail trade, restaurants and hotels	163	173	233	295	759	1046	3246	5878	8864	20469	30202	...
7 Transport, storage and communication	197	287	324	469	547	603	1871	2576	4451	8888	13292	...
8 Finance, insurance, real estate and business services	97	126	147	270	435	663	1751	2609	3684	6502	18504	...
9 Community, social and personal services [a]	52	64	74	98	103	125	263	419	459	505	555	...
Total, Industries	1187	1503	1773	2602	4577	7185	18645	27710	41299	80215	144127	...
Producers of Government Services	63	91	103	122	182	252	546	879	1065	1706	4525	...
Other Producers [a]	...	...	...	...	...	...	...	...	...	...	...	...
Subtotal	1250	1594	1876	2724	4758	7438	19191	28588	42364	81921	148652	...
Less: Imputed bank service charge	6	30	32	39	35	58	140	175	192	1606	3658	...
Plus: Import duties	49	40	32	45	62	102	649	666	1775	2523	5181	...
Plus: Value added tax	...	...	...	...	...	...	...	...	...	...	...	...
Equals: Gross Domestic Product	1292	1605	1876	2730	4785	7481	19701	29080	43947	82837	150175	...

a) Beginning 1980, item 'Other producers' is included in item 'Community, social and personal services'.

Sierra Leone

1.11 Gross Domestic Product by Kind of Activity, in Constant Prices

Million Sierra Leone leones

At constant prices of: 1972 (1980–1984) and 1984 (1984 onward). The 1984 column shows both (1972 prices / 1984 prices).

	1980	1981	1982	1983	1984	1985	1986	1987	1988	1989	1990	1991
1 Agriculture, hunting, forestry and fishing	139	146	140	143	174 / 2075	2013	2158	2311	2228	2344	2361	...
2 Mining and quarrying	26	22	20	23	21 / 296	342	358	359	406	447	469	...
3 Manufacturing	42	50	42	45	38 / 229	213	188	215	170	158	249	...
4 Electricity, gas and water	2	3	3	3	- / 6	7	10	8	8	9	8	...
5 Construction	22	17	13	16	19 / 128	132	137	100	147	138	124	...
6 Wholesale and retail trade, restaurants and hotels	65	65	74	62	81 / 759	763	783	798	881	966	1062	...
7 Transport, storage and communication	50	60	59	60	53 / 547	442	402	362	416	449	283	...
8 Finance, insurance, real estate and business services	41	46	47	49	46 / 435	437	458	461	462	524	629	...
9 Community, social and personal services [a]	23	24	26	30	22 / 103	107	108	110	109	109	109	...
Total, Industries	410	433	424	429	453 / 4577	4456	4599	4724	4827	5144	5294	...
Producers of Government Services	46	58	65	63	72 / 182	192	219	238	226	226	226	...
Other Producers [a]	...	...	...	...	...	...	...	...	...	...	...	...
Subtotal	456	491	489	492	525 / 4758	4648	4818	4961	5052	5370	5519	...
Less: Imputed bank service charge	2	14	15	18	10 / 35	37	38	39	40	74	84	...
Plus: Import duties	20	20	16	22	18 / 62	58	143	133	156	106	119	...
Plus: Value added tax	...	...	...	...	...	...	...	...	...	...	...	...
Equals: Gross Domestic Product	473	497	490	496	533 / 4785	4668	4923	5055	5169	5402	5554	...

a) Beginning 1980, item 'Other producers' is included in item 'Community, social and personal services'.

1.12 Relations Among National Accounting Aggregates

Million Sierra Leone leones

	1980	1981	1982	1983	1984	1985	1986	1987	1988	1989	1990	1991
Gross Domestic Product	1292	1605	1876	2730	4785	7481	19701	29080	43947	82837	150175	...
Plus: Net factor income from the rest of the world	-23	-43	-43	-40	-82	61	1862	-1979	395	681	-7572	...
Factor income from the rest of the world	1	1	-	1	3	4	2	5	5	20	156	...
Less: Factor income to the rest of the world	24	43	44	40	85	-56	-1860	1984	-389	-661	7728	...
Equals: Gross National Product	1269	1562	1833	2690	4703	7542	21563	27101	44341	83518	142603	...
Less: Consumption of fixed capital	124	153	183	280	360	507	1385	1947	2537	4882	8411	...
Equals: National Income	1145	1409	1650	2410	4343	7035	20178	25154	41804	78636	134192	...
Plus: Net current transfers from the rest of the world	56	51	62	69	83	101	99	231	283	435	1046	...
Current transfers from the rest of the world	60	52	67	74	87	108	104	252	305	475	1082	...
Less: Current transfers to the rest of the world	4	1	5	5	4	7	5	21	22	40	36	...
Equals: National Disposable Income	1201	1460	1713	2479	4426	7136	20277	25384	42087	79071	135238	...
Less: Final consumption	1262	1553	1814	2431	4348	6736	17477	26685	41428	75631	132712	...
Equals: Net Saving	-61	-93	-101	48	79	400	2800	-1300	659	3440	2526	...
Less: Surplus of the nation on current transactions	-191	-165	-199	-33	-57	38	2076	-748	147	-517	-7325	...
Statistical discrepancy	-8	-10	-12	-14	-19	-30	-50	902	2861	2798	-349	...
Equals: Net Capital Formation	123	62	85	67	117	332	673	350	3373	6755	9503	...

2.1 Government Final Consumption Expenditure by Function, in Current Prices

Million Sierra Leone leones   Fiscal year beginning 1 July

	1980	1981	1982	1983	1984	1985	1986	1987	1988	1989	1990	1991
1 General public services	43	49	43	55	56	136	503	611	719	1097	3853	...
2 Defence	14	18	18	20	22	35	110	159	281	554	1827	...
3 Public order and safety	...	...	...	...	...	...	...	...	...	...	...	...
4 Education	47	72	58	74	75	91	261	348	514	776	1996	...
5 Health	26	28	22	34	28	39	147	228	230	380	693	...
6 Social security and welfare	2	2	2	5	3	3	15	19	38	107	205	...
7 Housing and community amenities	4	7	4	5	3	7	44	40	33	103	339	...
8 Recreational, cultural and religious affairs	-	-	-	-	4	5	37	33	-	-	2	...
9 Economic services	123	111	139	121	147	348	816	683	1088	3496	9033	...
A Fuel and energy	15	...	...	...	20	38	44	40	228	2029	5003	...
B Agriculture, forestry, fishing and hunting	40	...			50	76	187	199	316	395	1006	...
C Mining, manufacturing and construction, except fuel and energy	5	...	...	...	1	9	5	34	13	58	129	...
D Transportation and communication	33	...	...	...	53	202	556	343	368	528	499	...
E Other economic affairs	30	...	...	...	22	23	25	67	163	485	2397	...
10 Other functions	145	95	57	58	151	235	288	144	980	1107	14391	...
Total Government Final Consumption Expenditure ab	405	382	344	370	489	900	2219	2264	3883	7620	32337	...

a) Item 'Total government final consumption expenditure' includes development expenditure.
b) Only central government data are included in the general government estimates.

2.5 Private Final Consumption Expenditure by Type and Purpose, in Current Prices

Million Sierra Leone leones   Fiscal year beginning 1 July

	1980	1981	1982	1983	1984	1985	1986	1987	1988	1989	1990	1991
Final Consumption Expenditure of Resident Households												
1 Food, beverages and tobacco	...	696	912	1242	2550	4024	10848	...	...	64232	...	...
A Food	...	...	...	...	...	...	...	...	...	60072	...	...
B Non-alcoholic beverages	...	...	...	...	...	...	...	...	...	693	...	...
C Alcoholic beverages	...	...	...	...	...	...	...	...	...	1099	...	...
D Tobacco	...	...	...	...	...	...	...	...	...	2367	...	...
2 Clothing and footwear	...	127	121	145	158	190	446	...	...	9654	...	...
3 Gross rent, fuel and power	...	144	178	299	598	932	2255	...	...	5645	...	...
A Fuel and power	...	...	...	...	...	...	...	...	...	3881	...	...
B Other	...	...	...	...	...	...	...	...	...	79	...	...
4 Furniture, furnishings and household equipment and operation	...	90	106	107	131	170	353	...	...	3853	...	...
5 Medical care and health expenses	...	16	21	35	38	57	173	...	...	3435	...	...
6 Transport and communication	...	209	237	340	322	429	1322	...	...	4221	...	...
7 Recreational, entertainment, education and cultural services	...	50	53	72	88	110	223	...	...	3652	...	...
8 Miscellaneous goods and services	...	25	24	27	30	51	150	...	...	2296	...	...
Statistical discrepancy	...	...	...	...	59	246	264	...	...	...	...	...
Total Final Consumption Expenditure in the Domestic Market by Households, of which	...	1355	1651	2267	3973	6209	16033	...	...	96989	...	...
Plus: Direct purchases abroad by resident households	...	4	6	7	8	11	81	...	...			
Less: Direct purchases in the domestic market by non-resident households	...	6	7	10	11	21	142	...	...			
Equals: Final Consumption Expenditure of Resident Households a	...	1353	1650	2264	3970	6199	15972	...	...			
Final Consumption Expenditure of Private Non-profit Institutions Serving Households												
Equals: Final Consumption Expenditure of Private Non-profit Organisations Serving Households	...	...	...	...	...	...	...	...	...	...	...	...
Statistical discrepancy	...	63	-3	-22	33	40	296	...	...	...	...	...
Private Final Consumption Expenditure	...	1416	1647	2242	4002	6238	16267	...	...	...	...	...

a) Item 'Final consumption expenditure of resident households' includes consumption expenditure of private non-profit institutions serving households.

Sierra Leone

2.6 Private Final Consumption Expenditure by Type and Purpose, in Constant Prices

Million Sierra Leone leones

	1980	1981	1982	1983	1984	1985	1986	1987	1988	1989	1990	1991
					At constant prices of:							
			1972						1984			

Final Consumption Expenditure of Resident Households

	1980	1981	1982	1983	1984	1985	1986	1987	1988	1989	1990	1991
1 Food, beverages and tobacco	...	214	213	204	200 / 2550	2694	2908	...	...	...	...	...
2 Clothing and footwear	...	44	41	40	38 / 158	162	168	...	...	...	...	...
3 Gross rent, fuel and power	...	54	56	55	57 / 598	608	603	...	...	...	...	...
4 Furniture, furnishings and household equipment and operation	...	30	30	29	19 / 131	113	124	...	...	...	...	...
5 Medical care and health expenses	...	5	5	4	5 / 38	39	39	...	...	...	...	...
6 Transport and communication	...	30	28	28	26 / 322	270	256	...	...	...	...	...
7 Recreational, entertainment, education and cultural services	...	19	18	23	26 / 88	87	94	...	...	...	...	...
8 Miscellaneous goods and services	...	7	7	7	4 / 30	31	32	...	...	...	...	...
Statistical discrepancy	...	19	-1	-4	-4 / 59	165	70	...	...	...	...	...
Total Final Consumption Expenditure in the Domestic Market by Households, of which	...	419	396	386	372 / 3973	4168	4295	...	...	...	...	...
Plus: Direct purchases abroad by resident households	...	1	1	1	1 / 8	6	18	...	...	...	...	...
Less: Direct purchases in the domestic market by non-resident households	...	1	2	2	2 / 11	12	31	...	...	...	...	...
Equals: Final Consumption Expenditure of Resident Households [a]	...	419	396	385	372 / 3970	4162	4281	...	...	...	...	...

Final Consumption Expenditure of Private Non-profit Institutions Serving Households

	1980	1981	1982	1983	1984	1985	1986	1987	1988	1989	1990	1991
Equals: Final Consumption Expenditure of Private Non-profit Organisations Serving Households	...	...	...	...	... / ...	...	...	...	...	...	...	...
Private Final Consumption Expenditure	...	419	396	385	372 / 3970	4162	4281	...	...	...	...	...

a) Item 'Final consumption expenditure of resident households' includes consumption expenditure of private non-profit institutions serving households.

2.7 Gross Capital Formation by Type of Good and Owner, in Current Prices

Million Sierra Leone leones

	1980				1981				1982			
	TOTAL	Total Private	Public Enterprises	General Government	TOTAL	Total Private	Public Enterprises	General Government	TOTAL	Total Private	Public Enterprises	General Government
Increase in stocks, total	11	3	8	...	10	20	-10	...	33	23	9	...
Gross Fixed Capital Formation, Total	236	147	35	54	205	124	20	61	235	165	13	58
1 Residential buildings												
2 Non-residential buildings	121	76	10	35	114	62	13	39	110	68	5	38
3 Other construction												
4 Land improvement and plantation and orchard development	11	-	-	11	14	-	-	14	15	-	-	15
5 Producers' durable goods	105	71	25	8	77	63	7	7	110	97	8	5
A Transport equipment	49	40	2	7	42	34	3	5	48	40	4	4
Passenger cars	23	...	...	...	19	...	...	...	19	...	...	...
Other	26	...	...	...	22	...	...	...	29	...	...	...
B Machinery and equipment	56	32	23	1	35	29	4	2	62	57	4	2
6 Breeding stock, dairy cattle, etc.	...	...	...	...	...	...	...	...	...	...	...	...
Total Gross Capital Formation	247	150	43	54	215	144	10	61	268	188	22	58

2.7 Gross Capital Formation by Type of Good and Owner, in Current Prices

Million Sierra Leone leones   Fiscal year beginning 1 July

	1983				1984				1985			
	TOTAL	Total Private	Public Enterprises	General Government	TOTAL	Total Private	Public Enterprises	General Government	TOTAL	Total Private	Public Enterprises	General Government
Increase in stocks, total	15	18	-3	...	53	16	37	...	109	72	37	...
Gross Fixed Capital Formation, Total	332	296	14	22	424	...	...	...	730	...	...	...
1 Residential buildings												
2 Non-residential buildings	184	165	3	15	238	...	...	...	402	...	...	...
3 Other construction												
4 Land improvement and plantation and orchard development	4	-	-	4	15	-	-	15	24	-	-	24
5 Producers' durable goods	144	131	11	3	171	...	...	...	304	...	...	...
A Transport equipment	54	47	5	2	62	...	...	...	153	...	...	...
Passenger cars	24	...	...	...	26	...	...	...	49	...	...	...
Other	30	...	...	...	36	...	...	...	104	...	...	...
B Machinery and equipment	90	84	6	1	109	...	...	...	151	...	...	...
6 Breeding stock, dairy cattle, etc.	...	...	...	...	...	...	...	...	...	...	...	...
Total Gross Capital Formation	347	314	11	22	477	...	...	...	839	...	...	...

4.1 Derivation of Value Added by Kind of Activity, in Current Prices

Million Sierra Leone leones   Fiscal year beginning 1 July

	1984			1985			1986			1987		
	Gross Output	Intermediate Consumption	Value Added	Gross Output	Intermediate Consumption	Value Added	Gross Output	Intermediate Consumption	Value Added	Gross Output	Intermediate Consumption	Value Added
All Producers												
1 Agriculture, hunting, forestry and fishing	2435	365	2070	3420	532	2888	9104	1405	7698	13848	2183	11665
A Agriculture and hunting	1563	225	1337	2070	298	1771	6542	964	5577	8921	1283	7639
B Forestry and logging	258	26	232	317	32	285	624	62	561	935	94	842
C Fishing	614	114	500	1034	202	832	1938	379	1560	3992	807	3185
2 Mining and quarrying	420	130	290	1753	447	1306	2860	725	2135	4082	1885	2198
3 Manufacturing	639	473	166	784	528	256	2931	2024	907	7438	6083	1355
4 Electricity, gas and water	39	27	12	48	26	21	160	51	109	279	171	108
A Electricity, gas and steam	30	22	8	37	23	14	118	35	83	188	138	50
B Water works and supply	9	4	5	11	3	7	42	16	27	91	33	58
5 Construction	238	110	128	402	228	174	965	547	418	1150	650	500
6 Wholesale and retail trade, restaurants and hotels	977	219	758	1344	302	1042	4088	846	3242	7400	1530	5870
7 Transport, storage and communication	892	346	546	1041	441	600	5073	3212	1862	6939	4372	2567
A Transport and storage	876	337	539	1012	427	585	4995	3179	1816	6770	4308	2462
B Communication	16	9	7	29	14	15	78	33	45	169	64	105
8 Finance, insurance, real estate and business services	472	38	434	770	108	662	1885	135	1750	3000	392	2608
A Financial institutions	129	24	105	212	84	128	546	79	467	874	302	572
B Insurance												
C Real estate and business services	344	15	329	558	24	535	1339	56	1283	2126	90	2036
9 Community, social and personal services [a]	141	38	103	169	44	125	359	97	262	574	157	417
A Sanitary and similar services	...	...	...	...	...	...	...	...	...	...	...	...
B Social and related community services	118	36	82	136	41	95	302	92	210	505	151	354
Educational services	73	21	52	84	24	60	179	51	128	367	105	262
Medical, dental, other health and veterinary services	45	15	30	52	17	35	123	41	82	138	46	92
C Recreational and cultural services	...	...	...	...	...	...	...	...	...	...	...	...
D Personal and household services	...	...	...	...	...	...	...	...	...	...	...	...
Total, Industries	6252	1746	4507	9730	2656	7074	27425	9042	18383	44712	17424	27288
Producers of Government Services	297	115	182	400	148	252	1072	526	546	1350	471	879

Sierra Leone

4.1 Derivation of Value Added by Kind of Activity, in Current Prices
(Continued)

Million Sierra Leone leones

Fiscal year beginning 1 July

	1984 Gross Output	1984 Intermediate Consumption	1984 Value Added	1985 Gross Output	1985 Intermediate Consumption	1985 Value Added	1986 Gross Output	1986 Intermediate Consumption	1986 Value Added	1987 Gross Output	1987 Intermediate Consumption	1987 Value Added
Other Producers a	...	...	...	...	...	...	...	...	...	...	...	...
Total b	6549	1861	4688	10130	2804	7327	28496	9568	18929	46062	17895	28166
Less: Imputed bank service charge	...	-35	35	...	-58	58	...	-140	140	...	-175	175
Import duties	...	...	...	...	...	...	...	...	...	...	...	...
Value added tax	...	...	...	...	...	...	...	...	...	...	...	...
Other adjustments c	132	...	132	213	...	213	912	...	912	1088	...	1088
Total	6681	1896	4785	10343	2862	7481	29408	9708	19701	47150	18070	29080

	1988 Gross Output	1988 Intermediate Consumption	1988 Value Added	1989 Gross Output	1989 Intermediate Consumption	1989 Value Added	1990 Gross Output	1990 Intermediate Consumption	1990 Value Added
All Producers									
1 Agriculture, hunting, forestry and fishing	19568	2942	16626	...	...	30497	60833	8341	52492
A Agriculture and hunting	14424	2036	12388	...	...	24062	43160	5857	37304
B Forestry and logging	1169	117	1052	...	...	1315	1900	190	1710
C Fishing	3974	789	3185	...	...	5120	15773	2294	13478
2 Mining and quarrying	...	...	2622	...	...	5677	...	...	13823
3 Manufacturing	...	...	2778	...	...	5240	...	...	6776
4 Electricity, gas and water	...	...	134	...	...	194	...	...	78
A Electricity, gas and steam	...	...	...	...	...	...	...	...	...
B Water works and supply	...	...	...	...	...	...	...	...	...
5 Construction	...	...	1100	...	...	1555	...	...	1869
6 Wholesale and retail trade, restaurants and hotels	...	...	8805	...	...	20413	...	...	30113
7 Transport, storage and communication	...	...	4428	...	...	8863	...	...	13284
A Transport and storage	...	...	...	...	...	...	...	...	...
B Communication	...	...	...	...	...	...	...	...	...
8 Finance, insurance, real estate and business services	...	...	3684	...	...	6502	...	...	18504
A Financial institutions	...	...	...	...	...	...	...	...	...
B Insurance	...	...	...	...	...	...	...	...	...
C Real estate and business services	...	...	...	...	...	...	...	...	...
9 Community, social and personal services a	...	...	459	...	...	505	...	...	555
A Sanitary and similar services	...	...	...	...	...	...	...	...	...
B Social and related community services	...	...	...	...	...	...	...	...	...
Educational services									
Medical, dental, other health and veterinary services									
C Recreational and cultural services	...	...	...	...	...	...	...	...	...
D Personal and household services	...	...	...	...	...	...	...	...	...
Total, Industries	...	...	40635	...	...	79445	...	...	137494
Producers of Government Services	...	...	1065	...	...	1706	...	...	4525
Other Producers a	...	...	...	...	...	...	...	...	...
Total b	...	...	41701	...	...	81151	...	...	142019
Less: Imputed bank service charge	...	...	192	...	...	1606	...	...	3658
Import duties	...	...	...	...	...	...	...	...	...
Value added tax	...	...	...	...	...	...	...	...	...
Other adjustments c	2438	...	2438	3293	...	3293	...	...	11815
Total	...	...	43947	...	...	82837	...	...	150175

a) Beginning 1980, item 'Other producers' is included in item 'Community, social and personal services'.
b) Gross domestic product in factor values.
c) Item 'Other adjustments' refers to indirect taxes net of subsidies.

1650

4.3 Cost Components of Value Added

Million Sierra Leone leones

Fiscal year beginning 1 July

All Producers

	1981						1982					
	Compensation of Employees	Capital Consumption	Net Operating Surplus	Indirect Taxes	Less: Subsidies Received	Value Added	Compensation of Employees	Capital Consumption	Net Operating Surplus	Indirect Taxes	Less: Subsidies Received	Value Added
1 Agriculture, hunting, forestry and fishing	61	19	459	14	...	552	92	25	569	5	...	691
A Agriculture and hunting	...	...	...	...	...	...	...	...	...	...	...	...
B Forestry and logging	...	...	...	...	...	...	...	...	...	...	...	...
C Fishing	...	...	...	...	...	...	...	...	...	...	...	...
2 Mining and quarrying	34	9	51	2	...	95	33	9	58	2	...	101
3 Manufacturing	18	6	77	43	...	143	21	7	80	37	...	145
4 Electricity, gas and water	4	3	2	...	-	8	5	3	3	...	-	11
A Electricity, gas and steam	...	...	...	...	...	...	...	...	...	...	...	...
B Water works and supply	...	...	...	...	...	...	...	...	...	...	...	...
5 Construction	29	4	22	...	...	55	20	4	24	...	...	48
6 Wholesale and retail trade, restaurants and hotels	50	17	105	1	...	173	68	23	141	1	...	233
7 Transport, storage and communication	52	77	157	1	-	287	62	90	173	1	-	324
A Transport and storage	...	...	...	...	...	...	...	...	...	...	...	...
B Communication	...	...	...	...	...	...	...	...	...	...	...	...
8 Finance, insurance, real estate and business services	21	18	87	...	...	126	26	22	99	...	...	147
A Financial institutions	...	...	...	...	...	...	...	...	...	...	...	...
B Insurance	...	...	...	...	...	...	...	...	...	...	...	...
C Real estate and business services	...	...	...	...	...	...	...	...	...	...	...	...
9 Community, social and personal services [a]	51	1	13	-	...	64	60	1	14	-	...	74
A Sanitary and similar services	...	...	...	...	...	...	...	...	...	...	...	...
B Social and related community services	...	...	...	...	...	...	...	...	...	...	...	...
Educational services	...	...	...	...	...	...	...	...	...	...	...	...
Medical, dental, other health and veterinary services	...	...	...	...	...	...	...	...	...	...	...	...
C Recreational and cultural services	...	...	...	...	...	...	...	...	...	...	...	...
D Personal and household services	...	...	...	...	...	...	...	...	...	...	...	...
Total, Industries	319	153	972	60	...	1503	386	183	1160	45	-	1773
Producers of Government Services	91	...	...	...	...	91	103	...	...	...	...	103
Other Producers [a]	...	...	...	...	...	...	...	...	...	...	...	...
Total [b]	410	153	972	60	-	1594	489	183	1160	45	-	1876
Less: Imputed bank service charge	-	-	30	...	...	30	-	-	32	...	...	32
Import duties	...	...	...	40	...	40	...	...	...	...	...	32
Value added tax	...	...	...	40	...	40	...	...	...	32	...	32
Other adjustments [c]	...	...	...	...	...	...	...	...	...	...	...	...
Total	410	153	942	101	-	1605	489	183	1128	77	-	1876

All Producers

	1983						1984					
	Compensation of Employees	Capital Consumption	Net Operating Surplus	Indirect Taxes	Less: Subsidies Received	Value Added	Compensation of Employees	Capital Consumption	Net Operating Surplus	Indirect Taxes	Less: Subsidies Received	Value Added
1 Agriculture, hunting, forestry and fishing	155	45	852	10	...	1062	264	...	1806	...	...	2070
A Agriculture and hunting	...	...	...	...	...	...	78	...	1259	...	...	1337
B Forestry and logging	...	...	...	...	...	...	13	...	220	...	...	232
C Fishing	...	...	...	...	...	...	173	...	327	...	...	500
2 Mining and quarrying	48	9	81	3	...	141	47	...	243	...	...	290
3 Manufacturing	30	8	97	47	...	182	40	...	126	...	...	166
4 Electricity, gas and water	7	3	4	...	-	14	8	...	4	...	-	12
A Electricity, gas and steam	...	...	...	...	...	...	7	...	1	...	...	8
B Water works and supply	...	...	...	...	...	...	1	...	4	...	...	5
5 Construction	32	7	32	...	...	71	55	...	73	...	...	128
6 Wholesale and retail trade, restaurants and hotels	89	30	176	1	...	295	64	...	694	...	...	758
7 Transport, storage and communication	94	135	240	1	1	469	86	...	460	...	...	546
A Transport and storage	...	...	...	...	...	...	81	...	458	...	...	539

Sierra Leone

Million Sierra Leone leones   Fiscal year beginning 1 July

	1983						1984					
	Compensation of Employees	Capital Consumption	Net Operating Surplus	Indirect Taxes	Less: Subsidies Received	Value Added	Compensation of Employees	Capital Consumption	Net Operating Surplus	Indirect Taxes	Less: Subsidies Received	Value Added
B Communication	...	...	...	...	...	...	5	...	2	...	...	7
8 Finance, insurance, real estate and business services	51	43	175	...	...	270	35	...	399	...	...	434
A Financial institutions	...	...	...	...	...	...	35	...	70	...	...	105
B Insurance	...	...	...	...	...	...		...		...	...	
C Real estate and business services	...	...	...	...	...	...	-	...	329	...	...	329
9 Community, social and personal services [a]	83	1	15	...	...	98	103	...	...	...	...	103
A Sanitary and similar services	...	...	...	...	...	...	...	...	...	...	...	...
B Social and related community services	...	...	...	...	...	...	82	...	-	...	...	82
Educational services	...	...	...	...	...	...	52	...	-	...	...	52
Medical, dental, other health and veterinary services	...	...	...	...	...	...	30	...	-	...	...	30
C Recreational and cultural services	...	...	...	...	...	...	...	...	...	...	...	...
D Personal and household services	...	...	...	...	...	...	...	...	...	...	...	...
Total, Industries	589	280	1673	61	1	2602	702	...	3804	...	...	4507
Producers of Government Services	122	...	...	...	...	122	182	...	...	...	...	182
Other Producers [a]	...	...	...	...	...	...	...	...	...	...	...	...
Total [b]	711	280	1673	61	1	2724	884	...	3804	...	...	4688
Less: Imputed bank service charge	-	-	39	...	...	39	-	-	35	...	...	35
Import duties	...	...	...	45	...	45	...	...	...	...	...	...
Value added tax	...	...	...	...	...	...	...	...	...	...	...	...
Other adjustments [c]	...	...	...	...	...	...	...	...	...	...	...	132
Total	711	280	1634	106	1	2730	884	...	3769	...	...	4785

	1985						1986					
	Compensation of Employees	Capital Consumption	Net Operating Surplus	Indirect Taxes	Less: Subsidies Received	Value Added	Compensation of Employees	Capital Consumption	Net Operating Surplus	Indirect Taxes	Less: Subsidies Received	Value Added
				All Producers								
1 Agriculture, hunting, forestry and fishing	380	...	2508	...	...	2888	854	...	6844	...	...	7698
A Agriculture and hunting	104	...	1668	...	...	1771	327	...	5250	...	...	5577
B Forestry and logging	16	...	270	...	...	285	31	...	530	...	...	561
C Fishing	261	...	571	...	...	832	496	...	1064	...	...	1560
2 Mining and quarrying	122	...	1184	...	...	1306	329	...	1806	...	...	2135
3 Manufacturing	65	...	192	...	...	256	172	...	736	...	...	907
4 Electricity, gas and water	9	...	12	...	-	21	11	...	98	...	-	109
A Electricity, gas and steam	8	...	6	...	...	14	9	...	74	...	...	83
B Water works and supply	1	...	6	...	...	7	3	...	24	...	...	27
5 Construction	142	...	31	...	...	174	345	...	74	...	...	418
6 Wholesale and retail trade, restaurants and hotels	101	...	942	...	...	1042	294	...	2948	...	...	3242
7 Transport, storage and communication	104	...	496	...	...	600	286	...	1576	...	...	1862
A Transport and storage	98	...	487	...	...	585	273	...	1544	...	...	1816
B Communication	6	...	9	...	...	15	14	...	32	...	...	45
8 Finance, insurance, real estate and business services	53	...	609	...	...	662	111	...	1639	...	...	1750
A Financial institutions	52	...	75	...	...	128	110	...	357	...	...	467
B Insurance		...		...	...			...		...	...	
C Real estate and business services	1	...	534	...	...	535	1	...	1282	...	...	1283
9 Community, social and personal services [a]	125	...	-	...	...	125	262	...	-	...	...	262
A Sanitary and similar services	...	...	...	...	...	...	...	...	...	...	...	...
B Social and related community services	95	...	-	...	...	95	210	...	-	...	...	210

4.3 Cost Components of Value Added
(Continued)

Million Sierra Leone leones

	1985						1986					
	Compensation of Employees	Capital Consumption	Net Operating Surplus	Indirect Taxes	Less: Subsidies Received	Value Added	Compensation of Employees	Capital Consumption	Net Operating Surplus	Indirect Taxes	Less: Subsidies Received	Value Added
Educational services	60	...	-	...	...	60	128	...	-	...	...	128
Medical, dental, other health and veterinary services	35	...	-	...	...	35	82	...	-	...	...	82
C Recreational and cultural services	...	...	...	...	...	...	...	...	...	...	...	...
D Personal and household services	...	...	...	...	...	...	...	...	...	...	...	...
Total, Industries	1100	...	5975	...	...	7074	2663	...	15720	...	...	18383
Producers of Government Services	252	...	...	...	...	252	546	...	...	...	...	546
Other Producers a	...	...	...	...	...	...	...	...	...	...	...	...
Total b	1352	...	5975	...	...	7327	3209	...	15720	...	...	18929
Less: Imputed bank service charge	-	-	58	...	...	58	-	-	140	...	...	140
Import duties	...	...	...	...	...	...	...	...	...	...	...	...
Value added tax	...	...	...	...	...	...	...	...	...	...	...	...
Other adjustments c	...	...	...	...	...	213	...	...	...	...	...	912
Total	1352	...	5917	...	...	7481	3209	...	15580	...	...	19701

	1987						1988					
	Compensation of Employees	Capital Consumption	Net Operating Surplus	Indirect Taxes	Less: Subsidies Received	Value Added	Compensation of Employees	Capital Consumption	Net Operating Surplus	Indirect Taxes	Less: Subsidies Received	Value Added

All Producers

	Compensation of Employees	Capital Consumption	Net Operating Surplus	Indirect Taxes	Less: Subsidies Received	Value Added	Compensation of Employees	Capital Consumption	Net Operating Surplus	Indirect Taxes	Less: Subsidies Received	Value Added
1 Agriculture, hunting, forestry and fishing	1440	...	10233	...	...	11673	1761	701	14164	25	...	16651
A Agriculture and hunting	446	...	7195	...	...	7641	721	355	11312	7	...	12395
B Forestry and logging	47	...	796	...	...	842	59	29	965	-	...	1053
C Fishing	947	...	2243	...	...	3190	982	317	1887	18	...	3203
2 Mining and quarrying	366	...	1858	...	...	2225	365	143	2115	66	...	2688
3 Manufacturing	247	...	1476	...	...	1722	556	222	2000	489	...	3267
4 Electricity, gas and water	42	...	66	...	-	108	46	17	71	...	-	134
A Electricity, gas and steam	38	...	12	...	...	50	...	...	...	...	...	...
B Water works and supply	4	...	54	...	...	58	...	...	...	...	...	...
5 Construction	412	...	89	...	...	501	531	103	466	2	...	1102
6 Wholesale and retail trade, restaurants and hotels	470	...	5407	...	...	5878	881	440	7484	59	...	8864
7 Transport, storage and communication	286	...	2290	...	...	2576	664	867	2897	29	6	4451
A Transport and storage	273	...	2199	...	...	2471	...	...	...	...	...	...
B Communication	14	...	91	...	...	105	...	...	...	...	...	...
8 Finance, insurance, real estate and business services	164	...	2445	...	...	2609	241	43	3400	...	...	3684
A Financial institutions	163	...	409	...	...	572	...	...	...	...	...	...
B Insurance		...			...		...	...	...	...	...	...
C Real estate and business services	2	...	2035	...	...	2036	...	...	...	...	...	...
9 Community, social and personal services a	364	...	55	...	...	419	458	1	-	-	...	459
A Sanitary and similar services	...	...	...	...	...	...	...	...	...	...	...	...
B Social and related community services	354	...	...	...	...	354	...	...	...	...	...	...
Educational services	262	...	-	...	...	262	...	...	...	...	...	...
Medical, dental, other health and veterinary services	92	...	-	...	...	92	...	...	...	...	...	...
C Recreational and cultural services	...	...	...	...	...	...	...	...	...	...	...	...
D Personal and household services	...	...	...	...	...	...	...	...	...	...	...	...
Total, Industries	3790	...	23919	...	...	27710	5502	2537	32596	670	6	41299
Producers of Government Services	879	...	...	...	...	879	1065	...	...	...	...	1065
Other Producers a	...	...	...	...	...	...	...	...	...	...	...	...
Total b	4669	...	23919	...	...	28588	6567	2537	32596	670	6	42364
Less: Imputed bank service charge	-	-	175	...	...	175	-	-	192	...	...	192
Import duties	...	...	...	666	...	666	...	...	...	1775	...	1775
Value added tax	...	...	...	...	...	...	...	...	...	...	...	...
Other adjustments c	...	...	...	...	...	...	...	...	...	...	...	...
Total	4669	...	24411	...	...	29080	6567	2537	32404	2445	6	43947

Sierra Leone

4.3 Cost Components of Value Added

Million Sierra Leone leones

Fiscal year beginning 1 July

	1989						1990					
	Compensation of Employees	Capital Consumption	Net Operating Surplus	Indirect Taxes	Less: Subsidies Received	Value Added	Compensation of Employees	Capital Consumption	Net Operating Surplus	Indirect Taxes	Less: Subsidies Received	Value Added
All Producers												
1 Agriculture, hunting, forestry and fishing	2801	1114	26583	57	...	30553	6555	2327	43610	3	...	52494
A Agriculture and hunting	1156	567	22338	30	...	24092	2158	1061	34085	2	...	37306
B Forestry and logging	73	37	1206	1	...	1316	95	48	1568	-	...	1710
C Fishing	1571	510	3039	26	...	5146	4302	1219	7958	-	...	13478
2 Mining and quarrying	943	674	4060	91	...	5768	2217	1616	9990	310	...	14133
3 Manufacturing	879	352	4010	541	...	5781	1355	542	4879	6224	...	13000
4 Electricity, gas and water	90	265	-160	...	-	194	159	111	-192	...	-	78
A Electricity, gas and steam	...	...	...	...	...	...	...	...	...	...	...	...
B Water works and supply	...	...	...	...	...	...	...	...	...	...	...	...
5 Construction	896	179	479	1	...	1555	977	243	649	1	...	1870
6 Wholesale and retail trade, restaurants and hotels	887	440	19086	56	...	20469	1585	792	27736	89	...	30202
7 Transport, storage and communication	1355	1773	5735	32	7	8888	2019	2659	8606	8	-	13292
A Transport and storage	...	...	...	...	...	...	...	...	...	...	...	...
B Communication	...	...	...	...	...	...	...	...	...	...	...	...
8 Finance, insurance, real estate and business services	534	84	5883	...	...	6502	911	120	17473	...	...	18504
A Financial institutions	...	...	...	...	...	...	...	...	...	...	...	...
B Insurance	...	...	...	...	...	...	...	...	...	...	...	...
C Real estate and business services	...	...	...	...	...	...	...	...	...	...	...	...
9 Community, social and personal services [a]	505	1	-1	-	...	505	555	1	-1	-	...	555
A Sanitary and similar services	...	...	...	...	...	...	...	...	...	...	...	...
B Social and related community services	...	...	...	...	...	...	...	...	...	...	...	...
Educational services	...	...	...	...	...	...	...	...	...	...	...	...
Medical, dental, other health and veterinary services	...	...	...	...	...	...	...	...	...	...	...	...
C Recreational and cultural services	...	...	...	...	...	...	...	...	...	...	...	...
D Personal and household services	...	...	...	...	...	...	...	...	...	...	...	...
Total, Industries	8889	4882	65674	777	7	80215	16333	8411	112749	6633	-	144127
Producers of Government Services	1706	...	...	...	...	1706	4525	...	...	...	...	4525
Other Producers [a]	...	...	...	...	...	...	...	...	...	...	...	...
Total [b]	10594	4882	65674	777	7	81921	20858	8411	112749	6633	-	148652
Less: Imputed bank service charge	-	-	1606	...	...	1606	-	-	3658	...	...	3658
Import duties	...	...	...	2523	-	2523	...	...	...	5181	...	5181
Value added tax	...	...	...	...	...	...	...	...	...	...	...	...
Other adjustments [c]	...	...	...	...	...	...	...	...	...	...	...	...
Total	10594	4882	64068	3300	7	82837	20858	8411	109091	11815	-	150175

a) Beginning 1980, item 'Other producers' is included in item 'Community, social and personal services'.

b) Gross domestic product in factor values.

c) Item 'Other adjustments' refers to indirect taxes net of subsidies.

Singapore

General note. The preparation of national accounts statistics in Singapore is undertaken by the Department of Statistics, Singapore. The official estimates together with a comprehensive description of the sources and methods used for the national accounts estimation is found in 'Singapore National Accounts, 1987' published by the Department of Statistics in March 1988. The estimates are generally in accordance with the classifications and definitions recommended in the United Nations System of National Accounts (SNA). The following tables have been prepared from successive replies to the United Nations national accounts questionnaire. When the scope and coverage of the estimates differ for conceptual or statistical reasons from the definitions and classifications recommended in SNA, a footnote is indicated to the relevant tables.

Sources and methods :

(a) Gross domestic product. Gross domestic product is estimated mainly through the production approach.

(b) Expenditure on the gross domestic product. The expenditure approach is used to estimate all components of GDP by expenditure type except private final expenditure on goods and capital expenditure on plant, machinery and equipment, for which the commodity-flow approach is used. The basic sources for estimating government final consumption expenditure are the annual financial statements of the Accountant-General, detailed income and expenditure statements of statutory boards and data collected from educational institutions. The estimates of private expenditure on goods are based on external trade statistics, data from the annual census of industrial production and on agricultural prduction data supplied by the Primary Production Department. Transport cost and distributor's margin are added to imports and local production values to arrive at market values of the commodities. Adjustments are made for stocks changes and for commodities with mulitple uses. Private expenditure on services are derived mainly from the results of surveys which are used as bench-mark estimates. Data used for the estimates of increase in stocks are derived from the annual censuses of industrial production and annual surveys of stocks conducted by the Department of Statistics. Capital formation in construction is estimated from the survey of capital expenditure on buildings, other construction and w orks. The estimates for capital formation of transport equipment are based on trade and prduction data as well as registration figures. The estimates of exports and imports of goods and services are based on balance-of-payments statistics. For the constant price estimates, all components of GDP by expenditure type are deflated by appropriate price indexes.

(c) Cost-structure of the gross domestic product. Estimates of the cost-structure of GDP are not made.

(d) Gross domestic product by kind of economic activity. The table of gross domestic product by kind of economic activity is prepared at market prices, i.e. producers' values. The production approach is used to estimate the value added of most industries. The income approach is used in the case of community, social and personal services and the transport sectors. Production data for the agricultural activities are estimated by the Primary Production Department based on two surveys conducted annually - the sample survey on pigs and poultry and the sample survey on vegetables. Fish production is based on fish caught and landed by locally registered fishing vessels while the estimates of output of live plants, flowers and aquarium fish are based on external trade statistics. Value added is calculated separately for each component as a fixed percentage of the value of production derived from the information available from the Department of Primary Production. Value added of the mining sector is derived from the annual census of industrial production with adjustments made to conform to the national income concept. For manufacturing, basic data for establishments employing 10 or more workers are obtained from the annual census of industrial production. For smaller establishments, estimates are based on the censuses of industrial production for establishments with five to nine workers supplemented by estimates made from employment data and per capita value added referring to establishments engaging less than five workers. The data used for the estimates of electricity, gas and water are taken from detailed accounts provided by the Public Utilities Board. Since April 1986, the Ministry of National Development has taken over the inquiries to collect expenditure data on new construction and major extensions and alteration works. Value added is estimated as a fixed ratio of the total cost of work done, the ratio calculated from detailed cost estimates of Housing and Development Board Construction and the margin earned by the contractors. The wholesale and retail trades are divided into entrepot trade and domestic trade activities. Value added of the entrepot trade is taken as the gross margin on re-export, which is the difference between re-exports in f.o.b. values and the corresponding imports in c.i.f. values, less an allowance for transport and other costs. The data are extracted from the external trade statistics. For the domestic trade activities, estimates for retained imports are compiled from the external trade statistics while estimates for local production are based on agricultural output and the sales of the manufacturing sector to wholesalers and retailers. Value added is taken as the gross mark-up margin on the value of retained imports or local production less the costs of transport and other intermediate expenses. Data gathered in the surveys of wholesale and retail trade, restaurants and hotels were also used. Bench-mark value added of the transport and communications sector is derived from the surveys of services and detailed accounts from airlines, Port of Singapore Authority, telecoms etc. Value added of banks is equal to the sum of actual and imputed bank charges minus purchases of goods and services for intermediate consumption. The data are based on detailed accounts submitted by the respective banks. Value added of finance companies is equal to the net interest income received less intermediate inputs. Other financial institutions are estimated on the basis of bench-mark value added data computed from the survey of services, employment data and other appropriate indicators. Value added estimates of insurance are based on income and expenditure data contained in the annual report of the Insurance Commissioner. For real estate and business services, the estimates for the private establishments are based on the surveys of services. The estimates of owner-occupied dwellings are based on the annual value of properties as assessed for property tax. Government output is valued at the cost of producing its services and value added is analysed from government financial statements, income and expenditure accounts of statutory boards and data provided by educational institutions and the Ministry of Education. The value added of domestic services consists of wages only and is estimated on the basis of the numbers employed and average earnings. For the constant price estimates, price deflation is used for agriculture, mining and quarrying, construction, trade, communication and services sectors. For manufacturing, electricity, gas and water and private services, value added is extrapolated by various output indicators. For transport, value added is either extrapolated by various indicators or deflated by price indexes.

1.1 Expenditure on the Gross Domestic Product, in Current Prices

Million Singapore dollars

	1980	1981	1982	1983	1984	1985	1986	1987	1988	1989	1990	1991
1 Government final consumption expenditure	2447.4	2788.6	3570.4	3995.3	4333.0	5548.5	5270.2	5314.6	5336.9	5872.0	6638.2	7263.4
2 Private final consumption expenditure	12911.3	14329.3	15282.5	16202.1	17569.5	17552.9	18191.8	20249.4	23415.1	25870.5	28136.4	29949.0
3 Gross capital formation	11627.6	13587.0	15658.8	17595.8	19417.3	16551.2	14894.8	16636.6	18435.0	19782.1	24918.1	25838.0
A Increase in stocks	1424.5	802.3	153.1	131.6	295.1	126.4	584.6	1471.7	1090.9	-755.5	1170.5	-1690.9
B Gross fixed capital formation	10203.1	12784.7	15505.7	17464.2	19122.2	16424.8	14310.2	15164.9	17344.1	20537.6	23747.6	27528.9
Residential buildings	1438.4	2060.7	3395.5	5516.8	6591.2	5265.4	3569.9	3021.0	3199.7	3254.5	3541.3	4228.2
Non-residential buildings	2069.7	3149.4	3912.4	4336.7	4200.5	3284.8	2133.7	1772.6	2054.4	2813.4	3596.2	4971.3
Other construction and land improvement etc.	801.4	897.0	972.2	1023.1	1162.9	1457.2	2205.3	2192.7	1412.2	1345.4	1209.9	1480.7
Other	5893.6	6677.6	7225.6	6587.6	7167.6	6417.4	6401.3	8178.6	10677.8	13124.3	15400.2	16848.7
4 Exports of goods and services	-2215.8	-1633.5	-1440.6	-663.8	-1113.0	-945.7	143.1	589.1	2527.2	5042.5	3870.3	6517.9
5 Less: Imports of goods and services												
Statistical discrepancy	320.2	268.0	-401.2	-396.6	-158.9	216.6	163.6	-153.9	283.8	277.1	109.9	-492.3
Equals: Gross Domestic Product	25090.7	29339.4	32669.9	36732.8	40047.9	38923.5	38663.5	42635.8	49998.0	56844.2	63672.9	69076.0

1.2 Expenditure on the Gross Domestic Product, in Constant Prices

Million Singapore dollars

	1980	1981	1982	1983	1984	1985	1986	1987	1988	1989	1990	1991
					At constant prices of:1985							
1 Government final consumption expenditure	3241.5	3411.6	3863.8	4235.9	4457.2	5548.5	5606.8	5653.9	5339.1	5594.8	6228.8	6730.7
2 Private final consumption expenditure	14809.7	15491.3	16086.4	16852.1	17711.6	17552.9	18287.7	20052.5	22757.8	24621.7	26252.2	27301.8
3 Gross capital formation	12642.7	13541.0	15549.7	17309.9	18950.4	16551.2	15177.6	16506.0	16838.0	18062.6	22640.5	23787.7
A Increase in stocks	1516.1	730.7	144.0	242.2	273.0	126.4	637.4	1478.0	578.4	-734.0	1015.1	-853.4
B Gross fixed capital formation	11126.6	12810.3	15405.7	17067.7	18677.4	16424.8	14540.2	15028.0	16259.6	18796.6	21625.4	24641.1

Singapore

1.2 Expenditure on the Gross Domestic Product, in Constant Prices
(Continued)

Million Singapore dollars

	1980	1981	1982	1983	1984	1985	1986	1987	1988	1989	1990	1991
	At constant prices of:1985											
Residential buildings	1573.1	1960.8	3403.2	5551.4	6549.5	5265.4	3722.8	3135.4	3186.2	2983.4	3026.6	3441.5
Non-residential buildings	2188.8	3000.8	3788.2	4123.8	4098.5	3284.8	2219.1	1849.9	2055.0	2586.9	3091.5	4046.1
Other construction and land improvement etc.	839.2	853.7	915.0	972.2	1132.7	1457.2	2290.6	2292.1	1420.3	1249.2	1054.1	1223.5
Other	6525.5	6995.0	7299.3	6420.3	6896.7	6417.4	6307.7	7750.6	9598.1	11977.1	14453.2	15930.0
4 Exports of goods and services	-1495.2	-1088.6	-2044.9	-1669.6	-1431.4	-945.7	349.3	1248.5	3489.0	4705.5	2207.4	3472.4
5 Less: Imports of goods and services												
Statistical discrepancy	-366.2	247.8	317.3	-191.1	-115.3	216.6	220.0	-73.4	-202.3	-306.6	-256.2	-396.7
Equals: Gross Domestic Product	28832.5	31603.1	33772.3	36537.2	39572.5	38923.5	39641.4	43387.5	48221.6	52678.0	57072.7	60895.9

1.10 Gross Domestic Product by Kind of Activity, in Current Prices

Million Singapore dollars

	1980	1981	1982	1983	1984	1985	1986	1987	1988	1989	1990	1991
1 Agriculture, hunting, forestry and fishing	310.8	342.8	332.6	312.7	320.0	272.7	226.5	204.3	185.5	170.9	159.6	147.2
2 Mining and quarrying	82.2	104.7	128.1	140.6	132.2	111.3	75.6	57.3	62.2	69.0	95.6	128.4
3 Manufacturing	7310.8	8359.4	8151.0	8905.1	9860.1	9180.7	10182.2	12087.5	14960.0	16687.8	18757.6	19984.5
4 Electricity, gas and water	555.0	477.5	600.9	702.7	773.0	796.0	1075.4	962.4	1155.5	1131.6	1250.0	1303.7
5 Construction	1583.2	2129.8	3102.7	4154.8	4892.4	4117.3	3098.5	2835.6	2757.1	3046.9	3564.7	4680.7
6 Wholesale and retail trade, restaurants and hotels	5435.1	5840.0	6387.5	6667.4	6885.5	6636.3	6516.3	7368.5	8877.4	9871.6	10983.4	11534.7
7 Transport, storage and communication	3517.3	4057.4	4429.0	4885.3	5213.6	5223.7	5269.3	5910.7	6864.8	7892.3	8467.2	9277.8
8 Finance, insurance, real estate and business services	4917.9	6631.4	7732.1	8845.6	9934.8	10622.3	9805.3	10843.1	12149.4	14957.0	17805.0	19025.4
9 Community, social and personal services	854.2	1022.6	1206.6	1402.7	1525.2	1500.2	1606.6	1707.8	1891.1	2198.4	2430.3	2842.2
Total, Industries	24566.5	28965.4	32070.5	36016.9	39536.8	38460.5	37855.7	41977.2	48903.0	56025.5	63513.4	68924.6
Producers of Government Services	1508.3	1724.7	2227.8	2511.7	2824.4	3191.4	3014.5	3092.1	3438.6	3780.4	4064.9	4331.8
Other Producers	...	...	...	...	...	...	...	...	...	...	...	...
Subtotal	26074.8	30690.1	34298.3	38528.6	42361.2	41651.9	40870.2	45069.3	52341.6	59805.9	67578.3	73256.4
Less: Imputed bank service charge	1410.9	1778.6	2109.9	2306.8	2827.4	3196.5	2600.3	2887.3	2939.9	3641.0	4514.3	4818.2
Plus: Import duties	426.8	427.9	481.5	511.0	514.1	468.1	393.6	453.8	596.3	679.3	608.9	637.8
Plus: Value added tax	...	...	...	...	...	...	...	...	...	...	...	...
Equals: Gross Domestic Product	25090.7	29339.4	32669.9	36732.8	40047.9	38923.5	38663.5	42635.8	49998.0	56844.2	63672.9	69076.0

1.11 Gross Domestic Product by Kind of Activity, in Constant Prices

Million Singapore dollars

	1980	1981	1982	1983	1984	1985	1986	1987	1988	1989	1990	1991
	At constant prices of:1985											
1 Agriculture, hunting, forestry and fishing	308.1	300.9	284.3	290.7	306.0	272.7	240.8	214.7	187.0	174.0	162.0	144.5
2 Mining and quarrying	65.0	83.5	104.0	122.0	120.2	111.3	94.3	93.4	88.1	89.4	81.4	94.7
3 Manufacturing	8497.3	9287.7	8962.5	9213.2	9904.2	9180.7	9952.1	11669.7	13770.2	15118.8	16554.5	17428.3
4 Electricity, gas and water	578.0	620.4	650.2	707.8	762.1	796.0	839.9	926.6	1012.1	1085.9	1203.3	1281.1
5 Construction	2010.5	2371.7	3248.8	4213.5	4873.6	4117.3	3177.9	2861.3	2749.1	2788.8	3003.8	3648.5
6 Wholesale and retail trade, restaurants and hotels	5452.8	5755.0	6091.9	6374.2	6738.9	6636.3	6641.8	7346.5	8560.8	9268.9	10026.4	10672.0
7 Transport, storage and communication	3441.2	3888.7	4343.7	4670.7	5122.7	5223.7	5647.0	6126.2	6773.6	7413.7	8066.0	8709.0
8 Finance, insurance, real estate and business services	5880.5	6843.2	7535.2	8370.5	9411.9	10622.3	10471.8	11570.3	12163.2	14012.7	15797.1	16650.3
9 Community, social and personal services	1175.3	1247.6	1354.8	1449.6	1516.9	1500.2	1584.8	1689.6	1834.5	2014.2	2165.5	2398.7
Total, Industries	27408.7	30398.7	32575.4	35412.2	38756.5	38460.5	38650.4	42498.3	47138.6	51966.4	57060.0	61027.1
Producers of Government Services	2268.6	2375.1	2593.8	2806.7	2971.1	3191.4	3341.3	3492.7	3518.5	3593.3	3735.9	3891.9
Other Producers	...	...	...	...	...	...	...	...	...	...	...	...
Subtotal	29677.3	32773.8	35169.2	38218.9	41727.6	41651.9	41991.7	45991.0	50657.1	55559.7	60795.9	64919.0
Less: Imputed bank service charge	1340.8	1653.8	1925.4	2191.7	2666.6	3196.5	2743.9	3001.5	2946.7	3466.1	4249.8	4555.0
Plus: Import duties	496.0	483.1	528.5	510.0	511.5	468.1	393.6	398.0	511.2	584.4	526.6	531.9
Plus: Value added tax	...	...	...	...	...	...	...	...	...	...	...	...
Equals: Gross Domestic Product	28832.5	31603.1	33772.3	36537.2	39572.5	38923.5	39641.4	43387.5	48221.6	52678.0	57072.7	60895.9

Singapore

1.12 Relations Among National Accounting Aggregates

Million Singapore dollars

	1980	1981	1982	1983	1984	1985	1986	1987	1988	1989	1990	1991
Gross Domestic Product	25090.7	29339.4	32669.9	36732.8	40047.9	38923.5	38663.5	42635.8	49998.0	56844.2	63672.9	69076.0
Plus: Net factor income from the rest of the world	-902.2	-1148.2	-894.2	-171.7	767.2	1406.9	949.0	-428.7	-136.0	433.9	794.5	1581.1
Equals: Gross National Product	24188.5	28191.2	31775.7	36561.1	40815.1	40330.4	39612.5	42207.1	49862.0	57278.1	64467.4	70657.1
Less: Consumption of fixed capital	3026.4	3551.8	4148.6	4900.4	5482.4	5789.5	6231.4	6751.7	7474.6	8182.8	8842.7	9797.1
Equals: National Income	21162.1	24639.4	27627.1	31660.7	35332.7	34540.9	33381.1	35455.4	42387.4	49095.3	55624.7	60860.0
Plus: Net current transfers from the rest of the world	-227.6	-322.8	-438.8	-454.2	-475.1	-469.0	-398.4	-492.2	-602.2	-740.2	-732.4	-829.4
Equals: National Disposable Income	20934.5	24316.6	27188.3	31206.5	34857.6	34071.9	32982.7	34963.2	41785.2	48355.1	54892.3	60030.6
Less: Final consumption	15358.7	17117.9	18852.9	20197.4	21902.5	23101.4	23462.0	25564.0	28752.0	31742.5	34774.6	37212.4
Statistical discrepancy	-320.2	-268.0	401.2	396.6	158.9	-216.6	-163.6	153.9	-283.8	-277.1	-109.9	492.3
Equals: Net Saving	5255.6	6930.7	8736.6	11405.7	13114.0	10753.9	9357.1	9553.1	12749.4	16335.5	20007.8	23310.5
Less: Surplus of the nation on current transactions	-3345.6	-3104.5	-2773.6	-1289.7	-820.9	-7.8	693.7	-331.8	1789.0	4736.2	3932.4	7269.6
Equals: Net Capital Formation	8601.2	10035.2	11510.2	12695.4	13934.9	10761.7	8663.4	9884.9	10960.4	11599.3	16075.4	16040.9

2.5 Private Final Consumption Expenditure by Type and Purpose, in Current Prices

Million Singapore dollars

	1980	1981	1982	1983	1984	1985	1986	1987	1988	1989	1990	1991
Final Consumption Expenditure of Resident Households												
1 Food, beverages and tobacco	3997.5	4561.8	4800.1	4932.0	5185.9	5121.5	5096.9	5430.2	6007.8	6241.4	6388.8	6739.2
A Food	3107.7	3583.6	3736.6	3723.7	3894.8	3818.3	3807.0	4105.2	4562.7	4749.4	4890.2	5134.4
B Non-alcoholic beverages	197.2	219.5	218.6	269.2	259.6	290.7	301.6	321.2	340.5	355.2	400.6	434.3
C Alcoholic beverages	343.5	364.9	417.4	453.4	498.6	465.2	442.3	496.4	560.3	575.3	563.5	567.2
D Tobacco	349.1	393.8	427.5	485.7	532.9	547.3	546.0	507.4	544.3	561.5	534.5	603.3
2 Clothing and footwear	1240.7	1408.4	1555.2	1681.8	1665.1	1569.4	1656.6	1870.4	2092.3	2225.6	2612.8	2616.9
3 Gross rent, fuel and power	1390.4	1493.1	1623.4	1745.3	1976.6	2184.9	2299.3	2430.4	2637.4	2786.3	3097.4	3404.7
4 Furniture, furnishings and household equipment and operation	1322.9	1525.8	1602.1	1719.3	1943.2	2015.3	2051.6	2157.1	2541.4	2736.7	2997.8	3208.2
A Household operation	251.7	297.3	336.3	418.0	458.9	489.1	516.8	569.5	655.7	696.7	764.1	849.7
B Other	1071.2	1228.5	1265.8	1301.3	1484.3	1526.2	1534.8	1587.6	1885.7	2040.0	2233.7	2358.5
5 Medical care and health expenses	411.7	445.3	502.8	567.4	643.1	702.2	898.1	962.8	1139.3	1265.7	1439.9	1629.7
6 Transport and communication	2198.3	2345.5	2560.2	2743.1	2816.7	2678.7	2609.3	2997.0	3696.2	4320.2	4786.0	4966.6
A Personal transport equipment	487.4	424.1	500.4	521.6	395.8	235.3	208.0	359.9	775.6	965.3	903.4	875.9
B Other	1710.9	1921.4	2059.8	2221.5	2420.9	2443.4	2401.3	2637.1	2920.6	3354.9	3882.6	4090.7
7 Recreational, entertainment, education and cultural services	1802.7	2153.8	2229.1	2421.0	2543.0	2453.5	2817.4	3258.9	4000.6	4479.6	5257.3	5771.9
A Education	95.1	102.3	147.3	167.5	183.5	192.5	213.7	243.1	271.9	329.3	376.1	439.5
B Other	1707.6	2051.5	2081.8	2253.5	2359.5	2261.0	2603.7	3015.8	3728.7	4150.3	4881.2	5332.4
8 Miscellaneous goods and services	3133.1	3638.4	3684.4	3829.6	3910.1	3562.4	3700.1	4532.7	5311.5	6399.7	7627.7	7642.9
A Personal care	288.7	330.4	408.4	432.5	474.3	456.1	457.6	502.0	589.6	706.5	785.0	857.1
B Expenditures in restaurants, cafes and hotels	1276.6	1449.9	1406.6	1432.6	1479.4	1423.3	1385.1	1556.3	1828.9	2222.7	2689.3	2794.7
C Other	1567.8	1858.1	1869.4	1964.5	1956.4	1683.0	1857.4	2474.4	2893.0	3470.5	4153.4	3991.1
Total Final Consumption Expenditure in the Domestic Market by Households, of which	15497.3	17572.1	18557.3	19639.5	20683.7	20287.9	21129.3	23639.5	27426.5	30455.2	34207.7	35980.1
Plus: Direct purchases abroad by resident households	585.7	651.2	843.3	973.4	1049.5	1103.5	1145.8	1362.3	1521.3	2106.9	2668.8	2820.9
Less: Direct purchases in the domestic market by non-resident households	3171.7	3894.0	4118.1	4410.8	4163.7	3838.5	4083.3	4752.4	5532.7	6691.6	8740.1	8852.0
Equals: Final Consumption Expenditure of Resident Households a	12911.3	14329.3	15282.5	16202.1	17569.5	17552.9	18191.8	20249.4	23415.1	25870.5	28136.4	29949.0
Final Consumption Expenditure of Private Non-profit Institutions Serving Households												
Equals: Final Consumption Expenditure of Private Non-profit Organisations Serving Households	...	...	...	...	...	...	...	...	...	...	...	...
Private Final Consumption Expenditure	12911.3	14329.3	15282.5	16202.1	17569.5	17552.9	18191.8	20249.4	23415.1	25870.5	28136.4	29949.0

a) Item 'Final consumption expenditure of resident households' includes consumption expenditure of private non-profit institutions serving households.

Singdapore

2.6 Private Final Consumption Expenditure by Type and Purpose, in Constant Prices

Million Singapore dollars

	1980	1981	1982	1983	1984	1985	1986	1987	1988	1989	1990	1991
					At constant prices of:1985							
					Final Consumption Expenditure of Resident Households							
1 Food, beverages and tobacco	4638.0	4810.1	4876.0	4962.4	5111.3	5121.5	5206.7	5469.0	5884.5	5976.9	6068.0	6332.6
A Food	3487.5	3643.3	3679.0	3663.2	3830.0	3818.3	3909.6	4209.7	4541.2	4670.3	4806.9	5055.3
B Non-alcoholic beverages	234.3	229.1	210.8	261.1	255.9	290.7	302.7	326.4	348.7	338.3	368.4	403.2
C Alcoholic beverages	428.1	428.5	475.7	501.8	495.1	465.2	448.5	467.3	502.5	499.2	475.5	467.7
D Tobacco	488.1	509.2	510.5	536.3	530.3	547.3	545.9	465.6	492.1	469.1	417.2	406.4
2 Clothing and footwear	1281.2	1457.0	1580.0	1642.4	1647.3	1569.4	1663.7	1852.5	2010.5	2112.6	2462.8	2442.1
3 Gross rent, fuel and power	1576.4	1630.9	1694.2	1794.9	1984.8	2184.9	2372.1	2559.4	2760.1	2862.4	3064.7	3208.8
4 Furniture, furnishings and household equipment and operation	1451.9	1609.4	1641.4	1747.1	1953.3	2015.3	2011.9	2099.0	2428.8	2577.5	2776.1	2956.4
A Household operation	329.8	369.6	385.4	435.9	459.9	489.1	491.9	541.5	613.1	648.7	702.5	775.4
B Other	1122.1	1239.8	1256.0	1311.2	1493.4	1526.2	1520.0	1557.5	1815.7	1928.8	2073.6	2181.0
5 Medical care and health expenses	550.9	570.0	620.1	633.1	654.6	702.2	902.1	967.5	1123.8	1225.7	1340.8	1388.7
6 Transport and communication	2618.4	2752.8	2861.2	2995.0	2967.3	2678.7	2698.7	2985.4	3553.5	4001.6	4296.7	4252.8
A Personal transport equipment	460.8	394.8	471.7	499.5	386.8	235.3	168.2	256.9	515.5	655.4	647.8	617.5
B Other	2157.6	2358.0	2389.5	2495.5	2580.5	2443.4	2530.5	2728.5	3038.0	3346.2	3648.9	3635.3
7 Recreational, entertainment, education and cultural services	1735.3	2047.0	2168.9	2480.4	2534.9	2453.5	2761.5	3155.8	3836.6	4287.6	5025.9	5518.4
A Education	124.6	127.9	177.8	180.2	192.6	192.5	209.5	229.8	242.9	287.9	308.1	334.8
B Other	1610.7	1919.1	1991.1	2300.2	2342.3	2261.0	2552.0	2926.0	3593.7	3999.7	4717.8	5183.6
8 Miscellaneous goods and services	3378.1	3523.8	3633.1	3779.3	3884.1	3562.4	3699.4	4465.1	5158.8	5983.7	6743.8	6594.3
A Personal care	351.5	364.2	407.9	445.0	484.0	456.1	452.8	488.8	557.5	666.3	735.2	780.9
B Expenditures in restaurants, cafes and hotels	1372.3	1390.9	1356.2	1386.5	1428.5	1423.3	1426.3	1642.8	1892.1	2086.4	2201.8	2275.1
C Other	1654.3	1768.7	1869.0	1947.8	1971.6	1683.0	1820.3	2333.5	2709.2	3231.0	3806.8	3538.3
Total Final Consumption Expenditure in the Domestic Market by Households, of which	17230.2	18401.0	19074.9	20034.6	20737.6	20287.9	21316.1	23553.7	26756.6	29028.0	31778.8	32694.1
Plus: Direct purchases abroad by resident households	699.0	729.6	896.0	992.2	1049.7	1103.5	1161.0	1366.1	1496.6	1993.1	2456.2	2525.8
Less: Direct purchases in the domestic market by non-resident households	3119.5	3639.3	3884.5	4174.7	4075.7	3838.5	4189.4	4867.3	5495.4	6399.4	7982.8	7918.1
Equals: Final Consumption Expenditure of Resident Households [a]	14809.7	15491.3	16086.4	16852.1	17711.6	17552.9	18287.7	20052.5	22757.8	24621.7	26252.2	27301.8
					Final Consumption Expenditure of Private Non-profit Institutions Serving Households							
Equals: Final Consumption Expenditure of Private Non-profit Organisations Serving Households	...	...	...	...	...	...	...	...	...	...	...	...
Private Final Consumption Expenditure	14809.7	15491.3	16086.4	16852.1	17711.6	17552.9	18287.7	20052.5	22757.8	24621.7	26252.2	27301.8

a) Item 'Final consumption expenditure of resident households' includes consumption expenditure of private non-profit institutions serving households.

Slovakia

Source. Reply to the United Nations national accounts questionnaire from the Statistical Office of the Slovak Republic.

General note. The estimates shown in the following tables are in accordance with the United Nations System of National Accounts (SNA) so far as the existing data would permit.

1.1 Expenditure on the Gross Domestic Product, in Current Prices

Million Koruna

	1980	1981	1982	1983	1984	1985	1986	1987	1988	1989	1990	1991
1 Government final consumption expenditure	33323	32096	34807	36049	39397	39840	43506	46025	47305	50610	53346	70711
2 Private final consumption expenditure	85246	87971	90565	93986	97360	101392	104804	108263	111438	116738	131330	141635
3 Gross capital formation	63972	56866	58236	59060	61715	64327	66706	63172	66969	69586	81470	101380
A Increase in stocks	9661	3843	5710	5250	3098	4581	5453	3799	5911	5079	5326	19723
B Gross fixed capital formation	54311	53023	52526	53810	58617	59746	61253	59373	61058	64507	76144	81657
4 Exports of goods and services								70188	72357	67526	64627	
5 Less: Imports of goods and services	-11014	-11546	-9835	-7025	-5372	-2301	-3308	78255	76546	75261	86584	-22526
Statistical discrepancy								7556	3489	4975	-639	
Equals: Gross Domestic Product	171527	165387	173773	182070	193100	203258	211708	216949	225012	234174	243550	291200

1.2 Expenditure on the Gross Domestic Product, in Constant Prices

Million Koruna

	1980	1981	1982	1983	1984	1985	1986	1987	1988	1989	1990	1991
				At constant prices of:1984								
1 Government final consumption expenditure	...	...	...	...	39397	40345	43737	45864	46612	50645	51086	...
2 Private final consumption expenditure	...	...	...	...	97360	98208	100908	105274	109460	113364	118342	...
3 Gross capital formation	...	...	...	...	61715	64118	66553	65283	68970	70696	78685	...
A Increase in stocks	...	...	...	...	3098	4620	5335	3740	5704	4900	5153	...
B Gross fixed capital formation	...	...	...	...	58617	59498	61218	61543	63266	65796	73532	...
4 Exports of goods and services	...	...	...	...				69230	70527	64391	55590	...
5 Less: Imports of goods and services	...	...	...	...	-5372	-1626	-1952	78627	80470	83146	87691	...
Statistical discrepancy	...	...	...	...				7556	3489	4975	-640	
Equals: Gross Domestic Product	...	...	...	...	193100	201045	209246	214580	218588	220925	215372	...

Slovenia

Source. Reply to the United Nations National Accounts Questionnaire from the Statistical Office of the Republic of Slovenia, Ljubljana.

General note. The estimates shown in the following tables are in accordance with the System of National Accounts (SNA) so far as the existing data would permit.

1.10 Gross Domestic Product by Kind of Activity, in Current Prices

Million Dinars

	1980	1981	1982	1983	1984	1985	1986	1987	1988	1989	1990	1991
1 Agriculture, hunting, forestry and fishing	...	...	...	...	...	...	...	36	109	1521	9233	19334
2 Mining and quarrying	...	...	...	...	...	...	...	14	34	284	2023	4016
3 Manufacturing	...	...	...	...	...	...	...	320	1013	12823	58363	115086
4 Electricity, gas and water	...	...	...	...	...	...	...	22	71	757	5084	16048
5 Construction	...	...	...	...	...	...	...	58	144	1584	8389	12882
6 Wholesale and retail trade, restaurants and hotels	...	...	...	...	...	...	...	99	270	3147	25873	36296
7 Transport, storage and communication	...	...	...	...	...	...	...	64	187	2203	12824	21250
8 Finance, insurance, real estate and business services	...	...	...	...	...	...	...	98	312	4339	29048	72264
9 Community, social and personal services	...	...	...	...	...	...	...	23	65	958	5786	7904
Total, Industries	...	...	...	...	...	...	...	732	2206	27616	156622	305078
Producers of Government Services	...	...	...	...	...	...	...	82	238	4381	21373	40844
Other Producers	...	...	...	...	...	...	...	7	21	300	1446	113
Subtotal	...	...	...	...	...	...	...	821	2464	32297	179440	346035
Less: Imputed bank service charge	...	...	...	...	...	...	...	18	62	751	5641	32623
Plus: Import duties	...	...	...	...	...	...	...	42	151	1214	9733	12555
Plus: Value added tax	...	...	...	...	...	...	...	...	...	...	...	...
Plus: Other adjustments	...	...	...	...	...	...	...	61	165	2045	12310	24682
Equals: Gross Domestic Product	...	...	...	...	...	...	...	905	2718	34805	195843	350649

1.11 Gross Domestic Product by Kind of Activity, in Constant Prices

Million Dinars

	1980	1981	1982	1983	1984	1985	1986	1987	1988	1989	1990	1991
				At constant prices of:1990								
1 Agriculture, hunting, forestry and fishing	...	...	...	...	...	...	...	9746	9392	9083	9233	...
2 Mining and quarrying	...	...	...	...	...	...	...	2366	2320	2316	2023	...
3 Manufacturing	...	...	...	...	...	...	...	67669	65705	65402	58363	...
4 Electricity, gas and water	...	...	...	...	...	...	...	5208	5066	5164	5084	...
5 Construction	...	...	...	...	...	...	...	9245	9256	9403	8389	...
6 Wholesale and retail trade, restaurants and hotels	...	...	...	...	...	...	...	31890	30419	27201	25873	...
7 Transport, storage and communication	...	...	...	...	...	...	...	12778	13111	13090	12824	...
8 Finance, insurance, real estate and business services	...	...	...	...	...	...	...	27208	27426	27776	29048	...
9 Community, social and personal services	...	...	...	...	...	...	...	5677	5827	5764	5786	...
Total, Industries	...	...	...	...	...	...	...	171787	168522	165199	156622	...
Producers of Government Services	...	...	...	...	...	...	...	21475	21340	21375	21372	...
Other Producers	...	...	...	...	...	...	...	1609	1715	1640	1446	...
Subtotal	...	...	...	...	...	...	...	194871	191577	188214	179440	...
Less: Imputed bank service charge	...	...	...	...	...	...	...					...
Plus: Import duties	...	...	...	...	...	...	...	17814	17513	17205	16403	...
Plus: Value added tax	...	...	...	...	...	...	...					...
Plus: Other adjustments	...	...	...	...	...	...	...					...
Equals: Gross Domestic Product	...	...	...	...	...	...	...	212685	209090	205419	195843	177600

Solomon Islands

Source. Reply to the United Nations National Accounts Questionnaire from the Statistics Division, Ministry of Finance, Honiara.

General note. The estimates have been adjusted by the United Nations Statistical Office to conform to the United Nations System of National Accounts so far as the existing data would permit.

1.1 Expenditure on the Gross Domestic Product, in Current Prices

Million Solomon Islands dollars

	1980	1981	1982	1983	1984	1985	1986	1987	1988	1989	1990	1991
1 Government final consumption expenditure	...	...	...	...	52.1	66.6	84.1	106.3	115.3	...	...	...
2 Private final consumption expenditure	118.1	...	...	...	122.0	152.0	159.3	184.9	251.7	...	...	...
3 Gross capital formation	...	...	...	...	50.9	62.1	66.1	67.5	120.0	...	...	...
A Increase in stocks	...	...	...	...	7.9	12.2	2.5	7.9	10.0	...	...	...
B Gross fixed capital formation	...	...	...	...	43.0	49.9	63.6	59.6	110.0	...	...	...
4 Exports of goods and services	60.8	...	...	...	135.2	121.1	132.9	163.6	192.2	...	...	...
5 Less: Imports of goods and services [a]	61.5	...	...	...	138.5	164.9	189.8	229.6	311.9	...	...	...
Equals: Gross Domestic Product [b] ..	119.1	140.6	158.5	141.4	221.7	236.9	252.5	292.8	367.0	...	...	...

a) Imports of merchandise, f.o.b. rather than c.i.f.
b) Data in this table have been revised, therefore they are not strictly comparable with the unrevised data in the other tables.

1.2 Expenditure on the Gross Domestic Product, in Constant Prices

Million Solomon Islands dollars

	1980	1981	1982	1983	1984	1985	1986	1987	1988	1989	1990	1991
					At constant prices of:1984							
1 Government final consumption expenditure	...	...	...	...	...	...	...	...	...	...	...	...
2 Private final consumption expenditure	...	...	...	...	...	...	...	...	...	...	...	...
3 Gross capital formation	...	...	...	...	...	...	...	...	...	...	...	...
4 Exports of goods and services	...	...	...	...	...	...	...	...	...	...	...	...
5 Less: Imports of goods and services	...	...	...	...	...	...	...	...	...	...	...	...
Equals: Gross Domestic Product	186.8	199.3	197.1	183.0	196.1	201.6	200.1	204.8	215.8	230.6	246.1	...

1.3 Cost Components of the Gross Domestic Product

Million Solomon Islands dollars

	1980	1981	1982	1983	1984	1985	1986	1987	1988	1989	1990	1991
1 Indirect taxes, net	10.8	14.5	18.0	18.0	25.8	26.9	31.4	40.0	...	...	...	...
A Indirect taxes	...	...	...	...	29.2	30.7	35.5	45.0	...	...	...	...
B Less: Subsidies	...	...	...	...	3.4	3.8	4.1	5.0	...	...	...	...
2 Consumption of fixed capital	14.2	18.1	22.0	24.0	13.1	15.8	19.1	21.0	...	...	...	...
3 Compensation of employees paid by resident producers to:	31.3	39.2	45.2	50.0	85.1	104.6	125.1	140.0	...	...	...	...
4 Operating surplus	63.0	68.9	73.3	83.0	96.8	88.1	74.7	93.0	...	...	...	...
Equals: Gross Domestic Product	119.4	140.6	158.5	175.0	220.8	235.3	250.4	294.0	...	...	...	...

1.4 General Government Current Receipts and Disbursements

Million Solomon Islands dollars

	1980	1981	1982	1983	1984	1985	1986	1987	1988	1989	1990	1991
					Receipts							
1 Operating surplus	...	...	...	...	1.2	1.5	1.1	...	...	...	...	...
2 Property and entrepreneurial income	...	...	...	...	2.4	3.2	4.2	...	...	...	...	...
3 Taxes, fees and contributions	...	...	...	...	44.6	49.0	56.1	...	...	...	...	...
A Indirect taxes	...	...	...	...	29.3	30.6	35.5	...	...	...	...	...
B Direct taxes	...	...	...	...	14.7	17.6	19.6	...	...	...	...	...
C Social security contributions	...	...	...	...	...	...	...	...	...	...	...	...
D Compulsory fees, fines and penalties	...	...	...	...	0.6	0.8	1.0	...	...	...	...	...
4 Other current transfers	...	...	...	...	23.4	22.8	62.2	...	...	...	...	...
Total Current Receipts of General Government	...	...	...	...	71.6	76.5	123.6	...	...	...	...	...
					Disbursements							
1 Government final consumption expenditure	...	...	...	...	51.7	66.1	83.6	...	...	...	...	...

Solomon Islands

1.4 General Government Current Receipts and Disbursements
(Continued)

Million Solomon Islands dollars

	1980	1981	1982	1983	1984	1985	1986	1987	1988	1989	1990	1991
2 Property income	...	...	...	...	1.8	3.4	4.8	...	...	...	...	...
A Interest	...	...	...	...	1.8	3.4	4.8	...	...	...	...	...
B Net land rent and royalties	...	...	...	...	...	...	...	...	...	...	...	...
3 Subsidies	...	...	...	...	3.4	3.8	4.1	...	...	...	...	...
4 Other current transfers	...	...	...	...	4.0	5.0	7.3	...	...	...	...	...
5 Net saving	...	...	...	...	10.7	-1.8	23.8	...	...	...	...	...
Total Current Disbursements and Net Saving of General Government	...	...	...	...	71.6	76.5	123.6	...	...	...	...	...

1.7 External Transactions on Current Account, Summary

Million Solomon Islands dollars

	1980	1981	1982	1983	1984	1985	1986	1987	1988	1989	1990	1991
Payments to the Rest of the World												
1 Imports of goods and services	...	...	...	...	138.5	164.9	189.8	...	...	...	...	...
2 Factor income to the rest of the world	...	...	...	...	17.9	16.8	22.4	...	...	...	...	...
A Compensation of employees	...	...	...	...	4.9	4.8	11.6	...	...	...	...	...
B Property and entrepreneurial income	...	...	...	...	13.0	12.0	10.8	...	...	...	...	...
3 Current transfers to the rest of the world	...	...	...	...	12.5	13.8	16.0	...	...	...	...	...
4 Surplus of the nation on current transactions	...	...	...	...	-0.7	-40.0	-15.2	...	...	...	...	...
Payments to the Rest of the World and Surplus of the Nation on Current Transactions	...	...	...	...	168.2	155.5	212.8	...	...	...	...	...
Receipts From The Rest of the World												
1 Exports of goods and services	...	...	...	...	135.2	121.1	132.8	...	...	...	...	...
2 Factor income from rest of the world	...	...	...	...	5.9	6.6	5.7	...	...	...	...	...
A Compensation of employees	...	...	...	...	...	...	...	...	...	...	...	...
B Property and entrepreneurial income	...	...	...	...	5.9	6.6	5.7	...	...	...	...	...
3 Current transfers from rest of the world	...	...	...	...	27.1	27.8	74.3	...	...	...	...	...
Receipts from the Rest of the World on Current Transactions	...	...	...	...	168.2	155.5	212.8	...	...	...	...	...

1.8 Capital Transactions of The Nation, Summary

Million Solomon Islands dollars

	1980	1981	1982	1983	1984	1985	1986	1987	1988	1989	1990	1991
Finance of Gross Capital Formation												
Gross saving	...	...	...	...	50.2	22.2	52.7	...	...	...	...	...
1 Consumption of fixed capital	...	...	...	...	13.1	15.8	19.1	...	...	...	...	...
A General government	...	...	...	...	0.2	0.3	0.5	...	...	...	...	...
B Corporate and quasi-corporate enterprises	...	...	...	...	...	...	...	...	...	...	...	...
Public	...	...	...	...	4.0	5.7	6.6	...	...	...	...	...
Private	...	...	...	...	...	...	...	...	...	...	...	...
C Other	...	...	...	...	...	...	...	...	...	...	...	...
2 Net saving	...	...	...	...	37.1	6.4	33.6	...	...	...	...	...
A General government	...	...	...	...	10.7	-1.8	23.8	...	...	...	...	...
B Corporate and quasi-corporate enterprises	...	...	...	...	...	...	...	...	...	...	...	...
Public	...	...	...	...	8.6	-2.5	-5.1	...	...	...	...	...
Private	...	...	...	...	...	...	...	...	...	...	...	...
C Other	...	...	...	...	...	...	...	...	...	...	...	...
Less: Surplus of the nation on current transactions	...	...	...	...	-0.7	-40.0	-15.2	...	...	...	...	...
Finance of Gross Capital Formation	...	...	...	...	50.9	62.2	67.9	...	...	...	...	...
Gross Capital Formation												
Increase in stocks	...	...	...	...	7.9	12.2	2.5	...	...	...	...	...

1.8 Capital Transactions of The Nation, Summary
(Continued)

Million Solomon Islands dollars

	1980	1981	1982	1983	1984	1985	1986	1987	1988	1989	1990	1991
Gross fixed capital formation	...	...	...	...	43.0	50.0	65.4	...	...	...	...	...
1 General government	...	...	...	...	12.2	14.3	29.6	...	...	...	...	...
2 Corporate and quasi-corporate enterprises	...	...	...	...	30.8	35.7	35.8	...	...	...	...	...
A Public	...	...	...	...	11.0	13.1	12.0	...	...	...	...	...
B Private	...	...	...	...	19.8	22.6	23.8	...	...	...	...	...
3 Other	...	...	...	...	...	...	...	...	...	...	...	...
Gross Capital Formation	...	...	...	...	50.9	62.2	67.9	...	...	...	...	...

1.9 Gross Domestic Product by Institutional Sectors of Origin

Million Solomon Islands dollars

	1980	1981	1982	1983	1984	1985	1986	1987	1988	1989	1990	1991
					Domestic Factor Incomes Originating							
1 General government	...	...	...	...	35.7	45.1	51.1	...	...	...	...	...
2 Corporate and quasi-corporate enterprises	...	...	...	...	84.1	78.9	79.4	...	...	...	...	...
3 Households and private unincorporated enterprises	...	...	...	...	60.4	66.5	67.0	...	...	...	...	...
4 Non-profit institutions serving households	...	...	...	...	1.7	2.1	2.3	...	...	...	...	...
Subtotal: Domestic Factor Incomes	...	...	...	...	181.9	192.6	199.9	...	...	...	...	...
Indirect taxes, net	...	...	...	...	25.8	26.9	31.4	...	...	...	...	...
A Indirect taxes	...	...	...	...	29.2	30.7	35.5	...	...	...	...	...
B Less: Subsidies	...	...	...	...	3.4	3.8	4.1	...	...	...	...	...
Consumption of fixed capital	...	...	...	...	13.1	15.8	19.1	...	...	...	...	...
Gross Domestic Product	...	...	...	...	220.8	235.3	250.4	...	...	...	...	...

1.10 Gross Domestic Product by Kind of Activity, in Current Prices

Million Solomon Islands dollars

	1980	1981	1982	1983	1984	1985	1986	1987	1988	1989	1990	1991
1 Agriculture, hunting, forestry and fishing	...	...	...	...	106.3	107.4	108.3	...	...	...	...	...
2 Mining and quarrying	...	...	...	...	-0.4	-1.5	-2.6	...	...	...	...	...
3 Manufacturing	...	...	...	...	7.2	8.0	10.1	...	...	...	...	...
4 Electricity, gas and water	...	...	...	...	1.7	2.2	2.6	...	...	...	...	...
5 Construction	...	...	...	...	7.6	9.0	11.4	...	...	...	...	...
6 Wholesale and retail trade, restaurants and hotels	...	...	...	...	21.1	22.1	18.9	...	...	...	...	...
7 Transport, storage and communication	...	...	...	...	10.4	10.8	13.0	...	...	...	...	...
8 Finance, insurance, real estate and business services	...	...	...	...	11.3	13.0	14.6	...	...	...	...	...
9 Community, social and personal services	...	...	...	...	33.6	42.0	48.0	...	...	...	...	...
Total, Industries	...	...	...	...	198.8	213.0	224.3	...	...	...	...	...
Producers of Government Services	...	...	...	...	...	...	...	...	...	...	...	...
Other Producers	...	...	...	...	...	...	...	...	...	...	...	...
Subtotal	...	...	...	...	198.8	213.0	224.3	...	...	...	...	...
Less: Imputed bank service charge	...	...	...	...	3.6	4.4	5.3	...	...	...	...	...
Plus: Import duties	...	...	...	...	...	...	...	...	...	...	...	...
Plus: Value added tax	...	...	...	...	...	...	...	...	...	...	...	...
Plus: Other adjustments	...	...	...	...	25.8	26.9	31.4	...	...	...	...	...
Equals: Gross Domestic Product	...	...	...	...	221.0	235.5	250.4	...	...	...	...	...

1.11 Gross Domestic Product by Kind of Activity, in Constant Prices

Million Solomon Islands dollars

	1980	1981	1982	1983	1984	1985	1986	1987	1988	1989	1990	1991
					At constant prices of:1984							
1 Agriculture, hunting, forestry and fishing	...	...	...	100.0	108.1	106.9	101.9	95.0	102.1	112.2	120.2	...
2 Mining and quarrying	...	...	...	-0.1	-0.4	-1.4	-2.5	-2.8	-0.7	-0.8	-0.7	...
3 Manufacturing	...	...	...	6.6	6.0	6.8	7.2	8.7	8.7	8.9	8.5	...
4 Electricity, gas and water	...	...	...	1.6	1.7	1.9	2.0	2.0	2.2	2.6	3.0	...
5 Construction	...	...	...	8.3	7.6	9.8	10.7	9.4	9.5	10.2	10.5	...

Solomon Islands

1.11 Gross Domestic Product by Kind of Activity, in Constant Prices
(Continued)

Million Solomon Islands dollars

	1980	1981	1982	1983	1984	1985	1986	1987	1988	1989	1990	1991
					At constant prices of:1984							
6 Wholesale and retail trade, restaurants and hotels	...	...	...	17.6	21.1	22.1	21.5	22.4	20.2	23.4	22.2	...
7 Transport, storage and communication	...	...	...	8.7	10.3	10.8	11.3	10.2	10.6	12.4	16.4	...
8 Finance, insurance, real estate and business services	...	...	...	4.7	5.5	5.4	6.2	7.1	7.2	7.8	7.7	...
9 Community, social and personal services	...	...	...	35.5	36.2	39.3	41.8	52.7	56.0	54.0	58.3	...
Total, Industries	...	...	...	183.0	196.1	201.6	200.1	204.8	215.8	230.6	246.1	...
Producers of Government Services	...	...	...	...	...	...	...	...	...	...	...	...
Other Producers	...	...	...	...	...	...	...	...	...	...	...	...
Subtotal	...	...	...	...	...	...	...	...	...	...	...	...
Less: Imputed bank service charge	...	...	...	...	...	...	...	...	...	...	...	...
Plus: Import duties	...	...	...	...	...	...	...	...	...	...	...	...
Plus: Value added tax	...	...	...	...	...	...	...	...	...	...	...	...
Equals: Gross Domestic Product	...	...	...	183.0	196.1	201.6	200.1	204.8	215.8	230.6	246.1	...

1.12 Relations Among National Accounting Aggregates

Million Solomon Islands dollars

	1980	1981	1982	1983	1984	1985	1986	1987	1988	1989	1990	1991
Gross Domestic Product	...	...	...	...	220.8	235.3	250.4	...	...	...	...	...
Plus: Net factor income from the rest of the world	...	...	...	...	-11.9	-10.2	-16.7	...	...	...	...	...
Equals: Gross National Product	...	...	...	...	208.9	225.1	233.7	...	...	...	...	...
Less: Consumption of fixed capital	...	...	...	...	13.1	15.8	19.1	...	...	...	...	...
Equals: National Income	...	...	...	...	195.8	209.3	214.6	...	...	...	...	...
Plus: Net current transfers from the rest of the world	...	...	...	...	14.6	14.0	58.4	...	...	...	...	...
Equals: National Disposable Income	...	...	...	...	210.4	223.4	273.0	...	...	...	...	...
Less: Final consumption	...	...	...	...	173.3	217.0	239.4	...	...	...	...	...
Equals: Net Saving	...	...	...	...	37.1	6.4	33.6	...	...	...	...	...
Less: Surplus of the nation on current transactions	...	...	...	...	-0.7	-40.0	-15.2	...	...	...	...	...
Equals: Net Capital Formation	...	...	...	...	37.8	46.4	48.8	...	...	...	...	...

2.7 Gross Capital Formation by Type of Good and Owner, in Current Prices

Million Solomon Islands dollars

	1984				1985				1986			
	TOTAL	Total Private	Public Enterprises	General Government	TOTAL	Total Private	Public Enterprises	General Government	TOTAL	Total Private	Public Enterprises	General Government
Increase in stocks, total	7.9	...	...	...	12.2	...	...	...	2.5	...	...	...
Gross Fixed Capital Formation, Total	43.0	19.8	10.9	12.3	49.9	22.6	13.0	14.3	65.3	23.7	12.0	29.6
1 Residential buildings	14.1	4.0	4.0	6.1	11.0	4.1	2.9	4.0	15.1	7.9	3.6	3.6
2 Non-residential buildings												
3 Other construction	2.4	-	0.9	1.5	5.6	-	0.4	5.2	11.0	-	0.7	10.3
4 Land improvement and plantation and orchard development	6.4	4.6	-	1.8	8.3	6.2	-	2.1	8.5	4.7	1.9	1.9
5 Producers' durable goods	20.1	11.2	6.0	2.9	25.0	12.3	9.7	3.0	30.7	11.1	5.8	13.8
A Transport equipment	7.0	2.6	3.4	1.0	11.6	5.0	7.2	-0.6	7.6	3.1	1.9	2.6
B Machinery and equipment	13.1	8.6	2.6	1.9	13.4	7.3	2.5	3.6	23.1	8.0	3.9	11.2
6 Breeding stock, dairy cattle, etc.	...	...	...	...	...	...	...	...	...	...	...	...
Total Gross Capital Formation	50.9	...	...	...	62.1	...	...	...	68.0	...	...	...

4.3 Cost Components of Value Added

Million Solomon Islands dollars

	1984						1985					
	Compensation of Employees	Capital Consumption	Net Operating Surplus	Indirect Taxes	Less: Subsidies Received	Value Added	Compensation of Employees	Capital Consumption	Net Operating Surplus	Indirect Taxes	Less: Subsidies Received	Value Added
All Producers												
1 Agriculture, hunting, forestry and fishing	22.1	7.2	76.9	...	...	106.2	27.1	8.6	71.7	...	...	107.4
2 Mining and quarrying	0.4	-	-0.8	...	...	-0.4	0.5	-	-2.1	...	...	-1.6
3 Manufacturing	4.5	0.9	1.8	...	...	7.2	5.4	1.0	1.6	...	...	8.0
4 Electricity, gas and water	1.2	0.4	0.1	...	...	1.7	1.2	0.5	0.5	...	...	2.2
5 Construction	4.0	0.2	3.4	...	...	7.6	5.8	0.3	2.9	...	...	9.0
6 Wholesale and retail trade, restaurants and hotels	7.7	1.5	11.9	...	...	21.1	9.2	1.9	11.0	...	...	22.1
7 Transport, storage and communication	6.0	1.6	2.8	...	...	10.4	7.3	1.7	1.7	...	...	10.7
A Transport and storage	4.6	1.3	2.1	...	...	8.0	5.4	1.4	1.1	...	...	7.9
B Communication	1.4	0.3	0.7	...	...	2.4	1.9	0.3	0.6	...	...	2.8
8 Finance, insurance, real estate and business services	6.0	0.9	4.3	...	...	11.2	6.7	1.3	5.1	...	...	13.1
9 Community, social and personal services	33.1	0.4	-	...	...	33.5	41.5	0.6	-	...	...	42.1
Total, Industries	85.0	13.1	100.4	...	...	198.5	104.7	15.9	92.4	...	...	213.0
Producers of Government Services	...	...	...	...	...	...	...	...	...	...	...	...
Other Producers	...	...	...	...	...	...	...	...	...	...	...	...
Total a	85.0	13.1	100.4	...	...	198.5	104.7	15.9	92.4	...	...	213.0
Less: Imputed bank service charge	...	...	3.6	...	...	3.6	...	...	4.4	...	...	4.4
Import duties	...	...	...	...	...	...	...	...	...	...	...	...
Value added tax	...	...	...	...	...	...	...	...	...	...	...	...
Other adjustments	...	...	...	29.2	3.4	25.8	...	...	...	30.7	3.8	26.9
Total	85.0	13.1	96.8	29.2	3.4	220.7	104.7	15.9	88.0	30.7	3.8	235.5

	1986					
	Compensation of Employees	Capital Consumption	Net Operating Surplus	Indirect Taxes	Less: Subsidies Received	Value Added
All Producers						
1 Agriculture, hunting, forestry and fishing	35.5	9.8	62.9	...	...	108.2
2 Mining and quarrying	0.6	0.4	-3.6	...	...	-2.6
3 Manufacturing	6.5	1.2	2.4	...	...	10.1
4 Electricity, gas and water	1.7	0.5	0.3	...	...	2.5
5 Construction	5.8	0.3	5.4	...	...	11.5
6 Wholesale and retail trade, restaurants and hotels	10.7	2.4	5.8	...	...	18.9
7 Transport, storage and communication	8.2	2.0	2.8	...	...	13.0
A Transport and storage	5.8	1.6	2.2	...	...	9.6
B Communication	2.4	0.4	0.6	...	...	3.4
8 Finance, insurance, real estate and business services	8.9	1.6	4.1	...	...	14.6
9 Community, social and personal services	47.2	0.8	-	...	...	48.0
Total, Industries	125.1	19.0	80.1	...	...	224.2
Producers of Government Services	...	...	...	...	...	...
Other Producers	...	...	...	...	...	...
Total a	125.1	19.0	80.1	...	...	224.2
Less: Imputed bank service charge	...	...	5.3	...	...	5.3
Import duties	...	...	...	...	...	...
Value added tax	...	...	...	...	...	...
Other adjustments	...	...	...	35.5	4.1	31.4
Total	125.1	19.0	74.8	35.5	4.1	250.3

a) Gross domestic product in factor values.

Somalia

Source. National Accounts estimates are published in 'National Accounts Aggregates of Somali Democratic Republic' by the Ministero Della Pianificazione Nazionale, Mogadishu.

General note. The estimates shown in the following tables have been prepared in accordance with the United Nations System of National Accounts so far as the existing data would permit.

1.1 Expenditure on the Gross Domestic Product, in Current Prices

Million Somali shillings

	1980	1981	1982	1983	1984	1985	1986	1987	1988	1989	1990	1991
1 Government final consumption expenditure a	2394	2570	3435	4722	5092	9222	11520	18810	...	...	...	...
2 Private final consumption expenditure b	15469	19974	27202	31764	57619	78986	105809	150551	...	...	...	...
3 Gross capital formation	1579	1428	1977	4032	6460	10299	21143	36524	...	...	...	...
A Increase in stocks c	-119	978	1224	-1376	897	2498	1203	8085	...	...	...	...
B Gross fixed capital formation a	1698	450	753	5408	5563	7801	19940	28439	...	...	...	...
4 Exports of goods and services d	845	718	1472	1578	1236	3647	6866	9925	...	...	...	...
5 Less: Imports of goods and services e	2946	2634	4975	6967	8154	14864	26557	46202	...	...	...	...
Equals: Gross Domestic Product	17341	22056	29111	35129	62253	87290	118781	169608	...	...	...	...

a) The value of Technical Assistance from abroad is included in 'Gross fixed capital formation' rather than 'Government final consumption expenditure'.
b) Item 'Private final consumption expenditure' has been obtained as a residual.
c) Item 'Increase in stocks' includes livestock only.
d) Item 'Exports of goods and services' includes exports of goods only.
e) Item 'Imports of goods and services' refers to imports of goods and non-factor services.

1.2 Expenditure on the Gross Domestic Product, in Constant Prices

Million Somali shillings

	1980	1981	1982	1983	1984	1985	1986	1987	1988	1989	1990	1991
					At constant prices of:1977							
1 Government final consumption expenditure	1388	1046	...	...	...	...	...	...	...	...	...	...
2 Private final consumption expenditure	4365	4633	...	...	...	...	...	...	...	...	...	...
3 Gross capital formation	527	1662	...	...	...	...	...	...	...	...	...	...
A Increase in stocks	-315	846	...	...	...	...	...	...	...	...	...	...
B Gross fixed capital formation	842	816	...	...	...	...	...	...	...	...	...	...
4 Exports of goods and services	754	686	...	...	...	...	...	...	...	...	...	...
5 Less: Imports of goods and services	1206	1035	...	...	...	...	...	...	...	...	...	...
Equals: Gross Domestic Product	5823	6992	...	...	...	...	...	...	...	...	...	...

1.7 External Transactions on Current Account, Summary

Million Somali shillings

	1980	1981	1982	1983	1984	1985	1986	1987	1988	1989	1990	1991
					Payments to the Rest of the World							
1 Imports of goods and services	3256	3080	...	...	...	...	...	...	...	...	...	...
A Imports of merchandise c.i.f.	2905	2681	...	...	...	...	...	...	...	...	...	...
B Other	351	399	...	...	...	...	...	...	...	...	...	...
2 Factor income to the rest of the world	41	104	...	...	...	...	...	...	...	...	...	...
A Compensation of employees	4	17	...	...	...	...	...	...	...	...	...	...
B Property and entrepreneurial income	37	88	...	...	...	...	...	...	...	...	...	...
3 Current transfers to the rest of the world	-	-	...	...	...	...	...	...	...	...	...	...
4 Surplus of the nation on current transactions	-1128	-634	...	...	...	...	...	...	...	...	...	...
Payments to the Rest of the World and Surplus of the Nation on Current Transactions	2169	2550	...	...	...	...	...	...	...	...	...	...
					Receipts From The Rest of the World							
1 Exports of goods and services	1221	1668	...	...	...	...	...	...	...	...	...	...

1.7 External Transactions on Current Account, Summary
(Continued)

Million Somali shillings

	1980	1981	1982	1983	1984	1985	1986	1987	1988	1989	1990	1991
A Exports of merchandise f.o.b.	839	1103	...	...	...	...	...	...	...	...	...	...
B Other	382	565	...	...	...	...	...	...	...	...	...	...
2 Factor income from rest of the world	51	82	...	...	...	...	...	...	...	...	...	...
A Compensation of employees	19	45	...	...	...	...	...	...	...	...	...	...
B Property and entrepreneurial income	31	37	...	...	...	...	...	...	...	...	...	...
3 Current transfers from rest of the world	897	800	...	...	...	...	...	...	...	...	...	...
Receipts from the Rest of the World on Current Transactions	2169	2550	...	...	...	...	...	...	...	...	...	...

1.10 Gross Domestic Product by Kind of Activity, in Current Prices

Million Somali shillings

	1980	1981	1982	1983	1984	1985	1986	1987	1988	1989	1990	1991
1 Agriculture, hunting, forestry and fishing	11162	13855	18346	21407	40561	55542	70413	105979	...	...	...	...
2 Mining and quarrying	43	69	77	110	212	291	396	507	...	...	...	...
3 Manufacturing	773	932	1423	1572	2805	4145	6240	8303	...	...	...	...
4 Electricity, gas and water	27	40	59	65	96	71	262	-891	...	...	...	...
5 Construction	461	514	633	642	1235	1889	3000	4800	...	...	...	...
6 Wholesale and retail trade, restaurants and hotels	1569	1768	2522	3171	6097	8452	11598	17418	...	...	...	...
7 Transport, storage and communication	717	958	1277	1807	3369	5667	8174	11109	...	...	...	...
8 Finance, insurance, real estate and business services	635	820	1312	1625	2125	3747	6608	8791	...	...	...	...
9 Community, social and personal services	353	526	664	932	1846	2620	3664	4833	...	...	...	...
Total, Industries	15740	19482	26312	31331	58346	82425	110354	160848	...	...	...	...
Producers of Government Services	810	1032	1090	1433	1807	1625	2230	2327	...	...	...	...
Other Producers	...	...	...	...	...	...	...	...	...	...	...	...
Subtotal a	16550	20514	27402	32764	60153	84050	112584	163175	...	...	...	...
Less: Imputed bank service charge	239	238	339	584	440	859	1000	1300	...	...	...	...
Plus: Import duties	...	...	...	...	...	...	...	...	...	...	...	...
Plus: Value added tax	...	...	...	...	...	...	...	...	...	...	...	...
Plus: Other adjustments b	1030	1780	2048	2949	2540	4099	7197	7733	...	...	...	...
Equals: Gross Domestic Product	17341	22056	29111	35129	62253	87290	118781	169608	...	...	...	...

a) Gross domestic product in factor values.
b) Item 'Other adjustments' refers to indirect taxes net of subsidies.

1.11 Gross Domestic Product by Kind of Activity, in Constant Prices

Million Somali shillings

	1980	1981	1982	1983	1984	1985	1986	1987	1988	1989	1990	1991
					At constant prices of:1977							
1 Agriculture, hunting, forestry and fishing	3844	4418	4495	3699	4220	4753	4426	5106	...	...	...	...
2 Mining and quarrying	20	22	20	21	21	21	21	21	...	...	...	...
3 Manufacturing	357	297	370	300	278	299	331	344	...	...	...	...
4 Electricity, gas and water	43	43	40	40	46	47	55	44	...	...	...	...
5 Construction	286	294	262	238	276	300	318	337	...	...	...	...
6 Wholesale and retail trade, restaurants and hotels	724	564	656	605	605	609	615	722	...	...	...	...
7 Transport, storage and communication	331	306	332	345	334	408	434	460	...	...	...	...
8 Finance, insurance, real estate and business services	367	332	349	370	327	337	340	351	...	...	...	...
9 Community, social and personal services	163	168	173	178	183	189	194	200	...	...	...	...
Total, Industries	6135	6444	6696	5796	6290	6963	6735	7585	...	...	...	...
Producers of Government Services	539	545	547	550	522	493	461	432	...	...	...	...

Somalia

1.11 Gross Domestic Product by Kind of Activity, in Constant Prices
(Continued)

Million Somali shillings

	1980	1981	1982	1983	1984	1985	1986	1987	1988	1989	1990	1991
	At constant prices of:1977											
Other Producers	...	...	...	...	...	...	...	...	...	...	...	...
Subtotal a	6674	6989	7243	6346	6812	7456	7196	8017	...	...	...	...
Less: Imputed bank service charge ...	110	76	88	111	44	62	53	54	...	...	...	...
Plus: Import duties	...	...	...	...	...	...	...	...	...	...	...	...
Plus: Value added tax	...	...	...	...	...	...	...	...	...	...	...	...
Plus: Other adjustments b	475	568	533	563	252	295	382	320	...	...	...	...
Equals: Gross Domestic Product	7040	7481	7688	6798	7020	7689	7524	8283	...	...	...	...

a) Gross domestic product in factor values.
b) Item 'Other adjustments' refers to indirect taxes net of subsidies.

1.12 Relations Among National Accounting Aggregates

Million Somali shillings

	1980	1981	1982	1983	1984	1985	1986	1987	1988	1989	1990	1991
Gross Domestic Product	17341	22056	29111	35129	62253	87290	118781	169608	...	...	...	...
Plus: Net factor income from the rest of the world	-6	-28	-131	-71	-875	-1922	-4372	-5490	...	...	...	...
Equals: Gross National Product	17335	22028	28980	35058	61378	85368	114409	164118	...	...	...	...
Less: Consumption of fixed capital ...	...	...	...	...	...	...	...	...	...	...	...	...
Equals: National Income	17335	22028	28980	35058	61378	85368	114409	164118	...	...	...	...
Plus: Net current transfers from the rest of the world	1259	1347	2225	3140	4903	8785	16871	36066	...	...	...	...
Equals: National Disposable Income	18594	23374	31205	38198	66281	94154	131280	200184	...	...	...	...
Less: Final consumption	17863	22544	30637	36486	62711	88208	117329	169361	...	...	...	...
Equals: Net Saving	731	830	568	1712	3570	5946	13951	30823	...	...	...	...
Less: Surplus of the nation on current transactions	-848	-598	-1409	-2320	-2890	-4353	-7192	-5701	...	...	...	...
Equals: Net Capital Formation	1579	1428	1977	4032	6460	10299	21143	36524	...	...	...	...

2.17 Exports and Imports of Goods and Services, Detail

Million Somali shillings

	1980	1981	1982	1983	1984	1985	1986	1987	1988	1989	1990	1991
	Exports of Goods and Services											
1 Exports of merchandise, f.o.b.	839	1103	...	...	...	...	...	...	...	...	...	...
2 Transport and communication	73	198	...	...	...	...	...	...	...	...	...	...
A In respect of merchandise imports ...	49	154	...	...	...	...	...	...	...	...	...	...
B Other	29	44	...	...	...	...	...	...	...	...	...	...
3 Insurance service charges	-	-	...	...	...	...	...	...	...	...	...	...
4 Other commodities	...	...	...	...	...	...	...	...	...	...	...	...
5 Adjustments of merchandise exports to change-of-ownership basis	-	-	...	...	...	...	...	...	...	...	...	...
6 Direct purchases in the domestic market by non-residential households	154	168	...	...	...	...	...	...	...	...	...	...
7 Direct purchases in the domestic market by extraterritorial bodies	145	198	...	...	...	...	...	...	...	...	...	...
Total Exports of Goods and Services	1221	1668	...	...	...	...	...	...	...	...	...	...
	Imports of Goods and Services											
1 Imports of merchandise, c.i.f.	2905	2681	...	...	...	...	...	...	...	...	...	...
By residents	1221	1668	...	...	...	...	...	...	...	...	...	...

2.17 Exports and Imports of Goods and Services, Detail
(Continued)

Million Somali shillings

	1980	1981	1982	1983	1984	1985	1986	1987	1988	1989	1990	1991
By non-residents	...	...	...	...	...	...	...	...	...	...	...	...
2 Adjustments of merchandise imports to change-of-ownership basis	-	-	...	...	...	...	...	...	...	...	...	...
3 Other transport and communication	80	37	...	...	...	...	...	...	...	...	...	...
4 Other insurance service charges	-	-	...	...	...	...	...	...	...	...	...	...
5 Other commodities	...	...	...	...	...	...	...	...	...	...	...	...
6 Direct purchases abroad by government	170	175	...	...	...	...	...	...	...	...	...	...
7 Direct purchases abroad by resident households	101	187	...	...	...	...	...	...	...	...	...	...
Total Imports of Goods and Services	3256	3080	...	...	...	...	...	...	...	...	...	...
Balance of Goods and Services	-2035	-1412	...	...	...	...	...	...	...	...	...	...
Total Imports and Balance of Goods and Services	1221	1668	...	...	...	...	...	...	...	...	...	...

South Africa

General note. The preparation of national accounts statistics in South Africa is undertaken by the South African Reserve Bank, Pretoria. The official estimates are published in the Bank's Quarterly Bulletin. A detailed description of the sources and methods used for the national accounts estimation is contained in a supplement to the Bulletin published in September 1991 entitled 'South Africa's national accounts, 1946 to 1990'. The estimates for the Republic of South Africa include the self-governing national states - the Republics of Transkei, Bophuthatswana, Venda and Ciskei. The estimates are generally in accordance with the classifications and definitions recommended in the United Nations System of National Accounts (SNA). Input-output tables have been published in 'The South African Journal of Economics'. The following tables have been prepared from successive replies to the United Nations national accounts questionnaire. When the scope and coverage of the estimates differ for conceptual or statistical reasons from the definitions and classifications recommended in SNA, a footnote is indicated to the relevant tables.

Sources and methods :

(a) Gross domestic product. Gross domestic product is estimated mainly through the income approach.

(b) Expenditure on the gross domestic product. All items of GDP by expenditure type are estimated through the expenditure approach. Government expenditure is estimated through the use of published annual accounts and monthly issues from the Exchequer Account for the central authorities quarterly returns submitted directly to the Reserve Bank for the provincial authorities, and annual and quarterly data collected by the Department of Statistics for the local authorities. Estimates of private consumption expenditure are based on a variety of sources such as quarterly data on the agricultural products marketed for food, monthly excise figures for beverages and tobacco, monthly retail sales data for clothing, medicine, entertainment, etc., number of motor vehicles and cycles sold for transport equipment, number of dwelling units and average rent and income of concerned enterprises. The estimates of increase in stocks are based on census results and quarterly surveys. Information on investment in the public sector is obtained from published accounts updated by quarterly returns submitted to the Reserve Bank by concerned authorities. For the private sector, data on investment by the different sectors are obtained from various sources -- censuses and quarterly surveys for agriculture, manufacturing and mining, the value of buildings completed in urban areas for the sectors of commerce, private transport, financial institutions, etc. All relevant information for exports and imports of goods and services is based on balance-of-payments data. Official statistics and sample surveys of financial and non-financial companies are also used for exports and imports of services. For the constant price estimates, price deflation is used for government expenditure on goods and services, increase in stocks except agricultural stocks, gross fixed capital formation and exports and imports of goods and services. The net value of gold exports at constant prices is obtained by extrapolating the value of 1970 on the basis of the number of kilograms of fine gold produced. The base-year values of government wages, salaries and allowances and private consumption expenditure are extrapolated by appropriate volume indexes. For agricultural stocks, values at constant prices are obtained by multiplying the change in the number of livestock by the average flock value.

(c) Cost-structure of the gross domestic product. Estimates of compensation of employees of all sectors of the economy are based on census results and monthly and quarterly data of wages, salaries and benefits paid to employees. Operating surplus is obtained from different sources for the different sectors of the economy - data obtained from the Department of Agricultural Economics and Marketing for the agricultural sector, census results and quarterly surveys of financial statistics for mining, manufacturing, construction and trade, information from concerned enterprises for electricity, gas and water, financial data for the financial institutions, annual and monthly statistics for trade and communication and data on the number of residential units and indexes of house and flat rents for real estate. The straight-line method based on the original cost of the original assets is used for estimating consumption of fixed capital. Depreciation is based on replacement cost. Indirect taxes and subsidies are estimated on the basis of an analysis of government accounts by the Reserve Bank.

(d) Gross domestic product by kind of economic activity. The table of GDP by kind of economic activity is prepared in factor values. The income approach is used to estimate the value added of all industries except agriculture for which the production approach is used. The estimates of agricultural production are obtained by valuing physical output at net producers' prices. Data pertaining to agricultural and livestock production are obtained from the census of agriculture and forestry and the Agricultural Control Boards. For forestry and fishing, estimates are obtained from the Department of Forestry and from the censuses of Fisheries, respectively. Estimates of income originating from gold, coal, diamond and other mines are obtained from triennial censuses. For non-census years, estimates are based on various sources such as reports of the Government Mining Engineer and quarterly sample surveys of financial statistics of mining. Estimates of manufacturing are based on biennial censuses covering establishments employing three or more full-time workers or using power equipment. For other years, estimates are based on quarterly sample surveys supplemented by financial reports for public corporations and Auditor-General's reports and anual surveys of local authorities for government enterprises. Intermediate consumption is estimated in census years only. For electricity, gas and water, estimates are based on annual financial statements for corporations and on results of annual censuses for local authorities and private enterprises. The estimates of construction are based on biennial censuses of construction. For non-census years, sample surveys of wages and salaries and analysis of financial statements of important companies are used. The basic information for trade is obtained from the five-yearly censuses of distribution. For other years, estimates are based on sample surveys of trading establishments. Estimates for the transport sector are obtained from published data of concerned establishments, annual surveys and for the private sector, on the results of the five-yearly censuses. For communication, estimates are obtained from the reports of the Auditor-General. Estimates for banking, insurance and real estate are based on quarterly data collected from the financial institutions. Estimates for ownership of dwellings are based on the results of inquiries into housing and rent as part of the decennial population censuses which are updated by monthly data. Data from the annual rent surveys and monthly data of dwellings completed are used for estimating owner-occupied dwelling rents. For government services, information is obtained from government accounts. For private services, estimates are based on annual surveys, inquiry conducted concurrently with the population censuses and on workmen's compensation statistics. Estimates of the contribution to the GDP at constant prices by each major industry division are made on a quarterly basis. The value added of most industries is extrapolated by quantity indicators. Double deflation is used for agriculture and forestry. For financial institutions, business services and part of private service, value added is deflated by appropriate indexes. Estimates are prepared by the South African Reserve Bank. These estimates include the Republic of South Africa (including the self-governing states), Transkei, Bophutatswana, Venda and Ciskei (TVBC countries), excluding Namibia.

1.1 Expenditure on the Gross Domestic Product, in Current Prices

Million South African rand

	1980	1981	1982	1983	1984	1985	1986	1987	1988	1989	1990	1991
1 Government final consumption expenditure	8158	9877	12361	14115	17927	21297	25672	30599	35276	43946	51421	61988
2 Private final consumption expenditure	30797	38086	44564	51596	59705	66167	77964	93353	111324	131940	154873	179283
A Households	30324	37518	43806	50739	58686	64989	76598	91707	109376	129400	151919	175798
B Private non-profit institutions serving households	473	568	758	857	1019	1178	1366	1646	1948	2540	2954	3485
3 Gross capital formation	18609	23545	20292	23605	26694	24981	27005	31852	42611	49536	50408	48046
A Increase in stocks	2569	3807	-2167	-893	485	-3734	-1702	355	3230	961	-2549	-5622
B Gross fixed capital formation	16040	19738	22459	24498	26209	28715	28707	31497	39381	48575	52957	53668
Residential buildings	1726	2228	2691	3506	4001	3851	3803	4291	5132	5973	6081	6592
Non-residential buildings	1939	2560	3176	3337	3487	4213	4325	4179	5179	6871	8547	8391
Other construction and land improvement etc. [a]	4573	4875	4719	5070	5390	5671	5751	6442	7906	10023	10781	10776
Other	7802	10075	11873	12585	13331	14980	14828	16585	21164	25708	27548	27909
4 Exports of goods and services	22022	20661	21778	23079	28182	39973	45856	48791	56923	66317	69487	74589
5 Less: Imports of goods and services	17034	21749	21897	19512	25982	28409	31981	35273	46544	53950	53984	59180
Statistical discrepancy	-2224	660	3433	-1426	695	-883	-2381	-4798	-1527	-4361	-8002	-6831
Equals: Gross Domestic Product	60328	71080	80531	91457	107221	123126	142135	164524	198063	233428	264203	297895

a) Land development includes transfer costs.

1.2 Expenditure on the Gross Domestic Product, in Constant Prices

Million South African rand

	1980	1981	1982	1983	1984	1985	1986	1987	1988	1989	1990	1991
					At constant prices of:1985							
1 Government final consumption expenditure	17477	17808	18934	19277	20589	21297	21785	22600	22975	23822	24432	26048
2 Private final consumption expenditure	58065	62306	63613	65525	68536	66167	66272	68827	72453	74478	76045	76282
3 Gross capital formation	34843	38855	29491	30516	31306	24981	21855	23220	27089	26779	22670	20977
A Increase in stocks	4356	5638	-3012	-836	421	-3734	-1638	291	2112	519	-3052	-2596
B Gross fixed capital formation	30487	33217	32503	31352	30885	28715	23493	22929	24977	26260	25722	23573
Residential buildings	3293	3699	3865	4145	4596	3851	3346	3344	3447	3428	3082	2977
Non-residential buildings	3713	4241	4471	4118	3931	4213	3732	3188	3384	3838	4223	3693
Other construction and land improvement etc. a	8728	8084	6764	6593	6145	5671	5000	4932	5201	5684	5381	4758
Other	14753	17193	17403	16496	16213	14980	11415	11465	12945	13310	13036	12145
4 Exports of goods and services	38150	36191	35948	33711	36609	39973	39288	39890	41391	45254	46799	47380
5 Less: Imports of goods and services	35061	39879	33485	27718	33274	28409	27769	29078	34844	35014	33938	34801
Statistical discrepancy	1640	6004	6319	-2722	870	-883	1717	276	1952	-1294	-2599	-2996
Equals: Gross Domestic Product	115114	121285	120820	118589	124636	123126	123148	125735	131016	134025	133409	132890

a) Land development includes transfer costs.

1.3 Cost Components of the Gross Domestic Product

Million South African rand

	1980	1981	1982	1983	1984	1985	1986	1987	1988	1989	1990	1991
1 Indirect taxes, net	3949	4815	6654	7048	8937	10678	12648	14593	19833	25418	27195	29945
A Indirect taxes	4761	5774	7717	8632	10929	13335	15785	18305	23825	30224	33048	35881
B Less: Subsidies	812	959	1063	1584	1992	2657	3137	3712	3992	4806	5853	5936
2 Consumption of fixed capital	8023	9688	11999	14216	16121	19645	24697	27998	32442	38402	43070	46990
3 Compensation of employees paid by resident producers to:	29106	36847	43970	49544	58481	65274	74581	87108	101610	119963	140746	160639
A Resident households	28355	35975	42984	48394	57187	63771	72815	85080	99318	117229	137861	157909
B Rest of the world	751	872	986	1150	1294	1503	1766	2028	2292	2734	2885	2730
4 Operating surplus	19250	19730	17908	20649	23682	27529	30209	34825	44178	49645	53192	60321
Equals: Gross Domestic Product	60328	71080	80531	91457	107221	123126	142135	164524	198063	233428	264203	297895

1.4 General Government Current Receipts and Disbursements

Million South African rand

	1980	1981	1982	1983	1984	1985	1986	1987	1988	1989	1990	1991
					Receipts							
1 Operating surplus	...	...	...	...	...	...	...	...	...	...	...	...
2 Property and entrepreneurial income	1785	1581	1179	1341	1751	1735	2062	2417	2518	2737	3178	3762
3 Taxes, fees and contributions	12163	14175	17336	20295	24066	29979	34978	39505	48749	61514	72525	79115
A Indirect taxes	4761	5774	7717	8632	10929	13335	15785	18305	23825	30224	33048	35881
B Direct taxes	7159	8124	9267	11267	12679	16104	18475	20342	24022	29861	37864	41110
C Social security contributions	153	178	227	263	303	368	523	597	640	1111	1251	1590
D Compulsory fees, fines and penalties	90	99	125	133	155	172	194	261	262	318	362	534
4 Other current transfers	279	345	276	277	269	373	426	431	400	455	459	323
Total Current Receipts of General Government	14227	16101	18791	21913	26086	32087	37466	42353	51667	64706	76162	83200
					Disbursements							
1 Government final consumption expenditure	8158	9877	12361	14115	17927	21297	25672	30599	35276	43946	51421	61988
2 Property income	1585	1796	2883	3394	4343	5456	5901	6721	7951	11001	11314	14203
A Interest	1585	1796	2883	3394	4343	5456	5901	6721	7951	11001	11314	14203
B Net land rent and royalties	...	...	...	...	...	...	...	...	...	...	...	...
3 Subsidies	812	959	1063	1584	1992	2657	3137	3712	3992	4806	5853	5936
4 Other current transfers	1306	1528	2155	2590	3020	3667	4424	5300	5695	6290	8684	9676
A Social security benefits	155	164	200	264	303	413	494	594	659	762	961	1075
B Social assistance grants	1136	1316	1731	2096	2417	2918	3590	4215	4706	5185	7562	8549
C Other	15	48	224	230	300	336	340	491	330	343	161	52
5 Net saving	2366	1941	329	230	-1196	-990	-1668	-3979	-1247	-1337	-1110	-8603
Total Current Disbursements and Net Saving of General Government	14227	16101	18791	21913	26086	32087	37466	42353	51667	64706	76162	83200

South Africa

1.6 Current Income and Outlay of Households and Non-Profit Institutions

Million South African rand

	1980	1981	1982	1983	1984	1985	1986	1987	1988	1989	1990	1991
Receipts												
1 Compensation of employees	28367	35990	43002	48414	57208	63794	72841	85108	99349	117276	137943	157995
A From resident producers	28355	35975	42984	48394	57187	63771	72815	85081	99318	117229	137861	157909
B From rest of the world	12	15	18	20	21	23	26	28	31	47	82	86
2 Operating surplus of private unincorporated enterprises	...	...	...	...	...	...	...	...	...	...	...	...
3 Property and entrepreneurial income	7176	4713	4796	7726	10052	12266	13269	20095	24588	30534	34360	44990
4 Current transfers	1503	1724	2229	2689	3090	3738	4509	5242	5808	6500	9019	10146
Total Current Receipts	37046	42427	50027	58829	70350	79798	90619	110445	129745	154310	181322	213131
Disbursements												
1 Private final consumption expenditure	30797	38086	44564	51596	59705	66167	77964	93353	111324	131940	154873	179283
2 Property income	...	...	...	...	...	...	...	...	...	...	...	...
3 Direct taxes and other current transfers n.e.c. to general government	2390	3418	4707	6211	7884	9139	10626	12506	14650	19908	24042	29463
A Social security contributions	...	...	...	...	...	...	...	...	...	...	...	...
B Direct taxes	2390	3418	4707	6211	7884	9139	10626	12506	14650	19908	24042	29463
C Fees, fines and penalties	...	...	...	...	...	...	...	...	...	...	...	...
4 Other current transfers	103	120	121	129	139	165	184	163	162	133	132	140
5 Net saving	3756	803	635	893	2622	4327	1844	4423	3609	2329	2276	4245
Total Current Disbursements and Net Saving	37046	42427	50027	58829	70350	79798	90618	110445	129745	154310	181322	213131

1.7 External Transactions on Current Account, Summary

Million South African rand

	1980	1981	1982	1983	1984	1985	1986	1987	1988	1989	1990	1991
Payments to the Rest of the World												
1 Imports of goods and services	17034	21749	21897	19512	25983	28409	31981	35273	46544	53950	53984	59180
A Imports of merchandise c.i.f.	15567	20089	20001	17498	23673	25969	28762	31627	42353	48902	48445	53047
B Other	1467	1660	1896	2014	2309	2440	3219	3646	4191	5048	5539	6132
2 Factor income to the rest of the world	3184	3835	4145	4702	5678	7939	9390	8898	9388	11229	11828	10737
A Compensation of employees	751	872	986	1151	1293	1503	1766	2028	2292	2734	2885	2730
B Property and entrepreneurial income	2433	2963	3159	3552	4385	6436	7624	6870	7096	8495	8943	8007
3 Current transfers to the rest of the world a	171	217	404	415	535	681	717	826	678	695	554	543
4 Surplus of the nation on current transactions	2539	-4174	-3696	-451	-2602	5087	6114	5995	2728	3108	5787	7422
Payments to the Rest of the World and Surplus of the Nation on Current Transactions	22928	21627	22750	24178	29593	42116	48202	50992	59338	68982	72153	77882
Receipts From The Rest of the World												
1 Exports of goods and services	22022	20661	21778	23079	28182	39973	45856	48791	56923	66317	69487	74589
A Exports of merchandise f.o.b.	19670	17949	18666	20004	24452	35437	41055	43619	50889	58313	60455	65566
B Other	2352	2712	3112	3075	3730	4536	4801	5172	6034	8004	9032	9023
2 Factor income from rest of the world	449	419	442	538	822	1421	1564	1412	1652	1750	1808	2555
A Compensation of employees	12	15	18	20	21	23	26	28	31	47	82	86
B Property and entrepreneurial income	437	404	424	518	801	1398	1538	1384	1621	1703	1726	2469
3 Current transfers from rest of the world	457	547	530	561	589	722	782	789	763	915	858	738
Receipts from the Rest of the World on Current Transactions	22928	21627	22750	24178	29593	42116	48202	50992	59338	68982	72153	77882

a) Item 'Current transfers to/from the rest of the world' includes also capital transfers.

1.8 Capital Transactions of The Nation, Summary

Million South African rand

	1980	1981	1982	1983	1984	1985	1986	1987	1988	1989	1990	1991
Finance of Gross Capital Formation												
Gross saving	21148	19371	16596	23154	24092	30068	33119	37847	45339	52644	56195	55468
1 Consumption of fixed capital	8023	9688	11999	14216	16121	19645	24697	27998	32442	38402	43070	46990
A General government	275	332	407	480	544	637	761	888	1065	1286	1493	1715
B Corporate and quasi-corporate enterprises	7748	9356	11592	13736	15577	19008	23937	27110	31377	37116	41578	45275
Public	2404	2955	3629	4303	4883	5859	7353	8374	9790	11457	12976	14017
Private	5344	6401	7963	9433	10694	13149	16584	18736	21587	25659	28602	31258
C Other	-	-	-	-	-	-	-	-	-	-	-	-
2 Net saving	13125	9683	4597	8938	7971	10423	8422	9849	12897	14242	13125	8478
A General government	2366	1941	329	230	-1196	-990	-1668	-3979	-1247	-1337	-1110	-8603
B Corporate and quasi-corporate enterprises	7003	6939	3633	7815	6545	7086	8246	9405	10535	13250	11960	12836
C Other	3756	803	635	893	2622	4327	1844	4423	3609	2329	2275	4245
Less: Surplus of the nation on current transactions	2539	-4174	-3696	-451	-2602	5087	6114	5995	2728	3108	5787	7422
Finance of Gross Capital Formation	18609	23545	20292	23605	26694	24981	27005	31852	42611	49536	50408	48046
Gross Capital Formation												
Increase in stocks	2569	3807	-2167	-893	485	-3734	-1702	355	3230	961	-2549	-5622
Gross fixed capital formation	16040	19738	22459	24498	26209	28715	28707	31497	39381	48575	52957	53668
1 General government	1760	2070	2172	2398	2607	2927	3331	3798	4411	5045	4836	4841
2 Corporate and quasi-corporate enterprises	14280	17668	20287	22100	23602	25788	25376	27699	34970	43530	48121	48827
A Public	6124	6656	7468	7800	7994	9665	8895	8288	8721	11259	12842	12036
B Private	8156	11012	12819	14300	15608	16123	16481	19411	26249	32271	35279	36791
3 Other	...	...	...	...	...	...	...	...	...	...	...	...
Gross Capital Formation	18609	23545	20292	23605	26694	24981	27005	31852	42611	49536	50408	48046

1.10 Gross Domestic Product by Kind of Activity, in Current Prices

Million South African rand

	1980	1981	1982	1983	1984	1985	1986	1987	1988	1989	1990	1991
1 Agriculture, hunting, forestry and fishing	2915	4706	4649	4150	5252	6526	7242	9430	11560	12649	12272	13039
2 Mining and quarrying	12112	10036	10007	11918	12949	16671	20214	19379	21903	23582	25079	27005
3 Manufacturing	12934	16552	18320	20844	23804	25928	30277	35752	44105	52859	59945	66567
4 Electricity, gas and water	1787	2156	2615	3220	3883	4836	5632	6827	8231	9225	10710	11710
5 Construction	1870	2556	3037	3485	3785	4144	4507	4915	5822	6571	7446	8201
6 Wholesale and retail trade, restaurants and hotels	6972	8784	9834	11353	12075	13254	15228	18995	22521	27029	31620	36173
7 Transport, storage and communication	5030	5827	6436	7391	9213	9935	11448	13217	15535	16825	19376	22687
8 Finance, insurance, real estate and business services	6373	7597	9145	11074	13311	15754	16686	19769	23768	28825	34192	39683
9 Community, social and personal services	819	944	1148	1464	1710	1897	2222	2604	2994	3446	4020	4645
Total, Industries	50812	59158	65191	74899	85982	98945	113456	130888	156439	181011	204660	229710
Producers of Government Services	5243	6595	8033	9372	12170	13901	16465	19636	22495	28006	33690	40012
Other Producers	1215	1427	1722	2044	2422	2802	3275	3787	4286	4876	5633	6416
Subtotal a	57270	67180	74946	86315	100574	115648	133196	154311	183220	213893	243983	276138
Less: Imputed bank service charge	891	915	1069	1906	2290	3200	3709	4380	4990	5883	6975	8188
Plus: Import duties	...	...	...	...	...	...	...	...	...	...	...	...
Plus: Value added tax	...	...	...	...	...	...	...	...	...	...	...	...
Plus: Other adjustments b	3949	4815	6654	7048	8937	10678	12648	14593	19833	25418	27195	29945
Equals: Gross Domestic Product c	60328	71080	80531	91457	107221	123126	142135	164524	198063	233428	264203	297895

a) Gross domestic product in factor values.
b) Item 'Other adjustments' refers to indirect taxes net of subsidies.
c) Estimates of GDP by economic activity are prepared by the Central Statistical Services.

South Africa

1.11 Gross Domestic Product by Kind of Activity, in Constant Prices

Million South African rand

	1980	1981	1982	1983	1984	1985	1986	1987	1988	1989	1990	1991
						At constant prices of:1985						
1 Agriculture, hunting, forestry and fishing	6503	6879	6298	4868	5423	6526	6956	7133	7333	8316	7698	7859
2 Mining and quarrying	16018	15928	15948	15994	16614	16671	16102	15356	15624	15470	15284	15049
3 Manufacturing	27342	29192	28307	26426	27480	25928	25886	26451	28155	28278	27910	27249
4 Electricity, gas and water	3610	4023	4260	4254	4528	4836	4967	5138	5395	5566	5661	5769
5 Construction	4441	4687	4502	4258	4363	4144	3809	3557	3672	3963	3956	3777
6 Wholesale and retail trade, restaurants and hotels	11171	12223	12241	12671	13844	13254	12771	13141	13689	13767	13936	13772
7 Transport, storage and communication	9380	9974	9665	9098	9813	9935	9765	9832	10302	10703	10723	10565
8 Finance, insurance, real estate and business services	13386	14086	14433	14912	15506	15754	16111	16705	17036	17397	17468	17692
9 Community, social and personal services	1429	1538	1633	1747	1864	1897	1935	1994	2048	2088	2118	2148
Total, Industries	93280	98530	97287	94228	99435	98945	98302	99307	103254	105548	104754	103880
Producers of Government Services	11952	12237	12721	13361	13880	13901	14387	15028	15489	15811	15954	16209
Other Producers	2412	2472	2546	2637	2739	2802	2879	2979	3091	3202	3210	3229
Subtotal a	107644	113239	112554	110226	116054	115648	115568	117314	121834	124561	123918	123318
Less: Imputed bank service charge	2523	2852	2920	2982	3195	3200	3109	3094	3276	3345	3430	3480
Plus: Import duties	...	...	...	...	...	...	...	...	...	...	...	...
Plus: Value added tax	...	...	...	...	...	...	...	...	...	...	...	...
Plus: Other adjustments b	9993	10898	11186	11345	11777	10678	10689	11515	12458	12809	12921	13052
Equals: Gross Domestic Product c	115114	121285	120820	118589	124636	123126	123148	125735	131016	134025	133409	132890

a) Gross domestic product in factor values.
b) Item 'Other adjustments' refers to indirect taxes net of subsidies.
c) Estimates of GDP by economic activity are prepared by the Central Statistical Services.

1.12 Relations Among National Accounting Aggregates

Million South African rand

	1980	1981	1982	1983	1984	1985	1986	1987	1988	1989	1990	1991
Gross Domestic Product	60328	71080	80531	91457	107221	123126	142135	164524	198063	233428	264203	297895
Plus: Net factor income from the rest of the world	-2735	-3416	-3703	-4164	-4856	-6518	-7826	-7486	-7736	-9479	-10020	-8182
Factor income from the rest of the world	449	419	442	538	822	1421	1564	1412	1652	1750	1808	2555
Less: Factor income to the rest of the world	3184	3835	4145	4702	5678	7939	9390	8898	9388	11229	11828	10737
Equals: Gross National Product	57593	67664	76828	87293	102365	116608	134309	157038	190327	223949	254183	289713
Less: Consumption of fixed capital	8023	9688	11999	14216	16121	19645	24697	27998	32442	38402	43070	46990
Equals: National Income	49570	57976	64829	73077	86244	96963	109612	129040	157885	185547	211113	242723
Plus: Net current transfers from the rest of the world	286	330	126	146	54	41	65	-37	85	220	304	195
Current transfers from the rest of the world	457	547	530	561	589	722	782	789	763	915	858	738
Less: Current transfers to the rest of the world a	171	217	404	415	535	681	717	826	678	695	554	543
Equals: National Disposable Income	49856	58306	64955	73223	86298	97004	109677	129003	157970	185767	211417	242918
Less: Final consumption	38955	47963	56925	65711	77632	87464	103636	123952	146600	175886	206294	241271
Statistical discrepancy	2224	-660	-3433	1426	-695	883	2381	4798	1527	4361	8002	6831
Equals: Net Saving	13125	9683	4597	8938	7971	10423	8422	9849	12897	14242	13125	8478
Less: Surplus of the nation on current transactions	2539	-4174	-3696	-451	-2602	5087	6114	5995	2728	3108	5787	7422
Equals: Net Capital Formation	10586	13857	8293	9389	10573	5336	2308	3854	10169	11134	7338	1056

a) Item 'Current transfers to/from the rest of the world' includes also capital transfers.

2.5 Private Final Consumption Expenditure by Type and Purpose, in Current Prices

Million South African rand

	1980	1981	1982	1983	1984	1985	1986	1987	1988	1989	1990	1991
					Final Consumption Expenditure of Resident Households							
1 Food, beverages and tobacco	10175	12549	14825	16764	19925	22528	27905	34157	40489	47333	56205	67439
A Food	7588	9570	10947	12576	14613	16618	20479	25373	29971	34875	40989	49057
B Non-alcoholic beverages	400	445	536	594	814	944	1280	1441	1764	1878	2349	2818
C Alcoholic beverages	1438	1755	2322	2541	3161	3447	4415	5255	6237	7488	9181	10696
D Tobacco	749	779	1020	1053	1337	1519	1731	2088	2517	3091	3686	4868
2 Clothing and footwear	2695	3297	3717	4021	4430	4641	5491	6740	8189	9950	11553	13366
3 Gross rent, fuel and power	2946	3846	4443	6210	7203	8001	9176	10516	12027	14031	15675	16785
4 Furniture, furnishings and household equipment and operation	3658	4452	5149	5899	6495	6907	8122	9724	12129	13925	16550	18167

2.5 Private Final Consumption Expenditure by Type and Purpose, in Current Prices
(Continued)

Million South African rand

	1980	1981	1982	1983	1984	1985	1986	1987	1988	1989	1990	1991
A Household operation	887	1105	1309	1558	1854	1899	2260	2530	2931	3330	3910	4027
B Other	2771	3347	3840	4341	4641	5008	5862	7194	9198	10595	12640	14140
5 Medical care and health expenses	1150	1369	1776	2038	2420	2802	3293	3837	4682	6083	7424	8798
6 Transport and communication [a]	5532	6781	7740	8749	9781	11033	12118	14774	17513	20471	23462	26761
A Personal transport equipment	1704	2190	2309	2605	2839	2404	2540	4032	4860	5433	5946	6854
B Other	3828	4591	5431	6144	6942	8629	9578	10742	12653	15038	17516	19907
7 Recreational, entertainment, education and cultural services	1936	2322	2673	3193	3580	3948	4448	5107	6362	8178	10021	11377
A Education	34	55	54	86	129	211	314	433	484	643	701	553
B Other	1902	2267	2619	3107	3451	3737	4134	4674	5878	7535	9320	10824
8 Miscellaneous goods and services	2753	3503	4140	4601	5755	6373	7049	8192	9613	11753	13821	15568
A Personal care	494	610	737	864	1000	1134	1307	1522	1829	2261	2718	3192
B Expenditures in restaurants, cafes and hotels	916	1213	1382	1385	1991	2101	2271	2715	3277	4041	4718	5293
C Other [a]	1343	1680	2021	2352	2764	3138	3471	3955	4507	5451	6385	7083
Total Final Consumption Expenditure in the Domestic Market by Households, of which	30845	38119	44464	51475	59589	66233	77602	93047	111004	131724	154711	178261
A Durable goods	3792	4799	5338	6003	6490	6034	6669	9054	11478	13171	15641	17836
B Semi-durable goods	5257	6461	7341	8332	9384	10352	12081	14594	18192	22053	25895	29434
C Non-durable goods	14013	17261	20348	22903	26836	30766	37234	44453	52552	62166	73620	86886
D Services	7783	9598	11437	14237	16879	19081	21618	24946	28782	34334	39555	44105
Plus: Direct purchases abroad by resident households	570	674	785	871	971	902	1327	1543	2214	2634	2953	3185
Less: Direct purchases in the domestic market by non-resident households [b]	1091	1275	1443	1607	1874	2146	2330	2883	3842	4957	5745	5648
Equals: Final Consumption Expenditure of Resident Households	30324	37518	43806	50739	58686	64989	76599	91707	109376	129401	151919	175798

Final Consumption Expenditure of Private Non-profit Institutions Serving Households

	1980	1981	1982	1983	1984	1985	1986	1987	1988	1989	1990	1991
1 Research and science	...	...	...	...	...	...	...	...	...	...	...	...
2 Education	349	429	583	656	782	906	1056	1281	1506	1962	2265	2672
3 Medical and other health services	69	78	104	122	145	167	190	222	274	364	446	530
4 Welfare services	...	...	...	...	...	...	...	...	...	...	...	...
5 Recreational and related cultural services	42	47	56	63	75	87	101	123	146	190	219	258
6 Religious organisations	...	...	...	...	...	...	...	...	...	...	...	...
7 Professional and labour organisations serving households	...	...	...	...	...	...	...	...	...	...	...	...
8 Miscellaneous	13	14	15	16	17	18	19	20	22	23	24	25
Equals: Final Consumption Expenditure of Private Non-profit Organisations Serving Households	473	568	758	857	1019	1178	1366	1646	1948	2539	2954	3485
Private Final Consumption Expenditure	30797	38086	44564	51596	59705	66167	77965	93353	111324	131940	154873	179283

a) Packaged tours is included in item 'Transport and communication'.
b) Item 'Direct purchases in the domestic market by non-resident households' includes a statistical discrepancy.

2.6 Private Final Consumption Expenditure by Type and Purpose, in Constant Prices

Million South African rand

	1980	1981	1982	1983	1984	1985	1986	1987	1988	1989	1990	1991
					At constant prices of:1985							
					Final Consumption Expenditure of Resident Households							
1 Food, beverages and tobacco	19138	19742	20646	20988	22428	22528	23401	23865	24337	25116	25566	25601
A Food	14319	14746	15188	15623	16353	16618	17008	17172	17531	18382	18619	18643
B Non-alcoholic beverages	833	815	841	816	940	944	1070	1010	1037	970	1039	1052
C Alcoholic beverages	2605	2844	3157	3168	3576	3448	3797	4065	4039	4010	4138	3991
D Tobacco	1381	1337	1460	1381	1559	1518	1526	1618	1730	1754	1770	1915
2 Clothing and footwear	4768	5202	5111	5032	4966	4641	4690	4828	5102	5346	5398	5567
3 Gross rent, fuel and power	5586	6367	6357	7394	7709	8001	8181	8409	8690	8978	9167	9290
4 Furniture, furnishings and household equipment and operation	6514	7009	7054	7116	7116	6907	6379	6628	7458	7661	7921	7680
A Household operation	1813	2045	2073	2126	2280	1899	1677	1606	1607	1557	1538	1305

2.6 Private Final Consumption Expenditure by Type and Purpose, in Constant Prices
(Continued)

Million South African rand

	1980	1981	1982	1983	1984	1985	1986	1987	1988	1989	1990	1991
				At constant prices of:1985								
B Other	4701	4964	4981	4990	4836	5008	4702	5022	5851	6104	6383	6375
5 Medical care and health expenses	2400	2526	2688	2678	2968	2969	2920	3057	3355	3498	3544	3503
6 Transport and communication a	10887	11845	11797	12059	12451	11033	10854	12082	12797	12645	12775	12675
A Personal transport equipment	3871	4295	4008	3774	3525	2404	1955	2490	2591	2448	2368	2073
B Other	7016	7550	7789	8285	8926	8629	8899	9592	10206	10197	10407	10602
7 Recreational, entertainment, education and cultural services	4555	4853	5003	5305	5387	4941	4583	4648	5106	5607	5896	5854
A Education	927	974	1050	1047	1121	1129	1078	1163	1185	1282	1228	1130
B Other	3628	3879	3953	4258	4266	3812	3505	3485	3921	4325	4668	4724
8 Miscellaneous goods and services	5445	5971	6083	6031	6634	6391	5985	6061	6303	6622	7024	6966
A Personal care	965	1072	1102	1124	1138	1109	1050	1036	1092	1181	1223	1241
B Expenditures in restaurants, cafes and hotels	1754	1902	1878	1762	2251	2109	1944	2005	2047	2165	2182	2009
C Other a	2726	2997	3103	3145	3245	3173	2991	3020	3164	3276	3619	3716
Total Final Consumption Expenditure in the Domestic Market by Households, of which	59293	63515	64739	66603	69659	67411	66993	69578	73148	75473	77291	77136
A Durable goods	7780	8518	8312	8149	7767	6034	5283	5983	6775	6817	7215	7047
B Semi-durable goods	9526	10423	10395	10640	10771	10352	10197	10525	11586	11939	12127	12112
C Non-durable goods	26029	27423	28605	29160	31209	30766	31516	32229	32947	34127	34777	34674
D Services	15958	17151	17427	18654	19912	20259	19997	20841	21840	22590	23172	23303
Plus: Direct purchases abroad by resident households	873	922	976	1008	1051	902	1241	1337	1773	1783	1576	1550
Less: Direct purchases in the domestic market by non-resident households b	2101	2131	2102	2086	2174	2146	1962	2088	2468	2778	2822	2404
Equals: Final Consumption Expenditure of Resident Households c	58065	62306	63613	65525	68536	66167	66272	68827	72453	74478	76045	76282

Final Consumption Expenditure of Private Non-profit Institutions Serving Households

	1980	1981	1982	1983	1984	1985	1986	1987	1988	1989	1990	1991
Equals: Final Consumption Expenditure of Private Non-profit Organisations Serving Households	...	...	...	...	...	...	...	...	...	...	...	...
Private Final Consumption Expenditure	58065	62306	63613	65525	68536	66167	66272	68827	72453	74478	76045	76282

a) Packaged tours is included in item 'Transport and communication'.
b) Item 'Direct purchases in the domestic market by non-resident households' includes a statistical discrepancy.
c) Item 'Final consumption expenditure of resident households' includes consumption expenditure of private non-profit institutions serving households.

2.7 Gross Capital Formation by Type of Good and Owner, in Current Prices

Million South African rand

	1980				1981				1982			
	TOTAL	Total Private	Public Enterprises	General Government	TOTAL	Total Private	Public Enterprises	General Government	TOTAL	Total Private	Public Enterprises	General Government
Increase in stocks, total abc	2569	2205	364	-	3807	3113	694	-	-2167	-1945	-222	-
1 Goods producing industries	332	...	...	...	857	...	...	...	-1311	...	...	...
2 Wholesale and retail trade c	1359	...	...	...	1744	...	...	...	-832	...	...	...
3 Other, except government stocks c	874	...	...	...	1155	...	...	...	-56	...	...	...
4 Government stocks c	4	...	...	...	50	...	...	...	32	...	...	...
Gross Fixed Capital Formation, Total	16040	8156	6124	1760	19738	11012	6656	2070	22459	12819	7468	2172
1 Residential buildings	1726	1155	...	...	2228	1577	...	...	2691	2036	...	...
2 Non-residential buildings	1939	932	...	...	2560	1378	...	...	3176	1938	...	...
3 Other construction	4224	639	...	...	4495	792	...	...	4290	848	...	...
4 Land improvement and plantation and orchard development d	349	349	...	...	380	380	...	...	429	429	...	...
5 Producers' durable goods	7802	5081	...	...	10075	6885	...	...	11873	7568	...	...
A Transport equipment	1857	1396	...	...	2535	1859	...	...	2855	1910	...	...
B Machinery and equipment	5945	3685	...	...	7540	5026	...	...	9018	5658	...	...
6 Breeding stock, dairy cattle, etc. a	...	...	...	...	...	...	...	...	...	...	...	...
Total Gross Capital Formation	18609	10361	6488	1760	23545	14125	7350	2070	20292	10874	7246	2172

2.7 Gross Capital Formation by Type of Good and Owner, in Current Prices

Million South African rand

	1983				1984				1985			
	TOTAL	Total Private	Public Enterprises	General Government	TOTAL	Total Private	Public Enterprises	General Government	TOTAL	Total Private	Public Enterprises	General Government
Increase in stocks, total abc	-893	-899	6	-	485	617	-132	-	-3734	-3210	-524	-
1 Goods producing industries	-453	...	...	...	330	...	...	...	-1616	...	...	...
2 Wholesale and retail trade c	-462	...	...	...	456	...	...	...	-919	...	...	...
3 Other, except government stocks c	109	...	...	...	-293	...	...	...	-1174	...	...	...
4 Government stocks c	-87	...	...	...	-9	...	...	...	-25	...	...	...
Gross Fixed Capital Formation, Total	24498	14300	7800	2398	26209	15608	7994	2607	28715	16123	9665	2927
1 Residential buildings	3506	2692	...	...	4001	3104	...	...	3851	3013	...	...
2 Non-residential buildings	3337	2003	...	...	3487	1900	...	...	4213	2320	...	...
3 Other construction	4593	1099	...	...	4668	1249	...	...	5040	1595	...	...
4 Land improvement and plantation and orchard development d	477	477	...	...	722	722	...	...	631	631	...	...
5 Producers' durable goods	12585	8029	...	...	13331	8633	...	...	14980	8564	...	...
A Transport equipment	3033	2000	...	...	2831	2247	...	...	2897	2242	...	...
B Machinery and equipment	9552	6029	...	...	10500	6386	...	...	12083	6322	...	...
6 Breeding stock, dairy cattle, etc. a	...	...	...	...	...	...	...	...	...	...	...	...
Total Gross Capital Formation	23605	13401	7806	2398	26694	16225	7862	2607	24981	12913	9141	2927

	1986				1987				1988			
	TOTAL	Total Private	Public Enterprises	General Government	TOTAL	Total Private	Public Enterprises	General Government	TOTAL	Total Private	Public Enterprises	General Government
Increase in stocks, total abc	-1702	-1617	-85	-	355	1442	-1087	-	3230	3063	167	-
1 Goods producing industries	-726	...	...	...	187	...	...	...	1249	...	...	...
2 Wholesale and retail trade c	-1350	...	...	...	754	...	...	...	1439	...	...	...
3 Other, except government stocks c	623	...	...	...	-466	...	...	...	590	...	...	...
4 Government stocks c	-249	...	...	...	-120	...	...	...	-48	...	...	...
Gross Fixed Capital Formation, Total	28707	16481	8895	3331	31497	19411	8288	3798	39381	26249	8721	4411
1 Residential buildings	3803	3064	...	...	4291	3545	...	...	5132	4267	...	...
2 Non-residential buildings	4325	2336	...	...	4179	2120	...	...	5179	2917	...	...
3 Other construction	5089	1618	...	...	5501	2032	...	...	6668	2342	...	...
4 Land improvement and plantation and orchard development d	662	662	...	...	941	941	...	...	1238	1238	...	...
5 Producers' durable goods	14828	8801	...	...	16585	10773	...	...	21164	15485	...	...
A Transport equipment	2835	2383	...	...	3751	3388	...	...	5502	5061	...	...
B Machinery and equipment	11993	6418	...	...	12834	7385	...	...	15662	10424	...	...
6 Breeding stock, dairy cattle, etc. a	...	...	...	...	...	...	...	...	...	...	...	...
Total Gross Capital Formation	27005	14864	8810	3331	31852	20853	7201	3798	42611	29312	8888	4411

	1989				1990				1991			
	TOTAL	Total Private	Public Enterprises	General Government	TOTAL	Total Private	Public Enterprises	General Government	TOTAL	Total Private	Public Enterprises	General Government
Increase in stocks, total abc	961	94	867	-	-2549	-178	-2371	-	-5622	-4941	-681	-
1 Goods producing industries	-625	...	...	...	-2700	...	...	...	-1969	...	...	...
2 Wholesale and retail trade c	333	...	...	...	-1970	...	...	...	-2187	...	...	...
3 Other, except government stocks c	1115	...	...	...	2350	...	...	...	-1373	...	...	...
4 Government stocks c	138	...	...	...	-229	...	...	...	-93	...	...	...
Gross Fixed Capital Formation, Total	48575	32271	11259	5045	52957	35279	12842	4836	53668	36791	12036	4841
1 Residential buildings	5973	4943	...	...	6081	5068	...	...	6592	5390	...	...
2 Non-residential buildings	6871	4110	...	...	8547	4868	...	...	8391	5410	...	...

South Africa

2.7 Gross Capital Formation by Type of Good and Owner, in Current Prices
(Continued)

Million South African rand

	1989				1990				1991			
	TOTAL	Total Private	Public Enterprises	General Government	TOTAL	Total Private	Public Enterprises	General Government	TOTAL	Total Private	Public Enterprises	General Government
3 Other construction	8640	2619	...	...	9173	2703	...	...	8891	2464	...	...
4 Land improvement and plantation and orchard development d	1383	1383			1608	1608	...	...	1885	1885		
5 Producers' durable goods	25708	19216	...	...	27548	21032	...	...	27909	21642	...	...
A Transport equipment	7061	6390	...	...	7124	6323	...	...	7874	6668	...	...
B Machinery and equipment	18647	12826	...	...	20424	14709	...	...	20035	14974	...	...
6 Breeding stock, dairy cattle, etc. a	...	...	...	...	...	...		...	...	...		
Total Gross Capital Formation	49536	32365	12126	5045	50408	35101	10471	4836	48046	31850	11355	4841

a) Item 'Breeding stocks, dairy cattle, etc.' is included in item 'Increase in stocks'.
b) Item 'Increase in stocks' excludes enterprises of commercial farms in business services, education, health and large unincorporated units of government enterprises.
c) The estimates of 'Increase in stocks' and their components are after inventory valuation adjustment.
d) Land development includes transfer costs.

2.8 Gross Capital Formation by Type of Good and Owner, in Constant Prices

Million South African rand

	1980				1981				1982			
	TOTAL	Total Private	Public Enterprises	General Government	TOTAL	Total Private	Public Enterprises	General Government	TOTAL	Total Private	Public Enterprises	General Government
At constant prices of:1985												
Increase in stocks, total abc	4356	3687	...	...	5638	4485	...	...	-3012	-2699	...	...
1 Goods producing industries	506	...	...	...	1393	...	...	...	-1818	...	...	...
2 Wholesale and retail trade c	2086	...	...	...	1365	...	...	...	-1084	...	...	...
3 Other, except government stocks c	1754	...	...	...	2798	...	...	...	-156	...	...	...
4 Government stocks c	10	...	...	...	82	...	...	...	46	...	...	...
Gross Fixed Capital Formation, Total	30487	15581	...	...	33217	18687	...	...	32502	18627	...	...
1 Residential buildings	3293	2200	...	...	3699	2621	...	...	3865	2926	...	...
2 Non-residential buildings	3713	1782	...	...	4241	2280	...	...	4471	2723	...	...
3 Other construction	8062	1211	...	...	7454	1311	...	...	6151	1225	...	...
4 Land improvement and plantation and orchard development d	666	666	...	...	630	630	...	...	613	613	...	...
5 Producers' durable goods	14753	9722	...	...	17193	11845	...	...	17403	11140	...	...
A Transport equipment	3762	2835	...	...	4522	3319	...	...	4300	2877	...	...
B Machinery and equipment	10991	6887	...	...	12671	8526	...	...	13103	8263	...	...
6 Breeding stock, dairy cattle, etc. a	...	...	...	...	...	...	...	...	...	...	...	...
Total Gross Capital Formation	34843	19268	...	...	38855	23172	...	...	29491	15928	...	...

	1983				1984				1985			
	TOTAL	Total Private	Public Enterprises	General Government	TOTAL	Total Private	Public Enterprises	General Government	TOTAL	Total Private	Public Enterprises	General Government
At constant prices of:1985												
Increase in stocks, total abc	-836	-843	...	...	421	572	...	...	-3734	-3210	...	...
1 Goods producing industries	-580	...	...	...	387	...	...	...	-1678	...	...	...
2 Wholesale and retail trade c	11	...	...	...	154	...	...	...	-1497	...	...	...
3 Other, except government stocks c	-154	...	...	...	-111	...	...	...	-535	...	...	...
4 Government stocks c	-113	...	...	...	-9	...	...	...	-24	...	...	...
Gross Fixed Capital Formation, Total	31352	18350	...	...	30885	18439	...	...	28715	16123	...	...
1 Residential buildings	4145	3126	...	...	4596	3567	...	...	3851	3013	...	...
2 Non-residential buildings	4118	2475	...	...	3931	2145	...	...	4213	2320	...	...
3 Other construction	5750	1374	...	...	5321	1420	...	...	5040	1595	...	...
4 Land improvement and plantation and orchard development d	843	843	...	...	824	824	...	...	631	631	...	...
5 Producers' durable goods	16496	10532	...	...	16213	10483	...	...	14980	8564	...	...
A Transport equipment	3939	2587	...	...	3367	2673	...	...	2897	2242	...	...
B Machinery and equipment	12557	7945	...	...	12846	7810	...	...	12083	6322	...	...
6 Breeding stock, dairy cattle, etc. a	...	...	...	...	...	...	...	...	...	...	...	...
Total Gross Capital Formation	30516	17507	...	...	31306	19011	...	...	24981	12913	...	...

2.8 Gross Capital Formation by Type of Good and Owner, in Constant Prices

Million South African rand

	1986				1987				1988			
	TOTAL	Total Private	Public Enterprises	General Government	TOTAL	Total Private	Public Enterprises	General Government	TOTAL	Total Private	Public Enterprises	General Government
	At constant prices of:1985											
Increase in stocks, total abc	-1638	-1550	...	...	291	1120	...	...	2112	2008	...	...
1 Goods producing industries	-637	...	...	...	128	...	...	...	848	...	...	...
2 Wholesale and retail trade c	-903	...	...	...	-194	...	...	...	1715	...	...	...
3 Other, except government stocks c	112	...	...	...	446	...	...	...	-418	...	...	...
4 Government stocks c	-210	...	...	...	-89	...	...	...	-33	...	...	...
Gross Fixed Capital Formation, Total	23493	13443	...	...	22929	13965	...	...	24977	16441	...	...
1 Residential buildings	3346	2697	...	...	3344	2760	...	...	3447	2867	...	...
2 Non-residential buildings	3732	2016	...	...	3188	1611	...	...	3384	1905	...	...
3 Other construction	4423	1398	...	...	4215	1551	...	...	4382	1531	...	...
4 Land improvement and plantation and orchard development d	577	577	...	...	717	717	...	...	819	819	...	...
5 Producers' durable goods	11415	6755	...	...	11465	7326	...	...	12945	9319	...	...
A Transport equipment	2134	1790	...	...	2260	2044	...	...	2846	2619	...	...
B Machinery and equipment	9281	4965	...	...	9205	5282	...	...	10099	6700	...	...
6 Breeding stock, dairy cattle, etc. a	...	...	...	...	...	...	...	...	...	...	...	...
Total Gross Capital Formation	21855	11893	...	...	23220	15085	...	...	27089	18449	...	...

	1989				1990				1991			
	TOTAL	Total Private	Public Enterprises	General Government	TOTAL	Total Private	Public Enterprises	General Government	TOTAL	Total Private	Public Enterprises	General Government
	At constant prices of:1985											
Increase in stocks, total abc	519	28	...	...	-3052	-1805	...	...	-2596	-2283	...	...
1 Goods producing industries	-269	...	...	...	-1374	...	...	...	-897	...	...	...
2 Wholesale and retail trade c	254	...	...	...	-269	...	...	...	-498	...	...	...
3 Other, except government stocks c	460	...	...	...	-1291	...	...	...	-1158	...	...	...
4 Government stocks c	74	...	...	...	-118	...	...	...	-43	...	...	...
Gross Fixed Capital Formation, Total	26260	17172	...	...	25722	16945	...	...	23573	16054	...	...
1 Residential buildings	3428	2835	...	...	3082	2568	...	...	2977	2436	...	...
2 Non-residential buildings	3838	2292	...	...	4223	2403	...	...	3693	2376	...	...
3 Other construction	4900	1476	...	...	4575	1344	...	...	3925	1086	...	...
4 Land improvement and plantation and orchard development d	784	784	...	...	806	806	...	...	833	833	...	...
5 Producers' durable goods	13310	9785	...	...	13036	9824	...	...	12145	9323	...	...
A Transport equipment	3012	2727	...	...	2702	2399	...	...	2683	2270	...	...
B Machinery and equipment	10298	7058	...	...	10334	7425	...	...	9462	7053	...	...
6 Breeding stock, dairy cattle, etc. a	...	...	...	...	...	...	...	...	...	...	...	...
Total Gross Capital Formation	26779	17200	...	...	22670	15140	...	...	20977	13771	...	...

a) Item 'Breeding stocks, dairy cattle, etc.' is included in item 'Increase in stocks'.
b) Item 'Increase in stocks' excludes enterprises of commercial farms in business services, education, health and large unincorporated units of government enterprises.
c) The estimates of 'Increase in stocks' and their components are after inventory valuation adjustment.
d) Land development includes transfer costs.

2.11 Gross Fixed Capital Formation by Kind of Activity of Owner, ISIC Divisions, in Current Prices

Million South African rand

	1980	1981	1982	1983	1984	1985	1986	1987	1988	1989	1990	1991
	All Producers											
1 Agriculture, hunting, forestry and fishing	938	1298	1102	1038	948	974	974	1027	1423	1841	1768	1863
2 Mining and quarrying	1822	2171	2347	2400	2705	3403	4198	4853	6080	6971	7088	6623
3 Manufacturing	4327	4741	4940	5350	4984	4398	4246	4806	6550	10207	14025	13649
4 Electricity, gas and water	1960	2277	3000	3609	4344	4871	4116	3957	3650	4243	4204	3695

South Africa

2.11 Gross Fixed Capital Formation by Kind of Activity of Owner, ISIC Divisions, in Current Prices
(Continued)

Million South African rand

	1980	1981	1982	1983	1984	1985	1986	1987	1988	1989	1990	1991
5 Construction	266	312	340	378	409	435	427	435	534	667	770	778
6 Wholesale and retail trade, restaurants and hotels	689	979	1308	1364	1633	2101	1678	1761	2612	3020	3184	3557
7 Transport, storage and communication	1652	2308	3133	2936	2656	3248	3026	2956	3297	3493	3849	4688
8 Finance, insurance, real estate and business services	2508	3397	3916	4799	5652	5970	6174	7478	10261	12441	12555	13065
9 Community, social and personal services a	118	185	201	226	271	388	537	426	563	647	678	909
Total Industries	14280	17668	20287	22100	23602	25788	25376	27699	34970	43530	48121	48827
Producers of Government Services	1760	2070	2172	2398	2607	2927	3331	3798	4411	5045	4836	4841
Private Non-Profit Institutions Serving Households a	...	...	...	...	...	...	...	...	...	...	...	...
Total	16040	19738	22459	24498	26209	28715	28707	31497	39381	48575	52957	53668

a) Item 'Private non-profit institutions serving households' is included in item 'Community, social and personal services'.

2.12 Gross Fixed Capital Formation by Kind of Activity of Owner, ISIC Divisions, in Constant Prices

Million South African rand

	1980	1981	1982	1983	1984	1985	1986	1987	1988	1989	1990	1991
At constant prices of:1985												
All Producers												
1 Agriculture, hunting, forestry and fishing	1957	2424	1729	1393	1137	974	795	722	854	929	814	792
2 Mining and quarrying	3394	3581	3369	3054	3165	3403	3435	3608	3961	3905	3543	2998
3 Manufacturing	8128	7885	7114	6906	5989	4398	3380	3439	4166	5582	6937	6175
4 Electricity, gas and water	3595	3756	4301	4642	5196	4871	3247	2869	2371	2363	2123	1718
5 Construction	499	527	491	488	492	435	333	303	331	353	368	344
6 Wholesale and retail trade, restaurants and hotels	1293	1634	1870	1740	1915	2101	1372	1263	1633	1597	1503	1538
7 Transport, storage and communication	3196	3923	4579	3788	3136	3248	2423	2063	2000	1748	1735	1930
8 Finance, insurance, real estate and business services	4831	5749	5670	6077	6582	5970	5164	5432	6394	6564	5953	5536
9 Community, social and personal services ab	228	308	289	278	308	388	449	318	363	360	340	452
Total Industries	27121	29787	29412	28366	27920	25788	20598	20017	22073	23401	23316	21483
Producers of Government Services a	3366	3430	3091	2986	2965	2927	2895	2912	2904	2859	2406	2090
Private Non-Profit Institutions Serving Households b	...	...	...	...	...	...	...	...	...	...	...	...
Total	30487	33217	32503	31352	30885	28715	23493	22929	24977	26260	25722	23573

a) Item 'Producers of government services' is included in item 'Community, social and personal services'.   b) Item 'Private non-profit institutions serving households' is included in item 'Community, social and personal services'.

2.17 Exports and Imports of Goods and Services, Detail

Million South African rand

	1980	1981	1982	1983	1984	1985	1986	1987	1988	1989	1990	1991
Exports of Goods and Services												
1 Exports of merchandise, f.o.b.	19670	17949	18666	20004	24452	35437	41055	43619	50889	58313	60455	65566
2 Transport and communication	842	879	1041	845	992	1364	1789	1689	2045	2517	2913	2998
3 Insurance service charges												
4 Other commodities	420	558	627	623	865	1026	683	600	147	530	374	377
5 Adjustments of merchandise exports to change-of-ownership basis	-			-		-			-		-	...
6 Direct purchases in the domestic market by non-residential households	1090	1275	1444	1607	1873	2146	2329	2883	3842	4957	5745	5648
7 Direct purchases in the domestic market by extraterritorial bodies	...	...	...	...	...	...	...	...	...	...	...	...
Total Exports of Goods and Services	22022	20661	21778	23079	28182	39973	45856	48791	56923	66317	69487	74589
Imports of Goods and Services												
1 Imports of merchandise, c.i.f.	15567	20089	20001	17498	23673	25969	28761	31627	42353	48902	48445	53048

2.17 Exports and Imports of Goods and Services, Detail
(Continued)

Million South African rand

	1980	1981	1982	1983	1984	1985	1986	1987	1988	1989	1990	1991
A Imports of merchandise, f.o.b.	14214	18211	18060	15908.	21519	23165	25636	28773	38940	44322	44100	48176
B Transport of services on merchandise imports	1353	1878	1941	1590	2154	2804	3125	2854	3413	4580	4345	4872
C Insurance service charges on merchandise imports												
2 Adjustments of merchandise imports to change-of-ownership basis	...	...	...	...	...	...	...	...	...	...	...	...
3 Other transport and communication	897	986	1111	1142	1338	1538	1893	2102	1977	2414	2586	2947
4 Other insurance service charges	...	...	...	...	...	...	...	...	...	...	...	...
5 Other commodities	...	...	...	...	...	...	...	...	...	...	...	...
6 Direct purchases abroad by government	...	...	...	...	...	...	...	...	...	...	...	...
7 Direct purchases abroad by resident households	570	674	785	872	971	902	1327	1544	2214	2634	2953	3185
Total Imports of Goods and Services	17034	21749	21897	19512	25982	28409	31981	35273	46544	53950	53984	59180
Balance of Goods and Services	4988	-1088	-119	3567	2200	11564	13875	13518	10379	12367	15503	15409
Total Imports and Balance of Goods and Services	22022	20661	21778	23079	28182	39973	45856	48791	56923	66317	69487	74589

Spain

General note. The preparation of national accounts statistics in Spain is undertaken by the Instituto Nacional de Estadistica (INE), Madrid. The official estimates are published by the Instituto in 'La Contabilidad Nacional de Espana'. A detailed description of the sources and methods used for the national accounts estimation is found in 'La Contabilidad Nacional de Espana, Base, 1980' published in 1986. The first input-output tables were elaborated and published by INE in 1985/1986 with reference to the year 1980. It was published in 'Contabilidad Nacional de Espana. Base 1980. Cuentas Nacionales y tabla input output', INE/MADRID 1986. The following tables have been prepared from successive replies to the United Nations national accounts questionnaire. When the scope and coverage of the estimates differ for conceptual or statistical reasons from the definitions and classifications recommended in SNA, a footnotes is indicated to the relevant tables.

Sources and methods :

(a) Gross domestic product. Gross domestic product is estimated mainly through the production approach.

(b) Expenditure on the gross domestic product. The expenditure approach is used to estimate government final consumption expenditure, increase in stocks and exports and imports of goods and services. This approach, in combination with the commodity-flow approach is used to estimate private consumption expenditure and gross fixed capital formation. Estimates of government expenditure are derived from the government accounts and for the social security funds, from basic accounting documents. Data obtained from the family budget expenditure surveys are used together with the commodity-flow method to arrive at the final estimates of private expenditure. For the estimation of changes in stocks, information is available from the Comisaria de Abastecimiento y Transportes and the Servicio Nacional de Cereales for the agricultural sector and from stock surveys for the industrial sectors. The basic data used for the estimation of gross fixed capital formation are obtained from various concerned agencies such as Ministerio de Agricultura for agricultural investments, Servicio Sindical de Estadistica for investments in the industrial sector, Comisaria del Plan de Desarrollo for public investments, reports from other enterprises, etc. The source of information for the estimation of exports and imports of goods and services is the balance of payments which is based on custom's statistics and information on external monetary flows. Supplementary information is obtained from the accounts of insurance companies and government accounts. For the constant prices estimates, all items of GDP by expenditure type are deflated by appropriate price indexes.

(c) Cost-structure of the gross domestic product. Wage statistics and social security data provided by the Instituto and the Ministerio de Sanidad u Seguridad Social are used to estimate compensation of employees. Operating surplus is obtained as a residual except interests of financial sector, rents of ownership of dwellings and imputed rents of public buildings for which separate estimates are made. The rate of consumption of fixed capital is based on average life of the existing stocks. Estimates of indirect taxes and subsidies are derived from the information used to compile the government accounts.

(d) Gross domestic product by kind of economic activity. The table of GDP by kind of economic activity is prepared in factor values. The production approach is used to estimate the value added of most industries. The income approach is used for government services and some service industries. Both production and income approaches are used for the trade sector, restaurants and hotels. The estimates of the agricultural sector are prepared by the Ministerio de Agricultura. Separate information on the volume and value of production of each subsector is available while intermediate consumption is estimated on a comprehensive basis. Value added of the fishing sector is estimated by using a fixed percentage between costs and value added based on data provided by the Sindicato Nacional de la Pescas. Annual mining statistics are obtained from the Direccion General de Minas y Combustibles supplemented by information obtained from the Ministerio de Industria. The estimates for manufacturing are based on industrial statistics compiled by the Ministerio de Industria, Ministerio de Agricultura and Servicio Sindical de Estadistica. The data used for estimating electricity, gas, and water are provided by the Ministerio de Industria, Servicio Sindical de Estadistica and Sindicato Nacional de Agua, Gas y Electricidad, respectively. The estimates of construction are based mainly on sample surveys supplemented by information on employment and material consumption obtained from the Ministerio de Obras Publicas and the Ministerio de Vivienda. For the trade sector, only scattered information is available on employment, wages and salaries, external trade and gross margins. However, a survey of domestic trade conducted for 1964 provided a detailed knowledge of the structure of this sector. For restaurants and hotels, estimates are based on information obtained from concerned agencies. The estimates for the transport sector are based on data supplied by the RENFE (a national enterprise) and other public and private companies for railways, data from the national airlines for air transport, passenger transport surveys and national surveys of goods transported for road transport and data from concerned maritime companies for water transport. The value added of communication is estimated directly on the basis of data provided by the State monopolies. For the financial and insurance sectors, the data are provided by the concerned institutions. For ownership of dwellings, the estimates are based on the resultes of family budget expenditure surveys. The rents are imputed by ascertaining the total dwelling costs, from which the net rent is derived as income on the capital. Estimates for producers of government services are based on data obtained from the Ministerio de Hacienda. The information for health and sanitary services in the private and public sectors is obtained from government accounts supplemented by information obtained from the family budget expenditure surveys and censuses of health establishments. For other services, estimates are based on the number of persons employed, derived from the population censuses and checked against the data of input-output tables. The value added of domestic services and business services is obtained from sample surveys of family budget and accounting documents, respectively. For the constant price estimates, current estimates of most industries are deflated by appropriate price indexes. For agriculture and construction, double deflation is used.

1.1 Expenditure on the Gross Domestic Product, in Current Prices

Thousand Million Spanish pesetas

	1980	1981	1982	1983	1984	1985	1986	1987	1988	1989	1990	1991
1 Government final consumption expenditure	2007.6	2369.9	2783.7	3280.2	3646.5	4151.7	4740.2	5451.8	5924.4	6831.3	7756.1	8587.7
2 Private final consumption expenditure	9991.5	11301.4	12939.2	14604.2	16304.6	18080.0	20437.7	22855.8	25179.6	28344.9	31284.4	34263.7
3 Gross capital formation	3524.8	3728.2	4379.5	4841.0	5033.1	5422.1	6458.8	7775.7	9502.4	11299.9	12780.2	13767.5
A Increase in stocks	156.6	-0.6	115.7	155.0	254.3	13.4	162.0	257.6	419.3	438.7	457.4	593.0
B Gross fixed capital formation	3368.2	3728.8	4263.8	4686.0	4778.8	5408.7	6296.8	7518.1	9083.1	10861.2	12322.8	13174.5
Residential buildings	934.9	1039.0	1147.3	1168.2	1187.7	1239.9	1423.9	1637.8	1992.6	2199.5	2513.1	2600.9
Non-residential buildings	1355.5	1478.1	1660.8	1917.3	2017.9	2293.6	2683.4	3107.7	3702.3	4702.6	5682.1	6447.6
Other construction and land improvement etc.												
Other	1077.8	1211.9	1455.8	1600.5	1573.3	1875.2	2189.5	2772.6	3388.1	3959.2	4127.6	4126.0
4 Exports of goods and services	2386.6	3041.9	3630.6	4666.9	5864.5	6407.2	6416.9	6995.8	7574.8	8150.4	8555.2	9300.3
5 Less: Imports of goods and services	2742.5	3396.7	4010.4	4860.5	5329.2	5860.1	5729.7	6935.1	8022.5	9620.6	10250.7	11128.1
Equals: Gross Domestic Product	15168.0	17044.7	19722.6	22531.8	25519.5	28200.9	32323.9	36144.0	40158.7	45005.9	50125.2	54791.1

1.2 Expenditure on the Gross Domestic Product, in Constant Prices

Thousand Million Spanish pesetas

	1980	1981	1982	1983	1984	1985	1986	1987	1988	1989	1990	1991
					At constant prices of:1986							
1 Government final consumption expenditure	3677.0	3805.9	4006.9	4162.3	4263.7	4498.0	4740.2	5159.9	5368.1	5812.9	6142.7	6401.2
2 Private final consumption expenditure	19357.9	19113.2	19092.1	19146.6	19106.3	19781.2	20437.7	21621.9	22683.7	23955.6	24849.7	25618.8
3 Gross capital formation	6315.2	5820.2	6073.9	6005.1	5658.1	5749.5	6458.8	7424.7	8563.8	9691.8	10338.3	10592.7
A Increase in stocks	343.3	-1.0	129.5	201.6	256.5	20.0	162.0	243.7	385.3	389.9	394.7	489.8
B Gross fixed capital formation	5971.9	5821.2	5944.4	5803.5	5401.6	5729.5	6296.8	7181.0	8178.5	9301.9	9943.6	10102.9

1.2 Expenditure on the Gross Domestic Product, in Constant Prices
(Continued)

Thousand Million Spanish pesetas

	1980	1981	1982	1983	1984	1985	1986	1987	1988	1989	1990	1991
	At constant prices of:1986											
Residential buildings	1507.0	1495.2	1465.5	1384.5	1309.4	1394.6	1423.9	1514.1	1687.0	1735.7	1855.9	1805.4
Non-residential buildings	2477.7	2362.6	2396.6	2431.2	2326.8	2390.1	2683.4	2979.6	3334.6	4008.2	4470.2	4782.3
Other construction and land improvement etc.												
Other	1987.4	1963.4	2082.3	1987.8	1765.3	1944.9	2189.5	2687.3	3157.0	3557.9	3617.5	3515.3
4 Exports of goods and services	4399.5	4761.4	4997.2	5495.1	6137.4	6300.1	6416.9	6823.1	7169.2	7383.9	7621.5	8121.1
5 Less: Imports of goods and services	4722.4	4524.7	4740.4	4726.2	4641.2	5007.1	5729.7	6882.0	7874.9	9230.0	9950.4	10837.3
Equals: Gross Domestic Product	29027.2	28976.0	29429.7	30082.9	30524.3	31321.7	32323.9	34147.6	35909.9	37614.2	39001.8	39896.5

1.3 Cost Components of the Gross Domestic Product

Thousand Million Spanish pesetas

	1980	1981	1982	1983	1984	1985	1986	1987	1988	1989	1990	1991
1 Indirect taxes, net	687.5	902.2	1024.7	1329.6	1572.1	1981.4	2817.7	3130.7	3283.5	3761.3	4081.8	4421.8
A Indirect taxes	1002.6	1236.6	1513.9	1885.3	2258.0	2668.7	3490.4	3908.3	4394.2	4897.5	5346.3	5807.4
B Less: Subsidies	315.1	334.4	489.2	555.7	685.9	687.3	672.7	777.6	1110.7	1136.2	1264.5	1385.6
2 Consumption of fixed capital	1722.3	2058.4	2402.8	2812.5	3230.1	3587.5	3857.9	4177.7	4599.8	5047.7	5558.0	6057.8
3 Compensation of employees paid by resident producers to:	7784.0	8714.9	9853.2	11132.4	11876.2	12904.7	14589.2	16307.1	18198.8	20413.3	23074.3	25270.0
A Resident households	7783.4	8714.6	9852.8	11132.0	11875.7	12903.8	14587.8	16305.6	18197.3	20411.5	23072.6	25268.1
B Rest of the world	0.6	0.3	0.4	0.4	0.5	0.9	1.4	1.5	1.5	1.8	1.7	1.9
4 Operating surplus	4974.2	5369.4	6442.0	7257.3	8841.1	9727.3	11059.2	12528.5	14076.6	15783.6	17411.1	19041.4
Statistical discrepancy	...	...	...	...	...	0.1	-	-	-	-	-	-
Equals: Gross Domestic Product	15168.0	17044.9	19722.7	22531.8	25519.5	28200.9	32324.0	36144.0	40158.7	45005.9	50125.2	54791.0

1.4 General Government Current Receipts and Disbursements

Thousand Million Spanish pesetas

	1980	1981	1982	1983	1984	1985	1986	1987	1988	1989	1990	1991
	Receipts											
1 Operating surplus	...	...	...	...	...	...	...	...	...	...	...	...
2 Property and entrepreneurial income	152.4	222.5	288.9	307.1	251.7	324.7 / 324.7	332.4	288.4	312.7	396.1	485.9	...
3 Taxes, fees and contributions	3879.6	4535.4	5236.3	6435.5	7368.0	8405.9 / 8403.7	9850.7	11748.7	13035.5	15484.2	17104.4	...
A Indirect taxes	1009.5	1243.0	1522.3	1900.1	2271.4	2686.9 / 2668.7	3401.3	3773.8	4162.1	4657.1	4975.9	...
B Direct taxes a	1059.0	1221.1	1332.6	1748.1	2085.6	2378.4 / 2394.4	2655.0	3705.3	4196.6	5430.4	6018.4	...
C Social security contributions	1811.1	2071.3	2381.4	2787.3	3011.0	3340.6 / 3340.6	3794.4	4269.6	4676.9	5396.7	6110.1	...
D Compulsory fees, fines and penalties a	...	...	...	...	...	... / ...	...	...	...	...	...	...
4 Other current transfers	489.1	536.3	611.8	696.0	729.7	884.0 / 917.7	1037.8	1130.7	1222.4	1276.9	1411.8	...
Total Current Receipts of General Government	4521.1	5294.2	6137.0	7438.6	8349.4	9614.6 / 9646.1	11220.9	13167.8	14570.6	17157.2	19002.1	...
	Disbursements											
1 Government final consumption expenditure	1929.3	2242.2	2619.5	3090.9	3448.3	3906.6 / 4151.7	4740.2	5451.8	5924.4	6831.2	7756.1	...
A Compensation of employees	1488.2	1747.2	2000.1	2364.9	2634.4	2975.1 / 1353.0	1470.2	1587.4	1733.1	1920.3	2185.5	...
B Consumption of fixed capital	77.1	89.7	105.6	126.6	148.1	168.8 / 180.0	194.1	208.4	225.4	244.7	269.7	...
C Purchases of goods and services, net	364.0	405.3	513.8	599.5	665.8	762.6 / 416.6	517.1	692.5	601.2	680.1	610.0	...
D Less: Own account fixed capital formation	...	...	...	...	...	...	...	...	...	...	...	...
E Indirect taxes paid, net	...	...	...	...	...	...	...	...	...	...	...	...
2 Property income	110.9	135.6	190.5	290.4	509.3	900.0 / 970.5	1278.5	1255.9	1345.9	1560.5	1775.5	...

Spain

1.4 General Government Current Receipts and Disbursements
(Continued)

Thousand Million Spanish pesetas

	1980	1981	1982	1983	1984	1985	1986	1987	1988	1989	1990	1991
3 Subsidies	315.1	334.4	489.0	575.8	703.6	738.7 / 687.3	634.8	654.2	829.6	888.9	960.6	...
4 Other current transfers	2156.3	2661.2	3045.6	3596.9	4015.9	4627.0 / 4515.4	5051.1	5561.4	6158.2	7016.6	7983.2	...
A Social security benefits	1926.3	2401.6	2747.5	3232.1	3642.9	4151.0 / 4039.5	4512.0	4990.4	5567.2	6276.6	7221.2	...
B Social assistance grants	...	...	...	...	...	...	...	...	...	...	...	...
C Other	230.0	259.6	298.2	364.8	372.9	476.0 / 476.0	539.0	571.1	590.9	739.9	762.0	...
5 Net saving	9.6	-79.1	-207.5	-115.4	-327.7	-557.7 / -678.8	-483.7	244.6	312.5	860.1	526.7	...
Total Current Disbursements and Net Saving of General Government	4521.2	5294.3	6137.1	7438.6	8349.4	9614.6 / 9646.1	11220.9	13167.9	14570.6	17157.3	19002.1	...

a) Item 'Fees, fines and penalties' is included in item 'Direct taxes'.

1.5 Current Income and Outlay of Corporate and Quasi-Corporate Enterprises, Summary

Thousand Million Spanish pesetas

	1980	1981	1982	1983	1984	1985	1986	1987	1988	1989	1990	1991
Receipts												
1 Operating surplus	1558.4	1484.4	1755.9	1812.2	2383.0	2695.5 / 3167.6	3512.6	4091.7	4668.8	5420.1	5805.6	...
2 Property and entrepreneurial income received	1925.2	2656.8	3485.9	3992.8	4939.9	5200.8 / 5324.6	5659.9	6695.7	7600.1	9358.3	11168.9	...
3 Current transfers	376.9	443.9	520.7	634.4	659.1	754.1 / 711.2	986.5	1153.4	1461.7	1611.0	1856.6	...
Total Current Receipts	3860.5	4585.1	5762.5	6439.4	7982.0	8650.4 / 9203.4	10159.0	11940.8	13730.6	16389.4	18831.1	...
Disbursements												
1 Property and entrepreneurial income	2485.7	3465.5	4393.8	4923.5	5710.0	5866.4 / 6354.6	6350.1	7388.1	8463.6	10236.0	12065.1	...
2 Direct taxes and other current payments to general government	259.4	295.2	351.1	434.1	481.5	556.0 / 560.1	694.9	963.7	1044.6	1571.2	1789.2	...
3 Other current transfers	449.9	539.3	675.1	800.6	814.6	937.3 / 729.7	961.0	1091.6	1195.7	1494.4	1753.3	...
Statistical discrepancy	10.4	2.2	1.5	-	25.3	47.0 / 47.0	168.2	154.6	396.6	262.4	252.7	...
4 Net saving	655.1	282.9	341.0	281.2	950.5	1243.7 / 1512.1	1984.8	2342.8	2630.0	2825.4	2970.7	...
Total Current Disbursements and Net Saving	3860.5	4585.1	5762.5	6439.4	7981.9	8650.4 / 9203.5	10159.0	11940.8	13730.5	16389.4	18831.0	...

1.6 Current Income and Outlay of Households and Non-Profit Institutions

Thousand Million Spanish pesetas

	1980	1981	1982	1983	1984	1985	1986	1987	1988	1989	1990	1991
Receipts												
1 Compensation of employees	7797.5	8734.4	9877.4	11162.3	11907.5	12922.5 / 12936.2	14626.1	16347.7	18235.8	20449.6	23108.0	...
A From resident producers	7783.3	8714.6	9852.8	11132.0	11875.6	12890.1 / 12903.8	14587.8	16305.6	18197.3	20411.5	23072.6	...
B From rest of the world	14.2	19.8	24.6	30.3	31.8	32.4 / 32.4	38.3	42.0	38.5	38.1	35.4	...
2 Operating surplus of private unincorporated enterprises	3557.0	3950.5	4671.3	5327.8	6254.8	7004.9 / 6559.6	7546.6	8436.8	9407.9	10363.6	11605.5	...
3 Property and entrepreneurial income	782.4	1077.1	1192.9	1324.0	1614.8	1922.8 / 2103.1	2258.1	2499.1	2927.6	3388.3	3883.9	...
4 Current transfers	2592.5	3181.3	3667.6	4279.5	4726.9	5405.8 / 5206.6	5850.8	6554.3	7278.1	8314.5	9466.5	...
A Social security benefits	2126.0	2639.2	3012.2	3509.2	3937.0	4480.1 / 4273.7	4767.7	5289.5	5860.3	6617.4	7699.7	...
B Social assistance grants	...	...	...	...	...	...	...	...	...	...	...	...
C Other	466.5	542.1	655.4	770.3	790.0	925.7 / 932.8	1083.2	1264.8	1417.8	1697.1	1766.8	...
Statistical discrepancy	10.4	2.2	1.5	-	25.3	47.0 / 47.0	168.1	154.6	396.5	262.5	252.9	...
Total Current Receipts	14739.8	16945.5	19410.7	22093.6	24529.3	27303.0 / 26852.5	30449.7	33992.5	38245.9	42778.5	48316.8	...

1.6 Current Income and Outlay of Households and Non-Profit Institutions
(Continued)

Thousand Million Spanish pesetas

	1980	1981	1982	1983	1984	1985	1986	1987	1988	1989	1990	1991
Disbursements												
1 Private final consumption expenditure	10080.4	11457.9	13143.3	14808.1	16370.0	18137.7 / 18080.0	20437.7	22855.8	25179.6	28344.9	31284.4	...
2 Property income	406.9	612.9	692.4	798.2	1015.2	1044.0 / 789.5	955.1	1184.3	1478.5	1766.4	2179.0	...
3 Direct taxes and other current transfers n.e.c. to general government	2683.3	3070.3	3439.1	4152.6	4661.5	5207.2 / 5225.1	5868.8	7162.1	7972.6	9385.0	10547.9	...
A Social security contributions	1883.7	2144.4	2457.6	2838.7	3057.4	3384.8 / 3390.8	3908.8	4420.5	4820.6	5525.9	6318.7	...
B Direct taxes	799.6	925.9	981.5	1313.9	1604.0	1822.4 / 1834.3	1960.0	2741.7	3152.0	3859.1	4229.2	...
C Fees, fines and penalties	...	...	...	...	...	...	...	...	...	...	...	...
4 Other current transfers	665.3	758.5	853.6	1006.3	1067.4	1248.9 / 1359.3	1565.0	1747.4	2088.4	2169.0	2428.6	...
5 Net saving	903.7	1045.9	1282.4	1328.5	1415.1	1665.3 / 1398.6	1623.1	1042.9	1526.8	1113.1	1877.0	...
Total Current Disbursements and Net Saving	14739.6	16945.5	19410.8	22093.7	24529.2	27303.1 / 26852.5	30449.7	33992.5	38245.9	42778.4	48316.9	...

1.7 External Transactions on Current Account, Summary

Thousand Million Spanish pesetas

	1980	1981	1982	1983	1984	1985	1986	1987	1988	1989	1990	1991
Payments to the Rest of the World												
1 Imports of goods and services	2758.5	3428.3	4024.3	4860.1	5363.3	5914.8 / 5860.1	5729.7	6935.1	8022.5	9620.6	10250.7	11128.1
A Imports of merchandise c.i.f.	2480.7	3045.6	3561.1	4300.4	4753.3	5205.2 / 5206.7	5035.9	6137.0	7101.3	8523.1	9024.6	9799.8
B Other	277.8	382.7	463.3	559.6	610.0	709.6 / 653.4	693.8	798.1	921.1	1097.5	1226.0	1328.3
2 Factor income to the rest of the world	256.9	429.3	496.3	552.4	641.5	645.2 / 868.9	703.9	684.4	887.4	1107.4	1299.7	1758.2
A Compensation of employees	0.6	0.3	0.4	0.4	0.5	0.9 / 0.9	1.4	1.5	1.5	1.8	1.7	1.9
B Property and entrepreneurial income	256.3	428.9	495.9	552.1	641.0	644.3 / 867.9	702.4	682.9	886.0	1105.6	1298.0	1756.3
3 Current transfers to the rest of the world	34.9	44.9	51.1	71.0	69.3	113.5 / 114.1	214.4	269.0	368.6	453.2	540.7	760.7
A Indirect taxes to supranational organizations	...	...	...	...	...	... / -	89.1	134.5	232.1	240.4	370.4	478.5
B Other current transfers	34.9	44.9	51.1	71.0	69.3	113.5 / 114.1	125.3	134.5	136.5	212.8	170.3	282.2
4 Surplus of the nation on current transactions	-364.3	-458.0	-487.1	-338.0	354.8	459.9 / 397.3	523.3	32.3	-433.3	-1453.6	-1847.8	-2090.2
Payments to the Rest of the World and Surplus of the Nation on Current Transactions	2686.0	3444.5	4084.6	5145.5	6428.9	7133.4 / 7240.4	7171.3	7920.8	8845.2	9727.6	10243.3	11556.8
Receipts From The Rest of the World												
1 Exports of goods and services	2409.8	3079.1	3672.2	4725.6	5943.5	6518.7 / 6407.2	6416.9	6995.8	7574.8	8150.4	8555.2	9300.3
A Exports of merchandise f.o.b.	1531.6	1976.2	2372.2	3066.8	3936.1	4296.2 / 4280.5	3939.8	4306.1	4738.8	5260.6	5681.0	6169.6

Spain

1.7 External Transactions on Current Account, Summary
(Continued)

Thousand Million Spanish pesetas

	1980	1981	1982	1983	1984	1985	1986	1987	1988	1989	1990	1991
B Other	878.2	1102.8	1300.0	1658.7	2007.4	2222.5 / 2126.7	2477.1	2689.7	2836.0	2889.8	2874.2	3130.7
2 Factor income from rest of the world	127.0	191.1	211.6	194.3	244.7	314.7 / 538.2	407.5	379.9	476.8	723.7	852.4	1189.8
A Compensation of employees	14.2	19.8	24.6	30.3	31.8	32.4 / 32.4	38.3	42.0	38.5	38.1	35.4	36.2
B Property and entrepreneurial income	112.8	171.3	187.0	163.9	212.9	282.3 / 505.7	369.1	337.9	438.4	685.6	817.0	1153.6
3 Current transfers from rest of the world	149.3	174.2	200.6	225.7	240.7	300.0 / 295.0	346.8	545.1	793.6	853.5	835.7	1066.6
A Subsidies from supranational organisations	...	...	...	...	...	... / -	37.9	123.5	281.1	247.3	304.0	455.9
B Other current transfers	149.3	174.2	200.6	225.7	240.7	300.0 / 295.0	308.9	421.6	512.5	606.2	531.7	610.7
Receipts from the Rest of the World on Current Transactions	2686.1	3444.4	4084.4	5145.6	6428.9	7133.4 / 7240.4	7171.2	7920.8	8845.2	9727.6	10243.3	11556.7

1.8 Capital Transactions of The Nation, Summary

Thousand Million Spanish pesetas

	1980	1981	1982	1983	1984	1985	1986	1987	1988	1989	1990	1991
Finance of Gross Capital Formation												
Gross saving	3183.8	3180.2	3669.5	4132.2	5067.6	5700.5 / 5819.5	6982.1	7808.1	9069.1	9846.3	10932.4	11677.2
1 Consumption of fixed capital	1615.4	1930.6	2253.7	2637.9	3029.6	3349.2 / 3587.5	3857.9	4177.7	4599.8	5047.7	5558.0	6057.8
A General government	77.1	89.7	105.6	126.6	148.1	168.8 / 289.0	321.9	355.2	395.4	445.2	508.5	...
B Corporate and quasi-corporate enterprises	1188.0	1415.4	1642.5	1932.4	2231.3	2489.0 / 2405.3	2505.8	2656.8	2892.6	3152.6	3448.6	...
C Other	350.2	425.5	505.6	578.9	650.3	691.4 / 893.1	1030.2	1165.7	1311.9	1449.9	1600.9	...
2 Net saving	1568.4	1249.6	1415.8	1494.3	2038.0	2351.3 / 2232.0	3124.2	3630.4	4469.3	4798.6	5374.4	5619.4
A General government	9.6	-79.1	-207.5	-115.4	-327.7	-557.7 / -678.8	-483.7	244.6	312.5	860.1	526.7	...
B Corporate and quasi-corporate enterprises	655.1	282.9	341.0	281.2	950.5	1243.7 / 1512.1	1984.8	2342.8	2630.0	2825.4	2970.7	...
C Other	903.7	1045.9	1282.4	1328.5	1415.1	1665.3 / 1398.6	1623.1	1042.9	1526.8	1113.1	1877.0	...
Less: Surplus of the nation on current transactions	-364.3	-458.0	-487.1	-338.0	354.8	459.9 / 397.3	523.3	32.3	-433.3	-1453.6	-1847.8	-2090.2
Statistical discrepancy	-	-	-	-	-	0.1 / -	-	-	-	-	-	...
Finance of Gross Capital Formation	3548.1	3638.2	4156.6	4470.2	4712.8	5240.7 / 5422.2	6458.8	7775.8	9502.4	11299.9	12780.2	13767.4
Gross Capital Formation												
Increase in stocks	179.9	-58.7	-14.4	-104.4	4.2	-34.9 / 13.4	162.0	257.6	419.3	438.7	457.4	593.0
Gross fixed capital formation	3368.2	3696.9	4171.0	4574.6	4708.6	5275.6 / 5408.7	6296.8	7518.1	9083.1	10861.2	12322.8	13174.5
Gross Capital Formation	3548.1	3638.2	4156.6	4470.2	4712.8	5240.7 / 5422.1	6458.8	7775.7	9502.4	11299.9	12780.2	13767.5

1.9 Gross Domestic Product by Institutional Sectors of Origin

Thousand Million Spanish pesetas

	1980	1981	1982	1983	1984	1985	1986	1987	1988	1989	1990	1991
Domestic Factor Incomes Originating												
1 General government	1488.2	1747.2	2000.1	2364.9	2634.4	2975.1 / 2978.6	3342.7	3751.6	4197.1	4805.5	5565.6	...
2 Corporate and quasi-corporate enterprises	11411.1	12402.7	14280.2	15907.5	17879.5	19616.3 / 19653.4	22305.7	25084.0	28078.3	31391.5	34919.9	...
A Non-financial	11116.6	12204.5	14160.4	15935.4	17838.0	19590.7 / 19736.3	22428.4	25236.1	28217.1	31604.2	35089.6	...
B Financial	294.6	198.1	119.8	-27.9	41.5	25.6 / -82.9	-122.7	-152.1	-138.9	-212.7	-169.8	...

1.9 Gross Domestic Product by Institutional Sectors of Origin
(Continued)

Thousand Million Spanish pesetas

	1980	1981	1982	1983	1984	1985	1986	1987	1988	1989	1990	1991
3 Households and private unincorporated enterprises	...	...	...	...	...	... ...						
4 Non-profit institutions serving households	...	...	...	...	...	... ...	...	...	...	...	...	...
Subtotal: Domestic Factor Incomes	12899.4	14149.8	16280.3	18272.4	20513.9	22591.4 22632.0	25648.4	28835.6	32275.4	36196.9	40485.4	44311.4
Indirect taxes, net	694.4	908.6	1033.3	1324.3	1567.8	1948.2 1981.4	2817.7	3130.7	3283.5	3761.3	4081.8	4421.8
A Indirect taxes	1009.5	1243.0	1522.3	1900.1	2271.4	2686.9 2668.7	3490.4	3908.3	4394.2	4897.5	5346.3	5807.4
B Less: Subsidies	315.1	334.4	489.0	575.8	703.6	738.7 687.3	672.7	777.6	1110.7	1136.2	1264.5	1385.6
Consumption of fixed capital	1615.4	1930.6	2253.7	2637.9	3029.6	3349.2 3587.5	3857.9	4177.7	4599.8	5047.7	5558.0	6057.8
Statistical discrepancy	-0.1	-	-	0.1	-	- 0.1	-	-	-	-	-	-
Gross Domestic Product	15209.1	16989.0	19567.3	22234.7	25111.3	27888.8 28200.9	32324.0	36144.0	40158.7	45005.9	50125.2	54791.0

1.10 Gross Domestic Product by Kind of Activity, in Current Prices

Thousand Million Spanish pesetas

	1980	1981	1982	1983	1984	1985	1986	1987	1988	1989	1990	1991
1 Agriculture, hunting, forestry and fishing	1073.4	1038.0	1225.9	1370.2	1642.7	1744.4 1668.9	1815.1	1969.6	2128.6	2159.9	2253.0	2179.8
2 Mining and quarrying	4284.3	4762.1	5326.2	6149.5	6903.6	7631.9a 274.6	246.1	223.8	226.0	261.2	10 1 722	10385.8
3 Manufacturing						... 7531.8	8322.4	9029.7	9679.1	10647.9		
4 Electricity, gas and water	309.0	426.7	562.2	591.7	765.8	860.9 816.5	858.6	1005.6	1156.9	1190.1	...	...
5 Construction	1283.7	1328.6	1527.9	1631.7	1635.6	1806.1 1895.2	2102.6	2486.7	3021.8	3774.3	4575.2	5111.6
6 Wholesale and retail trade, restaurants and hotels	2772.8	3192.0	3717.6	4329.8	5019.7	5665.1 5689.5	6492.9	7278.3	8143.9	9216.3	...	...
7 Transport, storage and communication	876.7	1036.2	1167.6	1362.3	1528.8	1661.9 1579.7	1755.1	1973.7	2206.0	2379.0	...	...
8 Finance, insurance, real estate and business services b ...	2010.6	2298.5	2547.8	2724.6	3376.5	3664.2 4996.4	5423.5	6037.4	6812.5	7721.8	...	...
9 Community, social and personal services bc	1297.5	1528.1	1895.7	2173.9	2460.6	2714.3 1360.0	1541.5	1728.0	1902.4	2197.2	...	...
Total, Industries	13908.0	15610.3	17970.8	20333.7	23333.3	25748.9 25812.8	28557.7	31732.9	35277.3	39547.7	44060.5	48215.8
Producers of Government Services	1565.3	1836.8	2105.6	2491.5	2782.5	3144.0 3267.6	3664.6	4106.8	4592.5	5250.7	6062.7	6748.8
Other Producers c	...	...	...	...	...	... 253.6	276.6	313.0	346.7	382.6	442.3	492.4
Subtotal	15473.4	17447.1	20076.4	22825.2	26115.8	28892.8 29334.1	32498.9	36152.6	40216.5	45181.0	50565.5	55457.0
Less: Imputed bank service charge	535.8	756.3	889.1	1043.0	1478.0	1560.4 1689.5	1971.9	2321.5	2682.8	3180.9	3581.5	4054.4
Plus: Import duties	271.5	298.2	379.9	452.5	473.5	556.4 556.4	329.2	396.4	440.4	413.6	372.8	345.5
Plus: Value added tax	...	...	...	...	...	... -	1467.8	1916.5	2184.6	2592.3	2768.5	3043.1
Plus: Other adjustments	0.1	-	0.1	-	-	-0.1	...	...	...	...	...	...
Equals: Gross Domestic Product	15209.1	16989.0	19567.3	22234.7	25111.3	27888.8 28200.9	32324.0	36144.1	40158.7	45006.0	50125.3	54791.2

a) Including item 'Manufacturing'.
b) Business services and real estate except dwellings are included in item 'Community, social and personal services'.
c) Item 'Other producers' is included in item 'Community, social and personal services'.

Spain

1.11 Gross Domestic Product by Kind of Activity, in Constant Prices

Thousand Million Spanish pesetas

	1980	1981	1982	1983	1984	1985	1986	1987	1988	1989	1990	1991
	At constant prices of: 1980						1986					
1 Agriculture, hunting, forestry and fishing	1073.4	971.7	956.9	1016.6	1104.1	1138.4	... 1815.1	2025.4	2091.7	1951.1	1999.0	1953.3
2 Mining and quarrying	4284.3	4278.8	4214.2	4287.3	4303.9	4384.1	... 246.1	224.2	226.1	249.6	8637.5	8623.7
3 Manufacturing							... 8322.4	8750.7	9127.5	9473.1		
4 Electricity, gas and water	309.0	303.6	312.2	312.5	345.8	362.9	... 858.6	899.3	968.5	950.3	...	...
5 Construction	1283.7	1281.1	1315.3	1316.6	1235.5	1263.2	... 2102.6	2277.8	2508.7	2855.2	3149.3	3259.7
6 Wholesale and retail trade, restaurants and hotels	2772.8	2766.5	2804.8	2854.1	2928.4	2985.5	... 6492.9	6824.5	7123.6	7463.7	...	...
7 Transport, storage and communication	876.7	900.3	906.5	930.1	956.0	991.5	... 1755.1	1829.2	1904.3	2020.0	...	...
8 Finance, insurance, real estate and business services [a]	2010.6	2034.8	2065.9	2077.6	2142.5	2186.6	... 5423.5	5697.4	6017.0	6328.3	...	...
9 Community, social and personal services [ab]	1297.5	1309.8	1378.8	1394.4	1413.7	1415.2	... 1541.5	1616.8	1675.9	1805.7	...	...
Total, Industries	13908.0	13846.7	13954.7	14189.3	14429.9	14727.5	... 28557.7	30145.4	31643.2	33097.1	34249.5	35002.0
Producers of Government Services	1565.3	1615.5	1683.0	1744.4	1798.5	1874.0	... 3664.6	3872.7	4111.8	4401.4	4713.4	4913.3
Other Producers [b]	...	...	...	...	...	...	... 276.6	292.7	307.7	323.6	343.9	358.5
Subtotal	15473.4	15462.1	15637.7	15933.7	16228.3	16601.5	... 32498.9	34310.8	36062.6	37822.1	39306.8	40273.8
Less: Imputed bank service charge	535.8	540.6	553.1	564.1	574.8	587.5	... 1971.9	2159.2	2311.8	2516.1	2652.1	2792.8
Plus: Import duties	271.5	249.8	271.3	263.6	261.0	268.8	... 329.2	418.6	499.7	532.5	520.7	533.0
Plus: Value added tax	...	...	...	...	...	...	... 1467.8	1577.4	1659.5	1775.6	1826.4	1882.5
Plus: Other adjustments	0.1	-0.1	-	-	-0.1	-	...	...	...	...	...	...
Equals: Gross Domestic Product	15209.1	15171.3	15355.9	15633.2	15914.5	16282.8	... 32324.0	34147.6	35910.1	37614.1	39001.8	39896.5

a) Business services and real estate except dwellings are included in item 'Community, social and personal services'.
b) Item 'Other producers' is included in item 'Community, social and personal services'.

1.12 Relations Among National Accounting Aggregates

Thousand Million Spanish pesetas

	1980	1981	1982	1983	1984	1985	1986	1987	1988	1989	1990	1991
Gross Domestic Product	15168.0	17044.8	19722.6	22531.8	25519.5	28200.9	32324.0	36144.0	40158.7	45006.0	50125.3	54791.1
Plus: Net factor income from the rest of the world	-130.0	-238.1	-284.7	-358.2	-396.9	-330.7	-296.4	-304.5	-410.6	-383.7	-447.2	-568.4
Factor income from the rest of the world	127.0	191.1	211.6	194.3	244.7	538.2	407.5	379.9	476.8	723.7	852.4	1189.8
Less: Factor income to the rest of the world	256.9	429.3	496.3	552.4	641.5	868.9	703.9	684.4	887.4	1107.4	1299.7	1758.2
Equals: Gross National Product	15038.0	16806.7	19438.0	22173.6	25122.7	27870.2	32027.6	35839.5	39748.2	44622.2	49678.0	54222.7
Less: Consumption of fixed capital	1722.3	2058.4	2402.8	2812.5	3230.1	3587.5	3857.9	4177.7	4599.8	5047.7	5558.0	6057.8
Equals: National Income	13315.7	14748.3	17035.2	19361.1	21892.6	24282.7	28169.7	31661.8	35148.3	39574.6	44120.0	48164.9
Plus: Net current transfers from the rest of the world	114.4	129.4	149.6	154.7	171.5	180.9	132.4	276.2	425.0	400.3	294.9	305.9
Current transfers from the rest of the world	...	...	...	...	...	295.0	346.8	545.1	793.5	853.5	835.6	1066.6
Less: Current transfers to the rest of the world	...	...	...	...	...	114.1	214.4	269.0	368.6	453.2	540.7	760.7
Equals: National Disposable Income	13430.1	14877.7	17184.8	19515.8	22064.0	24463.6	28302.1	31937.9	35573.3	39974.8	44414.9	48470.8
Less: Final consumption	11999.1	13671.3	15722.9	17884.4	19951.2	22231.7	25178.0	28307.6	31104.0	35176.2	39040.5	42851.4
Equals: Net Saving	1431.1	1206.4	1461.9	1631.4	2112.9	2232.0	3124.2	3630.4	4469.3	4798.6	5374.4	5619.4
Less: Surplus of the nation on current transactions	-371.5	-463.5	-514.8	-397.1	309.9	397.3	523.3	32.3	-433.3	-1453.6	-1847.8	-2090.2
Equals: Net Capital Formation	1802.6	1669.9	1976.7	2028.5	1803.0	1834.6	2600.9	3598.0	4902.5	6252.3	7222.2	7709.6

2.3 Total Government Outlays by Function and Type

Thousand Million Spanish pesetas

	Final Consumption Expenditures			Subsidies	Other Current Transfers & Property Income	Total Current Disbursements	Gross Capital Formation	Other Capital Outlays	Total Outlays
	Total	Compensation of Employees	Other						
1985									
1 General public services	163.4	...	...	27.3	319.5	510.2	92.8	39.2	642.1
2 Defence	553.4	...	...	-	0.7	554.1	-	7.0	561.2
3 Public order and safety	312.0	...	...	0.1	0.7	312.8	42.5	8.4	363.6
4 Education	741.4	...	...	137.2	64.3	942.9	105.7	10.3	1058.8
5 Health	978.6	...	...	0.6	272.1	1251.3	61.5	3.1	1315.8
6 Social security and welfare	453.0	...	...	0.7	3699.9	4153.6	12.6	1.9	4168.1
7 Housing and community amenities	243.1	...	...	6.9	4.8	254.8	191.1	119.7	565.7
8 Recreation, culture and religion	103.1	...	...	17.7	60.1	180.9	67.6	10.9	259.4
9 Economic services	243.3	...	...	462.4	111.2	816.9	390.7	485.0	1692.6
A Fuel and energy	1.8	...	...	43.6	43.8	89.2	4.0	10.6	103.8
B Agriculture, forestry, fishing and hunting	58.9	...	...	63.7	11.3	133.9	80.6	80.3	294.8
C Mining (except fuels), manufacturing and construction	14.9	...	...	4.2	9.5	28.6	18.9	260.4	307.9
D Transportation and communication	102.2	...	...	310.1	10.1	422.4	222.1	114.5	759.1
E Other economic affairs	65.6	...	...	40.8	36.5	142.9	65.1	19.2	227.1
10 Other functions	360.4	...	...	34.5	952.7	1347.6	29.7	5.7	1383.0
Total	4151.7	...	...	687.3	5485.9	10324.9	994.1	691.3	12010.3
1986									
1 General public services	200.9	...	...	18.6	33.1	252.6	114.4	51.4	418.3
2 Defence	670.9	...	...	0.4	0.9	672.2	-	8.1	680.4
3 Public order and safety	344.7	...	...	0.1	0.9	345.7	50.9	0.6	397.1
4 Education	828.3	...	...	143.9	114.1	1086.3	127.2	10.9	1224.4
5 Health	1106.8	...	...	0.6	296.0	1403.4	67.3	2.2	1472.9
6 Social security and welfare	520.2	...	...	0.7	4090.3	4611.2	19.1	2.0	4632.3
7 Housing and community amenities	277.4	...	...	21.4	3.9	302.7	239.2	53.0	594.9
8 Recreation, culture and religion	130.9	...	...	17.8	56.8	205.5	71.7	12.1	289.3
9 Economic services	271.3	...	...	412.4	154.3	838.0	404.8	641.5	1884.2
A Fuel and energy	5.3	...	...	37.3	38.3	80.9	5.4	20.1	106.5
B Agriculture, forestry, fishing and hunting	67.7	...	...	49.5	6.4	123.6	69.8	54.1	247.5
C Mining (except fuels), manufacturing and construction	17.2	...	...	4.1	0.2	21.5	35.4	421.5	478.4
D Transportation and communication	114.2	...	...	255.9	7.7	377.8	231.1	88.7	697.5
E Other economic affairs	66.8	...	...	65.6	101.7	234.1	63.1	57.1	354.3
10 Other functions	388.8	...	...	18.9	1579.3	1987.0	34.9	5.1	2027.0
Total	4740.2	...	...	634.8	6329.5	11704.5	1129.5	786.9	13620.9
1987									
1 General public services	274.9	...	...	34.0	36.6	345.5	68.8	46.3	460.6
2 Defence	788.9	...	...	0.7	1.0	790.6	-	6.8	797.4
3 Public order and safety	407.0	...	...	0.3	5.6	412.9	54.7	0.7	468.3
4 Education	1001.3	...	...	168.1	129.0	1298.4	118.7	18.4	1435.5
5 Health	1249.2	...	...	2.2	325.8	1577.2	75.8	1.9	1654.8
6 Social security and welfare	522.7	...	...	0.8	4459.8	4983.3	22.1	1.0	5006.3
7 Housing and community amenities	306.1	...	...	35.8	4.4	346.3	276.4	40.7	663.3
8 Recreation, culture and religion	148.0	...	...	20.6	66.9	235.5	82.1	13.0	330.6
9 Economic services	315.2	...	...	377.5	177.3	870.0	450.7	557.2	1878.0
A Fuel and energy	1.6	...	...	42.8	-	44.4	2.9	15.7	62.9
B Agriculture, forestry, fishing and hunting	69.6	...	...	29.3	6.5	105.4	69.3	58.2	232.9
C Mining (except fuels), manufacturing and construction	18.0	...	...	5.0	0.4	23.4	21.6	148.5	193.4
D Transportation and communication	131.1	...	...	234.5	8.2	373.8	278.2	103.2	755.2
E Other economic affairs	95.0	...	...	66.0	162.2	323.2	78.9	231.6	633.7
10 Other functions	438.5	...	...	14.2	1610.9	2063.6	39.8	4.2	2107.6
Total	5451.8	...	...	654.2	6817.3	12923.3	1189.1	690.2	14802.6

Spain

2.3 Total Government Outlays by Function and Type
(Continued)

Thousand Million Spanish pesetas

		Final Consumption Expenditures			Subsidies	Other Current Transfers & Property Income	Total Current Disbursements	Gross Capital Formation	Other Capital Outlays	Total Outlays
		Total	Compensation of Employees	Other						

1988

		Total	Compensation of Employees	Other	Subsidies	Other Current Transfers & Property Income	Total Current Disbursements	Gross Capital Formation	Other Capital Outlays	Total Outlays
1	General public services	324.0	...	...	31.1	30.4	385.5	114.7	48.5	548.7
2	Defence	729.2	...	...	1.2	1.4	731.8	-	5.2	736.9
3	Public order and safety	453.0	...	...	0.2	2.1	455.3	59.0	0.6	514.9
4	Education	1116.2	...	...	193.1	134.7	1444.0	132.7	9.0	1585.7
5	Health	1373.1	...	...	3.8	420.2	1797.1	82.0	4.1	1883.3
6	Social security and welfare	653.1	...	...	0.1	4922.7	5575.9	34.0	5.5	5615.5
7	Housing and community amenities	337.6	...	...	52.7	4.2	394.5	344.8	49.0	788.4
8	Recreation, culture and religion	160.6	...	...	45.0	70.9	276.5	124.3	26.4	427.3
9	Economic services	357.8	...	...	492.6	209.1	1059.5	574.3	605.7	2239.5
	A Fuel and energy	1.4			76.4	0.1	77.9	6.9	12.5	97.4
	B Agriculture, forestry, fishing and hunting	89.1	...	...	39.4	7.3	135.8	96.7	80.9	313.3
	C Mining (except fuels), manufacturing and construction	15.0			3.3	3.5	21.8	19.9	268.6	310.2
	D Transportation and communication	154.7	...	...	287.0	9.0	450.7	377.0	137.4	965.1
	E Other economic affairs	97.6	...	...	86.4	189.3	373.3	73.8	106.5	553.5
10	Other functions	419.8	...	...	9.7	1708.3	2137.8	10.4	8.4	2156.6
	Total	5924.4	...	...	829.6	7504.1	14258.1	1476.3	762.4	16496.8

2.5 Private Final Consumption Expenditure by Type and Purpose, in Current Prices

Thousand Million Spanish pesetas

		1980	1981	1982	1983	1984	1985	1986	1987	1988	1989	1990	1991
	Final Consumption Expenditure of Resident Households												
1	Food, beverages and tobacco	2918.7	3231.5	3656.7	3992.2	4507.7	4802.5	5395.6	5765.3	6022.4	6563.7	7120.8	7488.3
	A Food	...	...	...	...	...	4139.7	4651.2	4940.0	5147.1	5579.1	...	...
	B Non-alcoholic beverages	...	...	...	...	...	90.3	99.7	115.6	125.6	143.8	...	...
	C Alcoholic beverages	...	...	...	...	...	270.9	303.9	332.8	364.8	423.9	...	...
	D Tobacco	...	...	...	...	...	301.6	340.8	376.9	384.9	416.9	...	...
2	Clothing and footwear	839.8	973.6	1109.0	1269.2	1427.5	1665.8	1945.3	2172.6	2439.0	2694.7	2912.4	3137.6
3	Gross rent, fuel and power	1716.5	1961.0	2216.8	2431.5	2663.5	2794.8	2979.8	3191.8	3421.2	3749.7	4106.5	4491.4
	A Fuel and power	...	...	...	...	...	480.9	540.1	626.1	683.9	752.3	...	...
	B Other	...	...	...	...	...	2313.9	2439.6	2565.8	2737.3	2997.3	...	...
4	Furniture, furnishings and household equipment and operation	810.5	880.0	970.1	1093.4	1190.4	1298.6	1475.7	1620.1	1779.9	1971.5	2162.1	2334.6
5	Medical care and health expenses	371.4	386.6	443.9	492.0	528.1	681.0	749.5	825.2	951.1	1106.5	1276.0	1478.1
6	Transport and communication	1409.0	1606.8	1813.4	2144.0	2383.1	2611.3	3013.5	3613.6	4114.8	4667.5	5019.1	5435.9
	A Personal transport equipment	...	...	...	...	...	590.9	795.0	1144.3	1384.6	1542.4	...	...
	B Other	...	...	...	...	...	2020.4	2218.5	2469.4	2730.2	3125.1	...	...
7	Recreational, entertainment, education and cultural services	708.4	812.2	940.5	1070.7	1141.4	1266.2	1475.5	1605.8	1758.0	1941.4	2134.1	2354.1
	A Education	...	...	...	...	...	364.3	417.2	437.4	482.9	524.4	...	...
	B Other	...	...	...	...	...	901.8	1058.3	1168.5	1275.1	1417.0	...	...
8	Miscellaneous goods and services	1631.0	1983.1	2462.9	2971.4	3573.1	4154.6	4852.9	5640.4	6352.7	7202.0	7994.2	9056.5
	A Personal care	...	...	...	...	...	268.9	312.3	345.0	367.4	402.0	...	...
	B Expenditures in restaurants, cafes and hotels	...	...	...	...	...	2849.5	3351.8	3902.7	4432.3	5092.7	...	...

2.5 Private Final Consumption Expenditure by Type and Purpose, in Current Prices
(Continued)

Thousand Million Spanish pesetas

	1980	1981	1982	1983	1984	1985	1986	1987	1988	1989	1990	1991
C Other	...	...	...	...	...	1036.2	1188.9	1392.7	1552.9	1707.3	...	...
Total Final Consumption Expenditure in the Domestic Market by Households, of which	10405.3	11834.8	13613.4	15464.2	17414.7	19274.8	21887.7	24435.0	26839.1	29897.1	32725.3	35776.4
Plus: Direct purchases abroad by resident households	94.7	103.6	123.4	142.8	153.6	193.5	235.8	271.7	313.5	399.7	465.5	511.5
Less: Direct purchases in the domestic market by non-resident households	508.5	637.0	797.6	1002.8	1263.7	1388.3	1685.8	1851.0	1973.0	1951.9	1906.3	2024.2
Equals: Final Consumption Expenditure of Resident Households [a]	9991.5	11301.4	12939.2	14604.2	16304.6	18080.0	20437.7	22855.8	25179.6	28344.9	31284.4	34263.7

Final Consumption Expenditure of Private Non-profit Institutions Serving Households

	1980	1981	1982	1983	1984	1985	1986	1987	1988	1989	1990	1991
Equals: Final Consumption Expenditure of Private Non-profit Organisations Serving Households	...	...	...	...	...	...	...	...	...	...	...	...
Private Final Consumption Expenditure	9991.5	11301.4	12939.2	14604.2	16304.6	18080.0	20437.7	22855.8	25179.6	28344.9	31284.4	34263.7

a) Item 'Final consumption expenditure of resident households' includes consumption expenditure of private non-profit institutions serving households.

2.6 Private Final Consumption Expenditure by Type and Purpose, in Constant Prices

Thousand Million Spanish pesetas

At constant prices of:1986

Final Consumption Expenditure of Resident Households

	1980	1981	1982	1983	1984	1985	1986	1987	1988	1989	1990	1991
1 Food, beverages and tobacco	5831.3	5669.4	5548.8	5466.7	5429.6	5358.6	5395.6	5471.7	5508.3	5579.2	5689.9	5774.9
A Food	...	...	...	...	...	...	4651.2	4702.7	4734.4	4776.1	...	...
B Non-alcoholic beverages	...	...	...	...	...	...	99.7	111.3	116.4	124.6	...	...
C Alcoholic beverages	...	...	...	...	...	...	303.9	308.7	311.2	314.4	...	...
D Tobacco	...	...	...	...	...	...	340.8	348.9	346.2	364.2	...	...
2 Clothing and footwear	1646.0	1684.1	1697.7	1733.2	1739.7	1850.5	1945.3	1987.7	2073.4	2179.5	2246.2	2297.3
3 Gross rent, fuel and power	2995.5	2968.1	2949.5	2952.4	2958.6	2932.3	2979.8	3061.3	3134.4	3215.4	3293.0	3358.7
A Fuel and power	...	...	...	...	...	...	540.1	589.7	627.7	668.5	...	...
B Other	...	...	...	...	...	...	2439.6	2471.5	2506.8	2546.9	...	...
4 Furniture, furnishings and household equipment and operation	1541.9	1492.4	1442.8	1440.9	1415.2	1434.7	1475.7	1545.0	1628.7	1722.0	1793.9	1838.0
5 Medical care and health expenses	765.7	689.8	671.6	651.1	616.2	721.8	749.5	785.7	861.7	966.7	1079.5	1189.2
6 Transport and communication	2612.5	2534.3	2567.8	2609.8	2620.9	2746.9	3013.5	3422.9	3743.4	3992.3	4016.6	4021.9
A Personal transport equipment	...	...	...	...	...	...	795.0	1065.1	1230.2	1322.5	...	...
B Other	...	...	...	...	...	...	2218.5	2357.8	2513.2	2669.8	...	...
7 Recreational, entertainment, education and cultural services	1331.0	1344.0	1365.6	1391.4	1344.1	1380.1	1475.5	1535.1	1605.6	1702.2	1793.6	1881.1
A Education	...	...	...	...	...	...	417.2	418.5	432.6	440.4	...	...
B Other	...	...	...	...	...	...	1058.3	1116.6	1173.0	1261.8	...	...
8 Miscellaneous goods and services	3533.8	3741.8	3925.1	4102.3	4350.7	4687.2	4852.9	5288.3	5579.1	5838.9	5990.8	6284.3
A Personal care	...	...	...	...	...	...	312.3	328.0	335.5	349.0	...	...
B Expenditures in restaurants, cafes and hotels	...	...	...	...	...	...	3351.8	3643.0	3849.8	4061.5	...	...
C Other	...	...	...	...	...	...	1188.9	1317.3	1393.8	1428.5	...	...
Total Final Consumption Expenditure in the Domestic Market by Households, of which	20257.7	20123.9	20169.1	20347.9	20475.0	21112.1	21887.7	23097.7	24134.8	25196.1	25903.4	26645.5
Plus: Direct purchases abroad by resident households	197.5	178.5	187.7	174.5	175.5	203.2	235.8	263.8	301.1	378.5	428.4	452.6
Less: Direct purchases in the domestic market by non-resident households	1097.4	1189.1	1264.6	1375.7	1544.2	1534.1	1685.8	1739.7	1752.2	1619.1	1482.0	1479.3
Equals: Final Consumption Expenditure of Resident Households [a]	19357.9	19113.2	19092.1	19146.6	19106.3	19781.2	20437.7	21621.9	22683.7	23955.6	24849.7	25618.8

Final Consumption Expenditure of Private Non-profit Institutions Serving Households

	1980	1981	1982	1983	1984	1985	1986	1987	1988	1989	1990	1991
Equals: Final Consumption Expenditure of Private Non-profit Organisations Serving Households	...	...	...	...	...	...	...	...	...	...	...	...
Private Final Consumption Expenditure	19357.9	19113.2	19092.1	19146.6	19106.3	19781.2	20437.7	21621.9	22683.7	23955.6	24849.7	25618.8

a) Item 'Final consumption expenditure of resident households' includes consumption expenditure of private non-profit institutions serving households.

Spain

2.17 Exports and Imports of Goods and Services, Detail

Thousand Million Spanish pesetas

	1980	1981	1982	1983	1984	1985	1986	1987	1988	1989	1990	1991
Exports of Goods and Services												
1 Exports of merchandise, f.o.b.	1531.6	1976.2	2372.2	3066.8	3936.1	4296.2 / 4280.5	3939.8	4306.1	4738.8	5260.6	5681.0	6169.6
2 Transport and communication a	254.3	309.1	335.9	434.4	483.8	543.1 / 486.9	481.2	561.3	596.7	615.1	583.6	624.0
3 Insurance service charges	26.1	30.2	31.3	33.7	44.8	47.0 / 7.6	9.4	12.9	10.9	12.5	12.8	13.9
4 Other commodities a	89.2	126.5	135.3	187.9	215.2	244.1 / 243.9	300.7	264.5	255.4	310.3	371.5	468.6
5 Adjustments of merchandise exports to change-of-ownership basis	...	...				... / ...	...	...	...	...	...	...
6 Direct purchases in the domestic market by non-residential households	508.5	637.0	797.6	1002.8	1263.7	1388.3 / 1388.3	1685.8	1851.0	1973.0	1951.9	1906.3	2024.2
7 Direct purchases in the domestic market by extraterritorial bodies	...	...				... / ...	...	...	...	...	...	...
Total Exports of Goods and Services	2409.8	3079.1	3672.2	4725.6	5943.5	6518.7 / 6407.2	6416.9	6995.8	7574.8	8150.4	8555.2	9300.3
Imports of Goods and Services												
1 Imports of merchandise, c.i.f.	2480.7	3045.6	3561.1	4300.4	4753.3	5205.2 / 5206.7	5035.9	6137.0	7101.3	8523.1	9024.6	9799.8
2 Adjustments of merchandise imports to change-of-ownership basis	...	...				... / ...	...	...	...	...	...	...
3 Other transport and communication	55.9	93.4	108.2	142.4	164.9	155.3 / 129.7	133.0	169.8	182.3	206.0	232.5	248.2
4 Other insurance service charges	9.3	19.8	3.1	1.0	27.4	33.1 / 6.9	16.1	21.2	22.6	17.0	10.0	1.0
5 Other commodities	117.8	165.9	228.5	273.4	264.1	327.7 / 323.3	308.8	335.4	402.8	474.7	518.0	567.6
6 Direct purchases abroad by government	...	...	...	...		...	...	...	...	...	...	...
7 Direct purchases abroad by resident households	94.7	103.6	123.4	142.8	153.6	193.5 / 193.5	235.8	271.7	313.5	399.7	465.5	511.5
Total Imports of Goods and Services	2758.5	3428.3	4024.3	4860.1	5363.3	5914.8 / 5860.1	5729.7	6935.1	8022.5	9620.6	10250.7	11128.1
Balance of Goods and Services	-348.7	-349.2	-352.1	-134.5	580.2	603.9 / 547.1	687.2	60.7	-447.7	-1470.2	-1695.5	-1827.8
Total Imports and Balance of Goods and Services	2409.8	3079.1	3672.2	4725.6	5943.5	6518.7 / 6407.2	6416.9	6995.8	7574.8	8150.4	8555.2	9300.3

a) The estimates refer to transport only. Communication is included in item 'Other Commodities'.

3.11 General Government Production Account: Total and Subsectors

Thousand Million Spanish pesetas

	1985					1986				
	Total General Government	Central Government	State or Provincial Government	Local Government	Social Security Funds	Total General Government	Central Government	State or Provincial Government	Local Government	Social Security Funds
Gross Output										
1 Sales	268.1	37.1	...	190.2	40.8	293.6	48.8	...	205.2	39.6
2 Services produced for own use	4185.2	1974.4	...	1337.7	873.1	4775.6	2206.0	...	1559.9	1009.6
3 Own account fixed capital formation	...	...	...	...	...	...	...	...	...	...
Gross Output a	4453.3	2011.5	...	1527.9	913.9	5069.2	2254.8	...	1765.1	1049.2
Gross Input										
Intermediate Consumption	1185.7	478.4	...	456.8	250.4	1404.6	590.7	...	512.0	302.0
Subtotal: Value Added	3267.6	1533.0	...	1071.1	663.5	3664.6	1664.2	...	1253.1	747.3
1 Indirect taxes, net	...	...	...	...	...	...	...	...	...	...
2 Consumption of fixed capital	289.0	180.0	...	72.7	36.3	321.9	194.1	...	87.8	40.1
3 Compensation of employees	2978.6	1353.0	...	998.4	627.2	3342.7	1470.2	...	1165.4	707.2
4 Net Operating surplus	...	...	...	...	...	...	...	...	...	...
Gross Input a	4453.3	2011.4	...	1527.9	913.9	5069.2	2255.0	...	1765.2	1049.3

3.11 General Government Production Account: Total and Subsectors

Thousand Million Spanish pesetas

	1987					1988				
	Total General Government	Central Government	State or Provincial Government	Local Government	Social Security Funds	Total General Government	Central Government	State or Provincial Government	Local Government	Social Security Funds
Gross Output										
1 Sales	316.8	42.1	...	237.9	36.8	389.1	60.5	...	285.5	43.1
2 Services produced for own use	5494.3	2512.3	...	1824.7	1157.3	5972.6	2582.7	...	2035.5	1354.5
3 Own account fixed capital formation	...	...	...	...	...	...	...	...	...	...
Gross Output a	5811.1	2554.4	...	2062.6	1194.1	6361.7	2643.2	...	2321.0	1397.6
Gross Input										
Intermediate Consumption	1704.3	758.6	...	606.3	339.4	1769.3	684.6	...	690.6	394.0
Subtotal: Value Added	4106.8	1795.8	...	1456.3	854.7	4592.5	1958.5	...	1630.4	1003.6
1 Indirect taxes, net	...	...	...	...	...	...	...	...	...	...
2 Consumption of fixed capital	355.2	208.4	...	102.6	44.2	395.4	225.4	...	120.9	49.0
3 Compensation of employees	3751.6	1587.4	...	1353.7	810.5	4197.1	1733.1	...	1509.5	954.6
4 Net Operating surplus	...	...	...	...	...	...	...	...	...	...
Gross Input a	5811.1	2554.4	...	2062.6	1194.1	6361.8	2643.1	...	2321.0	1397.6
	1989					1990				
	Total General Government	Central Government	State or Provincial Government	Local Government	Social Security Funds	Total General Government	Central Government	State or Provincial Government	Local Government	Social Security Funds
Gross Output										
1 Sales	428.2	58.2	...	322.8	47.2	392.5	56.2	...	278.5	57.8
2 Services produced for own use	6887.8	2872.3	...	2381.4	1634.0	7817.6	3093.3	...	2863.6	1860.7
3 Own account fixed capital formation	...	...	...	...	...	...	...	...	...	...
Gross Output a	7316.0	2930.5	...	2704.2	1681.2	8210.1	3149.5	...	3142.1	1918.5
Gross Input										
Intermediate Consumption	2065.3	765.5	...	801.9	497.8	2136.0	694.3	...	900.0	541.7
Subtotal: Value Added	5250.7	2165.0	...	1902.3	1183.4	6074.1	2455.2	...	2242.1	1376.8
1 Indirect taxes, net	...	...	...	...	...	...	...	...	...	...
2 Consumption of fixed capital	445.2	244.7	...	145.0	55.5	508.5	269.7	...	175.1	63.7
3 Compensation of employees	4805.5	1920.3	...	1757.3	1127.8	5565.6	2185.5	...	2067.0	1313.1
4 Net Operating surplus	...	...	...	...	...	...	...	...	...	...
Gross Input a	7316.0	2930.5	...	2704.2	1681.1	8210.1	3149.5	...	3142.1	1918.5

a) Local Government includes provincial government and other regional government entities.

3.12 General Government Income and Outlay Account: Total and Subsectors

Thousand Million Spanish pesetas

	1985					1986				
	Total General Government	Central Government	State or Provincial Government	Local Government	Social Security Funds	Total General Government	Central Government	State or Provincial Government	Local Government	Social Security Funds
Receipts										
1 Operating surplus	...	...	...	...	...	...	...	...	...	...
2 Property and entrepreneurial income	324.7	266.0	...	45.4	13.2	332.4	275.1	...	45.1	12.2
A Withdrawals from public quasi-corporations	...	...	...	...	...	...	...	...	...	...
B Interest	201.7	153.8	...	38.4	9.5	218.1	167.4	...	39.5	11.2
C Dividends	123.0	112.2	...	7.0	3.7	114.3	107.7	...	5.7	1.0
D Net land rent and royalties	...	...	...	...	...	...	...	...	...	...
3 Taxes, fees and contributions	8403.7	3942.8	...	1130.3	3330.7	9850.7	5031.9	...	1063.3	3755.4
A Indirect taxes	2668.7	1977.6	...	670.5	20.7	3401.3	2845.6	...	555.6	-
B Direct taxes a	2394.4	1934.7	...	459.8	...	2655.0	2147.3	...	507.7	...
C Social security contributions	3340.6	30.5	...	-	3310.0	3794.4	39.0	...	-	3755.4
D Fees, fines and penalties a	...	...	...	...	...	...	...	...	...	...

Spain

3.12 General Government Income and Outlay Account: Total and Subsectors
(Continued)

Thousand Million Spanish pesetas

	1985					1986				
	Total General Government	Central Government	State or Provincial Government	Local Government	Social Security Funds	Total General Government	Central Government	State or Provincial Government	Local Government	Social Security Funds
4 Other current transfers	917.7	857.7	...	915.7	1150.0	1037.8	988.5	...	1246.2	1421.5
A Casualty insurance claims	...	...	...	...	...	...	...	...	...	...
B Transfers from other government subsectors	...	108.7	...	786.7	1110.3	...	112.3	...	1137.9	1368.3
C Transfers from the rest of the world	0.1	0.1	...	-	-	24.2	24.2	...	-	-
D Other transfers, except imputed	597.7	480.0	...	86.1	31.6	678.7	555.4	...	77.5	45.8
E Imputed unfunded employee pension and welfare contributions	319.9	268.9	...	42.9	8.1	334.8	296.5	...	30.9	7.5
Total Current Receipts b	9646.1	5066.5	...	2091.4	4493.9	11220.9	6295.5	...	2354.6	5189.1
Disbursements										
1 Government final consumption expenditure	4151.7	1949.7	...	1328.9	873.1	4740.2	2181.4	...	1549.3	1009.6
2 Property income	970.5	846.6	...	123.4	0.4	1278.5	1136.2	...	141.5	0.7
3 Subsidies	687.3	490.7	...	166.9	29.7	634.8	446.5	...	151.2	37.1
4 Other current transfers	4515.4	2603.1	...	260.1	3658.0	5051.1	3278.3	...	290.1	4101.1
A Casualty insurance premiums, net	...	...	...	...	...	...	...	...	...	...
B Transfers to other government subsectors	...	1848.2	...	84.1	73.5	...	2443.1	...	102.8	72.6
C Social security benefits	4039.5	370.3	...	88.0	3581.2	4512.0	401.0	...	93.8	4017.2
D Social assistance grants	...	...	...	...	...	...	...	...	...	...
E Unfunded employee pension and welfare benefits	461.9	370.6	...	88.1	3.2	519.2	414.4	...	93.6	11.3
F Transfers to private non-profit institutions serving households	...	...	...	...	...	...	...	...	...	...
G Other transfers n.e.c.	...	...	...	...	...	...	...	...	...	...
H Transfers to the rest of the world	14.1	14.1	...	...	-	19.8	19.8	...	...	-
Net saving	-678.8	-823.6	...	212.1	-67.3	-483.7	-746.9	...	222.6	40.6
Total Current Disbursements and Net Saving b	9646.1	5066.5	...	2091.4	4493.9	11220.9	6295.5	...	2354.7	5189.1

	1987					1988				
	Total General Government	Central Government	State or Provincial Government	Local Government	Social Security Funds	Total General Government	Central Government	State or Provincial Government	Local Government	Social Security Funds
Receipts										
1 Operating surplus	...	...	...	...	...	...	...	...	...	...
2 Property and entrepreneurial income	288.4	213.0	...	53.0	22.5	312.7	222.0	...	61.9	28.8
A Withdrawals from public quasi-corporations	...	...	...	...	...	...	...	...	...	...
B Interest	223.6	166.0	...	45.2	12.3	141.9	68.0	...	53.3	20.6
C Dividends	64.9	47.0	...	7.7	10.2	170.7	154.0	...	8.6	8.2
D Net land rent and royalties	...	...	...	...	...	...	...	...	...	...
3 Taxes, fees and contributions	11748.7	6292.8	...	1235.1	4220.8	13035.5	6881.6	...	1524.7	4629.4
A Indirect taxes	3773.8	3098.3	...	675.5	-	4162.1	3311.3	...	850.9	-
B Direct taxes a	3705.3	3145.7	...	559.6	...	4196.6	3522.9	...	673.6	...
C Social security contributions	4269.6	48.8	...	-	4220.8	4676.9	47.4	...	0.1	4629.4
D Fees, fines and penalties a	...	...	...	...	...	...	...	...	...	...
4 Other current transfers	1130.7	1088.1	...	1649.3	1664.1	1222.4	1167.2	...	1805.9	1891.2
A Casualty insurance claims	...	...	...	...	...	...	...	...	...	...
B Transfers from other government subsectors	...	102.7	...	1523.4	1644.7	...	136.1	...	1662.0	1843.7
C Transfers from the rest of the world	39.1	39.1	...	-	-	52.0	52.0	...	-	-
D Other transfers, except imputed	743.7	638.9	...	92.4	12.5	819.3	666.9	...	113.9	38.5
E Imputed unfunded employee pension and welfare contributions	347.8	307.4	...	33.5	6.9	351.1	312.0	...	30.0	9.0
Total Current Receipts b	13167.8	7593.9	...	2937.4	5907.4	14570.6	8270.8	...	3392.5	6549.4
Disbursements										
1 Government final consumption expenditure	5451.8	2488.3	...	1806.2	1157.3	5924.4	2559.8	...	2010.2	1354.5
2 Property income	1255.9	1082.0	...	173.1	0.7	1345.9	1155.8	...	190.0	0.2

3.12 General Government Income and Outlay Account: Total and Subsectors
(Continued)

Thousand Million Spanish pesetas

	1987					1988				
	Total General Government	Central Government	State or Provincial Government	Local Government	Social Security Funds	Total General Government	Central Government	State or Provincial Government	Local Government	Social Security Funds
3 Subsidies	654.2	410.7	...	196.7	46.8	829.6	529.0	...	242.7	57.9
4 Other current transfers	5561.4	4003.1	...	304.4	4524.7	6158.2	4322.1	...	391.7	5086.2
A Casualty insurance premiums, net	...	...	...	...	...	...	...	...	...	...
B Transfers to other government subsectors	...	3098.3	...	96.6	75.9	...	3373.8	...	174.2	93.8
C Social security benefits	4990.4	437.2	...	106.6	4446.6	5567.2	463.4	...	113.9	4989.9
D Social assistance grants	...	...	...	...	...	...	...	...	...	...
E Unfunded employee pension and welfare benefits	544.9	441.5	...	101.2	2.3	570.6	464.6	...	103.7	2.4
F Transfers to private non-profit institutions serving households	...	...	...	...	...	...	...	...	...	...
G Other transfers n.e.c.	...	...	...	...	...	...	...	...	...	...
H Transfers to the rest of the world	26.2	26.2	...	...	-	20.3	20.3	...	...	-
Net saving	244.6	-390.3	...	457.1	177.9	312.5	-296.0	...	557.8	50.7
Total Current Disbursements and Net Saving b	13167.9	7593.8	...	2937.5	5907.4	14570.6	8270.7	...	3392.4	6549.5

	1989					1990				
	Total General Government	Central Government	State or Provincial Government	Local Government	Social Security Funds	Total General Government	Central Government	State or Provincial Government	Local Government	Social Security Funds

Receipts

1 Operating surplus	...	...	...	...	...	...	...	...	...	...
2 Property and entrepreneurial income	396.1	281.6	...	87.6	27.0	485.9	326.1	...	125.9	33.9
A Withdrawals from public quasi-corporations	...	...	...	...	...	...	...	...	...	...
B Interest	164.8	67.1	...	78.3	19.3	204.9	59.9	...	111.5	33.6
C Dividends	231.4	214.5	...	9.3	7.7	281.0	266.3	...	14.4	0.3
D Net land rent and royalties	...	...	...	...	...	...	...	...	...	...
3 Taxes, fees and contributions	15484.2	8398.4	...	1747.7	5338.2	17104.4	8885.0	...	2171.1	6048.3
A Indirect taxes	4657.1	3665.3	...	991.8	-	4975.9	3726.8	...	1249.1	-
B Direct taxes a	5430.4	4674.6	...	755.7	...	6018.4	5096.6	...	921.8	...
C Social security contributions	5396.7	58.4	...	0.1	5338.2	6110.1	61.6	...	0.2	6048.3
D Fees, fines and penalties a	...	...	...	...	...	...	...	...	...	...
4 Other current transfers	1276.9	1277.9	...	2073.7	2188.5	1411.8	1361.3	...	2333.5	2362.6
A Casualty insurance claims	...	...	...	...	...	...	...	...	...	...
B Transfers from other government subsectors	...	160.0	...	1944.1	2159.1	...	201.2	...	2157.4	2287.1
C Transfers from the rest of the world	81.9	81.9	...	-	-	70.1	31.9	...	7.1	31.1
D Other transfers, except imputed	830.7	699.1	...	102.2	29.4	914.9	734.8	...	135.7	44.4
E Imputed unfunded employee pension and welfare contributions	364.3	336.8	...	27.5	-	426.8	393.4	...	33.3	-
Total Current Receipts b	17157.2	9957.9	...	3909.0	7553.7	19002.1	10572.4	...	4630.5	8444.8

Disbursements

1 Government final consumption expenditure	6831.2	2845.1	...	2352.1	1634.0	7756.1	3065.2	...	2830.2	1860.7
2 Property income	1560.5	1328.7	...	231.3	0.5	1775.5	1479.4	...	295.8	0.3
3 Subsidies	888.9	527.7	...	296.8	64.4	960.6	546.0	...	351.9	62.6

Spain

3.12 General Government Income and Outlay Account: Total and Subsectors
(Continued)

<u>Thousand Million Spanish pesetas</u>

	1989					1990				
	Total General Government	Central Government	State or Provincial Government	Local Government	Social Security Funds	Total General Government	Central Government	State or Provincial Government	Local Government	Social Security Funds
4 Other current transfers	7016.6	5031.0	...	503.6	5745.2	7983.2	5426.5	...	588.7	6613.7
A Casualty insurance premiums, net	...	...	...	...	...	...	...	...	...	...
B Transfers to other government subsectors	...	3929.6	...	221.9	111.7	...	4254.0	...	271.2	120.4
C Social security benefits	6276.6	517.7	...	126.8	5632.1	7221.2	585.2	...	143.3	6492.7
D Social assistance grants	...	...	...	...	...	...	...	...	...	...
E Unfunded employee pension and welfare benefits	679.1	523.0	...	154.8	1.3	737.5	562.8	...	174.1	0.5
F Transfers to private non-profit institutions serving households	...	...	...	...	...	...	...	...	...	...
G Other transfers n.e.c.	...	...	...	...	...	...	...	...	...	...
H Transfers to the rest of the world	60.8	60.8	...	...	-	24.5	24.5	...	...	-
Net saving	860.1	225.3	...	525.2	109.6	526.7	55.3	...	563.8	-92.4
Total Current Disbursements and Net Saving b	17157.3	9957.8	...	3909.0	7553.7	19002.1	10572.4	...	4630.4	8444.9

a) Item 'Fees, fines and penalties' is included in item 'Direct taxes'.
b) Local Government includes provincial government and other regional government entities.

3.13 General Government Capital Accumulation Account: Total and Subsectors

<u>Thousand Million Spanish pesetas</u>

	1985					1986				
	Total General Government	Central Government	State or Provincial Government	Local Government	Social Security Funds	Total General Government	Central Government	State or Provincial Government	Local Government	Social Security Funds
Finance of Gross Accumulation										
1 Gross saving	-389.8	-643.6	...	284.8	-31.0	-161.8	-552.8	...	310.4	80.7
A Consumption of fixed capital	289.0	180.0	...	72.7	36.3	321.9	194.1	...	87.8	40.1
B Net saving	-678.8	-823.6	...	212.1	-67.3	-483.7	-746.9	...	222.6	40.6
2 Capital transfers	118.2	31.0	...	300.3	6.0	148.1	115.0	...	352.4	9.4
A From other government subsectors	...	1.4	...	211.7	6.0	...	36.4	...	282.9	9.4
B From other resident sectors	118.1	29.5	...	88.6	-	107.5	38.0	...	69.5	-
C From rest of the world	0.1	0.1	...	-	-	40.6	40.6	...	-	-
Finance of Gross Accumulation a	-271.6	-612.6	...	585.1	-25.0	-13.7	-437.8	...	662.8	90.1
Gross Accumulation										
1 Gross capital formation	994.1	325.2	...	619.8	49.1	1129.5	330.1	...	740.7	58.7
A Increase in stocks	...	...	...	...	...	...	...	...	...	...
B Gross fixed capital formation	994.1	325.2	...	619.8	49.1	1129.5	330.1	...	740.7	58.7
2 Purchases of land, net	50.4	17.0	...	33.4	-	49.8	8.9	...	40.8	-
3 Purchases of intangible assets, net	...	...	...	...	...	...	...	...	...	...
4 Capital transfers	640.8	745.9	...	113.3	0.8	737.1	886.7	...	123.8	55.4
A To other government subsectors	...	217.2	...	1.4	0.5	...	292.3	...	1.3	35.1
B To other resident sectors	635.4	523.2	...	111.9	0.3	732.0	589.3	...	122.4	20.3
C To rest of the world	5.4	5.4	...	-	-	5.1	5.1	...	-	-
Net lending	-1957.0	-1700.6	...	-181.4	-74.9	-1930.1	-1663.6	...	-242.4	-24.1
Gross Accumulation a	-271.7	-612.5	...	585.1	-25.0	-13.7	-437.9	...	662.9	90.0

	1987					1988				
	Total General Government	Central Government	State or Provincial Government	Local Government	Social Security Funds	Total General Government	Central Government	State or Provincial Government	Local Government	Social Security Funds
Finance of Gross Accumulation										
1 Gross saving	599.8	-181.9	...	559.7	222.1	707.9	-70.6	...	678.7	99.7
A Consumption of fixed capital	355.2	208.4	...	102.6	44.2	395.4	225.4	...	120.9	49.0
B Net saving	244.6	-390.3	...	457.1	177.9	312.5	-296.0	...	557.8	50.7
2 Capital transfers	149.5	131.2	...	362.2	5.1	224.9	181.9	...	355.8	27.5
A From other government subsectors	...	54.5	...	289.4	5.1	...	51.3	...	264.9	24.2
B From other resident sectors	100.1	27.3	...	72.8	-	154.0	59.7	...	90.9	3.3
C From rest of the world	49.4	49.4	...	-	-	70.9	70.9	...	-	-
Finance of Gross Accumulation a	749.3	-50.7	...	921.9	227.2	932.8	111.3	...	1034.5	127.2
Gross Accumulation										
1 Gross capital formation	1189.1	384.2	...	736.1	68.8	1476.3	484.3	...	912.8	79.2

3.13 General Government Capital Accumulation Account: Total and Subsectors
(Continued)

Thousand Million Spanish pesetas

	1987					1988				
	Total General Government	Central Government	State or Provincial Government	Local Government	Social Security Funds	Total General Government	Central Government	State or Provincial Government	Local Government	Social Security Funds
A Increase in stocks	...	...	...	...	...	...	...	...	...	...
B Gross fixed capital formation	1189.1	384.2	...	736.1	68.8	1476.3	484.3	...	912.8	79.2
2 Purchases of land, net	56.3	17.5	...	38.8	-	64.8	19.0	...	45.7	-
3 Purchases of intangible assets, net	...	...	...	...	...	...	...	...	...	...
4 Capital transfers	634.0	797.8	...	133.9	51.3	697.6	781.2	...	204.2	52.6
A To other government subsectors	...	294.3	...	4.5	50.2	...	267.1	...	22.7	50.6
B To other resident sectors	632.0	501.5	...	129.4	1.1	695.5	511.9	...	181.6	2.0
C To rest of the world	2.0	2.0	...	-	-	2.1	2.1	...	-	-
Net lending	-1130.0	-1250.2	...	13.2	107.1	-1305.9	-1173.1	...	-128.3	-4.5
Gross Accumulation a	749.4	-50.7	...	922.0	227.2	932.8	111.4	...	1034.4	127.3

	1989					1990				
	Total General Government	Central Government	State or Provincial Government	Local Government	Social Security Funds	Total General Government	Central Government	State or Provincial Government	Local Government	Social Security Funds
Finance of Gross Accumulation										
1 Gross saving	1305.3	470.0	...	670.2	165.1	1035.2	325.0	...	738.9	-28.7
A Consumption of fixed capital	445.2	244.7	...	145.0	55.5	508.5	269.7	...	175.1	63.7
B Net saving	860.1	225.3	...	525.2	109.6	526.7	55.3	...	563.8	-92.4
2 Capital transfers	308.1	184.1	...	498.5	52.4	323.9	135.1	...	615.1	91.0
A From other government subsectors	...	1.9	...	372.6	52.4	...	2.3	...	424.0	91.0
B From other resident sectors	171.6	45.7	...	125.9	-	196.7	47.7	...	148.2	-
C From rest of the world	136.5	136.5	...	-	-	127.2	85.1	...	42.2	-
Finance of Gross Accumulation a	1613.4	654.1	...	1168.7	217.5	1359.1	460.1	...	1354.0	62.3
Gross Accumulation										
1 Gross capital formation	1975.2	620.9	...	1231.4	123.0	2492.3	852.9	...	1488.7	150.7
A Increase in stocks	...	...	...	...	...	...	...	...	...	...
B Gross fixed capital formation	1975.2	620.9	...	1231.4	123.0	2492.3	852.9	...	1488.7	150.7
2 Purchases of land, net	23.0	19.4	...	3.6	-	93.4	27.6	...	65.9	-
3 Purchases of intangible assets, net	...	...	...	...	...	...	...	...	...	...
4 Capital transfers	874.7	999.0	...	297.6	5.0	739.5	933.6	...	311.8	11.3
A To other government subsectors	...	380.1	...	44.4	2.4	...	478.6	...	34.0	4.7
B To other resident sectors	865.9	610.1	...	253.2	2.6	722.3	437.8	...	277.9	6.7
C To rest of the world	8.8	8.8	...	-	-	17.2	17.2	...	-	-
Net lending	-1259.6	-985.3	...	-363.8	89.6	-1966.1	-1354.0	...	-512.4	-99.8
Gross Accumulation a	1613.3	654.0	...	1168.8	217.6	1359.1	460.1	...	1354.0	62.2

a) Local Government includes provincial government and other regional government entities.

3.21 Corporate and Quasi-Corporate Enterprise Production Account: Total and Sectors

Thousand Million Spanish pesetas

	1985				1986				1987			
	Corporate and Quasi-Corporate Enterprises			ADDENDUM: Total,	Corporate and Quasi-Corporate Enterprises			ADDENDUM: Total,	Corporate and Quasi-Corporate Enterprises			ADDENDUM: Total,
	TOTAL	Non-Financial	Financial	including Unincorporated	TOTAL	Non-Financial	Financial	including Unincorporated	TOTAL	Non-Financial	Financial	including Unincorporated
Gross Output												
1 Output for sale	47857.6	47275.8	581.8	...	49957.7	49381.2	576.6	...	54575.7	53931.2	644.4	...
2 Imputed bank service charge	1689.5	...	1689.5	...	1971.9	...	1971.9	...	2321.5	...	2321.5	...
3 Own-account fixed capital formation	...	...	...	...	...	...	...	...	...	...	...	...
Gross Output	49547.1	47275.8	2271.3	...	51929.6	49381.2	2548.5	...	56897.2	53931.2	2965.9	...
Gross Input												
Intermediate consumption	25170.2	22972.3	2197.9	...	25067.2	22510.1	2557.1	...	27172.8	24154.5	3018.4	...
1 Imputed banking service charge	1689.5	...	1689.5	...	1971.9	...	1971.9	...	2321.5	...	2321.5	...
2 Other intermediate consumption	23480.7	22972.3	508.4	...	23095.3	22510.1	585.2	...	24851.3	24154.5	696.9	...
Subtotal: Value Added	24376.9	24303.5	73.4	...	26862.4	26871.1	-8.7	...	29724.3	29776.8	-52.4	...

Spain

Thousand Million Spanish pesetas

	1985				1986				1987			
	Corporate and Quasi-Corporate Enterprises			ADDENDUM: Total,	Corporate and Quasi-Corporate Enterprises			ADDENDUM: Total,	Corporate and Quasi-Corporate Enterprises			ADDENDUM: Total,
	TOTAL	Non-Financial	Financial	including Unincorporated	TOTAL	Non-Financial	Financial	including Unincorporated	TOTAL	Non-Financial	Financial	including Unincorporated
1 Indirect taxes, net	1425.1	1357.1	67.9	...	1020.7	1000.8	19.9	...	817.9	826.8	-8.9	...
A Indirect taxes	2112.4	2032.6	79.8	...	1693.4	1665.1	28.3	...	1590.2	1584.6.	5.6	...
B Less: Subsidies	687.3	675.5	11.9	...	672.7	664.3	8.4	...	772.3	757.8	14.5	...
2 Consumption of fixed capital	3298.4	3210.1	88.3	...	3536.0	3441.9	94.1	...	3822.5	3713.9	108.6	...
3 Compensation of employees	9926.1	9056.8	869.3	...	11246.5	10147.4	1099.0	...	12555.6	11383.7	1171.9	...
4 Net operating surplus	9727.3	10679.5	-952.2	...	11059.2	12280.9	-1221.7	...	12528.5	13852.5	-1324.0	...
Gross Input	49547.1	47275.8	2271.2	...	51929.6	49381.1	2548.4	...	56897.3	53931.4	2966.0	...

	1988				1989				1990			
	Corporate and Quasi-Corporate Enterprises			ADDENDUM: Total,	Corporate and Quasi-Corporate Enterprises			ADDENDUM: Total,	Corporate and Quasi-Corporate Enterprises			ADDENDUM: Total,
	TOTAL	Non-Financial	Financial	including Unincorporated	TOTAL	Non-Financial	Financial	including Unincorporated	TOTAL	Non-Financial	Financial	including Unincorporated
Gross Output												
1 Output for sale	60274.4	59462.2	812.2	...	66968.8	66123.3	845.4	...	74526.5	73408.7	1117.8	...
2 Imputed bank service charge	2682.8	...	2682.8	...	3180.9	...	3180.9	...	3581.5	...	3581.5	...
3 Own-account fixed capital formation	...	...	...	...	...	...	...	...	...	...	...	...
Gross Output	62957.2	59462.2	3495.0	...	70149.7	66123.3	4026.3	...	78108.0	73408.7	4699.3	...
Gross Input												
Intermediate consumption	30015.9	26495.2	3520.7	...	33400.2	29301.6	4098.6	...	37198.1	32499.7	4698.4	...
1 Imputed banking service charge	2682.8	...	2682.8	...	3180.9	...	3180.9	...	3581.5	...	3581.5	...
2 Other intermediate consumption	27333.2	26495.2	837.9	...	30219.4	29301.6	917.7	...	33616.6	32499.7	1116.9	...
Subtotal: Value Added	32941.2	32966.9	-25.7	...	36749.4	36821.7	-72.3	...	40909.9	40908.9	0.9	...
1 Indirect taxes, net	658.5	667.5	-9.0	...	755.5	759.9	-4.4	...	940.6	940.1	0.5	...
A Indirect taxes	1765.9	1760.2	5.7	...	1890.1	1884.0	6.1	...	2202.2	2196.0	6.2	...
B Less: Subsidies	1107.4	1092.7	14.7	...	1134.6	1124.1	10.5	...	1261.6	1255.9	5.7	...
2 Consumption of fixed capital	4204.5	4082.3	122.2	...	4602.5	4457.6	144.9	...	5049.5	4879.2	170.2	...
3 Compensation of employees	14001.7	12533.5	1468.2	...	15607.8	14121.0	1486.9	...	17508.7	15829.8	1678.9	...
4 Net operating surplus	14076.6	15683.6	-1607.0	...	15783.6	17483.2	-1699.6	...	17411.1	19259.8	-1848.7	...
Gross Input	62957.2	59462.1	3495.1	...	70149.6	66123.3	4026.4	...	78108.0	73408.6	4699.3	...

3.22 Corporate and Quasi-Corporate Enterprise Income and Outlay Account: Total and Sectors

Thousand Million Spanish pesetas

	1985			1986			1987			1988		
	TOTAL	Non-Financial	Financial	TOTAL	Non-Financial	Financial	TOTAL	Non-Financial	Financial	TOTAL	Non-Financial	Financial
Receipts												
1 Operating surplus	3167.6	4119.9	-952.2	3512.6	4734.3	-1221.7	4091.7	5415.7	-1324.0	4668.8	6275.8	-1607.0
2 Property and entrepreneurial income	5324.6	426.7	4897.9	5659.9	383.0	5276.9	6695.7	496.0	6199.7	7600.1	644.3	6955.8
A Withdrawals from quasi-corporate enterprises	...	...	...	...	...	...	...	...	...	...	...	...
B Interest	5216.3	379.5	4836.8	5524.2	304.4	5219.8	6493.5	372.9	6120.6	7322.8	453.5	6869.3
C Dividends	104.6	43.5	61.1	132.0	74.9	57.1	199.5	120.4	79.1	272.5	186.0	86.5
D Net land rent and royalties	3.7	3.7	-	3.7	3.7	-	2.7	2.7	-	4.8	4.8	-
3 Current transfers	711.2	243.8	467.4	986.5	258.0	728.5	1153.4	323.4	829.9	1461.7	352.5	1109.2
A Casualty insurance claims	95.6	94.5	1.1	120.0	118.8	1.1	160.0	158.8	1.2	186.7	185.4	1.4
B Casualty insurance premiums, net, due to be received by insurance companies	272.6	...	272.6	342.7	...	342.7	462.3		462.3	532.4		532.4
C Current transfers from the rest of the world	...	...	...	...	...	...	...		...	...		...
D Other transfers except imputed	96.8	3.5	93.3	188.5	2.7	185.8	202.1	7.2	194.9	203.9	3.5	200.4
E Imputed unfunded employee pension and welfare contributions	246.3	145.8	100.4	335.4	136.5	198.9	328.9	157.5	171.5	538.6	163.6	375.0
Total Current Receipts	9203.4	4790.4	4413.1	10159.0	5375.3	4783.7	11940.8	6235.1	5705.6	13730.6	7272.6	6458.0
Disbursements												
1 Property and entrepreneurial income	6354.6	2987.1	3367.5	6350.1	2918.0	3432.1	7388.1	3412.2	3976.0	8463.6	4018.4	4445.2
A Withdrawals from quasi-corporations	...	...	...	...	...	...	...	...	...	...	...	...
B Interest	5642.9	2449.2	3193.8	5532.5	2276.6	3255.9	6419.8	2605.9	3813.8	7005.8	2832.2	4173.6

3.22 Corporate and Quasi-Corporate Enterprise Income and Outlay Account: Total and Sectors
(Continued)

Thousand Million Spanish pesetas

	1985			1986			1987			1988		
	TOTAL	Non-Financial	Financial	TOTAL	Non-Financial	Financial	TOTAL	Non-Financial	Financial	TOTAL	Non-Financial	Financial
C Dividends	663.4	489.7	173.7	764.7	588.5	176.2	910.5	748.3	162.2	1368.3	1096.7	271.6
D Net land rent and royalties	48.2	48.2	...	52.9	52.9	...	57.9	57.9	...	89.5	89.5	...
2 Direct taxes and other current transfers n.e.c. to general government	560.1	481.8	78.3	694.9	558.3	136.6	963.7	807.9	155.7	1044.6	849.0	195.6
A Direct taxes	560.1	481.8	78.3	694.9	558.3	136.6	963.7	807.9	155.7	1044.6	849.0	195.6
B Fines, fees, penalties and other current transfers n.e.c.	...	...	...	...	...	...	...	...	...	...	...	...
3 Other current transfers	729.7	290.3	439.4	961.0	348.0	613.1	1091.6	390.5	701.0	1195.7	426.3	769.5
A Casualty insurance premiums, net	102.4	99.5	2.9	129.5	126.5	3.0	180.3	177.2	3.2	202.9	199.3	3.5
B Casualty insurance claims liability of insurance companies	272.6	...	272.6	342.7	...	342.7	462.3	...	462.3	532.4	...	532.4
C Transfers to private non-profit institutions	...	...	...	...	...	...	...	...	...	...	...	...
D Unfunded employee pension and welfare benefits	244.4	145.8	98.6	267.9	136.5	131.4	313.0	157.5	155.6	309.2	163.6	145.6
E Social assistance grants	...	...	...	...	...	...	...	...	...	...	...	...
F Other transfers n.e.c.	110.2	45.0	65.3	220.9	84.9	136.0	135.8	55.9	79.9	151.3	63.3	88.0
G Transfers to the rest of the world	...	...	...	...	...	...	...	...	...	...	...	...
Statistical discrepancy	47.0	...	47.0	168.2	...	168.2	154.6	...	154.6	396.6	...	396.6
Net saving	1512.1	1031.1	481.0	1984.8	1551.0	433.7	2342.8	1624.5	718.3	2630.0	1978.9	651.1
Total Current Disbursements and Net Saving	9203.5	4790.3	4413.2	10159.0	5375.3	4783.7	11940.8	6235.1	5705.6	13730.5	7272.6	6458.0

	1989			1990		
	TOTAL	Non-Financial	Financial	TOTAL	Non-Financial	Financial
Receipts						
1 Operating surplus	5420.1	7119.7	-1699.6	5805.6	7654.3	-1848.7
2 Property and entrepreneurial income	9358.3	787.5	8570.8	11168.9	992.8	10176.0
A Withdrawals from quasi-corporate enterprises	...	...	...	...	...	...
B Interest	9014.1	570.3	8443.8	10813.9	808.1	10005.8
C Dividends	332.3	205.3	127.0	342.3	172.2	170.2
D Net land rent and royalties	11.9	11.9	-	12.6	12.6	...
3 Current transfers	1611.0	452.5	1158.5	1856.6	583.2	1273.4
A Casualty insurance claims	245.9	244.4	1.5	273.8	271.8	2.0
B Casualty insurance premiums, net, due to be received by insurance companies	703.2	...	703.2	777.8	...	777.8
C Current transfers from the rest of the world	...	...	...	...	...	...
D Other transfers except imputed	195.3	2.8	192.5	273.1	1.2	271.9
E Imputed unfunded employee pension and welfare contributions	466.6	205.3	261.3	531.9	310.2	221.7
Total Current Receipts	16389.4	8359.7	8029.7	18831.1	9230.3	9600.7
Disbursements						
1 Property and entrepreneurial income	10236.0	4680.8	5555.2	12065.1	5182.4	6882.6
A Withdrawals from quasi-corporations	...	...	...	...	...	...
B Interest	8631.9	3376.0	5256.0	10388.1	3987.7	6400.4
C Dividends	1499.0	1199.9	299.2	1552.4	1070.2	482.2
D Net land rent and royalties	104.9	104.9	...	124.6	124.6	...
2 Direct taxes and other current transfers n.e.c. to general government	1571.2	1243.3	327.9	1789.2	1432.2	357.0
A Direct taxes	1571.2	1243.3	327.9	1789.2	1432.2	357.0
B Fines, fees, penalties and other current transfers n.e.c.	...	...	...	...	...	...

Spain

3.22 Corporate and Quasi-Corporate Enterprise Income and Outlay Account: Total and Sectors
(Continued)

Thousand Million Spanish pesetas

	1989			1990		
	TOTAL	Non-Financial	Financial	TOTAL	Non-Financial	Financial
3 Other current transfers	1494.4	539.9	954.5	1753.3	671.3	1082.1
A Casualty insurance premiums, net	267.1	263.3	3.9	295.7	290.4	5.3
B Casualty insurance claims liability of insurance companies	703.2	...	703.2	777.8	...	777.8
C Transfers to private non-profit institutions	...	...	...	...	...	...
D Unfunded employee pension and welfare benefits	359.7	205.3	154.4	498.7	310.2	188.5
E Social assistance grants	...	...	...	...	...	...
F Other transfers n.e.c.	164.3	71.3	93.0	181.1	70.6	110.5
G Transfers to the rest of the world	...	...	...	...	...	...
Statistical discrepancy	262.4	...	262.4	252.7	...	252.7
Net saving	2825.4	1895.8	929.7	2970.7	1944.4	1026.3
Total Current Disbursements and Net Saving	16389.4	8359.8	8029.7	18831.0	9230.3	9600.7

3.23 Corporate and Quasi-Corporate Enterprise Capital Accumulation Account: Total and Sectors

Thousand Million Spanish pesetas

	1985			1986			1987			1988		
	TOTAL	Non-Financial	Financial	TOTAL	Non-Financial	Financial	TOTAL	Non-Financial	Financial	TOTAL	Non-Financial	Financial
Finance of Gross Accumulation												
1 Gross saving	3917.4	3348.1	569.3	4490.6	3962.6	527.8	4999.6	4172.7	826.9	5522.6	4749.3	773.3
A Consumption of fixed capital	2405.3	2317.0	88.3	2505.8	2411.6	94.1	2656.8	2548.2	108.6	2892.6	2770.4	122.2
B Net saving	1512.1	1031.1	481.0	1984.8	1551.0	433.7	2342.8	1624.5	718.3	2630.0	1978.9	651.1
2 Capital transfers	649.1	601.5	47.7	735.3	685.8	49.5	629.3	579.1	50.2	664.9	624.9	40.0
Finance of Gross Accumulation	4566.5	3949.6	617.0	5225.9	4648.4	577.3	5628.9	4751.8	877.1	6187.5	5374.2	813.3
Gross Accumulation												
1 Gross capital formation	3162.8	3025.1	137.7	3870.2	3768.2	102.0	4854.6	4690.2	164.4	5859.6	5676.0	183.6
A Increase in stocks	...	...	...	...	...	...	...	...	...	...	...	...
B Gross fixed capital formation	3162.8	3025.1	137.7	3870.2	3768.2	102.0	4854.6	4690.2	164.4	5859.6	5676.0	183.6
2 Purchases of land, net	-	-	-	12.8	12.8	-	75.9	75.9	-	31.9	31.9	-
3 Purchases of intangible assets, net	...	...	-	...	...	...	...	...	-	...	...	...
4 Capital transfers	106.7	52.8	53.8	96.0	43.2	52.8	84.6	24.3	60.3	88.0	45.0	42.9
Net lending	1297.1	871.6	425.4	1246.8	824.2	422.5	613.9	-38.5	652.4	208.1	-378.7	586.8
Gross Accumulation	4566.6	3949.6	616.9	5225.8	4648.4	577.3	5629.0	4751.9	877.1	6187.6	5374.2	813.3

	1989			1990		
	TOTAL	Non-Financial	Financial	TOTAL	Non-Financial	Financial
Finance of Gross Accumulation						
1 Gross saving	5978.0	4903.5	1074.6	6419.3	5222.7	1196.5
A Consumption of fixed capital	3152.6	3007.7	144.9	3448.6	3278.3	170.2
B Net saving	2825.4	1895.8	929.7	2970.7	1944.4	1026.3
2 Capital transfers	817.3	764.5	52.8	734.0	642.3	91.7
Finance of Gross Accumulation	6795.3	5668.0	1127.4	7153.3	5865.0	1288.2
Gross Accumulation						
1 Gross capital formation	6884.7	6578.2	306.5	7530.7	7143.5	387.2
A Increase in stocks	...	...	...	...	...	...
B Gross fixed capital formation	6884.7	6578.2	306.5	7530.7	7143.5	387.2
2 Purchases of land, net	46.5	46.5	-	33.8	33.8	-
3 Purchases of intangible assets, net	...	...	-	...	...	...
4 Capital transfers	115.9	58.4	57.5	182.2	72.3	109.8
Net lending	-251.8	-1015.1	763.3	-593.4	-1384.6	791.2
Gross Accumulation	6795.3	5668.0	1127.3	7153.3	5865.0	1288.2

3.32 Household and Private Unincorporated Enterprise Income and Outlay Account

Thousand Million Spanish pesetas

	1980	1981	1982	1983	1984	1985	1986	1987	1988	1989	1990	1991
Receipts												
1 Compensation of employees	7797.5	8734.4	9877.4	11162.3	11907.5	12922.5 / 12936.2	14626.1	16347.7	18235.8	20449.6	23108.0	...
A Wages and salaries	6029.0	6698.7	7554.1	8494.5	9102.2	9757.5 / ...	...	...	...	...	...	...
B Employers' contributions for social security	1768.5	2035.7	2323.4	2667.8	2805.3	3165.0 / ...	...	...	...	...	...	
C Employers' contributions for private pension & welfare plans						...	...	...	...	...	...	
2 Operating surplus of private unincorporated enterprises	3557.0	3950.5	4671.3	5327.8	6254.8	7004.9 / 6559.6	7546.6	8436.8	9407.9	10363.6	11605.5	...
3 Property and entrepreneurial income	782.4	1077.1	1192.9	1324.0	1614.8	1922.8 / 2103.1	2258.1	2499.1	2927.6	3388.3	3883.9	...
A Withdrawals from private quasi-corporations	...	...	...	...	...	...						
B Interest	679.1	946.4	1030.4	1132.3	1434.1	1699.5 / 1753.8	1855.1	2011.1	2248.9	2681.9	3237.7	...
C Dividends	102.3	129.5	161.2	190.1	179.1	217.8 / 347.5	401.0	485.8	676.5	703.6	642.0	...
D Net land rent and royalties	0.9	1.2	1.3	1.5	1.7	5.6 / 1.8	2.0	2.2	2.3	2.8	4.2	...
3 Current transfers	2592.5	3181.3	3667.6	4279.5	4726.9	5405.8 / 5206.6	5850.8	6554.3	7278.1	8314.5	9466.5	...
A Casualty insurance claims	91.7	105.3	128.3	174.0	176.7	205.6 / 178.2	224.6	299.8	347.8	461.4	510.4	...
B Social security benefits	2126.0	2639.2	3012.2	3509.2	3937.0	4480.1 / 4273.7	4767.7	5289.5	5860.3	6617.4	7699.7	...
C Social assistance grants	...	...	...	...	...	...	...	...	...	...	...	...
D Unfunded employee pension and welfare benefits	...	...	...	...	...	...	...	...	...	...	...	...
E Transfers from general government	...	...	...	...	...	...	...	...	...	...	...	...
F Transfers from the rest of the world	116.7	133.4	143.9	156.2	157.0	168.5 / 187.3	175.5	167.9	183.5	195.1	197.1	...
G Other transfers n.e.c.	258.1	303.4	383.2	440.1	456.3	551.6 / 567.3	683.1	797.1	886.5	1040.6	1059.3	...
Statistical discrepancy a	10.4	2.2	1.5	-	25.3	47.0 / 47.0	168.1	154.6	396.5	262.5	252.9	...
Total Current Receipts b	14739.8	16945.5	19410.7	22093.6	24529.3	27303.0 / 26852.5	30449.7	33992.5	38245.9	42778.5	48316.8	...
Disbursements												
1 Final consumption expenditures	10080.4	11457.9	13143.3	14808.1	16370.0	18137.7 / 18080.0	20437.7	22855.8	25179.6	28344.9	31284.4	...
2 Property income	406.9	612.9	692.4	798.2	1015.2	1044.0 / 789.5	955.1	1184.3	1478.5	1766.4	2179.0	...
A Interest	406.9	612.9	692.4	798.2	1015.2	1044.0 / 789.5	955.1	1184.3	1478.5	1766.4	2179.0	...
B Net land rent and royalties	...	...	...	...	...	...	...	...	...	...	...	...
3 Direct taxes and other current transfers n.e.c. to government	2683.3	3070.3	3439.1	4152.6	4661.5	5207.2 / 5225.1	5868.8	7162.1	7972.6	9385.0	10547.9	...
A Social security contributions	1883.7	2144.4	2457.6	2838.7	3057.4	3384.8 / 3390.8	3908.8	4420.5	4820.6	5525.9	6318.7	...
B Direct taxes	799.6	925.9	981.5	1313.9	1604.0	1822.4 / 1834.3	1960.0	2741.7	3152.0	3859.1	4229.2	...
Income taxes	...	...	...	...	...	...	...	...	...	...	...	
Other	...	...	...	...	...	...	...	...	...	...	...	
C Fees, fines and penalties	...	...	...	...	...	...	...	...	...	...	...	

Spain

3.32 Household and Private Unincorporated Enterprise Income and Outlay Account
(Continued)

Thousand Million Spanish pesetas

	1980	1981	1982	1983	1984	1985	1986	1987	1988	1989	1990	1991
4 Other current transfers	665.3	758.5	853.6	1006.3	1067.4	1248.9 1359.3	1565.0	1747.4	2088.4	2169.0	2428.6	...
A Net casualty insurance premiums	75.5	86.6	104.5	141.5	143.9	165.1 164.3	209.7	282.0	327.9	433.9	478.5	...
B Transfers to private non-profit institutions serving households	1.3	3.3	3.6	3.0	4.4	3.7 ...	...	...	...	...	...	...
C Transfers to the rest of the world	0.5	0.9	1.5	2.1	3.2	21.5 21.5	17.2	15.0	17.8	28.0	21.6	...
D Other current transfers, except imputed	271.6	292.6	312.6	359.4	369.9	408.4 607.3	667.9	773.6	853.0	876.3	969.7	...
E Imputed employee pension and welfare contributions	316.4	375.1	431.5	500.4	546.1	650.3 566.2	670.2	676.8	889.7	830.9	958.7	...
Net saving	903.7	1045.9	1282.4	1328.5	1415.1	1665.3 1398.6	1623.1	1042.9	1526.8	1113.1	1877.0	...
Total Current Disbursements and Net Saving b	14739.6	16945.5	19410.8	22093.7	24529.2	27303.1 26852.5	30449.7	33992.5	38245.9	42778.4	48316.9	...

a) Item 'Statistical discrepancy' refers to the increase in the net equity of households in private pension and life insurance funds.　b) Private non-profit institutions serving households are included in household and private unincorporated enterprises.

3.33 Household and Private Unincorporated Enterprise Capital Accumulation Account

Thousand Million Spanish pesetas

	1980	1981	1982	1983	1984	1985	1986	1987	1988	1989	1990	1991
				Finance of Gross Accumulation								
1 Gross saving	1253.9	1471.4	1788.0	1907.4	2065.4	2356.7 2291.7	2653.3	2208.6	2838.7	2563.0	3477.9	...
A Consumption of fixed capital	350.2	425.5	505.6	578.9	650.3	691.4 893.1	1030.2	1165.7	1311.9	1449.9	1600.9	...
B Net saving	903.7	1045.9	1282.4	1328.5	1415.1	1665.3 1398.6	1623.1	1042.9	1526.8	1113.1	1877.0	...
2 Capital transfers	12.1	18.3	28.4	40.8	48.3	50.6 40.2	49.5	63.5	76.1	112.6	128.8	...
Total Finance of Gross Accumulation a	1266.0	1489.7	1816.4	1948.2	2113.7	2407.3 2331.9	2702.8	2272.1	2914.8	2675.6	3606.7	...
				Gross Accumulation								
1 Gross Capital Formation	902.7	994.8	1122.2	1149.1	1252.8	1321.9 1265.2	1459.1	1732.0	2166.5	2440.0	2757.2	...
A Increase in stocks	...	...	...	...	...	... ...	...	...	...	...	...	...
B Gross fixed capital formation	902.7	994.8	1122.2	1149.1	1252.8	1321.9 1265.2	1459.1	1732.0	2166.5	2440.0	2757.2	...
2 Purchases of land, net	-8.0	-24.8	-27.2	-24.3	-37.9	-50.4 -50.4	-62.6	-132.1	-96.6	-69.5	-127.2	...
3 Purchases of intangibles, net	...	...	...	...	...	... ...	...	...	...	...	...	...
4 Capital transfers	28.3	35.6	33.5	42.2	53.4	65.2 65.2	64.4	75.7	108.9	113.2	124.4	...
Net lending	343.0	484.1	688.0	781.4	845.5	1070.6 1051.9	1242.0	596.4	736.0	191.9	852.3	...
Total Gross Accumulation a	1266.0	1489.7	1816.5	1948.4	2113.8	2407.3 2331.9	2702.9	2272.0	2914.8	2675.6	3606.7	...

a) Private non-profit institutions serving households are included in household and private unincorporated enterprises.

3.51 External Transactions: Current Account: Detail

Thousand Million Spanish pesetas

	1980	1981	1982	1983	1984	1985	1986	1987	1988	1989	1990	1991
				Payments to the Rest of the World								
1 Imports of goods and services	2758.5	3428.3	4024.3	4860.1	5363.3	5914.8 5860.1	5729.7	6935.1	8022.5	9620.6	10250.7	11128.1
A Imports of merchandise c.i.f.	2480.7	3045.6	3561.1	4300.4	4753.3	5205.2 5206.7	5035.9	6137.0	7101.3	8523.1	9024.6	9799.8
B Other	277.8	382.7	463.3	559.6	610.0	709.6 653.4	693.8	798.1	921.1	1097.5	1226.0	1328.3
2 Factor income to the rest of the world	256.9	429.3	496.3	552.4	641.5	645.2 868.9	703.9	684.4	887.4	1107.4	1299.7	1758.2

3.51 External Transactions: Current Account: Detail
(Continued)

Thousand Million Spanish pesetas

	1980	1981	1982	1983	1984	1985	1986	1987	1988	1989	1990	1991
A Compensation of employees	0.6	0.3	0.4	0.4	0.5	0.9 / 0.9	1.4	1.5	1.5	1.8	1.7	1.9
B Property and entrepreneurial income	256.3	428.9	495.9	552.1	641.0	644.3 / 867.9	702.4	682.9	886.0	1105.6	1298.0	1756.3
3 Current transfers to the rest of the world	34.9	44.9	51.1	71.0	69.3	113.5 / 114.1	214.4	269.0	368.6	453.2	540.7	760.7
A Indirect taxes by general government to supranational organizations	...	...	...	...	...	... / -	89.1	134.5	232.1	240.4	370.4	478.5
B Other current transfers	34.9	44.9	51.1	71.0	69.3	113.5 / 114.1	125.3	134.5	136.5	212.8	170.3	282.2
By general government	3.4	3.7	6.9	9.6	8.8	14.1 / 14.1	19.8	26.2	20.3	60.8	24.5	86.5
By other resident sectors	31.5	41.2	44.2	61.4	60.4	99.4 / 100.0	105.4	108.3	116.2	151.9	145.8	195.7
4 Surplus of the nation on current transactions	-364.3	-458.0	-487.1	-338.0	354.8	459.9 / 397.3	523.3	32.3	-433.3	-1453.6	-1847.8	-2090.2
Payments to the Rest of the World, and Surplus of the Nation on Current Transfers	2686.0	3444.5	4084.6	5145.5	6428.9	7133.4 / 7240.4	7171.3	7920.8	8845.2	9727.6	10243.3	11556.8

Receipts From The Rest of the World

	1980	1981	1982	1983	1984	1985	1986	1987	1988	1989	1990	1991
1 Exports of goods and services	2409.8	3079.1	3672.2	4725.6	5943.5	6518.7 / 6407.2	6416.9	6995.8	7574.8	8150.4	8555.2	9300.3
A Exports of merchandise f.o.b.	1531.6	1976.2	2372.2	3066.8	3936.1	4296.2 / 4280.5	3939.8	4306.1	4738.8	5260.6	5681.0	6169.6
B Other	878.2	1102.8	1300.0	1658.7	2007.4	2222.5 / 2126.7	2477.1	2689.7	2836.0	2889.8	2874.2	3130.7
2 Factor income from the rest of the world	127.0	191.1	211.6	194.3	244.7	314.7 / 538.2	407.5	379.9	476.8	723.7	852.4	1189.8
A Compensation of employees	14.2	19.8	24.6	30.3	31.8	32.4 / 32.4	38.3	42.0	38.5	38.1	35.4	36.2
B Property and entrepreneurial income	112.8	171.3	187.0	163.9	212.9	282.3 / 505.7	369.1	337.9	438.4	685.6	817.0	1153.6
3 Current transfers from the rest of the world	149.3	174.2	200.6	225.7	240.7	300.0 / 295.0	346.8	545.1	793.6	853.5	835.7	1066.6
A Subsidies to general government from supranational organizations	...	...	...	...	...	... / -	37.9	123.5	281.1	247.3	304.0	455.9
B Other current transfers	149.3	174.2	200.6	225.7	240.7	300.0 / 295.0	308.9	421.6	512.5	606.2	531.7	610.7
To general government	-	0.1	0.2	0.4	0.1	0.1 / 0.1	24.2	39.1	52.0	81.9	70.1	171.8
To other resident sectors	149.3	174.1	200.4	225.3	240.6	299.9 / 294.9	284.7	382.5	460.4	524.2	461.6	438.9
Receipts from the Rest of the World on Current Transfers	2686.1	3444.4	4084.4	5145.6	6428.9	7133.4 / 7240.4	7171.2	7920.8	8845.2	9727.6	10243.3	11556.7

Spain

3.52 External Transactions: Capital Accumulation Account

Thousand Million Spanish pesetas

	1980	1981	1982	1983	1984	1985	1986	1987	1988	1989	1990	1991
Finance of Gross Accumulation												
1 Surplus of the nation on current transactions	-364.3	-458.0	-487.1	-338.0	354.8	459.9 397.3	523.3	32.3	-433.3	-1453.6	-1847.8	-2090.2
2 Capital transfers from the rest of the world	0.4	0.6	0.2	0.4	-	0.1 0.1	40.6	50.0	73.6	143.0	157.8	341.5
Total Finance of Gross Accumulation	-363.9	-457.4	-486.9	-337.6	354.8	460.0 397.4	563.9	82.3	-359.7	-1310.6	-1690.0	-1748.7
Gross Accumulation												
1 Capital transfers to the rest of the world	1.6	2.2	2.9	2.6	5.3	5.4 5.4	5.1	2.0	2.1	8.8	17.2	13.0
2 Purchases of intangible assets, n.e.c., net, from the rest of the world	...	...	...	...	...	... ...	...	...	...	...	...	...
Net lending to the rest of the world	-365.5	-459.7	-489.8	-340.2	349.5	454.6 392.0	558.7	80.4	-361.8	-1319.5	-1707.2	-1761.7
Total Gross Accumulation	-363.9	-457.5	-486.9	-337.6	354.8	460.0 397.4	563.8	82.4	-359.7	-1310.7	-1690.0	-1748.7

4.1 Derivation of Value Added by Kind of Activity, in Current Prices

Thousand Million Spanish pesetas

	1985			1986			1987			1988		
	Gross Output	Intermediate Consumption	Value Added	Gross Output	Intermediate Consumption	Value Added	Gross Output	Intermediate Consumption	Value Added	Gross Output	Intermediate Consumption	Value Added
All Producers												
1 Agriculture, hunting, forestry and fishing	3447.2	1778.3	1668.9	3623.5	1808.5	1815.1	3873.7	1904.1	1969.6	4173.1	2044.5	2128.6
2 Mining and quarrying	378.5	103.9	274.6	334.2	88.1	246.1	306.4	82.6	223.8	309.6	83.6	226.0
A Coal mining	243.1	71.3	171.8	246.1	69.3	176.8	223.5	67.5	156.0	223.8	68.4	155.4
B Crude petroleum and natural gas production	135.3	32.6	102.8	88.1	18.8	69.3	83.0	15.2	67.8	85.8	15.2	70.7
C Metal ore mining	...	...	...	...	...	...	...	...	...	...	...	...
D Other mining	...	...	...	...	...	...	...	...	...	...	...	...
3 Manufacturing	20793.4	13261.7	7531.8	20670.7	12348.3	8322.4	22179.0	13149.3	9029.7	23901.0	14221.9	9679.1
A Manufacture of food, beverages and tobacco	4578.5	3096.8	1481.7	4747.7	3137.1	1610.7	5087.3	3320.2	1767.1	5377.4	3518.2	1859.2
B Textile, wearing apparel and leather industries	1733.5	954.5	778.9	1801.1	961.7	839.5	1902.5	1012.9	889.6	1971.4	1063.6	907.8
C Manufacture of wood and wood products, including furniture	534.3	293.9	240.4	574.7	309.9	264.8	643.1	351.6	291.4	725.9	404.8	321.1
D Manufacture of paper and paper products, printing and publishing	895.0	508.9	386.1	974.7	529.5	445.2	1077.3	574.1	503.2	1185.2	646.7	538.5
E Manufacture of chemicals and chemical petroleum, coal, rubber and plastic products	4767.2	3214.9	1552.3	4148.9	2279.9	1869.0	4325.2	2365.5	1959.7	4375.4	2364.7	2010.7
F Manufacture of non-metallic mineral products, except products of petroleum and coal	983.3	476.5	506.8	1048.8	477.3	571.4	1137.1	511.5	625.6	1326.6	603.9	722.7
G Basic metal industries	2140.1	1701.2	438.9	1845.9	1402.1	443.8	1769.2	1330.5	438.7	1922.7	1435.8	487.0
H Manufacture of fabricated metal products, machinery and equipment	4901.2	2862.5	2038.7	5261.4	3096.1	2165.3	5958.4	3522.4	2436.0	6722.4	4016.4	2706.0
I Other manufacturing industries	260.5	152.5	108.0	267.4	154.7	112.7	279.0	160.5	118.4	294.0	167.9	126.1
4 Electricity, gas and water	1434.8	618.3	816.5	1435.5	576.9	858.6	1582.4	576.8	1005.6	1725.3	568.4	1156.9
A Electricity, gas and steam	1322.6	587.3	735.3	1316.0	544.0	772.1	1448.9	540.2	908.8	1575.0	526.8	1048.2
B Water works and supply	112.3	31.1	81.2	119.4	32.9	86.5	133.5	36.7	96.8	150.3	41.5	108.7
5 Construction	3604.1	1708.9	1895.2	4021.2	1918.5	2102.6	4597.3	2110.6	2486.7	5510.2	2488.4	3021.8
6 Wholesale and retail trade, restaurants and hotels	8692.5	3003.0	5689.5	9716.7	3223.8	6492.9	10882.1	3603.7	7278.3	12200.0	4056.1	8143.9
A Wholesale and retail trade	5278.0	1271.4	4006.6	5906.6	1346.6	4560.1	6493.5	1482.4	5011.1	7210.2	1673.9	5536.3
B Restaurants and hotels	3414.6	1731.6	1682.9	3810.0	1877.2	1932.8	4388.6	2121.3	2267.3	4989.8	2382.2	2607.6
7 Transport, storage and communication	2853.7	1274.0	1579.7	2945.4	1190.3	1755.1	3281.4	1307.7	1973.7	3644.6	1438.7	2206.0
A Transport and storage	2295.6	1209.8	1085.9	2372.3	1121.7	1250.6	2651.0	1233.9	1417.1	2911.3	1355.0	1556.3
B Communication	558.0	64.2	493.8	573.1	68.6	504.5	630.4	73.8	556.6	733.3	83.7	649.6
8 Finance, insurance, real estate and business services [a] ..	6321.2	1324.9	4996.4	6904.6	1481.1	5423.5	7647.0	1609.6	6037.4	8686.0	1873.5	6812.5
A Financial institutions	2271.3	508.4	1762.9	2548.4	585.2	1963.2	2965.9	696.9	2269.1	3495.0	837.9	2657.0

4.1 Derivation of Value Added by Kind of Activity, in Current Prices
(Continued)

Thousand Million Spanish pesetas

	1985			1986			1987			1988		
	Gross Output	Intermediate Consumption	Value Added	Gross Output	Intermediate Consumption	Value Added	Gross Output	Intermediate Consumption	Value Added	Gross Output	Intermediate Consumption	Value Added
B Insurance	...	...	...	...	...	...	...	...	...	...	...	...
C Real estate and business services	4049.9	816.4	3233.5	4356.1	895.8	3460.3	4681.1	912.8	3768.3	5191.1	1035.6	4155.5
9 Community, social and personal services ab	1727.2	366.9	1360.3	1954.8	413.4	1541.5	2183.6	455.5	1728.0	2404.4	502.1	1902.4
A Sanitary and similar services	373.3	85.4	287.9	431.3	101.2	330.0	488.0	112.4	375.6	542.0	124.2	417.8
B Social and related community services	...	...	...	...	...	...	...	...	...	...	...	...
Educational services	285.3	73.1	212.3	319.0	79.0	240.0	341.7	83.7	258.0	373.7	94.2	279.5
Medical, dental, other health and veterinary services	...	...	...	...	...	...	...	...	...	...	...	...
C Recreational and cultural services	...	...	...	...	...	...	...	...	...	...	...	...
D Personal and household services	...	...	...	...	...	...	...	...	...	...	...	...
Total, Industries	49252.7	23439.9	25812.8	51606.4	23048.7	28557.7	56532.9	24800.1	31732.9	62554.3	27277.0	35277.3
Producers of Government Services	4453.3	1185.7	3267.6	5069.2	1404.6	3664.6	5811.0	1704.3	4106.8	6361.8	1769.3	4592.5
Other Producers b	294.4	40.8	253.6	323.2	46.6	276.6	364.3	51.2	313.0	402.8	56.2	346.7
Total	54000.4	24666.4	29334.1	56998.8	24499.9	32498.9	62708.2	26555.6	36152.6	69318.9	29102.5	40216.5
Less: Imputed bank service charge	...	-1689.5	1689.5	...	-1971.9	1971.9	...	-2321.5	2321.5	...	-2682.8	2682.8
Import duties	556.4	...	556.4	329.2	...	329.2	396.4	...	396.4	440.4	...	440.4
Value added tax	-	...	-	1467.8	...	1467.8	1916.5	...	1916.5	2184.6	...	2184.6
Total	54556.8	26355.9	28200.9	58795.8	26471.8	32324.0	65021.1	28877.1	36144.1	71943.9	31785.3	40158.7

a) Business services and real estate except dwellings are included in item 'Community, social and personal services'.

b) Item 'Other producers' is included in item 'Community, social and personal services'.

4.2 Derivation of Value Added by Kind of Activity, in Constant Prices

Thousand Million Spanish pesetas

	1986			1987			1988			1989		
	Gross Output	Intermediate Consumption	Value Added	Gross Output	Intermediate Consumption	Value Added	Gross Output	Intermediate Consumption	Value Added	Gross Output	Intermediate Consumption	Value Added
						At constant prices of:1986						
						All Producers						
1 Agriculture, hunting, forestry and fishing	...	...	1815.1	...	...	2025.4	...	...	2091.7	...	...	1951.1
2 Mining and quarrying	...	...	246.1	...	...	224.2	...	...	226.1	...	...	249.6
A Coal mining	...	...	176.8	...	...	152.3	...	...	146.6	...	...	157.5
B Crude petroleum and natural gas production	...	...	69.3	...	...	71.9	...	...	79.5	...	...	92.2
C Metal ore mining	...	...	...	...	...	...	...	...	...	...	...	...
D Other mining	...	...	...	...	...	...	...	...	...	...	...	...
3 Manufacturing	...	...	8322.4	...	...	8750.7	...	...	9127.5	...	...	9473.1
A Manufacture of food, beverages and tobacco	...	...	1610.7	...	...	1695.0	...	...	1753.9	...	...	1770.1
B Textile, wearing apparel and leather industries	...	...	839.5	...	...	865.3	...	...	840.8	...	...	840.9
C Manufacture of wood and wood products, including furniture	...	...	264.8	...	...	275.3	...	...	281.3	...	...	290.3
D Manufacture of paper and paper products, printing and publishing	...	...	445.2	...	...	481.4	...	...	473.0	...	...	506.9
E Manufacture of chemicals and chemical petroleum, coal, rubber and plastic products	...	...	1869.0	...	...	1978.1	...	...	2099.6	...	...	2178.5
F Manufacture of non-metallic mineral products, except products of petroleum and coal	...	...	571.4	...	...	598.5	...	...	650.1	...	...	667.3
G Basic metal industries	...	...	443.8	...	...	443.2	...	...	469.3	...	...	493.3
H Manufacture of fabricated metal products, machinery and equipment	...	...	2165.3	...	...	2300.5	...	...	2440.6	...	...	2604.2
I Other manufacturing industries	...	...	112.7	...	...	113.6	...	...	119.0	...	...	121.6
4 Electricity, gas and water	...	...	858.6	...	...	899.3	...	...	968.5	...	...	950.3
A Electricity, gas and steam	...	...	772.1	...	...	815.6	...	...	883.0	...	...	863.1
B Water works and supply	...	...	86.5	...	...	83.7	...	...	85.5	...	...	87.2

Spain

4.2 Derivation of Value Added by Kind of Activity, in Constant Prices
(Continued)

Thousand Million Spanish pesetas

	1986			1987			1988			1989		
	Gross Output	Intermediate Consumption	Value Added	Gross Output	Intermediate Consumption	Value Added	Gross Output	Intermediate Consumption	Value Added	Gross Output	Intermediate Consumption	Value Added
				At constant prices of:1986								
5 Construction	...	...	2102.6	...	...	2277.8	...	...	2508.7	...	...	2855.2
6 Wholesale and retail trade, restaurants and hotels	...	...	6492.9	...	...	6824.5	...	...	7123.6	...	...	7463.7
A Wholesale and retail trade	...	...	4560.1	...	...	4756.4	...	...	4967.6	...	...	5202.2
B Restaurants and hotels	...	...	1932.8	...	...	2068.1	...	...	2155.9	...	...	2261.5
7 Transport, storage and communication	...	...	1755.1	...	...	1829.2	...	...	1904.3	...	...	2020.0
A Transport and storage	...	...	1250.6	...	...	1323.7	...	...	1368.9	...	...	1429.6
B Communication	...	...	504.5	...	...	505.6	...	...	535.4	...	...	590.4
8 Finance, insurance, real estate and business services a	...	...	5423.5	...	...	5697.4	...	...	6017.0	...	...	6328.3
A Financial institutions	...	...	1963.2	...	...	2099.7	...	...	2265.0	...	...	2425.5
B Insurance	...	...	...	...	...	...	...	...	...	...	...	...
C Real estate and business services	...	...	3460.3	...	...	3597.8	...	...	3752.0	...	...	3902.9
9 Community, social and personal services ab	...	...	1541.5	...	...	1616.8	...	...	1675.9	...	...	1805.7
A Sanitary and similar services	...	...	330.0	...	...	347.9	...	...	362.3	...	...	394.5
B Social and related community services	...	...	...	...	...	...	...	...	...	...	...	...
Educational services	...	...	240.0	...	...	243.8	...	...	247.7	...	...	253.0
Medical, dental, other health and veterinary services	...	...	...	...	...	...	...	...	...	...	...	...
C Recreational and cultural services	...	...	...	...	...	...	...	...	...	...	...	...
D Personal and household services	...	...	...	...	...	...	...	...	...	...	...	...
Total, Industries	...	...	28557.7	...	...	30145.4	...	...	31643.2	...	...	33097.1
Producers of Government Services	...	...	3664.6	...	...	3872.7	...	...	4111.8	...	...	4401.4
Other Producers b	...	...	276.6	...	...	292.7	...	...	307.7	...	...	323.6
Total	...	...	32498.9	...	...	34310.8	...	...	36062.6	...	...	37822.1
Less: Imputed bank service charge	...	...	1971.9	...	...	2159.2	...	...	2311.8	...	...	2516.1
Import duties	...	...	329.2	...	...	418.6	...	...	499.7	...	...	532.5
Value added tax	...	...	1467.8	...	...	1577.4	...	...	1659.5	...	...	1775.6
Total	...	...	32324.0	...	...	34147.6	...	...	35910.1	...	...	37614.1

a) Business services and real estate except dwellings are included in item 'Community, social and personal services'.
b) Item 'Other producers' is included in item 'Community, social and personal services'.

4.3 Cost Components of Value Added

Thousand Million Spanish pesetas

	1985						1986					
	Compensation of Employees	Capital Consumption	Net Operating Surplus	Indirect Taxes	Less: Subsidies Received	Value Added	Compensation of Employees	Capital Consumption	Net Operating Surplus	Indirect Taxes	Less: Subsidies Received	Value Added
					All Producers							
1 Agriculture, hunting, forestry and fishing	475.7	...	1248.3	-55.0	...	1668.9	487.4	...	1397.9	-70.3	...	1815.1
2 Mining and quarrying	136.5	...	161.3	-23.3	...	274.6	148.0	...	125.0	-26.9	...	246.1
A Coal mining	128.6	...	70.4	-27.3	...	171.8	140.7	...	64.5	-28.4	...	176.8
B Crude petroleum and natural gas production	7.9	...	90.9	4.0	...	102.8	7.3	...	60.5	1.5	...	69.3
C Metal ore mining	...	...	...	...	...	...	...	...	...	...	...	...
D Other mining	...	...	...	...	...	...	...	...	...	...	...	...

4.3 Cost Components of Value Added
(Continued)

Thousand Million Spanish pesetas

	1985						1986					
	Compensation of Employees	Capital Consumption	Net Operating Surplus	Indirect Taxes	Less: Subsidies Received	Value Added	Compensation of Employees	Capital Consumption	Net Operating Surplus	Indirect Taxes	Less: Subsidies Received	Value Added
3 Manufacturing	3605.4	...	3021.9	904.4	...	7531.8	3964.9	...	3720.6	636.8	...	8322.4
A Manufacture of food, beverages and tobacco	493.9	...	723.8	264.0	...	1481.7	541.8	...	858.5	210.4	...	1610.7
B Textile, wearing apparel and leather industries	442.2	...	320.8	15.9	...	778.9	481.8	...	351.4	6.2	...	839.5
C Manufacture of wood and wood products, including furniture	146.4	...	81.8	12.2	...	240.4	161.9	...	96.6	6.3	...	264.8
D Manufacture of paper and paper products, printing and publishing	186.8	...	182.7	16.6	...	386.1	230.2	...	208.0	7.1	...	445.2
E Manufacture of chemicals and chemical petroleum, coal, rubber and plastic products	508.2	...	616.2	428.0	...	1552.3	555.8	...	956.3	356.9	...	1869.0
F Manufacture of non-metallic mineral products, except products of petroleum and coal	250.1	...	234.8	21.9	...	506.8	270.2	...	292.4	8.8	...	571.4
G Basic metal industries	234.4	...	228.1	-23.6	...	438.9	241.3	...	213.5	-11.0	...	443.8
H Manufacture of fabricated metal products, machinery and equipment	1285.2	...	598.0	155.5	...	2038.7	1412.7	...	703.8	48.8	...	2165.3
I Other manufacturing industries	58.3	...	35.7	14.0	...	108.0	69.2	...	40.1	3.4	...	112.7
4 Electricity, gas and water	229.7	...	498.7	88.1	...	816.5	251.1	...	580.8	26.6	...	858.6
A Electricity, gas and steam	198.2	...	442.2	94.9	...	735.3	216.4	...	520.2	35.4	...	772.1
B Water works and supply	31.6	...	56.5	-6.9	...	81.2	34.7	...	60.6	-8.8	...	86.5
5 Construction	961.8	...	817.4	116.0	...	1895.2	1142.5	...	907.8	52.4	...	2102.6
6 Wholesale and retail trade, restaurants and hotels	1593.1	...	3801.1	295.3	...	5689.5	1846.2	...	4252.8	393.9	...	6492.9
A Wholesale and retail trade	1156.0	...	2614.1	236.5	...	4006.6	1333.4	...	2878.3	348.4	...	4560.1
B Restaurants and hotels	437.1	...	1187.0	58.8	...	1682.9	512.7	...	1374.5	45.6	...	1932.8
7 Transport, storage and communication	854.5	...	908.4	-183.2	...	1579.7	923.8	...	1014.1	-182.7	...	1755.1
A Transport and storage	644.5	...	686.5	-245.2	...	1085.9	684.3	...	756.9	-190.6	...	1250.6
B Communication	210.0	...	221.8	62.0	...	493.8	239.5	...	257.2	7.8	...	504.5
8 Finance, insurance, real estate and business services a	1179.1	...	3502.5	314.8	...	4996.4	1481.9	...	3718.7	222.9	...	5423.5
A Financial institutions	869.3	...	825.6	68.0	...	1762.9	1099.0	...	844.3	19.9	...	1963.2
B Insurance	...	...	...	...	...	...	...	...	...	...	...	...
C Real estate and business services	309.8	...	2676.8	246.8	...	3233.5	382.9	...	2874.5	202.9	...	3460.3
9 Community, social and personal services ab	639.9	...	752.4	-32.0	...	1360.3	727.6	...	845.8	-32.0	...	1541.5
A Sanitary and similar services	128.5	...	156.0	3.3	...	287.9	150.8	...	178.1	1.2	...	330.0
B Social and related community services	...	...	...	...	...	...	...	...	...	...	...	...
Educational services	215.4	...	136.8	-139.9	...	212.3	238.8	...	148.6	-147.4	...	240.0
Medical, dental, other health and veterinary services	...	...	...	...	...	...	...	...	...	...	...	...
C Recreational and cultural services	...	...	...	...	...	...	...	...	...	...	...	...
D Personal and household services	...	...	...	...	...	...	...	...	...	...	...	...
Total, Industries cd	9675.8	...	14712.0	1425.1	...	25812.8	10973.4	...	16563.6	1020.8	...	28557.7
Producers of Government Services	2978.6	...	289.0	-	...	3267.6	3342.7	...	321.9	-	...	3664.6
Other Producers b	250.4	...	3.3	...	...	253.6	273.1	...	3.5	...	...	276.6
Total cd	12904.7	...	15004.3	1425.1	...	29334.1	14589.2	...	16889.0	1020.8	...	32498.9
Less: Imputed bank service charge	...	...	1689.5	...	...	1689.5	...	...	1971.9	...	...	1971.9
Import duties	...	...	...	556.4	...	556.4	...	...	...	329.2	...	329.2
Value added tax	...	...	...	-	...	-	...	...	...	1467.8	...	1467.8
Total cd	12904.7	...	13314.8	1981.5	...	28200.9	14589.2	...	14917.1	2817.8	...	32324.0

Spain

4.3 Cost Components of Value Added

Thousand Million Spanish pesetas

	1987						1988					
	Compensation of Employees	Capital Consumption	Net Operating Surplus	Indirect Taxes	Less: Subsidies Received	Value Added	Compensation of Employees	Capital Consumption	Net Operating Surplus	Indirect Taxes	Less: Subsidies Received	Value Added
All Producers												
1 Agriculture, hunting, forestry and fishing	534.0	...	1509.6	-74.0	...	1969.6	552.5	...	1720.9	-144.8	...	2128.6
2 Mining and quarrying	152.7	...	100.8	-29.7	...	223.8	160.1	...	135.8	-69.8	...	226.0
A Coal mining	144.0	...	41.9	-30.0	...	156.0	150.0	...	75.5	-70.1	...	155.4
B Crude petroleum and natural gas production	8.7	...	58.8	0.3	...	67.8	10.1	...	60.3	0.3	...	70.7
C Metal ore mining	...	...	...	...	...	...	...	...	...	...	...	...
D Other mining	...	...	...	...	...	...	...	...	...	...	...	...
3 Manufacturing	4342.5	...	3965.6	721.6	...	9029.7	4686.7	...	4273.6	718.9	...	9679.1
A Manufacture of food, beverages and tobacco	608.9	...	992.9	165.2	...	1767.1	653.6	...	1054.2	151.4	...	1859.2
B Textile, wearing apparel and leather industries	519.0	...	363.2	7.4	...	889.6	537.2	...	362.7	8.0	...	907.8
C Manufacture of wood and wood products, including furniture	178.0	...	110.4	3.1	...	291.4	203.4	...	113.4	4.2	...	321.1
D Manufacture of paper and paper products, printing and publishing	262.0	...	238.0	3.2	...	503.2	285.1	...	251.2	2.2	...	538.5
E Manufacture of chemicals and chemical petroleum, coal, rubber and plastic products	593.7	...	848.5	517.5	...	1959.7	620.7	...	859.0	531.0	...	2010.7
F Manufacture of non-metallic mineral products, except products of petroleum and coal	294.8	...	326.0	4.8	...	625.6	328.3	...	390.2	4.3	...	722.7
G Basic metal industries	236.3	...	202.4	-0.1	...	438.7	234.7	...	253.7	-1.4	...	487.0
H Manufacture of fabricated metal products, machinery and equipment	1577.8	...	838.5	19.7	...	2436.0	1746.6	...	941.3	18.2	...	2706.0
I Other manufacturing industries	71.9	...	45.7	0.8	...	118.4	77.2	...	47.9	1.0	...	126.1
4 Electricity, gas and water	266.5	...	739.1	-	...	1005.6	284.7	...	872.5	-0.3	...	1156.9
A Electricity, gas and steam	230.1	...	665.3	13.4	...	908.8	245.4	...	792.6	10.2	...	1048.2
B Water works and supply	36.4	...	73.8	-13.4	...	96.8	39.3	...	79.9	-10.5	...	108.7
5 Construction	1388.8	...	1052.6	45.3	...	2486.7	1656.8	...	1308.8	56.2	...	3021.8
6 Wholesale and retail trade, restaurants and hotels	2116.8	...	4968.5	193.0	...	7278.3	2359.9	...	5604.1	179.9	...	8143.9
A Wholesale and retail trade	1512.0	...	3345.3	153.8	...	5011.1	1681.4	...	3716.0	139.0	...	5536.3
B Restaurants and hotels	604.8	...	1623.2	39.3	...	2267.3	678.6	...	1888.1	40.9	...	2607.6
7 Transport, storage and communication	992.0	...	1178.4	-196.7	...	1973.7	1051.1	...	1397.2	-242.3	...	2206.0
A Transport and storage	729.4	...	888.5	-200.8	...	1417.1	762.8	...	1059.3	-265.8	...	1556.3
B Communication	262.6	...	289.9	4.1	...	556.6	288.3	...	337.8	23.5	...	649.6
8 Finance, insurance, real estate and business services [a]	1645.7	...	4187.8	203.9	...	6037.4	2015.5	...	4546.0	251.0	...	6812.5
A Financial institutions	1171.9	...	1106.2	-8.9	...	2269.1	1468.2	...	1197.9	-9.1	...	2657.0
B Insurance	...	...	...	...	...	...	...	...	...	...	...	...
C Real estate and business services	473.8	...	3081.6	212.9	...	3768.3	547.3	...	3348.1	260.1	...	4155.5
9 Community, social and personal services [ab]	809.2	...	964.6	-45.8	...	1728.0	896.5	...	1096.3	-90.3	...	1902.4
A Sanitary and similar services	169.7	...	205.4	0.5	...	375.6	181.7	...	236.1	-	...	417.8
B Social and related community services	...	...	...	...	...	...	...	...	...	...	...	...
Educational services	252.8	...	177.7	-172.5	...	258.0	274.0	...	207.0	-201.5	...	279.5
Medical, dental, other health and veterinary services					...						...	
C Recreational and cultural services	...	...	...	...	...	...	...	...	...	...	...	...
D Personal and household services	...	...	...	...	...	...	...	...	...	...	...	...

4.3 Cost Components of Value Added
(Continued)

Thousand Million Spanish pesetas

	1987						1988					
	Compensation of Employees	Capital Consumption	Net Operating Surplus	Indirect Taxes	Less: Subsidies Received	Value Added	Compensation of Employees	Capital Consumption	Net Operating Surplus	Indirect Taxes	Less: Subsidies Received	Value Added
Total, Industries cd	12248.1	...	18666.9	817.8	...	31732.9	13663.8	...	20955.1	658.4	...	35277.3
Producers of Government Services	3751.6	...	355.2	-	...	4106.8	4197.1	...	395.4	-	...	4592.5
Other Producers b	307.4	...	5.6	...	...	313.0	337.9	...	8.8	...	...	346.7
Total cd	16307.1	...	19027.7	817.8	...	36152.6	18198.8	...	21359.2	658.4	...	40216.5
Less: Imputed bank service charge	...	...	2321.5	...	...	2321.5	...	...	2682.8	...	...	2682.8
Import duties	...	...	...	396.4	...	396.4	...	...	...	440.4	...	440.4
Value added tax	...	...	...	1916.5	...	1916.5	...	...	...	2184.6	...	2184.6
Total cd	16307.1	...	16706.2	3130.7	...	36144.1	18198.8	...	18676.4	3283.4	...	40158.7

	1989						1990					
	Compensation of Employees	Capital Consumption	Net Operating Surplus	Indirect Taxes	Less: Subsidies Received	Value Added	Compensation of Employees	Capital Consumption	Net Operating Surplus	Indirect Taxes	Less: Subsidies Received	Value Added

All Producers

	Comp. Emp.	Cap. Cons.	Net Op. Surplus	Indirect Taxes	Less: Subsidies	Value Added	Comp. Emp.	Cap. Cons.	Net Op. Surplus	Indirect Taxes	Less: Subsidies	Value Added
1 Agriculture, hunting, forestry and fishing	558.7	...	1765.9	...	...	2159.9	599.5	...	1815.2	...	...	2253.0
2 Mining and quarrying	171.3	...	143.0	...	...	261.2	...	...	...	...	...	...
A Coal mining	158.6	...	71.6	...	...	176.6	...	...	...	...	...	...
B Crude petroleum and natural gas production	12.7	...	71.4	...	...	84.6	...	...	...	...	...	...
C Metal ore mining	...	...	...	...	...	...	...	...	...	...	...	...
D Other mining	...	...	...	...	...	...	...	...	...	...	...	...
3 Manufacturing	5177.1	...	4642.8	...	...	10647.9	5704.2	...	4260.6	...	...	10172.2
A Manufacture of food, beverages and tobacco	709.4	...	1113.7	...	...	2010.8	...	...	...	...	...	...
B Textile, wearing apparel and leather industries	557.6	...	371.7	...	...	937.3	...	...	...	...	...	...
C Manufacture of wood and wood products, including furniture	230.1	...	119.5	...	...	353.1	...	...	...	...	...	...
D Manufacture of paper and paper products, printing and publishing	340.7	...	268.5	...	...	612.5	...	...	...	...	...	...
E Manufacture of chemicals and chemical petroleum, coal, rubber and plastic products	677.7	...	913.8	...	...	2195.6	...	...	...	...	...	...
F Manufacture of non-metallic mineral products, except products of petroleum and coal	367.5	...	434.9	...	...	806.5	...	...	...	...	...	...
G Basic metal industries	254.0	...	314.4	...	...	566.7	...	...	...	...	...	...
H Manufacture of fabricated metal products, machinery and equipment	1956.0	...	1052.5	...	...	3026.2	...	...	...	...	...	...
I Other manufacturing industries	84.3	...	53.8	...	...	139.2	...	...	...	...	...	...
4 Electricity, gas and water	307.1	...	885.3	...	...	1190.1	...	...	...	...	...	...
A Electricity, gas and steam	263.8	...	808.6	...	...	1080.6	...	...	...	...	...	...
B Water works and supply	43.3	...	76.7	...	...	109.5	...	...	...	...	...	...
5 Construction	2059.0	...	1661.3	...	...	3774.3	2442.8	...	2006.9	...	...	4575.2
6 Wholesale and retail trade, restaurants and hotels	2671.0	...	6368.7	...	...	9216.3	...	...	...	...	...	...
A Wholesale and retail trade	1904.8	...	4157.1	...	...	6200.9	...	...	...	...	...	...
B Restaurants and hotels	766.2	...	2211.6	...	...	3015.4	...	...	...	...	...	...
7 Transport, storage and communication	1162.2	...	1514.3	...	...	2379.0	...	...	...	...	...	...
A Transport and storage	812.4	...	1122.9	...	...	1659.1	...	...	...	...	...	...
B Communication	349.8	...	391.4	...	...	719.8	...	...	...	...	...	...
8 Finance, insurance, real estate and business services a	2105.7	...	5303.1	...	...	7721.8	...	...	...	...	...	...
A Financial institutions	1486.9	...	1626.1	...	...	3108.6	...	...	...	...	...	...
B Insurance	...	...	...	...	...	...	...	...	...	...	...	...
C Real estate and business services	618.8	...	3677.0	...	...	4613.2	...	...	...	...	...	...
9 Community, social and personal services ab	1023.9	...	1271.7	...	...	2197.2	...	...	...	...	...	...
A Sanitary and similar services	207.0	...	289.0	...	...	496.8	...	...	...	...	...	...
B Social and related community services	...	...	...	...	...	...	...	...	...	...	...	...

Spain

4.3 Cost Components of Value Added
(Continued)

Thousand Million Spanish pesetas

	1989						1990					
	Compensation of Employees	Capital Consumption	Net Operating Surplus	Indirect Taxes	Less: Subsidies Received	Value Added	Compensation of Employees	Capital Consumption	Net Operating Surplus	Indirect Taxes	Less: Subsidies Received	Value Added
Educational services	300.0	...	231.9	...	...	306.8	...	...	...	...	...	...
Medical, dental, other health and veterinary services	...	...	...	...	...	...	...	...	...	...	...	...
C Recreational and cultural services	...	...	...	...	...	...	...	...	...	...	...	...
D Personal and household services	...	...	...	...	...	...	...	...	...	...	...	...
Total, Industries cd	15236.0	...	23556.2	755.4	...	39547.7	17091.2	...	26028.8	940.5	...	44060.5
Producers of Government Services	4805.5	...	445.2	-	...	5250.7	5554.5	...	508.2	-	...	6062.7
Other Producers b	371.8	...	10.8	...	...	382.6	428.6	...	13.6	...	...	442.3
Total cd	20413.3	...	24012.2	755.4	...	45181.0	23074.3	...	26550.6	940.5	...	50565.5
Less: Imputed bank service charge	...	...	3180.9	...	...	3180.9	...	...	3581.5	...	...	3581.5
Import duties	...	...	...	413.6	...	413.6	...	...	...	372.8	...	372.8
Value added tax	...	...	...	2592.3	...	2592.3	...	...	...	2768.5	...	2768.5
Total cd	20413.3	...	20831.3	3761.3	...	45006.0	23074.3	...	22969.1	4081.8	...	50125.3

	1991					
	Compensation of Employees	Capital Consumption	Net Operating Surplus	Indirect Taxes	Less: Subsidies Received	Value Added
All Producers						
1 Agriculture, hunting, forestry and fishing	639.4	...	1758.8	...	...	2179.8
2 Mining and quarrying	...	...	...	...	...	...
A Coal mining	...	...	...	...	...	...
B Crude petroleum and natural gas production	...	...	...	...	...	...
C Metal ore mining	...	...	...	...	...	...
D Other mining	...	...	...	...	...	...
3 Manufacturing	5974.4	...	4303.9	...	...	10385.8
A Manufacture of food, beverages and tobacco	...	...	...	...	...	...
B Textile, wearing apparel and leather industries	...	...	...	...	...	...
C Manufacture of wood and wood products, including furniture	...	...	...	...	...	...
D Manufacture of paper and paper products, printing and publishing	...	...	...	...	...	...
E Manufacture of chemicals and chemical petroleum, coal, rubber and plastic products	...	...	...	...	...	...
F Manufacture of non-metallic mineral products, except products of petroleum and coal	...	...	...	...	...	...
G Basic metal industries	...	...	...	...	...	...
H Manufacture of fabricated metal products, machinery and equipment	...	...	...	...	...	...
I Other manufacturing industries	...	...	...	...	...	...
4 Electricity, gas and water	...	...	...	...	...	...
A Electricity, gas and steam	...	...	...	...	...	...
B Water works and supply	...	...	...	...	...	...
5 Construction	2758.1	...	2235.4	...	...	5111.6
6 Wholesale and retail trade, restaurants and hotels	...	...	...	...	...	...
A Wholesale and retail trade	...	...	...	...	...	...
B Restaurants and hotels	...	...	...	...	...	...
7 Transport, storage and communication	...	...	...	...	...	...
A Transport and storage	...	...	...	...	...	...
B Communication	...	...	...	...	...	...
8 Finance, insurance, real estate and business services a	...	...	...	...	...	...
A Financial institutions	...	...	...	...	...	...

4.3 Cost Components of Value Added
(Continued)

Thousand Million Spanish pesetas

	1991					
	Compensation of Employees	Capital Consumption	Net Operating Surplus	Indirect Taxes	Less: Subsidies Received	Value Added
B Insurance	...	...	...	...	...	...
C Real estate and business services	...	...	...	...	...	...
9 Community, social and personal services ab	...	...	...	...	...	...
A Sanitary and similar services	...	...	...	...	...	...
B Social and related community services	...	...	...	...	...	...
Educational services	...	...	...	...	...	...
Medical, dental, other health and veterinary services	...	...	...	...	...	...
C Recreational and cultural services	...	...	...	...	...	...
D Personal and household services	...	...	...	...	...	...
Total, Industries cd	18623.6	...	28558.9	1033.2	...	48215.8
Producers of Government Services	6170.7	...	578.1	...	...	6748.8
Other Producers b	475.7	...	16.7	...	...	492.4
Total cd	25270.0	...	29153.7	1033.2	...	55457.0
Less: Imputed bank service charge	...	...	4054.5	...	...	4054.4
Import duties	...	...	...	345.5	...	345.5
Value added tax	...	...	...	3043.1	...	3043.1
Total cd	25270.0	...	25099.2	4421.8	...	54791.2

a) Business services and real estate except dwellings are included in item 'Community, social and personal services'.
b) Item 'Other producers' is included in item 'Community, social and personal services'.

c) Column 4 refers to indirect taxes less subsidies received.
d) Column 'Operating surplus' includes capital consumption and net indirect taxes.

Sri Lanka

General note. The preparation of national accounts statistics in Sri Lanka is undertaken by the Department of Census and Statistics, Colombo. The official estimates are published by the Department in 'National Accounts in Sri Lanka'. The following presentation on sources and methods is based mainly on a report by the U.N. Regional Adviser of National Accounts entitled 'Assessment of sources, methods and reliability of estimates of gross domestic product by kind of economic activity in Sri Lanka (1975)' and on a detailed and comprehensive information received from the Department of Census and Statistics in 1978. The estimates are generally in accordance with the classifications and definitions recommended in the United Nations System of National Accounts (SNA). The following tables have been prepared from successve replies to the United Nations national accounts questionnaire. When the scope and coverage of the estimates differ for conceptual or statistical reasons from the definitions and classifications recommended in SNA, a footnote is indicated to the relevant tables.

Sources and methods :

(a) Gross domestic product. Gross domestic product is estimated mainly through the production approach.

(b) Expenditure on the gross domestic product. The expenditure approach is used to estimate government final consumption expenditure, gross fixed capital formation in the public sector and exports and imports of goods and services. This approach, in combination with the commodity-flow approach is used to estimate private final consumption expenditure. The commodity-flow approach is used for gross fixed capital formation in the private sector. Changes in stocks are estimated as a residual. General government expenditure consists of actual expenditure made by central government and current expenditure by the local government on goods and services which are obtained from the Treasury Votes Ledgers and the Ministry of Local Government, respectively. Private consumption expenditure is estimated by using the commodity-flow method on the basis of imports as well as domestic goods available for consumption. Bench-mark estimates for selected consumer items are avilable in value terms through the use of household survey data. These estimates are extrapolated by using the increase in population and price levels. For gross fixed capital formation in the public sector, direct estimates are prepared on the basis of information available in the budegetary accounts. For building and other construction, the supply of locally produced building materials are first compiled, adding 45 per cent to the production values for trade and transport margins while data on imported materials are obtained from customs returns adding import duties and 45 per cent for trade and transport margins. It has been found that building materials constitute 45 per cent of the construction cost with wages and profits at 55 per cent. For machinery and equipment, import statistics are analyzed in detail. Estimates for exports and imports of goods and services are based on foreign trade statistics and balance of payments data. For the constant price estimates, all items of GDP by expenditure type are deflated by appropriate price indices or extrapolated by using quantum indices.

(c) Cost-structure of the gross domestic product. Data on wages and salaries in the government sector are obtained from Treasury records. In order to estimate compensation of employees in the private sector, the percentages of wage component for the key sectors, obtained from the socio-economic survey data for 1980/1981, are applied to the respective activity. Based on special inquiries made, depreciation is assumed to be 33.3 per cent of the value of fixed assets up to 1978 and 20 per cent for the years 1979, 1980 and 1981. Indirect taxes are obtained from government revenue records and subsidies from treasury records.

(d) Gross domestic product by kind of economic activity. The table of GDP by kind of economic activity is prepared in producers values. The production approach is used to estimate value added of most industries. For livestock and forestry, the expenditure approach is used and for some of the service sectors like banking and transport, the income approach is used. Estimates of value added for tea and rubber have been revised by using the production approach. The estimation of coconut production is based on domestic and industrial consumption and exports. The annual cost-of-production returns are used for estimating inputs. The volume of paddy prodcution is estimated on the basis of acreage statistics obtained from a multistage sample survey of crop-cutting. Own-account consumption is estimated as 10 per cent of production. Bench-mark estimates for fruits and vegetables are based on the 1973 consumer finance survey. These are extrapolated for current years by increase in population and price levels. For livestock products, the per capita estimate obtained from the 1973 consumer finance survey is multiplied by each year's mid-year population. Production data for the mining and quarrying sector are obtained from the Department of Geological Survey. The value of input is assumed to be 15 per cent of the value of gross putput. For large-scale manufacturing, quantities and values of gross output and values of inputs are submitted in annual returns furnished by the registered industrial establishments. Bench-mark estimates for small-scale industries are obtained from the 1971 survey on the unorganized sector conducted by the Industrial Development Board. Extrapolation is done by using the growth in the labour force and the wage index. Data on electricity, gas and water are obtained from the Ceylon Electricity Board and the Ministry of Industries. The value added of construction activity in the private sector is based on locally produced and imported building materials obtained from the annual returns of manufacturing establishments and the customs returns, respectively. For the government sector, value of materials used in building and other construction accounts for 45 per cent of the gross value. This estimate is deducted from the value of the total supply of materials to obtain the value of material used in the private sector. Value added for the distributive trade is measured by net trade margins earned by traders on various types of products. Gross trade margin estimates are made seperately for exports, local market production, government and private imports, etc. From these estimates 15 per cent is deducted for input. Bench-mark estimates for hotels and restaurants have been obtained from the 1969/70 socio-economic survey. These estimates are extrapolated by population growth and a specially constructed index for meals consumed outside homes. For trnasport in the government sector, the expenditure on personal employment is taken as value added. The gross value of goods, transport and trade is obtained by applying specified distribution margins to the c.i.f. value in the case of imports and to the producer value in the case of locally produced goods. Wherever retail and producer prices are available the difference between them is taken as the distribution margin. For the financial sector, value added is based on data obtained from the Central Bank and concerned institutions. Bench-mark data for gross rental values have been obtained from the 1980/81 socio-economic survey. These estimates are applied to the housing stock, with an allowance made for rental increases. The value added of government services is obtained from the Treasury Accounts. For the private sector, value added is based on expenditure data obtained from the 1980/81 consumer finance survey, extrapolated by the growth in the labour force adjusted for changes in wages. For the constant price estimates, price deflation is used for most of the industries. For some agricultural products, electricity, gas and water, transport and government services, value added is extrapolated by a quantity index.

1.1 Expenditure on the Gross Domestic Product, in Current Prices

Million Sri Lanka rupees

	1980	1981	1982	1983	1984	1985	1986	1987	1988	1989	1990	1991
1 Government final consumption expenditure	6667	7456	10407	12727	15442	19170	22990	26204	30331	32585	41836	50766
2 Private final consumption expenditure	53457	64581	77310	93075	108312	118101	130728	138754	163092	178509	233961	270927
3 Gross capital formation	22410	24286	28174	31374	34412	37876	38631	44096	48449	51441	65855	87413
A Increase in stocks a	167	331	248	-210	150	225	137	148	601	-473	1038	950
B Gross fixed capital formation	22243	23955	27926	31584	34262	37651	38494	43948	47848	50968	64817	86463
Residential buildings	3808	5048	6138	6950	7238	9525	10694	10492	11870	12499	16715	20878
Non-residential buildings	2839	2350	2356	2858	2399	3039	4167	4931	4671	5917	7224	7817
Other construction and land improvement etc.	5113	7211	7472	7836	11075	9294	8966	10846	12429	14555	16753	17579
Other	10483	9348	11960	13939	13550	15793	14667	17679	18877	17997	24125	40188
4 Exports of goods and services	21434	25892	27148	32016	44285	42394	42602	50763	57885	68666	97117	106386
5 Less: Imports of goods and services	36456	39558	45905	50381	54469	62396	63737	70694	81771	92587	122481	144701
Statistical discrepancy	825	1869	394	391	-639	2619	1228	-301	788	9616	1616	-1071
Equals: Gross Domestic Product	68338	84527	97528	119202	147344	157763	172440	188822	218774	248230	317904	369720

a) The estimates of 'Increase in stocks' for the years prior to 1975 include a statistical discrepancy.

1.2 Expenditure on the Gross Domestic Product, in Constant Prices

Million Sri Lanka rupees

	1980	1981	1982	1983	1984	1985	1986	1987	1988	1989	1990	1991
					At constant prices of:1975							
1 Government final consumption expenditure	3626	3593	4208	3919	3953	4876	5714	5846	5855	5531	5774	6184
2 Private final consumption expenditure	31610	35390	37720	39188	39598	41986	44192	44428	46906	48018	51081	56709
3 Gross capital formation	6986	7434	7516	7262	6722	6696	6501	6973	6547	6344	6692	7256
A Increase in stocks	75	127	91	-61	42	61	39	42	153	105	166	138
B Gross fixed capital formation	6911	7306	7425	7324	6680	6635	6462	6931	6394	6239	6526	7118

1.2 Expenditure on the Gross Domestic Product, in Constant Prices
(Continued)

Million Sri Lanka rupees

	1980	1981	1982	1983	1984	1985	1986	1987	1988	1989	1990	1991
					At constant prices of:1975							
Residential buildings	1178	1312	1527	1593	1505	1839	2050	1991	1879	1604	2094	2420
Non-residential buildings	1108	774	726	813	613	742	1017	1059	996	1062	1044	1044
Other construction and land improvement etc.	1808	2523	2516	2236	2686	2081	1987	2311	2335	2538	2469	2237
Other	2817	2698	2656	2682	1876	1973	1408	1570	1184	1035	919	1416
4 Exports of goods and services	8131	8375	9213	8936	10312	10828	11550	11735	12098	13090	14535	15141
5 Less: Imports of goods and services	13573	14061	15509	15420	15559	15062	16839	17243	17657	17109	16702	18890
Statistical discrepancy	-1473	-3464	-3949	-2824	-1891	-4024	-3882	-3737	-4413	-5564	-7932	-10384
Equals: Gross Domestic Product a	35308	37266	39199	41062	43136	45300	47236	48002	49336	50310	53449	56016

a) The estimates before 1975 for this table have been calculated on the basis of 1963 prices and linked to the estimates for the years beginning 1975.

1.3 Cost Components of the Gross Domestic Product

Million Sri Lanka rupees

	1980	1981	1982	1983	1984	1985	1986	1987	1988	1989	1990	1991
1 Indirect taxes, net	9174	10688	11163	15210	23102	22481	24318	27223	28242	35811	44460	46416
A Indirect taxes	10163	11884	12176	16937	25245	24402	26437	29274	30449	38224	48114	51498
B Less: Subsidies	988	1197	1013	1727	2143	1921	2119	2051	2207	2413	3654	5082
2 Consumption of fixed capital	4449	4791	5585	6317	6852	7530	7699	8790	9570	10194	12963	17293
3 Compensation of employees paid by resident producers to:	31031	37636	44561	53729	64265	70748	78741	86388	98695	110033	141645	161472
4 Operating surplus a	22692	29211	35577	43765	53614	54160	60317	66574	83656	87973	116182	144660
Statistical discrepancy b	992	2200	642	181	-489	2844	1365	-153	-1389	4219	2654	-121
Equals: Gross Domestic Product	68338	84527	97528	119202	147344	157763	172440	188822	218774	248230	317904	369720

a) Item 'Operating surplus' has been obtained as a residual.
b) Item 'Statistical discrepancy' includes 'Increase in stocks'.

1.4 General Government Current Receipts and Disbursements

Million Sri Lanka rupees

	1980	1981	1982	1983	1984	1985	1986	1987	1988	1989	1990	1991
					Receipts							
1 Operating surplus	...	...	...	...	...	...	...	...	...	...	...	...
2 Property and entrepreneurial income	1073	1360	1578	2149	3545	5168	5071	5523	4453	4156	5553	6372
3 Taxes, fees and contributions	12775	14267	15476	20765	31296	31095	32004	35968	37102	48640	61625	67928
A Indirect taxes	10163	11884	12176	16937	25245	24402	26437	29274	30449	38224	48114	51498
B Direct taxes	2515	2250	3180	3703	5887	6232	5292	6377	6325	9858	12944	16001
C Social security contributions	51	60	71	71	84	89	106	127	193	422	385	408
D Compulsory fees, fines and penalties	47	72	49	55	79	372	169	190	136	136	182	21
4 Other current transfers	286	357	573	2077	2270	2368	2796	2835	2435	3331	1641	2436
Total Current Receipts of General Government a	14134	15984	17627	24991	37110	38631	39871	44326	43990	56127	68819	76736
					Disbursements							
1 Government final consumption expenditure	6667	7456	10407	12727	15442	19170	22990	26204	30331	32585	41836	50766
A Compensation of employees	3573	4162	5379	7260	8237	9244	11124	12708	15915	19675	24123	28852
B Consumption of fixed capital	...	...	...	...	...	...	...	...	...	...	...	...
C Purchases of goods and services, net	3094	3294	5029	5467	7205	9926	11866	13495	14416	12910	17713	21914
D Less: Own account fixed capital formation	...	...	...	...	...	...	...	...	...	...	...	...
E Indirect taxes paid, net	...	...	...	...	...	...	...	...	...	...	...	...
2 Property income	2213	3738	5104	7369	7446	8488	9448	10671	12700	13737	20898	22119
A Interest	2213	3738	5104	7369	7446	8488	9448	10671	12700	13737	20898	22119
B Net land rent and royalties	...	...	...	...	...	...	...	...	...	...	...	...
3 Subsidies	988	1197	1013	1867	1463	1646	1548	1830	2240	3457	3654	5082
4 Other current transfers	4042	3638	3632	1731	3175	6378	2775	111	4967	8397	4870	6345
5 Net saving	223	-45	-2530	1297	9584	2949	3110	5510	-6245	-2049	-2439	-7577
Total Current Disbursements and Net Saving of General Government a	14134	15984	17627	24991	37110	38631	39871	44326	43990	56127	68819	76736

a) Prior to 1980, estimates are based on data extracted from Central Bank of Ceylon and from the Department of Census and Statistics (DC & S). Beginning 1980, the estimates are prepared by DC & S and are therefore, not comparable with the data prior to 1980.

Sri Lanka

1.6 Current Income and Outlay of Households and Non-Profit Institutions

Million Sri Lanka rupees

	1980	1981	1982	1983	1984	1985	1986	1987	1988	1989	1990	1991
Receipts												
1 Compensation of employees	31031	37636	44561	53729	64265	70748	78741	86388	98696	110033	141644	161472
2 Operating surplus of private unincorporated enterprises	...	...	...	...	...	...	...	...	...	...	...	...
3 Property and entrepreneurial income	21817	26033	30647	37935	41640	44772	51281	56292	70838	86060	115864	144287
4 Current transfers	6100	8985	11055	12232	13982	15177	16049	17262	20419	21859	24828	27459
Total Current Receipts	58948	72654	86263	103896	119887	130697	146071	159942	189953	217952	282336	333218
Disbursements												
1 Private final consumption expenditure	53457	64581	77310	93075	108312	118101	130728	138754	163092	178509	233961	270927
2 Property income	136	165	204	253	412	409	479	478	582	673	957	1375
3 Direct taxes and other current transfers n.e.c. to general government	1671	2080	2636	2884	3860	4837	5637	6109	6572	8583	10903	11544
A Social security contributions	498	601	722	795	1057	1264	1281	1450	1810	2256	2713	3141
B Direct taxes	1173	1479	1914	2089	2803	3573	4356	4659	4762	6327	8190	8403
C Fees, fines and penalties	...	...	...	...	...	...	...	...	...	...	...	...
4 Other current transfers	530	830	866	894	1140	1329	1566	1869	1949	2049	2682	3338
Statistical discrepancy	-602	-1273	-1205	-941	-4959	-7529	-7411	-6973	-4875	-2016	-9620	-377
5 Net saving a	3756	6271	6452	7731	11122	13550	15072	19705	22633	30154	43453	46411
Total Current Disbursements and Net Saving a	58948	72654	86263	103896	119887	130697	146071	159942	189953	217952	282336	333218

a) Item 'Net saving' includes consumption of fixed capital.

1.7 External Transactions on Current Account, Summary

Million Sri Lanka rupees

	1980	1981	1982	1983	1984	1985	1986	1987	1988	1989	1990	1991
Payments to the Rest of the World												
1 Imports of goods and services a	36456	39558	45905	50381	54469	62396	63737	70694	81771	92587	122481	144701
A Imports of merchandise c.i.f.	33915	36121	41420	45201	49046	55528	55284	61102	71253	80225	107605	125511
B Other	2541	3438	4486	5180	5423	6868	8454	9592	10518	12362	14876	19190
2 Factor income to the rest of the world	1206	2502	2871	4270	4881	5706	5764	6755	7463	7845	10412	11680
A Compensation of employees	...	...	...	...	...	...	...	...	...	...	...	...
B Property and entrepreneurial income	1206	2502	2871	4270	4881	5706	5764	6755	7463	7845	10412	11680
3 Current transfers to the rest of the world	258	512	530	475	622	708	890	1098	1199	990	1536	1785
4 Surplus of the nation on current transactions	-13193	-11616	-15223	-15138	-6554	-16235	-17024	-15404	-18965	-17820	-17531	-29297
Payments to the Rest of the World and Surplus of the Nation on Current Transactions	24726	30956	34084	39987	53418	52575	53367	63142	71469	83602	116898	128868
Receipts From The Rest of the World												
1 Exports of goods and services a	21434	25892	27148	32016	44285	42394	42602	50763	57885	68666	97117	106386
A Exports of merchandise f.o.b.	17603	20507	21098	25038	37198	35729	33893	41097	46985	56175	79481	84378
B Other	3831	5385	6050	6978	7088	6665	8708	9666	10900	12491	17636	22007
2 Factor income from rest of the world	774	634	912	1056	1480	2261	1893	2056	2197	2106	3727	4364
A Compensation of employees	...	...	...	...	...	...	...	...	...	...	...	...
B Property and entrepreneurial income	774	634	912	1056	1480	2261	1893	2056	2197	2106	3727	4364
3 Current transfers from rest of the world	2518	4430	6024	6916	7653	7920	8873	10324	11386	12830	16054	18119
Receipts from the Rest of the World on Current Transactions	24726	30956	34084	39987	53418	52575	53367	63142	71469	83602	116898	128868

a) Prior to 1978, estimates of imports and exports of goods and services are valued at the Foreign Exchange Entitlement Certificate Rate (FEECR) which is a proxy to the unitary rate.

1.8 Capital Transactions of The Nation, Summary

Million Sri Lanka rupees

	1980	1981	1982	1983	1984	1985	1986	1987	1988	1989	1990	1991
Finance of Gross Capital Formation												
Gross saving	9216	12670	12951	16236	27858	21641	21607	28692	29484	33622	48324	58116
1 Consumption of fixed capital a	4449	4791	5585	6317	6852	7530	7699	8790	9570	10194	12963	17293
2 Net saving	4768	7879	7366	9919	21006	14111	13908	19902	19914	23428	35361	40823
Less: Surplus of the nation on current transactions	-13193	-11616	-15223	-15138	-6554	-16235	-17024	-15404	-18965	-17820	-17531	-29297
Finance of Gross Capital Formation	22410	24286	28174	31374	34412	37876	38631	44096	48449	51441	65855	87413
Gross Capital Formation												
Increase in stocks	167	331	248	-210	150	225	137	148	601	473	1038	950
Gross fixed capital formation	22243	23955	27926	31584	34262	37651	38494	43948	47848	50968	64817	86463
1 General government b	5177	4242	4246	5428	6142	7758	8937	11328	11499	15579	15669	16530
2 Corporate and quasi-corporate enterprises	17066	19713	23680	26156	28121	29893	29557	32620	36349	35389	49148	69933
A Public	...	...	...	...	...	...	...	...	...	...	...	...
B Private	17066	19713	23680	26156	28121	29893	29557	32620	36349	35389	49148	69933
3 Other	...	...	...	...	...	...	...	...	...	...	...	...
Gross Capital Formation	22410	24286	28174	31374	34412	37876	38631	44096	48449	51441	65855	87413

a) Item 'Consumption of fixed capital' includes depreciation of all private corporations as well as
depreciation of fixed assets in other private unincorporated units.
b) Public enterprises is included in general government.

1.10 Gross Domestic Product by Kind of Activity, in Current Prices

Million Sri Lanka rupees

	1980	1981	1982	1983	1984	1985	1986	1987	1988	1989	1990	1991
1 Agriculture, hunting, forestry and fishing a	17900	22787	25258	30468	37293	38506	39529	43174	51074	56774	72788	81926
2 Mining and quarrying	910	1078	1159	1420	1209	1227	1670	2194	3024	3605	4570	4048
3 Manufacturing a	12422	14028	14644	17933	24301	26180	26914	29701	34852	41415	54943	62798
4 Electricity, gas and water	547	1003	1543	1611	2507	2999	3062	3457	3986	4250	5635	6499
5 Construction	6503	8037	8651	9902	11306	11939	13197	14207	15349	17505	21592	24858
6 Wholesale and retail trade, restaurants and hotels	11331	16168	19732	23901	26951	29061	32716	35373	41643	44563	60486	73074
7 Transport, storage and communication	6962	7383	9748	11635	15621	17429	19661	20236	22305	23877	30912	37443
8 Finance, insurance, real estate and business services	3620	4624	5884	7226	8623	9235	10628	11363	13322	14871	17732	21035
9 Community, social and personal services	1513	1873	2093	2762	3057	3246	3594	4362	5284	5484	6975	9324
Total, Industries	61708	76981	88711	106857	130868	139822	150971	164067	190839	212344	275633	321005
Producers of Government Services	3573	4162	5379	7260	8237	9244	11124	12708	15915	19675	24123	28852
Other Producers	133	158	215	249	294	300	331	364	421	503	618	703
Subtotal	65414	81302	94305	114366	139399	149366	162426	177139	207175	232522	300374	350560
Less: Imputed bank service charge	...	...	...	...	...	...	...	...	...	...	...	...
Plus: Import duties	2924	3225	3222	4836	7945	8397	10014	11683	11599	15708	17530	19160
Plus: Value added tax	...	...	...	...	...	...	...	...	...	...	...	...
Equals: Gross Domestic Product	68338	84527	97528	119202	147344	157763	172440	188822	218774	248230	317904	369720

a) The estimates on processing of tea and rubber are included in the agricultural sector prior to
1975. From 1975 onward, they are included in the manufacturing sector.

1.11 Gross Domestic Product by Kind of Activity, in Constant Prices

Million Sri Lanka rupees

	1980	1981	1982	1983	1984	1985	1986	1987	1988	1989	1990	1991
At constant prices of:1975												
1 Agriculture, hunting, forestry and fishing a	9357	10058	10372	10994	10200	11146	11224	10562	10837	10528	11454	11659
2 Mining and quarrying	475	500	479	575	693	673	918	1133	1465	1818	2018	1618
3 Manufacturing a	7071	7327	7281	7064	8300	8812	9345	9670	9911	10227	11178	11927
4 Electricity, gas and water	181	203	222	226	253	274	294	304	315	321	351	375
5 Construction	1947	2208	2157	2172	2200	2248	2419	2556	2596	2616	2638	2683
6 Wholesale and retail trade, restaurants and hotels	7564	8059	9408	10162	10907	11422	11983	12422	12772	13077	13533	14525
7 Transport, storage and communication	3460	3564	3658	4043	4531	4607	4718	4803	4828	4774	5121	5522
8 Finance, insurance, real estate and business services	1269	1357	1512	1566	1649	1719	1772	1834	1905	1982	2052	2149
9 Community, social and personal services	980	1076	1117	1196	1296	1299	1338	1377	1338	1341	1390	1590

Sri Lanka

1.11 Gross Domestic Product by Kind of Activity, in Constant Prices
(Continued)

Million Sri Lanka rupees

	1980	1981	1982	1983	1984	1985	1986	1987	1988	1989	1990	1991
					At constant prices of:1975							
Total, Industries	32305	34352	36206	37997	40029	42200	44011	44661	45967	46684	49735	52048
Producers of Government Services	2206	2236	2256	2272	2298	2334	2380	2475	2502	2750	2851	3029
Other Producers	83	84	102	104	105	106	108	111	112	127	129	129
Subtotal b	34594	36672	38564	40373	42432	44640	46499	47247	48581	49561	52715	55206
Less: Imputed bank service charge	...	...	...	...	...	...	...	...	...	...	...	...
Plus: Import duties	714	595	635	689	704	660	737	755	755	749	734	810
Plus: Value added tax	...	...	...	...	...	...	...	...	...	...	...	...
Equals: Gross Domestic Product b	35308	37266	39199	41062	43136	45300	47236	48002	49336	50310	53449	56016

a) The estimates on processing of tea and rubber are included in the agricultural sector prior to 1975. From 1975 onward, they are included in the manufacturing sector. b) The estimates before 1975 for this table have been calculated on the basis of 1963 prices and linked to the estimates for the years beginning 1975.

1.12 Relations Among National Accounting Aggregates

Million Sri Lanka rupees

	1980	1981	1982	1983	1984	1985	1986	1987	1988	1989	1990	1991
Gross Domestic Product	68338	84527	97528	119202	147344	157763	172440	188822	218774	248230	317904	369720
Plus: Net factor income from the rest of the world	-432	-1868	-1959	-3214	-3401	-3445	-3871	-4699	-5266	-5739	-6685	-7316
Factor income from the rest of the world	774	634	912	1056	1480	2261	1893	2056	2197	2106	3727	4364
Less: Factor income to the rest of the world	1206	2502	2871	4270	4881	5706	5764	6755	7463	7845	10412	11680
Equals: Gross National Product	67906	82659	95568	115988	143943	154318	168569	184123	213508	242492	311219	362404
Less: Consumption of fixed capital	4449	4791	5585	6317	6852	7530	7699	8790	9570	10194	12963	17293
Equals: National Income	63457	77868	89983	109671	137091	146788	160870	175333	203938	232298	298256	345111
Plus: Net current transfers from the rest of the world	2260	3918	5494	6441	7031	7212	7983	9226	10187	11840	14518	16334
Current transfers from the rest of the world	2518	4430	6024	6916	7653	7920	8873	10324	11386	12830	16054	18119
Less: Current transfers to the rest of the world	258	512	530	475	622	708	890	1098	1199	990	1536	1785
Equals: National Disposable Income	65717	81786	95477	116112	144122	154000	168853	184559	214125	244138	312774	361445
Less: Final consumption	60124	72038	87717	105802	123755	137271	153718	164958	193423	211094	275797	321693
Statistical discrepancy	-825	-1869	-394	-391	639	-2619	-1228	301	-788	-9616	-1616	1071
Equals: Net Saving	4768	7879	7366	9919	21006	14111	13908	19902	19914	23428	35361	40823
Less: Surplus of the nation on current transactions	-13193	-11616	-15223	-15138	-6554	-16235	-17024	-15404	-18965	-17820	-17531	-29297
Equals: Net Capital Formation a	17961	19495	22589	25057	27560	30346	30932	35306	38879	41247	52892	70120

a) Item 'Net capital formation' includes a statistical discrepancy.

2.1 Government Final Consumption Expenditure by Function, in Current Prices

Million Sri Lanka rupees

	1980	1981	1982	1983	1984	1985	1986	1987	1988	1989	1990	1991
1 General public services	1860	2644	4346	4701	5816	6126	5281	5711	6140	7538	8766	10057
2 Defence	585	625	687	1229	1748	4654	7877	9110	8806	6779	10033	11687
3 Public order and safety	...	...	...	...	...	...	...	...	...	...	...	...
4 Education	1171	1508	1872	2380	2662	3154	3457	3691	4458	5231	6206	6338
5 Health	738	823	954	1259	1521	1660	1733	2258	2293	3275	3430	4081
6 Social security and welfare	756	930	1203	1681	1950	2228	3053	3514	4764	4863	6765	12053
7 Housing and community amenities	61	67	87	133	130	83	73	74	84	99	90	110
8 Recreational, cultural and religious affairs	39	37	48	64	74	82	93	104	125	139	167	199
9 Economic services	1457	824	1211	1279	1541	1183	1423	1742	3661	4661	6379	6242
10 Other functions	...	...	...	...	...	...	...	...	...	...	...	...
Total Government Final Consumption Expenditure	6667	7456	10407	12727	15442	19170	22990	26204	30331	32585	41836	50767

2.2 Government Final Consumption Expenditure by Function, in Constant Prices

Million Sri Lanka rupees

	1980	1981	1982	1983	1984	1985	1986	1987	1988	1989	1990	1991
					At constant prices of:1975							
1 General public services	1012	1276	1757	1448	1490	1555	1314	1275	1185	1278	1207	1224
2 Defence	319	302	278	379	447	1185	1960	2035	1700	1150	1386	1422
3 Public order and safety	...	...	...	...	...	...	...	...	...	...	...	...
4 Education	638	726	757	733	680	804	857	824	861	890	854	773
5 Health	403	395	386	388	391	424	429	503	443	559	473	495
6 Social security and welfare	410	449	486	518	498	566	760	783	920	824	930	1472
7 Housing and community amenities	33	32	35	41	32	20	17	17	16	17	12	12
8 Recreational, cultural and religious affairs	22	18	19	20	20	20	23	23	24	22	23	25
9 Economic services	791	395	490	394	395	302	354	386	706	791	889	761
10 Other functions	...	...	...	...	...	...	...	...	...	...	...	...
Total Government Final Consumption Expenditure a	3626	3593	4208	3919	3953	4876	5714	5846	5855	5531	5774	6184

a) The estimates before 1975 for this table have been calculated on the basis of 1963 prices and
linked to the estimates for the years beginning 1975.

2.5 Private Final Consumption Expenditure by Type and Purpose, in Current Prices

Million Sri Lanka rupees

	1980	1981	1982	1983	1984	1985	1986	1987	1988	1989	1990	1991
					Final Consumption Expenditure of Resident Households							
1 Food, beverages and tobacco	33101	37270	44674	55616	62411	64194	69240	75284	89736	107642	131859	153673
A Food	27298	30626	36974	47137	51684	52457	57307	65470	75409	92074	110429	131079
B Non-alcoholic beverages	88	77	52	233	659	292	626	595	1309	1247	2849	3381
C Alcoholic beverages	1884	1847	2809	2993	3111	3832	3474	3679	3559	3568	4976	4289
D Tobacco	3831	4720	4839	5253	6957	7613	7833	5540	9460	10753	13604	14924
2 Clothing and footwear	3208	3923	4558	5794	6548	8044	9172	10999	12563	11529	14199	15976
3 Gross rent, fuel and power	3112	3635	4704	5177	6174	6710	7033	7307	8173	8617	10233	11955
A Fuel and power	1050	1215	2171	2611	3334	3517	3729	3905	4614	5058	6289	7421
B Other	2062	2419	2534	2566	2840	3193	3304	3402	3559	3559	3944	4534
4 Furniture, furnishings and household equipment and operation	2606	3281	3428	3492	3759	5312	5711	5975	7613	8410	11464	12890
A Household operation	805	1265	1472	1474	1452	1853	2000	1873	3314	2738	3851	4479
B Other	1801	2016	1956	2018	2307	3459	3711	4102	4299	5672	7613	8411
5 Medical care and health expenses	896	1088	1236	1224	1508	1829	2597	2544	2865	2205	3672	4025
6 Transport and communication	6467	9253	10696	12684	17678	18715	19959	21008	24097	26167	34320	38327
A Personal transport equipment	988	1199	1093	1466	1546	1630	1459	1624	1903	1850	2370	2222
B Other	5478	8055	9603	11217	16132	17085	18500	19384	22194	24317	31950	36105
7 Recreational, entertainment, education and cultural services	2064	2201	3393	3642	4189	5494	5411	6187	6695	6766	8032	10361
A Education	385	219	587	689	677	1387	1120	1371	1643	1808	2781	3164
B Other	1680	1982	2806	2953	3512	4107	4291	4816	5052	4958	5251	7197
8 Miscellaneous goods and services	2235	2259	2467	2455	2942	3476	5497	5099	6752	7836	9301	11195
A Personal care	1202	887	952	1173	1367	2212	3537	2770	4650	5584	6590	7708
B Expenditures in restaurants, cafes and hotels	724	967	1308	991	1422	1106	1731	2087	1817	1923	2328	3055

Sri Lanka

2.5 Private Final Consumption Expenditure by Type and Purpose, in Current Prices
(Continued)

Million Sri Lanka rupees

	1980	1981	1982	1983	1984	1985	1986	1987	1988	1989	1990	1991
C Other	309	405	208	291	153	158	228	242	285	329	383	432
Total Final Consumption Expenditure in the Domestic Market by Households, of which	53689	62910	75156	90083	105208	113774	124620	134404	158494	179172	223076	258402
Plus: Direct purchases abroad by resident households ab	1656	4300	5201	5945	6839	7468	9316	8128	8617	9863	16960	19709
Less: Direct purchases in the domestic market by non-resident households c	1888	2629	3048	2952	3734	3141	3208	3778	4019	4656	6075	7185
Equals: Final Consumption Expenditure of Resident Households d	53457	64581	77310	93075	108312	118101	130728	138754	163092	184379	233961	270927

Final Consumption Expenditure of Private Non-profit Institutions Serving Households

	1980	1981	1982	1983	1984	1985	1986	1987	1988	1989	1990	1991
Equals: Final Consumption Expenditure of Private Non-profit Organisations Serving Households	...	...	...	...	...	...	...	...	...	...	...	...
Private Final Consumption Expenditure	53457	64581	77310	93075	108312	118101	130728	138754	163092	184379	233961	270927

a) Estimates up to 1972 for 'Direct purchases abroad by resident households' have been obtained from the Central Bank. For 1973 and 1974, no estimates have been made. From 1975 onward, figures have been estimated independently by the Department of Census and Statistics.
b) For 1981 and 1982, transfers made by residents abroad are not included in item 'Direct Purchases Abroad by Resident Households' shown in table 2.17 but are included in the estimates shown in table 2.5.

c) Estimates up to 1974 for 'Direct purchases in the domestic market by non-resident households' have been obtained from the Central Bank. From 1975 onward, figures have been estimated independently by the Department of Census and Statistics.
d) Item 'Final consumption expenditure of resident households' includes consumption expenditure of private non-profit institutions serving households.

2.6 Private Final Consumption Expenditure by Type and Purpose, in Constant Prices

Million Sri Lanka rupees

	1980	1981	1982	1983	1984	1985	1986	1987	1988	1989	1990	1991
						At constant prices of:1975						
						Final Consumption Expenditure of Resident Households						
1 Food, beverages and tobacco	18799	19201	19303	19851	18306	18718	18612	19689	20233	20609	21696	23873
A Food	16055	16534	16609	17025	15134	16001	16138	17639	17846	18495	19377	21634
B Non-alcoholic beverages	44	31	20	37	284	119	120	179	367	339	427	437
C Alcoholic beverages	946	741	1089	1141	967	1115	859	821	704	617	740	650
D Tobacco	1755	1896	1585	1648	1921	1483	1495	1050	1316	1158	1152	1152
2 Clothing and footwear	2691	3169	3426	4144	4433	4628	4692	4878	4971	3938	3182	3399
3 Gross rent, fuel and power	1197	1217	1419	1473	1455	1525	1582	1589	1651	1657	1629	1699
A Fuel and power	441	452	644	690	710	772	814	840	891	888	851	920
B Other	755	765	775	783	745	753	768	749	760	769	778	779
4 Furniture, furnishings and household equipment and operation	1648	1912	1675	1527	1481	1878	1863	1882	2084	2139	908	982
A Household operation	526	694	748	652	560	678	640	552	666	441	305	341
B Other	1122	1218	927	876	921	1200	1223	1330	1418	1698	603	641
5 Medical care and health expenses	585	602	628	541	582	669	830	750	740	492	291	306
6 Transport and communication	3404	3982	4596	4182	4950	5223	5255	5531	6345	7167	5033	4982
A Personal transport equipment	520	516	470	479	430	454	384	426	501	507	348	289
B Other	2883	3466	4127	3703	4520	4769	4871	5105	5844	6660	4685	4693
7 Recreational, entertainment, education and cultural services	1347	1207	1335	1315	1264	1545	1312	1495	1583	1617	1696	2054
A Education	251	120	231	172	231	507	354	404	424	403	220	241
B Other	1096	1087	1104	1142	1033	1038	958	1091	1159	1214	1476	1813
8 Miscellaneous goods and services	1459	1103	1253	1086	1135	1271	1758	1503	1566	1515	736	852
A Personal care	785	433	483	432	528	591	1132	816	1078	1080	522	587
B Expenditures in restaurants, cafes and hotels	473	472	664	555	548	614	554	615	422	372	184	233

2.6 Private Final Consumption Expenditure by Type and Purpose, in Constant Prices
(Continued)

Million Sri Lanka rupees

	1980	1981	1982	1983	1984	1985	1986	1987	1988	1989	1990	1991
				At constant prices of:1975								
C Other	202	198	106	100	59	66	72	72	66	63	30	32
Total Final Consumption Expenditure in the Domestic Market by Households, of which	31130	32393	33635	34119	33609	35457	35903	37316	39173	39134	35173	38147
Plus: Direct purchases abroad by resident households ab	1656	4011	5201	5945	6839	7468	9316	8128	8616	9863	16960	19709
Less: Direct purchases in the domestic market by non-resident households c	1177	1014	1116	876	850	939	1026	1016	883	979	1051	1147
Equals: Final Consumption Expenditure of Resident Households de	31610	35390	37720	39188	39598	41986	44192	44428	46906	48018	51081	56709

Final Consumption Expenditure of Private Non-profit Institutions Serving Households

	1980	1981	1982	1983	1984	1985	1986	1987	1988	1989	1990	1991
Equals: Final Consumption Expenditure of Private Non-profit Organisations Serving Households	...	...	...	...	...	...	...	...	...	...	...	...
Private Final Consumption Expenditure e	31610	35390	37720	39188	39598	41986	44192	44428	46906	48018	51081	56709

a) Estimates up to 1972 for 'Direct purchases abroad by resident households' have been obtained from the Central Bank. For 1973 and 1974, no estimates have been made. From 1975 onward, figures have been estimated independently by the Department of Census and Statistics.
b) For 1981 and 1982, transfers made by residents abroad are not included in item 'Direct Purchases Abroad by Resident Households' shown in table 2.17 but are included in the estimates shown in table 2.5.
c) Estimates up to 1974 for 'Direct purchases in the domestic market by non-resident households'

have been obtained from the Central Bank. From 1975 onward, figures have been estimated independently by the Department of Census and Statistics.
d) Item 'Final consumption expenditure of resident households' includes consumption expenditure of private non-profit institutions serving households.
e) The estimates before 1975 for this table have been calculated on the basis of 1963 prices and linked to the estimates for the years beginning 1975.

2.7 Gross Capital Formation by Type of Good and Owner, in Current Prices

Million Sri Lanka rupees

	1980				1981				1982			
	TOTAL	Total Private	Public Enterprises	General Government	TOTAL	Total Private	Public Enterprises	General Government	TOTAL	Total Private	Public Enterprises	General Government
Increase in stocks, total a	167	128	...	39	331	272	...	59	248	210	...	38
Gross Fixed Capital Formation, Total	22243	17066	...	5177	23955	19713	...	4242	27926	23680	...	4246
1 Residential buildings	3808	3645	...	162	5048	4996	...	51	6138	5981	...	157
2 Non-residential buildings	2839	1388	...	1451	2350	1199	...	1151	2356	1359	...	997
3 Other construction	1661	520	...	1141	3147	2125	...	1022	3074	1722	...	1353
4 Land improvement and plantation and orchard development	3453	2755	...	698	4063	3156	...	908	4398	3315	...	1083
5 Producers' durable goods	10483	8759	...	1725	9348	8236	...	1111	11960	11303	...	657
A Transport equipment	3653	3158	...	495	2850	2430	...	420	6627	6257	...	369
B Machinery and equipment	6831	5600	...	1230	6497	5806	...	691	5333	5046	...	287
6 Breeding stock, dairy cattle, etc.	...	...	...	...	...	...	...	...	...	...	...	...
Total Gross Capital Formation b	22410	17194	...	5216	24286	19985	...	4301	28174	23890	...	4284

	1983				1984				1985			
	TOTAL	Total Private	Public Enterprises	General Government	TOTAL	Total Private	Public Enterprises	General Government	TOTAL	Total Private	Public Enterprises	General Government
Increase in stocks, total a	-210	-174	...	-36	150	123	...	27	225	178	...	47
Gross Fixed Capital Formation, Total	31584	26156	...	5428	34262	28121	...	6142	37651	29893	...	7758
1 Residential buildings	6950	6883	...	67	7238	7186	...	53	9525	9477	...	48
2 Non-residential buildings	2858	1564	...	1294	2399	1633	...	766	3039	2154	...	885
3 Other construction	3848	1981	...	1867	4633	2069	...	2565	6490	2728	...	3762
4 Land improvement and plantation and orchard development	3988	2798	...	1191	6442	4784	...	1658	2804	1096	...	1708
5 Producers' durable goods	13939	12930	...	1009	13550	12449	...	1101	15793	14437	...	1355
A Transport equipment	5753	5414	...	339	5621	5184	...	437	5328	4506	...	822
B Machinery and equipment	8186	7516	...	671	7929	7266	...	664	10465	9931	...	533
6 Breeding stock, dairy cattle, etc.	...	...	...	...	...	...	...	...	...	...	...	...
Total Gross Capital Formation b	31374	25982	...	5392	34412	28244	...	6168	37876	30071	...	7805

Sri Lanka

2.7 Gross Capital Formation by Type of Good and Owner, in Current Prices

Million Sri Lanka rupees

	1986				1987				1988			
	TOTAL	Total Private	Public Enterprises	General Government	TOTAL	Total Private	Public Enterprises	General Government	TOTAL	Total Private	Public Enterprises	General Government
Increase in stocks, total a	137	105	...	32	148	110	...	38	601	457	...	144
Gross Fixed Capital Formation, Total	38494	29557	...	8937	43948	32620	...	11328	47848	36349	...	11499
1 Residential buildings	10694	10495	...	199	10492	10286	...	206	11871	11649	...	222
2 Non-residential buildings	4167	2385	...	1782	4931	2961	...	1970	4671	2647	...	2024
3 Other construction	6197	3021	...	3176	6217	2338	...	3879	8116	3354	...	4762
4 Land improvement and plantation and orchard development	2769	1008	...	1761	4629	1960	...	2669	4313	2280	...	2033
5 Producers' durable goods	14667	12648	...	2019	17679	15075	...	2604	18877	16419	...	2458
A Transport equipment	4883	3682	...	1201	6049	4639	...	1410	6852	5664	...	1188
B Machinery and equipment	9784	8966	...	818	11630	10436	...	1194	12025	10755	...	1270
6 Breeding stock, dairy cattle, etc.	...	...	...	...	...	...	...	...	...	...	...	...
Total Gross Capital Formation b	38631	29662	...	8969	44096	32730	...	11366	48449	36806	...	11643

	1989				1990				1991			
	TOTAL	Total Private	Public Enterprises	General Government	TOTAL	Total Private	Public Enterprises	General Government	TOTAL	Total Private	Public Enterprises	General Government
Increase in stocks, total a	473	326	...	147	1038	789	...	249	950	770	...	180
Gross Fixed Capital Formation, Total	50968	35389	...	15579	64817	49148	...	15669	86463	69933	...	16530
1 Residential buildings	12500	12315	...	185	16716	16564	...	152	20878	20754	...	124
2 Non-residential buildings	5918	2799	...	3119	7223	3764	...	3459	7817	4717	...	3100
3 Other construction	11148	3545	...	7603	11012	4768	...	6244	10884	5975	...	4909
4 Land improvement and plantation and orchard development	3406	2439	...	967	5740	3504	...	2236	6696	3851	...	2845
5 Producers' durable goods	17996	14291	...	3705	24126	20548	...	3578	40188	34636	...	5552
A Transport equipment	6168	4843	...	1325	5755	4154	...	1601	18932	15374	...	3558
B Machinery and equipment	11828	9448	...	2380	18371	16394	...	1977	21256	19262	...	1994
6 Breeding stock, dairy cattle, etc.	...	...	...	...	...	...	...	...	...	...	...	...
Total Gross Capital Formation b	51441	35715	...	15726	65855	49937	...	15918	87413	70702	...	16711

a) The estimates of 'Increase in stocks' for the years prior to 1975 include a statistical discrepancy.
b) Column 'Public Enterprises' is included in column 'General Government'.

2.8 Gross Capital Formation by Type of Good and Owner, in Constant Prices

Million Sri Lanka rupees

	1980				1981				1982			
	TOTAL	Total Private	Public Enterprises	General Government	TOTAL	Total Private	Public Enterprises	General Government	TOTAL	Total Private	Public Enterprises	General Government
	At constant prices of:1975											
Increase in stocks, total	75	58	...	18	127	105	...	23	91	77	...	14
Gross Fixed Capital Formation, Total	6911	5103	...	1809	7306	5922	...	1384	7425	6169	...	1257
1 Residential buildings	1178	1128	...	50	1312	1299	...	13	1527	1488	...	39
2 Non-residential buildings	1108	542	...	566	774	395	...	379	726	419	...	307
3 Other construction	690	216	...	474	1161	784	...	377	1053	590	...	463
4 Land improvement and plantation and orchard development	1118	864	...	255	1361	1067	...	294	1463	1139	...	325
5 Producers' durable goods	2817	2354	...	464	2698	2377	...	321	2656	2533	...	123
A Transport equipment	982	849	...	133	823	701	...	121	1250	1182	...	68
B Machinery and equipment	1836	1505	...	331	1875	1676	...	199	1406	1352	...	54
6 Breeding stock, dairy cattle, etc.	...	...	...	...	...	...	...	...	...	...	...	...
Total Gross Capital Formation a	6986	5160	...	1826	7434	6027	...	1407	7516	6245	...	1270

2.8 Gross Capital Formation by Type of Good and Owner, in Constant Prices

Million Sri Lanka rupees

	1983				1984				1985			
	TOTAL	Total Private	Public Enterprises	General Government	TOTAL	Total Private	Public Enterprises	General Government	TOTAL	Total Private	Public Enterprises	General Government
						At constant prices of:1975						
Increase in stocks, total	-61	-51	...	-11	42	35	...	8	61	48	...	13
Gross Fixed Capital Formation, Total	7324	5852	...	1472	6680	5248	...	1432	6635	5016	...	1619
1 Residential buildings	1593	1577	...	15	1505	1494	...	11	1839	1830	...	9
2 Non-residential buildings	813	445	...	368	613	418	...	196	742	526	...	216
3 Other construction	1214	625	...	589	1288	575	...	713	1464	616	...	848
4 Land improvement and plantation and orchard development	1022	717	...	305	1398	1038	...	360	617	241	...	376
5 Producers' durable goods	2682	2488	...	194	1876	1723	...	152	1973	1804	...	169
A Transport equipment	1107	1042	...	65	778	718	...	61	666	563	...	103
B Machinery and equipment	1575	1446	...	129	1098	1006	...	92	1307	1241	...	66
6 Breeding stock, dairy cattle, etc.	...	...	...	...	...	...	...	...	...	...	...	...
Total Gross Capital Formation a	7262	5801	...	1461	6722	5282	...	1440	6696	5064	...	1632

	1986				1987				1988			
	TOTAL	Total Private	Public Enterprises	General Government	TOTAL	Total Private	Public Enterprises	General Government	TOTAL	Total Private	Public Enterprises	General Government
						At constant prices of:1975						
Increase in stocks, total	39	30	...	9	42	31	...	11	153	116	...	37
Gross Fixed Capital Formation, Total	6462	4704	...	1758	6931	4840	...	2091	6394	4490	...	1904
1 Residential buildings	2050	2012	...	38	1991	1952	...	39	1879	1844	...	35
2 Non-residential buildings	1017	582	...	435	1059	636	...	423	996	565	...	431
3 Other construction	1393	679	...	714	1388	522	...	866	1581	653	...	928
4 Land improvement and plantation and orchard development	594	216	...	378	923	391	...	532	754	399	...	355
5 Producers' durable goods	1408	1215	...	193	1570	1339	...	231	1184	1029	...	155
A Transport equipment	469	354	...	115	537	412	...	125	430	355	...	75
B Machinery and equipment	939	861	...	78	1033	927	...	106	754	674	...	80
6 Breeding stock, dairy cattle, etc.	...	...	...	...	...	...	...	...	...	...	...	...
Total Gross Capital Formation a	6501	4734	...	1767	6973	4871	...	2102	6547	4606	...	1941

	1989				1990				1991			
	TOTAL	Total Private	Public Enterprises	General Government	TOTAL	Total Private	Public Enterprises	General Government	TOTAL	Total Private	Public Enterprises	General Government
						At constant prices of:1975						
Increase in stocks, total	105	72	...	33	166	126	...	40	138	112	...	26
Gross Fixed Capital Formation, Total	6240	3918	...	2322	6526	4595	...	1931	7118	5500	...	1618
1 Residential buildings	1604	1580	...	24	2094	2075	...	19	2420	2406	...	14
2 Non-residential buildings	1063	503	...	560	1044	544	...	500	1044	630	...	414
3 Other construction	2020	642	...	1378	1741	754	...	987	1507	828	...	679
4 Land improvement and plantation and orchard development	518	371	...	147	729	445	...	284	730	420	...	310
5 Producers' durable goods	1035	822	...	213	918	777	...	141	1416	1217	...	199
A Transport equipment	355	279	...	76	251	181	...	70	704	572	...	132
B Machinery and equipment	680	543	...	137	667	596	...	71	712	645	...	67
6 Breeding stock, dairy cattle, etc.	...	...	...	...	...	...	...	...	...	...	...	...
Total Gross Capital Formation a	6345	3990	...	2355	6692	4721	...	1971	7256	5612	...	1644

a) Column 'Public Enterprises' is included in column 'General Government'.

2.17 Exports and Imports of Goods and Services, Detail

Million Sri Lanka rupees

	1980	1981	1982	1983	1984	1985	1986	1987	1988	1989	1990	1991
					Exports of Goods and Services							
1 Exports of merchandise, f.o.b. ab	17603	20507	21098	25038	37198	35729	33893	41097	46985	56175	79481	84378
2 Transport and communication	...	...	...	...	...	...	...	...	...	...	...	...
3 Insurance service charges	...	...	...	...	...	...	...	...	...	...	...	...
4 Other commodities c	1943	2756	3003	4026	3353	3524	5501	5894	6881	7835	11561	14823

2.17 Exports and Imports of Goods and Services, Detail
(Continued)

Million Sri Lanka rupees

	1980	1981	1982	1983	1984	1985	1986	1987	1988	1989	1990	1991
5 Adjustments of merchandise exports to change-of-ownership basis	...	...	...	...	...	...	...	...	...	...	...	...
6 Direct purchases in the domestic market by non-residential households d	1888	2629	3048	2952	3734	3141	3208	3778	4019	4656	6075	7185
7 Direct purchases in the domestic market by extraterritorial bodies	...	...	...	...	...	...	...	...	...	...	...	...
Total Exports of Goods and Services	21434	25892	27148	32016	44285	42394	42602	50763	57885	68666	97117	106386

Imports of Goods and Services

	1980	1981	1982	1983	1984	1985	1986	1987	1988	1989	1990	1991
1 Imports of merchandise, c.i.f. b	33915	36121	41420	45201	49046	55528	55284	61102	71253	80225	107605	125511
2 Adjustments of merchandise imports to change-of-ownership basis	...	...	...	...	...	...	...	...	...	...	...	...
3 Other transport and communication	483	659	884	1256	1409	2077	2724	3176	3657	4832	6072	6546
4 Other insurance service charges	41	55	114	185	261	278	867	526	537	631	590	402
5 Other commodities	361	189	217	-	-	-	-	-	-	-	-	-
6 Direct purchases abroad by government	...	...	...	...	...	...	...	...	...	...	...	...
7 Direct purchases abroad by resident households ef	1656	4300	5202	5945	6839	7468	9316	8128	8617	9863	16960	19709
Statistical discrepancy	...	-1766	-1930	-2206	-3086	-2955	-4454	-2238	-2293	-2964	-8746	-7467
Total Imports of Goods and Services	36456	39558	45905	50381	54469	62396	63737	70694	81771	92587	122481	144701
Balance of Goods and Services	-15022	-13667	-18758	-18365	-10184	-20002	-21135	-19931	-23886	-23921	-25364	-38315
Total Imports and Balance of Goods and Services	21434	25892	27148	32016	44285	42394	42602	50763	57885	68666	97117	106386

a) Item 'Exports of merchandise, f.o.b.' excludes merchandise purchases in the domestic market by non-resident households.
b) Prior to 1978, estimates of imports and exports of goods and services are valued at the Foreign Exchange Entitlement Certificate Rate (FEECR) which is a proxy to the unitary rate.
c) Item 'Other commodities' has been obtained as a residual.
d) Estimates up to 1974 for 'Direct purchases in the domestic market by non-resident households' have been obtained from the Central Bank. From 1975 onward, figures have been estimated independently by the Department of Census and Statistics.
e) Estimates up to 1972 for 'Direct purchases abroad by resident households' have been obtained from the Central Bank. For 1973 and 1974, no estimates have been made. From 1975 onward, figures have been estimated independently by the Department of Census and Statistics.
f) For 1981 and 1982, transfers made by residents abroad are not included in item 'Direct Purchases Abroad by Resident Households' shown in table 2.17 but are included in the estimates shown in table 2.5.

4.1 Derivation of Value Added by Kind of Activity, in Current Prices

Million Sri Lanka rupees

	1980			1981			1982			1983		
	Gross Output	Intermediate Consumption	Value Added	Gross Output	Intermediate Consumption	Value Added	Gross Output	Intermediate Consumption	Value Added	Gross Output	Intermediate Consumption	Value Added

All Producers

	Gross Output	Intermediate Consumption	Value Added	Gross Output	Intermediate Consumption	Value Added	Gross Output	Intermediate Consumption	Value Added	Gross Output	Intermediate Consumption	Value Added
1 Agriculture, hunting, forestry and fishing a	...	...	17900	27496	4709	22787	31091	5834	25258	38474	8006	30468
A Agriculture and hunting	...	...	15824	24476	3944	20532	27574	4978	22596	34177	6676	27501
B Forestry and logging	...	...	946	944	-	944	1091	14	1077	1254	20	1234
C Fishing	...	...	1130	2076	765	1311	2427	841	1586	3043	1311	1733
2 Mining and quarrying	...	...	910	1268	190	1078	1364	205	1159	1566	146	1420
A Coal mining	...	...	...	...	...	...	...	...	...	...	...	...
B Crude petroleum and natural gas production	...	...	...	...	...	...	...	...	...	...	...	...
C Metal ore mining	...	...	...	...	...	...	...	...	...	...	...	...
D Other mining	...	...	910	1268	190	1078	1364	205	1159	1566	146	1420

4.1 Derivation of Value Added by Kind of Activity, in Current Prices
(Continued)

Million Sri Lanka rupees

	1980			1981			1982			1983		
	Gross Output	Intermediate Consumption	Value Added	Gross Output	Intermediate Consumption	Value Added	Gross Output	Intermediate Consumption	Value Added	Gross Output	Intermediate Consumption	Value Added
3 Manufacturing a	...	...	12422	24837	10810	14028	35915	21271	14644	40913	22980	17933
A Manufacture of food, beverages and tobacco	...	...	6065	12956	6206	6750	14945	7421	7524	19718	10268	9451
B Textile, wearing apparel and leather industries	...	...	1550	2473	830	1643	2960	972	1988	2784	924	1860
C Manufacture of wood and wood products, including furniture	...	...	154	267	90	177	456	143	313	544	168	376
D Manufacture of paper and paper products, printing and publishing	...	...	255	448	156	292	414	144	270	426	148	278
E Manufacture of chemicals and chemical petroleum, coal, rubber and plastic products	...	...	1950	3577	1278	2299	13310	10633	2676	11332	8132	3200
F Manufacture of non-metallic mineral products, except products of petroleum and coal	...	...	925	1631	528	1103	1486	504	982	1534	518	1016
G Basic metal industries	...	...	108	192	67	125	119	42	77	243	85	158
H Manufacture of fabricated metal products, machinery and equipment	...	...	793	1278	447	831	331	116	215	612	214	398
I Other manufacturing industries	...	...	622	2015	1208	807	1895	1297	598	3721	2524	1197
4 Electricity, gas and water	...	...	547	1579	576	1003	2621	1078	1543	4145	2534	1611
A Electricity, gas and steam	...	...	547	1579	576	1003	2621	1078	1543	4145	2534	1611
B Water works and supply	...	...	...	...	...	...	...	...	...	...	...	...
5 Construction	...	...	6503	14536	6499	8037	15696	7045	8651	17686	7784	9902
6 Wholesale and retail trade, restaurants and hotels	...	...	11331	19725	3557	16168	23384	3653	19732	28408	4508	23901
A Wholesale and retail trade	...	...	10895	18753	3168	15585	22058	3139	18919	27398	4110	23288
B Restaurants and hotels	...	...	436	972	389	583	1326	513	812	1010	398	612
Restaurants	...	...	...	...	...	...	527	207	321	568	224	344
Hotels and other lodging places	...	...	...	...	...	...	799	307	492	442	174	268
7 Transport, storage and communication	...	...	6962	15592	8209	7383	20240	10492	9748	23711	12075	11635
A Transport and storage	...	...	...	15362	8209	7153	19814	10492	9322	22803	12075	10727
B Communication	...	...	...	230	-	230	426	-	426	908	-	908
8 Finance, insurance, real estate and business services	...	...	3620	5246	623	4624	6509	625	5884	7925	699	7226
A Financial institutions	...	...	1877	2689	113	2576	3848	115	3732	5149	117	5032
B Insurance	...	...										
C Real estate and business services	...	...	1743	2557	510	2047	2662	510	2152	2776	582	2194
Real estate, except dwellings	...	...	84	100	-	100	114	-	114	131	-	131
Dwellings	...	...	1659	2457	510	1947	2548	510	2039	2645	582	2063
9 Community, social and personal services	...	...	1513	2524	651	1873	2731	638	2093	3477	715	2762
A Sanitary and similar services	...	...	...	...	...	...	...	...	...	...	...	...
B Social and related community services	...	...	217	312	73	239	742	222	519	1003	267	736
C Recreational and cultural services	...	...	800	1302	461	840	1143	325	818	1323	336	987
D Personal and household services	...	...	496	911	117	794	847	91	756	1151	111	1039
Total, Industries	...	...	61708	112805	35824	76981	139551	50840	88711	166304	59447	106857
Producers of Government Services	...	...	3573	7456	3294	4162	10407	5029	5379	12733	5473	7260
Other Producers	...	...	133	158	-	158	215	-	215	249	-	249
Total	...	...	65414	120419	39118	81302	150174	55869	94305	179286	64920	114366
Less: Imputed bank service charge	...	...	...	...	...	...	...	...	...	...	...	...
Import duties	...	...	2924	3225	-	3225	3222	-	3222	4836	-	4836
Value added tax	...	...	...	...	...	...	...	...	...	...	...	...
Total	...	...	68338	123644	39118	84527	153396	55869	97528	184121	64920	119202

Sri Lanka

Million Sri Lanka rupees

	1984			1985			1986			1987		
	Gross Output	Intermediate Consumption	Value Added	Gross Output	Intermediate Consumption	Value Added	Gross Output	Intermediate Consumption	Value Added	Gross Output	Intermediate Consumption	Value Added
All Producers												
1 Agriculture, hunting, forestry and fishing a	45132	7839	37293	47008	8502	38506	48918	9389	39529	53460	10286	43174
A Agriculture and hunting	40222	6950	33272	41663	7457	34206	42773	8112	34661	46393	8764	37629
B Forestry and logging	1444	13	1431	1652	15	1637	1723	13	1710	1797	18	1779
C Fishing	3466	876	2590	3693	1030	2663	4422	1264	3158	5270	1504	3766
2 Mining and quarrying	1344	135	1209	1372	145	1227	1869	199	1670	2412	218	2194
A Coal mining	...	...	...	...	...	...	...	...	...	...	...	...
B Crude petroleum and natural gas production	...	...	...	...	...	...	...	...	...	...	...	...
C Metal ore mining	...	...	...	...	...	...	...	...	...	...	...	...
D Other mining	1344	135	1209	1372	145	1227	1869	199	1670	2412	218	2194
3 Manufacturing a	57899	33598	24301	58938	32758	26180	59866	32952	26914	69165	39464	29701
A Manufacture of food, beverages and tobacco	29679	14423	15256	25868	11841	14027	28762	13905	14857	33481	17037	16444
B Textile, wearing apparel and leather industries	8416	5323	3093	9731	5634	4097	10527	6217	4310	13912	8233	5679
C Manufacture of wood and wood products, including furniture	655	207	448	980	317	663	913	292	621	945	301	644
D Manufacture of paper and paper products, printing and publishing	34	11	23	680	236	444	354	122	232	504	175	329
E Manufacture of chemicals and chemical petroleum, coal, rubber and plastic products	13834	11184	2650	12625	10345	2280	10596	8495	2101	13571	10536	3035
F Manufacture of non-metallic mineral products, except products of petroleum and coal	964	313	651	1865	627	1238	1748	587	1161	903	291	612
G Basic metal industries	84	30	54	147	51	96	180	63	117	115	40	75
H Manufacture of fabricated metal products, machinery and equipment	1335	467	868	2894	1013	1881	3108	1087	2021	1989	696	1293
I Other manufacturing industries	2898	1640	1258	4148	2694	1454	3678	2184	1494	3745	2155	1590
4 Electricity, gas and water	3304	797	2507	3369	370	2999	3520	458	3062	4435	978	3457
A Electricity, gas and steam	3304	797	2507	3369	370	2999	3520	458	3062	4435	978	3457
B Water works and supply	...	...	...	...	...	...	...	...	...	...	...	...
5 Construction	20411	9105	11306	21550	9611	11939	23667	10470	13197	25547	11340	14207
6 Wholesale and retail trade, restaurants and hotels	32114	5163	26951	36616	7555	29061	41323	8607	32716	44739	9366	35373
A Wholesale and retail trade	30683	4602	26081	35410	7082	28328	39565	7913	31652	42650	8530	34120
B Restaurants and hotels	1431	561	870	1206	473	733	1758	694	1064	2089	836	1253
Restaurants	1012	397	615	804	315	489	1288	508	780	1539	616	923
Hotels and other lodging places	419	164	255	402	158	244	470	196	284	550	220	330
7 Transport, storage and communication	31730	16109	15621	34413	16984	17429	36972	17311	19661	38481	18245	20236
A Transport and storage	30772	16109	14663	33365	16984	16381	35827	17311	18516	37248	18245	19003
B Communication	958	-	958	1048	-	1048	1145	-	1145	1233	-	1233
8 Finance, insurance, real estate and business services	9370	747	8623	10059	824	9235	11499	871	10628	12237	874	11363
A Financial institutions	6357	118	6239	6693	118	6575	8006	141	7865	8639	124	8515
B Insurance												
C Real estate and business services	3013	629	2384	3366	706	2660	3493	730	2763	3597	749	2848
Real estate, except dwellings	155	-	155	158	-	158	175	-	175	192	-	192
Dwellings	2858	629	2229	3208	706	2502	3318	730	2588	3405	749	2656
9 Community, social and personal services	3840	783	3057	4055	809	3246	4507	913	3594	5370	1008	4362
A Sanitary and similar services	...	...	...	...	...	...	...	...	...	...	...	...
B Social and related community services	1053	290	763	1127	303	824	1237	329	908	1413	351	1062
C Recreational and cultural services	1469	364	1105	1456	374	1082	1576	388	1188	1852	425	1427
D Personal and household services	1318	129	1189	1472	132	1340	1694	196	1498	2105	232	1873

4.1 Derivation of Value Added by Kind of Activity, in Current Prices
(Continued)

Million Sri Lanka rupees

	1984 Gross Output	1984 Intermediate Consumption	1984 Value Added	1985 Gross Output	1985 Intermediate Consumption	1985 Value Added	1986 Gross Output	1986 Intermediate Consumption	1986 Value Added	1987 Gross Output	1987 Intermediate Consumption	1987 Value Added
Total, Industries	205144	74276	130868	217380	77558	139822	232141	81170	150971	255846	91779	164067
Producers of Government Services	15442	7205	8237	19170	9926	9244	22990	11866	11124	26204	13496	12708
Other Producers	294	-	294	300	-	300	331	-	331	364	-	364
Total	220880	81481	139399	236850	87484	149366	255462	93036	162426	282414	105275	177139
Less: Imputed bank service charge	...	...	...	...	...	...	...	...	...	...	...	...
Import duties	7945	-	7945	8397	-	8397	10014	-	10014	11683	-	11683
Value added tax	...	...	...	...	...	...	...	...	...	...	...	...
Total	228825	81481	147344	245247	87484	157763	265476	93036	172440	294097	105275	188822

	1988 Gross Output	1988 Intermediate Consumption	1988 Value Added	1989 Gross Output	1989 Intermediate Consumption	1989 Value Added	1990 Gross Output	1990 Intermediate Consumption	1990 Value Added	1991 Gross Output	1991 Intermediate Consumption	1991 Value Added
All Producers												
1 Agriculture, hunting, forestry and fishing a	63408	12334	51074	70537	13763	56774	90129	17341	72788	101901	19975	81926
A Agriculture and hunting	54792	10456	44336	60793	11322	49471	78378	14389	63989	87335	16179	71156
B Forestry and logging	2010	12	1998	2521	13	2508	2961	21	2940	3221	16	3205
C Fishing	6606	1866	4740	7223	2428	4795	8790	2931	5859	11345	3780	7565
2 Mining and quarrying	3295	271	3024	3961	356	3605	5004	434	4570	4463	415	4048
A Coal mining	...	...	...	...	...	...	...	...	...	...	...	...
B Crude petroleum and natural gas production	...	...	...	...	...	...	...	...	...	...	...	...
C Metal ore mining	...	...	...	...	...	...	...	...	...	...	...	...
D Other mining	3295	271	3024	3961	356	3605	5004	434	4570	4463	415	4048
3 Manufacturing a	77378	42526	34852	87457	46042	41415	115025	60082	54943	110436	47638	62798
A Manufacture of food, beverages and tobacco	38436	19089	19347	44912	22523	22389	54684	28064	26620	58485	27482	31003
B Textile, wearing apparel and leather industries	16049	9333	6716	19374	11396	7978	25465	15373	10092	18892	6473	12419
C Manufacture of wood and wood products, including furniture	947	297	650	920	285	635	1206	372	834	1310	404	906
D Manufacture of paper and paper products, printing and publishing	476	165	311	358	123	235	462	159	303	524	180	344
E Manufacture of chemicals and chemical petroleum, coal, rubber and plastic products	13714	10432	3282	10874	6618	4256	19824	10485	9339	17135	7710	9425
F Manufacture of non-metallic mineral products, except products of petroleum and coal	1413	466	947	2627	888	1739	3287	1099	2188	3520	1173	2347
G Basic metal industries	255	89	166	315	110	205	400	140	260	511	179	332
H Manufacture of fabricated metal products, machinery and equipment	3000	1050	1950	3374	1181	2193	4453	1558	2895	5263	1841	3422
I Other manufacturing industries	3088	1605	1483	4703	2918	1785	5244	2832	2412	4796	2196	2600
4 Electricity, gas and water	5036	1050	3986	4602	352	4250	6210	575	5635	7448	949	6499
A Electricity, gas and steam	4754	855	3899	4460	264	4196	5768	310	5458	6566	420	6146
B Water works and supply	282	195	87	142	88	54	442	265	177	882	529	353
5 Construction	27590	12241	15349	31422	13917	17505	38738	17146	21592	44334	19476	24858
6 Wholesale and retail trade, restaurants and hotels	52501	10858	41643	56179	11616	44563	76250	15764	60486	92106	19032	73074
A Wholesale and retail trade	50654	10131	40523	54234	10847	43387	73681	14736	58945	89051	17810	71241
B Restaurants and hotels	1847	727	1120	1945	769	1176	2569	1028	1541	3055	1222	1833
Restaurants	1258	495	763	1479	585	894	1555	622	933	1703	681	1022
Hotels and other lodging places	589	232	357	466	184	282	1014	406	608	1352	541	811
7 Transport, storage and communication	41707	19402	22305	45636	21759	23877	57686	26774	30912	68606	31163	37443
A Transport and storage	40082	19402	20680	43872	21759	22113	56388	26774	29614	66432	31163	35269
B Communication	1625	-	1625	1764	-	1764	1298	-	1298	2174	-	2174
8 Finance, insurance, real estate and business services	14231	909	13322	15822	951	14871	18728	996	17732	22156	1121	21035
A Financial institutions	10448	126	10322	11862	138	11724	14575	154	14421	17428	162	17266
B Insurance												
C Real estate and business services	3783	783	3000	3960	813	3147	4153	842	3311	4728	959	3769
Real estate, except dwellings	222	-	222	265	-	265	326	-	326	371	-	371

Sri Lanka

Million Sri Lanka rupees

	1988			1989			1990			1991		
	Gross Output	Intermediate Consumption	Value Added	Gross Output	Intermediate Consumption	Value Added	Gross Output	Intermediate Consumption	Value Added	Gross Output	Intermediate Consumption	Value Added
Dwellings	3561	783	2778	3695	813	2882	3827	842	2985	4357	959	3398
9 Community, social and personal services	6442	1158	5284	6826	1342	5484	8799	1824	6975	11620	2296	9324
A Sanitary and similar services	...	...	...	...	...	...	...	...	...	...	...	...
B Social and related community services	1588	378	1210	1685	427	1258	2188	576	1612	3514	779	2735
C Recreational and cultural services	2088	485	1603	2416	567	1849	3323	819	2504	4288	1049	3239
D Personal and household services	2766	295	2471	2725	348	2377	3288	429	2859	3818	469	3349
Total, Industries	291588	100749	190839	322442	110098	212344	416569	140936	275633	463070	142065	321005
Producers of Government Services	30331	14416	15915	32585	12910	19675	41836	17713	24123	50776	21924	28852
Other Producers	421	-	421	503	-	503	618	-	618	703	-	703
Total	322340	115165	207175	355530	123008	232522	459023	158649	300374	514549	163989	350560
Less: Imputed bank service charge	...	...	...	...	...	...	...	...	...	...	...	...
Import duties	11599	-	11599	15708	-	15708	17530	-	17530	19160	-	19160
Value added tax	...	...	...	...	...	...	...	...	...	...	...	...
Total	333939	115165	218774	371238	123008	248230	476553	158649	317904	533709	163990	369720

a) The estimates on processing of tea and rubber are included in the agricultural sector prior to 1975. From 1975 onward, they are included in the manufacturing sector.

4.2 Derivation of Value Added by Kind of Activity, in Constant Prices

Million Sri Lanka rupees

	1980			1981			1982			1983		
	Gross Output	Intermediate Consumption	Value Added	Gross Output	Intermediate Consumption	Value Added	Gross Output	Intermediate Consumption	Value Added	Gross Output	Intermediate Consumption	Value Added
				At constant prices of:1975								
				All Producers								
1 Agriculture, hunting, forestry and fishing a	...	...	9357	...	...	10058	...	...	10372	...	...	10994
A Agriculture and hunting	...	...	8542	...	...	9177	...	...	9411	...	...	9962
B Forestry and logging	...	...	287	...	...	279	...	...	317	...	...	373
C Fishing	...	...	528	...	...	602	...	...	644	...	...	660
2 Mining and quarrying	...	...	475	...	...	500	...	...	479	...	...	575
A Coal mining	...	...	...	...	...	...	...	...	...	...	...	...
B Crude petroleum and natural gas production	...	...	...	...	...	...	...	...	...	...	...	...
C Metal ore mining	...	...	...	...	...	...	...	...	...	...	...	...
D Other mining	...	...	475	...	...	500	...	...	479	...	...	575
3 Manufacturing a	...	...	7071	...	...	7327	...	...	7281	...	...	7064
A Manufacture of food, beverages and tobacco	...	...	3452	...	...	3526	...	...	3741	...	...	3973
B Textile, wearing apparel and leather industries	...	...	882	...	...	858	...	...	989	...	...	651
C Manufacture of wood and wood products, including furniture	...	...	88	...	...	92	...	...	156	...	...	151
D Manufacture of paper and paper products, printing and publishing	...	...	145	...	...	153	...	...	134	...	...	94
E Manufacture of chemicals and chemical petroleum, coal, rubber and plastic products	...	...	1110	...	...	1201	...	...	1331	...	...	1148
F Manufacture of non-metallic mineral products, except products of petroleum and coal	...	...	527	...	...	576	...	...	488	...	...	285
G Basic metal industries	...	...	62	...	...	65	...	...	38	...	...	61
H Manufacture of fabricated metal products, machinery and equipment	...	...	451	...	...	434	...	...	107	...	...	236
I Other manufacturing industries	...	...	354	...	...	421	...	...	297	...	...	465
4 Electricity, gas and water	...	...	181	...	...	203	...	...	222	...	...	226
A Electricity, gas and steam	...	...	181	...	...	203	...	...	...	...	...	...
B Water works and supply	...	...	...	...	...	...	...	...	...	...	...	...

4.2 Derivation of Value Added by Kind of Activity, in Constant Prices
(Continued)

Million Sri Lanka rupees

	1980			1981			1982			1983		
	Gross Output	Intermediate Consumption	Value Added	Gross Output	Intermediate Consumption	Value Added	Gross Output	Intermediate Consumption	Value Added	Gross Output	Intermediate Consumption	Value Added
					At constant prices of:1975							
5 Construction	...	...	1947	...	...	2208	...	...	2157	...	...	2172
6 Wholesale and retail trade, restaurants and hotels	...	...	7564	...	...	8059	...	...	9408	...	...	10162
A Wholesale and retail trade	...	...	7267	...	...	7719	...	...	8999	...	...	9731
B Restaurants and hotels	...	...	297	...	...	340	...	...	409	...	...	430
7 Transport, storage and communication	...	...	3460	...	...	3564	...	...	3658	...	...	4043
A Transport and storage	...	...	...	...	...	...	...	...	...	...	...	...
B Communication	...	...	...	...	...	...	...	...	...	...	...	...
8 Finance, insurance, real estate and business services	...	...	1269	...	...	1357	...	...	1512	...	...	1566
A Financial institutions	...	...	541	...	...	622	...	...	762	...	...	805
B Insurance	...	...		...	...		...	...		...	...	
C Real estate and business services	...	...	728	...	...	735	...	...	750	...	...	761
Real estate, except dwellings	...	...	52	...	...	53	...	...	54	...	...	55
Dwellings	...	...	675	...	...	682	...	...	696	...	...	706
9 Community, social and personal services	...	...	980	...	...	1076	...	...	1117	...	...	1196
A Sanitary and similar services	...	...	...	...	...	...	...	...	...	...	...	...
B Social and related community services	...	...	138	...	...	133	...	...	309	...	...	367
C Recreational and cultural services	...	...	530	...	...	504	...	...	461	...	...	488
D Personal and household services	...	...	312	...	...	439	...	...	347	...	...	340
Total, Industries b	...	...	32305	...	...	34352	...	...	36206	...	...	37997
Producers of Government Services	...	...	2206	...	...	2236	...	...	2256	...	...	2272
Other Producers	...	...	83	...	...	84	...	...	102	...	...	104
Total b	...	...	34594	...	...	36672	...	...	38564	...	...	40373
Less: Imputed bank service charge	...	...	...	...	...	...	...	...	...	...	...	...
Import duties	...	...	714	...	...	595	...	...	635	...	...	689
Value added tax	...	...	...	...	...	...	...	...	...	...	...	...
Total b	...	...	35308	...	...	37266	...	...	39199	...	...	41062

	1984			1985			1986			1987		
	Gross Output	Intermediate Consumption	Value Added	Gross Output	Intermediate Consumption	Value Added	Gross Output	Intermediate Consumption	Value Added	Gross Output	Intermediate Consumption	Value Added
					At constant prices of:1975							
					All Producers							
1 Agriculture, hunting, forestry and fishing a	...	...	10200	...	...	11146	...	...	11224	...	...	10562
A Agriculture and hunting	...	...	9359	...	...	10249	...	...	10276	...	...	9589
B Forestry and logging	...	...	351	...	...	399	...	...	415	...	...	419
C Fishing	...	...	490	...	...	498	...	...	533	...	...	554
2 Mining and quarrying	...	...	693	...	...	673	...	...	918	...	...	1133
A Coal mining	...	...	...	...	...	...	...	...	...	...	...	...
B Crude petroleum and natural gas production	...	...	...	...	...	...	...	...	...	...	...	...
C Metal ore mining	...	...	...	...	...	...	...	...	...	...	...	...
D Other mining	...	...	693	...	...	673	...	...	918	...	...	1133

Sri Lanka

Million Sri Lanka rupees

	1984			1985			1986			1987		
	Gross Output	Intermediate Consumption	Value Added	Gross Output	Intermediate Consumption	Value Added	Gross Output	Intermediate Consumption	Value Added	Gross Output	Intermediate Consumption	Value Added
				At constant prices of:1975								
3 Manufacturing a	...	...	8300	...	...	8812	...	...	9345	...	...	9670
A Manufacture of food, beverages and tobacco	...	...	4737	...	...	4435	...	...	5248	...	...	5721
B Textile, wearing apparel and leather industries	...	...	1381	...	...	1497	...	...	1303	...	...	1586
C Manufacture of wood and wood products, including furniture	...	...	126	...	...	175	...	...	168	...	...	169
D Manufacture of paper and paper products, printing and publishing	...	...	7	...	...	117	...	...	63	...	...	87
E Manufacture of chemicals and chemical petroleum, coal, rubber and plastic products	...	...	1298	...	...	1216	...	...	1185	...	...	1186
F Manufacture of non-metallic mineral products, except products of petroleum and coal	...	...	125	...	...	231	...	...	226	...	...	125
G Basic metal industries	...	...	17	...	...	29	...	...	36	...	...	22
H Manufacture of fabricated metal products, machinery and equipment	...	...	272	...	...	563	...	...	617	...	...	390
I Other manufacturing industries	...	...	337	...	...	549	...	...	499	...	...	384
4 Electricity, gas and water	...	...	253	...	...	274	...	...	294	...	...	304
A Electricity, gas and steam	...	...	...	...	...	...	...	...	...	...	...	...
B Water works and supply	...	...	...	...	...	...	...	...	...	...	...	...
5 Construction	...	...	2200	...	...	2248	...	...	2419	...	...	2556
6 Wholesale and retail trade, restaurants and hotels	...	...	10907	...	...	11422	...	...	11983	...	...	12422
A Wholesale and retail trade	...	...	10291	...	...	10926	...	...	11421	...	...	11876
B Restaurants and hotels	...	...	616	...	...	496	...	...	562	...	...	546
7 Transport, storage and communication	...	...	4531	...	...	4607	...	...	4718	...	...	4803
A Transport and storage	...	...	...	...	...	...	...	...	...	...	...	...
B Communication	...	...	...	...	...	...	...	...	...	...	...	...
8 Finance, insurance, real estate and business services	...	...	1649	...	...	1719	...	...	1772	...	...	1834
A Financial institutions	...	...	879	...	...	938	...	...	976	...	...	1026
B Insurance	...	...		...	...		...	...		...	...	
C Real estate and business services	...	...	770	...	...	781	...	...	795	...	...	808
Real estate, except dwellings	...	...	55	...	...	56	...	...	57	...	...	58
Dwellings	...	...	715	...	...	726	...	...	738	...	...	750
9 Community, social and personal services	...	...	1296	...	...	1299	...	...	1338	...	...	1377
A Sanitary and similar services	...	...	...	...	...	...	...	...	...	...	...	...
B Social and related community services	...	...	372	...	...	393	...	...	413	...	...	438
C Recreational and cultural services	...	...	532	...	...	488	...	...	517	...	...	543
D Personal and household services	...	...	392	...	...	418	...	...	408	...	...	396
Total, Industries b	...	...	40029	...	...	42200	...	...	44011	...	...	44661
Producers of Government Services	...	...	2298	...	...	2334	...	...	2380	...	...	2475
Other Producers	...	...	105	...	...	106	...	...	108	...	...	111
Total b	...	...	42432	...	...	44640	...	...	46499	...	...	47247
Less: Imputed bank service charge	...	...	...	...	...	...	...	...	...	...	...	...
Import duties	...	...	704	...	...	660	...	...	737	...	...	755
Value added tax	...	...	...	...	...	...	...	...	...	...	...	...
Total b	...	...	43136	...	...	45300	...	...	47236	...	...	48002

Sri Lanka

4.2 Derivation of Value Added by Kind of Activity, in Constant Prices

Million Sri Lanka rupees

	1988 Gross Output	1988 Intermediate Consumption	1988 Value Added	1989 Gross Output	1989 Intermediate Consumption	1989 Value Added	1990 Gross Output	1990 Intermediate Consumption	1990 Value Added	1991 Gross Output	1991 Intermediate Consumption	1991 Value Added
At constant prices of:1975												
All Producers												
1 Agriculture, hunting, forestry and fishing a	...	...	10837	...	...	10528	...	...	11454	...	...	11659
A Agriculture and hunting	...	...	9869	...	...	9514	...	...	10495	...	...	10638
B Forestry and logging	...	...	393	...	...	417	...	...	428	...	...	440
C Fishing	...	...	575	...	...	597	...	...	531	...	...	581
2 Mining and quarrying	...	...	1465	...	...	1818	...	...	2018	...	...	1618
A Coal mining	...	...	...	...	...	...	...	...	...	...	...	...
B Crude petroleum and natural gas production	...	...	...	...	...	...	...	...	...	...	...	...
C Metal ore mining	...	...	...	...	...	...	...	...	...	...	...	...
D Other mining	...	...	1465	...	...	1818	...	...	2018	...	...	1618
3 Manufacturing a	...	...	9911	...	...	10227	...	...	11178	...	...	11927
A Manufacture of food, beverages and tobacco	...	...	5766	...	...	6162	...	...	6769	...	...	7179
B Textile, wearing apparel and leather industries	...	...	1659	...	...	1728	...	...	1968	...	...	2250
C Manufacture of wood and wood products, including furniture	...	...	163	...	...	134	...	...	139	...	...	144
D Manufacture of paper and paper products, printing and publishing	...	...	78	...	...	50	...	...	54	...	...	61
E Manufacture of chemicals and chemical petroleum, coal, rubber and plastic products	...	...	1209	...	...	934	...	...	976	...	...	879
F Manufacture of non-metallic mineral products, except products of petroleum and coal	...	...	175	...	...	296	...	...	321	...	...	330
G Basic metal industries	...	...	45	...	...	47	...	...	51	...	...	67
H Manufacture of fabricated metal products, machinery and equipment	...	...	529	...	...	499	...	...	548	...	...	625
I Other manufacturing industries	...	...	287	...	...	377	...	...	352	...	...	392
4 Electricity, gas and water	...	...	315	...	...	321	...	...	351	...	...	375
A Electricity, gas and steam	...	...	299	...	...	306	...	...	337	...	...	358
B Water works and supply	...	...	16	...	...	15	...	...	14	...	...	17
5 Construction	...	...	2596	...	...	2616	...	...	2638	...	...	2683
6 Wholesale and retail trade, restaurants and hotels	...	...	12772	...	...	13077	...	...	13533	...	...	14525
A Wholesale and retail trade	...	...	12384	...	...	12672	...	...	13207	...	...	14190
B Restaurants and hotels	...	...	388	...	...	405	...	...	326	...	...	335
7 Transport, storage and communication	...	...	4828	...	...	4774	...	...	5121	...	...	5522
A Transport and storage	...	...	4528	...	...	4453	...	...	4926	...	...	5210
B Communication	...	...	300	...	...	321	...	...	195	...	...	312
8 Finance, insurance, real estate and business services	...	...	1905	...	...	1982	...	...	2052	...	...	2149
A Financial institutions	...	...	[1086]	...	...	[1145]	...	...	[1214]	...	...	[1291]
B Insurance	...	...		...	...		...	...		...	...	
C Real estate and business services	...	...	819	...	...	837	...	...	838	...	...	858
Real estate, except dwellings	...	...	59	...	...	67	...	...	68	...	...	68
Dwellings	...	...	760	...	...	770	...	...	770	...	...	790
9 Community, social and personal services	...	...	1338	...	...	1341	...	...	1390	...	...	1590
A Sanitary and similar services	...	...	...	...	...	...	...	...	...	...	...	...
B Social and related community services	...	...	384	...	...	372	...	...	396	...	...	527
C Recreational and cultural services	...	...	495	...	...	538	...	...	539	...	...	594
D Personal and household services	...	...	459	...	...	431	...	...	455	...	...	469

Sri Lanka

4.2 Derivation of Value Added by Kind of Activity, in Constant Prices
(Continued)

Million Sri Lanka rupees

	1988			1989			1990			1991		
	Gross Output	Intermediate Consumption	Value Added	Gross Output	Intermediate Consumption	Value Added	Gross Output	Intermediate Consumption	Value Added	Gross Output	Intermediate Consumption	Value Added
				At constant prices of:1975								
Total, Industries b	...	...	45967	...	...	46684	...	...	49735	...	...	52048
Producers of Government Services	...	...	2502	...	...	2750	...	...	2851	...	...	3029
Other Producers	...	...	112	...	...	127	...	...	129	...	...	129
Total b	...	...	48581	...	...	49561	...	...	52715	...	...	55206
Less: Imputed bank service charge	...	...	...	...	...	...	...	...	...	...	...	...
Import duties	...	...	755	...	...	749	...	...	734	...	...	810
Value added tax	...	...	...	...	...	...	...	...	...	...	...	...
Total b	...	...	49336	...	...	50310	...	...	53449	...	...	56016

a) The estimates on processing of tea and rubber are included in the agricultural sector prior to 1975. From 1975 onward, they are included in the manufacturing sector.   b) The estimates before 1975 for this table have been calculated on the basis of 1963 prices and linked to the estimates for the years beginning 1975.

4.3 Cost Components of Value Added

Million Sri Lanka rupees

	1983						1984					
	Compensation of Employees	Capital Consumption	Net Operating Surplus	Indirect Taxes	Less: Subsidies Received	Value Added	Compensation of Employees	Capital Consumption	Net Operating Surplus	Indirect Taxes	Less: Subsidies Received	Value Added
	All Producers											
1 Agriculture, hunting, forestry and fishing a	11898	...	17263	1461	154	30468	15269	...	22156	65	197	37293
A Agriculture and hunting	...	...	...	...	...	...	...	...	...	...	...	...
B Forestry and logging	...	...	...	...	...	...	...	...	...	...	...	...
C Fishing	...	...	...	...	...	...	...	...	...	...	...	...
2 Mining and quarrying	451	...	954	16	-	1420	381	...	806	22	-	1209
3 Manufacturing a	8509	...	3276	6930	782	17933	11417	...	4396	9368	880	24301
4 Electricity, gas and water	329	...	1178	104	-	1611	541	...	1942	24	-	2507
5 Construction	6809	...	2918	189	14	9902	7835	...	3358	116	3	11306
6 Wholesale and retail trade, restaurants and hotels b	8334	...	13590	6812	-	28736	8057	...	13145	13694	-	34896
7 Transport, storage and communication	4409	...	7851	152	776	11635	5956	...	10588	140	1063	15621
8 Finance, insurance, real estate and business services c	3790	...	2923	246	-	6960	4617	...	3277	456	-	8350
9 Community, social and personal services dc	1941	...	308	1029	-	3277	1955	...	310	1359	-	3624
Total, Industries e	46469	...	50262	16937	1727	111942	56028	...	59978	25244	2143	139107
Producers of Government Services	7260	...	...	...	...	7260	8237	...	...	...	...	8237
Other Producers d	...	...	...	...	...	...	...	...	...	...	...	...
Total e	53729	...	50262	16937	1727	119202	64265	...	59978	25244	2143	147344
Less: Imputed bank service charge	...	...	...	...	...	...	...	...	...	...	...	...
Import duties b	...	...	...	...	...	...	...	...	...	...	...	...
Value added tax	...	...	...	...	...	...	...	...	...	...	...	...
Total e	53729	...	50262	16937	1727	119202	64265	...	59977	25245	2143	147344

	1985						1986					
	Compensation of Employees	Capital Consumption	Net Operating Surplus	Indirect Taxes	Less: Subsidies Received	Value Added	Compensation of Employees	Capital Consumption	Net Operating Surplus	Indirect Taxes	Less: Subsidies Received	Value Added
	All Producers											
1 Agriculture, hunting, forestry and fishing a	15805	...	22932	54	285	38506	16245	...	23571	57	344	39529
A Agriculture and hunting	...	...	...	...	...	...	...	...	...	...	...	...
B Forestry and logging	...	...	...	...	...	...	...	...	...	...	...	...
C Fishing	...	...	...	...	...	...	...	...	...	...	...	...
2 Mining and quarrying	386	...	816	24	-	1227	530	...	1121	19	-	1670
3 Manufacturing a	14841	...	5715	6446	822	26180	16556	...	6375	4830	847	26914
4 Electricity, gas and water	645	...	2313	41	-	2999	656	...	2354	52	-	3062
5 Construction	8273	...	3545	124	3	11939	9031	...	3870	299	3	13197
6 Wholesale and retail trade, restaurants and hotels b	8448	...	13783	15227	-	37458	9060	...	14781	18889	-	42730
7 Transport, storage and communication	6506	...	11565	149	791	17429	7322	...	13016	231	908	19661
8 Finance, insurance, real estate and business services c	4653	...	3558	747	-	8957	5893	...	3927	512	-	10332
9 Community, social and personal services dc	1929	...	307	1588	-	3824	2307	...	366	1548	-	4221

4.3 Cost Components of Value Added
(Continued)

Million Sri Lanka rupees

	Compensation of Employees	Capital Consumption	Net Operating Surplus	Indirect Taxes	Less: Subsidies Received	Value Added	Compensation of Employees	Capital Consumption	Net Operating Surplus	Indirect Taxes	Less: Subsidies Received	Value Added
	1985						1986					
Total, Industries [e]	61486	...	64534	24402	1901	148519	67600	...	69381	26437	2102	161316
Producers of Government Services	9264	...	...	...	20	9244	11141	...	...	...	17	11124
Other Producers [d]	...	...	...	...	...	...	...	...	...	...	...	...
Total [e]	70750	...	64534	24402	1921	157763	78741	...	69381	26437	2119	172440
Less: Imputed bank service charge	...	...	...	...	...	...	...	...	...	...	...	...
Import duties [b]	...	...	...	...	...	...	...	...	...	...	...	...
Value added tax	...	...	...	...	...	...	...	...	...	...	...	...
Total [e]	70748	...	64534	24402	1921	157763	78741	...	69381	26437	2119	172440

	Compensation of Employees	Capital Consumption	Net Operating Surplus	Indirect Taxes	Less: Subsidies Received	Value Added	Compensation of Employees	Capital Consumption	Net Operating Surplus	Indirect Taxes	Less: Subsidies Received	Value Added
	1987						1988					
	All Producers											
1 Agriculture, hunting, forestry and fishing [a]	17741	...	25742	51	360	43174	20024	...	31338	1	289	51074
A Agriculture and hunting	...	...	...	...	...	...	17382	...	27205	1	252	44336
B Forestry and logging	...	...	...	...	...	...	779	...	1219	-	-	1998
C Fishing	...	...	...	...	...	...	1863	...	2914	-	37	4740
2 Mining and quarrying	699	...	1479	16	-	2194	910	...	2092	22	-	3024
3 Manufacturing [a]	17879	...	6884	5532	594	29701	20852	...	9279	5417	696	34852
4 Electricity, gas and water	726	...	2605	126	-	3457	828	...	3116	42	-	3986
5 Construction	9760	...	4183	269	5	14207	10095	...	5015	241	2	15349
6 Wholesale and retail trade, restaurants and hotels [b]	9987	...	16294	20775	-	47056	11585	...	20275	21382	-	53242
7 Transport, storage and communication	7570	...	13457	279	1071	20235	8026	...	15247	218	1186	22305
8 Finance, insurance, real estate and business services [c]	6368	...	4102	556	-	11026	7364	...	4824	742	-	12930
9 Community, social and personal services [dc]	2929	...	465	1670	-	5064	3062	...	651	2384	-	6097
Total, Industries [e]	73659	...	75211	29274	2030	176114	82746	...	91837	30449	2173	202859
Producers of Government Services	12729	...	...	...	21	12708	15949	...	...	...	34	15915
Other Producers [d]	...	...	...	...	...	...	...	...	...	...	...	...
Total [e]	86388	...	75211	29274	2051	188822	98695	...	91837	30449	2207	218774
Less: Imputed bank service charge	...	...	...	...	...	...	...	...	...	...	...	...
Import duties [b]	...	...	...	...	...	...	...	...	...	...	...	...
Value added tax	...	...	...	...	...	...	...	...	...	...	...	...
Total [e]	86388	...	75211	29274	2051	188822	98695	...	91837	30449	2207	218774

	Compensation of Employees	Capital Consumption	Net Operating Surplus	Indirect Taxes	Less: Subsidies Received	Value Added	Compensation of Employees	Capital Consumption	Net Operating Surplus	Indirect Taxes	Less: Subsidies Received	Value Added
	1989						1990					
	All Producers											
1 Agriculture, hunting, forestry and fishing [a]	21680	...	35379	1	286	56774	27961	...	45007	4	184	72788
A Agriculture and hunting	18827	...	30915	1	272	49471	...	...	...	...	...	...
B Forestry and logging	978	...	1530	-	-	2508	...	...	...	...	...	...
C Fishing	1875	...	2934	-	14	4795	...	...	...	...	...	...
2 Mining and quarrying	1073	...	2519	13	-	3605	1367	...	3176	27	-	4570
3 Manufacturing [a]	24160	...	11768	6054	567	41415	31203	...	14806	9317	383	54943
4 Electricity, gas and water	833	...	3264	153	-	4250	1122	...	4344	169	-	5635
5 Construction	11172	...	5969	366	2	17505	13801	...	7197	594	-	21592
6 Wholesale and retail trade, restaurants and hotels [b]	11190	...	20433	28648	-	60271	15823	...	27221	34973	-	78017
7 Transport, storage and communication	8415	...	16680	310	1528	23877	10951	...	22731	262	3032	30912
8 Finance, insurance, real estate and business services [c]	8273	...	5512	682	-	14467	10575	...	6225	452	-	17252
9 Community, social and personal services [dc]	3532	...	862	1997	-	6391	4663	...	1093	2316	-	8072

Sri Lanka

4.3 Cost Components of Value Added
(Continued)

__Million Sri Lanka rupees__

	1989						1990					
	Compensation of Employees	Capital Consumption	Net Operating Surplus	Indirect Taxes	Less: Subsidies Received	Value Added	Compensation of Employees	Capital Consumption	Net Operating Surplus	Indirect Taxes	Less: Subsidies Received	Value Added
Total, Industries e	90328	...	102386	38224	2383	228555	117466	...	131800	48114	3599	293781
Producers of Government Services	19705	...	...	...	30	19675	24178	...	-	-	55	24123
Other Producers d	...	...	...	...	...	...	...	...	...	...	...	...
Total e	110033	...	102386	38224	2413	248230	141644	...	131800	48114	3654	317904
Less: Imputed bank service charge	...	...	...	...	...	...	...	...	...	...	...	...
Import duties b	...	...	...	...	...	...	...	...	...	...	...	...
Value added tax	...	...	...	...	...	...	...	...	...	...	...	...
Total e	110033	...	102386	38224	2413	248230	141644	...	131800	48114	3654	317904

	1991					
	Compensation of Employees	Capital Consumption	Net Operating Surplus	Indirect Taxes	Less: Subsidies Received	Value Added
	All Producers					
1 Agriculture, hunting, forestry and fishing a	31306	...	50968	3	351	81926
A Agriculture and hunting	...	...	...	...	...	...
B Forestry and logging	...	...	...	...	...	...
C Fishing	...	...	...	...	...	...
2 Mining and quarrying	1204	...	2828	16	-	4048
3 Manufacturing a	37013	...	17952	9008	1175	62798
4 Electricity, gas and water	1290	...	5040	169	-	6499
5 Construction	15917	...	8466	475	-	24858
6 Wholesale and retail trade, restaurants and hotels b	19697	...	33704	38833	-	92234
7 Transport, storage and communication	13007	...	27909	20	3494	37442
8 Finance, insurance, real estate and business services c ..	12724	...	7416	362	-	20502
9 Community, social and personal services dc	6400	...	1549	2612	-	10561
Total, Industries e	138558	...	155832	51498	5020	340868
Producers of Government Services	28914	...	...	...	62	28852
Other Producers d	...	...	...	...	...	...
Total e	167472	...	155832	51498	5082	369720
Less: Imputed bank service charge	...	...	...	...	...	...
Import duties b	...	...	...	...	...	...
Value added tax	...	...	...	...	...	...
Total e	...	...	...	...	...	...

a) The estimates on processing of tea and rubber are included in the agricultural sector prior to 1975. From 1975 onward, they are included in the manufacturing sector.
b) Item 'Import duties' is included in item 'Wholesale and retail trade'.
c) Finance is included in item 'Community, social and personal services'.
d) Item 'Other producers' is included in item 'Community, social and personal services'.
e) Column 'Consumption of fixed capital' is included in column 'Net operating surplus'.

Sudan

General note. The preparation of national accounts statistics in Sudan is undertaken by the Department of Statistics, Khartoum. The official estimates together with the sources and methods used for the national accounts estimates are published in a series of publications entitled 'National Accounts and Supporting Tables'. The estimates are generally in accordance with the classifications and definitions recommended in the United Nations System of National Accounts (SNA). Input-output tables were published in 1964 in 'National Income of Sudan in 1961/62 (with preliminary estimates for 1962/63)'. The following tables have been prepared from successive replies to the United Nations national accounts questionnaire. From 1969 estimates relate to fiscal year beginning 1 July. When the scope and coverage of the estimates differ for conceptual or statistical reasons from the definitions and classifications recommended in SNA, a footnote is indicated to the relevant tables.

Sources and methods :

(a) Gross domestic product. Gross domestic product is estimated mainly through the production approach.

(b) Expenditure on the gross domestic product. All components of GDP by expenditure type are estimated through the expenditure approach except the estimates of gross fixed capital formation which are based partly on the commodity-flow method and partly on the expenditure approach. The sources of data for government final consumption expenditure are the actual figures available at Ministry of Treasury, Ministry of Local Government, different government units and public entities. For the central government, current and capital expenditure budgets are available, while for the local government figures on receipts and expenditures are available only for the six northern provinces, for the three southern provinces, budget figures have to be used. The estimates of private fixed consumption expenditure are based on the Household Budget Sample Survey 1967/68 which provided for the six northern provinces, data on average income and expenditure of households in the urban, semi-urban and rural areas. The number of households in these areas is based on the result of the 1973 Population Census. For the three southern provinces, which were not included in the Household Budget Sample Survey 1967/68, certain assumptions have been made to estimate their average expenditure per household. The expenditure by object per household has been calculated for 1967/68 to 1970/71 by multiplying an estimated rate of consumption increase by the number of urban, semi-urban and rural households in the North and the South. Increase in stocks is estimated partly on the basis of replies to questionnaires sent to public enterprises, producing industries and wholesale and retail trade companies. Capital formation estimates for central government and public entities are extracted from government capital expenditure accounts and for local government from the accounts of local councils. Total private expenditure on construction is obtained as a residual after deducting public expenditure on construction from total output of the construction sector. The expenditure on machinery and equipment is obtained from the statistics of imports classified by end-use. The data on external transactions are provided by the Bank of Sudan. The estimates of direct purchases by non-residents are based on a survey of the non-residents in Sudan. GDP by expenditure type at constant prices is not estimated.

(c) Cost-structure of the gross domestic product. In estimating the cost-structure components of GDP, compensation of employees is taken as the wage bill reported by manufacturing establishments and companies in the various economic activities. For the agriculture and primary sectors, compensation of employees is imputed from the employment side. Operating surplus is in most cases taken as the residual of gross output over total costs. Depreciation estimates of public corporations and private manufacturing enterprises are based on actual information available. Indirect taxes consist mainly of import and excise duties and are obtained from government budgets and accounts.

(d) Gross domestic product by kind of economic activity. The table of GDP by kind of economic activity is prepared at market prices, i.e. producers' values. Value added of most industries is estimated through the production approach. The income approach is used for government services and for electricity, gas and water. The commodity-flow method is used for the construction and trade sectors, while the expenditure approach is used for private services. For the agricultural sector, information on crop production is based on rough estimates furnished by the Ministry of Agriculture. To obtain the value of most crops, production figures are multiplied by auction or wholesale prices reduced by 10 per cent for transport and distribution margins. The estimates of value added of cotton, wheat, durra and ground-nuts are based on the records of Sudan Gezira Board which provides data on production, value and cost of production. The value of animal production is obtained through multiplying the assumed production per species by average producer price per head, supplied by the Department of Animal Resources. In the calculation of input and value added of livestock, dairy and poultry products, certain percentages have been adopted. There is a considerable difficulty in estimating the non-marketed production and own consumption in agriculture, as such information is only available from supply and disposition surveys which unfortunately have not been recently conducted. For forestry, hunting and fishing, data are supplied by the respective departments. The intermediate consumption of hunting and fishing is assumed to be a certain percentage of gross output. The gross output and value added of manufacturing are based on the Industrial Survey 1970/71 and on computed indexes of the value of production. The value added of industrial corporations are obtained from the balance sheets and profit and loss accounts of the corporations. Gross output of construction is estimated indirectly by calculating the total supplies of cement and the imported building materials. Intermediate consumption constitute 60 per cent of gross output. The market value of imported building materials is calculated by adding estimated margins to the c.i.f. value. For the domestic production of cement, an assumed average price per ton is applied. The construction of traditional buildings is estimated based on the 1973 Population Census and certain assumptions. For the trade sector, the trade margin of imported goods is calculated on the basis of c.i.f. value plus 5 per cent covering assumed duties and transport margin. For local production, it is assumed that 20 per cent of agricultural production represents own consumption. For the remaining marketable agricultural and industrial production, the trade margin is assumed to be 21.2 per cent. A rough estimate of the intermediate consumption is obtained by applying certain percentages and ratios. For transport, detailed data on receipts and expenditure are obtained from the accounts of the large public enterprises and by means of questionnaires and special surveys for other enterprises. Information on banks and insurance companies are obtained from the enterprises concerned. Gross output of banks is equated to the sum of actual service charges received plus imputed service charges. Data on intermediate consumption and factor income of banks and insurance companies are obtained from their balance sheet and profit and loss statements. The estimates of producers of government services are obtained from the Ordinary Budget or the extra-budgetary funds. For health services, entertainment and personal care, information is obtained from the institutions concerned and from the Household Sample Survey 1967/68 and the Population Census 1973. GDP by kind of economic activity at constant prices is not estimated.

1.1 Expenditure on the Gross Domestic Product, in Current Prices

Million Sudanese pounds — Fiscal year beginning 1 July

		1980	1981	1982	1983	1984	1985	1986	1987	1988	1989	1990	1991
1	Government final consumption expenditure	648.2	719.9	853.5	1112.5	...	...	...	...	...	...	...	...
2	Private final consumption expenditure	4211.5	5431.0	7956.8	9464.7	...	...	...	...	...	...	...	...
	A Households	4176.5	5386.3	7897.2	9385.0	...	...	...	...	...	...	...	...
	B Private non-profit institutions serving households	35.0	44.7	59.6	79.7	...	...	...	...	...	...	...	...
3	Gross capital formation	1078.2	1648.1	1627.3	1630.9	...	...	...	...	...	...	...	...
	A Increase in stocks	80.4	372.7	32.9	-234.4	...	...	...	...	...	...	...	...
	B Gross fixed capital formation	997.8	1275.4	1594.4	1865.3	...	...	...	...	...	...	...	...
	Residential buildings	156.0	198.7	387.3	396.2	...	...	...	...	...	...	...	...
	Non-residential buildings	85.3	123.3	179.0	192.6	...	...	...	...	...	...	...	...
	Other construction and land improvement etc.	276.1	336.5	481.0	545.1	...	...	...	...	...	...	...	...
	Other	480.4	616.9	547.1	731.4	...	...	...	...	...	...	...	...
4	Exports of goods and services	504.9	630.9	1095.8	1306.7	...	...	...	...	...	...	...	...
5	Less: Imports of goods and services	1356.9	1709.4	2347.6	2185.4	...	...	...	...	...	...	...	...
	Equals: Gross Domestic Product	5085.9	6720.5	9185.8	11329.4	13913.0	22009.0	31157.0	...	...	...	...	...

Sudan

1.2 Expenditure on the Gross Domestic Product, in Constant Prices

Fiscal year beginning 1 July

	1980	1981	1982	1983	1984	1985	1986	1987	1988	1989	1990	1991
				At constant prices of:1981								
1 Government final consumption expenditure	...	719.9	617.3	626.8	...	...	...	...	...	...	...	...
2 Private final consumption expenditure	...	5431.0	5869.1	5352.7	...	...	...	...	...	...	...	...
A Households	...	5386.3	5822.3	5303.8	...	...	...	...	...	...	...	...
B Private non-profit institutions serving households	...	44.7	46.8	48.9	...	...	...	...	...	...	...	...
3 Gross capital formation	...	1648.1	1109.4	872.6	...	...	...	...	...	...	...	...
A Increase in stocks	...	372.7	47.5	-116.0	...	...	...	...	...	...	...	...
B Gross fixed capital formation	...	1275.4	1061.9	988.6	...	...	...	...	...	...	...	...
4 Exports of goods and services	...	630.9	822.2	807.1	...	...	...	...	...	...	...	...
5 Less: Imports of goods and services	...	1709.4	1656.7	1153.8	...	...	...	...	...	...	...	...
Statistical discrepancy	...	-	4.1	-27.7	...	...	...	...	...	...	...	...
Equals: Gross Domestic Product	...	6720.5	6765.4	6477.7	...	...	...	...	...	...	...	...

1.3 Cost Components of the Gross Domestic Product

Fiscal year beginning 1 July

	1980	1981	1982	1983	1984	1985	1986	1987	1988	1989	1990	1991
1 Indirect taxes, net	427.8	483.8	847.2	895.9	...	...	...	...	...	...	...	...
A Indirect taxes	437.0	500.9	852.4	895.9	...	...	...	...	...	...	...	...
B Less: Subsidies	9.2	17.1	5.2	-	...	...	...	...	...	...	...	...
2 Consumption of fixed capital	458.0	640.9	1012.3	1245.0	...	...	...	...	...	...	...	...
3 Compensation of employees paid by resident producers to:	1757.1	2347.8	3084.0	3895.1	...	...	...	...	...	...	...	...
A Resident households	1757.1	2347.8	3084.0	3895.1	...	...	...	...	...	...	...	...
B Rest of the world	-	-	-	-	...	...	...	...	...	...	...	...
4 Operating surplus	2443.0	3248.0	4242.3	5293.4	...	...	...	...	...	...	...	...
Equals: Gross Domestic Product	5085.9	6720.5	9185.8	11329.4	...	...	...	...	...	...	...	...

1.4 General Government Current Receipts and Disbursements

Fiscal year beginning 1 July

	1980	1981	1982	1983	1984	1985	1986	1987	1988	1989	1990	1991
				Receipts								
1 Operating surplus	...	...	...	...	...	...	...	...	...	...	...	...
2 Property and entrepreneurial income	55.6	9.7	61.5	33.9	...	...	...	...	...	...	...	...
3 Taxes, fees and contributions	704.1	795.3	1243.7	1337.6	...	...	...	...	...	...	...	...
A Indirect taxes	460.2	503.0	833.8	869.3	...	...	...	...	...	...	...	...
B Direct taxes	134.8	160.1	198.9	229.9	...	...	...	...	...	...	...	...
C Social security contributions	21.0	24.4	31.0	34.7	...	...	...	...	...	...	...	...
D Compulsory fees, fines and penalties	88.1	107.8	180.0	203.7	...	...	...	...	...	...	...	...
4 Other current transfers	-	-	-	-	...	...	...	...	...	...	...	...
Total Current Receipts of General Government	759.7	805.0	1305.2	1371.5	...	...	...	...	...	...	...	...
				Disbursements								
1 Government final consumption expenditure	648.2	719.9	853.5	1112.5	...	...	...	...	...	...	...	...
A Compensation of employees	417.0	464.7	593.9	767.8	...	...	...	...	...	...	...	...
B Consumption of fixed capital	77.0	80.3	155.7	214.7	...	...	...	...	...	...	...	...
C Purchases of goods and services, net	154.2	174.9	103.9	130.0	...	...	...	...	...	...	...	...
D Less: Own account fixed capital formation	...	...	...	...	...	...	...	...	...	...	...	...
E Indirect taxes paid, net	...	...	...	...	...	...	...	...	...	...	...	...

1.4 General Government Current Receipts and Disbursements
(Continued)

	1980	1981	1982	1983	1984	1985	1986	1987	1988	1989	1990	1991
2 Property income	153.5	179.3	256.6	321.5	...	...	...	...	...	...	...	...
A Interest	153.5	179.3	256.6	321.5	...	...	...	...	...	...	...	...
B Net land rent and royalties	...	...	...	...	...	...	...	...	...	...	...	...
3 Subsidies	9.2	17.1	5.2	-	...	...	...	...	...	...	...	...
4 Other current transfers	26.4	35.2	53.6	73.5	...	...	...	...	...	...	...	...
5 Net saving	-77.6	-146.5	136.3	-136.0	...	...	...	...	...	...	...	...
Total Current Disbursements and Net Saving of General Government	759.7	805.0	1305.2	1371.5	...	...	...	...	...	...	...	...

1.7 External Transactions on Current Account, Summary

	1980	1981	1982	1983	1984	1985	1986	1987	1988	1989	1990	1991
Payments to the Rest of the World												
1 Imports of goods and services	1356.9	1709.4	2347.6	2185.4	...	...	...	...	...	...	...	...
A Imports of merchandise c.i.f.	1235.1	1514.4	2118.2	1900.6	...	...	...	...	...	...	...	...
B Other	121.8	195.0	229.4	284.8	...	...	...	...	...	...	...	...
2 Factor income to the rest of the world	52.6	147.2	187.4	316.8	...	...	...	...	...	...	...	...
A Compensation of employees	-	-	-	-	...	...	...	...	...	...	...	...
B Property and entrepreneurial income	52.6	147.2	187.4	316.8	...	...	...	...	...	...	...	...
3 Current transfers to the rest of the world	33.4	34.0	40.0	51.6	...	...	...	...	...	...	...	...
4 Surplus of the nation on current transactions	-518.0	-795.3	-1100.1	-675.0	...	...	...	...	...	...	...	...
Payments to the Rest of the World and Surplus of the Nation on Current Transactions	924.9	1095.3	1474.9	1878.8	...	...	...	...	...	...	...	...
Receipts From The Rest of the World												
1 Exports of goods and services	504.9	630.9	1095.8	1306.7	...	...	...	...	...	...	...	...
A Exports of merchandise f.o.b.	326.5	340.8	589.4	873.3	...	...	...	...	...	...	...	...
B Other	178.4	290.1	506.4	433.4	...	...	...	...	...	...	...	...
2 Factor income from rest of the world	16.6	36.1	48.1	12.4	...	...	...	...	...	...	...	...
A Compensation of employees	-	-	-	-	...	...	...	...	...	...	...	...
B Property and entrepreneurial income	16.6	36.1	48.1	12.4	...	...	...	...	...	...	...	...
3 Current transfers from rest of the world	403.4	428.3	331.0	559.7	...	...	...	...	...	...	...	...
Receipts from the Rest of the World on Current Transactions	924.9	1095.3	1474.9	1878.8	...	...	...	...	...	...	...	...

1.8 Capital Transactions of The Nation, Summary

	1980	1981	1982	1983	1984	1985	1986	1987	1988	1989	1990	1991
Finance of Gross Capital Formation												
Gross saving	560.2	852.8	527.2	955.9	...	...	...	...	...	...	...	...
1 Consumption of fixed capital	458.0	640.9	1012.3	1245.0	...	...	...	...	...	...	...	...
A General government	77.0	80.3	155.7	214.7	...	...	...	...	...	...	...	...
B Corporate and quasi-corporate enterprises	...	...	...	...	...	...	...	...	...	...	...	...
C Other	...	...	...	...	...	...	...	...	...	...	...	...
2 Net saving	102.2	211.9	-485.1	-289.1	...	...	...	...	...	...	...	...
A General government	-77.6	-146.5	136.3	-136.0	...	...	...	...	...	...	...	...
B Corporate and quasi-corporate enterprises	...	...	...	...	...	...	...	...	...	...	...	...
C Other	...	...	...	...	...	...	...	...	...	...	...	...
Less: Surplus of the nation on current transactions	-518.0	-795.3	-1100.1	-675.0	...	...	...	...	...	...	...	...
Finance of Gross Capital Formation	1078.2	1648.1	1627.3	1630.9	...	...	...	...	...	...	...	...

Sudan

1.8 Capital Transactions of The Nation, Summary
(Continued)

Fiscal year beginning 1 July

	1980	1981	1982	1983	1984	1985	1986	1987	1988	1989	1990	1991
					Gross Capital Formation							
Increase in stocks	80.4	372.7	32.9	-234.4	...	...	...	...	...	...	...	...
Gross fixed capital formation	997.8	1275.4	1594.4	1865.3	...	...	...	...	...	...	...	...
1 General government	86.0	118.3	77.6	101.5	...	...	...	...	...	...	...	...
2 Corporate and quasi-corporate enterprises	...	...	...	...	...	...	...	...	...	...	...	...
3 Other	...	...	...	...	...	...	...	...	...	...	...	...
Gross Capital Formation	1078.2	1648.1	1627.3	1630.9	...	...	...	...	...	...	...	...

1.10 Gross Domestic Product by Kind of Activity, in Current Prices

Million Sudanese pounds

Fiscal year beginning 1 July

	1980	1981	1982	1983	1984	1985	1986	1987	1988	1989	1990	1991
1 Agriculture, hunting, forestry and fishing	1665.3	2401.9	2788.2	3339.4	...	...	...	...	...	...	...	...
2 Mining and quarrying	4.1	3.7	5.1	5.5	...	...	...	...	...	...	...	...
3 Manufacturing	394.6	466.1	670.1	869.7	...	...	...	...	...	...	...	...
4 Electricity, gas and water	69.4	76.4	93.6	175.3	...	...	...	...	...	...	...	...
5 Construction	296.0	381.9	604.9	666.7	...	...	...	...	...	...	...	...
6 Wholesale and retail trade, restaurants and hotels	791.5	949.3	1418.4	1978.6	...	...	...	...	...	...	...	...
7 Transport, storage and communication	488.1	691.4	927.1	1071.9	...	...	...	...	...	...	...	...
8 Finance, insurance, real estate and business services	551.8	795.0	1159.3	1383.0	...	...	...	...	...	...	...	...
9 Community, social and personal services	72.0	101.5	140.0	180.0	...	...	...	...	...	...	...	...
Total, Industries	4332.8	5867.2	7806.7	9670.1	...	...	...	...	...	...	...	...
Producers of Government Services	494.0	545.0	749.6	982.5	...	...	...	...	...	...	...	...
Other Producers	58.7	79.2	108.7	150.8	...	...	...	...	...	...	...	...
Subtotal	4885.5	6491.4	8665.0	10803.4	...	...	...	...	...	...	...	...
Less: Imputed bank service charge	79.6	107.8	132.9	142.4	...	...	...	...	...	...	...	...
Plus: Import duties	280.0	336.9	653.7	668.4	...	...	...	...	...	...	...	...
Plus: Value added tax	...	...	...	...	...	...	...	...	...	...	...	...
Equals: Gross Domestic Product	5085.9	6720.5	9185.8	11329.4	...	...	...	...	...	...	...	...

1.11 Gross Domestic Product by Kind of Activity, in Constant Prices

Million Sudanese pounds

Fiscal year beginning 1 July

	1980	1981	1982	1983	1984	1985	1986	1987	1988	1989	1990	1991
					At constant prices of:1981							
1 Agriculture, hunting, forestry and fishing	...	2401.9	2220.1	2164.3	...	...	...	...	...	...	...	...
2 Mining and quarrying	...	3.7	5.0	5.0	...	...	...	...	...	...	...	...
3 Manufacturing	...	466.1	511.5	503.6	...	...	...	...	...	...	...	...
4 Electricity, gas and water	...	76.4	94.5	102.2	...	...	...	...	...	...	...	...
5 Construction	...	381.9	460.7	399.4	...	...	...	...	...	...	...	...
6 Wholesale and retail trade, restaurants and hotels	...	949.3	979.5	905.5	...	...	...	...	...	...	...	...
7 Transport, storage and communication	...	691.4	706.9	672.3	...	...	...	...	...	...	...	...
8 Finance, insurance, real estate and business services	...	795.0	800.8	837.9	...	...	...	...	...	...	...	...
9 Community, social and personal services	...	101.5	110.0	110.3	...	...	...	...	...	...	...	...
Total, Industries	...	5867.2	5889.0	5700.5	...	...	...	...	...	...	...	...
Producers of Government Services	...	545.0	546.2	558.3	...	...	...	...	...	...	...	...
Other Producers	...	79.2	82.9	86.6	...	...	...	...	...	...	...	...
Subtotal	...	6491.4	6518.1	6345.4	...	...	...	...	...	...	...	...
Less: Imputed bank service charge	...	107.8	93.3	101.8	...	...	...	...	...	...	...	...
Plus: Import duties	...	336.9	340.6	234.1	...	...	...	...	...	...	...	...
Plus: Value added tax	...	...	...	...	...	...	...	...	...	...	...	...
Equals: Gross Domestic Product	...	6720.5	6765.4	6477.7	...	...	...	...	...	...	...	...

1.12 Relations Among National Accounting Aggregates

Million Sudanese pounds — Fiscal year beginning 1 July

	1980	1981	1982	1983	1984	1985	1986	1987	1988	1989	1990	1991
Gross Domestic Product	5085.9	6720.5	9185.8	11329.4	...	...	...	...	...	...	...	...
Plus: Net factor income from the rest of the world	-36.0	-111.1	-139.3	-304.4	...	...	...	...	...	...	...	...
Factor income from the rest of the world	16.6	36.1	48.1	12.4	...	...	...	...	...	...	...	...
Less: Factor income to the rest of the world	52.6	147.2	187.4	316.8	...	...	...	...	...	...	...	...
Equals: Gross National Product	5049.9	6609.4	9046.5	11025.0	...	...	...	...	...	...	...	...
Less: Consumption of fixed capital	458.0	640.9	1012.3	1245.0	...	...	...	...	...	...	...	...
Equals: National Income	4591.9	5968.5	8034.2	9780.0	...	...	...	...	...	...	...	...
Plus: Net current transfers from the rest of the world	370.0	394.3	291.0	508.1	...	...	...	...	...	...	...	...
Current transfers from the rest of the world	403.4	428.3	331.0	559.7	...	...	...	...	...	...	...	...
Less: Current transfers to the rest of the world	33.4	34.0	40.0	51.6	...	...	...	...	...	...	...	...
Equals: National Disposable Income	4961.9	6362.8	8325.2	10288.1	...	...	...	...	...	...	...	...
Less: Final consumption	4859.7	6150.9	8810.3	10577.2	...	...	...	...	...	...	...	...
Equals: Net Saving	102.2	211.9	-485.1	-289.1	...	...	...	...	...	...	...	...
Less: Surplus of the nation on current transactions	-518.0	-795.3	-1100.1	-675.0	...	...	...	...	...	...	...	...
Equals: Net Capital Formation	620.2	1007.2	615.0	385.9	...	...	...	...	...	...	...	...

2.1 Government Final Consumption Expenditure by Function, in Current Prices

Million Sudanese pounds — Fiscal year beginning 1 July

	1980	1981	1982	1983	1984	1985	1986	1987	1988	1989	1990	1991
1 General public services [a]	193.9	181.2	236.1	360.4	...	...	...	...	...	...	...	...
2 Defence	124.3	133.6	161.8	250.4	...	...	...	...	...	...	...	...
3 Public order and safety [a]	...	...	...	...	...	...	...	...	...	...	...	...
4 Education	178.9	222.4	236.8	263.8	...	...	...	...	...	...	...	...
5 Health	38.6	70.1	73.1	56.2	...	...	...	...	...	...	...	...
6 Social security and welfare	...	...	...	...	...	...	...	...	...	...	...	...
7 Housing and community amenities	0.6	0.7	0.4	-2.0	...	...	...	...	...	...	...	...
8 Recreational, cultural and religious affairs	16.4	22.7	22.3	24.0	...	...	...	...	...	...	...	...
9 Economic services [b]	95.5	89.2	123.0	159.7	...	...	...	...	...	...	...	...
10 Other functions [b]	...	...	...	...	...	...	...	...	...	...	...	...
Total Government Final Consumption Expenditure	648.2	719.9	853.5	1112.5	...	...	...	...	...	...	...	...

a) Item 'Public order and safety' is included in item 'General public services'.
b) Item 'Other functions' is included in item 'Economic services'.

2.2 Government Final Consumption Expenditure by Function, in Constant Prices

Million Sudanese pounds — Fiscal year beginning 1 July

At constant prices of:1981

	1980	1981	1982	1983	1984	1985	1986	1987	1988	1989	1990	1991
1 General public services	...	181.2	170.2	204.3	...	...	...	...	...	...	...	...
2 Defence	...	133.6	122.0	143.5	...	...	...	...	...	...	...	...
3 Public order and safety	...	...	...	...	...	...	...	...	...	...	...	...
4 Education	...	222.4	178.5	151.7	...	...	...	...	...	...	...	...
5 Health	...	70.1	53.9	31.0	...	...	...	...	...	...	...	...
6 Social security and welfare	...	...	...	...	...	...	...	...	...	...	...	...
7 Housing and community amenities	...	0.7	0.4	-1.0	...	...	...	...	...	...	...	...
8 Recreational, cultural and religious affairs	...	22.7	15.6	13.2	...	...	...	...	...	...	...	...
9 Economic services	...	89.2	76.7	84.1	...	...	...	...	...	...	...	...
10 Other functions	...	...	...	...	...	...	...	...	...	...	...	...
Total Government Final Consumption Expenditure	...	719.9	617.3	626.8	...	...	...	...	...	...	...	...

Sudan

2.3 Total Government Outlays by Function and Type

		Final Consumption Expenditures			Subsidies	Other Current Transfers & Property Income	Total Current Disbursements	Gross Capital Formation	Other Capital Outlays	Total Outlays
		Total	Compensation of Employees	Other						
	1980									
1	General public services [a]	193.9	129.5	64.4	...	11.7	...	73.1	...	...
2	Defence	124.3	92.6	31.7	...	...	...	-	...	...
3	Public order and safety [a]	...	...	...	...	...	...	...	...	...
4	Education	178.8	116.5	62.3	...	5.0	...	5.0	...	...
5	Health	38.6	20.3	18.3	...	0.3	...	4.4	...	...
6	Social security and welfare	...	...	...	...	...	...	...	...	...
7	Housing and community amenities	0.6	0.5	0.1	...	...	...	0.4	...	...
8	Recreation, culture and religion	16.4	3.7	12.7	...	1.8	...	0.3	...	...
9	Economic services [b]	95.5	53.9	41.6	9.2	0.2	...	29.0	...	...
	A Fuel and energy	...	...	...	...	...	...	...	...	...
	B Agriculture, forestry, fishing and hunting	18.8	16.5	2.3	...	...	...	15.8	...	...
	C Mining (except fuels), manufacturing and construction	29.5	8.1	21.4	...	...	...	0.9	...	...
	D Transportation and communication	-7.8	4.6	-12.4	...	...	...	4.4	...	...
	E Other economic affairs	55.0	24.7	30.3	...	...	...	7.9	...	...
10	Other functions [b]	...	...	...	...	7.4	...	...	...	...
	Total	648.1	417.0	231.1	9.2	26.4	...	112.2	...	...
	1981									
1	General public services [a]	181.2	120.0	61.2	...	13.5	...	110.0	...	...
2	Defence	133.6	100.9	32.7	...	...	...	-	...	...
3	Public order and safety [a]	...	...	...	...	...	...	...	...	...
4	Education	222.4	141.8	80.6	...	12.5	...	5.8	...	...
5	Health	70.1	41.1	29.0	...	0.3	...	5.1	...	...
6	Social security and welfare	...	...	...	...	...	...	...	...	...
7	Housing and community amenities	0.7	0.5	0.2	...	...	...	0.4	...	...
8	Recreation, culture and religion	22.7	6.8	15.9	...	0.2	...	1.4	...	...
9	Economic services [b]	89.2	53.6	35.6	17.1	-	...	33.3	...	...
	A Fuel and energy	...	...	...	...	...	...	...	...	...
	B Agriculture, forestry, fishing and hunting	20.1	18.2	1.9	...	...	...	18.3	...	...
	C Mining (except fuels), manufacturing and construction	28.1	8.9	19.2	...	...	...	1.3	...	...
	D Transportation and communication	-8.6	0.3	-8.9	...	...	...	5.6	...	...
	E Other economic affairs	49.6	26.2	23.4	...	...	...	8.1	...	...
10	Other functions [b]	...	...	...	...	8.7	...	...	...	...
	Total	719.7	464.7	255.2	17.1	35.2	...	156.0	...	...
	1982									
1	General public services [a]	236.1	157.0	79.1	...	34.2	...	57.7	...	...
2	Defence	161.8	122.6	39.2	...	...	...	-	...	...
3	Public order and safety [a]	...	...	...	...	...	...	...	...	...
4	Education	236.8	188.4	48.4	...	2.9	...	13.6	...	...
5	Health	73.1	50.4	22.7	...	-	...	10.9	...	...
6	Social security and welfare	...	...	...	...	...	...	...	...	...
7	Housing and community amenities	0.4	0.9	-0.5	...	...	...	0.4	...	...
8	Recreation, culture and religion	22.3	10.9	11.4	...	1.1	...	1.4	...	...
9	Economic services [b]	123.0	63.7	59.3	5.2	0.7	...	48.3	...	...
	A Fuel and energy	...	...	...	...	...	...	...	...	...
	B Agriculture, forestry, fishing and hunting	18.1	23.5	-5.4	...	...	...	24.1	...	...
	C Mining (except fuels), manufacturing and construction	40.7	10.3	30.4	...	...	...	2.7	...	...
	D Transportation and communication	-9.0	3.4	-12.4	...	...	...	9.9	...	...
	E Other economic affairs	73.2	26.5	46.7	...	...	...	11.6	...	...
10	Other functions [b]	...	...	...	...	14.7	...	...	...	...
	Total	853.5	593.9	259.6	5.2	53.6	...	132.3	...	...

2.3 Total Government Outlays by Function and Type
(Continued)

Million Sudanese pounds

	Final Consumption Expenditures			Subsidies	Other Current Transfers & Property Income	Total Current Disbursements	Gross Capital Formation	Other Capital Outlays	Total Outlays
	Total	Compensation of Employees	Other						
				1983					
1 General public services a	360.4	262.8	97.6	...	51.4	...	75.6	...	...
2 Defence	250.4	188.5	61.9	...	...	...	-	...	...
3 Public order and safety a	...	...	...	...	...	...	...	...	...
4 Education	263.8	211.0	52.8	...	0.3	...	15.7	...	...
5 Health	56.2	26.6	29.6	...	0.4	...	9.6	...	...
6 Social security and welfare	...	...	...	...	...	...	...	...	...
7 Housing and community amenities	-1.0	1.0	-3.0	...	...	...	0.3	...	...
8 Recreation, culture and religion	24.0	12.2	11.8	...	1.3	...	0.9	...	...
9 Economic services b	159.7	65.7	94.0	...	0.4	...	59.4	...	...
A Fuel and energy	...	...	...	...	...	...	...	...	...
B Agriculture, forestry, fishing and hunting	22.3	24.5	-2.2	...	...	...	26.9	...	...
C Mining (except fuels), manufacturing and construction	49.0	10.2	38.8	...	...	...	3.3	...	...
D Transportation and communication	-11.1	3.7	-14.8	...	...	...	14.6	...	...
E Other economic affairs	99.5	27.3	72.2	...	...	...	14.6	...	...
10 Other functions b	...	...	...	...	19.7	...	...	...	...
Total	1112.5	767.8	344.7	-	73.5	...	161.5	...	

a) Item 'Public order and safety' is included in item 'General public services'.
b) Item 'Other functions' is included in item 'Economic services'.

2.5 Private Final Consumption Expenditure by Type and Purpose, in Current Prices

Million Sudanese pounds

	1980	1981	1982	1983	1984	1985	1986	1987	1988	1989	1990	1991
				Final Consumption Expenditure of Resident Households								
1 Food, beverages and tobacco	2670.5	3384.8	4767.8	6073.4	...	...	...	...	...	...	...	...
A Food	2575.8	3251.1	4600.7	5905.8	...	...	...	...	...	...	...	...
B Non-alcoholic beverages	16.5	22.0	32.9	52.8	...	...	...	...	...	...	...	...
C Alcoholic beverages	26.3	34.4	27.4	2.4	...	...	...	...	...	...	...	...
D Tobacco	51.9	77.3	106.8	112.4	...	...	...	...	...	...	...	...
2 Clothing and footwear	229.0	300.7	595.8	500.4	...	...	...	...	...	...	...	...
3 Gross rent, fuel and power	650.8	850.0	1209.6	1429.2	...	...	...	...	...	...	...	...
A Fuel and power	212.1	250.1	315.6	352.7	...	...	...	...	...	...	...	...
B Other	438.7	599.9	894.0	1076.5	...	...	...	...	...	...	...	...
4 Furniture, furnishings and household equipment and operation	179.5	250.0	444.0	513.0	...	...	...	...	...	...	...	...
A Household operation	130.3	198.8	351.4	437.8	...	...	...	...	...	...	...	...
B Other	49.2	51.2	92.6	75.2	...	...	...	...	...	...	...	...
5 Medical care and health expenses	185.3	282.4	420.5	385.8	...	...	...	...	...	...	...	...
6 Transport and communication	91.2	127.6	199.7	143.4	...	...	...	...	...	...	...	...
7 Recreational, entertainment, education and cultural services	54.3	58.6	91.0	69.4	...	...	...	...	...	...	...	...
8 Miscellaneous goods and services	111.3	142.5	191.2	259.7	...	...	...	...	...	...	...	...
Total Final Consumption Expenditure in the Domestic Market by Households, of which	4171.9	5396.6	7919.6	9374.3	...	...	...	...	...	...	...	...
Plus: Direct purchases abroad by resident households	29.8	22.1	24.8	58.3	...	...	...	...	...	...	...	...
Less: Direct purchases in the domestic market by non-resident households	25.2	32.4	47.2	47.6	...	...	...	...	...	...	...	...
Equals: Final Consumption Expenditure of Resident Households	4176.5	5386.3	7897.2	9385.0	...	...	...	...	...	...	...	...
				Final Consumption Expenditure of Private Non-profit Institutions Serving Households								
Equals: Final Consumption Expenditure of Private Non-profit Organisations Serving Households	35.0	44.7	59.6	79.7	...	...	...	...	...	...	...	...
Private Final Consumption Expenditure	4211.5	5431.0	7956.8	9464.7	...	...	...	...	...	...	...	...

Sudan

2.6 Private Final Consumption Expenditure by Type and Purpose, in Constant Prices

Million Sudanese pounds   Fiscal year beginning 1 July

	1980	1981	1982	1983	1984	1985	1986	1987	1988	1989	1990	1991
					At constant prices of:1981							
					Final Consumption Expenditure of Resident Households							
1 Food, beverages and tobacco	...	3384.8	3595.3	3486.2	...	...	...	...	...	...	...	...
A Food	...	3251.1	3473.8	3392.9	...	...	...	...	...	...	...	...
B Non-alcoholic beverages	...	22.0	23.0	22.9	...	...	...	...	...	...	...	...
C Alcoholic beverages	...	34.4	20.0	1.5	...	...	...	...	...	...	...	...
D Tobacco	...	77.3	78.5	68.9	...	...	...	...	...	...	...	...
2 Clothing and footwear	...	300.7	355.5	226.5	...	...	...	...	...	...	...	...
3 Gross rent, fuel and power	...	850.0	898.1	898.9	...	...	...	...	...	...	...	...
A Fuel and power	...	250.1	269.8	247.2	...	...	...	...	...	...	...	...
B Other	...	599.9	628.3	651.7	...	...	...	...	...	...	...	...
4 Furniture, furnishings and household equipment and operation	...	250.0	305.0	181.8	...	...	...	...	...	...	...	...
A Household operation	...	30.1	31.5	32.9	...	...	...	...	...	...	...	...
B Other	...	219.9	273.5	148.9	...	...	...	...	...	...	...	...
5 Medical care and health expenses	...	282.4	329.6	235.9	...	...	...	...	...	...	...	...
6 Transport and communication	...	127.6	137.9	77.0	...	...	...	...	...	...	...	...
7 Recreational, entertainment, education and cultural services	...	58.6	71.6	42.6	...	...	...	...	...	...	...	...
8 Miscellaneous goods and services	...	142.5	147.9	152.6	...	...	...	...	...	...	...	...
Total Final Consumption Expenditure in the Domestic Market by Households, of which	...	5396.6	5840.9	5301.5	...	...	...	...	...	...	...	...
Plus: Direct purchases abroad by resident households	...	22.1	16.2	29.2	...	...	...	...	...	...	...	...
Less: Direct purchases in the domestic market by non-resident households	...	32.4	34.8	26.9	...	...	...	...	...	...	...	...
Equals: Final Consumption Expenditure of Resident Households	...	5386.3	5822.3	5303.8	...	...	...	...	...	...	...	...
					Final Consumption Expenditure of Private Non-profit Institutions Serving Households							
Equals: Final Consumption Expenditure of Private Non-profit Organisations Serving Households	...	...	...	...	...	...	...	...	...	...	...	...
Private Final Consumption Expenditure	...	...	...	...	...	...	...	...	...	...	...	...

2.7 Gross Capital Formation by Type of Good and Owner, in Current Prices

Million Sudanese pounds   Fiscal year beginning 1 July

	1980				1981				1982			
	TOTAL	Total Private	Public Enterprises	General Government	TOTAL	Total Private	Public Enterprises	General Government	TOTAL	Total Private	Public Enterprises	General Government
Increase in stocks, total	80.4	...	...	...	372.7	...	...	...	32.9	...	...	...
1 Goods producing industries	105.2	...	...	...	506.0	...	...	...	222.0	...	...	...
A Materials and supplies	...	...	...	...	...	...	...	...	...	...	...	...
B Work in progress	35.9	...	...	...	416.9	...	...	...	129.4	...	...	...
C Livestock, except breeding stocks, dairy cattle, etc.	69.3	...	...	...	89.1	...	...	...	92.6	...	...	...
D Finished goods	...	...	...	...	...	...	...	...	...	...	...	...
2 Wholesale and retail trade	19.4	...	...	...	-122.3	...	...	...	-93.0	...	...	...
3 Other, except government stocks	-44.2	...	...	...	-11.0	...	...	...	-96.1	...	...	...
4 Government stocks	...	...	...	...	...	...	...	...	...	...	...	...
Gross Fixed Capital Formation, Total	997.8	754.2	131.4	112.2	1275.4	908.5	211.1	155.8	1594.4	1144.3	317.9	132.2
1 Residential buildings	156.0	149.5	3.2	3.3	198.7	188.3	2.5	7.9	387.3	374.1	9.2	4.0
2 Non-residential buildings	85.3	21.6	22.5	41.2	123.3	28.4	43.7	51.2	179.0	68.9	57.8	52.3

2.7 Gross Capital Formation by Type of Good and Owner, in Current Prices
(Continued)

Million Sudanese pounds

Fiscal year beginning 1 July

	1980				1981				1982			
	TOTAL	Total Private	Public Enterprises	General Government	TOTAL	Total Private	Public Enterprises	General Government	TOTAL	Total Private	Public Enterprises	General Government
3 Other construction	251.4	149.8	58.5	43.1	316.7	204.3	47.5	64.9	428.8	313.4	88.4	27.0
4 Land improvement and plantation and orchard development	24.7	-	20.3	4.4	19.8	-	16.3	3.5	52.2	-	30.0	22.2
5 Producers' durable goods	480.4	433.3	26.9	20.2	616.9	487.5	101.1	28.3	547.1	387.9	132.5	26.7
A Transport equipment	188.0	181.2	4.6	2.2	333.2	279.4	51.5	2.3	124.4	78.7	40.8	4.9
B Machinery and equipment	292.4	252.1	22.3	18.0	283.7	208.1	49.6	26.0	422.7	309.2	91.7	21.8
6 Breeding stock, dairy cattle, etc.	-	-	-	...	-	-	-	...	-	-	-	...
Total Gross Capital Formation	1078.2	...	...	112.2	1648.1	...	...	155.8	1627.3	...	...	132.2

	1983			
	TOTAL	Total Private	Public Enterprises	General Government
Increase in stocks, total	-234.4	...	...	...
1 Goods producing industries	-71.1	...	...	...
A Materials and supplies	...	...	...	...
B Work in progress	-86.7	...	...	...
C Livestock, except breeding stocks, dairy cattle, etc.	15.6	...	...	...
D Finished goods	...	...	...	...
2 Wholesale and retail trade	-157.6	...	...	...
3 Other, except government stocks	-5.7	...	...	...
4 Government stocks	...	...	...	...
Gross Fixed Capital Formation, Total	1865.3	1390.7	312.8	161.8
1 Residential buildings	396.2	388.7	3.2	4.3
2 Non-residential buildings	192.6	60.0	55.9	76.7
3 Other construction	484.9	369.6	82.0	33.3
4 Land improvement and plantation and orchard development	60.2	-	51.9	8.3
5 Producers' durable goods	731.4	572.4	119.8	39.2
A Transport equipment	237.0	196.3	28.8	11.9
B Machinery and equipment	494.4	376.1	91.0	27.3
6 Breeding stock, dairy cattle, etc.	-	-	-	...
Total Gross Capital Formation	1630.9	...	...	161.8

2.11 Gross Fixed Capital Formation by Kind of Activity of Owner, ISIC Divisions, in Current Prices

Million Sudanese pounds

Fiscal year beginning 1 July

	1980	1981	1982	1983	1984	1985	1986	1987	1988	1989	1990	1991
				All Producers								
1 Agriculture, hunting, forestry and fishing	...	...	154.4	130.4	...	...	...	...	...	...	...	...
2 Mining and quarrying	...	...	0.5	0.6	...	...	...	...	...	...	...	...
3 Manufacturing	...	...	227.1	280.3	...	...	...	...	...	...	...	...
4 Electricity, gas and water	...	...	77.6	77.9	...	...	...	...	...	...	...	...
A Electricity, gas and steam	...	...	66.4	65.5	...	...	...	...	...	...	...	...
B Water works and supply	...	...	11.2	12.4	...	...	...	...	...	...	...	...
5 Construction	...	...	98.6	35.5	...	...	...	...	...	...	...	...
6 Wholesale and retail trade, restaurants and hotels	...	...	106.6	120.7	...	...	...	...	...	...	...	...
7 Transport, storage and communication	...	...	34.6	38.3	...	...	...	...	...	...	...	...
A Transport and storage	...	...	31.1	34.5	...	...	...	...	...	...	...	...
B Communication	...	...	3.5	3.8	...	...	...	...	...	...	...	...
8 Finance, insurance, real estate and business services	...	...	756.4	818.3	...	...	...	...	...	...	...	...
A Financial institutions	...	...	...	...	...	...	...	...	...	...	...	...

Sudan

2.11 Gross Fixed Capital Formation by Kind of Activity of Owner, ISIC Divisions, in Current Prices
(Continued)

Million Sudanese pounds

	1980	1981	1982	1983	1984	1985	1986	1987	1988	1989	1990	1991
B Insurance	...	...	...	...	...	...	...	...	...	...	...	...
C Real estate and business services	...	...	756.4	818.3	...	...	...	...	...	...	...	...
9 Community, social and personal services	...	...	...	...	...	...	...	...	...	...	...	...
Total Industries	...	...	1455.8	1502.0	...	...	...	...	...	...	...	...
Producers of Government Services	...	...	132.2	161.8	...	...	...	...	...	...	...	...
Private Non-Profit Institutions Serving Households	...	...	6.4	201.5	...	...	...	...	...	...	...	...
Total	...	...	1594.4	1865.3	...	...	...	...	...	...	...	...

2.17 Exports and Imports of Goods and Services, Detail

Million Sudanese pounds

	1980	1981	1982	1983	1984	1985	1986	1987	1988	1989	1990	1991
Exports of Goods and Services												
1 Exports of merchandise, f.o.b.	326.5	340.8	589.4	873.3	...	...	...	...	...	...	...	...
2 Transport and communication	13.1	14.8	31.6	8.8	...	...	...	...	...	...	...	...
3 Insurance service charges	0.3	0.5	0.6	0.2	...	...	...	...	...	...	...	...
4 Other commodities	139.8	242.4	427.0	376.8	...	...	...	...	...	...	...	...
5 Adjustments of merchandise exports to change-of-ownership basis	...	...	...	...	...	...	...	...	...	...	...	...
6 Direct purchases in the domestic market by non-residential households	25.2	32.4	47.2	47.6	...	...	...	...	...	...	...	...
7 Direct purchases in the domestic market by extraterritorial bodies	...	...	...	...	...	...	...	...	...	...	...	...
Total Exports of Goods and Services	504.9	630.9	1095.8	1306.7	...	...	...	...	...	...	...	...
Imports of Goods and Services												
1 Imports of merchandise, c.i.f.	1235.1	1514.4	2118.2	1900.6	...	...	...	...	...	...	...	...
A Imports of merchandise, f.o.b.	1218.7	1488.3	2093.5	1880.7	...	...	...	...	...	...	...	...
B Transport of services on merchandise imports	16.1	25.5	23.7	19.1	...	...	...	...	...	...	...	...
C Insurance service charges on merchandise imports	0.3	0.6	1.0	0.8	...	...	...	...	...	...	...	...
2 Adjustments of merchandise imports to change-of-ownership basis	...	...	...	...	...	...	...	...	...	...	...	...
3 Other transport and communication	16.1	25.5	23.7	19.1	...	...	...	...	...	...	...	...
4 Other insurance service charges	0.3	0.6	1.0	0.8	...	...	...	...	...	...	...	...
5 Other commodities	75.6	146.8	179.9	206.6	...	...	...	...	...	...	...	...
6 Direct purchases abroad by government	...	...	...	...	...	...	...	...	...	...	...	...
7 Direct purchases abroad by resident households	29.8	22.1	24.8	58.3	...	...	...	...	...	...	...	...
Total Imports of Goods and Services	1356.9	1709.4	2347.6	2185.4	...	...	...	...	...	...	...	...
Balance of Goods and Services	-852.0	-1078.5	-1251.8	-878.7	...	...	...	...	...	...	...	...
Total Imports and Balance of Goods and Services	504.9	630.9	1095.8	1306.7	...	...	...	...	...	...	...	...

4.1 Derivation of Value Added by Kind of Activity, in Current Prices

Million Sudanese pounds

	1980			1981			1982			1983		
	Gross Output	Intermediate Consumption	Value Added	Gross Output	Intermediate Consumption	Value Added	Gross Output	Intermediate Consumption	Value Added	Gross Output	Intermediate Consumption	Value Added
All Producers												
1 Agriculture, hunting, forestry and fishing	2070.7	405.4	1665.3	2955.1	553.2	2401.9	3610.3	822.1	2788.2	4499.6	1160.2	3339.4
A Agriculture and hunting	1953.8	395.4	1558.4	2804.4	540.0	2264.4	3431.1	806.8	2624.3	4276.2	1140.1	3136.1
B Forestry and logging	88.7	5.8	82.9	110.6	7.2	103.4	135.5	8.8	126.7	156.2	10.1	146.1
C Fishing	28.2	4.2	24.0	40.1	6.0	34.1	43.7	6.5	37.2	67.2	10.0	57.2
2 Mining and quarrying	5.8	1.7	4.1	5.3	1.6	3.7	7.2	2.1	5.1	7.7	2.2	5.5
A Coal mining	...	...	...	...	...	...	...	...	...	...	...	...
B Crude petroleum and natural gas production	...	...	...	...	...	...	...	...	...	...	...	...
C Metal ore mining	...	...	...	...	...	...	...	...	...	...	...	...

4.1 Derivation of Value Added by Kind of Activity, in Current Prices
(Continued)

Million Sudanese pounds

Fiscal year beginning 1 July

	1980			1981			1982			1983		
	Gross Output	Intermediate Consumption	Value Added	Gross Output	Intermediate Consumption	Value Added	Gross Output	Intermediate Consumption	Value Added	Gross Output	Intermediate Consumption	Value Added
D Other mining	5.8	1.7	4.1	5.3	1.6	3.7	7.2	2.1	5.1	7.7	2.2	5.5
3 Manufacturing	1001.7	607.1	394.6	1523.7	1057.6	466.1	2266.1	1595.9	670.2	2891.7	2022.0	869.7
A Manufacture of food, beverages and tobacco	423.8	246.1	177.7	581.1	342.2	238.9	815.8	485.1	330.7	1174.6	706.3	468.3
B Textile, wearing apparel and leather industries	127.4	80.3	47.1	373.4	319.8	53.6	594.9	507.6	87.3	735.4	633.7	101.7
C Manufacture of wood and wood products, including furniture	29.4	11.5	17.9	17.3	6.8	10.5	22.3	8.9	13.4	28.5	10.4	18.1
D Manufacture of paper and paper products, printing and publishing	34.4	17.6	16.8	34.8	23.1	11.7	57.8	40.6	17.2	62.3	43.5	18.8
E Manufacture of chemicals and chemical petroleum, coal, rubber and plastic products	269.2	183.1	86.1	343.3	270.8	72.5	519.5	408.8	110.7	572.4	447.8	124.6
F Manufacture of non-metallic mineral products, except products of petroleum and coal	37.3	19.6	17.7	45.3	23.1	22.2	85.7	45.4	40.3	124.8	66.9	57.9
G Basic metal industries	17.8	12.4	5.4	19.4	13.2	6.2	34.0	23.6	10.4	49.0	33.1	15.9
H Manufacture of fabricated metal products, machinery and equipment	57.5	34.5	23.0	102.6	53.4	49.2	127.1	68.7	58.4	132.7	70.7	62.0
I Other manufacturing industries	4.9	2.0	2.9	6.5	5.2	1.3	9.0	7.2	1.8	12.0	9.6	2.4
4 Electricity, gas and water	96.6	27.2	69.4	116.4	40.0	76.4	146.7	53.1	93.6	248.4	73.1	175.3
A Electricity, gas and steam	38.7	17.6	21.1	44.6	30.8	13.8	53.3	41.1	12.2	118.7	59.2	59.5
B Water works and supply	57.9	9.6	48.3	71.8	9.2	62.6	93.4	12.0	81.4	129.7	13.9	115.8
5 Construction	587.6	291.6	296.0	753.3	371.4	381.9	1193.8	588.9	604.9	1306.3	639.6	666.7
6 Wholesale and retail trade, restaurants and hotels	1150.4	358.9	791.5	1421.9	472.6	949.3	2100.9	682.5	1418.4	2717.8	739.2	1978.6
A Wholesale and retail trade	1064.1	310.4	753.7	1325.0	418.1	906.9	1982.2	618.9	1363.3	2569.6	660.1	1909.5
B Restaurants and hotels	86.3	48.5	37.8	96.9	54.5	42.4	118.7	63.6	55.1	148.2	79.1	69.1
Restaurants	49.1	30.4	18.7	54.9	34.0	20.9	74.6	46.2	28.4	99.4	61.6	37.8
Hotels and other lodging places	37.2	18.1	19.1	42.0	20.5	21.5	44.1	17.4	26.7	48.8	17.5	31.3
7 Transport, storage and communication	761.5	273.4	488.1	1089.2	397.8	691.4	1536.6	609.5	927.1	1880.3	808.4	1071.9
A Transport and storage	740.9	268.6	472.3	1065.0	392.6	672.4	1511.5	604.3	907.2	1847.8	799.1	1048.7
B Communication	20.6	4.8	15.8	24.2	5.2	19.0	25.1	5.2	19.9	32.5	9.3	23.2
8 Finance, insurance, real estate and business services	719.4	167.6	551.8	1076.7	281.7	795.0	1609.1	449.8	1159.3	1869.2	486.2	1383.0
A Financial institutions	139.3	17.3	122.0	193.3	21.2	172.1	253.0	31.6	221.4	306.4	46.7	259.7
B Insurance	11.6	0.7	10.9	13.2	0.8	12.4	16.5	1.3	15.2	23.5	1.9	21.6
C Real estate and business services	568.5	149.6	418.9	870.2	259.7	610.5	1339.6	416.9	922.7	1539.3	437.6	1101.7
9 Community, social and personal services	107.3	35.3	72.0	154.6	53.1	101.5	208.1	68.1	140.0	269.2	89.2	180.0
Total, Industries	6501.0	2168.2	4332.8	9096.2	3229.0	5867.2	12678.8	4872.0	7806.8	15690.2	6020.1	9670.1
Producers of Government Services	727.2	233.2	494.0	819.9	274.9	545.0	1011.4	261.8	749.6	1294.0	311.5	982.5
Other Producers	88.6	29.9	58.7	117.0	37.8	79.2	156.5	47.8	108.7	211.3	60.5	150.8
Total	7316.8	2431.3	4885.5	10033.1	3541.7	6491.4	13846.7	5181.6	8665.1	17195.5	6392.1	10803.4
Less: Imputed bank service charge	...	-79.6	79.6	...	-107.8	107.8	...	-132.9	132.9	...	-142.4	142.4
Import duties	280.0	-	280.0	336.9	-	336.9	653.7	-	653.7	668.4	-	668.4
Value added tax	...	...	...	...	...	...	...	...	...	...	...	...
Total	7596.8	2510.9	5085.9	10370.0	3649.5	6720.5	14500.4	5314.5	9185.9	17863.9	6534.5	11329.4

4.2 Derivation of Value Added by Kind of Activity, in Constant Prices

Million Sudanese pounds

Fiscal year beginning 1 July

	1981			1982			1983		
	Gross Output	Intermediate Consumption	Value Added	Gross Output	Intermediate Consumption	Value Added	Gross Output	Intermediate Consumption	Value Added
	At constant prices of:1981								
	All Producers								
1 Agriculture, hunting, forestry and fishing	...	...	2401.9	...	...	2220.1	...	...	2164.3
A Agriculture and hunting	...	...	2264.4	...	...	2088.5	...	...	2021.3
B Forestry and logging	...	...	103.4	...	...	98.9	...	...	108.8
C Fishing	...	...	34.1	...	...	32.7	...	...	34.2
2 Mining and quarrying	...	...	3.7	...	...	5.0	...	...	5.0

Sudan

4.2 Derivation of Value Added by Kind of Activity, in Constant Prices
(Continued)

	1981			1982			1983		
	Gross Output	Intermediate Consumption	Value Added	Gross Output	Intermediate Consumption	Value Added	Gross Output	Intermediate Consumption	Value Added
					At constant prices of:1981				
A Coal mining	...	...	...	...	...	...	...	...	...
B Crude petroleum and natural gas production	...	...	...	...	...	...	...	...	...
C Metal ore mining	...	...	...	...	...	...	...	...	...
D Other mining	...	...	3.7	...	...	5.0	...	...	5.0
3 Manufacturing	...	...	466.1	...	...	511.5	...	...	503.6
A Manufacture of food, beverages and tobacco	...	...	238.9	...	...	266.5	...	...	280.9
B Textile, wearing apparel and leather industries	...	...	53.6	...	...	59.2	...	...	53.9
C Manufacture of wood and wood products, including furniture	...	...	10.5	...	...	10.8	...	...	10.8
D Manufacture of paper and paper products, printing and publishing	...	...	11.7	...	...	12.2	...	...	12.8
E Manufacture of chemicals and chemical petroleum, coal, rubber and plastic products	...	...	72.5	...	...	78.4	...	...	75.9
F Manufacture of non-metallic mineral products, except products of petroleum and coal	...	...	22.2	...	...	29.5	...	...	31.1
G Basic metal industries	...	...	6.2	...	...	4.6	...	...	5.3
H Manufacture of fabricated metal products, machinery and equipment	...	...	49.2	...	...	48.9	...	...	31.5
I Other manufacturing industries	...	...	1.3	...	...	1.4	...	...	1.4
4 Electricity, gas and water	...	...	76.4	...	...	94.5	...	...	102.2
A Electricity, gas and steam	...	...	13.8	...	...	25.9	...	...	29.2
B Water works and supply	...	...	62.6	...	...	68.6	...	...	73.0
5 Construction	...	...	381.9	...	...	460.7	...	...	399.4
6 Wholesale and retail trade, restaurants and hotels	...	...	949.3	...	...	979.5	...	...	905.5
A Wholesale and retail trade	...	...	906.9	...	...	940.9	...	...	868.3
B Restaurants and hotels	...	...	42.4	...	...	38.6	...	...	37.2
7 Transport, storage and communication	...	...	691.4	...	...	706.9	...	...	672.3
A Transport and storage	...	...	672.4	...	...	691.5	...	...	658.7
B Communication	...	...	19.0	...	...	15.4	...	...	13.6
8 Finance, insurance, real estate and business services	...	...	795.0	...	...	800.3	...	...	837.9
A Financial institutions	...	...	172.1	...	...	148.4	...	...	162.6
B Insurance	...	...	12.4	...	...	17.6	...	...	17.6
C Real estate and business services	...	...	610.5	...	...	634.3	...	...	657.7
9 Community, social and personal services	...	...	101.5	...	...	110.0	...	...	110.3
Total, Industries	...	...	5867.2	...	...	5889.0	...	...	5700.5
Producers of Government Services	...	...	545.0	...	...	546.2	...	...	558.3
Other Producers	...	...	79.2	...	...	82.9	...	...	86.6
Total	...	...	6491.4	...	...	6518.1	...	...	6345.4
Less: Imputed bank service charge	...	...	107.8	...	...	93.3	...	...	101.8
Import duties	...	...	336.9	...	...	340.6	...	...	234.1
Value added tax	...	...	...	...	...	...	...	...	...
Total	...	...	6720.5	...	...	6765.4	...	...	6477.7

4.3 Cost Components of Value Added

	1980						1981					
	Compensation of Employees	Capital Consumption	Net Operating Surplus	Indirect Taxes	Less: Subsidies Received	Value Added	Compensation of Employees	Capital Consumption	Net Operating Surplus	Indirect Taxes	Less: Subsidies Received	Value Added
					All Producers							
1 Agriculture, hunting, forestry and fishing	434.3	52.0	1169.5	9.5	...	1665.3	669.5	69.9	1656.2	6.3	...	2401.9
A Agriculture and hunting	382.2	48.1	1119.3	8.8	...	1558.4	601.6	64.6	1592.7	5.5	...	2264.4
B Forestry and logging	35.4	2.2	44.8	0.5	...	82.9	44.2	2.8	55.8	0.6	...	103.4
C Fishing	16.7	1.7	5.4	0.2	...	24.0	23.7	2.5	7.7	0.2	...	34.1

4.3 Cost Components of Value Added
(Continued)

Million Sudanese pounds Fiscal year beginning 1 July

	1980						1981					
	Compensation of Employees	Capital Consumption	Net Operating Surplus	Indirect Taxes	Less: Subsidies Received	Value Added	Compensation of Employees	Capital Consumption	Net Operating Surplus	Indirect Taxes	Less: Subsidies Received	Value Added
2 Mining and quarrying	2.7	0.4	0.9	0.1	...	4.1	2.4	0.4	0.8	0.1	...	3.7
A Coal mining	...	...	...	...	...	...	...	...	...	...	...	...
B Crude petroleum and natural gas production	...	...	...	...	...	...	...	...	...	...	...	...
C Metal ore mining	...	...	...	...	...	...	...	...	...	...	...	...
D Other mining	2.7	0.4	0.9	0.1	...	4.1	2.4	0.4	0.8	0.1	...	3.7
3 Manufacturing	108.8	35.1	156.1	94.6	...	394.6	133.0	75.6	156.2	101.3	...	466.1
A Manufacture of food, beverages and tobacco	33.3	14.0	96.2	34.2	...	177.7	42.7	32.7	128.2	35.3	...	238.9
B Textile, wearing apparel and leather industries	22.3	6.8	10.5	7.5	...	47.1	43.4	25.1	-22.2	7.3	...	53.6
C Manufacture of wood and wood products, including furniture	6.1	0.9	10.3	0.6	...	17.9	4.1	0.8	5.0	0.6	...	10.5
D Manufacture of paper and paper products, printing and publishing	6.5	2.0	6.0	2.3	...	16.8	6.4	1.5	1.1	2.7	...	11.7
E Manufacture of chemicals and chemical petroleum, coal, rubber and plastic products	22.1	6.7	21.7	35.6	...	86.1	11.8	10.3	12.7	37.7	...	72.5
F Manufacture of non-metallic mineral products, except products of petroleum and coal	8.5	1.5	4.9	2.8	...	17.7	5.8	1.7	11.3	3.4	...	22.2
G Basic metal industries	1.4	0.6	1.1	2.3	...	5.4	1.9	0.3	2.0	2.0	...	6.2
H Manufacture of fabricated metal products, machinery and equipment	8.1	2.3	3.5	9.1	...	23.0	16.3	3.1	17.8	12.0	...	49.2
I Other manufacturing industries	0.5	0.3	1.9	0.2	...	2.9	0.6	0.1	0.3	0.3	...	1.3
4 Electricity, gas and water	51.9	5.1	12.4	-	...	69.4	66.7	7.0	2.7	-	...	76.4
A Electricity, gas and steam	8.5	3.7	8.9	-	...	21.1	12.4	4.4	-3.0	-	...	13.8
B Water works and supply	43.4	1.4	3.5	-	...	48.3	54.3	2.6	5.7	-	...	62.6
5 Construction	143.9	16.1	133.0	3.0	...	296.0	184.3	20.4	173.5	3.7	...	381.9
6 Wholesale and retail trade, restaurants and hotels	252.5	20.5	487.1	31.4	...	791.5	339.2	27.8	560.4	21.9	...	949.3
A Wholesale and retail trade	242.9	16.4	466.7	27.7	...	753.7	327.7	23.2	538.3	17.7	...	906.9
B Restaurants and hotels	9.6	4.1	20.4	3.7	...	37.8	11.5	4.6	22.1	4.2	...	42.4
Restaurants	4.1	-	14.6	-	...	18.7	4.6	-	16.3	-	...	20.9
Hotels and other lodging places	5.5	4.1	5.8	3.7	...	19.1	6.9	4.6	5.8	4.2	...	21.5
7 Transport, storage and communication	202.5	66.7	213.3	5.6	...	488.1	277.3	89.9	316.2	8.0	...	691.4
A Transport and storage	188.0	66.6	212.2	5.5	...	472.3	259.6	89.8	315.0	8.0	...	672.4
B Communication	14.5	0.1	1.1	0.1	...	15.8	17.7	0.1	1.2	-	...	19.0
8 Finance, insurance, real estate and business services	57.9	182.8	308.5	2.6	...	551.8	84.8	263.0	443.0	4.2	...	795.0
A Financial institutions	33.2	2.5	86.3	-	...	122.0	39.9	4.1	128.1	-	...	172.1
B Insurance	0.9	-	10.0	-	...	10.9	1.2	0.1	11.1	-	...	12.4
C Real estate and business services	23.8	180.3	212.2	2.6	...	418.9	43.7	258.8	303.8	4.2	...	610.5
9 Community, social and personal services	27.6	1.6	41.8	1.0	...	72.0	47.6	5.7	46.8	1.4	...	101.5
Total, Industries a	1282.1	380.3	2522.6	147.8	...	4332.8	1804.8	559.7	3355.8	146.9	...	5867.2
Producers of Government Services	417.0	77.0	-	-	...	494.0	464.7	80.3	-	-	...	545.0
Other Producers	58.0	0.7	-	-	...	58.7	78.3	0.9	-	-	...	79.2
Total a	1757.1	458.0	2522.6	147.8	...	4885.5	2347.8	640.9	3355.8	146.9	...	6491.4
Less: Imputed bank service charge	...	...	79.6	...		79.6	...	...	107.8	...		107.8
Import duties	...	...	...	280.0		280.0	...	...	...	336.9		336.9
Value added tax	...	...	...	...		...	...	...	...	...		...
Total a	1757.1	458.0	2443.0	427.8	...	5085.9	2347.8	640.9	3248.0	483.8	...	6720.5

Sudan

4.3 Cost Components of Value Added

Million Sudanese pounds
Fiscal year beginning 1 July

	1982						1983					
	Compensation of Employees	Capital Consumption	Net Operating Surplus	Indirect Taxes	Less: Subsidies Received	Value Added	Compensation of Employees	Capital Consumption	Net Operating Surplus	Indirect Taxes	Less: Subsidies Received	Value Added
All Producers												
1 Agriculture, hunting, forestry and fishing	788.2	110.8	1880.5	8.7	...	2788.2	1062.6	135.0	2130.5	11.3	...	3339.4
A Agriculture and hunting	708.2	104.7	1803.7	7.7	...	2624.3	960.4	126.9	2038.7	10.1	...	3136.1
B Forestry and logging	54.2	3.4	68.4	0.7	...	126.7	62.5	3.9	78.9	0.8	...	146.1
C Fishing	25.8	2.7	8.4	0.3	...	37.2	39.7	4.2	12.9	0.4	...	57.2
2 Mining and quarrying	3.3	0.5	1.2	0.1	...	5.1	3.6	0.5	1.3	0.1	...	5.5
A Coal mining	...	...	...	...	...	...	...	...	...	...	...	...
B Crude petroleum and natural gas production	...	...	...	...	...	...	...	...	...	...	...	...
C Metal ore mining	...	...	...	...	...	...	...	...	...	...	...	...
D Other mining	3.3	0.5	1.2	0.1	...	5.1	3.6	0.5	1.3	0.1	...	5.5
3 Manufacturing	199.6	114.2	232.2	124.2	...	670.2	261.4	157.9	310.1	140.3	...	869.7
A Manufacture of food, beverages and tobacco	60.4	46.3	181.3	42.7	...	330.7	87.8	67.6	262.6	50.3	...	468.3
B Textile, wearing apparel and leather industries	68.0	40.5	-24.2	3.0	...	87.3	82.4	56.3	-40.4	3.4	...	101.7
C Manufacture of wood and wood products, including furniture	5.4	0.8	6.8	0.4	...	13.4	6.7	1.2	8.9	1.3	...	18.1
D Manufacture of paper and paper products, printing and publishing	11.3	2.6	1.9	1.4	...	17.2	12.1	2.8	2.0	1.9	...	18.8
E Manufacture of chemicals and chemical petroleum, coal, rubber and plastic products	17.9	15.6	19.2	58.0	...	110.7	21.9	19.1	23.4	60.2	...	124.6
F Manufacture of non-metallic mineral products, except products of petroleum and coal	11.4	3.4	20.9	4.6	...	40.3	22.9	5.3	25.3	4.4	...	57.9
G Basic metal industries	3.4	0.6	3.5	2.9	...	10.4	4.8	0.9	4.8	5.4	...	15.9
H Manufacture of fabricated metal products, machinery and equipment	20.9	4.0	22.8	10.7	...	58.4	21.6	4.1	23.5	12.8	...	62.0
I Other manufacturing industries	0.9	0.4	-	0.5	...	1.8	1.2	0.6	-	0.6	...	2.4
4 Electricity, gas and water	86.1	18.5	-11.0	-	...	93.6	118.3	21.5	35.5	-	...	175.3
A Electricity, gas and steam	15.2	13.3	-16.3	-	...	12.2	20.0	15.0	24.5	-	...	59.5
B Water works and supply	70.9	5.2	5.3	-	...	81.4	98.3	6.5	11.0	-	...	115.8
5 Construction	287.7	33.2	278.0	6.0	...	604.9	325.9	31.7	303.2	5.9	...	666.7
6 Wholesale and retail trade, restaurants and hotels	489.5	33.7	856.2	39.0	...	1418.4	573.1	36.2	1317.1	51.2	...	1978.6
A Wholesale and retail trade	469.6	29.9	829.6	34.2	...	1363.3	547.5	31.9	1283.2	45.9	...	1909.5
B Restaurants and hotels	19.9	3.8	26.6	4.8	...	55.1	25.6	4.3	33.9	5.3	...	69.1
Restaurants	13.0	1.1	14.0	0.3	...	28.4	17.3	1.5	18.6	0.4	...	37.8
Hotels and other lodging places	6.9	2.7	12.6	4.5	...	26.7	8.3	2.8	15.3	4.9	...	31.3
7 Transport, storage and communication	351.1	129.0	439.4	7.6	...	927.1	405.4	153.6	505.5	7.4	...	1071.9
A Transport and storage	339.1	128.5	432.0	7.6	...	907.2	391.5	152.1	497.7	7.4	...	1048.7
B Communication	12.0	0.5	7.4	-	...	19.9	13.9	1.5	7.8	-	...	23.2
8 Finance, insurance, real estate and business services	120.3	408.4	624.6	6.0	...	1159.3	155.6	481.8	736.6	9.0	...	1383.0
A Financial institutions	44.6	5.9	170.8	0.1	...	221.4	64.0	9.0	186.2	0.5	...	259.7
B Insurance	2.2	0.2	12.8	-	...	15.2	2.9	0.3	18.4	-	...	21.6
C Real estate and business services	73.5	402.3	441.0	5.9	...	922.7	88.7	472.5	532.0	8.5	...	1101.7
9 Community, social and personal services	56.8	7.1	74.2	1.9	...	140.0	72.0	10.7	95.0	2.3	...	180.0
Total, Industries a	2382.6	855.4	4375.3	193.5	...	7806.8	2977.9	1028.9	5435.8	227.5	...	9670.1
Producers of Government Services	593.9	155.7	-	-	...	749.6	767.8	214.7	-	-	...	982.5
Other Producers	107.5	1.2	-	-	...	108.7	149.4	1.4	-	-	...	150.8
Total a	3084.0	1012.3	4375.3	193.5	...	8665.1	3895.1	1245.0	5435.8	227.5	...	10803.4
Less: Imputed bank service charge	...	...	132.9	...	...	132.9	...	...	142.4	...	...	142.4
Import duties	...	...	...	653.7	...	653.7	...	...	...	668.4	...	668.4
Value added tax	...	...	...	...	...	...	...	...	...	...	...	...
Total a	3084.0	1012.3	4242.4	847.2	...	9185.9	3895.1	1245.0	5293.4	895.9	...	11329.4

a) Column 4 refers to indirect taxes less subsidies received.

Suriname

Source. Reply to the United Nations National Accounts Questionnaire from the Algemeen Bureau Voor de Statistiek, Parmaribo. The official estimates based on the present SNA are published by the Bureau in 'Nationale Rekeningen van Suriname'.

General note. The estimates shown in the following table have been prepared in accordance with the United Nations System of National Accounts so far as the existing data would permit.

1.1 Expenditure on the Gross Domestic Product, in Current Prices

Million Suriname guilders

	1980	1981	1982	1983	1984	1985	1986	1987	1988	1989	1990	1991
1 Government final consumption expenditure	338.5	430.7	520.1	437.2	498.8	588.5	655.8	736.5	848.3	814.5	777.0	1069.4
2 Private final consumption expenditure	915.6	1040.7	1084.3	1314.0	1119.3	961.0	757.8	622.1	971.3	1058.7	1640.9	1713.3
3 Gross capital formation	420.6	555.0	507.3	275.6	203.9	252.2	391.2	508.8	387.3	565.2	636.2	695.6
A Increase in stocks	78.3	73.6	-8.8	-81.9	-110.1	-60.0	50.5	195.6	57.8	115.8	64.0	69.6
B Gross fixed capital formation	342.2	481.4	516.1	357.6	314.0	312.2	340.7	313.3	329.5	449.4	572.2	626.0
Residential buildings	211.7	229.2	254.0	187.4	181.2	214.8	219.2	217.9	222.2	...	...	...
Non-residential buildings										...	...	...
Other construction and land improvement etc.										...	...	...
Other	130.5	252.2	262.2	170.1	132.8	97.5	121.5	95.4	107.3	...	...	...
4 Exports of goods and services	1094.2	1009.8	909.5	775.5	749.4	641.7	581.0	608.8	680.6	1022.6	868.6	657.3
5 Less: Imports of goods and services	1179.2	1258.1	1190.8	1035.1	843.1	696.9	582.9	502.1	566.2	754.7	844.4	793.9
Equals: Gross Domestic Product	1589.7	1778.1	1830.4	1767.2	1728.3	1746.5	1802.8	1974.1	2321.3	2706.6	3078.3	3341.7

1.3 Cost Components of the Gross Domestic Product

Million Suriname guilders

	1980	1981	1982	1983	1984	1985	1986	1987	1988	1989	1990	1991
1 Indirect taxes, net	247.7	269.6	245.1	226.4	214.1	183.0	146.5	139.3	182.0	224.5	285.2	317.1
A Indirect taxes	273.8	298.7	277.9	259.2	245.2	204.0	178.0	164.1	205.1	256.5	318.5	350.2
B Less: Subsidies	26.1	29.1	32.8	32.8	31.1	21.0	31.5	24.8	23.1	32.0	33.3	33.1
2 Consumption of fixed capital	171.6	186.4	182.3	182.5	173.0	161.9	156.9	187.9	185.7	287.2	359.4	375.5
3 Compensation of employees paid by resident producers to:	782.4	878.9	1024.4	1063.4	1085.7	1128.6	1154.4	1182.7	1253.9	1322.3	1410.4	1591.1
4 Operating surplus	388.0	443.2	378.5	294.9	255.6	272.9	345.2	464.2	699.6	872.6	1023.4	1057.9
Equals: Gross Domestic Product	1589.7	1778.1	1830.4	1767.2	1728.3	1746.5	1802.8	1974.1	2321.3	2706.6	3078.3	3341.7

1.7 External Transactions on Current Account, Summary

Million Suriname guilders

	1980	1981	1982	1983	1984	1985	1986	1987	1988	1989	1990	1991
Payments to the Rest of the World												
1 Imports of goods and services	1179.2	1258.1	1190.8	1035.1	843.1	696.9	582.9	502.1	566.2	754.7	844.4	793.9
A Imports of merchandise c.i.f.	900.3	1013.7	921.2	806.0	639.4	553.2	443.2	378.4	430.2	592.5	668.3	610.4
B Other	278.9	244.4	269.6	229.1	203.7	143.7	139.7	123.7	136.0	162.2	176.1	183.5
2 Factor income to the rest of the world	76.1	41.7	51.1	49.4	6.4	5.8	8.3	10.4	17.7	12.7	19.2	22.5
A Compensation of employees	7.5	6.6	5.4	2.8	2.2	1.7	1.6	1.9	3.0	1.5	2.2	3.1
B Property and entrepreneurial income	68.6	35.1	45.7	46.6	4.2	4.1	6.7	8.5	14.7	11.3	17.0	19.4
3 Current transfers to the rest of the world	22.6	20.2	25.3	31.8	24.8	15.7	12.6	10.4	12.8	13.1	15.9	19.3
4 Surplus of the nation on current transactions	-103.7	-218.7	-273.2	-293.8	-104.4	-65.2	-16.1	91.8	90.9	246.8	-3.3	-169.7
Payments to the Rest of the World and Surplus of the Nation on Current Transactions	1174.2	1101.3	994.0	822.5	769.9	653.2	587.7	614.7	687.6	1027.4	876.2	666.0
Receipts From The Rest of the World												
1 Exports of goods and services	1094.2	1009.8	909.5	775.5	749.4	641.7	581.0	608.8	680.6	1022.6	868.6	657.3
A Exports of merchandise f.o.b.	918.2	845.7	765.1	654.7	650.8	562.7	535.2	464.4	640.1	980.3	831.6	617.5
B Other	176.0	164.1	144.4	120.8	98.6	79.0	45.8	144.4	40.5	42.3	37.0	39.8
2 Factor income from rest of the world	45.7	64.7	63.9	29.5	8.9	4.9	2.9	2.2	2.4	1.7	4.0	2.5
A Compensation of employees	1.2	1.9	0.7	1.4	1.2	1.0	0.1	0.1	0.1	-	-	...
B Property and entrepreneurial income	44.5	62.8	63.2	28.1	7.7	3.9	2.8	2.1	2.3	1.7	4.0	2.5
3 Current transfers from rest of the world	34.3	26.8	20.6	17.5	11.6	6.6	3.8	3.7	4.6	3.1	3.6	6.2
Receipts from the Rest of the World on Current Transactions	1174.2	1101.3	994.0	822.5	769.9	653.2	587.7	614.7	687.6	1027.4	876.2	666.0

Suriname

1.10 Gross Domestic Product by Kind of Activity, in Current Prices

Million Suriname guilders

	1980	1981	1982	1983	1984	1985	1986	1987	1988	1989	1990	1991
1 Agriculture, hunting, forestry and fishing	122.7	140.1	144.3	126.9	134.5	142.7	165.6	204.2	233.9	243.6	310.7	362.8
2 Mining and quarrying	96.8	123.6	132.0	95.7	92.7	94.6	79.0	62.5	79.7	89.9	91.4	88.9
3 Manufacturing	249.1	271.2	225.8	195.3	197.4	206.6	224.0	200.9	256.5	292.3	311.5	276.8
4 Electricity, gas and water	87.1	73.4	69.7	92.9	88.0	72.8	73.6	89.3	136.4	116.8	135.6	160.2
5 Construction	88.6	106.8	110.2	99.7	106.5	97.2	107.3	117.9	128.9	177.9	225.7	259.8
6 Wholesale and retail trade, restaurants and hotels	273.3	286.7	314.5	310.6	271.2	267.8	286.0	311.5	378.6	514.2	572.5	522.9
7 Transport, storage and communication	71.5	78.4	81.7	86.5	94.9	113.8	115.5	138.0	160.2	166.5	178.8	209.2
8 Finance, insurance, real estate and business services	176.5	219.7	222.9	202.5	204.4	239.7	276.5	338.4	400.2	540.9	621.1	676.1
9 Community, social and personal services a	21.9	26.4	29.5	32.1	25.2	21.0	32.7	33.8	36.8	35.1	34.6	36.3
Total, Industries	1187.5	1326.3	1331.5	1242.2	1214.8	1256.2	1360.2	1496.5	1811.2	2177.2	2481.9	2593.0
Producers of Government Services	225.9	276.1	346.3	373.9	374.1	396.6	408.7	472.6	506.8	514.0	527.1	677.5
Other Producers a	...	...	...	...	...	...	...	...	...	...	...	...
Subtotal b	1413.4	1602.4	1677.8	1616.1	1588.9	1652.8	1768.9	1969.1	2318.0	2691.2	3009.0	3270.5
Less: Imputed bank service charge	71.3	93.9	92.5	75.3	74.7	89.3	112.5	134.3	178.8	209.0	215.9	245.9
Plus: Import duties	...	...	...	...	...	...	...	...	...	...	...	...
Plus: Value added tax	...	...	...	...	...	...	...	...	...	...	...	...
Plus: Other adjustments c	247.7	269.6	245.1	226.4	214.1	183.0	146.4	139.3	182.1	224.4	285.2	317.1
Equals: Gross Domestic Product	1589.8	1778.1	1830.4	1767.2	1728.3	1746.5	1802.8	1974.1	2321.3	2706.6	3078.3	3341.7

a) Item 'Other producers' is included in item 'Community, social and personal services'.
b) Gross domestic product in factor values.
c) Item 'Other adjustments' refers to indirect taxes net of subsidies.

1.11 Gross Domestic Product by Kind of Activity, in Constant Prices

Million Suriname guilders

	1980	1981	1982	1983	1984	1985	1986	1987	1988	1989	1990	1991
	At constant prices of:1980											
1 Agriculture, hunting, forestry and fishing	122.7	138.9	134.7	122.9	127.6	129.4	126.1	133.0	132.3	129.1	129.9	139.5
2 Mining and quarrying	96.8	102.6	80.6	60.4	77.3	91.7	104.0	85.6	123.1	131.2	128.9	137.3
3 Manufacturing	249.1	256.1	214.0	193.6	187.5	199.6	205.1	160.2	183.9	186.9	174.1	158.5
4 Electricity, gas and water	87.1	78.0	63.3	64.0	63.9	67.8	81.8	76.2	102.2	110.0	122.4	121.8
5 Construction	88.6	106.3	104.5	94.4	98.1	87.0	93.4	77.2	75.9	68.1	67.0	71.8
6 Wholesale and retail trade, restaurants and hotels	273.3	263.8	269.7	255.2	214.9	191.3	172.0	122.2	138.4	182.9	170.6	123.7
7 Transport, storage and communication	71.5	67.8	69.2	69.1	68.2	70.8	71.3	80.9	80.8	76.9	74.4	77.5
8 Finance, insurance, real estate and business services	176.5	216.2	197.2	175.1	170.2	194.5	194.2	218.9	230.3	245.7	244.5	238.6
9 Community, social and personal services a	21.9	21.6	20.9	22.1	20.4	21.6	19.7	18.9	20.7	19.0	20.0	15.9
Total, Industries	1187.5	1251.3	1154.1	1056.8	1028.1	1053.4	1067.5	973.2	1087.6	1149.8	1131.8	1084.6
Producers of Government Services	225.9	276.1	298.5	322.3	322.5	333.2	342.6	371.5	370.8	375.5	382.1	462.4
Other Producers a	...	...	...	...	...	...	...	...	...	...	...	...
Subtotal	1413.4	1527.4	1452.6	1379.1	1350.6	1386.6	1410.1	1344.7	1458.3	1525.3	1513.9	1547.0
Less: Imputed bank service charge	71.3	90.1	75.6	56.2	52.6	62.4	75.8	92.5	103.8	113.8	115.3	109.5
Plus: Import duties	...	...	...	...	...	...	...	...	...	...	...	...
Plus: Value added tax	...	...	...	...	...	...	...	...	...	...	...	...
Equals: Gross Domestic Product b	1342.1	1437.3	1377.0	1322.9	1298.0	1324.2	1334.3	1252.2	1354.5	1411.5	1398.6	1437.5

a) Item 'Other producers' is included in item 'Community, social and personal services'.
b) Gross domestic product in factor values.

1.12 Relations Among National Accounting Aggregates

Million Suriname guilders

	1980	1981	1982	1983	1984	1985	1986	1987	1988	1989	1990	1991
Gross Domestic Product	1589.7	1778.1	1830.4	1767.2	1728.3	1746.5	1802.8	1974.1	2321.3	2706.6	3078.3	3341.7
Plus: Net factor income from the rest of the world	-30.4	23.0	12.8	-19.9	2.5	-0.9	-5.4	-8.2	-15.3	-11.1	-15.2	-20.0
Factor income from the rest of the world	45.7	64.7	63.9	29.5	8.9	4.9	2.9	2.2	2.4	1.7	4.0	2.5
Less: Factor income to the rest of the world	76.1	41.7	51.1	49.4	6.4	5.8	8.3	10.4	17.7	12.7	19.2	22.5
Equals: Gross National Product	1559.3	1801.1	1843.2	1747.3	1730.8	1745.6	1797.4	1965.9	2306.0	2695.5	3063.1	3321.7
Less: Consumption of fixed capital	171.6	186.4	182.3	182.5	173.0	161.9	156.9	187.9	185.7	287.2	359.4	375.5

1.12 Relations Among National Accounting Aggregates
(Continued)

Million Suriname guilders

	1980	1981	1982	1983	1984	1985	1986	1987	1988	1989	1990	1991
Equals: National Income	1387.7	1614.7	1660.9	1564.8	1557.8	1583.7	1640.5	1778.0	2120.3	2408.3	2703.8	2946.2
Plus: Net current transfers from the rest of the world	11.7	6.6	-4.7	-14.3	-13.2	-9.1	-8.8	-6.7	-8.2	-10.0	-12.3	-13.1
Current transfers from the rest of the world	34.3	26.8	20.6	17.5	11.6	6.6	3.8	3.7	4.6	3.1	3.6	6.2
Less: Current transfers to the rest of the world	22.6	20.2	25.3	31.8	24.8	15.7	12.6	10.4	12.8	13.1	15.9	19.3
Equals: National Disposable Income	1399.4	1621.3	1656.2	1550.5	1544.6	1574.6	1631.7	1771.3	2112.1	2398.3	2691.5	2933.1
Less: Final consumption	1254.1	1471.4	1604.4	1751.2	1618.1	1549.5	1413.6	1358.6	1819.6	1873.4	2417.9	2782.6
Equals: Net Saving	145.3	149.9	51.8	-200.6	-73.5	25.1	218.2	412.8	292.6	524.8	273.5	150.4
Less: Surplus of the nation on current transactions	-103.7	-218.7	-273.2	-293.8	-104.4	-65.2	-16.1	91.8	90.9	246.8	-3.3	-169.7
Equals: Net Capital Formation	249.0	368.6	325.0	93.2	30.9	90.3	234.3	321.0	201.7	278.1	276.8	320.1

Swaziland

Source. Reply to the United Nations National Accounts Questionnaire from the Central Statistical Office, Mbabane. Official estimates are published annually in 'National Accounts Report', issued by the same Office.

General note. The official estimates of Swaziland have been prepared by the Statistical Office to conform to the United Nations System of National Accounts so far as the existing data would permit.

1.1 Expenditure on the Gross Domestic Product, in Current Prices

Million Swaziland emalangeni — Fiscal year ending 30 June

	1980	1981	1982	1983	1984	1985	1986	1987	1988	1989	1990	1991
1 Government final consumption expenditure	86.5	105.9	121.8	132.5	155.6	182.9	226.3	220.3	272.5	...	...	...
2 Private final consumption expenditure a	337.6	360.9	394.6	451.3	495.4	582.0	653.8	578.1	562.1	...	...	...
3 Gross capital formation	137.4	154.6	188.8	185.4	244.0	210.4	204.8	176.7	374.0	...	...	...
A Increase in stocks	23.8	14.6	20.0	-13.2	12.2	12.8	41.2	-19.5	20.0			
B Gross fixed capital formation	113.6	140.0	168.8	198.6	231.8	197.6	163.6	196.2	354.0			
4 Exports of goods and services b	315.0	375.2	385.5	382.9	403.4	452.8	703.2	957.0	1180.7			
5 Less: Imports of goods and services b	423.0	498.8	506.7	533.4	568.9	625.6	736.7	814.1	1064.2			
Equals: Gross Domestic Product	453.5	497.8	584.0	618.7	729.5	802.5	1051.4	1118.0	1325.1	...	...	...

a) Item 'Private final consumption expenditure' shows significant increases from 1975 due to the sharp increases in salary. Estimates also include errors and omissions.   b) The estimates for imports and exports of goods and services and for the External Transaction Account are on calendar year basis.

1.3 Cost Components of the Gross Domestic Product

Million Swaziland emalangeni — Fiscal year ending 30 June

	1980	1981	1982	1983	1984	1985	1986	1987	1988	1989	1990	1991
1 Indirect taxes, net	96.5	72.4	112.7	117.5	130.7	144.0	148.0	166.5	...	...	...	...
2 Consumption of fixed capital	24.6	30.0	37.3	46.6	47.1	55.1	68.4	75.2	...	...	...	...
3 Compensation of employees paid by resident producers to:	187.3	232.9	265.0	300.5	324.1	374.0	458.8	499.1	...	...	...	...
4 Operating surplus	145.1	162.2	169.1	154.0	227.5	229.5	376.1	377.1	...	...	...	...
Equals: Gross Domestic Product	453.5	497.5	584.1	618.7	729.4	802.5	1051.3	1118.0	...	...	...	...

1.4 General Government Current Receipts and Disbursements

Million Swaziland emalangeni — Fiscal year ending 30 June

	1980	1981	1982	1983	1984	1985	1986	1987	1988	1989	1990	1991
Receipts												
1 Operating surplus	...	...	...	...	...	...	...	...	...	...	...	...
2 Property and entrepreneurial income	4.3	6.2	8.9	7.9	13.8	11.5	12.6	16.2	27.7	...	...	...
3 Taxes, fees and contributions	141.7	122.0	164.7	167.6	191.6	216.9	226.0	307.9	382.6	...	...	...
A Indirect taxes	102.9	77.8	121.6	123.0	137.0	151.8	154.7	176.1	234.7			
B Direct taxes	35.7	42.0	40.6	42.1	51.6	59.4	67.3	125.2	143.9			
C Social security contributions	-	-	-	-	-	-	-	-	-			
D Compulsory fees, fines and penalties	3.1	2.2	2.5	2.5	3.0	5.7	4.0	6.6	4.0			
4 Other current transfers	10.5	8.0	8.5	9.7	7.9	16.4	16.5	13.2	17.9	...	...	...
Total Current Receipts of General Government	156.5	136.2	182.1	185.2	213.3	244.8	255.1	337.3	428.2			
Disbursements												
1 Government final consumption expenditure	86.5	105.9	121.8	132.5	155.6	182.9	226.3	220.3	272.5	...	...	...
A Compensation of employees	45.9	59.2	66.6	75.6	83.0	87.5	106.8	118.7	144.3			
B Consumption of fixed capital	-	-	-	-	-	-	-	-	-			
C Purchases of goods and services, net	40.6	46.7	55.2	56.9	72.6	95.4	119.5	101.6	128.2			
D Less: Own account fixed capital formation	...	...	...	...	...	...	...	...	...			
E Indirect taxes paid, net	...	...	...	...	...	...	...	...	...			
2 Property income	4.6	5.8	7.9	8.7	10.3	15.7	21.6	20.2	22.2	...	...	...
3 Subsidies	...	...	...	...	...	...	...	...	...	...	...	...
4 Other current transfers	7.1	12.6	13.3	15.3	16.8	20.0	32.6	38.9	45.5	...	...	...
5 Net saving	58.3	11.9	39.1	28.7	30.6	26.2	-25.4	57.7	88.0	...	...	...
Total Current Disbursements and Net Saving of General Government	156.5	136.2	182.1	185.2	213.3	244.8	255.1	337.1	428.2	...	...	...

1.7 External Transactions on Current Account, Summary

Million Swaziland emalangeni   **Fiscal year ending 30 June**

	1980	1981	1982	1983	1984	1985	1986	1987	1988	1989	1990	1991
Payments to the Rest of the World												
1 Imports of goods and services	423.0	498.8	506.7	533.4	568.9	625.6	736.7	814.1	1064.2	...	...	...
A Imports of merchandise c.i.f.	379.1	425.7	419.9	459.8	480.6	541.2	642.0	716.8	956.7	...	...	...
B Other	43.9	73.1	86.8	73.6	88.3	84.4	94.7	97.3	107.5	...	...	...
2 Factor income to the rest of the world	32.7	43.9	45.0	32.7	47.3	73.5	130.2	198.8	229.2	...	...	...
A Compensation of employees	4.2	5.4	6.3	9.2	13.3	18.3	22.1	29.0	38.0	...	...	...
B Property and entrepreneurial income	28.5	38.5	38.7	23.5	34.0	55.2	108.1	169.8	191.2	...	...	...
3 Current transfers to the rest of the world	9.8	10.5	13.7	15.0	16.9	25.0	34.0	30.6	37.8	...	...	...
4 Surplus of the nation on current transactions	-107.1	-88.7	-119.3	-114.5	-107.9	-75.9	43.1	181.0	203.6	...	...	...
Payments to the Rest of the World and Surplus of the Nation on Current Transactions a	358.4	464.5	446.1	466.6	525.2	648.2	944.0	1224.5	1534.8	...	...	...
Receipts From The Rest of the World												
1 Exports of goods and services	314.1	375.2	385.5	382.9	403.4	452.8	703.2	957.0	1180.7	...	...	...
A Exports of merchandise f.o.b.	285.9	340.3	351.8	338.5	340.5	392.9	635.5	862.4	1059.9	...	...	...
B Other	28.2	34.9	33.7	44.4	62.9	59.9	67.7	94.6	120.8	...	...	...
2 Factor income from rest of the world	36.1	60.2	59.4	74.6	104.6	150.0	161.4	200.1	280.1	...	...	...
A Compensation of employees	27.5	35.0	40.4	59.1	77.7	105.7	125.7	160.0	214.9	...	...	...
B Property and entrepreneurial income	8.6	25.2	19.0	15.5	26.9	44.3	35.7	40.1	65.2	...	...	...
3 Current transfers from rest of the world	8.2	29.1	1.2	9.1	17.2	45.4	79.4	67.4	74.0	...	...	...
Receipts from the Rest of the World on Current Transactions a	358.4	464.5	446.1	466.6	525.2	648.2	944.0	1224.5	1534.8	...	...	...

a) The estimates for imports and exports of goods and services and for the External Transaction Account are on calendar year basis.

1.10 Gross Domestic Product by Kind of Activity, in Current Prices

Million Swaziland emalangeni   **Fiscal year ending 30 June**

	1980	1981	1982	1983	1984	1985	1986	1987	1988	1989	1990	1991
1 Agriculture, hunting, forestry and fishing	84.6	96.6	95.8	86.2	129.7	136.0	194.7	152.9	183.1	...	...	...
2 Mining and quarrying	14.1	15.1	14.4	15.7	12.4	18.0	15.1	19.5	16.0	...	...	...
3 Manufacturing	79.6	89.1	100.8	89.7	111.3	106.5	190.2	236.0	265.1	...	...	...
4 Electricity, gas and water	4.4	7.2	8.7	9.3	15.9	22.0	24.4	30.4	34.7	...	...	...
5 Construction	16.2	17.0	15.8	25.3	24.6	24.8	29.0	31.0	37.1	...	...	...
6 Wholesale and retail trade, restaurants and hotels	35.6	42.3	54.7	63.8	73.7	83.1	102.0	112.6	141.7	...	...	...
7 Transport, storage and communication	20.5	24.8	32.0	36.8	41.3	43.5	53.5	73.7	82.2	...	...	...
8 Finance, insurance, real estate and business services	39.2	57.1	66.8	80.1	82.7	101.0	123.8	141.4	154.0	...	...	...
9 Community, social and personal services	5.7	7.4	9.4	10.8	9.2	9.8	11.4	13.4	13.9	...	...	...
Total, Industries	299.9	356.6	398.4	417.7	500.8	544.7	744.1	810.9	927.8	...	...	...
Producers of Government Services	61.3	76.0	87.4	98.5	111.7	137.9	172.7	166.3	198.9	...	...	...
Other Producers	6.7	9.3	9.1	10.5	11.3	11.6	14.3	16.8	19.0	...	...	...
Subtotal a	367.7	441.9	495.0	526.7	623.8	694.2	931.1	994.0	1145.7	...	...	...
Less: Imputed bank service charge	10.9	16.5	23.6	25.5	25.0	35.7	27.7	42.5	44.9	...	...	...
Plus: Import duties	...	...	...	...	...	...	...	...	...	...	...	...
Plus: Value added tax	...	...	...	...	...	...	...	...	...	...	...	...
Plus: Other adjustments b	96.5	72.4	112.7	117.5	130.7	144.0	148.0	166.5	224.3	...	...	...
Equals: Gross Domestic Product	453.5	497.8	584.0	618.7	729.5	802.5	1051.4	1118.0	1325.1	...	...	...

a) Gross domestic product in factor values.
b) Item 'Other adjustments' refers to indirect taxes net of subsidies.

Swaziland

1.11 Gross Domestic Product by Kind of Activity, in Constant Prices

	1980	1981	1982	1983	1984	1985	1986	1987	1988	1989	1990	1991
					At constant prices of:1985							
1 Agriculture, hunting, forestry and fishing	132.5	139.5	123.7	113.4	137.4	136.0	160.6	138.6	136.8	...	...	...
2 Mining and quarrying	17.5	20.4	17.1	15.4	17.0	18.0	19.2	23.7	22.0	...	...	...
3 Manufacturing	91.8	102.0	107.3	108.5	107.9	106.5	122.7	128.8	147.8	...	...	...
4 Electricity, gas and water	17.6	19.6	16.8	15.2	20.4	22.0	25.2	28.0	31.2	...	...	...
5 Construction	30.0	27.6	22.0	31.3	27.8	24.8	24.2	22.8	23.9	...	...	...
6 Wholesale and retail trade, restaurants and hotels	66.4	76.2	78.3	75.0	86.3	83.1	89.2	88.2	101.1	...	...	...
7 Transport, storage and communication	34.9	36.6	36.8	38.9	40.1	43.5	49.0	49.4	55.0	...	...	...
8 Finance, insurance, real estate and business services	63.9	70.9	71.8	72.9	74.7	70.5	73.1	75.6	79.1	...	...	...
9 Community, social and personal services	7.6	8.3	8.9	9.3	9.0	9.8	10.8	10.5	10.7	...	...	...
Total, Industries	462.2	501.1	482.7	479.9	520.6	514.2	574.0	565.6	607.6	...	...	...
Producers of Government Services	82.8	89.3	98.9	104.3	110.5	137.9	133.3	125.3	129.0	...	...	...
Other Producers	9.8	10.1	10.6	10.9	11.3	11.6	12.0	12.5	12.9	...	...	...
Subtotal	554.8	600.5	592.2	595.1	642.4	663.7	719.3	703.4	749.5	...	...	...
Less: Imputed bank service charge	33.3	37.8	36.9	37.8	38.1	35.7	34.5	36.3	38.4	...	...	...
Plus: Import duties	...	...	...	...	...	...	...	...	...	...	...	...
Plus: Value added tax	...	...	...	...	...	...	...	...	...	...	...	...
Plus: Other adjustments	120.5	127.4	128.0	130.6	138.8	144.0	156.3	152.6	162.3	...	...	...
Equals: Gross Domestic Product	642.0	690.1	683.3	687.9	743.1	772.0	841.1	819.7	873.4	...	...	...

1.12 Relations Among National Accounting Aggregates

	1980	1981	1982	1983	1984	1985	1986	1987	1988	1989	1990	1991
Gross Domestic Product	453.5	497.6	584.0	618.7	729.5	802.5	1051.4	1118.0	1325.1	...	...	...
Plus: Net factor income from the rest of the world	3.4	16.3	14.4	41.9	57.3	76.5	31.2	1.3	50.9	...	...	...
Factor income from the rest of the world	36.1	60.2	59.4	74.6	104.6	150.0	161.4	200.1	280.1	...	...	...
Less: Factor income to the rest of the world	32.7	43.9	45.0	32.7	47.3	73.5	130.2	198.8	229.2	...	...	...
Equals: Gross National Product	456.9	513.9	598.4	660.6	786.8	879.0	1082.6	1119.3	1376.0	...	...	...
Less: Consumption of fixed capital	...	...	...	...	...	...	...	...	...	...	...	...
Equals: National Income	...	...	...	...	...	...	...	...	...	...	...	...
Plus: Net current transfers from the rest of the world	-1.6	18.6	-12.5	-5.9	0.3	20.4	45.4	36.8	36.2	...	...	...
Current transfers from the rest of the world	8.2	29.1	1.2	9.1	17.2	45.4	79.4	67.4	74.0	...	...	...
Less: Current transfers to the rest of the world	9.8	10.5	13.7	15.0	16.9	25.0	34.0	30.6	37.8	...	...	...
Equals: National Disposable Income a	455.3	532.7	585.9	654.7	787.1	899.4	1128.0	1156.1	1412.2	...	...	...
Less: Final consumption	424.1	466.8	516.4	583.8	651.0	764.9	880.1	798.4	834.6	...	...	...
Equals: Net Saving b	31.2	65.9	69.5	70.9	136.1	134.5	247.9	357.7	577.6	...	...	...
Less: Surplus of the nation on current transactions	-107.1	-88.7	-119.3	-114.5	-107.9	-75.9	43.1	181.0	203.6	...	...	...
Equals: Net Capital Formation c	138.3	154.6	188.8	185.4	244.0	210.4	204.8	176.7	374.0	...	...	...

a) Item 'National disposable income' includes consumption of fixed capital.
b) Item 'Net saving' includes consumption of fixed capital.
c) Item 'Net capital formation' includes consumption of fixed capital.

4.1 Derivation of Value Added by Kind of Activity, in Current Prices

	1980			1981			1982			1983		
	Gross Output	Intermediate Consumption	Value Added	Gross Output	Intermediate Consumption	Value Added	Gross Output	Intermediate Consumption	Value Added	Gross Output	Intermediate Consumption	Value Added
						All Producers						
1 Agriculture, hunting, forestry and fishing	141.8	57.2	84.6	158.5	61.9	96.6	156.7	60.9	95.8	154.6	68.4	86.2
A Agriculture and hunting	128.2	50.7	77.5	143.6	54.6	89.0	140.5	52.6	87.9	138.5	59.9	78.6
B Forestry and logging	13.6	6.5	7.1	14.9	7.3	7.6	16.2	8.3	7.9	16.1	8.5	7.6
C Fishing	...	...	...	...	...	...	...	...	...	...	...	...
2 Mining and quarrying	23.9	9.8	14.1	25.8	10.7	15.1	25.0	10.6	14.4	26.7	11.0	15.7

4.1 Derivation of Value Added by Kind of Activity, in Current Prices
(Continued)

Million Swaziland emalangeni

Fiscal year ending 30 June

	1980			1981			1982			1983		
	Gross Output	Intermediate Consumption	Value Added	Gross Output	Intermediate Consumption	Value Added	Gross Output	Intermediate Consumption	Value Added	Gross Output	Intermediate Consumption	Value Added
3 Manufacturing	296.2	216.5	79.7	373.0	284.0	89.0	404.4	303.6	100.8	403.2	313.5	89.7
A Manufacture of food, beverages and tobacco	148.4	115.1	33.3	174.1	131.5	42.6	182.5	137.9	44.6	208.9	159.5	49.4
B Textile, wearing apparel and leather industries	12.5	10.3	2.2	21.7	19.3	2.4	19.0	16.7	2.3	17.6	16.0	1.6
C Manufacture of wood and wood products, including furniture	16.0	9.9	6.1	20.0	13.9	6.1	22.2	14.1	8.1	20.7	15.2	5.5
D Manufacture of paper and paper products, printing and publishing	60.8	36.4	24.4	63.7	45.7	18.0	67.6	49.3	18.3	68.2	54.4	13.8
E Manufacture of chemicals and chemical petroleum, coal, rubber and plastic products	35.5	26.9	8.5	55.6	43.7	11.9	67.4	48.9	18.5	52.3	42.1	10.2
F Manufacture of non-metallic mineral products, except products of petroleum and coal	3.1	2.2	0.9	6.7	5.4	1.3	9.8	8.3	1.5	7.9	5.5	2.4
G Basic metal industries	...	...	...	...	...	...	...	...	...	...	...	...
H Manufacture of fabricated metal products, machinery and equipment	19.2	15.2	4.0	30.8	24.2	6.6	35.5	28.0	7.5	26.9	20.4	6.5
I Other manufacturing industries	0.7	0.5	0.2	0.5	0.3	0.2	0.5	0.4	0.1	0.6	0.3	0.3
4 Electricity, gas and water	11.3	6.9	4.4	14.9	7.7	7.2	20.5	11.8	8.7	22.9	13.6	9.3
5 Construction	54.8	38.6	16.2	60.0	43.0	17.0	62.6	46.8	15.8	71.9	46.6	25.3
6 Wholesale and retail trade, restaurants and hotels	84.0	48.4	35.6	115.5	73.2	42.3	118.6	63.7	54.9	121.0	57.2	63.8
A Wholesale and retail trade	65.6	38.6	27.0	90.4	58.8	31.6	90.4	48.1	42.2	96.7	45.7	51.0
B Restaurants and hotels	18.4	9.8	8.6	25.1	14.4	10.7	28.2	15.6	12.5	24.3	11.5	12.8
7 Transport, storage and communication	45.8	25.3	20.5	64.5	39.7	24.8	78.9	46.9	32.0	83.2	46.5	36.7
A Transport and storage	39.7	22.4	17.3	53.5	34.3	19.2	67.9	41.4	26.5	69.4	41.1	28.3
B Communication	6.1	2.9	3.2	10.9	5.4	5.6	11.0	5.5	5.5	13.8	5.4	8.5
8 Finance, insurance, real estate and business services	61.8	22.6	39.2	83.1	26.0	57.1	114.2	47.4	66.8	107.3	27.2	80.1
A Financial institutions	28.6	16.4	12.3	37.9	15.7	22.2	58.2	34.5	23.8	36.9	10.9	26.0
B Insurance	3.1	1.8	1.4	4.3	2.5	1.9	6.3	3.9	2.5	8.7	2.8	6.0
C Real estate and business services	30.0	4.5	25.6	40.9	7.9	33.0	49.7	9.1	40.6	61.7	13.5	48.2
Real estate, except dwellings	5.4	1.2	4.3	10.0	2.0	8.0	13.4	2.5	10.9	20.7	5.8	14.8
Dwellings a	16.4	0.8	15.6	18.5	0.9	17.6	22.2	1.1	21.1	25.3	1.3	24.0
9 Community, social and personal services	11.8	6.0	5.8	15.3	7.9	7.4	21.7	12.3	9.4	24.2	13.4	10.8
A Sanitary and similar services	...	...	...	...	...	...	...	...	...	...	...	...
B Social and related community services	1.3	0.6	0.8	3.2	1.7	1.5	...	...	...	...	...	...
C Recreational and cultural services	2.7	1.3	1.4	3.3	1.6	1.7	...	...	...	...	...	...
D Personal and household services	7.7	4.2	3.5	8.9	4.6	4.2	...	...	...	...	...	...
Total, Industries	731.4	431.3	300.1	910.6	554.1	356.5	1002.7	604.0	398.7	1015.0	597.4	417.6
Producers of Government Services	88.9	27.6	61.3	108.4	32.4	76.0	124.3	37.0	87.4	135.1	36.7	98.5
Other Producers	9.9	3.2	6.7	13.9	4.6	9.3	14.6	5.5	9.1	18.0	7.6	10.5
Total b	830.2	462.1	368.1	1032.9	591.1	441.8	1141.3	646.5	495.0	1168.1	641.7	526.7
Less: Imputed bank service charge	...	-10.9	10.9	...	-16.5	16.5	...	-23.6	23.6	...	-25.5	25.5
Import duties	...	...	...	...	...	...	...	...	...	...	...	...
Value added tax	...	...	...	...	...	...	...	...	...	...	...	...
Other adjustments c	96.5	...	96.5	72.4	...	72.4	112.7	...	112.7	117.5	...	117.5
Total	926.7	473.0	453.7	1105.3	607.6	497.7	1254.0	670.1	584.1	1285.6	667.2	618.7

of which General Government:

1 Agriculture, hunting, forestry and fishing	...	...	...	...	...	...	...	...	...	...	...	...
2 Mining and quarrying	...	...	...	...	...	...	...	...	...	...	...	...
3 Manufacturing	...	...	...	...	...	...	...	...	...	...	...	...
4 Electricity, gas and water	...	...	...	...	...	...	...	...	...	...	...	...

Swaziland

4.1 Derivation of Value Added by Kind of Activity, in Current Prices
(Continued)

Million Swaziland emalangeni   Fiscal year ending 30 June

	1980			1981			1982			1983		
	Gross Output	Intermediate Consumption	Value Added	Gross Output	Intermediate Consumption	Value Added	Gross Output	Intermediate Consumption	Value Added	Gross Output	Intermediate Consumption	Value Added
5 Construction	5.5	2.9	2.7	5.9	2.6	3.3	8.0	3.1	4.9	8.9	3.9	5.0
6 Wholesale and retail trade, restaurants and hotels	...	...	...	...	...	...	...	...	...	...	...	...
7 Transport and communication	7.1	5.9	1.2	8.6	7.1	1.5	11.7	9.9	1.8	10.4	8.6	1.8
8 Finance, insurance, real estate and business services	...	...	...	...	...	...	...	...	...	...	...	...
9 Community, social and personal services	...	...	...	...	...	...	...	...	...	...	...	...
Total, Industries of General Government	12.6	8.8	3.9	14.5	9.7	4.8	...	...	...	...	...	...
Producers of Government Services	88.9	27.6	61.3	108.4	32.4	76.0	124.4	37.0	87.4	135.2	36.7	98.5
Total, General Government	101.5	36.4	65.2	122.9	42.1	80.8	...	...	...	...	...	...

	1984			1985			1986			1987		
	Gross Output	Intermediate Consumption	Value Added	Gross Output	Intermediate Consumption	Value Added	Gross Output	Intermediate Consumption	Value Added	Gross Output	Intermediate Consumption	Value Added
	All Producers											
1 Agriculture, hunting, forestry and fishing	210.9	81.2	129.7	234.4	98.4	136.0	319.0	124.3	194.7	281.8	128.9	152.9
A Agriculture and hunting	194.0	71.9	122.1	212.8	86.7	126.1	294.5	111.1	183.4	252.4	113.3	139.1
B Forestry and logging	16.9	9.3	7.6	21.6	11.7	9.9	24.5	13.2	11.3	29.4	15.6	13.8
C Fishing	...	...	...	...	...	...	...	...	...	...	...	...
2 Mining and quarrying	27.8	15.3	12.4	41.9	23.8	18.1	40.3	25.2	15.1	47.7	28.2	19.5
3 Manufacturing	405.0	293.8	111.2	427.3	320.8	106.5	647.3	457.1	190.2	712.9	476.9	236.0
A Manufacture of food, beverages and tobacco	235.6	172.8	62.7	249.0	185.4	63.5	355.4	249.3	106.1	382.1	261.8	120.3
B Textile, wearing apparel and leather industries	21.8	17.9	3.9	22.1	18.8	3.4	56.4	43.8	12.6	60.3	42.1	18.2
C Manufacture of wood and wood products, including furniture	19.4	13.7	5.7	21.3	15.9	5.4	34.0	25.9	8.1	38.8	28.0	10.8
D Manufacture of paper and paper products, printing and publishing	88.3	58.8	29.5	101.3	76.9	24.4	147.2	98.5	48.7	172.6	101.3	71.3
E Manufacture of chemicals and chemical petroleum, coal, rubber and plastic products	7.4	6.4	1.1	5.7	4.3	1.4	10.8	9.1	1.7	12.3	10.0	2.3
F Manufacture of non-metallic mineral products, except products of petroleum and coal	6.9	5.1	1.8	6.0	4.9	1.2	6.5	5.0	1.5	3.5	2.7	0.8
G Basic metal industries	...	...	...	...	...	...	...	...	...	...	...	...
H Manufacture of fabricated metal products, machinery and equipment	24.9	18.6	6.3	21.2	14.3	6.9	36.7	25.4	11.3	43.1	30.8	12.3
I Other manufacturing industries	0.7	0.4	0.3	0.6	0.3	0.3	0.2	0.1	0.1	0.2	0.1	0.1
4 Electricity, gas and water	19.5	3.6	15.9	26.6	4.6	22.0	30.6	6.2	24.4	36.6	6.1	30.5
5 Construction	78.1	53.5	24.6	85.3	60.5	24.8	100.2	71.2	29.0	112.0	81.0	31.0
6 Wholesale and retail trade, restaurants and hotels	170.2	96.5	73.7	179.8	96.7	83.1	232.3	130.4	101.9	303.2	190.6	112.6
A Wholesale and retail trade	116.0	60.3	55.7	129.7	66.7	63.0	173.4	90.3	83.1	230.7	139.6	91.1
B Restaurants and hotels	54.2	36.2	18.0	50.1	30.0	20.1	58.9	40.1	18.8	72.5	51.0	21.5
7 Transport, storage and communication	101.7	60.4	41.3	114.3	70.8	43.5	130.0	76.5	53.5	160.6	86.9	73.7
A Transport and storage	85.2	53.6	31.6	94.0	62.9	31.2	103.1	66.1	37.0	129.6	77.3	52.3
B Communication	16.5	6.8	9.7	20.3	7.9	12.4	26.9	10.4	16.5	31.0	9.6	21.4
8 Finance, insurance, real estate and business services	113.5	31.1	82.7	144.0	43.0	101.0	162.1	38.3	123.8	190.9	49.5	141.4
A Financial institutions	40.6	13.8	26.8	56.7	23.6	33.1	70.6	19.3	51.3	71.7	24.1	47.6
B Insurance	4.4	3.9	0.5	9.7	5.0	4.7	5.8	2.0	3.8	15.2	5.2	10.1
C Real estate and business services	68.8	13.4	55.4	77.6	14.4	63.2	85.7	17.0	68.7	104.0	20.2	83.7
Real estate, except dwellings	26.9	6.6	20.3	30.3	7.3	22.9	20.3	9.3	10.9	21.8	9.6	12.2

4.1 Derivation of Value Added by Kind of Activity, in Current Prices
(Continued)

Million Swaziland emalangeni   Fiscal year ending 30 June

	1984			1985			1986			1987		
	Gross Output	Intermediate Consumption	Value Added	Gross Output	Intermediate Consumption	Value Added	Gross Output	Intermediate Consumption	Value Added	Gross Output	Intermediate Consumption	Value Added
Dwellings a	27.9	1.4	26.5	32.1	1.6	30.5	38.3	2.0	36.3	44.1	2.2	41.9
9 Community, social and personal services	27.8	18.6	9.2	27.8	18.0	9.8	31.8	20.4	11.4	36.8	23.4	13.4
A Sanitary and similar services	...	...	...	...	...	...	...	...	...	...	...	...
B Social and related community services	...	...	...	...	...	...	...	...	...	...	...	...
C Recreational and cultural services	...	...	...	...	...	...	...	...	...	...	...	...
D Personal and household services	...	...	...	...	...	...	...	...	...	...	...	...
Total, Industries	1154.5	654.0	500.8	1281.4	736.6	544.7	1693.6	949.6	744.1	1882.5	1071.5	810.9
Producers of Government Services	158.7	47.1	111.7	186.3	48.4	137.9	230.5	57.9	172.6	225.6	59.3	166.3
Other Producers	19.5	8.2	11.3	20.0	8.4	11.6	29.5	15.2	14.3	34.8	18.0	16.8
Total b	1332.7	709.3	623.8	1487.7	793.4	694.2	1953.6	1022.7	931.1	2142.9	1148.8	994.0
Less: Imputed bank service charge	...	-25.0	25.0	...	-35.7	35.7	...	-27.7	27.7	...	-42.5	42.5
Import duties	...	...	...	...	...	...	...	...	...	...	...	...
Value added tax	...	...	...	...	...	...	...	...	...	...	...	...
Other adjustments c	130.7	...	130.7	144.0	...	144.0	148.0	...	148.0	166.5	...	166.5
Total	1463.4	734.3	729.5	1631.7	829.1	802.5	2101.6	1050.4	1051.4	2309.4	1191.3	1118.0
of which General Government:												
1 Agriculture, hunting, forestry and fishing	...	...	...	...	...	...	...	...	...	...	...	...
2 Mining and quarrying	...	...	...	...	...	...	...	...	...	...	...	...
3 Manufacturing	...	...	...	...	...	...	...	...	...	...	...	...
4 Electricity, gas and water	...	...	...	...	...	...	...	...	...	...	...	...
5 Construction	7.5	4.0	3.5	7.1	4.0	3.1	...	...	...	...	...	...
6 Wholesale and retail trade, restaurants and hotels	...	...	...	...	...	...	...	...	...	...	...	...
7 Transport and communication	14.1	12.2	1.9	17.8	15.9	2.0	...	...	...	...	...	...
8 Finance, insurance, real estate and business services	...	...	...	...	...	...	...	...	...	...	...	...
9 Community, social and personal services	...	...	...	...	...	...	...	...	...	...	...	...
Total, Industries of General Government	...	...	...	...	...	...	...	...	...	...	...	...
Producers of Government Services	158.8	47.1	111.7	186.3	48.4	137.9	230.6	57.9	172.7	225.6	59.3	166.3
Total, General Government	...	...	...	...	...	...	...	...	...	...	...	...

a) Rented and owner-occupied dwellings are included in the category 'Dwelling' of item 'Finance, insurance, real estate and business services'. b) Gross domestic product in factor values.
c) Item 'Other adjustments' refers to indirect taxes net of subsidies.

4.3 Cost Components of Value Added

Million Swaziland emalangeni   Fiscal year ending 30 June

	1980						1981					
	Compensation of Employees	Capital Consumption	Net Operating Surplus	Indirect Taxes	Less: Subsidies Received	Value Added	Compensation of Employees	Capital Consumption	Net Operating Surplus	Indirect Taxes	Less: Subsidies Received	Value Added
All Producers												
1 Agriculture, hunting, forestry and fishing	22.2	5.8	56.6	...	...	84.6	23.6	6.0	67.0	...	...	96.6
A Agriculture and hunting	16.3	4.6	56.6	...	...	77.5	18.2	5.1	65.7	...	...	89.0
B Forestry and logging	5.9	1.2	-	...	...	7.1	5.4	0.9	1.3	...	...	7.6
C Fishing	...	...	...	...	...	...	...	...	...	...	...	...
2 Mining and quarrying	7.9	0.6	5.6	...	...	14.1	10.0	0.4	4.8	...	...	15.2

Swaziland

4.3 Cost Components of Value Added
(Continued)

Million Swaziland emalangeni

Fiscal year ending 30 June

	1980						1981					
	Compensation of Employees	Capital Consumption	Net Operating Surplus	Indirect Taxes	Less: Subsidies Received	Value Added	Compensation of Employees	Capital Consumption	Net Operating Surplus	Indirect Taxes	Less: Subsidies Received	Value Added
3 Manufacturing	30.3	9.2	40.1	...	...	79.6	38.9	10.8	39.4	...	...	89.1
A Manufacture of food, beverages and tobacco	13.0	5.0	15.3	...	...	33.3	16.2	5.1	21.3	...	...	42.6
B Textile, wearing apparel and leather industries	1.1	0.1	1.0	...	...	2.2	2.0	0.3	0.1	...	...	2.4
C Manufacture of wood and wood products, including furniture	2.6	0.4	3.1	...	...	6.1	4.0	0.3	1.8	...	...	6.1
D Manufacture of paper and paper products, printing and publishing	8.2	1.7	14.5	...	...	24.4	8.8	2.2	6.9	...	...	18.0
E Manufacture of chemicals and chemical petroleum, coal, rubber and plastic products	1.5	1.0	6.0	...	...	8.5	3.3	1.2	7.3	...	...	11.9
F Manufacture of non-metallic mineral products, except products of petroleum and coal	0.4	0.1	0.4	...	...	0.9	0.8	0.2	0.3	...	...	1.3
G Basic metal industries	...	...	...	...	...	...	...	...	...	...	...	...
H Manufacture of fabricated metal products, machinery and equipment	3.1	0.9	-	...	...	4.0	3.5	1.3	1.7	...	...	6.6
I Other manufacturing industries	0.3	-	-0.1	...	...	0.2	0.2	-	-	...	...	0.2
4 Electricity, gas and water	1.3	1.8	1.3	...	...	4.4	3.6	1.7	1.9	...	...	7.2
5 Construction	14.4	0.3	1.5	...	...	16.4	15.5	0.4	0.9	...	...	16.8
6 Wholesale and retail trade, restaurants and hotels	18.4	1.4	15.9	...	...	35.7	22.9	2.4	17.0	...	...	42.3
A Wholesale and retail trade	12.9	0.8	13.3	...	...	27.0	15.8	1.7	14.1	...	...	31.6
B Restaurants and hotels	5.5	0.6	2.6	...	...	8.6	7.1	0.6	2.9	...	...	10.7
7 Transport, storage and communication	10.0	3.3	7.1	...	...	20.4	12.4	4.7	7.8	...	...	24.9
A Transport and storage	8.2	2.7	6.4	...	...	17.3	10.2	3.5	5.5	...	...	19.2
B Communication	1.8	0.6	0.7	...	...	3.2	2.2	1.2	2.2	...	...	5.6
8 Finance, insurance, real estate and business services	10.8	1.4	27.1	...	...	39.3	15.7	3.0	38.5	...	...	57.2
A Financial institutions	6.9	0.9	4.5	...	...	12.3	9.5	1.9	10.8	...	...	22.2
B Insurance	0.6	-	0.8	...	...	1.4	0.8	-	1.1	...	...	1.9
C Real estate and business services	3.3	0.5	21.8	...	...	25.6	5.5	1.0	26.6	...	...	33.0
Real estate, except dwellings	...	...	...	...	...	...	0.4	0.7	6.8	...	...	7.9
Dwellings a	...	...	15.6	...	...	15.6	-	-	17.6	...	...	17.6
9 Community, social and personal services	4.2	0.5	1.0	...	...	5.7	5.1	0.7	1.6	...	...	7.4
Total, Industries	119.5	24.5	156.2	...	...	300.1	147.7	30.1	178.9	...	...	356.7
Producers of Government Services	61.3	-	-	...	...	61.3	76.0	-	-	...	...	76.0
Other Producers	6.6	0.1	-	...	...	6.7	9.2	0.1	-	...	...	9.3
Total b	187.4	24.6	156.2	...	...	368.1	232.9	30.2	178.9	...	...	442.0
Less: Imputed bank service charge	...	...	10.9	...	...	10.9	...	...	16.5	...	...	16.5
Import duties	...	...	...	...	...	...	...	...	...	...	...	...
Value added tax	...	...	...	...	...	...	...	...	...	...	...	...
Other adjustments c	...	...	...	...	...	96.5	...	...	...	...	...	72.4
Total	187.4	24.6	145.3	96.5	...	453.7	232.9	30.2	162.4	72.4	...	497.9

	1982						1983					
	Compensation of Employees	Capital Consumption	Net Operating Surplus	Indirect Taxes	Less: Subsidies Received	Value Added	Compensation of Employees	Capital Consumption	Net Operating Surplus	Indirect Taxes	Less: Subsidies Received	Value Added
				All Producers								
1 Agriculture, hunting, forestry and fishing	23.9	6.1	65.5	...	...	95.8	30.1	9.9	46.2	...	...	86.2
A Agriculture and hunting	18.5	5.2	64.2	...	...	87.9	25.0	9.1	44.5	...	...	78.6
B Forestry and logging	5.4	0.9	1.3	...	...	7.9	5.1	0.8	1.7	...	...	7.6
C Fishing	...	...	...	...	...	...	...	...	...	...	...	...
2 Mining and quarrying	10.0	0.2	4.2	...	...	14.4	9.8	0.2	5.8	...	...	15.8

4.3 Cost Components of Value Added
(Continued)

Million Swaziland emalangeni   Fiscal year ending 30 June

	1982						1983					
	Compensation of Employees	Capital Consumption	Net Operating Surplus	Indirect Taxes	Less: Subsidies Received	Value Added	Compensation of Employees	Capital Consumption	Net Operating Surplus	Indirect Taxes	Less: Subsidies Received	Value Added
3 Manufacturing	47.4	12.1	41.3	...	...	100.8	48.3	13.0	28.4	...		89.7
A Manufacture of food, beverages and tobacco	21.0	6.1	17.6	...	...	44.7	19.8	6.4	23.2	...	...	49.4
B Textile, wearing apparel and leather industries	1.6	0.3	0.4	...	...	2.3	1.6	0.3	-0.3	...	...	1.6
C Manufacture of wood and wood products, including furniture	5.1	0.5	2.6	...	...	8.2	5.2	0.9	-0.5	...	...	5.5
D Manufacture of paper and paper products, printing and publishing	10.3	2.5	5.6	...	...	18.4	11.1	2.4	0.3	...	...	13.8
E Manufacture of chemicals and chemical petroleum, coal, rubber and plastic products	4.1	1.2	13.2	...	...	18.5	5.5	1.3	3.4	...	...	10.2
F Manufacture of non-metallic mineral products, except products of petroleum and coal	0.9	0.8	-0.2	...	...	1.5	0.7	0.6	1.2	...	...	2.4
G Basic metal industries	...	...	...	...	...	...	...	...	...	...	...	...
H Manufacture of fabricated metal products, machinery and equipment	4.2	0.9	2.4	...	...	7.5	4.1	1.1	1.3	...	...	6.5
I Other manufacturing industries	0.3	-	-0.2	...	...	0.1	0.3	-	-0.1	...	...	0.2
4 Electricity, gas and water	4.2	1.9	2.5	...	...	8.6	4.3	2.1	2.9	...	...	9.3
5 Construction	15.4	0.6	-0.1	...	...	15.9	21.6	2.0	1.7	...	...	25.3
6 Wholesale and retail trade, restaurants and hotels	28.1	2.5	24.1	...	...	54.7	32.1	2.8	28.9	...	...	63.8
A Wholesale and retail trade	19.3	1.8	21.1	...	...	42.2	22.4	2.0	26.7	...	...	51.0
B Restaurants and hotels	8.8	0.7	3.0	...	...	12.5	9.8	0.8	2.2	...	...	12.8
7 Transport, storage and communication	15.6	7.7	8.7	...	...	32.0	17.3	9.2	10.2	...	...	36.7
A Transport and storage	13.1	6.2	7.1	...	...	26.5	14.5	7.2	6.6	...	...	28.3
B Communication	2.5	1.5	1.5	...	...	5.5	2.8	2.1	3.6	...	...	8.5
8 Finance, insurance, real estate and business services	17.8	5.2	43.8	...	...	66.8	21.4	6.4	52.3	...	...	80.1
A Financial institutions	10.9	4.3	8.6	...	...	23.8	13.1	4.1	8.8	...	...	26.0
B Insurance	1.0	0.1	1.4	...	...	2.5	1.1	0.1	4.8	...	...	6.0
C Real estate and business services	5.9	0.9	33.7	...	...	40.6	7.2	2.2	38.7	...	...	48.2
Real estate, except dwellings	0.5	0.5	9.9	...	...	10.9	0.9	1.8	12.2	...	...	14.8
Dwellings a	-	-	21.1	...	...	21.1	-	-	24.0	...	...	24.0
9 Community, social and personal services	5.9	0.7	2.7	...	...	9.3	6.8	0.7	3.2	...	...	10.7
Total, Industries	168.3	37.0	192.7	...	...	398.7	191.7	46.3	179.6	...	...	417.6
Producers of Government Services	87.4	-	-			87.4	98.5	-	-	...		98.5
Other Producers	9.0	0.1	-			9.1	10.2	0.2	-			10.4
Total b	264.7	37.1	192.7			495.0	300.4	46.5	179.6	...		526.5
Less: Imputed bank service charge	...	...	23.6			23.6	...	...	25.5			25.5
Import duties	...	...	...	...		...	...	...	...	...		...
Value added tax	...	...	...	...		...	...	...	...	...		...
Other adjustments c	...	...	...	...	...	112.7	...	...	...	...	...	117.5
Total	264.7	37.1	169.1	112.7		584.1	300.4	46.5	154.1	117.5	...	618.5

	1984						1985					
	Compensation of Employees	Capital Consumption	Net Operating Surplus	Indirect Taxes	Less: Subsidies Received	Value Added	Compensation of Employees	Capital Consumption	Net Operating Surplus	Indirect Taxes	Less: Subsidies Received	Value Added
					All Producers							
1 Agriculture, hunting, forestry and fishing	28.9	6.9	93.9	...	...	129.7	35.0	7.7	93.3	...	...	136.0
A Agriculture and hunting	23.3	6.0	92.8	...	...	122.1	26.9	6.4	92.8	...	...	126.1
B Forestry and logging	5.6	0.9	1.1	...	...	7.6	8.1	1.3	0.5	...	...	9.9
C Fishing	...	...	...			...	...	...	...			...
2 Mining and quarrying	9.1	0.1	3.2	...	...	12.4	11.4	0.8	5.8	...	...	18.0

Swaziland

Million Swaziland emalangeni   Fiscal year ending 30 June

	1984						1985					
	Compensation of Employees	Capital Consumption	Net Operating Surplus	Indirect Taxes	Less: Subsidies Received	Value Added	Compensation of Employees	Capital Consumption	Net Operating Surplus	Indirect Taxes	Less: Subsidies Received	Value Added
3 Manufacturing	44.9	11.9	54.5	...	...	111.3	51.2	12.7	42.7	...	...	106.6
A Manufacture of food, beverages and tobacco	22.6	6.7	33.4	...	...	62.7	26.0	6.9	30.5	...	...	63.5
B Textile, wearing apparel and leather industries	1.1	0.1	2.6	...	...	3.9	1.5	0.3	1.6	...	...	3.4
C Manufacture of wood and wood products, including furniture	3.4	0.9	1.4	...	...	5.7	5.2	0.8	-0.6	...	...	5.4
D Manufacture of paper and paper products, printing and publishing	11.7	2.5	15.4	...	...	29.5	13.2	3.1	8.1	...	...	24.4
E Manufacture of chemicals and chemical petroleum, coal, rubber and plastic products	0.6	0.1	0.4	...	...	1.1	0.8	0.2	0.5	...	...	1.5
F Manufacture of non-metallic mineral products, except products of petroleum and coal	1.8	0.5	-0.4	...	...	1.8	1.0	0.2	-	...	...	1.2
G Basic metal industries	...	...	...	...	...	...	...	...	...	...	...	...
H Manufacture of fabricated metal products, machinery and equipment	3.5	1.1	1.6	...	...	6.3	3.3	1.2	2.4	...	...	6.9
I Other manufacturing industries	0.3	-	-	...	...	0.3	0.2	-	-	...	...	0.3
4 Electricity, gas and water	5.5	2.9	7.5	...	...	15.9	5.8	4.2	12.0	...	...	22.0
5 Construction	20.3	1.3	3.0	...	...	24.6	20.9	1.2	2.7	...	...	24.8
6 Wholesale and retail trade, restaurants and hotels	39.5	3.8	30.4	...	...	73.7	41.6	3.9	37.6	...	...	83.1
A Wholesale and retail trade	26.2	2.7	26.9	...	...	55.8	30.2	2.8	29.9	...	...	63.0
B Restaurants and hotels	13.3	1.1	3.5	...	...	17.9	11.5	1.0	7.6	...	...	20.1
7 Transport, storage and communication	19.7	10.8	10.8	...	...	41.3	21.3	13.2	9.1	...	...	43.6
A Transport and storage	16.8	8.4	6.4	...	...	31.6	18.0	10.5	2.6	...	...	31.2
B Communication	2.9	2.4	4.4	...	...	9.7	3.3	2.7	6.5	...	...	12.4
8 Finance, insurance, real estate and business services	25.0	8.6	49.1	...	...	82.7	29.4	10.5	61.1	...	...	101.0
A Financial institutions	15.3	4.9	6.6	...	...	26.8	18.0	6.6	8.5	...	...	33.1
B Insurance	1.4	0.1	-1.0	...	...	0.5	1.8	0.1	2.8	...	...	4.7
C Real estate and business services	8.4	3.7	43.5	...	...	55.4	9.6	3.8	49.7	...	...	63.1
Real estate, except dwellings	2.1	3.2	15.0	...	...	20.3	2.3	3.2	17.4	...	...	22.9
Dwellings a	-	-	26.5	...	...	26.5	-	-	30.5	...	...	30.5
9 Community, social and personal services	8.1	0.7	0.3	...	...	9.1	8.2	0.6	1.0	...	...	9.8
Total, Industries	201.0	47.0	252.7	...	...	500.8	224.8	54.8	265.3	...	...	544.7
Producers of Government Services	111.7	-	-	...	...	111.7	137.9	-	-	...	...	137.9
Other Producers	11.1	0.2	-	...	...	11.3	11.3	0.3	-	...	...	11.6
Total b	323.8	47.2	252.7	...	...	623.8	374.0	55.1	265.3	...	...	694.2
Less: Imputed bank service charge	...	...	25.0	...	...	25.0	...	...	35.7	...	...	35.7
Import duties	...	...	...	...	...	...	...	...	...	...	...	...
Value added tax	...	...	...	...	...	...	...	...	...	...	...	...
Other adjustments c	...	...	...	...	...	130.7	...	...	...	...	...	144.0
Total	323.8	47.2	227.7	130.7	...	729.5	374.0	55.1	229.5	144.0	...	802.5

	1986						1987					
	Compensation of Employees	Capital Consumption	Net Operating Surplus	Indirect Taxes	Less: Subsidies Received	Value Added	Compensation of Employees	Capital Consumption	Net Operating Surplus	Indirect Taxes	Less: Subsidies Received	Value Added
					All Producers							
1 Agriculture, hunting, forestry and fishing	51.4	12.9	130.4	...	...	194.7	43.0	10.2	99.7	...	...	152.9
A Agriculture and hunting	41.8	11.3	130.3	...	...	183.4	31.3	8.3	99.5	...	...	139.1
B Forestry and logging	9.6	1.6	0.1	...	...	11.3	11.7	1.9	0.2	...	...	13.8
C Fishing	...	...	...	...	...	...	...	...	...	...	...	...
2 Mining and quarrying	14.4	1.8	-1.2	...	...	15.0	14.8	2.1	2.5	...	...	19.4

4.3 Cost Components of Value Added
(Continued)

Million Swaziland emalangeni

Fiscal year ending 30 June

	1986						1987					
	Compensation of Employees	Capital Consumption	Net Operating Surplus	Indirect Taxes	Less: Subsidies Received	Value Added	Compensation of Employees	Capital Consumption	Net Operating Surplus	Indirect Taxes	Less: Subsidies Received	Value Added
3 Manufacturing	62.1	14.1	114.0	...	...	190.2	86.7	18.4	130.8	...	...	235.9
A Manufacture of food, beverages and tobacco	29.3	7.3	69.5	...	...	106.1	39.2	8.6	72.4	...	...	120.3
B Textile, wearing apparel and leather industries	4.5	1.7	6.4	...	...	12.6	5.9	2.1	10.2	...	...	18.2
C Manufacture of wood and wood products, including furniture	5.2	0.6	2.3	...	...	8.1	6.5	0.7	3.6	...	...	10.8
D Manufacture of paper and paper products, printing and publishing	15.0	2.9	30.8	...	...	48.7	27.2	5.4	38.7	...	...	71.3
E Manufacture of chemicals and chemical petroleum, coal, rubber and plastic products	0.9	0.2	0.6	...	...	1.7	1.3	0.3	0.7	...	...	2.3
F Manufacture of non-metallic mineral products, except products of petroleum and coal	1.6	0.4	-0.5	...	...	1.5	0.6	0.1	0.1	...	...	0.8
G Basic metal industries	...	...	...	...	...	...	...	...	...	...	...	...
H Manufacture of fabricated metal products, machinery and equipment	5.5	1.0	4.8	...	...	11.3	6.1	1.1	5.1	...	...	12.3
I Other manufacturing industries	0.1	-	-	...	...	0.1	0.1	-	-	...	...	0.1
4 Electricity, gas and water	6.0	4.6	13.8	...	...	24.4	7.3	5.0	18.1	...	...	30.4
5 Construction	23.9	1.0	4.2	...	...	29.1	25.7	2.3	3.0	...	...	31.0
6 Wholesale and retail trade, restaurants and hotels	47.1	6.4	48.4	...	...	101.9	60.6	6.9	45.0	...	...	112.5
A Wholesale and retail trade	36.6	4.7	41.9	...	...	83.2	46.9	5.2	39.0	...	...	91.1
B Restaurants and hotels	10.5	1.7	6.5	...	...	18.8	13.7	1.7	6.0	...	...	21.5
7 Transport, storage and communication	23.5	16.0	14.1	...	...	53.6	26.6	15.1	32.0	...	...	73.7
A Transport and storage	19.1	13.4	4.5	...	...	37.0	21.8	12.5	18.0	...	...	52.3
B Communication	4.4	2.6	9.6	...	...	16.5	4.8	2.6	14.0	...	...	21.4
8 Finance, insurance, real estate and business services	33.8	10.3	79.5	...	...	123.8	40.6	14.1	86.9	...	...	141.4
A Financial institutions	21.4	6.7	23.2	...	...	51.3	25.4	8.2	13.9	...	...	47.5
B Insurance	2.0	-	2.0	...	...	3.8	2.3	0.1	7.6	...	...	10.1
C Real estate and business services	10.5	3.6	54.3	...	...	68.7	12.9	5.8	65.4	...	...	83.7
Real estate, except dwellings	8.1	0.4	2.4	...	...	10.9	9.1	0.4	2.8	...	...	12.2
Dwellings a	-	-	36.3	...	...	36.3	-	-	41.9	...	...	41.9
9 Community, social and personal services	10.0	0.8	0.6	...	...	11.4	11.1	0.7	1.6	...	...	13.4
Total, Industries	272.2	67.9	403.8	...	...	744.1	316.4	74.8	419.6	...	...	810.9
Producers of Government Services	172.7	...	...	...	...	172.7	166.3	...	...	...	...	166.3
Other Producers	13.9	0.4	...	...	...	14.3	16.4	0.4	-	...	...	16.8
Total b	458.8	68.3	403.8	...	...	931.1	499.1	75.2	419.6	...	...	994.0
Less: Imputed bank service charge	...	...	27.7	...	...	27.7	...	...	42.5	...	...	42.5
Import duties	...	...	...	...	...	...	...	...	...	...	...	...
Value added tax	...	...	...	...	...	...	...	...	...	...	...	...
Other adjustments c	...	...	...	...	...	148.0	...	...	...	...	...	166.5
Total	458.8	68.3	376.1	148.0	...	1051.4	499.1	75.2	377.1	166.5	...	1118.0

a) Rented and owner-occupied dwellings are included in the category 'Dwelling' of item 'Finance, insurance, real estate and business services'.
b) Gross domestic product in factor values.
c) Item 'Other adjustments' refers to indirect taxes net of subsidies.

Sweden

General note. The preparation of national accounts statistics in Sweden is undertaken by Statistics Sweden. The annual estimates of certain standard tables are published in a series of Statistical Reports entitled 'Nationalrakenskaper - National Accounts'. Supplementary and supporting tables are published separately in a set of five appendixes. Each series of the Statistical Reports contains some methodological notes. The Swedish National Accounts System corresponds closely to the United Nations System of National Accounts. Separate input-output tables have been published for the years 1964, 1968, 1969, 1975, 1980 and 1985 in 'Input-Output tabeller for Sverige'. The following tables have been prepared from successive replies to the United Nations national accounts questionnaire. When the scope and coverage of the estimates differ for conceptual or statistical reasons from the definitions and classifications recommended in SNA, a footnote is indicated to the relevant tables.

Sources and methods Sources and methods:

(a) Gross domestic product. (a) Gross domestic product. Gross domestic product is estimated mainly through the expenditure approach.

(b) Expenditure on the gross domestic product. (b) Expenditure on the gross domestic product. All components of GDP by expenditure type are estimated through the expenditure approach. Government final consumption expenditure is calculated from the cost side. The calculations for the central government are based on the semi-annual groupings made by the National Accounting and Audit Bureau and on reports of the central government revenue. For local government the calculations are based on finance statistics compiled by Statistics Sweden. Private consumption expenditure consists of approximately 90 items, for which a number of estimation methods are used. The Swedish Board of Agriculture is the source for the estimate of food consumption, and for most of the remaining goods, the estimates are based on a combination of the Family Expenditure Survey and turnover statistics of retail trade. Gross capital formation estimates are derived from investment inquiries from the different sectors of economic activity and from government accounts data. Exports and imports of goods and services are mainly estimated from foreign trade statistics and balance of payment statistics of the Swedish Central Bank. For the constant price estimates, price deflation is used for most of the expenditure items, the current values being deflated by various price indexes such as weighted consumer price indexes, adjusted export and import price indexes, price indexes for different capital goods, etc. Components of government consumption expenditure are deflated by relevant price indexes, except wages and salaries which are extrapolated by employment indexes.

(c) Cost-structure of the gross domestic product. (c) Cost-structure of the gross domestic product. Estimates of the cost components of the GDP are for compensation of employees based on statistics on income verifications from employers with addition for employers' contribution to social security schemes etc. Consumption of fixed capital is calculated from capital stock values. Data on indirect taxes and subsidies are based on government finance statistics. Operating surplus is a residual item.

(d) Gross domestic product by kind of economic activity. (d) Gross domestic product by kind of economic activity. The table on gross domestic product by kind of economic activity is calculated in basic values. Value added is derived from the input-output tables. The input-output tables are calculated annually in current and constant prices starting from 1980. Statistics from the Board of Agriculture is the main source of information for the estimation of the agriculture sector. Estimates of output and intermediate consumption of mining, manufacturing and electricity, gas and water are based on annual censuses. Special calculations are made to include establishments not included in the census. Output of construction is calculated mainly from the demand side. Production of the trade sector (trade margins) is calculated within the input-output tables. For the rest of the service sectors production statistics for services and financial accounting statistics are mostly used. The source for central government services is statistics from the National Accounting and Audit Bureau, estimates on local government are based on finance statistics. The general approach for the constant price estimates for most industries is double deflation. Different kinds of price indexes have been used, such as producer's price indexes, consumer price indexes, implicit price indexes, etc. For producers of government services base-year values on compensation of employees are extrapolated by employment statistics (hours worked), which is also the kind of statistics used for estimating value added of financing and insurance. In addition those values are adjusted for 2 per cent increase in productivity per year.

1.1 Expenditure on the Gross Domestic Product, in Current Prices

Million Swedish kronor

	1980	1981	1982	1983	1984	1985	1986	1987	1988	1989	1990	1991
1 Government final consumption expenditure	153764	170161	185672	203506	221060	239156	257246	269880	286809	317214	366716	387066
2 Private final consumption expenditure	274745	307050	342013	371866	407295	447931	492753	542541	589270	638772	698827	777285
A Households	266672	297825	331799	360702	395145	434685	478082	526293	571453	618700	675276	751425
B Private non-profit institutions serving households	8073	9225	10214	11164	12150	13246	14671	16248	17817	20072	23551	25860
3 Gross capital formation	109824	102894	109475	119362	136823	163292	165716	188466	216056	263592	280386	245686
A Increase in stocks	5923	-4073	-6286	-10263	-7757	-484	-5840	-4503	-3090	179	-1195	-25040
B Gross fixed capital formation	103901	106967	115761	129625	144580	163776	171556	192969	219146	263413	281581	270726
Residential buildings	24490	25776	26947	28856	33070	35211	35695	42594	52749	63948	75989	90432
Non-residential buildings	39180	40421	42568	45842	49195	52187	57211	61500	66778	80101	84527	75220
Other construction and land improvement etc.												
Other a	40231	40770	46246	54927	62315	76378	78650	88875	99619	119364	121065	105074
4 Exports of goods and services	156469	174107	204756	253260	289819	306595	311091	332298	359690	394470	406831	404561
5 Less: Imports of goods and services	166547	175299	208234	238142	260699	291186	281223	313638	341354	387735	403863	381669
Equals: Gross Domestic Product	528255	578913	633682	709852	794298	865788	945583	1019547	1110471	1226313	1348897	1432929

a) For years 1970-80 of the first series, item 'Other' of gross capital formation includes a statistical discrepancy.

1.2 Expenditure on the Gross Domestic Product, in Constant Prices

Million Swedish kronor

	1980	1981	1982	1983	1984	1985	1986	1987	1988	1989	1990	1991
					At constant prices of:1985							
1 Government final consumption expenditure	219215	224238	226532	228291	233542	239156	242387	244916	246456	251225	258386	258988
2 Private final consumption expenditure	437767	435384	438380	428553	435765	447931	471055	492581	504812	511983	510507	515608
A Households	...	...	...	...	...	434685	457303	478157	489883	496741	494091	498885
B Private non-profit institutions serving households	...	...	...	...	...	13246	13752	14424	14929	15242	16416	16723
3 Gross capital formation	159756	135287	133428	131544	144410	163292	160081	170641	182984	207437	207654	170379

1.2 Expenditure on the Gross Domestic Product, in Constant Prices
(Continued)

Million Swedish kronor

	1980	1981	1982	1983	1984	1985	1986	1987	1988	1989	1990	1991
					At constant prices of:1985							
A Increase in stocks	9282	-6425	-7864	-12369	-8155	-484	-4761	-6762	-4671	-2346	-1047	-20965
B Gross fixed capital formation	150474	141712	141292	143913	152565	163776	164842	177403	187655	209783	208701	191344
Residential buildings	...	...	...	...	...	35211	34000	38039	41681	43957	46076	47081
Non-residential buildings	...	...	...	...	...	52187	54999	55799	55899	61144	59443	53380
Other construction and land improvement etc.	...	...	...	...	...							
Other	...	...	...	...	...	76378	75843	83565	90075	104682	103182	90883
4 Exports of goods and services	238645	243481	257346	282813	302223	306595	316380	328831	338656	348770	353921	346251
5 Less: Imports of goods and services	261273	246060	254471	256462	270190	291186	304909	326766	342076	366534	370516	348824
Statistical discrepancy	-3110	-1071	-1167	-196	1226	...	...	...	...	...	...	...
Equals: Gross Domestic Product	791000	791259	800048	814543	846976	865788	884994	910203	930832	952881	959952	942402

1.3 Cost Components of the Gross Domestic Product

Million Swedish kronor

	1980	1981	1982	1983	1984	1985	1986	1987	1988	1989	1990	1991
1 Indirect taxes, net	48619	55929	57998	71766	86254	99154	112708	128870	133847	149800	170094	184663
A Indirect taxes	71446	82758	89247	108262	125764	142565	158958	176860	182766	205536	233362	257254
B Less: Subsidies	22827	26829	31249	36496	39510	43411	46250	47990	48919	55736	63268	72591
2 Consumption of fixed capital	59421	66479	74675	84339	91752	99464	107219	116475	127835	140084	153737	164935
3 Compensation of employees paid by resident producers to:	338187	369991	391347	424037	463722	505570	554233	598688	653766	732154	830736	883355
A Resident households	338157	369920	391341	423307	463368	505155	553319	597686	652614	730773	829268	881311
B Rest of the world	30	71	6	730	354	415	914	1002	1152	1381	1468	2044
4 Operating surplus	82028	86514	109662	129710	152570	161600	171423	175514	195023	204275	194330	199976
A Corporate and quasi-corporate enterprises	24527	27248	36837	47391	65669	67396	74892	84995	97159	102350	87953	91700
B Private unincorporated enterprises	55501	56956	70083	77912	82592	89567	91526	85189	91794	94366	98389	101494
C General government	2000	2310	2742	4407	4309	4637	5005	5330	6070	7559	7988	6782
Equals: Gross Domestic Product	528255	578913	633682	709852	794298	865788	945583	1019547	1110471	1226313	1348897	1432929

1.4 General Government Current Receipts and Disbursements

Million Swedish kronor

	1980	1981	1982	1983	1984	1985	1986	1987	1988	1989	1990	1991
					Receipts							
1 Operating surplus	2000	2310	2742	4407	4309	4637	5005	5330	6070	7559	7988	6782
2 Property and entrepreneurial income	27175	32836	38976	45714	50958	58345	62299	60431	61266	73821	79929	86987
3 Taxes, fees and contributions	260694	291205	313210	359687	400543	434728	492062	560991	610674	696985	762770	765178
A Indirect taxes	71446	82758	89247	108262	125764	142565	158958	176860	182766	205536	233362	257254
B Direct taxes	113925	121835	136230	154440	169294	181551	205979	243686	270319	310961	318612	284449
C Social security contributions	74647	85838	86634	95655	103781	108206	124456	137284	153799	176732	205867	218901
D Compulsory fees, fines and penalties	676	774	1099	1330	1704	2406	2669	3161	3790	3756	4929	4574
4 Other current transfers	7632	7001	12413	13139	14242	17375	12130	7954	7682	8770	9375	8937
Total Current Receipts of General Government	297501	333352	367341	422947	470052	515085	571496	634706	685692	787135	860062	867884
					Disbursements							
1 Government final consumption expenditure	153764	170161	185672	203506	221060	239156	257246	269880	286809	317214	366716	387066
A Compensation of employees [a]	110185	120388	130781	141543	153506	163563	177472	185037	197869	219117	255402	272861
B Consumption of fixed capital [a]	5367	6118	6915	7797	8509	9189	9768	10319	11252	12192	13412	14297
C Purchases of goods and services, net	36135	41090	45211	48425	53380	60189	62887	66594	71536	78335	88993	91891
D Less: Own account fixed capital formation	-	-	-	-	-	-	-	-	-	-	-	-
E Indirect taxes paid, net	2077	2565	2765	5741	5665	6215	7119	7930	6152	7570	8909	8017
2 Property income	21887	31144	43953	51457	60991	73159	70803	66747	63175	67377	69293	75904
A Interest	21591	30771	43496	51063	60464	72579	69899	66077	62110	66173	67972	74422
B Net land rent and royalties	296	373	457	394	527	580	904	670	1065	1204	1321	1482

Sweden

1.4 General Government Current Receipts and Disbursements
(Continued)

Million Swedish kronor

		1980	1981	1982	1983	1984	1985	1986	1987	1988	1989	1990	1991
3	Subsidies	22827	26829	31249	36496	39510	43411	46250	47990	48919	55736	63268	72591
4	Other current transfers	101876	114947	126606	141897	151983	171757	189334	207566	235027	260721	289988	329783
	A Social security benefits	73396	84729	92730	104640	112335	125050	139547	153639	176140	194247	214478	240972
	B Social assistance grants	16161	16436	19034	21025	22395	27734	28209	31513	33838	38286	43553	55698
	C Other	12319	13782	14842	16232	17253	18973	21578	22414	25049	28188	31957	33113
5	Net saving	-2853	-9729	-20139	-10409	-3492	-12398	7863	42523	51762	86087	70797	2540
	Total Current Disbursements and Net Saving of General Government	297501	333352	367341	422947	470052	515085	571496	634706	685692	787135	860062	867884

a) The estimates of 'compensation of employees' and 'consumption of fixed capital' of the government sector shown in this table 1.4 are different from those in table 3.11. The difference consists of those parts of general government that are included in Industries.

1.5 Current Income and Outlay of Corporate and Quasi-Corporate Enterprises, Summary

Million Swedish kronor

		1980	1981	1982	1983	1984	1985	1986	1987	1988	1989	1990	1991
	Receipts												
1	Operating surplus	24527	27248	36837	47391	65669	67396	74892	84995	97159	102350	87954	91700
2	Property and entrepreneurial income received	86631	111528	129034	141584	164432	192357	205756	230229	271187	335879	423703	480729
3	Current transfers	25856	32434	40018	40340	45386	56847	65080	67384	75203	83438	105136	135324
	Total Current Receipts	137014	171210	205889	229315	275487	316600	345728	382608	443549	521667	616793	707753
	Disbursements												
1	Property and entrepreneurial income	90562	114063	128751	146888	169415	193842	210440	229574	271441	344846	442642	503066
2	Direct taxes and other current payments to general government	6424	6171	8549	12776	14289	13469	16226	27058	28561	33893	27333	12824
3	Other current transfers	17855	24133	31577	33248	39361	48092	56800	58470	64286	71438	95420	121160
	Statistical discrepancy	2479	9856	8099	5855	8333	9373	14146	27928	27305	40693	38829	43225
4	Net saving	19694	16987	28913	30548	44089	51824	48116	39578	51956	30797	12569	27478
	Total Current Disbursements and Net Saving	137014	171210	205889	229315	275487	316600	345728	382608	443549	521667	616793	707753

1.6 Current Income and Outlay of Households and Non-Profit Institutions

Million Swedish kronor

		1980	1981	1982	1983	1984	1985	1986	1987	1988	1989	1990	1991
	Receipts												
1	Compensation of employees	338440	370353	391342	423525	463594	505417	553471	597974	652924	731131	829755	882084
	A From resident producers	338157	369920	391341	423307	463368	505155	553319	597686	652614	730773	829268	881311
	B From rest of the world	283	433	1	218	226	262	152	288	310	358	487	773
2	Operating surplus of private unincorporated enterprises	55501	56956	70083	77912	82592	89567	91526	85189	91794	94366	98389	101494
3	Property and entrepreneurial income	27267	33364	34417	37967	43978	52587	55161	57092	63559	72295	82229	83900
4	Current transfers	106748	121086	133374	150315	161962	183356	202795	223983	252791	278157	307987	351162
	A Social security benefits	73396	84729	92730	104640	112335	125050	139547	153639	176140	194247	214478	240972
	B Social assistance grants	20121	21421	23623	26537	28360	33918	35918	40072	43455	47974	53729	67442
	C Other	13231	14936	17021	19138	21267	24388	27330	30272	33196	35936	39780	42748
	Statistical discrepancy	2479	9856	8099	5855	8333	9373	14146	27928	27305	40693	38829	43225
	Total Current Receipts	530435	591615	637315	695574	760459	840300	917099	992166	1088373	1216642	1357189	1461865
	Disbursements												
1	Private final consumption expenditure	274745	307050	342013	371866	407295	447931	492753	542541	589270	638772	698827	777285
2	Property income	32900	41531	43004	42996	48640	57227	61228	67183	81635	96573	111290	110668
3	Direct taxes and other current transfers n.e.c. to general government	184165	204135	218360	241316	263295	281105	317734	358906	400766	457813	500032	492977
	A Social security contributions	74647	85838	86634	95655	103781	108206	124456	137284	153799	176732	205867	218901
	B Direct taxes	107614	115701	127773	141798	155060	167951	189557	216383	241570	276720	291053	271316
	C Fees, fines and penalties	1904	2596	3953	3863	4454	4948	3721	5239	5397	4361	3112	2760
4	Other current transfers	23967	25208	30420	32662	34905	44285	42447	40555	44574	49593	52976	58885
5	Net saving	14658	13691	3518	6734	6324	9752	2937	-17019	-27872	-26109	-5936	22050
	Total Current Disbursements and Net Saving	530435	591615	637315	695574	760459	840300	917099	992166	1088373	1216642	1357189	1461865

1.7 External Transactions on Current Account, Summary

Million Swedish kronor

	1980	1981	1982	1983	1984	1985	1986	1987	1988	1989	1990	1991
Payments to the Rest of the World												
1 Imports of goods and services	166547	175299	208234	238142	260699	291186	281223	313638	341354	387735	403863	381669
A Imports of merchandise c.i.f.	143281	148041	176671	201663	220361	246121	232949	257813	279341	315162	322360	300042
B Other	23266	27258	31563	36479	40338	45065	48274	55825	62013	72573	81503	81627
2 Factor income to the rest of the world	11947	20388	26996	30621	35523	40635	38207	38408	42391	58878	85793	97344
A Compensation of employees	30	71	6	730	354	415	914	1002	1152	1381	1468	2044
B Property and entrepreneurial income	11917	20317	26990	29891	35169	40220	37293	37406	41239	57497	84325	95300
By general government a	2981	6717	9168	11542	13295	14857	11983	12283	9308	8446	9552	11413
By corporate and quasi-corporate enterprises	...	...	...	...	...	...	...	...	...	...	...	...
By other	...	...	...	...	...	...	...	...	...	...	...	...
3 Current transfers to the rest of the world	6903	11986	14943	16085	16911	20727	21943	22776	24239	27278	30072	31515
A Indirect taxes to supranational organizations												
B Other current transfers	6903	11986	14943	16085	16911	20727	21943	22776	24239	27278	30072	31515
4 Surplus of the nation on current transactions	-18904	-15466	-22508	-8150	1850	-14650	419	-6909	-12375	-32733	-49219	-28683
Payments to the Rest of the World and Surplus of the Nation on Current Transactions	166493	192207	227665	276698	314983	337898	341792	367913	395609	441158	470509	481845
Receipts From The Rest of the World												
1 Exports of goods and services	156469	174107	204756	253260	289819	306595	311091	332298	359690	394470	406831	404561
A Exports of merchandise f.o.b.	131026	144683	168245	210893	242746	260146	263844	280153	303370	330803	336790	330143
B Other	25443	29424	36511	42367	47073	46449	47247	52145	56320	63667	70041	74418
2 Factor income from rest of the world	7924	11740	13710	14033	15717	19543	18190	21942	21310	31054	47448	58051
A Compensation of employees	283	433	1	218	226	262	152	288	310	358	487	773
B Property and entrepreneurial income	7641	11307	13709	13815	15491	19281	18038	21654	21000	30696	46961	57278
By general government a	1626	3091	3729	3350	3646	4493	5334	4767	2971	4835	6335	12100
By corporate and quasi-corporate enterprises	...	...	...	...	...	...	...	...	...	...	...	...
By other	...	...	...	...	...	...	...	...	...	...	...	...
3 Current transfers from rest of the world	2100	6360	9199	9405	9447	11760	12511	13673	14609	15634	16230	19233
A Subsidies from supranational organisations	...	...	...	...	...	...	...	...	...	...	...	...
B Other current transfers	2100	6360	9199	9405	9447	11760	12511	13673	14609	15634	16230	19233
Receipts from the Rest of the World on Current Transactions	166493	192207	227665	276698	314983	337898	341792	367913	395609	441158	470509	481845

a) Only central government data are included in the general government estimates.

1.8 Capital Transactions of The Nation, Summary

Million Swedish kronor

	1980	1981	1982	1983	1984	1985	1986	1987	1988	1989	1990	1991
Finance of Gross Capital Formation												
Gross saving	90920	87428	86967	111212	138673	148642	166135	181557	203681	230859	231167	217003
1 Consumption of fixed capital	59421	66479	74675	84339	91752	99464	107219	116475	127835	140084	153737	164935
A General government	6733	7654	8660	9747	10637	11410	12294	12973	14077	16222	17775	18701
B Corporate and quasi-corporate enterprises	37890	42178	47775	54433	58826	64484	70013	76714	83974	90364	98396	104249
C Other	14798	16647	18240	20159	22289	23570	24912	26788	29784	33498	37566	41985
2 Net saving	31499	20949	12292	26873	46921	49178	58916	65082	75846	90775	77430	52068
A General government	-2853	-9729	-20139	-10409	-3492	-12398	7863	42523	51762	86087	70797	2540
B Corporate and quasi-corporate enterprises	19694	16987	28913	30548	44089	51824	48116	39578	51956	30797	12569	27478
C Other	14658	13691	3518	6734	6324	9752	2937	-17019	-27872	-26109	-5936	22050
Less: Surplus of the nation on current transactions	-18904	-15466	-22508	-8150	1850	-14650	419	-6909	-12375	-32733	-49219	-28683
Finance of Gross Capital Formation	109824	102894	109475	119362	136823	163292	165716	188466	216056	263592	280386	245686

Sweden

1.8 Capital Transactions of The Nation, Summary
(Continued)

Million Swedish kronor

	1980	1981	1982	1983	1984	1985	1986	1987	1988	1989	1990	1991
					Gross Capital Formation							
Increase in stocks	5923	-4073	-6286	-10263	-7757	-484	-5840	-4503	-3090	179	-1195	-25040
Gross fixed capital formation	103901	106967	115761	129625	144580	163776	171556	192969	219146	263413	281581	270726
1 General government a	21835	23255	23813	25889	26893	27366	27294	27939	31339	39062	41191	43211
2 Corporate and quasi-corporate enterprises	59165	62445	71787	82621	95184	113046	121551	139848	157555	189887	202830	190819
3 Other	22901	21267	20161	21115	22503	23364	22711	25182	30252	34464	37560	36696
Gross Capital Formation	109824	102894	109475	119362	136823	163292	165716	188466	216056	263592	280386	245686

a) The estimates of government's gross fixed capital formation shownin this table are different from those in table 2.7. The difference consistsof those parts of general government that are included in Industries.

1.10 Gross Domestic Product by Kind of Activity, in Current Prices

Million Swedish kronor

	1980	1981	1982	1983	1984	1985	1986	1987	1988	1989	1990	1991
1 Agriculture, hunting, forestry and fishing	17734	19745	21722	24551	27066	28350	29845	30473	31473	34918	34637	30774
2 Mining and quarrying	2387	2287	2413	3019	3843	4340	3762	3516	4004	4948	5244	4666
3 Manufacturing	111464	116307	129624	148524	171339	186825	207034	220629	236217	258791	266071	259135
4 Electricity, gas and water	13674	15227	15271	17786	20948	22637	26767	28258	30050	32083	34342	37953
5 Construction	35230	37581	41197	42933	47424	50767	54594	60835	68392	82387	92774	96517
6 Wholesale and retail trade, restaurants and hotels	55526	58618	64964	74817	85671	93948	100617	109773	120032	128967	130402	136028
7 Transport, storage and communication	32578	35474	37592	40120	42706	46715	51503	57862	64320	70880	78645	81941
8 Finance, insurance, real estate and business services a	74798	87808	100820	114071	127403	138184	161120	177462	198504	219336	248218	287475
9 Community, social and personal services	16123	18825	20853	22829	25104	27548	30936	33838	37633	42629	46858	50492
Total, Industries	359514	391872	434456	488650	551504	599314	666178	722646	790625	874939	937191	984981
Producers of Government Services	117629	129071	140461	155081	167680	178967	194359	203286	215273	238879	277723	295175
Other Producers	6876	7829	8481	9318	9891	10629	11673	12870	14238	16182	18740	20491
Subtotal b	484019	528772	583398	653049	729075	788910	872210	938802	1020136	1130000	1233654	1300647
Less: Imputed bank service charge a	13825	17477	19680	23264	26966	31079	39282	43686	48247	52278	63086	63483
Plus: Import duties	1759	1909	2143	2180	2508	2724	3038	4057	4705	4605	4652	4781
Plus: Value added tax c	54804	63295	69507	79248	90129	103708	112533	124723	137694	149265	177801	193633
Plus: Other adjustments	1498	2414	-1686	-1361	-448	1525	-2916	-4349	-3817	-5279	-4124	-2649
Equals: Gross Domestic Product	528255	578913	633682	709852	794298	865788	945583	1019547	1110471	1226313	1348897	1432929
Memorandum Item: Mineral fuels and power d	12859	13524	14058	17285	20150	22578	30758	28780	30178	32853	35799	39761

a) For the years 1970-1980 of the first series, item 'Less: Imputed bank service charge' is netted out of item 'Finance, insurance, real estate and business services'.
b) Gross domestic product in basic values.
c) Item 'Value added tax' relates to value added tax and other taxes and subsidies on sales and production of commodities.
d) Item 'Mineral fuels and power' refers to ISIC categories 353 (Petroleum refineries), 354 (Manufacture of miscellaneous products of petroleum and coal) and 41 (Electricity, gas and steam). Beginning 1990, categories 353 and 354 are included in manufacturing (ISIC code 3) on an aggregated level.

1.11 Gross Domestic Product by Kind of Activity, in Constant Prices

Million Swedish kronor

	1980	1981	1982	1983	1984	1985	1986	1987	1988	1989	1990	1991
					At constant prices of:1985							
1 Agriculture, hunting, forestry and fishing	24761	24772	26131	28331	28939	28350	28138	26638	26378	30093	30751	28319
2 Mining and quarrying	4774	4041	3307	3206	4000	4340	4320	4346	4351	4311	4604	4495
3 Manufacturing	164850	160459	161152	170341	183224	186825	188842	193550	198168	201658	197286	187081
4 Electricity, gas and water	14911	15942	15182	17040	20620	22637	23822	25163	25201	24328	24781	24972
5 Construction	48277	46593	48448	47247	49616	50767	52913	54961	55347	58484	58608	56591
6 Wholesale and retail trade, restaurants and hotels	87892	86168	86257	88380	91634	93948	98016	103234	106701	109701	107494	105360
7 Transport, storage and communication	44331	45713	46343	44686	45235	46715	48551	52465	56018	58574	64959	64247
8 Finance, insurance, real estate and business services	119880	124254	129895	133500	135071	138184	142283	147628	153122	156806	160460	161762
9 Community, social and personal services	26099	27081	27274	27445	27627	27548	28544	29899	30052	29833	29521	29252
Total, Industries	535775	535023	543989	560176	585966	599314	615429	637884	655338	673788	678464	662079
Producers of Government Services	164434	168103	170412	173856	177530	178967	180931	182468	183729	187544	191165	191054
Other Producers	9977	10540	10952	10994	10503	10629	10932	11395	11901	12134	12929	13188

1.11 Gross Domestic Product by Kind of Activity, in Constant Prices
(Continued)

Million Swedish kronor

	1980	1981	1982	1983	1984	1985	1986	1987	1988	1989	1990	1991
					At constant prices of:1985							
Subtotal	710186	713666	725353	745026	773999	788910	807292	831747	850968	873466	882558	866321
Less: Imputed bank service charge	24067	24542	25622	27655	28551	31079	32526	35068	36514	37875	39045	41001
Plus: Import duties	103211	99763	101251	99933	102190	2724	2845	3333	3505	3627	3696	3665
Plus: Value added tax						103708	109182	113689	116091	118241	115374	115352
Plus: Other adjustments	1670	2372	-934	-2761	-662	1525	-1799	-3498	-3218	-4578	-2631	-1935
Equals: Gross Domestic Product	791000	791259	800048	814543	846976	865788	884994	910203	930832	952881	959952	942402
Memorandum Item: Mineral fuels and power	...	...	...	...	...	22578	24268	25172	25220	24211	24319	24706

1.12 Relations Among National Accounting Aggregates

Million Swedish kronor

	1980	1981	1982	1983	1984	1985	1986	1987	1988	1989	1990	1991
Gross Domestic Product	528255	578913	633682	709852	794298	865788	945583	1019547	1110471	1226313	1348897	1432929
Plus: Net factor income from the rest of the world	-4023	-8648	-13286	-16588	-19806	-21092	-20017	-16466	-21081	-27824	-38345	-39293
Factor income from the rest of the world	7924	11740	13710	14033	15717	19543	18190	21942	21310	31054	47448	58051
Less: Factor income to the rest of the world	11947	20388	26996	30621	35523	40635	38207	38408	42391	58878	85793	97344
Equals: Gross National Product	524232	570265	620396	693264	774492	844696	925566	1003081	1089390	1198489	1310552	1393636
Less: Consumption of fixed capital	59421	66479	74675	84339	91752	99464	107219	116475	127835	140084	153737	164935
Equals: National Income	464811	503786	545721	608925	682740	745232	818347	886606	961555	1058405	1156815	1228701
Plus: Net current transfers from the rest of the world	-4803	-5626	-5744	-6680	-7464	-8967	-9432	-9103	-9630	-11644	-13842	-12282
Current transfers from the rest of the world	2100	6360	9199	9405	9447	11760	12511	13673	14609	15634	16230	19233
Less: Current transfers to the rest of the world	6903	11986	14943	16085	16911	20727	21943	22776	24239	27278	30072	31515
Equals: National Disposable Income	460008	498160	539977	602245	675276	736265	808915	877503	951925	1046761	1142973	1216419
Less: Final consumption	428509	477211	527685	575372	628355	687087	749999	812421	876079	955986	1065543	1164351
Equals: Net Saving	31499	20949	12292	26873	46921	49178	58916	65082	75846	90775	77430	52068
Less: Surplus of the nation on current transactions	-18904	-15466	-22508	-8150	1850	-14650	419	-6909	-12375	-32733	-49219	-28683
Equals: Net Capital Formation	50403	36415	34800	35023	45071	63828	58497	71991	88221	123508	126649	80751

2.1 Government Final Consumption Expenditure by Function, in Current Prices

Million Swedish kronor

	1980	1981	1982	1983	1984	1985	1986	1987	1988	1989	1990	1991
1 General public services ab	20256	22716	23775	26836	29314	21448	23049	24373	25943	28562	33872	...
2 Defence	16031	17901	19089	19446	20738	23036	25489	24853	26313	30141	35113	...
3 Public order and safety b	...	...	...	...	...	11127	11974	12654	13690	16124	18918	...
4 Education a	31179	34183	37670	40856	43222	48889	52093	54138	56724	60911	70610	...
5 Health	38541	42603	46811	51776	56885	57638	60411	65835	71292	78714	88292	...
6 Social security and welfare	25415	27710	31401	35889	39547	40711	45261	48099	52970	59584	70630	...
7 Housing and community amenities	2988	3231	3109	3188	3371	2815	3060	3244	4598	4778	6596	...
8 Recreational, cultural and religious affairs	8159	9085	10017	10867	11917	13175	14475	14761	14616	15556	17410	...
9 Economic services	7470	8382	9309	10202	11287	19138	20214	20455	19720	21615	23887	...
A Fuel and energy	...	...	...	...	...	301	320	328	294	349	600	...
B Agriculture, forestry, fishing and hunting	...	...	...	...	...	1251	1302	1353	1464	1544	1521	...
C Mining, manufacturing and construction, except fuel and energy	...	...	...	...	...	742	801	753	771	681	784	...
D Transportation and communication	...	...	...	...	...	7836	8062	8067	7828	9461	9805	...
E Other economic affairs	...	...	...	...	...	9008	9729	9954	9363	9580	11177	...
10 Other functions	3725	4350	4491	4446	4779	1179	1220	1468	943	1229	1388	...
Total Government Final Consumption Expenditure c	153764	170161	185672	203506	221060	239156	257246	269880	286809	317214	366716	387066

a) General research is included in item 'General public services' for the years 1970-1981, and in item 'Education' for the years 1982-1985.
b) Item 'Public order and safety' is included in item 'General public services'.
c) This table is classified according to the SNA purpose classification for the period 1970-1984 and according to COFOG from 1985 onwards.

Sweden

2.2 Government Final Consumption Expenditure by Function, in Constant Prices

Million Swedish kronor

	1980	1981	1982	1983	1984	1985	1986	1987	1988	1989	1990	1991
					At constant prices of:							
				1980					1985			
1 General public services	20256ab	20974ab	21006ab	21682ab	21818ab	22138ab / 21448a	21314a	21783a	22219a	22800a	23739a	...
2 Defence	16031	15959	15469	14586	14664	14994 / 23036	24023	22682	22834	24366	25948	...
3 Public order and safety b	...	...	...	...	...	11127	10999	11197	11230	11682	11956	...
4 Education a	31179	31817	32194	32299	32733	32505 / 48889	47628	45522	44188	44992	45981	...
5 Health	38541	39822	40332	41085	42399	43983 / 57638	58351	59570	60448	61524	62571	...
6 Social security and welfare	25415	26090	27267	28222	28883	30041 / 40711	42820	44801	46667	47285	47303	...
7 Housing and community amenities	2988	2922	2551	2366	2353	2298 / 2815	2871	2914	3555	3588	4367	...
8 Recreational, cultural and religious affairs	8159	8305	8331	8258	8585	8846 / 13175	13447	13556	12878	12442	13074	...
9 Economic services	7470	7480	7579	7534	7821	7705 / 19138	19709	21758	21578	21488	22379	...
A Fuel and energy	...	...	...	...	...	301	301	285	243	256	421	...
B Agriculture, forestry, fishing and hunting	...	...	...	...	...	1251	1129	1145	1158	1112	1250	...
C Mining, manufacturing and construction, except fuel and energy	...	...	...	...	...	742	750	674	647	533	592	...
D Transportation and communication	...	...	...	...	...	7836	8270	8101	8129	8142	7788	...
E Other economic affairs	...	...	...	...	...	9008	9259	11553	11401	11445	12328	...
10 Other functions	3725	4193	4259	4066	4504	4761 / 1179	1225	1133	859	1058	1068	...
Total Government Final Consumption Expenditure c	153764	157562	158988	160098	163760	167271 / 239156	242387	244916	246456	251225	258386	258988

a) General research is included in item 'General public services' for the years 1970-1981, and in item 'Education' for the years 1982-1985.
b) Item 'Public order and safety' is included in item 'General public services'.
c) This table is classified according to the SNA purpose classification for the period 1970-1984 and according to COFOG from 1985 onwards.

2.3 Total Government Outlays by Function and Type

Million Swedish kronor

	Final Consumption Expenditures			Subsidies	Other Current Transfers & Property Income	Total Current Disbursements	Gross Capital Formation	Other Capital Outlays	Total Outlays
	Total	Compensation of Employees	Other						
				1980					
1 General public services ab	20256	15035	5221	...	...	...	2832	...	...
2 Defence	16031	5522	10509	...	...	...	1910	...	...
3 Public order and safety b	...	...	...	...	...	...	...	...	...
4 Education a	31179	23724	7455	...	...	...	3112	...	...
5 Health	38541	30669	7872	...	...	...	3357	...	...
6 Social security and welfare	25415	21811	3604	...	...	...	1519	...	...
7 Housing and community amenities	2988	1579	1409	...	...	...	3179	...	...
8 Recreation, culture and religion	8159	5173	2986	...	...	...	1224	...	...
9 Economic services	7470	4382	3088	...	...	...	5717	...	...
A Fuel and energy	...	...	...	...	...	...	...	...	...
B Agriculture, forestry, fishing and hunting	...	...	...	...	...	...	...	...	...
C Mining (except fuels), manufacturing and construction	...	...	...	...	...	...	...	...	...
D Transportation and communication	...	...	...	...	...	...	...	...	...
E Other economic affairs	...	...	...	...	...	...	...	...	...
10 Other functions	3725	2290	1435	...	...	...	...	...	...
Total c	153764	110185	43579	22827	123763	300354	22850	3963	327167
				1981					
1 General public services ab	22716	16290	6426	...	...	...	2897	...	...
2 Defence	17901	6178	11723	...	...	...	1576	...	...
3 Public order and safety b	...	...	...	...	...	...	...	...	...
4 Education a	34183	25840	8343	...	...	...	3522	...	...
5 Health	42603	33400	9203	...	...	...	3862	...	...

2.3 Total Government Outlays by Function and Type
(Continued)

Million Swedish kronor

	Final Consumption Expenditures			Subsidies	Other Current Transfers & Property Income	Total Current Disbursements	Gross Capital Formation	Other Capital Outlays	Total Outlays
	Total	Compensation of Employees	Other						
6 Social security and welfare	27710	24053	3657	...	...	...	1425	...	...
7 Housing and community amenities	3231	1672	1559	...	...	...	3245	...	...
8 Recreation, culture and religion	9085	5701	3384	...	...	...	1443	...	...
9 Economic services	8382	4759	3623	...	...	...	5821	...	...
A Fuel and energy	...	...	...	...	...	...	...	...	...
B Agriculture, forestry, fishing and hunting	...	...	...	...	...	...	...	...	...
C Mining (except fuels), manufacturing and construction	...	...	...	...	...	...	...	...	...
D Transportation and communication	...	...	...	...	...	...	...	...	...
E Other economic affairs	...	...	...	...	...	...	...	...	...
10 Other functions	4350	2495	1855	...	...	...	...	...	...
Total c	170161	120388	49773	26829	146091	343081	23791	6396	373268

1982

	Total	Compensation of Employees	Other	Subsidies	Other Current Transfers & Property Income	Total Current Disbursements	Gross Capital Formation	Other Capital Outlays	Total Outlays
1 General public services ab	23775	16898	6877	...	...	...	3045	...	...
2 Defence	19089	6695	12394	...	...	...	1527	...	...
3 Public order and safety b	...	...	...	...	...	...	...	...	...
4 Education a	37670	27918	9752	...	...	...	...	...	...
5 Health	46811	36682	10129	...	...	...	3487	...	...
6 Social security and welfare	31401	27014	4387	...	...	...	4374	...	...
7 Housing and community amenities	3109	1732	1377	...	...	...	1209	...	...
8 Recreation, culture and religion	10017	6125	3892	...	...	...	3108	...	...
9 Economic services	9309	5167	4142	...	...	...	1475	...	...
A Fuel and energy	...	...	...	...	...	...	6142	...	...
B Agriculture, forestry, fishing and hunting	...	...	...	...	...	...	...	...	...
C Mining (except fuels), manufacturing and construction	...	...	...	...	...	...	...	...	...
D Transportation and communication	...	...	...	...	...	...	...	...	...
E Other economic affairs	...	...	...	...	...	...	...	...	...
10 Other functions	4491	2550	1941	...	...	...	...	...	...
Total c	185672	130781	54891	31249	170559	387480	24367	10236	422083

1983

	Total	Compensation of Employees	Other	Subsidies	Other Current Transfers & Property Income	Total Current Disbursements	Gross Capital Formation	Other Capital Outlays	Total Outlays
1 General public services ab	26836	18338	8498	...	...	...	3325	...	...
2 Defence	19446	6617	12829	...	...	...	872	...	...
3 Public order and safety b	...	...	...	...	...	...	...	...	...
4 Education a	40856	29781	11075	...	...	...	3405	...	...
5 Health	51776	39884	11892	...	...	...	4901	...	...
6 Social security and welfare	35889	30415	5474	...	...	...	1146	...	...
7 Housing and community amenities	3188	1819	1369	...	...	...	3093	...	...
8 Recreation, culture and religion	10867	6548	4319	...	...	...	1732	...	...
9 Economic services	10202	5519	4683	...	...	...	7454	...	...
A Fuel and energy	...	...	...	...	...	...	...	...	...
B Agriculture, forestry, fishing and hunting	...	...	...	...	...	...	...	...	...
C Mining (except fuels), manufacturing and construction	...	...	...	...	...	...	...	...	...
D Transportation and communication	...	...	...	...	...	...	...	...	...
E Other economic affairs	...	...	...	...	...	...	...	...	...
10 Other functions	4446	2622	1824	...	...	...	...	...	...
Total c	203506	141543	61963	36496	193354	433356	25928	11110	470394

1984

	Total	Compensation of Employees	Other	Subsidies	Other Current Transfers & Property Income	Total Current Disbursements	Gross Capital Formation	Other Capital Outlays	Total Outlays
1 General public services ab	29314	19858	9456	...	...	...	3675	...	...
2 Defence	20738	6826	13912	...	...	...	-20	...	...
3 Public order and safety b	...	...	...	...	...	...	...	...	...
4 Education a	43222	31682	11540	...	...	...	3427	...	...
5 Health	56885	43913	12972	...	...	...	5435	...	...

Sweden

2.3 Total Government Outlays by Function and Type
(Continued)

Million Swedish kronor

		Final Consumption Expenditures			Subsidies	Other Current Transfers & Property Income	Total Current Disbursements	Gross Capital Formation	Other Capital Outlays	Total Outlays
		Total	Compensation of Employees	Other						
6	Social security and welfare	39547	33439	6108	...	...	...	1064	...	...
7	Housing and community amenities	3371	1922	1449	...	...	...	2882	...	...
8	Recreation, culture and religion	11917	7214	4703	...	...	...	1773	...	...
9	Economic services	11287	5838	5449	...	...	...	7822	...	...
	A Fuel and energy	...	...	...	...	...	...	...	...	...
	B Agriculture, forestry, fishing and hunting	...	...	...	...	...	...	...	...	...
	C Mining (except fuels), manufacturing and construction	...	...	...	...	...	...	...	...	...
	D Transportation and communication	...	...	...	...	...	...	...	...	...
	E Other economic affairs	...	...	...	...	...	...	...	...	...
10	Other functions	4779	2814	1965	...	...	...	...	...	...
	Total c	221060	153506	67554	39510	212974	473544	26058	6627	506229
	1985									
1	General public services ab	21448	12965	8483	...	...	...	3686	...	...
2	Defence	23036	7818	15218	...	...	...	268	...	...
3	Public order and safety b	11127	8280	2847	...	...	...	540	...	...
4	Education a	48889	35580	13309	...	...	...	3034	...	...
5	Health	57638	43543	14095	...	...	...	5094	...	...
6	Social security and welfare	40711	34112	6599	...	...	...	1417	...	...
7	Housing and community amenities	2815	1861	954	...	...	...	818	...	...
8	Recreation, culture and religion	13175	7982	5193	...	...	...	2082	...	...
9	Economic services	19138	10489	8649	...	...	...	9450	...	...
	A Fuel and energy	301	59	242	...	...	...	4444	...	...
	B Agriculture, forestry, fishing and hunting	1251	1038	213	...	...	...	90	...	...
	C Mining (except fuels), manufacturing and construction	742	375	367	...	...	...	14	...	...
	D Transportation and communication	7836	2556	5280	...	...	...	4022	...	...
	E Other economic affairs	9008	6461	2547	...	...	...	880	...	...
10	Other functions	1179	933	246	...	...	...	265	...	...
	Total c	239156	163563	75593	43411	244916	527483	26654	7979	562116
	1986									
1	General public services ab	23049	14093	8956	...	...	...	3257	...	...
2	Defence	25489	8743	16746	...	...	...	897	...	...
3	Public order and safety b	11974	8999	2975	...	...	...	492	...	...
4	Education a	52093	38394	13699	...	...	...	3421	...	...
5	Health	60411	45572	14839	...	...	...	5325	...	...
6	Social security and welfare	45261	38601	6660	...	...	...	1484	...	...
7	Housing and community amenities	3060	2012	1048	...	...	...	989	...	...
8	Recreation, culture and religion	14475	8936	5539	...	...	...	2188	...	...
9	Economic services	20214	11103	9111	...	...	...	8857	...	...
	A Fuel and energy	320	59	261	...	...	...	4059	...	...
	B Agriculture, forestry, fishing and hunting	1302	1123	179	...	...	...	68	...	...
	C Mining (except fuels), manufacturing and construction	801	418	383	...	...	...	10	...	...
	D Transportation and communication	8062	2594	5468	...	...	...	3943	...	...
	E Other economic affairs	9729	6909	2820	...	...	...	777	...	...
10	Other functions	1220	1019	201	...	...	...	262	...	...
	Total c	257246	177472	79774	46250	260137	563633	27172	7035	597840
	1987									
1	General public services ab	24373	14796	9577	...	...	...	4129	...	...
2	Defence	24853	8810	16043	...	...	...	2413	...	...
3	Public order and safety b	12654	9392	3262	...	...	...	594	...	...
4	Education a	54138	39249	14889	...	...	...	3284	...	...
5	Health	65835	49487	16348	...	...	...	4945	...	...

2.3 Total Government Outlays by Function and Type
(Continued)

Million Swedish kronor

	Final Consumption Expenditures			Subsidies	Other Current Transfers & Property Income	Total Current Disbursements	Gross Capital Formation	Other Capital Outlays	Total Outlays
	Total	Compensation of Employees	Other						
6 Social security and welfare	48099	40378	7721	...	...	...	1689	...	...
7 Housing and community amenities	3244	2057	1187	...	...	...	1256	...	...
8 Recreation, culture and religion	14761	8790	5971	...	...	...	2127	...	...
9 Economic services	20455	10896	9559	...	...	...	8550	...	...
A Fuel and energy	328	79	249	...	...	...	3355	...	...
B Agriculture, forestry, fishing and hunting	1353	1144	209	...	...	...	74	...	...
C Mining (except fuels), manufacturing and construction	753	359	394	...	...	...	9	...	...
D Transportation and communication	8067	2471	5596	...	...	...	4260	...	...
E Other economic affairs	9954	6843	3111	...	...	...	852	...	...
10 Other functions	1468	1182	286	...	...	...	230	...	...
Total c	269880	185037	84843	47990	274313	592183	29217	918	622318
1988									
1 General public services ab	25943	15144	10799	...	...	...	4498	...	...
2 Defence	26313	9311	17002	...	...	...	401	...	...
3 Public order and safety b	13690	10260	3430	...	...	...	691	...	...
4 Education a	56724	42075	14649	...	...	...	3915	...	...
5 Health	71292	53719	17573	...	...	...	5503	...	...
6 Social security and welfare	52970	44898	8072	...	...	...	1869	...	...
7 Housing and community amenities	4598	2735	1863	...	...	...	2128	...	...
8 Recreation, culture and religion	14616	8717	5899	...	...	...	2318	...	...
9 Economic services	19720	10270	9450	...	...	...	8851	...	...
A Fuel and energy	294	85	209	...	...	...	3423	...	...
B Agriculture, forestry, fishing and hunting	1464	1196	268	...	...	...	95	...	...
C Mining (except fuels), manufacturing and construction	771	345	426	...	...	...	13	...	...
D Transportation and communication	7828	1779	6049	...	...	...	4779	...	...
E Other economic affairs	9363	6865	2498	...	...	...	541	...	...
10 Other functions	943	740	203	...	...	...	613	...	...
Total c	286809	197869	88940	48919	298202	633930	30787	-1573	663144
1989									
1 General public services ab	28562	16328	12234	...	...	...	5104	...	...
2 Defence	30141	10508	19633	...	...	...	705	...	...
3 Public order and safety b	16124	11950	4174	...	...	...	905	...	...
4 Education a	60911	45579	15332	...	...	...	4817	...	...
5 Health	78714	59283	19431	...	...	...	5142	...	...
6 Social security and welfare	59584	50864	8720	...	...	...	2730	...	...
7 Housing and community amenities	4778	2603	2175	...	...	...	3256	...	...
8 Recreation, culture and religion	15556	9893	5663	...	...	...	2638	...	...
9 Economic services	21615	11152	10463	...	...	...	12619	...	...
A Fuel and energy	349	109	240	...	...	...	3555	...	...
B Agriculture, forestry, fishing and hunting	1544	1218	326	...	...	...	68	...	...
C Mining (except fuels), manufacturing and construction	681	293	388	...	...	...	29	...	...
D Transportation and communication	9461	2769	6692	...	...	...	8306	...	...
E Other economic affairs	9580	6763	2817	...	...	...	661	...	...
10 Other functions	1229	957	272	...	...	...	748	...	...
Total c	317214	219117	98097	55736	328098	701048	38664	-4826	734886
1990									
1 General public services ab	33872	19476	14396	...	...	...	5632	...	...
2 Defence	35113	12124	22989	...	...	...	1066	...	...
3 Public order and safety b	18918	14421	4497	...	...	...	812	...	...
4 Education a	70610	53720	16890	...	...	...	4582	...	...
5 Health	88292	67784	20508	...	...	...	4591	...	...

Sweden

2.3 Total Government Outlays by Function and Type
(Continued)

Million Swedish kronor

		Final Consumption Expenditures			Subsidies	Other Current Transfers & Property Income	Total Current Disbursements	Gross Capital Formation	Other Capital Outlays	Total Outlays
		Total	Compensation of Employees	Other						
6	Social security and welfare	70630	60894	9737	...	...	...	3033	...	...
7	Housing and community amenities	6596	2879	3717	...	...	...	3576	...	...
8	Recreation, culture and religion	17410	10748	6662	...	...	...	2660	...	...
9	Economic services	23887	12330	11557	...	...	...	14110	...	...
	A Fuel and energy	600	140	460	...	...	...	3695	...	...
	B Agriculture, forestry, fishing and hunting	1521	1352	169	...	...	...	81	...	...
	C Mining (except fuels), manufacturing and construction	784	299	485	...	...	...	23	...	...
	D Transportation and communication	9805	3017	6788	...	...	...	9519	...	...
	E Other economic affairs	11177	7522	3655	...	...	...	792	...	...
10	Other functions	1388	1027	361	...	...	...	913	...	...
	Total c	366716	255402	111314	63268	359281	789265	40975	-5775	824465
					1991					
1	General public services ab	...	...	...	...	...	...	...	...	...
2	Defence	...	...	...	...	...	...	...	...	...
3	Public order and safety b	...	...	...	...	...	...	...	...	...
4	Education a	...	...	...	...	...	...	...	...	...
5	Health	...	...	...	...	...	...	...	...	...
6	Social security and welfare	...	...	...	...	...	...	...	...	...
7	Housing and community amenities	...	...	...	...	...	...	...	...	...
8	Recreation, culture and religion	...	...	...	...	...	...	...	...	...
9	Economic services	...	...	...	...	...	...	...	...	...
	A Fuel and energy	...	...	...	...	...	...	...	...	...
	B Agriculture, forestry, fishing and hunting	...	...	...	...	...	...	...	...	...
	C Mining (except fuels), manufacturing and construction	...	...	...	...	...	...	...	...	...
	D Transportation and communication	...	...	...	...	...	...	...	...	...
	E Other economic affairs	...	...	...	...	...	...	...	...	...
10	Other functions	...	...	...	...	...	...	...	...	...
	Total c	387066	272861	114205	72591	405687	865344	43548	-5951	902941

a) General research is included in item 'General public services' for the years 1970-1981, and in item 'Education' for the years 1982-1985.

b) Item 'Public order and safety' is included in item 'General public services'.

c) This table is classified according to the SNA purpose classification for the period 1970-1984 and according to COFOG from 1985 onwards.

2.5 Private Final Consumption Expenditure by Type and Purpose, in Current Prices

Million Swedish kronor

	1980	1981	1982	1983	1984	1985	1986	1987	1988	1989	1990	1991
					Final Consumption Expenditure of Resident Households							
1 Food, beverages and tobacco	64687	71682	80219	88120	96644	103433	111551	117262	124523	134009	145396	154880
A Food	47086	53055	59783	66023	72887	77934	84561	88530	93308	99390	107415	114657
B Non-alcoholic beverages	1228	1326	1484	1544	1628	1868	2148	2503	3061	3627	4004	4284
C Alcoholic beverages	10552	11161	12221	13183	13879	14964	15982	16843	17699	19529	21391	22621
D Tobacco	5821	6140	6731	7370	8250	8667	8860	9386	10455	11463	12586	13318
2 Clothing and footwear	20446	21884	23629	25684	28342	31969	35730	40040	42636	44600	47468	49548
3 Gross rent, fuel and power	66148	75099	85841	94057	102392	113456	120230	129824	137526	149637	170341	215676
A Fuel and power	14523	16763	18717	19553	21116	24980	23681	24729	22726	24398	30023	38472
B Other	51625	58336	67124	74504	81276	88476	96549	105095	114800	125239	140318	177204
4 Furniture, furnishings and household equipment and operation	18424	19357	21002	22785	25142	26757	29311	32702	35808	40045	42613	44888
A Household operation	3226	3498	3815	4195	4494	4849	5270	5654	6153	6702	7301	7847
B Other	15198	15859	17187	18590	20648	21908	24041	27048	29655	33343	35312	37041
5 Medical care and health expenses	5467	6806	7853	8842	9754	10949	12057	13215	14497	15741	17242	19775
6 Transport and communication	40760	46594	53172	57554	62411	70484	80690	93853	106880	111662	119550	127869
A Personal transport equipment	8267	8819	11178	11503	12339	14230	19721	27865	32632	30073	23420	24225

2.5 Private Final Consumption Expenditure by Type and Purpose, in Current Prices
(Continued)

Million Swedish kronor

	1980	1981	1982	1983	1984	1985	1986	1987	1988	1989	1990	1991
B Other	32493	37775	41994	46051	50072	56254	60969	65988	74248	81589	96130	103644
7 Recreational, entertainment, education and cultural services	26515	29168	31638	34096	37432	41058	46076	50622	54716	60332	64241	67846
A Education	464	479	504	564	636	672	682	719	799	868	978	1110
B Other	26051	28689	31134	33532	36796	40386	45394	49903	53917	59464	63263	66736
8 Miscellaneous goods and services	20050	22415	24732	27369	30323	33458	37062	41610	46466	52151	55400	56905
A Personal care	7147	8021	8862	9653	10423	11333	12446	13397	14315	15555	16611	17904
B Expenditures in restaurants, cafes and hotels	9485	10681	11908	13452	15376	17367	18944	21750	24198	27845	29728	29163
C Other	3418	3713	3962	4264	4524	4758	5672	6463	7953	8751	9061	9838
Total Final Consumption Expenditure in the Domestic Market by Households, of which	262497	293005	328086	358507	392440	431564	472707	519128	563052	608177	662251	737387
A Durable goods	25009	26636	30715	32180	35032	38514	46794	58232	66096	67647	63271	65559
B Semi-durable goods	44507	48181	52582	57598	63854	70620	78908	87722	95737	103966	111325	116292
C Non-durable goods	100991	113487	126340	137244	148871	163679	170947	179633	188034	202544	228646	250093
D Services	91990	104701	118449	131485	144683	158751	176058	193541	213185	234020	259009	305443
Plus: Direct purchases abroad by resident households	8594	10069	10519	11048	12629	14378	17504	20928	23738	27933	31412	32000
Less: Direct purchases in the domestic market by non-resident households	4419	5249	6806	8853	9924	11257	12129	13763	15337	17410	18387	17962
Equals: Final Consumption Expenditure of Resident Households	266672	297825	331799	360702	395145	434685	478082	526293	571453	618700	675276	751425

Final Consumption Expenditure of Private Non-profit Institutions Serving Households

Equals: Final Consumption Expenditure of Private Non-profit Organisations Serving Households	8073	9225	10214	11164	12150	13246	14671	16248	17817	20072	23551	25860
Private Final Consumption Expenditure	274745	307050	342013	371866	407295	447931	492753	542541	589270	638772	698827	777285

2.6 Private Final Consumption Expenditure by Type and Purpose, in Constant Prices

Million Swedish kronor

	1980	1981	1982	1983	1984	1985	1986	1987	1988	1989	1990	1991
				At constant prices of: 1980					1985			

Final Consumption Expenditure of Resident Households

	1980	1981	1982	1983	1984	1985	1986	1987	1988	1989	1990	1991
1 Food, beverages and tobacco	64687	63173	64393	63132	63535	63536 / 103433	106236	106407	107304	108542	108846	110815
A Food	47086	46541	47099	46535	47094	47085 / 77934	79902	80450	80651	81547	82351	84196
B Non-alcoholic beverages	1228	1190	1246	1251	1275	1372 / 1868	2063	2205	2493	2598	2578	2512
C Alcoholic beverages	10552	9838	10126	9634	9438	9459 / 14964	15602	15212	15469	15874	15637	15721
D Tobacco	5821	5604	5922	5712	5728	5620 / 8667	8669	8540	8691	8523	8280	8386
2 Clothing and footwear	20446	19539	19506	18628	18975	19881 / 31969	35982	39390	40506	40969	42262	43259
3 Gross rent, fuel and power	66148	66550	66903	67038	68023	70505 / 113456	114303	115446	114457	114243	114818	117678
A Fuel and power	14523	14062	13732	13374	13733	15592 / 24980	24827	25007	23125	22087	21821	23219
B Other	51625	52488	53171	53664	54290	54913 / 88476	89476	90439	91332	92156	92997	94459
4 Furniture, furnishings and household equipment and operation	18424	17717	17940	17516	17940	18005 / 26757	27798	29799	31032	33068	33570	33507
A Household operation	3226	3179	3175	3127	3082	3155 / 4849	5031	5177	5301	5408	5538	5636
B Other	15198	14538	14765	14389	14858	14850 / 21908	22767	24622	25731	27660	28032	27871
5 Medical care and health expenses	5467	5576	5800	5974	6177	6381 / 10949	11301	11929	12640	13177	13501	14031
6 Transport and communication	40760	41444	43382	42295	43548	45705 / 70484	78429	86388	90887	88398	83966	82200
A Personal transport equipment	8267	8263	9711	8751	8634	9355 / 14230	18057	23050	24873	21502	16012	15800

Sweden

2.6 Private Final Consumption Expenditure by Type and Purpose, in Constant Prices
(Continued)

Million Swedish kronor

	1980	1981	1982	1983	1984	1985	1986	1987	1988	1989	1990	1991
					At constant prices of:							
				1980					1985			
B Other	32493	33181	33671	33544	34914	36350 / 56254	60372	63338	66014	66896	67954	66400
7 Recreational, entertainment, education and cultural services	26515	26514	26583	26176	26888	27929 / 41058	43834	46852	48808	51181	50814	51078
A Education	464	460	449	431	437	439 / 672	651	655	669	652	632	658
B Other	26051	26054	26134	25745	26451	27490 / 40386	43183	46197	48139	50529	50182	50420
8 Miscellaneous goods and services	20050	20493	21007	20798	21246	21977 / 33458	34238	35907	36985	38771	36481	35294
A Personal care	7147	7487	7822	7518	7382	7643 / 11333	11840	12207	12365	12746	12803	12912
B Expenditures in restaurants, cafes and hotels	9485	9464	9418	9487	9600	9780 / 17367	17157	18329	18995	20091	18201	16647
C Other	3418	3542	3767	3793	4264	4554 / 4758	5241	5371	5625	5934	5477	5735
Total Final Consumption Expenditure in the Domestic Market by Households, of which	262497	261006	265514	261557	266332	273919 / 431564	452121	472118	482619	488349	484258	487862
A Durable goods	25009	24974	27160	25139	25514	26710 / 38514	44465	51834	55656	55073	50404	50597
B Semi-durable goods	44507	43451	43625	42447	43658	45299 / 70620	76867	82970	86174	88606	89635	90247
C Non-durable goods	100991	98776	99635	98099	99125	101590 / 163679	167517	169093	168854	169979	170641	174634
D Services	91990	93805	95094	95872	98035	100320 / 158751	163272	168221	171935	174691	173578	172384
Plus: Direct purchases abroad by resident households	8594	8947	7690	6776	7425	8091 / 14378	16811	18701	20598	22610	23423	23168
Less: Direct purchases in the domestic market by non-resident households	4419	4682	5592	6680	6930	7324 / 11257	11629	12662	13334	14218	13590	12145
Equals: Final Consumption Expenditure of Resident Households	266672	265271	267612	261653	266827	274686 / 434685	457303	478157	489883	496741	494091	498885

Final Consumption Expenditure of Private Non-profit Institutions Serving Households

	1980	1981	1982	1983	1984	1985	1986	1987	1988	1989	1990	1991
Equals: Final Consumption Expenditure of Private Non-profit Organisations Serving Households	8073	8485	8964	8959	8817	8985 / 13246	13752	14424	14929	15242	16416	16723
Private Final Consumption Expenditure	274745	273756	276576	270612	275644	283671 / 447931	471055	492581	504812	511983	510507	515608

2.7 Gross Capital Formation by Type of Good and Owner, in Current Prices

Million Swedish kronor

	1980				1981				1982			
	TOTAL	Total Private	Public Enterprises	General Government	TOTAL	Total Private	Public Enterprises	General Government	TOTAL	Total Private	Public Enterprises	General Government
Increase in stocks, total	5923	...	...	1015	-4073	...	...	536	-6286	...	...	554
1 Goods producing industries	3391	...	...	...	-1007	...	...	...	-6170	...	...	...
A Materials and supplies	643	...	...	...	-1058	...	...	...	-616	...	...	...
B Work in progress	-30	...	...	...	-1741	...	...	...	-3194	...	...	...
C Livestock, except breeding stocks, dairy cattle, etc.	10	...	...	...	-2	...	...	...	-51	...	...	...
D Finished goods	2768	...	...	...	1794	...	...	...	-2309	...	...	...
2 Wholesale and retail trade	1517	...	...	...	-3602	...	...	...	-670	...	...	...
3 Other, except government stocks	...	...	...	...	...	...	...	...	...	...	...	...
4 Government stocks	1015	...	...	1015	536	...	...	536	554	...	...	554
Gross Fixed Capital Formation, Total ab	103901	86264	(...)	17637	106967	88320	(...)	18647	115761	96696	(...)	19065

2.7 Gross Capital Formation by Type of Good and Owner, in Current Prices
(Continued)

Million Swedish kronor

	1980				1981				1982			
	TOTAL	Total Private	Public Enterprises	General Government	TOTAL	Total Private	Public Enterprises	General Government	TOTAL	Total Private	Public Enterprises	General Government
1 Residential buildings	24490	18971	5519	-	25776	19189	6587	-	26947	19478	7469	-
2 Non-residential buildings a	37927	24137	...	13790	39120	24299	...	14821	41150	26169	...	14981
3 Other construction			...				...				...	
4 Land improvement and plantation and orchard development a	1253	623	...	630	1301	664	...	637	1418	835	...	583
5 Producers' durable goods a	39873	36656	...	3217	40376	37187	...	3189	45878	42377	...	3501
6 Breeding stock, dairy cattle, etc.	358	358	...	...	394	394	...	...	368	368	...	...
Total Gross Capital Formation a	109824	...	...	18652	102894	...	...	19183	109475	...	...	19619

	1983				1984				1985			
	TOTAL	Total Private	Public Enterprises	General Government	TOTAL	Total Private	Public Enterprises	General Government	TOTAL	Total Private	Public Enterprises	General Government
Increase in stocks, total	-10263	...	...	39	-7757	...	...	-835	-484	...	...	-712
1 Goods producing industries	-8542	...	...	...	-6680	...	...	...	809	...	...	...
A Materials and supplies	-2320	...	...	...	-4111	...	...	...	-1147	...	...	...
B Work in progress	-2683	...	...	...	197	...	...	...	1118	...	...	...
C Livestock, except breeding stocks, dairy cattle, etc.	-61	...	...	...	-1	...	...	...	-57	...	...	...
D Finished goods	-3478	...	...	...	-2765	...	...	...	895	...	...	...
2 Wholesale and retail trade	-1760	...	...	...	-242	...	...	...	-581	...	...	...
3 Other, except government stocks	...	...	...	...	...	...	...	...	...	...	...	...
4 Government stocks	39	...	...	39	-835	...	...	-835	-712	...	...	-712
Gross Fixed Capital Formation, Total ab	129625	109020	...	20605	144580	123206	...	21374	163776	122939	19020	21817
1 Residential buildings	28856	21410	7446	-	33070	25208	7862	-	35211	34712	499	-
2 Non-residential buildings a	44317	28243	...	16074	47601	31104	...	16497	50917	23857	10851	16209
3 Other construction			...				...					
4 Land improvement and plantation and orchard development a	1525	985	...	540	1594	1129	...	465	1270	1038	232	-
5 Producers' durable goods a	54515	50524	...	3991	61894	57482	...	4412	75995	62949	7438	5608
6 Breeding stock, dairy cattle, etc.	412	412	...	...	421	421	...	...	383	383	...	...
Total Gross Capital Formation a	119362	...	...	20644	136823	...	...	20539	163292	...	...	21105

	1986				1987				1988			
	TOTAL	Total Private	Public Enterprises	General Government	TOTAL	Total Private	Public Enterprises	General Government	TOTAL	Total Private	Public Enterprises	General Government
Increase in stocks, total	-5841	...	...	-126	-4503	...	...	1278	-3090	...	...	-551
1 Goods producing industries	-5884	...	...	...	-3417	...	...	...	-2053	...	...	...
A Materials and supplies	-1124	...	...	...	-1828	...	...	...	-515	...	...	...
B Work in progress	-1974	...	...	...	-40	...	...	...	216	...	...	...
C Livestock, except breeding stocks, dairy cattle, etc.	-150	...	...	...	-36	...	...	...	12	...	...	...
D Finished goods	-2636	...	...	...	-1513	...	...	...	-1766	...	...	...
2 Wholesale and retail trade	169	...	...	...	-2364	...	...	...	-486	...	...	...
3 Other, except government stocks	...	...	...	...	...	...	...	...	...	...	...	...
4 Government stocks	-126	...	...	-126	1278	...	...	1278	-551	...	...	-551
Gross Fixed Capital Formation, Total ab	171556	129148	20212	22196	192969	147782	21694	23493	219146	170865	21577	26704
1 Residential buildings	35695	35278	417	-	42594	42174	420	-	52749	52341	408	-
2 Non-residential buildings a	55828	28285	11420	16123	60067	32112	11523	16432	65243	34521	12225	18497
3 Other construction												
4 Land improvement and plantation and orchard development a	1383	1130	253	-	1433	1178	255	-	1535	1302	233	-
5 Producers' durable goods a	78156	63961	8122	6073	88194	71637	9496	7061	98611	81693	8711	8207
6 Breeding stock, dairy cattle, etc.	494	494	...	...	681	681	...	...	1008	1008	...	...
Total Gross Capital Formation a	165715	...	...	22070	188466	...	...	24771	216056	...	...	26153

Sweden

2.7 Gross Capital Formation by Type of Good and Owner, in Current Prices

Million Swedish kronor

	1989				1990				1991			
	TOTAL	Total Private	Public Enterprises	General Government	TOTAL	Total Private	Public Enterprises	General Government	TOTAL	Total Private	Public Enterprises	General Government
Increase in stocks, total	179	...	...	-400	-1195	...	...	-216	-25040	...	...	337
1 Goods producing industries	1178	...	...	...	1172	...	...	...	-15570	...	...	...
A Materials and supplies	198	...	...	...	-660	...	...	...	-7667	...	...	...
B Work in progress	-480	...	...	...	-350	...	...	...	-8442	...	...	...
C Livestock, except breeding stocks, dairy cattle, etc.	79	...	...	...	72	...	...	...	25	...	...	...
D Finished goods	1381	...	...	...	2110	...	...	...	514	...	...	...
2 Wholesale and retail trade	-599	...	...	...	-2151	...	...	...	-9807	...	...	...
3 Other, except government stocks	...	...	...	...	...	...	...	...	...	...	...	...
4 Government stocks	-400	...	...	-400	-216	...	...	-216	337	...	...	337
Gross Fixed Capital Formation, Total ab	263413	208016	23791	31606	281581	222936	25503	33142	270726	211029	25986	33711
1 Residential buildings	63948	63362	586	-	75989	75580	409	-	90432	89731	701	-
2 Non-residential buildings a	78419	42430	13549	22440	82883	44170	14778	23935	73516	35369	15175	22972
3 Other construction												
4 Land improvement and plantation and orchard development a	1682	1448	234	-	1644	1418	226	-	1704	1514	190	-
5 Producers' durable goods a	118302	99714	9422	9166	120264	100967	10090	9207	104237	83578	9920	10739
6 Breeding stock, dairy cattle, etc.	1062	1062	...	...	801	801	...	...	837	837	...	...
Total Gross Capital Formation a	263592	...	...	31206	280386	...	...	32926	245686	...	...	34048

a) For 1980-1984, public enterprises is included in column 'Total private'.
b) The estimates of government's gross fixed capital formation shownin this table are different from those in table 2.7. The difference consistsof those parts of general government that are included in Industries.

2.8 Gross Capital Formation by Type of Good and Owner, in Constant Prices

Million Swedish kronor

	1985				1986				1987			
	TOTAL	Total Private	Public Enterprises	General Government	TOTAL	Total Private	Public Enterprises	General Government	TOTAL	Total Private	Public Enterprises	General Government
	At constant prices of:1985											
Increase in stocks, total	-484	...	...	-712	-4760	...	...	-537	-6762	...	...	1239
1 Goods producing industries	809	...	...	...	-4601	...	...	...	-3499	...	...	...
A Materials and supplies	-1147	...	...	...	174	...	...	...	-1730	...	...	...
B Work in progress	1118	...	...	...	-1991	...	...	...	-510	...	...	...
C Livestock, except breeding stocks, dairy cattle, etc.	-57	...	...	...	-155	...	...	...	-27	...	...	...
D Finished goods	895	...	...	...	-2629	...	...	...	-1232	...	...	...
2 Wholesale and retail trade	-581	...	...	...	378	...	...	...	-4502	...	...	...
3 Other, except government stocks	...	...	...	...	...	...	...	...	...	...	...	...
4 Government stocks	-712	...	...	-712	-537	...	...	-537	1239	...	...	1239
Gross Fixed Capital Formation, Total a	163776	122939	19020	21817	164842	123845	19588	21409	177403	135078	20530	21795
1 Residential buildings	35211	34712	499	-	34000	33607	393	-	38039	37672	367	-
2 Non-residential buildings a	50917	23857	10851	16209	53699	27087	11187	15425	54520	28800	10833	14887
3 Other construction												
4 Land improvement and plantation and orchard development a	1270	1038	232	-	1300	1062	238	-	1279	1052	227	-
5 Producers' durable goods a	75995	62949	7438	5608	75347	61593	7770	5984	82942	66931	9103	6908
6 Breeding stock, dairy cattle, etc.	383	383	...	...	496	496	...	...	623	623	...	...
Total Gross Capital Formation a	163292	...	...	21105	160082	...	...	20872	170641	...	...	23034

	1988				1989				1990			
	TOTAL	Total Private	Public Enterprises	General Government	TOTAL	Total Private	Public Enterprises	General Government	TOTAL	Total Private	Public Enterprises	General Government
	At constant prices of:1985											
Increase in stocks, total	-4671	...	...	-1232	-2346	...	...	-970	-1047	...	...	-461
1 Goods producing industries	-2466	...	...	...	226	...	...	...	1328	...	...	...
A Materials and supplies	-897	...	...	...	-490	...	...	...	-217	...	...	...
B Work in progress	304	...	...	...	-376	...	...	...	-207	...	...	...
C Livestock, except breeding stocks, dairy cattle, etc.	11	...	...	...	56	...	...	...	56	...	...	...

2.8 Gross Capital Formation by Type of Good and Owner, in Constant Prices
(Continued)

Million Swedish kronor

	1988				1989				1990			
	TOTAL	Total Private	Public Enterprises	General Government	TOTAL	Total Private	Public Enterprises	General Government	TOTAL	Total Private	Public Enterprises	General Government
	At constant prices of:1985											
D Finished goods	-1884	...	...	...	1036	...	...	...	1696	...	...	...
2 Wholesale and retail trade	-973	...	...	...	-1602	...	...	...	-1914	...	...	...
3 Other, except government stocks	...	...	...	...	...	...	...	...	...	...	...	...
4 Government stocks	-1232	...	...	-1232	-970	...	...	-970	-461	...	...	-461
Gross Fixed Capital Formation, Total a	187655	144752	19615	23288	209783	163529	20589	25665	208701	162297	21133	25271
1 Residential buildings	41681	41369	312	-	43957	43567	390	-	46076	45836	240	-
2 Non-residential buildings a	54602	28404	10769	15429	59790	31567	11096	17127	58183	30144	11282	16757
3 Other construction												
4 Land improvement and plantation and orchard development a	1297	1101	196	-	1354	1167	187	-	1260	1087	173	-
5 Producers' durable goods a	89233	73036	8338	7859	103775	86321	8916	8538	102452	84500	9438	8514
6 Breeding stock, dairy cattle, etc.	842	842	...	...	907	907	...	...	730	730	...	...
Total Gross Capital Formation a	182984	...	...	22056	207437	...	...	24695	207654	...	...	24810

	1991			
	TOTAL	Total Private	Public Enterprises	General Government
	At constant prices of:1985			
Increase in stocks, total	-20965	...	...	288
1 Goods producing industries	-12877	...	...	...
A Materials and supplies	-6856	...	...	...
B Work in progress	-6520	...	...	...
C Livestock, except breeding stocks, dairy cattle, etc.	21	...	...	...
D Finished goods	478	...	...	...
2 Wholesale and retail trade	-8376	...	...	...
3 Other, except government stocks	...	...	...	...
4 Government stocks	288	...	...	288
Gross Fixed Capital Formation, Total a	191344	141508	21802	28034
1 Residential buildings	47081	46659	422	-
2 Non-residential buildings a	52130	23729	11499	16902
3 Other construction				
4 Land improvement and plantation and orchard development a	1250	1111	139	-
5 Producers' durable goods a	90244	69370	9742	11132
6 Breeding stock, dairy cattle, etc.	639	639	...	...
Total Gross Capital Formation a	170379	...	...	28322

a) For 1980-1984, public enterprises is included in column 'Total private'.

2.9 Gross Capital Formation by Kind of Activity of Owner, ISIC Major Divisions, in Current Prices

Million Swedish kronor

	1980			1981			1982			1983		
	Total Gross Capital Formation	Increase in Stocks	Gross Fixed Capital Formation	Total Gross Capital Formation	Increase in Stocks	Gross Fixed Capital Formation	Total Gross Capital Formation	Increase in Stocks	Gross Fixed Capital Formation	Total Gross Capital Formation	Increase in Stocks	Gross Fixed Capital Formation
	All Producers											
1 Agriculture, hunting, fishing and forestry	4248	-156	4404	4923	116	4807	5835	364	5471	6206	66	6140
2 Mining and quarrying	1055	169	886	1004	304	700	675	8	667	56	-418	474
3 Manufacturing	20936	3331	17605	16283	-1351	17634	10655	-6053	16708	11673	-7572	19245
4 Electricity, gas and water	8528	47	8481	10167	-76	10243	11660	-489	12149	13292	-618	13910

Sweden

2.9 Gross Capital Formation by Kind of Activity of Owner, ISIC Major Divisions, in Current Prices
(Continued)

Million Swedish kronor

	1980			1981			1982			1983		
	Total Gross Capital Formation	Increase in Stocks	Gross Fixed Capital Formation	Total Gross Capital Formation	Increase in Stocks	Gross Fixed Capital Formation	Total Gross Capital Formation	Increase in Stocks	Gross Fixed Capital Formation	Total Gross Capital Formation	Increase in Stocks	Gross Fixed Capital Formation
5 Construction	1818	...	1818	1891	...	1891	1884	...	1884	2477	...	2477
6 Wholesale and retail trade, restaurants and hotels	6574	1517	5057	1527	-3602	5129	5260	-670	5930	5604	-1760	7364
7 Transport, storage and communication	10322	...	10322	10045	...	10045	12424	...	12424	11797	...	11797
8 Finance, insurance, real estate and business services	35090	...	35090	34907	...	34907	38050	...	38050	43745	...	43745
9 Community, social and personal services	1757	...	1757	2022	...	2022	2285	...	2285	2861	...	2861
Statistical discrepancy [a]	844	...	844	942	...	942	1128	...	1128	1007	...	1007
Total Industries	91172	4908	86264	83711	-4609	88320	89856	-6840	96696	98718	-10302	109020
Producers of Government Services	18652	1015	17637	19183	536	18647	19619	554	19065	20644	39	20605
Private Non-Profit Institutions Serving Households	...	...	...	...	...	...	...	...	...	...	...	...
Total	109824	5923	103901	102894	-4073	106967	109475	-6286	115761	119362	-10263	129625
Memorandum Item: Mineral Fuels and Power [b]	...	...	6698	...	...	8585	...	...	10913	...	...	12921

	1984			1985			1986			1987		
	Total Gross Capital Formation	Increase in Stocks	Gross Fixed Capital Formation	Total Gross Capital Formation	Increase in Stocks	Gross Fixed Capital Formation	Total Gross Capital Formation	Increase in Stocks	Gross Fixed Capital Formation	Total Gross Capital Formation	Increase in Stocks	Gross Fixed Capital Formation
						All Producers						
1 Agriculture, hunting, fishing and forestry	6255	-314	6569	6262	-498	6760	6185	-232	6417	6937	45	6892
2 Mining and quarrying	284	-249	533	539	-105	644	531	-87	618	378	-274	652
3 Manufacturing	18405	-4836	23241	34181	2839	31342	26483	-6292	32775	35592	-2636	38228
4 Electricity, gas and water	12546	-1281	13827	12539	-1427	13966	12838	727	12111	10220	-552	10772
5 Construction	2771	...	2771	2887	...	2887	3244	...	3244	3765	...	3765
6 Wholesale and retail trade, restaurants and hotels	8450	-242	8692	12829	-581	13410	14865	169	14696	14710	-2364	17074
7 Transport, storage and communication	15765	...	15765	17471	...	17471	20690	...	20690	22952	...	22952
8 Finance, insurance, real estate and business services	48002	...	48002	50503	...	50503	53236	...	53236	62914	...	62914
9 Community, social and personal services	2658	...	2658	3567	...	3567	4120	...	4120	4626	...	4626
Statistical discrepancy [a]	1148	...	1148	1409	...	1409	1453	...	1453	1601	...	1601
Total Industries	116284	-6922	123206	142187	228	141959	143645	-5715	149360	163695	-5781	169476
Producers of Government Services	20539	-835	21374	21105	-712	21817	22070	-126	22196	24771	1278	23493
Private Non-Profit Institutions Serving Households	...	...	...	...	...	...	...	...	...	...	...	...
Total	136823	-7757	144580	163292	-484	163776	165715	-5841	171556	188466	-4503	192969
Memorandum Item: Mineral Fuels and Power [b]	...	...	12319	...	...	12486	...	...	10552	...	...	9576

	1988			1989			1990			1991		
	Total Gross Capital Formation	Increase in Stocks	Gross Fixed Capital Formation	Total Gross Capital Formation	Increase in Stocks	Gross Fixed Capital Formation	Total Gross Capital Formation	Increase in Stocks	Gross Fixed Capital Formation	Total Gross Capital Formation	Increase in Stocks	Gross Fixed Capital Formation
						All Producers						
1 Agriculture, hunting, fishing and forestry	7974	-84	8058	9687	652	9035	8142	16	8126	6170	-742	6912
2 Mining and quarrying	936	-164	1100	1307	109	1198	1505	52	1453	1055	-32	1087
3 Manufacturing	39977	-1883	41860	51020	1409	49611	48810	899	47911	26089	-14073	40162
4 Electricity, gas and water	11926	78	11848	12504	-992	13496	13114	205	12909	12740	-723	13463

2.9 Gross Capital Formation by Kind of Activity of Owner, ISIC Major Divisions, in Current Prices
(Continued)

Million Swedish kronor

	1988			1989			1990			1991		
	Total Gross Capital Formation	Increase in Stocks	Gross Fixed Capital Formation	Total Gross Capital Formation	Increase in Stocks	Gross Fixed Capital Formation	Total Gross Capital Formation	Increase in Stocks	Gross Fixed Capital Formation	Total Gross Capital Formation	Increase in Stocks	Gross Fixed Capital Formation
5 Construction	4990	...	4990	6954	...	6954	7851	...	7851	5339	...	5339
6 Wholesale and retail trade, restaurants and hotels	18798	-486	19284	21924	-599	22523	21638	-2151	23789	10489	-9807	20296
7 Transport, storage and communication	22486	...	22486	27759	...	27759	29511	...	29511	29396		29396
8 Finance, insurance, real estate and business services	75987	...	75987	93118		93118	109521	...	109521	113938	...	113938
9 Community, social and personal services	5241	...	5241	6413	...	6413	5453	...	5453	4362	...	4362
Statistical discrepancy a	1588	...	1588	1700	...	1700	1915	...	1915	2060	...	2060
Total Industries	189903	-2539	192442	232386	579	231807	247460	-979	248439	211638	-25377	237015
Producers of Government Services	26153	-551	26704	31206	-400	31606	32926	-216	33142	34048	337	33711
Private Non-Profit Institutions Serving Households	...	...	...	...	...	...	...	...	...	...	...	...
Total	216056	-3090	219146	263592	179	263413	280386	-1195	281581	245686	-25040	270726
Memorandum Item: Mineral Fuels and Power b	...	...	10654	...	...	11503	...	...	11276	...	...	...

a) Beginning 1980 of the new series, item 'Statistical discrepancy' is reduced to insurance payments for fixed capital formation.
b) Item 'Mineral fuels and power' refers to ISIC categories 353 (Petroleum refineries), 354 (Manufacture of miscellaneous products of petroleum and coal) and 41 (Electricity, gas and steam). Beginning 1990, categories 353 and 354 are included in manufacturing (ISIC code 3) on an aggregated level.

2.10 Gross Capital Formation by Kind of Activity of Owner, ISIC Major Divisions, in Constant Prices

Million Swedish kronor

	1985			1986			1987			1988		
	Total Gross Capital Formation	Increase in Stocks	Gross Fixed Capital Formation	Total Gross Capital Formation	Increase in Stocks	Gross Fixed Capital Formation	Total Gross Capital Formation	Increase in Stocks	Gross Fixed Capital Formation	Total Gross Capital Formation	Increase in Stocks	Gross Fixed Capital Formation
At constant prices of:1985												
All Producers												
1 Agriculture, hunting, fishing and forestry	6262	-498	6760	5805	-228	6033	6218	41	6177	6694	-92	6786
2 Mining and quarrying	539	-105	644	508	-85	593	262	-339	601	779	-181	960
3 Manufacturing	34181	2839	31342	25646	-5922	31568	33354	-2419	35773	35123	-2249	37372
4 Electricity, gas and water	12539	-1427	13966	13511	1634	11877	9462	-782	10244	10660	56	10604
5 Construction	2887	...	2887	3065	...	3065	3364	...	3364	4228	...	4228
6 Wholesale and retail trade, restaurants and hotels	12829	-581	13410	14436	378	14058	11050	-4502	15552	15676	-973	16649
7 Transport, storage and communication	17471	...	17471	19738	...	19738	21235	...	21235	19786	...	19786
8 Finance, insurance, real estate and business services	50503	...	50503	51171	...	51171	57024	...	57024	62168	...	62168
9 Community, social and personal services	3567	...	3567	3946	...	3946	4206	...	4206	4505	...	4505
Statistical discrepancy a	1409	...	1409	1384	...	1384	1432	...	1432	1309	...	1309
Total Industries	142187	228	141959	139210	-4223	143433	147607	-8001	155608	160928	-3439	164367
Producers of Government Services	21105	-712	21817	20872	-537	21409	23034	1239	21795	22056	-1232	23288
Private Non-Profit Institutions Serving Households	...	...	...	...	...	...	...	...	...	...	...	...
Total	163292	-484	163776	160082	-4760	164842	170641	-6762	177403	182984	-4671	187655
Memorandum Item: Mineral Fuels and Power	...	...	12486	...	...	10333	...	...	9127	...	...	9577

	1989			1990			1991		
	Total Gross Capital Formation	Increase in Stocks	Gross Fixed Capital Formation	Total Gross Capital Formation	Increase in Stocks	Gross Fixed Capital Formation	Total Gross Capital Formation	Increase in Stocks	Gross Fixed Capital Formation
At constant prices of:1985									
All Producers									
1 Agriculture, hunting, fishing and forestry	7941	557	7384	6263	69	6194	4407	-707	5114
2 Mining and quarrying	1089	102	987	1186	37	1149	817	-21	838
3 Manufacturing	43200	752	42448	40266	1110	39156	20676	-11460	32136
4 Electricity, gas and water	10027	-1185	11212	10132	112	10020	9368	-689	10057

Sweden

2.10 Gross Capital Formation by Kind of Activity of Owner, ISIC Major Divisions, in Constant Prices
(Continued)

Million Swedish kronor

	1989			1990			1991		
	Total Gross Capital Formation	Increase in Stocks	Gross Fixed Capital Formation	Total Gross Capital Formation	Increase in Stocks	Gross Fixed Capital Formation	Total Gross Capital Formation	Increase in Stocks	Gross Fixed Capital Formation
				At constant prices of:1985					
5 Construction	5589	...	5589	5935	...	5935	4025	...	4025
6 Wholesale and retail trade, restaurants and hotels	16734	-1602	18336	16606	-1914	18520	7211	-8376	15587
7 Transport, storage and communication	23627	...	23627	24284	...	24284	24738	...	24738
8 Finance, insurance, real estate and business services	67854	...	67854	72390	...	72390	65779	...	65779
9 Community, social and personal services	5407	...	5407	4454	...	4454	3576	...	3576
Statistical discrepancy a	1274	...	1274	1328	...	1328	1460	...	1460
Total Industries	182742	-1376	184118	182844	-586	183430	142057	-21253	163310
Producers of Government Services	24695	-970	25665	24810	-461	25271	28322	288	28034
Private Non-Profit Institutions Serving Households	...	...	...	...	...	...	...	...	...
Total	207437	-2346	209783	207654	-1047	208701	170379	-20965	191344
Memorandum Item: Mineral Fuels and Power	...	...	9583	...	...	8802	...	...	...

a) Beginning 1980 of the new series, item 'Statistical discrepancy' is reduced to insurance payments for fixed capital formation.

2.11 Gross Fixed Capital Formation by Kind of Activity of Owner, ISIC Divisions, in Current Prices

Million Swedish kronor

	1980	1981	1982	1983	1984	1985	1986	1987	1988	1989	1990	1991
						All Producers						
1 Agriculture, hunting, forestry and fishing	4404	4807	5471	6140	6569	6760	6417	6892	8058	9035	8126	6912
A Agriculture and hunting	3115	3328	3821	4285	4418	4258	3951	4258	5169	5619	4898	3966
B Forestry and logging	1233	1432	1588	1789	2084	2363	2398	2531	2848	3301	3184	2919
C Fishing	56	47	62	66	67	139	68	103	41	115	44	27
2 Mining and quarrying	886	700	667	474	533	644	618	652	1100	1198	1453	1087
A Coal mining	...	...	...	...	...	...	...	...	...	...	...	...
B Crude petroleum and natural gas production	...	...	...	...	...	...	...	...	...	...	...	...
C Metal ore mining	742	630	566	332	358	389	371	325	576	792	...	...
D Other mining	144	70	101	142	175	255	247	327	524	406	...	...
3 Manufacturing	17605	17634	16708	19245	23241	31342	32775	38228	41860	49611	47911	40162
A Manufacturing of food, beverages and tobacco	1967	1773	1635	1980	2106	2631	2671	3092	3738	4097	...	...
B Textile, wearing apparel and leather industries	456	388	360	318	392	422	538	709	763	886	...	...
C Manufacture of wood, and wood products, including furniture	1419	1154	1021	1380	1750	1690	1850	1875	2812	3363	...	...
D Manufacture of paper and paper products, printing and publishing	3378	4182	3950	4235	5047	7788	6982	8603	9835	11628	...	...
E Manufacture of chemicals and chemical petroleum, coal, rubber and plastic products	2041	1857	2351	3289	3002	3998	4194	4806	4920	5017	...	...
F Manufacture of non-metalic mineral products except products of petroleum and coal	615	506	440	417	493	636	850	837	1180	1769	...	...
G Basic metal industries	2018	1674	1025	930	1334	1795	1641	2013	2468	2967	...	...
H Manufacture of fabricated metal products, machinery and equipment	5661	6056	5875	6630	9032	12172	13919	16192	15990	19744	...	...
I Other manufacturing industries	50	44	51	66	85	210	130	101	154	140	...	...
4 Electricity, gas and water	8481	10243	12149	13910	13827	13966	12111	10772	11848	13496	12909	13463
A Electricity, gas and steam	6544	8313	10338	11956	12102	12209	10281	8957	9933	11175	10710	10942
B Water works and supply	1937	1930	1811	1954	1725	1757	1830	1815	1915	2321	2199	2521
5 Construction	1818	1891	1884	2477	2771	2887	3244	3765	4990	6954	7851	5339
6 Wholesale and retail trade, restaurants and hotels	5057	5129	5930	7364	8692	13410	14696	17074	19284	22523	23789	20296
A Wholesale and retail trade	4554	4715	5299	6060	7141	10886	11831	13731	15564	18262	19937	17507
B Restaurants and hotels	503	414	631	1304	1551	2524	2865	3343	3720	4261	3852	2789
7 Transport, storage and communication	10322	10045	12424	11797	15765	17471	20690	22952	22486	27759	29511	29396
A Transport and storage	6797	5940	7403	6672	10476	9844	12170	13527	13846	18386	18914	19076

1778

2.11 Gross Fixed Capital Formation by Kind of Activity of Owner, ISIC Divisions, in Current Prices
(Continued)

Million Swedish kronor

	1980	1981	1982	1983	1984	1985	1986	1987	1988	1989	1990	1991
B Communication	3525	4105	5021	5125	5289	7627	8520	9425	8640	9373	10597	10320
8 Finance, insurance, real estate and business services	35090	34907	38050	43745	48002	50503	53236	62914	75987	93118	109521	113938
A Financial institutions	680	602	594	555	1015	1219	1996	1741	1712	2122	2217	1525
B Insurance	144	181	200	180	268	585	433	391	409	743	828	1214
C Real estate and business services	34266	34124	37256	43010	46719	48699	50807	60782	73866	90253	106476	111199
Real estate except dwellings a	19174	17522	15799	15261	16156	14291	14315	16756	23367	29222	35219	37872
Dwellings b	10749	12674	16012	18723	22393	27417	29817	36616	41521	50732	58040	62557
9 Community, social and personal services	1757	2022	2285	2861	2658	3567	4120	4626	5241	6413	5453	4362
A Sanitary and similar services	303	353	390	359	438	572	706	850	744	970	...	...
B Social and related community services	366	374	382	406	499	614	732	978	899	1194	...	...
Educational services c	37	40	56	34	41	44	157	167	221	282	...	...
Medical, dental, other health and veterinary services	161	174	210	215	238	262	246	457	491	754	...	...
C Recreational and cultural services	657	793	862	1335	1095	1271	1598	1788	2191	2534	...	...
D Personal and household services	431	502	651	761	626	1110	1084	1010	1407	1715	...	...
Statistical discrepancy d	844	942	1128	1007	1148	1409	1453	1601	1588	1700	1915	2060
Total Industries	86264	88320	96696	109020	123206	141959	149360	169476	192442	231807	248439	237015
Producers of Government Services	17637	18647	19065	20605	21374	21817	22196	23493	26704	31606	33142	33711
Private Non-Profit Institutions Serving Households	...	...	...	...	...	...	...	...	...	...	...	...
Total	103901	106967	115761	129625	144580	163776	171556	192969	219146	263413	281581	270726

a) One-or two-dwelling houses including country lodges.
b) Multi-dwelling buildings and other real estate.
c) Item 'Educational services' includes research and scientific institutes (ISIC category 932).
d) Beginning 1980 of the new series, item 'Statistical discrepancy' is reduced to insurance payments for fixed capital formation.

2.12 Gross Fixed Capital Formation by Kind of Activity of Owner, ISIC Divisions, in Constant Prices

Million Swedish kronor

	1980	1981	1982	1983	1984	1985	1986	1987	1988	1989	1990	1991
					At constant prices of:							
				1980					1985			
					All Producers							
1 Agriculture, hunting, forestry and fishing	4404	4454	4702	4665	4807	4627 / 6760	6033	6177	6786	7384	6194	5114
A Agriculture and hunting	3115	3087	3288	3254	3257	3002 / 4258	3719	3818	4362	4628	3726	2945
B Forestry and logging	1233	1324	1362	1359	1499	1535 / 2363	2248	2261	2389	2656	2432	2147
C Fishing	56	43	52	52	51	90 / 139	66	98	35	100	36	22
2 Mining and quarrying	886	649	558	364	401	425 / 644	593	601	960	987	1149	838
A Coal mining	...	...	...	...	...	... / ...	...	...	...	...	...	...
B Crude petroleum and natural gas production	...	...	...	...	...	... / ...	...	...	...	...	...	...
C Metal ore mining	742	581	473	249	269	254 / 389	355	302	502	655	...	...
D Other mining	144	68	85	115	132	171 / 255	238	299	458	332	...	...

Sweden

2.12 Gross Fixed Capital Formation by Kind of Activity of Owner, ISIC Divisions, in Constant Prices
(Continued)

Million Swedish kronor

	1980	1981	1982	1983	1984	1985	1986	1987	1988	1989	1990	1991
			At constant prices of:									
			1980						1985			
3 Manufacturing	17605	16253	13788	14286	16817	20218 / 31342	31568	35773	37372	42448	39156	32136
A Manufacturing of food, beverages and tobacco	1967	1621	1339	1459	1515	1697 / 2631	2615	2919	3365	3537	...	...
B Textile, wearing apparel and leather industries	456	363	298	232	275	270 / 422	505	635	634	695	...	...
C Manufacture of wood, and wood products, including furniture	1419	1065	850	1043	1286	1118 / 1690	1771	1723	2441	2776	...	...
D Manufacture of paper and paper products, printing and publishing	3378	3840	3244	3131	3635	5038 / 7788	6721	8101	8892	10097	...	...
E Manufacture of chemicals and chemical petroleum, coal, rubber and plastic products	2041	1715	1921	2393	2146	2561 / 3998	4058	4513	4382	4204	...	...
F Manufacture of non-metalic mineral products except products of petroleum and coal	615	473	369	330	372	442 / 636	820	770	1038	1470	...	...
G Basic metal industries	2018	1548	845	683	948	1138 / 1795	1586	1936	2262	2600	...	...
H Manufacture of fabricated metal products, machinery and equipment	5661	5585	4879	4966	6580	7813 / 12172	13368	15084	14227	16955	...	...
I Other manufacturing industries	50	43	43	49	60	141 / 210	124	92	131	114	...	...
4 Electricity, gas and water	8481	9338	10160	10497	9833	9338 / 13966	11877	10244	10604	11212	10020	10057
A Electricity, gas and steam	6544	7588	8648	9009	8610	8166 / 12209	10061	8506	8868	9275	8327	8132
B Water works and supply	1937	1750	1512	1488	1223	1172 / 1757	1816	1738	1736	1937	1693	1925
5 Construction	1818	1762	1618	1979	2090	1706 / 2887	3065	3364	4228	5589	5935	4025
6 Wholesale and retail trade, restaurants and hotels	5057	4719	5021	5601	6297	7719 / 13410	14058	15552	16649	18336	18520	15587
A Wholesale and retail trade	4554	4336	4492	4633	5185	6598 / 10886	11308	12483	13432	14877	15456	13362
B Restaurants and hotels	503	383	529	968	1112	1121 / 2524	2750	3069	3217	3459	3064	2225
7 Transport, storage and communication	10322	9322	10653	9253	11817	11314 / 17471	19738	21235	19786	23627	24284	24738
A Transport and storage	6797	5587	6370	5280	7859	6634 / 9844	11573	12274	11672	14968	14717	14721
B Communication	3525	3735	4283	3973	3958	4680 / 7627	8165	8961	8114	8659	9567	10017
8 Finance, insurance, real estate and business services	35090	31673	32120	33651	34967	39138 / 50503	51171	57024	62168	67854	72390	65779
A Financial institutions	680	552	489	405	711	906 / 1219	1981	1711	1650	1975	1946	1348
B Insurance	144	167	167	139	193	398 / 585	431	345	373	611	675	924
C Real estate and business services	34266	30954	31464	33107	34063	37834 / 48699	48759	54968	60145	65268	69769	63507
Real estate except dwellings a	19174	15930	13442	11942	11629	9708 / 14291	13666	14815	17811	19436	20633	19109
Dwellings b	10749	11378	13586	14702	16688	19285 / 27417	28385	32787	33635	36052	36338	34025
9 Community, social and personal services	1757	1860	1916	2179	1922	2320 / 3567	3946	4206	4505	5407	4454	3576
A Sanitary and similar services	303	326	330	274	316	395 / 572	681	793	655	833	...	...
B Social and related community services	366	345	320	309	366	432 / 614	705	910	814	1054	...	...

2.12 Gross Fixed Capital Formation by Kind of Activity of Owner, ISIC Divisions, in Constant Prices
(Continued)

Million Swedish kronor

	1980	1981	1982	1983	1984	1985	1986	1987	1988	1989	1990	1991
					At constant prices of:							
			1980						1985			
Educational services	37c	37c	49c	26c	26c	30c						
						44	146	144	175	212	...	...
Medical, dental, other health and veterinary services	161	161	172	157	170	180						
						262	246	449	483	724	...	...
C Recreational and cultural services	657	722	719	1019	791	886						
						1271	1554	1638	1894	2218	...	...
D Personal and household services	431	467	547	577	449	607						
						1110	1006	865	1142	1302	...	...
Statistical discrepancy d	844	865	968	808	868	1015						
						1409	1384	1432	1309	1274	1328	1460
Total Industries	86264	80895	81504	83283	89819	97820						
						141959	143433	155608	164367	184118	183430	163310
Producers of Government Services	17637	16972	16180	16012	15693	15166						
						21817	21409	21795	23288	25665	25271	28034
Private Non-Profit Institutions Serving Households	...	...	...	...	...	...						
						...	...	...	...	...	...	...
Total	103901	97867	97684	99295	105512	112986						
						163776	164842	177403	187655	209783	208701	191344

a) One-or two-dwelling houses including country lodges.
b) Multi-dwelling buildings and other real estate.
c) Item 'Educational services' includes research and scientific institutes (ISIC category 932).

d) Beginning 1980 of the new series, item 'Statistical discrepancy' is reduced to insurance payments for fixed capital formation.

2.14 Stocks of Reproducible Fixed Assets, by Type of Good and Owner, in Constant Prices

Million Swedish kronor

	TOTAL		Total Private		Public Enterprises		General Government	
	Gross	Net	Gross	Net	Gross	Net	Gross	Net
			At constant prices of:1985					
			1985					
1 Residential buildings	1206715	603535	...	...	...	...	...	...
2 Non-residential buildings			...	...	...	...		
3 Other construction	1562384	1080381				...	548007	438380
4 Land improvement and plantation and orchard development			...	...	...	...		
5 Producers' durable goods	763009	393798	...	...	...	...	44348	22233
6 Breeding stock, dairy cattle, etc.	...	...	...	...	...	...	...	...
Total a	3532108	2077714	...	...	...	...	592355	460613
			1986					
1 Residential buildings	1228078	614494	...	...	...	...	...	...
2 Non-residential buildings			...	...	...	...		
3 Other construction	1597702	1098404				...	559555	444129
4 Land improvement and plantation and orchard development			...	...	...	...		
5 Producers' durable goods	794127	414488	...	...	...	...	46204	23471
6 Breeding stock, dairy cattle, etc.	...	...	...	...	...	...	...	...
Total a	3619907	2127386	...	...	...	...	605759	467600
			1987					
1 Residential buildings	1248969	625217	...	...	...	...	...	...
2 Non-residential buildings			...	...	...	...		
3 Other construction	1635244	1118273				...	570068	448742
4 Land improvement and plantation and orchard development			...	...	...	...		
5 Producers' durable goods	821779	430829	...	...	...	...	48428	24964
6 Breeding stock, dairy cattle, etc.	...	...	...	...	...	...	...	...
Total a	3705992	2174319	...	...	...	...	618496	473706

Sweden

2.14 Stocks of Reproducible Fixed Assets, by Type of Good and Owner, in Constant Prices
(Continued)

Million Swedish kronor

	TOTAL		Total Private		Public Enterprises		General Government	
	Gross	Net	Gross	Net	Gross	Net	Gross	Net
At constant prices of:1985								
1988								
1 Residential buildings	1279351	641189	...	...	...	...	...	...
2 Non-residential buildings			...	...	...	...		
3 Other construction	1673276	1137915	...	...	...	...	579686	452376
4 Land improvement and plantation and orchard development			...	...	...	...		
5 Producers' durable goods	858824	452657	...	...	...	...	51513	27174
6 Breeding stock, dairy cattle, etc.	...	...	...	...	...	...	...	...
Total a	3811451	2231761	...	...	...	...	631199	479550
1989								
1 Residential buildings	1319269	662028	...	...	...	...	...	...
2 Non-residential buildings			...	...	...	...		
3 Other construction	1710161	1156293	...	...	...	...	589449	456077
4 Land improvement and plantation and orchard development			...	...	...	...		
5 Producers' durable goods	897289	477286	...	...	...	...	55483	30054
6 Breeding stock, dairy cattle, etc.	...	...	...	...	...	...	...	...
Total a	3926719	2295607	...	...	...	...	644932	486131
1990								
1 Residential buildings	1361304	683900	...	...	...	...	...	...
2 Non-residential buildings			...	...	...	...		
3 Other construction	1752818	1179711	...	...	...	...	600294	460785
4 Land improvement and plantation and orchard development			...	...	...	...		
5 Producers' durable goods	952294	511532	...	...	...	...	60025	33224
6 Breeding stock, dairy cattle, etc.	...	...	...	...	...	...	...	...
Total a	4066416	2375143	...	...	...	...	660319	494009

a) At 1980 prices, leased machinery is part of branch 8320 (lessor). At 1985 prices, leased machinery is redistributed to branch of use (lessee).

2.16 Stocks of Reproducible Fixed Assets by Kind of Activity, in Constant Prices

Million Swedish kronor

	1985		1986		1987		1988		1989		1990	
	Gross	Net	Gross	Net	Gross	Net	Gross	Net	Gross	Net	Gross	Net
At constant prices of:1985												
1 Residential buildings	1206715	603535	1228078	614494	1248969	625217	1279351	641189	1319269	662028	1361304	683900
2 Non-residential buildings ab	1562384	1080381	1597702	1098404	1635244	1118273	1673276	1137915	1710161	1156293	1752818	1179711
A Industries	1014377	642001	1038147	654275	1065176	669531	1093590	685539	1120712	700216	1152524	718926
1 Agriculture	62584	52341	63039	52829	63423	53246	63874	53728	64394	54277	65021	54928
2 Mining and quarrying	9764	4635	9534	4368	9358	4174	9253	4065	9194	4020	9071	3924
3 Manufacturing	199200	108842	201631	109130	204788	110197	208529	111894	211767	113142	215159	114593
4 Electricity, gas and water	274616	191223	283181	195472	290678	198583	296848	200315	302902	201894	308840	203323
5 Construction	13508	8189	14003	8425	14896	9044	15899	9759	16869	10427	17931	11172
6 Wholesale and retail trade	79486	54164	82364	55738	85561	57593	88632	59286	91469	60715	94599	62405
7 Transport and communication	157693	93534	161122	95500	165269	98167	169720	101109	174044	103898	178853	107146
8 Finance, etc.	198408	116138	203555	119558	210828	124908	219623	131232	228130	137277	240308	146399
9 Community, social and personal services	19118	12935	19718	13255	20375	13619	21212	14151	21943	14566	22742	15036
B Producers of government services	548007	438380	559555	444129	570068	448742	579686	452376	589449	456077	600294	460785
C Other producers	...	...	...	...	...	...	...	...	...	...	...	...
3 Other construction b	...	...	...	...	...	...	...	...	...	...	...	...
4 Land improvement and development and plantation and orchard development a	...	...	...	...	...	...	...	...	...	...	...	...
5 Producers' durable goods	763009	393798	794127	414488	821779	430829	858824	452657	897289	477286	952294	511532
A Industries	718661	371565	747923	391017	773351	405865	807311	425483	841806	447232	892269	478308
1 Agriculture	62403	31160	63426	31618	63640	31417	63701	31131	64240	31304	65436	31885
2 Mining and quarrying	8757	3772	8503	3609	8120	3366	7667	3091	7522	3134	7477	3269

2.16 Stocks of Reproducible Fixed Assets by Kind of Activity, in Constant Prices
(Continued)

Million Swedish kronor

	1985 Gross	1985 Net	1986 Gross	1986 Net	1987 Gross	1987 Net	1988 Gross	1988 Net	1989 Gross	1989 Net	1990 Gross	1990 Net
					At constant prices of:1985							
3 Manufacturing	292876	150752	302337	156864	310627	161682	321833	169122	334628	177765	351695	189936
4 Electricity, gas and water	71338	40937	73555	41820	74579	41546	75122	40867	75956	40539	77317	40779
5 Construction	27768	13134	27862	13272	27650	13104	27596	13075	28462	13871	30617	15755
6 Wholesale and retail trade	56467	29424	61917	33641	67290	37401	74209	42185	82256	47500	91562	53410
7 Transport and communication	147281	74243	151678	77793	156626	81566	166044	86737	170531	89623	181522	94408
8 Finance, etc.	38398	21157	44095	24539	48991	27073	53991	29776	59508	33068	65710	36965
9 Community, social and personal services	13373	6986	14550	7861	15828	8710	17148	9499	18703	10428	20933	11901
B Producers of government services	44348	22233	46204	23471	48428	24964	51513	27174	55483	30054	60025	33224
C Other producers	...	...	...	...	...	...	...	...	...	...	...	...
6 Breeding stock, dairy cattle, etc.	...	...	...	...	...	...	...	...	...	...	...	...
Total c	3532108	2077714	3619907	2127386	3705992	2174319	3811451	2231761	3926719	2295607	4066416	2375143

a) Item 'Land improvement and plantation and orchard development' is included in item 'Non-residential buildings'.
b) Item 'Other construction' is included in item 'Non-residential buildings'.
c) At 1980 prices, leased machinery is part of branch 8320 (lessor). At 1985 prices, leased machinery is redistributed to branch of use (lessee).

2.17 Exports and Imports of Goods and Services, Detail

Million Swedish kronor

	1980	1981	1982	1983	1984	1985	1986	1987	1988	1989	1990	1991
					Exports of Goods and Services							
1 Exports of merchandise, f.o.b.	131026	144683	168245	210893	242746	260146	263844	280153	303370	330803	336790	330143
2 Transport and communication	13746	16605	17916	20088	21223	22328	19740	21525	24055	27079	28802	30109
A In respect of merchandise imports a	7103	8256	8967	9535	9947	10950	9445	8993	10250	13257	...	...
B Other	6643	8349	8949	10553	11276	11378	10295	12532	13805	13822	...	...
3 Insurance service charges b	...	...	...	...	...	...	...	...	...	...	...	...
4 Other commodities	7278	7570	11789	13426	15926	12864	15378	16857	16928	19178	22852	26347
5 Adjustments of merchandise exports to change-of-ownership basis	-	-	-	-	-	-	-	-	-	-	-	-
6 Direct purchases in the domestic market by non-residential households c	4419	5249	6806	8853	9924	11257	12129	13763	15337	17410	18387	17962
7 Direct purchases in the domestic market by extraterritorial bodies	...	...	...	...	...	...	...	...	...	...	...	...
Total Exports of Goods and Services	156469	174107	204756	253260	289819	306595	311091	332298	359690	394470	406831	404561
					Imports of Goods and Services							
1 Imports of merchandise, c.i.f.	143281	148041	176671	201663	220361	246121	232949	257813	279341	315162	322360	300042
A Imports of merchandise, f.o.b.	139475	144097	171981	196938	215407	241340	227016	251909	270130	...	...	...
B Transport of services on merchandise imports	3310	3433	4081	4023	4189	3900	5096	4977	8201	...	...	...
By residents	968	1097	1262	1183	1282	1631	1664	1415	2180	...	...	...
By non-residents	2342	2336	2819	2840	2907	2269	3432	3562	6021	...	...	...
C Insurance service charges on merchandise imports	496	511	609	702	765	881	837	927	1010	...	...	...
By residents	145	164	189	206	234	368	274	188	283	...	...	...

2.17 Exports and Imports of Goods and Services, Detail
(Continued)

Million Swedish kronor

	1980	1981	1982	1983	1984	1985	1986	1987	1988	1989	1990	1991
By non-residents	351	347	420	496	531	513	563	739	727	...	...	...
2 Adjustments of merchandise imports to change-of-ownership basis	...	...	...	...	...	...	...	...	...	...	...	...
3 Other transport and communication	6310	7237	8122	7588	9901	10391	9452	11175	14061	15631	17682	17828
4 Other insurance service charges [b]	...	...	...	...	...	...	...	...	...	...	...	...
5 Other commodities	7196	8480	11138	15927	15721	17240	17983	19791	19106	23943	26647	25930
6 Direct purchases abroad by government	...	...	...	...	...	...	...	...	...	...	...	...
7 Direct purchases abroad by resident households [c]	9760	11541	12303	12964	14716	17434	20839	24859	28846	32999	37174	37869
Total Imports of Goods and Services	166547	175299	208234	238142	260699	291186	281223	313638	341354	387735	403863	381669
Balance of Goods and Services	-10078	-1192	-3478	15118	29120	15409	29868	18660	18336	6735	2968	22892
Total Imports and Balance of Goods and Services	156469	174107	204756	253260	289819	306595	311091	332298	359690	394470	406831	404561

a) Transport and communication in respect of merchandise imports includes all freight services provided by Swedish transporters abroad.
b) Insurance service charges paid and received are calculated net.
c) Beginning 1975, items 'Direct purchases in the domestic market by non-residential households' and 'Direct purchase abroad by resident households' include gross amounts of Swedish bank-notes used for direct purchases abroad by residents and direct purchases in the domestic market.

3.11 General Government Production Account: Total and Subsectors

Million Swedish kronor

	1980					1981				
	Total General Government	Central Government	State or Provincial Government	Local Government	Social Security Funds	Total General Government	Central Government	State or Provincial Government	Local Government	Social Security Funds
Gross Output										
1 Sales	...	...	...	...	...	...	...	...	...	...
2 Services produced for own use	...	...	...	...	...	...	...	...	...	...
3 Own account fixed capital formation	...	...	...	...	...	...	...	...	...	...
Gross Output	...	...	...	...	...	...	...	...	...	...
Gross Input										
Intermediate Consumption	...	...	...	...	...	...	...	...	...	...
Subtotal: Value Added	...	...	...	...	...	...	...	...	...	...
1 Indirect taxes, net	...	...	...	...	...	...	...	...	...	...
2 Consumption of fixed capital [a] ...	6733	1460	...	5255	18	7654	1643	...	5990	21
3 Compensation of employees [a] ...	112806	...	...	...	...	123159	...	...	...	...
4 Net Operating surplus	2000	141	...	1859	-	2310	135	...	2175	-
Gross Input	...	...	...	...	...	...	...	...	...	...

	1982					1983				
	Total General Government	Central Government	State or Provincial Government	Local Government	Social Security Funds	Total General Government	Central Government	State or Provincial Government	Local Government	Social Security Funds
Gross Output										
1 Sales	...	...	...	...	...	...	...	...	...	...
2 Services produced for own use	...	...	...	...	...	...	...	...	...	...
3 Own account fixed capital formation	...	...	...	...	...	...	...	...	...	...
Gross Output	...	...	...	...	...	...	...	...	...	...
Gross Input										
Intermediate Consumption	...	...	...	...	...	...	...	...	...	...
Subtotal: Value Added	...	...	...	...	...	...	...	...	...	...
1 Indirect taxes, net	...	...	...	...	...	...	...	...	...	...
2 Consumption of fixed capital [a] ...	8660	1860	...	6776	24	9747	2066	...	7651	30
3 Compensation of employees [a] ...	133710	...	...	...	...	144621	...	...	...	...
4 Net Operating surplus	2742	145	...	2597	-	4407	145	...	4262	-
Gross Input	...	...	...	...	...	...	...	...	...	...

	1984					1985				
	Total General Government	Central Government	State or Provincial Government	Local Government	Social Security Funds	Total General Government	Central Government	State or Provincial Government	Local Government	Social Security Funds
Gross Output										
1 Sales	...	...	...	...	...	...	...	...	...	...
2 Services produced for own use	...	...	...	...	...	...	...	...	...	...
3 Own account fixed capital formation	...	...	...	...	...	...	...	...	...	...
Gross Output	...	...	...	...	...	...	...	...	...	...

3.11 General Government Production Account: Total and Subsectors
(Continued)

Million Swedish kronor

	1984					1985				
	Total General Government	Central Government	State or Provincial Government	Local Government	Social Security Funds	Total General Government	Central Government	State or Provincial Government	Local Government	Social Security Funds
Gross Input										
Intermediate Consumption	...	...	...	...	...	...	...	...	...	...
Subtotal: Value Added	...	...	...	...	...	...	...	...	...	...
1 Indirect taxes, net	...	...	...	...	...	...	...	...	...	...
2 Consumption of fixed capital a	10637	2251	...	8358	28	11410	2339	...	9040	31
3 Compensation of employees a	157064	...	...	...	...	167176	...	...	...	...
4 Net Operating surplus	4309	174	...	4135	-	4637	177	...	4460	-
Gross Input	...	...	...	...	...	...	...	...	...	...

	1986					1987				
	Total General Government	Central Government	State or Provincial Government	Local Government	Social Security Funds	Total General Government	Central Government	State or Provincial Government	Local Government	Social Security Funds
Gross Output										
1 Sales	...	...	...	...	...	...	...	...	...	...
2 Services produced for own use	...	...	...	...	...	...	...	...	...	...
3 Own account fixed capital formation	...	...	...	...	...	...	...	...	...	...
Gross Output	...	...	...	...	...	...	...	...	...	...
Gross Input										
Intermediate Consumption	...	...	...	...	...	...	...	...	...	...
Subtotal: Value Added	...	...	...	...	...	...	...	...	...	...
1 Indirect taxes, net	...	...	...	...	...	...	...	...	...	...
2 Consumption of fixed capital a	12294	2654	...	9610	30	12973	2607	...	10336	30
3 Compensation of employees a	181199	...	...	...	...	188891	...	...	...	...
4 Net Operating surplus	5005	103	...	4902	-	5330	181	...	5149	-
Gross Input	...	...	...	...	...	...	...	...	...	...

	1988					1989				
	Total General Government	Central Government	State or Provincial Government	Local Government	Social Security Funds	Total General Government	Central Government	State or Provincial Government	Local Government	Social Security Funds
Gross Output										
1 Sales	...	...	...	...	...	...	...	...	...	...
2 Services produced for own use	...	...	...	...	...	...	...	...	...	...
3 Own account fixed capital formation	...	...	...	...	...	...	...	...	...	...
Gross Output	...	...	...	...	...	...	...	...	...	...
Gross Input										
Intermediate Consumption	...	...	...	...	...	...	...	...	...	...
Subtotal: Value Added	...	...	...	...	...	...	...	...	...	...
1 Indirect taxes, net	...	...	...	...	...	...	...	...	...	...
2 Consumption of fixed capital a	14077	2733	...	11313	31	16222	4056	...	12135	31
3 Compensation of employees a	201363	...	...	...	...	223775	...	...	...	...
4 Net Operating surplus	6070	205	...	5865	-	7559	185	...	7374	-
Gross Input	...	...	...	...	...	...	...	...	...	...

	1990					1991				
	Total General Government	Central Government	State or Provincial Government	Local Government	Social Security Funds	Total General Government	Central Government	State or Provincial Government	Local Government	Social Security Funds
Gross Output										
1 Sales	...	...	...	...	...	...	...	...	...	...
2 Services produced for own use	...	...	...	...	...	...	...	...	...	...
3 Own account fixed capital formation	...	...	...	...	...	...	...	...	...	...
Gross Output	...	...	...	...	...	...	...	...	...	...

Sweden

3.11 General Government Production Account: Total and Subsectors
(Continued)

Million Swedish kronor

	1990					1991				
	Total General Government	Central Government	State or Provincial Government	Local Government	Social Security Funds	Total General Government	Central Government	State or Provincial Government	Local Government	Social Security Funds
					Gross Input					
Intermediate Consumption	...	...	...	...	...	...	...	...	...	...
Subtotal: Value Added	...	...	...	...	...	...	...	...	...	...
1 Indirect taxes, net	...	...	...	...	...	...	...	...	...	...
2 Consumption of fixed capital a ...	17775	4602	...	13142	31	18701	4747	...	13922	32
3 Compensation of employees a ...	258768	...	...	...	...	278011	...	...	...	...
4 Net Operating surplus	7988	182	...	7806	-	6782	230	...	6552	-
Gross Input	...	...	...	...	...	...	...	...	...	...

a) The estimates of 'compensation of employees' and 'consumption of fixed capital' of the government sector shown in this table 1.4 are different from those in table 3.11. The difference consists of those parts of general government that are included in Industries.

3.12 General Government Income and Outlay Account: Total and Subsectors

Million Swedish kronor

	1980					1981				
	Total General Government	Central Government	State or Provincial Government	Local Government	Social Security Funds	Total General Government	Central Government	State or Provincial Government	Local Government	Social Security Funds
					Receipts					
1 Operating surplus	2000	141	...	1859	-	2310	135	...	2175	-
2 Property and entrepreneurial income	27175	8288	...	4869	14018	32836	10473	...	5558	16805
A Withdrawals from public quasi-corporations	2246	2246	...	-	-	2736	2736	...	-	-
B Interest	23860	5927	...	3972	13961	28924	7621	...	4564	16739
C Dividends	196	92	...	47	57	197	95	...	36	66
D Net land rent and royalties	873	23	...	850	-	979	21	...	958	-
3 Taxes, fees and contributions	260694	133586	...	77668	49440	291205	147665	...	86946	56594
A Indirect taxes	71446	69696	...	1750	-	82758	80495	...	2263	-
B Direct taxes	113925	38007	...	75918	-	121835	37152	...	84683	-
C Social security contributions	74647	25207	...	-	49440	85838	29244	...	-	56594
D Fees, fines and penalties	676	676	...	-	-	774	774	...	-	-
4 Other current transfers	7632	3572	...	51520	2944	7001	2367	...	56762	1655
A Casualty insurance claims	-	-	...	-	-	-	-	...	-	-
B Transfers from other government subsectors	...	3620	...	43840	2944	...	3451	...	48677	1655
C Transfers from the rest of the world	-	-	...	-	-	-	-	...	-	-
D Other transfers, except imputed	1483	161	...	1322	-	1760	80	...	1680	-
E Imputed unfunded employee pension and welfare contributions	6149	-209	...	6358	-	5241	-1164	...	6405	-
Total Current Receipts	297501	145587	...	135916	66402	333352	160640	...	151441	75054
					Disbursements					
1 Government final consumption expenditure	153764	47654	...	103753	2357	170161	51716	...	115921	2524
2 Property income	21887	17057	...	4814	16	31144	25512	...	5604	28
A Interest	21591	17057	...	4518	16	30771	25512	...	5231	28
B Net land rent and royalties	296	-	...	296	-	373	-	...	373	-
3 Subsidies	22827	14742	...	3915	4170	26829	17732	...	4800	4297

3.12 General Government Income and Outlay Account: Total and Subsectors
(Continued)

Million Swedish kronor

	1980					1981				
	Total General Government	Central Government	State or Provincial Government	Local Government	Social Security Funds	Total General Government	Central Government	State or Provincial Government	Local Government	Social Security Funds
4 Other current transfers	101876	94216	...	15103	42961	114947	103122	...	15993	49615
A Casualty insurance premiums, net	-124	-124	...	-	-	-177	-177	...	-	-
B Transfers to other government subsectors	...	39526	...	5356	5522	...	42238	...	5508	6037
C Social security benefits	73396	36238	...	-	37158	84729	41470	...	-	43259
D Social assistance grants	16161	10607	...	5273	281	16436	10678	...	5439	319
E Unfunded employee pension and welfare benefits	3440	1650	...	1790	-	3580	1691	...	1889	-
F Transfers to private non-profit institutions serving households	4882	2198	...	2684	-	6068	2911	...	3157	-
G Other transfers n.e.c.	...	...	...	...	...	...	...	...	...	...
H Transfers to the rest of the world	4121	4121	...	-	-	4311	4311	...	-	-
Net saving	-2853	-28082	...	8331	16898	-9729	-37442	...	9123	18590
Total Current Disbursements and Net Saving	297501	145587	...	135916	66402	333352	160640	...	151441	75054

	1982					1983				
	Total General Government	Central Government	State or Provincial Government	Local Government	Social Security Funds	Total General Government	Central Government	State or Provincial Government	Local Government	Social Security Funds
Receipts										
1 Operating surplus	2742	145	...	2597	-	4407	145	...	4262	-
2 Property and entrepreneurial income	38976	13778	...	5783	19415	45714	17698	...	5848	22168
A Withdrawals from public quasi-corporations	4146	4146	...	-	-	6631	6631	...	-	-
B Interest	33504	9489	...	4683	19332	37702	10935	...	4693	22074
C Dividends	246	121	...	42	83	254	123	...	37	94
D Net land rent and royalties	1080	22	...	1058	-	1127	9	...	1118	-
3 Taxes, fees and contributions	313210	158333	...	97393	57484	359687	191842	...	107363	60482
A Indirect taxes	89247	86868	...	2379	-	108262	105801	...	2461	-
B Direct taxes	136230	41216	...	95014	-	154440	49140	...	104902	398
C Social security contributions	86634	29150	...	-	57484	95655	35571	...	-	60084
D Fees, fines and penalties	1099	1099	...	-	-	1330	1330	...	-	-
4 Other current transfers	12413	4675	...	61452	5494	13139	4404	...	67394	8936
A Casualty insurance claims	-	-	...	-	-	-	-	...	-	-
B Transfers from other government subsectors	...	3150	...	50564	5494	...	3239	...	55420	8936
C Transfers from the rest of the world	-		...	-	-	-		...	-	-
D Other transfers, except imputed	2912	146	...	2766	-	3325	224	...	3101	-
E Imputed unfunded employee pension and welfare contributions	9501	1379	...	8122	-	9814	941	...	8873	-
Total Current Receipts	367341	176931	...	167225	82393	422947	214089	...	184867	91586
Disbursements										
1 Government final consumption expenditure	185672	55109	...	127877	2686	203506	57496	...	143187	2823
2 Property income	43953	37653	...	6256	44	51457	44997	...	6424	36
A Interest	43496	37653	...	5799	44	51063	44997	...	6030	36
B Net land rent and royalties	457	-	...	457	-	394	-	...	394	-
3 Subsidies	31249	20983	...	5357	4909	36496	25637	...	5400	5459

Sweden

Million Swedish kronor

	1982					1983				
	Total General Government	Central Government	State or Provincial Government	Local Government	Social Security Funds	Total General Government	Central Government	State or Provincial Government	Local Government	Social Security Funds
4 Other current transfers	126606	111789	...	17943	56082	141897	125384	...	19900	64208
A Casualty insurance premiums, net	-210	-210	...	-	-	-242	-242	...	-	-
B Transfers to other government subsectors	...	47258		5124	6826	...	54677	...	5615	7303
C Social security benefits	92730	43834		-	48896	104640	48148	...	-	56492
D Social assistance grants	19034	11514		7160	360	21025	12726	...	7886	413
E Unfunded employee pension and welfare benefits	3944	1899	...	2045	-	4362	2090	...	2272	-
F Transfers to private non-profit institutions serving households	6343	2729	...	3614	-	7196	3069	...	4127	-
G Other transfers n.e.c.	...	...	...	...	...	...	...	...	...	
H Transfers to the rest of the world	4765	4765	...	-	-	4916	4916	...		
Net saving	-20139	-48603	...	9792	18672	-10409	-39425	...	9956	19060
Total Current Disbursements and Net Saving	367341	176931	...	167225	82393	422947	214089	...	184867	91586

	1984					1985				
	Total General Government	Central Government	State or Provincial Government	Local Government	Social Security Funds	Total General Government	Central Government	State or Provincial Government	Local Government	Social Security Funds
Receipts										
1 Operating surplus	4309	174	...	4135	-	4637	177	...	4460	-
2 Property and entrepreneurial income	50958	19242	...	6476	25240	58345	23116	...	6829	28400
A Withdrawals from public quasi-corporations	7921	7921	...	-	-	9743	9743	...	-	-
B Interest	41377	11079	...	5179	25119	46605	12981	...	5377	28247
C Dividends	382	217	...	44	121	571	361	...	57	153
D Net land rent and royalties	1278	25	...	1253	-	1426	31	...	1395	-
3 Taxes, fees and contributions	400543	218441	...	115534	66568	434728	242348	...	123084	69296
A Indirect taxes	125764	122579	...	2564	621	142565	140108	...	1780	677
B Direct taxes	169294	55699	...	112970	625	181551	59710	...	121304	537
C Social security contributions	103781	38459	...	-	65322	108206	40124	...	-	68082
D Fees, fines and penalties	1704	1704	...	-	-	2406	2406	...	-	-
4 Other current transfers	14242	4027	...	74211	10449	17375	6909	...	79586	19775
A Casualty insurance claims	-	-	...	-	-	-	-	...	-	-
B Transfers from other government subsectors	...	3470	...	60526	10449	...	3781	...	65339	19775
C Transfers from the rest of the world	-	-	...	-	-	-	-	...	-	-
D Other transfers, except imputed	4038	159	...	3879	-	4133	8	...	4125	-
E Imputed unfunded employee pension and welfare contributions	10204	398	...	9806	-	13242	3120	...	10122	-
Total Current Receipts	470052	241884	...	200356	102257	515085	272550	...	213959	117471
Disbursements										
1 Government final consumption expenditure	221060	61210	...	156944	2906	239156	64977	...	171006	3173
2 Property income	60991	54034	...	6849	108	73159	65656	...	7326	177
A Interest	60464	54034	...	6322	108	72579	65656	...	6746	177
B Net land rent and royalties	527	-	...	527	-	580	-	...	580	-
3 Subsidies	39510	28115	...	5575	5820	43411	30779	...	6340	6292

3.12 General Government Income and Outlay Account: Total and Subsectors
(Continued)

Million Swedish kronor

	1984					1985				
	Total General Government	Central Government	State or Provincial Government	Local Government	Social Security Funds	Total General Government	Central Government	State or Provincial Government	Local Government	Social Security Funds
4 Other current transfers	151983	133740	...	21794	70894	171757	150107	...	24343	86202
A Casualty insurance premiums, net	-327	-327	...	-	-	-328	-328	...	-	-
B Transfers to other government subsectors	...	60568	...	6198	7679	...	69193	...	6605	13097
C Social security benefits	112335	49579	...	-	62756	125050	52515	...	-	72535
D Social assistance grants	22395	13309	...	8627	459	27734	16770	...	10394	570
E Unfunded employee pension and welfare benefits	4706	2265	...	2441	-	4973	2297	...	2676	-
F Transfers to private non-profit institutions serving households	7773	3245	...	4528	-	8509	3841	...	4668	-
G Other transfers n.e.c.	...	...	...	...	...	...	...	...	...	...
H Transfers to the rest of the world	5101	5101	...	-	-	5819	5819	...	-	-
Net saving	-3492	-35215	...	9194	22529	-12398	-38969	...	4944	21627
Total Current Disbursements and Net Saving	470052	241884	...	200356	102257	515085	272550	...	213959	117471

	1986					1987				
	Total General Government	Central Government	State or Provincial Government	Local Government	Social Security Funds	Total General Government	Central Government	State or Provincial Government	Local Government	Social Security Funds
Receipts										
1 Operating surplus	5005	103		4902	-	5330	181	...	5149	-
2 Property and entrepreneurial income	62299	25487	...	6140	30672	60431	22285	...	5980	32166
A Withdrawals from public quasi-corporations	11050	11050	...	-	-	9437	9437	...	-	-
B Interest	48927	14006	...	4528	30393	48203	12292	...	4131	31780
C Dividends	759	396	...	84	279	1023	532	...	105	386
D Net land rent and royalties	1563	35	...	1528	-	1768	24	...	1744	-
3 Taxes, fees and contributions	492062	273544	...	138063	80455	560991	317511	...	153360	90120
A Indirect taxes	158958	156319	...	1832	807	176860	175530	...	429	901
B Direct taxes	205979	67845	...	136231	1903	243686	87298	...	152931	3457
C Social security contributions	124456	46711	...	-	77745	137284	51522	...	-	85762
D Fees, fines and penalties	2669	2669	...	-	-	3161	3161	...	-	-
4 Other current transfers	12130	5416	...	76892	18343	7954	7797	...	76928	21417
A Casualty insurance claims	-	-	...	-	-	...	...	...	-	-
B Transfers from other government subsectors	...	3996	...	66182	18343	...	6510	...	70261	21417
C Transfers from the rest of the world	-	-				-	-			
D Other transfers, except imputed	2159	8	...	2151	-	4402	-	...	4402	-
E Imputed unfunded employee pension and welfare contributions	9971	1412	...	8559	-	3552	1287	...	2265	-
Total Current Receipts	571496	304550	...	225997	129470	634706	347774	...	241417	143703
Disbursements										
1 Government final consumption expenditure	257246	70598	...	183322	3326	269880	72063	...	194159	3658
2 Property income	70803	62748	...	7960	95	66747	58384	...	8311	52
A Interest	69899	62748	...	7056	95	66077	58384	...	7641	52
B Net land rent and royalties	904	-	...	904	-	670	-	...	670	-
3 Subsidies	46250	32608	...	6663	6979	47990	32894	...	7139	7957

Sweden

3.12 General Government Income and Outlay Account: Total and Subsectors
(Continued)

Million Swedish kronor

	1986					1987				
	Total General Government	Central Government	State or Provincial Government	Local Government	Social Security Funds	Total General Government	Central Government	State or Provincial Government	Local Government	Social Security Funds
4 Other current transfers	189334	156742	...	25820	95293	207566	171067	...	28960	105727
A Casualty insurance premiums, net	-398	-398		-	-	-380	-380	...	-	-
B Transfers to other government subsectors	...	69397	...	6897	12227	...	75995	...	9684	12509
C Social security benefits	139547	56647		-	82900	153639	60540	...	-	93099
D Social assistance grants	28209	17320		10723	166	31513	20766	...	10628	119
E Unfunded employee pension and welfare benefits	5933	2801		3132	-	5996	2601	...	3395	-
F Transfers to private non-profit institutions serving households	9937	4869	...	5068	-	10366	5113	...	5253	-
G Other transfers n.e.c.	...	...	...	...	...	...	...	...	...	
H Transfers to the rest of the world	6106	6106		-	-	6432	6432	...	-	-
Net saving	7863	-18146	...	2232	23777	42523	13366	...	2848	26309
Total Current Disbursements and Net Saving	571496	304550	...	225997	129470	634706	347774	...	241417	143703

	1988					1989				
	Total General Government	Central Government	State or Provincial Government	Local Government	Social Security Funds	Total General Government	Central Government	State or Provincial Government	Local Government	Social Security Funds
Receipts										
1 Operating surplus	6070	205	...	5865	-	7559	185	...	7374	-
2 Property and entrepreneurial income	61266	20467	...	6216	34583	73821	29766	...	6654	37401
A Withdrawals from public quasi-corporations	6556	6556	...	-	-	8293	8293	...	-	-
B Interest	51466	13297	...	4129	34040	61813	20702	...	4443	36668
C Dividends	1250	590	...	117	543	1655	743	...	179	733
D Net land rent and royalties	1994	24	...	1970	-	2060	28	...	2032	-
3 Taxes, fees and contributions	610674	343272	...	165093	102309	696985	391185	...	181142	124658
A Indirect taxes	182766	181154	...	679	933	205536	203807	...	640	1089
B Direct taxes	270319	101496	...	164414	4409	310961	125125	...	180502	5334
C Social security contributions	153799	56832	...	-	96967	176732	58497	...	-	118235
D Fees, fines and penalties	3790	3790	...	-	-	3756	3756	...	-	-
4 Other current transfers	7682	8420	...	76412	25072	8770	7550	...	84066	20375
A Casualty insurance claims	-	-	...	-	-	-	-	...	-	-
B Transfers from other government subsectors	...	7012	...	70138	25072	...	5420	...	77288	20375
C Transfers from the rest of the world	-	-	...	-	-	-	-	...	-	-
D Other transfers, except imputed	4724	-	...	4724		4140	-	...	4278	
E Imputed unfunded employee pension and welfare contributions	2958	1408	...	1550	-	4630	2130	...	2500	-
Total Current Receipts	685692	372364	...	253586	161964	787135	428686	...	279236	182434
Disbursements										
1 Government final consumption expenditure	286809	75941	...	206947	3921	317214	85735	...	227324	4155
2 Property income	63175	55818	...	7284	73	67377	58843	...	8401	133
A Interest	62110	55818	...	6219	73	66173	58843	...	7197	133
B Net land rent and royalties	1065	-	...	1065	-	1204	-	...	1204	-
3 Subsidies	48919	33761	...	7110	8048	55736	37404	...	8266	10066

3.12 General Government Income and Outlay Account: Total and Subsectors
(Continued)

Million Swedish kronor

	1988					1989				
	Total General Government	Central Government	State or Provincial Government	Local Government	Social Security Funds	Total General Government	Central Government	State or Provincial Government	Local Government	Social Security Funds
4 Other current transfers	235027	183163	...	32180	121906	260721	194467	...	34084	135391
A Casualty insurance premiums, net	-364	-364	...	-	-	-390	-390	...	-	-
B Transfers to other government subsectors	...	78865	...	10389	12968	...	79938	...	8843	14302
C Social security benefits	176140	67202	...	-	108938	194247	73158	...	-	121089
D Social assistance grants	33838	21947	...	11891	-	38286	24324	...	13962	-
E Unfunded employee pension and welfare benefits	6251	2758	...	3493	-	6474	2972	...	3502	-
F Transfers to private non-profit institutions serving households	12143	5736	...	6407	-	13480	5841	...	7777	-
G Other transfers n.e.c.	...	...	...	...	...	...	...	...	...	...
H Transfers to the rest of the world	7019	7019	...	-	-	8624	8624	...	-	-
Net saving	51762	23681	...	65	28016	86087	52237	...	1161	32689
Total Current Disbursements and Net Saving	685692	372364	...	253586	161964	787135	428686	...	279236	182434

	1990					1991				
	Total General Government	Central Government	State or Provincial Government	Local Government	Social Security Funds	Total General Government	Central Government	State or Provincial Government	Local Government	Social Security Funds
					Receipts					
1 Operating surplus	7988	182	...	7806	-	6782	230	...	6552	-
2 Property and entrepreneurial income	79929	30162	...	7702	42065	86987	31132	...	8545	47310
A Withdrawals from public quasi-corporations	9042	9042	...	-	-	9072	9072	...	-	-
B Interest	66141	20086	...	5007	41048	72442	21614	...	5075	45753
C Dividends	2197	1003	...	177	1017	2388	417	...	414	1557
D Net land rent and royalties	2549	31	...	2518	-	3085	29	...	3056	-
3 Taxes, fees and contributions	762770	401704	...	204890	156176	765178	367861	...	232359	164958
A Indirect taxes	233362	231256	...	868	1238	257254	256330	...	796	128
B Direct taxes	318612	110716	...	204022	3874	284449	49546	...	231563	3340
C Social security contributions	205867	54803	...	-	151064	218901	57411	...	-	161490
D Fees, fines and penalties	4929	4929	...	-	-	4574	4574	...	-	-
4 Other current transfers	9375	15054	...	91455	20794	8937	11381	...	91389	18248
A Casualty insurance claims	-	-	...	-	-	-	-	...	-	-
B Transfers from other government subsectors	...	12451	...	84683	20794	...	9440	...	84393	18248
C Transfers from the rest of the world	-	-	...	-	-	-	-	...	-	-
D Other transfers, except imputed	3353	-	...	3353	-	3257	-	...	3257	-
E Imputed unfunded employee pension and welfare contributions	6022	2603	...	3419	-	5680	1941	...	3739	-
Total Current Receipts	860062	447102	...	311853	219035	867884	410604	...	338845	230516
					Disbursements					
1 Government final consumption expenditure	366716	100193	...	261579	4945	387066	106856	...	274863	5347
2 Property income	69293	60588	...	8465	240	75904	64299	...	11116	489
A Interest	67972	60588	...	7144	240	74422	64299	...	9634	489
B Net land rent and royalties	1321	-	...	1321	-	1482	-	...	1482	-
3 Subsidies	63268	42808	...	9166	11294	72591	49836	...	9985	12770

Sweden

Million Swedish kronor

	1990					1991				
	Total General Government	Central Government	State or Provincial Government	Local Government	Social Security Funds	Total General Government	Central Government	State or Provincial Government	Local Government	Social Security Funds
4 Other current transfers	289988	213075	...	38852	155989	329783	229198	...	45024	167642
A Casualty insurance premiums, net	-358	-358	...	-	-	-263	-263	...	-	-
B Transfers to other government subsectors	...	86349	...	10063	21516	...	81723	...	12676	17682
C Social security benefits	214478	80005	...	-	134473	240972	91412	...	-	149560
D Social assistance grants	43553	27025	...	16528	-	55698	35327	...	20371	-
E Unfunded employee pension and welfare benefits	7506	3316	...	4190	-	8325	4209	...	4116	-
F Transfers to private non-profit institutions serving households	15100	7029	...	8071	-	14925	7064	...	7861	-
G Other transfers n.e.c.	...	...	...	...		...	...	...	...	
H Transfers to the rest of the world	9709	9709	...	-		10126	9726	...	-	400
Net saving	70797	30438	...	-6209	46567	2540	-39585	...	-2143	44268
Total Current Disbursements and Net Saving	860062	447102	...	311853	219035	867884	410604	...	338845	230516

3.13 General Government Capital Accumulation Account: Total and Subsectors

Million Swedish kronor

	1980					1981				
	Total General Government	Central Government	State or Provincial Government	Local Government	Social Security Funds	Total General Government	Central Government	State or Provincial Government	Local Government	Social Security Funds
Finance of Gross Accumulation										
1 Gross saving	3880	-26622	...	13586	16916	-2075	-35799	...	15113	18611
A Consumption of fixed capital	6733	1460	...	5255	18	7654	1643	...	5990	21
B Net saving	-2853	-28082	...	8331	16898	-9729	-37442	...	9123	18590
2 Capital transfers	1633	580	...	2909	-	1705	631	...	3332	-
A From other government subsectors	...	-	...	1856	-	...	-	...	2258	-
B From other resident sectors	1633	580	...	1053	-	1705	631	...	1074	-
C From rest of the world	...	...	...	...	...	...	...	...	...	...
Finance of Gross Accumulation	5513	-26042	...	16495	16916	-370	-35168	...	18445	18611
Gross Accumulation										
1 Gross capital formation	22850	5814	...	16996	40	23791	5081	...	18656	54
A Increase in stocks	1015	1015	...	-	-	536	536	...	-	-
B Gross fixed capital formation	21835	4799	...	16996	40	23255	4545	...	18656	54
2 Purchases of land, net	-526	151	...	-677	-	-78	118	...	-196	-
3 Purchases of intangible assets, net	...	...	...	...	...	...	...	...	...	...
4 Capital transfers	4489	6239	...	106		6474	8571	...	161	
A To other government subsectors	...	1822	...	34	-	...	2177	...	81	-
B To other resident sectors	4489	4417	...	72	-	6474	6394	...	80	-
C To rest of the world	...	...	...	...	...	...	...	...	...	...
Net lending a	-21300	-38246	...	70	16876	-30557	-48938	...	-176	18557
Gross Accumulation	5513	-26042	...	16495	16916	-370	-35168	...	18445	18611

	1982					1983				
	Total General Government	Central Government	State or Provincial Government	Local Government	Social Security Funds	Total General Government	Central Government	State or Provincial Government	Local Government	Social Security Funds
Finance of Gross Accumulation										
1 Gross saving	-11479	-46743	...	16568	18696	-662	-37359	...	17607	19090
A Consumption of fixed capital	8660	1860	...	6776	24	9747	2066	...	7651	30
B Net saving	-20139	-48603	...	9792	18672	-10409	-39425	...	9956	19060
2 Capital transfers	1842	710	...	3263	-	1966	835	...	3334	-
A From other government subsectors	...	-	...	2131	-	...	-	...	2203	-
B From other resident sectors	1842	710	...	1132	-	1966	835	...	1131	-
C From rest of the world	...	...	...	...	...	...	...	...	...	...
Finance of Gross Accumulation	-9637	-46033	...	19831	18696	1304	-36524	...	20941	19090
Gross Accumulation										
1 Gross capital formation	24367	5455	...	18832	80	25928	5685	...	20198	45

3.13 General Government Capital Accumulation Account: Total and Subsectors
(Continued)

Million Swedish kronor

	1982					1983				
	Total General Government	Central Government	State or Provincial Government	Local Government	Social Security Funds	Total General Government	Central Government	State or Provincial Government	Local Government	Social Security Funds
A Increase in stocks	554	554	...	-	-	39	39	...	-	-
B Gross fixed capital formation	23813	4901	...	18832	80	25889	5646	...	20198	45
2 Purchases of land, net	-6	116	...	-122	-	81	115	...	-34	-
3 Purchases of intangible assets, net	...	...	...	...	...	...	...	...	...	...
4 Capital transfers	10242	12189	...	184	-	11029	13030	...	202	-
A To other government subsectors	...	2027	...	104	-	...	2090	...	113	-
B To other resident sectors	10242	10162	...	80	-	11029	10940	...	89	-
C To rest of the world	...	...	...	...	...	...	...	...	...	...
Net lending a	-44240	-63793	...	937	18616	-35734	-55354	...	575	19045
Gross Accumulation	-9637	-46033	...	19831	18696	1304	-36524	...	20941	19090

	1984					1985				
	Total General Government	Central Government	State or Provincial Government	Local Government	Social Security Funds	Total General Government	Central Government	State or Provincial Government	Local Government	Social Security Funds
Finance of Gross Accumulation										
1 Gross saving	7145	-32964	...	17552	22557	-988	-36630	...	13984	21658
A Consumption of fixed capital	10637	2251	...	8358	28	11410	2339	...	9040	31
B Net saving	-3492	-35215	...	9194	22529	-12398	-38969	...	4944	21627
2 Capital transfers	2127	1059	...	3707	-	2291	1183	...	3351	-
A From other government subsectors	...	-	...	2639	-	...	-	...	2243	-
B From other resident sectors	2127	1059	...	1068	-	2291	1183	...	1108	-
C From rest of the world	...	...	...	...	...	...	...	...	...	...
Finance of Gross Accumulation	9272	-31905	...	21259	22557	1303	-35447	...	17335	21658
Gross Accumulation										
1 Gross capital formation	26058	5360	...	20652	46	26654	5227	...	21375	52
A Increase in stocks	-835	-835	...	-	-	-712	-712	...	-	-
B Gross fixed capital formation	26893	6195	...	20652	46	27366	5939	...	21375	52
2 Purchases of land, net	238	109	...	129	-	-84	-6	...	-78	-
3 Purchases of intangible assets, net	...	...	...	...	...	...	...	...	...	...
4 Capital transfers	6389	8867	...	161	-	8063	10208	...	98	-
A To other government subsectors	...	2574	...	65	-	...	2243	...	-	-
B To other resident sectors	6389	6293	...	96	-	8063	7965	...	98	-
C To rest of the world	...	...	...	...	...	...	...	...	...	...
Net lending a	-23413	-46241	...	317	22511	-33330	-50876	...	-4060	21606
Gross Accumulation	9272	-31905	...	21259	22557	1303	-35447	...	17335	21658

	1986					1987				
	Total General Government	Central Government	State or Provincial Government	Local Government	Social Security Funds	Total General Government	Central Government	State or Provincial Government	Local Government	Social Security Funds
Finance of Gross Accumulation										
1 Gross saving	20157	-15492	...	11842	23807	55496	15973	...	13184	26339
A Consumption of fixed capital	12294	2654	...	9610	30	12973	2607	...	10336	30
B Net saving	7863	-18146	...	2232	23777	42523	13366	...	2848	26309
2 Capital transfers	2163	1252	...	3003	-	18514	17500	...	2774	-
A From other government subsectors	...	-	...	2092	-	...	-	...	1760	-
B From other resident sectors	2163	1252	...	911	-	18514	17500	...	1014	-
C From rest of the world	...	...	...	...	...	...	...	...	...	...
Finance of Gross Accumulation	22320	-14240	...	14845	23807	74010	33473	...	15958	26339
Gross Accumulation										
1 Gross capital formation	27172	5278	...	21841	53	29217	7948	...	21208	61
A Increase in stocks	-122	-122	...	-	-	1278	1278	...	-	-
B Gross fixed capital formation	27294	5400	...	21841	53	27939	6670	...	21208	61

Sweden

3.13 General Government Capital Accumulation Account: Total and Subsectors
(Continued)

Million Swedish kronor

	1986					1987				
	Total General Government	Central Government	State or Provincial Government	Local Government	Social Security Funds	Total General Government	Central Government	State or Provincial Government	Local Government	Social Security Funds
2 Purchases of land, net	-2083	-806	...	-1277	-	-2944	-1165	...	-1779	-
3 Purchases of intangible assets, net	...	...	...	...	...	...	...	...	...	...
4 Capital transfers	9118	11023	...	187	-	3862	5455	...	167	-
A To other government subsectors	...	2005	...	87	-	...	1694	...	66	-
B To other resident sectors	9118	9018	...	100	-	3862	3761	...	101	-
C To rest of the world	...	...	...	...	...	...	...	...	...	...
Net lending a	-11887	-29735	...	-5906	23754	43875	21235	...	-3638	26278
Gross Accumulation	22320	-14240	...	14845	23807	74010	33473	...	15958	26339

	1988					1989				
	Total General Government	Central Government	State or Provincial Government	Local Government	Social Security Funds	Total General Government	Central Government	State or Provincial Government	Local Government	Social Security Funds
Finance of Gross Accumulation										
1 Gross saving	65839	26414	...	11378	28047	102309	56293	...	13296	32720
A Consumption of fixed capital	14077	2733	...	11313	31	16222	4056	...	12135	31
B Net saving	51762	23681	...	65	28016	86087	52237	...	1161	32689
2 Capital transfers	2410	1286	...	2802	-	668	-912	...	2879	-
A From other government subsectors	...	-	...	1678	-	...	-	...	1299	-
B From other resident sectors	2410	1286	...	1124	-	668	-912	...	1580	-
C From rest of the world	...	...	...	...	...	...	...	...	...	...
Finance of Gross Accumulation	68249	27700	...	14180	28047	102977	55381	...	16175	32720
Gross Accumulation										
1 Gross capital formation	30787	6517	...	24203	67	38664	10834	...	27753	77
A Increase in stocks	-552	-552	...	-	-	-398	-398	...	-	-
B Gross fixed capital formation	31339	7069	...	24203	67	39062	11232	...	27753	77
2 Purchases of land, net	-4709	-447	...	-4262	-	-8416	-1075	...	-7341	-
3 Purchases of intangible assets, net	...	...	...	...	...	...	...	...	...	...
4 Capital transfers	3136	4557	...	257	-	3590	4543	...	346	-
A To other government subsectors	...	1584	...	94	-	...	1174	...	125	-
B To other resident sectors	3136	2973	...	163	-	3590	3369	...	221	-
C To rest of the world	...	...	...	...	...	...	...	...	...	...
Net lending a	39035	17073	...	-6018	27980	69139	41079	...	-4583	32643
Gross Accumulation	68249	27700	...	14180	28047	102977	55381	...	16175	32720

	1990					1991				
	Total General Government	Central Government	State or Provincial Government	Local Government	Social Security Funds	Total General Government	Central Government	State or Provincial Government	Local Government	Social Security Funds
Finance of Gross Accumulation										
1 Gross saving	88572	35040	...	6934	46598	21241	-34838	...	11779	44300
A Consumption of fixed capital	17775	4602	...	13142	31	18701	4747	...	13922	32
B Net saving	70797	30438	...	-6208	46567	2540	-39585	...	-2143	44268
2 Capital transfers	3314	1560	...	3640	-	-219	-1655	...	3627	-
A From other government subsectors	...	-	...	1886	-	...	-	...	2191	-
B From other resident sectors	3314	1560	...	1754	-	-219	-1655	...	1436	-
C From rest of the world	...	...	...	...	...	...	...	...	...	...
Finance of Gross Accumulation	91886	36600	...	10574	46598	21022	-36493	...	15406	44300
Gross Accumulation										
1 Gross capital formation	40975	13596	...	27291	88	43548	14310	...	29144	94
A Increase in stocks	-216	-216	...	-	-	337	337	...	-	-
B Gross fixed capital formation	41191	13812	...	27291	88	43211	13973	...	29144	94

3.13 General Government Capital Accumulation Account: Total and Subsectors
(Continued)

Million Swedish kronor

	1990					1991				
	Total General Government	Central Government	State or Provincial Government	Local Government	Social Security Funds	Total General Government	Central Government	State or Provincial Government	Local Government	Social Security Funds
2 Purchases of land, net	-8300	340	...	-8740	100	-10641	-121	...	-11049	529
3 Purchases of intangible assets, net	...	...	...	...	...	...	...	...	...	...
4 Capital transfers	2525	3990	...	421	-	4690	6407	...	474	-
A To other government subsectors	...	1706	...	180	-	...	1991	...	200	-
B To other resident sectors	2525	2284	...	241	-	4690	4416	...	274	-
C To rest of the world	...	...	...	...	...	...	...	...	...	...
Net lending ᵃ	56686	18674	...	-8398	46410	-16575	-57089	...	-3163	43677
Gross Accumulation	91886	36600	...	10574	46598	21022	-36493	...	15406	44300

a) Net lending of the capital accumulation account and the capital finance account have not been reconciled and are different due to different statistical sources.

3.14 General Government Capital Finance Account, Total and Subsectors

Million Swedish kronor

	1980					1981				
	Total General Government	Central Government	State or Provincial Government	Local Government	Social Security Funds	Total General Government	Central Government	State or Provincial Government	Local Government	Social Security Funds
Acquisition of Financial Assets										
1 Gold and SDRs	...	...	...	...	...	...	...	...	...	...
2 Currency and transferable deposits	1933	812	...	1003	118	2841	551	...	2382	-92
3 Other deposits ᵃ	868	-	...	868	-	86	-	...	86	-
4 Bills and bonds, short term ᵇ	100	-	...	100	-	-100	-	...	-100	-
5 Bonds, long term ᶜ	11200	-39	...	52	11187	14263	-12	...	228	14047
6 Corporate equity securities	1564	1238	...	232	94	2375	2054	...	167	154
7 Short-term loans, n.e.c.	14656	11622	...	1746	1288	13516	10365	...	2094	1057
8 Long-term loans, n.e.c.	...	...	...	...	...	...	...	...	...	...
9 Other receivables	...	...	...	...	...	...	...	...	...	...
10 Other assets	9917	4091	...	1643	4183	639	-2431	...	-275	3345
Total Acquisition of Financial Assets	40238	17724	...	5644	16870	33620	10527	...	4582	18511
Incurrence of Liabilities										
1 Currency and transferable deposits	...	...	...	...	...	...	...	...	...	...
2 Other deposits ᵃ	-	-	...	-	-	-	-	...	-	...
3 Bills and bonds, short term ᵇ	7444	7444	...	-	-	-743	-743	...	-	-
4 Bonds, long term ᶜ	35805	35821	...	-16	-	59731	58734	...	997	-
5 Short-term loans, n.e.c.	14766	12110	...	2656	-	7419	3437	...	3973	9
6 Long-term loans, n.e.c.	...	...	...	...	...	...	...	...	...	...
7 Other payables	...	...	...	...	...	...	...	...	...	...
8 Other liabilities	1337	-200	...	1538	-1	-979	15	...	-1053	59
Total Incurrence of Liabilities	59352	55175	...	4178	-1	65428	61443	...	3917	68
Net Lending ᵈ	-19114	-37451	...	1466	16871	-31808	-50916	...	665	18443
Incurrence of Liabilities and Net Worth	40238	17724	...	5644	16870	33620	10527	...	4582	18511

	1982					1983				
	Total General Government	Central Government	State or Provincial Government	Local Government	Social Security Funds	Total General Government	Central Government	State or Provincial Government	Local Government	Social Security Funds
Acquisition of Financial Assets										
1 Gold and SDRs	...	...	...	...	...	...	...	...	...	...
2 Currency and transferable deposits	617	1310	...	-487	-206	-1493	-79	...	-1055	-359
3 Other deposits ᵃ	562	-	...	562	-	389	2	...	387	-
4 Bills and bonds, short term ᵇ	2159	-	...	2012	147	1291	164	...	774	353
5 Bonds, long term ᶜ	15285	58	...	-161	15388	17952	-281	...	1333	16900
6 Corporate equity securities	2037	1582	...	333	122	5473	5360	...	250	-137
7 Short-term loans, n.e.c.	12740	10185	...	914	1641	11239	9700	...	1077	462
8 Long-term loans, n.e.c.	...	...	...	...	...	...	...	...	...	...
9 Other receivables	...	...	...	...	...	...	...	...	...	...
10 Other assets	6450	1561	...	2768	2121	7283	4184	...	1631	1468
Total Acquisition of Financial Assets	39850	14696	...	5941	19213	42134	19050	...	4397	18687
Incurrence of Liabilities										
1 Currency and transferable deposits	...	...	...	...	...	...	...	...	...	...

Sweden

3.14 General Government Capital Finance Account, Total and Subsectors
(Continued)

Million Swedish kronor

	1982					1983				
	Total General Government	Central Government	State or Provincial Government	Local Government	Social Security Funds	Total General Government	Central Government	State or Provincial Government	Local Government	Social Security Funds
2 Other deposits a	-	-	...	-	-	205	-	...	205	-
3 Bills and bonds, short term b	33741	33741	...	-	-	-5784	-5784	...	-	-
4 Bonds, long term c	26996	27105	...	-109	-	81395	81033	...	362	-
5 Short-term loans, n.e.c.	13932	11440	...	2489	3	4626	4031	...	591	4
6 Long-term loans, n.e.c.	...	...	...	...	...	...	...	...	...	...
7 Other payables	...	...	...	...	...	...	...	...	...	...
8 Other liabilities	5526	3165	...	2048	313	-911	-3180	...	2224	45
Total Incurrence of Liabilities	80195	75451	...	4428	316	79531	76100	...	3382	49
Net Lending d	-40345	-60755	...	1513	18897	-37397	-57050	...	1015	18638
Incurrence of Liabilities and Net Worth	39850	14696	...	5941	19213	42134	19050	...	4397	18687

	1984					1985				
	Total General Government	Central Government	State or Provincial Government	Local Government	Social Security Funds	Total General Government	Central Government	State or Provincial Government	Local Government	Social Security Funds
Acquisition of Financial Assets										
1 Gold and SDRs	...	...	...	...	...	...	...	...	...	...
2 Currency and transferable deposits	1184	1781	...	-840	243	-1927	2364	...	-4482	191
3 Other deposits a	63	-2	...	-192	257	1627	779	...	440	408
4 Bills and bonds, short term b	768	264	...	-1042	1546	123	-148	...	643	-372
5 Bonds, long term c	16218	166	...	150	15902	14264	556	...	-311	14019
6 Corporate equity securities	2750	440	...	770	1540	2955	1258	...	543	1154
7 Short-term loans, n.e.c.	11838	9470	...	2357	11	7767	8529	...	-635	-127
8 Long-term loans, n.e.c.	...	...	...	...	...	...	...	...	...	...
9 Other receivables	...	...	...	...	...	...	...	...	...	...
10 Other assets	8506	4714	...	1455	2337	77	-10083	...	4271	5889
Total Acquisition of Financial Assets	41327	16833	...	2658	21836	24886	3255	...	469	21162
Incurrence of Liabilities										
1 Currency and transferable deposits	...	...	...	...	...	...	...	...	...	...
2 Other deposits a	6556	6517	...	39	-	11008	10678	...	330	-
3 Bills and bonds, short term b	38900	38900	...	-	-	21625	21625	...	-	-
4 Bonds, long term c	49724	49544	...	180	-	27092	26909	...	183	-
5 Short-term loans, n.e.c.	-31177	-32962	...	1782	3	1943	-3371	...	5312	2
6 Long-term loans, n.e.c.	...	...	...	...	...	...	...	...	...	...
7 Other payables	...	...	...	...	...	...	...	...	...	...
8 Other liabilities	-2	-	...	-17	15	-1256	-	...	-870	-386
Total Incurrence of Liabilities	64001	61999	...	1984	18	60412	55841	...	4955	-384
Net Lending d	-22674	-45166	...	674	21818	-35526	-52586	...	-4486	21546
Incurrence of Liabilities and Net Worth	41327	16833	...	2658	21836	24886	3255	...	469	21162

	1986					1987				
	Total General Government	Central Government	State or Provincial Government	Local Government	Social Security Funds	Total General Government	Central Government	State or Provincial Government	Local Government	Social Security Funds
Acquisition of Financial Assets										
1 Gold and SDRs	...	...	...	...	...	...	...	...	...	...
2 Currency and transferable deposits	541	1961	...	-1615	195	-6572	-4756	...	-1847	31
3 Other deposits a	957	-499	...	-845	2301	2338	-123	...	803	1658
4 Bills and bonds, short term b	-2422	-50	...	-1764	-608	584	191	...	453	-60
5 Bonds, long term c	18542	1422	...	521	16599	23253	1591	...	465	21197
6 Corporate equity securities	4733	1833	...	401	2499	5952	2088	...	466	3398
7 Short-term loans, n.e.c.	-3654	-3775	...	-1560	1681	9603	11196	...	368	-1961
8 Long-term loans, n.e.c.	...	...	...	...	...	...	...	...	...	...
9 Other receivables	...	...	...	...	...	...	...	...	...	...
10 Other assets	10862	2668	...	5837	2357	1375	1271	...	-1116	1220
Total Acquisition of Financial Assets	29559	3560	...	975	25024	36533	11458	...	-408	25483
Incurrence of Liabilities										
1 Currency and transferable deposits	...	...	...	...	...	...	...	...	...	...
2 Other deposits a	17639	15813	...	1826	-	11632	9679	...	1953	-
3 Bills and bonds, short term b	-6625	-6625	...	-	-	-21200	-21200	...	-	-

3.14 General Government Capital Finance Account, Total and Subsectors
(Continued)

Million Swedish kronor

	1986					1987				
	Total General Government	Central Government	State or Provincial Government	Local Government	Social Security Funds	Total General Government	Central Government	State or Provincial Government	Local Government	Social Security Funds
4 Bonds, long term c	22297	20960	...	1337	-	-1242	-672	...	-570	-
5 Short-term loans, n.e.c.	4383	2570	...	1814	-1	-530	1065	...	-1589	-6
6 Long-term loans, n.e.c.	...	...	...	...	...	...	...	...	...	...
7 Other payables	...	...	...	...	...	...	...	...	...	...
8 Other liabilities	2458	-	...	873	1585	1598	-	...	2783	-1185
Total Incurrence of Liabilities	40152	32718	...	5850	1584	-9742	-11128	...	2577	-1191
Net Lending d	-10593	-29158	...	-4875	23440	46275	22586	...	-2985	26674
Incurrence of Liabilities and Net Worth	29559	3560	...	975	25024	36533	11458	...	-408	25483

	1988					1989				
	Total General Government	Central Government	State or Provincial Government	Local Government	Social Security Funds	Total General Government	Central Government	State or Provincial Government	Local Government	Social Security Funds
Acquisition of Financial Assets										
1 Gold and SDRs	...	...	...	...	...	...	...	...	...	...
2 Currency and transferable deposits	-5	712	...	-1099	382	1045	2183	...	-371	-767
3 Other deposits a	-685	2403	...	255	-3343	1259	-704	...	193	1770
4 Bills and bonds, short term b	-1039	-	...	-109	-930	563	902	...	-392	53
5 Bonds, long term c	36567	1651	...	867	34049	27520	2452	...	-204	25272
6 Corporate equity securities	-10951	-14237	...	553	2733	10127	1160	...	4401	4566
7 Short-term loans, n.e.c.	16371	15489	...	2398	-1516	11385	7422	...	1353	2610
8 Long-term loans, n.e.c.	...	...	...	...	...	...	...	...	...	...
9 Other receivables	...	...	...	...	...	...	...	...	...	...
10 Other assets	-3179	7985	...	-8307	-2857	8652	7672	...	1049	-69
Total Acquisition of Financial Assets	37079	14003	...	-5442	28518	60551	21087	...	6029	33435
Incurrence of Liabilities										
1 Currency and transferable deposits	...	...	...	...	...	...	...	...	...	...
2 Other deposits a	15335	14411	...	924	-	9912	9636	...	276	-
3 Bills and bonds, short term b	5151	5151	...	-	-	-25869	-25869	...	-	-
4 Bonds, long term c	-19060	-19034	...	-26	-	-37070	-36657	...	-413	-
5 Short-term loans, n.e.c.	-6217	-5829	...	-388	-	6885	704	...	6171	10
6 Long-term loans, n.e.c.	...	...	...	...	...	...	...	...	...	...
7 Other payables	...	...	...	...	...	...	...	...	...	...
8 Other liabilities	427	-	...	469	-42	38329	30860	...	7376	93
Total Incurrence of Liabilities	-4364	-5301	...	979	-42	-7813	-21326	...	13410	103
Net Lending d	41443	19304	...	-6421	28560	68364	42413	...	-7381	33332
Incurrence of Liabilities and Net Worth	37079	14003	...	-5442	28518	60551	21087	...	6029	33435

	1990					1991				
	Total General Government	Central Government	State or Provincial Government	Local Government	Social Security Funds	Total General Government	Central Government	State or Provincial Government	Local Government	Social Security Funds
Acquisition of Financial Assets										
1 Gold and SDRs	...	...	...	...	...	...	...	...	...	...
2 Currency and transferable deposits	1192	1461	...	-266	-3	90905	89647	...	966	292
3 Other deposits a	11043	4854	...	773	5416	10912	1106	...	546	9260
4 Bills and bonds, short term b	4306	3564	...	33	709	9802	-3188	...	1175	11815
5 Bonds, long term c	32623	3789	...	-987	29821	33554	3557	...	-629	30626
6 Corporate equity securities	11712	304	...	2203	9205	-902	2187	...	-3921	832
7 Short-term loans, n.e.c.	17030	10272	...	2034	4724	8823	1322	...	6317	1184
8 Long-term loans, n.e.c.	...	...	...	...	...	...	...	...	...	...
9 Other receivables	...	...	...	...	...	...	...	...	...	...
10 Other assets	-1983	101	...	2065	-4149	-8538	-2847	...	1702	-7393
Total Acquisition of Financial Assets	75923	24345	...	5855	45723	144556	91784	...	6156	46616
Incurrence of Liabilities										
1 Currency and transferable deposits	...	...	...	...	...	...	...	...	...	...
2 Other deposits a	-3914	-8100	...	4186	-	9291	7073	...	2218	-
3 Bills and bonds, short term b	61144	61144	...	-	-	170435	170435	...	-	-

Sweden

3.14 General Government Capital Finance Account, Total and Subsectors
(Continued)

Million Swedish kronor

	1990					1991				
	Total General Government	Central Government	State or Provincial Government	Local Government	Social Security Funds	Total General Government	Central Government	State or Provincial Government	Local Government	Social Security Funds
4 Bonds, long term c	-33271	-33321	...	50	-	12178	12774	...	-596	-
5 Short-term loans, n.e.c.	28087	12785	...	15306	-4	-3385	-6246	...	2863	-2
6 Long-term loans, n.e.c.	...	...	...	...	...	...	...	...	...	...
7 Other payables	...	...	...	...	...	...	...	...	...	...
8 Other liabilities	-24407	-15586	...	-8753	-68	-9353	-14683	...	5328	2
Total Incurrence of Liabilities	27639	16922	...	10789	-72	179166	169353	...	9813	-
Net Lending d	48284	7423	...	-4934	45795	-34610	-77569	...	-3657	46616
Incurrence of Liabilities and Net Worth	75923	24345	...	5855	45723	144556	91784	...	6156	46616

a) Item 'Other deposits' refers to certificates and general public scheme.
b) 'Bills and bonds' refer to treasury bills and special treasury bills.
c) Item 'Bonds, long-term' includes both short-term and long-term bonds.

d) Net lending of the capital accumulation account and the capital finance account have not been reconciled and are different due to different statistical sources.

3.21 Corporate and Quasi-Corporate Enterprise Production Account: Total and Sectors

Million Swedish kronor

	1980			ADDENDUM: Total, including Unincorporated	1981			ADDENDUM: Total, including Unincorporated	1982			ADDENDUM: Total, including Unincorporated
	Corporate and Quasi-Corporate Enterprises				Corporate and Quasi-Corporate Enterprises				Corporate and Quasi-Corporate Enterprises			
	TOTAL	Non-Financial	Financial		TOTAL	Non-Financial	Financial		TOTAL	Non-Financial	Financial	
Gross Output												
1 Output for sale	...	...	...	...	...	...	...	...	...	...	...	...
2 Imputed bank service charge	...	...	...	...	...	...	...	...	...	...	...	...
3 Own-account fixed capital formation	...	...	...	...	...	...	...	...	...	...	...	...
Gross Output	...	...	...	...	...	...	...	...	...	...	...	...
Gross Input												
Intermediate consumption	...	...	...	...	...	...	...	...	...	...	...	...
Subtotal: Value Added	...	...	...	...	...	...	...	...	...	...	...	...
1 Indirect taxes, net	...	...	...	...	...	...	...	...	...	...	...	...
2 Consumption of fixed capital	37890	37358	532	52688	42178	41574	604	58825	47775	47090	685	66018
3 Compensation of employees	213693	206230	7463	220065	234071	225880	8191	240560	...	...	...	...
4 Net operating surplus	24527	27403	-2876	80028	27248	30369	-3121	84204	36837	40344	-3507	106920
Gross Input	...	...	...	...	...	...	...	...	...	...	...	...

	1983			ADDENDUM: Total, including Unincorporated	1984			ADDENDUM: Total, including Unincorporated	1985			ADDENDUM: Total, including Unincorporated
	Corporate and Quasi-Corporate Enterprises				Corporate and Quasi-Corporate Enterprises				Corporate and Quasi-Corporate Enterprises			
	TOTAL	Non-Financial	Financial		TOTAL	Non-Financial	Financial		TOTAL	Non-Financial	Financial	
Gross Output												
1 Output for sale	...	...	...	...	...	...	...	...	...	...	...	...
2 Imputed bank service charge	...	...	...	...	...	...	...	...	...	...	...	...
3 Own-account fixed capital formation	...	...	...	...	...	...	...	...	...	...	...	...
Gross Output	...	...	...	...	...	...	...	...	...	...	...	...
Gross Input												
Intermediate consumption	...	...	...	...	...	...	...	...	...	...	...	...
Subtotal: Value Added	...	...	...	...	...	...	...	...	...	...	...	...
1 Indirect taxes, net	...	...	...	...	...	...	...	...	...	...	...	...
2 Consumption of fixed capital	54433	53662	771	74592	58826	57975	851	81115	64484	63538	946	88054
3 Compensation of employees	...	...	...	...	...	...	...	...	...	...	...	...
4 Net operating surplus	47391	52250	-4859	125303	65669	73079	-7410	148261	67396	77269	-9873	156963
Gross Input	...	...	...	...	...	...	...	...	...	...	...	...

	1986			ADDENDUM: Total, including Unincorporated	1987			ADDENDUM: Total, including Unincorporated	1988			ADDENDUM: Total, including Unincorporated
	Corporate and Quasi-Corporate Enterprises				Corporate and Quasi-Corporate Enterprises				Corporate and Quasi-Corporate Enterprises			
	TOTAL	Non-Financial	Financial		TOTAL	Non-Financial	Financial		TOTAL	Non-Financial	Financial	
Gross Output												
1 Output for sale	...	...	...	...	...	...	...	...	...	...	...	...
2 Imputed bank service charge	...	...	...	...	...	...	...	...	...	...	...	...
3 Own-account fixed capital formation	...	...	...	...	...	...	...	...	...	...	...	...
Gross Output	...	...	...	...	...	...	...	...	...	...	...	...

3.21 Corporate and Quasi-Corporate Enterprise Production Account: Total and Sectors
(Continued)

Million Swedish kronor

	1986				1987				1988			
	Corporate and Quasi-Corporate Enterprises			ADDENDUM: Total, including Unincorporated	Corporate and Quasi-Corporate Enterprises			ADDENDUM: Total, including Unincorporated	Corporate and Quasi-Corporate Enterprises			ADDENDUM: Total, including Unincorporated
	TOTAL	Non-Financial	Financial		TOTAL	Non-Financial	Financial		TOTAL	Non-Financial	Financial	
Gross Input												
Intermediate consumption	...	...	...	...	...	...	...	...	...	...	...	...
Subtotal: Value Added	...	...	...	...	...	...	...	...	...	...	...	...
1 Indirect taxes, net	...	...	...	...	...	...	...	...	...	...	...	...
2 Consumption of fixed capital	70013	68994	1019	94925	76714	75608	1106	103502	83974	82745	1229	113758
3 Compensation of employees	...	...	...	...	...	...	...	...	...	...	...	...
4 Net operating surplus	74892	85300	-10408	166418	84995	99800	-14805	170184	97159	111397	-14238	188953
Gross Input	...	...	...	...	...	...	...	...	...	...	...	...

	1989				1990				1991			
	Corporate and Quasi-Corporate Enterprises			ADDENDUM: Total, including Unincorporated	Corporate and Quasi-Corporate Enterprises			ADDENDUM: Total, including Unincorporated	Corporate and Quasi-Corporate Enterprises			ADDENDUM: Total, including Unincorporated
	TOTAL	Non-Financial	Financial		TOTAL	Non-Financial	Financial		TOTAL	Non-Financial	Financial	
Gross Output												
1 Output for sale	...	...	...	...	...	...	...	...	...	...	...	...
2 Imputed bank service charge	...	...	...	...	...	...	...	...	...	...	...	...
3 Own-account fixed capital formation	...	...	...	...	...	...	...	...	...	...	...	...
Gross Output	...	...	...	...	...	...	...	...	...	...	...	...
Gross Input												
Intermediate consumption	...	...	...	...	...	...	...	...	...	...	...	...
Subtotal: Value Added	...	...	...	...	...	...	...	...	...	...	...	...
1 Indirect taxes, net	...	...	...	...	...	...	...	...	...	...	...	...
2 Consumption of fixed capital	90364	89004	1360	123862	98396	96889	1507	135962	104249	102632	1617	146234
3 Compensation of employees	...	...	...	...	...	...	...	...	...	...	...	...
4 Net operating surplus	102350	120194	-17844	196716	87954	108483	-20529	186343	91700	113839	-22139	193194
Gross Input	...	...	...	...	...	...	...	...	...	...	...	...

3.22 Corporate and Quasi-Corporate Enterprise Income and Outlay Account: Total and Sectors

Million Swedish kronor

	1980			1981			1982			1983		
	TOTAL	Non-Financial	Financial	TOTAL	Non-Financial	Financial	TOTAL	Non-Financial	Financial	TOTAL	Non-Financial	Financial
Receipts												
1 Operating surplus	24527	27403	-2876	27248	30369	-3121	36837	40344	-3507	47391	52250	-4859
2 Property and entrepreneurial income	86631	3911	82720	111528	4063	107465	129034	5839	123195	141584	6110	135474
A Withdrawals from quasi-corporate enterprises	...	...	...	...	...	...	...	...	...	...	...	...
B Interest	81630	...	81630	106227	...	106227	121406	...	121406	133555	...	133555
C Dividends	4813	3723	1090	4804	3566	1238	7117	5328	1789	7142	5223	1919
D Net land rent and royalties	188	188	...	497	497	...	511	511	...	887	887	...
3 Current transfers	25856	12216	13640	32434	12345	20089	40018	14979	25039	40340	14919	25421
A Casualty insurance claims	3683	3683	...	3836	3836	...	4414	4414	...	4569	4569	...
B Casualty insurance premiums, net, due to be received by insurance companies	5725	...	5725	11358	...	11358	15731	...	15731	15239	...	15239
C Current transfers from the rest of the world	884	884	...	-	-	-	-	-	...	-	-	...
D Other transfers except imputed	1901	1552	349	2163	1952	211	4290	3945	345	4149	3472	677
E Imputed unfunded employee pension and welfare contributions	13663	6097	7566	15077	6557	8520	15583	6620	8963	16383	6878	9505
Total Current Receipts	137014	43530	93484	171210	46777	124433	205889	61162	144727	229315	73279	156036
Disbursements												
1 Property and entrepreneurial income	90562	30268	60294	114063	35800	78263	128751	38910	89841	146888	47831	99057
A Withdrawals from quasi-corporations	3683	2933	750	4251	3401	850	6089	4089	2000	9499	5499	4000
Public	2246	1496	750	2736	1886	850	4146	2146	2000	6631	2631	4000
Private	1437	1437	...	1515	1515	...	1943	1943	...	2868	2868	...
B Interest	79070	20519	58551	102240	25949	76291	112596	26150	86446	125296	32015	93281

Sweden

3.22 Corporate and Quasi-Corporate Enterprise Income and Outlay Account: Total and Sectors
(Continued)

Million Swedish kronor

	1980 TOTAL	Non-Financial	Financial	1981 TOTAL	Non-Financial	Financial	1982 TOTAL	Non-Financial	Financial	1983 TOTAL	Non-Financial	Financial
C Dividends	6733	5740	993	6331	5209	1122	8412	7017	1395	10298	8522	1776
D Net land rent and royalties	1076	1076	...	1241	1241	...	1654	1654	...	1795	1795	...
2 Direct taxes and other current transfers n.e.c. to general government	6424	5248	1176	6171	4585	1586	8549	6727	1822	12776	9825	2951
A Direct taxes	6263	5248	1015	6091	4585	1506	8403	6727	1676	12552	9825	2727
B Fines, fees, penalties and other current transfers n.e.c.	161	-	161	80	-	80	146	-	146	224	-	224
3 Other current transfers	17855	8240	9615	24133	7827	16306	31577	9645	21932	33248	11032	22216
A Casualty insurance premiums, net	3991	3991	...	3531	3531	...	4709	4709	...	4659	4659	...
B Casualty insurance claims liability of insurance companies	5825	...	5825	11700	...	11700	15205	...	15205	15372	...	15372
C Transfers to private non-profit institutions	...	...	...	...	...	...	...	...	...	...	...	...
D Unfunded employee pension and welfare benefits	5937	2607	3330	6803	2916	3887	7902	3256	4646	8779	3568	5211
E Social assistance grants	...	...	...	...	...	...	...	...	...	...	...	...
F Other transfers n.e.c.	2102	1642	460	2099	1380	719	3761	1680	2081	4438	2805	1633
G Transfers to the rest of the world	...	...	...	...	...	...	...	...	...	...	...	...
Statistical discrepancy	2479	2479	...	9856	9856	...	8099	8099	...	5855	5855	...
Net saving	19694	-2705	22399	16987	-11291	28278	28913	-2219	31132	30548	-1264	31812
Total Current Disbursements and Net Saving	137014	43530	93484	171210	46777	124433	205889	61162	144727	229315	73279	156036

	1984 TOTAL	Non-Financial	Financial	1985 TOTAL	Non-Financial	Financial	1986 TOTAL	Non-Financial	Financial	1987 TOTAL	Non-Financial	Financial
Receipts												
1 Operating surplus	65669	73079	-7410	67396	77269	-9873	74892	85300	-10408	84995	99800	-14805
2 Property and entrepreneurial income	164432	7456	156976	192357	9790	182567	205756	14583	191173	230229	18316	211913
A Withdrawals from quasi-corporate enterprises	...	...	...	...	...	...	...	...	...	...	...	...
B Interest	154152	...	154152	179842	...	179842	187851	...	187851	206904	...	206904
C Dividends	9478	6654	2824	11299	8574	2725	16895	13573	3322	21588	16579	5009
D Net land rent and royalties	802	802	...	1216	1216	...	1010	1010	...	1737	1737	...
3 Current transfers	45386	17076	28310	56847	20032	36815	65080	22831	42249	67384	22246	45138
A Casualty insurance claims	5805	5805	...	6335	6335	...	7022	7022	...	6017	6017	...
B Casualty insurance premiums, net, due to be received by insurance companies	16958	...	16958	21984	...	21984	25171	...	25171	24440	...	24440
C Current transfers from the rest of the world	-	-	...	-	-	...	-	-	...	-	-	...
D Other transfers except imputed	5128	4424	704	8002	6025	1977	11878	8077	3801	12965	8453	4512
E Imputed unfunded employee pension and welfare contributions	17495	6847	10648	20526	7672	12854	21009	7732	13277	23962	7776	16186
Total Current Receipts	275487	97611	177876	316600	107091	209509	345728	122714	223014	382608	140362	242246
Disbursements												
1 Property and entrepreneurial income	169415	55521	113894	193842	58893	134949	210440	75190	135250	229574	78628	150946
A Withdrawals from quasi-corporations	12550	8550	4000	14643	7982	6661	16631	9008	7623	14599	8758	5841
Public	7921	3921	4000	9743	3082	6661	11050	3427	7623	9437	3596	5841
Private	4629	4629	...	4900	4900	...	5581	5581	...	5162	5162	...
B Interest	142704	35381	107323	161401	36775	124626	169759	47743	122016	184253	45785	138468
C Dividends	11996	9425	2571	15009	11347	3662	20642	15031	5611	27485	20848	6637
D Net land rent and royalties	2165	2165	...	2789	2789	...	3408	3408	...	3237	3237	...
2 Direct taxes and other current transfers n.e.c. to general government	14289	11967	2322	13469	11570	1899	16226	10288	5938	27058	23496	3562
A Direct taxes	14130	11967	2163	13461	11570	1891	16218	10288	5930	27058	23496	3562
B Fines, fees, penalties and other current transfers n.e.c.	159	-	159	8	-	8	8	-	8	-	-	-

3.22 Corporate and Quasi-Corporate Enterprise Income and Outlay Account: Total and Sectors
(Continued)

Million Swedish kronor

	1984			1985			1986			1987		
	TOTAL	Non-Financial	Financial	TOTAL	Non-Financial	Financial	TOTAL	Non-Financial	Financial	TOTAL	Non-Financial	Financial
3 Other current transfers	39361	13013	26348	48092	15983	32109	56800	18985	37815	58470	19301	39169
A Casualty insurance premiums, net	5733	5733	...	6718	6718	...	7696	7696	...	5634	5634	...
B Casualty insurance claims liability of insurance companies	17806	...	17806	22190	...	22190	24975	...	24975	25022	...	25022
C Transfers to private non-profit institutions	...	...	...	...	...	...	...	...	...	...	...	...
D Unfunded employee pension and welfare benefits	9796	3750	6046	10434	3872	6562	11372	4082	7290	12090	4163	7927
E Social assistance grants	...	...	...	...	...	...	...	...	...	...	...	...
F Other transfers n.e.c.	6026	3530	2496	8750	5393	3357	12757	7207	5550	15724	9504	6220
G Transfers to the rest of the world	...	...	...	...	...	...	...	...	...	...	...	...
Statistical discrepancy	8333	8333	...	9373	9373	...	14146	14146	...	27928	27928	...
Net saving	44089	8777	35312	51824	11272	40552	48116	4105	44011	39578	-8991	48569
Total Current Disbursements and Net Saving	275487	97611	177876	316600	107091	209509	345728	122714	223014	382608	140362	242246

	1988			1989			1990			1991		
	TOTAL	Non-Financial	Financial	TOTAL	Non-Financial	Financial	TOTAL	Non-Financial	Financial	TOTAL	Non-Financial	Financial
Receipts												
1 Operating surplus	97159	111397	-14238	102350	120194	-17844	87954	108483	-20529	91700	113839	-22139
2 Property and entrepreneurial income	271187	24263	246924	335879	25059	310820	423703	30748	392955	480729	32241	448488
A Withdrawals from quasi-corporate enterprises	...	...	...	...	...	...	...	...	...	...	...	...
B Interest	241230	...	241230	304147	...	304147	384785	...	384785	439609	...	439609
C Dividends	27838	22144	5694	29059	22386	6673	35766	27596	8170	37122	28243	8879
D Net land rent and royalties	2119	2119	...	2673	2673	...	3152	3152	...	3998	3998	...
3 Current transfers	75203	25270	49933	83438	28819	54619	105136	46835	58301	135324	61957	73367
A Casualty insurance claims	6853	6853	...	7152	7152	...	8398	8398	...	7636	7636	...
B Casualty insurance premiums, net, due to be received by insurance companies	26201	...	26201	28798	...	28798	31351	...	31351	33969	...	33969
C Current transfers from the rest of the world	-	-	-	-	-	-	-	-	-	-	-	-
D Other transfers except imputed	15386	9410	5976	20224	11904	8320	37300	25049	12251	59926	41279	18647
E Imputed unfunded employee pension and welfare contributions	26763	9007	17756	27264	9763	17501	28087	13388	14699	33793	13042	20751
Total Current Receipts	443549	160930	282619	521667	174072	347595	616793	186066	430727	707753	208037	499716
Disbursements												
1 Property and entrepreneurial income	271441	94537	176904	344846	108993	235853	442642	136109	306533	503066	149116	353950
A Withdrawals from quasi-corporations	12017	8017	4000	14585	7985	6600	15699	8699	7000	15962	8962	7000
Public	6556	2556	4000	8293	1693	6600	9042	2042	7000	9072	2072	7000
Private	5461	5461	...	6292	6292	...	6657	6657	...	6890	6890	...
B Interest	222026	55299	166727	289748	67255	222493	381214	89341	291873	440753	99288	341465
C Dividends	33313	27136	6177	36118	29358	6760	40806	33146	7660	41485	36000	5485
D Net land rent and royalties	4085	4085	...	4395	4395	...	4923	4923	...	4866	4866	...
2 Direct taxes and other current transfers n.e.c. to general government	28561	22948	5613	33893	30982	2911	27333	24901	2432	12824	7808	5016
A Direct taxes	28561	22948	5613	33893	30982	2911	27333	24901	2432	12824	7808	5016
B Fines, fees, penalties and other current transfers n.e.c.	-	-	-	-	-	-	-	-	-	-	-	-

Sweden

3.22 Corporate and Quasi-Corporate Enterprise Income and Outlay Account: Total and Sectors
(Continued)

Million Swedish kronor

	1988			1989			1990			1991		
	TOTAL	Non-Financial	Financial	TOTAL	Non-Financial	Financial	TOTAL	Non-Financial	Financial	TOTAL	Non-Financial	Financial
3 Other current transfers	64286	22437	41849	71438	26109	45329	95420	33229	62191	121160	39089	82071
A Casualty insurance premiums, net	5863	5863	...	5830	5830	...	6362	6362	...	3836	3836	...
B Casualty insurance claims liability of insurance companies	26785	...	26785	28215	...	28215	32785	...	32785	35709	...	35709
C Transfers to private non-profit institutions	...	...	...	...	...	...	...	...	...	...	...	...
D Unfunded employee pension and welfare benefits	13028	4401	8627	14264	4521	9743	14844	4737	10107	16882	5242	11640
E Social assistance grants	...	...	...	...	...	...	...	...	...	...	...	...
F Other transfers n.e.c.	18610	12173	6437	23129	15758	7371	41429	22130	19299	64733	30011	34722
G Transfers to the rest of the world	...	...	...	...	...	...	...	...	...	...	...	...
Statistical discrepancy	27305	27305	...	40693	40693	...	38829	38829	...	43225	43225	...
Net saving	51956	-6297	58253	30797	-32705	63502	12569	-47002	59571	27478	-31201	58679
Total Current Disbursements and Net Saving	443549	160930	282619	521667	174072	347595	616793	186066	430727	707753	208037	499716

3.23 Corporate and Quasi-Corporate Enterprise Capital Accumulation Account: Total and Sectors

Million Swedish kronor

	1980			1981			1982			1983		
	TOTAL	Non-Financial	Financial	TOTAL	Non-Financial	Financial	TOTAL	Non-Financial	Financial	TOTAL	Non-Financial	Financial
Finance of Gross Accumulation												
1 Gross saving	57584	34653	22931	59165	30283	28882	76688	44871	31817	84981	52398	32583
A Consumption of fixed capital	37890	37358	532	42178	41574	604	47775	47090	685	54433	53662	771
B Net saving	19694	-2705	22399	16987	-11291	28278	28913	-2219	31132	30548	-1264	31812
2 Capital transfers	3822	3822	...	5881	5881	...	9599	9599	...	10193	10193	...
A From resident sectors	3822	3822	...	5881	5881	...	9599	9599	...	10193	10193	...
B From the rest of the world	...	...	...	...	...	...	...	...	...	...	...	...
Finance of Gross Accumulation	61406	38475	22931	65046	36164	28882	86287	54470	31817	95174	62591	32583
Gross Accumulation												
1 Gross capital formation	64073	63037	1036	57836	56780	1056	64947	63848	1099	72319	71292	1027
A Increase in stocks	4908	4908	...	-4609	-4609	...	-6840	-6840	...	-10302	-10302	...
B Gross fixed capital formation	59165	58129	1036	62445	61389	1056	71787	70688	1099	82621	81594	1027
2 Purchases of land, net	-2352	-2451	99	-2560	-2739	179	-2051	-4002	1951	-1971	-4003	2032
3 Purchases of intangible assets, net	...	...	...	...	...	...	...	...	...	...	...	...
4 Capital transfers	275	275	-	275	275	-	297	297	-	294	294	-
A To resident sectors	275	275	-	275	275	-	297	297	-	294	294	-
B To the rest of the world	...	...	...	...	...	...	...	...	...	...	...	...
Net lending ab	-590	-22386	21796	9495	-18152	27647	23094	-5673	28767	24532	-4992	29524
Gross Accumulation	61406	38475	22931	65046	36164	28882	86287	54470	31817	95174	62591	32583

	1984			1985			1986			1987		
	TOTAL	Non-Financial	Financial	TOTAL	Non-Financial	Financial	TOTAL	Non-Financial	Financial	TOTAL	Non-Financial	Financial
Finance of Gross Accumulation												
1 Gross saving	102915	66752	36163	116308	74810	41498	118129	73099	45030	116292	66617	49675
A Consumption of fixed capital	58826	57975	851	64484	63538	946	70013	68994	1019	76714	75608	1106
B Net saving	44089	8777	35312	51824	11272	40552	48116	4105	44011	39578	-8991	48569
2 Capital transfers	5503	5503	...	7008	7008	...	7976	7976	...	2633	2633	...
A From resident sectors	5503	5503	...	7008	7008	...	7976	7976	...	2633	2633	...
B From the rest of the world	...	...	...	...	...	...	...	...	...	...	...	...
Finance of Gross Accumulation	108418	72255	36163	123316	81818	41498	126105	81075	45030	118925	69250	49675
Gross Accumulation												
1 Gross capital formation	88262	86539	1723	113274	110981	2293	115833	112793	3040	134067	131361	2706
A Increase in stocks	-6922	-6922	...	228	228	...	-5718	-5718	...	-5781	-5781	...
B Gross fixed capital formation	95184	93461	1723	113046	110753	2293	121551	118511	3040	139848	137142	2706

3.23 Corporate and Quasi-Corporate Enterprise Capital Accumulation Account: Total and Sectors
(Continued)

Million Swedish kronor

	1984			1985			1986			1987		
	TOTAL	Non-Financial	Financial	TOTAL	Non-Financial	Financial	TOTAL	Non-Financial	Financial	TOTAL	Non-Financial	Financial
2 Purchases of land, net	-1932	-3988	2056	-1432	-3229	1797	723	184	539	1259	-1446	2705
3 Purchases of intangible assets, net	...	...	...	...	...	...	...	...	...	...	...	...
4 Capital transfers	281	281	-	294	294	-	246	246	-	10301	274	10027
A To resident sectors	281	281	-	294	294	-	246	246	-	10301	274	10027
B To the rest of the world	...	...	...	...	...	...	...	...	...	...	...	...
Net lending ab	21807	-10577	32384	11180	-26228	37408	9303	-32148	41451	-26702	-60939	34237
Gross Accumulation	108418	72255	36163	123316	81818	41498	126105	81075	45030	118925	69250	49675

	1988			1989			1990			1991		
	TOTAL	Non-Financial	Financial	TOTAL	Non-Financial	Financial	TOTAL	Non-Financial	Financial	TOTAL	Non-Financial	Financial
Finance of Gross Accumulation												
1 Gross saving	135930	76448	59482	121161	56299	64862	110965	49887	61078	131727	71431	60296
A Consumption of fixed capital	83974	82745	1229	90364	89004	1360	98396	96889	1507	104249	102632	1617
B Net saving	51956	-6297	58253	30797	-32705	63502	12569	-47002	59571	27478	-31201	58679
2 Capital transfers	2084	2084	...	3891	3891	...	1716	1716	...	2739	2739	...
A From resident sectors	2084	2084	...	3891	3891	...	1716	1716	...	2739	2739	...
B From the rest of the world	...	...	...	...	...	...	...	...	...	...	...	...
Finance of Gross Accumulation	138014	78532	59482	125052	60190	64862	112681	51603	61078	134466	74170	60296
Gross Accumulation												
1 Gross capital formation	155017	151172	3845	190464	185407	5057	201851	197436	4415	165442	161711	3731
A Increase in stocks	-2538	-2538	...	577	577	...	-979	-979	...	-25377	-25377	...
B Gross fixed capital formation	157555	153710	3845	189887	184830	5057	202830	198415	4415	190819	187088	3731
2 Purchases of land, net	2284	-1020	3304	5354	2401	2953	4322	2713	1609	6982	5839	1143
3 Purchases of intangible assets, net	...	...	...	...	...	...	...	...	...	...	...	...
4 Capital transfers	374	304	70	6493	408	6085	645	645	-	-270	-270	-
A To resident sectors	374	304	70	6493	408	6085	645	645	-	-270	-270	-
B To the rest of the world	...	...	...	...	...	...	...	...	...	...	...	...
Net lending ab	-19661	-71924	52263	-77259	-128026	50767	-94137	-149191	55054	-37688	-93110	55422
Gross Accumulation	138014	78532	59482	125052	60190	64862	112681	51603	61078	134466	74170	60296

a) Net lending of the capital accumulation account and the capital finance account have not been reconciled and are different due to different statistical sources.
b) Net lending excludes net acquisition of SDR.

3.24 Corporate and Quasi-Corporate Enterprise Capital Finance Account: Total and Sectors

Million Swedish kronor

	1980			1981			1982			1983		
	TOTAL	Non-Financial	Financial	TOTAL	Non-Financial	Financial	TOTAL	Non-Financial	Financial	TOTAL	Non-Financial	Financial
Acquisition of Financial Assets												
1 Gold and SDRs	-253	-	-253	8	-	8	53	-	53	-920	-	-920
2 Currency and transferable deposits	10918	145	10773	20985	14121	6864	13031	5258	7773	12162	7612	4550
3 Other deposits a	12903	5413	7490	156	306	-150	23893	19093	4800	4840	7189	-2349
4 Bills and bonds, short term b	6312	-	6312	-3057	-	-3057	10252	-	10252	-2733	1484	-4217
5 Bonds, long term c	23805	32	23773	61620	3066	58554	20937	1005	19932	64502	14944	49558
6 Corporate equity securities	7017	5467	1550	13687	11430	2257	13327	9075	4252	14410	9605	4805
7 Short term loans, n.e.c.	66108	10615	55493	66889	9052	57837	87955	20483	67472	110744	36455	74289
8 Long term loans, n.e.c.	...	...	...	...	...	...	...	...	...	...	...	...
9 Trade credits and advances	9444	9444	-	9842	9842	-	12328	12328	-	18041	18041	-
10 Other receivables	...	...	...	...	...	...	...	...	...	...	...	...
11 Other assets	7634	7291	343	28230	1468	26762	19973	872	19101	25991	383	25608
Total Acquisition of Financial Assets d	143888	38407	105481	198360	49285	149075	201749	68114	133635	247037	95713	151324
Incurrence of Liabilities												
1 Currency and transferable deposits	27432	-	27432	43415	-	43415	27729	-	27729	26418	-	26418
2 Other deposits a	14661	-	14661	298	-	298	4281	-	4281	4948	378	4570
3 Bills and bonds, short term	...	...	...	...	...	...	...	...	...	...	...	...
4 Bonds, long term c	15378	-481	15859	24372	957	23415	26941	2863	24078	31901	3501	28400
5 Corporate equity securities	4120	3826	294	9194	7285	1909	11465	7211	4254	18296	11632	6664
6 Short-term loans, n.e.c.	64585	43027	21558	60458	35989	24469	65892	37615	28277	77306	54953	22353

Sweden

Million Swedish kronor

	1980			1981			1982			1983		
	TOTAL	Non-Financial	Financial	TOTAL	Non-Financial	Financial	TOTAL	Non-Financial	Financial	TOTAL	Non-Financial	Financial
7 Long-term loans, n.e.c.	...	...	...	...	...	...	...	...	...	...	...	...
8 Net equity of households in life insurance and pension fund reserves	3182	-	3182	4140	-	4140	4914	-	4914	9071	-	9071
9 Proprietors' net additions to the accumulation of quasi-corporations	1208	1208	-	1308	1308	-	1525	1525	-	1910	1910	-
10 Trade credit and advances e	7274	7274	-	8170	8170	-	10079	10079	-	13994	13994	-
11 Other accounts payable	...	...	...	...	...	...	...	...	...	...	...	...
12 Other liabilities	13248	10496	2752	34431	9887	24544	27027	11918	15109	40330	15548	24782
Total Incurrence of Liabilities	151088	65350	85738	185786	63596	122190	179853	71211	108642	224174	101916	122258
Net Lending f	-7200	-26943	19743	12574	-14311	26885	21896	-3097	24993	22863	-6203	29066
Incurrence of Liabilities and Net Lending	143888	38407	105481	198360	49285	149075	201749	68114	133635	247037	95713	151324

	1984			1985			1986			1987		
	TOTAL	Non-Financial	Financial	TOTAL	Non-Financial	Financial	TOTAL	Non-Financial	Financial	TOTAL	Non-Financial	Financial
Acquisition of Financial Assets												
1 Gold and SDRs	486	-	486	313	-	313	330	-	330	-434	-	-434
2 Currency and transferable deposits	17995	16401	1594	163	-7785	7948	24828	14566	10262	15926	-8863	24789
3 Other deposits a	-2376	-7666	5290	-3815	-315	-3500	8916	-677	9593	21835	19343	2492
4 Bills and bonds, short term b	33576	-2912	36488	31100	17923	13177	-2460	-29986	27526	-15572	4345	-19917
5 Bonds, long term c	25920	1649	24271	37380	2729	34651	88617	62194	26423	33027	11648	21379
6 Corporate equity securities	25162	20094	5068	27791	23174	4617	34418	24273	10145	33059	17208	15851
7 Short term loans, n.e.c.	121168	41003	80165	116996	38610	78386	238243	53488	184755	218050	60299	157751
8 Long term loans, n.e.c.	...	...	...	...	...	...	...	...	...	...	...	...
9 Trade credits and advances	17225	17225	-	10554	10554	-	7788	7788	-	14693	14693	-
10 Other receivables	...	...	...	...	...	...	...	...	...	...	...	...
11 Other assets	44953	15514	29439	46397	13986	32411	77134	16598	60536	51120	-2229	53349
Total Acquisition of Financial Assets d	284109	101308	182801	266879	98876	168003	477814	148244	329570	371704	116444	255260
Incurrence of Liabilities												
1 Currency and transferable deposits	38119	-	38119	11748	-	11748	60457	-	60457	11626	-	11626
2 Other deposits a	-1793	4464	-6257	-1968	4218	-6186	7681	3432	4249	25835	-2120	27955
3 Bills and bonds, short term	...	...	...	...	...	...	...	...	...	...	...	...
4 Bonds, long term c	36590	4287	32303	52322	5481	46841	98621	14128	84493	68115	7911	60204
5 Corporate equity securities	23837	16025	7812	20703	13228	7475	33851	13216	20635	14395	17748	-3353
6 Short-term loans, n.e.c.	99072	63325	35747	89537	73955	15582	162570	118116	44454	190045	130948	59097
7 Long-term loans, n.e.c.	...	...	...	...	...	...	...	...	...	...	...	...
8 Net equity of households in life insurance and pension fund reserves	9433	-	9433	10741	-	10741	13312	-	13312	9823	-	9823
9 Proprietors' net additions to the accumulation of quasi-corporations	332	332	-	1948	1948	-	2454	2454	-	1957	1957	-
10 Trade credit and advances e	16609	16609	-	13725	13725	-	9473	9473	-	14543	14543	-
11 Other accounts payable	...	...	...	...	...	...	...	...	...	...	...	...
12 Other liabilities	49066	12648	36418	52337	6150	46187	89414	27727	61687	71937	15419	56518
Total Incurrence of Liabilities	271265	117690	153575	251093	118705	132388	477833	188546	289287	408276	186406	221870
Net Lending f	12844	-16382	29226	15786	-19829	35615	-19	-40302	40283	-36572	-69962	33390
Incurrence of Liabilities and Net Lending	284109	101308	182801	266879	98876	168003	477814	148244	329570	371704	116444	255260

	1988			1989			1990			1991		
	TOTAL	Non-Financial	Financial	TOTAL	Non-Financial	Financial	TOTAL	Non-Financial	Financial	TOTAL	Non-Financial	Financial
Acquisition of Financial Assets												
1 Gold and SDRs	759	-	759	-320	-	-320	-492	-	-492	690	-	690
2 Currency and transferable deposits	13037	5527	7510	32276	20766	11510	21082	27470	-6388	-23510	-3609	-19901
3 Other deposits a	1735	-1771	3506	35898	11905	23993	21867	12514	9353	3065	11122	-8057
4 Bills and bonds, short term b	10114	2270	7844	-17745	-4684	-13061	102316	41330	60986	157883	65044	92839
5 Bonds, long term c	31474	17622	13852	36217	-13934	50151	-19578	-6448	-13130	7409	-31449	38858
6 Corporate equity securities	59665	45384	14281	80069	43806	36263	95781	54118	41663	53862	14498	39364
7 Short term loans, n.e.c.	318824	46091	272733	406064	83053	323011	278400	-9574	287974	-24717	-42586	17869
8 Long term loans, n.e.c.	...	...	...	...	...	...	...	...	...	...	...	...
9 Trade credits and advances	21501	21501	-	24594	24594	-	32495	32495	-	-25256	-25256	-

3.24 Corporate and Quasi-Corporate Enterprise Capital Finance Account: Total and Sectors
(Continued)

Million Swedish kronor

	1988			1989			1990			1991		
	TOTAL	Non-Financial	Financial	TOTAL	Non-Financial	Financial	TOTAL	Non-Financial	Financial	TOTAL	Non-Financial	Financial
10 Other receivables	...	...	...	...	...	...	...	...	...	...	...	...
11 Other assets	182387	27264	155123	133819	50158	83661	266760	101535	165225	-66457	8679	-75136
Total Acquisition of Financial Assets d	639496	163888	475608	730872	215664	515208	798631	253440	545191	82969	-3557	86526
Incurrence of Liabilities												
1 Currency and transferable deposits	44955	-	44955	73310	-	73310	61905	-	61905	103827	-	103827
2 Other deposits a	1549	-1540	3089	37193	4744	32449	30253	-1197	31450	12644	-3261	15905
3 Bills and bonds, short term	...	...	...	...	...	...	...	...	...	...	...	...
4 Bonds, long term c	104939	3419	101520	116511	-4035	120546	93320	-5130	98450	72750	-7353	80103
5 Corporate equity securities	44600	15198	29402	32681	15823	16858	-2713	8261	-10974	11706	-4650	16356
6 Short-term loans, n.e.c.	249229	172827	76402	435901	315751	120150	341243	184166	157077	11706	-4650	16356
7 Long-term loans, n.e.c.	...	...	...	...	...	...	...	...	...	-64103	43822	-107925
8 Net equity of households in life insurance and pension fund reserves	14517	-	14517	23730	-	23730	22210	-	22210	19060	-	19060
9 Proprietors' net additions to the accumulation of quasi-corporations	-14188	-14188	-	722	722	-	76	76	-	700	700	-
10 Trade credit and advances e	23679	23679	-	23761	23761	-	29186	29186	-	-25256	-25256	-
11 Other accounts payable	...	...	...	...	...	...	...	...	...	...	...	...
12 Other liabilities	196498	38788	157710	93463	23628	69835	320032	192158	127874	-69793	25105	-94898
Total Incurrence of Liabilities	665778	238183	427595	837272	380394	456878	895512	407520	487992	61535	29107	32428
Net Lending f	-26282	-74295	48013	-106400	-164730	58330	-96881	-154080	57199	21434	-32664	54098
Incurrence of Liabilities and Net Lending	639496	163888	475608	730872	215664	515208	798631	253440	545191	82969	-3557	86526

a) Item 'Other deposits' refers to certificates and general public scheme.
b) 'Bills and bonds' refer to treasury bills and special treasury bills.
c) Item 'Bonds, long-term' includes both short-term and long-term bonds.
d) Item 'Total acquisition of financial assets' excludes net acquisition of SDRS except for 1982.

e) Item 'Trade credit advances' includes trade bills.
f) Net lending of the capital accumulation account and the capital finance account have not been reconciled and are different due to different statistical sources.

3.31 Household and Private Unincorporated Enterprise Production Account

Million Swedish kronor

	1980	1981	1982	1983	1984	1985	1986	1987	1988	1989	1990	1991
Gross Output												
1 Output for sale	...	...	...	...	...	...	...	...	...	...	...	...
2 Non-marketed output	...	...	...	...	...	...	...	...	...	...	...	...
Gross Output	...	...	...	...	...	...	...	...	...	...	...	...
Gross Input												
Intermediate consumption	...	...	...	...	...	...	...	...	...	...	...	...
Subtotal: Value Added	...	...	...	...	...	...	...	...	...	...	...	...
1 Indirect taxes net liability of unincorporated enterprises	...	...	...	...	...	...	...	...	...	...	...	...
2 Consumption of fixed capital	14798	16647	18240	20159	22289	23570	24912	26788	29784	33498	37566	41985
3 Compensation of employees	...	...	...	...	...	...	...	...	...	...	...	...
4 Net operating surplus	55501	56956	70083	77912	82592	89567	91526	85189	91794	94366	98389	101494
Gross Input	...	...	...	...	...	...	...	...	...	...	...	...

3.32 Household and Private Unincorporated Enterprise Income and Outlay Account

Million Swedish kronor

	1980	1981	1982	1983	1984	1985	1986	1987	1988	1989	1990	1991
Receipts												
1 Compensation of employees	338440	370353	391342	423525	463594	505417	553471	597974	652924	731131	829755	882084
A Wages and salaries	247026	267451	283171	305710	336631	368347	403237	438704	475283	530727	598741	631008
B Employers' contributions for social security	71602	82584	83087	91618	99264	103302	119254	131756	147920	168510	196905	211603
C Employers' contributions for private pension & welfare plans	19812	20318	25084	26197	27699	33768	30980	27514	29721	31894	34109	39473
2 Operating surplus of private unincorporated enterprises	55501	56956	70083	77912	82592	89567	91526	85189	91794	94366	98389	101494
3 Property and entrepreneurial income	27267	33364	34417	37967	43978	52587	55161	57092	63559	72295	82229	83900
A Withdrawals from private quasi-corporations	1437	1515	1943	2868	4629	4900	5581	5162	5461	6292	6657	6890
B Interest	22723	29604	30129	30446	35416	42631	44940	44272	50358	57106	65402	66217
C Dividends	2623	1719	1759	3806	3389	4466	3687	6904	6564	7552	8684	9100
D Net land rent and royalties	484	526	586	847	544	590	953	754	1176	1345	1486	1693

Sweden

3.32 Household and Private Unincorporated Enterprise Income and Outlay Account
(Continued)

Million Swedish kronor

	1980	1981	1982	1983	1984	1985	1986	1987	1988	1989	1990	1991
3 Current transfers	106748	121086	133374	150315	161962	183356	202795	223983	252791	278157	307987	351162
A Casualty insurance claims	2469	2818	3241	3517	4319	6405	7288	8436	9206	10442	11603	12412
B Social security benefits	73396	84729	92730	104640	112335	125050	139547	153639	176140	194247	214478	240972
C Social assistance grants	20121	21421	23623	26537	28360	33918	35918	40072	43455	47974	53729	67442
D Unfunded employee pension and welfare benefits	9377	10383	11846	13141	14502	15407	17305	18086	19279	20738	22350	25207
E Transfers from general government	1029	1161	1313	1405	1577	1490	2008	2242	2633	3162	3882	3347
F Transfers from the rest of the world	356	574	621	1075	869	1086	729	1508	2078	1594	1945	1782
G Other transfers n.e.c.	...	...	...	...	...	...	...	...	...	...	...	...
Statistical discrepancy	2479	9856	8099	5855	8333	9373	14146	27928	27305	40693	38829	43225
Total Current Receipts [a]	530435	591615	637315	695574	760459	840300	917099	992166	1088373	1216642	1357189	1461865

Disbursements

	1980	1981	1982	1983	1984	1985	1986	1987	1988	1989	1990	1991
1 Final consumption expenditures	274745	307050	342013	371866	407295	447931	492753	542541	589270	638772	698827	777285
A Market purchases	240874	268438	297357	322040	352939	388888	428536	472892	513075	555411	605810	660193
B Gross rents of owner-occupied housing	33871	38612	44656	49826	54356	59043	64217	69649	76195	83361	93017	117092
C Consumption from own-account production	...	...	...	...	...	...	...	...	...	...	...	...
2 Property income	32900	41531	43004	42996	48640	57227	61228	67183	81635	96573	111290	110668
A Interest	32230	40777	42170	42116	47655	56132	60030	65818	80095	94981	109322	108284
B Net land rent and royalties	670	754	834	880	985	1095	1198	1365	1540	1592	1968	2384
3 Direct taxes and other current transfers n.e.c. to government	184165	204135	218360	241316	263295	281105	317734	358906	400766	457813	500032	492977
A Social security contributions	74647	85838	86634	95655	103781	108206	124456	137284	153799	176732	205867	218901
B Direct taxes	107614	115701	127773	141798	155060	167951	189557	216383	241570	276720	291053	271316
Income taxes	...	...	...	...	...	...	...	...	...	...	...	...
Other	...	...	...	...	...	...	...	...	...	...	...	...
C Fees, fines and penalties	1904	2596	3953	3863	4454	4948	3721	5239	5397	4361	3112	2760
4 Other current transfers	23967	25208	30420	32662	34905	44285	42447	40555	44574	49593	52976	58885
A Net casualty insurance premiums	2527	2803	2992	3259	3861	6079	7278	8388	9706	11172	12924	14888
B Transfers to private non-profit institutions serving households	...	...	...	...	...	...	...	...	...	...	...	...
C Transfers to the rest of the world	1628	2087	2344	3206	3345	4438	4189	4653	5147	6527	5943	4524
D Other current transfers, except imputed	...	...	...	...	...	...	...	...	...	...	...	...
E Imputed employee pension and welfare contributions	19812	20318	25084	26197	27699	33768	30980	27514	29721	31894	34109	39473
Net saving	14658	13691	3518	6734	6324	9752	2937	-17019	-27872	-26109	-5936	22050
Total Current Disbursements and Net Saving [a]	530435	591615	637315	695574	760459	840300	917099	992166	1088373	1216642	1357189	1461865

a) Private non-profit institutions serving households are included in household and private unincorporated enterprises.

3.33 Household and Private Unincorporated Enterprise Capital Accumulation Account

Million Swedish kronor

	1980	1981	1982	1983	1984	1985	1986	1987	1988	1989	1990	1991
					Finance of Gross Accumulation							
1 Gross saving	29456	30338	21758	26893	28613	33322	27849	9769	1912	7389	31630	64035
A Consumption of fixed capital	14798	16647	18240	20159	22289	23570	24912	26788	29784	33498	37566	41985
Owner-occupied housing	9075	10169	11156	12147	13519	14453	15046	16416	18634	21522	24620	28054
Other unincorported enterprises	5723	6478	7084	8012	8770	9117	9866	10372	11150	11976	12946	13931
B Net saving	14658	13691	3518	6734	6324	9752	2937	-17019	-27872	-26109	-5936	22050
2 Capital transfers	667	593	643	836	886	1055	1142	1229	1052	8001	809	4634
A From resident sectors	667	593	643	836	886	1055	1142	1229	1052	8001	809	4634
B From the rest of the world	...	...	...	...	...	...	...	...	...	...	...	...
Total Finance of Gross Accumulation [a]	30123	30931	22401	27729	29499	34377	28991	10998	2964	15390	32439	68669
					Gross Accumulation							
1 Gross Capital Formation	22901	21267	20161	21115	22503	23364	22711	25182	30252	34464	37560	36696

3.33 Household and Private Unincorporated Enterprise Capital Accumulation Account
(Continued)

Million Swedish kronor

	1980	1981	1982	1983	1984	1985	1986	1987	1988	1989	1990	1991
A Increase in stocks	...	...	...	...	...	...	...	...	...	...	...	...
B Gross fixed capital formation	22901	21267	20161	21115	22503	23364	22711	25182	30252	34464	37560	36696
Owner-occupied housing b	16628	14442	12390	11757	12637	10778	10498	11453	15267	18683	23244	24497
Other gross fixed capital formation	6273	6825	7771	9358	9866	12586	12213	13729	14985	15781	14316	12199
2 Purchases of land, net	2878	2638	2057	1890	1694	1516	1360	1685	2425	3062	3978	3659
3 Purchases of intangibles, net	...	...	...	...	...	...	...	...	...	...	...	...
4 Capital transfers	1358	1430	1545	1672	1846	1997	1917	8213	2036	2477	2669	2734
A To resident sectors	1358	1430	1545	1672	1846	1997	1917	8213	2036	2477	2669	2734
B To the rest of the world	...	...	...	...	...	...	...	...	...	...	...	...
Net lending c	2986	5596	-1362	3052	3456	7500	3003	-24082	-31749	-24613	-11768	25580
Total Gross Accumulation a	30123	30931	22401	27729	29499	34377	28991	10998	2964	15390	32439	68669

a) Private non-profit institutions serving households are included in household and private unincorporated enterprises.
b) One-or two-dwelling houses including country lodges.
c) Net lending of the capital accumulation account and the capital finance account have not been reconciled and are different due to different statistical sources.

3.34 Household and Private Unincorporated Enterprise Capital Finance Account

Million Swedish kronor

	1980	1981	1982	1983	1984	1985	1986	1987	1988	1989	1990	1991
Acquisition of Financial Assets												
1 Gold	...	...	...	...	...	...	...	...	...	...	...	...
2 Currency and transferable deposits	22848	25530	19383	16029	16837	14059	31996	14755	27626	32401	24638	37114
3 Other deposits a	...	...	...	...	6517	10678	15813	9679	14411	9636	-8100	7073
4 Bills and bonds, short term	38	-9	-14	-17	4500	2100	-600	-1200	-800	...	-	-
A Corporate and quasi-corporate	...	...	...	...	...	...	...	...	...	...	...	...
B Government	38	-9	-14	-17	4500	2100	-600	-1200	-800	...	...	...
C Rest of the world	...	...	...	...	...	...	...	...	...	...	...	...
5 Bonds, long term b	9512	2272	4620	8406	8334	9645	16076	10314	1440	-11227	-3579	-9420
6 Corporate equity securities	-1708	-2494	-267	-128	-730	-8448	6467	-14830	5889	3901	-35385	-12213
7 Short term loans, n.e.c.	3389	1758	3874	412	4078	64	5276	1299	3068	-1604	12096	-6845
8 Long term loans, n.e.c.	...	...	...	...	...	...	...	...	...	...	...	...
9 Trade credit and advances c	52	101	107	114	121	129	166	147	-	-	176	...
10 Net equity of households in life insurance and pension fund reserves	3182	4140	4914	9071	9433	10741	13312	9823	14517	23730	22210	19060
11 Proprietors' net additions to the accumulation of quasi-corporations	...	...	...	...	...	...	...	...	...	...	...	...
12 Other c	-2966	4583	6130	6145	-4395	4607	3876	21040	17873	-10523	24334	-11982
Total Acquisition of Financial Assets	34347	35881	38747	40032	44695	43575	92382	51027	84024	46314	36390	22787
Incurrence of Liabilities												
1 Short term loans, n.e.c.	31252	30096	39861	36781	40955	35801	88816	73941	114532	70644	47623	-2770
2 Long term loans, n.e.c.	...	...	...	...	...	...	...	...	...	...	...	...
3 Trade credit and advances	90	219	232	245	259	274	289	306	323	342	361	-
4 Other accounts payable	...	...	...	...	...	...	...	...	...	...	...	...
5 Other liabilities	...	...	...	...	...	...	...	...	...	...	...	...
Total Incurrence of Liabilities	31342	30315	40093	37026	41214	36075	89105	74247	114855	70986	47984	-2770
Net Lending d	3005	5566	-1346	3006	3481	7500	3277	-23220	-30831	-24672	-11594	25557
Incurrence of Liabilities and Net Lending	34347	35881	38747	40032	44695	43575	92382	51027	84024	46314	36390	22787

a) Item 'Other deposits' refers to certificates and general public scheme.
b) Item 'Bonds, long-term' includes both short-term and long-term bonds.
c) Acquisition are reported net of incurrence of liabilities.

d) Net lending of the capital accumulation account and the capital finance account have not been reconciled and are different due to different statistical sources.

Sweden

3.41 Private Non-Profit Institutions Serving Households: Production Account

Million Swedish kronor

	1980	1981	1982	1983	1984	1985	1986	1987	1988	1989	1990	1991
					Gross Output							
1 Sales	...	...	...	...	...	...	...	...	...	...	...	...
2 Non-marketed output	...	...	...	...	...	...	...	...	...	...	...	...
Gross Output	9675	10832	11869	13060	14215	15436	16914	18604	20403	22951	26652	29304
					Gross Input							
Intermediate consumption	2799	3004	3388	3742	4324	4807	5241	5734	6165	6769	7912	8813
Subtotal: Value Added	6876	7828	8481	9318	9891	10629	11673	12870	14238	16182	18740	20491
1 Indirect taxes, net	132	170	184	376	365	394	428	520	420	530	741	531
2 Consumption of fixed capital	...	...	...	...	...	...	...	...	...	...	...	...
3 Compensation of employees	6744	7659	8297	8942	9526	10235	11245	12350	13818	15652	17999	19960
4 Net operating surplus	...	...	...	...	...	...	...	...	...	...	...	...
Gross Input	9675	10833	11869	13060	14215	15436	16914	18604	20403	22951	26652	29304

3.51 External Transactions: Current Account: Detail

Million Swedish kronor

	1980	1981	1982	1983	1984	1985	1986	1987	1988	1989	1990	1991
					Payments to the Rest of the World							
1 Imports of goods and services	166547	175299	208234	238142	260699	291186	281223	313638	341354	387735	403863	381669
A Imports of merchandise c.i.f.	143281	148041	176671	201663	220361	246121	232949	257813	279341	315162	322360	300042
B Other	23266	27258	31563	36479	40338	45065	48274	55825	62013	72573	81503	81627
2 Factor income to the rest of the world	11947	20388	26996	30621	35523	40635	38207	38408	42391	58878	85793	97344
A Compensation of employees	30	71	6	730	354	415	914	1002	1152	1381	1468	2044
B Property and entrepreneurial income	11917	20317	26990	29891	35169	40220	37293	37406	41239	57497	84325	95300
By general government a	2981	6717	9168	11542	13295	14857	11983	12283	9308	8446	9552	11413
By corporate and quasi-cororate enterprises	...	...	...	...	...	...	...	...	...	...	...	...
By other	...	...	...	...	...	...	...	...	...	...	...	...
3 Current transfers to the rest of the world	6903	11986	14943	16085	16911	20727	21943	22776	24239	27278	30072	31515
A Indirect taxes by general government to supranational organizations	...	...	...	...	...	...	...	...	...	...	...	...
B Other current transfers	6903	11986	14943	16085	16911	20727	21943	22776	24239	27278	30072	31515
By general government	4121	4311	4765	4916	5101	5819	6106	6432	7019	8624	9709	10126
By other resident sectors	2782	7675	10178	11169	11810	14908	15837	16344	17220	18654	20363	21389
4 Surplus of the nation on current transactions	-18904	-15466	-22508	-8150	1850	-14650	419	-6909	-12375	-32733	-49219	-28683
Payments to the Rest of the World, and Surplus of the Nation on Current Transfers	166493	192207	227665	276698	314983	337898	341792	367913	395609	441158	470509	481845
					Receipts From The Rest of the World							
1 Exports of goods and services	156469	174107	204756	253260	289819	306595	311091	332298	359690	394470	406831	404561
A Exports of merchandise f.o.b.	131026	144683	168245	210893	242746	260146	263844	280153	303370	330803	336790	330143
B Other	25443	29424	36511	42367	47073	46449	47247	52145	56320	63667	70041	74418
2 Factor income from the rest of the world	7924	11740	13710	14033	15717	19543	18190	21942	21310	31054	47448	58051
A Compensation of employees	283	433	1	218	226	262	152	288	310	358	487	773
B Property and entrepreneurial income	7641	11307	13709	13815	15491	19281	18038	21654	21000	30696	46961	57278
By general government a ...	1626	3091	3729	3350	3646	4493	5334	4767	2971	4835	6335	12100
By corporate and quasi-corporate enterprises	...	...	...	...	...	...	...	...	...	...	...	...
By other	...	...	...	...	...	...	...	...	...	...	...	...
3 Current transfers from the rest of the world	2100	6360	9199	9405	9447	11760	12511	13673	14609	15634	16230	19233
A Subsidies to general government from supranational organizations	...	...	...	...	...	...	...	...	...	...	...	...
B Other current transfers	2100	6360	9199	9405	9447	11760	12511	13673	14609	15634	16230	19233
To general government	...	...	...	...	...	...	...	...	...	...	...	...
To other resident sectors	2100	6360	9199	9405	9447	11760	12511	13673	14609	15634	16230	19233
Receipts from the Rest of the World on Current Transfers	166493	192207	227665	276698	314983	337898	341792	367913	395609	441158	470509	481845

a) Only central government data are included in the general government estimates.

3.52 External Transactions: Capital Accumulation Account

Million Swedish kronor

	1980	1981	1982	1983	1984	1985	1986	1987	1988	1989	1990	1991
Finance of Gross Accumulation												
1 Surplus of the nation on current transactions	-18904	-15466	-22508	-8150	1850	-14650	419	-6909	-12375	-32733	-49219	-28683
2 Capital transfers from the rest of the world	...	...	...	...	...	...	...	...	...	...	...	...
Total Finance of Gross Accumulation	-18904	-15466	-22508	-8150	1850	-14650	419	-6909	-12375	-32733	-49219	-28683
Gross Accumulation												
1 Capital transfers to the rest of the world	...	...	...	...	...	...	...	...	...	...	...	...
2 Purchases of intangible assets, n.e.c., net, from the rest of the world	...	...	...	...	...	...	...	...	...	...	...	...
Net lending to the rest of the world	-18904	-15466	-22508	-8150	1850	-14650	419	-6909	-12375	-32733	-49219	-28683
Total Gross Accumulation	-18904	-15466	-22508	-8150	1850	-14650	419	-6909	-12375	-32733	-49219	-28683

3.53 External Transactions: Capital Finance Account

Million Swedish kronor

	1980	1981	1982	1983	1984	1985	1986	1987	1988	1989	1990	1991
Acquisitions of Foreign Financial Assets												
1 Gold and SDR's	-253	8	53	-920	486	313	330	-434	759	-320	-492	690
2 Currency and transferable deposits	9252	8289	5363	5056	-56	6023	4036	21888	12961	10764	-12265	-17686
3 Other deposits a	...	...	...	...	...	...	...	...	...	...	...	2641
4 Bills and bonds, short term b	-992	-2410	-1060	4325	-56	11698	1143	5012	3124	8687	45478	-2750
5 Bonds, long term c	378	457	679	1069	531	671	3305	2034	-2182	6966	3229	6770
6 Corporate equity securities	1836	3467	3455	5470	5201	4880	11661	4558	21426	59039	78424	33742
7 Short-term loans, n.e.c.	3024	5813	12004	12222	7162	3169	8263	16099	44781	45095	62631	14730
8 Long-term loans	...	...	...	...	...	...	...	...	...	...	...	...
9 Prproprietors' net additions to accumulation of quasi-corporate, non-resident enterprises	...	...	...	...	...	...	...	...	...	...	...	...
10 Trade credit and advances	373	3513	2474	3129	1607	401	-100	2529	-992	2082	-322	-67
11 Other	...	...	...	...	...	...	...	...	...	...	...	...
Total Acquisitions of Foreign Financial Assets d	13618	19137	22968	30351	14875	27155	28638	51686	79877	132313	176683	38070
Incurrence of Foreign Liabilities												
1 Currency and transferable deposits	985	2348	61	4776	2047	5476	7128	9405	17258	18352	2728	-18368
2 Other deposits a	892	69	110	-76	559	550	-366	3615	1423	312	7561	21380
3 Bills and bonds, short term b	-	-	-	-	-	-	-	-	-	-	-	-
4 Bonds, long term c	7044	6405	13774	23505	36373	18796	988	2313	14216	33897	53812	60155
5 Corporate equity securities	291	401	1348	5921	2188	5233	2348	-3271	-2765	-1655	890	-1209
6 Short-term loans, n.e.c.	29474	21623	27120	8540	-21072	5623	24167	50603	64062	142680	174703	-32789
7 Long-term loans	...	...	...	...	...	...	...	...	...	...	...	...
8 Non-resident proprietors' net additions to accumulation of resident quasi-corporate enterprises	...	...	...	...	...	...	...	...	...	...	...	...
9 Trade credit and advances	-1759	1959	350	-787	1129	3717	1708	2538	1353	1435	-3446	-722
10 Other	...	...	...	...	...	...	...	...	...	...	...	...
Total Incurrence of Liabilities d	36927	32805	42763	41879	21224	39395	35973	65203	95547	195021	236248	28447
Statistical discrepancy	-4405	1798	2713	-3378	-8199	2410	-7754	-6608	-3295	-29975	-10346	38306
Net Lending d	-18904	-15466	-22508	-8150	1850	-14650	419	-6909	-12375	-32733	-49219	-28683
Total Incurrence of Liabilities and Net Lending d	13618	19137	22968	30351	14875	27155	28638	51686	79877	132313	176683	38070

a) Item 'Other deposits' refers to certificates and general public scheme.
b) 'Bills and bonds' refer to treasury bills and special treasury bills.
c) Item 'Bonds, long-term' includes both short-term and long-term bonds.
d) Beginning 1970 estimates of acquisition and incurrence of foreign liabilities are reported according to the financial accounts calculated by the Central Bureau of Statistics. Prior to 1970 estimates are based on the capital accounts of the balance of payment calculated by the Central Bank.

4.1 Derivation of Value Added by Kind of Activity, in Current Prices

Million Swedish kronor

	1980			1981			1982			1983		
	Gross Output	Intermediate Consumption	Value Added	Gross Output	Intermediate Consumption	Value Added	Gross Output	Intermediate Consumption	Value Added	Gross Output	Intermediate Consumption	Value Added
All Producers												
1 Agriculture, hunting, forestry and fishing	29620	11886	17734	33216	13471	19745	37111	15389	21722	41307	16756	24551
A Agriculture and hunting	19180	9987	9193	21394	11318	10076	24361	12703	11658	26076	14003	12073
B Forestry and logging	9843	1672	8171	11213	1913	9300	12065	2442	9623	14409	2466	11943
C Fishing	597	227	370	609	240	369	685	244	441	822	287	535

Sweden

Million Swedish kronor

	1980			1981			1982			1983		
	Gross Output	Intermediate Consumption	Value Added	Gross Output	Intermediate Consumption	Value Added	Gross Output	Intermediate Consumption	Value Added	Gross Output	Intermediate Consumption	Value Added
2 Mining and quarrying	4599	2212	2387	4317	2030	2287	4531	2118	2413	5438	2419	3019
A Coal mining	...	...	...	...	...	...	...	...	...	...	...	...
B Crude petroleum and natural gas production	...	...	...	...	...	...	...	...	...	...	...	...
C Metal ore mining	3325	1652	1673	2996	1492	1504	3245	1536	1709	4113	1782	2331
D Other mining	1274	560	714	1321	538	783	1286	582	704	1325	637	688
3 Manufacturing	330689	219225	111464	351141	234834	116307	390240	260616	129624	449469	300945	148524
A Manufacture of food, beverages and tobacco	43788	33004	10784	48752	36619	12133	56061	42533	13528	61201	46415	14786
B Textile, wearing apparel and leather industries	9576	5460	4116	9336	5325	4011	9604	5701	3903	10640	6451	4189
C Manufacture of wood and wood products, including furniture	26817	17290	9527	25389	16517	8872	26927	17668	9259	31664	20498	11166
D Manufacture of paper and paper products, printing and publishing	48241	32098	16143	52487	36036	16451	56602	37338	19264	66382	42756	23626
E Manufacture of chemicals and chemical petroleum, coal, rubber and plastic products	48264	37060	11204	50979	40670	10309	57830	45346	12484	70499	56017	14482
F Manufacture of non-metallic mineral products, except products of petroleum and coal	8565	4605	3960	8668	4740	3928	9628	5141	4487	10408	5521	4887
G Basic metal industries	26499	19943	6556	25435	19719	5716	28849	21917	6932	33931	26130	7801
H Manufacture of fabricated metal products, machinery and equipment	116348	68016	48332	127309	73367	53942	141612	82943	58669	161408	94833	66575
I Other manufacturing industries	2591	1749	842	2786	1841	945	3127	2029	1098	3336	2324	1012
4 Electricity, gas and water	22582	8908	13674	25812	10585	15227	27965	12694	15271	30786	13000	17786
A Electricity, gas and steam	19153	7647	11506	21977	9265	12712	23558	11192	12366	25941	11362	14579
B Water works and supply	3429	1261	2168	3835	1320	2515	4407	1502	2905	4845	1638	3207
5 Construction	71512	36282	35230	74915	37334	37581	82522	41325	41197	86820	43887	42933
6 Wholesale and retail trade, restaurants and hotels	89335	33809	55526	95982	37364	58618	107430	42466	64964	122064	47247	74817
A Wholesale and retail trade	77437	27368	50069	82668	30161	52507	92345	34403	57942	105153	38367	66786
B Restaurants and hotels	11898	6441	5457	13314	7203	6111	15085	8063	7022	16911	8880	8031
7 Transport, storage and communication	64046	31468	32578	71757	36283	35474	79614	42022	37592	87620	47500	40120
A Transport and storage	49209	26740	22469	54765	30920	23845	60961	35534	25427	66698	39957	26741
B Communication	14837	4728	10109	16992	5363	11629	18653	6488	12165	20922	7543	13379
8 Finance, insurance, real estate and business services [a]	112193	37395	74798	130031	42223	87808	148811	47991	100820	168284	54213	114071
A Financial institutions	16486	4033	12453	21317	4968	16349	24085	5776	18309	28929	7866	21063
B Insurance	5864	1250	4614	6100	1524	4576	5896	1776	4120	5995	1837	4158
C Real estate and business services	89843	32112	57731	102614	35731	66883	118830	40439	78391	133360	44510	88850
Real estate, except dwellings [b]	33871	7283	26588	38612	7892	30720	44656	8343	36313	49826	9277	40549
Dwellings [c]	27513	11042	16471	31707	12493	19214	36934	14295	22639	41437	16043	25394
9 Community, social and personal services	26137	10014	16123	29793	10968	18825	33030	12177	20853	36358	13529	22829
A Sanitary and similar services	4613	1775	2838	5332	2115	3217	5659	2163	3496	6001	2287	3714
B Social and related community services	4481	1424	3057	5239	1621	3618	5947	1743	4204	6668	2033	4635
C Recreational and cultural services	5982	2174	3808	7210	2255	4955	7746	2658	5088	8453	2953	5500
D Personal and household services	11061	4641	6420	12012	4977	7035	13678	5613	8065	15236	6256	8980
Total, Industries	750713	391199	359514	816964	425092	391872	911254	476798	434456	1028146	539496	488650
Producers of Government Services	...	...	117629	...	...	129071	...	...	140461	...	...	155081
Other Producers	...	...	6876	...	...	7829	...	...	8481	...	...	9318

4.1 Derivation of Value Added by Kind of Activity, in Current Prices
(Continued)

Million Swedish kronor

	1980			1981			1982			1983		
	Gross Output	Intermediate Consumption	Value Added	Gross Output	Intermediate Consumption	Value Added	Gross Output	Intermediate Consumption	Value Added	Gross Output	Intermediate Consumption	Value Added
Total d	...	...	484019	...	...	528772	...	...	583398	...	...	653049
Less: Imputed bank service charge a	...	...	13825	...	...	17477	...	...	19680	...	...	23264
Import duties	...	...	1759	...	...	1909	...	...	2143	...	...	2180
Value added tax e	...	...	54804	...	...	63295	...	...	69507	...	...	79248
Other adjustments	...	...	1498	...	...	2414	...	...	-1686	...	...	-1361
Total	...	...	528255	...	...	578913	...	...	633682	...	...	709852
Memorandum Item: Mineral fuels and power f	40316	27457	12859	44456	30932	13524	49437	35379	14058	57820	40535	17285

	1984			1985			1986			1987		
	Gross Output	Intermediate Consumption	Value Added	Gross Output	Intermediate Consumption	Value Added	Gross Output	Intermediate Consumption	Value Added	Gross Output	Intermediate Consumption	Value Added
All Producers												
1 Agriculture, hunting, forestry and fishing	45270	18204	27066	47014	18664	28350	48547	18702	29845	49529	19056	30473
A Agriculture and hunting	28268	15205	13063	28828	15340	13488	29297	15450	13847	29130	15641	13489
B Forestry and logging	16119	2690	13429	17279	2984	14295	18337	2966	15371	19447	3140	16307
C Fishing	883	309	574	907	340	567	913	286	627	952	275	677
2 Mining and quarrying	6447	2604	3843	7198	2858	4340	6580	2818	3762	6420	2904	3516
A Coal mining	...	...	...	...	...	...	...	...	...	...	...	...
B Crude petroleum and natural gas production	...	...	...	...	...	...	...	...	...	...	...	...
C Metal ore mining	4965	1920	3045	5694	2153	3541	5067	2098	2969	4867	2207	2660
D Other mining	1482	684	798	1504	705	799	1513	720	793	1553	697	856
3 Manufacturing	509693	338354	171339	545296	358471	186825	564381	357347	207034	603586	382957	220629
A Manufacture of food, beverages and tobacco	69079	52639	16440	74248	54858	19390	77710	56064	21646	80225	56522	23703
B Textile, wearing apparel and leather industries	11937	7054	4883	12866	7447	5419	13274	7346	5928	13973	7584	6389
C Manufacture of wood and wood products, including furniture	35950	23032	12918	35811	23520	12291	38042	25268	12774	41828	26975	14853
D Manufacture of paper and paper products, printing and publishing	78011	50697	27314	80973	54029	26944	86857	57205	29652	97473	63798	33675
E Manufacture of chemicals and chemical petroleum, coal, rubber and plastic products	76571	60061	16510	80426	61321	19105	71640	45376	26264	75436	50400	25036
F Manufacture of non-metallic mineral products, except products of petroleum and coal	11188	6018	5170	11909	6369	5540	12603	6271	6332	14074	7050	7024
G Basic metal industries	38605	29599	9006	40534	31647	8887	39312	29807	9505	40419	30635	9784
H Manufacture of fabricated metal products, machinery and equipment	184527	106743	77784	204314	116829	87485	220399	127563	92836	235382	137445	97937
I Other manufacturing industries	3825	2511	1314	4215	2451	1764	4544	2447	2097	4776	2548	2228
4 Electricity, gas and water	34245	13297	20948	39313	16676	22637	41251	14484	26767	44043	15785	28258
A Electricity, gas and steam	29079	11524	17555	33894	14560	19334	35436	12312	23124	37749	13383	24366
B Water works and supply	5166	1773	3393	5419	2116	3303	5815	2172	3643	6294	2402	3892
5 Construction	95764	48340	47424	102074	51307	50767	109444	54850	54594	121020	60185	60835
6 Wholesale and retail trade, restaurants and hotels	136615	50944	85671	151315	57367	93948	162593	61976	100617	179236	69463	109773
A Wholesale and retail trade	117272	41129	76143	129642	46510	83132	138916	50535	88381	152001	56358	95643
B Restaurants and hotels	19343	9815	9528	21673	10857	10816	23677	11441	12236	27235	13105	14130
7 Transport, storage and communication	96634	53928	42706	106096	59381	46715	113459	61956	51503	124572	66710	57862
A Transport and storage	72809	44735	28074	79310	47996	31314	83623	49079	34544	91762	52835	38927
B Communication	23825	9193	14632	26786	11385	15401	29836	12877	16959	32810	13875	18935
8 Finance, insurance, real estate and business services a ..	187758	60355	127403	205879	67695	138184	238766	77646	161120	266988	89526	177462
A Financial institutions	35327	9867	25460	39179	10783	28396	51721	13440	38281	57987	16560	41427
B Insurance	5677	2147	3530	5687	2245	3442	7255	2803	4452	8128	3046	5082
C Real estate and business services	146754	48341	98413	161013	54667	106346	179790	61403	118387	200873	69920	130953
Real estate, except dwellings b	54359	9966	44393	59043	10896	48147	64217	12542	51675	69649	14181	55468

Sweden

Million Swedish kronor

	1984			1985			1986			1987		
	Gross Output	Intermediate Consumption	Value Added	Gross Output	Intermediate Consumption	Value Added	Gross Output	Intermediate Consumption	Value Added	Gross Output	Intermediate Consumption	Value Added
Dwellings c	45719	18059	27660	50462	20332	30130	56092	22083	34009	62077	24517	37560
9 Community, social and personal services	39653	14549	25104	44032	16484	27548	48957	18021	30936	54476	20638	33838
A Sanitary and similar services	6528	2479	4049	7276	2910	4366	7824	2963	4861	8763	3322	5441
B Social and related community services	7152	2106	5046	8186	2623	5563	8966	2864	6102	10376	3280	7096
C Recreational and cultural services	9336	3226	6110	10368	3631	6737	11741	4101	7640	13041	4730	8311
D Personal and household services	16637	6738	9899	18202	7320	10882	20426	8093	12333	22296	9306	12990
Total, Industries	1152079	600575	551504	1248217	648903	599314	1333978	667800	666178	1449870	727224	722646
Producers of Government Services	...	...	167680	...	...	178967	...	...	194359	...	...	203286
Other Producers	...	...	9891	...	...	10629	...	...	11673	...	...	12870
Total d	...	...	729075	...	...	788910	...	...	872210	...	...	938802
Less: Imputed bank service charge a	...	...	26966	...	...	31079	...	...	39282	...	...	43686
Import duties	...	...	2508	...	...	2724	...	...	3038	...	...	4057
Value added tax e	...	...	90129	...	...	103708	...	...	112533	...	...	124723
Other adjustments	...	...	-448	...	...	1525	...	...	-2916	...	...	-4349
Total	...	...	794298	...	...	865788	...	...	945583	...	...	1019547
Memorandum Item: Mineral fuels and power f	61847	41697	20150	67731	45153	22578	59351	28593	30758	59584	30804	28780

	1988			1989			1990			1991		
	Gross Output	Intermediate Consumption	Value Added	Gross Output	Intermediate Consumption	Value Added	Gross Output	Intermediate Consumption	Value Added	Gross Output	Intermediate Consumption	Value Added
All Producers												
1 Agriculture, hunting, forestry and fishing	51355	19882	31473	56612	21694	34918	...	...	34637	...	...	30774
A Agriculture and hunting	30573	16263	14310	33821	17266	16555	...	...	15804	...	...	13443
B Forestry and logging	19731	3300	16431	21767	4065	17702	...	...	18041	...	...	16520
C Fishing	1051	319	732	1024	363	661	...	...	792	...	...	811
2 Mining and quarrying	7148	3144	4004	8512	3564	4948	...	...	5244	...	...	4666
A Coal mining	...	...	...	...	...	...	...	...	...	...	...	...
B Crude petroleum and natural gas production	...	...	...	...	...	...	...	...	...	...	...	...
C Metal ore mining	5468	2388	3080	6371	2539	3832	...	...	3913	...	...	3242
D Other mining	1680	756	924	2141	1025	1116	...	...	1331	...	...	1424
3 Manufacturing	655948	419731	236217	724327	465536	258791	...	...	266071	...	...	259135
A Manufacture of food, beverages and tobacco	85903	61473	24430	94213	66108	28105	...	...	31895	...	...	30882
B Textile, wearing apparel and leather industries	14073	7516	6557	14046	7446	6600	...	...	6596	...	...	6154
C Manufacture of wood and wood products, including furniture	46403	29950	16453	53184	33690	19494	...	...	21333	...	...	19246
D Manufacture of paper and paper products, printing and publishing	106905	68922	37983	115781	74608	41173	...	...	39296	...	...	39633
E Manufacture of chemicals and chemical petroleum, coal, rubber and plastic products	78556	51499	27057	85588	57544	28044	...	...	28901	...	...	29384
F Manufacture of non-metallic mineral products, except products of petroleum and coal	15393	7840	7553	17719	9100	8619	...	...	9069	...	...	8741
G Basic metal industries	48089	37841	10248	56222	44765	11457	...	...	12162	...	...	10119
H Manufacture of fabricated metal products, machinery and equipment	255266	151660	103606	282094	169194	112900	...	...	114208	...	...	112211
I Other manufacturing industries	5360	3030	2330	5480	3081	2399	...	...	2611	...	...	2765
4 Electricity, gas and water	45898	15848	30050	49507	17424	32083	...	...	34342	...	...	37953
A Electricity, gas and steam	38887	13176	25711	41617	13986	27631	...	...	29519	...	...	32331
B Water works and supply	7011	2672	4339	7890	3438	4452	...	...	4823	...	...	5622
5 Construction	135678	67286	68392	162388	80001	82387	...	...	92774	...	...	96517
6 Wholesale and retail trade, restaurants and hotels	196861	76829	120032	215735	86768	128967	...	...	130402	...	...	136028
A Wholesale and retail trade	166494	62286	104208	180813	70110	110703	...	...	112323	...	...	117934
B Restaurants and hotels	30367	14543	15824	34922	16658	18264	...	...	18079	...	...	18094
7 Transport, storage and communication	140431	76111	64320	157697	86817	70880	...	...	78645	...	...	81941

4.1 Derivation of Value Added by Kind of Activity, in Current Prices
(Continued)

Million Swedish kronor

	1988			1989			1990			1991		
	Gross Output	Intermediate Consumption	Value Added	Gross Output	Intermediate Consumption	Value Added	Gross Output	Intermediate Consumption	Value Added	Gross Output	Intermediate Consumption	Value Added
A Transport and storage	103263	59719	43544	115693	68621	47072	...	...	51117	...	...	53042
B Communication	37168	16392	20776	42004	18196	23808	...	...	27528	...	...	28899
8 Finance, insurance, real estate and business services a	304942	106438	198504	341233	121897	219336	...	...	248218	...	...	287475
A Financial institutions	65519	19429	46090	71912	21978	49934	...	...	58529	...	...	57061
B Insurance	10320	3526	6794	11334	4057	7277	...	...	8240	...	...	8806
C Real estate and business services	229103	83483	145620	257987	95862	162125	...	...	181449	...	...	221608
Real estate, except dwellings b	76195	15845	60350	83139	17774	65365	...	...	72440	...	...	93929
Dwellings c	69018	27862	41156	76667	31304	45363	...	...	50517	...	...	65635
9 Community, social and personal services	60583	22950	37633	67491	24862	42629	...	...	46858	...	...	50492
A Sanitary and similar services	10107	3947	6160	11673	4574	7099	...	...	7887	...	...	8623
B Social and related community services	11122	3623	7499	12302	4035	8267	...	...	9107	...	...	10064
C Recreational and cultural services	14017	5142	8875	15354	5428	9926	...	...	10524	...	...	10855
D Personal and household services	25337	10238	15099	28162	10825	17337	...	...	19340	...	...	20950
Total, Industries	1598844	808219	790625	1783502	908563	874939	...	...	937191	...	...	984981
Producers of Government Services	...	...	215273	...	...	238879	...	...	277723	...	...	295175
Other Producers	...	...	14238	...	...	16182	...	...	18740	...	...	20491
Total d	...	...	1020136	...	...	1130000	...	...	1233654	...	...	1300647
Less: Imputed bank service charge a	...	...	48247	...	...	52278	...	...	63086	...	...	63483
Import duties	...	...	4705	...	...	4605	...	...	4652	...	...	4781
Value added tax e	...	...	137694	...	...	149265	...	...	177801	...	...	193633
Other adjustments	...	...	-3817	...	...	-5279	...	...	-4124	...	...	-2649
Total	...	...	1110471	...	...	1226313	...	...	1348897	...	...	1432929
Memorandum Item: Mineral fuels and power f	56841	26663	30178	64836	31983	32853	...	...	35799	...	...	39761

a) Item 'Less: Imputed bank service charge' is netted out of item 'Finance, insurance, real estate and business services'.
b) One-or two-dwelling houses including country lodges.
c) Multi-dwelling buildings and other real estate.
d) Gross domestic product in basic values.
e) Item 'Value added tax' relates to value added tax and other taxes and subsidies on sales and production of commodities.
f) Item 'Mineral fuels and power' refers to ISIC categories 353 (Petroleum refineries), 354 (Manufacture of miscellaneous products of petroleum and coal) and 41 (Electricity, gas and steam). Beginning 1990, categories 353 and 354 are included in manufacturing (ISIC code 3) on an aggregated level.

4.2 Derivation of Value Added by Kind of Activity, in Constant Prices

Million Swedish kronor

	1985			1986			1987			1988		
	Gross Output	Intermediate Consumption	Value Added	Gross Output	Intermediate Consumption	Value Added	Gross Output	Intermediate Consumption	Value Added	Gross Output	Intermediate Consumption	Value Added
	At constant prices of:1985											
	All Producers											
1 Agriculture, hunting, forestry and fishing	47014	18664	28350	46752	18614	28138	44965	18327	26638	44998	18620	26378
A Agriculture and hunting	28828	15340	13488	28560	15339	13221	26488	15032	11456	26638	15301	11337
B Forestry and logging	17279	2984	14295	17355	2944	14411	17646	2983	14663	17334	2972	14362
C Fishing	907	340	567	837	331	506	831	312	519	1026	347	679
2 Mining and quarrying	7198	2858	4340	7176	2856	4320	7221	2875	4346	7191	2840	4351
A Coal mining	...	...	...	...	...	...	...	...	...	...	...	...
B Crude petroleum and natural gas production	...	...	...	...	...	...	...	...	...	...	...	...
C Metal ore mining	5694	2153	3541	5699	2150	3549	5820	2225	3595	5794	2173	3621
D Other mining	1504	705	799	1477	706	771	1401	650	751	1397	667	730

Sweden

4.2 Derivation of Value Added by Kind of Activity, in Constant Prices
(Continued)

Million Swedish kronor

	1985			1986			1987			1988		
	Gross Output	Intermediate Consumption	Value Added	Gross Output	Intermediate Consumption	Value Added	Gross Output	Intermediate Consumption	Value Added	Gross Output	Intermediate Consumption	Value Added
				At constant prices of:1985								
3 Manufacturing	545296	358471	186825	556729	367887	188842	573359	379809	193550	587452	389284	198168
A Manufacture of food, beverages and tobacco	74248	54858	19390	73351	54287	19064	73404	53857	19547	74522	55079	19443
B Textile, wearing apparel and leather industries	12866	7447	5419	12509	7180	5329	12844	7406	5438	11985	6892	5093
C Manufacture of wood and wood products, including furniture	35811	23520	12291	36538	24197	12341	38176	24993	13183	39798	26380	13418
D Manufacture of paper and paper products, printing and publishing	80973	54029	26944	83128	55293	27835	87442	57813	29629	88068	58288	29780
E Manufacture of chemicals and chemical petroleum, coal, rubber and plastic products	80426	61321	19105	83779	64235	19544	87125	66828	20297	87523	66327	21196
F Manufacture of non-metallic mineral products, except products of petroleum and coal	11909	6369	5540	11846	6265	5581	12593	6801	5792	13017	7106	5911
G Basic metal industries	40534	31647	8887	39983	31435	8548	41184	32574	8610	43922	34589	9333
H Manufacture of fabricated metal products, machinery and equipment	204314	116829	87485	211209	122556	88653	216132	127071	89061	223969	132005	91964
I Other manufacturing industries	4215	2451	1764	4386	2439	1947	4459	2466	1993	4648	2618	2030
4 Electricity, gas and water	39313	16676	22637	39901	16079	23822	41678	16515	25163	41361	16160	25201
A Electricity, gas and steam	33894	14560	19334	34232	13931	20301	35920	14241	21679	35200	13777	21423
B Water works and supply	5419	2116	3303	5669	2148	3521	5758	2274	3484	6161	2383	3778
5 Construction	102074	51307	50767	105479	52566	52913	110250	55289	54961	113037	57690	55347
6 Wholesale and retail trade, restaurants and hotels	151315	57367	93948	157110	59094	98016	166112	62878	103234	171928	65227	106701
A Wholesale and retail trade	129642	46510	83132	135696	48193	87503	143112	51036	92076	147922	52782	95140
B Restaurants and hotels	21673	10857	10816	21414	10901	10513	23000	11842	11158	24006	12445	11561
7 Transport, storage and communication	106096	59381	46715	112275	63724	48551	117461	64996	52465	126351	70333	56018
A Transport and storage	79310	47996	31314	84160	51712	32448	87561	52624	34937	94287	56730	37557
B Communication	26786	11385	15401	28115	12012	16103	29900	12372	17528	32064	13603	18461
8 Finance, insurance, real estate and business services [a]	205879	67695	138184	215863	73580	142283	227980	80352	147628	241940	88818	153122
A Financial institutions	39179	10783	28396	42648	12151	30497	46544	14351	32193	49568	15682	33886
B Insurance	5687	2245	3442	6268	2584	3684	6520	2678	3842	6831	2890	3941
C Real estate and business services	161013	54667	106346	166947	58845	108102	174916	63323	111593	185541	70246	115295
Real estate, except dwellings [b]	59043	10896	48147	59515	11971	47544	60011	12746	47265	60570	13297	47273
Dwellings [c]	50462	20332	30130	51558	21590	29968	53291	22631	30660	55016	23751	31265
9 Community, social and personal services	44032	16484	27548	45696	17152	28544	48105	18206	29899	49234	19182	30052
A Sanitary and similar services	7276	2910	4366	7381	2839	4542	7819	3037	4782	8325	3422	4903
B Social and related community services	8186	2623	5563	8431	2773	5658	9162	2992	6170	9318	3135	6183
C Recreational and cultural services	10368	3631	6737	10968	3881	7087	11537	4166	7371	11512	4274	7238
D Personal and household services	18202	7320	10882	18916	7659	11257	19587	8011	11576	20079	8351	11728
Total, Industries	1248217	648903	599314	1286981	671552	615429	1337131	699247	637884	1383492	728154	655338
Producers of Government Services	...	...	178967	...	...	180931	...	...	182468	...	...	183729
Other Producers	...	...	10629	...	...	10932	...	...	11395	...	...	11901
Total [d]	...	...	788910	...	...	807292	...	...	831747	...	...	850968
Less: Imputed bank service charge	...	...	31079	...	...	32526	...	...	35068	...	...	36514
Import duties	...	...	2724	...	...	2845	...	...	3333	...	...	3505
Value added tax [e]	...	...	103708	...	...	109182	...	...	113689	...	...	116091
Other adjustments	...	...	1525	...	...	-1799	...	...	-3498	...	...	-3218
Total	...	...	865788	...	...	884994	...	...	910203	...	...	930832
Memorandum Item: Mineral fuels and power [f]	67731	45153	22578	71382	47114	24268	72504	47332	25172	69676	44456	25220

4.2 Derivation of Value Added by Kind of Activity, in Constant Prices

Million Swedish kronor

	1989			1990			1991		
	Gross Output	Intermediate Consumption	Value Added	Gross Output	Intermediate Consumption	Value Added	Gross Output	Intermediate Consumption	Value Added
At constant prices of:1985									
All Producers									
1 Agriculture, hunting, forestry and fishing	48782	18689	30093	...	...	30751	...	...	28319
A Agriculture and hunting	29392	14992	14400	...	...	15129	...	...	13449
B Forestry and logging	18320	3348	14972	...	...	14889	...	...	14176
C Fishing	1070	349	721	...	...	733	...	...	694
2 Mining and quarrying	7279	2968	4311	...	...	4604	...	...	4495
A Coal mining	...	...	...	...	...	...	...	...	...
B Crude petroleum and natural gas production	...	...	...	...	...	...	...	...	...
C Metal ore mining	5671	2127	3544	...	...	3765	...	...	3668
D Other mining	1608	841	767	...	...	839	...	...	827
3 Manufacturing	603235	401577	201658	...	...	197286	...	...	187081
A Manufacture of food, beverages and tobacco	76338	56902	19436	...	...	19192	...	...	18555
B Textile, wearing apparel and leather industries	11527	6553	4974	...	...	4544	...	...	4080
C Manufacture of wood and wood products, including furniture	42110	27996	14114	...	...	14437	...	...	13433
D Manufacture of paper and paper products, printing and publishing	88114	58666	29448	...	...	28366	...	...	27754
E Manufacture of chemicals and chemical petroleum, coal, rubber and plastic products	88627	67844	20783	...	...	20797	...	...	19969
F Manufacture of non-metallic mineral products, except products of petroleum and coal	13807	7623	6184	...	...	5843	...	...	5424
G Basic metal industries	45384	35717	9667	...	...	9204	...	...	8897
H Manufacture of fabricated metal products, machinery and equipment	232861	137827	95034	...	...	92872	...	...	86963
I Other manufacturing industries	4467	2449	2018	...	...	2031	...	...	2006
4 Electricity, gas and water	41760	17432	24328	...	...	24781	...	...	24972
A Electricity, gas and steam	35146	14644	20502	...	...	20857	...	...	21104
B Water works and supply	6614	2788	3826	...	...	3924	...	...	3868
5 Construction	121843	63359	58484	...	...	58608	...	...	56591
6 Wholesale and retail trade, restaurants and hotels	177461	67760	109701	...	...	107494	...	...	105360
A Wholesale and retail trade	151939	54612	97327	...	...	96026	...	...	94729
B Restaurants and hotels	25522	13148	12374	...	...	11468	...	...	10631
7 Transport, storage and communication	131203	72629	58574	...	...	64959	...	...	64247
A Transport and storage	96359	58650	37709	...	...	42407	...	...	41016
B Communication	34844	13979	20865	...	...	22552	...	...	23231
8 Finance, insurance, real estate and business services [a]	250887	94081	156806	...	...	160460	...	...	161762
A Financial institutions	52099	16780	35319	...	...	35235	...	...	37454
B Insurance	7211	3114	4097	...	...	4145	...	...	4327
C Real estate and business services	191577	74187	117390	...	...	121080	...	...	119981
Real estate, except dwellings [b]	61088	13856	47232	...	...	47312	...	...	48033
Dwellings [c]	55963	24345	31618	...	...	33203	...	...	32803
9 Community, social and personal services	49213	19380	29833	...	...	29521	...	...	29252
A Sanitary and similar services	8621	3585	5036	...	...	5111	...	...	4909
B Social and related community services	9326	3129	6197	...	...	6356	...	...	6633
C Recreational and cultural services	11359	4315	7044	...	...	6692	...	...	6712
D Personal and household services	19907	8351	11556	...	...	11362	...	...	10998
Total, Industries	1431663	757875	673788	...	...	678464	...	...	662079
Producers of Government Services	...	...	187544	...	...	191165	...	...	191054
Other Producers	...	...	12134	...	...	12929	...	...	13188

Sweden

4.2 Derivation of Value Added by Kind of Activity, in Constant Prices
(Continued)

Million Swedish kronor

	1989			1990			1991		
	Gross Output	Intermediate Consumption	Value Added	Gross Output	Intermediate Consumption	Value Added	Gross Output	Intermediate Consumption	Value Added
			At constant prices of:1985						
Total d	...	...	873466	...	...	882558	...	...	866321
Less: Imputed bank service charge	...	...	37875	...	...	39045	...	...	41001
Import duties	...	...	3627	...	...	3696	...	...	3665
Value added tax e	...	...	118241	...	...	115374	...	...	115352
Other adjustments	...	...	-4578	...	...	-2631	...	...	-1935
Total	...	...	952881	...	...	959952	...	...	942402
Memorandum Item: Mineral fuels and power f	72063	47852	24211	...	...	24319	...	...	24706

a) Item 'Less: Imputed bank service charge' is netted out of item 'Finance, insurance, real estate and business services'.
b) One-or two-dwelling houses including country lodges.
c) Multi-dwelling buildings and other real estate.
d) Gross domestic product in basic values.
e) Item 'Value added tax' relates to value added tax and other taxes and subsidies on sales and production of commodities.
f) Item 'Mineral fuels and power' refers to ISIC categories 353 (Petroleum refineries), 354 (Manufacture of miscellaneous products of petroleum and coal) and 41 (Electricity, gas and steam). Beginning 1990, categories 353 and 354 are included in manufacturing (ISIC code 3) on an aggregated level.

4.3 Cost Components of Value Added

Million Swedish kronor

	1980						1981					
	Compensation of Employees	Capital Consumption	Net Operating Surplus	Indirect Taxes	Less: Subsidies Received	Value Added	Compensation of Employees	Capital Consumption	Net Operating Surplus	Indirect Taxes	Less: Subsidies Received	Value Added
						All Producers						
1 Agriculture, hunting, forestry and fishing	5017	...	12524	444	251	17734	5662	...	13935	507	359	19745
A Agriculture and hunting	2195	...	6941	306	249	9193	2313	...	7778	336	351	10076
B Forestry and logging	2790	...	5250	133	2	8171	3323	...	5819	166	8	9300
C Fishing	32	...	333	5	-	370	26	...	338	5	-	369
2 Mining and quarrying	1444	...	940	32	29	2387	1506	...	755	32	6	2287
A Coal mining	...	...	...	...	...	...	...	...	...	...	...	...
B Crude petroleum and natural gas production	...	...	...	...	...	...	...	...	...	...	...	...
C Metal ore mining	1151	...	502	23	3	1673	1212	...	275	23	6	1504
D Other mining	293	...	438	9	26	714	294	...	480	9	...	783
3 Manufacturing	88276	...	24415	1825	3052	111464	94879	...	22728	1924	3224	116307
A Manufacture of food, beverages and tobacco	6741	...	3871	172	...	10784	7297	...	4649	187	...	12133
B Textile, wearing apparel and leather industries	3364	...	988	69	305	4116	3426	...	790	70	275	4011
C Manufacture of wood and wood products, including furniture	5806	...	3620	126	25	**9527**	5978	...	2791	129	26	8872
D Manufacture of paper and paper products, printing and publishing	12619	...	3627	247	350	16143	13407	...	3191	260	407	16451
E Manufacture of chemicals and chemical petroleum, coal, rubber and plastic products	5962	...	5117	157	32	11204	6669	...	3520	143	23	10309
F Manufacture of non-metallic mineral products, except products of petroleum and coal	2998	...	913	62	13	3960	3020	...	859	62	13	3928
G Basic metal industries	6225	...	235	117	21	6556	6561	...	-926	124	43	5716
H Manufacture of fabricated metal products, machinery and equipment	42333	...	5242	832	75	48332	46246	...	6892	905	101	53942
I Other manufacturing industries	2228	...	802	43	2231	842	2275	...	962	44	2336	945
4 Electricity, gas and water	2342	...	11466	102	236	13674	2568	...	12852	115	308	15227
A Electricity, gas and steam	1692	...	9888	89	163	11506	1905	...	10924	102	219	12712
B Water works and supply	650	...	1578	13	73	2168	663	...	1928	13	89	2515
5 Construction	26300	...	8299	633	2	35230	29123	...	7797	663	2	37581
6 Wholesale and retail trade, restaurants and hotels	43688	...	10643	1210	15	55526	46997	...	10352	1269	...	58618
A Wholesale and retail trade	39691	...	9290	1088	...	50069	42573	...	8795	1139	...	52507
B Restaurants and hotels	3997	...	1353	122	15	5457	4424	...	1557	130	...	6111
7 Transport, storage and communication	22472	...	12349	1338	3581	32578	24608	...	13735	1471	4340	35474
A Transport and storage	16448	...	8411	1191	3581	22469	17821	...	9022	1312	4310	23845
B Communication	6024	...	3938	147	-	10109	6787	...	4713	159	30	11629
8 Finance, insurance, real estate and business services ab	22729	...	54960	1779	4670	74798	24942	...	67132	2314	6580	87808
A Financial institutions	4702	...	7647	104	-	12453	5165	...	11070	117	3	16349

4.3 Cost Components of Value Added
(Continued)

Million Swedish kronor

	1980 Compensation of Employees	Capital Consumption	Net Operating Surplus	Indirect Taxes	Less: Subsidies Received	Value Added	1981 Compensation of Employees	Capital Consumption	Net Operating Surplus	Indirect Taxes	Less: Subsidies Received	Value Added
B Insurance	2504	...	2055	55	...	4614	2715	...	1801	60	...	4576
C Real estate and business services	15523	...	45258	1620	4670	57731	17062	...	54261	2137	6577	66883
Real estate, except dwellings c	...	...	27264	778	1454	26588	...	...	32094	1255	2629	30720
Dwellings d	3446	...	15431	601	3007	16471	3525	...	18798	614	3723	19214
9 Community, social and personal services	10811	...	6550	1166	2404	16123	11884	...	8106	1399	2564	18825
A Sanitary and similar services	2146	...	713	59	80	2838	2331	...	922	62	98	3217
B Social and related community services	3576	...	1347	83	1949	3057	3925	...	1629	89	2025	3618
C Recreational and cultural services	1643	...	1617	911	363	3808	1954	...	2305	1129	433	4955
D Personal and household services	3446	...	2873	113	12	6420	3674	...	3250	119	8	7035
Total, Industries e	223079	...	142146	8529	14240	359514	242169	...	157392	9694	17383	391872
Producers of Government Services	110185	...	5367	2077	-	117629	120388	...	6118	2565	-	129071
Other Producers	6744	...	-	132	-	6876	7659	...	-	170	-	7829
Total fe	340008	...	147513	10738	14240	484019	370216	...	163510	12429	17383	528772
Less: Imputed bank service charge a	...	...	13825	...	...	13825	...	...	17477	...	...	17477
Import duties	...	...	...	1759	...	1759	...	...	...	1909	...	1909
Value added tax g	...	...	...	62155	7351	54804	...	...	...	71127	7832	63295
Other adjustments	-1821	...	7761	-3206	1236	1498	-225	...	6960	-2707	1614	2414
Total eh	338187	...	141449	71446	22827	528255	369991	...	152993	82758	26829	578913

	1982 Compensation of Employees	Capital Consumption	Net Operating Surplus	Indirect Taxes	Less: Subsidies Received	Value Added	1983 Compensation of Employees	Capital Consumption	Net Operating Surplus	Indirect Taxes	Less: Subsidies Received	Value Added
All Producers												
1 Agriculture, hunting, forestry and fishing	5799	...	15706	569	352	21722	6114	...	17775	1026	364	24551
A Agriculture and hunting	2455	...	9206	349	352	11658	2569	...	9334	530	360	12073
B Forestry and logging	3311	...	6098	214	-	9623	3509	...	7952	486	4	11943
C Fishing	33	...	402	6	-	441	36	...	489	10	-	535
2 Mining and quarrying	1500	...	1226	37	350	2413	1578	...	1763	68	390	3019
A Coal mining	...	...	...	...	...	...	...	...	...	...	...	...
B Crude petroleum and natural gas production	...	...	...	...	...	...	...	...	...	...	...	...
C Metal ore mining	1199	...	833	27	350	1709	1257	...	1412	52	390	2331
D Other mining	301	...	393	10	...	704	321	...	351	16	...	688
3 Manufacturing	98100	...	32410	2285	3171	129624	104929	...	42834	4415	3654	148524
A Manufacture of food, beverages and tobacco	7674	...	5641	213	...	13528	8301	...	6087	398	...	14786
B Textile, wearing apparel and leather industries	3310	...	777	77	261	3903	3501	...	791	152	255	4189
C Manufacture of wood and wood products, including furniture	6051	...	3091	145	28	9259	6556	...	4358	288	36	11166
D Manufacture of paper and paper products, printing and publishing	13850	...	5508	302	396	19264	15152	...	8312	621	459	23626
E Manufacture of chemicals and chemical petroleum, coal, rubber and plastic products	7092	...	5186	233	27	12484	7978	...	6164	357	17	14482
F Manufacture of non-metallic mineral products, except products of petroleum and coal	2976	...	1464	69	22	4487	3045	...	1727	129	14	4887
G Basic metal industries	6477	...	459	137	141	6932	6601	...	1063	265	128	7801
H Manufacture of fabricated metal products, machinery and equipment	48213	...	9593	1055	192	58669	50981	...	13867	2089	362	66575
I Other manufacturing industries	2457	...	691	54	2104	1098	2814	...	465	116	2383	1012
4 Electricity, gas and water	2975	...	12498	143	345	15271	3797	...	14219	244	474	17786
A Electricity, gas and steam	2231	...	10230	127	222	12366	3037	...	11654	213	325	14579
B Water works and supply	744	...	2268	16	123	2905	760	...	2565	31	149	3207

Sweden

Million Swedish kronor

	1982						1983					
	Compensation of Employees	Capital Consumption	Net Operating Surplus	Indirect Taxes	Less: Subsidies Received	Value Added	Compensation of Employees	Capital Consumption	Net Operating Surplus	Indirect Taxes	Less: Subsidies Received	Value Added
5 Construction	30307	...	10146	749	5	41197	31102	...	10458	1382	9	42933
6 Wholesale and retail trade, restaurants and hotels	49339	...	14230	1453	58	64964	53725	...	18481	2667	56	74817
A Wholesale and retail trade	44534	...	12145	1307	44	57942	48086	...	16352	2387	39	66786
B Restaurants and hotels	4805	...	2085	146	14	7022	5639	...	2129	280	17	8031
7 Transport, storage and communication	25825	...	15615	1608	5456	37592	27306	...	16818	2266	6270	40120
A Transport and storage	18489	...	10914	1423	5399	25427	19478	...	11569	1913	6219	26741
B Communication	7336	...	4701	185	57	12165	7828	...	5249	353	51	13379
8 Finance, insurance, real estate and business services ab	26725	...	81360	2484	9749	100820	31180	...	91270	3232	11611	114071
A Financial institutions	5555	...	13701	140	1087	18309	6407	...	16110	275	1729	21063
B Insurance	2976	...	1072	72	...	4120	3382	...	629	147	...	4158
C Real estate and business services	18194	...	66587	2272	8662	78391	21391	...	74531	2810	9882	88850
Real estate, except dwellings c	...	...	38702	1296	3685	36313	...	...	43413	1340	4204	40549
Dwellings d	3834	...	22888	659	4742	22639	4607	...	25440	784	5437	25394
9 Community, social and personal services	12341	...	9599	1559	2646	20853	13231	...	10391	2038	2831	22829
A Sanitary and similar services	2350	...	1185	70	109	3496	2568	...	1152	126	132	3714
B Social and related community services	4103	...	2062	102	2063	4204	4424	...	2154	202	2145	4635
C Recreational and cultural services	2060	...	2236	1256	464	5088	2132	...	2443	1465	540	5500
D Personal and household services	3828	...	4116	131	10	8065	4107	...	4642	245	14	8980
Total, Industries e	252911	...	192790	10887	22132	434456	272962	...	224009	17338	25659	488650
Producers of Government Services	130781	...	6915	2765	-	140461	141543	...	7797	5741	-	155081
Other Producers	8297	...	-	184	-	8481	8942	...	-	376	-	9318
Total fe	391989	...	199705	13836	22132	583398	423447	...	231806	23455	25659	653049
Less: Imputed bank service charge a	...	...	19680	...	...	19680	...	...	23264	...	...	23264
Import duties	...	...	...	2143	...	2143	...	...	...	2180	...	2180
Value added tax g	...	...	...	77345	7838	69507	...	...	...	88264	9016	79248
Other adjustments	-642	...	4312	-4077	1279	-1686	590	...	5507	-5637	1821	-1361
Total eh	391347	...	184337	89247	31249	633682	424037	...	214049	108262	36496	709852

	1984						1985					
	Compensation of Employees	Capital Consumption	Net Operating Surplus	Indirect Taxes	Less: Subsidies Received	Value Added	Compensation of Employees	Capital Consumption	Net Operating Surplus	Indirect Taxes	Less: Subsidies Received	Value Added
						All Producers						
1 Agriculture, hunting, forestry and fishing	6570	...	19952	1120	576	27066	6795	...	20954	1088	487	28350
A Agriculture and hunting	2855	...	10232	546	570	13063	2869	...	10543	560	484	13488
B Forestry and logging	3666	...	9205	564	6	13429	3859	...	9924	515	3	14295
C Fishing	49	...	515	10	-	574	67	...	487	13	-	567
2 Mining and quarrying	1718	...	2128	67	70	3843	1912	...	2394	77	43	4340
A Coal mining	...	...	...	...	...	...	...	...	...	...	...	...
B Crude petroleum and natural gas production	...	...	...	...	...	...	...	...	...	...	...	...
C Metal ore mining	1342	...	1681	49	27	3045	1467	...	2061	56	43	3541
D Other mining	376	...	447	18	43	798	445	...	333	21	...	799

4.3 Cost Components of Value Added
(Continued)

Million Swedish kronor

	Compensation of Employees	Capital Consumption	Net Operating Surplus	Indirect Taxes	Less: Subsidies Received	Value Added	Compensation of Employees	Capital Consumption	Net Operating Surplus	Indirect Taxes	Less: Subsidies Received	Value Added
	1984						1985					
3 Manufacturing	117116	...	53481	4478	3736	171339	129919	...	55606	5169	3869	186825
A Manufacture of food, beverages and tobacco	9166	...	6888	386	...	16440	9973	...	8953	464	...	19390
B Textile, wearing apparel and leather industries	3749	...	1236	149	251	4883	4009	...	1477	163	230	5419
C Manufacture of wood and wood products, including furniture	7285	...	5376	292	35	12918	7803	...	4193	322	27	12291
D Manufacture of paper and paper products, printing and publishing	17248	...	9874	644	452	27314	19234	...	7477	738	505	26944
E Manufacture of chemicals and chemical petroleum, coal, rubber and plastic products	9155	...	6998	375	18	16510	10351	...	8335	471	52	19105
F Manufacture of non-metallic mineral products, except products of petroleum and coal	3189	...	1875	122	16	5170	3503	...	1911	139	13	5540
G Basic metal industries	6586	...	2230	242	52	9006	7201	...	1452	273	39	8887
H Manufacture of fabricated metal products, machinery and equipment	57732	...	18174	2155	277	77784	64442	...	20802	2468	227	87485
I Other manufacturing industries	3006	...	830	113	2635	1314	3403	...	1006	131	2776	1764
4 Electricity, gas and water	4710	...	16442	266	470	20948	4857	...	18353	324	897	22637
A Electricity, gas and steam	3912	...	13716	236	309	17555	3980	...	15767	290	703	19334
B Water works and supply	798	...	2726	30	161	3393	877	...	2586	34	194	3303
5 Construction	33171	...	12932	1363	42	47424	36827	...	12428	1552	40	50767
6 Wholesale and retail trade, restaurants and hotels	59967	...	23107	2779	182	85671	67805	...	23206	3255	318	93948
A Wholesale and retail trade	53454	...	20355	2482	148	76143	60280	...	20230	2906	284	83132
B Restaurants and hotels	6513	...	2752	297	34	9528	7525	...	2976	349	34	10816
7 Transport, storage and communication	30353	...	16944	2214	6805	42706	33329	...	18461	2471	7546	46715
A Transport and storage	21775	...	11198	1861	6760	28074	23846	...	12913	2062	7507	31314
B Communication	8578	...	5746	353	45	14632	9483	...	5548	409	39	15401
8 Finance, insurance, real estate and business services ab	36827	...	98532	4232	12188	127403	39571	...	104406	8359	14152	138184
A Financial institutions	7731	...	17949	1137	1357	25460	8458	...	19616	1515	1193	28396
B Insurance	3781	...	-401	150	...	3530	4173	...	-898	167	...	3442
C Real estate and business services	25315	...	80984	2945	10831	98413	26940	...	85688	6677	12959	106346
Real estate, except dwellings c	...	...	47353	1368	4328	44393	...	...	50700	2489	5042	48147
Dwellings d	5587	...	27502	845	6274	27660	5456	...	28970	3368	7664	30130
9 Community, social and personal services	14160	...	11871	2132	3059	25104	15748	...	12716	2255	3171	27548
A Sanitary and similar services	2950	...	1108	130	139	4049	3210	...	1168	147	159	4366
B Social and related community services	4864	...	2322	202	2342	5046	5403	...	2403	231	2474	5563
C Recreational and cultural services	2365	...	2732	1568	555	6110	2592	...	3056	1614	525	6737
D Personal and household services	3981	...	5709	232	23	9899	4543	...	6089	263	13	10882
Total, Industries e	304592	...	255389	18651	27128	551504	336763	...	268524	24550	30523	599314
Producers of Government Services	153506	...	8509	5665	-	167680	163563	...	9189	6215	-	178967
Other Producers	9526	...	-	365	-	9891	10235	...	-	394	-	10629
Total fe	467624	...	263898	24681	27128	729075	510561	...	277713	31159	30523	788910
Less: Imputed bank service charge a	...	...	26966	...	...	26966	...	...	31079	...	...	31079
Import duties	...	...	...	2508	...	2508	...	...	...	2724	...	2724
Value added tax g	...	...	...	99872	9743	90129	...	...	...	114437	10729	103708
Other adjustments	-3902	...	7390	-1297	2639	-448	-4991	...	14430	-5755	2159	1525
Total eh	463722	...	244322	125764	39510	794298	505570	...	261064	142565	43411	865788

Sweden

4.3 Cost Components of Value Added

Million Swedish kronor

	1986						1987					
	Compensation of Employees	Capital Consumption	Net Operating Surplus	Indirect Taxes	Less: Subsidies Received	Value Added	Compensation of Employees	Capital Consumption	Net Operating Surplus	Indirect Taxes	Less: Subsidies Received	Value Added
All Producers												
1 Agriculture, hunting, forestry and fishing	7301	...	22202	1318	976	29845	7508	...	22222	1377	634	30473
A Agriculture and hunting	3106	...	11045	650	954	13847	3316	...	10119	661	607	13489
B Forestry and logging	4107	...	10633	653	22	15371	4077	...	11557	700	27	16307
C Fishing	88	...	524	15	-	627	115	...	546	16	-	677
2 Mining and quarrying	1944	...	1760	81	23	3762	1935	...	1518	83	20	3516
A Coal mining	...	...	...	...	...	...	...	...	...	...	...	...
B Crude petroleum and natural gas production	...	...	...	...	...	...	...	...	...	...	...	...
C Metal ore mining	1485	...	1449	58	23	2969	1428	...	1194	58	20	2660
D Other mining	459	...	311	23	...	793	507	...	324	25	...	856
3 Manufacturing	139534	...	65775	5879	4154	207034	151173	...	66978	6509	4031	220629
A Manufacture of food, beverages and tobacco	10649	...	10482	515	...	21646	11701	...	11431	571	...	23703
B Textile, wearing apparel and leather industries	4094	...	1822	176	164	5928	4231	...	2079	186	107	6389
C Manufacture of wood and wood products, including furniture	8181	...	4277	353	37	12774	9072	...	5411	400	30	14853
D Manufacture of paper and paper products, printing and publishing	20859	...	8592	833	632	29652	22531	...	10737	928	521	33675
E Manufacture of chemicals and chemical petroleum, coal, rubber and plastic products	11262	...	14426	631	55	26264	12388	...	12004	680	36	25036
F Manufacture of non-metallic mineral products, except products of petroleum and coal	3732	...	2452	156	8	6332	4041	...	2819	172	8	7024
G Basic metal industries	7311	...	1972	287	65	9505	7604	...	1899	309	28	9784
H Manufacture of fabricated metal products, machinery and equipment	69788	...	20517	2781	250	92836	75613	...	19424	3098	198	97937
I Other manufacturing industries	3658	...	1235	147	2943	2097	3992	...	1174	165	3103	2228
4 Electricity, gas and water	5098	...	22180	327	838	26767	5786	...	22708	364	600	28258
A Electricity, gas and steam	4183	...	19268	290	617	23124	4856	...	19568	323	381	24366
B Water works and supply	915	...	2912	37	221	3643	930	...	3140	41	219	3892
5 Construction	39656	...	13248	1754	64	54594	45095	...	13789	2004	53	60835
6 Wholesale and retail trade, restaurants and hotels	73229	...	24186	3501	299	100617	81728	...	24710	3905	570	109773
A Wholesale and retail trade	65148	...	20394	3104	265	88381	72253	...	20390	3448	448	95643
B Restaurants and hotels	8081	...	3792	397	34	12236	9475	...	4320	457	122	14130
7 Transport, storage and communication	37218	...	18923	2919	7557	51503	40160	...	22952	2990	8240	57862
A Transport and storage	26536	...	13093	2439	7524	34544	28770	...	15895	2472	8210	38927
B Communication	10682	...	5830	480	33	16959	11390	...	7057	518	30	18935
8 Finance, insurance, real estate and business services [ab]	45007	...	119226	11441	14554	161120	51101	...	129446	11697	14782	177462
A Financial institutions	9761	...	26344	3042	866	38281	10973	...	26671	4238	455	41427
B Insurance	4645	...	-388	195	...	4452	5261	...	-411	232	...	5082
C Real estate and business services	30601	...	93270	8204	13688	118387	34867	...	103186	7227	14327	130953
Real estate, except dwellings [c]	...	...	54294	2857	5476	51675	...	...	58563	2193	5288	55468
Dwellings [d]	6244	...	31348	4378	7961	34009	6546	...	35881	3880	8747	37560
9 Community, social and personal services	17479	...	14171	2767	3481	30936	19732	...	14811	3236	3941	33838
A Sanitary and similar services	3581	...	1263	172	155	4861	4015	...	1398	193	165	5441
B Social and related community services	6197	...	2454	274	2823	6102	7241	...	2774	324	3243	7096
C Recreational and cultural services	2826	...	3281	2023	490	7640	3146	...	3291	2398	524	8311
D Personal and household services	4875	...	7173	298	13	12333	5330	...	7348	321	9	12990
Total, Industries [e]	366466	...	301671	29987	31946	666178	404218	...	319134	32165	32871	722646
Producers of Government Services	177472	...	9768	7119	-	194359	185037	...	10319	7930	-	203286

4.3 Cost Components of Value Added
(Continued)

Million Swedish kronor

	1986						1987					
	Compensation of Employees	Capital Consumption	Net Operating Surplus	Indirect Taxes	Less: Subsidies Received	Value Added	Compensation of Employees	Capital Consumption	Net Operating Surplus	Indirect Taxes	Less: Subsidies Received	Value Added
Other Producers	11245	...	-	428	-	11673	12350	...	-	520	-	12870
Total fe	555183	...	311439	37534	31946	872210	601605	...	329453	40615	32871	938802
Less: Imputed bank service charge a	...	...	39282	...	...	39282	...	...	43686	...		43686
Import duties	...	...	...	3038	...	3038	...	...	...	4057	...	4057
Value added tax g	...	...	...	123980	11447	112533	...	...	...	136770	12047	124723
Other adjustments	-950	...	6485	-5594	2857	-2916	-2917	...	6222	-4582	3072	-4349
Total eh	554233	...	278642	158958	46250	945583	598688	...	291989	176860	47990	1019547

	1988						1989					
	Compensation of Employees	Capital Consumption	Net Operating Surplus	Indirect Taxes	Less: Subsidies Received	Value Added	Compensation of Employees	Capital Consumption	Net Operating Surplus	Indirect Taxes	Less: Subsidies Received	Value Added
					All Producers							
1 Agriculture, hunting, forestry and fishing	7917	...	23671	1190	1305	31473	8658	...	25806	1209	755	34918
A Agriculture and hunting	3622	...	11422	557	1291	14310	3941	...	12726	592	704	16555
B Forestry and logging	4190	...	11634	621	14	16431	4611	...	12538	604	51	17702
C Fishing	105	...	615	12	-	732	106	...	542	13	-	661
2 Mining and quarrying	2196	...	1747	73	12	4004	2485	...	2404	90	31	4948
A Coal mining	...	...	...	...	...	...	...	...	...	...	...	...
B Crude petroleum and natural gas production	...	...	...	...	...	...	...	...	...	...	...	...
C Metal ore mining	1519	...	1526	47	12	3080	1730	...	2070	58	26	3832
D Other mining	677	...	221	26	...	924	755	...	334	32	5	1116
3 Manufacturing	164029	...	71045	5320	4177	236217	179414	...	77183	6479	4285	258791
A Manufacture of food, beverages and tobacco	13055	...	10883	492	...	24430	14242	...	13277	586	...	28105
B Textile, wearing apparel and leather industries	4401	...	2098	142	84	6557	4382	...	2117	156	55	6600
C Manufacture of wood and wood products, including furniture	10158	...	5987	334	26	16453	11300	...	7824	408	38	19494
D Manufacture of paper and paper products, printing and publishing	24738	...	13040	748	543	37983	27383	...	13362	918	490	41173
E Manufacture of chemicals and chemical petroleum, coal, rubber and plastic products	14204	...	12280	633	60	27057	15637	...	11631	809	33	28044
F Manufacture of non-metallic mineral products, except products of petroleum and coal	4563	...	2848	146	4	7553	5116	...	3328	180	5	8619
G Basic metal industries	8126	...	1890	243	11	10248	8891	...	2279	298	11	11457
H Manufacture of fabricated metal products, machinery and equipment	80499	...	20799	2452	144	103606	87832	...	22282	2968	182	112900
I Other manufacturing industries	4285	...	1220	130	3305	2330	4631	...	1083	156	3471	2399
4 Electricity, gas and water	6235	...	23770	323	278	30050	6720	...	26481	306	1424	32083
A Electricity, gas and steam	5371	...	20094	293	47	25711	5792	...	22648	275	1084	27631
B Water works and supply	864	...	3676	30	231	4339	928	...	3833	31	340	4452
5 Construction	51015	...	15601	1787	11	68392	58674	...	21517	2201	5	82387
6 Wholesale and retail trade, restaurants and hotels	90276	...	26443	3400	87	120032	101581	...	23387	4087	88	128967
A Wholesale and retail trade	79598	...	21659	2972	21	104208	89301	...	17860	3568	26	110703
B Restaurants and hotels	10678	...	4784	428	66	15824	12280	...	5527	519	62	18264
7 Transport, storage and communication	43414	...	25976	2843	7913	64320	48628	...	28039	3186	8973	70880
A Transport and storage	31268	...	17748	2414	7886	43544	34930	...	18399	2660	8917	47072
B Communication	12146	...	8228	429	27	20776	13698	...	9640	526	56	23808
8 Finance, insurance, real estate and business services ab	57734	...	144274	11818	15322	198504	67158	...	155434	14182	17438	219336
A Financial institutions	12080	...	30016	4405	411	46090	13886	...	29938	6339	229	49934
B Insurance	5847	...	754	193	...	6794	6577	...	469	231	...	7277
C Real estate and business services	39807	...	113504	7220	14911	145620	46695	...	125027	7612	17209	162125
Real estate, except dwellings c	...	...	62795	2219	4664	60350	...	...	68392	2172	5199	65365

Sweden

4.3 Cost Components of Value Added
(Continued)

Million Swedish kronor

	1988						1989					
	Compensation of Employees	Capital Consumption	Net Operating Surplus	Indirect Taxes	Less: Subsidies Received	Value Added	Compensation of Employees	Capital Consumption	Net Operating Surplus	Indirect Taxes	Less: Subsidies Received	Value Added
Dwellings d	7259	...	39812	3991	9906	41156	8516	...	44280	4130	11563	45363
9 Community, social and personal services	21874	...	17112	3078	4431	37633	25153	...	18487	3920	4931	42629
A Sanitary and similar services	4549	...	1617	177	183	6160	5506	...	1582	223	212	7099
B Social and related community services	7925	...	2936	267	3629	7499	8959	...	2998	328	4018	8267
C Recreational and cultural services	3520	...	3602	2359	606	8875	4049	...	3517	3047	687	9926
D Personal and household services	5880	...	8957	275	13	15099	6639	...	10390	322	14	17337
Total, Industries e	444690	...	349639	29832	33536	790625	498471	...	378738	35660	37930	874939
Producers of Government Services	197869	...	11252	6152	-	215273	219117	...	12192	7570	-	238879
Other Producers	13818	...	-	420	-	14238	15652	...	-	530	-	16182
Total fe	656377	...	360891	36404	33536	1020136	733240	...	390930	43760	37930	1130000
Less: Imputed bank service charge a	...	...	48247	...	...	48247	...	...	52278	...	...	52278
Import duties	...	...	...	4705	...	4705	...	...	...	4605	...	4605
Value added tax g	...	...	...	148763	11069	137694	...	...	...	161497	12232	149265
Other adjustments	-2611	...	10214	-7106	4314	-3817	-1086	...	5707	-4326	5574	-5279
Total eh	653766	...	322858	182766	48919	1110471	732154	...	344359	205536	55736	1226313

	1990						1991					
	Compensation of Employees	Capital Consumption	Net Operating Surplus	Indirect Taxes	Less: Subsidies Received	Value Added	Compensation of Employees	Capital Consumption	Net Operating Surplus	Indirect Taxes	Less: Subsidies Received	Value Added
All Producers												
1 Agriculture, hunting, forestry and fishing	9186	...	27911	1310	3770	34637	9402	...	23489	1315	3432	30774
A Agriculture and hunting	4188	...	14696	627	3707	15804	4483	...	11668	661	3369	13443
B Forestry and logging	4878	...	12557	669	63	18041	4787	...	11157	639	63	16520
C Fishing	120	...	658	14	-	792	132	...	664	15	-	811
2 Mining and quarrying	2559	...	2624	92	31	5244	2776	...	1840	81	31	4666
A Coal mining	...	...	...	...	...	...	...	...	...	...	...	...
B Crude petroleum and natural gas production	...	...	...	...	...	...	...	...	...	...	...	...
C Metal ore mining	1678	...	2205	56	26	3913	1837	...	1382	49	26	3242
D Other mining	881	...	419	36	5	1331	939	...	458	32	5	1424
3 Manufacturing	191320	...	72271	6891	4411	266071	198823	...	59852	5703	5243	259135
A Manufacture of food, beverages and tobacco	15266	...	16023	620	14	31895	16283	...	14040	585	26	30882
B Textile, wearing apparel and leather industries	4193	...	2295	150	42	6596	4027	...	2077	119	69	6154
C Manufacture of wood and wood products, including furniture	12463	...	8468	443	41	21333	12628	...	6296	363	41	19246
D Manufacture of paper and paper products, printing and publishing	29104	...	9746	986	540	39296	30892	...	8518	813	590	39633
E Manufacture of chemicals and chemical petroleum, coal, rubber and plastic products	16491	...	11589	854	33	28901	17549	...	11161	707	33	29384
F Manufacture of non-metallic mineral products, except products of petroleum and coal	5431	...	3444	198	4	9069	5803	...	2773	169	4	8741
G Basic metal industries	9445	...	2392	335	10	12162	10027	...	-154	256	10	10119
H Manufacture of fabricated metal products, machinery and equipment	93713	...	17488	3132	125	114208	95953	...	13840	2543	125	112211
I Other manufacturing industries	5214	...	826	173	3602	2611	5661	...	1301	148	4345	2765
4 Electricity, gas and water	7776	...	27616	344	1394	34342	8013	...	30839	307	1206	37953
A Electricity, gas and steam	6830	...	23473	312	1096	29519	7012	...	25906	280	867	32331
B Water works and supply	946	...	4143	32	298	4823	1001	...	4933	27	339	5622
5 Construction	68171	...	22123	2482	2	92774	72495	...	21836	2188	2	96517
6 Wholesale and retail trade, restaurants and hotels	111358	...	15027	4415	398	130402	116185	...	15674	4567	398	136028
A Wholesale and retail trade	98187	...	10583	3878	325	112323	103750	...	10395	4114	325	117934
B Restaurants and hotels	13171	...	4444	537	73	18079	12435	...	5279	453	73	18094
7 Transport, storage and communication	54461	...	30241	3727	9784	78645	56986	...	31270	3634	9949	81941

4.3 Cost Components of Value Added
(Continued)

Million Swedish kronor

	1990						1991					
	Compensation of Employees	Capital Consumption	Net Operating Surplus	Indirect Taxes	Less: Subsidies Received	Value Added	Compensation of Employees	Capital Consumption	Net Operating Surplus	Indirect Taxes	Less: Subsidies Received	Value Added
A Transport and storage	39285	...	18326	3137	9631	51117	40232	...	19562	3113	9865	53042
B Communication	15176	...	11915	590	153	27528	16754	...	11708	521	84	28899
8 Finance, insurance, real estate and business services ab	78284	...	173842	17326	21234	248218	88826	...	204630	21997	27978	287475
A Financial institutions	15688	...	36248	6684	91	58529	17471	...	35220	4450	80	57061
B Insurance	7216	...	787	237	...	8240	7956	...	676	174	...	8806
C Real estate and business services	55380	...	136807	10405	21143	181449	63399	...	168734	17373	27898	221608
Real estate, except dwellings c	...	...	75585	3226	6371	72440	...	...	94722	7824	8617	93929
Dwellings d	10095	...	49000	5659	14237	50517	11708	...	64336	8146	18555	65635
9 Community, social and personal services	28377	...	20924	2974	5417	46858	31317	...	21815	3425	6065	50492
A Sanitary and similar services	6374	...	1483	248	218	7887	7210	...	1418	237	242	8623
B Social and related community services	10077	...	3129	360	4459	9107	11655	...	3090	342	5023	10064
C Recreational and cultural services	4603	...	4640	2021	740	10524	4935	...	4195	2525	800	10855
D Personal and household services	7323	...	11672	345	-	19340	7517	...	13112	321	-	20950
Total, Industries e	551492	...	392579	39561	46441	937191	584823	...	411245	43217	54304	984981
Producers of Government Services	255402	...	13412	8909	-	277723	272861	...	14297	8017	-	295175
Other Producers	17999	...	-	741	-	18740	19960	...	-	531	-	20491
Total fe	824893	...	405991	49211	46441	1233654	877644	...	425542	51765	54304	1300647
Less: Imputed bank service charge a	...	...	63086	...	...	63086	...	...	63483	...	...	63483
Import duties	...	...	...	4652	...	4652	...	...	...	4781	...	4781
Value added tax g	...	...	...	190897	13096	177801	...	...	...	206537	12904	193633
Other adjustments	5843	...	5162	-11398	3731	-4124	5711	...	2852	-5829	5383	-2649
Total eh	830736	...	348067	233362	63268	1348897	883355	...	364911	257254	72591	1432929

a) Item 'Less: Imputed bank service charge' is netted out of item 'Finance, insurance, real estate and business services'.
b) Column 'Operating Surplus' is reduced for imputed bank service charges.
c) One-or two-dwelling houses including country lodges.
d) Multi-dwelling buildings and other real estate.
e) Column 'Consumption of fixed capital' is included in column 'Net operating surplus'.

f) Gross domestic product in basic values.
g) Item 'Value added tax' relates to value added tax and other taxes and subsidies on sales and production of commodities.
h) There is a break in the series between 1987 and 1988 in the estimates of compensation of employees by kind of economic activity. This is the result of new and better source available for the estimates.

Switzerland

Source. Reply to the United Nations National Accounts Questionnaire from the Federal Bureau of Statistics, Bern. The official estimates are published annually by the Bureau in the September issue of 'La Vie Economique', and in 'Series revisees de la compatabilite nationale suisse, 1948-1976'.

General note. The estimates shown in the following tables have been adjusted to conform to the United Nations System of National Accounts so far as the existing data would permit.

1.1 Expenditure on the Gross Domestic Product, in Current Prices

Million Swiss francs

	1980	1981	1982	1983	1984	1985	1986	1987	1988	1989	1990	1991
1 Government final consumption expenditure	21685	23545	25555	27355	28500	30420	31845	32520	34860	37900	42200	46500
2 Private final consumption expenditure	108335	116020	122440	127755	134035	141015	145405	150715	157515	166735	178300	191145
3 Gross capital formation	46320	47010	47095	48845	51300	55565	63365	69345	74835	86295	91855	90435
A Increase in stocks	5820	2450	1795	1345	1500	1365	4370	4975	3355	6435	7310	5625
B Gross fixed capital formation	40500	44560	45300	47500	49800	54200	58995	64370	71480	79860	84545	84810
Residential buildings												
Non-residential buildings	27500	30800	31800	32750	34200	35900	38590	41870	46470	52325	55990	55880
Other construction and land improvement etc.												
Other	13000	13760	13500	14750	15600	18300	20405	22500	25010	27535	28555	28930
4 Exports of goods and services	62580	69100	69550	71760	80550	89015	89115	90525	97990	110510	115050	116740
5 Less: Imports of goods and services	68590	70920	68660	71850	81155	88065	86380	88420	96790	111080	113415	112135
Equals: Gross Domestic Product	170330	184755	195980	203865	213230	227950	243350	254685	268410	290360	313990	332685

1.2 Expenditure on the Gross Domestic Product, in Constant Prices

Million Swiss francs

	1980	1981	1982	1983	1984	1985	1986	1987	1988	1989	1990	1991
					At constant prices of:1980							
1 Government final consumption expenditure	21685	22225	22455	23315	23605	24365	25270	25720	26820	27940	29250	30070
2 Private final consumption expenditure	108335	108880	108855	110685	112410	114035	117250	119685	122260	124985	126875	128735
3 Gross capital formation	46320	43790	42090	43355	45225	47415	53715	57955	60055	64755	66545	62495
A Increase in stocks	5820	2200	1565	1165	1290	1155	3805	4335	2715	4105	4335	1810
B Gross fixed capital formation	40500	41590	40525	42190	43935	46260	49910	53620	57340	60650	62210	60685
Residential buildings												
Non-residential buildings	27500	28645	28175	29025	30205	31100	32415	34155	36340	38830	39585	38340
Other construction and land improvement etc.												
Other	13000	12945	12350	13165	13730	15160	17495	19465	21000	21820	22625	22345
4 Exports of goods and services	62580	65590	63715	64395	68480	74170	74445	75695	80090	84090	86630	86065
5 Less: Imports of goods and services	68590	67705	65935	68850	73760	77500	82965	87530	92145	97080	99905	98195
Equals: Gross Domestic Product	170330	172780	171180	172900	175960	182485	187715	191525	197080	204690	209395	209170

1.3 Cost Components of the Gross Domestic Product

Million Swiss francs

	1980	1981	1982	1983	1984	1985	1986	1987	1988	1989	1990	1991
1 Indirect taxes, net	9660	10510	10720	11320	11850	12630	14060	14795	15390	16160	15940	15695
A Indirect taxes	11910	12670	13315	14145	14895	15875	17375	18290	19245	20415	20685	20880
B Less: Subsidies	2250	2160	2595	2825	3045	3245	3315	3495	3855	4255	4745	5185
2 Consumption of fixed capital	17960	19550	20400	20900	21700	23400	24395	25640	27745	30520	32765	34220
3 Compensation of employees paid by resident producers to:	104650	114120	122700	128155	133425	141525	150455	158155	168015	180240	196655	211615
A Resident households	101740	110670	118910	124330	129490	137300	145765	152925	162010	173250	188665	202800
B Rest of the world	2910	3450	3790	3825	3935	4225	4690	5230	6005	6990	7990	8815
4 Operating surplus	38060	40575	42160	43490	46255	50395	54440	56095	57260	63440	68630	71155
Equals: Gross Domestic Product	170330	184755	195980	203865	213230	227950	243350	254685	268410	290360	313990	332685

1.4 General Government Current Receipts and Disbursements

Million Swiss francs

	1980	1981	1982	1983	1984	1985	1986	1987	1988	1989	1990	1991
						Receipts						
1 Operating surplus	-	-	-	-	-	-	-	-	-	-	-	-
2 Property and entrepreneurial income	2505	2940	3020	2975	2995	3210	3490	3645	3760	4175	4745	5005
3 Taxes, fees and contributions	51925	56070	60330	63995	68640	72520	78735	81085	86725	91405	98810	104545
A Indirect taxes	11910	12670	13315	14145	14895	15875	17375	18290	19245	20415	20685	20880

1.4 General Government Current Receipts and Disbursements
(Continued)

Million Swiss francs

	1980	1981	1982	1983	1984	1985	1986	1987	1988	1989	1990	1991
B Direct taxes	23340	25480	27720	29085	31070	32500	35650	35905	38765	40165	44680	47380
C Social security contributions	15550	16710	18035	19390	21165	22495	23900	25020	26715	28625	30815	33405
D Compulsory fees, fines and penalties	1125	1210	1260	1375	1510	1650	1810	1870	2000	2200	2630	2880
4 Other current transfers	1480	1655	1905	2155	2430	2765	3040	3190	3380	3530	3450	3525
Total Current Receipts of General Government	55910	60665	65255	69125	74065	78495	85265	87920	93865	99110	107005	113075
					Disbursements							
1 Government final consumption expenditure	21685	23545	25555	27355	28500	30420	31845	32520	34860	37900	42205	46500
2 Property income	3130	3375	3535	3630	3590	3695	3750	3725	3760	3960	4500	5035
3 Subsidies	2250	2160	2595	2825	3045	3245	3315	3495	3855	4255	4745	5185
4 Other current transfers	22795	24245	27365	29085	31790	33320	35350	36870	39485	41660	45605	50835
A Social security benefits	17575	18600	21050	22425	24595	25555	27140	28145	30035	31180	33595	37485
B Social assistance grants	4000	4355	4835	5050	5395	5780	6070	6380	6875	7735	8955	9900
C Other	1220	1290	1480	1610	1800	1985	2140	2345	2575	2745	3055	3450
5 Net saving	6050	7340	6205	6230	7140	7815	11005	11310	11905	11335	9950	5520
Total Current Disbursements and Net Saving of General Government	55910	60665	65255	69125	74065	78495	85265	87920	93865	99110	107005	113075

1.6 Current Income and Outlay of Households and Non-Profit Institutions

Million Swiss francs

	1980	1981	1982	1983	1984	1985	1986	1987	1988	1989	1990	1991
					Receipts							
1 Compensation of employees	102760	111540	119810	125310	130490	138335	146745	153900	163030	174295	189755	204015
A From resident producers	101740	110670	118910	124330	129490	137300	145765	152925	162010	173250	188665	202800
B From rest of the world	1020	870	900	980	1000	1035	980	975	1020	1045	1090	1215
2 Operating surplus of private unincorporated enterprises a	...	...	...	...	...	...	...	...	...	...	...	...
3 Property and entrepreneurial income ba	34115	37785	39395	40685	43750	45500	46650	48465	52365	56945	61775	64695
4 Current transfers	21915	23295	26225	27830	30345	31710	33595	34910	37295	39290	42925	47775
A Social security benefits	17575	18600	21050	22425	24595	25555	27140	28145	30035	31180	33595	37485
B Social assistance grants	...	...	4835	5050	5395	5780	6070	6380	6875	7735	8955	9900
C Other	4340	4695	340	355	355	375	385	385	385	375	375	390
Total Current Receipts	158790	172620	185430	193825	204585	215545	226990	237275	252690	270530	294455	316485
					Disbursements							
1 Private final consumption expenditure	108335	116020	122440	127755	134035	141015	145405	150715	157515	166735	178300	191145
2 Property income b	...	...	...	...	...	...	...	...	...	...	...	...
3 Direct taxes and other current transfers n.e.c. to general government	36710	39730	42940	45475	49220	51755	55615	56950	60990	64355	70410	75775
A Social security contributions	15550	16710	18035	19390	21165	22495	23900	25020	26715	28625	30815	33405
B Direct taxes	21160	23020	24905	26085	28055	29260	31715	31930	34275	35730	39595	42370
C Fees, fines and penalties	...	...	...	...	...	...	...	...	...	...	...	...
4 Other current transfers	1835	2120	2260	2295	2345	2490	2605	2750	2940	3150	3455	3700
5 Net saving	11910	14750	17790	18300	18985	20285	23365	26860	31245	36290	42290	45865
Total Current Disbursements and Net Saving	158790	172620	185430	193825	204585	215545	226990	237275	252690	270530	294455	316485

a) Item 'Operating surplus of private unincorporated enterprises' is included in item 'Property and entrepreneurial income'.
b) Item 'Property and entrepreneurial income' received is net of item 'Property income' paid.

1.7 External Transactions on Current Account, Summary

Million Swiss francs

	1980	1981	1982	1983	1984	1985	1986	1987	1988	1989	1990	1991
					Payments to the Rest of the World							
1 Imports of goods and services	68590	70920	68660	71850	81155	88065	86380	88420	96790	111080	113415	112135
2 Factor income to the rest of the world	4235	5290	5950	6650	6965	7845	9020	9495	9645	13200	14535	14965
A Compensation of employees	2910	3450	3790	3825	3935	4225	4690	5230	6005	6990	7990	8815
B Property and entrepreneurial income	1325	1840	2160	2825	3030	3620	4330	4265	3640	6210	6545	6150

Switzerland

1.7 External Transactions on Current Account, Summary
(Continued)

Million Swiss francs

	1980	1981	1982	1983	1984	1985	1986	1987	1988	1989	1990	1991
3 Current transfers to the rest of the world	3055	3410	3740	3905	4145	4475	4745	5095	5515	5895	6510	7150
A Indirect taxes to supranational organizations	...	...	...	...	...	...	...	...	...	...	...	...
B Other current transfers	3055	3410	3740	3905	4145	4475	4745	5095	5515	5895	6510	7150
4 Surplus of the nation on current transactions	-795	5430	8010	8075	10260	12375	12350	11265	13230	11485	11995	14620
Payments to the Rest of the World and Surplus of the Nation on Current Transactions	75085	85050	86360	90480	102525	112760	112495	114275	125180	141660	146455	148870

Receipts From The Rest of the World

	1980	1981	1982	1983	1984	1985	1986	1987	1988	1989	1990	1991
1 Exports of goods and services	62580	69100	69550	71760	80550	89015	89115	90525	97990	110510	115050	116740
2 Factor income from rest of the world	11250	14510	15140	16735	19795	21250	20595	20900	24185	28010	28130	28740
A Compensation of employees	1020	870	900	980	1000	1035	980	975	1020	1045	1090	1215
B Property and entrepreneurial income	10230	13640	14240	15755	18795	20215	19615	19925	23165	26965	27040	27525
3 Current transfers from rest of the world	1255	1440	1670	1985	2180	2495	2785	2850	3005	3140	3275	3390
A Subsidies from supranational organisations	...	...	...	...	...	...	...	...	...	...	...	...
B Other current transfers	1255	1440	1670	1985	2180	2495	2785	2850	3005	3140	3275	3390
Receipts from the Rest of the World on Current Transactions	75085	85050	86360	90480	102525	112760	112495	114275	125180	141660	146455	148870

1.8 Capital Transactions of The Nation, Summary

Million Swiss francs

	1980	1981	1982	1983	1984	1985	1986	1987	1988	1989	1990	1991
Finance of Gross Capital Formation												
Gross saving	45525	52440	55105	56920	61560	67940	75715	80610	88065	97780	103850	105055
1 Consumption of fixed capital	17960	19550	20400	20900	21700	23400	24395	25640	27745	30520	32765	34220
2 Net saving	27565	32890	34705	36020	39860	44540	51320	54970	60320	67260	71085	70835
A General government	6050	7340	6205	6230	7140	7815	11005	11310	11905	11335	9950	5520
B Corporate and quasi-corporate enterprises	9605	10800	10710	11490	13735	16440	16950	16800	17170	19635	18840	19450
C Other	11910	14750	17790	18300	18985	20285	23365	26860	31245	36290	42295	45865
Less: Surplus of the nation on current transactions	-795	5430	8010	8075	10260	12375	12350	11265	13230	11485	11995	14620
Finance of Gross Capital Formation	46320	47010	47095	48845	51300	55565	63365	69345	74835	86295	91855	90435
Gross Capital Formation												
Increase in stocks	5820	2450	1795	1345	1500	1365	4370	4975	3355	6435	7310	5625
Gross fixed capital formation	40500	44560	45300	47500	49800	54200	58995	64370	71480	79860	84545	84810
Gross Capital Formation	46320	47010	47095	48845	51300	55565	63365	69345	74835	86295	91855	90435

1.10 Gross Domestic Product by Kind of Activity, in Current Prices

Million Swiss francs

	1980	1981	1982	1983	1984	1985	1986	1987	1988	1989	1990	1991
1 Agriculture, hunting, forestry and fishing	...	...	...	...	...	8180	...	...	...	...	...	...
2 Mining and quarrying	...	...	...	...	...	-	...	...	...	...	...	...
3 Manufacturing	...	...	...	...	...	58625	...	...	...	...	...	...
4 Electricity, gas and water	...	...	...	...	...	5023	...	...	...	...	...	...
5 Construction	...	...	...	...	...	17325	...	...	...	...	...	...
6 Wholesale and retail trade, restaurants and hotels	...	...	...	...	...	44077	...	...	...	...	...	...
7 Transport, storage and communication	...	...	...	...	...	14763	...	...	...	...	...	...
8 Finance, insurance, real estate and business services	...	...	...	...	...	36994	...	...	...	...	...	...
9 Community, social and personal services	...	...	...	...	...	18943	...	...	...	...	...	...

1.10 Gross Domestic Product by Kind of Activity, in Current Prices
(Continued)

Million Swiss francs

	1980	1981	1982	1983	1984	1985	1986	1987	1988	1989	1990	1991
Total, Industries	...	...	...	...	...	203930	...	...	...	...	...	...
Producers of Government Services	...	...	...	...	...	26065	...	...	...	...	...	...
Other Producers	...	...	...	...	...	4655	...	...	...	...	...	...
Subtotal	...	...	...	...	...	234650	...	...	...	...	...	...
Less: Imputed bank service charge	...	...	...	...	...	10400	...	...	...	...	...	...
Plus: Import duties	...	...	...	...	...	3700	...	...	...	...	...	...
Plus: Value added tax	...	...	...	...	...	...	...	...	...	...	...	...
Equals: Gross Domestic Product	...	...	...	...	...	227950	...	...	...	...	...	...

1.12 Relations Among National Accounting Aggregates

Million Swiss francs

	1980	1981	1982	1983	1984	1985	1986	1987	1988	1989	1990	1991
Gross Domestic Product	170330	184755	195980	203865	213230	227950	243350	254685	268410	290360	313990	332685
Plus: Net factor income from the rest of the world	7015	9220	9190	10085	12830	13405	11575	11405	14540	14810	13595	13775
Factor income from the rest of the world	11250	14510	15140	16735	19795	21250	20595	20900	24185	28010	28130	28740
Less: Factor income to the rest of the world	4235	5290	5950	6650	6965	7845	9020	9495	9645	13200	14535	14965
Equals: Gross National Product	177345	193975	205170	213950	226060	241355	254925	266090	282950	305170	327585	346460
Less: Consumption of fixed capital	17960	19550	20400	20900	21700	23400	24395	25640	27745	30520	32765	34220
Equals: National Income	159385	174425	184770	193050	204360	217955	230530	240450	255205	274650	294820	312240
Plus: Net current transfers from the rest of the world	-1800	-1970	-2070	-1920	-1965	-1980	-1960	-2245	-2510	-2755	-3235	-3760
Current transfers from the rest of the world	1255	1440	1670	1985	2180	2495	2785	2850	3005	3140	3275	3395
Less: Current transfers to the rest of the world	3055	3410	3740	3905	4145	4475	4745	5095	5515	5895	6510	7155
Equals: National Disposable Income	157585	172455	182700	191130	202395	215975	228570	238205	252695	271895	291585	308480
Less: Final consumption	130020	139565	147995	155110	162535	171435	177250	183235	192375	204635	220500	237645
Equals: Net Saving	27565	32890	34705	36020	39860	44540	51320	54970	60320	67260	71085	70835
Less: Surplus of the nation on current transactions	-795	5430	8010	8075	10260	12375	12350	11265	13230	11485	11995	14620
Equals: Net Capital Formation	28360	27460	26695	27945	29600	32165	38970	43705	47090	55775	59090	56215

2.5 Private Final Consumption Expenditure by Type and Purpose, in Current Prices

Million Swiss francs

	1980	1981	1982	1983	1984	1985	1986	1987	1988	1989	1990	1991
Final Consumption Expenditure of Resident Households												
1 Food, beverages and tobacco	29900	32085	33940	35330	36960	38655	40135	41000	42390	43755	46550	49220
A Food	21750	23290	24470	25530	26985	28250	29360	29945	31035	31935	34105	36015
B Non-alcoholic beverages												
C Alcoholic beverages	8150	8795	9470	9800	9975	10405	10775	11055	11355	11820	12445	13205
D Tobacco												
2 Clothing and footwear	5220	5555	5640	5855	6045	6340	6735	6880	7005	7165	7510	7840
3 Gross rent, fuel and power	20990	22270	23855	25120	26470	27805	27065	27600	28105	29810	32560	36380
A Fuel and power	7630	8095	8105	8235	8890	9380	7625	7225	6770	7300	7725	8740
B Other	13360	14175	15750	16885	17580	18425	19440	20375	21335	22510	24835	27640
4 Furniture, furnishings and household equipment and operation	6315	6550	6625	6735	6925	7125	7435	7630	7970	8320	8700	8825
A Household operation	1790	1845	1905	1960	2005	2050	2095	2130	2200	2285	2420	2535
B Other	4525	4705	4720	4775	4920	5075	5340	5500	5770	6035	6280	6290
5 Medical care and health expenses	8585	9280	10070	10815	11400	12130	12965	13820	14610	15625	17000	19040
6 Transport and communication	12775	13925	14240	14400	14770	15310	15800	16355	17155	18800	20080	21290
A Personal transport equipment	3825	4135	4215	4090	4100	4195	4880	5065	5445	5960	5935	5825
B Other	8950	9790	10025	10310	10670	11115	10920	11290	11710	12840	14145	15465
7 Recreational, entertainment, education and cultural services [a]	9925	10700	11315	11870	12620	13325	14020	14695	15430	16530	17555	18725
8 Miscellaneous goods and services	9820	10530	11230	11850	12435	13240	14165	15110	16280	17400	18810	20170
A Personal care	2075	2195	2340	2440	2560	2710	2845	2960	3100	3240	3445	3670
B Expenditures in restaurants, cafes and hotels [a]	...	...	...	...	...	...	...	...	...	...	...	...

Switzerland

2.5 Private Final Consumption Expenditure by Type and Purpose, in Current Prices
(Continued)

Million Swiss francs

	1980	1981	1982	1983	1984	1985	1986	1987	1988	1989	1990	1991
C Other	7745	8335	8890	9410	9875	10530	11320	12150	13180	14160	15365	16500
Total Final Consumption Expenditure in the Domestic Market by Households, of which	103530	110895	116915	121975	127625	133930	138320	143090	148945	157405	168765	181490
Plus: Direct purchases abroad by resident households	4805	5125	5525	5780	6410	7085	7085	7625	8570	9330	9535	9655
Less: Direct purchases in the domestic market by non-resident households [b]	...	...	...	...	...	...	...	...	...	...	...	...
Equals: Final Consumption Expenditure of Resident Households [c]	108335	116020	122440	127755	134035	141015	145405	150715	157515	166735	178300	191145

Final Consumption Expenditure of Private Non-profit Institutions Serving Households

	1980	1981	1982	1983	1984	1985	1986	1987	1988	1989	1990	1991
Equals: Final Consumption Expenditure of Private Non-profit Organisations Serving Households	...	...	...	...	...	...	...	...	...	...	...	...
Private Final Consumption Expenditure	108335	116020	122440	127755	134035	141015	145405	150715	157515	166735	178300	191145

a) Item 'Expenditure in restaurants, cafes and hotels' is included in item 'Recreational, entertainment, education and cultural services'.
b) Item 'Direct purchases in the domestic market by non-resident households' is netted out from the appropriate items above.
c) Item 'Final consumption expenditure of resident households' includes consumption expenditure of private non-profit institutions serving households.

2.6 Private Final Consumption Expenditure by Type and Purpose, in Constant Prices

Million Swiss francs

	1980	1981	1982	1983	1984	1985	1986	1987	1988	1989	1990	1991
At constant prices of:1980												
Final Consumption Expenditure of Resident Households												
1 Food, beverages and tobacco	29900	29475	29315	29765	30210	30605	31285	31635	32040	32430	32800	33090
A Food	21750	21265	21035	21490	21885	22245	22825	23035	23290	23560	23870	24120
B Non-alcoholic beverages												
C Alcoholic beverages	8150	8210	8280	8275	8325	8360	8460	8600	8750	8870	8930	8970
D Tobacco												
2 Clothing and footwear	5220	5315	5185	5220	5230	5280	5415	5420	5425	5430	5490	5510
3 Gross rent, fuel and power	20990	21145	21205	21850	22385	22690	23160	23630	23795	24145	24365	25400
A Fuel and power	7630	7565	7405	7825	8135	8220	8455	8670	8555	8640	8615	9450
B Other	13360	13580	13800	14025	14250	14470	14705	14970	15240	15505	15750	15950
4 Furniture, furnishings and household equipment and operation	6315	6275	6070	6020	6100	6135	6270	6345	6520	6640	6640	6465
A Household operation	1790	1780	1750	1750	1750	1740	1740	1740	1745	1750	1760	1765
B Other	4525	4495	4320	4270	4350	4395	4530	4605	4775	4890	4880	4700
5 Medical care and health expenses	8585	8755	8845	9050	9195	9385	9625	9855	10025	10590	11125	11770
6 Transport and communication	12775	13150	13170	13145	13125	13085	13840	14285	14865	15585	15835	15940
A Personal transport equipment	3820	3905	3900	3735	3650	3585	4305	4430	4655	4940	4680	4360
B Other	8955	9245	9270	9410	9475	9500	9535	9855	10210	10645	11155	11580
7 Recreational, entertainment, education and cultural services [a]	9925	10175	10245	10460	10655	10915	11160	11325	11565	12015	12190	12245
8 Miscellaneous goods and services	9820	9955	10015	10225	10425	10675	11075	11505	11995	12195	12480	12570
A Personal care	2075	2120	2165	2190	2260	2340	2415	2470	2545	2500	2560	2605
B Expenditures in restaurants, cafes and hotels [a]	...	...	...	...	...	...	...	...	...	...	...	...
C Other	7745	7835	7850	8035	8165	8335	8660	9035	9450	9695	9920	9965
Total Final Consumption Expenditure in the Domestic Market by Households, of which	103530	104245	104050	105735	107325	108770	111830	114000	116230	119030	120925	122990
Plus: Direct purchases abroad by resident households	4805	4635	4805	4950	5085	5265	5420	5685	6030	5955	5950	5745
Less: Direct purchases in the domestic market by non-resident households [b]	...	...	...	...	...	...	...	...	...	...	...	...
Equals: Final Consumption Expenditure of Resident Households [c]	108335	108880	108855	110685	112410	114035	117250	119685	122260	124985	126875	128735

Final Consumption Expenditure of Private Non-profit Institutions Serving Households

	1980	1981	1982	1983	1984	1985	1986	1987	1988	1989	1990	1991
Equals: Final Consumption Expenditure of Private Non-profit Organisations Serving Households	...	...	...	...	...	...	...	...	...	...	...	...
Private Final Consumption Expenditure	108335	108880	108855	110685	112410	114035	117250	119685	122260	124985	126875	128735

a) Item 'Expenditure in restaurants, cafes and hotels' is included in item 'Recreational, entertainment, education and cultural services'.
b) Item 'Direct purchases in the domestic market by non-resident households' is netted out from the appropriate items above.
c) Item 'Final consumption expenditure of resident households' includes consumption expenditure of private non-profit institutions serving households.

Syrian Arab Republic

General note. The preparation of national accounts statistics in Syrian Arab Republic is undertaken by the Directorate of National Accounts, Central Bureau of Statistics, Damascus. The official estimates are published annually in the 'Statistical Abstract', issued by the Central Bureau of Statistics. The following presentation of sources and methods is based on a report entitled: 'National Accounts of the Syrian Arab Republic and Syria's First Effort at Implementing Stages of the New United Nations System of National Accounts (SNA)'. The estimates are generally in accordance with the classifications and definitions recommended in the United Nations System of National Accounts. The following tables have been prepared from successive replies to the United Nations national accounts questionnaire. When the scope and coverage of the estimates differ for conceptual or statisitcal reasons from the definitions and classifications recommended in SNA, a footnote is indicated to the relevant tables.

Sources and methods :

(a) Gross domestic product. Gross domestic product is estimated mainly through the production approach.

(b) Expenditure on the gross domestic product. The expenditure approach is used to estimate government final consumption expenditure, exports and imports of goods and services, and part of changes in stocks. This approach, in combination with the commodity-flow approach, is used to estimate gross fixed capital formation. Private final consumption expenditure is obtained as a residual. The basic data for government final consumption expenditure estimates are available from the budgets of the State, the municipalities and religious endowment administrations. Stock fluctuations are not estimated. For gross fixed capital formation, detailed classification of import statistics are utilized for machinery and equipment. Added to the c.i.f. values are import duties, other indirect taxes and estimated trade margins. For construction in the private sector, estimates are obtained by multiplying the area of floor space indicated in the annual census by the average price per square metre and by adding thereto the value of repairs carried out. The estimates of exports and imports of goods and services are based on foreign trade statistics and balance-of-payments data. For the constant price estimates, price deflation is used for government final consumption expenditure and gross fixed capital formation. Price deflation and extrapolation by volume index are used for exports and imports of merchandise. Private consumption expenditure is obtained as a residual and no estimates for increase in stocks are made.

(c) Cost-structure of the gross domestic product. The cost-structure table of the GDP is not being estimated.

(d) Gross domestic product by kind of economic activity. The table of gross domestic product by kind of economic activity is prepared at market prices, i.e., producers' values. The production approach is used to estimate the value added of most industries. The income aproach is used for some private services and for producers of government services. The commodity-flow approach is used to estimate the gross output of the trade sector. The data on field and animal agricultural production are collected by the Ministry of Agriculture. Gross output and intermediate input are compiled per individual commodity group, estimated

from figures gathered separately on quantities and prices. The agricultural prices were obtained through a census for the year 1971. For other years, only wholesale prices are known while producers' prices are derived on the basis of varying assumptions. Own-account consumption of agricultural production is mainly based on the sample survey conducted in 1970 and the 1968 family budget survey. Data for extractive industries, such as crude oil and phosphates, owned by the State are obtained from reports that include the size and value of production and intermediate consumption. Extractive industries in the private sector are based on industrial surveys. Data concerning industrial public enterprises are available from the Union of Industries. For the private sector, the Central Bureau of Statistics has undertaken a general economic survey for 1971, which covers all establishments employing more than nine persons and includes a sample of the smaller establishments. The frame for the survey was based on the 1970 population census. Other data sources has been used to cover establishments created after 1970. In the manufacture of food, the value of flour is multiplied by the ratio between the value of bread and the value of flour derived from the economic survey. Similar ratios between gross output and intermediate consumption and compensation of employees are used for the estimation of intermediate consumption and compensation of employees. The sources of data on the electricity and water industries are the accounts of the concerned enterprises. For construction, estimates of production values and intermediate consumption in the private sector are made by determining the value of construction projects completed during the year and adding to it the value of the completed portions of unfinished buildings and construction projects. The progress reports issued by the State Planning Commission are the prime source of data for construction in the public sector. For trade, gross margins are estimated as percentage mark-ups on commodity-flow values. The value of intermediate consumption is estimated as 8 percent of the production value. Information on railway and air transport and communication activities is supplied entirely by public enterprises. Gross output of road transport are based on the registration of licenses issued, and on gross revenue and cost data by type of unit, based on ad hoc transport sample surveys. Estimates of pipeline and sea transport are obtained from concerned enterprises. For banks, the production value is calculated by adding to actual expenditure imputed service charges. Estimates of insurance and real estate activities are derived from the concerned companies. The production value of the housing sector is estimated as rents paid to others for house leases plus the estimated rental value of owner-occupied houses. For community services, the basic data are available from the accounting records of public enterprises and the budgets of public authorities. The results of the 1971 general economic survey are used for some private services while proxy output indicators derived from the results of the 1970 population census and administrative records are used for other services. For the constant price estimates, double deflation is used for agriculture. Value added of all other economic activity sectors of GDP, except trade, is extrapolated by a quantity index. To obtain wholesale and retail trade margin at constant prices, the same percentages as those used for current prices are applied to the production values of the agricultural, mining and quarrying and manufacturing sectors.

1.1 Expenditure on the Gross Domestic Product, in Current Prices

Million Syrian pounds

	1980	1981	1982	1983	1984	1985	1986	1987	1988	1989	1990	1991
1 Government final consumption expenditure	11870	13656	15103	16154	18448	19785	21440	22945	24529	33433	38502	42779
2 Private final consumption expenditure	33858	48031	44749	49464	47535	54650	67026	98496	152683	142213	187433	237488
3 Gross capital formation	14365	15487	16513	17508	18082	20016	22443	23223	25992	33312	41351	49231
A Increase in stocks	...	...	...	...	...	...	...	...	...	...	...	...
B Gross fixed capital formation	14365	15487	16513	17508	18082	20016	22443	23223	25992	33312	41351	49231
Residential buildings	4271	4897	4877	4070	4678	5347	8971	9407	8587	9957	12075	14282
Non-residential buildings	1175	1058	1682	1834	2268	2344	2266	2048	2205	2647	3310	4085
Other construction and land improvement etc.	4271	4458	5582	6319	6706	7505	7017	6799	9033	9942	12392	14924
Other	4648	5074	4372	5285	4430	4820	4189	4969	6167	10766	13574	15940
4 Exports of goods and services	9345	10290	9572	9714	9360	9949	11256	20003	31212	62811	76042	76038
5 Less: Imports of goods and services	18168	21687	17149	19549	18083	21175	22232	36955	48369	62877	75000	99931
Equals: Gross Domestic Product	51270	65777	68788	73291	75342	83225	99933	127712	186047	208892	268328	305605

1.2 Expenditure on the Gross Domestic Product, in Constant Prices

Million Syrian pounds

	1980	1981	1982	1983	1984	1985	1986	1987	1988	1989	1990	1991
					At constant prices of:1985							
1 Government final consumption expenditure	16880	17698	18707	19705	21385	19785	17788	13762	12909	15203	14964	15874
2 Private final consumption expenditure	49642	53914	50732	49305	44287	54650	53246	66379	76166	65727	74000	80605
3 Gross capital formation	17006	17352	17838	18878	19090	20016	17736	11951	11469	10235	10761	10370
A Increase in stocks	...	...	...	...	...	...	...	...	...	...	...	...
B Gross fixed capital formation	17006	17352	17838	18878	19090	20016	17736	11951	11469	10235	10761	10370

Syrian Arab Republic

1.2 Expenditure on the Gross Domestic Product, in Constant Prices
(Continued)

Million Syrian pounds

	1980	1981	1982	1983	1984	1985	1986	1987	1988	1989	1990	1991
	At constant prices of:1985											
Residential buildings	5060	5353	5262	4246	4776	5347	5446	3839	2353	2183	2756	2870
Non-residential buildings	1431	1702	1809	1900	2306	2344	2172	968	956	803	742	806
Other construction and land improvement etc.	4912	4816	5999	6547	6825	7505	6811	3282	3847	2879	2778	2961
Other	5603	5481	4768	6185	5183	4820	3307	3862	4313	4370	4485	3733
4 Exports of goods and services	8714	8487	8934	9263	8875	9949	9196	10816	12343	14666	12653	13801
5 Less: Imports of goods and services	20164	18520	15605	15393	15208	21175	18857	22290	21574	22698	22893	23160
Equals: Gross Domestic Product	72078	78931	80606	81758	78429	83225	79109	80618	91313	83133	89485	97490

1.3 Cost Components of the Gross Domestic Product

Million Syrian pounds

	1980	1981	1982	1983	1984	1985	1986	1987	1988	1989	1990	1991
1 Indirect taxes, net	1420	400	867	1094	361	919	-190	-5359	-9149	-13361	-13749	-11952
2 Consumption of fixed capital	1443	1969	2115	2243	2334	2731	3065	4212	6299	7843	9824	10824
3 Compensation of employees paid by resident producers to:	...	...	...	...	...	...	...	...	...	...	...	...
4 Operating surplus	...	...	...	...	...	...	...	...	...	...	...	...
Equals: Gross Domestic Product	51270	65777	68788	73291	75342	83225	99933	127712	186047	208892	268328	305605

1.10 Gross Domestic Product by Kind of Activity, in Current Prices

Million Syrian pounds

	1980	1981	1982	1983	1984	1985	1986	1987	1988	1989	1990	1991
1 Agriculture, hunting, forestry and fishing	10369	12759	13854	15627	14805	17463	23816	32479	56575	49548	76514	94124
2 Mining and quarrying	6154	7004	6480	6024	6043	5948	3050	9662	15593	25099	40154	39339
3 Manufacturing	1825	5500	5176	5788	6047	6382	12298	8322	13329	16491	14111	16683
4 Electricity, gas and water	394	526	-47	201	-55	191	206	110	1306	-209	-208	-158
5 Construction	3574	3759	4327	4460	5006	5692	6692	6692	7177	8172	10128	12127
6 Wholesale and retail trade, restaurants and hotels	12693	16274	16846	17813	17701	18509	20045	31716	45690	52845	60875	69728
7 Transport, storage and communication	3555	4810	5513	5968	6254	8196	9883	11770	16830	21974	25542	28081
8 Finance, insurance, real estate and business services	3266	4113	4328	4202	4402	4180	4883	5912	6616	7810	9996	10966
9 Community, social and personal services	926	1154	1407	1468	1818	2195	2734	3168	3861	3891	4986	6011
Total, Industries	42756	55899	57884	61551	62022	68757	83607	109831	166977	185621	242098	276901
Producers of Government Services	8480	9840	10861	11693	13268	14408	16260	17808	18987	23176	26127	28586
Other Producers	34	38	43	47	52	60	66	73	83	95	103	118
Subtotal	51270	65777	68788	73291	75342	83225	99933	127712	186047	208892	268328	305605
Less: Imputed bank service charge	...	...	...	...	...	...	...	...	...	...	...	...
Plus: Import duties	...	...	...	...	...	...	...	...	...	...	...	...
Plus: Value added tax	...	...	...	...	...	...	...	...	...	...	...	...
Equals: Gross Domestic Product	51270	65777	68788	73291	75342	83225	99933	127712	186047	208892	268328	305605

1.11 Gross Domestic Product by Kind of Activity, in Constant Prices

Million Syrian pounds

	1980	1981	1982	1983	1984	1985	1986	1987	1988	1989	1990	1991
	At constant prices of:1985											
1 Agriculture, hunting, forestry and fishing	18071	18617	18074	18021	16461	17463	18590	15999	21131	14800	17891	19073
2 Mining and quarrying	5218	5918	5784	6032	6073	5948	6790	9166	11063	15442	20765	25115
3 Manufacturing	4550	3882	4722	5351	3379	6383	3897	4619	7553	6626	4883	5179
4 Electricity, gas and water	99	116	112	135	156	190	132	176	177	804	786	739
5 Construction	4209	4356	4690	4615	5121	5693	5355	2989	2676	2207	2257	2416
6 Wholesale and retail trade, restaurants and hotels	16359	19883	19626	18949	17571	18509	15644	21946	23163	17139	16032	17329
7 Transport, storage and communication	5948	6973	6914	7338	7704	8196	8312	8860	9107	9197	9436	9600
8 Finance, insurance, real estate and business services	4804	5226	5302	4896	4383	4180	4612	3936	4028	3614	3974	4091
9 Community, social and personal services	1724	1822	2181	2279	2132	2195	2005	1498	1328	1155	1315	1510

1.11 Gross Domestic Product by Kind of Activity, in Constant Prices
(Continued)

Million Syrian pounds

	1980	1981	1982	1983	1984	1985	1986	1987	1988	1989	1990	1991
					At constant prices of:1985							
Total, Industries	60982	66793	67405	67616	62980	68757	65337	69189	80226	70984	77339	85052
Producers of Government Services	11057	12095	13155	14091	15394	14408	13709	11362	11016	12070	12063	12348
Other Producers	39	43	46	51	55	60	63	67	71	79	83	90
Subtotal	72078	78931	80606	81758	78429	83225	79109	80618	91313	83133	89485	97490
Less: Imputed bank service charge	...	...	...	...	...	...	...	...	...	...	...	...
Plus: Import duties	...	...	...	...	...	...	...	...	...	...	...	...
Plus: Value added tax	...	...	...	...	...	...	...	...	...	...	...	...
Equals: Gross Domestic Product	72078	78931	80606	81758	78429	83225	79109	80618	91313	83133	89485	97490

2.11 Gross Fixed Capital Formation by Kind of Activity of Owner, ISIC Divisions, in Current Prices

Million Syrian pounds

	1980	1981	1982	1983	1984	1985	1986	1987	1988	1989	1990	1991
					All Producers							
1 Agriculture, hunting, forestry and fishing	527	923	942	1473	2065	2608	2613	2498	3528	6831	8930	9955
2 Mining and quarrying												
3 Manufacturing	3573	4350	4743	4573	3220	3732	3374	4550	7096	6763	7894	8968
4 Electricity, gas and water												
5 Construction	...	...	...	...	...	...	...	...	...	...	...	...
6 Wholesale and retail trade, restaurants and hotels	...	...	...	...	...	...	...	...	...	...	...	...
7 Transport, storage and communication	1168	1770	2065	2785	2212	2311	2151	2122	1822	2302	2795	4101
8 Finance, insurance, real estate and business services	9097	8444	8763	8677	10585	11365	14305	14053	13546	17416	21732	26207
9 Community, social and personal services												
Total Industries	14365	15487	16513	17508	18082	20016	22443	23223	25992	33312	41351	49231
Producers of Government Services	...	...	...	...	...	...	...	...	...	...	...	...
Private Non-Profit Institutions Serving Households	...	...	...	...	...	...	...	...	...	...	...	...
Total	14365	15487	16513	17508	18082	20016	22443	23223	25992	33312	41351	49231

2.12 Gross Fixed Capital Formation by Kind of Activity of Owner, ISIC Divisions, in Constant Prices

Million Syrian pounds

	1980	1981	1982	1983	1984	1985	1986	1987	1988	1989	1990	1991
					At constant prices of:1985							
					All Producers							
1 Agriculture, hunting, forestry and fishing	622	1107	1013	1542	2124	2608	2457	1338	1659	2255	2359	2114
2 Mining and quarrying												
3 Manufacturing	4241	4817	4949	4823	3356	3732	2907	3028	4131	2521	2291	1971
4 Electricity, gas and water												
5 Construction	...	...	...	...	...	...	...	...	...	...	...	...
6 Wholesale and retail trade, restaurants and hotels	...	...	...	...	...	...	...	...	...	...	...	...
7 Transport, storage and communication	1373	2072	2437	3271	2591	2311	1955	1276	980	811	803	881
8 Finance, insurance, real estate and business services	10770	9356	9439	9242	11019	11365	10417	6309	4699	4648	5308	5404
9 Community, social and personal services												
Total Industries	17006	17352	17838	18878	19090	20016	17736	11951	11469	10235	10761	10370
Producers of Government Services	...	...	...	...	...	...	...	...	...	...	...	...
Private Non-Profit Institutions Serving Households	...	...	...	...	...	...	...	...	...	...	...	...
Total	17006	17352	17838	18878	19090	20016	17736	11951	11469	10235	10761	10370

Syrian Arab Republic

4.1 Derivation of Value Added by Kind of Activity, in Current Prices

Million Syrian pounds

	1980			1981			1982			1983		
	Gross Output	Intermediate Consumption	Value Added	Gross Output	Intermediate Consumption	Value Added	Gross Output	Intermediate Consumption	Value Added	Gross Output	Intermediate Consumption	Value Added
All Producers												
1 Agriculture, hunting, forestry and fishing	12804	2435	10369	16270	3511	12759	17870	4016	13854	19492	3866	15626
2 Mining and quarrying	...	...	6154	...	...	7004	...	...	6480	...	...	6023
3 Manufacturing	...	...	1825	...	...	5500	...	...	5176	...	...	5788
A Manufacture of food, beverages and tobacco	...	...	716	...	...	382	...	...	-443	...	...	-275
B Textile, wearing apparel and leather industries	...	...	1837	...	...	1997	...	...	1225	...	...	1249
C Manufacture of wood and wood products, including furniture	...	...	530	...	...	452	...	...	421	...	...	453
D Manufacture of paper and paper products, printing and publishing	...	...	43	...	...	54	...	...	125	...	...	90
E Manufacture of chemicals and chemical petroleum, coal, rubber and plastic products	...	...	-2098	...	...	1626	...	...	1462	...	...	1181
F Manufacture of non-metallic mineral products, except products of petroleum and coal	...	...	213	...	...	289	...	...	707	...	...	965
G Basic metal industries	...	...	69	...	...	141	...	...	46	...	...	66
H Manufacture of fabricated metal products, machinery and equipment	...	...	474	...	...	516	...	...	1476	...	...	1670
I Other manufacturing industries	...	...	41	...	...	43	...	...	157	...	...	389
4 Electricity, gas and water	...	...	394	...	...	526	...	...	-47	...	...	201
5 Construction	9717	6143	3574	10413	6654	3759	12141	7814	4327	12223	7763	4460
6 Wholesale and retail trade, restaurants and hotels	14340	1647	12693	18341	2067	16274	18992	2146	16846	20094	2281	17813
7 Transport, storage and communication	5642	2087	3555	7718	2908	4810	8733	3220	5513	9538	3570	5968
8 Finance, insurance, real estate and business services	3478	212	3266	4368	255	4113	4558	230	4328	4506	304	4202
9 Community, social and personal services	1219	293	926	1584	430	1154	1890	483	1407	2019	551	1468
Total, Industries	70912	28156	42756	92401	36502	55899	100400	42516	57884	106514	44963	61551
Producers of Government Services	11989	3509	8480	13803	3963	9840	15214	4353	10861	16269	4576	11693
Other Producers	46	12	34	51	13	38	57	14	43	63	16	47
Total	82947	31677	51270	106255	40478	65777	115671	46883	68788	122846	49555	73291
Less: Imputed bank service charge	...	...	...	...	...	...	...	...	...	...	...	...
Import duties	...	...	...	...	...	...	...	...	...	...	...	...
Value added tax	...	...	...	...	...	...	...	...	...	...	...	...
Total	...	...	...	...	...	...	...	...	...	...	...	...

	1984			1985			1986			1987		
	Gross Output	Intermediate Consumption	Value Added	Gross Output	Intermediate Consumption	Value Added	Gross Output	Intermediate Consumption	Value Added	Gross Output	Intermediate Consumption	Value Added
All Producers												
1 Agriculture, hunting, forestry and fishing	19338	4533	14805	22517	5054	17463	30883	7067	23816	42723	10244	32479
2 Mining and quarrying	...	...	6043	6593	645	5948	4092	1042	3050	10407	745	9662
3 Manufacturing	...	...	6047	31223	24841	6382	35912	23614	12298	42247	33925	8322
A Manufacture of food, beverages and tobacco	...	...	517	...	...	215	...	...	730	10357	8379	1978

1832

4.1 Derivation of Value Added by Kind of Activity, in Current Prices
(Continued)

Million Syrian pounds

	1984			1985			1986			1987		
	Gross Output	Intermediate Consumption	Value Added	Gross Output	Intermediate Consumption	Value Added	Gross Output	Intermediate Consumption	Value Added	Gross Output	Intermediate Consumption	Value Added
B Textile, wearing apparel and leather industries	...	...	976	...	...	1249	...	...	1634	8605	6362	2243
C Manufacture of wood and wood products, including furniture	...	...	595	...	...	540	...	...	806	1361	968	393
D Manufacture of paper and paper products, printing and publishing	...	...	84	...	...	138	...	...	183	279	175	104
E Manufacture of chemicals and chemical petroleum, coal, rubber and plastic products	...	...	1836	...	...	1690	...	...	6475	15255	14469	786
F Manufacture of non-metallic mineral products, except products of petroleum and coal	...	...	1129	...	...	1066	...	...	1492	3344	1740	1604
G Basic metal industries	...	...	81	...	...	157	...	...	120	242	151	91
H Manufacture of fabricated metal products, machinery and equipment	...	...	723	...	...	1198	...	...	729	2762	1663	1099
I Other manufacturing industries	...	...	106	...	...	129	...	...	129	42	18	24
4 Electricity, gas and water	...	...	-55	1977	1786	191	2213	2007	206	2503	2393	110
5 Construction	13653	8647	5006	15195	9503	5692	18254	11562	6692	18254	11562	6692
6 Wholesale and retail trade, restaurants and hotels	19751	2049	17702	20604	2095	18509	22334	2289	20045	35277	3561	31716
7 Transport, storage and communication	10095	3841	6254	12612	4416	8196	15166	5283	9883	18209	6439	11770
8 Finance, insurance, real estate and business services	4708	306	4402	4508	327	4181	5252	369	4883	6349	437	5912
9 Community, social and personal services	2604	786	1818	3301	1106	2195	4397	1663	2734	5606	2438	3168
Total, Industries	109953	47931	62022	118530	49773	68757	138503	54896	83607	181575	71744	109831
Producers of Government Services	18569	5301	13268	19915	5507	14408	21698	5438	16260	23089	5281	17808
Other Producers	70	18	52	80	20	60	88	22	66	97	24	73
Total	128592	53250	75342	138525	55300	83225	160289	60356	99933	204761	77049	127712
Less: Imputed bank service charge	...	...	...	...	...	...	...	...	...	...	...	...
Import duties	...	...	...	...	...	...	...	...	...	...	...	...
Value added tax	...	...	...	...	...	...	...	...	...	...	...	...
Total	...	...	...	...	...	...	...	...	...	...	...	...

	1988			1989			1990			1991		
	Gross Output	Intermediate Consumption	Value Added	Gross Output	Intermediate Consumption	Value Added	Gross Output	Intermediate Consumption	Value Added	Gross Output	Intermediate Consumption	Value Added
						All Producers						
1 Agriculture, hunting, forestry and fishing	74734	18159	56575	80618	31070	49548	118343	41829	76514	136507	42383	94124
2 Mining and quarrying	16799	1206	15593	26430	1331	25099	41597	1443	40154	40651	1312	39339
3 Manufacturing	68370	55041	13329	81489	64998	16491	100664	86553	14111	118120	101437	16683
A Manufacture of food, beverages and tobacco	18416	18612	-196	19849	17342	2507	28501	27045	1456	34882	34393	489
B Textile, wearing apparel and leather industries	15452	10798	4654	20816	15494	5322	24008	18734	5274	32939	24859	8080
C Manufacture of wood and wood products, including furniture	2176	1401	775	3271	2239	1032	2741	1778	963	3285	2133	1152
D Manufacture of paper and paper products, printing and publishing	640	489	151	1054	814	240	1134	880	254	1487	1150	337
E Manufacture of chemicals and chemical petroleum, coal, rubber and plastic products	22590	17754	4836	25440	21773	3667	29409	27397	2012	29003	26883	2120
F Manufacture of non-metallic mineral products, except products of petroleum and coal	3565	2239	1326	4223	2613	1610	4594	3367	1227	4774	3536	1238
G Basic metal industries	299	235	64	538	395	143	1930	1653	277	2222	1914	308
H Manufacture of fabricated metal products, machinery and equipment	5149	3460	1689	6072	4152	1920	7918	5337	2581	8924	6059	2865
I Other manufacturing industries	83	53	30	226	176	50	429	362	67	604	510	94
4 Electricity, gas and water	3275	1969	1306	3352	3561	-209	4716	4924	-208	4618	4776	-158

Syrian Arab Republic

4.1 Derivation of Value Added by Kind of Activity, in Current Prices
(Continued)

Million Syrian pounds

		1988			1989			1990			1991		
		Gross Output	Intermediate Consumption	Value Added	Gross Output	Intermediate Consumption	Value Added	Gross Output	Intermediate Consumption	Value Added	Gross Output	Intermediate Consumption	Value Added
5	Construction	19825	12648	7177	22546	14374	8172	27777	17649	10128	33291	21164	12127
6	Wholesale and retail trade, restaurants and hotels	50661	4971	45690	59787	6942	52845	68043	7168	60875	76323	6595	69728
7	Transport, storage and communication	28649	11819	16830	37271	15297	21974	44590	19048	25542	48978	20897	28081
8	Finance, insurance, real estate and business services	7183	567	6616	8396	586	7810	10798	802	9996	11840	874	10966
9	Community, social and personal services	7369	3508	3861	7804	3913	3891	9429	4443	4986	11374	5363	6011
	Total, Industries	276865	109888	166977	327693	142072	185621	425957	183859	242098	481702	204801	276901
	Producers of Government Services	24681	5694	18987	33656	10480	23176	38821	12694	26127	43185	14599	28586
	Other Producers	110	27	83	126	31	95	136	33	103	156	38	118
	Total	301656	115609	186047	361475	152583	208892	464914	196586	268328	525043	219438	305605
	Less: Imputed bank service charge	...	...	...	...	...	...	...	...	...	...	...	...
	Import duties	...	...	...	...	...	...	...	...	...	...	...	...
	Value added tax	...	...	...	...	...	...	...	...	...	...	...	...
	Total	...	...	...	...	...	...	...	...	...	...	...	...

4.2 Derivation of Value Added by Kind of Activity, in Constant Prices

Million Syrian pounds

		1980			1981			1982			1983		
		Gross Output	Intermediate Consumption	Value Added	Gross Output	Intermediate Consumption	Value Added	Gross Output	Intermediate Consumption	Value Added	Gross Output	Intermediate Consumption	Value Added
						At constant prices of:1985								
						All Producers								
1	Agriculture, hunting, forestry and fishing	22470	4399	18071	23835	5218	18617	23336	5262	18074	23384	5363	18021
2	Mining and quarrying	6370	1152	5218	7217	1299	5918	6328	544	5784	6650	618	6032
3	Manufacturing	23337	18787	4550	26759	22877	3882	29985	25263	4722	32559	27208	5351
	A Manufacture of food, beverages and tobacco	5953	4569	1384	6573	5431	1142	6127	5570	557	6861	5938	923
	B Textile, wearing apparel and leather industries	5548	3912	1636	5590	3954	1636	4429	3328	1101	5370	4287	1083
	C Manufacture of wood and wood products, including furniture	1288	430	858	1074	356	718	947	329	618	970	363	607
	D Manufacture of paper and paper products, printing and publishing	191	112	79	189	110	79	259	152	107	352	215	137
	E Manufacture of chemicals and chemical petroleum, coal, rubber and plastic products	7303	8007	-704	9994	11196	-1202	11086	11966	-880	11164	12481	-1317
	F Manufacture of non-metallic mineral products, except products of petroleum and coal	1100	740	360	1233	828	405	2069	1426	643	2396	1497	899
	G Basic metal industries	235	169	66	338	241	97	282	220	62	332	260	72
	H Manufacture of fabricated metal products, machinery and equipment	1608	793	815	1651	699	952	3825	1491	2334	4133	1602	2531
	I Other manufacturing industries	111	55	56	117	62	55	961	781	180	981	565	416
4	Electricity, gas and water	905	806	99	1021	905	116	1144	1032	112	1467	1332	135
5	Construction	11403	7194	4209	11871	7515	4356	13070	8380	4690	12693	8078	4615
6	Wholesale and retail trade, restaurants and hotels	18502	2143	16359	22322	2439	19883	21899	2273	19626	21332	2383	18949
7	Transport, storage and communication	9400	3452	5948	11067	4094	6973	11035	4121	6914	11613	4275	7338
8	Finance, insurance, real estate and business services	5133	329	4804	5569	343	5226	5672	370	5302	5276	380	4896
9	Community, social and personal services	2273	549	1724	2458	636	1822	2931	750	2181	3132	853	2279
	Total, Industries	99793	38811	60982	112119	45326	66793	115400	47995	67405	118106	50490	67616
	Producers of Government Services	17049	5992	11057	17888	5793	12095	18844	5689	13155	19845	5754	14091
	Other Producers	53	14	39	57	14	43	63	17	46	70	19	51
	Total	116895	44817	72078	130064	51133	78931	134307	53701	80606	138021	56263	81758
	Less: Imputed bank service charge	...	...	...	...	...	...	...	...	...	...	...	...
	Import duties	...	...	...	...	...	...	...	...	...	...	...	...
	Value added tax	...	...	...	...	...	...	...	...	...	...	...	...
	Total	...	...	...	...	...	...	...	...	...	...	...	...

4.2 Derivation of Value Added by Kind of Activity, in Constant Prices

Million Syrian pounds

	1984			1985			1986			1987		
	Gross Output	Intermediate Consumption	Value Added	Gross Output	Intermediate Consumption	Value Added	Gross Output	Intermediate Consumption	Value Added	Gross Output	Intermediate Consumption	Value Added
	At constant prices of:1985											
	All Producers											
1 Agriculture, hunting, forestry and fishing	21526	5065	16461	22517	5054	17463	24102	5512	18590	21345	5346	15999
2 Mining and quarrying	6723	650	6073	6593	645	5948	8028	1238	6790	9715	549	9166
3 Manufacturing	32035	28656	3379	31223	24840	6383	32023	28126	3897	31584	26965	4619
A Manufacture of food, beverages and tobacco	6710	6163	547	5509	5294	215	5949	5678	271	5868	6256	-388
B Textile, wearing apparel and leather industries	5609	4741	868	5505	4255	1250	5927	4786	1141	5833	4562	1271
C Manufacture of wood and wood products, including furniture	1163	295	868	1281	741	540	1137	261	876	775	374	401
D Manufacture of paper and paper products, printing and publishing	350	242	108	503	364	139	498	357	141	155	109	46
E Manufacture of chemicals and chemical petroleum, coal, rubber and plastic products	11973	13403	-1430	12754	11064	1690	13175	13764	-589	14559	13135	1424
F Manufacture of non-metallic mineral products, except products of petroleum and coal	2731	1570	1161	2409	1343	1066	2438	1391	1047	2508	1289	1219
G Basic metal industries	324	272	52	458	303	155	353	241	112	133	101	32
H Manufacture of fabricated metal products, machinery and equipment	2779	1681	1098	2383	1184	1199	2105	1331	774	1727	1120	607
I Other manufacturing industries	396	289	107	421	292	129	441	317	124	26	19	7
4 Electricity, gas and water	1792	1636	156	1977	1787	190	1650	1518	132	1891	1715	176
5 Construction	13907	8786	5121	15196	9503	5693	14429	9074	5355	8089	5100	2989
6 Wholesale and retail trade, restaurants and hotels	19600	2029	17571	20604	2095	18509	17355	1711	15644	24286	2340	21946
7 Transport, storage and communication	12347	4643	7704	12612	4416	8196	12743	4431	8312	14807	5947	8860
8 Finance, insurance, real estate and business services	4699	316	4383	4507	327	4180	4939	327	4612	4213	277	3936
9 Community, social and personal services	3052	920	2132	3301	1106	2195	3225	1220	2005	2646	1148	1498
Total, Industries	115681	52701	62980	118530	49773	68757	118494	53157	65337	118576	49387	69189
Producers of Government Services	21525	6131	15394	19915	5507	14408	18002	4293	13709	13848	2486	11362
Other Producers	77	22	55	80	20	60	85	22	63	90	23	67
Total	137283	58854	78429	138525	55300	83225	136581	57472	79109	132514	51896	80618
Less: Imputed bank service charge	...	...	...	...	...	...	...	...	...	...	...	...
Import duties	...	...	...	...	...	...	...	...	...	...	...	...
Value added tax	...	...	...	...	...	...	...	...	...	...	...	...
Total	...	...	...	...	...	...	...	...	...	...	...	...

	1988			1989			1990			1991		
	Gross Output	Intermediate Consumption	Value Added	Gross Output	Intermediate Consumption	Value Added	Gross Output	Intermediate Consumption	Value Added	Gross Output	Intermediate Consumption	Value Added
	At constant prices of:1985											
	All Producers											
1 Agriculture, hunting, forestry and fishing	28109	6978	21131	24425	9625	14800	28710	10819	17891	29950	10877	19073
2 Mining and quarrying	11963	900	11063	16380	938	15442	21743	978	20765	26163	1048	25115
3 Manufacturing	38068	30515	7553	36403	29777	6626	34947	30064	4883	37414	32235	5179
A Manufacture of food, beverages and tobacco	9051	8116	935	6095	6658	-563	7018	7768	-750	8654	9054	-400

Syrian Arab Republic

4.2 Derivation of Value Added by Kind of Activity, in Constant Prices
(Continued)

Million Syrian pounds

	1988 Gross Output	1988 Intermediate Consumption	1988 Value Added	1989 Gross Output	1989 Intermediate Consumption	1989 Value Added	1990 Gross Output	1990 Intermediate Consumption	1990 Value Added	1991 Gross Output	1991 Intermediate Consumption	1991 Value Added
				At constant prices of:1985								
B Textile, wearing apparel and leather industries	6965	5376	1589	7329	5649	1680	6696	5152	1544	6704	5242	1462
C Manufacture of wood and wood products, including furniture	1053	761	292	1894	1338	556	1042	675	367	1011	656	355
D Manufacture of paper and paper products, printing and publishing	325	160	165	187	94	93	181	154	27	237	196	41
E Manufacture of chemicals and chemical petroleum, coal, rubber and plastic products	15538	13036	2502	15360	13042	2318	15434	13157	2277	16326	13922	2404
F Manufacture of non-metallic mineral products, except products of petroleum and coal	2401	1333	1068	2827	1333	1494	2083	1431	652	2062	1439	623
G Basic metal industries	149	107	42	227	120	107	315	258	57	310	256	54
H Manufacture of fabricated metal products, machinery and equipment	2544	1608	936	2372	1494	878	2010	1327	683	1877	1272	605
I Other manufacturing industries	42	18	24	112	49	63	168	142	26	233	198	35
4 Electricity, gas and water	1996	1819	177	2051	1247	804	2412	1626	786	2311	1572	739
5 Construction	7156	4480	2676	5867	3660	2207	6197	3940	2257	6637	4221	2416
6 Wholesale and retail trade, restaurants and hotels	25701	2538	23163	18991	1852	17139	17922	1890	16032	18971	1642	17329
7 Transport, storage and communication	15194	6087	9107	15213	6016	9197	15633	6197	9436	15903	6303	9600
8 Finance, insurance, real estate and business services	4358	330	4028	3846	232	3614	4242	268	3974	4376	285	4091
9 Community, social and personal services	2548	1220	1328	2318	1163	1155	2488	1173	1315	2860	1350	1510
Total, Industries	135093	54867	80226	125494	54510	70984	134294	56955	77339	144585	59533	85052
Producers of Government Services	12989	1973	11016	15305	3235	12070	15088	3025	12063	16025	3677	12348
Other Producers	95	24	71	105	26	79	110	27	83	119	29	90
Total	148177	56864	91313	140904	57771	83133	149492	60007	89485	160729	63239	97490
Less: Imputed bank service charge	...	...	...	...	...	...	...	...	...	...	...	...
Import duties	...	...	...	...	...	...	...	...	...	...	...	...
Value added tax	...	...	...	...	...	...	...	...	...	...	...	...
Total	...	...	...	...	...	...	...	...	...	...	...	...

Tajikistan

Source. Reply to the United Nations national accounts questionnaire from the State Committee of Republic of Tajikistan on Statistics.
General note. The estimates shown in the following table are in accordance with the United Nations System of National Accounts so far as the existing data would permit.

1.12 Relations Among National Accounting Aggregates

Million Roubles

	1980	1981	1982	1983	1984	1985	1986	1987	1988	1989	1990	1991
Gross Domestic Product	...	...	...	...	...	...	...	6027	6716	6639	7347	13407
Plus: Net factor income from the rest of the world	...	...	...	...	...	...	...	173	165	265	407	127
Equals: Gross National Product	...	...	...	...	...	...	...	6200	6881	6904	7754	13534
Less: Consumption of fixed capital	...	...	...	...	...	...	...	1032	1052	1133	1080	1141
Equals: National Income	...	...	...	...	...	...	...	5168	5829	5771	6674	12393
Plus: Net current transfers from the rest of the world	...	...	...	...	...	...	...	...	...	...	...	...
Equals: National Disposable Income	...	...	...	...	...	...	...	...	...	...	...	...
Less: Final consumption	...	...	...	...	...	...	...	...	...	...	...	...
Equals: Net Saving	...	...	...	...	...	...	...	...	...	...	...	...
Less: Surplus of the nation on current transactions	...	...	...	...	...	...	...	...	...	...	...	...
Equals: Net Capital Formation	...	...	...	...	...	...	...	...	...	...	...	...

Thailand

General note. The preparation of national accounts statistics in Thailand is undertaken by the Office of the National Economic Development Board, Bangkok. The official estimates together with methodological notes are published annually by the same office in 'National Income of Thailand'. The estimates are generally in accordance with the classifications and definitions recommended in the United Nations System of National Accounts (SNA). The following tables have been prepared from successive replies to the United Nations national accounts questionnaire. When the scope and coverage of the estimates differ from conceptual of statistical reasons from the definitions and classifications recommended in SNA, a footnote is indicated to the relevant tables.

Sources and methods :

(a) Gross domestic product. Gross domestic product is estimated mainly through the production approach.

(b) Expenditure on the gross domestic product. The expenditure approach is used to estimate government final consumption expenditure, increase in stocks and exports and imports of goods and services. The commodity-flow approach, supplemented by the expenditure approach, is used for the estimation of private final consumption expenditure and gross fixed capital formation. Estimates of government consumption expenditure are compiled from government accounts. Expenditure financed by foreign aids is added. For the main items of private consumption expenditure, the commodity-flow method is used. The per capita consumption of other items such as flour and chicken is based on family expenditure inquiries extrapolated by population and price changes. Stock changes in the private sector are estimated on the basis of commodity balance accounts. The estimate of private building activity is based on building permits issued for the urban areas and on municipal building construction costs. Additions are made for the imput profit of builders based on sample surveys, for permanent fixtures and fittings and for construction for own use. For the public sector questionnaires are sent to various government departments and enterprises. Estimates of other capital formation are based on foreign trade statistics. To the import values are added import duties, mark-ups and installation costs. Exports and imports of goods and services are derived directly from the balance-of-payments. For the constant price estimates, current values of most of the expenditure items are deflated by appropriate price indexes. For private consumption expenditure, direct revaluation at base-year prices is used when information is available on quantities of commodities consumed.

(c) Cost-structure of the gross domestic product. Estimates of compensation of employees are derived from the cost of production estimated through surveys for the agricultural sector, from data on the average wage per worker multiplied by the construction sector, and for the public and financial sectors, the estimates are obtained from their records. Depreciation is estimated as 6.67 per cent and 10 per cent of GDP for building construction and equipment, respectively. Indirect taxes net of subsidies are estimated by the Comptroller-General's Department. Operating surplus is obtained as a residual.

(d) Gross domestic product by kind of economic activity. The table of GDP by kind of economic activity is prepared at market prices, i.e., producers' values. The production approach is used to estimate value added of most industries. However, the expenditure approach is used to estimate part of the agricultural sector, the income approach for public administration and defence and part of the private services and the commodity-flow approach for gross output of the trade sector. For the agricultural sector, annual production figures of paddy and 19 other principal crops are reported by the Department of Agriculture while vegetables and fruit production is based on consumption estimates. The production figure of each crop is multiplied by the average ex-farm prices. Annual livestock production estimates are based on inventory changes and the number of animals that are exported or slaughtered while cost estimates are based on information from the Department of Livestock Development. Own-account consumption of rice and fish, vegetables and fruits is based on the quantity consumed multiplied by local prices and on the 1962 household expenditure survey, respectively. The value of forestry production is estimated by multiplying the average price per unit by the total quantity produced. For mining and quarrying, the total production quantity of each mineral is multiplied by its average price to obtain the production value. Data on the gross value of production, intermediate consumption and value added in manufacturing by both private and public enterprises and registered partnership are obtained from reports submitted to the Comptroller-General's Department, the Ministry of Industry, the Department of Revenue and the Budget Bureau. For other manufacturing, value added is estimated by applying approximate value-added ratios to the gross value of production derived from financial statements and tax returns. The estimates of electricity, gas and water are computed directly from the financial statements of the various agencies. Construction expenditure in the public sector is reported directly to the National Statistical Office. Adjustments are made for non-reported construction. For the private sector, it is based on reported data such as building permits of municipalities or on average price of new houses. Intermediate cost for each type of construction is derived from questionnaires sent to contractors and information received from architects and engineers. The income originating in the trade sector is estimated by the commodity-flow method which traces the flows of consumer and producer goods of both domestic and foreign origin through the distribution channel. Gross margins are derived from the differences between retail prices and producers' prices. For the public transport and communications sectors, information is obtained directly from the financial statements of the agencies concerned. In the private sector, information is obtained from various sources such as the operating accounts of enterprises, registration and licence data and information on the earnings of companies that supply data. Value added of travel agencies is calculated from a tourist expenditure survey. For the financial sector, estimates are based on profit and loss statements for banking and insurance and on income tax returns for real-estate brokers and warehouse operators. Value added of ownership of dwelling represents the estimated rental value after expenses. Net rent is estimated by multiplying the estimated average net rent per dwelling by the estimated number of dwellings. For business services, value added of legal services for the base year is estimated from the number of lawyers practicing while average income is based on the labour survey and extrapolated by the growth rate of total criminal and civiL cases. Other services such as auditing and engineering are estimated from auditing fees paid and the value of dwellings construction in the municipal area, respectively. Value added of public administration and defence are supplied by the Comptroller-General's Department. For other private services, including restaurants and hotels, data from the Department of Revenue licensing statistics and other data collected by the National Statistical Office are used. Both public and private education estimates are based on wages and salaries data of teachers. For the constant price estimates, price deflation is used to estimate the value added for most industries. For agriculture, when quantity figures of agricultural products are available, the base-year of mining and quarrying are extrapolated by quantity indicators. For public administration and defence, the number of employees by civil classification is used as an indicator of value added in real terms.

1.1 Expenditure on the Gross Domestic Product, in Current Prices

Million Thai baht

	1980	1981	1982	1983	1984	1985	1986	1987	1988	1989	1990	1991
1 Government final consumption expenditure	81433	97007	110167	118577	130100	142923	144564	147224	156710	176753	206824	237078
2 Private final consumption expenditure	433585	496417	534991	599560	628937	657365	695784	781064	885008	1039002	1249651	1420297
3 Gross capital formation	193060	225638	223155	276069	291215	298404	293236	362347	508354	651175	895735	1069434
A Increase in stocks	9073	12817	-3573	13931	8616	11405	1043	3078	29820	8299	19363	20908
B Gross fixed capital formation	183987	212821	226728	262138	282599	286999	292193	359269	478534	642876	876372	1048526
Residential buildings	28794	40434	48437	60702	66785	67993	80119	100613	115308	158374	201718	249651
Non-residential buildings	40262	40666	34462	35856	37657	36007	31339	37326	54083	84672	116738	138989
Other construction and land improvement etc.	30645	33925	46456	53891	61163	65262	61975	56039	69628	85432	117764	159895
Other	84286	97796	97373	111689	116994	117737	118760	165291	239515	314398	440152	499991
4 Exports of goods and services	159734	181325	192870	185222	216401	245252	290170	375597	514922	648488	745285	886577
5 Less: Imports of goods and services	201180	229029	207282	251184	258557	274073	267131	368317	536596	695882	909310	1063333
Statistical discrepancy	-4150	-11002	-12332	-7255	-20026	-13375	-23226	1998	31406	36940	-6085	-40626
Equals: Gross Domestic Product	662482	760356	841569	920989	988070	1056496	1133397	1299913	1559804	1856476	2182100	2509427

1.2 Expenditure on the Gross Domestic Product, in Constant Prices

Million Thai baht

	1980	1981	1982	1983	1984	1985	1986	1987	1988	1989	1990	1991
	At constant prices of:1988											
1 Government final consumption expenditure	106938	122904	124424	130959	141572	151252	150208	150637	156710	160778	173306	187924
2 Private final consumption expenditure	607226	620549	634507	682669	712971	723199	748896	813783	885008	990929	1127428	1208971
3 Gross capital formation	276079	299594	279223	340859	358564	345874	331495	394184	508354	594750	778624	879379
A Increase in stocks	6452	12424	-6561	13450	11921	12230	142	1776	29820	8432	23649	19333
B Gross fixed capital formation	269627	287170	285784	327409	346643	333644	331353	392408	478534	586318	754975	860046

1.2 Expenditure on the Gross Domestic Product, in Constant Prices
(Continued)

Million Thai baht

	1980	1981	1982	1983	1984	1985	1986	1987	1988	1989	1990	1991
	At constant prices of:1988											
Residential buildings	38623	49360	56464	68706	75329	74376	87191	108037	115308	146615	170298	195766
Non-residential buildings	53548	49403	39956	40484	42338	39380	34127	40209	54083	78205	98792	109220
Other construction and land improvement etc.	40616	41137	53778	60191	68236	71136	67540	60299	69628	79462	100449	125185
Other	136840	147270	135586	158028	160740	148752	142495	183863	239515	282036	385436	429875
4 Exports of goods and services	195231	213116	237964	223726	262337	288017	332419	404905	514922	624808	702531	813422
5 Less: Imports of goods and services	271199	272724	232838	309125	332452	290571	287873	384479	536596	653154	812936	928910
Statistical discrepancy	-542	-15733	-23779	7344	-4372	-26516	-17968	-2183	31406	33404	-14724	-52537
Equals: Gross Domestic Product	913733	967706	1019501	1076432	1138353	1191255	1257177	1376847	1559804	1751515	1954229	2108249

1.3 Cost Components of the Gross Domestic Product

Million Thai baht

	1980	1981	1982	1983	1984	1985	1986	1987	1988	1989	1990	1991
1 Indirect taxes, net	76233	84725	87338	104502	115719	113965	127029	149669	202842	236110	291137	322866
A Indirect taxes	81672	88722	93429	114158	119100	120749	133129	159561	208261	254206	311606	338743
B Less: Subsidies	5439	3997	6091	9656	3381	6784	6100	9892	5419	18096	20469	15877
2 Consumption of fixed capital	46659	54584	63140	72442	82543	92958	104016	116507	133421	157125	191123	234467
3 Compensation of employees paid by resident producers to:	164594	188611	221684	243261	257542	273066	290715	324025	372245	437348	525860	613205
4 Operating surplus	374996	432436	469407	500784	532266	576507	611637	709712	851296	1025893	1173980	1338889
Equals: Gross Domestic Product	662482	760356	841569	920989	988070	1056496	1133397	1299913	1559804	1856476	2182100	2509427

1.4 General Government Current Receipts and Disbursements

Million Thai baht

	1980	1981	1982	1983	1984	1985	1986	1987	1988	1989	1990	1991
	Receipts											
1 Operating surplus	...	...	...	...	...	...	...	...	...	...	...	...
2 Property and entrepreneurial income	5315	8075	7884	13224	8493	13273	15737	17325	17045	19985	23210	34160
3 Taxes, fees and contributions	99128	111836	119131	143104	152021	157162	169178	198513	262771	325544	417531	474524
A Indirect taxes [a]	81672	88722	93429	114158	119100	120749	133129	159561	208261	254206	311606	338743
B Direct taxes	17304	22927	25498	28722	32672	36145	35764	38648	54177	70944	105484	131230
C Social security contributions	152	187	204	224	249	268	285	304	333	394	441	4551
D Compulsory fees, fines and penalties	...	...	...	...	...	...	...	...	...	...	...	...
4 Other current transfers	4865	5808	5670	5149	6520	7689	7728	8766	9108	9786	10422	9899
Total Current Receipts of General Government	109308	125719	132685	161477	167034	178124	192643	224604	288924	355315	451163	518583
	Disbursements											
1 Government final consumption expenditure	81433	97007	110167	118577	130100	142923	144564	147224	156710	176753	206824	237078
A Compensation of employees	50828	55037	68074	76792	79391	85971	90425	94509	101413	118015	138725	155578
B Consumption of fixed capital	...	...	...	...	...	...	...	...	...	...	...	...
C Purchases of goods and services, net	30605	41970	42093	41785	50709	56952	54139	52715	55297	58738	68099	81500
D Less: Own account fixed capital formation	...	...	...	...	...	...	...	...	...	...	...	...
E Indirect taxes paid, net	...	...	...	...	...	...	...	...	...	...	...	...
2 Property income	10905	14600	18778	22275	26762	30519	35959	36695	40061	44421	39971	32172
A Interest	10905	14600	18778	22275	26762	30519	35959	36695	40061	44421	39971	32172
B Net land rent and royalties	...	...	...	...	...	...	...	...	...	...	...	...
3 Subsidies [a]	5439	3997	6091	9656	3381	6784	6100	9892	5419	18096	20469	15877
4 Other current transfers	1000	941	1033	903	1088	1218	1270	1389	1361	3086	3466	6312
A Social security benefits	98	148	151	205	247	233	218	268	347	397	443	1602
B Social assistance grants	-	-	-	-	-	-	-	-	-	-	-	1097
C Other	902	793	882	698	841	985	1052	1121	1014	2689	3023	3613
5 Net saving	10531	9174	-3384	10066	5703	-3320	4750	29404	85373	112959	180433	227144
Total Current Disbursements and Net Saving of General Government	109308	125719	132685	161477	167034	178124	192643	224604	288924	355315	451163	518583

a) For years before 1974, item 'Subsidies' is netted out of item 'Indirect taxes'.

Thailand

1.6 Current Income and Outlay of Households and Non-Profit Institutions

Million Thai baht

	1980	1981	1982	1983	1984	1985	1986	1987	1988	1989	1990	1991
Receipts												
1 Compensation of employees	171561	198172	233235	261644	277252	294853	309794	343902	393083	458191	545388	631819
A From resident producers	164594	188611	220181	243261	257542	273066	290715	324025	372245	437414	525937	613320
B From rest of the world	6967	9561	13054	18383	19710	21787	19079	19877	20838	20777	19451	18499
2 Operating surplus of private unincorporated enterprises	287108	316092	342127	350968	362836	381976	412472	492888	590666	693082	721134	781617
3 Property and entrepreneurial income	59559	73883	88078	100544	119148	134008	135094	132953	150216	188666	241534	306643
4 Current transfers	3331	2828	3610	5511	3651	3681	4143	5361	4216	6444	7624	14990
A Social security benefits	98	148	151	205	247	233	218	268	347	397	443	1602
B Social assistance grants	...	...	...	...	...	...	...	...	...	...	...	...
C Other	3233	2680	3459	5306	3404	3448	3925	5093	3869	6047	7181	13388
Total Current Receipts	521559	590975	667050	718667	762887	814518	861503	975104	1138181	1346383	1515680	1735069
Disbursements												
1 Private final consumption expenditure	433585	496417	534991	599560	628937	657365	695784	781064	885008	1039002	1249651	1420297
2 Property income	3765	4489	5135	6062	7910	9243	8298	9514	12544	16911	23529	33614
3 Direct taxes and other current transfers n.e.c. to general government	7831	9647	12821	15621	18168	20887	20344	20949	26602	31186	44323	55419
A Social security contributions	152	187	204	224	249	268	285	304	333	394	441	3454
B Direct taxes	7679	9460	12617	15397	17919	20619	20059	20645	26269	30792	43882	51965
C Fees, fines and penalties	...	...	...	...	...	...	...	...	...	...	...	...
4 Other current transfers	1122	1187	1092	1322	1898	2214	2348	2353	2889	2858	4280	5902
5 Net saving	75256	79235	113011	96102	105974	124809	134729	161224	211138	256426	193897	219837
Total Current Disbursements and Net Saving	521559	590975	667050	718667	762887	814518	861503	975104	1138181	1346383	1515680	1735069

1.7 External Transactions on Current Account, Summary

Million Thai baht

	1980	1981	1982	1983	1984	1985	1986	1987	1988	1989	1990	1991
Payments to the Rest of the World												
1 Imports of goods and services	201180	229029	207282	251184	258557	274073	267131	368317	536596	695882	909310	1063333
2 Factor income to the rest of the world	18438	28290	32843	31541	38139	48176	50126	51321	58165	64635	80108	97683
3 Current transfers to the rest of the world	395	317	359	444	461	693	680	612	948	1091	1950	3956
4 Surplus of the nation on current transactions	-42107	-54916	-22008	-66018	-48669	-40532	6885	-6865	-40238	-63696	-185832	-206597
Payments to the Rest of the World and Surplus of the Nation on Current Transactions	177906	202720	218476	217151	248488	282410	324822	413385	555471	697912	805536	958375
Receipts From The Rest of the World												
1 Exports of goods and services	159734	181325	192870	185222	216401	245252	290170	375597	514922	648488	745285	886577
2 Factor income from rest of the world	13044	16255	19921	24840	26688	30578	27688	28926	33395	41288	52990	58999
3 Current transfers from rest of the world	5128	5140	5685	7089	5399	6580	6963	8861	7154	8136	7261	12799
Receipts from the Rest of the World on Current Transactions	177906	202720	218476	217151	248488	282410	324821	413384	555471	697912	805536	958375

1.8 Capital Transactions of The Nation, Summary

Million Thai baht

	1980	1981	1982	1983	1984	1985	1986	1987	1988	1989	1990	1991
Finance of Gross Capital Formation												
Gross saving	146803	159720	188815	202796	222520	244497	276895	357480	499522	624419	703818	822211
1 Consumption of fixed capital	46659	54584	63140	72442	82543	92958	104016	116507	133421	157125	191123	234467
2 Net saving	100144	105136	125675	130354	139977	151539	172879	240973	366101	467294	512695	587744
A General government	10531	9174	-3384	10066	5703	-3320	4750	29404	85373	112959	180433	227144
B Corporate and quasi-corporate enterprises	14357	16727	16048	24186	28300	30050	33400	50345	69590	97909	138365	140763
Public	901	2003	2731	7393	11583	14455	15420	18530	25328	33730	41984	46368
Private	13456	14724	13317	16793	16717	15595	17980	31815	44262	64179	96381	94395
C Other	75256	79235	113011	96102	105974	124809	134729	161224	211138	256426	193897	219837
Less: Surplus of the nation on current transactions	-42107	-54916	-22008	-66018	-48669	-40532	6885	-6865	-40238	-63696	-185832	-206597

1.8 Capital Transactions of The Nation, Summary
(Continued)

Million Thai baht

	1980	1981	1982	1983	1984	1985	1986	1987	1988	1989	1990	1991
Statistical discrepancy	4150	11002	12332	7255	20026	13375	23226	-1998	-31406	-36940	6085	40626
Finance of Gross Capital Formation	193060	225638	223155	276069	291215	298404	293236	362347	508354	651175	895735	1069434
Gross Capital Formation												
Increase in stocks	9073	12817	-3573	13931	8616	11405	1043	3078	29820	8299	19363	20908
Gross fixed capital formation	183987	212821	226728	262138	282599	286999	292193	359269	478534	642876	876372	1048526
1 General government	58611	67986	66402	73645	82076	91919	83579	77482	78713	93689	134021	180954
2 Corporate and quasi-corporate enterprises	125376	144835	160326	188493	200523	195080	208614	281787	399821	549187	742351	867572
A Public	...	...	...	...	...	...	...	...	...	...	...	...
B Private	125376	144835	160326	188493	200523	195080	208614	281787	399821	549187	742351	867572
3 Other	...	...	...	...	...	...	...	...	...	...	...	...
Gross Capital Formation	193060	225638	223155	276069	291215	298404	293236	362347	508354	651175	895735	1069434

1.10 Gross Domestic Product by Kind of Activity, in Current Prices

Million Thai baht

	1980	1981	1982	1983	1984	1985	1986	1987	1988	1989	1990	1991
1 Agriculture, hunting, forestry and fishing	153960	162390	156098	184752	173642	167026	177537	204521	252346	279690	279081	321356
2 Mining and quarrying	11727	11208	13416	14106	18543	25962	19753	22221	26599	31805	34362	39331
3 Manufacturing	142504	172143	179438	203837	226360	231598	270605	315291	403034	497053	595873	706561
4 Electricity, gas and water	6373	10814	15601	17093	18609	24955	28888	33279	35298	42465	47687	52941
5 Construction	29383	34696	39890	46632	52427	53903	55715	62641	74449	102124	133438	170893
6 Wholesale and retail trade, restaurants and hotels	151210	178356	207605	201757	228879	252659	254753	302452	359226	421826	514656	573735
7 Transport, storage and communication	34894	41648	54350	56613	65078	78075	88202	99344	116611	138085	157319	175686
8 Finance, insurance, real estate and business services	45793	51296	59718	70865	78220	84283	90217	107204	128427	156687	199586	220116
9 Community, social and personal services	55920	64444	75638	80630	81222	89356	97046	100234	107326	122120	143538	162325
Total, Industries	631764	726995	801754	876285	942980	1007817	1082716	1247187	1503316	1791855	2105540	2422944
Producers of Government Services	30718	33361	39815	44704	45090	48679	50681	52726	56488	64621	76560	86483
Other Producers	...	...	...	...	...	...	...	...	...	...	...	...
Subtotal	662482	760356	841569	920989	988070	1056496	1133397	1299913	1559804	1856476	2182100	2509427
Less: Imputed bank service charge	...	...	...	...	...	...	...	...	...	...	...	...
Plus: Import duties	...	...	...	...	...	...	...	...	...	...	...	...
Plus: Value added tax	...	...	...	...	...	...	...	...	...	...	...	...
Equals: Gross Domestic Product	662482	760356	841569	920989	988070	1056496	1133397	1299913	1559804	1856476	2182100	2509427

1.11 Gross Domestic Product by Kind of Activity, in Constant Prices

Million Thai baht

	1980	1981	1982	1983	1984	1985	1986	1987	1988	1989	1990	1991
					At constant prices of:1988							
1 Agriculture, hunting, forestry and fishing	184576	194023	198825	208312	217518	227324	228191	228346	252346	276729	266414	278063
2 Mining and quarrying	6861	8327	11022	11659	16167	21553	21511	24107	26599	28404	31457	35542
3 Manufacturing	211031	224294	230235	255995	271855	268133	294521	341750	403034	467666	542169	606763
4 Electricity, gas and water	15614	17525	20732	21171	23230	26959	29890	31515	35298	42259	48233	50246
5 Construction	41882	44690	48008	53772	59390	59269	60138	66060	74449	95554	114420	135240
6 Wholesale and retail trade, restaurants and hotels	202067	221530	232111	229880	243382	262804	282136	318146	359226	392703	440088	461780
7 Transport, storage and communication	65669	60230	69607	72308	80548	85922	92046	100585	116611	128754	147103	155329
8 Finance, insurance, real estate and business services	75187	75506	79420	86237	90754	93071	95594	110065	128427	149610	180311	189125
9 Community, social and personal services	73090	80127	86027	89024	88061	95307	100821	102556	107326	112559	122668	131234
Total, Industries	875977	926252	975987	1028358	1090905	1140342	1204848	1323130	1503316	1694238	1892863	2043322
Producers of Government Services	37756	41454	43514	48074	47448	50913	52329	53717	56488	57277	61366	64927
Other Producers	...	...	...	...	...	...	...	...	...	...	...	...
Subtotal	913733	967706	1019501	1076432	1138353	1191255	1257177	1376847	1559804	1751515	1954229	2108249
Less: Imputed bank service charge	...	...	...	...	...	...	...	...	...	...	...	...
Plus: Import duties	...	...	...	...	...	...	...	...	...	...	...	...
Plus: Value added tax	...	...	...	...	...	...	...	...	...	...	...	...
Equals: Gross Domestic Product	913733	967706	1019501	1076432	1138353	1191255	1257177	1376847	1559804	1751515	1954229	2108249

Thailand

1.12 Relations Among National Accounting Aggregates

Million Thai baht

	1980	1981	1982	1983	1984	1985	1986	1987	1988	1989	1990	1991
Gross Domestic Product	662482	760356	841569	920989	988070	1056496	1133397	1299913	1559804	1856476	2182100	2509427
Plus: Net factor income from the rest of the world	-5394	-12035	-12922	-6701	-11451	-17598	-22437	-22394	-24770	-23347	-27118	-38684
Factor income from the rest of the world	13044	16255	19921	24840	26688	30578	27688	28926	33395	41288	52990	58999
Less: Factor income to the rest of the world	18438	28290	32843	31541	38139	48176	50126	51321	58165	64635	80108	97683
Equals: Gross National Product	657088	748321	828647	914288	976619	1038898	1110960	1277519	1535034	1833129	2154982	2470743
Less: Consumption of fixed capital	46659	54584	63140	72442	82543	92958	104016	116507	133421	157125	191123	234467
Equals: National Income	610429	693737	765507	841846	894076	945940	1006944	1161012	1401613	1676004	1963859	2236276
Plus: Net current transfers from the rest of the world	4733	4823	5326	6645	4938	5887	6283	8249	6206	7045	5311	8843
Current transfers from the rest of the world	5128	5140	5685	7089	5399	6580	6963	8861	7154	8136	7261	12799
Less: Current transfers to the rest of the world	395	317	359	444	461	693	680	612	948	1091	1950	3956
Equals: National Disposable Income	615162	698560	770833	848491	899014	951827	1013227	1169261	1407819	1683049	1969170	2245119
Less: Final consumption	515018	593424	645158	718137	759037	800288	840348	928288	1041718	1215755	1456475	1657375
Equals: Net Saving	100144	105136	125675	130354	139977	151539	172879	240973	366101	467294	512695	587744
Less: Surplus of the nation on current transactions	-42107	-54916	-22008	-66018	-48669	-40532	6885	-6865	-40238	-63696	-185832	-206597
Statistical discrepancy	4150	11002	12332	7255	20026	13375	23226	-1998	-31406	-36940	6085	40626
Equals: Net Capital Formation	146401	171054	160015	203627	208672	205446	189220	245840	374933	494050	704612	834967

2.1 Government Final Consumption Expenditure by Function, in Current Prices

Million Thai baht

		1980	1981	1982	1983	1984	1985	1986	1987	1988	1989	1990	1991
1	General public services [a]	19308	23586	24234	25469	26806	28264	28555	29083	30777	35937	41158	48699
2	Defence [a]	32564	40443	43865	47372	52557	60385	57125	57393	60218	63830	75525	85281
3	Public order and safety												
4	Education	20740	22651	29540	32270	36154	38777	41938	43139	46178	54035	63052	71389
5	Health	4551	5467	6877	8164	8880	10118	10324	10933	11868	13847	17005	20508
6	Social security and welfare	419	466	607	610	704	728	860	891	924	1407	1263	1443
7	Housing and community amenities	...	...	...	...	...	...	...	...	...	...	...	...
8	Recreational, cultural and religious affairs	...	...	...	...	...	...	...	...	...	...	...	...
9	Economic services	2739	3224	3485	3290	3191	3025	3294	3201	3711	4166	4739	4905
	A Fuel and energy	...	...	...	...	...	...	...	...	...	...	...	...
	B Agriculture, forestry, fishing and hunting	...	...	...	...	...	...	...	...	...	...	...	...
	C Mining, manufacturing and construction, except fuel and energy	...	...	...	...	...	...	...	...	...	...	...	...
	D Transportation and communication	2739	3224	3485	3290	3191	3025	3294	3201	3711	4166	4739	4905
	E Other economic affairs	...	...	...	...	...	...	...	...	...	...	...	...
10	Other functions [b]	1112	1170	1559	1402	1808	1626	2468	2584	3034	3531	4082	4853
	Total Government Final Consumption Expenditure	81433	97007	110167	118577	130100	142923	144564	147224	156710	176753	206824	237078

a) Justice and police are included in item 'Defence'.
b) Item 'Other functions' includes items 'Housing and community amenities' and 'Recreational, cultural and religious affairs'.

2.2 Government Final Consumption Expenditure by Function, in Constant Prices

Million Thai baht

		1980	1981	1982	1983	1984	1985	1986	1987	1988	1989	1990	1991
						At constant prices of:1988							
1	General public services	24871	29620	27169	27988	28967	29842	29632	29717	30777	32881	34624	38735
2	Defence	44851	52373	50929	53559	58720	64650	59787	58965	60218	58815	64876	69471
3	Public order and safety												
4	Education	25619	27950	32153	34569	38082	40399	43200	43950	46178	48160	51056	54455
5	Health	5963	6862	7738	8985	9610	10684	10708	11171	11868	12614	14318	16417
6	Social security and welfare	552	585	686	667	766	769	892	910	924	1296	1051	1137
7	Housing and community amenities	...	...	...	...	...	...	...	...	...	...	...	...
8	Recreational, cultural and religious affairs	...	...	...	...	...	...	...	...	...	...	...	...
9	Economic services	3600	4036	3964	3635	3447	3184	3423	3281	3711	3781	3934	3834

2.2 Government Final Consumption Expenditure by Function, in Constant Prices
(Continued)

Million Thai baht

	1980	1981	1982	1983	1984	1985	1986	1987	1988	1989	1990	1991
					At constant prices of:1988							
A Fuel and energy	...	...	...	...	...	...	...	...	...	...	...	...
B Agriculture, forestry, fishing and hunting	...	...	...	...	...	...	...	...	...	...	...	...
C Mining, manufacturing and construction, except fuel and energy	...	...	...	...	...	...	...	...	...	...	...	...
D Transportation and communication	3600	4036	3964	3635	3447	3184	3423	3281	3711	3781	3934	3834
E Other economic affairs	...	...	...	...	...	...	...	...	...	...	...	...
10 Other functions	1482	1478	1785	1556	1980	1724	2566	2643	3034	3231	3447	3875
Total Government Final Consumption Expenditure	106938	122904	124424	130959	141572	151252	150208	150637	156710	160778	173306	187924

2.5 Private Final Consumption Expenditure by Type and Purpose, in Current Prices

Million Thai baht

	1980	1981	1982	1983	1984	1985	1986	1987	1988	1989	1990	1991
					Final Consumption Expenditure of Resident Households							
1 Food, beverages and tobacco	208826	231439	240059	261959	256421	254289	261478	281824	323073	366841	410906	456443
A Food	165950	184925	188904	204275	193134	192633	194265	208590	234486	262236	285616	321196
B Non-alcoholic beverages	12442	13382	15011	17557	19538	21201	24125	27340	31762	37813	45064	47843
C Alcoholic beverages	18368	19256	21437	23582	26402	23042	25055	27102	36081	43480	53283	57880
D Tobacco	12066	13876	14707	16545	17347	17413	18033	18792	20744	23312	26943	29524
2 Clothing and footwear	41078	48477	52696	60720	66914	73962	80404	93620	104643	122416	149954	170406
3 Gross rent, fuel and power	40822	47599	54046	61635	68079	75608	81127	87977	92661	100470	109997	118538
A Fuel and power	12006	14141	14811	16468	17492	18207	19116	20225	20548	21757	23454	25428
B Other	28816	33458	39235	45167	50587	57401	62011	67752	72113	78713	86543	93110
4 Furniture, furnishings and household equipment and operation	30595	35818	38539	46594	49121	52718	56936	67848	79826	104067	131509	160295
A Household operation	8054	9034	10024	11155	12442	13684	14579	15924	18003	20001	21910	24240
B Other	22541	26784	28515	35439	36679	39034	42357	51924	61823	84066	109599	136055
5 Medical care and health expenses	17150	21229	23109	27469	36951	42715	48432	57258	69955	86756	107687	117236
6 Transport and communication	42372	53300	60694	66645	70830	73759	77742	90022	112531	135576	175852	189428
A Personal transport equipment	9836	11172	12376	14689	14653	11835	13104	19128	31356	42867	60676	55824
B Other	32536	42128	48318	51956	56177	61924	64638	70894	81175	92709	115176	133604
7 Recreational, entertainment, education and cultural services	19094	21945	24499	26932	28892	30180	33336	36464	41795	49212	60905	69534
A Education	2834	3460	3735	4225	4257	4339	4187	4271	4606	5332	6418	7814
B Other	16260	18485	20764	22707	24635	25841	29149	32193	37189	43880	54487	61720
8 Miscellaneous goods and services	46424	52039	59077	64760	71756	78280	85852	106173	124130	150846	176879	189925
A Personal care	8596	9606	10632	11774	12940	14159	15605	16917	18488	20235	21860	24056
B Expenditures in restaurants, cafes and hotels	33854	38199	43275	46673	52310	57185	62720	79896	93168	115143	133998	144249
C Other	3974	4234	5170	6313	6506	6936	7527	9360	12474	15468	21021	21620
Total Final Consumption Expenditure in the Domestic Market by Households, of which	446361	511846	552719	616714	648964	681511	725307	821186	948614	1116184	1323689	1471805
A Durable goods	32167	37327	40045	49715	52444	49585	53113	67500	91589	125533	173146	193785
B Semi-durable goods	316340	360959	382477	421995	437292	458905	485732	545943	638190	738202	841454	908735
C Non-durable goods												
D Services	97854	113560	130197	145004	159228	173021	186462	207743	218835	252449	309089	369285
Plus: Direct purchases abroad by resident households	4989	6027	6151	7896	7290	7622	7798	9902	15253	19204	36534	48497
Less: Direct purchases in the domestic market by non-resident households	17765	21456	23879	25050	27317	31768	37321	50024	78859	96386	110572	100005
Equals: Final Consumption Expenditure of Resident Households a	433585	496417	534991	599560	628937	657365	695784	781064	885008	1039002	1249651	1420297
					Final Consumption Expenditure of Private Non-profit Institutions Serving Households							
Equals: Final Consumption Expenditure of Private Non-profit Organisations Serving Households	...	...	...	...	...	...	...	...	...	...	...	...
Private Final Consumption Expenditure	433585	496417	534991	599560	628937	657365	695784	781064	885008	1039002	1249651	1420297

a) Item 'Final consumption expenditure of resident households' includes consumption expenditure of private non-profit institutions serving households.

Thailand

2.6 Private Final Consumption Expenditure by Type and Purpose, in Constant Prices

Million Thai baht

	1980	1981	1982	1983	1984	1985	1986	1987	1988	1989	1990	1991
						At constant prices of:1988						
					Final Consumption Expenditure of Resident Households							
1 Food, beverages and tobacco	267346	270424	269783	283093	286595	286381	292189	301528	323073	351808	377879	389429
A Food	203823	207400	208080	211383	209758	219420	219992	224349	234486	248463	260409	267664
B Non-alcoholic beverages	17512	17302	16801	18984	21217	22815	25117	27879	31762	37426	43295	45187
C Alcoholic beverages	28658	27805	29586	35527	37480	27959	29256	30495	36081	42003	49446	51200
D Tobacco	17353	17917	15316	17199	18140	16187	17824	18805	20744	23916	24729	25378
2 Clothing and footwear	61386	67011	71006	75956	79780	83663	87465	97381	104643	117760	135206	142606
3 Gross rent, fuel and power	69122	71284	73279	76548	79965	83147	86225	89451	92661	96247	100761	104773
A Fuel and power	15520	15763	16169	17142	17949	18493	19377	20229	20548	21171	22250	23471
B Other	53602	55521	57110	59406	62016	64654	66848	69222	72113	75076	78511	81302
4 Furniture, furnishings and household equipment and operation	41211	41004	40786	48385	51488	53393	58099	69224	79826	100438	122521	143838
A Household operation	11723	11468	11775	12730	14041	14576	15006	16352	18003	19492	20215	21647
B Other	29488	29536	29011	35655	37447	38817	43093	52872	61823	80946	102306	122191
5 Medical care and health expenses	23127	26524	27233	31553	40828	46611	50699	58388	69955	82139	94542	96667
6 Transport and communication	72156	69300	74206	80687	83788	78401	81370	92660	112531	132190	163598	167669
A Personal transport equipment	18518	19263	20468	23384	22047	16954	17058	21844	31356	40033	53797	50539
B Other	53638	50037	53738	57303	61741	61447	64312	70816	81175	92157	109801	117130
7 Recreational, entertainment, education and cultural services	28890	31019	31907	34435	35632	35792	35310	38201	41795	44764	51892	57514
A Education	3730	4353	4459	4750	4685	4628	4404	4397	4606	4922	5437	5868
B Other	25160	26666	27448	29685	30947	31164	30906	33804	37189	39842	46455	51646
8 Miscellaneous goods and services	61746	63229	67846	72585	78940	83543	90553	110216	124130	135453	143272	147743
A Personal care	10967	11392	11916	13090	13564	14006	15567	16941	18488	19852	20421	21601
B Expenditures in restaurants, cafes and hotels	44974	46364	49654	52158	57973	61904	66879	83511	93168	100956	103969	107699
C Other	5805	5473	6276	7337	7403	7633	8107	9764	12474	14645	18882	18443
Total Final Consumption Expenditure in the Domestic Market by Households, of which	624984	639795	656046	703242	737016	750931	781928	857049	948614	1060799	1189671	1250239
A Durable goods	49705	49802	50321	60248	62736	55787	58311	70733	91589	120660	160655	176515
B Semi-durable goods	419696	435275	442579	470018	490535	507098	530222	574468	638190	704202	760070	767870
C Non-durable goods												
D Services	155583	154718	163146	172976	183745	188046	193395	211848	218835	235937	268946	305854
Plus: Direct purchases abroad by resident households	6884	7432	7161	8863	8093	8243	8282	10269	15253	18242	32764	41136
Less: Direct purchases in the domestic market by non-resident households	24642	26678	28700	29436	32138	35975	41314	53535	78859	88112	95007	82404
Equals: Final Consumption Expenditure of Resident Households	607226	620549	634507	682669	712971	723199	748896	813783	885008	990929	1127428	1208971
			Final Consumption Expenditure of Private Non-profit Institutions Serving Households									
Equals: Final Consumption Expenditure of Private Non-profit Organisations Serving Households	...	...	...	...	...	...	...	...	...	...	...	...
Private Final Consumption Expenditure	607226	620549	634507	682669	712971	723199	748896	813783	885008	990929	1127428	1208971

4.1 Derivation of Value Added by Kind of Activity, in Current Prices

Million Thai baht

	1980			1981			1982			1983		
	Gross Output	Intermediate Consumption	Value Added	Gross Output	Intermediate Consumption	Value Added	Gross Output	Intermediate Consumption	Value Added	Gross Output	Intermediate Consumption	Value Added
						All Producers						
1 Agriculture, hunting, forestry and fishing	...	...	153960	...	...	162390	...	...	156098	...	...	184752
A Agriculture and hunting	...	...	136835	...	...	141975	...	...	136306	...	...	163006
B Forestry and logging	...	...	8775	...	...	9695	...	...	8846	...	...	9338
C Fishing	...	...	8350	...	...	10720	...	...	10946	...	...	12408
2 Mining and quarrying	...	...	11727	...	...	11208	...	...	13416	...	...	14106
A Coal mining	...	...	73	...	...	144	...	...	162	...	...	245
B Crude petroleum and natural gas production	...	...	-	...	...	807	...	...	3519	...	...	5158
C Metal ore mining	...	...	8897	...	...	6783	...	...	5412	...	...	3954
D Other mining	...	...	2757	...	...	3474	...	...	4323	...	...	4749

4.1 Derivation of Value Added by Kind of Activity, in Current Prices
(Continued)

Million Thai baht

	1980			1981			1982			1983		
	Gross Output	Intermediate Consumption	Value Added	Gross Output	Intermediate Consumption	Value Added	Gross Output	Intermediate Consumption	Value Added	Gross Output	Intermediate Consumption	Value Added
3 Manufacturing	...	...	142504	...	...	172143	...	...	179438	...	...	203837
A Manufacture of food, beverages and tobacco	...	...	35841	...	...	50909	...	...	51710	...	...	54394
B Textile, wearing apparel and leather industries	...	...	32032	...	...	37738	...	...	39793	...	...	43223
C Manufacture of wood and wood products, including furniture	...	...	10174	...	...	9293	...	...	9263	...	...	10159
D Manufacture of paper and paper products, printing and publishing	...	...	4333	...	...	5114	...	...	5686	...	...	6151
E Manufacture of chemicals and chemical petroleum, coal, rubber and plastic products	...	...	20324	...	...	21779	...	...	22716	...	...	28283
F Manufacture of non-metallic mineral products, except products of petroleum and coal	...	...	6779	...	...	8739	...	...	9774	...	...	11613
G Basic metal industries	...	...	4999	...	...	4642	...	...	4266	...	...	4389
H Manufacture of fabricated metal products, machinery and equipment	...	...	22444	...	...	26480	...	...	27661	...	...	34856
I Other manufacturing industries	...	...	5578	...	...	7449	...	...	8569	...	...	10769
4 Electricity, gas and water	...	...	6373	...	...	10814	...	...	15601	...	...	17093
A Electricity, gas and steam	...	...	4994	...	...	9267	...	...	13061	...	...	14372
B Water works and supply	...	...	1379	...	...	1547	...	...	2540	...	...	2721
5 Construction	...	...	29383	...	...	34696	...	...	39890	...	...	46632
6 Wholesale and retail trade, restaurants and hotels	...	...	151210	...	...	178356	...	...	207605	...	...	201757
A Wholesale and retail trade	...	...	116711	...	...	138594	...	...	161738	...	...	152380
B Restaurants and hotels	...	...	34499	...	...	39762	...	...	45867	...	...	49377
Restaurants	...	...	29439	...	...	34582	...	...	39575	...	...	42739
Hotels and other lodging places	...	...	5060	...	...	5180	...	...	6292	...	...	6638
7 Transport, storage and communication	...	...	34894	...	...	41648	...	...	54350	...	...	56613
A Transport and storage	...	...	31286	...	...	37036	...	...	48544	...	...	50642
B Communication	...	...	3608	...	...	4612	...	...	5806	...	...	5971
8 Finance, insurance, real estate and business services	...	...	45793	...	...	51296	...	...	59718	...	...	70865
A Financial institutions	...	...	15584	...	...	17736	...	...	20249	...	...	24326
B Insurance	...	...	1820	...	...	2090	...	...	2382	...	...	2882
C Real estate and business services	...	...	28389	...	...	31470	...	...	37087	...	...	43657
Real estate, except dwellings	...	...	3099	...	...	2007	...	...	2911	...	...	3667
Dwellings	...	...	22682	...	...	26344	...	...	30922	...	...	35732
9 Community, social and personal services	...	...	55920	...	...	64444	...	...	75638	...	...	80630
A Sanitary and similar services	...	...	...	...	...	...	...	...	...	...	...	...
B Social and related community services	...	...	29827	...	...	33501	...	...	41754	...	...	46668
Educational services	...	...	22027	...	...	24308	...	...	30683	...	...	34161
Medical, dental, other health and veterinary services	...	...	7800	...	...	9193	...	...	11071	...	...	12507
C Recreational and cultural services	...	...	4154	...	...	4463	...	...	4777	...	...	5008
D Personal and household services	...	...	21939	...	...	26480	...	...	29107	...	...	28954
Total, Industries	...	...	631764	...	...	726995	...	...	801754	...	...	876285
Producers of Government Services	...	...	30718	...	...	33361	...	...	39815	...	...	44704
Other Producers	...	...	...	...	...	...	...	...	...	...	...	...
Total	...	...	662482	...	...	760356	...	...	841569	...	...	920989
Less: Imputed bank service charge	...	...	...	...	...	...	...	...	...	...	...	...
Import duties	...	...	...	...	...	...	...	...	...	...	...	...
Value added tax	...	...	...	...	...	...	...	...	...	...	...	...
Total	...	...	662482	...	...	760356	...	...	841569	...	...	920989

Thailand

4.1 Derivation of Value Added by Kind of Activity, in Current Prices

Million Thai baht

	1984			1985			1986			1987		
	Gross Output	Intermediate Consumption	Value Added	Gross Output	Intermediate Consumption	Value Added	Gross Output	Intermediate Consumption	Value Added	Gross Output	Intermediate Consumption	Value Added
All Producers												
1 Agriculture, hunting, forestry and fishing	...	...	173642	...	...	167026	...	...	177537	...	...	204521
A Agriculture and hunting	...	...	152090	...	...	144414	...	...	151918	...	...	173361
B Forestry and logging	...	...	9692	...	...	9497	...	...	9985	...	...	11045
C Fishing	...	...	11860	...	...	13115	...	...	15634	...	...	20115
2 Mining and quarrying	...	...	18543	...	...	25962	...	...	19753	...	...	22221
A Coal mining	...	...	476	...	...	2115	...	...	2314	...	...	2899
B Crude petroleum and natural gas production	...	...	8309	...	...	14290	...	...	10577	...	...	12165
C Metal ore mining	...	...	4320	...	...	3678	...	...	1312	...	...	1209
D Other mining	...	...	5438	...	...	5879	...	...	5550	...	...	5948
3 Manufacturing	...	...	226360	...	...	231598	...	...	270605	...	...	315291
A Manufacture of food, beverages and tobacco	...	...	64856	...	...	67228	...	...	66714	...	...	69098
B Textile, wearing apparel and leather industries	...	...	49210	...	...	53645	...	...	64562	...	...	83353
C Manufacture of wood and wood products, including furniture	...	...	10714	...	...	10658	...	...	11472	...	...	14861
D Manufacture of paper and paper products, printing and publishing	...	...	6399	...	...	6611	...	...	7597	...	...	8843
E Manufacture of chemicals and chemical petroleum, coal, rubber and plastic products	...	...	26955	...	...	26215	...	...	43906	...	...	41517
F Manufacture of non-metallic mineral products, except products of petroleum and coal	...	...	13863	...	...	14653	...	...	15123	...	...	17565
G Basic metal industries	...	...	5116	...	...	5414	...	...	4959	...	...	5683
H Manufacture of fabricated metal products, machinery and equipment	...	...	38230	...	...	35408	...	...	40862	...	...	53284
I Other manufacturing industries	...	...	11017	...	...	11766	...	...	15410	...	...	21087
4 Electricity, gas and water	...	...	18609	...	...	24955	...	...	28888	...	...	33279
A Electricity, gas and steam	...	...	15885	...	...	20474	...	...	24298	...	...	27662
B Water works and supply	...	...	2724	...	...	4481	...	...	4590	...	...	5617
5 Construction	...	...	52427	...	...	53903	...	...	55715	...	...	62641
6 Wholesale and retail trade, restaurants and hotels	...	...	228879	...	...	252659	...	...	254753	...	...	302452
A Wholesale and retail trade	...	...	175026	...	...	193810	...	...	189986	...	...	223129
B Restaurants and hotels	...	...	53853	...	...	58849	...	...	64767	...	...	79323
Restaurants	...	...	46791	...	...	51660	...	...	55320	...	...	66327
Hotels and other lodging places	...	...	7062	...	...	7189	...	...	9447	...	...	12996
7 Transport, storage and communication	...	...	65078	...	...	78075	...	...	88202	...	...	99344
A Transport and storage	...	...	57639	...	...	68768	...	...	75239	...	...	85614
B Communication	...	...	7439	...	...	9307	...	...	12963	...	...	13730
8 Finance, insurance, real estate and business services	...	...	78220	...	...	84283	...	...	90217	...	...	107204
A Financial institutions	...	...	26802	...	...	27810	...	...	28374	...	...	39143
B Insurance	...	...	3077	...	...	3805	...	...	4626	...	...	5093
C Real estate and business services	...	...	48341	...	...	52668	...	...	57217	...	...	62968
Real estate, except dwellings	...	...	3612	...	...	3656	...	...	4102	...	...	5744
Dwellings	...	...	39728	...	...	43934	...	...	47899	...	...	51773
9 Community, social and personal services	...	...	81222	...	...	89356	...	...	97046	...	...	100234
A Sanitary and similar services	...	...	...	...	...	...	...	...	...	...	...	...
B Social and related community services	...	...	50189	...	...	54586	...	...	57859	...	...	60989
Educational services	...	...	36788	...	...	39722	...	...	42067	...	...	44036
Medical, dental, other health and veterinary services	...	...	13401	...	...	14864	...	...	15792	...	...	16953
C Recreational and cultural services	...	...	5834	...	...	5979	...	...	6211	...	...	7027
D Personal and household services	...	...	25199	...	...	28791	...	...	32976	...	...	32218

4.1 Derivation of Value Added by Kind of Activity, in Current Prices
(Continued)

Million Thai baht

	1984			1985			1986			1987		
	Gross Output	Intermediate Consumption	Value Added	Gross Output	Intermediate Consumption	Value Added	Gross Output	Intermediate Consumption	Value Added	Gross Output	Intermediate Consumption	Value Added
Total, Industries	...	...	942980	...	...	1007817	...	...	1082716	...	...	1247187
Producers of Government Services	...	...	45090	...	...	48679	...	...	50681	...	...	52726
Other Producers	...	...	...	...	...	...	...	...	...	...	...	...
Total	...	...	988070	...	...	1056496	...	...	1133397	...	...	1299913
Less: Imputed bank service charge	...	...	...	...	...	...	...	...	...	...	...	...
Import duties	...	...	...	...	...	...	...	...	...	...	...	...
Value added tax	...	...	...	...	...	...	...	...	...	...	...	...
Total	...	...	988070	...	...	1056496	...	...	1133397	...	...	1299913

	1988			1989			1990			1991		
	Gross Output	Intermediate Consumption	Value Added	Gross Output	Intermediate Consumption	Value Added	Gross Output	Intermediate Consumption	Value Added	Gross Output	Intermediate Consumption	Value Added
						All Producers						
1 Agriculture, hunting, forestry and fishing	...	...	252346	...	...	279690	...	...	279081	...	...	321356
A Agriculture and hunting	...	...	216603	...	...	243645	...	...	239831	...	...	280615
B Forestry and logging	...	...	10489	...	...	8584	...	...	6972	...	...	5194
C Fishing	...	...	25254	...	...	27461	...	...	32278	...	...	35547
2 Mining and quarrying	...	...	26599	...	...	31805	...	...	34362	...	...	39331
A Coal mining	...	...	3036	...	...	3721	...	...	5108	...	...	5929
B Crude petroleum and natural gas production	...	...	13233	...	...	13861	...	...	15754	...	...	18671
C Metal ore mining	...	...	1393	...	...	2039	...	...	1035	...	...	508
D Other mining	...	...	8937	...	...	12184	...	...	12465	...	...	14223
3 Manufacturing	...	...	403034	...	...	497053	...	...	595873	...	...	706561
A Manufacture of food, beverages and tobacco	...	...	88171	...	...	109958	...	...	113539	...	...	127401
B Textile, wearing apparel and leather industries	...	...	102095	...	...	122434	...	...	150094	...	...	186380
C Manufacture of wood and wood products, including furniture	...	...	18427	...	...	23612	...	...	29466	...	...	32472
D Manufacture of paper and paper products, printing and publishing	...	...	10306	...	...	11699	...	...	13173	...	...	15902
E Manufacture of chemicals and chemical petroleum, coal, rubber and plastic products	...	...	50314	...	...	51563	...	...	54947	...	...	73364
F Manufacture of non-metallic mineral products, except products of petroleum and coal	...	...	20939	...	...	26978	...	...	37130	...	...	46317
G Basic metal industries	...	...	7016	...	...	9063	...	...	10529	...	...	10597
H Manufacture of fabricated metal products, machinery and equipment	...	...	79863	...	...	107868	...	...	139267	...	...	154919
I Other manufacturing industries	...	...	25903	...	...	33878	...	...	47728	...	...	59209
4 Electricity, gas and water	...	...	35298	...	...	42465	...	...	47687	...	...	52941
A Electricity, gas and steam	...	...	29579	...	...	35824	...	...	39838	...	...	44520
B Water works and supply	...	...	5719	...	...	6641	...	...	7849	...	...	8421
5 Construction	...	...	74449	...	...	102124	...	...	133438	...	...	170893
6 Wholesale and retail trade, restaurants and hotels	...	...	359226	...	...	421826	...	...	514656	...	...	573735
A Wholesale and retail trade	...	...	266257	...	...	306725	...	...	377527	...	...	426233
B Restaurants and hotels	...	...	92969	...	...	115101	...	...	137129	...	...	147502
Restaurants	...	...	75050	...	...	89091	...	...	104097	...	...	116220
Hotels and other lodging places	...	...	17919	...	...	26010	...	...	33032	...	...	31282
7 Transport, storage and communication	...	...	116611	...	...	138085	...	...	157319	...	...	175686
A Transport and storage	...	...	100389	...	...	117941	...	...	132356	...	...	146426
B Communication	...	...	16222	...	...	20144	...	...	24963	...	...	29260
8 Finance, insurance, real estate and business services	...	...	128427	...	...	156687	...	...	199586	...	...	220116
A Financial institutions	...	...	48559	...	...	64686	...	...	89956	...	...	103493
B Insurance	...	...	7771	...	...	11033	...	...	14127	...	...	17275
C Real estate and business services	...	...	72097	...	...	80968	...	...	95503	...	...	99348
Real estate, except dwellings	...	...	9890	...	...	11484	...	...	17980	...	...	13574

Thailand

4.1 Derivation of Value Added by Kind of Activity, in Current Prices
(Continued)

Million Thai baht

	1988			1989			1990			1991		
	Gross Output	Intermediate Consumption	Value Added	Gross Output	Intermediate Consumption	Value Added	Gross Output	Intermediate Consumption	Value Added	Gross Output	Intermediate Consumption	Value Added
Dwellings	...	...	55416	...	...	60457	...	...	66238	...	...	71589
9 Community, social and personal services	...	...	107326	...	...	122120	...	...	143538	...	...	162325
A Sanitary and similar services	...	...	...	...	...	...	...	...	...	...	...	...
B Social and related community services	...	...	65190	...	...	76871	...	...	90543	...	...	103103
Educational services	...	...	46889	...	...	54669	...	...	63873	...	...	71514
Medical, dental, other health and veterinary services	...	...	18301	...	...	22202	...	...	26670	...	...	31589
C Recreational and cultural services	...	...	7919	...	...	8885	...	...	10506	...	...	12570
D Personal and household services	...	...	34217	...	...	36364	...	...	42489	...	...	46652
Total, Industries	...	...	1503316	...	...	1791855	...	...	2105540	...	...	2422944
Producers of Government Services	...	...	56488	...	...	64621	...	...	76560	...	...	86483
Other Producers	...	...	...	...	...	...	...	...	...	...	...	...
Total	...	...	1559804	...	...	1856476	...	...	2182100	...	...	2509427
Less: Imputed bank service charge	...	...	...	...	...	...	...	...	...	...	...	...
Import duties	...	...	...	...	...	...	...	...	...	...	...	...
Value added tax	...	...	...	...	...	...	...	...	...	...	...	...
Total	...	...	1559804	...	...	1856476	...	...	2182100	...	...	2509427

4.2 Derivation of Value Added by Kind of Activity, in Constant Prices

Million Thai baht

	1980			1981			1982			1983		
	Gross Output	Intermediate Consumption	Value Added	Gross Output	Intermediate Consumption	Value Added	Gross Output	Intermediate Consumption	Value Added	Gross Output	Intermediate Consumption	Value Added

At constant prices of:1988

All Producers

	Gross Output	Intermediate Consumption	Value Added	Gross Output	Intermediate Consumption	Value Added	Gross Output	Intermediate Consumption	Value Added	Gross Output	Intermediate Consumption	Value Added
1 Agriculture, hunting, forestry and fishing	...	...	184576	...	...	194023	...	...	198825	...	...	208312
A Agriculture and hunting	...	...	155121	...	...	162756	...	...	166724	...	...	176035
B Forestry and logging	...	...	13217	...	...	11992	...	...	11254	...	...	11241
C Fishing	...	...	16238	...	...	19275	...	...	20847	...	...	21036
2 Mining and quarrying	...	...	6861	...	...	8327	...	...	11022	...	...	11659
A Coal mining	...	...	582	...	...	695	...	...	810	...	...	770
B Crude petroleum and natural gas production	...	...	-	...	...	643	...	...	2946	...	...	3824
C Metal ore mining	...	...	2430	...	...	2365	...	...	2027	...	...	1570
D Other mining	...	...	3849	...	...	4624	...	...	5239	...	...	5495
3 Manufacturing	...	...	211031	...	...	224294	...	...	230235	...	...	255995
A Manufacture of food, beverages and tobacco	...	...	55183	...	...	59855	...	...	62178	...	...	65798
B Textile, wearing apparel and leather industries	...	...	45851	...	...	49531	...	...	51853	...	...	56252
C Manufacture of wood and wood products, including furniture	...	...	12867	...	...	11643	...	...	11923	...	...	13282
D Manufacture of paper and paper products, printing and publishing	...	...	7047	...	...	7328	...	...	7718	...	...	8498
E Manufacture of chemicals and chemical petroleum, coal, rubber and plastic products	...	...	31527	...	...	32024	...	...	33193	...	...	35943
F Manufacture of non-metallic mineral products, except products of petroleum and coal	...	...	10002	...	...	10738	...	...	10881	...	...	12381
G Basic metal industries	...	...	5919	...	...	5348	...	...	4827	...	...	4920
H Manufacture of fabricated metal products, machinery and equipment	...	...	34926	...	...	38567	...	...	37627	...	...	46763
I Other manufacturing industries	...	...	7709	...	...	9260	...	...	10035	...	...	12158
4 Electricity, gas and water	...	...	15614	...	...	17525	...	...	20732	...	...	21171
A Electricity, gas and steam	...	...	11555	...	...	13281	...	...	15729	...	...	16227
B Water works and supply	...	...	4059	...	...	4244	...	...	5003	...	...	4944

4.2 Derivation of Value Added by Kind of Activity, in Constant Prices
(Continued)

Million Thai baht

	1980			1981			1982			1983		
	Gross Output	Intermediate Consumption	Value Added	Gross Output	Intermediate Consumption	Value Added	Gross Output	Intermediate Consumption	Value Added	Gross Output	Intermediate Consumption	Value Added
			At constant prices of:1988									
5 Construction	...	...	41882	...	...	44690	...	...	48008	...	...	53772
6 Wholesale and retail trade, restaurants and hotels	...	...	202067	...	...	221530	...	...	232111	...	...	229880
A Wholesale and retail trade	...	...	163680	...	...	177866	...	...	183928	...	...	181627
B Restaurants and hotels	...	...	38387	...	...	43664	...	...	48183	...	...	48253
Restaurants	...	...	31449	...	...	36402	...	...	39495	...	...	39266
Hotels and other lodging places	...	...	6938	...	...	7262	...	...	8688	...	...	8987
7 Transport, storage and communication	...	...	65669	...	...	60230	...	...	69607	...	...	72308
A Transport and storage	...	...	62301	...	...	55908	...	...	64249	...	...	66915
B Communication	...	...	3368	...	...	4322	...	...	5358	...	...	5393
8 Finance, insurance, real estate and business services	...	...	75187	...	...	75506	...	...	79420	...	...	86237
A Financial institutions	...	...	21504	...	...	21870	...	...	23575	...	...	27305
B Insurance	...	...	2512	...	...	2577	...	...	2773	...	...	3235
C Real estate and business services	...	...	51171	...	...	51059	...	...	53072	...	...	55697
Real estate, except dwellings	...	...	4276	...	...	2475	...	...	3390	...	...	4117
Dwellings	...	...	43299	...	...	44740	...	...	45896	...	...	46804
9 Community, social and personal services	...	...	73090	...	...	80127	...	...	86027	...	...	89024
A Sanitary and similar services	...	...	...	...	...	...	...	...	...	...	...	...
B Social and related community services	...	...	37500	...	...	41696	...	...	46381	...	...	50584
Educational services	...	...	27467	...	...	30356	...	...	33888	...	...	36927
Medical, dental, other health and veterinary services	...	...	10033	...	...	11340	...	...	12493	...	...	13657
C Recreational and cultural services	...	...	5228	...	...	5760	...	...	5861	...	...	6059
D Personal and household services	...	...	30362	...	...	32671	...	...	33785	...	...	32381
Total, Industries	...	...	875977	...	...	926252	...	...	975987	...	...	1028358
Producers of Government Services	...	...	37756	...	...	41454	...	...	43514	...	...	48074
Other Producers	...	...	...	...	...	...	...	...	...	...	...	...
Total	...	...	913733	...	...	967706	...	...	1019501	...	...	1076432
Less: Imputed bank service charge	...	...	...	...	...	...	...	...	...	...	...	...
Import duties	...	...	...	...	...	...	...	...	...	...	...	...
Value added tax	...	...	...	...	...	...	...	...	...	...	...	...
Total	...	...	913733	...	...	967706	...	...	1019501	...	...	1076432

	1984			1985			1986			1987		
	Gross Output	Intermediate Consumption	Value Added	Gross Output	Intermediate Consumption	Value Added	Gross Output	Intermediate Consumption	Value Added	Gross Output	Intermediate Consumption	Value Added
			At constant prices of:1988									
			All Producers									
1 Agriculture, hunting, forestry and fishing	...	...	217518	...	...	227324	...	...	228191	...	...	228346
A Agriculture and hunting	...	...	185586	...	...	195707	...	...	194101	...	...	192043
B Forestry and logging	...	...	11503	...	...	11424	...	...	12274	...	...	11745
C Fishing	...	...	20429	...	...	20193	...	...	21816	...	...	24558
2 Mining and quarrying	...	...	16167	...	...	21553	...	...	21511	...	...	24107
A Coal mining	...	...	969	...	...	2132	...	...	2311	...	...	2892
B Crude petroleum and natural gas production	...	...	6436	...	...	9990	...	...	9755	...	...	11865
C Metal ore mining	...	...	1735	...	...	1401	...	...	1549	...	...	1376
D Other mining	...	...	7027	...	...	8030	...	...	7896	...	...	7974

Thailand

4.2 Derivation of Value Added by Kind of Activity, in Constant Prices
(Continued)

Million Thai baht

	1984			1985			1986			1987		
	Gross Output	Intermediate Consumption	Value Added	Gross Output	Intermediate Consumption	Value Added	Gross Output	Intermediate Consumption	Value Added	Gross Output	Intermediate Consumption	Value Added
					At constant prices of:1988	268133			294521			341750
3 Manufacturing	...	...	271855	...	...		...	...		...	...	
A Manufacture of food, beverages and tobacco	...	...	71735	...	...	69874	...	...	73024	...	...	76652
B Textile, wearing apparel and leather industries	...	...	59276	...	...	61992	...	...	70527	...	...	86328
C Manufacture of wood and wood products, including furniture	...	...	14506	...	...	15389	...	...	16837	...	...	18115
D Manufacture of paper and paper products, printing and publishing	...	...	8834	...	...	8924	...	...	9343	...	...	10006
E Manufacture of chemicals and chemical petroleum, coal, rubber and plastic products	...	...	35188	...	...	37944	...	...	42418	...	...	46727
F Manufacture of non-metallic mineral products, except products of petroleum and coal	...	...	14340	...	...	14867	...	...	15285	...	...	17828
G Basic metal industries	...	...	5797	...	...	5592	...	...	5849	...	...	6557
H Manufacture of fabricated metal products, machinery and equipment	...	...	49866	...	...	40734	...	...	44766	...	...	57513
I Other manufacturing industries	...	...	12313	...	...	12817	...	...	16472	...	...	22024
4 Electricity, gas and water	...	...	23230	...	...	26959	...	...	29890	...	...	31515
A Electricity, gas and steam	...	...	18255	...	...	21857	...	...	24389	...	...	26259
B Water works and supply	...	...	4975	...	...	5102	...	...	5501	...	...	5256
5 Construction	...	...	59390	...	...	59269	...	...	60138	...	...	66060
6 Wholesale and retail trade, restaurants and hotels	...	...	243382	...	...	262804	...	...	282136	...	...	318146
A Wholesale and retail trade	...	...	189102	...	...	197432	...	...	207211	...	...	229859
B Restaurants and hotels	...	...	54280	...	...	65372	...	...	74925	...	...	88287
Restaurants	...	...	44271	...	...	55000	...	...	61755	...	...	71823
Hotels and other lodging places	...	...	10009	...	...	10372	...	...	13170	...	...	16464
7 Transport, storage and communication	...	...	80548	...	...	85922	...	...	92046	...	...	100585
A Transport and storage	...	...	73645	...	...	76659	...	...	80646	...	...	88462
B Communication	...	...	6903	...	...	9263	...	...	11400	...	...	12123
8 Finance, insurance, real estate and business services	...	...	90754	...	...	93071	...	...	95594	...	...	110065
A Financial institutions	...	...	29754	...	...	30076	...	...	30135	...	...	40595
B Insurance	...	...	3416	...	...	4115	...	...	4913	...	...	5282
C Real estate and business services	...	...	57584	...	...	58880	...	...	60546	...	...	64188
Real estate, except dwellings	...	...	4011	...	...	3954	...	...	4356	...	...	5957
Dwellings	...	...	48023	...	...	49433	...	...	50647	...	...	52575
9 Community, social and personal services	...	...	88061	...	...	95307	...	...	100821	...	...	102556
A Sanitary and similar services	...	...	...	...	...	...	...	...	...	...	...	...
B Social and related community services	...	...	53173	...	...	57196	...	...	59884	...	...	62178
Educational services	...	...	38906	...	...	41612	...	...	43497	...	...	44922
Medical, dental, other health and veterinary services	...	...	14267	...	...	15584	...	...	16387	...	...	17256
C Recreational and cultural services	...	...	7064	...	...	7124	...	...	6015	...	...	6890
D Personal and household services	...	...	27824	...	...	30987	...	...	34922	...	...	33488
Total, Industries	...	...	1090905	...	...	1140342	...	...	1204848	...	...	1323130
Producers of Government Services	...	...	47448	...	...	50913	...	...	52329	...	...	53717
Other Producers	...	...	...	...	...	...	...	...	...	...	...	...
Total	...	...	1138353	...	...	1191255	...	...	1257177	...	...	1376847
Less: Imputed bank service charge	...	...	...	...	...	...	...	...	...	...	...	...
Import duties	...	...	...	...	...	...	...	...	...	...	...	...
Value added tax	...	...	...	...	...	...	...	...	...	...	...	...
Total	...	...	1138353	...	...	1191255	...	...	1257177	...	...	1376847

4.2 Derivation of Value Added by Kind of Activity, in Constant Prices

Million Thai baht

At constant prices of:1988

All Producers

	1988 Gross Output	1988 Intermediate Consumption	1988 Value Added	1989 Gross Output	1989 Intermediate Consumption	1989 Value Added	1990 Gross Output	1990 Intermediate Consumption	1990 Value Added	1991 Gross Output	1991 Intermediate Consumption	1991 Value Added
1 Agriculture, hunting, forestry and fishing	...	...	252346	...	...	276729	...	...	266414	...	...	278063
A Agriculture and hunting	...	...	216603	...	...	240242	...	...	229958	...	...	242038
B Forestry and logging	...	...	10489	...	...	8551	...	...	6389	...	...	4752
C Fishing	...	...	25254	...	...	27936	...	...	30067	...	...	31273
2 Mining and quarrying	...	...	26599	...	...	28404	...	...	31457	...	...	35542
A Coal mining	...	...	3036	...	...	3716	...	...	5180	...	...	6137
B Crude petroleum and natural gas production	...	...	13233	...	...	13444	...	...	14418	...	...	17184
C Metal ore mining	...	...	1393	...	...	1408	...	...	1300	...	...	994
D Other mining	...	...	8937	...	...	9836	...	...	10559	...	...	11227
3 Manufacturing	...	...	403034	...	...	467666	...	...	542169	...	...	606763
A Manufacture of food, beverages and tobacco	...	...	88171	...	...	99807	...	...	102838	...	...	110018
B Textile, wearing apparel and leather industries	...	...	102095	...	...	116507	...	...	133815	...	...	155319
C Manufacture of wood and wood products, including furniture	...	...	18427	...	...	19069	...	...	21995	...	...	23237
D Manufacture of paper and paper products, printing and publishing	...	...	10306	...	...	11255	...	...	12810	...	...	14274
E Manufacture of chemicals and chemical petroleum, coal, rubber and plastic products	...	...	50314	...	...	56044	...	...	61219	...	...	63828
F Manufacture of non-metallic mineral products, except products of petroleum and coal	...	...	20939	...	...	25726	...	...	30910	...	...	34920
G Basic metal industries	...	...	7016	...	...	7581	...	...	8507	...	...	9090
H Manufacture of fabricated metal products, machinery and equipment	...	...	79863	...	...	99456	...	...	126910	...	...	145153
I Other manufacturing industries	...	...	25903	...	...	32221	...	...	43165	...	...	50924
4 Electricity, gas and water	...	...	35298	...	...	42259	...	...	48233	...	...	50246
A Electricity, gas and steam	...	...	29579	...	...	35729	...	...	40565	...	...	41738
B Water works and supply	...	...	5719	...	...	6530	...	...	7668	...	...	8508
5 Construction	...	...	74449	...	...	95554	...	...	114420	...	...	135240
6 Wholesale and retail trade, restaurants and hotels	...	...	359226	...	...	392703	...	...	440088	...	...	461780
A Wholesale and retail trade	...	...	266257	...	...	295668	...	...	341084	...	...	361243
B Restaurants and hotels	...	...	92969	...	...	97035	...	...	99004	...	...	100537
Restaurants	...	...	75050	...	...	78010	...	...	79942	...	...	81405
Hotels and other lodging places	...	...	17919	...	...	19025	...	...	19062	...	...	19132
7 Transport, storage and communication	...	...	116611	...	...	128754	...	...	147103	...	...	155329
A Transport and storage	...	...	100389	...	...	106012	...	...	117634	...	...	120533
B Communication	...	...	16222	...	...	22742	...	...	29469	...	...	34796
8 Finance, insurance, real estate and business services	...	...	128427	...	...	149610	...	...	180311	...	...	189125
A Financial institutions	...	...	48559	...	...	61445	...	...	80674	...	...	87786
B Insurance	...	...	7771	...	...	10481	...	...	12669	...	...	14654
C Real estate and business services	...	...	72097	...	...	77684	...	...	86968	...	...	86685
Real estate, except dwellings	...	...	9890	...	...	10908	...	...	16124	...	...	11514
Dwellings	...	...	55416	...	...	58213	...	...	60756	...	...	63181
9 Community, social and personal services	...	...	107326	...	...	112559	...	...	122668	...	...	131234
A Sanitary and similar services	...	...	...	...	...	...	...	...	...	...	...	...
B Social and related community services	...	...	65190	...	...	69024	...	...	73932	...	...	78894

Thailand

4.2 Derivation of Value Added by Kind of Activity, in Constant Prices
(Continued)

Million Thai baht

	1988			1989			1990			1991		
	Gross Output	Intermediate Consumption	Value Added	Gross Output	Intermediate Consumption	Value Added	Gross Output	Intermediate Consumption	Value Added	Gross Output	Intermediate Consumption	Value Added
				At constant prices of:1988								
Educational services	...	...	46889	...	...	48653	...	...	51538	...	...	53939
Medical, dental, other health and veterinary services	...	...	18301	...	...	20371	...	...	22394	...	...	24955
C Recreational and cultural services	...	...	7919	...	...	9002	...	...	10636	...	...	12760
D Personal and household services	...	...	34217	...	...	34533	...	...	38100	...	...	39580
Total, Industries	...	...	1503316	...	...	1694238	...	...	1892863	...	...	2043322
Producers of Government Services	...	...	56488	...	...	57277	...	...	61366	...	...	64927
Other Producers	...	...	...	...	...	...	...	...	...	...	...	...
Total	...	...	1559804	...	...	1751515	...	...	1954229	...	...	2108249
Less: Imputed bank service charge	...	...	...	...	...	...	...	...	...	...	...	...
Import duties	...	...	...	...	...	...	...	...	...	...	...	...
Value added tax	...	...	...	...	...	...	...	...	...	...	...	...
Total	...	...	1559804	...	...	1751515	...	...	1954229	...	...	2108249

4.3 Cost Components of Value Added

Million Thai baht

	1980						1981					
	Compensation of Employees	Capital Consumption	Net Operating Surplus	Indirect Taxes	Less: Subsidies Received	Value Added	Compensation of Employees	Capital Consumption	Net Operating Surplus	Indirect Taxes	Less: Subsidies Received	Value Added
						All Producers						
1 Agriculture, hunting, forestry and fishing	14018	...	139942	...	...	153960	15286	...	147104	...	...	162390
A Agriculture and hunting	12388	...	124447	...	...	136835	13041	...	128934	...	...	141975
B Forestry and logging	307	...	8468	...	...	8775	333	...	9362	...	...	9695
C Fishing	1323	...	7027	...	...	8350	1912	...	8808	...	...	10720
2 Mining and quarrying	2798	...	8929	...	...	11727	3268	...	7940	...	...	11208
A Coal mining	...	...	...	...	...	73	...	...	...	...	...	144
B Crude petroleum and natural gas production	...	...	...	...	...	-	...	...	...	...	...	807
C Metal ore mining	...	...	...	...	...	8897	...	...	...	...	...	6783
D Other mining	...	...	...	...	...	2757	...	...	...	...	...	3474
3 Manufacturing	35685	...	106819	...	...	142504	42836	...	129307	...	...	172143
A Manufacture of food, beverages and tobacco	...	...	...	...	...	35841	...	...	...	...	...	50909
B Textile, wearing apparel and leather industries	...	...	...	...	...	32032	...	...	...	...	...	37738
C Manufacture of wood and wood products, including furniture	...	...	...	...	...	10174	...	...	...	...	...	9293
D Manufacture of paper and paper products, printing and publishing	...	...	...	...	...	4333	...	...	...	...	...	5114
E Manufacture of chemicals and chemical petroleum, coal, rubber and plastic products	...	...	...	...	...	20324	...	...	...	...	...	21779
F Manufacture of non-metallic mineral products, except products of petroleum and coal	...	...	...	...	...	6779	...	...	...	...	...	8739
G Basic metal industries	...	...	...	...	...	4999	...	...	...	...	...	4642
H Manufacture of fabricated metal products, machinery and equipment	...	...	...	...	...	22444	...	...	...	...	...	26480
I Other manufacturing industries	...	...	...	...	...	5578	...	...	...	...	...	7449
4 Electricity, gas and water	2850	...	3523	...	...	6373	3643	...	7171	...	...	10814
A Electricity, gas and steam	...	...	...	...	...	4994	...	...	...	...	...	9267
B Water works and supply	...	...	...	...	...	1379	...	...	...	...	...	1547
5 Construction	17015	...	12368	...	...	29383	18664	...	16032	...	...	34696
6 Wholesale and retail trade, restaurants and hotels	12155	...	139055	...	...	151210	15815	...	162541	...	...	178356
A Wholesale and retail trade	10125	...	106586	...	...	116711	13115	...	125479	...	...	138594
B Restaurants and hotels	2030	...	32469	...	...	34499	2700	...	37062	...	...	39762

4.3 Cost Components of Value Added
(Continued)

Million Thai baht

	1980						1981					
	Compensation of Employees	Capital Consumption	Net Operating Surplus	Indirect Taxes	Less: Subsidies Received	Value Added	Compensation of Employees	Capital Consumption	Net Operating Surplus	Indirect Taxes	Less: Subsidies Received	Value Added
Restaurants	884	...	28555	...	...	29439	1253	...	33329	...	...	34582
Hotels and other lodging places	1146	...	3914	...	...	5060	1447	...	3733	...	...	5180
7 Transport, storage and communication	10955	...	23939	...	...	34894	12458	...	29190	...	...	41648
A Transport and storage	...	...	...	...	...	31286	...	...	...	...	...	37036
B Communication	...	...	...	...	...	3608	...	...	...	...	...	4612
8 Finance, insurance, real estate and business services	8787	...	37006	...	...	45793	10237	...	41059	...	...	51296
A Financial institutions	...	...	...	...	...	15584	...	...	...	...	...	17736
B Insurance	...	...	...	...	...	1820	...	...	...	...	...	2090
C Real estate and business services	...	...	...	...	...	28389	...	...	...	...	...	31470
Real estate, except dwellings	...	...	...	...	...	3099	...	...	...	...	...	2007
Dwellings	...	...	...	...	...	22682	...	...	...	...	...	26344
9 Community, social and personal services	30777	...	25143	...	...	55920	34597	...	29847	...	...	64444
A Sanitary and similar services	...	...	...	...	...	...	...	...	...	...	...	...
B Social and related community services	...	...	...	...	...	29827	...	...	...	...	...	33501
Educational services	...	...	...	...	...	22027	...	...	...	...	...	24308
Medical, dental, other health and veterinary services	...	...	...	...	...	7800	...	...	...	...	...	9193
C Recreational and cultural services	...	...	...	...	...	4154	...	...	...	...	...	4463
D Personal and household services	...	...	...	...	...	21939	...	...	...	...	...	26480
Total, Industries a	135040	...	496724	...	...	631764	156804	...	570191	...	...	726995
Producers of Government Services	29554	...	1164	...	...	30718	31807	...	1554	...	...	33361
Other Producers	...	...	...	...	...	...	...	...	...	...	...	...
Total a	164594	...	497888	...	...	662482	188611	...	571745	...	...	760356
Less: Imputed bank service charge	...	...	...	...	...	...	...	...	...	...	...	...
Import duties	...	...	...	...	...	...	...	...	...	...	...	...
Value added tax	...	...	...	...	...	...	...	...	...	...	...	...
Total a	164594	...	497888	...	...	662482	188611	...	571745	...	...	760356

	1982						1983					
	Compensation of Employees	Capital Consumption	Net Operating Surplus	Indirect Taxes	Less: Subsidies Received	Value Added	Compensation of Employees	Capital Consumption	Net Operating Surplus	Indirect Taxes	Less: Subsidies Received	Value Added

All Producers

1 Agriculture, hunting, forestry and fishing	15331	...	140767	...	...	156098	15923	...	168829	...	...	184752
A Agriculture and hunting	12737	...	123569	...	...	136306	13018	...	149988	...	...	163006
B Forestry and logging	368	...	8478	...	...	8846	419	...	8919	...	...	9338
C Fishing	2226	...	8720	...	...	10946	2486	...	9922	...	...	12408
2 Mining and quarrying	3631	...	9785	...	...	13416	3678	...	10428	...	...	14106
A Coal mining	...	...	...	...	...	162	...	...	...	...	...	245
B Crude petroleum and natural gas production	...	...	...	...	...	3519	...	...	...	...	...	5158
C Metal ore mining	...	...	...	...	...	5412	...	...	...	...	...	3954
D Other mining	...	...	...	...	...	4323	...	...	...	...	...	4749

Thailand

4.3 Cost Components of Value Added
(Continued)

Million Thai baht

		1982						1983					
		Compensation of Employees	Capital Consumption	Net Operating Surplus	Indirect Taxes	Less: Subsidies Received	Value Added	Compensation of Employees	Capital Consumption	Net Operating Surplus	Indirect Taxes	Less: Subsidies Received	Value Added
3	Manufacturing	49253	...	130185	...	...	179438	56070	...	147767	...	...	203837
	A Manufacture of food, beverages and tobacco	...	...	...	...	...	51710	...	...	...	...	...	54394
	B Textile, wearing apparel and leather industries	...	...	...	...	...	39793	...	...	...	...	...	43223
	C Manufacture of wood and wood products, including furniture	...	...	...	...	...	9263	...	...	...	...	...	10159
	D Manufacture of paper and paper products, printing and publishing	...	...	...	...	...	5686	...	...	...	...	...	6151
	E Manufacture of chemicals and chemical petroleum, coal, rubber and plastic products	...	...	...	...	...	22716	...	...	...	...	...	28283
	F Manufacture of non-metallic mineral products, except products of petroleum and coal	...	...	...	...	...	9774	...	...	...	...	...	11613
	G Basic metal industries	...	...	...	...	...	4266	...	...	...	...	...	4389
	H Manufacture of fabricated metal products, machinery and equipment	...	...	...	...	...	27661	...	...	...	...	...	34856
	I Other manufacturing industries	...	...	...	...	...	8569	...	...	...	...	...	10769
4	Electricity, gas and water	4521	...	11080	...	...	15601	5084	...	12009	...	...	17093
	A Electricity, gas and steam	...	...	...	...	...	13061	...	...	...	...	...	14372
	B Water works and supply	...	...	...	...	...	2540	...	...	...	...	...	2721
5	Construction	20565	...	19325	...	...	39890	22444	...	24188	...	...	46632
6	Wholesale and retail trade, restaurants and hotels	18457	...	189148	...	...	207605	19616	...	182141	...	...	201757
	A Wholesale and retail trade	15122	...	146616	...	...	161738	16195	...	136185	...	...	152380
	B Restaurants and hotels	3335	...	42532	...	...	45867	3421	...	45956	...	...	49377
	Restaurants	1629	...	37946	...	...	39575	1645	...	41094	...	...	42739
	Hotels and other lodging places	1706	...	4586	...	...	6292	1776	...	4862	...	...	6638
7	Transport, storage and communication	14538	...	39812	...	...	54350	16218	...	40395	...	...	56613
	A Transport and storage	...	...	...	...	...	48544	...	...	...	...	...	50642
	B Communication	...	...	...	...	...	5806	...	...	...	...	...	5971
8	Finance, insurance, real estate and business services	13566	...	46152	...	...	59718	13566	...	57299	...	...	70865
	A Financial institutions	...	...	...	...	...	20249	...	...	...	...	...	24326
	B Insurance	...	...	...	...	...	2382	...	...	...	...	...	2882
	C Real estate and business services	...	...	...	...	...	37087	...	...	...	...	...	43657
	Real estate, except dwellings	...	...	...	...	...	2911	...	...	...	...	...	3667
	Dwellings	...	...	...	...	...	30922	...	...	...	...	...	35732
9	Community, social and personal services	43892	...	31746	...	...	75638	48048	...	32582	...	...	80630
	A Sanitary and similar services	...	...	...	...	...	...	...	...	...	...	...	...
	B Social and related community services	...	...	...	...	...	41754	...	...	...	...	...	46668
	Educational services	...	...	...	...	...	30683	...	...	...	...	...	34161
	Medical, dental, other health and veterinary services	...	...	...	...	...	11071	...	...	...	...	...	12507
	C Recreational and cultural services	...	...	...	...	...	4777	...	...	...	...	...	5008
	D Personal and household services	...	...	...	...	...	29107	...	...	...	...	...	28954
	Total, Industries a	183754	...	618000	...	...	801754	200647	...	675638	...	...	876285
	Producers of Government Services	37930	...	1885	...	...	39815	42614	...	2090	...	...	44704
	Other Producers	...	...	...	...	...	...	...	...	...	...	...	...
	Total a	221684	...	619885	...	...	841569	243261	...	677728	...	...	920989
	Less: Imputed bank service charge	...	...	...	...	...	...	...	...	...	...	...	...
	Import duties	...	...	...	...	...	...	...	...	...	...	...	...
	Value added tax	...	...	...	...	...	...	...	...	...	...	...	...
	Total a	221684	...	619885	...	...	841569	243261	...	677728	...	...	920989

4.3 Cost Components of Value Added

Million Thai baht

All Producers

	1984						1985					
	Compensation of Employees	Capital Consumption	Net Operating Surplus	Indirect Taxes	Less: Subsidies Received	Value Added	Compensation of Employees	Capital Consumption	Net Operating Surplus	Indirect Taxes	Less: Subsidies Received	Value Added
1 Agriculture, hunting, forestry and fishing	16228	...	157414	...	...	173642	16983	...	150043	...	...	167026
A Agriculture and hunting	13458	...	138632	...	...	152090	13861	...	130553	...	...	144414
B Forestry and logging	450	...	9242	...	...	9692	471	...	9026	...	...	9497
C Fishing	2320	...	9540	...	...	11860	2651	...	10464	...	...	13115
2 Mining and quarrying	3989	...	14554	...	...	18543	3732	...	22230	...	...	25962
A Coal mining	...	...	...	...	...	476	...	...	...	...	...	2115
B Crude petroleum and natural gas production	...	...	...	...	...	8309	...	...	...	...	...	14290
C Metal ore mining	...	...	...	...	...	4320	...	...	...	...	...	3678
D Other mining	...	...	...	...	...	5438	...	...	...	...	...	5879
3 Manufacturing	61877	...	164483	...	...	226360	62735	...	168863	...	...	231598
A Manufacture of food, beverages and tobacco	...	...	...	...	...	64856	...	...	...	...	...	67228
B Textile, wearing apparel and leather industries	...	...	...	...	...	49210	...	...	...	...	...	53645
C Manufacture of wood and wood products, including furniture	...	...	...	...	...	10714	...	...	...	...	...	10658
D Manufacture of paper and paper products, printing and publishing	...	...	...	...	...	6399	...	...	...	...	...	6611
E Manufacture of chemicals and chemical petroleum, coal, rubber and plastic products	...	...	...	...	...	26955	...	...	...	...	...	26215
F Manufacture of non-metallic mineral products, except products of petroleum and coal	...	...	...	...	...	13863	...	...	...	...	...	14653
G Basic metal industries	...	...	...	...	...	5116	...	...	...	...	...	5414
H Manufacture of fabricated metal products, machinery and equipment	...	...	...	...	...	38230	...	...	...	...	...	35408
I Other manufacturing industries	...	...	...	...	...	11017	...	...	...	...	...	11766
4 Electricity, gas and water	5644	...	12965	...	...	18609	6391	...	18564	...	...	24955
A Electricity, gas and steam	...	...	...	...	...	15885	...	...	...	...	...	20474
B Water works and supply	...	...	...	...	...	2724	...	...	...	...	...	4481
5 Construction	23613	...	28814	...	...	52427	24678	...	29225	...	...	53903
6 Wholesale and retail trade, restaurants and hotels	20620	...	208259	...	...	228879	21905	...	230754	...	...	252659
A Wholesale and retail trade	16704	...	158322	...	...	175026	17369	...	176441	...	...	193810
B Restaurants and hotels	3916	...	49937	...	...	53853	4536	...	54313	...	...	58849
Restaurants	1906	...	44885	...	...	46791	2399	...	49261	...	...	51660
Hotels and other lodging places	2010	...	5052	...	...	7062	2137	...	5052	...	...	7189
7 Transport, storage and communication	17397	...	47681	...	...	65078	19264	...	58811	...	...	78075
A Transport and storage	...	...	...	...	...	57639	...	...	...	...	...	68768
B Communication	...	...	...	...	...	7439	...	...	...	...	...	9307
8 Finance, insurance, real estate and business services	15223	...	62997	...	...	78220	16690	...	67593	...	...	84283
A Financial institutions	...	...	...	...	...	26802	...	...	...	...	...	27810
B Insurance	...	...	...	...	...	3077	...	...	...	...	...	3805
C Real estate and business services	...	...	...	...	...	48341	...	...	...	...	...	52668
Real estate, except dwellings	...	...	...	...	...	3612	...	...	...	...	...	3656
Dwellings	...	...	...	...	...	39728	...	...	...	...	...	43934
9 Community, social and personal services	50208	...	31014	...	...	81222	54745	...	34611	...	...	89356
A Sanitary and similar services	...	...	...	...	...	...	...	...	...	...	...	...
B Social and related community services	...	...	...	...	...	50189	...	...	...	...	...	54586

Thailand

(Continued)

Million Thai baht

	1984						1985					
	Compensation of Employees	Capital Consumption	Net Operating Surplus	Indirect Taxes	Less: Subsidies Received	Value Added	Compensation of Employees	Capital Consumption	Net Operating Surplus	Indirect Taxes	Less: Subsidies Received	Value Added
Educational services	...	...	...	...	...	36788	...	...	...	...	...	39722
Medical, dental, other health and veterinary services	...	...	...	...	...	13401	...	...	...	...	...	14864
C Recreational and cultural services	...	...	...	...	...	5834	...	...	...	...	...	5979
D Personal and household services	...	...	...	...	...	25199	...	...	...	...	...	28791
Total, Industries a	214799	...	728181	...	...	942980	227123	...	780694	...	...	1007817
Producers of Government Services	42743	...	2347	...	...	45090	45943	...	2736	...	...	48679
Other Producers	...	...	...	...	...	...	...	...	...	...	...	...
Total a	257542	...	730528	...	...	988070	273066	...	783430	...	...	1056496
Less: Imputed bank service charge	...	...	...	...	...	...	...	...	...	...	...	...
Import duties	...	...	...	...	...	...	...	...	...	...	...	...
Value added tax	...	...	...	...	...	...	...	...	...	...	...	...
Total a	257542	...	730528	...	...	988070	273066	...	783430	...	...	1056496

	1986						1987					
	Compensation of Employees	Capital Consumption	Net Operating Surplus	Indirect Taxes	Less: Subsidies Received	Value Added	Compensation of Employees	Capital Consumption	Net Operating Surplus	Indirect Taxes	Less: Subsidies Received	Value Added
					All Producers							
1 Agriculture, hunting, forestry and fishing	16913	...	160624	...	...	177537	17432	...	187089	...	...	204521
A Agriculture and hunting	13205	...	138713	...	...	151918	12891	...	160470	...	...	173361
B Forestry and logging	479	...	9506	...	...	9985	490	...	10555	...	...	11045
C Fishing	3229	...	12405	...	...	15634	4051	...	16064	...	...	20115
2 Mining and quarrying	2985	...	16768	...	...	19753	2979	...	19242	...	...	22221
A Coal mining	...	...	...	...	...	2314	...	...	...	...	...	2899
B Crude petroleum and natural gas production	...	...	...	...	...	10577	...	...	...	...	...	12165
C Metal ore mining	...	...	...	...	...	1312	...	...	...	...	...	1209
D Other mining	...	...	...	...	...	5550	...	...	...	...	...	5948
3 Manufacturing	69810	...	200795	...	...	270605	84544	...	230747	...	...	315291
A Manufacture of food, beverages and tobacco	...	...	...	...	...	66714	...	...	...	...	...	69098
B Textile, wearing apparel and leather industries	...	...	...	...	...	64562	...	...	...	...	...	83353
C Manufacture of wood and wood products, including furniture	...	...	...	...	...	11472	...	...	...	...	...	14861
D Manufacture of paper and paper products, printing and publishing	...	...	...	...	...	7597	...	...	...	...	...	8843
E Manufacture of chemicals and chemical petroleum, coal, rubber and plastic products	...	...	...	...	...	43906	...	...	...	...	...	41517
F Manufacture of non-metallic mineral products, except products of petroleum and coal	...	...	...	...	...	15123	...	...	...	...	...	17565
G Basic metal industries	...	...	...	...	...	4959	...	...	...	...	...	5683
H Manufacture of fabricated metal products, machinery and equipment	...	...	...	...	...	40862	...	...	...	...	...	53284
I Other manufacturing industries	...	...	...	...	...	15410	...	...	...	...	...	21087
4 Electricity, gas and water	7176	...	21712	...	...	28888	7896	...	25383	...	...	33279
A Electricity, gas and steam	...	...	...	...	...	24298	...	...	...	...	...	27662
B Water works and supply	...	...	...	...	...	4590	...	...	...	...	...	5617
5 Construction	25565	...	30150	...	...	55715	30689	...	31952	...	...	62641
6 Wholesale and retail trade, restaurants and hotels	22809	...	231944	...	...	254753	26161	...	276291	...	...	302452
A Wholesale and retail trade	17835	...	172151	...	...	189986	19811	...	203318	...	...	223129
B Restaurants and hotels	4974	...	59793	...	...	64767	6350	...	72973	...	...	79323
Restaurants	2746	...	52574	...	...	55320	3246	...	63081	...	...	66327
Hotels and other lodging places	2228	...	7219	...	...	9447	3104	...	9892	...	...	12996
7 Transport, storage and communication	20566	...	67636	...	...	88202	22204	...	77140	...	...	99344
A Transport and storage	...	...	...	...	...	75239	...	...	...	...	...	85614

4.3 Cost Components of Value Added
(Continued)

Million Thai baht

	1986						1987					
	Compensation of Employees	Capital Consumption	Net Operating Surplus	Indirect Taxes	Less: Subsidies Received	Value Added	Compensation of Employees	Capital Consumption	Net Operating Surplus	Indirect Taxes	Less: Subsidies Received	Value Added
B Communication	...	...	...	...	...	12963	...	...	...	...	...	13730
8 Finance, insurance, real estate and business services	18353	...	71864	...	...	90217	20744	...	86460	...	...	107204
A Financial institutions	...	...	...	...	...	28374	...	...	...	...	...	39143
B Insurance	...	...	...	...	...	4626	...	...	...	...	...	5093
C Real estate and business services	...	...	...	...	...	57217	...	...	...	...	...	62968
Real estate, except dwellings	...	...	...	...	...	4102	...	...	...	...	...	5744
Dwellings	...	...	...	...	...	47899	...	...	...	...	...	51773
9 Community, social and personal services	58864	...	38182	...	...	97046	61877	...	38357	...	...	100234
A Sanitary and similar services	...	...	...	...	...	...	...	...	...	...	...	...
B Social and related community services	...	...	...	...	...	57859	...	...	...	...	...	60989
Educational services	...	...	...	...	...	42067	...	...	...	...	...	44036
Medical, dental, other health and veterinary services	...	...	...	...	...	15792	...	...	...	...	...	16953
C Recreational and cultural services	...	...	...	...	...	6211	...	...	...	...	...	7027
D Personal and household services	...	...	...	...	...	32976	...	...	...	...	...	32218
Total, Industries a	243041	...	839675	...	...	1082716	274526	...	972661	...	...	1247187
Producers of Government Services	47674	...	3007	...	...	50681	49499	...	3227	...	...	52726
Other Producers	...	...	...	...	...	...	...	...	...	...	...	...
Total a	290715	...	842682	...	...	1133397	324025	...	975888	...	...	1299913
Less: Imputed bank service charge	...	...	...	...	...	...	...	...	...	...	...	...
Import duties	...	...	...	...	...	...	...	...	...	...	...	...
Value added tax	...	...	...	...	...	...	...	...	...	...	...	...
Total a	290715	...	842682	...	...	1133397	324025	...	975888	...	...	1299913

	1988						1989					
	Compensation of Employees	Capital Consumption	Net Operating Surplus	Indirect Taxes	Less: Subsidies Received	Value Added	Compensation of Employees	Capital Consumption	Net Operating Surplus	Indirect Taxes	Less: Subsidies Received	Value Added
All Producers												
1 Agriculture, hunting, forestry and fishing	19752	...	232594	...	...	252346	20922	...	258768	...	...	279690
A Agriculture and hunting	14760	...	201843	...	...	216603	15402	...	228243	...	...	243645
B Forestry and logging	503	...	9986	...	...	10489	417	...	8167	...	...	8584
C Fishing	4489	...	20765	...	...	25254	5103	...	22358	...	...	27461
2 Mining and quarrying	3183	...	23416	...	...	26599	3495	...	28310	...	...	31805
A Coal mining	...	...	...	...	...	3036	...	...	...	...	...	3721
B Crude petroleum and natural gas production	...	...	...	...	...	13233	...	...	...	...	...	13861
C Metal ore mining	...	...	...	...	...	1393	...	...	...	...	...	2039
D Other mining	...	...	...	...	...	8937	...	...	...	...	...	12184

Thailand

Million Thai baht

	1988						1989					
	Compensation of Employees	Capital Consumption	Net Operating Surplus	Indirect Taxes	Less: Subsidies Received	Value Added	Compensation of Employees	Capital Consumption	Net Operating Surplus	Indirect Taxes	Less: Subsidies Received	Value Added
3 Manufacturing	104407	...	298627	...	...	403034	127958	...	369095	...	...	497053
A Manufacture of food, beverages and tobacco	...	...	...	...	...	88171	...	...	...	...	...	109958
B Textile, wearing apparel and leather industries	...	...	...	...	...	102095	...	...	...	...	...	122434
C Manufacture of wood and wood products, including furniture	...	...	...	...	...	18427	...	...	...	...	...	23612
D Manufacture of paper and paper products, printing and publishing	...	...	...	...	...	10306	...	...	...	...	...	11699
E Manufacture of chemicals and chemical petroleum, coal, rubber and plastic products	...	...	...	...	...	50314	...	...	...	...	...	51563
F Manufacture of non-metallic mineral products, except products of petroleum and coal	...	...	...	...	...	20939	...	...	...	...	...	26978
G Basic metal industries	...	...	...	...	...	7016	...	...	...	...	...	9063
H Manufacture of fabricated metal products, machinery and equipment	...	...	...	...	...	79863	...	...	...	...	...	107868
I Other manufacturing industries	...	...	...	...	...	25903	...	...	...	...	...	33878
4 Electricity, gas and water	8570	...	26728	...	...	35298	10171	...	32294	...	...	42465
A Electricity, gas and steam	...	...	...	...	...	29579	...	...	...	...	...	35824
B Water works and supply	...	...	...	...	...	5719	...	...	...	...	...	6641
5 Construction	37427	...	37022	...	...	74449	42220	...	59904	...	...	102124
6 Wholesale and retail trade, restaurants and hotels	30122	...	329104	...	...	359226	34610	...	387216	...	...	421826
A Wholesale and retail trade	22928	...	243329	...	...	266257	26523	...	280202	...	...	306725
B Restaurants and hotels	7194	...	85775	...	...	92969	8087	...	107014	...	...	115101
Restaurants	3540	...	71510	...	...	75050	3895	...	85196	...	...	89091
Hotels and other lodging places	3654	...	14265	...	...	17919	4192	...	21818	...	...	26010
7 Transport, storage and communication	24776	...	91835	...	...	116611	28966	...	109119	...	...	138085
A Transport and storage	...	...	...	...	...	100389	...	...	...	...	...	117941
B Communication	...	...	...	...	...	16222	...	...	...	...	...	20144
8 Finance, insurance, real estate and business services	24488	...	103939	...	...	128427	30652	...	126035	...	...	156687
A Financial institutions	...	...	...	...	...	48559	...	...	...	...	...	64686
B Insurance	...	...	...	...	...	7771	...	...	...	...	...	11033
C Real estate and business services	...	...	...	...	...	72097	...	...	...	...	...	80968
Real estate, except dwellings	...	...	...	...	...	9890	...	...	...	...	...	11484
Dwellings	...	...	...	...	...	55416	...	...	...	...	...	60457
9 Community, social and personal services	66396	...	40930	...	...	107326	77259	...	44861	...	...	122120
A Sanitary and similar services	...	...	...	...	...	...	...	...	...	...	...	...
B Social and related community services	...	...	...	...	...	65190	...	...	...	...	...	76871
Educational services	...	...	...	...	...	46889	...	...	...	...	...	54669
Medical, dental, other health and veterinary services	...	...	...	...	...	18301	...	...	...	...	...	22202
C Recreational and cultural services	...	...	...	...	...	7919	...	...	...	...	...	8885
D Personal and household services	...	...	...	...	...	34217	...	...	...	...	...	36364
Total, Industries a	319121	...	1184195	...	...	1503316	376253	...	1415602	...	...	1791855
Producers of Government Services	53124	...	3364	...	...	56488	61095	...	3526	...	...	64621
Other Producers	...	...	...	...	...	...	...	...	...	...	...	...
Total a	372245	...	1187559	...	...	1559804	437348	...	1419128	...	...	1856476
Less: Imputed bank service charge	...	...	...	...	...	...	...	...	...	...	...	...
Import duties	...	...	...	...	...	...	...	...	...	...	...	...
Value added tax	...	...	...	...	...	...	...	...	...	...	...	...
Total a	372245	...	1187559	...	...	1559804	437348	...	1419128	...	...	1856476

4.3 Cost Components of Value Added

Million Thai baht

		1990						1991					
		Compensation of Employees	Capital Consumption	Net Operating Surplus	Indirect Taxes	Less: Subsidies Received	Value Added	Compensation of Employees	Capital Consumption	Net Operating Surplus	Indirect Taxes	Less: Subsidies Received	Value Added
	All Producers												
1	Agriculture, hunting, forestry and fishing	19809	...	259272	...	...	279081	21744	...	299612	...	...	321356
	A Agriculture and hunting	14122	...	225709	...	...	239831	15242	...	265373	...	...	280615
	B Forestry and logging	392	...	6580	...	...	6972	402	...	4792	...	...	5194
	C Fishing	5295	...	26983	...	...	32278	6100	...	29447	...	...	35547
2	Mining and quarrying	3880	...	30482	...	...	34362	4322	...	35009	...	...	39331
	A Coal mining	...	...	...	...	...	5108	...	...	...	...	...	5929
	B Crude petroleum and natural gas production	...	...	...	...	...	15754	...	...	...	...	...	18671
	C Metal ore mining	...	...	...	...	...	1035	...	...	...	...	...	508
	D Other mining	...	...	...	...	...	12465	...	...	...	...	...	14223
3	Manufacturing	161335	...	434538	...	...	595873	194400	...	512161	...	...	706561
	A Manufacture of food, beverages and tobacco	...	...	...	...	...	113539	...	...	...	...	...	127401
	B Textile, wearing apparel and leather industries	...	...	...	...	...	150094	...	...	...	...	...	186380
	C Manufacture of wood and wood products, including furniture	...	...	...	...	...	29466	...	...	...	...	...	32472
	D Manufacture of paper and paper products, printing and publishing	...	...	...	...	...	13173	...	...	...	...	...	15902
	E Manufacture of chemicals and chemical petroleum, coal, rubber and plastic products	...	...	...	...	...	54947	...	...	...	...	...	73364
	F Manufacture of non-metallic mineral products, except products of petroleum and coal	...	...	...	...	...	37130	...	...	...	...	...	46317
	G Basic metal industries	...	...	...	...	...	10529	...	...	...	...	...	10597
	H Manufacture of fabricated metal products, machinery and equipment	...	...	...	...	...	139267	...	...	...	...	...	154919
	I Other manufacturing industries	...	...	...	...	...	47728	...	...	...	...	...	59209
4	Electricity, gas and water	12046	...	35641	...	...	47687	13428	...	39513	...	...	52941
	A Electricity, gas and steam	...	...	...	...	...	39838	...	...	...	...	...	44520
	B Water works and supply	...	...	...	...	...	7849	...	...	...	...	...	8421
5	Construction	51914	...	81524	...	...	133438	61676	...	109217	...	...	170893
6	Wholesale and retail trade, restaurants and hotels	40454	...	474202	...	...	514656	46661	...	527074	...	...	573735
	A Wholesale and retail trade	31528	...	345999	...	...	377527	36802	...	389431	...	...	426233
	B Restaurants and hotels	8926	...	128203	...	...	137129	9859	...	137643	...	...	147502
	Restaurants	4262	...	99835	...	...	104097	4612	...	111608	...	...	116220
	Hotels and other lodging places	4664	...	28368	...	...	33032	5247	...	26035	...	...	31282
7	Transport, storage and communication	35093	...	122226	...	...	157319	40526	...	135160	...	...	175686
	A Transport and storage	...	...	...	...	...	132356	...	...	...	...	...	146426
	B Communication	...	...	...	...	...	24963	...	...	...	...	...	29260
8	Finance, insurance, real estate and business services	38855	...	160731	...	...	199586	46871	...	173245	...	...	220116
	A Financial institutions	...	...	...	...	...	89956	...	...	...	...	...	103493
	B Insurance	...	...	...	...	...	14127	...	...	...	...	...	17275
	C Real estate and business services	...	...	...	...	...	95503	...	...	...	...	...	99348
	Real estate, except dwellings	...	...	...	...	...	17980	...	...	...	...	...	13574
	Dwellings	...	...	...	...	...	66238	...	...	...	...	...	71589
9	Community, social and personal services	90302	...	53236	...	...	143538	102226	...	60099	...	...	162325
	A Sanitary and similar services	...	...	...	...	...	...	...	...	...	...	...	...
	B Social and related community services	...	...	...	...	...	90543	...	...	...	...	...	103103

Thailand

Million Thai baht

	1990						1991					
	Compensation of Employees	Capital Consumption	Net Operating Surplus	Indirect Taxes	Less: Subsidies Received	Value Added	Compensation of Employees	Capital Consumption	Net Operating Surplus	Indirect Taxes	Less: Subsidies Received	Value Added
Educational services	...	...	...	...	...	63873	...	...	...	...	...	71514
Medical, dental, other health and veterinary services	...	...	...	...	...	26670	...	...	...	...	...	31589
C Recreational and cultural services	...	...	...	...	...	10506	...	...	...	...	...	12570
D Personal and household services	...	...	...	...	...	42489	...	...	...	...	...	46652
Total, Industries a	453688	...	1651852	...	...	2105540	531854	...	1891090	...	...	2422944
Producers of Government Services	72172	...	4388	...	...	76560	81351	...	5132	...	...	86483
Other Producers	...	...	...	...	...	...	...	...	...	...	...	...
Total a	525860	...	1656240	...	...	2182100	613205	...	1896222	...	...	2509427
Less: Imputed bank service charge	...	...	...	...	...	...	...	...	...	...	...	...
Import duties	...	...	...	...	...	...	...	...	...	...	...	...
Value added tax	...	...	...	...	...	...	...	...	...	...	...	...
Total a	525860	...	1656240	...	...	2182100	613205	...	1896222	...	...	2509427

a) Column 'Operating surplus' includes capital consumption and net indirect taxes.

Togo

Source. Reply to the United Nations National Accounts Questionnaire from the Haut Commissariat du Plan, Lome. The official estimates and descriptions are published by the Commissariat in 'Comptes Nationaux'.

General note. The estimates shown in the following tables have been prepared in accordance with the United Nations System of National Accounts so far as the existing data would permit.

1.1 Expenditure on the Gross Domestic Product, in Current Prices

Million CFA francs

	1980	1981	1982	1983	1984	1985	1986	1987	1988	1989	1990	1991
1 Government final consumption expenditure	34655	38700	41800	40600	42600	47200	52500	...	...	...	...	...
2 Private final consumption expenditure	157193	180600	194900	201500	201200	219500	250900	...	...	...	...	...
3 Gross capital formation	86729	79100	70900	63300	60000	93700	105900	...	...	...	...	...
A Increase in stocks	16600	11400	7300	7000	-4600	17400	19200	...	...	...	...	...
B Gross fixed capital formation	70129	67700	63600	56300	64600	76300	86700	...	...	...	...	...
4 Exports of goods and services	90562	103400	110700	104600	158200	160500	129500	...	...	...	...	...
5 Less: Imports of goods and services	130267	143800	148600	128700	157200	188400	175200	...	...	...	...	...
Equals: Gross Domestic Product	238872	258000	269700	281300	304800	332500	363600	...	...	...	...	...

1.2 Expenditure on the Gross Domestic Product, in Constant Prices

Million CFA francs

	1980	1981	1982	1983	1984	1985	1986	1987	1988	1989	1990	1991
				At constant prices of:1970								
1 Government final consumption expenditure	18211	18152	...	...	...	...	...	...	...	...	...	...
2 Private final consumption expenditure	60297	60772	...	...	...	...	...	...	...	...	...	...
3 Gross capital formation	34627	24263	...	...	...	...	...	...	...	...	...	...
A Increase in stocks	6217	5372	...	...	...	...	...	...	...	...	...	...
B Gross fixed capital formation	28410	18891	...	...	...	...	...	...	...	...	...	...
4 Exports of goods and services	33541	35847	...	...	...	...	...	...	...	...	...	...
5 Less: Imports of goods and services	52394	50589	...	...	...	...	...	...	...	...	...	...
Equals: Gross Domestic Product	94282	88445	...	...	...	...	...	...	...	...	...	...

1.3 Cost Components of the Gross Domestic Product

Million CFA francs

	1980	1981	1982	1983	1984	1985	1986	1987	1988	1989	1990	1991
1 Indirect taxes, net	33065	35325	...	...	...	...	...	...	...	...	...	...
2 Consumption of fixed capital	17900	19124	...	...	...	...	...	...	...	...	...	...
3 Compensation of employees paid by resident producers to:	67112	71699	...	...	...	...	...	...	...	...	...	...
4 Operating surplus	120795	129052	...	...	...	...	...	...	...	...	...	...
Equals: Gross Domestic Product	238872	255200	...	...	...	...	...	...	...	...	...	...

1.7 External Transactions on Current Account, Summary

Million CFA francs

	1980	1981	1982	1983	1984	1985	1986	1987	1988	1989	1990	1991
				Payments to the Rest of the World								
1 Imports of goods and services	138862	...	...	...	...	...	...	...	...	...	...	...
2 Factor income to the rest of the world	6600	...	...	...	...	...	...	...	...	...	...	...
A Compensation of employees	100	...	...	...	...	...	...	...	...	...	...	...
B Property and entrepreneurial income	6500	...	...	...	...	...	...	...	...	...	...	...
3 Current transfers to the rest of the world	3500	...	...	...	...	...	...	...	...	...	...	...
4 Surplus of the nation on current transactions	-37700	...	...	...	...	...	...	...	...	...	...	...
Payments to the Rest of the World and Surplus of the Nation on Current Transactions	111262	...	...	...	...	...	...	...	...	...	...	...

Togo

1.7 External Transactions on Current Account, Summary
(Continued)

Million CFA francs

	1980	1981	1982	1983	1984	1985	1986	1987	1988	1989	1990	1991
Receipts From The Rest of the World												
1 Exports of goods and services	90562	...	...	...	...	...	...	...	...	...	...	...
2 Factor income from rest of the world	2200	...	...	...	...	...	...	...	...	...	...	...
A Compensation of employees	500	...	...	...	...	...	...	...	...	...	...	...
B Property and entrepreneurial income	1700	...	...	...	...	...	...	...	...	...	...	...
3 Current transfers from rest of the world	18500	...	...	...	...	...	...	...	...	...	...	...
Receipts from the Rest of the World on Current Transactions	111262	...	...	...	...	...	...	...	...	...	...	...

1.10 Gross Domestic Product by Kind of Activity, in Current Prices

Million CFA francs

	1980	1981	1982	1983	1984	1985	1986	1987	1988	1989	1990	1991
1 Agriculture, hunting, forestry and fishing	63640	69300	...	...	...	...	...	...	...	...	...	...
2 Mining and quarrying	21876	22600	...	...	...	...	...	...	...	...	...	...
3 Manufacturing	16633	16300	...	...	...	...	...	...	...	...	...	...
4 Electricity, gas and water	4057	4100	...	...	...	...	...	...	...	...	...	...
5 Construction	13948	11000	...	...	...	...	...	...	...	...	...	...
6 Wholesale and retail trade, restaurants and hotels	45977	52900	...	...	...	...	...	...	...	...	...	...
7 Transport, storage and communication	15331	17200	...	...	...	...	...	...	...	...	...	...
8 Finance, insurance, real estate and business services	12656	15111	...	...	...	...	...	...	...	...	...	...
9 Community, social and personal services	...	...	...	...	...	...	...	...	...	...	...	...
Total, Industries	...	...	...	...	...	...	...	...	...	...	...	...
Producers of Government Services	...	...	...	...	...	...	...	...	...	...	...	...
Other Producers	...	...	...	...	...	...	...	...	...	...	...	...
Subtotal	223479	242311	...	...	...	...	...	...	...	...	...	...
Less: Imputed bank service charge	1756	1711	...	...	...	...	...	...	...	...	...	...
Plus: Import duties	17149	17400	...	...	...	...	...	...	...	...	...	...
Plus: Value added tax	...	...	...	...	...	...	...	...	...	...	...	...
Equals: Gross Domestic Product	238872	258000	269700	281300	304800	332500	363600	...	...	...	...	...

1.12 Relations Among National Accounting Aggregates

Million CFA francs

	1980	1981	1982	1983	1984	1985	1986	1987	1988	1989	1990	1991
Gross Domestic Product	238872	258000	269700	281300	304800	332500	363600	...	...	...	...	...
Plus: Net factor income from the rest of the world	-4400	...	...	...	...	...	...	...	...	...	...	...
Factor income from the rest of the world	2200	...	...	...	...	...	...	...	...	...	...	...
Less: Factor income to the rest of the world	6600	...	...	...	...	...	...	...	...	...	...	...
Equals: Gross National Product	234472	...	...	...	...	...	...	...	...	...	...	...
Less: Consumption of fixed capital	17900	...	...	...	...	...	...	...	...	...	...	...
Equals: National Income	216572	224300	230000	234500	256400	281800	311700	...	...	...	...	...
Plus: Net current transfers from the rest of the world	15000	...	...	...	...	...	...	...	...	...	...	...
Current transfers from the rest of the world	18500	...	...	...	...	...	...	...	...	...	...	...
Less: Current transfers to the rest of the world	3500	...	...	...	...	...	...	...	...	...	...	...
Equals: National Disposable Income	231572	...	...	...	...	...	...	...	...	...	...	...
Less: Final consumption	191848	...	...	...	...	...	...	...	...	...	...	...
Equals: Net Saving	39724	...	...	...	...	...	...	...	...	...	...	...
Less: Surplus of the nation on current transactions	-29105	...	...	...	...	...	...	...	...	...	...	...
Equals: Net Capital Formation	68829	...	...	...	...	...	...	...	...	...	...	...

Tonga

Source. Reply to the United Nations National Accounts Questionnaire from the Statistics Department, Nuku'alofa.
General note. The estimates shown in the following tables have been prepared in accordance with the United Nations System of National Accounts so far as the existing data would permit.

1.1 Expenditure on the Gross Domestic Product, in Current Prices

Million Tongan pa'anga

	1980	1981	1982	1983	1984	1985	1986	1987	1988	1989	1990	1991
1 Government final consumption expenditure	6.9	7.7	10.8	10.3	...	...	...	...	...	...	...	...
2 Private final consumption expenditure	49.8	66.8	77.7	91.5	...	...	...	...	...	...	...	...
3 Gross capital formation	13.8	14.2	15.7	21.1	...	...	...	...	...	...	...	...
A Increase in stocks	1.2	1.2	0.9	0.7	...	...	...	...	...	...	...	...
B Gross fixed capital formation	12.6	13.0	14.8	20.4	...	...	...	...	...	...	...	...
Residential buildings	3.9	2.1	3.2	6.6	...	...	...	...	...	...	...	...
Non-residential buildings	5.3	6.5	6.4	9.0	...	...	...	...	...	...	...	...
Other construction and land improvement etc.	0.1	0.1	0.1	0.2	...	...	...	...	...	...	...	...
Other	3.3	4.3	5.1	4.6	...	...	...	...	...	...	...	...
4 Exports of goods and services	14.1	14.3	16.5	14.3	...	...		...	...	.		...
5 Less: Imports of goods and services	31.7	36.6	41.0	50.9	...	...	...	...		...		...
Equals: Gross Domestic Product	52.9	54.4	64.2	72.7	74.5	80.0	100.0	...	...	...	...	...

1.3 Cost Components of the Gross Domestic Product

Million Tongan pa'anga

	1980	1981	1982	1983	1984	1985	1986	1987	1988	1989	1990	1991
1 Indirect taxes, net	6.1	7.1	8.4	9.3	...	...	...	...	...	...	...	...
A Indirect taxes	...	7.3	8.7	9.7	...	...	...	...	...	...	...	...
B Less: Subsidies	...	0.2	0.3	0.4	...	...	...	...	...	...	...	...
2 Consumption of fixed capital	2.2	2.5	2.9	2.9	...	...	...	...	...	...	...	...
3 Compensation of employees paid by resident producers to:	18.6	24.1	28.5	32.2	...	...	...	...	...	...	...	...
4 Operating surplus	25.9	32.5	39.5	41.5	...	...	...	...	...	...	...	...
Equals: Gross Domestic Product	52.8	54.4	64.2	72.7	...	...	...	...	...	...	...	...

1.4 General Government Current Receipts and Disbursements

Million Tongan pa'anga

	1980	1981	1982	1983	1984	1985	1986	1987	1988	1989	1990	1991
Receipts												
1 Operating surplus	0.2	0.4	0.9	...	...	...	...	...	...	...	...	...
2 Property and entrepreneurial income	0.3	0.3	0.4	0.5	0.7	1.0	1.3	1.5	...	...		...
3 Taxes, fees and contributions	7.8	9.1	10.7	12.2	12.7	16.1	19.0	19.5	...	...	...	...
A Indirect taxes	6.2	7.3	8.7	9.7	10.1	13.5	15.8	16.4	...	...	...	...
B Direct taxes	1.5	1.7	1.9	2.4	2.4	2.4	2.9	2.8	...	...	...	...
C Social security contributions	-	-	-	-	-	-	-	-	...	...		...
D Compulsory fees, fines and penalties	0.1	0.1	0.1	0.1	0.2	0.2	0.3	0.3	...	...	...	...
4 Other current transfers	2.5	0.2	0.3	0.4	0.2	0.5	0.4	0.7	...	...	...	...
Total Current Receipts of General Government a	10.8	12.5	15.8	18.2	18.0	22.5	26.5	27.5	...	...	...	...
Disbursements												
1 Government final consumption expenditure	7.2	8.1	12.3	12.5	12.9	14.7	17.7	21.3	...	...	...	...
A Compensation of employees	4.3	4.4	6.0	6.3	6.8	8.3	10.0	11.9	...	...	...	...
B Consumption of fixed capital	...	...	...	...	...	...	...	...	...	...	...	...
C Purchases of goods and services, net	2.9	3.7	6.3	6.2	6.1	6.4	7.7	9.4	...	...	...	...
D Less: Own account fixed capital formation	...	...	...	...	...	...	...	...	...	...	...	...
E Indirect taxes paid, net	...	...	...	...	...	...	...	...	...	...	...	...
2 Property income	0.2	0.2	0.5	0.5	0.3	0.7	0.5	1.8	...	...	...	...
A Interest	0.2	0.2	0.4	0.4	0.2	0.6	0.5	1.8	...	...	...	...
B Net land rent and royalties	-	-	0.1	0.1	0.1	0.1	-	-	...	...	...	...

Tonga

1.4 General Government Current Receipts and Disbursements
(Continued)

Million Tongan pa'anga | | | | | | | | | | | Fiscal year ending 30 June | |

	1980	1981	1982	1983	1984	1985	1986	1987	1988	1989	1990	1991
3 Subsidies	-	-	-	-	-	-	-	-	...	...	...	...
4 Other current transfers	0.5	0.7	0.8	1.0	1.1	1.1	3.1	2.2	...	...	...	...
A Social security benefits	...	...	...	...	...	...	...	...	...	...	...	...
B Social assistance grants	0.2	0.2	0.2	0.2	0.2	0.2	0.2	0.2	...	...	...	...
C Other	2.0	2.1	2.3	2.5	2.6	3.8	4.6	4.6	...	...	...	...
5 Net saving b	0.6	1.2	-0.3	1.5	0.9	2.0	0.4	-2.6	...	...	...	...
Total Current Disbursements and Net Saving of General Government a	10.8	12.5	15.8	18.2	18.0	22.5	26.5	27.5	...	...	...	...

a) Data in this table have been revised, therefore they are not strictly comparable with the unrevised data in the other tables.
b) Item 'Net saving' includes consumption of fixed capital.

1.7 External Transactions on Current Account, Summary

Million Tongan pa'anga | | | | | | | | | | | Fiscal year ending 30 June | |

	1980	1981	1982	1983	1984	1985	1986	1987	1988	1989	1990	1991
Payments to the Rest of the World												
1 Imports of goods and services	31.7	36.7	41.0	50.9	...	...	...	...	...	...	...	...
A Imports of merchandise c.i.f.	27.2	32.2	36.2	43.8	...	...	...	...	...	...	...	...
B Other	4.5	4.5	4.8	7.1	...	...	...	...	...	...	...	...
2 Factor income to the rest of the world	0.4	0.5	0.9	0.1	...	...	...	...	...	...	...	...
A Compensation of employees	0.3	0.5	0.8	0.1	...	...	...	...	...	...	...	...
B Property and entrepreneurial income	0.2	-	0.1	-	...	...	...	...	...	...	...	...
3 Current transfers to the rest of the world	1.0	2.0	2.9	6.2	...	...	...	...	...	...	...	...
4 Surplus of the nation on current transactions	-4.7	-6.1	2.9	-13.7	...	...	...	...	...	...	...	...
Payments to the Rest of the World and Surplus of the Nation on Current Transactions	28.5	33.0	47.7	43.6	...	...	...	...	...	...	...	...
Receipts From The Rest of the World												
1 Exports of goods and services	14.1	14.3	16.4	14.3	...	...	...	...	...	...	...	...
A Exports of merchandise f.o.b.	7.7	7.1	6.7	3.8	...	...	...	...	...	...	...	...
B Other	6.4	7.2	9.7	10.6	...	...	...	...	...	...	...	...
2 Factor income from rest of the world	2.7	3.9	5.3	3.3	...	...	...	...	...	...	...	...
A Compensation of employees	0.8	2.7	2.8	3.3	...	...	...	...	...	...	...	...
B Property and entrepreneurial income	1.9	1.2	2.5	-	...	...	...	...	...	...	...	...
3 Current transfers from rest of the world	11.7	14.9	25.9	25.9	...	...	...	...	...	...	...	...
Receipts from the Rest of the World on Current Transactions	28.5	33.0	47.7	43.6	...	...	...	...	...	...	...	...

1.8 Capital Transactions of The Nation, Summary

Million Tongan pa'anga | | | | | | | | | | | Fiscal year ending 30 June | |

	1980	1981	1982	1983	1984	1985	1986	1987	1988	1989	1990	1991
Finance of Gross Capital Formation												
Gross saving	10.9	10.2	18.9	...	...	...	...	...	...	...	...	...
1 Consumption of fixed capital	2.2	2.5	2.8	...	...	...	...	...	...	...	...	...
2 Net saving	8.7	7.8	16.1	...	...	...	...	...	...	...	...	...
Less: Surplus of the nation on current transactions	-4.6	-6.6	2.5	...	...	...	...	...	...	...	...	...
Finance of Gross Capital Formation	15.5	16.8	16.3	...	...	...	...	...	...	...	...	...
Gross Capital Formation												
Increase in stocks	2.0	2.0	1.3	...	...	...	...	...	...	...	...	...
Gross fixed capital formation	13.6	14.8	15.0	...	...	...	...	...	...	...	...	...
1 General government	6.0	4.2	6.4	...	...	...	...	...	...	...	...	...
2 Corporate and quasi-corporate enterprises	7.5	10.6	8.6	...	...	...	...	...	...	...	...	...
A Public	1.3	2.1	0.9	...	...	...	...	...	...	...	...	...
B Private	6.2	8.5	7.7	...	...	...	...	...	...	...	...	...
3 Other	...	...	...	...	...	...	...	...	...	...	...	...
Gross Capital Formation	15.5	16.8	16.3	...	...	...	...	...	...	...	...	...

1.9 Gross Domestic Product by Institutional Sectors of Origin

Million Tongan pa'anga

Fiscal year ending 30 June

	1980	1981	1982	1983	1984	1985	1986	1987	1988	1989	1990	1991
Domestic Factor Incomes Originating												
1 General government	4.5	4.5	6.2	...	...	...	...	...	...	...	...	...
2 Corporate and quasi-corporate enterprises	11.3	13.1	14.7	...	...	...	...	...	...	...	...	...
A Non-financial a	11.3	13.1	14.7	...	...	...	...	...	...	...	...	...
Public	5.4	5.5	6.1	...	...	...	...	...	...	...	...	...
Private	5.9	7.6	8.6	...	...	...	...	...	...	...	...	...
B Financial a	...	...	...	...	...	...	...	...	...	...	...	...
3 Households and private unincorporated enterprises	22.7	26.4	27.9	...	...	...	...	...	...	...	...	...
4 Non-profit institutions serving households	2.1	2.3	2.5	...	...	...	...	...	...	...	...	...
Subtotal: Domestic Factor Incomes	40.6	46.3	51.2	...	...	...	...	...	...	...	...	...
Indirect taxes, net	6.1	7.3	8.7	...	...	...	...	...	...	...	...	...
Consumption of fixed capital	...	...	...	...	...	...	...	...	...	...	...	...
Gross Domestic Product	46.8	53.5	59.9	...	...	...	...	...	...	...	...	...

a) Item 'Non-financial' includes also financial corporate and quasi-corporate enterprises.

1.10 Gross Domestic Product by Kind of Activity, in Current Prices

Million Tongan pa'anga

Fiscal year ending 30 June

	1980	1981	1982	1983	1984	1985	1986	1987	1988	1989	1990	1991
1 Agriculture, hunting, forestry and fishing	21.3	17.8	21.1	24.3	...	...	...	...	...	...	...	...
2 Mining and quarrying	0.3	0.4	0.4	0.4	...	...	...	...	...	...	...	...
3 Manufacturing	2.8	4.5	5.2	5.0	...	...	...	...	...	...	...	...
4 Electricity, gas and water	0.3	0.3	8.4	0.4	...	...	...	...	...	...	...	...
5 Construction	1.8	2.0	1.9	2.5	...	...	...	...	...	...	...	...
6 Wholesale and retail trade, restaurants and hotels	6.8	7.4	10.6	12.4	...	...	...	...	...	...	...	...
7 Transport, storage and communication	3.1	4.5	4.7	4.9	...	...	...	...	...	...	...	...
8 Finance, insurance, real estate and business services	3.8	2.9	3.2	4.0	...	...	...	...	...	...	...	...
9 Community, social and personal services a	6.5	7.5	8.3	9.5	...	...	...	...	...	...	...	...
Statistical discrepancy	...	-6.3	0.2	-9.1	...	...	...	...	...	...	...	...
Total, Industries	...	...	...	...	...	...	...	...	...	...	...	...
Producers of Government Services a	...	-0.2	-2.7	4.6	...	...	...	...	...	...	...	...
Other Producers a	...	...	...	...	...	...	...	...	...	...	...	...
Subtotal b	46.7	47.3	55.8	63.4	...	...	...	...	...	...	...	...
Less: Imputed bank service charge	0.3	0.4	0.5	0.7	...	...	...	...	...	...	...	...
Plus: Import duties	...	...	...	...	...	...	...	...	...	...	...	...
Plus: Value added tax	...	...	...	...	...	...	...	...	...	...	...	...
Plus: Other adjustments c	6.1	7.1	8.4	9.3	...	...	...	...	...	...	...	...
Equals: Gross Domestic Product	52.9	64.4	64.2	72.7	...	...	...	...	...	...	...	...

a) Items 'Other producers' and 'Producers of government services' are included in item 'Community, social and personal services'. b) Gross domestic product in factor values. c) Item 'Other adjustments' refers to indirect taxes net of subsidies.

1.11 Gross Domestic Product by Kind of Activity, in Constant Prices

Million Tongan pa'anga

Fiscal year ending 30 June

	1980	1981	1982	1983	1984	1985	1986	1987	1988	1989	1990	1991
At constant prices of: 1975												
1 Agriculture, hunting, forestry and fishing	13.5	17.2	18.6	20.2	...	...	...	...	...	...	...	...
2 Mining and quarrying	0.2	0.3	0.2	0.3	...	...	...	...	...	...	...	...
3 Manufacturing	1.7	2.1	2.2	1.5	...	...	...	...	...	...	...	...
4 Electricity, gas and water	0.3	0.3	0.4	0.4	...	...	...	...	...	...	...	...
5 Construction	0.9	0.8	0.8	0.8	...	...	...	...	...	...	...	...
6 Wholesale and retail trade, restaurants and hotels	3.3	3.3	4.3	4.6	...	...	...	...	...	...	...	...
7 Transport, storage and communication	2.0	2.1	2.5	2.8	...	...	...	...	...	...	...	...
8 Finance, insurance, real estate and business services	2.5	2.5	3.3	3.6	...	...	...	...	...	...	...	...
9 Community, social and personal services a	3.9	3.8	5.0	5.3	...	...	...	...	...	...	...	...
Total, Industries	...	...	...	...	...	...	...	...	...	...	...	...
Producers of Government Services a	...	...	...	...	...	...	...	...	...	...	...	...

Tonga

1.11 Gross Domestic Product by Kind of Activity, in Constant Prices
(Continued)

Million Tongan pa'anga

	1980	1981	1982	1983	1984	1985	1986	1987	1988	1989	1990	1991
					At constant prices of:1975							
Other Producers a	...	...	...		...	...	...	...	...	...	...	...
Subtotal b	28.3	32.5	37.3	39.5	...	...	...	...	...	...	...	...
Less: Imputed bank service charge	...	...	...	...	...	...	...	...	...	...	...	...
Plus: Import duties	...	...	...	...	...	...	...	...	...	...	...	...
Plus: Value added tax	...	...	...	...	...	...	...	...	...	...	...	...
Plus: Other adjustments c	3.2	3.4	3.9	4.2	...	...	...	...	...	...	...	...
Equals: Gross Domestic Product	31.5	35.9	41.2	43.6	...	...	...	...	...	...	...	...

a) Items 'Other producers' and 'Producers of government services' are included in item 'Community, social and personal services'. b) Gross domestic product in factor values.
c) Item 'Other adjustments' refers to indirect taxes net of subsidies.

1.12 Relations Among National Accounting Aggregates

Million Tongan pa'anga

	1980	1981	1982	1983	1984	1985	1986	1987	1988	1989	1990	1991
Gross Domestic Product	52.9	54.4	64.2	72.7	...	...	...	...	...	...	...	...
Plus: Net factor income from the rest of the world	2.3	3.4	4.4	3.2	...	...	...	...	...	...	...	...
Factor income from the rest of the world	2.7	3.9	5.3	3.3	...	...	...	...	...	...	...	...
Less: Factor income to the rest of the world	0.4	0.5	0.9	0.1	...	...	...	...	...	...	...	...
Equals: Gross National Product	55.2	57.8	68.6	75.9	...	...	...	...	...	...	...	...
Less: Consumption of fixed capital	2.2	2.5	2.9	2.9	...	...	...	...	...	...	...	...
Equals: National Income	53.0	55.3	65.7	73.0	...	...	...	...	...	...	...	...
Plus: Net current transfers from the rest of the world	10.7	12.9	23.0	19.7	...	...	...	...	...	...	...	...
Current transfers from the rest of the world	11.7	14.9	25.9	25.9	...	...	...	...	...	...	...	...
Less: Current transfers to the rest of the world	1.0	2.0	2.9	6.2	...	...	...	...	...	...	...	...
Equals: National Disposable Income	63.7	68.2	88.7	92.0	...	...	...	...	...	...	...	...
Less: Final consumption	56.7	74.5	88.5	101.8	...	...	...	...	...	...	...	...
Equals: Net Saving	7.0	5.7	15.7	4.5	...	...	...	...	...	...	...	...
Less: Surplus of the nation on current transactions	-4.7	-6.1	2.9	-13.7	...	...	...	...	...	...	...	...
Equals: Net Capital Formation	11.7	11.8	12.8	18.2	...	...	...	...	...	...	...	...

2.1 Government Final Consumption Expenditure by Function, in Current Prices

Million Tongan pa'anga

	1980	1981	1982	1983	1984	1985	1986	1987	1988	1989	1990	1991
1 General public services	2.1	2.3	3.6	3.1	3.7	4.4	6.1	8.6	...	...	...	...
2 Defence	0.4	0.4	0.6	0.6	0.7	0.9	1.0	1.1	...	...	...	...
3 Public order and safety	0.8	1.0	1.2	1.3	1.3	1.5	1.9	2.2	...	...	...	...
4 Education	1.6	1.8	2.2	2.3	2.4	2.9	3.7	4.2	...	...	...	...
5 Health	1.4	1.6	2.1	2.2	2.3	2.6	3.2	3.3	...	...	...	...
6 Social security and welfare	0.3	0.2	0.3	0.3	0.4	0.4	0.5	0.6	...	...	...	...
7 Housing and community amenities	...	...	...	...	...	...	...	...	...	...	...	...
8 Recreational, cultural and religious affairs	...	...	...	...	...	...	...	...	...	...	...	...
9 Economic services	3.3	3.9	5.5	6.0	5.9	6.8	7.8	8.4	...	...	...	...
A Fuel and energy	...	...	...	...	...	...	...	...	...	...	...	...
B Agriculture, forestry, fishing and hunting	1.1	1.2	1.4	1.2	1.2	1.4	1.6	1.6	...	...	...	...
C Mining, manufacturing and construction, except fuel and energy	1.0	1.2	2.3	2.6	2.2	2.1	3.7	3.9	...	...	...	...
D Transportation and communication	0.8	1.0	1.2	1.5	1.5	1.3	1.5	1.7	...	...	...	...
E Other economic affairs	0.4	0.5	0.6	0.7	1.0	1.0	1.1	1.2	...	...	...	...
10 Other functions	0.6	0.7	0.8	1.1	1.1	1.8	2.6	3.6	...	...	...	...
Total Government Final Consumption Expenditure a	10.5	11.8	16.3	17.0	17.8	21.3	26.9	32.0	...	...	...	...

a) Data in this table have been revised, therefore they are not strictly comparable with the unrevised data in the other tables.

2.11 Gross Fixed Capital Formation by Kind of Activity of Owner, ISIC Divisions, in Current Prices

Million Tongan pa'anga

Fiscal year ending 30 June

	1980	1981	1982	1983	1984	1985	1986	1987	1988	1989	1990	1991
					All Producers							
1 Agriculture, hunting, forestry and fishing	1.4	1.6	4.0	...	...	...	...	...	...	...	...	...
A Agriculture and hunting	1.4	1.6	4.0	...	...	...	...	...	...	...	...	...
B Forestry and logging	...	...	...	...	...	...	...	...	...	...	...	...
C Fishing	...	...	...	...	...	...	...	...	...	...	...	...
2 Mining and quarrying	0.1	-	-	...	...	...	...	...	...	...	...	...
A Coal mining	...	...	...	...	...	...	...	...	...	...	...	...
B Crude petroleum and natural gas production	...	...	...	...	...	...	...	...	...	...	...	...
C Metal ore mining	...	...	...	...	...	...	...	...	...	...	...	...
D Other mining	0.1	-	-	...	...	...	...	...	...	...	...	...
3 Manufacturing	1.1	0.9	1.5	...	...	...	...	...	...	...	...	...
4 Electricity, gas and water	0.8	2.1	0.6	...	...	...	...	...	...	...	...	...
5 Construction	1.5	1.2	0.5	...	...	...	...	...	...	...	...	...
6 Wholesale and retail trade, restaurants and hotels	0.9	1.1	1.0	...	...	...	...	...	...	...	...	...
7 Transport, storage and communication	2.5	4.0	3.1	...	...	...	...	...	...	...	...	...
8 Finance, insurance, real estate and business services	2.3	2.8	3.1	...	...	...	...	...	...	...	...	...
9 Community, social and personal services	2.9	1.1	1.3	...	...	...	...	...	...	...	...	...
Total Industries	13.6	14.8	15.0	...	...	...	...	...	...	...	...	...
Producers of Government Services	...	...	...	...	...	...	...	...	...	...	...	...
Private Non-Profit Institutions Serving Households	...	...	...	...	...	...	...	...	...	...	...	...
Total	13.6	14.8	15.0	...	...	...	...	...	...	...	...	...

Trinidad and Tobago

Source. Reply to the United Nations National Accounts Questionnaire from the Central Statistical Office, Port-of-Spain. The official estimates are published by the Office in the 'National Income of Trinidad and Tobago' and in the 'Annual Statistical Digest'.

General note. The official estimates of Trinidad and Tobago have been adjusted by the Central Statistical Office to conform to the United Nations System of National Accounts so far as the existing data would permit. It should be noted that interest on the public debt is treated as a factor payment and is therefore included in National Income.

1.1 Expenditure on the Gross Domestic Product, in Current Prices

Million Trinidad and Tobago dollars

	1980	1981	1982	1983	1984	1985	1986	1987	1988	1989	1990	1991
1 Government final consumption expenditure	1805	2110	4032	3907	4179	4109	4042	3730	3424	3099	3315	3391
2 Private final consumption expenditure	6865	8197	11103	11594	10224	9494	10621	9853	10765	10784	12067	14129
3 Gross capital formation	4580	4541	5417	5069	4514	3451	3824	3444	2258	3034	2713	3024
A Increase in stocks	376	199	228	30	97	-276	130	129	73	331	-43	-20
B Gross fixed capital formation	4204	4342	5189	5038	4416	3726	3694	3315	2185	2703	2756	3044
Residential buildings	1257	1415	1725	2149	2044	1668	1150	831	...	...	...	...
Non-residential buildings									...	...	...	...
Other construction and land improvement etc.	735	917	1360	952	505	279	623	382	...	...	...	...
Other	2212	2011	2105	1937	1868	1780	1921	2102	...	...	...	...
4 Exports of goods and services	7550	7542	6694	5756	5981	5883	5740	5854	6727	7834	9771	9264
5 Less: Imports of goods and services	5834	5952	8070	7606	6283	5136	6967	5610	5889	6378	6126	7388
Equals: Gross Domestic Product a	14966	16438	19176	18719	18615	17801	17260	17272	17285	18373	21741	22420

a) Data in this table have been revised, therefore they are not strictly comparable with the unrevised data in the other tables.

1.2 Expenditure on the Gross Domestic Product, in Constant Prices

Million Trinidad and Tobago dollars

	1980	1981	1982	1983	1984	1985	1986	1987	1988	1989	1990	1991
		At constant prices of: 1970					1985					
1 Government final consumption expenditure	529	607	737	568 / 4032	4225	4109	4008	3975	3652	3769	3881	...
2 Private final consumption expenditure	2021	2110	2565	2426 / 14156	11006	9494	9861	8284	7861	7145	7039	...
3 Gross capital formation	1774	1479	1558	1389 / 5084	4383	3451	3035	2448	2005	2048	2021	...
4 Exports of goods and services	839	826	749	744 / 5333	5806	5883	5804	5546	6115	5912	6682	...
5 Less: Imports of goods and services	2380	2175	2815	2694 / 6146	5404	5136	5568	4105	3773	3575	3866	...
Statistical discrepancy	-33	28	197	283 / -2356	-1166	-	360	480	198	730	378	...
Equals: Gross Domestic Product	2748	2874	2990	2715 / 20104	18850	17801	17500	16627	16057	16030	16135	...

1.3 Cost Components of the Gross Domestic Product

Million Trinidad and Tobago dollars

	1980	1981	1982	1983	1984	1985	1986	1987	1988	1989	1990	1991
1 Indirect taxes, net	-588	-537	-856	-665	-37	82	454	419	635	843	607	...
A Indirect taxes	637	681	819	968	1038	1172	1088	1066	1160	1308	1057	...
B Less: Subsidies	1225	1218	1675	1633	1075	1090	634	646	525	465	450	...
2 Consumption of fixed capital	848	930	1142	1458	1619	1634	1797	1834	1931	2018	2073	...
3 Compensation of employees paid by resident producers to:	6110	7652	10612	11235	11678	10849	10774	10293	10332	10400	10855	...
4 Operating surplus	8597	8394	8278	6691	5354	5236	4235	4756	4434	5180	7252	...
Statistical discrepancy a	-	-	-	-	-	-	-	-	-	-	863	...
Equals: Gross Domestic Product	14966	16438	19176	18719	18615	17801	17260	17301	17333	18440	21650	...

a) Item 'Statistical Discrepancy' refers to value added tax.

1.4 General Government Current Receipts and Disbursements

Million Trinidad and Tobago dollars

	1980	1981	1982	1983	1984	1985	1986	1987	1988	1989	1990	1991
					Receipts							
1 Operating surplus	...	...	...	...	...	...	...	...	...	...	...	...
2 Property and entrepreneurial income	781	908	851	897	823	870	924	764	623	683	677	...
3 Taxes, fees and contributions	5258	6037	6132	5526	5552	5397	4139	4243	3947	3970	3985	...
A Indirect taxes	637	681	819	968	1038	1172	1088	1066	1160	1272	1128	...

1.4 General Government Current Receipts and Disbursements
(Continued)

Million Trinidad and Tobago dollars

	1980	1981	1982	1983	1984	1985	1986	1987	1988	1989	1990	1991
B Direct taxes	4537	5225	5183	4395	4372	4021	2899	3004	2650	2552	2742	...
C Social security contributions	...	...	...	...	...	...	...	...	...	...	...	...
D Compulsory fees, fines and penalties	84	131	131	163	141	204	151	174	137	146	115	...
4 Other current transfers	37	39	49	50	80	104	80	75	-	-	-	...
Statistical discrepancy	5	4	8	46	48	68	45	121	87	153	1009	...
Total Current Receipts of General Government	6082	6989	7039	6519	6503	6439	5187	5203	4657	4806	5673	...

Disbursements

	1980	1981	1982	1983	1984	1985	1986	1987	1988	1989	1990	1991
1 Government final consumption expenditure	1805	2110	4032	3907	4179	4109	4042	3730	3424	3099	3315	...
A Compensation of employees	1522	1807	3577	3339	3558	3519	3571	3301	3114	2799	2881	...
B Consumption of fixed capital	1	2	2	2	3	3	3	4	3	3	12	...
C Purchases of goods and services, net	282	302	452	566	618	588	468	425	306	297	422	...
D Less: Own account fixed capital formation	...	...	...	...	...	...	...	...	...	...	...	...
E Indirect taxes paid, net	...	...	...	...	...	...	...	...	...	...	...	...
2 Property income [a]	125	179	161	197	264	282	478	561	672	845	1001	...
3 Subsidies	1225	1218	1675	1633	1075	1090	634	646	525	448	431	...
4 Other current transfers	294	346	456	708	690	639	588	632	513	479	599	...
A Social security benefits	93	101	139	221	222	210	238	218	236	234	264	...
B Social assistance grants												...
C Other	201	245	317	487	468	428	350	414	277	244	335	...
5 Net saving	2633	3135	716	73	295	320	-555	-366	-476	-64	326	...
Total Current Disbursements and Net Saving of General Government	6082	6989	7039	6519	6503	6439	5187	5203	4657	4806	5673	...

a) Item 'Property income' relates to interest on loans.

1.7 External Transactions on Current Account, Summary

Million Trinidad and Tobago dollars

	1980	1981	1982	1983	1984	1985	1986	1987	1988	1989	1990	1991
Payments to the Rest of the World												
1 Imports of goods and services	5834	5952	8070	7606	6283	5136	6967	5610	5889	6378	6497	...
2 Factor income to the rest of the world	1314	1309	1011	891	1105	1338	1263	1064	1254	1773	1770	...
3 Current transfers to the rest of the world	162	222	340	290	302	177	144	162	127	128	130	...
4 Surplus of the nation on current transactions	803	891	-1865	-2464	-1337	-263	-2275	-891	-452	-284	1754	...
Payments to the Rest of the World and Surplus of the Nation on Current Transactions	8112	8374	7556	6324	6352	6388	6099	5944	6818	7996	10151	...
Receipts From The Rest of the World												
1 Exports of goods and services	7550	7542	6694	5756	5981	5883	5740	5854	6727	7834	9986	...
2 Factor income from rest of the world	558	827	857	553	340	480	352	61	78	138	134	...
3 Current transfers from rest of the world	4	5	5	15	32	25	7	29	14	24	30	...
Receipts from the Rest of the World on Current Transactions	8112	8374	7556	6324	6352	6388	6099	5944	6818	7996	10151	...

1.10 Gross Domestic Product by Kind of Activity, in Current Prices

Million Trinidad and Tobago dollars

	1980	1981	1982	1983	1984	1985	1986	1987	1988	1989	1990	1991
1 Agriculture, hunting, forestry and fishing	337	386	433	615	491	546	510	515	502	485	539	546
2 Mining and quarrying	5928	5801	4760	3946	4047	3990	3051	3430	2707	3580	4580	3582
3 Manufacturing	1338	1118	1349	1541	1712	1572	1662	1767	2189	2335	3098	3160
4 Electricity, gas and water	26	31	-4	-5	177	181	198	254	294	259	269	258
5 Construction	1885	2639	3152	2817	2502	2188	1836	1675	1785	1843	1983	2146

Trinidad and Tobago

1.10 Gross Domestic Product by Kind of Activity, in Current Prices
(Continued)

Million Trinidad and Tobago dollars

	1980	1981	1982	1983	1984	1985	1986	1987	1988	1989	1990	1991
6 Wholesale and retail trade, restaurants and hotels	1431	1793	2313	2470	2367	2296	2719	2682	3001	3163	3092	3706
7 Transport, storage and communication	1444	1624	2005	1845	1725	1588	1690	1700	1707	1702	1754	1981
8 Finance, insurance, real estate and business services	1434	1841	2167	2296	2179	2185	2160	2059	1950	2073	2295	2526
9 Community, social and personal services	728	809	1301	1325	1418	1324	1433	1326	1361	1419	1471	1622
Total, Industries	14551	16042	17476	16849	16617	15870	15259	15408	15496	16859	19081	19527
Producers of Government Services	1174	1475	2868	2617	2776	2741	2765	2552	2441	2194	2298	2482
Other Producers	...	...	...	...	...	...	...	...	...	...	...	...
Subtotal	15725	17517	20344	19466	19392	18611	18024	17960	17937	19053	21379	22009
Less: Imputed bank service charge	758	1079	1168	747	778	810	766	687	652	680	564	640
Plus: Import duties	...	...	...	...	...	...	...	...	...	...		
Plus: Value added tax	...	...	...	-	-	-	-	-	-	-	927	1052
Equals: Gross Domestic Product a	14966	16438	19176	18719	18615	17801	17260	17272	17285	18373	21741	22419

a) Data in this table have been revised, therefore they are not strictly comparable with the unrevised data in the other tables.

1.11 Gross Domestic Product by Kind of Activity, in Constant Prices

Million Trinidad and Tobago dollars

	1980	1981	1982	1983	1984	1985	1986	1987	1988	1989	1990	1991
			At constant prices of:									
		1970					1985					
1 Agriculture, hunting, forestry and fishing	67	66	68	66 521	410	410	413	556	534	543	647	597
2 Mining and quarrying	207	185	174	157 3698	3856	3990	3819	3500	3407	3366	3387	3279
3 Manufacturing	471	440	450	445 1955	1917	1708	1792	1518	1539	1640	1669	1863
4 Electricity, gas and water	66	75	89	96 174	180	181	198	208	208	207	215	226
5 Construction	410	474	486	399 3238	2609	2188	1722	1534	1495	1372	1402	1539
6 Wholesale and retail trade, restaurants and hotels	489	533	560	483 3121	2420	2296	2433	2426	2199	2068	1895	2128
7 Transport, storage and communication	440	468	515	438 1502	1740	1586	1627	1665	1628	1654	1687	1743
8 Finance, insurance, real estate and business services	429	481	508	449 2761	2346	2185	2029	1726	1517	1448	1443	1530
9 Community, social and personal services	176	184	175	179 1416	1434	1324	1414	1327	1318	1372	1360	1400
Total, Industries	2755	2906	3025	2712 18385	16911	15868	15447	14460	13845	13670	13705	14305
Producers of Government Services	223	249	238	238 2617	2776	2741	2765	2795	2674	2670	2792	2718
Other Producers	...	...	...	... ...	...	...	...	...	...	...	...	...
Subtotal	2978	3155	3263	2950 21002	19687	18609	18212	17255	16519	16340	16497	17023
Less: Imputed bank service charge	227	282	274	234 898	837	810	712	576	507	475	355	388
Plus: Import duties	...	...	...	...	...	...	...	...	...	...	...	...
Plus: Value added tax	...	...	...	...	...	...	...	...	...	...	...	...
Equals: Gross Domestic Product	2748	2874	2990	2715 20104 a	18850 a	17800 a	17500 a	16678 a	16012 a	15865 a	16142 a	16634 a

a) Data in this table have been revised, therefore they are not strictly comparable with the unrevised data in the other tables.

1.12 Relations Among National Accounting Aggregates

Million Trinidad and Tobago dollars

	1980	1981	1982	1983	1984	1985	1986	1987	1988	1989	1990	1991
Gross Domestic Product	14966	16438	19176	18719	18615	17801	17260	17272	17285	18373	21741	22419
Plus: Net factor income from the rest of the world	-756	-481	-154	-339	-765	-859	-911	-1003	-1176	-1635	-1710	-1903
Factor income from the rest of the world	558	827	857	553	340	480	352	61	78	138	...	...
Less: Factor income to the rest of the world	1314	1309	1011	891	1105	1338	1263	1064	1254	1773	...	...
Equals: Gross National Product	14210	15957	19022	18381	17850	16942	16349	16269	16109	16738	20031	20516

1.12 Relations Among National Accounting Aggregates
(Continued)

Million Trinidad and Tobago dollars

	1980	1981	1982	1983	1984	1985	1986	1987	1988	1989	1990	1991
Less: Consumption of fixed capital	848	930	1142	1458	1619	1634	1797	1834	1931	2018	...	...
Equals: National Income	13362	15027	17880	16923	16231	15309	14552	14435	14178	14720	...	...
Plus: Net current transfers from the rest of the world	-157	-218	-335	-275	-270	-151	-137	-132	-114	-105	...	...
Current transfers from the rest of the world	4	5	5	15	32	25	7	29	14	24		
Less: Current transfers to the rest of the world	162	222	340	290	302	177	144	162	127	129		
Equals: National Disposable Income	13205	14809	17544	16648	15961	15157	14415	14303	14064	14615	...	...
Less: Final consumption	8670	10307	15134	15501	14403	13603	14663	13583	14189	13883	...	...
Equals: Net Saving	4536	4502	2410	1146	1558	1554	-248	720	-125	732	...	...
Less: Surplus of the nation on current transactions	803	891	-1865	-2464	-1337	-263	-2275	-891	-452	-284		
Equals: Net Capital Formation	3733	3610	4275	3610	2895	1817	2027	1611	327	1016	...	...

2.1 Government Final Consumption Expenditure by Function, in Current Prices

Million Trinidad and Tobago dollars

	1980	1981	1982	1983	1984	1985	1986	1987	1988	1989	1990	1991
1 General public services	...	306	787	519	584	606	617	666	671	739	781	...
2 Defence	...	...	...	...	...	...	...	...	...	...	...	...
3 Public order and safety	...	284	562	543	582	565	577	520	499	456	465	...
4 Education	...	374	792	751	794	802	799	729	692	619	619	...
5 Health	...	354	620	658	701	698	690	633	595	532	584	...
6 Social security and welfare	...	12	17	17	17	19	19	18	18	16	15	...
7 Housing and community amenities	...	139	218	236	255	257	272	218	207	190	186	...
8 Recreational, cultural and religious affairs	...	...	...	...	...	...	...	...	...	...	...	...
9 Economic services	...	628	1032	1184	1245	1163	1069	949	744	675	715	...
A Fuel and energy a	...	149	248	214	213	202	217	187	146	160	191	...
B Agriculture, forestry, fishing and hunting	...	101	162	200	170	180	143	125	114	98	115	...
C Mining, manufacturing and construction, except fuel and energy	...	40	52	71	69	71	65	52	64	56	55	...
D Transportation and communication	...	277	460	569	499	431	419	365	273	234	237	...
E Other economic affairs	...	61	110	129	294	279	224	218	147	127	117	...
10 Other functions	...	15	5	...	...	...	...	...	...	...	...	...
Total Government Final Consumption Expenditure	...	2110	4032	3907	4179	4109	4042	3730	3424	3227	3368	...

a) Item 'Fuel and energy' includes general administration of economic services.

2.11 Gross Fixed Capital Formation by Kind of Activity of Owner, ISIC Divisions, in Current Prices

Million Trinidad and Tobago dollars

	1980	1981	1982	1983	1984	1985	1986	1987	1988	1989	1990	1991
					All Producers							
1 Agriculture, hunting, forestry and fishing	68	62	60	50	93	46	49	29	...	...	...	...
2 Mining and quarrying	513	544	816	417	431	560	906	775	...	...	...	...
3 Manufacturing	1012	740	625	344	593	342	635	661	...	...	...	...
A Manufacturing of food, beverages and tobacco	122	120	143	102	133	130	157	181	...	...	...	...

Trinidad and Tobago

2.11 Gross Fixed Capital Formation by Kind of Activity of Owner, ISIC Divisions, in Current Prices
(Continued)

Million Trinidad and Tobago dollars

	1980	1981	1982	1983	1984	1985	1986	1987	1988	1989	1990	1991
B Textile, wearing apparel and leather industries	24	11	3	16	18	8	23	24	...	...	...	...
C Manufacture of wood, and wood products, including furniture	21	9	16	15	11	5	6	4	...	...	...	...
D Manufacture of paper and paper products, printing and publishing	41	20	38	26	23	25	38	42	...	...	...	...
E Manufacture of chemicals and chemical petroleum, coal, rubber and plastic products	709	483	265	106	241	153	305	301	...	...	...	...
F Manufacture of non-metalic mineral products except products of petroleum and coal									...	...	...	...
G Basic metal industries	81	83	145	65	152	13	98	91	...	...	...	...
H Manufacture of fabricated metal products, machinery and equipment									...	...	...	...
I Other manufacturing industries	15	15	16	14	15	9	8	17	...	...	...	...
4 Electricity, gas and water	225	220	241	347	192	127	64	59	...	...	...	...
5 Construction	132	98	58	118	44	64	64	24	...	...	...	...
6 Wholesale and retail trade, restaurants and hotels	378	286	812	669	352	18	316	328	...	...	...	...
A Wholesale and retail trade	355	268	792	635	321	13	260	176	...	...	...	...
B Restaurants and hotels	23	18	20	34	30	5	56	151	...	...	...	...
7 Transport, storage and communication	530	504	392	583	691	496	419	530	...	...	...	...
8 Finance, insurance, real estate and business services	850	840	902	1133	1172	1031	932	636	...	...	...	...
9 Community, social and personal services	152	181	195	242	134	232	144	180	...	...	...	...
Total Industries a	3858	3474	4101	3903	3702	2918	3529	3222	...	...	...	...
Producers of Government Services	722	1067	1316	1166	812	533	295	222	...	...	...	...
Private Non-Profit Institutions Serving Households	...	...	...	...	...	...	...	...	...	...	...	...
Total a	4580	4541	5417	5069	4514	3451	3824	3444	...	...	...	...

a) The estimates of this table (Gross Fixed Capital Formation by kind of activity of owner) include increase in stocks.

4.3 Cost Components of Value Added

Million Trinidad and Tobago dollars

	1980						1981					
	Compensation of Employees	Capital Consumption	Net Operating Surplus	Indirect Taxes	Less: Subsidies Received	Value Added	Compensation of Employees	Capital Consumption	Net Operating Surplus	Indirect Taxes	Less: Subsidies Received	Value Added
All Producers												
1 Agriculture, hunting, forestry and fishing	181	10	165	...	18	337	210	11	188	...	23	386
2 Mining and quarrying	213	245	5460	10	...	5928	260	249	5284	8	...	5801
3 Manufacturing	779	130	634	63	268	1338	950	156	256	69	312	1118
A Manufacture of food, beverages and tobacco	217	36	204	50	210	296	258	50	192	49	258	291
B Textile, wearing apparel and leather industries	56	3	11	3	...	73	71	4	18	-	...	93
C Manufacture of wood and wood products, including furniture	37	9	15	...	...	61	42	8	-	...	...	49
D Manufacture of paper and paper products, printing and publishing	46	4	-4	...	...	46	61	6	8	...	...	75
E Manufacture of chemicals and chemical petroleum, coal, rubber and plastic products	293	64	310	7	59	614	336	68	-49	7	53	309
F Manufacture of non-metallic mineral products, except products of petroleum and coal												
G Basic metal industries	119	11	89	3	...	222	166	18	72	11	...	267
H Manufacture of fabricated metal products, machinery and equipment					...						...	
I Other manufacturing industries	12	3	10	1	...	25	15	4	15	1	...	35
4 Electricity, gas and water	175	21	11	1	183	26	210	17	13	1	209	31

4.3 Cost Components of Value Added
(Continued)

Million Trinidad and Tobago dollars

	Compensation of Employees	Capital Consumption	Net Operating Surplus	Indirect Taxes	Less: Subsidies Received	Value Added	Compensation of Employees	Capital Consumption	Net Operating Surplus	Indirect Taxes	Less: Subsidies Received	Value Added
	1980						1981					
5 Construction	1115	68	680	22	...	1885	1479	62	1065	33	...	2639
6 Wholesale and retail trade, restaurants and hotels	660	71	510	497	306	1431	768	83	765	522	345	1793
A Wholesale and retail trade	583	60	461	495	306	1293	679	69	706	520	345	1628
B Restaurants and hotels	77	11	49	2	...	138	90	13	59	3	...	164
7 Transport, storage and communication	978	204	685	27	450	1444	1329	231	363	30	329	1624
8 Finance, insurance, real estate and business services	319	97	1016	2	...	1434	412	117	1309	3	...	1841
9 Community, social and personal services	518	2	194	14	...	728	560	4	230	15	...	809
Total, Industries	4938	848	9355	636	1225	14551	6178	930	9473	681	1218	16042
Producers of Government Services	1172	1	...	...	...	1174	1474	2	...	...	...	1475
Other Producers	...	...	...	...	...	...	...	...	...	...	...	...
Total	6110	849	9355	636	1225	15725	7652	932	9473	681	1218	17517
Less: Imputed bank service charge	...	...	758	...	...	758	...	...	1079	...	...	1079
Import duties	...	...	...	...	...	...	...	...	...	...	...	...
Value added tax	...	...	...	...	...	...	...	...	...	...	...	...
Total	6110	848	8597	637	1225	14966	7652	930	8394	681	1218	16438

	Compensation of Employees	Capital Consumption	Net Operating Surplus	Indirect Taxes	Less: Subsidies Received	Value Added	Compensation of Employees	Capital Consumption	Net Operating Surplus	Indirect Taxes	Less: Subsidies Received	Value Added
	1982						1983					
	All Producers											
1 Agriculture, hunting, forestry and fishing	241	13	207	...	28	433	299	9	352	...	45	615
2 Mining and quarrying	338	327	4084	11	...	4760	374	327	3226	20	...	3946
3 Manufacturing	1097	201	352	79	379	1349	1297	268	287	116	426	1541
A Manufacture of food, beverages and tobacco	298	56	261	56	290	381	341	68	224	61	422	272
B Textile, wearing apparel and leather industries	72	4	7	1	...	83	73	4	20	1	...	98
C Manufacture of wood and wood products, including furniture	47	9	3	...	...	59	49	14	8	1	...	72
D Manufacture of paper and paper products, printing and publishing	69	7	14	...	...	90	70	7	31	...	...	109
E Manufacture of chemicals and chemical petroleum, coal, rubber and plastic products	403	101	-26	6	90	394	442	113	69	17	4	636
F Manufacture of non-metallic mineral products, except products of petroleum and coal												
G Basic metal industries	194	21	82	15	...	311	300	60	-76	34	...	318
H Manufacture of fabricated metal products, machinery and equipment					...							
I Other manufacturing industries	15	3	13	1	...	32	22	2	11	2	...	36
4 Electricity, gas and water	305	23	52	1	384	-4	356	25	-4	2	384	-5
5 Construction	1745	50	1318	39	...	3152	1695	54	1032	36	...	2817
6 Wholesale and retail trade, restaurants and hotels	1001	110	947	622	367	2313	1061	111	738	721	160	2470
A Wholesale and retail trade	899	94	881	618	367	2125	925	89	704	719	160	2277
B Restaurants and hotels	103	16	66	4	...	188	136	22	34	2	...	193
7 Transport, storage and communication	1524	287	666	45	516	2005	1728	481	215	38	618	1845
8 Finance, insurance, real estate and business services	524	127	1513	4	...	2167	807	152	1326	11	...	2296
9 Community, social and personal services	972	3	307	19	...	1301	1004	30	266	25	...	1325

Trinidad and Tobago

4.3 Cost Components of Value Added
(Continued)

Million Trinidad and Tobago dollars

	1982						1983					
	Compensation of Employees	Capital Consumption	Net Operating Surplus	Indirect Taxes	Less: Subsidies Received	Value Added	Compensation of Employees	Capital Consumption	Net Operating Surplus	Indirect Taxes	Less: Subsidies Received	Value Added
Total, Industries	7747	1141	9446	820	1674	17476	8620	1456	7438	968	1633	16849
Producers of Government Services	2866	2	...	...	...	2868	2615	2	...	...	...	2617
Other Producers	...	...	...	...	...	...	...	...	...	...	...	...
Total	10612	1143	9446	820	1674	20344	11235	1458	7438	968	1633	19466
Less: Imputed bank service charge	...	...	1168	...	...	1168	...	...	747	...	...	747
Import duties	...	...	...	...	...	...	...	...	...	...	...	...
Value added tax	...	...	...	...	...	...	...	...	...	...	...	...
Total	10612	1142	8278	819	1675	19176	11235	1458	6691	968	1633	18719

	1984						1985					
	Compensation of Employees	Capital Consumption	Net Operating Surplus	Indirect Taxes	Less: Subsidies Received	Value Added	Compensation of Employees	Capital Consumption	Net Operating Surplus	Indirect Taxes	Less: Subsidies Received	Value Added
	All Producers											
1 Agriculture, hunting, forestry and fishing	313	13	194	3	33	491	370	14	177	3	19	546
2 Mining and quarrying	366	330	3329	21	...	4047	392	350	3229	19	...	3990
3 Manufacturing	1278	319	350	139	374	1712	1242	373	162	165	370	1572
A Manufacture of food, beverages and tobacco	351	69	153	78	374	277	362	71	197	90	273	446
B Textile, wearing apparel and leather industries	71	4	13	2	...	91	57	5	5	2	...	69
C Manufacture of wood and wood products, including furniture	49	11	18	2	...	80	27	6	5	1	...	38
D Manufacture of paper and paper products, printing and publishing	75	8	32	1	...	116	78	12	21	2	...	112
E Manufacture of chemicals and chemical petroleum, coal, rubber and plastic products	447	166	152	22	-	787	445	204	-1	25	97	575
F Manufacture of non-metallic mineral products, except products of petroleum and coal												
G Basic metal industries	278	62	-10	35	...	364	252	71	-86	45	...	283
H Manufacture of fabricated metal products, machinery and equipment					...						...	
I Other manufacturing industries	26	3	3	2	...	34	25	4	6	1	...	36
4 Electricity, gas and water	387	29	7	2	248	177	359	35	64	2	278	181
5 Construction	1504	52	934	12	...	2502	1460	43	675	9	...	2188
6 Wholesale and retail trade, restaurants and hotels	1446	157	-7	787	17	2367	1388	267	-261	924	21	2296
A Wholesale and retail trade	1321	140	-25	784	17	2203	1270	244	-277	921	21	2137
B Restaurants and hotels	125	19	19	3	-	164	118	22	16	3	-	158
7 Transport, storage and communication	1678	500	-91	41	403	1725	1017	320	616	38	403	1588
8 Finance, insurance, real estate and business services	847	174	1154	4	...	2179	816	195	1173	1	...	2185
9 Community, social and personal services	1085	41	263	29	...	1418	1065	35	211	12	...	1324
Total, Industries	8904	1615	6132	1038	1075	16615	8109	1632	6046	1172	1090	15870
Producers of Government Services	2773	2	...	...	...	2776	2740	2	...	...	...	2741
Other Producers	...	...	...	...	...	...	...	...	...	...	...	...
Total	11679	1619	6132	1038	1075	19393	10849	1634	6046	1172	1090	18611
Less: Imputed bank service charge	...	...	778	...	...	778	...	...	810	...	...	810
Import duties	...	...	...	...	...	...	...	...	...	...	...	...
Value added tax	...	...	...	...	...	...	...	...	...	...	...	...
Total	11678	1619	5354	1038	1075	18615	10849	1634	5236	1172	1090	17801

4.3 Cost Components of Value Added

Million Trinidad and Tobago dollars

All Producers

	1986						1987					
	Compensation of Employees	Capital Consumption	Net Operating Surplus	Indirect Taxes	Less: Subsidies Received	Value Added	Compensation of Employees	Capital Consumption	Net Operating Surplus	Indirect Taxes	Less: Subsidies Received	Value Added
1 Agriculture, hunting, forestry and fishing	341	14	168	4	17	510	340	14	175	3	17	515
2 Mining and quarrying	387	332	2315	18	...	3051	435	378	2600	16	...	3430
3 Manufacturing	1251	362	10	194	155	1662	1226	379	112	206	156	1767
A Manufacture of food, beverages and tobacco	383	79	343	101	308	598	419	87	190	111	136	671
B Textile, wearing apparel and leather industries	57	5	11	2	...	74	39	4	25	3	...	71
C Manufacture of wood and wood products, including furniture	26	4	2	1	...	33	30	5	-4	1	...	31
D Manufacture of paper and paper products, printing and publishing	81	13	27	1	...	122	87	15	23	1	...	126
E Manufacture of chemicals and chemical petroleum, coal, rubber and plastic products	462	192	-224	21	...	450	472	186	-18	22	...	662
F Manufacture of non-metallic mineral products, except products of petroleum and coal												
G Basic metal industries	248	77	-52	39	...	313	225	84	-101	19	...	226
H Manufacture of fabricated metal products, machinery and equipment												
I Other manufacturing industries	29	4	8	2	...	43	31	5	9	2	...	46
4 Electricity, gas and water	365	46	-8	3	207	198	347	88	-44	4	140	254
5 Construction	1325	44	463	5	...	1836	1217	42	413	3	...	1675
6 Wholesale and retail trade, restaurants and hotels	1480	250	339	809	9	2869	1453	200	464	763	15	2864
A Wholesale and retail trade	1360	244	318	807	9	2719	1332	191	412	762	15	2682
B Restaurants and hotels	120	7	21	2	...	150	121	8	52	1	...	182
7 Transport, storage and communication	1005	488	404	39	247	1690	951	474	549	48	319	1702
8 Finance, insurance, real estate and business services	819	225	1112	5	...	2160	798	231	1016	14	...	2059
9 Community, social and personal services	1039	34	199	12	...	1284	975	27	160	9	...	1171
Total, Industries	8010	1795	5002	1088	634	15260	7742	1832	5443	1065	646	15436
Producers of Government Services	2764	2	...	...	...	2765	2550	2	...	...	...	2552
Other Producers	...	...	...	...	...	...	...	...	...	...	...	...
Total	10774	1797	5002	1088	634	18025	10292	1834	5443	1065	646	17988
Less: Imputed bank service charge	...	...	767	...	...	767	...	...	687	...	...	687
Import duties	...	...	...	...	...	...	...	...	...	...	...	...
Value added tax	...	...	...	...	...	...	...	...	...	...	...	...
Total	10774	1797	4235	1088	634	17260	10292	1834	4756	1066	646	17301

All Producers

	1988						1989					
	Compensation of Employees	Capital Consumption	Net Operating Surplus	Indirect Taxes	Less: Subsidies Received	Value Added	Compensation of Employees	Capital Consumption	Net Operating Surplus	Indirect Taxes	Less: Subsidies Received	Value Added
1 Agriculture, hunting, forestry and fishing	343	12	157	4	23	493	347	11	73	3	15	420
2 Mining and quarrying	411	390	1889	16	...	2707	411	375	2520	17	...	3323
3 Manufacturing	1244	418	502	241	155	2250	1289	442	563	273	125	2443
A Manufacture of food, beverages and tobacco	...	...	...	...	...	...	...	...	...	...	...	...

Trinidad and Tobago

4.3 Cost Components of Value Added
(Continued)

Million Trinidad and Tobago dollars

	1988						1989					
	Compensation of Employees	Capital Consumption	Net Operating Surplus	Indirect Taxes	Less: Subsidies Received	Value Added	Compensation of Employees	Capital Consumption	Net Operating Surplus	Indirect Taxes	Less: Subsidies Received	Value Added
B Textile, wearing apparel and leather industries	37	5	9	2	...	53	...	...	...	...	...	...
C Manufacture of wood and wood products, including furniture	25	4	5	1	...	35	...	...	...	...	...	...
D Manufacture of paper and paper products, printing and publishing	82	15	24	3	...	123	...	...	...	...	...	...
E Manufacture of chemicals and chemical petroleum, coal, rubber and plastic products	...	...	...	...	...	...	...	...	...	...	...	...
F Manufacture of non-metallic mineral products, except products of petroleum and coal	...	...	...	...	...	...	...	...	...	...	...	...
G Basic metal industries	...	...	...	...			...	...	...	...	...	...
H Manufacture of fabricated metal products, machinery and equipment	...	...	...	...			...	...	...	...	...	...
I Other manufacturing industries	...	...	...	...	...	...	...	...	...	...	...	...
4 Electricity, gas and water	352	91	-95	8	63	294	321	88	-102	9	44	272
5 Construction	1267	45	467	4	...	1782	1340	54	483	9	...	1887
6 Wholesale and retail trade, restaurants and hotels	1675	242	474	818	23	3187	1772	257	532	934	84	3412
A Wholesale and retail trade	1537	225	462	800	23	3001	1624	238	518	915	84	3211
B Restaurants and hotels	138	17	12	18	-	186	148	19	14	19	...	201
7 Transport, storage and communication	872	463	563	54	262	1690	912	506	526	48	198	1793
8 Finance, insurance, real estate and business services	759	240	946	5	...	1950	766	253	1110	5	...	2135
9 Community, social and personal services	970	29	184	10	...	1192	909	29	176	10	...	1124
Total, Industries	7892	1930	5088	1160	525	15546	8068	2016	5884	1308	465	16809
Producers of Government Services	2440	1	...	...	...	2441	2332	2	...	...	...	2334
Other Producers	...	...	...	...	...	...	...	...	...	...	...	...
Total	10332	1931	5088	1160	525	17987	10400	2018	5884	1308	465	19143
Less: Imputed bank service charge	...	...	654	...	...	654	...	...	704	...	...	704
Import duties	...	...	...	...	...	...	...	...	...	...	...	...
Value added tax	...	...	...	...	...	...	...	...	...	...	...	...
Total	10332	1931	4434	1160	525	17333	10400	2018	5180	1308	465	18440

	1990					
	Compensation of Employees	Capital Consumption	Net Operating Surplus	Indirect Taxes	Less: Subsidies Received	Value Added
	All Producers					
1 Agriculture, hunting, forestry and fishing	396	12	121	3	35	497
2 Mining and quarrying	460	368	4003	18	...	4851
3 Manufacturing	1382	450	834	112	104	2675
A Manufacture of food, beverages and tobacco	...	...	...	...	...	...

4.3 Cost Components of Value Added
(Continued)

Million Trinidad and Tobago dollars

	1990					
	Compensation of Employees	Capital Consumption	Net Operating Surplus	Indirect Taxes	Less: Subsidies Received	Value Added
B Textile, wearing apparel and leather industries	...	...	...	...	...	...
C Manufacture of wood and wood products, including furniture	...	...	...	...	...	...
D Manufacture of paper and paper products, printing and publishing	...	...	...	...	...	...
E Manufacture of chemicals and chemical petroleum, coal, rubber and plastic products	...	...	...	...	...	...
F Manufacture of non-metallic mineral products, except products of petroleum and coal	...	...	...	...	...	...
G Basic metal industries	...	...	...	...	...	...
H Manufacture of fabricated metal products, machinery and equipment	...	...	...	...	...	...
I Other manufacturing industries	...	...	...	...	...	...
4 Electricity, gas and water	330	92	-37	9	43	349
5 Construction	1354	55	567	-70	-1	1903
6 Wholesale and retail trade, restaurants and hotels	1871	267	691	901	87	3643
A Wholesale and retail trade	1726	249	674	881	87	3443
B Restaurants and hotels	145	18	17	20	...	200
7 Transport, storage and communication	942	535	510	67	180	1874
8 Finance, insurance, real estate and business services	797	262	1106	6	...	2171
9 Community, social and personal services	921	30	178	11	...	1140
Total, Industries	8453	2071	7973	1057	450	19103
Producers of Government Services	2402	...	2	...	...	2404
Other Producers	...	...	...	...	...	...
Total	10855	2073	7973	1057	450	21507
Less: Imputed bank service charge	...	...	721	...	...	721
Import duties	...	...	...	...	...	...
Value added tax	...	...	...	...	...	863
Total	10855	2073	7252	1057	450	21650

Tunisia

Source. Reply to the United Nations National Accounts Questionnaire from the Direction de la Planification, Ministere du Plan, Tunis. The official estimates are published annually by the same Office in 'l'Economie de la Tunisie en Chiffres'.

General note. The estimates shown in the following tables have been prepared in accordance with the United Nations System of National Accounts so far as the existing data would permit.

1.1 Expenditure on the Gross Domestic Product, in Current Prices

Million Tunisian dinars

	1980	1981	1982	1983	1984	1985	1986	1987	1988	1989	1990	1991
1 Government final consumption expenditure	512.2	615.7	793.8	926.8	1030.0	1142.0	1217.0	1305.4	1386.6	1608.1	...	...
2 Private final consumption expenditure	2178.7	2553.7	2997.2	3434.2	3944.0	4356.0	4670.0	5120.0	5562.0	6168.0	...	...
3 Gross capital formation	1039.5	1345.5	1519.3	1610.0	1995.0	1835.0	1649.5	1615.9	1614.6	2155.6	...	...
A Increase in stocks	37.5	55.5	-115.7	-140.0	75.0	-15.0	-35.5	-4.1	-65.4	155.6	...	...
B Gross fixed capital formation	1002.0	1290.0	1635.0	1750.0	1920.0	1850.0	1685.0	1620.0	1680.0	2000.0	...	...
Residential buildings	188.0	198.0	266.0	327.0	365.0	378.0	391.0	403.0	370.0	410.0	...	...
Non-residential buildings	...	...	...	...	...	...	...	...	...	...	...	...
Other construction and land improvement etc.	...	...	...	...	...	...	...	...	...	...	...	...
Other	...	...	...	...	...	...	...	...	...	...	...	...
4 Exports of goods and services	1424.6	1721.9	1773.3	1947.8	2114.0	2253.0	2161.2	2796.1	3659.5	4067.0	...	...
5 Less: Imports of goods and services	1614.5	2074.3	2279.2	2421.4	2843.0	2676.0	2693.7	2878.4	3618.1	4502.0	...	...
Equals: Gross Domestic Product	3540.5	4162.0	4804.4	5497.4	6240.0	6910.0	7004.0	7959.0	8604.6	9496.7	...	...

1.2 Expenditure on the Gross Domestic Product, in Constant Prices

Million Tunisian dinars

	1980	1981	1982	1983	1984	1985	1986	1987	1988	1989	1990	1991
					At constant prices of:1980							
1 Government final consumption expenditure	512.2	554.8	596.0	631.0	668.0	696.0	690.0	695.8	697.7	722.9	...	...
2 Private final consumption expenditure	2178.7	2336.0	2403.0	2514.0	2664.0	2733.0	2760.0	2795.0	2830.0	2904.0	...	...
3 Gross capital formation	1039.5	1196.1	1188.0	1162.0	1263.0	1104.0	902.2	796.7	639.7	906.0	...	...
A Increase in stocks	37.5	51.7	-50.0	-18.0	27.0	-30.0	-23.8	-33.7	-148.4	51.3	...	...
B Gross fixed capital formation	1002.0	1144.4	1238.0	1180.0	1236.0	1134.0	926.0	830.4	788.1	854.7	...	...
4 Exports of goods and services	1424.6	1473.7	1372.0	1385.0	1422.0	1469.0	1546.0	1765.8	2199.3	2171.9	...	...
5 Less: Imports of goods and services	1614.5	1824.6	1841.0	1800.0	1902.0	1654.0	1620.0	1527.5	1775.0	1971.6	...	...
Equals: Gross Domestic Product	3540.5	3736.0	3718.0	3892.0	4115.0	4348.0	4278.2	4525.8	4591.7	4733.2	...	...

1.3 Cost Components of the Gross Domestic Product

Million Tunisian dinars

	1980	1981	1982	1983	1984	1985	1986	1987	1988	1989	1990	1991
1 Indirect taxes, net	476.4	521.3	573.0	738.0	821.0	865.8	935.0	1012.0	1097.8	1092.6	...	...
A Indirect taxes	553.6	651.0	...	...	...	...	...	...	...	...	...	...
B Less: Subsidies	77.2	129.7	...	...	...	...	...	...	...	...	...	...
2 Consumption of fixed capital	325.0	380.0	464.0	563.0	672.0	784.0	860.8	949.5	962.9	1020.9	...	...
3 Compensation of employees paid by resident producers to:	2739.1	3260.7	3767.4	4196.4	4747.0	5260.2	5208.2	5997.5	6543.9	7383.2	...	...
4 Operating surplus											...	...
Equals: Gross Domestic Product	3540.5	4162.0	4804.4	5497.4	6240.0	6910.0	7004.0	7959.0	8604.6	9496.7	...	...

1.4 General Government Current Receipts and Disbursements

Million Tunisian dinars

	1980	1981	1982	1983	1984	1985	1986	1987	1988	1989	1990	1991
					Receipts							
1 Operating surplus	...	...	...	...	...	...	...	...	...	...	...	...
2 Property and entrepreneurial income	75.5	76.3	90.8	134.8	158.1	164.4	193.0	201.5	206.2	241.5	...	...
3 Taxes, fees and contributions	1062.7	1321.4	1628.0	1825.5	2105.3	2270.9	2335.8	2373.2	2607.0	2795.4	...	...
A Indirect taxes	553.6	651.0	798.6	983.2	1126.8	1214.6	1243.8	1280.6	1415.4	1563.2	...	...
B Direct taxes	386.5	503.1	645.6	615.1	742.3	808.6	778.7	813.5	839.4	862.3	...	...
C Social security contributions	122.6	167.3	183.8	227.2	236.2	247.7	313.3	279.1	352.2	369.9	...	...
D Compulsory fees, fines and penalties	...	...	...	...	...	...	...	...	...	...	...	...
4 Other current transfers	44.8	28.2	21.8	28.7	28.9	14.2	31.3	42.1	67.5	126.2	...	...
Total Current Receipts of General Government	1183.0	1425.9	1740.6	1989.0	2292.3	2449.5	2560.1	2616.8	2880.7	3163.1	...	...

1.4 General Government Current Receipts and Disbursements
(Continued)

Million Tunisian dinars

	1980	1981	1982	1983	1984	1985	1986	1987	1988	1989	1990	1991
Disbursements												
1 Government final consumption expenditure	533.9	634.7	815.1	950.9	1067.7	1140.9	1217.0	1305.4	1386.6	1608.1	...	...
2 Property income	57.6	63.3	87.9	105.8	130.9	145.8	179.2	220.1	244.0	285.6	...	...
A Interest	57.6	63.3	87.9	105.8	130.9	145.8	179.2	220.1	244.0	285.6	...	...
B Net land rent and royalties	...	...	...	...	...	...	...	...	...	...	...	...
3 Subsidies	77.2	129.7	190.8	183.2	280.6	273.7	282.2	272.9	290.3	512.5	...	...
4 Other current transfers	119.3	200.5	196.1	220.6	267.8	326.9	375.9	392.8	484.5	582.5	...	...
A Social security benefits	78.7	108.5	128.0	155.7	187.4	187.1	230.6	273.6	327.5	430.6	...	...
B Social assistance grants	29.8	77.7	59.0	58.2	73.1	78.8	93.1	96.8	109.3	115.1	...	...
C Other	10.8	14.3	9.1	6.7	7.3	61.0	52.2	22.4	47.7	36.8	...	...
5 Net saving	395.0	397.7	450.7	528.5	545.3	562.2	505.8	425.6	475.3	174.4	...	...
Total Current Disbursements and Net Saving of General Government	1183.0	1425.9	1740.6	1989.0	2292.3	2449.5	2560.1	2616.8	2880.7	3163.1	...	...

1.7 External Transactions on Current Account, Summary

Million Tunisian dinars

	1980	1981	1982	1983	1984	1985	1986	1987	1988	1989	1990	1991
Payments to the Rest of the World												
1 Imports of goods and services	1614.5	2074.3	2279.2	2421.4	2842.5	2676.3	2693.7	2878.4	3618.1	4502.0	...	...
A Imports of merchandise c.i.f.	1467.1	1866.0	2002.0	2106.4	2511.0	2287.0	2303.7	2509.1	3167.1	3990.0	...	...
B Other	147.4	208.3	277.2	315.0	331.5	389.3	390.0	369.3	451.0	512.0	...	...
2 Factor income to the rest of the world	166.2	213.0	250.6	259.8	291.2	351.0	371.6	424.4	483.0	545.0	...	...
A Compensation of employees	8.1	5.7	6.9	6.3	5.2	5.3	4.0	3.1	2.5	...	...	...
B Property and entrepreneurial income	158.1	207.3	243.7	253.5	286.0	345.7	367.6	421.3	480.5	...	...	...
3 Current transfers to the rest of the world	...	...	...	...	...	...	...	...	...	...	...	...
4 Surplus of the nation on current transactions	-167.7	-320.5	-453.3	-409.5	-680.0	-491.2	-582.4	-67.6	90.9	-370.0	...	...
Payments to the Rest of the World and Surplus of the Nation on Current Transactions	1613.0	1966.8	2076.5	2271.7	2453.7	2536.1	2482.9	3235.2	4192.0	4677.0	...	...
Receipts From The Rest of the World												
1 Exports of goods and services	1424.6	1721.9	1773.3	1947.8	2113.7	2253.0	2161.2	2796.1	3659.5	4067.0	...	...
A Exports of merchandise f.o.b.	970.0	1212.4	1169.4	1262.6	1399.1	1443.0	1403.8	1770.7	2055.5	2595.0	...	...
B Other	454.6	509.5	603.9	685.2	714.6	810.1	757.4	1025.4	1604.1	1472.0	...	...
2 Factor income from rest of the world	188.4	244.9	303.2	323.9	340.0	283.0	321.7	439.1	532.5	610.0	...	...
A Compensation of employees	122.8	178.3	219.6	243.8	245.9	225.8	287.1	403.0	466.2	470.0	...	...
B Property and entrepreneurial income	65.6	66.6	83.6	80.1	94.1	57.2	34.6	36.1	66.3	140.0	...	...
3 Current transfers from rest of the world	...	...	...	...	...	...	...	...	...	...	...	...
Receipts from the Rest of the World on Current Transactions	1613.0	1966.8	2076.5	2271.7	2453.7	2536.1	2482.9	3235.2	4192.0	4677.0	...	...

1.10 Gross Domestic Product by Kind of Activity, in Current Prices

Million Tunisian dinars

	1980	1981	1982	1983	1984	1985	1986	1987	1988	1989	1990	1991
1 Agriculture, hunting, forestry and fishing	500.3	568.8	632.0	673.0	863.0	1048.0	933.0	1226.0	1018.0	1153.0	...	...
2 Mining and quarrying	422.9	514.2	560.7	609.5	668.7	701.1	576.5	669.7	683.8	757.8	...	...
3 Manufacturing	417.3	493.9	534.1	615.6	733.7	818.0	920.3	1049.6	1212.3	1375.1	...	...
4 Electricity, gas and water a	53.5	62.4	66.0	81.3	95.4	116.1	127.5	135.3	144.5	152.2	...	...
5 Construction	207.8	262.0	331.0	370.0	406.0	423.0	385.0	370.1	379.8	446.0	...	...
6 Wholesale and retail trade, restaurants and hotels b	621.7	745.4	905.9	1010.4	1147.2	1280.2	1365.6	1450.0	1761.9	1935.7	...	...
7 Transport, storage and communication	170.2	191.3	220.0	273.1	327.5	361.0	379.3	471.4	569.0	625.7	...	...
8 Finance, insurance, real estate and business services cd	163.0	194.3	221.1	239.9	249.4	265.8	302.4	330.0	349.2	377.9	...	...
9 Community, social and personal services d	138.9	160.6	184.6	212.8	196.8	225.5	210.0	304.2	374.0	400.0	...	...

Tunisia

1.10 Gross Domestic Product by Kind of Activity, in Current Prices
(Continued)

Million Tunisian dinars

	1980	1981	1982	1983	1984	1985	1986	1987	1988	1989	1990	1991
Total, Industries	2695.6	3192.9	3655.4	4085.6	4687.4	5238.7	5199.6	6006.3	6492.5	7223.4	...	...
Producers of Government Services	368.5	447.8	571.3	674.4	731.6	805.5	869.4	940.7	1014.3	1180.7	...	...
Other Producers	...	...	...	...	...	...	...	...	...	...	...	...
Subtotal e	3064.1	3640.7	4226.7	4760.0	5419.0	6044.2	6069.0	6947.0	7506.8	8404.1		
Less: Imputed bank service charge	...	...	...	...	...	...	...	...	...	...		
Plus: Import duties	...	...	...	...	...	...	...	...	...	...		
Plus: Value added tax	...	...	...	...	...	...	...	...	...	...		
Plus: Other adjustments f	476.4	521.3	577.7	737.4	821.0	865.8	935.0	1012.0	1097.8	1092.6	...	...
Equals: Gross Domestic Product	3540.5	4162.0	4804.4	5497.4	6240.0	6910.0	7004.0	7959.0	8604.6	9496.7	...	...

a) Item 'Electricity, gas and water' excludes gas.
b) Restaurants and hotels are included in item 'Community, social and personal services'.
c) Real estate refers to owner-occupied dwellings and rent only.
d) Finance, insurance and business services are included in item 'Community, social and personal services'.
e) Gross domestic product in factor values.
f) Item 'Other adjustments' refers to indirect taxes net of subsidies.

1.11 Gross Domestic Product by Kind of Activity, in Constant Prices

Million Tunisian dinars

	1980	1981	1982	1983	1984	1985	1986	1987	1988	1989	1990	1991
					At constant prices of:1980							
1 Agriculture, hunting, forestry and fishing	500.3	533.0	478.0	490.0	553.0	649.0	570.0	670.0	510.0	531.0	...	...
2 Mining and quarrying	422.9	412.8	393.0	428.1	421.7	408.6	410.0	393.9	388.8	386.0	...	...
3 Manufacturing	417.3	458.9	482.0	521.8	556.0	584.6	612.6	637.5	681.6	714.7	...	...
4 Electricity, gas and water a	53.5	58.5	61.7	67.3	72.0	76.9	80.4	85.4	89.8	94.4	...	...
5 Construction	207.8	236.7	241.7	240.2	254.9	257.9	219.0	202.5	189.9	202.6	...	...
6 Wholesale and retail trade, restaurants and hotels b	621.7	665.8	688.9	720.6	763.8	786.7	805.1	827.6	929.4	949.9	...	...
7 Transport, storage and communication	170.2	173.5	174.2	180.9	198.3	207.1	200.5	219.6	237.6	248.5	...	...
8 Finance, insurance, real estate and business services cd	163.0	170.0	176.3	183.3	190.5	197.2	206.0	217.8	225.0	231.9	...	...
9 Community, social and personal services d	138.9	143.8	130.1	121.2	121.0	148.0	147.0	201.6	225.2	229.0	...	...
Total, Industries	2695.6	2863.0	2825.9	2953.4	3131.2	3316.0	3250.6	3455.9	3477.3	3588.0	...	...
Producers of Government Services	368.5	405.6	426.7	451.4	468.6	487.3	492.2	503.9	515.0	528.4	...	...
Other Producers	...	...	...	...	...	...	...	...	...	...	...	...
Subtotal e	3064.1	3268.6	3252.6	3404.8	3599.8	3803.3	3742.8	3959.8	3992.3	4116.4		
Less: Imputed bank service charge	...	...	...	...	...	...	...	...	...	...		
Plus: Import duties	...	...	...	...	...	...	...	...	...	...		
Plus: Value added tax	...	...	...	...	...	...	...	...	...	...		
Plus: Other adjustments f	476.4	467.4	465.1	486.9	514.9	544.2	535.4	566.0	599.4	616.8	...	...
Equals: Gross Domestic Product	3540.5	3736.0	3717.7	3891.7	4114.7	4347.5	4278.2	4525.8	4591.7	4733.2	...	...

a) Item 'Electricity, gas and water' excludes gas.
b) Restaurants and hotels are included in item 'Community, social and personal services'.
c) Real estate refers to owner-occupied dwellings and rent only.
d) Finance, insurance and business services are included in item 'Community, social and personal services'.
e) Gross domestic product in factor values.
f) Item 'Other adjustments' refers to indirect taxes net of subsidies.

1.12 Relations Among National Accounting Aggregates

Million Tunisian dinars

	1980	1981	1982	1983	1984	1985	1986	1987	1988	1989	1990	1991
Gross Domestic Product	3540.5	4162.0	4804.4	5497.4	6240.0	6910.0	7004.0	7959.0	8604.6	9496.7	...	...
Plus: Net factor income from the rest of the world	22.2	31.9	52.6	64.1	48.8	-68.0	-49.9	14.7	49.5	65.0	...	...
Factor income from the rest of the world	188.4	244.9	303.2	323.9	340.0	283.0	321.7	439.1	532.5	610.0	...	...
Less: Factor income to the rest of the world	166.2	213.0	250.6	259.8	291.2	351.0	371.6	424.4	483.0	545.0	...	...
Equals: Gross National Product	3562.7	4193.9	4857.0	5561.4	6288.8	6842.0	6954.1	7973.7	8654.1	9561.7	...	...
Less: Consumption of fixed capital	325.0	380.0	464.0	563.0	672.0	784.0	860.8	949.5	962.9	1020.9	...	...
Equals: National Income	3237.7	3813.9	4393.0	4998.4	5616.8	6058.0	6093.3	7024.2	7691.2	8540.8	...	...
Plus: Net current transfers from the rest of the world	...	...	...	...	...	...	...	...	...	...	...	...
Equals: National Disposable Income	3237.7	3813.9	4393.0	4998.4	5616.8	6058.0	6093.3	7024.2	7691.2	8540.8	...	...
Less: Final consumption	2690.9	3168.9	3791.0	4361.0	4974.0	5498.0	5887.0	6425.4	6948.6	7776.1	...	...
Equals: Net Saving	546.8	645.0	602.0	637.4	642.8	560.0	206.3	598.8	742.6	764.7	...	...
Less: Surplus of the nation on current transactions	-167.7	-320.5	-453.3	-409.5	-680.0	-491.0	-582.4	-67.6	91.0	-370.0	...	...
Equals: Net Capital Formation	714.5	965.5	1055.3	1046.9	1322.8	1051.0	788.7	666.4	651.6	1134.7	...	...

2.11 Gross Fixed Capital Formation by Kind of Activity of Owner, ISIC Divisions, in Current Prices

Million Tunisian dinars

	1980	1981	1982	1983	1984	1985	1986	1987	1988	1989	1990	1991
					All Producers							
1 Agriculture, hunting, forestry and fishing	149.5	178.1	204.7	261.7	265.5	303.0	274.7	260.5	282.0	328.0	...	...
2 Mining and quarrying	120.1	226.6	300.0	197.8	191.4	224.4	182.3	151.0	134.1	157.0	...	...
3 Manufacturing	133.9	216.0	289.5	362.4	364.3	274.1	290.0	255.2	265.8	320.0	...	...
4 Electricity, gas and water	71.9	89.4	113.1	150.7	206.7	152.7	111.1	99.0	78.8	91.0	...	...
5 Construction	10.2	12.0	13.0	15.0	20.0	5.0	5.0	10.0	15.0	20.0	...	...
6 Wholesale and retail trade, restaurants and hotels a	6.5	36.5	55.0	82.8	114.6	118.1	101.9	87.1	154.3	195.0	...	...
7 Transport, storage and communication	211.0	235.4	288.7	219.8	230.7	231.7	181.0	185.2	197.0	273.0	...	...
8 Finance, insurance, real estate and business services	188.0	198.0	266.0	327.0	365.0	378.0	391.0	403.0	370.0	410.0	...	...
9 Community, social and personal services a	25.5	...	...	...	...	...	...	...	...	...	...	...
Total Industries	916.6	1192.0	1530.0	1617.2	1758.2	1687.0	1537.0	1451.0	1497.0	1794.0	...	...
Producers of Government Services	...	...	...	...	...	...	...	...	...	...	...	...
Private Non-Profit Institutions Serving Households	85.4	98.0	105.0	132.8	161.8	163.0	148.0	169.0	183.0	206.0	...	...
Total	1002.0	1290.0	1635.0	1750.0	1920.0	1850.0	1685.0	1620.0	1680.0	2000.0	...	...

a) Beginning 1981, item 'Community, social and personal services' is included in item 'Wholesale and retail trade, restaurants and hotels'.

2.17 Exports and Imports of Goods and Services, Detail

Million Tunisian dinars

	1980	1981	1982	1983	1984	1985	1986	1987	1988	1989	1990	1991
					Exports of Goods and Services							
1 Exports of merchandise, f.o.b.	970.0	1212.4	1169.4	1262.6	1399.1	1443.0	1403.8	1770.7	2055.5	2595.0	...	...
2 Transport and communication	104.0	122.3	150.1	153.1	157.6	155.3	150.9	218.2	247.0	290.0	...	...
3 Insurance service charges											...	...
4 Other commodities	276.5	312.3	367.2	416.0	389.4	466.4	437.0	629.1	1145.2	926.5	...	...
5 Adjustments of merchandise exports to change-of-ownership basis	...	...	...	...	...	...	...	...	...	...	...	...
6 Direct purchases in the domestic market by non-residential households a	29.5	44.2	46.5	62.5	102.9	120.9	101.4	111.5	137.7	143.2	...	...
7 Direct purchases in the domestic market by extraterritorial bodies	44.6	30.7	40.1	53.6	64.7	67.5	68.1	66.6	74.1	112.3	...	...
Total Exports of Goods and Services	1424.6	1721.9	1773.3	1947.8	2113.7	2253.1	2161.2	2796.1	3659.5	4067.0	...	...
					Imports of Goods and Services							
1 Imports of merchandise, c.i.f.	1467.1	1866.0	2002.0	2106.4	2511.0	2287.0	2303.7	2509.1	3167.1	3990.0	...	...
A Imports of merchandise, f.o.b.	1398.6	1771.2	1900.8	1986.6	2353.9	2166.0	2183.9	2377.3	3004.1	3784.5	...	...
B Transport of services on merchandise imports	68.5	94.8	101.2	119.8	128.0	121.0	119.8	131.8	163.0	205.5	...	...
C Insurance service charges on merchandise imports											...	...
2 Adjustments of merchandise imports to change-of-ownership basis	...	...	...	...	...	...	...	...	...	...	...	...
3 Other transport and communication	132.8	78.3	99.5	98.1	102.1	109.4	81.0	102.0	126.0	150.0	...	...
4 Other insurance service charges	...	...	...	...	...	...	...	...	...	...	...	...
5 Other commodities b	43.2	54.0	87.2	92.0	109.9	105.3	90.0	77.9	97.1	110.0	...	...
6 Direct purchases abroad by government	...	49.0	62.6	90.1	98.6	136.8	156.0	132.4	158.2	170.0	...	...
7 Direct purchases abroad by resident households	...	27.0	27.9	34.8	50.0	37.8	63.0	57.0	69.7	82.0	...	...
Total Imports of Goods and Services	1614.5	2074.3	2279.2	2421.4	2842.5	2676.3	2693.7	2878.4	3618.1	4502.0	...	...
Balance of Goods and Services	-189.9	-352.4	-505.9	-473.6	-728.8	-423.2	-532.5	-82.3	41.5	-435.0	...	...
Total Imports and Balance of Goods and Services	1424.6	1721.9	1773.3	1947.8	2113.7	2253.1	2161.2	2796.1	3659.6	4067.0	...	...

a) Item 'Direct purchases in the domestic market by non-residential households' refers to governmental and other services.
b) Item 'Other commodities' refers to tourism and travel.

Turkey

Source. Reply to the United Nations National Accounts Questionnaire from the State Institute of Statistics, Ankara. Methods of estimation, explanatory notes and primary sources are described annually in 'National Income of Turkey'.

General note. The official estimates have been prepared by the Institute to conform to the United Nations System of National Accounts so far as the existing data would permit.

1.1 Expenditure on the Gross Domestic Product, in Current Prices

Thousand Million Turkish liras

	1980	1981	1982	1983	1984	1985	1986	1987	1988	1989	1990	1991
1 Government final consumption expenditure	440	861	994	1454	1964	3139	4592	7254	12128	26791	...	...
2 Private final consumption expenditure	3468	4465	6204	8431	13632	19212	25916	37487	61954	103335	...	...
3 Gross capital formation	751	1416	1683	2092	3290	5960	9841	14512	24231	38138	...	...
A Increase in stocks [a]	61	198	47	-56	-87	136	409	-156	49	-166	...	...
B Gross fixed capital formation [a]	690	1218	1636	2148	3377	5824	9432	14668	24182	38304	...	...
Residential buildings	174	236	221	319	500	919	2049	3374	...	...	...	...
Non-residential buildings	119	243	403	346	580	928	1973	1656		...	...	...
Other construction and land improvement etc.	171	252	229	542	725	1415	680	2839	...	...	...	...
Other	226	487	784	942	1572	2562	4730	6799	...	...	...	...
4 Exports of goods and services	284	666	1274	1814	3574	5762	7043	12110	24747	38365	...	...
5 Less: Imports of goods and services	615	993	1535	2258	4248	6522	8104	13064	22235	39173	...	...
Equals: Gross Domestic Product	4328	6414	8620	11532	18212	27552	39288	58299	100825	167456	...	...

a) Item 'Breeding stocks, dairy cattle, etc.' is included in item 'Increase in stocks'.

1.2 Expenditure on the Gross Domestic Product, in Constant Prices

Million Turkish liras

	1980	1981	1982	1983	1984	1985	1986	1987	1988	1989	1990	1991
					At constant prices of:1968							
1 Government final consumption expenditure	23661	35215	31478	36696	37386	42666	46613	51014	51047	59201	...	...
2 Private final consumption expenditure	158563	141087	156638	164487	176847	174678	189482	202501	205272	210548	...	...
3 Gross capital formation	33931	44939	40038	36914	36935	44404	47415	49271	49802	45560	...	...
A Increase in stocks	2654	5856	1881	-1537	-875	1947	1493	-571	311	-1885	...	...
B Gross fixed capital formation	31277	39083	38157	38451	37810	42457	45922	49842	49491	47445	...	...
Residential buildings	8916	9219	6921	7115	7571	9494	13793	14553	...	...	...	...
Non-residential buildings	5866	9507	12511	7935	8652	8228	13166	7107	...	...	...	...
Other construction and land improvement etc.	8682	10084	7187	12313	10815	13925	4389	12183	...	...	...	...
Other	7813	10273	11538	11088	10772	10810	14574	15999	...	...	...	...
4 Exports of goods and services	10453	17085	22900	25904	32492	31864	30239	40585	50664	52364	...	...
5 Less: Imports of goods and services	22652	25485	27586	32259	38622	36066	34794	43784	45522	53467	...	...
Equals: Gross Domestic Product	203956	212841	223468	231742	245038	257546	278955	299587	311263	314206	...	...

1.3 Cost Components of the Gross Domestic Product

Thousand Million Turkish liras

	1980	1981	1982	1983	1984	1985	1986	1987	1988	1989	1990	1991
1 Indirect taxes, net [a]	230	390	540	714	863	2026	3660	5371	9085	15969	...	...
A Indirect taxes [a]	306	498	648	911	1206	2479	4003	5856	9923	17262	...	...
B Less: Subsidies [a]	76	108	108	197	343	453	343	485	838	1293	...	...
2 Consumption of fixed capital	242	358	477	630	1001	1515	2146	3186	5472	9300	...	...
3 Compensation of employees paid by resident producers to:	1075	1454	1840	2467	3704	5468	7651	11566	18997	47943	...	...
4 Operating surplus	2781	4213	5764	7721	12644	18544	25831	38176	67272	94244	...	...
Equals: Gross Domestic Product	4328	6414	8620	11532	18212	27552	39288	58299	100826	167456	...	...

a) The estimates of indirect taxes and subsidies are entered on accrual payment basis.

1.7 External Transactions on Current Account, Summary

Thousand Million Turkish liras

	1980	1981	1982	1983	1984	1985	1986	1987	1988	1989	1990	1991
					Payments to the Rest of the World							
1 Imports of goods and services	614	993	1535	2258	4248	6522	8104	13064	22235	39173	...	...
A Imports of merchandise c.i.f.	601	984	1423	2069	3925	6019	7497	12261	20412	35674	...	...
B Other	13	9	112	189	323	503	607	803	1823	3499	...	...
2 Factor income to the rest of the world	89	164	261	351	602	959	1485	2111	4102	6386	...	...

1.7 External Transactions on Current Account, Summary
(Continued)

Thousand Million Turkish liras

	1980	1981	1982	1983	1984	1985	1986	1987	1988	1989	1990	1991
3 Current transfers to the rest of the world	-	-	-	-	-	-	-	-	-	-	...	...
A Indirect taxes to supranational organizations	-	-	-	-	-	-	-	-	-	-	...	...
B Other current transfers	-	-	-	-	-	-	-	-	-	-	...	...
4 Surplus of the nation on current transactions	-259	-211	-151	-424	-513	-525	-1041	-689	2267	2048		
Payments to the Rest of the World and Surplus of the Nation on Current Transactions	444	946	1645	2185	4337	6956	8548	14486	28604	47607		

Receipts From The Rest of the World

	1980	1981	1982	1983	1984	1985	1986	1987	1988	1989	1990	1991
1 Exports of goods and services	283	666	1274	1814	3574	5762	7043	12110	24747	38365	...	...
A Exports of merchandise f.o.b.	221	518	925	1283	2603	4125	4992	8719	16569	24661		
B Other	62	148	349	531	971	1637	2051	3391	8178	13704		
2 Factor income from rest of the world	161	280	371	371	763	1194	1505	2376	3857	9242	...	...
3 Current transfers from rest of the world	-	-	-	-	-	-	-	-	-	-	...	...
A Subsidies from supranational organisations	-	-	-	-	-	-	-	-	-	-	...	...
B Other current transfers	-	-	-	-	-	-	-	-	-	-	...	...
Receipts from the Rest of the World on Current Transactions	444	946	1645	2185	4337	6956	8548	14486	28604	47607	...	...

1.10 Gross Domestic Product by Kind of Activity, in Current Prices

Thousand Million Turkish liras

	1980	1981	1982	1983	1984	1985	1986	1987	1988	1989	1990	1991
1 Agriculture, hunting, forestry and fishing	1281	1819	2255	2778	4533	6740	9932	13259	22250	38302	71174	105100
2 Mining and quarrying	74	134	186	260	396	561	828	1475	2578	5163	7639	11895
3 Manufacturing	1003	1618	2228	2860	4342	6819	11820	17207	32016	54280	87168	140139
4 Electricity, gas and water	42	64	111	126	264	636	838	1482	2829	5107	8332	14889
5 Construction	296	411	487	761	1185	2052	3446	4974	10506	15109	23958	39908
6 Wholesale and retail trade, restaurants and hotels	874	1362	1891	2580	4324	6797	9314	14553	25282	42943	72640	112494
7 Transport, storage and communication	595	991	1424	1995	3289	5014	6713	10386	18233	31443	53626	84627
8 Finance, insurance, real estate and business services	536	777	1038	1391	2064	3304	4695	6672	10137	14889	26087	48621
9 Community, social and personal services	138	212	282	377	557	829	1203	1753	3094	5176	8760	13957
Total, Industries	4839	7388	9902	13128	20954	32752	48789	71761	126925	212412	359385	571630
Producers of Government Services	464	546	630	820	1126	1788	2394	3899	6552	16109	33653	58878
Other Producers	...	...	...	...	...	...	...	...	...	...	...	...
Subtotal	5303	7934	10532	13948	22080	34540	51183	75660	133477	228521	393038	630508
Less: Imputed bank service charge	84	127	105	154	29	-327	729	1997	3613	3116	10712	26245
Plus: Import duties	71	114	153	289	496	855	1504	2652	4246	6854	13397	22206
Plus: Value added tax	...	...	...	...	...		...	...	...	...	...	...
Equals: Gross Domestic Product a	5290	7918	10580	14084	22545	35720	51958	76316	134109	232260	395722	626471

a) Data in this table have been revised, therefore they are not strictly comparable with the unrevised data in the other tables.

1.11 Gross Domestic Product by Kind of Activity, in Constant Prices

Thousand Million Turkish liras

	1980	1981	1982	1983	1984	1985	1986	1987	1988	1989	1990	1991
					At constant prices of:1987							
1 Agriculture, hunting, forestry and fishing	12028	11840	12362	12259	12428	12443	13114	13259	14307	13252	14198	13991
2 Mining and quarrying	1031	1108	1112	1089	1127	1258	1439	1475	1407	1590	1550	1620
3 Manufacturing	9790	10714	11402	12252	13386	14149	15634	17207	17474	17985	19723	20181
4 Electricity, gas and water	882	955	896	920	1154	1232	1401	1482	1636	1763	1915	2001
5 Construction	3097	3161	2866	3365	3761	4273	4661	4974	5086	4768	4761	4683
6 Wholesale and retail trade, restaurants and hotels	8285	9053	9722	10453	11462	12115	12840	14553	14899	14737	16647	16743
7 Transport, storage and communication	5907	6604	7183	7644	8483	8586	8943	10386	10348	10572	11787	11789
8 Finance, insurance, real estate and business services	5708	5802	5941	6042	6135	6254	6438	6672	6776	6951	7112	7241
9 Community, social and personal services	1173	1235	1291	1354	1452	1511	1616	1753	1793	1783	1934	1951

Turkey

1.11 Gross Domestic Product by Kind of Activity, in Constant Prices
(Continued)

Thousand Million Turkish liras

	1980	1981	1982	1983	1984	1985	1986	1987	1988	1989	1990	1991
					At constant prices of:1987							
Total, Industries	47901	50472	52775	55378	59388	61821	66086	71761	73726	73401	79627	80200
Producers of Government Services	3265	3337	3336	3384	3600	3700	3795	3899	3972	4019	4136	4237
Other Producers	...	...	...	...	...	...	...	...	...	...	...	...
Subtotal	51166	53809	56111	58762	62988	65521	69881	75660	77698	77420	83763	84437
Less: Imputed bank service charge	1669	1689	1753	1786	1807	1848	1924	1997	2079	2122	2161	2166
Plus: Import duties	609	678	669	980	1051	1303	2068	2652	2379	2322	3436	3556
Plus: Value added tax	...	...	...	...	...	...	...	...	...	...	...	...
Equals: Gross Domestic Product a	50105	52799	55026	57955	62233	64976	70026	76316	77998	77620	85037	85827

a) Data in this table have been revised, therefore they are not strictly comparable with the unrevised data in the other tables.

1.12 Relations Among National Accounting Aggregates

Thousand Million Turkish liras

	1980	1981	1982	1983	1984	1985	1986	1987	1988	1989	1990	1991
Gross Domestic Product	4328	6414	8620	11532	18212	27552	39288	58299	100826	167456	...	...
Plus: Net factor income from the rest of the world	107	140	115	20	163	245	82	266	-244	2956	...	...
Factor income from the rest of the world	161	286	381	378	773	1214	1590	2408	4053	9432	...	...
Less: Factor income to the rest of the world	89	164	261	351	602	959	1485	2111	4102	6386	...	...
Equals: Gross National Product	4435	6554	8735	11552	18375	27797	39370	58565	100582	170412	...	...
Less: Consumption of fixed capital	242	358	477	630	1001	1515	2146	3186	5472	9300	...	...
Equals: National Income	4193	6196	8258	10922	17373	26282	37224	55379	95110	161112	...	...
Plus: Net current transfers from the rest of the world	-	-	-	-	-	-	-	-	-	-	...	...
Equals: National Disposable Income	4193	6196	8258	10922	17373	26282	37224	55379	95110	161112	...	...
Less: Final consumption	3908	5325	7198	9885	15596	22352	30508	44741	74082	130126	...	...
Equals: Net Saving	285	871	1060	1037	1777	3931	6716	10638	21028	30986	...	...
Less: Surplus of the nation on current transactions	-224	-187	-146	-425	-511	-515	-979	-688	2269	2148	...	...
Equals: Net Capital Formation	509	1058	1206	1462	2289	4446	7695	11326	18759	28838	...	...

2.7 Gross Capital Formation by Type of Good and Owner, in Current Prices

Thousand Million Turkish liras

	1980				1981				1982			
	TOTAL	Total Private	Public Enterprises	General Government	TOTAL	Total Private	Public Enterprises	General Government	TOTAL	Total Private	Public Enterprises	General Government
Increase in stocks, total	61	16	45	45	198	66	131	131	47	-7	51	51
1 Goods producing industries ab	43	16	27	27	167	66	101	101	5	-7	10	10
A Materials and supplies	15	-3	18	18	68	23	45	45	43	12	24	24
B Work in progress	3	6	-3	-3	-8	-12	4	4	53	56	-3	-3
C Livestock, except breeding stocks, dairy cattle, etc. b	-	-	-	-	-	-	-	-	-	-	-	-
D Finished goods	25	12	12	12	108	56	52	52	-90	-75	-11	-11
2 Wholesale and retail trade c	18	-	18	18	24	-	24	24	32	-	32	32
3 Other, except government stocks	-	-	-	-	7	-	7	7	9	-	9	9
4 Government stocks	...	...	...	...	...	...	...	...	...	...	...	...
Gross Fixed Capital Formation, Total	690	211	479	479	1218	474	744	744	1636	659	977	977
1 Residential buildings	174	169	5	5	236	221	14	14	221	194	27	27
2 Non-residential buildings	119	27	92	92	243	35	208	208	403	42	360	360
3 Other construction	171	1	170	170	252	1	251	251	229	4	225	225
4 Land improvement and plantation and orchard development	...	...	...	...	...	...	...	...	...	...	...	...
5 Producers' durable goods	226	15	211	211	487	217	270	270	784	419	365	365
6 Breeding stock, dairy cattle, etc. b	...	...	...	...	...	...	...	...	...	...	...	...
Total Gross Capital Formation	751	227	524	524	1416	541	875	875	1683	652	1028	1028

2.7 Gross Capital Formation by Type of Good and Owner, in Current Prices

Thousand Million Turkish liras

	1983				1984				1985			
	TOTAL	Total Private	Public Enterprises	General Government	TOTAL	Total Private	Public Enterprises	General Government	TOTAL	Total Private	Public Enterprises	General Government
Increase in stocks, total	-56	61	-117	-117	-87	-32	-55	-55	136	87	49	49
1 Goods producing industries ab	25	61	-36	-36	-147	-32	-115	-115	162	87	76	76
A Materials and supplies	38	56	-19	-19	-75	-69	-7	-7	55	24	31	31
B Work in progress	15	-	15	15	-48	-10	-38	-38	46	18	28	28
C Livestock, except breeding stocks, dairy cattle, etc. b	-	-	-	-	-	-	-	-	-	-	-	-
D Finished goods	-27	5	-32	-32	-23	47	-70	-70	62	45	17	17
2 Wholesale and retail trade c	-60	-	-60	-60	56	-	56	56	-28	-	-28	-28
3 Other, except government stocks	-21	-	-21	-21	4	-	4	4	1	-	1	1
4 Government stocks	...	...	...	...	...	...	...	...	...	...	...	...
Gross Fixed Capital Formation, Total	2148	726	1422	1422	3377	1488	1889	1889	5824	2453	3372	3372
1 Residential buildings	319	298	20	20	500	472	28	28	919	879	40	40
2 Non-residential buildings	346	76	270	270	580	91	489	489	928	152	777	777
3 Other construction	542	4	537	537	725	3	721	721	1415	4	1411	1411
4 Land improvement and plantation and orchard development	...	...	...	...	...	...	...	...	...	...	...	...
5 Producers' durable goods	942	348	594	594	1572	922	650	650	2562	1418	1144	1144
6 Breeding stock, dairy cattle, etc. b	...	...	...	...	...	...	...	...	...	...	...	...
Total Gross Capital Formation	2092	787	1305	1305	3290	1456	1834	1834	5960	2540	3421	3421

	1986				1987			
	TOTAL	Total Private	Public Enterprises	General Government	TOTAL	Total Private	Public Enterprises	General Government
Increase in stocks, total	409	388	21	21	-156	154	-310	-310
1 Goods producing industries ab	244	388	-144	-144	-235	154	-389	-389
A Materials and supplies	50	161	-111	-111	-47	292	-339	-339
B Work in progress	76	43	33	33	-56	20	-76	-76
C Livestock, except breeding stocks, dairy cattle, etc. b	-1	-	-1	-1	13	-	13	13
D Finished goods	119	184	-65	-65	-145	-158	13	13
2 Wholesale and retail trade c	108	-	108	108	87	-	87	87
3 Other, except government stocks	57	-	57	57	-8	-	-8	-8
4 Government stocks	...	...	...	...	...	...	...	...
Gross Fixed Capital Formation, Total	9432	4200	5232	5232	14668	7113	7555	7555
1 Residential buildings	2049	1987	62	62	3374	3298	76	76
2 Non-residential buildings	1973	348	1624	1624	1656	650	1006	1006
3 Other construction	680	5	675	675	2839	7	2832	2832
4 Land improvement and plantation and orchard development	...	...	...	...	...	...	...	...
5 Producers' durable goods	4730	1860	2871	2871	6799	3158	3641	3641
6 Breeding stock, dairy cattle, etc. b	...	...	...	...	...	...	...	...
Total Gross Capital Formation	9841	4588	5253	5253	14512	7267	7245	7245

a) Item 'Goods producing industries' excludes the stock changes of private agriculture.
b) Item 'Breeding stocks, dairy cattle, etc.' is included in item 'Increase in stocks'.
c) Item 'Wholesale and retail trade' excludes changes in stocks of private trade.

2.8 Gross Capital Formation by Type of Good and Owner, in Constant Prices

Million Turkish liras

	1980				1981				1982			
	TOTAL	Total Private	Public Enterprises	General Government	TOTAL	Total Private	Public Enterprises	General Government	TOTAL	Total Private	Public Enterprises	General Government
	At constant prices of:1968											
Increase in stocks, total	2654	832	1822	1822	5856	1821	4035	4035	1881	47	1834	1834
1 Goods producing industries ab	2091	832	1259	1259	4834	1821	3013	3013	438	47	391	391
A Materials and supplies	840	13	827	827	1777	455	1322	1322	1190	541	649	649
B Work in progress	172	258	-86	-86	-188	-284	96	96	1190	1249	-59	-59
C Livestock, except breeding stocks, dairy cattle, etc. b	-2	-	-2	-2	-	-	-	-	-13	-	-13	-13

Turkey

2.8 Gross Capital Formation by Type of Good and Owner, in Constant Prices
(Continued)

Million Turkish liras

	1980				1981				1982			
	TOTAL	Total Private	Public Enterprises	General Government	TOTAL	Total Private	Public Enterprises	General Government	TOTAL	Total Private	Public Enterprises	General Government
	At constant prices of:1968											
D Finished goods	1081	561	520	520	3245	1650	1595	1595	-1929	-1743	-186	-186
2 Wholesale and retail trade c	545	-	545	545	834	-	834	834	1206	-	1206	1206
3 Other, except government stocks	18	-	18	18	188	-	188	188	237	-	237	237
4 Government stocks	...	...	...	...	...	...	...	...	...	...	...	...
Gross Fixed Capital Formation, Total	31277	10511	20765	20765	39083	14685	24398	24398	38157	13680	24476	24476
1 Residential buildings	8916	8646	270	270	9219	8653	566	566	6921	6070	850	850
2 Non-residential buildings	5866	1325	4541	4541	9507	1358	8149	8149	12511	1316	11195	11195
3 Other construction	8682	36	8646	8646	10084	94	9990	9990	7187	129	7058	7058
4 Land improvement and plantation and orchard development	...	...	...	...	...	...	...	...	...	...	...	...
5 Producers' durable goods	7813	504	7308	7308	10273	4580	5693	5693	11538	6165	5373	5373
6 Breeding stock, dairy cattle, etc. b	...	...	...	...	...	...	...	...	...	...	...	...
Total Gross Capital Formation	33931	11343	22587	22587	44939	16506	28433	28433	40038	13727	26310	26310

	1983				1984				1985			
	TOTAL	Total Private	Public Enterprises	General Government	TOTAL	Total Private	Public Enterprises	General Government	TOTAL	Total Private	Public Enterprises	General Government
	At constant prices of:1968											
Increase in stocks, total	-1537	999	-2536	-2536	-875	-209	-666	-666	1947	1195	752	752
1 Goods producing industries ab	391	999	-608	-608	-1693	-209	-1484	-1484	2337	1195	1142	1142
A Materials and supplies	663	947	-284	-284	-834	-745	-89	-89	956	456	500	500
B Work in progress	287	-13	300	300	-611	-117	-494	-494	486	197	289	289
C Livestock, except breeding stocks, dairy cattle, etc. b	-1	-	-1	-1	-	-	-	-	2	-	2	2
D Finished goods	-558	65	-623	-623	-248	653	-901	-901	893	542	351	351
2 Wholesale and retail trade c	-1549	-	-1549	-1549	765	-	765	765	-421	-	-421	-421
3 Other, except government stocks	-379	-	-379	-379	53	-	53	53	31	-	31	31
4 Government stocks	...	...	...	...	...	...	...	...	...	...	...	...
Gross Fixed Capital Formation, Total	38451	12586	25866	25866	37810	14870	22941	22941	42457	16446	26010	26010
1 Residential buildings	7115	6661	454	454	7571	7150	421	421	9494	9077	417	417
2 Non-residential buildings	7935	1737	6199	6199	8652	1356	7296	7296	8228	1344	6884	6884
3 Other construction	12313	95	12219	12219	10815	49	10767	10767	13925	41	13883	13883
4 Land improvement and plantation and orchard development	...	...	...	...	...	...	...	...	...	...	...	...
5 Producers' durable goods	11088	4093	6994	6994	10772	6315	4457	4457	10810	5984	4826	4826
6 Breeding stock, dairy cattle, etc. b	...	...	...	...	...	...	...	...	...	...	...	...
Total Gross Capital Formation	36914	13585	23330	23330	36935	14661	22275	22275	44404	17641	26762	26762

	1986				1987			
	TOTAL	Total Private	Public Enterprises	General Government	TOTAL	Total Private	Public Enterprises	General Government
	At constant prices of:1968							
Increase in stocks, total	1493	1533	-40	-40	-571	563	-1134	-1134
1 Goods producing industries ab	-287	1533	-1820	-1820	-859	563	-1422	-1422
A Materials and supplies	-741	521	-1262	-1262	-171	1066	-1237	-1237
B Work in progress	232	149	83	83	-205	75	-280	-280
C Livestock, except breeding stocks, dairy cattle, etc. b	-	-	-	-	46	-	46	46
D Finished goods	222	863	-641	-641	-529	-578	49	49
2 Wholesale and retail trade c	1468	-	1468	1468	316	-	316	316
3 Other, except government stocks	312	-	312	312	-28	-	-28	-28
4 Government stocks	...	...	...	...	...	...	...	...
Gross Fixed Capital Formation, Total	45922	21477	24445	24445	49842	24515	25327	25327

1886

2.8 Gross Capital Formation by Type of Good and Owner, in Constant Prices
(Continued)

Million Turkish liras

	1986				1987			
	TOTAL	Total Private	Public Enterprises	General Government	TOTAL	Total Private	Public Enterprises	General Government
				At constant prices of:1968				
1 Residential buildings	13793	13379	414	414	14552	14261	291	291
2 Non-residential buildings	13166	2370	10796	10796	7107	2772	4335	4335
3 Other construction	4389	44	4345	4345	12183	122	12061	12061
4 Land improvement and plantation and orchard development	...	...	...	...	...	...	...	...
5 Producers' durable goods ....,..........	14575	5684	8891	8891	15999	7359	8640	8640
6 Breeding stock, dairy cattle, etc. [b]	...	...	...	...	...	...	...	...
Total Gross Capital Formation	47415	23010	24405	24405	49271	25078	24193	24193

a) Item 'Goods producing industries' excludes the stock changes of private agriculture.
b) Item 'Breeding stocks, dairy cattle, etc.' is included in item 'Increase in stocks'.
c) Item 'Wholesale and retail trade' excludes changes in stocks of private trade.

Uganda

General note. The preparation of national accounts statistics in Uganda is undertaken by the Statistics Division, Ministry of Planning and Economic Development, Entebbe. The official estimates are published in the 'Statistical Abstract'. The following presentation of sources and methods is mainly based on information received by the United Nations from the Statistical Division of Uganda. The estimates are generally in accordance with the classifications and definitions recommended in the United Nations System of National Accounts (SNA). On May 15, 1987 the new shilling equal to 100 old shilling, was introduced. The following tables have been prepared from successive replies to the United Nations national accounts questionnaire. When the scope and coverage of the estimates differ for conceptual or statistical reasons from the difinitions and classifications recommended in SNA, a footnote is indicated to the relevant tables.

Sources and methods :

(a) Gross domestic product. Gross domestic product is estimated mainly through the production approach.

(b) Expenditure on the gross domestic product. The expenditure approach is used to estimate government final consumption expenditure and exports and imports of goods and services. The commodity-flow approach is used to estimate gross capital formation. Private final consumption expenditure is obtained as a residual. Government final consumption expenditure is obtained from accounts of the government bodies. The estimates are recorded on a cash basis and are classified by purpose. Estimates of changes in stocks are prepared for coffee and livestock only, for which average prices are used. The value of capital expenditure on plant, machinery and transport equipment is estimated on the basis of import values, adding import duties, mark-ups for trade, transport and other miscellaneous charges. The estimates of construction are prepared on the basis of the estimated value of building materials as well as on wages and salaries paid. Own-account rural residential construction is estimated on the assumption that it keeps pace with the population growth. Estimates of government gross fixed capital formation are derived from the government fiscal and operating accounts. For exports and imports of goods and services, the Annual Trade Reports issued by the East African Customs Department and the balance-of-payments statistics are used. GDP by expenditure type at constant prices is not estimated.

(c) Cost-structure of the gross domestic product. For the government sector, wages and salaries are derived from the government accounts, for large-scale manufacturing they are obtained from the surveys of industrial production, for trade they are based on the 1966 census of distribution, with a constant ratio to total value added for other years and for services, they are taken from accounts of the services establishments or from the enumeration of employees. The estimates of consumption of fixed capital are built up by branch from various sources such as the annual surveys of industrial production and the accounts of enterprises in mining, electricity and water supply. Estimates of indirect taxes and subsidies are obtained from government accounts. Operating surplus is in most cases derived as a residual.

(d) Gross domestic product by kind of economic activity. The table of GDP by kind of economic activity is prepared in factor values. The production approach is used to estimate the value added of the goods-commodity-producing sectors. The income approach is used for the service-producing sectors except the trade sector, for which the commodity-flow approach is used. For the five major commercial agricultural crops: coffee, cotton, tea, tobacco and sugar cane, statistics of production and value

are available annually from sources such as the Coffee Marketing Board, the annual surveys of industrial production and the Produce Marketing Board. For other crops, bench-mark estimates are based on the results of the census of agriculture in 1964/65. Production figures for other years are obtained by using population growth as an indicator. Estimates of subsistence production are based on ad hoc statistical inquiries conducted during the 1960s. Crop prices are collected monthly by the Ministry of Agriculture from selected markets. For intermediate consumption, input ratios are used. Livestock slaughtered for own consumption is evaluated at annual average auction prices while the marketed meat is evaluated at annual average retail prices adjusted for trade and transport margins. For forestry, the gross value of output of the public forests is taken to be equal to the gross revenue earned by the government from this activity. The main sources for estimating the mining industry are the annual surveys of industrial production. For manufacturing, the Statistics Division conducts annual surveys of industrial production covering all establishments employing 10 or more workers. The 1965 survey also covered small establishments employing 5 to 9 workers. The price data applicable for the large-scale sector are also used for the small-scale sector. The input ratios are mainly based on the 1965 survey results and assumed to remain constant. Estimates of electricity and water are obtained from the annual reports and accounts of the agencies involved. For construction, a bench-mark survey of building and construction activities was carried out in 1964 covering both small and large construction units and own-account construction in the organized sector. For trade, annual gross sales are determined by applying mark-ups based on the 1966 census of distribution and assuming stocks to remain constant. The value of gross sales is then related to inputs, wages and operating surplus on the basis of global norms derived from the 1966 census results. These norms are assumed to remain constant over the years. For restaurants and hotels, bench-mark information has been collected for 1967 from the profit and loss accounts of 50 hotels and resturants. The information collected are projected by means of either sales-tax data or data on wages and salaries. The estimates of railways, air transport and communications are obtained from the relevant corporations which are managed by the East African Community. For financial institutions, bench-mark information in terms of profit and loss accounts and balance-sheets of individual banks and other financial institutions has been analysed and estimates have been complied for 1969. For other years, these relationships have been applied to the number of employees in these institutions. Bench-mark information on insurance companies is available for 1967 and extrapolated by using management expenses. For real estate and ownership of dwellings, the estimates of rental values in urban areas are based on the records of the Land and Survey Department and the annual reports of the town councils. Bench-mark estimates for business services were collected in 1967 and are projected using as indicator the number of persons engaged in these services. For producers of government services, sources of data are the annual reports of government agencies and accounts of non-profit institutions. For other services, 1967 bench-mark estimates are extrapolated by the results of the annual enumeration of employees. For the constant price estimates, double deflation is used for agriculture, mining and quarrying, electricity, gas and water and trade sectors. For manufacturing and transport, value added is extrapolated by a quantity index for output. Price deflation is used for construction, restaurants and hotels and for financial and services sectors.

1.1 Expenditure on the Gross Domestic Product, in Current Prices

Million Uganda new shillings

	1980	1981	1982	1983	1984	1985	1986	1987	1988	1989	1990	1991
1 Government final consumption expenditure	...	1462	3011	4353	5804	...	...	...	...	...	...	...
2 Private final consumption expenditure	...					...	...	...	...	...	...	...
3 Gross capital formation	...	48	183	411	841	...	...	...	...	...	...	...
A Increase in stocks	...	28	123	319	653	...	...	...	...	...	...	...
B Gross fixed capital formation	...	20	71	92	188	...	...	...	...	...	...	...
4 Exports of goods and services	...	63	219	488	1104	...	...	...	...	...	...	...
5 Less: Imports of goods and services	...	166	414	499	1267	...	...	...	...	...	...	...
Equals: Gross Domestic Product	...	1406	2999	4752	6482	...	...	...	...	...	...	...

1.10 Gross Domestic Product by Kind of Activity, in Current Prices

Million Uganda new shillings

	1980	1981	1982	1983	1984	1985	1986	1987	1988	1989	1990	1991
1 Agriculture, hunting, forestry and fishing	...	1472	2070	3380	5109	14625	35955	122294	330052	666217	...	...
2 Mining and quarrying	...	2	3	4	8	14	24	34	35	37	...	...
3 Manufacturing	...	45	155	192	254	518	1655	6734	22630	40840	...	...
4 Electricity, gas and water	...	1	4	5	15	32	37	130	558	1459	...	...
5 Construction	...	18	27	51	122	244	422	3261	13814	29210	...	...
6 Wholesale and retail trade, restaurants and hotels	...	397	493	696	862	2382	5830	18977	61829	122680	...	...
7 Transport, storage and communication	...	33	110	182	317	620	1413	5812	14700	39919	...	...
8 Finance, insurance, real estate and business services a	...	94	116	148	214	495	1432	4975	14509	27212	...	...
9 Community, social and personal services	...	305	372	520	1399	2572	3876	12226	33305	68005	...	...

1.10 Gross Domestic Product by Kind of Activity, in Current Prices
(Continued)

Million Uganda new shillings

	1980	1981	1982	1983	1984	1985	1986	1987	1988	1989	1990	1991
Total, Industries	...	2367	3350	5178	8300	21502	50644	174443	491432	995579	...	...
Producers of Government Services	...	...	...	...	...	...	...	...	...	...	...	...
Other Producers	...	...	...	...	...	...	...	...	...	...	...	...
Subtotal	...	...	...	...	...	...	...	...	...	...	...	...
Less: Imputed bank service charge	...	...	...	...	...	...	...	...	...	...	...	...
Plus: Import duties	...	...	...	...	...	...	...	...	...	...	...	...
Plus: Value added tax	...	...	...	...	...	...	...	...	...	...	...	...
Equals: Gross Domestic Product [b]	...	2367	3350	5178	8300	21502	50644	174443	491432	995579	...	...

a) Item 'Finance, insurance, real estate and business services' includes only rented and owner-occupied dwellings.
b) Gross domestic product in factor values.

1.11 Gross Domestic Product by Kind of Activity, in Constant Prices

Million Uganda new shillings

	1980	1981	1982	1983	1984	1985	1986	1987	1988	1989	1990	1991
					At constant prices of:1987							
1 Agriculture, hunting, forestry and fishing	...	110374	116673	125773	112631	115278	116000	122294	129358	136598	...	...
2 Mining and quarrying	...	53	53	46	42	34	28	34	33	33	...	...
3 Manufacturing	...	5588	6482	7020	6795	6129	5767	6734	8262	9793	...	...
4 Electricity, gas and water	...	113	116	108	118	108	126	130	105	113	...	...
5 Construction	...	2474	2759	3332	3214	2904	2438	3261	4154	4524	...	...
6 Wholesale and retail trade, restaurants and hotels	...	17893	18590	19593	17198	17750	17389	18977	21091	22943	...	...
7 Transport, storage and communication	...	3835	4010	4384	4759	5137	5596	5812	6230	6979	...	...
8 Finance, insurance, real estate and business services [a]	...	4215	4324	4455	4580	4708	4841	4975	5115	5259	...	...
9 Community, social and personal services	...	9748	10119	10528	11006	11433	11820	12226	12619	13005	...	...
Total, Industries	...	154293	163126	175239	160343	163481	164005	174443	186967	199247	...	...
Producers of Government Services	...	...	...	...	...	...	...	...	...	...	...	...
Other Producers	...	...	...	...	...	...	...	...	...	...	...	...
Subtotal	...	...	...	...	...	...	...	...	...	...	...	...
Less: Imputed bank service charge	...	...	...	...	...	...	...	...	...	...	...	...
Plus: Import duties	...	...	...	...	...	...	...	...	...	...	...	...
Plus: Value added tax	...	...	...	...	...	...	...	...	...	...	...	...
Equals: Gross Domestic Product [b]	...	...	...	...	...	...	...	...	...	...	...	...

a) Item 'Finance, insurance, real estate and business services' includes only rented and owner-occupied dwellings.
b) Gross domestic product in factor values.

Ukraine

Source. Communication from the Central Statistical Board of the Council of Ministers. The official estimates are published annually in 'Narodue Gospodarstvo Ukrainskoi SSR' (National Economy of the Ukrainian SSR).
General note. Except for Gross Domestic Product (GDP) in table 1.1, the estimates shown in the following tables have been prepared in accordance with the System of Material Product Balances. Therefore, these estimates are not comparable in concept and coverage with those conforming to the United Nations System of National Accounts.

1.1 Expenditure on the Gross Domestic Product, in Current Prices

Thousand Million Roubles

	1980	1981	1982	1983	1984	1985	1986	1987	1988	1989	1990	1991
1 Government final consumption expenditure	...	...	...	...	...	...	...	...	...	...	...	...
2 Private final consumption expenditure	...	...	...	...	...	...	...	...	...	...	...	...
3 Gross capital formation	...	...	...	...	...	...	...	...	...	...	...	...
4 Exports of goods and services	...	...	...	...	...	...	...	...	...	...	...	...
5 Less: Imports of goods and services	...	...	...	...	...	...	...	...	...	...	...	...
Equals: Gross Domestic Product	105.7	111.9	117.8	124.0	129.7	128.3	130.6	136.3	142.2	154.1	164.8	...

1a Net Material Product by Use at Current Market Prices

Thousand Million Roubles

	1980	1981	1982	1983	1984	1985	1986	1987	1988	1989	1990	1991
1 Personal consumption	53.7	56.0	57.7	59.7	61.8	63.8	64.9	66.4	69.5	75.4	85.9	153.4
2 Material consumption in the units of the non-material sphere serving individuals	5.5	5.7	6.0	6.2	6.4	6.7	6.9	7.1	7.2	7.9	8.6	16.4
Consumption of the Population	59.2	61.7	63.7	65.9	68.2	70.5	71.8	73.5	76.7	83.3	94.5	169.8
3 Material consumption in the units of the non-material sphere serving the community as a whole	1.5	1.5	1.6	1.7	1.8	1.6	2.0	2.2	2.3	2.4	2.8	5.7
4 Net fixed capital formation	7.9	7.3	8.3	8.2	9.6	9.4	9.9	11.4	11.1	12.1	9.7	1.3
5 Increase in material circulating assets and in stocks	5.5	8.5	10.6	11.2	11.7	10.3	10.1	9.0	7.0	10.1	11.4	24.8
6 Losses												
7 Exports of goods and material services	3.4	3.6	3.3	5.3	4.9	2.2	1.2	2.6	5.4	1.0	-0.4	9.0
8 Less: Imports of goods and material services												
Net Material Product	77.5	82.6	87.5	92.3	96.2	94.0	95.0	98.7	102.5	108.9	118.0	210.6

1b Net Material Product by Use at Constant Market Prices

Thousand Million Roubles

	1980	1981	1982	1983	1984	1985	1986	1987	1988	1989	1990	1991
		At constant prices of: 1973				At constant prices of: 1983						
1 Personal consumption	50.2	51.4	51.9	53.5	55.6	57.0 / 64.4	64.8	65.3	67.9	... 72.9	77.0	79.5
2 Material consumption in the units of the non-material sphere serving individuals	5.4	5.5	5.8	6.0	6.3	6.5 / 6.7	6.9	7.1	7.2	... 7.8	8.2	8.6
Consumption of the Population	55.6	56.9	57.7	59.5	61.9	63.5 / 71.1	71.7	72.4	75.1	... 80.7	85.2	88.1
3 Material consumption in the units of the non-material sphere serving the community as a whole	1.5	1.6	1.6	1.7	1.8	1.9 / 1.6	2.1	2.3	2.4	... 2.4	2.7	2.7
4 Net fixed capital formation	7.9	7.4	8.1	8.0	7.9	7.2 / 9.7	9.9	11.1	10.3	... 10.9	8.3	6.1
5 Increase in material circulating assets and in stocks	5.9	7.4	8.1	9.0	9.0	8.8 / 9.3	9.8	9.6	7.1	... 9.0	8.9	8.7
6 Losses												
7 Exports of goods and material services	8.4	8.1	10.5	12.4	13.0	12.5 / 4.5	4.2	7.5	10.4	... 3.6	0.1	-0.9
8 Less: Imports of goods and material services												
Net Material Product [a]	79.3	81.4	86.0	90.6	93.6	93.9 / 96.2	97.7	102.9	105.3	... 106.6	105.2	104.7

a) Beginning 1989, the base year is the preceding year (T-1).

2a Net Material Product by Kind of Activity of the Material Sphere in Current Market Prices

Thousand Million Roubles

	1980	1981	1982	1983	1984	1985	1986	1987	1988	1989	1990	1991
1 Agriculture and forestry	14.2	16.6	18.2	21.8	23.5	22.7	24.0	25.5	25.7	30.6	35.9	60.6
A Agriculture and livestock	14.1	16.5	18.1	21.7	23.4	22.6	23.9	25.4	25.6	30.5	35.8	60.4
B Forestry	0.1	0.1	0.1	0.1	0.1	0.1	0.1	0.1	0.1	0.1	0.1	0.2
C Other	...	...	...	...	...	...	...	...	...	...	...	...
2 Industrial activity	38.7	39.9	41.6	41.5	42.4	41.6	41.1	44.0	46.4	46.4	48.7	90.8
3 Construction	6.9	7.0	7.3	7.7	8.7	9.4	10.1	10.3	10.8	11.4	11.5	29.0
4 Wholesale and retail trade and restaurants and other eating and drinking places	4.2	4.4	4.4	4.5	4.6	4.7	4.7	4.6	5.3	5.8	6.5	10.2
5 Transport and communication	4.2	4.3	4.9	5.2	5.2	5.4	5.4	5.2	5.4	5.6	7.1	9.4
A Transport	4.0	4.1	4.7	5.0	4.9	5.1	5.1	4.9	5.1	5.2	6.7	8.8
B Communication	0.2	0.2	0.2	0.2	0.3	0.3	0.3	0.3	0.3	0.4	0.4	0.6
6 Other activities of the material sphere	9.3	10.4	11.1	11.6	11.8	10.2	9.7	9.1	8.9	9.1	8.3	10.6
Net material product	77.5	82.6	87.5	92.3	96.2	94.0	95.0	98.7	102.5	108.9	118.0	210.6

2b Net Material Product by Kind of Activity of the Material Sphere in Constant Market Prices

Thousand Million Roubles

	1980	1981	1982	1983	1984	1985	1986	1987	1988	1989	1990	1991
			1973					**1983**			**1988**	
			At constant prices of:									
1 Agriculture and forestry	12.2	12.3	13.3	13.5	13.6	12.7 / 24.7	25.3	26.4	26.3	... 27.5	28.5	31.1
A Agriculture and livestock	12.1	12.2	13.2	13.4	13.5	12.6 / 24.6	25.2	26.3	26.2	... 27.4	28.4	31.0
B Forestry	0.1	0.1	0.1	0.1	0.1	0.1 / 0.1	0.1	0.1	0.1	... 0.1	0.1	0.1
C Other	...	...	...	...	...	... / ...	...	...	...	... ...	...	...
2 Industrial activity	43.4	44.1	46.5	49.3	51.0	50.5 / 41.7	42.6	47.2	49.0	... 48.0	46.0	44.1
3 Construction	7.0	7.1	7.2	7.7	7.8	8.5 / 9.6	10.1	10.1	10.8	... 10.8	11.4	10.7
4 Wholesale and retail trade and restaurants and other eating and drinking places	3.6	3.8	3.8	3.9	4.0	4.2 / 4.8	4.9	4.8	5.1	... 5.8	6.5	5.8
5 Transport and communication	4.3	4.4	4.6	4.8	4.9	4.9 / 5.4	5.4	5.2	5.3	... 5.3	4.9	7.1
A Transport	...	...	...	...	...	... / ...	...	...	...	... ...	4.5	6.6
B Communication	...	...	...	...	...	... / ...	...	...	...	... ...	0.4	0.5
6 Other activities of the material sphere	8.8	9.7	10.6	11.4	12.3	13.1 / 10.0	9.4	9.2	8.8	... 9.2	7.9	5.9
Net material product ᵃ	79.3	81.4	86.0	90.6	93.6	93.9 / 96.2	97.7	102.9	105.3	... 106.6	105.2	104.7

a) Beginning 1989, the base year is the preceding year (T-1).

2b Net Material Product by Kind of Activity of the Material Sphere in Constant Market Prices

Index numbers 1960=100

	1980	1981	1982	1983	1984	1985	1986	1987	1988	1989	1990	1991
						At constant prices of:1960						
1 Agriculture and forestry	...	...	...	...	...	...	...	...	...	...	...	...
A Agriculture and livestock	85	85	93	93	95	88	91	94	94	101	94	81
B Forestry	109	106	110	109	108	109	109	110	110	131	117	117
C Other	...	...	...	...	...	...	...	...	...	...	...	564
2 Industrial activity	444	451	474	503	520	515	526	583	607	628	623	...

Ukraine

2b Net Material Product by Kind of Activity of the Material Sphere in Constant Market Prices
(Continued)

Index numbers 1960=100

	1980	1981	1982	1983	1984	1985	1986	1987	1988	1989	1990	1991
					At constant prices of:1960							
3 Construction	193	196	197	212	214	234	246	246	263	261	262	245
4 Wholesale and retail trade and restaurants and other eating and drinking places	348	361	361	371	387	399	403	395	424	461	518	462
5 Transport and communication	324	336	348	368	368	374	374	360	371	369	324	321
A Transport	...	...	...	...	...	...	...	...	...	...	...	...
B Communication	...	...	...	...	...	...	...	...	...	...	...	...
6 Other activities of the material sphere	451	498	549	584	633	673	631	618	590	617	516	367
Net material product	287	295	311	327	338	339	345	363	372	387	373	331

United Arab Emirates

Source. Reply to the United Nations National Accounts Questionnaire from the Ministry of Foreign Affairs, Abu Dhabi.
General note. The estimates shown in the following tables have been prepared in accordance with the United Nations System of National Accounts so far as the existing data would permit.

1.1 Expenditure on the Gross Domestic Product, in Current Prices

Million U.A.E Dirhams

	1980	1981	1982	1983	1984	1985	1986	1987	1988	1989	1990	1991
1 Government final consumption expenditure	11992	21475	22000	19030	17696	19554	17581	17762	18722	19798	20250	21400
2 Private final consumption expenditure	18968	24946	26846	28051	27485	28317	31640	33852	38605	42510	47874	51500
3 Gross capital formation	31155	31801	32163	32203	29403	24933	23872	20956	21770	23526	25323	26500
A Increase in stocks	1000	1158	480	535	280	475	500	650	868	1150	1220	1300
B Gross fixed capital formation	30155	30643	31683	31668	29123	24458	23372	20306	20902	22376	24103	25200
4 Exports of goods and services	85592	83662	71576	60289	59755	57672	37901	48562	46879	59853	81151	84200
5 Less: Imports of goods and services	37874	40784	40152	36664	32496	31060	31428	33766	38870	44711	50590	59400
Equals: Gross Domestic Product	109833	121100	112433	102909	101843	99416	79566	87366	87106	100976	124008	126000

1.2 Expenditure on the Gross Domestic Product, in Constant Prices

Million U.A.E Dirhams

	1980	1981	1982	1983	1984	1985	1986	1987	1988	1989	1990	1991
				At constant prices of:								
			1980						1985			
1 Government final consumption expenditure	11992	20300	20042	18225	17996	19185 / 19554	17668	16756	17790	18395	18578	...
2 Private final consumption expenditure	18968	23262	25669	26322	27662	29007 / 28317	32032	32368	36294	39424	43425	...
3 Gross capital formation	31155	30114	29615	30527	29810	25496 / 24933	24113	20543	20785	22010	23572	...
A Increase in stocks	1000	1064	455	515	292	490 / 475	505	635	844	1060	1130	...
B Gross fixed capital formation	30155	29050	29160	30012	29518	25006 / 24458	23608	19908	19941	20950	22442	...
4 Exports of goods and services	85592	77835	66714	57916	60583	58537 / 57672	39230	48713	45796	57263	73430	...
5 Less: Imports of goods and services	37874	38557	38405	34565	33375	32002 / 31060	32481	32776	37114	42235	47310	...
Equals: Gross Domestic Product	109833	112954	103635	98425	102676	100223 / 99416	80562	85604	83551	94857	111695	...

1.3 Cost Components of the Gross Domestic Product

Million U.A.E Dirhams

	1980	1981	1982	1983	1984	1985	1986	1987	1988	1989	1990	1991
1 Indirect taxes, net	-1637	-2954	-3221	-2595	-2700	-2574	-2266	-1852	-1695	-1768	-1699	...
2 Consumption of fixed capital	9035	10384	13622	16582	17649	17027	14622	13363	14382	15127	16078	...
3 Compensation of employees paid by resident producers to:	16011	21123	23300	24297	24573	24997	24007	24426	25226	26769	27996	...
A Resident households	11639	14673	16300	16997	17761	18097	16980	17272	17816	19179	19096	...
B Rest of the world	4372	6450	7000	7300	6812	6900	7027	7154	7410	7590	8900	...
4 Operating surplus	86424	92547	78732	64625	62321	59966	43203	51429	49193	60848	81633	...
Equals: Gross Domestic Product	109833	121100	112433	102909	101843	99416	79566	87366	87106	100976	124008	...

1.7 External Transactions on Current Account, Summary

Million U.A.E Dirhams

	1980	1981	1982	1983	1984	1985	1986	1987	1988	1989	1990	1991
					Payments to the Rest of the World							
1 Imports of goods and services	37874	40784	40152	36664	32496	31060	31428	33766	38870	44711	50590	...
A Imports of merchandise c.i.f.	34116	35594	34795	30969	25925	24760	24878	26786	31790	36971	42510	...
B Other	3758	5190	5357	5695	6571	6300	6550	6980	7080	7740	8080	...
2 Factor income to the rest of the world	10306	12770	12076	11600	10157	9800	8927	9354	9690	10178	12200	...

United Arab Emirates

1.7 External Transactions on Current Account, Summary
(Continued)

Million U.A.E Dirhams

	1980	1981	1982	1983	1984	1985	1986	1987	1988	1989	1990	1991
A Compensation of employees	4372	6450	7000	7300	6812	6900	7027	7154	7410	7590	8900	...
B Property and entrepreneurial income	5934	6320	5076	4300	3345	2900	1900	2200	2280	2588	3300	...
3 Current transfers to the rest of the world	6757	4016	2510	800	1064	1012	1675	1190	1040	744	11000	...
4 Surplus of the nation on current transactions	38909	34842	26138	21125	26638	26000	5671	12752	7219	14820	18261	...
Payments to the Rest of the World and Surplus of the Nation on Current Transactions	93846	92412	80876	70189	70355	67872	47701	57062	56819	70453	92051	...

Receipts From The Rest of the World

	1980	1981	1982	1983	1984	1985	1986	1987	1988	1989	1990	1991
1 Exports of goods and services	85592	83662	71576	60289	59755	57672	37901	48562	46879	59853	81151	...
A Exports of merchandise f.o.b.	84512	82142	69980	58669	58187	56172	36281	46862	45033	57703	78771	...
B Other	1080	1520	1596	1620	1568	1500	1620	1700	1846	2150	2380	...
2 Factor income from rest of the world	8254	8750	9300	9900	10600	10200	9800	8500	9940	10600	10900	...
A Compensation of employees	...	...	...	...	...	...	...	...	...	...	...	...
B Property and entrepreneurial income	8254	8750	9300	9900	10600	10200	9800	8500	9940	10600	10900	...
3 Current transfers from rest of the world	...	...	...	...	...	...	...	...	...	...	...	...
Receipts from the Rest of the World on Current Transactions	93846	92412	80876	70189	70355	67872	47701	57062	56819	70453	92051	...

1.10 Gross Domestic Product by Kind of Activity, in Current Prices

Million U.A.E Dirhams

	1980	1981	1982	1983	1984	1985	1986	1987	1988	1989	1990	1991
1 Agriculture, hunting, forestry and fishing	827	1036	1144	1198	1349	1440	1540	1593	1664	1895	2012	...
2 Mining and quarrying	70767	70071	56280	46454	46942	45016	26453	32672	29905	39073	57939	...
3 Manufacturing	4191	8077	9436	9584	9761	9255	7172	8151	8188	8646	9242	...
4 Electricity, gas and water	1297	1547	1851	1746	2076	2143	2132	2063	2117	2243	2313	...
5 Construction	9834	10475	10168	10520	9860	8882	8945	8400	8850	9570	9987	...
6 Wholesale and retail trade, restaurants and hotels	9094	10849	10913	9701	9154	8715	9385	9625	10215	10705	11285	...
7 Transport, storage and communication	3731	4950	5465	4780	4459	4224	4582	4746	5030	5654	5931	...
8 Finance, insurance, real estate and business services a	6129	9132	11375	12107	10617	10330	9972	10076	9886	11922	13135	...
9 Community, social and personal services b	814	1174	1380	1556	1602	1645	1758	1841	1994	2210	2467	...
Total, Industries	106684	117311	108012	97646	95820	91650	71939	79167	77849	91918	114311	...
Producers of Government Services	5989	8910	9632	9847	10356	11001	10542	10972	11854	12347	12927	...
Other Producers b	200	234	253	298	335	364	380	403	434	465	499	...
Subtotal c	112873	126455	117897	107791	106511	103015	82861	90542	90137	104730	127737	...
Less: Imputed bank service charge a	1403	2401	2243	2287	1968	1025	1029	1324	1336	1986	2030	...
Plus: Import duties	...	...	...	...	...	...	...	...	...	...	...	...
Plus: Value added tax	...	...	...	...	...	...	...	...	...	...	...	...
Plus: Other adjustments d	-1637	-2954	-3221	-2595	-2700	-2574	-2266	-1852	-1695	-1768	-1699	...
Equals: Gross Domestic Product	109833	121100	112433	102909	101843	99416	79566	87366	87106	100976	124008	...

a) Beginning 1987 of the new series, item 'Import duties' includes all taxes linked to imports (excluding VAT) less import subsidies.
b) Beginning 1987 of the second series, item 'Other producers' includes only domestic services of households; private non-profit services to households are included in various industries above.
c) Gross domestic product in factor values.
d) Item 'Other adjustments' refers to indirect taxes net of subsidies.

1.11 Gross Domestic Product by Kind of Activity, in Constant Prices

Million U.A.E Dirhams

	1980	1981	1982	1983	1984	1985	1986	1987	1988	1989	1990	1991
						At constant prices of: 1980					1985	
1 Agriculture, hunting, forestry and fishing	827	1020	1079	1236	1400	1525 / 1440	1673	1626	1693	1915	2033	...
2 Mining and quarrying	70767	65504	53487	45255	47327	45606 / 45016	26643	32214	28754	36444	50462	...
3 Manufacturing	4191	7990	9251	9116	9655	9443 / 9255	7470	8054	7950	8275	8720	...
4 Electricity, gas and water	1297	1509	1710	1742	2025	2225 / 2143	2110	2023	2095	2177	2245	...
5 Construction	9834	9615	9692	10250	11650	9022 / 8882	9221	8462	8581	9252	9505	...

1.11 Gross Domestic Product by Kind of Activity, in Constant Prices
(Continued)

Million U.A.E Dirhams

	1980	1981	1982	1983	1984	1985	1986	1987	1988	1989	1990	1991
				1980	At constant prices of:				1985			
6 Wholesale and retail trade, restaurants and hotels	9094	10384	10295	9574	9251	9025 / 8715	9528	9202	9552	9904	10251	...
7 Transport, storage and communication	3731	3909	3880	3647	3890	3950 / 4224	4493	4608	4838	5416	5504	...
8 Finance, insurance, real estate and business services	6129a	8484a	8966a	10907a	10505a	10290a / 10330	10530	10064	9568	10991	11935	...
9 Community, social and personal services	814b	1126b	1234b	1472b	1475b	1580b / 1645	1674	1789	1866	2046	2245	...
Total, Industries	106684	109541	99594	93199	97178	92666 / 91650	73342	78042	74897	86420	102900	...
Producers of Government Services	5989	8104	8830	9491	9865	10792 / 11001	10137	10240	11095	11497	11712	...
Other Producers	200b	223b	233b	307b	359b	410b / 364	410	400	421	450	477	...
Subtotal c	112873	117868	108657	102997	107402	103868 / 103015	83889	88682	86413	98367	115089	...
Less: Imputed bank service charge	1403a	2180a	2050a	2130a	1996a	1064a / 1025	1040	1261	1243	1853	1915	...
Plus: Import duties	...	...	...	...	...	...	...	...	...	...	...	...
Plus: Value added tax	...	...	...	...	...	...	...	...	...	...	...	...
Plus: Other adjustments d	-1637	-2734	-2972	-2442	-2730	-2581 / -2574	-2287	-1817	-1619	-1657	-1479	...
Equals: Gross Domestic Product	109833	112954	103635	98425	102676	100223 / 99416	80562	85604	83551	94857	111695	...

a) Beginning 1987 of the new series, item 'Import duties' includes all taxes linked to imports (excluding VAT) less import subsidies.
b) Beginning 1987 of the second series, item 'Other producers' includes only domestic services of households; private non-profit services to households are included in various industries above.
c) Gross domestic product in factor values.
d) Item 'Other adjustments' refers to indirect taxes net of subsidies.

1.12 Relations Among National Accounting Aggregates

Million U.A.E Dirhams

	1980	1981	1982	1983	1984	1985	1986	1987	1988	1989	1990	1991
Gross Domestic Product	109833	121100	112433	102909	101843	99416	79566	87366	87106	100976	124008	...
Plus: Net factor income from the rest of the world	-2052	-4020	-2776	-1700	443	400	873	-854	250	422	-1300	...
Factor income from the rest of the world	8254	8750	9300	9900	10600	10200	9800	8500	9940	10600	10900	...
Less: Factor income to the rest of the world	10306	12770	12076	11600	10157	9800	8927	9354	9690	10178	12200	...
Equals: Gross National Product	107781	117080	109657	101209	102286	99816	80439	86512	87356	101398	122708	...
Less: Consumption of fixed capital	9035	10384	13622	16582	17649	17027	14622	13363	14382	15127	16078	...
Equals: National Income	98746	106696	96035	84627	84637	82789	65817	73149	72974	86271	106630	...
Plus: Net current transfers from the rest of the world	-6757	-4016	-2510	-800	-1064	-1012	-1675	-1190	-1040	-744	-11000	...
Current transfers from the rest of the world	-	-	-	-	-	-	-	-	-	-	-	...
Less: Current transfers to the rest of the world	6757	4016	2510	800	1064	1012	1675	1190	1040	744	11000	...
Equals: National Disposable Income	91989	102680	93525	83827	83573	81777	64142	71959	71934	85527	95630	...
Less: Final consumption	30960	46421	48846	47081	45181	47871	49221	51614	57327	62308	68124	...
Equals: Net Saving	61029	56259	44679	36746	38392	33906	14921	20345	14607	23219	27506	...
Less: Surplus of the nation on current transactions	38909	34842	26138	21125	26638	26000	5671	12752	7219	14820	18261	...
Equals: Net Capital Formation	22120	21417	18541	15621	11754	7906	9250	7593	7388	8399	9245	...

2.11 Gross Fixed Capital Formation by Kind of Activity of Owner, ISIC Divisions, in Current Prices

Million U.A.E Dirhams

	1980	1981	1982	1983	1984	1985	1986	1987	1988	1989	1990	1991
					All Producers							
1 Agriculture, hunting, forestry and fishing	560	472	482	430	392	319	199	202	191	235	247	...
2 Mining and quarrying	5463	3949	3839	7724	8201	6955	6420	6565	6968	7316	7738	...
3 Manufacturing	9983	11855	12800	7633	6970	5700	4785	2770	3150	3334	3422	...
4 Electricity, gas and water	2663	1900	2033	3565	3253	2599	2106	2328	2228	2310	2444	...

United Arab Emirates

2.11 Gross Fixed Capital Formation by Kind of Activity of Owner, ISIC Divisions, in Current Prices
(Continued)

Million U.A.E Dirhams

	1980	1981	1982	1983	1984	1985	1986	1987	1988	1989	1990	1991
5 Construction	715	1016	1006	1080	736	592	600	435	800	830	871	...
6 Wholesale and retail trade, restaurants and hotels	749	611	733	685	732	480	702	1011	1059	1268	1467	...
7 Transport, storage and communication	4139	4779	4612	4928	4547	3948	3704	3673	3470	3545	3550	...
8 Finance, insurance, real estate and business services	2483	2101	2070	2239	1335	1061	1014	792	787	1065	1153	...
9 Community, social and personal services	15	30	40	45	41	80	100	115	121	133	144	...
Total Industries	26770	26713	27615	28329	26207	21734	19630	17891	18774	20036	21036	...
Producers of Government Services	3385	3930	4068	3339	2916	2724	3742	2415	2128	2340	3067	...
Private Non-Profit Institutions Serving Households	...	...	...	...	...	...	...	...	...	...	...	...
Total	30155	30643	31683	31668	29123	24458	23372	20306	20902	22376	24103	...

2.12 Gross Fixed Capital Formation by Kind of Activity of Owner, ISIC Divisions, in Constant Prices

Million U.A.E Dirhams

	1980	1981	1982	1983	1984	1985	1986	1987	1988	1989	1990	1991
					At constant prices of:1985							
					All Producers							
1 Agriculture, hunting, forestry and fishing	...	...	...	...	...	...	...	...	...	...	...	...
2 Mining and quarrying	...	...	...	...	...	...	...	...	...	...	...	...
3 Manufacturing	...	...	...	...	...	...	...	...	...	...	...	...
4 Electricity, gas and water	...	...	...	...	...	...	...	...	...	...	...	...
5 Construction	...	...	...	...	...	...	...	...	...	...	...	...
6 Wholesale and retail trade, restaurants and hotels	...	...	...	...	...	...	...	...	...	...	...	...
7 Transport, storage and communication	...	...	...	...	...	...	...	...	...	...	...	...
8 Finance, insurance, real estate and business services	...	...	...	...	...	...	...	...	...	...	...	...
9 Community, social and personal services	...	...	...	...	...	...	...	...	...	...	...	...
Total Industries	...	...	...	...	...	...	...	...	...	...	...	...
Producers of Government Services	...	...	...	...	...	...	...	...	...	...	...	...
Private Non-Profit Institutions Serving Households	...	...	...	...	...	...	...	...	...	...	...	...
Total	...	...	...	...	...	24458	23608	19908	19941	20950	22442	...

2.17 Exports and Imports of Goods and Services, Detail

Million U.A.E Dirhams

	1980	1981	1982	1983	1984	1985	1986	1987	1988	1989	1990	1991
					Exports of Goods and Services							
1 Exports of merchandise, f.o.b.	84512	82142	69980	58669	58187	56172	36281	46862	45033	57703	78771	...
2 Transport and communication	659	900	950	850	900	800	850	885	936	1104	1210	...
3 Insurance service charges	...	...	...	...	...	...	...	...	...	...	...	...
4 Other commodities a	219	320	331	390	318	350	370	390	440	516	570	...
5 Adjustments of merchandise exports to change-of-ownership basis	...	...	...	...	...	...	...	...	...	...	...	...
6 Direct purchases in the domestic market by non-residential households	202	300	315	380	350	350	400	425	470	530	600	...
7 Direct purchases in the domestic market by extraterritorial bodies	...	...	...	...	...	...	...	...	...	...	...	...
Total Exports of Goods and Services	85592	83662	71576	60289	59755	57672	37901	48562	46879	59853	81151	...
					Imports of Goods and Services							
1 Imports of merchandise, c.i.f.	34116	35594	34795	30969	25925	24760	24878	26786	31790	36971	42510	...

2.17 Exports and Imports of Goods and Services, Detail
(Continued)

Million U.A.E Dirhams

	1980	1981	1982	1983	1984	1985	1986	1987	1988	1989	1990	1991
2 Adjustments of merchandise imports to change-of-ownership basis	...	...	...	...	...	...	...	...	...	...	...	...
3 Other transport and communication	976	1250	1438	1015	1463	1400	1500	1580	1595	1700	1800	...
4 Other insurance service charges	...	...	...	...	...	...	...	...	...	...	...	...
5 Other commodities a	2507	3570	3519	4280	4708	4500	4600	5000	5075	5580	5800	...
6 Direct purchases abroad by government	275	370	400	400	400	400	450	400	410	460	480	...
7 Direct purchases abroad by resident households	...	...	...	...	...	...	...	...	...	...	...	...
Total Imports of Goods and Services	37874	40784	40152	36664	32496	31060	31428	33766	38870	44711	50590	...
Balance of Goods and Services	47718	42878	31424	23625	27259	26612	6473	14796	8009	15142	30561	...
Total Imports and Balance of Goods and Services	85592	83662	71576	60289	59755	57672	37901	48562	46879	59853	81151	...

a) Item 'Other commodities' refers to tourism and travel.

4.1 Derivation of Value Added by Kind of Activity, in Current Prices

Million U.A.E Dirhams

	1983			1984			1985			1986		
	Gross Output	Intermediate Consumption	Value Added	Gross Output	Intermediate Consumption	Value Added	Gross Output	Intermediate Consumption	Value Added	Gross Output	Intermediate Consumption	Value Added
						All Producers						
1 Agriculture, hunting, forestry and fishing	1477	365	1112	1645	392	1254	1760	476	1284	1869	490	1379
2 Mining and quarrying	49206	2746	46460	49617	2666	46951	47387	2365	45022	28538	2080	26458
3 Manufacturing	18625	9058	9567	19906	10149	9757	18660	9413	9247	14173	7031	7142
4 Electricity, gas and water	1335	2552	-1217	1384	2400	-1016	1472	2206	-734	1629	2081	-452
5 Construction	19886	9274	10612	17250	7280	9970	15100	6120	8980	15250	6215	9035
6 Wholesale and retail trade, restaurants and hotels	11460	1732	9728	10694	1410	9284	10132	1317	8815	11080	1600	9480
7 Transport, storage and communication	6880	2085	4795	6521	2052	4469	6320	2090	4230	6426	1827	4599
8 Finance, insurance, real estate and business services	13303	1177	12126	11963	1320	10643	11517	1159	10358	11124	1124	10000
9 Community, social and personal services	1895	335	1560	1951	344	1607	2003	353	1650	2146	382	1764
Total, Industries	124067	29324	94743	120932	28013	92919	114351	25499	88852	92235	22830	69405
Producers of Government Services	16810	6963	9847	17696	7340	10356	19484	8483	11001	17089	6547	10542
Other Producers	299	-	299	336	-	336	366	-	366	382	-	382
Total	141176	36287	104889	138964	35353	103611	134201	33982	100219	109706	29377	80329
Less: Imputed bank service charge	-	-2287	2287	-	-1968	1968	-	-1025	1025	-	-1029	1029
Import duties	307	-	307	200	-	200	222	-	222	266	-	266
Value added tax	...	...	...	...	...	...	...	...	...	...	...	...
Total	141483	38574	102909	139164	37321	101843	134423	35007	99416	109972	30406	79566

	1987			1988			1989			1990		
	Gross Output	Intermediate Consumption	Value Added	Gross Output	Intermediate Consumption	Value Added	Gross Output	Intermediate Consumption	Value Added	Gross Output	Intermediate Consumption	Value Added
						All Producers						
1 Agriculture, hunting, forestry and fishing	1956	446	1510	2052	470	1582	2248	457	1791	2387	482	1905
2 Mining and quarrying	35129	2452	32677	32446	2536	29910	42440	3363	39077	61813	3870	57943
3 Manufacturing	16300	8156	8144	15693	7512	8181	17294	8643	8651	18836	9586	9250
4 Electricity, gas and water	1787	2084	-297	1978	2166	-188	2290	2282	8	2406	2328	78
5 Construction	14275	5784	8491	14980	6032	8948	15730	6056	9674	16850	6750	10100
6 Wholesale and retail trade, restaurants and hotels	11583	1814	9769	12308	1941	10367	13066	2214	10852	13854	2409	11445
7 Transport, storage and communication	6693	1928	4765	7190	2130	5060	7595	2060	5535	7967	2145	5822
8 Finance, insurance, real estate and business services	11221	1115	10106	11049	1131	9918	13295	1337	11958	14635	1463	13172
9 Community, social and personal services	2246	399	1847	2438	438	2000	2700	484	2216	3010	536	2474

United Arab Emirates

4.1 Derivation of Value Added by Kind of Activity, in Current Prices
(Continued)

Million U.A.E Dirhams

	1987			1988			1989			1990		
	Gross Output	Intermediate Consumption	Value Added	Gross Output	Intermediate Consumption	Value Added	Gross Output	Intermediate Consumption	Value Added	Gross Output	Intermediate Consumption	Value Added
Total, Industries	101190	24178	77012	100134	24356	75778	116658	26896	89762	141758	29569	112189
Producers of Government Services	17658	6686	10972	18661	6807	11854	19224	6877	12347	19967	7040	12927
Other Producers	404	-	404	435	-	435	466	-	466	500	-	500
Total	119252	30864	88388	119230	31163	88067	136348	33773	102575	162225	36609	125616
Less: Imputed bank service charge	-	-1324	1324	-	-1336	1336	-	-1986	1986	-	-2030	2030
Import duties	302	-	302	375	-	375	387	-	387	422	-	422
Value added tax	...	...	...	...	...	...	...	...	...	...	...	...
Total	119554	32188	87366	119605	32499	87106	136735	35759	100976	162647	38639	124008

4.3 Cost Components of Value Added

Million U.A.E Dirhams

	1983						1984					
	Compensation of Employees	Capital Consumption	Net Operating Surplus	Indirect Taxes	Less: Subsidies Received	Value Added	Compensation of Employees	Capital Consumption	Net Operating Surplus	Indirect Taxes	Less: Subsidies Received	Value Added
	All Producers											
1 Agriculture, hunting, forestry and fishing	258	178	762	4	90	1112	261	205	883	3	98	1254
2 Mining and quarrying	1537	7086	37831	6	-	46460	1437	7725	37780	9	-	46951
3 Manufacturing	1900	2060	5624	15	32	9567	1810	2012	5939	26	30	9757
4 Electricity, gas and water	810	936	-	2	2965	-1217	934	1142	-	3	3095	-1016
5 Construction	4045	980	5495	92	-	10612	3950	1020	4890	110	-	9970
6 Wholesale and retail trade, restaurants and hotels	1794	673	7234	137	110	9728	1790	850	6514	157	27	9284
7 Transport, storage and communication	2210	1550	1020	35	20	4795	2102	1705	652	49	39	4469
8 Finance, insurance, real estate and business services	1178	2304	8625	19	-	12126	1174	2139	7304	26	-	10643
9 Community, social and personal services	1220	15	321	4	-	1560	1256	19	327	5	-	1607
Total, Industries	14952	15782	66912	314	3217	94743	14714	16817	64289	388	3289	92919
Producers of Government Services	9047	800	-	-	-	9847	9524	832	-	-	-	10356
Other Producers	298	-	-	1	-	299	335	-	-	1	-	336
Total	24297	16582	66912	315	3217	104889	24573	17649	64289	389	3289	103611
Less: Imputed bank service charge	-	-	2287	-	-	2287	-	-	1968	-	-	1968
Import duties	-	-	-	307	-	307	-	-	-	200	-	200
Value added tax	...	...	...	...	...	...	...	...	...	...	...	...
Total	24297	16582	64625	622	3217	102909	24573	17649	62321	589	3289	101843

	1985						1986					
	Compensation of Employees	Capital Consumption	Net Operating Surplus	Indirect Taxes	Less: Subsidies Received	Value Added	Compensation of Employees	Capital Consumption	Net Operating Surplus	Indirect Taxes	Less: Subsidies Received	Value Added
	All Producers											
1 Agriculture, hunting, forestry and fishing	263	203	974	2	158	1284	410	282	848	4	165	1379
2 Mining and quarrying	1393	7200	36422	6	-	45022	1167	4320	20966	5	-	26458
3 Manufacturing	1800	1830	5625	29	37	9247	1834	1950	3388	10	40	7142
4 Electricity, gas and water	928	1215	-	2	2879	-734	851	1281	-	1	2585	-452
5 Construction	3765	1350	3767	98	-	8980	3490	1200	4255	90	-	9035
6 Wholesale and retail trade, restaurants and hotels	1840	878	5997	135	35	8815	1895	1180	6310	130	35	9480
7 Transport, storage and communication	2068	1716	440	42	36	4230	2000	1720	862	52	35	4599
8 Finance, insurance, real estate and business services	1173	1726	7431	28	-	10358	1083	1414	7475	28	-	10000
9 Community, social and personal services	1287	24	334	5	-	1650	1380	250	128	6	-	1764
Total, Industries	14517	16142	60991	347	3145	88852	14110	13597	44232	326	2860	69405
Producers of Government Services	10116	885	-	-	-	11001	9517	1025	-	-	-	10542
Other Producers	364	-	-	2	-	366	380	-	-	2	-	382
Total	24997	17027	60991	349	3145	100219	24007	14622	44232	328	2860	80329
Less: Imputed bank service charge	-	-	1025	-	-	1025	-	-	1029	-	-	1029
Import duties	-	-	-	222	-	222	-	-	-	266	-	266
Value added tax	...	...	...	...	...	...	...	...	...	...	...	...
Total	24997	17027	59966	571	3145	99416	24007	14622	43203	594	2860	79566

4.3 Cost Components of Value Added

Million U.A.E Dirhams

	1987						1988					
	Compensation of Employees	Capital Consumption	Net Operating Surplus	Indirect Taxes	Less: Subsidies Received	Value Added	Compensation of Employees	Capital Consumption	Net Operating Surplus	Indirect Taxes	Less: Subsidies Received	Value Added
All Producers												
1 Agriculture, hunting, forestry and fishing	408	188	997	2	85	1510	405	186	1073	3	85	1582
2 Mining and quarrying	1130	4060	27482	5	-	32677	1051	3672	25182	5	-	29910
3 Manufacturing	1930	1650	4571	28	35	8144	1920	1812	4456	32	39	8181
4 Electricity, gas and water	836	1227	-	2	2362	-297	778	1339	-	2	2307	-188
5 Construction	3430	850	4120	91	-	8491	3680	700	4470	98	-	8948
6 Wholesale and retail trade, restaurants and hotels	1910	1300	6415	194	50	9769	1924	1415	6876	222	70	10367
7 Transport, storage and communication	2009	1833	904	52	33	4765	2040	1770	1220	57	27	5060
8 Finance, insurance, real estate and business services	1068	1110	7898	30	-	10106	1114	1915	6857	32	-	9918
9 Community, social and personal services	1450	25	366	6	-	1847	1569	30	395	6	-	2000
Total, Industries	14171	12243	52753	410	2565	77012	14481	12839	50529	457	2528	75778
Producers of Government Services	9852	1120	-	-	-	10972	10311	1543	-	-	-	11854
Other Producers	403	-	-	1	-	404	434	-	-	1	-	435
Total	24426	13363	52753	411	2565	88388	25226	14382	50529	458	2528	88067
Less: Imputed bank service charge	-	-	1324	-	-	1324	-	-	1336	-	-	1336
Import duties	-	-	-	302	-	302	-	-	-	375	-	375
Value added tax	...	...	...	...	...	...	...	...	...	...	...	...
Total	24426	13363	51429	713	2565	87366	25226	14382	49193	833	2528	87106

	1989						1990					
	Compensation of Employees	Capital Consumption	Net Operating Surplus	Indirect Taxes	Less: Subsidies Received	Value Added	Compensation of Employees	Capital Consumption	Net Operating Surplus	Indirect Taxes	Less: Subsidies Received	Value Added
All Producers												
1 Agriculture, hunting, forestry and fishing	464	329	1102	3	107	1791	480	330	1202	3	110	1905
2 Mining and quarrying	1128	3896	34049	4	-	39077	1230	4062	52647	4	-	57943
3 Manufacturing	1961	1843	4842	42	37	8651	2042	1990	5210	48	40	9250
4 Electricity, gas and water	915	1328	-	2	2237	8	945	1368	-	2	2237	78
5 Construction	3895	750	4925	104	-	9674	4068	860	5059	113	-	10100
6 Wholesale and retail trade, restaurants and hotels	2018	1645	7042	232	85	10852	2105	1812	7368	250	90	11445
7 Transport, storage and communication	2236	1751	1667	51	170	5535	2273	1892	1766	55	164	5822
8 Finance, insurance, real estate and business services	1188	1965	8769	36	-	11958	1201	2008	9926	37	-	13172
9 Community, social and personal services	1736	36	438	6	-	2216	1923	59	485	7	-	2474
Total, Industries	15541	13543	62834	480	2636	89762	16267	14381	83663	519	2641	112189
Producers of Government Services	10763	1584	-	-	-	12347	11230	1697	-	-	-	12927
Other Producers	465	-	-	1	-	466	499	-	-	1	-	500
Total	26769	15127	62834	481	2636	102575	27996	16078	83663	520	2641	125616
Less: Imputed bank service charge	-	-	1986	-	-	1986	-	-	2030	-	-	2030
Import duties	-	-	-	387	-	387	-	-	-	422	-	422
Value added tax	...	...	...	...	...	...	...	...	...	...	...	...
Total	26769	15127	60848	868	2636	100976	27996	16078	81633	942	2641	124008

United Kingdom

General note. The preparation of national accounts statistics in United Kingdom is undertaken by the Central Statistical Office, London. Official estimates are published annually in 'National Income and Expenditure'. A comprehensive descripton of the sources and methods used in the preparation of the estimates is given in 'National Accounts Statistics, Sources and Methods', H.M.S.O., London, 1968. A new source of reference is 'The National Accounts - A Short Guide', H.M.S.O. London, 1981. Input-output tables for selected years are produced and published by the Central Statistical Office. The following tables have been prepared from successive replies to the United Nations national accounts questionnaire. When the scope and coverage of the estimates differ for conceptual or statistical reasons from the definitions and classifications recommended in SNA, a footnote is indicated to the relevant tables.

Sources and methods :

(a) Gross domestic product. GDP is calculated as average estimate of the three component measures of income, expenditure and output.

(b) Expenditure on the gross domestic product. The expenditure approach is used to estimate all types of expenditure. Government final consumption expenditure is based on accounting data and departmental returns. Estimates for the central government are derived from the various exchequer and departmental accounts. Both the central government and the local government data are extensively rearranged to fit the concepts used in the national accounts. The estimates of private final consumption expenditure are built up commodity by commodity from a variety of independent sources. The sources available are statistics of supplies, sample surveys of consumers' expenditure, and statistics of sales by retail shops and other outlets. The major sources for estimating gross fixed capital formation in private industries are the annual censuses of production and annual inquiries into the distributive and service trades. Base-year estimates of dwellings are, however, based on the number of houses under construction and average prices. Changes are estimated from building output data obtained from contractors. The estimates of capital formation for the public sector are based on accounts. The statistics of exports and imports of goods and services are taken from the balance of payments accounts. Government final consumption expenditures referring to wages and salaries are estimated at constant prices partly by deflating by indexes of changes in rates of pay, but mostly by the use of volume indicators based on numbers employed. Goods and services are mainly deflated by composite base-weighted price indexes. No single-approach is used for all components of private final consumption expenditure. Most food, beverages and tobacco are revalued item by item at average base-year prices. Deflators constructed from components of the General Index of Retail Prices are used for other items. Price deflation is used for gross fixed capital formation. For buildings and other construction out-turn price indexes of successful tenders are used. For exports and imports of goods and services base-year figures on a balance of payments basis are extrapolated by means of volume changes for many goods. For other goods and services, however, mainly price deflation is used.

(c) Cost-structure of the gross domestic product. Information about wages and salaries paid in cash is obtained from the PAYE (Pay-As-You-Earn) system. The estimates of employers' contributions to national insurance and health are taken from the central government accounts. Estimates of operating surplus are provided through tax assessment data for profit incomes. Since they, however, are not available for the latest periods, the quarterly sample inquiry on company trading profits undertaken by the Inland Revenue is also used. Statistics of the trading surplus of public corporations, central government and local authority trading enterprises are taken from their accounts. The method used for estimating capital consumption is mainly the perpetual inventory method. Estimates of total taxes on expenditure and subsidies are available from government accounts.

(d) Gross domestic product by kind of economic activity. The income approach is used to estimate value added of most of the various economic activities. The production approach is applied in connexion with the estimates of agricultural income. The production figures of agriculture are based on estimates prepared by the departments concerned. Agricultural earnings, including payments in kind, are estimated by these departments from regular sample surveys. The estimate of income from farming is built up from very detailed estimates of output and expenditure. Information about crop areas and livestock numbers is collected from farmers by means of questionnaires, and estimates on the quantity harvested are based on the production acreage and the yield per acre. The estimates of mining and quarrying, manufacturing, electricity, gas and water and construction are built up from tax assessment data and production censuses. The censuses of production which are conducted annually, provide information on sales, employment, wages and salaries, purchases, expenditure, etc. For electricity, gas and water annual accounts data are also used, while for construction government accounts are among the sources. The estimates for the distributive trade are calculated from tax assessment data, number in employment and changes in average earnings. In the transport, storage and communication group, income data for the nationalized industries and public corporations are obtained from their annual reports, whereas for the remainder tax assessment data, annual censuses of employment and earnings inquiries are used. Tax assessment data and PAYE (Pay-As-You-Earn) statistics are mainly used as sources for financial institutions. Rents are based on the estimated rent income from various groups of property. Business services are mainly estimated from Inland Revenue data. The figures of central government wages and salaries are obtained from departments, while for local authorities they are derived from official publications. Tax assessment data are utilized to estimate the wage and salary bill for most services. Estimates at constant prices for the agricultural sector are obtained through double deflation. Output is valued at base-year prices, while input is valued at pre-subsidy base-year prices. Value added of all other sectors is obtained through extrapolation by indexes of production, volume or output.

1.1 Expenditure on the Gross Domestic Product, in Current Prices

Million Pounds Sterling

	1980	1981	1982	1983	1984	1985	1986	1987	1988	1989	1990	1991
1 Government final consumption expenditure	48959	55395	60387	65814	69788	73834	79413	85381	91763	99068	109919	121943
2 Private final consumption expenditure	138863	154551	169604	185817	198944	217436	241432	265879	300330	328700	348533	365930
A Households	136074	151281	165910	181653	194256	212087	235212	258904	292111	319123	337640	354414
B Private non-profit institutions serving households	2789	3270	3694	4164	4688	5349	6220	6975	8219	9577	10893	11516
3 Gross capital formation	38989	38536	43636	50080	56263	61174	65230	75465	94639	106400	104566	90139
A Increase in stocks	-2572	-2768	-1188	1465	1296	821	716	1388	4782	3138	-1462	-5303
B Gross fixed capital formation	41561	41304	44824	48615	54967	60353	64514	74077	89857	103262	106028	95442
Residential buildings	8674	8138	8920	10447	11718	11854	13622	15274	19354	20986	19906	16645
Non-residential buildings	11802	12471	13386	13306	14646	15218	16514	19874	24694	31189	34736	32366
Other construction and land improvement etc.	1561	1782	1937	2397	2673	2972	3466	4051	5456	4381	4255	4163
Other	19524	18913	20581	22465	25930	30309	30912	34878	40353	46706	47131	42268
4 Exports of goods and services	63097	67837	73184	80511	92402	102706	98817	107621	108316	122756	134225	135871
5 Less: Imports of goods and services	57900	60607	68030	77737	92940	99054	101213	112061	125379	143325	148347	141037
Statistical discrepancy	-775	-1515	-694	-1108	330	-	-	-	-	-	-277	-445
Equals: Gross Domestic Product a	231233	254197	278087	303377	324787	356096	383679	422285	469669	513599	548619	572401

a) The estimates are averages derived from three independent GDP measures constructed from the aggregates of expenditure, income and outputs.

1.2 Expenditure on the Gross Domestic Product, in Constant Prices

Million Pounds Sterling

	1980	1981	1982	1983	1984	1985	1986	1987	1988	1989	1990	1991
					At constant prices of:1985							
1 Government final consumption expenditure	71012	71213	71791	73117	73820	73834	75138	76066	76518	77216	79721	81963
2 Private final consumption expenditure	194560	194774	196672	205537	209522	217436	231439	244220	262418	271144	272927	267186
A Households	190661	190714	192389	200931	204581	212087	225598	237948	255365	263336	264663	259187
B Private non-profit institutions serving households	3899	4060	4283	4606	4941	5349	5841	6272	7053	7808	8264	7999
3 Gross capital formation a	50045	45098	49634	54833	59118	61174	62550	68911	81405	85654	79354	68955

1.2 Expenditure on the Gross Domestic Product, in Constant Prices
(Continued)

Million Pounds Sterling

	1980	1981	1982	1983	1984	1985	1986	1987	1988	1989	1990	1991
					At constant prices of:1985							
A Increase in stocks	-3371	-3200	-1281	1357	1084	821	737	1158	4010	2657	-1110	-3507
B Gross fixed capital formation a	53416	48298	50915	53476	58034	60353	61813	67753	77395	82997	80464	72462
Residential buildings	12379	10247	10899	12247	12550	11854	12901	13475	15548	15296	13594	11020
Non-residential buildings	13086	12527	13815	13878	15181	15218	15825	18400	21283	23745	24772	24149
Other construction and land improvement etc.	2170	2295	2521	2773	2975	2972	3068	3287	3596	2588	2337	2248
Other	25917	23164	23503	24578	27328	30309	30019	32591	36968	41368	39761	35045
4 Exports of goods and services	89231	88491	89323	91091	97096	102706	107565	113718	113655	117972	123775	124155
5 Less: Imports of goods and services	81145	78838	82728	87941	96672	99054	105832	114165	128484	137933	139364	135103
Statistical discrepancy	-1271	-2543	-1116	-1231	348	-	-	-	-	-	-207	-314
Equals: Gross Domestic Product b	322432	318195	323576	335406	343232	356096	370860	388750	405512	414053	416206	406842

a) For years prior to 1983 in constant 1985 prices, components do not add up to total due to the method used to rebase to 1985 prices.   b) The estimates are averages derived from three independent GDP measures constructed from the aggregates of expenditure, income and outputs.

1.3 Cost Components of the Gross Domestic Product

Million Pounds Sterling

	1980	1981	1982	1983	1984	1985	1986	1987	1988	1989	1990	1991
1 Indirect taxes, net	30029	35256	39634	42046	43750	47885	55194	61289	68522	72388	69061	75266
A Indirect taxes	35802	41809	45637	48450	51428	55207	61536	67800	74649	78438	75388	81372
B Less: Subsidies	5773	6553	6003	6404	7678	7322	6342	6511	6127	6050	6327	6106
2 Consumption of fixed capital	27952	31641	33653	36150	38758	41883	45084	48149	52596	56632	61126	63968
3 Compensation of employees paid by resident producers to:	137970	149923	159060	170094	181685	197168	212729	230233	255932	283319	312166	330220
A Resident households	137714	149665	158762	169774	181335	196783	212299	229746	255535	282829	311645	329708
B Rest of the world	256	258	298	320	350	385	430	487	397	490	521	512
4 Operating surplus a	34507	36633	45231	55334	59243	69160	70672	82614	92619	101260	105938	102930
A Corporate and quasi-corporate enterprises	11514	10857	16382	24127	24938	31552	27662	34763	37218	37072	32274	27906
B Private unincorporated enterprises	21080	23754	26932	29802	33126	35914	41519	46650	54578	63434	72786	74650
C General government	1913	2022	1917	1403	1178	1694	1492	1200	1110	1078	1193	653
Statistical discrepancy	775	744	509	-247	1351	-	-	-	-	-	328	17
Equals: Gross Domestic Product	231233	254197	278087	303377	324787	356096	383679	422285	469669	513599	548619	572401

a) This item includes an adjustment to compensate for balance of payments coverage of the Channel Islands and Isle of Man from 1988. These islands are not considered to be part of the U.K. economic territory.

1.4 General Government Current Receipts and Disbursements

Million Pounds Sterling

	1980	1981	1982	1983	1984	1985	1986	1987	1988	1989	1990	1991
					Receipts							
1 Operating surplus	1913	2022	1917	1403	1178	1694	1492	1200	1110	1078	1193	653
2 Property and entrepreneurial income	5111	5817	6865	6956	7608	8639	6785	6990	6939	7591	7026	6556
3 Taxes, fees and contributions	82349	95631	106209	115065	123056	134157	143597	156144	173699	186945	192122	197462
A Indirect taxes	35802	41809	45637	48450	51428	55207	61536	67800	74649	78438	75388	81372
B Direct taxes	32415	37701	42257	45573	49046	54466	55583	59292	66499	75118	81523	79017
C Social security contributions	13944	15923	18104	20793	22337	24226	26180	28657	32123	32919	34666	36659
D Compulsory fees, fines and penalties	188	198	211	249	245	258	298	395	428	470	545	414
4 Other current transfers	2958	3610	4057	4431	4658	5210	5548	6250	6463	7372	16326	16976
Total Current Receipts of General Government	92331	107080	119048	127855	136500	149700	157422	170584	188211	202986	216667	221647
					Disbursements							
1 Government final consumption expenditure	48959	55395	60387	65814	69788	73834	79413	85381	91763	99068	109919	121943
A Compensation of employees	31159	35500	37972	41432	43677	46095	49550	53892	58402	62711	68493	73892
B Consumption of fixed capital	3110	3515	3573	3677	3806	4087	4406	4725	5262	5915	6150	7077
C Purchases of goods and services, net	15600	16417	18310	20492	22196	23561	25125	26101	27405	29797	36321	42815
D Less: Own account fixed capital formation	451	431	484	556	467	467	556	665	754	830	659	542
E Indirect taxes paid, net	-459	394	1016	769	576	558	888	1328	1448	1475	-386	-1299
2 Property income	10888	12718	13925	14180	15755	17711	17257	18003	18255	18943	18793	17097

United Kingdom

1.4 General Government Current Receipts and Disbursements
(Continued)

Million Pounds Sterling

	1980	1981	1982	1983	1984	1985	1986	1987	1988	1989	1990	1991
A Interest	10888	12718	13925	14180	15755	17711	17257	18003	18255	18943	18793	17097
B Net land rent and royalties	...	...	...	...	...	...	...	...	...	...	...	...
3 Subsidies	5773	6553	6003	6404	7678	7322	6342	6511	6127	6050	6327	6106
4 Other current transfers	30267	36466	42439	46230	49792	55466	58780	62036	63816	67874	74311	81646
A Social security benefits	14804	17859	19348	20832	21927	23421	25756	26287	27149	28735	31284	35382
B Social assistance grants	9276	11793	15404	16866	18820	20878	22378	23222	23542	25034	27901	33271
C Other	6187	6814	7687	8532	9045	11167	10646	12527	13125	14105	15126	12993
5 Net saving	-3556	-4052	-3706	-4772	-6513	-4633	-4370	-1347	8251	11051	7317	-5145
Total Current Disbursements and Net Saving of General Government	92331	107080	119048	127856	136500	149700	157422	170584	188212	202986	216667	221647

1.5 Current Income and Outlay of Corporate and Quasi-Corporate Enterprises, Summary

Million Pounds Sterling

	1980	1981	1982	1983	1984	1985	1986	1987	1988	1989	1990	1991
Receipts												
1 Operating surplus	11514	10857	16382	24127	24938	31552	27662	34763	37218	37072	32274	27906
2 Property and entrepreneurial income received	44405	52179	56653	56293	63130	73882	78475	83470	99560	151385	172718	165741
3 Current transfers	...	...	...	...	88068	105434	106137	118233	136778	188457	204992	193647
Total Current Receipts	55919	63036	73035	80420	88068	105434	106137	118233	136778	188457	204992	193647
Disbursements												
1 Property and entrepreneurial income	46653	53457	58784	57816	65690	77176	79944	86800	106384	158981	182225	175139
2 Direct taxes and other current payments to general government	6839	8740	10746	12323	14418	17045	15338	16562	18808	23110	22270	18409
3 Other current transfers	52	62	69	86	107	123	158	184	232	324	334	314
4 Net saving	2375	777	3436	10195	7853	11090	10697	14687	11354	6042	163	-215
Total Current Disbursements and Net Saving	55919	63036	73035	80420	88068	105434	106137	118233	136778	188457	204992	193647

1.6 Current Income and Outlay of Households and Non-Profit Institutions

Million Pounds Sterling

	1980	1981	1982	1983	1984	1985	1986	1987	1988	1989	1990	1991
Receipts												
1 Compensation of employees	137783	149737	158838	169847	181406	196858	212374	229836	255625	282919	311745	329808
A From resident producers	137714	149665	158762	169774	181335	196783	212299	229746	255535	282829	311645	329708
B From rest of the world	69	72	76	73	71	75	75	90	90	90	100	100
2 Operating surplus of private unincorporated enterprises	21080	23754	26932	29802	33126	35914	41519	46650	54578	63434	72786	74650
3 Property and entrepreneurial income	18674	20341	22765	23990	29597	36377	38153	41019	47424	61404	70801	67686
4 Current transfers	26511	32421	37901	41470	44777	48707	52861	54320	56002	58827	64101	73955
A Social security benefits	14689	17674	19151	20582	21630	23085	25383	25878	26698	28216	30702	34709
B Social assistance grants	9260	11782	15413	16892	18824	20909	22425	23253	23532	25030	27878	33246
C Other	2562	2965	3337	3996	4323	4713	5053	5189	5772	5581	5521	6000
Total Current Receipts	204048	226253	246436	265109	288906	317856	344907	371825	413629	466584	519433	546099
Disbursements												
1 Private final consumption expenditure	138863	154551	169604	185817	198944	217436	241432	265879	300330	328700	348533	365930
2 Property income	10236	11359	12678	13424	17085	22538	24531	26912	30799	44397	53306	51325
3 Direct taxes and other current transfers n.e.c. to general government	39703	45075	49817	54279	57193	61885	66695	71743	80193	85926	103043	105801
A Social security contributions	13939	15916	18095	20780	22322	24210	26165	28642	32106	32902	34651	36643
B Direct taxes	25576	28961	31511	33250	34628	37421	40245	42730	47691	52008	59253	60608
C Fees, fines and penalties	188	198	211	249	243	254	285	371	396	430	510	388
4 Other current transfers	1139	1057	1200	1191	1283	1459	1656	1789	1985	2050	2100	2200
5 Net saving	14107	14211	13137	10398	14401	14538	10593	5502	322	5511	12451	20843
Total Current Disbursements and Net Saving	204048	226253	246436	265109	288906	317856	344907	371825	413629	466584	519433	546099

1.7 External Transactions on Current Account, Summary

Million Pounds Sterling

	1980	1981	1982	1983	1984	1985	1986	1987	1988	1989	1990	1991
Payments to the Rest of the World												
1 Imports of goods and services	57900	60607	68030	77737	92940	99054	101213	112061	125379	143325	148347	141037
A Imports of merchandise c.i.f.	48319	49980	55974	64784	78283	83952	84783	93372	105013	120226	124035	117031
B Other	9581	10627	12056	12953	14657	15102	16430	18689	20366	23099	24312	24006
2 Factor income to the rest of the world	21890	34953	42100	38725	45280	46334	41891	41391	50223	67328	75208	74752
A Compensation of employees	256	258	298	320	350	385	430	487	397	490	521	512
B Property and entrepreneurial income	21634	34695	41802	38405	44930	45949	41461	40904	49826	66838	74687	74240
By general government	895	940	1090	1188	1342	1494	1677	2046	2323	2510	2237	1897
By corporate and quasi-corporate enterprises	20739	33755	40712	37217	43588	44455	39784	38858	47503	64328	72450	72343
By other	...	...	...	...	...	...	...	...	...	...	...	...
3 Current transfers to the rest of the world	3936	4530	5344	5504	5930	6759	6197	7701	7574	8756	9202	8387
A Indirect taxes to supranational organizations	1837	2372	3070	3129	3354	3516	2967	4404	3150	4709	4927	3546
B Other current transfers	2099	2158	2274	2375	2576	3243	3230	3297	4424	4047	4275	4841
4 Surplus of the nation on current transactions	3439	6300	4087	2753	-742	1704	-3226	-8472	-22401	-27486	-23219	-10503
Payments to the Rest of the World and Surplus of the Nation on Current Transactions	87165	106390	119561	124719	143408	153851	146075	152681	160775	191923	209538	213673
Receipts From The Rest of the World												
1 Exports of goods and services	63097	67837	73184	80511	92402	102706	98817	107621	108316	122756	134225	135871
A Exports of merchandise f.o.b.	47149	50668	55331	60700	70265	77991	72627	79153	80306	92108	101683	103394
B Other	15948	17169	17853	19811	22137	24715	26190	28468	28010	30648	32542	32477
2 Factor income from rest of the world	22116	35570	42774	40297	46806	47497	43218	40759	48403	64989	71008	70764
A Compensation of employees	69	72	76	73	71	75	75	90	90	90	100	100
B Property and entrepreneurial income	22047	35498	42698	40224	46735	47422	43143	40669	48313	64899	70908	70664
By general government	946	971	979	765	818	735	765	931	1456	1949	1812	1763
By corporate and quasi-corporate enterprises	21101	34527	41719	39459	45917	46687	42378	39738	46857	62950	69096	68901
By other												
3 Current transfers from rest of the world	1952	2983	3603	3911	4200	3648	4040	4301	4056	4178	4305	7038
A Subsidies from supranational organisations	604	867	983	1217	1494	1248	1540	1683	1588	1583	1754	1989
B Other current transfers	1348	2116	2620	2694	2706	2400	2500	2618	2468	2595	2551	5049
Receipts from the Rest of the World on Current Transactions	87165	106390	119561	124719	143408	153851	146075	152681	160775	191923	209538	213673

1.8 Capital Transactions of The Nation, Summary

Million Pounds Sterling

	1980	1981	1982	1983	1984	1985	1986	1987	1988	1989	1990	1991
Finance of Gross Capital Formation												
Gross saving	40878	42577	46520	51972	54500	62878	62004	66993	72238	78914	80742	79174
1 Consumption of fixed capital	27952	31641	33653	36150	38758	41883	45084	48149	52596	56632	61126	63968
A General government	3110	3515	3573	3677	3806	4087	4406	4725	5262	5915	6150	7077
B Corporate and quasi-corporate enterprises	18753	21206	22671	24272	25829	27790	29625	31084	32762	35509	38303	39670
Public	5998	6728	7012	7296	7576	6300	6482	5672	5819	5751	5166	3487
Private	12787	14478	15659	16976	18253	21490	23143	25412	26943	29758	33137	36183
C Other	6089	6920	7409	8201	9124	10006	11052	12341	14572	15209	16673	17220
2 Net saving [a]	12926	10936	12867	15822	15742	20995	16920	18844	19642	22282	19616	15206
A General government	-3556	-4052	-3706	-4772	-6513	-4633	-4370	-1347	8251	11051	7317	-5145
B Corporate and quasi-corporate enterprises	2375	777	3436	10195	7853	11090	10697	14687	11354	6042	163	-215
Public	-2154	-1454	-810	179	-1402	-1018	-542	-638	-31	-543	-1637	-1170
Private	4876	2231	4246	10016	9255	12108	11239	15325	11385	6585	1800	955
C Other	14107	14211	13137	10398	14401	14538	10593	5502	322	5511	12451	20843
Less: Surplus of the nation on current transactions	3439	6300	4087	2753	-742	1704	-3226	-8472	-22401	-27486	-23219	-10503

United Kingdom

1.8 Capital Transactions of The Nation, Summary
(Continued)

Million Pounds Sterling

	1980	1981	1982	1983	1984	1985	1986	1987	1988	1989	1990	1991
Statistical discrepancy	1550	2259	1203	861	1021	-	-	-	-	-	605	462
Finance of Gross Capital Formation	38989	38536	43636	50080	56263	61174	65230	75465	94639	106400	104566	90139
Gross Capital Formation												
Increase in stocks	-2572	-2768	-1188	1465	1296	821	716	1388	4782	3138	-1462	-5303
Gross fixed capital formation	41561	41304	44824	48615	54967	60353	64514	74077	89857	103262	106028	95442
1 General government	5652	4672	4437	5869	6719	6872	7509	7577	6506	9582	12659	12173
2 Corporate and quasi-corporate enterprises	26510	26792	28341	28819	33464	37820	38814	44744	54606	65687	66611	59790
A Public	6653	6924	7314	8065	7441	5931	5548	4609	4619	5513	4985	3928
B Private	20125	19868	21027	20754	26023	31889	33266	40135	49987	60174	61626	55862
3 Other	9399	9840	12046	13927	14784	15661	18191	21756	28745	27993	26758	23479
Gross Capital Formation	38989	38536	43636	50080	56263	61174	65230	75465	94639	106400	104566	90139

a) This item includes an adjustment to compensate for balance of payments coverage of the Channel Islands and Isle of Man from 1988. These islands are not considered to be part of the U.K. economic territory.

1.9 Gross Domestic Product by Institutional Sectors of Origin

Million Pounds Sterling

	1980	1981	1982	1983	1984	1985	1986	1987	1988	1989	1990	1991
Domestic Factor Incomes Originating												
1 General government	33072	37522	39889	42835	44855	47789	51042	55092	59512	63789	69686	74545
2 Corporate and quasi-corporate enterprises	107406	113134	124254	138402	146795	164069	169497	186912	206810	224820	238668	243457
A Non-financial	106382	113572	124452	135863	145786	161517	165645	180982	203145	218965	233448	238974
Public	15672	17781	19890	20863	18397	16798	18801	15836	15436	14957	12556	12810
Private	90710	95791	104562	115000	127389	144719	146844	165146	187709	204008	220892	226164
B Financial	1024	-438	-198	2539	1009	2552	3852	5930	3665	5855	5220	4483
Public	12	8	1	-4	12	3	8	-12	-1	11	-	26
Private	1012	-446	-199	2543	997	2549	3844	5942	3666	5844	5220	4457
3 Households and private unincorporated enterprises	31999	35900	40148	44190	49277	54470	62863	70842	82516	96294	110065	115427
A Owner-occupied housing	7830	9114	10160	11264	11863	12880	13993	15280	17272	19633	23251	26995
B Subsistence production	-	-	-	-	-	-	-	-	-	-	-	-
C Other	24169	26786	29988	32926	37414	41590	48870	55562	65244	76661	86814	88432
4 Non-profit institutions serving households	...	...	...	...	...	...	...	...	...	...	...	...
Subtotal: Domestic Factor Incomes	172477	186556	204291	225427	240928	266328	283401	312846	348551	384578	418104	433150
Indirect taxes, net	30029	35256	39634	42047	43750	47885	55194	61289	68522	72388	69061	75266
A Indirect taxes	35802	41809	45637	48451	51428	55207	61536	67800	74649	78438	75388	81372
B Less: Subsidies	5773	6553	6003	6404	7678	7322	6342	6511	6127	6050	6327	6106
Consumption of fixed capital	27952	31641	33653	36150	38758	41883	45084	48149	52596	56632	61126	63968
Statistical discrepancy	775	744	509	-247	1351	-	-	-	-	-	328	17
Gross Domestic Product a	231233	254197	278087	303377	324787	356096	383679	422284	469669	513598	548619	572401

a) This item includes an adjustment to compensate for balance of payments coverage of the Channel Islands and Isle of Man from 1988. These islands are not considered to be part of the U.K. economic territory.

1.10 Gross Domestic Product by Kind of Activity, in Current Prices

Million Pounds Sterling

	1980	1981	1982	1983	1984	1985	1986	1987	1988	1989	1990	1991
1 Agriculture, hunting, forestry and fishing	4247	4839	5508	5346	6456	5941	6565	6918	7008	8139	8753	8772
2 Mining and quarrying	12405	15901	18138	20584	22197	23174	12940	13541	...	...	...	...
3 Manufacturing a	54139	55069	59465	62619	65769	73459	79065	83675	...	...	...	...
4 Electricity, gas and water b	6460	7377	7996	9048	7671	8871	10019	10918	11204	11850	13294	15993
5 Construction	12269	13027	14100	15733	17183	18399	20718	24083	28988	32084	35616	33686
6 Wholesale and retail trade, restaurants and hotels a	25942	27469	30356	33409	36743	41376	46435	50557	58510	64651	71865	73024
7 Transport, storage and communication	14584	16182	17481	18530	20433	21799	23601	25968	28465	31073	33487	34755
8 Finance, insurance, real estate and business services	35380	38908	43766	50553	53502	61988	71101	80499	90531	108691	117405	123018
9 Community, social and personal services a	9468	10496	11089	12549	14300	16410	18732	20893	24824	26901	27301	32629
Total, Industries	174894	189268	207899	228371	244254	271417	289176	317052	353816	395012	425691	438440
Producers of Government Services	31055	35189	37336	40845	43165	45225	49164	53810	58729	62353	68167	72999
Other Producers	2944	3445	3856	4255	4757	5394	6178	7131	8248	10223	11846	13128

1.10 Gross Domestic Product by Kind of Activity, in Current Prices
(Continued)

Million Pounds Sterling

	1980	1981	1982	1983	1984	1985	1986	1987	1988	1989	1990	1991
Subtotal c	208893	227902	249091	273471	292176	322036	344518	377993	420793	467588	505704	524567
Less: Imputed bank service charge	8464	9705	11147	11893	12490	13825	16033	16997	19359	26052	26159	27171
Plus: Import duties d	18132	22200	25326	25830	25473	27281	31957	35473	39183	40749	36060	37199
Plus: Value added tax	11897	13056	14308	16216	18277	20604	23237	25816	29339	31639	33001	38067
Plus: Other adjustments e	775	744	509	-247	1351	-	-	-	-287	-325	13	-261
Equals: Gross Domestic Product f	231233	254197	278087	303377	324787	356096	383679	422285	469669	513599	548619	572401
Memorandum Item: Mineral fuels and power g	19416	23521	26127	30100	29662	32966	24386	25266	23122	23771	25456	28273

a) Repairs to consumer durables other than clothing are included in item 'Wholesale and retail trade, restaurants and hotels'.
b) Item 'Electricity, gas and water' includes nuclear fuel production.
c) Gross domestic product in factor values.
d) Item 'Import duties' refers to indirect taxes net of subsidies less value added tax.
e) Item 'Other adjustments' refers to statistical discrepancy.
f) This item includes an adjustment to compensate for balance of payments coverage of the Channel Islands and Isle of Man from 1988. These islands are not considered to be part of the U.K. economic territory.
g) Item 'Mineral fuels and Power' includes water supply.

1.12 Relations Among National Accounting Aggregates

Million Pounds Sterling

	1980	1981	1982	1983	1984	1985	1986	1987	1988	1989	1990	1991
Gross Domestic Product	231233	254197	278087	303377	324787	356096	383679	422285	469669	513599	548619	572401
Plus: Net factor income from the rest of the world	226	617	674	1572	1526	1163	1327	-632	-1820	-2339	-4200	-3988
Factor income from the rest of the world	22116	35570	42774	40297	46806	47497	43218	40759	48403	64989	71008	70764
Less: Factor income to the rest of the world	21890	34953	42100	38725	45280	46334	41891	41391	50223	67328	75208	74752
Equals: Gross National Product	231460	254814	278763	304949	326313	357260	385005	421651	467848	511257	544417	568411
Less: Consumption of fixed capital	27952	31641	33653	36150	38758	41883	45084	48149	52596	56632	61126	63968
Equals: National Income	203507	223173	245108	268799	287555	315376	339922	373504	415253	454628	483293	504445
Plus: Net current transfers from the rest of the world	-1984	-1547	-1741	-1593	-1730	-3111	-2157	-3400	-3518	-4578	-4897	-1349
Current transfers from the rest of the world	1952	2983	3603	3911	4200	3648	4040	4301	4056	4178	4305	7038
Less: Current transfers to the rest of the world	3936	4530	5344	5504	5930	6759	6197	7701	7574	8756	9202	8387
Equals: National Disposable Income	201523	221626	243367	267206	285825	312265	337765	370104	411735	450050	478396	503096
Less: Final consumption	187047	208431	229297	250523	269062	291270	320845	351260	392093	427768	458175	487428
Statistical discrepancy	-1550	-2259	-1203	-861	-1021	-	-	-	-	-	-605	-462
Equals: Net Saving	12926	10936	12867	15822	15742	20995	16920	18844	19642	22282	19616	15206
Less: Surplus of the nation on current transactions a	3439	6300	4087	2753	-742	1704	-3226	-8472	-22401	-27486	-23219	-10503
Statistical discrepancy	1550	2259	1203	861	1021	-	-	-	-	-	605	462
Equals: Net Capital Formation	11037	6895	9983	13930	17505	19291	20146	27316	42043	49768	43440	26171

a) Item 'Surplus of the nations on current transactions' includes capital transfers abroad, net, of 59 million pounds in 1973 and 75 million pounds in 1974.

2.1 Government Final Consumption Expenditure by Function, in Current Prices

Million Pounds Sterling

	1980	1981	1982	1983	1984	1985	1986	1987	1988	1989	1990	1991
1 General public services	2747	2961	3237	3345	3366	3750	4050	4233	4636	5751	6653	7014
2 Defence	11325	12532	14284	15596	16852	17872	18613	18683	19306	20474	22211	24432
3 Public order and safety	3407	4050	4517	4961	5530	5783	6401	6997	7772	8607	9723	11548
4 Education	9851	11122	12026	12817	13229	13534	15225	16487	17925	18808	20119	22278
5 Health	10971	12631	13199	14994	15741	16763	17956	19765	21771	23577	25853	29076
6 Social security and welfare	3143	3658	4115	4436	4758	5118	5253	6099	6818	7427	8332	9532
7 Housing and community amenities	1589	1734	1923	2113	2245	2376	2599	2887	2847	2803	3301	3626
8 Recreational, cultural and religious affairs	1058	1159	1265	1449	1535	1546	1737	1894	2130	2308	2650	2906
9 Economic services	3120	3600	3804	4022	4345	4720	4996	5532	5448	5865	7271	7641
A Fuel and energy	183	163	153	206	243	264	304	281	167	303	237	280
B Agriculture, forestry, fishing and hunting	430	456	479	495	444	526	552	664	647	588	640	656
C Mining, manufacturing and construction, except fuel and energy	173	374	385	365	405	465	437	446	512	464	466	670
D Transportation and communication	1324	1502	1686	1742	1744	1890	1927	2096	2094	2344	2702	2796
E Other economic affairs	1010	1105	1101	1214	1509	1575	1776	2045	2028	2166	3226	3239
10 Other functions	1748	1948	2017	2081	2187	2372	2583	2804	3110	3448	3806	3890
Total Government Final Consumption Expenditure	48959	55395	60387	65814	69788	73834	79413	85381	91763	99068	109919	121943

United Kingdom

2.3 Total Government Outlays by Function and Type

Million Pounds Sterling

	Final Consumption Expenditures			Subsidies	Other Current Transfers & Property Income	Total Current Disbursements	Gross Capital Formation	Other Capital Outlays	Total Outlays
	Total	Compensation of Employees	Other						
1980									
1 General public services	2747	...	...	-	1032	3779	447	40	4266
2 Defence	11325	...	...	-	38	11363	70	11	11444
3 Public order and safety	3407	...	...	-	98	3505	188	-	3693
4 Education	9851	...	...	-	2147	11998	585	184	12767
5 Health	10971	...	...	-	46	11017	616	-	11633
6 Social security and welfare	3143	...	...	-	25407	28550	95	1	28646
7 Housing and community amenities	1589	...	...	2557	264	4410	1919	846	7175
8 Recreation, culture and religion	1058	...	...	-	128	1186	238	14	1438
9 Economic services	3120	...	...	2612	529	6261	1537	1357	9155
A Fuel and energy	183	...	...	289	17	489	28	3	520
B Agriculture, forestry, fishing and hunting	430	...	...	149	43	622	215	229	1066
C Mining (except fuels), manufacturing and construction	173	...	...	213	56	442	60	643	1145
D Transportation and communication	1324	...	...	1135	-	2459	1066	429	3954
E Other economic affairs	1010	...	...	826	413	2249	168	53	2470
10 Other functions	1748	...	...	-	10636	12384	-	-	12384
Total	48959	...	...	5169	40325	94453	5695	2453	102601
1981									
1 General public services	2961	...	...	-	1141	4102	373	33	4508
2 Defence	12532	...	...	-	54	12586	46	10	12642
3 Public order and safety	4050	...	...	-	92	4142	200	-	4342
4 Education	11122	...	...	-	2434	13556	567	201	14324
5 Health	12631	...	...	-	43	12674	700	-	13374
6 Social security and welfare	3658	...	...	-	31494	35152	99	1	35252
7 Housing and community amenities	1734	...	...	2164	383	4281	967	759	6007
8 Recreation, culture and religion	1159	...	...	-	156	1315	248	13	1576
9 Economic services	3600	...	...	3522	688	7810	1379	4864	14053
A Fuel and energy	163	...	...	551	38	752	-5	10	757
B Agriculture, forestry, fishing and hunting	456	...	...	153	44	653	101	218	972
C Mining (except fuels), manufacturing and construction	374	...	...	268	117	759	52	4406	5217
D Transportation and communication	1502	...	...	1348	-	2850	1083	162	4095
E Other economic affairs	1105	...	...	1202	489	2796	148	68	3012
10 Other functions	1948	...	...	-	12311	14259	-	-	14259
Total	55395	...	...	5686	48796	109877	4579	5881	120337
1982									
1 General public services	3237	...	...	-	1105	4342	545	37	4924
2 Defence	14284	...	...	-	60	14344	72	35	14451
3 Public order and safety	4517	...	...	-	99	4616	251	-	4867
4 Education	12026	...	...	-	2564	14590	512	187	15289
5 Health	13199	...	...	-	61	13260	817	4	14081
6 Social security and welfare	4115	...	...	-	36851	40966	102	-	41068
7 Housing and community amenities	1923	...	...	1553	497	3973	3	1140	5116
8 Recreation, culture and religion	1265	...	...	-	162	1427	273	4	1704
9 Economic services	3804	...	...	3467	914	8185	2017	2475	12677
A Fuel and energy	153	...	...	565	72	790	-33	11	768
B Agriculture, forestry, fishing and hunting	479	...	...	55	50	584	419	245	1248
C Mining (except fuels), manufacturing and construction	385	...	...	312	147	844	32	1792	2668
D Transportation and communication	1686	...	...	1589	72	3347	1384	352	5083
E Other economic affairs	1101	...	...	946	573	2620	215	75	2910
10 Other functions	2017	...	...	-	13468	15485	-	-	15485
Total	60387	...	...	5020	55781	121188	4592	3882	129662

2.3 Total Government Outlays by Function and Type
(Continued)

Million Pounds Sterling

	Final Consumption Expenditures			Subsidies	Other Current Transfers & Property Income	Total Current Disbursements	Gross Capital Formation	Other Capital Outlays	Total Outlays
	Total	Compensation of Employees	Other						
1983									
1 General public services	3345	...	...	-	1250	4595	470	43	5108
2 Defence	15596	...	...	-	48	15644	173	23	15840
3 Public order and safety	4961	...	...	-	99	5060	266	-	5326
4 Education	12817	...	...	-	2772	15589	566	179	16334
5 Health	14994	...	...	-	76	15070	854	4	15928
6 Social security and welfare	4436	...	...	-	39922	44358	105	-	44463
7 Housing and community amenities	2113	...	...	1393	462	3968	1163	1933	7064
8 Recreation, culture and religion	1449	...	...	-	182	1631	332	3	1966
9 Economic services	4022	...	...	3794	1396	9212	2186	1405	12803
A Fuel and energy	206	...	...	946	152	1304	38	-	1342
B Agriculture, forestry, fishing and hunting	495	...	...	101	54	650	338	270	1258
C Mining (except fuels), manufacturing and construction	365	...	...	313	101	779	81	787	1647
D Transportation and communication	1742	...	...	1613	87	3442	1501	304	5247
E Other economic affairs	1214	...	...	821	1002	3037	228	44	3309
10 Other functions	2081	...	...	-	13622	15703	-	-	15703
Total	65814	...	...	5187	59829	130830	6115	3590	140535
1984									
1 General public services	3366	...	...	-	1418	4784	564	49	5397
2 Defence	16852	...	...	-	61	16913	203	17	17133
3 Public order and safety	5530	...	...	-	108	5638	305	-	5943
4 Education	13229	...	...	-	2865	16094	623	187	16904
5 Health	15741	...	...	-	91	15832	945	4	16781
6 Social security and welfare	4758	...	...	-	42940	47698	126	1	47825
7 Housing and community amenities	2245	...	...	1402	528	4175	1566	2272	8013
8 Recreation, culture and religion	1535	...	...	-	193	1728	414	1	2143
9 Economic services	4345	...	...	4782	1721	10848	2253	1307	14408
A Fuel and energy	243	...	...	1941	206	2390	34	5	2429
B Agriculture, forestry, fishing and hunting	444	...	...	49	49	542	370	277	1189
C Mining (except fuels), manufacturing and construction	405	...	...	291	101	797	50	670	1517
D Transportation and communication	1744	...	...	1568	96	3408	1594	299	5301
E Other economic affairs	1509	...	...	933	1269	3711	205	56	3972
10 Other functions	2187	...	...	-	15129	17316	-	-	17316
Total	69788	...	...	6184	65054	141026	6999	3838	151863
1985									
1 General public services	3750	...	...	-	1470	5220	689	54	5963
2 Defence	17872	...	...	-	51	17923	269	21	18213
3 Public order and safety	5783	...	...	-	98	5881	344	-	6225
4 Education	13534	...	...	-	2926	16460	618	208	17286
5 Health	16763	...	...	-	117	16880	1005	4	17889
6 Social security and welfare	5118	...	...	-	47193	52311	159	-	52470
7 Housing and community amenities	2376	...	...	1456	572	4404	1334	1685	7423
8 Recreation, culture and religion	1546	...	...	-	298	1844	401	3	2248
9 Economic services	4720	...	...	4618	1726	11064	2503	1344	14911
A Fuel and energy	264	...	...	1501	421	2186	49	-	2235
B Agriculture, forestry, fishing and hunting	526	...	...	160	49	735	519	220	1474
C Mining (except fuels), manufacturing and construction	465	...	...	250	86	801	77	797	1675
D Transportation and communication	1890	...	...	1534	82	3506	1709	285	5500
E Other economic affairs	1575	...	...	1173	1088	3836	149	42	4027
10 Other functions	2372	...	...	-	17352	19724	-	-	19724
Total	73834	...	...	6074	71803	151711	7322	3319	162352

United Kingdom

2.3 Total Government Outlays by Function and Type
(Continued)

Million Pounds Sterling

		Final Consumption Expenditures			Subsidies	Other Current Transfers & Property Income	Total Current Disbursements	Gross Capital Formation	Other Capital Outlays	Total Outlays
		Total	Compensation of Employees	Other						
	1986									
1	General public services	4050	...	...	-	1580	5630	587	66	6283
2	Defence	18613	...	...	-	82	18695	359	12	19066
3	Public order and safety	6401	...	...	-	107	6508	318	-	6826
4	Education	15225	...	...	-	3147	18372	668	235	19275
5	Health	17956	...	...	-	125	18081	1078	5	19164
6	Social security and welfare	5253	...	...	-	51237	56490	190	-	56680
7	Housing and community amenities	2599	...	...	1411	800	4810	1688	3072	9570
8	Recreation, culture and religion	1737	...	...	-	290	2027	420	1	2448
9	Economic services	4996	...	...	3391	1923	10310	1964	1235	13509
	A Fuel and energy	304	...	...	712	593	1609	4	3	1616
	B Agriculture, forestry, fishing and hunting	552	...	...	138	21	711	-183	170	698
	C Mining (except fuels), manufacturing and construction	437	...	...	226	94	757	50	845	1652
	D Transportation and communication	1927	...	...	1376	88	3391	1914	303	5608
	E Other economic affairs	1776	...	...	939	1127	3842	179	-86	3935
10	Other functions	2583	...	...	-	16430	19013	-	-	19013
	Total	79413	...	...	4802	75721	159936	7272	4626	171834
	1987									
1	General public services	4233	...	...	-	1669	5902	552	70	6524
2	Defence	18683	...	...	-	84	18767	351	-	19118
3	Public order and safety	6997	...	...	-	138	7135	389	-	7524
4	Education	16487	...	...	-	3299	19786	798	245	20829
5	Health	19765	...	...	-	138	19903	998	4	20905
6	Social security and welfare	6099	...	...	-	53018	59117	221	-1	59337
7	Housing and community amenities	2887	...	...	1363	1263	5513	1667	1749	8929
8	Recreation, culture and religion	1894	...	...	-	301	2195	399	3	2597
9	Economic services	5532	...	...	3465	1296	10293	1704	1146	13143
	A Fuel and energy	281	...	...	664	482	1427	-	-	1427
	B Agriculture, forestry, fishing and hunting	664	...	...	618	14	1296	-442	169	1023
	C Mining (except fuels), manufacturing and construction	446	...	...	301	35	782	30	562	1374
	D Transportation and communication	2096	...	...	1194	94	3384	1978	317	5679
	E Other economic affairs	2045	...	...	688	671	3404	138	98	3640
10	Other functions	2804	...	...	-	17120	19924	-	-	19924
	Total	85381	...	...	4828	78326	168535	7079	3216	178830
	1988									
1	General public services	4636	...	...	-	2083	6719	789	73	7581
2	Defence	19306	...	...	-	99	19405	358	-	19763
3	Public order and safety	7772	...	...	-	179	7951	455	-	8406
4	Education	17925	...	...	-	3576	21501	622	455	22578
5	Health	21771	...	...	-	158	21929	994	13	22936
6	Social security and welfare	6818	...	...	-	54581	61399	256	-2	61653
7	Housing and community amenities	2847	...	...	1482	1102	5431	378	1967	7776
8	Recreation, culture and religion	2130	...	...	-	293	2423	407	6	2836
9	Economic services	5448	...	...	3057	1291	9796	1925	5274	16995
	A Fuel and energy	167	...	...	610	159	936	-	7	943
	B Agriculture, forestry, fishing and hunting	647	...	...	631	1	1279	-239	71	1111
	C Mining (except fuels), manufacturing and construction	512	...	...	297	18	827	22	4957	5806
	D Transportation and communication	2094	...	...	1065	86	3245	2142	299	5686
	E Other economic affairs	2028	...	...	454	1027	3509	-	-60	3449
10	Other functions	3110	...	...	-	17957	21067	-	-	21067
	Total	91763	...	...	4539	81319	177621	6184	7786	191591

2.3 Total Government Outlays by Function and Type
(Continued)

Million Pounds Sterling

	Final Consumption Expenditures			Subsidies	Other Current Transfers & Property Income	Total Current Disbursements	Gross Capital Formation	Other Capital Outlays	Total Outlays
	Total	Compensation of Employees	Other						
1989									
1 General public services	5751	...	...	-	2248	7999	1338	80	9417
2 Defence	20474	...	...	-	79	20553	408	-	20961
3 Public order and safety	8607	...	...	-	187	8794	639	-	9433
4 Education	18808	...	...	-	4537	23345	922	570	24837
5 Health	23577	...	...	-	173	23750	1352	13	25115
6 Social security and welfare	7427	...	...	-	57171	64598	426	-3	65021
7 Housing and community amenities	2803	...	...	1538	165	4506	876	7173	12555
8 Recreation, culture and religion	2308	...	...	-	205	2513	663	6	3182
9 Economic services	5865	...	...	2929	1751	10545	2795	1422	14762
A Fuel and energy	303	...	...	740	157	1200	-	7	1207
B Agriculture, forestry, fishing and hunting	588	...	...	57	3	648	-71	80	657
C Mining (except fuels), manufacturing and construction	464	...	...	226	9	699	31	505	1235
D Transportation and communication	2344	...	...	1000	89	3433	2666	405	6504
E Other economic affairs	2166	...	...	906	1493	4565	169	425	5159
10 Other functions	3448	...	...	-	17873	21321	-	-	21321
Total	99068	...	...	4467	84389	187924	9419	9261	206604
1990									
1 General public services	6653	...	...	-	2603	9256	1296	91	10643
2 Defence	22211	...	...	-	39	22250	622	-	22872
3 Public order and safety	9723	...	...	-	236	9959	973	-	10932
4 Education	20119	...	...	-	4871	24990	1051	659	26700
5 Health	25853	...	...	-	245	26098	1548	25	27671
6 Social security and welfare	8332	...	...	-	62780	71112	544	-	71656
7 Housing and community amenities	3301	...	...	1613	146	5060	1734	4462	11256
8 Recreation, culture and religion	2650	...	...	-	223	2873	784	9	3666
9 Economic services	7271	...	...	2960	1725	11956	4263	5761	21980
A Fuel and energy	237	...	...	226	103	566	-	4301	4867
B Agriculture, forestry, fishing and hunting	640	...	...	137	3	780	281	85	1146
C Mining (except fuels), manufacturing and construction	466	...	...	152	11	629	36	435	1100
D Transportation and communication	2702	...	...	1105	94	3901	3587	490	7978
E Other economic affairs	3226	...	...	1340	1514	6080	359	450	6889
10 Other functions	3806	...	...	-	17682	21488	-	-	21488
Total	109919	...	...	4573	90550	205042	12815	11007	228864
1991									
1 General public services	7014	...	...	-	832	7846	1203	88	9137
2 Defence	24432	...	...	-	-2002	22430	696	-	23126
3 Public order and safety	11548	...	...	-	301	11849	951	-	12800
4 Education	22278	...	...	-	5520	27798	921	721	29440
5 Health	29076	...	...	-	172	29248	1669	17	30934
6 Social security and welfare	9532	...	...	-	73897	83429	572	-	84001
7 Housing and community amenities	3626	...	...	1675	177	5478	1266	4909	11653
8 Recreation, culture and religion	2906	...	...	-	302	3208	684	10	3902
9 Economic services	7641	...	...	2442	1156	11239	4362	1442	17043
A Fuel and energy	280	...	...	389	63	732	-	107	839
B Agriculture, forestry, fishing and hunting	656	...	...	-340	6	322	261	82	665
C Mining (except fuels), manufacturing and construction	670	...	...	233	46	949	71	368	1388
D Transportation and communication	2796	...	...	1312	27	4135	3495	405	8035
E Other economic affairs	3239	...	...	848	1014	5101	535	480	6116
10 Other functions	3890	...	...	-	19906	23796	-	-	23796
Total	121943	...	...	4117	100261	226321	12324	7187	245832

United Kingdom

2.5 Private Final Consumption Expenditure by Type and Purpose, in Current Prices

Million Pounds Sterling

	1980	1981	1982	1983	1984	1985	1986	1987	1988	1989	1990	1991
Final Consumption Expenditure of Resident Households												
1 Food, beverages and tobacco	38431	41613	44374	47540	50212	53314	56436	59533	63286	67248	72290	77354
A Food	22472	23744	25236	26601	27694	28960	30599	32207	34088	36426	38667	40708
B Non-alcoholic beverages	1183	1202	1254	1460	1580	1697	1962	2222	2499	2838	3202	3345
C Alcoholic beverages a	9955	11152	12003	13270	14316	15651	16404	17451	18754	19809	21738	23555
D Tobacco	4821	5515	5881	6209	6622	7006	7471	7653	7945	8175	8683	9746
2 Clothing and footwear	9873	10155	10925	12120	13168	14912	16661	17684	19034	19943	20875	21034
3 Gross rent, fuel and power	25285	30420	34754	37393	39095	43159	47058	50705	55665	60388	59914	65886
A Fuel and power	6355	7727	8696	9348	9492	10560	10885	10905	11115	11459	12321	14272
B Other	18930	22693	26058	28045	29603	32599	36173	39800	44550	48929	47593	51614
4 Furniture, furnishings and household equipment and operation	9883	10522	11104	12131	12861	14108	15765	17573	20112	21605	21907	22796
A Household operation	2171	2436	2608	2787	3077	3439	3800	4317	4832	5510	5836	6037
B Other	7712	8086	8496	9344	9784	10669	11965	13256	15280	16095	16071	16759
5 Medical care and health expenses	1305	1562	1860	2140	2392	2679	3085	3335	3786	4317	4869	5568
6 Transport and communication	22754	25348	27780	31185	33048	36448	39897	45108	52367	57681	60854	60656
A Personal transport equipment	6510	6557	7407	9112	8978	9853	11485	13429	17384	19926	18877	16426
B Other	16244	18791	20373	22073	24070	26595	28412	31679	34983	37755	41977	44230
7 Recreational, entertainment, education and cultural services	12902	14239	15647	16988	18365	20130	22364	24671	27624	30569	33458	34915
A Education	1135	1337	1442	1432	1524	1638	1785	1959	2185	2620	3255	4008
B Other	11767	12900	14205	15556	16841	18492	20579	22712	25439	27949	30203	30907
8 Miscellaneous goods and services	16429	17805	19774	22962	26179	29171	34748	40811	49808	56731	63301	65435
A Personal care	2180	2427	2713	3000	3393	3788	4301	4875	5568	6119	6602	7103
B Expenditures in restaurants, cafes and hotels b	8288	8820	9461	10928	12509	13876	16195	18307	22942	26027	29398	31049
C Other	5961	6558	7600	9034	10277	11508	14252	17629	21298	24585	27301	27283
Total Final Consumption Expenditure in the Domestic Market by Households, of which	136862	151664	166218	182459	195320	213921	236014	259420	291682	318482	337468	353644
A Durable goods	13495	13942	15439	18250	18638	20166	22836	26238	32176	35343	34246	32268
B Semi-durable goods	22605	23579	25362	27812	30185	33923	38137	41743	46429	50647	54922	56629
C Non-durable goods	52961	59189	64042	68757	72634	77881	81112	85104	90214	96126	103883	112267
D Services	47801	54952	61375	67635	73860	81954	93932	106335	122860	136367	144416	152480
Plus: Direct purchases abroad by resident households	2648	3131	3483	3855	4275	4440	5651	6702	7605	8668	9052	8978
Less: Direct purchases in the domestic market by non-resident households	3436	3513	3792	4661	5336	6276	6455	7217	7172	8026	8878	8207
Equals: Final Consumption Expenditure of Resident Households	136074	151282	165909	181653	194259	212085	235210	258905	292115	319124	337642	354415
Final Consumption Expenditure of Private Non-profit Institutions Serving Households												
Equals: Final Consumption Expenditure of Private Non-profit Organisations Serving Households	2789	3270	3694	4164	4688	5349	6220	6975	8219	9577	10893	11516
Private Final Consumption Expenditure	138863	154552	169603	185817	198947	217434	241430	265880	300334	328701	348535	365931

a) Item 'Alcoholic beverages' includes expenditure in catering establishments.
b) Item 'Expenditure in restaurants, cafes and hotels' excludes expenditure on alcoholic beverages.

2.6 Private Final Consumption Expenditure by Type and Purpose, in Constant Prices

Million Pounds Sterling

	1980	1981	1982	1983	1984	1985	1986	1987	1988	1989	1990	1991
At constant prices of:1985												
Final Consumption Expenditure of Resident Households												
1 Food, beverages and tobacco a	54249	53047	52314	53316	52840	53314	54053	55111	56306	56889	56410	55805
A Food	29218	28996	28984	29256	28668	28960	29572	30153	30961	31379	30906	30968
B Non-alcoholic beverages	1254	1268	1346	1545	1608	1697	1969	2171	2164	2353	2431	2441
C Alcoholic beverages b	15408	14875	14503	15059	15363	15651	15699	16024	16401	16377	16359	15827
D Tobacco	8806	8167	7541	7456	7201	7006	6813	6763	6780	6780	6714	6569
2 Clothing and footwear	11903	11788	12227	13071	13767	14912	16220	16933	17621	17566	17616	17305
3 Gross rent, fuel and power a	39652	39978	40263	41060	41510	43159	44453	45686	46568	46714	46764	47512
A Fuel and power	10282	10246	10047	9916	9851	10560	10798	10930	10868	10564	10573	11378

2.6 Private Final Consumption Expenditure by Type and Purpose, in Constant Prices
(Continued)

Million Pounds Sterling

	1980	1981	1982	1983	1984	1985	1986	1987	1988	1989	1990	1991
					At constant prices of:1985							
B Other	29398	29756	30229	31144	31659	32599	33655	34756	35700	36150	36191	36134
4 Furniture, furnishings and household equipment and operation a	12389	12389	12525	13178	13439	14108	15236	16562	18139	18644	17909	17459
A Household operation	3105	3162	3133	3132	3270	3439	3633	3924	4139	4392	4267	4005
B Other	9303	9253	9409	10046	10169	10669	11603	12638	14000	14252	13642	13454
5 Medical care and health expenses	1938	2039	2210	2393	2532	2680	2951	3028	3236	3440	3618	3844
6 Transport and communication a	30121	30571	30976	33869	34627	36448	39506	42331	46331	48586	48682	45355
A Personal transport equipment	7623	7754	8005	9965	9362	9853	10735	11241	12907	14011	13060	10657
B Other	22741	23059	23187	23904	25265	26595	28771	31090	33424	34575	35622	34698
7 Recreational, entertainment, education and cultural services a	17082	17225	17595	18547	19363	20130	21645	23222	25142	26501	27255	26885
A Education	1778	1883	1740	1636	1623	1638	1640	1652	1671	1851	2109	2409
B Other	15351	15403	15888	16911	17740	18492	20005	21570	23471	24650	25146	24476
8 Miscellaneous goods and services a	24664	24284	24819	26476	27873	29173	32523	35619	41165	44013	45775	43887
A Personal care	3150	3218	3296	3440	3670	3788	4083	4438	4813	4950	4908	4839
B Expenditures in restaurants, cafes and hotels c	12904	12261	12002	12710	13309	13875	15208	16089	18674	19914	20742	20028
C Other	8679	8844	9526	10326	10894	11510	13232	15092	17678	19149	20125	19020
Statistical discrepancy	-295	-284	-222	-	-	-	-	-	-	-	-	-
Total Final Consumption Expenditure in the Domestic Market by Households, of which a	191703	191037	192707	201910	205951	213924	226587	238492	254508	262353	264029	258052
A Durable goods	15417	15707	16504	19448	19261	20166	22100	24079	27488	28952	27564	25208
B Semi-durable goods	28442	28274	29182	30610	31828	33922	36748	39309	42192	43954	44969	43878
C Non-durable goods	77249	76198	75456	76509	76501	77881	79537	81138	83113	83880	83656	83556
D Services	71666	71843	72203	75342	78360	81952	88205	93966	101716	105568	107839	105408
Plus: Direct purchases abroad by resident households	4038	4277	4267	4344	4354	4440	5064	5836	6744	7109	6862	6523
Less: Direct purchases in the domestic market by non-resident households	5134	4646	4602	5323	5722	6276	6053	6381	5886	6127	6227	5385
Equals: Final Consumption Expenditure of Resident Households a	190619	190630	192332	200931	204583	212088	225598	237947	255366	263335	264664	259190

Final Consumption Expenditure of Private Non-profit Institutions Serving Households

	1980	1981	1982	1983	1984	1985	1986	1987	1988	1989	1990	1991
Equals: Final Consumption Expenditure of Private Non-profit Organisations Serving Households	3899	4060	4283	4606	4941	5349	5841	6272	7053	7808	8264	7999
Statistical discrepancy	42	84	57	-	-3	-1	-	1	-	2	-	-
Private Final Consumption Expenditure a	194560	194774	196672	205537	209521	217436	231439	244220	262419	271145	272928	267189

a) For years prior to 1983 in constant 1985 prices, components do not add up to total due to the method used to rebase to 1985 prices.
b) Item 'Alcoholic beverages' includes expenditure in catering establishments.
c) Item 'Expenditure in restaurants, cafes and hotels' excludes expenditure on alcoholic beverages.

2.7 Gross Capital Formation by Type of Good and Owner, in Current Prices

Million Pounds Sterling

	1980				1981				1982			
	TOTAL	Total Private	Public Enterprises	General Government	TOTAL	Total Private	Public Enterprises	General Government	TOTAL	Total Private	Public Enterprises	General Government
Increase in stocks, total	-2572	-2834	219	43	-2768	-2735	60	-93	-1188	-1604	261	155
1 Goods producing industries	-2359	-2579	220	-	-2155	-2250	95	-	-1165	-1467	302	-
A Materials and supplies	-1292	-1394	102	-	-1307	-1386	79	-	-360	-743	383	-
B Work in progress	-1031	-964	-67	-	-124	-159	35	-	-526	-495	-31	-
C Livestock, except breeding stocks, dairy cattle, etc.	-42	-42	...	...	-15	-15	...	...	46	46	...	...
D Finished goods	7	-177	184	-	-708	-689	-19	-	-325	-276	-49	-
2 Wholesale and retail trade	-861	-863	2	-	-644	-652	8	-	16	13	3	-
3 Other, except government stocks	604	607	-3	-	123	166	-43	-	-194	-150	-44	-
4 Government stocks	43	...	...	43	-93	...	...	-93	155	...	...	155
Statistical discrepancy	1	1	...	...	1	1	...	...	-	...	...	...
Gross Fixed Capital Formation, Total	41561	29081	6828	5652	41304	29708	6924	4672	44824	33073	7314	4437
1 Residential buildings	8674	6115	335	2224	8138	6174	309	1655	8920	6850	301	1769
2 Non-residential buildings	11802	6020	2637	3145	12471	6460	2700	3311	13386	6415	3034	3937

United Kingdom

2.7 Gross Capital Formation by Type of Good and Owner, in Current Prices
(Continued)

Million Pounds Sterling

	1980				1981				1982			
	TOTAL	Total Private	Public Enterprises	General Government	TOTAL	Total Private	Public Enterprises	General Government	TOTAL	Total Private	Public Enterprises	General Government
3 Other construction	...	...	...	...	...	...	...	...	...	...	...	...
4 Land improvement and plantation and orchard development	1561	2418	-173	-684	1782	2982	-42	-1158	1937	4254	-91	-2226
5 Producers' durable goods	19559	14563	4029	967	18910	14089	3957	864	20553	15526	4070	957
A Transport equipment	4566	3557	800	209	3846	3199	473	174	4285	3735	359	191
B Machinery and equipment	14993	11006	3229	758	15064	10890	3484	690	16268	11791	3711	766
6 Breeding stock, dairy cattle, etc.	-35	-35	...	...	3	3	...	...	28	28	...	...
Total Gross Capital Formation	38989	26247	7047	5695	38536	26973	6984	4579	43636	31469	7575	4592

	1983				1984				1985			
	TOTAL	Total Private	Public Enterprises	General Government	TOTAL	Total Private	Public Enterprises	General Government	TOTAL	Total Private	Public Enterprises	General Government
Increase in stocks, total	1465	883	336	246	1296	1459	-443	280	821	375	-4	450
1 Goods producing industries	647	298	349	-	435	920	-485	-	-234	-248	14	-
A Materials and supplies	28	-340	368	-	-370	179	-549	-	479	178	301	-
B Work in progress	623	663	-40	-	334	298	36	-	-344	-403	59	-
C Livestock, except breeding stocks, dairy cattle, etc.	-12	-12	...	...	-17	-17	...	...	-73	-73	...	...
D Finished goods	-71	-55	-16	-	483	499	-16	...	-326	20	-346	-
2 Wholesale and retail trade	449	447	2	-	589	589	-	-	553	553	-	-
3 Other, except government stocks	161	176	-15	-	-8	-50	42	-	53	71	-18	-
4 Government stocks	246	...	...	246	280	...	...	280	450	...	...	450
Statistical discrepancy	-38	-38	...	...	-	-	...	...	-1	-1	...	...
Gross Fixed Capital Formation, Total	48615	34681	8065	5869	54967	40807	7441	6719	60353	47550	5931	6872
1 Residential buildings	10447	7757	326	2364	11718	8972	318	2428	11854	9318	280	2256
2 Non-residential buildings	13306	6269	3082	3955	14646	7237	2868	4541	15218	7793	2703	4722
3 Other construction	...	...	...	...	...	...	...	...	...	...	...	...
4 Land improvement and plantation and orchard development	2397	4292	-156	-1739	2673	4638	-316	-1649	2972	5151	-381	-1798
5 Producers' durable goods	22472	16370	4813	1289	25958	19988	4571	1399	30296	25275	3329	1692
A Transport equipment	4530	3745	535	250	5664	4785	630	249	6439	5522	657	260
B Machinery and equipment	17942	12625	4278	1039	20294	15203	3941	1150	23857	19753	2672	1432
6 Breeding stock, dairy cattle, etc.	-7	-7	...	...	-28	-28	...	...	13	13	...	...
Total Gross Capital Formation	50080	35564	8401	6115	56263	42266	6998	6999	61174	47925	5927	7322

	1986				1987				1988			
	TOTAL	Total Private	Public Enterprises	General Government	TOTAL	Total Private	Public Enterprises	General Government	TOTAL	Total Private	Public Enterprises	General Government
Increase in stocks, total	716	1418	-465	-237	1388	2107	-221	-498	4782	5088	16	-322
1 Goods producing industries	-346	97	-443	-	76	268	-192	-	2246	2181	65	-
A Materials and supplies	-60	8	-68	-	-96	15	-111	-	...	...	...	...
B Work in progress	-12	132	-144	-	-21	-84	63	-	...	...	...	...
C Livestock, except breeding stocks, dairy cattle, etc.	-32	-32	...	...	-87	-87	...	...	-36	-36	...	...
D Finished goods	-368	-318	-50	-	287	369	-82	-	...	...	...	...
2 Wholesale and retail trade	1410	1410	-	-	2011	2011	-	-	2981	2981	-	-
3 Other, except government stocks	-112	-90	-22	-	-202	-173	-29	-	-123	-74	-49	-
4 Government stocks	-237	...	...	-237	-498	...	...	-498	-322	...	...	-322
Statistical discrepancy	1	1	...	...	1	1	...	...	-	-	...	...
Gross Fixed Capital Formation, Total	64514	51457	5548	7509	74077	61891	4609	7577	89857	78732	4619	6506
1 Residential buildings	13622	11008	242	2372	15274	12358	253	2663	19354	16440	246	2668
2 Non-residential buildings	16514	8596	2762	5156	19874	12043	2483	5348	24694	15713	2779	6202

2.7 Gross Capital Formation by Type of Good and Owner, in Current Prices
(Continued)

Million Pounds Sterling

	1986				1987				1988			
	TOTAL	Total Private	Public Enterprises	General Government	TOTAL	Total Private	Public Enterprises	General Government	TOTAL	Total Private	Public Enterprises	General Government
3 Other construction	...	...	...	...	...	...	...	...	...	...	...	...
4 Land improvement and plantation and orchard development	3466	5798	-408	-1924	4051	7353	-901	-2401	5456	11138	-1277	-4405
5 Producers' durable goods	30907	26050	2952	1905	34908	30167	2774	1967	40319	35407	2871	2041
A Transport equipment	6222	5445	487	290	7805	7044	458	303	8849	8059	466	324
B Machinery and equipment	24685	20605	2465	1615	27103	23123	2316	1664	31470	27348	2405	1717
6 Breeding stock, dairy cattle, etc.	5	5	...	...	-30	-30	...	...	34	34	...	...
Total Gross Capital Formation	65230	52875	5083	7272	75465	63998	4388	7079	94639	83820	4635	6184

	1989				1990				1991			
	TOTAL	Total Private	Public Enterprises	General Government	TOTAL	Total Private	Public Enterprises	General Government	TOTAL	Total Private	Public Enterprises	General Government
Increase in stocks, total	3138	3094	207	-163	-1462	-1354	-264	156	-5303	-5462	8	151
1 Goods producing industries	1213	987	226	-	-1690	-1450	-240	-	-3769	-3787	18	-
A Materials and supplies	...	...	...	-	...	...	...	-	...	...	...	-
B Work in progress	...	...	...	-	...	...	...	-	...	...	...	-
C Livestock, except breeding stocks, dairy cattle, etc.	-30	-30	...	...	-48	-48	...	...	-16	-16	...	...
D Finished goods	...	...	...	...	...	...	...	...	...	...	...	...
2 Wholesale and retail trade	2115	2115	-	-	162	162	-	-	-1790	-1790	-	-
3 Other, except government stocks	-28	-9	-19	-	-90	-66	-24	-	105	115	-10	-
4 Government stocks	-163	...	...	-163	156	...	...	156	151	...	...	151
Statistical discrepancy	1	1	...	...	-	-	...	...	-	-	...	...
Gross Fixed Capital Formation, Total	103262	88167	5513	9582	106028	88384	4985	12659	95442	79341	3928	12173
1 Residential buildings	20986	17140	256	3590	19906	15679	247	3980	16645	13806	234	2605
2 Non-residential buildings	31189	20141	3236	7812	34736	23132	2215	9389	32366	20990	2167	9209
3 Other construction	...	...	...	...	...	...	...	...	...	...	...	...
4 Land improvement and plantation and orchard development	4381	9979	-1171	-4427	4255	8697	-845	-3597	4163	6893	-608	-2122
5 Producers' durable goods	46661	40862	3192	2607	47100	40845	3368	2887	42303	37687	2135	2481
A Transport equipment	10324	9298	585	441	9969	8926	616	427	8452	7522	551	379
B Machinery and equipment	36337	31564	2607	2166	37131	31919	2752	2460	33851	30165	1584	2102
6 Breeding stock, dairy cattle, etc.	45	45	...	...	31	31	...	...	-35	-35	...	...
Total Gross Capital Formation	106400	91261	5720	9419	104566	87030	4721	12815	90139	73879	3936	12324

2.8 Gross Capital Formation by Type of Good and Owner, in Constant Prices

Million Pounds Sterling

	1980				1981				1982			
	TOTAL	Total Private	Public Enterprises	General Government	TOTAL	Total Private	Public Enterprises	General Government	TOTAL	Total Private	Public Enterprises	General Government
	At constant prices of:1985											
Increase in stocks, total [a]	-3371	-3800	219	56	-3200	-3244	36	-104	-1281	-1729	194	151
1 Goods producing industries [a]	-3108	-3525	221	-	-2754	-2893	83	-	-1208	-1679	242	-
A Materials and supplies	-1717	-1871	134	-	-1652	-1785	73	-	-326	-892	418	-
B Work in progress	-1341	-1277	-89	-	-174	-197	36	-	-579	-550	-34	-
C Livestock, except breeding stocks, dairy cattle, etc.	-53	-53	...	...	-19	-19	...	...	51	51	...	...
D Finished goods	65	13	244	-	-879	-858	-25	-	-353	-299	-78	-
2 Wholesale and retail trade	-1142	-1144	2	-	-785	-793	8	-	113	111	2	-
3 Other, except government stocks	312	316	-4	-	101	156	-55	-	-136	-86	-50	-
4 Government stocks	56	...	...	56	-104	...	...	-104	151	...	...	151
Statistical discrepancy	511	511	...	...	342	342	...	...	-201	-201	...	...
Gross Fixed Capital Formation, Total [a]	53416	38174	8719	6465	48298	35726	7941	4730	50915	38556	8115	4440
1 Residential buildings	12379	9134	419	2778	10247	8149	339	1817	10899	8680	333	1949
2 Non-residential buildings	13086	6486	3013	3570	12527	6418	2729	3352	13815	6616	3128	4066

United Kingdom

2.8 Gross Capital Formation by Type of Good and Owner, in Constant Prices
(Continued)

Million Pounds Sterling

	1980				1981				1982			
	TOTAL	Total Private	Public Enterprises	General Government	TOTAL	Total Private	Public Enterprises	General Government	TOTAL	Total Private	Public Enterprises	General Government
	At constant prices of:1985											
3 Other construction	...	...	...	...	...	...	...	...	...	...	...	...
4 Land improvement and plantation and orchard development	2170	3359	-240	-950	2295	3838	-53	-1491	2521	5544	-118	-2905
5 Producers' durable goods a	25963	19144	5329	1080	23160	17141	4800	952	23470	17626	4531	957
A Transport equipment	6296	4899	1105	292	4895	4077	592	226	5028	4374	425	229
B Machinery and equipment	19706	14269	4450	965	18265	13063	4373	825	18447	13259	4316	856
6 Breeding stock, dairy cattle, etc.	-47	-47	...	...	4	4	...	...	32	32	...	...
Statistical discrepancy	-135	98	198	-13	65	176	126	100	178	58	241	373
Total Gross Capital Formation	50045	34374	8938	6521	45098	32482	7977	4626	49634	36827	8309	4591

	1983				1984				1985			
	TOTAL	Total Private	Public Enterprises	General Government	TOTAL	Total Private	Public Enterprises	General Government	TOTAL	Total Private	Public Enterprises	General Government
	At constant prices of:1985											
Increase in stocks, total a	1357	919	202	236	1084	1593	-781	272	821	375	-4	450
1 Goods producing industries a	454	280	174	-	179	1004	-825	-	-234	-248	14	-
A Materials and supplies	-149	-384	235	-	-700	133	-833	-	456	40	416	-
B Work in progress	702	739	-37	-	376	337	39	-	-334	-392	58	-
C Livestock, except breeding stocks, dairy cattle, etc.	-12	-12	...	...	-17	-17	...	...	-73	-73	...	...
D Finished goods	-84	-95	11	-	523	509	14	-	-313	-253	-60	-
2 Wholesale and retail trade	460	458	2	-	636	636	-	-	553	553	-	-
3 Other, except government stocks	157	131	26	-	-3	-47	44	-	53	71	-18	-
4 Government stocks	236	...	...	236	272	...	...	272	450	...	...	450
Statistical discrepancy	50	50	...	...	-	-	...	...	-1	-1	...	...
Gross Fixed Capital Formation, Total a	53476	38724	8683	6069	58034	43419	7772	6843	60353	47550	5931	6872
1 Residential buildings	12247	9323	354	2570	12550	9725	327	2498	11854	9318	280	2256
2 Non-residential buildings	13878	6560	3197	4121	15181	7516	2950	4715	15218	7793	2703	4722
3 Other construction	...	...	...	...	...	...	...	...	...	...	...	...
4 Land improvement and plantation and orchard development	2773	4972	-176	-2023	2975	5164	-351	-1838	2972	5151	-381	-1798
5 Producers' durable goods a	24586	17877	5308	1401	27360	21046	4846	1468	30296	25275	3329	1692
A Transport equipment	5177	4298	593	286	6101	5161	673	267	6439	5522	657	260
B Machinery and equipment	19409	13579	4715	1115	21259	15885	4173	1201	23857	19753	2672	1432
6 Breeding stock, dairy cattle, etc.	-8	-8	...	...	-32	-32	...	...	13	13	...	...
Statistical discrepancy	...	...	...	...	...	...	...	...	...	...	...	...
Total Gross Capital Formation	54833	39643	8885	6305	59118	45012	6991	7115	61174	47925	5927	7322

	1986				1987				1988			
	TOTAL	Total Private	Public Enterprises	General Government	TOTAL	Total Private	Public Enterprises	General Government	TOTAL	Total Private	Public Enterprises	General Government
	At constant prices of:1985											
Increase in stocks, total a	737	949	23	-235	1158	2019	-364	-497	4010	4286	14	-290
1 Goods producing industries a	-225	-270	45	-	20	355	-335	-	1846	1788	58	-
A Materials and supplies	76	-46	122	-	-178	7	-185	-	...	...	...	-
B Work in progress	-22	99	-121	-	51	13	38	-	...	...	...	-
C Livestock, except breeding stocks, dairy cattle, etc.	-32	-32	...	...	-87	-87	...	...	-36	-36	...	...
D Finished goods	-421	-407	-14	-	300	315	-15	-	...	...	...	...
2 Wholesale and retail trade	1417	1417	-	-	1879	1879	-	-	2615	2615	-	-
3 Other, except government stocks	-190	-168	-22	-	-244	-215	-29	-	-161	-117	-44	-
4 Government stocks	-235	...	...	-235	-497	...	...	-497	-290	...	...	-290
Statistical discrepancy	-30	-30	...	...	-	-	...	...	-	-	...	...
Gross Fixed Capital Formation, Total a	61813	48937	5416	7460	67753	55807	4476	7470	77395	66361	4385	6649
1 Residential buildings	12901	10365	234	2302	13475	10734	237	2504	15548	12999	214	2335
2 Non-residential buildings	15825	8137	2697	4991	18400	10947	2394	5059	21283	13552	2420	5311

2.8 Gross Capital Formation by Type of Good and Owner, in Constant Prices
(Continued)

Million Pounds Sterling

	1986				1987				1988			
	TOTAL	Total Private	Public Enterprises	General Government	TOTAL	Total Private	Public Enterprises	General Government	TOTAL	Total Private	Public Enterprises	General Government
	At constant prices of:1985											
3 Other construction	...	...	...	...	...	...	...	...	...	...	...	...
4 Land improvement and plantation and orchard development	3068	5138	-361	-1709	3287	5990	-731	-1972	3596	7338	-843	-2899
5 Producers' durable goods a	30014	25292	2846	1876	32619	28164	2576	1879	36936	32440	2594	1902
A Transport equipment	5769	5042	456	271	6648	5978	407	263	7113	6442	404	267
B Machinery and equipment	24245	20250	2390	1605	25971	22186	2169	1616	29823	25998	2190	1635
6 Breeding stock, dairy cattle, etc.	5	5	...	...	-28	-28	...	...	32	32	...	...
Statistical discrepancy	...	...	...	...	...	...	...	...	...	...	...	...
Total Gross Capital Formation	62550	49886	5439	7225	68911	57826	4112	6973	81405	70647	4399	6359

	1989				1990				1991			
	TOTAL	Total Private	Public Enterprises	General Government	TOTAL	Total Private	Public Enterprises	General Government	TOTAL	Total Private	Public Enterprises	General Government
	At constant prices of:1985											
Increase in stocks, total a	2657	2624	196	-163	-1110	-1098	-176	164	-3507	-3764	123	134
1 Goods producing industries a	971	760	211	-	-1438	-1282	-156	-	-2574	-2706	132	-
A Materials and supplies	...	...	...	-	...	...	...	-	...	...	...	-
B Work in progress	...	...	...	-	...	...	...	-	...	...	...	-
C Livestock, except breeding stocks, dairy cattle, etc.	-28	-28	...	...	-43	-43	...	...	-14	-14	...	...
D Finished goods	...	...	...	-	...	...	...	-	...	...	...	...
2 Wholesale and retail trade	1838	1838	-	-	153	153	-	-	-1296	-1296	-	-
3 Other, except government stocks	-53	-38	-15	-	11	31	-20	-	230	239	-9	-
4 Government stocks	-163	...	...	-163	164	...	...	164	134	...	...	134
Statistical discrepancy	64	64	...	...	-	-	...	...	-1	-1	...	...
Gross Fixed Capital Formation, Total a	82997	70046	4659	8292	80464	66647	3983	9834	72462	59701	3215	9546
1 Residential buildings	15296	12290	200	2806	13594	10506	180	2908	11020	8942	172	1906
2 Non-residential buildings	23745	15503	2462	5780	24772	16781	1575	6416	24149	15858	1630	6661
3 Other construction	...	...	...	...	...	...	...	...	...	...	...	...
4 Land improvement and plantation and orchard development	2588	5927	-696	-2643	2337	4796	-467	-1992	2248	3723	-328	-1147
5 Producers' durable goods a	41339	36297	2693	2349	39734	34537	2695	2502	35063	31196	1741	2126
A Transport equipment	7777	6963	477	337	7022	6220	497	305	5684	4974	450	260
B Machinery and equipment	33562	29334	2216	2012	32712	28317	2198	2197	29379	26222	1291	1866
6 Breeding stock, dairy cattle, etc.	29	29	...	...	27	27	...	...	-18	-18	...	...
Statistical discrepancy	...	...	...	...	...	...	...	...	...	...	...	...
Total Gross Capital Formation	85654	72670	4855	8129	79354	65549	3807	9998	68955	55937	3338	9680

a) For years prior to 1983 in constant 1985 prices, components do not add up to total due to the method used to rebase to 1985 prices.

2.9 Gross Capital Formation by Kind of Activity of Owner, ISIC Major Divisions, in Current Prices

Million Pounds Sterling

	1980			1981			1982			1983		
	Total Gross Capital Formation	Increase in Stocks	Gross Fixed Capital Formation	Total Gross Capital Formation	Increase in Stocks	Gross Fixed Capital Formation	Total Gross Capital Formation	Increase in Stocks	Gross Fixed Capital Formation	Total Gross Capital Formation	Increase in Stocks	Gross Fixed Capital Formation
	All Producers											
1 Agriculture, hunting, fishing and forestry	1042	-51	1093	1007	-33	1040	1338	39	1299	1457	28	1429
2 Mining and quarrying a	3647	84	3563	3556	-522	4078	3672	-439	4111	3658	-274	3932
3 Manufacturing	4874	-2321	7195	4589	-1565	6154	5126	-1291	6417	6843	129	6714
4 Electricity, gas and water a	2254	128	2126	2569	76	2493	3124	424	2700	3569	473	3096

2.9 Gross Capital Formation by Kind of Activity of Owner, ISIC Major Divisions, in Current Prices
(Continued)

Million Pounds Sterling

	1980			1981			1982			1983		
	Total Gross Capital Formation	Increase in Stocks	Gross Fixed Capital Formation	Total Gross Capital Formation	Increase in Stocks	Gross Fixed Capital Formation	Total Gross Capital Formation	Increase in Stocks	Gross Fixed Capital Formation	Total Gross Capital Formation	Increase in Stocks	Gross Fixed Capital Formation
5 Construction	286	-198	484	354	-110	464	685	102	583	844	218	626
6 Wholesale and retail trade, restaurants and hotels	2582	-861	3443	2809	-644	3453	3896	16	3880	4482	449	4033
7 Transport, storage and communication	4184	-3	4187	3613	-43	3656	3478	-44	3522	4120	20	4100
8 Finance, insurance, real estate and business services	13294	607	12687	12927	116	12811	13930	-150	14080	15885	176	15709
9 Community, social and personal services	3431	47	3384	3333	-133	3466	3824	87	3737	4260	238	4022
Statistical discrepancy	1614	-6	1620	1959	50	1909	2091	-	2091	2492	-	2492
Total Industries	37219	-2574	39793	36729	-2808	39537	41182	-1256	42438	47619	1457	46162
Producers of Government Services	1770	2	1768	1807	40	1767	2454	68	2386	2461	8	2453
Private Non-Profit Institutions Serving Households	...	...	...	...	...	...	...	...	...	...	...	...
Total	38989	-2572	41561	38536	-2768	41304	43636	-1188	44824	50080	1465	48615
Memorandum Item: Mineral Fuels and Power	5587	212	5375	5799	-448	6247	6443	-15	6458	6833	199	6634

	1984			1985			1986			1987		
	Total Gross Capital Formation	Increase in Stocks	Gross Fixed Capital Formation	Total Gross Capital Formation	Increase in Stocks	Gross Fixed Capital Formation	Total Gross Capital Formation	Increase in Stocks	Gross Fixed Capital Formation	Total Gross Capital Formation	Increase in Stocks	Gross Fixed Capital Formation
	All Producers											
1 Agriculture, hunting, fishing and forestry	1558	94	1464	939	-242	1181	1237	41	1196	1079	-186	1265
2 Mining and quarrying [a]	3470	-200	3670	3314	-397	3711	3211	-260	3471	2949	-7	2884
3 Manufacturing	9331	1010	8321	9675	-443	10118	9312	-419	9731	10552	-262	10814
4 Electricity, gas and water [a]	2611	-461	3072	3439	406	3033	3264	-22	3286	3100	-178	3343
5 Construction	565	-8	573	1067	441	626	924	315	609	1473	710	763
6 Wholesale and retail trade, restaurants and hotels	5518	589	4929	6292	553	5739	7679	1410	6269	9698	2011	7687
7 Transport, storage and communication	5190	48	5142	5858	-9	5867	5692	18	5674	6766	-74	6840
8 Finance, insurance, real estate and business services	17685	-56	17741	19049	62	18987	21698	-130	21828	26683	-128	26811
9 Community, social and personal services	4762	277	4485	5286	443	4843	5037	-237	5274	5365	-498	5863
Statistical discrepancy	2955	-	2955	3391	-	3391	4051	-	4051	4787	-	4787
Total Industries	53673	1293	52380	58359	814	57545	62150	716	61434	72465	1388	71077
Producers of Government Services	2590	3	2587	2815	7	2808	3080	-	3080	3000	-	3000
Private Non-Profit Institutions Serving Households	...	...	...	...	...	...	...	...	...	...	...	...
Total	56263	1296	54967	61174	821	60353	65230	716	64514	75465	1388	74077
Memorandum Item: Mineral Fuels and Power	5662	-661	6323	6368	17	6351	6012	-289	6301	5580	-94	5674

	1988			1989			1990			1991		
	Total Gross Capital Formation	Increase in Stocks	Gross Fixed Capital Formation	Total Gross Capital Formation	Increase in Stocks	Gross Fixed Capital Formation	Total Gross Capital Formation	Increase in Stocks	Gross Fixed Capital Formation	Total Gross Capital Formation	Increase in Stocks	Gross Fixed Capital Formation
	All Producers											
1 Agriculture, hunting, fishing and forestry	1281	-139	1420	1396	-89	1485	1327	-41	1368	1197	-2	1199
2 Mining and quarrying [a]	3000	-63	3063	3625	202	3423	3918	-361	4279	5701	1	5700
3 Manufacturing	13260	979	12281	14147	-134	14281	12375	-1953	14328	8758	-3920	12678
4 Electricity, gas and water [a]	3763	44	3719	4647	108	4539	5211	-134	5345	6389	174	6215

2.9 Gross Capital Formation by Kind of Activity of Owner, ISIC Major Divisions, in Current Prices
(Continued)

Million Pounds Sterling

	1988			1989			1990			1991		
	Total Gross Capital Formation	Increase in Stocks	Gross Fixed Capital Formation	Total Gross Capital Formation	Increase in Stocks	Gross Fixed Capital Formation	Total Gross Capital Formation	Increase in Stocks	Gross Fixed Capital Formation	Total Gross Capital Formation	Increase in Stocks	Gross Fixed Capital Formation
5 Construction	2567	1425	1142	2238	1127	1111	1764	799	965	597	-22	619
6 Wholesale and retail trade, restaurants and hotels	12437	2981	9456	11583	2115	9468	9113	162	8951	6857	-1790	8647
7 Transport, storage and communication	8094	-58	8152	9599	-2	9601	9067	-87	9154	9140	-25	9165
8 Finance, insurance, real estate and business services	34451	-65	34516	41159	-26	41185	41260	-3	41263	...	130	...
9 Community, social and personal services	5866	-322	6188	7929	-162	8091	9297	156	9141	...	151	...
Statistical discrepancy	6920	-	6920	5525	-1	5526	5073	-	5073	4495	-	4495
Total Industries	91639	4782	86857	101848	3138	98710	98405	-1462	99867	83613	-5303	88916
Producers of Government Services	3000	-	3000	4552	-	4552	6161	-	6161	6526	-	6526
Private Non-Profit Institutions Serving Households	...	...	...	...	...	...	...	...	...	...	...	...
Total	94639	4782	89857	106400	3138	103262	104566	-1462	106028	90139	-5303	95442
Memorandum Item: Mineral Fuels and Power	6046	-	6046	7457	309	7148	7936	-506	8442	10794	181	10613

a) Item 'Electricity, gas and water' is included in item 'Mining and Quarrying'.

2.10 Gross Capital Formation by Kind of Activity of Owner, ISIC Major Divisions, in Constant Prices

Million Pounds Sterling

	1980			1981			1982			1983		
	Total Gross Capital Formation	Increase in Stocks	Gross Fixed Capital Formation	Total Gross Capital Formation	Increase in Stocks	Gross Fixed Capital Formation	Total Gross Capital Formation	Increase in Stocks	Gross Fixed Capital Formation	Total Gross Capital Formation	Increase in Stocks	Gross Fixed Capital Formation
At constant prices of:1985												
All Producers												
1 Agriculture, hunting, fishing and forestry	1228	-65	1293	1114	-34	1148	1443	41	1402	1545	34	1511
2 Mining and quarrying a	4423	71	4352	3888	-686	4574	4006	-510	4516	3896	-295	4191
3 Manufacturing	6733	-3048	9781	5683	-1989	7672	6021	-1461	7482	7545	135	7410
4 Electricity, gas and water a	2947	215	2732	2978	105	2873	3595	593	3002	3657	336	3321
5 Construction	349	-281	630	417	-150	567	782	129	653	985	294	691
6 Wholesale and retail trade, restaurants and hotels	3199	-1142	4341	3239	-785	4024	4464	113	4351	4887	460	4427
7 Transport, storage and communication	5472	-4	5476	4283	-55	4338	3943	-50	3993	4550	26	4524
8 Finance, insurance, real estate and business services	18912	316	18596	17278	156	17122	18446	-86	18532	19868	131	19737
9 Community, social and personal services	3860	60	3800	3440	-148	3588	3880	108	3772	4216	181	4035
Statistical discrepancy	2755	505	2250	2802	346	2456	2500	-223	2723	1110	46	1064
Total Industries b	48019	-3373	51392	43285	-3240	46525	47076	-1346	48422	52268	1348	50920
Producers of Government Services	2075	2	2073	1863	40	1823	2553	65	2488	2565	9	2556
Private Non-Profit Institutions Serving Households	...	...	...	...	...	...	...	...	...	...	...	...
Statistical discrepancy	-49	-	-49	-50	-	-50	5	-	5	...	-	...
Total b	50045	-3371	53416	45098	-3200	48298	49634	-1281	50915	54833	1357	53476
Memorandum Item: Mineral Fuels and Power	7019	286	6733	6557	-581	7138	7252	82	7170	7144	40	7104

	1984			1985			1986			1987		
	Total Gross Capital Formation	Increase in Stocks	Gross Fixed Capital Formation	Total Gross Capital Formation	Increase in Stocks	Gross Fixed Capital Formation	Total Gross Capital Formation	Increase in Stocks	Gross Fixed Capital Formation	Total Gross Capital Formation	Increase in Stocks	Gross Fixed Capital Formation
At constant prices of:1985												
All Producers												
1 Agriculture, hunting, fishing and forestry	1615	108	1507	939	-242	1181	1215	59	1156	1000	-196	1196
2 Mining and quarrying a	3620	-185	3805	3314	-397	3711	3002	-350	3352	2799	41	2717
3 Manufacturing	9880	1057	8823	9675	-443	10118	9020	-403	9423	9827	-221	10048
4 Electricity, gas and water a	2406	-800	3206	3439	406	3033	3321	134	3187	2855	-251	3141
5 Construction	608	-1	609	1067	441	626	887	305	582	1334	647	687
6 Wholesale and retail trade, restaurants and hotels	5873	636	5237	6292	553	5739	7373	1417	5956	8874	1879	6995
7 Transport, storage and communication	5473	50	5423	5858	-9	5867	5495	17	5478	6209	-72	6281
8 Finance, insurance, real estate and business services	21399	-53	21452	22531	62	22469	23380	-207	23587	27231	-172	27403
9 Community, social and personal services	4601	269	4332	4861	443	4418	4318	-235	4553	4380	-497	4877

United Kingdom

2.10 Gross Capital Formation by Kind of Activity of Owner, ISIC Major Divisions, in Constant Prices
(Continued)

Million Pounds Sterling

	1984			1985			1986			1987		
	Total Gross Capital Formation	Increase in Stocks	Gross Fixed Capital Formation	Total Gross Capital Formation	Increase in Stocks	Gross Fixed Capital Formation	Total Gross Capital Formation	Increase in Stocks	Gross Fixed Capital Formation	Total Gross Capital Formation	Increase in Stocks	Gross Fixed Capital Formation
			At constant prices of:1985									
Statistical discrepancy	951	-	951	334	-	334	1391	-	1391	1345	-	1345
Total Industries b	56454	1081	55373	58359	814	57545	59454	737	58717	65893	1158	64735
Producers of Government Services	2664	3	2661	2815	7	2808	3096	-	3096	3018	-	3018
Private Non-Profit Institutions Serving Households	...	...	...	...	...	...	...	...	...	...	...	...
Statistical discrepancy	...	-	...	...	-	...	...	-	...	...	-	...
Total b	59118	1084	58034	61174	821	60353	62550	737	61813	68911	1158	67753
Memorandum Item: Mineral Fuels and Power	5596	-985	6581	6368	17	6351	5879	-223	6102	5220	-128	5348

	1988			1989			1990			1991		
	Total Gross Capital Formation	Increase in Stocks	Gross Fixed Capital Formation	Total Gross Capital Formation	Increase in Stocks	Gross Fixed Capital Formation	Total Gross Capital Formation	Increase in Stocks	Gross Fixed Capital Formation	Total Gross Capital Formation	Increase in Stocks	Gross Fixed Capital Formation
			At constant prices of:1985									
			All Producers									
1 Agriculture, hunting, fishing and forestry	1105	-146	1251	1136	-75	1211	1015	-34	1049	924	-	924
2 Mining and quarrying a	2557	-161	2718	2988	216	2772	2856	-432	3288	4520	24	4496
3 Manufacturing	12085	887	11198	12373	-22	12395	10264	-1495	11759	7565	-2782	10347
4 Electricity, gas and water a	3372	53	3319	3777	36	3741	4051	-74	4125	5001	226	4775
5 Construction	2211	1213	998	1789	881	908	1333	597	736	415	-43	458
6 Wholesale and retail trade, restaurants and hotels	10975	2615	8360	9650	1838	7812	7151	153	6998	5642	-1296	6938
7 Transport, storage and communication	7177	-51	7228	8128	-	8128	7435	5	7430	7299	-22	7321
8 Finance, insurance, real estate and business services	29260	-110	29370	32518	-53	32571	30814	6	30808	...	252	...
9 Community, social and personal services	5063	-290	5353	6123	-164	6287	6805	164	6641	...	134	...
Statistical discrepancy	4563	-	4563	3278	-	3278	2795	-	2795	2427	-	2427
Total Industries b	78368	4010	74358	81760	2657	79103	74519	-1110	75629	63778	-3507	67285
Producers of Government Services	3037	-	3037	3894	-	3894	4835	-	4835	5177	-	5177
Private Non-Profit Institutions Serving Households	...	...	...	...	...	...	...	...	...	...	...	...
Statistical discrepancy	...	-	...	...	-	...	...	-	...	...	-	...
Total b	81405	4010	77395	85654	2657	82997	79354	-1110	80464	68955	-3507	72462
Memorandum Item: Mineral Fuels and Power	5381	-	5381	6119	251	5868	5996	-515	6511	8502	256	8246

a) Item 'Electricity, gas and water' is included in item 'Mining and Quarrying'.
b) For years prior to 1983 in constant 1985 prices, components do not add up to total due to the method used to rebase to 1985 prices.

2.11 Gross Fixed Capital Formation by Kind of Activity of Owner, ISIC Divisions, in Current Prices

Million Pounds Sterling

	1980	1981	1982	1983	1984	1985	1986	1987	1988	1989	1990	1991
					All Producers							
1 Agriculture, hunting, forestry and fishing	1093	1040	1299	1429	1464	1181	1196	1265	1420	1485	1368	1199
A Agriculture and hunting	949	862	1052	1171	1103	845	791	847	1254	1326	1214	1082
B Forestry and logging	66	77	74	84	108	128	136	140	164	154	153	115
C Fishing	8	1	3	4	8	13	5	9	2	5	1	2
2 Mining and quarrying a	3563	4078	4111	3932	3670	3711	3471	2884	3063	3423	4279	5700
A Coal mining	784	766	820	783	328	627	595	569	524	411	373	288
B Crude petroleum and natural gas production	2779	3312	3291	3149	3342	3084	2876	2315	2539	3012	3906	5412
C Metal ore mining	...	...	...	...	...	...	...	...	...	...	...	...
D Other mining	...	...	...	...	...	...	...	...	...	...	...	...

2.11 Gross Fixed Capital Formation by Kind of Activity of Owner, ISIC Divisions, in Current Prices
(Continued)

Million Pounds Sterling

	1980	1981	1982	1983	1984	1985	1986	1987	1988	1989	1990	1991
3 Manufacturing	7195	6154	6417	6714	8321	10118	9731	10814	12281	14281	14328	12678
A Manufacturing of food, beverages and tobacco	961	900	1002	996	1235	1395	1297	1407	1759	1851	2004	2127
B Textile, wearing apparel and leather industries	235	181	238	249	336	384	449	517	559	504	437	319
C Manufacture of wood, and wood products, including furniture	171	105	113	136	157	192	190	259	340	363	310	233
D Manufacture of paper and paper products, printing and publishing	542	446	432	497	694	828	954	1202	1729	1732	1373	1239
E Manufacture of chemicals and chemical petroleum, coal, rubber and plastic products	256	196	205	233	360	391	406	534	637	726	701	595
F Manufacture of non-metalic mineral products except products of petroleum and coal	443	333	361	373	507	542	462	639	852	1044	870	554
G Basic metal industries	389	297	263	251	239	360	418	543	611	700	1093	474
H Manufacture of fabricated metal products, machinery and equipment	3414	2813	2799	3062	3799	4590	4596	4783	5714	7270	7428	7052
I Other manufacturing industries	67	52	73	62	55	53	57	65	80	91	112	85
4 Electricity, gas and water a	2126	2493	2700	3096	3072	3033	3286	3343	3719	4539	5345	6215
A Electricity, gas and steam	1812	2169	2347	2702	2653	2640	2830	2792	2983	3725	4163	4913
B Water works and supply	314	324	353	394	418	393	456	551	736	814	1182	1302
5 Construction	484	464	583	626	573	626	609	763	1142	1111	965	619
6 Wholesale and retail trade, restaurants and hotels	3443	3453	3880	4033	4929	5739	6269	7687	9456	9468	8951	8647
A Wholesale and retail trade	2573	2559	2886	3051	3743	4235	4543	5787	7650	7420	6959	7054
B Restaurants and hotels	666	664	693	725	771	945	1212	1421	1806	2048	1992	1593
7 Transport, storage and communication	4187	3656	3522	4100	5142	5867	5674	6840	8152	9601	9154	9165
A Transport and storage	2426	1896	1721	2100	2756	2790	2568	2949	3923	4505	4444	5385
B Communication	1456	1465	1491	1685	1858	2301	2572	2881	4229	5096	4710	3780
8 Finance, insurance, real estate and business services	12687	12811	14080	15709	17741	18987	21828	26811	34516	41185	41263	...
A Financial institutions	2977	3161	3778	3655	4976	6383	5915	7660	4078	5245	4803	...
B Insurance	604	660	695	794	711	706	811	967	1565	1955	2349	...
C Real estate and business services	10633	10653	11598	13142	14613	15380	17715	21489	28873	33985	34111	25835
Real estate except dwellings	1959	2515	2678	2695	2895	3526	4192	5980	9519	12999	14205	9190
Dwellings	8674	8138	8920	10447	11718	11854	13523	15509	19354	20986	19906	16645
9 Community, social and personal services	3384	3466	3737	4022	4485	4843	5274	5863	6188	8091	9141	...
A Sanitary and similar services	605	553	610	633	660	637	733	844	1027	1203	1247	1074
B Social and related community services	1556	1695	1812	1924	2128	2326	2511	2690	3039	3793	4096	4133
Educational services	845	874	839	894	979	1063	1152	1311	1387	1757	1873	1776
Medical, dental, other health and veterinary services	711	821	973	1030	1149	1263	1359	1379	1652	2036	2223	2357
C Recreational and cultural services	1019	1048	1094	1218	1346	1455	1434	1609	2122	3095	3798	...
D Personal and household services												...
Statistical discrepancy	1620	1909	2091	2492	2955	3391	4051	4787	6920	5526	5073	4495
Total Industries	39793	39537	42438	46162	52380	57545	61434	71077	86857	98710	99867	88916
Producers of Government Services	1768	1767	2386	2453	2587	2808	3080	3000	3000	4552	6161	6526
Private Non-Profit Institutions Serving Households	...	...	...	...	...	...	...	...	...	...	...	...
Total	41561	41304	44824	48615	54967	60353	64514	74077	89857	103262	106028	95442

a) Item 'Electricity, gas and water' is included in item 'Mining and Quarrying'.

United Kingdom

2.12 Gross Fixed Capital Formation by Kind of Activity of Owner, ISIC Divisions, in Constant Prices

Million Pounds Sterling

	1980	1981	1982	1983	1984	1985	1986	1987	1988	1989	1990	1991
					At constant prices of:1985							
					All Producers							
1 Agriculture, hunting, forestry and fishing	1293	1148	1402	1511	1507	1181	1156	1196	1251	1211	1049	924
A Agriculture and hunting	1122	953	1143	1245	1139	845	757	787	1103	1077	926	830
B Forestry and logging	82	88	82	89	111	128	131	128	146	129	122	92
C Fishing	11	3	4	4	8	13	5	8	2	5	1	2
2 Mining and quarrying a	4352	4574	4516	4191	3805	3711	3352	2717	2718	2772	3288	4496
A Coal mining	1025	889	923	836	344	627	578	543	473	344	300	233
B Crude petroleum and natural gas production	3340	3683	3594	3355	3461	3084	2774	2174	2245	2428	2988	4263
C Metal ore mining	...	...	...	...	...	...	...	...	...	...	...	...
D Other mining	...	...	...	...	...	...	...	...	...	...	...	...
3 Manufacturing	9781	7672	7482	7410	8823	10118	9423	10048	11198	12395	11759	10347
A Manufacturing of food, beverages and tobacco	1304	1118	1157	1102	1316	1395	1248	1291	1584	1602	1624	1710
B Textile, wearing apparel and leather industries	308	217	269	276	355	384	432	468	500	427	347	256
C Manufacture of wood, and wood products, including furniture	233	129	133	152	167	192	183	233	305	306	245	182
D Manufacture of paper and paper products, printing and publishing	751	569	518	563	740	828	919	1093	1551	1480	1123	1022
E Manufacture of chemicals and chemical petroleum, coal, rubber and plastic products	341	240	237	256	379	391	395	492	579	625	577	489
F Manufacture of non-metalic mineral products except products of petroleum and coal	588	404	414	407	534	542	445	588	770	890	699	435
G Basic metal industries	516	363	304	275	251	360	403	504	570	603	884	368
H Manufacture of fabricated metal products, machinery and equipment	4631	3474	3246	3322	4006	4590	4467	4452	5267	6380	6169	5816
I Other manufacturing industries	89	65	82	69	57	53	55	59	72	82	91	69
4 Electricity, gas and water a	2732	2873	3002	3321	3206	3033	3187	3141	3319	3741	4125	4775
A Electricity, gas and steam	2356	2540	2636	2913	2776	2640	2742	2611	2663	3096	3223	3750
B Water works and supply	372	335	366	408	430	393	445	530	656	645	902	1025
5 Construction	630	567	653	691	609	626	582	687	998	908	736	458
6 Wholesale and retail trade, restaurants and hotels	4341	4024	4351	4427	5237	5739	5956	6995	8360	7812	6998	6938
A Wholesale and retail trade	3275	3006	3244	3364	3986	4235	4311	5249	6790	6173	5494	...
B Restaurants and hotels	817	753	775	789	818	945	1148	1275	1570	1639	1504	...
7 Transport, storage and communication	5476	4338	3993	4524	5423	5867	5478	6281	7228	8128	7430	7321
A Transport and storage	3149	2234	1973	2309	2895	2790	2453	2679	3384	3620	3427	4231
B Communication	1916	1749	1670	1877	1976	2301	2478	2660	3844	4508	4003	3090
8 Finance, insurance, real estate and business services	18596	17122	18532	19737	21452	22469	23587	27403	29370	32571	30808	...
A Financial institutions	3587	3533	4064	3856	5167	6383	5784	7208	3772	4753	4119	...
B Insurance	654	665	718	825	746	706	770	891	1379	1579	1762	...
C Real estate and business services	14391	12913	13709	15056	15539	15380	16882	19272	24219	26239	24927	...
Real estate except dwellings	2164	2608	2753	2809	2989	3526	4077	5575	8671	10943	11333	...
Dwellings	12379	10247	10899	12247	12550	11854	12805	13697	15548	15296	13594	11020
9 Community, social and personal services	3800	3588	3772	4035	4332	4418	4553	4877	5353	6287	6641	...
A Sanitary and similar services	725	583	641	663	682	637	717	818	908	947	937	833
B Social and related community services	1832	1825	1935	2059	2235	2326	2386	2442	2571	2870	2865	3035

2.12 Gross Fixed Capital Formation by Kind of Activity of Owner, ISIC Divisions, in Constant Prices
(Continued)

Million Pounds Sterling

	1980	1981	1982	1983	1984	1985	1986	1987	1988	1989	1990	1991
					At constant prices of:1985							
Educational services	994	941	898	953	1024	1063	1099	1197	1189	1333	1280	1276
Medical, dental, other health and veterinary services	837	883	1038	1106	1211	1263	1287	1245	1382	1537	1585	1759
C Recreational and cultural services	1245	1181	1195	1313	1415	1455	1367	1476	1874	2470	2839	...
D Personal and household services												...
Statistical discrepancy	2250	2456	2723	1064	951	334	1391	1345	4563	3278	2795	2427
Total Industries b	51392	46525	48422	50920	55373	57545	58717	64735	74358	79103	75629	67285
Producers of Government Services	2073	1823	2488	2556	2661	2808	3096	3018	3037	3894	4835	5177
Private Non-Profit Institutions Serving Households	...	...	...	...	...	...	...	...	...	...	...	...
Statistical discrepancy	-49	-50	5	...	...	...	...	...	...	...	...	...
Total	53416	48298	50915	53476	58034	60353	61813	67753	77395	82997	80464	72462

a) Item 'Electricity, gas and water' is included in item 'Mining and Quarrying'.
b) For years prior to 1983 in constant 1985 prices, components do not add up to total due to the
method used to rebase to 1985 prices.

2.13 Stocks of Reproducible Fixed Assets, by Type of Good and Owner, in Current Prices

Thousand Million Pounds Sterling

	TOTAL		Total Private		Public Enterprises		General Government	
	Gross	Net	Gross	Net	Gross	Net	Gross	Net
					1980			
1 Residential buildings	359.8	248.6	242.1	157.6	10.1	8.7	107.6	82.3
2 Non-residential buildings	...	...	...	...	...	...	...	...
3 Other construction	449.2	306.2	198.4	131.8	107.8	63.4	142.2	111.0
4 Land improvement and plantation and orchard development	...	...	...	...	...	...	...	...
5 Producers' durable goods	348.6	197.4	224.0	129.3	112.1	60.3	12.4	7.8
A Transport equipment	56.1	29.5	41.0	22.9	13.4	5.8	1.7	0.9
B Machinery and equipment	292.5	167.9	183.0	106.4	98.7	54.5	10.7	6.9
6 Breeding stock, dairy cattle, etc.	...	...	...	...	...	...	...	...
Total a	1157.6	752.2	664.5	418.7	230.0	132.4	262.2	201.1
					1981			
1 Residential buildings	389.6	268.1	264.8	172.6	11.0	9.4	113.8	86.1
2 Non-residential buildings	...	...	...	...	...	...	...	...
3 Other construction	474.4	322.5	208.1	137.2	114.1	67.1	151.3	118.1
4 Land improvement and plantation and orchard development	...	...	...	...	...	...	...	...
5 Producers' durable goods	383.2	214.1	249.1	141.8	120.4	63.7	13.6	8.5
A Transport equipment	58.3	30.1	43.2	23.5	13.4	5.6	1.8	0.9
B Machinery and equipment	324.8	184.0	205.9	118.3	107.1	58.1	11.8	7.6
6 Breeding stock, dairy cattle, etc.	...	...	...	...	...	...	...	...
Total a	1247.2	804.7	722.0	451.6	245.5	140.2	278.7	212.7
					1982			
1 Residential buildings	406.9	278.7	283.4	185.0	11.4	9.7	112.2	84.0
2 Non-residential buildings	...	...	...	...	...	...	...	...
3 Other construction	475.0	322.2	208.6	136.9	113.6	66.8	152.0	118.5
4 Land improvement and plantation and orchard development	...	...	...	...	...	...	...	...
5 Producers' durable goods	414.9	228.7	272.3	153.2	127.8	66.4	14.7	9.1
A Transport equipment	60.1	30.4	44.9	24.1	13.4	5.4	1.8	0.9
B Machinery and equipment	354.8	198.3	227.4	129.1	114.4	61.0	12.9	8.2
6 Breeding stock, dairy cattle, etc.	...	...	...	...	...	...	...	...
Total a	1296.8	829.6	764.3	475.1	252.8	142.9	278.9	211.6

2.13 Stocks of Reproducible Fixed Assets, by Type of Good and Owner, in Current Prices
(Continued)

Thousand Million Pounds Sterling

	TOTAL		Total Private		Public Enterprises		General Government	
	Gross	Net	Gross	Net	Gross	Net	Gross	Net
1983								
1 Residential buildings	440.5	300.5	312.9	204.5	12.1	10.2	115.5	85.7
2 Non-residential buildings	...	...	...	...	...	...	...	...
3 Other construction	483.2	327.1	213.6	139.3	113.9	67.2	154.8	120.7
4 Land improvement and plantation and orchard development	...	...	...	...	...	...	...	...
5 Producers' durable goods	442.9	241.3	292.1	162.1	135.0	69.4	15.8	10.0
A Transport equipment	62.1	30.8	46.5	24.3	13.7	5.6	1.8	1.0
B Machinery and equipment	380.9	210.5	245.6	137.8	121.3	63.8	14.0	9.0
6 Breeding stock, dairy cattle, etc.	...	...	...	...	...	...	...	...
Total a	1366.6	868.9	818.6	505.9	261.0	146.8	286.1	216.4
1984								
1 Residential buildings	478.5	325.3	345.9	230.9	12.9	10.8	119.7	83.5
2 Non-residential buildings	...	...	...	...	...	...	...	...
3 Other construction	503.9	341.7	228.2	148.6	112.8	66.1	162.9	127.0
4 Land improvement and plantation and orchard development	...	...	...	...	...	...	...	...
5 Producers' durable goods	475.1	256.5	348.3	189.7	109.8	55.9	17.0	11.0
A Transport equipment	65.9	32.2	50.4	25.5	13.5	5.5	1.9	1.2
B Machinery and equipment	409.2	224.4	297.9	164.2	96.2	50.4	15.1	9.8
6 Breeding stock, dairy cattle, etc.	...	...	...	...	...	...	...	...
Total a	1457.5	923.5	922.4	569.2	235.5	132.8	299.6	221.5
1985								
1 Residential buildings	516.3	349.2	383.9	251.3	13.6	11.3	118.9	86.6
2 Non-residential buildings	...	...	...	...	...	...	...	...
3 Other construction	534.5	361.8	244.4	158.9	116.9	68.6	173.1	134.3
4 Land improvement and plantation and orchard development	...	...	...	...	...	...	...	...
5 Producers' durable goods	507.8	273.3	374.9	203.5	114.5	57.7	18.5	11.9
A Transport equipment	71.0	34.2	55.1	27.4	13.9	5.6	2.1	1.2
B Machinery and equipment	436.8	239.1	319.8	176.1	100.6	52.1	16.4	10.7
6 Breeding stock, dairy cattle, etc.	...	...	...	...	...	...	...	...
Total a	1558.6	984.3	1003.2	613.7	245.0	137.6	310.5	232.8
1986								
1 Residential buildings	563.9	379.1	422.8	277.6	14.2	11.8	126.9	89.8
2 Non-residential buildings	...	...	...	...	...	...	...	...
3 Other construction	563.6	387.6	276.3	185.8	105.0	61.1	182.4	140.7
4 Land improvement and plantation and orchard development	...	...	...	...	...	...	...	...
5 Producers' durable goods	538.5	289.4	405.7	220.3	113.1	55.9	19.7	13.2
A Transport equipment	74.3	36.0	58.4	29.0	13.9	5.7	2.0	1.4
B Machinery and equipment	464.1	253.4	347.3	191.3	99.1	50.2	17.7	11.8
6 Breeding stock, dairy cattle, etc.	...	...	...	...	...	...	...	...
Total a	1666.0	1056.1	1104.8	683.7	232.3	128.8	329.0	243.7
1987								
1 Residential buildings	633.7	423.2	484.5	315.1	15.3	12.5	133.9	95.5
2 Non-residential buildings	...	...	...	...	...	...	...	...
3 Other construction	612.7	421.5	304.1	204.9	109.3	63.9	199.0	152.7
4 Land improvement and plantation and orchard development	...	...	...	...	...	...	...	...
5 Producers' durable goods	571.2	307.9	436.9	238.0	113.2	55.6	21.1	14.3
A Transport equipment	79.0	39.1	65.6	33.0	11.3	4.6	2.1	1.5
B Machinery and equipment	492.3	268.8	371.3	205.0	102.0	51.0	19.0	12.8
6 Breeding stock, dairy cattle, etc.	...	...	...	...	...	...	...	...
Total a	1817.6	1152.6	1225.5	758.0	237.8	132.0	354.0	262.5

2.13 Stocks of Reproducible Fixed Assets, by Type of Good and Owner, in Current Prices
(Continued)

Thousand Million Pounds Sterling

	TOTAL		Total Private		Public Enterprises		General Government	
	Gross	Net	Gross	Net	Gross	Net	Gross	Net
1988								
1 Residential buildings	733.7	488.1	567.5	369.0	17.1	13.8	149.2	105.3
2 Non-residential buildings	...	...	...	...	...	...	...	...
3 Other construction	712.9	486.0	361.6	237.3	121.9	72.1	229.4	176.7
4 Land improvement and plantation and orchard development	...	...	...	...	...	...	...	...
5 Producers' durable goods	602.0	327.3	462.5	255.2	116.9	56.9	22.6	15.2
A Transport equipment	84.1	42.6	70.8	36.6	11.0	4.5	2.3	1.5
B Machinery and equipment	517.9	284.7	391.7	218.6	105.9	52.4	20.3	13.7
6 Breeding stock, dairy cattle, etc.	...	...	...	...	...	...	...	...
Total a	2048.6	1301.4	1391.6	861.5	255.9	142.8	401.2	297.2
1989								
1 Residential buildings	831.8	551.2	647.0	419.9	18.9	15.2	166.0	116.1
2 Non-residential buildings	...	...	...	...	...	...	...	...
3 Other construction	798.4	546.4	454.1	300.9	86.6	47.5	257.7	197.9
4 Land improvement and plantation and orchard development	...	...	...	...	...	...	...	...
5 Producers' durable goods	653.4	359.9	507.1	284.3	121.0	58.6	25.3	17.0
A Transport equipment	91.2	47.5	78.4	41.6	10.1	4.2	2.7	1.7
B Machinery and equipment	562.2	312.4	428.7	242.7	110.9	54.4	22.6	15.3
6 Breeding stock, dairy cattle, etc.	...	...	...	...	...	...	...	...
Total a	2283.6	1457.5	1608.2	1005.1	226.5	121.3	449.0	331.0
1990								
1 Residential buildings	886.5	584.8	721.6	468.4	19.7	15.7	145.2	100.6
2 Non-residential buildings	...	...	...	...	...	...	...	...
3 Other construction	823.7	566.7	475.3	316.8	83.6	46.1	264.9	203.7
4 Land improvement and plantation and orchard development	...	...	...	...	...	...	...	...
5 Producers' durable goods	697.5	387.6	595.6	333.5	73.9	35.1	27.9	18.8
A Transport equipment	98.5	52.1	85.5	45.8	10.0	4.3	3.0	1.9
B Machinery and equipment	598.9	335.5	510.1	287.7	64.0	30.8	24.9	16.9
6 Breeding stock, dairy cattle, etc.	...	...	...	...	...	...	...	...
Total a	2407.7	1539.1	1792.5	1118.7	177.2	96.9	438.0	323.1
1991								
1 Residential buildings	897.0	587.9	735.0	474.7	19.4	15.3	142.9	97.8
2 Non-residential buildings	...	...	...	...	...	...	...	...
3 Other construction	812.9	561.4	483.8	322.8	71.9	41.0	257.2	197.6
4 Land improvement and plantation and orchard development	...	...	...	...	...	...	...	...
5 Producers' durable goods	714.6	399.1	630.6	353.0	54.8	26.4	29.2	19.6
A Transport equipment	100.9	53.4	88.2	47.2	9.5	4.2	3.2	2.0
B Machinery and equipment	613.7	345.7	542.4	305.8	45.3	22.2	26.1	17.6
6 Breeding stock, dairy cattle, etc.	...	...	...	...	...	...	...	...
Total a	2424.5	1548.4	1849.4	1150.5	146.1	82.7	429.3	315.0

a) The total includes statistical adjustment not allocated to the components.

2.14 Stocks of Reproducible Fixed Assets, by Type of Good and Owner, in Constant Prices

Thousand Million Pounds Sterling

	TOTAL		Total Private		Public Enterprises		General Government	
	Gross	Net	Gross	Net	Gross	Net	Gross	Net
At constant prices of:1985								
1980								
1 Residential buildings	450.5	311.4	313.2	205.2	11.7	10.1	125.6	96.1
2 Non-residential buildings	...	...	...	...	...	...	...	...
3 Other construction	473.5	322.8	204.9	136.1	116.2	68.2	151.5	118.5
4 Land improvement and plantation and orchard development	...	...	...	...	...	...	...	...
5 Producers' durable goods	453.6	256.5	291.4	168.8	146.4	78.1	15.8	9.6
A Transport equipment	73.4	38.8	54.4	30.9	16.8	6.8	2.2	1.1
B Machinery and equipment	380.2	217.7	237.0	137.9	129.6	71.2	13.6	8.5
6 Breeding stock, dairy cattle, etc.	...	...	...	...	...	...	...	...
Total a	1377.6	890.7	809.5	510.1	274.3	156.4	292.9	224.2
1981								
1 Residential buildings	459.7	316.2	322.6	211.2	12.1	10.3	125.0	94.7
2 Non-residential buildings	...	...	...	...	...	...	...	...
3 Other construction	482.3	327.8	210.7	138.9	116.5	68.6	154.2	120.3
4 Land improvement and plantation and orchard development	...	...	...	...	...	...	...	...
5 Producers' durable goods	461.6	257.5	299.8	171.4	145.7	76.4	16.1	9.6
A Transport equipment	71.7	37.1	53.4	29.7	16.2	6.4	2.1	1.0
B Machinery and equipment	389.9	220.4	246.4	141.7	129.5	70.1	14.0	8.6
6 Breeding stock, dairy cattle, etc.	...	...	...	...	...	...	...	...
Total a	1403.6	901.5	833.1	521.5	274.3	155.3	295.3	224.6
1982								
1 Residential buildings	469.4	321.4	334.3	219.0	12.4	10.5	122.7	91.9
2 Non-residential buildings	...	...	...	...	...	...	...	...
3 Other construction	492.2	333.9	216.4	142.0	117.2	68.9	157.7	122.9
4 Land improvement and plantation and orchard development	...	...	...	...	...	...	...	...
5 Producers' durable goods	469.3	258.3	307.6	173.8	145.3	74.7	16.4	9.7
A Transport equipment	70.0	35.5	52.6	28.7	15.4	5.8	2.1	1.0
B Machinery and equipment	399.3	222.8	255.0	145.1	130.0	68.9	14.3	8.7
6 Breeding stock, dairy cattle, etc.	...	...	...	...	...	...	...	...
Total a	1430.9	913.6	858.3	534.8	274.9	154.1	296.8	224.5
1983								
1 Residential buildings	480.2	327.7	345.6	226.4	12.7	10.8	121.9	90.5
2 Non-residential buildings	...	...	...	...	...	...	...	...
3 Other construction	502.0	339.9	222.4	145.1	117.5	69.4	161.2	125.4
4 Land improvement and plantation and orchard development	...	...	...	...	...	...	...	...
5 Producers' durable goods	477.2	259.6	314.4	175.5	145.9	74.1	17.0	10.0
A Transport equipment	68.5	34.0	51.7	27.5	14.7	5.5	2.1	1.0
B Machinery and equipment	408.7	225.6	262.7	148.0	131.2	68.6	14.9	9.0
6 Breeding stock, dairy cattle, etc.	...	...	...	...	...	...	...	...
Total a	1459.4	927.2	882.4	547.0	276.1	154.3	300.1	225.9
1984								
1 Residential buildings	490.7	333.7	356.3	233.5	13.1	11.0	121.3	89.2
2 Non-residential buildings	...	...	...	...	...	...	...	...
3 Other construction	512.7	347.8	232.5	151.5	114.3	67.0	166.0	129.3
4 Land improvement and plantation and orchard development	...	...	...	...	...	...	...	...
5 Producers' durable goods	487.4	263.2	357.2	196.4	112.7	56.4	17.5	10.4
A Transport equipment	68.3	33.4	52.4	27.2	13.9	5.2	2.0	1.0
B Machinery and equipment	419.1	229.8	304.7	169.1	98.8	51.3	15.5	9.4
6 Breeding stock, dairy cattle, etc.	...	...	...	...	...	...	...	...
Total a	1490.8	944.7	946.0	581.4	240.1	134.4	304.8	228.9

2.14 Stocks of Reproducible Fixed Assets, by Type of Good and Owner, in Constant Prices
(Continued)

Thousand Million Pounds Sterling

	TOTAL		Total Private		Public Enterprises		General Government	
	Gross	Net	Gross	Net	Gross	Net	Gross	Net
	At constant prices of:1985							
	1985							
1 Residential buildings	501.0	339.2	366.5	239.9	13.3	11.1	121.1	88.2
2 Non-residential buildings	...	...	...	...	...	...	...	...
3 Other construction	523.7	354.9	238.3	154.7	115.2	67.8	170.1	132.4
4 Land improvement and plantation and orchard development	...	...	...	...	...	...	...	...
5 Producers' durable goods	499.5	269.1	369.0	202.8	112.2	55.5	18.2	10.8
A Transport equipment	68.2	33.0	52.9	27.1	13.4	5.1	2.0	1.0
B Machinery and equipment	431.3	236.1	316.1	175.7	98.8	50.5	16.3	9.8
6 Breeding stock, dairy cattle, etc.	...	...	...	...	...	...	...	...
Total a	1524.2	963.2	973.8	597.4	240.7	134.4	309.4	231.4
	1986							
1 Residential buildings	512.3	345.4	380.0	248.7	13.6	11.2	118.8	85.6
2 Non-residential buildings	...	...	...	...	...	...	...	...
3 Other construction	535.1	362.3	259.5	167.6	101.8	59.3	173.9	135.3
4 Land improvement and plantation and orchard development	...	...	...	...	...	...	...	...
5 Producers' durable goods	508.4	273.8	383.1	210.8	106.5	51.7	18.8	11.2
A Transport equipment	65.3	31.4	50.8	25.8	12.7	4.8	1.8	0.9
B Machinery and equipment	443.1	242.5	332.3	185.0	93.8	47.0	17.0	10.3
6 Breeding stock, dairy cattle, etc.	...	...	...	...	...	...	...	...
Total a	1555.8	981.5	1022.6	627.1	221.9	122.2	311.5	232.1
	1987							
1 Residential buildings	524.2	352.2	389.6	254.7	13.8	11.3	120.8	86.2
2 Non-residential buildings	...	...	...	...	...	...	...	...
3 Other construction	548.8	371.9	269.8	174.2	100.7	58.9	178.3	138.7
4 Land improvement and plantation and orchard development	...	...	...	...	...	...	...	...
5 Producers' durable goods	520.2	281.2	398.0	220.1	102.7	49.5	19.5	11.6
A Transport equipment	65.0	31.9	53.3	27.4	9.9	3.6	1.7	0.9
B Machinery and equipment	455.2	249.2	344.7	192.7	92.8	45.9	17.7	10.8
6 Breeding stock, dairy cattle, etc.	...	...	...	...	...	...	...	...
Total a	1593.2	1005.3	1057.4	649.0	217.2	119.7	318.6	236.5
	1988							
1 Residential buildings	538.0	360.8	401.3	262.8	14.0	11.4	122.7	86.6
2 Non-residential buildings	...	...	...	...	...	...	...	...
3 Other construction	564.5	383.4	281.6	182.1	100.0	59.0	182.9	142.3
4 Land improvement and plantation and orchard development	...	...	...	...	...	...	...	...
5 Producers' durable goods	536.0	292.6	413.7	231.5	101.8	48.7	20.6	12.4
A Transport equipment	65.5	32.9	54.3	28.4	9.4	3.5	1.8	0.9
B Machinery and equipment	470.5	259.7	359.4	203.1	92.3	45.2	18.8	11.5
6 Breeding stock, dairy cattle, etc.	...	...	...	...	...	...	...	...
Total a	1638.5	1036.8	1096.6	676.4	215.8	119.1	326.2	241.3
	1989							
1 Residential buildings	551.6	368.7	412.4	269.9	14.2	11.4	125.0	87.4
2 Non-residential buildings	...	...	...	...	...	...	...	...
3 Other construction	582.5	397.2	328.9	215.2	65.5	35.7	188.1	146.4
4 Land improvement and plantation and orchard development	...	...	...	...	...	...	...	...
5 Producers' durable goods	555.3	307.6	434.0	246.8	99.1	47.2	22.1	13.6
A Transport equipment	66.6	34.5	56.2	30.2	8.4	3.2	1.9	1.1
B Machinery and equipment	488.7	273.1	377.8	216.5	90.7	44.0	20.2	12.6
6 Breeding stock, dairy cattle, etc.	...	...	...	...	...	...	...	...
Total a	1689.4	1073.5	1175.3	731.9	178.8	94.3	335.2	247.4

2.14 Stocks of Reproducible Fixed Assets, by Type of Good and Owner, in Constant Prices
(Continued)

Thousand Million Pounds Sterling

	TOTAL		Total Private		Public Enterprises		General Government	
	Gross	Net	Gross	Net	Gross	Net	Gross	Net
At constant prices of:1985								
1990								
1 Residential buildings	563.3	374.7	442.9	289.8	14.4	11.5	106.0	73.5
2 Non-residential buildings	...	...	...	...	...	...	...	...
3 Other construction	601.7	412.4	344.2	226.4	63.5	34.8	194.1	151.2
4 Land improvement and plantation and orchard development	...	...	...	...	...	...	...	...
5 Producers' durable goods	572.6	320.2	490.1	278.2	58.7	27.2	23.7	14.8
A Transport equipment	67.0	35.1	56.9	30.7	8.1	3.3	2.0	1.1
B Machinery and equipment	505.6	285.1	433.3	247.4	50.6	24.0	21.7	13.7
6 Breeding stock, dairy cattle, etc.	...	...	...	...	...	...	...	...
Total a	1737.6	1107.3	1277.2	794.4	136.6	73.5	323.8	239.5
1991								
1 Residential buildings	572.5	378.0	450.7	293.0	14.6	11.5	107.3	73.5
2 Non-residential buildings	...	...	...	...	...	...	...	...
3 Other construction	620.1	425.6	362.4	237.6	57.6	32.6	200.1	155.5
4 Land improvement and plantation and orchard development	...	...	...	...	...	...	...	...
5 Producers' durable goods	585.0	327.9	516.2	291.8	43.9	20.5	24.9	15.6
A Transport equipment	66.2	34.4	56.4	30.0	7.8	3.3	2.1	1.1
B Machinery and equipment	518.8	293.5	459.8	261.8	36.1	17.2	22.8	14.5
6 Breeding stock, dairy cattle, etc.	...	...	...	...	...	...	...	...
Total a	1777.6	1131.5	1329.3	822.4	116.1	64.6	332.3	244.6

a) The total includes statistical adjustment not allocated to the components.

2.15 Stocks of Reproducible Fixed Assets by Kind of Activity, in Current Prices

Thousand Million Pounds Sterling

	1980		1981		1982		1983		1984		1985	
	Gross	Net	Gross	Net	Gross	Net	Gross	Net	Gross	Net	Gross	Net
1 Residential buildings	359.8	248.6	389.6	268.1	406.9	278.7	440.5	300.5	478.5	325.3	516.3	349.2
2 Non-residential buildings a	...	...	...	...	...	...	...	...	...	...	...	...
3 Other construction ba	449.2	306.2	474.4	322.5	475.0	322.2	483.2	327.1	503.9	341.7	534.5	361.8
A Industries	385.4	246.2	405.7	258.0	405.2	256.9	411.3	260.0	428.4	271.3	454.9	287.9
1 Agriculture	13.6	8.1	14.2	8.3	14.3	8.3	14.8	8.5	15.6	8.9	16.4	9.2
2 Mining and quarrying	21.3	13.5	23.6	14.8	24.6	15.3	25.9	16.0	27.7	17.0	29.6	17.9
3 Manufacturing	75.2	43.0	76.7	43.4	74.9	41.9	75.1	41.4	77.0	42.0	79.8	43.2
4 Electricity, gas and water	43.6	26.4	46.8	28.1	47.0	28.1	47.8	28.5	49.1	29.1	50.8	30.0
5 Construction	3.2	2.3	3.3	2.3	3.3	2.3	3.3	2.3	3.4	2.3	3.6	2.4
6 Wholesale and retail trade	34.7	25.8	36.4	27.0	36.6	27.1	37.3	27.6	39.5	29.1	43.4	32.0
7 Transport and communication	45.1	23.2	47.5	24.5	46.8	24.2	46.9	24.4	47.9	25.1	49.4	26.1
8 Finance, etc.	48.3	36.5	51.2	38.7	52.1	39.4	53.6	40.5	56.9	43.0	62.8	47.3
9 Community, social and personal services	100.4	67.4	106.0	70.9	105.7	70.3	106.7	70.8	111.4	74.8	119.2	79.7
B Producers of government services	63.8	60.0	68.7	64.5	69.8	65.3	71.9	67.2	75.5	70.4	79.6	73.9
C Other producers	...	...	...	...	...	...	...	...	...	...	...	...
4 Land improvement and development and plantation and orchard development	...	...	...	...	...	...	...	...	...	...	...	...
5 Producers' durable goods	348.6	197.4	383.2	214.1	414.9	228.7	442.9	241.3	475.1	256.5	507.8	273.3
A Industries	344.4	195.0	378.6	211.5	409.8	225.9	437.5	238.5	469.1	253.1	501.2	269.4
1 Agriculture	11.6	7.0	12.1	7.2	12.8	7.6	13.3	8.0	13.3	7.8	13.3	7.9
2 Mining and quarrying	12.0	7.5	14.2	8.7	16.5	9.9	18.5	10.8	19.7	11.0	21.0	11.4
3 Manufacturing	136.6	73.7	149.3	78.9	160.8	83.2	170.1	86.3	179.9	90.3	190.0	94.8
4 Electricity, gas and water	54.2	30.2	59.3	32.7	63.9	34.8	67.9	36.7	71.8	38.5	75.6	40.0

2.15 Stocks of Reproducible Fixed Assets by Kind of Activity, in Current Prices
(Continued)

Thousand Million Pounds Sterling

	1980		1981		1982		1983		1984		1985	
	Gross	Net	Gross	Net	Gross	Net	Gross	Net	Gross	Net	Gross	Net
5 Construction	9.7	5.3	10.5	5.6	11.2	5.8	11.5	5.9	11.9	6.0	12.2	6.0
6 Wholesale and retail trade	28.0	17.0	31.4	18.9	34.6	20.7	37.5	22.3	41.3	24.6	45.6	27.3
7 Transport and communication	55.4	29.2	58.0	30.1	59.3	30.1	61.1	30.5	65.2	31.9	67.0	32.4
8 Finance, etc.	23.0	16.7	28.2	20.2	33.5	23.7	38.7	26.9	45.4	31.2	54.1	37.0
9 Community, social and personal services	13.9	8.3	15.5	9.2	17.2	10.0	18.8	10.9	20.6	11.8	22.4	12.8
B Producers of government services	4.1	2.4	4.6	2.6	5.0	2.8	5.4	3.1	6.0	3.4	6.7	3.9
C Other producers	...	...	...	...	...	...	...	...	...	...	...	...
6 Breeding stock, dairy cattle, etc.	...	...	...	...	...	...	...	...	...	...	...	...
Total c	1157.6	752.2	1247.2	804.7	1296.8	829.6	1366.6	868.9	1457.5	923.5	1558.6	984.3

	1986		1987		1988		1989		1990		1991	
	Gross	Net	Gross	Net	Gross	Net	Gross	Net	Gross	Net	Gross	Net
1 Residential buildings	563.9	379.1	633.7	423.2	733.7	488.1	831.8	551.2	886.5	584.8	897.0	587.9
2 Non-residential buildings a	...	...	...	...	...	...	...	...	...	...	...	...
3 Other construction ba	563.6	387.6	612.7	421.5	712.9	486.0	798.4	546.4	823.7	566.7	812.9	561.4
A Industries	480.5	310.8	522.2	338.1	607.1	388.8	680.0	438.0	700.7	454.2	690.9	449.8
1 Agriculture	17.0	9.4	18.2	9.8	20.2	10.7	22.0	11.5	22.1	11.3	21.1	...
2 Mining and quarrying	31.1	18.4	33.5	19.3	37.8	21.5	41.5	23.3	42.5	23.8	...	...
3 Manufacturing	82.1	44.0	86.7	46.1	96.1	50.9	104.7	55.4	105.2	55.4	...	...
4 Electricity, gas and water	52.2	30.7	56.0	32.5	63.2	36.9	68.8	39.9	69.2	40.0	...	...
5 Construction	3.7	2.5	4.0	2.6	4.5	3.0	5.0	3.3	5.1	3.4	...	...
6 Wholesale and retail trade	47.6	35.1	53.6	39.9	63.0	47.2	71.7	54.0	74.8	56.5	...	...
7 Transport and communication	50.6	33.7	54.0	36.2	70.3	41.5	77.7	46.4	79.7	48.4	...	...
8 Finance, etc.	69.1	52.1	77.7	59.3	93.0	71.3	109.6	85.2	118.9	93.4	...	...
9 Community, social and personal services	127.1	84.9	138.6	92.3	159.0	105.8	179.0	119.1	183.2	122.0	...	...
B Producers of government services	83.2	76.8	90.5	83.4	105.8	97.3	118.4	108.4	123.0	112.5	122.0	111.6
C Other producers	...	...	...	...	...	...	...	...	...	...	...	...
4 Land improvement and development and plantation and orchard development	...	...	...	...	...	...	...	...	...	...	...	...
5 Producers' durable goods	538.5	289.4	571.2	307.9	602.0	327.3	653.4	359.9	697.5	387.6	714.6	399.1
A Industries	531.0	285.0	563.0	302.9	592.8	321.6	642.6	353.0	685.1	379.6	701.1	390.3
1 Agriculture	13.6	8.1	13.7	8.2	14.0	8.7	14.5	9.3	14.6	9.5	...	...
2 Mining and quarrying	22.0	11.6	22.2	11.3	22.3	10.9	22.8	10.8	22.9	10.7	...	...
3 Manufacturing	199.4	98.9	208.4	103.2	214.7	107.3	229.9	116.3	242.5	123.6	...	...
4 Electricity, gas and water	79.1	41.4	83.0	43.1	87.5	45.1	94.4	48.5	100.8	51.8	...	...
5 Construction	12.6	6.1	13.0	6.3	13.7	6.8	14.7	7.4	15.5	7.7	...	...
6 Wholesale and retail trade	49.6	29.7	53.5	32.2	58.4	35.9	64.9	40.3	69.5	43.2	...	...
7 Transport and communication	68.3	33.3	71.0	35.2	74.9	38.3	80.6	42.9	84.1	46.0	...	...
8 Finance, etc.	62.3	42.1	72.4	48.9	79.9	53.1	90.4	60.0	101.4	67.1	...	...
9 Community, social and personal services	24.1	13.7	25.8	14.6	27.3	15.5	30.4	17.6	34.0	20.1	...	...
B Producers of government services	7.5	4.4	8.3	5.0	9.3	5.7	10.8	6.9	12.4	8.0	13.4	8.8
C Other producers	...	...	...	...	...	...	...	...	...	...	...	...
6 Breeding stock, dairy cattle, etc.	...	...	...	...	...	...	...	...	...	...	...	...
Total c	1666.0	1056.1	1817.6	1152.6	2048.6	1301.4	2283.6	1457.5	2407.7	1539.1	2424.5	1548.4

a) Item 'Non-residential buildings' is included in item 'Other construction'.
b) Item 'Land improvement and plantation and orchard development' is included in item 'Other construction'.
c) The total includes statistical adjustment not allocated to the components.

United Kingdom

2.16 Stocks of Reproducible Fixed Assets by Kind of Activity, in Constant Prices

Thousand Million Pounds Sterling

	1980 Gross	1980 Net	1981 Gross	1981 Net	1982 Gross	1982 Net	1983 Gross	1983 Net	1984 Gross	1984 Net	1985 Gross	1985 Net
						At constant prices of:1985						
1 Residential buildings	450.5	311.4	459.7	316.2	469.4	321.4	480.2	327.7	490.7	333.7	501.0	339.2
2 Non-residential buildings a	...	...	...	...	...	...	...	...	...	...	...	...
3 Other construction ba	473.5	322.8	482.3	327.8	492.2	333.9	502.0	339.9	512.7	347.8	523.7	354.9
A Industries	405.1	258.5	412.4	262.2	420.1	266.3	427.7	270.5	436.0	276.3	444.5	281.2
1 Agriculture	14.4	8.4	14.8	8.4	14.8	8.6	15.3	8.8	15.8	9.0	16.1	9.1
2 Mining and quarrying	22.4	14.2	24.1	15.1	25.6	15.9	26.7	16.5	28.1	17.2	29.2	17.7
3 Manufacturing	77.9	44.5	78.0	44.1	78.0	43.6	77.9	42.9	78.0	42.5	78.3	42.4
4 Electricity, gas and water	47.3	28.6	47.8	28.7	48.4	29.0	49.1	29.3	49.7	29.5	50.3	29.7
5 Construction	3.3	2.3	3.4	2.3	3.4	2.3	3.4	2.4	3.5	2.4	3.5	2.4
6 Wholesale and retail trade	35.7	26.6	36.7	27.3	37.8	28.0	39.0	28.8	40.4	29.8	42.0	31.0
7 Transport and communication	48.6	25.0	48.5	25.0	48.4	25.1	48.4	25.2	48.6	25.5	48.6	25.6
8 Finance, etc.	49.7	37.5	51.6	39.0	53.9	40.7	56.2	42.4	58.4	44.1	60.6	45.7
9 Community, social and personal services	105.8	71.4	107.5	72.3	109.7	73.1	111.6	74.2	113.5	76.3	115.9	77.6
B Producers of government services	68.4	64.3	69.9	65.6	72.2	67.5	74.3	69.4	76.7	71.5	79.2	73.7
C Other producers	...	...	...	...	...	...	...	...	...	...	...	...
4 Land improvement and development and plantation and orchard development	...	...	...	...	...	...	...	...	...	...	...	...
5 Producers' durable goods	453.6	256.5	461.6	257.5	469.3	258.3	477.2	259.6	487.4	263.2	499.5	269.1
A Industries	448.4	253.5	456.2	254.5	463.7	255.2	471.4	256.3	481.3	259.7	492.9	265.3
1 Agriculture	14.9	9.1	14.6	8.7	14.2	8.5	13.9	8.3	13.5	8.0	13.0	7.7
2 Mining and quarrying	16.0	10.0	17.3	10.6	18.6	11.1	19.7	11.5	20.2	11.3	20.7	11.2
3 Manufacturing	180.8	97.6	182.2	96.3	183.2	94.8	183.9	93.4	185.2	93.0	187.0	93.3
4 Electricity, gas and water	71.8	40.0	72.2	39.8	72.6	39.6	73.3	39.6	73.8	39.6	74.2	39.3
5 Construction	12.2	6.6	12.2	6.5	12.2	6.3	12.3	6.3	12.2	6.1	12.1	6.0
6 Wholesale and retail trade	36.5	22.2	37.9	22.8	39.4	23.6	40.9	24.3	42.7	25.4	44.6	26.7
7 Transport and communication	71.3	37.8	69.8	36.4	68.0	34.6	66.6	33.3	66.2	32.4	65.8	31.8
8 Finance, etc.	27.2	19.6	31.6	22.6	36.2	25.5	40.6	28.1	46.3	31.8	53.5	36.7
9 Community, social and personal services	17.6	10.5	18.3	10.8	19.2	11.2	20.2	11.7	21.2	12.2	22.1	12.6
B Producers of government services	5.2	3.0	5.4	3.1	5.6	3.1	5.8	3.3	6.1	3.5	6.6	3.8
C Other producers	...	...	...	...	...	...	...	...	...	...	...	...
6 Breeding stock, dairy cattle, etc.	...	...	...	...	...	...	...	...	...	...	...	...
Total	1377.6	890.7	1403.6	901.5	1430.9	913.6	1459.4	927.2	1490.8	944.7	1524.2	963.2

	1986 Gross	1986 Net	1987 Gross	1987 Net	1988 Gross	1988 Net	1989 Gross	1989 Net	1990 Gross	1990 Net	1991 Gross	1991 Net
						At constant prices of:1985						
1 Residential buildings	512.3	345.4	524.2	352.2	538.0	360.8	551.6	368.7	563.3	374.7	572.5	378.0
2 Non-residential buildings a	...	...	...	...	...	...	...	...	...	...	...	...
3 Other construction ba	535.1	362.3	548.8	371.9	564.5	383.4	582.5	397.2	601.7	412.4	620.1	425.6
A Industries	453.2	286.2	464.1	293.3	477.0	302.3	491.7	313.3	507.0	324.8	521.2	334.3
1 Agriculture	16.3	9.0	16.5	9.0	16.7	8.9	16.8	8.7	16.9	8.6	...	...
2 Mining and quarrying	30.0	17.7	30.6	17.7	31.2	17.7	31.7	17.8	32.5	18.2	...	...
3 Manufacturing	78.5	42.1	78.8	41.9	79.2	42.0	79.8	42.2	80.2	42.3	...	...
4 Electricity, gas and water	51.0	30.0	51.2	30.2	51.4	29.6	51.6	29.4	51.9	29.4	...	...
5 Construction	3.6	2.4	3.6	2.4	3.7	2.5	3.8	2.5	3.9	2.6	...	...
6 Wholesale and retail trade	43.8	32.4	46.5	34.7	49.5	37.2	52.3	39.5	54.9	41.5	...	...
7 Transport and communication	48.7	25.9	48.8	26.2	49.2	26.5	49.7	27.1	50.1	27.5	...	...
8 Finance, etc.	63.3	47.8	67.3	50.7	72.6	55.7	79.4	61.7	86.6	68.0	...	...
9 Community, social and personal services	118.3	78.9	120.9	80.5	123.6	82.3	126.7	84.5	130.1	86.7	...	...
B Producers of government services	81.9	76.1	84.7	78.6	87.5	81.0	90.8	83.9	94.8	87.5	98.9	91.3

1928

2.16 Stocks of Reproducible Fixed Assets by Kind of Activity, in Constant Prices
(Continued)

Thousand Million Pounds Sterling

	1986		1987		1988		1989		1990		1991	
	Gross	Net	Gross	Net	Gross	Net	Gross	Net	Gross	Net	Gross	Net
At constant prices of:1985												
C Other producers	...	...	...	...	...	...	...	...	...	...	...	...
4 Land improvement and development and plantation and orchard development	...	...	...	...	...	...	...	...	...	...	...	...
5 Producers' durable goods	508.4	273.8	520.2	281.2	536.0	292.6	555.3	307.6	572.6	320.2	585.0	327.9
A Industries	501.3	269.6	512.5	276.0	527.5	287.3	545.7	301.5	561.9	313.2	573.3	320.3
1 Agriculture	12.6	7.5	12.1	7.3	12.0	7.4	12.0	7.6	11.8	7.7	...	...
2 Mining and quarrying	20.9	11.0	20.5	10.4	19.8	9.7	19.2	9.1	18.6	8.7	...	...
3 Manufacturing	188.5	93.5	189.9	94.1	193.0	96.6	196.9	99.8	200.5	102.4	...	...
4 Electricity, gas and water	74.5	39.1	74.6	38.9	74.8	38.3	75.3	38.4	76.0	38.6	...	...
5 Construction	11.9	5.8	11.8	5.8	12.1	6.0	12.3	6.2	12.3	6.2	...	...
6 Wholesale and retail trade	46.5	27.9	48.6	29.4	52.1	32.2	55.1	34.5	57.7	36.2	...	...
7 Transport and communication	63.4	31.0	63.2	30.9	64.8	33.1	66.9	35.5	68.2	37.2	...	...
8 Finance, etc.	60.0	40.8	68.0	45.9	74.0	50.0	81.6	55.1	88.6	59.6	...	...
9 Community, social and personal services	23.0	13.0	23.8	13.4	24.9	14.1	26.5	15.4	28.3	16.7	...	...
B Producers of government services	7.1	4.3	7.7	4.6	8.5	5.3	9.6	6.1	10.7	7.0	11.7	7.6
C Other producers	...	...	...	...	...	...	...	...	...	...	...	...
6 Breeding stock, dairy cattle, etc.	...	...	...	...	...	...	...	...	...	...	...	...
Total	1555.8	981.5	1593.2	1005.3	1638.5	1036.8	1689.4	1073.5	1737.6	1107.3	1777.6	1131.5

a) Item 'Non-residential buildings' is included in item 'Other construction'.
b) Item 'Land improvement and plantation and orchard development' is included in item 'Other construction'.

2.17 Exports and Imports of Goods and Services, Detail

Million Pounds Sterling

	1980	1981	1982	1983	1984	1985	1986	1987	1988	1989	1990	1991
Exports of Goods and Services												
1 Exports of merchandise, f.o.b.	47149	50668	55331	60700	70265	77991	72627	79153	80306	92108	101683	103394
2 Transport and communication	6940	6923	6665	6730	7512	7603	7333	7955	8324	9475	10165	9806
A In respect of merchandise imports	538	459	549	523	610	532	541	653	717	826	847	867
B Other	6402	6464	6116	6207	6902	7071	6792	7302	7607	8649	9318	8939
3 Insurance service charges	662	919	1019	1199	1372	2239	3200	3047	1882	990	431	720
A In respect of merchandise imports	12	18	17	5	11	41	32	27	16	8	3	-2
B Other	650	901	1002	1194	1361	2198	3168	3020	1866	982	428	722
4 Other commodities	4910	5814	6377	7221	7917	8597	9202	10249	10632	12157	13068	13744
5 Adjustments of merchandise exports to change-of-ownership basis	...	...	...	...	...	...	...	...	...	...	...	...
6 Direct purchases in the domestic market by non-residential households	3436	3513	3792	4661	5336	6276	6455	7217	7172	8026	8878	8207
7 Direct purchases in the domestic market by extraterritorial bodies	...	...	...	...	...	...	...	...	...	...	...	...
Total Exports of Goods and Services	63097	67837	73184	80511	92402	102706	98817	107621	108316	122756	134225	135871
Imports of Goods and Services												
1 Imports of merchandise, c.i.f.	48319	49980	55974	64784	78283	83952	84783	93372	105013	120226	124035	117031
A Imports of merchandise, f.o.b.	45792	47416	53421	62237	75601	81336	82186	90735	101866	116883	120562	113722
B Transport of services on merchandise imports	2387	2425	2371	2337	2430	2377	2342	2357	2800	2954	3065	2926
By residents	538	459	549	523	610	532	541	653	717	826	847	867
By non-residents	1849	1966	1822	1814	1820	1845	1801	1704	2083	2128	2218	2059
C Insurance service charges on merchandise imports	140	139	182	210	252	239	255	280	347	389	408	383
By residents	12	18	17	5	11	41	32	27	16	8	3	-2

2.17 Exports and Imports of Goods and Services, Detail
(Continued)

Million Pounds Sterling

	1980	1981	1982	1983	1984	1985	1986	1987	1988	1989	1990	1991
By non-residents	128	121	165	205	241	198	223	253	331	381	405	385
2 Adjustments of merchandise imports to change-of-ownership basis	...	...	...	...	...	...	...	...	...	...	...	...
3 Other transport and communication	3993	4166	4322	4655	5075	5305	5442	6135	6353	6852	7186	7056
4 Other insurance service charges	...	...	...	...	...	...	...	...	...	...	...	...
5 Other commodities	2940	3330	4251	4443	5307	5357	5337	5852	6408	7579	8074	7972
6 Direct purchases abroad by government	...	...	...	...	...	...	...	...	...	...	...	...
7 Direct purchases abroad by resident households	2648	3131	3483	3855	4275	4440	5651	6702	7605	8668	9052	8978
Total Imports of Goods and Services	57900	60607	68030	77737	92940	99054	101213	112061	125379	143325	148347	141037
Balance of Goods and Services	5197	7230	5154	2774	-538	3652	-2396	-4440	-17063	-20569	-14122	-5166
Total Imports and Balance of Goods and Services	63097	67837	73184	80511	92402	102706	98817	107621	108316	122756	134225	135871

3.11 General Government Production Account: Total and Subsectors

Million Pounds Sterling

	1980					1981				
	Total General Government	Central Government	State or Provincial Government	Local Government	Social Security Funds	Total General Government	Central Government	State or Provincial Government	Local Government	Social Security Funds
Gross Output										
1 Sales	...	...	...	...	...	...	...	...	...	...
2 Services produced for own use	55715	31456	...	23657	602	63946	35751	...	27472	723
3 Own account fixed capital formation	451	144	...	307	...	431	164	...	267	...
Gross Output	56166	31600	...	23964	602	64377	35915	...	27739	723
Gross Input										
Intermediate Consumption	20443	15087	...	5049	307	22946	17235	...	5344	367
Subtotal: Value Added	35723	16513	...	18915	295	41431	18680	...	22395	356
1 Indirect taxes, net	-459	513	...	-978	6	394	614	...	-228	8
A Indirect taxes	2398	556	...	1836	6	2902	666	...	2228	8
B Less: Subsidies	2857	43	...	2814	...	2508	52	...	2456	...
2 Consumption of fixed capital	3110	713	...	2397	...	3515	806	...	2709	...
3 Compensation of employees	31159	15321	...	15549	289	35500	17245	...	17907	348
A To residents	30903	15065	...	15549	289	35242	16987	...	17907	348
B To the rest of the world	256	256	...	...	...	258	258	...	...	...
4 Net Operating surplus	1913	-34	...	1947	...	2022	15	...	2007	...
Gross Input	56166	31600	...	23964	602	64377	35915	...	27739	723

	1982					1983				
	Total General Government	Central Government	State or Provincial Government	Local Government	Social Security Funds	Total General Government	Central Government	State or Provincial Government	Local Government	Social Security Funds
Gross Output										
1 Sales	...	...	...	...	...	...	...	...	...	...
2 Services produced for own use	70364	39284	...	30328	752	76287	43139	...	32399	749
3 Own account fixed capital formation	484	190	...	294	...	556	212	...	344	...
Gross Output	70848	39474	...	30622	752	76843	43351	...	32743	749
Gross Input										
Intermediate Consumption	26370	19731	...	6261	378	29562	22099	...	7095	368
Subtotal: Value Added	44478	19743	...	24361	374	47281	21252	...	25648	381
1 Indirect taxes, net	1016	605	...	404	7	769	467	...	297	5
A Indirect taxes	3139	659	...	2473	7	2783	522	...	2256	5
B Less: Subsidies	2123	54	...	2069	...	2014	55	...	1959	...
2 Consumption of fixed capital	3573	848	...	2725	...	3677	889	...	2788	...
3 Compensation of employees	37972	18381	...	19224	367	41432	20153	...	20903	376
A To residents	37674	18083	...	19224	367	41112	19833	...	20903	376
B To the rest of the world	298	298	...	...	...	320	320	...	...	...
4 Net Operating surplus	1917	-91	...	2008	...	1403	-257	...	1660	...
Gross Input	70848	39474	...	30622	752	76843	43351	...	32743	749

3.11 General Government Production Account: Total and Subsectors

Million Pounds Sterling

	1984					1985				
	Total General Government	Central Government	State or Provincial Government	Local Government	Social Security Funds	Total General Government	Central Government	State or Provincial Government	Local Government	Social Security Funds
Gross Output										
1 Sales	...	...		...	...	...	...		...	...
2 Services produced for own use	80472	45447	...	34286	739	84859	47559	...	36373	927
3 Own account fixed capital formation	467	195	...	272	...	467	233	...	234	...
Gross Output	80939	45642	...	34558	739	85326	47792	...	36607	927
Gross Input										
Intermediate Consumption	31702	23792	...	7549	361	32892	24252	...	8162	478
Subtotal: Value Added	49237	21850	...	27009	378	52434	23540	...	28445	449
1 Indirect taxes, net	576	361	...	212	3	558	275	...	283	-
A Indirect taxes	2571	427	...	2141	3	2446	340	...	2106	-
B Less: Subsidies	1995	66	...	1929	...	1888	65	...	1823	...
2 Consumption of fixed capital	3806	933	...	2873	...	4087	1021	...	3066	...
3 Compensation of employees	43677	21007	...	22295	375	46095	22356	...	23290	449
A To residents	43327	20657	...	22295	375	45710	21971	...	23290	449
B To the rest of the world	350	350	...	...	...	385	385	...	...	...
4 Net Operating surplus	1178	-451	...	1629	...	1694	-112	...	1806	...
Gross Input	80939	45642	...	34558	739	85326	47792	...	36607	927

	1986					1987				
	Total General Government	Central Government	State or Provincial Government	Local Government	Social Security Funds	Total General Government	Central Government	State or Provincial Government	Local Government	Social Security Funds
Gross Output										
1 Sales	...	...		...	...	...	...		...	...
2 Services produced for own use	90191	50297	...	39097	797	96492	53555	...	42110	827
3 Own account fixed capital formation	556	337	...	219	...	665	463	...	202	...
Gross Output	90747	50634	...	39316	797	97157	54018	...	42312	827
Gross Input										
Intermediate Consumption	34411	25648	...	8344	419	36012	26873	...	8727	412
Subtotal: Value Added	56336	24986	...	30972	378	61145	27145	...	33585	415
1 Indirect taxes, net	888	300	...	588	-	1328	327	...	1001	-
A Indirect taxes	2639	368	...	2271	-	2849	397	...	2452	-
B Less: Subsidies	1751	68	...	1683	...	1521	70	...	1451	...
2 Consumption of fixed capital	4406	1117	...	3289	...	4725	1224	...	3501	...
3 Compensation of employees	49550	23785	...	25387	378	53892	25950	...	27527	415
A To residents	49120	23355	...	25387	378	53405	25463	...	27527	415
B To the rest of the world	430	430	...	...	...	487	487	...	...	...
4 Net Operating surplus	1492	-216	...	1708	...	1200	-356	...	1556	...
Gross Input	90747	50634	...	39316	797	97157	54018	...	42312	827

	1988					1989				
	Total General Government	Central Government	State or Provincial Government	Local Government	Social Security Funds	Total General Government	Central Government	State or Provincial Government	Local Government	Social Security Funds
Gross Output										
1 Sales	...	...	...	...	...	...	...	...	...	...
2 Services produced for own use	103751	57308	...	45570	873	111959	62478	...	48619	862
3 Own account fixed capital formation	754	575	...	179	...	830	655	...	175	...
Gross Output	104505	57883	...	45749	873	112789	63133	...	48794	862
Gross Input										
Intermediate Consumption	38283	28769	...	9080	434	41610	31042	...	10137	431
Subtotal: Value Added	66222	29114	...	36669	439	71179	32091	...	38657	431
1 Indirect taxes, net	1448	355	...	1093	-	1475	377	...	1098	-
A Indirect taxes	3120	420	...	2700	-	3239	445	...	2794	-
B Less: Subsidies	1672	65	...	1607	...	1764	68	...	1696	...
2 Consumption of fixed capital	5262	1342	...	3920	...	5915	1543	...	4372	...
3 Compensation of employees	58402	27763	...	30200	439	62711	30445	...	31835	431
A To residents	58005	27366	...	30200	439	62221	29955	...	31835	431
B To the rest of the world	397	397	...	...	...	490	490	...	...	...
4 Net Operating surplus	1110	-346	...	1456	...	1078	-274	...	1352	...
Gross Input	104505	57883	...	45749	873	112789	63133	...	48794	862

3.11 General Government Production Account: Total and Subsectors

Million Pounds Sterling

	1990					1991				
	Total General Government	Central Government	State or Provincial Government	Local Government	Social Security Funds	Total General Government	Central Government	State or Provincial Government	Local Government	Social Security Funds
Gross Output										
1 Sales	...	...	...	...	...	...	...	...	...	...
2 Services produced for own use	123388	68861	...	53526	1001	136268	76213	...	59031	1024
3 Own account fixed capital formation	659	530	...	129	...	542	417	...	125	...
Gross Output	124047	69391	...	53655	1001	136810	76630	...	59156	1024
Gross Input										
Intermediate Consumption	48597	34283	...	13814	500	56487	39406	...	16569	512
Subtotal: Value Added	75450	35108	...	39841	501	80323	37224	...	42587	512
1 Indirect taxes, net	-386	417	...	-803	-	-1299	429	...	-1728	-
A Indirect taxes	1481	487	...	994	-	532	504	...	28	-
B Less: Subsidies	1867	70	...	1797	...	1831	75	...	1756	...
2 Consumption of fixed capital	6150	1737	...	4413	...	7077	1825	...	5252	...
3 Compensation of employees	68493	33471	...	34521	501	73892	35480	...	37900	512
A To residents	67972	32950	...	34521	501	73380	34968	...	37900	512
B To the rest of the world	521	521	...	...	...	512	512	...	...	...
4 Net Operating surplus	1193	-517	...	1710	...	653	-510	...	1163	...
Gross Input	124047	69391	...	53655	1001	136810	76630	...	59156	1024

3.12 General Government Income and Outlay Account: Total and Subsectors

Million Pounds Sterling

	1980					1981				
	Total General Government	Central Government	State or Provincial Government	Local Government	Social Security Funds	Total General Government	Central Government	State or Provincial Government	Local Government	Social Security Funds
Receipts										
1 Operating surplus	1913	-34	...	1947	...	2022	15	...	2007	...
2 Property and entrepreneurial income	5111	6028	...	707	625	5817	6896	...	738	618
A Withdrawals from public quasi-corporations	...	-	...	...	...	...	-	...	...	...
B Interest	3789	4706	...	707	625	4276	5355	...	738	618
C Dividends	166	166	...	...	...	179	179	...	...	...
D Net land rent and royalties	1156	1156	...	...	...	1362	1362	...	...	...
3 Taxes, fees and contributions	82349	60144	...	8261	13944	95631	69514	...	10194	15923
A Indirect taxes	35802	27541	...	8261	...	41809	31615	...	10194	...
B Direct taxes	32415	32415	...	...	...	37701	37701	...	...	...
Income	31689	31689	...	...	...	36861	36861	...	...	...
Other	726	726	...	...	...	840	840	...	...	...
C Social security contributions	13944	...	...	...	13944	15923	...	...	...	15923
D Fees, fines and penalties	188	188	...	...	...	198	198	...	...	...
4 Other current transfers	2958	2865	...	14326	2802	3610	3607	...	16492	2988
A Casualty insurance claims	...	-	...	-	-	...	-	...	-	...
B Transfers from other government subsectors	...	1034	...	13233	2768	...	1333	...	15201	2943
C Transfers from the rest of the world	...	-	...	...	...	...	-	...	-	...
D Other transfers, except imputed	-	...	...	...	...	...	...	...	...	...
E Imputed unfunded employee pension and welfare contributions	2958	1831	...	1093	34	3610	2274	...	1291	45
Total Current Receipts	92331	69003	...	25241	17371	107080	80032	...	29431	19529
Disbursements										
1 Government final consumption expenditure	48959	29406	...	18951	602	55395	33177	...	21495	723
2 Property income	10888	8889	...	4248	-	12718	10739	...	4413	1
A Interest	10888	8889	...	4248	-	12718	10739	...	4413	1
B Net land rent and royalties	...	-	...	-	...	...	-	...	-	...
3 Subsidies	5773	4674	...	1099	...	6553	5355	...	1198	...

3.12 General Government Income and Outlay Account: Total and Subsectors
(Continued)

Million Pounds Sterling

	1980					1981				
	Total General Government	Central Government	State or Provincial Government	Local Government	Social Security Funds	Total General Government	Central Government	State or Provincial Government	Local Government	Social Security Funds
4 Other current transfers	30267	29232	...	2198	15872	36466	34273	...	2433	19237
A Casualty insurance premiums, net	-	-	...	-	-	-	-	...	-	-
B Transfers to other government subsectors	...	16001	...	...	1034	...	18144	...	...	1333
C Social security benefits	14804	...	...	...	14804	17859	...	...	...	17859
D Social assistance grants	9276	8176	...	1100	...	11793	10662	...	1131	...
E Unfunded employee pension and welfare benefits	2958	1831	...	1093	34	3610	2274	...	1291	45
F Transfers to private non-profit institutions serving households	1575	1570	...	5	...	1786	1775	...	11	...
G Other transfers n.e.c.	...	...	...	...	...	...	...	...	...	...
H Transfers to the rest of the world	1654	1654	...	...	...	1418	1418	...	...	...
Net saving	-3556	-3198	...	-1255	897	-4052	-3512	...	-108	-432
Total Current Disbursements and Net Saving	92331	69003	...	25241	17371	107080	80032	...	29431	19529

	1982					1983				
	Total General Government	Central Government	State or Provincial Government	Local Government	Social Security Funds	Total General Government	Central Government	State or Provincial Government	Local Government	Social Security Funds
	Receipts									
1 Operating surplus	1917	-91	...	2008	...	1403	-257	...	1660	...
2 Property and entrepreneurial income	6865	7840	...	818	512	6956	8253	...	745	463
A Withdrawals from public quasi-corporations	...	-	...	...	...	...	-	...	...	...
B Interest	5006	5981	...	818	512	4762	6059	...	745	463
C Dividends	259	259	...	...	...	307	307	...	...	...
D Net land rent and royalties	1600	1600	...	...	...	1887	1887	...	...	...
3 Taxes, fees and contributions	106209	76373	...	11732	18104	115065	82052	...	12219	20793
A Indirect taxes	45637	33905	...	11732	...	48450	36230	...	12219	...
B Direct taxes	42257	42257	...	...	...	45573	45573	...	...	...
Income	41235	41235	...	...	...	44389	44389	...	...	...
Other	1022	1022	...	...	...	1184	1184	...	...	...
C Social security contributions	18104	...	...	...	18104	20793	...	...	...	20793
D Fees, fines and penalties	211	211	...	...	...	249	249	...	...	...
4 Other current transfers	4057	4177	...	17603	2308	4431	4616	...	20207	2841
A Casualty insurance claims	...	-	...	-	...	...	-	...	-	-
B Transfers from other government subsectors	...	1582	...	16190	2259	...	1741	...	18703	2789
C Transfers from the rest of the world	...	-	...	...	...	...	-	...	...	...
D Other transfers, except imputed	-	...	...	-	...	-	...	...	-	...
E Imputed unfunded employee pension and welfare contributions	4057	2595	...	1413	49	4431	2875	...	1504	52
Total Current Receipts	119048	88299	...	32161	20924	127855	94664	...	34831	24097
	Disbursements									
1 Government final consumption expenditure	60387	36272	...	23363	752	65814	39932	...	25133	749
2 Property income	13925	11905	...	4298	27	14180	12698	...	3959	28
A Interest	13925	11905	...	4298	27	14180	12698	...	3959	28
B Net land rent and royalties	...	-	...	-	...	...	-	...	-	...
3 Subsidies	6003	4578	...	1425	...	6404	4878	...	1525	...

3.12 General Government Income and Outlay Account: Total and Subsectors
(Continued)

Million Pounds Sterling

	1982					1983				
	Total General Government	Central Government	State or Provincial Government	Local Government	Social Security Funds	Total General Government	Central Government	State or Provincial Government	Local Government	Social Security Funds
4 Other current transfers	42439	38782	...	2709	20979	46230	42153	...	4685	22625
A Casualty insurance premiums, net		·		-			·	...	-	
B Transfers to other government subsectors	...	18449	...	...	1582	...	21492	...	...	1741
C Social security benefits	19348	...	...	...	19348	20832	...	...	...	20832
D Social assistance grants	15404	14131	...	1273	...	16866	13719	...	3147	...
E Unfunded employee pension and welfare benefits	4057	2595	...	1413	49	4431	2875	...	1504	52
F Transfers to private non-profit institutions serving households	2020	1997	...	23	...	2382	2348	...	34	...
G Other transfers n.e.c.	...	...	...	...	...	...	...	...	...	...
H Transfers to the rest of the world	1610	1610	...	...	...	1719	1719	...	...	...
Net saving	-3706	-3238	...	366	-834	-4772	-4996	...	-471	695
Total Current Disbursements and Net Saving	119048	88299	...	32161	20924	127856	94665	...	34831	24097

	1984					1985				
	Total General Government	Central Government	State or Provincial Government	Local Government	Social Security Funds	Total General Government	Central Government	State or Provincial Government	Local Government	Social Security Funds
Receipts										
1 Operating surplus	1178	-451	...	1629	...	1694	-112	...	1806	...
2 Property and entrepreneurial income	7608	9225	...	777	483	8639	10503	...	838	538
A Withdrawals from public quasi-corporations	...	-	...	...	...	...	-	...	...	...
B Interest	4831	6448	...	777	483	5661	7525	...	838	538
C Dividends	318	318	...	...	...	612	612	...	...	...
D Net land rent and royalties	2459	2459	...	...	...	2366	2366	...	...	...
3 Taxes, fees and contributions	123056	87952	...	12767	22337	134157	96293	...	13638	24226
A Indirect taxes	51428	38661	...	12767	...	55207	41569	...	13638	...
B Direct taxes	49046	49046	...	...	...	54466	54466	...	...	...
Income	47757	47757	...	...	...	52984	52984	...	...	...
Other	1289	1289	...	...	...	1482	1482	...	...	...
C Social security contributions	22337	...	...	...	22337	24226	...	...	...	24226
D Fees, fines and penalties	245	245	...	...	...	258	258	...	...	...
4 Other current transfers	4658	4759	...	21600	2773	5210	5369	...	22231	2508
A Casualty insurance claims	...	-	...	-	-	...	-	...	-	...
B Transfers from other government subsectors	...	1846	...	19908	2720	...	2016	...	20438	2444
C Transfers from the rest of the world	...	-	...	-	...	...	-	...	...	...
D Other transfers, except imputed	-	...	...	-	...	-	...	...	-	...
E Imputed unfunded employee pension and welfare contributions	4658	2913	...	1692	53	5210	3353	...	1793	64
Total Current Receipts	136500	101485	...	36773	25593	149700	112053	...	38513	27272
Disbursements										
1 Government final consumption expenditure	69788	42431	...	26618	739	73834	44981	...	27926	927
2 Property income	15755	14575	...	4039	18	17711	16258	...	4689	4
A Interest	15755	14575	...	4039	18	17711	16258	...	4689	4
B Net land rent and royalties	...	-	...	-	...	...	-	...	-	...
3 Subsidies	7678	6181	...	1497	...	7322	6036	...	1286	...

3.12 General Government Income and Outlay Account: Total and Subsectors
(Continued)

Million Pounds Sterling

	1984					1985				
	Total General Government	Central Government	State or Provincial Government	Local Government	Social Security Funds	Total General Government	Central Government	State or Provincial Government	Local Government	Social Security Funds
4 Other current transfers	49792	45012	...	5428	23826	55466	48989	...	5874	25501
A Casualty insurance premiums, net	-	-	...	-			-	...	-	-
B Transfers to other government subsectors	...	22628	...	...	1846	...	22882	...	...	2016
C Social security benefits	21927	...	...	...	21927	23421	...	...	...	23421
D Social assistance grants	18820	15112	...	3708	...	20878	16834	...	4044	...
E Unfunded employee pension and welfare benefits	4658	2913	...	1692	53	5210	3353	...	1793	64
F Transfers to private non-profit institutions serving households	2566	2538	...	28	...	2819	2782	...	37	...
G Other transfers n.e.c.	...	...	...	...	...	...	...	...	...	...
H Transfers to the rest of the world	1821	1821	...	...	...	3138	3138	...	...	...
Net saving	-6513	-6714	...	-809	1010	-4633	-4211	...	-1262	840
Total Current Disbursements and Net Saving	136500	101485	...	36773	25593	149700	112053	...	38513	27272

	1986					1987				
	Total General Government	Central Government	State or Provincial Government	Local Government	Social Security Funds	Total General Government	Central Government	State or Provincial Government	Local Government	Social Security Funds
Receipts										
1 Operating surplus	1492	-216	...	1708	...	1200	-356	...	1556	...
2 Property and entrepreneurial income	6785	9195	...	801	577	6990	9843	...	851	556
A Withdrawals from public quasi-corporations	...	-	...	...	...	...	-	...	...	...
B Interest	5112	7522	...	801	577	5105	7958	...	851	556
C Dividends	732	732	...	...	...	734	734	...	...	...
D Net land rent and royalties	941	941	...	...	...	1151	1151	...	...	...
3 Taxes, fees and contributions	143597	102166	...	15251	26180	156144	110710	...	16777	28657
A Indirect taxes	61536	46285	...	15251	...	67800	51023	...	16777	...
B Direct taxes	55583	55583	...	...	...	59292	59292	...	...	...
Income	54017	54017	...	...	...	57680	57680	...	...	...
Other	1566	1566	...	...	...	1612	1612	...	...	...
C Social security contributions	26180	...	...	...	26180	28657	...	...	...	28657
D Fees, fines and penalties	298	298	...	...	...	395	395	...	...	...
4 Other current transfers	5548	5751	...	23784	2342	6250	6792	...	25403	2291
A Casualty insurance claims	...	-	...	-	-	...	-	...	-	-
B Transfers from other government subsectors	...	2228	...	21813	2288	...	2725	...	23277	2234
C Transfers from the rest of the world	...	-	...	-	...	...	-	...	-	...
D Other transfers, except imputed	-	...	...	-	...	-	...	...	-	...
E Imputed unfunded employee pension and welfare contributions	5548	3523	...	1971	54	6250	4067	...	2126	57
Total Current Receipts	157422	116896	...	41544	29099	170584	126989	...	44587	31504
Disbursements										
1 Government final consumption expenditure	79413	48036	...	30580	797	85381	51245	...	33309	827
2 Property income	17257	16523	...	4522	-	18003	17626	...	4637	-
A Interest	17257	16523	...	4522	-	18003	17626	...	4637	-
B Net land rent and royalties	...	-	...	-	...	...	-	...	-	...
3 Subsidies	6342	5180	...	1162	...	6511	5561	...	950	...

United Kingdom

3.12 General Government Income and Outlay Account: Total and Subsectors
(Continued)

Million Pounds Sterling

	1986					1987				
	Total General Government	Central Government	State or Provincial Government	Local Government	Social Security Funds	Total General Government	Central Government	State or Provincial Government	Local Government	Social Security Funds
4 Other current transfers	58780	50712	...	6359	28038	62036	54468	...	6735	29069
A Casualty insurance premiums, net	-	-	...	-	-	-	-	...	-	-
B Transfers to other government subsectors	...	24101	...	...	2228	...	25511	...	...	2725
C Social security benefits	25756	...	...	...	25756	26287	...	...	...	26287
D Social assistance grants	22378	18024	...	4354	...	23222	18637	...	4585	...
E Unfunded employee pension and welfare benefits	5548	3523	...	1971	54	6250	4067	...	2126	57
F Transfers to private non-profit institutions serving households	3176	3142	...	34	...	3363	3339	...	24	...
G Other transfers n.e.c.	...	...	...	...	...	...	...	...	...	...
H Transfers to the rest of the world	1922	1922	...	...	...	2914	2914	...	...	...
Net saving	-4370	-3555	...	-1079	264	-1347	-1911	...	-1044	1608
Total Current Disbursements and Net Saving	157422	116896	...	41544	29099	170584	126989	...	44587	31504

	1988					1989				
	Total General Government	Central Government	State or Provincial Government	Local Government	Social Security Funds	Total General Government	Central Government	State or Provincial Government	Local Government	Social Security Funds
Receipts										
1 Operating surplus	1110	-346	...	1456	...	1078	-274	...	1352	...
2 Property and entrepreneurial income	6939	9993	...	915	684	7591	10592	...	1435	1026
A Withdrawals from public quasi-corporations	...	-	...	...	...	...	...	...	...	...
B Interest	5663	8717	...	915	684	6533	9534	...	1435	1026
C Dividends	453	453	...	...	...	502	502	...	...	...
D Net land rent and royalties	823	823	...	...	...	556	556	...	...	...
3 Taxes, fees and contributions	173699	122850	...	18726	32123	186945	134113	...	19913	32919
A Indirect taxes	74649	55923	...	18726	...	78438	58525	...	19913	...
B Direct taxes	66499	66499	...	...	...	75118	75118	...	...	...
Income	64806	64806	...	...	...	73325	73325	...	...	...
Other	1693	1693	...	...	...	1793	1793	...	...	...
C Social security contributions	32123	...	...	...	32123	32919	...	...	...	32919
D Fees, fines and penalties	428	428	...	...	...	470	470	...	...	...
4 Other current transfers	6463	7496	...	25778	1985	7372	8456	...	27181	662
A Casualty insurance claims	...	-	...	-	-	...	...	...	-	-
B Transfers from other government subsectors	...	3419	...	23452	1925	...	4117	...	24200	610
C Transfers from the rest of the world	...	...	...	...	...	...	...	...	-	...
D Other transfers, except imputed	-	...	...	-	...	586	...	...	586	...
E Imputed unfunded employee pension and welfare contributions	6463	4077	...	2326	60	6786	4339	...	2395	52
Total Current Receipts	188211	139993	...	46875	34792	202986	152887	...	49881	34607
Disbursements										
1 Government final consumption expenditure	91763	54771	...	36119	873	99068	59704	...	38502	862
2 Property income	18255	18035	...	4873	-	18943	19011	...	5394	-
A Interest	18255	18035	...	4873	-	18943	19011	...	5394	-
B Net land rent and royalties	...	-	...	-	...	...	-	...	-	...
3 Subsidies	6127	5097	...	1030	...	6050	5042	...	1008	...

3.12 General Government Income and Outlay Account: Total and Subsectors
(Continued)

Million Pounds Sterling

	1988					1989				
	Total General Government	Central Government	State or Provincial Government	Local Government	Social Security Funds	Total General Government	Central Government	State or Provincial Government	Local Government	Social Security Funds
4 Other current transfers	63816	54791	...	7193	30628	67874	56144	...	7753	32904
A Casualty insurance premiums, net	-	-	...	-	-			...	-	-
B Transfers to other government subsectors	...	25377	...	...	3419	...	24810	...	...	4117
C Social security benefits	27149	...	...	...	27149	28735	...	...	...	28735
D Social assistance grants	23542	18698	...	4844	...	25034	19700	...	5334	...
E Unfunded employee pension and welfare benefits	6463	4077	...	2326	60	6786	4339	...	2395	52
F Transfers to private non-profit institutions serving households	3857	3834	...	23	...	3547	3523	...	24	...
G Other transfers n.e.c.	...	...	...	...	...	...	...	...	...	...
H Transfers to the rest of the world	2805	2805	...	...	...	3772	3772	...	...	...
Net saving	8251	7300	...	-2340	3291	11051	12986	...	-2776	841
Total Current Disbursements and Net Saving	188212	139994	...	46875	34792	202986	152887	...	49881	34607

	1990					1991				
	Total General Government	Central Government	State or Provincial Government	Local Government	Social Security Funds	Total General Government	Central Government	State or Provincial Government	Local Government	Social Security Funds
	Receipts									
1 Operating surplus	1193	-517	...	1710	...	653	-510	...	1163	...
2 Property and entrepreneurial income	7026	10353	...	1309	1025	6556	10246	...	962	1096
A Withdrawals from public quasi-corporations	...	-	...	...	...	...	-	...	...	...
B Interest	5870	9197	...	1309	1025	5150	8840	...	962	1096
C Dividends	502	502	...	...	...	825	825	...	...	...
D Net land rent and royalties	654	654	...	...	...	581	581	...	...	...
3 Taxes, fees and contributions	192122	152327	...	5129	34666	197462	160685	...	118	36659
A Indirect taxes	75388	70259	...	5129	...	81372	81254	...	118	...
B Direct taxes	81523	81523	...	...	...	79017	79017	...	...	...
Income	79686	79686	...	...	...	77138	77138	...	...	...
Other	1837	1837	...	...	...	1879	1879	...	...	...
C Social security contributions	34666	...	...	...	34666	36659	...	...	...	36659
D Fees, fines and penalties	545	545	...	...	...	414	414	...	...	...
4 Other current transfers	16326	9318	...	49543	644	16976	10351	...	58823	1761
A Casualty insurance claims	...	-	...	-	-	...	-	...	-	-
B Transfers from other government subsectors	...	4261	...	38333	585	...	4533	...	47730	1696
C Transfers from the rest of the world	...	-	...	-	...	...	-	...	-	...
D Other transfers, except imputed	8629	...	...	8629	...	8162	...	...	8162	...
E Imputed unfunded employee pension and welfare contributions	7697	5057	...	2581	59	8814	5818	...	2931	65
Total Current Receipts	216667	171481	...	57691	36335	221647	180772	...	61066	39516
	Disbursements									
1 Government final consumption expenditure	109919	66092	...	42826	1001	121943	73462	...	47457	1024
2 Property income	18793	18902	...	5552	-	17097	17436	...	5409	-
A Interest	18793	18902	...	5552	-	17097	17436	...	5409	-
B Net land rent and royalties	...	-	...	-	...	...	-	...	-	...
3 Subsidies	6327	5662	...	665	...	6106	5526	...	580	...

United Kingdom

3.12 General Government Income and Outlay Account: Total and Subsectors
(Continued)

Million Pounds Sterling

	1990					1991				
	Total General Government	Central Government	State or Provincial Government	Local Government	Social Security Funds	Total General Government	Central Government	State or Provincial Government	Local Government	Social Security Funds
4 Other current transfers	74311	73308	...	8578	35604	81646	84893	...	10732	39980
A Casualty insurance premiums, net	-	-	...	-	-	-	-	...	-	-
B Transfers to other government subsectors	...	38918	...	...	4261	...	49426	...	...	4533
C Social security benefits	31284	...	...	...	31284	35382	...	...	...	35382
D Social assistance grants	27901	21929	...	5972	...	33271	25495	...	7776	...
E Unfunded employee pension and welfare benefits	7697	5057	...	2581	59	8814	5818	...	2931	65
F Transfers to private non-profit institutions serving households	3422	3397	...	25	...	3812	3787	...	25	...
G Other transfers n.e.c.	...	...	...	...	...	...	...	...	...	...
H Transfers to the rest of the world	4007	4007	...	...	...	367	367	...	...	...
Net saving	7317	7517	...	70	-270	-5145	-545	...	-3112	-1488
Total Current Disbursements and Net Saving	216667	171481	...	57691	36335	221647	180772	...	61066	39516

3.13 General Government Capital Accumulation Account: Total and Subsectors

Million Pounds Sterling

	1980					1981				
	Total General Government	Central Government	State or Provincial Government	Local Government	Social Security Funds	Total General Government	Central Government	State or Provincial Government	Local Government	Social Security Funds
Finance of Gross Accumulation										
1 Gross saving	-446	-2485	...	1142	897	-537	-2706	...	2601	-432
A Consumption of fixed capital	3110	713	...	2397	...	3515	806	...	2709	...
B Net saving	-3556	-3198	...	-1255	897	-4052	-3512	...	-108	-432
2 Capital transfers	494	451	...	338	...	780	745	...	352	...
A From other government subsectors	...	...	...	295	...	...	...	...	317	...
B From other resident sectors	494	451	...	43	...	780	745	...	35	...
C From rest of the world	...	...	...	...	...	...	...	...	...	...
Finance of Gross Accumulation	48	-2034	...	1480	897	243	-1961	...	2953	-432
Gross Accumulation										
1 Gross capital formation	5695	1804	...	3891	...	4579	1775	...	2804	...
A Increase in stocks	43	43	...	...	...	-93	-93	...	...	...
B Gross fixed capital formation	5652	1761	...	3891	...	4672	1868	...	2804	...
2 Purchases of land, net	...	...	...	...	...	...	...	...	...	...
3 Purchases of intangible assets, net	...	...	...	...	...	...	...	...	...	...
4 Capital transfers	2453	2490	...	258	...	5881	5888	...	310	...
A To other government subsectors	...	295	...	...	...	...	317	...	...	...
B To other resident sectors	2453	2195	...	258	...	5881	5571	...	310	...
C To rest of the world	-	-	...	...	...	-	-	...	...	...
Net lending	-8100	-6328	...	-2669	897	-10217	-9624	...	-161	-432
Gross Accumulation	48	-2034	...	1480	897	243	-1961	...	2953	-432

	1982					1983				
	Total General Government	Central Government	State or Provincial Government	Local Government	Social Security Funds	Total General Government	Central Government	State or Provincial Government	Local Government	Social Security Funds
Finance of Gross Accumulation										
1 Gross saving	-133	-2390	...	3091	-834	-1095	-4107	...	2317	695
A Consumption of fixed capital	3573	848	...	2725	...	3677	889	...	2788	...
B Net saving	-3706	-3238	...	366	-834	-4772	-4996	...	-471	695
2 Capital transfers	665	623	...	370	...	615	573	...	358	...
A From other government subsectors	...	...	...	328	...	...	...	...	316	...
B From other resident sectors	665	623	...	42	...	615	573	...	42	...
C From rest of the world	...	...	...	...	...	...	...	...	...	...
Finance of Gross Accumulation	532	-1767	...	3461	-834	-480	-3534	...	2675	695
Gross Accumulation										
1 Gross capital formation	4592	2385	...	2207	...	6115	2743	...	3372	...

3.13 General Government Capital Accumulation Account: Total and Subsectors
(Continued)

Million Pounds Sterling

	1982					1983				
	Total General Government	Central Government	State or Provincial Government	Local Government	Social Security Funds	Total General Government	Central Government	State or Provincial Government	Local Government	Social Security Funds
A Increase in stocks	155	155	...	...	...	246	246	...	...	...
B Gross fixed capital formation	4437	2230	...	2207	...	5869	2497	...	3372	...
2 Purchases of land, net	...	...	...	...	...	...	...	...	...	...
3 Purchases of intangible assets, net	...	...	...	...	...	...	...	...	...	...
4 Capital transfers	3882	3666	...	544	...	3590	2773	...	1133	...
A To other government subsectors	...	328	...	...	...	...	316	...	...	...
B To other resident sectors	3882	3338	...	544	...	3590	2457	...	1133	...
C To rest of the world	-	-	...	...	...	-	-	...	...	...
Net lending	-7942	-7818	...	710	-834	-10185	-9050	...	-1830	695
Gross Accumulation	532	-1767	...	3461	-834	-480	-3534	...	2675	695

	1984					1985				
	Total General Government	Central Government	State or Provincial Government	Local Government	Social Security Funds	Total General Government	Central Government	State or Provincial Government	Local Government	Social Security Funds
Finance of Gross Accumulation										
1 Gross saving	-2707	-5781	...	2064	1010	-546	-3190	...	1804	840
A Consumption of fixed capital	3806	933	...	2873	...	4087	1021	...	3066	...
B Net saving	-6513	-6714	...	-809	1010	-4633	-4211	...	-1262	840
2 Capital transfers	709	664	...	722	...	928	877	...	801	...
A From other government subsectors	...	...	...	677	...	...	...	...	750	...
B From other resident sectors	709	664	...	45	...	928	877	...	51	...
C From rest of the world	...	...	...	...	...	...	...	...	...	...
Finance of Gross Accumulation	-1998	-5117	...	2786	1010	382	-2313	...	2605	840
Gross Accumulation										
1 Gross capital formation	6999	3008	...	3991	...	7322	3576	...	3746	...
A Increase in stocks	280	280	...	...	...	450	450	...	...	...
B Gross fixed capital formation	6719	2728	...	3991	...	6872	3126	...	3746	...
2 Purchases of land, net	...	...	...	...	...	...	...	...	...	...
3 Purchases of intangible assets, net	...	...	...	...	...	...	...	...	...	...
4 Capital transfers	3838	3179	...	1336	...	3319	3298	...	771	...
A To other government subsectors	...	677	...	...	...	...	750	...	...	...
B To other resident sectors	3838	2502	...	1336	...	3319	2548	...	771	...
C To rest of the world	-	-	...	...	...	-	-	...	...	...
Net lending	-12835	-11304	...	-2541	1010	-10259	-9187	...	-1912	840
Gross Accumulation	-1998	-5117	...	2786	1010	382	-2313	...	2605	840

	1986					1987				
	Total General Government	Central Government	State or Provincial Government	Local Government	Social Security Funds	Total General Government	Central Government	State or Provincial Government	Local Government	Social Security Funds
Finance of Gross Accumulation										
1 Gross saving	36	-2438	...	2210	264	3378	-687	...	2457	1608
A Consumption of fixed capital	4406	1117	...	3289	...	4725	1224	...	3501	...
B Net saving	-4370	-3555	...	-1079	264	-1347	-1911	...	-1044	1608
2 Capital transfers	1159	976	...	1120	...	1266	1058	...	1210	...
A From other government subsectors	...	...	...	937	...	...	...	...	1002	...
B From other resident sectors	1159	976	...	183	...	1266	1058	...	208	...
C From rest of the world	...	...	...	...	...	...	...	...	...	...
Finance of Gross Accumulation	1195	-1462	...	3330	264	4644	371	...	3667	1608
Gross Accumulation										
1 Gross capital formation	7272	3114	...	4158	...	7079	2860	...	4219	...
A Increase in stocks	-237	-237	...	...	...	-498	-498	...	...	...
B Gross fixed capital formation	7509	3351	...	4158	...	7577	3358	...	4219	...

United Kingdom

3.13 General Government Capital Accumulation Account: Total and Subsectors
(Continued)

Million Pounds Sterling

	1986					1987				
	Total General Government	Central Government	State or Provincial Government	Local Government	Social Security Funds	Total General Government	Central Government	State or Provincial Government	Local Government	Social Security Funds
2 Purchases of land, net	...	...	...	...	...	...	...	...	...	...
3 Purchases of intangible assets, net	...	...	...	...	...	...	...	...	...	...
4 Capital transfers	4626	4966	...	597	...	3216	3436	...	782	...
A To other government subsectors	...	937	...	...	...	...	1002	...	...	...
B To other resident sectors	4626	4029	...	597	...	3216	2434	...	782	...
C To rest of the world	-	-	...	...	...	-	-	...	...	...
Net lending	-10703	-9542	...	-1425	264	-5651	-5925	...	-1334	1608
Gross Accumulation	1195	-1462	...	3330	264	4644	371	...	3667	1608

	1988					1989				
	Total General Government	Central Government	State or Provincial Government	Local Government	Social Security Funds	Total General Government	Central Government	State or Provincial Government	Local Government	Social Security Funds
Finance of Gross Accumulation										
1 Gross saving	13513	8642	...	1580	3291	16966	14529	...	1596	841
A Consumption of fixed capital	5262	1342	...	3920	...	5915	1543	...	4372	...
B Net saving	8251	7300	...	-2340	3291	11051	12986	...	-2776	841
2 Capital transfers	1321	1110	...	1248	...	1438	1195	...	2387	...
A From other government subsectors	...	...	...	1037	...	...	...	...	2144	...
B From other resident sectors	1321	1110	...	211	...	1438	1195	...	243	...
C From rest of the world	...	...	...	...	...	...	...	...	...	...
Finance of Gross Accumulation	14834	9752	...	2828	3291	18404	15724	...	3983	841
Gross Accumulation										
1 Gross capital formation	6184	3387	...	2797	...	9419	4788	...	4631	...
A Increase in stocks	-322	-322	...	...	...	-163	-163	...	...	...
B Gross fixed capital formation	6506	3709	...	2797	...	9582	4951	...	4631	...
2 Purchases of land, net	...	...	...	...	...	...	...	...	...	...
3 Purchases of intangible assets, net	...	...	...	...	...	...	...	...	...	...
4 Capital transfers	7786	7973	...	850	...	9261	10531	...	874	...
A To other government subsectors	...	1037	...	...	...	...	2144	...	...	...
B To other resident sectors	7786	6936	...	850	...	9261	8387	...	874	...
C To rest of the world	-	-	...	...	...	-	-	...	...	...
Net lending	864	-1608	...	-819	3291	-276	405	...	-1522	841
Gross Accumulation	14834	9752	...	2828	3291	18404	15724	...	3983	841

	1990					1991				
	Total General Government	Central Government	State or Provincial Government	Local Government	Social Security Funds	Total General Government	Central Government	State or Provincial Government	Local Government	Social Security Funds
Finance of Gross Accumulation										
1 Gross saving	13467	9254	...	4483	-270	1932	1280	...	2140	-1488
A Consumption of fixed capital	6150	1737	...	4413	...	7077	1825	...	5252	...
B Net saving	7317	7517	...	70	-270	-5145	-545	...	-3112	-1488
2 Capital transfers	1544	1315	...	2039	...	1509	1263	...	2667	...
A From other government subsectors	...	...	...	1810	...	...	...	...	2421	...
B From other resident sectors	1544	1315	...	229	...	1509	1263	...	246	...
C From rest of the world	...	...	...	...	...	...	...	...	...	...
Finance of Gross Accumulation	15011	10569	...	6522	-270	3441	2543	...	4807	-1488
Gross Accumulation										
1 Gross capital formation	12815	6571	...	6244	...	12324	7193	...	5131	...
A Increase in stocks	156	156	...	...	...	151	151	...	...	...
B Gross fixed capital formation	12659	6415	...	6244	...	12173	7042	...	5131	...

3.13 General Government Capital Accumulation Account: Total and Subsectors
(Continued)

Million Pounds Sterling

	1990					1991				
	Total General Government	Central Government	State or Provincial Government	Local Government	Social Security Funds	Total General Government	Central Government	State or Provincial Government	Local Government	Social Security Funds
2 Purchases of land, net	...	...	...	...	...	...	...	...	...	...
3 Purchases of intangible assets, net	...	...	...	...	...	...	...	...	...	...
4 Capital transfers	11005	11951	...	864	...	7187	8524	...	1084	...
A To other government subsectors	...	1810	...	...	...	...	2421	...	...	...
B To other resident sectors	11005	10141	...	864	...	7187	6103	...	1084	...
C To rest of the world	-	-	...	...	...	-	-	...	...	...
Net lending	-8809	-7953	...	-586	-270	-16070	-13174	...	-1408	-1488
Gross Accumulation	15011	10569	...	6522	-270	3441	2543	...	4807	-1488

3.14 General Government Capital Finance Account, Total and Subsectors

Million Pounds Sterling

	1980					1981				
	Total General Government	Central Government	State or Provincial Government	Local Government	Social Security Funds	Total General Government	Central Government	State or Provincial Government	Local Government	Social Security Funds
Acquisition of Financial Assets										
1 Gold and SDRs	...	...	...	...	...	...	...	...	...	...
2 Currency and transferable deposits	489	474	...	15	...	-2500	-2550	...	50	...
3 Other deposits	-110	-142	...	32	...	-124	-189	...	65	...
4 Bills and bonds, short term	403	403	...	-	...	2559	2559	...	-	...
A Corporate and quasi-corporate enterprises, resident	403	403	...	-	...	2559	2559	...	-	...
B Other government subsectors	...	...	...	...	...	...	...	...	...	...
C Rest of the world	...	...	...	...	...	...	...	...	...	...
5 Bonds, long term	12	8	...	4	...	8	-6	...	14	...
A Corporations	...	...	...	...	...	...	...	...	...	...
B Other government subsectors	12	8	...	4	...	8	-6	...	14	...
C Rest of the world	...	...	...	...	...	...	...	...	...	...
6 Corporate equity securities	152	148	...	4	...	1664	1649	...	15	...
7 Short-term loans, n.e.c.	-147	-562	...	33	382	-2006	-482	...	9	-1533
8 Long-term loans, n.e.c.	4835	4430	...	405	...	-2569	-2787	...	218	...
A Mortgages	456	...	...	456	...	271	...	...	271	...
B Other	4379	4430	...	-51	...	-2840	-2787	...	-53	...
9 Other receivables	1328	1098	...	-279	509	3471	2708	...	-326	1089
10 Other assets	9	9	...	...	...	-7	-7	...	...	...
Total Acquisition of Financial Assets	6971	5866	...	214	891	496	895	...	45	-444
Incurrence of Liabilities										
1 Currency and transferable deposits	266	266	...	...	...	527	527	...	...	...
2 Other deposits	1635	1738	...	-103	...	4138	4375	...	-237	...
3 Bills and bonds, short term	546	276	...	270	...	-986	-1160	...	174	...
4 Bonds, long term	10541	10678	...	-137	...	7958	8135	...	-177	...
5 Short-term loans, n.e.c.	285	-441	...	726	...	-202	-1786	...	1584	...
6 Long-term loans, n.e.c.	1268	-991	...	2259	...	-2179	-1229	...	-950	...
7 Other payables	-17	-154	...	137	...	359	132	...	227	...
8 Other liabilities	667	667	...	...	...	1405	1405	...	...	...
Total Incurrence of Liabilities	15191	12039	...	3152	...	11020	10399	...	621	...
Statistical discrepancy	-194	148	...	-342	...	-389	36	...	-425	...
Net Lending	-8026	-6321	...	-2596	891	-10135	-9540	...	-151	-444
Incurrence of Liabilities and Net Worth	6971	5866	...	214	891	496	895	...	45	-444

	1982					1983				
	Total General Government	Central Government	State or Provincial Government	Local Government	Social Security Funds	Total General Government	Central Government	State or Provincial Government	Local Government	Social Security Funds
Acquisition of Financial Assets										
1 Gold and SDRs	...	...	...	...	...	...	...	...	...	...
2 Currency and transferable deposits	-1416	-1497	...	81	...	-533	-577	...	44	...
3 Other deposits	714	300	...	414	...	-45	-52	...	7	...
4 Bills and bonds, short term	4714	4714	...	-	...	-725	-725	...	-	...

United Kingdom

3.14 General Government Capital Finance Account, Total and Subsectors
(Continued)

Million Pounds Sterling

	1982 Total General Government	Central Government	State or Provincial Government	Local Government	Social Security Funds	1983 Total General Government	Central Government	State or Provincial Government	Local Government	Social Security Funds
A Corporate and quasi-corporate enterprises, resident	4714	4714	...	-	...	-725	-725	...	-	...
B Other government subsectors	...	...	...	...	...	...	...	...	...	...
C Rest of the world	...	...	...	...	...	...	...	...	...	...
5 Bonds, long term	-240	-242	...	2	...	134	116	...	18	...
A Corporations	...	...	...	...	...	...	...	...	...	...
B Other government subsectors	-240	-242	...	2	...	134	116	...	18	...
C Rest of the world	...	...	...	...	...	...	...	...	...	...
6 Corporate equity securities	-11	-60	...	49	...	-490	-505	...	15	...
7 Short-term loans, n.e.c.	-62	-484	...	-13	435	-350	-250	...	-1	-99
8 Long-term loans, n.e.c.	3387	2996	...	391	...	5135	5507	...	-372	...
A Mortgages	555	...	...	555	...	-306	...	...	-306	...
B Other	2832	2996	...	-164	...	5441	5507	...	-66	...
9 Other receivables	-1725	135	...	-578	-1282	1899	976	...	131	792
10 Other assets	-10	-10	...	...	...	-8	-8	...	...	...
Total Acquisition of Financial Assets	5351	5852	...	346	-847	5017	4482	...	-158	693

Incurrence of Liabilities

	Total General Government	Central Government	State or Provincial Government	Local Government	Social Security Funds	Total General Government	Central Government	State or Provincial Government	Local Government	Social Security Funds
1 Currency and transferable deposits	300	300	...	...	...	787	787	...	...	...
2 Other deposits	3993	4995	...	-1002	...	3251	3262	...	-11	...
3 Bills and bonds, short term	-758	-323	...	-435	...	241	142	...	99	...
4 Bonds, long term	6290	6457	...	-167	...	9254	9490	...	-236	...
5 Short-term loans, n.e.c.	1015	521	...	494	...	-1109	-189	...	-920	...
6 Long-term loans, n.e.c.	822	29	...	793	...	1520	-844	...	2364	...
7 Other payables	6	151	...	-145	...	690	515	...	175	...
8 Other liabilities	1148	1148	...	...	...	585	585	...	...	...
Total Incurrence of Liabilities	12816	13278	...	-462	...	15219	13748	...	1471	...
Statistical discrepancy	447	342	...	105	...	-113	-251	...	138	...
Net Lending	-7912	-7768	...	703	-847	-10089	-9015	...	-1767	693
Incurrence of Liabilities and Net Worth	5351	5852	...	346	-847	5017	4482	...	-158	693

	1984 Total General Government	Central Government	State or Provincial Government	Local Government	Social Security Funds	1985 Total General Government	Central Government	State or Provincial Government	Local Government	Social Security Funds

Acquisition of Financial Assets

	Total General Government	Central Government	State or Provincial Government	Local Government	Social Security Funds	Total General Government	Central Government	State or Provincial Government	Local Government	Social Security Funds
1 Gold and SDRs	...	...	...	...	...	...	...	...	...	...
2 Currency and transferable deposits	-823	-757	...	-66	...	1743	1592	...	151	...
3 Other deposits	32	-92	...	124	...	368	-155	...	523	...
4 Bills and bonds, short term	3062	3062	...	-	...	1143	1129	...	14	...
A Corporate and quasi-corporate enterprises, resident	3062	3062	...	-	...	1143	1129	...	14	...
B Other government subsectors	...	...	...	...	...	...	...	...	...	...
C Rest of the world	...	...	...	...	...	...	...	...	...	...
5 Bonds, long term	-9	-22	...	13	...	-25	-28	...	3	...
A Corporations	...	...	...	...	...	...	...	...	...	...
B Other government subsectors	-9	-22	...	13	...	-25	-28	...	3	...
C Rest of the world	...	...	...	...	...	...	...	...	...	...
6 Corporate equity securities	-2427	-2431	...	4	...	-2334	-2344	...	10	...
7 Short-term loans, n.e.c.	849	-3	...	148	704	692	62	...	121	509
8 Long-term loans, n.e.c.	3475	3691	...	-216	...	5336	5971	...	-635	...
A Mortgages	-195	...	...	-195	...	-502	...	...	-502	...
B Other	3670	3691	...	-21	...	5838	5971	...	-133	...
9 Other receivables	1472	1206	...	-2	268	1295	757	...	208	330
10 Other assets	-9	-9	...	...	...	1	1	...	...	...
Total Acquisition of Financial Assets	5622	4645	...	5	972	8219	6985	...	395	839

Incurrence of Liabilities

	Total General Government	Central Government	State or Provincial Government	Local Government	Social Security Funds	Total General Government	Central Government	State or Provincial Government	Local Government	Social Security Funds
1 Currency and transferable deposits	617	617	...	...	...	429	429	...	...	...

3.14 General Government Capital Finance Account, Total and Subsectors
(Continued)

Million Pounds Sterling

	1984					1985				
	Total General Government	Central Government	State or Provincial Government	Local Government	Social Security Funds	Total General Government	Central Government	State or Provincial Government	Local Government	Social Security Funds
2 Other deposits	4386	3723	...	663	...	2803	3171	...	-368	...
3 Bills and bonds, short term	94	-12	...	106	...	231	100	...	131	...
4 Bonds, long term	8220	8558	...	-338	...	8926	9555	...	-629	...
5 Short-term loans, n.e.c.	332	545	...	-213	...	-765	615	...	-1380	...
6 Long-term loans, n.e.c.	1902	-399	...	2301	...	5659	1034	...	4625	...
7 Other payables	1684	1591	...	93	...	502	434	...	68	...
8 Other liabilities	759	759	...	...	...	712	712	...	...	...
Total Incurrence of Liabilities	17994	15382	...	2612	...	18497	16050	...	2447	...
Statistical discrepancy	357	469	...	-112	...	-589	-130	...	-459	...
Net Lending	-12729	-11206	...	-2495	972	-9689	-8935	...	-1593	839
Incurrence of Liabilities and Net Worth	5622	4645	...	5	972	8219	6985	...	395	839

	1986					1987				
	Total General Government	Central Government	State or Provincial Government	Local Government	Social Security Funds	Total General Government	Central Government	State or Provincial Government	Local Government	Social Security Funds
Acquisition of Financial Assets										
1 Gold and SDRs	...	...	...	...	...	...	...	...	...	...
2 Currency and transferable deposits	3335	3184	...	151	...	12448	11903	...	545	...
3 Other deposits	881	-149	...	1030	...	1162	-111	...	1273	...
4 Bills and bonds, short term	509	523	...	-14	...	-5735	-5735	...	-	...
A Corporate and quasi-corporate enterprises, resident	509	523	...	-14	...	-5735	-5735	...	-	...
B Other government subsectors	...	...	...	...	...	...	...	...	...	...
C Rest of the world	...	...	...	...	...	...	...	...	...	...
5 Bonds, long term	82	75	...	7	...	-183	-187	...	4	...
A Corporations	...	...	...	...	...	...	...	...	...	...
B Other government subsectors	82	75	...	7	...	-183	-187	...	4	...
C Rest of the world	...	...	...	...	...	...	...	...	...	...
6 Corporate equity securities	-3761	-3810	...	49	...	-5678	-5929	...	251	...
7 Short-term loans, n.e.c.	875	-75	...	619	331	1824	39	...	604	1181
8 Long-term loans, n.e.c.	3882	4670	...	-788	...	4738	5316	...	-578	...
A Mortgages	-506	...	...	-506	...	-445	...	...	-445	...
B Other	4388	4670	...	-282	...	5183	5316	...	-133	...
9 Other receivables	-1600	-1270	...	-192	-138	862	686	...	-115	291
10 Other assets	-9	-9	...	...	...	-3	-3	...	...	...
Total Acquisition of Financial Assets	4194	3139	...	862	193	9435	5979	...	1984	1472
Incurrence of Liabilities										
1 Currency and transferable deposits	674	674	...	...	...	1089	1089	...	...	...
2 Other deposits	1175	2190	...	-1015	...	1153	2093	...	-940	...
3 Bills and bonds, short term	-128	1	...	-129	...	2551	2460	...	91	...
4 Bonds, long term	6640	6870	...	-230	...	4509	4648	...	-139	...
5 Short-term loans, n.e.c.	-880	256	...	-1136	...	655	1428	...	-773	...
6 Long-term loans, n.e.c.	7385	2416	...	4969	...	4952	-240	...	5192	...
7 Other payables	-175	-156	...	-19	...	512	469	...	43	...
8 Other liabilities	870	870	...	...	...	903	903	...	...	...
Total Incurrence of Liabilities	15561	13121	...	2440	...	16324	12850	...	3474	...
Statistical discrepancy	-661	-149	...	-512	...	-1009	-741	...	-268	...
Net Lending	-10706	-9833	...	-1066	193	-5880	-6130	...	-1222	1472
Incurrence of Liabilities and Net Worth	4194	3139	...	862	193	9435	5979	...	1984	1472

United Kingdom

3.22 Corporate and Quasi-Corporate Enterprise Income and Outlay Account: Total and Sectors

Million Pounds Sterling

	1980			1981			1982			1983		
	TOTAL	Non-Financial	Financial	TOTAL	Non-Financial	Financial	TOTAL	Non-Financial	Financial	TOTAL	Non-Financial	Financial
Receipts												
1 Operating surplus	11514	16766	-5252	10857	18486	-7629	16382	24837	-8455	24127	31049	-6922
2 Property and entrepreneurial income	44405	7526	36879	52179	8541	43638	56653	8848	47805	56293	9649	46644
A Withdrawals from quasi-corporate enterprises	44405	7526	36879	52179	8541	43638	56653	8848	47805	56293	9649	46644
B Interest	...	...	...	...	...	...	...	...	...	...	...	...
C Dividends	...	...	...	...	...	...	...	...	...	...	...	...
D Net land rent and royalties	...	...	...	...	...	...	...	...	...	...	...	...
3 Current transfers	...	...	...	...	...	...	...	...	...	...	...	...
Total Current Receipts	55919	24292	31627	63036	27027	36009	73035	33685	39350	80420	40698	39722
Disbursements												
1 Property and entrepreneurial income	46653	18407	28246	53457	19554	33903	58784	21777	37007	57816	23017	34799
2 Direct taxes and other current transfers n.e.c. to general government	6839	5781	1058	8740	7856	884	10746	9753	993	12323	11329	994
A Direct taxes	6839	5781	1058	8740	7856	884	10746	9753	993	12323	11329	994
B Fines, fees, penalties and other current transfers n.e.c.	...	...	...	...	...	...	...	...	...	...	...	...
3 Other current transfers	52	43	9	62	51	11	69	57	12	86	71	15
A Casualty insurance premiums, net	...	...	...	...	...	...	...	...	...	...	...	...
B Casualty insurance claims liability of insurance companies	...	...	...	...	...	...	...	...	...	...	...	...
C Transfers to private non-profit institutions	52	43	9	62	51	11	69	57	12	86	71	15
D Unfunded employee pension and welfare benefits	...	...	...	...	...	...	...	...	...	...	...	...
E Social assistance grants	...	...	...	...	...	...	...	...	...	...	...	...
F Other transfers n.e.c.	-	-	-	-	-	-	-	-	-	-	-	-
G Transfers to the rest of the world	...	...	...	...	...	...	...	...	...	...	...	...
Net saving	2375	61	2314	777	-434	1211	3436	2098	1338	10195	6281	3914
Total Current Disbursements and Net Saving	55919	24292	31627	63036	27027	36009	73035	33685	39350	80420	40698	39722

	1984			1985			1986			1987		
	TOTAL	Non-Financial	Financial	TOTAL	Non-Financial	Financial	TOTAL	Non-Financial	Financial	TOTAL	Non-Financial	Financial
Receipts												
1 Operating surplus	24938	34670	-9732	31552	41205	-9653	27662	37636	-9974	34763	44589	-9826
2 Property and entrepreneurial income	63130	8719	54411	73882	9850	64032	78475	11516	66959	83470	11783	71687
A Withdrawals from quasi-corporate enterprises	63130	8719	54411	73882	9850	64032	78475	11516	66959	83470	11783	71687
B Interest	...	...	...	...	...	...	...	...	...	...	...	...
C Dividends	...	...	...	...	...	...	...	...	...	...	...	...
D Net land rent and royalties	...	...	...	...	...	...	...	...	...	...	...	...
3 Current transfers	...	...	...	...	...	...	...	...	...	...	...	...
Total Current Receipts	88068	43389	44679	105434	51055	54379	106137	49152	56985	118233	56372	61861
Disbursements												
1 Property and entrepreneurial income	65690	23578	42112	77176	26906	50270	79944	28675	51269	86800	32423	54377
2 Direct taxes and other current transfers n.e.c. to general government	14418	13255	1163	17045	15766	1279	15338	13586	1752	16562	13999	2563
A Direct taxes	14418	13255	1163	17045	15766	1279	15338	13586	1752	16562	13999	2563
B Fines, fees, penalties and other current transfers n.e.c.	...	...	...	...	...	...	...	...	...	...	...	...

3.22 Corporate and Quasi-Corporate Enterprise Income and Outlay Account: Total and Sectors
(Continued)

Million Pounds Sterling

	1984			1985			1986			1987		
	TOTAL	Non-Financial	Financial	TOTAL	Non-Financial	Financial	TOTAL	Non-Financial	Financial	TOTAL	Non-Financial	Financial
3 Other current transfers	107	88	19	123	102	21	158	128	30	184	141	43
A Casualty insurance premiums, net	...	...	...	...	...	...	...	...	...	...	...	...
B Casualty insurance claims liability of insurance companies	...	...	...	...	...	...	...	...	...	...	...	...
C Transfers to private non-profit institutions	105	86	19	119	98	21	145	118	27	160	127	33
D Unfunded employee pension and welfare benefits	...	...	...	...	...	...	...	...	...	...	...	...
E Social assistance grants	...	...	...	...	...	...	...	...	...	...	...	...
F Other transfers n.e.c.	2	2	-	4	4	-	13	10	3	24	14	10
G Transfers to the rest of the world	...	...	...	...	...	...	...	...	...	...	...	...
Net saving	7853	6468	1385	11090	8281	2809	10697	6763	3934	14687	9809	4878
Total Current Disbursements and Net Saving	88068	43389	44679	105434	51055	54379	106137	49152	56985	118233	56372	61861

	1988			1989			1990			1991		
	TOTAL	Non-Financial	Financial	TOTAL	Non-Financial	Financial	TOTAL	Non-Financial	Financial	TOTAL	Non-Financial	Financial
Receipts												
1 Operating surplus	37218	51768	-14550	37072	52620	-15548	32274	51537	-19263	27906	49163	-21257
2 Property and entrepreneurial income	99560	14421	85139	151385	25897	125488	172718	26835	145883	165741	28715	137026
A Withdrawals from quasi-corporate enterprises	99560	14421	85139	151385	25897	125488	172718	26835	145883	165741	28715	137026
B Interest	...	...	...	...	...	...	...	...	...	...	...	...
C Dividends	...	...	...	...	...	...	...	...	...	...	...	...
D Net land rent and royalties	...	...	...	...	...	...	...	...	...	...	...	...
3 Current transfers	...	...	...	...	...	...	...	...	...	...	...	...
Total Current Receipts	136778	66189	70589	188457	78517	109940	204992	78372	126620	193647	77878	115769
Disbursements												
1 Property and entrepreneurial income	106384	40889	65495	158981	59476	99505	182225	63422	118803	175139	66180	108959
2 Direct taxes and other current transfers n.e.c. to general government	18808	16228	2580	23110	20208	2902	22270	19859	2411	18409	16730	1679
A Direct taxes	18808	16228	2580	23110	20208	2902	22270	19859	2411	18409	16730	1679
B Fines, fees, penalties and other current transfers n.e.c.	...	...	...	...	...	...	...	...	...	...	...	...
3 Other current transfers	232	181	51	324	260	64	334	265	69	314	258	56
A Casualty insurance premiums, net	...	...	...	...	...	...	...	...	...	...	...	...
B Casualty insurance claims liability of insurance companies	...	...	...	...	...	...	...	...	...	...	...	...
C Transfers to private non-profit institutions	200	164	36	284	239	45	299	249	50	288	249	39
D Unfunded employee pension and welfare benefits	...	...	...	...	...	...	...	...	...	...	...	...
E Social assistance grants	...	...	...	...	...	...	...	...	...	...	...	...
F Other transfers n.e.c.	32	17	15	40	21	19	35	16	19	26	9	17
G Transfers to the rest of the world	...	...	...	...	...	...	...	...	...	...	...	...
Net saving	11354	8891	2463	6042	-1427	7469	163	-5174	5337	-215	-5290	5075
Total Current Disbursements and Net Saving	136778	66189	70589	188457	78517	109940	204992	78372	126620	193647	77878	115769

3.23 Corporate and Quasi-Corporate Enterprise Capital Accumulation Account: Total and Sectors

Million Pounds Sterling

	1980			1981			1982			1983		
	TOTAL	Non-Financial	Financial	TOTAL	Non-Financial	Financial	TOTAL	Non-Financial	Financial	TOTAL	Non-Financial	Financial
Finance of Gross Accumulation												
1 Gross saving	21128	17959	3169	21983	19785	2198	26107	23697	2410	34467	29341	5126
A Consumption of fixed capital	18753	17898	855	21206	20219	987	22671	21599	1072	24272	23060	1212
B Net saving	2375	61	2314	777	-434	1211	3436	2098	1338	10195	6281	3914
2 Capital transfers	1343	1343	-	4873	4873	-	2339	2339	-	1428	1428	-

United Kingdom

3.23 Corporate and Quasi-Corporate Enterprise Capital Accumulation Account: Total and Sectors
(Continued)

Million Pounds Sterling

	1980			1981			1982			1983		
	TOTAL	Non-Financial	Financial	TOTAL	Non-Financial	Financial	TOTAL	Non-Financial	Financial	TOTAL	Non-Financial	Financial
A From resident sectors	1343	1343	-	4873	4873	-	2339	2339	-	1428	1428	-
B From the rest of the world	...	...	...	...	...	...	...	...	...	...	...	...
Finance of Gross Accumulation	22471	19302	3169	26856	24658	2198	28446	26036	2410	35895	30769	5126
Gross Accumulation												
1 Gross capital formation	24135	20886	3249	24328	20876	3452	26940	23224	3716	29890	26789	3101
A Increase in stocks	-2375	-2381	6	-2464	-2473	9	-1401	-1405	4	1071	1033	38
B Gross fixed capital formation	26510	23267	3243	26792	23349	3443	28341	24629	3712	28819	25756	3063
2 Purchases of land, net	...	...	...	...	...	...	...	...	...	...	...	...
3 Purchases of intangible assets, net	...	...	...	...	...	...	...	...	...	...	...	...
4 Capital transfers	150	150	-	411	144	267	185	97	88	222	222	-
A To resident sectors	150	150	-	411	144	267	185	97	88	222	222	-
B To the rest of the world	...	...	...	...	...	...	...	...	...	...	...	...
Net lending	-1814	-1734	-80	2117	3638	-1521	1321	2715	-1394	5783	3758	2025
Gross Accumulation	22471	19302	3169	26856	24658	2198	28446	26036	2410	35895	30769	5126

	1984			1985			1986			1987		
	TOTAL	Non-Financial	Financial	TOTAL	Non-Financial	Financial	TOTAL	Non-Financial	Financial	TOTAL	Non-Financial	Financial
Finance of Gross Accumulation												
1 Gross saving	33682	30999	2683	38880	34600	4280	40322	34764	5558	45771	39083	6688
A Consumption of fixed capital	25829	24531	1298	27790	26319	1471	29625	28001	1624	31084	29274	1810
B Net saving	7853	6468	1385	11090	8281	2809	10697	6763	3934	14687	9809	4878
2 Capital transfers	1303	1303	-	1375	1375	-	3009	3009	-	1352	1352	-
A From resident sectors	1303	1303	-	1375	1375	-	3009	3009	-	1352	1352	-
B From the rest of the world	...	...	...	...	...	...	...	...	...	...	...	...
Finance of Gross Accumulation	34985	32302	2683	40255	35975	4280	43331	37773	5558	47123	40435	6688
Gross Accumulation												
1 Gross capital formation	34292	30522	3770	38236	34880	3356	39412	35613	3799	46313	42135	4178
A Increase in stocks	828	804	24	416	416	-	598	598	-	1569	1569	-
B Gross fixed capital formation	33464	29718	3746	37820	34464	3356	38814	35015	3799	44744	40566	4178
2 Purchases of land, net	...	...	...	...	...	...	...	...	...	...	...	...
3 Purchases of intangible assets, net	...	...	...	...	...	...	...	...	...	...	...	...
4 Capital transfers	245	245	-	258	258	-	375	375	-	372	372	-
A To resident sectors	245	245	-	258	258	-	375	375	-	372	372	-
B To the rest of the world	...	...	...	...	...	...	...	...	...	...	...	...
Net lending	448	1535	-1087	1761	837	924	3544	1785	1759	438	-2072	2510
Gross Accumulation	34985	32302	2683	40255	35975	4280	43331	37773	5558	47123	40435	6688

	1988			1989			1990			1991		
	TOTAL	Non-Financial	Financial	TOTAL	Non-Financial	Financial	TOTAL	Non-Financial	Financial	TOTAL	Non-Financial	Financial
Finance of Gross Accumulation												
1 Gross saving	44116	39659	4457	41551	31934	9617	38466	30817	7649	39455	31968	7487
A Consumption of fixed capital	32762	30768	1994	35509	33361	2148	38303	35991	2312	39670	37258	2412
B Net saving	11354	8891	2463	6042	-1427	7469	163	-5174	5337	-215	-5290	5075
2 Capital transfers	5952	5952	-	7042	7042	-	8199	8199	-	3393	3393	-
A From resident sectors	5952	5952	-	7042	7042	-	8199	8199	-	3393	3393	-
B From the rest of the world	...	...	...	...	...	...	...	...	...	...	...	...
Finance of Gross Accumulation	50068	45611	4457	48593	38976	9617	46665	39016	7649	42848	35361	7487
Gross Accumulation												
1 Gross capital formation	59111	52580	6531	68559	60687	7872	64909	58116	6793	54629	48432	6197
A Increase in stocks	4505	4505	-	2872	2872	-	-1702	-1702	-	-5161	-5161	-
B Gross fixed capital formation	54606	48075	6531	65687	57815	7872	66611	59818	6793	59790	53593	6197

3.23 Corporate and Quasi-Corporate Enterprise Capital Accumulation Account: Total and Sectors
(Continued)

Million Pounds Sterling

	1988			1989			1990			1991		
	TOTAL	Non-Financial	Financial	TOTAL	Non-Financial	Financial	TOTAL	Non-Financial	Financial	TOTAL	Non-Financial	Financial
2 Purchases of land, net	...	...	...	...	...	...	...	...	...	...	...	...
3 Purchases of intangible assets, net	...	...	...	...	...	...	...	...	...	...	...	...
4 Capital transfers	419	419	-	467	467	-	453	453	-	402	402	-
A To resident sectors	419	419	-	467	467	-	453	453	-	402	402	-
B To the rest of the world	...	...	...	...	...	...	...	...	...	...	...	...
Net lending	-9462	-7388	-2074	-20433	-22178	1745	-18697	-19553	856	-12183	-13473	1290
Gross Accumulation	50068	45611	4457	48593	38976	9617	46665	39016	7649	42848	35361	7487

3.24 Corporate and Quasi-Corporate Enterprise Capital Finance Account: Total and Sectors

Million Pounds Sterling

	1980			1981			1982			1983		
	TOTAL	Non-Financial	Financial	TOTAL	Non-Financial	Financial	TOTAL	Non-Financial	Financial	TOTAL	Non-Financial	Financial
Acquisition of Financial Assets												
1 Gold and SDRs	...	...	...	...	...	...	...	...	...	...	...	...
2 Currency and transferable deposits	-442	-224	-218	2573	1629	944	1224	368	856	2594	2066	528
3 Other deposits	26842	3298	23544	29418	3972	25446	12818	2506	10312	20035	3477	16558
4 Bills and bonds, short term	2131	388	1743	-113	69	-182	-1869	46	-1915	2127	325	1802
A Corporate and quasi-corporate, resident	1411	383	1028	845	80	765	-943	-24	-919	1904	227	1677
B Government	720	5	715	-958	-11	-947	-926	70	-996	223	98	125
C Rest of the world	...	...	...	...	...	...	...	...	...	...	...	...
5 Bonds, long term	8903	412	8491	7871	-54	7925	8661	546	8115	12205	406	11799
A Corporate, resident	...	...	...	...	...	...	...	...	...	...	...	...
B Government	214	214	...	-339	-339	...	403	403	...	377	377	...
C Rest of the world	...	...	...	...	...	...	...	...	...	...	...	...
6 Corporate equity securities	7669	2225	5444	7649	1382	6267	9472	1920	7552	9277	1794	7483
7 Short term loans, n.e.c.	19635	68	19567	24198	98	24100	21334	-3	21337	9305	44	9261
8 Long term loans, n.e.c.	10397	2004	8393	13938	3549	10389	17180	2523	14657	20183	3803	16380
A Mortgages	6615	37	6578	8896	29	8867	13201	-30	13231	14753	-57	14810
B Other	3782	1967	1815	5042	3520	1522	3979	2553	1426	5430	3860	1570
9 Trade credits and advances	746	746	...	3698	3698	...	556	556	...	1508	1508	...
A Consumer credit	-126	-126	...	378	378	...	32	32	...	109	109	...
B Other	872	872	...	3320	3320	...	524	524	...	1399	1399	...
10 Other receivables	...	...	...	...	...	...	...	...	...	...	...	...
11 Other assets	-71	-124	53	81	34	47	357	169	188	728	515	213
Total Acquisition of Financial Assets	75810	8793	67017	89313	14377	74936	69733	8631	61102	77962	13938	64024
Incurrence of Liabilities												
1 Currency and transferable deposits	2737	...	2737	6961	...	6961	6599	...	6599	7441	...	7441
2 Other deposits	47970	-145	48115	37364	-31	37395	29747	-3	29750	31972	18	31954
3 Bills and bonds, short term	2788	500	2288	15347	428	14919	8949	412	8537	4389	-595	4984
4 Bonds, long term	267	56	211	298	87	211	420	-75	495	1055	405	650
5 Corporate equity securities	1808	1329	479	3520	2282	1238	2465	1328	1137	4000	2014	1986
6 Short-term loans, n.e.c.	7349	5843	1506	7312	5931	1381	8261	6330	1931	4862	2058	2804
7 Long-term loans, n.e.c.	3715	3631	84	-2020	-2082	62	2767	2219	548	4432	3224	1208
8 Net equity of households in life insurance and pension fund reserves	12147	...	12147	14217	...	14217	14935	...	14935	15931	...	15931
9 Proprietors' net additions to the accumulation of quasi-corporations	...	...	...	...	...	...	...	...	...	...	...	...
10 Trade credit and advances	569	521	48	2258	2310	-52	170	142	28	1497	1477	20
11 Other accounts payable	...	...	...	...	...	...	...	...	...	...	...	...
12 Other liabilities	1617	679	938	3274	2744	530	-484	-1412	928	2474	1550	924
Total Incurrence of Liabilities	80967	12414	68553	88531	11669	76862	73829	8941	64888	78053	10151	67902
Statistical discrepancy	-3218	-2479	-739	-2299	-1042	-1257	-6538	-3572	-2966	-5941	-1235	-4706
Net Lending	-1939	-1142	-797	3081	3750	-669	2442	3262	-820	5850	5022	828
Incurrence of Liabilities and Net Lending	75810	8793	67017	89313	14377	74936	69733	8631	61102	77962	13938	64024

United Kingdom

3.24 Corporate and Quasi-Corporate Enterprise Capital Finance Account: Total and Sectors

Million Pounds Sterling

	1984 TOTAL	1984 Non-Financial	1984 Financial	1985 TOTAL	1985 Non-Financial	1985 Financial	1986 TOTAL	1986 Non-Financial	1986 Financial	1987 TOTAL	1987 Non-Financial	1987 Financial
Acquisition of Financial Assets												
1 Gold and SDRs	...	...	...	...	...	...	...	...	...	...	...	...
2 Currency and transferable deposits	4659	1832	2827	3599	1778	1821	6347	3557	2790	11284	5384	5900
3 Other deposits	18878	866	18012	33297	3735	29562	68046	7378	60668	65291	1726	63565
4 Bills and bonds, short term	197	-281	478	1376	173	1203	3970	471	3499	11301	3380	7921
A Corporate and quasi-corporate, resident	227	-154	381	1178	205	973	4039	425	3614	10132	2834	7298
B Government	-30	-127	97	198	-32	230	-69	46	-115	1169	546	623
C Rest of the world	...	...	...	...	...	...	...	...	...	...	...	...
5 Bonds, long term	17568	333	17235	21249	-292	21541	23318	341	22977	-5999	128	-6127
A Corporate, resident	...	...	...	...	...	...	...	...	...	...	...	...
B Government	-143	-143	...	-409	-409	...	-78	-78	...	-351	-351	...
C Rest of the world	...	...	...	...	...	...	...	...	...	...	...	...
6 Corporate equity securities	11991	4566	7425	19077	5898	13179	26917	5995	20922	22455	7353	15102
7 Short term loans, n.e.c.	16460	65	16395	12562	22	12540	27196	274	26922	41129	-23	41152
8 Long term loans, n.e.c.	20849	2023	18826	23858	993	22865	26082	-1705	27787	38311	6126	32185
A Mortgages	17248	-62	17310	19466	-93	19559	26906	-120	27026	29887	-265	30152
B Other	3601	2085	1516	4392	1086	3306	-824	-1585	761	8424	6391	2033
9 Trade credits and advances	459	459	...	612	612	...	617	617	...	739	739	...
A Consumer credit	200	200	...	118	118	...	-103	-103	...	49	49	...
B Other	259	259	...	494	494	...	720	720	...	690	690	...
10 Other receivables	...	...	...	...	...	...	...	...	...	...	...	...
11 Other assets	2051	1669	382	922	342	580	1229	500	729	1447	751	696
Total Acquisition of Financial Assets	93112	11532	81580	116552	13261	103291	183722	17428	166294	185958	25564	160394
Incurrence of Liabilities												
1 Currency and transferable deposits	11362	...	11362	19238	...	19238	4226	...	4226	24482	...	24482
2 Other deposits	40170	-	40170	48891	-	48891	90918	18	90900	66549	432	66117
3 Bills and bonds, short term	830	-191	1021	-4890	26	-4916	16815	991	15824	20675	1590	19085
4 Bonds, long term	1362	230	1132	8154	797	7357	6322	698	5624	4173	645	3528
5 Corporate equity securities	3462	1457	2005	6966	4239	2727	14886	7105	7781	25845	17495	8350
6 Short-term loans, n.e.c.	14594	8204	6390	11129	6739	4390	24518	8373	16145	30033	12131	17902
7 Long-term loans, n.e.c.	-2835	-2328	-507	2404	-31	2435	-986	-639	-347	1276	-42	1318
8 Net equity of households in life insurance and pension fund reserves	17755	...	17755	18420	...	18420	18756	...	18756	19669	...	19669
9 Proprietors' net additions to the accumulation of quasi-corporations	...	...	...	...	...	...	...	...	...	...	...	...
10 Trade credit and advances	259	239	20	496	476	20	725	705	20	689	669	20
11 Other accounts payable	...	...	...	...	...	...	...	...	...	...	...	...
12 Other liabilities	3019	852	2167	3522	229	3293	1639	275	1364	3857	785	3072
Total Incurrence of Liabilities	89978	8463	81515	114330	12475	101855	177819	17526	160293	197248	33705	163543
Statistical discrepancy	-11	-1003	992	-3808	-4094	286	-4064	-5913	1849	-22771	-14723	-8048
Net Lending	3145	4072	-927	6030	4880	1150	9967	5815	4152	11481	6582	4899
Incurrence of Liabilities and Net Lending	93112	11532	81580	116552	13261	103291	183722	17428	166294	185958	25564	160394

3.32 Household and Private Unincorporated Enterprise Income and Outlay Account

Million Pounds Sterling

	1980	1981	1982	1983	1984	1985	1986	1987	1988	1989	1990	1991
Receipts												
1 Compensation of employees	137783	149737	158838	169847	181406	196858	212374	229836	255625	282919	311745	329808
A Wages and salaries	119149	128037	136462	145737	156067	170364	184581	200413	223753	248568	274903	289741
B Employers' contributions for social security	8210	8814	9344	10536	11269	12245	13540	14878	16817	17912	20076	21362
C Employers' contributions for private pension & welfare plans	10424	12886	13032	13574	14070	14249	14253	14545	15055	16439	16766	18705
2 Operating surplus of private unincorporated enterprises	21080	23754	26932	29802	33126	35914	41519	46650	54578	63434	72786	74650
3 Property and entrepreneurial income	18674	20341	22765	23990	29597	36377	38153	41019	47424	61404	70801	67686
A Withdrawals from private quasi-corporations	...	...	...	...	...	...	...	...	...	...	...	...
B Interest	18674	20341	22765	23990	29597	36377	38153	41019	47424	61404	70801	67686

3.32 Household and Private Unincorporated Enterprise Income and Outlay Account
(Continued)

Million Pounds Sterling

	1980	1981	1982	1983	1984	1985	1986	1987	1988	1989	1990	1991
C Dividends	...	...	...	...	...	...	...	...	...	...	...	...
D Net land rent and royalties	...	...	...	...	...	...	...	...	...	...	...	...
3 Current transfers	26511	32421	37901	41470	44777	48707	52861	54320	56002	58827	64101	73955
A Casualty insurance claims	-	-	-	-	-	-	-	-	-	-	-	-
B Social security benefits	14689	17674	19151	20582	21630	23085	25383	25878	26698	28216	30702	34709
C Social assistance grants	9260	11782	15413	16892	18824	20909	22425	23253	23532	25030	27878	33246
D Unfunded employee pension and welfare benefits	-	-	-	-	-	-	-	-	-	-	-	-
E Transfers from general government	1575	1786	2020	2382	2566	2819	3176	3363	3857	3547	3422	3812
F Transfers from the rest of the world	935	1117	1248	1528	1652	1775	1732	1666	1715	1750	1800	1900
G Other transfers n.e.c.	52	62	69	86	105	119	145	160	200	284	299	288
Total Current Receipts	204048	226253	246436	265109	288906	317856	344907	371825	413629	466584	519433	546099

Disbursements

	1980	1981	1982	1983	1984	1985	1986	1987	1988	1989	1990	1991
1 Final consumption expenditures	138863	154551	169604	185817	198944	217436	241432	265879	300330	328700	348533	365930
2 Property income	10236	11359	12678	13424	17085	22538	24531	26912	30799	44397	53306	51325
A Interest	10236	11359	12678	13424	17085	22538	24531	26912	30799	44397	53306	51325
Consumer debt	...	...	...	...	...	...	...	...	...	...	...	...
Mortgage	6175	6847	7599	7544	11744	15841	17154	18933	21833	31696	38772	37631
Other	...	...	...	...	...	...	...	...	...	...	...	...
B Net land rent and royalties	...	...	...	...	...	...	...	...	...	...	...	...
3 Direct taxes and other current transfers n.e.c. to government	39703	45075	49817	54279	57193	61885	66695	71743	80193	85926	103043	105801
A Social security contributions	13939	15916	18095	20780	22322	24210	26165	28642	32106	32902	34651	36643
B Direct taxes	25576	28961	31511	33250	34628	37421	40245	42730	47691	52008	59253	60608
Income taxes	24850	28121	30489	32066	33339	35939	38679	41118	45998	50215	57416	58729
Other	726	840	1022	1184	1289	1482	1566	1612	1693	1793	1837	1879
C Fees, fines and penalties	188	198	211	249	243	254	285	371	396	430	510	388
4 Other current transfers	1139	1057	1200	1191	1283	1459	1656	1789	1985	2050	2100	2200
A Net casualty insurance premiums	-	-	-	-	-	-	-	-	-	-	-	-
B Transfers to private non-profit institutions serving households	...	...	...	...	...	...	...	...	...	...	...	...
C Transfers to the rest of the world	1139	1057	1200	1191	1283	1459	1656	1789	1985	2050	2100	2200
D Other current transfers, except imputed	...	...	...	...	...	...	...	...	...	...	...	...
E Imputed employee pension and welfare contributions	-	-	-	-	-	-	-	-	-	-	-	-
Net saving	14107	14211	13137	10398	14401	14538	10593	5502	322	5511	12451	20843
Total Current Disbursements and Net Saving	204048	226253	246436	265109	288906	317856	344907	371825	413629	466584	519433	546099

3.33 Household and Private Unincorporated Enterprise Capital Accumulation Account

Million Pounds Sterling

	1980	1981	1982	1983	1984	1985	1986	1987	1988	1989	1990	1991
Finance of Gross Accumulation												
1 Gross saving	20196	21131	20546	18599	23525	24544	21645	17843	14894	20720	29124	38063
A Consumption of fixed capital	6089	6920	7409	8201	9124	10006	11052	12341	14572	15209	16673	17220
B Net saving	14107	14211	13137	10398	14401	14538	10593	5502	322	5511	12451	20843
2 Capital transfers	1278	1178	1645	2410	2809	2206	1870	2098	2107	2509	3124	3966
A From resident sectors	1278	1178	1645	2410	2809	2206	1870	2098	2107	2509	3124	3966
B From the rest of the world	...	...	...	...	...	...	...	...	...	...	...	...
Total Finance of Gross Accumulation	21474	22309	22191	21009	26334	26750	23515	19941	17001	23229	32248	42029
Gross Accumulation												
1 Gross Capital Formation	9159	9629	12104	14075	14972	15616	18546	22073	29344	28422	26842	23186
A Increase in stocks	-240	-211	58	148	188	-45	355	317	599	429	84	-293
B Gross fixed capital formation	9399	9840	12046	13927	14784	15661	18191	21756	28745	27993	26758	23479

United Kingdom

3.33 Household and Private Unincorporated Enterprise Capital Accumulation Account
(Continued)

Million Pounds Sterling

	1980	1981	1982	1983	1984	1985	1986	1987	1988	1989	1990	1991
2 Purchases of land, net	...	...	...	...	...	...	...	...	...	...	...	...
3 Purchases of intangibles, net	...	...	...	...	...	...	...	...	...	...	...	...
4 Capital transfers	512	539	582	641	738	932	1037	1128	1175	1261	1407	1279
A To resident sectors	512	539	582	641	738	932	1037	1128	1175	1261	1407	1279
B To the rest of the world	...	...	...	...	...	...	...	...	...	...	...	...
Net lending	11803	12141	9505	6294	10624	10202	3932	-3260	-13518	-6454	3999	17564
Total Gross Accumulation	21474	22309	22191	21010	26334	26750	23515	19941	17001	23229	32248	42029

3.34 Household and Private Unincorporated Enterprise Capital Finance Account

Million Pounds Sterling

	1980	1981	1982	1983	1984	1985	1986	1987	1988	1989	1990	1991
Acquisition of Financial Assets												
1 Gold	...	...	...	...	...	...	...	...				...
2 Currency and transferable deposits	1345	1538	2977	2546	3476	6986	7566	7716	...	...	...	...
3 Other deposits	15285	14315	14940	14413	16716	14514	15970	16624	...	...	...	...
4 Bills and bonds, short term	...	...	...	...	...	...	...	...	...	...	...	...
5 Bonds, long term	1419	1381	1762	1401	1178	4766	3320	3754	...	...	...	...
A Corporate	92	-220	-193	289	-77	1233	173	56	...	...	...	...
B Government	1412	1969	1981	820	1113	1381	2061	2821	...	...	...	...
C Rest of the world	-85	-368	-26	292	142	2152	1086	877	...	...	...	...
6 Corporate equity securities	-3012	-1492	-2717	-1497	-4976	-3672	1189	4510	...	...	...	...
7 Short term loans, n.e.c.	99	126	75	292	380	333	267	660	...	...	...	...
8 Long term loans, n.e.c.	149	176	-622	-389	-180	-496	-676	-737	...	...	...	...
A Mortgages	...	...	...	...	...	...	...	...	...	...	...	...
B Other	149	176	-622	-389	-180	-496	-676	-737	...	...	...	...
9 Trade credit and advances	...	...	...	...	...	...	...	...	...	...	...	...
10 Net equity of households in life insurance and pension fund reserves	12846	14863	15556	16622	18523	19133	19640	20574	...	...	...	...
11 Proprietors' net additions to the accumulation of quasi-corporations	...	...	...	...	...	...	...	...	...	...	...	...
12 Other	347	263	636	699	1187	1824	1826	2079	...	...	...	...
Total Acquisition of Financial Assets	28478	31170	32607	34087	36304	43388	49102	55180	...	...	...	...
Incurrence of Liabilities												
1 Short term loans, n.e.c.	2966	3975	5015	4892	4075	6528	5059	8216	...	...	...	...
2 Long term loans, n.e.c.	7970	10088	14516	15335	17661	20566	27455	31887	...	...	...	...
A Mortgages	7368	9483	14127	14501	17030	19032	26468	29504	...	...	...	...
B Other	602	605	389	834	631	1534	987	2383	...	...	...	...
3 Trade credit and advances	-126	378	32	109	200	118	-103	49	...	...	...	...
A Consumer credit	-126	378	32	109	200	118	-103	49	...	...	...	...
B Other	...	...	...	...	...	...	...	...	...	...	...	...
4 Other accounts payable	4	182	-254	162	7	17	-9	19	...	...	...	...
5 Other liabilities	-1	16	-29	-2	-1	4	75	24	...	...	...	...
Total Incurrence of Liabilities	10813	14639	19280	20496	21942	27233	32477	40195	...	...	...	...
Statistical discrepancy	5056	4007	2659	5635	4832	9080	16413	21659	...	...	...	...
Net Lending	12609	12524	10668	7956	9530	7075	212	-6674	...	...	...	...
Incurrence of Liabilities and Net Lending	28478	31170	32607	34087	36304	43388	49102	55180	...	...	...	...

3.51 External Transactions: Current Account: Detail

Million Pounds Sterling

	1980	1981	1982	1983	1984	1985	1986	1987	1988	1989	1990	1991
Payments to the Rest of the World												
1 Imports of goods and services	57900	60607	68030	77737	92940	99054	101213	112061	125379	143325	148347	141037
A Imports of merchandise c.i.f.	48319	49980	55974	64784	78283	83952	84783	93372	105013	120226	124035	117031
B Other	9581	10627	12056	12953	14657	15102	16430	18689	20366	23099	24312	24006
2 Factor income to the rest of the world	21890	34953	42100	38725	45280	46334	41891	41391	50223	67328	75208	74752

3.51 External Transactions: Current Account: Detail
(Continued)

Million Pounds Sterling

	1980	1981	1982	1983	1984	1985	1986	1987	1988	1989	1990	1991
A Compensation of employees	256	258	298	320	350	385	430	487	397	490	521	512
B Property and entrepreneurial income	21634	34695	41802	38405	44930	45949	41461	40904	49826	66838	74687	74240
By general government	895	940	1090	1188	1342	1494	1677	2046	2323	2510	2237	1897
By corporate and quasi-corporate enterprises	20739	33755	40712	37217	43588	44455	39784	38858	47503	64328	72450	72343
By other												
3 Current transfers to the rest of the world	3936	4530	5344	5504	5930	6759	6197	7701	7574	8756	9202	8387
A Indirect taxes by general government to supranational organizations	1837	2372	3070	3129	3354	3516	2967	4404	3150	4709	4927	3546
B Other current transfers	2099	2158	2274	2375	2576	3243	3230	3297	4424	4047	4275	4841
By general government	960	1101	1074	1184	1293	1784	1574	1508	2439	1997	2175	2641
By other resident sectors	1139	1057	1200	1191	1283	1459	1656	1789	1985	2050	2100	2200
4 Surplus of the nation on current transactions	3439	6300	4087	2753	-742	1704	-3226	-8472	-22401	-27486	-23219	-10503
Payments to the Rest of the World, and Surplus of the Nation on Current Transfers	87165	106390	119561	124719	143408	153851	146075	152681	160775	191923	209538	213673

Receipts From The Rest of the world

	1980	1981	1982	1983	1984	1985	1986	1987	1988	1989	1990	1991
1 Exports of goods and services	63097	67837	73184	80511	92402	102706	98817	107621	108316	122756	134225	135871
A Exports of merchandise f.o.b.	47149	50668	55331	60700	70265	77991	72627	79153	80306	92108	101683	103394
B Other	15948	17169	17853	19811	22137	24715	26190	28468	28010	30648	32542	32477
2 Factor income from the rest of the world	22116	35570	42774	40297	46806	47497	43218	40759	48403	64989	71008	70764
A Compensation of employees	69	72	76	73	71	75	75	90	90	90	100	100
B Property and entrepreneurial income	22047	35498	42698	40224	46735	47422	43143	40669	48313	64899	70908	70664
By general government	946	971	979	765	818	735	765	931	1456	1949	1812	1763
By corporate and quasi-corporate enterprises	21101	34527	41719	39459	45917	46687	42378	39738	46857	62950	69096	68901
By other												
3 Current transfers from the rest of the world	1952	2983	3603	3911	4200	3648	4040	4301	4056	4178	4305	7038
A Subsidies to general government from supranational organizations	604	867	983	1217	1494	1248	1540	1683	1588	1583	1754	1989
B Other current transfers	1348	2116	2620	2694	2706	2400	2500	2618	2468	2595	2551	5049
To general government	413	999	1372	1166	1054	625	768	952	753	845	751	3149
To other resident sectors	935	1117	1248	1528	1652	1775	1732	1666	1715	1750	1800	1900
Receipts from the Rest of the World on Current Transfers	87165	106390	119561	124719	143408	153851	146075	152681	160775	191923	209538	213673

3.52 External Transactions: Capital Accumulation Account

Million Pounds Sterling

	1980	1981	1982	1983	1984	1985	1986	1987	1988	1989	1990	1991
				Finance of Gross Accumulation								
1 Surplus of the nation on current transactions	3439	6300	4087	2753	-742	1704	-3226	-8472	-22401	-27486	-23219	-10503
2 Capital transfers from the rest of the world	...	...	...	...	...	...	...	...	...	...	...	...
Total Finance of Gross Accumulation	3439	6300	4087	2753	-742	1704	-3226	-8472	-22401	-27486	-23219	-10503
				Gross Accumulation								
1 Capital transfers to the rest of the world	-	-	-	-	-	-	-	-	-	-	-	-
A By general government	-	-	-	-	-	-	-	-	-	-	-	-
B By other resident sectors	...	...	...	...	...	...	...	...	...	...	...	...
2 Purchases of intangible assets, n.e.c., net, from the rest of the world	...	...	...	...	...	...	...	...	...	...	...	...
Net lending to the rest of the world	3439	6300	4087	2753	-742	1704	-3226	-8472	-22401	-27486	-23219	-10503
Total Gross Accumulation	3439	6300	4087	2753	-742	1704	-3226	-8472	-22401	-27486	-23219	-10503

United Kingdom

3.53 External Transactions: Capital Finance Account

Million Pounds Sterling

	1980	1981	1982	1983	1984	1985	1986	1987	1988	1989	1990	1991
Acquisitions of Foreign Financial Assets												
1 Gold and SDR's	...	...	...	...	...	...	...	...	...	...	...	...
2 Currency and transferable deposits	291	-2419	-1421	-607	-908	1758	2891	12012	...	...	...	...
3 Other deposits	22435	24805	9125	13642	13433	24478	53212	49338	...	...	...	...
4 Bills and bonds, short term	312	1746	2029	579	1213	-460	983	-2644	...	...	...	...
5 Bonds, long term	1038	1459	3903	4305	10086	14406	18179	-5574	...	...	...	...
6 Corporate equity securities	4044	5412	4575	4769	2466	8120	13734	3632	...	...	...	...
7 Short-term loans, n.e.c.	8985	11232	6941	599	-1655	-3305	-358	4698	...	...	...	...
8 Long-term loans	3468	5681	3421	6061	3543	1690	-2667	5173	...	...	...	...
9 Prpoprietors' net additions to accumulation of quasi-corporate, non-resident enterprises	...	...	...	...	...	...	...	...	...	...	...	...
10 Trade credit and advances	313	530	-290	-	-	-	-	-	...	...	...	...
11 Other	...	...	...	...	...	...	...	...	...	...	...	...
Total Acquisitions of Foreign Financial Assets	40886	48446	28283	29348	28178	46687	85974	66635	...	...	...	...
Incurrence of Foreign Liabilities												
1 Currency and transferable deposits	1902	3458	2693	3014	3759	9097	-9457	6135	...	...	...	...
2 Other deposits	30023	22698	14393	14462	22363	27993	60408	33963	...	...	...	...
3 Bills and bonds, short term	1111	13677	7346	3805	-1123	-7634	13266	15040	...	...	...	...
4 Bonds, long term	1512	455	430	874	931	5496	4421	5536	...	...	...	...
5 Corporate equity securities	1043	1111	296	1479	1340	2015	4275	8190	...	...	...	...
6 Short-term loans, n.e.c.	-2	-1	-115	-3	-343	-	1	-11	...	...	...	...
7 Long-term loans	1040	25	1581	2419	-3873	1621	1899	976	...	...	...	...
8 Non-resident proprietors' net additions to accumulation of resident quasi-corporate enterprises	...	...	...	...	...	...	...	...	...	...	...	...
9 Trade credit and advances	-211	76	-107	-	-	-	-	-	...	...	...	...
10 Other	180	158	-	-	-	-	-	-	...	...	...	...
Total Incurrence of Liabilities	36598	41657	26517	26050	23054	38588	74813	69829	...	...	...	...
Statistical discrepancy	1644	1319	-3432	-419	5178	4683	11688	-2121	...	...	...	...
Net Lending	2644	5470	5198	3717	-54	3416	-527	-1073	...	...	...	...
Total Incurrence of Liabilities and Net Lending	40886	48446	28283	29348	28178	46687	85974	66635	...	...	...	...

4.3 Cost Components of Value Added

Million Pounds Sterling

	1980						1981					
	Compensation of Employees	Capital Consumption	Net Operating Surplus	Indirect Taxes	Less: Subsidies Received	Value Added	Compensation of Employees	Capital Consumption	Net Operating Surplus	Indirect Taxes	Less: Subsidies Received	Value Added
All Producers												
1 Agriculture, hunting, forestry and fishing	1452	1121	1674	...	...	4247	1564	1204	2071	...	...	4839
2 Mining and quarrying	3245	1984	7176	...	...	12405	3528	2349	10024	...	...	15901
3 Manufacturing a	43391	6586	4162	...	...	54139	44697	7286	3086	...	...	55069
4 Electricity, gas and water b	3147	2253	1060	...	...	6460	3588	2517	1272	...	...	7377
5 Construction	7635	551	4083	...	...	12269	7836	593	4598	...	...	13027
6 Wholesale and retail trade, restaurants and hotels a	18205	1874	5863	...	...	25942	20163	2104	5202	...	...	27469
7 Transport, storage and communication	10633	3976	-25	...	...	14584	11490	4508	184	...	...	16182
8 Finance, insurance, real estate and business services	12637	5586	17157	...	...	35380	14485	6522	17901	...	...	38908
9 Community, social and personal services a	5742	406	3320	...	...	9468	6289	496	3711	...	...	10496
Total, Industries c	106087	25836	42971	...	...	174894	113640	29290	46338	...	...	189268
Producers of Government Services	29307	1748	-	...	...	31055	33241	1948	-	...	...	35189
Other Producers	2576	368	-	...	...	2944	3042	403	-	...	...	3445
Total d	137970	27952	42971	...	...	208893	149923	31641	46338	...	...	227902
Less: Imputed bank service charge	...	...	8464	...	...	8464	...	...	9705	...	...	9705
Import duties e	...	...	...	...	...	18132	...	...	...	...	...	22200
Value added tax	...	...	...	11897	...	11897	...	...	...	13056	...	13056
Other adjustments f	...	...	...	23905	5773	775	...	...	...	28753	6553	744
Total	137970	27952	34507	35802	5773	231233	149923	31641	36633	41809	6553	254197

4.3 Cost Components of Value Added

Million Pounds Sterling

All Producers

	1982						1983					
	Compensation of Employees	Capital Consumption	Net Operating Surplus	Indirect Taxes	Less: Subsidies Received	Value Added	Compensation of Employees	Capital Consumption	Net Operating Surplus	Indirect Taxes	Less: Subsidies Received	Value Added
1 Agriculture, hunting, forestry and fishing	1691	1243	2574	...	...	5508	1828	1294	2224	...	...	5346
2 Mining and quarrying	3771	2566	11801	...	...	18138	3665	2783	14136	...	...	20584
3 Manufacturing a	46274	7805	5386	...	...	59465	47307	8231	7081	...	...	62619
4 Electricity, gas and water b	3768	2655	1573	...	...	7996	3805	2784	2459	...	...	9048
5 Construction	8105	637	5358	...	...	14100	8675	650	6408	...	...	15733
6 Wholesale and retail trade, restaurants and hotels a	21461	2299	6596	...	...	30356	23110	2438	7861	...	...	33409
7 Transport, storage and communication	11957	4655	869	...	...	17481	12738	5001	791	...	...	18530
8 Finance, insurance, real estate and business services	16646	6941	20179	...	...	43766	19090	7544	23919	...	...	50553
9 Community, social and personal services a	6621	567	3901	...	...	11089	7274	626	4648	...	...	12549
Total, Industries c	120294	31227	56378	...	...	207899	127492	33652	67227	...	...	228371
Producers of Government Services	35319	2017	-	...	...	37336	38764	2081	-	...	...	40845
Other Producers	3447	409	-	...	...	3856	3838	417	-	...	...	4255
Total d	159060	33653	56378	...	...	249091	170094	36150	67227	...	...	273471
Less: Imputed bank service charge	...	...	11147	...	...	11147	...	...	11893	...	...	11893
Import duties e	...	...	...	...	...	25326	...	...	...	...	...	25830
Value added tax	...	...	...	14308	...	14308	...	...	...	16216	...	16216
Other adjustments f	...	...	...	31329	6003	509	...	...	...	32235	6404	-247
Total	159060	33653	45231	45637	6003	278087	170094	36150	55334	48451	6404	303377

All Producers

	1984						1985					
	Compensation of Employees	Capital Consumption	Net Operating Surplus	Indirect Taxes	Less: Subsidies Received	Value Added	Compensation of Employees	Capital Consumption	Net Operating Surplus	Indirect Taxes	Less: Subsidies Received	Value Added
1 Agriculture, hunting, forestry and fishing	1952	1331	3173	...	...	6456	2157	1358	2426	...	...	5941
2 Mining and quarrying	1917	2950	17330	...	...	22197	3434	3133	16607	...	...	23174
3 Manufacturing a	50327	8620	6822	...	...	65769	54200	9217	10042	...	...	73459
4 Electricity, gas and water b	3967	2903	801	...	...	7671	4183	3066	1622	...	...	8871
5 Construction	9157	668	7358	...	...	17183	9484	698	8217	...	...	18399
6 Wholesale and retail trade, restaurants and hotels a	25126	2622	8995	...	...	36743	27167	2915	11294	...	...	41376
7 Transport, storage and communication	13785	5407	1241	...	...	20433	14354	5702	1743	...	...	21799
8 Finance, insurance, real estate and business services	21684	8380	23438	...	...	53502	24666	9318	28004	...	...	61988
9 Community, social and personal services a	8467	692	5141	...	...	14300	9734	793	5883	...	...	16410
Total, Industries c	136382	36139	71733	...	...	244254	149379	39053	82985	...	...	271417
Producers of Government Services	40978	2187	-	...	...	43165	42853	2372	-	...	...	45225
Other Producers	4325	432	-	...	...	4757	4936	458	-	...	...	5394
Total d	181685	38758	71733	...	...	292176	197168	41883	82985	...	...	322036
Less: Imputed bank service charge	...	...	12490	...	...	12490	...	...	13825	...	...	13825
Import duties e	...	...	...	...	...	25473	...	...	...	...	...	27281
Value added tax	...	...	...	18277	...	18277	...	...	...	20604	...	20604
Other adjustments f	...	...	...	33151	7678	1351	...	...	...	34603	7322	-
Total	181685	38758	59243	51428	7678	324787	197168	41883	69160	55207	7322	356096

All Producers

	1986						1987					
	Compensation of Employees	Capital Consumption	Net Operating Surplus	Indirect Taxes	Less: Subsidies Received	Value Added	Compensation of Employees	Capital Consumption	Net Operating Surplus	Indirect Taxes	Less: Subsidies Received	Value Added
1 Agriculture, hunting, forestry and fishing	2261	1394	2910	...	...	6565	2398	1432	3088	...	...	6918
2 Mining and quarrying	3479	3293	6168	...	...	12940	3234	3357	6950	...	...	13541
3 Manufacturing a	56820	9637	12608	...	...	79065	59874	10216	13585	...	...	83675
4 Electricity, gas and water b	4354	3201	2464	...	...	10019	4480	3297	3141	...	...	10918

4.3 Cost Components of Value Added
(Continued)

Million Pounds Sterling

	1986						1987					
	Compensation of Employees	Capital Consumption	Net Operating Surplus	Indirect Taxes	Less: Subsidies Received	Value Added	Compensation of Employees	Capital Consumption	Net Operating Surplus	Indirect Taxes	Less: Subsidies Received	Value Added
5 Construction	9962	720	10036	...	...	20718	10897	756	12430	...	...	24083
6 Wholesale and retail trade, restaurants and hotels [a]	29093	3202	14140	...	...	46435	31318	3498	15741	...	...	50557
7 Transport, storage and communication	15010	6056	2535	...	...	23601	15956	5878	4134	...	...	25968
8 Finance, insurance, real estate and business services	27948	10295	32858	...	...	71101	31863	11521	37115	...	...	80499
9 Community, social and personal services [a]	11528	892	6312	...	...	18732	12579	997	7317	...	...	20893
Total, Industries [c]	160455	42016	86705	...	...	289176	172599	44842	99611	...	...	317052
Producers of Government Services	46581	2583	-	...	...	49164	51006	2804	-	...	...	53810
Other Producers	5693	485	-	...	...	6178	6628	503	-	...	...	7131
Total [d]	212729	45084	86705	...	...	344518	230233	48149	99611	...	...	377993
Less: Imputed bank service charge	...	...	16033	...	...	16033	...	...	16997	...	...	16997
Import duties [e]	...	...	...	...	...	31957	...	...	...	...	...	35473
Value added tax	...	...	...	23237	...	23237	...	...	...	25816	...	25816
Other adjustments [f]	...	...	...	38299	6342	-	...	...	...	41984	6511	-
Total	212729	45084	70672	61536	6342	383679	230233	48149	82614	67800	6511	422285

	1988						1989					
	Compensation of Employees	Capital Consumption	Net Operating Surplus	Indirect Taxes	Less: Subsidies Received	Value Added	Compensation of Employees	Capital Consumption	Net Operating Surplus	Indirect Taxes	Less: Subsidies Received	Value Added
					All Producers							
1 Agriculture, hunting, forestry and fishing	2633	1471	2904	...	...	7008	2808	1578	3753	...	...	8139
2 Mining and quarrying	...	3471	...	...	...	...	...	3701	...	...	...	...
3 Manufacturing [a]	...	10464	...	...	...	...	...	11264	...	...	...	...
4 Electricity, gas and water [b]	4597	3575	3032	...	...	11204	4994	3948	2908	...	...	11850
5 Construction	12444	787	15757	...	...	28988	14299	850	16935	...	...	32084
6 Wholesale and retail trade, restaurants and hotels [a]	36237	3766	18507	...	...	58510	40741	4167	19743	...	...	64651
7 Transport, storage and communication	17491	5864	5110	...	...	28465	19232	6202	5639	...	...	31073
8 Finance, insurance, real estate and business services	36851	13206	40474	...	...	90531	43349	15363	49979	...	...	108691
9 Community, social and personal services [a]	15018	1121	8685	...	...	24824	16407	1348	9146	...	...	26901
Total, Industries [c]	192589	48962	112265	...	...	353816	214748	52627	127637	...	...	395012
Producers of Government Services	55619	3110	-	...	...	58729	58905	3448	-	...	...	62353
Other Producers	7724	524	-	...	...	8248	9666	557	-	...	...	10223
Total [d]	255932	52596	112265	...	...	420793	283319	56632	127637	...	...	467588
Less: Imputed bank service charge	...	...	19359	...	...	19359	...	...	26052	...	...	26052
Import duties [e]	...	...	...	...	...	39183	...	...	...	...	...	40749
Value added tax	...	...	...	29339	...	29339	...	...	...	31639	...	31639
Other adjustments [f]	...	...	-287	45310	6127	-287	...	...	-325	46799	6050	-325
Total	255932	52596	92619	74649	6127	469669	283319	56632	101260	78438	6050	513599

	1990						1991					
	Compensation of Employees	Capital Consumption	Net Operating Surplus	Indirect Taxes	Less: Subsidies Received	Value Added	Compensation of Employees	Capital Consumption	Net Operating Surplus	Indirect Taxes	Less: Subsidies Received	Value Added
					All Producers							
1 Agriculture, hunting, forestry and fishing	3083	1629	4041	...	...	8753	3199	1592	3981	...	...	8772
2 Mining and quarrying	...	3955	...	...	...	...	...	...	...	...	...	...
3 Manufacturing [a]	...	10650	...	...	...	...	...	...	...	...	...	...
4 Electricity, gas and water [b]	5440	5478	2376	...	...	13294	5986	...	...	...	...	15993
5 Construction	15792	910	18914	...	...	35616	15306	...	...	...	...	33686
6 Wholesale and retail trade, restaurants and hotels [a]	44778	4522	22565	...	...	71865	47294	...	...	...	...	73024
7 Transport, storage and communication	21435	6672	5380	...	...	33487	22676	...	...	...	...	34755
8 Finance, insurance, real estate and business services	49743	17327	50335	...	...	117405	52409	...	...	...	...	123018
9 Community, social and personal services [a]	17113	1505	8683	...	...	27301	21843	...	...	...	...	32629
Total, Industries [c]	236544	56735	132412	...	...	425691	248583	59478	130379	...	...	438440
Producers of Government Services	64361	3806	-	...	...	68167	69109	3890	-	...	...	72999

1954

4.3 Cost Components of Value Added
(Continued)

Million Pounds Sterling

	1990						1991					
	Compensation of Employees	Capital Consumption	Net Operating Surplus	Indirect Taxes	Less: Subsidies Received	Value Added	Compensation of Employees	Capital Consumption	Net Operating Surplus	Indirect Taxes	Less: Subsidies Received	Value Added
Other Producers	11261	585	-	...	...	11846	12528	600	-	...	...	13128
Total d	312166	61126	132412	...	...	505704	330220	63968	130379	...	...	524567
Less: Imputed bank service charge	...	...	26159	...	...	26159	...	...	27171	...	...	27171
Import duties e	...	...	...	...	...	36060	...	...	...	...	...	37199
Value added tax	...	...	...	33001	...	33001	...	...	...	38067	...	38067
Other adjustments f	...	...	-315	42387	6327	13	...	...	-278	43305	6106	-261
Total	312166	61126	105938	75388	6327	548619	330220	63968	102930	81372	6106	572401

a) Repairs to consumer durables other than clothing are included in item 'Wholesale and retail trade, restaurants and hotels'.
b) Item 'Electricity, gas and water' includes nuclear fuel production.
c) Capital consumption for total industries includes transfer costs of land and buildings which cannot be allocated to individual industries, therefore, net operating surplus shown for individual industries is overestimated by this amount.
d) Gross domestic product in factor values.
e) Item 'Import duties' refers to indirect taxes net of subsidies less value added tax.
f) Item 'Other adjustments' refers to statistical discrepancy.

United Rep.of Tanzania

General note. The preparation of National Accounts Statistics in the United Republic of Tanzania is undertaken by the Bureau of Statistics, President's Office, Planning Commission, Dar es Salaam. Official estimates are published in a series of reports entitled 'National Accounts of Tanzania'. Detailed and comprehensive report on the sources and methods employed for the computation of the national accounts estimation is found in the report entitled 'National Accounts of Tanzania, 1976 to 1984: Sources and Methods ' published in 1985. The estimates follow closely the classifications and definitions recommended in the United Nations System of National Accounts (SNA). Input-output tables have been compiled for 1969, 1970 and 1976. The following tables have been prepared from successive replies to the United Nations national accounts questionnaire. The estimates presented relate to Tanzania (mainland) only, i.e., the former territory of Tanganyika and excluding Zanzibar. When the scope and coverage of the estimates differ for conceptual or statistical reasons from the definitions and classifications recommended in SNA, a footnote is indicated to the relevant tables.

Sources and methods :

(a) Gross domestic product. Gross domestic product is estimated mainly through the income approach.

(b) Expenditure on the gross domestic product. Government final consumption expenditure and exports and imports of goods and services are estimated through the expenditure approach, while private final consumption expenditure and gross capital formation are compiled by using a combination of the commodity-flow and expenditure approaches. For government expenditure, actual central government revenue and expenditure, classified by purpose, are available from government documents. Revenue and expenditure details of local authorities are obtained from the Prime Minister's Office and from the local authorities themselves. For private consumption expenditure, estimates of domestic production of all commodities are compiled and allowances made for various intermediate uses and government and business purposes. The estimates are then marked up for distribution costs and adjusted for imports and exports. Data from the 1976/77 Household Budget Survey are used with regard to most expenditures on services. The estimate of change in stocks only covers the parastatal enterprises, export crops, livestock and those factories which were included in the survey of manufacturing industries. Estimates of gross fixed capital formation for the public sector are derived from detailed analysis of the accounts of the agencies concerned and from detailed statistics on imports of capital equipment. Own account rural residential construction has been estimated on the basis of building costs data, rental values and data on population growth. Exports and imports of goods and services are obtained from the balance of payment statements of the Bank of Tanzania. GDP by expenditure at constant prices is not estimated.

(c) Cost-structure of the gross domestic product. In estimating the cost structure components of GDP, estimates of compensation of employees are obtained from each industry group separately. In addition, information obtained from Employment and Earnings survey is used for the non-primary and mining industries groups. For agriculture, animal husbandry, forestry and fishing, the wage component of value added is fixed at 4.3 per cent of its value added based on the results of various farm surveys. Operating surplus estimates for each industrial sector is obtained from the companies concerned. Estimates of depreciation for fixed assets of the parastatal enterprises are provided by the establishments themselves and for other sectors, estimates are based on percentages obtained from previous surveys. Data on indirect taxes and subsidies are obtained by analyzing government recurrent revenue and expenditure.

(d) Gross domestic product by kind of economic activity. The table of gross domestic product by kind of economic activity is prepared at factor costs. The value added of agriculture, mining and manufacturing is estimated through the production approach while for the remaining industries, the income approach is used. For agriculture, the data on production, prices and cost of production of each export crop, available with the respective commodity boards, are utilized to derive estimates of their value added. For the non-export crops, similar data available from the Ministry of Agriculture and Livestock Development, Marketing Development Bureau, Bureau of Statistics and data collected through Economic and Household Budget Surveys and the 1976 Input-Output Table have been used. The 1969 and 1976-77 Household Budget Surveys provided information on the quantities of crops harvested and the value and quantity of crops sold for a number of food crops. Based on some assumptions regarding conversion factors for differing physical units and the adjustment from retail to producer prices, approximate values of the crop harvested at producers' prices have been worked out in a number of cases. For livestock, forestry and fishing, data are obtained from the concerned departments or sections of the Ministry of Agriculture and from the household budget surveys. The production costs incurred by producers of livestocks are based on scattered data available, from farm studies and informal discussions. For some minor crops and by-products, a very rough mark-up is established to cover their production. Data on mining are available in the annual Economic Surveys, obtained directly from Mines Division, Dodoma. The data obtained from Employment and Earnings Survey, census reports and monthly surveys are utilized for manufacturing. Bench-mark estimates of value added of manufacturing establishments were obtained from the Census of Industrial Production 1978 while current estimates are prepared mainly on the basis of annual surveys of manufacturing industries. The Annual Accounts and Supporting Schedules of Tanzania's electric company gives full details of its activities. Total volume of construction activity is estimated from a variety of sources and the estimates of factor incomes are specially collected from a large sample of contractors and building firms. Data collected through the 1969 and 1976/77 Household Budget Survey were used to re-examine estimates made for rural own account construction. For trade, transport and service industries, the data provided by the Employment and Earnings Surveys and the data on income and expenditure, specially collected from a large sample of such enterprises, together with the estimated gross trade margins, number of trade licenses, vehicle licenses, etc. provide the basis for estimation. Rental value of houses in the urban and rural areas are compiled on the basis of information on rented houses collected through the 1967 Population Census and the 1969 Household Budget Survey. For government services, data are collected from the agencies concerned and detailed analysis of their revenue and expenditure are undertaken. Information on the activities of East African Community are obtained from the East African Statistical Department. For the constant price estimates, double deflation is used for the agricultural, mining and quarrying, and construction sectors with current year quantities revalued at base-year prices. For the manufacturing, electricity, trade and transport sectors, value added is extrapolated by various quantity indicators and indexes. For the financial and service sectors, value added is deflated by different indexes such as employment index.

1.1 Expenditure on the Gross Domestic Product, in Current Prices

Million Tanzanian shillings

	1980	1981	1982	1983	1984	1985	1986	1987	1988	1989	1990	1991
1 Government final consumption expenditure	5494	6105	8046	9443	13844	18555	23621	25433	35855	58914	71015	92920
2 Private final consumption expenditure	32486	37035	42261	55128	68652	93130	127307	175555	311325	329592	366437	526831
3 Gross capital formation	9685	10130	12235	9588	13618	18963	31166	68760	101423	140097	235426	282376
A Increase in stocks	1055	1498	1410	1836	1645	2091	2487	3685	4122	11075	18022	19998
B Gross fixed capital formation	8630	8632	10825	7752	11973	16872	28679	65075	97301	129022	217404	262378
Residential buildings	709	1001	1043	949	1291	1708	1789	2886	3643	3907	14730	16578
Non-residential buildings	1126	1446	1373	898	1219	1388	2550	3171	3159	7711	4693	5523
Other construction and land improvement etc.	2524	2230	2985	1687	2203	2762	4665	13020	28089	20492	48039	56871
Other	4271	3955	5424	4218	7260	11014	19675	45998	62410	96912	149942	183406
4 Exports of goods and services	5540	5994	4546	5111	6321	7453	14580	26452	45541	73705	102963	122002
5 Less: Imports of goods and services	11087	10162	8862	8761	13543	17480	37026	69250	162928	195767	280842	333709
Equals: Gross Domestic Product	42118	49102	58226	70509	88892	120621	159648	226950	331217	406542	494999	690421

1.2 Expenditure on the Gross Domestic Product, in Constant Prices

Million Tanzanian shillings

	1980	1981	1982	1983	1984	1985	1986	1987	1988	1989	1990	1991
	At constant prices of:1976											
1 Government final consumption expenditure	...	...	...	...	...	...	...	...	...	...	...	...
2 Private final consumption expenditure	...	...	...	...	...	...	...	...	...	...	...	...
3 Gross capital formation	6103	6368	6563	4632	6333	7635	7397	9387	9233	9418	12632	12453
A Increase in stocks	488	562	511	590	442	414	390	423	410	870	1190	1190
B Gross fixed capital formation	5615	5806	6052	4042	5891	7221	7007	8964	8823	8548	11442	11263

1.2 Expenditure on the Gross Domestic Product, in Constant Prices
(Continued)

Million Tanzanian shillings

	1980	1981	1982	1983	1984	1985	1986	1987	1988	1989	1990	1991
						At constant prices of:1976						
Residential buildings	439	551	516	412	478	519	456	389	542	525	1277	1230
Non-residential buildings	700	799	683	394	467	397	551	486	291	606	310	329
Other construction and land improvement etc.	1569	1232	1485	740	844	789	1007	1997	2587	1609	3173	3063
Other	2907	3224	3369	2496	4102	5517	4993	6092	5403	5808	6682	6641
4 Exports of goods and services	...	...	...	...	...	...	...	...	...	...	...	...
5 Less: Imports of goods and services	...	...	...	...	...	...	...	...	...	...	...	...
Equals: Gross Domestic Product a ..	23419	23301	23439	22882	23656	24278	25070	26345	27460	28376	29368	30484

a) Gross domestic product in factor values.

1.3 Cost Components of the Gross Domestic Product

Million Tanzanian shillings

	1980	1981	1982	1983	1984	1985	1986	1987	1988	1989	1990	1991
1 Indirect taxes, net	4664	5196	5680	7901	10749	12538	18855	27079	46065	71037	94280	116885
A Indirect taxes	4963	5730	6594	8391	11016	12855	19018	26573	47081	72283	95608	117821
B Less: Subsidies	299	534	914	490	267	317	163	-506	1016	1246	1328	936
2 Consumption of fixed capital	1540	1542	1568	1619	1879	2482	3761	5340	6896	13957	14364	14737
3 Compensation of employees paid by resident producers to:	7940	9047	10168	12906	14713	17816	20185	25633	36251	40470	53554	59278
4 Operating surplus	27974	33317	40810	48083	61551	87785	116847	168896	242005	281078	332801	499521
Equals: Gross Domestic Product	42118	49102	58226	70509	88892	120621	159648	226950	331217	406542	494999	690421

1.7 External Transactions on Current Account, Summary

Million Tanzanian shillings

	1980	1981	1982	1983	1984	1985	1986	1987	1988	1989	1990	1991
						Payments to the Rest of the World						
1 Imports of goods and services	11087	10162	8862	8761	13543	17480	37026	69250	162928	195767	280842	333709
A Imports of merchandise c.i.f.	10003	9120	8392	8192	12960	16470	34329	62143	150078	176354	262545	309446
B Other	1084	1042	470	569	583	1010	2697	7107	12850	19413	18297	24263
2 Factor income to the rest of the world	226	266	257	232	190	734	3697	11399	18853	29593	40981	42180
3 Current transfers to the rest of the world	209	192	168	270	303	286	917	1772	2178	4273	5852	23626
4 Surplus of the nation on current transactions	-4604	-2456	-3440	-2715	-5968	-7660	-10225	-15579	-73558	-57595	-83094	-62911
Payments to the Rest of the World and Surplus of the Nation on Current Transactions	6918	8164	5847	6548	8068	10840	31415	66842	110401	172038	244581	336604
						Receipts From The Rest of the World						
1 Exports of goods and services	5540	5994	4546	5111	6321	7453	14580	26452	45540	73705	102963	122002
A Exports of merchandise f.o.b.	4187	4373	3484	4001	5125	5718	11391	19686	33830	56663	75935	89586
B Other	1353	1621	1062	1110	1196	1735	3189	6766	11710	17042	27028	32416
2 Factor income from rest of the world	114	90	26	21	17	30	416	361	311	550	495	495
3 Current transfers from rest of the world	1264	2080	1275	1416	1730	3357	16419	40029	64549	97783	141123	214107
Receipts from the Rest of the World on Current Transactions	6918	8164	5847	6548	8068	10840	31415	66842	110401	172038	244581	336604

1.10 Gross Domestic Product by Kind of Activity, in Current Prices

Million Tanzanian shillings

	1980	1981	1982	1983	1984	1985	1986	1987	1988	1989	1990	1991
1 Agriculture, hunting, forestry and fishing	16636	20338	26449	32737	41295	61231	84153	117982	178760	207059	233804	358693
2 Mining and quarrying	329	299	266	249	337	251	474	645	723	1129	4815	6975
3 Manufacturing a	4097	4501	4361	4869	5932	6665	8551	14792	15187	15197	18301	20680
4 Electricity, gas and water	424	423	421	514	551	1071	1488	4992	4628	4842	7438	8395
5 Construction	1498	1614	1863	1252	1661	2061	3131	6511	11808	9720	12650	14416
6 Wholesale and retail trade, restaurants and hotels	4713	5479	6814	8148	10447	14195	19476	25963	41591	50392	56638	83325
7 Transport, storage and communication	3019	3133	3395	3507	4789	7021	7797	11584	14259	23854	36242	47017
8 Finance, insurance, real estate and business services	3744	4507	4891	5252	6028	6659	8127	11061	14132	19187	24123	28757
9 Community, social and personal services b	3959	4732	5446	7372	8614	10735	10213	13291	16952	22168	31968	34478

1.10 Gross Domestic Product by Kind of Activity, in Current Prices
(Continued)

Million Tanzanian shillings

	1980	1981	1982	1983	1984	1985	1986	1987	1988	1989	1990	1991
Total, Industries	38419	45026	53906	63900	79654	109889	143410	206821	298040	353548	425979	602736
Producers of Government Services b	...	...	...	...	...	...	...	...	...	...	...	...
Other Producers b	...	...	...	...	...	...	...	...	...	...	...	...
Subtotal c	38419	45026	53906	63900	79654	109889	143410	206821	298040	353548	425979	602736
Less: Imputed bank service charge	965	1120	1360	1292	1511	1806	2544	6444	12888	18043	25260	29200
Plus: Import duties	...	...	...	...	...	...	...	...	...	...	...	...
Plus: Value added tax	...	...	...	...	...	...	...	...	...	...	...	...
Plus: Other adjustments d	4664	5196	5680	7901	10749	12538	18855	27079	46065	71037	94280	116885
Equals: Gross Domestic Product	42118	49102	58226	70509	88892	120621	159648	226950	331217	406542	494999	690421

a) Item 'Manufacturing' includes handicrafts.
b) Items 'Other producers' and 'Producers of government services' are included in item 'Community, social and personal services'.
c) Gross domestic product in factor values.
d) Item 'Other adjustments' refers to indirect taxes net of subsidies.

1.11 Gross Domestic Product by Kind of Activity, in Constant Prices

Million Tanzanian shillings

	1980	1981	1982	1983	1984	1985	1986	1987	1988	1989	1990	1991
					At constant prices of:1976							
1 Agriculture, hunting, forestry and fishing	9418	9511	9639	9914	10312	10931	11557	12066	12606	13183	14055	14696
2 Mining and quarrying	189	193	193	174	186	174	154	149	138	139	165	240
3 Manufacturing a	2683	2382	2304	2103	2159	2075	1991	2081	2228	2399	2338	2439
4 Electricity, gas and water	400	417	420	413	439	461	544	584	574	506	512	535
5 Construction	932	890	930	549	660	601	705	1052	1177	858	937	962
6 Wholesale and retail trade, restaurants and hotels	2839	2725	2668	2612	2640	2662	2958	3112	3236	3549	3520	3662
7 Transport, storage and communication	1818	1652	1694	1473	1482	1509	1504	1588	1643	1663	1697	1747
8 Finance, insurance, real estate and business services	2483	2529	2702	2817	2984	3046	3318	3332	3435	3554	3630	3724
9 Community, social and personal services b	3188	3551	3556	3543	3549	3616	3225	3243	3343	3475	3552	3619
Total, Industries	23950	23850	24106	23598	24411	25075	25956	27207	28380	29326	30406	31624
Producers of Government Services b	...	...	...	...	...	...	...	...	...	...	...	...
Other Producers b	...	...	...	...	...	...	...	...	...	...	...	...
Subtotal c	23950	23850	24106	23598	24411	25075	25956	27207	28380	29326	30406	31624
Less: Imputed bank service charge	531	549	667	716	755	797	886	862	920	950	1038	1140
Plus: Import duties	...	...	...	...	...	...	...	...	...	...	...	...
Plus: Value added tax	...	...	...	...	...	...	...	...	...	...	...	...
Equals: Gross Domestic Product c	23419	23301	23439	22882	23656	24278	25070	26345	27460	28376	29368	30484

a) Item 'Manufacturing' includes handicrafts.
b) Items 'Other producers' and 'Producers of government services' are included in item 'Community, social and personal services'.
c) Gross domestic product in factor values.

1.12 Relations Among National Accounting Aggregates

Million Tanzanian shillings

	1980	1981	1982	1983	1984	1985	1986	1987	1988	1989	1990	1991
Gross Domestic Product	42118	49102	58226	70509	88892	120621	159648	226950	331217	406542	494999	690421
Plus: Net factor income from the rest of the world	-112	-176	-231	-211	-173	-704	-3281	-11038	-18542	-29043	-40486	-41685
Factor income from the rest of the world	114	90	26	21	17	30	416	361	311	550	495	495
Less: Factor income to the rest of the world	226	266	257	232	190	734	3697	11399	18853	29593	40981	42180
Equals: Gross National Product	42006	48926	57995	70298	88719	119917	156367	215912	312675	377499	454513	648736
Less: Consumption of fixed capital	1540	1542	1568	1619	1879	2482	3761	5340	6896	13957	14364	14737
Equals: National Income	40466	47384	56427	68679	86840	117435	152606	210572	305779	363542	440149	633999
Plus: Net current transfers from the rest of the world	1055	1888	1107	1146	1427	3071	15502	38257	62371	93510	135271	190481
Current transfers from the rest of the world	1264	2080	1275	1416	1730	3357	16419	40029	64549	97783	141123	214107
Less: Current transfers to the rest of the world	209	192	168	270	303	286	917	1772	2178	4273	5852	23626
Equals: National Disposable Income	41521	49272	57534	69825	88267	120506	168108	248829	368150	457052	575420	824480
Less: Final consumption	37980	43140	50307	64571	82496	111685	150928	200988	347180	388506	437452	619751
Equals: Net Saving	3541	6132	7227	5254	5771	8821	17180	47841	20970	68546	137968	204729
Less: Surplus of the nation on current transactions	-4604	-2456	-3440	-2715	-5968	-7660	-10225	-15579	-73559	-57595	-83094	-62911
Equals: Net Capital Formation	8145	8588	10667	7969	11739	16481	27405	63420	94529	126141	221062	267640

2.1 Government Final Consumption Expenditure by Function, in Current Prices

Million Tanzanian shillings

Fiscal year beginning 1 July

		1980	1981	1982	1983	1984	1985	1986	1987	1988	1989	1990	1991
1	General public services	1584	1712	2380	2257	3463	5873	7686	10131	15592	22763	31585	35613
2	Defence	1110	1862	2308	2557	2744	3659	4979	7200	7636	10074	11572	12820
3	Public order and safety	558	719	927	1040	1265	2130	2204	3468	4767	6705	10530	12913
4	Education	1653	1782	2298	2543	2503	1795	2303	3191	3990	6133	8868	14383
5	Health	739	813	992	983	1171	1329	1492	2257	3273	4985	6632	10213
6	Social security and welfare	52	44	51	61	62	125	54	133	215	349	578	854
7	Housing and community amenities	147	187	189	209	212	258	268	328	667	860	1113	1197
8	Recreational, cultural and religious affairs	277	322	381	385	440	589	697	1100	1896	2450	2162	4356
9	Economic services	5222	5354	5495	5213	5563	6463	6567	9283	11916	18723	21461	45838
	A Fuel and energy a	647	545	677	647	712	680	489	1000	1434	2486	3103	5589
	B Agriculture, forestry, fishing and hunting	1328	1272	1282	1233	1580	1654	1951	3198	3880	6037	5903	11880
	C Mining, manufacturing and construction, except fuel and energy	1406	1340	1555	1399	1492	1674	1487	1410	1803	2368	2554	6290
	D Transportation and communication	1109	1379	1482	1439	1295	1678	1777	2684	3526	5175	5808	16875
	E Other economic affairs	732	819	500	494	484	769	865	992	1273	2659	4096	5204
10	Other functions	1195	1802	3406	4042	4029	5219	7052	12631	23345	37453	40190	68813
	Total Government Final Consumption Expenditure b	12537	14597	18427	19289	21451	27440	33302	49722	73298	110494	134691	207000

a) Item 'Fuel and energy' includes water supply.
b) Only central government data are included in the general government estimates.

2.11 Gross Fixed Capital Formation by Kind of Activity of Owner, ISIC Divisions, in Current Prices

Million Tanzanian shillings

		1980	1981	1982	1983	1984	1985	1986	1987	1988	1989	1990	1991
						All Producers							
1	Agriculture, hunting, forestry and fishing	698	677	846	972	1490	2197	1907	1918	2668	2992	6577	8093
2	Mining and quarrying	46	41	41	104	134	109	154	134	167	219	381	555
3	Manufacturing	1955	1961	3022	1724	2584	4289	5095	18423	27708	36119	62606	74714
4	Electricity, gas and water	779	652	403	776	1430	1680	8707	7499	12402	19759	24043	28226
	A Electricity, gas and steam	508	410	209	511	1163	1473	8268	...	...	...	...	...
	B Water works and supply	271	242	194	265	267	207	439	...	...	...	...	...
5	Construction	500	680	1051	645	1319	1589	2358	7106	9707	10301	24576	30325
6	Wholesale and retail trade, restaurants and hotels	151	105	504	131	340	396	324	749	1372	2466	2343	2616
7	Transport, storage and communication	1913	1927	2162	1887	2854	4176	7717	25004	37349	49097	83992	101269
8	Finance, insurance, real estate and business services	687	771	884	305	374	436	749	937	1715	3083	2929	3270
9	Community, social and personal services ab	1901	1818	1912	1208	1448	2000	1668	3304	4213	4986	10957	13310
	Total Industries	8630	8632	10825	7752	11973	16872	28679	65075	97301	129022	217404	262378
	Producers of Government Services a	...	...	...	...	...	...	...	...	...	...	...	...
	Private Non-Profit Institutions Serving Households b	...	...	...	...	...	...	...	...	...	...	...	...
	Total	8630	8632	10825	7752	11973	16872	28679	65075	97301	129022	217404	262378

a) Item 'Producers of government services' is included in item 'Community, social and personal services'.   b) Item 'Private non-profit institutions serving households' is included in item 'Community, social and personal services'.

United States

General note. The Bureau of Economic Analysis (BEA), an agency of the Department of Commerce, is responsible for the preparation of national income account statistics in the United States. The official estimates are published in the survey of current business, (survey). A selected set of tables appears monthly and the full set appears normally in the July issue. The capital finance accounts and balance sheets are published by the Board of Governors of the Federal Reserve System. The official estimates are not totally consistent with the classifications and definitions used in the United Nations System of National Accounts (SNA). See 'The United Nations System of National Accounts: An Introduction', which was published in the June 1990 survey. A summary explanation of the accounting framework appears in BEA's 1985 publication, Methodlogy Paper No.1, An Introduction to National Economic Accounting. Subsequent modifications are described in the September and October 1991 surveys. Information on sources and methods used to estimate the national accounts appears in BEA's 1987 publication, Methodology Paper No. 4, GNP: An Overview of Source Data and Estimating Methods. The July 1992 survey updates this publication. See also the February 1993 survey for additional information about the national income and product accounts. Information on U.S. capital finance accounts and balance sheets is found in Guide to Flow of Funds, 1993, a publication of the Federal Reserve System. The most recent benchmark input-output accounts were published in 1991 in the 1982 Benchmark Input-Output Accounts of the United States. Annual update input-output tables also are prepared: See the April 1992 survey for the 1987 accounts. The following tables have been prepared from national accounts questionnaires provided to the United Nations. The United States converts its official estimates as closely as possible to SNA definitions. When differences in scope and coverage from the SNA recommendations remain, footnotes are attached to the appropriate tables.

Sources and methods :
(a) Gross domestic product. Both the expenditure and income approach are used.
(b) Expenditure on the gross domestic product. The estimates of central government final consumption expenditures are based largely on budgetary and admnistrative information. Estimates of state and local government expenditures are based largely on census bureau and quinquennial and annual surveys of these governments. Benchmark estimates of private final consumption expenditures are taken from the detailed input-output tables prepared every five years to coincide with comprehensive economic censuses. In addition, major statistical sources include the Census Bureau, Decennial Census of Housing and Survey of Residential Finance for housing services; Department of Energy and private trade sources for household utilities; various federal regulatory agencies for imputed bank service charges; the Securities and Exchange Commission for various personal business expenses; and private trade sources for various insurance expenses. Estimates for non-benchmark years are extrapolations and interpolations of the benchmark data using Census Bureau surveys of retail trade sales, service receipts, rental payments, and other public and private data sources. Benchmark estimates of gross fixed capital formation are summations of residential buildings (estimates are based on Census Bureau construction surveys and other government and other private trade surces), non-residential buildings and other construction (estimates from the census of construction industries and other Census Bureau surveys, other government agencies statistics, and private trade data), and producers' durable goods (estimates are mainly from the Census Bureau census of manufactures shipments data, Census Bureau of merchandise trade data, and private trade sources). Estimates for non-benchmark years are extrapolations of the benchmark data using Census

Bureau annual and monthly survey data, merchandise trade statistics and various trade sources. Estimates of exports and imports of merchandise, taken from U.S Balance of Payment Accounts are based on customs documents tabulated by the Census Bureau. Service transactions are taken from the U.S. Balance of Payments Accounts based on Bureau of Economic Analysis surveys and other government sources. Constant-dollar government final consumption expenditures - central as well as state and local - are calculated in three parts. Employee compensation is obtained by extrapolating base-year compensation with full-time equivalent employment measures with detail by level of pay or experience. Purchases of many defense goods are derived by developing base-year prices for specific items and applying those prices to actual deliveries of goods. Purchases of most other goods and services are obtained by deflation. The price indexes used include components of the Consumer Price Index (CPI) and the Producer Price Index (PPI), selected construction price indexes, and a variety of other indexes. Constant-dollar government final consumption expenditures are deflated mainly by components of the CPI. To deflate several service components, BEA composite indexes of input prices are used. Constant-dollar gross fixed capital formation are deflated by various price indexes. For residential buildings, hedonic price indexes from the Census Bureau and from BEA are the major sources. Non-residential buildings and other construction are deflated using cost indexes from government agencies and trade sources. For most of producers durable goods, components of the PPI are used; for computers and related equipment, a BEA hedonic price index is used. Purchases of imports are deflated with components of the Bureau of Labor Statistics (BLS) import price index. Constant-dollar exports and imports of goods and services are deflated mainly by components of the BLS export and import price indexes. Other indexes used include the PPI, CPI, various BEA price indexes, indexes from other government agencies and other sources.

(c) Cost-structure of the gross domestic product. Indirect taxes for the federal government include excise taxes and customs duties; estimates are based on administrative records. Indirect taxes for state and local government include sales taxes and property taxes and are derived from census bureau sources. Subsidies paid by the federal government are mainly payments to farmers and housing subsidies. Subsidies are estimated using the same sources as used for government final consumption. Consumption of fixed capital, which consists of depreciation and accidental damage, is derived from perpetual inventory calculations from BEA's capital stock estimates. The annual estimates of compensation of employees are taken mainly from administrative records of government agencies. The operating surplus is estimated in four separate parts: income of unincorporated enterprises, corporate profits, net interest, and rental income of persons. Tabulations of tax returns are the primary source of non-farm proprietors' income, corpporate profits and net interest. Farm income is based on data compiled by the Department of Agriculture. Rental income of persons which covers only rental income of persons not primarily engaged in the real estate business and royalty payments, is based primarily on the decennial census and a biennial survey of housing. Imputed rental receipts of owner-occupants of non-farm dwellings are estimated using the rental-equivalency method. Rental receipts for both tenant-occupied and owner-occupied housing are adjusted to exclude expenses. Royalty type income based on tax information, is also included.

(d) Gross domestic product by kind of economic activity. The GDP by kind of economic activity program is being revised. A summary of sources and methods will be provided when revised estimates are completed.

1.1 Expenditure on the Gross Domestic Product, in Current Prices

Million United States dollars

	1980	1981	1982	1983	1984	1985	1986	1987	1988	1989	1990	1991
1 Government final consumption expenditure a	476343	529385	579269	620821	669749	727869	781950	830972	876420	915832	975725	1023260
2 Private final consumption expenditure	1708277	1887328	2016947	2201908	2401883	2598435	2764716	2960584	3198135	3420469	3633800	3762819
3 Gross capital formation	539898	635396	579247	626957	799150	811584	822803	855515	895221	955536	932341	855275
A Increase in stocks bc	-6535	31562	-11411	593	71341	28599	14937	25641	8361	34980	11754	-7203
B Gross fixed capital formation b	546433	603834	590658	626364	727809	782985	807866	829874	886860	920556	920587	862478
Residential buildings	122012	121356	104523	150641	177480	184481	215345	223609	229981	228380	213078	188355
Non-residential buildings	94227	108266	115513	108524	127932	148847	144306	150767	160511	175512	183929	163920
Other construction and land improvement etc. d	98515	117274	118302	100044	106053	112827	101600	98732	100477	105616	108637	109732
Other	231679	256938	252320	267155	316344	336830	346615	356766	395891	411048	414943	400471
4 Exports of goods and services e	277525	301373	280227	272738	297795	296384	313052	356553	436394	500380	548832	589418
5 Less: Imports of goods and services e	293896	317686	303194	328126	405110	417623	451737	507050	552208	587708	625903	619972
Equals: Gross Domestic Product	2708147	3035796	3152496	3394298	3763467	4016649	4230784	4496574	4853962	5204509	5464795	5610800

a) Includes consumption of fixed capital of roads, dams or other forms of construction except structures.
b) All livestock are included in increase in stocks.
c) Inventories valued at current replacement cost.
d) Land improvement is not included in item 'Other construction and land improvement, etc.'.
e) Merchandise valued at Free Along Side (F.A.S.).

1.2 Expenditure on the Gross Domestic Product, in Constant Prices

Million United States dollars

	1980	1981	1982	1983	1984	1985	1986	1987	1988	1989	1990	1991
					At constant prices of:1985							
1 Government final consumption expenditure a	629457	640324	655417	669786	694005	727869	763738	793890	805363	803767	815947	832171
2 Private final consumption expenditure	2221193	2249412	2270600	2371810	2489309	2598435	2696329	2773372	2879226	2939006	2972703	2956064
3 Gross capital formation	647750	690336	599353	655890	813676	811584	804492	816792	831834	867853	839880	761402
A Increase in stocks bc	-7301	31536	-12267	8614	71472	28599	17109	21842	7542	31853	18863	-4803
B Gross fixed capital formation b	655051	658800	611620	647276	742204	782985	787383	794950	824292	836000	821017	766205

1.2 Expenditure on the Gross Domestic Product, in Constant Prices
(Continued)

Million United States dollars

	1980	1981	1982	1983	1984	1985	1986	1987	1988	1989	1990	1991
	At constant prices of:1985											
Residential buildings	150287	138346	113208	159043	182212	184481	206915	205538	202812	194470	176494	154288
Non-residential buildings	120891	127198	128125	116442	132118	148847	139518	140446	143897	151571	154034	135396
Other construction and land improvement etc. d	112702	117445	111910	102482	110267	112827	102149	101434	98049	98705	99868	98798
Other	271171	275811	258377	269309	317607	336830	338801	347532	379534	391254	390621	377723
4 Exports of goods and services e	307479	313533	285534	273720	293355	296384	315983	351039	409104	459331	497920	528992
5 Less: Imports of goods and services e	281841	292061	287105	320373	396274	417623	452215	479419	502194	526097	545718	550543
Equals: Gross Domestic Product	3524038	3601544	3523799	3650833	3894071	4016649	4128327	4255674	4423333	4543860	4580732	4528086

a) Includes consumption of fixed capital of roads, dams or other forms of construction except structures.
b) All livestock is included in increase in stocks.
c) Inventories valued at current replacement cost.
d) Land improvement is not included in item 'Other construction and land improvement, etc.'.
e) Merchandise valued at Free Along Side (F.A.S.).

1.3 Cost Components of the Gross Domestic Product

Million United States dollars

	1980	1981	1982	1983	1984	1985	1986	1987	1988	1989	1990	1991
1 Indirect taxes, net	201346	237099	240942	258006	287004	307411	318621	332966	354079	385613	416357	445734
A Indirect taxes	211957	249277	256425	280104	309480	329910	345500	364986	385343	414691	444193	475215
B Less: Subsidies a	10611	12178	15483	22098	22476	22499	26879	32020	31264	29078	27836	29481
2 Consumption of fixed capital b	364559	418944	457926	478744	496187	521533	548330	574345	610783	662612	687571	714665
3 Compensation of employees paid by resident producers to:	1652530	1825399	1927107	2041148	2237670	2395159	2536519	2712491	2936165	3115476	3307213	3407000
A Resident households	1651967	1824732	1926355	2040387	2236813	2394276	2535634	2711553	2935144	3114389	3306051	3405806
B Rest of the world	563	667	752	761	857	883	885	938	1021	1087	1162	1194
4 Operating surplus	476075	543463	533951	606235	751644	806433	826068	901589	981350	1039776	1048277	1021579
A Corporate and quasi-corporate enterprises	235161	259686	239016	294800	357790	372883	367905	414922	461979	488648	481365	452831
B Private unincorporated enterprises	240914	283777	294935	311435	393854	433550	458163	486667	519371	551128	566912	568748
C General government	...	...	...	...	...	...	...	...	...	...	...	...
Statistical discrepancy	13638	10891	-7429	10166	-9038	-13887	1246	-24817	-28415	1075	5419	21866
Equals: Gross Domestic Product	2708148	3035796	3152497	3394299	3763467	4016649	4230784	4496574	4853962	5204509	5464795	5610800

a) Excludes subsidies to public corporations received from the same level of general government.
b) Includes consumption of fixed capital of roads, dams or other forms of construction except structures.

1.4 General Government Current Receipts and Disbursements

Million United States dollars

	1980	1981	1982	1983	1984	1985	1986	1987	1988	1989	1990	1991
	Receipts											
1 Operating surplus	...	...	...	...	...	...	...	...	...	...	...	...
2 Property and entrepreneurial income	33816	43384	50362	55742	64445	72076	76902	76435	82165	87028	92019	92729
3 Taxes, fees and contributions	767085	877596	890029	944198	1048155	1136368	1204981	1316821	1399501	1523840	1598205	1635537
A Indirect taxes	211957	249277	256425	280104	309480	329910	345500	364986	385343	414691	444193	475215
B Direct taxes	383165	425813	417277	429664	471551	513811	543576	616168	639600	706630	725656	709395
C Social security contributions	166696	196217	209232	226334	257904	282101	304007	322861	360740	387146	412020	433266
D Compulsory fees, fines and penalties	5267	6289	7095	8096	9220	10546	11898	12806	13818	15373	16336	17661
4 Other current transfers	27987	31701	34366	36068	36134	39735	40596	42273	44761	46982	54085	94615
Total Current Receipts of General Government	828888	952681	974757	1036008	1148734	1248179	1322479	1435529	1526427	1657850	1744309	1822881
	Disbursements											
1 Government final consumption expenditure	476343	529385	579270	620821	669749	727868	781951	830972	876420	915832	975724	1023260
A Compensation of employees	295633	325519	353763	377273	401371	432213	458641	488303	521784	559515	602790	638580
B Consumption of fixed capital a	40576	43279	44829	45764	47708	50809	52781	54477	57840	62048	63500	66422
C Purchases of goods and services, net	141634	162114	182244	199369	222427	246824	272742	290576	299361	297039	312393	321253
D Less: Own account fixed capital formation	1500	1527	1566	1585	1757	1978	2213	2384	2565	2770	2959	2995
E Indirect taxes paid, net	...	...	...	...	...	...	...	...	...	...	...	...
2 Property income	85406	112113	132954	149433	178100	200376	212999	222106	237413	258669	278525	294595
A Interest	85406	112113	132954	149433	178100	200376	212999	222106	237413	258669	278525	294595
B Net land rent and royalties	...	...	...	...	...	...	...	...	...	...	...	...

United States

1.4 General Government Current Receipts and Disbursements
(Continued)

Million United States dollars

	1980	1981	1982	1983	1984	1985	1986	1987	1988	1989	1990	1991
3 Subsidies	10611	12178	15483	22098	22476	22499	26879	32020	31264	29078	27836	29481
4 Other current transfers	300660	340767	379981	408853	418906	449512	475985	494784	525822	571434	634969	710694
A Social security benefits	180310	208974	242058	261088	265334	283925	301360	314320	332123	359192	391682	433431
B Social assistance grants	89310	97367	99653	106972	111493	117563	125076	130996	141571	157115	178914	213580
C Other	31040	34426	38270	40793	42079	48024	49549	49468	52128	55127	64373	63683
5 Net saving	-44132	-41762	-132931	-165197	-140497	-152076	-175335	-144353	-144492	-117163	-172745	-235149
Total Current Disbursements and Net Saving of General Government	828888	952681	974757	1036008	1148734	1248179	1322479	1435529	1526427	1657850	1744309	1822881

a) Includes consumption of fixed capital of roads, dams or other forms of construction except structures.

1.5 Current Income and Outlay of Corporate and Quasi-Corporate Enterprises, Summary

Million United States dollars

	1980	1981	1982	1983	1984	1985	1986	1987	1988	1989	1990	1991
					Receipts							
1 Operating surplus	235161	259686	239016	294800	357790	372883	367905	414922	461979	488648	481365	452831
2 Property and entrepreneurial income received	499437	640292	707891	693183	794686	861813	901590	960546	1115977	1314606	1319848	1262393
3 Current transfers	5369	6063	6639	7120	7321	8140	8217	9374	10470	10021	10596	11913
Total Current Receipts a	739967	906041	953546	995103	1159797	1242836	1277712	1384842	1588426	1813275	1811809	1727137
					Disbursements							
1 Property and entrepreneurial income	612845	781646	856854	845867	955742	1026559	1084144	1138022	1300703	1543670	1558147	1477793
2 Direct taxes and other current payments to general government	84785	81143	63081	77241	94037	96512	106487	127089	137014	141309	136681	124041
3 Other current transfers	14418	17086	19371	20997	23287	25598	28594	29555	32353	33310	33586	36256
4 Net saving	27919	26166	14240	50998	86731	94167	58487	90176	118356	94986	83395	89047
Total Current Disbursements and Net Saving a	739967	906041	953546	995103	1159797	1242836	1277712	1384842	1588426	1813275	1811809	1727137

a) This table, Corporate and Quasi-corporate Enterprises, does not include private quasi-corporate enterprises.

1.6 Current Income and Outlay of Households and Non-Profit Institutions

Million United States dollars

	1980	1981	1982	1983	1984	1985	1986	1987	1988	1989	1990	1991
					Receipts							
1 Compensation of employees	1652432	1825243	1926895	2040961	2237432	2394922	2536327	2712378	2936005	3115240	3306983	3406760
A From resident producers	1651967	1824732	1926355	2040387	2236813	2394276	2535634	2711553	2935144	3114389	3306051	3405806
B From rest of the world	465	511	540	574	619	646	693	825	861	851	932	954
2 Operating surplus of private unincorporated enterprises	171801	180801	170715	186656	235974	259899	283715	310235	324312	347270	366919	367965
3 Property and entrepreneurial income	320065	403276	447954	470571	536831	571099	599546	604019	644650	731378	763641	757469
4 Current transfers	306878	348792	388017	418233	428319	459056	487959	509702	541599	588561	646394	727946
A Social security benefits	180310	208974	242058	261088	265334	283925	301360	314320	332123	359192	391682	433431
B Social assistance grants	89310	97367	99653	106972	111493	117563	125076	130996	141571	157115	178914	213580
C Other	37258	42451	46306	50173	51492	57568	61523	64386	67905	72254	75798	80935
Total Current Receipts a	2451176	2758112	2933581	3116421	3438556	3684976	3907547	4136334	4446566	4782449	5083937	5260140
					Disbursements							
1 Private final consumption expenditure	1708277	1887328	2016947	2201908	2401883	2598435	2764716	2960584	3198135	3420469	3633800	3762819
2 Property income	49404	54584	58802	65713	74955	83582	90928	92290	93732	102981	109609	112542
3 Direct taxes and other current transfers n.e.c. to general government	470343	547176	570523	586853	644638	709946	752994	824746	877144	967840	1017331	1036281
A Social security contributions	166696	196217	209232	226334	257904	282101	304007	322861	360740	387146	412020	433266
B Direct taxes	298380	344670	354196	352423	377514	417299	437089	489079	502586	565321	588975	585354
C Fees, fines and penalties	5267	6289	7095	8096	9220	10546	11898	12806	13818	15373	16336	17661
4 Other current transfers	34921	39422	42330	44661	45323	49232	50556	53672	56553	66469	70558	74675
5 Net saving	188231	229602	244979	217286	271757	243781	248353	205042	221002	224690	252639	273823
Total Current Disbursements and Net Saving a	2451176	2758112	2933581	3116421	3438556	3684976	3907547	4136334	4446566	4782449	5083937	5260140

a) This table, Households and Non-profit Institutions, includes also private unincorporated enterprises and private quasi-corporate enterprises.

1.7 External Transactions on Current Account, Summary

Million United States dollars

	1980	1981	1982	1983	1984	1985	1986	1987	1988	1989	1990	1991
Payments to the Rest of the World												
1 Imports of goods and services	293896	317686	303194	328126	405110	417623	451737	507050	552208	587708	625903	619972
A Imports of merchandise c.i.f. a	248638	267742	250604	272700	336337	343310	370023	414796	452127	485068	507837	499910
B Other	45258	49944	52590	55426	68773	74313	81714	92254	100081	102640	118066	120062
2 Factor income to the rest of the world	44131	58611	64128	62317	79071	76679	80633	93014	112976	133850	131543	116782
A Compensation of employees	563	667	752	761	857	883	885	938	1021	1087	1162	1194
B Property and entrepreneurial income	43568	57944	63376	61556	78214	75796	79748	92076	111955	132763	130381	115588
By general government	12684	17313	19282	18993	21155	22972	24071	25291	30164	35856	37870	38986
By corporate and quasi-corporate enterprises	30884	40631	44094	42563	57059	52824	55677	66785	81791	96907	92511	76602
By other	...	...	...	...	...	...	...	...	...	...	...	...
3 Current transfers to the rest of the world	12942	13657	14874	15248	18057	20081	21289	19889	21806	29949	37076	34292
A Indirect taxes to supranational organizations	...	...	...	...	...	...	...	...	...	...	...	...
B Other current transfers	12942	13657	14874	15248	18057	20081	21289	19889	21806	29949	37076	34292
4 Surplus of the nation on current transactions	10316	8445	-2462	-34961	-94010	-118067	-141721	-155122	-117987	-89337	-76062	8977
Payments to the Rest of the World and Surplus of the Nation on Current Transactions	361285	398399	379734	370730	408228	396316	411938	464831	569003	662170	718460	780023
Receipts From The Rest of the World												
1 Exports of goods and services	277525	301373	280227	272738	297795	296384	313052	356553	436394	500380	548832	589418
A Exports of merchandise f.o.b. a	225635	238918	214833	207096	225413	221911	225751	257260	325336	371100	397515	422504
B Other	51890	62455	65394	65642	72382	74473	87301	99293	111058	129280	151317	166914
2 Factor income from rest of the world	80583	94088	97293	95834	108118	97262	95960	105051	128701	157490	160590	143464
A Compensation of employees	465	511	540	574	619	646	693	825	861	851	932	954
B Property and entrepreneurial income	80118	93577	96753	95260	107499	96616	95267	104226	127840	156639	159658	142510
By general government	2562	3680	4118	4832	5227	5499	6413	5311	6703	5635	10508	8104
By corporate and quasi-corporate enterprises	77556	89897	92635	90428	102272	91117	88854	98915	121137	151004	149150	134406
By other	...	...	...	...	...	...	...	...	...	...	...	...
3 Current transfers from rest of the world	3177	2938	2214	2158	2315	2670	2926	3227	3908	4300	9038	47141
A Subsidies from supranational organisations	...	...	...	...	...	...	...	...	...	...	...	...
B Other current transfers	3177	2938	2214	2158	2315	2670	2926	3227	3908	4300	9038	47141
Receipts from the Rest of the World on Current Transactions	361285	398399	379734	370730	408228	396316	411938	464831	569003	662170	718460	780023

a) Merchandise valued at Free Along Side (F.A.S.).

1.8 Capital Transactions of The Nation, Summary

Million United States dollars

	1980	1981	1982	1983	1984	1985	1986	1987	1988	1989	1990	1991
Finance of Gross Capital Formation												
Gross saving	536576	632950	584214	581830	714178	707404	679836	725210	805649	865124	850860	842386
1 Consumption of fixed capital	364559	418944	457926	478744	496187	521533	548330	574345	610783	662612	687571	714665
A General government a	40576	43279	44828	45764	47708	50810	52780	54477	57840	62048	63501	66422
B Corporate and quasi-corporate enterprises	197187	232699	257750	272229	281091	294035	311177	325433	346577	372593	389506	405157
Public	12107	13300	14042	14537	15234	16199	17000	17718	18938	20211	21256	22152
Private b	185080	219399	243708	257692	265857	277836	294177	307715	327639	352382	368250	383005
C Other b	126795	142966	155347	160750	167388	176688	184373	194435	206366	227970	234565	243086
2 Net saving	172017	214006	126288	103086	217991	185871	131506	150865	194866	202512	163289	127721
A General government	-44132	-41762	-132930	-165197	-140497	-152077	-175334	-144353	-144492	-117163	-172746	-235149
B Corporate and quasi-corporate enterprises	27919	26166	14240	50998	86731	94167	58487	90176	118356	94986	83395	89047
Public	-4757	-4088	-2148	-1780	857	2980	3095	4371	7347	10256	9709	15289
Private b	32676	30254	16388	52778	85874	91187	55392	85805	111009	84730	73686	73758

United States

1.8 Capital Transactions of The Nation, Summary
(Continued)

Million United States dollars

	1980	1981	1982	1983	1984	1985	1986	1987	1988	1989	1990	1991
C Other b	188231	229602	244979	217286	271757	243781	248353	205042	221002	224690	252639	273823
Less: Surplus of the nation on current transactions	10316	8445	-2462	-34961	-94010	-118067	-141721	-155122	-117987	-89337	-76062	8977
Statistical discrepancy	13638	10891	-7429	10166	-9038	-13887	1246	-24817	-28415	1075	5419	21866
Finance of Gross Capital Formation	539898	635396	579247	626957	799150	811584	822803	855515	895221	955536	932341	855275
Gross Capital Formation												
Increase in stocks b	-6535	31562	-11411	593	71341	28599	14937	25641	8361	34980	11754	-7203
Gross fixed capital formation	546433	603834	590658	626364	727809	782985	807866	829874	886860	920556	920587	862478
1 General government	47253	46940	48828	51174	56233	66176	69067	75001	76781	87461	91223	96701
2 Corporate and quasi-corporate enterprises	297316	343667	349231	338188	393319	424184	415385	417803	457798	472991	488617	464533
A Public	22083	24354	22487	22981	23775	26892	29842	31865	32710	34163	36185	34433
B Private b	275233	319313	326744	315207	369544	397292	385543	385938	425088	438828	452432	430100
3 Other b	201864	213227	192599	237002	278257	292625	323414	337070	352281	360104	340747	301244
Gross Capital Formation	539898	635396	579247	626957	799150	811584	822803	855515	895221	955536	932341	855275

a) Item 'Public order and safety' is included in item 'General public services'.
b) Private quasi-corporate enterprises are included with item 'other'.

1.9 Gross Domestic Product by Institutional Sectors of Origin

Million United States dollars

	1980	1981	1982	1983	1984	1985	1986	1987	1988	1989	1990	1991
Domestic Factor Incomes Originating												
1 General government	295633	325519	353763	377273	401371	432213	458641	488303	521784	559515	602790	638580
2 Corporate and quasi-corporate enterprises	1743665	1942889	1995649	2148816	2455955	2627697	2750631	2955316	3208096	3389639	3524949	3543932
3 Households and private unincorporated enterprises a	6103	6163	6250	6283	7292	7341	7730	7709	8315	8922	9351	9184
A Owner-occupied housing	...	...	...	...	...	...	...	...	...	...	...	...
B Subsistence production	...	...	...	...	...	...	...	...	...	...	...	...
C Other a	6103	6163	6250	6283	7292	7341	7730	7709	8315	8922	9351	9184
4 Non-profit institutions serving households	83204	94291	105396	115011	124696	134341	145585	162752	179320	197176	218400	236883
Subtotal: Domestic Factor Incomes	2128605	2368862	2461058	2647383	2989314	3201592	3362587	3614080	3917515	4155252	4355490	4428579
Indirect taxes, net	201346	237099	240942	258006	287004	307411	318621	332966	354079	385613	416357	445734
A Indirect taxes	211957	249277	256425	280104	309480	329910	345500	364986	385343	414691	444193	475215
B Less: Subsidies	10611	12178	15483	22098	22476	22499	26879	32020	31264	29078	27836	29481
Consumption of fixed capital	364559	418944	457926	478744	496187	521533	548330	574345	610783	662612	687571	714665
Statistical discrepancy	13638	10891	-7429	10166	-9038	-13887	1246	-24817	-28415	1075	5419	21866
Gross Domestic Product	2708148	3035796	3152497	3394299	3763467	4016649	4230784	4496574	4853962	5204509	5464795	5610800

a) Private quasi-corporate enterprises are included with item 'other'.

1.12 Relations Among National Accounting Aggregates

Million United States dollars

	1980	1981	1982	1983	1984	1985	1986	1987	1988	1989	1990	1991
Gross Domestic Product	2708147	3035796	3152496	3394298	3763467	4016649	4230784	4496574	4853962	5204509	5464795	5610800
Plus: Net factor income from the rest of the world	36452	35477	33165	33517	29047	20583	15327	12037	15725	23640	29047	26682
Factor income from the rest of the world	80583	94088	97293	95834	108118	97262	95960	105051	128701	157490	160590	143464
Less: Factor income to the rest of the world	44131	58611	64128	62317	79071	76679	80633	93014	112976	133850	131543	116782
Equals: Gross National Product	2744599	3071273	3185661	3427815	3792514	4037232	4246111	4508611	4869687	5228149	5493842	5637482
Less: Consumption of fixed capital	364559	418944	457926	478744	496187	521533	548330	574345	610783	662612	687571	714665

1.12 Relations Among National Accounting Aggregates
(Continued)

Million United States dollars

	1980	1981	1982	1983	1984	1985	1986	1987	1988	1989	1990	1991
Equals: National Income	2380040	2652329	2727735	2949071	3296327	3515699	3697781	3934266	4258904	4565537	4806271	4922817
Plus: Net current transfers from the rest of the world	-9765	-10719	-12660	-13090	-15742	-17411	-18363	-16662	-17898	-25649	-28038	12849
Current transfers from the rest of the world	3177	2938	2214	2158	2315	2670	2926	3227	3908	4300	9038	47141
Less: Current transfers to the rest of the world	12942	13657	14874	15248	18057	20081	21289	19889	21806	29949	37076	34292
Equals: National Disposable Income	2370275	2641610	2715075	2935981	3280585	3498288	3679418	3917604	4241006	4539888	4778233	4935666
Less: Final consumption	2184620	2416713	2596216	2822729	3071632	3326304	3546666	3791556	4074555	4336301	4609525	4786079
Statistical discrepancy a	-13638	-10891	7429	-10166	9038	13887	-1246	24817	28415	-1075	-5419	-21866
Equals: Net Saving	172017	214006	126288	103086	217991	185871	131506	150865	194866	202512	163289	127721
Less: Surplus of the nation on current transactions	10316	8445	-2462	-34961	-94010	-118067	-141721	-155122	-117987	-89337	-76062	8977
Statistical discrepancy a	13638	10891	-7429	10166	-9038	-13887	1246	-24817	-28415	1075	5419	21866
Equals: Net Capital Formation	175339	216452	121321	148213	302963	290051	274473	281170	284438	292924	244770	140610

a) Statistical Discrepancy is defined as the difference between GNP less charges against GNP other than Statistical Discrepancy. It arises because GNP and charges against GNP are independently derived by different methodologies. This Statistical Discrepancy after item 'Final consumption' is treated as a negative item and after item 'Surplus of the nations on current transactions', it is treated as a positive item.

2.3 Total Government Outlays by Function and Type

Million United States dollars

	Final Consumption Expenditures			Subsidies	Other Current Transfers & Property Income	Total Current Disbursements	Gross Capital Formation	Other Capital Outlays	Total Outlays	
	Total	Compensation of Employees	Other							
					1980					
1 General public services	...	...	...	...	...	...	...	...	...	
2 Defence	...	...	...	...	...	...	...	...	...	
3 Public order and safety	...	...	...	...	...	...	...	...	...	
4 Education	...	...	...	...	...	...	...	...	...	
5 Health	...	...	...	...	...	...	...	...	...	
6 Social security and welfare	...	...	...	...	...	...	...	...	...	
7 Housing and community amenities	...	...	...	...	...	...	...	...	...	
8 Recreation, culture and religion	...	...	...	...	...	...	...	...	...	
9 Economic services	...	...	...	...	...	...	...	...	...	
10 Other functions	...	...	...	...	...	...	...	...	...	
Total	476343	295633	180710	10611	386066	873020	50016	-2422	920614	
					1981					
1 General public services	...	...	...	...	...	...	...	...	...	
2 Defence	...	...	...	...	...	...	...	...	...	
3 Public order and safety	...	...	...	...	...	...	...	...	...	
4 Education	...	...	...	...	...	...	...	...	...	
5 Health	...	...	...	...	...	...	...	...	...	
6 Social security and welfare	...	...	...	...	...	...	...	...	...	
7 Housing and community amenities	...	...	...	...	...	...	...	...	...	
8 Recreation, culture and religion	...	...	...	...	...	...	...	...	...	
9 Economic services	...	...	...	...	...	...	...	...	...	
10 Other functions	...	...	...	...	...	...	...	...	...	
Total	529385	325519	203866	12178	452880	994443	52973	-3586	1043830	
					1982					
1 General public services	...	...	...	...	...	...	...	...	...	
2 Defence	...	...	...	...	...	...	...	...	...	
3 Public order and safety	...	...	...	...	...	...	...	...	...	
4 Education	...	...	...	...	...	...	...	...	...	
5 Health	...	...	...	...	...	...	...	...	...	
6 Social security and welfare	...	...	...	...	...	...	...	...	...	
7 Housing and community amenities	...	...	...	...	...	...	...	...	...	
8 Recreation, culture and religion	...	...	...	...	...	...	...	...	...	
9 Economic services	...	...	...	...	...	...	...	...	...	
10 Other functions	...	...	...	...	...	...	...	...	...	
Total	579269	353763	225507	15483	512935	1107688	53265	-1589	1159363	

United States

2.3 Total Government Outlays by Function and Type
(Continued)

	Final Consumption Expenditures			Subsidies	Other Current Transfers & Property Income	Total Current Disbursements	Gross Capital Formation	Other Capital Outlays	Total Outlays
	Total	Compensation of Employees	Other						
1983									
1 General public services	...	...	...	...	...	...	...	...	...
2 Defence	...	...	...	...	...	...	...	...	...
3 Public order and safety	...	...	...	...	...	...	...	...	...
4 Education	...	...	...	...	...	...	...	...	...
5 Health	...	...	...	...	...	...	...	...	...
6 Social security and welfare	...	...	...	...	...	...	...	...	...
7 Housing and community amenities	...	...	...	...	...	...	...	...	...
8 Recreation, culture and religion	...	...	...	...	...	...	...	...	...
9 Economic services	...	...	...	...	...	...	...	...	...
10 Other functions	...	...	...	...	...	...	...	...	...
Total	620821	377273	243548	22098	558286	1201205	57149	-2741	1255613
1984									
1 General public services	...	...	...	...	...	...	...	...	...
2 Defence	...	...	...	...	...	...	...	...	...
3 Public order and safety	...	...	...	...	...	...	...	...	...
4 Education	...	...	...	...	...	...	...	...	...
5 Health	...	...	...	...	...	...	...	...	...
6 Social security and welfare	...	...	...	...	...	...	...	...	...
7 Housing and community amenities	...	...	...	...	...	...	...	...	...
8 Recreation, culture and religion	...	...	...	...	...	...	...	...	...
9 Economic services	...	...	...	...	...	...	...	...	...
10 Other functions	...	...	...	...	...	...	...	...	...
Total	669749	401371	268378	22476	597006	1289231	56530	-1422	1344339
1985									
1 General public services	...	...	...	...	...	...	...	...	...
2 Defence	...	...	...	...	...	...	...	...	...
3 Public order and safety	...	...	...	...	...	...	...	...	...
4 Education	...	...	...	...	...	...	...	...	...
5 Health	...	...	...	...	...	...	...	...	...
6 Social security and welfare	...	...	...	...	...	...	...	...	...
7 Housing and community amenities	...	...	...	...	...	...	...	...	...
8 Recreation, culture and religion	...	...	...	...	...	...	...	...	...
9 Economic services	...	...	...	...	...	...	...	...	...
10 Other functions	...	...	...	...	...	...	...	...	...
Total	727869	432213	295655	22499	649888	1400255	70138	1824	1472218
1986									
1 General public services	...	...	...	...	...	...	...	...	...
2 Defence	...	...	...	...	...	...	...	...	...
3 Public order and safety	...	...	...	...	...	...	...	...	...
4 Education	...	...	...	...	...	...	...	...	...
5 Health	...	...	...	...	...	...	...	...	...
6 Social security and welfare	...	...	...	...	...	...	...	...	...
7 Housing and community amenities	...	...	...	...	...	...	...	...	...
8 Recreation, culture and religion	...	...	...	...	...	...	...	...	...
9 Economic services	...	...	...	...	...	...	...	...	...
10 Other functions	...	...	...	...	...	...	...	...	...
Total	781950	458641	323310	26879	688984	1497814	75575	651	1574039

2.3 Total Government Outlays by Function and Type
(Continued)

Million United States dollars

	Final Consumption Expenditures			Subsidies	Other Current Transfers & Property Income	Total Current Disbursements	Gross Capital Formation	Other Capital Outlays	Total Outlays
	Total	Compensation of Employees	Other						
1987									
1 General public services	...	...	...	...	...	...	...	...	...
2 Defence	...	...	...	...	...	...	...	...	...
3 Public order and safety	...	...	...	...	...	...	...	...	...
4 Education	...	...	...	...	...	...	...	...	...
5 Health	...	...	...	...	...	...	...	...	...
6 Social security and welfare	...	...	...	...	...	...	...	...	...
7 Housing and community amenities	...	...	...	...	...	...	...	...	...
8 Recreation, culture and religion	...	...	...	...	...	...	...	...	...
9 Economic services	...	...	...	...	...	...	...	...	...
10 Other functions	...	...	...	...	...	...	...	...	...
Total	830972	488303	342669	32020	716890	1579882	74179	3773	1657834
1988									
1 General public services	...	...	...	...	...	...	...	...	...
2 Defence	...	...	...	...	...	...	...	...	...
3 Public order and safety	...	...	...	...	...	...	...	...	...
4 Education	...	...	...	...	...	...	...	...	...
5 Health	...	...	...	...	...	...	...	...	...
6 Social security and welfare	...	...	...	...	...	...	...	...	...
7 Housing and community amenities	...	...	...	...	...	...	...	...	...
8 Recreation, culture and religion	...	...	...	...	...	...	...	...	...
9 Economic services	...	...	...	...	...	...	...	...	...
10 Other functions	...	...	...	...	...	...	...	...	...
Total	876420	521784	354636	31264	763235	1670919	68867	4247	1744033
1989									
1 General public services	...	...	...	...	...	...	...	...	...
2 Defence	...	...	...	...	...	...	...	...	...
3 Public order and safety	...	...	...	...	...	...	...	...	...
4 Education	...	...	...	...	...	...	...	...	...
5 Health	...	...	...	...	...	...	...	...	...
6 Social security and welfare	...	...	...	...	...	...	...	...	...
7 Housing and community amenities	...	...	...	...	...	...	...	...	...
8 Recreation, culture and religion	...	...	...	...	...	...	...	...	...
9 Economic services	...	...	...	...	...	...	...	...	...
10 Other functions	...	...	...	...	...	...	...	...	...
Total	915832	559515	356317	29078	830103	1775013	89045	4195	1868253
1990									
1 General public services	...	...	...	...	...	...	...	...	...
2 Defence	...	...	...	...	...	...	...	...	...
3 Public order and safety	...	...	...	...	...	...	...	...	...
4 Education	...	...	...	...	...	...	...	...	...
5 Health	...	...	...	...	...	...	...	...	...
6 Social security and welfare	...	...	...	...	...	...	...	...	...
7 Housing and community amenities	...	...	...	...	...	...	...	...	...
8 Recreation, culture and religion	...	...	...	...	...	...	...	...	...
9 Economic services	...	...	...	...	...	...	...	...	...
10 Other functions	...	...	...	...	...	...	...	...	...
Total	975725	602790	372934	27836	913494	1917054	96545	4445	2018045

United States

2.3 Total Government Outlays by Function and Type
(Continued)

Million United States dollars

	Final Consumption Expenditures			Subsidies	Other Current Transfers & Property Income	Total Current Disbursements	Gross Capital Formation	Other Capital Outlays	Total Outlays
	Total	Compensation of Employees	Other						
					1991				
1 General public services	...	...	...	...	...	...	...	...	...
2 Defence	...	...	...	...	...	...	...	...	...
3 Public order and safety	...	...	...	...	...	...	...	...	...
4 Education	...	...	...	...	...	...	...	...	...
5 Health	...	...	...	...	...	...	...	...	...
6 Social security and welfare	...	...	...	...	...	...	...	...	...
7 Housing and community amenities	...	...	...	...	...	...	...	...	...
8 Recreation, culture and religion	...	...	...	...	...	...	...	...	...
9 Economic services	...	...	...	...	...	...	...	...	...
10 Other functions	...	...	...	...	...	...	...	...	...
Total	1023260	638580	384680	29481	1005289	2058030	99729	5351	2163110

2.4 Composition of General Government Social Security Benefits and Social Assistance Grants to Households

Million United States dollars

	1980		1981		1982		1983		1984		1985	
	Social Security Benefits	Social Assistance Grants	Social Security Benefits	Social Assistance Grants	Social Security Benefits	Social Assistance Grants	Social Security Benefits	Social Assistance Grants	Social Security Benefits	Social Assistance Grants	Social Security Benefits	Social Assistance Grants
1 Education benefits	...	9318	...	10332	...	9716	...	10507	...	10489	...	10967
2 Health benefits	...	26671	...	31041	...	33982	...	37267	...	40554	...	44228
3 Social security and welfare benefits	180310	51848	208974	54829	242058	55083	261088	58111	265334	59669	283925	62123
4 Housing and community amenities	...	167	...	163	...	96	...	16	...	16	...	83
5 Recreation and cultural benefits	...	312	...	408	...	264	...	425	...	520	...	326
6 Other	...	994	...	594	...	512	...	646	...	245	...	-164
Total	180310	89310	208974	97367	242058	99653	261088	106972	265334	111493	283925	117563

	1986		1987		1988		1989		1990		1991	
	Social Security Benefits	Social Assistance Grants	Social Security Benefits	Social Assistance Grants	Social Security Benefits	Social Assistance Grants	Social Security Benefits	Social Assistance Grants	Social Security Benefits	Social Assistance Grants	Social Security Benefits	Social Assistance Grants
1 Education benefits	...	10945	...	11180	...	11564	...	13953	...	14258	...	14566
2 Health benefits	...	48774	...	53467	...	59393	...	67853	...	81247	...	106540
3 Social security and welfare benefits	301360	64286	314320	65708	332123	70166	359192	74420	391682	81963	433431	90494
4 Housing and community amenities	...	319	...	352	...	367	...	168	...	211	...	169
5 Recreation and cultural benefits	...	472	...	390	...	423	...	406	...	487	...	508
6 Other	...	280	...	-101	...	-342	...	315	...	748	...	1303
Total	301360	125076	314320	130996	332123	141571	359192	157115	391682	178914	433431	213580

2.5 Private Final Consumption Expenditure by Type and Purpose, in Current Prices

Million United States dollars

	1980	1981	1982	1983	1984	1985	1986	1987	1988	1989	1990	1991
					Final Consumption Expenditure of Resident Households							
1 Food, beverages and tobacco	269281	288255	301505	316967	334367	349966	365688	377640	398078	425044	453351	466938
A Food	196160	208963	215529	222509	235784	245862	254980	265426	281313	300974	323007	330019
B Non-alcoholic beverages	22523	24252	27263	29720	31676	33434	36928	36523	38773	40037	40366	41239
C Alcoholic beverages	29738	32210	34410	36387	36774	38937	40709	40653	41828	43546	46615	47912
D Tobacco	20860	22830	24303	28351	30133	31733	33071	35038	36164	40487	43363	47768
2 Clothing and footwear	114524	124779	128181	139326	151300	161621	173224	185086	199324	214643	223326	226242
3 Gross rent, fuel and power	329252	369220	401922	433191	465931	500915	527624	559701	597221	633650	668722	701899
A Fuel and power	71751	79214	87104	94446	98859	102827	99095	100437	105489	109922	110266	115264
B Other	257501	290006	314818	338745	367072	398088	428529	459264	491732	523728	558456	586635
4 Furniture, furnishings and household equipment and operation	110896	119137	122777	134650	149498	159502	173986	184473	197184	210221	217399	215579
A Household operation	32168	35318	38098	41198	45945	49439	54047	57808	61604	65210	69355	70110

2.5 Private Final Consumption Expenditure by Type and Purpose, in Current Prices
(Continued)

__Million United States dollars__

	1980	1981	1982	1983	1984	1985	1986	1987	1988	1989	1990	1991
B Other	78728	83819	84679	93452	103553	110063	119939	126665	135580	145011	148044	145469
5 Medical care and health expenses	207231	242852	272771	302174	331711	364698	396701	440373	487745	536390	595871	656021
6 Transport and communication	274976	302768	311858	343190	384208	423808	434239	450669	483014	509800	528194	514488
A Personal transport equipment	73222	80764	86859	108394	132688	155505	173165	170908	183922	190813	186544	168967
B Other	201754	222004	224999	234796	251520	268303	261074	279761	299092	318987	341650	345521
7 Recreational, entertainment, education and cultural services	147593	164652	178343	197597	218332	237328	257577	283053	313379	340758	362628	378055
A Education	33616	37879	41743	45808	49763	54470	58988	64076	71618	79415	86410	92760
B Other	113977	126773	136600	151789	168569	182858	198589	218977	241761	261343	276218	285295
8 Miscellaneous goods and services	250984	276048	298652	331175	361950	395214	434019	476215	522503	557943	597013	621898
A Personal care	50640	54206	55146	61997	68318	73364	80793	88169	95214	102356	107771	109658
B Expenditures in restaurants, cafes and hotels	101223	110187	117395	127261	136683	144743	156639	172329	187138	196610	207886	215233
C Other	99121	111655	126111	141917	156949	177107	196587	215717	240151	258977	281356	297007
Total Final Consumption Expenditure in the Domestic Market by Households, of which	1704737	1887711	2016009	2198270	2397297	2593052	2763058	2957210	3198448	3428449	3646504	3781120
A Durable goods	164377	176647	182264	215618	253728	286291	318568	327892	353286	369793	369057	348768
B Semi-durable goods	215974	234669	243000	264005	287296	304816	326542	350339	378588	406930	425619	431694
C Non-durable goods	500311	546734	571626	603358	637720	669031	674415	704838	743925	796663	851565	875937
D Services	824075	929661	1019119	1115289	1218553	1332914	1443533	1574141	1722649	1855063	2000263	2124721
Plus: Direct purchases abroad by resident households a	15098	16253	17672	19356	26889	28674	28018	33371	35767	36347	39893	39818
Less: Direct purchases in the domestic market by non-resident households	11558	16636	16734	15718	22303	23291	26360	29997	36080	44325	52596	58118
Equals: Final Consumption Expenditure of Resident Households b	1708277	1887328	2016947	2201908	2401883	2598435	2764716	2960584	3198135	3420471	3633801	3762820

Final Consumption Expenditure of Private Non-profit Institutions Serving Households

	1980	1981	1982	1983	1984	1985	1986	1987	1988	1989	1990	1991
Equals: Final Consumption Expenditure of Private Non-profit Organisations Serving Households	...	...	...	...	...	...	...	...	...	...	...	...
Private Final Consumption Expenditure	1708277	1887328	2016947	2201908	2401883	2598435	2764716	2960584	3198135	3420471	3633801	3762820

a) Item 'Direct purchases abroad by resident households' includes direct purchases abroad by resident households less value of gifts in kind, sent abroad, net.   b) Item 'Final consumption expenditure of resident households' includes consumption expenditure of private non-profit institutions serving households.

2.6 Private Final Consumption Expenditure by Type and Purpose, in Constant Prices

__Million United States dollars__

	1980	1981	1982	1983	1984	1985	1986	1987	1988	1989	1990	1991
At constant prices of:1985												
Final Consumption Expenditure of Resident Households												
1 Food, beverages and tobacco	330741	328965	330474	336574	341660	349966	354175	352558	356983	357448	360360	355827
A Food	235106	231551	231187	235439	239774	245862	248831	247850	251608	252057	255263	253800
B Non-alcoholic beverages	25701	26555	29026	31055	32293	33434	34888	35441	37609	37531	37091	37702
C Alcoholic beverages	36118	36610	37467	38082	37681	38937	39512	38680	38809	39125	40120	36825
D Tobacco	33814	34247	32792	31997	31911	31733	30942	30585	28955	28734	27885	27498
2 Clothing and footwear	131468	137243	137401	146070	156089	161621	172752	176913	182925	192082	191548	187255
3 Gross rent, fuel and power	464482	467941	470314	478062	489348	500915	506597	518384	531418	539858	542001	548692
A Fuel and power	101062	97002	96863	99481	100115	102827	102423	105135	109528	110563	106806	109108
B Other	363419	370939	373450	378581	389232	398088	404174	413249	421890	429295	435194	439583
4 Furniture, furnishings and household equipment and operation	135626	135094	131574	139829	152442	159502	170582	176544	184874	193028	194251	188504
A Household operation	40772	40937	41574	43449	47373	49439	52200	53883	56048	57058	58430	57023
B Other	94854	94157	90000	96380	105068	110063	118382	122660	128825	135970	135820	131480
5 Medical care and health expenses	312718	328064	333053	342680	353263	364698	378543	397175	411206	419667	435045	448727
6 Transport and communication	328811	329838	331886	358022	392377	423808	445502	446067	468137	474562	472903	449474
A Personal transport equipment	92793	94613	96764	115736	136636	155505	167499	157801	167168	168035	163284	143678
B Other	236018	235225	235122	242285	255740	268303	278003	288265	300968	306526	309618	305796
7 Recreational, entertainment, education and cultural services	184809	191080	195685	208850	224121	237328	253234	271313	291438	306017	315696	319317
A Education	47153	48009	49236	51022	52236	54470	56587	58627	62055	65215	67631	68631

United States

2.6 Private Final Consumption Expenditure by Type and Purpose, in Constant Prices
(Continued)

Million United States dollars

	1980	1981	1982	1983	1984	1985	1986	1987	1988	1989	1990	1991
				At constant prices of:1985								
B Other	137655	143071	146449	157827	171884	182858	196647	212685	229383	240802	248064	250685
8 Miscellaneous goods and services	334280	337410	343129	360376	377123	395214	415757	435655	456834	467321	476547	477018
A Personal care	62310	61976	60368	65090	69790	73364	78915	82565	85017	87061	86987	85312
B Expenditures in restaurants, cafes and hotels	133501	133160	133996	139026	142692	144743	150238	158761	165112	165825	166766	164993
C Other	138468	142272	148764	156258	164640	177107	186602	194328	206703	214435	222793	226713
Total Final Consumption Expenditure in the Domestic Market by Households, of which	2222938	2255640	2273520	2370466	2486426	2593052	2697146	2774613	2883818	2949988	2988354	2974818
A Durable goods	192946	194451	192984	222332	256855	286291	314323	313906	333071	341835	339296	318277
B Semi-durable goods	254214	260478	259132	274699	294591	304816	323731	335774	350569	366506	369690	363288
C Non-durable goods	624546	621301	623317	638205	653475	669031	682173	691220	705912	711031	712219	707371
D Services	1151230	1179409	1198086	1235228	1281505	1332914	1376917	1433712	1494264	1530616	1567148	1585880
Plus: Direct purchases abroad by resident households a	14053	14603	16510	18776	26274	28674	24792	26594	27306	26838	26366	24408
Less: Direct purchases in the domestic market by non-resident households	15798	20831	19431	17432	23391	23292	25609	27835	31898	37820	42018	43162
Equals: Final Consumption Expenditure of Resident Households b	2221193	2249412	2270600	2371810	2489309	2598434	2696329	2773372	2879226	2939006	2972703	2956064

Final Consumption Expenditure of Private Non-profit Institutions Serving Households

	1980	1981	1982	1983	1984	1985	1986	1987	1988	1989	1990	1991
Equals: Final Consumption Expenditure of Private Non-profit Organisations Serving Households	...	...	...	...	...	...	...	...	...	...	...	...
Private Final Consumption Expenditure	2221193	2249412	2270600	2371810	2489309	2598434	2696329	2773372	2879226	2939006	2972703	2956064

a) Item 'Direct purchases abroad by resident households' includes direct purchases abroad by resident households less value of gifts in kind, sent abroad, net. b) Item 'Final consumption expenditure of resident households' includes consumption expenditure of private non-profit institutions serving households.

2.7 Gross Capital Formation by Type of Good and Owner, in Current Prices

Million United States dollars

	1980				1981				1982			
	TOTAL	Total Private	Public Enterprises	General Government	TOTAL	Total Private	Public Enterprises	General Government	TOTAL	Total Private	Public Enterprises	General Government
Increase in stocks, total ab	-6535	-9490	192	2763	31562	25436	93	6033	-11411	-15946	98	4437
1 Goods producing industries c	-6088	-6088	...	...	12781	12781	...	...	-7211	-7211	...	...
A Materials and supplies	-586	-586	...	...	473	473	...	...	-5268	-5268	...	...
B Work in progress	47	47	...	...	-1770	-1770	...	...	-5432	-5432	...	...
C Livestock, except breeding stocks, dairy cattle, etc. a	1339	1339	...	...	287	287	...	...	-646	-646	...	...
D Finished goods	-6888	-6888	...	...	13791	13791	...	...	4135	4135	...	...
2 Wholesale and retail trade	-1306	-1306	...	...	7640	7640	...	...	-6196	-6196	...	...
3 Other, except government stocks	-1904	-2096	192	...	5108	5015	93	...	-2441	-2539	98	...
4 Government stocks	2763	...	...	2763	6033	...	...	6033	4437	...	...	4437
Gross Fixed Capital Formation, Total	546433	477097	22083	47253	603834	532540	24354	46940	590658	519343	22487	48828
1 Residential buildings d	122012	119877	1291	844	121356	118932	1512	912	104523	101991	1483	1049
2 Non-residential buildings	94227	77455	754	16018	108266	90939	903	16424	115513	98496	476	16541
3 Other construction	98515	60003	18143	20369	117274	78203	19334	19737	118302	80308	17824	20170
4 Land improvement and plantation and orchard development	...				...				...			
5 Producers' durable goods	231679	219762	1895	10022	256938	244466	2605	9867	252320	238548	2704	11068
A Transport equipment e	53023	48385	...	4638	55905	50556	...	5349	52060	46821	...	5239
Passenger cars	15640	14258	...	1382	18224	16711	...	1513	18168	16594	...	1574
Other	37383	34127	...	3256	37681	33845	...	3836	33892	30227	...	3665
B Machinery and equipment e	178656	171377	1895	5384	201033	193910	2605	4518	200260	191727	2704	5829
6 Breeding stock, dairy cattle, etc. a	...				...				...			
Total Gross Capital Formation	539898	467607	22275	50016	635396	557976	24447	52973	579247	503397	22585	53265

2.7 Gross Capital Formation by Type of Good and Owner, in Current Prices

Million United States dollars

	1983				1984				1985			
	TOTAL	Total Private	Public Enterprises	General Government	TOTAL	Total Private	Public Enterprises	General Government	TOTAL	Total Private	Public Enterprises	General Government
Increase in stocks, total [ab]	593	-5532	150	5975	71341	71081	-37	297	28599	24629	8	3962
1 Goods producing industries [c]	-15254	-15254	...	...	33604	33604	...	...	1682	1682	...	...
A Materials and supplies	670	670	...	...	6952	6952	...	...	-2296	-2296	...	...
B Work in progress	624	624	...	...	13064	13064	...	...	-806	-806	...	...
C Livestock, except breeding stocks, dairy cattle, etc. [a]	-378	-378	...	...	-1646	-1646	...	...	-1819	-1819	...	...
D Finished goods	-16170	-16170	...	...	15234	15234	...	...	6603	6603	...	...
2 Wholesale and retail trade	8969	8969	...	...	32917	32917	...	...	15732	15732	...	...
3 Other, except government stocks	903	753	150	...	4523	4560	-37	...	7223	7215	8	...
4 Government stocks	5975	...	...	5975	297	...	...	297	3962	...	...	3962
Gross Fixed Capital Formation, Total	626364	552209	22981	51174	727809	647801	23775	56233	782985	689917	26892	66176
1 Residential buildings [d]	150641	147804	1552	1285	177480	174173	2029	1278	184481	180859	2014	1608
2 Non-residential buildings	108524	90876	559	17089	127932	109813	480	17639	148847	127425	555	20867
3 Other construction	100044	62215	17652	20177	106053	65828	17509	22716	112827	65984	19754	27089
4 Land improvement and plantation and orchard development	...	...	...	...	...	...	...	...	...	...	...	...
5 Producers' durable goods	267155	251314	3218	12623	316344	297987	3757	14600	336830	315649	4569	16612
A Transport equipment [e]	59374	54030	...	5344	72291	65586	...	6705	79184	71313	...	7871
Passenger cars	23775	22110	...	1665	28121	26157	...	1964	29695	27704	...	1991
Other	35599	31920	...	3679	44170	39429	...	4741	49489	43609	...	5880
B Machinery and equipment [e]	207781	197284	3218	7279	244053	232401	3757	7895	257646	244336	4569	8741
6 Breeding stock, dairy cattle, etc. [a]	...	...	...	...	...	...	...	...	...	...	...	...
Total Gross Capital Formation	626957	546677	23131	57149	799150	718882	23738	56530	811584	714546	26900	70138

	1986				1987				1988			
	TOTAL	Total Private	Public Enterprises	General Government	TOTAL	Total Private	Public Enterprises	General Government	TOTAL	Total Private	Public Enterprises	General Government
Increase in stocks, total [ab]	14937	8643	-214	6508	25641	26280	183	-822	8361	16231	44	-7914
1 Goods producing industries [c]	-3679	-3679	...	...	220	220	...	...	4505	4505	...	...
A Materials and supplies	-539	-539	...	...	1243	1243	...	...	4936	4936	...	...
B Work in progress	-2162	-2162	...	...	4734	4734	...	...	5796	5796	...	...
C Livestock, except breeding stocks, dairy cattle, etc. [a]	-1461	-1461	...	...	-831	-831	...	...	-867	-867	...	...
D Finished goods	483	483	...	...	-4926	-4926	...	...	-5360	-5360	...	...
2 Wholesale and retail trade	9257	9257	...	...	23876	23876	...	...	12390	12390	...	...
3 Other, except government stocks	2851	3065	-214	...	2367	2184	183	...	-620	-664	44	...
4 Government stocks	6508	...	...	6508	-822	...	...	-822	-7914	...	...	-7914
Gross Fixed Capital Formation, Total	807866	708957	29842	69067	829874	723008	31865	75001	886860	777369	32710	76781
1 Residential buildings [d]	215345	211103	2648	1594	223609	219428	2233	1948	229981	225698	2287	1996
2 Non-residential buildings	144306	120682	580	23044	150767	124528	814	25425	160511	133746	767	25998
3 Other construction	101600	53276	21687	26637	98732	46791	23462	28479	100477	48236	24442	27799
4 Land improvement and plantation and orchard development	...	...	...	...	...	...	...	...	...	...	...	...
5 Producers' durable goods	346615	323896	4927	17792	356766	332261	5356	19149	395891	369689	5214	20988
A Transport equipment [e]	79945	72639	...	7306	80431	73608	...	6823	88370	80489	...	7881
Passenger cars	32260	30243	...	2017	31030	28901	...	2129	34538	32309	...	2229
Other	47685	42396	...	5289	49401	44707	...	4694	53832	48180	...	5652
B Machinery and equipment [e]	266670	251257	4927	10486	276335	258653	5356	12326	307521	289200	5214	13107
6 Breeding stock, dairy cattle, etc. [a]	...	...	...	...	...	...	...	...	...	...	...	...
Total Gross Capital Formation	822803	717600	29628	75575	855515	749288	32048	74179	895221	793600	32754	68867

United States

2.7 Gross Capital Formation by Type of Good and Owner, in Current Prices

Million United States dollars

	1989 TOTAL	1989 Total Private	1989 Public Enterprises	1989 General Government	1990 TOTAL	1990 Total Private	1990 Public Enterprises	1990 General Government	1991 TOTAL	1991 Total Private	1991 Public Enterprises	1991 General Government
Increase in stocks, total ab	34980	33326	70	1584	11754	6314	118	5322	-7203	-10235	4	3028
1 Goods producing industries c	21316	21316	...	...	6829	6829	...	...	-7470	-7470	...	...
A Materials and supplies	3985	3985	...	...	667	667	...	...	-1839	-1839	...	...
B Work in progress	10082	10082	...	...	-334	-334	...	...	-4616	-4616	...	...
C Livestock, except breeding stocks, dairy cattle, etc. a	-30	-30	...	...	452	452	...	...	962	962	...	...
D Finished goods	7279	7279	...	...	6044	6044	...	...	-1977	-1977	...	...
2 Wholesale and retail trade	15517	15517	...	...	690	690	...	...	3108	3108	...	...
3 Other, except government stocks	-3437	-3507	70	...	-1087	-1205	118	...	-5869	-5873	4	...
4 Government stocks	1584	...	...	1584	5322	...	...	5322	3028	...	...	3028
Gross Fixed Capital Formation, Total	920556	798932	34163	87461	920587	793179	36185	91223	862478	731344	34433	96701
1 Residential buildings d	228380	224224	2211	1945	213078	208829	2153	2096	188355	183658	2497	2200
2 Non-residential buildings	175512	143694	916	30902	183929	149965	1021	32943	163920	127042	863	36015
3 Other construction	105616	49611	25621	30384	108637	51123	26063	31451	109732	53085	24945	31702
4 Land improvement and plantation and orchard development	...	...	...	...	...	...	...	...	...	...	...	...
5 Producers' durable goods	411048	381403	5415	24230	414943	383262	6948	24733	400471	367559	6128	26784
A Transport equipment e	84531	76574	...	7957	85454	83062	...	2392	86797	85071	...	1726
Passenger cars	33264	31111	...	2153	37867	35475	...	2392	38288	36562	...	1726
Other	51267	45463	...	5804	47587	47587	...	-	48509	48509	...	-
B Machinery and equipment e	326517	304829	5415	16273	329489	300200	6948	22341	313674	282488	6128	25058 i
6 Breeding stock, dairy cattle, etc. a	...	...	...	...	...	...	...	...	...	...	...	...
Total Gross Capital Formation	955536	832258	34233	89045	932341	799493	36303	96545	855275	721109	34437	99729

a) All livestock are included in increase in stocks.
b) Inventories valued at current replacement cost.
c) Item 'Goods producing industries' includes only manufacturing and farming.
d) The estimates of residential buildings of government enterprises and general government are included in the respective columns of item 'Residential buildings' in tables 2.7 and 2.8, These estimates are included in item 'Real estate' in tables 2.9-2.12 and are therefore excluded from the estimates of government enterprises and general government of these tables. This latter classification is followed in tables 2.13-2.16.
e) Item 'Machinery and equipment' includes all producers durable goods of public enterprises.

2.8 Gross Capital Formation by Type of Good and Owner, in Constant Prices

Million United States dollars

	1980 TOTAL	1980 Total Private	1980 Public Enterprises	1980 General Government	1981 TOTAL	1981 Total Private	1981 Public Enterprises	1981 General Government	1982 TOTAL	1982 Total Private	1982 Public Enterprises	1982 General Government
	At constant prices of:1985											
Increase in stocks, total ab	-7301	-9631	397	1932	31536	25553	192	5790	-12267	-16709	202	4239
1 Goods producing industries c	-4996	-4996	...	...	11777	11777	...	...	-7912	-7912	...	...
A Materials and supplies	-623	-623	...	...	390	390	...	...	-5349	-5349	...	...
B Work in progress	47	47	...	...	-1557	-1557	...	...	-5102	-5102	...	...
C Livestock, except breeding stocks, dairy cattle, etc. a	1069	1069	...	...	90	90	...	...	-554	-554	...	...
D Finished goods	-5489	-5489	...	...	12853	12853	...	...	3093	3093	...	...
2 Wholesale and retail trade	-1985	-1985	...	...	8456	8456	...	...	-6478	-6478	...	...
3 Other, except government stocks	-2253	-2650	397	...	5513	5321	192	...	-2117	-2319	202	...
4 Government stocks	1932	...	...	1932	5790	...	...	5790	4239	...	...	4239
Gross Fixed Capital Formation, Total	655051	573289	26301	55461	658800	579457	27231	52112	611620	534331	24049	53240
1 Residential buildings d	150287	147761	1537	989	138346	135723	1647	976	113208	110662	1504	1042
2 Non-residential buildings	120891	99360	1359	20172	127198	106834	1494	18870	128125	109244	748	18133
3 Other construction	112702	69397	21110	22195	117445	74939	21168	21338	111910	70344	18990	22576
4 Land improvement and plantation and orchard development	...	...	...	...	...	...	...	...	...	...	...	...
5 Producers' durable goods	271171	256771	2295	12105	275811	261961	2922	10928	258377	244081	2807	11489
A Transport equipment e	63617	57574	...	6043	62779	56515	...	6264	55845	50060	...	5785
Passenger cars	15912	14154	...	1758	19010	17203	...	1807	19051	17270	...	1781
Other	47704	43419	...	4285	43768	39311	...	4457	36793	32789	...	4004
B Machinery and equipment e	207554	199197	2295	6062	213032	205446	2922	4664	202532	194021	2807	5704
6 Breeding stock, dairy cattle, etc. a	...	...	...	...	...	...	...	...	...	...	...	...
Total Gross Capital Formation	647750	563658	26698	57393	690336	605010	27423	57902	599353	517622	24251	57479

2.8 Gross Capital Formation by Type of Good and Owner, in Constant Prices

Million United States dollars

	1983				1984				1985			
	TOTAL	Total Private	Public Enterprises	General Government	TOTAL	Total Private	Public Enterprises	General Government	TOTAL	Total Private	Public Enterprises	General Government
	At constant prices of:1985											
Increase in stocks, total ab	8614	-331	310	8635	71472	70361	-76	1188	28588	24618	8	3962
1 Goods producing industries c	-11162	-11162	...	...	31575	31575	...	...	1681	1681	...	...
A Materials and supplies	731	731	...	...	6910	6910	...	...	-2296	-2296	...	...
B Work in progress	736	736	...	...	13153	13153	...	...	-805	-805	...	...
C Livestock, except breeding stocks, dairy cattle, etc. a	-447	-447	...	...	-1770	-1770	...	...	-1819	-1819	...	...
D Finished goods	-12183	-12183	...	...	13281	13281	...	...	6603	6603	...	...
2 Wholesale and retail trade	9768	9768	...	...	34189	34189	...	...	15729	15729	...	...
3 Other, except government stocks	1374	1064	310	...	4522	4598	-76	...	7214	7206	8	...
4 Government stocks	8635	...	...	8635	1188	...	...	1188	3962	...	...	3962
Gross Fixed Capital Formation, Total	647276	567682	24360	55234	742204	658662	24649	58893	782986	689918	26892	66176
1 Residential buildings d	159043	156132	1607	1304	182212	178789	2090	1333	184481	180859	2014	1608
2 Non-residential buildings	116442	97493	863	18086	132118	113396	727	17995	148847	127425	555	20867
3 Other construction	102482	61030	18598	22854	110267	67366	18014	24887	112827	65984	19754	27089
4 Land improvement and plantation and orchard development	...	...	...	...	...	...	...	...	...	...	...	...
5 Producers' durable goods	269309	253027	3292	12990	317607	299111	3818	14678	336831	315650	4569	16612
A Transport equipment e	62469	56777	...	5692	74721	67882	...	6839	79128	71312	...	7816
Passenger cars	24929	23124	...	1805	29661	27614	...	2047	29695	27704	...	1991
Other	37539	33652	...	3887	45059	40267	...	4792	49433	43608	...	5825
B Machinery and equipment e	206840	196250	3292	7298	242886	231229	3818	7839	257703	244338	4569	8796
6 Breeding stock, dairy cattle, etc. a	...	...	...	...	...	...	...	...	...	...	...	...
Total Gross Capital Formation	655890	567351	24670	63869	813676	729023	24573	60081	811574	714536	26900	70138

	1986				1987				1988			
	TOTAL	Total Private	Public Enterprises	General Government	TOTAL	Total Private	Public Enterprises	General Government	TOTAL	Total Private	Public Enterprises	General Government
	At constant prices of:1985											
Increase in stocks, total ab	17109	10004	-443	7548	21842	23312	378	-1849	7542	16327	91	-8876
1 Goods producing industries c	-3050	-3050	...	...	-2036	-2036	...	...	5221	5221	...	...
A Materials and supplies	-594	-594	...	...	1435	1435	...	...	4763	4763	...	...
B Work in progress	-2144	-2144	...	...	4777	4777	...	...	5666	5666	...	...
C Livestock, except breeding stocks, dairy cattle, etc. a	-1386	-1386	...	...	-734	-734	...	...	-606	-606	...	...
D Finished goods	1075	1075	...	...	-7516	-7516	...	...	-4601	-4601	...	...
2 Wholesale and retail trade	10437	10437	...	...	22997	22997	...	...	11796	11796	...	...
3 Other, except government stocks	2173	2616	-443	...	2731	2353	378	...	-600	-691	91	...
4 Government stocks	7548	...	...	7548	-1849	...	...	-1849	-8876	...	...	-8876
Gross Fixed Capital Formation, Total	787383	690517	29396	67470	794950	691553	31133	72264	824292	722273	30816	71203
1 Residential buildings d	206915	202721	2554	1640	205538	201657	2048	1833	202812	198989	2021	1802
2 Non-residential buildings	139518	116678	840	22000	140446	115991	1163	23292	143897	119888	1062	22947
3 Other construction	102149	54497	21121	26531	101434	50018	22675	28741	98049	48659	22728	26662
4 Land improvement and plantation and orchard development	...	...	...	...	...	...	...	...	...	...	...	...
5 Producers' durable goods	338801	316621	4881	17299	347532	323887	5247	18398	379534	354737	5005	19792
A Transport equipment e	69404	67518	...	1886	68368	66483	...	1885	78424	70929	...	7495
Passenger cars	28994	27108	...	1886	26433	24548	...	1885	28985	27054	...	1931
Other	40410	40410	...	-	41935	41935	...	-	49438	43874	...	5564
B Machinery and equipment e	269397	249103	4881	15413	279164	257404	5247	16513	301110	283808	5005	12297
6 Breeding stock, dairy cattle, etc. a	...	...	...	...	...	...	...	...	...	...	...	...
Total Gross Capital Formation	804492	700521	28953	75018	816792	714865	31511	70415	831834	738600	30907	62327

United States

2.8 Gross Capital Formation by Type of Good and Owner, in Constant Prices

Million United States dollars

	1989				1990				1991			
	TOTAL	Total Private	Public Enterprises	General Government	TOTAL	Total Private	Public Enterprises	General Government	TOTAL	Total Private	Public Enterprises	General Government
	At constant prices of:1985											
Increase in stocks, total [ab]	31853	28623	144	3085	18863	7642	244	10976	-4803	-9677	8	4865
1 Goods producing industries [c]	18499	18499	...	...	7334	7334	...	...	-7206	-7206	...	...
A Materials and supplies	3620	3620	...	...	905	905	...	...	-1640	-1640	...	...
B Work in progress	9534	9534	...	...	-30	-30	...	...	-3458	-3458	...	...
C Livestock, except breeding stocks, dairy cattle, etc. [a]	-42	-42	...	...	324	324	...	...	665	665	...	...
D Finished goods	5387	5387	...	...	6135	6135	...	...	-2773	-2773	...	...
2 Wholesale and retail trade	13956	13956	...	...	1057	1057	...	...	2537	2537	...	...
3 Other, except government stocks	-3688	-3832	144	...	-505	-749	244	...	-5000	-5008	8	...
4 Government stocks	3085	...	...	3085	10976	...	...	10976	4865	...	...	4865
Gross Fixed Capital Formation, Total	836000	726058	31347	78595	821017	708171	32675	80171	766205	651774	30774	83657
1 Residential buildings [d]	194470	190941	1882	1647	176494	173042	1780	1672	154288	150451	2061	1776
2 Non-residential buildings	151571	124088	1222	26261	154034	125516	1324	27194	135396	104926	1099	29371
3 Other construction	98705	47068	23167	28470	99868	47471	23185	29212	98798	47764	22091	28943
4 Land improvement and plantation and orchard development	...	...	...	...	...	...	...	...	...	...	...	...
5 Producers' durable goods	391254	363961	5076	22217	390621	362142	6386	22093	377723	348633	5523	23567
A Transport equipment [e]	73190	65513	...	7677	76563	69168	...	7395	73463	67120	...	6343
Passenger cars	27392	25591	...	1801	30159	28224	...	1935	28340	27011	...	1329
Other	45797	39921	...	5876	46404	40944	...	5460	45123	40109	...	5014
B Machinery and equipment [e]	318064	298448	5076	14540	314058	292974	6386	14698	304260	281513	5523	17224
6 Breeding stock, dairy cattle, etc. [a]	...	...	...	...	...	...	...	...	...	...	...	...
Total Gross Capital Formation	867853	754681	31491	81680	839880	715813	32919	91147	761402	642097	30782	88522

a) All livestock are included in increase in stocks.
b) Inventories valued at current replacement cost.
c) Item 'Goods producing industries' includes only manufacturing and farming.
d) The estimates of residential buildings of government enterprises and general government are included in the respective columns of item 'Residential buildings' in tables 2.7 and 2.8. These

estimates are included in item 'Real estate' in tables 2.9-2.12 and are therefore excluded from the estimates of government enterprises and general government of these tables. This latter classification is followed in tables 2.13-2.16.
e) Item 'Machinery and equipment' includes all producers durable goods of public enterprises.

2.9 Gross Capital Formation by Kind of Activity of Owner, ISIC Major Divisions, in Current Prices

Million United States dollars

	1980			1981			1982			1983		
	Total Gross Capital Formation	Increase in Stocks	Gross Fixed Capital Formation	Total Gross Capital Formation	Increase in Stocks	Gross Fixed Capital Formation	Total Gross Capital Formation	Increase in Stocks	Gross Fixed Capital Formation	Total Gross Capital Formation	Increase in Stocks	Gross Fixed Capital Formation
	All Producers											
1 Agriculture, hunting, fishing and forestry	13863	-6111	19974	27572	8761	18811	19944	5754	14190	-988	-15356	14368
2 Mining and quarrying	42988	-303	43291	67259	2015	65244	65935	153	65782	42071	-2838	44909
3 Manufacturing	79535	23	79512	96898	4020	92878	76236	-12965	89201	71586	102	71484
4 Electricity, gas and water	28256	-1037	29293	30517	-323	30840	28307	-2323	30630	27406	-1645	29051
5 Construction	4896	-500	5396	5979	335	5644	4753	233	4520	5936	1462	4474
6 Wholesale and retail trade, restaurants and hotels	36306	-1306	37612	51564	7640	43924	42455	-6196	48651	70896	8969	61927
7 Transport, storage and communication	45278	-114	45392	45818	-455	46273	41570	-964	42534	44757	940	43817
8 Finance, insurance, real estate and business services [a]	181818	189	181629	189761	795	188966	175182	-494	175676	232793	986	231807
9 Community, social and personal services	17714	-331	18045	21070	2648	18422	20883	856	20027	26069	1848	24221
Statistical discrepancy [ba]	20984	192	20792	22935	93	22842	21102	98	21004	21579	150	21429
Total Industries [cde]	475822	-9298	485120	566718	25529	541189	507874	-15848	523722	549814	-5382	555196
Producers of Government Services [a]	49172	2763	46409	52061	6033	46028	52216	4437	47779	55864	5975	49889
Private Non-Profit Institutions Serving Households	14904	-	14904	16617	-	16617	19157	-	19157	21279	-	21279
Total [cd]	539898	-6535	546433	635396	31562	603834	579247	-11411	590658	626957	593	626364

1974

2.9 Gross Capital Formation by Kind of Activity of Owner, ISIC Major Divisions, in Current Prices

Million United States dollars

	1984			1985			1986			1987		
	Total Gross Capital Formation	Increase in Stocks	Gross Fixed Capital Formation	Total Gross Capital Formation	Increase in Stocks	Gross Fixed Capital Formation	Total Gross Capital Formation	Increase in Stocks	Gross Fixed Capital Formation	Total Gross Capital Formation	Increase in Stocks	Gross Fixed Capital Formation

All Producers

1 Agriculture, hunting, fishing and forestry	20525	5729	14796	19053	5755	13298	10140	-1452	11592	7246	-6419	13665
2 Mining and quarrying	45102	-1123	46225	44245	1346	42899	22811	-1730	24541	20785	-76	20861
3 Manufacturing	113995	27875	86120	93646	-4073	97719	83898	-2227	86125	102131	6639	95492
4 Electricity, gas and water	35686	814	34872	52428	1758	50670	46880	-921	47801	48728	1169	47559
5 Construction	8610	3084	5526	9305	2734	6571	9046	2400	6646	7296	-176	7472
6 Wholesale and retail trade, restaurants and hotels	110749	32917	77832	93565	15732	77833	87108	9257	77851	89332	23876	65456
7 Transport, storage and communication	47868	1646	46222	47946	121	47825	56274	942	55332	48793	-841	49634
8 Finance, insurance, real estate and business services a	283302	-192	283494	302482	-149	302631	340821	672	340149	352571	340	352231
9 Community, social and personal services	25992	331	25661	29560	1405	28155	32948	1702	31246	35684	1768	33916
Statistical discrepancy ba	21709	-37	21746	24886	8	24878	26980	-214	27194	29815	183	29632
Total Industries cde	721530	71044	650486	720169	24637	695532	724124	8429	715695	754908	26463	728445
Producers of Government Services a	55252	297	54955	68530	3962	64568	73981	6508	67473	72231	-822	73053
Private Non-Profit Institutions Serving Households	22368	-	22368	22885	-	22885	24698	-	24698	28376	-	28376
Total cd	799150	71341	727809	811584	28599	782985	822803	14937	807866	855515	25641	829874

	1988			1989			1990			1991		
	Total Gross Capital Formation	Increase in Stocks	Gross Fixed Capital Formation	Total Gross Capital Formation	Increase in Stocks	Gross Fixed Capital Formation	Total Gross Capital Formation	Increase in Stocks	Gross Fixed Capital Formation	Total Gross Capital Formation	Increase in Stocks	Gross Fixed Capital Formation

All Producers

1 Agriculture, hunting, fishing and forestry	2894	-11292	14186	17796	1488	16308	20707	3060	17647	15598	26	15572
2 Mining and quarrying	25008	252	24756	22144	24	22120	24743	376	24367	24965	1274	23691
3 Manufacturing	113909	15797	98112	140866	19828	121038	131513	3769	127744	112757	-7496	120253
4 Electricity, gas and water	46052	-49	46101	40808	-1586	42394	50392	87	50305	47861	-102	47963
5 Construction	8932	1265	7667	7823	116	7707	5809	-1129	6938	1275	-4739	6014
6 Wholesale and retail trade, restaurants and hotels	91505	12390	79115	99442	15517	83925	88824	690	88134	90151	3108	87043
7 Transport, storage and communication	50403	-607	51010	52328	-1782	54110	51949	-627	52576	46197	-634	46831
8 Finance, insurance, real estate and business services a	363826	-63	363889	372553	673	371880	345194	-195	345389	301059	-298	301357
9 Community, social and personal services	35842	-1462	37304	38990	-952	39942	38161	283	37878	37426	-1374	38800
Statistical discrepancy ba	30467	44	30423	32022	70	31952	34150	118	34032	31940	4	31936
Total Industries cde	796802	16275	780527	834049	33396	800653	801355	6432	794923	720388	-10231	730619
Producers of Government Services a	66871	-7914	74785	87100	1584	85516	94449	5322	89127	97529	3028	94501
Private Non-Profit Institutions Serving Households	31548	-	31548	34387	-	34387	36537	-	36537	37358	-	37358
Total cd	895221	8361	886860	955536	34980	920556	932341	11754	920587	855275	-7203	862478

a) The estimates of residential buildings of government enterprises and general government are included in the respective columns of item 'Residential buildings' in tables 2.7 and 2.8. These estimates are included in item 'Real estate' in tables 2.9-2.12 and are therefore excluded from the estimates of government enterprises and general government of these tables. This latter classification is followed in tables 2.13-2.16.
b) Item 'Statistical discrepancy' refers to government enterprises.
c) Item 'Goods producing industries' includes only manufacturing and farming.
d) Inventories valued at current replacement cost.
e) The sub-items do not add-up to 'Total industries', the difference is 'Statistical discrepancy' which is not shown explicitly.

2.10 Gross Capital Formation by Kind of Activity of Owner, ISIC Major Divisions, in Constant Prices

Million United States dollars

	1980			1981			1982			1983		
	Total Gross Capital Formation	Increase in Stocks	Gross Fixed Capital Formation	Total Gross Capital Formation	Increase in Stocks	Gross Fixed Capital Formation	Total Gross Capital Formation	Increase in Stocks	Gross Fixed Capital Formation	Total Gross Capital Formation	Increase in Stocks	Gross Fixed Capital Formation

At constant prices of:1985

All Producers

1 Agriculture, hunting, fishing and forestry	20818	-5236	26054	29694	7564	22130	20335	4796	15539	3490	-11611	15101
2 Mining and quarrying	51439	-339	51778	64793	2037	62756	55846	163	55683	40184	-2814	42998
3 Manufacturing	98481	240	98241	108046	4212	103834	81443	-12708	94151	74170	448	73722
4 Electricity, gas and water	35817	-1283	37100	34820	-428	35248	30026	-2224	32250	28116	-1577	29693

United States

2.10 Gross Capital Formation by Kind of Activity of Owner, ISIC Major Divisions, in Constant Prices
(Continued)

Million United States dollars

	1980			1981			1982			1983		
	Total Gross Capital Formation	Increase in Stocks	Gross Fixed Capital Formation	Total Gross Capital Formation	Increase in Stocks	Gross Fixed Capital Formation	Total Gross Capital Formation	Increase in Stocks	Gross Fixed Capital Formation	Total Gross Capital Formation	Increase in Stocks	Gross Fixed Capital Formation
At constant prices of:1985												
5 Construction	6267	-665	6932	6908	386	6522	5062	231	4831	6202	1553	4649
6 Wholesale and retail trade, restaurants and hotels	44101	-1985	46086	57562	8456	49106	44830	-6478	51308	72515	9768	62747
7 Transport, storage and communication	57890	-146	58036	53022	-429	53451	44821	-862	45683	46453	924	45529
8 Finance, insurance, real estate and business services a	218278	229	218049	209479	878	208601	184801	-519	185320	241033	1055	239978
9 Community, social and personal services	21590	-446	22036	23067	2877	20190	21462	892	20570	26438	1923	24515
Statistical discrepancy ba	26030	397	25633	27060	192	26868	22934	202	22732	23484	310	23174
Total Industries cde	577274	-9233	586507	615374	25746	589628	522201	-16506	538707	571139	-21	571160
Producers of Government Services a	55572	1932	53640	55656	5790	49866	56188	4239	51949	62125	8635	53490
Private Non-Profit Institutions Serving Households	14904	-	14904	19306	-	19306	20964	-	20964	22626	-	22626
Total cd	647750	-7301	655051	690336	31536	658800	599353	-12267	611620	655890	8614	647276

	1984			1985			1986			1987		
	Total Gross Capital Formation	Increase in Stocks	Gross Fixed Capital Formation	Total Gross Capital Formation	Increase in Stocks	Gross Fixed Capital Formation	Total Gross Capital Formation	Increase in Stocks	Gross Fixed Capital Formation	Total Gross Capital Formation	Increase in Stocks	Gross Fixed Capital Formation
At constant prices of:1985												
All Producers												
1 Agriculture, hunting, fishing and forestry	18757	3636	15121	19054	5756	13298	10190	-1012	11202	3940	-8985	12925
2 Mining and quarrying	45749	-1115	46864	44245	1346	42899	23392	-1974	25366	23581	-85	23666
3 Manufacturing	114765	27938	86827	93646	-4073	97719	81765	-2037	83802	97659	6947	90712
4 Electricity, gas and water	35755	754	35001	52428	1758	50670	46040	-1085	47125	47816	1400	46416
5 Construction	8753	3149	5604	9305	2734	6571	8827	2404	6423	6830	-173	7003
6 Wholesale and retail trade, restaurants and hotels	111545	34189	77356	93562	15729	77833	86844	10437	76407	85924	22997	62927
7 Transport, storage and communication	48700	1678	47022	47937	112	47825	55511	912	54599	47255	-834	48089
8 Finance, insurance, real estate and business services a	286214	-200	286414	302482	-149	302631	332240	666	331574	332998	327	332671
9 Community, social and personal services	25742	332	25410	29560	1405	28155	32609	1693	30916	34836	1718	33118
Statistical discrepancy ba	22723	-76	22799	24886	8	24878	26717	-443	27160	30311	378	29933
Total Industries cde	732297	70284	662013	720159	24626	695533	707585	9561	698024	722455	23691	698764
Producers of Government Services a	58404	1188	57216	68530	3962	64568	72949	7548	65401	67675	-1849	69524
Private Non-Profit Institutions Serving Households	22975	-	22975	22885	-	22885	23958	-	23958	26662	-	26662
Total cd	813676	71472	742204	811574	28588	782986	804492	17109	787383	816792	21842	794950

	1988			1989			1990			1991		
	Total Gross Capital Formation	Increase in Stocks	Gross Fixed Capital Formation	Total Gross Capital Formation	Increase in Stocks	Gross Fixed Capital Formation	Total Gross Capital Formation	Increase in Stocks	Gross Fixed Capital Formation	Total Gross Capital Formation	Increase in Stocks	Gross Fixed Capital Formation
At constant prices of:1985												
All Producers												
1 Agriculture, hunting, fishing and forestry	2948	-10148	13096	14445	1	14444	18210	3015	15195	11928	-1064	12992
2 Mining and quarrying	26062	311	25751	22055	28	22027	23915	397	23518	23131	1322	21809
3 Manufacturing	106703	15370	91333	127463	18498	108965	116905	4319	112586	98653	-6142	104795
4 Electricity, gas and water	44088	-62	44150	36823	-1904	38727	45003	186	44817	41491	-143	41634

2.10 Gross Capital Formation by Kind of Activity of Owner, ISIC Major Divisions, in Constant Prices
(Continued)

Million United States dollars

	1988			1989			1990			1991		
	Total Gross Capital Formation	Increase in Stocks	Gross Fixed Capital Formation	Total Gross Capital Formation	Increase in Stocks	Gross Fixed Capital Formation	Total Gross Capital Formation	Increase in Stocks	Gross Fixed Capital Formation	Total Gross Capital Formation	Increase in Stocks	Gross Fixed Capital Formation
						At constant prices of:1985						
5 Construction	8132	1153	6979	6848	99	6749	4899	-993	5892	748	-4226	4974
6 Wholesale and retail trade, restaurants and hotels	86687	11796	74891	91612	13956	77656	81621	1057	80564	82496	2537	79959
7 Transport, storage and communication	47791	-672	48463	48465	-1763	50228	47614	-413	48027	41569	-520	42089
8 Finance, insurance, real estate and business services a ..	334454	-55	334509	331662	560	331102	300363	-161	300524	262067	-246	262313
9 Community, social and personal services	34764	-1366	36130	36890	-852	37742	35562	235	35327	34832	-1195	36027
Statistical discrepancy ba	29545	91	29454	30585	144	30441	33002	244	32758	29853	8	29845
Total Industries cde	743487	16418	727069	758581	28768	729813	721116	7887	713229	644212	-9668	653880
Producers of Government Services a	59659	-8876	68535	79043	3085	75958	87551	10976	76575	85709	4865	80844
Private Non-Profit Institutions Serving Households	28688	-	28688	30229	-	30229	31213	-	31213	31481	-	31481
Total cd	831834	7542	824292	867853	31853	836000	839880	18863	821017	761402	-4803	766205

a) The estimates of residential buildings of government enterprises and general government are included in the respective columns of item 'Residential buildings' in tables 2.7 and 2.8. These estimates are included in item 'Real estate' in tables 2.9-2.12 and are therefore excluded from the estimates of government enterprises and general government of these tables. This latter classification is followed in tables 2.13-2.16.
b) Item 'Statistical discrepancy' refers to government enterprises.
c) Item 'Goods producing industries' includes only manufacturing and farming.
d) Inventories valued at current replacement cost.
e) The sub-items do not add-up to 'Total industries', the difference is 'Statistical discrepancy' which is not shown explicitly.

2.11 Gross Fixed Capital Formation by Kind of Activity of Owner, ISIC Divisions, in Current Prices

Million United States dollars

	1980	1981	1982	1983	1984	1985	1986	1987	1988	1989	1990	1991
					All Producers							
1 Agriculture, hunting, forestry and fishing	19974	18811	14190	14368	14796	13298	11592	13665	14186	16308	17647	15572
2 Mining and quarrying	43291	65244	65782	44909	46225	42899	24541	20861	24756	22120	24367	23691
A Coal mining	2670	3094	4234	3334	2909	2813	2279	1819	2098	1679	1799	1573
B Crude petroleum and natural gas production	36986	58923	58600	38968	40438	37161	20058	17126	19304	17697	19582	18664
C Metal ore mining	2017	1476	1627	1712	1917	1442	1096	915	1169	853	1105	1180
D Other mining	1619	1751	1320	895	960	1484	1108	1001	2185	1892	1881	2274
3 Manufacturing	79512	92878	89201	71484	86120	97719	86125	95492	98112	121038	127744	120253
A Manufacturing of food, beverages and tobacco	6703	7977	8647	7223	7625	8481	7957	9691	9887	11634	12342	12551
B Textile, wearing apparel and leather industries	2602	3063	2476	2573	3257	2999	2551	3218	3386	3650	3703	3212
C Manufacture of wood, and wood products, including furniture	3015	2924	2270	2097	2775	2758	2664	3163	3174	3447	3360	2876
D Manufacture of paper and paper products, printing and publishing	7996	8011	8630	8008	9208	11344	10606	12118	13778	18497	19499	14333
E Manufacture of chemicals and chemical petroleum, coal, rubber and plastic products	17314	21075	22944	16846	17701	19194	15947	18535	21710	28117	29042	32691
F Manufacture of non-metalic mineral products except products of petroleum and coal	3272	2848	2546	1878	2462	2956	2360	2584	2444	3123	3076	2519
G Basic metal industries	5810	6888	5014	4446	4171	4789	2817	4141	4997	6190	6702	5645
H Manufacture of fabricated metal products, machinery and equipment	32036	39432	36001	27867	38288	44556	40645	41194	37855	45396	48980	45323
I Other manufacturing industries	764	660	673	547	634	641	579	847	882	984	1041	1101
4 Electricity, gas and water	29293	30840	30630	29051	34872	50670	47801	47559	46101	42394	50305	47963
5 Construction	5396	5644	4520	4474	5526	6571	6646	7472	7667	7707	6938	6014
6 Wholesale and retail trade, restaurants and hotels	37612	43924	48651	61927	77832	77833	77851	65456	79115	83925	88134	87043
A Wholesale and retail trade	34301	40013	43678	56407	72083	72003	71700	59588	73837	77971	81277	82655
B Restaurants and hotels	3311	3912	4973	5520	5748	5831	6151	5868	5277	5954	6858	4388
Restaurants	...	...	...	...	...	...	...	...	...	...	...	...
Hotels and other lodging places	3311	3912	4973	5520	5748	5831	6151	5868	5277	5954	6858	4388
7 Transport, storage and communication	45392	46273	42534	43817	46222	47825	55332	49634	51010	54110	52576	46831
A Transport and storage	19557	18227	14993	18850	19956	18210	23719	18139	20305	22191	19731	16197

2.11 Gross Fixed Capital Formation by Kind of Activity of Owner, ISIC Divisions, in Current Prices
(Continued)

Million United States dollars

	1980	1981	1982	1983	1984	1985	1986	1987	1988	1989	1990	1991
B Communication	25835	28046	27541	24968	26266	29615	31613	31495	30705	31919	32845	30634
8 Finance, insurance, real estate and business services	181629	188966	175676	231807	283494	302631	340149	352231	363889	371880	345389	301357
A Financial institutions	20466	24250	25525	26973	32605	36076	40953	42759	47604	53036	50150	46594
B Insurance	3735	4541	4934	7293	10686	10894	12344	14396	14187	16185	16248	15231
C Real estate and business services	157428	160174	145216	197541	240202	255660	286853	295076	302098	302659	278991	239532
Real estate except dwellings	29090	33965	36052	41826	57248	65060	64533	64598	64699	66192	57199	42825
Dwellings	128338	126209	109164	155715	182954	190600	222319	230478	237399	236467	221792	196707
9 Community, social and personal services	18045	18422	20027	24221	25661	28155	31246	33916	37304	39942	37878	38800
A Sanitary and similar services	...	...	...	...	...	...	...	...	...	...	...	...
B Social and related community services	6511	7102	7481	9828	11235	11826	12827	13779	15186	16322	16297	16344
Educational services	269	294	280	277	289	303	337	388	403	430	398	432
Medical, dental, other health and veterinary services	3783	4327	4584	6868	7636	7930	8500	9238	10035	10773	10831	11045
C Recreational and cultural services	2265	2352	2398	2566	2908	3164	3089	4148	4871	5150	4955	6792
D Personal and household services	9268	8968	10148	11826	11518	13166	15330	15989	17247	18469	16626	15664
Statistical discrepancy a	20792	22842	21004	21429	21746	24878	27194	29632	30423	31952	34032	31936
Total Industries b	485120	541189	523722	555196	650486	695532	715695	728445	780527	800653	794923	730619
Producers of Government Services	46409	46028	47779	49889	54955	64568	67473	73053	74785	85516	89127	94501
Private Non-Profit Institutions Serving Households	14904	16617	19157	21279	22368	22885	24698	28376	31548	34387	36537	37358
Total c	546433	603834	590658	626364	727809	782985	807866	829874	886860	920556	920587	862478

a) Item 'Statistical discrepancy' refers to government enterprises.
b) The sub-items do not add-up to 'Total industries', the difference is 'Statistical discrepancy' which is not shown explicitly.
c) The estimates of residential buildings of government enterprises and general government are included in the respective columns of item 'Residential buildings' in tables 2.7 and 2.8. These estimates are included in item 'Real estate' in tables 2.9-2.12 and are therefore excluded from the estimates of government enterprises and general government of these tables. This latter classification is followed in tables 2.13-2.16.

2.12 Gross Fixed Capital Formation by Kind of Activity of Owner, ISIC Divisions, in Constant Prices

Million United States dollars

	1980	1981	1982	1983	1984	1985	1986	1987	1988	1989	1990	1991
					At constant prices of: 1985							
					All Producers							
1 Agriculture, hunting, forestry and fishing	26054	22130	15539	15101	15121	13298	11202	12925	13096	14444	15195	12992
2 Mining and quarrying	51778	62756	55683	42998	46864	42899	25366	23666	25751	22027	23518	21809
A Coal mining	3388	3543	4530	3497	2989	2813	2213	1720	1917	1481	1543	1321
B Crude petroleum and natural gas production	43695	55480	48005	36767	40916	37161	21001	20126	20748	18117	19414	17581
C Metal ore mining	2588	1717	1747	1801	1974	1442	1072	875	1082	761	959	1009
D Other mining	2108	2015	1401	933	984	1484	1079	946	2005	1667	1602	1898
3 Manufacturing	98241	103834	94151	73722	86827	97719	83802	90712	91333	108965	112586	104795
A Manufacturing of food, beverages and tobacco	8397	9084	9266	7574	7758	8481	7648	9010	8944	10136	10453	10433
B Textile, wearing apparel and leather industries	3297	3514	2681	2723	3337	2999	2441	2962	3021	3151	3098	2619
C Manufacture of wood, and wood products, including furniture	3667	3275	2456	2218	2843	2758	2576	2980	2910	3060	2913	2450
D Manufacture of paper and paper products, printing and publishing	10052	9019	9077	8255	9261	11344	10259	11412	12679	16418	16904	12345
E Manufacture of chemicals and chemical petroleum, coal, rubber and plastic products	21502	23897	24533	17559	18024	19194	15388	17398	19827	24760	24894	27431
F Manufacture of non-metalic mineral products except products of petroleum and coal	3881	3040	2560	1875	2409	2956	2325	2528	2380	2976	2922	2435
G Basic metal industries	7348	7866	5342	4641	4248	4789	2723	3916	4612	5508	5792	4758
H Manufacture of fabricated metal products, machinery and equipment	39138	43390	37520	28306	38306	44556	39883	39709	36150	42080	44710	41384
I Other manufacturing industries	960	747	717	571	642	641	559	797	810	876	901	941
4 Electricity, gas and water	37100	35248	32250	29693	35001	50670	47125	46416	44150	38727	44817	41634

2.12 Gross Fixed Capital Formation by Kind of Activity of Owner, ISIC Divisions, in Constant Prices
(Continued)

Million United States dollars

	1980	1981	1982	1983	1984	1985	1986	1987	1988	1989	1990	1991
					At constant prices of:1985							
5 Construction	6932	6522	4831	4649	5604	6571	6423	7003	6979	6749	5892	4974
6 Wholesale and retail trade, restaurants and hotels	46086	49106	51308	62747	77356	77833	76407	62927	74891	77656	80564	79959
A Wholesale and retail trade	41923	44589	45868	56922	71484	72003	70422	57381	70061	72380	74636	76215
B Restaurants and hotels	4163	4518	5441	5825	5872	5831	5985	5546	4830	5276	5928	3744
Restaurants	...	...	...	...	...	...	...	...	...	...	...	...
Hotels and other lodging places	4163	4518	5441	5825	5872	5831	5985	5546	4830	5276	5928	3744
7 Transport, storage and communication	58036	53451	45683	45529	47022	47825	54599	48089	48463	50228	48027	42089
A Transport and storage	25414	20946	16261	19762	20349	18210	23486	17677	19384	20594	17934	14326
B Communication	32622	32504	29423	25767	26673	29615	31113	30412	29079	29634	30092	27763
8 Finance, insurance, real estate and business services	218049	208601	185320	239978	286414	302631	331574	332671	334509	331102	300524	262313
A Financial institutions	23843	25912	26190	26804	31989	36076	40759	42159	46882	50804	47306	44220
B Insurance	3945	4639	4940	6877	9844	10894	12597	14853	14866	16633	17008	17110
C Real estate and business services	190261	178051	154191	206296	244582	255660	278218	275658	272761	263664	236209	200983
Real estate except dwellings	36499	38392	38117	43086	57733	65060	63045	61502	60191	59612	50322	37266
Dwellings	153762	139659	116074	163210	186849	190600	215173	214156	212571	204052	185888	163718
9 Community, social and personal services	22036	20190	20570	24515	25410	28155	30916	33118	36130	37742	35327	36027
A Sanitary and similar services	...	...	...	...	...	...	...	...	...	...	...	...
B Social and related community services	7939	7863	7808	10094	11216	11826	12681	13405	14600	15322	15097	15085
Educational services	311	313	286	278	284	303	337	384	390	405	371	406
Medical, dental, other health and veterinary services	4698	4910	4912	7184	7749	7930	8318	8818	9372	9782	9611	9637
C Recreational and cultural services	2727	2600	2519	2611	2928	3164	3022	3991	4617	4730	4488	6282
D Personal and household services	11370	9727	10243	11810	11266	13166	15213	15721	16913	17690	15743	14660
Statistical discrepancy a	25633	26868	22732	23174	22799	24878	27160	29933	29454	30441	32758	29845
Total Industries b	586507	589628	538707	571160	662013	695533	698024	698764	727069	729813	713229	653880
Producers of Government Services	53640	49866	51949	53490	57216	64568	65401	69524	68535	75958	76575	80844
Private Non-Profit Institutions Serving Households	14904	19306	20964	22626	22975	22885	23958	26662	28688	30229	31213	31481
Total c	655051	658800	611620	647276	742204	782986	787383	794950	824292	836000	821017	766205

a) Item 'Statistical discrepancy' refers to government enterprises.
b) The sub-items do not add-up to 'Total industries', the difference is 'Statistical discrepancy' which is not shown explicitly.
c) The estimates of residential buildings of government enterprises and general government are included in the respective columns of item 'Residential buildings' in tables 2.7 and 2.8. These estimates are included in item 'Real estate' in tables 2.9-2.12 and are therefore excluded from the estimates of government enterprises and general government of these tables. This latter classification is followed in tables 2.13-2.16.

2.13 Stocks of Reproducible Fixed Assets, by Type of Good and Owner, in Current Prices

Thousand Million United States dollars

	TOTAL		Total Private		Public Enterprises		General Government	
	Gross	Net	Gross	Net	Gross	Net	Gross	Net
					1980			
1 Residential buildings a	4361	2894	4263	2824	57	40	42	30
2 Non-residential buildings	2216	1383	1573	980	41	28	602	375
3 Other construction	2663	1619	1110	634	512	333	1040	652
4 Land improvement and plantation and orchard development	...	...	...	...	...	...	...	...
5 Producers' durable goods	2609	1472	2418	1376	25	14	167	82
A Transport equipment	...	...	560	321	...	...	...	...
Passenger cars	...	...	92	63	...	...	...	...
Other	...	...	468	258	...	...	...	...
B Machinery and equipment	...	...	1858	1055	...	...	...	...
6 Breeding stock, dairy cattle, etc.	...	...	...	...	...	...	...	...
Total	11849	7368	9364	5814	635	415	1850	1139

2.13 Stocks of Reproducible Fixed Assets, by Type of Good and Owner, in Current Prices
(Continued)

Thousand Million United States dollars

	TOTAL		Total Private		Public Enterprises		General Government	
	Gross	Net	Gross	Net	Gross	Net	Gross	Net
1981								
1 Residential buildings a	4712	3113	4599	3031	62	43	51	38
2 Non-residential buildings	2466	1533	1764	1097	45	30	657	406
3 Other construction	2850	1724	1268	727	547	355	1035	643
4 Land improvement and plantation and orchard development	...	...	...	...	...	...	...	...
5 Producers' durable goods	2965	1662	2756	1558	28	16	180	88
A Transport equipment	...	...	619	350	...	...	...	...
Passenger cars	...	...	100	68	...	...	...	...
Other	...	...	519	282	...	...	...	...
B Machinery and equipment	...	...	2137	1208	...	...	...	...
6 Breeding stock, dairy cattle, etc.	...	...	...	...	...	...	...	...
Total	12993	8031	10387	6413	682	444	1924	1174
1982								
1 Residential buildings a	4900	3212	4783	3129	64	44	53	39
2 Non-residential buildings	2665	1648	1920	1191	47	31	698	426
3 Other construction	2918	1758	1327	761	565	364	1025	632
4 Land improvement and plantation and orchard development	...	...	...	...	...	...	...	...
5 Producers' durable goods	3193	1765	2975	1657	31	18	187	91
A Transport equipment	...	...	645	357	...	...	...	...
Passenger cars	...	...	105	70	...	...	...	...
Other	...	...	540	287	...	...	...	...
B Machinery and equipment	...	...	2330	1299	...	...	...	...
6 Breeding stock, dairy cattle, etc.	...	...	...	...	...	...	...	...
Total	13675	8384	11005	6737	708	458	1963	1188
1983								
1 Residential buildings a	5118	3345	4996	3260	67	46	55	40
2 Non-residential buildings	2840	1743	2057	1267	49	32	734	443
3 Other construction	2958	1772	1319	752	585	374	1053	646
4 Land improvement and plantation and orchard development	...	...	...	...	...	...	...	...
5 Producers' durable goods	3328	1820	3104	1708	34	19	190	93
A Transport equipment	...	...	669	366	...	...	...	...
Passenger cars	...	...	116	78	...	...	...	...
Other	...	...	553	288	...	...	...	...
B Machinery and equipment	...	...	2436	1342	...	...	...	...
6 Breeding stock, dairy cattle, etc.	...	...	...	...	...	...	...	...
Total	14244	8680	11477	6987	735	471	2032	1222
1984								
1 Residential buildings a	5385	3517	5256	3427	71	48	58	42
2 Non-residential buildings	3039	1856	2217	1362	51	33	770	460
3 Other construction	3105	1853	1356	772	614	389	1135	692
4 Land improvement and plantation and orchard development	...	...	...	...	...	...	...	...
5 Producers' durable goods	3484	1905	3253	1787	37	21	194	97
A Transport equipment	...	...	698	383	...	...	...	...
Passenger cars	...	...	127	88	...	...	...	...
Other	...	...	571	296	...	...	...	...
B Machinery and equipment	...	...	2555	1403	...	...	...	...
6 Breeding stock, dairy cattle, etc.	...	...	...	...	...	...	...	...
Total	15013	9130	12082	7348	773	492	2158	1291

2.13 Stocks of Reproducible Fixed Assets, by Type of Good and Owner, in Current Prices
(Continued)

Thousand Million United States dollars

	TOTAL		Total Private		Public Enterprises		General Government	
	Gross	Net	Gross	Net	Gross	Net	Gross	Net
1985								
1 Residential buildings [a]	5684	3710	5549	3617	75	50	61	43
2 Non-residential buildings	3257	1985	2395	1472	53	35	809	479
3 Other construction	3244	1929	1388	789	645	405	1211	735
4 Land improvement and plantation and orchard development	...	...	...	...	...	...	...	...
5 Producers' durable goods	3655	2001	3415	1874	40	24	200	104
A Transport equipment	...	...	730	403	...	...	...	...
Passenger cars	...	...	139	98	...	...	...	...
Other	...	...	591	306	...	...	...	...
B Machinery and equipment	...	...	2685	1471	...	...	...	...
6 Breeding stock, dairy cattle, etc.	...	...	...	...	...	...	...	...
Total	15840	9626	12747	7752	813	513	2281	1361
1986								
1 Residential buildings [a]	6087	3978	5942	3878	81	54	65	46
2 Non-residential buildings	3478	2111	2572	1575	55	36	850	501
3 Other construction	3277	1939	1379	779	667	417	1231	743
4 Land improvement and plantation and orchard development	...	...	...	...	...	...	...	...
5 Producers' durable goods	3895	2130	3643	1993	44	26	208	111
A Transport equipment	...	...	764	422	...	...	...	...
Passenger cars	...	...	154	109	...	...	...	...
Other	...	...	610	314	...	...	...	...
B Machinery and equipment	...	...	2879	1570	...	...	...	...
6 Breeding stock, dairy cattle, etc.	...	...	...	...	...	...	...	...
Total	16737	10158	13536	8224	847	532	2354	1401
1987								
1 Residential buildings [a]	6567	4294	6410	4187	87	57	70	49
2 Non-residential buildings	3708	2240	2751	1676	58	37	899	528
3 Other construction	3370	1985	1404	787	696	433	1270	765
4 Land improvement and plantation and orchard development	...	...	...	...	...	...	...	...
5 Producers' durable goods	4087	2226	3822	2079	48	29	217	119
A Transport equipment	...	...	778	429	...	...	...	...
Passenger cars	...	...	162	114	...	...	...	...
Other	...	...	616	315	...	...	...	...
B Machinery and equipment	...	...	3044	1650	...	...	...	...
6 Breeding stock, dairy cattle, etc.	...	...	...	...	...	...	...	...
Total	17733	10745	14388	8729	888	556	2457	1460
1988								
1 Residential buildings [a]	6697	4376	6538	4269	88	58	71	49
2 Non-residential buildings	3972	2387	2963	1796	61	39	947	552
3 Other construction	3593	2100	1515	840	738	458	1340	801
4 Land improvement and plantation and orchard development	...	...	...	...	...	...	...	...
5 Producers' durable goods	4346	2364	4061	2203	53	32	232	129
A Transport equipment	...	...	826	455	...	...	...	...
Passenger cars	...	...	173	121	...	...	...	...
Other	...	...	653	334	...	...	...	...
B Machinery and equipment	...	...	3235	1747	...	...	...	...
6 Breeding stock, dairy cattle, etc.	...	...	...	...	...	...	...	...
Total	18608	11227	15078	9108	941	586	2589	1532

2.13 Stocks of Reproducible Fixed Assets, by Type of Good and Owner, in Current Prices
(Continued)

Thousand Million United States dollars

	TOTAL		Total Private		Public Enterprises		General Government	
	Gross	Net	Gross	Net	Gross	Net	Gross	Net
1989								
1 Residential buildings a	7122	4647	6954	4535	94	61	74	51
2 Non-residential buildings	4234	2535	3168	1912	65	41	1002	581
3 Other construction	3746	2176	1588	874	774	479	1384	823
4 Land improvement and plantation and orchard development	...	...	...	...	...	...	...	...
5 Producers' durable goods	4619	2506	4313	2330	57	34	249	142
A Transport equipment	...	...	861	470	...	...	...	...
Passenger cars	...	...	180	126	...	...	...	...
Other	...	...	681	345	...	...	...	...
B Machinery and equipment	...	...	3452	1860	...	...	...	...
6 Breeding stock, dairy cattle, etc.	...	...	...	...	...	...	...	...
Total	19721	11864	16022	9650	990	615	2709	1598
1990								
1 Residential buildings a	7503	4879	7327	4762	99	63	78	54
2 Non-residential buildings	4438	2646	3331	2002	68	43	1040	601
3 Other construction	3860	2230	1634	892	803	495	1424	843
4 Land improvement and plantation and orchard development	...	...	...	...	...	...	...	...
5 Producers' durable goods	4933	2666	4603	2473	64	38	266	154
A Transport equipment	...	...	897	487	...	...	...	...
Passenger cars	...	...	189	132	...	...	...	...
Other	...	...	708	354	...	...	...	...
B Machinery and equipment	...	...	3706	1987	...	...	...	...
6 Breeding stock, dairy cattle, etc.	...	...	...	...	...	...	...	...
Total	20734	12421	16894	10130	1032	639	2808	1651
1991								
1 Residential buildings a	7829	5062	7645	4940	103	66	81	56
2 Non-residential buildings	4584	2713	3437	2047	70	44	1077	621
3 Other construction	3963	2276	1673	907	824	506	1465	863
4 Land improvement and plantation and orchard development	...	...	...	...	...	...	...	...
5 Producers' durable goods	5091	2725	4734	2517	69	41	288	167
A Transport equipment	...	...	956	513	...	...	...	...
Passenger cars	...	...	196	137	...	...	...	...
Other	...	...	760	376	...	...	...	...
B Machinery and equipment	...	...	3778	2004	...	...	...	...
6 Breeding stock, dairy cattle, etc.	...	...	...	...	...	...	...	...
Total	21466	12775	17489	10412	1066	657	2911	1707

a) The estimates of residential buildings of government enterprises and general government are included in the respective columns of item 'Residential buildings' in tables 2.7 and 2.8. These estimates are included in item 'Real estate' in tables 2.9-2.12 and are therefore excluded from the estimates of government enterprises and general government of these tables. This latter classification is followed in tables 2.13-2.16.

2.14 Stocks of Reproducible Fixed Assets, by Type of Good and Owner, in Constant Prices

Thousand Million United States dollars

	TOTAL		Total Private		Public Enterprises		General Government	
	Gross	Net	Gross	Net	Gross	Net	Gross	Net
At constant prices of:1985								
1980								
1 Residential buildings a	5023	3332	4911	3252	65	45	47	34
2 Non-residential buildings	2685	1677	1896	1182	46	31	744	464
3 Other construction	2932	1787	1281	739	558	363	1093	685
4 Land improvement and plantation and orchard development	...	...	...	...	...	...	...	...
5 Producers' durable goods	3202	1805	2982	1694	28	16	192	95
A Transport equipment	...	...	668	383	...	...	...	...
Passenger cars	...	...	107	74	...	...	...	...
Other	...	...	561	309	...	...	...	...
B Machinery and equipment	...	...	2314	1311	...	...	...	...
6 Breeding stock, dairy cattle, etc.	...	...	...	...	...	...	...	...
Total	13841	8600	11070	6868	696	456	2075	1277
1981								
1 Residential buildings a	5128	3388	5007	3301	66	46	55	41
2 Non-residential buildings	2792	1736	1991	1238	47	32	754	466
3 Other construction	2993	1820	1312	760	574	372	1107	688
4 Land improvement and plantation and orchard development	...	...	...	...	...	...	...	...
5 Producers' durable goods	3321	1859	3099	1748	30	17	192	94
A Transport equipment	...	...	679	383	...	...	...	...
Passenger cars	...	...	110	75	...	...	...	...
Other	...	...	569	308	...	...	...	...
B Machinery and equipment	...	...	2420	1364	...	...	...	...
6 Breeding stock, dairy cattle, etc.	...	...	...	...	...	...	...	...
Total	14234	8803	11409	7047	717	467	2108	1288
1982								
1 Residential buildings a	5202	3412	5079	3324	67	46	56	41
2 Non-residential buildings	2893	1790	2080	1291	48	32	765	467
3 Other construction	3050	1848	1342	777	583	376	1125	695
4 Land improvement and plantation and orchard development	...	...	...	...	...	...	...	...
5 Producers' durable goods	3402	1879	3179	1767	32	18	191	93
A Transport equipment	...	...	681	377	...	...	...	...
Passenger cars	...	...	113	75	...	...	...	...
Other	...	...	569	302	...	...	...	...
B Machinery and equipment	...	...	2498	1390	...	...	...	...
6 Breeding stock, dairy cattle, etc.	...	...	...	...	...	...	...	...
Total	14548	8928	11680	7159	731	473	2137	1296
1983								
1 Residential buildings a	5321	3480	5195	3392	69	47	57	42
2 Non-residential buildings	2981	1830	2157	1329	49	32	775	468
3 Other construction	3100	1866	1363	785	593	378	1145	702
4 Land improvement and plantation and orchard development	...	...	...	...	...	...	...	...
5 Producers' durable goods	3485	1904	3260	1791	34	19	192	94
A Transport equipment	...	...	690	378	...	...	...	...
Passenger cars	...	...	121	81	...	...	...	...
Other	...	...	569	296	...	...	...	...
B Machinery and equipment	...	...	2570	1413	...	...	...	...
6 Breeding stock, dairy cattle, etc.	...	...	...	...	...	...	...	...
Total	14888	9080	11975	7296	745	477	2169	1307

2.14 Stocks of Reproducible Fixed Assets, by Type of Good and Owner, in Constant Prices
(Continued)

Thousand Million United States dollars

	TOTAL		Total Private		Public Enterprises		General Government	
	Gross	Net	Gross	Net	Gross	Net	Gross	Net
At constant prices of:1985								
1984								
1 Residential buildings a	5462	3570	5334	3480	71	48	58	42
2 Non-residential buildings	3085	1884	2250	1383	50	33	785	469
3 Other construction	3157	1891	1391	799	603	382	1163	710
4 Land improvement and plantation and orchard development	...	...	...	...	...	...	...	...
5 Producers' durable goods	3602	1967	3371	1849	36	21	194	97
A Transport equipment	...	...	704	387	...	...	...	...
Passenger cars	...	...	129	89	...	...	...	...
Other	...	...	575	298	...	...	...	...
B Machinery and equipment	...	...	2668	1462	...	...	...	...
6 Breeding stock, dairy cattle, etc.	...	...	...	...	...	...	...	...
Total	15306	9312	12346	7511	760	483	2200	1317
1985								
1 Residential buildings a	5603	3659	5471	3568	73	49	59	42
2 Non-residential buildings	3205	1953	2357	1449	51	33	797	472
3 Other construction	3220	1922	1421	816	615	387	1184	719
4 Land improvement and plantation and orchard development	...	...	...	...	...	...	...	...
5 Producers' durable goods	3730	2041	3494	1917	39	23	197	102
A Transport equipment	...	...	720	398	...	...	...	...
Passenger cars	...	...	137	96	...	...	...	...
Other	...	...	583	302	...	...	...	...
B Machinery and equipment	...	...	2774	1519	...	...	...	...
6 Breeding stock, dairy cattle, etc.	...	...	...	...	...	...	...	...
Total	15758	9575	12744	7749	778	491	2237	1335
1986								
1 Residential buildings a	5770	3771	5634	3678	75	50	60	43
2 Non-residential buildings	3310	2009	2451	1500	52	33	807	476
3 Other construction	3271	1940	1438	820	628	393	1205	728
4 Land improvement and plantation and orchard development	...	...	...	...	...	...	...	...
5 Producers' durable goods	3853	2107	3610	1975	42	25	200	107
A Transport equipment	...	...	732	404	...	...	...	...
Passenger cars	...	...	144	102	...	...	...	...
Other	...	...	588	302	...	...	...	...
B Machinery and equipment	...	...	2878	1571	...	...	...	...
6 Breeding stock, dairy cattle, etc.	...	...	...	...	...	...	...	...
Total	16204	9827	13133	7973	798	501	2273	1353
1987								
1 Residential buildings a	5933	3878	5794	3784	77	51	62	44
2 Non-residential buildings	3414	2061	2541	1546	53	34	820	481
3 Other construction	3320	1959	1452	821	641	398	1228	739
4 Land improvement and plantation and orchard development	...	...	...	...	...	...	...	...
5 Producers' durable goods	3968	2164	3716	2024	46	27	206	112
A Transport equipment	...	...	742	408	...	...	...	...
Passenger cars	...	...	149	104	...	...	...	...
Other	...	...	593	304	...	...	...	...
B Machinery and equipment	...	...	2974	1616	...	...	...	...
6 Breeding stock, dairy cattle, etc.	...	...	...	...	...	...	...	...
Total	16635	10063	13502	8175	817	511	2316	1377

2.14 Stocks of Reproducible Fixed Assets, by Type of Good and Owner, in Constant Prices
(Continued)

Thousand Million United States dollars

	TOTAL		Total Private		Public Enterprises		General Government	
	Gross	Net	Gross	Net	Gross	Net	Gross	Net
	At constant prices of:1985							
	1988							
1 Residential buildings a	6093	3981	5950	3885	79	52	63	44
2 Non-residential buildings	3521	2114	2633	1593	55	35	833	486
3 Other construction	3363	1973	1460	820	657	408	1246	746
4 Land improvement and plantation and orchard development	...	...	...	...	...	...	...	...
5 Producers' durable goods	4097	2232	3835	2084	49	29	213	119
A Transport equipment	...	...	754	415	...	...	...	...
Passenger cars	...	...	154	108	...	...	...	...
Other	...	...	600	306	...	...	...	...
B Machinery and equipment	...	...	3081	1669	...	...	...	...
6 Breeding stock, dairy cattle, etc.	...	...	...	...	...	...	...	...
Total	17074	10300	13878	8382	840	523	2356	1394
	1989							
1 Residential buildings a	6237	4069	6092	3972	81	52	65	44
2 Non-residential buildings	3631	2171	2725	1642	56	36	850	493
3 Other construction	3404	1987	1468	818	673	417	1263	752
4 Land improvement and plantation and orchard development	...	...	...	...	...	...	...	...
5 Producers' durable goods	4236	2305	3961	2147	52	31	223	127
A Transport equipment	...	...	762	415	...	...	...	...
Passenger cars	...	...	159	111	...	...	...	...
Other	...	...	603	305	...	...	...	...
B Machinery and equipment	...	...	3199	1732	...	...	...	...
6 Breeding stock, dairy cattle, etc.	...	...	...	...	...	...	...	...
Total	17509	10532	14246	8580	862	536	2400	1416
	1990							
1 Residential buildings a	6368	4140	6219	4042	82	53	66	45
2 Non-residential buildings	3742	2227	2817	1690	58	37	868	501
3 Other construction	3451	2005	1478	820	690	426	1283	760
4 Land improvement and plantation and orchard development	...	...	...	...	...	...	...	...
5 Producers' durable goods	4365	2366	4076	2198	56	34	232	135
A Transport equipment	...	...	771	418	...	...	...	...
Passenger cars	...	...	163	114	...	...	...	...
Other	...	...	608	304	...	...	...	...
B Machinery and equipment	...	...	3306	1780	...	...	...	...
6 Breeding stock, dairy cattle, etc.	...	...	...	...	...	...	...	...
Total	17926	10739	14590	8749	886	549	2449	1441
	1991							
1 Residential buildings a	6472	4186	6320	4087	84	54	68	46
2 Non-residential buildings	3829	2262	2884	1714	59	37	886	511
3 Other construction	3496	2022	1488	822	705	433	1302	767
4 Land improvement and plantation and orchard development	...	...	...	...	...	...	...	...
5 Producers' durable goods	4469	2402	4164	2224	59	35	246	143
A Transport equipment	...	...	774	416	...	...	...	...
Passenger cars	...	...	164	115	...	...	...	...
Other	...	...	609	301	...	...	...	...
B Machinery and equipment	...	...	3391	1808	...	...	...	...
6 Breeding stock, dairy cattle, etc.	...	...	...	...	...	...	...	...
Total	18266	10872	14857	8846	908	559	2501	1467

a) The estimates of residential buildings of government enterprises and general government are included in the respective columns of item 'Residential buildings' in tables 2.7 and 2.8. These estimates are included in item 'Real estate' in tables 2.9-2.12 and are therefore excluded from the estimates of government enterprises and general government of these tables. This latter classification is followed in tables 2.13-2.16.

United States

2.15 Stocks of Reproducible Fixed Assets by Kind of Activity, in Current Prices

Thousand Million United States dollars

	1980 Gross	1980 Net	1981 Gross	1981 Net	1982 Gross	1982 Net	1983 Gross	1983 Net	1984 Gross	1984 Net	1985 Gross	1985 Net
1 Residential buildings a	4361	2894	4712	3113	4900	3212	5118	3345	5385	3517	5684	3710
2 Non-residential buildings b	2216	1383	2466	1533	2665	1648	2840	1743	3039	1856	3257	1985
A Industries	2932	1780	3288	1995	3498	2119	3623	2182	3827	2299	4044	2430
1 Agriculture	149	90	163	97	171	100	178	102	185	104	193	107
2 Mining and quarrying	310	168	402	223	414	232	377	210	385	214	392	215
3 Manufacturing	416	253	469	287	514	315	547	332	587	354	631	380
4 Electricity, gas and water	456	282	503	310	538	329	562	341	584	352	604	363
5 Construction	22	16	24	18	27	19	28	19	30	20	32	21
6 Wholesale and retail trade	217	141	246	159	268	173	290	186	319	205	352	228
7 Transport and communication	398	211	423	225	441	234	450	238	459	242	464	246
8 Finance, etc.	269	173	308	198	342	221	374	241	415	270	467	307
9 Community, social and personal services	142	85	158	94	171	101	183	108	197	115	211	123
Statistical discrepancy c	553	361	592	385	612	396	634	406	665	423	698	440
B Producers of government services	1642	1027	1692	1048	1723	1058	1787	1089	1906	1152	2020	1214
C Other producers d	304	195	336	213	362	228	387	243	412	257	437	271
3 Other construction b	2663	1619	2850	1724	2918	1758	2958	1772	3105	1853	3244	1929
4 Land improvement and development and plantation and orchard development	...	...	...	...	...	...	...	...	...	...	...	...
5 Producers' durable goods	2609	1472	2965	1662	3193	1765	3328	1820	3484	1905	3655	2001
A Industries	2407	1370	2743	1550	2959	1647	3086	1697	3233	1775	3393	1861
1 Agriculture	184	99	204	107	212	106	216	104	213	98	205	91
2 Mining and quarrying	93	56	120	73	137	83	140	82	144	81	150	82
3 Manufacturing	729	413	828	467	888	495	906	494	932	502	968	518
4 Electricity, gas and water	190	109	218	123	235	131	242	132	251	137	271	152
5 Construction	70	34	74	35	73	34	69	31	66	30	65	30
6 Wholesale and retail trade	203	114	230	129	250	141	276	160	309	185	337	203
7 Transport and communication	455	253	512	281	548	295	568	299	587	304	601	305
8 Finance, etc.	311	190	363	222	406	246	444	269	493	304	542	337
9 Community, social and personal services	148	85	167	95	179	100	192	107	202	113	214	120
Statistical discrepancy c	25	14	28	16	31	18	34	19	37	21	40	24
B Producers of government services	167	82	180	88	187	91	190	93	194	97	200	104
C Other producers d	36	21	42	25	47	28	52	31	57	34	62	37
6 Breeding stock, dairy cattle, etc.	...	...	...	...	...	...	...	...	...	...	...	...
Total	11849	7368	12993	8031	13675	8384	14244	8680	15013	9130	15840	9626

	1986 Gross	1986 Net	1987 Gross	1987 Net	1988 Gross	1988 Net	1989 Gross	1989 Net	1990 Gross	1990 Net	1991 Gross	1991 Net
1 Residential buildings a	6087	3978	6567	4294	6697	4376	7122	4647	7503	4879	7829	5062
2 Non-residential buildings b	3478	2111	3708	2240	3972	2387	4234	2535	4438	2646	4584	2713
A Industries	4209	2520	4415	2630	4748	2810	5031	2964	5244	3075	5393	3136
1 Agriculture	200	108	206	109	214	111	220	112	223	111	224	109
2 Mining and quarrying	359	190	344	176	374	185	381	182	387	180	393	179
3 Manufacturing	670	400	711	420	759	444	811	473	854	498	884	512
4 Electricity, gas and water	626	375	655	390	714	422	754	443	781	454	800	462
5 Construction	34	22	36	22	38	23	40	24	42	24	42	24
6 Wholesale and retail trade	385	249	415	266	454	290	487	309	516	326	535	334
7 Transport and communication	468	249	482	257	506	270	534	286	545	291	555	296
8 Finance, etc.	518	342	571	378	628	415	686	453	734	482	762	494
9 Community, social and personal services	227	132	242	141	261	152	279	162	293	171	302	175
Statistical discrepancy c	723	453	753	470	800	497	839	520	870	538	894	550
B Producers of government services	2081	1244	2170	1292	2287	1353	2386	1405	2464	1443	2543	1484
C Other producers d	465	286	494	303	530	323	564	342	591	357	611	368

2.15 Stocks of Reproducible Fixed Assets by Kind of Activity, in Current Prices
(Continued)

Thousand Million United States dollars

	1986 Gross	1986 Net	1987 Gross	1987 Net	1988 Gross	1988 Net	1989 Gross	1989 Net	1990 Gross	1990 Net	1991 Gross	1991 Net
3 Other construction b	3277	1939	3370	1985	3593	2100	3746	2176	3860	2230	3963	2276
4 Land improvement and development and plantation and orchard development	...	...	...	...	...	...	...	...	...	...	...	...
5 Producers' durable goods	3895	2130	4087	2226	4346	2364	4619	2506	4933	2666	5091	2725
A Industries	3617	1977	3791	2060	4025	2181	4269	2303	4552	2442	4678	2483
1 Agriculture	201	86	196	83	188	80	190	82	193	85	190	85
2 Mining and quarrying	150	78	149	74	151	72	150	69	149	67	143	63
3 Manufacturing	1024	539	1068	559	1115	579	1185	615	1251	651	1295	671
4 Electricity, gas and water	292	164	311	176	335	188	355	196	393	216	413	223
5 Construction	65	31	66	33	67	34	70	36	72	37	74	38
6 Wholesale and retail trade	371	224	391	231	429	252	458	267	501	291	530	306
7 Transport and communication	625	316	637	317	661	324	668	324	705	338	688	324
8 Finance, etc.	612	381	677	419	759	466	846	513	915	542	951	548
9 Community, social and personal services	232	131	248	141	270	155	290	167	310	178	325	185
Statistical discrepancy c	44	26	48	29	53	32	57	34	64	38	69	41
B Producers of government services	208	111	217	119	232	129	249	142	266	154	288	167
C Other producers d	70	42	79	47	89	54	101	61	114	69	125	75
6 Breeding stock, dairy cattle, etc.	...	...	...	...	...	...	...	...	...	...	...	...
Total	16737	10158	17733	10745	18608	11227	19721	11864	20734	12421	21466	12775

a) The estimates of residential buildings of government enterprises and general government are included in the respective columns of item 'Residential buildings' in tables 2.7 and 2.8. These estimates are included in item 'Real estate' in tables 2.9-2.12 and are therefore excluded from the estimates of government enterprises and general government of these tables. This latter classification is followed in tables 2.13-2.16. b) The sub-items of 'Other constructions' are included in the sub-items of 'Non-residential buildings'. c) Item 'Statistical discrepancy' refers to government enterprises. d) Item 'Other producers' consists of non-profit institutions serving individuals.

2.16 Stocks of Reproducible Fixed Assets by Kind of Activity, in Constant Prices

Thousand Million United States dollars

	1980 Gross	1980 Net	1981 Gross	1981 Net	1982 Gross	1982 Net	1983 Gross	1983 Net	1984 Gross	1984 Net	1985 Gross	1985 Net
					At constant prices of:1985							
1 Residential buildings a	5023	3332	5128	3388	5202	3412	5321	3480	5462	3570	5603	3659
2 Non-residential buildings b	2685	1677	2792	1736	2893	1790	2981	1830	3085	1884	3205	1953
A Industries	3407	2076	3541	2159	3659	2227	3755	2269	3875	2335	4015	2418
1 Agriculture	183	111	187	112	188	110	188	108	190	107	191	106
2 Mining and quarrying	328	180	353	199	376	214	391	221	409	230	420	232
3 Manufacturing	511	313	537	330	562	346	578	352	598	362	622	376
4 Electricity, gas and water	531	330	547	338	560	344	570	347	582	352	599	361
5 Construction	27	20	28	20	29	21	30	21	31	21	32	21
6 Wholesale and retail trade	268	174	281	182	293	190	306	197	325	209	348	226
7 Transport and communication	451	236	454	239	457	242	460	243	463	246	468	249
8 Finance, etc.	330	212	351	227	374	242	395	255	424	276	461	304
9 Community, social and personal services	175	105	181	108	187	111	194	114	201	118	209	122
Statistical discrepancy c	603	394	621	404	632	408	642	411	653	415	666	420
B Producers of government services	1836	1148	1861	1154	1890	1162	1920	1171	1948	1178	1981	1191
C Other producers d	373	239	383	243	395	249	407	256	419	262	430	267
3 Other construction b	2932	1787	2993	1820	3050	1848	3100	1866	3157	1891	3220	1922
4 Land improvement and development and plantation and orchard development	...	...	...	...	...	...	...	...	...	...	...	...
5 Producers' durable goods	3202	1805	3321	1859	3402	1879	3485	1904	3602	1967	3730	2041
A Industries	2968	1685	3083	1738	3162	1757	3240	1779	3350	1836	3471	1903
1 Agriculture	231	124	232	121	228	114	222	107	216	100	206	91
2 Mining and quarrying	115	69	130	79	140	85	144	84	148	83	151	83
3 Manufacturing	906	512	938	527	959	532	966	525	980	526	998	532
4 Electricity, gas and water	230	132	236	134	241	134	246	135	253	138	271	152

United States

2.16 Stocks of Reproducible Fixed Assets by Kind of Activity, in Constant Prices
(Continued)

Thousand Million United States dollars

	1980		1981		1982		1983		1984		1985	
	Gross	Net	Gross	Net	Gross	Net	Gross	Net	Gross	Net	Gross	Net
At constant prices of:1985												
5 Construction	91	45	87	42	82	37	76	34	72	32	68	32
6 Wholesale and retail trade	249	140	259	146	271	152	292	168	323	192	348	209
7 Transport and communication	569	317	584	322	591	318	597	315	602	312	606	308
8 Finance, etc.	364	224	394	242	422	257	458	278	508	313	560	347
9 Community, social and personal services	185	107	191	108	197	110	206	114	214	119	224	126
Statistical discrepancy c	28	16	30	17	32	18	34	19	36	21	39	23
B Producers of government services	192	95	192	94	191	93	192	94	194	97	197	102
C Other producers d	42	25	46	27	49	29	53	31	57	34	62	37
6 Breeding stock, dairy cattle, etc.	...	...	...	...	...	...	...	...	...	...	...	...
Total	13841	8600	14234	8803	14548	8928	14888	9080	15306	9312	15758	9575

	1986		1987		1988		1989		1990		1991	
	Gross	Net	Gross	Net	Gross	Net	Gross	Net	Gross	Net	Gross	Net
At constant prices of:1985												
1 Residential buildings a	5770	3771	5933	3878	6093	3981	6237	4069	6368	4140	6472	4186
2 Non-residential buildings b	3310	2009	3414	2061	3521	2114	3631	2171	3742	2227	3829	2262
A Industries	4129	2475	4233	2522	4338	2571	4443	2621	4549	2673	4630	2701
1 Agriculture	192	105	191	102	191	100	190	97	189	95	189	93
2 Mining and quarrying	418	223	415	213	410	204	401	193	392	184	381	176
3 Manufacturing	639	383	656	390	673	396	696	408	721	423	741	432
4 Electricity, gas and water	616	370	630	377	644	383	658	389	670	392	682	397
5 Construction	33	21	34	21	34	21	35	21	36	21	36	20
6 Wholesale and retail trade	367	238	383	247	402	258	418	267	435	277	449	282
7 Transport and communication	472	253	477	255	481	258	486	261	490	263	493	264
8 Finance, etc.	495	328	528	352	558	371	590	392	621	411	641	418
9 Community, social and personal services	217	127	224	131	232	136	240	140	248	145	254	148
Statistical discrepancy c	680	426	694	433	712	442	729	452	748	462	765	470
B Producers of government services	2012	1203	2048	1221	2079	1231	2113	1245	2151	1261	2188	1278
C Other producers d	441	272	453	278	466	284	479	291	493	299	506	305
3 Other construction b	3271	1940	3320	1959	3363	1973	3404	1987	3451	2005	3496	2022
4 Land improvement and development and plantation and orchard development	...	...	...	...	...	...	...	...	...	...	...	...
5 Producers' durable goods	3853	2107	3968	2164	4097	2232	4236	2305	4365	2366	4469	2402
A Industries	3585	1960	3688	2007	3803	2064	3924	2124	4035	2173	4117	2195
1 Agriculture	194	83	185	78	175	74	168	72	161	71	154	69
2 Mining and quarrying	149	78	145	71	141	67	135	63	129	58	122	54
3 Manufacturing	1006	529	1020	534	1032	536	1054	549	1074	560	1089	567
4 Electricity, gas and water	285	160	300	170	313	176	319	176	333	183	342	185
5 Construction	66	31	64	32	64	33	63	33	63	33	62	32
6 Wholesale and retail trade	374	225	389	230	414	243	437	255	465	269	495	287
7 Transport and communication	615	311	617	306	617	302	618	300	615	295	606	286
8 Finance, etc.	617	384	675	418	738	453	801	486	849	502	886	509
9 Community, social and personal services	236	133	248	141	262	151	277	160	289	166	300	171
Statistical discrepancy c	42	25	46	27	49	29	52	31	56	34	59	35
B Producers of government services	200	107	206	112	213	119	223	127	232	135	246	143
C Other producers d	67	40	74	44	81	49	90	54	98	59	106	64
6 Breeding stock, dairy cattle, etc.	...	...	...	...	...	...	...	...	...	...	...	...
Total	16204	9827	16635	10063	17074	10300	17509	10532	17926	10739	18266	10872

a) The estimates of residential buildings of government enterprises and general government are included in the respective columns of item 'Residential buildings' in tables 2.7 and 2.8. These estimates are included in item 'Real estate' in tables 2.9-2.12 and are therefore excluded from the estimates of government enterprises and general government of these tables. This latter classification is followed in tables 2.13-2.16.

b) The sub-items of 'Other constructions' are included in the sub-items of 'Non-residential buildings'.

c) Item 'Statistical discrepancy' refers to government enterprises.

d) Item 'Other producers' consists of non-profit institutions serving individuals.

2.17 Exports and Imports of Goods and Services, Detail

Million United States dollars

	1980	1981	1982	1983	1984	1985	1986	1987	1988	1989	1990	1991
Exports of Goods and Services												
1 Exports of merchandise, f.o.b. a	225635	238918	214833	207096	225413	221911	225751	257260	325336	371100	397515	422504
2 Transport and communication	14209	15671	15491	16200	17867	19056	21329	24300	28381	31620	38082	39252
3 Insurance service charges	...	...	...	...	...	...	...	...	...	...	...	...
4 Other commodities	26123	30148	33169	33724	32212	32126	39612	44996	46597	53335	60639	69544
5 Adjustments of merchandise exports to change-of-ownership basis	...	...	...	...	...	...	...	...	...	...	...	...
6 Direct purchases in the domestic market by non-residential households	11558	16636	16734	15718	22303	23291	26360	29997	36080	44325	52596	58118
7 Direct purchases in the domestic market by extraterritorial bodies	...	...	...	...	...	...	...	...	...	...	...	...
Total Exports of Goods and Services	277525	301373	280227	272738	297795	296384	313052	356553	436394	500380	548832	589418
Imports of Goods and Services												
1 Imports of merchandise, c.i.f. a	248638	267742	250604	272700	336337	343310	370023	414796	452127	485068	507837	499910
A Imports of merchandise, f.o.b. a	248638	267742	250604	272700	336337	343310	370023	414796	452127	485068	507837	499910
B Transport of services on merchandise imports	...	...	...	...	...	...	...	...	...	...	...	...
C Insurance service charges on merchandise imports	...	...	...	...	...	...	...	...	...	...	...	...
2 Adjustments of merchandise imports to change-of-ownership basis	...	...	...	...	...	...	...	...	...	...	...	...
3 Other transport and communication	11790	12474	11710	12222	14843	15643	16715	17788	19534	20664	23401	23297
4 Other insurance service charges	...	...	...	...	...	...	...	...	...	...	...	...
5 Other commodities	17992	20804	22810	23451	26647	29487	36531	40630	44328	45148	54235	56391
6 Direct purchases abroad by government	...	...	...	...	...	...	...	...	...	...	...	...
7 Direct purchases abroad by resident households	15476	16666	18070	19753	27283	29183	28468	33836	36219	36828	40430	40374
Total Imports of Goods and Services	293896	317686	303194	328126	405110	417623	451737	507050	552208	587708	625903	619972
Balance of Goods and Services	-16371	-16313	-22967	-55388	-107315	-121239	-138685	-150497	-115814	-87328	-77071	-30554
Total Imports and Balance of Goods and Services	277525	301373	280227	272738	297795	296384	313052	356553	436394	500380	548832	589418

a) Merchandise valued at Free Along Side (F.A.S.).

3.12 General Government Income and Outlay Account: Total and Subsectors

Million United States dollars

	1980					1981				
	Total General Government	Central Government	State or Provincial Government	Local Government	Social Security Funds	Total General Government	Central Government	State or Provincial Government	Local Government	Social Security Funds
Receipts										
1 Operating surplus	...	...	...	...	...	...	...	...	...	...
2 Property and entrepreneurial income	33816	11470	...	21497	849	43384	15242	...	27154	988
A Withdrawals from public quasi-corporations	...	...	...	...	...	...	...	...	...	...
B Interest	33719	11470	...	21400	849	43258	15242	...	27028	988
C Dividends	97	...	...	97	...	126	...	...	126	...
D Net land rent and royalties	...	...	...	...	...	...	...	...	...	...
3 Taxes, fees and contributions	767085	359689	...	240700	166696	877596	413286	...	268093	196217
A Indirect taxes	211957	39649	...	172308	...	249277	57271	...	192006	...
B Direct taxes	383165	319808	...	63357	...	425813	355756	...	70057	...
Income	376868	319808	...	57060	...	419110	355756	...	63354	...
Other	6297	...	...	6297	...	6703	...	...	6703	...
C Social security contributions	166696		...	...	166696	196217	...	...	...	196217
D Fees, fines and penalties	5267	232	...	5035	...	6289	259	...	6030	...

3.12 General Government Income and Outlay Account: Total and Subsectors
(Continued)

Million United States dollars

	1980					1981				
	Total General Government	Central Government	State or Provincial Government	Local Government	Social Security Funds	Total General Government	Central Government	State or Provincial Government	Local Government	Social Security Funds
4 Other current transfers	27987	33275	...	88990	5631	31701	37465	...	88257	6428
A Casualty insurance claims	...	...	...	...	...	...	...	...	...	...
B Transfers from other government subsectors	...	5288	...	88990	5631	...	5764	...	88257	6428
C Transfers from the rest of the world	1618	1618	...	-	...	1551	1551	...	-	...
D Other transfers, except imputed	2723	2723	...	...	...	2917	2917	...	...	...
E Imputed unfunded employee pension and welfare contributions	23646	23646	...	...	...	27233	27233	...	...	...
Total Current Receipts [a]	828888	404434	...	351187	173176	952681	465993	...	383504	203633

Disbursements

	1980					1981				
	Total General Government	Central Government	State or Provincial Government	Local Government	Social Security Funds	Total General Government	Central Government	State or Provincial Government	Local Government	Social Security Funds
1 Government final consumption expenditure	476343	208005	...	268338	5600	529385	237681	...	291704	6128
2 Property income	85406	66048	...	19358	...	112113	89269	...	22844	...
A Interest	85406	66048	...	19358	...	112113	89269	...	22844	...
B Net land rent and royalties	...	...	...	...	...	...	...	...	...	...
3 Subsidies	10611	10257	...	354	...	12178	11776	...	402	...
4 Other current transfers	300660	166810	...	47849	180310	340767	172866	...	53248	208974
A Casualty insurance premiums, net	...	...	...	...	...	...	...	...	...	...
B Transfers to other government subsectors	...	94309	...	...	...	...	94321	...	...	...
C Social security benefits	180310	...	...	...	180310	208974	...	...	...	208974
D Social assistance grants	89310	41501	...	47809	...	97367	44119	...	53248	...
E Unfunded employee pension and welfare benefits [b]	23686	23646	...	40	...	27174	27174	...	-	...
F Transfers to private non-profit institutions serving households	...	...	...	...	...	...	...	...	...	...
G Other transfers n.e.c.	...	...	...	...	...	...	...	...	...	...
H Transfers to the rest of the world	7354	7354	...	...	...	7252	7252	...	...	...
Net saving	-44132	-46686	...	15288	-12734	-41762	-45599	...	15306	-11469
Total Current Disbursements and Net Saving [a]	828888	404434	...	351187	173176	952681	465993	...	383504	203633

	1982					1983				
	Total General Government	Central Government	State or Provincial Government	Local Government	Social Security Funds	Total General Government	Central Government	State or Provincial Government	Local Government	Social Security Funds

Receipts

	1982					1983				
	Total General Government	Central Government	State or Provincial Government	Local Government	Social Security Funds	Total General Government	Central Government	State or Provincial Government	Local Government	Social Security Funds
1 Operating surplus	...	...	...	...	...	...	...	...	...	...
2 Property and entrepreneurial income	50362	18595	...	30512	1255	55742	21125	...	33120	1497
A Withdrawals from public quasi-corporations	...	...	...	...	...	...	...	...	...	...
B Interest	50208	18595	...	30358	1255	55566	21125	...	32944	1497
C Dividends	154	...	...	154	...	176	...	...	176	...
D Net land rent and royalties	...	...	...	...	...	...	...	...	...	...
3 Taxes, fees and contributions	890029	394082	...	286715	209232	944198	401628	...	316236	226334
A Indirect taxes	256425	49675	...	206750	...	280104	53484	...	226620	...
B Direct taxes	417277	344096	...	73181	...	429664	347663	...	82001	...
Income	410017	344096	...	65921	...	421844	347663	...	74181	...
Other	7260	...	...	7260	...	7820	...	...	7820	...
C Social security contributions	209232	...	...	...	209232	226334	...	...	...	226334
D Fees, fines and penalties	7095	311	...	6784	...	8096	481	...	7615	...
4 Other current transfers	34366	40360	...	84270	6350	36068	42606	...	87430	5994
A Casualty insurance claims	...	...	...	...	...	...	...	...	...	...
B Transfers from other government subsectors	...	5994	...	84270	6350	...	6538	...	87430	5994
C Transfers from the rest of the world	1489	1489	...	-	...	1246	1246	...	-	...
D Other transfers, except imputed	3099	3099	...	...	...	3218	3218	...	...	...
E Imputed unfunded employee pension and welfare contributions	29778	29778	...	...	...	31604	31604	...	...	...

3.12 General Government Income and Outlay Account: Total and Subsectors
(Continued)

Million United States dollars

	1982					1983				
	Total General Government	Central Government	State or Provincial Government	Local Government	Social Security Funds	Total General Government	Central Government	State or Provincial Government	Local Government	Social Security Funds
Total Current Receipts a	974757	453037	...	401497	216837	1036008	465359	...	436786	233825
Disbursements										
1 Government final consumption expenditure	579270	266762	...	312508	6408	620821	290715	...	330106	6989
2 Property income	132954	105829	...	27125	...	149433	117138	...	32295	...
A Interest	132954	105829	...	27125	...	149433	117138	...	32295	...
B Net land rent and royalties	...	...	...	...	...	...	...	...	...	...
3 Subsidies	15483	15029	...	454	...	22098	21656	...	442	...
4 Other current transfers	379981	171218	...	56911	242058	408853	179334	...	61404	261088
A Casualty insurance premiums, net	...	...	...	...	...	...	...	...	...	...
B Transfers to other government subsectors	...	90206	...	...	...	...	92973	...	...	...
C Social security benefits	242058	...	...	...	242058	261088	...	...	...	261088
D Social assistance grants	99653	42742	...	56911	...	106972	45568	...	61404	...
E Unfunded employee pension and welfare benefits b	29782	29782	...	-	...	32049	32049	...	-	...
F Transfers to private non-profit institutions serving households	...	...	...	...	...	...	...	...	...	...
G Other transfers n.e.c.	...	...	...	...	...	...	...	...	...	...
H Transfers to the rest of the world	8488	8488	...	...	...	8744	8744	...	...	...
Net saving	-132931	-105801	...	4499	-31629	-165197	-143484	...	12539	-34252
Total Current Disbursements and Net Saving a	974757	453037	...	401497	216837	1036008	465359	...	436786	233825

	1984					1985				
	Total General Government	Central Government	State or Provincial Government	Local Government	Social Security Funds	Total General Government	Central Government	State or Provincial Government	Local Government	Social Security Funds
Receipts										
1 Operating surplus	...	...	...	...	...	...	...	...	...	...
2 Property and entrepreneurial income	64445	24005	...	38792	1648	72076	26206	...	44033	1837
A Withdrawals from public quasi-corporations	...	...	...	...	...	...	...	...	...	...
B Interest	64281	24005	...	38628	1648	71920	26206	...	43877	1837
C Dividends	164	...	...	164	...	156	...	...	156	...
D Net land rent and royalties	...	...	...	...	...	...	...	...	...	...
3 Taxes, fees and contributions	1048155	435048	...	355203	257904	1136368	471270	...	382997	282101
A Indirect taxes	309480	57829	...	251651	...	329910	58557	...	271353	...
B Direct taxes	471551	376729	...	94822	...	513811	412102	...	101709	...
Income	462999	376729	...	86270	...	504471	412102	...	92369	...
Other	8552	...	...	8552	...	9340	...	...	9340	...
C Social security contributions	257904	...	...	...	257904	282101	...	...	...	282101
D Fees, fines and penalties	9220	490	...	8730	...	10546	611	...	9935	...
4 Other current transfers	36134	42841	...	94860	9056	39735	46929	...	100781	11683
A Casualty insurance claims	...	...	...	...	...	...	...	...	...	...
B Transfers from other government subsectors	...	6707	...	94860	9056	...	7194	...	100781	11683
C Transfers from the rest of the world	1374	1374	...	-	...	2024	2024	...	-	...
D Other transfers, except imputed	3386	3386	...	...	...	3408	3408	...	...	...
E Imputed unfunded employee pension and welfare contributions	31374	31374	...	...	...	34303	34303	...	...	...
Total Current Receipts a	1148734	501894	...	488855	268608	1248179	544405	...	527811	295621
Disbursements										
1 Government final consumption expenditure	669749	313931	...	355818	7181	727868	341425	...	386443	7700
2 Property income	178100	141109	...	36991	...	200376	158281	...	42095	...
A Interest	178100	141109	...	36991	...	200376	158281	...	42095	...
B Net land rent and royalties	...	...	...	...	...	...	...	...	...	...
3 Subsidies	22476	22091	...	385	...	22499	22172	...	327	...

3.12 General Government Income and Outlay Account: Total and Subsectors
(Continued)

Million United States dollars

	1984					1985				
	Total General Government	Central Government	State or Provincial Government	Local Government	Social Security Funds	Total General Government	Central Government	State or Provincial Government	Local Government	Social Security Funds
4 Other current transfers	418906	191482	...	65532	265334	449512	206723	...	70822	283925
A Casualty insurance premiums, net	...	...	...	...	...	...	...	...	...	...
B Transfers to other government subsectors	...	103442	...	...	...	...	111958	...	...	...
C Social security benefits	265334	...	...	...	265334	283925	...	...	...	283925
D Social assistance grants	111493	45961	...	65532	...	117563	46741	...	70822	...
E Unfunded employee pension and welfare benefits [b]	31154	31154	...	-	...	34533	34533	...	-	...
F Transfers to private non-profit institutions serving households	...	...	...	...	...	...	...	...	...	...
G Other transfers n.e.c.	...	...	...	...	...	...	...	...	...	...
H Transfers to the rest of the world	10925	10925	...	...	...	13491	13491	...	...	...
Net saving	-140497	-166719	...	30129	-3907	-152076	-184196	...	28124	3996
Total Current Disbursements and Net Saving [a]	1148734	501894	...	488855	268608	1248179	544405	...	527811	295621

	1986					1987				
	Total General Government	Central Government	State or Provincial Government	Local Government	Social Security Funds	Total General Government	Central Government	State or Provincial Government	Local Government	Social Security Funds
Receipts										
1 Operating surplus	...	...	...	...	...	...	...	...	...	...
2 Property and entrepreneurial income	76902	28346	...	46627	1929	76435	26835	...	47568	2032
A Withdrawals from public quasi-corporations	...	...	...	...	...	...	...	...	...	...
B Interest	76752	28346	...	46477	1929	76273	26835	...	47406	2032
C Dividends	150	...	...	150	...	162	...	...	162	...
D Net land rent and royalties	...	...	...	...	...	...	...	...	...	...
3 Taxes, fees and contributions	1204981	487726	...	413248	304007	1316821	555065	...	438895	322861
A Indirect taxes	345500	53464	...	292036	...	364986	58441	...	306545	...
B Direct taxes	543576	433728	...	109848	...	616168	495717	...	120451	...
Income	533838	433728	...	100110	...	605577	495717	...	109860	...
Other	9738		...	9738	...	10591		...	10591	...
C Social security contributions	304007	...	...	...	304007	322861	...	...	...	322861
D Fees, fines and penalties	11898	534	...	11364	...	12806	907	...	11899	...
4 Other current transfers	40596	47860	...	108207	12702	42273	49401	...	103509	15189
A Casualty insurance claims	...	...	...	...	...	...	...	...	...	...
B Transfers from other government subsectors	...	7264	...	108207	12702	...	7128	...	103509	15189
C Transfers from the rest of the world	1844	1844	...	-	...	2105	2105	...	-	...
D Other transfers, except imputed	3398	3398	...	...	...	3273	3273	...	...	...
E Imputed unfunded employee pension and welfare contributions	35354	35354	...	...	...	36895	36895	...	...	...
Total Current Receipts [a]	1322479	563932	...	568082	318638	1435529	631301	...	589972	340082
Disbursements										
1 Government final consumption expenditure	781951	364592	...	417359	7834	830972	388065	...	442907	7790
2 Property income	212999	165044	...	47955	...	222106	170180	...	51926	...
A Interest	212999	165044	...	47955	...	222106	170180	...	51926	...
B Net land rent and royalties	...	...	...	...	...	...	...	...	...	...
3 Subsidies	26879	26573	...	306	...	32020	31745	...	275	...

3.12 General Government Income and Outlay Account: Total and Subsectors
(Continued)

Million United States dollars

	1986					1987				
	Total General Government	Central Government	State or Provincial Government	Local Government	Social Security Funds	Total General Government	Central Government	State or Provincial Government	Local Government	Social Security Funds
4 Other current transfers	475985	217939	...	77025	301360	494784	216309	...	82191	314320
A Casualty insurance premiums, net	...	...	...	...	...	...	...	...	...	...
B Transfers to other government subsectors	...	120339	...	...	...	...	118036	...	...	...
C Social security benefits	301360	...	...	...	301360	314320	...	...	...	314320
D Social assistance grants	125076	48051	...	77025	...	130996	48805	...	82191	...
E Unfunded employee pension and welfare benefits b ..	35354	35354	...	-	...	36895	36895	...	-	...
F Transfers to private non-profit institutions serving households	...	...	...	...	...	...	...	...	...	...
G Other transfers n.e.c.	...	...	...	...	...	...	...	...	...	...
H Transfers to the rest of the world	14195	14195	...	...	...	12573	12573	...	...	...
Net saving	-175335	-210216	...	25437	9444	-144353	-174998	...	12673	17972
Total Current Disbursements and Net Saving a	1322479	563932	...	568082	318638	1435529	631301	...	589972	340082

	1988					1989				
	Total General Government	Central Government	State or Provincial Government	Local Government	Social Security Funds	Total General Government	Central Government	State or Provincial Government	Local Government	Social Security Funds
	Receipts									
1 Operating surplus	...	...	...	...	...	...	...	...	...	
2 Property and entrepreneurial income	82165	28915	...	51134	2116	87028	27947	...	56885	2196
A Withdrawals from public quasi-corporations	...	...	...	...	...	...	...	...	...	...
B Interest	81989	28915	...	50958	2116	86851	27947	...	56708	2196
C Dividends	176	...	...	176	...	177	...	...	177	...
D Net land rent and royalties	...	...	...	...	...	...	...	...	...	...
3 Taxes, fees and contributions	1399501	574307	...	464454	360740	1523840	631918	...	504776	387146
A Indirect taxes	385343	60854	...	324489	...	414691	61888	...	352803	...
B Direct taxes	639600	512328	...	127272	...	706630	568780	...	137850	...
Income	628255	512328	...	115927	...	694442	568780	...	125662	...
Other	11345	...	...	11345	...	12188	...	...	12188	...
C Social security contributions	360740	...	...	...	360740	387146	...	...	...	387146
D Fees, fines and penalties	13818	1125	...	12693	...	15373	1250	...	14123	...
4 Other current transfers	44761	52728	...	112022	20436	46982	55309	...	119144	27962
A Casualty insurance claims	...	...	...	...	...	...	...	...	...	...
B Transfers from other government subsectors	...	7967	...	112022	20436	...	8327	...	119144	27962
C Transfers from the rest of the world	2619	2619	...	-	...	1850	1850	...	-	...
D Other transfers, except imputed	3082	3082	...	...	...	3194	3194	...	...	...
E Imputed unfunded employee pension and welfare contributions	39060	39060	...	...	...	41938	41938	...	...	...
Total Current Receipts a	1526427	655950	...	627610	383292	1657850	715174	...	680805	417304
	Disbursements									
1 Government final consumption expenditure	876420	401786	...	474634	8727	915832	404060	...	511772	9255
2 Property income	237413	183025	...	54388	...	258669	201093	...	57576	...
A Interest	237413	183025	...	54388	...	258669	201093	...	57576	...
B Net land rent and royalties	...	...	...	...	...	...	...	...	...	...
3 Subsidies	31264	30911	...	353	...	29078	28701	...	377	...

United States

3.12 General Government Income and Outlay Account: Total and Subsectors
(Continued)

Million United States dollars

	1988 Total General Government	Central Government	State or Provincial Government	Local Government	Social Security Funds	1989 Total General Government	Central Government	State or Provincial Government	Local Government	Social Security Funds
4 Other current transfers	525822	236368	...	89029	332123	571434	259419	...	99001	359192
A Casualty insurance premiums, net	...	...	...	...	...			...	...	...
B Transfers to other government subsectors	...	131698	...	...	...	...	146178	...	...	...
C Social security benefits	332123	...	...	...	332123	359192	...	...	...	359192
D Social assistance grants	141571	52542	...	89029	...	157115	58114	...	99001	...
E Unfunded employee pension and welfare benefits [b]	39060	39060	...	-	...	41938	41938	...	-	...
F Transfers to private non-profit institutions serving households	...	...	...	...	...	...	...	...	...	...
G Other transfers n.e.c.	...	...	...	...	...	...	...	...	...	...
H Transfers to the rest of the world	13068	13068	...	...	...	13189	13189	...	...	...
Net saving	-144492	-196140	...	9206	42442	-117163	-178099	...	12079	48857
Total Current Disbursements and Net Saving [a]	1526427	655950	...	627610	383292	1657850	715174	...	680805	417304

	1990 Total General Government	Central Government	State or Provincial Government	Local Government	Social Security Funds	1991 Total General Government	Central Government	State or Provincial Government	Local Government	Social Security Funds
Receipts										
1 Operating surplus	...	...	...	...	...	...	...	...	...	...
2 Property and entrepreneurial income	92019	31767	...	57910	2342	92729	32974	...	57287	2468
A Withdrawals from public quasi-corporations	...	...	...	...	...	...	...	...	...	...
B Interest	91838	31767	...	57729	2342	92545	32974	...	57103	2468
C Dividends	181	...	...	181	...	184	...	...	184	...
D Net land rent and royalties	...	...	...	...	...	...	...	...	...	...
3 Taxes, fees and contributions	1598205	650865	...	535320	412020	1635537	643062	...	559209	433266
A Indirect taxes	444193	65954	...	378239	...	475215	78174	...	397041	...
B Direct taxes	725656	584039	...	141617	...	709395	563900	...	145495	...
Income	712787	584039	...	128748	...	695725	563900	...	131825	...
Other	12869	...	...	12869	...	13670	...	...	13670	...
C Social security contributions	412020	...	...	...	412020	433266	...	...	...	433266
D Fees, fines and penalties	16336	872	...	15464	...	17661	988	...	16673	...
4 Other current transfers	54085	62575	...	133415	34713	94615	103800	...	154553	39386
A Casualty insurance claims	...	...	...	...	...	...	...	...	...	...
B Transfers from other government subsectors	...	8490	...	133415	34713	...	9185	...	154553	39386
C Transfers from the rest of the world	6213	6213	...	-	...	44346	44346	...	-	...
D Other transfers, except imputed	3210	3210	...	...	...	3163	3163	...	...	...
E Imputed unfunded employee pension and welfare contributions	44662	44662	...	...	...	47106	47106	...	...	...
Total Current Receipts [a]	1744309	745207	...	726645	449075	1822881	779836	...	771049	475120
Disbursements										
1 Government final consumption expenditure	975724	426368	...	549356	9633	1023260	447654	...	575606	10436
2 Property income	278525	217826	...	60699	...	294595	230877	...	63718	...
A Interest	278525	217826	...	60699	...	294595	230877	...	63718	...
B Net land rent and royalties	...	...	...	...	...	...	...	...	...	...
3 Subsidies	27836	27458	...	378	...	29481	29091	...	390	...

3.12 General Government Income and Outlay Account: Total and Subsectors
(Continued)

Million United States dollars

	1990 Total General Government	Central Government	State or Provincial Government	Local Government	Social Security Funds	1991 Total General Government	Central Government	State or Provincial Government	Local Government	Social Security Funds
4 Other current transfers	634969	294728	...	115544	391682	710694	326334	...	143617	433431
A Casualty insurance premiums, net	...	...	...	...	...	...	...	...	...	...
B Transfers to other government subsectors	...	166985	...	...	...	...	192688	...	...	...
C Social security benefits	391682	...	...	...	391682	433431	...	...	...	433431
D Social assistance grants	178914	63370	...	115544	...	213580	69963	...	143617	...
E Unfunded employee pension and welfare benefits b	44612	44612	...	-	...	47156	47156	...	-	...
F Transfers to private non-profit institutions serving households	...	...	...	...	...	...	...	...	...	...
G Other transfers n.e.c.	...	...	...	...	...	...	...	...	...	...
H Transfers to the rest of the world	19761	19761	...	...	...	16527	16527	...	...	...
Net saving	-172745	-221173	...	668	47760	-235149	-254120	...	-12282	31253
Total Current Disbursements and Net Saving a	1744309	745207	...	726645	449075	1822881	779836	...	771049	475120

a) State or provincial government is included in local government.
b) Item 'Unfunded employee pension and welfare benefits' also includes wage accruals less disbursements.

3.13 General Government Capital Accumulation Account: Total and Subsectors

Million United States dollars

	1980 Total General Government	Central Government	State or Provincial Government	Local Government	Social Security Funds	1981 Total General Government	Central Government	State or Provincial Government	Local Government	Social Security Funds
Finance of Gross Accumulation										
1 Gross saving	-3556	-38278	...	47456	-12734	1517	-36416	...	49402	-11469
A Consumption of fixed capital a	40576	8408	...	32168	...	43279	9183	...	34096	...
B Net saving	-44132	-46686	...	15288	-12734	-41762	-45599	...	15306	-11469
2 Capital transfers	9930	7666	...	2264	...	10355	7984	...	2371	...
A From other government subsectors	...	...	...	...	...	...	...	...	...	...
B From other resident sectors	8778	6514	...	2264	...	9262	6891	...	2371	...
C From rest of the world	1152	1152	...	...	...	1093	1093	...	...	...
Finance of Gross Accumulation b	6374	-30612	...	49720	-12734	11872	-28432	...	51773	-11469
Gross Accumulation										
1 Gross capital formation	50016	11560	...	38456	...	52973	14792	...	38181	...
A Increase in stocks c	2763	2532	...	231	...	6033	5885	...	148	...
B Gross fixed capital formation	47253	9028	...	38225	...	46940	8907	...	38033	...
Own account	1500	107	...	1393	...	1527	98	...	1429	...
Other	45753	8921	...	36832	...	45413	8809	...	36604	...
2 Purchases of land, net	2377	342	...	2035	...	2441	222	...	2219	...
3 Purchases of intangible assets, net	-4799	-4376	...	-423	...	-6027	-5706	...	-321	...
4 Capital transfers	-	-	...	...	...	-	-	...	...	...
A To other government subsectors	...	...	...	...	...	...	...	...	...	...
B To other resident sectors	...	...	...	...	...	...	...	...	...	...
C To rest of the world	-	-	...	...	...	-	-	...	...	...
Net lending d	-41220	-38138	...	9652	-12734	-37515	-37740	...	11694	-11469
Gross Accumulation b	6374	-30612	...	49720	-12734	11872	-28432	...	51773	-11469

	1982 Total General Government	Central Government	State or Provincial Government	Local Government	Social Security Funds	1983 Total General Government	Central Government	State or Provincial Government	Local Government	Social Security Funds
Finance of Gross Accumulation										
1 Gross saving	-88102	-95781	...	39308	-31629	-119433	-133340	...	48159	-34252
A Consumption of fixed capital a	44829	10020	...	34809	...	45764	10144	...	35620	...
B Net saving	-132931	-105801	...	4499	-31629	-165197	-143484	...	12539	-34252
2 Capital transfers	10103	7515	...	2588	...	8287	5770	...	2517	...

United States

3.13 General Government Capital Accumulation Account: Total and Subsectors
(Continued)

Million United States dollars

	1982					1983				
	Total General Government	Central Government	State or Provincial Government	Local Government	Social Security Funds	Total General Government	Central Government	State or Provincial Government	Local Government	Social Security Funds
A From other government subsectors	...	...	...	...	...		...	...	...	...
B From other resident sectors	10103	7515	...	2588	...	8287	5770	...	2517	...
C From rest of the world	-	-	...	...	...	-		...	...	...
Finance of Gross Accumulation b	-77999	-88266	...	41896	-31629	-111146	-127570	...	50676	-34252
Gross Accumulation										
1 Gross capital formation	53265	15210	...	38055		57149	17154	...	39995	
A Increase in stocks c	4437	4400	...	37		5975	5606		369	
B Gross fixed capital formation	48828	10810	...	38018	...	51174	11548	...	39626	...
Own account	1566	90	...	1476	...	1585	89	...	1496	...
Other	47262	10720	...	36542	...	49589	11459	...	38130	
2 Purchases of land, net	2391	183	...	2208	...	2443	153	...	2290	
3 Purchases of intangible assets, net	-3980	-3813	...	-167	...	-5184	-5052	...	-132	...
4 Capital transfers	-	-	...	...	...	-	...	...	...	...
A To other government subsectors	...	...	...	...	...	...	...	...	...	...
B To other resident sectors	...	...	...	...	...	...	...	...	...	...
C To rest of the world	-	-	...	...	...	-	...	...	...	...
Net lending d	-129675	-99846	...	1800	-31629	-165554	-139825	...	8523	-34252
Gross Accumulation b	-77999	-88266	...	41896	-31629	-111146	-127570	...	50676	-34252

	1984					1985				
	Total General Government	Central Government	State or Provincial Government	Local Government	Social Security Funds	Total General Government	Central Government	State or Provincial Government	Local Government	Social Security Funds
Finance of Gross Accumulation										
1 Gross saving	-92789	-156369	...	67487	-3907	-101267	-173603	...	68340	3996
A Consumption of fixed capital a	47708	10350	...	37358	...	50809	10593	...	40216	...
B Net saving	-140497	-166719	...	30129	-3907	-152076	-184196	...	28124	3996
2 Capital transfers	8363	5973	...	2390	...	8931	6370	...	2561	...
A From other government subsectors	...	...	...	...	...	...	...	...	...	...
B From other resident sectors	8363	5973	...	2390	...	8931	6370	...	2561	...
C From rest of the world	-	-	...	...	...	-	...	...	...	...
Finance of Gross Accumulation b	-84426	-150396	...	69877	-3907	-92336	-167233	...	70901	3996
Gross Accumulation										
1 Gross capital formation	56530	11950	...	44580	...	70138	19240	...	50898	...
A Increase in stocks c	297	165	...	132	...	3962	3744	...	218	...
B Gross fixed capital formation	56233	11785	...	44448	...	66176	15496	...	50680	...
Own account	1757	84	...	1673	...	1978	85	...	1893	...
Other	54476	11701	...	42775	...	64198	15411	...	48787	...
2 Purchases of land, net	2817	177	...	2640	...	3307	218	...	3089	...
3 Purchases of intangible assets, net	-4239	-4083	...	-156	...	-1483	-1370	...	-113	...
4 Capital transfers	-	-	...	...	...	-	-	...	...	...
A To other government subsectors	...	...	...	...	...	...	...	...	...	...
B To other resident sectors	...	...	...	...	...	...	...	...	...	...
C To rest of the world	-	-	...	...	...	...	...	...	...	...
Net lending d	-139534	-158440	...	22813	-3907	-164298	-185321	...	17027	3996
Gross Accumulation b	-84426	-150396	...	69877	-3907	-92336	-167233	...	70901	3996

	1986					1987				
	Total General Government	Central Government	State or Provincial Government	Local Government	Social Security Funds	Total General Government	Central Government	State or Provincial Government	Local Government	Social Security Funds
Finance of Gross Accumulation										
1 Gross saving	-122554	-199409	...	67411	9444	-89876	-163963	...	56115	17972
A Consumption of fixed capital a	52781	10807	...	41974	...	54477	11035	...	43442	...
B Net saving	-175335	-210216	...	25437	9444	-144353	-174998	...	12673	17972
2 Capital transfers	10011	6963	...	3048	...	10580	7212	...	3368	...

3.13 General Government Capital Accumulation Account: Total and Subsectors
(Continued)

Million United States dollars

	1986					1987				
	Total General Government	Central Government	State or Provincial Government	Local Government	Social Security Funds	Total General Government	Central Government	State or Provincial Government	Local Government	Social Security Funds
A From other government subsectors	...	...	...	...	...	...	...	...	...	...
B From other resident sectors	10011	6963	...	3048	...	10580	7212	...	3368	...
C From rest of the world	-	-	...	...	...	-	-	...	...	...
Finance of Gross Accumulation b	-112543	-192446	...	70459	9444	-79296	-156751	...	59483	17972
Gross Accumulation										
1 Gross capital formation	75575	19441	...	56134	...	74179	13016	...	61163	...
A Increase in stocks c	6508	6933	...	-425	...	-822	-1119	...	297	...
B Gross fixed capital formation	69067	12508	...	56559	...	75001	14135	...	60866	...
Own account	2213	80	...	2133	...	2384	86	...	2298	...
Other	66854	12428	...	54426	...	72617	14049	...	58568	...
2 Purchases of land, net	3879	193	...	3686	...	4428	202	...	4226	...
3 Purchases of intangible assets, net	-3228	-3173	...	-55	...	-655	-600	...	-55	...
4 Capital transfers	-	-	...	...	...	-	-	...	...	...
A To other government subsectors	...	...	...	...	...	...	...	...	...	...
B To other resident sectors	...	...	...	...	...	...	...	...	...	...
C To rest of the world	-	-	...	...	...	-	-	...	...	...
Net lending d	-188769	-208907	...	10694	9444	-157248	-169369	...	-5851	17972
Gross Accumulation b	-112543	-192446	...	70459	9444	-79296	-156751	...	59483	17972

	1988					1989				
	Total General Government	Central Government	State or Provincial Government	Local Government	Social Security Funds	Total General Government	Central Government	State or Provincial Government	Local Government	Social Security Funds
Finance of Gross Accumulation										
1 Gross saving	-86652	-184683	...	55589	42442	-55115	-166506	...	62534	48857
A Consumption of fixed capital a	57840	11457	...	46383	...	62048	11593	...	50455	...
B Net saving	-144492	-196140	...	9206	42442	-117163	-178099	...	12079	48857
2 Capital transfers	11327	7637	...	3690	...	12611	8903	...	3708	...
A From other government subsectors	...	...	...	...	...	...	...	...	...	...
B From other resident sectors	11327	7637	...	3690	...	12611	8903	...	3708	...
C From rest of the world	-	-	...	...	...	-	-	...	...	...
Finance of Gross Accumulation b	-75325	-177046	...	59279	42442	-42504	-157603	...	66242	48857
Gross Accumulation										
1 Gross capital formation	68867	2685	...	66182	...	89045	15196	...	73849	...
A Increase in stocks c	-7914	-8104	...	190	...	1584	1219	...	365	...
B Gross fixed capital formation	76781	10789	...	65992	...	87461	13977	...	73484	...
Own account	2565	89	...	2476	...	2770	87	...	2683	...
Other	74216	10700	...	63516	...	84691	13890	...	70801	...
2 Purchases of land, net	5623	1196	...	4427	...	5112	169	...	4943	...
3 Purchases of intangible assets, net	-1376	-1310	...	-66	...	-917	-856	...	-61	...
4 Capital transfers	-	-	...	...	...	-	-	...	...	...
A To other government subsectors	...	...	...	...	...	...	...	...	...	...
B To other resident sectors	...	...	...	...	...	...	...	...	...	...
C To rest of the world	-	-	...	...	...	-	-	...	...	...
Net lending d	-148439	-179617	...	-11264	42442	-135744	-172112	...	-12489	48857
Gross Accumulation b	-75325	-177046	...	59279	42442	-42504	-157603	...	66242	48857

	1990					1991				
	Total General Government	Central Government	State or Provincial Government	Local Government	Social Security Funds	Total General Government	Central Government	State or Provincial Government	Local Government	Social Security Funds
Finance of Gross Accumulation										
1 Gross saving	-109245	-209179	...	52174	47760	-168727	-241812	...	41832	31253
A Consumption of fixed capital a	63500	11994	...	51506	...	66422	12308	...	54114	...
B Net saving	-172745	-221173	...	668	47760	-235149	-254120	...	-12282	31253
2 Capital transfers	15970	11595	...	4375	...	15703	10977	...	4726	...

United States

3.13 General Government Capital Accumulation Account: Total and Subsectors
(Continued)

Million United States dollars

	1990					1991				
	Total General Government	Central Government	State or Provincial Government	Local Government	Social Security Funds	Total General Government	Central Government	State or Provincial Government	Local Government	Social Security Funds
A From other government subsectors	...	...	...	...	...	...	...	...	...	...
B From other resident sectors	15970	11595	...	4375	...	15703	10977	...	4726	...
C From rest of the world	-	-	...	...	...	-	...	...	...	...
Finance of Gross Accumulation b	-93275	-197584	...	56549	47760	-153024	-230835	...	46558	31253
Gross Accumulation										
1 Gross capital formation	96545	16702	...	79843	...	99729	17437	...	82292	...
A Increase in stocks c	5322	5118	...	204	...	3028	2890	...	138	...
B Gross fixed capital formation	91223	11584	...	79639	...	96701	14547	...	82154	...
Own account	2959	82	...	2877	...	2995	79	...	2916	...
Other	88264	11502	...	76762	...	93706	14468	...	79238	...
2 Purchases of land, net	5682	169	...	5513	...	5919	197	...	5722	...
3 Purchases of intangible assets, net	-1237	-1174	...	-63	...	-568	-500	...	-68	...
4 Capital transfers	-	-	...	...	...	-	...	...	...	...
A To other government subsectors	...	...	...	...	...	...	...	...	...	...
B To other resident sectors	...	...	...	...	...	...	...	...	...	...
C To rest of the world	-	-	...	...	...	-	...	...	...	...
Net lending d	-194265	-213281	...	-28744	47760	-258104	-247969	...	-41388	31253
Gross Accumulation b	-93275	-197584	...	56549	47760	-153024	-230835	...	46558	31253

a) Includes consumption of fixed capital of roads, dams or other forms of construction except structures.
b) State or provincial government is included in local government.
c) Inventories valued at current replacement cost.
d) Net lending of the capital accumulation account and the capital finance account have not been reconciled and are different due to different statistical sources.

3.14 General Government Capital Finance Account, Total and Subsectors

Million United States dollars

	1980					1981				
	Total General Government	Central Government	State or Provincial Government	Local Government	Social Security Funds	Total General Government	Central Government	State or Provincial Government	Local Government	Social Security Funds
Acquisition of Financial Assets										
1 Gold and SDRs	4961	4961	...	-	...	4736	4736	...	-	...
2 Currency and transferable deposits	-3143	-2536	...	-607	...	-1099	375	...	-1474	...
3 Other deposits	-2177	-210	...	-1967	...	2097	-142	...	2239	...
4 Bills and bonds, short term	-4794	-	...	-4794	...	894	-	...	894	...
5 Bonds, long term			...		...			...		...
6 Corporate equity securities	...	...	...	...	...	...	...	...	...	...
7 Short-term loans, n.e.c.	21397	16181	...	5216	...	18271	19107	...	-836	...
8 Long-term loans, n.e.c.	17288	7506	...	9782	...	12621	4939	...	7682	...
9 Other receivables	3778	3778	...	-	...	2542	2542	...	...	...
10 Other assets	-1370	-4353	...	2983	...	-10966	-9107	...	-1859	...
Total Acquisition of Financial Assets a	35940	25327	...	10613	...	29096	22450	...	6646	...
Incurrence of Liabilities										
1 Currency and transferable deposits	...	...	...	...	...	...	...	...	...	...
2 Other deposits	...	...	...	...	...	...	...	...	...	...
3 Bills and bonds, short term	-	...	...	...	...	-	...	...	-	...
4 Bonds, long term	87409	77455	...	9954	...	100629	85587	...	15042	...
5 Short-term loans, n.e.c.	924	-	...	924	...	1238	-	...	1238	...
6 Long-term loans, n.e.c.	-104	-104	...	-	...	-109	-109	...	-	...
7 Other payables	3277	1296	...	1981	...	1598	491	...	1107	...
8 Other liabilities	8187	8187	...	-	...	12334	12334	...	-	...
Total Incurrence of Liabilities	99693	86834	...	12859	...	115690	98303	...	17387	...
Net Lending b	-63753	-61507	...	-2246	...	-86594	-75853	...	-10741	...
Incurrence of Liabilities and Net Worth a	35940	25327	...	10613	...	29096	22450	...	6646	...

3.14 General Government Capital Finance Account, Total and Subsectors

Million United States dollars

	1982					1983				
	Total General Government	Central Government	State or Provincial Government	Local Government	Social Security Funds	Total General Government	Central Government	State or Provincial Government	Local Government	Social Security Funds
Acquisition of Financial Assets										
1 Gold and SDRs	4438	4438	...	-	...	2892	2892	...	-	...
2 Currency and transferable deposits	4874	6429	...	-1555	...	-8943	-8263	...	-680	...
3 Other deposits	4300	472	...	3828	...	-6711	-451	...	-6260	...
4 Bills and bonds, short term	16535	-	...	16535	...	21042	-	...	21042	...
5 Bonds, long term			...		...			...		...
6 Corporate equity securities	...	...	...	...	...	...	...	...	...	...
7 Short-term loans, n.e.c.	15997	13572	...	2425	...	25289	8435	...	16854	...
8 Long-term loans, n.e.c.	7603	2364	...	5239	...	9106	1220	...	7886	...
9 Other receivables	4792	4792	...	-	...	3766	3766	...	-	...
10 Other assets	-7035	-8551	...	1516	...	8728	5957	...	2771	...
Total Acquisition of Financial Assets [a]	51504	23516	...	27988	...	55169	13556	...	41613	...
Incurrence of Liabilities										
1 Currency and transferable deposits	...	...	...	...	...	...	...	...	...	...
2 Other deposits	...	...	...	...	...	...	...	...	...	...
3 Bills and bonds, short term	-	-	...	-	...	-	-	...	-	...
4 Bonds, long term	190837	161424	...	29413	...	218816	185290	...	33526	...
5 Short-term loans, n.e.c.	967	-	...	967	...	1109	-	...	1109	...
6 Long-term loans, n.e.c.	-119	-119	...	-	...	-81	-81	...	-	...
7 Other payables	2850	1912	...	938	...	3744	2952	...	792	...
8 Other liabilities	13734	13734	...	-	...	16720	16720	...	-	...
Total Incurrence of Liabilities	208269	176951	...	31318	...	240308	204881	...	35427	...
Net Lending [b]	-156765	-153435	...	-3330	...	-185139	-191325	...	6186	...
Incurrence of Liabilities and Net Worth [a]	51504	23516	...	27988	...	55169	13556	...	41613	...

	1984					1985				
	Total General Government	Central Government	State or Provincial Government	Local Government	Social Security Funds	Total General Government	Central Government	State or Provincial Government	Local Government	Social Security Funds
Acquisition of Financial Assets										
1 Gold and SDRs	2596	2596	...	-	...	1907	1907	...	-	...
2 Currency and transferable deposits	10294	5263	...	5031	...	14062	12991	...	1071	...
3 Other deposits	761	532	...	229	...	7066	40	...	7026	...
4 Bills and bonds, short term	16292	-	...	16292	...	120581	-	...	120581	...
5 Bonds, long term			...		...			...		...
6 Corporate equity securities	...	...	...	...	...	...	...	...	...	...
7 Short-term loans, n.e.c.	25971	16612	...	9359	...	24102	15923	...	8179	...
8 Long-term loans, n.e.c.	10704	469	...	10235	...	11649	1841	...	9808	...
9 Other receivables	5082	5082	...	-	...	3679	3679	...	-	...
10 Other assets	3043	2048	...	995	...	1271	-2699	...	3970	...
Total Acquisition of Financial Assets [a]	74743	32602	...	42141	...	184317	33682	...	150635	...
Incurrence of Liabilities										
1 Currency and transferable deposits	...	...	...	...	...	...	...	...	...	...
2 Other deposits	...	...	...	...	...	...	...	...	...	...
3 Bills and bonds, short term	-	-	...	-	...	-	-	...	-	...
4 Bonds, long term	225286	197302	...	27984	...	351550	225758	...	125792	...
5 Short-term loans, n.e.c.	7741	-	...	7741	...	8179	-	...	8179	...
6 Long-term loans, n.e.c.	-100	-100	...	-	...	-69	-69	...	-	...
7 Other payables	4253	3271	...	982	...	5713	4630	...	1083	...
8 Other liabilities	23615	23615	...	-	...	20174	20174	...	-	...
Total Incurrence of Liabilities	260795	224088	...	36707	...	385547	250493	...	135054	...
Net Lending [b]	-186052	-191486	...	5434	...	-201230	-216811	...	15581	...
Incurrence of Liabilities and Net Worth [a]	74743	32602	...	42141	...	184317	33682	...	150635	...

United States

Million United States dollars

3.14 General Government Capital Finance Account, Total and Subsectors

	1986					1987				
	Total General Government	Central Government	State or Provincial Government	Local Government	Social Security Funds	Total General Government	Central Government	State or Provincial Government	Local Government	Social Security Funds
Acquisition of Financial Assets										
1 Gold and SDRs	-741	-741	...	-	...	-5363	-5363	...	-	...
2 Currency and transferable deposits	3915	408	...	3507	...	-7305	-8074	...	769	...
3 Other deposits	-4403	185	...	-4588	...	1686	218	...	1468	...
4 Bills and bonds, short term	47080	-	...	47080	...	35159	-	...	35159	...
5 Bonds, long term			...		...			...		...
6 Corporate equity securities	...	...	...	...	...	...	...	...	...	...
7 Short-term loans, n.e.c.	17187	9153	...	8034	...	18131	-2593	...	20724	...
8 Long-term loans, n.e.c.	12315	517	...	11798	...	3404	-5288	...	8692	...
9 Other receivables	-2322	-2322	...	-	...	8341	8341	...	-	...
10 Other assets	3066	318	...	2748	...	40	-442	...	482	...
Total Acquisition of Financial Assets [a]	76097	7518	...	68579	...	54093	-13201	...	67294	...
Incurrence of Liabilities										
1 Currency and transferable deposits	...	...	...	...	...	...	...	...	...	...
2 Other deposits	...	...	...	...	...	...	...	...	...	...
3 Bills and bonds, short term	...	...	...	-	...	-	-	...	-	...
4 Bonds, long term	273785	216017	...	57768	...	229255	143914	...	85341	...
5 Short-term loans, n.e.c.	1437	-	...	1437	...	-2359	-	...	-2359	...
6 Long-term loans, n.e.c.	-36	-36	...	-	...	-15	-15	...	-	...
7 Other payables	11459	9824	...	1635	...	4408	2449	...	1959	...
8 Other liabilities	25025	25025	...	-	...	10274	10274	...	-	...
Total Incurrence of Liabilities	311670	250830	...	60840	...	241563	156622	...	84941	...
Net Lending [b]	-235573	-243312	...	7739	...	-187470	-169823	...	-17647	...
Incurrence of Liabilities and Net Worth [a]	76097	7518	...	68579	...	54093	-13201	...	67294	...

	1988					1989				
	Total General Government	Central Government	State or Provincial Government	Local Government	Social Security Funds	Total General Government	Central Government	State or Provincial Government	Local Government	Social Security Funds
Acquisition of Financial Assets										
1 Gold and SDRs	1391	1391	...	-	...	12680	12680	...	-	...
2 Currency and transferable deposits	11044	8996	...	2048	...	-14739	-14179	...	-560	...
3 Other deposits	-3762	-247	...	-3515	...	-934	-143	...	-791	...
4 Bills and bonds, short term	14661	-	...	14661	...	9156	-	...	9156	...
5 Bonds, long term			...		...			...		...
6 Corporate equity securities	...	...	...	...	...	...	...	...	...	...
7 Short-term loans, n.e.c.	15066	-9594	...	24660	...	8599	-2321	...	10920	...
8 Long-term loans, n.e.c.	2898	-1052	...	3950	...	8002	-758	...	8760	...
9 Other receivables	153	153	...	-	...	3424	3424	...	-	...
10 Other assets	1087	-2548	...	3635	...	15086	11605	...	3481	...
Total Acquisition of Financial Assets [a]	42538	-2901	...	45439	...	41274	10308	...	30966	...
Incurrence of Liabilities										
1 Currency and transferable deposits	...	...	...	...	...	...	...	...	...	...
2 Other deposits	...	...	...	...	...	...	...	...	...	...
3 Bills and bonds, short term	-	-	...	-	...	-	-	...	-	...
4 Bonds, long term	207353	155126	...	52227	...	209761	146353	...	63408	...
5 Short-term loans, n.e.c.	-3298	-	...	-3298	...	-230	-	...	-230	...
6 Long-term loans, n.e.c.	-5	-5	...	-	...	-3	-3	...	-	...
7 Other payables	4529	2285	...	2244	...	11861	9164	...	2697	...
8 Other liabilities	30110	30110	...	-	...	41396	41396	...	-	...
Total Incurrence of Liabilities	238689	187516	...	51173	...	262785	196910	...	65875	...
Net Lending [b]	-196151	-190417	...	-5734	...	-221511	-186602	...	-34909	...
Incurrence of Liabilities and Net Worth [a]	42538	-2901	...	45439	...	41274	10308	...	30966	...

3.14 General Government Capital Finance Account, Total and Subsectors

Million United States dollars

	1990					1991				
	Total General Government	Central Government	State or Provincial Government	Local Government	Social Security Funds	Total General Government	Central Government	State or Provincial Government	Local Government	Social Security Funds
Acquisition of Financial Assets										
1 Gold and SDRs	813	813	...	-	...	-2608	-2608	...	-	...
2 Currency and transferable deposits	3866	4840	...	-974	...	32451	27400	...	5051	...
3 Other deposits	-934	142	...	-1076	...	-7315	148	...	-7463	...
4 Bills and bonds, short term	20885	-	...	20885	...	12882	-	...	12882	...
5 Bonds, long term			...		...			...		...
6 Corporate equity securities	...	...	...	...	...	...	...	...	...	...
7 Short-term loans, n.e.c.	-18131	-1911	...	-16220	...	-20384	-5441	...	-14943	...
8 Long-term loans, n.e.c.	40918	35575	...	5343	...	18812	15429	...	3383	...
9 Other receivables	-1760	-1760	...	-	...	-5020	-5020	...	-	...
10 Other assets	27339	27631	...	-292	...	19582	19687	...	-105	...
Total Acquisition of Financial Assets [a]	72996	65330	...	7666	...	48400	49595	...	-1195	...
Incurrence of Liabilities										
1 Currency and transferable deposits	...	...	...	...	...	...	...	...	...	...
2 Other deposits	...	...	...	...	...	...	...	...	...	...
3 Bills and bonds, short term	-	-	...	-	...	-	-	...	-	...
4 Bonds, long term	294327	246897	...	47430	...	316400	278235	...	38165	...
5 Short-term loans, n.e.c.	878	-	...	878	...	363	-	...	363	...
6 Long-term loans, n.e.c.	-3	-3	...	-	...	-	-	...	-	...
7 Other payables	-3208	-6261	...	3053	...	-3578	-4726	...	1148	...
8 Other liabilities	7390	7390	...	-	...	39917	39917	...	-	...
Total Incurrence of Liabilities	299384	248023	...	51361	...	353102	313426	...	39676	...
Net Lending [b]	-226388	-182693	...	-43695	...	-304702	-263831	...	-40871	...
Incurrence of Liabilities and Net Worth [a]	72996	65330	...	7666	...	48400	49595	...	-1195	...

a) State or provincial government is included in local government.
b) Net lending of the capital accumulation account and the capital finance account have not been reconciled and are different due to different statistical sources.

3.15 General Government Balance Sheet, Total and Subsectors

Million United States dollars

	1980					1981				
	Total General Government	Central Government	State or Provincial Government	Local Government	Social Security Funds	Total General Government	Central Government	State or Provincial Government	Local Government	Social Security Funds
Assets										
Non-financial assets	...	...	...	...		...	...	...	...	...
Financial assets	494859	247911	...	246948	...	522729	269135	...	253594	...
1 Gold and SDRs	29750	29750	...	-	...	33134	33134	...	-	...
2 Currency and transferable deposits	28614	16176	...	12438	...	28331	17367	...	10964	...
3 Other deposits	59623	797	...	58826	...	61720	655	...	61065	...
4 Bills and bonds, short term	108701	-	...	108701	...	109595	-	...	109595	...
5 Bonds, long term			...		...			...		...
7 Short term loans, n.e.c.	135716	121719	...	13997	...	153902	140741	...	13161	...
8 Long term loans, n.e.c.	75430	42073	...	33357	...	88051	47012	...	41039	...
9 Other receivables	15091	15091	...	-	...	17633	17633	...	-	...
10 Other assets	41934	22305	...	19629	...	30363	12593	...	17770	...
Total Assets	...	...	...	...	...	...	...	...	...	...
Liabilities and Net Worth										
Liabilities	1183897	855394	...	328503	...	1298538	952648	...	345890	...
1 Currency and transferable deposits	...	...	...	...	...	...	...	...	...	...
2 Other deposits	...	...	...	...	...	...	...	...	...	...
3 Other deposits	-	-	...	-	...	-	-	...	-	...
4 Bonds, long term	1037279	734451	...	302828	...	1137908	820038	...	317870	...
5 Short term loans, n.e.c.	7586	-	...	7586	...	8824	-	...	8824	...
6 Long term loans, n.e.c.	550	550	...	-	...	441	441	...	-	...
7 Other payables	39396	21307	...	18089	...	40994	21798	...	19196	...
8 Other liabilities	99086	99086	...	-	...	110371	110371	...	-	...
Net worth	...	...	...	...	...	...	...	...	...	...
Total Liabilities and Net Worth	...	...	...	...	...	...	...	...	...	...

United States

3.15 General Government Balance Sheet, Total and Subsectors

Million United States dollars

1982 / 1983

	1982					1983				
	Total General Government	Central Government	State or Provincial Government	Local Government	Social Security Funds	Total General Government	Central Government	State or Provincial Government	Local Government	Social Security Funds
Assets										
Non-financial assets	...	...	...	...	...	...	...	...	...	...
Financial assets	581996	300414	...	281582	...	633157	309962	...	323195	...
1 Gold and SDRs	36376	36376	...	-	...	38286	38286	...	-	...
2 Currency and transferable deposits	33922	24513	...	9409	...	25173	16444	...	8729	...
3 Other deposits	66020	1127	...	64893	...	59309	676	...	58633	...
4 Bills and bonds, short term	126130	-	...	126130	...	147172	-	...	147172	...
5 Bonds, long term			...		...			...		...
7 Short term loans, n.e.c.	169811	154225	...	15586	...	195074	162634	...	32440	...
8 Long term loans, n.e.c.	95654	49376	...	46278	...	104760	50596	...	54164	...
9 Other receivables	22425	22425	...	-	...	26191	26191	...	-	...
10 Other assets	31658	12372	...	19286	...	37192	15135	...	22057	...
Total Assets	...	...	...	...	...	...	...	...	...	...
Liabilities and Net Worth										
Liabilities	1506663	1129455	...	377208	...	1744948	1332313	...	412635	...
1 Currency and transferable deposits	...	...	...	...	...	...	...	...	...	...
2 Other deposits	...	...	...	...	...	...	...	...	...	...
3 Other deposits	-	-	...	-	...	-	-	...	-	...
4 Bonds, long term	1328745	981462	...	347283	...	1547561	1166752	...	380809	...
5 Short term loans, n.e.c.	9791	-	...	9791	...	10900	-	...	10900	...
6 Long term loans, n.e.c.	322	322	...	-	...	241	241	...	-	...
7 Other payables	43850	23716	...	20134	...	47584	26658	...	20926	...
8 Other liabilities	123955	123955	...	-	...	138662	138662	...	-	...
Net worth	...	...	...	...	...	...	...	...	...	...
Total Liabilities and Net Worth	...	...	...	...	...	...	...	...	...	...

1984 / 1985

	1984					1985				
	Total General Government	Central Government	State or Provincial Government	Local Government	Social Security Funds	Total General Government	Central Government	State or Provincial Government	Local Government	Social Security Funds
Assets										
Non-financial assets	...	...	...	...	...	...	...	...	...	...
Financial assets	712299	346963	...	365336	...	906920	390949	...	515971	...
1 Gold and SDRs	39607	39607	...	-	...	44429	44429	...	-	...
2 Currency and transferable deposits	35588	21828	...	13760	...	48804	33973	...	14831	...
3 Other deposits	60070	1208	...	58862	...	67136	1248	...	65888	...
4 Bills and bonds, short term	163464	-	...	163464	...	284045	-	...	284045	...
5 Bonds, long term			...		...			...		...
7 Short term loans, n.e.c.	220459	178660	...	41799	...	245271	195293	...	49978	...
8 Long term loans, n.e.c.	115862	51463	...	64399	...	127511	53304	...	74207	...
9 Other receivables	31273	31273	...	-	...	34952	34952	...	-	...
10 Other assets	45976	22924	...	23052	...	54772	27750	...	27022	...
Total Assets	...	...	...	...	...	...	...	...	...	...
Liabilities and Net Worth										
Liabilities	2000868	1551526	...	449342	...	2385807	1801411	...	584396	...
1 Currency and transferable deposits	...	...	...	...	...	...	...	...	...	...
2 Other deposits	...	...	...	...	...	...	...	...	...	...
3 Other deposits	-	-	...	-	...	-	-	...	-	...
4 Bonds, long term	1772847	1364054	...	408793	...	2124397	1589812	...	534585	...
5 Short term loans, n.e.c.	18641	-	...	18641	...	26820	-	...	26820	...
6 Long term loans, n.e.c.	141	141	...	-	...	72	72	...	-	...
7 Other payables	51838	29930	...	21908	...	57551	34560	...	22991	...
8 Other liabilities	157401	157401	...	-	...	176967	176967	...	-	...
Net worth	...	...	...	...	...	...	...	...	...	...
Total Liabilities and Net Worth	...	...	...	...	...	...	...	...	...	...

3.15 General Government Balance Sheet, Total and Subsectors

Million United States dollars

	1986					1987				
	Total General Government	Central Government	State or Provincial Government	Local Government	Social Security Funds	Total General Government	Central Government	State or Provincial Government	Local Government	Social Security Funds
Assets										
Non-financial assets	...	...	...	...	...	...	...	...	...	...
Financial assets	989248	404698	...	584550	...	1041662	389818	...	651844	...
1 Gold and SDRs	47338	47338	...	-	...	48412	48412	...	-	...
2 Currency and transferable deposits	51178	32840	...	18338	...	40517	21410	...	19107	...
3 Other deposits	62733	1433	...	61300	...	68208	1651	...	66557	...
4 Bills and bonds, short term	331125	-	...	331125	...	362495	-	...	362495	...
5 Bonds, long term			...		...			...		...
7 Short term loans, n.e.c.	258821	200809	...	58012	...	269518	190782	...	78736	...
8 Long term loans, n.e.c.	140362	54357	...	86005	...	143766	49069	...	94697	...
9 Other receivables	32630	32630	...	-	...	40971	40971	...	-	...
10 Other assets	65061	35291	...	29770	...	67775	37523	...	30252	...
Total Assets	...	...	...	...	...	...	...	...	...	...
Liabilities and Net Worth										
Liabilities	2694312	2049076	...	645236	...	2946412	2216235	...	730177	...
1 Currency and transferable deposits	...	...	...	...	...	...	...	...	...	...
2 Other deposits	...	...	...	...	...	...	...	...	...	...
3 Other deposits	-	-	...	-	...	-	-	...	...	...
4 Bonds, long term	2399182	1805829	...	593353	...	2628437	1949743	...	678694	...
5 Short term loans, n.e.c.	27257	-	...	27257	...	24898	-	...	24898	...
6 Long term loans, n.e.c.	36	36	...	-	...	21	21	...	-	...
7 Other payables	69010	44384	...	24626	...	73418	46833	...	26585	...
8 Other liabilities	198827	198827	...	-	...	219638	219638	...	...	...
Net worth	...	...	...	...	...	...	...	...	...	...
Total Liabilities and Net Worth	...	...	...	...	...	...	...	...	...	...

	1988					1989				
	Total General Government	Central Government	State or Provincial Government	Local Government	Social Security Funds	Total General Government	Central Government	State or Provincial Government	Local Government	Social Security Funds
Assets										
Non-financial assets	...	...	...	...	...	...	...	...	...	...
Financial assets	1076981	379698	...	697283	...	1115872	387623	...	728249	...
1 Gold and SDRs	46971	46971	...	-	...	51038	51038	...	-	...
2 Currency and transferable deposits	53273	32118	...	21155	...	46702	26107	...	20595	...
3 Other deposits	64446	1404	...	63042	...	63512	1261	...	62251	...
4 Bills and bonds, short term	377156	-	...	377156	...	386312	-	...	386312	...
5 Bonds, long term			...		...			...		...
7 Short term loans, n.e.c.	268569	165173	...	103396	...	272130	157814	...	114316	...
8 Long term loans, n.e.c.	146664	48017	...	98647	...	154666	47259	...	107407	...
9 Other receivables	41124	41124	...	-	...	44548	44548	...	-	...
10 Other assets	78778	44891	...	33887	...	96964	59596	...	37368	...
Total Assets	...	...	...	...	...	...	...	...	...	...
Liabilities and Net Worth										
Liabilities	3180115	2398765	...	781350	...	3428690	2581465	...	847225	...
1 Currency and transferable deposits	...	...	...	...	...	...	...	...	...	...
2 Other deposits	...	...	...	...	...	...	...	...	...	...
3 Other deposits	-	-	...	-	...	-	-	...	...	...
4 Bonds, long term	2848390	2104869	...	743521	...	3058151	2251222	...	806929	...
5 Short term loans, n.e.c.	9000	-	...	9000	...	8770	-	...	8770	...
6 Long term loans, n.e.c.	16	16	...	-	...	13	13	...	-	...
7 Other payables	77947	49118	...	28829	...	89808	58282	...	31526	...
8 Other liabilities	244762	244762	...	-	...	271948	271948	...	-	...
Net worth	...	...	...	...	...	...	...	...	...	...
Total Liabilities and Net Worth	...	...	...	...	...	...	...	...	...	...

United States

3.15 General Government Balance Sheet, Total and Subsectors

Million United States dollars

	1990					1991				
	Total General Government	Central Government	State or Provincial Government	Local Government	Social Security Funds	Total General Government	Central Government	State or Provincial Government	Local Government	Social Security Funds
Assets										
Non-financial assets	...	...	...	...	...	...	...	...	...	...
Financial assets	1195748	459833	...	735915	...	1252047	517327	...	734720	...
1 Gold and SDRs	58984	58984	...	-	...	59223	59223	...	-	...
2 Currency and transferable deposits	45038	25417	...	19621	...	74762	50090	...	24672	...
3 Other deposits	62578	1403	...	61175	...	55263	1551	...	53712	...
4 Bills and bonds, short term	410067	-	...	410067	...	422949	-	...	422949	...
5 Bonds, long term								...		
7 Short term loans, n.e.c.	253977	155881	...	98096	...	231032	147879	...	83153	...
8 Long term loans, n.e.c.	192740	82860	...	109880	...	211552	98289	...	113263	...
9 Other receivables	42788	42788	...	-	...	37768	37768	...	-	...
10 Other assets	129576	92500	...	37076	...	159498	122527	...	36971	...
Total Assets	...	...	...	...	...	...	...	...	...	...
Liabilities and Net Worth										
Liabilities	3745079	2846493	...	898586	...	4083160	3144898	...	938262	...
1 Currency and transferable deposits	...	...	...	...	...	...	...	...	...	...
2 Other deposits	...	...	...	...	...	...	...	...	...	...
3 Other deposits	-	-	...	...	...	...	...	...	...	...
4 Bonds, long term	3352478	2498119	...	854359	...	3668878	2776354	...	892524	...
5 Short term loans, n.e.c.	9648	-	...	9648	...	10011	-	...	10011	...
6 Long term loans, n.e.c.	10	10	...	-	...	10	10	...	-	...
7 Other payables	86600	52021	...	34579	...	83022	47295	...	35727	...
8 Other liabilities	296343	296343	...	-	...	321239	321239	...	-	...
Net worth	...	...	...	...	...	...	...	...	...	...
Total Liabilities and Net Worth	...	...	...	...	...	...	...	...	...	...

3.22 Corporate and Quasi-Corporate Enterprise Income and Outlay Account: Total and Sectors

Million United States dollars

	1980			1981			1982			1983		
	TOTAL	Non-Financial	Financial	TOTAL	Non-Financial	Financial	TOTAL	Non-Financial	Financial	TOTAL	Non-Financial	Financial
Receipts												
1 Operating surplus	235161	212684	22477	259686	243500	16186	239016	227933	11083	294800	271081	23719
2 Property and entrepreneurial income	499437	111387	388050	640292	136459	503833	707891	146822	561069	693183	140600	552583
A Withdrawals from quasi-corporate enterprises	...	...	...	...	...	...	...	...	...	...	...	...
B Interest	446942	77736	369206	588355	103710	484645	647336	108195	539141	636023	105083	530940
C Dividends	52495	33651	18844	51937	32749	19188	60555	38627	21928	57160	35517	21643
D Net land rent and royalties	...	...	...	...	...	...	...	...	...	...	...	...
3 Current transfers	5369	5369	...	6063	6063	...	6639	6639	...	7120	7120	...
A Casualty insurance claims	...	...	...	...	...	...	...	...	...	...	...	...
B Casualty insurance premiums, net, due to be received by insurance companies												
C Current transfers from the rest of the world	...	...	...	...	...	...	...	...	...	...	...	...
D Other transfers except imputed	1053	1053	...	1096	1096	...	1175	1175	...	1237	1237	...
E Imputed unfunded employee pension and welfare contributions	4316	4316	...	4967	4967	...	5464	5464	...	5883	5883	...
Total Current Receipts a	739967	329440	410527	906041	386022	520019	953546	381394	572152	995103	418801	576302
Disbursements												
1 Property and entrepreneurial income	612845	228961	383884	781646	279020	502626	856854	302093	554761	845867	291776	554091
A Withdrawals from quasi-corporations	...	...	...	...	...	...	...	...	...	...	...	...
B Interest	503222	133560	369662	662797	177834	484963	729238	190989	538249	710884	178138	532746

3.22 Corporate and Quasi-Corporate Enterprise Income and Outlay Account: Total and Sectors
(Continued)

Million United States dollars

	1980			1981			1982			1983		
	TOTAL	Non-Financial	Financial	TOTAL	Non-Financial	Financial	TOTAL	Non-Financial	Financial	TOTAL	Non-Financial	Financial
C Dividends	109623	95401	14222	118849	101186	17663	127616	111104	16512	134983	113638	21345
D Net land rent and royalties	...	...	...	...	...	...	...	...	...	...	...	...
2 Direct taxes and other current transfers n.e.c. to general government	84785	67006	17779	81143	63887	17256	63081	46258	16823	77241	59437	17804
A Direct taxes	84785	67006	17779	81143	63887	17256	63081	46258	16823	77241	59437	17804
On income	84785	67006	17779	81143	63887	17256	63081	46258	16823	77241	59437	17804
Other	...	...	...	...	...	...	...	...	...	...	...	...
B Fines, fees, penalties and other current transfers n.e.c.	...	...	...	...	...	...	...	...	...	...	...	...
3 Other current transfers	14418	12913	1505	17086	15302	1784	19371	17227	2144	20997	18683	2314
A Casualty insurance premiums, net	...	...	...	...	...	...	...	...	...	...	...	...
B Casualty insurance claims liability of insurance companies	...	...	...	...	...	...	...	...	...	...	...	...
C Transfers to private non-profit institutions	2359	2124	235	2514	2305	209	2906	2692	214	3627	3319	308
D Unfunded employee pension and welfare benefits	4316	4316	...	4967	4967	...	5464	5464	...	5883	5883	...
E Social assistance grants	935	406	529	1311	616	695	1805	923	882	1841	964	877
F Other transfers n.e.c.	4403	3789	614	5098	4384	714	5624	4835	789	5861	5036	825
G Transfers to the rest of the world	2405	2278	127	3196	3030	166	3572	3313	259	3785	3481	304
Net saving	27919	20560	7359	26166	27813	-1647	14240	15816	-1576	50998	48905	2093
Total Current Disbursements and Net Saving [a]	739967	329440	410527	906041	386022	520019	953546	381394	572152	995103	418801	576302

	1984			1985			1986			1987		
	TOTAL	Non-Financial	Financial	TOTAL	Non-Financial	Financial	TOTAL	Non-Financial	Financial	TOTAL	Non-Financial	Financial
						Receipts						
1 Operating surplus	357790	335511	22279	372883	338909	33974	367905	325302	42603	414922	368485	46437
2 Property and entrepreneurial income	794686	160544	634142	861813	177128	684685	901590	186717	714873	960546	192278	768268
A Withdrawals from quasi-corporate enterprises	...	...	...	...	...	...	...	...	...	...	...	...
B Interest	732724	123152	609572	798354	141544	656810	832049	147271	684778	890231	152255	737976
C Dividends	61962	37392	24570	63459	35584	27875	69541	39446	30095	70315	40023	30292
D Net land rent and royalties	...	...	...	...	...	...	...	...	...	...	...	...
3 Current transfers	7321	7321	...	8140	8140	...	8217	8217	...	9374	9374	...
A Casualty insurance claims	...	...	...	...	...	...	...	...	...	...	...	...
B Casualty insurance premiums, net, due to be received by insurance companies	...	...	...	...	...	...	...	...	...	...	...	...
C Current transfers from the rest of the world	...	...	...	...	...	...	...	...	...	...	...	...
D Other transfers except imputed	1275	1275	...	1376	1376	...	1338	1338	...	1409	1409	...
E Imputed unfunded employee pension and welfare contributions	6046	6046	...	6764	6764	...	6879	6879	...	7965	7965	...
Total Current Receipts [a]	1159797	503376	656421	1242836	524177	718659	1277712	520236	757476	1384842	570137	814705
						Disbursements						
1 Property and entrepreneurial income	955742	319336	636406	1026559	333140	693419	1084144	349312	734832	1138022	349669	788353
A Withdrawals from quasi-corporations	...	...	...	...	...	...	...	...	...	...	...	...
B Interest	814982	200993	613989	875224	211999	663225	909952	216777	693175	967348	217038	750310
C Dividends	140760	118343	22417	151335	121141	30194	174192	132535	41657	170674	132631	38043
D Net land rent and royalties	...	...	...	...	...	...	...	...	...	...	...	...
2 Direct taxes and other current transfers n.e.c. to general government	94037	73650	20387	96512	69934	26578	106487	75580	30907	127089	93450	33639
A Direct taxes	94037	73650	20387	96512	69934	26578	106487	75580	30907	127089	93450	33639
On income	94037	73650	20387	96512	69934	26578	106487	75580	30907	127089	93450	33639
Other	...	...	...	...	...	...	...	...	...	...	...	...
B Fines, fees, penalties and other current transfers n.e.c.	...	...	...	...	...	...	...	...	...	...	...	...

3.22 Corporate and Quasi-Corporate Enterprise Income and Outlay Account: Total and Sectors
(Continued)

Million United States dollars

	1984			1985			1986			1987		
	TOTAL	Non-Financial	Financial	TOTAL	Non-Financial	Financial	TOTAL	Non-Financial	Financial	TOTAL	Non-Financial	Financial
3 Other current transfers	23287	20694	2593	25598	22725	2873	28594	25031	3563	29555	25946	3609
A Casualty insurance premiums, net	...	...	...	...	...	...	...	...	...	...	...	...
B Casualty insurance claims liability of insurance companies	...	...	...	...	...	...	...	...	...	...	...	...
C Transfers to private non-profit institutions	4059	3706	353	4472	4090	382	5179	4582	597	4980	4383	597
D Unfunded employee pension and welfare benefits	6046	6046	...	6764	6764	...	6879	6879	...	7965	7965	...
E Social assistance grants	2081	1136	945	2862	1751	1111	3126	1911	1215	3207	1950	1257
F Other transfers n.e.c.	7211	6194	1017	8291	7120	1171	9903	8504	1399	10217	8770	1447
G Transfers to the rest of the world	3890	3612	278	3209	3000	209	3507	3155	352	3186	2878	308
Net saving	86731	89696	-2965	94167	98378	-4211	58487	70313	-11826	90176	101072	-10896
Total Current Disbursements and Net Saving a	1159797	503376	656421	1242836	524177	718659	1277712	520236	757476	1384842	570137	814705

	1988			1989			1990			1991		
	TOTAL	Non-Financial	Financial	TOTAL	Non-Financial	Financial	TOTAL	Non-Financial	Financial	TOTAL	Non-Financial	Financial
						Receipts						
1 Operating surplus	461979	419712	42267	488648	436548	52100	481365	434890	46475	452831	412573	40258
2 Property and entrepreneurial income	1115977	230032	885945	1314606	266787	1047819	1319848	274703	1045145	1262393	266741	995652
A Withdrawals from quasi-corporate enterprises	...	...	...	...	...	...	...	...	...	...	...	...
B Interest	1016424	172047	844377	1206614	205632	1000982	1212990	217330	995660	1158152	215095	943057
C Dividends	99553	57985	41568	107992	61155	46837	106858	57373	49485	104241	51646	52595
D Net land rent and royalties	...	...	...	...	...	...	...	...	...	...	...	...
3 Current transfers	10470	10470	...	10021	10021	...	10596	10596	...	11913	11913	...
A Casualty insurance claims	...	...	...	...	...	...	...	...	...	...	...	...
B Casualty insurance premiums, net, due to be received by insurance companies	...	...	...	...	...	...	...	...	...	...	...	...
C Current transfers from the rest of the world	...	...	...	...	...	...	...	...	...	...	...	...
D Other transfers except imputed	1426	1426	...	1310	1310	...	1322	1322	...	1422	1422	...
E Imputed unfunded employee pension and welfare contributions	9044	9044	...	8711	8711	...	9274	9274	...	10491	10491	...
Total Current Receipts a	1588426	660214	928212	1813275	713356	1099919	1811809	720189	1091620	1727137	691227	1035910
						Disbursements						
1 Property and entrepreneurial income	1300703	414191	886512	1543670	490923	1052747	1558147	508881	1049266	1477793	486840	990953
A Withdrawals from quasi-corporations	...	...	...	...	...	...	...	...	...	...	...	...
B Interest	1092704	245036	847668	1309189	301289	1007900	1310956	312918	998038	1236566	299661	936905
C Dividends	207999	169155	38844	234481	189634	44847	247191	195963	51228	241227	187179	54048
D Net land rent and royalties	...	...	...	...	...	...	...	...	...	...	...	...
2 Direct taxes and other current transfers n.e.c. to general government	137014	101748	35266	141309	99535	41774	136681	92769	43912	124041	81137	42904
A Direct taxes	137014	101748	35266	141309	99535	41774	136681	92769	43912	124041	81137	42904
On income	137014	101748	35266	141309	99535	41774	136681	92769	43912	124041	81137	42904
Other	...	...	...	...	...	...	...	...	...	...	...	...
B Fines, fees, penalties and other current transfers n.e.c.	...	...	...	...	...	...	...	...	...	...	...	...

3.22 Corporate and Quasi-Corporate Enterprise Income and Outlay Account: Total and Sectors
(Continued)

Million United States dollars

	1988			1989			1990			1991		
	TOTAL	Non-Financial	Financial	TOTAL	Non-Financial	Financial	TOTAL	Non-Financial	Financial	TOTAL	Non-Financial	Financial
3 Other current transfers	32353	28570	3783	33310	29313	3997	33586	29515	4071	36256	31906	4350
A Casualty insurance premiums, net	...	...	...	...	...	...	...	...	...	...	...	...
B Casualty insurance claims liability of insurance companies	...	...	...	...	...	...	...	...	...	...	...	...
C Transfers to private non-profit institutions	4893	4279	614	4893	4240	653	4637	4011	626	5065	4383	682
D Unfunded employee pension and welfare benefits	9044	9044	...	8711	8711	...	9274	9274	...	10491	10491	...
E Social assistance grants	3354	2025	1329	3251	1841	...	3347	1759	1588	4080	2308	1772
F Other transfers n.e.c.	10265	8800	1465	11011	9463	1548	11103	9543	1560	11348	9752	1596
G Transfers to the rest of the world	4797	4422	375	5444	5058	386	5225	4928	297	5272	4972	300
Net saving	118356	115705	2651	94986	93585	1401	83395	89024	-5629	89047	91344	-2297
Total Current Disbursements and Net Saving a	1588426	660214	928212	1813275	713356	1099919	1811809	720189	1091620	1727137	691227	1035910

a) This table, Corporate and Quasi-corporate Enterprises, does not include private quasi-corporate enterprises.

3.23 Corporate and Quasi-Corporate Enterprise Capital Accumulation Account: Total and Sectors

Million United States dollars

	1980			1981			1982			1983		
	TOTAL	Non-Financial	Financial	TOTAL	Non-Financial	Financial	TOTAL	Non-Financial	Financial	TOTAL	Non-Financial	Financial
Finance of Gross Accumulation												
1 Gross saving	225106	207427	17679	258865	248139	10726	271990	259268	12722	323227	305535	17692
A Consumption of fixed capital	197187	186867	10320	232699	220326	12373	257750	243452	14298	272229	256630	15599
B Net saving	27919	20560	7359	26166	27813	-1647	14240	15816	-1576	50998	48905	2093
2 Capital transfers	...	...	...	...	...	...	...	...	...	...	...	...
Finance of Gross Accumulation a	225106	207427	17679	258865	248139	10726	271990	259268	12722	323227	305535	17692
Gross Accumulation												
1 Gross capital formation	294870	272571	22299	359269	332831	26438	328058	300219	27839	346793	315228	31565
A Increase in stocks b	-2446	-2446	-	15602	15602	-	-21173	-21173	-	8605	8605	-
B Gross fixed capital formation	297316	275017	22299	343667	317229	26438	349231	321392	27839	338188	306623	31565
2 Purchases of land, net	-2377	-2377	...	-2441	-2441	...	-2391	-2391	...	-2443	-2443	...
3 Purchases of intangible assets, net	4799	4799	...	6027	6027	...	3980	3980	...	5184	5184	...
4 Capital transfers	...	...	...	...	...	...	...	...	...	...	...	...
Net lending c	-72186	-67566	-4620	-103990	-88278	-15712	-57657	-42540	-15117	-26307	-12434	-13873
Gross Accumulation ad	225106	207427	17679	258865	248139	10726	271990	259268	12722	323227	305535	17692

	1984			1985			1986			1987		
	TOTAL	Non-Financial	Financial	TOTAL	Non-Financial	Financial	TOTAL	Non-Financial	Financial	TOTAL	Non-Financial	Financial
Finance of Gross Accumulation												
1 Gross saving	367822	353073	14749	388202	372623	15579	369664	358691	10973	415609	400194	15415
A Consumption of fixed capital	281091	263377	17714	294035	274245	19790	311177	288378	22799	325433	299122	26311
B Net saving	86731	89696	-2965	94167	98378	-4211	58487	70313	-11826	90176	101072	-10896
2 Capital transfers	...	...	...	...	...	...	...	...	...	...	...	...
Finance of Gross Accumulation a	367822	353073	14749	388202	372623	15579	369664	358691	10973	415609	400194	15415
Gross Accumulation												
1 Gross capital formation	455479	415045	40434	440826	396450	44376	424502	374105	50397	448443	394276	54167
A Increase in stocks b	62160	62160	-	16642	16642	-	9117	9117	-	30640	30640	-
B Gross fixed capital formation	393319	352885	40434	424184	379808	44376	415385	364988	50397	417803	363636	54167
2 Purchases of land, net	-2817	-2817	...	-3307	-3307	...	-3879	-3879	...	-4428	-4428	...
3 Purchases of intangible assets, net	4239	4239	...	1483	1483	...	3228	3228	...	655	655	...
4 Capital transfers	...	...	...	...	...	...	...	...	...	...	...	...
Net lending c	-89079	-63394	-25685	-50800	-22003	-28797	-54187	-14763	-39424	-29061	9691	-38752
Gross Accumulation ad	367822	353073	14749	388202	372623	15579	369664	358691	10973	415609	400194	15415

United States

3.23 Corporate and Quasi-Corporate Enterprise Capital Accumulation Account: Total and Sectors

Million United States dollars

	1988			1989			1990			1991		
	TOTAL	Non-Financial	Financial	TOTAL	Non-Financial	Financial	TOTAL	Non-Financial	Financial	TOTAL	Non-Financial	Financial
Finance of Gross Accumulation												
1 Gross saving	464933	432112	32821	467579	431146	36433	472901	439571	33330	494204	454732	39472
A Consumption of fixed capital	346577	316407	30170	372593	337561	35032	389506	350547	38959	405157	363388	41769
B Net saving	118356	115705	2651	94986	93585	1401	83395	89024	-5629	89047	91344	-2297
2 Capital transfers	...	...	...	...	...	...	...	...	...	...	...	...
Finance of Gross Accumulation a	464933	432112	32821	467579	431146	36433	472901	439571	33330	494204	454732	39472
Gross Accumulation												
1 Gross capital formation	484349	424902	59447	503311	436382	66929	492481	427866	64615	454865	394589	60276
A Increase in stocks b	26551	26551	-	30320	30320	-	3864	3864	-	-9668	-9668	-
B Gross fixed capital formation	457798	398351	59447	472991	406062	66929	488617	424002	64615	464533	404257	60276
2 Purchases of land, net	-5623	-5623	...	-5112	-5112	...	-5682	-5682	...	-5919	-5919	...
3 Purchases of intangible assets, net	1376	1376	...	917	917	...	1237	1237	...	568	568	...
4 Capital transfers	...	...	...	...	...	...	...	...	...	44690	65494	-20804
Net lending c	-15169	11457	-26626	-31537	-1041	-30496	-15135	16150	-31285	494204	454732	39472
Gross Accumulation ad	464933	432112	32821	467579	431146	36433	472901	439571	33330			

a) This table, Corporate and Quasi-corporate Enterprises, does not include private quasi-corporate enterprises.
b) Inventories valued at current replacement cost.
c) Net lending of the capital accumulation account and the capital finance account have not been reconciled and are different due to different statistical sources.
d)

3.24 Corporate and Quasi-Corporate Enterprise Capital Finance Account: Total and Sectors

Million United States dollars

	1980			1981			1982			1983		
	TOTAL	Non-Financial	Financial	TOTAL	Non-Financial	Financial	TOTAL	Non-Financial	Financial	TOTAL	Non-Financial	Financial
Acquisition of Financial Assets												
1 Gold and SDRs	-43	-	-43	10	-	10	6	-	6	-45	-	-45
2 Currency and transferable deposits	9782	6762	3020	-7407	-9698	2291	13083	5879	7204	9174	8691	483
3 Other deposits	32744	11288	21456	62623	19670	42953	34444	11474	22970	4893	6865	-1972
4 Bills and bonds, short term	165773	-1940	167713	211383	8962	202421	249565	20264	229301	243480	13333	230147
5 Bonds, long term												
6 Corporate equity securities	62532	22194	40338	55845	11477	44368	49433	10756	38677	66991	8151	58840
7 Short term loans, n.e.c.	89313	10005	79308	133972	5785	128187	98969	9110	89859	96595	10155	86440
8 Long term loans, n.e.c.	98150	-	98150	81488	-	81488	71310	-	71310	179203	-	179203
9 Trade credits and advances	50006	48022	1984	26918	24269	2649	-13372	-15497	2125	53653	51656	1997
10 Other receivables	...	...	...	...	...	...	...	...	...	80529	21557	58972
11 Other assets	21132	719	20413	50411	35449	14962	87978	5571	82407			
Total Acquisition of Financial Assets	529389	97050	432339	615243	95914	519329	591416	47557	543859	734473	120408	614065
Incurrence of Liabilities												
1 Currency and transferable deposits	17058	-	17058	27904	-	27904	37659	-	37659	40379	-	40379
2 Other deposits	173500	-	173500	218901	-	218901	195970	-	195970	163113	-	163113
3 Bills and bonds, short term	20127	7202	12925	51748	19068	32680	3021	-6907	9928	27424	6136	21288
4 Bonds, long term	92875	38519	54356	92041	36192	55849	118013	33809	84204	118579	25414	93165
5 Corporate equity securities	31261	23563	7698	16445	7124	9321	28209	11363	16846	63647	29451	34196
6 Short-term loans, n.e.c.	64289	33409	30880	96086	48147	47939	96248	61618	34630	34024	29357	4667
7 Long-term loans, n.e.c.	-13015	-12975	-40	7941	7921	20	-36329	-36442	113	-802	-827	25
8 Net equity of households in life insurance and pension fund reserves	109710	-	109710	107871	-	107871	141563	-	141563	166466	-	166466
9 Proprietors' net additions to the accumulation of quasi-corporations	...	...	...	...	...	...	...	...	...	...	...	...
10 Trade credit and advances	37994	37994	-	28622	28622	-	4914	4914	-	38026	37003	1023
11 Other accounts payable	...	...	...	...	...	...	...	...	...	...	...	...
12 Other liabilities	20977	2878	18099	42933	-4000	46933	30955	732	30223	102415	4488	97927
Total Incurrence of Liabilities	554776	130590	424186	690492	143074	547418	620223	69087	551136	753271	131022	622249
Net Lending a	-25387	-33540	8153	-75249	-47160	-28089	-28807	-21530	-7277	-18798	-10614	-8184
Incurrence of Liabilities and Net Lending	529389	97050	432339	615243	95914	519329	591416	47557	543859	734473	120408	614065

3.24 Corporate and Quasi-Corporate Enterprise Capital Finance Account: Total and Sectors

Million United States dollars

	1984			1985			1986			1987		
	TOTAL	Non-Financial	Financial	TOTAL	Non-Financial	Financial	TOTAL	Non-Financial	Financial	TOTAL	Non-Financial	Financial
Acquisition of Financial Assets												
1 Gold and SDRs	-43	-	-43	16	-	16	-42	-	-42	8	-	8
2 Currency and transferable deposits	14926	12682	2244	31825	19418	12407	27719	18789	8930	5760	9648	-3888
3 Other deposits	18876	3549	15327	28815	2629	26186	45479	16747	28732	-1364	2385	-3749
4 Bills and bonds, short term	307921	7450	300471	296949	-2302	299251	524316	13109	511207	308495	11859	296636
5 Bonds, long term												
6 Corporate equity securities	20562	11969	8593	71141	8742	62399	82692	12069	70623	36794	21859	14935
7 Short term loans, n.e.c.	220605	3067	217538	189367	13306	176061	199905	16354	183551	85864	7457	78407
8 Long term loans, n.e.c.	207993	-	207993	230571	-	230571	316654	-	316654	306580	-	306580
9 Trade credits and advances	50255	47494	2761	41789	39599	2190	30235	25363	4872	49222	45633	3589
10 Other receivables	...	...	...	...	...	...	...	...	...	...	...	...
11 Other assets	112931	17613	95318	151244	1561	149683	154658	48018	106640	92937	9535	83402
Total Acquisition of Financial Assets	954026	103824	850202	1041717	82953	958764	1381616	150449	1231167	884296	108376	775920
Incurrence of Liabilities												
1 Currency and transferable deposits	47371	-	47371	83464	-	83464	126988	-	126988	4085	-	4085
2 Other deposits	292241	-	292241	169307	-	169307	177386	-	177386	150910	-	150910
3 Bills and bonds, short term	48533	24506	24027	44514	12489	32025	14700	-9536	24236	32955	6045	26910
4 Bonds, long term	187050	66620	120430	235768	96776	138992	393278	117215	276063	289451	77851	211600
5 Corporate equity securities	-20358	-59652	39294	36484	-65683	102167	119723	-56487	176210	65951	-23335	89286
6 Short-term loans, n.e.c.	135607	81019	54588	90818	44155	46663	145686	74781	70905	38068	28841	9227
7 Long-term loans, n.e.c.	5273	4862	411	-10362	-10417	55	32421	32342	79	30790	30411	379
8 Net equity of households in life insurance and pension fund reserves	164767	-	164767	198797	-	198797	227895	-	227895	111343	-	111343
9 Proprietors' net additions to the accumulation of quasi-corporations	...	...	...	...	...	...	...	...	...	...	...	...
10 Trade credit and advances	34220	33698	522	34830	34039	791	14750	13690	1060	39716	39865	-149
11 Other accounts payable	...	...	...	...	...	...	...	...	...	...	...	...
12 Other liabilities	125674	5758	119916	206175	2497	203678	163130	7224	155906	185235	5094	180141
Total Incurrence of Liabilities	1020378	156811	863567	1089795	113856	975939	1415957	179229	1236728	948504	164772	783732
Net Lending a	-66352	-52987	-13365	-48078	-30903	-17175	-34341	-28780	-5561	-64208	-56396	-7812
Incurrence of Liabilities and Net Lending	954026	103824	850202	1041717	82953	958764	1381616	150449	1231167	884296	108376	775920

	1988			1989			1990			1991		
	TOTAL	Non-Financial	Financial	TOTAL	Non-Financial	Financial	TOTAL	Non-Financial	Financial	TOTAL	Non-Financial	Financial
Acquisition of Financial Assets												
1 Gold and SDRs	-10	-	-10	-1	-	-1	-2	-	-2	-3	-	-3
2 Currency and transferable deposits	22845	17031	5814	-3413	-3782	369	12469	-1937	14406	3841	10417	-6576
3 Other deposits	18032	-530	18562	26567	2740	23827	13057	18046	-4989	37032	15815	21217
4 Bills and bonds, short term	254024	-855	254879	319718	10800	308918	379389	3390	375999	526147	21906	504241
5 Bonds, long term												
6 Corporate equity securities	18941	5780	13161	51328	20951	30377	41718	27679	14039	160372	26661	133711
7 Short term loans, n.e.c.	174880	14749	160131	145291	-1915	147206	50739	1293	49446	-82853	-4594	-78259
8 Long term loans, n.e.c.	287233	-	287233	277704	-	277704	184649	-	184649	96361	-	96361
9 Trade credits and advances	75105	68296	6809	47279	44463	2816	13277	11315	1962	-9727	-11590	1863
10 Other receivables	...	...	...	...	...	...	...	...	...	...	...	...
11 Other assets	113765	55296	58469	191654	32915	158739	16986	27503	-10517	97974	5398	92576
Total Acquisition of Financial Assets	964815	159767	805048	1056127	106172	949955	712282	87289	624993	829144	64013	765131
Incurrence of Liabilities												
1 Currency and transferable deposits	43215	-	43215	6105	-	6105	44172	-	44172	75756	-	75756
2 Other deposits	196296	-	196296	204484	-	204484	63513	-	63513	-2880	-	-2880
3 Bills and bonds, short term	66784	11953	54831	55965	24617	31348	11711	3118	8593	-56235	-24233	-32002
4 Bonds, long term	239318	103302	136016	270734	72928	197806	248632	46751	201881	282949	77469	205480
5 Corporate equity securities	-64179	-78607	14428	-17869	-72218	54349	56703	-22277	78980	177647	21886	155761
6 Short-term loans, n.e.c.	107886	64078	43808	128189	59049	69140	-15395	31775	-47170	-95690	-44470	-51220

3.24 Corporate and Quasi-Corporate Enterprise Capital Finance Account: Total and Sectors
(Continued)

Million United States dollars

	1988			1989			1990			1991		
	TOTAL	Non-Financial	Financial	TOTAL	Non-Financial	Financial	TOTAL	Non-Financial	Financial	TOTAL	Non-Financial	Financial
7 Long-term loans, n.e.c.	19754	19497	257	17025	16980	45	5033	4774	259	-7777	-8355	578
8 Net equity of households in life insurance and pension fund reserves	198953	-	198953	228966	-	228966	190416	-	190416	264466	-	264466
9 Proprietors' net additions to the accumulation of quasi-corporations	...	...	...	...	...	...	...	...	...	...	...	...
10 Trade credit and advances	63411	59141	4270	36796	30530	6266	41823	40317	1506	5459	10747	-5288
11 Other accounts payable	...	...	...	...	...	...	...	...	...	...	...	...
12 Other liabilities	137927	5023	132904	149001	398	148603	94896	-574	95470	157379	-5582	162961
Total Incurrence of Liabilities	1009365	184387	824978	1079396	132284	947112	741504	103884	637620	801074	27462	773612
Net Lending a	-44550	-24620	-19930	-23269	-26112	2843	-29222	-16595	-12627	28070	36551	-8481
Incurrence of Liabilities and Net Lending	964815	159767	805048	1056127	106172	949955	712282	87289	624993	829144	64013	765131

a) Net lending of the capital accumulation account and the capital finance account have not been reconciled and are different due to different statistical sources.

3.25 Corporate and Quasi-Corporate Enterprise Balance Sheet: Total and Sectors

Million United States dollars

	1980			1981			1982			1983		
	TOTAL	Non-Financial	Financial	TOTAL	Non-Financial	Financial	TOTAL	Non-Financial	Financial	TOTAL	Non-Financial	Financial
Assets												
Non-financial assets	3442904	3278661	164243	3866584	3674476	192108	4078520	3860370	218150	4221277	3979658	241619
1 Tangible assets	3442904	3278661	164243	3866584	3674476	192108	4078520	3860370	218150	4221277	3979658	241619
A Stocks	644031	644031	-	699912	699912	-	679359	679359	-	689998	689998	-
B Reproducible fixed assets	2257077	2126669	130408	2557550	2403402	154148	2734580	2560568	174012	2822536	2630271	192265
C Land and other non-reproducible tangible assets	541796	507961	33835	609122	571162	37960	664581	620443	44138	708743	659389	49354
2 Intangible assets	...	...	...	...	...	...	...	...	...	...	...	...
Financial assets	5758352	1191242	4567110	6349698	1294112	5055586	7025468	1322203	5703265	7828971	1422926	6406045
1 Gold and SDRs	11102	-	11102	11112	-	11112	11118	-	11118	11073	-	11073
2 Currency and transferable deposits	88115	57071	31044	80690	47373	33317	93213	53252	39961	102387	61943	40444
3 Other deposits	150287	69469	80818	212505	89139	123366	265913	100613	165300	270382	107478	162904
4 Bills and bonds, short term	1358594	41547	1317047	1569039	50509	1518530	1828760	70773	1757987	2069240	84106	1985134
5 Bonds, long term												
6 Corporate equity securities	844075	384287	459788	871634	402859	468775	1005491	393816	611675	1141496	382047	759449
7 Short-term loans, n.e.c.	1076897	53575	1023322	1209769	59360	1150409	1279574	68469	1211105	1379169	78624	1300545
8 Long-term loans, n.e.c.	1278834	-	1278834	1360453	-	1360453	1421950	-	1421950	1600792	-	1600792
9 Trade credits and allowances	497907	482332	15575	524718	506601	18117	511347	491105	20242	565000	542761	22239
10 Other receivables	...	...	...	...	...	...	...	...	...	...	...	...
11 Other assets	452541	102961	349580	509778	138271	371507	608102	144175	463927	689432	165967	523465
Total Assets	9201256	4469903	4731353	216282	4968588	5247694	1103988	5182573	5921415	2050248	5402584	6647664
Liabilities and Net Worth												
Liabilities	5719708	1376838	4342870	6388913	1536531	4852382	7132455	1637145	5495310	7945269	1766658	6178611
1 Currency and transferable deposits	471741	-	471741	499645	-	499645	537319	-	537319	577698	-	577698
2 Other deposits	1540959	-	1540959	1759860	-	1759860	1949574	-	1949574	2112687	-	2112687
3 Bills and bonds, short term	173941	45102	128839	225689	64170	161519	232455	58280	174175	259879	64416	195463
4 Bonds, long term	805738	411462	394276	897073	447654	449419	1015221	481463	533758	1134157	506877	627280
5 Corporate equity securities	61808	-	61808	59841	-	59841	76851	-	76851	112121	-	112121
6 Short-term loans, n.e.c.	482217	287240	194977	577035	334286	242749	672941	395473	277468	709963	427828	282135
7 Long-term loans, n.e.c.	133086	131176	1910	135867	133937	1930	95786	93743	2043	114896	112828	2068
8 Net equity of households in life insurance and pension fund reserves	1047006	-	1047006	1127044	-	1127044	1404617	-	1404617	1639929	-	1639929
9 Proprietors' net equity in quasi-corporations	...	...	...	...	...	...	...	...	...	...	...	...
1 Trade credit and advances	347749	347749	-	376371	376371	-	381285	381285	-	419311	418288	1023
1 Other accounts payable	...	...	...	...	...	...	...	...	...	...	...	...
12 Other liabilities	655463	154109	501354	730488	180113	550375	766406	226901	539505	864628	236421	628207
Net worth	3481548	3093065	388483	3827369	3432057	395312	3971533	3545428	426105	4104979	3635926	469053
Total Liabilities and Net Worth	9201256	4469903	4731353	216282	4968588	5247694	1103988	5182573	5921415	2050248	5402584	6647664

3.25 Corporate and Quasi-Corporate Enterprise Balance Sheet: Total and Sectors

Million United States dollars

	1984			1985			1986			1987		
	TOTAL	Non-Financial	Financial	TOTAL	Non-Financial	Financial	TOTAL	Non-Financial	Financial	TOTAL	Non-Financial	Financial
Assets												
Non-financial assets	4488709	4215671	273038	4708042	4399322	308720	4902713	4547251	355462	5153842	4751381	402461
1 Tangible assets	4488709	4215671	273038	4708042	4399322	308720	4902713	4547251	355462	5153842	4751381	402461
A Stocks	760526	760526	-	768090	768090	-	758926	758926	-	817721	817721	-
B Reproducible fixed assets	2971160	2753221	217939	3136202	2890390	245812	3295217	3013861	281356	3437408	3120937	316471
C Land and other non-reproducible tangible assets	757023	701924	55099	803750	740842	62908	848570	774464	74106	898713	812723	85990
2 Intangible assets	...	...	...	...	...	...	...	...	...	...	...	...
Financial assets	8792558	1506459	7286099	9972250	1600697	8371553	1495253	1765854	9729399	2453657	1911648	542009
1 Gold and SDRs	11030	-	11030	11046	-	11046	11004	-	11004	11012	-	11012
2 Currency and transferable deposits	117313	74625	42688	149138	94043	55095	176857	112832	64025	180913	120399	60514
3 Other deposits	288590	111027	177563	318890	113656	205234	366358	130403	235955	363281	134869	228412
4 Bills and bonds, short term	2376826	91556	2285270	2676364	89254	2587110	3199725	102363	3097362	3519285	114222	3405063
5 Bonds, long term												
6 Corporate equity securities	1113845	373880	739965	1325285	393968	931317	1559895	419625	1140270	1672416	479081	1193335
7 Short-term loans, n.e.c.	1595080	81692	1513388	1785446	94997	1690449	1984567	111351	1873216	2067783	118808	1948975
8 Long-term loans, n.e.c.	1812085	-	1812085	2042656	-	2042656	2360969	-	2360969	2676774	-	2676774
9 Trade credits and allowances	615254	590254	25000	657044	629854	27190	687279	655217	32062	736501	700850	35651
10 Other receivables	...	...	...	...	...	...	...	...	...	...	...	...
11 Other assets	862535	183425	679110	1006381	184925	821456	1148599	234063	914536	1225692	243419	982273
Total Assets	3281267	5722130	7559137	4680292	6000019	8680273	6397966	6313105	84861	7607499	6663029	944470
Liabilities and Net Worth												
Liabilities	9015850	2007612	7008238	262128	2208146	8053982	1833827	2466026	9367801	2920108	2741445	178663
1 Currency and transferable deposits	625075	-	625075	708539	-	708539	835527	-	835527	839612	-	839612
2 Other deposits	2404922	-	2404922	2574229	-	2574229	2747423	-	2747423	2891098	-	2891098
3 Bills and bonds, short term	308412	88922	219490	352926	100530	252396	375626	90994	284632	429252	106343	322909
4 Bonds, long term	1321127	573497	747630	1558088	670273	887815	1950927	787488	1163439	2237284	865339	1371945
5 Corporate equity securities	136679	-	136679	240230	-	240230	413473	-	413473	460144	-	460144
6 Short-term loans, n.e.c.	848865	508844	340021	945934	559249	386685	1087480	629890	457590	1127516	655308	472208
7 Long-term loans, n.e.c.	123770	121291	2479	112442	109774	2668	144358	141611	2747	203959	200833	3126
8 Net equity of households in life insurance and pension fund reserves	1804415	-	1804415	2089615	-	2089615	2408445	-	2408445	2571576	-	2571576
9 Proprietors' net equity in quasi-corporations	...	...	...	...	...	...	...	...	...	...	...	...
1 Trade credit and advances	453531	451986	1545	488361	486025	2336	503111	499715	3396	542827	539580	3247
1 Other accounts payable	...	...	...	...	...	...	...	...	...	...	...	...
12 Other liabilities	989054	263072	725982	1191764	282295	909469	1367457	316328	1051129	1616840	374042	1242798
Net worth	4265417	3714518	550899	4418164	3791873	626291	4564139	3847079	717060	4687391	3921584	765807
Total Liabilities and Net Worth	3281267	5722130	7559137	4680292	6000019	8680273	6397966	6313105	84861	7607499	6663029	944470

	1988			1989			1990			1991		
	TOTAL	Non-Financial	Financial	TOTAL	Non-Financial	Financial	TOTAL	Non-Financial	Financial	TOTAL	Non-Financial	Financial
Assets												
Non-financial assets	5514594	5056566	458028	5842801	5334975	507826	5863802	5333803	529999	5587897	5049860	538037
1 Tangible assets	5514594	5056566	458028	5842801	5334975	507826	5863802	5333803	529999	5587897	5049860	538037
A Stocks	883120	883120	-	936040	936040	-	961590	961590	-	942020	942020	-
B Reproducible fixed assets	3659199	3300109	359090	3864035	3461575	402460	4061154	3619790	441364	4148381	3682373	466008
C Land and other non-reproducible tangible assets	972275	873337	98938	1042726	937360	105366	841058	752423	88635	497496	425467	72029
2 Intangible assets	...	...	...	...	...	...	...	...	...	...	...	...
Financial assets	3583384	2074028	1509356	4949464	2189893	2759571	5595796	2310689	3285107	6848617	2378952	4469665
1 Gold and SDRs	11002	-	11002	11001	-	11001	10999	-	10999	10996	-	10996
2 Currency and transferable deposits	204832	137430	67402	201419	133648	67771	213888	131711	82177	217729	142128	75601

United States

3.25 Corporate and Quasi-Corporate Enterprise Balance Sheet: Total and Sectors
(Continued)

Million United States dollars

	1988			1989			1990			1991		
	TOTAL	Non-Financial	Financial	TOTAL	Non-Financial	Financial	TOTAL	Non-Financial	Financial	TOTAL	Non-Financial	Financial
3 Other deposits	382233	134339	247894	418927	137079	281848	431399	155125	276274	465752	170940	294812
4 Bills and bonds, short term	3772112	113367	3658745	4081252	124167	3957085	4442014	127557	4314457	4968161	149463	4818698
5 Bonds, long term												
6 Corporate equity securities	1830815	486930	1343885	2206757	514887	1691870	2165431	576738	1588693	2752455	604755	2147700
7 Short-term loans, n.e.c.	2249444	133558	2115886	2412657	131642	2281015	2456219	132935	2323284	2373366	128341	2245025
8 Long-term loans, n.e.c.	2958939	-	2958939	3242035	-	3242035	3465492	-	3465492	3561853	-	3561853
9 Trade credits and allowances	835605	793145	42460	882885	837609	45276	896162	848924	47238	886435	837334	49101
10 Other receivables	...	...	...	...	...	...	...	...	...	...	...	...
11 Other assets	1338402	275259	1063143	1492531	310861	1181670	1514192	337699	1176493	1611870	345991	1265879
Total Assets	9097978	7130594	1967384	792265	7524868	3267397	1459598	7644492	3815106	2436514	7428812	5007702
Liabilities and Net Worth												
Liabilities	4165710	3047064	1118646	5630995	3296079	2334916	6293410	3446033	2847377	7440933	3465424	3975509
1 Currency and transferable deposits	882827	-	882827	888588	-	888588	932760	-	932760	1008516	-	1008516
2 Other deposits	3104049	-	3104049	3308877	-	3308877	3372390	-	3372390	3369510	-	3369510
3 Bills and bonds, short term	496036	118296	377740	552001	142913	409088	563712	146031	417681	507477	121798	385679
4 Bonds, long term	2477086	968641	1508445	2777854	1041569	1736285	3030050	1088320	1941730	3317362	1165789	2151573
5 Corporate equity securities	478262	-	478262	566172	-	566172	602119	-	602119	812406	-	812406
6 Short-term loans, n.e.c.	1241213	722887	518326	1369402	781936	587466	1354006	813709	540297	1258316	769240	489076
7 Long-term loans, n.e.c.	210489	207106	3383	232280	228852	3428	229531	225320	4211	221754	216965	4789
8 Net equity of households in life insurance and pension fund reserves	2861326	-	2861326	3324462	-	3324462	3420629	-	3420629	3996301	-	3996301
9 Proprietors'net equity in quasi-corporations	...	...	...	...	...	...	...	...	...	...	...	...
1 Trade credit and advances	606238	598721	7517	643034	629251	13783	684857	669568	15289	690316	680315	10001
1 Other accounts payable	...	...	...	...	...	...	...	...	...	...	...	...
12 Other liabilities	1808184	431413	1376771	1968325	471558	1496767	2103356	503085	1600271	2258975	511317	1747658
Net worth	4932268	4083530	848738	5161270	4228789	932481	5166188	4198459	967729	4995581	3963388	1032193
Total Liabilities and Net Worth	9097978	7130594	1967384	792265	7524868	3267397	1459598	7644492	3815106	2436514	7428812	5007702

3.26 Financial Transactions of Financial Institutions: Detail

Million United States dollars

	1980					1981				
	ALL FINANCIAL INSTITUTIONS	Central Bank	Other Monetary Institutions	Insurance	Other Financial Institutions	ALL FINANCIAL INSTITUTIONS	Central Bank	Other Monetary Institutions	Insurance	Other Financial Institutions
Acquisition of Financial Assets										
1 Gold and SDRs	-43	-43	-	-	-	10	10	-	-	-
A Gold	-12	-12	-	-	-	-9	-9	-	-	-
B Net acquisitions of SDRs	-31	-31	-	-	-	19	19	-	-	-
2 Currency and transferable deposits	3020	-	2047	-221	1194	2291	-	2454	414	-577
A Liability of resident institutions	3020	-	2047	-221	1194	2291	-	2454	414	-577
B Liability of rest of the world	-	-	-	-	-	-	-	-	-	-
3 Other deposits	21456	3236	4954	2572	10694	42953	430	-703	8305	34921
A Liability of resident institutions	18220	-	4954	2572	10694	42523	-	-703	8305	34921
B Liability of rest of the world	3236	3236	-	-	-	430	430	-	-	-
4 Bills and bonds, short term	167713	3531	68901	72353	22928	202421	8825	35886	73781	83929
5 Bonds, long term										
6 Corporate equity securities	40338	-	13952	27906	-1520	44368	-	16415	27816	137
7 Short-term loans, n.e.c.	79308	966	44075	6586	27681	128187	350	68533	7395	51909
A Liability of: resident sectors	66562	-	32295	6586	27681	124810	-	65506	7395	51909
B Liability of: rest of the world	12746	966	11780	-	-	3377	350	3027	-	-
8 Long-term loans, n.e.c.	98150	-	47049	14714	36387	81488	-	38661	8996	33831
9 Trade credit and advances	1984	-	-	1984	-	2649	-	-	2649	-
10 Other assets	20413	-666	5905	5584	9590	14962	-1483	10121	1330	4994
Total Acquisition of Financial Assets	432339	7024	186883	131478	106954	519329	8132	171367	130686	209144

3.26 Financial Transactions of Financial Institutions: Detail
(Continued)

Million United States dollars

1980 / 1981

	ALL FINANCIAL INSTITUTIONS	Central Bank	Other Monetary Institutions	Insurance	Other Financial Institutions	ALL FINANCIAL INSTITUTIONS	Central Bank	Other Monetary Institutions	Insurance	Other Financial Institutions
Incurrence of Liabilities										
1 Currency and transferable deposits	17058	9024	8034	-	-	27904	10884	17020	-	-
2 Other deposits	173500	-	142669	-	30831	218901	-	109105	-	109796
3 Bills and bonds, short term	12925	-	13691	-	-766	32680	-	18749	-	13931
4 Bonds, long term	54356	-	1663	-	52693	55849	-	3172	-	52677
5 Corporate equity securities	7698	-	1442	1551	4705	9321	-	2422	1580	5319
6 Short-term loans, n.e.c.	30880	-	29649	-	1231	47939	-	36671	-	11268
7 Long-term loans, n.e.c.	-40	-	-	-	-40	20	-	-	-	20
8 Net equity of households in life insurance and pension fund reserves	109710	-	-	109710	-	107871	-	-	107871	-
9 Other liabilities	18099	-2000	-12015	16812	15302	46933	-2752	13253	19020	17412
Total Incurrence of liabilities	424186	7024	185133	128073	103956	547418	8132	200392	128471	210423
Statistical discrepancy	432339	7024	186883	131478	106954	519329	8132	171367	130686	209144
Net Lending	...	...	...	...	...	...	...	...	...	...
Incurrence of Liabilities and Net Lending	8153	-	1750	3405	2998	-28089	-	-29025	2215	-1279

1982 / 1983

	ALL FINANCIAL INSTITUTIONS	Central Bank	Other Monetary Institutions	Insurance	Other Financial Institutions	ALL FINANCIAL INSTITUTIONS	Central Bank	Other Monetary Institutions	Insurance	Other Financial Institutions
Acquisition of Financial Assets										
1 Gold and SDRs	6	6	-	-	-	-45	-45	-	-	-
A Gold	-3	-3	-	-	-	-27	-27	-	-	-
B Net acquisitions of SDRs	9	9	-	-	-	-18	-18	-	-	-
2 Currency and transferable deposits	7204	-	3545	892	2767	483	-	1402	-389	-530
A Liability of resident institutions	7204	-	3545	892	2767	483	-	1402	-389	-530
B Liability of rest of the world	-	-	-	-	-	-	-	-	-	-
3 Other deposits	22970	520	14585	6026	1839	-1972	-1652	2812	15468	-18600
A Liability of resident institutions	22450	-	14585	6026	1839	-320	-	2812	15468	-18600
B Liability of rest of the world	520	520	-	-	-	-1652	-1652	-	-	-
4 Bills and bonds, short term	229301	7681	85633	84620	51367	230147	14659	130933	97540	-12985
5 Bonds, long term										
6 Corporate equity securities	38677	-	8849	25191	4637	58840	-	4136	36042	18662
7 Short-term loans, n.e.c.	89859	2093	65379	8231	14156	86440	-3763	67540	10743	11920
A Liability of: resident sectors	93274	-	70887	8231	14156	86580	-	63917	10743	11920
B Liability of: rest of the world	-3415	2093	-5508	-	-	-140	-3763	3623	-	-
8 Long-term loans, n.e.c.	71310	-	-8518	7040	72788	179203	-	82797	11275	85131
9 Trade credit and advances	2125	-	-	2125	-	1997	-	-	1997	-
10 Other assets	82407	2007	40940	30624	8836	58972	206	23349	22019	13398
Total Acquisition of Financial Assets	543859	12307	210413	164749	156390	614065	9405	312969	194695	96996
Incurrence of Liabilities										
1 Currency and transferable deposits	37659	10153	27506	-	-	40379	12995	27384	-	-
2 Other deposits	195970	-	163263	-	32707	163113	-	203557	-	-40444
3 Bills and bonds, short term	9928	-	12485	-	-2557	21288	-	8722	-	12566
4 Bonds, long term	84204	-	6728	-	77476	93165	-	9755	-	83410
5 Corporate equity securities	16846	-	2108	3076	11662	34196	-	1638	1983	30575
6 Short-term loans, n.e.c.	34630	-	8044	-	26586	4667	-	21099	-	-16432
7 Long-term loans, n.e.c.	113		-	-	113	25	-	-	-	25
8 Net equity of households in life insurance and pension fund reserves	141563	-	-	141563	-	166466	-	-	166466	-
9 Other liabilities	30223	2154	-464	17859	10674	97927	-3590	51386	21392	28739
Total Incurrence of liabilities	551136	12307	219670	162498	156661	622249	9405	323541	189841	99462
Statistical discrepancy	543859	12307	210413	164749	156390	614065	9405	312969	194695	96996
Net Lending	...	...	...	...	...	...	...	...	...	...
Incurrence of Liabilities and Net Lending	-7277	-	-9257	2251	-271	-8184	-	-10572	4854	-2466

United States

3.26 Financial Transactions of Financial Institutions: Detail

Million United States dollars

	1984 ALL FINANCIAL INSTITUTIONS	Central Bank	Other Monetary Institutions	Insurance	Other Financial Institutions	1985 ALL FINANCIAL INSTITUTIONS	Central Bank	Other Monetary Institutions	Insurance	Other Financial Institutions
Acquisition of Financial Assets										
1 Gold and SDRs	-43	-43	-	-	-	16	16	-	-	-
A Gold	-25	-25	-	-	-	-6	-6	-	-	-
B Net acquisitions of SDRs	-18	-18	-	-	-	22	22	-	-	-
2 Currency and transferable deposits	2244	-	-340	2199	385	12407	-	1963	3892	6552
A Liability of resident institutions	2244	-	-340	2199	385	12407	-	1963	3892	6552
B Liability of rest of the world	-	-	-	-	-	-	-	-	-	-
3 Other deposits	15327	577	-6691	22544	-1103	26186	1934	7239	25998	-8985
A Liability of resident institutions	14750	-	-6691	22544	-1103	24252	-	7239	25998	-8985
B Liability of rest of the world	577	577	-	-	-	1934	1934	-	-	-
4 Bills and bonds, short term	300471	8409	55871	133732	102459	299251	18413	66050	112455	102333
5 Bonds, long term										
6 Corporate equity securities	8593	-	1932	1440	5221	62399	-	-4221	53441	13179
7 Short-term loans, n.e.c.	217538	5	146438	4639	66456	176061	3208	103310	5567	63976
A Liability of: resident sectors	224150	-	153055	4639	66456	175699	-	106156	5567	63976
B Liability of: rest of the world	-6612	5	-6617	-	-	362	3208	-2846	-	-
8 Long-term loans, n.e.c.	207993	-	131221	6725	70047	230571	-	108192	16273	106106
9 Trade credit and advances	2761	-	-	2761	-	2190	-	-	2190	-
10 Other assets	95318	5614	64076	21104	4524	149683	1308	84023	28951	35401
Total Acquisition of Financial Assets	850202	14562	392507	195144	247989	958764	24879	366556	248767	318562
Incurrence of Liabilities										
1 Currency and transferable deposits	47371	10285	37086	-	-	83464	16560	66904	-	-
2 Other deposits	292241	-	238080	-	54161	169307	-	159059	-	10248
3 Bills and bonds, short term	24027	-	9830	-	14197	32025	-	-7120	-	39145
4 Bonds, long term	120430	-	15417	-	105013	138992	-	23465	-	115527
5 Corporate equity securities	39294	-	2753	3687	32854	102167	-	2811	8087	91269
6 Short-term loans, n.e.c.	54588	-	36557	-	18031	46663	-	44415	-	2248
7 Long-term loans, n.e.c.	411	-	-	-	411	55	-	-	-	55
8 Net equity of households in life insurance and pension fund reserves	164767	-	-	164767	-	198797	-	-	198797	-
9 Other liabilities	119916	4277	60108	29427	26104	203678	8319	73454	51420	70485
Total Incurrence of liabilities	863567	14562	399831	197881	251293	975939	24879	362988	258304	329768
Statistical discrepancy	850202	14562	392507	195144	246989	958764	24879	366556	248767	318562
Net Lending	...	...	...	...	...	...	...	...	...	...
Incurrence of Liabilities and Net Lending	-13365		-7324	-2737	-3304	-17175	-	3568	-9537	-11206

	1986 ALL FINANCIAL INSTITUTIONS	Central Bank	Other Monetary Institutions	Insurance	Other Financial Institutions	1987 ALL FINANCIAL INSTITUTIONS	Central Bank	Other Monetary Institutions	Insurance	Other Financial Institutions
Acquisition of Financial Assets										
1 Gold and SDRs	-42	-42	-	-	-	8	8	-	-	-
A Gold	-26	-26	-	-	-	14	14	-	-	-
B Net acquisitions of SDRs	-16	-16	-	-	-	-6	-6	-	-	-
2 Currency and transferable deposits	8930	-	1077	1302	6551	-3888	-	-3086	-112	-690
A Liability of resident institutions	8930	-	1077	1302	6551	-3888	-	-3086	-112	-690
B Liability of rest of the world	-	-	-	-	-	-	-	-	-	-

3.26 Financial Transactions of Financial Institutions: Detail
(Continued)

Million United States dollars

	1986					1987				
	ALL FINANCIAL INSTITUTIONS	Central Bank	Other Monetary Institutions	Insurance	Other Financial Institutions	ALL FINANCIAL INSTITUTIONS	Central Bank	Other Monetary Institutions	Insurance	Other Financial Institutions
3 Other deposits	28732	470	11017	11828	5417	-3749	-3794	-8108	-5730	13883
A Liability of resident institutions	28262	-	11017	11828	5417	45	-	-8108	-5730	13883
B Liability of rest of the world	470	470	-	-	-	-3794	-3794	-	-	-
4 Bills and bonds, short term	511207	19429	96664	181125	213989	296636	24650	94953	136182	40851
5 Bonds, long term										
6 Corporate equity securities	70623	-	7340	40517	22766	14935	-	-13930	8103	20762
7 Short-term loans, n.e.c.	183551	10782	105687	-188	67270	78407	-14689	22856	447	69793
A Liability of: resident sectors	173799	-	106717	-188	67270	96702	-	26462	447	69793
B Liability of: rest of the world	9752	10782	-1030	-	-	-18295	-14689	-3606	-	-
8 Long-term loans, n.e.c.	316654	-	99508	23133	194013	306580	-	151792	17784	137004
9 Trade credit and advances	4872	-	-	4872	-	3589	-	-	3589	-
10 Other assets	106640	1228	57406	19681	28325	83402	4532	64063	12220	2587
Total Acquisition of Financial Assets	1231167	31867	378699	282270	538331	775920	10707	308540	172483	284190

Incurrence of Liabilities

	ALL FINANCIAL INSTITUTIONS	Central Bank	Other Monetary Institutions	Insurance	Other Financial Institutions	ALL FINANCIAL INSTITUTIONS	Central Bank	Other Monetary Institutions	Insurance	Other Financial Institutions
1 Currency and transferable deposits	126988	12366	114622	-	-	4085	16692	-12607	-	-
2 Other deposits	177386	-	129079	-	48307	150910	-	126924	-	23986
3 Bills and bonds, short term	24236	-	-9112	-	33348	26910	-	7052	-	19858
4 Bonds, long term	276063	-	21047	-	255016	26910	-	7052	-	19858
5 Corporate equity securities	176210	-	2916	7266	166028	211600	-	17839	-	193761
6 Short-term loans, n.e.c.	70905	-	55484	-	15421	89286	-	3148	4998	81140
7 Long-term loans, n.e.c.	79	-	-	-	79	9227	-	62193	-	-52966
8 Net equity of households in life insurance and pension fund reserves	227895	-	-	227895	-	379	-	-	-	379
9 Other liabilities	155906	19501	53927	47525	34953	111343	-	-	111343	-
						180141	-5985	94289	46903	44934
Total Incurrence of liabilities	1236728	31867	367963	282686	554212	783732	10707	298838	163244	310943
Statistical discrepancy	1231167	31867	378699	282270	538331	775920	10707	308540	172483	284190
Net Lending	...	...	...	...	...	...	...	...	...	...
Incurrence of Liabilities and Net Lending	-5561	-	10736	-416	-15881	-7812	-	9702	9239	-26753

	1988					1989				
	ALL FINANCIAL INSTITUTIONS	Central Bank	Other Monetary Institutions	Insurance	Other Financial Institutions	ALL FINANCIAL INSTITUTIONS	Central Bank	Other Monetary Institutions	Insurance	Other Financial Institutions

Acquisition of Financial Assets

	ALL FINANCIAL INSTITUTIONS	Central Bank	Other Monetary Institutions	Insurance	Other Financial Institutions	ALL FINANCIAL INSTITUTIONS	Central Bank	Other Monetary Institutions	Insurance	Other Financial Institutions
1 Gold and SDRs	-10	-10	-	-	-	-1	-1	-	-	-
A Gold	-18	-18	-	-	-	-1	-1	-	-	-
B Net acquisitions of SDRs	8	8	-	-	-	-	-	-	-	-
2 Currency and transferable deposits	5814	-	378	1463	3973	369	-	-512	85	796
A Liability of resident institutions	5814	-	378	1463	3973	369	-	-512	85	796
B Liability of rest of the world	-	-	-	-	-	-	-	-	-	-
3 Other deposits	18562	2533	-3411	12155	7285	23827	12614	-4785	10860	5138
A Liability of resident institutions	16029	-	-3411	12155	7285	11213	-	-4785	10860	5138
B Liability of rest of the world	2533	2533	-	-	-	12614	12614	-	-	-
4 Bills and bonds, short term	254879	10524	26772	164427	53156	308918	-7327	-57504	190531	183218
5 Bonds, long term										
6 Corporate equity securities	13161	-	4798	22567	-14204	30377	-	2328	27065	984
7 Short-term loans, n.e.c.	160131	5545	86900	3907	63779	147206	-4744	66305	3128	82517
A Liability of: resident sectors	156386	-	88700	3907	63779	152092	-	66447	3128	82517
B Liability of: rest of the world	3745	5545	-1800	-	-	-4886	-4744	-142	-	-
8 Long-term loans, n.e.c.	287233	-	165149	21145	100939	277704	-	84069	13975	179660
9 Trade credit and advances	6809	-	-	6809	-	2816	-	-	2816	-
10 Other assets	58469	-177	22118	16601	19927	158739	10612	107843	22187	18097
Total Acquisition of Financial Assets	805048	18415	302704	249074	234855	949955	11154	197744	270647	470410

Incurrence of Liabilities

	ALL FINANCIAL INSTITUTIONS	Central Bank	Other Monetary Institutions	Insurance	Other Financial Institutions	ALL FINANCIAL INSTITUTIONS	Central Bank	Other Monetary Institutions	Insurance	Other Financial Institutions
1 Currency and transferable deposits	43215	18086	25129	-	-	6105	9547	-3442	-	-

3.26 Financial Transactions of Financial Institutions: Detail
(Continued)

Million United States dollars

	1988					1989				
	ALL FINANCIAL INSTITUTIONS	Central Bank	Other Monetary Institutions	Insurance	Other Financial Institutions	ALL FINANCIAL INSTITUTIONS	Central Bank	Other Monetary Institutions	Insurance	Other Financial Institutions
2 Other deposits	196296	-	174438	-	21858	204484	-	114344	-	90140
3 Bills and bonds, short term	54831	-	-2937	-	57768	31348	-	126	-	31222
4 Bonds, long term	136016	-	6969	-	129047	197806	-	1250	-	196556
5 Corporate equity securities	14428	-	5225	2892	6311	54349	-	3820	4603	45926
6 Short-term loans, n.e.c.	43808	-	56537	-	-12729	69140	-	-19953	-	89093
7 Long-term loans, n.e.c.	257	-	-	-	257	45	-	-	-	45
8 Net equity of households in life insurance and pension fund reserves	198953	-	-	198953	-	228966	-	-	228966	-
9 Other liabilities	132904	329	62673	39111	30791	148603	1607	90614	42794	13588
Total Incurrence of liabilities	824978	18415	328034	240956	237573	947112	11154	186759	276363	472836
Statistical discrepancy	805048	18415	302704	249074	234855	949955	11154	197744	270647	470410
Net Lending	...	...	...	...	...	...	...	...	...	...
Incurrence of Liabilities and Net Lending	-19930	-	-25330	8118	-2718	2843	-	10985	-5716	-2426

	1990					1991				
	ALL FINANCIAL INSTITUTIONS	Central Bank	Other Monetary Institutions	Insurance	Other Financial Institutions	ALL FINANCIAL INSTITUTIONS	Central Bank	Other Monetary Institutions	Insurance	Other Financial Institutions
Acquisition of Financial Assets										
1 Gold and SDRs	-2	-2	-	-	-	-3	-3	-	-	-
A Gold	-1	-1	-	-	-	1	1	-	-	-
B Net acquisitions of SDRs	-1	-1	-	-	-	-4	-4	-	-	-
2 Currency and transferable deposits	14406	-	-476	1933	12949	-6576	-	1807	-881	-7502
A Liability of resident institutions	14406	-	-476	1933	12949	-6576	-	1807	-881	-7502
B Liability of rest of the world	-	-	-	-	-	-	-	-	-	-
3 Other deposits	-4989	1348	360	12850	-19547	21217	-3154	4718	13022	6631
A Liability of resident institutions	-6337	-	360	12850	-19547	24371	-	4718	13022	6631
B Liability of rest of the world	1348	1348	-	-	-	-3154	-3154	-	-	-
4 Bills and bonds, short term	375999	8131	-3088	170347	200609	504241	31099	53955	209434	209753
5 Bonds, long term										
6 Corporate equity securities	14039	-	-3941	7893	10087	133711	-	9342	75746	48623
7 Short-term loans, n.e.c.	49446	16237	-14987	7276	40920	-78259	-2456	-63584	-255	-11964
A Liability of: resident sectors	36074	-	-12122	7276	40920	-78910	-	-66691	-255	-11964
B Liability of: rest of the world	13372	16237	-2865	-	-	651	-2456	3107	-	-
8 Long-term loans, n.e.c.	184649	-	-8851	13999	179501	96361	-	-59269	1185	154445
9 Trade credit and advances	1962	-	-	1962	-	1863	-	-	1863	-
10 Other assets	10517	2212	-11554	1185	-2360	92576	-3219	-6186	26786	75195
Total Acquisition of Financial Assets	624993	27926	-42537	217445	422159	765131	22267	-59217	326900	475181
Incurrence of Liabilities										
1 Currency and transferable deposits	44172	25209	18963	-	-	75756	29237	46519	-	-
2 Other deposits	63513	-	-6768	-	70281	-2880	-	-44134	-	41254
3 Bills and bonds, short term	8593	-	-23971	-	32564	-32002	-	-20057	-	-11945
4 Bonds, long term	201881	-	-10366	-	212247	205480	-	146	-	205334
5 Corporate equity securities	78980	-	2883	6477	69620	155761	-	2838	3870	149053
6 Short-term loans, n.e.c.	-47170	-	-65134	-	17964	-51220	-	-80886	-	29666
7 Long-term loans, n.e.c.	259	-	-	-	259	578	-	-	-	578
8 Net equity of households in life insurance and pension fund reserves	190416	-	-	190416	-	264466	-	-	264466	-
9 Other liabilities	95470	2717	51071	19844	21838	162961	-6970	50719	40000	79212
Total Incurrence of liabilities	637620	27926	-33322	216737	426279	773612	22267	-44855	308336	487864
Statistical discrepancy	624993	27926	-42537	217445	422159	765131	22267	-59217	326900	475181
Net Lending	...	...	...	...	...	...	...	...	...	...
Incurrence of Liabilities and Net Lending	-12627	-	-9215	708	-4120	-8481	-	-14362	18564	-12683

3.32 Household and Private Unincorporated Enterprise Income and Outlay Account

Million United States dollars

	1980	1981	1982	1983	1984	1985	1986	1987	1988	1989	1990	1991
Receipts												
1 Compensation of employees	1652432	1825243	1926895	2040961	2237432	2394922	2536327	2712378	2936005	3115240	3306983	3406760
A Wages and salaries	1378461	1517645	1595490	1686854	1852914	1989545	2109026	2265184	2447161	2590719	2747354	2816805
B Employers' contributions for social security	88940	103610	109769	119834	138998	147771	157665	165568	183261	193714	206285	215079
C Employers' contributions for private pension & welfare plans	185031	203988	221636	234273	245520	257606	269636	281626	305583	330807	353344	374876
2 Operating surplus of private unincorporated enterprises	171801	180801	170715	186656	235974	259899	283715	310235	324312	347270	366919	367965
3 Property and entrepreneurial income	320065	403276	447954	470571	536831	571099	599546	604019	644650	731378	763641	757469
A Withdrawals from private quasi-corporations	...	...	...	...	...	...	...	...	...	...	...	...
B Interest	249776	315542	358961	370682	434700	464476	486244	500478	531871	618380	635569	630891
C Dividends	57128	66912	67061	77823	78798	87876	104651	100359	108446	126489	140333	136986
D Net land rent and royalties	13161	20822	21932	22066	23333	18747	8651	3182	4333	-13491	-12261	-10408
3 Current transfers	306878	348792	388017	418233	428319	459056	487959	509702	541599	588561	646394	727946
A Casualty insurance claims	...	...	...	...	...	...	...	...	...	...	...	...
B Social security benefits	180310	208974	242058	261088	265334	283925	301360	314320	332123	359192	391682	433431
C Social assistance grants	89310	97367	99653	106972	111493	117563	125076	130996	141571	157115	178914	213580
D Unfunded employee pension and welfare benefits [a]	28002	32141	35246	37932	37200	41297	42233	44860	48104	50649	53886	57647
E Transfers from general government	...	...	...	...	...	...	...	...	...	...	...	...
F Transfers from the rest of the world	1559	1387	725	912	941	646	1082	1122	1289	2450	2825	2795
G Other transfers n.e.c.	7697	8923	10335	11329	13351	15625	18208	18404	18512	19155	19087	20493
Total Current Receipts	2451176	2758112	2933581	3116421	3438556	3684976	3907547	4136334	4446566	4782449	5083937	5260140
Disbursements												
1 Final consumption expenditures	1708277	1887328	2016947	2201908	2401883	2598435	2764716	2960584	3198135	3420469	3633800	3762819
A Market purchases	1524059	1680536	1793346	1962494	2143564	2321958	2468909	2643525	2858846	3059378	3248586	3358193
B Gross rents of owner-occupied housing	182985	205578	222472	238365	257302	275551	294911	316316	338558	360423	384525	404002
C Consumption from own-account production	1233	1214	1129	1049	1017	926	896	743	731	668	689	624
2 Property income	49404	54584	58802	65713	74955	83582	90928	92290	93732	102981	109609	112542
A Interest	49404	54584	58802	65713	74955	83582	90928	92290	93732	102981	109609	112542
Consumer debt	49404	54584	58802	65713	74955	83582	90928	92290	93732	102981	109609	112542
Mortgage	...	...	...	...	...	...	...	...	...	...	...	...
Other	...	...	...	...	...	...	...	...	...	...	...	...
B Net land rent and royalties	...	...	...	...	...	...	...	...	...	...	...	...
3 Direct taxes and other current transfers n.e.c. to government	470343	547176	570523	586853	644638	709946	752994	824746	877144	967840	1017331	1036281
A Social security contributions	166696	196217	209232	226334	257904	282101	304007	322861	360740	387146	412020	433266
B Direct taxes	298380	344670	354196	352423	377514	417299	437089	489079	502586	565321	588975	585354
Income taxes	292083	337967	346936	344603	368962	407959	427351	478488	491241	553133	576106	571684
Other	6297	6703	7260	7820	8552	9340	9738	10591	11345	12188	12869	13670
C Fees, fines and penalties	5267	6289	7095	8096	9220	10546	11898	12806	13818	15373	16336	17661
4 Other current transfers	34921	39422	42330	44661	45323	49232	50556	53672	56553	66469	70558	74675
A Net casualty insurance premiums	...	...	...	...	...	...	...	...	...	...	...	...
B Transfers to private non-profit institutions serving households	...	...	...	...	...	...	...	...	...	...	...	...
C Transfers to the rest of the world	3183	3209	2814	2719	3242	3381	3587	4130	3941	11316	12090	12493
D Other current transfers, except imputed	3776	4013	4274	4455	4661	4784	4736	4682	4508	4504	4532	4585
E Imputed employee pension and welfare contributions	27962	32200	35242	37487	37420	41067	42233	44860	48104	50649	53936	57597
Net saving	188231	229602	244979	217286	271757	243781	248353	205042	221002	224690	252639	273823
Total Current Disbursements and Net Saving	2451176	2758112	2933581	3116421	3438556	3684976	3907547	4136334	4446566	4782449	5083937	5260140

a) Item 'Unfunded employee pension and welfare benefits' also includes wage accruals less disbursements.

United States

3.33 Household and Private Unincorporated Enterprise Capital Accumulation Account

Million United States dollars

	1980	1981	1982	1983	1984	1985	1986	1987	1988	1989	1990	1991
					Finance of Gross Accumulation							
1 Gross saving	315026	372568	400326	378036	439145	420469	432726	399477	427368	452660	487204	516909
A Consumption of fixed capital	126795	142966	155347	160750	167388	176688	184373	194435	206366	227970	234565	243086
Owner-occupied housing	51016	55997	59567	61691	64068	68393	70770	75527	80509	92520	93510	97808
Other unincorported enterprises	75779	86969	95780	99059	103320	108295	113603	118908	125857	135450	141055	145278
B Net saving	188231	229602	244979	217286	271757	243781	248353	205042	221002	224690	252639	273823
2 Capital transfers	...	...	...	...	...	...	...	...	...	...	...	...
Total Finance of Gross Accumulation a	315026	372568	400326	378036	439145	420469	432726	399477	427368	452660	487204	516909
					Gross Accumulation							
1 Gross Capital Formation	195012	223154	197924	223015	287141	300620	322726	332893	342005	363180	343315	300681
A Increase in stocks bc	-6852	9927	5325	-13987	8884	7995	-688	-4177	-10276	3076	2568	-563
B Gross fixed capital formation	201864	213227	192599	237002	278257	292625	323414	337070	352281	360104	340747	301244
Owner-occupied housing	79878	82084	78472	116976	137433	139473	168545	176392	185100	185435	174927	155110
Other gross fixed capital formation	121986	131143	114127	120026	140824	153152	154869	160678	167181	174669	165820	146134
2 Purchases of land, net	...	...	...	...	...	...	...	...	...	...	...	...
3 Purchases of intangibles, net	...	...	...	...	...	...	...	...	...	...	...	...
4 Capital transfers	8778	9262	10103	8287	8363	8931	10011	10580	11327	12611	15970	15703
A To resident sectors	8778	9262	10103	8287	8363	8931	10011	10580	11327	12611	15970	15703
B To the rest of the world	...	...	...	...	...	...	...	...	...	...	...	...
Net lending d	111236	140152	192299	146734	143641	110918	99989	56004	74036	76869	127919	200525
Total Gross Accumulation a	315026	372568	400326	378036	439145	420469	432726	399477	427368	452660	487204	516909

a) This table, Households and Non-profit Institutions, includes also private unincorporated enterprises and private quasi-corporate enterprises.
b) Item 'Goods producing industries' includes only manufacturing and farming.
c) Inventories valued at current replacement cost.
d) Net lending of the capital accumulation account and the capital finance account have not been reconciled and are different due to different statistical sources.

3.34 Household and Private Unincorporated Enterprise Capital Finance Account

Million United States dollars

	1980	1981	1982	1983	1984	1985	1986	1987	1988	1989	1990	1991
					Acquisition of Financial Assets							
1 Gold	...	...	...	...	...	...	...	...	...	...	...	...
2 Currency and transferable deposits	9197	36342	24841	34336	21599	33910	102192	6625	7406	19268	22351	51930
3 Other deposits	149434	162760	155434	164044	262836	127717	148508	142793	178376	194493	65883	-33776
4 Bills and bonds, short term	30407	36777	45841	94450	108004	182175	16741	151520	165690	153247	143484	-43326
5 Bonds, long term												
6 Corporate equity securities	-10606	-37024	-15608	-4077	-49418	-52925	5162	-32100	-119674	-97187	23580	60517
7 Short term loans, n.e.c.	-63	18	51	667	396	330	312	383	344	-23	253	32
8 Long term loans, n.e.c.	19158	19032	14324	5062	11487	8043	21334	15372	27415	17330	18703	15436
9 Trade credit and advances	1618	4376	7581	6795	6489	4105	6353	8304	11755	7659	4896	5573
10 Net equity of households in life insurance and pension fund reserves	118503	117911	153490	180705	182953	217901	248966	130519	218910	250135	212442	290051
11 Proprietors' net additions to the accumulation of quasi-corporations	...	...	...	...	...	...	...	...	...	...	...	...
12 Other	9228	-17476	830	20901	20737	60681	59430	33351	45038	48932	30496	65061
Total Acquisition of Financial Assets	326876	322716	386784	502883	565083	581937	608998	456767	535260	593854	522088	411498
					Incurrence of Liabilities							
1 Short term loans, n.e.c.	31894	62065	24252	67761	120255	109539	88124	57530	73856	69160	40078	-11863
2 Long term loans, n.e.c.	147715	105309	129685	194254	225011	260694	317918	294581	297797	286014	239240	138386
3 Trade credit and advances	8331	8543	7543	2329	6937	6274	2361	10738	13904	7977	6724	4005
4 Other accounts payable	...	...	...	...	...	...	...	...	...	...	...	...
5 Other liabilities	16810	13156	25058	36178	28164	60676	9105	-6914	15191	16365	10278	34982
Total Incurrence of Liabilities	204750	189073	186538	300522	380367	437183	417508	355935	400748	379516	296320	165510
Net Lending a	122126	133643	200246	202361	184716	144754	191490	100832	134512	214338	225768	245988
Incurrence of Liabilities and Net Lending	326876	322716	386784	502883	565083	581937	608998	456767	535260	593854	522088	411498

a) Net lending of the capital accumulation account and the capital finance account have not been reconciled and are different due to different statistical sources.

3.35 Household and Private Unincorporated Enterprise Balance Sheet

Million United States dollars

	1980	1981	1982	1983	1984	1985	1986	1987	1988	1989	1990	1991
Assets												
Non-financial assets	7174002	7750918	8097572	8528737	9075537	9626871	225647	966486	1572987	2372593	2342204	2740343
1 Tangible assets	7174002	7750918	8097572	8528737	9075537	9626871	225647	966486	1572987	2372593	2342204	2740343
A Stocks of household enterprises	140169	136188	137741	137602	138274	136210	128874	132879	140681	145107	144004	139755
B Dwellings	2807318	3015431	3113366	3244259	3411800	3600611	3861683	4170370	4255032	4521352	4749904	4926641
C Other reproducible fixed assets of unincorporated enterprises	1764167	1926146	2023046	2114002	2246540	2406045	2594924	2780849	3002430	3194529	3349679	3459222
D Land and other non-reproducible tangible assets	2462348	2673153	2823419	3032874	3278923	3484005	3640166	3882388	4174844	4511605	4098617	4214725
2 Intangible assets	...	...	...	...	...	...	...	...	...	...	...	...
Financial assets	4699976	5009038	5603854	6352745	6973420	8117597	9086107	9546865	447856	1775505	2043049	3394835
1 Gold	...	...	...	...	...	...	...	...	...	...	...	...
2 Currency and transferable deposits	298855	335215	360631	395095	416592	450502	552694	561023	567317	585838	608189	660119
3 Other deposits	1341724	1504484	1634813	1798857	2061687	2189404	2333720	2469278	2664309	2859146	2925029	2891253
4 Bills and bonds, short term	385022	419942	458186	556398	656940	831147	843279	1014121	1200715	1387684	1550707	1500008
5 Bonds, long term												
6 Corporate equity securities	1163384	1103870	1195134	1365752	1382166	1818258	2107601	2006523	2136939	2495644	2355989	3060846
7 Short-term loans, n.e.c.	4391	4409	4461	5128	5523	5854	6166	6549	6892	6870	7123	7155
8 Long-term loans, n.e.c.	119198	137685	151043	156378	167099	171392	187871	206008	225141	254215	253239	268675
9 Trade credit and advances of unincorporated enterprises	36512	40888	48469	55264	61753	65858	72211	80515	92270	99929	104825	110398
1 Net equity in life insurance and pension fund reserves	1132492	1222570	1512070	1761621	1944293	2248597	2588498	2770805	3080512	3564817	3683010	4284267
1 Proprietors' equity in quasi-corporations	...	...	...	...	...	...	...	...	...	...	...	...
12 Other	218398	239975	239047	258252	277367	336585	394067	432043	473761	521362	554938	612114
Total Assets	1873978	2759956	3701426	4881482	6048957	7744468	9311754	513351	2020843	4148098	4385253	6135178
Memorandum Item: Consumer Durable Goods	1014341	1086193	1133710	1193796	1281469	1391103	1527490	1659528	1808389	1929632	2030688	2122669
Liabilities and Net Worth												
Liabilities	2166937	2360476	2539242	2819269	3193872	3623984	4033591	4361170	4765880	5171571	5484876	5652496
1 Short-term loans, n.e.c.	658567	720632	744660	812423	927986	1033024	1116365	1167272	1242278	1324361	1357263	1342839
2 Long-term loans, n.e.c.	...	...	...	...	...	...	...	...	...	...	...	...
A Mortgages	75767	84310	91853	94182	101119	107393	109754	120492	134796	142773	149497	158225
B Other	...	...	...	...	...	...	...	...	...	...	...	...
3 Trade credit and advances	...	...	...	...	...	...	...	...	...	...	...	...
4 Other accounts payable	92777	105653	130190	165871	193632	254522	262664	250838	268567	285814	296186	331116
5 Other liabilities	9707041	399480	1162184	2062213	2855085	4120484	5278163	6152181	7254963	8976527	8900377	482682
Net worth	1873978	2759956	3701426	4881482	6048957	7744468	9311754	513351	2020843	4148098	4385253	6135178
Total Liabilities and Net Worth	...	...	...	...	...	...	...	...	...	...	...	...

3.51 External Transactions: Current Account: Detail

Million United States dollars

	1980	1981	1982	1983	1984	1985	1986	1987	1988	1989	1990	1991
Payments to the Rest of the World												
1 Imports of goods and services	293896	317686	303194	328126	405110	417623	451737	507050	552208	587708	625903	619972
A Imports of merchandise c.i.f. [a]	248638	267742	250604	272700	336337	343310	370023	414796	452127	485068	507837	499910
B Other	45258	49944	52590	55426	68773	74313	81714	92254	100081	102640	118066	120062
2 Factor income to the rest of the world	44131	58611	64128	62317	79071	76679	80633	93014	112976	133850	131543	116782
A Compensation of employees	563	667	752	761	857	883	885	938	1021	1087	1162	1194
B Property and entrepreneurial income	43568	57944	63376	61556	78214	75796	79748	92076	111955	132763	130381	115588
By general government	12684	17313	19282	18993	21155	22972	24071	25291	30164	35856	37870	38986
By corporate and quasi-corporate enterprises	30884	40631	44094	42563	57059	52824	55677	66785	81791	96907	92511	76602

3.51 External Transactions: Current Account: Detail
(Continued)

Million United States dollars

	1980	1981	1982	1983	1984	1985	1986	1987	1988	1989	1990	1991
By other	...	...	...	...	...	...	...	...	...	...	...	...
3 Current transfers to the rest of the world	12942	13657	14874	15248	18057	20081	21289	19889	21806	29949	37076	34292
A Indirect taxes by general government to supranational organizations	...	...	...	...	...	...	...	...	...	...	...	...
B Other current transfers	12942	13657	14874	15248	18057	20081	21289	19889	21806	29949	37076	34292
By general government	7354	7252	8488	8744	10925	13491	14195	12573	13068	13189	19761	16527
By other resident sectors	5588	6405	6386	6504	7132	6590	7094	7316	8738	16760	17315	17765
4 Surplus of the nation on current transactions	10316	8445	-2462	-34961	-94010	-118067	-141721	-155122	-117987	-89337	-76062	8977
Payments to the Rest of the World, and Surplus of the Nation on Current Transfers	361285	398399	379734	370730	408228	396316	411938	464831	569003	662170	718460	780023

Receipts From The Rest of the World

	1980	1981	1982	1983	1984	1985	1986	1987	1988	1989	1990	1991
1 Exports of goods and services	277525	301373	280227	272738	297795	296384	313052	356553	436394	500380	548832	589418
A Exports of merchandise f.o.b. [a]	225635	238918	214833	207096	225413	221911	225751	257260	325336	371100	397515	422504
B Other	51890	62455	65394	65642	72382	74473	87301	99293	111058	129280	151317	166914
2 Factor income from the rest of the world	80583	94088	97293	95834	108118	97262	95960	105051	128701	157490	160590	143464
A Compensation of employees	465	511	540	574	619	646	693	825	861	851	932	954
B Property and entrepreneurial income	80118	93577	96753	95260	107499	96616	95267	104226	127840	156639	159658	142510
By general government	2562	3680	4118	4832	5227	5499	6413	5311	6703	5635	10508	8104
By corporate and quasi-corporate enterprises	77556	89897	92635	90428	102272	91117	88854	98915	121137	151004	149150	134406
By other	...	...	...	...	...	...	...	...	...	...	...	...
3 Current transfers from the rest of the world	3177	2938	2214	2158	2315	2670	2926	3227	3908	4300	9038	47141
A Subsidies to general government from supranational organizations	...	...	...	...	...	...	...	...	...	...	...	...
B Other current transfers	3177	2938	2214	2158	2315	2670	2926	3227	3908	4300	9038	47141
To general government	1618	1551	1489	1246	1374	2024	1844	2105	2619	1850	6213	44346
To other resident sectors	1559	1387	725	912	941	646	1082	1122	1289	2450	2825	2795
Receipts from the Rest of the World on Current Transfers	361285	398399	379734	370730	408228	396316	411938	464831	569003	662170	718460	780023

a) Merchandise valued at Free Along Side (F.A.S.).

3.52 External Transactions: Capital Accumulation Account

Million United States dollars

	1980	1981	1982	1983	1984	1985	1986	1987	1988	1989	1990	1991
Finance of Gross Accumulation												
1 Surplus of the nation on current transactions	10316	8445	-2462	-34961	-94010	-118067	-141721	-155122	-117987	-89337	-76062	8977
2 Capital transfers from the rest of the world	1152	1093	-	-	-	-	-	-	-	-	-	-
A By general government	1152	1093	-	-	-	-	-	-	-	-	-	-
B By other resident sectors	...	...	...	...	...	...	...	...	...	...	...	...
Total Finance of Gross Accumulation	11468	9538	-2462	-34961	-94010	-118067	-141721	-155122	-117987	-89337	-76062	8977
Gross Accumulation												
1 Capital transfers to the rest of the world	-	-	-	-	-	-	-	-	-	-	-	-
A By general government	-	-	-	-	-	-	-	-	-	-	-	-
B By other resident sectors	...	...	...	...	...	...	...	...	...	...	...	...
2 Purchases of intangible assets, n.e.c., net, from the rest of the world	...	...	...	...	...	...	...	...	...	...	...	...
Net lending to the rest of the world [a]	11468	9538	-2462	-34961	-94010	-118067	-141721	-155122	-117987	-89337	-76062	8977
Total Gross Accumulation	11468	9538	-2462	-34961	-94010	-118067	-141721	-155122	-117987	-89337	-76062	8977

a) Net lending of the capital accumulation account and the capital finance account have not been reconciled and are different due to different statistical sources.

3.53 External Transactions: Capital Finance Account

Million United States dollars

	1980	1981	1982	1983	1984	1985	1986	1987	1988	1989	1990	1991
Acquisitions of Foreign Financial Assets												
1 Gold and SDR's	16	1823	1372	65	979	897	246	510	-127	535	193	176
2 Currency and transferable deposits	8138	3353	3592	1130	2151	2960	-559	-9659	4041	24758	1966	-5941
3 Other deposits	4479	10419	4501	1279	-5785	-3935	9069	-3076	-3129	1118	12640	1464
4 Bills and bonds, short term	4091	6922	8517	-122	969	-7351	-5376	980	-2374	-5319	-3212	-4350
5 Bonds, long term	1202	5487	6616	3081	3813	3794	3118	7381	6936	4857	21361	14861
6 Corporate equity securities	27497	15244	14287	14761	15545	12933	13322	21254	10984	41246	35039	58408
A Subsidiaries abroad	25131	15031	12917	11078	14601	9245	12169	23384	10075	24033	27635	28252
B Other	2366	213	1370	3683	944	3688	1153	-2130	909	17213	7404	30156
7 Short-term loans, n.e.c.	16464	7240	-1011	7892	-2601	-1451	484	-5960	-6890	-2460	-6602	-2790
8 Long-term loans	...	...	...	...	...	...	...	...	...	...	...	...
9 Prporietors' net additions to accumulation of quasi-corporate, non-resident enterprises	...	...	...	...	...	...	...	...	...	...	...	...
10 Trade credit and advances	5360	681	-3908	-943	-1633	-133	-1189	2884	7395	3402	-1283	5301
11 Other	-14865	1955	-305	4385	987	3405	9527	1374	22319	19769	11175	-21222
Total Acquisitions of Foreign Financial Assets	52382	53124	33661	31528	14425	11119	28642	15688	39155	87906	71277	45907
Incurrence of Foreign Liabilities												
1 Currency and transferable deposits	17	-3785	-3660	1605	1940	1565	2679	-1403	-560	-233	-310	-1403
2 Other deposits	1214	2270	6813	514	4560	3708	-2659	925	3054	-1910	-505	-511
3 Bills and bonds, short term	922	-1293	-1712	792	1150	-152	1061	267	539	2322	-1818	606
4 Bonds, long term	23701	20121	27471	22802	44441	55190	78812	54646	77907	43847	32567	50504
5 Corporate equity securities	21150	30025	17111	17927	24074	24339	52789	73806	56801	74831	30617	21625
A Subsidiaries of non-resident incorporated units	16918	25196	13792	11947	25359	20010	35623	58219	57279	67873	45137	11498
B Other	4232	4829	3319	5980	-1285	4329	17166	15587	-478	6958	-14520	10127
6 Short-term loans, n.e.c.	...	...	...	...	...	...	...	...	...	...	...	...
7 Long-term loans	...	...	...	...	...	...	...	...	...	...	...	...
8 Non-resident proprietors' net additions to accumulation of resident quasi-corporate enterprises	...	...	...	...	...	...	...	...	...	...	...	...
9 Trade credit and advances	3494	-207	27	-1340	1506	477	834	375	3140	1084	6184	971
10 Other	-23789	-25650	-42307	13748	9544	22887	27247	54642	25057	66712	47601	-21126
Total Incurrence of Liabilities	26709	21481	3743	56048	87215	108014	160763	183258	165938	186653	114336	50666
Net Lending [a]	25673	31643	29918	-24520	-72790	-96895	-132121	-167570	-126783	-98747	-43059	-4759
Total Incurrence of Liabilities and Net Lending	52382	53124	33661	31528	14425	11119	28642	15688	39155	87906	71277	45907

a) Net lending of the capital accumulation account and the capital finance account have not been reconciled and are different due to different statistical sources.

Uruguay

General note. The preparation of national accounts statistics in Uruguay is undertaken by the Banco Central del Uruguay, Montevideo. The official estimates together with some methological notes are published annually by the Banco Central in 'Producto e Ingreso Nacionales'. The following presentation of sources and methods is mainly based on a report entitled 'Metodologia del Calculo de las cuentas de actividades, a precios corrientes'. The estimates are generally in accordance with the classifications and definitions recommended in the United Nations System of National Accounts (SNA). The following tables have been prepared from successive replies to the United Nations national accounts questionnaire. When the scope and coverage of the estimates differ for conceptual or statistical reasons from the definitions and classifications recommended in SNA, a footnote is indicated to the relevant tables.

Sources and methods :

(a) Gross domestic product. Gross domestic product is estimated mainly through the production approach.

(b) Expenditure on the gross domestic product. All components of GDP by expenditure type are estimated through the expenditure approach except private final consumption expenditure and gross investment in machinery and equipments which are estimated by the commodity-flow approach. The estimates of government final consumption expenditure are based on the budgetary programmes of the different institutional subsectors. The items are analyzed in accordance with government disbursements which are classified into ten different items. The commodity-flow approach is used to estimate private final consumption expenditure by separating the current products according to their origin and source. These estimates are periodically checked by surveys of homes and of family budgets. The estimates of increase in stocks refer to stock variations for meat and wool only. The estimates of imported machinery and equipment are based on c.i.f. import values classified by industry of origin, principal groups of goods and sectors of destination. Customs duties, indirect taxes, trade margins, etc. are then added. Domestically produced capital goods are estimated in the same manner. The estimates of exports and imports of goods and services are based on the foreign trade statistics which are adjusted for unregistered transactions. The balance-of-payments data are also used. For the constant price estimates, price deflation is used for government purchases of goods and services, public construction and exports and imports of services. For government compensation of employees, increase in stocks, private construction, investment in machinery and equipment and exports and imports of goods, the base-year estimates are extrapolated by quantity index. Private consumption expenditure is obtained as a residual.

(c) Cost-structure of the gross domestic product. The estimates of wages and salaries in the agricultural sector are estimated by using employment data and average wages obtained from censuses and extrapolated and interpolated by using indices of physical volumes. For private construction, the ratio of wages and salaries to the value of building is determined for the different types of construction work. For the trade sector, wages and salaries are measured from employment data obtained from the 1963 population census and extrapolated by volume index of commercialized merchandise. For the public sectors, compensation of employees is obtained directly from the government enterprises. In general, consumption of fixed capital is valued at original cost. Information of indirect taxes and subsidies is available directly for registered tax classifications by economic branch. Profits of government monopoly enterprises are treated as indirect taxes while deficits are

treated as subsidies. Operating surplus is obtained as a residual.

(d) Gross domestic product by kind of economic activity. The table of GDP by kind of economic activity is prepared in factor values. The production approach is used to estimate the value added of most industries. However, the income approach is used for producers of government services, part of the construction sector and part of the services sector. The Ministerio de Ganaderia y Agricultura conducts censuses and surveys every four years, covering agricultural establishments of over one hectare. The censuses include various type of information such as ownership, locations, land tenure conditions, production, stocks, etc. The Ministerio also conducts annual sample surveys on principal crops, wool production, etc. The gross value of livestock production is based on the number of livestock, adjusted for imports and exports and changes in stocks. Data on mining production and prices are provided by the Instituto Geologico del Uruguay and the Camara de la Construccion, respectively. The estimates of intermediate consumption are based on the 1968 national economic census. For manufacturing, quarterly and annual surveys are conducted. They provide data on labour force, salaries and wages, raw materials, manufactured products, costs, etc. The value of electricity and water production is obtained directly from the concerned enterprises which are government monopolies. The data of gas production are furnished by the concerned companies. Basic information used to estimate the gross vaue of production in the building sector is obtained from the administrative records of the public sector. For private building, the municipal records provide data on approved licences, quantity, size and type of construction. This information is adjusted on the basis of surveys on time extension of buildings and areas. The accounting records of the central government and public enterprises supply the information used to estimate the gross production value of public buildings. The estimates of the trade sector are based on the gross value of commercialized production while intermediate consumption is obtained from an analysis of the accounts of certain enterprises. The Banco Central del Uruguay conducts surveys of trade channels and trade margins. For restaurants and hotels, the estimates are based on studies carried out in 1962 extrapolated by price and volume indexes. The production values of railways, air transport and ports are estimated from the data supplied by the respective government enterprises. For other transport, data are obtained directly from concerned enterprises and from licence permits issued. Bench-mark estimates of cargo transport were prepared for 1961. These estimates are projected by the use of an index of receipts. Information on water transport, storage and communication is obtained directly from a special maritime commission, from the Mercado de Frutos, and from the accounts of government enterprises, respectively. The estimates of banking services are obtained from administrative records. For real estate, the value of production is determined as the amount of gross rents paid or imputed for housing services. Owner-occupied dwellings are imputed in accordance with the average rents for rented houses. The estimates of business services are based on the number of persons employed and average wages. For producers of government services, the estimates are based on budgetary programmes of the institutional subsectors. For domestic service, data from the 1963 population census are extrapolated on the basis of information from employment agencies. For other private services, bench-mark studies referring to 1961 are extrapolated by the most suitable indicators. For the constant price estimates, value added of most industries is extrapolated by a quantity index. Double deflation is used for all components of the agricultural sector and price deflation is used for public construction.

1.1 Expenditure on the Gross Domestic Product, in Current Prices

Million Uruguayan new pesos

	1980	1981	1982	1983	1984	1985	1986	1987	1988	1989	1990	1991
1 Government final consumption expenditure	11482	17336	20100	25653 25486	36851	69154	127586	219727	358572	647000	1287228	2551896
2 Private final consumption expenditure	69890	91147	94076	137826 121252	187259	327975	610346	1163696	1880389	3342603	6575082	13385879
3 Gross capital formation	15994	18802	18555	18427 24995	32804	54485	99569	237467	359281	545949	1110936	2480088
A Increase in stocks a	572	-403	-827	-1902 953	3175	8367	11467	48218	34300	-13943	20468	197102
B Gross fixed capital formation	15422	19205	19382	20329 24042	29629	46118	88102	189249	324981	559892	1090468	2282986
Residential buildings	10324	13880	14931	14568 16323	22349	31183	52690	113037	192705	350857	659597	1372271
Non-residential buildings												
Other construction and land improvement etc.	227	157	178	289 445	545	817	1797	3167	7546	10150	18340	37875
Other	4871	5168	4273	5472 7274	6735	14118	33615	73045	124730	198885	412531	872840
4 Exports of goods and services	13861	17987	18072	44700 45057	72059	128076	233432	359700	649519	1231570	2599588	4498664
5 Less: Imports of goods and services	19023	22819	22107	41600 41373	57948	101049	180482	319113	522254	927834	1874798	3781059
Equals: Gross Domestic Product	92204	122453	128696	185006 175417	271025	478641	890451	1661477	2725507	4839288	9698036	19135468

a) Item 'Increase in stocks' refers to increase in stocks of wool and livestock in the private sector, and to stocks held by the public sector.

1.2 Expenditure on the Gross Domestic Product, in Constant Prices

Million Uruguayan new pesos

	1980	1981	1982	1983	1984	1985	1986	1987	1988	1989	1990	1991
			At constant prices of: 1978					At constant prices of: 1983				
1 Government final consumption expenditure	4244	4562	4452	4322 / 25486	25443	25875	28190	29709	29034	29493	30732	31998
2 Private final consumption expenditure	26232	26854	24257	21926 / 121252	118315	119585	134560	155826	153973	153702	145644	153552
3 Gross capital formation	6461	5888	4815	3052 / 24995	20870	18675	21873	25899	24046	21845	23059	27254
A Increase in stocks a	206	-179	-350	-419 / 953	2339	3828	5122	4570	1774	-313	2211	3374
B Gross fixed capital formation	6255	6067	5165	3471 / 24042	18531	14847	16751	21329	22272	22158	20848	23880
Residential buildings	3757	3840	3638	2412 / 16323	14047	9955	10291	12863	13590	13867	12445	12627
Non-residential buildings												
Other construction and land improvement etc.	91	54	54	46 / 445	326	293	411	450	705	511	423	542
Other	2407	2173	1473	1013 / 7274	4158	4599	6049	8016	7977	7780	7980	10711
4 Exports of goods and services	6106	6483	5801	6697 / 45057	44320	47000	52402	47965	52352	57761	63822	63173
5 Less: Imports of goods and services	8235	8318	7187	5740 / 41373	35447	35074	45371	52541	52565	53302	51839	60620
Equals: Gross Domestic Product	34808	35469	32138	30257 / 175417	173501	176061	191654	206858	206840	209499	211418	215357

a) Item 'Increase in stocks' refers to increase in stocks of wool and livestock in the private sector, and to stocks held by the public sector.

1.3 Cost Components of the Gross Domestic Product

Million Uruguayan new pesos

	1980	1981	1982	1983	1984	1985	1986	1987	1988	1989	1990	1991
1 Indirect taxes, net	12665	16550	16735	22874 / 22817	39161	77054	154675	274236	442996	732864	1690698	3598731
A Indirect taxes	14552	19239	20181	27787 / 27429	44877	85048	168543	299915	487203	800509	1782734	3755171
B Less: Subsidies	1887	2689	3446	4913 / 4612	5716	7994	13868	25679	44207	67645	92036	156440
2 Consumption of fixed capital a	4858	6050	6105	6404	...	...	...	...	...	...	...	...
3 Compensation of employees paid to resident producers to:	28367	39890	45956	55671 / 61070	89431	182407	352982	628269	1044425	1942953	3880885	8397386
4 Operating surplus a	46314	59963	59900	100057 / 91530	142433	219180	382794	758972	1238086	2163471	4126453	7139351
Equals: Gross Domestic Product	92204	122453	128696	185006 / 175417	271025	478641	890451	1661477	2725507	4839288	9698036	1 9135468

a) Item 'Operating surplus' includes consumption of fixed capital.

1.4 General Government Current Receipts and Disbursements

Million Uruguayan new pesos

	1980	1981	1982	1983	1984	1985	1986	1987	1988	1989	1990	1991
					Receipts							
1 Operating surplus	...	...	...	...	...	...	...	...	...	...	...	...
2 Property and entrepreneurial income	185	169	447	193 / 193	294	323	527	899	399	486	1057	...
3 Taxes, fees and contributions	24119	30563	33390	46553 / 44817	66600	130121	264950	486649	803489	1332409	2904570	...
A Indirect taxes	14552	19239	20181	27787 / 27429	44877	85048	168543	299915	487203	800509	1782734	3755171
B Direct taxes	3680	3885	4320	6980 / 5602	5396	12457	27893	62539	109301	173064	310067	...
C Social security contributions	5887	7439	8889	11786 / 11786	16327	32616	68514	124195	206985	358836	811769	1841438
D Compulsory fees, fines and penalties	...	...	...	...	...	...	...	...	...	...	...	...
4 Other current transfers	...	...	...	378	559	1093	3829	1797	7630	4829	9461	51842
Total Current Receipts of General Government	24304	30732	33837	46746 / 45388	67453	131537	269306	489345	811518	1337724	2915088	...

Uruguay

1.4 General Government Current Receipts and Disbursements
(Continued)

Million Uruguayan new pesos

	1980	1981	1982	1983	1984	1985	1986	1987	1988	1989	1990	1991
Disbursements												
1 Government final consumption expenditure	11482	17336	20100	25653 / 25486	36851	69154	127586	219727	358572	647000	1287228	2551896
2 Property income a	290	412	1769	3556 / 3556	4823	6080	16967	25024	45986	102716	195000	...
3 Subsidies	1887	2689	3446	4913 / 4612	5716	7994	13868	25679	44207	67645	92036	156440
4 Other current transfers	6722	12419	15662	18637 / 18935	25612	44044	87905	167596	289630	519685	1174981	...
A Social security benefits	6783	12501	15776	18935 / 18935	25612	44044	87905	167596	289630	519685	1174981	...
B Social assistance grants	...	...	...	... / ...	...	...	...	...	...	...	...	...
C Other	-61	-82	-114	-298 / ...	...	...	...	...	...	...	...	...
5 Net saving	3923	-2124	-7140	-6013 / -7201	-5549	4265	22980	51319	73123	678	165843	...
Total Current Disbursements and Net Saving of General Government	24304	30732	33837	46746 / 45388	67453	131537	269306	489345	811518	1337724	2915088	...

a) Item 'Property income' relates to interest on public debt.

1.7 External Transactions on Current Account, Summary

Million Uruguayan new pesos

	1980	1981	1982	1983	1984	1985	1986	1987	1988	1989	1990	1991
Payments to the Rest of the World												
1 Imports of goods and services	19023	22819	22107	41600 / 41373	57948	101049	180482	319113	522254	927834	1874798	3781059
A Imports of merchandise c.i.f.	15620	18746	15160	26947 / 29021	44155	73511	137888	265842	434366	760001	1602295	3341160
B Other	3403	4073	6947	14653 / 12352	13793	27538	42594	53271	87888	167833	272503	439899
2 Factor income to the rest of the world	1527	2372	4768	12043 / 12103	25182	43460	58376	91366	153593	334302	678741	942986
3 Current transfers to the rest of the world	23	30	42	107 / 107	168	447	653	1474	1689	4239	9017	20188
4 Surplus of the nation on current transactions	-5995	-5524	-6619	-6415 / -5892	-5639	-7511	12444	-25765	22414	96979	357119	299199
Payments to the Rest of the World and Surplus of the Nation on Current Transactions	14578	19697	20298	47335 / 47691	77659	137445	251955	386188	699950	1363354	2919675	5043432
Receipts From The Rest of the World												
1 Exports of goods and services	13861	17987	18072	44700 / 45057	72059	128076	233432	359700	649519	1231570	2599588	4498664
A Exports of merchandise f.o.b.	9611	13114	14167	35931 / 36295	51959	88510	167570	272986	514001	991640	2081572	3343111
B Other	4250	4873	3905	8769 / 8762	20100	39566	65862	86714	135518	239930	518016	1155553
2 Factor income from rest of the world	615	1575	2039	2148 / 2149	4874	7831	14040	23216	41112	122716	301609	472738
3 Current transfers from rest of the world	102	135	187	487 / 485	726	1538	4483	3272	9319	9068	18478	72031
Receipts from the Rest of the World on Current Transactions	14578	19697	20298	47335 / 47691	77659	137445	251955	386188	699950	1363354	2919675	5043433

1.10 Gross Domestic Product by Kind of Activity, in Current Prices

Million Uruguayan new pesos

	1980	1981	1982	1983	1984	1985	1986	1987	1988	1989	1990	1991
1 Agriculture, hunting, forestry and fishing	8860	9987	9942	16686 / 23505	39656	65076	112658	227827	363644	605393	1114269	1870210
2 Mining and quarrying	1191	1613	1465	2425 / 511	647	781	1697	3678	4439	10307	17005	34632
3 Manufacturing	20603	24152	21724	38336 / 44474	73949	140720	264601	480951	769612	1267155	2544332	4812491
4 Electricity, gas and water a	1185	1774	2587	4209 / 5663	8790	16223	31853	56582	77747	112658	274902	535656
5 Construction	4182	5965	6494	5621 / 7479	9904	14347	24424	54163	93380	183482	302408	726369

1.10 Gross Domestic Product by Kind of Activity, in Current Prices
(Continued)

Million Uruguayan new pesos

	1980	1981	1982	1983	1984	1985	1986	1987	1988	1989	1990	1991
6 Wholesale and retail trade, restaurants and hotels	14910	19150	16401	24839 / 18899	34001	59951	111937	202278	321466	578155	1181359	2391110
7 Transport, storage and communication	5083	6982	7898	11617 / 10698	15905	28749	56812	96470	160824	318262	630971	1219852
8 Finance, insurance, real estate and business services	10241	16315	21480	28585 / 41394	67072	109266	175954	293447	559125	1168602	2465675	4961558
9 Community, social and personal services b	3053	4493	5430	7269 / 12936	18752	35488	69404	126891	215269	407490	867303	1971179
Total, Industries	69308	90431	93421	139587 / 165559	268676	470601	849340	1542287	2565506	4651504	9398224	18523057
Producers of Government Services	8490	12958	15406	18956 / 18901	25765	48147	91649	162924	264248	474682	899512	1683800
Other Producers b	1741	2514	3134	3589 / ...	...	...	...	...	...	...	...	...
Subtotal c	79539	105903	111961	162132 / 184460	294441	518748	940989	1705211	2829754	5126186	10297736	20206857
Less: Imputed bank service charge	...	...	...	... / 13901	32511	56124	85628	107814	212687	466354	1009204	1895156
Plus: Import duties	...	...	...	4858	9095	16017	35090	64080	108440	179456	409504	823767
Plus: Value added tax	...	...	...	...	...	...	...	...	...	...	...	...
Plus: Other adjustments d	12665	16550	16735	22874 / ...	...	...	...	...	...	...	...	...
Equals: Gross Domestic Product	92204	122453	128696	185006 / 175417	271025	478641	890451	1661477	2725507	4839288	9698036	19135468

a) Item 'Electricity, gas and water' includes sewage services.
b) Item 'Other producers' is included in item 'Community, social and personal services'.
c) For the first series, gross domestic product in factor values.
d) Item 'Other adjustments' refers to indirect taxes net of subsidies.

1.11 Gross Domestic Product by Kind of Activity, in Constant Prices

Million Uruguayan new pesos

	1980	1981	1982	1983	1984	1985	1986	1987	1988	1989	1990	1991
	At constant prices of:											
		1978						1983				
1 Agriculture, hunting, forestry and fishing	3408	3596	3332	3402 / 23505	20489	23061	22483	23510	23139	23938	24267	24262
2 Mining and quarrying	374	367	290	248 / 511	434	346	404	462	369	371	290	285
3 Manufacturing	6980	6662	5536	5148 / 44474	46466	45740	51108	56156	55667	55560	54750	54464
4 Electricity, gas and water a	408	430	435	444 / 5663	5613	5796	6041	6837	7415	6680	7456	8069
5 Construction	1546	1593	1545	1026 / 7479	6496	4659	4823	5956	6356	6494	5719	5717
6 Wholesale and retail trade, restaurants and hotels	6214	6341	5063	4591 / 18899	20068	21166	23122	24899	24503	24279	24271	25800
7 Transport, storage and communication	2041	2025	1802	1717 / 10698	10098	10595	12138	12795	13434	14565	14535	14946
8 Finance, insurance, real estate and business services	3645	3909	4070	4047 / 41394	40106	41315	42230	45068	47202	50043	50949	50477
9 Community, social and personal services	1104	1139	1118	1039 / 31837 bc	31534 bc	32000 bc	34880 bc	37319 bc	36735 bc	37421 bc	38393 bc	38240 bc
Total, Industries	25720	26062	23191	21662 / 184460	181304	184678	197229	213002	214820	219351	220630	222260
Producers of Government Services	3147	3365	3373	3427 / ...	...	...	...	...	...	...	...	...

Uruguay

1.11 Gross Domestic Product by Kind of Activity, in Constant Prices
(Continued)

Million Uruguayan new pesos

	1980	1981	1982	1983	1984	1985	1986	1987	1988	1989	1990	1991
				At constant prices of:								
		1978						1983				
Other Producers	733	746	755	631 ...	...	...	...	...	...	...	...	...
Subtotal	29600 d	30173 d	27319 d	25720 d 184460	181304	184678	197229	213002	214820	219351	220630	222260
Less: Imputed bank service charge	...	...	...	... ...	...	...	...	...	...	...	...	...
Plus: Import duties	...	...	...	... ...	...	...	...	...	...	...	...	...
Plus: Value added tax	...	...	...	... ...	...	...	...	...	...	...	...	...
Plus: Other adjustments	5208 e	5296 e	4819 e	4537 e ...	...	...	...	...	...	...	...	...
Equals: Gross Domestic Product	34808	35469	32138	30257 175417	173501	176061	191654	206858	206840	209499	211418	215357

a) Item 'Electricity, gas and water' includes sewage services.
b) Item 'Producers of government services' is included in item 'Community, social and personal services'.
c) Item 'Other producers' is included in item 'Community, social and personal services'.
d) Gross domestic product in factor values.
e) Item 'Other adjustments' refers to indirect taxes net of subsidies.

1.12 Relations Among National Accounting Aggregates

Million Uruguayan new pesos

	1980	1981	1982	1983	1984	1985	1986	1987	1988	1989	1990	1991
Gross Domestic Product	92204	122453	128696	185006 175417	271025	478641	890451	1661477	2725507	4839288	9698036	19135468
Plus: Net factor income from the rest of the world	-912	-797	-2729	-9895 -9954	-20308	-35629	-44336	-68150	-112481	-211586	-377132	-470248
Factor income from the rest of the world	615	1575	2039	2148 2149	4874	7831	14040	23216	41112	122716	301609	472738
Less: Factor income to the rest of the world	1527	2372	4768	12043 12103	25182	43460	58376	91366	153593	334302	678741	942986
Equals: Gross National Product	91292	121656	125967	175111 165463	250717	443012	846115	1593327	2613026	4627702	9320904	18665220
Less: Consumption of fixed capital	4858	6050	6105	6404 ...	...	...	...	...	...	...	...	...
Equals: National Income a	86434	115606	119862	168707 165463	250717	443012	846115	1593327	2613026	4627702	9320904	18665220
Plus: Net current transfers from the rest of the world	79	105	145	380 378	558	1091	3830	1798	7630	4829	9461	51842
Current transfers from the rest of the world	102	135	187	487 485	726	1538	4483	3272	9319	9068	18478	72030
Less: Current transfers to the rest of the world	23	30	42	107 107	168	447	653	1474	1689	4239	9017	20188
Equals: National Disposable Income b	86513	115711	120007	169087 165841	251275	444103	849945	1595125	2620656	4632531	9330365	18717062
Less: Final consumption	81372	108483	114176	163479 146738	224110	397129	737932	1383423	2238961	3989603	7862310	5937775
Equals: Net Saving c	5141	7228	5831	5608 19103	27165	46974	112013	211702	381695	642928	1468055	12779287
Less: Surplus of the nation on current transactions	-5995	-5524	-6619	-6415 -5892	-5639	-7511	12444	-25765	22414	96979	357119	299199
Equals: Net Capital Formation d	11136	12752	12450	12023 24995	32804	54485	99569	237467	359281	545949	1110936	12480088

a) Item 'National income' includes consumption of fixed capital.
b) Item 'National disposable income' includes consumption of fixed capital.
c) Item 'Net saving' includes consumption of fixed capital.
d) Item 'Net capital formation' includes consumption of fixed capital.

2.7 Gross Capital Formation by Type of Good and Owner, in Current Prices

Million Uruguayan new pesos

	1983 TOTAL	1983 Total Private	1983 Public Enterprises	1983 General Government	1984 TOTAL	1984 Total Private	1984 Public Enterprises	1984 General Government	1985 TOTAL	1985 Total Private	1985 Public Enterprises	1985 General Government
Increase in stocks, total a	953	953	-	...	3175	3175	-	...	8367	8367	-	...
Gross Fixed Capital Formation, Total	24042	15069	8973	...	29629	17474	12155	...	46118	29402	16716	...
1 Residential buildings				...				...				...
2 Non-residential buildings	16323	10014	6309	...	22349	11533	10816	...	31183	18322	12861	...
3 Other construction				...				...				...
4 Land improvement and plantation and orchard development	445	445	-	...	545	545	-	...	817	817	-	...
5 Producers' durable goods	7274	4610	2664	...	6735	5396	1339	...	14118	10263	3855	...
6 Breeding stock, dairy cattle, etc.	...	...	...	...	...	...	...	...	...	...	...	...
Total Gross Capital Formation	24995	16022	8973	...	32804	20649	12155	...	54485	37769	16716	...

	1986 TOTAL	1986 Total Private	1986 Public Enterprises	1986 General Government	1987 TOTAL	1987 Total Private	1987 Public Enterprises	1987 General Government	1988 TOTAL	1988 Total Private	1988 Public Enterprises	1988 General Government
Increase in stocks, total a	11467	11467	-	...	48218	48218	-	...	34300	34300	-	...
Gross Fixed Capital Formation, Total	88102	55473	32629	...	189249	122688	66561	...	324981	214754	110227	...
1 Residential buildings				...				...				...
2 Non-residential buildings	52690	29823	22867	...	113037	61549	51488	...	192705	98282	94423	...
3 Other construction				...				...				...
4 Land improvement and plantation and orchard development	1797	1797	-	...	3167	3167	-	...	7546	7546	-	...
5 Producers' durable goods	33615	23853	9762	...	73045	57972	15073	...	124730	108926	15804	...
6 Breeding stock, dairy cattle, etc.	...	...	...	...	...	...	...	...	...	...	...	...
Total Gross Capital Formation	99569	66940	32629	...	237467	170906	66561	...	359281	249054	110227	...

	1989 TOTAL	1989 Total Private	1989 Public Enterprises	1989 General Government	1990 TOTAL	1990 Total Private	1990 Public Enterprises	1990 General Government	1991 TOTAL	1991 Total Private	1991 Public Enterprises	1991 General Government
Increase in stocks, total a	-13943	-13943	-	...	20468	20468	-	...	197102	197102	-	...
Gross Fixed Capital Formation, Total	559892	350601	209291	...	1090468	745508	344960	...	2282986	1483709	799277	...
1 Residential buildings				...				...				...
2 Non-residential buildings	350857	165879	184978	...	659597	357235	302362	...	1372271	790630	581641	...
3 Other construction				...				...				...
4 Land improvement and plantation and orchard development	10150	10150	-	...	18340	18340	-	...	37875	37875	-	...
5 Producers' durable goods	198885	174572	24313	...	412531	369933	42598	...	872840	655204	217636	...
6 Breeding stock, dairy cattle, etc.	...	...	...	...	...	...	...	...	...	...	...	...
Total Gross Capital Formation	545949	336658	209291	...	1110936	765976	344960	...	2480088	1680811	799277	...

a) Item 'Increase in stocks' refers to increase in stocks of wool and livestock in the private sector, and to stocks held by the public sector.

2.8 Gross Capital Formation by Type of Good and Owner, in Constant Prices

Million Uruguayan new pesos

At constant prices of:1983

	1983 TOTAL	1983 Total Private	1983 Public Enterprises	1983 General Government	1984 TOTAL	1984 Total Private	1984 Public Enterprises	1984 General Government	1985 TOTAL	1985 Total Private	1985 Public Enterprises	1985 General Government
Increase in stocks, total a	953	953	-	...	2339	2339	-	...	3828	3828	-	...
Gross Fixed Capital Formation, Total	24042	15069	8973	...	18531	10688	7843	...	14847	9098	5749	...
1 Residential buildings				...				...				...
2 Non-residential buildings	16323	10014	6309	...	14047	7126	6921	...	9955	5569	4386	...
3 Other construction				...				...				...
4 Land improvement and plantation and orchard development	445	445	-	...	326	326	-	...	293	293	-	...
5 Producers' durable goods	7274	4610	2664	...	4158	3236	922	...	4599	3236	1363	...
6 Breeding stock, dairy cattle, etc.	...	...	...	...	...	...	...	...	...	...	...	...
Total Gross Capital Formation	24995	16022	8973	...	20870	13027	7843	...	18675	12926	5749	...

Uruguay

2.8 Gross Capital Formation by Type of Good and Owner, in Constant Prices

Million Uruguayan new pesos

	1986				1987				1988			
	TOTAL	Total Private	Public Enterprises	General Government	TOTAL	Total Private	Public Enterprises	General Government	TOTAL	Total Private	Public Enterprises	General Government
At constant prices of:1983												
Increase in stocks, total a	5122	5122	-	...	4570	4570	-	...	1774	1774	-	...
Gross Fixed Capital Formation, Total	16751	10035	6716	...	21329	13224	8105	...	22272	14164	8108	...
1 Residential buildings				...				...				...
2 Non-residential buildings	10291	5722	4569	...	12863	6812	6051	...	13590	6686	6904	...
3 Other construction				...				...				...
4 Land improvement and plantation and orchard development	411	411	-	...	450	450	-	...	705	705	-	...
5 Producers' durable goods	6049	3902	2147	...	8016	5962	2054	...	7977	6773	1204	...
6 Breeding stock, dairy cattle, etc.	...	...	...	...	...	...	...	...	...	...	...	...
Total Gross Capital Formation	21873	15157	6716	...	25899	17794	8105	...	24046	15938	8108	...

	1989				1990				1991			
	TOTAL	Total Private	Public Enterprises	General Government	TOTAL	Total Private	Public Enterprises	General Government	TOTAL	Total Private	Public Enterprises	General Government
At constant prices of:1983												
Increase in stocks, total a	-313	-313	-	...	2211	2211	-	...	3374	3374	-	...
Gross Fixed Capital Formation, Total	22158	13425	8733	...	20848	13905	6943	...	23880	15348	8532	...
1 Residential buildings				...				...				...
2 Non-residential buildings	13867	6305	7562	...	12445	6507	5938	...	12627	7121	5506	...
3 Other construction				...				...				...
4 Land improvement and plantation and orchard development	511	511	-	...	423	423	-	...	542	542	-	...
5 Producers' durable goods	7780	6609	1171	...	7980	6975	1005	...	10711	7685	3026	...
6 Breeding stock, dairy cattle, etc.	...	...	...	...	...	...	...	...	...	...	...	...
Total Gross Capital Formation	21845	13112	8733	...	23059	16116	6943	...	27254	18722	8532	...

a) Item 'Increase in stocks' refers to increase in stocks of wool and livestock in the private sector, and to stocks held by the public sector.

4.1 Derivation of Value Added by Kind of Activity, in Current Prices

Million Uruguayan new pesos

	1983			1984			1985			1986		
	Gross Output	Intermediate Consumption	Value Added	Gross Output	Intermediate Consumption	Value Added	Gross Output	Intermediate Consumption	Value Added	Gross Output	Intermediate Consumption	Value Added
All Producers												
1 Agriculture, hunting, forestry and fishing	33005	9500	23505	56548	16892	39656	97582	32506	65076	162126	49468	112658
A Agriculture and hunting	31952	8924	23028	54677	15890	38787	94508	30615	63893	156880	46634	110246
B Forestry and logging	...	...	...	...	...	...	...	...	...	...	...	...
C Fishing	1053	576	477	1871	1002	869	3074	1891	1183	5246	2834	2412
2 Mining and quarrying	801	290	511	1037	390	647	1373	592	781	2649	952	1697
3 Manufacturing	118796	74322	44474	199154	125205	73949	350291	209571	140720	604502	339901	264601
A Manufacture of food, beverages and tobacco	50162	31965	18196	72183	50626	21556	129572	87698	41874	210042	139624	70416
B Textile, wearing apparel and leather industries	14941	9647	5294	30692	19205	11488	51372	29713	21659	93287	51988	41301
C Manufacture of wood and wood products, including furniture	5868	4151	1717	10423	6917	3506	14489	8774	5716	24364	16748	7617
D Manufacture of paper and paper products, printing and publishing	4427	2521	1905	8551	4445	4106	15628	7933	7695	29060	14509	14552
E Manufacture of chemicals and chemical petroleum, coal, rubber and plastic products	28136	18975	9160	48418	29916	18500	89338	52314	37025	140898	68735	72163
F Manufacture of non-metallic mineral products, except products of petroleum and coal	4211	1782	2428	6210	2522	3688	10017	4634	5384	19779	8100	11679
G Basic metal industries	1019	499	521	1811	861	950	3186	1450	1736	5301	2734	2567
H Manufacture of fabricated metal products, machinery and equipment	7172	3248	3924	15465	7926	7539	29268	13301	15965	67369	30625	36743
I Other manufacturing industries	2861	1532	1329	5403	2786	2617	7421	3756	3665	14400	6838	7562
4 Electricity, gas and water a	8001	2338	5663	12046	3256	8790	21836	5613	16223	41016	9163	31853
A Electricity, gas and steam	6998	1957	5041	10492	2617	7875	18403	4584	13819	33978	7272	26706
B Water works and supply	1003	381	622	1554	639	915	3433	1029	2404	7038	1891	5147

2028

4.1 Derivation of Value Added by Kind of Activity, in Current Prices
(Continued)

Million Uruguayan new pesos

	1983			1984			1985			1986		
	Gross Output	Intermediate Consumption	Value Added	Gross Output	Intermediate Consumption	Value Added	Gross Output	Intermediate Consumption	Value Added	Gross Output	Intermediate Consumption	Value Added
5 Construction	19404	11925	7479	26985	17081	9904	40264	25917	14347	69785	45361	24424
6 Wholesale and retail trade, restaurants and hotels	27071	8172	18899	48806	14805	34001	89146	29195	59951	163824	51887	111937
A Wholesale and retail trade	19478	3330	16148	34660	5927	28733	58598	10020	48578	111752	19110	92642
B Restaurants and hotels	7593	4842	2751	14146	8878	5268	30548	19175	11373	52072	32777	19295
7 Transport, storage and communication	19396	8698	10698	30339	14434	15905	55207	26458	28749	101333	44521	56812
A Transport and storage	16204	7937	8267	25254	13349	11905	45697	23922	21775	84100	39987	44113
B Communication	3192	761	2431	5085	1085	4000	9510	2536	6974	17233	4534	12699
8 Finance, insurance, real estate and business services	47396	6002	41394	76083	9011	67072	126178	16912	109266	206682	30728	175954
A Financial institutions	16476	1935	14541	34489	3041	31448	59132	5657	53475	92566	9818	82748
B Insurance	2219	1034	1185	3727	1506	2221	7779	3182	4597	13737	6020	7717
C Real estate and business services	28701	3033	25668	37867	4464	33403	59267	8073	51194	100379	14890	85489
Real estate, except dwellings	25467	2290	23177	33434	3434	30000	51267	6217	45050	83573	11160	72413
Dwellings	3234	743	2491	4433	1030	3403	8000	1856	6144	16806	3730	13076
9 Community, social and personal services [b]	19775	6839	12936	28897	10145	18752	54131	18643	35488	101993	32589	69404
A Sanitary and similar services	...	...	...	...	...	...	...	...	...	...	...	...
B Social and related community services	8078	3513	4565	12574	5499	7075	24977	10312	14665	47522	17797	29725
C Recreational and cultural services	4415	753	3662	6393	1221	5172	11164	2240	8924	20469	3601	16868
D Personal and household services	7282	2573	4709	9930	3425	6505	17990	6091	11899	34002	11191	22811
Total, Industries	293645	128086	165559	479895	211219	268676	836008	365407	470601	1453910	604570	849340
Producers of Government Services	25486	6585	18901	36851	11086	25765	69154	21007	48147	127586	35937	91649
Other Producers [b]	...	...	...	...	...	...	...	...	...	...	...	...
Total	319131	134671	184460	516746	222305	294441	905162	386414	518748	1581496	640507	940989
Less: Imputed bank service charge	...	-13901	13901	...	-32511	32511	...	-56124	56124	...	-85628	85628
Import duties	4858	...	4858	9095	...	9095	16017	...	16017	35090	...	35090
Value added tax	...	...	...	...	...	...	...	...	...	...	...	...
Total	323989	148572	175417	525841	254816	271025	921179	442538	478641	1616586	726135	890451

	1987			1988			1989			1990		
	Gross Output	Intermediate Consumption	Value Added	Gross Output	Intermediate Consumption	Value Added	Gross Output	Intermediate Consumption	Value Added	Gross Output	Intermediate Consumption	Value Added
						All Producers						
1 Agriculture, hunting, forestry and fishing	309170	81343	227827	496804	133160	363644	837101	231708	605393	1583069	468800	1114269
A Agriculture and hunting	299588	76764	222824	486756	128993	357763	815082	222599	592483	1547412	455975	1091437
B Forestry and logging	...	...	...	...	...	...	...	...	...	...	...	...
C Fishing	9582	4579	5003	10048	4167	5881	22019	9109	12910	35657	12825	22832
2 Mining and quarrying	5310	1632	3678	7875	3436	4439	15266	4959	10307	25419	8414	17005

Uruguay

Million Uruguayan new pesos

	1987			1988			1989			1990		
	Gross Output	Intermediate Consumption	Value Added	Gross Output	Intermediate Consumption	Value Added	Gross Output	Intermediate Consumption	Value Added	Gross Output	Intermediate Consumption	Value Added
3 Manufacturing	1089589	608638	480951	1743571	973959	769612	3127595	1860440	1267155	6279926	3735594	2544332
A Manufacture of food, beverages and tobacco	351531	225894	125637	...	...	...	...	...	...	...	...	...
B Textile, wearing apparel and leather industries	172258	98964	73294	...	...	...	...	...	...	...	...	...
C Manufacture of wood and wood products, including furniture	47639	33382	14256	...	...	...	...	...	...	...	...	...
D Manufacture of paper and paper products, printing and publishing	54950	28530	26420	...	...	...	...	...	...	...	...	...
E Manufacture of chemicals and chemical petroleum, coal, rubber and plastic products	240899	126031	114868	...	...	...	...	...	...	...	...	...
F Manufacture of non-metallic mineral products, except products of petroleum and coal	38880	15019	23862	...	...	...	...	...	...	...	...	...
G Basic metal industries	9796	5073	4722	...	...	...	...	...	...	...	...	...
H Manufacture of fabricated metal products, machinery and equipment	150093	63892	86200	...	...	...	...	...	...	...	...	...
I Other manufacturing industries	23543	11851	11692	...	...	...	...	...	...	...	...	...
4 Electricity, gas and water a	78007	21425	56582	124089	46342	77747	225378	112720	112658	553104	278202	274902
A Electricity, gas and steam	66503	18138	48365	106419	40531	65888	193508	101607	91901	483877	254062	229815
B Water works and supply	11504	3287	8217	17670	5811	11859	31870	11113	20757	69227	24140	45087
5 Construction	147190	93027	54163	254007	160627	93380	457669	274187	183482	883127	580719	302408
6 Wholesale and retail trade, restaurants and hotels	291620	89342	202278	473325	151859	321466	848278	270123	578155	1767506	586147	1181359
A Wholesale and retail trade	206237	35267	170970	319881	54700	265181	578201	98872	479329	1158353	198079	960274
B Restaurants and hotels	85383	54075	31308	153444	97159	56285	270077	171251	98826	609153	388068	221085
7 Transport, storage and communication	172436	75966	96470	291868	131044	160824	548156	229894	318262	1094751	463780	630971
A Transport and storage	143497	67312	76185	241768	114303	127465	446572	204584	241988	869428	407462	461966
B Communication	28939	8654	20285	50100	16741	33359	101584	25310	76274	225323	56318	169005
8 Finance, insurance, real estate and business services	345833	52386	293447	644450	85325	559125	1319925	151323	1168602	2785415	319740	2465675
A Financial institutions	135169	16671	118498	275868	27467	248401	583504	48978	534526	1417338	134697	1282641
B Insurance	23238	8440	14798	41291	10580	30711						
C Real estate and business services	187426	27275	160151	327291	47278	280013	659845	88717	571128	1368077	185043	1183034
Real estate, except dwellings	157361	20456	136905	273264	34625	238639	546205	64028	482177	1116152	130839	985313
Dwellings	30065	6819	23246	54027	12653	41374	113640	24689	88951	251925	54204	197721
9 Community, social and personal services b	185379	58488	126891	317488	102219	215269	593616	186126	407490	1272289	404986	867303
A Sanitary and similar services	...	...	...	...	...	...	...	...	...	...	...	...
B Social and related community services	87377	32513	54864	149586	57478	92108	289011	107258	181753	648479	239456	409023
C Recreational and cultural services	36554	6393	30161	60364	9902	50462	104132	16122	88010	202980	31416	171564
D Personal and household services	61448	19582	41866	107538	34839	72699	200473	62746	137727	420830	134114	286716
Total, Industries	2624534	1082247	1542287	4353477	1787971	2565506	7972984	3321480	4651504	16244606	6846382	9398224
Producers of Government Services	219727	56803	162924	358572	94324	264248	647000	172318	474682	1287228	387716	899512
Other Producers b	...	...	...	...	...	...	...	...	...	...	...	...
Total	2844261	1139050	1705211	4712049	1882295	2829754	8619984	3493798	5126186	17531834	7234098	10297736
Less: Imputed bank service charge	...	-107814	107814	...	-212687	212687	...	-466354	466354	...	1009204	1009204
Import duties	64080	...	64080	108440	...	108440	179456	...	179456	409504	...	409504
Value added tax	...	...	...	...	...	...	...	...	...	...	...	...
Total	2908341	1246864	1661477	4820489	2094982	2725507	8799440	3960152	4839288	7941338	8243302	9698036

4.1 Derivation of Value Added by Kind of Activity, in Current Prices

Million Uruguayan new pesos

All Producers

		1991		
		Gross Output	Intermediate Consumption	Value Added
1	Agriculture, hunting, forestry and fishing	2640764	770554	1870210
A	Agriculture and hunting	2522681	728081	1794600
B	Forestry and logging	...	...	...
C	Fishing	118083	42473	75610
2	Mining and quarrying	51767	17135	34632
3	Manufacturing	1878202	7065711	4812491
A	Manufacture of food, beverages and tobacco	...	...	...
B	Textile, wearing apparel and leather industries	...	...	...
C	Manufacture of wood and wood products, including furniture	...	...	...
D	Manufacture of paper and paper products, printing and publishing	...	...	...
E	Manufacture of chemicals and chemical petroleum, coal, rubber and plastic products	...	...	...
F	Manufacture of non-metallic mineral products, except products of petroleum and coal	...	...	...
G	Basic metal industries	...	...	...
H	Manufacture of fabricated metal products, machinery and equipment	...	...	...
I	Other manufacturing industries	...	...	...
4	Electricity, gas and water a	1068439	532783	535656
A	Electricity, gas and steam	907591	476694	430897
B	Water works and supply	160848	56089	104759
5	Construction	1858048	1131679	726369
6	Wholesale and retail trade, restaurants and hotels	3696119	1305009	2391110
A	Wholesale and retail trade	2244285	383773	1860512
B	Restaurants and hotels	1451834	921236	530598
7	Transport, storage and communication	2117465	897613	1219852
A	Transport and storage	1650008	781078	868930
B	Communication	467457	116535	350922
8	Finance, insurance, real estate and business services	5613959	652401	4961558
A	Financial institutions	2659647	252760	2406887
B	Insurance			
C	Real estate and business services	2954312	399641	2554671
	Real estate, except dwellings	2403894	281793	2122101
	Dwellings	550418	117848	432570
9	Community, social and personal services b	2911121	939942	1971179
A	Sanitary and similar services	...	...	...
B	Social and related community services	1579044	577904	1001140
C	Recreational and cultural services	416273	64388	351885
D	Personal and household services	915804	297650	618154
	Total, Industries	21835884	3312827	18523057
	Producers of Government Services	2551896	868096	1683800
	Other Producers b	...	...	...
	Total	24387780	4180923	20206857
	Less: Imputed bank service charge	...	1895156	1895156
	Import duties	823767	...	823767
	Value added tax	...	...	...
	Total	25211547	6076079	19135468

a) Item 'Electricity, gas and water' includes sewage services.
b) Item 'Other producers' is included in item 'Community, social and personal services'.

Uruguay

4.2 Derivation of Value Added by Kind of Activity, in Constant Prices

Million Uruguayan new pesos

	1983			1984			1985			1986		
	Gross Output	Intermediate Consumption	Value Added	Gross Output	Intermediate Consumption	Value Added	Gross Output	Intermediate Consumption	Value Added	Gross Output	Intermediate Consumption	Value Added
						At constant prices of:1983						
						All Producers						
1 Agriculture, hunting, forestry and fishing	...	...	23505	...	...	20489	...	...	23061	...	...	22483
A Agriculture and hunting	...	...	23028	...	...	19951	...	...	22522	...	...	22080
B Forestry and logging	...	...	...	...	...	...	...	...	...	...	...	...
C Fishing	...	...	477	...	...	538	...	...	539	...	...	403
2 Mining and quarrying	...	...	511	...	...	434	...	...	346	...	...	404
3 Manufacturing	...	...	44474	...	...	46466	...	...	45740	...	...	51108
A Manufacture of food, beverages and tobacco	...	...	18196	...	...	15808	...	...	16464	...	...	17086
B Textile, wearing apparel and leather industries	...	...	5294	...	...	6618	...	...	6320	...	...	7266
C Manufacture of wood and wood products, including furniture	...	...	1717	...	...	1753	...	...	1408	...	...	1578
D Manufacture of paper and paper products, printing and publishing	...	...	1905	...	...	2186	...	...	2046	...	...	2379
E Manufacture of chemicals and chemical petroleum, coal, rubber and plastic products	...	...	9160	...	...	9833	...	...	9850	...	...	11081
F Manufacture of non-metallic mineral products, except products of petroleum and coal	...	...	2428	...	...	2463	...	...	2081	...	...	2652
G Basic metal industries	...	...	521	...	...	603	...	...	558	...	...	588
H Manufacture of fabricated metal products, machinery and equipment	...	...	3924	...	...	5439	...	...	5673	...	...	6918
I Other manufacturing industries	...	...	1329	...	...	1762	...	...	1338	...	...	1561
4 Electricity, gas and water [a]	...	...	5663	...	...	5613	...	...	5796	...	...	6041
A Electricity, gas and steam	...	...	5041	...	...	5005	...	...	5157	...	...	5377
B Water works and supply	...	...	622	...	...	608	...	...	639	...	...	664
5 Construction	...	...	7479	...	...	6496	...	...	4659	...	...	4823
6 Wholesale and retail trade, restaurants and hotels	...	...	18899	...	...	20068	...	...	21166	...	...	23122
A Wholesale and retail trade	...	...	16148	...	...	16671	...	...	17028	...	...	19179
B Restaurants and hotels	...	...	2751	...	...	3397	...	...	4138	...	...	3943
7 Transport, storage and communication	...	...	10698	...	...	10098	...	...	10595	...	...	12138
A Transport and storage	...	...	8267	...	...	7754	...	...	8152	...	...	9480
B Communication	...	...	2431	...	...	2344	...	...	2443	...	...	2658
8 Finance, insurance, real estate and business services	...	...	41394	...	...	40106	...	...	41315	...	...	42230
9 Community, social and personal services [b]	...	...	31837	...	...	31534	...	...	32000	...	...	34880
Total, Industries	...	...	184460	...	...	181304	...	...	184678	...	...	197229
Producers of Government Services	...	...	...	...	...	...	...	...	...	...	...	...
Other Producers	...	...	...	...	...	...	...	...	...	...	...	...
Total	...	...	...	...	...	...	...	...	...	...	...	...
Less: Imputed bank service charge	...	...	...	...	...	...	...	...	...	...	...	...
Import duties	...	...	...	...	...	...	...	...	...	...	...	...
Value added tax	...	...	...	...	...	...	...	...	...	...	...	...
Total	...	...	175417	...	...	173501	...	...	176061	...	...	191654

	1987			1988			1989			1990		
	Gross Output	Intermediate Consumption	Value Added	Gross Output	Intermediate Consumption	Value Added	Gross Output	Intermediate Consumption	Value Added	Gross Output	Intermediate Consumption	Value Added
						At constant prices of:1983						
						All Producers						
1 Agriculture, hunting, forestry and fishing	...	...	23510	...	...	23139	...	...	23938	...	...	24267
A Agriculture and hunting	...	...	23140	...	...	22877	...	...	23614	...	...	23991
B Forestry and logging	...	...	...	...	...	...	...	...	...	...	...	...
C Fishing	...	...	370	...	...	262	...	...	324	...	...	276
2 Mining and quarrying	...	...	462	...	...	369	...	...	371	...	...	290

4.2 Derivation of Value Added by Kind of Activity, in Constant Prices
(Continued)

Million Uruguayan new pesos

	1987			1988			1989			1990		
	Gross Output	Intermediate Consumption	Value Added	Gross Output	Intermediate Consumption	Value Added	Gross Output	Intermediate Consumption	Value Added	Gross Output	Intermediate Consumption	Value Added
At constant prices of:1983												
3 Manufacturing	...	...	56156	...	...	55667	...	...	55560	...	...	54750
A Manufacture of food, beverages and tobacco	...	...	17118	...	...	18864	...	...	19790	...	...	19536
B Textile, wearing apparel and leather industries	...	...	7808	...	...	7051	...	...	8829	...	...	8051
C Manufacture of wood and wood products, including furniture	...	...	1709	...	...	1488	...	...	1068	...	...	1052
D Manufacture of paper and paper products, printing and publishing	...	...	2625	...	...	2406	...	...	2212	...	...	2166
E Manufacture of chemicals and chemical petroleum, coal, rubber and plastic products	...	...	12406	...	...	12369	...	...	11892	...	...	12206
F Manufacture of non-metallic mineral products, except products of petroleum and coal	...	...	3573	...	...	3478	...	...	3669	...	...	3775
G Basic metal industries	...	...	688	...	...	670	...	...	668	...	...	624
H Manufacture of fabricated metal products, machinery and equipment	...	...	8804	...	...	7948	...	...	7139	...	...	7062
I Other manufacturing industries	...	...	1427	...	...	1396	...	...	294	...	...	262
4 Electricity, gas and water [a]	...	...	6837	...	...	7415	...	...	6680	...	...	7456
A Electricity, gas and steam	...	...	6152	...	...	6693	...	...	5939	...	...	6711
B Water works and supply	...	...	685	...	...	722	...	...	741	...	...	745
5 Construction	...	...	5956	...	...	6356	...	...	6494	...	...	5719
6 Wholesale and retail trade, restaurants and hotels	...	...	24899	...	...	24503	...	...	24279	...	...	24271
A Wholesale and retail trade	...	...	21193	...	...	20515	...	...	20345	...	...	20364
B Restaurants and hotels	...	...	3706	...	...	3988	...	...	3934	...	...	3907
7 Transport, storage and communication	...	...	12795	...	...	13434	...	...	14565	...	...	14535
A Transport and storage	...	...	9884	...	...	10359	...	...	10660	...	...	9963
B Communication	...	...	2911	...	...	3075	...	...	3905	...	...	4572
8 Finance, insurance, real estate and business services	...	...	45068	...	...	47202	...	...	50043	...	...	50949
9 Community, social and personal services [b]	...	...	37319	...	...	36735	...	...	37421	...	...	38393
Total, Industries	...	...	213002	...	...	214820	...	...	219351	...	...	220630
Producers of Government Services	...	...	...	...	...	...	...	...	...	...	...	...
Other Producers	...	...	...	...	...	...	...	...	...	...	...	...
Total	...	...	...	...	...	...	...	...	...	...	...	...
Less: Imputed bank service charge	...	...	...	...	...	...	...	...	...	...	...	...
Import duties	...	...	...	...	...	...	...	...	...	...	...	...
Value added tax	...	...	...	...	...	...	...	...	...	...	...	...
Total	...	...	206858	...	...	206840	...	...	209499	...	...	211418

	1991		
	Gross Output	Intermediate Consumption	Value Added
At constant prices of:1983			
All Producers			
1 Agriculture, hunting, forestry and fishing	...	...	24262
A Agriculture and hunting	...	...	23889
B Forestry and logging	...	...	...
C Fishing	...	...	373
2 Mining and quarrying	...	...	285

Uruguay

Million Uruguayan new pesos

	1991		
	Gross Output	Intermediate Consumption	Value Added
			At constant prices of:1983
3 Manufacturing	...	...	54464
A Manufacture of food, beverages and tobacco	...	...	19759
B Textile, wearing apparel and leather industries	...	...	8407
C Manufacture of wood and wood products, including furniture	...	...	1047
D Manufacture of paper and paper products, printing and publishing	...	...	2587
E Manufacture of chemicals and chemical petroleum, coal, rubber and plastic products	...	...	11747
F Manufacture of non-metallic mineral products, except products of petroleum and coal	...	...	3432
G Basic metal industries	...	...	627
H Manufacture of fabricated metal products, machinery and equipment	...	...	6572
I Other manufacturing industries	...	...	266
4 Electricity, gas and water a	...	...	8069
A Electricity, gas and steam	...	...	7290
B Water works and supply	...	...	779
5 Construction	...	...	5717
6 Wholesale and retail trade, restaurants and hotels	...	...	25800
A Wholesale and retail trade	...	...	21384
B Restaurants and hotels	...	...	4416
7 Transport, storage and communication	...	...	14946
A Transport and storage	...	...	9973
B Communication	...	...	4973
8 Finance, insurance, real estate and business services	...	...	50477
9 Community, social and personal services b	...	...	38240
Total, Industries	...	...	222260
Producers of Government Services	...	...	...
Other Producers	...	...	...
Total	...	...	...
Less: Imputed bank service charge	...	...	...
Import duties	...	...	...
Value added tax	...	...	...
Total	...	...	215357

a) Item 'Electricity, gas and water' includes sewage services.
b) Items 'Other producers' and 'Producers of government services' are included in item 'Community, social and personal services'.

USSR (Former)

Source. Communication from the Central Statistical Office of the former USSR, Moscow. The official estimates and descriptions are published annually in 'Narodnoe Khozyaistvo SSSR' (National Economy of the USSR).

General note. The estimates shown in the following tables have been prepared in accordance with the System of Material Product Balances. Therefore, these estimates are not comparable in concept and coverage with those conforming to the United Nations System of National Accounts. In addition, the table 'Expenditure on the Gross Domestic Product, in Current Prices' in accordance with the United Nations System of National Accounts (SNA) is also shown. It should be noted that the estimates for the former USSR include those for the Belarus and Ukraine. Separate country chapters for those two States are shown in this Yearbook.

1.1 Expenditure on the Gross Domestic Product, in Current Prices

Thousand Million Roubles

	1980	1981	1982	1983	1984	1985	1986	1987	1988	1989	1990	1991
1 Government final consumption expenditure [a]	...	...	...	...	...	159.3	166.0	172.0	188.1	...	...	...
2 Private final consumption expenditure	...	...	...	...	...	369.3	377.0	388.2	411.2	...	...	...
3 Gross capital formation	...	...	...	...	...	248.4	255.5	264.8	276.1	...	...	...
4 Exports of goods and services	...	...	...	...	...							
5 Less: Imports of goods and services	...	...	...	...	...	...	...	...	...			
Equals: Gross Domestic Product [b]	...	...	...	...	...	777.0	798.5	825.0	875.4	...	...	...

a) Item 'Government final consumption expenditure' includes net exports and net income from abroad.
b) Gross national product rather than gross domestic product.

1a Net Material Product by Use at Current Market Prices

Thousand Million Roubles

	1980	1981	1982	1983	1984	1985	1986	1987	1988	1989	1990	1991
1 Personal consumption	297.7	314.8	325.0	336.4	348.4	356.9	363.6	373.5	393.0	426.4	...	...
2 Material consumption in the units of the non-material sphere serving individuals	33.5	35.0	37.5	39.3	40.6	41.8	43.5	45.8	48.2	51.8	...	...
Consumption of the Population	331.2	349.8	362.5	375.7	389.0	398.7	407.1	419.3	441.2	478.2		
3 Material consumption in the units of the non-material sphere serving the community as a whole	14.3	15.1	16.0	17.3	18.4	19.7	20.5	22.6	24.5	26.0	...	...
4 Net fixed capital formation [ab]	108.6	113.0	134.4	143.4	151.8	150.3	148.4	143.9	153.4	161.8		
5 Increase in material circulating assets and in stocks [abc]											...	...
6 Losses	...	...	...	...	...	...	...	...	...	...		
7 Exports of goods and material services	...	...	...	...	...	...	...	...	...			
8 Less: Imports of goods and material services	...	...	...	...	...	...	...	...	...			
Net Material Product	454.1	477.9	512.9	536.4	559.0	568.7	576.0	585.8	619.1	666.0		

a) Changes in work-in-progress on construction are included in item 'Increase in material circulating assets and in stocks'.
b) Increase in productive livestock and draught animals is included in item 'Net fixed capital formation'.
c) Item 'Increase in material circulating assets and in stocks' includes increase in value of young animals.

1b Net Material Product by Use at Constant Market Prices

Thousand Million Roubles

	1980	1981	1982	1983	1984	1985	1986	1987	1988	1989	1990	1991
				At constant prices of: 1983					1988			
1 Personal consumption	314.1	326.0	327.3	336.1	349.3	355.9	358.0	363.0	377.2 / 393.0	412.9	...	...
2 Material consumption in the units of the non-material sphere serving individuals	33.2	34.7	36.8	38.7	40.2	41.8	43.5	45.8	48.1 / 48.2	51.1	...	...
Consumption of the Population	347.3	360.7	364.1	374.8	389.5	397.7	401.5	408.8	425.3 / 441.2	464.0	...	...
3 Material consumption in the units of the non-material sphere serving the community as a whole	15.4	16.1	16.6	17.9	18.8	19.8	21.0	23.6	25.4 / 24.5	25.5	...	...
4 Net fixed capital formation [ab]	123.2	124.9	138.4	144.6	139.9	142.5	146.7	140.5	148.4 / 153.4	151.0		
5 Increase in material circulating assets and in stocks [abc]											...	...
6 Losses	...	...	...	...	...	...	...	...	...			
7 Exports of goods and material services	...								...			
8 Less: Imports of goods and material services	...								...			
Net Material Product	485.9	501.7	519.1	537.3	548.2	560.0	569.2	572.9	599.1 / 619.1	640.5	...	...

a) Changes in work-in-progress on construction are included in item 'Increase in material circulating assets and in stocks'.
b) Increase in productive livestock and draught animals is included in item 'Net fixed capital formation'.
c) Item 'Increase in material circulating assets and in stocks' includes increase in value of young animals.

USSR (Former)

2a Net Material Product by Kind of Activity of the Material Sphere in Current Market Prices

Thousand Million Roubles

	1980	1981	1982	1983	1984	1985	1986	1987	1988	1989	1990	1991
1 Agriculture and forestry	69.5	73.7	81.7	112.0	116.6	113.5	121.9	123.3	144.0	158.4	184.3	...
A Agriculture and livestock	68.9	73.1	80.9	111.1	115.7	112.8	121.2	122.6	143.3	157.7	183.5	...
B Forestry	0.6	0.6	0.8	0.9	0.9	0.7	0.7	0.7	0.7	0.7	0.8	...
C Other	...	...	...	...	...	...	...	...	...	...	...	...
2 Industrial activity [a]	238.1	248.0	266.6	253.8	262.1	263.1	258.0	268.6	269.5	282.0	290.6	...
3 Construction	47.6	49.0	51.9	53,2	59.4	62.3	70.3	74.7	80.6	86.4	92.6	...
4 Wholesale and retail trade and restaurants and other eating and drinking places [b]	80.0	87.9	92.1	96.1	98.7	104.6	100.7	96.4	98.0	109.0	114.7	...
5 Transport and communication	27.0	28.1	31.6	33.2	33.7	35.0	36.5	36.6	38.7	37.9	48.2	...
A Transport	25.8	26.9	30.3	31.7	32.1	33.3	34.7	34.6	36.6	35.6	45.8	...
B Communication	1.1	1.2	1.3	1.5	1.6	1.7	1.8	2.0	2.1	2.3	2.4	...
6 Other activities of the material sphere	...	...	...	...	...	...	...	...	...	...	...	...
Net material product	462.2	486.7	523.9	548.3	570.5	578.5	587.4	599.6	630.8	673.7	730.4	...

a) Item 'Industrial activity' includes turnover taxes realized in prices on industrial goods.
b) Item 'Wholesale and retail trade, restaurants and other eating and drinking places', refers to trade and procurement.

2b Net Material Product by Kind of Activity of the Material Sphere in Constant Market Prices

Index numbers 1975=100

At constant prices of:1983

	1980	1981	1982	1983	1984	1985	1986	1987	1988	1989	1990	1991
1 Agriculture and forestry	99	97 / 98	104	111	107	105	113	111	114	116	112	...
A Agriculture and livestock	99	97 / 98	104	111	107	105	113	111	114	116	112	...
B Forestry	102	101 / 99	99	109	109	110	110	111	114	127	128	...
C Other	...	...	...	...	...	...	...	...	...	...	...	...
2 Industrial activity	127	132 / 104	107	110	114	115	116	120	128	131	128	...
3 Construction	117	120 / 103	105	110	113	117	131	138	149	151	142	...
4 Wholesale and retail trade and restaurants and other eating and drinking places [a]	121	125 / 104	104	107	111	113	114	113	119	128	132	...
5 Transport and communication	120	125 / 104	107	112	113	116	120	121	128	119	109	...
A Transport	119	124 / 104	107	111	112	115	120	119	126	117	107	...
B Communication	148	157 / 106	111	122	127	133	141	152	165	178	166	...
6 Other activities of the material sphere	...	...	...	...	...	...	...	...	...	...	...	...
Net material product	124	128 / 103	107	112	115	117	120	122	127	130	125	...

a) Item 'Wholesale and retail trade, restaurants and other eating and drinking places', refers to trade and procurement.

6b Capital Formation by Kind of Activity of the Material and Non-Material Spheres in Constant Market Prices

Thousand Million Roubles

At constant prices of:1984

Net Fixed Capital Formation

	1980	1981	1982	1983	1984	1985	1986	1987	1988	1989	1990	1991
1 Agriculture and forestry	...	...	...	...	...	...	...	...	...	...	...	...
2 Industrial activity	...	...	...	...	...	...	...	...	...	...	...	...
3 Construction	...	...	...	...	...	...	...	...	...	...	...	...
4 Wholesale and retail trade, restaurants and other eating and drinking places	...	...	...	...	...	...	...	...	...	...	...	...
5 Transport and communication	...	...	...	...	...	...	...	...	...	...	...	...
6 Other activities of the material sphere	...	...	...	...	...	...	...	...	...	...	...	...
Total Material Sphere	...	...	...	...	...	...	...	...	...	...	...	...
7 Housing except owner-occupied, communal and miscellaneous personal services	...	...	...	...	...	...	...	...	...	...	...	...
8 Education, culture and art	...	...	...	...	...	...	...	...	...	...	...	...
9 Health and social welfare services and sports	...	...	...	...	...	...	...	...	...	...	...	...
Total Non-Material Sphere Serving Individuals	...	...	...	...	...	...	...	...	...	...	...	...

6b Capital Formation by Kind of Activity of the Material and Non-Material Spheres in Constant Market Prices
(Continued)

Thousand Million Roubles

	1980	1981	1982	1983	1984	1985	1986	1987	1988	1989	1990	1991
					At constant prices of:1984							
10 Government	...	...	...	...	...	...	...	...	...	...	...	...
11 Finance, credit and insurance	...	...	...	...	...	...	...	...	...	...	...	...
12 Research, scientific and technological institutes	...	...	...	...	...	...	...	...	...	...	...	...
13 Other activities of the non-material sphere	...	...	...	...	...	...	...	...	...	...	...	...
Total Non-Material Sphere Serving the Community as a Whole	...	...	...	...	...	...	...	...	...	...	...	...
14 Owner-occupied dwellings	...	...	...	...	...	...	...	...	...	...	...	...
Total Net Fixed Capital Formation	150.9	156.5	161.9	171.0	174.3	179.5	194.4	205.4	218.2	228.5	229.8	...
					Gross Fixed Capital Formation							
1 Agriculture and forestry	30.0	30.8	31.2	32.3	31.4	31.8	33.8	34.6	36.7	38.9	41.6	...
2 Industrial activity	53.3	55.3	56.8	60.4	62.7	65.5	71.0	75.0	79.5	85.7	78.9	...
3 Construction	6.0	5.9	6.4	6.2	5.8	6.1	6.8	6.9	8.3	10.6	9.9	...
4 Wholesale and retail trade and restaurants and other eating and drinking places	3.3	3.7	3.9	4.0	3.8	4.1	4.6	2.9	2.8	3.1	3.8	...
5 Transport and communcation	18.1	18.8	19.8	21.5	22.3	21.9	22.8	24.0	25.1	21.6	24.2	...
6 Other activities of the material sphere	0.5	0.5	0.5	0.5	0.5	0.4	0.5	1.8	1.8	1.5	1.7	...
Total Material Sphere	111.2	115.0	118.6	124.9	126.5	129.8	139.5	145.2	154.2	161.4	160.1	...
7 Housing except owner-occupied, communal and miscellaneous personal services	21.1	22.5	24.0	25.8	27.3	28.1	30.9	33.5	35.6	37.7	39.1	...
8 Education, culture and art	4.6	4.5	4.3	4.5	4.9	5.3	5.9	7.1	8.0	8.2	8.0	...
9 Health and social welfare services and sports	2.3	2.2	2.2	2.4	2.5	2.6	3.0	3.5	3.9	4.5	4.7	...
Total Non-Material Sphere Serving Individuals	28.0	29.2	30.5	32.7	34.7	36.0	39.8	44.1	47.5	50.4	51.8	...
10 Government												...
11 Finance, credit and insurance	11.7	12.3	12.8	13.4	13.1	13.7	15.1	16.1	16.5	16.7	17.9	...
12 Research, scientific and technological institutes												...
13 Other activities of the non-material sphere	...	...	...	...	...	...	...	...	...	...	...	...
Total Non-Material Sphere Serving the Community as a Whole	11.7	12.3	12.8	13.4	13.1	13.7	15.1	16.1	16.5	16.7	17.9	...
14 Owner-occupied dwellings	...	...	...	...	...	...	...	...	...	...	...	...
Total Gross Fixed Capital Formation	150.9	156.5	161.9	171.0	174.3	179.5	194.4	205.4	218.2	228.5	229.8	...

Vanuatu

Source. Reply to the United Nations National Accounts Questionnaire from the National Planing and Statistical Office, Vila. The estimates are published in 'National Income Accounts of Vanuatu, 1983 to 1987'.

General note. The estimates shown in the following tables have been prepared in accordance with the United Nations System of National Accounts so far as the existing data would permit.

1.1 Expenditure on the Gross Domestic Product, in Current Prices

Million Vanuatu francs

	1980	1981	1982	1983	1984	1985	1986	1987	1988	1989	1990	1991
1 Government final consumption expenditure	...	...	...	3660	4068	4501	4604	4544	4969	4881	5054	...
2 Private final consumption expenditure	...	...	...	5450	6306	7091	7406	8198	9562	10545	11267	...
3 Gross capital formation	...	...	...	2605	2949	3544	4200	4737	4611	6076	7799	...
A Increase in stocks	...	...	...	463	458	695	620	320	441	606	488	...
B Gross fixed capital formation	...	...	...	2142	2491	2849	3580	4417	4170	5470	7311	...
4 Exports of goods and services	...	...	...	5934	7757	6391	4417	5144	5508	6008	8301	...
5 Less: Imports of goods and services	...	...	...	7326	8424	9067	8253	9084	9213	10588	13714	...
Statistical discrepancy	...	...	...	-173	-317	74	-195	-135	-431	-555	-808	...
Equals: Gross Domestic Product	...	...	...	10150	12339	12534	12179	13404	15006	16367	17899	...

1.2 Expenditure on the Gross Domestic Product, in Constant Prices

Million Vanuatu francs

	1980	1981	1982	1983	1984	1985	1986	1987	1988	1989	1990	1991
				At constant prices of:1983								
1 Government final consumption expenditure	...	...	...	3660	3928	4237	4123	3814	3817	3461	...	...
2 Private final consumption expenditure	...	...	...	5450	6035	6079	6118	6051	6330	6591	...	...
3 Gross capital formation	...	...	...	2605	2805	3253	3742	3588	3197	3811	...	...
A Increase in stocks	...	...	...	463	435	634	559	267	350	433	...	...
B Gross fixed capital formation	...	...	...	2142	2370	2619	3183	3321	2847	3378	...	...
4 Exports of goods and services	...	...	...	5934	6309	5652	5001	4421	4232	4314	...	...
5 Less: Imports of goods and services	...	...	...	7326	8245	8737	7754	7696	7362	7407	...	...
Statistical discrepancy	...	...	...	-173	12	482	-486	611	637	573	...	...
Equals: Gross Domestic Product	...	...	...	10150	10846	10966	10743	10789	10850	11343	...	...

1.3 Cost Components of the Gross Domestic Product

Million Vanuatu francs

	1980	1981	1982	1983	1984	1985	1986	1987	1988	1989	1990	1991
1 Indirect taxes, net	...	...	...	1561	2068	2410	2387	2879	3116	3352	...	...
2 Consumption of fixed capital	...	...	...	...	...	...	...	...	...	...	...	...
3 Compensation of employees paid by resident producers to:	...	...	...	4255	4922	5370	5365	5586	6423	6785	...	...
4 Operating surplus	...	...	...	4335	5350	4755	4428	4940	5467	6230	...	...
Equals: Gross Domestic Product	...	...	...	10150	12339	12534	12179	13404	15006	16367	...	...

1.4 General Government Current Receipts and Disbursements

Million Vanuatu francs

	1980	1981	1982	1983	1984	1985	1986	1987	1988	1989	1990	1991
				Receipts								
1 Operating surplus	...	...	...	109	115	123	139	180	-38	55	...	...
2 Property and entrepreneurial income	...	...	...	156	159	160	146	73	194	253	...	...
3 Taxes, fees and contributions	...	...	...	1617	2142	2498	2444	2939	3178	3416	...	...
A Indirect taxes	...	...	...	1561	2068	2410	2387	2879	3116	3352	...	...
B Direct taxes	...	...	...	56	74	88	57	60	62	64	...	...
C Social security contributions	...	...	...	...	...	...	...	...	...	...	...	...
D Compulsory fees, fines and penalties	...	...	...	...	...	...	...	...	...	...	...	...
4 Other current transfers	...	...	...	2715	3319	2819	2509	5128	3920	2532	...	...
Total Current Receipts of General Government	...	...	...	4597	5735	5600	5237	8319	7254	6256	...	...
				Disbursements								
1 Government final consumption expenditure	...	...	...	3660	4068	4501	4604	4544	4969	4881	...	...

1.4 General Government Current Receipts and Disbursements
(Continued)

Million Vanuatu francs

	1980	1981	1982	1983	1984	1985	1986	1987	1988	1989	1990	1991
A Compensation of employees	...	...	...	1393	1597	1710	1893	1909	2144	2037	...	...
B Consumption of fixed capital	...	...	...	...	...	...	...	...	...	...	...	...
C Purchases of goods and services, net	...	...	...	2267	2471	2791	2711	2635	2825	2844	...	...
D Less: Own account fixed capital formation	...	...	...	...	...	...	...	...	...	...	...	...
E Indirect taxes paid, net	...	...	...	...	...	...	...	...	...	...	...	...
2 Property income	...	...	...	...	...	...	...	...	...	...	...	...
3 Subsidies	...	...	...	...	...	...	...	...	...	...	...	...
4 Other current transfers	...	...	...	73	73	53	90	124	136	141	...	...
5 Net saving	...	...	...	864	1594	1046	543	3651	2149	1234	...	...
Total Current Disbursements and Net Saving of General Government	...	...	...	4597	5735	5600	5237	8319	7254	6256	...	...

1.6 Current Income and Outlay of Households and Non-Profit Institutions

Million Vanuatu francs

	1980	1981	1982	1983	1984	1985	1986	1987	1988	1989	1990	1991
Receipts												
1 Compensation of employees	...	...	...	4255	4922	5370	5365	5586	6423	6785	...	...
2 Operating surplus of private unincorporated enterprises	...	...	...	...	...	...	...	...	...	...	...	...
3 Property and entrepreneurial income	...	...	...	2460	3138	3483	3531	2326	3120	4267	...	...
4 Current transfers	...	...	...	750	880	964	1177	1213	1339	923	...	...
Total Current Receipts	...	...	...	7465	8940	9816	10072	9124	10882	11975	...	...
Disbursements												
1 Private final consumption expenditure	...	...	...	5450	6306	7091	7406	8198	9562	10545	...	...
2 Property income	...	...	...	...	...	...	...	...	...	...	...	...
3 Direct taxes and other current transfers n.e.c. to general government	...	...	...	212	262	320	504	651	398	486	...	...
4 Other current transfers	...	...	...	...	...	...	...	...	...	...	...	...
Statistical discrepancy	...	...	...	-172	-316	74	-195	-135	-431	-555	...	...
5 Net saving	...	...	...	1976	2688	2331	2357	410	1353	1499	...	...
Total Current Disbursements and Net Saving	...	...	...	7465	8940	9816	10072	9124	10882	11975	...	...

1.7 External Transactions on Current Account, Summary

Million Vanuatu francs

	1980	1981	1982	1983	1984	1985	1986	1987	1988	1989	1990	1991
Payments to the Rest of the World												
1 Imports of goods and services	...	...	...	7326	8424	9067	8253	9084	9213	10588	...	...
A Imports of merchandise c.i.f.	...	...	...	4618	5174	5575	5014	6202	6106	7077	...	...
B Other	...	...	...	2708	3250	3492	3239	2882	3107	3511	...	...
2 Factor income to the rest of the world	...	...	...	2275	2818	2427	3816	4291	2857	1995	...	...
3 Current transfers to the rest of the world	...	...	...	226	266	303	522	701	459	550	...	...
4 Surplus of the nation on current transactions	...	...	...	1291	2798	1136	-233	761	595	-1199	...	...
Payments to the Rest of the World and Surplus of the Nation on Current Transactions	...	...	...	11118	14306	12933	12358	14837	13124	11934	...	...
Receipts From The Rest of the World												
1 Exports of goods and services	...	...	...	5934	7757	6391	4417	5144	5508	6008	...	...
A Exports of merchandise f.o.b.	...	...	...	2709	4201	3017	1449	1691	1719	1727	...	...
B Other	...	...	...	3225	3556	3374	2968	3453	3789	4281	...	...
2 Factor income from rest of the world	...	...	...	1778	2419	2829	4327	3426	2432	2548	...	...
3 Current transfers from rest of the world	...	...	...	3406	4130	3713	3614	6267	5184	3378	...	...
Receipts from the Rest of the World on Current Transactions	...	...	...	11118	14306	12933	12358	14837	13124	11934	...	...

Vanuatu

1.8 Capital Transactions of The Nation, Summary

Million Vanuatu francs

	1980	1981	1982	1983	1984	1985	1986	1987	1988	1989	1990	1991
Finance of Gross Capital Formation												
Gross saving	...	...	...	3896	5747	4680	3967	5498	5206	4877	...	...
1 Consumption of fixed capital	...	...	...	...	...	...	...	...	...	...	...	...
2 Net saving	...	...	...	3896	5747	4680	3967	5498	5206	4877	...	...
A General government	...	...	...	864	1594	1046	543	3651	2149	1234	...	...
B Corporate and quasi-corporate enterprises	...	...	...	1057	1464	1303	1066	1436	1704	2144	...	...
C Other	...	...	...	1976	2688	2331	2357	411	1353	1499	...	...
Less: Surplus of the nation on current transactions	...	...	...	1291	2798	1136	-233	761	595	-1199	...	...
Finance of Gross Capital Formation	...	...	...	2605	2949	3544	4200	4737	4611	6076	...	...
Gross Capital Formation												
Increase in stocks	...	...	...	463	458	695	620	320	441	606	...	...
Gross fixed capital formation	...	...	...	2142	2491	2849	3580	4417	4170	5470	...	...
Gross Capital Formation	...	...	...	2605	2949	3544	4200	4737	4611	6076	...	...

1.10 Gross Domestic Product by Kind of Activity, in Current Prices

Million Vanuatu francs

	1980	1981	1982	1983	1984	1985	1986	1987	1988	1989	1990	1991
1 Agriculture, hunting, forestry and fishing	...	...	...	2649	3542	3693	2958	2881	2933	3149	...	...
2 Mining and quarrying	...	...	...	...	...	...	...	...	...	...	...	...
3 Manufacturing	...	...	...	311	430	481	471	613	702	880	...	...
4 Electricity, gas and water	...	...	...	158	196	202	200	189	206	254	...	...
5 Construction	...	...	...	303	324	335	445	696	859	945	...	...
6 Wholesale and retail trade, restaurants and hotels	...	...	...	3627	4301	4046	3802	4393	4967	5254	...	...
7 Transport, storage and communication	...	...	...	757	868	873	909	1085	1216	1375	...	...
8 Finance, insurance, real estate and business services	...	...	...	1346	1425	1686	2227	1839	2445	2766	...	...
9 Community, social and personal services	...	...	...	72	80	90					...	...
Total, Industries	...	...	...	9223	11167	11407	11013	11696	13328	14623	...	...
Producers of Government Services	...	...	...	1393	1597	1710	1893	1909	2144	2037	...	...
Other Producers	...	...	...	...	...	...	...	...	...	...	...	...
Subtotal	...	...	...	10616	12764	13117	12906	13605	15472	16660	...	...
Less: Imputed bank service charge	...	...	...	465	425	583	727	201	466	293	...	...
Plus: Import duties	...	...	...	...	...	...	...	...	...	...	...	...
Plus: Value added tax	...	...	...	...	...	...	...	...	...	...	...	...
Equals: Gross Domestic Product	...	...	...	10150	12339	12534	12179	13404	15006	16367	...	...

1.11 Gross Domestic Product by Kind of Activity, in Constant Prices

Million Vanuatu francs

	1980	1981	1982	1983	1984	1985	1986	1987	1988	1989	1990	1991
At constant prices of:1983												
1 Agriculture, hunting, forestry and fishing	...	...	...	2649	2831	2771	2539	2383	2148	2350	...	...
2 Mining and quarrying	...	...	...	...	...	...	...	...	...	...	...	...
3 Manufacturing	...	...	...	311	419	466	467	588	684	774	...	...
4 Electricity, gas and water	...	...	...	158	191	192	190	180	191	214	...	...
5 Construction	...	...	...	303	293	282	368	514	598	638	...	...
6 Wholesale and retail trade, restaurants and hotels	...	...	...	3627	3740	3753	3378	3452	3460	3482	...	...
7 Transport, storage and communication	...	...	...	757	808	770	741	735	776	847	...	...
8 Finance, insurance, real estate and business services	...	...	...	1346	1359	1577	1993	1484	1769	1846	...	...
9 Community, social and personal services	...	...	...	72	72	74					...	...

1.11 Gross Domestic Product by Kind of Activity, in Constant Prices
(Continued)

Million Vanuatu francs

	1980	1981	1982	1983	1984	1985	1986	1987	1988	1989	1990	1991
				At constant prices of:1983								
Total, Industries	...	...	...	9223	9714	9886	9676	9335	9626	10151	...	...
Producers of Government Services	...	...	...	1393	1542	1629	1721	1614	1564	1390	...	...
Other Producers	...	...	...	...	...	...	...	...	...	...	...	...
Subtotal	...	...	...	10616	11256	11515	11397	10949	11190	11541	...	...
Less: Imputed bank service charge	...	...	...	465	410	548	654	160	340	198	...	...
Plus: Import duties	...	...	...	...	...	...	...	...	...	...	...	...
Plus: Value added tax	...	...	...	...	...	...	...	...	...	...	...	...
Equals: Gross Domestic Product	...	...	...	10150	10846	10966	10743	10789	10850	11343	...	...

1.12 Relations Among National Accounting Aggregates

Million Vanuatu francs

	1980	1981	1982	1983	1984	1985	1986	1987	1988	1989	1990	1991
Gross Domestic Product	...	...	...	10150	12339	12534	12179	13404	15006	16367	17899	...
Plus: Net factor income from the rest of the world	...	...	...	-497	-399	402	511	-865	-425	553	1283	...
Factor income from the rest of the world	...	...	...	1778	2419	2829	4327	3426	2432	2548	...	...
Less: Factor income to the rest of the world	...	...	...	2275	2818	2427	3816	4291	2857	1995	...	...
Equals: Gross National Product	...	...	...	9653	11940	12936	12690	12539	14581	16920	19182	...
Less: Consumption of fixed capital	...	...	...	...	...	...	...	...	...	...	...	...
Equals: National Income	...	...	...	9653	11940	12936	12690	12539	14581	16920	19182	...
Plus: Net current transfers from the rest of the world	...	...	...	3180	3864	3410	3092	5566	4725	2828	...	...
Current transfers from the rest of the world	...	...	...	3406	4130	3713	3614	6267	5184	3378	...	...
Less: Current transfers to the rest of the world	...	...	...	226	266	303	522	701	459	550	...	...
Equals: National Disposable Income	...	...	...	12833	15804	16346	15782	18105	19306	19748	...	...
Less: Final consumption	...	...	...	9110	10374	11592	12010	12742	14531	15426	...	...
Statistical discrepancy	...	...	...	172	316	-74	195	135	431	555	...	...
Equals: Net Saving	...	...	...	3896	5747	4680	3967	5498	5206	4877	...	...
Less: Surplus of the nation on current transactions	...	...	...	1291	2798	1136	-233	761	595	-1199	...	...
Equals: Net Capital Formation	...	...	...	2604	2949	3544	4200	4737	4611	6076	...	...

2.1 Government Final Consumption Expenditure by Function, in Current Prices

Million Vanuatu francs

	1980	1981	1982	1983	1984	1985	1986	1987	1988	1989	1990	1991
1 General public services	...	...	...	514	563	688	663	656	849	776	...	...
2 Defence	...	...	...	226	240	247	270	276	338	375	...	...
3 Public order and safety	...	...	...								...	...
4 Education	...	...	...	651	692	785	886	889	1046	854	...	...
5 Health	...	...	...	355	390	414	407	376	417	393	...	...
6 Social security and welfare	...	...	...								...	...
7 Housing and community amenities	...	...	...	15	18	19	20	15	25	13	...	...
8 Recreational, cultural and religious affairs	...	...	...	25	39	48	38	28	33	31	...	...
9 Economic services	...	...	...	521	614	665	697	675	910	1200	...	...
A Fuel and energy	...	...	...	32	33	48	54	58 .	109	520	...	...
B Agriculture, forestry, fishing and hunting	...	...	...	92	105	125	120	122	157	125	...	...
C Mining, manufacturing and construction, except fuel and energy	...	...	...	239	275	265	291	274	291	279	...	...
D Transportation and communication	...	...	...	94	127	130	133	136	157	141	...	...
E Other economic affairs	...	...	...	64	74	97	99	85	196	135	...	...
10 Other functions	...	...	...	1353	1512	1635	1625	1630	1351	1239	...	...
Total Government Final Consumption Expenditure	...	...	...	3660	4068	4501	4604	4544	4969	4881	...	...

Vanuatu

2.2 Government Final Consumption Expenditure by Function, in Constant Prices

Million Vanuatu francs

	1980	1981	1982	1983	1984	1985	1986	1987	1988	1989	1990	1991
					At constant prices of:1983							
1 General public services	...	...	...	...	...	305	306	318	395	373	...	...
2 Defence	...	...	...	...	...	132	230	223	247	278	...	...
3 Public order and safety	...	...	...	...	...						...	...
4 Education	...	...	...	...	...	558	627	647	724	661	...	...
5 Health	...	...	...	...	...	290	303	291	311	306	...	...
6 Social security and welfare	...	...	...	...	...						...	...
7 Housing and community amenities	...	...	...	...	...	11	12	13	12	4	...	...
8 Recreational, cultural and religious affairs	...	...	...	...	...	29	24	24	20	19	...	...
9 Economic services	...	...	...	...	...	385	390	392	435	396	...	...
A Fuel and energy						36	40	40	42	33		
B Agriculture, forestry, fishing and hunting	...	...	...	...	...	90	86	86	100	90	...	...
C Mining, manufacturing and construction, except fuel and energy	...	...	...	...	...	114	119	121	127	128	...	...
D Transportation and communication						74	74	78	90	80		
E Other economic affairs	...	...	...	...	...	71	71	67	76	65		
10 Other functions	...	...	...	...	...	...	...	...	...	...		
Total Government Final Consumption Expenditure	...	...	...	...	...	4237	4123	3814	3817	3461		

2.5 Private Final Consumption Expenditure by Type and Purpose, in Current Prices

Million Vanuatu francs

	1980	1981	1982	1983	1984	1985	1986	1987	1988	1989	1990	1991
			Final Consumption Expenditure of Resident Households									
1 Food, beverages and tobacco	...	...	...	2784	3144	3237	3585	3900	4453	4855	...	...
A Food	...	...	...	2165	2427	2469	2775	3089	3585	3848	...	...
B Non-alcoholic beverages	...	...	...								...	...
C Alcoholic beverages	...	...	...	619	717	768	810	811	868	1007	...	...
D Tobacco	...	...	...								...	...
2 Clothing and footwear	...	...	...	409	450	493	452	426	530	518	...	...
3 Gross rent, fuel and power	...	...	...	517	586	589	622	611	703	833	...	...
A Fuel and power	...	...	...	280	285	250	281	282	304	366	...	...
B Other	...	...	...	237	301	339	341	329	399	467	...	...
4 Furniture, furnishings and household equipment and operation	...	...	...	155	184	204	204	223	255	298	...	...
A Household operation	...	...	...	155	184	204	204	223	255	298	...	...
B Other				...	...	...	...	...	...	...		
5 Medical care and health expenses	...	...	...	135	173	...	...	...	...	...	...	...
6 Transport and communication	...	...	...	892	1083	1300	1398	1628	2151	2417	...	...
A Personal transport equipment	...	...	...	75	77	...	...	...	...	...	...	...
B Other	...	...	...	817	1006	...	...	...	...	...	...	...
7 Recreational, entertainment, education and cultural services	...	...	...	66	89	...	...	...	...	...	...	...
A Education	...	...	...	30	32	...	...	...	...	...	...	...
B Other	...	...	...	36	57	...	...	...	...	...	...	...
8 Miscellaneous goods and services	...	...	...	493	597	792	688	815	869	942	...	...
Total Final Consumption Expenditure in the Domestic Market by Households, of which	...	...	...	5450	6306	7091	7406	8198	9562	10545	...	...
Plus: Direct purchases abroad by resident households	...	...	...	...	...	...	...	...	...	...	...	...
Less: Direct purchases in the domestic market by non-resident households	...	...	...	...	...	...	...	...	...	...	...	...
Equals: Final Consumption Expenditure of Resident Households	...	...	...	5450	6306	7091	7406	8198	9562	10545	...	...
			Final Consumption Expenditure of Private Non-profit Institutions Serving Households									
Equals: Final Consumption Expenditure of Private Non-profit Organisations Serving Households	...	...	...	...	...	...	...	...	...	...	...	...
Private Final Consumption Expenditure	...	...	...	5450	6306	7091	7406	8198	9562	10545	...	...

2.6 Private Final Consumption Expenditure by Type and Purpose, in Constant Prices

Million Vanuatu francs

	1980	1981	1982	1983	1984	1985	1986	1987	1988	1989	1990	1991
At constant prices of:1983												
Final Consumption Expenditure of Resident Households												
1 Food, beverages and tobacco	...	...	...	2784	3020	2919	3105	3056	3100	3147	...	...
A Food	...	...	...	2165	2356	2328	2491	2499	2556	2567	...	...
B Non-alcoholic beverages	...	...	...		...						...	...
C Alcoholic beverages	...	...	...	619	...	591	614	557	544	580	...	...
D Tobacco	...	...	...		...						...	...
2 Clothing and footwear	...	...	...	409	436	475	435	395	467	453	...	...
3 Gross rent, fuel and power	...	...	...	517	586	564	559	559	631	734	...	...
A Fuel and power	...	...	...	280	308	253	269	258	274	325	...	...
B Other	...	...	...	237	278	311	290	301	357	409	...	...
4 Furniture, furnishings and household equipment and operation	...	...	...	155	173	167	169	149	161	172	...	...
A Household operation	...	...	...	155	173	167	169	149	161	172	...	...
B Other	...	...	...	...	...	...	...	...	...	...	...	...
5 Medical care and health expenses	...	...	...	135	166	...	...	...	...	...	...	...
6 Transport and communication	...	...	...	892	1001	907	945	876	1060	1168	...	...
A Personal transport equipment	...	...	...	75	77	...	...	...	...	...	...	...
B Other	...	...	...	817	924	...	...	...	...	...	...	...
7 Recreational, entertainment, education and cultural services	...	...	...	66	86	...	...	...	...	...	...	...
A Education	...	...	...	30	32	...	...	...	...	...	...	...
B Other	...	...	...	36	54	...	...	...	...	...	...	...
8 Miscellaneous goods and services	...	...	...	493	570	647	537	606	532	537	...	...
Total Final Consumption Expenditure in the Domestic Market by Households, of which	...	...	...	5450	6035	6079	6118	6051	6331	6591	...	...
Plus: Direct purchases abroad by resident households	...	...	...	...	...		...	...	...	...	...	...
Less: Direct purchases in the domestic market by non-resident households	...	...	...	...	...	...	...	...	...	...	...	...
Equals: Final Consumption Expenditure of Resident Households	...	...	...	5450	6035	6079	6118	6051	6331	6591	...	...
Final Consumption Expenditure of Private Non-profit Institutions Serving Households												
Equals: Final Consumption Expenditure of Private Non-profit Organisations Serving Households	...	...	...	...	...	...	...	...	...	...	...	...
Private Final Consumption Expenditure	...	...	...	5450	6035	6079	6118	6051	6331	6591	...	...

Venezuela

General note. The preparation of national accounts statistics in Venezuela is undertaken by the Banco Central de Venezuela. The official estimates are published annually by the Banco in 'Memorias o Informes Economicas'. A detailed description of the sources and methods used for the national accounts estimation is found in 'Metodologia de las Cuentas Nacionales de Venezuela' and in 'Practicas en materia de cuentas' published by the Banco. The estimates are generally in accordance with the classifications and difininitions recommended in the United Nations System of National Accounts (SNA). The following tables have been prepared from successive replies to the United Nations national accounts questionnaire. When the scope and coverage of the estimates differ for conceptual or statistical reasons from the definitions and classifications recommended in SNA, a footnote is indicated to the relevant tables.

Sources and methods :

(a) Gross domestic product. Gross domestic product is estimated mainly through the production approach.

(b) Expenditure on the gross domestic product. The expenditure approach is used to estimate government final consumption expenditure and exports and imports of goods and services. The commodity-flow approach is used for private consumption expenditure and gross fixed capital formation. Increase in stocks is obtained as a residual. The estimates of government final consumption expenditures are based on information obtained from government budgets and financial statements of the government entities. For private consumption expenditure on imported goods, estimates are based on the value of imports f.o.b. Values of locally produced goods are based on the production account of agriculture, manufacturing and the services. Trade margins based on surveys are used to estimate purchasers' values. The information used to estimate gross fixed capital formation include data on construction, manufacturing production, sales of vechiles and livestock and imported capital goods. The data on petroleum and iron-ore exports are obtained from the Ministerio de Energia y Minas while exports of other merchandise are obtained from the Oficina Central de Estadisticas e Informatica. The Corporacion de turismo, the embassies as well as companies engaged in transports, communication and insurance also provide export data. Import data are mainly provided by the Oficina Central de Estadisticas e Informatica. For the constant price estimates, only information for gross fixed capital formation is available. The item is deflated by price indexes constructed separately for construction, machinery and equipment and transport equipment. For other aggregates of this item, the estimates are obtained directly at constant prices.

(c) Cost-structure of the gross domestic product. In estimating the cost structure components of GDP, estimates of compensation of employees, operating surplus and depreciation are obtained for each industry group separately. For agriculture, forestry and fishing, they are estimated as a percentage of the gross value of production based on factore and coefficients from a 1968 study. For the mining sector, information from the Ministerio de Energia e Minas are used for petroleum activity and iron-ore mining. For manufacturing, estimates are based on cost structure data by the Ministerio de Hacienda supplemented by information from public enterprises and petroleum refineries. A survey conducted by the Banco in 1968-70 provides coefficients for the trade sector. Financial statements are used for public enterprises railway transport, communication, financial institutions and insurance. Input coefficients obtained from surveys are used for road transport and private services. Data on indirect taxes and subsidies are obtained from government sources.

(d) Gross domestic product by kind of economic activity. The table of GDP by kind of economic activity at market prices, i.e., producers' values. The production approach is used to estimate the value added of most industries. The income approach is used to estimate producers of government services. domestic services and part of other private services. The information on gross output in the agricultural sector is furnished annually by the Ministerio de Agricultura y Cria on the basis of field survey conducted during the summer (January-April) and the winter(May-December). These surveys give information on cultivated areas and physical production of the principal crops. The value of production is first calculated in constant prices by multiplying the physical production of each item by the respective producers' prices in 1968 and then converting it to current values by using the producers' price index estimated by the Banco. Value added is obtained by applying the cost structure estimated for 1968. For crude petroleum and refinery products, a production account covering all enterprises in the petroleum sector is constructed on the basis of information provided by the Ministerio de Energia y Minas. Crude petroleum is separated from refinery production on the basis of annual survey data. During the period 1968-1975, exports were calculated at official fiscal prices for export as declared by foreign concessionaires while from 1976 onwards, the prices reported by the nationalized enterprises have been used. Value added for the manufacturing industries is estimated by applying to the gross value of production by kind of economic activity the cost structure information on companies. Bench-mark estimates on gross value of manufacturing production have been prepared based on the third industrial survey conducted in 1971. These estimates are extrapolated by the annual changes in the index of industrial production through annual surveys. The Instituto Nacional de Obras Sanitarias provides information on production and cost structure of water supply. For public construction, information is obtained from censuses conducted by the Banco. For private construction requiring permits, estimates are based on construction coefficients per capita which are available for 14 urben centres through a Survey. The estimates for the federal district are calculated independently through a survey and through using information on construction permits. Non-permit construction estimates are agriculture. Bench-mark estimates for each of the activities in the trade sector have been prepared for 1968-1970 by using the results of a national survey conducted by the Banco. Since 1970, over-all estimates are made by extrapolating the total value of production by an index of market sales. Adjustments are made to account for the public enterprises by using their respective financial statements. Value added in the private transport sector is estimated by applying the sample coefficient, obtained through surveys, to the receipts for each type of services. For the public sector, information is obtained directly from concerned enterprises. The value added of the financial institutions is obtained as the difference between the value of production and intermediate consumption. For ownership of dwellings, the value of production is estimated from the total number of occupied dwellings and the annual average rent, adjusted by the rent item in the cost-of-living index. For real estate and business services, the production value is estimated by projecting the annual changes of incomes obtained from surveys. The value added of government services constitutes the renumeration of employees of the various government agencies and the consumption of fixed capital of the administrative organizations. For private services, coefficients of value added obtained from surveys are used. For the constant price estimates, value added of agriculture and mining is extrapolated by quantum indexes. For other industries, current values are deflated by various price indexes.

1.1 Expenditure on the Gross Domestic Product, in Current Prices

Million Venezuelan bolivares

	1980	1981	1982	1983	1984	1985	1986	1987	1988	1989	1990	1991
1 Government final consumption expenditure	35123	42643	42594	41339	43565 / 43311	48547	54712	71116	91945	144371	191816	285784
2 Private final consumption expenditure	135375	160533	182239	183435	209834 / 256327	287321	337106	450347	597737	977280	1415385	2040126
A Households	...	...	...	...	251639	281722	329942	441276	584818	959478	1387507	2000986
B Private non-profit institutions serving households	...	...	...	...	... / 4688	5599	7164	9071	12919	17802	27878	39140
3 Gross capital formation	62791	65409	75330	34149	51345 / 73523	85982	102417	171120	244142	191826	232939	567575
A Increase in stocks	-1354	-4374	5167	-21197	1751 / 6230	5430	2593	23208	44815	-63216	-89185	26351
B Gross fixed capital formation	64145	69783	70163	55346	49594 / 67293	80552	99824	147912	199327	255042	322124	541224
Residential buildings	17228	16272	12354	10209	8095 / 17549	17730	19597	25101	31589	40147	31463	41337
Non-residential buildings	20548	23452	27412	24319	18227 / 24129	27097	31992	44429	62796	80439	140872	232222
Other construction and land improvement etc.	451	707	748	786	437 / 1010	1300	2080	2926	5080	3155	5201	9650
Other	25918	29352	29649	20032	22835 / 24605	34425	46155	75456	99862	131301	144588	258015
4 Exports of goods and services	85463	89614	75197	74067	105159 / 115946	116154	96047	154151	178970	515387	899169	939444
5 Less: Imports of goods and services	64551	72991	84092	42498	62373 / 69035	73263	101110	150313	239511	318503	460048	796654
Equals: Gross Domestic Product	254201	285208	291268	290492	347530 / 420072	464741	489172	696421	873283	1510361	2279261	3036275

1.2 Expenditure on the Gross Domestic Product, in Constant Prices

Million Venezuelan bolivares

	1980	1981	1982	1983	1984	1985	1986	1987	1988	1989	1990	1991
			At constant prices of: 1968						1984			
1 Government final consumption expenditure	...	...	...	...	43311	42664	44962	46480	51573	50404	52932	57978
2 Private final consumption expenditure	...	...	...	...	256327	256958	264570	275130	289013	271793	279590	304167
A Households	...	...	...	...	251639	252088	259120	269145	282568	265554	272858	296984
B Private non-profit institutions serving households	...	...	...	...	4688	4870	5450	5985	6445	6239	6732	7183
3 Gross capital formation	...	...	...	...	73523	76597	80128	91426	105361	49969	46046	83568
A Increase in stocks	...	...	...	...	6230	4898	2081	12971	19949	-13663	-13770	3290
B Gross fixed capital formation	22290	22959	22102	16280	13209 / 67293	71699	78047	78455	85412	63632	59816	80278
Residential buildings	5403	4669	3290	2552	1830 / 17549	16166	16452	16428	15458	12202	7866	8181
Non-residential buildings	6583	6814	7228	6075	4149 / 24129	24166	26146	26954	30375	23005	30248	40831
Other construction and land improvement etc.	143	205	198	197	100 / 1010	1116	1657	1769	2485	1035	1292	1824
Other	10161	11271	11386	7456	7130 / 24605	30251	33792	33304	37094	27390	20410	29442
4 Exports of goods and services	...	...	...	...	115946	111149	124759	123123	133756	135365	154722	162518
5 Less: Imports of goods and services	...	...	...	...	69035	66484	66134	71818	88331	58269	54970	80304
Equals: Gross Domestic Product	75857	75628	76144	71867	70894 / 420072	420884	448285	464341	491372	449262	478320	527927

1.3 Cost Components of the Gross Domestic Product

Million Venezuelan bolivares

	1980	1981	1982	1983	1984	1985	1986	1987	1988	1989	1990	1991
1 Indirect taxes, net	7996	8416	9776	20387	20395 / 24920	30352	17783	41630	26122	48569	33794	108500
A Indirect taxes	11378	12013	12910	22693	22568 / 27975	33925	21682	52513	41972	77483	69487	125459
B Less: Subsidies	3382	3597	3134	2306	2173 / 3055	3573	3899	10883	15850	28914	35693	16959
2 Consumption of fixed capital	17104	19869	21666	24031	26628 / 32719	36499	43183	56157	71619	107345	154230	220222
3 Compensation of employees paid by resident producers to:	105143	119642	124529	123625	128398 / 144371	163383	183550	244444	321148	518295	699402	1011412
A Resident households	105143	119642	124529	123578	128334 / 144344	163353	183500	244351	321023	518178	698928	1010954
B Rest of the world	-	-	-	47	64 / 27	30	50	93	125	117	474	458
4 Operating surplus	123958	137281	135297	122449	172109 / 218062	234507	244656	354190	454394	836152	1391835	1696141
Equals: Gross Domestic Product	254201	285208	291268	290492	347530 / 420072	464741	489172	696421	873283	1510361	2279261	3036275

1.4 General Government Current Receipts and Disbursements

Million Venezuelan bolivares

	1980	1981	1982	1983	1984	1985	1986	1987	1988	1989	1990	1991
					Receipts							
1 Operating surplus	88	91	106	94	112 / 213	258	377	426	444	614	873	630
2 Property and entrepreneurial income	14342	18290	21482	26983	29871 / 28359	27793	31212	38091	48141	78408	159180	245708
3 Taxes, fees and contributions	72296	80393	68287	66978	110993 / 85215	86395	75834	126282	140937	294364	407639	554064
A Indirect taxes	11378	12013	12910	20863	19588 / 13657	18211	24642	35531	44190	52659	69487	125459

Venezuela

1.4 General Government Current Receipts and Disbursements
(Continued)

Million Venezuelan bolivares

	1980	1981	1982	1983	1984	1985	1986	1987	1988	1989	1990	1991
B Direct taxes	54910	61996	48491	41014	84667 / 66387	62588	44975	83308	88216	231667	302545	387275
C Social security contributions	4258	4397	4734	4735	4879 / 4943	5363	5917	7084	8177	9722	35152	40530
D Compulsory fees, fines and penalties	1750	1987	2152	366	1859 / 228	233	300	359	354	316	455	800
4 Other current transfers	13758	17804	17785	16569	18003 / 16518	20557	21181	36710	38298	62779	100396	144599
Statistical discrepancy a	...	...	...	...	10017	15489	6916	...	...	...	...	...
Total Current Receipts of General Government	100484	116578	107660	110624	158979 / 140322	150492	135520	201509	227820	436165	668088	945001

Disbursements

	1980	1981	1982	1983	1984	1985	1986	1987	1988	1989	1990	1991
1 Government final consumption expenditure	35123	42643	42594	41339	43565 / 43311	48547	54712	71116	91945	144371	191816	285784
A Compensation of employees	30030	34851	35171	34421	35788 / 35239	39733	43920	55967	66528	107877	140434	207335
B Consumption of fixed capital	48	52	51	82	97 / 166	196	229	220	251	270	330	388
C Purchases of goods and services, net	5045	7740	7372	6836	7680 / 7894	8616	10560	14928	25164	36222	51050	78059
D Less: Own account fixed capital formation	...	...	...	...	...	...	...	...	...	...	...	...
E Indirect taxes paid, net	...	...	...	...	... / 12	2	3	1	2	2	2	2
2 Property income	5585	5992	6399	7231	11619 / 11241	12470	13005	25137	23927	57185	98936	143997
A Interest	5585	5992	6399	7231	11619 / 11241	12470	13005	25137	23927	57185	98936	143997
B Net land rent and royalties	...	...	...	...	...	...	...	...	...	...	...	...
3 Subsidies b	3382	3597	3134	2306	2173 / 3055	3573	3899	22845	38194	66754	35693	16959
4 Other current transfers	17046	20720	23760	27446	37232 / 35549	40348	36972	53056	58125	99998	168659	227470
A Social security benefits	1298	1584	1783	1759	1864 / 2578	2885	3245	3975	4347	4847	11093	20051
B Social assistance grants	1081	955	906	2805	3261 / 3175	3457	4794	5513	7081	13348	17967	50195
C Other	14667	18181	21071	22882	32107 / 29796	34006	28933	43568	46697	81803	139599	157224
5 Net saving	39348	43626	31773	32302	64390 / 47166	45554	26932	29355	15629	67857	172984	270791
Total Current Disbursements and Net Saving of General Government	100484	116578	107660	110624	158979 / 140322	150492	135520	201509	227820	436165	668088	945001

a) Item 'Statistical discrepancy' refers to earnings from the used of unified market-determined exchange rate.
b) Beginning 1987, item 'Subsidies' includes subsidies to cover the differences in exchange rates.

1.7 External Transactions on Current Account, Summary

Million Venezuelan bolivares

	1980	1981	1982	1983	1984	1985	1986	1987	1988	1989	1990	1991
Payments to the Rest of the World												
1 Imports of goods and services	64551	72991	84092	42498	62373 / 69035	73263	101110	150313	239511	318503	460048	796654
A Imports of merchandise c.i.f.	50783	56218	62977	33082	49365 / 55692	63146	87707	132945	214767	266495	370256	659552
B Other	13768	16773	21115	9416	13008 / 13343	10117	13403	17368	24744	52008	89792	137102
2 Factor income to the rest of the world	8487	13080	17539	16957	22279 / 28519	30416	32217	37074	50491	124484	170802	170870

1.7 External Transactions on Current Account, Summary
(Continued)

__Million Venezuelan bolivares__

	1980	1981	1982	1983	1984	1985	1986	1987	1988	1989	1990	1991
A Compensation of employees	-	-	-	47	64 / 27	30	50	93	125	117	474	458
B Property and entrepreneurial income	8487	13080	17539	16910	22215 / 28492	30386	32167	36981	50366	124367	170328	170412
3 Current transfers to the rest of the world	1879	1750	2738	988	863 / 1683	1880	2176	3333	4283	14872	33866	39666
A Indirect taxes to supranational organizations	...	...	...	...	... / ...	...	...	...	...	...	...	...
B Other current transfers	1879	1750	2738	988	863 / 1683	1880	2176	3333	4283	14872	33866	39666
4 Surplus of the nation on current transactions	20236	17120	-18186	20720	33389 / 32131	25549	-21069	-15297	-87960	127222	358038	61383
Payments to the Rest of the World and Surplus of the Nation on Current Transactions	95153	104941	86183	81163	118904 / 131368	131108	114434	175423	206325	585081	1022754	1068573

Receipts From The Rest of the World

	1980	1981	1982	1983	1984	1985	1986	1987	1988	1989	1990	1991
1 Exports of goods and services	85463	89614	75197	74067	105159 / 115946	116154	96047	154151	178970	515387	899169	939444
A Exports of merchandise f.o.b.	82497	86374	70738	69078	99871 / 109961	108464	85760	140301	159743	474397	830764	857597
B Other	2966	3240	4459	4989	5288 / 5985	7690	10287	13850	19227	40990	68405	81847
2 Factor income from rest of the world	9690	15327	10986	7096	13745 / 14731	14332	17497	18736	25667	62065	103102	109045
A Compensation of employees	-	-	-	75	50 / -	7	-	-	-	57	47	114
B Property and entrepreneurial income	9690	15327	10986	7021	13695 / 14731	14325	17497	18736	25667	62008	103055	108931
3 Current transfers from rest of the world	-	-	-	-	- / 691	622	890	2536	1688	7629	20483	20084
A Subsidies from supranational organisations	...	...	...	...	... / ...	...	...	...	...	...	...	...
B Other current transfers	...	...	...	...	... / 691	622	890	2536	1688	7629	20483	20084
Receipts from the Rest of the World on Current Transactions	95153	104941	86183	81163	118904 / 131368	131108	114434	175423	206325	585081	1022754	1068573

1.9 Gross Domestic Product by Institutional Sectors of Origin

__Million Venezuelan bolivares__

	1980	1981	1982	1983	1984	1985	1986	1987	1988	1989	1990	1991

Domestic Factor Incomes Originating

	1980	1981	1982	1983	1984	1985	1986	1987	1988	1989	1990	1991
1 General government	...	...	...	...	35452	39991	44297	56393	66972	108491	141307	207965
2 Corporate and quasi-corporate enterprises	...	...	...	...	177850	188866	193442	289292	376130	712443	1226617	1454639
A Non-financial	...	...	...	...	176755	187926	192796	285853	367913	701449	1214052	1441744
Public	...	...	...	...	98051	95484	74907	116829	137759	370734	714315	772250
Private	...	...	...	...	78704	92442	117889	169024	230154	330715	499737	669494
B Financial	...	...	...	...	1095	940	646	3439	8217	10994	12565	12895
Public	...	...	...	...	226	29	-134	210	-86	1107	775	-1756
Private	...	...	...	...	869	911	780	3229	8303	9887	11790	14651
3 Households and private unincorporated enterprises	...	...	...	...	144371	163383	183550	244444	321148	518295	699402	1011412
4 Non-profit institutions serving households	...	...	...	...	4760	5650	6917	8505	11292	15218	23911	33537
Subtotal: Domestic Factor Incomes	...	...	...	...	362433	397890	428206	598634	775542	1354447	2091237	2707553
Indirect taxes, net	...	...	...	...	24920	30352	17783	41630	26122	48569	33794	108500
A Indirect taxes	...	...	...	...	27975	33925	21682	52513	41972	77483	69487	125459
B Less: Subsidies	...	...	...	...	3055	3573	3899	10883	15850	28914	35693	16959
Consumption of fixed capital	...	...	...	...	32719	36499	43183	56157	71619	107345	154230	220222
Gross Domestic Product	...	...	...	...	420072	464741	489172	696421	873283	1510361	2279261	3036275

Venezuela

1.10 Gross Domestic Product by Kind of Activity, in Current Prices

Million Venezuelan bolivares

	1980	1981	1982	1983	1984	1985	1986	1987	1988	1989	1990	1991
1 Agriculture, hunting, forestry and fishing	14436	16413	17676	19536	23886 21502	26927	32454	42574	57881	92044	122765	167418
2 Mining and quarrying a	62188	66944	54389	46922	69662 67385	62810	44373	83273	95805	271136	530565	562687
3 Manufacturing b	41197	43089	46784	49293	67675 89927	101796	113812	143315	179412	314339	467778	602706
4 Electricity, gas and water c	2579	3977	4900	5398	5773 6086	6907	7627	10822	12867	22622	43218	64223
5 Construction	14479	15683	15657	14317	10335 25812	28119	32447	44641	62238	71060	102896	166763
6 Wholesale and retail trade, restaurants and hotels	20834	23245	25704	33339	38292 63254	73860	87366	124012	170859	275780	400861	556792
7 Transport, storage and communication	25184	30769	35631	33266	37725 21167	24673	30557	40187	51358	73285	104158	173238
8 Finance, insurance, real estate and business services	37883	46277	49953	51820	57999 57257	61932	71733	93333	123324	180768	256069	357382
9 Community, social and personal services	9579	10981	11166	11421	13197 17343	19803	23692	32482	42908	63518	94901	136389
Total, Industries	228359	257378	261860	265312	324544 369733	406827	444061	614639	796652	1364552	2123211	2787598
Producers of Government Services	30078	34903	35222	34503	35885 35236	39785	43875	55861	66428	107824	140382	207300
Other Producers	2499	2966	3187	3777	3994 4866	5775	7077	8708	11580	15615	24533	34411
Subtotal	260936	295247	300269	303592	364423 409835	452387	495013	679208	874660	1487991	2288126	3029309
Less: Imputed bank service charge	13104	16378	15879	16101	19916 8546	9652	11718	15489	20318	26619	42178	53272
Plus: Import duties	6369	6339	6878	3001	3023 4465	6292	8837	15720	21159	24165	33313	60238
Plus: Value added tax	...	...	...	...	...	...	...	...	...	...	...	...
Plus: Other adjustments	...	...	...	...	... 14318	15714	-2960	16982	-2218	24824	-	...
Equals: Gross Domestic Product	254201	285208	291268	290492	347530 420072	464741	489172	696421	873283	1510361	2279261	3036275

a) Item 'Mining and quarrying' also includes crude petroleum and natural gas production.
b) Item 'Manufacturing' includes petroleum refining
c) Item 'Electricity, gas and water' excludes gas.

1.11 Gross Domestic Product by Kind of Activity, in Constant Prices

Million Venezuelan bolivares

	1980	1981	1982	1983	1984	1985	1986	1987	1988	1989	1990	1991
					At constant prices of:							
				1968			1984					
1 Agriculture, hunting, forestry and fishing	4765	4676	4843	4863	4901 21502	23250	25127	26126	27338	25937	25483	26303
2 Mining and quarrying	6103	5948	5340	5002	5098 67385a	61100a	66585a	70575a	74155a	73995a	86737a	94344a
3 Manufacturing	13660	13322	13863	13626	14247 89927b	94405b	101147b	103645b	110755b	97654b	103614b	115476b
4 Electricity, gas and water c	1950	2256	2533	2635	2634 6086	6364	6726	7086	7612	7726	8123	8854
5 Construction	4609	4511	4131	3583	2350 25812	25400	26977	27822	30019	21884	23576	30826
6 Wholesale and retail trade, restaurants and hotels	6907	6724	6897	7012	6643 63254	66423	68665	71644	75525	63581	66013	70931
7 Transport, storage and communication	9805	10155	10508	9080	8806 21167	21978	23073	24980	27015	25297	25233	27215
8 Finance, insurance, real estate and business services	14023	15133	14645	14600	15660 57257	57787	61014	64912	69203	64854	66020	69283
9 Community, social and personal services	4872	4848	4492	4226	4330 17343	18318	19962	21135	22681	22551	24025	26048
Total, Industries	66694	67573	67252	64627	64669 369733	375025	399276	417925	444303	403479	428824	469280
Producers of Government Services	10498	10586	10593	10399	10357 35236	35042	36467	37365	39095	40682	43781	47313

1.11 Gross Domestic Product by Kind of Activity, in Constant Prices
(Continued)

Million Venezuelan bolivares

	1980	1981	1982	1983	1984	1985	1986	1987	1988	1989	1990	1991
			1968		At constant prices of:			**1984**				
Other Producers	835	847	863	861	843 4866	5257	5692	6094	6306	6227	7024	7591
Subtotal	78027	79006	78708	75887	75869 409835	415324	441435	461384	489704	450388	479629	524184
Less: Imputed bank service charge	4777	5697	4910	4904	5637 8546	8716	8699	8577	9023	6559	6675	7484
Plus: Import duties	2607	2319	2346	884	662 4465	4926	4872	4546	4896	3719	5366	11227
Plus: Value added tax	...	...	...	...	... ...	...	...	...	...	...	...	...
Plus: Other adjustments	...	...	...	...	14318	9350	10677	6988	5795	1714	-	-
Equals: Gross Domestic Product	75857	75628	76144	71867	70894 420072	420884	448285	464341	491372	449262	478320	527927

a) Item 'Mining and quarrying' also includes crude petroleum and natural gas production.
b) Item 'Manufacturing' includes petroleum refining
c) Item 'Electricity, gas and water' excludes gas.

1.12 Relations Among National Accounting Aggregates

Million Venezuelan bolivares

	1980	1981	1982	1983	1984	1985	1986	1987	1988	1989	1990	1991
Gross Domestic Product	254201	285208	291268	290492	347530 420072	464741	489172	696421	873283	1510361	2279261	3036275
Plus: Net factor income from the rest of the world	1203	2247	-6553	-9861	-8534 -13788	-16084	-14720	-18338	-24824	-62419	-67700	-61825
Factor income from the rest of the world	9690	15327	10986	7096	13745 14731	14332	17497	18736	25667	62065	103102	109045
Less: Factor income to the rest of the world	8487	13080	17539	16957	22279 28519	30416	32217	37074	50491	124484	170802	170870
Equals: Gross National Product	255404	287455	284715	280631	338996 406284	448657	474452	678083	848459	1447942	2211561	2974450
Less: Consumption of fixed capital	17104	19869	21666	24031	26628 32719	36499	43183	56157	71619	107345	154230	220222
Equals: National Income	238300	267586	263049	256600	312368 373565	412158	431269	621926	776840	1340597	2057331	2754228
Plus: Net current transfers from the rest of the world	-1879	-1750	-2738	-988	-863 -992	-1258	-1286	-797	-2595	-7243	-13383	-19582
Current transfers from the rest of the world	-	-	-	-	- 691	622	890	2536	1688	7629	20483	20084
Less: Current transfers to the rest of the world	1879	1750	2738	988	863 1683	1880	2176	3333	4283	14872	33866	39666
Equals: National Disposable Income	236421	265836	260311	255612	311505 372573	410900	429983	621129	774245	1333354	2043948	2734646
Less: Final consumption	170498	203176	224833	224774	253399 299638	335868	391818	521463	689682	1121651	1607201	2325910
Equals: Net Saving	65923	62660	35478	30838	58106 72935	75032	38165	99666	84563	211703	436747	408736
Less: Surplus of the nation on current transactions	20236	17120	-18186	20720	33389 32131	25549	-21069	-15297	-87960	127222	358038	61383
Equals: Net Capital Formation	45687	45540	53664	10118	24717 40804	49483	59234	114963	172523	84481	78709	347353

Venezuela

2.1 Government Final Consumption Expenditure by Function, in Current Prices

Million Venezuelan bolivares

	1980	1981	1982	1983	1984	1985	1986	1987	1988	1989	1990	1991
1 General public services	9469	9524	8316	8373	7277 ...	...	...	...	...	...	...	...
2 Defence	3240	3905	4903	4220	6033 ...	...	...	...	...	...	...	...
3 Public order and safety	...	...	...	...	... ...	...	...	...	...	...	...	...
4 Education	11449	13239	14068	13482	15381 / 13355	14121	15360	18214	21658	40166	48375	61579
5 Health	3925	5397	5484	7244	7416 / 4877	5433	6867	9292	10696	18194	26730	31303
6 Social security and welfare	2605	4371	4322	2466	3190	...	...	...	...	...	...	...
7 Housing and community amenities	737	1078	1162	1116	1267 ...	...	...	...	...	...	...	...
8 Recreational, cultural and religious affairs	662	791	988	964	705 ...	...	...	...	...	...	...	...
9 Economic services	3036	4163	3351	3474	2296 ...	...	...	...	...	...	...	...
10 Other functions	...	175	-	-	- ...	...	...	...	...	...	...	...
Total Government Final Consumption Expenditure	35123	42643	42594	41339	43565 / 43311	48547	54712	71116	91945	144371	191816	285784

2.2 Government Final Consumption Expenditure by Function, in Constant Prices

Million Venezuelan bolivares

	1980	1981	1982	1983	1984	1985	1986	1987	1988	1989	1990	1991
					At constant prices of:1984							
1 General public services	...	...	...	...	...	...	...	...	...	...	...	...
2 Defence	...	...	...	...	...	...	...	...	...	...	...	...
3 Public order and safety	...	...	...	...	...	...	...	...	...	...	...	...
4 Education	...	...	...	...	13355	13747	14229	14359	15085	15739	16534	18423
5 Health	...	...	...	...	4877	5217	6251	6815	7175	7261	7334	7979
6 Social security and welfare	...	...	...	...	...	...	...	...	...	...	...	...
7 Housing and community amenities	...	...	...	...	...	...	...	...	...	...	...	...
8 Recreational, cultural and religious affairs	...	...	...	...	...	...	...	...	...	...	...	...
9 Economic services	...	...	...	...	...	...	...	...	...	...	...	...
10 Other functions	...	...	...	...	...	...	...	...	...	...	...	...
Total Government Final Consumption Expenditure	...	...	...	...	43311	42664	44962	46480	51573	50404	52932	57978

2.5 Private Final Consumption Expenditure by Type and Purpose, in Current Prices

Million Venezuelan bolivares

	1980	1981	1982	1983	1984	1985	1986	1987	1988	1989	1990	1991
					Final Consumption Expenditure of Resident Households							
1 Food, beverages and tobacco	59004	74727	85767	97157	111230 / 79693	92229	108838	146965	199599	394741	567106	797715
A Food	42517	52258	60004	69953	82572 / 65822	75430	89289	122410	167810	340746	490014	687364
B Non-alcoholic beverages	2525	3855	5342	3533	4036 / 9236[a]	9635	12005	15498	21094	35911	55252	78757
C Alcoholic beverages	11775	15917	17777	20660	21999 / ...							
D Tobacco	2187	2687	2644	3011	2623 / 4635	7164	7544	9057	10695	18084	21840	31594
2 Clothing and footwear	7467	7758	8379	7596	8275 / 25223	29565	34001	46030	62444	89598	113059	158408
3 Gross rent, fuel and power	11178	14107	15996	17665	18569 / 37218	40620	45906	54382	64221	90654	127764	180515
A Fuel and power [b]	989	1686	1757	2046	2163 / 8159	9130	10892	11771	12602	18450	24083	32736

2050

2.5 Private Final Consumption Expenditure by Type and Purpose, in Current Prices
(Continued)

Million Venezuelan bolivares

	1980	1981	1982	1983	1984	1985	1986	1987	1988	1989	1990	1991
B Other	10189	12421	14239	15619	16406 29059	31490	35014	42611	51619	72204	103681	147779
4 Furniture, furnishings and household equipment and operation	9660	9318	10090	8302	10293 8718	9986	12006	18436	24575	34374	49802	79980
5 Medical care and health expenses	4917	5326	5864	7595	8880 5943	6789	8068	10959	13957	20722	30354	42476
6 Transport and communication	14413	17197	21255	20138	21595 17663	20730	24048	32976	40785	49220	74588	126945
A Personal transport equipment	2887	3802	4132	4765	2624 ...	...	...	...	...	...	...	...
B Other	11526	13395	17123	15373	18971 ...	...	...	...	...	...	...	...
7 Recreational, entertainment, education and cultural services	12763	12955	13170	10246	11908 7704	8813	10223	12469	16505	24625	37099	49700
A Education	...	...	...	...	... 2187	2397	2584	3009	3628	4834	8528	12000
B Other	...	...	...	...	5517	6416	7639	9460	12877	19791	28571	37700
8 Miscellaneous goods and services	8072	9138	9661	7949	9403 60924	70844	85374	117067	156316	246255	362740	515499
A Personal care	...	...	...	...	... ...	...	...	...	...	...	...	...
B Expenditures in restaurants, cafes and hotels	...	...	...	...	... 29550	34707	41572	54253	76380	124755	180534	251823
C Other	...	...	...	...	... 31374	36137	43802	62814	79936	121500	182206	263676
Total Final Consumption Expenditure in the Domestic Market by Households, of which	127474	150526	170182	176648	200153 243086	279576	328464	439284	578402	950189	1362512	1951238
A Durable goods	10970	11122	11322	6437	6831 12490	14581	17789	27472	34626	45137	70028	125487
B Semi-durable goods	14948	15738	17288	15055	17284 132490c	153245	181417	246108	328260	581128	822205	1160495
C Non-durable goods	67990	84226	97951	109663	126327 ...							
D Services	33566	39440	43621	45493	49711 98106	111750	129258	165704	215516	323924	470279	665256
Plus: Direct purchases abroad by resident households	8046	9651	12052	8592	13001 13250	7891	10189	13715	16940	25504	...	...
Less: Direct purchases in the domestic market by non-resident households	1168	920	1482	3302	4697 4697	5745	8711	11723	10524	16215	...	...
Equals: Final Consumption Expenditure of Resident Households	134352	159257	180752	181938	208457 251639	281722	329942	441276	584818	959478	1387507	2000986

Final Consumption Expenditure of Private Non-profit Institutions Serving Households

	1980	1981	1982	1983	1984	1985	1986	1987	1988	1989	1990	1991
Equals: Final Consumption Expenditure of Private Non-profit Organisations Serving Households	1023	1276	1487	1497	1377 4688	5599	7164	9071	12919	17802	27878	39140
Private Final Consumption Expenditure	135375	160533	182239	183435	209834 256327	287321	337106	450347	597737	977280	1415385	2040126

a) Including item 'Alcoholic beverages'.
b) Beginning 1984 of the second series, item 'Fuel and power' includes water.
c) Including item 'Non-durable goods'.

2.6 Private Final Consumption Expenditure by Type and Purpose, in Constant Prices

Million Venezuelan bolivares

	1980	1981	1982	1983	1984	1985	1986	1987	1988	1989	1990	1991
					At constant prices of:1984							
					Final Consumption Expenditure of Resident Households							
1 Food, beverages and tobacco	...	...	...	...	79693	79001	81016	84854	89462	87773	87564	92039
A Food	...	...	...	...	65822	65981	67464	70569	74425	74521	73237	77906
B Non-alcoholic beverages	...	...	...	...	9236	7990	8737	9257	10202	8741	9676	9831
C Alcoholic beverages	...	...	...	...								
D Tobacco	...	...	...	...	4635	5030	4815	5028	4835	4511	4651	4302
2 Clothing and footwear	...	...	...	...	25223	27415	27760	28686	29603	26312	26088	29208
3 Gross rent, fuel and power	...	...	...	...	37218	38094	39133	40633	42048	42160	42736	44192

Venezuela

2.6 Private Final Consumption Expenditure by Type and Purpose, in Constant Prices
(Continued)

Million Venezuelan bolivares

	1980	1981	1982	1983	1984	1985	1986	1987	1988	1989	1990	1991
					At constant prices of:1984							
A Fuel and power a	...	...	...	...	8159	8394	8154	8494	8858	8402	8440	8737
B Other	...	...	...	...	29059	29700	30979	32139	33190	33758	34296	35455
4 Furniture, furnishings and household equipment and operation	...	...	...	...	8718	9138	9810	10388	10804	7951	9112	11830
5 Medical care and health expenses	...	...	...	...	5943	6253	6696	7335	7776	8001	8456	8982
6 Transport and communication	...	...	...	...	17663	18884	20071	20284	20817	17237	17808	19705
7 Recreational, entertainment, education and cultural services	...	...	...	...	7704	8166	8691	8757	9205	9159	10653	11151
A Education	...	...	...	...	2187	2293	2391	2512	2536	2495	2852	2988
B Other	...	...	...	...	5517	5873	6300	6245	6669	6664	7801	8163
8 Miscellaneous goods and services	...	...	...	...	60924	63882	67756	71164	74228	67137	68901	75886
A Personal care	...	...	...	...	...	...	...	...	...	...	...	...
B Expenditures in restaurants, cafes and hotels	...	...	...	...	29550	31314	33280	33328	35124	32861	32845	34807
C Other	...	...	...	...	31374	32568	34476	37836	39104	34276	36056	41079
Total Final Consumption Expenditure in the Domestic Market by Households, of which	...	...	...	...	243086	250833	260933	272101	283943	265730	271318	292993
A Durable goods	...	...	...	...	12490	13394	14684	14702	14786	9910	11904	16306
B Semi-durable goods	...	...	...	...	132490	134765	138027	145491	152267	140908	140909	151849
C Non-durable goods	...	...	...	...								
D Services	...	...	...	...	98106	102674	108222	111908	116890	114912	118505	124838
Plus: Direct purchases abroad by resident households	...	...	...	...	13250	6412	5195	4408	3731	4089	6481	7978
Less: Direct purchases in the domestic market by non-resident households	...	...	...	...	4697	5157	7008	7364	5106	4265	4941	3987
Equals: Final Consumption Expenditure of Resident Households	...	...	...	...	251639	252088	259120	269145	282568	265554	272858	296984

Final Consumption Expenditure of Private Non-profit Institutions Serving Households

	1980	1981	1982	1983	1984	1985	1986	1987	1988	1989	1990	1991
Equals: Final Consumption Expenditure of Private Non-profit Organisations Serving Households	...	...	...	...	4688	4870	5450	5985	6445	6239	6732	7183
Private Final Consumption Expenditure	...	...	...	...	256327	256958	264570	275130	289013	271793	279590	304167

a) Beginning 1984 of the second series, item 'Fuel and power' includes water.

2.11 Gross Fixed Capital Formation by Kind of Activity of Owner, ISIC Divisions, in Current Prices

Million Venezuelan bolivares

	1980	1981	1982	1983	1984	1985	1986	1987	1988	1989	1990	1991
					All Producers							
1 Agriculture, hunting, forestry and fishing	2091	2651	2131	1270	1794	3357	...	...	...	...	...	...
2 Mining and quarrying	9116	12338	15645	12344	9589	10044	...	...	...	...	...	...
3 Manufacturing a	4262	2843	2642	903	913	1869	...	...	...	...	...	...
4 Electricity, gas and water	6301	10495	14355	12434	7876	8764	...	...	...	...	...	...
5 Construction b	...	...	...	...	...	...	...	...	...	...	...	...
6 Wholesale and retail trade, restaurants and hotels a	120	65	14	30	56	-14	...	...	...	...	...	...
7 Transport, storage and communication	5455	5747	6352	6124	4450	6606	...	...	...	...	...	...
8 Finance, insurance, real estate and business services c	2633	4023	4410	4242	3413	4865	...	...	...	...	...	...
9 Community, social and personal services bc	26616	20874	14609	5970	14754	12417	...	...	...	...	...	...
Total Industries	56594	59036	60158	43317	42845	47908	...	...	...	...	...	...
Producers of Government Services	6806	9816	8911	10935	5562	8237	...	...	...	...	...	...
Private Non-Profit Institutions Serving Households	745	931	1094	1094	1187	1325	...	...	...	...	...	...
Total	64145	69783	70163	55346	49594	57470	...	...	...	...	...	...

a) Beginning 1977, items 'Manufacturing', 'Wholesale and retail trade', 'Restaurant and hotels', refer only to gross fixed public investment.
b) Item 'Construction' is included in item 'Community, social and personal services'.
c) Business services and real estate except dwellings are included in item 'Community, social and personal services'.

2.12 Gross Fixed Capital Formation by Kind of Activity of Owner, ISIC Divisions, in Constant Prices

Million Venezuelan bolivares

	1980	1981	1982	1983	1984	1985	1986	1987	1988	1989	1990	1991
					At constant prices of:1968							
					All Producers							
1 Agriculture, hunting, forestry and fishing	727	872	671	365	478	827	...	...	...	...	...	...
2 Mining and quarrying	3168	4059	4928	3542	2553	2475	...	...	...	...	...	...
3 Manufacturing a	1481	935	832	259	243	461	...	...	...	...	...	...
4 Electricity, gas and water	2189	3453	4522	3569	2098	2160	...	...	...	...	...	...
5 Construction b	...	...	...	...	...	...	...	...	...	...	...	...
6 Wholesale and retail trade, restaurants and hotels a	42	21	4	9	15	-3	...	...	...	...	...	...
7 Transport, storage and communication	1895	1891	2001	1757	1185	1628	...	...	...	...	...	...
8 Finance, insurance, real estate and business services c	915	1324	1389	1217	909	1199	...	...	...	...	...	...
9 Community, social and personal services bc	9249	6868	4602	2110	3931	3062	...	...	...	...	...	...
Total Industries	19666	19423	18949	12828	11412	11809	...	...	...	...	...	...
Producers of Government Services	2365	3230	2808	3138	1481	2030	...	...	...	...	...	...
Private Non-Profit Institutions Serving Households	259	306	345	314	316	327	...	...	...	...	...	...
Total	22290	22959	22102	16280	13209	14166	...	...	...	...	...	...

a) Beginning 1977, items 'Manufacturing', 'Wholesale and retail trade', 'Restaurant and hotels', refer only to gross fixed public investment.
b) Item 'Construction' is included in item 'Community, social and personal services'.
c) Business services and real estate except dwellings are included in item 'Community, social and personal services'.

2.17 Exports and Imports of Goods and Services, Detail

Million Venezuelan bolivares

	1980	1981	1982	1983	1984	1985	1986	1987	1988	1989	1990	1991
					Exports of Goods and Services							
1 Exports of merchandise, f.o.b.	82497	86374	70738	69078	99871 / 109961	108464	85760	140301	159743	474397	830764	857597
2 Transport and communication	1181	1571	1885	2246	2748 / 3221	3886	5025	7104	13208	22380	34400	49287
A In respect of merchandise imports	137	180	364	439	914 / 1566	1879	2226	3094	6518	8798	12020	17256
B Other	1044	1391	1521	1807	1834 / 1655	2007	2799	4010	6690	13582	22380	32031
3 Insurance service charges	463	364	869	280	57 / 14	15	79	186	266	543	190	228
A In respect of merchandise imports	56	43	167	23	13 / 7	7	20	27	16	36	71	154
B Other	407	321	702	257	44 / 7	8	59	159	250	507	119	74
4 Other commodities	154	385	223	1012	227 / 96	397	455	704	891	2860	7347	3671
5 Adjustments of merchandise exports to change-of-ownership basis	-	-	-	-	-	-	-	-	-	-	-	-
6 Direct purchases in the domestic market by non-residential households	1040	800	1323	1451	2256 / 2449	3115	4392	5524	4846	15171	26426	28616
7 Direct purchases in the domestic market by extraterritorial bodies	128	120	159	-	- / 205	277	336	332	16	36	42	45
Total Exports of Goods and Services	85463	89614	75197	74067	105159 / 115946	116154	96047	154151	178970	515387	899169	939444
					Imports of Goods and Services							
1 Imports of merchandise, c.i.f.	50783	56218	62977	33082	49365 / 55692	63146	87707	132945	214767	266495	370256	659552
A Imports of merchandise, f.o.b.	46554	51887	58180	29997	45767 / 50214	56662	78172	118538	190225	241743	328023	586700
B Transport of services on merchandise imports	4163	4295	4664	3047	3573 / 5444	6447	9486	14327	24448	24452	41219	71669
By residents	...	...	...	...	... / 1566	1879	2226	3094	6518	8798	12020	13840
By non-residents	4163	4295	4664	3047	3573 / 3878	4568	7260	11233	17930	15654	29199	57829
C Insurance service charges on merchandise imports	66	36	133	38	25 / 34	37	49	80	94	300	1014	1183

Venezuela

Million Venezuelan bolivares

	1980	1981	1982	1983	1984	1985	1986	1987	1988	1989	1990	1991
By residents	...	...	...	...	7	7	20	27	16	36	71	154
By non-residents	66	36	133	38	25 / 27	30	29	53	78	264	943	1029
2 Adjustments of merchandise imports to change-of-ownership basis	-	-	-	-	-			-	-	-	-	-
3 Other transport and communication	1968	2375	1730	1268	3674 / 3631	2479	3017	4475	7785	13105	15735	24754
4 Other insurance service charges	449	501	1041	191	164 / 96	83	138	93	234	636	443	764
5 Other commodities	2582	3570	5247	2724	2275 / 2168	2628	4362	5656	7987	12881	18360	29045
6 Direct purchases abroad by government	723	676	1045	805	624 / 246	554	693	199	562	936	3833	4175
7 Direct purchases abroad by resident households	8046	9651	12052	4428	6271 / 7202	4373	5193	6945	8176	24450	51421	78364
Total Imports of Goods and Services	64551	72991	84092	42498	62373 / 69035	73263	101110	150313	239511	318503	460048	796654
Balance of Goods and Services	20912	16623	-8895	31569	42786 / 46911	42891	-5063	3838	-60541	196884	439121	142790
Total Imports and Balance of Goods and Services	85463	89614	75197	74067	105159 / 115946	116154	96047	154151	178970	515387	899169	939444

4.1 Derivation of Value Added by Kind of Activity, in Current Prices

Million Venezuelan bolivares

	1984			1985			1986			1987		
	Gross Output	Intermediate Consumption	Value Added	Gross Output	Intermediate Consumption	Value Added	Gross Output	Intermediate Consumption	Value Added	Gross Output	Intermediate Consumption	Value Added
All Producers												
1 Agriculture, hunting, forestry and fishing	31111	9609	21502	38705	11778	26927	46962	14508	32454	60897	18323	42574
A Agriculture and hunting [a]	29293	9411	19882	36124	11486	24638	43307	14095	29212	55323	17710	37613
B Forestry and logging	211	33	178	258	40	218	372	55	317	630	92	538
C Fishing	1607	165	1442	2323	252	2071	3283	358	2925	4944	521	4423
2 Mining and quarrying	76071	8686	67385	70777	7967	62810	55124	10751	44373	100208	16935	83273
A Coal mining	4	1	3	4	1	3	5	1	4	36	6	30
B Crude petroleum and natural gas production	73389	7926	65463	67516	7008	60508	50055	9359	40696	91041	14281	76760
C Metal ore mining	1723	482	1241	2190	656	1534	3635	1024	2611	7271	2144	5127
D Other mining	955	277	678	1067	302	765	1429	367	1062	1860	504	1356
3 Manufacturing	235538	145611	89927	272227	170431	101796	310930	197118	113812	425448	282133	143315
A Manufacture of food, beverages and tobacco	62211	43436	18775	73642	50147	23495	84683	58829	25854	107648	75794	31854
B Textile, wearing apparel and leather industries	22478	14847	7631	26687	17378	9309	31054	20532	10522	42832	28661	14171
C Manufacture of wood and wood products, including furniture	6299	4006	2293	7149	4552	2597	8470	5390	3080	11265	7214	4051
D Manufacture of paper and paper products, printing and publishing	10923	6842	4081	12350	7715	4635	13578	8511	5067	20197	13229	6968
E Manufacture of chemicals and chemical petroleum, coal, rubber and plastic products	69734	38244	31490	78358	43733	34625	79142	44936	34206	111274	69417	41857
F Manufacture of non-metallic mineral products, except products of petroleum and coal	7920	3868	4052	8837	4438	4399	11467	5872	5595	15836	8190	7646
G Basic metal industries	19510	10153	9357	22487	13795	8692	30180	18021	12159	39761	25114	14647
H Manufacture of fabricated metal products, machinery and equipment	34746	23137	11609	40510	27329	13181	49606	33371	16235	71869	51516	20353
I Other manufacturing industries	1717	1078	639	2207	1344	863	2750	1656	1094	4766	2998	1768
4 Electricity, gas and water	9141	3055	6086	10653	3746	6907	11740	4113	7627	15982	5160	10822
A Electricity, gas and steam [b]	7914	2562	5352	9511	3289	6222	10455	3620	6835	14637	4599	10038
B Water works and supply	1227	493	734	1142	457	685	1285	493	792	1345	561	784

4.1 Derivation of Value Added by Kind of Activity, in Current Prices
(Continued)

Million Venezuelan bolivares

	1984			1985			1986			1987		
	Gross Output	Intermediate Consumption	Value Added	Gross Output	Intermediate Consumption	Value Added	Gross Output	Intermediate Consumption	Value Added	Gross Output	Intermediate Consumption	Value Added
5 Construction	40101	14289	25812	43781	15662	28119	51264	18817	32447	70032	25391	44641
6 Wholesale and retail trade, restaurants and hotels	102041	38787	63254	119887	46027	73860	142440	55074	87366	200113	76101	124012
A Wholesale and retail trade	69417	19663	49754	81410	23710	57700	96716	28475	68241	140323	41533	98790
B Restaurants and hotels	32624	19124	13500	38477	22317	16160	45724	26599	19125	59790	34568	25222
Restaurants	24990	15008	9982	30012	17752	12260	35794	21403	14391	44942	26693	18249
Hotels and other lodging places	7634	4116	3518	8465	4565	3900	9930	5196	4734	14848	7875	6973
7 Transport, storage and communication	36125	14958	21167	43159	18486	24673	53490	22933	30557	69509	29322	40187
A Transport and storage	31152	14500	16652	37181	17772	19409	45956	21915	24041	60281	27788	32493
B Communication	4973	458	4515	5978	714	5264	7534	1018	6516	9228	1534	7694
8 Finance, insurance, real estate and business services	72509	15252	57257	79957	18025	61932	93658	21925	71733	122086	28753	93333
A Financial institutions	12982	3751	9231	14519	4466	10053	17335	5296	12039	25871	7358	18513
B Insurance	4083	2486	1597	4997	3134	1863	5809	3846	1963	7884	5492	2392
C Real estate and business services	55444	9015	46429	60441	10425	50016	70514	12783	57731	88331	15903	72428
Real estate, except dwellings	9104	1356	7748	9967	1443	8524	11953	1602	10351	16927	2286	14641
Dwellings	29058	2877	26181	31488	3117	28371	35011	3466	31545	42610	4218	38392
9 Community, social and personal services	27037	9694	17343	31246	11443	19803	36983	13291	23692	51332	18850	32482
A Sanitary and similar services	1638	607	1031	2072	939	1133	2518	1192	1326	3021	1550	1471
B Social and related community services c	8517	1867	6650	9632	2105	7527	11407	2454	8953	14825	3177	11648
Educational services	2213	620	1593	2398	671	1727	2564	718	1846	2968	831	2137
Medical, dental, other health and veterinary services	5978	1101	4877	6823	1250	5573	8218	1502	6716	11130	2074	9056
C Recreational and cultural services	4408	1323	3085	5474	1619	3855	6568	2051	4517	8585	2534	6051
D Personal and household services	12474	5897	6577	14068	6780	7288	16490	7594	8896	24901	11589	13312
Total, Industries	629674	259941	369733	710392	303565	406827	802591	358530	444061	1115607	500968	614639
Producers of Government Services	44122	8886	35236	49498	9713	39785	55689	11814	43875	72329	16468	55861
Other Producers	7184	2318	4866	8532	2757	5775	10596	3519	7077	13163	4455	8708
Total	680980	271145	409835	768422	316035	452387	868876	373863	495013	1201099	521891	679208
Less: Imputed bank service charge	...	-8546	8546	...	-9652	9652	...	-11718	11718	...	-15489	15489
Import duties	4465	...	4465	6292	...	6292	8837	...	8837	15720	...	15720
Value added tax	...	...	...	...	...	...	...	...	...	...	...	...
Other adjustments	14318	...	14318	15714	...	15714	-2960	...	-2960	16982	...	16982
Total	699763	279691	420072	790428	325687	464741	874753	385581	489172	1233801	537380	696421

	1988			1989			1990			1991		
	Gross Output	Intermediate Consumption	Value Added	Gross Output	Intermediate Consumption	Value Added	Gross Output	Intermediate Consumption	Value Added	Gross Output	Intermediate Consumption	Value Added

All Producers

	1988			1989			1990			1991		
1 Agriculture, hunting, forestry and fishing	80769	22888	57881	127985	35941	92044	174090	51325	122765	247439	80021	167418
A Agriculture and hunting a	72996	22065	50931	115031	34604	80427	159307	49548	109759	227015	77778	149237
B Forestry and logging	989	141	848	1716	246	1470	1854	267	1587	2620	392	2228
C Fishing	6784	682	6102	11238	1091	10147	12929	1510	11419	17804	1851	15953
2 Mining and quarrying	119065	23260	95805	321441	50305	271136	617077	86512	530565	684230	121543	562687
A Coal mining	393	65	328	2823	468	2355	3402	880	2522	4032	1016	3016
B Crude petroleum and natural gas production	105582	19235	86347	300768	42892	257876	586081	74967	511114	641585	103251	538334
C Metal ore mining	10756	3319	7437	13737	5796	7941	20848	8868	11980	28112	14393	13719
D Other mining	2334	641	1693	4113	1149	2964	6746	1797	4949	10501	2883	7618

Venezuela

Million Venezuelan bolivares

	1988			1989			1990			1991		
	Gross Output	Intermediate Consumption	Value Added	Gross Output	Intermediate Consumption	Value Added	Gross Output	Intermediate Consumption	Value Added	Gross Output	Intermediate Consumption	Value Added
3 Manufacturing	533330	353918	179412	916796	602457	314339	1329835	862057	467778	1775795	1173089	602706
A Manufacture of food, beverages and tobacco	133415	93785	39630	231067	163421	67646	330542	232970	97572	461667	324851	136816
B Textile, wearing apparel and leather industries	57361	38378	18983	80512	53752	26760	103998	68963	35035	145230	96255	48975
C Manufacture of wood and wood products, including furniture	15389	9873	5516	18032	11403	6629	21546	13635	7911	30612	19408	11204
D Manufacture of paper and paper products, printing and publishing	26515	17485	9030	42859	28841	14018	59963	39484	20479	77346	50906	26440
E Manufacture of chemicals and chemical petroleum, coal, rubber and plastic products	137859	87176	50683	291093	181519	109574	...	...	188811	...	...	225185
F Manufacture of non-metallic mineral products, except products of petroleum and coal	20358	11050	9308	29352	15178	14174	...	...	19976	...	...	29159
G Basic metal industries	51824	32708	19116	104034	67943	36091	...	...	45619	...	...	46872
H Manufacture of fabricated metal products, machinery and equipment	84646	59708	24938	110110	74294	35816	...	...	47249	...	...	70752
I Other manufacturing industries	5963	3755	2208	9737	6106	3631	...	...	5126	...	...	7303
4 Electricity, gas and water	19000	6133	12867	32752	10130	22622	58608	15390	43218	86627	22404	64223
A Electricity, gas and steam b	17637	5508	12129	31259	9445	21814	56834	14421	42413	83934	20934	63000
B Water works and supply	1363	625	738	1493	685	808	1774	969	805	2693	1470	1223
5 Construction	96206	33968	62238	116630	45570	71060	161195	58299	102896	260257	93494	166763
6 Wholesale and retail trade, restaurants and hotels	277475	106616	170859	450788	175008	275780	653390	252529	400861	906173	349381	556792
A Wholesale and retail trade	193324	57795	135529	314129	94582	219547	450578	133258	317320	623198	183296	439902
B Restaurants and hotels	84151	48821	35330	136659	80426	56233	202812	119271	83541	282975	166085	116890
Restaurants	65477	38902	26575	117716	70343	47373	173421	103630	69791	237682	141981	95701
Hotels and other lodging places	18674	9919	8755	18943	10083	8860	29391	15641	13750	45293	24104	21189
7 Transport, storage and communication	88995	37637	51358	128862	55577	73285	196662	92504	104158	309141	135903	173238
A Transport and storage	78260	35116	43144	113582	51599	61983	174810	87909	86901	271419	128735	142684
B Communication	10735	2521	8214	15280	3978	11302	21852	4595	17257	37722	7168	30554
8 Finance, insurance, real estate and business services	162918	39594	123324	239966	59198	180768	343566	87497	256069	481499	124117	357382
A Financial institutions	37897	10513	27384	51771	16499	35272	76551	24341	52210	95932	32250	63682
B Insurance	11979	8182	3797	19606	13332	6274	26253	17937	8316	34585	23596	10989
C Real estate and business services	113042	20899	92143	168589	29367	139222	240762	45219	195543	350982	68271	282711
Real estate, except dwellings	22365	3095	19270	33879	4392	29487	46033	5787	40246	64824	9217	55607
Dwellings	51611	5109	46502	71988	7127	64861	103673	10264	93409	147711	14624	133087
9 Community, social and personal services	68139	25231	42908	104320	40802	63518	156585	61684	94901	220228	83839	136389
A Sanitary and similar services	3816	1979	1837	6895	4842	2053	10148	7118	3030	15503	7472	8031
B Social and related community services c	18633	3961	14672	27057	5702	21355	40748	8735	32013	57530	12280	45250
Educational services	3590	1005	2585	4790	1342	3448	8059	2321	5738	11790	3301	8489
Medical, dental, other health and veterinary services	14181	2634	11547	21055	3908	17147	30843	5725	25118	43126	8003	35123
C Recreational and cultural services	11463	3432	8031	14742	4520	10222	21478	6809	14669	26911	8280	18631
D Personal and household services	34227	15859	18368	55626	25738	29888	84211	39022	45189	120284	55807	64477
Total, Industries	1445897	649245	796652	2439540	1074988	1364552	3691008	1567797	2123211	4971389	2183791	2787598
Producers of Government Services	93250	26822	66428	145768	37944	107824	195144	54762	140382	292302	85002	207300

4.1 Derivation of Value Added by Kind of Activity, in Current Prices
(Continued)

Million Venezuelan bolivares

	1988			1989			1990			1991		
	Gross Output	Intermediate Consumption	Value Added	Gross Output	Intermediate Consumption	Value Added	Gross Output	Intermediate Consumption	Value Added	Gross Output	Intermediate Consumption	Value Added
Other Producers	17917	6337	11580	24350	8735	15615	38207	13674	24533	53609	19198	34411
Total	1557064	682404	874660	2609658	1121667	1487991	3924359	1636233	2288126	5317300	2287991	3029309
Less: Imputed bank service charge	...	-20318	20318	...	-26619	26619	...	-42178	42178	...	-53272	53272
Import duties	21159	...	21159	24165	...	24165	33313	...	33313	60238	...	60238
Value added tax	...	...	...	...	...	...	...	...	...	...	...	...
Other adjustments	-2218	...	-2218	24824	...	24824	...	...	...	...	...	...
Total	1576005	702722	873283	2658647	1148286	1510361	3957672	1678411	2279261	5377538	2341263	3036275

a) Item 'Agriculture and hunting' includes agricultural products and improvements and other non-agricultural products.
b) Item 'Electricity, gas and water' excludes gas.
c) Social and related community services includes in addition to Educational and health services (item 33 and 34) also the services of commercial and professional associations.

4.2 Derivation of Value Added by Kind of Activity, in Constant Prices

Million Venezuelan bolivares

	1984			1985			1986			1987		
	Gross Output	Intermediate Consumption	Value Added	Gross Output	Intermediate Consumption	Value Added	Gross Output	Intermediate Consumption	Value Added	Gross Output	Intermediate Consumption	Value Added

At constant prices of:1984

All Producers

1 Agriculture, hunting, forestry and fishing	31111	9609	21502	33510	10260	23250	36172	11045	25127	37659	11533	26126
A Agriculture and hunting a	29293	9411	19882	31371	10016	21355	33700	10766	22934	34895	11228	23667
B Forestry and logging	211	33	178	258	40	218	312	47	265	381	56	325
C Fishing	1607	165	1442	1881	204	1677	2160	232	1928	2383	249	2134
2 Mining and quarrying	76071	8686	67385	69095	7995	61100	75345	8760	66585	79967	9392	70575
A Coal mining	4	1	3	3	1	2	4	1	3	35	6	29
B Crude petroleum and natural gas production	73389	7926	65463	66100	7139	58961	71864	7761	64103	75627	8168	67459
C Metal ore mining	1723	482	1241	2025	569	1456	2306	650	1656	3093	865	2228
D Other mining	955	277	678	967	286	681	1171	348	823	1212	353	859
3 Manufacturing	235538	145611	89927	247132	152727	94405	263695	162548	101147	269448	165803	103645
A Manufacture of food, beverages and tobacco	62211	43436	18775	61871	43448	18423	63747	44652	19095	67268	47002	20266
B Textile, wearing apparel and leather industries	22478	14847	7631	24685	16288	8397	26055	17136	8919	27719	18144	9575
C Manufacture of wood and wood products, including furniture	6299	4006	2293	6610	4201	2409	7260	4610	2650	7356	4679	2677
D Manufacture of paper and paper products, printing and publishing	10923	6842	4081	10464	6522	3942	10734	6686	4048	12326	7688	4638
E Manufacture of chemicals and chemical petroleum, coal, rubber and plastic products	69734	38244	31490	74338	40769	33569	79783	43755	36028	76318	41947	34371
F Manufacture of non-metallic mineral products, except products of petroleum and coal	7920	3868	4052	8174	3998	4176	9438	4615	4823	10072	4926	5146
G Basic metal industries	19510	10153	9357	21838	11445	10393	23556	12344	11212	26405	13792	12613
H Manufacture of fabricated metal products, machinery and equipment	34746	23137	11609	37062	24774	12288	40746	27282	13464	38997	25748	13249
I Other manufacturing industries	1717	1078	639	2090	1282	808	2376	1468	908	2987	1877	1110
4 Electricity, gas and water	9141	3055	6086	9545	3181	6364	10086	3360	6726	10623	3537	7086
A Electricity, gas and steam b	7914	2562	5352	8399	2721	5678	8865	2869	5996	9366	3032	6334
B Water works and supply	1227	493	734	1146	460	686	1221	491	730	1257	505	752
5 Construction	40101	14289	25812	39335	13935	25400	42367	15390	26977	43504	15682	27822
6 Wholesale and retail trade, restaurants and hotels	102041	38787	63254	107387	40964	66423	112430	43765	68665	116558	44914	71644
A Wholesale and retail trade	69417	19663	49754	72768	20646	52122	75080	21844	53236	79856	23426	56430
B Restaurants and hotels	32624	19124	13500	34619	20318	14301	37350	21921	15429	36702	21488	15214
Restaurants	24990	15008	9982	26913	16163	10750	29000	17420	11580	27695	16634	11061
Hotels and other lodging places	7634	4116	3518	7706	4155	3551	8350	4501	3849	9007	4854	4153
7 Transport, storage and communication	36125	14958	21167	37981	16003	21978	39682	16609	23073	43148	18168	24980
A Transport and storage	31152	14500	16652	32706	15527	17179	34047	16102	17945	36930	17610	19320
B Communication	4973	458	4515	5275	476	4799	5635	507	5128	6218	558	5660
8 Finance, insurance, real estate and business services	72509	15252	57257	73433	15646	57787	77437	16423	61014	82754	17842	64912
A Financial institutions	12982	3751	9231	13072	3788	9284	13194	3908	9286	14086	4279	9807

Venezuela

Million Venezuelan bolivares

	1984			1985			1986			1987		
	Gross Output	Intermediate Consumption	Value Added	Gross Output	Intermediate Consumption	Value Added	Gross Output	Intermediate Consumption	Value Added	Gross Output	Intermediate Consumption	Value Added
				At constant prices of:1984								
B Insurance	4083	2486	1597	4513	2748	1765	4499	2739	1760	4828	2939	1889
C Real estate and business services	55444	9015	46429	55848	9110	46738	59744	9776	49968	63840	10624	53216
Real estate, except dwellings	9104	1356	7748	8934	1443	7491	9586	1438	8148	10737	1666	9071
Dwellings	29058	2877	26181	29697	2940	26757	30976	3067	27909	32138	3182	28956
9 Community, social and personal services	27037	9694	17343	28878	10560	18318	31514	11552	19962	33457	12322	21135
A Sanitary and similar services	1638	607	1031	1820	859	961	2258	982	1276	2453	1177	1276
B Social and related community services c	8517	1867	6650	9005	1993	7012	9774	2183	7591	10479	2324	8155
Educational services	2213	620	1593	2293	643	1650	2371	665	1706	2466	692	1774
Medical, dental, other health and veterinary services	5978	1101	4877	6284	1158	5126	6826	1259	5567	7445	1377	6068
C Recreational and cultural services	4408	1323	3085	4764	1430	3334	5284	1698	3586	5205	1574	3631
D Personal and household services	12474	5897	6577	13289	6278	7011	14198	6689	7509	15320	7247	8073
Total, Industries	629674	259941	369733	646296	271271	375025	688728	289452	399276	717118	299193	417925
Producers of Government Services	44122	8886	35236	43615	8573	35042	45939	9472	36467	47693	10328	37365
Other Producers	7184	2318	4866	7646	2389	5257	8355	2663	5692	9013	2919	6094
Total	680980	271145	409835	697557	282233	415324	743022	301587	441435	773824	312440	461384
Less: Imputed bank service charge	...	-8546	8546	...	-8716	8716	...	-8699	8699	...	-8577	8577
Import duties	4465	...	4465	4926	...	4926	4872	...	4872	4546	...	4546
Value added tax	...	...	...	...	...	...	...	...	...	...	...	...
Other adjustments	14318	...	14318	9350	...	9350	10677	...	10677	6988	...	6988
Total	699763	279691	420072	711833	290949	420884	758571	310286	448285	785358	321017	464341

	1988			1989			1990			1991		
	Gross Output	Intermediate Consumption	Value Added	Gross Output	Intermediate Consumption	Value Added	Gross Output	Intermediate Consumption	Value Added	Gross Output	Intermediate Consumption	Value Added
				At constant prices of:1984								
				All Producers								
1 Agriculture, hunting, forestry and fishing	39491	12153	27338	36666	10729	25937	35831	10348	25483	37660	11357	26303
A Agriculture and hunting a	36550	11834	24716	33583	10399	23184	33167	10064	23103	35077	11085	23992
B Forestry and logging	418	62	356	376	54	322	338	50	288	339	51	288
C Fishing	2523	257	2266	2707	276	2431	2326	234	2092	2244	221	2023
2 Mining and quarrying	84261	10106	74155	84046	10051	73995	98984	12247	86737	107406	13062	94344
A Coal mining	184	31	153	558	93	465	574	95	479	556	93	463
B Crude petroleum and natural gas production	78717	8501	70216	78727	8503	70224	92788	10022	82766	101474	10960	90514
C Metal ore mining	4013	1189	2824	3500	1091	2409	3549	1109	2440	3288	1037	2251
D Other mining	1347	385	962	1261	364	897	2073	1021	1052	2088	972	1116

4.2 Derivation of Value Added by Kind of Activity, in Constant Prices
(Continued)

Million Venezuelan bolivares

At constant prices of:1984

	1988			1989			1990			1991		
	Gross Output	Intermediate Consumption	Value Added	Gross Output	Intermediate Consumption	Value Added	Gross Output	Intermediate Consumption	Value Added	Gross Output	Intermediate Consumption	Value Added
3 Manufacturing	287472	176717	110755	250612	152958	97654	266892	163278	103614	299749	184273	115476
A Manufacture of food, beverages and tobacco	71175	49422	21753	66665	46886	19779	71126	49700	21426	75941	53572	22369
B Textile, wearing apparel and leather industries	29481	19476	10005	25964	17044	8920	28627	18770	9857	34700	22692	12008
C Manufacture of wood and wood products, including furniture	7839	4967	2872	5872	3677	2195	5944	3724	2220	6778	4256	2522
D Manufacture of paper and paper products, printing and publishing	13481	8434	5047	9608	6000	3608	10862	6801	4061	10595	6645	3950
E Manufacture of chemicals and chemical petroleum, coal, rubber and plastic products	86034	47558	38476	79365	43600	35765	82466	45273	37193	94786	52166	42620
F Manufacture of non-metallic mineral products, except products of petroleum and coal	10387	5304	5083	8462	4122	4340	8718	4252	4466	9666	4702	4964
G Basic metal industries	27466	14309	13157	26677	13674	13003	28550	15013	13537	28668	15074	13594
H Manufacture of fabricated metal products, machinery and equipment	38765	25477	13288	25415	16341	9074	27598	17870	9728	34784	22774	12010
I Other manufacturing industries	2844	1770	1074	2584	1614	970	3001	1875	1126	3831	2392	1439
4 Electricity, gas and water	11410	3798	7612	11581	3855	7726	12165	4042	8123	13283	4429	8854
A Electricity, gas and steam b	10107	3274	6833	10241	3317	6924	10789	3489	7300	11580	3745	7835
B Water works and supply	1303	524	779	1340	538	802	1376	553	823	1703	684	1019
5 Construction	46654	16635	30019	34170	12286	21884	36084	12508	23576	46936	16110	30826
6 Wholesale and retail trade, restaurants and hotels	122930	47405	75525	105634	42053	63581	109170	43157	66013	117299	46368	70931
A Wholesale and retail trade	84240	24748	59492	69468	20744	48724	72168	21379	50789	78102	23316	54786
B Restaurants and hotels	38690	22657	16033	36166	21309	14857	37002	21778	15224	39197	23052	16145
Restaurants	29230	17557	11673	29437	17681	11756	29826	17909	11917	31382	18839	12543
Hotels and other lodging places	9460	5100	4360	6729	3628	3101	7176	3869	3307	7815	4213	3602
7 Transport, storage and communication	46718	19703	27015	42897	17600	25297	41861	16628	25233	45405	18190	27215
A Transport and storage	40344	19126	21218	36021	16969	19052	35036	16001	19035	39180	17614	21566
B Communication	6374	577	5797	6876	631	6245	6825	627	6198	6225	576	5649
8 Finance, insurance, real estate and business services	88566	19363	69203	82787	17933	64854	84093	18073	66020	90032	20749	69283
A Financial institutions	15567	4588	10979	11847	3607	8240	12619	3842	8777	13063	3727	9336
B Insurance	5433	3308	2125	5402	3289	2113	5215	3175	2040	5066	3085	1981
C Real estate and business services	67566	11467	56099	65538	11037	54501	66259	11056	55203	71903	13937	57966
Real estate, except dwellings	11387	1841	9546	10619	1814	8805	10654	1780	8874	11369	3225	8144
Dwellings	33184	3285	29899	33678	3334	30344	34288	3394	30894	35410	3505	31905
9 Community, social and personal services	35974	13293	22681	36392	13841	22551	39388	15363	24025	41582	15534	26048
A Sanitary and similar services	2596	1241	1355	2676	1676	1000	3054	1913	1141	3783	1679	2104
B Social and related community services c	10877	2380	8497	10979	2374	8605	11630	2516	9114	12306	2662	9644
Educational services	2491	699	1792	2438	684	1754	2592	726	1866	2742	768	1974
Medical, dental, other health and veterinary services	7890	1458	6432	8117	1499	6618	8583	1585	6998	9082	1677	7405
C Recreational and cultural services	5609	1670	3939	5194	1486	3708	5999	2093	3906	5946	1976	3970
D Personal and household services	16892	8002	8890	17543	8305	9238	18705	8841	9864	19547	9217	10330
Total, Industries	763476	319173	444303	684785	281306	403479	724468	295644	428824	799352	330072	469280
Producers of Government Services	52878	13783	39095	51801	11119	40682	56087	12306	43781	63624	16311	47313

Venezuela

4.2 Derivation of Value Added by Kind of Activity, in Constant Prices
(Continued)

Million Venezuelan bolivares

	1988			1989			1990			1991		
	Gross Output	Intermediate Consumption	Value Added	Gross Output	Intermediate Consumption	Value Added	Gross Output	Intermediate Consumption	Value Added	Gross Output	Intermediate Consumption	Value Added
						At constant prices of:1984						
Other Producers	9445	3139	6306	9265	3038	6227	10302	3278	7024	11091	3500	7591
Total	825799	336095	489704	745851	295463	450388	790857	311228	479629	874067	349883	524184
Less: Imputed bank service charge	...	-9023	9023	...	-6559	6559	...	-6675	6675	...	-7484	7484
Import duties	4896	...	4896	3719	...	3719	5366	...	5366	11227	...	11227
Value added tax	...	...	...				...	...	...	...	...	...
Other adjustments	5795	...	5795	1714	...	1714	...	...	...	...	...	...
Total	836490	345118	491372	751284	302022	449262	796223	317903	478320	885294	357367	527927

a) Item 'Agriculture and hunting' includes agricultural products and improvements and other non-agricultural products.
b) Item 'Electricity, gas and water' excludes gas.

c) Social and related community services includes in addition to Educational and health services (item 33 and 34) also the services of commercial and professional associations.

4.3 Cost Components of Value Added

Million Venezuelan bolivares

	1984						1985					
	Compensation of Employees	Capital Consumption	Net Operating Surplus	Indirect Taxes	Less: Subsidies Received	Value Added	Compensation of Employees	Capital Consumption	Net Operating Surplus	Indirect Taxes	Less: Subsidies Received	Value Added
					All Producers							
1 Agriculture, hunting, forestry and fishing	5179	1896	14564	...	137	21502	6467	2412	18428	...	380	26927
A Agriculture and hunting a	4654	1826	13539	...	137	19882	5726	2307	16985	...	380	24638
B Forestry and logging	30	8	140	...	...	178	38	11	169	...	...	218
C Fishing	495	62	885	...	...	1442	703	94	1274	...	...	2071
2 Mining and quarrying	5395	3293	58399	298	...	67385	6897	3544	52033	336	...	62810
A Coal mining	3	...	...	...	...	3	3	...	...	...	...	3
B Crude petroleum and natural gas production	4761	3072	57332	298	...	65463	6238	3309	50635	326	...	60508
C Metal ore mining	426	110	705	...	...	1241	453	117	954	10	...	1534
D Other mining	205	111	362	...	...	678	203	118	444	...	...	765
3 Manufacturing	28565	7489	50987	5334	2448	89927	33279	8010	55562	7484	2539	101796
A Manufacture of food, beverages and tobacco	5698	1468	9685	3430	1506	18775	7532	1596	9831	5269	733	23495
B Textile, wearing apparel and leather industries	3499	413	3678	42	1	7631	4178	541	4554	64	28	9309
C Manufacture of wood and wood products, including furniture	1002	163	1114	14	...	2293	1154	184	1241	18	...	2597
D Manufacture of paper and paper products, printing and publishing	1971	297	1782	36	5	4081	2153	319	2124	47	8	4635
E Manufacture of chemicals and chemical petroleum, coal, rubber and plastic products	6378	1930	22045	1643	506	31490	7052	2106	24444	1889	866	34625
F Manufacture of non-metallic mineral products, except products of petroleum and coal	1732	562	1737	31	10	4052	1865	518	2010	31	25	4399
G Basic metal industries	2835	1639	5266	20	403	9357	3329	1529	4671	21	858	8692
H Manufacture of fabricated metal products, machinery and equipment	5190	979	5345	112	17	11609	5698	1165	6202	137	21	13181
I Other manufacturing industries	260	38	335	6	...	639	318	52	485	8	...	863
4 Electricity, gas and water	2546	1190	2075	275	...	6086	2641	1420	2501	345	...	6907
A Electricity, gas and steam b	1772	1167	2138	275	...	5352	1857	1375	2645	345	...	6222
B Water works and supply	774	23	-63	...	...	734	784	45	-144	...	...	685
5 Construction	8067	3167	14463	115	...	25812	9115	3806	15082	116	...	28119
6 Wholesale and retail trade, restaurants and hotels	27375	3701	30844	1341	7	63254	30397	4706	37246	1518	7	73860
A Wholesale and retail trade	22512	2290	23817	1142	7	49754	24642	3032	28788	1245	7	57700
B Restaurants and hotels	4863	1411	7027	199	...	13500	5755	1674	8458	273	...	16160
Restaurants	3960	1162	4690	170	...	9982	4756	1396	5872	236	...	12260
Hotels and other lodging places	903	249	2337	29	...	3518	999	278	2586	37	...	3900
7 Transport, storage and communication	7586	2919	10681	123	142	21167	7991	3049	13616	149	132	24673
A Transport and storage	5554	2393	8724	123	142	16652	6124	2504	10764	149	132	19409
B Communication	2032	526	1957	...	...	4515	1867	545	2852	...	...	5264
8 Finance, insurance, real estate and business services	11444	7564	36834	1415	...	57257	12020	8390	40037	1485	...	61932
A Financial institutions	5399	650	2822	360	...	9231	5855	705	3092	401	...	10053

4.3 Cost Components of Value Added
(Continued)

Million Venezuelan bolivares

	1984						1985					
	Compensation of Employees	Capital Consumption	Net Operating Surplus	Indirect Taxes	Less: Subsidies Received	Value Added	Compensation of Employees	Capital Consumption	Net Operating Surplus	Indirect Taxes	Less: Subsidies Received	Value Added
B Insurance	1055	98	394	50	...	1597	1245	117	433	68	...	1863
C Real estate and business services	4990	6816	33618	1005	...	46429	4920	7568	36512	1016	...	50016
Real estate, except dwellings	1117	1102	4851	678	...	7748	1023	1325	5501	675	...	8524
Dwellings	142	5219	20563	257	...	26181	154	5655	22308	254	...	28371
9 Community, social and personal services	8381	1236	7761	286	321	17343	9334	850	9654	480	515	19803
A Sanitary and similar services	1229	15	-218	5	...	1031	1415	18	-308	8	...	1133
B Social and related community services c	2548	311	4097	15	321	6650	2842	260	4932	8	515	7527
Educational services	1374	71	467	2	321	1593	1489	110	643	...	515	1727
Medical, dental, other health and veterinary services	1039	228	3599	11	...	4877	1183	134	4251	5	...	5573
C Recreational and cultural services	1318	393	1156	218	...	3085	1407	115	1955	378	...	3855
D Personal and household services	3286	517	2726	48	...	6577	3670	457	3075	86	...	7288
Total, Industries	104538	32455	226608	9187	3055	369733	118141	36187	244159	11913	3573	406827
Producers of Government Services	35073	163	...	...	...	35236	39592	193	...	...	...	39785
Other Producers	4760	101	...	5	...	4866	5650	119	...	6	...	5775
Total	144371	32719	226608	9192	3055	409835	163383	36499	244159	11919	3573	452387
Less: Imputed bank service charge	...	...	8546	...	...	8546	...	...	9652	...	...	9652
Import duties	...	...	...	4465	...	4465	...	...	...	6292	...	6292
Value added tax	...	...	...	...	...	...	...	...	...	...	...	...
Other adjustments	...	...	...	14318	...	14318	...	...	...	15714	...	15714
Total	144371	32719	218062	27975	3055	420072	163383	36499	234507	33925	3573	464741

	1986						1987					
	Compensation of Employees	Capital Consumption	Net Operating Surplus	Indirect Taxes	Less: Subsidies Received	Value Added	Compensation of Employees	Capital Consumption	Net Operating Surplus	Indirect Taxes	Less: Subsidies Received	Value Added

All Producers

	Comp. of Empl. 1986	Cap. Cons.	Net Op. Surplus	Indirect Taxes	Less: Subsidies	Value Added	Comp. of Empl. 1987	Cap. Cons.	Net Op. Surplus	Indirect Taxes	Less: Subsidies	Value Added
1 Agriculture, hunting, forestry and fishing	7875	2852	22054	...	327	32454	10339	3684	28974	...	423	42574
A Agriculture and hunting a	6827	2706	20006	...	327	29212	8678	3475	25883	...	423	37613
B Forestry and logging	52	14	251	...	...	317	87	22	429	...	...	538
C Fishing	996	132	1797	...	...	2925	1574	187	2662	...	...	4423
2 Mining and quarrying	5514	4022	34704	133	...	44373	6964	4649	71239	431	10	83273
A Coal mining	7	1	-4	...	...	4	12	6	12	...	...	30
B Crude petroleum and natural gas production	4640	3710	32243	103	...	40696	5668	4156	66677	259	...	76760
C Metal ore mining	630	171	1784	26	...	2611	972	300	3767	98	10	5127
D Other mining	237	140	681	4	...	1062	312	187	783	74	...	1356
3 Manufacturing	35170	9257	61271	11023	2909	113812	45934	11469	81527	13908	9523	143315
A Manufacture of food, beverages and tobacco	7898	1817	11430	5985	1276	25854	8988	1996	18212	7302	4644	31854
B Textile, wearing apparel and leather industries	4360	631	5438	102	9	10522	5974	884	7132	225	44	14171
C Manufacture of wood and wood products, including furniture	1285	220	1547	28	...	3080	1567	235	2224	25	...	4051
D Manufacture of paper and paper products, printing and publishing	2351	384	2296	63	27	5067	3074	463	3447	55	71	6968
E Manufacture of chemicals and chemical petroleum, coal, rubber and plastic products	6860	2265	21109	4505	533	34206	9538	2480	27062	5678	2901	41857
F Manufacture of non-metallic mineral products, except products of petroleum and coal	1994	563	3084	41	87	5595	2775	610	4337	37	113	7646
G Basic metal industries	3975	1974	7069	85	944	12159	5246	3068	7637	397	1701	14647
H Manufacture of fabricated metal products, machinery and equipment	6068	1338	8657	200	28	16235	8183	1638	10397	177	42	20353
I Other manufacturing industries	379	65	641	14	5	1094	589	95	1079	12	7	1768
4 Electricity, gas and water	2409	1704	3099	415	...	7627	4154	2522	3648	498	...	10822
A Electricity, gas and steam b	1843	1679	2898	415	...	6835	3169	2492	3879	498	...	10038
B Water works and supply	566	25	201	...	...	792	985	30	-231	...	...	784

Venezuela

Million Venezuelan bolivares

	1986						1987					
	Compensation of Employees	Capital Consumption	Net Operating Surplus	Indirect Taxes	Less: Subsidies Received	Value Added	Compensation of Employees	Capital Consumption	Net Operating Surplus	Indirect Taxes	Less: Subsidies Received	Value Added
5 Construction	10657	5290	16306	194	...	32447	14699	7708	22044	190	...	44641
6 Wholesale and retail trade, restaurants and hotels	37683	4945	43121	1618	1	87366	53780	6561	61662	2186	177	124012
A Wholesale and retail trade	30808	2946	33159	1329	1	68241	44895	3980	48262	1830	177	98790
B Restaurants and hotels	6875	1999	9962	289	...	19125	8885	2581	13400	356	...	25222
Restaurants	5673	1664	6804	250	...	14391	7124	2089	8736	300	...	18249
Hotels and other lodging places	1202	335	3158	39	...	4734	1761	492	4664	56	...	6973
7 Transport, storage and communication	9070	3748	17463	391	115	30557	11979	5150	22867	376	185	40187
A Transport and storage	7248	3288	13229	391	115	24041	9826	4385	18091	376	185	32493
B Communication	1822	460	4234	...	...	6516	2153	765	4776	...	...	7694
8 Finance, insurance, real estate and business services	13602	9722	46803	1606	...	71733	17253	12188	62124	1768	...	93333
A Financial institutions	6481	912	4182	464	...	12039	8171	1124	8681	537	...	18513
B Insurance	1402	164	357	40	...	1963	1720	208	373	91	...	2392
C Real estate and business services	5719	8646	42264	1102	...	57731	7362	10856	53070	1140	...	72428
Real estate, except dwellings	1196	1648	6753	754	...	10351	1698	2305	9758	880	...	14641
Dwellings	172	6288	24896	189	...	31545	209	7653	30458	72	...	38392
9 Community, social and personal services	11007	1262	11553	417	547	23692	15193	1816	15594	444	565	32482
A Sanitary and similar services	1911	21	-615	9	...	1326	2285	41	-866	11	...	1471
B Social and related community services c	3196	417	5840	47	547	8953	4016	536	7604	57	565	11648
Educational services	1592	133	668	...	547	1846	1843	154	705	...	565	2137
Medical, dental, other health and veterinary services	1431	230	5048	7	...	6716	1972	319	6755	10	...	9056
C Recreational and cultural services	1593	183	2442	299	...	4517	2283	271	3208	289	...	6051
D Personal and household services	4307	641	3886	62	...	8896	6609	968	5648	87	...	13312
Total, Industries	132987	42802	256374	15797	3899	444061	180295	55747	369679	19801	10883	614639
Producers of Government Services	43646	229	...	...	...	43875	55644	217	...	...	...	55861
Other Producers	6917	152	...	8	...	7077	8505	193	...	10	...	8708
Total	183550	43183	256374	15805	3899	495013	244444	56157	369679	19811	10883	679208
Less: Imputed bank service charge	...	...	11718	...	...	11718	...	...	15489	...	...	15489
Import duties	...	...	...	8837	...	8837	...	...	...	15720	...	15720
Value added tax	...	...	...	...	...	...	...	...	...	...	...	...
Other adjustments	...	...	...	-2960	...	-2960	...	...	...	16982	...	16982
Total	183550	43183	244656	21682	3899	489172	244444	56157	354190	52513	10883	696421

	1988						1989					
	Compensation of Employees	Capital Consumption	Net Operating Surplus	Indirect Taxes	Less: Subsidies Received	Value Added	Compensation of Employees	Capital Consumption	Net Operating Surplus	Indirect Taxes	Less: Subsidies Received	Value Added
					All Producers							
1 Agriculture, hunting, forestry and fishing	14164	4805	39365	...	453	57881	22648	7313	63381	...	1298	92044
A Agriculture and hunting a	11845	4523	35016	...	453	50931	18898	6824	56003	...	1298	80427
B Forestry and logging	134	38	676	...	...	848	233	65	1172	...	...	1470
C Fishing	2185	244	3673	...	...	6102	3517	424	6206	...	...	10147
2 Mining and quarrying	10159	5922	79728	233	237	95805	21814	7453	242630	1063	1824	271136
A Coal mining	132	66	132	...	2	328	944	476	1350	...	415	2355
B Crude petroleum and natural gas production	8014	5144	72984	205	...	86347	17810	6034	233100	932	...	257876
C Metal ore mining	1487	451	5709	25	235	7437	2331	496	6414	109	1409	7941
D Other mining	526	261	903	3	...	1693	729	447	1766	22	...	2964

4.3 Cost Components of Value Added
(Continued)

Million Venezuelan bolivares

	1988						1989					
	Compensation of Employees	Capital Consumption	Net Operating Surplus	Indirect Taxes	Less: Subsidies Received	Value Added	Compensation of Employees	Capital Consumption	Net Operating Surplus	Indirect Taxes	Less: Subsidies Received	Value Added
3 Manufacturing	60860	13528	101969	16329	13274	179412	106857	22152	187159	20296	22125	314339
A Manufacture of food, beverages and tobacco	11426	2493	20830	9049	4168	39630	20710	4320	36251	12643	6278	67646
B Textile, wearing apparel and leather industries	8014	1200	9003	914	148	18983	15400	1690	10101	264	695	26760
C Manufacture of wood and wood products, including furniture	2137	324	3032	23	...	5516	3598	383	2621	27	...	6629
D Manufacture of paper and paper products, printing and publishing	4024	605	4706	52	357	9030	6841	977	6375	64	239	14018
E Manufacture of chemicals and chemical petroleum, coal, rubber and plastic products	13782	2906	32113	5579	3697	50683	21827	4424	80211	5914	2802	109574
F Manufacture of non-metallic mineral products, except products of petroleum and coal	3388	735	5457	35	307	9308	5692	1111	7704	39	372	14174
G Basic metal industries	7499	3212	12420	481	4496	19116	13367	6518	22491	1130	7415	36091
H Manufacture of fabricated metal products, machinery and equipment	9802	1935	13109	186	94	24938	17040	2536	19375	203	3338	35816
I Other manufacturing industries	788	118	1299	10	7	2208	2382	193	2030	12	986	3631
4 Electricity, gas and water	5624	3053	3601	589	...	12867	8516	5348	7802	956	...	22622
A Electricity, gas and steam b	4179	3034	4327	589	...	12129	6934	5327	8597	956	...	21814
B Water works and supply	1445	19	-726	...	...	738	1582	21	-795	...	...	808
5 Construction	20701	10573	30683	281	...	62238	24075	11487	35174	324	...	71060
6 Wholesale and retail trade, restaurants and hotels	74336	9182	85587	2224	470	170859	124089	15758	134538	1894	499	275780
A Wholesale and retail trade	61774	5509	66879	1837	470	135529	100687	8975	108834	1550	499	219547
B Restaurants and hotels	12562	3673	18708	387	...	35330	23402	6783	25704	344	...	56233
Restaurants	10360	3069	12815	331	...	26575	18650	5477	22972	274	...	47373
Hotels and other lodging places	2202	604	5893	56	...	8755	4752	1306	2732	70	...	8860
7 Transport, storage and communication	16991	6402	28117	441	593	51358	24290	11241	39377	523	2146	73285
A Transport and storage	13229	5584	24505	419	593	43144	20090	8038	35501	500	2146	61983
B Communication	3762	818	3612	22	...	8214	4200	3203	3876	23	...	11302
8 Finance, insurance, real estate and business services	22742	15244	82892	2446	...	123324	35557	22347	119995	2869	...	180768
A Financial institutions	10601	1511	14592	680	...	27384	17004	2381	14929	958	...	35272
B Insurance	2578	271	821	127	...	3797	3776	393	1916	189	...	6274
C Real estate and business services	9563	13462	67479	1639	...	92143	14777	19573	103150	1722	...	139222
Real estate, except dwellings	2051	3043	12929	1247	...	19270	2989	4811	20434	1253	...	29487
Dwellings	253	9269	36781	199	...	46502	353	12929	51285	294	...	64861
9 Community, social and personal services	18100	2388	22770	473	823	42908	27675	3602	32715	548	1022	63518
A Sanitary and similar services	2874	51	-1098	10	...	1837	5267	108	-3329	7	...	2053
B Social and related community services c	4972	665	9791	67	823	14672	7026	958	14219	87	935	21355
Educational services	2229	187	992	...	823	2585	2970	254	1159	...	935	3448
Medical, dental, other health and veterinary services	2505	404	8627	11	...	11547	3721	600	12818	8	...	17147
C Recreational and cultural services	2850	362	4516	303	...	8031	3567	442	5925	375	87	10222
D Personal and household services	7404	1310	9561	93	...	18368	11815	2094	15900	79	...	29888
Total, Industries	243677	71097	474712	23016	15850	796652	395521	106701	862771	28473	28914	1364552
Producers of Government Services	66179	249	...	...	...	66428	107556	268	...	...	...	107824
Other Producers	11292	273	...	15	...	11580	15218	376	...	21	...	15615
Total	321148	71619	474712	23031	15850	874660	518295	107345	862771	28494	28914	1487991
Less: Imputed bank service charge	...	...	20318	...	...	20318	...	...	26619	...	...	26619
Import duties	...	...	...	21159	...	21159	...	...	...	24165	...	24165
Value added tax	...	...	...	...	...	...	...	...	...	...	...	...
Other adjustments	...	...	...	-2218	...	-2218	...	...	...	24824	...	24824
Total	321148	71619	454394	41972	15850	873283	518295	107345	836152	77483	28914	1510361

Venezuela

4.3 Cost Components of Value Added

Million Venezuelan bolivares

	1990						1991					
	Compensation of Employees	Capital Consumption	Net Operating Surplus	Indirect Taxes	Less: Subsidies Received	Value Added	Compensation of Employees	Capital Consumption	Net Operating Surplus	Indirect Taxes	Less: Subsidies Received	Value Added
All Producers												
1 Agriculture, hunting, forestry and fishing	29743	9876	84669	...	1523	122765	40921	13819	113011	...	333	167418
A Agriculture and hunting [a]	25419	9312	76551	...	1523	109759	34904	13056	101610	...	333	149237
B Forestry and logging	251	70	1266	...	...	1587	365	100	1763	...	...	2228
C Fishing	4073	494	6852	...	...	11419	5652	663	9638	...	...	15953
2 Mining and quarrying	32760	10454	489153	542	2345	530565	49878	14302	499157	675	1325	562687
A Coal mining	194	163	2401	-	237	2522	310	227	2641	1	163	3016
B Crude petroleum and natural gas production	28700	8947	473292	175	...	511114	43965	12088	482119	162	...	538334
C Metal ore mining	2693	635	10428	332	2108	11980	3577	827	10016	461	1162	13719
D Other mining	1173	709	3032	35	...	4949	2026	1160	4381	51	...	7618
3 Manufacturing	118164	30211	321204	24178	25979	467778	166325	39688	374566	33340	11213	602706
A Manufacture of food, beverages and tobacco	21763	4256	61241	15033	4721	97572	30497	5974	79028	21984	667	136816
B Textile, wearing apparel and leather industries	13909	2805	18098	1027	804	35035	20037	3961	23274	1826	123	48975
C Manufacture of wood and wood products, including furniture	3037	477	4363	34	...	7911	4365	667	6110	62	...	11204
D Manufacture of paper and paper products, printing and publishing	7740	1362	11501	78	202	20479	9966	1745	14752	137	160	26440
E Manufacture of chemicals and chemical petroleum, coal, rubber and plastic products	28918	6348	149307	6250	2012	188811	43941	8607	169946	6933	4242	225185
F Manufacture of non-metallic mineral products, except products of petroleum and coal	6628	1913	11910	52	527	19976	9744	2821	16745	92	243	29159
G Basic metal industries	17994	9068	27611	1427	10481	45619	20021	9835	19546	1774	4304	46872
H Manufacture of fabricated metal products, machinery and equipment	16840	3679	32993	263	6526	47249	25882	5648	40162	506	1446	70752
I Other manufacturing industries	1335	303	4180	14	706	5126	1872	430	5003	26	28	7303
4 Electricity, gas and water	11731	5431	24698	1358	...	43218	18317	8347	35529	2030	...	64223
A Electricity, gas and steam [b]	9705	5413	25937	1358	...	42413	15242	8320	37408	2030	...	63000
B Water works and supply	2026	18	-1239	...	...	805	3075	27	-1879	...	...	1223
5 Construction	39829	20472	42153	442	...	102896	64125	34686	67198	754	...	166763
6 Wholesale and retail trade, restaurants and hotels	176919	23706	196846	3665	275	400861	245430	32963	268858	9665	124	556792
A Wholesale and retail trade	142096	13593	158971	2935	275	317320	196396	18751	217211	7668	124	439902
B Restaurants and hotels	34823	10113	37875	730	...	83541	49034	14212	51647	1997	...	116890
Restaurants	27475	8070	33654	592	...	69791	37710	11064	45298	1629	...	95701
Hotels and other lodging places	7348	2043	4221	138	...	13750	11324	3148	6349	368	...	21189
7 Transport, storage and communication	33698	15946	56297	1044	2827	104158	53042	23450	97639	1253	2146	173238
A Transport and storage	27608	12074	49050	996	2827	86901	42029	19523	82025	1253	2146	142684
B Communication	6090	3872	7247	48	...	17257	11013	3927	15614	-	...	30554
8 Finance, insurance, real estate and business services	51038	31792	170169	4101	1031	256069	74101	44170	228997	10114	-	357382
A Financial institutions	25232	3493	21878	1607	...	52210	35304	4777	20801	2800	...	63682
B Insurance	5246	510	2397	163	...	8316	7352	708	2717	212	...	10989
C Real estate and business services	20560	27789	145894	2331	1031	195543	31445	38685	205479	7102	-	282711
Real estate, except dwellings	3571	6627	29386	1693	1031	40246	5206	8368	37547	4486	-	55607
Dwellings	508	18620	73950	331	...	93409	724	26529	104071	1763	...	133087
9 Community, social and personal services	41555	5422	48824	813	1713	94901	58821	7580	64458	7348	1818	136389
A Sanitary and similar services	7752	159	-4896	15	...	3030	10762	152	-2932	49	...	8031
B Social and related community services [c]	11103	1476	21013	134	1713	32013	15656	2077	28839	196	1518	45250

4.3 Cost Components of Value Added
(Continued)

Million Venezuelan bolivares

	1990						1991					
	Compensation of Employees	Capital Consumption	Net Operating Surplus	Indirect Taxes	Less: Subsidies Received	Value Added	Compensation of Employees	Capital Consumption	Net Operating Surplus	Indirect Taxes	Less: Subsidies Received	Value Added
Educational services	5142	439	1869	1	1713	5738	7312	624	2069	2	1518	8489
Medical, dental, other health and veterinary services	5451	879	18775	13	...	25118	7622	1229	26248	24	...	35123
C Recreational and cultural services	4869	630	8667	503	-	14669	6999	858	4399	6675	300	18631
D Personal and household services	17831	3157	24040	161	...	45189	25404	4493	34152	428	...	64477
Total, Industries	535437	153310	1434013	36143	35693	2123211	770960	219005	1749413	65179	16959	2787598
Producers of Government Services	140054	328	...	...	...	140382	206915	385	...	...	...	207300
Other Producers	23911	592	...	30	...	24533	33537	832	...	42	...	34411
Total	699402	154230	1434013	36174	35693	2288126	1011412	220222	1749413	65221	16959	3029309
Less: Imputed bank service charge	...	...	42178	...	...	42178	...	...	53272	...	...	53272
Import duties	...	...	...	33313	...	33313	...	...	...	60238	...	60238
Value added tax	...	...	...	...	...	...	...	...	...	...	...	...
Other adjustments	...	...	...	...	...	...	...	...	...	...	...	...
Total	699402	154230	1391835	69487	35693	2279261	1011412	220222	1696141	125459	16959	3036275

a) Item 'Agriculture and hunting' includes agricultural products and improvements and other non-agricultural products.

b) Item 'Electricity, gas and water' excludes gas.

c) Social and related community services includes in addition to Educational and health services (item 33 and 34) also the services of commercial and professional associations.

Viet Nam

Source. Reply to the United Nations National Accounts Questionnaire from the General Statistical Office, Hanoi. The official estimates are published in: System of National Accounts of Viet Nam, 1986-1990'.

General note. The estimates shown in the following tables have been prepared in accordance with the United Nations System of National Accounts (SNA) so far as the existing data would permit.

1.1 Expenditure on the Gross Domestic Product, in Current Prices

Thousand Million Dongs

	1980	1981	1982	1983	1984	1985	1986	1987	1988	1989	1990	1991
1 Government final consumption expenditure	...	...	...	...	...	...	525	2520	13291	4213	... 6491	10397
2 Private final consumption expenditure	...	...	...	...	...	...				20144	... 30885	56213
3 Gross capital formation	...	...	...	...	...	...	60	270	1906	2817	... 4385	8128
A Increase in stocks	...	...	...	...	...	...	...	...	...	411	...	...
B Gross fixed capital formation	...	...	...	...	...	...	...	...	...	2406	...	...
Residential buildings	...	...	...	...	...	...	...	...	...	1007	...	...
Non-residential buildings	...	...	...	...	...	...	...	...	...		...	...
Other construction and land improvement etc.	...	...	...	...	...	...	...	...	...	36	...	...
Other	...	...	...	...	...	...	...	...	...	1363	...	...
4 Exports of goods and services	...	...	...	...	...	...	40	172	608	6700	-2935	-3925
5 Less: Imports of goods and services	...	...	...	...	...	...	99	425	2314	9567		
Statistical discrepancy	...	...	...	...	...	...	-13	-69	-225	-	... -660	-854
Equals: Gross Domestic Product	...	...	...	...	...	...	512	2469	13266	24308	... 38166	69959

1.3 Cost Components of the Gross Domestic Product

Thousand Million Dongs

	1980	1981	1982	1983	1984	1985	1986	1987	1988	1989	1990	1991
1 Indirect taxes, net	...	...	...	...	...	...	...	...	...	2759	...	...
A Indirect taxes	...	...	...	...	...	...	...	...	...	2924	...	...
B Less: Subsidies	...	...	...	...	...	...	...	...	...	165	...	...
2 Consumption of fixed capital	...	...	...	...	...	...	...	...	...	1657	...	...
3 Compensation of employees paid by resident producers to:										14436	...	...
A Resident households	...	...	...	...	...	...	...	...	...	14422	...	...
B Rest of the world	...	...	...	...	...	...	...	...	...	14	...	...
4 Operating surplus	...	...	...	...	...	...	...	...	...	5455	...	...
A Corporate and quasi-corporate enterprises	...	...	...	...	...	...	...	...	...	1624	...	...
B Private unincorporated enterprises	...	...	...	...	...	...	...	...	...	3552	...	...
C General government	...	...	...	...	...	...	...	...	...	279	...	...
Equals: Gross Domestic Product	...	...	...	...	...	...	...	...	...	24308	...	...

1.4 General Government Current Receipts and Disbursements

Thousand Million Dongs

	1980	1981	1982	1983	1984	1985	1986	1987	1988	1989	1990	1991
					Receipts							
1 Operating surplus	...	...	...	...	...	...	...	...	...	279	...	...
2 Property and entrepreneurial income	...	...	...	...	...	...	...	...	...	14	...	...
3 Taxes, fees and contributions	...	...	...	...	...	...	...	...	...	3322	...	...
A Indirect taxes	...	...	...	...	...	...	...	...	...	2924	...	...
B Direct taxes	...	...	...	...	...	...	...	...	...	398	...	...
C Social security contributions	...	...	...	...	...	...	...	...	...		...	...
D Compulsory fees, fines and penalties	...	...	...	...	...	...	...	...	...		...	...
4 Other current transfers	...	...	...	...	...	...	...	...	...	1011	...	...
Total Current Receipts of General Government	...	...	...	...	...	...	...	...	...	4626	...	...
					Disbursements							
1 Government final consumption expenditure	...	...	...	...	...	...	...	...	...	4214	...	...

1.4 General Government Current Receipts and Disbursements
(Continued)

Thousand Million Dongs

	1980	1981	1982	1983	1984	1985	1986	1987	1988	1989	1990	1991
A Compensation of employees	...	...	...	...	...	...	...	...	...	1809	...	...
B Consumption of fixed capital	...	...	...	...	...	...	...	...	...	358	...	...
C Purchases of goods and services, net	...	...	...	...	...	...	...	...	...	1675	...	...
D Less: Own account fixed capital formation	...	...	...	...	...	...	...	...	...	-	...	...
E Indirect taxes paid, net	...	...	...	...	...	...	...	...	...	372	...	...
2 Property income	...	...	...	...	...	...	...	...	...	569	...	...
A Interest	...	...	...	...	...	...	...	...	...	21	...	...
B Net land rent and royalties	...	...	...	...	...	...	...	...	...	548	...	...
3 Subsidies	...	...	...	...	...	...	...	...	...	165	...	...
4 Other current transfers	...	...	...	...	...	...	...	...	...	1767	...	...
A Social security benefits	...	...	...	...	...	...	...	...	...	473	...	...
B Social assistance grants	...	...	...	...	...	...	...	...	...	1261	...	...
C Other	...	...	...	...	...	...	...	...	...	33	...	...
5 Net saving	...	...	...	...	...	...	...	...	...	-2088	...	...
Total Current Disbursements and Net Saving of General Government	...	...	...	...	...	...	...	...	...	4626	...	...

1.5 Current Income and Outlay of Corporate and Quasi-Corporate Enterprises, Summary

Thousand Million Dongs

	1980	1981	1982	1983	1984	1985	1986	1987	1988	1989	1990	1991
					Receipts							
1 Operating surplus	...	...	...	...	...	...	...	...	...	1624	...	...
2 Property and entrepreneurial income received	...	...	...	...	...	...	...	...	...	1217	...	...
3 Current transfers	...	...	...	...	...	...	...	...	...	502	...	...
Total Current Receipts	...	...	...	...	...	...	...	...	...	3343	...	...
					Disbursements							
1 Property and entrepreneurial income	...	...	...	...	...	...	...	...	...	1133	...	...
2 Direct taxes and other current payments to general government	...	...	...	...	...	...	...	...	...	56	...	...
3 Other current transfers	...	...	...	...	...	...	...	...	...	483	...	...
4 Net saving	...	...	...	...	...	...	...	...	...	1671	...	...
Total Current Disbursements and Net Saving	...	...	...	...	...	...	...	...	...	3343	...	...

1.6 Current Income and Outlay of Households and Non-Profit Institutions

Thousand Million Dongs

	1980	1981	1982	1983	1984	1985	1986	1987	1988	1989	1990	1991
					Receipts							
1 Compensation of employees	...	...	...	...	...	...	...	...	...	3787	...	...
2 Operating surplus of private unincorporated enterprises	...	...	...	...	...	...	...	...	...	14187	...	...
3 Property and entrepreneurial income	...	...	...	...	...	...	...	...	...	117	...	...
4 Current transfers	...	...	...	...	...	...	...	...	...	3871	...	...
A Social security benefits	...	...	...	...	...	...	...	...	...	472	...	...
B Social assistance grants	...	...	...	...	...	...	...	...	...	97	...	...
C Other	...	...	...	...	...	...	...	...	...	3302	...	...
Total Current Receipts	...	...	...	...	...	...	...	...	...	21962	...	...
					Disbursements							
1 Private final consumption expenditure	...	...	...	...	...	...	...	...	...	20144	...	...

Viet Nam

1.6 Current Income and Outlay of Households and Non-Profit Institutions
(Continued)

Thousand Million Dongs

	1980	1981	1982	1983	1984	1985	1986	1987	1988	1989	1990	1991
2 Property income	...	...	...	...	...	...	...	...	...	130	...	...
3 Direct taxes and other current transfers n.e.c. to general government	...	...	...	...	...	...	...	...	...	730	...	...
A Social security contributions	...	...	...	...	...	...	...	...	...	388	...	...
B Direct taxes	...	...	...	...	...	...	...	...	...	342	...	...
C Fees, fines and penalties	...	...	...	...	...	...	...	...	...	...	...	...
4 Other current transfers	...	...	...	...	...	...	...	...	...	453	...	...
5 Net saving	...	...	...	...	...	...	...	...	...	505	...	...
Total Current Disbursements and Net Saving	...	...	...	...	...	...	...	...	...	21962		

1.7 External Transactions on Current Account, Summary

Thousand Million Dongs

	1980	1981	1982	1983	1984	1985	1986	1987	1988	1989	1990	1991
Payments to the Rest of the World												
1 Imports of goods and services	...	...	...	...	...	...	...	...	...	9567	...	...
A Imports of merchandise c.i.f.	...	...	...	...	...	...	...	...	...	7017	...	...
B Other	...	...	...	...	...	...	...	...	...	2550	...	...
2 Factor income to the rest of the world	...	...	...	...	...	...	...	...	...	732	...	...
A Compensation of employees	...	...	...	...	...	...	...	...	...	14	...	...
B Property and entrepreneurial income	...	...	...	...	...	...	...	...	...	718	...	...
By general government	...	...	...	...	...	...	...	...	...	534	...	...
By corporate and quasi-corporate enterprises	...	...	...	...	...	...	...	...	...	100	...	...
By other	...	...	...	...	...	...	...	...	...	84	...	...
3 Current transfers to the rest of the world	...	...	...	...	...	...	...	...	...	33	...	...
A Indirect taxes to supranational organizations	...	...	...	...	...	...	...	...	...	32	...	...
B Other current transfers	...	...	...	...	...	...	...	...	...	1	...	...
4 Surplus of the nation on current transactions	...	...	...	...	...	...	...	...	...	-1072	...	...
Payments to the Rest of the World and Surplus of the Nation on Current Transactions	...	...	...	...	...	...	...	...	...	9260	...	...
Receipts From The Rest of the World												
1 Exports of goods and services	...	...	...	...	...	...	...	...	...	6700	...	...
A Exports of merchandise f.o.b.	...	...	...	...	...	...	...	...	...	6161	...	...
B Other	...	...	...	...	...	...	...	...	...	539	...	...
2 Factor income from rest of the world	...	...	...	...	...	...	...	...	...	234	...	...
A Compensation of employees	...	...	...	...	...	...	...	...	...	17	...	...
B Property and entrepreneurial income	...	...	...	...	...	...	...	...	...	217	...	...
3 Current transfers from rest of the world	...	...	...	...	...	...	...	...	...	2326	...	...
A Subsidies from supranational organisations	...	...	...	...	...	...	...	...	...	497	...	...
B Other current transfers	...	...	...	...	...	...	...	...	...	1829	...	...
Receipts from the Rest of the World on Current Transactions	...	...	...	...	...	...	...	...	...	9260	...	...

1.8 Capital Transactions of The Nation, Summary

Thousand Million Dongs

	1980	1981	1982	1983	1984	1985	1986	1987	1988	1989	1990	1991
Finance of Gross Capital Formation												
Gross saving	...	...	...	...	...	...	...	...	...	1745	...	...
1 Consumption of fixed capital	...	...	...	...	...	...	...	...	...	1657	...	...
A General government	...	...	...	...	...	...	...	...	...	375	...	...
B Corporate and quasi-corporate enterprises	...	...	...	...	...	...	...	...	...	1282	...	...
Public	...	...	...	...	...	...	...	...	...	906	...	...

1.8 Capital Transactions of The Nation, Summary
(Continued)

Thousand Million Dongs

	1980	1981	1982	1983	1984	1985	1986	1987	1988	1989	1990	1991
Private	...	...	...	...	...	...	...	...	...	376	...	...
C Other	...	...	...	...	...	...	...	...	...	...	...	...
2 Net saving	...	...	...	...	...	...	...	...	...	88	...	...
A General government	...	...	...	...	...	...	...	...	...	-2088	...	...
B Corporate and quasi-corporate enterprises	...	...	...	...	...	...	...	...	...	2176	...	...
Public	...	...	...	...	...	...	...	...	...	1671	...	...
Private	...	...	...	...	...	...	...	...	...	505	...	...
C Other	...	...	...	...	...	...	...	...	...	...	...	...
Less: Surplus of the nation on current transactions	...	...	...	...	...	...	...	...	...	-1072	...	...
Finance of Gross Capital Formation	...	...	...	...	...	...	...	...	...	2817	...	...

Gross Capital Formation

	1980	1981	1982	1983	1984	1985	1986	1987	1988	1989	1990	1991
Increase in stocks	...	...	...	...	...	...	...	...	...	411	...	...
Gross fixed capital formation	...	...	...	...	...	...	...	...	...	2406	...	...
Gross Capital Formation	...	...	...	...	...	...	...	...	...	2817	...	...

1.10 Gross Domestic Product by Kind of Activity, in Current Prices

Thousand Million Dongs

	1980	1981	1982	1983	1984	1985	1986	1987	1988	1989	1990	1991
1 Agriculture, hunting, forestry and fishing	...	...	...	...	...	...	185	966	5927	9841	... 14717	28551
2 Mining and quarrying	...	...	...	...	...	...						
3 Manufacturing	...	...	...	...	...	...	141	655	2918	4783	... 7596	14202
4 Electricity, gas and water	...	...	...	...	...	...						
5 Construction	...	...	...	...	...	...	14	59	352	872	... 1468	2328
6 Wholesale and retail trade, restaurants and hotels	...	...	...	...	...	...	66	286	1276	2754	... 4614	8173
7 Transport, storage and communication	...	...	...	...	...	...	7	33	274	599	... 1233	2652
8 Finance, insurance, real estate and business services	...	...	...	...	...	...	38	191	982	1957	... 4456	7359
9 Community, social and personal services	...	...	...	...	...	...	56	261	1442	3260	... 3641	6034
Total, Industries	...	...	...	...	...	...	507	2451	13171	24066	... 37725	69299
Producers of Government Services	...	...	...	...	...	...	...	...	...	...	...	...
Other Producers	...	...	...	...	...	...	...	...	...	...	...	...
Subtotal	...	...	...	...	...	...	507	2451	13171	24066	... 37725	69299
Less: Imputed bank service charge	...	...	...	...	...	...	...	...	...	...	...	...
Plus: Import duties	...	...	...	...	...	...	6	17	95	241	... 442	660
Plus: Value added tax	...	...	...	...	...	...	...	...	...	...	...	...
Equals: Gross Domestic Product	...	...	...	...	...	...	512	2469	13266	24308	... 38166	69959

1.11 Gross Domestic Product by Kind of Activity, in Constant Prices

Thousand Million Dongs

	1980	1981	1982	1983	1984	1985	1986	1987	1988	1989	1990	1991
						At constant prices of:1989						
1 Agriculture, hunting, forestry and fishing	...	...	...	...	...	...	8900	8850	9202	9841	... 9987	...
2 Mining and quarrying	...	...	...	...	...	...						...
3 Manufacturing	...	...	...	...	...	...	4345	4806	4969	4783	... 4905	...
4 Electricity, gas and water	...	...	...	...	...	...						...
5 Construction	...	...	...	...	...	...	825	868	841	872	... 913	...

1.11 Gross Domestic Product by Kind of Activity, in Constant Prices
(Continued)

Thousand Million Dongs

	1980	1981	1982	1983	1984	1985	1986	1987	1988	1989	1990	1991
						At constant prices of:1989						
6 Wholesale and retail trade, restaurants and hotels	...	...	...	...	...	...	2587	2693	2830	2995	3153	...
7 Transport, storage and communication	...	...	...	...	...	...	548	596	598	599	628	...
8 Finance, insurance, real estate and business services	...	...	...	...	...	...	1378	1453	1538	1957	2194	...
9 Community, social and personal services	...	...	...	...	...	...	1997	2129	2518	3260	3756	...
Total, Industries	...	...	...	...	...	...	20579	21395	22497	24308	25536	...
Producers of Government Services	...	...	...	...	...	...	...	...	...	...	...	
Other Producers	...	...	...	...	...	...	...	...	...	...	...	...
Subtotal	...	...	...	...	...	...	20579	21395	22497	24308	25536	...
Less: Imputed bank service charge	...	...	...	...	...	...	...	...	...	...	...	...
Plus: Import duties	...	...	...	...	...	...	...	...	...	...	...	...
Plus: Value added tax	...	...	...	...	...	...	...	...	...	...	...	...
Equals: Gross Domestic Product	...	...	...	...	...	...	20579	21395	22497	24308	25536	...

1.12 Relations Among National Accounting Aggregates

Thousand Million Dongs

	1980	1981	1982	1983	1984	1985	1986	1987	1988	1989	1990	1991
Gross Domestic Product	...	...	...	...	...	...	...	...	...	24308	...	...
Plus: Net factor income from the rest of the world	...	...	...	...	...	...	...	...	...	-498	...	...
Factor income from the rest of the world	...	...	...	...	...	...	...	...	...	234	...	...
Less: Factor income to the rest of the world	...	...	...	...	...	...	...	...	...	732	...	...
Equals: Gross National Product	...	...	...	...	...	...	...	...	...	23810	...	...
Less: Consumption of fixed capital	...	...	...	...	...	...	...	...	...	1657	...	...
Equals: National Income	...	...	...	...	...	...	...	...	...	22153	...	...
Plus: Net current transfers from the rest of the world	...	...	...	...	...	...	...	...	...	2293	...	...
Current transfers from the rest of the world	...	...	...	...	...	...	...	...	...	2326	...	...
Less: Current transfers to the rest of the world	...	...	...	...	...	...	...	...	...	33	...	...
Equals: National Disposable Income	...	...	...	...	...	...	...	...	...	24446	...	...
Less: Final consumption	...	...	...	...	...	...	...	...	...	24358	...	...
Equals: Net Saving	...	...	...	...	...	...	...	...	...	88	...	...
Less: Surplus of the nation on current transactions	...	...	...	...	...	...	...	...	...	-1072	...	...
Equals: Net Capital Formation	...	...	...	...	...	...	...	...	...	1160	...	...

4.1 Derivation of Value Added by Kind of Activity, in Current Prices

Thousand Million Dongs

	1986			1987			1988			1989		
	Gross Output	Intermediate Consumption	Value Added	Gross Output	Intermediate Consumption	Value Added	Gross Output	Intermediate Consumption	Value Added	Gross Output	Intermediate Consumption	Value Added
						All Producers						
1 Agriculture, hunting, forestry and fishing	269	84	185	1400	434	966	8563	2635	5927	14668	4827	9841
2 Mining and quarrying												
3 Manufacturing	320	179	141	1481	825	655	6992	4075	2918	12613	7831	4783
4 Electricity, gas and water												

4.1 Derivation of Value Added by Kind of Activity, in Current Prices
(Continued)

Thousand Million Dongs

	1986			1987			1988			1989		
	Gross Output	Intermediate Consumption	Value Added	Gross Output	Intermediate Consumption	Value Added	Gross Output	Intermediate Consumption	Value Added	Gross Output	Intermediate Consumption	Value Added
5 Construction	36	23	14	147	88	59	904	550	352	2270	1398	872
6 Wholesale and retail trade, restaurants and hotels	91	25	66	391	106	286	1774	498	1276	3780	1026	2754
7 Transport, storage and communication	13	6	7	65	32	33	538	263	274	1215	616	599
8 Finance, insurance, real estate and business services	43	4	38	212	21	191	1129	147	982	2218	261	1957
9 Community, social and personal services	102	46	56	470	210	261	2411	970	1442	5390	2130	3260
Total, Industries	874	367	507	4166	1715	2451	22311	9139	13171	42155	18088	24066
Producers of Government Services	...	...	...	...	...	...	...	...	...	...	...	...
Other Producers	...	...	...	...	...	...	...	...	...	...	...	...
Total	874	367	507	4166	1715	2451	22311	9139	13171	42155	18088	24066
Less: Imputed bank service charge	...	...	...	...	...	...	...	...	...	...	...	...
Import duties	6	...	6	17	...	17	95	...	95	241	...	241
Value added tax	...	...	...	...	...	...	...	...	...	...	...	...
Total	880	367	512	4184	1715	2469	22405	9139	13266	42395	18088	24308

4.2 Derivation of Value Added by Kind of Activity, in Constant Prices

Thousand Million Dongs

	1986			1987			1988			1989		
	Gross Output	Intermediate Consumption	Value Added	Gross Output	Intermediate Consumption	Value Added	Gross Output	Intermediate Consumption	Value Added	Gross Output	Intermediate Consumption	Value Added
	At constant prices of:1989											
	All Producers											
1 Agriculture, hunting, forestry and fishing	12936	4036	8900	13189	4339	8850	13696	4494	9202	14668	4827	9841
2 Mining and quarrying												
3 Manufacturing	10850	6505	4345	11688	6882	4806	12702	7733	4969	12613	7830	4783
4 Electricity, gas and water												
5 Construction	2099	1274	825	2207	1339	868	2192	1351	841	2270	1398	872
6 Wholesale and retail trade, restaurants and hotels	3482	895	2587	3623	930	2693	3804	974	2830	4021	1026	2995
7 Transport, storage and communication	1155	607	548	1206	610	596	1212	614	598	1215	616	599
8 Finance, insurance, real estate and business services	1552	174	1378	1638	185	1453	1781	243	1538	2218	261	1957
9 Community, social and personal services	3401	1404	1997	3737	1608	2129	4302	1784	2518	5390	2130	3260
Total, Industries	35474	14895	20579	37289	15894	21395	39690	17193	22497	42395	18087	24308
Producers of Government Services	...	...	...	...	...	...	...	...	...	...	...	...
Other Producers	...	...	...	...	...	...	...	...	...	...	...	...
Total	35474	14895	20579	37289	15894	21395	39690	17193	22497	42395	18087	24308
Less: Imputed bank service charge	...	...	...	...	...	...	...	...	...	...	...	...
Import duties	...	...	...	...	...	...	...	...	...	...	...	...
Value added tax	...	...	...	...	...	...	...	...	...	...	...	...
Total	35474	14895	20579	37289	15894	21395	39690	17193	22497	42395	18087	24308

4.3 Cost Components of Value Added

Thousand Million Dongs

	1989					
	Compensation of Employees	Capital Consumption	Net Operating Surplus	Indirect Taxes	Less: Subsidies Received	Value Added
	All Producers					
1 Agriculture, hunting, forestry and fishing	7097	239	1674	831	...	9841
2 Mining and quarrying	2583	612	785	803	...	4783
3 Manufacturing	...	...	...	...	...	...
4 Electricity, gas and water	...	...	...	...	...	...

Viet Nam

4.3 Cost Components of Value Added
(Continued)

Thousand Million Dongs

	1989					
	Compensation of Employees	Capital Consumption	Net Operating Surplus	Indirect Taxes	Less: Subsidies Received	Value Added
5 Construction	718	46	92	16	...	872
6 Wholesale and retail trade, restaurants and hotels a	1111	150	1169	565	...	2995
7 Transport, storage and communication	289	126	82	102	...	599
8 Finance, insurance, real estate and business services	309	78	1302	268	...	1957
9 Community, social and personal services	2328	407	350	176	...	3260
Total, Industries	14436	1657	5455	2760	...	24308
Producers of Government Services	...	...	...	...	...	...
Other Producers	...	...	...	...	...	...
Total	14436	1657	5455	2760	...	24308
Less: Imputed bank service charge	...	...	...	...	...	...
Import duties	...	...	...	...	...	...
Value added tax	...	...	...	...	...	...
Total	14436	1657	5455	2760	...	24308

a) Item 'Import duties' is included in item 'Wholesale and retail trade'.

Yemen

On 22 May 1990 , Yemen and Democratic Yemen merged to form a single State. Since that date they have been represented as one country with the name "Yemen".

National Accounts estimates for Yemen are available for the years 1989 and 1990. These estimates are followed by the estimates for the former Yemen and the former Democratic Yemen..

Yemen

Source. Reply to the United Nations National Accounts Questionnaire from the Central Statistical Organization, Sana'a.
General note. The estimates shown in the following tables have been prepared in accordance with the United Nations System of National Accounts so far as the existing data would permit.

1.1 Expenditure on the Gross Domestic Product, in Current Prices

Million Yemeni rials

	1980	1981	1982	1983	1984	1985	1986	1987	1988	1989	1990	1991
1 Government final consumption expenditure	...	...	...	...	...	...	...	...	...	16470	21154	...
2 Private final consumption expenditure	...	...	...	...	...	...	...	...	...	48322	58030	...
3 Gross capital formation	...	...	...	...	...	...	...	...	...	11490	12670	...
A Increase in stocks	...	...	...	...	...	...	...	...	...	134	700	...
B Gross fixed capital formation	...	...	...	...	...	...	...	...	...	11356	11970	...
4 Exports of goods and services	...	...	...	...	...	...	...	...	...	10205	10471	...
5 Less: Imports of goods and services	...	...	...	...	...	...	...	...	...	25081	25166	...
Equals: Gross Domestic Product	...	...	...	...	...	...	...	...	...	61406	77159	...

1.3 Cost Components of the Gross Domestic Product

Million Yemeni rials

	1980	1981	1982	1983	1984	1985	1986	1987	1988	1989	1990	1991
1 Indirect taxes, net	...	...	...	...	...	...	...	...	...	6809	6947	...
2 Consumption of fixed capital	...	...	...	...	...	...	...	...	...	2499	4202	...
3 Compensation of employees paid by resident producers to:	...	...	...	...	...	...	...	...	...	52098	66010	...
4 Operating surplus	...	...	...	...	...	...	...	...	...			...
Equals: Gross Domestic Product	...	...	...	...	...	...	...	...	...	61406	77159	...

1.7 External Transactions on Current Account, Summary

Million Yemeni rials

	1980	1981	1982	1983	1984	1985	1986	1987	1988	1989	1990	1991
Payments to the Rest of the World												
1 Imports of goods and services	...	...	...	...	...	...	...	...	...	25081	25166	...
2 Factor income to the rest of the world	...	...	...	...	...	...	...	...	...	...	...	...
3 Current transfers to the rest of the world	...	...	...	...	...	...	...	...	...	...	...	...
4 Surplus of the nation on current transactions	...	...	...	...	...	...	...	...	...	-9717	-2162	...
Payments to the Rest of the World and Surplus of the Nation on Current Transactions	...	...	...	...	...	...	...	...	...	15364	23004	...
Receipts From The Rest of the World												
1 Exports of goods and services	...	...	...	...	...	...	...	...	...	10205	10471	...
2 Factor income from rest of the world	...	...	...	...	...	...	...	...	...	1454	1658	...
3 Current transfers from rest of the world	...	...	...	...	...	...	...	...	...	3706	10875	...
Statistical discrepancy	...	...	...	...	...	...	...	...	...	-1	-	...
Receipts from the Rest of the World on Current Transactions	...	...	...	...	...	...	...	...	...	15364	23004	...

1.10 Gross Domestic Product by Kind of Activity, in Current Prices

Million Yemeni rials

	1980	1981	1982	1983	1984	1985	1986	1987	1988	1989	1990	1991
1 Agriculture, hunting, forestry and fishing	...	...	...	...	...	...	...	...	...	14682	16101	...
2 Mining and quarrying	...	...	...	...	...	...	...	...	...	3912	7030	...
3 Manufacturing	...	...	...	...	...	...	...	...	...	5861	6586	...
4 Electricity, gas and water	...	...	...	...	...	...	...	...	...	1191	1400	...
5 Construction	...	...	...	...	...	...	...	...	...	2838	3394	...
6 Wholesale and retail trade, restaurants and hotels	...	...	...	...	...	...	...	...	...	7784	9590	...
7 Transport, storage and communication	...	...	...	...	...	...	...	...	...	5202	6015	...
8 Finance, insurance, real estate and business services	...	...	...	...	...	...	...	...	...	4154	4929	...
9 Community, social and personal services	...	...	...	...	...	...	...	...	...	483	572	...

Yemen

1.10 Gross Domestic Product by Kind of Activity, in Current Prices
(Continued)

Million Yemeni rials

	1980	1981	1982	1983	1984	1985	1986	1987	1988	1989	1990	1991
Total, Industries	...	...	...	...	...	...	...	...	...	46107	55617	...
Producers of Government Services	...	...	...	...	...	...	...	...	...	10875	18201	...
Other Producers	...	...	...	...	...	...	...	...	...	79	95	...
Subtotal	...	...	...	...	...	...	...	...	...	57061	73913	...
Less: Imputed bank service charge	...	...	...	...	...	...	...	...	...	655	750	...
Plus: Import duties	...	...	...	...	...	...	...	...	...	5000	3996	...
Plus: Value added tax	...	...	...	...	...	...	...	...	...	...	...	...
Equals: Gross Domestic Product	...	...	...	...	...	...	...	...	...	61406	77159	...

1.12 Relations Among National Accounting Aggregates

Million Yemeni rials

	1980	1981	1982	1983	1984	1985	1986	1987	1988	1989	1990	1991
Gross Domestic Product	...	...	...	...	...	...	...	...	...	61406	77159	...
Plus: Net factor income from the rest of the world	...	...	...	...	...	...	...	...	...	1454	1658	...
Equals: Gross National Product	...	...	...	...	...	...	...	...	...	62860	78817	...
Less: Consumption of fixed capital	...	...	...	...	...	...	...	...	...	2499	4202	...
Equals: National Income	...	...	...	...	...	...	...	...	...	60361	74615	...
Plus: Net current transfers from the rest of the world	...	...	...	...	...	...	...	...	...	3706	10875	...
Equals: National Disposable Income	...	...	...	...	...	...	...	...	...	64067	85490	...
Less: Final consumption	...	...	...	...	...	...	...	...	...	64792	79184	...
Equals: Net Saving	...	...	...	...	...	...	...	...	...	-725	6306	...
Less: Surplus of the nation on current transactions	...	...	...	...	...	...	...	...	...	-9717	-2162	...
Equals: Net Capital Formation	...	...	...	...	...	...	...	...	...	8992	8468	...

Yemen (Former)

Source. Reply to the United Nations National Accounts Questionnaire from the Central Planning Organization, Sanaa. The official estimates and descriptions are published in the 'National Accounts of Yemen Arab Republic', issued by the same Organization.

General note. The official estimates of Yemen have been prepared in accordance with the United Nations System of National Accounts so far as the existing data would permit.

1.1 Expenditure on the Gross Domestic Product, in Current Prices

Million Yemeni rials

Fiscal year beginning 1 July

	1980	1981	1982	1983	1984	1985	1986	1987	1988	1989	1990	1991
1 Government final consumption expenditure	3007	3891	6416	7449	7135	... 5543	6898	...	...	...	...	...
2 Private final consumption expenditure	12910	12467	13530	14189	14837	... 29404	33999	...	...	...	...	...
3 Gross capital formation	5005	5530	5362	3981	3755	... 4472	4988	...	...	...	...	...
A Increase in stocks	107	219	240	-148	-90	... -75	50	...	...	...	...	...
B Gross fixed capital formation	4898	5311	5122	4129	3845	... 4547	4938	...	...	...	...	...
4 Exports of goods and services	805	1130	958	1126	1178	... 1164	1155	...	...	...	...	...
5 Less: Imports of goods and services	9046	9636	10397	9575	8955	... 9644	9568	...	...	...	...	...
Equals: Gross Domestic Product a	12681	13382	15869	17170	17950	... 30939	37472	...	...	...	...	...

a) Beginning 1981, estimates relate to calendar year.

1.2 Expenditure on the Gross Domestic Product, in Constant Prices

Million Yemeni rials

Fiscal year beginning 1 July

	1980	1981	1982	1983	1984	1985	1986	1987	1988	1989	1990	1991
					At constant prices of:1981							
1 Government final consumption expenditure	3103	3891	5263	5762	5493	... 3791	4290	...	...	...	...	...
2 Private final consumption expenditure	12120	12467	13308	13541	13696	... 17206	16984	...	...	...	...	...
3 Gross capital formation	6433	5530	5155	3673	3370	... 3344	3108	...	...	...	...	...
A Increase in stocks	110	219	235	-140	-81	... -42	23	...	...	...	...	...
B Gross fixed capital formation	6323	5311	4920	3813	3451	... 3386	3085	...	...	...	...	...
4 Exports of goods and services	824	1130	939	1023	1038	... 711	560	...	...	...	...	...
5 Less: Imports of goods and services	9529	9636	9949	8769	8001	... 5913	4688	...	...	...	...	...
Equals: Gross Domestic Product a	12951	13382	14716	15230	15596	... 19139	20254	...	...	...	...	...

a) Beginning 1981, estimates relate to calendar year.

1.3 Cost Components of the Gross Domestic Product

Million Yemeni rials

Fiscal year beginning 1 July

	1980	1981	1982	1983	1984	1985	1986	1987	1988	1989	1990	1991
1 Indirect taxes, net	1868	1792	1943	2327	2397	... 2974	2863	...	...	...	...	...
2 Consumption of fixed capital	309	313	360	393	421	... 839	1038	...	...	...	...	...
3 Compensation of employees paid by resident producers to:	10504	11277	13566	14450	15132	... 27126	33571	...	...	...	...	...
4 Operating surplus	...	...	...	...	...	... ...	...	...	...	...	...	...
Equals: Gross Domestic Product a	12681	13382	15869	17170	17950	... 30939	37472	...	...	...	...	...

a) Beginning 1981, estimates relate to calendar year.

Yemen (Former)

1.7 External Transactions on Current Account, Summary

Million Yemeni rials

Fiscal year beginning 1 July

	1980	1981	1982	1983	1984	1985	1986	1987	1988	1989	1990	1991
Payments to the Rest of the World												
1 Imports of goods and services	9046	9636	10397	9575	8955	... 9644	9568	...	...	...	...	...
2 Factor income to the rest of the world	...	...	...	...	...	... ...		...	...	...	...	...
3 Current transfers to the rest of the world	...	...	...	...	...	... ...		...	...	...	...	...
4 Surplus of the nation on current transactions	-2980	-2990	-2665	-2451	-1663	... -2210	-1158	...	...			
Payments to the Rest of the World and Surplus of the Nation on Current Transactions [a]	6066	6646	7732	7124	7292	... 7434	8410	...	...	...	...	...
Receipts From The Rest of the World												
1 Exports of goods and services	805	1130	958	1126	1178	... 1164	1155	...	...	...	...	...
2 Factor income from rest of the world [b]	1899	1938	6774	5998	6114	... 6270	7255	...	...	...	...	...
A Compensation of employees	1356	1484	...	...	...	... ...		...	...	...	...	...
B Property and entrepreneurial income	543	454	...	...	...	... ...	...	...	...	...	...	...
3 Current transfers from rest of the world [b]	3362	3579	...	...	...	... ...	...	...	...	...	...	...
Receipts from the Rest of the World on Current Transactions [a]	6066	6646	7732	7124	7292	... 7434	8410	...	...	...	...	...

a) Beginning 1981, estimates relate to calendar year.
b) Net factor income and net current transfers are shown in items 2 and 3, respectively, of the receipt from the rest of the world.

1.10 Gross Domestic Product by Kind of Activity, in Current Prices

Million Yemeni rials

Fiscal year beginning 1 July

	1980	1981	1982	1983	1984	1985	1986	1987	1988	1989	1990	1991
1 Agriculture, hunting, forestry and fishing	3579	3685	3799	3596	3712	... 8033	10680	...	...	...	...	...
2 Mining and quarrying [a]	149	156	168	190	210	... 241	506	...	...	...	...	...
3 Manufacturing	730	820	1043	1254	1453	... 3365	4620	...	...	...	...	...
4 Electricity, gas and water	80	117	138	173	226	... 257	320	...	...	...	...	...
5 Construction	1110	1098	1215	1255	1365	... 1541	1285	...	...	...	...	...
6 Wholesale and retail trade, restaurants and hotels	2131	2185	2369	2476	2614	... 4169	4896	...	...	...	...	...
7 Transport, storage and communication	461	497	610	665	710	... 3489	4106	...	...	...	...	...
8 Finance, insurance, real estate and business services	946	1117	1274	1503	1635	... 3598	4166	...	...	...	...	...
9 Community, social and personal services	130	131	155	162	182	... 242	286	...	...	...	...	...
Total, Industries	9316	9806	10771	11274	12107	... 24935	30865	...	...	...	...	...
Producers of Government Services	1906	2129	3477	3912	3857	... 3643	4410	...	...	...	...	...
Other Producers	24	24	27	31	34	... 38	50	...	...	...	...	...
Subtotal	11246	11959	14275	15217	15998	... 28616	35325	...	...	...	...	...
Less: Imputed bank service charge	274	211	246	260	288	... 651	716	...	...	...	...	...
Plus: Import duties	1709	1634	1840	2213	2240	... 2974	2863	...	...	...	...	...
Plus: Value added tax	...	...	...	...	...	... ...	...	...	...	...	...	...
Equals: Gross Domestic Product [b]	12681	13382	15869	17170	17950	... 30939	37472	...	...	...	...	...

a) For 1986, item 'Mining and Quarrying' includes crude petroleum production.
b) Beginning 1981, estimates relate to calendar year.

1.11 Gross Domestic Product by Kind of Activity, in Constant Prices

Million Yemeni rials   Fiscal year beginning 1 July

	1980	1981	1982	1983	1984	1985	1986	1987	1988	1989	1990	1991
					At constant prices of:1981							
1 Agriculture, hunting, forestry and fishing	3578	3685	3854	3418	3414	... 3704	4126	...	...	...	...	...
2 Mining and quarrying a	154	156	163	178	187	... 172	397	...	...	...	...	...
3 Manufacturing	741	820	987	1216	1345	... 2404	2662	...	...	...	...	...
4 Electricity, gas and water	91	117	138	173	216	... 239	286	...	...	...	...	...
5 Construction	1196	1098	1167	1159	1225	... 1101	857	...	...	...	...	...
6 Wholesale and retail trade, restaurants and hotels	2131	2185	2303	2259	2317	... 2553	2728	...	...	...	...	...
7 Transport, storage and communication	465	497	596	593	620	... 2406	2549	...	...	...	...	...
8 Finance, insurance, real estate and business services	969	1117	1274	1477	1556	... 2436	2597	...	...	...	...	...
9 Community, social and personal services	127	131	154	154	160	... 138	159	...	...	...	...	...
Total, Industries	9452	9806	10636	10627	11040	... 15153	16361	...	...	...	...	...
Producers of Government Services	1963	2129	2472	2763	2724	... 2291	2314	...	...	...	...	...
Other Producers	24	24	27	31	32	36	40	...	...	...	...	...
Subtotal	11439	11959	13135	13421	13796	... 17480	18715	...	...	...	...	...
Less: Imputed bank service charge	295	211	251	248	260	465	482	...	...	...	...	...
Plus: Import duties	1807	1634	1832	2057	2060	... 2124	2021	...	...	...	...	...
Plus: Value added tax	...	...	...	...	...	...	...	...	...	...	...	...
Equals: Gross Domestic Product b	12951	13382	14716	15230	15596	... 19139	20254	...	...	...	...	...

a) For 1986, item 'Mining and Quarrying' includes crude petroleum production.
b) Beginning 1981, estimates relate to calendar year.

1.12 Relations Among National Accounting Aggregates

Million Yemeni rials   Fiscal year beginning 1 July

	1980	1981	1982	1983	1984	1985	1986	1987	1988	1989	1990	1991
Gross Domestic Product	12681	13382	15869	17170	17950	... 30939	37472	...	...	...	...	...
Plus: Net factor income from the rest of the world a	1899	1938	6774	5998	6114	... 6270	7255	...	...	...	...	...
Equals: Gross National Product	14580	15320	...	...	...	...	...	...	...	...	...	...
Less: Consumption of fixed capital	309	313	360	393	421	... 839	1038	...	...	...	...	...
Equals: National Income	14271	15007	...	...	...	...	...	...	...	...	...	...
Plus: Net current transfers from the rest of the world a	3362	3579	...	...	...	...	...	...	...	...	...	...
Equals: National Disposable Income	17633	18586	22283	22775	23643	... 36370	43689	...	...	...	...	...
Less: Final consumption	15917	16358	19946	21638	21972	... 34947	40897	...	...	...	...	...
Equals: Net Saving	1716	2227	2337	1137	1671	... 1423	2792	...	...	...	...	...
Less: Surplus of the nation on current transactions	-2980	-2990	-2665	-2451	-1663	... -2210	-1158	...	...	...	...	...
Equals: Net Capital Formation b	4696	5217	5002	3588	3334	... 3633	3950	...	...	...	...	...

a) Beginning 1982, item 'Net factor income from abroad' includes item 'Net current transfers from the rest of the world'.
b) Beginning 1981, estimates relate to calendar year.

Yemen (Former)

2.11 Gross Fixed Capital Formation by Kind of Activity of Owner, ISIC Divisions, in Current Prices

Million Yemeni rials　　　　　　　　　　　　　　　　　　　　　　　　　　　　　Fiscal year beginning 1 July

	1980	1981	1982	1983	1984	1985	1986	1987	1988	1989	1990	1991
					All Producers							
1 Agriculture, hunting, forestry and fishing	383	269	341	402	416	... 619	526	...	...	...	...	...
2 Mining and quarrying	44	60	66	67	70	... 35	52	...	...	...	...	...
3 Manufacturing	372	364	237	187	168	... 578	451	...	...	...	...	...
4 Electricity, gas and water	609	768	661	552	505	... 839	801	...	...	...	...	...
5 Construction	303	80	52	54	56	... 104	116	...	...	...	...	...
6 Wholesale and retail trade, restaurants and hotels	...	430	229	227	219	... 269	257	...	...	...	...	...
7 Transport, storage and communication	1506	941	1053	531	445	... 322	571	...	...	...	...	...
8 Finance, insurance, real estate and business services	965	817	700	840	792	... 864	1001	...	...	...	...	...
A Financial institutions	...	27	22	68	59	... 44	78	...	...	...	...	...
B Insurance	...	...	...	...	...	...	...	...	...	...	...	...
C Real estate and business services	965	790	678	772	733	... 820	923	...	...	...	...	...
9 Community, social and personal services	716	1583	1783	1271	1174	... 917	1163	...	...	...	...	...
Total Industries [a]	4898	5311	5122	4129	3845	... 4547	4938	...	...	...	...	...
Producers of Government Services	...	...	...	...	...	...	...	...	...	...	...	...
Private Non-Profit Institutions Serving Households	...	...	...	...	...	...	...	...	...	...	...	...
Total	...	...	...	...	...	...	...	...	...	...	...	...

a) Beginning 1981, estimates relate to calendar year.

2.12 Gross Fixed Capital Formation by Kind of Activity of Owner, ISIC Divisions, in Constant Prices

Million Yemeni rials　　　　　　　　　　　　　　　　　　　　　　　　　　　　　Fiscal year beginning 1 July

	1980	1981	1982	1983	1984	1985	1986	1987	1988	1989	1990	1991
					At constant prices of:1981							
					All Producers							
1 Agriculture, hunting, forestry and fishing	526	269	328	373	371	... 461	329	...	...	...	...	...
2 Mining and quarrying	66	59	64	60	65	... 26	32	...	...	...	...	...
3 Manufacturing	573	364	227	172	147	... 430	282	...	...	...	...	...
4 Electricity, gas and water	897	768	635	509	464	... 625	500	...	...	...	...	...
5 Construction	476	80	50	50	49	... 77	72	...	...	...	...	...
6 Wholesale and retail trade, restaurants and hotels	...	430	220	209	191	... 200	161	...	...	...	...	...
7 Transport, storage and communication	1905	941	1012	490	394	... 240	357	...	...	...	...	...
8 Finance, insurance, real estate and business services	930	817	672	775	690	... 644	626	...	...	...	...	...
A Financial institutions	...	27	21	62	54	... 32	49	...	...	...	...	...

2.12 Gross Fixed Capital Formation by Kind of Activity of Owner, ISIC Divisions, in Constant Prices
(Continued)

Million Yemeni rials — Fiscal year beginning 1 July

	1980	1981	1982	1983	1984	1985	1986	1987	1988	1989	1990	1991
					At constant prices of:1981							
B Insurance	...	...	...	...	...	...						
							...	...	...	...	...	...
C Real estate and business services	930	790	651	713	636	...						
						612	577	...	...	...	...	...
9 Community, social and personal services	950	1583	1712	1175	1080	...						
						683	726	...	...	...	...	...
Total Industries a	6323	5311	4920	3813	3451	...						
						3386	3085	...	...	...	...	...
Producers of Government Services	...	...	...	...	...	...						
						...	...	...	...	...	...	...
Private Non-Profit Institutions Serving Households	...	...	...	...	...	...						
						...	...	...	...	...	...	...
Total	...	...	...	...	...	...						
						...	...	...	...	...	...	...

a) Beginning 1981, estimates relate to calendar year.

4.1 Derivation of Value Added by Kind of Activity, in Current Prices

Million Yemeni rials — Fiscal year beginning 1 July

	1985			1986		
	Gross Output	Intermediate Consumption	Value Added	Gross Output	Intermediate Consumption	Value Added
			All Producers			
1 Agriculture, hunting, forestry and fishing	11476	3443	8033	16430	5750	10680
2 Mining and quarrying	330	89	241	662	156	506
A Coal mining	...	...	...	...	...	...
B Crude petroleum and natural gas production	...	...	...	325	65	260
C Metal ore mining	...	...	...	...	...	...
D Other mining	...	...	...	337	91	246
3 Manufacturing	7692	4327	3365	10675	6055	4620
4 Electricity, gas and water	492	235	257	685	365	320
5 Construction	3436	1895	1541	3022	1737	1285
6 Wholesale and retail trade, restaurants and hotels	5072	903	4169	5968	1072	4896
7 Transport, storage and communication	4743	1254	3489	5583	1477	4106
8 Finance, insurance, real estate and business services	3957	359	3598	4570	404	4166
9 Community, social and personal services	303	61	242	359	73	286
Total, Industries a	37501	12566	24935	47954	17089	30865
Producers of Government Services	5609	1966	3643	7010	2600	4410
Other Producers	45	7	38	65	15	50
Total	43155	14539	28616	55029	19704	35325
Less: Imputed bank service charge	...	-651	651	...	-716	716
Import duties	2974	...	2974	2863	...	2863
Value added tax	...	...	...	...	...	...
Total a	46129	15190	30939	57892	20420	37472

a) Beginning 1981, estimates relate to calendar year.

4.2 Derivation of Value Added by Kind of Activity, in Constant Prices

Million Yemeni rials — Fiscal year beginning 1 July

	1985			1986		
	Gross Output	Intermediate Consumption	Value Added	Gross Output	Intermediate Consumption	Value Added
			At constant prices of:1981			
			All Producers			
1 Agriculture, hunting, forestry and fishing	5292	1588	3704	6347	2221	4126
2 Mining and quarrying	235	63	172	512	115	397
A Coal mining	...	...	...	...	...	...
B Crude petroleum and natural gas production	...	...	...	325	65	260
C Metal ore mining	...	...	...	...	...	...
D Other mining	...	...	...	187	50	137
3 Manufacturing	5495	3091	2404	6201	3539	2662
4 Electricity, gas and water	457	218	239	612	326	286

Yemen (Former)

Million Yemeni rials Fiscal year beginning 1 July

	1985			1986		
	Gross Output	Intermediate Consumption	Value Added	Gross Output	Intermediate Consumption	Value Added
				At constant prices of:1981		
5 Construction	2455	1354	1101	2015	1158	857
6 Wholesale and retail trade, restaurants and hotels	3115	562	2553	3326	598	2728
7 Transport, storage and communication	3271	865	2406	3466	917	2549
8 Finance, insurance, real estate and business services	2686	250	2436	2858	261	2597
9 Community, social and personal services	173	35	138	200	41	159
Total, Industries a	23179	8026	15153	25537	9176	16361
Producers of Government Services	3837	1546	2291	4359	2045	2314
Other Producers	43	7	36	52	12	40
Total	27059	9579	17480	29948	11233	18715
Less: Imputed bank service charge	...	-465	465	...	-482	482
Import duties	2124	...	2124	2021	...	2021
Value added tax	...	...	...	...	...	...
Total a	29183	10044	19139	31969	11715	20254

a) Beginning 1981, estimates relate to calendar year.

4.3 Cost Components of Value Added

Million Yemeni rials Fiscal year beginning 1 July

	1980						1981					
	Compensation of Employees	Capital Consumption	Net Operating Surplus	Indirect Taxes	Less: Subsidies Received	Value Added	Compensation of Employees	Capital Consumption	Net Operating Surplus	Indirect Taxes	Less: Subsidies Received	Value Added
	All Producers											
1 Agriculture, hunting, forestry and fishing	421	...	3016	...	...	3579	428	...	3069	...	...	3648
2 Mining and quarrying	36	...	106	...	...	149	38	...	112	...	...	156
3 Manufacturing	133	...	398	...	...	730	275	...	411	...	...	854
4 Electricity, gas and water	19	...	58	...	...	80	26	...	81	...	...	111
5 Construction	617	...	420	...	...	1088	603	...	410	...	...	1080
6 Wholesale and retail trade, restaurants and hotels	224	...	1930	...	...	2260	231	...	1878	...	...	2188
7 Transport, storage and communication	78	...	234	...	...	461	84	...	229	...	...	470
8 Finance, insurance, real estate and business services	133	...	1346	...	...	1536	134	...	1370	...	...	1565
9 Community, social and personal services	8	...	111	...	...	130	9	...	103	...	...	131
Total, Industries ab	1670	...	7619	...	...	10013	1828	...	7662	...	...	10203
Producers of Government Services	1741	...	...	...	...	1748	1958	...	...	...	...	1965
Other Producers	24	...	...	...	...	24	24	...	...	...	...	24
Total	3435	...	7619	...	...	11785	3810	...	7662	...	...	12192
Less: Imputed bank service charge	...	...	864	...	...	864	...	...	705	...	...	705
Import duties	...	...	...	...	...	1709	...	...	...	...	...	1633
Value added tax	...	...	...	...	...	...	...	...	...	...	...	...
Total ab	3435	...	6755	...	...	12630	3810	...	6957	...	...	13120

	1982					
	Compensation of Employees	Capital Consumption	Net Operating Surplus	Indirect Taxes	Less: Subsidies Received	Value Added
	All Producers					
1 Agriculture, hunting, forestry and fishing	447	...	3209	...	...	3813
2 Mining and quarrying	41	...	120	...	...	167
3 Manufacturing	320	...	478	...	...	991
4 Electricity, gas and water	36	...	114	...	...	155
5 Construction	649	...	441	...	...	1161
6 Wholesale and retail trade, restaurants and hotels	258	...	2094	...	...	2445
7 Transport, storage and communication	96	...	261	...	...	525
8 Finance, insurance, real estate and business services	128	...	1379	...	...	1569
9 Community, social and personal services	10	...	116	...	...	146

4.3 Cost Components of Value Added
(Continued)

	1982					
	Compensation of Employees	Capital Consumption	Net Operating Surplus	Indirect Taxes	Less: Subsidies Received	Value Added
Total, Industries ab	1985	...	8212	...	...	10972
Producers of Government Services	2454	...	...	...	...	2463
Other Producers	26	...	...	...	...	26
Total	4465	...	8212	...	...	13461
Less: Imputed bank service charge	...	...	670	...	...	670
Import duties	...	...	...	...	...	1846
Value added tax	...	...	...	...	...	...
Total ab	4465	...	7542	...	...	14637

a) Beginning 1981, estimates relate to calendar year.
b) Data for this table have not been revised, therefore, data for some years are not comparable with those of other tables.

Yemen Democratic Yemen (Former)

Source. Reply to the United Nations National Accounts Questionnaire from the Central Statistical Organization. The official estimates are published by the same office in 'Statistical Yearbook' of the People's Republic of Yemen.

General note. The estimates shown in the following tables have been prepared in accordance with the United Nations System of National Accounts so far as the existing data would permit.

1.1 Expenditure on the Gross Domestic Product, in Current Prices

Million Yemeni rials

	1980	1981	1982	1983	1984	1985	1986	1987	1988	1989	1990	1991
1 Government final consumption expenditure	79.7	147.5	160.3	174.2	188.5	195.6	180.0	...	...	...	...	...
2 Private final consumption expenditure	244.7	261.0	293.1	305.4	332.4	349.0	327.0	...	...	...	...	...
3 Gross capital formation	112.7	104.4	132.6	152.0	162.1	159.1	108.5	...	...	...	...	...
A Increase in stocks	26.5	...	...	...	...	...	...	...	...	...	...	...
B Gross fixed capital formation	86.2	...	...	...	...	...	...	...	...	...	...	...
4 Exports of goods and services	33.4	33.8	36.9	40.3	45.2	40.1	22.6	...	...	...	...	...
5 Less: Imports of goods and services	239.9	284.6	302.6	321.0	354.3	374.4	327.5	...	...	...	...	...
Equals: Gross Domestic Product	230.6	262.1	320.3	350.9	373.9	369.4	310.6	...	...	...	...	...

1.3 Cost Components of the Gross Domestic Product

Million Yemeni rials

	1980	1981	1982	1983	1984	1985	1986	1987	1988	1989	1990	1991
1 Indirect taxes, net	36.8	50.0	58.1	63.3	63.1	56.4	28.6	...	...	...	...	...
2 Consumption of fixed capital	17.4	18.0	19.6	20.0	21.0	21.8	22.8	...	...	...	...	...
3 Compensation of employees paid by resident producers to:	133.1	149.0	177.0	208.0	218.7	228.9	235.0	...	...	...	...	...
4 Operating surplus	43.3	45.1	65.6	59.6	71.1	62.3	24.2	...	...	...	...	...
Equals: Gross Domestic Product	230.6	262.1	320.3	350.9	373.9	369.4	310.6	...	...	...	...	...

1.7 External Transactions on Current Account, Summary

Million Yemeni rials

	1980	1981	1982	1983	1984	1985	1986	1987	1988	1989	1990	1991
Payments to the Rest of the World												
1 Imports of goods and services	239.9	284.6	302.6	321.0	354.3	374.4	...	...	...	...	...	...
2 Factor income to the rest of the world	1.7	2.4	...	...	...	...	...	...	...	...	...	...
A Compensation of employees	...	...	...	...	...	...	...	...	...	...	...	...
B Property and entrepreneurial income	1.7	2.4	...	...	...	...	...	...	...	...	...	...
3 Current transfers to the rest of the world	1.7	1.7	4.5	4.0	5.0	4.5	...	...	...	...	...	...
4 Surplus of the nation on current transactions	-57.3	-62.5	-60.9	-106.7	-131.2	-176.7	...	...	...	...	...	...
Payments to the Rest of the World and Surplus of the Nation on Current Transactions	186.0	226.2	246.2	218.3	228.1	202.2	...	...	...	...	...	...
Receipts From The Rest of the World												
1 Exports of goods and services	33.4	33.8	36.9	40.3	45.2	40.1	...	...	...	...	...	...
2 Factor income from rest of the world	12.0	17.7	17.1	11.3	6.0	7.0	...	...	...	...	...	...
3 Current transfers from rest of the world	140.6	174.7	192.2	166.7	176.9	155.1	...	...	...	...	...	...
Receipts from the Rest of the World on Current Transactions	186.0	226.2	246.2	218.3	228.1	202.2	...	...	...	...	...	...

1.10 Gross Domestic Product by Kind of Activity, in Current Prices

Million Yemeni rials

	1980	1981	1982	1983	1984	1985	1986	1987	1988	1989	1990	1991
1 Agriculture, hunting, forestry and fishing	25.2	31.5	29.5	33.9	36.3	39.5	40.5	46.7	52.5	...	...	...
2 Mining and quarrying										...	...	...
3 Manufacturing	16.7	17.9	18.6	21.2	22.0	29.0	27.6	28.5	29.8	...	...	...
4 Electricity, gas and water										...	...	...
5 Construction	25.1	33.3	41.1	43.3	48.0	40.5	28.4	31.9	39.0	...	...	...
6 Wholesale and retail trade, restaurants and hotels	32.4	37.7	42.4	44.5	48.8	45.8	36.1	50.6	46.8	...	...	...
7 Transport, storage and communication	21.0	26.6	27.1	29.8	32.5	31.8	27.4	32.2	35.0	...	...	...
8 Finance, insurance, real estate and business services	9.2	10.0	11.0	12.5	23.6	18.2	15.1	14.5	10.3	...	...	...
9 Community, social and personal services	1.8	2.0	2.2	2.5	2.7	2.7	2.8	2.8	2.8	...	...	...

1.10 Gross Domestic Product by Kind of Activity, in Current Prices
(Continued)

Million Yemeni rials

	1980	1981	1982	1983	1984	1985	1986	1987	1988	1989	1990	1991
Total, Industries a	131.4	159.0	171.9	187.7	213.9	207.5	177.9	207.2	216.2	...	...	...
Producers of Government Services	52.3	64.0	70.7	80.9	86.1	91.0	90.9	98.6	106.7	...	...	...
Other Producers	...	...	...	...	...	...	...	...	...	...	...	...
Subtotal a	183.7	223.0	242.6	268.6	300.0	298.5	268.8	305.8	322.9	...	...	...
Less: Imputed bank service charge	.	...	...	...	...	...	...	...	...	...	...	...
Plus: Import duties b	44.4	52.9	58.1	63.3	66.9	61.7	51.3	53.6	55.4	...	...	...
Plus: Value added tax	...	...	...	...	...	...	...	...	...	...	...	...
Plus: Other adjustments c	18.6	19.0	19.6	20.0	20.9	21.8	22.8	31.7	32.4	...	...	...
Equals: Gross Domestic Product d	246.7	294.9	320.3	351.9	387.8	382.0	342.9	391.1	410.7	...	...	...

a) The estimates of GDP by industries are at net domestic product in factor values.
b) Item 'Import duties' refers to indirect taxes net of subsidies.
c) Item 'Other adjustments' refers to consumption of fixed capital.

d) Data in this table have been revised, therefore they are not strictly comparable with the unrevised data in the other tables.

1.12 Relations Among National Accounting Aggregates

Million Yemeni rials

	1980	1981	1982	1983	1984	1985	1986	1987	1988	1989	1990	1991
Gross Domestic Product	230.6	262.1	320.3	350.9	373.9	369.4	...	...	...	...	...	...
Plus: Net factor income from the rest of the world	10.3	15.3	17.1	11.3	6.0	7.0	...	...	...	...	...	...
Equals: Gross National Product	240.9	277.4	337.4	362.2	379.9	376.4	...	...	...	...	...	...
Less: Consumption of fixed capital	17.4	18.0	19.6	20.0	21.0	21.8	...	...	...	...	...	...
Equals: National Income	223.5	259.4	317.8	342.2	358.9	354.6	...	...	...	...	...	...
Plus: Net current transfers from the rest of the world	138.9	173.0	187.7	162.7	171.9	150.6	...	...	...	...	...	...
Equals: National Disposable Income	362.4	432.4	505.5	504.9	530.8	505.2	...	...	...	...	...	...
Less: Final consumption	324.4	408.5	453.4	479.6	520.9	544.6	...	...	...	...	...	...
Equals: Net Saving	38.0	23.9	52.1	25.3	9.9	-39.4	...	...	...	...	...	...
Less: Surplus of the nation on current transactions	-57.3	-62.5	-60.9	-106.7	-131.2	-176.7	...	...	...	...	...	...
Equals: Net Capital Formation	95.3	86.4	113.0	132.0	141.1	137.3	...	...	...	...	...	...

Yugoslavia, Socialist Fed.Rep of(Former)

Source. Reply to the United Nations National Accounts Questionnaire from the Federal Institute for Statistics, Belgrade. The official estimates and descriptions are published annually in 'Statisticki Godisnjak' (Statistical Yearbook), issued by the same Office.

General note. The estimates shown in the following tables have been prepared in accordance with the United Nations System of National Accounts so far as the existing data would permit. On January 1, 1990, the new dinar, equal to 10,000 old dinars was introduced.

1.1 Expenditure on the Gross Domestic Product, in Current Prices

Million New Dinars

	1980	1981	1982	1983	1984	1985	1986	1987	1988	1989	1990	1991
1 Government final consumption expenditure	29	38	50	64	93	167	335	752	2252	34005	201991	...
2 Private final consumption expenditure	88	123	162	224	339	595	1178	2644	7925	111594	758812	...
3 Gross capital formation	73	98	123	166	269	470	900	1955	5873	99991	253153	
A Increase in stocks	19	30	37	63	123	209	395	964	3154	65799	83908	
B Gross fixed capital formation	55	68	85	103	146	261	505	991	2719	34192	169245	
4 Exports of goods and services a	32	45	60	85	170	264	376	1235	4664	59580	271664	
5 Less: Imports of goods and services a	48	57	74	95	186	277	393	1304	4806	68655	337833	
Statistical discrepancy	-3	-6	-5	-16	-20	-23	-56	-48	-76	-1120	-	
Equals: Gross Domestic Product	172	241	316	428	665	1195	2340	5234	15833	235395	1147787	

a) Beginning 1987, the data are estimated at current prices. Prior to 1987, they are estimated at prices established by the Executive Council.

1.3 Cost Components of the Gross Domestic Product

Million New Dinars

	1980	1981	1982	1983	1984	1985	1986	1987	1988	1989	1990	1991
1 Indirect taxes, net	15	22	26	40	60	88	175	362	1188	10711	181367	...
A Indirect taxes	20	27	34	51	77	119	236	515	1566	16009	200116	...
B Less: Subsidies	4	5	8	11	17	32	62	152	378	5297	18749	...
2 Consumption of fixed capital	17	24	37	53	78	133	249	666	1930	28514	128299	...
3 Compensation of employees paid by resident producers to:	...	...	...	...	...	...	...	...	...	...	...	...
4 Operating surplus	...	...	...	...	...	...	...	...	...	...	...	...
Statistical discrepancy	140	196	252	335	527	975	1916	4205	12715	196170	838121	...
Equals: Gross Domestic Product	172	241	316	428	665	1195	2340	5234	15833	235395	1147787	...

1.9 Gross Domestic Product by Institutional Sectors of Origin

Million New Dinars

	1980	1981	1982	1983	1984	1985	1986	1987	1988	1989	1990	1991
Domestic Factor Incomes Originating												
1 General government	...	...	...	...	...	...	...	...	...	...	...	
2 Corporate and quasi-corporate enterprises	...	...	...	...	...	...	...	...	...	...	...	
3 Households and private unincorporated enterprises	...	...	...	...	...	...	...	...	...	...	...	
4 Non-profit institutions serving households	...	...	...	...	...	...	...	...	...	...	...	
Subtotal: Domestic Factor Incomes	140	196	252	335	527	975	1916	4205	12715	196170	838121	...
Indirect taxes, net	15	22	26	40	60	88	175	362	1188	10711	181367	...
A Indirect taxes	20	27	34	51	77	119	236	515	1566	16009	200116	...
B Less: Subsidies	4	5	8	11	17	32	62	152	378	5297	18749	...
Consumption of fixed capital	17	24	37	53	78	133	249	666	1930	28514	128299	...
Statistical discrepancy	-	-	-	-	-	-	-	-	-	-	-	...
Gross Domestic Product	172	241	316	428	665	1195	2340	5234	15833	235395	1147787	...

1.10 Gross Domestic Product by Kind of Activity, in Current Prices

Million New Dinars

	1980	1981	1982	1983	1984	1985	1986	1987	1988	1989	1990	1991
1 Agriculture, hunting, forestry and fishing	20	30	44	62	90	138	290	568	1644	25451	124201	...
2 Mining and quarrying	4	6	8	10	20	34	51	136	393	5494	24503	...
3 Manufacturing	48	70	92	126	206	413	762	1819	5895	92948	301150	...
4 Electricity, gas and water	5	6	8	9	14	26	56	124	326	3755	16783	...
5 Construction	17	23	27	32	45	82	159	347	911	14406	75921	...
6 Wholesale and retail trade, restaurants and hotels	20	26	36	50	77	131	261	375	1119	14900	82250	...
7 Transport, storage and communication	13	18	23	31	47	89	174	551	1628	23527	118756	...
8 Finance, insurance, real estate and business services	6	8	11	13	22	42	89	243	760	12841	67927	...
9 Community, social and personal services	26	32	42	53	84	154	323	709	1970	31362	154929	...
Statistical discrepancy	-	-	-	-	-	-	-	-	-	-	-	...

1.10 Gross Domestic Product by Kind of Activity, in Current Prices
(Continued)

Million New Dinars

	1980	1981	1982	1983	1984	1985	1986	1987	1988	1989	1990	1991
Total, Industries	157	219	290	388	605	1107	2165	4872	14645	224684	966420	...
Producers of Government Services	...	...	...	...	...	...	...	...	...	...	...	...
Other Producers	...	...	...	...	...	...	...	...	...	...	...	...
Subtotal	157	219	290	388	605	1107	2165	4872	14645	224684	966420	...
Less: Imputed bank service charge	...	...	...	...	...	...	...	...	...	...	...	...
Plus: Import duties ᵃ	15	22	26	40	60	88	175	362	1188	10711	181367	...
Plus: Value added tax	...	...	...	...	...	...	...	...	...	...	...	...
Plus: Other adjustments	-	-	-	-	-	-	-	-	-	-	-	...
Equals: Gross Domestic Product	172	241	316	428	665	1195	2340	5234	15833	235395	1147787	...

a) Item 'Import duties' refers to indirect taxes net of subsidies.

1.12 Relations Among National Accounting Aggregates

Million New Dinars

	1980	1981	1982	1983	1984	1985	1986	1987	1988	1989	1990	1991
Gross Domestic Product	172	241	316	428	665	1195	2340	5234	15833	235395	1147787	...
Plus: Net factor income from the rest of the world	9	10	12	12	22	29	42	196	784	16233	100030	...
Factor income from the rest of the world	13	16	21	23	46	65	92	344	1327	21915	119482	...
Less: Factor income to the rest of the world	4	6	9	11	24	36	50	147	543	5683	19452	...
Equals: Gross National Product	181	251	328	440	688	1224	2382	5430	16617	251628	1247817	...
Less: Consumption of fixed capital	17	24	37	53	78	133	249	666	1930	28514	128299	...
Equals: National Income	164	228	291	387	610	1092	2133	4764	14687	223114	1119518	...
Plus: Net current transfers from the rest of the world	...	...	...	...	...	...	...	...	...	...	...	...
Equals: National Disposable Income	...	...	...	...	...	...	...	...	...	...	...	...
Less: Final consumption	117	161	212	289	432	762	1513	3396	10177	145599	960803	...
Equals: Net Saving	...	...	...	...	...	...	...	...	...	...	...	...
Less: Surplus of the nation on current transactions	...	...	...	...	...	...	...	...	...	...	...	...
Equals: Net Capital Formation	56	75	85	113	191	338	650	1289	3942	71477	124854	...

Zaire

General note. The preparation of national accounts statistics in Zaire is undertaken by Institut de Recherche Scientifique, Kinshasa. Official estimates are published by the Banque du Zaire in 'Rapport Annuel'. The estimates are generally in accordance with the classifications and definitions recommended in the United Nations System of National Accounts (SNA). The following tables have been prepared from successive replies to the United Nations national accounts questionnaire. When the scope and coverage of the estimates differ from conceptual or statistical reasons from the definitions and classifications recommend in SNA, a footnote is indicated to the relevant tables.

Sources and methods :

(a) Gross domestic product. Gross domestic product is estimated mainly through the production approach.

(b) Expenditure on the gross domestic product. The expenditure approach is used to estimate government final consumption expenditure and exports and imports of goods and services. This approach, together with the commodity flow approach, is used to estimate private final consumption expenditure and gross capital formation. The estimates of government consumption expenditure are derived from the government accounts. Information on private consumption expenditure is obtained from household sample surveys on expenditure conducted by the Institut National de la Statistique in the principal urban centres. The results of these surveys are extrapolated to cover the whole country. Some items are calculated as residuals by using the commodity-flow approach. For increase in stocks, information on the value of stocks at the beginning and end of the accounting year are obtained from the annual surveys of enterprises. For gross fixed capital formation, the estimates, using the commodity-flow approach, are based on information on acquisition of capital goods obtained from the surveys of enterprises. The estimates of capital formation by the general government, public enterprises and public corporations are derived from accounts while information from external trade statistics are used for machinery and equipment. The estimates of exports and imports of goods and services are derived from the balance of payments. The estimates of GDP by expenditure type at constant prices are obtained by applying to the value added at current prices the corresponding implicit price indexes.

1.1 Expenditure on the Gross Domestic Product, in Current Prices

Million Zaires

	1980	1981	1982	1983	1984	1985	1986	1987	1988	1989	1990	1991
1 Government final consumption expenditure	2756	4190	5948	8676	14999	17134	38567	73147	231979	309686	...	...
2 Private final consumption expenditure	10426	15275	17094	36794	34363	70360	97841	251916	...	...	...	...
3 Gross capital formation	4277	5967	7493	11492	29322	43364	63585	83764	140857	356149	...	...
A Increase in stocks	842	1292	1225	2010	8523	11378	16824	17324	22815	68542	...	...
B Gross fixed capital formation	3435	4675	6268	9482	20799	31986	46761	66440	118042	287607	...	...
4 Exports of goods and services	6102	8349	10013	23387	76783	106269	124847	206485	504615	998106	...	...
5 Less: Imports of goods and services	6379	10001	9437	21214	55883	89911	121268	288365	...	...	...	...
Equals: Gross Domestic Product a ..	17183	23781	31110	59134	99723	147263	203416	326946	622822	146811	...	...

a) Data in this table have been revised, therefore they are not strictly comparable with the unrevised data in the other tables.

1.12 Relations Among National Accounting Aggregates

Million Zaires

	1980	1981	1982	1983	1984	1985	1986	1987	1988	1989	1990	1991
Gross Domestic Product	17183.0	23781.0	31110.0	59134.0	99723.0	47263.0	...	...	...	...	...	...
Plus: Net factor income from the rest of the world	-742.0	-935.0	-1647.0	-2562.0	11452.0	-4084.0	...	...	...	...	...	...
Equals: Gross National Product	16441.0	22846.0	29463.0	56572.0	88271.0	43179.0	...	...	...	...	...	...
Less: Consumption of fixed capital	548.0	837.0	1220.0	1725.0	2501.0	4331.0	...	...	...	...	...	...
Equals: National Income	15893.0	22009.0	28243.0	54847.0	85770.0	38848.0	...	...	...	...	...	...
Plus: Net current transfers from the rest of the world	...	...	...	...	...	...	...	...	...	...	...	...
Equals: National Disposable Income	...	...	...	...	...	...	...	...	...	...	...	...
Less: Final consumption	...	...	...	...	...	...	...	...	...	...	...	...
Equals: Net Saving	...	...	...	...	...	...	...	...	...	...	...	...
Less: Surplus of the nation on current transactions	...	...	...	...	...	...	...	...	...	...	...	...
Equals: Net Capital Formation	...	...	...	...	...	...	...	...	...	...	...	...

Zambia

General note. The preparation of national accounts statistics in Zambia is undertaken by the Central Statistical Office (CSO), Lusaka. The official estimates are published in November-December issue of the Monthly Digest of Statistics. A description of the sources and methods used for the National Accounts estimation is found in 'National Accounts and Input-Output Tables, 1971' and 'National Accounts, 1972' published in August 1975 and June 1978, respectively. The estimates are generally in accordance with the classifications and definitions recommended in the United Nations System of National Accounts (SNA). The following tables have been prepared from successive replies to the United Nations national accounts questionnaire. When the scope and coverage of the estimates differ for conceptual or statistical reasons from the definitions and classifications recommended in SNA, a footnote is indicated to the relevant tables.

Sources and methods :

(a) Gross domestic product. Gross domestic product is estimated mainly through the production approach.

(b) Expenditure on the gross domestic product. All components of GDP by expenditure type are estimated through the expenditure approach except for the total estimate of private consumption expenditure which is obtained as a residual. However, a detailed breakdown is obtained through the use of the expenditure approach. Data used to estimate government expenditure are contained in 'Financial Statistics of the Government Sector' supplemented by detailed tabulations prepared by the CSO. The 'Urban Household Budget Survey in Low-cost Housing Areas, 1966-1968' and the household budget surveys 1974/75 for the urban and rural areas provide a detailed breakdown for the private consumption expenditure. Data on changes in stocks are collected through the annual national income inquiries and the balance sheets supplied by the enterprises. These two sources as well as government accounts are also used to estimate gross fixed capital formation. For transport equipment and machinery, furniture etc., the estimates are based closely on end-use groupings of imports and domestic products. Transactions with the rest of the world are estimated from the balance of payments statistics. Data on exports and imports are obtained from the annual statements of external trade prepared by the CSO. The CSO also undertakes a special inquiry on international transactions of all major private and public sector enterprises. For the constant price estimates, the current values of the expenditure items are deflated by various price indexes such as weighted index of wages and prices, consumer price index, implicit price index, etc.

(c) Cost-structure of the gross domestic product. The estimates of compensation of employees are based on information obtained through the annual income inquiries, the annual censuses of production and construction and other sources. Grossing-up factors to account for non-responding units are worked out on the basis of employment data collected through the quarterly employment surveys. Compensation of employees includes an estimated figure for domestic servant based on the 1969 population census data projected by an assumed 5 per cent annual growth rate. Consumption of fixed capital figures are obtained from the balance sheets of enterprises. Depreciation is imputed for some government enterprises and government administration and for owner-occupied buildings in urban and rural areas. Indirect taxes estimates are derived from the annual national income inquiries, the annual censuses of industrial production and construction data.

Operating surplus is obtained as a residual.

(d) Gross domestic product by kind of economic activity. The table of GDP by kind of economic activity is prepared at market prices, i.e., producers' values. The production approach is used to estimate the value added of nearly all industries. The income approach is used for the value added of producers of government services. The accounts of the agricultural sector have been divided into a commercial sector and a subsistence sector. The commercial sector includes all surplus production of the rural areas, the output of agricultural extension services, own-account capital formation and retentions by commercial farmers. The estimates for the subsistence sector are restricted to own consumption by traditional producers. The Quarterly Agricultural Statistical Bulletin gives information on intakes of agricultural products, official producer prices and input prices. Intake data are used for estimating surplus productions of commercial and non-commercial farmers. The output of agricultural extension services relates to tenant schemes of the Tobacco Board of Zambia and the extension services of the government. The estimates of own-account capital formation of livestocks are based on the annual surveys of agricultural and pastoral production and on annual censuses of livestock. The estimates of retentions by commercial farmers are also based on the annual surveys of agricultural and pastoral production. The 1971/72 survey included, for the first time, information on intermediate inputs of commercial farmers. This information is used for non-commercial farmers as well. The average input-output ratio for 1972 has been applied to agricultural output for earlier years. For later years, a constant real input-output ratio is assumed. Estimates of the subsistence sector's own-consumed production are derived from total production estimates by subtracting surplus production, covered by the commercial sector estimates. This is done for crops on the basis of the first sample census of non-commercial farms held during the crop year 1970/71. The annual censuses of industrial production provide the data for the estimates of mining and quarrying, manufacturing and electricity and water. For mining, the financial statements of the mining companies are also used. For manufacturing, extensive data on output and input of goods and services are available from the censuses. Provisions for non-responding establishments are made on the basis of employment data. The annual censuses of construction by contractors provide data for the construction sector. For own-account construction by households, the Ministry of Local Government and Housing provides information on the number, type and cost of houses. The principal source for the services sectors-trade, transport, communication, financial and community services - is the annual national income inquiry. Questionnaires are sent out annually to all large and medium-sized establishments and on a sample basis for small establishments using a short form. Information by kind of economic activity, is requested on employment, earnings, operating and non-operating incomes and expenditure, appropriation of surplus, capital investment and input and output of materials. For owner-occupied dwellings, rents are estimated on the basis of cost of houses and their life and on data from the household budget surveys. For producers of government services, estimates are based on financial statistics of the government sector. For constant price estimates, double deflation is used for the agricultural and mining sectors. For the remaining sectors, the current values are deflated by various price indexes.

1.1 Expenditure on the Gross Domestic Product, in Current Prices

Million Zambian kwacha

	1980	1981	1982	1983	1984	1985	1986	1987	1988	1989	1990	1991
1 Government final consumption expenditure	2325	2509	2910	3702	3921	6174	11031	10671	17725	43008	67579	141677
2 Private final consumption expenditure	782	986	996	1009	1240	1687	3481	4581	4470	7904	17421	33430
3 Gross capital formation	672	693	677	737	873	1453	3261	5494	6428	11667	37911	57695
A Increase in stocks	...	...	...	...	...	...	...	...	...	...	...	...
B Gross fixed capital formation	672	693	677	737	873	1453	3261	5494	6428	11667	37911	57695
Residential buildings												
Non-residential buildings	281	324	291	332	401	511	811	1226	1691	4255	9466	16017
Other construction and land improvement etc.												
Other	391	369	386	405	472	943	2450	4268	4737	7412	28445	41678
4 Exports of goods and services	1268	998	995	1281	1807	2740	5759	8512	10266	14792	42302	61950
5 Less: Imports of goods and services	1391	1434	1312	1329	1619	2703	5915	7694	8066	18665	41726	60248
Equals: Gross Domestic Product a	3656	3752	4266	5400	6222	9351	17617	21564	30823	58706	123487	234504

a) Data in this table have been revised, therefore they are not strictly comparable with the unrevised data in the other tables.

Zambia

1.2 Expenditure on the Gross Domestic Product, in Constant Prices

Million Zambian kwacha

	1980	1981	1982	1983	1984	1985	1986	1987	1988	1989	1990	1991
	At constant prices of:1977											
1 Government final consumption expenditure	531.3	611.3	541.5	454.6	483.8	460.1	464.4	377.6	331.3	438.7	427.8	...
2 Private final consumption expenditure	1104.0	1176.4	1089.0	1102.1	1113.5	1236.9	1224.6	1498.5	1660.0	1505.5	1226.8	...
3 Gross capital formation	439.1	390.5	298.9	226.5	242.0	261.2	384.3	233.9	245.0	228.2	339.5	...
A Increase in stocks	94.0	38.1	-10.6	-21.1	30.1	62.4	216.7	75.0	100.1	105.0	210.0	...
B Gross fixed capital formation	345.1	352.4	309.5	247.6	211.9	198.8	168.6	158.9	144.9	123.2	129.5	...
4 Exports of goods and services	632.7	552.0	640.4	567.3	536.9	527.8	537.8	505.9	476.3	469.6	544.5	...
5 Less: Imports of goods and services	710.4	596.4	465.4	392.7	383.0	465.2	526.9	541.4	540.4	452.7	423.7	...
Statistical discrepancy	-0.9	-14.9	-45.1	61.0	18.3	23.7	-25.9	39.8	74.0	34.9	98.9	...
Equals: Gross Domestic Product	1995.8	2118.9	2059.3	2018.8	2011.5	2044.5	2059.3	2114.3	2247.1	2224.2	2213.6	...

1.3 Cost Components of the Gross Domestic Product

Million Zambian kwacha

	1980	1981	1982	1983	1984	1985	1986	1987	1988	1989	1990	1991
1 Indirect taxes, net a	221.0	357.3	345.2	632.1	666.9	738.5	1345.6	2337.3	1310.7	1143.1	8133.8	...
A Indirect taxes a	417.8	467.5	502.1	714.3	758.5	926.9	1915.5	3014.7	2706.6	2645.9	12048.9	...
B Less: Subsidies a	196.8	110.2	156.9	82.2	91.6	188.4	569.9	677.4	1396.0	1502.8	3915.1	...
2 Consumption of fixed capital	339.1	383.4	405.8	426.4	630.3	932.8	2233.1	3429.3	4264.4	5248.6	10556.9	...
3 Compensation of employees paid by resident producers to:	1436.8	1722.7	1920.1	1974.2	2162.9	2818.6	4207.2	5922.8	8306.6	30640.6	64896.0	...
A Resident households	1436.8	1722.7	1920.1	1974.2	2162.9	2818.6	4207.3	5922.8	8306.6	30640.6	64896.0	...
B Rest of the world	-	-	-	-	-	-	-	-	-	-	-	...
4 Operating surplus	1066.7	1022.0	924.2	1148.5	1470.9	2582.0	5177.2	8089.0	16139.1	22992.2	29754.2	...
Equals: Gross Domestic Product	3063.6	3485.4	3595.3	4181.2	4931.0	7071.9	12963.1	19778.9	30020.8	60024.5	13340.9	...

a) The estimates of indirect taxes and subsidies are entered on accrual payment basis.

1.7 External Transactions on Current Account, Summary

Million Zambian kwacha

	1980	1981	1982	1983	1984	1985	1986	1987	1988	1989	1990	1991
	Payments to the Rest of the World											
1 Imports of goods and services	1391.2	1434.1	1311.5	1328.8	1636.7	2702.6	5915.6	7694.9	8065.5	...	...	...
A Imports of merchandise c.i.f.	1085.8	1097.3	1083.9	1067.2	1345.1	2103.6	4447.7	6627.4	6898.1	...	...	...
B Other	305.4	336.8	227.6	261.6	291.6	599.0	1467.9	1067.5	1167.4	...	...	...
2 Factor income to the rest of the world	233.8	115.3	230.9	250.0	380.0	714.1	2350.5	2258.6	3937.4	...	...	...
A Compensation of employees	-	-	-	-	-	-	-	-	-	...	...	...
B Property and entrepreneurial income	233.8	115.3	230.9	250.0	380.0	714.1	2350.5	2258.6	3937.4	...	...	...
3 Current transfers to the rest of the world	166.1	140.4	67.1	59.5	89.5	109.8	338.7	203.6	242.7	...	...	...
4 Surplus of the nation on current transactions	-490.3	-648.5	-570.9	-298.5	-317.0	...	...	...	...	...	...	...
Payments to the Rest of the World and Surplus of the Nation on Current Transactions	1300.8	1041.3	1038.6	1340.0	1789.2	...	...	...	...	...	...	...
	Receipts From The Rest of the World											
1 Exports of goods and services	1268.0	998.0	993.1	1280.7	1755.1	2740.2	5759.3	8512.4	10266.2	...	...	...
A Exports of merchandise f.o.b.	1149.2	866.3	877.6	1150.4	1618.4	2447.5	5247.0	8058.6	9786.2	...	...	...
B Other	118.8	131.7	115.5	130.1	136.7	292.7	512.3	453.8	480.0	...	...	...
2 Factor income from rest of the world	5.2	17.4	11.7	3.6	8.6	5.0	10.0	...	...	...	...	...
A Compensation of employees	-	-	-	-	-	-	...	...	...	...	...	...
B Property and entrepreneurial income	5.2	17.4	11.7	3.6	8.6	5.0	10.0	10.0	12.5	...	...	...
By general government	0.5	0.2	0.9	0.9	1.3	1.0	...	...	...	...	...	...
By corporate and quasi-corporate enterprises	-	0.2	-	-	-	-	...	...	...	...	...	...
By other	4.7	17.0	10.8	3.0	7.3	4.0	...	...	...	...	...	...
3 Current transfers from rest of the world	27.6	25.9	31.0	55.7	25.5	23.6	177.8	294.9	525.0	...	...	...
Receipts from the Rest of the World on Current Transactions	1300.8	1041.3	1038.6	1340.0	1789.2	...	...	...	...	...	...	...

1.10 Gross Domestic Product by Kind of Activity, in Current Prices

Million Zambian kwacha

	1980	1981	1982	1983	1984	1985	1986	1987	1988	1989	1990	1991
1 Agriculture, hunting, forestry and fishing	287	328	393	514	625	817	1969	2347	3905	6390	14175	28132
2 Mining and quarrying	634	332	366	778	974	2324	4559	4665	6280	10042	25272	33755
3 Manufacturing	485	615	812	1007	1040	1764	3067	4053	6865	13027	25510	61725
4 Electricity, gas and water	78	83	92	88	86	109	245	277	334	308	635	1909
5 Construction	196	228	204	238	299	378	611	882	1338	3019	6300	10911
6 Wholesale and retail trade, restaurants and hotels	542	513	533	587	687	849	1617	2320	3697	8963	13148	24021
7 Transport, storage and communication	301	315	327	405	418	539	1503	1826	2237	3116	6861	15812
8 Finance, insurance, real estate and business services	580	625	762	828	971	1130	1706	1989	2313	6837	13290	24832
9 Community, social and personal services a	426	449	534	540	644	789	1059	1721	2728	4148	9484	19254
Total, Industries	3529	3488	4023	4985	5744	8699	16336	20080	29697	55850	114675	220351
Producers of Government Services a	...	...	...	...	...	...	...	...	...	...	...	...
Other Producers	...	...	...	...	...	...	...	...	...	...	...	...
Subtotal b	3529	3488	4023	4985	5744	8699	16336	20080	29697	55850	114675	220351
Less: Imputed bank service charge	63	68	85	92	109	126	194	219	239	768	1471	2726
Plus: Import duties	...	...	...	...	...	...	...	...	...	...	...	...
Plus: Value added tax	...	...	...	...	...	...	...	...	...	...	...	...
Plus: Other adjustments c	190	332	328	507	587	778	1475	1703	1365	3624	10283	16879
Equals: Gross Domestic Product d	3656	3752	4266	5400	6222	9351	17617	21564	30823	58706	123487	234504

a) Item 'Producers of government services' is included in item 'Community, social and personal services'.
b) Gross domestic product in factor values.
c) Item 'Other adjustments' refers to indirect taxes net of subsidies.
d) Data in this table have been revised, therefore they are not strictly comparable with the unrevised data in the other tables.

1.11 Gross Domestic Product by Kind of Activity, in Constant Prices

Million Zambian kwacha

	1980	1981	1982	1983	1984	1985	1986	1987	1988	1989	1990	1991
					At constant prices of:1985							
1 Agriculture, hunting, forestry and fishing	685	668	690	786	787	817	1089	994	1205	1188	1097	1159
2 Mining and quarrying	2909	2612	2726	2723	2532	2324	2242	2435	2203	2186	2092	1858
3 Manufacturing	1358	1482	1483	1612	1636	1764	1656	1732	1874	1903	2034	1879
4 Electricity, gas and water	100	106	114	109	106	109	106	91	90	72	86	94
5 Construction	496	505	403	392	411	378	397	393	386	380	376	338
6 Wholesale and retail trade, restaurants and hotels	653	689	723	769	810	849	902	954	1007	1068	1126	1184
7 Transport, storage and communication	468	485	497	509	524	539	553	568	585	604	622	641
8 Finance, insurance, real estate and business services	944	995	1112	1078	1116	1130	1191	1199	1177	1205	1234	1331
9 Community, social and personal services a	736	745	757	767	777	789	797	809	820	831	843	855
Total, Industries	8349	8287	8505	8745	8699	8699	8933	9175	9347	9437	9510	9339
Producers of Government Services a	...	...	...	...	...	...	...	...	...	...	...	...
Other Producers	...	...	...	...	...	...	...	...	...	...	...	...
Subtotal b	8349	8287	8505	8745	8699	8699	8933	9175	9347	9437	9510	9339
Less: Imputed bank service charge	105	111	126	120	124	126	133	133	129	131	134	146
Plus: Import duties	...	...	...	...	...	...	...	...	...	...	...	...
Plus: Value added tax	...	...	...	...	...	...	...	...	...	...	...	...
Plus: Other adjustments c	748	742	760	783	778	778	799	821	837	845	851	834
Equals: Gross Domestic Product d	8992	8918	9139	9408	9353	9351	9599	9863	10055	10151	10227	10027

a) Item 'Producers of government services' is included in item 'Community, social and personal services'.
b) Gross domestic product in factor values.
c) Item 'Other adjustments' refers to indirect taxes net of subsidies.
d) Data in this table have been revised, therefore they are not strictly comparable with the unrevised data in the other tables.

1.12 Relations Among National Accounting Aggregates

Million Zambian kwacha

	1980	1981	1982	1983	1984	1985	1986	1987	1988	1989	1990	1991
Gross Domestic Product	3063.6	3485.4	3595.3	4181.2	4931.0	7071.9	12963.1	19778.4	27724.9	...	...	...
Plus: Net factor income from the rest of the world	-228.6	-97.9	-219.2	-246.1	-375.0	-709.1	-2340.5	-2248.6	-3924.9	...	...	...
Factor income from the rest of the world	5.2	17.4	11.7	3.6	8.6	5.0	10.0	10.0	12.5	...	...	...
Less: Factor income to the rest of the world	233.8	115.3	230.9	250.0	380.0	714.1	2350.5	2258.6	3937.4	...	...	...
Equals: Gross National Product	2835.0	3387.5	3376.1	3934.8	4556.0	6362.8	10622.6	17529.8	23800.0	...	...	...
Less: Consumption of fixed capital	339.1	383.4	405.8	426.4	630.3	932.8	2233.1	3429.3	4016.4	...	...	...

Zambia

1.12 Relations Among National Accounting Aggregates
(Continued)

Million Zambian kwacha

	1980	1981	1982	1983	1984	1985	1986	1987	1988	1989	1990	1991
Equals: National Income	2495.9	3004.1	2970.3	3508.4	3925.7	5430.0	8389.5	14100.5	19783.6	...	...	...
Plus: Net current transfers from the rest of the world	-138.5	-114.5	-36.1	-3.8	-64.0	-86.2	-160.9	91.3	282.3	...	...	...
Current transfers from the rest of the world	27.6	25.9	31.0	55.7	25.5	23.6	177.8	294.9	525.0	...	...	...
Less: Current transfers to the rest of the world	166.1	140.4	67.1	59.5	89.5	109.8	338.7	203.6	242.7	...	...	...
Equals: National Disposable Income	2357.4	2889.6	2934.2	3504.6	3865.3	5343.8	8228.6	14191.8	20065.9	...	...	...
Less: Final consumption	2473.3	3248.2	3308.0	3654.3	4088.6	5981.3	10032.9	16219.3	22111.2	...	...	...
Equals: Net Saving	-115.9	-358.6	-373.8	-149.7	-223.3	-637.5	-1804.3	-2027.4	-2045.3	...	...	...
Less: Surplus of the nation on current transactions	-490.3	-648.5	-570.9	-298.7	-317.0	...	...	...	...	...	...	...
Equals: Net Capital Formation	374.2	289.9	197.1	148.8	93.7	...	...	...	...	...	...	...

2.17 Exports and Imports of Goods and Services, Detail

Million Zambian kwacha

	1980	1981	1982	1983	1984	1985	1986	1987	1988	1989	1990	1991
Exports of Goods and Services												
1 Exports of merchandise, f.o.b.	1038.5	950.9	969.7	1061.8	1192.0	1494.7	5247.0	...	...	...	...	...
2 Transport and communication	72.7	69.4	64.9	80.0	87.6	118.3	234.4	...	...	...	...	...
A In respect of merchandise imports	48.5	35.8	27.3	37.0	41.1	52.3	157.4	...	...	...	...	...
B Other	24.2	33.6	37.6	43.0	46.5	66.0	77.0	...	...	...	...	...
3 Insurance service charges	...	...	...	...	...	...	...	...	...	...	...	...
4 Other commodities	9.5	14.1	2.0	2.0	2.5	4.0	5.0	...	...	...	...	...
5 Adjustments of merchandise exports to change-of-ownership basis	110.7	-84.6	-89.5	100.4	426.4	952.8	-	...	...	...	...	...
6 Direct purchases in the domestic market by non-residential households	16.6	27.0	23.0	23.3	23.0	24.0	48.0	...	...	...	...	...
7 Direct purchases in the domestic market by extraterritorial bodies	20.0	21.2	23.0	25.0	23.6	34.0	68.0	...	...	...	...	...
Total Exports of Goods and Services [a]	1268.0	998.0	993.1	1292.5	1755.1	2627.8	5602.4	...	...	...	...	...
Imports of Goods and Services												
1 Imports of merchandise, c.i.f.	1085.8	1097.3	1083.9	1067.2	1345.1	2103.6	5224.6	...	...	...	...	...
A Imports of merchandise, f.o.b.	878.7	926.4	932.0	895.2	1109.9	1790.0	4294.1	...	...	...	...	...
B Transport of services on merchandise imports	207.1	170.9	151.9	172.0	235.2	313.6	930.5	...	...	...	...	...
By residents	...	...	...	...	...	...	...	...	...	...	...	...
By non-residents	207.1	170.9	151.9	172.0	235.2	313.6	930.5	...	...	...	...	...
C Insurance service charges on merchandise imports	...	...	...	...	...	...	...	...	...	...	...	...
2 Adjustments of merchandise imports to change-of-ownership basis	...	...	...	...	...	...	...	...	...	...	...	...
3 Other transport and communication	88.4	77.6	79.4	100.0	110.3	157.0	183.3	...	...	...	...	...
4 Other insurance service charges	...	...	...	...	...	...	...	...	...	...	...	...
5 Other commodities	164.5	180.0	50.6	118.7	120.0	126.4	109.0	...	...	...	...	...
6 Direct purchases abroad by government	10.0	19.3	17.8	16.6	17.6	27.0	130.0	...	...	...	...	...
7 Direct purchases abroad by resident households	42.5	59.9	79.7	26.3	43.5	51.7	146.6	...	...	...	...	...
Total Imports of Goods and Services	1391.2	1434.1	1311.4	1328.4	1636.5	2465.7	5793.5	...	...	...	...	...
Balance of Goods and Services	-123.2	-436.1	-318.3	-36.3	118.6	162.1	-191.1	...	...	...	...	...
Total Imports and Balance of Goods and Services [a]	1268.0	998.0	993.1	1292.1	1755.1	2627.8	5602.4	...	...	...	...	...

a) Data for this table have not been revised, therefore, data for some years are not comparable with those of other tables.

4.1 Derivation of Value Added by Kind of Activity, in Current Prices

Million Zambian kwacha

	1980			1981			1982			1983		
	Gross Output	Intermediate Consumption	Value Added	Gross Output	Intermediate Consumption	Value Added	Gross Output	Intermediate Consumption	Value Added	Gross Output	Intermediate Consumption	Value Added
All Producers												
1 Agriculture, hunting, forestry and fishing	...	...	435.3	...	...	553.8	...	...	492.2	...	...	593.7
A Agriculture and hunting	...	...	386.8	...	...	504.2	...	...	426.5	...	...	521.5
B Forestry and logging	...	...	27.8	...	...	29.4	...	...	32.4	...	...	34.2
C Fishing	...	...	20.7	...	...	20.2	...	...	33.3	...	...	38.0
2 Mining and quarrying	...	...	501.7	...	...	488.4	...	...	396.6	...	...	641.6
A Coal mining	...	...	...	...	...	...	...	...	...	...	...	...
B Crude petroleum and natural gas production	...	...	...	...	...	...	...	...	...	...	...	...
C Metal ore mining	...	...	490.1	...	...	472.7	...	...	381.6	...	...	619.1
D Other mining	...	...	11.6	...	...	15.7	...	...	15.0	...	...	22.5
3 Manufacturing	...	...	566.1	...	...	684.1	...	...	740.4	...	...	829.8
A Manufacture of food, beverages and tobacco	...	...	266.0	...	...	317.5	...	...	351.3	...	...	393.9
B Textile, wearing apparel and leather industries	...	...	72.1	...	...	89.3	...	...	100.3	...	...	104.0
C Manufacture of wood and wood products, including furniture	...	...	19.1	...	...	33.3	...	...	32.3	...	...	16.2
D Manufacture of paper and paper products, printing and publishing	...	...	20.4	...	...	20.6	...	...	19.6	...	...	23.2
E Manufacture of chemicals and chemical petroleum, coal, rubber and plastic products	...	...	69.5	...	...	87.1	...	...	74.9	...	...	83.4
F Manufacture of non-metallic mineral products, except products of petroleum and coal	...	...	27.0	...	...	48.5	...	...	58.9	...	...	81.2
G Basic metal industries	...	...	8.1	...	...	8.2	...	...	6.0	...	...	11.8
H Manufacture of fabricated metal products, machinery and equipment	...	...	78.3	...	...	73.0	...	...	89.6	...	...	107.5
I Other manufacturing industries	...	...	5.6	...	...	6.6	...	...	7.5	...	...	8.6
4 Electricity, gas and water	...	...	61.0	...	...	66.3	...	...	72.2	...	...	70.4
5 Construction	...	...	136.5	...	...	111.7	...	...	127.0	...	...	133.1
6 Wholesale and retail trade, restaurants and hotels	...	...	361.2	...	...	410.9	...	...	452.9	...	...	524.9
A Wholesale and retail trade	...	...	301.5	...	...	328.0	...	...	355.5	...	...	401.6
B Restaurants and hotels	...	...	59.7	...	...	82.9	...	...	97.4	...	...	123.3
7 Transport, storage and communication	...	...	161.5	...	...	171.1	...	...	193.2	...	...	227.4
A Transport and storage	...	...	135.1	...	...	142.8	...	...	161.1	...	...	189.2
B Communication	...	...	26.4	...	...	28.3	...	...	32.1	...	...	38.2
8 Finance, insurance, real estate and business services	...	...	290.9	...	...	325.0	...	...	363.3	...	...	403.6
A Financial institutions	...	...	110.0]	...	...	119.2]	...	...	137.3]	...	...	156.6]
B Insurance	...	...		...	...		...	...		...	...	
C Real estate and business services	...	...	180.9	...	...	205.8	...	...	226.0	...	...	247.0
9 Community, social and personal services [a]	...	...	468.0	...	...	586.8	...	...	665.2	...	...	708.9
A Sanitary and similar services	...	...	202.8	...	...	262.0	...	...	290.0	...	...	281.0
B Social and related community services	...	...	196.4	...	...	244.4	...	...	287.7	...	...	324.7
Educational services	...	...	148.2	...	...	180.2	...	...	211.2	...	...	237.0
Medical, dental, other health and veterinary services	...	...	48.2	...	...	64.2	...	...	76.5	...	...	87.7
C Recreational and cultural services	...	...	18.8	...	...	24.9	...	...	25.6	...	...	30.0
D Personal and household services	...	...	50.0	...	...	55.5	...	...	61.9	...	...	73.0

Zambia

4.1 Derivation of Value Added by Kind of Activity, in Current Prices
(Continued)

Million Zambian kwacha

	1980			1981			1982			1983		
	Gross Output	Intermediate Consumption	Value Added	Gross Output	Intermediate Consumption	Value Added	Gross Output	Intermediate Consumption	Value Added	Gross Output	Intermediate Consumption	Value Added
Total, Industries	...	...	...	...	...	...	...	...	...	...	...	...
Producers of Government Services a	...	...	...	...	...	...	...	...	...	...	...	...
Other Producers a	...	...	...	...	...	...	...	...	...	...	...	...
Total	...	...	2982.2	...	...	3398.1	...	...	3503.0	...	...	4133.4
Less: Imputed bank service charge	...	...	31.1			33.7			38.8			44.9
Import duties	...	...	112.5	...	...	121.0	...	...	131.1	...	...	92.7
Value added tax	...	...	...	...	...	...	...	...	...	...	...	...
Total	...	...	3063.6	...	...	3485.4	...	...	3595.3	...	...	4181.2

	1984			1985			1986			1987		
	Gross Output	Intermediate Consumption	Value Added	Gross Output	Intermediate Consumption	Value Added	Gross Output	Intermediate Consumption	Value Added	Gross Output	Intermediate Consumption	Value Added
All Producers												
1 Agriculture, hunting, forestry and fishing	...	...	717.2	...	...	925.2	...	...	1577.8	...	...	2180.4
A Agriculture and hunting	...	...	624.1	...	...	775.3	...	...	...	...	...	...
B Forestry and logging	...	...	44.5	...	...	72.2	...	...	...	...	...	...
C Fishing	...	...	48.6	...	...	77.6	...	...	148.9	...	...	293.6
2 Mining and quarrying	...	...	673.8	...	...	1101.9	...	...	2354.9	...	...	2689.0
A Coal mining	...	...	...	...	...	...	...	...	...	...	...	...
B Crude petroleum and natural gas production	...	...	...	...	...	...	...	...	...	...	...	...
C Metal ore mining	...	...	644.8	...	...	1056.8	...	...	2280.4	...	...	2584.5
D Other mining	...	...	29.0	...	...	45.1	...	...	74.5	...	...	104.5
3 Manufacturing	...	...	1010.6	...	...	1616.5	...	...	2936.3	...	...	5547.9
A Manufacture of food, beverages and tobacco	...	...	442.2	...	...	600.2	...	...	843.3	...	...	1283.9
B Textile, wearing apparel and leather industries	...	...	130.5	...	...	212.6	...	...	289.8	...	...	459.5
C Manufacture of wood and wood products, including furniture	...	...	22.8	...	...	43.8	...	...	88.4	...	...	74.0
D Manufacture of paper and paper products, printing and publishing	...	...	34.9	...	...	95.4	...	...	166.4	...	...	344.9
E Manufacture of chemicals and chemical petroleum, coal, rubber and plastic products	...	...	108.6	...	...	194.8	...	...	370.5	...	...	592.1
F Manufacture of non-metallic mineral products, except products of petroleum and coal	...	...	69.8	...	...	129.7	...	...	153.7	...	...	200.5
G Basic metal industries	...	...	13.0	...	...	13.2	...	...	23.9	...	...	59.3
H Manufacture of fabricated metal products, machinery and equipment	...	...	177.6	...	...	309.0	...	...	960.7	...	...	2448.7
I Other manufacturing industries	...	...	11.2	...	...	17.8	...	...	39.6	...	...	85.0
4 Electricity, gas and water	...	...	69.7	...	...	71.0	...	...	166.2	...	...	238.5
5 Construction	...	...	153.3	...	...	183.2	...	...	292.0	...	...	393.8
6 Wholesale and retail trade, restaurants and hotels	...	...	646.8	...	...	944.1	...	...	1899.9	...	...	3205.7
A Wholesale and retail trade	...	...	520.8	...	...	763.0	...	...	1638.2	...	...	2778.3
B Restaurants and hotels	...	...	126.0	...	...	181.1	...	...	261.7	...	...	427.4
7 Transport, storage and communication	...	...	251.3	...	...	342.3	...	...	594.3	...	...	839.6
A Transport and storage	...	...	205.5	...	...	261.9	...	...	458.7	...	...	649.0
B Communication	...	...	45.8	...	...	80.4	...	...	135.6	...	...	190.6
8 Finance, insurance, real estate and business services	...	...	517.2	...	...	683.5	...	...	1197.0	...	...	1891.0
A Financial institutions	...	...	[172.9	...	...	[228.9	...	...	[445.2	...	...	[735.1
B Insurance	...	...		...	...		...	...		...	...	
C Real estate and business services	...	...	344.3	...	...	454.6	...	...	751.8	...	...	1155.9
9 Community, social and personal services a	...	...	800.3	...	...	934.3	...	...	1169.2	...	...	1487.6
A Sanitary and similar services	...	...	318.5	...	...	391.7	...	...	472.8	...	...	623.8
B Social and related community services	...	...	360.2	...	...	404.7	...	...	508.7	...	...	585.4

Zambia

4.1 Derivation of Value Added by Kind of Activity, in Current Prices
(Continued)

Million Zambian kwacha

	1984 Gross Output	1984 Intermediate Consumption	1984 Value Added	1985 Gross Output	1985 Intermediate Consumption	1985 Value Added	1986 Gross Output	1986 Intermediate Consumption	1986 Value Added	1987 Gross Output	1987 Intermediate Consumption	1987 Value Added
Educational services	...	...	259.0	...	...	292.1	...	...	384.1	...	...	436.2
Medical, dental, other health and veterinary services	...	...	101.2	...	...	112.6	...	...	124.6	...	...	149.2
C Recreational and cultural services	...	...	34.0	...	...	41.8	...	...	187.7	...	...	278.4
D Personal and household services	...	...	87.6	...	...	96.1	...	...		...	...	
Total, Industries	...	...	...	...	...	...	...	...	...	...	...	...
Producers of Government Services [a]	...	...	...	...	...	...	...	...	...	...	...	...
Other Producers [a]	...	...	...	...	...	...	...	...	...	...	...	...
Total	...	...	4840.2	...	...	6802.0	...	...	12187.6	...	...	18473.5
Less: Imputed bank service charge	...	...	49.6	...	...	64.2	...	...	124.9	...	...	202.0
Import duties	...	...	140.4	...	...	334.1	...	...	900.2	...	...	1506.4
Value added tax	...	...	...	...	...	...	...	...	...	...	...	...
Total	...	...	4931.0	...	...	7071.9	...	...	12963.1	...	...	19778.9

a) Items 'Other producers' and 'Producers of government services' are included in item 'Community, social and personal services'.

4.2 Derivation of Value Added by Kind of Activity, in Constant Prices

Million Zambian kwacha

	1980 Gross Output	1980 Intermediate Consumption	1980 Value Added	1981 Gross Output	1981 Intermediate Consumption	1981 Value Added	1982 Gross Output	1982 Intermediate Consumption	1982 Value Added	1983 Gross Output	1983 Intermediate Consumption	1983 Value Added
					At constant prices of:1977							
					All Producers							
1 Agriculture, hunting, forestry and fishing	...	...	303.9	...	...	328.7	...	...	290.3	...	...	314.6
A Agriculture and hunting	...	...	273.8	...	...	299.3	...	...	257.7	...	...	279.8
B Forestry and logging	...	...	14.5	...	...	14.9	...	...	15.3	...	...	15.8
C Fishing	...	...	15.6	...	...	14.5	...	...	17.3	...	...	19.0
2 Mining and quarrying	...	...	205.2	...	...	214.8	...	...	215.2	...	...	221.7
A Coal mining	...	...	...	...	...	...	...	...	...	...	...	...
B Crude petroleum and natural gas production	...	...	...	...	...	...	...	...	...	...	...	...
C Metal ore mining	...	...	198.2	...	...	206.3	...	...	206.1	...	...	215.0
D Other mining	...	...	7.0	...	...	8.5	...	...	9.1	...	...	6.7
3 Manufacturing	...	...	383.5	...	...	430.2	...	...	415.1	...	...	384.5
A Manufacture of food, beverages and tobacco	...	...	180.7	...	...	203.4	...	...	196.0	...	...	182.8
B Textile, wearing apparel and leather industries	...	...	62.2	...	...	69.4	...	...	73.3	...	...	63.1
C Manufacture of wood and wood products, including furniture	...	...	11.8	...	...	16.0	...	...	13.8	...	...	6.7
D Manufacture of paper and paper products, printing and publishing	...	...	11.7	...	...	11.1	...	...	12.0	...	...	11.3
E Manufacture of chemicals and chemical petroleum, coal, rubber and plastic products	...	...	45.7	...	...	58.8	...	...	47.5	...	...	44.5
F Manufacture of non-metallic mineral products, except products of petroleum and coal	...	...	14.9	...	...	17.6	...	...	16.5	...	...	19.6
G Basic metal industries	...	...	4.5	...	...	3.9	...	...	3.3	...	...	3.6
H Manufacture of fabricated metal products, machinery and equipment	...	...	48.4	...	...	45.8	...	...	48.7	...	...	49.3
I Other manufacturing industries	...	...	3.6	...	...	4.2	...	...	4.0	...	...	3.8
4 Electricity, gas and water	...	...	65.8	...	...	71.0	...	...	75.8	...	...	72.2
5 Construction	...	...	102.8	...	...	78.9	...	...	84.0	...	...	88.6
6 Wholesale and retail trade, restaurants and hotels	...	...	236.3	...	...	248.6	...	...	231.8	...	...	227.6
A Wholesale and retail trade	...	...	196.2	...	...	195.2	...	...	178.5	...	...	171.8
B Restaurants and hotels	...	...	40.1	...	...	53.4	...	...	53.3	...	...	55.8
7 Transport, storage and communication	...	...	117.5	...	...	118.3	...	...	118.8	...	...	119.4
A Transport and storage	...	...	96.1	...	...	97.3	...	...	97.1	...	...	95.6

Zambia

4.2 Derivation of Value Added by Kind of Activity, in Constant Prices
(Continued)

Million Zambian kwacha

	1980			1981			1982			1983		
	Gross Output	Intermediate Consumption	Value Added	Gross Output	Intermediate Consumption	Value Added	Gross Output	Intermediate Consumption	Value Added	Gross Output	Intermediate Consumption	Value Added
At constant prices of:1977												
B Communication	...	...	21.4	...	...	21.0	...	...	21.7	...	...	23.8
8 Finance, insurance, real estate and business services	...	...	211.3	...	...	218.3	...	...	226.5	...	...	234.5
A Financial institutions	...	...	66.8	...	...	65.0	...	...	70.8	...	...	66.2
B Insurance	...	...		...	...		...	...		...	...	
C Real estate and business services	...	...	144.5	...	...	153.3	...	...	155.7	...	...	168.3
9 Community, social and personal services a	...	...	346.0	...	...	391.9	...	...	393.9	...	...	355.7
A Sanitary and similar services	...	...	147.8	...	...	172.2	...	...	168.6	...	...	138.5
B Social and related community services	...	...	143.1	...	...	160.7	...	...	167.3	...	...	159.9
Educational services	...	...	108.0	...	...	118.5	...	...	122.8	...	...	116.7
Medical, dental, other health and veterinary services	...	...	35.1	...	...	42.2	...	...	44.5	...	...	43.2
C Recreational and cultural services	...	...	13.7	...	...	16.4	...	...	14.9	...	...	14.8
D Personal and household services	...	...	41.4	...	...	42.6	...	...	43.1	...	...	42.5
Total, Industries	...	...	...	...	...	...	...	...	...	...	...	...
Producers of Government Services a												
Other Producers a	...	...	...	...	...	...	...	...	...	...	...	...
Total	...	...	1972.3	...	...	2100.7	...	...	2051.4	...	...	2018.8
Less: Imputed bank service charge	...	...	18.8	...	...	18.2	...	...	19.8	...	...	18.5
Import duties	...	...	42.3	...	...	36.4	...	...	27.1	...	...	18.5
Value added tax	...	...	...	...	...	...	...	...	...	...	...	...
Total	...	...	1995.8	...	...	2118.9	...	...	2059.3	...	...	2018.8

	1984			1985			1986			1987		
	Gross Output	Intermediate Consumption	Value Added	Gross Output	Intermediate Consumption	Value Added	Gross Output	Intermediate Consumption	Value Added	Gross Output	Intermediate Consumption	Value Added
At constant prices of:1977												
All Producers												
1 Agriculture, hunting, forestry and fishing	...	...	332.2	...	...	343.8	...	...	373.8	...	...	365.6
A Agriculture and hunting	...	...	294.2	...	...	...	...	...	...	...	...	...
B Forestry and logging	...	...	15.3	...	...	...	...	...	...	...	...	...
C Fishing	...	...	22.7	...	...	24.3	...	...	27.7	...	...	25.2
2 Mining and quarrying	...	...	200.0	...	...	185.8	...	...	176.5	...	...	184.2
A Coal mining	...	...	...	...	...	...	...	...	...	...	...	...
B Crude petroleum and natural gas production	...	...	...	...	...	...	...	...	...	...	...	...
C Metal ore mining	...	...	193.5	...	...	179.0	...	...	167.6	...	...	...
D Other mining	...	...	6.5	...	...	6.4	...	...	6.3	...	...	...
3 Manufacturing	...	...	389.3	...	...	421.6	...	...	425.3	...	...	462.9
A Manufacture of food, beverages and tobacco	...	...	180.2	...	...	176.9	...	...	179.8	...	...	189.2
B Textile, wearing apparel and leather industries	...	...	60.5	...	...	74.3	...	...	63.5	...	...	68.1
C Manufacture of wood and wood products, including furniture	...	...	8.0	...	...	9.3	...	...	9.1	...	...	8.1
D Manufacture of paper and paper products, printing and publishing	...	...	11.5	...	...	15.3	...	...	19.3	...	...	29.9
E Manufacture of chemicals and chemical petroleum, coal, rubber and plastic products	...	...	46.1	...	...	42.9	...	...	41.7	...	...	39.0
F Manufacture of non-metallic mineral products, except products of petroleum and coal	...	...	15.1	...	...	26.1	...	...	19.1	...	...	21.2
G Basic metal industries	...	...	3.8	...	...	3.6	...	...	3.3	...	...	2.6
H Manufacture of fabricated metal products, machinery and equipment	...	...	60.2	...	...	68.9	...	...	85.1	...	...	100.2
I Other manufacturing industries	...	...	3.9	...	...	4.3	...	...	4.4	...	...	4.6
4 Electricity, gas and water	...	...	70.9	...	...	72.7	...	...	71.1	...	...	62.2

4.2 Derivation of Value Added by Kind of Activity, in Constant Prices
(Continued)

Million Zambian kwacha

	1984			1985			1986			1987		
	Gross Output	Intermediate Consumption	Value Added	Gross Output	Intermediate Consumption	Value Added	Gross Output	Intermediate Consumption	Value Added	Gross Output	Intermediate Consumption	Value Added
At constant prices of:1977												
5 Construction	...	...	88.6	...	...	77.1	...	...	81.1	...	...	77.3
6 Wholesale and retail trade, restaurants and hotels	...	...	216.9	...	...	226.0	...	...	221.2	...	...	228.0
A Wholesale and retail trade	...	...	167.9	...	...	174.7	...	...	174.4	...	...	181.5
B Restaurants and hotels	...	...	49.0	...	...	51.3	...	...	46.8	...	...	46.5
7 Transport, storage and communication	...	...	116.2	...	...	109.2	...	...	110.1	...	...	114.5
A Transport and storage	...	...	91.2	...	...	82.9	...	...	81.7	...	...	...
B Communication	...	...	25.0	...	...	25.8	...	...	25.4	...	...	...
8 Finance, insurance, real estate and business services	...	...	242.0	...	...	239.6	...	...	235.4	...	...	240.0
A Financial institutions	...	...	62.5	...	...	60.6	...	...	56.8	...	...	50.8
B Insurance	...	...		...	...		...	...		...	...	
C Real estate and business services	...	...	179.5	...	...	179.0	...	...	178.6	...	...	189.2
9 Community, social and personal services [a]	...	...	354.9	...	...	365.6	...	...	357.9	...	...	370.6
A Sanitary and similar services	...	...	137.4	...	...	141.3	...	...	137.3	...	...	142.2
B Social and related community services	...	...	158.7	...	...	163.1	...	...	158.6	...	...	164.4
Educational services	...	...	115.8	...	...	119.0	...	...	115.7	...	...	120.0
Medical, dental, other health and veterinary services	...	...	42.9	...	...	44.1	...	...	42.9	...	...	44.4
C Recreational and cultural services	...	...	14.7	...	...	15.1	...	...	14.7	...	...	...
D Personal and household services	...	...	44.1	...	...	46.1	...	...	50.8	...	...	...
Total, Industries	...	...	...	...	...	...	...	...	...	...	...	...
Producers of Government Services [a]	...	...	...	...	...	...	...	...	...	...	...	...
Other Producers [a]	...	...	...	...	...	...	...	...	...	...	...	...
Total	...	...	2011.0	...	...	2038.4	...	...	2047.0	...	...	...
Less: Imputed bank service charge	...	...	17.5	...	...	16.8	...	...	15.8	...	...	14.1
Import duties	...	...	18.0	...	...	19.9	...	...	22.5	...	...	23.1
Value added tax	...	...	...	...	...	...	...	...	...	...	...	...
Total	...	...	2011.5	...	...	2044.5	...	...	2059.3	...	...	2114.3

	1988		
	Gross Output	Intermediate Consumption	Value Added
At constant prices of:1977			
All Producers			
1 Agriculture, hunting, forestry and fishing	...	...	436.2
A Agriculture and hunting	...	...	...
B Forestry and logging	...	...	...
C Fishing	...	...	29.8
2 Mining and quarrying	...	...	160.4
A Coal mining	...	...	...
B Crude petroleum and natural gas production	...	...	...
C Metal ore mining	...	...	154.2
D Other mining	...	...	6.2

Zambia

Million Zambian kwacha

	Gross Output	Intermediate Consumption	Value Added	
		1988		
3 Manufacturing	...	...	547.0	At constant prices of:1977
A Manufacture of food, beverages and tobacco	...	...	249.6	
B Textile, wearing apparel and leather industries	...	...	76.4	
C Manufacture of wood and wood products, including furniture	...	...	8.0	
D Manufacture of paper and paper products, printing and publishing	...	...	34.7	
E Manufacture of chemicals and chemical petroleum, coal, rubber and plastic products	...	...	39.5	
F Manufacture of non-metallic mineral products, except products of petroleum and coal	...	...	25.2	
G Basic metal industries	...	...	2.8	
H Manufacture of fabricated metal products, machinery and equipment	...	...	100.2	
I Other manufacturing industries	...	...	10.6	
4 Electricity, gas and water	...	...	61.3	
5 Construction	...	...	70.3	
6 Wholesale and retail trade, restaurants and hotels	...	...	233.9	
A Wholesale and retail trade	...	...	185.3	
B Restaurants and hotels	...	...	48.6	
7 Transport, storage and communication	...	...	113.3	
A Transport and storage	...	...	86.9	
B Communication	...	...	26.4	
8 Finance, insurance, real estate and business services	...	...	251.1	
A Financial institutions	...	...	60.0	
B Insurance	...	...		
C Real estate and business services	...	...	191.1	
9 Community, social and personal services [a]	...	...	373.5	
A Sanitary and similar services	...	...	143.2	
B Social and related community services	...	...	64.9	
Educational services	...	...	120.7	
Medical, dental, other health and veterinary services	...	...	44.7	
C Recreational and cultural services	...	...	...	
D Personal and household services	...	...	...	
Total, Industries	...	...	...	
Producers of Government Services [a]	...	...	...	
Other Producers [a]	...	...	...	
Total	...	...	...	
Less: Imputed bank service charge	...	...	16.6	
Import duties	...	...	16.7	
Value added tax	...	...		
Total	...	...	2247.1	

a) Items 'Other producers' and 'Producers of government services' are included in item 'Community, social and personal services'.

Zimbabwe

General note. The prepration of national accounts statistics in Zimbabwe is undertaken by the Central Statistical Office, Hararel. The official estimates together with methodological notes are published annually in 'National Accounts of Zimbabwe Rhodesia'. The estimates are generally in accordance with the classifications and definitions recommended in the United Nations System of National AccoUnts (SNA). The following tables have been prepared from successive replies to the United Nations national accounts questionnaire. When the scope and coverage of the estimates differ for conceptual or statistical reasons from the definitions and classifications recommended in SNA, a footnote is indicated to the relevant tables.

Sources and methods :

(a) Gross domestic product. Gross domestic product is estimated mainly through the production approach.

(b) Expenditure on the gross domestic product. All items of GDP by expenditure type are estimated through the use of the expenditure approach combined with the commodity-flow approach except private consumption expenditure which is derived as a residual. In general, the commodity-flow approach determines to which consuming sector or group the commodities would be allocated. For government expenditure, detailed accounts are available from each department of the central government while the local authorities and certain controlled organizations and funds provide copies of their annual financial statement. Total private consumption expenditure is to a large extent derived as a residual. However, suplementary information is obtained from returns of major suppliers of consumer products and from family budget surveys. The estimates are checked by turnover statistics of retailers. Data on changes in stocks are available from the annual censuses of production, agriculture and livestock and from the 1975 census of road transport and for the trade sector, from turnover indexes. Expenditure on capital goods are available in the anual censuses of agriculture and production, the annual analysis of public sector accounts and the annual surveys of financial institutions. The data from these sources are classified by industry, sector and type of asset. The value of new buildings construction is estimated from monthly surveys of private contractors and public sector producers. The estimates include own-account construction of dwellings and service charges of capital nature. Tabulations of exports and imports classified by industry of origin and commodity are used to determine the proportion of each group's output sold abroad and the value of imports at the border. Valuation adjustments are made to bring all trade to a uniform f.o.b. or free-on-rail valuation at the border of the exporting country. For the constant price estimates of all expenditure items deflation is done with the use of appropriate price indexes.

(c) Cost-structure of the gross domestic product. Wages and salaries paid in the industrial activity sectors are obtained from the annual censuses of industrial production. The estimates are adjusted from fiscal to calendar year and projected using ratios derived from the quarterly employment inquiries. This latter soUrce also provides wage data for the financial, trade and service sectors. Wages and salaries paid in the agricultural sector are taken from the results of qUarterly censuses of farmers. Estimates of indirect taxes and subsidies are obtained from government accounts. Gross operating surplus, including depreciation, is estimated as a residual.

(d) Gross domestic product by kind of economic activity. The table of GDP by kind of economic activity is prepared in factor values. The production approach is used to estimate value added of most industries. For the service sector, the income approach is used while for the trade sector, the estimates are made by projecting the results of the latest census of distribution. Information on the gross output of agriculture is available either from regular annual censuses or from records of sales to official marketing authorities. ValUe of own-accout consumption for some items is estimated on the basis of forecasts of total production less recorded sales and for other items, on the basis of assumed average consumption rates. The gross output of forestry and logging is estimated to include the cost of plantation development, sales and increase in stocks of cut timber, etc. For agricultural services, estimates are based on a survey held in 1974 of the main estalishments. For the industrial activity sector and construction, complete output and input accounts are available from the annual censuses of production. The results are converted from fiscal to calendary-year basis and extrapolated by indcators such as turnover, mineral output, construction work done and prices. The gross output of establishments classified to manufacturing which also engage in distribution activity includes the sales margin only on goods purchased for resale without further processing. Estimates of output and input of the trade sector are made by extrapolating the results of the 1969 census of distribution, using turnover indicators. For transport, the production account is based on the results of the 1975 census of road transport supplemented by the accounts of concerned companies. Estimates of financial institutions are based on the results of annual surveys taken together with statutory statistical returns rendered by registered institutions. The 1969 census of population provided information on the number of dwellings by type of dwelling, as well as the average gross rents paid for rented dwellings and these are updated using the consumer price rent index. The ratio between rented and owner-occupied dwellings are assumed to have remained constant since 1969. Cost of inputs into dwellings are estimated on a unit basis from annual surveys. Value added of private domestic services is estimated as wages in cash and in kind paid. Value added of education, health and other services are based on income tax statistics and wage data collected through the quarterly employment inquiries. GDP by kind of economic activity is estimated at constant prices mainly by the use of volume indices at commodity group levels for goods producing industries, trade (volume of goods handled), transport (volume of traffic by types) and services like education (combined index of students and teachers). In the case of the rest of the services, the total employment in each year is used as the indicator for constant price estimates.

1.1 Expenditure on the Gross Domestic Product, in Current Prices

Million Zimbabwean dollars

	1980	1981	1982	1983	1984	1985	1986	1987	1988	1989	1990	1991
1 Government final consumption expenditure	677	763	1027	1159	1364	1566	1830	2531	3004	...	...	...
2 Private final consumption expenditure	2219	2969	3378	4341	3792	4198	4561	4503	5348	...	...	...
A Households	2184	2934	3341	4302	3746	4142	4492	4416	5251	...	...	...
B Private non-profit institutions serving households	35	35	37	39	46	56	69	87	97	...	...	...
3 Gross capital formation	648	1026	1102	1002	1213	1445	1541	1539	2490	...	...	...
A Increase in stocks	120	196	63	-236	28	312	229	-134	459	...	...	...
B Gross fixed capital formation	528	830	1039	1238	1185	1133	1312	1673	2031	...	...	...
Residential buildings	34	53	57	59	58	67	52	85	80	...	...	...
Non-residential buildings	107	183	203	239	241	224	270	391	535	...	...	...
Other construction and land improvement etc.	109	193	398	396	98	216	225	341	447	...	...	...
Other	278	401	381	544	788	626	765	857	969	...	...	...
4 Exports of goods and services	1043	1117	1141	1345	1708	2101	2559	2789	3434	...	...	...
5 Less: Imports of goods and services	1146	1442	1450	1542	1673	2015	2202	2423	2835	...	...	...
Equals: Gross Domestic Product	3441	4433	5197	6306	6404	7295	8289	8939	11441	13583	16466	21234

1.2 Expenditure on the Gross Domestic Product, in Constant Prices

Million Zimbabwean dollars

	1980	1981	1982	1983	1984	1985	1986	1987	1988	1989	1990	1991
					At constant prices of:1980							
1 Government final consumption expenditure	677	791	892	942	1020	1058	1195	1350	1608	...	...	...
2 Private final consumption expenditure	2219	2601	2557	2982	2254	2271	2161	1741	2207	...	...	...
A Households	2184	2570	2530	2954	2225	2239	2126	1700	2167	...	...	...
B Private non-profit institutions serving households	35	31	27	28	29	32	35	41	40	...	...	...
3 Gross capital formation	646	950	816	599	661	760	688	433	965	...	...	...

1.2 Expenditure on the Gross Domestic Product, in Constant Prices
(Continued)

Million Zimbabwean dollars

	1980	1981	1982	1983	1984	1985	1986	1987	1988	1989	1990	1991
					At constant prices of:1980							
A Increase in stocks	118	228	28	-166	43	255	170	-168	279	...	...	...
B Gross fixed capital formation	528	722	788	765	618	505	518	601	686	...	...	...
Residential buildings	34	43	40	35	30	31	21	32	28	...	...	...
Non-residential buildings	107	147	141	143	128	105	110	145	187	...	...	...
Other construction and land improvement etc.	109	160	279	235	52	104	98	131	162	...	...	...
Other	278	372	328	352	408	266	290	293	309	...	...	...
4 Exports of goods and services	1042	1123	1151	1155	1078	1376	1602	1524	1415	...	...	...
5 Less: Imports of goods and services	1146	1450	1463	1325	1056	1320	1379	1249	1320	...	...	...
Statistical discrepancy a	2	-143	20	-316	3	90	80	494	-180	...	...	...
Equals: Gross Domestic Product	3441	3872	3974	4037	3960	4235	4347	4293	4695	5001	5100	5198

a) Item 'Statistical discrepancy' refers to the difference between gross domestic product obtained by the product approach and that obtained by the expenditure approach.

1.3 Cost Components of the Gross Domestic Product

Million Zimbabwean dollars

	1980	1981	1982	1983	1984	1985	1986	1987	1988	1989	1990	1991
1 Indirect taxes, net	217	384	540	874	755	792	881	920	1257	1680	1972	2231
A Indirect taxes	317	504	709	956	1051	1148	1251	1346	1645	...	...	...
B Less: Subsidies	100	120	169	82	296	356	370	426	388	...	...	...
2 Consumption of fixed capital a	...	...	...	...	...	...	...	...	...	...	...	...
3 Compensation of employees paid by resident producers to:	1902	2325	2798	3134	3418	3829	4351	4859	5611	...	...	...
4 Operating surplus a	1322	1727	1859	2298	2230	2675	3058	3160	4573	...	...	...
Equals: Gross Domestic Product	3441	4433	5197	6306	6405	7297	8289	8939	11441	13583	16466	21234

a) Item 'Operating surplus' includes consumption of fixed capital.

1.4 General Government Current Receipts and Disbursements

Million Zimbabwean dollars

	1980	1981	1982	1983	1984	1985	1986	1987	1988	1989	1990	1991
					Receipts							
1 Operating surplus	...	...	...	...	...	...	...	...	...	...	...	...
2 Property and entrepreneurial income a	56	56	79	107	124	135	185	...	...	...	...	...
3 Taxes, fees and contributions	705	1052	1424	1753	1913	2112	2455	...	...	...	...	...
A Indirect taxes	316	504	709	956	1051	1148	1251	...	...	...	...	...
B Direct taxes	383	539	707	783	856	955	1196	...	...	...	...	...
C Social security contributions	5	5	7	13	6	9	8	...	...	...	...	...
D Compulsory fees, fines and penalties	1	1	1	1	-	-	-	...	...	...	...	...
4 Other current transfers	54	72	62	68	86	95	125	...	...	...	...	...
Total Current Receipts of General Government b	815	1180	1565	1928	2123	2342	2765	...	...	...	...	...
					Disbursements							
1 Government final consumption expenditure	663	750	1007	1138	1334	1559	1834	...	...	...	...	...
2 Property income	93	125	193	242	310	396	460	...	...	...	...	...
3 Subsidies	100	120	169	82	296	356	370	...	...	...	...	...
4 Other current transfers	158	184	269	370	364	360	414	...	...	...	...	...
A Social security benefits	3	4	4	6	5	6	7	...	...	...	...	...
B Social assistance grants c	74	71	77	75	79	85	101	...	...	...	...	...
C Other	81	109	188	289	280	269	309	...	...	...	...	...
Statistical discrepancy d	33	46	46	18	28	9	-1	...	...	...	...	...
5 Net saving e	-232	-45	-119	78	-209	-338	-312	...	...	...	...	...
Total Current Disbursements and Net Saving of General Government b	815	1180	1565	1928	2123	2342	2765	...	...	...	...	...

a) Item 'Property and entrepreneural income' includes consumption of fixed capital.
b) Estimates of general government cover central & local government.
c) Item 'Social assistance grants' refers to pensions.

d) Item 'Statistical discrepancy' represents unclassified estimates.
e) Item 'Net saving' includes consumption of fixed capital.

1.7 External Transactions on Current Account, Summary

Million Zimbabwean dollars

	1980	1981	1982	1983	1984	1985	1986	1987	1988	1989	1990	1991
Payments to the Rest of the World												
1 Imports of goods and services	1146	1442	1450	1542	1673	2015	2202	2423	2835	...	...	...
A Imports of merchandise c.i.f.	861	1059	1114	1087	1237	1486	1686	1781	...	...	...	...
B Other	285	383	336	455	436	530	515	642	...	...	...	...
2 Factor income to the rest of the world	115	187	272	339	287	365	480	463	533	...	...	...
A Compensation of employees	23	31	36	44	51	58	71	90	112	...	...	...
B Property and entrepreneurial income	92	156	236	295	236	307	410	373	421	...	...	...
By general government	5	20	63	94	128	147	154	163	205	...	...	...
By corporate and quasi-corporate enterprises	57	98	125	150	74	112	196	197	198	...	...	...
By other	31	38	48	52	34	48	59	13	19	...	...	...
3 Current transfers to the rest of the world	71	86	97	116	127	136	137	145	185	...	...	...
4 Surplus of the nation on current transactions	-157	-439	-533	-454	-102	-159	15	82	211	...	...	...
Payments to the Rest of the World and Surplus of the Nation on Current Transactions	1175	1276	1286	1543	1984	2358	2834	3112	3764	...	...	...
Receipts From The Rest of the World												
1 Exports of goods and services	1043	1118	1141	1345	1708	2101	2559	2789	3439	...	...	...
A Exports of merchandise f.o.b.	929	1001	998	1174	1484	1811	2206	2416	...	...	...	...
B Other	114	117	143	164	226	290	353	373	...	...	...	...
2 Factor income from rest of the world	68	72	78	91	92	81	96	108	56	...	...	...
A Compensation of employees	2	4	14	16	19	15	27	50	18	...	...	...
B Property and entrepreneurial income	66	68	64	75	73	66	69	58	38	...	...	...
By general government	-	8	14	12	12	12	13	18	23	...	...	...
By corporate and quasi-corporate enterprises	50	44	37	43	42	43	43	34	6	...	...	...
By other	15	17	13	20	19	12	13	6	9	...	...	...
3 Current transfers from rest of the world	64	86	67	107	184	175	179	215	274	...	...	...
Receipts from the Rest of the World on Current Transactions	1175	1276	1286	1543	1984	2358	2834	3112	3764	...	...	...

1.8 Capital Transactions of The Nation, Summary

Million Zimbabwean dollars

	1980	1981	1982	1983	1984	1985	1986	1987	1988	1989	1990	1991
Finance of Gross Capital Formation												
Gross saving	492	587	568	549	1110	1286	1556	1620	2700	...	...	...
1 Consumption of fixed capital	...	...	...	...	...	...	...	...	...	...	...	...
2 Net saving	492	587	568	549	1110	1286	1556	1620	2700	...	...	...
A General government	-232	-44	-119	79	-209	-338	-312	...	...	...	...	...
B Corporate and quasi-corporate enterprises	47	67	64	148	185	35	99	...	...	...	...	...
C Other	677	564	623	322	1134	1590	1769	...	...	...	...	...
Less: Surplus of the nation on current transactions	-157	-439	-533	-455	-102	-159	15	82	211	...	...	...
Finance of Gross Capital Formation	648	1026	1102	1002	1213	1445	1541	1539	2490	...	...	...
Gross Capital Formation												
Increase in stocks	120	196	63	-236	28	312	229	-134	459	...	...	...
Gross fixed capital formation	528	830	1039	1238	1185	1133	1312	1673	2031	...	...	...
1 General government	117	155	239	304	329	349	274	476	613	...	...	...
2 Corporate and quasi-corporate enterprises	411	675	800	933	856	784	1038	1197	1418	...	...	...
A Public	45	82	277	430	299	319	328	279	348	...	...	...
B Private	366	593	523	503	557	465	710	917	1070	...	...	...
3 Other	...	...	...	...	...	...	...	...	...	...	...	...
Gross Capital Formation	648	1026	1102	1002	1213	1445	1541	1539	2490	...	...	...

Zimbabwe

1.9 Gross Domestic Product by Institutional Sectors of Origin

Million Zimbabwean dollars

	1980	1981	1982	1983	1984	1985	1986	1987	1988	1989	1990	1991
	Domestic Factor Incomes Originating											
1 General government	563	692	852	984	1115	1263	1283	1519	2446	...	...	...
2 Corporate and quasi-corporate enterprises	2020	2551	2963	3620	3670	3509	4434	4970	6024	...	...	...
A Non-financial	1969	2487	2881	3517	3599	3371	4281	4759	5789	...	...	...
Public	198	234	298	605	657	459	611	902	918	...	...	...
Private	1771	2253	2583	2912	2942	2912	3670	3857	4871	...	...	...
B Financial	51	64	82	103	71	138	153	211	235	...	...	...
Public	45	41	41	53	-7	93	91	140	86	...	...	...
Private	6	23	41	50	78	45	62	71	149	...	...	...
3 Households and private unincorporated enterprises	551	743	757	732	765	1583	1494	1393	1608	...	...	...
A Owner-occupied housing	18	24	25	26	25	30	30	43	98	...	...	...
B Subsistence production	...	...	...	...	...	...	...	...	...	...	...	...
C Other	533	719	732	706	740	1553	1464	1350	1510	...	...	...
4 Non-profit institutions serving households	88	63	85	96	100	150	197	137	106	...	...	...
Subtotal: Domestic Factor Incomes a	3224	4049	4657	5432	5649	6505	7408	8019	10186	...	...	...
Indirect taxes, net	217	384	540	874	755	792	881	920	1257	...	...	...
A Indirect taxes	317	504	709	956	1051	1148	1251	1346	1645	...	...	...
B Less: Subsidies	100	120	169	82	296	356	370	426	388	...	...	...
Consumption of fixed capital	...	...	...	...	...	...	...	...	...	...	...	...
Gross Domestic Product	3441	4433	5197	6306	6404	7297	8289	8939	11441	...	...	...

a) Item 'Domestic factor incomes' includes consumption of fixed capital.

1.10 Gross Domestic Product by Kind of Activity, in Current Prices

Million Zimbabwean dollars

	1980	1981	1982	1983	1984	1985	1986	1987	1988	1989	1990	1991
1 Agriculture, hunting, forestry and fishing	451	640	669	544	748	1314	1179	1123	1596	1753	2391	3709
2 Mining and quarrying	285	252	217	393	320	335	446	335	681	827	923	1175
3 Manufacturing	802	1016	1121	1441	1475	1488	1832	2089	2518	3162	3691	4849
4 Electricity, gas and water a	70	78	73	195	142	144	229	276	307	391	417	567
5 Construction	91	138	190	258	205	154	168	225	243	284	323	368
6 Wholesale and retail trade, restaurants and hotels	451	603	741	783	742	777	971	1001	1152	1258	1569	1898
7 Transport, storage and communication	211	306	365	403	434	431	582	671	787	930	1067	1243
8 Finance, insurance, real estate and business services b	202	240	283	334	342	411	441	570	736	863	977	1133
9 Community, social and personal services b	478	588	777	856	965	1178	1275	1399	1652	1878	2423	3197
Total, Industries	3041	3861	4436	5207	5373	6234	7123	7689	9672	11346	13781	18139
Producers of Government Services	291	309	367	398	444	476	518	614	810	895	1057	1230
Other Producers	...	...	...	...	...	...	...	...	...	...	...	...
Subtotal c	3332	4170	4803	5605	5817	6710	7641	8303	10482	12241	14838	19369
Less: Imputed bank service charge	108	121	146	173	168	205	233	284	299	338	344	366
Plus: Import duties	...	...	...	...	...	...	...	...	...	...	...	...
Plus: Value added tax	...	...	...	...	...	...	...	...	...	...	...	...
Plus: Other adjustments d	217	384	540	874	755	792	881	920	1257	1680	1972	2231
Equals: Gross Domestic Product	3441	4433	5197	6306	6404	7295	8289	8939	11441	13583	16466	21234

a) Item 'Electricity, gas and water' excludes gas.
b) Business services are included in item 'Community, social and personal services'.
c) Gross domestic product in factor values.
d) Item 'Other adjustments' refers to indirect taxes net of subsidies.

1.11 Gross Domestic Product by Kind of Activity, in Constant Prices

Million Zimbabwean dollars

	1980	1981	1982	1983	1984	1985	1986	1987	1988	1989	1990	1991
	At constant prices of:1980											
1 Agriculture, hunting, forestry and fishing	451	515	478	403	496	614	576	472	592	587	548	565
2 Mining and quarrying	285	278	284	280	291	288	293	300	295	307	310	327
3 Manufacturing	802	881	877	852	809	902	933	949	996	1055	1119	1147
4 Electricity, gas and water a	70	70	63	68	70	79	94	123	127	150	146	143
5 Construction	91	105	101	93	86	64	67	62	61	63	57	48

1.11 Gross Domestic Product by Kind of Activity, in Constant Prices
(Continued)

Million Zimbabwean dollars

	1980	1981	1982	1983	1984	1985	1986	1987	1988	1989	1990	1991
					At constant prices of:1980							
6 Wholesale and retail trade, restaurants and hotels	451	456	451	392	366	386	418	428	451	483	512	522
7 Transport, storage and communication	211	221	226	224	226	237	244	234	248	254	260	266
8 Finance, insurance, real estate and business services b	202	217	251	247	233	231	226	245	257	278	283	290
9 Community, social and personal services b	478	561	637	674	703	750	782	795	829	855	870	925
Total, Industries	3041	3304	3368	3233	3280	3551	3633	3608	3856	4032	4105	4233
Producers of Government Services	291	339	333	338	364	372	370	386	409	423	425	442
Other Producers	...	...	...	...	...	...	...	...	...	...	...	...
Subtotal c	3332	3643	3701	3571	3644	3923	4003	3994	4265	4455	4530	4675
Less: Imputed bank service charge	108	106	112	110	105	120	122	133	122	118	105	88
Plus: Import duties	...	...	...	...	...	...	...	...	...	...	...	...
Plus: Value added tax	...	...	...	...	...	...	...	...	...	...	...	...
Plus: Other adjustments d	217	336	385	576	421	431	466	432	552	664	674	611
Equals: Gross Domestic Product	3441	3873	3974	4037	3960	4235	4347	4293	4695	5001	5100	5198

a) Item 'Electricity, gas and water' excludes gas.
b) Business services are included in item 'Community, social and personal services'.
c) Gross domestic product in factor values.
d) Item 'Other adjustments' refers to indirect taxes net of subsidies.

1.12 Relations Among National Accounting Aggregates

Million Zimbabwean dollars

	1980	1981	1982	1983	1984	1985	1986	1987	1988	1989	1990	1991
Gross Domestic Product	3441	4433	5197	6306	6404	7295	8289	8939	11441	...	...	...
Plus: Net factor income from the rest of the world	-47	-115	-194	-248	-195	-284	-384	-355	-478	...	...	...
Factor income from the rest of the world	68	72	78	91	92	81	96	108	55	...	...	...
Less: Factor income to the rest of the world	115	187	272	339	287	365	480	463	533	...	...	...
Equals: Gross National Product	3394	4318	5003	6058	6209	7011	7905	8584	10963	...	...	...
Less: Consumption of fixed capital	...	...	...	...	...	...	...	...	...	...	...	...
Equals: National Income a	3394	4318	5003	6058	6209	7011	7905	8584	10963	...	...	...
Plus: Net current transfers from the rest of the world	-6	1	-30	-9	57	39	42	70	89	...	...	...
Current transfers from the rest of the world	64	87	67	107	184	175	179	215	274	...	...	...
Less: Current transfers to the rest of the world	70	86	97	116	127	136	137	145	185	...	...	...
Equals: National Disposable Income b	3388	4319	4973	6049	6266	7050	7947	8654	11052	...	...	...
Less: Final consumption	2896	3732	4405	5500	5156	5764	6391	7034	8352	...	...	...
Equals: Net Saving c	492	587	568	549	1110	1286	1556	1620	2700	...	...	...
Less: Surplus of the nation on current transactions	-157	-439	-533	-454	-102	-159	15	81	210	...	...	...
Equals: Net Capital Formation d	648	1026	1102	1002	1213	1445	1541	1539	2490	...	...	...

a) Item 'National income' includes consumption of fixed capital.
b) Item 'National disposable income' includes consumption of fixed capital.
c) Item 'Net saving' includes consumption of fixed capital.
d) Item 'Net capital formation' includes consumption of fixed capital.

2.1 Government Final Consumption Expenditure by Function, in Current Prices

Million Zimbabwean dollars

	1980	1981	1982	1983	1984	1985	1986	1987	1988	1989	1990	1991
1 General public services										345	...	...
2 Defence	487	439	510	541	653	745	870	1110	1221	872	...	...
3 Public order and safety										330	...	...
4 Education	99	144	260	300	363	447	554	605	666	1370	...	...
5 Health	54	70	95	106	128	164	176	196	216	449	...	...
6 Social security and welfare	...	...	...	...	...	...	...	...	...	146	...	...
7 Housing and community amenities	26	35	34	53	46	53	67	64	70	67	...	...
8 Recreational, cultural and religious affairs	13	18	32	38	37	32	35	41	45	76	...	...
9 Economic services	53	75	101	93	92	148	160	176	194	784	...	...

Zimbabwe

2.1 Government Final Consumption Expenditure by Function, in Current Prices
(Continued)

Million Zimbabwean dollars

	1980	1981	1982	1983	1984	1985	1986	1987	1988	1989	1990	1991
A Fuel and energy	...	...	...	...	...	...	...	...	...	5	...	...
B Agriculture, forestry, fishing and hunting	...	...	...	...	...	...	...	...	...	58	...	...
C Mining, manufacturing and construction, except fuel and energy	...	...	...	...	...	...	...	...	...	77	...	...
D Transportation and communication	...	...	...	...	...	...	...	...	...	404	...	...
E Other economic affairs	...	...	...	...	...	...	...	...	...	240	...	...
10 Other functions	-69	-31	-25	7	15	-30	16	18	20	934	...	...
Total Government Final Consumption Expenditure [a]	663	750	1007	1138	1334	1559	1878	2210	2431	5373	...	...

a) Estimates of general government cover central & local government.

2.3 Total Government Outlays by Function and Type

Million Zimbabwean dollars

	Final Consumption Expenditures			Subsidies	Other Current Transfers & Property Income	Total Current Disbursements	Gross Capital Formation	Other Capital Outlays	Total Outlays
	Total	Compensation of Employees	Other						
1980									
1 General public services		...	...	...					
2 Defence	487	...	...	...	7	494	24	2	520
3 Public order and safety		...	...	...					
4 Education	99	...	...	...	103	202	6	-	208
5 Health	54	...	...	...	9	63	7	-	70
6 Social security and welfare	...	...	...	...	...	...	...	...	...
7 Housing and community amenities	26	...	...	...	-	26	35	-	61
8 Recreation, culture and religion	13	...	...	...	89	102	1	-	103
9 Economic services	53	...	...	100	13	166	37	...	203
10 Other functions	-69	...	...	...	40	-29	10	2	-17
Total [ab]	663	518	145	100	261	1025	120	4	1148
1981									
1 General public services		...	...	...					
2 Defence	439	...	...	...	4	443	30	5	478
3 Public order and safety		...	...	...					
4 Education	144	...	...	...	156	300	10	-	310
5 Health	70	...	...	...	23	93	7	-	100
6 Social security and welfare	...	...	...	...	...	...	...	...	...
7 Housing and community amenities	35	...	...	...	-	35	39	-	74
8 Recreation, culture and religion	18	...	...	...	92	110	1	-	111
9 Economic services	75	...	...	120	17	212	56	...	268
10 Other functions	-31	...	...	...	5	-26	12	2	-12
Total [ab]	750	626	124	120	297	1167	155	7	1329
1982									
1 General public services		...	...	...					
2 Defence	510	...	...	...	2	512	37	14	563
3 Public order and safety		...	...	...					
4 Education	260	...	...	...	263	523	22	-	545
5 Health	95	...	...	...	32	127	6	1	134
6 Social security and welfare	...	...	...	...	...	...	...	...	...
7 Housing and community amenities	34	...	...	...	-	34	45	-	79
8 Recreation, culture and religion	32	...	...	...	136	168	10	-	178
9 Economic services	101	...	...	169	26	296	140	...	436
10 Other functions	-25	...	...	...	10	-15	10	5	-
Total [ab]	1007	829	178	169	469	1645	270	20	1935

2.3 Total Government Outlays by Function and Type
(Continued)

Million Zimbabwean dollars

	Final Consumption Expenditures			Subsidies	Other Current Transfers & Property Income	Total Current Disbursements	Gross Capital Formation	Other Capital Outlays	Total Outlays
	Total	Compensation of Employees	Other						
1983									
1 General public services		...	...	...					
2 Defence	541	...	...	...	3	544	51	5	600
3 Public order and safety		...	...	...					
4 Education	300	...	...	...	279	579	33	-	612
5 Health	106	...	...	...	29	135	8	5	148
6 Social security and welfare	...	...	...	...	...	...	...	...	...
7 Housing and community amenities	53	...	...	...	2	55	42	-	97
8 Recreation, culture and religion	38	...	...	...	216	254	7	-	261
9 Economic services	93	...	...	82	40	215	153	1	369
10 Other functions	7	...	...	...	9	16	7	6	29
Total ab	1138	925	213	82	578	1798	301	17	2116
1984									
1 General public services		...	...	...					
2 Defence	653	...	...	...	12	665	61	12	738
3 Public order and safety		...	...	...					
4 Education	363	...	...	...	324	687	33	-	720
5 Health	128	...	...	...	39	167	12	3	182
6 Social security and welfare	...	...	...	...	...	...	...	...	...
7 Housing and community amenities	46	...	...	...	-	46	43	-	89
8 Recreation, culture and religion	37	...	...	...	166	203	8	-	211
9 Economic services	92	...	...	296	51	439	168	-	607
10 Other functions	15	...	...	...	8	23	2	4	29
Total ab	1334	1064	270	296	600	2230	327	19	2576
1985									
1 General public services		...	...	...					
2 Defence	745	...	...	...	6	751	63	-13	801
3 Public order and safety		...	...	...					
4 Education	447	...	...	...	410	857	35	-	892
5 Health	164	...	...	...	32	196	19	-2	213
6 Social security and welfare	...	...	...	...	...	...	...	...	...
7 Housing and community amenities	53	...	...	...	-	53	33	-	86
8 Recreation, culture and religion	32	...	...	...	109	141	5	-	146
9 Economic services	148	...	...	356	115	619	175	-	794
10 Other functions	-30	...	...	...	12	-18	2	6	-10
Total ab	1559	1190	369	356	684	2599	332	-9	2922
1986									
1 General public services		...	...	...					
2 Defence	870	...	...	...	12	882	71	3	956
3 Public order and safety		...	...	...					
4 Education	554				483	1037	32	-	1069
5 Health	176				61	237	20	-2	255
6 Social security and welfare	...	...	...	...	...	...	...	...	...
7 Housing and community amenities	67				-	67	46	2	115
8 Recreation, culture and religion	35				117	152	3	-	155
9 Economic services	160			370	129	659	199	-	858
10 Other functions	16				17	33	2	6	41
Total ab	1878	1342	536	370	819	3067	373	9	3449

Zimbabwe

2.3 Total Government Outlays by Function and Type
(Continued)

	Final Consumption Expenditures			Subsidies	Other Current Transfers & Property Income	Total Current Disbursements	Gross Capital Formation	Other Capital Outlays	Total Outlays
	Total	Compensation of Employees	Other						
1987									
1 General public services		...	...	...					
2 Defence	1110	...	...	...	74	1184	86	3	1273
3 Public order and safety		...	...	...					
4 Education	605	...	...	...	225	830	49	-	879
5 Health	196	...	...	...	105	300	26	-	326
6 Social security and welfare	...	...	...	...	...	...	...	...	...
7 Housing and community amenities	64	...	...	...	32	96	41	-	137
8 Recreation, culture and religion	41	...	...	...	28	69	9	2	80
9 Economic services	176	...	...	426	150	752	199	48	999
10 Other functions	18	...	...	...	21	39	3	-	42
Total ab	2210	1905	305	426	634	3270	413	53	3736
1988									
1 General public services		...	...	...					
2 Defence	1221	...	...	...	81	1302	95	3	1400
3 Public order and safety		...	...	...					
4 Education	666	...	...	...	248	913	54	-	967
5 Health	216	...	...	...	114	330	29	-	359
6 Social security and welfare	...	...	...	...	...	...	...	...	...
7 Housing and community amenities	70	...	...	...	35	106	45	-	151
8 Recreation, culture and religion	45	...	...	...	31	76	10	2	88
9 Economic services	194	...	...	469	165	827	219	53	1099
10 Other functions	20	...	...	...	23	43	3	-	46
Total ab	2431	2091	340	469	697	3597	454	58	4110

a) Estimates of general government cover central & local government.
b) Property income and net of inter-governmental transfers in column 5 are included in the total and not in the breakdowns. Also included in the same total are some unclassified estimates.

2.5 Private Final Consumption Expenditure by Type and Purpose, in Current Prices

	1980	1981	1982	1983	1984	1985	1986	1987	1988	1989	1990	1991
Final Consumption Expenditure of Resident Households												
1 Food, beverages and tobacco	795	956	1069	1347	1089	1346	1437	1301	...	...	...	...
A Food	457	512	520	534	467	629	590	580	...	...	...	...
B Non-alcoholic beverages	105	133	202	349	266	348	450	303	...	...	...	...
C Alcoholic beverages	233	311	347	464	356	369	397	418	...	...	...	...
D Tobacco									...	...	...	...
2 Clothing and footwear	289	414	462	518	406	444	478	446	...	...	...	...
3 Gross rent, fuel and power	307	423	475	758	761	657	701	664	...	...	...	...
A Fuel and power	127	190	249	466	468	390	426	383	...	...	...	...
B Other	180	233	226	292	293	267	275	281	...	...	...	...
4 Furniture, furnishings and household equipment and operation	280	371	363	416	386	298	525	556	...	...	...	...
A Household operation	219	272	294	325	307	235	427	445	...	...	...	...
B Other	61	99	69	91	79	63	98	111	...	...	...	...
5 Medical care and health expenses	93	118	130	166	147	163	237	307	...	...	...	...
6 Transport and communication a	55	96	112	133	76	75	57	46	...	...	...	...
7 Recreational, entertainment, education and cultural services	92	127	155	228	220	253	263	284	...	...	...	...
A Education	53	79	104	157	159	201	236	259	...	...	...	...
B Other	39	48	51	71	61	52	27	25	...	...	...	...
8 Miscellaneous goods and services a	331	507	546	726	658	618	732	720	...	...	...	...
A Personal care	...	...	...	...	...	...	...	...	...	...	...	...
B Expenditures in restaurants, cafes and hotels	149	263	293	398	365	344	401	377	...	...	...	...
C Other	182	244	253	328	293	274	331	343	...	...	...	...
Total Final Consumption Expenditure in the Domestic Market by Households, of which	2242	3009	3310	4289	3743	3851	4431	4324	...	...	...	...

2.5 Private Final Consumption Expenditure by Type and Purpose, in Current Prices
(Continued)

Million Zimbabwean dollars

	1980	1981	1982	1983	1984	1985	1986	1987	1988	1989	1990	1991
A Durable goods	270	394	389	461	375	275	451	482	...	...	...	...
B Semi-durable goods	...	...	...	...	...	...	...	...	...	...	...	...
C Non-durable goods	1364	1739	1975	2572	2170	2392	2640	2420	...	...	...	...
D Services	609	877	946	1258	1198	1184	1340	1421	...	...	...	...
Plus: Direct purchases abroad by resident households	...	...	...	...	...	...	...	...				
Less: Direct purchases in the domestic market by non-resident households	58	75	-31	-12	-3	9	-33	4	...	...	...	...
Equals: Final Consumption Expenditure of Resident Households	2184	2934	3341	4302	3745	3842	4464	4324	...	...	...	...

Final Consumption Expenditure of Private Non-profit Institutions Serving Households

	1980	1981	1982	1983	1984	1985	1986	1987	1988	1989	1990	1991
1 Research and science	...	...	...	...					...	...	...	...
2 Education	17	17	17	16	...	...	...	...	...	...	...	...
3 Medical and other health services	6	6	3	3	...	...	...	...	...	...	...	...
4 Welfare services	...	...	...	...	...	...	...	...	...	...	...	...
5 Recreational and related cultural services	...	...	...	...	...	...	...	...	...	...		
6 Religious organisations	...	...	...	...	...	...	...	...	...	...		
7 Professional and labour organisations serving households	...	...	...	...	...	...	...	...	...	...		...
8 Miscellaneous	12	12	17	20								
Equals: Final Consumption Expenditure of Private Non-profit Organisations Serving Households	35	35	37	39	46	52	57	63	...	...	...	...
Private Final Consumption Expenditure b	2219	2969	3378	4341	3791	3894	4521	4387	...	...	...	...

a) Item 'Transport and communication' includes personal transport equipment only. Communication is included in item 'Miscellaneous good and services'. b) Data for this table have not been revised, therefore, data for some years are not comparable with those of other tables.

2.6 Private Final Consumption Expenditure by Type and Purpose, in Constant Prices

Million Zimbabwean dollars

	1980	1981	1982	1983	1984	1985	1986	1987	1988	1989	1990	1991
					At constant prices of:1980							
				Final Consumption Expenditure of Resident Households								
1 Food, beverages and tobacco	795	816	815	869	610	695	664	512	...	...	...	...
A Food	457	431	395	334	255	312	253	217	...	...	...	...
B Non-alcoholic beverages	105	105	139	203	131	144	270	156	...	...	...	...
C Alcoholic beverages	233	280	281	332	224	239	141	139	...	...	...	...
D Tobacco									...	...	...	...
2 Clothing and footwear	289	364	358	355	244	214	225	161	...	...	...	...
3 Gross rent, fuel and power	307	367	356	543	398	325	304	280	...	...	...	...
A Fuel and power	127	155	193	296	231	166	140	122	...	...	...	...
B Other	180	212	163	247	167	159	164	158	...	...	...	...
4 Furniture, furnishings and household equipment and operation	280	322	271	287	236	198	288	265	...	...	...	...
A Household operation	219	236	218	222	192	163	239	219	...	...	...	...
B Other	61	86	53	65	44	35	49	46	...	...	...	...
5 Medical care and health expenses	93	109	103	122	100	103	125	142	...	...	...	...
6 Transport and communication a	55	93	104	91	42	41	21	14	...	...	...	...
7 Recreational, entertainment, education and cultural services	92	133	140	194	170	174	162	157	...	...	...	...
A Education	53	87	96	143	129	139	147	145	...	...	...	...
B Other	39	46	44	51	41	35	15	12	...	...	...	...
8 Miscellaneous goods and services a	331	430	405	501	424	342	362	327	...	...	...	...
A Personal care	...	...	...	...	...	...	...	...	...	...	...	...
B Expenditures in restaurants, cafes and hotels	149	215	208	255	220	168	196	171	...	...	...	...
C Other	182	215	197	246	204	174	166	156	...	...	...	...
Total Final Consumption Expenditure in the Domestic Market by Households, of which	2242	2633	2553	2961	2224	2093	2150	1858	...	...	...	...
A Durable goods	270	360	332	339	242	180	249	228	...	...	...	...
B Semi-durable goods	...	...	...	...	...	...	...	...	...	...	...	...
C Non-durable goods	1364	1501	1526	1702	1234	1229	1169	913	...	...	...	...

Zimbabwe

2.6 Private Final Consumption Expenditure by Type and Purpose, in Constant Prices
(Continued)

Million Zimbabwean dollars

	1980	1981	1982	1983	1984	1985	1986	1987	1988	1989	1990	1991
				At constant prices of:1980								
D Services	609	772	695	920	747	684	732	716	...	...	...	...
Plus: Direct purchases abroad by resident households	...	...	...	...	...	...	...	...	...	...	...	...
Less: Direct purchases in the domestic market by non-resident households	58	63	22	7	-2	4	-14	...	...	...	...	...
Equals: Final Consumption Expenditure of Resident Households	2184	2570	2531	2954	2225	2089	2164	1858	...	...	...	...
Final Consumption Expenditure of Private Non-profit Institutions Serving Households												
Equals: Final Consumption Expenditure of Private Non-profit Organisations Serving Households	35	31	27	28	29	31	29	30	...	...	...	...
Private Final Consumption Expenditure b	2219	2601	2558	2982	2254	2120	2193	1888	...	...	...	...

a) Item 'Transport and communication' includes personal transport equipment only. Communication is included in item 'Miscellaneous good and services'. b) Data for this table have not been revised, therefore, data for some years are not comparable with those of other tables.

2.7 Gross Capital Formation by Type of Good and Owner, in Current Prices

Million Zimbabwean dollars

	1980				1981				1982			
	TOTAL	Total Private	Public Enterprises	General Government	TOTAL	Total Private	Public Enterprises	General Government	TOTAL	Total Private	Public Enterprises	General Government
Increase in stocks, total	120	...	...	...	196	...	...	...	63	...	...	...
1 Goods producing industries	164	...	...	...	377	...	...	...	378	...	...	...
A Materials and supplies	63	...	...	...	96	...	...	...	48	...	...	...
B Work in progress	...	...	...	...		...	...	...		...	...	...
C Livestock, except breeding stocks, dairy cattle, etc.	67	...	...	...	199	...	...	...	256	...	...	...
D Finished goods	34	...	...	...	82	...	...	...	74	...	...	...
2 Wholesale and retail trade	104	...	...	...	262	...	...	...	69	...	...	...
3 Other, except government stocks	9	...		...	15	...	...	...	43	...	...	...
4 Government stocks		...	...	...		...	...	...		...	...	...
Statistical discrepancy a	-157	...	...	...	-458	...	...	...	-427	...	...	...
Gross Fixed Capital Formation, Total	528	366	45	117	830	593	82	155	1039	523	277	239
1 Residential buildings	34	6	2	26	53	17	2	34	57	11	-	46
2 Non-residential buildings	107	90	1	16	183	158	2	23	203	139	14	50
3 Other construction	109	37	19	53	193	92	38	63	398	59	244	96
4 Land improvement and plantation and orchard development	...	...	...	...	...	...	...	...	...	...	...	...
5 Producers' durable goods	278	233	23	22	401	326	40	35	381	314	19	47
A Transport equipment	84	75	2	7	106	90	4	12	136	113	6	17
B Machinery and equipment	194	158	21	15	295	236	36	23	245	201	13	30
6 Breeding stock, dairy cattle, etc.	...	...	...	...	...	...	...	...	...	...	...	...
Total Gross Capital Formation	648	...	...	...	1026	...	...	...	1102	...	...	...

	1983				1984				1985			
	TOTAL	Total Private	Public Enterprises	General Government	TOTAL	Total Private	Public Enterprises	General Government	TOTAL	Total Private	Public Enterprises	General Government
Increase in stocks, total	-236	...	...	...	28	...	...	...	312	...	...	...
1 Goods producing industries	609	...	...	...	122	...	...	...	527	...	...	...
A Materials and supplies	76	...	...	...	293	...	...	...	302	...	...	...
B Work in progress	...	...	...	...	...	...	...	...	...	...	...	...
C Livestock, except breeding stocks, dairy cattle, etc.	455	...	...	...	-96	...	...	...	150	...	...	...
D Finished goods	78	...	...	...	-75	...	...	...	75	...	...	...
2 Wholesale and retail trade	-6	...	...	...	49	...	...	...	177	...	...	...
3 Other, except government stocks	33	...	...	...	47	...	...	...	16	...	...	...
4 Government stocks		...	...	...		...	...	...		...	...	...
Statistical discrepancy a	-872	...	...	...	-191	...	...	...	-409	...	...	...
Gross Fixed Capital Formation, Total	1238	503	430	304	1185	556	299	329	1133	465	319	349
1 Residential buildings	60	15	5	40	58	14	2	42	67	19	2	46
2 Non-residential buildings	240	126	34	80	241	143	29	69	224	130	17	77

2.7 Gross Capital Formation by Type of Good and Owner, in Current Prices
(Continued)

Million Zimbabwean dollars

	1983				1984				1985			
	TOTAL	Total Private	Public Enterprises	General Government	TOTAL	Total Private	Public Enterprises	General Government	TOTAL	Total Private	Public Enterprises	General Government
3 Other construction	395	47	222	126	98	40	-109	167	216	23	23	170
4 Land improvement and plantation and orchard development	...	...	...	...	...	...	...	...	...	...	...	...
5 Producers' durable goods	542	315	169	58	788	360	377	51	626	293	277	56
A Transport equipment	133	103	14	17	138	120	11	7	114	98	9	7
B Machinery and equipment	411	212	155	41	650	240	366	44	512	195	268	49
6 Breeding stock, dairy cattle, etc.	...	...	...	...	...	...	...	...	...	...	...	...
Total Gross Capital Formation	1002	...	...	...	1213	...	...	...	1445	...	...	...

	1986				1987				1988			
	TOTAL	Total Private	Public Enterprises	General Government	TOTAL	Total Private	Public Enterprises	General Government	TOTAL	Total Private	Public Enterprises	General Government
Increase in stocks, total	229	...	...	...	-134	...	...	...	459	...	...	...
1 Goods producing industries	600	...	...	...	-346	...	...	...	682	...	...	...
A Materials and supplies	301	...	...	...	-10	...	...	...	371	...	...	...
B Work in progress	...	...	...	...	...	...	...	...	...	...	...	...
C Livestock, except breeding stocks, dairy cattle, etc.	245	...	...	...	-418	...	...	...	157	...	...	...
D Finished goods	54	...	...	...	82	...	...	...	154	...	...	...
2 Wholesale and retail trade	247	...	...	...	14	...	...	...	273	...	...	...
3 Other, except government stocks	30	...	...	...	33	...	...	...	47	...	...	...
4 Government stocks		...	...	...		...	...	...		...	...	...
Statistical discrepancy a	-649	...	...	...	165	...	...	...	-543	...	...	...
Gross Fixed Capital Formation, Total	1312	710	328	274	1673	917	279	476	2031	1070	348	613
1 Residential buildings	52	15	1	36	85	38	3	45	80	41	10	29
2 Non-residential buildings	269	199	14	56	391	226	59	106	535	215	91	229
3 Other construction	225	46	38	141	341	87	71	180	447	79	85	284
4 Land improvement and plantation and orchard development	...	...	...	...	...	...	...	...	...	...	...	...
5 Producers' durable goods	766	450	275	41	857	566	146	145	968	735	162	71
A Transport equipment	175	155	13	7	235	191	29	15	292	243	38	11
B Machinery and equipment	591	295	262	34	622	375	117	130	676	492	124	60
6 Breeding stock, dairy cattle, etc.	...	...	...	...	...	...	...	...	...	...	...	...
Total Gross Capital Formation	1541	...	...	...	1539	...	...	...	2490	...	...	...

a) Item 'Statistical discrepancy' refers to revaluation adjustment.

2.8 Gross Capital Formation by Type of Good and Owner, in Constant Prices

Million Zimbabwean dollars

	1980				1981				1982			
	TOTAL	Total Private	Public Enterprises	General Government	TOTAL	Total Private	Public Enterprises	General Government	TOTAL	Total Private	Public Enterprises	General Government
At constant prices of:1980												
Increase in stocks, total	118	...	...	...	228	...	...	...	28	...	...	...
1 Goods producing industries	45	...	...	...	76	...	...	...	34	...	...	...
A Materials and supplies	40	...	...	...	38	...	...	...	-3	...	...	...
B Work in progress	...	...	...	...	...	...	...	...	...	...	...	...
C Livestock, except breeding stocks, dairy cattle, etc.	-7	...	...	...	8	...	...	...	16	...	...	...
D Finished goods	11	...	...	...	30	...	...	...	21	...	...	...
2 Wholesale and retail trade	72	...	...	...	149	...	...	...	-32	...	...	...
3 Other, except government stocks	3	...	...	...	3	...	...	...	25	...	...	...
4 Government stocks		...	...	...		...	...	...		...	...	...
Gross Fixed Capital Formation, Total	528	...	...	...	722	...	...	...	788	...	...	...
1 Residential buildings	34	...	...	...	43	...	...	...	40	...	...	...
2 Non-residential buildings	107	...	...	...	147	...	...	...	141	...	...	...

Zimbabwe

2.8 Gross Capital Formation by Type of Good and Owner, in Constant Prices
(Continued)

Million Zimbabwean dollars

	1980				1981				1982			
	TOTAL	Total Private	Public Enterprises	General Government	TOTAL	Total Private	Public Enterprises	General Government	TOTAL	Total Private	Public Enterprises	General Government
	At constant prices of:1980											
3 Other construction	109	...	...	...	160	...	...	...	279	...	...	...
4 Land improvement and plantation and orchard development	...	...	...	...	...	...	...	...	...	...	...	...
5 Producers' durable goods	278	...	...	...	372	...	...	...	328	...	...	...
A Transport equipment	84	...	...	...	105	...	...	...	126	...	...	...
B Machinery and equipment	194	...	...	...	267	...	...	...	202	...	...	...
6 Breeding stock, dairy cattle, etc.	...	...	...	...	...	...	...	...	...	...	...	...
Total Gross Capital Formation	646	...	...	...	950	...	...	...	816	...	...	...

	1983				1984				1985			
	TOTAL	Total Private	Public Enterprises	General Government	TOTAL	Total Private	Public Enterprises	General Government	TOTAL	Total Private	Public Enterprises	General Government
	At constant prices of:1980											
Increase in stocks, total	-166	...	...	...	43	...	...	...	255	...	...	...
1 Goods producing industries	-25	...	...	...	49	...	...	...	211	...	...	...
A Materials and supplies	-5	...	...	...	130	...	...	...	181	...	...	...
B Work in progress	...	...	...	...	...	...	...	...	...	...	...	...
C Livestock, except breeding stocks, dairy cattle, etc.	-19	...	...	...	2	...	...	...	18	...	...	...
D Finished goods	-1	...	...	...	-83	...	...	...	12	...	...	...
2 Wholesale and retail trade	-149	...	...	...	-23	...	...	...	48	...	...	...
3 Other, except government stocks	8	...	...	...	16	...	...	...	-4	...	...	...
4 Government stocks		...	...	...		...	...	...		...	...	...
Gross Fixed Capital Formation, Total	765	...	...	...	618	...	...	...	505	...	...	...
1 Residential buildings	35	...	...	...	30	...	...	...	31	...	...	...
2 Non-residential buildings	143	...	...	...	128	...	...	...	104	...	...	...
3 Other construction	235	...	...	...	52	...	...	...	104	...	...	...
4 Land improvement and plantation and orchard development	...	...	...	...	...	...	...	...	...	...	...	...
5 Producers' durable goods	352	...	...	...	408	...	...	...	266	...	...	...
A Transport equipment	102	...	...	...	83	...	...	...	65	...	...	...
B Machinery and equipment	250	...	...	...	325	...	...	...	201	...	...	...
6 Breeding stock, dairy cattle, etc.	...	...	...	...	...	...	...	...	...	...	...	...
Total Gross Capital Formation	600	...	...	...	661	...	...	...	760	...	...	...

	1986				1987				1988			
	TOTAL	Total Private	Public Enterprises	General Government	TOTAL	Total Private	Public Enterprises	General Government	TOTAL	Total Private	Public Enterprises	General Government
	At constant prices of:1980											
Increase in stocks, total	170	...	...	...	-168	...	...	...	279	...	...	...
1 Goods producing industries	107	...	...	...	-127	...	...	...	196	...	...	...
A Materials and supplies	99	...	...	...	-174	...	...	...	169	...	...	...
B Work in progress	...	...	...	...	...	...	...	...	...	...	...	...
C Livestock, except breeding stocks, dairy cattle, etc.	1	...	...	...	39	...	...	...	-15	...	...	...
D Finished goods	7	...	...	...	8	...	...	...	42	...	...	...
2 Wholesale and retail trade	57	...	...	...	-48	...	...	...	73	...	...	...
3 Other, except government stocks	6	...	...	...	6	...	...	...	10	...	...	...
4 Government stocks		...	...	...		...	...	...		...	...	...
Gross Fixed Capital Formation, Total	518	...	...	...	601	...	...	...	686	...	...	...
1 Residential buildings	21	...	...	...	32	...	...	...	28	...	...	...
2 Non-residential buildings	110	...	...	...	145	...	...	...	187	...	...	...

2.8 Gross Capital Formation by Type of Good and Owner, in Constant Prices
(Continued)

Million Zimbabwean dollars

	1986				1987				1988			
	TOTAL	Total Private	Public Enterprises	General Government	TOTAL	Total Private	Public Enterprises	General Government	TOTAL	Total Private	Public Enterprises	General Government
	At constant prices of:1980											
3 Other construction	98	...	...	...	131	...	...	...	162	...	...	...
4 Land improvement and plantation and orchard development	...	...	...	...	...	...	...	...	...	...	...	...
5 Producers' durable goods	290	...	...	...	293	...	...	...	309	...	...	...
A Transport equipment	83	...	...	...	98	...	...	...	118	...	...	...
B Machinery and equipment	207	...	...	...	195	...	...	...	191	...	...	...
6 Breeding stock, dairy cattle, etc.	...	...	...	...	...	...	...	...	...	...	...	...
Total Gross Capital Formation	688	...	...	...	433	...	...	...	965	...	...	...

2.11 Gross Fixed Capital Formation by Kind of Activity of Owner, ISIC Divisions, in Current Prices

Million Zimbabwean dollars

	1980	1981	1982	1983	1984	1985	1986	1987	1988	1989	1990	1991
					All Producers							
1 Agriculture, hunting, forestry and fishing	53	91	116	96	90	74	142	174	164	...	...	...
2 Mining and quarrying	83	133	94	86	81	30	55	117	167	...	...	...
3 Manufacturing	123	201	168	192	169	171	294	398	501	...	...	...
4 Electricity, gas and water a	26	47	133	288	163	189	218	233	173	...	...	...
5 Construction	12	26	35	33	23	29	31	37	130	...	...	...
6 Wholesale and retail trade, restaurants and hotels	43	50	47	28	100	65	58	56	83	...	...	...
7 Transport, storage and communication	48	60	160	137	125	140	113	140	160	...	...	...
8 Finance, insurance, real estate and business services b	49	87	95	113	117	120	121	161	157	...	...	...
9 Community, social and personal services b	29	62	78	84	115	105	114	147	189	...	...	...
A Sanitary and similar services	...	...	...	...	...	...	...	...	...	...	...	...
B Social and related community services	15	25	38	42	59	72	92	102	133	...	...	...
Educational services	8	18	30	31	46	59	69	76	80	...	...	...
Medical, dental, other health and veterinary services	7	7	8	11	13	13	23	26	53	...	...	...
C Recreational and cultural services	14	37	40	42	56	33	22	45	56	...	...	...
D Personal and household services	...	...	...	...	...	...	...	...	...	...	...	...
Total Industries	466	757	926	1057	982	923	1146	1465	1724	...	...	...
Producers of Government Services	62	73	113	181	203	210	166	209	307	...	...	...
Private Non-Profit Institutions Serving Households	...	...	...	...	...	...	...	...	...	...	...	...
Total	528	830	1039	1238	1185	1133	1312	1673	2031	...	...	...

a) Item 'Electricity, gas and water' excludes gas.
b) Business services are included in item 'Community, social and personal services'.

2.12 Gross Fixed Capital Formation by Kind of Activity of Owner, ISIC Divisions, in Constant Prices

Million Zimbabwean dollars

	1980	1981	1982	1983	1984	1985	1986	1987	1988	1989	1990	1991
				At constant prices of:1980								
					All Producers							
1 Agriculture, hunting, forestry and fishing	53	82	93	64	50	36	61	67	59	...	...	...
2 Mining and quarrying	83	114	72	53	42	13	21	41	54	...	...	...
3 Manufacturing	123	179	135	121	88	74	112	139	157	...	...	...
4 Electricity, gas and water a	26	41	94	174	78	76	77	81	60	...	...	...

Zimbabwe

2.12 Gross Fixed Capital Formation by Kind of Activity of Owner, ISIC Divisions, in Constant Prices
(Continued)

Million Zimbabwean dollars

	1980	1981	1982	1983	1984	1985	1986	1987	1988	1989	1990	1991
						At constant prices of:1980						
5 Construction	12	24	29	21	12	13	12	14	45	...	...	...
6 Wholesale and retail trade, restaurants and hotels	43	44	37	18	53	30	23	20	27	...	...	...
7 Transport, storage and communication	48	54	123	88	66	30	47	58	56	...	...	...
8 Finance, insurance, real estate and business services b	49	71	67	67	62	55	49	60	55	...	...	...
9 Community, social and personal services b	29	52	57	51	60	47	46	54	64	...	...	...
A Sanitary and similar services	...	...	...	...	...	...	...	...	...	...	...	...
B Social and related community services	16	21	28	25	31	33	37	38	45	...	...	...
Educational services	8	15	22	19	24	27	28	28	27	...	...	...
Medical, dental, other health and veterinary services	8	6	6	6	7	6	9	10	18	...	...	...
C Recreational and cultural services	14	31	29	26	29	14	9	16	19	...	...	...
D Personal and household services	...	...	...	...	...	...	...	...	...	...	...	...
Total Industries	466	661	707	657	511	405	448	521	577	...	...	...
Producers of Government Services	62	61	81	108	107	100	70	80	109	...	...	...
Private Non-Profit Institutions Serving Households	...	...	...	...	...	...	...	...	...	...	...	...
Total	528	722	788	765	618	505	518	601	686	...	...	...

a) Item 'Electricity, gas and water' excludes gas.
b) Business services are included in item 'Community, social and personal services'.

4.1 Derivation of Value Added by Kind of Activity, in Current Prices

Million Zimbabwean dollars

	1980			1981			1982			1983		
	Gross Output	Intermediate Consumption	Value Added	Gross Output	Intermediate Consumption	Value Added	Gross Output	Intermediate Consumption	Value Added	Gross Output	Intermediate Consumption	Value Added
						All Producers						
1 Agriculture, hunting, forestry and fishing	769	319	451	1089	449	640	1178	509	669	1104	560	544
2 Mining and quarrying	468	183	285	485	233	252	440	223	217	629	235	393
3 Manufacturing	2204	1402	802	2837	1821	1016	3219	2098	1121	3429	1989	1441
A Manufacture of food, beverages and tobacco	638	461	177	785	573	211	1053	778	275	1185	758	427
B Textile, wearing apparel and leather industries	400	262	138	546	350	197	550	355	195	517	306	211
C Manufacture of wood and wood products, including furniture	74	42	32	111	63	48	110	64	46	98	51	47
D Manufacture of paper and paper products, printing and publishing	115	67	48	157	88	68	179	101	78	207	100	106
E Manufacture of chemicals and chemical petroleum, coal, rubber and plastic products	284	181	103	380	236	144	412	265	147	499	317	182
F Manufacture of non-metallic mineral products, except products of petroleum and coal	63	30	33	88	55	33	118	55	63	114	49	66
G Basic metal industries	289	169	120	263	168	95	230	155	75	325	182	143
H Manufacture of fabricated metal products, machinery and equipment	311	173	138	465	262	202	522	299	223	453	212	241
I Other manufacturing industries	30	18	13	42	25	17	45	26	19	30	14	16
4 Electricity, gas and water a	163	93	70	186	108	78	181	108	73	331	136	195
A Electricity, gas and steam	146	87	59	169	101	68	156	98	58	319	126	193
B Water works and supply	17	6	10	17	7	10	25	10	15	12	10	2

4.1 Derivation of Value Added by Kind of Activity, in Current Prices
(Continued)

Million Zimbabwean dollars

	1980			1981			1982			1983		
	Gross Output	Intermediate Consumption	Value Added	Gross Output	Intermediate Consumption	Value Added	Gross Output	Intermediate Consumption	Value Added	Gross Output	Intermediate Consumption	Value Added
5 Construction	255	168	91	341	203	138	463	273	190	536	278	258
6 Wholesale and retail trade, restaurants and hotels	893	438	451	1176	573	603	1262	521	741	1254	471	783
A Wholesale and retail trade	837	404	433	1112	537	575	1178	464	714	1152	412	740
B Restaurants and hotels	52	34	18	64	36	28	84	57	27	102	59	43
7 Transport, storage and communication	410	199	211	548	243	306	659	294	365	779	376	403
8 Finance, insurance, real estate and business services b ..	269	67	202	311	71	240	382	99	283	439	104	334
A Financial institutions	184	25	159	211	26	185	267	39	228	315	39	276
B Insurance												
C Real estate and business services	85	42	43	100	45	55	115	60	55	124	65	59
Real estate, except dwellings	85	42	43	100	45	55	115	60	55	124	65	59
Dwellings	...	...	...	...	...	...	...	...	...	...	...	...
9 Community, social and personal services b	619	141	478	756	166	588	1004	227	777	1173	317	856
A Sanitary and similar services	...	...	...	...	...	...	...	...	...	...	...	...
B Social and related community services	309	69	240	366	68	297	498	83	415	598	147	451
Educational services	213	44	169	249	33	215	351	42	309	437	95	343
Medical, dental, other health and veterinary services	96	25	71	117	35	82	147	41	106	161	52	108
C Recreational and cultural services	245	72	173	318	98	219	421	144	277	487	170	317
D Personal and household services	65	...	65	72	...	72	85	...	85	88	...	88
Total, Industries	6050	3010	3041	7729	3867	3861	8788	4352	4438	9674	4466	5207
Producers of Government Services	586	295	291	603	294	309	730	363	367	820	422	398
Other Producers	...	...	...	...	...	...	...	...	...	...	...	...
Total c	6636	3305	3332	8332	4161	4170	9518	4715	4803	10494	4888	5605
Less: Imputed bank service charge	...	-108	108	...	-121	121	...	-146	146	...	-173	173
Import duties	...	...	...	...	...	...	...	...	...	...	...	...
Value added tax	...	...	...	...	...	...	...	...	...	...	...	...
Other adjustments d	217	...	217	384	...	384	540	...	540	874	...	874
Total	6853	3420	3441	8716	4282	4433	10058	4861	5197	11368	5061	6306

	1984			1985			1986			1987		
	Gross Output	Intermediate Consumption	Value Added	Gross Output	Intermediate Consumption	Value Added	Gross Output	Intermediate Consumption	Value Added	Gross Output	Intermediate Consumption	Value Added
All Producers												
1 Agriculture, hunting, forestry and fishing	1384	635	748	2031	716	1314	2103	924	1179	2118	995	1123
2 Mining and quarrying	613	293	320	704	369	335	780	334	446	819	484	335
3 Manufacturing	3883	2408	1475	4451	2963	1488	5171	3340	1832	6218	4131	2089
A Manufacture of food, beverages and tobacco	1289	857	432	1381	1059	322	1577	1186	391	2024	1525	499

Zimbabwe

Million Zimbabwean dollars

	1984			1985			1986			1987		
	Gross Output	Intermediate Consumption	Value Added	Gross Output	Intermediate Consumption	Value Added	Gross Output	Intermediate Consumption	Value Added	Gross Output	Intermediate Consumption	Value Added
B Textile, wearing apparel and leather industries	714	454	260	852	592	260	947	634	313	1157	758	399
C Manufacture of wood and wood products, including furniture	102	63	39	100	60	40	146	81	65	178	102	76
D Manufacture of paper and paper products, printing and publishing	205	114	91	243	135	108	283	150	133	315	155	160
E Manufacture of chemicals and chemical petroleum, coal, rubber and plastic products	571	372	199	679	413	266	865	520	345	928	572	356
F Manufacture of non-metallic mineral products, except products of petroleum and coal	101	56	45	111	73	38	160	84	76	198	115	85
G Basic metal industries	362	200	162	486	278	208	434	264	170	559	411	148
H Manufacture of fabricated metal products, machinery and equipment	510	276	234	569	335	234	727	405	322	824	475	349
I Other manufacturing industries	28	16	12	31	18	13	32	17	15	35	18	17
4 Electricity, gas and water a	500	358	142	597	453	144	521	292	229	456	180	276
A Electricity, gas and steam	465	343	122	565	436	129	490	278	212	...	...	...
B Water works and supply	35	15	20	32	17	15	31	13	18	...	...	...
5 Construction	462	257	205	452	298	154	444	276	168	538	313	225
6 Wholesale and retail trade, restaurants and hotels	1441	699	742	1883	1106	777	2197	1226	971	2144	1143	1001
A Wholesale and retail trade	1327	626	701	1763	1015	746	2046	1113	931	1933	1006	927
B Restaurants and hotels	114	73	41	132	103	29	152	113	39	211	137	74
7 Transport, storage and communication	880	446	434	922	491	431	1140	557	582	1359	688	671
8 Finance, insurance, real estate and business services b	483	141	342	592	180	412	627	186	441	808	237	570
A Financial institutions	341	59	282	424	80	344	440	74	366	596	119	476
B Insurance												
C Real estate and business services	142	82	60	168	100	68	187	112	75	212	118	94
Real estate, except dwellings	142	82	60	168	100	68	187	112	75	212	118	94
Dwellings	...	...	...	...	...	...	...	...	...	...	...	...
9 Community, social and personal services b	1324	359	965	1573	396	1178	1824	546	1275	1946	546	1400
A Sanitary and similar services	...	...	...	...	...	...	...	...	...	...	...	...
B Social and related community services	675	144	532	860	198	663	1022	248	774	1081	221	860
Educational services	515	99	416	658	139	520	796	186	610	827	151	676
Medical, dental, other health and veterinary services	160	45	116	202	59	143	226	62	164	254	70	184
C Recreational and cultural services	562	215	346	617	198	419	671	298	372	723	326	397
D Personal and household services	87	...	87	96	...	96	129	...	129	142	...	142
Total, Industries	10970	5595	5373	13204	6972	6232	14804	7681	7123	16407	8717	7690
Producers of Government Services	835	391	444	1052	576	476	1014	496	518	1201	587	614
Other Producers	...	...	...	...	...	...	...	...	...	...	...	...
Total c	11805	5986	5817	14256	7548	6708	15818	8177	7641	17608	9304	8304
Less: Imputed bank service charge	...	-168	168	...	-205	205	...	-233	233	...	-284	284
Import duties	...	...	...	...	...	...	...	...	...	...	...	...
Value added tax	...	...	...	...	...	...	...	...	...	...	...	...
Other adjustments d	755	...	755	792	...	792	881	...	881	920	...	920
Total	12560	6154	6404	15048	7753	7295	16699	8410	8289	18528	9588	8940

4.1 Derivation of Value Added by Kind of Activity, in Current Prices

Million Zimbabwean dollars

	Gross Output	Intermediate Consumption	Value Added
	1988		
	All Producers		
1 Agriculture, hunting, forestry and fishing	2657	1061	1596
2 Mining and quarrying	1156	475	681
3 Manufacturing	7250	4732	2518
A Manufacture of food, beverages and tobacco	2063	1554	509
B Textile, wearing apparel and leather industries	1440	889	551
C Manufacture of wood and wood products, including furniture	203	122	80
D Manufacture of paper and paper products, printing and publishing	393	213	179
E Manufacture of chemicals and chemical petroleum, coal, rubber and plastic products	1128	659	469
F Manufacture of non-metallic mineral products, except products of petroleum and coal	222	119	102
G Basic metal industries	738	527	211
H Manufacture of fabricated metal products, machinery and equipment	1020	622	398
I Other manufacturing industries	43	27	18
4 Electricity, gas and water a	466	159	307
A Electricity, gas and steam	...	...	...
B Water works and supply	...	...	...
5 Construction	697	454	243
6 Wholesale and retail trade, restaurants and hotels	2651	1499	1152
A Wholesale and retail trade	2429	1346	1082
B Restaurants and hotels	223	153	70
7 Transport, storage and communication	1564	777	787
8 Finance, insurance, real estate and business services b	1004	268	736
A Financial institutions	674	141	533
B Insurance			
C Real estate and business services	330	127	203
Real estate, except dwellings	330	127	203
Dwellings	...	...	...
9 Community, social and personal services b	2223	571	1652
A Sanitary and similar services	...	...	...
B Social and related community services	1285	210	1075
Educational services	987	133	854
Medical, dental, other health and veterinary services	298	77	221
C Recreational and cultural services	782	361	421
D Personal and household services	156	...	156
Total, Industries	19668	9996	9672
Producers of Government Services	1456	646	810
Other Producers	...	...	...
Total c	21124	10641	10482
Less: Imputed bank service charge	...	-299	299
Import duties	...	...	...
Value added tax	...	...	...
Other adjustments d	1257	...	1257
Total	22381	10940	11440

a) Item 'Electricity, gas and water' excludes gas.
b) Business services are included in item 'Community, social and personal services'.
c) Gross domestic product in factor values.
d) Item 'Other adjustments' refers to indirect taxes net of subsidies.

Zimbabwe

4.3 Cost Components of Value Added

Million Zimbabwean dollars

	1980						1981					
	Compensation of Employees	Capital Consumption	Net Operating Surplus	Indirect Taxes	Less: Subsidies Received	Value Added	Compensation of Employees	Capital Consumption	Net Operating Surplus	Indirect Taxes	Less: Subsidies Received	Value Added
All Producers												
1 Agriculture, hunting, forestry and fishing	146	...	305	...	...	451	210	...	430	...	...	640
2 Mining and quarrying	116	...	169	...	...	285	158	...	94	...	...	252
3 Manufacturing	402	...	400	...	...	802	541	...	475	...	...	1016
A Manufacture of food, beverages and tobacco	90	...	86	...	...	176	115	...	96	...	...	211
B Textile, wearing apparel and leather industries	62	...	76	...	...	138	89	...	108	...	...	197
C Manufacture of wood and wood products, including furniture	18	...	14	...	...	32	26	...	22	...	...	48
D Manufacture of paper and paper products, printing and publishing	31	...	16	...	...	47	41	...	27	...	...	68
E Manufacture of chemicals and chemical petroleum, coal, rubber and plastic products	45	...	59	...	...	104	59	...	85	...	...	144
F Manufacture of non-metallic mineral products, except products of petroleum and coal	15	...	18	...	...	33	22	...	11	...	...	33
G Basic metal industries	51	...	69	...	...	120	69	...	26	...	...	95
H Manufacture of fabricated metal products, machinery and equipment	83	...	56	...	...	139	113	...	89	...	...	202
I Other manufacturing industries	7	...	6	...	...	13	7	...	10	...	...	17
4 Electricity, gas and water a	27	...	43	...	...	70	30	...	48	...	...	78
A Electricity, gas and steam	25	...	34	...	...	59	28	...	40	...	...	68
B Water works and supply	2	...	9	...	...	11	2	...	8	...	...	10
5 Construction	81	...	9	...	...	91	110	...	28	...	...	138
6 Wholesale and retail trade, restaurants and hotels	203	...	248	...	...	451	197	...	406	...	...	603
A Wholesale and retail trade	185	...	249	...	...	434	176	...	399	...	...	575
B Restaurants and hotels	19	...	-1	...	...	18	21	...	7	...	...	28
7 Transport, storage and communication	194	...	17	...	...	211	218	...	88	...	...	306
8 Finance, insurance, real estate and business services b	78	...	124	...	...	202	100	...	140	...	...	240
A Financial institutions	74	...	85	...	...	159	95	...	90	...	...	185
B Insurance		...		...	...			...		...	...	
C Real estate and business services	4	...	39	...	...	43	5	...	50	...	...	55
Real estate, except dwellings	4	...	39	...	...	43	5	...	50	...	...	55
Dwellings	...	...	...	...	...	...	...	...	...	...	...	...
9 Community, social and personal services b	392	...	86	...	...	478	479	...	109	...	...	586
A Sanitary and similar services	...	...	...	...	...	...	...	...	...	...	...	...
B Social and related community services	218	...	22	...	...	240	272	...	29	...	...	301
Educational services	169	...	-	...	...	169	216	...	1	...	...	215
Medical, dental, other health and veterinary services	49	...	22	...	...	71	56	...	26	...	...	82
C Recreational and cultural services	110	...	63	...	...	173	135	...	84	...	...	219
D Personal and household services	65	...	-	...	...	65	72	...	-	...	...	72
Total, Industries	1639	...	1405	...	...	3041	2043	...	1818	...	...	3860
Producers of Government Services	263	...	27	...	...	291	281	...	28	...	...	309
Other Producers	...	...	...	...	...	...	...	...	...	...	...	...
Total c	1902	...	1432	...	...	3332	2324	...	1846	...	...	4170
Less: Imputed bank service charge	...	...	108	...	...	108	...	...	121	...	...	121
Import duties	...	...	...	...	...	...	...	...	...	...	...	...
Value added tax	...	...	...	...	...	...	...	...	...	...	...	...
Other adjustments d	...	...	...	217	...	217	...	...	...	384	...	384
Total c	1902	...	1322	217	...	3441	2324	...	1725	384	...	4433

4.3 Cost Components of Value Added
(Continued)

Million Zimbabwean dollars

	1980						1981					
	Compensation of Employees	Capital Consumption	Net Operating Surplus	Indirect Taxes	Less: Subsidies Received	Value Added	Compensation of Employees	Capital Consumption	Net Operating Surplus	Indirect Taxes	Less: Subsidies Received	Value Added
of which General Government:												
1 Agriculture, hunting, forestry and fishing	5	...	-1	...	...	4	4	...	-	...	...	4
2 Mining and quarrying	...	...	...	...	...	...	...	...	...	...	...	...
3 Manufacturing	4	...	5	...	...	9	5	...	4	...	...	9
4 Electricity, gas and water	17	...	28	...	...	45	19	...	34	...	...	53
5 Construction	35	...	-2	...	...	33	40	...	3	...	...	43
6 Wholesale and retail trade, restaurants and hotels	3	...	4	...	...	7	4	...	4	...	...	8
7 Transport and communication	8	...	...	...	...	8	8	...	...	...	...	8
8 Finance, insurance, real estate & business services	...	...	28	...	...	28	...	...	28	...	...	28
9 Community, social and personal services	170	...	...	...	...	170	258	...	...	...	...	258
Total, Industries of General Government	242	...	62	...	...	304	338	...	73	...	...	411
Producers of Government Services	263	...	...	...	...	263	281	...	...	...	...	281
Total, General Government	505	...	62	...	...	567	619	...	73	...	...	692

	1982						1983					
	Compensation of Employees	Capital Consumption	Net Operating Surplus	Indirect Taxes	Less: Subsidies Received	Value Added	Compensation of Employees	Capital Consumption	Net Operating Surplus	Indirect Taxes	Less: Subsidies Received	Value Added
All Producers												
1 Agriculture, hunting, forestry and fishing	248	...	421	...	...	669	280	...	264	...	...	544
2 Mining and quarrying	179	...	38	...	...	217	161	...	232	...	...	393
3 Manufacturing	649	...	472	...	...	1121	702	...	739	...	...	1441
A Manufacture of food, beverages and tobacco	148	...	127	...	...	275	160	...	267	...	...	427
B Textile, wearing apparel and leather industries	110	...	85	...	...	195	128	...	83	...	...	211
C Manufacture of wood and wood products, including furniture	31	...	15	...	...	46	33	...	15	...	...	48
D Manufacture of paper and paper products, printing and publishing	50	...	28	...	...	78	53	...	53	...	...	106
E Manufacture of chemicals and chemical petroleum, coal, rubber and plastic products	71	...	77	...	...	148	84	...	97	...	...	181
F Manufacture of non-metallic mineral products, except products of petroleum and coal	27	...	36	...	...	63	27	...	38	...	...	65
G Basic metal industries	67	...	7	...	...	74	79	...	64	...	...	143
H Manufacture of fabricated metal products, machinery and equipment	134	...	89	...	...	223	129	...	113	...	...	242
I Other manufacturing industries	11	...	8	...	...	19	9	...	7	...	...	16
4 Electricity, gas and water a	34	...	39	...	...	73	35	...	160	...	...	195
A Electricity, gas and steam	32	...	26	...	...	58	34	...	159	...	...	193
B Water works and supply	2	...	13	...	...	15	2	...	1	...	...	3
5 Construction	142	...	48	...	...	190	134	...	125	...	...	258
6 Wholesale and retail trade, restaurants and hotels	189	...	551	...	...	741	336	...	446	...	...	783
A Wholesale and retail trade	169	...	544	...	...	714	314	...	425	...	...	739
B Restaurants and hotels	20	...	7	...	...	27	22	...	21	...	...	43
7 Transport, storage and communication	263	...	101	...	...	365	295	...	108	...	...	403
8 Finance, insurance, real estate and business services b	122	...	161	...	...	283	144	...	190	...	...	334
A Financial institutions	117	...	111	...	...	228	138	...	137	...	...	275
B Insurance												
C Real estate and business services	5	...	50	...	...	55	6	...	53	...	...	59
Real estate, except dwellings	5	...	50	...	...	55	6	...	53	...	...	59

Zimbabwe

Million Zimbabwean dollars

	1982						1983					
	Compensation of Employees	Capital Consumption	Net Operating Surplus	Indirect Taxes	Less: Subsidies Received	Value Added	Compensation of Employees	Capital Consumption	Net Operating Surplus	Indirect Taxes	Less: Subsidies Received	Value Added
Dwellings	...	...	...	...	...	...	...	...	...	...	...	...
9 Community, social and personal services b	642	...	136	...	...	778	700	...	157	...	...	857
A Sanitary and similar services	...	...	...	...	...	...	...	...	...	...	...	...
B Social and related community services	386	...	30	...	...	416	420	...	32	...	...	452
Educational services	310	...	-1	...	...	309	344	...	-1	...	...	343
Medical, dental, other health and veterinary services	76	...	30	...	...	106	76	...	32	...	...	108
C Recreational and cultural services	171	...	106	...	...	277	192	...	125	...	...	317
D Personal and household services	85	...	-	...	...	85	88	...	-	...	...	88
Total, Industries	2468	...	1966	...	...	4434	2787	...	2420	...	...	5207
Producers of Government Services	330	...	37	...	...	367	348	...	50	...	...	398
Other Producers	...	...	...	...	...	...	...	...	...	...	...	...
Total c	2798	...	2003	...	...	4801	3135	...	2470	...	...	5605
Less: Imputed bank service charge	...	...	146	...	...	146	...	...	173	...	...	173
Import duties	...	...	...	...	...	...	...	...	...	...	...	...
Value added tax	...	...	...	...	...	...	...	...	...	...	...	...
Other adjustments d	...	...	...	540	...	540	...	...	...	874	...	874
Total c	2798	...	1859	540	...	5197	3135	...	2297	874	...	6306

of which General Government:

	1982						1983					
	Compensation of Employees	Capital Consumption	Net Operating Surplus	Indirect Taxes	Less: Subsidies Received	Value Added	Compensation of Employees	Capital Consumption	Net Operating Surplus	Indirect Taxes	Less: Subsidies Received	Value Added
1 Agriculture, hunting, forestry and fishing	20	...	-2	...	...	18	18	...	-5	...	...	13
2 Mining and quarrying	...	...	...	...	...	...	...	...	...	...	...	...
3 Manufacturing	7	...	5	...	...	12	44	...	8	...	...	52
4 Electricity, gas and water	22	...	19	...	...	41	26	...	141	...	...	167
5 Construction	52	...	-4	...	...	48	44	...	36	...	...	80
6 Wholesale and retail trade, restaurants and hotels	5	...	3	...	...	8	5	...	8	...	...	13
7 Transport and communication	9	...	...	...	...	9	10	...	...	...	...	10
8 Finance, insurance, real estate & business services	...	...	37	...	...	37	...	...	50	...	...	50
9 Community, social and personal services	363	...	...	...	...	363	392	...	...	...	...	392
Total, Industries of General Government	478	...	58	...	...	536	539	...	238	...	...	777
Producers of Government Services	330	...	...	...	...	330	348	...	...	...	...	348
Total, General Government	808	...	58	...	...	866	887	...	238	...	...	1125

	1984						1985					
	Compensation of Employees	Capital Consumption	Net Operating Surplus	Indirect Taxes	Less: Subsidies Received	Value Added	Compensation of Employees	Capital Consumption	Net Operating Surplus	Indirect Taxes	Less: Subsidies Received	Value Added

All Producers

	1984						1985					
1 Agriculture, hunting, forestry and fishing	313	...	436	...	...	748	227	...	1087	...	...	1314
2 Mining and quarrying	170	...	149	...	...	320	188	...	147	...	...	335
3 Manufacturing	742	...	732	...	...	1475	854	...	634	...	...	1488
A Manufacture of food, beverages and tobacco	184	...	248	...	...	432	206	...	116	...	...	322

4.3 Cost Components of Value Added
(Continued)

Million Zimbabwean dollars

	1984						1985					
	Compensation of Employees	Capital Consumption	Net Operating Surplus	Indirect Taxes	Less: Subsidies Received	Value Added	Compensation of Employees	Capital Consumption	Net Operating Surplus	Indirect Taxes	Less: Subsidies Received	Value Added
B Textile, wearing apparel and leather industries	125	...	135	...	...	260	153	...	107	...	...	260
C Manufacture of wood and wood products, including furniture	32	...	6	...	...	38	31	...	10	...	...	41
D Manufacture of paper and paper products, printing and publishing	60	...	31	...	...	91	66	...	42	...	...	108
E Manufacture of chemicals and chemical petroleum, coal, rubber and plastic products	91	...	108	...	...	199	104	...	161	...	...	265
F Manufacture of non-metallic mineral products, except products of petroleum and coal	29	...	16	...	...	45	32	...	5	...	...	37
G Basic metal industries	80	...	82	...	...	162	102	...	106	...	...	208
H Manufacture of fabricated metal products, machinery and equipment	134	...	100	...	...	234	152	...	82	...	...	234
I Other manufacturing industries	7	...	5	...	...	12	8	...	5	...	...	13
4 Electricity, gas and water [a]	44	...	98	...	...	142	69	...	75	...	...	144
A Electricity, gas and steam	42	...	80	...	...	122	67	...	62	...	...	129
B Water works and supply	2	...	15	...	...	17	2	...	13	...	...	15
5 Construction	131	...	74	...	...	205	129	...	26	...	...	154
6 Wholesale and retail trade, restaurants and hotels	356	...	386	...	...	742	409	...	368	...	...	777
A Wholesale and retail trade	327	...	374	...	...	701	377	...	372	...	...	749
B Restaurants and hotels	29	...	12	...	...	41	32	...	-4	...	...	28
7 Transport, storage and communication	308	...	126	...	...	434	328	...	103	...	...	431
8 Finance, insurance, real estate and business services [b]	158	...	184	...	...	342	221	...	191	...	...	411
A Financial institutions	151	...	131	...	...	282	163	...	181	...	...	343
B Insurance		...		...	...			...		...	...	
C Real estate and business services	7	...	53	...	...	60	58	...	10	...	...	68
Real estate, except dwellings	7	...	53	...	...	60	58	...	10	...	...	68
Dwellings	...	...	...	...	...	...	...	...	...	...	...	...
9 Community, social and personal services [b]	805	...	160	...	...	965	975	...	202	...	...	1178
A Sanitary and similar services	...	...	...	...	...	...	...	...	...	...	...	...
B Social and related community services	507	...	25	...	...	532	631	...	31	...	...	663
Educational services	416	...	-1	...	...	416	524	...	-5	...	...	520
Medical, dental, other health and veterinary services	91	...	25	...	...	116	107	...	36	...	...	143
C Recreational and cultural services	211	...	135	...	...	346	248	...	171	...	...	419
D Personal and household services	87	...	-	...	...	87	96	...	-	...	...	96
Total, Industries	3027	...	2345	...	...	5373	3400	...	2833	...	...	6233
Producers of Government Services	391	...	53	...	...	444	429	...	47	...	...	476
Other Producers	...	...	...	...	...	...	...	...	...	...	...	...
Total [c]	3418	...	2398	...	...	5817	3829	...	2880	...	...	6709
Less: Imputed bank service charge	...	...	168	...	...	168	...	...	205	...	...	205
Import duties	...	...	...	...	...	...	...	...	...	...	...	...
Value added tax	...	...	...	...	...	...	...	...	...	...	...	...
Other adjustments [d]	...	...	...	755	...	755	...	...	...	792	...	792
Total [c]	3418	...	2230	755	...	6404	3829	...	2675	792	...	7295
of which General Government:												
1 Agriculture, hunting, forestry and fishing	11	...	4	...	...	15	15	...	-5	...	...	10
2 Mining and quarrying	...	...	...	...	...	...	...	...	...	...	...	...
3 Manufacturing	49	...	-18	...	...	31	59	...	-19	...	...	40
4 Electricity, gas and water	10	...	42	...	...	52	7	...	62	...	...	69

Zimbabwe

4.3 Cost Components of Value Added
(Continued)

Million Zimbabwean dollars

	1984						1985					
	Compensation of Employees	Capital Consumption	Net Operating Surplus	Indirect Taxes	Less: Subsidies Received	Value Added	Compensation of Employees	Capital Consumption	Net Operating Surplus	Indirect Taxes	Less: Subsidies Received	Value Added
5 Construction	49	...	15	...	...	64	50	...	26	...	...	76
6 Wholesale and retail trade, restaurants and hotels	6	...	7	...	...	13	5	...	5	...	...	10
7 Transport and communication	12	...	...	...	...	12	14	...	...	...	...	14
8 Finance, insurance, real estate & business services	...	...	53	...	...	53	...	...	47	...	...	47
9 Community, social and personal services	484	...	...	...	...	484	571	...	...	...	...	571
Total, Industries of General Government	621	...	103	...	...	724	721	...	116	...	...	837
Producers of Government Services	391	...	...	...	...	391	429	...	...	...	...	429
Total, General Government	1012	...	103	...	...	1115	1150	...	116	...	...	1266

	1986						1987					
	Compensation of Employees	Capital Consumption	Net Operating Surplus	Indirect Taxes	Less: Subsidies Received	Value Added	Compensation of Employees	Capital Consumption	Net Operating Surplus	Indirect Taxes	Less: Subsidies Received	Value Added

All Producers

	Comp.	Cap. Cons.	Net Op. Surplus	Ind. Taxes	Less: Subs.	Value Added	Comp.	Cap. Cons.	Net Op. Surplus	Ind. Taxes	Less: Subs.	Value Added
1 Agriculture, hunting, forestry and fishing	281	...	898	...	...	1179	389	...	734	...	...	1123
2 Mining and quarrying	201	...	245	...	...	446	288	...	47	...	...	335
3 Manufacturing	993	...	839	...	...	1832	1089	...	1002	...	...	2089
A Manufacture of food, beverages and tobacco	239	...	153	...	...	392	255	...	244	...	...	499
B Textile, wearing apparel and leather industries	176	...	137	...	...	313	209	...	191	...	...	400
C Manufacture of wood and wood products, including furniture	39	...	26	...	...	65	44	...	32	...	...	76
D Manufacture of paper and paper products, printing and publishing	73	...	60	...	...	133	63	...	96	...	...	160
E Manufacture of chemicals and chemical petroleum, coal, rubber and plastic products	122	...	223	...	...	345	160	...	196	...	...	356
F Manufacture of non-metallic mineral products, except products of petroleum and coal	42	...	34	...	...	76	52	...	33	...	...	85
G Basic metal industries	111	...	59	...	...	170	135	...	13	...	...	148
H Manufacture of fabricated metal products, machinery and equipment	181	...	140	...	...	321	162	...	188	...	...	350
I Other manufacturing industries	9	...	6	...	...	15	9	...	9	...	...	18
4 Electricity, gas and water [a]	56	...	172	...	...	229	55	...	221	...	...	276
A Electricity, gas and steam	54	...	159	...	...	213	...	...	...	...	...	...
B Water works and supply	2	...	13	...	...	15	...	...	...	...	...	...
5 Construction	120	...	48	...	...	168	140	...	84	...	...	225
6 Wholesale and retail trade, restaurants and hotels	443	...	528	...	...	971	488	...	513	...	...	1001
A Wholesale and retail trade	406	...	526	...	...	932	444	...	483	...	...	927
B Restaurants and hotels	37	...	2	...	...	39	44	...	30	...	...	74
7 Transport, storage and communication	396	...	186	...	...	582	425	...	246	...	...	671
8 Finance, insurance, real estate and business services [b]	246	...	195	...	...	441	197	...	372	...	...	570
A Financial institutions	184	...	182	...	...	366	189	...	286	...	...	476
B Insurance		...		...	...			...		...	...	
C Real estate and business services	62	...	13	...	...	75	8	...	86	...	...	94
Real estate, except dwellings	62	...	13	...	...	75	8	...	86	...	...	94
Dwellings	...	...	...	...	...	...	...	...	...	...	...	...
9 Community, social and personal services [b]	1150	...	127	...	...	1275	1252	...	147	...	...	1399
A Sanitary and similar services	...	...	...	...	...	...	...	...	...	...	...	...
B Social and related community services	741	...	33	...	...	772	814	...	45	...	...	860

4.3 Cost Components of Value Added
(Continued)

__Million Zimbabwean dollars__

	1986						1987					
	Compensation of Employees	Capital Consumption	Net Operating Surplus	Indirect Taxes	Less: Subsidies Received	Value Added	Compensation of Employees	Capital Consumption	Net Operating Surplus	Indirect Taxes	Less: Subsidies Received	Value Added
Educational services	616	...	-6	...	...	610	682	...	-7	...	...	676
Medical, dental, other health and veterinary services	125	...	39	...	...	164	132	...	52	...	...	184
C Recreational and cultural services	278	...	94	...	...	372	296	...	102	...	...	397
D Personal and household services	131	...	-2	...	...	129	142	...	-	...	...	142
Total, Industries	3886	...	3238	...	...	7123	4323	...	3366	...	...	7689
Producers of Government Services	465	...	53	...	...	518	536	...	78	...	...	614
Other Producers	...	...	...	...	...	...	...	...	...	...	...	...
Total c	4351	...	3291	...	...	7641	4859	...	3444	...	...	8303
Less: Imputed bank service charge	...	...	233	...	...	233	...	...	284	...	...	284
Import duties	...	...	...	...	...	...	...	...	...	...	...	...
Value added tax	...	...	...	...	...	...	...	...	...	...	...	...
Other adjustments d	...	...	...	881	...	881	...	...	...	920	...	920
Total c	4351	...	3058	881	...	8289	4859	...	3160	920	...	8939

of which General Government:

	1986						1987					
	Compensation of Employees	Capital Consumption	Net Operating Surplus	Indirect Taxes	Less: Subsidies Received	Value Added	Compensation of Employees	Capital Consumption	Net Operating Surplus	Indirect Taxes	Less: Subsidies Received	Value Added
1 Agriculture, hunting, forestry and fishing	23	...	-7	...	...	16	28	...	-10	...	...	18
2 Mining and quarrying	...	...	...	...	...	...	...	...	...	...	...	...
3 Manufacturing	66	...	-20	...	...	46	8	...	1	...	...	9
4 Electricity, gas and water	9	...	26	...	...	35	4	...	9	...	...	13
5 Construction	38	...	-5	...	...	33	47	...	4	...	...	51
6 Wholesale and retail trade, restaurants and hotels	6	...	5	...	...	11	9	...	5	...	...	14
7 Transport and communication	18	...	...	...	...	18	21	...	...	...	...	21
8 Finance, insurance, real estate & business services	...	...	53	...	...	53	...	...	78	...	...	78
9 Community, social and personal services	644	...	...	...	...	644	779	...	...	...	...	779
Total, Industries of General Government	804	...	52	...	...	856	896	...	87	...	...	983
Producers of Government Services	465	...	...	...	...	465	536	...	...	...	...	536
Total, General Government	1269	...	52	...	...	1321	1432	...	87	...	...	1519

	1988					
	Compensation of Employees	Capital Consumption	Net Operating Surplus	Indirect Taxes	Less: Subsidies Received	Value Added
	All Producers					
1 Agriculture, hunting, forestry and fishing	444	...	1152	...	...	1596
2 Mining and quarrying	245	...	436	...	...	681
3 Manufacturing	1333	...	1185	...	...	2518
A Manufacture of food, beverages and tobacco	303	...	206	...	...	508
B Textile, wearing apparel and leather industries	249	...	302	...	...	551
C Manufacture of wood and wood products, including furniture	49	...	31	...	...	80
D Manufacture of paper and paper products, printing and publishing	88	...	91	...	...	179
E Manufacture of chemicals and chemical petroleum, coal, rubber and plastic products	175	...	294	...	...	469
F Manufacture of non-metallic mineral products, except products of petroleum and coal	59	...	42	...	...	102
G Basic metal industries	176	...	35	...	...	211
H Manufacture of fabricated metal products, machinery and equipment	224	...	175	...	...	398
I Other manufacturing industries	9	...	9	...	...	18
4 Electricity, gas and water a	68	...	238	...	...	307
A Electricity, gas and steam	64	...	212	...	...	276
B Water works and supply	4	...	26	...	...	31

Zimbabwe

4.3 Cost Components of Value Added
(Continued)

__Million Zimbabwean dollars__

	Compensation of Employees	Capital Consumption	Net Operating Surplus	Indirect Taxes	Less: Subsidies Received	Value Added
	1988					
5 Construction	144	...	99	...	...	243
6 Wholesale and retail trade, restaurants and hotels	570	...	582	...	...	1152
A Wholesale and retail trade	523	...	559	...	...	1082
B Restaurants and hotels	47	...	23	...	. ...	70
7 Transport, storage and communication	474	...	313	...	...	787
8 Finance, insurance, real estate and business services b	266	...	470	...	...	736
A Financial institutions	254	...	279	...	...	533
B Insurance		...			...	
C Real estate and business services	12	...	191	...	...	203
Real estate, except dwellings	12	...	191	...	...	203
Dwellings	...	...	...	...	...	...
9 Community, social and personal services b	1476	...	175	...	...	1652
A Sanitary and similar services	...	...	...	...	...	...
B Social and related community services	1024	...	50	...	...	1075
Educational services	861	...	-7	...	...	854
Medical, dental, other health and veterinary services	163	...	57	...	...	221
C Recreational and cultural services	296	...	125	...	...	421
D Personal and household services	156	...	-	...	...	156
Total, Industries	5020	...	4650	...	...	9672
Producers of Government Services	590	...	221	...	...	811
Other Producers	...	...	...	...	...	...
Total c	5610	...	4871	...	...	10483
Less: Imputed bank service charge	...	...	299	...	...	299
Import duties	...	...	...	...	...	...
Value added tax	...	...	...	...	...	...
Other adjustments d	...	...	...	1257	...	1257
Total c	5610	...	4575	1257	...	11441

of which General Government:

1 Agriculture, hunting, forestry and fishing	35	...	2	...	...	37
2 Mining and quarrying	...	...	...	...	...	...
3 Manufacturing	12	...	6	...	...	18
4 Electricity, gas and water	-	...	-	...	...	-
5 Construction	23	...	34	...	...	57
6 Wholesale and retail trade, restaurants and hotels	9	...	-1	...	...	8
7 Transport and communication	23	...	...	...	...	23
8 Finance, insurance, real estate & business services	...	...	221	...	...	221
9 Community, social and personal services	992	...	...	...	...	992
Total, Industries of General Government	1094	...	262	...	...	1356
Producers of Government Services	590	...	...	...	...	590
Total, General Government	1684	...	262	...	...	1946

a) Item 'Electricity, gas and water' excludes gas.
b) Business services are included in item 'Community, social and personal services'.
c) Column 'Consumption of fixed capital' is included in column 'Net operating surplus'.
d) Item 'Other adjustments' refers to indirect taxes net of subsidies.